Psychology 3RD
AUSTRALIAN AND NEW ZEALAND EDITION

Psychology 3RD

AUSTRALIAN AND NEW ZEALAND EDITION

LORELLE BURTON

DREW WESTEN

ROBIN KOWALSKI

John Wiley & Sons Australia, Ltd

Third edition published 2012 by
John Wiley & Sons Australia, Ltd
42 McDougall Street, Milton Qld 4064

First edition published 2006
Second edition published 2009

Typeset in 10/12.5 pt Times LT

National Library of Australia
Cataloguing-in-Publication entry

Author:	Burton, Lorelle, 1971–
Title:	Psychology / Lorelle Burton, Drew Westen, Robin Kowalski.
Edition:	3rd Australian and New Zealand ed.
ISBN:	9781742166445 (pbk.)
Notes:	Includes bibliographical references and index.
Subjects:	Psychology — Australia — Textbooks. Psychology — New Zealand — Textbooks.
Other Authors/Contributors:	Westen, Drew, 1959– Kowalski, Robin M.
Dewey Number:	150.994

Typeset in India by diacriTech

Printed in China by
1010 Printing

10 9 8 7 6 5 4

Brief contents

Contents

Preface

My teaching philosophy is all about challenging students to become critical thinkers and self-directed learners. My aim is to arouse their passion and interest in the material they are studying. I believe this is the key to success. I feel that I am successful when students become totally engaged in the learning process and take on more responsibility for motivating and directing their own search for knowledge.

As the author of *Psychology: 3rd Australian and New Zealand Edition*, my philosophy of writing an introductory psychology book reflects this same teaching philosophy. I have drawn on my expertise in the teaching of foundation psychology and individual differences courses. Additionally, my primary research interests focus on how teachers may best respond to issues of student diversity in their teaching.

A major objective is to consider the various individual and sociocultural factors that students bring with them to the learning environment and to explore methods for enhancing learning for all students, regardless of their location, cultural background or experience. Given my areas of expertise and research interests, it will not surprise you to learn that this edition includes more extensive coverage of research related to cross-cultural issues and continues to draw on research emerging from Australia, New Zealand and other parts of the Asia–Pacific region. A new section on conservation psychology (chapter 17) has also been included, reflecting the emerging importance of this topic to the discipline. Additionally, the positive and negative psychological implications of social media are comprehensively covered throughout this current edition.

The principal aim of *Psychology: 3rd Australian and New Zealand Edition* is to enhance the quality of the learning experience for all Australian and New Zealand students, by including material that is both relevant and interesting to them. First, the text provides a local cultural context that will help students to better relate to the subject matter and engage in the learning process. For example, the inclusion of local examples and research that reflect students' personal experiences will help them to understand the psychological concepts they are studying. Second, the text is compatible with the way undergraduate psychology is taught in Australian and New Zealand universities today.

My goal has also been to try to give students a sense of the 'big picture' of how we think, feel and behave, and how our evolving science continually addresses and readdresses the central questions that brought most of us into the field — questions about the relationship between psychological events and their neural underpinnings, between cognition and emotion, between cultural processes and human evolution, between nature and nurture and so forth. Introductory psychology is probably the last time most students — and psychologists — get a broad view of our field. In fact, I suspect one of the greatest personal benefits for those of us who teach introductory psychology is that we are continually exposed to new information, often in domains far from our own areas of expertise, which stretches and challenges our imaginations.

Writing a textbook is always a balancing act, with each edition adjusting scales that were tipped a bit too far in one direction with the previous one. Probably the most difficult balance to achieve in writing an introductory text is how to cover what we know (at least for now) and what is on the cutting edge, without making an encyclopaedia, particularly in a field that is moving forward so rapidly. Another challenge is to help those who might desire more structure to learn the material, without placing roadblocks in the path of students who would find most pedagogical devices contrived and distracting. A final balancing act involves presenting solid research in a manner that is accessible, lively and thought-provoking. I believe that this third edition of *Psychology* successfully achieves equilibrium across these different issues. The revisions have served to complement the original text, while maintaining its integrity and pedagogy. The text still speaks with one voice — albeit a voice with a trace of an Australian accent. I am very grateful for the strong support the textbook has received from students and my academic colleagues across Australasia. I am sure you will find the third edition even more useful and enjoyable than the second.

Features of this edition

Additional local research and examples in each chapter

Adapting the text to the Australian and Asia–Pacific landscape involved drawing on the considerable body of research emerging from Australia and New Zealand, as well as including statistics relevant to local experience. I believe that presenting research and literature relevant to students' own countries considerably enhances the quality of the learning experience. The adaptation was an exciting opportunity to optimise the benefits of the original text, by placing it in a cultural context familiar to local students. In this third edition I have continued to focus on citing recent work that provides up-to-date information and examples for each chapter. The **Australian and New Zealand content at a glance** section on pages xix–xxiii briefly outlines the extensive local content contained in this edition.

Enhanced cross-cultural and indigenous psychology coverage

Cross-cultural and indigenous psychology issues are covered both where relevant throughout the entire text, and also in a stand-alone chapter (chapter 19). Such coverage allows for maximum flexibility in teaching cross-cultural and indigenous psychology in an Introductory Psychology course.

Chapter 19 embeds a contextual analysis of indigenous issues in psychology. In this chapter, I explain the issues, psychological concepts, history and research of this broad and complex field. The chapter has been written to be relevant to readers in both Australia and New Zealand, yet maintains substantial contact with the broader, international literature. Some of the key issues addressed in this edition include:

- examining the National Indigenous Reform Agreement and efforts to close the gap between Indigenous and non-Indigenous Australians
- exploring the mental health and wellbeing needs of refugees and asylum seekers
- recognising the need for cultural awareness training and developing culturally competent psychologists.

A proven pedagogical framework: an integrated study package

Several key conceptual features remain from earlier editions that give *Psychology: 3rd Australian and New Zealand Edition* its distinctive 'signature'. They arose from five objectives in creating this book:

- to focus on both the biological basis of psychology and the role of culture in shaping basic psychological processes
- to provide a conceptual orientation that would capture the excitement and tensions in the field
- to help students understand the logic of scientific discovery and hypothesis testing as applied to psychological questions
- to suggest ways of integrating psychological theories and knowledge across subfields
- to employ language that would be sophisticated but engaging.

Balanced coverage of multiple perspectives

Earlier editions have endeavoured to acquaint students not just with seminal research but with the conceptual frameworks that guide that research across subdisciplines. With this edition, I have once again tried to describe the strengths and limitations of the major perspectives, with increased emphasis on humanistic, cognitive and evolutionary perspectives and on potential integrations across perspectives.

From the start, students are challenged to think about psychological phenomena from multiple perspectives. Chapter 1 is not perfunctory;

it introduces five perspectives — cognitive, evolutionary, behaviourist, humanistic and psychodynamic — in enough depth to allow students to begin conceptualising psychological data rather than simply memorising a list of facts, names or studies. At the same time, I have avoided slavishly introducing paragraphs on each perspective in every chapter, since some perspectives obviously apply better to certain phenomena than to others.

Biology and culture: a micro to macro approach

A consistent theme of the book, introduced in the first chapter, is that biology and culture form the boundaries of psychology. Understanding people means attending simultaneously to biological processes, psychological experience, and cultural and historical context. The focus on biological and neural underpinnings echoes one of the major trends in contemporary psychological science, as technological developments allow progressively more sophisticated understanding of the neural substrates of psychological experience. The focus on culture has been a central feature of *Psychology* since the publication of the first edition.

One of the key features of this text is the integration of both neuroscientific and cross-cultural research into the fabric of the narrative. Each chapter of this book contains two extended discussions that show the way psychological experience is situated between the nervous system and cultural experience, called **From brain to behaviour** and **A global vista**. These special features flow integrally from the text and are not presented as isolated 'boxes'. Thus, students will get the message that biological and cultural material is integral to understanding psychology, not somehow superfluous or added on.

Conceptual orientation

The book is conceptually oriented. It attempts, within the limits of my objectivity and expertise (considerable limits, no doubt), to give a fair and compelling account of the different perspectives psychologists take in understanding psychological phenomena. I have a healthy respect for each approach and assume that if thousands of my colleagues find an approach compelling, it probably contains something that students should know.

Research focus

This book is about psychological science. A student should come out of an Introductory Psychology class not only with a sense of the questions and frameworks for answering them, but also with an appreciation for how to obtain psychological knowledge. Thus, chapter 2 is devoted to research methods, and the style reflects an effort to engage, not intimidate, so that students can see how methods actually make a difference. The statistical supplement that immediately follows it, which even the most seriously maths-phobic can understand, is included in the body of the text rather than cast off at the end as an impenetrable appendix. From start to finish, students read about specific studies so that they can learn about the logic of scientific investigation.

Language

Above all, I wanted to avoid writing in 'textese', a language that presents dry summaries of data for students to memorise instead of engaging them in thinking about psychology. *Psychology: 3rd Australian and New Zealand Edition* offers a solid and comprehensive account of the principles of psychology in what I hope is an accessible, lively and thought-provoking style. Throughout the book, I aim for clarity and introduce terminology only when it enlightens, not obscures. I am not shy about using metaphor or weaving a narrative, but not a single term in this book is defined by context alone. If students need to understand a concept, they will see the definition in the same sentence in which the word is boldfaced. I have also tried to keep the language at a level appropriate to first-year university students, but if they have to look up an occasional word, I will not lose sleep over it. (I had to look up a few in writing it!)

As a teacher and writer, I try to make use of one of the most robust findings in psychology: that memory and understanding are enhanced when target information is associated with vivid and personally relevant material. Each chapter begins with a case or an event that lets students know why the topic is important and why anyone might be excited about it. None of the cases is invented; this is real Australian and New Zealand material, and the questions raised in the opening vignette re-emerge throughout each chapter.

Learning aids

I have tried to avoid pedagogy that is condescending or unnecessary. In my experience, students never follow up on annotated recommendations for future reading, so I have not cluttered the ends of chapters with them. On the other hand, most students need guidance in studying the material. Therefore, I have retained the learning aids from the last edition that have proven effective in helping students learn: **Central questions**, **Making connections**, **Apply & discuss**, boldfaced **key terms**, **interim summaries** and **chapter summaries**. The inclusion of the interim summaries reflects both feedback from lecturers and the results of research suggesting that distributing conceptual summaries throughout a chapter and presenting them shortly after students have read the material is likely to optimise learning. Additionally, the review, discussion, and application questions at the end of each chapter enable students to actively engage with the material and self-test their understanding of the key concepts.

Organisation

I tried to organise *Psychology: 3rd Australian and New Zealand Edition* in a way that would be convenient for most instructors and yet follow a coherent design. Of course, different instructors organise things differently, but I do not think many will find the organisation idiosyncratic.

Illustration and design

Consistent with earlier editions, I took tremendous care to select and design only figures and tables that actually add something and that do not just make the pages look less ominous. Consistent with the goal of providing students with a more integrative perspective on psychology, and with the goal of creating 'the thinking student's introduction to psychology', this edition again includes an integrated study package built into the structure of the text, without cluttering the margins and distracting from the narrative.

In this edition, I continue to integrate photos with the text in a way that fosters critical thinking and helps students see the connections between concepts presented in different chapters. Instead of using photos primarily to brighten the book or provide interesting diversions (both lofty aims, of course), I have used them to link concepts and visual images, through the two pedagogical features called **Making connections** and **Apply & discuss**.

Dr Lorelle Burton
May 2011

About the authors

Lorelle Burton is Associate Professor of Psychology and Associate Dean (Learning and Teaching) in the Faculty of Sciences at the University of Southern Queensland (USQ). Lorelle is a fully registered psychologist and a full member of the Australian Psychological Society (APS). She commenced full-time teaching in 1996, with her primary areas of interest including foundation psychology and individual differences. Lorelle's passion for teaching psychology has been recognised with a number of teaching excellence awards, both locally and nationally. She received the USQ Award for Teaching Excellence in 2001, and the Dean's Award for Outstanding Contribution to the Faculty of Sciences in 2005 and 2006. In 2004, she was awarded the 2004 Pearson Education and APS Psychology Early Career Teaching Award, and in 2006 she received a Carrick Australian Award for Teaching Excellence (Social Sciences) and a Carrick Australian Citation for Outstanding Contributions to Student Learning. One of the keys to Lorelle's success as a teacher is her commitment to developing innovative approaches to course design and delivery. She is deeply committed to the quality of learning experiences and the success of her students, and has passionately embraced new technologies as a means of creating exciting, interesting and meaningful learning environments. Via online discussion forums, interactive online exercises and multimedia delivery, she engages her students and enables them to become active and satisfied participants in their learning experiences. For example, she authored the widely used text entitled *An Interactive Approach to Writing Essays and Research Reports in Psychology*, currently in its third edition, which includes interactive practice exercises to help students quickly master the core referencing requirements in psychology and better manage their own learning needs. She also adapted the Study Guide to accompany this latest edition of the text. Lorelle's current research focus is on better understanding the factors that impact on student learning. She has presented and published multiple papers at national and international conferences in her specialised areas of teaching and research. Psychology is second to her main love in life — her family. Lorelle is married to Andrew Fox and they have two children, Emily and Benjamin.

Drew Westen is Professor in the Department of Psychology and Department of Psychiatry and Behavioral Sciences at Emory University. He received his BA at Harvard University, an MA in Social and Political Thought at the University of Sussex (England) and his PhD in Clinical Psychology at the University of Michigan, where he subsequently taught for six years. While at the University of Michigan, he was honoured two years in a row by the *Michigan Daily* as the best teaching professor at the university, and was the recipient of the first Golden Apple Award for outstanding undergraduate teaching. More recently, he was selected as a G. Stanley Hall Lecturer by the American Psychological Association. Drew is an active researcher who is on the editorial boards of multiple journals, including *Clinical Psychology: Science and Practice*, *Psychological Assessment* and the *Journal of Personality Disorders*. His major areas of research are personality disorders, eating disorders, emotion regulation, implicit processes, psychotherapy effectiveness and adolescent psychopathology. His series of videotaped lectures on abnormal psychology, called *Is Anyone Really Normal*?, was published by the Teaching Company, in collaboration with the Smithsonian Institution. Drew also provides psychological commentaries on political issues for *All Things Considered* on National Public Radio. His main loves outside of psychology are his wife, Laura, and his daughter, Mackenzie. He also writes comedy music, has performed as a stand-up comic in Boston, and has performed and directed improvisational comedy for the President of the United States.

Robin Kowalski is Professor of Psychology in the Department of Psychology at Clemson University. She received her BA at Furman University, an MA in General Psychology at Wake Forest University and her PhD in Social Psychology at the University of North Carolina at Greensboro. Robin spent the first 13 years of her career at Western Carolina University in Cullowhee, North Carolina. While there, she received the Botner Superior Teaching Award and the University Teaching-Research Award. She came to Clemson in 2003, where she has received the College of Business and Behavioral Science Undergraduate Teaching Excellence Award, the Board of Trustee's Award for Faculty Excellence and the National Scholar's Mentoring Award. She is also an active researcher who served on the editorial board for the *Journal of Social and Clinical Psychology*. She has written or edited nine books and has published in many professional journals, including *Psychological Bulletin* and the *Journal of Experimental Social Psychology*. Robin has two primary research interests. The first focuses on aversive interpersonal behaviours, specifically cyber bullying and complaining. Her research on complaining has received international attention, including an appearance on NBC's *Today Show*. Her book, *Complaining, Teasing, and Other Annoying Behaviors*, was featured on National Public Radio's *All Things Considered*, and in an article in *USA Weekend*. Her book on cyber bullying entitled *Cyber Bullying: Bullying in the Digital Age* has an accompanying website: www.cyberbullyhelp.com. Her second research focus is health psychology, with a particular focus on organ donation and transplantation. Robin has ten-year-old twin boys, Noah and Jordan.

How to use this book

Learning objectives
At the start of each chapter, learning objectives are provided to guide you through the material to be learned. These objectives are revisited in the end-of-chapter summary.

Concept maps
Each chapter opens with a concept map, outlining the key psychological topics and concepts to be explored. This provides a visual overview of the chapter as a whole.

Central questions
A number of questions central to the chapter topic are posed at the beginning of each chapter. These questions are revisited at the end of each chapter.

Another feature provided by Australian and New Zealand academics, ***One step further*** is an advanced discussion of an aspect of the topic being covered. It is intended for students who find the topic especially intriguing and want to learn more about it.

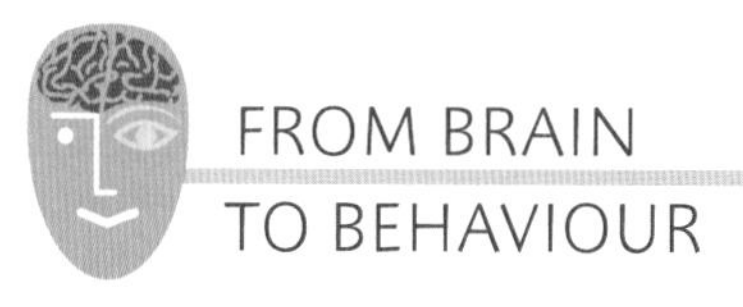

From brain to behaviour focuses on concepts and findings from biopsychology and the neurosciences, providing a detailed discussion of a specific issue.

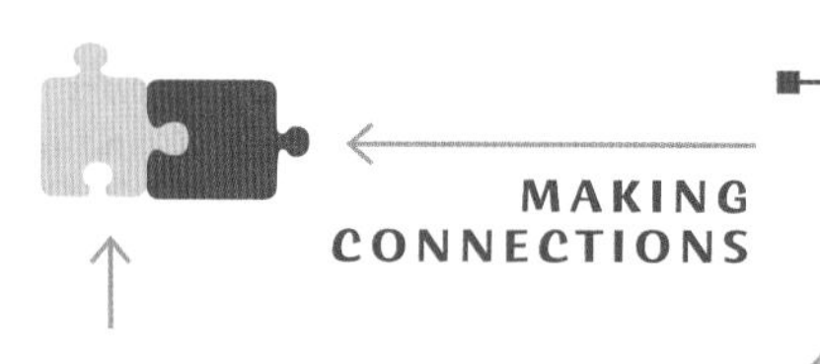

Making connections illustrates and links material from different chapters so that you can see the threads that tie the psychology discipline together. Key concepts are highlighted in a different colour to help you better establish these links.

At the end of major sections, ***interim summaries*** recap the 'gist' of what has been presented. The inclusion of these summaries reflects both feedback from lecturers and the results of research suggesting that distributing conceptual summaries throughout a chapter and presenting them shortly after students have read the material is likely to optimise learning.

Australian and New Zealand academics have provided expert ***commentary*** on one or two key issues covered in each chapter, often presenting both sides of a debate, or letting the reader know their personal opinions on an issue. They will often challenge you to extend your thinking as you consider the relevance of the topic to the Australian and Asia-Pacific region.

A ***global vista*** uses ethnographic material and cross-cultural studies to explore psychological phenomena in other cultures, with an eye to addressing the universality or culture-specificity of psychological theories and observations.

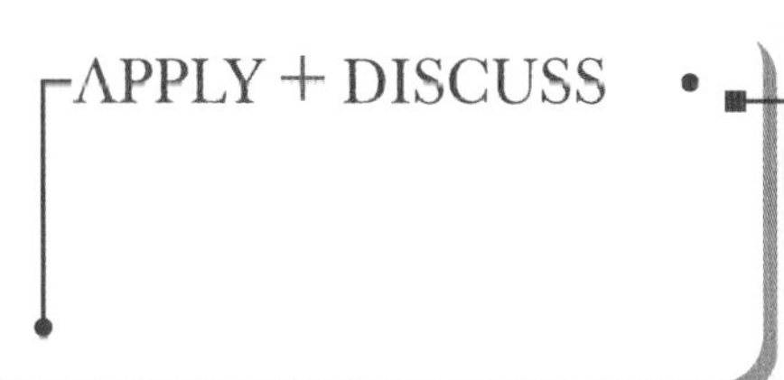

Apply + discuss combines visual imagery with questions to encourage higher order thinking, analysis and application of key concepts.

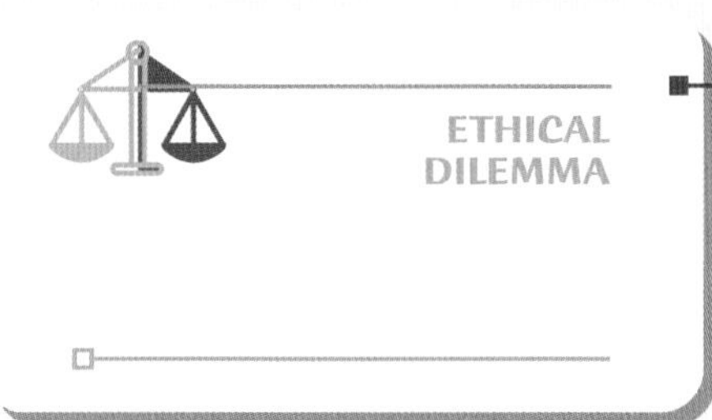

In each chapter, an ***ethical dilemma*** is posed to help you better understand and apply the APS code of ethics.

Chapter summaries

Each chapter concludes with a summary of the major points, which are organised under the learning objectives introduced at the start of the chapter.

End-of-chapter review, discussion and application questions

Each chapter contains review, discussion and application questions to test not only knowledge and understanding, but also higher order thinking and analysis in relation to key concepts.

Accompanying resources

Psychology: 3rd Australian and New Zealand Edition is accompanied by a comprehensive range of teaching and learning resources. These resources — including print-, software- and web-based materials — are integrated with the text and take an active learning approach to help build students' ability to think clearly and critically. They have been specifically designed to facilitate a dynamic and innovative learning environment for both lecturers and students.

For students

Cyberpsych multimedia

The *Cyberpsych* multimedia resource is available as an *option* to accompany the text. *Cyberpsych* contains extensive rich media content, authored by Dr Natalie Gasson (Curtin University), Dr Mara Blosfelds (Curtin University), Dr Vivienne Lewis (University of Canberra), Dr Greg Tooley (Deakin University), Dr Liam Hendry (University of Southern Queensland) and Dr Helen Correia (University of Western Sydney). The multimedia resources include:

- interactive modules
- concept animations
- Australian video cases
- international video clips provided by ScienCentral and selected for relevance by Dr Majella Albion (University of Southern Queensland).

Cyberpsych may be purchased as a stand-alone item, or packaged with the text.

An Interactive Approach to Writing Essays and Research Reports in Psychology

Also written by adapting text author Lorelle Burton, this is a practical and thorough overview of writing in the psychology discipline, based on the latest edition of the *APA Publication Manual*.

Study Guide

Written by the adapting text author Lorelle Burton and Alistair Younger (University of Ottawa), the *Study Guide* is the perfect companion to the text. It allows students to efficiently review materials, and to test and apply their knowledge. Each chapter in the *Study Guide* corresponds to a chapter in the text, and contains short-answer and multiple-choice self-test questions, fill-in exercises, crossword puzzles and applied activities. The *Study Guide* may be purchased as a stand-alone item, or packaged with the text.

For instructors

Instructor's Resource Guide

Prepared by Dr Kate Mulgrew (University of the Sunshine Coast), this comprehensive resource includes, for each text chapter:

- introductory statements/questions to stimulate thought about focus topics
- student learning objectives
- a brief chapter overview
- chapter outline (indicating the major headings in the chapter)
- extensive chapter notes, featuring enhancements such as lecture/tutorial activities to help extend students and stimulate their interest in the topic
- chapter summary
- key terms
- suggested responses for end-of-chapter questions, including review, discussion and application questions
- materials for additional class activity, including supplementary topics, practical class exercises or written projects, suggested web links and so on.

PowerPoint presentation slides

Prepared by Dr Tania Signal (Central Queensland University), these PowerPoint presentations contain an average of 30 slides per chapter and feature a combination of key concepts, images and problems from the textbook for use during lectures. The presentations are designed according to the organisation of the material in the textbook and can easily be customised to suit particular lectures.

Computerised test bank

Prepared by Dr Kate Mulgrew (University of the Sunshine Coast), this test bank is made up of approximately 2000 questions including true/false, multiple-choice, fill-in and essay questions. All questions include answers, page references and brief answer descriptions. They have been grouped as 'factual' (facts found directly in text), 'conceptual' (students utilise conceptual knowledge gained to work out an appropriate answer) or 'applied' (students apply their knowledge to a real-life situation). This allows for testing of students, in areas from fundamental knowledge and understanding through to higher order thinking skills, such as the application and analysis of key concepts.

Art files CD

All images from the text can be provided on CD-ROM for easy integration into lecturers' own resources.

Online resources for Course Management Systems

The resources for *Psychology: 3rd Australian and New Zealand Edition* are all available to be loaded into any contemporary online teaching and learning platform, such as BlackBoard, WebCT and Moodle. John Wiley & Sons Australia provides rich content based on the extensive range of text and accompanying resource material. Instructors have the option of uploading additional material and customising existing content to meet their needs.

Australian and New Zealand content at a glance

1 Psychology: the study of mental processes and behaviour

- Psychology as a field of scientific research in Australasia
- Australasian focus on education, training and accreditation issues in Psychology
- The national registration and accreditation scheme for psychologists in Australia
- Careers and professional associations in Australasia
- Psychologist services covered by Medicare in Australia
- A review of the Port Arthur tragedy
- Australian research on having a home advantage in elite sport
- An Australian forensic psychology research group examined
- Forensic psychology: perceptions on television shows versus reality
- Australian research on successful learning approaches

2 Research methods in psychology

- New Zealand road safety research
- Children's exposure to violence in electronic media — the Australian Government's inquiry
- Australian Psychological Society (APS) Code of Ethics
- Australian internet research
- Australian social media use research

3 Biological bases of mental life and behaviour

- A physical trauma account (David Keohane)
- Research on reading difficulties of Australian children
- An analysis of Steve Hooker's brain function at the height of competition
- The Morris brothers — Australian twins' sporting success

4 Sensation and perception

- Research on Australian cancer patients and their attitudes to pain management
- Sensory adaptation at Rotorua, New Zealand
- The Australian Bureau of Statistics' National Health Survey
- Poker player Joe Hachem and the eye as a cue
- Sensory positioning in sport — pole vault champion Steve Hooker
- AC/DC and the nature of sound
- Use of monocular cues for depth perception in a painting of the Gallipoli landing
- Australian research on visual cliff experiments with toddlers and water
- Graeme Clark and the cochlear implant
- Triathlete Emma Snowsill and pain perception
- Australian theme park rides and the proprioceptive senses
- The moon perception over Q1 Resort and Spa on the Gold Coast
- Linear perspective cues and the city of Adelaide

5 Consciousness

- The Strutt sisters: living with synaesthesia in an Australian community
- Australian research on synaesthesia
- Australian tennis player Bernard Tomic and the teenage body clock
- Findings of a study of Australian ecstasy users
- A New Zealand study about the effects of ecstasy on rats
- Australasian sleep studies on babies, children, students and adults
- Australian work patterns and statistics
- Australians' use of prescription drugs (sleeping tablets)
- The cost of insomnia to the Australian community
- Australian research on smoke alarm effectiveness
- Hypnosis in Australasia — entertainment versus science, registration requirements and its effectiveness as a source of pain relief
- Research on alcohol use
- Australian research on alcohol-related homicides
- Statistics on illicit drug use
- Young Australians' views about the environment and drug and alcohol use compared
- Australian research on pregnancy and drug use
- Statistics on hallucinogens
- Cannabis use among teenagers in New Zealand

6 Learning

- Successful New Zealand initiatives to decrease unsafe driving behaviour and graffiti
- How did crows learn to eat cane toads without being poisoned?
- Child learning in Aboriginal communities
- Australian research on needle phobias among chemotherapy patients
- Australian research on locus of control and relationship quality at work
- New Zealand research on autistic behaviour
- Findings of an Australian study examining punishment styles
- Two-process learning theory and fear appeals such as the Grim Reaper AIDS campaign on Australian television
- Discriminative stimuli and aggression on the AFL sporting field
- Research discussions about Aboriginal belief systems and individuality

- New Zealand research on long-term potentiation (LTP)
- Australian research on the association between maternal facial expressions and social learning among toddlers

7 Memory

- Australian entertainer Patti Newton's memory loss
- Missing for four days — a Brisbane manager's amnesia experience
- Findings from a Queensland study of primary school students' memory and cognitive functioning
- New Zealand research on the effects of drugs on the brain
- Australian research on shallow and deep learning (and processing) and achievement
- Australian research on teaching methods and assessment processes and shallow learning
- The Australian World Cup cricket team: a recall and recognition task
- Levels of processing in a professional theatre production: Australian actor Hugh Jackman
- New Zealand research on false memories
- Flashbulb memories and the death of Crocodile Hunter Steve Irwin
- An Australian example of the hierarchical organisation of information
- A discussion about recall in young children
- Child memory limitations study
- Research into the accuracy of child witness testimony
- Australian research on schemas and eyewitness testimony
- Australian research on forgetfulness during pregnancy: a link or a myth?

8 Thought and language

- Phonic reading instruction in Australian schools
- How do children learn to recognise spoken words?
- Semantics on the Australian television show *Talkin' 'bout your Generation*
- Analogies — Iraq and Vietnam war involvement for Australians
- Australian research on intelligence, gender and positive thinking as predictors of academic performance in youth
- Australian research on self-perceived efficacy of problem solving and productive coping strategies
- Australian language statistics
- An Australian mother's research into infant communication
- Australian research on tone perception and discrimination in infants
- Indigenous language use in Australia

9 Intelligence

- Intelligence types — Aboriginal trackers possess a unique form of intelligence
- Musical genius — pianist David Helfgott
- Monitoring standards in education — Western Australia's approach
- Research into the learning styles of Indigenous Australians
- Australian research on intellectual impairments
- Australian research on intellectual and physical impairments and class attendance
- Studies on emotional intelligence
- Royal commission into Aboriginal deaths in custody
- Intelligence tests (e.g. the Koori IQ Test)
- Australian research on emotional intelligence and leadership
- Melissa Wu — a gifted diver
- Australian research on giftedness in chess prodigies
- Singer–songwriter Missy Higgins and Wallaby halfback Will Genia: differences in intelligence examined (Gardiner's theory of multiple intelligences)
- Australian research on early risk factors for adolescent antisocial behaviour
- The search for new cognitive abilities and unique intelligence measurement approaches

10 Motivation and emotion

- *The Biggest Loser* — Alison Braun's story
- Solo sailor Jessica Watson — achieving a difficult goal
- Paralympian Kurt Fearnley — conquering the Kokoda Track
- Goal setting and expectancies — NRL player Preston Campbell as a role model for Indigenous Australian children
- Australian research using the Thematic Apperception Test to measure how travellers' unconscious motives influence interpretations and preferences
- Australian study on health and relationships, including adolescent sexual activity statistics
- New Zealand sexual activity statistics
- Social values in culturally diverse university students
- Attitudes on body shape
- Cultural perceptions of body type (Jennifer Hawkins as a modern standard of beauty)
- Australasian research and statistics on weight, dieting, obesity and health issues
- Australasian research into cross-cultural differences in eating and body image issues
- Studies from the Australian Research Centre in Sex, Health and Society
- Sexual health statistics for Australian students
- Cathy Freeman as an example of self-actualisation
- Child rearing practices of Australians
- Australasian research findings on murders
- Implicit egotism as a behavioural influence: an Australian study
- Motivation and emotion in Australian sport
- Australian supermodel Kristy Hinze and billionaire Jim Clark: a likely or unlikely duo?
- Cross-cultural study on the relationship between emotion and behaviour

11 Personality

- Steve and Mark Waugh and the 'Twinnies' — an analysis of the personalities of twins
- The Dunedin Multidisciplinary Health and Development Study findings on the correlation between behaviour traits in early childhood and adulthood

- Australian research on the association between self-efficacy and motivation to engage in physical activity
- Cricket Australia's decision to ban the Mexican wave and personality dynamics in a group setting
- Australia Day riots and the situational causes of behaviour
- Discussions on Eckermann's analysis of the notion of creation stories known as 'The Dreaming' in traditional Aboriginal societies

12 Physical and cognitive development

- The Wiggles and preschool children's preoperational thought processes
- Australian research contributions on infant sensory and perceptual development
- Australian research on the consequences of emotional neglect and physical abuse in childhood
- Cultural diversity, the 'Aussie' beach culture and the reliability of cross-cultural studies
- Challenges for the Australian Government in ensuring Indigenous mental health needs are effectively met
- Australian research comparing theory of mind development in children with a disability and children without a disability
- A maternal influence on theory of mind development
- Australian research on language development and theory of mind
- Australian study on Foetal Alcohol Syndrome
- Hockey player Jamie Dwyer: psychomotor speed and ageing in an elite athlete
- Research into motor development in Indigenous children
- Study of behaviour problems in Australian primary school children
- Research on memory impairment during pregnancy
- Dementia and the ageing population
- New Zealand research on memory problems among people with Alzheimer's disease
- Dementia rates in some rural and remote Indigenous communities versus general population rates
- Dorothy De Low: the experience of ageing in an Australian centenarian
- Longitudinal study of ageing in Adelaide

13 Social development

- An Australian teenager's experience with cyber bullying
- An ongoing inequity in life opportunities between Indigenous versus non-Indigenous populations in Australia and measures to close the gap
- An international comparison on life expectancies
- Research on attachment in Aboriginal children
- Western Australian research on children and their concept of community
- Australian research on maternal sensitivity in the caregiving role as a determinant of infant attachment security
- Parental employment and use of childcare as influences of attachment formation
- An Australian longitudinal study on maternal attitudes and the development of behavioural problems during childhood
- Australasian studies on temperament and later life
- Burns victim Jandamarra O'Shane: resiliency after a traumatic childhood experience
- Australian research on young children's concepts of community
- Research on age and the value placed on different relationships by Australians
- Australian research on the value of independence during adolescence
- Cultural variations in temperament
- Australian researchers' strategies to combat cyber bullying
- TOMNET and the Toowoomba Flexi School: an intergenerational mentoring problem
- Culture and social learning: reactions to Julia Gillard's rise to power as Australia's first female Prime Minister
- Australian research on risk factors for body dissatisfaction
- Moral values among fathers and sons in Australia's media dynasties
- Discussion and comparison of teaching strategies for boys and girls
- Research into socialisation and learning in Aboriginal cultures
- Australasian statistics on marriage and divorce

14 Health, stress and coping

- Geoff Huegill — weight loss, mental toughness and winning in the pool
- Catastrophes in the Asia–Pacific region, including the 2011 Queensland floods, Cyclone Yasi and Cyclone Larry, the Victorian bushfire crisis and the 2010 and 2011 Christchurch earthquakes — as well as the Japanese earthquake, tsunami, and nuclear crisis
- New Zealand and Australian HIV/AIDS statistics
- Trends in major causes of deaths in Australia in recent history
- A ranking of leading underlying specific causes of death for men and women in Australia
- Australian research on the rising prevalence of diabetes
- A review supporting health psychology in Australia
- Australian and New Zealand overweight and obesity statistics, including a comparison of rates for at-risk groups
- Fruit and vegetable consumption among Australian children
- Environmental contributors to obesity: a reflection on traditional and Western approaches adopted by Aboriginal groups in Australia
- The Walking School Bus program in Australian communities
- Australian Government health initiatives
- Breast cancer: risk factors, screening statistics and publicity generated by Australian celebrities and charities
- Government screening programs for bowel and cervical cancer in Australia
- Australian smoking statistics
- Australian alcohol use statistics and associated health issues and costs
- Sexually transmitted diseases in Australia: statistics and treatment
- Associations between self-assessed health and other health indicators
- Indigenous and non-Indigenous health in Australia: a comparison and the specific targets set to close the gap
- Skin cancer in Australia

- The Condom Tree program in the Kimberley region, Western Australia
- Private health insurance statistics
- The impact of random breath testing programs on driver behaviour
- Australian research on student transitions to university
- The Dunedin Multidisciplinary Health and Development Study findings on work-related stress and the correlation between children's television viewing habits and health issues
- The Australian National Children's Nutrition and Physical Activity Survey: findings on children's real versus recommended time spent engaging in screen-based activities
- Government health campaigns — recent Australian tobacco campaigns and the earlier 'Life. Be in it.' campaign
- Swine flu cases in Australia
- Australasian study on performance at school — Maori, Aboriginal and migrant students

15 Psychological disorders

- A former NSW policewoman's experience with post-traumatic stress disorder
- Seasonal affective disorder in tropical north Queensland
- The lifetime prevalence of mental disorders among Australians
- Lifetime prevalence for anxiety disorders — an Australian gender comparison
- Illicit drug use statistics and the cost of alcohol misuse to the Australian public
- James and Erica Packer and evolutionary views about mate selection
- The cost of weight loss initiatives for Australians and New Zealanders
- Medicare statistics on psychologist consultations in Australia
- Bulimia nervosa and other eating disorder statistics
- New Zealand research into the cognitive emotional experiences of women with eating disorders
- Personality and addiction: the connection for Australian actor Matthew Newton
- Andrew Johns (former NRL star) and his battle with bipolar disorder
- Indigenous spirituality
- Australian attention-deficit hyperactivity disorder (ADHD) statistics
- Schizophrenia in Australia
- Australian anxiety and depression statistics
- Depression among Australian ethnic minority groups and the relationship between culture and treatment for mental health issues
- New Zealand research on schizophrenia and child abuse
- Bipolar disorder in the Australian population
- Do Australians have unique psychological characteristics?
- High-risk groups for mental health issues
- Colonisation — the psychological legacy for Indigenous groups

16 Treatment of psychological disorders

- Mental health statistics, including the 10 mental health issues most commonly managed by GPs
- Mental health issues among Indigenous groups in Australia and New Zealand
- Use of services by Indigenous groups in Australia and New Zealand
- Mental illness treatment statistics
- Use of antidepressants by age group in Australia
- Self-help groups in Australia and New Zealand
- The Medicare Benefits Scheme program and access to mental health services in Australia
- The use of electroconvulsive therapy in Australia
- Post-traumatic stress disorder and drug use problems
- The Royal Australian and New Zealand College of Psychiatrists' findings on treating depression with psychosis
- Australia's national depression initiative 'beyondblue'
- Study on drug treatment services for ethnic communities in Victoria
- Comparative study on the respective drug policies of Australia and the United States
- New Zealand study on the most effective patient–health care professional relationships
- Clinical psychologists — roles in the workplace
- Scientist–practitioner model in Australia
- The Triple P — Positive Parenting Program in practice at an Australian Parenting and Family Support Centre

17 Attitudes and social cognition

- The politics of asylum seekers — 'boat people' — arriving in Australia
- New Zealand study of text messaging (SMS)
- Australian research on conservation psychology
- A New Zealand academic's perspective on persuasion and climate change
- An Australian academic's experience growing up in Africa: distinguishing between attitudes and stereotypes
- Ingroups and outgroups: racial tension at the Australian Open
- Why do some people become so parochial during rugby league's annual State of Origin series?
- The Australian Socceroos' poor World Cup performance and the public backlash: an example of the 'us-versus-them' divide
- Bicultural (Maori–Pakeha) research in New Zealand
- Stereotypes in Australasia
- Fatalism and emergency preparations: an earlier study of attitudes towards earthquakes in New Zealand
- Contemporary New Zealand research on preparation as a variable in the 2010 and 2011 Christchurch earthquakes
- The self-serving bias in play at the Melbourne Cup
- Elle 'The Body' Macpherson and self-monitoring in society

18 Interpersonal processes

- Situational variables in practice: an Australian woman's decision to save a swimmer near a circling white pointer shark
- The power of physical attractiveness: did looks help celebrity chef Curtis Stone achieve success?
- Australian online dating statistics and the role of social media as Cupid for many modern couples

- The top five criteria for finding a partner and gender differences in mate selection
- Australian research on the leading causes of relationship breakdowns
- Australian research on positive and negative correlations between both attachment and conflict resolution styles and emotional intelligence and satisfaction in long-term marital relationships
- Gift-giving as big business in Australia and theories of altruism
- Altruism during the 2011 Queensland floods
- Altruism after the tragic Bali bombings
- Research on bystander interventions during drug overdoses
- The media habits of Australian youths
- The impact of violence in the media on children
- Low self-esteem and aggression: is there a link? A study including samples of New Zealand adolescents and college students
- Australian and New Zealand codes of ethics for the profession of psychology
- Discussion of the actions of Australian Boer War soldier Harry 'Breaker' Morant
- New Zealand study on the mating preferences of university students
- Australian Institute of Family Studies research on creating and maintaining long and enduring marriages
- Relationship education programs in Australia
- Cross-cultural murder rate data for Canada, the United States, Australia and New Zealand
- Study of the attachment styles and conflict resolution patterns of long-term heterosexual couples
- New Zealand research into the societal aspects of physical and sexual abuse to better understand violence against women
- Antisocial group behaviour at the Star Hotel in NSW

19 Cross-cultural and Indigenous psychology

This entire chapter focuses on cross-cultural and Indigenous psychology in Australia and New Zealand, including:

- The National Indigenous Reform Agreement and closing the gap between Indigenous and non-Indigenous Australians
- A feature on Tania Major, Indigenous advocate/campaigner and former Young Australian of the Year
- The role of the Australian Indigenous Psychologists Association
- Australian and New Zealand birth statistics
- New Zealand ethnic group statistics
- Depth perception in Torres Strait Islanders
- Australian Department of Immigration and Citizenship statistics
- The survival of Indigenous languages in Australia
- The impact of multiculturalism on society
- Cross-cultural self-esteem studies
- Spirituality and functionality in traditional art: a defining feature of Aboriginal culture
- The haka in traditional Maori culture
- Features of Australian culture
- The *Building bridges: learning from experts* project
- Australian Indigenous cultures — Aboriginal peoples and Torres Strait Islanders
- Indigenous cultures in Aotearoa/New Zealand
- The individualist–collectivist dichotomy in an Australian school context
- A discussion of the 2011 Department of Education and Training (Queensland) guidelines titled 'Embedding Aboriginal and Torres Strait Islander perspectives in schools'
- Findings of an Australian study comparing the performance on cognitive tests of people from both English-speaking backgrounds and non-English speaking backgrounds
- Cultural bias and Indigenous and non-Indigenous Australian students' performances on IQ tests
- The mental health and wellbeing needs of refugees and asylum seekers and the presence of xenophobic and hostile attitudes towards these groups in some Australian communities
- International student statistics for Australia and New Zealand
- Cultural awareness training: an expert's opinions on best practice
- New Zealand research into Maori psychology and a discussion of a *New Zealand Journal of Psychology* special feature edition on Maori psychological issues
- Culture clashes on the sporting field in an Indian cricket tour of Australia
- The 2005 Cronulla riots in Sydney
- Discursive psychology research in New Zealand on preventing racism by understanding the power of conversation
- The Australian Government's apology to the Stolen Generation
- Discussion of the award-winning Australian film about the Stolen Generation, *Rabbit-Proof Fence*
- Indigenous health statistics
- *The Tracker* and *Once Were Warriors*: stories about minority cultures within mainstream Australia and New Zealand
- The Australian Government's intervention into the running of Aboriginal communities in the Northern Territory
- Comparison of Indigenous versus non-Indigenous Australian suicide statistics
- Indigenous psychology courses in Australia
- Culturally competent psychologists from Australia and their assistance with catastrophes and natural disasters

Acknowledgements

I am especially grateful to the many academics from Australia and New Zealand who provided the insightful **Commentary**, **One step further** and **A Global Vista** features contained in the text. These contributions greatly enhance each chapter's content.

Commentary contributors (in order of chapter) — Dr Andrea Chester, RMIT; Professor Donald Hine, University of New England; Dr Tony Marks, University of New England; Professor Simon Crowe, La Trobe University; Professor Peter Wenderoth, Macquarie University; Professor Kevin McConkey, University of Newcastle; Professor Ottmar Lipp, University of Queensland; Professor Stephan Lewandowsky, University of Western Australia; Professor Catherine Best, University of Western Sydney; Dr Christine Kitamura, University of Western Sydney; Professor Con Stough, Swinburne University of Technology; Professor Timothy C. Bates, University of Edinburgh; Professor Peter Terry, University of Southern Queensland; Professor Greg Boyle, Bond University; Professor Janet Fletcher, University of Western Australia; Professor Susan Paxton, La Trobe University; Professor Keithia Wilson, Griffith University; Associate Professor Alf Lizzio, Griffith University; Professor David Kavanagh, Queensland University of Technology; Professor Matthew Sanders, University of Queensland; Dr Niki Harre, Auckland University; Professor Stuart C. Carr, Massey University; Professor Dennis M. McInerney, The Hong Kong Institute of Education; and Arief Liem, University of Sydney.

One step further contributors (in order of chapter) — Dr Sharon Casey, Deakin University; Dr Kenneth Mavor, Australian National University; Dr Nick Burns, University of Adelaide; Associate Professor Ulrich Schall, University of Newcastle; Associate Professor Catherine Stevens, University of Western Sydney; Professor Dorothy Bruck, Victoria University; Dr Steve Provost, Southern Cross University; Professor Craig Speelman, Edith Cowan University; Dr Damian Birney, University of New South Wales; Dr Richard Roberts, Center for New Constructs, Educational Testing Service (USA); Dr Guy Curtis, Murdoch University; Dr Carolyn MacCann, University of Sydney; Professor Jan Piek, Curtin University; Dr Julie-Ann Pooley, Edith Cowan University; Professor John Toumbourou, Deakin University; Professor Gordon Parker, University of New South Wales; Professor Patrick McGorry, University of Melbourne; Professor Louise Sharpe, University of Sydney; Dr Stefania Paolini, University of Newcastle; Dr Bruce Findlay, Swinburne University of Technology; and Pat Dudgeon, University of Western Australia.

In addition, Emeritus Professor Graham R. Richardson, University of the Sunshine Coast provided a **Global Vista** feature for chapter 19.

My sincere thanks also to my colleagues who have produced some fantastic additional resources for both lecturers and students: Dr Natalie Gasson, Curtin University; Dr Mara Blosfelds, Curtin University; Dr Vivienne Lewis, University of Canberra; Dr Greg Tooley, Deakin University; Dr Helen Correia, University of Western Sydney; Dr Liam Hendry, University of Southern Queensland; Dr Majella Albion, University of Southern Queensland; Dr Tania Signal, Central Queensland University; and Dr Kate Mulgrew, University of the Sunshine Coast.

Finally, I'd like to thank the team at John Wiley & Sons, including John Coomer, Jacqui Belesky, Dan Logovik, Emma Knight, Belinda Rose, Jo Hawthorne and Delia Sala for all their hard work on the project.

Dr Lorelle Burton
May 2011

The authors and publisher would like to thank the following copyright holders, organisations and individuals for their permission to reproduce copyright material in this book.

Images

• © Shutterstock: p. 3 (middle left)/Vibrant Image Studio; p. 7 (bottom left)/R_R; p. 19 (bottom right)/Monkey Business Images; p. 19 (middle right)/Thorsten Rust; p. 22 (middle left)/Monkey Business Images; p. 25 (middle right)/Leah-Anne Thompson; p. 34 (middle left)/Dean Mitchell; p. 41 (middle left)/Marcin Balcerzak; p. 42 (middle left)/light-poet; p. 44 (middle left)/Piotr Marcinski; p. 66 (top left)/Iculig; p. 83 (top right)/Lynne Carpenter; p. 106 (bottom left)/Elena Elisseeva; p. 130 (bottom left)/lev dolgachov; p. 145 (bottom right)/Perutskyi Petro; p. 145 (middle right)/Kim Reinick; p. 155 (top right)/Ji Zhou; p. 184 (middle left)/szefei; p. 185 (bottom left)/Anelina; p. 188 (top left)/Konstantin Chagin; p. 198 (bottom left)/Yuri Arcurs; p. 201 (bottom right)/Ramona Heim; p. 203 (top right)/Yuri Arcurs; p. 210 (middle left)/Piotr Marcinski; p. 212 (top left)/Oliver Hoffmann; p. 220 (bottom left)/Nate A.; p. 221 (middle right)/Yuri Arcurs; p. 222 (middle left)/Art_man; p. 228 (bottom left)/orionmystery@flickr; p. 235 (bottom right)/Andrejs Pidjass; p. 259 (middle right)/Andrey Chmelyov; p. 263 (middle right)/Karen Roach; p. 267 (top right)/Charlie Hutton; p. 267 (top right)/Claudiu Mihai Badea; p. 267 (top right)/Davor Ratkovic; p. 267 (top right)/Nataliia Natykach; p. 274 (top left)/S.Borisov; p. 286 (bottom right)/Rob Marmion; p. 297 (middle right)/Golbay; p. 297 (top left)/Miau; p. 301 (bottom left)/Leah-Anne Thompson; p. 301 (bottom right)/Susan Flashman; p. 314 (middle left)/Phil Date; p. 325 (middle right)/Lev Dolgachov; p. 327 (middle right)/Lana K; p. 328 (bottom left)/Andrew Chin; p. 331 (bottom right)/Petro Feketa; p. 341 (middle left)/Otna Ydur; p. 345 (middle right [bottom])/Alexander Raths; p. 345 (middle right [top])/Sudheer Sakthan; p. 358 (bottom left)/Voronin76; p. 362 (top left)/tomas del amo; p. 364 (bottom left)/Neo Edmund; p. 381 (middle right)/Thor Jorgen Udvang; p. 382 (top left)/Tracy Whiteside; p. 382 (top middle)/Shawn Hempel; p. 389 (top right)/Tish1; p. 392 (top left)/michaeljung; p. 394 (middle left)/vgstudio; p. 395 (top right)/Zdorov Kirill Vladimirovich; p. 407 (middle right)/Yuri Arcurs; p. 408 (top left)/Fred Goldstein; p. 412 (top left)/Monkey Business Images; p. 422 (top left)/Liv Rriis-Larsen; p. 433 (middle right)/Belinda Pretorius; p. 438 (middle left)/VojtechVlk; p. 456 (middle left)/Melanie DeFazio; p. 465 (middle right)/T-Design; p. 466 (middle left)/Songquan Deng; p. 476 (top right)/Losevsky Pavel; p. 479 (top right)/Lev Dolgachov; p. 481 (middle right)/Maresol; p. 502 (bottom right)/Monkey Business Images; p. 506 (middle left)/michaeljung; p. 506 (middle right)/Henk Bentlage; p. 517 (bottom right)/Denis Nata; p. 518 (middle left)/Norman Pogson; p. 519 (bottom right)/Monkey Business Images; p. 521 (top right)/Miroslav K; p. 538 (middle left)/Konstantin Sutyagin; p. 548 (bottom left)/Junial Enterprises; p. 549 (top left)/James Peragine; p. 556 (middle left)/auremar; p. 557 (bottom right)/Monkey Business Images; p. 560 (middle left)/Peter Elvidge; p. 587 (middle right)/Elena Elisseeva; p. 589 (middle right)/iofoto; p. 590 (bottom left)/Liudmila P. Sundikova; p. 593 (top right)/Pinkcandy; p. 600 (middle right)/Olena Mykhaylova; p. 601 (top right)/Cameramannz; p. 608 (top left)/Monkey Business Images; p. 636 (bottom left)/Jackie Smithson; p. 641 (bottom right)/mikeledray; p. 654 (middle left)/sniegirova mariia; p. 659 (middle right)/Lindsay Schoon; p. 670 (top left)/Anatoliy Samara; p. 692 (bottom right)/Poznyakov; p. 697 (middle right)/Kirill P; p. 702 (middle left)/Alex Staroseltsev; p. 707 (top right)/mamahoohooba; p. 708 (bottom left)/wavebreakmedia Ltd; p. 721 (bottom left)/Kzenon; p. 734 (bottom left)/Phil Date; p. 735 (middle right)/Sean De Burca; p. 738 (bottom left)/Orchidflower; p. 741 (middle right)/StockLite; p. 744 (bottom left)/USTIN; p. 758 (bottom left)/Losevsky Pavel; p. 764 (bottom left)/RoxyFer; p. 768 (top left)/Monkey Business Images; p. 786 (top left)/cjpdesigns; • © The Kobal Collection:p. 4 (middle left)/Hollywood Pictures/Ron Phillips; p. 28 (bottom left)/CBS-TV/Staedler, Lance; p. 107 (middle right)/Summit Entertainment/Danny Rothenberg; p. 108 (bottom left)/Focus Features/David Lee; p. 258 (bottom left)/Universal; p. 351 (middle left)/United Artists; p. 525 (top right)/Polygram Australia/Australian Film Finance/Elise Lockwood; p. 626 (top left)/Dreamworks/Universal/Eli Reed;

p. 753 (middle right)/ITV Global; p. 761 (top right)/S. Australia Film Corp./Australian Film Commission; p. 807 (top right)/Mirimax/Dimension Films; • © Photolibrary: p. 6 (middle)/SPL/Department of Cognitive Neurology; p. 17 (top right)/SuperStock; p. 46 (top left)/Stockbroker: p. 56 (bottom left)/Oxford Scientific/Jackie Le Fevre; p. 61 (middle right)/SPL; p. 62 (top left)/NIH/Science Source; p. 62 (top right)/NIH/Science Source; p. 90 (middle left)/SPL/Manfred Kage; p. 90 (top right)/SPL/CNRI; p. 130 (top left)/jspix jspix; p. 134 (top left); p. 154 (bottom left)/Corbis; p. 189 (top right)/Photononstop/Anais Mai; p. 227 (top right)/JW.Alker; p. 301 (top right)/SPL/David Gifford; p. 348 (top left)/Image Source; p. 390 (middle right); p. 393 (bottom right)/B. Boissonnet; p. 446 (bottom left)/Antoine Juliette; p. 457 (bottom left)/D H Webster; p. 464 (bottom right)/panoramaMedia; p. 472 (middle)/Science Photo Library/Dr G Moscoso; p. 472 (middle left)/David Phillips; p. 483 (middle right)/Photo Researchers; p. 504 (middle left)/Stockbroker; p. 579 (middle left) com/James Stevenson; p. 741 (top right)/Dom Emerson; • © Getty Images: p. 7 (top right)/Fotoseach; p. 8 (middle left)/Imagno; p. 10 (top left)/Hulton Archive/Stringer; p. 12 (top left)/Clemens Bilan/Stringer/AFP; p. 13 (bottom right)/Bachrach; p. 50 (middle left)/National Institute of Health/Martin Rogers; p. 111 (middle right)/Mark Dadswell; p. 120 (top left)/Matthew Lewis; p. 167 (top left)/Jeremy Woodhouse; p. 234 (top left)/Time & Life Pictures/Nina Leen; p. 247 (middle right)/Popperfoto; p. 248 (bottom left)/Penny Tweedie/The Image Bank; p. 271 (middle right)/Mark Nolan/Stringer; p. 276 (top left)/William West/AFP; p. 316 (top left)/Magictorch; p. 321 (middle right)/Ashlee Ralla; p. 360 (bottom right)/Bradley Kanaris; p. 402 (bottom left)/Sean Garnsworthy; p. 415 (bottom right)/Stone; p. 415 (middle right)/Stone; p. 427 (middle right)/Roger Viollet Collection; p. 429 (top left)/Steve Granitz/WireImage; p. 451 (top right)/Lori Moffett/Bloomberg; p. 472 (middle right)/The Image Bank/Steve Allen; p. 477 (bottom right)/Tom Raymond; p. 495 (top right)/for Sydney 2009 World Masters Games/Craig Golding; p. 505 (bottom left)/Time Life Pictures/Nina Leen; p. 561 (top right)/WireImage/JAB Promotions; p. 575 (middle right)/Fred Duval; p. 585 (bottom right)/Nicole Alayne/HAMMERMEISTER/AFP; p. 653 (middle left)/Manchan/Digital Vision; p. 660 (middle left)/Ian Waldie; p. 711 (middle right)/Handout; p. 739 (top right); p. 791 (bottom right)/Hamish Blair; p. 815 (bottom right)/Phil Walter; p. 816 (bottom left)/Phil Walter; • © Corbis Australia: p. 16 (top left)/Roger Ressmeyer; p. 20 (top left)/Bettmann; p. 60 (bottom right)/Mika; p. 95 (bottom right)/Paul Taylor; p. 167 (bottom left)/Archivo Iconografico, S.A./Giotto di Bondone; p. 171 (middle left)/Morton Beebe; p. 171 (middle right)/Morton Beebe; p. 205 (bottom right)/Joel Sartore/National Geographic Society; p. 326 (top left)/Pete Souza/White House/Handout/CNP; p. 376 (middle left)/Scott Stulberg; p. 384 (top left)/Stonehill; p. 390 (bottom right)/Bettmann; p. 430 (top left)/Katy Winn; p. 496 (top left)/Gabriela Hasbun/Aurora Photos; p. 667 (middle right)/David Woods; p. 728 (top right)/Edward Le Poulin; p. 758 (middle left)/Oliver Rossi; p. 821 (bottom right)/Christine Schneider; p. 825 (top right)/George Steinmetz; • © Copyright Clearance Center: p. 17 (bottom right)/Cave, C. B (1997). Very long-lasting priming in picture naming. *Psychological Science, 8*, 322–325. Reprinted by permission of SAGE Publications; p. 187 (bottom left)/Macdonald, A. W.,Cohen, J. D., Stenger, V. A. & Carter, C. S., (2000). Dissociating the role of the dorsolateral prefrontal and anterior cingulate cortex in cognitive control. *Science, 288*, 1835–1838. Reprinted with permission from AAAS; p. 277 (top right)/Bahrick, Hall & Berger (1993). Maintenance of foreign language vocabulary and the spacing effect. *Psychological Science, 4*, 319. Reprinted by permission of SAGE Publications; p. 285 (top right)/Adapted from Bahrick, Hall and Berger (1996). Accuracy and distortion in memory for high school grades. *Psychological Science, 7*, 266. © 1996 by SAGE. Reprinted by permission of SAGE Publications; p. 306 (top left)/Wason, P. C. (1968). Reasoning about a rule. *Quarterly Journal of Experimental Psychology, 20*, 273–281. Reprinted by permission of the Taylor & Francis Group, www.informaworld.com; p. 316 (bottom left)/Adapted from Rumelhart, D. (1984). Schemata and the cognitive system. In R. S. Wyler & T. K. Strull (eds.), *Handbook of Social Cognition*, 1st edn. Reproduced with permission from Lawrence Erlbaum Associates via Copyright Clearance Center; p. 355 (top right)/Adapted from Duncan, J., Seitz, R., Kolodny, J., Bor, D., Herzog, H., Ahmed, A., Newell, F.N., & Emslie, H. (2000). A neural basis for general intelligence. *Science, 289*, 457–460. Reprinted with permission from AAAS; p. 393 (top left)/Butler, C.A. (1976). New data about female sexual response. *Journal of Sex & Marital Therapy 2*(1, Jan). Reprinted with permission from Taylor & Francis Ltd via Copyright Clearance Center; p. 396 (middle left)/Gladue, B. A., Green, R., & Hellman, R. E. (1984). Neuroendocrine response to estrogen and sexual orientation. *Science, 225*, 1496. Reprinted with permission from AAAS via Rightslink; p. 405 (top right)/Ekman, P., et al. (1983). Automatic nervous system activity distinguishes among emotions. *Science, 221*, 1209. Reprinted with permission from AAAS via Rightslink; p. 408 (middle)/Fischer, K. W., Shaver, P. R., & Carnochan, P. (1990). How emotions develop and how they organize development. *Cognition and Emotion, 4*, 90. Reproduced with permission from Lawrence Erlbaum Associates via Copyright Clearance Centre; p. 410 (middle left)/LeDoux, J. E (1995). Emotion: Clues from the brain. *Annual Review of Psychology, 46*, 225; p. 416 (middle left)/Buss, D. M., Larsen, R., Westen, D., & Semmelroth, J. (1992). Sex differences in jealousy: Evolution, physiology and psychology. *Psychological Science, 3*, 251–255. © 1992 by SAGE. Reprinted by permission of SAGE Publications; p. 480 (bottom right)/A.N. Meltzoff & M.K. Moore (1977). Imitation of facial and manual gestures by human neonates. *Science, 198*, 75–78. Reprinted with permision from AAAS via Rightslink; p. 480 (middle left)/Meltzoff, A. N., & Borton, R.W. (1979). Intermodal matching by human neonates, *Nature, 282*. Reprinted by permission from Macmillan Publishers Ltd; p. 489 (bottom right)/Fry, A., & Hale, S. (1996). Processing speed, working memory and fluid intelligence: Evidence for a developmental cascade, *Psychological Science, 7*, 328. © 1996 by SAGE. Reprinted by permission of SAGE Publications; p. 531 (middle left)/Darley, J. M. & Shultz, T. R. (1990). Moral rules: Their content and acquisition. *Annual Review of Psychology, 41*, 532; p. 561 (bottom right)/Kopelman, P. G. (2000). Obesity as a medical problem. *Nature, 404*. Reprinted by permission from Macmillan Publishers Ltd; p. 562 (middle)/Friedman, J. M. (2000). Obesity in the new millennium. *Nature, 404*. Reprinted by permission from Macmillan Publishers Ltd; p. 662 (top left)/Adapted from Ventis, et al. (2001). Using humour in systematic desensitization to reduce fear. *The Journal of General Psychology, 128*(2), 241–53. Reprinted by permission of Taylor & Francis Group, http://www.informaworld.com; • © Cook, Dr Lawrence: p. 20 (top middle)/J. A. Bishop & L. M. Cook; p. 20 (top right)/Dr. Laurence Cook; • © Todd Dekay: p. 23 (middle)/Based on Dekay, T. (1988). *An evolutionary-computational approach to social cognition: Grandparental investment as a test case* (Unpublished doctoral dissertation). University of Michigan; p. 23 (top)/Based on DeKay, T. (1988). *An evolutionary-computational approach to social cognition: Grandparental investment as a test case* (Unpublished doctoral dissertation). University of Michigan; • © Newspix: p. 25 (top right)/Michael Klein; p. 47 (middle right)/Noel Kessel; p. 49 (top right)/Nicole Garmston; p. 88 (top left); p. 148 (top left)/Adam Smith; p. 148 (top right)/Adam Ward; p. 150 (bottom left)/Katrina Tepper; p. 160 (bottom left)/David Sproule; p. 169 (bottom right)/Mike Batterham; p. 171 (middle left)/Joanna Robinson; p. 199 (middle right)/George Salpigtidis; p. 237 (middle right); p. 239 (middle right)/Sarah Reed; p. 278 (bottom left)/Brett Hartwig; p. 281 (bottom right)/Chris Hyde; p. 285 (middle left)/Rob Maccoll; p. 285 (middle right)/Steve Pohlner; p. 324 (top left)/Rob Baird; p. 340 (middle left)/Jodie Campbell; p. 342 (middle left)/Stephen Harman; p. 374 (middle left)/Allen Stewart; p. 379 (top right)/Anthony Reginato; p. 387 (bottom left)/Sam Rosewarne; p. 400 (middle left); p. 424 (bottom left)/John Wilson; p. 446 (top left)/Phil Hillyard; p. 449 (middle right)/Braden Fastier; p. 470 (bottom left)/Hilton Stone; p. 488 (top left)/Nellie Ireland; p. 511 (middle right)/Veronica Sagredo; p. 513 (bottom right)/Brooke Whatnall; p. 550 (bottom left)/Steve Pohlner; p. 550 (bottom right)/Phil Hillyard; p. 564 (top left)/Raoul Kochanowski; p. 578 (bottom left)/Leon Meade; p. 579 (middle right)/

Cameron Tandy; p. 585 (middle right)/Amos Aikman; p. 694 (middle left)/Colin Murty; p. 704 (middle left)/Brad Hunter; p. 715 (top left)/Peter Wallis: p. 715 (top right)/Jay Town; p. 716 (top left)/Craig Greenhill; p. 718 (bottom left)/Mark Mitchell; p. 719 (middle right)/Philip Norrish; p. 720 (top left)/Craig Borrow; p. 736 (top left)/Ken Matts; p. 747 (middle right)/Ian Baker; p. 770 (bottom left)/Gary Graham; p. 778 (middle left)/Chris Hyde; p. 780 (middle left)/Cairns Post; p. 808 (top middle)/Phil Hillyard; p. 814 (middle right); • © Australian Psychological Society: p. 29 (middle right); • © New Zealand Psychological Society: p. 29 (bottom right); • © John Wiley & Sons, Australia: p. 30 (top left)/Renee Bryon; p. 127 (bottom left)/Renee Bryon; p. 298 (top left)/Renee Bryon; p. 309 (middle right); p. 310 (top left)/Vikki Steele; p. 700 (middle left)/Renee Bryon; p. 763 (top right)/The Estate of Sara Love; • © iStockphoto: p. 59 (top right)/Daniel Rodriguez; p. 60 (bottom left)/Darrell Scott; p. 104 (middle left)/Carlos Santa Maria; p. 352 (bottom left)/Kerrie Kerr; p. 467 (bottom right)/pamspix; p. 485 (top right)/Isabelle Limbach; p. 570 (middle left)/Brian Toro; p. 634/kickers; p. 652 (middle right)/Alexander Raths; p. 671 (top right)/ilkeryuksel; p. 693 (middle right)/Varvara Mikhaleva; p. 737 (top right)/franckreporter; p. 779 (middle left)/Bartosz Hadyniak; p. 783 (top left)/best-photo; p. 796 (middle left)/Steve Debenport; p. 819 (middle right)/mphotoi; • © D'Esposito, Professor Mark: p. 62 (bottom left)/Courtesy Mark D'Esposito, University of California, Berkeley; • © Twitter: p. 63 (middle); • © Clatworthy family: p. 87 (bottom right); p. 155 (middle right); p. 287 (middle right); p. 509 (middle right); p. 517 (bottom left); • © Picture Media: p. 94 (middle left)/Reuters/Lucas Jackson; • © Eidelberg, Dr David: p. 95 (top right [left])/Courtesy Dr David Eidelberg — NorthShore LIJ Health System, New York University Medical College; p. 95 (top right [right])/Courtesy Dr David Eidelberg– The Feinstein Institute for Medical Research, North Shore LIJ Health System; • © W. H. Freeman: p. 100 (middle)/Adapted from Kolb, B. @ Whishaw, I. Q. (1996). *Fundamentals of human neuropsychology*. W.H. Freeman and Company. Used with permission; • © W. W. Norton: p. 100 (bottom left)/Gleitman, H., Reisberg, D. & Cross, J (2007). *Psychology,* 7th edn, p. 88 (fig. 3.8); p. 106 (middle)/Gleitman, H., Reisberg, D. & Cross, J (2007). *Psychology*, 7th edn, p. 89 (fig. 3.12); p. 308 (middle left)/Gazzaniga, M. S., Halpern, D. & Heatherton, T. F. (2009). *Psychological science,* 3rd edn, (fig. 8.16); p. 310 (middle)/Gazzaniga, M. S., Halpern, D. & Heatherton, T. F. (2009). *Psychological science,* 3rd edn; p. 443 (top right)/Gazzaniga, M. & Heatherton, T. F. (2003). Psychological science: the mind, brain and behaviour, p. 509 (fig. 15.11); • © AAP Image: p. 101 (top right)/Mark Graham; p. 111 (middle right [right])/AFP Photo/Adrian Dennis; p. 114 (middle right)/Harvard Medical School/©AP/Wide World Photos; p. 137 (middle right)/AP Photo/Joe Cavaretta; p. 158 (bottom left)/Alan Porritt; p. 158 (bottom right)/Alan Porritt; p. 166 (top left)/AP Photo/Shizuo Kambayashi; p. 197 (bottom right)/Dean Lewins; p. 260 (top left)/Adrian Buman; p. 349 (bottom right)/AP Photo/Domenico Stinellis; p. 351 (middle right)/AP Photo/Barton Glasser; p. 360 (bottom left)/Marilia Ogayar; p. 390 (bottom left)/Tracey Nearmy; p. 416 (middle left)/Supplied by the Lantern Group; p. 424 (middle left)/AFP Photo/Manan Vatsyayana; p. 424 (middle right)/Sergio Dionisio; p. 492 (middle left)/Hockey Australia/Grant Treeby; p. 527 (top right)/POOL/Alan Porritt; p. 532 (middle left)/Dean Lewins; p. 566 (top left)/Dave Hunt; p. 569 (middle right); p. 612 (top left); p. 663 (top right)/AP/Wide World Photos/Christopher A. Record; p. 728 (top left)/Tracey Nearmy; p. 748 (top left)/AFP photo/Mark Ralston; p. 790 (top left)/Rod McGuirk; p. 793 (top right)/EPA/Irham Mast; p. 798 (bottom left)/AFP Photo/Torston Blackwood; p. 800 (middle left)/Mary Evans; p. 803 (bottom right)/Dave Hunt; p. 805 (top right)/Penny Tweedie/Wildlight; • © John Wiley & Sons, Inc: p. 103 (bottom)/Huffman, K. (2007). *Psychology in action*, p. 69 (fig. 2.11); p. 111 (top)/Huffman, K. (2007). *Psychology in action,* p. 76 (fig. 2.17); p. 169 (top left)/Schiffman, H. R., (1996). *Sensation and perception: An integrated approach,* 4th edn, p. 197; p. 359 (middle left)/Adapted from Figure 10.2 Sternberg's triarchic theory of intelligence. Comer & Gould (2010). Psychology around us, p. 315. New York: John Wiley & Sons; p. 377 (middle left)/Comer & Gould (2010). Psychology around us, p. 354 (Figure 11.1). New York: John Wiley & Sons; p. 434 (bottom left); • © Moonrunner Design Ltd: p. 107 (bottom left)/Carter, R. *Mapping the mind*, p. 161; • © Wikipedia: p. 114 (middle left)/From the collection of Jack and Beverly Wilgus; • © Shaywitz, Dr Sally: p. 116 (bottom left)/Shaywitz, et al. (1995). NMR Research/Yale Medical School; • © Fairfax Photo Library: p. 117 (bottom right)/Glenn Campbell; p. 186 (top left)/Marco Del Grande/The Sydney Morning Herald; p. 266 (top left)/Nicole Emanuel; p. 618 (middle left)/Janie Barrett; p. 698 (middle left)/Joe Castro; p. 715 (bottom right)/Simon Alekna; • © Stock Boston: p. 119 (middle right)/Peter Menzel; • © Image Source: p. 127 (bottom left); • © Optometric Extension: p. 128 (bottom left)/Courtesy Optometric Extension Program Foundation, Santa Ana, CA, www.oepf.org; p. 128: (bottom right)/Courtesy Optometric Extension Program Foundation, Santa Ana, CA, www.oepf.org; • © Raichle, Dr Marcus: p. 134 (bottom left)/Courtesy of Professor Michael Posner University of Oregon and Dr. Marcus Raichle,Washington University in St. Louis; • © Destination Rotorua Tourism: p. 135 (bottom left)/Destination Rotorua Tourism Marketing. All rights reserved. Reproduced with permission; • © McGraw-Hill Education: p. 140 (middle left)/Sekuler, R., & Blake, R. (1994). *Perception,* 3rd edn. New York: McGraw-Hill, Inc; p. 144 (top right)/Sekuler, R., & Blake, R. (1994). *Perception*, 3rd edn. New York: McGraw-Hill, Inc; p. 151 (middle right)/Sekuler, R., & Blake,R (1994). *Perception*, 3rd edn. New York: McGraw-Hill, Inc; p. 506 (top left)/Kagan, J. (1983). Stress and coping in early development. In N. Garmezy & M. Rutter (eds.), *Stress, coping and development in children*, p. 198. New York: McGraw-Hill, Inc; • © Graham-Field Health Products: p. 147 (top right)/Courtesy Graham-Field Surgical Company; • © Photo Researchers, Inc: p. 155 (bottom)/Omikron; • © MIT Press: p. 163 (middle left)/Osherson, D. (1990). 1 figure, Recognition by components. In *An invitation to cognitive science, volume 2: visual cognition*; • © Elsevier: p. 164 (top)/Reprinted from Beiderman, I. (1987). Recognition by components. *Computer Visions, Graphics and Image Processing, 32,* 29–73; p. 319 (top left)/Frith & Dolan (1996). The role of the prefrontal cortex in higher cognitive functions. *Cognitive Brain Research, 5*, 178; p. 493 (top right)/Adapted from Cerella, J. (1990). Ageing and information processing rate. In J. Birren & K. W. Schaie (eds), *Handbook of the Psychology of Ageing (3rd edition),* p. 203. Orlando, FL: Academic Press; p. 494 (bottom middle)/Adapted from Schaie, K. W. (1990). Intellectual development in adulthood. In J. Birren & K. W. Schaie (eds), *Handbook of the Psychology of Ageing (3rd edition),* p. 297. Orlando, FL: Academic Press; • © M. C. Escher Company: p. 164 (bottom middle)/M. C. Escher's 'Convex and Concave'. All rights reserved. www.mcescher.com; • © Australian War Memorial: p. 167 (bottom right)/Australian War Memorial Neg number ART02161; • © David and Jean Rosenberg: p. 172 (bottom left)/Gibson, E. J, & Walk, R. D (1960). The visual cliff. *Scientific American, 202* (April), 67–71. With permission of Jean Gibson Rosenberg; • © Susannah Tye: p. 172 (middle); • © Blakemore, Professor Colin: p. 173 (middle right); • © Stephen M. Kosslyn, Prof: p. 175 (top left); • © Wiley Blackwell Publishers: p. 181 (middle right)/Reprinted from Finke et al. (1989). Reinterpreting visual patterns in mental imagery. In *Cognitive Science, 13*, 51–78. Reproduced with permission from Taylor & Francis Ltd via Copyright Clearance Center; p. 274 (bottom left)/Hermann, D. J., Crawford, M. & Holdsworth, M. (1992). Gender-linked differences in everyday memory performance. *The British Journal of Psychology*, 83, 221–231; p. 306 (middle left)/Adapted from Griggs, R. A. & Cox, J. R. (1982). The elusive thematic-materials effect in Watson's selection task. *The British Journal of Psychology, 73*, 407–420; p. 362 (bottom left)/Sameroff, A., Baldwin, A., & Baldwin, C. (1993). Stability of intelligence from preschool to adolescence: The influence of social and family risk factors. *Child Development, 64*, 89; p. 539 (top right)/Rosenblum, G. D., & Lewis, M. (1999). The relations among body image, physical attractiveness and body mass in adolescence. *Child Development, 70*, 54; • © Rosalind Cartwright, Ph.D: p. 201 (top left)/Adapted from Cartwright, R.D. (1978). *A primer on sleep and dreaming*. Addison Wesley; • © Dept of Health & Ageing:

p. 213 (bottom right)/National Drugs Campaign ecstasy 'girl' advertisement, reproduced with permission from the Commonwealth of Australia as represented by the Department of Health and Ageing; • © Photodisc: p. 220 (middle left); p. 231 (top right); p. 267 (top right); p. 494 (bottom left); • © The Granger Collection: p. 224 (top middle); • © Oxford University Press: p. 224 (middle left); • © Harris, Professor Ben: p. 226 (bottom left)/Courtesy of Benjamin Harris, University of New Hampshire; • © American Psychological Association: p. 237 (bottom right)/Adapted from Williams, C.D. (1959). The elimination of tantrum behaviour by extinction procedures. *Journal of Abnormal and Social Psychology, 50*, 269; p. 358 (top middle)/Adapted from Mumaw, R., & Pellegrino, J. (1984). Individual differences in complex spatial processing. *Journal of Educational Psychology, 76,* 923; p. 411 (top right)/Adapted from Tomarken, Davidson, Wheeler & Doss (1992). Individual differences in interior brain asymmetry and fundamental dimensions of emotion. *Journal of Personality and Social Psychology, 62*, 681; p. 412 (bottom middle)/Adapted from Shedler, J., Mayman, M., & Manis, M. (1993). The illusion of mental health. *American Psychologist, 48*, 1123; p. 439 (bottom middle)/Wood, R., & Bandura, A. (1989). Impact of conceptions of ability on self-regulatory mechanisms and complex decision making. *Journal of Personality and Social Psychology, 56*, 411–413; p. 447 (middle)/Adapted from Caspi, A. (2000). The child is father of the Man: Personality continuities from childhood to adulthood. *Journal of Personality and Social Psychology, 78*, 158–172; p. 565 (middle left)/Wadden, T. A., Brownell, K. D., & Foster, G. D. (2002). Obesity: Responding to the global epidemic. *Journal of Consulting and Clinical Psychology, 70*, 510–525; p. 587 (bottom left)/Adapted from Cohen S., & Williamson, G. M. (1991). Stress and infectious diseases in humans. *Psychological Bulletin, 109*, 5; p. 620 (middle left)/Adapted from Shedler, J., & Block, J. (1990). Adolescent drug use and emotional health: A longitudinal perspective. *American Psychologist, 45*, 624; p. 620 (middle right)/Adapted from Shedler, J., & Block, J. (1990). Adolescent drug use and emotional health: A longitudinal perspective. *American Psychologist, 45*, 624; p. 630 (top left)/De La Ronde, C., & Swann, W. B., Jr. (1998). Partner verification: Reporting shattered images of our intimates. *Journal of Personality and Social Psychology, 74*, 374–382; p. 637 (top left)/Rapee, Brown, Anthony & Barlow (1992). Response to hyperventilation and inhalation of 5.5% carbon dioxide-enriched air across the DSM-IIIR anxiety disorders. *Journal of Abnormal Psychology, 101*, 545; p. 681 (middle right)/Adapted from Smith, M. L., & Glass, G. V. (September 1977). Meta-analysis of psychotherapy outcome studies. *American Psychologist, 32*, 754; p. 712 (top left)/Adapted from Macrae, C. N, Bodenhausen, G. V., & Milne, A. B. (1998). Saying no to unwanted thoughts: Self-focus and the regulation of mental life. *Journal of Personality and Social Psychology, 74*, 585; p. 742 (middle left)/Adapted from Buss, D. M., & Schmitt, D. P. (1993). Sexual strategies theory: An evolutionary perspective on human mating. *Psychological Review, 100*(2), 224; p. 742 (middle right)/Adapted from Buss, D. M., & Schmidt, D. P. (1993). Sexual strategies theory: An evolutionary perspective on human mating. Psychological Review, 100 (2), 220; • © Slattery Media Group: p. 240 (middle left)/Greg Ford/GSP Images; • © Kaku Kurita: p. 242 (middle left); • © Belesky family: p. 242 (middle right); • © Dr Albert Bandura: p. 249 (middle right)/Dr Albert Bandura; • © National Associationfor the Education of Young Children: p. 249 (bottom left)/Bandura, A. (1967). In Hartup and Smothergill's (eds), *The young child: Reviews of research,* 1st edn, pp.42–58; • © Oxford University Press UK: p. 265 (bottom right)/Adapted from Baddeley, A. (1986). *Working memory*, p. 67; p. 266 (bottom)/Adapted from Logie, R. (1996). The seven ages of working memory. In John T. E. Richardson et al, *Working memory and human cognition*; • © Cognitive Evolution Group: p. 304 (middle left)/Photo courtesy of Cognitive Evolution Group, University of Louisiana at Lafayette; • © William Brewer, Prof: p. 282 (top left)/Courtesy of Professor William Brewer, University of Illinois; • © Springer: p. 299 (bottom left)/Adapted from Cooper, L. A., & Shepard, R. N. (1973). The time required to prepare for a rotated stimulus. *Memory & Cognition, 1*(3), 246–250. © 1973 The Psychonomic Society, with kind permission from Springer Science+Business Media B.V.; • © Emerald City Images: p. 313 (top)/John & Lorraine Carnemolla; • © Scientific American: p. 334 (middle left)/Premack, A. J., & Premack, D. (October 1972). Teaching language to an ape. *Scientific American, 227*(4), 93; • © Language Research Center: p. 335 (top)/Courtesy of the Language Research Center, Georgia State University; • © ANTPhoto.com.au: p. 343 (bottom right)/Rik Thwaites; p. 541: (middle right); p. 818 (middle left)/Peter Cowan; • © Pearson Education US: p. 348 (middle)/Anastasi, A. & Urbina, S. (1997). *Psychological testing, 7th Edition*, Adapted by permission of Pearson Education, Inc., Upper Saddle River, NJ; • © Guilford Press: p. 356 (top middle)/Adapted from Horn, J. & Noll, J. (1997). Human cognitive capacity: Gf-Gc theory. In D. P. Flanagan, J. L. Gerchaft, & P. L. Harrison (eds), *Contemporary intellectual assessment*; • © Jill Tait: p. 363 (top right); • © Channel 7 — Sydney: p. 372 (top right); • © Kit de Guymer photography: p. 373 (middle left); • © Hachette Book Group USA: p. 392 (middle left)/Masters, W. H., & Johnson, V. E. (1966). *Human sexual response*, p. 5. Boston: Little, Brown and Company. ©1966 by the Masters and Johnson Institute; p. 392 (middle right)/Masters, W. H., & Johnson, V. E. (1966). *Human sexual response*, p. 5. Boston: Little, Brown and Company. ©1966 by the Masters and Johnson Institute; • © Paul Ekman PhD: p. 405 (top left)/Paul Ekman Group, LLC; p. 406 (middle left)/Paul Ekman Group, LLC; p. 406 (middle left)/Paul Ekman Group, LLC; p. 406 (top left)/Paul Ekman Goup, LLC; p. 406 (top left)/Paul Ekman Group, LLC; p. 406 (top left)/Paul Ekman Group, LLC; p. 406 (top left)/Paul Ekman Group, LLC; • © PhotoEdit: p. 430 (bottom left)/Davis Barber; p. 637 (bottom right)/Tony Freeman; • © Rorschach Museum: p. 434 (middle left)/Rorschach Museum Switzerland; • © Allyn & Bacon: p. 455 (top right)/Carver, C. S., & Scheier, M. F. (1991). *Perspectives on personality*, 2e. Boston, MA: Allyn & Bacon. © 1992 by Pearson Education; • © Alamy Limited: p. 490 (top left)/CoverSpot; • © Corbis Royalty Free: p. 491 (top right)/Digital Stock; • © Hofer, Professor Scott: p. 494 (top left)/Horn, J., & Hofer, S. (1992). Major abilities and development in the adult period. In R. Sternberg & C. Berg (eds.), *Intellectual Development*, p.79. New York: Cambridge University Press; • © Cengage Learning: p. 515 (top right)/Bukatko & Daehler (2004). *Child development: A thematic approach*, 5th edn. Wadsworth, a part of Cengage Learning, Inc; p. 526(middle left)/Bukatko & Daehler (2004). *Child development: A thematic approach*, 5th edn. Wadsworth, a part of Cengage Learning, Inc; p. 822 (middle left)/Matsumoto & Juang (2004). *Culture and psychology (with InfoTrac)* 3rd edn (Fig. 10.20, 268). Wadsworth, a part of Cengage Learning, Inc; • © AIHW: p. 553 (middle)/Australian Institute of Health and Welfare. *Chronic disease mortality*. www.aihw.gov.au; • © *Journal of New England:* p. 588 (middle)/Cohen et al. (1991). Psychological stress and susceptibility to the common cold. *New England Journal of Medicine, 325*, 609–610. Massachusetts Medical Society. All rights reserved; • © Penguin Books Aus — Adult Pub: p. 602 (middle left)/Cover of McKay, E. (2010). Forensic Investigator: True stories from the life of a country crime scene cop; • © Australasian Medical Pub Co: p. 675 (middle left) Page, A. N. et al. (2009). Sociodemographic correlates of antidepressant utilisation in Australia. *Medical Journal of Australia, 190,* 479–483; • © Renato Sabbatini, PhD: p. 678 (top left)/Renato M.E. Sabbatini (1997). *Brain and Mind Magazine*, June; • © American Psychiatric Pub, Inc: p. 681 (top right)/Maj et al. (1992). Pattern of recurrence of illness after recovery from an episode of major depression: a prospective study. Reprinted with permission from the *American Journal of Psychiatry, 149* (June); • © Beyond Blue: p. 683 (middle right); • © John Coomer: p. 699 (top right); • © Psychology Today: p. 750 (bottom)/Darley & Latane (1968). A decision making model of bystander intervention. *Psychology Today*, December, 70–71; • © Banana Stock: p. 755 (middle right); • © Mark Levings: p. 758 (middle left); • © Alexandra Milgram: p. 762 (top middle)/Based on Table 2 in Milgram, S. (1963). Behavioural study of obedience. *Journal of Abnormal and Social Psychology, 65*, 371–378; • © Philip Zimbardo Emeritus Prof: p. 765 (bottom right); • © National Health and Medical Research Council: p. 785 (middle left)/National

Health and Medical Research Council (2003). *Guidelines for ethical conduct in Aboriginal and Torres Strait Islander health research*, p. 9. www.nhmrc.gov.au; • © Statistics New Zealand: p. 792 (middle left)/ This work is based on/includes Statistics New Zealand's data which are licensed by Statistics New Zealand for re-use under the Creative Commons Attribution-Noncommercial 3.0 New Zealand license; • © Anne-Katrin Eckermann: p. 804 (bottom middle)/Eckerman, A. (1995). *Introduction to traditional Aboriginal societies* (29). Armidale, NSW: University of New England Press; • © Harold Thomas: p. 806 (middle right)/Design of the Aboriginal Flag by Harold Thomas © 1971; • © Spatial Vision: p. 812 (top left); • © Torres Strait Island Regional: p. 814 (middle left)/Designed by Mr. Bernard Namok;

Text

• © American Psychological Association: p. 42/Lumley & Provenzano (2003). Stress management through written emotional disclosure improves academic performance among college students. *Journal of Educational Psychology, 95*(3), 641–649; • © *American Journal of Pharmaceutical Education:* p. 53/Sansgiry, S. S., PhD & Sail, K., BS (2006). Effect of students' perceptions of course load on test anxiety. *American Journal of Pharmaceutical Education, April 15; 70(2),* Article 26; • © American Psychological Association: p. 60/Adapted from Shiner, R. L. (2000). Linking childhood personality with adaptation: Evidence for continuity and change across time in late adolescence. *Journal of Personality and Social Psychology, 78*, 316; p. 443/ Adapted from McCrae, R.R., & Costa, P.T., Jr. (1997). Personality trait structure as a human universal. *American Psychologist, 52*, 513; p. 448/ Adapted from Block, J.M., Gjerde, P., & Block, J.H. (1991). Personality antecedents of depressive tendencies in 18-year-olds: A prospective study. *Journal of Personality and Social Psychology, 60*, 726–738; p. 455/Adapted from Tellegan, A., & Lykken, D.T., Bouchard, T.J., Jr., Wilcox, K.J., & Rich, S. (1988). Personality similarity in twins reared apart and together. *Journal of Personality and Social Psychology, 54*, 1031–1039; p. 523/Adapted from Montemayor, R., & Eisen, M. (1977). A developmental sequence of self-conceptions from childhood to adolescence. *Developmental Psychology, 13,* 317–318; • © Psychology Today: p. 246/Rooter, J. (1971). Internal control – external control: A sampler. *Psychology Today, June*, 42; • © Copyright Clearance Center: p. 363/Henderson, N. D. (1982). Moral behavior genetics. *Annual Reveiw of Psychology, 33*, 410; p. 453/Jonas, E., et al. (2002). The scrooge effect: Evidence that morality salience increases prosocial attitudes and behaviour. *Personality and Social Psychology Bulletin, 28*, 1345. Reproduced with permission from Sage Publications Inc; p. 526/Williams, J. E. & Best, D. L. (1982). Measuring sex stereotypes: A thirty nation study, p. 77. Reproduced with permission from Sage Publications Inc; p. 583./Reprinted from Holmes and Rahe (1976). The social readjustment rating scale. *Journal of Psychosomatic Research, 11*(2), 213–218. Permission from Elselvier; p. 660/Strupp, H. H. (1984). Psychotherapy in a new key. Reprinted by permission of Basic Books, a member of the Perseus Books Group; • © Cengage Learning: p. 309/Berstein, D. A. (1997). Psychology. 4th Edition. © Wadsworth, a part of Cengage Learning, Inc; p. 330/Weitan (2010). Psychology, 8th Edition, p. 320. © 2010 Wadsworth, a part of Cengage Learning, Inc; p. 766/Forsyth (1990). Group dynamics 2nd Edition. © Wadsworth, a part of Cengage Learning, Inc; p. 767/From Janis, Irving L. (1982). Groupthink: Psychological studies of policy decisions and fiascoes, 2nd Edition. © Wadsworth, a part of Cengage Learning, Inc; • © Pearson Clinical Assessment: p. 347/*Wechsler Adult Intelligence Scale, Third Edition (WAIS_III).* © 1997 NCS Pearson, Inc. and Wechsler Adult Intelligence Scale, fourth Edition (WAIS_IV); • © John Wiley & Sons, Inc: p. 360/Comer & Gould (2010). Psychology around us, p. 315. New York: John Wiley & Sons, 2010; • © Yale University Press: p. 395/Green, R. (1987). *The "sissy boy" syndrome and the development of homosexuality*. New Haven, Ct: Yale University Press; p. 708/ Luchins, A. S. (1957). Primacy-recency in impression formation. In C.I. Hovland (eds.), *The Order of Presentation in Persuasion*, pp. 34–35. New Haven, CT: Yale UniversityPress; • © Allyn & Bacon: p. 415/ From Plutchik, R. (1979). *Emotion: a psychoevolutionary synthesis.* Boston, MA: Allyn & Bacon; • © D. G. Paterson: p. 450/Forer, B. R. (1949). The fallacy of personal validation: A classroom demonstration of gullibility. *Journal of Abnormal and Social Psychology, 44*, 118–23; • © Karger Publishing: p. 529/Kohlberg, L. (1963). *Vita Humana, 6*: 11–33. Reproduced with the permission of S. Karger AG, Basel; • © David Goslin: p. 530/Adapted from Kohlberg, L., (1969). Stage and sequence: The cognitive-developmental approach to socialization. In D. A. Goslin (Ed.), *Handbook of Socialization and Research*, 347–380. Boston: Houghton-Mifflin; • © AIHW: p. 542/'How Australia compares'; p. 554, 559/'Australia's health 2010' © Australian Institute of Health and Welfare, pp. 38, 50; p. 619/(2006) Statistics on drug use in Australia, *Australian Institute of Health and Welfare*, cat. no. PHE 80; • © Sheridan Content Services: p. 584/Martikainen & Valkonen (1996). Mortality after the death of a spouse: Rates and causes of death in a large Finnish cohort. *American Journal of Public Health, 86*, 1090. © American Public Health Association, via Sheridan Content Services; • © W W Norton: p. 622/Gazzaniga, M. & Heatherton, T. F. (2003). *Psychological science: The mind brain, and behavior*, p. 539; • © W H Freeman: p. 623/Adapted from Gottesman, I. I. (1991). *Schizophrenia genesis: The origin of madness*. Used with permission of Worth Publishers; • © Australian Bureau of Statistics: p. 633/'Lifetime Mental Disorders (a)' from 'National Survey of Mental Health and Wellbeing: Summary of Results', *Australian Bureau of Statistics*, 2007, p. 27, Cat. 4326.0; • © International Universities: p. 666/Beck, A. T. (1976). *Cognitive therapy and the emotional disorders*, p. 289–290; • © Robert Sternberg, Dr: p. 740/Sternberg, R. J. (1987). The triangle of love: Intimacy, passion, commitment; • © Alexandra Milgram: p. 761/Milgram, S. (1974). *Obedience to authority: An experimental view* (p. 35). New York: Harper & Row; • © Linda Waimarie Nikora: p. 827/Waldegrave, C. (1993). Cultural justice & ethics. Proceedings of a symposium held at the Annual Conference of the New Zealand Psychological Society, University of Victoria, Wellington, 23–24 August. © 2000 National Standing Committee on Bicultural Issues; p. 827/Waldegrave, C. (1993). Cultural justice & ethics. Proceedings of a symposium held at the Annual Conference of the New Zealand Psychological Society, University of Victoria, Wellington, 23–24 August. © 2000 National Standing Committee on Bicultural Issues.

Every effort has been made to trace the ownership of copyright material. Information that will enable the publisher to rectify any error or omission in subsequent editions will be welcome. In such cases, please contact the Permissions Section of John Wiley & Sons Australia, Ltd.

Psychology: the study of mental processes and behaviour

1

LEARNING OBJECTIVES

After studying this chapter you should be able to:

1 define psychology

2 discuss the contributions of biopsychology

3 outline the history of psychology

4 distinguish among the major theoretical perspectives in psychology

5 discuss the educational requirements for psychologists and outline their most common work settings

6 understand how to study effectively.

Psychology is the scientific investigation of mental processes (thinking, remembering and feeling) and behaviour. Understanding a person requires attention to the individual's biology, psychological experience and cultural context.

The boundaries and borders of psychology

- *Biopsychology* examines the physical basis of psychological phenomena such as motivation, emotion and stress.
- *Cross-cultural psychology* tries to distinguish universal psychological processes from those that are specific to particular cultures.

History of psychology

Philosophical roots of psychological questions

- *Free will or determinism:* do we freely choose our actions or is our behaviour caused — determined — by things outside our control?
- *Mind–body problem:* the question of how mental and physical events interact.

From philosophical speculation to scientific investigation

- Wilhelm Wundt founded the first psychological laboratory in 1879.
- Two prominent early schools of thought were *structuralism* (uncover the basic elements of consciousness through *introspection*) and *functionalism* (explain psychological processes in terms of the role, or function, they serve).
- Edward Titchener initiated the school of thought known as structuralism; William James was one of the founders of functionalism.

Psychology in Australia and New Zealand

Education and training to become a psychologist

- Currently, a registered psychologist in Australia has completed a minimum of six years study in an APS-accredited psychology program. To practise as a psychologist in Australia, there is a legal requirement that you be registered with the National Psychology Board, a single registration scheme enabling registered psychologists to practise anywhere in Australia.
- In New Zealand, psychologists working in the public sector must be registered with the New Zealand Psychologists Board, which also involves a period of supervision on top of university training.

Major subdisciplines in psychology

- Within the broad discipline of psychology there are many fields of specialisation, including developmental, social, clinical, cognitive, health, forensic and sport psychology, among others.
- Different psychologists adopt different perspectives in their approach to the study of human behaviour.

How to study effectively

- Managing your time effectively is extremely important if you are to be successful in your studies. Set up a weekly schedule filled with specific study tasks (e.g. lectures, tutorials, assignments and exams) to help you stay on track with your studies.
- It is important that you learn how to get the most out of your study by becoming an active learner. Effectively preparing for the final exam involves setting up a revision timetable and applying a systematic approach to answering questions in an exam.

Professional associations for psychologists

- Both Australia and New Zealand also have peak bodies that represent the profession and its members — the Australian Psychological Society (APS), established in 1944, and the New Zealand Psychological Society (NZPsS) established in 1967.

Careers in psychology

- There are a wide range of career options available to psychologists. Psychologists may work in private practice. They may also gain employment in many other government and private sector organisations.
- There is a predicted strong employment growth within the next five years.

Perspectives in psychology

The psychodynamic perspective

- The *psychodynamic perspective* relies on several key premises:
  1. People's actions are determined by the way thoughts, feelings and wishes are connected in their minds.
  2. Many of these mental events occur outside conscious awareness.
  3. These mental processes may conflict with one another, leading to compromises among competing motives.
  4. Sigmund Freud emphasised unconscious mental forces in his psychoanalytic theory.
  5. According to psychoanalytic theory, many of the associations between feelings and behaviours or situations that guide our behaviour are expressed unconsciously.

The behaviourist perspective

- The *behaviourist perspective* focuses on the way objects or events in the environment come to control behaviour through learning.
- B. F. Skinner observed that behaviour can be controlled by environmental consequences that either increase (reinforce) or decrease (punish) their likelihood of occurring.

The cognitive perspective

- The *cognitive perspective* focuses on the way people perceive, process and retrieve information.
- Rene Descartes' early philosophical questions led many cognitive psychologists to emphasise the role of reason in creating knowledge.
- Modern-day cognitive psychologists use experimental procedures to infer the underlying mental processes in operation.

The humanistic perspective

- The *humanistic perspective* focuses on the uniqueness of the individual — it assumes that people are motivated to become *self-actualised* (reach their full potential).
- Carl Rogers' client-centred therapy emphasised conscious, goal-directed choices and the need for individuals to realise their true potential — to self-actualise.

The evolutionary perspective

- The *evolutionary perspective* argues that many behavioural tendencies in humans, from the need to eat to concern for our children, evolved because they helped our ancestors survive and rear healthy offspring.
- Evolutionary psychologists support Charles Darwin's theory of natural selection — the most adaptive behavioural traits are those that helped our ancestors adjust and survive in their environment.

Central questions: facts, theories and perspectives in psychology

- The way psychologists and other scientists understand any phenomenon depends on their interpretation of the whole — on their perspectives.
- Although the different perspectives offer radically different ways of approaching psychology, each has made distinctive contributions.

Workers at the emergency clinic of a metropolitan hospital were on a first-name basis with Bernard, a 36-year-old man who had become a regular visitor. Bernard lived alone and worked as a labourer in a nearby factory. He had a long history of presentations to the hospital for a range of ailments. Often, he sought treatment and drugs for what he claimed were viral infections. He would fast for days beforehand, and induce vomiting in the hospital room, to make his condition deteriorate.

On numerous other occasions, Bernard presented with wounds that required stitching. Initially they were confined to the extremities of the body — the arms and legs. Bernard had undergone partial amputations of three of his fingers and full amputations of nearly all of his toes after they had become intractably infected as a result of apparent self-mutilation. While he denied it, the hospital staff believed the wounds were self-inflicted. Adding weight to the suspicions were the odd times that Bernard would arrive at the hospital — often when relief doctors or staff who had not previously treated him were rostered on. The visits continued over a 12-month period, with the wounds progressively worsening.

Finally, Bernard presented with a severe abdominal wound, which required emergency surgery and almost cost him his life. No family came to visit Bernard while he was in care. His recovery was delayed when Bernard pulled out stitches and re-opened the wound several times during his hospitalisation (adapted from McEwan, 1998).

How could Bernard inflict such self-induced injury? What could have motivated him to do this? The answer: Munchausen's syndrome, a psychological illness that falls within the spectrum of factitious illnesses, in which people fabricate or induce illness in themselves. Some people, like Bernard, go to extreme lengths to endure repeated hospitalisations and unnecessary surgeries. For example, imagine the woman who cut her eyes to 'blind herself' to the sexual abuse she was experiencing at home. Or the woman who cut her tonsils out with scissors. (For further information on Munchausen's syndrome, including other stories, refer to Feldman, 2004; Feldman & Ford, 1994). In fact, some people perpetrate Munchausen's syndrome by proxy, in which they fabricate or induce illness in others. Typically a mother does this to her child. For example, in the film *The Sixth Sense*, a young boy is able to converse with the ghost of a young girl, locating a video tape that reveals the young girl's mother had been poisoning her with cleaning fluid in her food, making her a victim of Munchausen's syndrome by proxy. (For a look inside the world of Munchausen's by proxy as told by the victim, read Gregory's (2003) book *Sickened*.). Although the cause of Munchausen's syndrome remains unknown, researchers believe it is motivated in part by a desire for attention. In *The Sixth Sense*, the mother embraces the attention given to her at the young girl's wake and wears a bright red dress for the occasion. Health care providers acknowledge that people with Munchausen's syndrome are often difficult to treat due to patient resistance; however, early recognition and intervention is often the best initial treatment approach.

In the film *The Sixth Sense*, which starred Australian actress Toni Collette, a young boy is able to converse with the ghost of a young girl, locating a video tape that reveals the young girl's mother had been poisoning her with cleaning fluid in her food, making her a victim of Munchausen's syndrome by proxy.

Perhaps because the true cause remains elusive, many questions are raised by Munchausen's syndrome or Munchausen's syndrome by proxy. Are these people mentally ill? Are their brains the same as those of other people? Does an environmental stimulus activate neural pathways in the brain that lead to such behaviour? Is this phenomenon limited to Western cultures or do other cultures display similar types of bizarre behaviour? Bernard's case, as well as those of others who perpetrate factitious illness, illustrates a central issue that has vexed philosophers for over two millennia and psychologists for over a century — the relationship between mental and physical events, between meaning and mechanism.

Psychology seeks to answer questions about why we do the things we do. In trying to understand why things happen, we must be cautious not to be to too quick in looking for a single cause of behaviour or an event. Humans are complex creatures whose psychological experience lies at the intersection of biology and culture. To paraphrase one theorist, Erik Erikson (1963), psychologists must practise 'triple bookkeeping' to understand an individual at any given time, simultaneously tracking biological events, psychological experience, and the cultural and historical context.

Psychology lies at the intersection of biology and culture. ***Psychology*** is the scientific investigation of mental processes (thinking, remembering and feeling) and behaviour. All psychological processes occur through the interaction of cells in the nervous system, and all human action occurs in the context of cultural beliefs and values that render it meaningful. Psychological understanding requires a constant movement between the micro-level of biology and the macro-level of culture.

This chapter begins by exploring the biological and cultural boundaries and borders that frame human psychology. We then examine the theoretical perspectives that have focused, and often divided, the attention of the scientific community for more than a century. The chapter closes by looking at psychology as a discipline in the twenty-first century. We will examine the major subdisciplines in psychology and consider the various career options for psychology graduates in Australia and New Zealand. Importantly, the issue of 'how to study effectively' is introduced, to help put you on the pathway to success with your psychology studies.

INTERIM SUMMARY

Psychology is the scientific investigation of mental processes (thinking, remembering and feeling) and behaviour. Understanding a person requires attention to the individual's biology, psychological experience and cultural context.

Central questions

- How does our theoretical perspective influence the way we interpret the world?
- Can we dispense with theory and simply look at the facts?

The boundaries and borders of psychology

Biology and culture establish both the possibilities and the constraints within which people think, feel and act. On the one hand, the structure of the brain sets the parameters, or limits, of human potential. Most 10-year-olds cannot solve algebra problems because the neural circuitry essential for abstract thought has not yet matured. Similarly, the capacity for love has its roots in the innate tendency of infants to develop an emotional attachment to their caretakers. These are biological givens.

On the other hand, most adults throughout human history would find algebra problems as mystifying as would a preschooler because their culture never provided the groundwork for this kind of reasoning. And though love may be a basic potential, the way people love depends on the values, beliefs and practices of their society. In some cultures, people seek and expect romance in their marriages, whereas in others, they do not select a spouse based on affection or attraction at all.

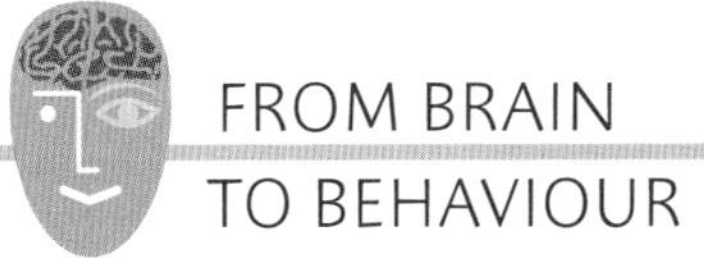

The boundary with biology

The biological boundary of psychology is the province of ***biopsychology*** (or ***behavioural neuroscience***), which investigates the physical basis of psychological phenomena such as memory, emotion and stress. Instead of studying thoughts, feelings or fears, behavioural neuroscientists (some of whom are doctors or biologists rather than psychologists) investigate the electrical and chemical processes in the nervous system that underlie these mental events. Their aim is to link mind and body, psyche and brain.

The connection between brain and behaviour became increasingly clear during the nineteenth century, when doctors began observing patients with severe head injuries. These patients often showed deficits in language and memory, or dramatic changes in their personality. For example, following a severe blow to the head, a genteel, socially adept businessman and devoted father could suddenly become lewd, cantankerous and unable to care about the people he had loved just days earlier.

Such observations led researchers to experiment by *producing* lesions surgically in animals in different neural regions to observe the effects on behaviour. This method is still used today, as in research on emotion, which has begun to identify the neural pathways involved in fear reactions

(LeDoux, 1995). In this research, psychologists create lesions in one brain structure at a time along pathways hypothesised to be involved when rats learn to fear an object associated with pain. When a lesion disrupts learning, the researcher knows that the damaged area, or other areas connected to it, is involved in fear.

Since its origins in the nineteenth century, one of the major issues in behavioural neuroscience has been ***localisation of function***, or the extent to which different parts of the brain control different aspects of functioning. In 1836, a doctor named Marc Dax presented a paper suggesting that lesions on the left side of the brain were associated with aphasia, or language disorders. The notion that language was localised to the left side of the brain (the left hemisphere) developed momentum, with new discoveries linking specific language functions to specific regions of the left hemisphere. Paul Broca (1824–1880) discovered that brain-injured people with lesions in the front section of the left hemisphere were often unable to speak fluently but could comprehend language. Carl Wernicke (1848–1904) showed that damage to an area a few centimetres behind the section Broca had discovered could lead to another kind of aphasia. These individuals can speak fluently and follow rules of grammar, but they can neither understand language nor speak in a way that is comprehensible to others (figure 1.1). Individuals with this form of aphasia might speak fluently, apparently following rules of grammar, but their words make little sense (e.g. 'I saw the bats and cuticles as the dog lifted the hoof, the pauser.').

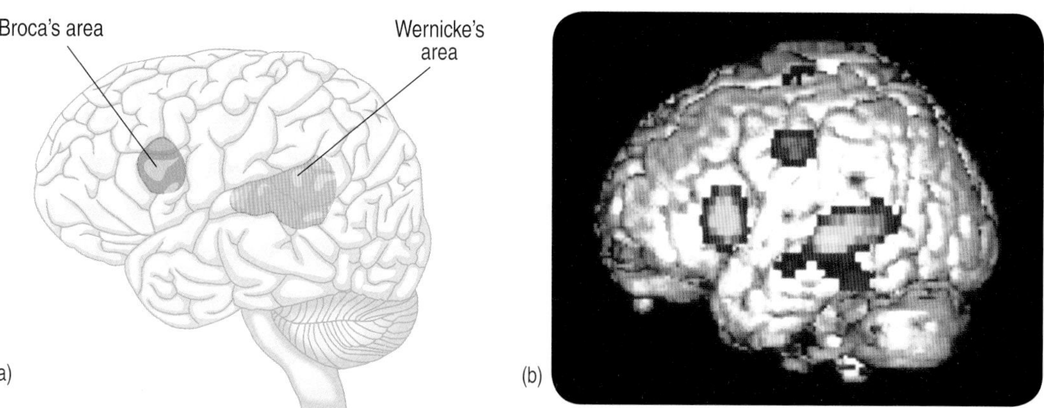

FIGURE 1.1
Broca's and Wernicke's areas. (a) Broca's aphasia involves difficulty producing speech, whereas Wernicke's aphasia typically involves difficulty comprehending language. (b) Positron emission tomography (PET) is a computerised imaging technique that allows researchers to study the functioning of the brain as the person responds to stimuli. The PET scan here shows activity in Wernicke's area (right), Broca's area (left) and a motor region producing speech, during an exercise in which the participant was asked to repeat words.

One of the metaphors that underlies neuropsychological thinking compares the brain to an electronic device with a complex series of circuits. Particular experiences or behaviours reflect patterns or sequences of activated cells that are 'wired' together. Just as no single point on a television screen means anything on its own, because each pixel or dot can be used in millions of different configurations, the pattern in which that dot is activated gives it meaning. Similarly, the pattern of firing cells determines the meaning of a neural event.

Contemporary neuroscientists no longer believe that complex psychological functions 'happen' exclusively in a single localised part of the brain. Rather, the circuits for psychological events, such as emotions or thoughts, are distributed throughout the brain, with each part contributing to the total experience. A man who sustains lesions to one area may be unable consciously to distinguish his wife's face from the face of any other woman — a disabling condition indeed — but may react physiologically to her face with a higher heart rate or pulse (Bruyer, 1991; Young, 1994). Technological advances over the last two decades have allowed researchers to pinpoint lesions precisely, and even to watch computerised portraits of the brain light up with activity (or fail to light up, in cases of neural damage) as people perform psychological tasks (chapter 2). In large part as a result of these technological advances, psychology has become increasingly biological over the last decade, as behavioural neuroscience has extended into virtually all areas of psychology.

MAKING CONNECTIONS

Patients with damage to circuits in the **brain** linking thoughts with feelings may 'know' something is risky but do it anyway. They cannot seem to connect actions with their **emotional** consequences (chapters 3 and 10).

A GLOBAL VISTA

The boundary with culture

Humans are not only collections of cells; they are also themselves the 'cells' of larger groups, such as tribes or nations, which similarly impose their stamp on psychological functioning. The emergence of agriculture and cities, generally known as civilisation, occurred less than ten thousand years ago. Before that time, and until well into the twentieth century in much of this planet's southern hemisphere, humans lived in small bands composed largely of their own kin. Several bands often joined together into larger tribes in order to trade mates, protect territory, wage war on other groups, or participate in communal rituals.

The anthropologists who first studied these native cultures in Africa, Australia, North America and elsewhere were struck by how different these cultures were from their own. Their observations raised a central issue that psychology has been slow to address: to what extent do cultural differences create psychological differences? How can we understand someone who becomes terrified because he believes that a quarrel with kin has offended the forest and may bring disaster upon his family? Does he share our psychological nature, or does each society produce its own psychology?

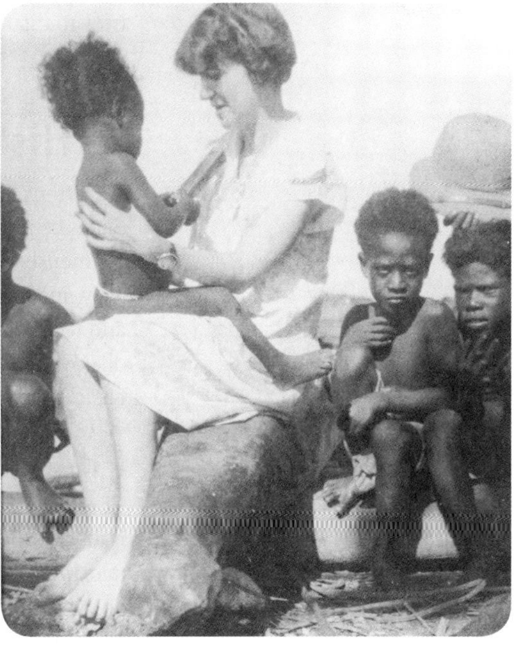

Margaret Mead was a leading figure among anthropologists and psychologists trying to understand the relationship between personality and culture. Here she is pictured with children of Manus Island, circa 1930s.

The first theorists to address this issue were psychologically sophisticated anthropologists such as Margaret Mead and Ruth Benedict, who were interested in the relationship between culture and personality (LeVine, 1982). They argued that individual psychology is fundamentally shaped by cultural values, ideals and ways of thinking. As children develop, they learn to behave in ways that conform to cultural standards. The openly competitive, confident, self-interested style generally rewarded in Western societies is unthinkable in Japan, where communal sentiments are much stronger. Japanese manufacturing companies do not lay off workers during economic downturns as do their Western counterparts because they believe corporations are like families and should treat their employees accordingly.

In the middle of the twentieth century, ***psychological anthropologists***, who study psychological phenomena in other cultures by observing people in their natural settings (see Shimizu & LeVine, 2001; Suarez-Orozco, Spindler, & Spindler, 1994), began studying the way economic realities shape child-rearing practices, which in turn mould personality (Kardiner, 1945; Whiting & Child, 1953). Then, as now, people in much of the developing world were leaving their ancestral homelands seeking work in large cities. Working as a labourer in a factory requires different attitudes towards time, mobility and individuality from farming or foraging. A labourer must punch a time clock, move where the work is, work for wages and spend all day away from family (see Inkeles & Smith, 1974). Notions we take for granted — such as arriving at work within a prescribed span of minutes — are not 'natural' to human beings. Punctuality is necessary for shift-work in a factory or for changing from class to class in a modern school, and we consider it an aspect of character or personality. Yet punctuality was probably not even recognised as a dimension of personality in most cultures before the contemporary era and was certainly not a prime concern of parents in rearing their children.

After the 1950s, interest in the relationship between culture and psychological attributes waned for decades. Within psychology, however, a small group of researchers developed the field of ***cross-cultural psychology***, which tests psychological hypotheses in different cultures (see Berry, Dasen, & Saraswathi, 1997; Berry, Poortinga, Segall, & Dasen, 1992; Lonner & Malpass, 1994a, 1994b; Triandis, 1980, 1994). Interest in cross-cultural psychology has blossomed recently as issues of diversity have come to the fore in the political arena. Psychologists are now pondering the extent to which decades of research on topics such as memory, motivation, psychological disorders or obedience have yielded results about *people* or about a particular *group* of people (chapter 19). Do individuals in all cultures experience depression? Do toddlers learn to walk and talk at the same rate cross-culturally? Do people dream in all cultures and, if so, what is the function of dreaming? Only cross-cultural comparisons can distinguish between universal and culturally specific psychological processes.

APPLY + DISCUSS

- How do parents in an industrial society teach their children to value punctuality? What aspects of life — at home, in school and later in life — foster a belief in the value of being on time? Do these all require *intentional* teaching or do some 'just happen' as the child goes through the course of a day?
- Why are some people chronically late?

INTERIM SUMMARY

Biopsychology (or ***behavioural neuroscience***) examines the physical basis of psychological phenomena such as motivation, emotion and stress. Although different neural regions perform different functions, the neural circuits that underlie psychological events are distributed throughout the brain and cannot be 'found' in one location. At another boundary of psychology, cross-cultural investigation tries to distinguish universal psychological processes from those that are specific to particular cultures.

History of psychology

Questions about human nature, such as whether psychological attributes are the same everywhere, were once the province of philosophy. Early in the twentieth century, however, philosophers entered a period of intense self-doubt, wrestling with the limitations of what they could know about topics such as morality, justice and the nature of knowledge. At the same time, psychologists began to apply the methods and technologies of natural science to psychological questions. They reasoned that if physicists could discover the atom and industrialists could mass produce cars, psychological scientists could uncover basic laws of human and animal behaviour.

Philosophical roots of psychological questions

The fact that psychology was born from the womb of philosophy is of no small consequence. Many issues at the heart of contemporary psychological research and controversy are classic philosophical questions. One of these is whether human action is the product of ***free will*** or ***determinism***; that is, do we freely choose our actions or is our behaviour caused — determined — by things outside our control?

Philosopher René Descartes contended human action follows on from human intention; that is, people choose a course of action and act on it.

Champions of free will follow in the footsteps of seventeenth-century French philosopher René Descartes (1596–1650), who contended that human action follows from human intention — that people choose a course of action and act on it. Proponents of determinism, from the Greek philosopher Democritus onwards, assert, however, that behaviour follows lawful patterns like everything else in the universe, from falling rocks to orbiting planets. Psychological determinists believe that the actions of humans and other animals are determined by physical forces — internally by genetic processes and externally by environmental events.

This debate has no easy resolution. Subjectively, we have the experience of free will. We could choose to stop writing — or you to stop reading — at this very moment. Yet here we are, continuing into the next sentence. Why? What determined our decision to forge ahead? And how can mental processes exercise control over physical processes such as moving a pen or turning a page?

Humans are material beings, part of nature, like birds, plants and water. When we choose to move, our limbs exert a force that counters gravity and disturbs molecules of air. How can a non-material force — will — displace material forces? No-one has ever proposed a satisfactory solution to the ***mind–body problem***, the question of how mental and physical events interact. However, psychological phenomena put the mind–body problem in a new light by drawing attention to the way psychological meaning can be transformed into mechanism (physiological events).

Psychologists do not tackle philosophical issues such as free will directly, but classic philosophical questions reverberate through many contemporary psychological discussions. Research into the genetics of personality and personality disturbances provides an intriguing, if disquieting, example. People with antisocial personality disorder have minimal conscience and a tendency towards aggressive or criminal behaviour. In an initial psychiatric evaluation one man boasted that he had terrorised his former girlfriend for an hour by brandishing a knife and telling her in exquisite detail the ways he intended to slice her flesh. This man could undoubtedly have exercised his free will to continue or discontinue his behaviour at any moment and hence was morally (and legally) responsible for his acts. He knew what he was doing, he was not hearing voices commanding him to behave aggressively and he thoroughly enjoyed his victim's terror. A determinist, however, could offer an equally compelling case. Like many violent men, he was the son of violent, alcoholic parents who had beaten him severely as a child. Both physical abuse in childhood and parental alcoholism (which can exert both genetic and environmental influences) render an individual more likely to develop antisocial personality disorder (see Cadoret, Yates, Troughton, Woodworth, & Stewart, 1995; Zanarini, Gunderson, Marino, Schwartz, & Frankenburg, 1990). In the immediate moment, perhaps, he had free will, but over the long run, he may have had no choice but to be the person he was.

Other philosophical questions set the stage for psychology and are central to contemporary psychological theory and research. Many of these questions, such as free will versus determinism, take the apparent form of choices between polar opposites, neither of which can be entirely true. Does human behaviour reflect nature (biology) or nurture (environmental influence)? Does knowledge come from observing the world or from thinking about it? Several of these fundamental questions are summarised in table 1.1.

TABLE **1.1 Philosophical issues and psychological questions**

Philosophical issue	Examples of contemporary psychological questions
Free will versus determinism: Do people make free choices or are their actions determined by forces outside their control?	What causes patients with antisocial personality disorder to produce criminal behaviour?
Nature versus nurture: To what extent do psychological processes reflect biological or environmental influences?	To what extent is intelligence inherited, and how do genes and environment interact to influence intellectual functioning?
Rationalism versus empiricism: To what extent does knowledge about the world come from observation and experience or from logic and reasoning?	How do children come to understand that other people have thoughts and feelings?
Reason versus emotion: To what extent are people guided by their knowledge or by their feelings (and to what extent should they be)?	Should people choose their mates based on 'gut' feelings, or should they carefully weigh a potential partner's costs and benefits if they want to have a happy, long-lasting marriage?
Continuity versus discontinuity with other animals: To what extent are humans similar to other animals (that is, to what extent is human psychology continuous with the psychology of other animals)?	To what degree can studying fear responses in rats inform psychologists about the nature of human emotions?
Individualism versus relationality: To what extent are humans fundamentally self-interested or oriented towards relating to and helping other people?	Do people ever really help others without any benefit to themselves or are they motivated by other considerations, such as desires to feel good about themselves or avoid guilt?
Conscious versus unconscious: To what extent are people conscious of the contents of their mind and the causes of their behaviour?	Can people describe themselves accurately or are they unaware of many aspects of their personality?
Mental versus physical: To what extent can we understand psychological events independent of their neural basis?	How many kinds of memory are there? When we hold a phone number in mind briefly as we reach for the phone, are we using different neural 'hardware' than when we store that number 'for keeps'?

APPLY + DISCUSS

In 1996, Martin Bryant shot dead 35 people at Port Arthur in Tasmania. Mental health professionals who evaluated Bryant testified that he was of limited intellectual ability, had severe developmental problems and suffered a significant personality disorder. Serial killer Ivan Milat murdered seven backpackers between 1989 and 1992, burying their bodies in the Belanglo State Forest south-west of Sydney. Milat came from a poor immigrant family and spent time in juvenile detention facilities during his teenage years; however, he was considered of sound enough mind to be convicted of the murders.

- Were Bryant and Milat responsible for their actions?
- Was one any less responsible than the other?
- Was either more responsible than a person who has a heart attack while driving and consequently kills a pedestrian? If so, why?

From philosophical speculation to scientific investigation

Philosophical questions have been around throughout human history — they were the province of religion and, later, philosophy. They have survived because they allowed people to better understand themselves.

Philosophical arguments have thus set the agenda for many issues confronting psychologists and, in our lifetimes, psychological research may shed light on questions that have seemed unanswerable for 2500 years. The emergence of psychology as a science has provided a new means for answering these long-asked questions. The fact that psychology emerged from philosophy, however, has had another monumental influence on the discipline. Philosophers searched for answers to questions about the nature of thought, feeling and behaviour in their minds, using logic and argumentation. By the late nineteenth century an alternative approach emerged: if we want to understand the mind and behaviour, we should investigate it scientifically, just as physicists study the nature of light or gravity through systematic observation and experimentation. Thus, in 1879, Wilhelm Wundt (1832–1920), often described as the 'father of psychology', founded the first psychological laboratory in Leipzig, Germany.

Wilhelm Wundt is often called the father of psychology for his pioneering laboratory research. This portrait was painted in Leipzig, where he founded the first psychological laboratory.

Wundt's scientific psychology

Wundt hoped to use scientific methods to uncover the elementary units of human consciousness that combine to form more complex ideas, much as atoms combine into molecules in chemistry. Foremost among the methods he and his students used was ***introspection***, the process of looking inward and reporting on one's conscious experience. The kind of introspection Wundt had in mind, however, was nothing like the introspection of philosophers, who speculated freely on their experiences and observations. Instead, Wundt trained observers to report verbally everything that went through their minds when presented with a stimulus or task. By varying the objects presented to his observers and recording their responses, he concluded that the basic elements of consciousness are sensations (such as colours) and feelings. These elements combine into more meaningful perceptions (such as of a face or a cat), which can be combined into still *more* complex ideas by focusing attention on them and mentally manipulating them.

Wundt never believed that experimentation was the *only* route to psychological knowledge. He considered it essential for studying the basic elements of the mind, but other methods — such as the study of myths, religion and language in various cultures — were essential for understanding higher mental processes. The next generation of experimental psychologists, however, took a different view, motivated by their wish to divorce themselves from philosophical speculation and establish a fully scientific psychology.

Structuralism and functionalism

Wundt's student, Edward Titchener (1867–1927), advocated the use of introspection in experiments with the hope of devising a periodic table of the elements of human consciousness, much like the periodic table developed by chemists. Because of his interest in studying the structure of consciousness, the school of thought Titchener initiated was known as ***structuralism***. Unlike Wundt, Titchener believed that experimentation was the only appropriate method for a science of psychology and that concepts such as 'attention' implied too much free will to be scientifically useful. As we will see, the generation of experimental psychologists who followed Titchener went even further, viewing the study of consciousness itself as unscientific because the data — sensations and feelings — could not be observed by anyone except the person reporting them.

Structuralism was one of two schools of thought that dominated psychology in its earliest years. The other was functionalism. Instead of focusing on the contents of the mind, ***functionalism*** emphasised the role — or function — of psychological processes in helping individuals adapt to their environment. A functionalist would not be content to state that the idea of running comes into consciousness in the presence of a snake raising its head to strike. From a functionalist perspective, it is no accident that this particular idea enters consciousness when a person sees a snake but not when he sees a flower.

One of the founders of functionalism, Harvard psychologist William James (1842–1910), penned the first textbook in psychology in 1890. (If you think *this* one is long, try reading James' 1400-page, two-volume set.) James believed that knowledge about human psychology could come from many sources, including not only introspection and experimentation but also the study of children, other animals (whose introspective reports may not be very useful) and people whose minds do *not* function adequately (such as the mentally ill). James thought the structuralists' efforts to catalogue the elements of consciousness were not only misguided but profoundly boring! Consciousness exists because it serves a function, and the task of the psychologist is to understand that function. James was interested in explaining, not simply describing, the contents of the mind. As we will see, functionalism bore the imprint of Charles Darwin's evolutionary theory, which has again come to play a central role in psychological thought a century later.

Structuralism and functionalism were two early 'camps' in psychology that attracted passionate advocates and opponents. But they were not the last.

INTERIM SUMMARY

Although many contemporary psychological questions derive from age-old philosophical questions, by the end of the nineteenth century psychology emerged as a discipline that aimed to answer questions about human nature through scientific investigation. Two prominent early schools of thought were ***structuralism*** and ***functionalism***. Structuralism attempted to uncover the basic elements of consciousness through ***introspection***. Functionalism attempted to explain psychological processes in terms of the role, or function, they serve.

Perspectives in psychology

Thomas Kuhn, a philosopher of science, studied the history of science and found some remarkable convergences across disciplines in the way schools of thought come and go and knowledge is generated. Kuhn (1970) observed that science does not progress, as many believe, primarily through the accumulation of 'facts'. Rather, scientific progress depends as much, or more, on the development of better and better paradigms.

A ***paradigm*** is a broad system of theoretical assumptions that a scientific community uses to make sense of its domain of study. A paradigm has several components. First, it includes a set of theoretical assertions that provide a model, or an abstract picture, of the object of study. Chemists, for example, have models of the way atoms combine to form molecules — something the structuralists hoped to emulate, by identifying basic 'elements' of consciousness and discovering the ways they combine into thoughts and perceptions. Second, a paradigm includes a set of shared metaphors that compare the object under investigation to something else that is readily apprehended (such as 'the mind is like a computer'). Metaphors provide mental models for thinking about a phenomenon in a way that makes the unfamiliar seem familiar. Third, a paradigm includes a set of methods that members of the scientific community agree will, if properly executed, produce valid and useful data. Astronomers, for example, agree that telescopic investigation provides a window to events in space.

According to Kuhn, the social sciences and psychology differ from the older natural sciences (such as physics and biology) in that they lack an accepted paradigm upon which most members of the scientific community agree. Instead, he proposes, these young sciences are still splintered into several schools of thought, or what we will call ***perspectives***.

In this chapter and throughout the book, we examine five perspectives that guide current psychological thinking, offering sometimes competing and sometimes complementary points of view on phenomena ranging from antisocial personality disorder to the way people make decisions when choosing a mate. The five psychological perspectives we examine offer the same kind of broad, orienting approach as a scientific paradigm, and they share its three essential features. Focusing on these particular perspectives does not mean that other less comprehensive approaches have not contributed to psychological knowledge, or that nothing can be studied without them. A researcher interested in a specific question, such as whether preschool programs for economically disadvantaged children will improve their functioning later in life (Reynolds, Mehana, & Temple, 1995; Zigler & Styfco, 2000), does not need to employ a broader outlook. But perspectives generally guide psychological investigations.

APPLY + DISCUSS

- To what extent has integration between the different theoretical perspectives occurred?
- What are the main benefits of an approach that accepts many behaviourist principles but also emphasises the role of thought processes in learning?

In the following sections we examine the psychodynamic, behaviourist, humanistic, cognitive and evolutionary perspectives. In many respects, these perspectives have evolved independently, and at the centre of each are phenomena the others tend to ignore.

INTERIM SUMMARY

A ***paradigm*** is a broad system of theoretical assumptions employed by a scientific community that includes shared models, metaphors and methods. Psychology lacks a unified paradigm but has a number of schools of thought, or ***perspectives***, that can be used to understand psychological events.

The psychodynamic perspective

A friend has been going out with a man for five months and has even jokingly tossed around the idea of marriage. Suddenly, her boyfriend tells her he has found someone else. She is shocked and angry and cries uncontrollably but a day later declares that 'he didn't mean that much to me anyway'. When you try to console her about the rejection she must be feeling, she says, 'Rejection? Hey, I don't know why I put up with him for as long as I did', and jokes that 'bad character is a genetic abnormality carried on the Y chromosome' (more on that later). You know she really cared about him, and you conclude that she is being defensive — that she really feels rejected. You draw these conclusions because you have grown up in a culture influenced by the psychoanalytic theory of Sigmund Freud.

In the late nineteenth century, Sigmund Freud (1856–1939), a Viennese physician, developed a theory of mental life and behaviour and an approach to treating psychological disorders known as psychoanalysis. Since then, many psychologists have continued Freud's emphasis on ***psychodynamics***,

The Couch! Sigmund Freud's signature therapy procedure was to have patients lie on a couch and say whatever came to mind, while he took notes behind them. This wax recreation has been displayed at museums.

or the dynamic interplay of mental forces. The ***psychodynamic perspective*** rests on three key premises. First, people's actions are determined by the way thoughts, feelings and wishes are connected in their minds. Second, many of these mental events occur outside of conscious awareness. And third, these mental processes may conflict with one another, leading to compromises among competing motives. Thus, people are unlikely to know precisely the chain of psychological events that leads to their conscious thoughts, intentions, feelings or behaviours.

As we will see, Freud and many of his followers failed to take seriously the importance of using scientific methods to test and refine their hypotheses. As a result, many psychodynamic concepts that could have proven useful to researchers, such as ideas about unconscious processes, remained outside the mainstream of psychology until brought into the laboratory by contemporary researchers (Westen, 1998; Wilson, Lindsey, & Schooler, 2000). In this book, we will emphasise those aspects of psychodynamic thinking for which the scientific evidence is strongest.

Origins of the psychodynamic perspective

Freud originated his theory in response to patients whose symptoms, although real, were not based on physiological malfunctioning. At the time, scientific thinking had no way to explain patients who were preoccupied with irrational guilt after the death of a parent or were so paralysed with fear that they could not leave their homes. Freud made a deceptively simple deduction, but one that changed the face of intellectual history: if the symptoms were not consciously created and maintained, and if they had no physical basis, only one possibility remained — their basis must be unconscious.

Just as people have conscious motives or wishes, Freud argued, they also have powerful unconscious motives that underlie their conscious intentions. Each of us has undoubtedly had the infuriating experience of waiting for half an hour as traffic crawls on the highway, only to find that nothing was blocking the road at all — just an accident in the opposite lane. Why do people slow down and gawk at accidents on the highway? Is it because they are concerned? Perhaps. But Freud would suggest that people derive an unconscious titillation or excitement, or at least satisfy a morbid curiosity, from viewing a gruesome scene, even though they may deny such socially unacceptable feelings.

Many have likened the relationship between conscious awareness and unconscious mental forces to the visible tip of an iceberg and the vast, submerged hulk that lies out of sight beneath the water. For example, one patient, an economics student, went to see a psychologist because of a pattern of failing to hand in assignments. She would spend hours researching a topic, write two-thirds of the assignment, and then suddenly find herself unable to finish. She was perplexed by her own behaviour because she consciously wanted to succeed.

So what lay beneath the surface? The patient came from a very traditional working-class family that expected girls to get married, not to develop a career. She had always outshone her brothers in school but had to hide her successes because of the discomfort this caused in the family. When she would show her report card to her mother, her mother would glance anxiously around to make sure her brothers did not see it; eventually she learned to keep her grades to herself.

Years later, finding herself succeeding in a largely male course put her back in a familiar position, although she had not realised the link. The closer she came to success, the more difficulty she had finishing her assignments. She was caught in a conflict between her conscious desire to succeed and her unconscious association of discomfort with success. Research confirms that most psychological processes occur outside of awareness and that many of the associations between feelings and behaviours or situations that guide our behaviour are expressed implicitly or unconsciously (Bargh, 1997; Westen, 1998; Wilson, Lindsey, & Schooler, 2000).

APPLY + DISCUSS

Experimental research finds that homophobic men — men who report particularty negative attitudes towards homosexuality — show more sexual arousal when viewing photos of homosexual intercourse than do their less homophobic peers (Adams, Wright, & Lohr, 1996).

- How might a psychodynamic psychologist explain this?

Methods and data of the psychodynamic perspective

The methods used by psychodynamic psychologists flow from their aims. Psychodynamic understanding seeks to interpret meanings — to infer underlying wishes, fears and patterns of thought from an individual's conscious, verbalised thought and behaviour. Accordingly, a psychodynamic clinician observes a patient's dreams, fantasies, posture and subtle behaviour towards the therapist. The psychodynamic perspective thus relies substantially on the case study method, which entails in-depth observation of a small number of people (chapter 2).

The most important legacy of the psychodynamic perspective is its emphasis on unconscious processes. The data of psychoanalysis can be thoughts, feelings and actions that occur anywhere, from a CEO jockeying for power in a corporate boardroom to a young child biting his brother for refusing to give him a tricycle. The use of any and all forms of information about a person reflects the psychodynamic assumption that people reveal themselves in everything they do (which is why psychoanalysts may not always be the most welcome guests at dinner parties).

Psychodynamic psychologists have typically relied primarily on clinical data to support their theories. Because clinical observations are open to many interpretations, many psychologists have been sceptical about psychodynamic ideas. In recent years, however, a number of researchers who are both committed to scientific method and interested in psychodynamic concepts have been subjecting psychodynamic ideas to experimental tests and trying to integrate them with the body of scientific knowledge in psychology (see Fisher & Greenberg, 1985, 1996; Shedler, Mayman, & Manis, 1993; Westen & Gabbard, 1999). For example, several studies have documented that people who avoid conscious awareness of their negative feelings are at increased risk for a range of health problems such as asthma, heart disease and cancer (Weinberger, 1990).

INTERIM SUMMARY

The ***psychodynamic perspective*** proposes that people's actions reflect the way thoughts, feelings and wishes are associated in their minds; that many of these processes are unconscious; and that mental processes can conflict with one another, leading to compromises among competing motives. Although their primary method has been the analysis of case studies, reflecting the goal of interpreting the meanings hypothesised to underlie people's actions, psychodynamic psychologists are increasingly making use of experimental methods to try to integrate psychodynamic thinking with scientific psychology.

The behaviourist perspective

You are enjoying an intimate dinner at a little Italian place on Main Street when your partner springs on you an unexpected piece of news: the relationship is over. Your stomach turns and you leave in tears. One evening a year or two later, your new partner suggests dining at that same restaurant. Just as before, your stomach turns and your appetite disappears.

The second broad perspective that developed in psychology early in the twentieth century, behaviourism, argues that the aversion to that quaint Italian restaurant, like many reactions, is the result of learning — changes in behaviour based on experience — in this case, instant, one-trial learning. Whereas the psychodynamic perspective emphasises internal mental events, the ***behaviourist*** (or ***behavioural***) ***perspective***, also called ***behaviourism***, focuses on the way objects or events in the environment (stimuli) come to control behaviour through learning. Thus, the behaviourist perspective focuses on the relationship between external (environmental) events and observable behaviours. Indeed, John Watson (1878–1958), a pioneer of American behaviourism, considered mental events entirely outside the province of a scientific psychology, and B. F. Skinner (1904–1990), who developed behaviourism into a fully-fledged perspective years later, stated, 'There is no place in a scientific analysis of behavior for a mind or self' (1990, p. 1209).

Psychologist B. F. Skinner developed behaviourism as a fully-fledged perspective during the twentieth century.

Origins of the behaviourist perspective

At the same time that Freud was developing psychoanalytic theory, Ivan Pavlov (1849–1936), a Russian physiologist, was conducting experiments on the digestive system of dogs. During the course of his experiments, Pavlov made an important and quite accidental discovery. Once his dogs became accustomed to hearing a particular sound at mealtime, they began to salivate automatically whenever they heard it, much as they would salivate if food were presented. The process that had shaped this new response was learning. Behaviourists argue that human and animal behaviours — from salivation in Pavlov's laboratory to losing one's appetite upon hearing the name of a restaurant associated with rejection — are largely acquired by learning. Indeed, psychologists today have begun to identify biochemical changes in brain cells and neural circuits involved in learning (Martinez & Derrick, 1996).

The behaviourist perspective, particularly as it developed in the United States, sought to do away with two ideas propounded by the philosopher Descartes. Descartes stressed the role of reason in human affairs; he believed that thought can generate knowledge that is not derived from experience. To be human is to reflect upon one's experience, and to reflect is to create new insights about oneself and the world. Descartes also proposed a dualism of mind and body, in which mental events and physical events can have different causes. The mind, or soul, is free to think and choose, while the body is constrained by the laws of nature.

Behaviourists asserted that the behaviour of humans, like other animals, can be understood entirely without reference to internal states such as thoughts and feelings. They therefore attempted to counter ***Cartesian dualism*** (the doctrine of dual spheres of mind and body) by demonstrating that human conduct follows laws of behaviour, just as the law of gravity explains why things fall down instead of up.

The task for behaviourists was to discover how environmental events, or stimuli, control behaviour. John Locke (1632–1704), a seventeenth-century British philosopher, had contended that at birth the mind is a *tabula rasa*, or blank slate, upon which experience writes itself. In a similar vein, John Watson later claimed that if he were given 12 healthy infants at birth, he could turn them into whatever he wanted, doctors or thieves, regardless of any innate dispositions or talents, simply by controlling their environments (Watson, 1925).

The environment and behaviour

The dramatic progress of the natural sciences in the nineteenth century led many psychologists to believe that the time had come to wrest the study of human nature away from philosophers and put it into the hands of scientists. For behaviourists, psychology is the science of behaviour, and the proper procedure for conducting psychological research should be the same as for other sciences — rigorous application of the scientific method, particularly experimentation.

Scientists can directly observe a rat running through a maze, a baby sucking on a plastic nipple to make a mobile turn, and even the increase in a rat's heart rate at the sound of a bell that has previously preceded a painful electric shock. But no-one can directly observe unconscious motives. Science, behaviourists argued, entails making observations on a reliable and calibrated instrument that others can use to make precisely the same observations. If two observers can view the same data differently, as often occurs with psychodynamic inferences, how can a scientist test a hypothesis?

According to behaviourists, psychologists cannot even study conscious thoughts in a scientific way because no-one has access to them except the person reporting them. Structuralists such as Titchener had used introspection to understand the way conscious sensations, feelings and images fit together. But behaviourists such as Watson questioned the scientific value of this research, since the observations on which it relied could not be independently verified. They proposed an alternative to psychodynamic and introspective methods: study observable behaviours and environmental events and build a science around the way people and animals *behave*. Hence the term behaviourism. Today, many behaviourists acknowledge the existence of mental events but do not believe these events play a *causal* role in human affairs. Rather, from the behaviourist perspective, mental processes are byproducts of environmental events.

Probably the most systematic behaviourist approach was developed by B. F. Skinner. Building on the work of earlier behaviourists, Skinner observed that the behaviour of organisms can be controlled by environmental consequences that either increase (reinforce) or decrease (punish) their likelihood of occurring. Subtle alterations in these conditions, such as the timing of an aversive consequence, can have dramatic effects on behaviour. Most dog owners can attest that swatting a dog with a rolled-up newspaper after it grabs a piece of steak from the dinner table can be very useful in suppressing the dog's unwanted behaviour, but not if the punishment comes an hour later.

Behaviourist researchers have discovered that this kind of learning by consequences can be used to control some very unlikely behaviours in humans. For example, by giving people feedback on their biological or physiological processes (biofeedback), psychologists can help them to learn to control 'behaviours' such as headaches, chronic pain and blood pressure (Carmagnani & Carmagnani, 1999; Lisspers & Ost, 1990; Nakao, Nomura, Shimosawa, Fujita, & Kuboki, 1999).

Metaphors, methods and data of behaviourism

A primary metaphor of behaviourism is that humans and other animals are like machines. Just as pushing a button starts the coffee maker brewing, presenting food triggered an automatic or reflexive response in Pavlov's dogs. Similarly, opening this book probably triggered the learned behaviour of underlining and note taking. Some behaviourists also view the mind as a 'black box' whose mechanisms can never be observed. A stimulus enters the box, and a response comes out; what happens inside is not the behaviourist's business. Other behaviourists are interested in what might occur in that box but are not convinced that it is accessible to scientific investigation with current technologies. Consequently, they prefer to study what *can* be observed — the relationship between what goes in and what comes out.

The primary method of behaviourism is experimental. The experimental method entails framing a hypothesis, or prediction, about the way certain environmental events will affect behaviour and then creating a laboratory situation to test that hypothesis. Consider two rats placed in simple mazes shaped like the letter T, as shown in figure 1.2. The two mazes are identical in all respects but one: pellets of food lie at the end of the left arm of the first rat's maze but not of the second. After a few trials (efforts at running through the maze), the rat that obtains the reward will be more likely to turn to the left and run the maze faster. The experimenter can now systematically modify the situation, again observing the results over several trials. What happens if the rat is rewarded only every third time? Every fourth time? Will it run faster or slower? Because these data can be measured quantitatively, experimenters can test the accuracy of their predictions and they can apply them to practical questions, such as how an employer can maximise the rate at which employees produce a product.

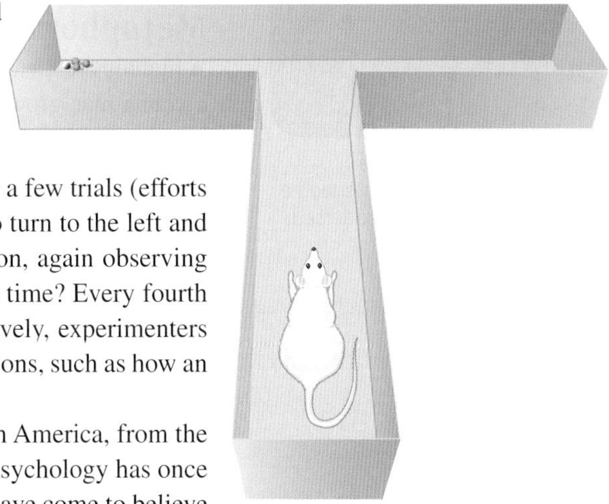

FIGURE 1.2
A standard T-maze from a behaviourist experiment. The experimenter controls the rat's behaviour by giving or eliminating rewards in one arm or the other of the T.

Behaviourism was the dominant perspective in psychology, particularly in North America, from the 1920s to the 1960s. In its purest form it has lost favour in the last two decades as psychology has once again become concerned with the study of mental processes. Many psychologists have come to believe that thoughts *about* the environment are just as important in controlling behaviour as the environment itself (Bandura, 1977a, 1977b, 1999; Mischel, 1990; Mischel & Shoda, 1995; Rotter, 1966, 1990). Some contemporary behaviourists even define behaviour broadly to include thoughts as private behaviours. Nevertheless, traditional behaviourist theory continues to have widespread applications, from helping people to quit smoking to enhancing children's learning in school.

Among the contributions of the behaviourist perspective to psychology are two that cannot be overestimated. The first is its focus on learning and its postulation of a mechanism for many kinds of learning: reward and punishment. Behaviourists offer a fundamental insight into the psychology of humans and other animals that can be summarised in a simple but remarkably important formula: behaviour follows its consequences. The notion that the consequences of our actions shape the way we behave has a long philosophical history, but the behaviourists were the first to develop a sophisticated, scientifically based set of principles that describe the way environmental events shape behaviour. The second major contribution of the behaviourist approach is its emphasis on ***empiricism*** — the belief that the path to scientific knowledge is systematic observation and, ideally, experimental observation.

INTERIM SUMMARY

The ***behaviourist perspective*** focuses on learning and studies the way environmental events control behaviour. Behaviourists reject the concept of 'mind', viewing mental events as the contents of a black box that cannot be known or studied scientifically. Scientific knowledge comes from using experimental methods to study the relationship between environmental events and behaviour.

The humanistic perspective

Humanistic theories focus on the uniqueness of the individual. Abraham Maslow (1908–1970) and Carl Rogers (1902–1987) are two key figures in humanistic psychology. They both emphasised ***self-actualisation*** — the idea that people are motivated to reach their full potential. The humanistic perspective represents an optimistic view of human experience. It assumes that people are innately good and will almost always choose adaptive, goal-directed and self-actualising behaviours.

Abraham Maslow, a key figure in humanistic psychology, emphasised the idea that people are motivated to reach their full potential.

Origins of the humanistic perspective

During the 1950s and especially the 1960s, an approach to personality emerged as an alternative to psychoanalysis and behaviourism. Unlike these approaches, humanistic approaches to personality focus on aspects of personality that are distinctly human, not shared by other animals. How do people find meaning in life, and how can they remain true to themselves in the midst of pressures experienced from the first days of life to accommodate other people's wishes and preconceptions? Many humanistic psychologists argue that scientific methods borrowed from the natural sciences are inappropriate for studying people, whose actions, unlike those of fish or asteroids, reflect the way they understand and experience themselves and the world.

Metaphors, methods and data of the humanistic perspective

A humanistic metaphor is that life is like a bottle of milk — the cream always rises to the top. Imagine a young man growing up in a poverty-stricken home environment. He longs to study at university but does not have any financial support or resources to assist him. The young man enjoys studying and does very well in school, despite the barriers presented by his home environment. He wishes to pursue a university degree in law, to fulfil his lifelong dream of becoming a lawyer to help underprivileged children. Why will this man strive hard to realise his goals and ambitions? According to humanistic theory, he will strive to become a self-fulfilled individual and achieve what he knows he is capable of achieving in life. He is driven by a desire to reach his full potential — it does not matter that he comes from a disadvantaged home environment.

The focus of the humanistic approach is on the individual's unique perspective and experience. Humanistic theorists believe that people are not powerless victims of external forces but have an innate desire to improve themselves and fulfil their own potential. The goals people set for themselves are influenced by their own personal and subjective experiences. These goals can be chosen consciously as people strive to self-actualise. As a result, humanistic methods typically centre on helping individuals to understand their unique frame of reference and work towards achieving their desire to be the 'best' that they can be. The humanistic approach is very much ***person-centred*** and relies on the therapist showing ***empathy***. The idea is to treat people with respect and warmth, stressing every individual's freedom to make their own choices in life. Behaviour can be modified by helping people to consciously and deliberately set self-actualisation goals.

The data of humanistic theory include the thoughts, motives and actions that reflect a person's inner drive to realise their full potential. Humanistic psychologists assume that people will act in ways to help them to achieve their life goals. They emphasise the central role of consciousness in shaping our behaviours, assuming that personal experience is a powerful medium for people to become more self-aware and self-directed in life.

The humanistic perspective emphasises the uniqueness of individuals and their potential for personal growth. Both Rogers (1959) and Maslow (1962) asserted that the prime motivator of all human behaviour is self-actualisation — an innate tendency that we have towards growth and the fulfilment of our potential. According to this perspective, behaviour is determined by the way in which people perceive their own worlds. Humanistic theorists believe that people experience problems when there is a discrepancy between our ***self-concept*** and the ***ideal self***. This can occur when our expectations exceed our achievements. The humanistic approach readily lends itself to therapy because it focuses on the person's immediate experience. However, some critics have viewed this perspective as naive because it assumes that people are basically 'good' and will grow if given the opportunity. That there are people incarcerated in countries all around the world is testament to the fact that people do not always act in ways that promote inner growth.

INTERIM SUMMARY

The ***humanistic perspective*** emphasises the uniqueness of the individual and focuses on the person's immediate experience. Humanistic theorists assert that people have free will — the freedom to make choices so that they can fulfil their potential. According to this perspective, people are motivated to achieve personal goals so that they can fulfil their true potential.

The cognitive perspective

In the past 30 years, psychology has undergone a 'cognitive revolution'. Today the study of ***cognition***, or thought, dominates psychology in the same way that the study of behaviour dominated in the middle of the twentieth century. When chairpersons of psychology departments were asked to rank the 10 most important contemporary psychologists, eight were cognitive psychologists (Korn, Davis, & Davis, 1991). Indeed, the history of psychology could be viewed as a series of shifts: from the 'philosophy of the mind' of the Western philosophers, to the 'science of the mind' in the work of the structuralists, to the 'science of behaviour' in the research of the behaviourists, to the 'science of behaviour and mental processes' in contemporary, cognitively informed psychology. The humanistic approach of the 1950s and 1960s was a shift away from the 'science' of psychology towards a focus on the unique experiences of each individual.

The ***cognitive perspective*** focuses on the way people perceive, process and retrieve information. Cognitive psychology has roots in experiments conducted by Wundt and others in the late nineteenth century that examined phenomena such as the influence of attention on perception and the ability to remember lists of words. Gestalt psychology, too, was arguably a cognitive psychology, in its focus on the way people organise sensory information into meaningful units.

MAKING CONNECTIONS

How do people recognise this abstract object as a dog? According to cognitive psychologists, people categorise an object that resembles a dog by comparing it to examples of dogs, generalised knowledge about dogs, or defining features of dogs stored in memory (chapter 8).

In large measure, though, the cognitive perspective owes its contemporary form to a technological development — the computer. Many cognitive psychologists use the metaphor of the computer to understand and model the way the mind works. From this perspective, thinking is ***information processing***: the environment provides inputs, which are transformed, stored and retrieved using various mental 'programs', leading to specific response outputs. Just as the computer database of a bookstore codes its inventory according to topic, title, author and so on, human memory systems encode information in order to store and retrieve it. The coding systems we use affect how easily we can later access information. Thus, most people would find it hard to name the tenth prime minister of Australia (but easy to name the prime minister responsible for introducing the goods and services tax) because they do not typically code prime ministers numerically.

To test hypotheses about memory, researchers need ways of measuring it. One way is simple: ask a question like, 'Do you remember seeing this object?' A second method is more indirect: see how quickly people can name an object they saw some time ago. Our memory system evolved to place frequently used and more recent information at the front of our memory 'files' so that we can get to it faster. This makes sense, since dusty old information is less likely to tell us about our immediate environment. Thus, response time is a useful measure of memory.

For example, one investigator used both direct questions and response time to test memory for objects seen weeks or months before (Cave, 1997). In an initial session, she rapidly flashed more than 100 drawings on a computer screen and asked participants to name them as quickly as they could. That was the participants' only exposure to the pictures. In a second session, weeks or months later, she mixed some of the drawings in with other drawings the students had *not* seen and asked them either to tell her whether they recognised them from the earlier session or to name them.

When asked directly, participants were able to distinguish the old pictures from new ones with better-than-chance accuracy as many as 48 weeks later; that is, they correctly identified which drawings they had seen previously more than half the time. Perhaps more striking, as figure 1.3 shows, almost a year later they were also faster at naming the pictures they had seen previously than those they had not seen. Thus, exposure to a visual image appears to keep it towards the front of our mental files for a very long time.

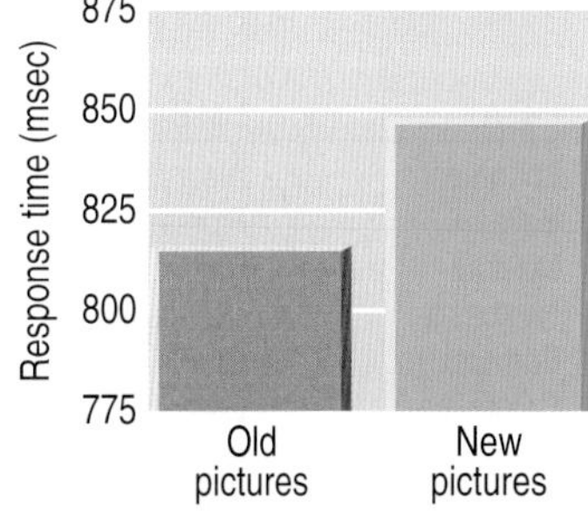

FIGURE 1.3
Response time in naming drawings 48 weeks after initial exposure. This graph shows the length of time participants took to name drawings they saw 48 weeks earlier ('old' drawings) versus similar drawings they were seeing for the first time. Response time was measured in milliseconds (thousandths of a second). As can be seen, at 48 weeks — nearly a year — participants were faster at naming previously seen pictures.

SOURCE: Cave (1997).

The cognitive perspective is useful not only in examining memory but also in understanding processes such as decision making. When people enter a car showroom, they have a set of attributes in their minds: for example, smooth ride, sleek look, good fuel economy, affordable price. At the same time, they must process a great deal of new information (the salesman's description of one car as a 'real steal', for instance) and match it with stored linguistic knowledge. This allows them to comprehend the meaning of the dealer's speech, such as the connotation of 'real steal' (from both his viewpoint and theirs). In deciding which car to buy, they must somehow integrate information about multiple attributes and weigh their importance. As we will see, some of these processes are conscious or explicit, whereas others happen through the silent whirring of our neural 'engines'.

APPLY + DISCUSS

A four-year-old is about to grab a lolly off the shelf at a shop, and his older sister says, 'No, don't take that. That would be stealing'.

- How would a psychologist from a behaviourist perspective explain both children's behaviour? How did their learning history shape their actions?
- How would a psychologist from a cognitive perspective explain their behaviour? What made the four-year-old think that inside this lolly wrapper would be something tasty? How did the older child learn to resist such temptations and to view stealing as wrong?

Origins of the cognitive perspective

The philosophical roots of the cognitive perspective lie in a series of questions about where knowledge comes from that were first raised by the ancient Greek philosophers and pondered by British and European philosophers over the last four centuries (see Gardner, 1985). Descartes, like Plato, reflected on the remarkable truths of arithmetic and geometry and noted that the purest and most useful abstractions — such as a hypotenuse, pi or a square root — could never be observed by the senses. Rather, this kind of knowledge appeared to be generated by the mind itself. Other philosophers, beginning with Aristotle, emphasised the role of experience in generating knowledge. Locke proposed that complex ideas arise from the mental manipulation of simple ideas and that these simple ideas are products of the senses, of observation.

The behaviourists roundly rejected Descartes' view of an active, reasoning mind that can arrive at knowledge independently of experience. Cognitive psychologists, in contrast, are interested in many of the questions raised by Descartes and other ***rationalist philosophers***, who emphasised the role of reason in creating knowledge. For example, cognitive psychologists have studied the way people form abstract concepts or categories. These concepts are derived in part from experience, but they often differ from any particular instance the person has ever perceived, which means that they must be mentally constructed (Medin & Heit, 1999; Smith, 1995). Children can recognise that a bulldog is a dog, even if they have never seen one before, because they have formed an abstract concept of 'dog' that goes beyond the details of any specific dogs they have seen.

Metaphors, methods and data of cognitive psychology

Both the cognitive and behaviourist perspectives view organisms as machines that respond to environmental input with predictable output. Some cognitive theories even propose that a stimulus evokes a series of mini-responses inside the head, much like the responses that behaviourists study outside the head (Anderson, 1983). However, most cognitive psychologists rely on different metaphors than their behaviourist colleagues. When the cognitive perspective emerged, perhaps what differentiated it most was that it filled the black box of the behaviourists with software — mental programs that produce output.

Recently, cognitive psychologists have begun using the brain itself as a metaphor for the mind (e.g. Burgess & Hitch, 1999; McClelland, 1995; Rumelhart, McClelland, & the PDP Research Group, 1986). According to this view, an idea can be conceived as a network of brain cells that are activated together. Thus, whenever a person thinks of the concept 'bird', a certain set of nerve cells becomes active. When confronted with a stimulus that resembles a bird, part of the network is activated; if enough of the network becomes active, the person concludes that the animal is a bird. A person is likely to recognise a sparrow as a bird quickly because it resembles most other birds and hence immediately activates most of the 'bird' network. Correctly classifying a penguin takes longer because it is less typically 'birdlike' and activates less of the network.

In only four decades since the introduction of the first textbook on cognition (Neisser, 1967), the cognitive perspective has transformed our understanding of thought and memory in a way that 2500 years of philosophical speculation could not approach. Like the behaviourist perspective, the contributions of the cognitive perspective reflect its commitment to empiricism and experimental methods. As with behaviourism, the primary method of the cognitive perspective is experimental, but with one important difference. Cognitive psychologists use experimental procedures to infer mental processes at work. For example, when people try to retrieve information from a list (such as the names of cities or towns), do they scan all the relevant information in memory until they hit the right item?

List A	List B
Longreach	Albury
Ballarat	Fremantle
Mackay	Dalby
Newcastle	Launceston
Bathurst	Charleville
Caloundra	Lismore
Woomera	Nambour
Tamworth	Warwick
Emerald	Winton
Cessnock	

FIGURE 1.4
Two lists of words used in a study of memory scanning. Giving participants in a study two lists of city names provides a test of the memory-scanning hypothesis. Dubbo is not on either list. If an experimenter asks whether Dubbo was on the list, participants take longer to respond to list A than to list B because they have to scan more items in memory.

One way psychologists have explored this question is by presenting subjects with a series of word lists of varying lengths to memorise, such as those in figure 1.4. Then they ask the participants in the study if particular words were on the lists. If participants take longer to recognise that a word was *not* on a longer list — which they do — they must be scanning the lists sequentially (that is, item by item), because additional words on the list take additional time to scan (Lalor, 2002; Sternberg, 1975).

Cognitive psychologists primarily study processes such as memory and decision making. In recent years, however, some have attempted to use cognitive concepts and metaphors to explain a much wider range of phenomena (Cantor & Kihlstrom, 1987; Sorrentino & Higgins, 1996). Cognitive research on emotion, for example, documents that the way people think about events plays a substantial role in generating emotions (Ferguson, 2000; Lazarus, 1999a, 1999b; Roseman, Dhawan, Rettek, Naidu, & Thapa, 1995).

INTERIM SUMMARY

The ***cognitive perspective*** focuses on the way people perceive, process and retrieve information. Cognitive psychologists are interested in how memory works, how people solve problems and make decisions, and similar questions. The primary metaphor originally underlying the cognitive perspective was the mind as a computer. In recent years, many cognitive psychologists have turned to the brain itself as a source of metaphors. The primary method of the cognitive perspective is experimental.

The evolutionary perspective

- The impulse to eat in humans has a biological basis.
- The sexual impulse in humans has a biological basis.
- Caring for offspring has a biological basis.
- The fact that most males are interested in sex with females, and vice versa, has a biological basis.
- The higher incidence of aggressive behaviour in males than in females has a biological basis.
- The tendency to care more for one's own offspring than for the offspring of other people has a biological basis.

Most people fully agree with the first few of these statements, but many have growing doubts as the list proceeds. The degree to which inborn processes determine human behaviour is a classic issue in psychology, called the ***nature–nurture controversy***. Advocates of the 'nurture' position maintain that behaviour is primarily learned and not biologically ordained. Other psychologists, however, point to the similarities in behaviour between humans and other animals, from chimpanzees to birds, and argue that some behavioural similarities are so striking that they must reflect shared tendencies rooted in biology. Indeed, anyone who believes the sight of two male teenagers brawling behind the local high school for the attention of a popular girl is distinctively human should observe the behaviour of rams and baboons. As we will see, many, if not most, psychological processes reflect an *interaction* of nature and nurture.

The ***evolutionary perspective*** argues that many behavioural tendencies in humans, from the need to eat to concern for our children, evolved because they helped our ancestors survive and rear healthy offspring. Why, for example, are young children so upset by separation from their parents? From an evolutionary perspective, a deep emotional bond between parents and children prevents them from straying too far from each other while children are immature and vulnerable. Breaking this bond leads to tremendous distress.

Like the functionalists at the turn of the century, evolutionary psychologists believe that most enduring human attributes at some time served a function for humans as biological organisms (Buss, 1991, 2000). They argue that this is as true for physical traits — such as the presence of two eyes (rather than one), which allows us to perceive depth and distance — as for cognitive and emotional tendencies such as a child's distress over the absence of her caregivers. The implication for psychological theory is that understanding human mental processes and behaviours requires insight into their evolution.

APPLY + DISCUSS

Humans, like other animals, take care of their young.

- Is this behaviour instinctive?
- How might a behaviourist explain the same phenomenon?

Origins of the evolutionary perspective

The evolutionary perspective is rooted in the writings of Charles Darwin (1859). Darwin did not invent the concept of evolution, but he was the first to propose a mechanism that could account for it — ***natural selection***. Darwin argued that natural forces select traits in organisms that are adaptive and are likely to be passed on to their offspring. ***Adaptive traits*** are characteristics that help organisms to adjust and survive in their environment. Selection of organisms occurs 'naturally' because organisms not endowed with features that help them adapt to their particular environmental circumstances, or niche, are less likely to survive and reproduce. In turn, they have fewer offspring to survive and reproduce.

A classic example of natural selection occurred in Birmingham, Liverpool, Manchester and other industrial cities in England (Bishop & Cook, 1975). A light-coloured variety of peppered moth that was common in rural areas of Britain also populated most cities. But as England industrialised in the

Charles Darwin revolutionised human self-understanding in 1859 by rewriting the family tree.

nineteenth century, light-coloured moths became scarce in industrial regions and dark-coloured moths predominated.

How did this happen? With industrialisation, the air became sooty, darkening the bark of the trees on which these moths spent much of their time. Light-coloured moths were thus easily noticed and eaten by predators. Before industrialisation, moths that had darker colouration were selected *against* by nature because they were conspicuous on light-coloured bark. Now, however, they were *better* able to blend into the background of the dark tree trunks (figure 1.5). As a result, they survived to pass on their colouration to the next generation. Over decades, the moth population changed to reflect the differential selection of light and dark varieties. Since England has been cleaning up its air through more stringent pollution controls in the past 30 years, the trend has begun to reverse.

(a)

(b)

FIGURE 1.5

The natural selection of moth colour. As environmental conditions changed in industrial England, so, too, did the moth population. In (a), where two pepper moths rest on the dark bark of an oak tree in Manchester, the darker moth is better camouflaged. With industrialisation, darker moths were better adapted to their environments. In contrast, (b) shows a light-coloured oak bark typical of rural Wales, where the light moth is extremely difficult to see and hence better able to evade its predators.

The peppered moth story highlights a crucial point about evolution: because adaptation is always relative to a specific niche, evolution is not synonymous with progress. A trait or behaviour that is highly adaptive can suddenly become maladaptive in the face of even a seemingly small change in the environment. A new insect that enters a geographical region can eliminate a flourishing crop, just as the arrival of a warlike tribe (or nation) in a previously peaceful region can render prior attitudes towards war and peace maladaptive. People have used Darwinian ideas to justify racial and class prejudices ('people on welfare must be naturally unfit'), but sophisticated evolutionary arguments contradict the idea that adaptation or fitness can ever be absolute. Adaptation is always relative to a niche.

Ethology, sociobiology and evolutionary psychology

If Darwin's theory of natural selection can be applied to characteristics such as the colour of a moth, can it also apply to behaviours? It stands to reason that certain behaviours, such as the tendency of moths to rest on trees in the first place, evolved because they helped members of the species to survive. In the middle of the twentieth century the field of ***ethology***, which studies animal behaviour from a biological and evolutionary perspective (Hinde, 1982), began to apply this sort of evolutionary approach to understanding animal behaviour.

For example, several species of birds emit warning cries to alert their flock about approaching predators; some even band together to attack. Konrad Lorenz, an ethologist who befriended a flock of black jackdaws, was once attacked by the flock while carrying a wet black bathing suit. Convinced that the birds were not simply offended by the style, Lorenz hypothesised that jackdaws have an inborn, or innate, tendency to become distressed whenever they see a creature dangling a black object resembling a jackdaw, and they respond by attacking (Lorenz, 1979).

If animal behaviours can be explained by their adaptive advantage, can the same logic be applied to human behaviour? Harvard biologist E. O. Wilson (1975) christened a new and controversial field called ***sociobiology***, which explores possible evolutionary and biological bases of human social behaviour. Sociobiologists and ***evolutionary psychologists***, who apply evolutionary thinking to a wide range of psychological phenomena, propose that genetic transmission is not limited to physical traits such as height, body type or vulnerability to heart disease. Parents also pass onto their children behavioural and mental tendencies. Some of these are universal, such as the need to eat and sleep or the capacity to perceive certain wavelengths of light. Others differ across individuals.

As we will see in later chapters, research in ***behavioural genetics*** — a field that examines the genetic and environmental bases of differences among individuals on psychological traits — suggests that heredity is a surprisingly strong determinant of many personality traits and intellectual skills. The tendencies to be outgoing, aggressive or musically talented, for example, are all under partial genetic control (Loehlin, 1992; Plomin, DeFries, McClearn, & Rutter, 1997).

Perhaps the fundamental concept in all contemporary evolutionary theories is that evolution selects organisms that maximise their reproductive success. ***Reproductive success*** refers to the capacity to survive and produce offspring. Over many generations, organisms with greater reproductive success will have many more descendants because they will survive and reproduce more than other organisms, including other members of their own species. Central to evolutionary psychology is the notion that the human brain, like the eye or the heart, has evolved through natural selection to solve certain problems associated with survival and reproduction, such as selecting mates, using language, competing for scarce resources, and cooperating with kin and neighbours who might be helpful in the future (Tooby & Cosmides, 1992).

For example, we take for granted that people usually tend to care more about, and do more for, their children, parents and siblings than for their second cousins or non-relatives. Most of you have probably received more financial support from your parents in the last five years than from your aunts and uncles. This seems natural — and we rarely wonder about it — but *why* does it seem so natural? And what are the causes of this behavioural tendency?

From an evolutionary perspective, individuals who care for others who share their genes will have more of their genes in the gene pool generations later. And the genes involved in promoting that caring tendency in those individuals will be preferentially passed on as well. As a result, the caring trait (or predisposition for it) will also be passed on. Thus, evolutionary theorists have expanded the concept of reproductive success to encompass ***inclusive fitness***, which refers not only to an individual's own reproductive success but also to his or her influence on the reproductive success of genetically related individuals (Daly & Wilson, 1988; Hamilton, 1964).

According to the theory of inclusive fitness, natural selection favours animals whose concern for kin is proportional to their degree of biological relatedness. In other words, animals should devote more resources and offer more protection to close relatives than to more distant kin. The reasons for this preference are strictly mathematical. Imagine you are sailing with your brother or sister and with your cousin, and the ship capsizes. Neither your sibling nor your cousin can swim, and you can save only one of them. Who will you save?

Most readers, after perhaps a brief, gleeful flicker of sibling rivalry, opt for the sibling because first-degree relatives such as siblings share much more genetic material than more distant relatives such as cousins. Siblings share half of their genes, whereas cousins share only one-eighth. In crass evolutionary terms, two siblings are worth eight cousins. Evolution selects the neural mechanisms that make this preference feel natural — so natural that psychologists have rarely even thought to explain it.

At this point you might object that the real reason for saving the sibling over the cousin is that you know the sibling better; you grew up together, and you have more bonds of affection. This poses no problem for the evolutionary theorist, since familiarity and bonds of affection are probably the psychological mechanisms selected by nature to help you in your choice. When human genes were evolving, close relatives typically lived together. People who were familiar and loved were more often than not relatives. Humans who protected others based on familiarity and affection would be more prevalent in the gene pool thousands of years later because more of their genes would be available.

Metaphors, methods and data of the evolutionary perspective

Darwin's theory of natural selection is part of a tradition of Western thought since the Renaissance that emphasises individual self-interest and competition for scarce resources. Perhaps the major metaphor underlying the evolutionary perspective is borrowed from another member of that tradition, sixteenth-century philosopher Thomas Hobbes (1588–1679). According to Hobbes, wittingly or unwittingly, we are all runners in a race, competing for survival, sexual access to partners and resources for our kin and ourselves.

Evolutionary methods are frequently deductive; that is, they begin with an observation of something that already exists in nature and try to explain it with logical arguments. For instance, evolutionists might begin with the fact that people care for their kin and try to deduce an explanation. This method is very different from experimentation, in which investigators create circumstances in the laboratory and test the effect of changing these conditions on behaviour. Many psychologists have challenged the deductive methods of evolutionary psychologists, just as they criticise psychodynamic explanations of individual cases. They argue that predicting behaviour in the laboratory is much more difficult and therefore convincing than explaining what has already happened.

One of the most distinctive features of evolutionary psychology in recent years has been its application of experimental and other procedures that involve *prediction* of behaviour in the laboratory, rather than after-the-fact explanation (Buss, Larsen, Westen, & Semmelroth, 1992). For example, recent studies from the United States, Canada and Germany have used evolutionary theory to predict the extent to which grandparents will invest in their grandchildren (DeKay, 1998; Euler & Weitzel, 1996). According to evolutionary theory, one of the major problems facing males in many animal species, including our own, is paternity uncertainty — the lack of certainty that their presumed offspring are really theirs. Female primates (monkeys, apes and humans) are always certain that their children are their own because they bear them. Males, on the other hand, can never be certain of paternity because their mate could have copulated with another male.

If a male is going to invest time, energy and resources in a child, he wants to be certain that the child is his own. Not surprisingly, males of many species develop elaborate ways to minimise the possibility of accidentally investing in another male's offspring, such as guarding their mates during fertile periods and killing off an infant born too close to the time at which they began copulating with the infant's mother. In humans, infidelity (and suspicion of infidelity) is one of the major causes of spouse battering and homicide committed by men cross-culturally (Daly & Wilson, 1988).

Evolutionary psychologists have used the concept of paternity uncertainty to make some very specific and novel predictions about patterns of *grandparental* investment in children. As shown in figure 1.6a, the father's father is the least certain of all grandparents that his grandchildren are really his own, since he did not bear his son, who did not bear his child. The mother's mother is the most certain of all grandparents because she is sure that her daughter is hers, and her daughter is equally certain that she is the mother of her children. The other two grandparents (father's mother and mother's father) are intermediate in certainty. This analysis leads to a hypothesis about the extent to which grandparents will invest in their grandchildren: the greatest investment should be seen in maternal grandmothers, the least in paternal grandfathers, and intermediate levels in paternal grandmothers and maternal grandfathers.

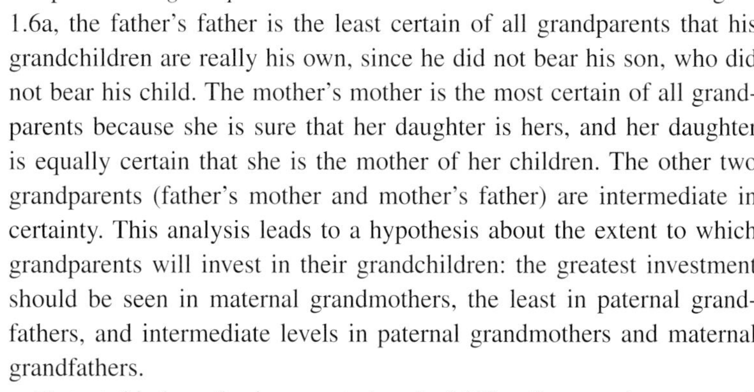

Research suggests that grandparental investment may be highest in maternal grandmothers and lowest in paternal grandfathers.

To test this hypothesis, one study asked US college students to rank their grandparents on a number of dimensions, including emotional closeness and amount of time and resources their grandparents invested in them (DeKay, 1998). On each dimension, the pattern was as predicted: maternal grandmothers, on the average, were ranked most invested of all four grandparents and paternal grandfathers least invested. Figure 1.6b shows the percentage of college students who ranked each grandparent a 1 — that is, most invested or most emotionally close. A similar pattern emerged in a German study (Euler & Weitzel, 1996), and in a Canadian study by Boon and Brussoni (1996), who found that maternal grandmothers are most often chosen as the closest grandparent. Although a critic could generate alternative explanations, these studies are powerful because the investigators tested hypotheses that were not intuitively obvious or readily predictable from other perspectives. Thus, according to the evolutionary perspective, individuals are simply acting according to their genetic make-up and inherent tendencies.

The evolutionary perspective asks a basic question about psychological processes that direct our attention to phenomena we might easily take for granted. *Why* do we think, feel or behave the way we do as opposed to some other way? The evolutionary perspective suggests a single and deceptively simple principle: we think, feel and behave in ways that helped our ancestors adapt to their environments, and hence to survive and reproduce.

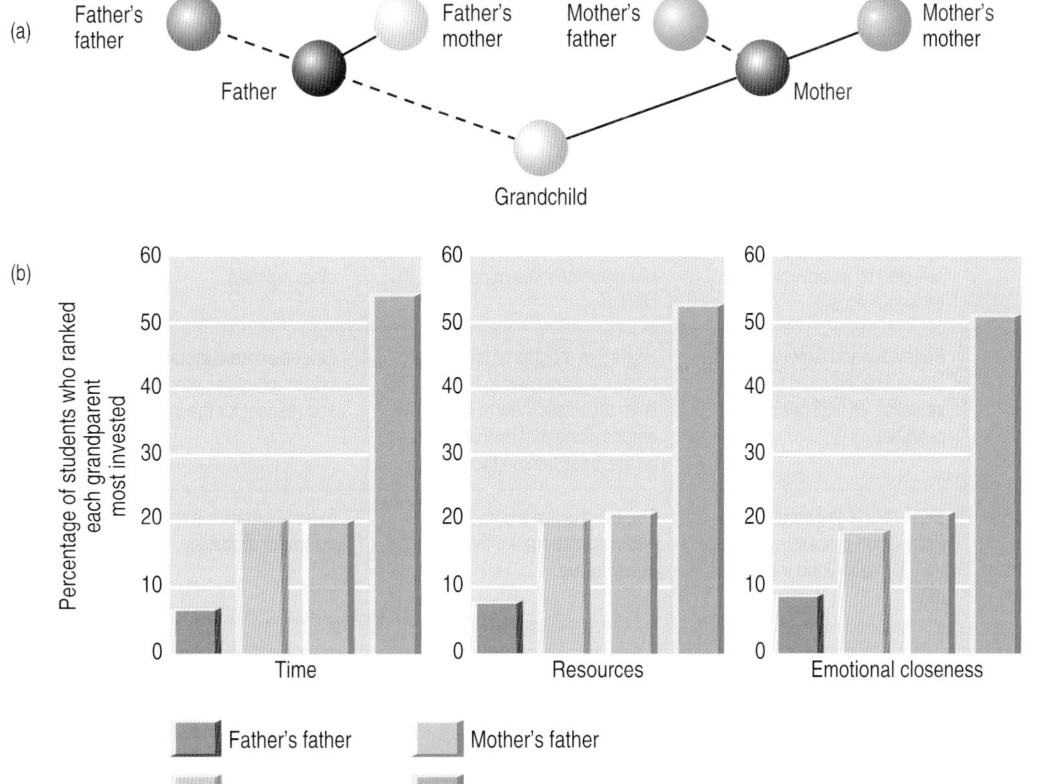

FIGURE 1.6
(a) Certainty of genetic relatedness. Dashed lines indicate uncertainty of genetic relatedness, whereas solid lines indicate certainty. As can be seen, the father's father is least certain that his presumed grandchild is his own (dashed lines between both himself and his son and his son and the son's child), whereas the mother's mother is most certain. Each of the other two grandparents is sure of one link but unsure of the other. (b) Rankings of grandparental investment. This graph shows the percentage of participants in the study who ranked each grandparent the highest of all four grandparents on investment (measured two ways) and on emotional closeness. Students ranked their maternal grandmothers most invested and close and their paternal grandfathers least invested and close on all three dimensions (based on DeKay, 1998).

INTERIM SUMMARY

The ***evolutionary perspective*** argues that many human behavioural tendencies evolved because they helped our ancestors to survive and reproduce. Psychological processes have evolved through the natural selection of traits that help organisms adapt to their environment. Evolution selects organisms that maximise their reproductive success, defined as the capacity to survive and reproduce as well as to maximise the reproductive success of genetically related individuals. Although the methods of evolutionary theorists have traditionally been deductive and comparative, evolutionary psychologists are increasingly using experimental methods.

It is interesting to compare the five perspectives on psychology. Consider, as a start, the following summary.

- The psychodynamic perspective originates from the work of Sigmund Freud and argues that behaviour is largely the result of unconscious motives and early experiences. Psychoanalytic therapy involves inferring underlying wishes, motives and fears from an individual's conscious, verbalised thought and behaviour.
- The behaviourist perspective originates from the early work of Pavlov and Skinner and focuses on learning — examining the way the environment shapes behaviour. Behaviour therapists advocate that experimental methods are needed to advance scientific understanding of human behaviour.
- The humanistic perspective represents an optimistic view of human behaviour and focuses on the uniqueness of the individual. Both Maslow and Rogers emphasised self-actualisation — the belief that people are motivated to reach their full potential. Humanistic therapists are person-centred, showing empathy to help individuals realise their potential for personal growth.
- Cognitive psychology focuses on the way people perceive, process and retrieve information. Descartes' interest in the role of reasoning in creating knowledge prompted cognitive psychologists to examine how memory works and how people form abstract ideas, solve problems and make decisions.
- The evolutionary perspective stems from the work of Darwin and emphasises natural selection, whereby adaptive behavioural traits are passed through generations to help individuals adapt and survive in their environments.

The key figures, basic principles, metaphors and methods of the five perspectives on psychology are also described in table 1.2 (see overleaf).

TABLE 1.2 Key perspectives on psychology

Perspective	Key figures	Basic principles	Metaphors	Methods
Psychodynamic	Sigmund Freud	Behaviour is largely the result of unconscious processes, motivation and early experiences.	Consciousness is like the tip of an iceberg; the mind is like a battleground for warring factions.	Interpretation of verbal discourse, slips of the tongue, dreams, fantasies, actions and postures; case studies; limited experimentation
Behaviourist	B. F. Skinner	Behaviour is learned and selected by its environmental consequences.	Humans and other animals are like machines; the mind is like a black box.	Experimentation with humans and other animals
Humanistic	Carl Rogers	Behaviour and experience are shaped by the need to self-actualise, to fulfil one's inner potential.	Life is like a bottle of milk — the cream always rises to the top. This is an optimistic view of behaviour, emphasising that everyone aims to be the 'best' person they can be.	Person-centred therapeutic approach that emphasises empathy, acceptance and respect for the individual
Cognitive	René Descartes (Descartes' early philosophical questions led many cognitive psychologists to emphasise the role of reason in creating knowledge.)	Behaviour is the product of information processing: storage, transformation and retrieval of data.	The mind is like a computer; enduring patterns of thought are like software.	Experimentation with humans; computer modelling
Evolutionary	Charles Darwin	Psychological processes reflect evolutionary process of natural selection.	Life is like a race for survival and reproduction.	Deduction of explanations for traits and behaviours; cross-species and cross-cultural comparisons; limited experimentation

Putting psychological perspectives in perspective

By Associate Professor Andrea Chester, RMIT University

This chapter introduces the five major schools of thought in psychology: psychodynamic, behaviourist, humanistic, cognitive and evolutionary. Most psychologists have been influenced by these schools of thought, and frequently work in ways that are informed by at least one of these primary perspectives.

Consider, for example, the question of what makes a successful sportsperson. Psychodynamic approaches can offer insight into unconscious processes that both enhance and inhibit performance. Behaviourists, by focusing on conscious processes, can help shape behaviour through reinforcement. Humanists add to the picture by articulating the conditions under which motivation is enhanced and sportspeople flourish. Cognitive psychologists have explored the roles of visualisation and positive self-talk in sport to enhance attitude and performance. Finally, evolutionary psychology can explain how some responses in sporting competition may be hardwired in the brain. Each perspective offers important information, but only provides part of the answer to the question of what makes a successful sportsperson.

Many psychologists take an integrated or pluralistic approach to their work — drawing on a range of perspectives to explain, research and treat psychological phenomena. The value of an integrative approach is emphasised in Erik Erikson's (1963) notion of 'triple bookkeeping'. Erikson's recommendation to simultaneously recognise the processes at biological, psychological and contextual levels acknowledges the inherent limitations of any of these explanations on their own. This integrative approach has been formalised more recently in the biopsychosocial model (Suls & Rothman, 2004). The biopsychosocial model can help with appreciating the layers of processes (biological, psychological and social) that operate in any human behaviour.

Consider, for example, the success that swimmer Michael Phelps experienced at the 2008 Beijing Olympics: Phelps won a staggering eight gold medals and set seven world records. Any one of the three levels of the biopsychosocial model is unlikely to be able to account adequately for Phelp's success, but together they can build a picture that explains his extraordinary achievement.

At the *biological level* of analysis, much was made of the 50 000 kilojoules Phelps was said to consume each day, including eggs, sandwiches, grits, French toast, pancakes and coffee. And that was just for breakfast! Phelps' physique was also described as uniquely suited to swimming: he has an unusually large arm span and proportionally short legs. At a *psychological level*, the unique set of circumstances that saw Phelps take up swimming as child and the interrelated processes of learning and memory that allowed him to develop his technique were speculated upon. Also at a psychological level are the individual differences in how people cope with stress. Successful sportspeople, like Phelps, develop strategies to harness the autonomic arousal that is a natural response to competition. The *social level* of analysis helps to complete the picture. Swinburne mathematician Stephen Clarke (2005) has demonstrated a home advantage in 80 percent of Australian rules football games. Familiarity with the ground, as well as a large and vocal support group, explain this advantage. Phelps, however, had no home advantage in Beijing. He was swimming in an unfamiliar pool in another country.

A home-crowd advantage has been demonstrated in 80 percent of AFL games.

INTERIM SUMMARY

Although the different perspectives offer radically different ways of approaching psychology, each has made distinctive contributions. These perspectives have often developed in mutual isolation, but efforts to integrate aspects of them are likely to continue to be fruitful, particularly in clinical psychology.

APPLY + DISCUSS

Patriotic feelings — deep affection for one's nation, tribe or group — are cross-culturally universal. How might psychologists from the following perspectives explain this:

- Psychodynamic?
- Behaviourist?
- Humanistic?
- Cognitive?
- Evolutionary?

Psychology in Australia and New Zealand

We began this chapter with a look at the history of psychology and how psychology developed from philosophy. We considered the contributions of different theoretical perspectives and showed how each approach can be used to explain human experience. Now that you are aware of where psychology came from, you can better appreciate where psychology is heading as we move further into the twenty-first century. In the following sections, we examine the educational qualifications required to become a fully registered psychologist and consider the main goals of professional associations for psychologists working in Australia and New Zealand. We will outline the major specialisations in the discipline and consider the various career options for psychology graduates. To help put you on the pathway to academic success, we will also outline some strategies to help you learn effectively. We will discuss how to better manage your time, how to prepare your study schedule, how to engage in active learning and how to prepare for exams.

Education and training to become a psychologist

At the time of writing, becoming a registered psychologist able to practise in Australia takes a minimum of six years. You must first complete a university degree in psychology. This involves a minimum four years of study — typically a four-year Bachelor of Psychology or a three-year degree followed by an honours program — plus an additional two years of supervised practice or higher degree studies in psychology. These programs must be accredited by the Australian Psychology Accreditation Council (APAC).

There is international pressure to review Australian psychology training to achieve global education and uniformity of registration standards for professional practice (see Littlefield, Giese, & Katsikitis, 2007 for a review). It is necessary that the review of training requirements for psychologists in Australia be informed by developments in international higher education (see Lipp et al., 2007). However, the

APAC and the psychology profession are resolute that any pressures for change will not be to the detriment of the high standards of professional training and practice (Littlefield et al., 2007).

To practise as a psychologist in Australia, there is a legal requirement that you be registered with the national registration scheme that came into place in 2010 (www.nhwt.gov.au/natreg.asp), replacing the former state registration board scheme. You cannot call yourself a psychologist (or legally use the title) until you are fully registered with the national psychology board. The new national registration and accreditation system applies to 10 health professions, including psychologists. According to the National Health Workforce Taskforce (2010), this new scheme will enable health professionals to move around Australia more easily, provide greater safeguards for the public, and promote a more flexible, responsive and sustainable health workforce.

In New Zealand, psychologists working in the public sector must be registered with the New Zealand Psychologists Board, which also involves a period of supervision on top of university training. Clinical psychologists registered with the New Zealand Psychologists Board have completed a minimum of a Masters in Psychology and a postgraduate diploma or equivalent in clinical psychology. Registration is not compulsory for other psychologists, but is highly recommended.

Under Australian and New Zealand laws, people in the same registered occupations can work and move freely between the two countries. As a result, becoming a registered psychologist in one of these countries entitles you to practise in the other.

The differences between psychologists and psychiatrists

ETHICAL DILEMMA

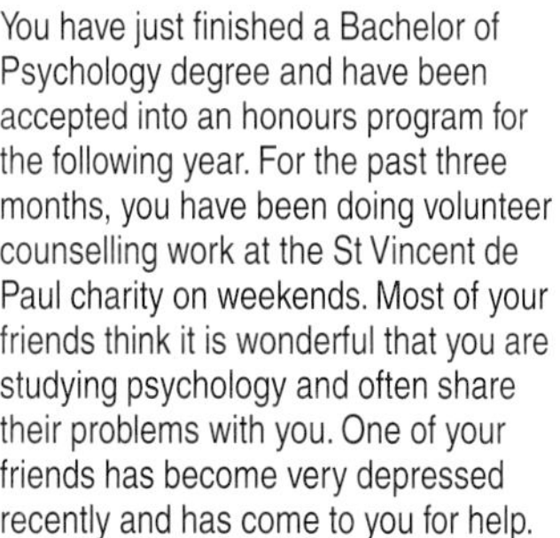

You have just finished a Bachelor of Psychology degree and have been accepted into an honours program for the following year. For the past three months, you have been doing volunteer counselling work at the St Vincent de Paul charity on weekends. Most of your friends think it is wonderful that you are studying psychology and often share their problems with you. One of your friends has become very depressed recently and has come to you for help.

- Are you qualified to give professional psychological advice to your depressed friend?
- What advice can you give to your friend?

People are often unsure about the differences between psychologists and ***psychiatrists***, or think they are the same. The two disciplines are both concerned with mental health issues but there are important distinctions between them.

Psychology is defined as the study of human behaviour and mental processes. A key aspect of this definition is the connection between the body (human behaviour) and the mind (mental processes). Now let us move one step further and look at the broad range of activities undertaken by psychologists. ***Psychologists*** are concerned with why people behave the way they do — the thought processes that underpin behaviour. They base their understanding of behaviour on the results of scientific research and investigations. Broadly speaking, psychologists are interested in the thought processes that govern human behaviour in general. Psychiatrists are interested more in the narrower field of mental illness.

There are important differences in the training and qualifications needed for both disciplines. Psychiatrists are medical doctors. They first complete a general medical degree, then do further specialist study in the field of psychiatry. Because they are medical doctors, they are able to prescribe medication to treat mental illnesses. Psychologists do not have medical degrees. They typically undertake tertiary study in the field of human behaviour. After completing their studies, they then carry out a set amount of supervised work to gain registration as a qualified psychologist. Psychologists are not able to prescribe medication.

INTERIM SUMMARY

A registered ***psychologist*** in Australia has completed a minimum of six years' study in an APS-accredited psychology course. Psychologists are concerned with why people behave the way they do; they study human behaviour in tertiary institutions and complete a period of supervised work to gain registration.

Psychiatrists are medical doctors who specialise in the study of psychiatry. Clinical psychologists and psychiatrists will often deal with the same types of person, but their methods of treatment will differ. Psychologists do not use medication to treat mental illnesses. In contrast, psychiatrists typically adhere to the medical model of treatment and may prescribe medication to their clients.

Major subdisciplines in psychology

Psychologists can apply their understanding of human behaviour to a wide variety of areas. A common misperception is that psychologists only treat people with mental illnesses and disorders. This is far from the truth. Much of the time, psychologists work with mentally healthy people to help them improve the way they function. This can often involve helping people to deal with stressful or difficult situations. For example, a person may need assistance in coping with family problems such as the death of a loved one. Or an elite athlete may need help in mental preparation for an important sporting event.

However, psychologists do not just work with people one-on-one to provide counselling for their personal problems. They also deal with group processes, such as interactions in families and large companies and organisations. In these cases, psychologists help to analyse why people behave the way they do in group situations, so that adjustments can be made. For example, psychologists may provide counselling to a couple experiencing relationship problems. They may work with a sporting team to develop strategies for improving motivation. They may also work with companies to identify working arrangements that help staff to become more productive.

Within the broad discipline of psychology there are many fields of specialisation, including a relatively new field of specialisation, ***conservation psychology***. Different psychologists adopt different perspectives in their approach to the study of human behaviour. The major subdisciplines are summarised in table 1.3.

TABLE 1.3 Major subdisciplines in psychology

Subdiscipline	Examples of questions asked
Biopsychology: investigates the physical basis of psychological phenomena such as thought, emotion and stress	How are memories stored in the brain? Do hormones influence whether an individual is heterosexual or homosexual?
Developmental psychology: studies the way thought, feeling and behaviour develop through the life span, from infancy to death	Can children remember experiences from their first year of life? Do children in daycare tend to be more or less well adjusted than children reared at home?
Social psychology: examines interactions of individual psychology and group phenomena; examines the influence of real or imagined others on the way people behave	When and why do people behave aggressively? Can people behave in ways indicating racial prejudice without knowing it?
Clinical psychology: focuses on the nature and treatment of psychological processes that lead to emotional distress	What causes depression? What impact does childhood sexual abuse have on later functioning?
Cognitive psychology: examines the nature of thought, memory, sensation perception and language	What causes amnesia, or memory loss? How are people able to drive a car while engrossed in thought about something else?
Personality psychology: examines people's enduring ways of responding in different kinds of situation and how individuals differ in the way they tend to think, feel and behave	To what extent does the tendency to be outgoing, anxious or conscientious reflect genetic and environmental influences?
Industrial/organisational (I/O) psychology: examines the behaviour of people in organisations and attempts to help solve organisational problems	Are some forms of leadership more effective than others? What motivates workers to do their jobs efficiently?
Educational psychology: examines psychological processes in learning and applies psychological knowledge in educational settings	Why do some children have trouble learning to read? What causes some teenagers to drop out of school?
Health psychology: examines psychological factors involved in health and disease	Are certain personality types more vulnerable to disease? What factors influence people to take risks with their health, such as smoking or not using condoms?
Counselling psychology: provides diagnosis and assessment, short- and long-term counselling and therapy to individuals, couples, families, groups and organisations	How do interests and scholastic abilities influence career decision making? How does stress affect behaviour?
Sport psychology: focuses on ways to enhance performance in individual athletes	Why do some athletes 'choke' under pressure? How can competition bring out the 'best' in an athlete?
Forensic psychology: provides services in criminal, civil and family legal contexts relevant to the prevention and treatment of criminal behaviour	How does psychological abuse suffered as a child relate to crimes committed in adulthood? Can victims of such abuse be considered psychologically unfit if they commit crimes in adulthood?
Conservation psychology: studying the reciprocal relationships between humans and nature, with a focus on changing attitudes and behaviours to encourage conservation of the environment	Why do people recycle? How can society change to help conserve the environment?

Thus, psychologists may undertake any number of activities, including the following:

- counselling individuals, couples and groups
- administering psychological tests to assess people's thought processes and state of mind
- planning treatment programs to address problems identified
- providing services to organisations such as analysing staff morale and motivation

- assessing people's suitability for particular roles, such as job selection processes
- carrying out academic research to help better understand human thought processes
- planning programs to effect social change.

However, people who study psychology at university are not always intending to work as a psychologist. For example, students from a variety of other disciplines, including nursing, education, human resources, occupational therapy, physiotherapy, social work and dental therapy, may take psychology courses as electives towards their degrees. An understanding of human behaviour and thought processes can be extremely valuable to people in many such situations and roles. Many people therefore study psychology as a way to improve their performance in other jobs and occupations.

ONE STEP FURTHER

The subdisciplines of psychology

By Doctor Sharon Casey, Deakin University

Psychology can be broadly defined as the scientific investigation of mental processes and behaviour. As a discipline, it includes an extensive array of subdisciplines, including how brain structure and function is related to specific psychological processes (neuropsychology), the psychological changes that occur over the life span (developmental psychology) and understanding the nature, causes and treatment of mental disorders (abnormal psychology). It also includes less obvious subdisciplines, such as the role of human thought, emotion and behaviour in politics (political psychology); the relationship between behaviour and experience and the built and natural environment (environmental psychology); and the study of when, why, how and where people choose to buy a particular product (consumer psychology).

One subdiscipline that has gained popularity over the past decade is forensic psychology. Unfortunately, it is also one of the most misunderstood! Thanks to television programs, such as *The Mentalist*, *Criminal Minds* and the *CSI* franchise, the term *forensic psychology* frequently evokes images of people assisting police by helping to identify the perpetrator of a crime, and professionals examining crime scenes for clues. While some psychologists do work with the police to profile suspects, this is more often the province of police officers specially trained in offender profiling techniques (e.g. FBI agents who train at the National Center for the Analysis of Violent Crime, NCAVC, at Quantico in the United States). Similarly, while a profiler may examine a crime scene, this task is typically undertaken by forensic pathologists.

Television programs, such as *Criminal Minds, CSI* and *The Mentalist* — starring Australian actor Simon Baker — frequently evoke images of people assisting police by helping to identify the perpetrator of a crime, and professionals examining crime scenes for clues.

So, what is meant by the term forensic psychology? At its very broadest, forensic psychology has been defined by Gudjonsson and Haward (1998) as a branch of applied psychology concerned with 'the collection, examination and presentation of evidence for judicial purposes' (p. 1). While this definition covers some aspects of forensic psychology, it fails to account for psychological work undertaken in prisons or forensic mental health facilities, which is clearly relevant to the courts. A more comprehensive definition is that offered by Fulero and Wrightsman (2009), who state that forensic psychology is 'any application of psychological research, methods, theory, and practice to a task faced by the legal system' (p. 1). This definition also covers the main areas of work typically undertaken by those working in this subdiscipline: *psychology in the law*, which refers to specific applications of psychological research and practice in legal contexts (e.g. eyewitness testimony reliability, a defendant's mental state); *psychology of the law*, which examines legal questions and processes (e.g. jury dynamics, legal decision making, police line-up procedures); *psychology and the law*, which investigates how people understand the law and the processes by which that understanding occurs (e.g. moral development and offending, public perceptions and attitudes towards penal sanctions); and *psychology by the law*, which refers to the rules and laws governing practice and how the law influences clinical practice, academia, and research (e.g. professional standards of care, legal parameters).

Many academics working within the forensic psychology field belong to what are called research concentrations, or research groups. At Deakin University, academics researching in the field of forensic psychology are members of the Centre for Mental Health and Wellbeing Research. Their research domains cover a diverse range of topics, including clinical forensic psychology (with a focus on sexual offenders, violent offenders, substance abuse, working with marginalised groups), procedural justice (policing, police attitudes, and attitudes toward police, witness testimony), and the reintegration of offenders within the community (with a focus on conditions that promote and constrain successful offender re-integration within the community). In addition to conducting their own research, these academics are also involved in research training, the training of scientist–practitioner clinicians, professional training to practising clinicians and other correctional services professionals, the provision of expert advice to government and non-government organisations with respect to offender reintegration, and the provision of expert evidence in court.

Professional associations for psychologists

Both Australia and New Zealand have peak bodies that represent the profession and its members — the Australian Psychological Society (APS), established in 1944, and the New Zealand Psychological Society (NZPsS), established in 1967. The APS (www.psychology.org.au) has more than 19 000 members. Its principal aim is to represent, promote and advance psychology within the context of improving community wellbeing and scientific knowledge. People studying in an APS-accredited university course are eligible for student membership. The APS is not involved in the registration process and membership of the APS is not compulsory. Registration with the Psychology Board of Australia is compulsory if you want to practise psychology in Australia.

The NZPsS (www.psychology.org.nz) is the profession's peak body in New Zealand and has more than 1000 members. To be eligible for full membership you must have an honours degree or higher in psychology, an approved postgraduate degree in education, or equivalent qualifications or experience approved by the society. People studying in an approved university course are eligible for student membership.

There are many benefits of belonging to the professional bodies that represent psychologists in Australia and New Zealand. These bodies help establish and enforce high standards for the profession. They act as the profession's peak body and speak on behalf of members to groups such as governments and the media. Membership allows you to play a part in ensuring that standards of education and conduct remain high. Membership also provides opportunities to network with other psychologists, access a wide range of resources and support services, remain up to date on the current knowledge in specialist areas and contribute to the future of the profession. Consequently, many psychologists also seek full membership of one or more of the nine colleges of the APS. Each college represents a specialist area in psychology: Clinical Psychology, Clinical Neuropsychology, Community Psychology, Counselling Psychology, Educational and Developmental Psychology, Forensic Psychology, Health Psychology, Organisational Psychology and Exercise Psychology.

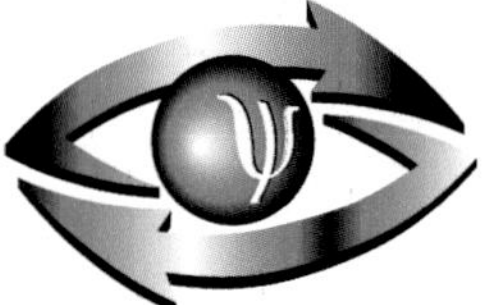

The Australian Psychological Society and the New Zealand Psychological Society are the peak bodies that represent psychologists in Australia and New Zealand.

INTERIM SUMMARY

There are many fields of specialisation within the discipline of psychology, including clinical psychology, developmental psychology and sport psychology. Each major subdiscipline asks different questions about human behaviour. The APS and NZPsS are the peak professional bodies that represent psychologists in Australia and New Zealand. These professional associations help establish and enforce high standards in the profession.

Careers in psychology

There are a wide range of career options available to psychologists. The stereotype of a psychologist is someone who provides personal counselling to individuals in a private practice. In reality, this is only one of a huge number of roles that psychologists can play. You can find psychologists working not only in private practice, but also for many public and private sector organisations. There are psychologists in such places as hospitals, prisons, human resource departments, defence organisations, sporting teams, universities, job recruitment agencies, community health services and government departments.

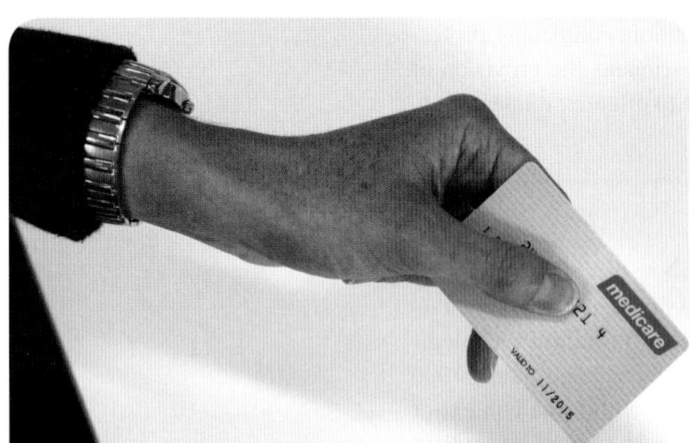

Australians can access treatment from registered psychologists under the Medicare system.

As shown in table 1.4, the major employer of psychologists in Australia is the private sector (Graduate Careers Council of Australia [GCCA], 2009). A smaller proportion of psychologists are also employed in education, government and health positions. This trend is expected to continue due to the Australian government's psychology Medicare initiative released in late 2006. This initiative allows all registered psychologists to provide services under the Medicare system, ensuring that all Australians can access effective treatment for mental health problems under the nation's health system (APS, 2006a; see also chapter 16).

Similarly, in New Zealand, clinical psychology represents one of the fastest growing fields in the discipline, with the majority of psychologists employed as clinical psychologists (Evans, 2002).

TABLE 1.4 **Employment of psychologists in Australia by sector**

Sector	% share
Private	29.6
Education	18.5
Health	16.5
Government	13.2
Other	22.2

SOURCE: Data from GCCA (2009).

Many people who study psychology work in jobs in which they are not called 'psychologists' but still apply the knowledge they have gained through their studies. For example, a company might look for someone with psychological qualifications to employ as its human resources manager. You may not need to be a fully registered psychologist to work in these roles.

Each year, the Graduate Careers Council of Australia (GCCA) conducts the Graduate Destination Survey to examine the activities of new university graduates. In 2008, the survey showed that about 88 percent of psychology bachelor degree graduates seeking full-time employment had found it within four months of completing their course. This figure rises to more than 94 percent for graduates of higher research degrees (GCCA, 2009). The median salaries for psychology bachelor degree graduates were $43 000 (GCCA, 2009). For postgraduate diploma in psychology graduates the median salary was $50 000, for master's coursework graduates the median salary was $59 000 and for PhDs the median salary was $65 000.

The job prospects for people with psychology qualifications in Australia are very good. There has been continued strong demand for psychologists in a range of different jobs. Figure 1.7 summarises the key indicators for the profession of psychology.

- There are about 22 000 people employed as psychologists in Australia.
- 60% of these people work full-time and earn on average $1190 per week (before tax).
- There is predicted strong employment growth over the next five years.
- Job prospects for psychologists are good as there is currently a very high vacancy level.

FIGURE 1.7
Fact box about psychologists

SOURCE: Australian Job Search at http://jobsearch.gov.au/joboutlook/

INTERIM SUMMARY

There are a wide range of career options available to psychologists and a number of websites provide useful information about graduate destination and industry employment trends. Contemporary psychologists can work in a variety of settings, including hospitals, organisations, private practice and universities.

How to study effectively

This chapter has introduced you to the major theoretical perspectives in the discipline of psychology and you have learned about the major educational qualifications required to practice as a psychologist in Australia and in New Zealand. Now that we have introduced you to these requirements, let us look at how we can help you to experience academic success. The reality is that you need to perform well in your studies to be accepted into an honours program to become a psychologist. It is going to take hard work and commitment to realise this goal. The next sections will outline some strategies on how to build effective study schedules that actively engage you in learning and help equip you with the skills for success. We will discuss how to develop time management skills, how to design your study schedule, how to be an active learner and how to prepare for exams.

Researchers have long been interested in how students go about learning, what strategies they use and why they choose particular approaches (Vermunt, 2007). Approaches to learning reflect the individual differences in strategies used to achieve a particular learning task (Diseth, 2003). The student approach to learning (SAL) tradition distinguishes between deep, surface and strategic learning approaches (see Entwistle & Peterson, 2004 for a review). A ***deep learning approach*** involves finding meaning in what is being studied to maximise understanding. A ***surface learning approach*** involves investing little time in the academic task and memorising information with rote learning. A ***strategic learning approach*** involves being guided by the assessment criteria and enhancing self-esteem through competition.

Recent research from an Australian regional university shows that successful first-year students are strategic in their approaches to learning (see Burton, Taylor, Dowling, & Lawrence, 2009). Strategic students monitor and regulate their use of time more effectively than students who apply a more shallow approach to learning (Burton et al., 2009). School leavers score high on the surface approach, suggesting that they are more syllabus-bound and use more unrelated memorising in their learning than do non-school leavers (Entwistle & Peterson, 2004). In contrast, 'mature-age' students score higher than school leavers on the strategic approach, reflecting an intention to do well in the course by organising and planning their study in response to assessment requirements and criteria. Mature-age students manage time and effort effectively (Burton et al., 2009). Thus, students who adopt a strategic approach intend to succeed and are motivated to obtain the best possible mark by effectively organising their study time and learning environments. Together, these findings support the view that all students should seek to develop an active interest in, and engagement with, subject material (see the *Study Guide* as a starting point for improving your understanding of the material that is covered in this textbook).

Developing effective time management skills

Managing your time effectively is extremely important if you are to be successful in your studies. For everyone, study is just one aspect of life that has to be fitted into often busy schedules. We all have family commitments, work commitments, sports, hobbies and social lives that demand our time. Unless you are organised, time can slip away. Unfortunately, when assignment deadlines and exams loom, there is no way to get that time back. Here are a few tips on how you can better manage the time required for your studies.

- *Plan out your semester*. Sit down at the start of term and develop a plan that will keep you on track. Mark out when assignments are due, and exams take place, so you are aware of what is ahead. Do not forget to allow for other commitments — for example, you might want to give yourself a night off on your birthday!
- *Set milestones and review your progress*. Write down where you want to be at a certain point in time — for instance, aim to have the first draft of an assignment completed within a certain week of the semester.
- *Do not procrastinate and leave things until the last minute*. End-of-semester exams may be months away but that does not mean you only start thinking of them the day before. It is impossible to make up for lost time.
- *In particular, do the toughest tasks first*. The temptation is to do all the easy things and leave the hardest ones until the end — and risk running out of time to do them properly.
- *Be realistic in the way you plan*. For instance, it is better to study for two hours a night, than to do nothing during the week and expect to spend 10 hours on Saturday making up for it.
- *Allow time for study breaks*. It is very hard to study for hours on end without a break. Do not pretend you are superhuman.

- *Prioritise where you need to spend your time.* Try to estimate the time required to complete those assessment pieces that you will be marked on. For instance, an assignment in a course that you have difficulty with may require more time than a course at which you excel.
- *Give yourself some room to move.* Do not commit every moment of your time. There will always be emergencies or unexpected diversions that threaten your schedule, so you need to have some flexibility to make adjustments.
- *Set goals and reward yourself when you achieve them.* It is always more motivating to study when there is a reward on offer.
- *Develop a routine.* Get into the habit of studying at the same time each day, so you plan other activities around it. Make sure you study in the right environment — if possible, a quiet place where you will have minimum interruptions. Trying to study in front of the television while your flatmate practises the guitar may not be the best move!
- *Break up large tasks into smaller, more achievable goals.* A major assignment may seem daunting at first, but becomes much more manageable if you plan to complete it in sections. This also helps you to set mini-deadlines and remain on track.
- *Do not spend all your time studying.* If you plan properly there will be plenty of time to socialise and enjoy yourself away from the desk. In fact, you will perform better if you have a balance in your life, so clear some time in your schedule to have some fun!

Setting a study schedule

The previous section on time management skills emphasised just how important it is for you to develop a study schedule. So, exactly how do you do that? While there is no right way to pull a schedule together, here are a few ideas that might help (see the example of a weekly study schedule in the *Study Guide*, the Study Guides and Strategies website at www.studygs.net and The Augustine Club at the Columbia University website, www.columbia.edu/cu/augustine, for more information).

- *Sit down at the start of the semester with a diary.* Alternatively, you could use some paper ruled up — one page for each day of each week, and each day marked off in hours.
- *Look at the assignment due dates and the exam periods.* Mark them on your schedule. Check the course materials that you have been given. They may also have suggested study schedules that give you an idea of where you need to be at any given point in the semester.
- *Next, block off the study periods that are already committed.* For example, the scheduled lectures and tutorials that you are required to attend. It is also a good idea to allow some time before and after classes to review and absorb the material.
- *Now, block off the other regular commitments you might have.* For example, regular work shifts or nights you are committed to sports training.
- *Also, mark off any other less regular or one-off commitments you might have.* The reasons can be many and varied — a trip away for a long weekend, or a loved one's birthday.
- *Now, build a regular study schedule around these commitments.* Wherever possible, make the study pattern regular so you can settle into a routine. There is more chance of sticking with a consistent schedule than doing something different every day.
- *Be realistic.* There will be times when you simply cannot stick to a schedule. Try to look ahead and see if there are times that will cause problems, and adjust your overall schedule to allow for it.
- *Spread out your studies over the available time.* Do not try to cram in long hours of hunching over the desk one night and do nothing the rest of the week.
- *Review your progress periodically.* It is important to check how you are going against you milestones and to see whether you need to adjust your schedule.
- *Also, remember to schedule some down time, when you have the chance to exercise or relax and recharge the battery.* If you have allowed for it in your overall plan, then you can enjoy a study-free weekend at the beach with no feelings of guilt!

Becoming an active learner

You may have come to study psychology straight after finishing high school, or perhaps after many years without ever touching a textbook. Whatever your background, one thing is true of tertiary education — as an adult learner, you are responsible for your own success. You must be proactive in becoming a self-directed learner and developing the required study skills. You will get plenty of guidance and raw information from your lecturers — but it is up to you to take control and be responsible for what you do with your learning materials.

As a student, you will be expected to read and absorb large amounts of written material. You will also sit through many lectures or listen to lots of recorded material online. It is important that you learn how to get the most out of these activities by becoming an active reader and an active listener.

Active reading

Reading through long passages about complex concepts can be taxing for anyone. Simply reading through from start to finish and then expecting to absorb the information is extremely difficult. But there are techniques you can use to help you to get the most out of reading.

One popular approach is the ***SQ4R method***, which stands for survey, question, read, recite, review and write). If you *survey* (skim through a chapter, looking at headings and the summary), *question* (at the beginning of each section, turn the heading into a question), *read* (as you read, try to answer the question you posed), *recite* (mentally or orally answer your question), *review* (at end of the chapter, recall your questions and relate what you have learned to your real life) and *write* (as you read or listen, actively write answers to questions and take notes), you have a better chance of retaining crucial information (see chapter 7 for more information on the SQ4R method).

A good idea is to apply the SQ4R method to chunks of the reading material as you go. That is, do not wait until you get through the whole book to try to absorb all the concepts. You might review at the end of each paragraph, or section, or chapter. A useful idea is to use a pencil to tick off each paragraph once you are sure you understand its meaning. Or, once you get to the end of a chapter, you might like to close the book and jot down in your own words what the key points and concepts are. This is an effective way to check that you have not missed anything and that you fully understand the material. Asking yourself questions is also a good way to check your comprehension. How does this material relate to other concepts you have learned? Can you apply this to your own experience? Can you think of examples that illustrate the themes? Many textbooks contain study aids that are specifically designed to help you become an active learner. Look closely at this book. The authors have gone to a lot of time and trouble to include concept maps; interim summaries; 'apply and discuss' questions; 'making connections' boxes and 'from brain to behaviour' features. Make the most of them!

Active listening

Active listening skills are important to gain the most from sitting in a crowded lecture room listening to your teacher talk for an hour or so. But they can also be used in a smaller tutorial setting, while talking one-on-one with a fellow student, or when listening in to a teleconference. There are some similarities to active reading, but also some important differences.

Active listening requires that you focus your attention on the person speaking and take on board their whole message. That means not just listening but (where possible) watching closely to pick up nonverbal clues, and tuning your other senses into the situation. Even in a lecture, you can play an active part in the presentation by maintaining eye contact and providing your own nonverbal feedback to the speaker — for example, slumping your head onto the desk is not going to help you absorb what is being said; nor is it going to encourage an enthusiastic response from the lecturer. Conversely, if you do not understand something, displaying a puzzled look on your face may prompt the speaker to try a different explanation. Asking questions is also a good way to be an active listener — you can take the opportunity to check that your understanding of a topic is accurate.

In lectures, it is advisable that you take notes along the way. But do not simply try to record exactly what the lecturer has said. Jot down the key ideas and concepts in your own words. That will help you absorb the meaning and also make it easier to recall when you go back to review the notes.

Effectively preparing for exams

As a student starting out on the path of tertiary education, it is guaranteed that you will be taking plenty of exams in the next few years. For some, exams are no big deal. For others, they are a bit like fingernails on a blackboard. But regardless of how you feel about them, there are a few simple tips that can help you survive and thrive in the examination environment.

Before the exam

Preparations for an exam do not start with sharpening a pencil or two the night before it takes place. Of course, the best preparation is to ensure that you have kept up with the study workload consistently throughout the semester. But you do need to do some revision, especially of the topics that you covered at the start of the course.

About a month before the exam, sit down and draw up a revision timetable. If you are taking multiple courses, ensure that you allow for the different exam dates and adjust the revision schedule accordingly. Be smart about allocating your time — you might find some courses harder than others, so you might need to spend a bit more time on them. Look through your lecture notes, and review the key concepts in your textbooks. Take notice of any guidance that the lecturer might provide about what to concentrate on. Review past exam papers to get an idea of the type of questions to expect. If possible, get together with other students to test each other and ensure that you have not interpreted anything incorrectly.

Allow enough time to revise the work. Cramming just does not work — plus, it is extremely stressful. The night before the exam you should skim the key concepts one last time, get your pencils, pens and paper together, and get a good night's sleep. On the day of the exam, eat a decent breakfast and give yourself plenty of time to reach the venue.

During the exam

When the exam paper hits your desk, the most important thing to do is to stay calm and relaxed. Read the entire exam paper through carefully so you understand exactly what you have been asked to do. Sometimes, there are a number of sections in an exam — for example, multiple choice, short answer and/or short essay sections. Look at how the marks have been allocated and calculate how much time you should be spending on each section. There is no point spending most of your time on short answer questions if they are worth only half the marks of the multiple choice section!

There are many tips and techniques that can help you take a more systematic approach to an exam:

- *Identify the key words in the question.* They are a clue to what you need to focus on.
- *Read the question carefully to make sure you know exactly what you are being asked to do.* For example, a request to 'analyse' topics is different to a request to 'compare' them.
- *Try not to get bogged down on questions you simply cannot answer.* If you do not know the answer, take a guess and move on. Mark the question and come back to it if time permits.

There are also some handy techniques for multiple choice questions:

- *Try to answer the question first without looking at the choices.* Often your immediate response will be correct.
- *Take a first pass and answer the questions you are confident about.* Mark them off so you do not have to look at them again.
- *Take a second pass, and look at the choices for each question.* Immediately strike out the options you know are definitely incorrect.
- *Go back and look again at each question.* If more than one answer still seems plausible, compare them and decide which appears the most accurate.
- *Choices that offer sweeping generalisations are often incorrect.* Look for words such as 'never' or 'always' as a clue.
- *Do not leave an answer blank.* If all else fails, take a guess.

APPLY + DISCUSS

One of the many ways that you can help manage your time is to create a study schedule or a 'to-do' list to prioritise your study tasks. On your university course website for this subject, you should be able to complete an exercise and create your own personal to-do list.

- What are the key tasks you need to do?
- Why is each task important to you?
- What reward would you expect after completing each task?
- What dates should each task be completed by?

After the exam

It is common practice after an exam for students to agonise over every answer and second-guess everything they have done. But the simple truth is that worrying about it excessively is never going to change the result. What is done is done.

The best thing to do is to put the exam out of your mind. Once you have received your final grade, you can then review your performance to see whether the preparation strategy and schedule you had was appropriate or needs to be adjusted the next time an exam day looms. Good luck!

INTERIM SUMMARY

Managing your time effectively is extremely important if you are to be successful in your studies. Set up a weekly schedule filled with specific study tasks (e.g. lectures, tutorials, assignments and exams) to help you stay on track with your studies. It is important that you learn how to get the most out of your study by becoming an active reader and an active listener. The SQ4R study method will help you to chunk the reading material into key concepts. Active listening will enable you to check that your understanding of a topic is accurate. Effectively preparing for the final exam involves setting up a revision timetable and applying a systematic approach to answering questions in an exam.

Central questions revisited

◆ Facts, theories and perspectives in psychology

A tale is told of several blind men in India who came upon an elephant. They had no knowledge of what an elephant was and, eager to understand the beast, they reached out to explore it. One man grabbed its trunk and concluded, 'An elephant is like a snake'. Another touched its ear and proclaimed, 'An elephant is like a leaf'. A third, examining its leg, disagreed: 'An elephant', he announced, 'is like the trunk of a tree.'

Psychologists are in some ways like those blind men, struggling with imperfect instruments to try to understand the beast we call human nature, and typically touching only part of the animal while trying to grasp the whole. So why do we not just look at 'the facts', instead of relying on perspectives that lead us to grasp only the trunk or the tail? Because we are cognitively incapable of seeing reality without imposing some kind of order on what otherwise seems like chaos.

The importance of perspective can be illustrated by a simple perceptual phenomenon. Consider figure 1.8. Does it depict a vase? The profiles of two faces? The answer depends on your perspective on the whole picture. Were we not to impose some perspective on this figure, we would see nothing but patches of black and white.

FIGURE 1.8
An ambiguous figure. The indentation in the middle could be either an indentation in a vase or a nose. In science, as in everyday perception, knowledge involves understanding 'facts' in the context of a broader interpretive framework.

This picture was used by a German school of psychology in the early twentieth century, known as ***Gestalt psychology***. The Gestalt psychologists argued that perception is not a passive experience akin to taking photographic snapshots. Rather, perception is an active experience of imposing order on an overwhelming panorama of details by seeing them as parts of larger wholes (or gestalts).

On simple perceptual tasks, then, the way people understand specific details depends on their interpretation of the object as a whole. This is equally true of complex scientific observations, which always occur within the context of a broader view, a theoretical perspective. We have seen earlier how each perspective offers insights into why psychologists believe what they believe.

To take a clinical example (an example from the therapeutic practice of psychology), a patient with an irrational fear, or phobia, of elevators is told by one psychologist that her problem stems from the way thoughts and feelings were connected in her mind as a child. A second psychologist informs her that her problem is a result of an unfortunate connection between something in her environment, an elevator, and her learned response — avoidance of elevators. A third — examining the data, no less — concludes that she has faulty wiring in her brain that leads to irrational anxiety.

What can we make of this state of affairs, in which experts disagree on the meaning and implications of a simple symptom? And what confidence could anyone have in seeking psychological help? The alternative is even less attractive: a psychologist with no perspective at all would be totally baffled and could only recommend to this patient that she take the stairs. Perspectives are like imperfect lenses through which we view some aspect of reality. Often they are too convex or too concave, leaving their wearers blind to data on the periphery of their understanding. Without them, however, we are totally blind.

◆

SUMMARY

1 Psychology

- ***Psychology*** is the scientific investigation of mental processes and behaviour. Understanding a person means practising 'triple bookkeeping' — simultaneously examining the person's biological makeup, psychological experience and functioning, and cultural and historical moment.

2 The contributions of biopsychology

- ***Biopsychology*** (or ***behavioural neuroscience***) examines the physical basis of psychological phenomena such as motivation, emotion and stress. ***Cross-cultural psychology*** tests psychological hypotheses in different cultures. Biology and culture form the boundaries, or constraints, within which psychological processes operate.

3 The history of psychology

- A classic question inherited from philosophy is whether human action is characterised by ***free will*** or ***determinism*** — that is, whether people freely choose their actions or whether behaviour follows lawful patterns. A related issue is the ***mind–body problem*** — the question of how mental and physical events interact.
- The field of psychology began in the late nineteenth century as experimental psychologists attempted to wrest questions about the mind from philosophers. Most shared a strong belief in the scientific method as a way of avoiding philosophical debates about the way the mind works. Among the earliest schools of thought were structuralism and functionalism. ***Structuralism***, developed by Edward Titchener, attempted to use introspection to uncover the basic elements of consciousness and the way they combine with one another into ideas (i.e. the structure of consciousness). ***Functionalism*** looked for explanations of psychological processes in their role, or function, in helping the individual adapt to the environment.

4 Perspectives in psychology

- A ***paradigm*** is a broad system of theoretical assumptions employed by a scientific community to make sense of a domain of experience. Psychology lacks a unified paradigm but has a number of schools of thought, or ***perspectives***, which are broad ways of understanding psychological phenomena. A psychological perspective, like a paradigm, includes theoretical propositions, shared metaphors and accepted methods of observation.
- The ***psychodynamic perspective*** originated with Sigmund Freud. From a psychodynamic perspective, most psychological processes that guide behaviour are unconscious. Thus, consciousness is like the tip of an iceberg. Because a primary aim is to interpret the meanings or motives of human behaviour, psychodynamic psychologists have relied primarily on case study methods, although ongoing efforts to apply more rigorous methods to psychodynamic concepts are likely to prove fruitful in integrating these concepts into scientific psychology.
- The ***behaviourist perspective*** focuses on the relation between environmental events (or ***stimuli***) and the responses of the organism. Skinner proposed that all behaviour can ultimately be understood as learned responses and that behaviours are selected on the basis of their consequences. A primary metaphor underlying behaviourism is the machine; many behaviourists also consider the 'mind' to be an unknowable black box because its contents cannot be studied scientifically. The primary method of behaviourists is laboratory experimentation.
- The ***humanistic perspective*** emphasises the uniqueness of the individual and focuses on the person's immediate experience. According to this perspective, people are motivated to achieve personal goals so that they can fulfil their true potential. As a result, humanistic methods typically focus on helping individuals to understand their own unique frame of reference and work towards achieving ***self-actualisation***, defined as the fulfilment of the whole range of needs.
- The ***cognitive perspective*** focuses on the way people process, store and retrieve information. ***Information processing*** refers to taking input from the environment and transforming it into meaningful output. A metaphor underlying the cognitive perspective is the mind as a computer, complete with software. In recent years, however, many cognitive psychologists have used the brain itself as a metaphor for the way mental processes operate.
- The ***evolutionary perspective*** argues that many human behavioural proclivities exist because they helped our ancestors survive and produce offspring that would be more likely to survive. ***Natural selection*** is the mechanism by which natural forces select traits in organisms that are adaptive in their environmental niche. The basic notion of evolutionary theory is that evolution selects organisms that maximise their ***reproductive success***, defined as the capacity to survive and reproduce, and maximise the reproductive success of genetically related individuals. The primary methods are deductive and comparative, although evolutionary psychologists are increasingly relying on experimental methods.
- Although the five major perspectives largely developed independently, each has made distinctive contributions.

5 Psychology in Australia and New Zealand

- You must register with a psychologists' registration board to practise as a psychologist in Australia and New Zealand. The career prospects for psychologists are very good. Psychologists work in a variety of settings, including health and community services, education, government administration and private practice. The vast majority of psychologists have chosen to become members of the peak bodies that represent psychologists, to help establish and enforce high standards in the profession.

6 How to study effectively

- You need to perform well in your studies to be accepted into an honours program to become a psychologist. It is going to take hard work and commitment to realise this goal. Managing your time effectively, and suitable exam preparation, are both extremely important if you are to be successful in your studies. As an adult learner, you are responsible for your own success. If you want to succeed, you need to be proactive in becoming a self-directed learner and developing the required study skills, which include active learning and active reading skills.
- Approaches to learning reflect the individual differences in strategies used to achieve a particular learning task. A ***deep learning approach*** involves finding meaning in what is being studied to maximise understanding. A ***surface learning approach*** involves investing little time in the academic task and memorising information with rote learning. A ***strategic learning approach*** involves being guided by the assessment criteria and enhancing self-esteem through competition. Strategic students monitor and regulate their use of time more effectively than students who apply a more shallow approach to learning. Recent research shows that successful first-year students are strategic in their approaches to learning. Students who adopt a strategic approach intend to succeed and are motivated to obtain the best possible mark by effectively organising their study time and learning environments.

KEY TERMS

adaptive traits, *p. 19*
behavioural genetics, *p. 21*
behaviourism, *p. 13*
behaviourist *or* behavioural perspective, *p. 13*
biopsychology *or* behavioural neuroscience, *p. 5*
Cartesian dualism, *p. 14*
cognition, *p. 17*
cognitive perspective, *p. 17*
conservation psychology, *p. 27*
cross-cultural psychology, *p. 7*
deep learning approach, *p. 31*
empathy, *p. 16*
empiricism, *p. 15*
ethology, *p. 20*
evolutionary perspective, *p. 19*
evolutionary psychologists, *p. 20*
free will or determinism, *p. 8*
functionalism, *p. 10*
Gestalt psychology, *p. 35*
humanistic, *p. 15*
ideal self, *p. 16*
inclusive fitness, *p. 21*
information processing, *p. 17*
introspection, *p. 10*
localisation of function, *p. 6*
mind–body problem, *p. 8*
natural selection, *p. 19*
nature–nurture controversy, *p. 19*
paradigm, *p. 11*
person-centred, *p. 16*
perspectives, *p. 11*
psychiatrists, *p. 26*
psychodynamic perspective, *p. 12*
psychodynamics, *p. 11*
psychological anthropologists, *p. 7*
psychologists, *p. 26*
psychology, *p. 5*
rationalist philosophers, *p. 18*
reproductive success, *p. 21*
self-actualisation, *p. 15*
self-concept, *p. 16*
sociobiology, *p. 20*
SQ4R method, *p. 33*
strategic learning approach, *p. 31*
structuralism, *p. 10*
surface learning approach, *p. 31*

REVIEW QUESTIONS

1. Define structuralism and explain how it differs from functionalism.
2. Describe the key premises of the psychodynamic perspective.
3. Compare and contrast the major contributions of the behaviourist and cognitive perspectives.
4. Describe the role of self-actualisation in the humanistic perspective.
5. Describe the basic premise of the evolutionary perspective.

DISCUSSION QUESTIONS

1. Comment on the nature–nurture debate. How much of our behaviour is inherited and how much is the result of the world in which we live?
2. Who are the most important figures in the history of psychology?
3. There are many competing theoretical perspectives in psychology. Which one is right?

APPLICATION QUESTIONS

1. Outline the benefits to be gained from membership of professional associations such as the Australian Psychological Society (APS) or the New Zealand Psychological Society (NZPsS).
2. Outline the current career prospects for psychologists in Australia and New Zealand.

The solutions to the application questions can be found on page 833.

MULTIMEDIA RESOURCES

The *Cyberpsych* multimedia resource is available *as an option* to accompany this textbook to further develop your understanding of many key psychology concepts. *Cyberpsych* contains a wealth of rich media content and activities, and for this chapter includes an interactive module on perspectives in modern psychology.

Research methods in psychology

2

LEARNING OBJECTIVES

After studying this chapter you should be able to:

1 describe the characteristics of scientific psychological research

2 outline the steps in conducting an experiment

3 describe the various descriptive research methods

4 explain the basic premise of correlational research

5 discuss the benefits and limitations of psychology research on the internet

6 summarise the ethical guidelines for the conduct of psychological research

7 outline the procedures for critically evaluating a study.

Characteristics of scientific psychological research

- Psychological research is generally guided by a ***theory*** — a systematic way of organising and explaining observations.
- ***Standardised procedures*** expose participants in a study to as similar procedures as possible.
- To be ***generalisable***, a study must have both ***internal validity*** (a valid design) and ***external validity*** (applicability to situations outside the laboratory).
- A measure is ***reliable*** if it produces consistent results. A measure is ***valid*** if it accurately assesses the construct it is intended to measure.

Experimental research

- In ***experimental research***, psychologists manipulate some aspect of a situation (the ***independent variables***) and examine the impact on the way participants respond (the ***dependent variables***) to assess cause and effect.
- Conducting an experiment requires systematically going through a series of steps: (1) framing a hypothesis; (2) operationalising variables; (3) developing a standardised procedure; (4) selecting and assigning participants; (5) applying statistical techniques; and (6) drawing conclusions.
- Limitations of experimentation include the difficulty of bringing some complex phenomena into the laboratory and the question of whether results apply to phenomena outside the laboratory.

Correlational research

- ***Correlational research*** assesses the degree to which two variables are related.
- A ***correlation coefficient*** quantifies the association between two variables, and ranges from −1.0 to +1.0. A correlation of 0 means that two variables are unrelated, whereas a high correlation (either positive or negative) means that participants' scores on one variable are good predictors of their scores on the other.
- Correlational research can shed important light on the relationships among variables, but correlation does not imply causation.

Descriptive research

- ***Descriptive research*** describes phenomena as they already exist rather than manipulating variables. Unlike experiments, descriptive methods cannot unambiguously establish causation.
- A ***case study*** is an in-depth observation of one person or a group of people; it is useful in generating hypotheses and in exploring complex phenomena that are not well understood or are difficult to examine experimentally.
- ***Naturalistic observation*** is the in-depth observation of a phenomenon in its natural setting; it is useful for describing complex phenomena as they exist outside the laboratory.
- ***Survey research*** involves asking a large sample of people questions, usually about their attitudes or behaviours, through ***interviews*** or ***questionnaires***.

Ethics in psychological research

- The Australian Psychological Society (2002, 2003, 2007a) developed a code of ethics that sets forth a series of principles of ethics and professional practice in psychology.
- ***Informed consent*** requires that participants be informed of the purpose of the study and the nature of the treatments before they agree (or refuse) to participate in the research.
- A small proportion of experiments involve ***deception*** (e.g. when participants are kept blind to the aims of the investigation until the end). When deception is used, experimenters need to debrief the participants afterwards, explaining the purposes of the study and removing any stressful after-effects.

The internet and psychology research

- Internet technologies are impacting on the way psychology research takes place.
- The benefits of using these technologies come from their ability to access, automate and process data quickly and easily.
- However, psychology research on the internet also raises some potential downsides, such as sampling bias, uncontrolled data collection procedures, protecting the welfare of participants and ensuring participants' right to confidentiality.

How to evaluate a study critically

- To evaluate a study, a critical reader should ask a number of questions regarding the theoretical framework, the sample, the measures and procedures, the results, the broader conclusions drawn and the ethics of the research.
- ***Critical thinking*** is essential in psychological research. It involves making a logical and rational assessment of information, assessing both its strengths and weaknesses.

Central questions: how do we know when we know something?

- Researchers often use multiple measures to advance psychological knowledge.
- Taking a scientific, empiricist approach means using whatever methods are available to study a phenomenon, continually testing hypotheses and applying experimental methods wherever possible to assess cause and effect.

RACHEL was 18 years old when she received a call that would change her life forever. Her best friend had been killed in a car accident. Initially, Rachel reacted with shock and tremendous grief, but over the course of the next year, she gradually regained her emotional equilibrium.

About a year after the accident, however, Rachel noticed that she was constantly ill with a cold, a sore throat or a bout of flu. After a few trips to a health service, an astute doctor asked her if anything out of the ordinary had happened in the last year. When she mentioned the death of her best friend, the doctor recommended that she see a psychologist. She did — and she was free from physical illness from the day she entered the psychologist's office until more than a year later.

Was it a coincidence that Rachel's health improved just as she began expressing her feelings about the loss of her best friend? Research by Lumley and Provenzano (2003) suggests not.

In one study, the researchers examined a stressful experience much less calamitous than Rachel's: the transition to university. For most people, including school leavers, entering university is an exciting event, but it can also be stressful, since it often means leaving home, breaking predictable routines, finding a new group of friends and having to make many more decisions independently. For non-school leavers, it can also mean finding time to balance study with work and family commitments. To assess the impact of emotional disclosure on academic performance, Lumley and Provenzano (2003) assigned first-year university students to one of two groups. Students in the emotional disclosure group were instructed to write for 15–20 minutes on four consecutive days about their deepest thoughts and feelings about a traumatic and upsetting experience. Students in the control group were asked to think about and write about how they planned to use their time to meet goals in the immediate and longer-term future. Students in this control group were explicitly instructed *not* to mention their emotions, feelings or opinions.

The results were dramatic (figure 2.1). Students in the emotional disclosure group had significantly better grade point averages (GPAs) the next semester than those who simply described how they would manage their time to reach their academic goals. Likewise, Pennebaker, Zech, and Rime (2001) examined the impact of emotional expression on health and showed that students who disclosed their deepest thoughts and feelings about the experience of coming to university made less visits to the health service than did those explicitly instructed not to disclose their emotions, feelings or opinions. Thus, thinking and writing about general life experiences appears to improve performance.

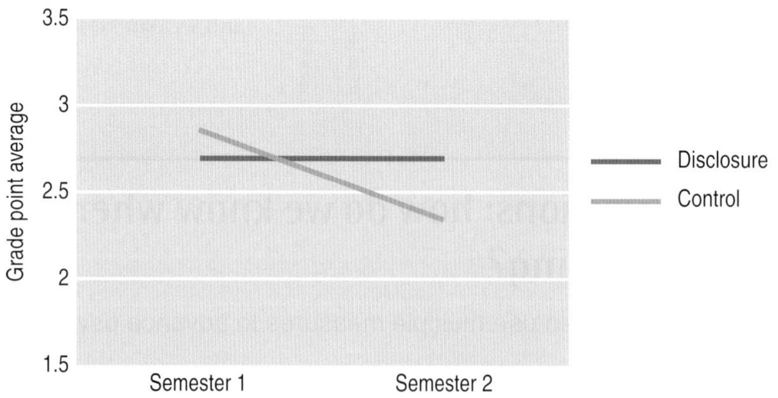

FIGURE 2.1
Emotional disclosure and academic performance. The figure compares the GPAs between the written emotional disclosure (disclosure) group and the control group for the semester of writing (Semester 1) and the following semester (Semester 2). The disclosure group had significantly higher GPAs than the control group in Semester 2.

SOURCE: Adapted from Lumley and Provenzano (2003, p. 645)

Philosophers have speculated for centuries about the relationship between mind and body. Yet here, psychologists were able to demonstrate empirically — that is, through systematic observation — how a psychological event (in this case, simply expressing feelings about a stressful experience) can affect the body's ability to protect itself from infection. In this chapter we address the ways psychologists use the scientific method to try to separate the scientific wheat from the speculative chaff — that is, to develop theories and answer practical questions using sound scientific procedures.

We begin by describing the features of good psychological research. How do researchers take a situation such as the sudden improvement in Rachel's health after seeing a psychologist and turn it into a researchable question? How do they know when the findings apply to the real world? Then we describe three major types of research: (1) experimental, (2) descriptive and (3) correlational. Next, we discuss how to distinguish a quality research study from a bad one.

Throughout, we address a central question: how do we know when we know something about people? What methods — or combination of methods — provide the most conclusive results? What do we gain and what do we lose when we 'domesticate' a psychological phenomenon and bring it into the laboratory? And how do we know when we have asked the right questions in the first place?

Central questions

- How do we know when we really know something psychological about people?
- What kinds of evidence are most conclusive?
- How do different methods contribute to our understanding of psychological phenomena?

Characteristics of scientific psychological research

The tasks of a psychological researcher trying to understand human nature are in some respects similar to the tasks we all face in our daily lives as we try to predict other people's behaviour. For example, a student named Marco is running behind on an assignment. He wants to ask his lecturer for an extension but does not want to risk her forming a negative impression of him. His task, then, is one of prediction: how will the lecturer behave?

To make his decision, he can rely on his observations of the way his lecturer normally behaves, or he can 'experiment', by saying something and seeing how she responds. Marco has observed his lecturer on many occasions, and his impression — or theory — about her is that she tends to be rigid. He has noticed that when students arrive late to class she looks angry and that when they ask to meet with her outside class she often seems inflexible in scheduling appointments. He thus expects — hypothesises — that she will not give him an extension.

Not sure, however, that his observations are accurate, he tests his hypothesis by speaking with her casually after class one day. He mentions a 'friend' who is having trouble finishing the assignment on time, and he carefully observes her reaction — her facial expressions, her words and the length of time she takes to respond. The lecturer surprises him by smiling and advising him that his 'friend' can have an extra week.

In this scenario, Marco is doing exactly what psychologists do: observing a psychological phenomenon (his lecturer's behaviour), constructing a theory, using the theory to develop a hypothesis, measuring psychological responses and testing the hypothesis. Psychologists are much more systematic in applying scientific methods, and they have more sophisticated tools, but the logic of investigation is basically the same.

Like carpenters, researchers attempting to lay a solid empirical foundation for a theory or hypothesis have a number of tools at their disposal. Just as a carpenter would not use a hammer to turn a screw or loosen a bolt, a researcher would not rely exclusively on any single method to lay a solid empirical foundation for a theory. Nevertheless, most of the methods psychologists use — the tools of their trade — share certain features: a theoretical framework, standardised procedures, generalisability and objective measurement. These typical characteristics of scientific psychological research are worthy of further consideration. The different aspects of these attributes are outlined in figure 2.2, which is shown overleaf.

A theoretical framework	A standardised procedure	Generalisability	Objective measurement
Systematic way of organising and explaining observations	Procedure that is the same for all participants except where variation is introduced to test a hypothesis	Sample that is representative of the population	Measures that are reliable (that produce consistent results)
Hypothesis that flows from the theory or from an important question		Procedure that is sensible and relevant to circumstances outside the laboratory	Measures that are valid (that assess the dimensions they purport to assess)

FIGURE 2.2
Characteristics of scientific psychological research. Studies vary tremendously in design, but most quality research shares certain attributes.

Theoretical framework

Psychologists study some phenomena because of their practical importance. They may, for example, research the impact of divorce on children (Martinez, Charles, & Forgatch, 2002; Wallerstein & Corbin, 1999) or the effect of poverty on children's psychological development (Duncan & Brooks, 2000). In most cases, however, research is grounded firmly in theory.

MAKING CONNECTIONS

Optimism and pessimism are linked to mental as well as physical health (chapters 6 and 15).

- To what extent is pessimism a cause or consequence of depression? Do people who are pessimistic become depressed more easily, or do people who are in a depressed mood just feel pessimistic because they are depressed?
- How might a researcher test the hypothesis that a pessimistic style predisposes people to later episodes of depression?

A ***theory*** is a systematic way of organising and explaining observations, which includes a set of propositions, or statements, about the relationships among various phenomena. For example, a psychologist might theorise that a pessimistic attitude promotes poor physical health for two reasons: pessimists do not take good care of themselves, and pessimism taxes the body's defences against disease by keeping the body in a constant state of alarm.

People frequently assume that a theory is simply a fact that has not yet been proven. As suggested in chapter 1, however, a theory is always a mental construction, an imperfect rendering of reality by a scientist or community of scientists, which can have more or less evidence to support it. The scientist's thinking is the mortar that holds the bricks of reality in place. Without that mortar, the entire edifice would crumble.

In most research, theory provides the framework for the researcher's specific hypothesis. A ***hypothesis*** is a tentative belief about the relationship between two or more variables. It predicts the findings that should be observed if the theory is correct. A ***variable*** is any phenomenon that can differ, or vary, from one situation to another or from one person to another; in other words, a variable is a characteristic that can take on different values (such as IQ scores of 115 or 125).

For example, a research team interested in the links between optimism and health decided to test the hypothesis that optimism (variable 1) is related to speed of recovery from heart surgery (variable 2). Their theory suggested that optimism should be related to health in general; their specific hypothesis focused on heart disease in particular. In fact, the researchers found that patients undergoing coronary artery bypass operations who are optimistic recover more quickly than patients who are pessimistic (Scheier & Carver, 1993; see also Kubzansky, Sparrow, Vokonas, & Kawachi, 2001).

In this case, optimism and health are variables, because different people are more or less optimistic (they vary on degree of optimism) and recover more or less quickly (they vary on recovery rate). A variable that can be placed on a continuum — such as degree of optimism, intelligence, shyness or rate of recovery — is called a ***continuous variable***. In contrast, a ***categorical variable*** is comprised of groupings or categories, such as gender, species or whether or not a person has had a heart attack. A categorical variable cannot easily be placed on a continuum; people are either male or female and cannot usually be located on a continuum between the two.

Standardised procedures

In addition to being grounded in theory, good psychological research uses ***standardised procedures***, which expose the participants in a study to as similar procedures as possible. For example, in the study of emotional disclosure and academic performance that opened this chapter, the experimenters instructed students in both groups to write for 15–20 minutes a day for four days. If instead they had let the students write for as long as they wanted, students in one group might have written more, and the experimenters would not have been able to tell whether differences in GPA reflected the content of their writing or simply the quantity.

Generalisability from a sample

Psychological research typically studies the behaviour of a subset of people in order to learn about a larger group to whom research findings should be applicable, called a ***population***. The population might be as broad as all humans or as narrow as preschool children with working mothers. A ***sample*** is a subgroup of the population that is likely to be ***representative*** of the population as a whole — that is, similar enough to other members of the population so that conclusions drawn from the sample are likely to be true of the rest of the population. The individuals who participate in a study are called ***participants*** or ***subjects***. Typically, researchers say 'participants' to refer to those individuals who provide informed consent and participate in an experiment. This is discussed in more detail later in the chapter, in the section on ethics in psychological research.

A representative sample contributes to the generalisability of a study's conclusions. ***Generalisability*** refers to the applicability of the findings to the entire population of interest to the researcher. Often researchers intend their findings to be generalisable to people as a whole. At other times, however, they are interested in generalising to specific subgroups, such as people over 65, married couples or women. A ***sampling bias*** occurs when the sample is not representative of the population as a whole. That is, certain elements or events have a greater (this leads to over-representation) or lesser chance (this leads to under-representation) of being selected than they should, given their frequency in the population (Reber & Reber, 2001).

For a study to be generalisable, its procedures must be sound, or ***valid***. To be valid, a study must meet two criteria. First, it must employ methods that convincingly test the hypothesis; this is called ***internal validity*** — validity of the design itself (i.e. validity internal to the study). If a study has fatal flaws — such as an unrepresentative sample or nonstandardised aspects of the design that affect the way participants respond — its internal validity is jeopardised.

Second, the study must establish ***external validity***, which means that the findings can be generalised to situations outside, or external to, the laboratory. Replicating results found in the laboratory using other data collection procedures is critical to establishing external validity (Winer, 2000). Such replication provides empirical support for the theory in various settings external to the laboratory (Winer, 2000). Does expressing feelings on paper for three days in a laboratory simulate what happens when people express feelings in their diary or to a close friend? Often researchers must strike a balance between internal and external validity, because the more tightly a researcher controls what participants experience, the less the situation may resemble life outside the laboratory.

APPLY + DISCUSS

Participants in the study of emotional disclosure and academic performance that opened this chapter were students from a university in the United States.

- Can these results be generalised to samples of Australian or New Zealand university students?
- Would the study have likely been different in a culture that discourages expression of emotions, feelings or opinions?

INTERIM SUMMARY

Psychological research is generally guided by a ***theory*** — a systematic way of organising and explaining observations. The theory helps generate a ***hypothesis***, or tentative belief, about the relationship between two or more variables. ***Variables*** are phenomena that differ or change across circumstances or individuals; they can be either ***continuous*** or ***categorical***, depending on whether they form a continuum or are comprised of categories. ***Standardised procedures*** expose participants in a study to as similar procedures as possible. Although psychologists are typically interested in knowing something about a ***population***, to do so they usually study a ***sample***, or subgroup, that is likely to be ***representative*** of the population. To be ***generalisable***, a study must have both ***internal validity*** (a valid design) and ***external validity*** (applicability to situations outside the laboratory).

Objective measurement

As in all scientific endeavours, objectivity is an important ideal in psychological research. Otherwise, the results of a study might simply reflect the experimenter's subjective impression. Researchers must therefore devise ways to quantify or categorise variables so they can be measured.

Consider a study in which the researchers hoped to challenge popular beliefs and theories about children's popularity (Rodkin, Farmer, Pearl, & Van Acker, 2000). Rather than viewing all popular children as 'model citizens', the researchers theorised that some popular children (in this study, boys) are actually aggressive kids who impress others with their 'toughness' more than with their good nature.

So how might a researcher turn a seemingly subjective variable such as 'popularity' in primary school boys into something that can be measured? One way is through quantifying teachers' observations. Contrary to many students' beliefs, teachers often have a keen eye for what is going on in their classrooms, and they tend to know which children are high or low on the schoolyard totem pole. Thus, in this study, teachers filled out an 18-item questionnaire that asked them to rate each boy in their class on items such as 'popular with girls', 'popular with boys' and 'lots of friends'. (Teachers also rated items about the boys' scholastic achievement, athletic ability and other variables.)

Research suggests that teachers have a keen eye for recognising variables such as popularity in the classroom.

Using statistical techniques that can sort people who are similar to each other and different from others into groups — in this case, sorting boys into groups based on their teachers' descriptions of them — the researchers discovered two kinds of boys who are popular. One kind was indeed the model citizen type — high in academic achievement, friendly, good looking and good at sports. The other kind, however, differed from the first type in one respect. These boys, too, were good looking and good at sports, but their other most striking quality was that they were *aggressive*.

To study a variable such as popularity, then, a researcher must first devise a technique to measure it. A ***measure*** is a concrete way of assessing a variable, a way of bringing an often abstract concept down to earth. In this study, the investigators used a rating scale — that is, a measure that assesses a variable on a numerical scale, such as 1–7, where 1 = not true and 7 = very true — to assess popularity. As a general measure of popularity, they actually took the average of each child's rating on three items (popularity with boys, popularity with girls and having many friends). In the study of emotional expression and health, the investigators obtained records of visits from the campus health service as a rough measure of illness. This was a better measure than simply asking students how often they got sick, because people may not be able to remember or report illness objectively. For example, one person's threshold for being 'sick' might be much lower than another's.

For some variables, measurement is not a problem. Researchers typically have little difficulty distinguishing males from females. However, for some characteristics, such as popularity, health or optimism, measurement is much more complex. In these cases, researchers need to know two characteristics of a measure: whether it is reliable and whether it is valid.

Reliability

Reliability refers to a measure's ability to produce consistent results. Using a measure is like stepping on a scale. The same person should not register 86 kilograms one moment and 102 a few minutes later. Similarly, a reliable psychological measure does not fluctuate substantially despite the presence of random factors that may influence results, such as whether the participant had a good night's sleep or who coded the data.

Reliability in this technical sense is not altogether different from reliability in its everyday meaning. A test is unreliable if we cannot count on it to behave consistently, just as a plumber is unreliable if we cannot count on him to consistently show up when he says he will. An unreliable measure may sometimes work, just as an unreliable plumber may sometimes work, but we can never predict when either will perform adequately.

Three kinds of reliability are especially important. ***Retest reliability*** refers to the tendency of a test to yield relatively similar scores for the same individual over time. The researchers interested in boys' popularity examined the retest reliability of their measure by readministering it three weeks later; they found that boys rated as popular or aggressive initially were rated very similarly three weeks later, confirming the measure's reliability.

Another kind of reliability is ***internal consistency***. A measure is internally consistent if several ways of asking the same question yield similar results. Thus, if being high on popularity with boys did not predict being high on popularity with girls, averaging these two items would not yield an internally consistent measure.

A third kind of reliability is ***interrater reliability*** — if two different interviewers rate an individual on some dimension, both should give the person similar scores. In the study of popularity, for example, one way to assess interrater reliability would have been to ask two different teachers who knew the same children to rate them and to see whether their ratings were similar. Although some variables can be rated quite easily with relatively high reliability, others, such as optimism as assessed from people's diaries, require the development of detailed coding manuals to guarantee that different raters are similarly 'calibrated', like two thermometers recording temperature in the same room.

The distinctions among these kinds of reliability can be clarified by returning to the plumbing analogy. A plumber establishes retest reliability by showing up when he says he will on different occasions and by performing competently on each occasion. He establishes internal consistency by fixing an overflowing toilet with as much dispatch as he would a blocked-up sink. He can boast interrater reliability if his customers agree in their assessment of his work. If he fails any of these reliability tests, he is unlikely to be called again, just as an unreliable measure will not be used in another study.

Validity

A study can be valid only if the measures it relies on are themselves valid. When the term ***validity*** is applied to a psychological measure, it refers to the measure's ability to assess the variable it is supposed to assess. For example, IQ tests are supposed to measure intelligence. One way psychologists have tried to demonstrate the validity of IQ test scores is to show that they consistently predict other phenomena that require intellectual ability, such as school performance. As we will see in chapter 9, IQ tests are, in general, highly predictive of school success (Anastasi & Urbina, 1997). Some of the measures people intuitively use in their daily lives have much less certain validity, as when Marco initially presumed that his lecturer's inflexibility in arranging meetings with students was a good index of her general flexibility (rather than, say, a tight schedule).

To ensure the validity of a psychological measure, researchers conduct validation research. ***Validation*** means demonstrating that a measure consistently relates to some objective criterion or to other measures that have themselves already demonstrated their validity. For example, the teacher report measure used to assess children's popularity, aggressiveness, academic achievement and other variables had been shown in several prior studies to agree with behavioural observations by people trained to watch children interact in the classroom. It also predicted children's functioning as many as eight years later (e.g. rates of school drop-out and teenage pregnancy). Showing that a measure of children's achievement, popularity and adjustment can predict how well they will do socially and academically several years later provides strong evidence for the validity of the measure, because a central characteristic of a valid measure is that it can predict other variables with which it should, theoretically, be related.

MAKING CONNECTIONS

Sometimes artistic geniuses are brilliant in other realms, and sometimes they are not.

- If an IQ test can predict school success but not artistic genius, is it a valid measure of intelligence?
- What assumptions about the meaning of **intelligence** underlie the use of paper-and-pencil IQ tests (chapter 9)?

Multiple measures

One of the best ways to obtain an accurate assessment of a variable is to employ multiple measures of it. Multiple measures are important because no psychological measure is perfect. A measure that assesses a variable accurately 80 percent of the time is excellent — but it is also inaccurate 20 percent of the time. In fact, built into every measure is a certain amount of ***error***, or discrepancy between the phenomenon as measured and the phenomenon as it really is. For example, IQ is a good predictor of school success *most* of the time, but for some people it overpredicts or underpredicts their performance. Multiple measures therefore provide a safety net for catching errors.

Virtually all good psychological studies share the ingredients of psychological research outlined here: a theoretical framework, standardised procedures, generalisability and objective measurement. Nevertheless, studies vary considerably in design and goals. The following sections examine three broad types of research (table 2.1; see overleaf): experimental, descriptive and correlational. In actuality, the lines separating these types are not hard and fast. Many studies categorised as descriptive include experimental components, and correlational questions are often built into experiments. The aim in designing research is scientific rigour and practicality, not purity; the best strategy is to use whatever systematic empirical methods are available to explore the hypothesis and to see whether different methods and designs converge on similar findings — that is, to see whether the finding is 'reliable' using different methods.

TABLE 2.1 **Comparison of research methods**

Method	Description	Uses and advantages	Potential limitations
Experimental	Manipulation of variables to assess cause and effect	• Demonstrates causal relationships • Replicability: study can be repeated to see if the same findings emerge • Maximises control over relevant variables	• Generalisability outside the laboratory • Some complex phenomena cannot be readily tested using pure experimental methods
Descriptive			
Case study	In-depth observation of a small number of cases	• Describes psychological processes as they occur in individual cases • Allows study of complex phenomena not easily reproduced experimentally • Provides data that can be useful in framing hypotheses	• Generalisability to the population • Replicability: study may not be repeatable • Researcher bias • Cannot establish causation
Naturalistic observation	In-depth observation of a phenomenon as it occurs in nature	• Reveals phenomena as they exist outside the laboratory • Allows study of complex phenomena not easily reproduced experimentally • Provides data that can be useful in framing hypotheses	• Generalisability to the population • Observer effects: the presence of an observer may alter the behaviour of the participants • Replicability • Researcher bias • Cannot establish causation
Survey research	Asking people questions about their attitudes, behaviour etc.	• Reveals attitudes or self-reported behaviours of a large sample of individuals • Allows quantification of attitudes or behaviours	• Self-report bias: people may not be able to report honestly or accurately • Cannot establish causation
Correlational	Examines the extent to which two or more variables are related and can be used to predict one another	• Reveals relationships among variables as they exist outside the laboratory • Allows quantification of relationships among variables	• Cannot establish causation

Step by step, until dancing with the concepts

By Doctor Kenneth I. Mavor, Australian National University

The advent of dancing reality television shows has made partner dancing popular again, and many people have made dancing into a new hobby. Learning particular dances, however, requires time and good instruction. There are some important similarities between learning to dance, and learning statistics and research methods. Ultimately, what makes dancing worth watching, and exhilarating to do, is the complex connection between the partners and the music. A good connection between partners, and good musicality, requires more than just learning the steps. They require a more complex understanding of the structure of the music and the range of ways that both partners respond to it. In learning research methods and statistics, this can be called the *relational* approach to learning (Skemp, 1976), in which particular statistical procedures and design methods form part of a larger and deeper understanding of how knowledge in psychology is developed and tested.

Like with learning to dance, everyone starts with the basics with learning research methods and statistics. All dancers start by learning the distinctive rhythm of a particular dance and the most basic steps; and repetition is used to make sure these basic steps are comfortable. Similarly, research methods and statistics are taught by giving the basic techniques for carrying out particular analyses. Pearson's correlation coefficient, for example, is a very basic step in the dance involving two continuous variables. As students progress through the levels of learning and skill, they will find more advanced steps in that particular dance, such as regression and factor analysis, but these advanced techniques benefit from a good understanding of the basic concept of correlation. To learn correlation involves some exercises and repetition — breaking down the steps into smaller segments, as would occur with learning to dance, and then using the steps in a range of research contexts (like dancing to a variety of music). It is important to remember, however, what is the ultimate purpose of early exercises.

There are some similarities between learning statistics and research methods and the process that participants on reality television shows, such as *Dancing with the Stars*, undergo in learning to dance.

Those who learn to dance just by learning and remembering steps and sequences of steps are much less interesting to dance with or to watch, because the dance is hollow and lifeless. Each new step they learn becomes increasingly difficult, as there is simply more and more to remember. However, someone who comes to understand the dance learns more complex steps as combinations of the simple steps and how they can be used to respond to the music, so learning new steps actually gets easier over time.

Similarly, some students take what is called an *instrumental* approach to learning. Such students only learn what is necessary to pass an exam, or to get an answer to simple exercises without really understanding why (Skemp, 1976). This is, ultimately, hollow and unsatisfying. When these students later try to learn more complex procedures, like regression or factor analysis, the effort just gets harder and harder for them. However, students who take the relational approach to the basic concepts will find that the more complex concepts become easier over time, because they fit into a larger picture of understanding. This approach is, ultimately, much more pleasing. It is pleasing to see students find a deeper appreciation for the concepts and to truly learn to dance with ideas.

INTERIM SUMMARY

Just as researchers take a sample of a population, they similarly take a 'sample' of a variable — that is, they use a ***measure*** of the variable, which provides a concrete way of assessing it. A measure is ***reliable*** if it produces consistent results — that is, if it does not show too much random fluctuation. A measure is ***valid*** if it accurately assesses or 'samples' the construct it is intended to measure. Because every measure includes some degree of error, researchers often use multiple measures (in order to assess more than one sample of the relevant behaviour).

Experimental research

Psychology takes a ***scientific approach*** to research, using empirical methodologies to gain knowledge (see Badcock, Hammond, Gillam, Brewer, & Andrews, 2007). Empirical methodologies involve a process where hypotheses are tested using experimentation and observation in order to further understanding of a topic. The scientific approach does not rely merely on intuition or gut feeling — it involves the rigorous testing of a theory, using methods that other researchers can replicate. The scientific approach has three main goals — ***description***, ***prediction*** and ***understanding*** (Shaughnessy & Zechmeister, 1997). Description involves being able to summarise the data your research has produced in a way that makes the events and their relationships easily understandable. Prediction involves using the outcome of your research to be able to identify what would happen in the future, given the same circumstances. Understanding involves identifying why that would happen — the causal factors that led to the results found in your research.

In ***experimental research***, investigators manipulate some aspect of a situation and examine the impact on the way participants respond. Experimental methods are important because they can establish cause and effect — causation — directly. An experiment can demonstrate causation by proving that manipulating one variable leads to predicted changes in another. The researchers studying the impact of emotional disclosure on academic performance could be confident that participants writing about their emotions relating to a stressful experience *caused* better performance, because participants who did so were better able to maintain their GPAs over time than those who did not. University students do not typically write for 15 to 20 minutes a day for four consecutive days about the experience of beginning university, but when researchers influenced their behaviour in this way, they found some very practical, and theoretically interesting, impacts on academic performance.

The logic of experimentation

The logic of experimentation is much more straightforward and intuitive than many people think. (Marco used it implicitly when he tested his lecturer's flexibility, as we all do multiple times a day in one situation after another.) An experimenter manipulates variables, called ***independent variables***, which are outside the participants' control (i.e. independent of their actions). The aim is to assess the impact of these manipulations on the way participants subsequently respond. Because participants' responses depend on their exposure to the independent variable, these responses are known as ***dependent variables***. The independent variable, then, is the variable the experimenter manipulates; the dependent variable is the response the experimenter measures to see whether the experimental manipulation had an effect.

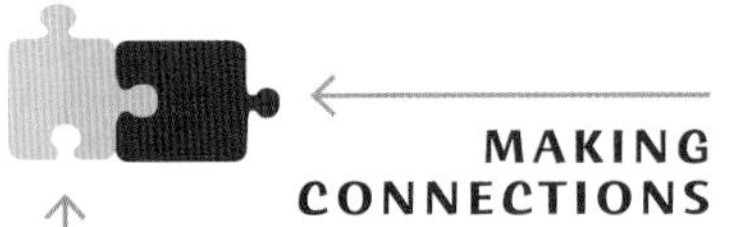

MAKING CONNECTIONS

In Harlow's classic studies of emotional attachment, monkeys were separated from birth from their mothers and given the choice of spending time with a wire mother or a cloth mother. Regardless of which 'mother' fed the baby monkey, it preferred the soft cloth mother, suggesting that security, not nourishment, is the basis of **attachment** in monkeys (chapter 13).

To assess cause and effect, experimenters present participants with different possible variations, or ***conditions***, of the independent variable and study the way participants react. In the study of emotional disclosure and academic performance that opened this chapter, the experimenters used an independent variable (the transition to university) with two conditions (disclosure or control). They then tested the impact on performance (dependent variable).

Consider a series of classic studies conducted in the 1950s by Harry Harlow and his colleagues (Harlow & Zimmerman, 1959). They were interested in determining which of two theories better explained why infant monkeys become emotionally attached to their mothers. One theory proposed that the basis for this attachment was the mother's role as the source of food. An alternative theory suggested that infant monkeys are drawn by the security and comfort mothers provide.

To compare these two theories, the researchers conducted an experiment in which infant monkeys were separated from their mothers and raised in social isolation. Each monkey shared its cage with two surrogate (replacement) 'mothers', one made of wire and the other also made of wire but covered with terry-towelling cloth (and hence softer and more 'maternal' to the touch).

The independent variable — the variable manipulated by the researchers — was the placement of the milk bottle. In one experimental condition, a bottle was attached to the wire mother, whereas in the other condition it was attached to the cloth mother. The dependent variable was the infant monkeys' response, notably the amount of time they spent holding onto each of the two mothers, and which mother they turned to when frightened. The researchers tested the hypothesis that the infant monkeys would cling to the cloth mother regardless of which mother held the bottle.

In fact, as predicted, whether the wire or the cloth surrogate was the source of milk did not matter. The infants showed a clear preference for the cloth surrogate. Harlow and Zimmerman (1959) concluded that security and comfort were more important than simple nourishment in the development of attachment (chapter 13).

INTERIM SUMMARY

The ***scientific approach*** to psychology uses empirical methodologies to gain knowledge. ***Description*** (summarising relationships between variables), ***prediction*** (anticipating future events) and ***understanding*** (identifying the causes of a phenomenon) are the three main goals of the scientific approach. In ***experimental research***, psychologists manipulate some aspect of a situation (the ***independent variables***) and examine the impact on the way participants respond (the ***dependent variables***). By comparing results in different experimental ***conditions***, researchers can assess cause and effect.

Steps in conducting an experiment

Experiments vary widely in both their design and their goals, but the steps in conceiving and executing them are roughly the same, from the starting point of framing a hypothesis to the ultimate evaluation of findings (figure 2.3). Although these steps relate specifically to the experimental method, many apply to descriptive and correlational methods as well.

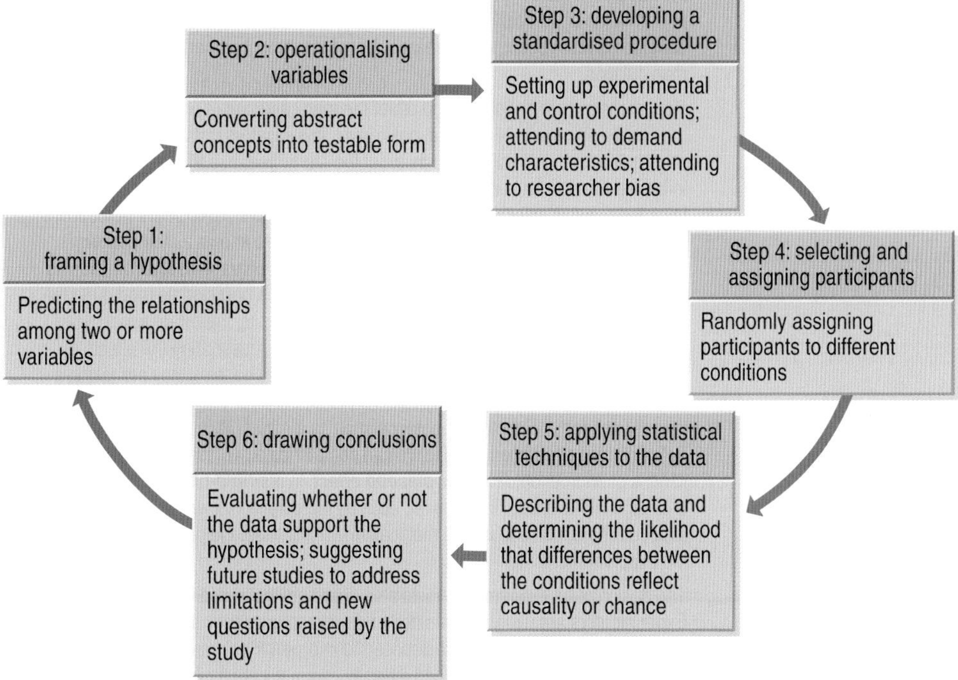

FIGURE 2.3
Conducting an experiment requires systematically going through a series of steps, from the initial framing of a hypothesis to drawing conclusions about the data. The process is circular, as the conclusion of one study is generally the origin of another.

Table 2.2 provides a more detailed guide to the different steps that are involved in conducting an experiment. An example of a research experiment is provided in the following figure.

TABLE 2.2 Guide to the steps in conducting an experiment

Step	Explanation
1. Framing a hypothesis	To conduct an experiment, a researcher must first frame a hypothesis that predicts the relationship between two or more variables. Usually that hypothesis is derived from a theory. Gordon Bower (1981, 1989) and his associates hypothesised that people who are in a positive mood while learning new information will be more likely to remember pleasant aspects of that information. Conversely, people in a negative mood while learning will be more likely to remember negative information. This hypothesis states a relationship between two variables: mood state when learning material (the independent variable) and later ability to recall that material (the dependent variable).
2. Operationalising variables	***Operationalising*** means turning an abstract concept into a concrete variable defined by some set of actions, or operations. Bower (1981) operationalised the independent variable, mood state, by hypnotising participants to feel either happy or sad (the two conditions of the independent variable). He then had participants read a psychiatric patient's descriptions of various happy and sad memories. Bower operationalised the dependent variable — the ability to recall either positive or negative information — as the number of positive and negative memories the participant could recall 20 minutes later.
3. Developing a standardised procedure	Standardised procedures maximise the likelihood that any differences observed in participants' behaviour can be attributed to the experimental manipulation, allowing the investigator to draw inferences about cause and effect. Experimental research

(continued)

TABLE 2.2 *(continued)*

Step	Explanation
3. Developing a standardised procedure *(continued)*	typically involves dividing participants into groups who experience different conditions of the independent variable and then comparing the responses of the different groups. Experiments often include another kind of group or condition, called a ***control group***. Instead of being exposed to the experimental manipulation, participants in the control group experience a neutral condition. Examining the performance of participants who have not been exposed to the experimental condition gives researchers a clearer view of the impact of the experimental manipulation. Researchers try to anticipate and offset the many sources of bias that can affect the results of a study. At the most basic level, investigators must ensure that participants do not know too much about the study, because this knowledge could influence their performance. Some participants try to respond in the way they think the experimenter wants them to respond. The ways participants' perceptions of the researcher's goals influence their responses are known as the ***demand characteristics*** of a study. To prevent these demand characteristics from biasing results, psychologists conduct ***blind studies***, in which participants (and often the researchers themselves) are kept unaware of, or blind to, important aspects of the research. Blind studies are especially valuable in researching the effects of medication on psychological symptoms. Participants who think they are taking a medication often find that their symptoms disappear after they have taken what is really an inert, or inactive, substance such as a sugar pill (a placebo). Simply believing that a treatment is effective can sometimes prove as effective as the drug itself, a phenomenon called the ***placebo effect***. In a ***single-blind study***, participants are kept blind to crucial information, such as the condition to which they are being exposed (here, placebo versus medication). In this case, the participant is blind, but the experimenter is not. The design of an experiment should also guard against researcher bias. Experimenters are usually committed to the hypotheses they set out to test and, being human, they might be predisposed to interpret their results in a positive light. Experimenters may also inadvertently communicate their expectations to participants — for example, by probing for improvement more in the medication group than in the control group. The best way to avoid the biases of both participants and investigators is to perform a ***double-blind study***. In this case, both the participants and the researchers who interact with them are blind to who has been exposed to which experimental condition until the research is completed.
4. Selecting and assigning participants	Experimenters typically place participants randomly in each of the experimental conditions. Random assignment is essential for internal validity, because it minimises the chance that participants in different groups will differ in some systematic way (e.g. gender or age) that might influence their responses and lead to mistaken conclusions about cause and effect. ***Confounding variables*** — variables that can produce effects that are confused, or confounded, with the effects of the independent variable — compromise the internal validity of a study by making inferences about causality impossible.
5. Applying statistical techniques to the data	Analysing data involves two tasks. The first consists of describing the findings in a way that summarises their essential features (***descriptive statistics***). The second involves drawing inferences from the sample to the population as a whole (***inferential statistics***). Descriptive statistics are a way of taking what may be a staggeringly large set of observations, sometimes made over months or years, and putting them into a summary form that others can comprehend in a table or graph. Almost *any* time two groups are compared, differences will appear between them simply because no two groups of people are exactly alike. Determining whether the differences are meaningful or simply random is the job of inferential statistics, which yield tests of statistical significance. The goal of inferential statistics is to see if the independent variable really has an impact on the way participants respond.
6. Drawing conclusions	Drawing conclusions involves evaluating whether or not the hypothesis is supported — that is, whether the independent and dependent variables are related as predicted. Researchers also try to interpret their findings in the light of the broader theoretical framework and assess their generalisability outside the laboratory. Part of drawing conclusions means determining what worked, what did not and where to go from here. Most published research reports conclude by acknowledging their limitations and point towards future research that might address unanswered questions.

Example of a research experiment

Introduction

Most teachers are keen to equip their students with the skills needed for academic success and to identify those factors that influence performance. One factor shown to have a negative impact on student performance is *test anxiety* (McDonald, 2001). Anxious students are typically distracted during the exam; they allow worry and negative thoughts to detrimentally impact on their memory and recall. Alternatively, ineffective study habits, low self-efficacy, or poor test-taking skills can cause students to become anxious, affecting their test performance.

Research evidence shows that students with high levels of test anxiety are more likely to procrastinate, use rote learning and perform poorly in exams (Cassady, 2004). Sansgiry and Sail (2006) argued that *perceived course load* could be a key factor that influences test anxiety. To explore this hypothesis, Sansgiry and Sail examined the relationship between student perceptions of course load, their ability to manage time and test anxiety.

Method

Participants: A total of 198 students completed the survey. The response rate for each year level was adequate (Year 1, 48 percent; Year 2, 52 percent; Year 3, 52 percent; and Year 4, 72 percent).
Procedure: A survey was self-administered to all students enrolled in the Doctor of Pharmacy (across years 1 through to 4) at the University of Houston. The survey measured the following key variables: test anxiety, perceived course load and ability to manage time.

Results

There was a significant difference in students' perception of course load, ability to manage time and test anxiety scores across the four years (see table 2.3). Second-year students perceived their course load to be the highest; the final-year students perceived their course load to be the lowest. Second-year students also indicated significantly higher test anxiety scores as compared with third-year students ($p < .05$). There was a significant difference in perception of course load among first-year and fourth-year students ($p < .05$). Test anxiety was positively correlated with students' perceptions of course load ($r = .24$, $p < .01$) and negatively correlated with students' ability to manage time with course work ($r = -.20$, $p < .01$)

TABLE 2.3 Test anxiety, students' perception of course load and ability to manage time among first-, second-, third- and fourth-year students

Variables	First-year	Second-year	Third-year	Fourth-year
Test anxiety*†	2.5 (0.9)	2.9 (1.0)	2.3 (0.7)	2.3 (0.8)
Perception of course load*‡	79.5 (17.5)	88.1 (12.9)	70.7 (16.4)	67.4 (21.2)
Ability to manage time*	68.3 (16.6)	60.2 (23.6)	72.2 (19.4)	78.5 (17.9)

*Second- and fourth-year students are significantly different ($p < .05$)
†Second- and third-year students are significantly different ($p < .05$)
‡First- and fourth-year students are significantly different ($p < .05$)

SOURCE: Adapted from Sansgiry and Sail (2006).

Discussion

This study revealed some interesting results about factors that influence test anxiety. The majority of students in this study experienced moderate test anxiety. Test anxiety scores were highest for those students who perceived they had a high workload. Students' perceptions of course load and their ability to manage time with their course work was associated with test anxiety. Thus, successfully managing a course load requires effective time management and study habits (see chapter 1).

INTERIM SUMMARY

The first step in conducting an experiment is to frame a hypothesis that predicts the relationships among two or more variables. The second is to operationalise variables — to turn abstract ideas or constructs into concrete form defined by a set of actions or operations. The third step is to develop a standardised procedure so that only the variables of interest vary. In experimental research, researchers often divide participants into different groups, which experience different conditions of the independent variable.

Some participants may be assigned to a ***control group*** — a neutral condition against which participants in various experimental conditions can be compared. The fourth step is to select samples that are as representative as possible of the population of interest. The fifth step is to analyse the data using statistical techniques. The final step is to conclude from the data whether the hypothesis was supported and whether the results are generalisable. Although these steps are best exemplified in experimental studies, most of them apply to other research designs as well.

Limitations of experimental research

Because experimenters can manipulate variables one at a time and observe the effects of each manipulation, experiments provide the 'cleanest' findings of any research method in psychology. No other method can determine cause and effect so unambiguously. Furthermore, experiments can be replicated, or repeated, to see whether the same findings emerge with a different sample; the results can thus be corroborated or refined.

Experimental methods do, however, have their limitations. First, for both practical and ethical reasons, many complex phenomena cannot be tested in the laboratory. A notable exception is the leading-edge research conducted by the Traffic and Road Safety (TARS) Research Group at the University of Waikato in New Zealand. The group uses innovative technologies, including an advanced driving simulator, to study a broad range of road-safety topics, including road design, driver behaviour and vehicle performance. The group received a prestigious national road-safety award because its research led to the development of various novice driver education and training programs that helped to lower the annual road toll in New Zealand. In contrast, a psychologist who wants to know whether divorce has a negative impact on children's intellectual development cannot manipulate people into divorcing in order to test the hypothesis. Researchers frequently have to examine phenomena as they exist in nature.

When experiments are impractical, psychologists sometimes employ ***quasi-experimental designs***, which share the logic and many features of the experimental method but do not allow as much control over all relevant variables, such as random assignment of participants to different conditions (Campbell & Stanley, 1963). An experimenter interested in the impact of divorce on memory, for example, might compare the ability of children from divorced and non-divorced families to retrieve positive and negative memories. In this case, the independent variable (divorced or non-divorced) is not really something the experimenter manipulates; it is a participant characteristic that is used to predict the dependent variable (memory). Because researchers have to 'take participants as they find them' in quasi-experimental designs, they have to be particularly careful to test to be sure the groups do not differ on other variables that might influence the results, such as age, gender or socioeconomic status (social class).

Quasi-experimental designs cannot provide the degree of certainty about cause-and-effect relationships that experiments offer. Because participants cannot be randomly assigned to divorced and non-divorced groups, experimenters can only observe differences, rather than create differences by 'bending nature'. Nevertheless, quasi-experimental designs are probably the most common designs used in psychology. Reality is, unfortunately, both the object of scientific inquiry and its major impediment.

APPLY + DISCUSS

Design a study to test the hypothesis that anxiety interferes with people's ability to solve problems.

- What is the independent variable?
- What is the dependent variable?
- How might you operationalise anxiety (i.e. how would you induce it)?
- How might you measure problem-solving ability?
- What are the limits to your study's generalisability?

A second limitation of the experimental method regards external validity. Researchers can never be certain how closely a phenomenon observed in a laboratory parallels its real-life counterparts. In some instances, such as the study that opened this chapter, the implications seem clear: if briefly writing about stressful events can improve health, imagine what talking about them with a professional over time might do. And, in fact, research shows that people who get help for psychological problems through psychotherapy tend to make fewer trips to the doctor for medical problems (Gabbard & Atkinson, 1996). In other cases, external validity is more problematic. For example, do the principles that operate in a laboratory study of decision making apply when a person decides whether to stay in a relationship (Ceci & Bronfenbrenner, 1991; Neisser, 1976; Rogoff & Lave, 1984)?

Despite its limitations, the experimental method is the bread and butter of psychology. No research method is more definitive than a well-executed experiment. Nevertheless, few would desire a steady diet of bread and butter, and scientific investigation is nourished by multiple methods and many sources of data.

INTERIM SUMMARY

Experimentation is the only research method in psychology that allows researchers to draw unambiguous conclusions about cause and effect. Limitations include the difficulty of bringing some complex phenomena into the laboratory and the question of whether results apply to phenomena outside the laboratory.

Descriptive research

The second major type of research, ***descriptive research***, attempts to describe phenomena as they exist rather than to manipulate variables. Do people in different cultures use similar terms to describe people's personalities, such as 'outgoing' or 'responsible' (McCrae, Costra, del Pilar, Rolland, & Parker, 1998; Paunonen, Jackson, Trzebinski, & Forsterling, 1992)? Do members of other primate species compete for status and form coalitions against powerful members of the group whose behaviour is becoming oppressive? To answer such questions, psychologists use a variety of descriptive methods, including case studies, naturalistic observation and survey research. Table 2.1 (p. 48) summarises the major uses and limitations of these descriptive methods as well as the other methods that psychologists use.

Case study methods

A ***case study*** is an in-depth observation of one person or a small group of individuals. Case study methods are useful when trying to learn about complex psychological phenomena that are not yet well understood and require exploration, or that are difficult to produce experimentally. For example, one study used the case of a four-year-old girl who had witnessed her mother's violent death three years earlier as a way of trying to explore the issue of whether, and if so in what ways, children can show effects of traumatic incidents they cannot explicitly recall (Gaensbauer, Chatoor, Drell, Siegel, & Zeanah, 1995). Single-case designs can also be used in combination with quantitative or experimental procedures (Blampied, 1999; Kazdin & Tuma, 1982), as when researchers studying patients with severe seizure disorders who have had the connecting tissue between the two sides of their brain surgically cut have presented information to one side of the brain to see whether the other side of the brain can work out what is going on (chapter 5).

Psychologists who take an interpretive (or hermeneutic) approach to methodology often use case studies; their aim is to examine the complex meanings that may underlie human behaviour (Martin & Sugarman, 1999; Messer, Sass, & Woolfolk, 1988). One person may commit suicide because he feels he is a failure; another may kill herself to get back at a relative or spouse; another may seek escape from intense or chronic psychic pain; and still another may take his life because cultural norms demand it in the face of a wrongdoing or humiliation. From an interpretive point of view, explaining a behaviour such as suicide means understanding the subjective meanings behind it. Interpreting meanings of this sort typically requires in-depth interviewing.

One major limitation of case study methods is sample size. Because case studies examine only a small group of participants, generalisation to a larger population is always uncertain. An investigator who conducts intensive research on one or several young women with anorexia and finds that their self-starvation behaviour appears tied to their wishes for control (in this case, demonstrating to themselves that they have complete control over their most intense desires) might be tempted to conclude that control issues are central to this disorder (e.g. Bruch, 1973). They may well be, but they may also be idiosyncratic to this particular study.

One way to minimise this limitation is to use a multiple-case-study method (Rosenwald, 1988), extensively examining a small sample of people individually and drawing generalisations across them. Another way is to follow up case studies with more systematic studies using other designs. We now know from several studies, for example, that patients with anorexia *do* tend to be preoccupied with control, a finding initially discovered through the careful analysis of individual cases (Serpell, Treasure, Teasdale, & Sullivan, 1999).

A second limitation of case studies is their susceptibility to ***researcher bias***, also known as ***observer bias***. Researcher bias results in systematic errors in measurement due to investigators seeing what they expect to see. According to Shaughnessy, Zechmeister, and Zechmeister (2000), observer bias is the systematic errors in observation or results that are influenced by the observer's expectations regarding the outcome of the study. For example, a psychotherapist who believes that anorexic patients have

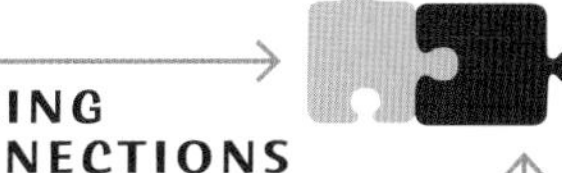

MAKING CONNECTIONS

Case studies are often useful when large numbers of participants are not available, either because they do not exist or because obtaining them would be extremely difficult. For example, extensive case studies of patients who have undergone surgery to sever the tissue connecting the right and left hemispheres of the brain (in order to control severe epileptic seizures) have yielded important information about the specific functions of the two hemispheres (chapters 3 and 5).

conflicts about sexuality will undoubtedly see such conflicts in his anorexic patients because they are operative in virtually everyone. In writing up the case, he may select examples that demonstrate these conflicts and miss other issues that might be just as salient to another observer. Because no-one else is privy to the data of a case, no other investigator can examine the data directly and draw different conclusions; unless the therapy sessions are videotaped, the data are always filtered through the psychologist's theoretical lens. In the following case study (see figure 2.4), the person outlines symptoms for anxiety disorder. This case study approach is typically used by clinical psychologists working with individual clients to diagnose and treat psychological problems (see chapters 15 and 16 for further information on the disorder and recommended treatment approaches). Although it remains questionable whether the results of one case can be generalised to the general population, exploring individual cases can help clinical psychologists to determine key questions to ask and to establish general conclusions by examining a series of case studies involving similar problems.

Carole was 25 when she was first visited her doctor complaining of feeling tense, restless and having heart palpitations. She told her doctor that at times she felt like something terrible had just happened, even when there was no apparent danger. She felt tense and jumpy almost all of the time. Carole reported that she had been like that all of her life, constantly worrying that something bad was going to happen. She was a perfectionist, taking a long time to complete tasks because she had to get everything absolutely correct. She told the doctor, 'Little things can set me off. The other day, I had a job interview. I practised my interview questions and possible responses for hours the day before and I couldn't sleep that night because I was going over everything to make sure nothing would go wrong. By the time I got to the interview I felt sick. I had a dry mouth, I was trembling, and I thought that I was going to faint. After the interview, I worried about my responses for the next week. I kept going over the interview in my mind, feeling terribly embarrassed at things I could have said better or things that I thought I got wrong. I felt sick. People don't understand how much I worry. I don't remember the last time I felt relaxed.'

FIGURE 2.4
A sample case study of a patient who is displaying symptoms for an anxiety disorder

Case studies are probably most useful at either the beginning or end of a series of studies that employ quantitative methods with larger samples. Exploring individual cases can be crucial in deciding what questions to ask or what hypotheses to test because they allow researchers to immerse themselves in the phenomenon as it appears in real life. A case study can also flesh out the meaning of quantitative findings by providing a detailed analysis of representative examples.

Naturalistic observation

A second descriptive method, ***naturalistic observation***, is the in-depth observation of a phenomenon in its natural setting, such as Jane Goodall's well-known studies of apes in the wilds of Africa. For example, Frans de Waal, like Goodall, has spent years both in the wild and at zoos observing the way groups of apes and monkeys behave.

De Waal (1989) describes an incident in which a dominant male chimpanzee in captivity made an aggressive charge at a female. The troop, clearly distressed by the male's behaviour, came to the aid of the female and then settled into an unusual silence. Suddenly, the room echoed with hoots and howls, during which two of the chimps kissed and embraced. To de Waal's surprise, the two chimps were the same ones who had been involved in the fight that had set off the episode! After several hours of pondering the incident, de Waal suddenly realised that he had observed something he had naively assumed was unique to humans: reconciliation. This led him to study the way primates maintain social relationships despite conflicts and acts of aggression. His research led him to conclude that for humans, as for our nearest neighbours, 'making peace is as natural as making war'.

Naturalistic observation can lead to novel insights, such as the importance of peacemaking in primates.

Psychologists also observe humans 'in the wild' using naturalistic methods, as did Swiss psychologist Jean Piaget in some classic studies of Genevan school children (1926). Piaget and his colleagues relied heavily on experimental methods, but they also conducted naturalistic research in playgrounds and classrooms, taking detailed notes on who spoke to whom, for how long and on what topics (chapter 12).

Piaget found that young children often speak in 'collective monologues', talking all at once; they may neither notice whether they are being listened to nor address their comments to a particular listener. An advantage of naturalistic observation over experimental methods is that its findings are clearly applicable outside the laboratory.

Most people behave somewhat differently when they are aware that someone is watching them; thus, a limitation of observational methods is that the very fact of being watched may influence behaviour, if only subtly. Researchers try to minimise this bias in one of two ways. One is simply to be as inconspicuous as possible — to blend into the woodwork. The other is to become a participant–observer, interacting naturally with subjects in their environment, much as Goodall did once she came to 'know' a troop over months or years.

Naturalistic observation shares other limitations with the case study method, such as the problem of generalisability. When can psychologists conclude that after they have seen one baboon troop they have seen them all? Researcher bias can also pose limitations since observers' theoretical biases can influence what they look for and therefore what they see. As with case studies, this limitation can be minimised by observing several groups of participants or by videotaping interactions, so that more than one judge can independently rate the data.

Finally, like other descriptive studies, naturalistic observation primarily *describes* behaviours; it cannot explain why they take place. Based on extensive observation, a psychologist can make a convincing argument about the way one variable influences another, but this method does not afford the luxury of doing something to participants and seeing what they do in response, as in experimental designs.

Survey research

A third type of descriptive research, ***survey research***, involves asking questions of a large sample of people, usually about their attitudes or behaviours. For example, a large corporation might call in an organisational psychologist to try to help the directors understand why morale is declining among workers in the factory. The psychologist begins by interviewing a small sample of employees, from executives to workers on the line, and then designs a survey, which is completed by a random sample of workers in randomly selected plants around the country. The survey asks workers to rate a series of statements, such as 'My job does not pay well', 'I do not receive enough holiday time' and 'I feel like I do not learn anything on the job', on a seven-point scale (where 1 = *strongly disagree* and 7 = *strongly agree*). The two most frequently used tools of survey researchers are ***interviews***, in which researchers ask questions using a standard format, usually to a large sample of participants; and ***questionnaires***, which participants fill out by themselves.

Selecting the sample is extremely important in survey research. For example, pollsters conducting voter exit interviews must be sure that their sample reflects a large and heterogeneous population if they are to predict election results accurately. Researchers typically want a ***random sample***, a sample selected from the general population in a relatively arbitrary way that does not introduce any systematic bias. In random sampling, every member of a population has an equal chance of being selected for the sample. The organisational psychologist seeking a random sample of factory workers in a company, for instance, might choose names randomly selected from payroll or personnel records.

Random selection, however, does not always guarantee that a sample will accurately reflect the demographic characteristics (qualities such as gender, race and socioeconomic status) of the population in which the researcher is interested. A survey sent to a random sample of workers in a company may, for example, lead to biased results if unhappy workers are afraid to answer, or if workers who are unhappy have higher absentee rates (and hence are not at work when the form arrives). Similarly, a political poll that randomly samples names from the phone book may over-represent people who happen to be home answering the phone during the day, such as older people, and may under-represent poor people who do not have a phone.

> **APPLY + DISCUSS**
> - In surveys, or in any other studies, can we ever justify studying only men or only women?
> - Under what circumstances can we assume or not assume that different groups of people (such as people of different ethnicities) will have similar psychological characteristics?

Where proportional representation of different subpopulations is important, researchers use a stratified random sample. A ***stratified random sample*** specifies the percentage of people to be drawn from each population category (age, race etc.) and then randomly selects participants from within each category. Figure 2.5 (see overleaf) demonstrates these concepts. In the proportional stratified sample, a sampling ratio of 1:5 was used for all four departments in the stratified population. In the disproportional stratified sample, there is an under-representation of students from the Departments of Psychology (1:8) and Nursing (1:6) and an over-representation of students from the Departments of Maths (1:2) and Biology (1:4).

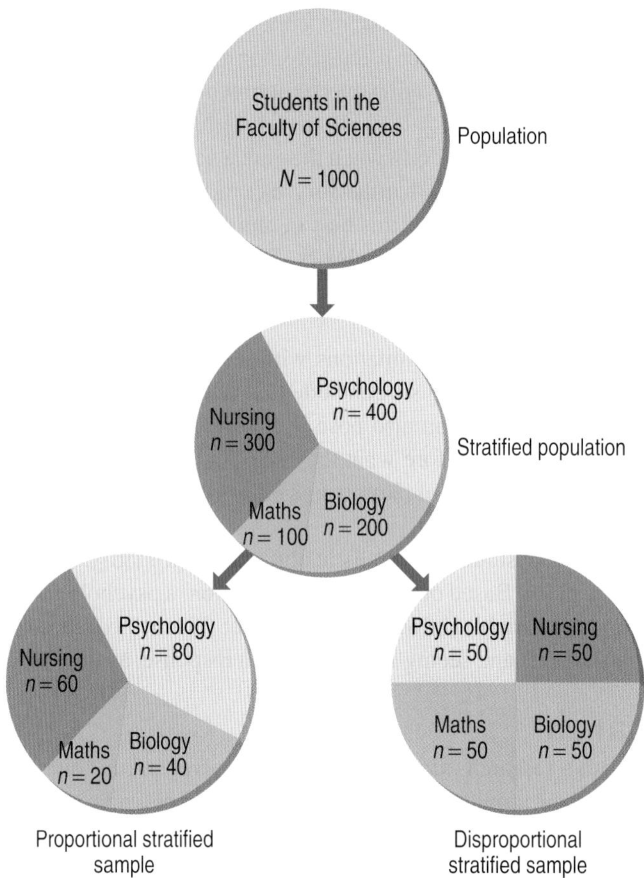

FIGURE 2.5
Proportional and disproportional stratified random sampling

Researchers often use census data to provide demographic information on the population of interest and then match this information as closely as possible in their sample. Thus, they may stratify a sample along a number of lines, such as age, gender, race, marital status, geographical region and education, to make sure that they provide an accurate picture of the population.

The major problem with survey methods is that they rely on participants to report on themselves truthfully and accurately, and even minor wording changes can sometimes dramatically alter their responses (Schwarz, 1999). For example, most people tend to describe their behaviours and attitudes in more flattering terms than others would use to describe them (Campbell & Sedikides, 1999; John & Robins, 1994). How many people are likely to admit their addiction to *Neighbours* reruns? In part, people's answers may be biased by conscious efforts to present themselves in the best possible light. However, they may also shade the truth without being aware of doing so because they want to feel intelligent or psychologically healthy (Shedler, Mayman, & Manis, 1993). In addition, participants may honestly misjudge themselves, or their conscious attitudes may differ from attitudes expressed in their behaviour (chapter 17). Measuring people's attitudes towards people with disabilities by questionnaire typically indicates much more positive attitudes than measuring how far they sit from a person with disabilities when entering a room (see Greenwald & Banaji, 1995; Wilson, Lindsey, & Schooler, 2000).

INTERIM SUMMARY

Descriptive research describes phenomena as they already exist rather than manipulating variables. A ***case study*** is an in-depth observation of one person or a group of people. Case studies are useful in generating hypotheses, exploring complex phenomena that are not yet well understood or difficult to examine experimentally, fleshing out the meaning of quantitative findings and interpreting behaviours with complex meanings. ***Naturalistic observation*** is the in-depth observation of a phenomenon in its natural setting. It is useful for describing complex phenomena as they exist outside the laboratory. ***Survey research*** involves asking a large sample of people questions, usually about their attitudes or behaviour, through ***interviews*** or ***questionnaires***. ***Random*** and ***stratified random samples*** allow psychologists to gather substantial information about the population by examining representative samples. Unlike experiments, descriptive methods cannot unambiguously establish causation.

Correlational research

Correlational research attempts to determine the degree to which two or more variables are related, so that knowing the value (or score) on one variable allows prediction of the other. Although correlational analyses can be applied to data from any kind of study, most often correlational designs rely on survey data such as self-report questionnaires.

For example, for years psychologists have studied the extent to which personality in childhood predicts personality in adulthood (chapter 11; Block, 1971; Caspi, 1998). Are we the same person at age 30 as we were at age four? In one study, researchers followed up children whose personalities were first assessed at around age nine, examining their personalities again 10 years later (Shiner, 2000). They then correlated childhood personality variables with personality characteristics in late adolescence. To ***correlate*** two variables means to assess the extent to which being high or low on one measure predicts being high or low on the other. The statistic that enables a researcher to do this is called a correlation coefficient. A ***correlation coefficient*** measures the extent to which two variables are related (literally, co-related, or related to each other).

A correlation can be either positive or negative. A ***positive correlation*** means that the higher individuals measure on one variable, the higher they are likely to measure on the other. This also means, of course, that the lower they score on one variable, the lower they will score on the other. A ***negative correlation*** means that the higher participants measure on one variable, the lower they will measure on the other. Correlations can be depicted on scatterplot graphs, which show the scores of every participant along two dimensions (figure 2.6).

Correlation coefficients vary between +1.0 and –1.0. A strong correlation — one with a value close to either positive or negative 1.0 — means that a psychologist who knows a person's score on one variable can confidently predict that person's score on the other. For instance, one might expect a high positive correlation between childhood aggressiveness at age nine and social problems at age 19 (i.e. the higher the aggressiveness, the higher the person's score on a measure of social dysfunction). One might equally expect a high negative correlation between childhood aggressiveness and adult academic success. A weak correlation (say, between childhood agreeableness and adult height) hovers close to zero, either on the positive or the negative side. Variables with a correlation close to zero are unrelated and thus cannot be used to predict one another.

Many people think they believe in equal treatment of men and women in the workplace. However, 'implicit' **attitudes** often show up in their behaviour — as when they assign women smaller offices than men with the same level of seniority or accomplishment. The recognition that people may be of 'two minds' in their attitudes towards women and men, ethnic minorities, and even themselves has led to new technologies for measuring attitudes people cannot easily report (chapter 17).

(a)

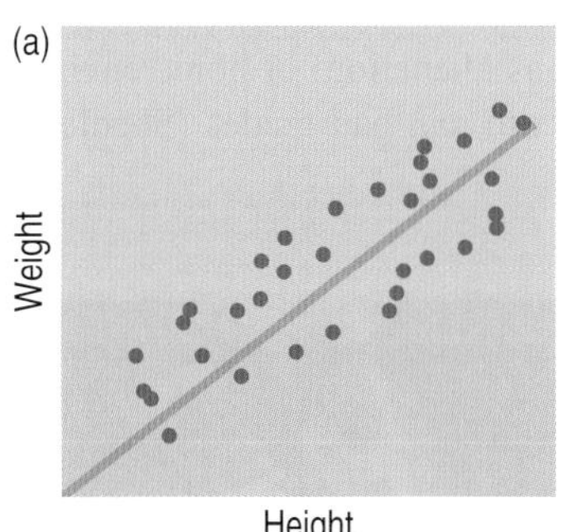

(b)

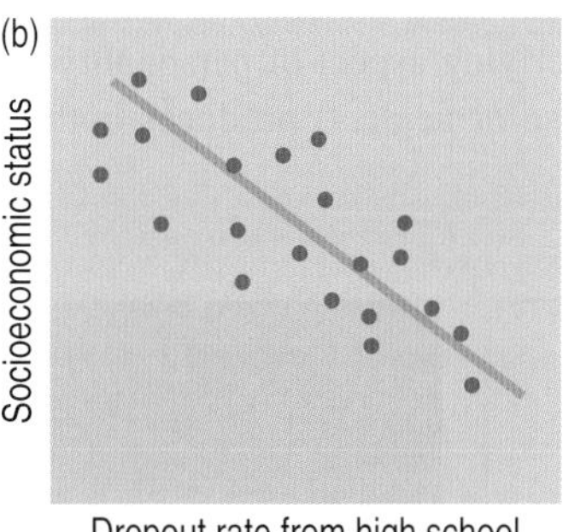

(c)

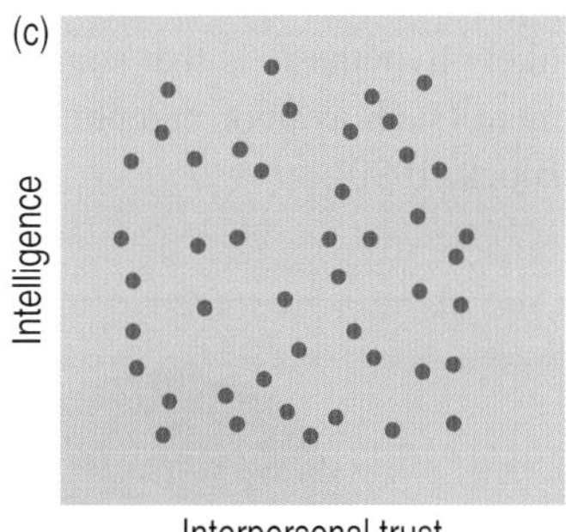

FIGURE 2.6
(a) Positive, (b) negative and (c) zero correlations. A correlation expresses the relationship between two variables. The panels depict three kinds of correlations on hypothetical scatterplot graphs, which show the way data points fall (are scattered) on two dimensions. Panel (a) shows a positive correlation, between height and weight. A comparison of the dots (which represent individual participants) on the right with those on the left shows that those on the left are lower on both variables. The dots scatter around the line that summarises them, which is the correlation coefficient. Panel (b) shows a negative correlation, between socioeconomic status and dropout rate from high school. The higher the socioeconomic status, the lower the dropout rate. Panel (c) shows a zero correlation, between intelligence and the extent to which an individual believes people can be trusted. Being high on one dimension predicts nothing about whether the participant is high or low on the other.

Table 2.4 (see overleaf) shows the correlations among three childhood personality variables — extroversion (sociability), agreeableness and achievement motivation — and three measures of functioning in late adolescence — academic achievement, conduct (e.g. not breaking rules or committing crimes) and social functioning. These correlations are arrayed as a ***correlation matrix*** — a table presenting the correlations among a number of variables. Childhood extroversion is not a strong predictor of academic functioning and conduct in late adolescence (if anything, extroverted

APPLY + DISCUSS

The Australian government established a Committee of Ministers to investigate and make recommendations relative to the portrayal of violence in the electronic media. This committee had to rely primarily on correlational evidence linking exposure to violence in computer games and increased aggression among children.

- Could the committee conclude that exposure to media violence will *cause* subsequent aggressive behaviour?
- What third variable might account for *both* high exposure to violent computer games and aggressive behaviours in children?
- If many children watch violent computer games but only some act aggressively, what might be the relationship between these two variables?

kids become rowdier adolescents; the correlation coefficient denoted by the letter $r = -.14$). However, extroverted children do tend to become socially well-adapted adults ($r = .35$). Childhood agreeableness and achievement motivation both tend to predict positive functioning in all three domains in late adolescence.

TABLE 2.4 The relationship between childhood personality and late adolescent functioning

	Late adolescent functioning		
Childhood personality trait	**Academic**	**Conduct**	**Social**
Extroversion	−.07	−.14	.35
Agreeableness	.23	.33	.19
Achievement motivation	.37	.26	.25

SOURCE: Adapted from Shiner (2000, p. 316).

In psychological research, theoretically meaningful correlations tend to hover around .3, and correlations above .5 are considered large (Cohen, 1983). Sometimes, however, seemingly tiny correlations can be meaningful. For example, a study of the impact of aspirin on heart disease in a sample of roughly 20 000 participants had to be discontinued on ethical grounds when researchers found a −.03 correlation between use of a single aspirin a day and risk of death by heart attack (Rosenthal, 1996)! This correlation translates to 15 out of 1000 people dying if they do not take an aspirin a day as a preventive measure.

The virtue of correlational research is that it allows investigators to study a whole range of phenomena that vary in nature — from personality characteristics to attitudes — but cannot be produced in the laboratory. Like other non-experimental methods, however, correlational research can only *describe* relationships among variables (which is why it is actually sometimes categorised as a descriptive method, rather than placed in its own category). When two variables correlate with each other, the researcher must infer the relationship between them. Does one cause the other, or does some *third variable* explain the correlation?

Media reports on scientific research often disregard or misunderstand the fact that *correlation does not imply causation*. If a study shows a correlation between drug use and poor grades, the media often reports that 'scientists have found that drug use leads to bad grades'. That *may* be true, but an equally likely hypothesis is that some underlying aspect of personality (such as alienation) or home environment (such as poor parenting, abuse or neglect) produces both drug use *and* bad grades (Shedler & Block, 1990).

The reported co-occurrence of two events (correlation) does not necessarily mean that one is causing the other. Children who eat ice cream, for example, tend to have bike accidents. It may be that eating ice cream while riding causes young bikers to have more accidents. Or, it may be that parents typically treat their children to ice cream whenever they have accidents. Or, perhaps hot summer days lead to increases in both ice cream eating and bike riding.

INTERIM SUMMARY

Correlational research assesses the degree to which two variables are related; a ***correlation coefficient*** quantifies the association between two variables, and ranges from −1.0 to +1.0. A correlation of 0 means that two variables are unrelated, whereas a high correlation (either positive or negative) means that subjects' scores on one variable are good predictors of their scores on the other. Correlational research can shed important light on the relationships among variables, but correlation does not imply causation.

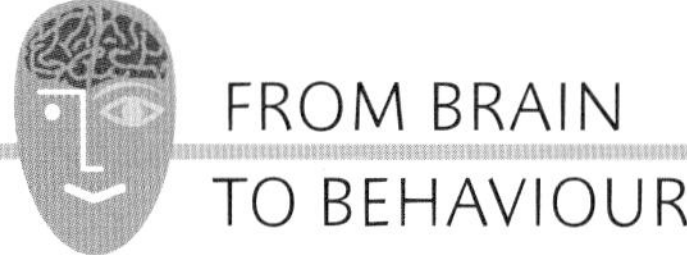

Researching the brain

The research methods psychologists use are only as powerful as the technologies and statistical tools that support them. For example, the development of a seemingly simple mathematical device — the correlation coefficient — set the stage for psychologists to begin answering questions about the influence of heredity on traits such as intelligence, anxiety and shyness that were previously mere topics of speculation.

In the last two decades, a powerful new set of technologies for studying the brain has revolutionised our understanding of human thought and memory (Posner & Raichle, 1996). Advances in these technologies are proceeding at such a bewildering rate that the next decade may well yield as much new knowledge about the basic mechanisms of thought, feeling and behaviour as humans have accumulated since the dawn of civilisation.

Scientists began studying the functioning of the brain more than a century ago by examining patients who had sustained damage or disease (lesions) to particular neural regions (chapter 1). A major advance came in the 1930s, with the development of the ***electroencephalogram***, or ***EEG***, which measures electrical activity towards the surface of the brain (near the skull). The EEG capitalises on the fact that every time a nerve cell fires it produces electrical activity. Researchers can measure this activity in a region of the brain's outer layers by placing electrodes on the scalp. The EEG is frequently used to diagnose disorders such as epilepsy as well as to study neural activity during sleep. It has also been used to examine questions such as whether the two hemispheres of the brain respond differently to stimuli that evoke positive versus negative emotions, which they do (Davidson, 1996).

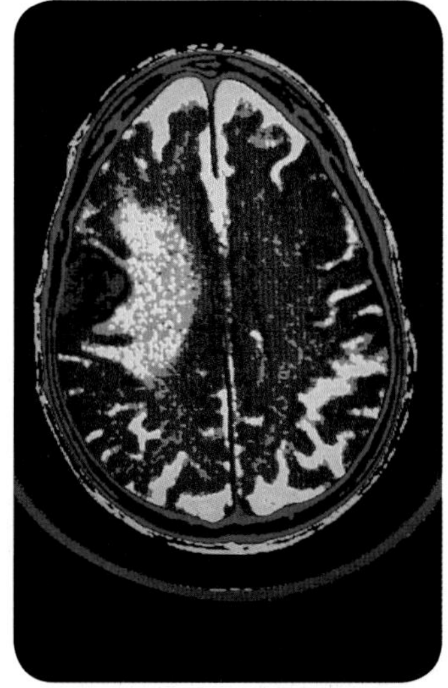

A CAT scan of a patient with a tumour (shown in blue)

A technological breakthrough that is revolutionising our understanding of brain and behaviour occurred when scientists discovered ways to use x-ray technology and other methods to produce pictures of soft tissue (rather than the familiar bone x-rays), such as the living brain. ***Neuroimaging techniques*** use computer programs to convert the data taken from brain-scanning devices into visual images of the brain. One of the first neuroimaging techniques to be developed was ***computerised axial tomography***, commonly known as a ***CAT scan***. A CAT scanner rotates an x-ray tube around a person's head, producing a series of x-ray pictures. A computer then combines these pictures into a composite visual image. Computerised tomography scans can pinpoint the location of abnormalities such as neuronal degeneration and abnormal tissue growths (tumours). A related technology, ***magnetic resonance imaging (MRI)***, is a neuroimaging technique that produces similar results without using x-rays.

It was only a matter of time before scientists developed two imaging techniques that actually allowed researchers to observe the brain in action rather than simply detect neural damage. These techniques rely on properties of cells in the brain that can be measured, such as the amount of blood that flows to cells that have just been activated. Thus, researchers can directly observe what occurs in the brain as participants solve mathematical problems, watch images or retrieve memories.

Positron emission tomography (PET) is a neuroimaging method that requires injection of a small quantity of radioactive glucose (too small a dose to be dangerous) into the bloodstream. Nerve cells use glucose for energy, and they replenish their supply from the bloodstream. As these cells use glucose that has been radioactively 'tagged', a computer produces a colour portrait of the brain, showing which parts are active. The results of such investigations are changing our understanding of diseases such as schizophrenia, as researchers can administer tasks to patients and find the neural pathways on which they diverge from individuals without the disorder (e.g. Andreasen, 1999; Heckers et al., 1999; Spence et al., 2000).

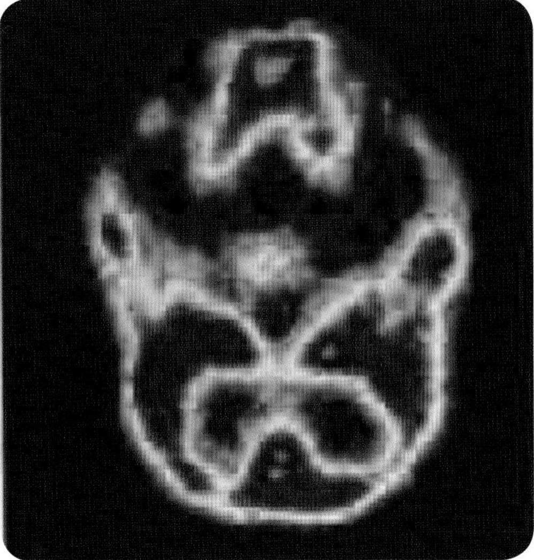

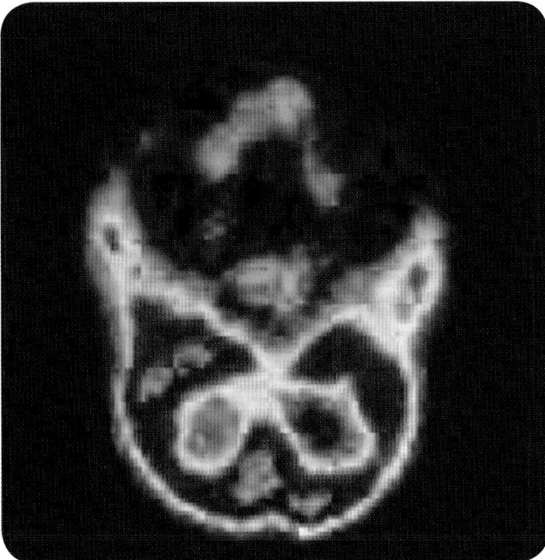

In these two scans, the left scan shows brain activity when the eyes are open, while the one on the right is with the eyes closed. Note the increased activity, red and yellow, in the top of the photo when the eyes are open.

The other technique, called ***functional magnetic resonance imaging (fMRI)***, uses MRI to watch the brain as an individual carries out tasks such as solving mathematical problems or looking at emotionally evocative pictures (Puce, Allison, Asgari, Gore, & McCarthy, 1996; Rickard et al., 2000). Functional MRI works by exposing the brain to pulses of a phenomenally strong magnet (strong enough to lift a truck) and measuring the response of chemicals in blood cells going to and from various regions, which become momentarily 'lined up' in the direction of the magnet.

For example, one research team used fMRI to study the parts of the brain that are active when people generate mental images, such as of a horse, an apple or a house (D'Esposito et al., 1997). When we conjure up a picture of a horse in our mind, do we activate different parts of the brain than when we simply hear about an object but do not picture it? In other words, how are memories represented in our brain? Do we actually form visual images or do we really think in words?

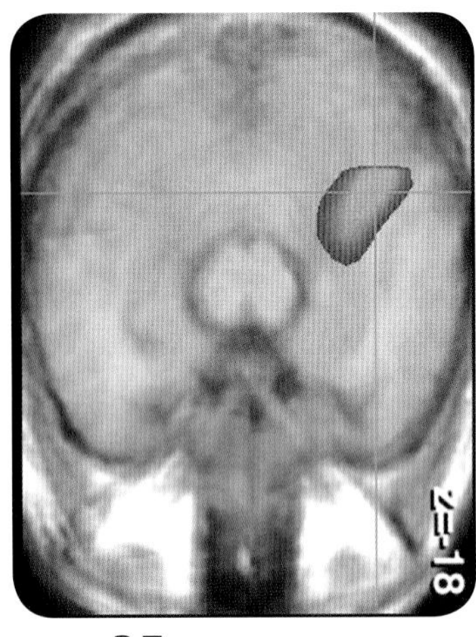

FIGURE 2.7
An averaged view of the working brain using fMRI. The red and yellow show the areas of the brain that were significantly more active while participants were forming mental images than when they were performing a control task. This scan shows a frontal view, sliced top to bottom roughly through the middle of the head.

The investigators set out to answer this question by asking seven participants to carry out two tasks with their eyes closed, while their heads were surrounded by the powerful magnet of the MRI scanner. In the first experimental condition, participants listened to 40 concrete words and were asked to try to picture them in their minds. In the second condition, they listened to 40 words that are difficult to picture (such as 'treaty' and 'guilt') and were asked simply to listen to them. (This is called a within-subjects experimental design, because instead of placing each subject in one condition or the other, each subject is exposed to both conditions. Differences in the way subjects respond to the two conditions are then compared within, rather than across, subjects.)

The experimenters then used fMRI to measure whether the same or different parts of the brain were activated under the two conditions. They hypothesised that when people actually picture objects, their brains would show activity in regions involved in forming and remembering visual images and their meanings, regions that are also activated when people actually see an object, such as a horse. When people just hear words, in contrast, these vision centres should not be active. That is precisely what the investigators found, as can be seen in figure 2.7.

Researchers are still a long way from mapping the micro-details of the brain. The resolution, or sharpness, of the images produced by most scanning techniques is still too fuzzy to enable psychologists to pinpoint, for example, the different neural networks activated when a person feels guilty versus sad or angry. Further, people's brains differ, so that a single map will not work precisely for every person; averaging the responses of several participants can thus sometimes lead to imprecise results. Nevertheless, if progress made in the last decade is any indication, imaging techniques will continue to increase in precision at a dazzling pace, and so will our knowledge of the brain and behaviour.

INTERIM SUMMARY

Researchers study the relationship between mental and neural processes using a number of methods, including case studies of patients with brain damage, experimental lesion studies with animals, ***EEGs*** and computerised ***neuroimaging techniques*** that enable researchers to study the brain in action, such as ***CAT scans***, ***PET*** and ***fMRI***. Cross-cultural research attempts to assess the extent to which psychological processes vary across cultures. Researchers studying psychological phenomena cross-culturally use various methods, including naturalistic observation, correlational studies linking one cultural trait to another and experiments.

The internet and psychology research

Online technology is rapidly changing the lifestyles of people in all corners of the globe. Consider this: In the year 2000, there were 3.8 million active internet subscribers in Australia (Australian Bureau of Statistics [ABS], 2008c). By 2010 — only a decade later — there were 9.6 million active internet subscribers in Australia. By 2010, nearly 92 percent of internet connections were non-dial-up, and mobile wireless (excluding mobile handset connections; e.g. via smartphones) was the fastest growing technology, with 3.5 million people choosing to access the internet wirelessly (an increase of more than 21 percent in less a year) (ABS, 2010).

High levels of penetration into Australian households mean a whole new world of connectivity and social interaction. Social networks like Facebook, Twitter and MySpace are quickly changing the way many people organise their lives. In recent years, people have gained access to the internet via smartphones to share information and content in real time. Those changes are happening so rapidly that the full implications for our world are still unclear.

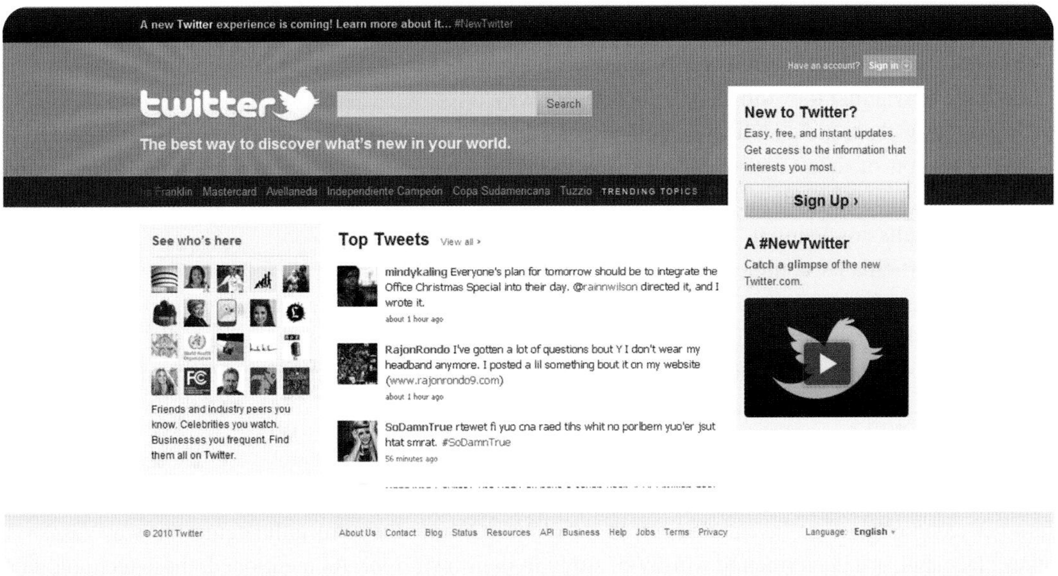

What is clear, however, is that just as internet technologies are changing all aspects of our life, so too are they impacting on the way psychology research takes place. In many ways, the opportunities that these technologies open up are extremely exciting. But just as in wider society, there are also some challenges that need to be considered as we adapt to the online universe.

Positive opportunities for psychology research

In many cases, internet technologies simply represent a new medium for carrying out what would be considered core research activities in psychology. The benefits of using these technologies come from their ability to access, automate and process data quickly and easily. Some key advantages include the following (British Psychological Society [BPS], 2007; Kraut et al., 2003):

1. Online sources provide easy access to existing research and data about your topic. Rather than physically visiting libraries to gather data from paper-based sources, the latest research from around the works is now literally available at your fingertips.

2. Internet technologies offer fantastic opportunities to recruit participants for testing. The wide penetration of internet access provides opportunities to more easily achieve sampling goals, with the ability to stratify across particular demographics.
3. There are cost and efficiency benefits from using this technology. Paper-based survey instruments can incur significance postage and collation costs, which the internet can overcome. Internet platforms can also avoid the need to bring people into a central location to be part of a test. This is not only less costly, but a more efficient way of reaching people who might be spread over wide geographic areas.
4. Automation of data entry and collection also cuts down on costs. Rather than transcribing people's written paper-based responses, digital data can be quickly collated, summarised and analysed.
5. Having people complete survey instruments or tests in their own environment may also encourage them to be completely unaffected by the presence of the researcher or other participants.

Challenges for psychology research

At the same time as offering advantages to the researcher, there are also some important potential downsides that must also be considered. They include the following (BPS, 2007; Kraut et al., 2003):

1. While the internet enables ready access to existing research data, the veracity of information sourced from the web is sometimes questionable. It is important that researchers apply the same standard of scrutiny to information sources on the web as they would to traditional sources.
2. Depending on the research topic, it is also important to consider that internet connectivity is not universal. For instance, access to the web in rural or remote areas of Australia, or in lower socio-economic households, may exclude some potential participants. As a result, true random sampling may not be possible.
3. Use of internet technologies may also reduce the control of the researcher over the process. For example, it may be difficult to verify whether the intended participant actually completed a research activity, or whether they did so in a meaningful way.
4. Importantly, there are a number of ethical considerations that need to be carefully considered. Digital collection of data is more efficient for the researcher, but also makes it easier for data to be shared. Particular attention must be paid to protecting the anonymity of participants and the ability to keep results confidential.
5. Having participants completing tasks remotely also makes it difficult for a researcher to assess whether participation is causing any stress or harm. Care must be taken to ensure there are mechanisms though which participants can withdraw from testing if they experience distress.
6. Debriefing is also an important consideration in many research activities. Mechanisms must be incorporated to ensure this takes place.

A phenomenon in its own right

Internet technologies are fascinating not just because of how they are influencing the way research takes place, but as a phenomenon worthy of study in their own right. As mentioned, these technologies are ushering in a whole new range of social networking capabilities. Are these web-enabled communication activities changing the way we interact with each other? Are there psychological constructs that affect the way we communicate via a social networking site rather than the phone or face-to-face? The web is delivering a whole new range of potential research topics and we explore these social aspects of behaviour more fully in chapters 17 and 18.

INTERIM SUMMARY

Internet technologies are impacting on the way psychology research takes place. The benefits of using these technologies come from a capacity to access, automate and process data quickly and easily. However, psychology research on the internet also raises some potential downsides, such as sampling bias, uncontrolled data collection procedures, protecting the welfare of participants and ensuring participants' right to confidentiality.

Ethics in psychological research

The Australian Psychological Society (2002, 2003, 2007a) developed a code of ethics that sets forth a series of principles of ethics and professional practice in psychology. The guidelines for the conduct of psychological research are now summarised.

- ***Informed consent*** is vital in carrying out ethical research. You must ensure that participants understand the purpose of the investigation and the nature of the treatments, including what they will be expected to do. You must also ensure that they consent voluntarily to their involvement, and are not being forced or coerced. You need to obtain this informed consent before carrying out your study. Participants must also be aware that they are free to withdraw from the research at any time, without prejudice.
- You must ensure that the welfare of participants is not compromised in any way by your study. Your research should not subject anyone to the risk of physical or emotional harm. Be careful to check that any equipment being used is not faulty and cannot cause injury. Ensure you respect the dignity of participants at all times.
- You should not offer excessive cash rewards or other inducements to take part in your study. Nor should you use a position of power to force people to participate. For example, it would be inappropriate for a university lecturer to force students to take part in a study.
- You must respect a participant's right to confidentiality. Do not disclose information about participants that you obtain through the research process. Ensure you have procedures in place to prevent information about individual participants from becoming public. Explain those procedures to participants before the study begins, so that they can participate without reservations.
- In some cases, it is necessary to carry out research without fully explaining its true purpose to participants before the study starts. This involves ***deception*** and, in these cases, participants must be informed of the true purpose of the investigation when the study finishes.
- Ensure that you take all reasonable steps to minimise any discomfort to any animals being used in your research.
- If you are carrying out research in an academic environment, you must ensure you have the approval of the university and the appropriate faculty or research review committee. You will normally have to make a submission that spells out the nature and purpose of your investigation.

The ethical issues involved in research are not always black and white. Two central issues concern the use of deception and the use of animals in research. Both relate to the issue of informed consent — the participant's ability to agree (or refuse) to participate in an informed manner.

APPLY + DISCUSS

- Is it possible to obtain informed consent from people who are seriously disturbed or intellectually impaired? If not, should we suspend all research on these populations, even if this research could lead to substantial improvements in their quality of life?
- What about research with children, who cannot be expected to understand the implications of participating or not participating?

Deception in psychological research

Many studies keep participants blind to the aims of the investigation until the end; some go further by giving participants a 'cover story' to make sure they do not 'catch on' to the hypothesis being tested. For example, in one experiment, researchers wanted to study the conditions under which people can be induced to make false confessions (Kassin & Kiechel, 1996). They led university student participants to believe that they would be taking a typing test with another participant, who was really an accomplice, or a confederate, of the experimenters. The experimenters explicitly instructed the participants not to touch the ALT key on the computer, since that would allegedly make the computer crash, and all data would be lost. Sixty seconds into the task, the computer seemed to stop functioning, and the experimenter rushed into the room accusing the participant of having hit the forbidden key.

To assess whether false incriminating evidence could convince people that they had actually done something wrong, in one condition the confederate (allegedly simply waiting to take the test) 'admitted' having seen the participant hit the ALT key. In a control condition, the accomplice denied having seen anything. The striking finding was that in the experimental condition about half of the participants came to believe that they *had* hit the key and destroyed the experiment. Obviously, if they had known what the experiment was really about, the experiment would not have worked.

Only a small proportion of experiments actually involve deception, and APS guidelines permit deception only if a study meets four conditions: (1) the research is of great importance and cannot be conducted without deception; (2) participants can be expected to find the procedures reasonable once they are informed after the experiment; (3) participants can withdraw from the experiment at any time; and (4) experimenters debrief the participants afterwards, explaining the purposes of the study

ETHICAL DILEMMA

A researcher intends to interview a number of new mothers about the early bonding experiences they share with their children. She tells them that she will use the data to prepare a new training program for first-time mothers. However, she has no intention of developing such a program — she is more interested in identifying the factors that influence a mother's decision on whether or not to breastfeed her child.

- Is the use of deception in this research proposal justified?
- Should the research be given ethical approval to proceed?

and removing any stressful after-effects. Many universities address the issue of deception by asking potential participants if they would object to being deceived temporarily in a study. That way, any participant who is deceived by an experimenter has given prior consent to be deceived.

Ethics and animal research

A larger ethical controversy concerns the use of non-human animals for psychological research (Bersoff, 1999; Petrinovich, 1999; Ulrich, 1991). By creating lesions in a region of a rat's brain, for example, researchers can sometimes learn a tremendous amount about the function of similar regions in the human brain. Such experiments, however, have an obvious cost to the animal, raising questions about the moral status of animals — that is, whether they have rights (Plous, 1996; Regan, 1997). Again the issue is how to balance costs and benefits: to what extent do the costs to animals justify the benefits to humans? The problem, of course, is that, unlike humans, animals cannot give informed consent.

The use of animals in psychological research is the topic of much ethical debate.

To what extent humans can use other sentient creatures (i.e. animals who feel) to solve human problems is a difficult moral question. Some animal rights groups argue that animal research in psychology has produced little of value to humans, especially considering the enormous suffering animals have undergone. Most psychologists, however, disagree (Miller, 1985). Animal research has led to important advances in behaviour therapy, treatments for serious disorders such as Alzheimer's disease (a degenerative brain illness that leads to loss of mental functions and ultimately death), and insight into nearly every area of psychological functioning, from stress and emotion to the effects of ageing on learning and memory. The difficulty lies in balancing the interests of humans with those of other animals and advancing science while staying within sensible ethical boundaries (Bowd, 1990). Accordingly, institutional review boards examine proposals for experiments with non-human animals as they do with human participants and similarly veto or require changes in proposals they deem unethical.

How to evaluate a study critically

Having explored the major research designs, we now turn to the question of how to be an informed consumer of research. In deciding whether to 'buy' the results of a study, the same maxim applies as in buying a car: *caveat emptor* — let the buyer beware. The popular media often reports that 'University studies indicate . . .' followed by conclusions that are tempting to take at face value. In reality, most studies have their limitations. To evaluate a study critically, the reader should examine the research carefully and attempt to answer seven broad questions.

1. **Does the theoretical framework make sense?** This question encompasses a number of others. Does the specific hypothesis make sense, and does it flow logically from the broader theory? Are terms defined logically and consistently? For example, if the study explores the relationship between social class and intelligence, does the article explain why social class and intelligence should have some relationship to each other? Are the two terms defined the same way throughout the study?
2. **Is the sample adequate and appropriate?** A second question is whether the sample represents the population of interest. If researchers want to know about emotional expression and health in undergraduates, then a sample of undergraduates is perfectly appropriate. If they truly want to generalise to other populations, however, they may need additional samples, such as adults drawn from the local community, or people from the wider community, to see if the effects hold. Another question is sample size. To test a hypothesis, the sample has to be large enough to determine whether the results are meaningful or accidental. A sample of six rolls of the dice that twice produces 'snake eyes' is not sufficient to conclude that the dice are loaded because the 'results' could easily happen by chance (chapter 2 Supplement).
3. **Are the measures and procedures adequate?** Once again, this question encompasses a number of issues. Do the measures assess what they were designed to assess? Were proper control groups chosen to rule out alternative explanations and to assure the validity of the study? Did the investigators carefully control for confounding variables? For example, if the study involved interviews, were some of the interviewers male and some female? If so, did the gender of the interviewer affect how participants responded?

4. **Are the data conclusive?** The central question here is whether the data demonstrate what the researcher claims. Typically, data in research articles are presented in a section entitled 'Results', usually in the form of graphs, charts or tables. To evaluate a study, carefully examine the data presented in these figures and ask whether any alternative interpretations could explain the results as well as or better than the researcher's explanation. Often, data permit many interpretations, and the findings may fit a pattern that the researcher rejected or did not consider.
5. **Are the broader conclusions warranted?** Even when the results 'come out' as hypothesised, researchers have to be careful to draw the right conclusions, particularly as they pertain to the broader theory or phenomenon. A researcher who finds that children who watch violent television shows are more likely to hit other children can conclude that the two are correlated, but not that watching violent shows causes aggressive behaviour. An equally plausible hypothesis is that aggressive children prefer to watch violent television shows — or perhaps that violent television shows trigger actual violence only in children who are already predisposed to violence.
6. **Does the study say anything meaningful?** This is the 'so what?' test. Does the study tell us anything we did not already know? Does it lead to questions for future research? How meaningful a study is depends in part on the importance, usefulness and adequacy of the theoretical perspective from which it derives. Important studies tend to produce findings that are in some way surprising or help choose between opposing theories (Abelson, 1995).
7. **Is the study ethical?** Finally, if the study uses animals or human participants, does it treat them humanely, and do the ends of the study — the incremental knowledge it produces — justify the means? Individual psychologists were once free to make ethical determinations on their own. Today, however, the Australian Psychological Society publishes guidelines that govern psychological research practices (APS, 2002, 2003, 2007a), and universities and other institutions have ethics committees and institutional review boards that review proposals for psychological studies, with the power to reject them or ask for substantial revisions to protect the welfare of participants. In fact, most people would be surprised to learn just how much effort is involved in getting institutional approval for the most benign studies, such as studies of memory or mathematical ability.

Critical thinking

Critical thinking is a skill that has wide application in life. It involves carefully examining and analysing information to judge its value as well as considering other views and explanations before accepting the truthfulness of that information. Critical thinking is essential in psychological research.

To apply critical thinking does not mean you are criticising another viewpoint. It simply means that you are making a logical and rational assessment of information, assessing both its strengths and weaknesses. It involves looking for the evidence that supports arguments put forward by other researchers, not accepting them on face value.

Critical thinking is a skill that is essential in allowing you to decide for yourself how to interpret and evaluate the worth of information you read in scholarly journals and books. Almost all research that you carry out in psychology will involve reading the works of others. It is crucial that you develop an ability to look critically at what other researchers have concluded, the evidence they have presented in support of those conclusions and the methods they used to obtain that evidence. Only by carrying out this critical analysis of past research can you ensure that your own research is built on sound foundations (Burton, 2007, 2010).

Three key principles underpin critical thinking: (1) scepticism, (2) objectivity and (3) open-mindedness. ***Scepticism*** means always questioning assumptions or conclusions and analysing whether the evidence presented supports the results. For example, you should not accept an assertion merely because it is in print or is delivered by a person in a position of authority. You should check the rigour of the process used to get to that assertion. ***Objectivity*** means taking an impartial and disinterested approach. You must judge what you are considering based on the logic and evidence presented, not on subjective beliefs or assumptions. You must put personal feelings or biases aside. ***Open-mindedness*** means considering all sides of an issue. Never ignore potential explanations or interpretations — be flexible and willing to accept evidence that might be contrary to your personal experience.

COMMENTARY

Evidence-based practice in psychology

By Professor Don Hine, University of New England, and Doctor Tony Marks, University of New England

> Throughout the history of psychology and medicine, untested fads, half-baked ideas and outright quackery have blown across the land, sweeping the ill-informed along, and leaving human wreckage in their path. (Meltzoff, 1998, p. xiii)

So, how can researchers tell the difference between untested fads, half-baked ideas and effective psychological therapies? The answer lies in learning about research methods and critical thinking. The science of psychology aspires to operate within a scientist–practitioner model, where practice drives research questions and research evidence informs psychological practice. Evidence-based practice in psychology involves identifying therapeutic interventions that 'maximise the chance of benefit, minimise the risk of harm, and deliver treatment at an acceptable cost' (APS, 2010).

What exactly constitutes evidence? According to the National Health and Medical Research Council (1999), three factors should be taken into account when evaluating evidence for the effectiveness of treatments:

1. *Level and quality of the evidence.* Reviews of relevant randomised controlled trial (RCT) studies are rated more highly than single RCTs, which, in turn, are rated more highly than studies involving no random assignment or control group. In science, it is a very dangerous proposition to draw strong conclusions based on the results of a single study (Mook, 2001). On the other hand, if a systematic review of the literature indicates that, say, 46 out of 50 studies have produced positive findings, researchers can be much more confident (but not 100 percent confident) that the therapy is effective.

   Random assignment ensures that groups are equivalent prior to administering a treatment, so researchers can properly conclude that post-treatment differences are caused by the intervention. The inclusion of a control group in experimental trials performs a similar function. Most people seek psychological treatment when they hit 'rock bottom'. If researchers measure someone at 'rock bottom' and then several weeks after they have seen a therapist, chances are that the person will be a 'happier camper' after seeing the therapist. Is this evidence that therapy is effective? Unfortunately, it is not. This simply reflects a principle called 'regression toward the mean' (Mook, 2001). If a person is extremely bummed out now, chances are, therapy or no therapy, they will feel better next week. Similarly, if a person is having an exceptionally good day, they are less likely to have as good a day the next day. Control groups help control for these confounds that influence outcomes independent of treatment effects.
2. *Relevance of the evidence.* Research evidence must address the clinical issue under investigation, and must be relevant (and, therefore, generalisable) to the population of interest. Randomised controlled trials do provide value; however, like any other research method, they also have important limitations. First, RCTs are conducted in highly controlled conditions. Researchers administer treatments in strict accordance with a manual to ensure that the therapies being evaluated are uniformly administered. Is this how psychological interventions are delivered in the real world? Probably not. Therapists differ considerably in terms of personality, warmth and competence, and most improvise based on situational factors and the personal values of their clients. It is not safe to assume that, since a therapy has been shown to be effective in an RCT, it will be equally effective (or even acceptable to therapists or clients) in actual clinical settings. There is growing pressure on researchers to incorporate therapist and client values into RCTs of the effectiveness of therapies (APS, 2010).
3. *Strength of effect.* Whereas tests of statistical significance tell researchers whether a treatment benefit is unlikely to be due to chance, effect size provides information about the actual magnitude of the benefit. Strength of effect is relevant for two reasons. First, most therapists and clients prefer highly effective interventions. Second, therapies that produce strong effects are more likely to be robust across different therapist and client populations.

Learning about methods and statistics provides the skills to critically evaluate research evidence. These skills are invaluable for university academics, as well as for practising psychologists who are searching for the best approaches to use when treating mental health problems.

Fallacies in arguments

Good psychological research sets out an argument to establish a conclusion. From a critical thinking perspective, it is important to be able to identify arguments that are not based on the evidence and do not flow logically. Four common fallacies in arguments are (1) straw man, (2) appeals to popularity, (3) appeals to authority and (4) arguments directed to the person.

1. A ***straw man*** approach involves authors deliberately attacking an opposing argument in order to strengthen their own argument. Authors create a decoy — the straw man — that will be deliberately destroyed. This straw man argument is weak and easily refuted, so it can be comprehensively discredited. However, destroying an opposing argument does not necessarily prove your own. The only way to validate an argument is to support it with evidence.
2. ***Appeals to popularity*** refers to the fallacy that a popular and widespread argument is true. Many years ago, people believed the earth was flat and you would sail off the edge if you went far enough. This argument was popular but untrue. It was accepted without evidence to support its truth. Just because an argument is widespread and popular, you should not accept it as true. Never accept a generalisation or a sweeping statement that echoes a popular sentiment. You must always analyse more deeply.
3. ***Appeals to authority*** refers to the fallacy that an argument must be true because of the authority of the person making it. Simply because an author is well known or has made compelling arguments in the past does not mean that any new arguments they make will be equally strong. Do not accept an argument simply because of the person putting it forward. When judging the strength of an argument, you should assess the evidence alone and disregard who has said it.
4. ***Arguments directed to the person*** refers to the approach in which authors try to strengthen their own position by attacking the authors of alternative arguments. In this case, an argument is rejected because of supposed failings of the person making it.

INTERIM SUMMARY

To evaluate a study, a critical reader should ask a number of questions regarding the theoretical framework, the sample, the measures and procedures, the results, the broader conclusions drawn and the ethics of the research. Critical thinking also requires you to identify arguments that are not based on the research evidence. Common fallacies in arguments include the ***straw man***, ***appeals to popularity***, ***appeals to authority*** and ***arguments directed to the person***.

Central questions revisited

◆ How do we know when we know something?

As we have seen, psychological research has the power to tackle questions that have seemed unanswerable for centuries. Can talking about unpleasant experiences reduce the risk of illness? Yes. Is the brain equipped to produce mental images that people can generate from memory and scan as they try to find their way around a new city? Yes. Is psychology essentially the same cross-culturally, or do humans think, feel and behave in entirely different ways depending on their culture? Neither. These are solid answers that only solid empirical procedures could have provided.

At the outset we posed a series of questions. What methods — or combination of methods — provide the most conclusive results? What do we gain and what do we lose when we 'domesticate' a psychological phenomenon and bring it into the laboratory? And how do we know when we have asked the right questions in the first place?

The philosopher of science Karl Popper (1963) argued that the criterion that distinguishes science from other practices (and from mere speculation) is the formulation and evaluation of testable hypotheses that can be refuted if they are untrue. Preferably, these hypotheses should not be intuitively obvious, so they can put a theory to the test. The strongest tests are experimental. That is why cognitive and behavioural psychologists have always emphasised experimental methods and why evolutionary and psychodynamic psychologists are increasingly doing so.

The phenomena that are most important to study do not, however, always lend themselves readily to experimental investigation. As we saw in chapter 1, researchers have offered competing theories for more than a century about the extent to which specific parts of the brain perform specific functions.

We now know that many functions are, in fact, localised to specific structures and pathways, although most functions are distributed across circuits in diverse parts of the brain, not just a single region. The question of how the brain is organised was no less important before the advent of brain imaging techniques than after, and researchers did the best they could with the technologies available, such as lesion and EEG studies. The same is true of the study of unconscious processes, for which the primary available data were once case studies, but which are increasingly coming under experimental scrutiny — allowing researchers to test more refined hypotheses about their functioning.

Should a hypothesis be discarded simply because it is difficult to assess? To do so would confuse the truth-value of a hypothesis with its testability. A sophisticated psychological theory may include many accurate propositions that are difficult to precisely empirically test, because humans are complex and psychology is only a century old. Science, like all human cognition, involves constructing a mental model or 'map' of a phenomenon we want to understand, using all the information at our disposal. That means tentatively accepting hypotheses supported by our strongest methods, even more tentatively holding other theoretical beliefs that have *some* basis in more limited methods, and gradually weeding out those beliefs that do not withstand closer scientific scrutiny when the technologies are available to test them.

In its broadest sense, a scientific, empiricist attitude in psychology means keeping your eyes wide open in as many settings as possible and constantly testing what you believe. Philosophers of science sometimes distinguish between the ***context of discovery*** (in which phenomena are observed, hypotheses are framed and theories are built) and the ***context of justification*** (in which hypotheses are tested empirically). Case studies, naturalistic observation and surveys are often most useful in the context of discovery precisely because the investigator is not structuring the situation. The more experimenters exert control, the less unconstrained behaviour — behaviour as it occurs in nature — they see.

Descriptive methods often foster the kind of exploration that leads researchers to ask the right questions. In contrast, in the context of justification, where hypotheses are put to the test, the best designs are experimental, quasi-experimental and sometimes correlational. By using inferential statistics, researchers can assess the likelihood that their findings are genuine and, by implication, that their theories and hypotheses may have merit.

The road to psychological knowledge is paved in many directions. Just as an optimal study uses multiple measures, so an optimal science of mental life and behaviour uses multiple methods of observation. The remainder of this text examines the discoveries to which the various methods have led, beginning with the biological bases of mental processes and behaviour.

◆

INTERIM SUMMARY

Descriptive methods tend to be most useful in the ***context of discovery***, whereas experimental methods tend to be most useful in the ***context of justification***. Taking a scientific, empiricist approach means using whatever methods you can to study a phenomenon, continually testing your hypotheses and applying experimental methods wherever possible to assess cause and effect.

SUMMARY

1 Characteristics of scientific psychological research

- Quality psychological research is characterised by a theoretical framework, standardised procedures, generalisability and objective measurement.
- A ***theory*** is a systematic way of organising and explaining observations that includes a set of propositions about the relationships among various phenomena. A ***hypothesis*** is a tentative belief or educated guess that purports to predict or explain the relationship between two or more variables; variables are phenomena that differ or change across circumstances or individuals. A ***variable*** that can be placed on a continuum is a ***continuous variable***. A variable comprised of groupings or categories is a ***categorical variable***.
- A ***sample*** is a subgroup of a ***population*** that is likely to be ***representative*** of the population as a whole. ***Generalisability*** refers to the applicability of findings based on a sample to the entire population of interest. For a study's findings to be generalisable, its methods must be sound, or ***valid***.
- A ***measure*** is a concrete way of assessing a variable. A good measure is both reliable and valid. ***Reliability*** refers to a measure's ability to produce consistent results. The ***validity*** of a measure refers to its ability to assess the construct it is intended to measure.

2 Steps in conducting an experiment

- The ***scientific approach*** uses empirical methodologies such as observation and experimentation to gain knowledge. The three main goals of the scientific approach are (1) ***description***, (2) ***prediction*** and (3) ***understanding***.
- In ***experimental research***, investigators manipulate some aspect of a situation and examine the impact on the way participants respond in order to assess cause and effect. ***Independent variables*** are the variables the experimenter manipulates; ***dependent variables*** are the participants' responses, which indicate if the manipulation had an effect.
- Conducting an experiment — or most other kinds of research — entails a series of steps: framing a hypothesis, operationalising variables, developing a standardised procedure, selecting participants, testing the results for statistical significance and drawing conclusions. ***Operationalising*** means turning an abstract concept into a concrete variable defined by some set of actions or operations.
- A ***control group*** is a neutral condition of an experiment in which participants are not exposed to the experimental manipulation. Researchers frequently perform ***blind studies***, in which participants are kept unaware of, or 'blind' to, important aspects of the research. In a ***single-blind study***, only participants are kept blind; in ***double-blind studies***, participants and researchers alike are blind.
- A ***confounding variable*** is a variable that could produce effects that might be confused with the effects of the independent variable.
- Experimental studies provide the strongest evidence in psychology because they can establish cause and effect. The major limitations of experimental studies include the difficulty bringing some important phenomena into the laboratory and issues of external validity (applicability of the results to phenomena outside the laboratory).

3 Descriptive research methods

- Unlike experimental studies, ***descriptive research*** cannot unambiguously demonstrate cause and effect. It describes phenomena as they already exist rather than manipulating variables to test the effects. Descriptive methods include case studies, naturalistic observation and survey research.
- A ***case study*** is an in-depth observation of one person or a small group of people. ***Naturalistic observation*** is the in-depth observation of a phenomenon in its natural setting. Both case studies and naturalistic observation are vulnerable to researcher bias — the tendency of investigators to see what they expect to see. ***Survey research*** involves asking a large sample of people questions, often about attitudes or behaviours, using ***questionnaires*** or ***interviews***.

4 Correlational research

- ***Correlational research*** assesses the degree to which two variables are related, in an effort to see whether knowing the value of one can lead to prediction of the other. A ***correlation coefficient*** measures the extent to which two variables are related. A ***positive correlation*** between two variables means that the higher individuals measure on one variable, the higher they are likely to measure on the other. A ***negative correlation*** means that the higher individuals measure on one variable, the lower they will measure on the other, and vice versa. Correlation does not demonstrate causation.
- Researchers studying the relationship between mental and neural processes use a number of methods, including case studies of patients with brain damage, experimental lesion studies with animals, ***EEGs*** and computerised ***neuroimaging techniques***, such as ***CAT scans***, ***PET*** and ***fMRI***.
- Researchers studying psychological phenomena cross-culturally use a variety of methods, including naturalistic observation, correlational studies linking one cultural trait to another and experiments.

5 The internet and psychology research

- Internet technologies are impacting on the way psychology research takes place. The benefits of using these technologies come from a capacity to access, automate and process data quickly and easily. Potential downsides include sampling bias, uncontrolled data collection procedures, protecting the welfare of participants and ensuring participants' right to confidentiality.

6 Ethical guidelines for the conduct of psychological research

- The Australian Psychological Society developed a code of ethics that sets forth a series of principles of ethics and professional practice in psychology.
- Two of the key ethical issues in psychological research include ***informed consent*** (the participant's ability to agree or refuse to participate in a study) and ***deception*** (where participants are not informed of the aims of the investigation until the end of the study).

7 Critically evaluating a study

- To evaluate a study, a critical reader should answer several broad questions: (1) Does the theory make sense, and do the hypotheses flow sensibly from it? (2) Is the sample adequate and appropriate? (3) Are the measures and procedures valid and reliable? (4) Are the data conclusive? (5) Are the broader conclusions warranted? (6) Does the study say anything meaningful? (7) Is the study ethical?

KEY TERMS

appeals to authority *p. 69*
appeals to popularity *p. 69*
arguments directed to the person *p. 69*
blind studies *p. 52*
case study *p. 55*
categorical variable *p. 44*
computerised axial tomography (CAT) scan *p. 61*
conditions *p. 50*
confounding variables *p. 52*
context of discovery *p. 70*
context of justification *p. 70*
continuous variable *p. 44*
control group *p. 54*
correlate *p. 59*
correlation coefficient *p. 59*
correlation matrix *p. 59*
correlational research *p. 59*
critical thinking *p. 67*
deception *p. 65*
demand characteristics *p. 52*
dependent variables *p. 50*
description *p. 49*
descriptive research *p. 55*
descriptive statistics *p. 52*
double-blind study *p. 52*
electroencephalogram (EEG) *p. 61*
error *p. 47*
experimental research *p. 49*
external validity *p. 45*
functional magnetic resonance imaging (fMRI) *p. 62*
generalisability *p. 45*
hypothesis *p. 44*
independent variables *p. 50*
inferential statistics *p. 52*
informed consent *p. 65*
internal consistency *p. 46*
internal validity *p. 45*
interrater reliability *p. 47*
interviews *p. 57*
magnetic resonance imaging (MRI) *p. 61*
measure *p. 46*
naturalistic observation *p. 56*
negative correlation *p. 59*
neuroimaging techniques *p. 61*
objectivity *p. 67*
observer bias *p. 55*
open-mindedness *p. 67*
operationalising *p. 51*
participants *or* subjects *p. 45*
placebo effect *p. 52*
population *p. 45*
positive correlation *p. 59*
positron emission tomography (PET) *p. 61*
prediction *p. 49*
quasi-experimental designs *p. 54*
questionnaires *p. 57*
random sample *p. 57*
reliability *p. 46*
representative *p. 45*
researcher bias *p. 55*
retest reliability *p. 46*
sample *p. 45*
sampling bias *p. 45*
scepticism *p. 67*
scientific approach *p. 49*
single-blind study *p. 52*
standardised procedures *p. 44*
stratified random sample *p. 57*
straw man *p. 69*
survey research *p. 57*
theory *p. 44*
understanding *p. 49*
valid *p. 45*
validation *p. 47*
validity *p. 47*
variable *p. 44*

REVIEW QUESTIONS

1. Describe some of the common flaws in psychological research.
2. Explain how experimental methods can be used by researchers to demonstrate causality.
3. Describe the three goals of the scientific approach to psychology.
4. Differentiate among the various descriptive methods used in psychological research.
5. Describe the advantages and limitations of correlational research.

DISCUSSION QUESTIONS

1. Why are the reliability and validity of a measure so important in psychological research?
2. When is it acceptable for psychologists to use animals in their research?
3. Is deception in psychological research an example of the 'end justifying the means'?

APPLICATION QUESTIONS

1. Consider the following research study and answer the questions that follow.
   A researcher is interested in whether the difficulty of examination questions affects students' course evaluations.
   (a) If she wants to determine whether setting a difficult exam produces less favourable comments in students' course evaluations (i.e. a cause-and-effect relationship), what type of research procedure should she use?
   (b) What procedures would she follow in setting up such a study?
   (c) What could she select for independent and dependent variables?
   (d) Do you think a control group would be important? Why or why not?
   (e) How could she control for possible demand characteristics in the study?
2. Identify the research method that best describes each of the examples of research studies that follow.
   (a) A team of researchers, interested in what makes two people attracted to each other, spends several weeks in bars and night clubs observing young adults interacting with one another.
   (b) A sport psychologist collects considerable information concerning each elite athlete that he sees, including information concerning their sporting performance in competition, to try to determine under what conditions they are most likely to exhibit their maximal performance.
   (c) The relationship between exercise, healthy diet and body weight is examined.
   (d) A researcher is interested in whether there are gender differences in the performance on a road map task. He compares the test scores of the male and female participants in the sample.
   (e) A local health and community psychologist is interested in learning about the relationships people have with their residential communities. She sends out a questionnaire to all people in the town asking them various questions about how they perceive life in their community.
   (f) A lecturer wants to determine whether students are more likely to participate in class discussions when group members are the same sex. She randomly assigns students to either same-sex or mixed-sex groups and monitors the discussion for each group.

3. In an experimental study on the effects of alcohol on memory performance:
   (a) What variable is the dependent variable?
   (b) What variable is the independent variable?
4. You want to see if there is a difference in the rate of water evaporation if the water is coloured. Red, green and blue food colouring is added to three vials of water and the millimetres of water in the vial is measured after 12 hours.
   (a) What is the theoretical independent variable?
   (b) How is the IV manipulated or operationalised?
   (c) What is the theoretical dependent variable?
   (d) How is the DV measured or operationalised?
5. What are the (a) advantages and (b) disadvantages of experimental research?
6. Prepare responses to the following questions about naturalistic observation.
   (a) What is naturalistic observation?
   (b) Give an example of naturalistic observation.
   (c) What are the advantages of naturalistic observation?
   (d) What are the disadvantages of naturalistic observation?
7. Prepare responses to the following instructions and questions about case studies:
   (a) Define the case study method and give an example.
   (b) What are the advantages of using a case study?
   (c) What are the disadvantages of using a case study?
8. Prepare responses to the following instructions and questions about collecting data:
   (a) Describe the survey method for collecting data and give an example.
   (b) What are the advantages of using a survey method for collecting data?
   (c) What are the disadvantages of using a survey method for collecting data?

The solutions to the application questions can be found on page 833.

MULTIMEDIA RESOURCES

The *Cyberpsych* multimedia resource is available *as an option* to accompany this textbook to further develop your understanding of many key psychology concepts. *Cyberpsych* contains a wealth of rich media content and activities, and for this chapter includes:

- video clips on overweight adults and exercise, gene therapy safety and sex cells
- concept animations on descriptive statistics, inferential statistics and the art of prediction.

Statistical principles in psychological research

SUPPLEMENT 

LEARNING OBJECTIVES

After studying this supplement you should be able to:

1. distinguish between the different measures of central tendency
2. describe the different measures of variability
3. define statistical significance
4. define effect size and explain why it is important in the reporting of data
5. outline some common tests of statistical significance.

Summarising the data: descriptive statistics

- ***Descriptive statistics*** allow researchers to summarise data in a readily understandable form. The first step in describing the data is often to provide a ***frequency distribution***, which shows how frequently participants received each of the many possible scores.
- ***Measures of central tendency*** provide an index of the way a typical participant responded on a measure. The three most common measures of central tendency are the ***mean*** (average of the scores of all participants), ***mode*** (most common score) and ***median*** (the score that falls in the middle of the distribution).
- ***Variability*** is the extent to which participants tend to differ from one another. The ***standard deviation*** describes how much the average participant deviates from the mean.
- In a ***normal distribution***, the scores of most participants fall in the middle of the bell-shaped distribution, and progressively fewer participants have scores at either extreme. Participants' scores on a normally distributed variable can be described in terms of the number of standard deviations from the mean or as ***percentile scores***, which indicate the percentage of scores that fall below them.

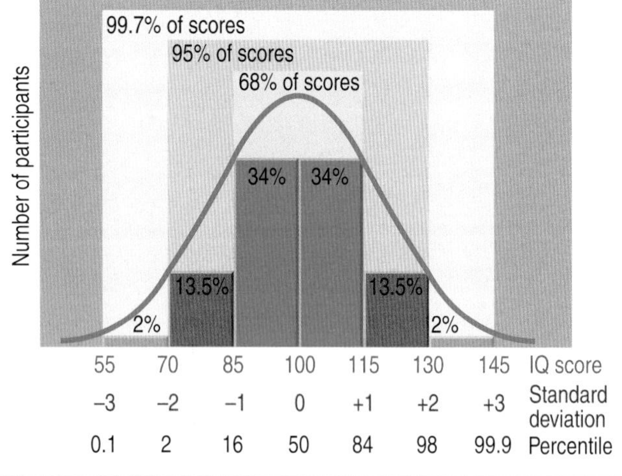

Testing the hypothesis: inferential statistics

- To assess whether the findings of a study are likely to reflect anything other than chance, psychologists use ***inferential statistics***, notably tests of ***statistical significance***. They usually report a ***probability value***, or ***p value***, which represents the probability that any positive findings obtained (such as a difference between groups, or a correlation coefficient that differs from zero) were accidental or just a matter of chance. By convention, psychologists accept *p* values that fall below .05 (that have a probability of being accidental of less than 5 percent). The best ways to protect against spurious findings are to use large samples and to try to replicate findings in other samples.
- The ***effect size*** indicates the magnitude of the experimental effect or the strength of a relationship.
- Choosing which inferential statistics to use depends on the design of the study and whether the variables assessed are continuous or categorical.
- A ***Chi-square test*** (or χ^2) is used if both the independent and dependent variables are categorical; it compares the observed data with the results that would be expected by chance and tests the likelihood that the differences observed and expected are accidental.
- A ***t test*** compares the mean scores of two groups and is a special case of a statistical procedure called an ***analysis of variance (ANOVA)***, which can be used to compare the means of two or more groups. ANOVA assesses the likelihood that differences in means among groups occurred by chance (or examines the extent to which variation in scores is attributable to the independent variable); if the variation between groups is substantially larger than the variation within groups, then the independent variable probably accounts for the difference.

Central questions: what does it mean to say that a finding is 'significant'?

- Inferential statistics are extremely important in trying to draw inferences from psychological research. But they are not foolproof, and are heavily dependent on sample size.

STATISTICS are far more intuitive than most people believe, even to people who do not consider mathematics their strong suit. As described in chapter 2, psychologists use ***descriptive statistics*** to summarise quantitative data in an understandable form. They employ ***inferential statistics*** to tell whether the results reflect anything other than chance. We discuss each in turn, and then return to one central question: what does it mean to describe a study's findings as 'significant'?

Central question

- **What does it mean to say that a psychological finding is 'significant'?**

■ Summarising the data: descriptive statistics

The first step in describing participants' responses on a variable is usually to chart a ***frequency distribution***. A frequency distribution is exactly what it sounds like — a method of organising the data to show how frequently participants received each of the many possible scores. In other words, a frequency distribution represents the way scores were distributed across the sample.

The kind of frequency distribution that a lecturer might observe on a mid semester examination (in a very small class, for illustration) is shown in figure 2S.1 and again graphically in figure 2S.2. The graph, called a ***histogram***, plots ranges of scores along the x axis and the frequency of scores in each range on the y axis. The rounded-out version of the histogram drawn with a line is the familiar 'curve'.

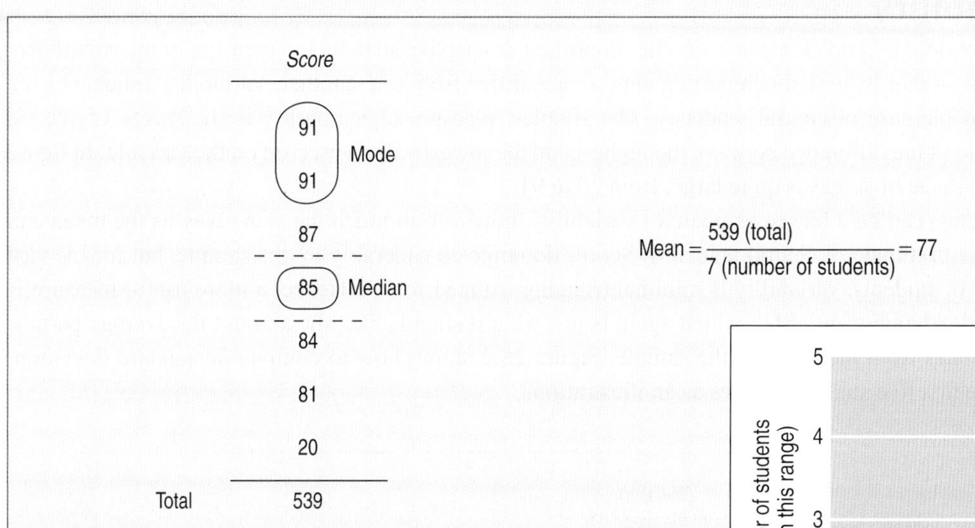

FIGURE 2S.1
Distribution of test scores on a mid-semester examination

FIGURE 2S.2
Histogram showing a frequency distribution of test scores. A frequency distribution shows graphically the frequency of each score (how many times it occurs) distributed across the sample.

Measures of central tendency

Perhaps the most important descriptive statistics are ***measures of central tendency***, which provide an index of the way a typical participant responded on a measure. The three most common measures of central tendency are the mean, the mode and the median.

The ***mean*** is simply the statistical average of the scores of all participants, calculated by adding up all the participants' scores and dividing by the number of participants. The mean is the most commonly reported measure of central tendency and is the most intuitively descriptive of the average participant.

Sometimes, however, the mean may be misleading. For example, consider the table of mid-semester exam scores presented in figure 2S.1. The mean grade is 77. Yet the mean falls below 6 of the 7 scores on the table. In fact, most students' scores fall somewhere between 81 and 91.

Why is the mean so low? It is pulled down by a single student's score — an outlier — who probably did not study. In this case, the median would be a more useful measure of central tendency, because a mean can be strongly influenced by extreme and unusual scores in a sample. The ***median*** refers to the score that falls in the middle of the distribution of scores, with half scoring below and half above it. Reporting the median essentially allows us to ignore extreme scores on each end of the distribution that would bias a portrait of the typical participant. In fact, the median in this case — 85 (which has three scores above and 3 below it) — makes more intuitive sense, in that it seems to capture the middle of the distribution, which is precisely what a measure of central tendency is supposed to do.

In other instances, a useful measure of central tendency is the ***mode*** (or modal score), which is the most common (i.e. most frequent) score observed in the sample. In this case, the mode is 91, because two students received a score of 91, whereas all other scores had a frequency of only 1. The problem with the mode in this case is that it is also the highest score, which is not a good estimate of central tendency.

INTERIM SUMMARY

Descriptive statistics allow researchers to summarise data in a readily understandable form. The first step in describing the data is often to provide a ***frequency distribution***, which shows how frequently participants received each of the many possible scores. The most important descriptive statistics are ***measures of central tendency***, which provide an index of the way a typical participant responded on a measure. The ***mean*** is the average of the scores of all participants; the ***mode*** is the most common score; the ***median*** is the score that falls in the middle of the distribution.

Variability

As the previous examples suggest, another important descriptive statistic is a measure of the ***variability*** of scores — that is, how much participants' scores differ from one another. Variability influences the choice of measure of central tendency. The simplest measure of variability is the ***range*** of scores, which shows the difference between the highest and the lowest value observed on the variable. In figure 2S.1, the range of scores is quite large, from 20 to 91.

The range can be a biased estimate of variability, however, in much the same way as the mean can be a biased estimate of central tendency. Scores do range considerably in this sample, but for the vast majority of students, variability is minimal (ranging from 81 to 91). Hence, a more useful measure is the ***standard deviation (SD)***, which again is just what it sounds like: the amount the average participant deviates from the mean of the sample. Figure 2S.3 shows how to compute a standard deviation, using the first five students' scores as an illustration.

APPLY + DISCUSS

In Indonesia, many people are very poor, whereas a small number are extremely wealthy.

- How might the mean, median and mode for family income provide realistic or misleading measures of central tendency in describing how poor or wealthy the *average* Indonesian is?

Score	*Deviation from the mean* (D)	D^2
91	91 − 87.6 = 3.4	11.56
91	91 − 87.6 = 3.4	11.56
87	87 − 87.6 = −.6	.36
85	85 − 87.6 = −2.6	6.76
84	84 − 87.6 = −3.6	12.96
Σ = sum = 438	0	43.20

$$Mean = \frac{\Sigma}{N} = 438/5 = 87.6$$

$$SD = \sqrt{\frac{\Sigma D^2}{N}} = \sqrt{\frac{43.2}{5}} = 2.94$$

NOTE: Computing a standard deviation (*SD*) is more intuitive than it might seem. The first step is to calculate the mean score, which in this case is 87.6. The next step is to calculate the difference, or deviation, between each participant's score and the mean score, as shown in column 2. The standard deviation is meant to capture the average deviation of participants from the mean. The only complication is that taking the average of the deviations would always produce a mean deviation of zero because the sum of deviations is by definition zero (see the total in column 2). Thus, the next step is to square the deviations (column 3). The standard deviation is then calculated by taking the square root of the sum (Σ) of all the squared differences divided by the number of participants (*N*).

FIGURE 2S.3
The standard deviation

The normal distribution

When researchers collect data on continuous variables (such as weight or IQ) and plot them on a histogram, the data usually approximate a normal distribution, like the distribution of IQ scores shown in figure 2S.4. In a ***normal distribution***, the scores of most participants fall in the middle of the bell-shaped distribution, and progressively fewer participants have scores at either extreme. In other words, most individuals are about average on most dimensions, and very few are extremely above or below average. Thus, most people have an IQ around average (100), whereas very few have an IQ of 70 or 130. In a distribution of scores that is completely normal, the mean, mode and median are all the same.

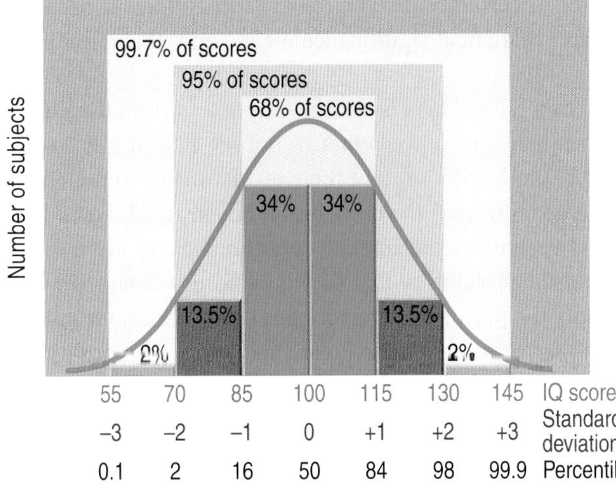

FIGURE 2S.4 A normal distribution. IQ scores approximate a normal distribution, which looks like a bell-shaped curve; 68 percent of scores fall within one standard deviation of the mean (represented by the area under the curve in blue). The curve is a smoothed-out version of a histogram. An individual's score can be represented alternatively by the number of standard deviations it diverges from the mean in either direction or by a percentile score, which shows the percentage of scores that fall below it (to the left on the graph).

Participants' scores on a variable that is normally distributed can be described in terms of how far they are from average — that is, their deviation from the mean. Thus, a person's IQ could be described either as 85 or as one standard deviation below the mean, because the standard deviation in IQ is about 15. A participant two standard deviations below the mean would have an IQ of 70, which is bordering on severe intellectual impairment. For normal data, 68 percent of participants fall within one standard deviation of the mean (34 percent on either side of it), 95 percent fall within two standard deviations, and more than 99.7 percent fall within three standard deviations. Thus, an IQ above 145 is a very rare occurrence.

Knowing the relationship between standard deviations and percentages of participants whose scores lie within different parts of a distribution allows researchers to report ***percentile scores***, which indicate the percentage of scores that fall below a score. Thus, a participant whose score is three standard deviations above the mean is in the 99.7th percentile, whereas an average participant (whose score does not deviate from the mean) is in the 50th percentile.

INTERIM SUMMARY

Variability is the extent to which participants tend to differ from one another. The ***standard deviation*** describes how much the average participant deviates from the mean. When psychologists collect data on continuous variables, they often find that the data approximate a ***normal distribution***, with most scores towards the middle. Participants' scores on a normally distributed variable can be described in terms of the number of standard deviations from the mean or as ***percentile scores***, which indicate the percentage of scores that fall below them.

Testing the hypothesis: inferential statistics

When researchers find a difference between the responses of participants in one condition and another, they must infer whether these differences occurred by chance or reflect a true causal relationship. Similarly, if they discover a correlation between two variables, they need to know the likelihood that the two variables simply correlated by chance.

As the philosopher David Hume (1711–1776) explained two centuries ago, we can never be entirely sure about the answer to questions like these. If someone believes that all swans are white and observes

99 swans that are white and none that are not, can the person conclude with certainty that the hundredth swan will also be white? The issue is one of probability. If the person has observed a representative sample of swans, what is the likelihood that, given 99 white swans, a black one will appear next?

Statistical significance

Psychologists typically deal with this issue in their research by using tests of ***statistical significance***, which help determine whether the results of a study are likely to have occurred simply by chance (and thus cannot be meaningfully generalised to a population) or whether they reflect true properties of the population. Statistical significance should not be confused with practical or theoretical significance. A researcher may demonstrate with a high degree of certainty that, on the average, females spend less time watching football than males, but who cares? Statistical significance means only that a finding is unlikely to be an accident of chance.

Beyond describing the data, then, the researcher's second task is to draw inferences from the sample to the population as a whole. Inferential statistics help sort out whether or not the findings of a study really show anything. Researchers usually report the likelihood that their results mean something in terms of a ***probability value*** (or ***p value***). A p value represents the probability that any positive findings obtained with the sample (such as differences between two experimental conditions) were just a matter of chance. In other words, a p value is an index of the probability that positive findings obtained would not apply to the population and instead reflect only the peculiar characteristics of the particular sample.

To illustrate, one study tested the hypothesis that children increasingly show signs of morality and empathy during their second year (Zahn-Waxler, Radke-Yarrow, Wagner, & Chapman, 1992). The investigators trained 27 mothers to tape-record reports of any episode in which their one-year-olds either witnessed distress (e.g. seeing the mother burn herself on the stove) or caused distress (e.g. pulling the cat's tail or biting the mother's breast while nursing). The mothers dictated descriptions of these events over the course of the next year; each report included the child's response to the other person's distress. Coders then rated the child's behaviour using categories such as prosocial behaviour, defined as efforts to help the person in distress.

Table 2S.1 shows the average percentage of times the children behaved prosocially during these episodes at each of three periods: time 1 (13 to 15 months of age), time 2 (18 to 20 months) and time 3 (23 to 25 months). As the table shows, the percentage of times children behaved prosocially increased dramatically over the course of the year, regardless of whether they witnessed or caused the distress. When the investigators analysed the changes in rates of prosocial responses over time to both types of distress (witnessed and caused), they found the differences statistically significant. A jump from 9 to 49 prosocial behaviours in 12 months was thus probably not a chance occurrence.

By convention, psychologists accept the results of a study whenever the probability of positive findings attributable to chance is less than 5 percent. This is typically expressed as $p < .05$. Thus, the *smaller* the p value, the more certain you can feel about the results. A researcher would rather be able to say that the chances that her findings are spurious (i.e. just accidental) are 1 in 1000 ($p < .001$) than 1 in 100 ($p < .01$).

TABLE **2S.1** **Children's prosocial response to another person's distress during the second year of life**

	Percentage of episodes in which the child behaved prosocially		
Type of incident	**Time 1**	**Time 2**	**Time 3**
Witnessed distress	9	21	49
Caused distress	7	10	52

SOURCE: Adapted from Zahn-Waxler et al. (1992).

Nevertheless, researchers can never be certain that their results are true of the population as a whole; a black swan could always be swimming in the next lake. Nor can they be sure that if they performed the study with 100 different participants they would not obtain different findings. This is why replication — repeating a study to see whether the same results occur again — is extremely important in science. For example, in his studies of mood and memory described in chapter 2, Bower hit an unexpected black swan. His initial series of studies yielded compelling results, but some of these findings failed to replicate in later experiments. He ultimately had to alter parts of his theory that the initial data had supported (Bower, 1989).

The best way to ensure that a study's results are not accidental is to use a large sample. The larger the sample, the more likely it reflects the actual properties of the population. Suppose 30 people in the world are over 115 years old, and researchers want to know about memory in this population. If the researchers test 25 of them, they can be much more certain that their findings are generalisable to this population than if they study a sample of only two of them. These two could have had poor memories in the first place or have had illnesses that affected their memory.

Most people intuitively understand the importance of large numbers in sampling, even if they do not realise it. For example, tennis fans recognise the logic behind matches comprised of multiple sets and would object if decisions about who moves on to the next round were made on the basis of a single game. Intuitively, they know that a variety of factors could influence the outcome of any single game other than the ability of the players, such as fluctuations in concentration, momentary physical condition (such as a dull pain in the foot), lighting, wind or which player served first. Because a single game is not a large enough set of observations to make a reliable assessment of who is the better player, many sports rely on a best-of-three, best-of-five or best-of-seven series.

Information about the ***effect size*** is required to understand the magnitude of the experimental effect or the strength of a relationship (Burton, 2007). Effect size indices are of two general types: (1) indices that compare differences between treatment means (e.g. Cohen's *d* and Glass's Δ — point biserial correlation); and (2) indices that are based on measures of association, such as correlation (e.g. Pearson's *r*) and explained variance. The effect size indicator should be reported immediately after the test of statistical significance (e.g. *p* value), followed by a short descriptive sentence about the nature of the effect. For example, 'with an alpha level of .01, the relationship between the personality trait "extroversion" and academic success was weak (Pearson's $r = .10$)'.

MAKING CONNECTIONS

Research using large samples of older people has dispelled many myths about 'senility'. Among other things, this research finds tremendous variation in cognitive abilities in **old age**, with some people showing substantial impairment and others very little (chapter 12).

ONE STEP FURTHER

Understanding inferential statistics

By Associate Professor Nick Burns, University of Adelaide

In George Orwell's classic novel, *Nineteen Eighty-Four*, the term *doublethink* refers to the act of holding two contradictory beliefs in one's mind simultaneously — and accepting both of them. An element of doublethink is required when considering inferential statistics.

The logic of statistical significance testing is as follows: Given that there is no effect of an independent variable, what is the probability that a researcher would have observed the data that they have, or data more extreme? The convention is that if this probability is less than .05 (i.e., $p < .05$), then the researcher can reject the null hypothesis that the independent variable has no effect, and can conclude that, indeed, it does affect the dependent variable. On the other hand, what if $p \geq .05$? Well, the result of the statistical test is deemed non-significant, and the null hypothesis of no effect is accepted (or not rejected). Recent commentary emphasises that this is illogical (Hurlbert & Lombardi, 2009) and that this illogicality has been recognised widely for a very long time — yet psychologists and scientists continue to behave as if all this was reasonable and sensible. Why is it so?

Null hypothesis significance testing sets up a decision framework around an arbitrary probability criterion ($p = .05$). This procedure has its roots in, and involves sensible practice in, industrial quality control settings. Questions that might be asked about its application in the context of basic science include: 'Once data is collected and analysed, is there really a need to make a decision?' 'Why do psychologists and scientists dichotomise the continuous distribution of probabilities associated with test statistics?' They really ought to report exact probabilities and interpret the outcome of a study in terms of the relative likelihood that an effect exists, or not. A so-called non-significant statistical test does not decide the issue.

Recent efforts (e.g., Wilkinson & Task Force on Statistical Inference, 1999) to influence the behaviour of psychologists in reporting the results of their studies have centred on encouraging the use of confidence intervals and effect sizes. Confidence intervals give an indication of the plausible range of values a statistic might take (e.g. a 95 percent confidence interval can loosely be interpreted as an interval for which researchers are 95 percent confident that it contains the population value of the parameter their sample statistic is estimating). Carefully considering the size of any observed effect is also very important. In statistical terms, any effect, no matter how trivial, will be statistically significant on a large enough sample size. Very large effects can be non-significant in a small sample. The substantive interpretation of an effect size is context dependent; what is large and important in one context may not be so in another.

The message is to not view statistical significance testing as a replacement for careful consideration of the story about the world that a researcher hopes that data can convey. Indeed, inferential statistics are perhaps no more than another form of descriptive statistics.

INTERIM SUMMARY

To assess whether the findings of a study are likely to reflect anything other than chance, psychologists use ***inferential statistics***, notably tests of ***statistical significance***. They usually report a ***probability value***, or ***p value***, which represents the probability that any positive findings obtained (such as a difference between groups, or a correlation coefficient that differs from zero) were accidental or just a matter of chance. By convention, psychologists accept p values that fall below .05 (that have a probability of being accidental of less than 5 percent). The best ways to protect against spurious findings are to use large samples and to try to replicate findings in other samples. The ***effect size*** indicates the magnitude of the experimental effect or the strength of a relationship.

Common tests of statistical significance

Choosing which inferential statistics to use depends on the design of the study and particularly on whether the variables to be assessed are continuous or categorical. If both sets of variables are continuous, the researcher simply correlates them to see whether they are related and tests the probability that a correlation of that magnitude could occur by chance.

For many kinds of research, however, the investigator wants to compare two or more groups, such as males and females, or participants exposed to several different experimental conditions. In this case, the independent variables are categorical (male/female, condition 1/condition 2). If both the independent and dependent variables are categorical, the appropriate statistic is a ***Chi-square test*** (or χ^2). A Chi-square test compares the observed data with the results that would be expected by chance and tests the likelihood that the differences between observed and expected are accidental.

	Scholastic performance	
	Failure	No failure
Antisocial	20	30
Normal	2	48

Note: A Chi-square is the appropriate statistic when testing the relationship between two categorical variables. In this case, the variables are diagnosis (presence or absence of antisocial personality disorder) and school failure (presence or absence of a failed grade). The Chi-square statistic tests the likelihood that the relative abundance of school failure in the antisocial group occurred by chance.

FIGURE 2S.5
Typical data appropriate for a Chi-square analysis

For example, suppose a researcher wants to know whether patients with antisocial personality disorder are more likely than the general population to have had academic difficulties in primary school. In other words, he wants to know whether one categorical variable (a diagnosis of antisocial versus normal personality) predicts another (presence or absence of academic difficulties, defined as having failed a grade in primary school). The researcher collects a sample of 50 male patients with the disorder (since the incidence is much higher in males and gender could be a confounding variable) and compares them with 50 males of similar socioeconomic status (since difficulties in school are correlated with social class) without the disorder. He finds that of his antisocial sample, 20 individuals failed a grade in primary school, whereas only two of the others did (figure 2S.5). The likelihood is extremely small that this difference could have occurred by chance, and the Chi-square test would therefore show that the difference between groups is statistically significant.

In many cases, the independent variables are categorical, but the dependent variables are continuous. This was the case in Pennebaker, Colder, and Sharp's (1990) study of emotional expression. In this study, the investigators placed participants in one of two conditions (writing about emotional events or about neutral events, a categorical variable) and compared the number of visits they subsequently made to the health service (a continuous variable). The question to be answered statistically was the likelihood that the mean number of visits to the doctor in the two conditions differed by chance. If participants who wrote about the transition to university made 0.73 visits to the health service on average whereas those who wrote about a neutral event made 1.56, is this discrepancy likely to be accidental or does it truly depend on the condition to which they were exposed?

When comparing the mean scores of two groups, researchers use a ***t test***. A t test is actually a special case of a statistical procedure called an ***analysis of variance (ANOVA)***, which can be used to compare the means of two or more groups. ANOVA assesses the likelihood that mean differences among groups occurred by chance. To put it another way, ANOVA assesses the extent to which variation in scores is attributable to the independent variable. The logic behind ANOVA is quite simple. If the variation *between* groups (the difference between the average member of one group versus another) is substantially larger than the variation *within* groups, then the independent variable probably accounts for the difference.

Once again, a larger sample is helpful in determining whether mean differences between groups are real or random. If Pennebaker and his colleagues tested only two participants in each condition and found mean differences, they could not be confident of the findings because the results could simply reflect the idiosyncrasies of these four participants. If they tested 30, however, and the differences between the two conditions were large and relatively consistent across participants, the ANOVA would be statistically significant.

Chi-square, *t* tests and analysis of variance are not the only statistics psychologists employ. They also use correlation coefficients and many others. In all cases, however, their aim is the same: to try to draw generalisations about a population without having to study every one of its members.

INTERIM SUMMARY

Whether you use inferential statistics such as ***Chi-square*** or ***ANOVA*** depends on the design of the study, particularly on whether the variables assessed are continuous or categorical.

APPLY + DISCUSS

A team of researchers wants to test the hypothesis that children who are physically abused by their parents will be more aggressive. They are considering analysing the data in three ways.

- First, they classify participants as abused or non-abused (the independent variable). They measure aggressiveness (the dependent variable) using a scale of 1 to 7 completed by their teacher (1 = not aggressive, 7 = very aggressive). What statistic are they likely to use to test the hypothesis?
- Next, they again classify patients as abused versus non-abused, but this time they measure whether the child has hit another child in school, coded yes or no (a categorical variable). What statistic are they likely to use?
- Now, the researchers decide to measure abuse on a scale of 1 to 7 (1 = no abuse, 7 = severe abuse). They also measure the child's aggressiveness on a scale of 1 to 7. What statistic are they likely to use?

Central question revisited

◆ What does it mean to say that a finding is 'significant'?

Inferential statistics are extremely important in trying to draw inferences from psychological research, but they are not foolproof. In fact, some psychologists are now debating just how useful significance testing really is (see Abelson, 1995; Hubbard et al., 2000; Hunter, 1997; Shrout, 1997).

One problem with significance testing is that *p* values are heavily dependent on sample size. With a large enough sample, a tiny correlation will become significant, even though the relationship between the two variables may be minuscule. Conversely, researchers often mistakenly infer from non-significant findings that no real difference exists between groups, when they simply have not used a large enough sample to know. If group differences *do* emerge, a *p* value is meaningful because it specifies the likelihood that the findings could have occurred by chance. If group differences *do not* emerge, however, a *p* value can be misleading because true differences between groups or experimental conditions may not show up simply because the sample was too small or the study was not conducted well enough.

For these reasons, some psychologists have called for other methods of reporting data that allow consumers of research to draw their own conclusions. One approach is to report the size of the effect of being in one group or another, such as how much difference an experimental manipulation made on the dependent variable. One way of reporting effect size puts the effect in standard deviation units — that is, how many standard deviations does the average participant in one condition differ from the average participant in another on the dependent variable?

For example, if participants who write about an emotional event for four days in a row go to the health service 0.73 times and those who write about a neutral event go 1.56 times, the meaning of that discrepancy is unclear unless we know the standard deviations (*SD*) of the means. If the *SD* is around 0.75, then students who write about emotional events are a full standard deviation better off than control participants — which is definitely a finding worth writing home about. If the *SD* is 0.25, the effect size is three standard deviations, which means that writing about emotional events would put the average participant in the experimental condition in the 99th percentile of health in comparison with participants in the control condition, which would be an extraordinary effect. This example illustrates why researchers always report *SD*s along with means: 0.73 vs. 1.56 is a meaningless difference if we do not know how much the average person normally fluctuates from these means.

A related problem is that people often confuse *statistical* significance with *practical* significance. For example, in the study of aspirin and heart disease described in chapter 2, the researchers discovered an effect of taking aspirin that translated into a correlation of .03. With a large enough sample (about 20 000, which is hundreds of times larger than the sample in most studies), they realised that this seemingly small effect was not only statistically significant but clinically significant, translating into large numbers of lives. But suppose they had tested the hypothesis on a sample of 300, which would have been a very small sample for this kind of research. In this case, a .03 correlation would *not* have been statistically significant, and the scientific community would never have known about the beneficial effects of aspirin on the heart.

In the final analysis, perhaps what statistics really do is to help a researcher tell a compelling story (Abelson, 1995). A good series of studies aims to solve a mystery, leading the reader step by step through all the possible scenarios, ruling out one suspect after another. Statistics can lend confidence to the conclusion, but they can never entirely rule out the possibility of a surprise ending.

SUMMARY

1 Central tendency

- The most important descriptive statistics are ***measures of central tendency***, which provide an index of the way a typical participant responded on a measure. The ***mean*** is the statistical average of the scores of all participants. The ***mode*** is the most common or frequent score or value of the variable observed in the sample. The ***median*** is the score that falls right in the middle of the distribution of scores; half the participants score below it and half above it.

2 Variability

- ***Variability*** refers to the extent to which participants tend to differ from one another in their scores. The ***standard deviation*** refers to the amount that the average participant deviates from the mean of the sample.

3 Statistical significance

- Psychologists apply tests of ***statistical significance*** to determine whether positive results are likely to have occurred simply by chance. A ***probability value***, or ***p value***, represents the probability that positive findings (such as group differences) were accidental or just a matter of chance. By convention, psychologists accept p values that fall below .05 (that have a probability of being accidental of less than 5 percent). The best way to ensure that a study's results are not accidental is to use a large enough sample that random fluctuations will cancel each other out.

4 Effect size

- Tests of statistical significance are not without their limitations. With a large enough sample size, significant differences are likely to appear whether or not they are meaningful, and p values do not adequately reflect the possibility that negative findings occurred by chance. Thus, some psychologists advocate other methods for making inferences from psychological data, such as effect size, to indicate the magnitude of the experimental effect or the strength of a relationship. Statistical techniques are useful ways of making an argument, not foolproof methods for establishing psychological truths.

5 Common tests of statistical significance

- The choice of which inferential statistics to use depends on the design of the study, particularly on whether the variables assessed are continuous or categorical. Common statistical tests are ***Chi-square*** and ***analysis of variance***.

KEY TERMS

analysis of variance (ANOVA), *p. 82*
Chi-square (*or* χ^2) test, *p. 82*
descriptive statistics, *p. 77*
effect size, *p. 81*
frequency distribution, *p. 77*
histogram, *p. 77*
inferential statistics, *p. 77*
mean, *p. 77*
measures of central tendency, *p. 77*
median, *p. 78*
mode, *p. 78*
normal distribution, *p. 79*
percentile scores, *p. 79*
probability value (*or p* value), *p. 80*
range, *p. 78*
standard deviation (*SD*), *p. 78*
statistical significance, *p. 80*
t test, *p. 82*
variability, *p. 78*

REVIEW QUESTIONS

1. Describe the different types of descriptive statistics used to summarise data.
2. Describe the characteristics of a normal distribution.
3. Explain what is meant by the 75th percentile.
4. Explain what is meant by the expression '$p < .05$'.
5. Distinguish between the Chi-square test and the analysis of variance.

DISCUSSION QUESTIONS

1. When can we be confident that a psychological finding is 'significant'?
2. What is the best way to ensure that the results of a study are not due to chance?
3. Why should psychologists report the effect size when reporting their results?

APPLICATION QUESTIONS

1. Calculate the mean, mode and median for the following set of scores: 10, 4, 8, 5, 3, 6, 8, 4, 8 and 9.
2. Calculate the standard deviation for the following data set: 31, 39, 46, 33, 42, 44 and 38.

The solutions to the application questions can be found on page 833.

Biological bases of mental life and behaviour

3

LEARNING OBJECTIVES

After studying this chapter you should be able to:

1. describe the basic units of the nervous system
2. describe the major structures and functions of the endocrine system
3. explain the major subdivisions of the peripheral nervous system
4. describe the major structures and functions of the central nervous system
5. describe the relative roles of genetics and environment in psychological functioning.

Neurons: basic units of the nervous system

- The nervous system consists of the *central nervous system (CNS)* and the *peripheral nervous system (PNS)*.
- *Sensory neurons* carry sensory information from sensory receptors to the central nervous system. *Motor neurons* transmit commands from the brain to the glands and muscles of the body. *Interneurons* connect neurons with one another.
- *Neurons* generally have a *cell body*, *dendrites* (branch-like extensions of the cell body) and an *axon* that carries information to other neurons.
- When a neuron is at rest (its *resting potential*), it is polarised, with a negative charge inside the cell membrane and a positive charge outside. *Graded potentials* are the spreading voltage changes along the cell membrane that occur as the neuron is excited by other neurons. An *action potential* is the 'firing' of the neuron, or a nerve impulse.
- *Neurotransmitters* transmit information from one neuron to another as they are released into the synapse. They bind with receptors in the membrane of the postsynaptic neuron, which produces graded potentials that can either excite or inhibit the postsynaptic neuron from firing.

The endocrine system

- The *endocrine system* is a collection of glands that control various bodily functions through the secretion of *hormones*.
- The endocrine system sends global messages through the bloodstream.

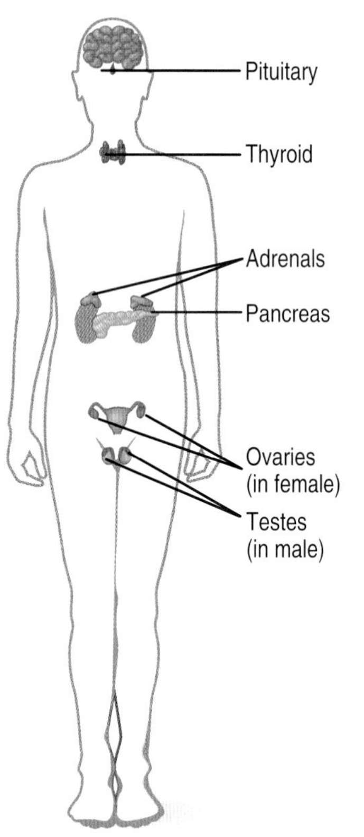

The peripheral nervous system

- Neurons of the PNS carry messages to and from the CNS. The PNS has two subdivisions: the *somatic nervous system* (carries sensory information to the brain and motor neurons that direct the action of skeletal muscles) and the *autonomic nervous system* (controls basic life processes such as heartbeat, digestive system and breathing).
- The autonomic nervous system consists of two parts: the *sympathetic nervous system* (activated in response to threats) and the *parasympathetic nervous system* (involved in routine activities).

The central nervous system

- The design of the human nervous system reflects its evolution. The most primitive vertebrate brain, or brainstem, included a forebrain, a midbrain and a hindbrain. The forebrain of humans includes an expanded *cerebrum* and *cortex*, which allows much more sophisticated sensory, cognitive and motor processes.
- The CNS consists of the brain and the spinal cord. The *spinal cord* carries out reflexes, transmits sensory information to the brain and transits messages from the brain to the muscles and organs.

  The *hindbrain* consists of the *medulla oblongata*, the *cerebellum* and parts of the *reticular formation*. These structures link the brain to the spinal cord, sustain life by controlling the supply of air and blood to cells in the body, and regulate arousal level.
- The *midbrain* consists of the *tectum* and *tegmentum*; these structures help humans orient to visual and auditory stimuli with eye and body movements.
- The *forebrain* is involved in complex sensory, emotional, cognitive and behavioural processes and consists of the *hypothalamus*, *thalamus*, the *subcortical structures* of the cerebrum and the cerebral cortex.
- The *cerebral cortex* consists of two hemispheres, each of which has four sets of lobes: *occipital lobes*, *parietal lobes*, *frontal lobes* and *temporal lobes*. The primary and association areas of the cerebral cortex are involved in complex mental processes such as perception and thinking.

Brain, gene and behaviour

- *Heritability* refers to the proportion of variability among individuals on an observed characteristic (phenotypic variance) that can be accounted for by genetic variability (genotypic variance).

Central questions: brain–behaviour relationships

- An understanding of the biological underpinnings of human mental life and behaviour adds to our psychological interpretation of people's thoughts and behaviours.

AUSTRALIA has long been a dream destination for many young people from the British Isles. They come to visit, to live and to work, drawn by the promise of a much different lifestyle, as well as a sense of shared history. Irishman David Keohane was no different. In 2008, the then 28-year-old flooring contractor was living the dream. He was working in Sydney and had been enjoying the Australian way of life for more than four years. David liked it so much he had applied for and been granted permanent residency in Australia. While happy with life down under, he retained close ties with the expatriate Irish community and played soccer in a social group with compatriots from the Emerald Isle. Life was good.

One night in August 2008, however, the dream turned sour.

After a night out on the town, David was dropped off at the beachside Coogee Bay Hotel in Sydney in the early hours of Saturday, 9 August. He was seen on closed circuit television footage in the hotel for a short time before he crossed the road and bought a pizza around 2.30 am. What happened after that was as brutal as it was unexpected.

At 3 am David was found lying unconscious in a pool of blood on the footpath a short distance away, presumably on his way home to his nearby apartment. He had been beaten beyond recognition and left with severe head injuries. He was rushed to hospital. At that stage, doctors were unsure whether the Irishman would ever regain consciousness. A male teenager was subsequently acquitted of attempted murder, and pleaded guilty to robbery in company and inflicting grievous bodily harm.

In the weeks after the incident, David remained in a coma on life support with family members maintaining a bedside vigil. In September, a month after the attack, the family flew him home to Ireland, unsure whether he would ever recover. The future looked bleak.

Then, in March 2009, came a breakthrough. Fittingly it was on St Patrick's Day, 17 March, that David opened his eyes for the first time in his Cork University Hospital bed, emerging from a coma. While unable to walk or talk, David was able to recognise family members and friends. While this was a major step forward, he still had a way to go in his recovery. Basically, David had to start learning many things all over again. Simple, everyday actions like walking and talking were skills that had to be reacquired. David has a long road ahead, working with the hospital's neurosurgery specialists to recover as best he can, with family there to support him all the way.

The physical trauma David suffered disrupted his nervous system, robbing him of the neural connections required to carry out simple tasks such as walking or talking. To comprehend David Keohane's experience requires an understanding of the ***nervous system*** — the interacting network of nerve cells that underlies all psychological activity. We begin by examining the neuron, or nerve cell, and the way neurons communicate with one another to produce thought, feeling and behaviour. After briefly exploring the hormones that work together with chemicals in the nervous system to create psychological experience, we then consider the extraordinary organisation of billions of neurons in the central nervous system (the brain and spinal cord) and in the peripheral nervous system (neurons in the rest of the body). We conclude with a brief discussion of the role of biology and genetics in understanding human mental processes and behaviour.

Throughout, we wrestle with some thorny questions about the way physical mechanisms are translated into psychological meanings. Indeed, a central question that runs throughout this chapter is the extent to which we can separate the mental and the physical. Can we study psychological processes — thoughts, feelings, wishes, hopes and dreams — as if they were independent of the brain that embodies them? Alternatively, can we reduce the pain of a jilted lover or a grieving widow to the neural circuits that regulate emotion? Is our subjective experience little more than a shadow cast by our neurons, hormones and genes?

Central questions

- To what extent can we understand psychological processes without reference to events in the brain?
- To what extent can we *reduce* psychological processes to events in the brain?

Neurons: basic units of the nervous system

Nerve cells, or ***neurons***, are the basic units of the nervous system. Appreciating a sunset, swaying to music, pining for a lover thousands of kilometres away or praying for forgiveness — all of these acts reflect the coordinated action of thousands or millions of neurons. We do not, of course, experience ourselves as systems of interacting nerve cells, any more than we experience hunger as the depletion of sugar in the bloodstream. We think, we feel, we hurt, we want. But we do all these things through the silent, behind-the-scenes activity of neurons, which carry information from cell to cell within the nervous system as well as to and from muscles and organs.

No-one knows how many neurons are in the nervous system; the best estimates range from 10 to 100 billion in the brain alone (Stevens, 1979). Some neurons connect with as many as 30 000 neurons, although the average neuron transmits information to about 1000 (Damasio, 1994).

The nervous system is composed of three kinds of neurons: sensory neurons, motor neurons and interneurons. ***Sensory neurons*** transmit information from sensory cells in the body called receptors (cells that receive sensory information) to the brain (either directly or by way of the spinal cord). Thus, sensory neurons might send information to the brain about the sensations perceived as a sunset or a sore throat. The output is received by ***interneurons***, nerve cells that connect other neurons with one another. The vast majority of neurons in the brain and spinal cord are interneurons. ***Motor neurons*** transmit commands from interneurons to the glands and muscles of the body, most often through the spinal cord. Motor neurons carry out both voluntary actions, such as grabbing a glass of water, and vital bodily functions, such as digestion and heartbeat. (Sensory neurons are sometimes called afferent neurons, and motor neurons are sometimes called efferent neurons. Interneurons, sadly, do not have nicknames.)

APPLY + DISCUSS

On your university course website for this subject, you should be able to access the following:

- a video clip about neurons
- an animation
- an online quiz to test your understanding of the anatomy of a neuron.

Consider the following question:

- What is the basic structure of the neuron?

Anatomy of a neuron

The same metaphor of input, computation and output also characterises the 'division of labour' within individual neurons. Branch-like extensions of the neuron, called ***dendrites*** (figure 3.1; see overleaf), receive inputs from other cells. The ***cell body*** includes a nucleus that contains the genetic material of the cell (the chromosomes). The nucleus, with its genetic blueprints, is the 'brains' of the operation, which determines how that particular neuron will manipulate the input from the dendrites. If a neuron receives enough stimulation through its dendrites and cell body, it passes the manipulated input to the dendrites of other neurons through its axon. The ***axon*** is a long extension from the cell body — occasionally as long as one metre — whose central function is to transmit information to other neurons. Axons often have two or more offshoots, or collateral branches.

The axons of most neurons in the nervous system are covered with a ***myelin sheath***, a tight coat of cells composed primarily of lipids (fats) that facilitates transmission of information to other neurons. Myelinated axons give some portions of the brain a white appearance (hence the term 'white matter'). The 'grey matter' of the brain gets its colour from cell bodies, dendrites and unmyelinated axons.

The myelin sheath insulates the axon from chemical and physical stimuli that might interfere with the transmission of nerve impulses, much as the coating of a wire prevents electrical currents from getting crossed. The myelin sheath also dramatically increases the speed of transmission of messages. It does this by capitalising on the fact that between the cells that form the sheath are small spaces of 'bare wire' called nodes of Ranvier. When a neuron fires (is activated enough to send information to other neurons), the electrical impulse is rapidly conducted from node to node, like an express train that does not have to stop at every station.

Not all axons are myelinated at birth. The transmission of impulses along these axons is slow and arduous, which helps explain why babies have such poor motor control. As myelination occurs in areas of the nervous system involved in motor action, an infant becomes capable of reaching and pointing. Such developmental achievements can be reversed in demyelinating diseases such as multiple sclerosis. In these disorders, degeneration of the myelin sheath on large clusters of axons can cause jerky, uncoordinated movement, although for reasons not well understood, the disease often goes into remission and the symptoms temporarily disappear. Multiple sclerosis and other diseases that progressively strip axons of their myelin may be fatal, particularly if they strike the neurons that control basic life-support processes such as the beating of the heart.

FIGURE 3.1
The anatomy of a neuron.
(a) Neurons differ in their shape throughout the nervous system.
Photo (1) shows a neuron in the most recently evolved part of the brain, the cerebral cortex, which is involved in the most complex psychological processes.
Photo (2) shows neurons in the spinal cord, which is a much older structure. (These images were magnified using an electron microscope.)
(b) The dendrites receive neural information from other neurons and pass it down the axon. The terminal buttons then release neurotransmitters, chemicals that transmit information to other cells.

(a)

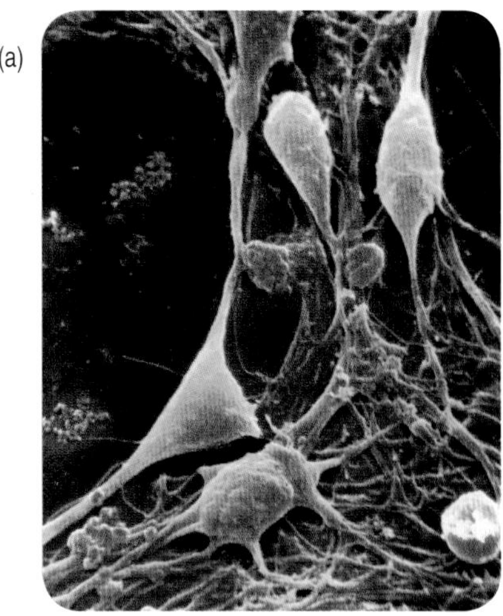

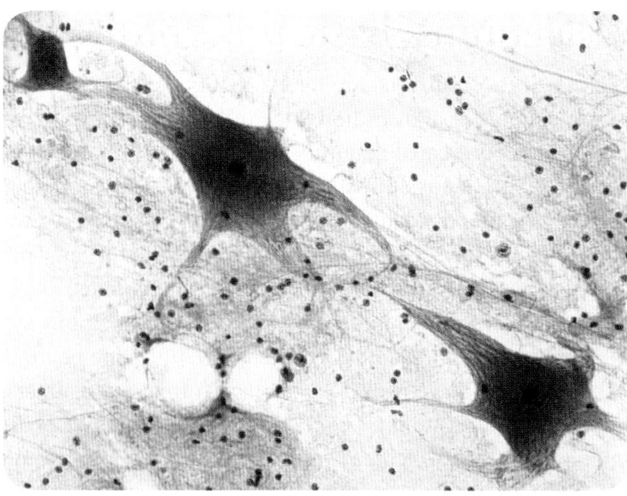

(b)

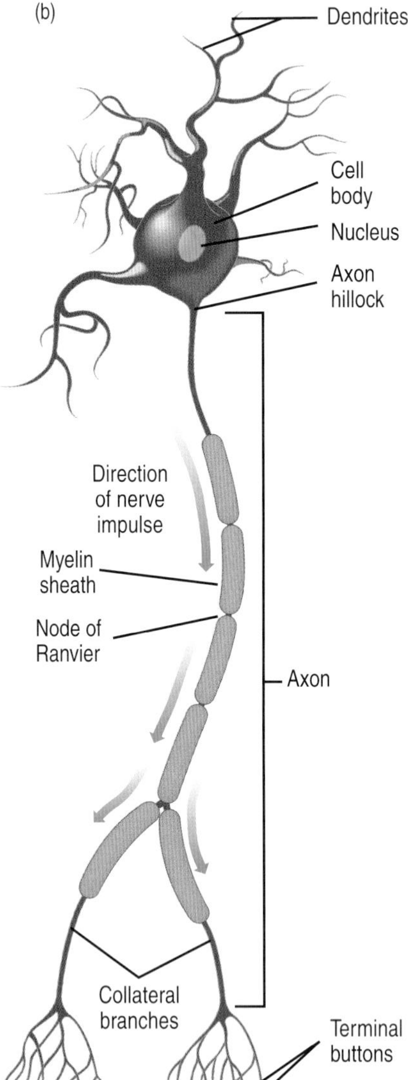

At the end of an axon are ***terminal buttons***, which send signals from a neuron to adjacent cells. These signals are triggered by the electrical impulse that has travelled down the axon and are then typically received by the dendrites or cell bodies of other neurons. Connections between neurons occur at ***synapses***. Two cells do not actually touch at a synapse; instead, a space exists between the two neurons, called the synaptic cleft. (Not all synapses work quite the same way. For example, in the brain, many synapses are located on parts of the cell other than the dendrites. Elsewhere in the nervous system, neurons may send their signals to glands or muscles rather than to other neurons.)

INTERIM SUMMARY

The nervous system is the interacting network of nerve cells that underlies all psychological activity. ***Neurons*** are the basic units of the nervous system. ***Sensory neurons*** carry sensory information from sensory receptors to the central nervous system. ***Motor neurons*** transmit commands from the brain to the glands and muscles of the body. ***Interneurons*** connect neurons with one another. Neurons generally have a ***cell body***, ***dendrites*** (branch-like extensions of the cell body) and an ***axon*** that carries information to other neurons. Neurons connect at ***synapses***.

Firing of a neuron

Most neurons communicate at the synapse through a process that involves the conversion of the electrical charge in one neuron to a chemical 'message'. When this message is released into the synapse, it alters the electrical charge of the next neuron. Most neurons receive inputs from many neurons and provide output to many neurons as well. The overall pattern of neural activation distributed across many thousands of neurons gives rise to the changes we experience in our thoughts and feelings.

Before we can hope to understand this cavalcade of neural fireworks, we must examine the events that energise a single resting neuron so that it fires off a chemical message to its neighbours.

Resting potentials

When a neuron is 'at rest', its membrane is polarised, like two sides of a battery. Inside the membrane has a negative electrical charge, whereas the fluid outside the cell has a positive charge. This polarised state reflects the fact that the cell membrane naturally lets some chemicals in, keeps others out, and actively pumps some in and out. (In a sense, neurons are never really at rest, since they use vast amounts of energy to pump chemicals across their membranes.)

A combination of chemicals normally exists inside and outside the membrane, the most important of which are sodium (Na^+), potassium (K^+) and chloride (Cl^-) ions. (An ion is an atom or a small molecule that carries an electrical charge.) Outside the cell is a fluid much like the seawater within which the most primitive cells appear to have evolved millions of years ago. Thus, sodium and chloride ions tend to concentrate on the outside of the cell. (Sodium chloride, or NaCl, is salt.) The cell membrane of a neuron is typically not permeable to positively charged sodium ions; that is, these ions cannot easily get through the membrane, so they tend to accumulate outside the neuron. The membrane is also completely impermeable to a variety of negatively charged protein ions inside the cell that are involved in carrying out its basic functions. As a result, the electrical charge is normally more negative on the inside than on the outside of the cell.

This 'resting' condition, in which the neuron is not firing, is called the ***resting potential***. (It is called a potential because the cell has a stored-up source of energy, which has the potential to be used.) At its resting potential, the difference between the electrical charge inside and outside the neuron is about −70 millivolts (mV). (A volt is a standard unit of electricity, and a millivolt is one-thousandth of a volt.) Researchers discovered this by inserting tiny electrodes (materials that conduct electricity) on the inside and outside of the cell membrane of animals with the largest neurons they could find and measuring the electrical potential across the membrane.

Graded potentials

When a neuron is stimulated by another, one of two things can happen. The stimulation can reduce the membrane's polarisation, decreasing the voltage discrepancy between the inside and the outside. For instance, the resting potential might move from −70 to −60 mV. This excites the neuron — that is, renders it more likely to fire with further stimulation. Alternatively, stimulation from another neuron can increase polarisation. This inhibits the neuron — that is, renders it less likely to fire.

Typically, a decrease in polarisation — called depolarisation — stems from an influx of positive sodium ions. As a result, the charge inside the cell membrane becomes less negative, making it more likely to fire if further stimulated. The opposite state of affairs — increasing the electrical difference between the inside and outside of the cell — is called hyperpolarisation. This condition usually results from an outflow of potassium ions, which are also positively charged, or an influx of negatively charged chloride ions; as a result, the potential across the membrane becomes even more negative, making the neuron less likely to fire.

Most of these brief voltage changes occur at synapses along the neuron's dendrites and cell body; they then spread down the cell membrane like ripples on a pond. These spreading voltage changes, which occur when the neural membrane receives a signal from another cell, are called ***graded potentials***. Graded potentials have two notable characteristics. First, their strength diminishes as they travel along the cell membrane away from the source of the stimulation, just as the ripples on a pond grow smaller with distance from a tossed stone's point of impact. Second, graded potentials are cumulative, or additive. If a neuron is simultaneously depolarised by +2 mV at one point on a dendrite and hyperpolarised by −2 mV at an adjacent point, the two graded potentials add up to zero and essentially cancel each other out. In contrast, if the membrane of a neuron is depolarised at multiple points, a progressively greater influx of positive ions occurs, producing a 'ripple' all the way down the cell body to the axon.

Action potentials

If this cumulative electrical 'ripple' crosses a certain threshold, depolarising the membrane at the axon from its resting state of −70 mV to about −50 mV, a sudden change occurs. For a flicker of an instant, the membrane is totally permeable to positive sodium ions, which have accumulated outside the membrane. These ions pour in, changing the potential across the membrane to about +40 mV (figure 3.2; see overleaf). Thus, the charge on the inside of the cell becomes momentarily positive. An outpouring of positive potassium ions then rapidly restores the neuron to its resting potential, rendering the charge inside the cell negative once again. This entire electrochemical process typically takes less than 2 milliseconds (msec, or thousandths of a second).

The shift in polarity across the membrane and subsequent restoration of the resting potential is called an ***action potential***, or the 'firing' of the neuron. The action potential rapidly spreads down the length of the axon to the terminal buttons, as ions pour in and out (figure 3.2a; see overleaf). Unlike a graded potential, an action potential (or nerve impulse) is not cumulative. Instead, it has an all-or-none quality: the action potential either occurs or does not. In this sense, the firing of a neuron is like the firing of a gun. Unless the trigger is pulled hard enough, the amount of pressure placed on the trigger below that threshold does not matter. Once the threshold is crossed, however, the trigger gives way, the gun fires and the trigger springs back, ready to be pulled once more.

Although action potentials seem more dramatic, in many ways the prime movers behind psychological processes are graded potentials. Graded potentials create new information at the cellular level by allowing the cell to integrate signals from multiple sources (multiple synapses). Action potentials, in contrast, can only pass along information already collected without changing it.

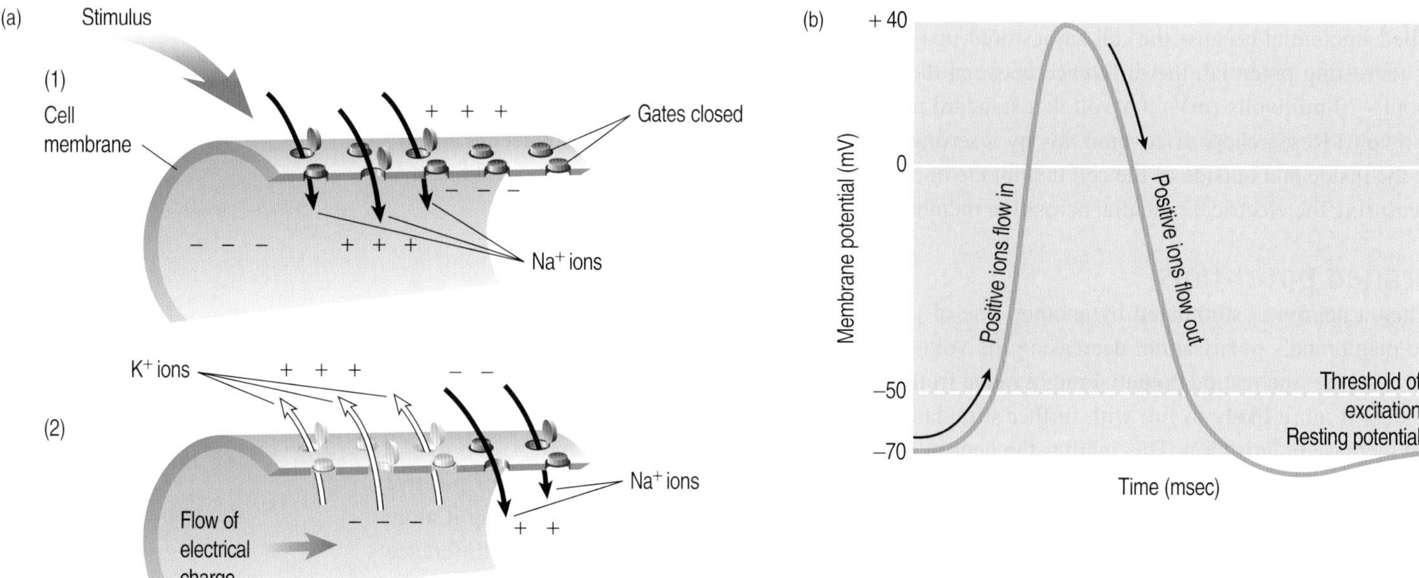

FIGURE 3.2
An action potential. (a) Initially, when the axon is depolarised at a specific locus (1), the 'floodgates' open, and sodium ions (Na^+) come rushing in. Immediately afterwards (2), the gates close to those ions and potassium ions (K^+) come rushing back out, restoring the potential to its resting negative state. This process, however, leads to depolarisation of the next segment of the cell's membrane, spreading down the axon. (b) This graph depicts the firing of a neuron as recorded by nearby electrodes. When a neuron is depolarised to about –50 mV (the threshold of excitation), an influx of positively charged ions briefly creates an action potential. An outpouring of positive ions then contributes to restoring the neuron to its resting potential. (This outpouring actually overshoots the mark briefly, so that for a brief instant after firing the potential across the membrane is slightly more negative than –70 mV.)

INTERIM SUMMARY

When a neuron is at rest (its ***resting potential***), it is polarised, with a negative charge inside the cell membrane and a positive charge outside. When a neuron is stimulated by another, its cell membrane is either depolarised or hyperpolarised. The spreading voltage changes along the cell membrane that occur as one neuron is excited by other neurons are called graded potentials. If the cell membrane is depolarised by enough ***graded potentials***, the neuron will fire. This is called an ***action potential***, or nerve impulse.

Transmission of information between cells

When a nerve impulse travels down an axon, it sets in motion a series of events that can lead to transmission of information to other cells (table 3.1). Figure 3.3 presents a simplified diagram of a synaptic connection between two neurons. The neuron that is sending an impulse is called the presynaptic neuron (i.e. before the synapse); the cell receiving the impulse is the postsynaptic neuron.

TABLE 3.1 **Communication from one neuron to another**

Stage	What happens
1. Resting state	Na^+ cannot enter, or is actively pumped out of, the neuron; the cell is negatively charged.
2. Depolarisation	Na^+ enters dendrites and cell body, making the cell less negatively charged.
3. Graded potential	Change in cell voltage is passed down dendrites and cell body.
4. Action potential	If the change in axon voltage surpasses a threshold, the axon suddenly lets in a surge of Na^+.
5. Neurotransmitter release	The action potential causes terminal buttons to release neurotransmitters into the synaptic cleft.
6. Chemical message transmitted	Depending on the facilitating or inhibitory nature of the neurotransmitter released, the voltage of the cell membrane receiving the message becomes depolarised or hyperpolarised, and the process repeats.

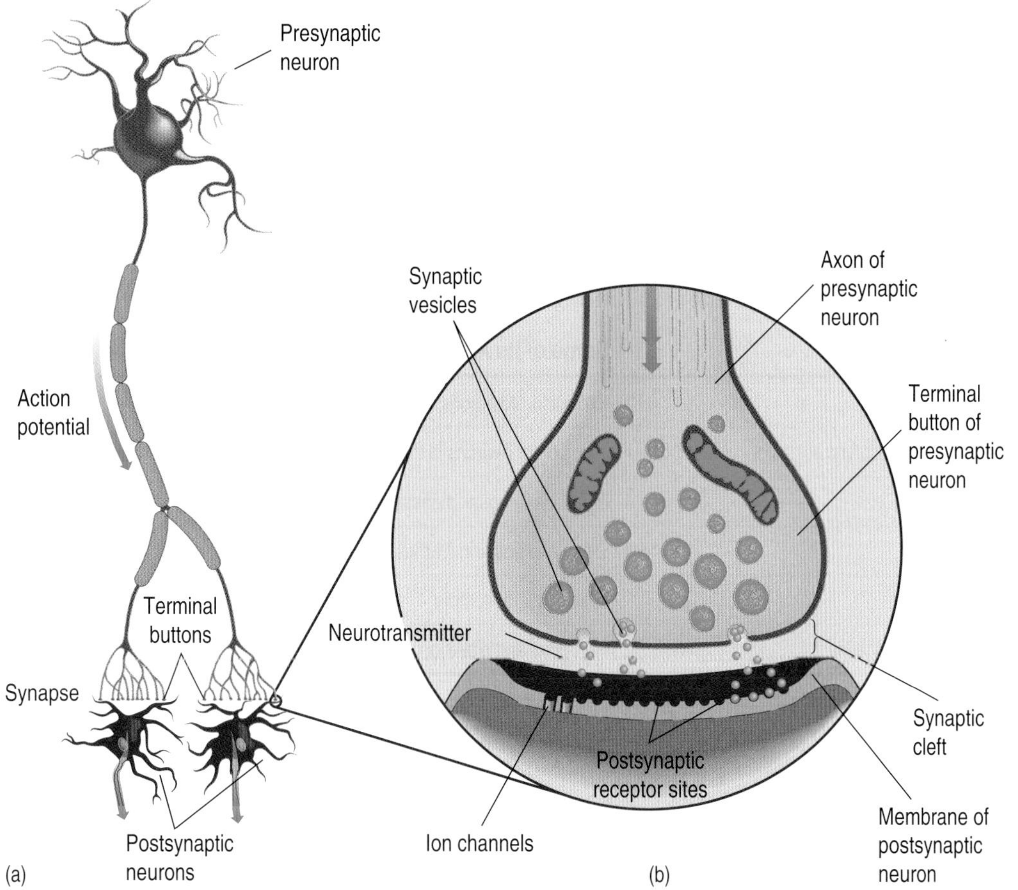

FIGURE 3.3
Transmission of a nerve impulse. (a) When an action potential occurs, the nerve impulse travels along the axon until it reaches the synaptic vesicles. The synaptic vesicles release neurotransmitters into the synaptic cleft. (b) The neurotransmitters then bind with postsynaptic receptors and produce a graded potential on the membrane of lhe postsynaptic neuron. Receptors are strings of amino acids (the building blocks of proteins) suspended in the fatty membrane of the postsynaptic neuron. Typically, several strands of these proteins extend outside the cell Into the synapse, where they detect the presence of neurotransmitters and may transport them through the membrane. Other strands remain on the inside of the cell and send information to the nucleus of the cell, alerting it, for example, to open or close channels in the membrane (called ion channels) in order to let various ions in or out.

Neurotransmitters and receptors

Within the terminal buttons of a neuron are small sacs called synaptic vesicles. These sacs contain ***neurotransmitters***, chemicals that transmit information from one cell to another. When the presynaptic neuron fires, the synaptic vesicles in its terminal buttons move towards the cell's membrane (the presynaptic membrane). Some of them adhere to the membrane and break open, releasing neurotransmitters into the synaptic cleft.

Once in the synaptic cleft, some of these neurotransmitters then bind with protein molecules in the postsynaptic membrane that receive their chemical messages; these molecules are called ***receptors***. Receptors act like locks that can be opened only by particular keys. In this case, the keys are neurotransmitters in the synaptic cleft. When a receptor binds with the neurotransmitter that fits it — in both molecular structure and electrical charge — the chemical and electrical balance of the postsynaptic cell membrane changes, producing a graded potential — a ripple in the neuronal pond.

APPLY + DISCUSS

Figure 3.3 outlines the transmission of a nerve impulse. On your university course website for this subject, you should be able to access a related animation.

- How do neurons communicate with other neurons?
- What is an action potential and how does it occur?

The effects of neurotransmitters

Neurotransmitters can either increase or decrease neural firing. Excitatory neurotransmitters depolarise the postsynaptic cell membrane, making an action potential more likely (i.e. they excite the neuron). In contrast, inhibitory neurotransmitters hyperpolarise the membrane (increase its polarisation); this reduces the likelihood that the postsynaptic neuron will fire (or inhibits firing). Excitatory neurotransmitters thus grease the wheels of neural communication, whereas inhibitory neurotransmitters put on the brakes. A neuron can also release more than one neurotransmitter, affecting the cells to which it is connected in various ways.

Aside from being excitatory or inhibitory, neurotransmitters differ in another important respect. Some, like the ones we have been describing, are released into a specific synapse and affect only the neuron at the other end of the synaptic cleft (the postsynaptic neuron). Others have a much wider radius of impact and remain active considerably longer. Once released, they find their way into multiple synapses, where they can affect any neuron within reach that has the appropriate chemicals in its membrane. The primary impact of these transmitter substances, called modulatory neurotransmitters (or neuromodulators), is to increase or decrease (that is, modulate) the impact of other neurotransmitters released into the synapse.

Types of neurotransmitters

Researchers have discovered more than 100 chemical substances that can transmit messages between neurons. Neurotransmitters that bind to receptor sites (much as a key fits into a lock) can have either excitatory or inhibitory effects. For example, the neurotransmitters norepinephrine (NE; noradrenaline) and epinephrine (adrenaline) are hormones of the adrenal medulla that affect emotional arousal, anxiety and fear. We will briefly examine some of the best understood neurotransmitters: glutamate, GABA, dopamine, serotonin, acetylcholine and endorphins (table 3.2).

TABLE 3.2 **Partial list of neurotransmitters**

Transmitter substance	Some of its known effects
Glutamate	Excitation of neurons throughout the nervous system
GABA (gamma-aminobutyric acid)	Inhibition of neurons in the brain
Dopamine	Emotional arousal, pleasure and reward; voluntary movement; attention
Serotonin	Sleep and emotional arousal; aggression; pain regulation; mood regulation
Acetylcholine (ACh)	Learning and memory
Endorphins and enkephalins	Pain relief and elevation of mood

NOTE: The effect of a neurotransmitter depends on the type of receptor it fits. Each neurotransmitter can activate different receptors, depending on where in the nervous system the receptor is located. Thus, the impact of any neurotransmitter depends less on the neurotransmitter itself than on the receptor it unlocks. In fact, some neurotransmitters can have an excitatory effect at one synapse and an inhibitory effect at another.

MAKING CONNECTIONS

Actor Michael J. Fox and boxer Muhammad Ali are two high-profile sufferers of Parkinson's disease. They are pictured here at a benefit for the Michael J. Fox Foundation for Parkinson's Research. Parkinson's disease is associated with decreased levels of dopamine. In contrast, dopamine overactivity in certain parts of the brain has been implicated in the hallucinations and delusions seen in **schizophrenia** (chapter 15). Medications that block dopamine receptors can reduce schizophrenic symptoms. However, because dopamine is also involved in movement, these **drugs** can have side effects, such as jerky movements or tics (chapter 16).

Glutamate and GABA

Glutamate (glutamic acid) is a neurotransmitter that can excite nearly every neuron in the nervous system. Although glutamate is involved in many psychological processes, it appears to play a particularly important role in learning (Blokland, 1997; Izquierdo & Medina, 1997; see also Antzoulatos & Byrne, 2004; Riedel, Platt, & Micheau, 2003). Some people respond to the MSG (monosodium glutamate) in Chinese food with neurological symptoms such as tingling and numbing because this ingredient activates glutamate receptors.

GABA (gamma-aminobutyric acid) has the opposite effect in the brain. It is a neurotransmitter that plays an inhibitory role. Glycine is another inhibitory neurotransmitter in the lower brain and spinal cord (Reber & Reber, 2001). Roughly one-third of all the neurons in the brain use GABA for synaptic communication (Petty, 1995). GABA is particularly important in regulating anxiety. Drugs such as valium and alcohol that bind with its receptors tend to reduce anxiety (chapter 5).

Dopamine

Dopamine is a neurotransmitter that has wide-ranging effects in the nervous system, involving thought, feeling, motivation and behaviour. Some neural pathways that rely on dopamine are involved in emotional arousal, the experience of pleasure and learning to associate particular behaviours with reward (Schultz, 1998; see also Schultz, 2002). Drugs ranging from marijuana to heroin increase the release of dopamine in some of these pathways and may play a part in addictions (Robbins & Everitt, 1999; see also Volkow, Fowler, Wang, & Swabsib, 2004). Other dopamine pathways are involved in movement, attention, decision making and various cognitive processes. Abnormally high levels of dopamine in some parts of the brain have been linked to schizophrenia (chapter 15; Stevens, 2002; Tsai & Coyle, 2002).

Degeneration of the dopamine-releasing neurons in a part of the brain called the substantia nigra (literally, 'dark substance', named for its colouration) causes ***Parkinson's disease***, a disorder characterised by uncontrollable tremors and difficulty both initiating behaviour (such as standing up) and stopping movements already in progress (such as walking forward). Other symptoms can include depression, reduced facial displays of emotion and a general slowing of thought that parallels the slowing of behaviour (Rao, Huber, & Bornstein, 1992; Tandberg, Larsen, Aarsland, & Cummings, 1996; see also Ehrt & Aarsland, 2005; Remy, Doder, Lees, Turjanski, & Brooks, 2005).

Parkinson's disease has been effectively treated using L-dopa, a chemical that readily converts to dopamine. Dopamine itself cannot be administered because it cannot cross the blood–brain barrier, which normally protects the brain from foreign substances in the blood. The blood–brain barrier results from the fact that the cells in the blood vessels of the brain tend to be so tightly packed that large molecules have difficulty entering.

The blood–brain barrier is a double-edged sword. On the one hand, it serves an adaptive function, preventing toxic substances from disrupting neural functioning. On the other hand, it rejects medications that could treat brain diseases. Due to its chemical structure, only a small percentage of L-dopa gets past the blood–brain barrier. The rest affects other cells throughout the body, causing side effects such as nausea, vomiting and shortness of breath. The L-dopa that *does* make its way into the brain can also have unwanted consequences because the brain uses dopamine for neural transmission in many regions and for different purposes. The L-dopa can thus reduce Parkinsonian symptoms, but it can also produce disordered thinking (such as hallucinations) or movement disorders other than Parkinson's.

MAKING CONNECTIONS

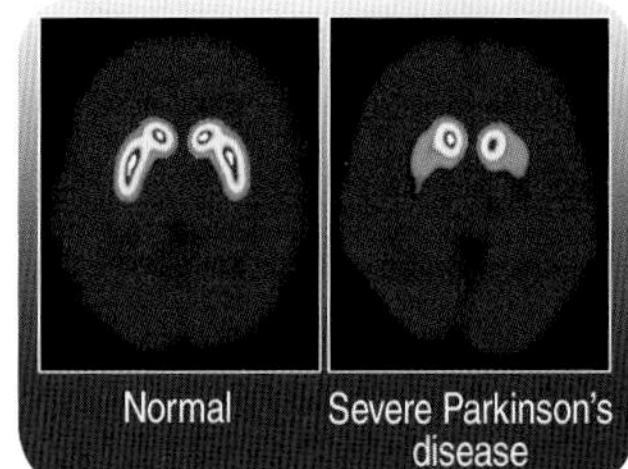

Developments in **neuroimaging** — taking computerised images of a live functioning nervous system — have revolutionised our understanding of the brain (chapter 2). These **PET scans** contrast the brain of a normal volunteer (left) with that of a patient with Parkinson's disease (right). Hotter (or brighter) areas indicate more activity. Areas of the brain that normally use dopamine and control movement are less active in the Parkinsonian brain. The red indicates the most intense activity, and the blue the least.

Serotonin

Serotonin is a neurotransmitter involved in the regulation of mood, sleep, eating, arousal and pain. Decreased serotonin in the brain is common in severe depression, which often responds to medications that increase serotonin activity. For example, popular antidepressants such as fluoxetine (Prozac) work by boosting serotonin levels (chapter 16; Margolis & Swartz, 2001). Serotonin usually plays an inhibitory role, affecting, for example, neural circuits involved in aggression, antisocial behaviour and other forms of social behaviour (Altamura, Pioli, Vitto, & Mannu, 1999; Chung, Martinez, & Herbert, 2000).

Acetylcholine

The neurotransmitter ***acetylcholine (ACh)*** is involved in learning and memory (Gold, 2003). Experiments show increased ACh activity while rats are learning to discriminate one stimulus from another (Butt, Testylier, & Dykes, 1997; see also Uzum, Diler, Bahcekapili, Tasyurekli, & Zivlan, 2004). A key piece of evidence linking ACh to learning and memory is the fact that patients with Alzheimer's disease, which destroys memory, show depleted ACh (Perry, Walker, Grace, & Perry, 1999).

Knowing about the functions of acetylcholine holds out the hope that scientists may eventually be able to transplant neural tissue rich in this neurotransmitter into the brains of patients with Alzheimer's disease. Some promising research with animals along these lines is ongoing (see Harper, 2000). For example, old rats with neural transplants perform substantially better on learning tasks than same-aged peers without the transplants (Bjorklund & Gage, 1985).

Endorphins

Endorphins are chemicals that elevate mood and reduce pain. They have a range of effects, from the numbness people often feel immediately after tearing a muscle (which wears off once these natural painkillers stop flowing) to the 'runner's high' athletes sometimes report after a prolonged period of exercise (Hoffman, 1997; see also Boecker et al., 2008).

The word 'endorphin' comes from endogenous (meaning 'produced within the body') and morphine (a chemical substance derived from the opium poppy that elevates mood and reduces pain). Opium and similar narcotic drugs kill pain and elevate mood because they stimulate receptors in the brain specialised for endorphins. Essentially, narcotics 'pick the locks' normally opened by endorphins.

Chocolate consumption has been associated with the release of neurotransmitters including serotonin, endorphins and dopamine, which may explain why some people experience such strong chocolate cravings.

INTERIM SUMMARY

Within the terminal buttons of the presynaptic neuron are ***neurotransmitters***, such as ***glutamate***, ***GABA***, ***dopamine***, ***serotonin***, ***acetylcholine*** and ***endorphins***. Neurotransmitters transmit information from one neuron to another as they are released into the synapse from the synaptic vesicles. They bind with receptors in the membrane of the postsynaptic neuron, which produces graded potentials that can either excite the postsynaptic neuron or inhibit it from firing.

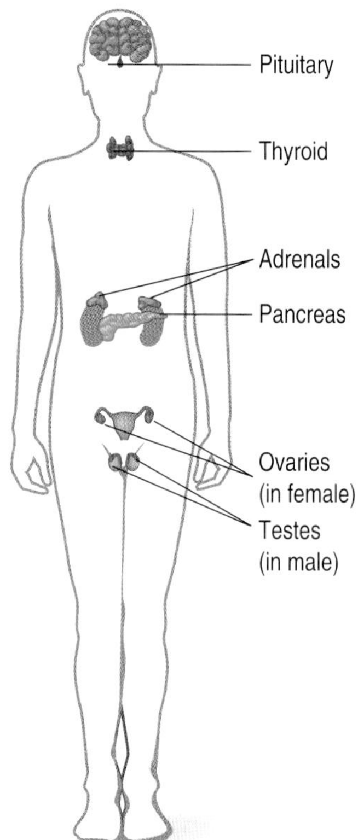

FIGURE 3.4
The major endocrine glands. The endocrine system is a series of glands that rely on hormonal communication to activate cells throughout the body.

The endocrine system

Neurotransmitters are not the only chemicals that transmit psychologically significant messages. The ***endocrine system*** is a collection of glands that secrete chemicals directly into the bloodstream. These chemicals are called ***hormones*** (figure 3.4). Like neurotransmitters, hormones bind with receptors in cell membranes, but because they travel through the bloodstream, they can simultaneously activate many cells in the body as long as these cells are equipped with the right receptors.

The chemical structure of some hormones is similar or even identical to that of some neurotransmitters. For example, the hormones ***adrenaline*** and ***noradrenaline*** trigger physiological arousal, particularly in potential danger situations. These two hormones are actually the same chemicals as the neurotransmitters epinephrine and norepinephrine, respectively, which are involved in anxiety, fear and emotional arousal. Similarly, another chemical, oxytocin, increases nurturing behaviours when released in the brain as a neurotransmitter. Oxytocin released into the body as a hormone facilitates breast milk production (MedlinePlus, 2004; Mendoza & Mason, 1997).

The endocrine system is thus a second system for intercellular communication, but it does not rely on the kind of intricate 'wiring' between cells used by the nervous system. The difference between the methods of communication used by the two systems is like the difference between word of mouth — which requires transmission from one person to the next — and mass media — which can communicate information to millions of people at once. The endocrine system 'broadcasts' its signals by releasing hormones into the bloodstream. Its messages are less specific but readily 'heard' throughout the body.

The ***pituitary gland***, an oval structure in the brain that is about the size of a pea, is often described as the 'master gland' because many of the hormones it releases stimulate and regulate the other glands. The pituitary gland is connected more directly to the central nervous system than any of the other endocrine glands.

The ***thyroid gland***, located in the neck, releases hormones that control growth and metabolism (transformation of food into energy). The thyroid gland also affects energy levels and mood (Hahn, Pawlyk, Whybrow, Gyulai, & Tejani-Butt, 1999). People with hypothyroidism, or an underactive thyroid (hypo means 'under'), sometimes require artificial replacement of thyroid hormones to relieve sluggishness and depression (Rack & Makela, 2000). In fact, roughly 10 percent of people who complain of depression actually have undiagnosed hypothyroidism (Gold & Pearsall, 1983; see also Tews, Shah, & Gossain, 2005).

The ***adrenal glands*** are located above the kidneys. (The Latin *ad renal* means 'towards the kidney'.) These glands secrete adrenalin and other hormones during emergencies. Another endocrine gland, the pancreas, is located near the stomach and produces hormones that control blood-sugar level.

The ***gonads*** are endocrine glands that influence sexual development and behaviour. The male gonads, or testes, are located in the testicles. The most important hormone they produce is ***testosterone***. ***Estrogens*** are hormones produced by the female gonads (ovaries). In both sexes, these hormones control not only sex drive but also the development of secondary sex characteristics such as growth of breasts in females, deepened voice in males and pubic hair in both sexes.

INTERIM SUMMARY

The ***endocrine system*** is a collection of glands that control various bodily functions through the secretion of ***hormones***. The endocrine system complements the cell-to-cell communication of the nervous system by sending global messages through the bloodstream. Hormones are like neurotransmitters, except that they travel through the bloodstream and can thus activate many cells simultaneously.

The peripheral nervous system

Although the endocrine system plays an important role in psychological functioning, the centre of our psychological experience is the nervous system. The nervous system has two major divisions: the central nervous system and the peripheral nervous system (figures 3.5 and 3.6). The ***central nervous system (CNS)*** consists of the brain and spinal cord. The ***peripheral nervous system (PNS)*** consists of neurons that convey messages to and from the central nervous system. We begin with the peripheral nervous system, which has two subdivisions: the somatic and the autonomic nervous systems.

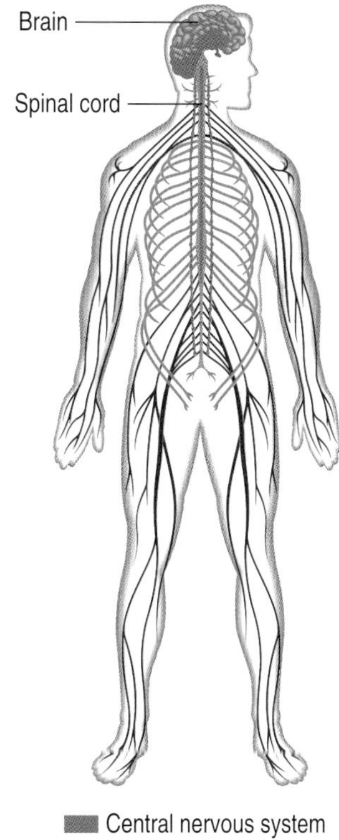

FIGURE 3.5
The nervous system. The nervous system consists of the brain, the spinal cord and the neurons of the peripheral nervous system that carry information to and from these central nervous system structures.

The somatic nervous system

The ***somatic nervous system*** transmits sensory information to the central nervous system and carries out its motor commands. Sensory neurons receive information through receptors in the eyes, ears, tongue, skin, muscles and other parts of the body. Motor neurons direct the action of skeletal muscles. Because the somatic nervous system is involved in intentional actions, such as standing up or shaking someone's hand, it is sometimes called the voluntary nervous system. However, the somatic nervous system also directs some involuntary or automatic actions, such as adjustments in posture and balance.

The autonomic nervous system

The ***autonomic nervous system*** conveys information to and from internal bodily structures that carry out basic life processes such as digestion and respiration. It consists of two parts: the sympathetic and the parasympathetic nervous systems. Although these systems work together, their functions are often opposed or complementary. In broadest strokes, one can think of the sympathetic nervous system as an emergency system and the parasympathetic nervous system as a 'business-as-usual' system (figure 3.7; see overleaf).

The ***sympathetic nervous system*** is typically activated in response to threats. Its job is to ready the body for fight or flight, which it does in several ways. It stops digestion, diverting blood away from the stomach and redirecting it to the muscles, which may need extra oxygen for an emergency response. It increases heart rate, dilates the pupils, and causes hairs on the body and head to stand erect. It is also involved in other states of intense activation, such as ejaculation in males.

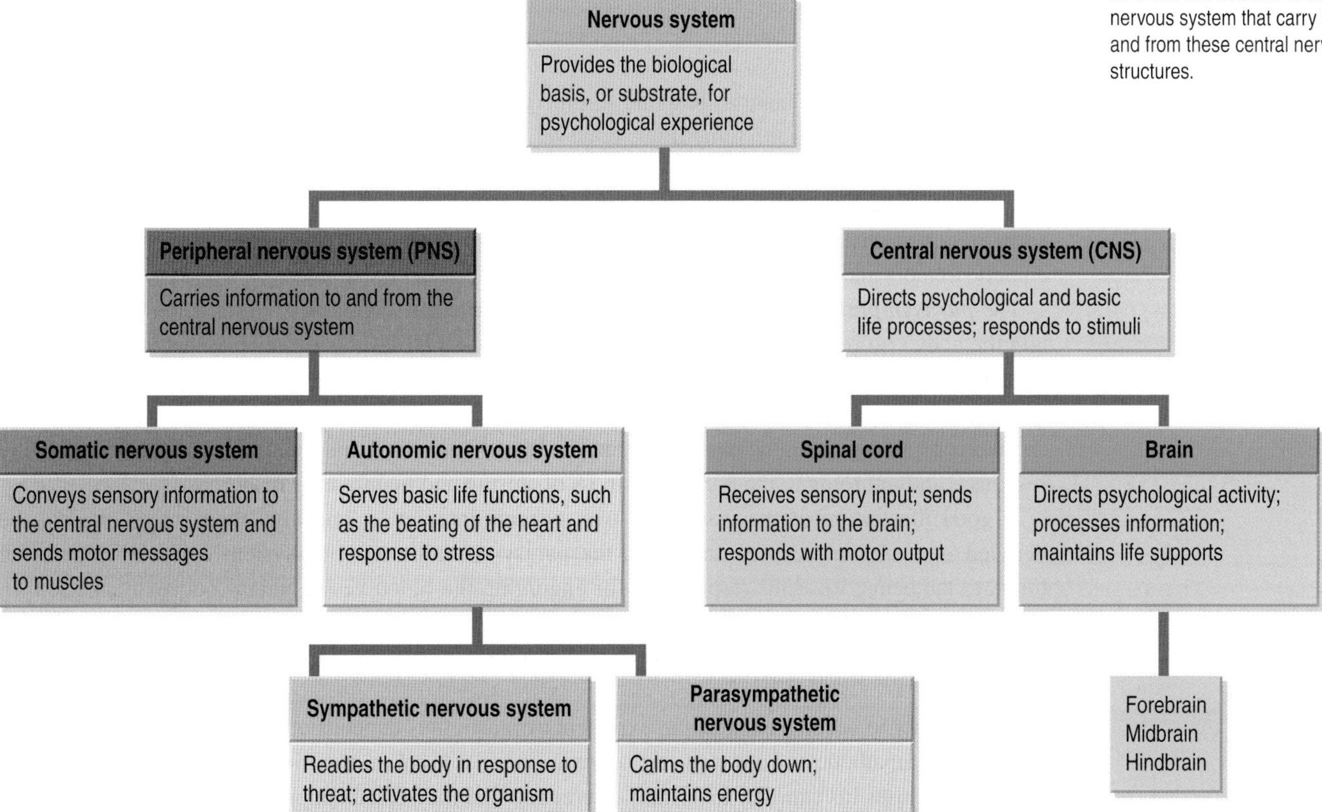

FIGURE 3.6
Divisions of the nervous system. See also the online *Brain Atlas*, which you should be able to access at your university course website for this subject.

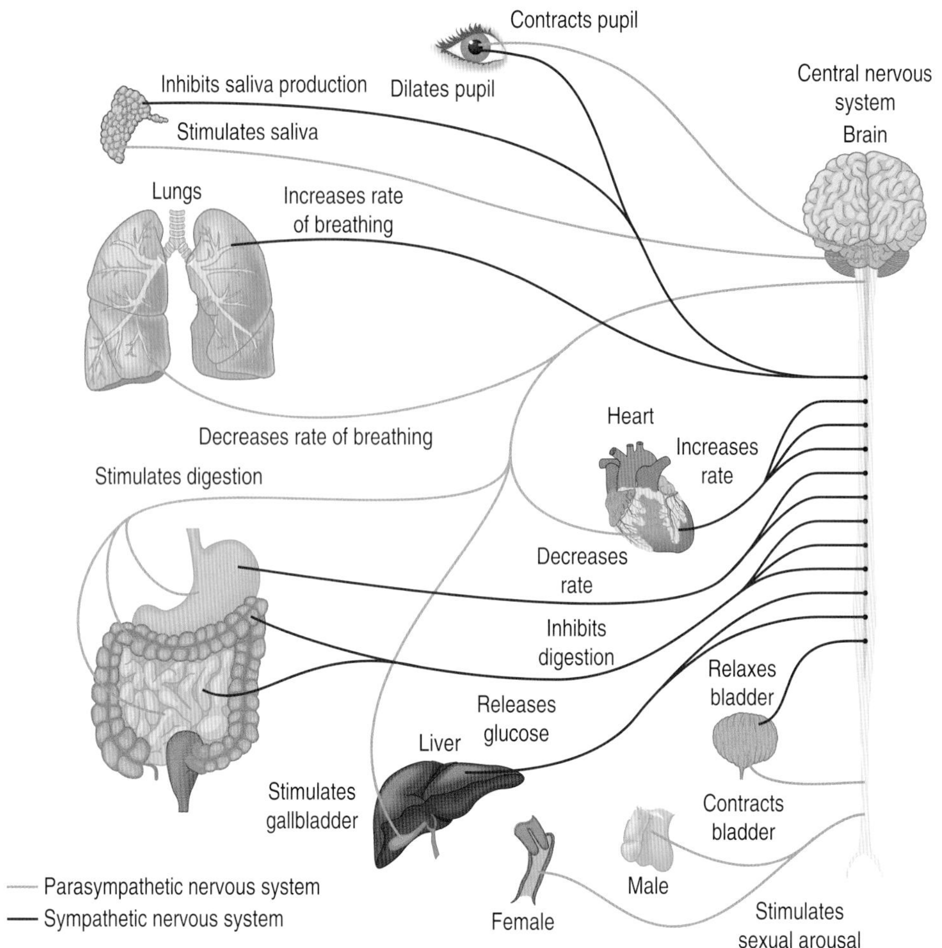

FIGURE 3.7
The sympathetic and parasympathetic divisions of the autonomic nervous system

By preparing the organism to respond to emergencies, the sympathetic nervous system serves an important adaptive function. Sometimes, however, the sympathetic cavalry comes to the rescue when least wanted. A surge of anxiety, tremors, sweating, dry mouth and a palpitating heart may have helped prepare our ancestors to flee from a hungry lion, but they are less welcome when trying to deliver a speech. Similar physiological reactions occur in panic attacks, which include symptoms such as intense anxiety, tremors and a palpitating heart (chapter 15).

The ***parasympathetic nervous system*** supports more mundane, or routine, activities that maintain the body's store of energy, such as regulating blood-sugar levels, secreting saliva and eliminating wastes. It also participates in functions such as regulating heart rate and pupil size. The relationship between the sympathetic and parasympathetic nervous systems is in many ways a balancing act. When an emergency has passed, the parasympathetic nervous system resumes control, reversing sympathetic responses and returning to the normal business of storing and maintaining resources.

A good illustration of the way these two systems interact — and how their interaction can be derailed — is sexual activity. In males, the parasympathetic nervous system controls the flow of blood to the penis; it is thus responsible for engorging the blood vessels that produce an erection. In females, parasympathetic processes are similarly involved in vaginal lubrication. Ejaculation, however, is controlled by the sympathetic nervous system, which is probably involved in female orgasm as well.

The capacity to become excited and experience orgasm thus depends on the synchronised activation of the parasympathetic and sympathetic nervous systems. If a man experiences sympathetic activation too early, he loses his capacity to sustain an erection and may ejaculate prematurely. Conversely, if he does not experience sympathetic activation, ejaculation will not take place (Kimble, 1992). In women, poor coordination of sympathetic and parasympathetic activity may inhibit vaginal lubrication and thus hinder sexual pleasure.

In a society that places a premium on sexual performance, a few disappointing sexual experiences can disrupt the delicate balance between sympathetic and parasympathetic activation. For example, a man who experiences a brief period of difficulty maintaining sexual excitement may begin to see himself as a failure sexually and become more anxious with each new encounter. The anxiety, in turn, can inhibit the parasympathetic activation that normally leads to erection, setting in motion a cycle in which sympathetic activation and feelings of anxiety fuel each other and create a fully-fledged problem in sexual functioning. This example illustrates the interaction of psychological experience, physiological processes and culture. Based on cultural standards of sexual performance, a transitory dysfunction (failure to sustain an erection) leads the person to feel anxious and inadequate, which then exacerbates the initial psychobiological condition.

INTERIM SUMMARY

The nervous system consists of the ***central nervous system (CNS)*** and the ***peripheral nervous system (PNS)***. Neurons of the PNS carry messages to and from the CNS. The PNS has two subdivisions: the somatic nervous system and the autonomic nervous system. The ***somatic nervous system*** consists of sensory neurons that carry sensory information to the brain and motor neurons that direct the action of skeletal muscles. The ***autonomic nervous system*** controls basic life processes such as the beating of the heart, workings of the digestive system and breathing. It consists of two parts, the ***sympathetic nervous system***, which is activated primarily in response to threats (but is also involved in general emotional arousal), and the ***parasympathetic nervous system***, which is involved in more routine activities such as maintaining the body's energy resources and restoring the system to an even keel following sympathetic activation.

■ The central nervous system

The peripheral nervous system reflects a complex job of neural wiring, but the human central nervous system is probably the most remarkable feat of electrical engineering ever accomplished. Understanding the way it functions requires some knowledge of its evolution.

The evolution of the central nervous system

If an engineer were to design the command centre for an organism like ours from scratch, it would probably not look much like the human central nervous system. The reason is that, at every evolutionary juncture, nature has had to work with the structures (collections of cells that perform particular functions) already in place. The modifications made by natural selection have thus been sequential, one building on the next. For example, initially no organisms had colour vision; the world of the ancestors of all contemporary sighted organisms was like a black-and-white movie. Gradually the capacity to perceive certain colours emerged in some species, conferring an adaptive advantage to organisms that could now, for instance, more easily distinguish one type of plant from another. The human central nervous system, like that of all animals, is like a living fossil record. The further down we go (almost literally, from the upper layers of the brain down to the spinal cord), the more we see ancient structures that evolved hundreds of millions of years ago and were shared — and continue to be shared — by most other vertebrates (animals with spinal cords).

It is tempting to think of nature's creatures as arranged on a scale from simple to complex, beginning with organisms such as amoebas, then moving up the ladder perhaps to pets and farm animals, and on to the highest form of life, ourselves (see Butler & Hodos, 1996). And in a sense, there is something to this; after all, *we* can dissect the brain of a frog, but a frog cannot return the favour.

One must always remember, however, that natural selection is a process that favours adaptation to a niche, and different niches require different adaptations. Nobody would trade their brain for that of their dog, no matter how endearing their pet might be, because we would all rather be the one throwing than fetching. But dogs have abilities we lack, either because we humans never acquired them or because over time we lost them as our brains evolved in a different direction. Dogs can hear things we cannot hear, and they do not need to call out in the dark 'Who's there?' because their noses tell them. And anyone who thinks humans and invertebrates are easy to place on a single, evolutionary scale has never stared a poisonous spider in the face and asked, 'Who is better adapted, you or I?' (Do not try this experiment at home.)

The evolution of vertebrates

Our understanding of the evolution of the human nervous system still contains heavy doses of guesswork, but a general outline looks something like the following (Butler & Hodos, 1996; Healy, 1996; Kolb & Whishaw, 1996; MacLean, 1982, 1990). The earliest precursors to vertebrate animals were probably fish-like creatures whose actions were less controlled by a central 'executive' like the human brain than by 'local' reactions at particular points along the body. These organisms were probably little more than stimulus–response machines whose actions were controlled by a simple fluid-filled tube of neurons that evolved into the spinal cord. Sensory information from the environment entered the upper side of the cord, and neurons exiting the underside produced automatic responses called ***reflexes***.

Through evolution, the front end of the spinal cord became specialised to allow more sophisticated processing of information and more flexible motor responses (figure 3.8). Presumably this end developed because our early ancestors moved forward, head first — which is why our brains are in our heads instead of our feet.

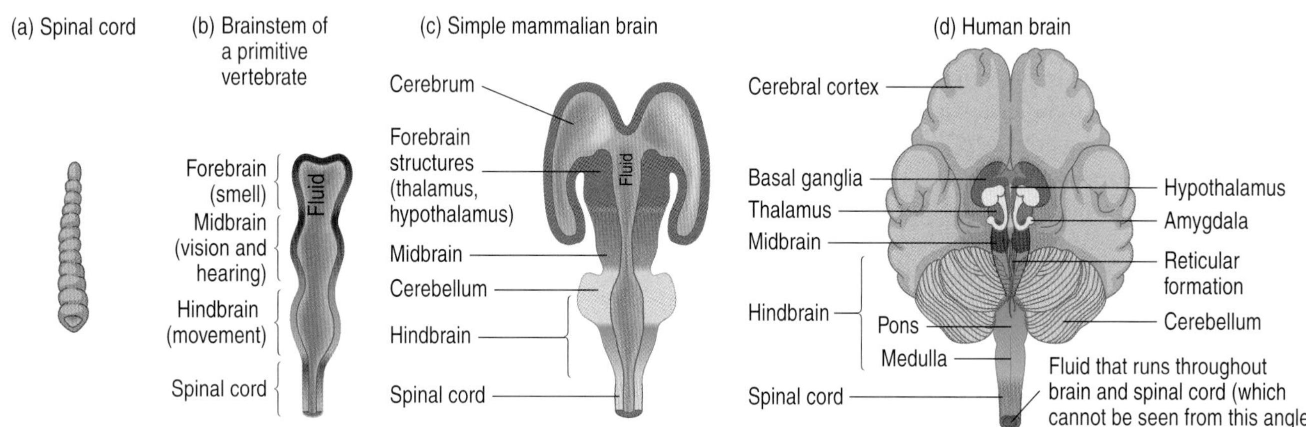

FIGURE 3.8
Evolution of the human brain. (a) The earliest central nervous system in the ancestors of contemporary vertebrates was probably a structure similar to the contemporary spinal cord. (b) The primitive brain, or brainstem, allowed more complex sensation and movement in vertebrates. (c) Among the most important evolutionary developments of mammals was the cerebrum. (d) The human brain is a storehouse of knowledge packed in a remarkably small container, the human skull.

SOURCE: Adapted from Kolb and Whishaw (1996).

The primitive vertebrate brain, or brainstem, appears to have had three parts (figure 3.9). The foremost section, called the forebrain, was specialised for sensation at a very immediate level — smell and eventually taste. The middle region, or midbrain, controlled sensation for distant stimuli — vision and hearing. The back of the brainstem, or hindbrain, was specialised for movement, particularly for balance (Sarnat & Netsky, 1974; see also Glynn, 2003).

The hindbrain was also the connecting point between the brain and spinal cord, allowing messages to travel between the two. This rough division of labour in the primitive central nervous system still applies in the spinal cord and brainstem of humans. Many human reflexes, for example, occur precisely as they did, and do, in the simplest vertebrates. Sensory information enters one side of the spinal cord (towards the back of the body in humans, who stand erect), and motor impulses exit from the other.

As animals, and particularly mammals, evolved, the most dramatic changes occurred in the hindbrain and forebrain. The hindbrain sprouted an expanded cerebellum, which increased the animal's capacity to put together complex movements and make sensory discriminations. The forebrain also evolved many new structures, most notably those that comprise the ***cerebrum***, the part of the brain most involved in complex thought, which greatly expanded the capacity for processing information and initiating movement (Finlay & Darlington, 1995; see also Marieb & Hoehn, 2007). Of particular significance is the evolution of the many-layered surface of the cerebrum known as the ***cortex*** (from the Latin word for 'bark'), which makes humans so 'cerebral'. In fact, 80 percent of the human brain's mass is cortex (Kolb & Whishaw, 1996).

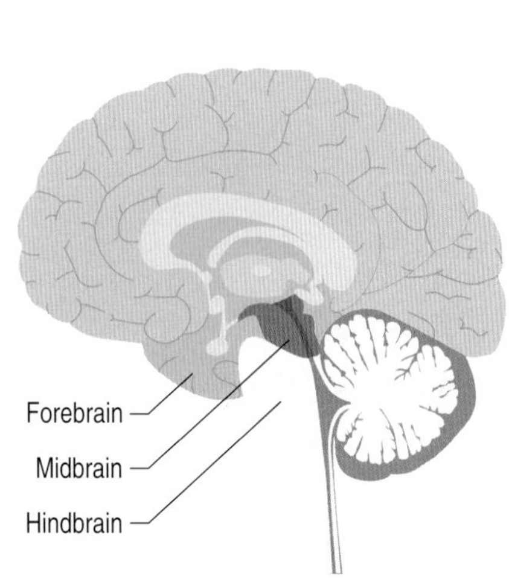

FIGURE 3.9
The brain has three main parts: the forebrain, the midbrain and the hindbrain. In this diagram, the brain is shown as if it were split down the middle, with the front of the person's head to the left.

SOURCE: Gleitman, Reisberg, and Gross (2007, p. 88).

The human nervous system

Although the human brain and the brains of its early vertebrate and mammalian ancestors differ dramatically, most of the differences are the result of additions to, rather than replacement of, the original brain structures. Two very important consequences flow from this.

First, as we have seen, many neural mechanisms are the same in humans and other animals; others differ across species that have evolved in different directions from common ancestors. Generalisations between humans and animals as seemingly different as cats or rats are likely to be more appropriate at lower levels of the nervous system, such as the spinal cord and brainstem, because these lower neural structures were already in place before these species diverged millions of years ago. The human brainstem (which includes most of the structures below the cerebrum) is almost identical to the brainstem of sheep (Kolb & Whishaw, 1996), but the two species differ tremendously in the size, structure and function of their cortex. Much of the sheep's cortex is devoted to processing sensory information, whereas a greater part of the human cortex is involved in forming complex thoughts, perceptions and plans for action.

The second implication is that human psychology bears the distinct imprint of the same relatively primitive structures that guide motivation, learning and behaviour in other animals. This is a sobering thought. It led Darwin to place species on our family tree that we might consider poor relations; Freud to view our extraordinary capacities to love, create and understand ourselves and the universe as a thin veneer (only a few millimetres thick, in fact) over primitive structures that motivate our greatest achievements and our most 'inhuman' atrocities; and Skinner to argue that the same laws of learning apply to humans as to other animals.

The human nervous system is thus a set of hierarchically organised structures built layer upon layer over millions of years of evolution. The most primitive centres send information to, and receive information from, higher centres; these higher centres are in turn integrated with, and regulated by, still more advanced areas of the brain. Behavioural and cognitive precision progressively increases from the lower to the higher and more recently evolved structures (Luria, 1973). Thus, the spinal cord can respond to a prick of the skin with a reflex without even consulting the brain, but more complex cognitive activity simultaneously occurs as the person makes sense of what has happened. We reflexively withdraw from a pinprick, but if the source is a vaccine injection, we inhibit our response — though often milliseconds later, since information travelling to and from the brain takes neural time. Responding appropriately requires the integrated functioning of structures from the spinal cord up through the cortex.

Before discussing the major structures of the central nervous system, an important caveat, or caution, is in order. A central debate since the origins of modern neuroscience in the nineteenth century has centred on the extent to which certain functions are localised to specific parts of the brain. One of the most enlightening things about watching a brain scan in action as a person performs even a simple task is just how much of the brain actually 'lights up'. Different regions are indeed specialised for different functions; a severe blow to the head that damages the back of the cortex is more likely to disrupt vision than speech. Knowing that a lesion at the back of the cortex can produce blindness thus suggests that this region is involved in visual processing and that it must be relatively intact for normal visual functioning to occur. But this does not mean that this region is the brain's 'centre' for vision. Every thought, feeling or psychological attribute is the result of a network of neurons acting in combination.

In the pages that follow, we describe a series of structures as if they were discrete entities. In reality, evolution did not produce a nervous system with neat boundaries. Distinctions among structures are not, of course, simply the whims of neuroanatomists; they are based on qualities such as the appearance, function and cellular structure of adjacent regions. Nevertheless, where one structure ends and another begins is to some extent arbitrary. Axons from the spinal cord synapse with neurons far into the brain, so that parts of the brain could actually be called spinal. Similarly, progress in the understanding of the brain has led to increased recognition of different functions served by particular clumps of neurons or axons *within* a given structure. Where researchers once asked questions such as 'What does the cerebellum do?' today they are more likely to ask about the functions of specific parts of the cerebellum.

APPLY + DISCUSS

- Are political contests any different from the competition for status, power or 'turf' seen in other animal species? How are they similar, and how are they different?
- To what extent can we 'rise above' the power of the primitive neural structures that motivate our behaviours? Are we anything more than sophisticated monkeys, pursuing what other animals pursue but with a little more wit and style?

INTERIM SUMMARY

The design of the human nervous system, like that of other animals, reflects its evolution. Early precursors to the first vertebrates (animals with spinal cords) probably reacted with reflexive responses to environmental stimulation at specific points of their bodies. The most primitive vertebrate brain, or brainstem, included a forebrain (specialised for sensing nearby stimuli, notably smells and tastes), a midbrain (specialised for sensation at a distance, namely vision and hearing) and a hindbrain (specialised for control of movement). This rough division of labour persists in contemporary vertebrates, including humans. The forebrain of humans and other contemporary vertebrates includes an expanded cerebrum, with a rich network of cells comprising its outer layers or cortex, which allows much more sophisticated sensory, cognitive and motor processes.

The spinal cord

As in all vertebrates, neurons in the human spinal cord produce reflexes, as sensory stimulation activates rapid, automatic motor responses. In humans, however, an additional, and crucial, function of the spinal cord is to transmit information between the brain and the rest of the body. The ***spinal cord*** sends information from sensory neurons in various parts of the body to the brain, and it relays motor commands back to muscles and organs (such as the heart and stomach) via motor neurons.

The spinal cord is segmented, with each segment controlling a different part of the body. By and large, the upper segments control the upper parts of the body and the lower segments control the lower body (figure 3.10). As in the earliest vertebrates, sensory information enters one side of the spinal cord (towards the back of the body), and motor impulses exit the other (towards the front).

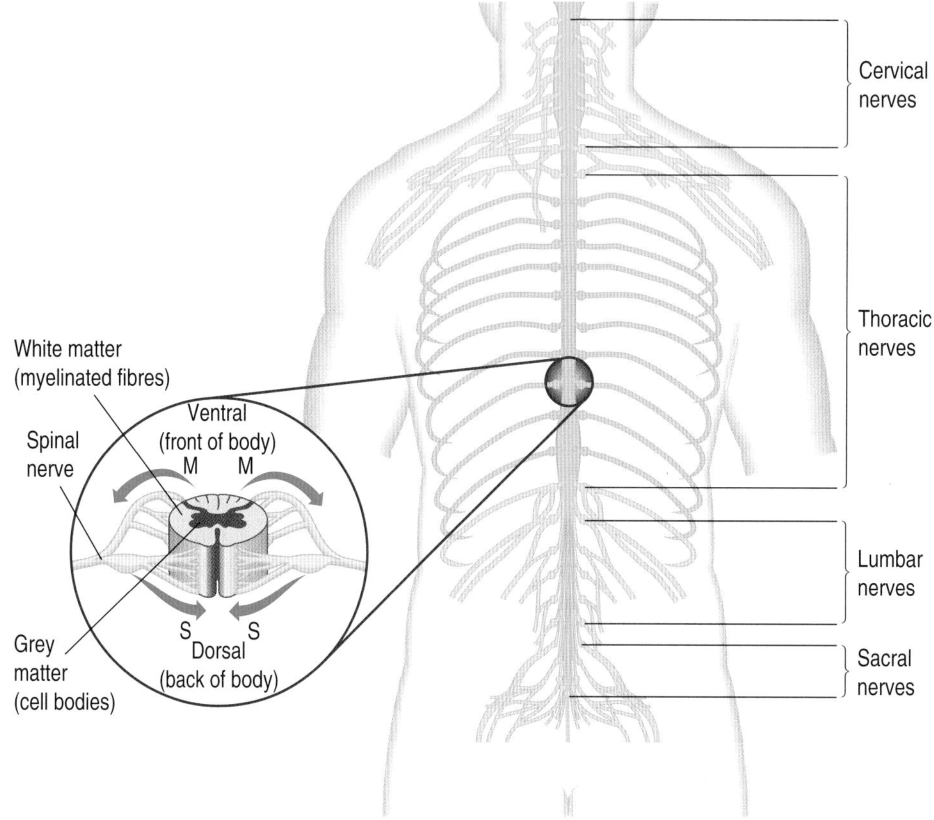

FIGURE 3.10
The spinal cord. Segments of the spinal cord relay information to and from different parts of the body. Sensory fibres (S) relay information to the back of the spine (dorsal), and motor neurons (M) transmit information from the front of the spinal cord (ventral) to the periphery.

Outside the cord, bundles of axons from these sensory and motor neurons join together to form 31 pairs (from the two sides of the body) of spinal nerves; these nerves carry information to and from the spinal cord to the periphery. Inside the spinal cord, other bundles of axons (spinal tracts, which comprise much of the white matter of the cord) send impulses to and from the brain, relaying sensory messages and motor commands. (Outside the central nervous system, bundles of axons are usually called nerves; within the brain and spinal cord, they are called tracts.)

When the spinal cord is severed, the result is loss of feeling and paralysis at all levels below the injury, which can no longer communicate with the brain. Even with less severe lesions, doctors can often pinpoint the location of spinal damage from patients' descriptions of their symptoms alone (figure 3.10). We recently heard from a colleague who learned about the spinal cord in a less academic way when he developed a nerve inflammation that rendered him unable to sit or lie down for much of five months. Although virtually all of the pain was on the right side, a perplexing symptom was severe pain in his left little toe. Shortly after, the doctor showed him a chart tracing the probable source of the pain in that toe up to the first sacral nerve (called S1, for short) and the report of the MRI scan came in: he had a bulging disc sitting on top of the S1 nerve. (Much as our colleague loves psychology, he could have lived without this extra training in neuroanatomy.)

INTERIM SUMMARY

The central nervous system (CNS) consists of the brain and spinal cord. The ***spinal cord*** carries out reflexes (automatic motor responses), transmits sensory information to the brain and transmits messages from the brain to the muscles and organs. Each of its segments controls sensation and movement in a different part of the body.

The brain

The human brain consists of three main parts: (1) the hindbrain, (2) the midbrain and (3) the forebrain. Each of these parts will be discussed in turn. The *Brain Atlas* describes the various parts of the brain in detail. You should be able to access it online from your university course website for this subject. Alternatively, you might like to watch a brief anatomy of the brain video clip that you should also be able to access via your university course website.

The hindbrain

Directly above the spinal cord in humans are several structures that comprise the ***hindbrain***: the medulla oblongata, the cerebellum and parts of the reticular formation. Another small hindbrain region, the pons, contains fibres that link the medulla oblongata and the cerebellum with the upper portion of the brainstem (Reber & Reber, 2001). The pons is involved in respiration, movement, sleep, waking and dreaming (figure 3.11).

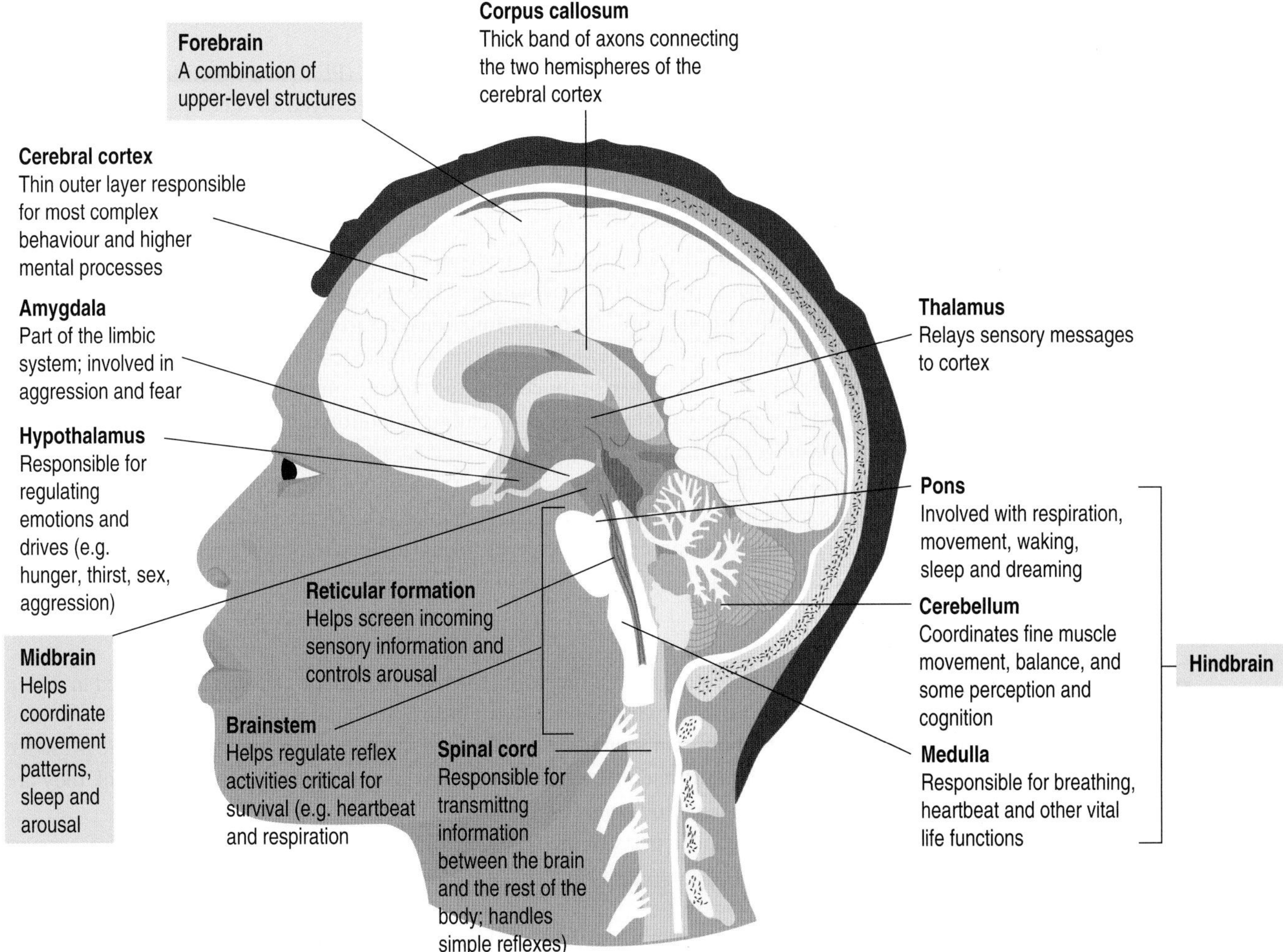

FIGURE 3.11
The human brain. The drawing shows a view of the inside surface of the left half of the brain, highlighting the key structures and some of their principal functions.

SOURCE: Huffman (2007, p. 69).

As in other animals, hindbrain structures link the brain to the spinal cord, sustain life by controlling the supply of air and blood to cells in the body, and regulate arousal level. With the exception of the cerebellum, which sits at the back of the brain and has a distinct appearance, the structures of the hindbrain merge into one another and perform multiple functions as information passes from one structure to the next on its way to higher brain regions.

Medulla oblongata

Anatomically, the lowest brainstem structure, the ***medulla oblongata*** (or simply ***medulla***), is actually an extension of the spinal cord that links the cord to the brain. Although quite small — about 3.5 centimetres long and 2 centimetres wide at its broadest part — the medulla is essential to life, controlling such vital physiological functions as heartbeat, circulation and respiration. Neither humans nor other animals can survive destruction of the medulla.

The medulla is the link between the spinal cord (and hence much of the body) and the rest of the brain. Here, many bundles of axons cross over from each side of the body to the opposite side of the brain. As a result, most of the sensations experienced on the right side of the body, as well as the capacity to move the right side, are controlled by the left side of the brain, and vice versa. Thus, if a person has weakness in the left side of the body following a stroke, the damage to the brain was probably on the right side of the brain.

The cerebellum is involved in coordinating smooth, well-sequenced movements and in maintaining balance and posture.

Cerebellum

The ***cerebellum*** (Latin for 'little cerebrum') is a large structure at the back of the brain involved in movement as well as other functions. For decades researchers believed that the cerebellum was exclusively involved in coordinating smooth, well-sequenced movements (such as riding a bike) and in maintaining balance and posture. Staggering and slurred speech after a few too many drinks stem in large part from the effects of alcohol on cerebellar functioning.

More recently, researchers using positron emission tomography (PET) and functional magnetic resonance imaging (fMRI) scans have found the cerebellum to be involved in other psychological processes as well. Among the most important are sensory and cognitive processes, such as learning to associate one stimulus with another (Drepper, Timmann, Kolb, & Diener, 1999).

Reticular formation

The ***reticular formation*** is a diffuse network of neurons that extends from the lowest parts of the medulla in the hindbrain to the upper end of the midbrain. The reticular formation sends axons to many parts of the brain and to the spinal cord. Its major functions are to maintain consciousness, regulate arousal levels and modulate the activity of neurons throughout the central nervous system. The reticular formation also appears to help higher brain centres to integrate information from different neural pathways (such as sounds and associated images) by calling attention to their simultaneous activation (Munk, Roelfsema, Konig, Engel, & Singer, 1996).

Reticular damage can affect sleep patterns as well as the ability to be alert or attentive. Damage to the reticular formation is a major cause of coma. In fact, humans can lose an entire side (or hemisphere) of the cerebrum — about 50 billion cells — without losing the capacity for consciousness, whereas lesions to the reticular formation can render all the information in the cortex useless (Baars, 1995).

MAKING CONNECTIONS

Visual processing in the tectum appears to be involved in an intriguing phenomenon called **blindsight**, in which damage to core visual processing circuits in the brain leaves the person blind — or seemingly blind (chapter 5). Although patients with blindsight may protest that they cannot see anything, they can nevertheless 'guess' correctly whether a visual stimulus is to their left or right, because the **tectum** is still intact.

The midbrain

The ***midbrain*** consists of the tectum and tegmentum. The ***tectum*** includes structures involved in vision and hearing. These structures largely help humans orient to visual and auditory stimuli with eye and body movements. When higher brain structures are lesioned, people can often still sense the presence of stimuli, but they cannot identify them, leading to a strange phenomenon: people may think they are blind but they can actually respond to visual stimuli (chapter 5).

The ***tegmentum***, which includes parts of the reticular formation and other neural structures, serves a variety of functions, many related to movement. The tegmentum includes the substantia nigra, which deteriorates in Parkinson's disease.

Research suggests that these midbrain structures also play an important role in learning to produce behaviours that minimise unpleasant (aversive) consequences and maximise rewards — a kind of learning studied for years by behaviourists (chapter 5). Neurons deep inside the tectum are part of a system of neurons involved in generating unpleasant feelings and linking them, through learning, to actions that can help the animal escape or avoid them (Brandao, Cardoso, Kelo, Motta, & Coimbra, 1994).

Chemical or electrical activation of these pathways in rats produces 'freezing' (a characteristic fear response) and efforts to escape.

Other nuclei (collections of neurons in a region of the brain that serve a shared function) in the tegmentum are involved in the experience of pleasure or reward, which is crucial to learning to produce actions that lead to positive consequences (Johnson, Churchill, Klitenick, & Hooks, 1996; Nader & van der Kooy, 1997). For example, rats will learn to perform behaviours that lead to morphine injections in regions of their tegmentum (Jaeger & van der Kooy, 1996).

INTERIM SUMMARY

The ***hindbrain*** includes the ***medulla oblongata***, the ***cerebellum*** and parts of the ***reticular formation***. The medulla regulates vital physiological functions, such as heartbeat, circulation and respiration, and forms a link between the spinal cord and the rest of the brain. The cerebellum has long been seen as the lowest brain structure involved in movement, but parts of it also appear to be involved in learning and sensory discrimination. The reticular formation is most centrally involved in consciousness and arousal. The ***midbrain*** consists of the tectum and tegmentum. The ***tectum*** is involved in orienting to visual and auditory stimuli. The ***tegmentum*** is involved, among other things, in movement and arousal. Midbrain structures are also part of neural circuits that help humans learn to approach or avoid stimuli associated with reward and punishment.

The forebrain

The ***forebrain***, which is involved in complex sensory, emotional, cognitive and behavioural processes, consists of the hypothalamus, thalamus and cerebrum. Within the cerebrum are the basal ganglia and limbic system, which are called ***subcortical structures*** (sub, or below, the cortex). The outer layers of the cerebrum, or cortex, are so complex that we will devote a separate section to them.

Hypothalamus

Situated in front of the midbrain and adjacent to the pituitary gland is the ***hypothalamus***. Although the hypothalamus accounts for only 0.3 percent of the brain's total weight, this tiny structure helps regulate behaviours ranging from eating and sleeping to sexual activity and emotional experience.

In non-human animals, the hypothalamus is involved in species-specific behaviours, such as responses to predators. For example, electrical stimulation of the hypothalamus in cats can produce rage attacks — including hissing, growling and biting (Bandler, 1982; Lu, Shaikh, & Siegel, 1992; Siegel, Roeling, Gregg, & Kruk, 1999).

The hypothalamus works closely with the pituitary gland and provides a key link between the nervous system and the endocrine system, largely by activating pituitary hormones. When people undergo stressful experiences (such as taking an exam or getting into a heated argument), the hypothalamus activates the pituitary, which in turn puts the body on alert by sending out hormonal messages. One of the most important functions of the hypothalamus is homeostasis — keeping vital processes such as body temperature, blood-sugar (glucose) level and metabolism (use and storage of energy) within a fairly narrow range (chapter 10). For example, as people ingest food, the hypothalamus detects a rise in glucose level and responds by shutting off hunger sensations. Chemically blocking glucose receptors (cells that detect glucose levels) in cats can produce ravenous eating, as the hypothalamus attempts to maintain homeostasis in the face of misleading information (Batuev & Gafurov, 1993; Berridge & Zajonc, 1991; Hagan et al., 1998).

Thalamus

The ***thalamus*** is a set of nuclei located above the hypothalamus. Its various nuclei perform a number of functions. One of its most important functions is to process sensory information as it arrives and transmit this information to higher brain centres. In some respects the thalamus is like a switchboard for routing information from neurons connected to visual, auditory, taste and touch receptors to appropriate regions of the brain. However, the thalamus plays a much more active role than a simple switchboard. Its function is not only to route messages to the appropriate structures but also to filter them, highlighting some and de-emphasising others.

The thalamus is ideally situated for performing this function, since it receives projections (i.e. axons leading to it) from several sensory systems, as well as feedback from higher cortical centres in the brain. Thus, the thalamus can collect information from multiple senses and determine the extent to which information is converging on something important that may require more detailed processing.

The thalamus also receives input from the reticular formation, which 'highlights' neural messages of potential importance. Recent studies using PET and other techniques suggest that the reticular formation and thalamus may be the anatomically 'lower' sections of a neural circuit that directs attention and consciousness towards potentially significant events (Fiset et al., 1999; Kinomura, Larsson, Gulyas, & Roland, 1996).

The limbic system

The ***limbic system*** is a set of structures with diverse functions involving emotion, motivation, learning and memory. The limbic system includes the septal area, the amygdala and the hippocampus (figure 3.12).

The role of the septal area is only gradually becoming clear, but it appears to be involved in some forms of emotionally significant learning. Early research linked it to the experience of pleasure. Stimulating a section of the septal area is such a powerful reinforcer for rats that they will walk across an electrified grid to receive the stimulation (Milner, 1991; Olds & Milner, 1954).

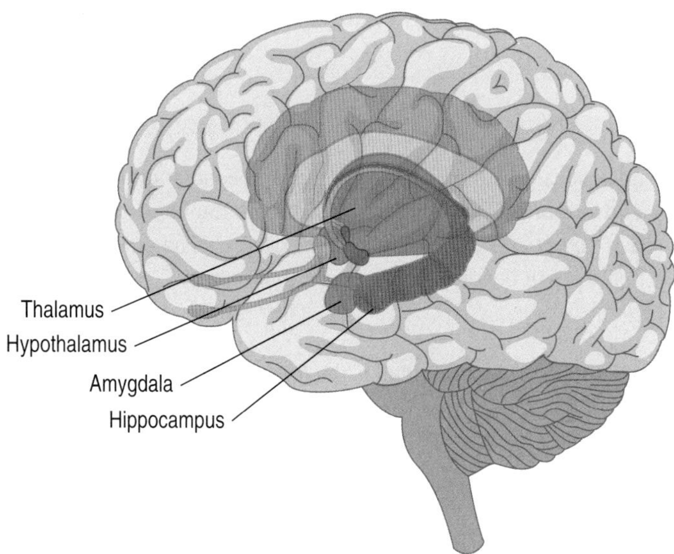

FIGURE 3.12
The hippocampus and amygdala are part of the limbic system.

SOURCE: Gleitman et al. (2007, p. 89).

MAKING CONNECTIONS

Learning a complex piece of music at first requires the involvement of some of our most advanced cortical circuits. However, over time, the basal ganglia come to regulate the movement of the fingers. In fact, we can 'remember' with our fingers far faster than we can consciously think about what our fingers are doing (chapters 5 and 6).

Other research suggests that, like most brain structures, different sections of the septal area are likely to have distinct, though related, functions. For example, one part of the septal area appears to be involved in relief from pain and other unpleasant emotional states (Yadin & Thomas, 1996). Another part seems to help animals learn to avoid situations that *lead* to aversive experiences, since injecting chemicals that temporarily block its functioning makes rats less able to learn to avoid stimuli associated with pain (Rashidy-Pour, Motaghed-Larijani, & Bures, 1995). These regions receive projections from midbrain and thalamic nuclei involved in learning.

The ***amygdala*** is an almond-shaped structure (amygdala is Latin for 'almond') involved in many emotional processes, especially learning and remembering emotionally significant events (Aggleton, 1992; LeDoux, 1995; Sarter & Markowitsch, 1985). One of its primary roles is to attach emotional significance to events. The amygdala appears to be particularly important in fear responses. Lesioning the amygdala in rats, for example, inhibits learned fear responses; that is, the rats no longer avoid a stimulus they had previously connected with pain (LaBar & LeDoux, 1996).

The amygdala is also involved in recognising emotion, particularly fearful emotion, in other people. One study using PET technology found that presenting pictures of fearful rather than neutral or happy faces activated the left amygdala and that the amount of activation strongly correlated with the amount of fear displayed in the pictures (Morris et al., 1996). From an evolutionary perspective, this suggests that humans have evolved particular mechanisms for detecting fear in others and that these 'fear detectors' are anatomically connected to neural circuits that produce fear. This makes sense, since fear in others is probably a signal of danger to oneself. In fact, infants as young as nine to 12 months show distress when they see distress on their parents' faces (Campos, Bertenthal, & Kermoian, 1992). Remarkably, the amygdala can respond to threatening stimuli even when the person has no awareness of seeing them. If researchers present a threatening stimulus so quickly that the person cannot report seeing it, the amygdala may nevertheless be activated, suggesting that it is detecting some very subtle cues for danger (Morris, Dehman, & Dolan, 1998).

The ***hippocampus*** is particularly important for storing new information in memory so that the person can later consciously remember it (e.g. see Eldridge, Knowlton, & Engel, 2000; Squire & Zola-Morgan, 1991). This was demonstrated dramatically in a famous case study by Brenda Milner and her colleagues (Milner, Corkin, & Teuber, 1968; Scoville & Milner, 1957). A man identified as H. M. underwent surgery to control life-threatening epileptic seizures. The surgeon removed sections of the patient's cortex and some underlying structures. Unfortunately, one of those structures was the hippocampus, and although H. M. was now free of seizures, he was also 'free' of the capacity to remember new information.

Actually, that is only half of H. M.'s story, and the other half has, in the last 15 years, changed our understanding of memory. H. M. *did* lose his memory in the sense that psychologists and laypeople alike have traditionally understood memory. For example, every time he met Dr Milner, who studied him over 20 years, he had to be reintroduced; invariably, he would smile politely and tell her it was a pleasure to make her acquaintance. But as we will see in chapter 7, we now know that certain kinds of memory do not involve the hippocampus, and H. M. retained those capacities. For example, on one occasion H. M.'s father took him to visit his mother in the hospital. Afterwards, H. M. did not remember anything of the visit, but he 'expressed a vague idea that something might have happened to his mother' (Milner, Corkin, & Teuber, 1968, p. 216). Amazingly, despite a lack of explicit knowledge of his mother's death, H. M. never responded to reminders of this event with the emotional response that would be expected from someone first hearing this news (Hirst, 1994). He did not 'remember' his mother's death, but it registered nonetheless. H. M. died in 2008 at the age of 82. You should be able to access his life story through your university course website for this subject.

The movie *Memento*, starring Australian actor Guy Pearce, depicted the problems associated with not being able to lay down new memories.

The basal ganglia

The ***basal ganglia*** are a set of structures, including the putamen and caudate nucleus (figure 3.13), located near the thalamus and hypothalamus that are involved in a wide array of functions, particularly movement and judgements that require minimal conscious thought. Damage to structures in the basal ganglia can affect posture and muscle tone or cause abnormal movements. The basal ganglia have been implicated in Parkinson's disease and in the epidemic of encephalitis lethargica that struck millions early in the twentieth century. The dopamine-rich neurons of the substantia nigra (in the midbrain) normally project to the basal ganglia. When these neurons die, as in Parkinson's, they stop sending signals to the basal ganglia, which in turn cease functioning properly. Some neural circuits involving the basal ganglia appear to inhibit movement, whereas others initiate it, since lesions in different sections of the basal ganglia can either release movements (leading to twitches or jerky movements) or block them (leading to Parkinsonian symptoms).

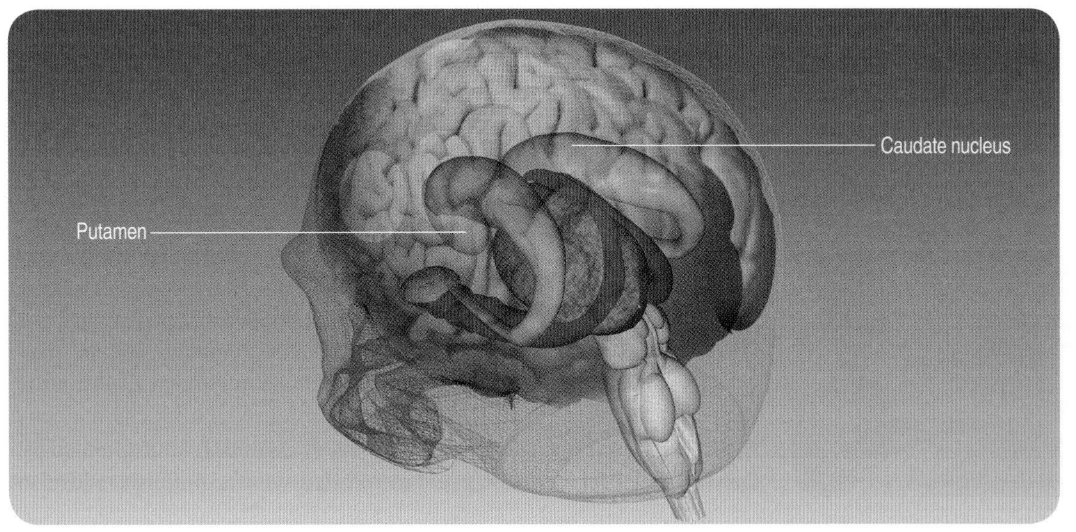

FIGURE 3.13
The putamen and caudate nucleus are part of the basal ganglia.

Damage to the basal ganglia can also lead to a variety of emotional, social and cognitive impairments (Knowlton, Mangels, & Squire, 1996; Lieberman, 2000; Postle & D'Esposito, 1999). For example, people with basal ganglia damage sometimes have difficulty making rapid, automatic judgements about how to classify or understand the meaning of things they see or hear. Thus, a person with damage to certain regions of the basal ganglia may have difficulty recognising that a subtle change in another person's tone of voice reflects sarcasm — the kind of judgement the rest of us make without a moment's thought.

Remembering that things have changed

By Professor Simon Crowe, La Trobe University

The level of sophistication of any organism is largely determined by its ability to learn from its experiences. Until the last few years, it has been one of the unshakeable orthodoxies of memory research that memory is initially laid down in a changeable form for only a short period of time following an experience and that, over time, memory trace becomes 'fixed' or 'consolidated' into the physical structure of the brain. Recent research, however, has turned this orthodoxy on its head, as a huge volume of evidence has developed indicating that a 'consolidated' memory may again be returned to a modifiable state, following retrieval of the material from the memory store.

The ability to update memory is at the heart of the adaptive success of any complex organism; however, the literature on the neurobiology of memory formation has, until only recently, not been able to identify how it might be neurally possible to add newly arising information to an existing record of events. The process of re-consolidation provides the mechanism by which this crucial memory process can occur. It now seems clear that the consolidation of memory cannot take place in a once-off fashion, and memories are, most probably, repeatedly consolidated and re-consolidated as people grow and experience throughout the life span. Many researchers now contend that it is re-consolidation, rather than consolidation, that is the most common form of memory processing.

There is no point, for example, forming an unchangeable record of where a person has parked their car in a carpark today — if they are going to park their car somewhere else tomorrow. So, if they park their car in bay 1 on the first day of the semester and form a long-term memory of this fact, how will they find their car when they come back on day 2, 3, 4 or 5 — when they have parked their car in bay 2, bay 14, bay 21 and bay 46 across the week? What they need to be able to do is to encode not just where they parked their car, but where they parked their car *today*, and then they need to amend and update this record of car parking for each new day that they park. A comprehensive account of the biology of memory formation must, therefore, permit the modifiability of the representation of the world, taking into account the fact that information changes and needs to be updated.

You might ask yourself what does all of this mean in the 'real' world? You may have seen the 2004 movie *Eternal Sunshine of the Spotless Mind*, starring Jim Carrey and Kate Winslet. Clementine Kruczynski (Winslet) and Joel Barish (Carrey) are lovers, and after a nasty argument, Clementine hires some (fictional) psychological researchers to 'erase' the memory of her heartbreak. They erase her total recall of Joel, along with all of their shared experiences. Upon discovering that Clementine has erased her memories of him, Joel decides to undergo the same experience. As the memories are erased, Joel re-experiences them in a reverse sequence, until no recall of Clementine is left. Clearly this represents a fictionalised account, but there are certainly some parallels with the re-consolidation phenomenon.

An excellent example of where this technique has been used in the clinic is in the area of the treatment of post-traumatic stress disorder (PTSD). In these patients, the individual is reminded of the initial trauma and is then given the drug propranolol, which blocks the acute stress response. The memory of the event is thus re-consolidated, so that the new record of the event is recalled with a diminished level of trauma. There is also a possible indication for this approach in the reversal of various forms of phobia. Contemporary memory research is suggesting that memory is modifiable, and that each time people revisit a memory, it can be modified and rewritten. Obviously, it is possible that with the further development and validation of this technique, it could be put to inappropriate usage (such as occurred in the film) and this brings the questions of how much one can remember and, most importantly, how much and under what circumstances one could be made to forget.

INTERIM SUMMARY

The ***forebrain*** consists of the ***hypothalamus***, the ***thalamus***, the ***subcortical structures*** of the cerebrum (the limbic system and basal ganglia) and the cerebral cortex. The hypothalamus helps regulate a wide range of behaviours, including eating, sleeping, sexual activity and emotional experience. Among its other functions, the thalamus processes incoming sensory information and transmits this information to higher brain centres. The ***limbic system*** includes the septal area, ***amygdala*** and hippocampus. The precise functions of the septal area are unclear, although it appears to be involved in learning to act in ways that avoid pain and produce pleasure. The amygdala is crucial to the experience of emotion. The hippocampus plays an important role in committing new information to memory. ***Basal ganglia*** structures are involved in the control of movement and also play a part in 'automatic' responses and judgements that may normally require little conscious attention.

The cerebral cortex

The cerebral cortex consists of a 3 millimetre thick layer of densely packed interneurons; it is greyish in colour and highly convoluted (i.e. filled with twists and turns). The convolutions appear to serve a purpose. Just as crumpling a piece of paper into a tight wad reduces its size, the folds and wrinkles of the cortex allow a relatively large area of cortical cells to fit into a compact region within the skull. The hills of these convolutions are known as gyri (plural of gyrus) and the valleys as sulci (plural of sulcus).

In humans, the ***cerebral cortex*** performs three functions. First, it allows the flexible construction of sequences of voluntary movements involved in activities such as changing a tyre or playing a piano concerto. Second, it permits subtle discriminations among complex sensory patterns; without a cerebral cortex, the words *gene* and *gem* would be indistinguishable. Third, it makes possible symbolic thinking — the ability to use symbols such as words or pictorial signs (like a flag) to represent an object or a concept with a complex meaning. The capacity to think symbolically enables people to have conversations about things that do not exist or are not presently in view; it is the foundation of human thought and language.

Primary and association areas

The cortex consists of areas specialised for different functions, such as vision, hearing and body sensation. Each of these areas can be divided roughly into two zones, called the primary cortex and the association cortex. The ***primary areas*** of the cortex process raw sensory information or (in one section of the brain, the frontal lobes) initiate movement. The ***association areas*** are involved in complex mental processes such as forming perceptions, ideas and plans; they were given this name in the nineteenth century because scientists believed that higher mental functioning revolved around the association of one idea with another.

The primary areas are responsible for the initial cortical processing of sensory information. Neurons in the primary and association areas receive sensory information, usually via the thalamus, from sensory receptors in the ears, eyes, skin and muscles. When a person sees a safety pin lying on her dresser, the primary or sensory areas receive the simple visual sensations that make up the contours of the safety pin. Activation of circuits in the visual association cortex enables the person to recognise the object as a safety pin rather than a needle or a formless shiny object.

Neurons in the primary areas tend to have more specific functions than neurons in the association cortex. Many of these neurons are wired to register very basic, and very specific, attributes of a stimulus. For example, some neurons in the primary visual cortex respond to horizontal lines but not to

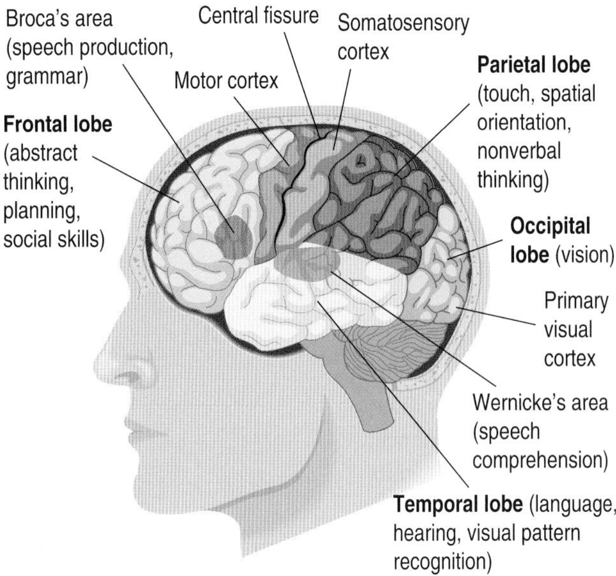

FIGURE 3.14
The lobes of the cerebral cortex. The cortex has four lobes, each specialised for different functions and each containing primary and association areas.

vertical lines; other neurons respond only to vertical lines (Hubel & Wiesel, 1963). Some neurons in the association cortex are equally specific in their functions, but many develop their functions through experience. The brain may be wired from birth to detect the contours of objects such as safety pins, but a person must learn what a safety pin is and what it does. From an evolutionary perspective, this combination of 'hard-wired' and 'flexible' neurons is very important. It guarantees that we have the capacity to detect features of *any* environment that are likely to be relevant to adaptation, but we can also learn the features of the *specific* environment in which we find ourselves.

Lobes of the cerebral cortex

The cerebrum is divided into two roughly symmetrical halves, or ***cerebral hemispheres***, which are separated by the longitudinal fissure. (A fissure is a deep sulcus, or valley.) A band of neural fibres called the ***corpus callosum*** connects the right and left hemispheres. Each hemisphere consists of four regions, or lobes: (1) occipital, (2) parietal, (3) frontal and (4) temporal. Thus, a person has a right and left occipital lobe, a right and left parietal lobe, and so forth (figure 3.14). Once again, it is important to bear in mind that nature did not create clearly bounded cortical regions and rope them off from one another; the functions of adjacent cortical regions tend to be related, even if some cells are called 'occipital' and others 'temporal'.

The occipital lobes

The ***occipital lobes***, located in the rear portion of the cortex, are specialised for vision. Primary areas of the occipital lobes receive visual input from the thalamus. The thalamus, in turn, receives information from the receptors in the retina via the optic nerve. The primary areas respond to relatively simple features of a visual stimulus, and the association areas organise these simple characteristics into more complex maps of features of objects and their position in space. Damage to the primary areas leads to partial or complete blindness.

The visual association cortex, which actually extends into neighbouring lobes, projects (i.e. sends axons carrying messages) to several regions throughout the cortex that receive other types of sensory information, such as auditory or tactile (touch). Areas that receive information from more than one sensory system are called polysensory areas. The existence of polysensory areas at various levels of the brain (including subcortical levels) helps us, for example, to associate the sight of a car stopping suddenly with the sound of squealing tyres.

The parietal lobes

The ***parietal lobes*** are located in front of the occipital lobes. They are involved in several functions, including the sense of touch, detecting movement in the environment, locating objects in space and experiencing one's own body as it moves through space. A person with damage to the primary area of the parietal lobes may be unable to feel a thimble on her finger, whereas damage to the association area could render her unable to recognise the object she was feeling as a thimble or to understand what the object does.

The primary area of the parietal lobe, called the ***somatosensory cortex***, lies directly behind the central fissure, which divides the parietal lobe from the frontal lobe. Different sections of the somatosensory cortex receive information from different parts of the body (figure 3.15). Thus, one section registers sensations from the hand, another from the foot, and so forth. The parietal lobes are also involved in complex visual processing, particularly the posterior (back) regions nearest to the occipital lobes.

MAKING CONNECTIONS

Circuits in the frontal lobes make possible some of the most extraordinary feats of the human intellect, from solving equations to understanding complex social situations (chapters 8 and 9).

The frontal lobes

The ***frontal lobes*** are involved in a number of functions, including movement, attention, planning, social skills, abstract thinking, memory and some aspects of personality (see Goldman-Rakic, 1995; Russell & Roxanas, 1990). Figure 3.15 shows the ***motor cortex***, the primary zone of the frontal lobe. Through its projections to the basal ganglia, cerebellum and spinal cord, the motor cortex initiates voluntary movement. The motor cortex and the adjacent somatosensory cortex send and receive information from the same parts of the body.

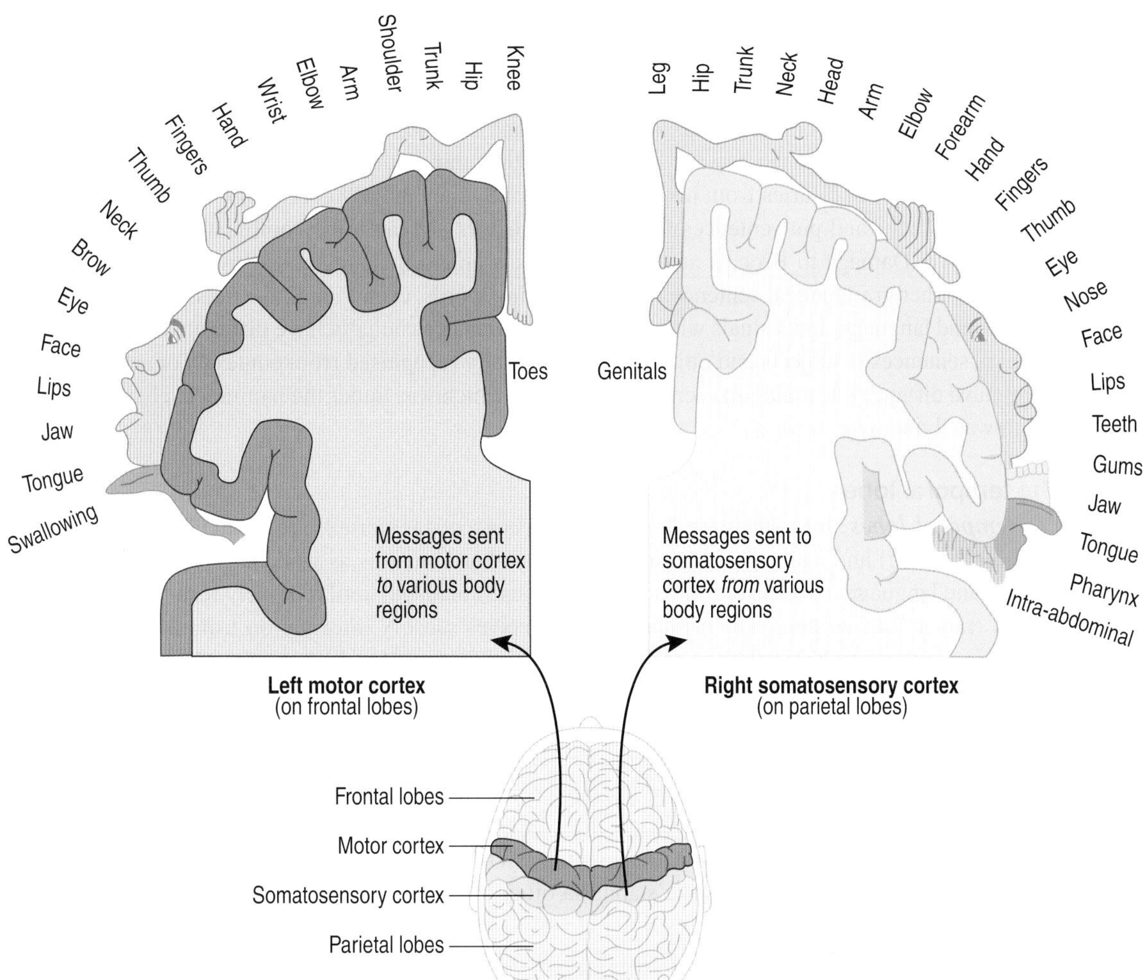

FIGURE 3.15
The motor and somatosensory cortex. The motor cortex initiates movement. The somatosensory cortex receives sensory information from the spinal cord, largely via the thalamus. Both the motor and somatosensory cortex devote space according to the importance, neural density (number of neurons) and complexity of the anatomical regions to which they are connected. At the top of the diagram we see a functional map of the motor cortex and somatosensory cortex.

SOURCE: Huffman (2007, p. 76).

As the figure indicates, the amount of space devoted to different parts of the body in the motor and somatosensory cortices is not directly proportional to their size. Parts of the body that produce fine motor movements or have particularly dense and sensitive receptors take up more space in the motor and somatosensory cortices. These body parts tend to serve important or complex functions and thus require more processing capacity. In humans, the hands, which are crucial to exploring objects and using tools, occupy considerable territory, whereas a section of the back of similar size occupies only a fraction of that space. Other species have different cortical 'priorities'; in cats, for example, input from the whiskers receives considerably more space than input from 'whiskers' on the face of human males.

In the frontal lobes, the primary area is motor rather than sensory. The association cortex is involved in planning and putting together sequences of behaviour. Neurons in the primary areas then issue specific commands to motor neurons throughout the body.

Damage to the frontal lobes can lead to a wide array of problems, from paralysis to difficulty thinking abstractly, focusing attention efficiently, coordinating complex sequences of behaviour and adjusting socially (Adolphs, 1999; Damasio, 1994). Lesions in other parts of the brain that project to the frontal lobes can produce similar symptoms because the frontal lobes fail to receive normal activation. For example, the victims of encephalitis lethargica could not initiate movements even though their frontal lobes were intact because projections from the basal ganglia that normally activate the frontal lobes were impaired by dopamine depletion.

After two failed attempts, Steve Hooker dramatically clinched the gold medal for Australia in the pole vault at the Beijing Olympics with a vault of 5.96 metres. Trace what would have been happening in Hooker's nervous system in this pressure situation.

- What cortical and subcortical circuits would have been activated in the photo of him on the left, as he was sizing up the task and its significance?
- What parts of the cortex would have become active first as he executed his vault? How would his intentions have been carried out by his muscles, as depicted in the above photo on the right?

In most individuals, the left frontal lobe is also involved in language. ***Broca's area***, located in the left frontal lobe at the base of the motor cortex, is specialised for movements of the mouth and tongue necessary for speech production. It also plays a pivotal role in the use and understanding of grammar. Speech problems from brain trauma are common, and vary in severity from mild and temporary to debilitating, depending on the location and extent of the brain injury. Thankfully, David Keohane, who suffered serious head injuries from his brutal attack in Sydney in 2008 (see p. 88), has since been able to recognise faces and put sentences together and doctors are cautiously optimistic that his progress will continue. Damage to Broca's area causes Broca's aphasia, characterised by difficulty speaking, putting together grammatical sentences and articulating words, even though the person remains able to comprehend language. Individuals with lesions to this area occasionally have difficulty comprehending complex sentences if subjects and objects cannot be easily recognised from context. For example, they might have difficulty decoding the sentence, 'The cat, which was under the hammock, chased the bird, which was flying over the dog'.

The temporal lobes

The ***temporal lobes***, located in the lower side portions of the cortex, are particularly important in audition (hearing) and language, although they have other functions as well. The connection between hearing and language makes evolutionary sense because language, until relatively recently, was always spoken (rather than written). The primary cortex receives sensory information from the ears, and the association cortex breaks the flow of sound into meaningful units (such as words). Cells in the primary cortex respond to particular frequencies of sound (i.e. to different tones) and are arranged anatomically from low (towards the front of the brain) to high frequencies (towards the back).

For most people the left hemisphere of the temporal lobe is specialised for language, although some linguistic functions are shared by the right hemisphere. ***Wernicke's area***, located in the left temporal lobe, is important in language comprehension. Damage to Wernicke's area may produce Wernicke's aphasia, characterised by difficulty understanding what words and sentences mean (see Wilshire & Saffran, 2005). Patients with Wernicke's aphasia often produce 'word salad': they may speak fluently and expressively, as if their speech were meaningful, but the words are tossed together so that they make little sense. In contrast, right temporal damage typically results in nonverbal deficits, such as difficulty recognising songs, faces or paintings.

Psychologists once believed that hearing and language were the primary functions of the temporal lobes; however, research suggests that the temporal lobes have multiple sections and that these different sections serve different functions (Rodman, 1997). For example, regions towards the back (posterior) of the temporal lobes respond to concrete visual features of objects such as colour and shape, whereas regions towards the front respond to more abstract knowledge (such as memory for objects, or the meaning of the concept 'democracy') (Graham, Patterson, & Hodges, 1999; Ishai, Ungerleier, Martin, Schouten, & Haxby, 1999; Srinivas, Breedin, Coslett, & Saffran, 1997). In general, information processed towards the back of the temporal lobes is more concrete and specific, whereas information processed towards the front is more abstract and integrated.

APPLY + DISCUSS

Neuroplasticity suggests that the brain is a dynamic organ that continues to develop and change over time. According to Dr Norman Doidge, a psychiatrist and psychoanalyst, our thoughts can change the structure and function of our brains. Dr Doidge has documented how patients suffering from neurological disorders can train their brains to learn new skills, in his popular book entitled, *The Brain That Changes Itself.* Essentially, the book outlines various neuroplastic interventions to show how healthy brain tissue can be trained to take over from damaged tissue.

- Can we train our brains to increase our IQs or change our personalities?
- How might the ever-expanding world of new technologies influence the way we train our brains?

ONE STEP FURTHER

A slow but conscious brain

By Associate Professor Ulrich Schall, The University of Newcastle

Think of our neocortex as a very powerful computer that generates a 'virtual reality' of ourselves in our personal here and now, by assessing our past experiences and combining them with the actual sensory input from the world around us. Importantly, this process is an active construction of our personal reality, rather than a physically accurate representation of sensory input. By doing this, our brains generate something that is probably best described as the biological basis of consciousness (Young & Pigott, 1999).

But why is it a construction of reality akin to a 'virtual reality'? The answer lies in the relatively slow speed of the brain when processing information. For example, becoming fully aware of something takes about 0.3 of a second. This means that our virtual here and now lags about 0.3 of a second behind the actual here and now. In order to compensate for this, the brain needs to compute the best possible prediction of what is going to happen 0.3 of a second into the future (Edelman, 2001). Otherwise, we would not be able to perform simple tasks like catching a ball or avoiding a collision with a moving object. As we all know, our brains perform better predictions with more experience, which helps us to perform complex tasks, such as driving a car, despite the relative slowness of our brains.

Speaking aloud is an example of the 'virtual synchronicity' of thinking, speaking and hearing. Imagine a conversation and think about all the steps involved and, in particular, the timing of the sequence from a thought to the spoken sentence. First, the thought needs to be translated into appropriate words and to be syntactically organised. This is then followed by the coordinated activation of the facial, mouth, larynx and breathing muscles, thus resulting in speaking aloud. This, in turn, is picked up by our auditory system and is monitored for correct execution. While this sequence takes considerable time, we perceive all this as happening virtually simultaneously: we speak — and hear ourselves speaking — as we think. A small disturbance of this process, such as feeding back our own voice with a subtle delay, derails our ability to speak fluently aloud: we start stuttering and even have trouble recognising the feedback voice as our own, because it sounds very different and alien to us. A failure of the underlying neural processes has been proposed to lead to auditory hallucinations (e.g. hearing voices; Ford & Mathalon, 2005).

Another example: catching a ball requires the brain to 'virtually' integrate the visual, auditory and tactile sensations with our intention to catch the ball in a way that all this is consistent with our experience of catching a ball.

The following experiment illustrates that we can artificially reverse intention and perception (Libet, 1965). Imagine a brain stimulation experiment in which we ask a subject during open brain surgery to grasp an object. We also place a stimulation electrode above the hand area of the somatosensory cortex. We are assured that stimulating this area induces the same tactile sensation as if the subject would grasp the object. We now activate our stimulation device the very moment our subject grasps the object. Since we bypass the tactile neural pathways and directly stimulate the hand region of the somatosensory cortex, our subject will report a very strange experience: feeling the (artificially induced) tactile sensation *before* actually grasping the object and, when asked to act quickly, even before *deciding* to initiate the grasping act! The inability of identifying a motor act as self-generated can also lead to clinical symptoms, such as delusions of being controlled by an alien force (Frith, 2005).

INTERIM SUMMARY

The ***cerebral cortex*** includes ***primary areas***, which usually process raw sensory data (except in the frontal lobes), and ***association areas***, which are involved in complex mental processes such as perception and thinking. The cortex consists of two hemispheres, each of which has four lobes. The ***occipital lobes*** are involved in vision. The ***parietal lobes*** are involved in the sense of touch, perception of movement and location of objects in space. The ***frontal lobes*** serve a variety of functions, such as coordinating and initiating movement, attention, planning, social skills, abstract thinking, memory and aspects of personality. Sections of the ***temporal lobes*** are important in hearing, language and recognising objects by sight.

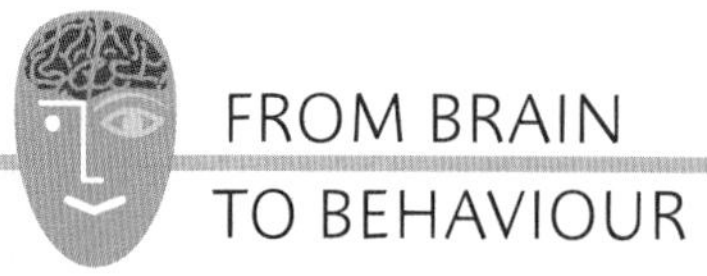

The impact of frontal lobe damage on personality

If damage to the brain can affect such specific functions as language, what can it do to the complex patterns of emotion, thought and behaviour that constitute an individual's personality? Psychologists define personality much as laypeople do, as both a person's reputation (the way people tend to perceive the person) and the enduring psychological attributes (mental processes) that create this reputation. Personality thus includes an individual's characteristic ways of feeling, of thinking about themselves and the world, and of behaving. We hold people responsible for their personalities and tend to associate personality more with the 'mind' or the 'soul' than with the brain. We condemn people for aspects of their personality or character in a way that we do not for intellectual impairment or physical disabilities.

But is personality really so independent of the brain that serves as its biological substrate? Can a damaged brain create a damaged soul for which a person bears no more responsibility than for paralysis caused by a car accident? In fact, damage to parts of the brain can alter personality so that someone literally becomes a different person. Lesions to the frontal lobes provide striking examples.

Patients with frontal lobe damage may become callous, grandiose, boastful, socially inappropriate and unable to understand other people's perspectives (Russell & Roxanas, 1990; Stuss, Gow, & Hetherington, 1992). A famous early report of such symptoms was the case of a construction worker named Phineas Gage. In 1848 an explosion sent a metal bar of more than an inch in diameter through Gage's skull, damaging association areas of his frontal lobes. Previously known as a decent, conscientious man, Gage was described following the accident as childish and irreverent. He was unable to control his impulses and was constantly devising plans that he would abandon within moments (Blumer & Benson, 1984; Damasio, 1994). According to his doctor, the accident disrupted the balance between Gage's intellect and his 'animal propensities'.

Phineas Gage holds the railroad spike that impaled his brain (left). A reconstruction (right) suggests how the spike likely entered Gage's head. After the accident, Gage's personality changed dramatically.

Another broad class of personality alterations associated with frontal lobe lesions includes indifference, apathy and loss of motivation. A 46-year-old man suffered a skull fracture in a car accident and consequently had a portion of his left frontal lobe removed. Although his physical and cognitive abilities returned to normal, his personality changed dramatically. Before the accident, his friends described him as friendly, active in the community, talkative, animated and happy. He was a warm, loving father and husband and a successful salesperson. After his injury, he became quiet, spent most of his time alone smoking and spoke only in response to questions. His altered behaviour makes sense neuropsychologically, since the frontal lobes are involved in initiating activity. The patient spoke in an intelligent but very 'matter of fact' manner, and he was completely indifferent to his wife and children. Eventually the family broke apart (Blumer & Benson, 1984).

ETHICAL DILEMMA

One of your patients recently survived a serious car accident. She suffered severe frontal lobe damage as a result, and was hospitalised for several months. Lately, you have noticed a change in her personality. You witness her making cold-blooded comments towards other patients in the waiting room and notice her displaying socially unconventional behaviours in public. She was recently brought up on criminal charges, and you have been asked to provide an expert character testimony at her court hearing.

- Can you respect the patient's right to confidentiality?
- Is she psychologically responsible for her inappropriate behaviours?

These cases challenge the way most of us intuitively understand ourselves and other people, particularly in the West, where cultural beliefs emphasise personal responsibility and the separation of mind and body (chapter 19). How does a person respond to a once loving spouse or father who no longer seems to care? Is he the same husband or father, or does the same body now house a different person? Is he accountable for the way he behaves? The courts were faced with just such a dilemma in sentencing children who survived encephalitis lethargica, some of whom developed sexual perversions and became sex offenders (Cheyette & Cummings, 1995). As we will see in chapter 11, the moral and philosophical issues become even more complex in the face of evidence that personality is partly innate and that some people are born with a tendency to behave antisocially or indifferently to others.

Cerebral lateralisation

We have seen that the left frontal and temporal lobes tend to play a more important role in speech and language than their right-hemisphere counterparts. This raises the question of whether other cortical functions are ***lateralised*** — that is, localised to one or the other side of the brain.

Global generalisations require caution because most functions that are popularly considered to be lateralised are actually represented on both sides of the brain in most people. However, some division of labour between the hemispheres does exist, with each side dominant for (i.e. in more control of) certain functions.

In general, at least for right-handed people, the left hemisphere tends to be dominant for language, logic, complex motor behaviour and aspects of consciousness (particularly verbal aspects). Many of these left-hemisphere functions are analytical, breaking down thoughts and perceptions into component parts and analysing the relationships among them. The right hemisphere tends to be dominant for non-linguistic functions, such as forming visual maps of the environment. Studies indicate that it is involved in the recognition of faces, places and non-linguistic sounds such as music.

The right hemisphere's specialisation for non-linguistic sounds seems to hold in non-human animals as well. Japanese macaque monkeys, for example, process vocalisations from other macaques on the left but other sounds in their environment on the right (Petersen et al., 1984). Recent research indicates that the region of the brain that constitutes Wernicke's area of the left temporal lobe in humans may have special significance in chimpanzees as well, since this region is larger in the left than in the right hemisphere in chimps, as in humans (Gannon, Holloway, Broadfield, & Braun, 1998).

Split-brain studies

A particularly important source of information about cerebral lateralisation has been case studies of ***split-brain*** patients — individuals whose corpus callosum has been surgically cut, blocking communication between the two hemispheres. Severing this connective tissue is a radical treatment for severe epileptic seizures that spread from one hemisphere to another and cannot be controlled by other means.

In their everyday behaviour, split-brain patients generally appear normal (Sperry, 1984). However, their two hemispheres can actually operate independently, and each may be oblivious to what the other is doing. Under certain experimental circumstances, the disconnection between the two minds housed in one brain becomes apparent.

To understand the results of these experiments, bear in mind that the left hemisphere, which is dominant for most speech functions, receives information from the right visual field and that the right hemisphere receives information from the left. Normally, whether the right or left hemisphere receives the information makes little difference because once the message reaches the brain, the two hemispheres freely pass information between them via the corpus callosum. Severing the corpus callosum, however, blocks this sharing of information (Gazzaniga, 1967).

Figure 3.16a depicts a typical split-brain experiment. A patient is seated at a table, and the surface of the table is blocked from view by a screen so the individual cannot see objects on it. The experimenter asks the person to focus on a point in the centre of the screen. A word (here, *key*) is quickly flashed on the left side of the screen (which is therefore processed in the right hemisphere). When information is flashed for only about 150 milliseconds, the eyes do not have time to move, ensuring that the information is sent to only one hemisphere. The patient is unable to identify the word verbally because the information never reached his left hemisphere, which is dominant for speech. He can, however, select a key with his left hand from the array of objects hidden behind the screen because the left hand receives information from the right hemisphere, which 'saw' the key. Thus, the right hand literally does not know what the left hand is doing, and neither does the left hemisphere. Figure 3.16b illustrates the way visual information from the left and right visual fields is transmitted to the brain in normal and split-brain patients.

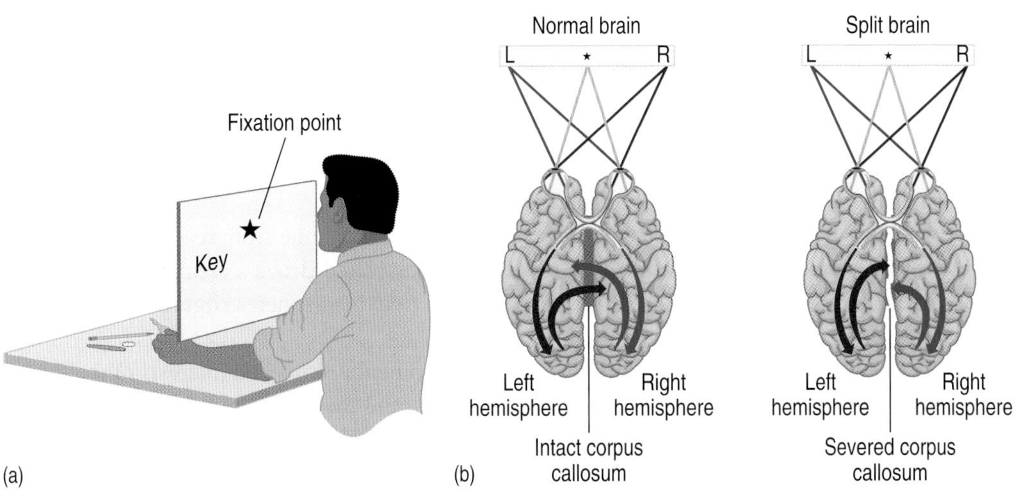

FIGURE 3.16
A split-brain experiment. In a typical split-brain study (a), a patient sees the word *key* flashed on the left portion of the screen. Although he cannot name what he has seen, because speech is lateralised to the left hemisphere, he is able to use his left hand to select the key from a number of objects because the right hemisphere, which has 'seen' the key, controls the left hand and has *some* language skills. Part (b) illustrates the way information from the left and right visual fields is transmitted to the brain in normal and split brains. When participants focus their vision on a point in the middle of the visual field (such as the star in the diagram), anything on the left of this fixation point (for instance, point L) is sensed by receptors on the right half of each eye. This information is subsequently processed by the right hemisphere. In the normal brain, information is readily transmitted via the corpus callosum between the two hemispheres. In the split-brain patient, the severed neural route means the right and left hemispheres 'see' different things.

SOURCE: Part (a) adapted from Gazzaniga (1967).

APPLY + DISCUSS

- If a close friend or roommate had a split brain, would you know?
- If it were not readily apparent, what subtle 'tests' could you perform to find out?
- You might like to watch a brief video clip that documents how the left and right hemispheres of the brain communicate (you should be able to access this via your university course website for this subject).

This research raises an intriguing question: can a person with two independent hemispheres be literally of two minds, with two centres of conscious awareness, like Siamese twins joined at the cortex? Consider the case of a 10-year-old boy with a split brain (LeDoux, Wilson, & Gazzaniga, 1977). In one set of tests, the boy was asked about his sense of himself, his future, and his likes and dislikes. The examiner asked the boy questions in which a word or words were replaced by the word *blank*. The missing words were then presented to one hemisphere or the other. For example, when the boy was asked, 'Who ______?' the missing words 'are you' were projected to the left or the right hemisphere. Not surprisingly, the boy could only answer verbally when enquiries were made to the left hemisphere. The right hemisphere could, however, answer by spelling out words with letter tiles with the left hand (because the right hemisphere is usually not entirely devoid of language) when the question was flashed to the right hemisphere. Thus, the boy could describe his feelings or moods with both hemispheres.

Many times the views expressed by the right and left hemispheres overlapped, but not always. One day, when the boy was in a pleasant mood, his hemispheres tended to agree (e.g. both reported high self-esteem). Another day, when the boy seemed anxious and behaved aggressively, the hemispheres were in disagreement. In general, his right-hemisphere responses were consistently more negative than those of the left, as if the right hemisphere tended to be in a worse mood.

Researchers using other methods have also reported that the two hemispheres differ in their processing of positive and negative emotions and that these differences may exist at birth (Davidson, 1995; Fox, 1991). Left frontal regions are generally more involved in processing positive feelings that motivate approach towards objects in the environment, whereas right frontal regions are more related to negative emotions that motivate avoidance or withdrawal. A patient of one of our colleagues received frontal lobe damage in a horse-riding accident and has unsuccessfully undergone every form of treatment for a severe and deadening depression possible, thus far to no avail. The damage was in the right hemisphere and appears to have destroyed inhibitory mechanisms that normally control right frontal emotional activation.

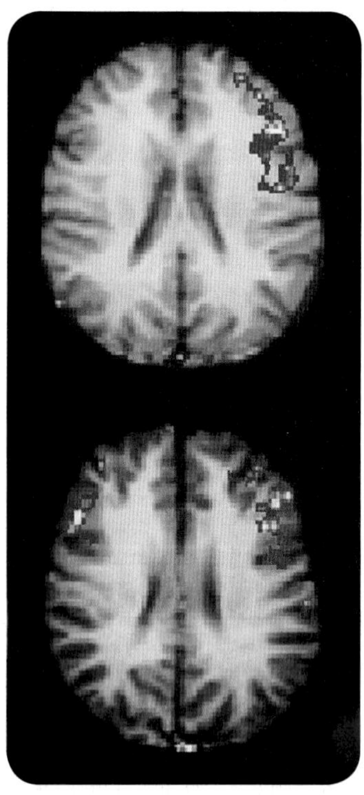

FIGURE 3.17
These composite fMRI images show the distribution of active areas in the brains of males (top) and females during a 'rhyming task'. In males, activation is lateralised (confined) to the left interior frontal regions but in females, the same region is active bilaterally. (From the angle at which these images were taken, left activation appears on the right.)

SOURCE: Shaywitz et al. (1995) NMR Research/Yale Medical School.

Gender differences in lateralisation

Psychologists have long known that females typically score higher on tests of verbal fluency, perceptual speed and manual dexterity than males, whereas males tend to score higher on tests of mathematical ability and spatial processing, particularly geometric thinking (Casey, Nuttall, & Pezaris, 1997; Maccoby & Jacklin, 1974). In a study of students under age 13 with exceptional mathematical ability, boys outnumbered girls 13 to 1 (Benbow & Stanley, 1983). On the other hand, males are much more likely than females to develop learning disabilities with reading and language comprehension.

Although most of these gender differences are not particularly large (Caplan, Crawford, Hyde, & Richardson, 1997; Hyde, 1990), they have been documented in several countries and have not consistently decreased over the last two decades despite social changes encouraging equality of the sexes (see Bradbury, 1989; Randhawa, 1991). Psychologists have thus debated whether such discrepancies in performance might be based in part on innate differences between the brains of men and women.

Some data suggest that women's and men's brains may indeed differ in ways that affect cognitive functioning. At a hormonal level, research with human and non-human primates indicates that the presence of testosterone and estrogen in the bloodstream early in development influences aspects of brain development (Clark & Goldman-Rakic, 1989; Gorski & Barraclough, 1963). One study found that level of exposure to testosterone during the second trimester of pregnancy predicted the speed with which children could rotate mental images in their minds at age seven (Grimshaw, Bryden, & Finegan, 1995). Some evidence even suggests that women's spatial abilities on certain tasks are lower during high-estrogen periods of the menstrual cycle, whereas motor skills, on which females typically have an advantage, are superior during high-estrogen periods (Kimura, 1987).

Perhaps the most definitive data on gender differences in the brain come from research using fMRI technology (Shaywitz et al., 1995). In males, a rhyming task activated Broca's area in the left frontal lobe. The same task in females produced frontal activation in *both* hemispheres (figure 3.17). Thus, in females, language appears less lateralised.

Cultural factors also appear to play a significant role in shaping the skills and interests of males and females (chapter 19). Parents tend to talk to little girls more, and they encourage boys to play with mechanical objects and discourage them from many verbal activities such as writing poetry. Girls also learn early that maths is 'supposed' to be their weak suit and become anxious about their abilities, which can actually lead to worse performance. For example, experimental research shows that telling men and women that their performance on an upcoming maths test will indicate whether they are particularly weak in maths has little influence on men but leads to substantially weaker performance by women (Brown & Josephs, 1999).

Some of the most interesting evidence of the impact of culture comes from a study that followed girls from ages 11 to 18 (Newcombe & Dubas, 1992). The best predictors of spatial ability at age 16 were two psychological attributes at age 11: (1) wishing to be a boy and (2) having a more stereotypically masculine view of what they would like to be. To what extent these psychological attributes themselves could be influenced by biology, however, is unknown.

INTERIM SUMMARY

Some psychological functions are ***lateralised***, or processed primarily by one hemisphere. In general, the left hemisphere is more verbal and analytic, and the right is ***specialised*** for non-linguistic functions. Although the differences tend to be relatively small, males and females tend to differ in cognitive strengths, which appears to be related in part to differences between their brains, including in the extent of lateralisation of functions such as language.

A GLOBAL VISTA

Environment, culture and the brain

The issue of how, and in what ways, cultural practices and beliefs influence cognitive abilities raises an intriguing question: since all abilities reflect the actions of neural circuits, can environmental and cultural factors actually affect the circuitry of the brain?

We have little trouble imagining that biological factors can alter the brain. Tumours, or abnormal tissue growths, can damage regions of the brain by putting pressure on them, leading to symptoms as varied as blurred vision, searing headaches or explosive emotional outbursts. High blood pressure or diseases of the blood vessels can lead to strokes, in which blood flow to regions of the brain is interrupted. If the interruption occurs for more than about 10 minutes, the cells in those areas die, which can result in paralysis, loss of speech or even death if the stroke destroys neural regions vital for life support such as the medulla or hypothalamus. Trauma to the nervous system caused by car accidents, blows to the head or falls that break the neck can have similar effects, as can infections caused by viruses, bacteria or parasites.

But what about psychological blows to the head, or, conversely, experiences that enrich the brain or steer it in one direction or another? In one study, young monkeys that were separated from their mothers for long periods of time developed abnormal electroencephalograms (EEGs), suggesting that social and environmental processes can indeed alter the structure of the brain (Berman, Berman, & Prescott, 1974).

A fascinating line of research indicates that early sensory enrichment or deprivation can affect the brain in fundamental ways (Heritch, Henderson, & Westfall, 1990; Rosenzweig, Bennett, & Diamond, 1972). In one series of studies, young male rats were raised in one of two conditions: an enriched environment, with six to 12 rats sharing an open-mesh cage filled with toys; or an impoverished one, in which rats lived alone without toys or companions (Cummins, Livesey, & Evans, 1977). Days or months later, the experimenters weighed the rats' forebrains. The brains of enriched rats tended to be heavier than those of the deprived rats, indicating that different environments can alter the course of neural development.

Is the same true of humans? And can cultural differences become translated into neurological differences? The human brain triples in weight in the first two years and quadruples to its adult weight by age 14 (Winson, 1985). This means that social, cultural and other environmental influences can become *built into* the brain (Shore, 1997), particularly into the more evolutionarily recent cortical regions involved in complex thought and learning (Damasio, 1994).

APPLY + DISCUSS

In strife-ravaged East Timor, children grew up for years knowing nothing of safety, subjected to constant threats to their lives and families.

- Could these experiences alter the way they think and feel without changing their brains?
- To what extent might chronic danger or loss of a parent alter the brain and literally become part of who a person *physically* is?

For instance, many native Asian language speakers have difficulty distinguishing *la* from *ra* because Asian languages do not distinguish these units of sound. One study found that Japanese people who heard sound frequencies between *la* and *ra* did not hear them as *either la or ra*, as do Australians (Goto, 1971). If children do not hear certain linguistic patterns in the first few years of life (such as the *la–ra* distinction, the French *r*, or the Hebrew *ch*), they may lose the capacity to do so. These patterns may then have to be laid down with different and much less efficient neural machinery later on (Lenneberg, 1967) (see chapter 8).

Brain, gene, behaviour

Having described the structure and function of the nervous system, we conclude with a brief discussion of the influence of genetics on psychological functioning. Few people would argue with the view that hair and eye colour are heavily influenced by genetics or that genetic vulnerabilities contribute to heart disease, cancer and diabetes. Is the same true of psychological qualities or disorders?

Genetics

Psychologists interested in genetics study the influence of genetic blueprints, or genotypes, on observable psychological attributes or qualities, or phenotypes. The phenotypes that interest psychologists are characteristics such as quickness of thought, extroverted behaviour and the tendency to become anxious or depressed. The ***gene*** is the unit of hereditary transmission. Although a single gene may control eye colour, genetic contributions to most complex phenomena, such as intelligence or personality, reflect the action of many genes.

Genes are encoded in the DNA (deoxyribonucleic acid) contained within the nucleus of every cell in the body. Genes are arranged along ***chromosomes*** — strands of paired DNA that spiral around each other. Human cells have 46 chromosomes, except sperm cells in males and egg cells in females, each of which has 23. The union of a sperm and an egg creates a cell with 46 chromosomes, half from the mother and half from the father. Children receive a somewhat random selection of half the genetic material of each parent, which means that the probability that a parent and child will share any particular gene that varies in the population (such as genes for eye colour) is 1 out of 2, or .50. The probability of sharing genes among relatives is termed the ***degree of relatedness***.

Because children and their parents are related and *their* parents are related by .50, the degree of relatedness between grandchildren and grandparents is .25 or .5 × .5. In other words, a grandmother passes on half of her genes to her daughter, who passes on half of those genes to her child; the likelihood that the grandchild receives any particular gene from her maternal grandmother through her mother is thus .25. Siblings are also related by .50 because they have a .25 chance of sharing a gene from their mother and a .25 chance from their father; added together, this means that they are related by .50 on the average. Table 3.3 shows the degree of relatedness for various relatives.

TABLE 3.3 **Degree of relatedness among selected relatives**

Relation	Degree of relatedness
Identical (MZ) twin	1.0
Fraternal (DZ) twin	.50
Parent/child	.50
Sibling	.50
Grandparent/grandchild	.25
Half-sibling	.25
First cousin	.125
Non-biological parent/adopted child	.0

The fact that relatives differ in degree of relatedness enables researchers to tease apart the relative contributions of heredity and environment to phenotypic differences between individuals. If the similarity between relatives on attributes such as intelligence or conscientiousness varies with their degree of relatedness, this suggests genetic influence, especially if the relatives did not share a common upbringing (such as siblings adopted into different families).

Particularly important for research on the genetic basis of behavioural differences are identical and fraternal twins. ***Monozygotic*** **(*MZ*, or *identical*) *twins*** develop from the union of the same sperm and egg. They share the same genetic make-up, so their degree of genetic relatedness is 1.0. In contrast, ***dizygotic*** **(*DZ*, or *fraternal*) *twins*** develop from the union of two sperm with two separate eggs. Like other siblings, their degree of relatedness is .50, since they have a 50 percent chance of sharing the same gene for any characteristic.

Behavioural genetics

A sub-field called behavioural genetics has made rapid advances in our understanding of the relative roles of genetics and environment in shaping mental processes and behaviour (chapter 1). Genetic influences are far greater than once believed in a number of domains, including personality, intelligence and mental illness (Gottesman, 1991; McGue, Bacon, & Lykken, 1993; Plomin, DeFries, McClean, & Rutter, 1997).

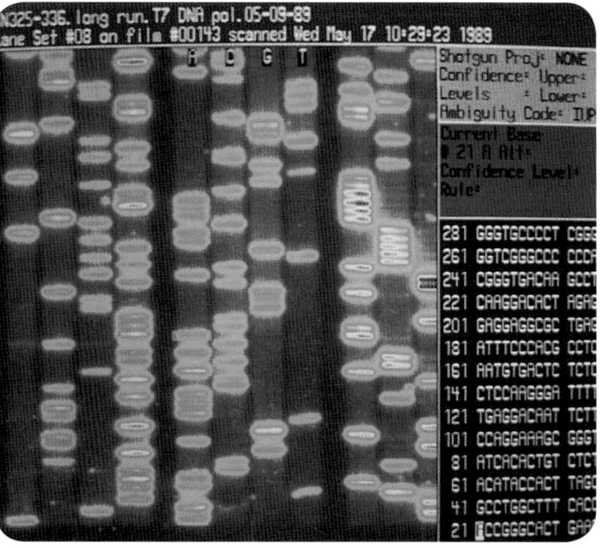

One of the most momentous occasions in the history of science occurred in the first years of the twenty-first century, as scientists working on the Human Genome Project, an international collaborative effort, mapped the genetic structure of all 46 human chromosomes. Although in many respects the most important work lies ahead, mapping the human genome is beginning to allow researchers to discover genes that lead to abnormal cellular responses and contribute to a variety of diseases, from cancer to schizophrenia.

Studies of twins provide psychologists a golden opportunity to examine the role of genetics because MZ and DZ twins typically share similar environments but differ in their degree of genetic relatedness. If a psychological attribute is genetically influenced, MZ twins should be more likely than DZ twins and other siblings to share it. This method is not free of bias; identical twins may receive more similar treatment than fraternal twins, because they look the same. Thus, behavioural geneticists also compare twins reared together in the same family with twins who were adopted separately and reared apart (Loehlin, 1992; Lykken, Bouchard, McGue, & Tellegen, 1992; Tellegen et al., 1988).

Findings from these studies have allowed psychologists to estimate the extent to which differences among individuals on psychological dimensions such as intelligence and personality are inherited or heritable. A ***heritability coefficient*** quantifies the extent to which variation in the trait across individuals (such as high or low levels of conscientiousness) can be accounted for by genetic variation. A coefficient of 0 indicates no heritability at all, while a coefficient of 1.0 indicates that a trait is completely heritable.

An important point — and one that is often misunderstood — is that ***heritability*** refers to genetic influences on variability among individuals; it says nothing about the extent to which a trait is genetically determined. An example makes this clear. The fact that humans have two eyes is genetically determined. For all practical purposes, however, humans show no variability in the expression of the trait of two-eyedness because virtually all humans are born with two eyes. Thus, the heritability of two-eyedness is 0; genetic variability is not correlated with phenotypic or observed variability because virtually no variability exists. In contrast, the trait of eye colour has a very high degree of heritability (approaching 1.0) in a heterogeneous population. Thus, heritability refers to the proportion of variability among individuals on an observed trait (phenotypic variance) that can be accounted for by variability in their genes (genotypic variance).

Genes influence both intellectual functioning (chapter 9) and personality (chapter 11). Several studies of the personality characteristics of twins have produced heritability estimates from .15 to .50 (that is, up to 50 percent heritability) on a broad spectrum of traits, including conservatism, neuroticism, nurturance, assertiveness and aggressiveness (Plomin, DeFries, McClearn, & Rutter, 1997). Some findings have been very surprising and counterintuitive. For example, identical twins reared apart, who may never even have met each other, tend to have very similar vocational interests and levels of job satisfaction (Arvey, McCall, & Bouchard, 1994; Moloney, Bouchard, & Segal, 1991). Researchers have even found a genetic influence on religious attitudes, beliefs and values (Waller, Kojetin, Bouchard, & Lykken, 1990). Remarkably, the likelihood of divorce is influenced by genetics, since personality traits such as the tendency to be unhappy are partly under genetic control and influence life events such as

Identical twins Brett and Josh Morris share a love for rugby league and the skills to play at the highest level of the game, having represented Australia together in recent times.

divorce (Jockin, McGue, & Lykken, 1996). Heritability estimates for IQ are over .50 (McGue & Bouchard, 1998).

In interpreting findings such as these, it is important to remember, as emphasised by leading behavioural geneticists but too readily forgotten, that heritability in the range of 50 percent means that environmental factors are equally important — they account for the other 50 percent (Kandel, 1998). Equally important in understanding heritability is that many genes require environmental input to 'turn them on'; otherwise, they are never expressed. Thus, even though a trait may be highly heritable, whether it even 'shows up' in behaviour may actually depend on the environment. As we will see throughout the book, in most domains, psychologists have become less interested in parcelling out the relative roles of genes and environment than in understanding the way genetic and environmental variables *interact*.

INTERIM SUMMARY

Psychologists interested in genetics study the influence of genetic blueprints (genotypes) on observable qualities (phenotypes). Research in behavioural genetics suggests that a surprisingly large percentage of the variation among individuals on psychological attributes such as intelligence and personality reflects genetic influences, which interact with environmental variables in very complex ways. ***Heritability*** refers to the proportion of variability among individuals on an observed characteristic (phenotypic variance) that can be accounted for by genetic variability (genotypic variance).

Central questions revisited

◆ Brain–behaviour relationships

APPLY + DISCUSS

According to Francis Crick (1993), who won the Nobel Prize for the discovery of DNA, 'You, your joys and your sorrows, your memories and your ambitions, your sense of identity and free will, are in fact no more than the behaviour of a vast assembly of nerve cells and their associated molecules' (p. 3).

- Is Crick correct?

Twenty years ago, a cognitive psychologist with minimal knowledge about the brain could develop hypotheses and design important experiments — because we knew so little about the function of the hippocampus in memory or the role of the frontal lobes in attention and problem solving. Now, we ask participants to rotate mental images in their minds and scan their brains to see where they show the most activation.

Scarcely an area of research in psychology has been left untouched by the explosion of new information about the brain, biology and behavioural genetics. We now know that different memory systems reflect different neural pathways, and we can no longer study 'memory' as if it were one system. And we know that genetic factors contribute substantially to success in school, work and marriage.

Do these new findings mean that psychological experiences are nothing but biological events dressed up in cognitive or emotional clothing? No. The grief of losing a parent or lover is not adequately explained as the activation of neural circuits in the hypothalamus, amygdala and cortex. And the most sophisticated brain-scanning techniques yield little of value if psychologists cannot associate what is happening in the brain with psychologically meaningful processes.

Thus, psychologists are increasingly focusing on brain–behaviour relationships. To study the biological side of human nature is not to commit to an image of a disembodied brain divorced from its psychological, social and cultural context. An understanding of the biological underpinnings of human mental life and behaviour should not *reduce* its richness; it should *add* to it. We have reached a new level of self-understanding, and we can never turn back.

◆

SUMMARY

1 The basic units of the nervous system

- The firing of billions of nerve cells provides the physiological basis for psychological processes.
- ***Neurons***, or nerve cells, are the basic units of the nervous system. ***Sensory neurons*** carry sensory information from sensory receptors to the central nervous system. ***Motor neurons*** transmit commands from the brain to the glands and muscles of the body. ***Interneurons*** connect neurons with one another.
- A neuron typically has a ***cell body***, ***dendrites*** (branch-like extensions of the cell body) and an ***axon*** that carries information to other neurons. Axons are often covered with ***myelin*** for more efficient electrical transmission. Located on the axons are ***terminal buttons***, which contain ***neurotransmitters***, chemicals that transmit information across the ***synapse*** (the space between neurons through which they communicate).
- The 'resting' voltage at which a neuron is not firing is called the ***resting potential***. When a neuron stimulates another neuron, it either depolarises the membrane (reducing its polarisation) or hyperpolarises it (increasing its polarisation). The spreading voltage changes that occur when the neural membrane receives signals from other cells are called ***graded potentials***. If enough depolarising graded potentials accumulate to cross a threshold, the neuron will fire. This ***action potential***, or nerve impulse, leads to the release of neurotransmitters (such as glutamate, GABA, dopamine, serotonin and acetylcholine). These chemical messages are received by ***receptors*** in the cell membrane of other neurons, which in turn can excite or inhibit those neurons. Modulatory neurotransmitters can increase or reduce the impact of other neurotransmitters released into the synapse.

2 The endocrine system

- The ***endocrine system*** is a collection of glands that control various bodily functions through the secretion of ***hormones***. The endocrine system complements the cell-to-cell communication of the nervous system by sending global messages through the bloodstream.

3 The peripheral nervous system

- The ***peripheral nervous system (PNS)*** consists of neurons that carry messages to and from the central nervous system. The peripheral nervous system has two subdivisions: the somatic nervous system and the autonomic nervous system. The ***somatic nervous system*** consists of the sensory neurons that receive information through sensory receptors in the skin, muscles and other parts of the body, such as the eyes, and the motor neurons that direct the action of skeletal muscles. The ***autonomic nervous system*** controls basic life processes such as the beating of the heart, workings of the digestive system and breathing. It consists of two parts, the ***sympathetic nervous system***, which is activated in response to threats, and the ***parasympathetic nervous system***, which returns the body to normal and works to maintain the body's energy resources.

4 The central nervous system

- The ***central nervous system (CNS)*** consists of the brain and spinal cord. It is hierarchically organised, with an overall structure that follows its evolution. Centres that have evolved more recently regulate many of the processes that occur at lower levels.
- Aside from carrying out ***reflexes***, the ***spinal cord*** transmits sensory information to the brain and transmits messages from the brain to the muscles and organs.
- Several structures comprise the ***hindbrain***. The ***medulla oblongata*** controls vital physiological functions, such as heartbeat, circulation and respiration, and forms a link between the spinal cord and the rest of the brain. The ***cerebellum*** appears to be involved in a variety of tasks, including learning, discriminating stimuli from one another and coordinating smooth movements. The ***reticular formation*** maintains consciousness and helps regulate activity and arousal states throughout the central nervous system, including sleep cycles.
- The ***midbrain*** consists of the tectum and tegmentum. The ***tectum*** includes structures involved in orienting to visual and auditory stimuli as well as others involved in linking unpleasant feelings to behaviours that can help the animal escape or avoid them. The ***tegmentum*** includes parts of the reticular formation and other nuclei with a variety of functions, of which two are particularly important: movement and the linking of pleasure to behaviours that help the animal to obtain reward.
- The ***forebrain*** consists of the hypothalamus, thalamus and cerebrum. The ***hypothalamus*** is involved in regulating a wide range of behaviours, including eating, sleeping, sexual activity and emotional experience. The ***thalamus*** is a complex of nuclei that perform a number of functions; one of the most important is to process arriving sensory information and transmit this information to higher brain centres.
- The ***cerebrum*** includes a number of ***subcortical structures*** as well as an outer layer, or ***cortex***. The subcortical structures are the limbic system and the basal ganglia. Structures of the ***limbic system*** (the septal area, ***amygdala*** and ***hippocampus***) are involved in emotion, motivation, learning and memory. ***Basal ganglia*** structures are involved in movement, mood and memory.
- In humans, the ***cerebral cortex*** allows the flexible construction of sequences of voluntary movements, enables people to discriminate complex sensory patterns, and provides the capacity to think symbolically. The ***primary areas*** of the cortex receive sensory information and initiate motor movements. The ***association areas*** are involved in putting together perceptions, ideas and plans.
- The right and left hemispheres of the cerebral cortex are connected by the ***corpus callosum***. Each hemisphere consists of four sections or lobes. The ***occipital lobes*** are specialised for vision. The ***parietal lobes*** are involved in a number of functions, including the sense of touch, movement and the experience of one's own body and other objects in space. The functions of the ***frontal lobes*** include coordination of movement, attention, planning, social skills, conscience, abstract thinking, memory and aspects of personality. Sections of the ***temporal lobes*** are important in hearing, language and visual object recognition. Some psychological functions are lateralised, or primarily processed by one hemisphere.
- Cultural and environmental factors can modify not only behaviour but also the structure of the brain.

5 Genetics and environment

- Environment and genes interact in staggeringly complex ways that psychologists are just beginning to understand. Psychologists interested in genetics study the influence of genetic blueprints (genotypes) on observable psychological attributes or qualities (phenotypes). Studies in behavioural genetics suggest that a substantial portion of the variation among individuals on many psychological attributes such as intelligence and personality is ***heritable***. Heritability refers to the proportion of variability among individuals on an observed trait (phenotypic variance) that can be accounted for by variability in their genes (genotypic variance).

KEY TERMS

acetylcholine (ACh), *p. 95*
action potential, *p. 91*
adrenal glands, *p. 96*
adrenaline, *p. 96*
amygdala, *p. 106*
association areas, *p. 109*
autonomic nervous system, *p. 97*
axon, *p. 89*
basal ganglia, *p. 107*
Broca's area, *p. 112*
cell body, *p. 89*
central nervous system (CNS), *p. 96*
cerebellum, *p. 104*
cerebral cortex, *p. 109*
cerebral hemispheres, *p. 110*
cerebrum, *p. 100*
chromosomes, *p. 118*
corpus callosum, *p. 110*
cortex, *p. 100*
degree of relatedness, *p. 118*
dendrites, *p. 89*
dizygotic (DZ, *or* fraternal) twins, *p. 119*
dopamine, *p. 94*
endocrine system, *p. 96*
endorphins, *p. 95*
estrogens, *p. 96*
forebrain, *p. 105*
frontal lobes, *p. 110*
GABA, *p. 94*
gene, *p. 118*
glutamate, *p. 94*
gonads, *p. 96*
graded potentials, *p. 91*
heritability, *p. 119*
heritability coefficient, *p. 119*
hindbrain, *p. 103*
hippocampus, *p. 107*
hormones, *p. 96*
hypothalamus, *p. 105*
interneurons, *p. 89*
lateralised, *p. 114*
limbic system, *p. 106*
medulla oblongata *or* medulla, *p. 104*
midbrain, *p. 104*
monozygotic (MZ, *or* identical) twins, *p. 119*
motor cortex, *p. 110*
motor neurons, *p. 89*
myelin sheath, *p. 89*
nervous system, *p. 88*
neurons, *p. 89*
neurotransmitters, *p. 93*
noradrenaline, *p. 96*
occipital lobes, *p. 110*
parasympathetic nervous system, *p. 98*
parietal lobes, *p. 110*
Parkinson's disease, *p. 94*
peripheral nervous system (PNS), *p. 96*
pituitary gland, *p. 96*
primary areas, *p. 109*
receptors, *p. 93*
reflexes, *p. 100*
resting potential, *p. 91*
reticular formation, *p. 104*
sensory neurons, *p. 89*
serotonin, *p. 95*
somatic nervous system, *p. 97*
somatosensory cortex, *p. 110*
spinal cord, *p. 102*
split brain, *p. 115*
subcortical structures, *p. 105*
sympathetic nervous system, *p. 97*
synapses, *p. 90*
tectum, *p. 104*
tegmentum, *p. 104*
temporal lobes, *p. 112*
terminal buttons, *p. 90*
testosterone, *p. 96*
thalamus, *p. 105*
thyroid gland, *p. 96*
Wernicke's area, *p. 112*

REVIEW QUESTIONS

1. Describe the functions of the three kinds of neurons.
2. Describe how the 'firing of a neuron' or an action potential works.
3. Describe how a nerve impulse is transmitted down the axon.
4. Define the role of neurotransmitters and explain the psychological functions of the following neurotransmitters: glutamate, GABA, dopamine, serotonin, acetylcholine and endorphins.
5. Describe the functions of the following endocrine glands: pituitary gland, thyroid gland, adrenal glands and gonads.
6. Distinguish between the functions of the somatic and autonomic nervous systems.

DISCUSSION QUESTIONS

1. How does the design of the human nervous system reflect its evolution?
2. What are the effects of recurring injuries to the cerebellum?
3. Can a brain lesion bring about a change in your personality?

APPLICATION QUESTIONS

1. In each of the following hypothetical examples, an individual has suffered an injury to some area of the brain. Try to determine where the injury may be.
   (a) Following a motorbike accident in which his head brutally struck the bitumen road, a man has poor control of his motor actions and sometimes displays jerky movements. He is not able to recognise when others are being cynical or sarcastic.
   (b) A boy was climbing a tree with his friend when he fell and hit his head. Before long, he was complaining of blurred vision. A visit to the optometrist showed no physiological evidence of defects in his eyes.
   (c) Following a stroke, a patient has difficulty holding a conversation with her friends. Although she knows what she wants to say, she has difficulty articulating her ideas and cannot put the right words together in a sentence.
2. You are shopping in the supermarket and see a friend down the aisle in front of you. You call out to him but he does not hear you, so you run to catch up with him before he goes through the checkout. Explain how the different lobes of the cortex are involved in this event.
3. Draw a map showing the divisions of the nervous system. Include the following sections: amygdala, autonomic nervous system, basal ganglia, brain, central nervous system, cerebral cortex, cerebellum, forebrain, hindbrain, hippocampus, hypothalamus, limbic system, medulla, midbrain, parasympathetic nervous system, peripheral nervous system, pons, septal area, somatic nervous system, spinal cord, sympathetic nervous system, tectum, tegmentum, thalamus.

4. Match the term with the correct description:

Term	Function
Amygdala	Abstract thinking, planning, and social skills
Broca's area	Necessary for speech production
Cerebellum	Controls vision
Frontal lobe	Touch, spatial orientation, and non-verbal thinking
Hippocampus	Receives sensory information
Hypothalamus	Language, hearing, and visual pattern recognition
Limbic system	Coordinates movement
Medulla	Speech comprehension
Midbrain	A relay centre
Occipital lobes	Involved in remembering emotionally significant events
Parietal lobes	Responsible for emotions, motivation, learning and memory
Somatosensory cortex	Controls basic life functions
Temporal lobe	Necessary for storing new memories
Thalamus	Helps regulates behaviour
Wernicke's area	Consists of the tectum and the tegmentum

The solutions to the application questions can be found on pages 833–4.

MULTIMEDIA RESOURCES

The *Cyberpsych* multimedia resource is available *as an option* to accompany this textbook to further develop your understanding of many key psychology concepts. *Cyberpsych* contains a wealth of rich media content and activities, and for this chapter includes:

- video clips on appetite, skin cells, genomes, the brain and learning
- a video case study on the topic of addiction
- an interactive module on the components of the brain
- a concept animation on the relationship between alcohol, neurotransmitters and the brain.

Sensation and perception

4

LEARNING OBJECTIVES

After studying this chapter you should be able to:

1 outline the three basic principles that apply across all senses

2 describe the processes common to all sensory systems

3 explain how light wavelengths are transformed into vision and colour

4 explain how sound waves are transformed into hearing

5 distinguish among the main functions of smell, taste, touch and the vestibular and kinaesthetic systems

6 describe the various ways in which perception is organised.

Basic principles

- ***Sensation*** is the process by which sense organs gather information about the environment and transmit it to the brain for initial processing.
- ***Perception*** is the process by which the brain selects, organises and interprets sensations.
- Three basic principles apply across all senses:
  (a) there is no one-to-one correspondence between physical and psychological reality
  (b) sensation and perception are active, not passive
  (c) sensory and perceptual processes reflect the impact of adaptive pressures over the course of evolution.

Hearing

- Sound travels in ***waves***, which occur as a vibrating object sets air particles in motion. The sound wave's ***frequency***, which is experienced as ***pitch***, refers to the number of times those particles oscillate per second. The loudness of a sound reflects the height and depth, or ***amplitude***, of the wave.
- Sound waves travel through the auditory canal to the ***eardrum***, which in turn sets the ossicles in motion, amplifying the sound. Transduction of sound occurs in the ear — the outer ear collects and magnifies sounds in the air; the middle ear converts waves of air pressure into movements of tiny bones; and the inner ear transforms these movements into waves in fluid that generate neural signals.
- From the auditory nerve, sensory information passes through the inferior colliculus in the midbrain and the medial geniculate nucleus of the thalamus on to the auditory cortex in the temporal lobes.

Vision

- Light is just one form of electromagnetic radiation, but it is a form to which the eye is sensitive.
- Two basic processes occur in the eyes:
  (a) light is focused on the ***retina*** by the ***cornea***, ***pupil*** and ***lens***
  (b) the retina transduces this visual image into a code that the brain can read.
- From the optic nerve, visual information travels along two pathways. One is the superior colliculus in the midbrain, which in humans is particularly involved in eye movements. The other is the lateral geniculate nucleus in the thalamus and on to the visual cortex. Beyond the primary visual cortex, visual information flows along two pathways (***'what' pathway*** and ***'where' pathway***).
- According to the ***Young–Helmholtz*** or ***trichromatic*** theory, the eye contains three types of receptors that are most sensitive to wavelengths experienced as red, green or blue. According to the ***opponent-process theory***, the colours we experience (and after-images we perceive) reflect three antagonistic colour systems — a blue–yellow, red–green and black–white system.

Other senses

- Transduction of smell, or ***olfaction***, occurs in the ***olfactory epithelium***, a thin pair of structures at the top of the nasal cavities.
- Transduction of taste occurs in the ***taste buds*** distributed throughout the mouth and throat.
- The ***proprioceptive*** senses (such as the ***vestibular sense*** and ***kinaesthesia***) register body position and movement.

Sensing the environment

- *Transduction* is the process of converting stimulus information into neural impulses.
- The *absolute threshold* is the minimum amount of energy needed for an observer to sense that a stimulus is present.
- The *difference threshold* is the lowest level of stimulation required to sense that a change in stimulation has occurred.
- *Sensory adaptation* is the tendency of sensory systems to respond less to stimuli that continue without change.

Perception

- *Perceptual organisation* integrates sensations into percepts, locates them in space and preserves their meaning as the perceiver examines them from different vantage points.
- There are four aspects of perceptual organisation: *form perception*, depth or *distance perception*, *motion perception* and *perceptual constancy*.
- *Perceptual interpretation* involves generating meaning from sensory experience.
- Perceptual interpretation lies at the intersection of sensation and memory, as the brain interprets current sensations in the light of past experience.
  - *Bottom-up processing* emphasises the role of sensory data in shaping perception.
  - *Top-down processing* emphasises the influence of prior experience on perception.

Central questions: physical reality and psychological reality

- Our sensory systems and perceptual processes reflect the combination of nature and nurture.

A WOMAN in her early twenties damaged her knee in a fall. Following surgery, she experienced sharp, burning pain so excruciating that she could not eat or sleep. The pain ran from her ankle to the middle of her thigh, and the slightest touch — even a light brush with a piece of cotton — provoked a feeling of intense burning. Surgical attempts to relieve her pain gave her no relief or only temporary relief followed by even more severe pain (Gracely, Lynch, & Bennett, 1992).

Another case had a happier ending. A 50-year-old man whose chronic back pain failed to respond to exercise and medication finally underwent surgery. Like roughly 1 percent of patients who undergo this procedure (Sachs, Zindrick, & Beasley, 1993), he, too, developed severe burning pain and extraordinary sensitivity to any kind of stimulation of the skin. Fortunately, however, the pain disappeared after three months of treatment.

These patients suffered from a disorder called painful neuropathy, which literally means a painful illness of the neurons. Painful neuropathy can result from either an accident or surgery. What happens is that the brain interprets signals from receptors in the skin or joints that normally indicate light touch, pressure or movement as excruciating pain.

More recently, research suggests that up to 60 percent of breast cancer patients receiving taxane therapy (i.e. chemotherapeutic drugs) experience symptoms such as numbness, tingling, burning and pain (Wampler, Hamolsky, Hamel, Melisko, & Topp, 2004). Similarly, painful diabetic neuropathy is commonly experienced by diabetics — affecting many aspects of their daily lives, including mood, sleep and interpersonal relationships, among others (Huizinga & Peltier, 2007). For example, a 52-year-old diabetic experiences sharp and needle-like pain when he stands. He also experiences pain with any touch, including fabric, on his skin.

This syndrome raises some intriguing questions about the way the nervous system translates information about the world into psychological experience. Does the intensity of sensory experience normally mirror the intensity of physical stimulation? In other words, when pain increases or the light in a theatre seems extremely bright following a movie, how much does this reflect changes in reality versus changes in our *perception* of reality? And if neurons can become accidentally rewired so that touch is misinterpreted as burning pain, could attaching neurons from the ear to the primary cortex of the occipital lobes produce visual images of sound?

Questions such as these are central to the study of sensation and perception. ***Sensation*** refers to the process by which the sense organs gather information about the environment and transmit this information to the brain for initial processing. ***Perception*** is the process by which the brain organises and interprets these sensations. Sensations are immediate experiences of qualities — red, hot, bright and so on — whereas perceptions are experiences of objects or events that appear to have form, order or meaning (figure 4.1). The distinction between sensation and perception is useful, though somewhat artificial, because sensory and perceptual processes form an integrated whole, translating physical reality into psychological reality.

(a)

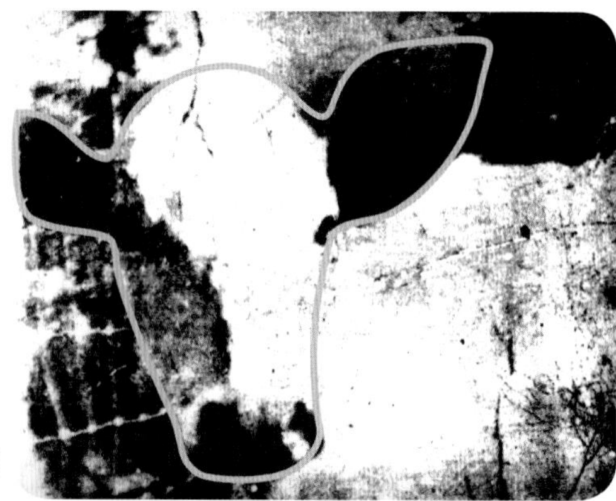
(b)

FIGURE 4.1
From sensation to perception. Take a careful look at the photo on the left before reading further, and try to figure out what it depicts. When people first look at the photo on the left, their eyes transmit information to the brain about which parts of the picture are white and which are black; this is sensation. Sorting out the pockets of white and black into a meaningful picture is perception. The photograph makes little sense until you recognise a cow, facing the viewer, as shown in the photo on the right.

SOURCE: Courtesy Optometric Extension Program Foundation, Santa Ana, CA, www.oepf.org.

Why do sensation and perception matter? When students first approach this topic, they often think, 'Oh, that rods-and-cones stuff I learned in fifth grade', and wonder what it has to do with psychology. What draws many students to psychology are questions such as how memory works and why people fall in love. It is only years later that a simple and obvious fact becomes clear: sensation and perception constitute the gateway from the world to our imagination.

Memory involves the mental reconstruction of past experience (chapter 7) — but what would we remember if we could not sense, perceive and store images or sounds to re-create in our minds? Consider love. What would love be if we could not feel another person's skin against ours? Could lovers experience the sense of comfort and security they feel when they mould into each other's arms if the skin were not laden with pressure detectors? (Okay, it isn't Shakespeare, but you get the point.) Without our senses, we are literally senseless — without the capacity to know or feel. And without knowledge or feeling, there is little left to being human.

We begin the chapter with sensation, exploring basic processes that apply to all the senses (or sensory modalities — the different senses that provide ways of knowing about stimuli). We then discuss each sense individually, focusing on the two that allow sensation at a distance, vision and hearing (or audition), and more briefly exploring smell (olfaction), taste (gustation), touch and proprioception (the sense of the body's position and motion). Next we turn to perception, beginning with the way the brain organises and interprets sensations and concluding with the influence of experience, expectations and needs on the way people make sense of sensations.

Throughout, we address two central questions. First, to what extent is our knowledge of the world *given by* our experiences or *constructed from* our experiences? In other words, does reality impress itself on our senses, so that we have no choice but to see things as they are, or does it merely provide the raw materials from which we piece together an internal 'map' of the world outside us?

Second, and related, is the question of the extent to which we are born with ways of viewing reality or have to discover them through experience. Do people learn to organise visual sensations into three-dimensional shapes or does our brain automatically experience the world in three dimensions? Does an x-ray of a finger actually give rise to a radiologist having sensations or perceptions that are different from a patient's, or does the radiologist just notice aspects of the x-ray that the patient is not trained to see as meaningful?

INTERIM SUMMARY

Sensation is the process by which sense organs gather information about the environment and transmit it to the brain for initial processing. ***Perception*** is the related process by which the brain selects, organises and interprets sensations.

Central questions

- To what extent is our knowledge of the world *given* by our experience or *constructed* from our experience?
- To what extent are we born with ways of viewing reality?

Basic principles

Throughout this discussion, three general principles repeatedly emerge. First, there is no one-to-one correspondence between physical and psychological reality. What is 'out there' is not directly reproduced 'in here'. Of course, the relationship between physical stimuli and our psychological experience of them is not random; as we will see, it is actually so orderly that it can be expressed as an equation.

Yet the inner world is not simply a photograph of the outer. The degree of pressure or pain experienced when a pin presses against the skin — even in those of us *without* painful neuropathy — does not precisely match the actual pressure exerted. Up to a certain point, light pressure is not experienced at all, and pressure only feels like pain when it crosses a certain threshold. The inexact correspondence between physical and psychological reality is one of the fundamental findings of ***psychophysics***, the branch of psychology that studies the relationship between attributes of the physical world and our psychological experience of them.

Sensation is an active process in which humans, like other animals, focus their senses on potentially important information.

Second, sensation and perception are active processes. Sensation may seem passive — images are cast on the retina at the back of the eye; pressure is imposed on the skin. Yet sensation is first and foremost an act of translation, converting external energy into an internal version, or *representation*, of it. People also orient themselves to stimuli to capture sights, sounds and smells that are relevant to them. We turn our ears towards potentially threatening sounds to magnify their impact on our senses, just as we turn our noses towards the smell of baking bread. We also selectively focus our consciousness on parts of the environment that are particularly relevant to our needs and goals (chapter 5).

Like sensation, perception is an active process: it organises and interprets sensations. The world as subjectively experienced by an individual — the phenomenological world — is a joint product of external reality and the person's creative efforts to understand and depict it mentally. People often assume that perception is like photographing a scene or tape recording a sound and that they need only open their eyes and ears to capture what is 'really' there. In fact, perception is probably more like stitching a quilt than taking a photograph. The phenomenological world must be constructed from sensory experience, just as the quilt maker creates something whole from thread and patches.

If perception is a creative, constructive process, to what extent do people perceive the world in the same way? Does red appear to one person as it does to another? If one person loves garlic and another hates it, are the two loving and hating the same taste, or does garlic have a different taste to each? To what extent do people see the world the way it really is?

Plato argued that what we perceive is little more than shadows on the wall of a cave, cast by the movement of an unseen reality in the dim light. What does it mean to say that a cup of coffee is hot? Relative to what? Do fish perceive the depths of the ocean as cold? And is grass *really* green? A person who is colour blind for green, whose visual system is unable to discriminate certain wavelengths of light, will not see the grass as green. Is greenness, then, an attribute of the object (grass), the perceiver, or some interaction between them? These are philosophical questions at the heart of sensation and perception.

APPLY + DISCUSS

- In what ways might an innate (inborn) tendency to pay attention to faces foster adaptation in human infants?

The third general principle is that sensation and perception are adaptive. From an evolutionary perspective, the ability to see, hear or touch is the product of millions of adaptations that left our senses exquisitely crafted to serve functions that facilitate survival and reproduction (Tooby & Cosmides, 1992). Frogs have 'bug detectors' in their visual systems that automatically fire in the presence of a potential meal. Similarly, humans have neural regions specialised for the perception of faces and facial expressions (Adolphs, Damasio, Tranel, & Damasio, 1996; Phillips et al., 1997). Human infants have an innate tendency to pay attention to forms that resemble the human face, and over the course of their first year they become remarkably expert at reading emotions from other people's faces (chapter 12).

INTERIM SUMMARY

Three basic principles apply across all the senses. There is no one-to-one correspondence between physical and psychological reality; sensation and perception are active, not passive; and sensory and perceptual processes reflect the impact of adaptive pressures over the course of evolution.

Sensing the environment

Although each sensory system is attuned to particular forms of energy, all the senses share certain common features. First, they must translate physical stimulation into sensory signals. Second, they all have thresholds below which a person does not sense anything despite external stimulation. Children know this intuitively when they tiptoe through a room to 'sneak up' on someone — who may suddenly hear them and turn around. The tiptoeing sounds increase gradually in intensity as the child approaches, but the person senses nothing until the sound crosses a threshold.

Third, sensation requires constant decision making, as the individual tries to distinguish meaningful from irrelevant stimulation. We are unaware of most of these sensory 'decisions' because they occur rapidly and unconsciously. Alone at night, people often wonder, 'Did I hear something?' Their answers depend not only on the intensity of the sound but also on their tendency to attach meaning to small variations in sound.

Fourth, sensing the world requires the ability to detect changes in stimulation — to notice when a bag of groceries has gotten heavier or a light has dimmed. Fifth and finally, efficient sensory processing means 'turning down the volume' on information that is redundant; the nervous system tunes out messages that continue without change. We examine each of these processes in turn.

Transduction

Sensation requires converting energy in the world into internal signals that are psychologically meaningful (Julius & King, 2005). The more the brain processes these signals — from sensation to perception to cognition — the more meaningful they become. Sensation typically begins with an environmental stimulus, a form of energy capable of exciting the nervous system. We actually register only a tiny fraction of the energy surrounding us, and different species have evolved the capacity to process different types of information. Honeybees, for example, can sense the Earth's magnetic field and re-locate important landmarks, such as places they have found food, by their compass coordinates (Collett & Baron, 1994; see also Collett, Harland, & Collett, 2002).

Creating a neural code

Specialised cells in the nervous system, called ***sensory receptors***, transform energy in the environment into neural impulses that can be interpreted by the brain (Loewenstein, 1960; Miller, Ratliff, & Hartline, 1961). Receptors respond to different forms of energy and generate action potentials in sensory neurons adjacent to them. In the eye, receptors respond to particles of light; in the ear, to the movement of molecules of air.

The process of converting physical energy or stimulus information into neural impulses is called ***transduction***. The brain then interprets the impulses generated by sensory receptors as light, sound, smell, taste, touch or motion. It reads a neural code — a pattern of neural firing — and translates it into a psychologically meaningful 'language'.

In 1826, Johannes Müller proposed the doctrine of specific nerve energies, which suggests that whether a neural message is experienced as light, sound or some other sensation results less from differences in stimuli than from the particular neurons excited by them. Müller's hypothesis is bolstered by reports of syndromes such as painful neuropathy. If a cotton ball produces a sensation of burning instead of a light touch, this means that sensory receptors may have been rewired to different neural fibres.

Extending and revising Müller's doctrine, psychologists now recognise that the nature of a sensation depends on the pathways in the brain that it activates. Electrical stimulation of the primary visual cortex produces visual sensations as surely as shining a light in the eye, whereas electrical stimulation of the auditory cortex produces sensations experienced as sound. The stimulus may be the same — electrical current — but the pathways are different.

Coding for intensity and quality of the stimulus

For each sense, the brain codes sensory stimulation for intensity and quality. The neural code for intensity, or strength, of a sensation varies by sensory modality but usually involves the number of sensory neurons that fire, the frequency with which they fire, or some combination of the two. The neural code for quality of the sensation (such as colour, pitch, taste or temperature) is often more complicated, relying on both the specific type of receptors involved and the pattern of neural impulses generated. For example, some receptors respond to warmth and others to cold, but a combination of both leads to the sensation of extreme heat. Remarkably, the brain synthesises millions of simple on-off decisions (made by sensory neurons that receive information from receptors and either fire or do not fire) to perceive the lines and shapes of a Brett Whitely painting or words on a printed page. It does this so quickly and automatically that we are unaware of anything but the end product.

INTERIM SUMMARY

Sensation begins with an environmental stimulus; all sensory systems have specialised cells called ***sensory receptors*** that respond to environmental stimuli and typically generate action potentials in adjacent sensory neurons. The process of converting stimulus information into neural impulses is called ***transduction***. Within each sensory modality, the brain codes sensory stimulation for intensity and quality.

Absolute thresholds

APPLY + DISCUSS

On your university course website for this subject you should be able to watch a video developed by Gary Fisk about absolute thresholds.

- What is an absolute threshold?
- What is the difference threshold?

Even if a sensory system has the capacity to respond to a stimulus, the individual may not experience the stimulus if it is too weak. The minimum amount of physical energy needed for an observer to notice a stimulus is called an ***absolute threshold***. One way psychologists measure absolute thresholds is by presenting a particular stimulus (light, sound, taste, odour, pressure) at varying intensities and determining the level of stimulation necessary for the person to detect it about 50 percent of the time.

A psychologist trying to identify the absolute threshold for sound of a particular pitch would present participants with sounds at that pitch, some so soft they would never hear them and others so loud they would never miss them. In between would be sounds they would hear some or most of the time. The volume at which most participants hear the sound half the time but miss it half the time is defined as the absolute threshold; above this point, people sense stimulation most of the time. The thresholds for the key senses are (Brown, Galanter, Hess, & Mandler, 1962):

- *hearing:* the ticking of a watch six metres away in a quiet place
- *smell:* one drop of perfume in a large house
- *taste:* one teaspoon of sugar dissolved in 10 litres of water
- *touch:* the wing of a fly falling on the cheek from a height of one centimetre
- *vision:* the flame of a candle 50 kilometres away on a dark, clear night.

APPLY + DISCUSS

- To what extent does a perceiver skilled in detecting the presence of enemy missiles actually *perceive* what a layperson would not see?
- How does the skilled perceiver recognise the signal in a sea of noise? What changes with perceptual practice and learning?

Despite the 'absolute' label, absolute thresholds vary from person to person and situation to situation. One reason for this variation is the presence of noise, which technically refers to irrelevant, distracting information (not just to loud sounds). Some noise is external; to pick out the ticking of a watch at a concert is far more difficult than in a quiet room. Other noise is internal, created by the random firing of neurons. Psychological events such as expectations, motivation, stress and level of fatigue can also affect the threshold at which a person can sense a low level of stimulation (see Fehm-Wolfsdorf et al., 1993; Pause, Bernfried, Krauel, Fehm-Wolfsdorf, & Ferstl, 1996). Someone whose home has been burgled, for example, is likely to be highly attuned to night-time sounds and to 'hear' suspicious noises more readily, whether or not they actually occur.

Signal detection

Is the absolute threshold, then, really absolute? Or perhaps sensation at low levels of stimulation actually requires the detection of a stimulus against a background of noise (Greene & Swets, 1966; Swets, 1992). According to ***signal detection theory***, sensation is not a passive process that occurs when the amount of stimulation exceeds a critical threshold; rather, experiencing a sensation means making a judgement about whether a stimulus is present or absent.

Does a noise downstairs, a blip on a radar screen or a small irregularity on a brain scan signal something dangerous? According to signal detection theory, two distinct processes are at work in detection tasks of this sort. The first is an initial sensory process, reflecting the observer's sensitivity to the stimulus — how well the person sees, hears or feels the stimulus. The second is a decision process, reflecting the observer's ***response bias*** (or decision criterion) — that is, the individual's readiness to report detecting a stimulus when uncertain.

Assessing response bias

To assess response bias, signal detection researchers present participants with stimuli at low intensities, as in the traditional procedure for measuring absolute thresholds, but they add trials with *no* stimulus presented. What participants experience on each trial is some mixture of stimulus energy (the signal), which may or may not be present, and noise, which randomly waxes and wanes. Sometimes the noise alone is enough to lead the person to say she heard or saw something because its effect crosses the decision criterion. At other times, the signal is present but too weak to be detected, and the noise level is too low to augment it. At still other times, noise, when added to a signal, increases the intensity of the signal enough to lead the participant to report a sensation (figure 4.2).

Participants in signal detection experiments can make two kinds of error. They may respond with a false alarm, reporting a stimulus when none was presented, or they may fail to report an actual stimulus (a miss). Similarly, they may give two kinds of correct response. They may hit, reporting an actual stimulus, or they may declare a correct negative, reporting no stimulus when none was presented. Accuracy in sensing a signal involves a trade-off between sensitivity to stimuli that are presented and vulnerability to reporting stimuli that have not been presented. Thus, an observer who tends to over-report sensations will have a high number of hits but also a high number of false alarms. An observer who tends to underreport will have a lower number of hits but also a lower number of false alarms.

	You say 'Yes'	You say 'No'
Signal is present	Hit	Miss
Signal is not present	False alarm	Correct rejection

FIGURE 4.2
Is the signal really there in signal detection experiments?

Factors affecting response bias

Whether a person has a low or high response bias for reporting 'yes' depends on many factors. One is expectations. If a patient complains of heart pain, shooting pain in his legs and shortness of breath, his doctor is more likely to hear an irregular heartbeat. Another factor that influences response bias is motivation. Two neurologists who review the MRI scan of a woman experiencing blinding headaches may come to different conclusions about a possible irregularity. The neurologist who recently lost a patient by mistaking a tumour for noise will have a low threshold for reporting 'yes' because the psychological cost of setting it higher is too great. The other, who recently performed exploratory surgery when in fact no tumour was present and accidentally left the patient with partial blindness, will have a much higher threshold for reporting a 'hit'.

To distinguish the relative contributions of sensitivity and response bias, psychologists experimentally manipulate the costs and benefits of over- or under-reporting stimulation by paying participants different amounts for different types of correct or incorrect responses (figure 4.3). These consequences can be described in a pay-off matrix, which shows the costs and benefits of each type of response. Researchers then plot the proportion of hits against the proportion of false alarms on a receiver operating characteristic (ROC) curve, which literally shows the way the receiver of the signal operates at different signal intensities. This allows the researcher to determine how well the participant can actually sense the stimulus, independent of response bias.

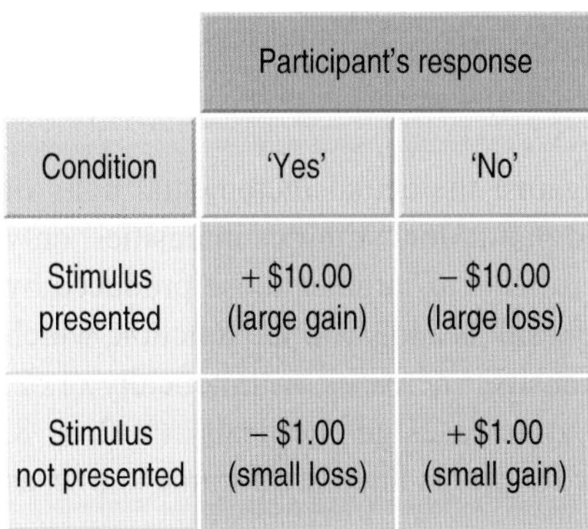

	Participant's response	
Condition	'Yes'	'No'
Stimulus presented	+ \$10.00 (large gain)	– \$10.00 (large loss)
Stimulus not presented	– \$1.00 (small loss)	+ \$1.00 (small gain)

(a) Matrix that will produce a 'yes' bias

	Participant's response	
Condition	'Yes'	'No'
Stimulus presented	+ \$1.00 (small gain)	– \$1.00 (small loss)
Stimulus not presented	– \$10.00 (large loss)	+ \$10.00 (large gain)

(b) Matrix that will produce a 'no' bias

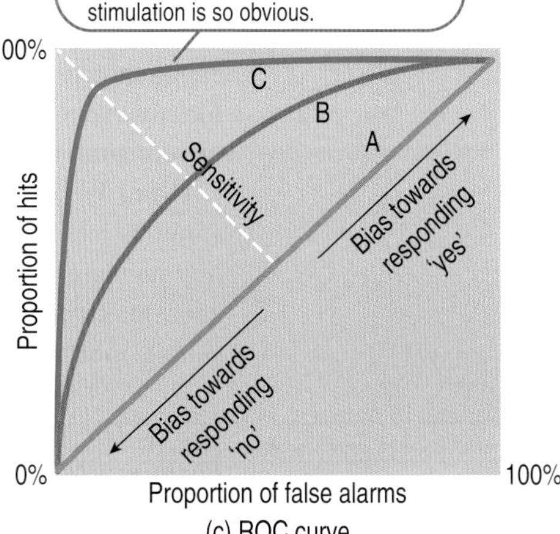

(c) ROC curve

FIGURE 4.3
Signal detection. Two pay-off matrices, one that leads to a 'yes' bias (a), and the other to a 'no' bias (b). To assess sensitivity to a stimulus (c), researchers plot the proportion of hits against the proportion of false alarms on an ROC curve. If the signal is so low that it is imperceptible (line A), the proportion of hits will equal the proportion of false alarms because the receiver's responses are random. At a somewhat higher stimulus intensity (line B) participants have a better ratio of hits to false alarms because their responses are influenced by the presence of a detectable signal, so they are no longer just guessing. At very high signal intensities (line C), people rarely give wrong answers. The sensitivity of the observer to different signal intensities (e.g. how well the person can hear) is represented by the dotted line, which shows how far the receiver's ROC curve diverges from the diagonal, which represents random responding.

Difference thresholds

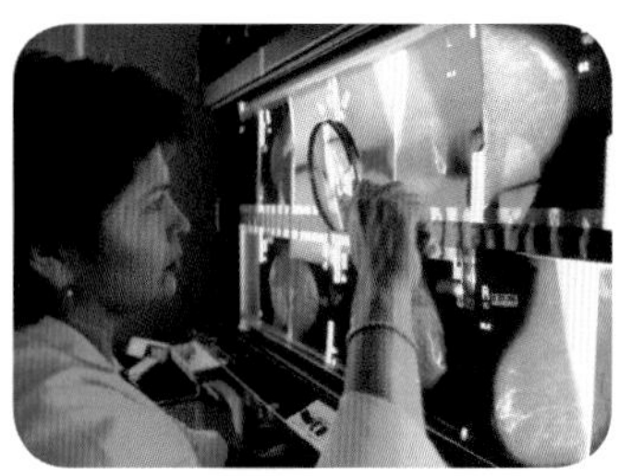

Here, a radiologist carefully examines a mammogram, looking for the slightest indication of a tumour. An individual's ability to detect a difference between two visual stimuli (such as normal versus abnormal tissue) can be increased by special training, practice and instruments, but it is still limited, to some degree, by sensory difference thresholds.

Thus far, we have focused on absolute thresholds, the lowest level of stimulation required to sense that a stimulus is present. Another important kind of threshold is the ***difference threshold*** — the lowest level of stimulation required to sense that a change in stimulation has occurred. In other words, the difference threshold is the difference in intensity between two stimuli that is necessary to produce a ***just noticeable difference*** (or ***jnd***), such as the difference between two light bulbs of slightly different wattage. (The absolute threshold is actually a special case of the difference threshold, in which the difference is between no intensity and a very weak stimulus.)

The jnd depends not only on the intensity of the new stimulus but also on the level of stimulation already present. The more intense the existing stimulus, the larger the change must be to be noticeable. A person carrying a one kilogram backpack will easily notice the addition of a half kilogram book, but adding the same book to a 30 kilogram backpack will not make the pack feel any heavier; that is, it will not produce a jnd.

Weber's law

In 1834, the German physiologist Ernst Weber recognised not only this lack of a one-to-one relationship between the physical and psychological worlds but also the existence of a consistent relationship between them. Regardless of the magnitude of two stimuli, the second must differ from the first by a constant proportion for it to be perceived as different. This relationship is called ***Weber's law***. That constant proportion — the ratio of change in intensity required to produce a jnd compared to the previous intensity of the stimulus — can be expressed as a fraction, called the Weber fraction. Weber was the first to show not only that subjective sensory experience and objective sensory stimulation were related but also that one could be predicted from the other mathematically. To put it another way, Weber was hot on the trail of a science of consciousness.

The Weber fraction varies depending on the individual, stimulus, context and sensory modality. For example, the Weber fraction for perceiving changes in heaviness is 1/50. This means that the average person can perceive an increase of one kilogram if added to a 50 kilogram bag, 2 kilograms added to 100 kilograms, and so on. The Weber fraction for a sound around middle C is 1/10, which means that a person can hear an extra voice in a chorus of 10 but would require two voices to notice an increase in loudness in a chorus of 20.

Fechner's law

Weber's brother-in-law, Gustav Fechner, took the field a 'just noticeable step' further in 1860 with the publication of his *Elements of Psychophysics*. He broadened the application of Weber's law by linking the subjective experience of intensity of stimulation with the actual magnitude of a stimulus. In other words, using Weber's law, Fechner was able to estimate precisely how intensely a person would report experiencing a sensation based on the amount of stimulus energy actually present. He assumed that for any given stimulus, all jnds are created equal; that is, each additional jnd feels subjectively like one incremental (additional) unit in intensity.

Using Weber's law, he then plotted these subjective units against the actual incremental units of stimulus intensity necessary to produce each jnd. He recognised that at low stimulus intensities, only tiny increases in stimulation are required to produce subjective effects as large as those produced by enormous increases in stimulation at high levels of intensity. The result is a logarithmic function, which simply means that as one variable (in this case, subjective intensity) increases arithmetically (1, 2, 3, 4, 5 …), the other variable (in this case, objective intensity) increases geometrically (1, 2, 4, 8, 16 …). The logarithmic relation between subjective and objective stimulus intensity became known as ***Fechner's law***.

Fechner's law means that people experience only a small percentage of actual increases in stimulus intensity but that this percentage is predictable. Knowing the Weber constant and the intensity of the stimulus, a psychologist can actually predict how strong a person's subjective sensation will be. Fechner's law is remarkable because it demonstrates that aspects of our subjective experience can be predicted mathematically.

Stevens' power law

Fechner's law held up for a century but was modified by S. S. Stevens (1961, 1975) because it did not quite apply to all stimuli and senses. For example, the relationship between perceived pain and stimulus intensity is the opposite of most other psychophysical relations: the greater the pain, the less additional intensity is required for a jnd. This makes adaptive sense, since increasing pain means increasing danger and therefore demands heightened attention.

In part on a dare from a colleague, Stevens (1956) set out to prove that people can accurately rate subjective intensity on a numerical scale. He instructed participants to listen to a series of tones of differing intensity and simply assign numbers to the tones to indicate their relative loudness. What he discovered was a lawful relation between self-reports and stimulus intensity across a much wider range of sensory modes and intensities than Fechner's law could accommodate.

According to ***Stevens' power law***, as the perceived intensity of a stimulus grows arithmetically, the actual magnitude of the stimulus grows exponentially — that is, by some power (squared, cubed, etc.). The exponent varies for different senses, just as the Weber fraction varies. Where the exponent is less than 1 (for example, for brightness it is 0.33), the results are generally similar to Fechner's law. Thus, to double the perceived brightness of a light, the physical stimulus has to increase by a factor of 8. Where the exponent is larger than 1, however, as for sensations produced by electric shock (where the exponent is 3.5), the magnitude of sensations grows quite rapidly as stimulation increases. Thus, Stevens' power law can predict subjective experiences of pain intensity as readily as brightness.

Although the formulae have become more precise, the message from Weber, Fechner and Stevens is fundamentally the same. Sensation bears an orderly, predictable relation to physical stimulation, but psychological experience is not a photograph, tape recording or wax impression of external reality.

Sensory adaptation

A final process shared by all sensory systems is adaptation. You walk into a crowded restaurant, and the noise level is overwhelming, yet within a few minutes, you do not even notice it. Similarly, at Rotorua in New Zealand, hot springs throughout the town emit a sulfur smell that is quite striking when you first arrive; however, it soon becomes something that you adjust to. These are examples of ***sensory adaptation*** — the tendency of sensory receptors to respond less to stimuli that continue without change.

APPLY + DISCUSS

- To what extent are we prisoners of our senses, constrained by sensory 'maps' of the world that only capture limited dimensions of it?
- What might we be able to know if we had evolved different, or keener, senses — such as a dog's ability to smell?
- What is gained and lost by increased sensory capacities? Would we be distracted or overloaded if we had a dog's sense of smell?

A distinct sulfur smell pervades the air at Rotorua in New Zealand — a destination that is renowned for its dramatic geyser eruptions and hot mud pools. Many visitors soon adjust to the strong smell through the process of sensory adaption, and can focus instead on enjoying the scenery.

Sensory adaptation makes sense from an evolutionary perspective. Constant sensory inputs provide no new information about the environment, so the nervous system ignores them. Given all the stimuli that bombard an organism at any particular moment, an animal that paid as much attention to constant stimulation as to changes that might be adaptively significant would be at a disadvantage. Sensory adaptation also performs the function of 'turning down the volume' on information that would overwhelm the brain by reducing its perceived intensity to a manageable level.

Although sensory adaptation generally applies across senses, the nervous system is wired to circumvent it in some important instances. For example, the visual system has ways to keep its receptors from adapting; otherwise, stationary objects would disappear from sight. The eyes are constantly making tiny quivering motions, which guarantees that the receptors affected by a given stimulus are constantly changing. The result is a steady flow of graded potentials on the sensory neurons that synapse with those receptors. Similarly, although we may adapt to mild pain, we generally do not adapt to severe pain (Miller & Kraus, 1990), an evolutionarily sensible design feature of a sensory system that responds to body damage.

INTERIM SUMMARY

The ***absolute threshold*** is the minimum amount of energy needed for an observer to sense that a stimulus is present. ***Signal detection theory*** asserts that judgements about the presence or absence of stimulus reflect the observer's sensitivity to the stimulus and the observer's response bias. The ***difference threshold*** is the lowest level of stimulation required to sense that a change in stimulation has occurred. According to ***Weber's law***, regardless of the magnitude of two stimuli, the second must differ by a constant proportion from the first for it to be perceived as different. According to ***Fechner's law***, the magnitude of a stimulus grows logarithmically as the subjective experience of intensity grows arithmetically, so that people subjectively experience only a fraction of actual increases in stimulation. According to ***Stevens' power law***, subjective intensity increases in a linear fashion as actual intensity grows exponentially. ***Sensory adaptation*** is the tendency of sensory systems to respond less to stimuli that continue without change.

Vision

Throughout this chapter we will use vision as our major example of sensory processes because it is the best understood of the senses. We begin by discussing the form of energy (light) transduced by the visual system. We then examine the organ responsible for transduction (the eye) and trace the neural pathways that take raw information from receptors and convert it into sensory knowledge.

The nature of light

Light is just one form of electromagnetic radiation, but it is the form to which the eye is sensitive. That humans and other animals respond to light is no accident, since cycles of light and dark have occurred over the course of 5 billion years of evolution. These cycles, and the mere presence of light as a medium for sensation, have shaped virtually every aspect of our psychology, from the times of day at which we are conscious to the way we choose mating partners (using visual appearance as a cue).

Indeed, light is so useful for tracking prey, avoiding predators and 'checking out' potential mates that a structure resembling the eye has apparently evolved independently over 40 times in different organisms (Fernald, 1996). Other forms of electromagnetic radiation to which humans are blind include infra-red, ultraviolet, radio and x-ray radiation.

Electromagnetic energy travels in waves characterised by patterned movement, or oscillation. Different forms of radiation have waves of different lengths, or ***wavelengths***. This simply means that their particles oscillate more or less frequently — that is, with higher or lower frequency. Some of these wavelengths, such as gamma rays, are as short or shorter than the diameter of an atom; others are quite long, such as radio waves, which may oscillate once in a kilometre. Wavelengths are measured in nanometres (nm), or billionths of a metre (figure 4.4). The receptors in the human eye are tuned to detect only a very restricted portion of the electromagnetic spectrum, from roughly 400 to 700 nm. Other organisms are sensitive to different regions of the spectrum. For example, many insects (such as ants and bees) and some vertebrate animals (such as iguanas and some bird species) see ultraviolet light (Alberts, 1989; Goldsmith, 1994; see also Salcedo, Zheng, Phistry, Bagg, & Britt, 2003).

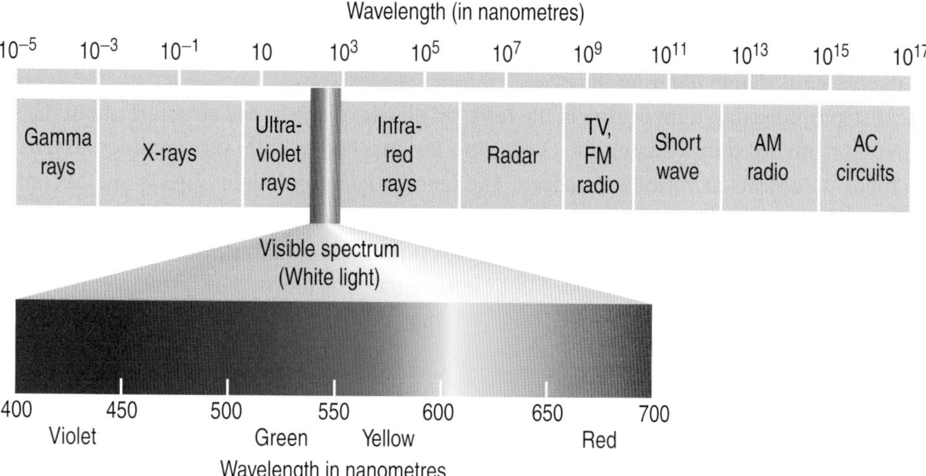

FIGURE 4.4
The electromagnetic spectrum. Humans sense only a small portion of the electromagnetic spectrum (enlarged in the figure), light. Light at different wavelengths is experienced as different colours.

The physical dimension of wavelength translates into the psychological dimension of colour, just as the physical intensity of light is related to the subjective sensation of brightness. Light is a useful form of energy to sense for a number of reasons (see Sekuler & Blake, 1994). Like other forms of electromagnetic radiation, light travels very quickly (roughly 300 000 kilometres per second), so sighted organisms can see things almost immediately after they happen. Light also travels in straight lines, which means that it preserves the geometric organisation of the objects it illuminates; the image an object casts on the retina resembles its actual structure. Perhaps most importantly, light interacts with the molecules on the surface of many objects and is either absorbed or reflected. The light that is reflected reaches the eyes and creates a visual pattern. Objects that reflect a lot of light appear brighter, whereas those that absorb much of the light that hits them appear dark.

The eye

Two basic processes occur in the eyes (figure 4.5). First, the cornea, pupil and lens focus light on the retina. Next, the retina transduces this visual image into neural impulses that are relayed to and interpreted by the brain.

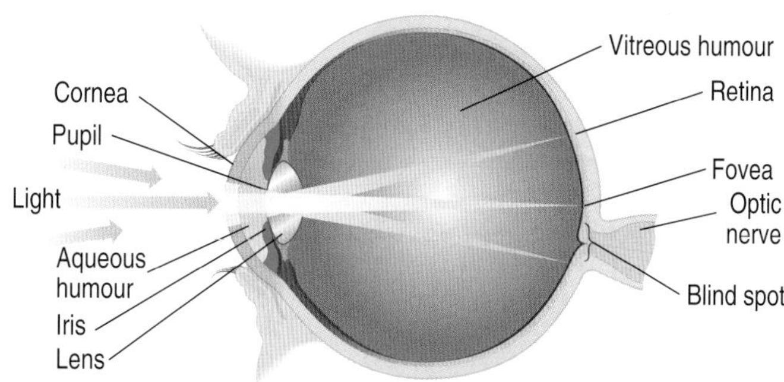

FIGURE 4.5
Anatomy of the human eye. The cornea, pupil and lens focus a pattern of light onto the retina, which then transduces the retinal image into neural signals carried to the brain by the optic nerve.

Focusing light

Light enters the eye through the ***cornea***, a tough, transparent tissue covering the front of the eyeball. Under water, people cannot see clearly because the cornea is constructed to bend (or refract) light rays travelling through air, not water. That is why a diving mask allows clearer vision: it puts a layer of air between the water and the cornea.

From the cornea, light passes through a chamber of fluid called aqueous humour, which supplies oxygen and other nutrients to the cornea and lens. Unlike blood, which performs this function in other parts of the body, the aqueous humour is a clear fluid, so light can pass through it. Next, light travels

MAKING CONNECTIONS

The size of the pupils changes not only with changes in light but also with changes in emotional state, such as fear, excitement, interest and sexual arousal. Skilled gamblers (or con artists) may literally be able to read other people's hands from their eyes. This may explain why Australia's Joe Hachem, a professional poker player who won $7.5 million in the World Series of Poker in Las Vegas, usually plays wearing sunglasses. Interestingly, gamblers and con artists may use pupil size as a cue, even though they have no **conscious awareness** that they are doing so (chapter 5).

through the ***pupil***, an opening in the centre of the ***iris*** (the pigmented tissue that gives the eye its blue, green or brown colour). Muscle fibres in the iris cause the pupil to expand (dilate) or constrict to regulate the amount of light entering the eye.

The next step in focusing light occurs in the ***lens***, an elastic, disc-shaped structure about the size of a lima bean that is involved in focusing the eyes. Muscles attached to cells surrounding the lens alter its shape to focus on objects at various distances. The lens flattens for distant objects and becomes more rounded or spherical for closer objects, a process known as ***accommodation***. The light is then projected through the vitreous humour (a clear, gelatinous liquid) onto the ***retina***, a light-sensitive layer of tissue at the back of the eye that transduces light into visual sensations. The retina receives a constant flow of images as people turn their heads and eyes or move through space.

The retina

The eye is like a camera, insofar as it has an opening to adjust the amount of incoming light, a lens to focus the light, and the equivalent of photosensitive film — the retina. (The analogy is incomplete, of course, because the eye, unlike a camera, works best when it is moving.) The retina translates light energy from illuminated objects into neural impulses, transforming a pattern of light reflected off objects into psychologically meaningful information.

Structure of the retina

The retina is a multilayered structure about as thick as a sheet of paper (figure 4.6). The innermost layer (at the back of the retina) contains two types of light receptors, or photoreceptors ('photo' is from the Greek word for light), called ***rods*** and ***cones***, which were named for their distinctive shapes. Each retina contains approximately 120 million rods and 8 million cones.

When a rod or cone absorbs light energy, it generates an electrical signal, stimulating the neighbouring ***bipolar cells***. These cells combine the information from many receptors and produce graded potentials on ***ganglion cells***, which integrate information from multiple bipolar cells. The long axons of these ganglion cells bundle together to form the ***optic nerve***, which carries visual information to the brain.

APPLY + DISCUSS

Watch the video clip about how light enters the eye that should be accessible from your university course website for this subject.

- How is light transduced by the eye?
- How does the retina transduce a visual image into a code that the brain can read?

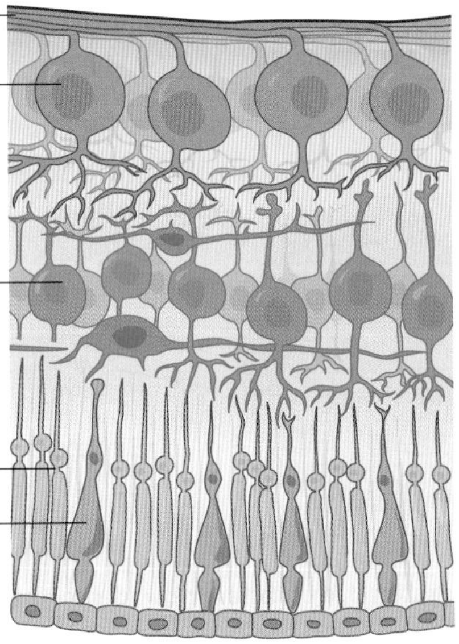

FIGURE 4.6
The retina. Light passes through layers of neurons to reach photoreceptors, called rods and cones, which respond to different wavelengths of light. These receptors in turn connect to bipolar cells, which pass information to the ganglion cells, whose axons form the optic nerve.

The central region of the retina, the ***fovea***, is most sensitive to small detail, so vision is sharpest for stimuli directly in sight. In contrast, the point on the retina where the optic nerve leaves the eye, called the ***blind spot*** (or optic disk), has no receptor cells.

People are generally unaware of their blind spots for several reasons. Different images usually fall on the blind spots of the two eyes so one eye sees what the other does not. In addition, the eyes are always moving, providing information about the missing area. To avoid perceiving an empty visual space, the brain also automatically uses visual information from the rest of the retina to fill in the gap. (To see the effects of the blind spot in action, see figure 4.7.)

FIGURE 4.7
The blind spot. Close your left eye, fix your gaze on the plus, and slowly move the book towards and away from you. The circle will disappear when it falls in the blind spot of the right retina.

Rods and cones

Rods and cones have distinct functions. Rods are more sensitive to light than cones, allowing vision in dim light. Rods only produce visual sensations in black, white and grey. Cones are, evolutionarily speaking, a more recent development than rods and respond to colour as well as black and white. They require more light to be activated, however, which is why we see little or no colour in dim light. Nocturnal animals such as owls have mostly rods, whereas animals that sleep at night (including most other birds) have mostly cones (Schiffman, 1996). Humans see both in black and white and in colour, depending on the amount of light available.

Rods and cones also differ in their distribution on the retina and in their connections to bipolar cells. Rods are concentrated off the centre of the retina. Thus, in dim light, objects are seen most clearly by looking slightly away from them. (You can test this yourself tonight by looking at the stars. Fix your eyes directly on a bright star and then focus your gaze slightly off to the side of it. The star will appear brighter when the image is cast away from the fovea.)

Several rods may also provide input to a single bipolar cell. Since the bipolar cell can be activated by many different rods or combinations of them, it cannot transmit fine details to the brain. On the other hand, the sum of the energy collected by many rods can easily cause an action potential in sensory neurons excited by them, so these cells can fire in very dim light.

In contrast, cones are concentrated in the centre of the retina in the fovea, although they are also found in smaller proportions in the periphery. Thus, in bright light an object is seen best if looked at directly, focusing the image on the fovea. Further, a single cone may connect with a single bipolar cell. This allows perception of fine detail, since precise information from each cone is preserved and passed on for higher processing.

Transforming light into sight

Both rods and cones contain photosensitive pigments that change chemical structure in response to light (Rushton, 1962; Wald, 1968). This process is called bleaching because the pigment breaks down when exposed to light, leading the photoreceptors to lose their characteristic colour. When photoreceptors bleach, they create graded potentials in the bipolar cells connected to them, which may then fire. Bleaching must be reversed before a photoreceptor is restored to full sensitivity. Pigment regeneration takes time, which is why people often have to feel their way around the seats when entering a dark theatre on a bright day.

Adjusting to a dimly illuminated setting is called dark adaptation. The cones adapt relatively quickly, usually within about five minutes, depending on the duration and intensity of light to which the eye was previously exposed. Rods, in contrast, take about 15 minutes to adapt. Since they are especially useful in dim light, vision may remain less than optimal in the theatre for some time. Light adaptation, the process of adjusting to bright light after exposure to darkness, is much faster; re-adapting to bright sunlight upon leaving a theatre takes only about a minute (Matlin, 1983).

Receptive fields

Once the rods and cones have responded to patterns of light, the nervous system must somehow convert these patterns into a neural code to allow the brain to reconstruct the scene. This is truly a remarkable process: waves of light reflected off, say, your friend's face, pass through the eye to the rods and cones of the retina. The pattern of light captured by those receptor cells translates your friend's face into a pattern of nerve impulses that the brain can 'read' with such precision that you know precisely who you are seeing.

APPLY + DISCUSS

Watch the brief video clip about how light is transformed into sight that should be accessible from your university course website for this subject.

- What role does the receptive field play in transforming light into sight?

This process begins with the ganglion cells. Each ganglion cell has a receptive field. A ***receptive field*** is a region within which a neuron responds to appropriate stimulation (that is, in which it is receptive to stimulation) (Hartline, 1938). Neurons at higher levels of the visual system (in the brain) also have receptive fields, which means that at higher and higher levels of processing, the visual system keeps creating maps of the scenes the eye has observed. The same basic principles apply in other sensory systems, as when neurons from the peripheral nervous system all the way up through the cortex map precisely where a mosquito has landed on the skin.

Psychologists have learned about receptive fields in ganglion cells through a technique called single-cell recording. In single-cell recording, researchers insert a tiny electrode into the brain or retina of an animal, close enough to a neuron to detect when it fires. Then, holding the animal's head still, they flash light to different parts of the visual field to see what kind of stimulation leads the ganglion cell to fire. By placing electrodes in many places, psychologists can map the receptive fields of the ganglion cells of the retina.

Using this method, researchers discovered that the receptive fields of some ganglion cells have a centre and a surrounding area, like a target (figure 4.8). Presenting light to the centre of the receptive field turns the cell 'on' (that is, excites the cell), whereas presenting light within the receptive field but outside the centre turns the cell 'off' (Kuffler, 1953). For other ganglion cells the pattern is just the opposite: light in the centre inhibits neural firing, whereas light in the periphery excites the neuron. The process by which adjacent visual units inhibit or suppress each other's level of activity is called lateral inhibition. Figure 4.9 (opposite) illustrates the way excitatory and inhibitory graded potentials from bipolar cells may be involved in this process.

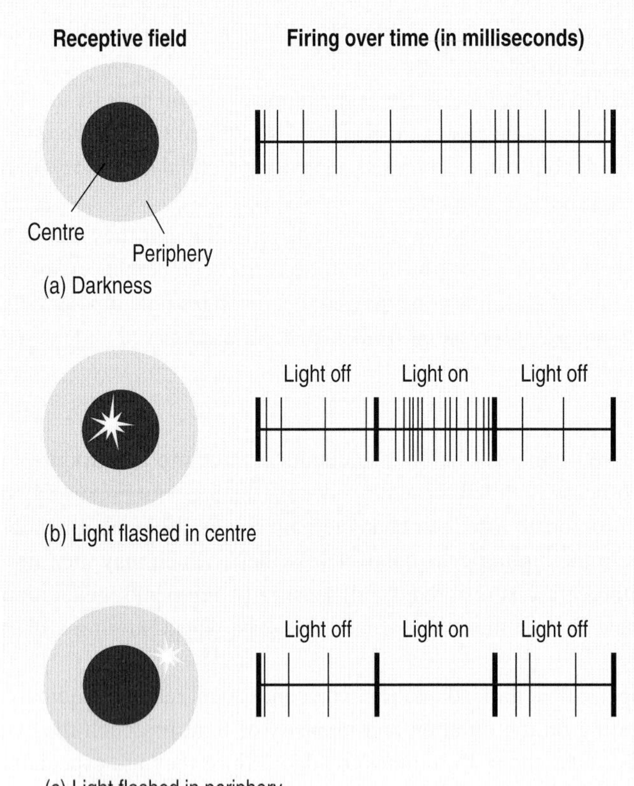

FIGURE 4.8
Single-cell recording. In (a), the neuron spontaneously fires (indicated by the thin vertical lines) randomly in darkness. In (b), it fires repeatedly when light is flashed to the centre of its receptive field. In (c), firing stops when light is flashed in the periphery of its receptive field; that is, light outside the centre inhibits firing.

SOURCE: From Sekuler and Blake (1994). Copyright © 1994, 1990, 1985 by McGraw-Hill, Inc. Reproduced with the permission of the McGraw-Hill Companies.

Why do receptive fields have this concentric circular organisation, with on and off regions that inhibit each other? As described at the beginning of the chapter, our sensory systems are attuned to changes and differences. The target-like organisation of ganglion cells allows humans and other animals to perceive edges and changes in brightness and texture that signal where one surface ends and another begins. A neuron that senses light in the centre of its receptive field will fire rapidly if the light is bright and covers much of the centre. To the extent that light is also present in the periphery of the receptive field, however, neural firing will be inhibited, essentially transmitting the information that the image is continuous in this region of space, with no edges.

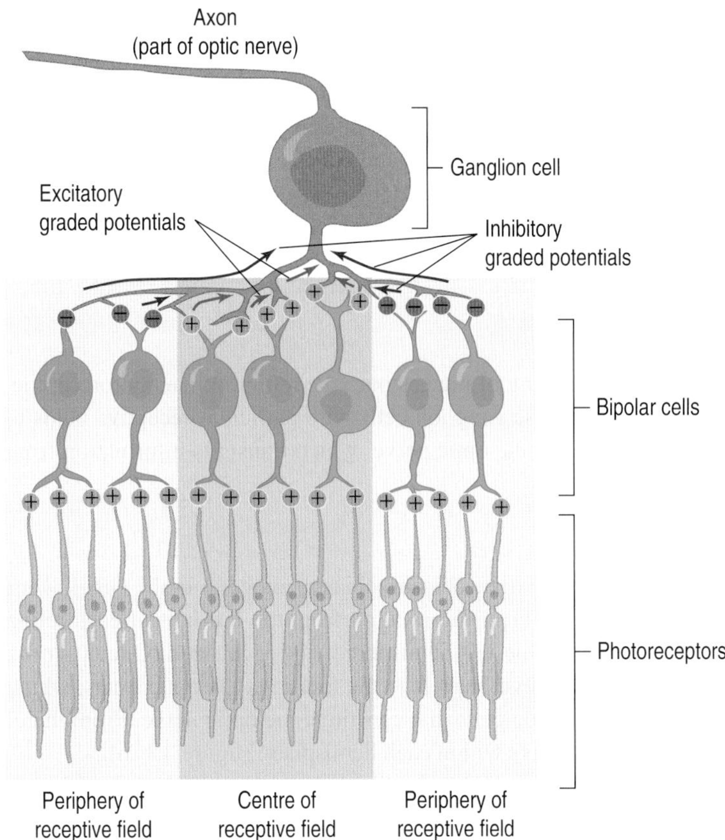

FIGURE 4.9
Activation of a centre-on/periphery-off ganglion cell. Transduction begins as photoreceptors that respond to light in the centre of the ganglion cell's receptive field excite bipolar cells, which in turn generate excitatory graded potentials (represented here by a +) on the dendrites of the ganglion cell. Photoreceptors that respond to light in the periphery of the ganglion cell's receptive field inhibit firing of the ganglion cell (represented by a –). If enough light is present in the centre, and little enough in the periphery of the receptive field, the excitatory graded potentials will depolarise the ganglion cell membrane. The axon of the ganglion cell is part of the optic nerve, which will then transmit information about light in this particular visual location to the brain.

Lateral inhibition appears to be responsible in part for the phenomenon seen in Hermann grids (figure 4.10), in which the intersections of white lines in a dark grid appear grey and the intersections of black lines in a white grid appear grey (Spillman, 1994). Essentially, white surrounded by white on all four sides appears darker than white surrounded by black on two sides, and vice versa. The receptive fields of neurons in the fovea tend to be very small, allowing for high visual acuity, whereas receptive fields increase in size with distance from the centre of the retina (Wiesel & Hubel, 1960). This is why looking straight at the illusory patches of darkness or lightness in Hermann grids makes them disappear. Receptive fields of neurons in the fovea can be so small that the middle of each line is surrounded primarily by the same shade regardless of whether it is at an intersection.

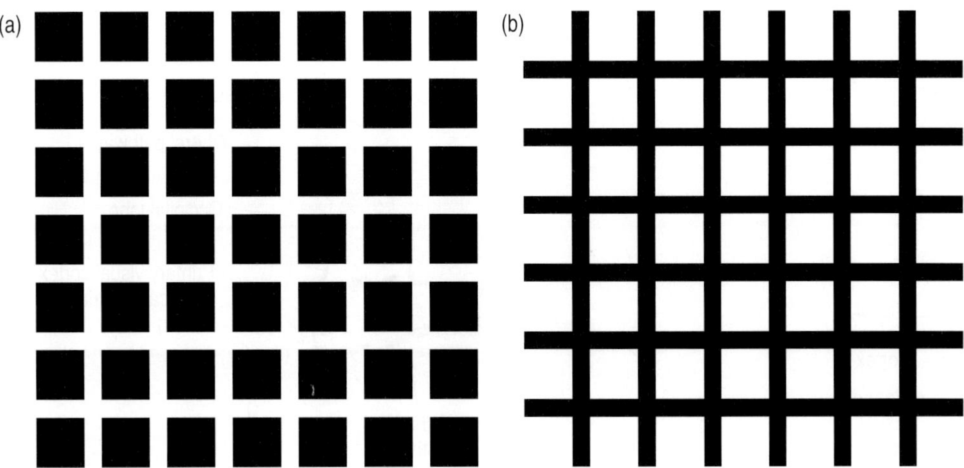

FIGURE 4.10
Hermann grids. White lines against a black grid appear to have grey patches at their intersections (a), as do black lines against a white grid (b).

INTERIM SUMMARY

Two basic processes occur in the eyes. Light is focused on the ***retina*** by the ***cornea***, ***pupil*** and ***lens***, and the retina transduces this visual image into a code that the brain can read. The retina includes two kinds of photoreceptors: ***rods*** (which produce sensations in black, white and grey and are very sensitive to light) and ***cones*** (which produce sensations of colour). Rods and cones excite ***bipolar cells***, which in turn excite or inhibit ***ganglion cells***, whose axons constitute the ***optic nerve***. Ganglion cells, like sensory cells higher up in the nervous system, have ***receptive fields***, areas that are excited or inhibited by the arriving sensory information.

Neural pathways

Transduction in the eye, then, starts with the focusing of images onto the retina. When photoreceptors bleach, they excite bipolar cells, which in turn cause ganglion cells with particular receptive fields to fire. The axons from these ganglion cells comprise the optic nerve, which transmits information from the retina to the brain.

From the eye to the brain

Impulses from the optic nerve first pass through the optic chiasm (chiasm comes from the Greek word for 'cross'), where the optic nerve splits (figure 4.11a). Information from the left half of each retina (which comes from the right visual field) goes to the left hemisphere, and vice versa. Once past the optic chiasm, combined information from the two eyes travels to the brain via the optic tracts, which are simply a continuation of the axons from ganglion cells that constitute the optic nerve. From there, visual information flows along two separate pathways within each hemisphere (figure 4.11b).

The first pathway projects to the lateral geniculate nucleus of the thalamus and then to the primary visual cortex in the occipital lobes. Neurons in the lateral geniculate nucleus preserve the map of visual space in the retina, that is, neighbouring ganglion cells transmit information to thalamic neurons next to each other, which in turn transmit this retinal map to the cortex. Neurons in the lateral geniculate nucleus have the same kind of concentric (target-like) receptive fields as retinal neurons. They also receive input from the reticular formation, which means that the extent to which an animal is attentive, aroused and awake may modulate the transmission of impulses from the thalamus to the visual cortex (Burke & Cole, 1978; Munk, Roelfsema, Konig, Engel, & Singer, 1996).

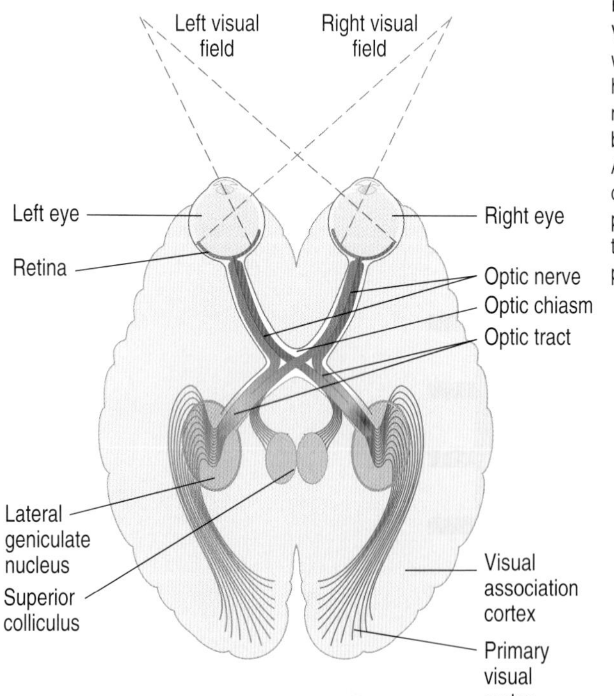

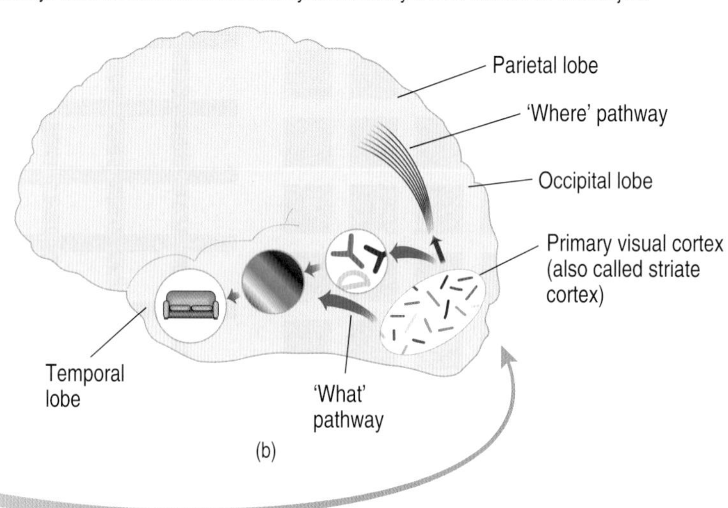

FIGURE 4.11

Visual pathways. (a) The optic nerve carries visual information from the retina to the optic chiasm, where the optic nerve splits. The brain processes information from the right visual field in the left hemisphere and vice versa because of the way some visual information crosses and some does not cross over to the opposite hemisphere at the optic chiasm. At the optic chiasm, the optic nerve becomes the optic tract (because bundles of axons within the brain itself are called tracts, not nerves). A small pathway from the optic tract carries information simultaneously to the superior colliculus. The optic tract then carries information to the lateral geniculate nucleus of the thalamus, where neurons project to the primary visual cortex. (b) From the primary visual cortex visual information flows along two pathways: the 'what' and 'where' pathways. You can also watch a brief video clip about visual pathways that should be accessible from your university course website for this subject.

A second, short pathway projects to a clump of neurons in the midbrain known as the superior colliculus, which in humans is involved in controlling eye movements. Its neurons respond to the presence or absence of visual stimulation in parts of the visual field but cannot identify specific objects. Neurons in the superior colliculus also integrate input from the eyes and the ears, so that weak stimulation from the two senses together can orient the person towards a region in space that neither sense alone could detect (Stein & Meredith, 1990).

The presence of two visual pathways from the optic nerve to the brain appears to be involved in an intriguing phenomenon known as ***blindsight***, in which individuals are unaware of their capacity to see (Sahraie et al., 1997; Weiskrantz, Warrington, Sanders, & Marshall, 1974; see also Trevethan, Sahraie, & Weiskrantz, 2007). Pursuing observations made by neurologists in the early part of the twentieth century, researchers have studied a subset of patients with lesions to the primary visual cortex, which receives input from the second visual pathway (through the lateral geniculate nucleus). These patients are, for all intents and purposes, blind. If shown an object, they deny that they have seen it. Yet if asked to describe its geometric form (e.g. triangle or square) or give its location in space (to the right or left, up or down), they do so with accuracy far better than chance — frequently protesting all the while that they cannot do the task because they cannot see! Visual processing in the superior colliculus, and perhaps at the level of the lateral geniculate nucleus, apparently leads to visual responses that can guide behaviour outside of awareness.

MAKING CONNECTIONS

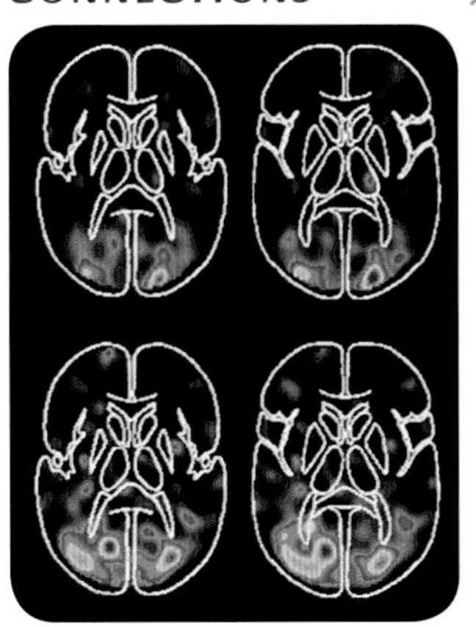

In the two lower PET scans, it can be observed that the primary visual cortex in the occipital lobes lights up when people actively view words. In contrast, the top two PET scans show less occipital lobe activity when the eyes are either closed or staring continuously at a black dot (chapter 3).

Visual cortex

From the lateral geniculate nucleus, then, visual information travels to the primary visual cortex in the occipital lobes. The primary visual cortex is sometimes called the striate cortex because of its striped ('striated') appearance; visual pathways outside the striate cortex to which its neurons project are thus called extrastriate cortex (because they are outside of, or extra to, the striate cortex).

Primary visual cortex

The size of a brain region that serves a particular function (in this case, vision) is a rough index of the importance of that function to the organism's adaptation over the course of evolution. Once again this simply reflects the 'logic' of natural selection. If vision was particularly useful for survival and reproduction in our primate ancestors, those animals with larger visual processing centres would be at an adaptive advantage, and larger and more sophisticated visual 'modules' would be likely to evolve over time. In fact, in many monkey species whose visual systems resemble those of humans, over half the cortex is devoted to visual processing (Van Essen, Anderson, & Felleman, 1992).

Within a sensory system, such as the visual system, the same principle also holds true. For example, in humans as in other primates, the primary visual cortex does not give 'equal time' to all regions of the person's visual field. Approximately 25 percent of the striate cortex is devoted to information from the central 2 percent of the visual field (Carlson, 1999; Drasdo, 1977), just as the somatosensory cortex in the parietal lobes over-represents regions such as the hands, which have many receptors and transmit especially important information (chapter 3). Additionally, much of the visual cortex is organised in such a way that adjacent groups of visual neurons receive input from adjacent areas of the retina.

The striate cortex is the 'first stop' in the cortex for all visual information. Neurons in this region begin to 'make sense' of visual information, in large measure through the action of neurons known as feature detectors. ***Feature detectors***, discovered by Nobel Prize winners David Hubel and Thorsten Wiesel (1959, 1979; see also Ferster & Miller, 2000), are neurons that fire only when stimulation in their receptive field matches a very specific pattern.

Simple cells are feature detectors that respond most vigorously to lines of a particular orientation, such as horizontal or vertical, in an exact location in the visual field (figure 4.12; see overleaf). Complex cells are feature detectors that generally cover a larger receptive field and respond when a stimulus of the proper orientation falls anywhere within their receptive field, not just at a particular location. They may also fire only when the stimulus moves in a particular direction. Still other cells, called hypercomplex cells, require that a stimulus be of a specific size or length to fire. Other neurons in the primary visual cortex respond selectively to colour, contrast and texture (Engel, Zhang, & Wandell, 1997; Livingstone & Hubel, 1988). This combination of cells allows us to recognise a vertical line as a vertical line despite its size and ultimately allows us to distinguish a pencil from an antenna, even though both may be vertical.

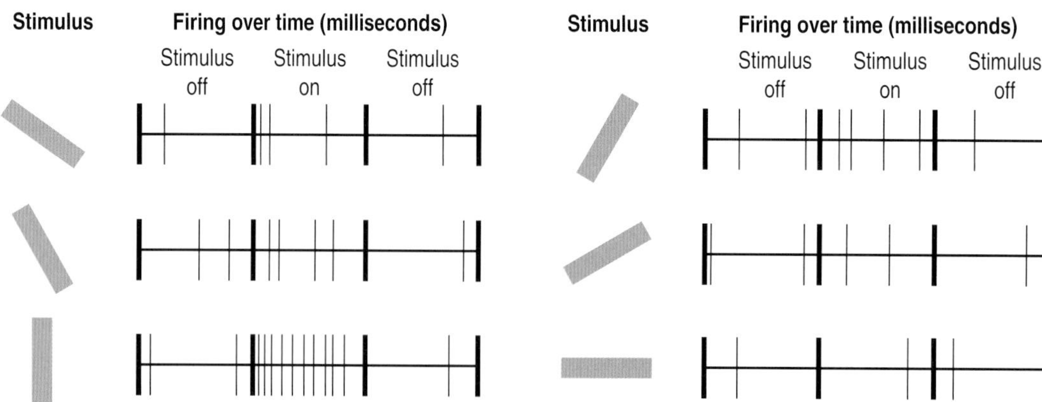

FIGURE 4.12
Feature detectors. A simple cell that responds maximally to vertical lines will show more rapid firing the closer a visual image in its receptive field matches its preferred orientation.

SOURCE: From Sekuler and Blake (1994). Copyright © 1994, 1990, 1985 by McGraw-Hill, Inc. Reproduced with the permission of the McGraw-Hill Companies.

The 'what' and the 'where' pathways

From the primary visual cortex, visual information appears to flow along two pathways, or processing streams (figure 4.11b) (Shapley, 1995; Ungerleider & Haxby, 1994; Van Essen et al., 1992). Much of what we know about these pathways comes from the study of macaque monkeys, although recent imaging studies using PET and fMRI confirm that the neural pathways underlying visual perception in the human and the macaque are very similar. Researchers have labelled these visual streams the 'what' and the 'where' pathways.

The ***'what' pathway***, which runs from the striate cortex in the occipital lobes through the lower part of the temporal lobes (or the inferior temporal cortex), is involved in determining what an object is. In this pathway, primitive features from the striate cortex (such as lines) are integrated into more complex combinations (such as cones or squares). At other locations along the pathway, the brain processes features of the object such as colour and texture. All of these processes occur simultaneously, as the striate cortex routes shape information to a shape-processing module, colour information to a colour-processing module, and so on.

Although some 'cross-talk' occurs among these different modules, each appears to create its own map of the visual field, such as a shape map and a colour map. Not until the information has reached the front, or anterior, sections of the temporal lobes does a fully integrated percept appear to exist. At various points along the stream, however, polysensory areas bring visual information in contact with information from other senses. For example, when a person shakes hands with another person, he not only sees the other's hand but also feels it, hears the person move towards him, and feels his own arm moving through space. This requires integrating information from all of the lobes of the cortex.

The second stream, the ***'where' pathway***, is involved in locating the object in space, following its movement, and guiding movement towards it. (Researchers could just as easily have labelled this the 'where and how' pathway because it guides movement and hence offers information on 'how to get there from here'.) This pathway runs from the striate cortex through the middle and upper (superior) regions of the temporal lobes and up into the parietal lobes.

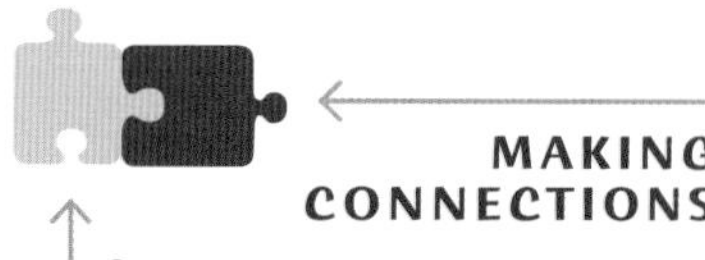

MAKING CONNECTIONS

Some patients with prosopagnosia, who cannot even recognise their spouse, nevertheless 'feel' different upon seeing their husband or wife. This suggests that some neural circuits are detecting that this is a familiar and loved person, even though these circuits have no direct access to consciousness (chapter 5).

Lesions that occur along these pathways produce disorders that would seem bizarre without understanding the neuroanatomy. For example, patients with lesions at various points along the 'what' pathway may be unable to recognise or name objects, to recognise colours or to recognise familiar faces (prosopagnosia). Patients with lesions in the 'where' pathway, in contrast, typically have little trouble recognising or naming objects, but they may constantly bump into things, have trouble grasping nearby objects or fail to respond to objects in a part of their visual field, even including their own limbs (a phenomenon called visual neglect). Interestingly, this neglect may occur even when they are picturing a scene from memory. When asked to draw a scene, patients with neglect may simply leave out an entire segment of the scene and have no idea that it is missing.

Anatomically, the location of these two pathways makes sense as well. Recognition of objects ('what') is performed by modules in the temporal lobes directly below those involved in language, particularly in naming objects. Knowing where objects are in space and tracking their movements, on the other hand, is important for guiding one's own movement towards or away from them. Circuits in the parietal lobes, adjacent to the 'where' pathway, process information about the position of the body in space.

INTERIM SUMMARY

From the optic nerve, visual information travels along two pathways. One is to the superior colliculus in the midbrain, which in humans is particularly involved in eye movements. The other is to the lateral geniculate nucleus in the thalamus and on to the visual cortex. ***Feature detectors*** in the primary visual cortex respond only when stimulation in their receptive field matches a particular pattern or orientation. Beyond the primary visual cortex, visual information flows along two pathways, the ***'what' pathway*** (involved in determining what an object is) and the ***'where' pathway*** (involved in locating the object in space, following its movement and guiding movement towards it).

Perceiving in colour

'Roses are red, violets are blue …' Well, not exactly. Colour is a psychological property, not a quality of the stimulus. All species of domestic animals have been shown to possess colour vision, though not to the same extent as humans. For example, dogs appear to see the world in shades of violet, blue and yellow — their vision is similar to that of a colour blind person who sees the green light as pale yellow, yellow as yellow and red as dark yellow (Houpt, 2004). Similarly, grazing animals, such as cows, also have partial colour blindness, finding it difficult to discriminate green from blue (Chenoweth & Sanderson, 2005); in contrast, most insects, reptiles, fish and birds have excellent colour vision (Nathans, 1987). As Sir Isaac Newton demonstrated in research with prisms in the sixteenth century, white light (such as sunlight and light from common indoor lamps) is composed of all the wavelengths that constitute the colours in the visual spectrum. A rose appears red because it absorbs certain wavelengths and reflects others, and humans have receptors that detect electromagnetic radiation in that range of the spectrum.

Actually, colour has three psychological dimensions: hue, saturation and lightness (Sewall & Wooten, 1991). ***Hue*** is what people commonly mean by colour — that is, whether an object appears blue, red, violet and so on. Saturation is a colour's purity (the extent to which it is diluted with white or black, or 'saturated' with its own wavelength, like a sponge in water). Lightness is the extent to which a colour is light or dark.

People of all cultures appear to perceive the same colours or hues, although cultures vary widely in the number of their colour labels (chapter 8). In the West, colour also appears to be gendered (i.e. to differ between the two genders). Few men would pass a test requiring them to label colours such as bone, taupe and magenta, despite their mastery of the English language.

APPLY + DISCUSS

A dog is likely to see a red rose as being dark yellow instead.

- How could dogs, such as this Australian cattle dog, compensate for their limited colour vision with other sensory abilities?
- What implications do you think that limited colour vision might have for dogs?

Retinal transduction of colour

How does the visual system translate wavelengths into the subjective experience of colour? The first step occurs in the retina, where cones with different photosensitive pigments respond to varying degrees to different wavelengths of the spectrum. In 1802, a British physician named Thomas Young proposed that human colour vision is trichromatic — that is, the colours we see reflect blends of three colours to which our retinas are sensitive. Developed independently 50 years later by Hermann von Helmholtz, the ***Young-Helmholtz*** (or ***trichromatic***) ***theory of colour*** holds that the eye contains three types of receptors, each maximally sensitive to wavelengths of light that produce sensations of blue, green or red.

Another century later, Nobel Prize winner George Wald and others confirmed the existence of three different types of cones in the retina (Brown & Wald, 1964; Schnapf, Kraft, Nunn, & Baylor, 1989). Each cone responds to a range of wavelengths but responds most persistently to waves of light at a particular point on the spectrum (figure 4.13; see overleaf). Short-wavelength cones (S-cones) are most sensitive to wavelengths of about 420 nm, which are perceived as blue. Middle-wavelength cones (M-cones), which produce the sensation of green, are most sensitive to wavelengths of about 535 nm. Long-wavelength cones (L-cones), which produce red sensations, are most sensitive to wavelengths of about 560 nm (Brown & Wald, 1964). Mixing these three primary colours of light — red, green and blue — produces the thousands of colour shades humans can discriminate and identify.

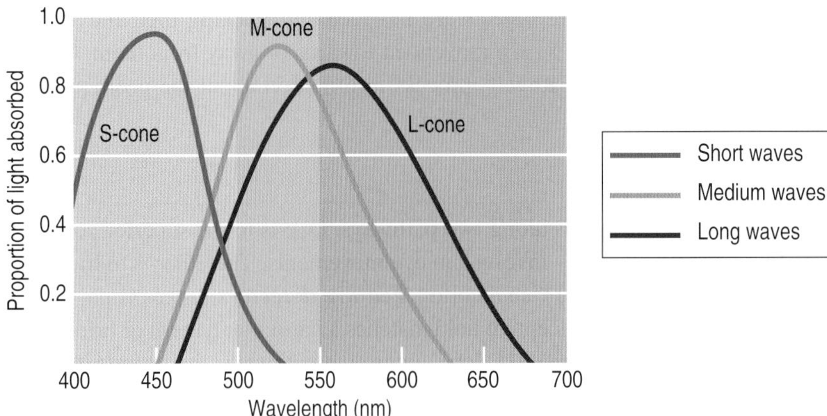

FIGURE 4.13
Cone response curves. All three kinds of cones respond to a range of frequencies — that is, they absorb light waves of many lengths, which contributes to bleaching — but they are maximally sensitive at particular frequencies and thus produce different colour sensations.

APPLY + DISCUSS

Watch a brief video clip about how wavelengths are transformed into colour that should be accessible from your university course website for this subject.

- How does mixing coloured paint differ from mixing coloured light?

This list of primary colours differs from the list of primary colours children learn in primary school from mixing paints (blue, red and yellow). The reason is that mixing paint and mixing light alter the wavelengths perceived in different ways, one subtracting and the other adding parts of the spectrum. Mixing paints is called subtractive colour mixture because each new paint added actually blocks out, or subtracts, wavelengths reflected onto the retina. For example, yellow paint appears yellow because its pigment absorbs most wavelengths and reflects only those perceived as yellow; the same is true of blue paint. When blue and yellow paints are mixed, only the wavelengths not absorbed by *either* the blue or yellow paint reach the eye; the wavelengths left are the ones we perceive as green.

Subtractive colour mixture, then, mixes wavelengths of light before they reach the eye. In contrast, additive colour mixture takes place in the eye itself, as light of differing wavelengths simultaneously strikes the retina and thus expands (adds to) the perceived section of the spectrum. Newton discovered additive colour mixture by using two prisms to funnel two colours simultaneously into the eye. Colour television works on an additive principle. A television picture is composed of tiny blue, green and red dots, which the eye blends from a distance. When struck by an electron beam inside the set, the spots light up. From a distance, the spots combine to produce multicoloured images, although the dots can be seen at very close range.

Processing colour in the brain

The trichromatic theory accurately predicted the nature of retinal receptors, but it was not a complete theory of colour perception. For example, the physiologist Ewald Hering noted that trichromatic theory could not alone explain a phenomenon that occurs with after-images, visual images that persist after a stimulus has been removed. Hering (1878, 1920) wondered why the colours of the after-image were different in predictable ways from those of the original image (figure 4.14). He proposed a theory, modified substantially by later researchers, known as opponent-process theory (DeValois & DeValois, 1975; Hurvich & Jameson, 1957). ***Opponent-process theory*** argues that all colours are derived from three antagonistic colour systems: black–white, blue–yellow and red–green. The black–white system contributes to brightness and saturation; the other two systems are responsible for hue.

Hering proposed his theory in opposition to trichromatic theory, but subsequent research suggests that the two theories are actually complementary. Trichromatic theory applies to the retina, where cones are, in fact, particularly responsive to red, blue or green. Opponent-process theory applies at higher visual centres in the brain.

FIGURE 4.14
After-image. Stare at the centre of the yellow and red globe for three minutes, then look at the white space on the page above it. The after-image is the traditional blue and green globe, reflecting the operation of antagonistic colour-opponent cells in the lateral geniculate nucleus.

Researchers have found that some neurons in the lateral geniculate nucleus of monkeys, whose visual system is similar to that of humans, are colour-opponent cells, excited by wavelengths that produce one colour but inhibited by wavelengths of the other member of the pair (DeValois & DeValois, 1975). For example, some red–green neurons increase their activity when wavelengths experienced as red are in their receptive fields and decrease their activity when exposed to wavelengths perceived as green; others are excited by green and inhibited by red. The pattern of activation of several colour-opponent neurons together determines the colour the person senses (Abramov & Gordon, 1994).

Opponent-process theory neatly explains after-images. Recall that in all sensory modalities the sensory system adapts, or responds less, to constant stimulation. In the visual system, adaptation begins with bleaching in the retina. Photoreceptors take time to resynthesise their pigments once they have bleached and thus cannot respond continuously to constant stimulation. During the period in which their pigment is returning, they cannot send inhibitory signals; this facilitates sensation of the opponent colour. The after-image of yellow therefore appears blue (and vice versa), red appears green and black appears white.

Opponent-process and trichromatic theory together explain another phenomenon that interested Hering: colour blindness (or, more accurately, colour deficiency). Few people are entirely blind to colour; those who are (because of genetic abnormalities that leave them with only one kind of cone) can only detect brightness, not colour. Most colour-deficient people confuse red and green (figure 4.15). Red–green colour blindness is sex linked, over 10 times more prevalent in males than females. It generally reflects a deficiency of either M- or L-cones, which makes red–green distinctions impossible at higher levels of the nervous system (Weale, 1982; Wertenbaker, 1981).

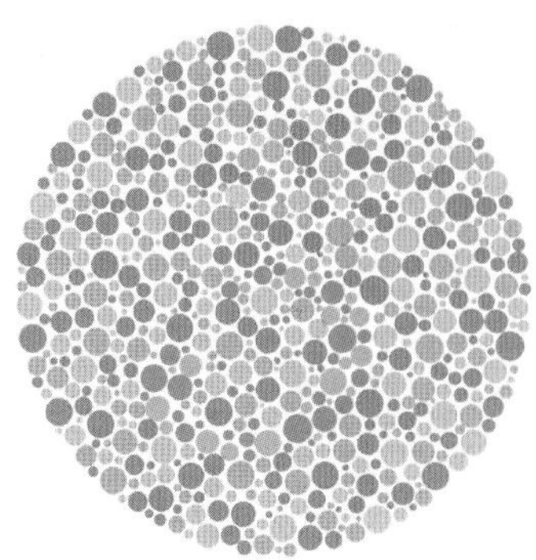

FIGURE 4.15
Colour blindness. In this common test for colour blindness, a green 3 is presented against a background of orange and yellow dots. The pattern of stimulation normally sent to the lateral geniculate nucleus by S-, M-, and L-cones allows discrimination of these colours. People who are red–green colour blind see only a random array of dots.

INTERIM SUMMARY

Two theories together explain what is known about colour vision. According to the ***Young–Helmholtz***, or ***trichromatic*, *theory***, the eye contains three types of receptors, which are most sensitive to wavelengths experienced as red, green or blue. According to ***opponent-process theory***, the colours we experience (and the after-images we perceive) reflect three antagonistic colour systems; a blue–yellow, red–green and black–white system. Trichromatic theory operates at the level of the retina, and opponent-process theory at higher neural levels.

How the world becomes represented in the brain

The processes by which objects in the external world become translated into an 'internal' portrait of them should now be growing clear. At the lowest level of the nervous system, neurons collect highly specific information from receptor cells — bits of information that, by themselves, would be meaningless. At each subsequent stage, through the thalamus to the most complex modules in the cortex, information is combined to provide a progressively richer, more integrated picture of the bits and pieces of knowledge collected at the prior stage. Through this process, isolated units of stimulus energy gradually undergo a remarkable metamorphosis, as the brain weaves sensory threads into complex and meaningful perceptual tapestries.

Hearing

If a tree falls in a forest, does it make a sound if no-one hears it? To answer this question requires an understanding of hearing, or ***audition***, and the physical properties it reflects. Like vision, hearing allows sensation at a distance and is thus of tremendous adaptive value. Hearing is also involved in the richest form of communication, spoken language. As with our discussion of vision, we begin by considering the stimulus energy underlying hearing — sound. Next we examine the organ that transduces it, the ear, and the neural pathways for auditory processing.

The nature of sound

When a tree falls in the forest, the crash produces vibrations in adjacent air molecules, which in turn collide with one another. A guitar string being plucked, a piece of paper rustling or a tree falling to the ground all produce sound because they create vibrations in the air. Like ripples on a pond, these rhythmic pulsations of acoustic energy (sound) spread outward from the vibrating object as ***sound waves***. Sound waves grow weaker with distance, but they travel at a constant speed, roughly 340 metres per second.

Sound differs from light in a number of respects. Sound travels more slowly, which is why fans hear the crack of a bat *after* seeing the bat hit the ball, or why thunder often appears to follow lightning even though the two occur at the same time. At close range, however, the difference between the speed of light and the speed of sound is imperceptible.

Residents in Brisbane would have seen this impressive lightning display before they heard the crackling thunder associated with it, as sound travels more slowly than light.

At close range, fans of AC/DC could not perceive a difference between the speed of light and the speed of sound during the legendary rockers' recent Australian tour. Noise complaints, however, were recorded from residents living several kilometres away. Definitely thunderstruck!

Unlike light, sound also travels *through* most objects, which explains why sound is more difficult to shut out. Like light, sound waves can be reflected off or absorbed by objects in the environment, but the impact on hearing is different from the impact on vision. When sound is reflected off an object, it produces an echo; when it is absorbed by an object, such as carpet, it is muffled. Everyone sounds like the great Italian tenor Luciano Pavarotti in the shower (or like Jimmy Barnes if they have a sore throat) because tile absorbs so little sound, creating echoes and resonance that give fullness to even a mediocre voice.

Frequency

APPLY + DISCUSS

Test the capacity of your auditory senses. Search for the mosquito ring tone online and download it. The high frequency sound of this ring tone is inaudible to most adults over the age of 25. Can you hear the ring tone?

- Do your results support the notion that hearing capacity diminishes with age?
- What explanation might the evolutionary perspective offer for this phenomenon?

Acoustic energy has three important properties: frequency, complexity and amplitude. When a person hits a tuning fork, the prongs of the fork move rapidly inward and outward, putting pressure on the air molecules around them, which collide with the molecules next to them. Each round of expansion and contraction of the distance between molecules of air is known as a ***cycle***.

The number of cycles per second determines the sound wave's frequency. ***Frequency*** is just what it sounds like — a measure of how often (that is, how frequently) a wave cycles. Frequency is expressed in ***hertz***, or ***Hz*** (named after the German physicist Heinrich Hertz). One hertz equals one cycle per second, so a 1500 Hz tone has 1500 cycles per second. The frequency of a simple sound wave corresponds to the psychological property of ***pitch*** (the quality of a tone, from low to high). Generally, the higher the frequency, the higher the pitch. When frequency is doubled — that is, when the number of cycles per second is twice as frequent — the pitch perceived is an octave higher.

The human auditory system is sensitive to a wide range of frequencies. Young adults can hear frequencies from about 15 to 20 000 Hz, but as with most senses, capacity diminishes with age. For example, Howard Stapleton created a text-message ring tone that emits the same pitch as the mosquito, about 17 000 Hz. This high-pitch frequency ring tone cannot usually be heard by people over the age of 30. Schoolchildren have been using this high-pitch ring tone, otherwise known as 'Teen Buzz', to text messages in class because their teachers usually cannot hear their mobile phones ring! Frequencies used in music range from the lowest note on an organ (16 Hz) to the highest note on a grand piano (over 4000 Hz). Human voices range from about 100 Hz to about 3500 Hz, and our ears are most sensitive to sounds in that frequency range. Other species are sensitive to different ranges. Dogs hear frequencies ranging from 15 to 50 000 Hz, which is why they are responsive to 'silent' whistles whose frequencies fall above the range humans can sense. Elephants can hear ultra-low frequencies over considerable distances.

So, does a tree falling in the forest produce a sound? It produces sound waves, but the waves only become perceptible as 'a sound' if creatures in the forest have receptors tuned to them.

Complexity

Sounds rarely consist of waves of uniform frequency. Rather, most sounds are a combination of sound waves, each with a different frequency. ***Complexity*** refers to the extent to which a sound is composed of multiple frequencies, and corresponds to the psychological property of ***timbre***, or texture of the sound. People recognise each other's voices, as well as the sounds of different musical instruments, from their characteristic timbre. The dominant part of each wave produces the predominant pitch, but overtones (additional frequencies) give a voice or musical instrument its distinctive timbre. (Synthesisers imitate conventional instruments by electronically adding the right overtones to pure frequencies.) The sounds instruments produce, whether in a rock band or a symphony, are music to our ears because we learn to interpret particular temporal patterns and combinations of sound waves as music. What people hear as music and as random auditory noise depends on their culture.

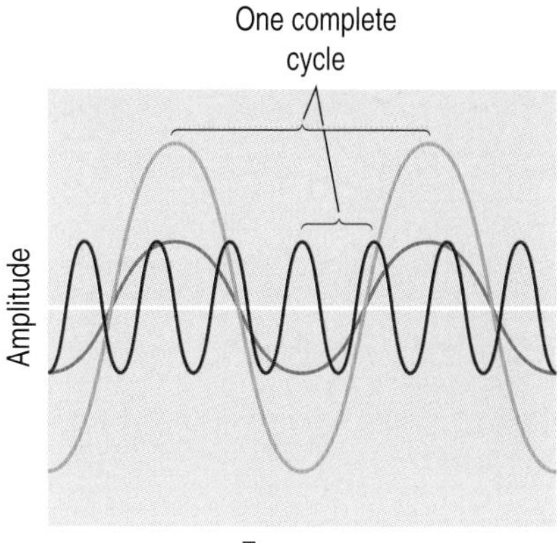

— High frequency, low amplitude (soft tenor or soprano)
— Low frequency, low amplitude (soft bass)
— Low frequency, high amplitude (loud bass)

FIGURE 4.16
Frequency and amplitude. Sound waves can differ in both frequency (pitch) and amplitude (loudness). A cycle can be represented as the length of time or distance between peaks of the curve.

Amplitude

In addition to frequency and complexity, sound waves have amplitude. ***Amplitude*** refers to the height and depth of a wave, that is, the difference between its maximum and minimum pressure level (figure 4.16). The amplitude of a sound wave corresponds to the psychological property of ***loudness***; the greater the amplitude, the louder the sound. Amplitude is measured in ***decibels (dB)***. Zero decibels is the absolute threshold above which most people can hear a 1000 Hz tone.

Like the visual system, the human auditory system has an astonishing range, handling energy levels that can differ by a factor of 10 billion or more (Bekesy & Rosenblith, 1951). The decibel scale is logarithmic, condensing a huge array of intensities into a manageable range, just as the auditory system does. A loud scream is 100 000 times more intense than a sound at the absolute threshold, but it is only 100 dB different. Conversation is usually held at 50 to 60 dB. Most people experience sounds over 130 dB as painful, and prolonged exposure to sounds over about 90 dB, such as amplifiers at a rock concert, can produce permanent hearing loss or ringing in the ears (figure 4.17).

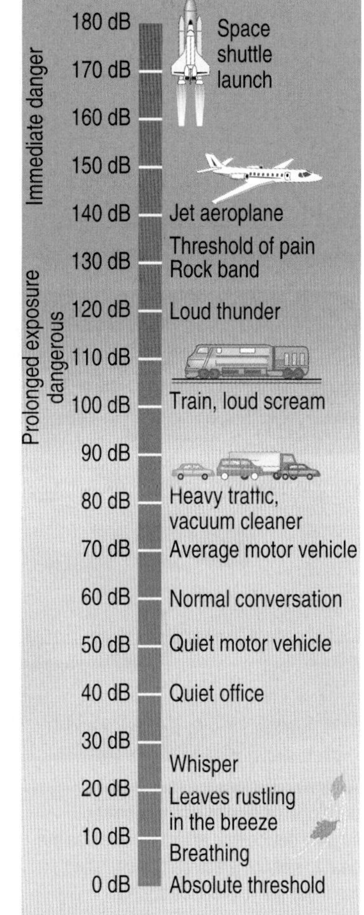

FIGURE 4.17
Loudness of various common sounds at close range, in decibels

INTERIM SUMMARY

Sound travels in ***waves***, which occur as a vibrating object sets air particles in motion. The sound wave's ***frequency***, which is experienced as ***pitch***, refers to the number of times those particles oscillate per second. Most sounds are actually composed of waves with many frequencies, which gives them their characteristic texture, or ***timbre***. The loudness of a sound reflects the height and depth, or ***amplitude***, of the wave.

The ear

Transduction of sound occurs in the ear, which consists of an outer, middle and inner ear (figure 4.18; see overleaf). The outer ear collects and magnifies sounds in the air; the middle ear converts waves of air pressure into movements of tiny bones; and the inner ear transforms these movements into waves in fluid that generate neural signals (Plack, 2005).

Transduction

The hearing process begins in the outer ear, which consists of the pinna and the auditory canal. Sound waves are funnelled into the ear by the pinna, the skin-covered cartilage that protrudes from the side of the head. The pinna is not essential for hearing, but its irregular shape helps locate sounds in space, which bounce off its folds differently when they come from various locations (Batteau, 1967). Just inside the skull is the auditory canal, a passageway about 2.5 centimetres long. As sound waves resonate in the auditory canal, they are amplified by up to a factor of 2.

The middle ear

At the end of the auditory canal is a thin, flexible membrane known as the ***eardrum***, or ***tympanic membrane***. The eardrum marks the outer boundary of the middle ear. When sound waves reach the eardrum, they set it in motion. The movements of the eardrum are extremely small — 0.000 000 01 centimetre, or about the width of a hydrogen molecule, in response to a whisper (Sekuler & Blake, 1994).

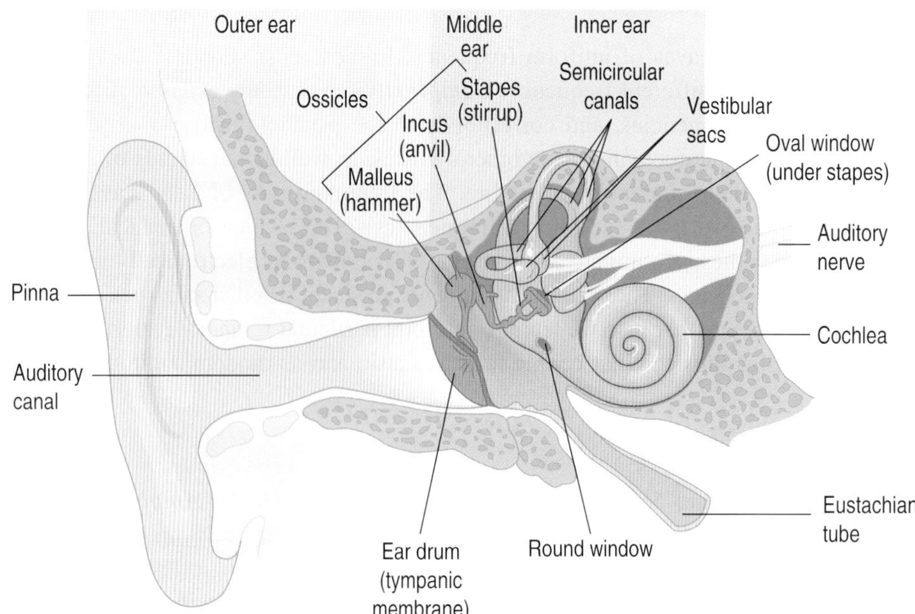

FIGURE 4.18
The ear consists of outer, middle and inner sections, which direct the sound, amplify it and turn mechanical energy into neural signals.

The eardrum reproduces the cyclical vibration of the object that created the noise on a microcosmic scale. This only occurs, however, if air pressure on both sides of it (in the outer and middle ear) is roughly the same. When an aeroplane begins its descent and a person's head is blocked by a head cold, the pressure is greater on the inside, which blunts the vibrations of the eardrum. The normal mechanism for equalising air pressure is the Eustachian tube, which connects the middle ear to the throat but can become blocked by mucus. When the eardrum vibrates, it sets in motion three tiny bones in the middle ear, called ossicles. These bones, named for their distinctive shapes, are called the malleus, incus and stapes, which translate from the Latin into hammer, anvil and stirrup, respectively. The ossicles further amplify the sound two or three times before transmitting vibrations to the inner ear. The stirrup vibrates against a membrane called the oval window, which forms the beginning of the inner ear.

The inner ear

The inner ear consists of two sets of fluid-filled cavities hollowed out of the temporal bone of the skull: the semicircular canals (involved in balance) and the cochlea (involved in hearing). The temporal bone is the hardest bone in the body and serves as natural soundproofing for its vibration-sensitive cavities. Chewing during a meeting sounds louder to the person doing the chewing than to those nearby because it rattles the temporal bone and thus augments the sounds from the ears.

Australian Professor Graeme Clark developed a revolutionary cochlear implant device that artificially enables the deaf to hear by electrically stimulating the inner ear to produce sound sensations. Shenae Hyland received a device at six months of age, making her one of the youngest babies to have a cochlear implant in Australia.

The ***cochlea*** (figure 4.19) is a three-chambered tube in the inner ear shaped like a snail and involved in transduction of sound. When the stirrup vibrates against the oval window, the oval window vibrates, causing pressure waves in the cochlear fluid. These waves disturb the basilar membrane, which separates two of the cochlea's chambers.

Attached to the basilar membrane are the ear's 15 000 receptors for sound, called ***hair cells*** (because they terminate in tiny bristles, or cilia). Above the hair cells is another membrane, the tectorial membrane, which also moves as waves of pressure travel through the cochlear fluid. The cilia bend as the basilar and tectorial membranes move in different directions. This triggers action potentials in sensory neurons forming the ***auditory nerve***, which transmits auditory information to the brain. Thus, mechanical energy — the movement of cilia and membranes — is transduced into neural energy.

Sensory deficits in hearing, as in other senses, can arise from problems either with parts of the sense organ that channel stimulus energy or with the receptors and neural circuits that convert this energy into psychological experience. Failure of the outer or middle ear to conduct sound to the receptors in the hair cells is called conduction loss; failure of receptors in the inner ear or of neurons in any auditory pathway in the brain is referred to as sensorineural loss.

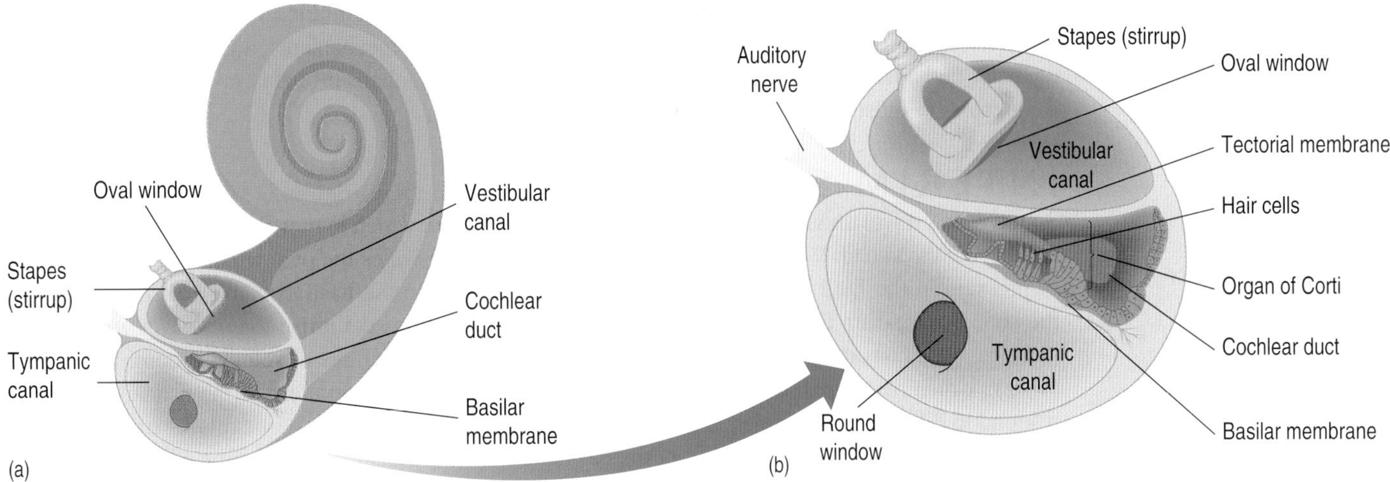

FIGURE 4.19
The anatomy of hearing. (a) The cochlea's chambers (the vestibular canal, the cochlear duct and the tympanic canal) are filled with fluid. When the stapes vibrates against the oval window, it vibrates, causing pressure waves in the fluid of the vestibular canal. These pressure waves spiral up the vestibular canal and down the tympanic canal, flexing the basilar membrane and, to a lesser extent, the tectorial membrane. (b) Transduction occurs in the organ of Corti, which includes these two membranes and the hair cells sandwiched between them. At the end of the tympanic canal is the round window, which pushes outward to relieve pressure when the sound waves have passed through the cochlea.

The most common problems with hearing result from exposure to noise or reflect changes in the receptors through ageing; similar age-related changes occur in most sensory systems (chapter 12). A single exposure to an extremely loud noise, such as a firecracker, an explosion or a gun firing at close range, can permanently damage the hair cell receptors in the inner ear. Many musicians who have spent years in front of loud amplifiers are functionally deaf or have lost a large portion of their hearing.

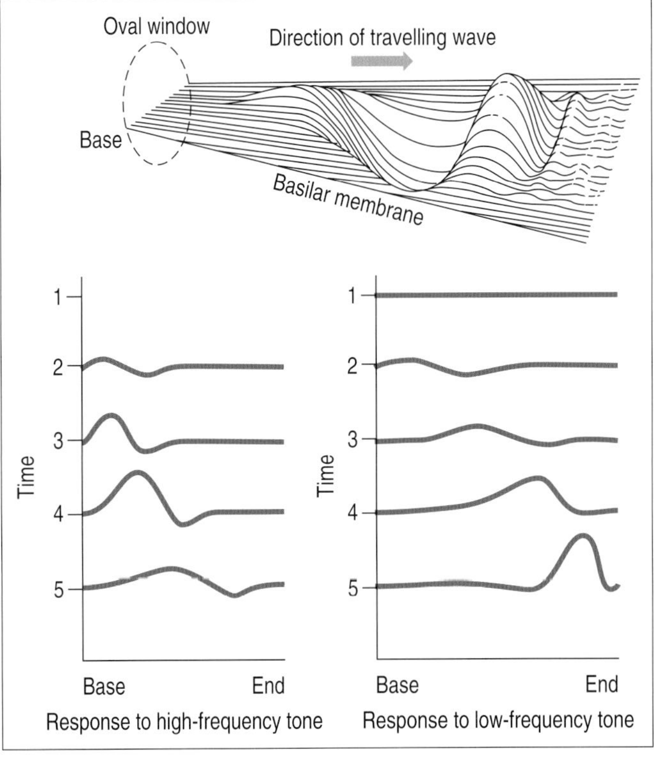

FIGURE 4.20
Place theory. The frequency with which the stapes strikes the oval window affects the location of peak vibration on the basilar membrane. The lower the tone, the farther the maximum displacement on the membrane is from the oval window.

SOURCE: From Sekuler and Blake (1994). Copyright © 1994, 1990, 1985 by McGraw-Hill, Inc. Reproduced with the permission of the McGraw-Hill Companies.

Sensing pitch

Precisely how does auditory transduction transform the physical properties of sound frequency and amplitude into the psychological experiences of pitch and loudness? Two theories, both proposed in the nineteenth century and once considered opposing explanations, together appear to explain the available data.

The first, called ***place theory***, holds that different areas of the basilar membrane are maximally sensitive to different frequencies (Bekesy, 1959, 1960; Helmholtz, 1863). Place theory was initially proposed by Herman von Helmholtz (of trichromatic colour fame), who had the wrong mechanism but the right idea. A Hungarian scientist named Georg von Bekesy discovered the mechanism a century after Helmholtz by recognising that when the stapes hits the oval window, a wave travels down the basilar membrane like a carpet being shaken at one end (figure 4.20). Shaking a carpet rapidly (i.e. at high frequency) produces an early peak in the wave of the carpet, whereas shaking it slowly produces a peak in the wave towards the other end of the carpet. Similarly, high-frequency tones, which produce rapid strokes of the stapes, produce the largest displacement of the basilar membrane close to the oval window, whereas low-frequency tones cause a peak in basilar movement towards the far end of the membrane. Peak vibration leads to peak firing of hair cells at a particular location. Hair cells at different points on the basilar membrane thus transmit information about different frequencies to the brain, just as rods and cones transduce electromagnetic energy at different frequencies.

Place theory has one major problem. At very low frequencies the entire basilar membrane vibrates fairly uniformly; thus, for very low tones, location of maximal vibration cannot account for pitch. The second theory of pitch, ***frequency theory***, overcomes this problem. It proposes that the more frequently a sound wave cycles, the more frequently the basilar membrane vibrates and its hair cells fire. Thus, pitch perception is probably mediated by two neural mechanisms: a place code at high frequencies and a frequency code at low frequencies. Both mechanisms probably operate at intermediate frequencies (Goldstein, 1989).

INTERIM SUMMARY

Sound waves travel through the auditory canal to the ***eardrum***, which in turn sets the ossicles in motion, amplifying the sound. When the stirrup (one of the ossicles) strikes the oval window, it creates waves of pressure in the fluid of the ***cochlea***. ***Hair cells*** attached to the basilar membrane then transduce the sound, triggering firing of the sensory neurons whose axons comprise the ***auditory nerve***. Two theories, once considered opposing, explain the psychological qualities of sound. According to ***place theory***, which best explains transduction at high frequencies, different areas of the basilar membrane respond to different frequencies. According to ***frequency theory***, which best explains transduction at low frequencies, the rate of vibration of the basilar membrane transforms frequency into pitch.

Neural pathways

Sensory information transmitted along the auditory nerves ultimately finds its way to the auditory cortex in the temporal lobes, but it makes several stops along the way (figure 4.21). The auditory nerve from each ear projects to the medulla, where the majority of its fibres cross over to the other hemisphere. (Recall from chapter 3 that the medulla is where sensory and motor neurons cross from one side of the body to the other.) From the medulla, bundles of axons project to the midbrain (to the inferior colliculus, just below the superior colliculus, which is involved in vision) and on to the thalamus (to the medial geniculate nucleus, just towards the centre of the brain from its visual counterpart, the lateral geniculate nucleus). The thalamus transmits information to the auditory cortex in the temporal lobes, which has sections devoted to different frequencies.

Just as the cortical region corresponding to the fovea is disproportionately large, so, too, is the region of the primary auditory cortex tuned to sound frequencies in the middle of the spectrum — the same frequencies involved in speech (Schreiner, Read, & Sutter, 2000). Indeed, in humans and other animals, some cortical neurons in the left temporal lobe respond exclusively to particular sounds characteristic of the 'language' of the species, whether monkey calls or human speech.

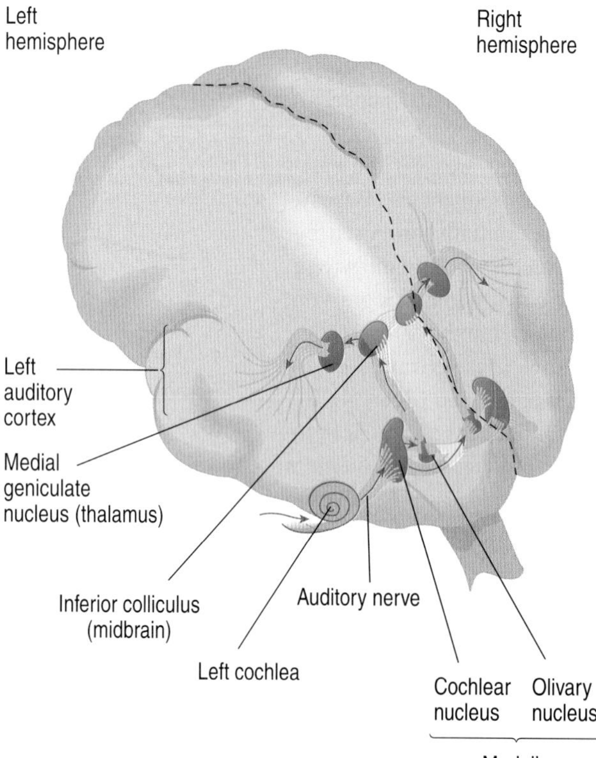

FIGURE 4.21
Auditory pathways. The drawing shows how the brain processes sensory information entering the left ear. Axons from neurons in the inner ear project to the cochlear nucleus in the medulla. From there, most cross over to a structure called the olivary nucleus on the opposite side, although some remain uncrossed. At the olivary nucleus, information from the two ears begins to be integrated. Information from the olivary nucleus then passes to a midbrain structure (the inferior colliculus) and on to the medial geniculate nucleus in the thalamus before reaching the auditory cortex.

APPLY + DISCUSS

- In what ways do systems of neurons in the auditory system resemble those in the visual system?
- How do the ears and brain process the 'size', 'colour' and 'brightness' of a sound, from the ear on up through the cortex?

Sound localisation

Humans use two main cues for ***sound localisation***, which means identifying the location of a sound in space: differences between the two ears in loudness and timing of the sound (Feng & Ratnam, 2000; King & Carlile, 1995; Stevens & Newman, 1934). Particularly for high-frequency sounds, relative loudness in the ear closer to the source provides information about its location because the head blocks some of the sound from hitting the other ear. At low frequencies, localisation relies less on loudness and more on the split-second difference in the arrival time of the sound at the two ears. Moving the head towards sounds is also crucial.

Neurologically, the basis for sound localisation lies in binaural neurons, neurons that respond to relative differences in the signals from two ears. Binaural neurons exist at nearly all levels of the auditory system in the brain, from the brainstem up through the cortex (King & Carlile, 1995). At higher levels of the brain, this information is connected with visual information about the location and distance of objects, which allows joint mapping of auditory and visual information.

Researchers have studied this process of 'coordinating maps' in the barn owl, an animal whose brain localises sound primarily through timing differences between the arrival of the sound at each ear (Feldman, Brainard, & Knudsen, 1996; Konishi, 1995). When these owls are raised wearing glasses that use prisms to distort the perceived location of objects, their auditory map essentially becomes linked to a visual map with different coordinates — leading to difficulty connecting what the eyes know with what the ears know.

INTERIM SUMMARY

From the auditory nerve, sensory information passes through the inferior colliculus in the midbrain and the medial geniculate nucleus of the thalamus on to the auditory cortex in the temporal lobes. ***Sound localisation*** — locating a sound in space — depends on binaural neurons that respond to relative differences in the loudness and timing of sensory signals transduced by the two ears.

APPLY + DISCUSS

Contemporary jazz would have been musically incomprehensible to Mozart, just as hip-hop is senseless noise to people (like parents and textbook authors) who grew up with rock 'n' roll.

- What makes some patterns of sound pleasurable and others 'noise'?
- How might a behaviourist explain the difference?

Other senses

Vision and audition are the most highly specialised senses in humans, occupying the greatest amount of brain space and showing the most cortical evolution. Our other senses, however, play important roles in adaptation as well. These include smell, taste, the skin senses (pressure, temperature and pain) and the proprioceptive senses (body position and motion).

MAKING CONNECTIONS

Vision and hearing are our most prominent senses. However, other senses such as taste and smell are also important in helping us to adapt to our environments. Blind children are thought to develop exceptional sensory abilities to compensate for their loss of sight. However, research by Wakefield, Homewood, and Taylor (2004) suggests that early-blind children develop superior **cognitive skills** that facilitate their **memory** for non-visual material and underlie their enhanced performance on odour naming tasks. In contrast, sighted children often rely on a visual strategy to complete **cognitive tasks** and under perform when unable to apply this strategy (chapters 7 and 8).

Smell

Smell (***olfaction***) serves a number of functions in humans. It enables us to detect danger (e.g. the smell of something burning), discriminate palatable from unpalatable or spoiled foods and recognise familiar others. Smell plays a less important role in humans than in most other animals, who rely heavily on olfaction to mark territory and track other animals. Many species communicate through ***pheromones*** (chapter 10), scent messages detected through an auxiliary olfactory system that regulate the sexual behaviour of many animals and direct a variety of behaviours in insects (Carolsfeld, Tester, Kreiberg, & Sherwood, 1997; Lepri, 2003; Sorensen, 1996).

We humans, in contrast, often try to 'cover our tracks' in the olfactory domain using perfumes and deodorants to mask odours that our mammalian ancestors might have found informative or appealing. Nevertheless, vestiges of this ancient reproductive mechanism remain. Humans appear both to secrete and sense olfactory cues related to reproduction. Experiments using sweaty hands or articles of clothing have shown that people can identify the gender of another person by smell alone with remarkable accuracy (Doty, Green, Ram, & Tandeil, 1982; Russell, 1976; Wallace, 1977). The synchronisation of menstrual cycles of women living in close proximity also appears to occur through smell and may reflect ancient pheromonal mechanisms (McClintock, 1971; Preti, Cutler, Garcia, Huggins, & Lawley, 1986; Stern & McClintock, 1998).

Transduction

The environmental stimuli for olfaction are invisible molecules of gas emitted by substances and suspended in the air. The thresholds for recognising most odours are remarkably low — as low as one molecule per 50 trillion molecules of air for some molecules (Geldard, 1972). Although the nose is the sense organ for smell, the vapours that give rise to olfactory sensations can enter the nasal cavities — the region hollowed out of the bone in the skull that contains smell receptors — through either the nose or the mouth (figure 4.22). When food is chewed, vapours travel up the back of the mouth into the nasal cavity; this process actually accounts for much of the flavour.

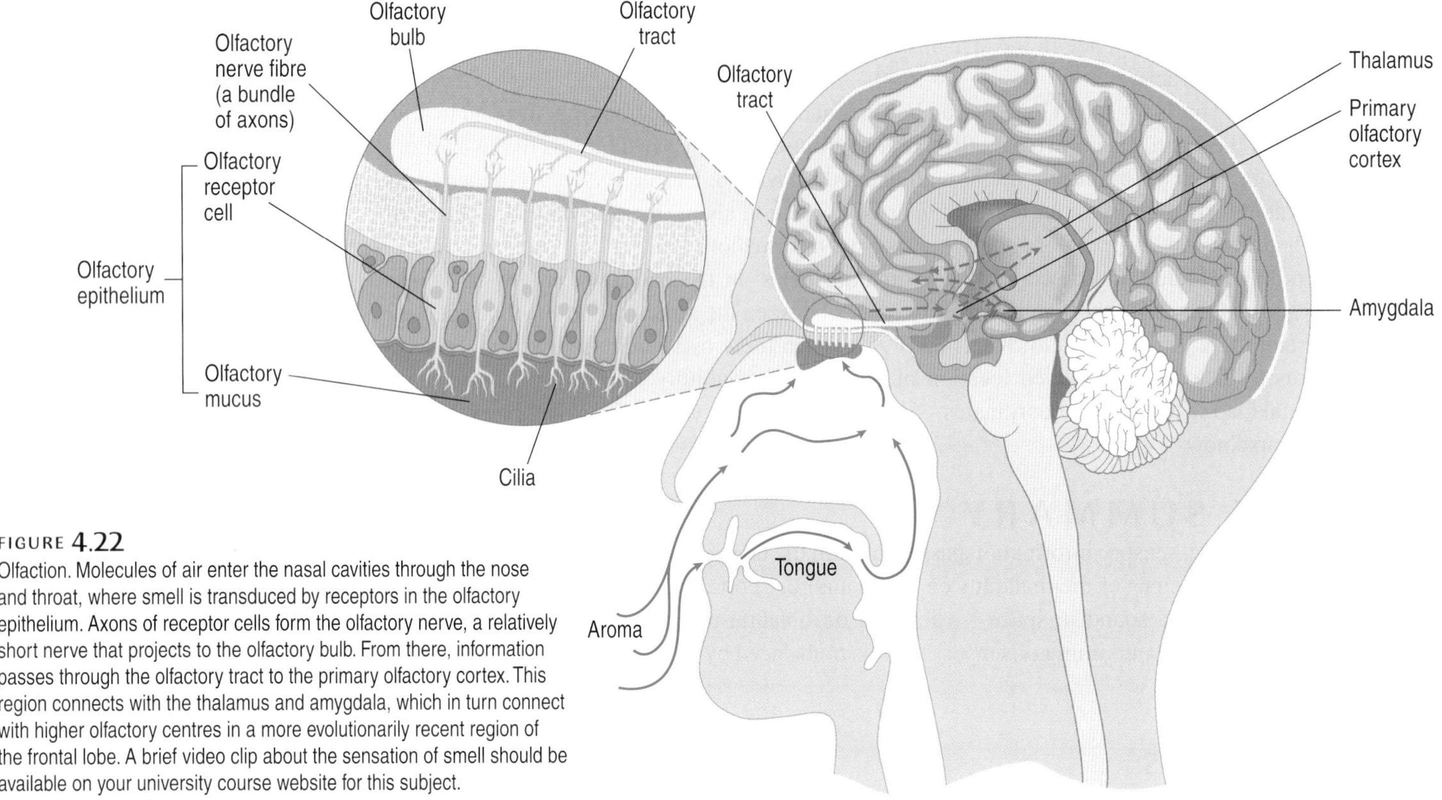

FIGURE 4.22
Olfaction. Molecules of air enter the nasal cavities through the nose and throat, where smell is transduced by receptors in the olfactory epithelium. Axons of receptor cells form the olfactory nerve, a relatively short nerve that projects to the olfactory bulb. From there, information passes through the olfactory tract to the primary olfactory cortex. This region connects with the thalamus and amygdala, which in turn connect with higher olfactory centres in a more evolutionarily recent region of the frontal lobe. A brief video clip about the sensation of smell should be available on your university course website for this subject.

APPLY + DISCUSS

- What senses do humans and other animals use in choosing mates?
- Do species differ in the senses they favour in picking a potential 'lover'?
- How might such differences have evolved?

Transduction of smell occurs in the ***olfactory epithelium***, a thin pair of structures (one on each side) less than 2.5 cm^2 in area at the top of the nasal cavities. Chemical molecules in the air become trapped in the mucus of the epithelium, where they make contact with olfactory receptor cells that transduce the stimulus into olfactory sensations. Humans have approximately 10 million olfactory receptors (Engen, 1982), in comparison with dogs, whose 200 million receptors enable them to track humans and other animals with their noses (Marshall & Moulton, 1981).

Neural pathways

The axons of olfactory receptor cells form the ***olfactory nerve***, which transmits information to the olfactory bulbs, multilayered structures that combine information from receptor cells. Olfactory information then travels to the primary olfactory cortex, a primitive region of the cortex deep in the frontal lobes. Unlike other senses, smell is not relayed through the thalamus on its way to the cortex; however, the olfactory cortex has projections to both the thalamus and the limbic system, so that smell is connected to both taste and emotion.

Many animals that respond to pheromonal cues have a second, or accessory, olfactory system that projects to the amygdala and on to the hypothalamus, which helps regulate reproductive behaviour. Although the data at this point are conflicting, some studies suggest that humans may have a similar secondary olfactory system, which, if operative, has no links to consciousness and thus influences reproductive behaviour without our knowing it (Bartoshuk & Beauchamp, 1994; Stern & McClintock, 1998).

INTERIM SUMMARY

The environmental stimuli for smell are gas molecules suspended in the air. These molecules flow through the nose into the ***olfactory epithelium***, where they are detected by hundreds of different types of receptors. The axons of these receptor cells comprise the ***olfactory nerve***, which transmits information to the olfactory bulbs and on to the primary olfactory cortex deep in the frontal lobes.

Taste

The sense of smell is sensitive to molecules in the air, whereas taste (***gustation***) is sensitive to molecules soluble in saliva. At the dinner table, the contributions of the nose and mouth to taste are indistinguishable, except when the nasal passages are blocked so that food loses much of its flavour.

From an evolutionary perspective, taste serves two functions: to protect the organism from ingesting toxic substances and to regulate intake of nutrients such as sugars and salt. For example, toxic substances often taste bitter, and foods high in sugar (which provides the body with energy) are usually sweet. The tendency to reject bitter substances and to ingest sweet ones is present even in newborns, despite their lack of experience with taste (Bartoshuk & Beauchamp, 1994; Ronenstein & Oster, 2005).

Transduction of taste occurs in the ***tastebuds*** (figure 4.23). Roughly 10 000 tastebuds are distributed throughout the mouth and throat (Miller, 1995), although most are located in the bumps on the surface of the tongue called papillae (Latin for 'pimple'). Soluble chemicals that enter the mouth penetrate tiny pores in the papillae and stimulate the taste receptors. Each tastebud contains between 50 and 150 receptor cells (Margolskee, 1995). Taste receptors, unlike sensory receptors in the eye or ear, wear out and are replaced every 10 or 11 days (Graziadei, 1969). Regeneration is essential, or a burn to the tongue would result in permanent loss of taste.

Taste receptors stimulate neurons that carry information to the medulla and pons and then along one of two pathways. The first leads to the thalamus and primary gustatory cortex and allows us to identify tastes. The second pathway is more primitive and has no access to consciousness. This pathway leads to the limbic system and produces immediate emotional and behavioural responses, such as spitting out a bitter substance or a substance previously associated with nausea. As in blindsight, people with damage to the first (cortical) pathway cannot identify substances by taste, but they react with appropriate facial expressions to bitter and sour substances if this second, more primitive pathway is intact.

The gustatory system responds to four basic tastes: sweet, sour, salty and bitter. Different receptors are most sensitive to one of these tastes, at least at low levels of stimulation. This appears to be cross-culturally universal: people of different cultures diverge in their taste preferences and beliefs about basic flavours, but they vary little in identifying substances as sweet, sour, salty or bitter (Laing, Prescott, Bell, & Gilmore, 1993).

More than one receptor, however, can produce the same sensation, at least for bitterness. Apparently, as plants and insects evolved toxic chemicals to protect against predation, animals that ate them evolved specific receptors for detecting these substances. The nervous system, however, continued to rely on the same sensation, bitterness, to discourage snacking on them (Bartoshuk & Beauchamp, 1994).

The tendency to reject bitter substances and to ingest sweet ones is present from a young age.

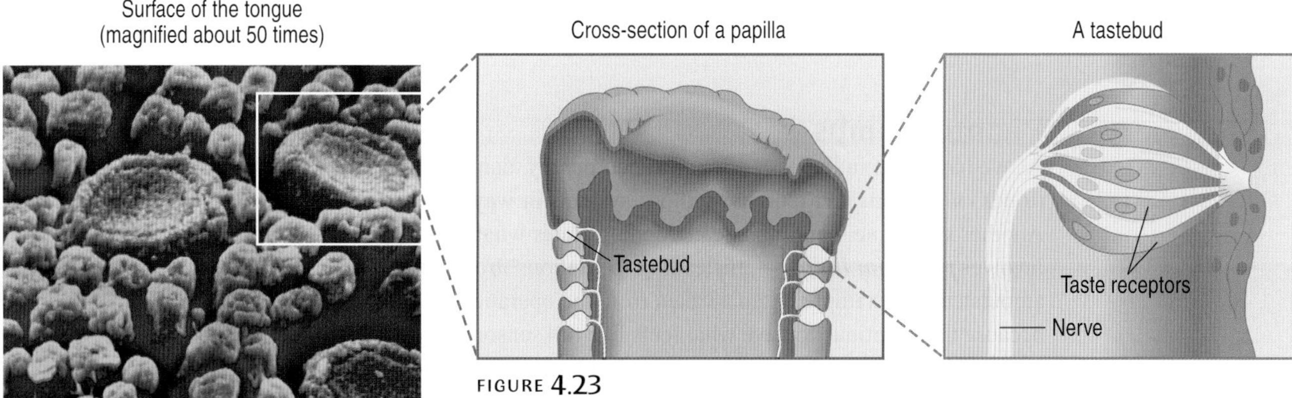

FIGURE 4.23
Tastebuds. The majority of tastebuds are located on the papillae of the tongue (shown in purple). Tastebuds contain receptor cells that bind with chemicals in the saliva and stimulate gustatory neurons. (The cells shown in blue are support cells.)

INTERIM SUMMARY

Taste occurs as receptors in the ***tastebuds*** transduce chemical information from molecules soluble in saliva into neural information, which is integrated with olfactory sensations in the brain. Taste receptors stimulate neurons that project to the medulla and pons in the hindbrain. From there, the information is carried along two neural pathways, one leading to the primary gustatory cortex, which allows identification of tastes, and the other leading to the limbic system, which allows initial gut-level reactions and learned responses to tastes. The gustatory system responds to four tastes: sweet, sour, salty and bitter.

Skin senses

The approximately two square metres of skin covering the human body constitutes a complex, multilayered organ. The skin senses help protect the body from injury, aid in identifying objects, help maintain body temperature and facilitate social interaction through hugs, kisses, holding and handshakes.

What we colloquially call the sense of touch is actually a mix of at least three qualities: pressure, temperature and pain. Approximately 5 million touch receptors in the skin respond to different aspects of these qualities, such as warm or cold or light or deep pressure (figure 4.24). Receptors are specialised for different qualities, but most skin sensations are complex, reflecting stimulation across many receptors.

The qualities that sensory neurons convey to the nervous system (such as soft pressure, warmth and cold) depend on the receptors to which they are connected. Thus, when receptors re-attach to the wrong nerve fibres, as appears to occur in some cases of painful neuropathy, sensory information can be misinterpreted. Like neurons in other sensory systems, those involved in touch also have receptive fields, which distinguish both where and how long the stimulation occurred on the skin.

Sensory neurons synapse with spinal interneurons that stimulate motor neurons, allowing animals to respond with rapid reflex actions. Sensory neurons also synapse with neurons that carry information up the spinal cord to the medulla, where neural tracts cross over. From there, sensory information travels to the thalamus and is subsequently routed to the primary touch centre in the brain, the somatosensory cortex (chapter 3).

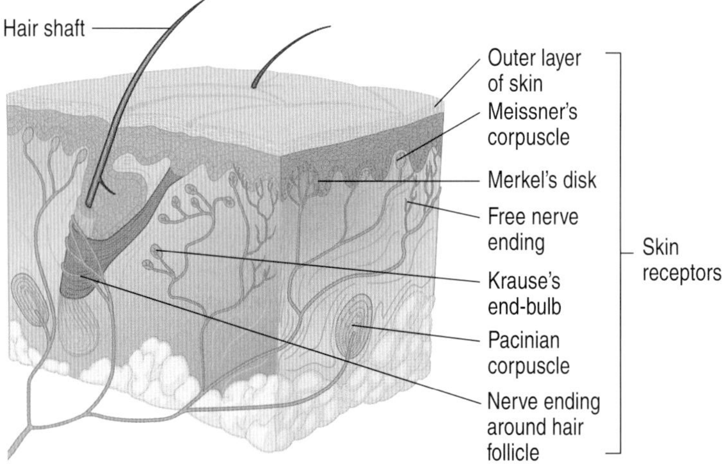

FIGURE **4.24**
The skin and its receptors. Several different types of receptors transduce tactile stimulation, such as Meissner's corpuscles, which respond to brief stimulation (as when a ball of cotton moves across the skin); Merkel's disks, which detect steady pressure; and the nerve endings around hair follicles, which explains why plucking eyebrows or pulling tape off the skin can be painful. A brief video clip about the skin and its receptors should be available from your university course website for this subject.

Phantom limbs

As we have seen in the case of painful neuropathy, damage to the sensory systems that control tactile (touch) sensations can reorganise those systems in ways that lead to an altered experience of reality. Another syndrome that dramatically demonstrates what can happen when those systems are disrupted involves ***phantom limbs*** — misleading 'sensations' from missing limbs. People who have had a limb amputated, for example, often awaken from the operation wondering why the surgeon did not operate, because they continue to have what feels like full sensory experiences from the limb (Katz & Melzack, 1990). Alternatively, they may experience phantom limb pain — pain felt in a limb that no longer exists, typically similar to the pain experienced before the limb was amputated (Chan, 2006). Even if the stump is completely anesthetised, the pain typically persists (Hill, 1999; Melzack, 1970), although hypnosis (chapter 16) is a promising treatment for pain (Chan, 2006).

Phantom limbs have some fascinating implications for our understanding of the way the brain processes sensory information. For example, although the experience of a phantom limb tends to be most pronounced in people who have more recently lost a limb, phantom experiences of this sort can occur even in people who lost a limb very early in life or were born without it (Melzack, 1993). This suggests that certain kinds of sensory 'expectations' throughout the body may be partly innate.

Another aspect of phantom limbs has begun to lead neuroscientists to a better understanding of how the brain reorganises after damage to a sensory system (Ramachandran & Hirstein, 1998). If a hand has been amputated, the person often experiences a touch of the face or shoulder as sensation in the fingers of the missing hand. The locations of sensations that occur with phantom limbs tend to be quite precise, forming a map of the hand on the face and shoulders — so that touching a specific part of the face may repeatedly lead to feelings in a particular part of the missing hand.

Why would this be? Recall from chapter 3 that the primary sensory cortex in the parietal lobes (the somatosensory cortex) contains a map of the body, with each part of the somatosensory cortex representing a specific part of the body. In fact, areas of the somatosensory cortex adjacent to the hand and arm are the face and shoulder. Because stimulation is no longer coming from the hand, these other areas begin to respond to input from the body to adjacent areas (Jones, 2000).

Although phantom limb phenomena certainly seem dysfunctional, the mechanism that produces them probably is not. The brain tends to make use of sensory tissue, and over time, unused cortex is more likely to be 'annexed' than thrown away. For instance, individuals born blind show activity in the visual cortex when reading Braille with their fingers (Hamilton & Pascual-Leone, 1998). Essentially, because the 'fingers' region of the parietal lobes is not large enough to store all the information necessary to read with the fingers, areas of the visual cortex usually involved in the complex sensory discriminations required in reading simply take on a different function. Lesions to the primary visual cortex can, in turn, impair the ability to read Braille (Pascual-Leone, Walsh, & Rothwell, 2000).

Transducing pressure, temperature and pain

Each of the skin senses transduces a distinct form of stimulation. Pressure receptors transduce mechanical energy (like the receptors in the ear). Temperature receptors respond to thermal energy (heat). Pain receptors do not directly transform external stimulation into psychological experience; rather, they respond to a range of internal and external bodily states, from strained muscles to damaged skin.

Pressure

People experience pressure when the skin is mechanically displaced, or moved. Sensitivity to pressure varies considerably over the surface of the body (Craig & Rollman, 1999). The most sensitive regions are the face and fingers, the least sensitive the back and legs, as reflected in the amount of space taken by neurons representing these areas in the somatosensory cortex (see chapter 3).

The hands are the skin's 'foveas', providing tremendous sensory acuity and the ability to make fine discriminations (e.g. between a coin and a button). The primary cortex thus devotes substantial space to the hands (see Johnson & Lamb, 1981). The hands turn what could be a passive sensory process — responding to indentations produced in the skin by external stimulation — into an active process. As the hands move over objects, pressure receptors register the indentations created in the skin and hence allow perception of texture. Just as eye movements allow people to read written words, finger movements allow blind people to read the raised dots that constitute Braille. In other animals, the somatosensory cortex emphasises other body zones that provide important information for adaptation, such as whiskers in cats (Kaas, 1987).

Temperature

When people sense the temperature of an object, they are largely sensing the difference between the temperature of the skin and the object, which is why a pool of 25° Celsius water feels warm to someone who has been standing in the cold rain but chilly to someone lying on a hot beach. Temperature sensation relies on two sets of receptors, one for cold and one for warmth. Cold receptors, however, not only detect coolness but also are involved in the experience of extreme temperatures, both hot and cold. Participants who grasp two pipes twisted together, one containing warm water and the other cold, experience intense heat (figure 4.25). Different neural circuits are, in fact, activated by the combination of cold and warm water than by either cold or warm alone (Craig, Reiman, Evans, & Bushnell, 1996).

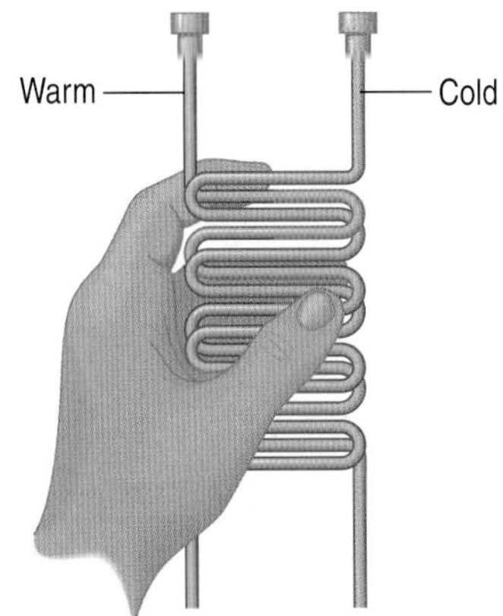

FIGURE 4.25
Experiencing intense heat. Warm and cold receptors activated simultaneously produce a sensation of intense heat.

Pain

People spend billions of dollars a year fighting pain, but pain serves an important function: preventing tissue damage. Indeed, people who are insensitive to pain because of nerve damage or genetic abnormalities are at serious risk of injury and infection (Nagasako, Oaklander, & Dworkin, 2003). Young children with congenital (inborn) pain insensitivity have bitten off their tongues, chewed off the tips of their fingers, and been severely burned leaning against hot stoves or climbing into scalding bathwater (Jewesbury, 1951). On the other hand, persistent pain can be debilitating. The National Health Survey conducted by the Australian Bureau of Statistics (ABS) in 2009 found that back pain is one of the top three medical conditions for Australians. The cost in suffering, lost productivity and dollars is immense (ABS, 2009d).

In contrast to other senses, pain has no specific physical stimulus; the skin does not transduce 'pain waves'. Sounds that are too loud, lights that are too bright, pressure that is too intense, temperatures that are too extreme and other stimuli can all elicit pain. Although pain transduction is not well understood, the most important receptors for pain in the skin appear to be the free nerve endings. According to one prominent theory, when cells are damaged, they release chemicals that stimulate the free nerve endings, which in turn transmit pain messages to the brain (Price, 1988).

Experiencing pain

Of all the senses, pain is probably the most affected by beliefs, expectations and emotional state, and the least reducible to level of stimulation (Sternbach, 1968). A large-scale Australian study of hospitalised cancer patients examined attitudinal barriers to effective pain management. Factors found to potentially influence participants' responses to pain included lack of knowledge about pain, low perceived control over pain and a deficit in communication about pain (Yates et al., 2002). (The next time you have a headache or a sore throat, try focusing your consciousness on the minute details of the sensation, and you will notice that you can momentarily kill the pain by 'reframing' it.) Anxiety can increase pain, whereas intense fear, stress or concentration on other things can inhibit it (al Absi & Rokke, 1991; Melzack & Wall, 1983).

The body's ability to inhibit pain perception makes it possible for endurance athletes, such as champion triathlete Emma Snowsill, to 'push through' pain. Snowsill captured the gold medal for Australia at the Beijing Olympics after completing the three 'legs' that make up this gruelling event — a 1.5 kilometre swim, 40 kilometre cycle and 10 kilometre run — in just under 2 hours.

Cultural norms and expectations also influence the subjective experience and behavioural expression of pain (Bates, 1987; Zatzick & Dimsdale, 1990). For example, on the island of Fiji, women of two subcultures appear to experience labour pain quite differently (Morse & Park, 1988). The native Fijian culture is sympathetic to women in labour and provides both psychological support and herbal remedies for labour pain. In contrast, an Indian subculture on the island considers childbirth contaminating and hence offers little sympathy or support. Interestingly, women from the Indian group rate the pain of childbirth significantly lower than native Fijians. Apparently, cultural recognition of pain influences the extent to which people recognise and acknowledge it.

Gate-control theory

How do cultural norms, expectations and competing sensory signals affect the experience of pain? One theory, ***gate-control theory***, emphasises the role of the central nervous system (the brain and spinal cord) in regulating pain. According to gate-control theory, when sensory neurons transmit information to the back (dorsal region) of the spinal cord, input from other nearby sensory neurons, as well as from messages descending from the brain, can inhibit or amplify their pain signals (Melzack, 1993; Melzack & Wall, 1965).

Gate-control theory distinguishes two kinds of neural fibres (axons from sensory neurons) that open and close spinal 'gateways' for pain. Large-diameter fibres (called A-fibres) transmit neural information very quickly, just as thick cables allow faster internet access than thin telephone wires. A-fibres carry information about many forms of tactile stimulation, including sharp pain. Once they transmit a message, they close the pain gate by inhibiting the firing of the neurons with which they synapse.

Small-diameter fibres (C-fibres) synapse with the same neurons, carrying information about dull pain and burning to the brain. Because their small axons transmit neural information more slowly, their messages may arrive at a closed gate if competing sensory input from A-fibres has inhibited pain transmission. (More accurately, the gate is only partially closed, since pain does not usually completely disappear.)

This theory may explain why rubbing the area around a burn or cut, or even pinching a nearby region of skin, can alleviate pain — because these actions stimulate A-fibres, which close the gates to incoming signals from C-fibres. According to gate-control theory, messages from the brain to the spinal cord can also close or open the gates, so that calm or anxious mental states can increase or decrease pain sensations arising from the peripheral nervous system.

Pain control

Because mental as well as physiological processes contribute to pain, treatment may require attention to both mind and matter — to both the psychology and neurophysiology of pain. The Lamaze method of childbirth, for example, teaches women to relax through deep breathing and muscle relaxation and to distract themselves by focusing their attention elsewhere. It also teaches the woman's 'coach' (her partner) to stimulate A-fibres through gentle massage.

These procedures can be quite effective: Lamaze-trained women tend to experience less pain during labour (Leventhal, Leventhal, Shacham, & Easterling, 1989), and they show a general increase in pain tolerance. For example, experiments show that they are able to keep their hands submerged in ice water longer than women without the training, especially if their coach provides encouragement (Whipple, Josimovich, & Komisaruk, 1990; Worthington, Martin, Shumate, & Carpenter, 1983). Many other techniques target the cognitive and emotional aspects of pain. Though not a magic potion or universal remedy, distraction is generally a useful strategy for increasing pain tolerance (Christenfeld, 1997; McCaul & Malott, 1984). Health care professionals often chatter away while giving patients injections in order to distract and relax them.

Something as simple as a pleasant view can affect pain tolerance as well. In one study, surgery patients whose rooms overlooked lush plant life had shorter hospital stays and required less medication than patients whose otherwise identical rooms looked out on a brick wall (Ulrich, 1984). Similarly, a Hong Kong study found that creating a pleasant environment using an eyeglass display changed the sensation and perception of pain (Tse, Ng, Chung, & Wong, 2002). Environmental psychologists, who apply psychological knowledge to building and landscape design, use such information to help architects design hospitals (Saegert & Winkel, 1990).

MAKING CONNECTIONS

Experimental data show that **hypnosis** can be extremely helpful to burn victims, whose bandages must be constantly removed and replaced to avoid infection — a process so painful that the strongest narcotics can often barely numb the pain (Patterson, Everett, Burns, & Marvin, 1992; see also Hoffman et al., 2004) (chapter 5).

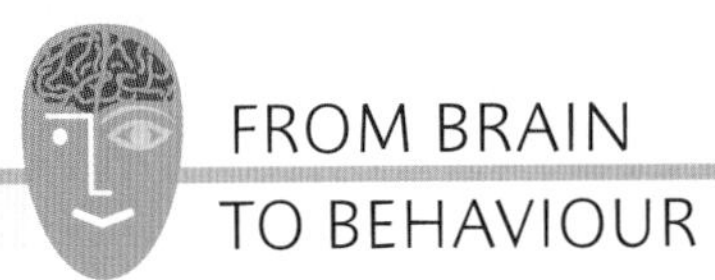

Personality and pain

If mental states can affect pain sensation, are some people vulnerable to chronic pain by virtue of their personalities? Despite long-standing controversy in this area, researchers have identified a personality style that appears to be shared by many chronic pain patients (Keller & Butcher, 1991). These patients often blame their physical condition for all life's difficulties and deny any emotional or interpersonal problems. They tend to have difficulty expressing anger and to be anxious, depressed, needy and dependent.

The difficulty in studying such patients, however, is distinguishing the causes from the effects of chronic pain, since unending pain could produce many of these personality traits (Gamsa, 1990). A team of researchers addressed this methodological problem by studying patients at risk for developing chronic pain before they actually developed it (Dworkin et al., 1992; see also Mogil, Yu, & Basbaum, 2000). The patients suffered from herpes zoster (shingles), a viral infection caused by reactivation of the chicken pox virus. The nature and duration of pain associated with herpes zoster vary widely, but some patients experience disabling chronic pain.

To see if they could predict which patients would develop chronic pain, the investigators gave a sample of recently diagnosed herpes zoster patients a series of questionnaires and tests, including measures of depression, anxiety, life stress, attitudes towards their illness and pain severity. Doctors provided data on the severity of the patients' initial outbreak of the disease. The researchers re-contacted the patients several times over the next year to distinguish those who reported ongoing pain three months after the acute outbreak from those who did not.

Although the two groups did not differ in the initial severity of their symptoms, they did differ significantly on a number of psychological dimensions assessed at the time of their initial diagnosis. Fitting the description of the 'chronic pain personality', those patients who would later experience continued pain were initially more depressed and anxious and less satisfied with their lives than patients without pain. They were also more likely to dwell on their illness and resist doctors' reassurances.

Chronic pain is by no means 'all in the head'. In many cases it likely reflects an interaction of psychological factors, physiological vulnerabilities and disease or injury. But this research suggests that the way people experience themselves and the world affects their vulnerability to their own sensory processes.

INTERIM SUMMARY

Touch includes three senses: pressure, temperature and pain. Sensory neurons synapse with spinal interneurons that stimulate motor neurons (producing reflexes) as well as with neurons that carry information up the spinal cord to the medulla. From there, nerve tracts cross over, and the information is conveyed through the thalamus to the somatosensory cortex, which contains a map of the body. The function of pain is to prevent tissue damage; the experience of pain is greatly affected by beliefs, expectations, emotional state and personality.

Proprioceptive senses

Part of the 'thrill' of amusement park rides comes from our vestibular sense becoming confused. This sense is used by the body to maintain visual fixation, and sometimes to change body orientation. Thrillseekers on The Claw at Dreamworld on the Gold Coast use their vestibular sense to recognise that they are defying gravity, albeit temporarily, on a ride.

Aside from the five traditional senses — vision, hearing, smell, taste and touch — two additional senses, called ***proprioceptive senses***, register body position and movement. The first, the ***vestibular sense***, provides information about the position of the body in space by sensing gravity and movement. The ability to sense gravity is a very early evolutionary development found in nearly all animals. The existence of this sense again exemplifies the way psychological characteristics have evolved to match characteristics of the environment that impact on adaptation. Gravity affects movement, so humans and other animals have receptors to transduce it, just as they have receptors for light.

The vestibular sense organs are in the inner ear, above the cochlea (see figure 4.18). Two organs transduce vestibular information: the semicircular canals and the vestibular sacs. The semicircular canals sense acceleration or deceleration in any direction as the head moves. The vestibular sacs sense gravity and the position of the head in space. Vestibular receptors are hair cells that register movement, much as hair cells in the ear transduce air movements. The neural pathways for the vestibular sense are not well understood, although impulses from the vestibular system travel to several regions of the hindbrain, notably the cerebellum, which is involved in smooth movement, and to a region deep in the temporal cortex.

The other proprioceptive sense, ***kinaesthesia***, provides information about the movement and position of the limbs and other parts of the body relative to one another. Kinaesthesia is essential in guiding every complex movement, from walking, which requires instantaneous adjustments of the two legs, to drinking a cup of coffee. Some receptors for kinaesthesia are in the joints; these cells transduce information about the position of the bones. Other receptors, in the tendons and muscles, transmit messages about muscle tension that signal body position (Neutra & LeBlond, 1969).

The vestibular and kinaesthetic senses work in tandem to communicate different aspects of movement and position. Proprioceptive sensations are also integrated with messages from other sensory systems, especially touch and vision. For example, even when the proprioceptive senses are intact, walking can be difficult if tactile stimulation from the feet is shut off, as when a person's legs 'fall asleep'. (To see the importance of vision to balance, try balancing on one foot while raising the other foot as high as you can, first with your eyes closed and then with your eyes open.)

INTERIM SUMMARY

The ***proprioceptive senses*** register body position and movement. The ***vestibular sense*** provides information on the position of the body in space by sensing gravity and movement. ***Kinaesthesia*** provides information about the movement and position of the limbs and other parts of the body relative to one another.

Perception

The line between sensation and perception is thin, and we probably have already crossed it in discussing the psychology of pain. The hallmarks of perception are organisation and interpretation. (Many psychologists consider attention a third aspect of perception, but since attention is also involved in memory, thought and emotion, we address it in chapter 5 on consciousness.)

Perception organises a continuous array of sensations into meaningful units. When we speak, we produce, on average, a dozen distinct units of sounds (called phonemes) per second (e.g. all the vowel and consonant sounds in a simple word, such as fascination) and are capable of understanding up to 40 phonemes per second (Pinker, 1994). This requires organisation of sensations into units. Beyond organisation, we must interpret the information organised. A scrawl on a piece of paper is not just a set of lines of particular orientation but a series of letters and words.

In this final section, we again emphasise the visual system, since the bulk of work in perception has used visual stimuli, but the same principles largely hold across the senses. We begin by describing several ways in which perception is organised and then examine the way people interpret sensory experiences.

Organising sensory experience

If you put this book on the floor, it does not suddenly look like part of the floor; if you walk slowly away from it, it does not seem to diminish in size. These are examples of perceptual organisation. ***Perceptual organisation*** integrates sensations into ***percepts*** (meaningful perceptual units, such as images of particular objects), locates them in space, and preserves their meaning as the perceiver examines them from different vantage points. Here we explore four aspects of perceptual organisation: form perception, depth or distance perception, motion perception and perceptual constancy.

Form perception

Form perception refers to the organisation of sensations into meaningful shapes and patterns. When you look at this book, you do not perceive it as a patternless collection of molecules. Nor do you perceive it as part of your leg, even though it may be resting in your lap, or think a piece of it has disappeared simply because your hand or pen is blocking your vision of it.

FIGURE 4.26
An ambiguous figure. Whether the perceiver forms a global image of a young or an old woman determines the meaning of each part of the picture; what looks like a young woman's nose from one perspective looks like a wart on an old woman's nose from another. The perception of the whole even leads to different inferences about the coat the woman is wearing. In one case, it appears to be a stylish fur, whereas in the other, it is more likely to be interpreted as an old overcoat.

SOURCE: Boring (1930, p. 42).

Gestalt principles

The first psychologists to study form perception systematically were the Gestalt psychologists of the early twentieth century. As noted in chapter 1, Gestalt is a German word that translates loosely to 'whole' or 'form'. Proponents of the Gestalt approach argued that in perception the whole (the percept) is greater than the sum of its sensory parts.

Consider the ambiguous picture in figure 4.26, which some people see as an old woman with a scarf over her head and others see as a young woman with a feather coming out of a stylish hat.

Depending on the perceiver's gestalt, or whole view of the picture, the short black line in the middle could be either the old woman's mouth or the young woman's necklace.

Based on experiments conducted in the 1920s and 1930s, the Gestalt psychologists proposed a small number of basic perceptual rules the brain automatically and unconsciously follows as it organises sensory input into meaningful wholes (figure 4.27).

- ***Figure–ground perception***. People inherently distinguish between figure (the object they are viewing) and ground (or background), such as words in black ink against a white page.
- ***Similarity***. The brain tends to group similar elements together, such as the circles that form the letter R in figure 4.27a.
- ***Proximity*** (nearness). The brain tends to group together objects that are close to one another. In figure 4.27b, the first six lines have no particular organisation, whereas the same six lines arranged somewhat differently in the second part of the panel are perceived as three pairs.
- ***Good continuation***. If possible, the brain organises stimuli into continuous lines or patterns rather than discontinuous elements. In figure 4.27c, the figure appears to show an X superimposed on a circle, rather than pieces of a pie with lines extending beyond the pie's perimeter.
- ***Simplicity***. People tend to perceive the simplest pattern possible. Most people perceive figure 4.27d as a heart with an arrow through it because that is the simplest interpretation.
- ***Closure***. Where possible, people tend to perceive incomplete figures as complete. If part of a familiar pattern or shape is missing, perceptual processes complete the pattern, as in the triangle shown in figure 4.27e. The second part of figure 4.27e demonstrates another type of closure (sometimes called illusory contour) (Albert, 1993; Kanizsa, 1976). People see two overlapping triangles, but in fact, neither one exists; the brain simply fills in the gaps to perceive familiar patterns. Covering the notched yellow circles reveals that the solid white triangle is entirely an illusion. The brain treats illusory contours as if they were real because illusory contours activate the same areas of early visual processing in visual cortex as real contours (Mendola, Dale, Fischl, Liu, & Tootell, 1999).

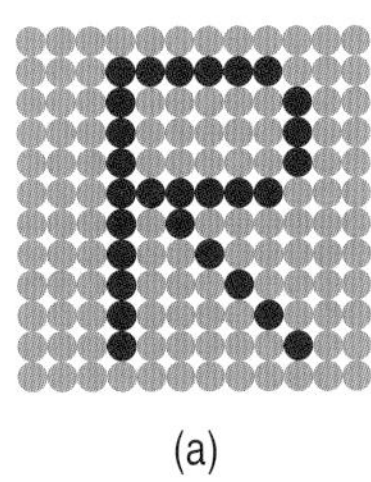
(a)

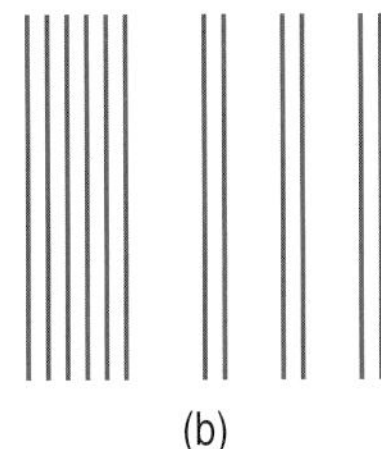
(b)

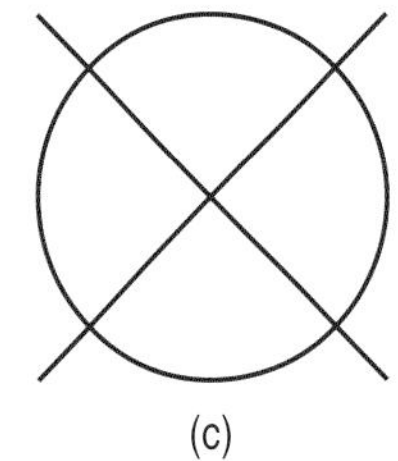
(c)

(d)

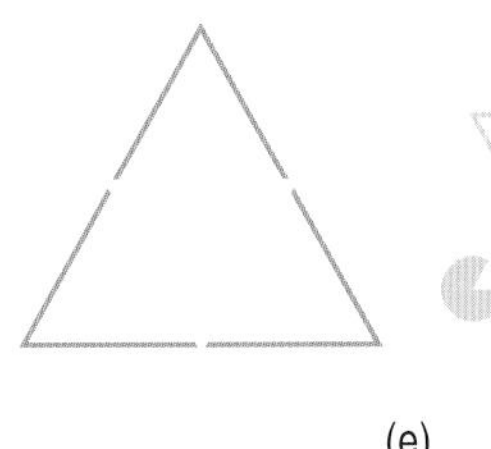
(e)

FIGURE 4.27
Gestalt principles of form perception. The Gestalt psychologists discovered a set of laws of perceptual organisation, including (a) similarity, (b) proximity, (c) good continuation, (d) simplicity and (e) closure.

SOURCE: Part (e) adapted from Kanizsa (1976).

Although the Gestalt principles are most obvious with visual perception, they apply to other senses as well. For example, the figure–ground principle applies when people attend to the voice of a server in a noisy restaurant; her voice becomes figure and all other sounds, ground. In music perception, good continuation allows people to hear a series of notes as a melody; similarity allows them to recognise a melody played on a violin while other instruments are playing; and proximity groups notes played together as a chord.

From an evolutionary perspective, the Gestalt principles exemplify the way the brain organises perceptual experience to reflect the regularities of nature. In nature, the parts of objects tend to be near one another and attached. Thus, the principles of proximity and good continuation are useful perceptual rules of thumb. Similarly, objects often partially block, or occlude, other objects, as when a possum crawls up the bark of a tree. The principle of closure leads humans and other animals to assume the existence of the part of the tree that is covered by the possum's body.

Combining features

More recent research has focused on the question of how the brain combines the simple features detected in primary areas of the cortex (particularly primary visual cortex) into larger units that can be used to identify objects. Object identification requires matching the current stimulus array against past percepts stored in memory to determine the identity of the object (such as a ball, a chair or a particular person's face). Imaging studies and research on patients and animals with temporal lobe lesions suggest that this process occurs along the 'what' visual pathway.

One prominent theory of how the brain forms and recognises images was developed by Irving Biederman (1987, 1990; Bar & Biederman, 1998). Consider the following common scenario. It is late at night, and you are channel surfing — rapidly pressing the television remote control in search of something to watch. From less than a second's glance, you can readily perceive what most shows are about and whether they might be interesting. How does the brain, in less than a second, recognise a complex visual array on a television screen in order to make such a rapid decision?

Biederman and his colleagues have shown that we do not even need a *half* a second to recognise most scenes; 100 milliseconds — a tenth of a second — will typically do. Biederman's theory, called ***recognition-by-components***, asserts that we perceive and categorise objects in our environment by breaking them down into component parts and then matching the components and the way they are arranged against similar 'sketches' stored in memory. According to this theory, the brain combines the simple features extracted by the primary cortex (such as lines of particular orientations) into a small number of elementary geometrical forms (called geons, for 'geometric ions'). From this geometrical 'alphabet' of 20 to 30 geons, the outlines of virtually any object can be constructed, just as millions of words can be constructed from an alphabet of 26 letters. Figure 4.28 presents examples of some of these geons.

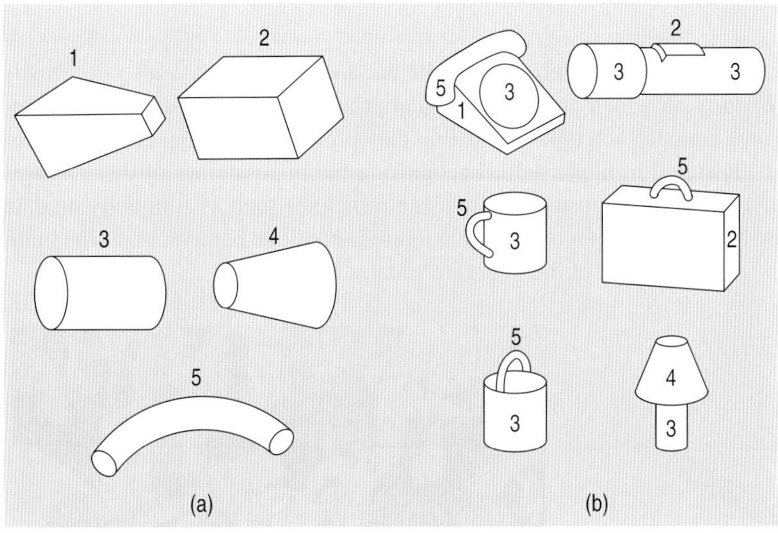

FIGURE 4.28
Recognition by components. The simple geons in (a) can be used to create thousands of different objects (b) simply by altering the relationships among them, such as their relative size and placement.

SOURCE: Biederman (1990, p. 49).

Biederman argues that combining primitive visual sensations into geons not only allows rapid identification of objects but also explains why we can recognise objects even when parts of them are blocked or missing. The reason is that the Gestalt principles, such as good continuation, apply to perception of geons. In other words, the brain fills in gaps in a segment of a geon, such as a blocked piece of a circle. The theory predicts, and research supports the prediction, that failures in identifying objects should occur if the lines where separate geons connect are missing or ambiguous, so that the brain can no longer tell where one component ends and another begins (figure 4.29; overleaf).

Recognition-by-components is not a complete theory of form perception. It was intended to explain how people make relatively rapid initial determinations about what they are seeing and what might be worth closer inspection. More subtle discriminations require additional analysis of qualities such as colour, texture and movement, as well as the integration of these different mental 'maps' (Ullman, 1995). For example, participants asked to find a triangle in a large array of geometric shapes can do so very quickly, whether the triangle is one of 10 or 50 other shapes (Triesman, 1986). If they are asked to find the *red* triangle, not only does their response time increase, but the length of time required is directly proportional to the number of other geometric shapes in view. Apparently, making judgements about the conjunction of two attributes — in this case, shape and colour — requires not only consulting two maps (one of shape and the other of colour) but also superimposing one on the other. That we can carry out such complex computations as quickly as we can is remarkable.

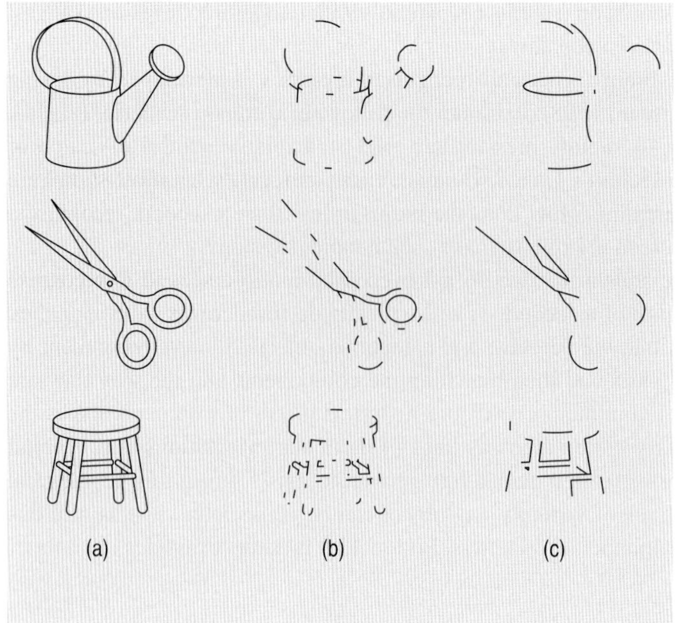

FIGURE 4.29
Identifiable and unidentifiable images. People can rapidly identify objects (a) even if many parts of them are missing, as long as the relationships among their components, or geons, remain clear (b). When they can no longer tell where one geon ends and another begins (c), the ability to identify the objects will disappear.

SOURCE: Biederman (1987, p. 135).

Perceptual illusions

Sometimes the brain's efforts to organise sensations into coherent and accurate percepts fail. This is the case with ***perceptual illusions***, in which normal perceptual processes produce perceptual misinterpretations. Impossible figures are one such type of illusion; they provide conflicting cues for three-dimensional organisation, as illustrated in figure 4.30. Recognising the impossibility of these figures takes time because the brain attempts to impose order by using principles such as simplicity on data that allow no simple solution. Each portion of an impossible figure is credible, but as soon as the brain organises sensations in one way, another part of the figure invalidates it.

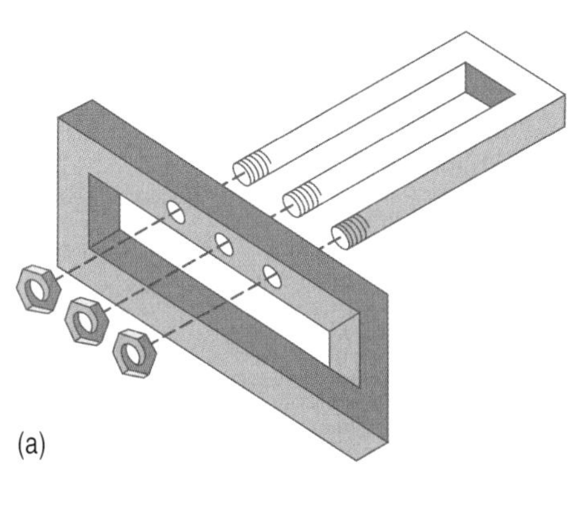

FIGURE 4.30
Impossible figures. The brain cannot form a stable percept because each time it does, another segment of the figure renders the percept impossible. Escher, who painted the impossible figure in (b), made use of perceptual research.

Perceptual illusions

By Professor Peter Wenderoth, Macquarie University

In this chapter there is a section titled 'Perceptual illusions', but it deals only with impossible figures (figure 4.30). Impossible figures can be seen as locally consistent but globally impossible. Thus, the 'object' in figure 4.30a appears to have two prongs at its right-hand end but three at its left-hand end. Each of these local views when examined in isolation is consistent with a particular 3D interpretation of the object, but the global percept (a left-hand middle prong that becomes an empty space on the right-hand side) is impossible. Yet the term 'illusion' is used in several other places in the chapter, referring, for example, to figures 4.27e, 4.32, 4.34, 4.35, 4.36 and 4.37, none of which exhibits an impossible figure. There is no definition of 'perceptual illusion' given in the chapter, so what might be an acceptable definition? And are impossible figures really examples of illusions?

Elsewhere, I have stated that 'A visual illusion occurs when there is a discrepancy between a physical stimulus and the perception of that stimulus, despite the normal functioning of the visual system' (*Encyclopedia of Neuroscience*, Springer, August 2008). This definition seems to apply adequately to the perceived triangle that is not really there (figure 4.27e); to the moon that normally appears small and far away when at the zenith but that sometimes appears very big and close near the horizon (figure 4.34); and to the equal lines that look unequal in geometrical drawings (figures 4.35 and 4.37). But the definition does not really apply to impossible figures, because there is no sense in which there is a discrepancy between the physical display and the perception: we correctly perceive two or three prongs if we attend only to one end or the other; and we correctly perceive that the figure is impossible if we attend to the whole figure at once. I would also argue that there is no illusion in figure 4.32: the various monocular depth cues give an impression of depth but there is no discrepancy between the stimulus and the percept. Despite the 'impression' of depth, the viewer does not actually *perceive* the boats as further away than the men in the foreground and the page correctly appears flat.

Perceptual illusions have proved useful to psychologists who seek to understand how perceptual systems function normally. Thus, neuropsychologists study patients with specific brain damage to learn about normal brain functioning; and perceptual scientists study illusions where perception fails, to understand the mechanisms of normal perceptual functioning (e.g. Wenderoth & Johnstone, 1988). Impossible figures reveal nothing about perceptual mechanisms.

Illusions occur when the part of the stimulus being judged — the test stimuli (e.g. the truly equal lines in figures 4.35 and 4.37) are presented *simultaneously* with the other components that cause the illusion — the inducing stimuli (the arrowheads in figure 4.35 and the converging lines in figure 4.37). But similar effects occur when the inducing stimuli are presented for a prolonged period and then replaced (i.e. *successively*) by the test stimuli. These are called after-effects. An example is the motion after-effect: staring at a waterfall for about 60 seconds causes the stationary surrounds to appear to drift upwards for a while (the same effect often occurs after watching rolling movie credits).

It is also important to remember that many perceptual illusions occur in more than one modality (e.g. vision and touch), including the Müller-Lyer illusion in figure 4.35. When this is true, purely *visual* explanations such as that offered here simply cannot be adequate.

INTERIM SUMMARY

Perception involves the organisation and interpretation of sensory experience. ***Form perception*** refers to the organisation of sensations into meaningful shapes and patterns (***percepts***). The Gestalt psychologists described several principles of form perception. More recently, a theory called ***recognition-by-components*** has argued that people perceive and categorise objects by first breaking them down into elementary units. The brain's efforts to organise percepts can sometimes produce ***perceptual illusions***.

Depth perception

A second aspect of perceptual organisation is ***depth*** or ***distance perception***, the organisation of perception in three dimensions. Depth perception is integral to the experience that a person has when watching a movie or television program that creates the illusion of three-dimensional viewing. The Hollywood blockbuster *Avatar* became the highest grossing film of all time after offering moviegoers the opportunity to enter a three-dimensional world, known as Pandora, in which the wonder of nature was on full display (Serjeant, 2010). Soon after *Avatar* was released, several leading television manufacturers announced plans to launch three-dimensional television sets that could be used, in conjunction with liquid crystal shutter glasses, to offer consumers a unique and interactive viewing experience. You are also making a three-dimensional judgement with this book — perceiving it as

Liquid crystal shutter glasses must be worn to create the illusion of a three-dimensional viewing experience on the flatscreen three-dimensional television sets that have recently been introduced to the market. The glass in each eye contains a liquid crystal layer that alternates between being dark and transparent, depending on the infrared instructions received from the display screen. The glasses artificially alter depth perception, ensuring each eye receives only the image specifically intended for it to create the desired viewing effect.

having height, width and breadth, and as being at a particular distance. Similarly, a skilled athlete might use depth perception to throw a ball 14 metres into a tiny hoop that is not much bigger than the ball. Three-dimensional judgements are made based on two-dimensional retinal images, and are done with such rapidity that we have no awareness of the computations our nervous system is making.

Although we focus again on the visual system, other sensory systems provide cues for depth perception as well, such as auditory cues and kinaesthetic sensations about the extension of the body. Two kinds of visual information provide particularly important information about depth and distance: ***binocular cues*** (visual input integrated from the two eyes) and ***monocular cues*** (visual input from one eye).

Binocular cues

Because the eyes are in slightly different locations, all but the most distant objects produce a different image on each retina, or a retinal disparity. To see this in action, hold your finger about 15 centimetres from your nose and alternately close your left and right eye. You will note that each eye sees your finger in a slightly different position. Now, do the same for a distant object; you will note only minimal differences between the views. Retinal disparity is greatest for close objects and diminishes with distance.

How does the brain translate retinal disparity into depth perception? Most cells in the primary visual cortex are ***binocular cells***; that is, they receive information from both eyes. Some of these cells respond most vigorously when the same input arrives from each eye, whether the input is a vertical line, a horizontal line or a line moving in one direction. Other binocular cells respond to disparities between the eyes.

Like many cells receptive to particular orientations, binocular cells require environmental input early in life to assume their normal functions. Researchers have learned about binocular cells by allowing kittens to see with only one eye at a time, covering one eye or the other on alternate days. As adults, these cats are unable to use binocular cues for depth perception (Blake & Hirsch, 1975; Crair, Gillespie, & Stryker, 1998; Packwood & Gordon, 1975).

Another binocular cue, convergence, is actually more kinaesthetic than visual. When looking at a close object (such as your finger 15 centimetres in front of your face), the eyes converge, whereas distant objects require ocular divergence. Convergence of the eyes towards each other thus creates a distance cue produced by muscle movements in the eyes.

Monocular cues

Although binocular cues are extremely important for depth perception, people do not crash their cars whenever an eyelash momentarily gets into one eye, because they can still rely on monocular cues. The photograph of the Taj Majal in figure 4.31 illustrates the main monocular depth cues involved even when looking at a non-moving scene:

- *Interposition.* When one object blocks part of another, the obstructed object is perceived as more distant.
- *Elevation.* Objects farther away are higher on a person's plane of view and thus appear higher up towards the horizon.
- *Texture gradient.* Textured surfaces, such as cobblestones or grained wood, appear coarser at close range, and finer and more densely packed at greater distances.
- *Linear perspective.* Parallel lines appear to converge in the distance.
- *Shading.* The brain assumes that light comes from above and hence interprets shading differently towards the top or the bottom of an object.
- *Aerial perspective.* Because light scatters as it passes through space, and especially through moist or polluted air, objects at greater distances appear fuzzier than those nearby.
- *Familiar size.* People tend to assume an object is its usual size and therefore perceive familiar objects that appear small as distant.
- *Relative size.* When looking at two objects known to be of similar size, people perceive the smaller object as farther away.

FIGURE 4.31
Monocular depth cues. The photo of the Taj Majal in India illustrates all of the monocular cues to depth perception: interposition (the trees blocking the sidewalk and the front of the building), elevation (the most distant object seems to be the highest), texture gradient (the relative clarity of the breaks in the walkways closer to the camera), linear perspective (the convergence of the lines of the walkways surrounding the water), shading (the indentation of the arches towards the top of the building), aerial perspective (the lack of detail of the towers in the distance), familiar size (the people standing on the balcony who seem tiny) and relative size (the diminishing size of the trees as they get further away).

Artists working in two-dimensional media rely on monocular depth cues to represent a three-dimensional world. Thus, people have used interposition and elevation to convey depth for thousands of years. Other cues, however, such as linear perspective, were not discovered until as late as the fifteenth century; as a result, art before that time appears flat to the modern eye (figure 4.32a). Although some monocular cues appear to be innate, cross-cultural research suggests that perceiving three dimensions in two-dimensional drawings is partially learned. For example, people in technologically less developed cultures who have never seen photography often initially have difficulty recognising even their own images in two-dimensional form (Berry, Poortinga, Segall, & Dasen, 1992).

(a)

(b)

Australian War Memorial neg. ART02161

FIGURE 4.32
Artistic use of monocular cues for depth perception has developed tremendously since Giotto's *Flight into Egypt* painted in the fifteenth century (a). In this painting of the Gallipoli landing (b), the artist had much greater mastery of monocular cues for depth perception, such as linear perspective, creating the illusion of depth.

A final monocular depth cue arises from movement. When people move, images of nearby objects sweep across their field of vision faster than objects farther away. This disparity in apparent velocity produces a depth cue called ***motion parallax***. The relative motion of nearby versus distant objects is particularly striking when looking out the window of a moving car or train. Nearby trees appear to speed by, whereas distant objects barely seem to move.

Motion perception

From an evolutionary perspective, just as important as identifying objects and their distance is identifying motion. A moving object is potentially a dangerous object — or, alternatively, a meal, a mate, or a friend or relative in distress. Thus, it is no surprise that humans, like other animals, developed the capacity for ***motion perception*** — the perception of movement in objects.

Motion perception occurs in multiple sensory modes. People can perceive the movement of a fly on the skin through touch, just as they can perceive the fly's trajectory through space by the sounds it makes. We focus here again, however, on the visual system.

Neural pathways

The visual perception of movement begins in the retina itself, with ganglion cells called ***motion detectors*** that are particularly sensitive to movement. These cells tend to be concentrated outside the fovea, to respond (and stop responding) very quickly and to have large receptive fields. These characteristics make adaptive sense. An object in the fovea is one we are already 'keeping a close eye on' through attention to it; motion detectors in the periphery of our vision, in contrast, provide an early warning system to turn the head or the eyes towards something potentially relevant. Without relatively quick onset and offset of motion-detecting neurons, many objects could escape detection by moving faster than these neurons could fire. Large receptive fields cover a large visual landscape, maximising the likelihood of detecting motion (Schiffman, 1996).

With each 'stop' along the processing stream in the brain, the receptive fields of neurons that detect motion grow larger. Several ganglion cells project to each motion-detecting neuron in the thalamus. Several of these thalamic neurons may then feed into motion-sensitive neurons in the primary visual cortex. From there, information travels along the 'where' pathway through a region in the temporal lobes called area MT (for medial temporal) and finally to the parietal lobes (see Barinaga, 1997; Rodman & Albright 1989; Tootell, Reppas, Kwong, & Malach, 1995). In area MT, receptive fields are even larger than in the primary visual cortex, and many neurons are direction sensitive, firing vigorously only if an object is moving in the direction to which the neuron is tuned. Interestingly, area MT can be activated by still photos that contain cues suggesting movement, such as a runner in midstride (Kourtzi & Kanwisher, 2000).

Two systems for processing movement

Tracking an object's movement is a tricky business because the perceiver may be moving as well. Thus, accurate perception requires distinguishing the motion of the perceiver from the motion of the perceived. Current developments in this field include using computational models to analyse properties of the primary visual cortex and MT neurons. For example, Perrone (2004) has constructed computer simulations of how the neurons in the MT area of the brain perceive movement.

Consider the perceptual task of a tennis player awaiting a serve. Most tennis players bob, fidget or move from side to side as they await a serve, which means that the image on their retina is changing every second, even before the ball is in the air. Once the ball is served, its retinal image becomes larger and larger as it approaches, and the brain must calculate its distance and velocity as it moves through space. Making matters more complex, the perceiver is likely to be running, all the while trying to keep the ball's image on the fovea. And the brain must integrate these cues — the size of the image on the retina, its precise location on the retina, the movement of the eyes and the movement of the body — all in a split second.

Two systems appear to be involved in motion perception (Gregory, 1978). The first calculates motion from the changing image projected by the object on the retina (figure 4.33a). This system operates when the eyes are relatively stable, as when an insect darts across the floor so quickly that the eyes cannot move fast enough to track it. In this case, the image of the insect moves across the retina, and motion detectors then fire as adjacent receptors in the retina bleach one after another in rapid succession.

The second system makes use of commands from the brain to the muscles in the eye that signal the presence of eye movements. This mechanism operates when people move their head and eyes to follow an object, as when fans watch a runner sprinting towards the finish line. In this case, the image of the object remains at roughly the same place on the retina; what moves is the position of the eyes (figure 4.33b). The brain calculates movement from a combination of the image on the retina and the movement of eye muscles. Essentially, if the eyes are moving but the object continues to cast the same retinal image, the object must be moving. (A third system, less well understood, probably integrates proprioceptive and other cues to offset the impact of body movements on the retinal image.)

APPLY + DISCUSS

- To what extent do we *learn* to perceive motion or are we *born* to perceive motion?
- Why can experienced drivers estimate their speed better than inexperienced drivers? How do they do it?
- Is motion a characteristic of reality, perceptual experience or both?

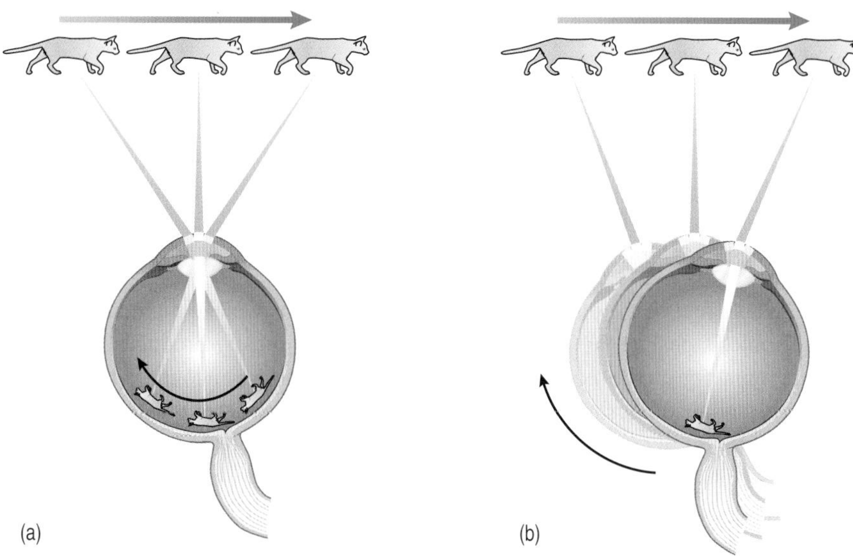

FIGURE 4.33
Two systems for processing movement. In (a), a stationary eye detects movement as an object moves across the person's visual field, progressively moving across the retina. In (b), the eye moves along with the object, which casts a relatively constant retinal image. What changes are the background and signals from the brain that control the muscles that move the eyes.

SOURCE: Adapted from Gregory (1970) and Schiffman (1996).

Perceptual constancy

A fourth form of perceptual organisation, ***perceptual constancy***, refers to the perception of objects as relatively stable despite changes in the stimulation of sensory receptors. As your grandmother walks away from you, you do not perceive her as shrinking, even though the image she casts on your retina is steadily decreasing in size (although you may notice that she has shrunk a little since you last saw her). You similarly recognise that a song on the radio is still the same even though the volume has been turned down. Here we examine three types of perceptual constancy, again focusing on vision: size, colour and shape constancy.

Size constancy

One type of perceptual constancy is ***size constancy***: objects do not appear to change in size when viewed from different distances. The closer an object is, the larger an image it casts on the retina. A car three metres away will cast a retinal image five times as large as the same car 15 metres away, yet people do not wonder how the car 15 metres away can possibly carry full-sized passengers. The reason is that the brain corrects for the size of the retinal image based on cues such as the size of objects in the background.

Helmholtz (1909/1962) was the first to recognise that the brain adjusts for distance when assessing the size of objects, just as it adjusts for colour and brightness. He called this process unconscious inference, because people have no consciousness of the computations involved. Although these computations generally lead to accurate inferences, they can also give rise to perceptual illusions. A classic example is the moon illusion, in which the moon seems larger on the horizon than at its zenith (figure 4.34). This illusion appears to result from the visual system interpreting objects on the horizon as farther away than objects overhead (Kaufman & Rock, 1989). For most objects, like birds and clouds, this is a good inference. Astronomical objects, including the moon and sun, are the only phenomena we encounter that occur both overhead and on the horizon without varying in distance.

FIGURE 4.34
The moon illusion. The moon appears larger against a city skyline than high in the sky, where, among other things, no depth cues exist. The retinal image is the same size in both cases, but in one case, depth cues signal that it must be further away.

Colour constancy

Colour constancy refers to the tendency to perceive the colour of objects as stable despite changing illumination. An apple appears the same colour in the kitchen as it does in the sunlight, even though the light illuminating it is very different. A similar phenomenon occurs with achromatic colour (black and white). Snow in moonlight appears whiter than coal appears in sunlight, even though the amount of light reflected off the coal may be greater (Schiffman, 1996).

In perceiving the brightness of an object, neural mechanisms adjust for the amount of light illuminating it. For chromatic colours, the mechanism is more complicated, but colour constancy does not work if the light contains only a narrow band of wavelengths. Being in a room with only red light bulbs causes even familiar objects to appear red.

A case study of a patient who lacked colour constancy shed light on the neural circuits involved in colour constancy. The patient had damage to an area at the border of the occipital and temporal lobes that responds to changing illumination and thus plays a central role in colour constancy (Zeki, Aglioti, McKeefry, & Berlucchi, 1999). The patient could see colours, but as the illumination surrounding objects changed, so did the patient's perception of the object's colour.

Shape constancy

Shape constancy, a remarkable feat of the engineering of the brain, means we can maintain constant perception of the shape of objects despite the fact that the same object typically produces a new and different impression on the retina (or on the receptors in our skin) every time we encounter it. The brain has to overcome several substantial sources of noise to recognise, for example, that the unkempt beast in the mirror whose hair is pointing in every direction is the same person you happily called 'me' the night before. When people see an object for the second time, they are likely to see it from a different position, with different lighting, in a different setting (e.g. against a different background), with different parts of it blocked from view (such as different locks of hair covering the face), and even in an altered shape (such as a body standing up versus on the couch) (see Ullman, 1995).

Recognition-by-components (geon) theory offers one possible explanation. As long as enough of the geons that define the form of the object remain the same, the object ought to be identifiable. Thus, if a person views a bee on a flower and then as it flies around her face, she will still recognise the insect as a bee as long as it still looks like a tube with a little cone at the back and thin waferlike wings flapping at its sides.

Other theorists, however, argue that geons are not the whole story. Some propose that each time we view an object from a different perspective, we form a mental image of it from that point of view. Each new viewpoint provides a new image stored in memory. The next time we see a similar object, we rotate it in our minds so that we can 'see' it from a previously seen perspective to determine if it looks like the same object, or we match it against an image generalised from our multiple 'snapshots' of it.

Research has shown that the more different a scene is from the way a person saw it before (e.g. if the image is 90 versus 15 degrees off from the earlier image), the longer the person will take to recognise it (DeLoache, Miller, & Rosengren, 1997; Tarr, Buelthoff, Zabinski, & Blanz, 1997; Ullman, 1989). This suggests that shape constancy does, to some extent, rely on rotating mental images (probably of both geons and finer perceptual details) and comparing them against perceptual experiences stored in memory.

Culture and perceptual illusions

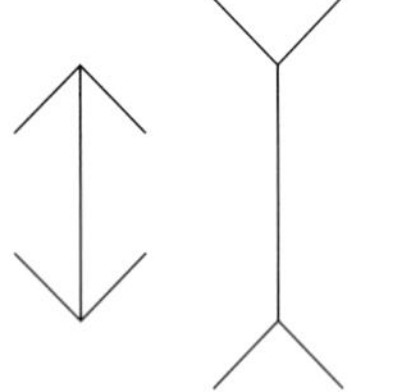

FIGURE 4.35
The Müller–Lyer illusion. The line on the right appears longer than the line on the left, when in fact they are exactly the same size.

Size constancy, like other processes of perceptual organisation, can sometimes produce perceptual illusions. This is likely the case with the ***Müller–Lyer illusion***, in which two lines of equal length appear to differ in size (figure 4.35). According to one theory, the angled lines provide linear perspective cues that make the vertical line appear closer or farther away (Gregory, 1978). The brain then adjusts for distance, interpreting the fact that the retinal images of the two vertical lines are the same size as evidence that the line on the right is longer.

If the Müller–Lyer illusion relies on depth cues such as linear perspective that are not recognised in all cultures, are people in some cultures more susceptible to the illusion than others (chapter 19)? That is, does vulnerability to an illusion depend on culture and experience (chapter 19), or is it rooted entirely in the structure of the brain? Four decades ago, a team of psychologists and anthropologists set out to answer these questions in what has become a classic study (Segall, Campbell, & Herskovitz, 1966).

Two hypotheses that guided the investigators are especially relevant. The first, called the carpentered world hypothesis, holds that the nature of architecture in a culture influences the tendency to experience particular illusions (see figure 4.36). People reared in cultures without roads that join at angles, rectangular buildings and houses with angled roofs lack experience with the kinds of cues that give rise to the Müller–Lyer illusion and hence should be less susceptible to it. The second hypothesis posits that individuals from cultures that do not use sophisticated two-dimensional cues (such as linear perspective) to represent three dimensions in pictures should also be less vulnerable to perceptual illusions of this sort.

The researchers presented individuals from 14 non-Western and three Western societies with several stimuli designed to elicit perceptual illusions. They found that Westerners were consistently more likely to experience the Müller–Lyer illusion than non-Westerners, but they were no more likely to experience other illusions unrelated to angles and sophisticated depth cues. Subsequent studies have replicated these findings with the Müller–Lyer illusion (Pedersen & Wheeler, 1983; Segall, Dasen, Berry, & Poortinga, 1990). Teasing apart the relative impact of architecture and simple exposure to pictures is difficult, but the available data support both hypotheses (Berry et al., 1992).

FIGURE 4.36
People from this Papua New Guinean village (a; see inset) are less susceptible to illusions involving straight lines than people who live in 'carpentered worlds', such as Adelaide (b), who are familiar with angled buildings and streets.

Size constancy is involved in another famous illusion, the Ponzo illusion, which also appears to be influenced by culture and experience (figure 4.37). Linear perspective cues indicate that the upper bar is larger because it seems farther away. Cross-culturally, people who live in environments in which lines converge in the distance (such as railroad tracks and long, straight highways) appear to be more susceptible to this illusion than people from environments with relatively few converging lines (Brislin & Keating, 1976).

FIGURE 4.37
The Ponzo illusion. Converging lines lead to the perception of the upper red bar as larger since it appears to be farther away. The bars are actually identical in length.

INTERIM SUMMARY

Depth perception is the organisation of perception in three dimensions; it is based on ***binocular*** and ***monocular visual cues***. ***Motion perception***, the perception of movement, relies on ***motion detectors*** from the retina through the cortex. It appears to involve two systems. The first calculates motion from the changing image on the retina, and the second uses information from eye muscles about the movement of the eyes. ***Perceptual constancy*** refers to the organisation of changing sensations into percepts that are relatively stable. Three types of perceptual constancy are ***colour***, ***shape*** and ***size constancy***.

Interpreting sensory experience

The processes of perceptual organisation we have examined — form perception, depth perception, motion perception and perceptual constancy — organise sensations into stable, recognisable forms. These perceptions do not, however, tell us what an object *is* or what its significance to us might be.

Generating meaning from sensory experience is the task of ***perceptual interpretation***. The line between organisation and interpretation is not, of course, hard and fast. The kind of object identification tasks studied by Biederman, for example, involve both, and in everyday life, organising perceptual experience is simply one step on the path to interpreting it.

Perceptual interpretation lies at the intersection of sensation and memory, as the brain interprets current sensations in the light of past experience. This can occur at a very primitive level — reacting to a bitter taste, recoiling from an object coming towards the face, or responding emotionally to a familiar voice — without either consciousness or cortical involvement. Much of the time, however, interpretation involves classifying stimuli — a moving object is a dog; a pattern of tactile stimulation is a soft caress. In this final section, we examine how experience, expectations and motivation shape perceptual interpretation.

The influence of experience

To what degree do our current perceptions rely on our past experience? This question leads back to the nature–nurture debate that runs through nearly every domain of psychology.

The German philosopher Immanuel Kant argued that humans innately experience the world using certain categories, such as time, space and causality. For example, when a person slams a door and the doorframe shakes, she naturally infers that slamming the door caused the frame to shake. According to Kant, people automatically infer causality, prior to any learning.

Direct perception

Whereas Kant emphasised the way the mind orders perception of the world, psychologist James Gibson (1966, 1979) emphasised the way the world organises perception, so that we detect the order that exists in nature. Gibson championed a theory known as ***direct perception***, which holds that the meaning of stimuli is often immediate and obvious, even to the 'untrained eye'. For example, we automatically perceive depth in an object that has patterned texture (such as a snake), because when the elements of the texture (in this case, the scales on the back of the snake) diminish in size, the brain interprets the change as a depth cue (Goodenough & Gillam, 1997).

MAKING CONNECTIONS

A typical dry visual cliff and a modified cliff with wet and dry edges are shown here. Infants are afraid to crawl over conventional 'cliffs' even when they have recently begun to crawl and therefore have little experience leading them to fear it. This perception is best demonstrated in the first two years of life, where infants learn about the world with their hands, mouths and senses (chapter 12). Recent research suggests infants are less cautious about exploring cliffs with wet and dry edges.

Gibson's theory is essentially evolutionary. The senses evolved to respond to aspects of the environment relevant to adaptation. An object coming rapidly towards the face is dangerous; food with a sweet taste affords energy; a loud, angry voice is threatening. In this view, we do not construct our reality; we perceive it directly. And we can often perceive reality with little experience.

Laboratory evidence of direct perception comes from studies using the ***visual cliff***. The visual cliff is a clear table with a checkerboard directly beneath it on one side and another checkerboard that appears to drop off like a cliff on the other. Infants are reluctant to crawl to the side of the table that looks deep even when they have recently begun crawling and have had little or no relevant experience with falling off surfaces (Gibson & Walk, 1960). In other words, the perceptual systems of infants are already adapted to make sense of the important features of the world before they have had an opportunity to learn what falling means (see Bertenthal, 1996). The infant directly perceives that certain situations signal danger.

More recently, Dr Merrilyn Hooley and Professor Boris Crassini at Deakin University have examined infants' behaviours to better understand why toddlers do not avoid wet 'falling-off' places, like the edges of swimming pools. Their quasi-naturalistic observations of toddlers showed that the tactual properties of edges and surfaces influenced infants' behaviours (Hooley & Crassini, 2008). In contrast to the traditional visual cliff experiments, infants were allowed to freely explore the visual cliff environment in the experiments and either avoid (as predicted by traditional visual cliff experiments) or approach and explore the wet and dry edges of a modified visual cliff. Using this method, over 80 percent of infants approached and explored the wet and dry visual cliff edges, which is not consistent with avoidance and fear predicted by earlier visual cliff studies. Infants soon moved away from the dry edge, but stayed and played at the wet edge, occasionally falling into the water while playing.

This research has important real-world implications for preventing the drowning of toddlers. Further research is currently underway to determine how infants behave in natural settings that include wet and dry 'falling-off' places and how actual depth influences infants' behaviour at the edges.

As we have seen, specific parts of the brain do appear to have evolved to allow some very specific kinds of perception. Some regions, for example, respond solely to faces (Critchley et al., 2000; Kanwisher, McDermott, & Chun, 1997). One area of the brain seems to be so specialised that it responds selectively to movements of the eyes and mouth that are involved in interpreting facial expressions, but not to faces in general (Puce, Alison, Bentin, Gore, & McCarthy, 1998).

When nurture activates nature

Although the nervous system has certain innate potentials — such as seeing in depth or recognising meaningful facial movements — most of these potentials require environmental input to develop. Where psychologists once asked, 'Which is more important, nature or nurture?' today they often ask, 'How do certain experiences activate certain innate potentials?'

In one set of studies, researchers reared kittens in darkness for their first five months except for five hours each day, during which time they placed the kittens in a cylinder with either horizontal or vertical stripes (Blakemore & Cooper, 1970). The kittens saw *only* the stripes, since they wore a big collar that kept them from seeing even their own bodies. As adults, kittens reared in horizontal environments were unable to perceive vertical lines, and they lacked cortical feature detectors responsive to vertical lines; the opposite was true of kittens reared in a vertical environment. Although these cats were genetically programmed to have both vertical and horizontal feature detectors, their brains adapted to a world without certain features to detect.

Researchers reared kittens in darkness for their first five months except for five hours each day. During this time they placed the kittens in a cylinder with either horizontal or vertical stripes. The kittens saw only the stripes since they wore a big collar that kept them from seeing even their own bodies. Their research showed that cats could adapt their brains to a world without certain features to detect (e.g. horizontal lines).

- Did the researchers take all reasonable steps to minimise any discomfort to the kittens being used in their research?
- Is the use of animals as research subjects justified here?

Photograph by Colin Blakemore.

Other studies have outfitted infant kittens and monkeys with translucent goggles that allow light to pass through but only in a blurry, diffuse, unpatterned form. When the animals are adults and the goggles are removed, they are able to perform simple perceptual tasks without difficulty, such as distinguishing colours, brightness and size. However, they have difficulty with other tasks; for example, they are unable to distinguish objects from one another or to track moving objects (Riesen, 1960; Wiesel, 1982).

Similar findings have emerged in studies of humans who were born blind but subsequently became sighted in adulthood through surgery (Gregory, 1978; Sacks, 1993; Von Senden, 1960). Most of these individuals can tell figure from ground, sense colours and follow moving objects, but many never learn to recognise objects they previously knew by touch and hence remain functionally blind. What these studies suggest, like studies described in chapter 3, is that the brain has evolved to 'expect' certain experiences, without which it will not develop normally.

Early experiences are not the only ones that shape the neural system's underlying sensation and perception. In one study, monkeys who were taught to make fine-pitch discriminations showed increases in the size of the cortical regions responsive to pitch (Recanzone, Schreiner, & Merzenich, 1993). Intriguing research with humans finds that practice at discriminating letters manually in Braille produces changes in the brain. A larger region of the cortex of Braille readers is devoted to the fingertips, with which they read (Pascual-Leone & Torres, 1993). Thus, experience can alter the structure of the brain, making it more or less responsive to subsequent sensory input.

Bottom-up and top-down processing

We have seen that experience can activate innate mechanisms or even affect the amount of cortical space devoted to certain kinds of sensory processing. But when we come upon a face that looks familiar or an animal that resembles one we have seen, does our past experience actually alter the way we perceive it, or do we only begin to categorise the face or the animal once we have identified its features? Similarly, does wine taste different to a wine connoisseur — does his knowledge about wine actually alter his perceptions — or does he just have fancier words to describe his experience after the fact?

Psychologists have traditionally offered two opposing answers to questions such as these, which now, as in many classic debates about sensation and perception, appear to be complementary. One view emphasises the role of sensory data in shaping perception, whereas the other emphasises the influence of prior experience (figure 4.38; overleaf). ***Bottom-up processing*** refers to processing that begins 'at the bottom' with raw sensory data that feed 'up' to the brain. A bottom-up explanation of visual perception argues that the brain forms perceptions by combining the responses of multiple feature detectors in the primary cortex, which themselves integrate input from neurons lower in the visual system.

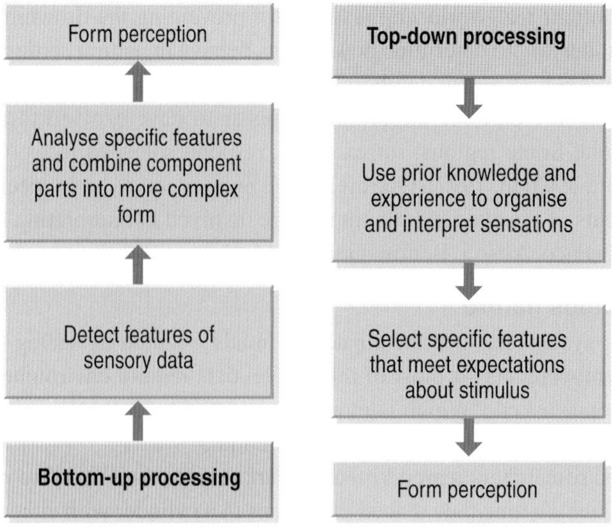

FIGURE 4.38
Bottom-up processing compared with top-down processing

Top-down processing, in contrast, starts 'at the top', with the observer's expectations and knowledge. Theorists who favour a top-down processing explanation typically work from a cognitive perspective. They maintain that the brain uses prior knowledge to begin organising and interpreting sensations as soon as the information starts coming in, rather than waiting for percepts to form based on sequential (step-by-step) analysis of their isolated features. Thus, like Gestalt theorists, these researchers presume that as soon as the brain has detected features resembling eyes, it begins to expect a face and thus to look for a nose and mouth.

Studies demonstrating bottom-up and top-down processing

Both approaches have empirical support. Research on motion perception provides an example of bottom-up processing. Psychologists trained monkeys to report the direction in which a display of dots moved. The researchers then observed the response of individual neurons previously identified as feature detectors for movement of a particular speed and direction while the monkeys performed the task (Newsome, Britten, & Movshan, 1989). They discovered that the 'decisions' made by individual neurons about the direction the dots moved were as accurate as — and sometimes even *more* accurate than — the decisions of the monkeys!

Perceptual decisions on simple tasks of the sort given to these monkeys may require little involvement of higher mental processes. On the other hand, reading these words provides a good example of top-down processing, since reading would be incredibly cumbersome if people had to detect every letter of every word from the bottom up rather than expecting and recognising patterns.

MAKING CONNECTIONS

Research suggests that many psychological processes — perception, **thought** and memory — occur through the simultaneous activation of multiple neural circuits. The perception or solution to a problem that 'comes to mind', in this view, is the one that best fits the data. We are typically not even aware that we have considered and ruled out multiple competing hypotheses; we are only aware of the 'conclusion' (chapter 8).

Recent evidence of top-down processing comes from studies using PET technology. In one study, participants viewed block letters presented in a grid, as in figure 4.39a (Kosslyn et al., 1993). Then they were shown the same grid without the letter and asked to decide whether the letter would cover an X placed in one of the boxes of the grid. This task required that they create a mental image of the letter in the grid and locate the X on the imaginary letter. Next, they performed the same task, except this time the block letter was actually present in the grid, so they could perceive it instead of having to imagine it. Participants in a control condition performed a simple task that essentially involved viewing the empty grid with and without an X.

The study relied on a 'method of subtraction' used in many imaging studies. The investigators measured the amount of neuronal activity in the imagery and perception conditions and subtracted the amount of brain activity seen in the control condition. The logic is to have the experimental and control conditions differ in as few respects as possible, so that what is left in the computerised image of brain activity after subtraction is a picture of only the neural activity connected with the operation being investigated (in this case, mental imagery and perception).

Predictably, both perception and mental imagery activated many parts of the visual system, such as visual association cortex. However, the most striking finding was that the mental imagery condition activated the same areas of the primary visual cortex activated by actual perception of the letters — normally believed to reflect bottom-up processing of sensory information (figure 4.39b). In fact, the primary cortex was even more active during mental imagery than during actual perception! Although these findings are controversial (D'Esposito et al., 1997), if they hold up with future replications, they suggest that when people picture an image in their minds, they actually create a visual image using the same neural pathways involved when they view a visual stimulus — a completely top-down activation of brain regions normally activated by sensory input.

(a)

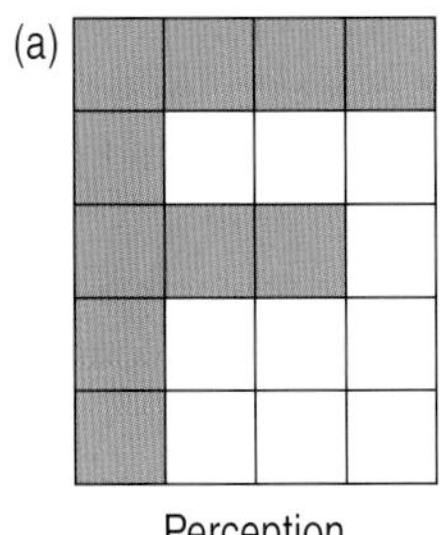

Perception

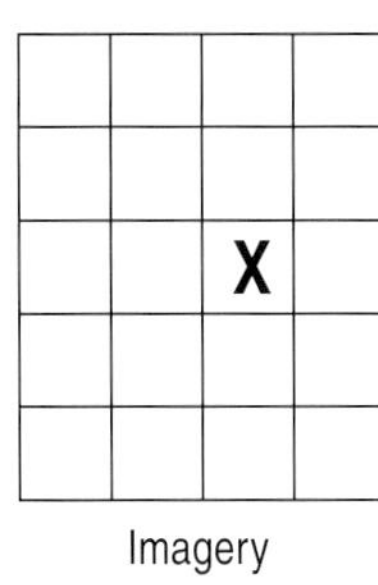

Imagery

(b)

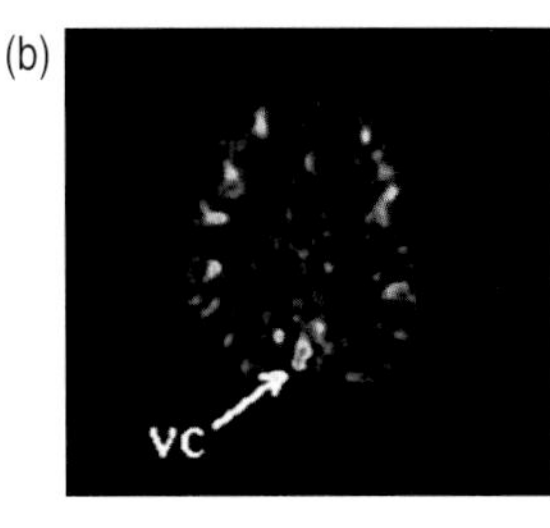

FIGURE 4.39
Visual imagery activates the primary visual cortex. (a) Participants viewed one of two stimulus patterns (left and centre). In one, they actually saw a letter on a grid along with a black X. In another, they had to imagine the letter to decide whether the X would fall on the letter. In a control condition, participants simply watch the X appear and disappear. (b) As can be seen from the small area of bright activation (marked 'vc') in the brain (right), the imaging condition activated the primary visual cortex, just as looking at the actual letter did.

Resolving the paradox: simultaneous processing in perception

Trying to explain perception by either bottom-up or top-down processes alone presents a paradox. You would not be able to identify the shapes in figure 4.40a unless you knew they were part of a dog. Yet you would not recognise figure 4.40b as a dog unless you could process information about the parts shown in the first panel. Without bottom-up processing, external stimuli would have no effect on perception; we would hallucinate rather than perceive. Without top-down processing, experience would have no effect on perception. How, then, do people ever recognise and classify objects?

According to current thinking, both types of processing occur simultaneously (Pollen, 1999; Rumelhart, McClelland, & the PDP Research Group, 1986). For example, features of the environment create patterns of stimulation in the primary visual cortex. These patterns in turn stimulate neural circuits in the visual association cortex that represent various objects, such as a friend's face. If the perceiver expects to see that face or if a large enough component of the neural network representing the face becomes activated, the brain essentially forms a 'hypothesis' about an incoming pattern of sensory stimulation, even though all the data are not yet in from the feature detectors. It may even entertain multiple hypotheses simultaneously, which are each tested against new incoming data until one hypothesis 'wins out' because it seems to provide the best fit to the data.

(a)

(b)

FIGURE 4.40
Top-down and bottom-up processing. In isolation (perceiving from the bottom up), the designs in (a) would have no meaning. Yet the broader design in (b), the dog, cannot be recognised without recognising component parts.

A pitch in time: perceiving dynamic events and acquiring expectations

By Associate Professor Catherine Stevens, University of Western Sydney

Anticipating and perceiving events as they unfold in time are at the core of human behaviour — speech perception and production, social behaviour, nonverbal communication, sport and the enjoyment and performance of music and dance. Most temporal events are structured, consisting of actions that have beginnings, rhythms, tempos and endings (Large & Jones, 1999). For example, it is easy to detect when unfamiliar music sounds are 'out of tune' or 'out of time'. The musical event, even though it may be unfamiliar, has cued certain expectations about pitch or temporal relations. One explanation is that through experience, humans learn the statistical regularities characteristic of their environment. Acquired sensitivity to statistical structure has been demonstrated for perception of speech (Pelucchi, Hay, & Saffran, 2009), musical pitch and time (Huron, 2006), and dance (Opacic, Stevens, & Tillmann, 2009).

What about perceiving unexpected events and change? In auditory perception, for example, there is evidence that a sound that increases in intensity (an 'up-ramp'), matched on all other acoustic features, is judged to change more in loudness than a sound that decreases in intensity (a 'down-ramp'). Perceived change in the up-ramp is overestimated relative to the down-ramp. One possibility is that the motion implied by a sound that increases rapidly in intensity elicits an adaptive response, enabling an organism to avoid a potentially dangerous, 'looming' sound source (Bach et al., 2008). Acoustic intensity is also a cue that listeners use when they are asked to judge emotion expressed in music from cultures other than their own (Balkwill & Thompson, 1999). These latter findings, when coupled with research on auditory looming (Olsen & Stevens, 2010) point not only to the fundamental role of intensity, but also to intensity change in music perception and emotional responses to music.

Dynamic events unfolding in time — epitomised in music, speech and movement — bring into relief the role of expectations; temporal structure; and change in human visual, auditory and multimodal perception.

INTERIM SUMMARY

Perceptual interpretation means generating meaning from sensory experience. According to the theory of ***direct perception***, the meaning or adaptive significance of a percept is often obvious, immediate and innate. Trying to distinguish the relative roles of nature and nurture in perception may in some ways be asking the wrong question, because the nervous system has innate potentials that require environmental input to develop. Perception simultaneously involves ***bottom-up processing***, which begins with raw sensory data that feed 'up' to the brain, and ***top-down processing***, which begins with the observer's expectations and knowledge.

Expectations and perception

Experience with the environment thus shapes perception by creating perceptual expectations, an important top-down influence on perception. These expectations, called perceptual set (i.e. the setting, or context, for a given perceptual 'decision'), make certain interpretations more likely. Two aspects of perceptual set are the current context and enduring knowledge.

Schemas

A person's enduring beliefs and expectations affect perceptual interpretation. One way knowledge is organised in memory is in ***schemas*** — patterns of thinking about a domain that render the environment relatively predictable (Neisser, 1976). We have schemas (organised knowledge) about objects (such as chairs and dogs), people (such as introverts and ministers) and situations (such as funerals and restaurants). The fact that people generally sit on chairs instead of on other people reflects their schemas about what chairs and people do.

Because schemas allow individuals to anticipate what they will encounter, they increase both the speed and efficiency of perception. For example, people process information extremely quickly when shown photographs of real-world scenes, such as a kitchen, a city street or a desk top. In one study, participants could recall almost half the objects in familiar scenes after viewing them for only one-tenth of a second (Biederman, Glass, & Stacy, 1973). In contrast, participants who viewed the same scenes cut into six equal pieces and randomly reassembled had difficulty both identifying and remembering the objects in the picture. Schemas can also induce perceptual errors, however, when individuals fail to notice what they do not expect to see, such as a new pothole in the street (Biederman, Mezzanotte, & Rabinowitz, 1982; Biederman, Mezzanotte, Rabinowitz, Francolini, & Plude, 1981).

Context

Context also plays a substantial role in perceptual interpretation. Consider, for example, how readily you understood the meaning of *substantial role* in the last sentence. Had someone uttered that phrase in a bakery, you would have assumed they meant *substantial roll*, unless the rest of the sentence provided a context suggesting otherwise. Context is important in perceiving spoken language (chapter 8) because even the most careful speaker drops syllables, slurs sounds or misses words altogether, and many words (such as role and roll) have the same sound but different meanings. Context is just as important with tactile sensations (touch). A hug from a relative or from a stranger may have entirely different meanings and may immediately elicit very different feelings, even if the pattern of sensory stimulation is identical. Figure 4.41 illustrates the importance of context in the visual mode.

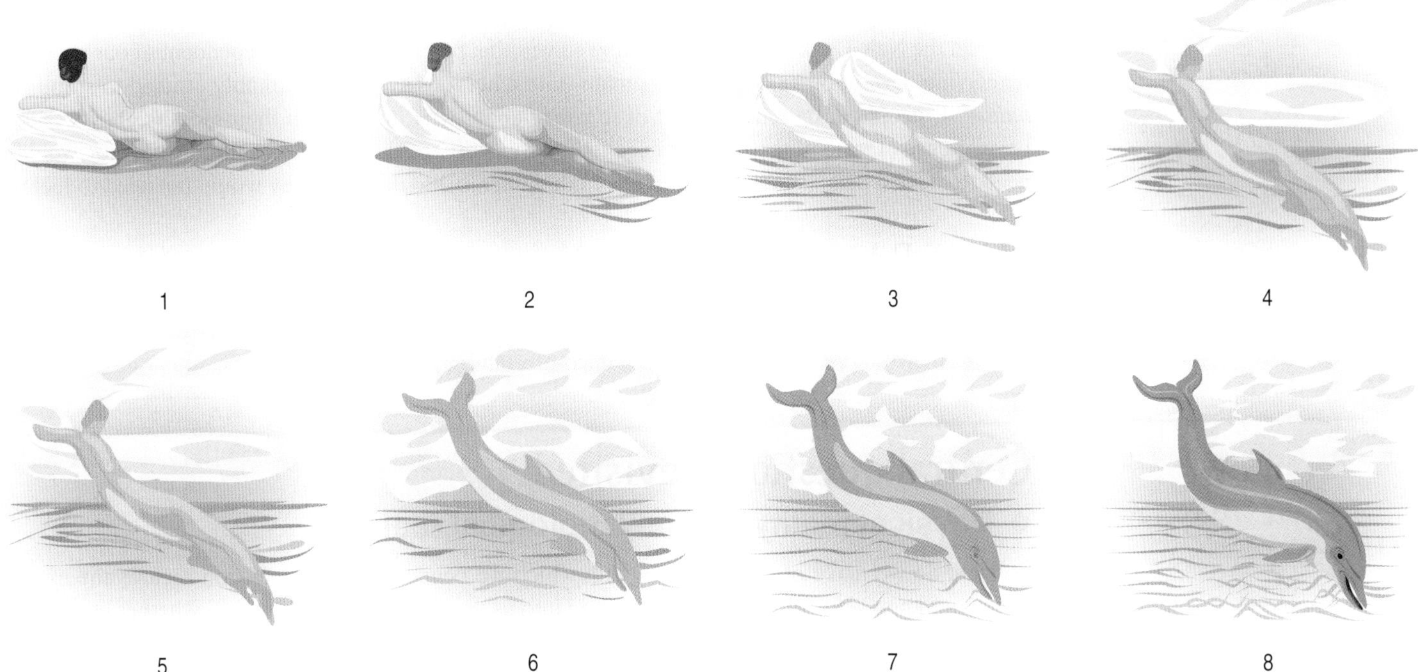

FIGURE **4.41**
The impact of context on perception. Look at drawings 1, 2, 3 and 4, in that order (top row, left to right). Now look at drawings 5, 6, 7 and 8, in reverse order (bottom row, right to left). Drawing 4 most likely seems to be a woman's body and drawing 5, a dolphin, yet drawings 4 and 5 are identical. The same pattern of stimulation can be interpreted in many ways depending on context.

Motivation and perception

As we have seen, expectations can lead people to see what they expect to see and hear what they expect to hear. But people also frequently hear the words they *want* to hear. In other words, motivation, like cognition, can exert a top-down influence on perception. This was the argument of a school of perceptual thought in the late 1940s called the New Look in perception, which focused on the impact of emotion, motivation and personality on perception (Dixon, 1981; Erdelyi, 1985). Many of the issues raised by New Look researchers are receiving renewed attention half a century later (e.g. see Bargh, 1997; Bruner, 1992).

One classic experiment examined the effects of food and water deprivation on identification of words (Wispe & Drambarean, 1953). The experimenters placed participants in one of three groups. Some went without food for 24 hours prior to the experiment; some ate nothing for 10 hours; and others ate just beforehand. The researchers then flashed two kinds of words on a screen so rapidly that they were barely perceptible: neutral words (e.g. serenade and hunch) and words related to food (e.g. lemonade and munch).

The three groups did not differ in their responses to the neutral words. However, both of the deprived groups perceived the need-related words more readily (i.e. when flashed more briefly) than non-deprived controls. A similar phenomenon occurs outside the laboratory. People are often intensely aware of the aroma of food outside a restaurant when they are hungry but oblivious to it when their stomachs are full.

Based on psychodynamic ideas, New Look researchers were also interested in the way emotional factors influence perception, as in the everyday experience of 'failing to see what we don't want to see' (see Broadbent, 1958; Dixon, 1971, 1981; Erdelyi, 1985). In one study, the researcher exposed participants to neutral and taboo words so quickly that they could barely recognise even a flash of light (Blum, 1954). (In the 1950s, obscenities were viewed as taboo and were not used in movies, music and so on. This experiment might be hard to replicate today!) When asked which stimuli seemed more salient — that is, which ones 'caught their eye' more — participants consistently chose the taboo words, even though they had no idea what they had seen. Yet when presented with words at speeds that could just barely allow recognition of them, participants could identify the neutral words more quickly and easily than the taboo ones. These findings suggest that more emotionally evocative taboo words attract attention even below the threshold of consciousness but are harder to recognise consciously than neutral words. Subsequent research has replicated and extended these findings (Erdelyi, 1985; Shevrin, 1980; Shevrin, Bond, Brakel, Hertel, & Williams, 1996).

What the New Look fundamentally showed was that perception is not independent of our reasons for perceiving. Evolution has equipped humans with a nervous system remarkably attuned to stimuli *that matter*. If people did not need to eat or to worry about what they put in their mouths, they would not have a sense of taste. If they did not need to find food, escape danger and communicate, they would not need to see and hear. And if their skin were not vulnerable to damage, they would not need to feel pain.

INTERIM SUMMARY

Expectations based on both the current context and enduring knowledge structures (schemas) influence the way people interpret ongoing sensory experience. Motives can also influence perception, including motives to avoid perceiving stimuli with uncomfortable content.

Central questions revisited

◆ Physical reality and psychological reality

So what do we make of the questions with which we began? The first question regards the extent to which our knowledge of the world is stamped into us or woven together by us — whether perception is more like photography or painting.

The answer, like so many psychological questions, is not either/or. Our sensory systems evolved to pick up regularities in the world. Wavelengths of light provide information about the world that our nervous systems transduce into colour sensations through processes that are built into the structure of the sense organs and brain, from the retina up through the cortex. At the same time, our perceptions reflect our expectations. Consider how much more easily you would have recognised the cow in figure 4.1 if the caption had simply read, 'A cow'.

A second and related question regards the extent to which perceptual processes are born or learned — the question of nature and nurture. The answer, once again, is both. As James Gibson argued, our senses have been exquisitely crafted by natural selection to help us sense things we need to sense. No-one needs to teach us to cover our ears when confronted with a loud noise. At the same time, the conductor of a symphony may be able to pick out a single note missed by one violinist that is imperceptible to a thousand symphony-goers. What experience does is to help us separate signal from noise — and perhaps most importantly, to focus on the signals that matter to us.

In summary, nature has endowed us with remarkable sensory instruments to create music out of noise. Experience teaches us how to tune those instruments.

◆

SUMMARY

1 Basic principles

- ***Sensation*** refers to the process by which sense organs gather information about the environment and transmit it to the brain for initial processing. ***Perception*** refers to the closely related process by which the brain selects, organises and interprets sensations.
- Three basic principles apply across all the senses. First, there is no one-to-one correspondence between physical and psychological reality. Second, sensation and perception are active, not passive. Third, sensation and perception are adaptive.

2 Processes common to sensory systems

- Sensation begins with an environmental stimulus; all sensory systems have specialised cells called ***sensory receptors*** that respond to environmental stimuli and typically generate action potentials in adjacent sensory neurons. This process is called ***transduction***. Within each sensory modality, the brain codes sensory stimulation for intensity and quality.
- The ***absolute threshold*** refers to the minimum amount of stimulation needed for an observer to notice a stimulus. The ***signal detection theory*** asserts that people make a judgement about whether a stimulus is present or absent. The ***difference threshold*** refers to the lowest level of stimulation required to sense that a change in stimulation has occurred (a ***just noticeable difference***, or ***jnd***).
- ***Weber's law*** states that regardless of the magnitude of two stimuli, the second must differ by a constant proportion from the first for it to be perceived as different. ***Fechner's law*** holds that the physical magnitude of a stimulus grows logarithmically as the subjective experience of intensity grows arithmetically; in other words, people only subjectively experience a small percentage of actual increases in stimulus intensity. ***Stevens' power law*** states that subjective intensity grows as a proportion of the actual intensity raised to some power; that is, that sensation increases in a linear fashion as actual intensity grows exponentially.
- ***Sensory adaptation*** is the tendency of sensory systems to respond less to stimuli that continue without change.

3 Vision and colour

- The eyes are sensitive to a small portion of the electromagnetic spectrum called light. In vision, light is focused on the retina by the ***cornea***, ***pupil*** and ***lens***. ***Rods*** are very sensitive to light, allowing vision in dim light; ***cones*** are especially sensitive to particular wavelengths, producing the psychological experience of colour. Cones are concentrated at the ***fovea***, the region of the retina most sensitive to detail.
- The ***ganglion cells*** of the retina transmit visual information via the ***optic nerve*** to the brain. Ganglion cells, like other neurons involved in sensation, have ***receptive fields***, a region of stimulation to which the neuron responds. ***Feature detectors*** are specialised cells in the cortex that respond only when stimulation in their receptive field matches a particular pattern or orientation, such as horizontal or vertical lines.
- From the primary visual cortex, visual information flows along two pathways, or processing streams, called the 'what' and the 'where' pathways. The ***'what' pathway*** is involved in determining what an object is; this network runs from the primary visual cortex in the occipital lobes through the lower part of the temporal lobes (the inferior temporal cortex). The second stream, the ***'where' pathway***, is involved in locating the object in space, following its movement, and guiding movement towards it. This pathway runs from the primary visual cortex through the middle and upper regions of the temporal lobes and up into the parietal lobes.
- The property of light that is transduced into colour is ***wavelength***. The ***Young–Helmholtz***, or ***trichromatic, theory*** proposes that the eye contains three types of sensory receptors, sensitive to red, green or blue. ***Opponent-process theory*** argues for the existence of pairs of opposite primary colours linked in three systems: a blue–yellow system, a red–green system and a black–white system. Both theories appear to be involved in colour perception; trichromatic theory is operative at the level of the retina and opponent-process theory at higher neural levels.

4 Hearing

- Hearing, or ***audition***, occurs as a vibrating object sets air particles in motion. Each round of expansion and contraction of the air is known as a ***cycle***. The number of cycles per second determines a sound wave's ***frequency***, which corresponds to the psychological property of ***pitch***. ***Amplitude*** refers to the height and depth of the wave and corresponds to the psychological property of ***loudness***.
- Sound waves travel through the auditory canal to the eardrum, where they are amplified. Transduction occurs by way of ***hair cells*** attached to the basilar membrane that respond to vibrations in the fluid-filled ***cochlea***. This mechanical process triggers action potentials in the ***auditory nerve***, which are then transmitted to the brain.
- Two theories, once considered opposing, explain the psychological qualities of sound. ***Place theory***, which holds that different areas of the basilar membrane respond to different frequencies, appears to be most accurate for high frequencies. ***Frequency theory***, which asserts that the basilar membrane's rate of vibration reflects the frequency with which a sound wave cycles, explains sensation of low-frequency sounds.

5 Smell, taste, touch and the vestibular and kinaesthetic systems

- The environmental stimuli for smell, or ***olfaction***, are invisible molecules of gas emitted by substances and suspended in the air. As air enters the nose, it flows into the ***olfactory epithelium***, where hundreds of different types of receptors respond to various kinds of molecules, producing complex smells. The axons of olfactory receptor cells constitute the ***olfactory nerve***, which transmits information to the olfactory bulbs under the frontal lobes and on to the primary olfactory cortex, a primitive region of the cortex deep in the frontal lobes.
- Taste, or ***gustation***, is sensitive to molecules soluble in saliva. Much of the experience of flavor, however, is really contributed by smell. Taste occurs as receptors in the ***tastebuds*** on the tongue and throughout the mouth transduce chemical information into neural information, which is integrated with olfactory information in the brain.
- Touch includes three senses: pressure, temperature and pain. The human body contains approximately five million touch receptors of at least seven different types. Sensory neurons synapse with spinal interneurons that stimulate motor neurons, allowing reflexive action. They also synapse with neurons that carry information up the spinal cord to the medulla, where nerve tracts cross over. From there, sensory information travels to the thalamus and is subsequently routed to the primary touch centre in the brain, the somatosensory cortex, which contains a map of the body.
- Pain is greatly affected by beliefs, expectations and emotional state. ***Gate-control theory*** holds that the experience of pain is heavily influenced by the central nervous system, through the action of neural

fibres that can 'close the gate' on pain, preventing messages from other fibres getting through.

- The ***proprioceptive senses*** provide information about the body's position and movement. The ***vestibular sense*** provides information on the position of the body in space by sensing gravity and movement. ***Kinaesthesia*** provides information about the movement and position of the limbs and other parts of the body relative to one another.

6 Perception

- The hallmarks of perception are organisation and interpretation. ***Perceptual organisation*** integrates sensations into meaningful units, locates them in space, tracks their movement and preserves their meaning as the perceiver observes them from different vantage points. ***Form perception*** refers to the organisation of sensations into meaningful shapes and patterns (***percepts***). The Gestalt psychologists described several principles of form perception, including figure–ground perception, similarity, proximity, good continuation, simplicity and closure. A more recent theory, called ***recognition-by-components***, asserts that we perceive and categorise objects in the environment by breaking them down into component parts, much like letters in words.
- ***Depth perception*** is the organisation of perception in three dimensions. Depth perception organises two-dimensional retinal images into a three-dimensional world, primarily through binocular and monocular visual cues.
- ***Motion perception*** refers to the perception of movement. Two systems appear to be involved in motion perception. The first calculates motion from the changing image projected by the object on the retina; the second makes use of commands from the brain to the muscles in the eye that signal eye movements.
- ***Perceptual constancy*** refers to the organisation of changing sensations into percepts that are relatively stable in size, shape and colour. Three types of perceptual constancy are ***size***, ***shape*** and ***colour constancy***, which refer to the perception of unchanging size, shape and colour despite momentary changes in the retinal image. The processes that organise perception leave perceivers vulnerable to ***perceptual illusions***, some of which appear to be innate and others of which depend on culture and experience.
- ***Perceptual interpretation*** involves generating meaning from sensory experience. Perceptual interpretation lies at the intersection of sensation and memory, as the brain interprets current sensations in the light of past experience. Perception is neither entirely innate nor entirely learned. The nervous system has certain innate potentials, but these potentials require environmental input to develop. Experience can alter the structure of the brain, making it more or less responsive to subsequent sensory input.
- ***Bottom-up processing*** refers to processing that begins 'at the bottom', with raw sensory data that feeds 'up' to the brain. ***Top-down processing*** starts 'at the top', from the observer's expectations and knowledge. According to current thinking, perception proceeds in both directions simultaneously.
- Experience with the environment shapes perceptual interpretation by creating perceptual expectations called perceptual set. Two aspects of perceptual set are current context and enduring knowledge structures called ***schemas***. Motives, like expectations, can influence perceptual interpretation.

KEY TERMS

REVIEW QUESTIONS

1. Describe how sensation differs from perception.
2. Discuss the features shared by all sensory modalities.
3. Compare and contrast the two theories of colour vision: trichromatic theory and the opponent-process theory.
4. Explain how the place theory and the frequency theory each account for the psychological experiences of pitch and loudness.
5. Distinguish among the four aspects of perceptual organisation: form perception, depth perception, movement perception and perceptual constancy.

DISCUSSION QUESTIONS

1. How do your beliefs, expectations and emotional state affect your experience of pain?
2. What senses, in addition to vision and hearing, will help you to adapt to your environment?
3. How do nature and nurture influence perception?

APPLICATION QUESTIONS

1. For each of the four scenarios listed, answer the question that follows.
   (a) Andrew is studying for a final exam. His mother brings him a cup of coffee to help him study through the night. He takes one mouthful of the coffee and says 'Thanks Mum, but you put one too many sugars in my coffee again!' Explain Andrew's comment using the principles of absolute threshold.
   (b) Karen has just returned home from holidays to find that her house has been burgled. That night, Karen tosses and turns in her sleep and wakes up in the early hours of the morning with a start, believing she heard footsteps outside her window. Discuss this scenario using the principles of signal detection theory.
   (c) Yong Wah is at the beach and has decided not to spend $15 for some fish and chips because he saw it advertised for $9 at another seafood shop down the road. Later in the week he goes shopping for a new electric razor and does not think twice about spending an extra $6 for an electric razor, valued at $90. Explain this scenario using the principles of Weber's Law.
   (d) Giovanni is cooking a surprise dinner for friends but forgets to turn off the oven and burns the roast. His friends arrive and later, when he opens the oven door, smoke and a charcoal odour fill the room. A short time later, he and his friends no longer notice the smoke or odour in the room. Discuss this scenario using the principles of sensory adaptation.
2. For each of the examples, identify and describe the Gestalt principle involved.
   (a) Stars in the sky form a constellation known as the Southern Cross.
   (b) People sitting in a stadium appear to be in clusters of colour.
   (c) A sequence of specks and squiggles on a scribble page appears to form a cat.
   (d) Figure 4.42 is most likely perceived as the letter 'A' superimposed onto an upside down triangle.

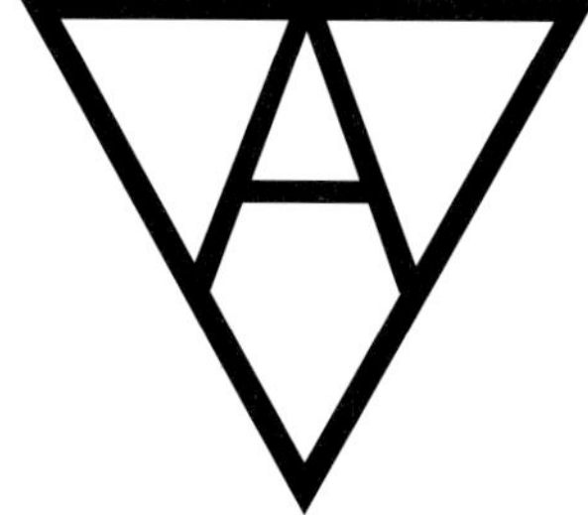

FIGURE 4.42
Explain the perception of this shape.

The solutions to the application questions can be found on page 834.

MULTIMEDIA RESOURCES

The *Cyberpsych* multimedia resource is available *as an option* to accompany this textbook to further develop your understanding of many key psychology concepts. *Cyberpsych* contains a wealth of rich media content and activities, and for this chapter includes:

- video clips on the sense of smell and the effect of smell on taste
- a concept animation on how we see and hear.

Consciousness 5

LEARNING OBJECTIVES

After studying this chapter you should be able to:

1 describe the two main functions of consciousness

2 distinguish among the different theoretical perspectives on consciousness

3 describe the functions of sleep and distinguish among the psychological views of dreaming

4 explain how people might experience altered states of consciousness.

The nature of consciousness

- *Consciousness* refers to the subjective awareness of mental events. Consciousness serves at least two functions: monitoring the self and the environment and controlling thought and behaviour.
- *Attention* refers to the process of focusing conscious awareness, providing heightened sensitivity to a limited range of experience requiring more extensive information processing.
- A major component of the normal flow of consciousness is *daydreaming* — turning attention away from external stimuli to internal thoughts and imagined scenarios.

Perspectives on consciousness

- The *psychodynamic perspective*. Freud distinguished three types of mental activities: *conscious* processes, of which the person is currently subjectively aware; *preconscious* processes, which are not presently conscious but could be readily brought into consciousness; and the *unconscious* processes, which are dynamically kept from consciousness because they are threatening.

Conscious

Preconscious

Repression

Wishes, fears, memories, emotions

Unconscious

- *The cognitive perspective*. The *cognitive unconscious* focuses on information-processing mechanisms that operate outside of awareness, such as procedural knowledge and implicit memory.
- The *behavioural perspective*. Consciousness was considered analogous to a continuously moving video camera, surveying potentially significant perceptions, thoughts, emotions, goals and problem-solving strategies. The two functions of consciousness — monitor and control — allow people to initiate and terminate thought and behaviour in order to attain goals.
- The *evolutionary perspective*. Consciousness evolved as a mechanism for directing behaviour in adaptive ways, which was superimposed on more primitive psychological processes such as conditioning. The primary function of consciousness is to foster adaptation.

Sleeping and dreaming

- The sleep cycle is governed by ***circadian rhythms***, cyclical biological 'clocks' that evolved around the daily cycles of light and dark.
- Sleep proceeds through a series of stages that can be assessed by EEG. The major distinction is between ***rapid eye movement (REM)*** and ***non-REM (NREM) sleep***. Most dreaming occurs in REM sleep, in which the eyes dart around and the EEG takes on an active pattern resembling waking consciousness.
- Three theories on dreaming:
  (1) Freud believed that dreams have meaning and distinguished between ***the manifest content*** (story line) and the ***latent content*** (underlying meaning) of the dream
  (2) the cognitive perspective suggests that dreams are the outcome of cognitive processes and that their content reflects the concerns and metaphors people express in their waking cognition
  (3) some theorists propose that dreams are biological phenomena with no meaning at all.

Altered states of consciousness

- ***Altered states of consciousness***, in which the usual conscious ways of perceiving, thinking and feeling are modified or disrupted, are often brought about through meditation, hypnosis, ingestion of drugs and religious experiences.
- ***Meditation*** creates a deep state of tranquillity by altering the normal flow of conscious thoughts.
- ***Hypnosis*** is characterised by deep relaxation and suggestibility.
- The most common way people alter their state of consciousness is by ingesting ***psychoactive substances*** — such as alcohol and other depressants, stimulants, hallucinogens and marijuana — that operate on the nervous system to alter mental activity.

Central questions: perpectives on consciousness

- Issues of consciousness and unconciousness continue to be a central focus of psychological attention. Future research will look to synthesise the varied tools and methods of the different psychological perspectives.

TWIN sisters Catherine and Jennifer Strutt, from the city of Newcastle in New South Wales, are talented artists who are known for pushing the boundaries of mixed media. They produce dioramas using characters from medical textbooks and vintage magazines; they create quirky jewellery inspired by Scandinavian themes; and they produce amazing artistic creations in aluminium, collage and painted wood. As well as seeing artistic possibilities in ordinary everyday objects, the sisters also have another special ability — they have synaesthesia. Around 10 000 Australians are thought to have synaesthesia — a condition in which the five senses of sight, sound, taste, smell and touch are mingled in some way. In the case of the Strutt sisters, playing music makes them see colours. For Jennifer, playing wind instruments conjures a fluffy blue colour, and the double bass is like a really deep red. For Catherine, a double bass or cello feels dark green, coming into purple. Many people with synaesthesia often see the letters of the alphabet as different colours (Ramachandran & Hubbard, 2005). Some can smell a musical note or hear different colours (cf. Cytowic, 2003). The condition does not affect people's day-to-day life. In fact, many people do not even realise they have a 'condition'. To them, hearing colours is perfectly normal.

Researchers like Dr Anina Rich at Macquarie University are currently looking to unravel the mystery of synaesthesia. Dr Rich has established one of the world's largest databases of people with synaesthesia. She and other researchers are posing questions, such as: Why do the brains of people with this condition process information from the senses this way? Can a better understanding of the way a synaesthete's brain works help us understand cognitive functions overall?

In attempting to understand the source of this additional dimension, researchers have looked at both basic visual ability and at more sophisticated central nervous system processing. Synaesthetes have normal vision and colour vision, and PET scans have revealed that the initial pathways for sensory information arrive at the correct areas of the brain (i.e. visual information goes to the visual cortex, not to the auditory cortex). However, when the information is relayed to the somatosensory cortex and association areas, there appears to be cross-communication in synaesthetes that does not occur in non-synaesthetes. Thus, a synaesthete receives the same sensory information as you or I, but, after initial processing, a different use of the information results in altered perception and, thus, an altered state of consciousness.

We begin this chapter by discussing the nature and functions of consciousness, examining the way attention focuses consciousness at any given time on a narrow subset of the thoughts and feelings of which a person could be aware. We then examine multiple perspectives on consciousness and explore the neural basis of consciousness. The remainder of the chapter is devoted to ***states of consciousness*** — qualitatively different patterns of subjective experience, including ways of experiencing both internal and external events. We start with the most basic distinction, between waking and sleeping, exploring the stages of sleep and the nature of dreaming. We conclude by examining several altered states of consciousness — deviations from the normal waking state — including meditation, religious experiences, hypnosis and drug-induced states.

Throughout, we focus on a central question. How do the psychodynamic, behavioural, cognitive and evolutionary perspectives in psychology contribute to our understanding of consciousness? To this end, we will examine how Freud's model of consciousness compares with cognitive models of consciousness and examine the neuropsychology of consciousness, identifying the neural structures that produce conscious awareness and regulate our states of consciousness. We will also examine how evolutionary psychologists argue that consciousness functions to maximise adaptation of the self and the environment. As we will see, these seemingly incompatible vantage points may be starting to find some common ground.

Central question

- What light do psychodynamic, behavioural, cognitive and evolutionary perspectives shed on consciousness?

The nature of consciousness

Consciousness, the subjective awareness of mental events, is easier to describe than to define. William James (1890) viewed consciousness as a constantly moving stream of thoughts, feelings and perceptions. Following in the footsteps of the French philosopher René Descartes, who offered the famous proposition *cogito ergo sum* ('I think, therefore I am'), James also emphasised a second aspect of consciousness, the consciousness of self. James argued that part of being conscious of any particular thought is a simultaneous awareness of oneself as the author or owner of it.

Functions of consciousness

Why do we have consciousness at all? Two of the functions of consciousness are readily apparent: consciousness monitors the self and the environment, and it regulates thought and behaviour (Kihlstrom, 1987). Consciousness as a monitor is analogous to a continuously moving video camera, surveying potentially significant perceptions, thoughts, emotions, goals and problem-solving strategies. The regulatory or control function of consciousness allows people to initiate and terminate thought and behaviour in order to attain goals. People often rehearse scenarios in their minds, such as asking for a raise or confronting a disloyal friend. Consciousness is often engaged when people choose between competing strategies for solving a problem (Mandler & Nakamura, 1987; Wegner & Bargh, 1998).

These two functions of consciousness — monitor and control — are intertwined, because consciousness monitors inner and outer experience to prevent and solve problems. For example, consciousness often 'steps in' when automatised processes (procedural knowledge) are not successful. In this sense, consciousness is like the inspector in a garment factory. It does not make the product, but it checks to make sure the product is made correctly. If it finds an imperfection, it institutes a remedy (Gilbert, 1989, p. 206).

Recent neuroimaging evidence suggests that the dorsolateral prefrontal cortex, which is involved in working memory and conscious decision making (chapters 7 and 8), is activated when people exercise conscious control. Researchers in one study (MacDonald, Cohen, Stenger, & Carter, 2000) demonstrated this using the Stroop task, in which participants are presented a word printed in colour and then have to name the colour quickly while ignoring the word. This task can be very difficult, particularly if the word itself is the name of a colour, because the participant has to name the colour of the ink and ignore the competing colour name — a task that requires considerable conscious attention (figure 5.1).

The researchers found that the Stroop task leads to activation of the dorsolateral prefrontal cortex, as participants 'put their mind to' the job of ignoring the words while naming the colour (figure 5.2; cf. Harrison et al., 2005). Interestingly, a different part of the cortex, the anterior cingulate, becomes active only when the colour of the ink and the word conflict but not when the colour of the ink is congruent with the word (e.g. 'red' printed in red ink). This suggests that the anterior cingulate is involved in consciously regulating conflicting cues and perhaps in inhibiting responses that are incorrect (cf. Imbrosciano & Berlach, 2005).

Red	Yellow	Green
Blue	Red	Yellow
Green	Blue	Red

FIGURE 5.1
The Stroop colour-naming task. The task is to name the colour of the ink in which each word is printed as quickly as possible while ignoring the words themselves. Try it yourself — the task is very difficult because the word interferes with colour naming when the word is printed in a different colour (e.g. when 'green' is written in red).

APPLY + DISCUSS

Self-test with the interactive Stroop Effect experiment that should be available to try out via your university course website for this subject.

- Why does interference occur?
- How might selection attention theory explain the Stroop Effect?

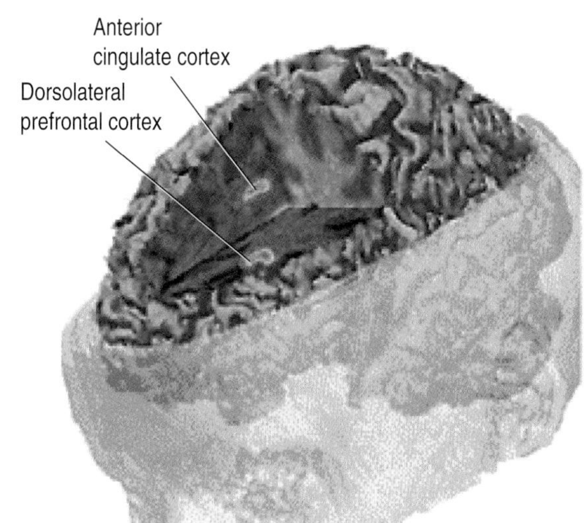

FIGURE 5.2
Neural pathways in controlling and monitoring tasks. Participants showed more activation in the dorsolateral prefrontal cortex when preparing to exert conscious control but showed more activation in the anterior cingulate when monitoring for conflicts.

SOURCE: From MacDonald, Cohen, Stenger, and Carter (2000). Reprinted with permission from AAAS.

APPLY + DISCUSS

- What is the role of consciousness in typing?
- To what extent is consciousness involved in knowing which keys to press while typing?

From an evolutionary standpoint, consciousness probably evolved as a mechanism for directing behaviour in adaptive ways that was superimposed on more primitive psychological processes such as conditioning (Reber, 1992). Indeed, William James, who was heavily influenced by Darwin, explained consciousness in terms of its function: fostering adaptation. Consciousness is often 'grabbed' by things that are unexpected, unusual, contradictory (as in the Stroop task), or contrary to expectations — precisely the things that could affect wellbeing or survival. Much of the time people respond automatically to the environment, learning and processing information without much attention. Important choices, however, require more careful conscious consideration.

INTERIM SUMMARY

Consciousness refers to the subjective awareness of mental events. ***States of consciousness*** are qualitatively different patterns of subjective experience, including ways of experiencing both internal and external events. Consciousness plays at least two functions: monitoring the self and the environment and controlling thought and behaviour. Consciousness probably evolved as a mechanism for directing behaviour in adaptive ways that was superimposed on more primitive psychological processes that continue to function without conscious awareness.

Consciousness and attention

At any given time, people are dimly aware of much more than what is conscious. For example, while watching the grand final, a person may have some vague awareness of the microwave humming, children's voices in the next room and the smell of freshly cut grass, but none of these is at the centre of awareness or consciousness.

Attention

Attention refers to the process of focusing conscious awareness, providing heightened sensitivity to a limited range of experience requiring more extensive information processing. Selection — of a particular object, a train of thought or a location in space where something important might be happening — is the essence of attention (Posner & DiGirolamo, 2000). Attention is generally guided by some combination of external stimulation, which naturally leads us to focus on relevant sensory information and activated goals, which lead us to attend to thoughts, feelings or stimuli relevant to obtaining these goals.

Filtering in and filtering out

Some psychologists have likened attention to a filtering process through which only more important information passes (Broadbent, 1958). For example, people frequently become so engrossed in conversation with one person that they tune out all the other conversations in the room — an important skill at a loud party. However, if they hear someone mention their name across the room, they may suddenly look up and focus attention on the person who has just spoken the magic word. This phenomenon, called the cocktail party phenomenon (Cherry, 1953), suggests that we implicitly process much more information than reaches consciousness (Haykin & Chen, 2005).

Mind wandering occurs when our conscious thoughts do not remain on topic and our brain processes additional, unrelated sensory information (Schooler, Reichle, & Halpern, 2004). People typically report having no awareness of what happened in the external environment when their mind wanders to another topic. Recent research indicates that mind wandering is a stable cognitive trait that can increase with stress, boredom, or sleepiness; it decreases with concentration, effort, successful and enjoyable tasks, or happiness (Kane et al., 2007; McVay, Kane, & Kwapil, 2009).

On the other hand, people also sometimes divert attention from information that may be relevant but emotionally upsetting, a process called ***selective inattention***. This can be highly adaptive, as when students divert their attention from the anxiety of taking a test to the task itself. It can also be maladaptive, as when people ignore a darkening birthmark on their arm that could be malignant.

Components of attention

Attention actually consists of at least three functions: orienting to sensory stimuli, controlling behaviour and the contents of consciousness and maintaining alertness (see Posner, 1995). Different neural networks, relying on different neurotransmitter systems, appear to be involved in these three functions (Robbins, 1997).

Orienting, which has been studied most extensively in the visual system (Robertson & Rafal, 2000), involves turning sensory organs such as the eyes and ears towards a stimulus. It also involves spreading extra activation to the parts of the cortex that are processing information about the stimulus and probably inhibiting activation of others. When we attend to a stimulus, such as a mosquito buzzing around the room, the brain uses the same circuits it normally uses to process information that is not the focus of attention. For example, watching the mosquito activates the 'what' and 'where' visual pathways in the occipital, temporal and parietal lobes. What attention does is to enhance processing at those cortical locations (Rees, Frackowiak, & Firth, 1997). Orienting to stimuli activates neural circuits in the midbrain (such as the superior colliculi, which help control eye movements), thalamus (which directs attention to particular sensory systems) and parietal lobes (which, among other functions, direct attention to particular locations).

A second function of attention is to control the contents of consciousness, such as deciding how much to listen as someone is talking. Despite our subjective experience of consciously controlling what we attend to, the situation is more the other way around. To notice something consciously, unconscious attentional mechanisms have to alert us to its potential significance. Thus, paradoxically, consciousness is, to a large degree, regulated *outside* of consciousness, by unconscious attentional mechanisms that focus conscious awareness. Controlling the contents of consciousness and controlling voluntary behaviour involve areas of the frontal lobes and basal ganglia known to be involved in thought, movement and self-control.

APPLY + DISCUSS

• What parts of the brain are involved as a person notices that her baby is playing with something, categorises the object as dangerous, and moves the baby away from the object?

The third function of attention, maintaining alertness, is crucial in tasks ranging from focusing on test items in the face of anxiety, to staying alert for hours while watching a radar screen to detect seemingly small but potentially meaningful changes. A whole network of neurons from the reticular formation (involved in regulating states of alertness) through the frontal lobes appear to be involved in alertness (Posner, 1995).

Divided attention

Everyone has had the experience of being on the telephone and having someone in the room begin talking at the same time. Trying to follow two such conversations is an example of ***divided attention***, splitting attention between two complex tasks (see Craik, Govoni, Naveh-Benjamin, & Anderson, 1996).

One way researchers study divided attention is through ***dichotic listening*** tasks, in which participants are fitted with earphones, and different information is simultaneously presented to the left and right ears (figure 5.3). Participants can be instructed to attend only to the information from one ear by repeating aloud what they hear in that ear, a procedure called shadowing.

Participants can become so adept at shadowing that they are completely unable to recognise information in the unattended channel. Nevertheless, the information does appear to be processed to some degree, as demonstrated in research on priming, in which exposure to a stimulus (such as a word) affects performance on tasks involving related stimuli (chapter 7). For example, participants who hear 'England' (the prime) in the unattended channel in a dichotic listening study may have no recollection of having heard the name of any country. When compared to control participants who have not been similarly primed, however, they are more likely to say 'London' if asked to name a capital city and will more quickly fill in the missing letters when asked for the name of a city when presented with LO—.

Divided attention can be seen in such everyday but remarkably complex events as listening to a lecture while simultaneously taking notes. Psychologists have even trained participants to take dictation while reading (Spelke, Hirst, & Neisser, 1976). Sometimes people accomplish such feats by rapidly shifting attention back and forth between the two tasks. Much of the time, however, they solve attentional dilemmas by automatising one task or the other (chapter 7). Automatisation develops through practice, as actions previously performed with deliberate conscious effort are eventually processed automatically. While students listen to a lecture, their primary focus of consciousness is on the lecturer's current words, while a largely automatic process, perhaps drawing on some subset of attentional processes, allows note taking.

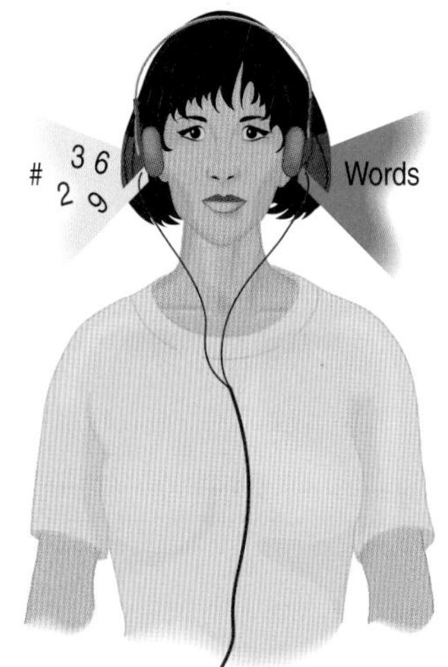

FIGURE 5.3
A dichotic listening task. Participants are fitted with earphones, and different information is transmitted into each ear simultaneously. Participants often show effects of information presented in the unattended channel, even when they have no conscious recognition of it.

INTERIM SUMMARY

Attention refers to the process of focusing conscious awareness, providing heightened sensitivity to a limited range of experience requiring more extensive information processing. Attention consists of at least three functions: orienting to sensory stimuli, controlling behaviour and the contents of consciousness and maintaining alertness. ***Divided attention***, which often involves automatising one or more tasks or rapidly shifting attention between them, refers to the capacity to split attention or cognitive resources between two or more tasks.

APPLY + DISCUSS

Consider the following quote from North American science writer Carl Zimmer, who has written numerous books and regularly contributes articles for various print and online media:

> I am going to do my best to hold your attention until the very last word of this column. Actually, I know it's futile. Along the way, your mind will wander off, then return, then drift away again. But I can console myself with some recent research on the subject of mind wandering. Mind wandering is not necessarily the sign of a boring column. It's just one of the things that makes us human . . . (Zimmer, 2009).

- Self-test yourself to see how often your mind wanders — randomly sample your thoughts at eight random times a day for a week. On average, how often were you not thinking about what you were doing?
- How might a wandering mind be important to setting goals, making discoveries and living a balanced life?
- What strategies might you employ to focus your attention on your textbook, your lectures and learning psychology?

The normal flow of consciousness

A major component of the normal flow of consciousness is ***daydreaming*** — turning attention away from external stimuli to internal thoughts and imagined scenarios. Some daydreams are pleasurable fantasies, whereas others involve planning for future actions or conversations with significant others. In one large-scale study of daydreaming, all participants reported daydreaming daily (Singer, 1975). Another research team found that university students daydream about half the time they are conscious, if daydreaming includes thoughts about something other than what is currently happening in the person's environment, such as thinking about an upcoming date while sitting in the library (Klinger, 1992).

Psychologists study the normal flow of consciousness using ***experience-sampling*** techniques, in which participants report on the contents of consciousness at specified times (Larson, 1997; Singer & Kolligian, 1987). For example, after being instructed simply to report the contents of their consciousness, they may come into the laboratory and talk aloud, often while performing a task. Psychologists then code their verbal responses into categories, such as emotional tone, relevance to the task at hand and ways of solving the task.

Beeper studies are an experience-sampling technique that has provided a more natural window to the flow of consciousness in everyday life. In these studies, participants carry pagers or personal digital assistants and report their experience when 'beeped' at various points during the day (Larsen, 1996). In one study, researchers randomly selected 75 high school students within several categories, such as sex, grade and social class (a stratified random sample; chapter 2) (Csikszentmihalyi & Larson, 1984). For an entire week, they beeped the students at some point during every two-hour period (except, of course, at night). Participants then immediately filled out a brief form reporting what they were doing and with whom, what they were thinking and feeling, and how intensely they were feeling it. Some of the results were quite unexpected. For example, when participants were with their families, their negative thoughts outnumbered their positive thoughts by about 10 to 1. In a more recent study, university students were sorted according to intellect, and the scientists beeped them at random intervals (eight times a day, between noon and midnight) for seven days (Herbert, 2007). The average intellect students reported 'wandering' not when they were bored, but rather when their minds were overtaxed by some unusually challenging task. Thus, such students' minds seemed to use 'escaping' as a coping mechanism.

INTERIM SUMMARY

Prominent in the normal flow of conscious experience are ***daydreams***, in which the person turns attention away from external stimuli to internal thoughts and imagined scenarios, often for pleasure or for problem solving. Psychologists learn about the normal flow of consciousness through ***experience-sampling*** techniques, such as ***beeper studies***, in which participants carry pagers or personal digital assistants and report on aspects of consciousness when they are paged at random intervals.

Perspectives on consciousness

While consciousness figured prominently in the work of early psychologists, it was considered less relevant by modern behaviourists. Until about a decade ago, cognitive psychologists paid little attention to consciousness either. As we will see in chapters 7 and 8, however, that all changed with the surge of research on implicit memory and cognition. Spurred by developments in neuroscience and neuroimaging that provide a new window on consciousness, cognitive scientists — as well as philosophers, neurologists, biologists and even physicists — have begun rethinking consciousness (e.g. Cohen &

Schooler, 1997; Edelman, 1989). In this section we examine psychodynamic and cognitive perspectives on consciousness and explore some emerging common ground.

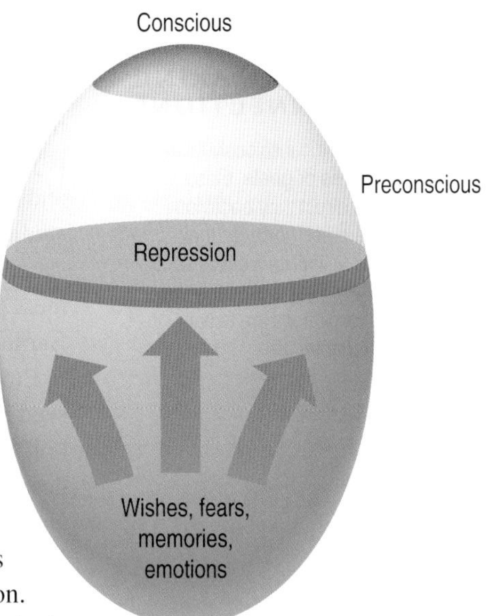

FIGURE 5.4
Freud's model of consciousness
Conscious mental processes are those of which a person is subjectively aware. Preconscious mental processes are not presently conscious but could readily be brought to consciousness. Unconscious mental processes are inaccessible to consciousness because they have been repressed.

The psychodynamic unconscious

Freud (1900/1965) defined consciousness as one of three mental systems called the conscious, preconscious and unconscious (figure 5.4). ***Conscious mental processes*** involve subjective awareness of stimuli, feelings or ideas (e.g. consciousness of the sentence you just read — if you were paying attention). ***Preconscious mental processes*** are not presently conscious but could be readily brought to consciousness if the need arose, such as the smell of bacon cooking in the background or the name of a city that is not currently in mind but could easily be retrieved. ***Unconscious mental processes*** are inaccessible to consciousness because they would be too anxiety provoking to acknowledge and thus have been repressed (chapter 11).

Freud likened repression to a censor: just as a repressive government censors ideas or wishes it considers threatening, so, too, does the mind censor threatening thoughts from consciousness. Thus, a person may remember an abusive parent with love and admiration and have little access to unhappy memories because admitting the truth would be painful. Unconscious processes of this sort are dynamically unconscious — that is, kept unconscious for a reason. According to Freud, keeping mental contents out of awareness requires continuing psychological effort or energy, a postulate that has received empirical support in recent years (Wegner & Wheatley, 1999). Other researchers have found that people can regulate their emotions outside of awareness by keeping distressing thoughts, feelings and memories out of consciousness (Paulhus, Fridlander, & Hayes, 1997; Vaillant, 1992). Freud (1915/1963) recognised that many other psychological processes are descriptively unconscious — that is, not conscious even though they are not threatening, such as the processes by which readers are converting symbols on this page into words with psychological meaning.

Subliminal perception

In the 1940s and 1950s, as part of the New Look in perception (chapter 4), researchers tested hypotheses derived from Freud's theory of consciousness. Studies of ***subliminal perception*** — perception of stimuli below the threshold of consciousness — used a device called a tachistoscope, which can flash images too quickly for conscious recognition but slowly enough to be registered outside awareness (Dixon, 1971, 1981; Erdelyi, 1985; Weinberger, 2004).

Although experiments in subliminal perception went out of favour for almost 30 years, more recently both cognitive and psychodynamic researchers have breathed new life into subliminal research, demonstrating that subliminal presentation of stimuli can indeed influence thought and emotion (Morris, Oehman, & Dolan, 1998; Shevrin, Bond, Brakel, Hertel, & Williams, 1996; Weinberger & Hardaway, 1990; Whalen et al., 1998). For instance, subliminal presentation of a happy or sad face directly prior to exposure to a novel visual stimulus (such as a Chinese character) affects the extent to which participants like it (Murphy & Zajonc, 1993). Subliminal presentation of the face seems to 'tag' the stimulus with an emotional connotation. Other studies have shown that participants subliminally primed with a word (e.g. 'beach') will more quickly recognise words semantically related to it (e.g. 'sand'), even though they never consciously registered the prime (Marcel, 1983).

Psychologists have not been the only people interested in subliminal processing. In the 1950s, rumours flew that movie theatres were manipulating consumers by subliminally presenting messages 'eat popcorn' and 'buy Coke'. In the 1980s, parents expressed fears about subliminal messages in rock music, such as backward messages encouraging violence. Since then there have been countless examples of companies allegedly including subliminal messages in advertisements — despite regulatory bodies such as the Australian Broadcasting Authority and legal authorities in many countries strictly prohibiting the use of such messages (Australian Broadcasting Authority, 2004). Although the impact of these messages on consumers is not likely to be particularly large, research on subliminal priming clearly demonstrates that presenting people with subliminal stimuli that are positive or negative can influence their emotional reactions and behaviours (Glassman & Andersen, 1997; Weinberger, 2004).

Unconscious emotion and motivation

The proposition that unconscious cognitive and perceptual processes can influence behaviour is no longer controversial. Historically, however, the most distinctively psychodynamic hypothesis is that

MAKING CONNECTIONS

When people are consciously focusing on their **motives** or **goals**, these goals tend to direct their behaviour. When they are not, however, their unconscious or implicit motives control their behaviour. That is probably why New Year's resolutions are usually short-lived (chapter 10).

motivational and emotional processes can be unconscious as well. This proposition has now also gained experimental support (see Bargh & Barndollar, 1996; Epstein, 1994; Westen, 1998).

With respect to motivation, research suggests a distinction between conscious and unconscious motivational systems similar to the distinction between implicit and explicit memory in cognitive psychology. Numerous studies have shown that when people are not attending to their conscious goals and values, they tend to act on implicit motives (McClelland, Koestner, & Weinberger, 1989). Other studies show that priming people with words associated with their motives (e.g. priming people with *success*, which is associated with the need for achievement) makes them more likely to act on these motives, even though they may be completely unaware that they have been primed (Bargh & Barndollar, 1996).

Emotional processes can also influence thought and behaviour without being conscious. This can be seen in research with patients with Korsakoff's disorder who have severe amnesia. In one study, Korsakoff's patients preferred a person described a week earlier as having positive traits over someone described more negatively, even though they had no recollection of having seen either one before (Johnson, Kim, & Risse, 1985). Similar findings emerge in subliminal priming studies of patients without neurological damage (see Lazarus & McCleary, 1951), using measures ranging from facial muscle movements indicating distress to brainwave activity assessed by EEG (see Ohman, 1994; Wong, Shevrin, & Williams, 1994). These findings are of particular relevance to the psychodynamic hypothesis that individuals can respond emotionally to people or situations without knowing why.

The cognitive unconscious

The ***cognitive unconscious*** of cognitive research refers to information-processing mechanisms that operate outside of awareness (such as implicit memory) rather than information the person is motivated to keep from awareness. In other words, the cognitive unconscious includes what Freud called *descriptively* but not *dynamically* unconscious processes. Information-processing models often use the terms *consciousness* and *working memory* interchangeably. Most models now distinguish explicit (conscious) and implicit (unconscious) memory (chapter 7) and cognition (chapter 8), such as conscious problem-solving strategies versus automatic, unconscious heuristics. Connectionist models further propose that information processing occurs simultaneously in multiple, relatively separate neural networks, most of which are unconscious (chapter 8). The brain synthesises a unitary conscious experience from the various activated unconscious networks, 'highlighting' those that best fit the data (Baars, 1988, 1997; Mandler, 1997; Searle, 2000).

The functions of conscious and unconscious processes

Some cognitive theorists have examined the complementary functions, strengths and weaknesses of conscious and unconscious processes in everyday behaviour. Unconscious processes, notably skills and associative processes such as priming and classical conditioning, are extremely fast and efficient (Baars & McGovern, 1996; Mandler, 1997). Since they are usually based on considerable learning, they tend to lead to adaptive responses that make sense in the light of observed regularities in the environment (such as avoiding stimuli that would lead to pain or danger).

Another strength of unconscious processes is that they can operate simultaneously. When solving a problem, for example, multiple networks can 'collect data' at the same time and come up with independent and 'well-researched' potential solutions. Consciousness, in contrast, has limited capacity. We can only form one 'scene' at a time in our conscious minds; we cannot, for example, see the classic ambiguous Gestalt figure as both two faces and a vase simultaneously (chapter 1). We can switch rapidly back and forth between two views of a scene or among tasks that require attention, but ultimately, each will draw conscious cognitive resources from the other. On the other hand, conscious processes are more flexible than unconscious processes, and because consciousness is not limited to quasi-independent networks operating in parallel in their own small domains, consciousness can survey the landscape and consider the 'big picture'.

One theory suggests that unconscious processes operating in parallel are like independent teams of 'experts', each offering its own advice on how to solve a problem or make a decision (Baars, 1988, 1997). A central role of consciousness is to redistribute activation among the tens, hundreds or thousands of networks ('team of experts') active at any given time (Mandler, 1997). When conscious goals are active, they spread extra activation to networks associated with goal attainment. If a person is trying to make a decision or solve a problem, the networks activated below consciousness all vie for conscious access. Those that seem to provide the best potential solutions become represented in consciousness. Becoming conscious in turn spreads further activation to them and inhibits activation of less compelling alternatives.

INTERIM SUMMARY

Freud distinguished types of mental activities: ***conscious*** processes, of which the person is currently subjectively aware; ***preconscious*** processes, which are not presently conscious but could be readily brought to consciousness; and ***unconscious*** processes, which are dynamically kept from consciousness because they are threatening. Studies of ***subliminal perception*** have shown that perception of stimuli below the threshold of consciousness can indeed have an impact on conscious thought and behaviour. Recent research also supports the psychodynamic hypothesis that emotional and motivational processes can occur outside of awareness. Researchers from a cognitive perspective have been studying the ***cognitive unconscious***, which focuses on information-processing mechanisms that operate outside of awareness, such as procedural knowledge and implicit memory. Implicit processes tend to be rapid and to operate simultaneously. Conscious processes are slower and less efficient for tasks that require instant responses but are useful for 'shining a spotlight' on problems that require more careful consideration.

APPLY + DISCUSS

- In what ways do cognitive and psychodynamic views of consciousness diverge or disagree?
- In what ways do these two views converge or agree?

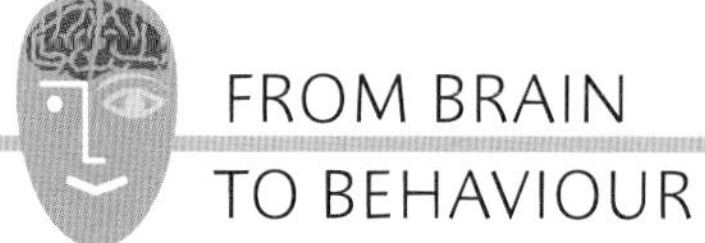

The neuropsychology of consciousness

Subjectively, consciousness is the seat of who we are; to lose consciousness permanently is to lose existence as a psychological being. So what neural structures produce conscious awareness and regulate states of consciousness?

Insights from neurological disorders

One way to learn about the neural pathways involved in consciousness is to examine neurological conditions that disrupt it. People with split brains, whose two hemispheres function independently following severing of the corpus callosum, provide one window to the neuropsychology of consciousness. An instructive case, described in chapter 3, concerned a 10-year-old boy who could only answer written questions orally when enquiries were made to the left hemisphere, suggesting that information presented to his right hemisphere lacked access to consciousness — although he could spell answers using his left hand when questions were addressed to his right hemisphere (LeDoux, Wilson, & Gazzaniga, 1977). The feelings spelled by his nonverbal right hemisphere were consistently more negative than those of his left hemisphere, raising questions about the unity of consciousness across the hemispheres.

Blindsight

Another phenomenon that bears on the neural underpinnings of consciousness is blindsight (chapter 4). Pursuing observations made by neurologists in the early part of the twentieth century, researchers have examined patients who are, in one sense, totally blind. If shown an object, they deny having seen it. They typically have lesions to the primary visual cortex in the occipital lobes, a region central to visual sensation, so their inability to see makes neurological sense. Yet, if asked to describe the object's geometric form (e.g. triangle or square) or give its location in space (to the right or left, up or down), they do so with accuracy far better than chance, frequently protesting all the while that they cannot do the task because they cannot see (Weiskrantz, 1997; Weiskrantz, Warrington, Sanders, & Marshall, 1974)!

The neural basis for blindsight is not entirely clear, but one hypothesis, derived in part from animal research, points to the role of two neural pathways involved in vision (figure 5.5; see overleaf). In the evolutionarily more recent pathway, neurons of the optic nerve carrying sensory information project to the thalamus via the optic tract; the information is subsequently transmitted to the primary visual cortex in the occipital lobes. This pathway is responsible for conscious visual perception and for determining the precise nature of stimuli.

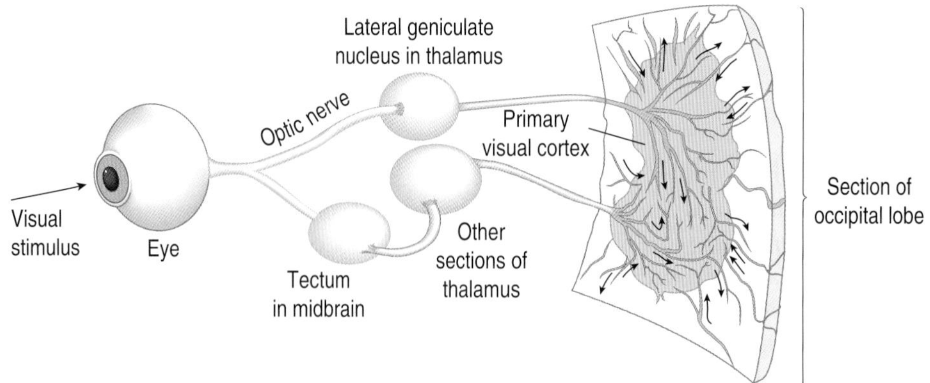

FIGURE 5.5
Blindsight. In blindsight, the neural pathway from the lateral geniculate nucleus in the thalamus to the primary visual cortex, which allows consciousness of visual images, is inoperative. However, a second, evolutionarily older pathway through the midbrain remains intact, permitting the implicit ability to locate visual stimuli.

The other pathway is evolutionarily older. Neurons carrying information from the retina project to a midbrain structure responsible for vision in animals such as frogs and birds that lack the highly specialised visual cortex of humans. From there the information passes through the thalamus and eventually on to the cortex. In blindsight, this second pathway appears to allow some visual processing at the midbrain level, even though the first pathway is rendered inoperative by damage to the visual cortex. Thalamic processing may also permit some recognition of what an object is, even though this thalamic knowledge cannot be consciously accessed — and may lead to emotional reactions to it even though the person has no idea what he has seen.

Amnesia

Studies with amnesics have shown that people can remember things implicitly even while lacking any consciousness of having seen them. In one series of studies (Squire, 1986), researchers showed amnesic and normal participants a word list and asked them to recall the words with and without cues. When later tested for explicit memory, amnesic participants were considerably impaired on both free-recall (recall without cues) and cued-recall tasks (in which participants were given the first three letters of the word). However, amnesics were as likely as neurologically intact participants to use words from the list when shown the first three letters of the word and simply asked to complete them with the first words that came to mind.

Implicit memory can show up in some unusual ways in amnesic patients. In one study, researchers had amnesic and normal participants play the computer game Tetris for several hours over three days (Stickgold, Malia, Maguire, Roddenberry, & O'Connor, 2000). Amnesics were just as likely to report Tetris-related imagery while nodding off to sleep those nights, even though they had no explicit recollection of having played! Similarly, a psychologist told a joke to a Korsakoff's patient whose ability to remember new experiences was virtually nonexistent (Jacoby & Kelley, 1987). Predictably, the man laughed, but the next time he heard the joke, he thought the joke was 'dumb'. The patient had apparently anticipated the punch line unconsciously, even though he had no conscious recollection of it.

Where is consciousness located?

So where is consciousness located in the brain? Research over the past two decades has made increasingly clear that this is probably not the right question to ask about any psychological phenomenon. Consciousness, like most psychological functions, involves a distributed network of neurons rather than a single 'centre'. The better question, then, is, 'What neural structures are involved in the experience of consciousness?'

The answer to this question, too, has a twist. It depends on which meaning of consciousness one has in mind. If one simply means the state of being conscious (as opposed to being unconscious or asleep), then hindbrain and midbrain structures, especially the reticular formation, are particularly important (Bogen, 1995; Franklin, Donohew, Dhoundiyal, & Cook, 1988; Szymusiak, Iriye, & McGinty, 1989). For example, neuroimaging of surgical patients undergoing anaesthesia finds reduced activity in the midbrain (as well as the thalamus, which plays an important role in conscious awareness) (Fiset et al., 1999). Similarly, damage to the reticular formation through head injury in humans or lesioning in animals can lead to loss of consciousness or coma. The pons and medulla are also involved in regulating states of conscious arousal (figure 5.6); in contrast, we can lose an entire cerebral hemisphere and remain conscious.

But consciousness has another meaning, which has been our focus thus far in this chapter: consciousness as the centre of subjective awareness. In this sense, consciousness is distributed across a number of neural pathways, most of them found in the cortex as well as the reticular formation and the thalamus (Newman, 1995). The reticular formation extends throughout much of the hindbrain and sends axons through the midbrain (in the tegmentum). These fibres then synapse with nuclei in the thalamus, which in turn synapse with parts of the cortex. A region of particular importance is the prefrontal cortex (Goldman-Rakic, 1995), which is involved in momentarily storing, manipulating or calling up information from various senses into working memory and hence making them conscious (chapter 7).

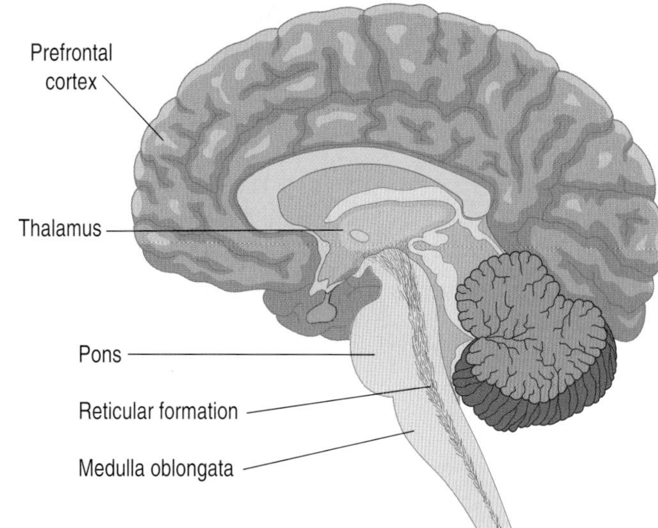

FIGURE 5.6
Neuropsychological basis of consciousness. The hindbrain and midbrain structures involved in conscious arousal and in shifts from waking to sleep include the reticular formation, pons and medulla. Midbrain reticular regions, the thalamus and the prefrontal cortex play a particular role in shining a conscious 'spotlight' on thoughts, feelings or perceptions.

Recent positron emission tomography (PET) data have in fact confirmed that when participants are consciously attending to stimuli, a pathway from the midbrain sections of the reticular formation through the region of the thalamus to which it projects becomes activated (Kinomura, Larsson, Gulyas, & Roland, 1996). Once the cortex is activated and the person attends to a stimulus, it sends messages back down to another region of the thalamus that signals the first region to limit its activation to the most relevant details of the stimulus, 'shining a spotlight' on information that needs to be highlighted and inhibiting attention to irrelevant details (see Crick & Koch, 1998). Thus, the thalamus and cortex appear to have a feedback loop, in which the thalamus and reticular formation 'illuminate' a large terrain, the cortex sends messages back to narrow the focus, and the thalamus in turn helps the cortex focus its conscious spotlight on a more specific target (Newman, 1995).

Not all areas of the cortex have direct access to consciousness. Some researchers have suggested that early sensory processing areas such as area V1 in the visual cortex (one of the first sensory 'stops' along the road to visual perception; chapter 4) do not have connections to the prefrontal cortex and hence cannot directly influence conscious experience (Crick & Koch, 1998). A series of creative neuroimaging studies supports this theory. The Necker cube (figure 5.7), the outline of a see through cube, produces two distinct conscious percepts that subjectively seem to alternate every few seconds. Because the Necker cube casts a constant image on the retina, and hence a constant 'image' on the primary visual cortex, this means that the subjective experience of alternating percepts or images is independent of sensory activation in V1. However, changes in conscious attention — even without moving the eyes — can alter activation levels in V1. This suggests that consciousness can focus the spotlight on the sensory building blocks of perception and hence alter perception of what is ultimately seen (Lumer & Rees, 1999; Watanabe et al., 1998).

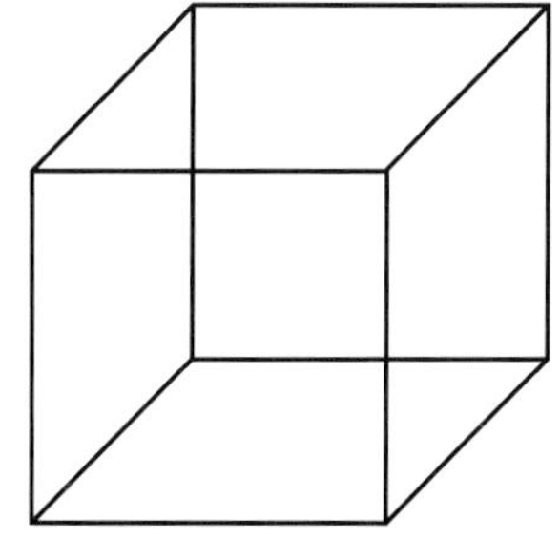

FIGURE 5.7
The Necker cube

INTERIM SUMMARY

An integrated view suggests that consciousness is a specialised processing function that monitors and controls current states for the purpose of maximising adaptation. Consciousness thus highlights or inhibits information based on its relevance to adaptation and its emotional consequences. Consciousness involves a network of neurons distributed throughout the brain. Damage to hindbrain structures, particularly the reticular formation, can lead to a complete loss of consciousness. The neural networks that 'shine a spotlight' on perceptions, thoughts, emotions or goals at any moment appear to involve the prefrontal cortex, the thalamus and midbrain regions of the reticular formation.

Sleep and dreaming

We have focused thus far on waking consciousness. We now turn to the major series of changes that occur in consciousness every 24 hours: the sleep–wake cycle. Those who lament that life is too short would be horrified to realise that they will sleep away roughly a third of their time on the Earth, about 25 years. A newborn infant typically sleeps about 70 percent of every 24 hours and typically results in 400–750 hours lost sleep for parents in the first year (The National Sleep Research Project, 2000). According to the National Sleep Research Project, Australians sleep an average of eight hours and one minute per day. Northern Territorians get the most sleep (eight hours and 16 minutes) compared with those in the Australian Capital Territory, Queensland and New South Wales, who all average less than eight hours. We sleep about one to 1.5 hours less than we did 100 years ago (An Intro to Sleep: What is Sleep, 2007). Anything less than five minutes to fall asleep at night means you are sleep deprived (The National Sleep Research Project, 2000). Ideally, you should take between 10 and 15 minutes to fall asleep.

An *Infant Sleep Study* in 2003 was a large Australian study that showed that babies' sleep and mothers' wellbeing could be improved into toddlerhood by a brief infant sleep program, involving a Maternal and Child Health nurse helping the mother to learn ways to manage their infant's sleep (Sleep Studies, 2009). A total of 695 babies (aged four to seven months) and their mothers from six Melbourne local government areas participated, and in 2009–10, the *Kids Sleep Study* followed up these children when they were six years old. Because of the success of this program, the Department of Education and Early Childhood Development funded the training of all Victorian Maternal and Child Health nurses in the program, which began mid 2008. The *Infant Sleep Study* findings are available in the 'Babies Sleep' pages of the Raising Children website (http://raisingchildren.net.au) which provides information for parents about children from birth to eight years of age.

APPLY + DISCUSS

- Why might sleep have evolved?
- Why might it make adaptive sense for our consciousness to wax and wane with the cycles of the sun?

The nature and evolution of sleep

Sleep evolved over 3 billion years ago in some organisms, and the mechanisms that govern the biological clock in humans are apparently over 500 million years old (Lavie, 1996). Although not all animals show the characteristic EEG signs of sleep (described on pages 199–201), nearly all animals show behavioural signs of sleeping: minimal movement, a stereotyped posture and a high degree of stimulation needed to arouse them. They differ, however, in how much they sleep (figure 5.8).

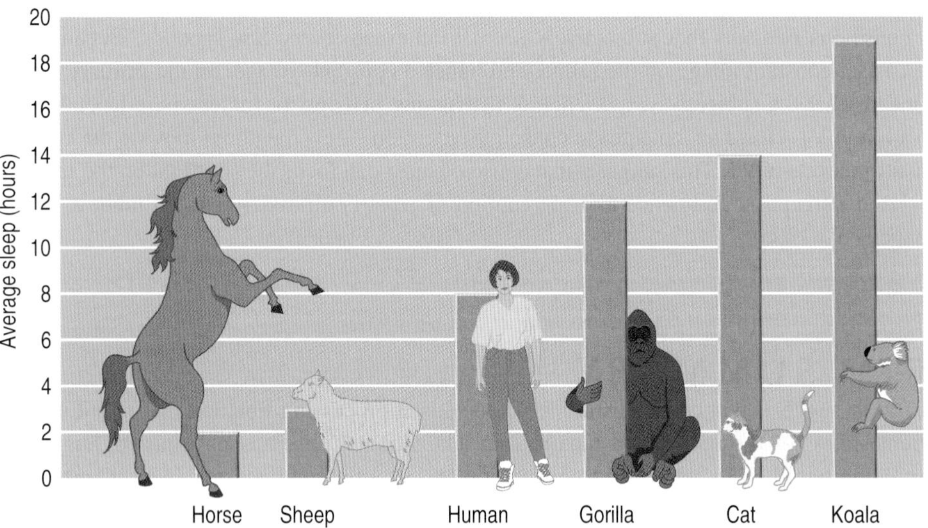

FIGURE 5.8
Average hours of sleep per night. Animals vary according to the amount of sleep they need; humans lie somewhere in the middle.

Individuals differ widely in the amount of sleep they both need and get, with most people sleeping between 6.5 and 8.5 hours a night (Lavie, 1996). As people get older, they tend to require less sleep. The number of hours people sleep is related to mortality rates, although the reasons for this are unclear. People who report sleeping for unusually long *or* unusually short durations are prone to die earlier than people whose reported sleep is closer to average. Researchers from the University of Warwick and University College London suggest that lack of sleep doubles the risk of death, but so can too much sleep. They found that those who had cut their sleeping from seven hours to five hours or less faced a 1.7 fold increased risk in mortality from all causes, and twice the increased risk of death from a cardiovascular problem in particular (Ferrie et al., 2007). Interestingly, the researchers also found that too much sleep also increased mortality. Those individuals who showed an increase in sleep duration to eight hours or more a night were more than twice as likely to die as those who had not changed their habit; however, cause of death was predominantly from non-cardiovascular diseases. The researchers suggest that consistently sleeping around seven hours per night is optimal for health and a sustained reduction (or increase) may predispose individuals to ill-health. University students should heed this warning, with research from the late 1960s to the early 1990s suggesting that such students sleep about an hour less on average per night (Hicks & Pelligrini, 1991). More recently, research from The George Institute for Global Health in Sydney, Australia, indicates that young adults sleeping less than five hours sleep per night are tripling their chances of developing a mental illness (Glozier et al., 2009). Chronic sleep deprivation is related to high levels of psychological distress and early intervention programs are needed to prevent these problems from persisting.

Researchers have documented rare cases of people who require minimal sleep with no adverse consequences, such as a 70-year-old English nurse who was observed to sleep only one hour every night (Borbély, 1986). Legend has it that Leonardo DaVinci had the unusual habit of sleeping 15 minutes every four hours.

Circadian rhythms

The cycle of sleep and waking in humans and other animals, like the ebb and flow of body temperature, hormones and other life support processes, is a circadian rhythm. A ***circadian rhythm*** (from the Latin, *circa*, meaning 'about', and *diem*, meaning 'day') is a cyclical biological process that evolved around the daily cycles of light and dark. Expectant mothers can attest to the fact that circadian rhythms begin before birth. Foetuses begin showing rhythms of sleep and activity by the sixth month in utero.

Rhythms akin to sleep–wake cycles may exist in daytime as well as in sleep. Research supports the distinction between 'day people' and 'night people', finding that people peak in their alertness and arousal at different times of the day (Wallace, 1993). Researchers studying mice have tracked down the genes responsible for controlling their internal 'clock' by examining mutant mice whose clocks do not tick correctly (Antoch et al., 1997; Shearman, Jin, Lee, Reppert, & Weaver, 2000). The 'natural alarm clock' which enables some people to wake up more or less when they want to is caused by a burst of the stress hormone adrenocorticotropin. Researchers say this reflects an unconscious anticipation of the stress of waking up (The National Sleep Research Project, 2000).

Human circadian rhythms are controlled largely by the hypothalamus but are influenced by light and dark. A special neural tract that projects from the retina to the hypothalamus responds only to relatively intense light, such as sunlight. During periods of darkness, the pineal gland in the middle of the brain produces a hormone called melatonin; melatonin levels gradually diminish during daylight hours. Melatonin influences not only sleep but also sexual arousal. Thus, during the winter months, when the number of daylight hours diminishes, so, too, does sexual arousal. The old saying that 'a young man's fancy turns to thoughts of love' in the springtime thus has more than a grain (or gram) of hormonal truth (see Lavie, 1996).

Circadian rhythms account for the difficulties people experience when they cross time zones (jet lag) or have frequently changing work shifts. Nurses, medical residents on call, police, pilots and flight attendants whose shifts change from day to day or week to week, suffer greater incidence of health problems, in part because of disrupted circadian rhythms (Monk, 1997; Tan, 1991). Although some people seem to function well despite these frequent disruptions in their sleep cycle, others become irritable and inefficient — not particularly comforting traits to see in pilots or doctors in training. Prescription melatonin has proven effective for some people in reducing jet lag, presumably by 'recalibrating' the body to the light–dark cycle of the new time zone (Arendt, Skene, Middleton, Lockley, & Deacon, 1997; Claustrat, Brun, David, Sassolas, & Chazot, 1992). Studies carried out in South Australia have illustrated the 'recalibration' process. Participants who went through a week of simulated night work were found to

MAKING CONNECTIONS

How many hours do you need to sleep each night for optimal health and performance? Most Australians sleep between 6.5 and 8.5 hours each night. The record for the longest period without sleep is 18 days, 21 hours and 40 minutes during a rocking chair marathon. The record holder reported **hallucinations**, **paranoia**, blurred vision, slurred speech and memory and concentration lapses (chapter 15). Politician Tony Abbott survived without sleep for 36 hours in the lead up to the 2010 federal election. He relied on 'catnaps' between campaign commitments, and managed to fit in a game of tennis with Liberal candidate and former professional tennis player John Alexander.

both sleep and work better at the end of the week, as their circadian rhythms adapted to the new arrangements (Lamond et al., 2003).

Sleep deprivation

No-one knows precisely what functions sleep serves. Some researchers emphasise its role in conserving energy, because sleep turns down the body's 'thermostat' at night (Berger & Phillips, 1995). Others emphasise a restorative function, in which sleep 'freshens' both body and mind; as we will see, still others point to a potential role in consolidating memories learned during the day (see Stickgold, 1998; Walsh & Lindblom, 1997).

People have known of the ill effects of extreme sleep deprivation for at least 2000 years. In Roman times and during the Middle Ages, sleep deprivation was used as a form of torture. Long-term sleep deprivation reduces the functioning of the immune system and makes the body more vulnerable to diseases ranging from common colds to cancer (Everson, 1997). Rats deprived of sleep die after two or three weeks (Rechtschaffen, Bergmann, Everson, Kushida, & Gilliland, 1989). Lack of sleep has been pinpointed as a key factor in road accidents in Australia and New Zealand. The Department of Transport in Queensland has identified fatigue as one of the 'Fatal Four' causes of road deaths in advertising campaigns. Yee, Campbell, Beasley, and Neill (2002) from the WellSleep Department of Medicine at Wellington School of Medicine in New Zealand also examined the role of fatigue in motor vehicle accidents. They found that a significant proportion of those involved in accidents reported feeling drowsy before the crash, had regularly slept less than six hours a night or suffered from a disorder that affected their sleep.

Sleep thus appears essential to physical and emotional wellness. When your body works well, you sleep well. No matter what age you are, limited sleep can affect every aspect of your lifestyle — from work to home to personal relationships (Chiropractors' Association of Australia, 2009). Pfizer Australia and the Australasian Sleep Association surveyed 1600 Australians aged 18 years and over and estimated that over 1.2 million Australians experience sleep disorders (Pfizer Australia, 2004b). On average, Australians feel sleepy for approximately five months of the year (Pfizer Australia, 2004a). More than 70 percent of those surveyed feel their ability to get to sleep is affected by the level of work/school or everyday stresses and that they sleep better when relaxed. According to research conducted by the Better Sleep Council, poor sleep is detrimental to performance at work — 44 percent of employees surveyed said they were likely to be in a bad mood at work as a result of poor sleep (Better Sleep Council, 2007).

Many Australians feel stressed and 'time poor', perhaps reflecting the fact that we work some of the longest hours in the developed world.

Many Australians feel stressed and 'time poor', perhaps reflecting the fact that we work some of the longest hours in the developed world! The average Australian works around 1855 hours annually, compared to an international average of 1643 hours (Eight Hour Day, 2003). In August 2002, around 1.7 million Australians worked 50 hours or more per week, twice as many as in 1982 (Eight Hour Day, 2003). Research at the Institute for Social Research at Swinburne University of Technology suggests that feeling tired and run down is a warning sign that work is interfering with home life. However, people are turning to shiftwork and doing casual work on Sundays because they need the income, forfeiting their time for relaxation and time with the family (Eight Hour Day, 2003). Today's '24 hour society', complete with the all-hours availability of the internet, has been viewed by many as disrupting sleeping patterns across the world. According to Millman (2005), adolescents and young adults are at risk of poor academic performance, mood swings and increased car crashes as a result of excessive sleepiness. Additionally, a survey of Australian university students showed that the most common sleep complaints were difficulty falling asleep (18 percent), early morning awakening (13 percent), general sleep difficulties (12 percent) and difficulty staying asleep (9 percent; Lack, 1986).

Research suggests that sleep deprivation is associated with impaired immune and motor function and psychological problems such as memory and attention deficits. Professor Tim Olds, from the University of South Australia, presented his research on the sleeping habits of 4000 Australian children, aged between nine and 18, at the 2010 Australasian Sleep Conference. According to Professor Olds, most teenagers commence the week with a sleep deficit that continues to grow as the week progresses. They make up for the sleep lost on a Saturday night, but then find it difficult to wake up on Monday morning because they typically go to bed late on a Sunday night, wanting the weekend to last as long as possible. This sleep deficit then continues throughout the week.

As anyone who has ever had a bad night's sleep knows, the time required to fall asleep drops substantially after even a single sleepless night (Carskadon & Dement, 1982). Researchers have recently discovered that a neurotransmitter substance (actually a modulatory neurotransmitter, which regulates the activity of other neurotransmitters) in the thalamus and in structures deep within the cerebrum increases with each additional hour an animal is awake (Porkka-Heiskanen, Strecker, Thakkar, & Bjorkam, 1997). This neurotransmitter, called adenosine, plays an inhibitory role in the brain, shutting down the systems that normally lead to arousal and hence fostering sleep when an animal has been awake too long.

Most people experience difficulty sleeping at some time. ***Insomnia***, or inability to sleep, affects virtually everyone at some point, but for some people it is a chronic problem. Reports suggest that up to one in three Australians suffer from insomnia at some stage, making it the second most common medical complaint, with almost one half of older adults experiencing symptoms of insomnia on a few nights each week (Sleep Disorders Australia, 2006). Despite this, few people seek help from their doctor. Insomnia costs the Australian community over half a billion dollars each year in direct medical costs, and as much as 10 times that amount in indirect costs, such as lost productivity or days off work (Sleep Disorders Australia, 2006). For both the community and the sufferer, it is an issue that should not be ignored.

Alarming statistics show that almost 10 percent of Australians are turning to sleeping tablets to help them cope, a third of which admit to taking them every night (Pfizer Australia, 2004b). This is a major public health issue, because over time, sleep deprivation can lead to an inability to deal with stress, ill health, irritability, and feeling distracted and unfocused (Pfizer Australia, 2004a). Additionally, sleeping tablets are problematic because they do not often address the cause of the sleeping problem. Thus, although sleeping pills are sometimes appropriate and may offer temporary relief, they should always be taken with caution. Sleeping pills can lead to more, rather than less, trouble sleeping, as the person becomes dependent on them or the brain develops a tolerance, requiring higher doses to achieve the same effect (Lavie, 1996). Some suggestions by a major sleep researcher for reducing or avoiding insomnia should also be available for you to view via your university course website for this subject.

APPLY + DISCUSS

Bernard Tomic lost an epic five-set encounter at the 2010 Australian Open, with his match lasting nearly four hours and not ending until after 2 am. After the match, Tomic complained to tournament organisers that he should not have been playing a match at that time.

- As a 17 year old when that particular match was played, would Tomic necessarily have been playing with a sleep deficit?
- If so, can we say with confidence that his sporting performance was impacted by the late timeslot?

INTERIM SUMMARY

People spend roughly one-third of their lives asleep. The sleep cycle is governed by ***circadian rhythms***, cyclical biological 'clocks' that evolved around the daily cycles of light and dark. The functions of sleep are not yet known, although sleep appears to be involved in restoration and maintenance of bodily processes such as homoeostasis, immune functioning and consolidation of memory.

ETHICAL DILEMMA

Researchers at a sleep institute are interested in learning more about how sleep deprivation interferes with simple problem-solving capacities. They propose to first keep participants awake for more than 24 hours. Following this period of sleep deprivation, participants will be allowed to sleep for periods of two to eight hours at a time. Participants will then be randomly woken at the different time intervals and asked to count backwards from 100 in threes. The researchers will record the participants' answers and note down any comments the participants make when they are awake.

- How should the researchers obtain informed consent from their participants?
- Is the welfare of participants compromised in any way by this study?

Stages of sleep

Sleep proceeds through a series of stages (figure 5.9; see overleaf). To study these stages, researchers use EEG (chapter 2), attaching electrodes to participants' heads to assess electrical activity in the brain. (They also attach electrodes at the corners of the eyes to track eye movements.) In general, as people move from a waking state through deeper stages of sleep, their brainwaves become slower and more rhythmic, decreasing from over 14 cycles per second (cps) in the waking state to as little as 0.5 cps in deep sleep (Dement & Kleitman, 1957). (The number of cycles per second is a gross measure of rate of neural firing and hence of mental activity.)

Early stages of sleep

As figure 5.9 shows, normal waking brain activity has an irregular pattern with a high mental activity level, evidenced in a large number of cycles per second (known as beta waves). As people close their eyes and relax, alpha waves (8 to 12 cps) emerge, signalling a slowing of mental activity and a transition into sleep.

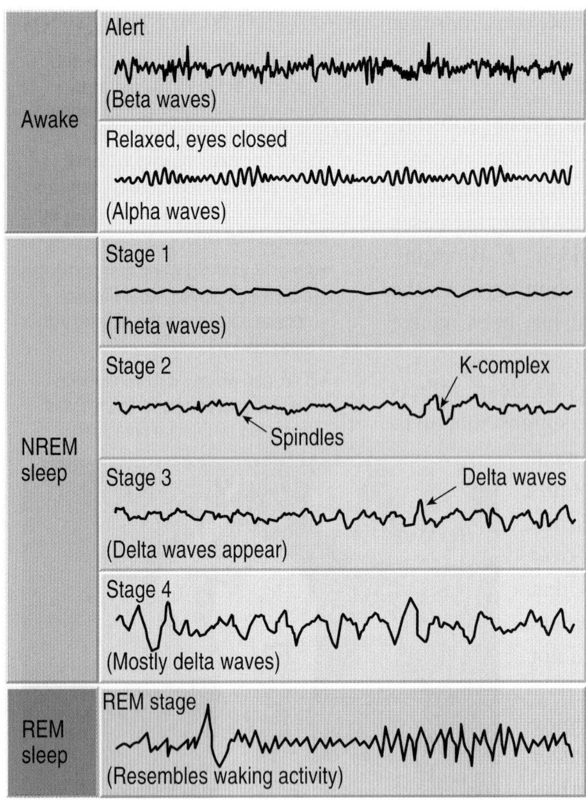

FIGURE 5.9
Stages of sleep. As people move from a waking state through deeper stages of sleep, their brainwaves become slower and more rhythmic, decreasing from over 14 cycles per second in the waking state to as little as half a cycle per second in deep sleep.

Stage 1 sleep is brief (only a few minutes), marked by the appearance of slower theta waves (3 to 7 cps). Physiological changes accompany this shift from drowsiness into sleep as eye movements slow, muscles relax and blood pressure drops, bringing the body into a calm, quiet state.

Stage 2 sleep is marked by an EEG pattern of slightly larger waves interrupted by bursts of low-amplitude activity (called sleep spindles) and slow, high-amplitude waves called K-complexes (Halasz, 1993). During stage 2, sleep deepens, as alpha activity disappears.

Stage 3 sleep is marked by large, slow, rhythmic delta waves (less than 1 cps). When delta waves comprise more than 50 percent of recorded brain activity, the person has entered stage 4 sleep. Together, stages 3 and 4 constitute what is called delta sleep, a deep sleep characterised by relaxed muscles, decreased rate of respiration and slightly lower body temperature. People aroused from delta sleep are groggy and disoriented. During delta sleep, muscles apparently rest and rejuvenate, since people deprived of it frequently complain of muscle aches and tension.

Rapid eye movement sleep

Delta sleep is followed by a kind of sleep that is qualitatively different from the preceding stages. Stage 4 sleep is interrupted, and the sleep stages occur in reverse order, through stages 3 and 2. But instead of entering stage 1, suddenly the eyes begin to dart around as if the sleeper were watching a play. At this point, the person enters ***rapid eye movement (REM) sleep***, a qualitatively different stage of sleep that is named for the darting eye movements that characterise it. Because REM sleep is so different, stages 1 to 4 are often collectively called simply ***non-REM*** (or ***NREM***) ***sleep***.

In REM sleep, autonomic activity increases. Pulse and blood pressure quicken, respiration becomes faster and irregular, and both males and females evidence signs of sexual arousal that may last for several minutes. At the same time, muscle movement is largely 'turned off' (which is a good thing, or we would act out our dreams). The EEG during REM sleep resembles the irregular, faster pattern of waking life, suggesting that, although the body is not moving, the brain is quite active. The function of REM sleep is not clear, but if a person is repeatedly awakened from it, the brain will return to it with increasing persistence.

The mental activity that occurs during REM sleep is dreaming. Roughly 80 percent of the time when people are awakened from REM sleep, they report dream activity. Although many people believe they do not dream, the evidence suggests that everyone dreams several times a night, even though they may not remember dreaming. Dreaming also occurs during NREM sleep, but less frequently (Suzuki et al., 2004), and the dreams often consist of a simple experience, such as 'I dreamed I smelled fish' (Antrobus, 1991; Foulkes, 1995).

PET studies find that a network of neurons, beginning at the pons and extending through the thalamus and amygdala, are active during REM sleep (Maquet, Peters, Aerts, & Delfiore, 1996). Visual association areas in the occipital and temporal lobes, which are active when people form mental images and identify objects, are also activated during REM sleep, but the primary visual cortex is not (Braun et al., 1998). At the same time, areas of the prefrontal cortex involved in consciousness and attention are inactive or inhibited.

These findings are particularly interesting in light of the fact that watching an event in normal waking consciousness (as opposed to 'watching' a dream) involves both primary visual cortex and prefrontal attentional mechanisms. Together, these findings suggest that dreaming involves a neurologically distinct kind of consciousness that does not rely on normal waking attentional mechanisms. These findings may also explain why dreams are often highly emotional — because the amygdala is very active — and why dreamers can uncritically accept bizarre story lines — because the frontal circuits involved in critical thinking and social judgement are shut off during dreaming.

After a period of REM sleep, the person descends again through stage 2 and on to delta sleep. A complete cycle of REM and NREM sleep occurs about every 90 minutes (figure 5.10). However, as the night progresses, the person spends less of the 90 minutes in delta sleep and more in REM sleep. Rapid eye movement sleep recurs four or five times a night and accounts for about 25 percent of all time asleep (on average, two hours per night). Thus, over the course of a lifetime, the average person spends an estimated 50 000 hours — 2000 days, or six full years — dreaming (Hobson, 1988).

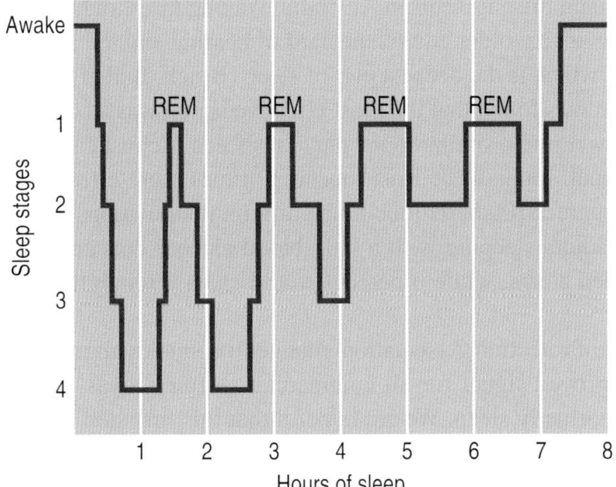

FIGURE 5.10
REM sleep. The stages of sleep follow a cyclical pattern that repeats about every 90 minutes, from stage 1 through delta sleep and back again. As the night progresses, the person spends less time in deeper sleep and more time in REM sleep.

SOURCE: Cartwright (1978).

Research by Dorothy Bruck and her colleagues at Victoria University has examined the effectiveness of smoke alarm signals in waking children, deep sleeping young adults, older adults, the hard of hearing, and the alcohol impaired. Bruck and Thomas (2008) found that a 520 Hz square signal is at least four to 12 times more effective in waking people than the current high-pitched signal, prompting the need to incorporate a new smoke alarm signal to wake the Australian population and prevent possible fatalities and injuries.

ONE STEP FURTHER

Sleeping through smoke alarms

By Professor Dorothy Bruck, Victoria University

You have probably burnt toast, set off your smoke alarm and thought that no one could possibly sleep through such a dreadful, high-pitched sound. This is what the developers of smoke alarms for sale back in the 1960s thought. The fire safety engineers put a lot of work into the technology to ensure the smoke alarms would detect smoke reliably, and simply put in a small signal device that emitted shrill, loud beeps. It took more than a decade for anyone to seriously consider whether the sound would actually wake people (Berry, 1978). The first test, on healthy young students who knew an alarm would go off once they were asleep, showed that under these experimental conditions, sleepers would wake up quickly (Nober, Peirce, & Well, 1981). However, the relevance of this finding was then questioned in a review (Bruck, 2001) for a number of reasons. First, the literature shows that some people need very loud sounds to wake up, older adults have trouble hearing high-pitch sounds, people will wake up more easily if they are expecting to be woken up and alcohol and sleeping tablets will raise waking thresholds. Second, some studies using smoke alarms at the volumes typically generated by a hallway placement (60 decibels) had raised concerns, finding that 94 percent of 6–12 year olds (Bruck, 1999) and 20 percent of young university students (Bruck & Horasan, 1995) would not reliably awaken to such a signal. Third, the most vulnerable groups for death by fire are the very young, elderly or intoxicated. The review argued that the waking thresholds of the healthy, young, unimpaired university students tested by Nober were not generalisable to the responsiveness of the people most likely to be the victims of fire occurring while they were asleep. Importantly, an alarm signal was needed that had the highest chance of waking those most at risk of dying.

A review (Bruck, 2001) found that a smoke alarm was needed that had the highest chance of waking those most at risk of dying, including the very young, elderly and intoxicated. Subsequent research has revealed that a complex sound with dominant frequencies at a low pitch, similar to the pitch of speech, is most effective at waking people from sleep.

The concerns raised in the review, and the knowledge that some fire tragedies occur during the sleeping period despite working smoke alarms, led to national and international support for studies to be conducted by a team combining psychologists and fire engineers in Australia. Waking thresholds of different auditory signals in deep-sleeping young adults, older adults, the hard of hearing and the alcohol impaired were tested during slow-wave sleep, which is the deepest part of sleep (Bruck, Ball, Thomas, & Rouillard, 2009; Thomas & Bruck, 2010). It was found that the most effective signal was a complex sound with dominant frequencies at a much lower pitch, similar to the pitch of speech. Acoustically this is described as the 520 hertz square-wave signal, found to be least four to 12 times more effective at waking people than the current high-pitched, pure, 3100 hertz tone in the different populations tested. So, for example, some 40 percent of young adults sleeping with a 0.05 blood alcohol concentration would sleep through a 75 decibel, high-pitched alarm, while 0 percent would sleep through the new signal at the same volume.

In response, the powerful US National Fire Protection Association changed its smoke alarm standards (NFPA 72, 2010) to introduce this improved signal for all commercial sleeping areas and all areas where people who are hard of hearing normally sleep. We are hopeful that this first step will be followed by changes internationally that extend to all residences.

INTERIM SUMMARY

Sleep proceeds through a series of stages that can be assessed by EEG. The major distinction is between ***rapid eye movement (REM)*** and ***non-REM (NREM) sleep***. Most dreaming occurs in REM sleep, in which the eyes dart around and the EEG takes on an active pattern resembling waking consciousness.

Three views of dreaming

For thousands of years, humans have speculated about the nature and significance of dreams. Some cultures view dreams as indices of the dreamer's deepest desires, revelations from the spiritual world or sources of supernatural power (Bourguignon, 1979). Here we address three contemporary psychological views of dreaming: psychodynamic, cognitive and biological.

A psychodynamic view

Freud (1900/1965) believed that dreams, like all mental events, have meaning but must be deciphered by someone skilled in dream interpretation. As communications spoken in the language of the unconscious, which is irrational and wishful, dreams are often vague, illogical or bizarre and thus require translation into the language of rational waking consciousness. For example, in dreams two people are often condensed into one, or thoughts about one person are displaced onto someone else (that is, attributed to the wrong person).

According to Freud, unconscious processes are associative processes. Thus, ideas are connected by their relationship to one another along networks of association, not by logic. During sleep, a person is not using conscious, rational processes to create or monitor the story, so one thought or image can easily be activated in place of another. Because associative thinking replaces logical thought, Freud saw dreams as 'the insanity of the night'. For example, a man who was angry at his father had a dream of murdering his father's best friend, presumably because anger and murder were associatively linked, as were his father and his father's friend.

Freud distinguished between the ***manifest content***, the story line of the dream, and the ***latent content***, the dream's underlying meaning. To uncover the latent content of a dream, the dreamer free-associates to each part of the dream (that is, simply says aloud whatever thoughts come to mind about it), while the dream analyst tries to trace the networks of association.

Freud proposed that the underlying meaning of every dream is an unconscious wish, typically a forbidden sexual or aggressive desire. He suggested that people often rapidly forget their dreams upon awakening because dreams contain anxiety-provoking thoughts that are repressed during normal waking consciousness. The empirical data do not support the hypothesis that dream content is generally associated with sexual and aggressive wishes (see Fisher & Greenberg, 1997). Most contemporary psychodynamic psychologists believe, instead, that the latent content of a dream can be a wish, a fear or anything else that is emotionally pressing (Flanagan, 2000). Probably the most central aspect of the psychodynamic approach today is its view of dreaming as associative thought laden with emotional concerns. This form of thought requires interpretation because the story line has not been constructed using the rational thought processes characteristic of conscious mental activity.

MAKING CONNECTIONS

If dreaming is a kind of **thought**, theories of thinking ought to be useful in understanding even this unusual form of cognition (chapter 8).

- How might events of the day before prime implicit 'thinking' at night? What could lead the content of a dream to bear a relation to the content of thoughts shortly before going to bed — or what Freud called the 'day residue' of the dream?
- How might activation of networks during the day result in 'problem solving' in dreams? Could dream activity be 'productive' even if the person is not consciously trying to solve the problem at night? If so, how might this occur?

A cognitive view

A cognitive perspective suggests that dreams are cognitive constructions that reflect the concerns and metaphors people express in their waking thought (Antrobus, 1991; Domhoff, 1996; Kerr, Foulkes, & Jurkovic, 1978). In other words, dreams are simply a form of thought. At times, they may even serve a problem-solving function, presenting dreamers with potential solutions to problems they faced during the day (e.g. Cartwright, 1996).

Dreams rely on the same metaphors people use in everyday thinking. However, conscious monitoring is deactivated during dreaming, so metaphoric thinking is relatively unconstrained, leading to images or events that may seem bizarre to the conscious mind (Lakoff, 1997). Dreams also show cognitive development. Children's dreams lack the sophistication of adult dreams (Foulkes, 1982).

A grammar of dreams

One cognitive view that shares many points with Freud's theory was proposed by dream researcher David Foulkes (1993; and in Kerr et al., 1978). Like many contemporary psychodynamic psychologists, Foulkes disagrees that the latent meaning of every dream is an unconscious wish. He proposes instead that dreams simply express current concerns of one sort or another, in a language with its own peculiar grammar. The manifest content is constructed from the latent content through rules of transformation — that is, rules for putting a thought or concern into the 'language' of dreaming.

Decoding dream language thus requires a knowledge of those rules of transformation, just as a transformational grammar allows linguists to transform the surface structure of a sentence into its deep structure, or meaning (chapter 7). In everyday language, the sentence 'The boy threw the ball' can be transformed into 'The ball was thrown by the boy'. In dream language, the thought 'I am worried about my upcoming exam' can be translated into a dream about falling off a cliff.

Dreams and current concerns

Empirical research supports the view that dreams are related to current concerns, whether wishes, fears or preoccupations of other sorts (Domhoff, 1996). A study of the dreams of Israeli medical students five weeks into the Gulf War, when Israel was under threat of missile attacks, found that over half the dream reports dealt with themes of war or attack (Lavie, 1996). Other research finds that the extent to which people's dreams express wishes for intimacy correlates with their desires for intimacy by day (Evans & Singer, 1994). Similarly, people who report high wellbeing during waking hours also report fewer nightmares (Zadra & Donderi, 2000). An Australian study, which compared people who reported frequent nightmares with a control group, came up with similar findings. The study indicated that those people who experienced numerous nightmares were more likely to suffer from anxiety, paranoia and depression. The study also found that feelings of stress increased the number and intensity of nightmares (Berquier & Ashton, 1992).

Gender and cross-cultural differences also support the view that dreams express concerns similar to those that people experience in their waking consciousness (Domhoff, 1996). Just as males tend to be more aggressive than females by day, their dreams show a greater ratio of aggressive to friendly interactions than women's dreams. Similarly, the Netherlands and Switzerland are two of the least violent technologically developed societies, whereas the United States is the most violent. Incidents involving physical aggression are about 20 percent more prevalent in the dreams of males and females in the US than among their Dutch and Swiss counterparts.

A biological view

Some dream researchers argue that dreams are biological phenomena with no meaning at all (e.g. Crick & Mitchison, 1983). According to one such theory (Hobson, 1988; Hobson & McCarley, 1977), dreams reflect cortical interpretations of random neural signals initiated in the midbrain during REM sleep.

These signals are relayed through the thalamus to the visual and association cortexes, which try to understand this information in their usual way — namely, by using existing knowledge structures (schemas) to process the information. Because the initial signals are essentially random, however, the interpretations proposed by the cortex rarely make logical sense.

Many dream researchers, however, criticise this view, arguing that the presence of dreams during NREM sleep challenges this explanation of dreaming. Further, the lack of evidence linking specific patterns of midbrain activation with specific patterns of dream content suggests that a biological interpretation is at least incomplete (Foulkes, 1995; Squier & Domhoff, 1998).

More recently, biologically oriented researchers have offered another view that emphasises the role of sleep and dreaming in learning and memory. If they are right, the next time you are tempted to stay up all night to prepare for a big exam, think again. Sleep appears to be involved in the consolidation of memory. Memories for newly learned material are stronger after eight hours of sleep than after eight hours of wakefulness (Smith, 1985). Researchers are just beginning to track down the mechanisms, but the data suggest that during sleep the cortex and hippocampus work together to consolidate newly learned material — that is, to solidify it so it 'sticks' (chapter 6). According to this view, during NREM sleep, the hippocampus 'replays' what it has 'learned' during the day and activates relevant parts of the cortex to consolidate the memory (Chrobak & Buzsaki, 1994; Wilson & McNaughton, 1994). During REM sleep, activity appears to flow in the other direction — from the cortex to the hippocampus — erasing old memories from the hippocampus that are now fully consolidated in the cortex (Holscher, Anwyl, & Rowan, 1997; Stickgold, 1998).

Integrating the alternative models

Are these three models of dreaming really incompatible? The psychodynamic and cognitive views converge on the notion that dreams express current ideas and concerns in a highly symbolic language that requires decoding. They differ over the extent to which those concerns involve motives and emotions, although dreams probably express motives (wishes and fears) as well as ideas. Many motives have cognitive components, such as representations of wished-for or feared states (chapter 10). Thus, a fear of failing an examination includes a representation of the feared scenario and its possible consequences. What applies to cognition, then, probably applies to many aspects of motivation as well, so dreams are as likely to express motives as beliefs.

Even the biological view of dreams as cortical interpretations of random midbrain events is not necessarily incompatible with either the psychodynamic or the cognitive view. The interpretive processes that occur at the cortical level involve the same structures of meaning — schemas, associational networks and emotional processes — posited by Freud and Foulkes. Hence, even random activation of these structures would produce dreams that reveal something about the organisation of thoughts and feelings in the person's mind, particularly those that have received chronic or recent activation. Further, neurons activated during the day should be more readily triggered at night, leading to likely similarities of content in daytime and night-time thoughts. The memory consolidation theory is even more congruent with psychodynamic and cognitive theories, because what matters during the day is what is likely to be replayed and consolidated by night.

INTERIM SUMMARY

Freud viewed dreams as a window to the language of unconscious associative thoughts, feelings and wishes. He distinguished the ***latent content***, or underlying meaning, from the ***manifest content***, or story line. Although Freud believed that the latent content of every dream is an unconscious sexual or aggressive wish that has been repressed, empirical data do not support this view. Most psychodynamic theorists instead believe that the latent content can be a wish, a fear or anything else that is emotionally pressing. The cognitive perspective suggests that dreams are the outcome of cognitive processes and that their content reflects the concerns and metaphors people express in their waking cognition. One biological view of dreaming proposes that dreams reflect cortical interpretations of random neural signals arising from the midbrain during REM sleep. Another points to the role of sleep and dreaming in memory consolidation, as the hippocampus and cortex work together to consolidate memories and then 'wipe the slate clean' in the hippocampus. These three perspectives are probably not incompatible.

Altered states of consciousness

Sleep is the most common example of a psychological state in which normal waking consciousness is suspended, but it is not the only one. In ***altered states of consciousness***, the usual conscious ways of perceiving, thinking, and feeling are modified or disrupted. Altered states are often culturally patterned and occur through meditation, hypnosis, ingestion of drugs and religious experiences.

Meditation

In ***meditation***, the meditator develops a deep state of tranquility by altering the normal flow of conscious thoughts. Many religions and belief systems, such as Buddhism, believe that meditation leads to a deepened understanding of reality (Ornstein, 1986). By focusing attention on a simple stimulus or by concentrating on stimuli that are usually in the background of awareness (such as one's breathing), meditation shuts down the normal flow of self-conscious inner dialogue (J. Weinberger, personal communication, 1992). With the usual goal-directed flow of consciousness disrupted, the procedures that normally direct conscious attention are 'de-automatised' or disrupted.

Meditation can produce a state of serenity that is reflected in altered brainwave activity. Some forms of meditation facilitate the alpha waves characteristic of the relaxed state of falling into sleep. Others produce beta activity, and still others even produce theta waves, which are rarely observed except in participants who are fully asleep (Jangid, Vyas, & Shukla, 1988; Matsuoka, 1990). As a result, some experienced meditators can perform remarkable feats, such as meditating for hours in the bitter cold.

APPLY + DISCUSS

Mindfulness is a state of focused awareness whereby an individual calls upon all senses to shift focus from external stimuli to internal awareness and develop the mental, emotional, physical, and social competencies needed to successfully handle life's challenges. A growing number of schools are using mindfulness training programs to combat increasing levels of anxiety and social conflict, and promote slowing down and calming behaviours, balance and stability in their students. Mindfulness training involves (a) learning how to focus attention to inner and outer experience, (b) learning to tolerate any emotional discomfort you experience in response to this focused attention and (c) purposefully responding to yourself and others in a kind and compassionate way.

- To what extent does mindfulness training represent a true altered state of consciousness versus a learned capacity to manipulate the brain?
- Discuss the physiological and psychological benefits to be gained from mindfulness training programs.

Hypnosis

Another type of altered state, hypnosis, was named after Hypnos, the Greek god of sleep, because of the superficial resemblance between the hypnotic state and sleep. ***Hypnosis*** is characterised by deep relaxation and suggestibility (proneness to follow the suggestions of the hypnotist). The participant is likely to experience a number of changes in consciousness, including an altered sense of time, self, volition (voluntary control over actions) and perception of the external world. For instance, a participant directed to raise her arm may have no sense of initiating the action but feel instead as if the arm has a mind of its own (Bowers, 1976).

Entertainers such as Grant Boddington in New Zealand and Martin St. James in Australia make a living through stage shows where they hypnotise people from the crowd and ask them to comply with humorous suggestions. Many sceptics go along to these shows believing they can never be hypnotised — only to find themselves up on stage becoming part of the night's entertainment. These 'hypnotists' are not psychologists. They use hypnosis to entertain and to make a living. However, there is a more serious side to hypnosis. Psychologists undergo comprehensive training to gain qualifications in hypnosis and use these skills to assist people with a variety of problems in living. For example, hypnosis is commonly used to assist people to stop smoking (Barabasz & Watkins, 2004; Elkins, Marcus, Bates, Rajab, & Cook, 2006) and to lose weight (Heinkel, Rosenfeld, & Sheikh, 2003). In Australia, clinical hypnotherapists can become registered members of the Australian National Hypnotherapy Register (ANHR) when they complete extensive education in hypnotherapy and associated disciplines and comply with a strict Code of Conduct and continuing professional education requirements (ANHR, 2009).

There is a superficial resemblance between the hypnotic state and sleep, with hypnosis characterised by deep relaxation and suggestibility. These volunteers entered a catatonic state with the click of a hypnotist's fingers.

Not everyone can be hypnotised. People differ in ***hypnotic susceptibility***, the capacity to enter into deep hypnotic states (Hilgard, 1965, 1986). People who are highly hypnotisable tend to be able to form vivid visual images and to become readily absorbed in fantasy, daydreams, movies and the like (see Kunzendorf, Spanos, & Wallace, 1996).

Hypnotic effects

Hypnosis can produce an array of unusual effects, although, as we will see, researchers disagree on the extent to which many of these effects are either genuine or unique to hypnosis. For example, if told they are about to smell a beautiful flower, participants will smile peacefully rather than reflexively turn their heads when ammonia is placed under their noses. Under hypnosis, people can experience amnesia (for example, for events that occurred while under hypnosis) or its opposite, hyperamnesia, the recall of forgotten memories. A hypnotist can induce age regression, in which hypnotic participants feel as if they are reliving an earlier experience. Under hypnosis, one participant spoke a language he did not consciously remember but was spoken in his home when he was a very young child (Nash, 1988).

Hypnosis has clear and well-documented therapeutic effects (Kirsch, Montgomery, & Sapirstein, 1995). Hypnotised participants often demonstrate hypnotic analgesia, an apparent lack of pain despite pain-inducing stimulation. Some hypnotic participants have undergone surgery without anaesthesia and shown no signs of conscious pain. Hypnosis can, in fact, be useful in minimising the experience of pain in many situations, ranging from the dentist's chair to the treatment of burn injuries (Mulligan, 1996; Patterson & Ptacek, 1997). A recent Australian study showed that hypnosis can also be used for effective pain relief during labour and childbirth (Cyna, McAuliffe, & Andrew, 2004). Controlled scientific studies have even shown that hypnotised participants can rid themselves of warts (Noll, 1994; Sinclair-Gieben & Chalmers, 1959) and stop blood from flowing profusely from lacerated skin (Bowers, 1976; Ornstein, 1986).

The hidden observer

Ernest Hilgard (1986) experimented extensively with hypnotic phenomena and told the story of a striking event that led him down a productive path of scientific research. In a class demonstration of hypnosis, he hypnotised a student to become deaf, telling him he could hear nothing until Hilgard touched his right shoulder. Hilgard then banged together large wooden blocks near the participant's ears and even fired off a starter pistol, to which the participant did not respond.

A student in the room wondered whether 'some part' of the participant could still hear him, so Hilgard, confident this was not the case, told the participant, 'Perhaps there is some part of you that is hearing my voice. If there is, I should like the index finger of your right hand to rise'. To the surprise of both instructor and students, the finger rose. The hypnotised student then asked Hilgard to restore his hearing and tell him what had just happened, explaining, 'I felt my finger rise in a way that was not a spontaneous twitch, so you must have done something to make it rise, and I want to know what you did' (Hilgard, 1986, p. 186).

Hilgard then instructed the student, 'When I place my hand on your arm ... I can be in touch with that part of you that listened to me before and made your finger rise ... But this hypnotised part of you, to whom I am now talking, will not know what you are saying'. The hidden observer — the part of the student's consciousness that raised the finger — then fully described what had happened, including hearing the slamming wooden blocks. When Hilgard lifted his hand and again asked what had happened in the last few minutes, the participant had no idea (pp. 187–188).

Hilgard's discovery of the hidden observer led him to conduct some fascinating experiments on hypnotic analgesia. In the basic design, the participant places her hand and forearm in ice water and reports the degree of pain produced, from 0 (no pain) to 10 (pain so severe that she wants to pull out her hand). In a normal waking state, the person usually hits 10 in less than a minute. When given a suggestion for hypnotic analgesia, participants often report no pain and would keep their arm in the water indefinitely if allowed. However, when given the suggestion for the hidden observer to rate the pain using the same 0 to 10 scale, participants report steadily increasing pain.

Hypnosis and memory

Some advocates of hypnosis have claimed that hypnosis can restore forgotten memories. In the late 1970s, a busload of children and their driver were kidnapped at gunpoint. Later, under hypnosis, the driver relived the experience from beginning to end and was able to recall the kidnappers' licence plate number with enough clarity to lead to their apprehension.

One researcher found that participants under hypnosis could even recall events that occurred under anaesthesia (Levinson, 1965). While a surgeon was removing a small lump from the lower lip of a patient, the doctor made the comment, 'Good gracious ... it may be a cancer!' For the next three weeks, the patient was inexplicably depressed. The investigator then hypnotised the woman and induced hypnotic regression to the day of the operation. She remembered the exclamation 'Good gracious' and then, crying profusely, recalled, 'He is saying this may be malignant' (p. 201). The researcher subsequently demonstrated the capacity for recall of similar events experimentally with a sample of dental patients. Since then, a number of memory researchers have demonstrated both implicit and explicit memory for events occurring during anaesthesia, such as later recognition of word lists presented while surgery patients were completely unconscious (Bonebakker, Bonke, Klein, & Wolters, 1996; Cork, 1996).

Despite such examples, many psychologists have expressed concern about the use of hypnosis to retrieve memories of crime scenes or experiences from childhood such as sexual abuse. Others have questioned the scientific validity of hypnosis as an aid to memory enhancement for legal purposes (Lynn, Lock, Myers, & Payne, 1997). One of the major problems is that people under hypnosis are highly suggestible, and a subtle inflection or leading question can lead hypnotised eyewitnesses to report more than they actually know (Wagstaff, 1984). Hypnosis may also lower the threshold for feeling confident enough to report a memory. This can increase the capacity to recall actual memories, such as the licence plate of the school bus kidnappers described above, but it can also increase the tendency to mistake beliefs, hypotheses, fantasies or suggestions for true memories (Malpass & Devine, 1980). Controversy continues over the conditions under which hypnosis leads to genuine or distorted memories and is likely to do so for some time (Applebaum, Uyehara, & Elin, 1997; Loftus, 2000; McConkey, 1995).

Is hypnosis real?

Hypnosis has drawn considerable scepticism since it first received scientific attention in the nineteenth century, in part because of a history of charlatans using stage hypnosis mixed with liberal doses of deception (such as planting participants). As we will see in chapter 17, research over many decades has demonstrated that social pressure can lead people to perform peculiar, deviant or destructive behaviour, even in a normal state of consciousness (see Kirsch & Lynn, 1998). Several researchers have produced evidence to suggest that hypnotic participants are simply playing the role they believe they are expected to play (Murrey, Cross, & Whipple, 1992; Spanos, Burgess, Wallace-Capretta, & Ouaida, 1996).

Other critics contend that aspects of hypnotic suggestion that are not unique to hypnosis, such as heavy reliance on imagery, actually account for hypnotic effects. For example, people instructed to use vivid visual images can often accomplish the same feats as hypnotised participants, such as eliminating warts (Spanos, Stenstrom, & Johnston, 1988).

Data supporting the validity of hypnosis, however, come from studies in which participants are given posthypnotic suggestions — commands to perform a behaviour on demand once they are out of the hypnotic trance. In a study designed to test the hypothesis that hypnotised participants are simply playing roles (and that they are not really in an altered state), the investigators compared the behaviour of participants instructed to act *as if* they were hypnotised with the behaviour of truly hypnotised participants (Orne, Sheehan, & Evans, 1968). When both groups of participants were distracted from assigned tasks and thus diverted from thinking about what they were supposed to do, hypnotised participants were three times as likely to carry out the posthypnotic suggestion as simulators.

Neuroscientific data also provide evidence for the validity of hypnosis as an altered state. Not only do studies find distinct EEG patterns in hypnotised participants (De Pascalis & Perrone, 1996), but also recent neuroimaging studies support the distinctness of hypnotic states. In one study, researchers suggested to hypnotised participants that they should see colour images in black and white (Kosslyn et al., 2000). Remarkably, their brain scans showed decreased activation in a part of the cortex that processes colour (at the borders of the occipital and temporal lobes; chapter 3), compared with activation while viewing colour images without the suggestion. When the researchers made the same suggestion to the same individuals *without* hypnosis, they showed no reduction in the colour area of the cortex. These findings suggest that hypnosis can, in fact, dramatically influence basic components of perceptual experience that psychologists have generally assumed to be independent of people's intentions.

Other strong evidence comes from studies in which hypnotic participants have endured painful medical procedures, including surgery, without anaesthesia. Although some sceptics argue that these patients may be 'faking it', it is difficult to imagine undergoing an operation without anaesthesia simply to please an experimenter (Bowers, 1976). (We wish the participants in our own studies were so compliant!)

At this juncture, the most appropriate conclusion is probably that hypnosis is, in fact, an altered state of consciousness, at least in highly hypnotisable people. However, some or many of its effects can be produced under other conditions, such as use of imagery, relaxation or social pressure.

Understanding hypnosis and hypnotisability

By Professor Kevin McConkey, The University of Newcastle

Scientific theory and method have been applied to understanding hypnosis and hypnotisability for over 225 years. There is much that is known, and much that is still to discover. This is what makes hypnosis so fascinating. So, what are some of the key questions that people ask about hypnosis and hypnotisability?

People often ask whether there is a 'special state of hypnosis'. Because this seemingly simple question typically gets an answer of 'well, yes and no', Woody and McConkey (2003) suggested that contemporary psychological scientists should really be asking: What diversity of states occurs within hypnosis? How can we characterise them? What are the important patterns of change in these states over time? These questions are consistent with the interactionist position that has been argued in the debate about whether hypnosis is a cognitive or a social phenomenon (McConkey, 2008).

The interactionist position is that hypnosis involves genuine and subjectively compelling alterations in conscious awareness, with these alterations being powerfully shaped by the social setting in which the hypnotist and the hypnotised person are interacting. From the interactionist perspective, the issue is to determine and explain the conditions under which internal, cognitive or external social processes are more influential in shaping the experience and behaviour of the hypnotised person.

In this respect, the experience and expression of hypnosis is no different from most other human experience and behaviour — in that the experience and the behaviour of the person are ultimately the result of a reciprocal interaction between internal personal factors (personal thoughts, feelings, abilities and so on) and external environmental factors (the social setting, the impact of other people, the possible consequences of behaviour and so on).

Nevertheless, hypnosis is distinctive in the sense that the hypnotised person's emotional conviction is that the world is as suggested by the hypnotist. This experience occurs in an agreed and collaborative interplay between the hypnotist and the hypnotised person, and is largely determined by the abilities of the hypnotised person. It is not determined by any 'power of the hypnotist'.

People often ask whether 'everyone can be hypnotised'. The answer is that most people can experience hypnosis to some degree — some people cannot experience it at all and some can experience hypnosis to a large degree. Science has known for many years that there are stable individual differences in response to hypnotic suggestion. There are many standardised measures that allow the reliable assessment of hypnotisability. To understand these individual differences in hypnotic ability, contemporary researchers are now asking questions such as: Which sets of abilities are related to which types of hypnotic behaviour? How do these abilities combine, or how are they organised? Is there a core, common underlying component, or components, of hypnotisability? If so, is this component unique to hypnosis, or shared with other, nonhypnotic phenomena?

Woody, Barnier, and McConkey (2005) showed that hypnotisability involved the four types, or components, of responding to hypnotic suggestions. These types of response are: direct motor (e.g. a hand held out getting too heavy to hold up), motor challenge (e.g. feeling unable to move the head from side-to-side), perceptual–cognitive (e.g. seeing or hearing something that is not present in reality) and posthypnotic amnesia (e.g. not being able to remember something that has just been learnt or a personal name). These components arguably point to the building blocks of hypnotic response. These four separate components of hypnotic response also arguably arise because the subjective phenomena that underlie them are very distinct.

In perceptual–cognitive hypnotic responses, for instance, the compelling subjective experience is one of a feeling of external reality that is inconsistent with actual reality. A visual or auditory hallucination is the prototypical example of this kind of experience. In contrast, with motor challenge responses, the core subjective experience is a feeling of involuntariness or ineffectiveness of one's will — trying but failing to do something physical is the prototype of this kind of experience. A hypnotised person who is experiencing a hallucination does not have the conviction of involuntariness, nor does the hypnotised person who tries to move but cannot move necessarily have the conviction of an external reality.

These brief comments about hypnosis and hypnotisability point to some things that are known, and to others that are not known, by psychological scientists. A very important point to underscore, however, is that — as with all aspects of human experience and behaviour — an understanding of hypnosis and hypnotisability must occur within, must reflect, and must inform the general psychological principles and evidence set out in this book.

INTERIM SUMMARY

Altered states of consciousness, in which the usual conscious ways of perceiving, thinking and feeling are modified or disrupted, are often brought about through meditation, hypnosis, ingestion of drugs and religious experiences. ***Meditation*** creates a deep state of tranquility by altering the normal flow of conscious thoughts. ***Hypnosis*** is an altered state characterised by deep relaxation and suggestibility.

Drug-induced states of consciousness

The most common way people alter their state of consciousness (other than by going to sleep, of course) is by ingesting ***psychoactive substances*** — drugs that operate on the nervous system to alter mental activity. In the West, people use many psychoactive substances, ranging from caffeine in coffee and nicotine in tobacco, to medications that relieve depression or anxiety (chapter 16), to drugs that seriously impair functioning, such as cocaine and heroin. Some psychoactive drugs resemble the molecular structure of naturally occurring neurotransmitters and thus have similar effects at synapses. Others alter the normal processes of synthesis, release, reuptake or breakdown of neurotransmitters (chapter 3) and consequently affect the rate of neural firing in various regions of the brain.

The action of psychoactive substances cannot, however, be reduced entirely to their chemical properties. Their impact also depends on cultural beliefs and expectations. Native Americans who use peyote (a potent consciousness-altering drug) in religious rituals typically experience visions congruent with their religious beliefs, as well as feelings of reverence or religious awe and relief from physical ailments. In contrast, Anglo-Americans using the same drug often experience frightening visions, extreme mood states and a breakdown in normal social inhibitions (Wallace, 1959). Similarly, the drug kava (drawn from the root of the kava plant) is a traditional drink widely used in Polynesian societies in the Pacific Ocean, from New Guinea to the Hawaiian Islands. While the substance has psychoactive properties, its consumption is usually part of a ritual that is an important component of those societies' culture and belief systems.

In Australia, there are approximately 20 species of 'magic mushrooms' that have hallucinogenic properties, including 'gold tops', 'blue meanies', and 'liberty caps' (National Drug & Alcohol Research Centre [NDARC], 2009). Fresh or dried magic mushrooms are usually taken orally, and may be eaten raw or added to a variety of foods including pasta, stews or teas. The effects produced by these substances can differ greatly among individual users, ranging from elation to terror (NDARC, 2009).

The major types of psychoactive substances in widespread use include alcohol and other depressants, stimulants, hallucinogens and marijuana. We briefly examine each in turn.

Alcohol and other depressants

Depressants are substances that depress, or slow down, the nervous system. Common depressants are barbiturates and benzodiazepines. Barbiturates ('downers') provide a sedative or calming effect and in higher doses can be used as sleeping pills. Benzodiazepines, or anti-anxiety agents, serve as tranquillisers; common examples are Valium and Xanax (chapter 16). Depressants can produce both psychological and physical dependence.

Heroin is also a depressant that slows down the activity of the central nervous system. Immediate effects of its use can range from an intense pleasure and a strong feeling of wellbeing to feeling confused, drowsiness, reduced coordination, nausea and vomiting. Long-term effects include dependence, depression and cognitive impairment. People who are physically dependent on heroin usually develop tolerance to the drug, making it necessary to take more and more to get the desired effects. Eventually, a dose plateau is reached, at which no amount of the drug is sufficient. When this level is achieved, the person may continue to use heroin, but largely for the purpose of delaying withdrawal symptoms (Australian Drug Foundation, 2006b).

Contrary to what many people who rely on alcohol to elevate their mood believe, alcohol is a depressant. Researchers are still tracking down the precise neural mechanisms by which alcohol slows down central nervous system activity, but like other sedatives, alcohol appears to enhance the activity of the neurotransmitter GABA (gamma-aminobutyric acid) (Buck, 1986). Because GABA inhibits norepinephrine, which is involved in anxiety reactions, alcohol can reduce anxiety. Alcohol also enhances the activity of dopamine and endorphins, which provide pleasurable feelings that reinforce behaviour (De Witte, 1996; Di Chiara, Acquas, & Tanda, 1996). Thus, alcohol derives its powerful effects from its capacity both to diminish unpleasant feelings and heighten pleasurable ones.

Cross-culturally, alcohol is the most widely used psychoactive substance. In moderate doses — wine with dinner or a drink after work — alcohol can enhance wellbeing and even have positive health consequences, but the social costs of abuse of alcohol and other substances are staggering. In an Australian study of 16- to 17-year-olds, 70 percent of participants said they drank alcohol, 17 percent of drinkers reported alcohol-related violence (accidents or injuries) and 15 percent reported problems related to sex under the influence of alcohol in the previous 12 months (Bonomo et al., 2001). A recent survey by Mission Australia that considered the views of 50 000 young Australians revealed that alcohol and drugs were the second most important issue, behind the environment, among young people. Drugs and alcohol were highlighted as an important issue by both younger and older respondents in the survey. A higher proportion of younger respondents (children aged 11–14), however, considered alcohol and drug use to be a serious issue, and more young male respondents than young female respondents were concerned about drug and alcohol use (Mission Australia, 2010). According to a recent National Drug Strategy Household Survey, more than 80 percent of the Australian population aged over 14 years consumed alcohol in the 12 months prior to the survey. The survey also showed that most Australians are 17 years old when they experience their first full serve of alcohol (Australian Institute of Health and Welfare [AIHW], 2007a). In the United States, approximately one in seven people abuse alcohol, and another one in 20 misuse other psychoactive substances. The number of people killed in alcohol-related accidents in the United States every year surpasses the total number killed in the entire Vietnam War (Group for the Advancement of Psychiatry [GAP], 1991). A Swedish study found that reported alcohol consumption in 1973 predicted mortality rates in a large sample followed up over the next 20 years (Andreasson & Brandt, 1997).

Teenage drinking is a serious problem in Australia.

APPLY + DISCUSS

- From a cognitive perspective, how do expectations and beliefs about alcohol affect the way people behave when they are under the influence (or *believe* they are under the influence) of alcohol? How do these expectations develop, and at what point(s) in the drinking process (e.g. before, during or after ingestion or intoxication) do they get activated?
- From a psychodynamic perspective, why might people be more likely to behave in deviant ways when they are under the influence (or believe they are under the influence) of alcohol?

Alcohol and expectations

As with psychoactive substances in general, expectations about alcohol's effects, shaped by culture and personal experience, can sometimes have as much impact on behaviour as the drug's direct effects on the nervous system (see Collins, Lapp, Emmons, & Isaac, 1990; Hittner, 1997). This appears to be true cross-culturally (Velez-Blasini, 1997).

Several studies have sought to distinguish the causal roles of two independent variables: whether participants are drinking alcohol and whether they *think* they are drinking alcohol. The researchers place participants in one of four groups. In one, participants drink an alcoholic beverage and are told they are drinking alcohol; in another, they drink alcohol but are told they are not. (The flavour of the drink makes alcohol detection impossible.) In the other two groups, participants drink a non-alcoholic beverage and are either informed or misinformed about what they are drinking.

The results of these investigations can help 'distill' the relative contributions of biology and beliefs to the effects of alcoholic consumption. For example, male participants who think they are drinking alcohol report greater sexual arousal and less guilt when exposed to sexually arousing stimuli, whether or not they have actually been drinking alcohol. This is even more likely to occur if they have strong beliefs about the impact of alcohol on arousal (see Abrams & Wilson, 1983; Hull & Bond, 1986). More generally, people are more likely to behave in ways that are deviant, dangerous or antisocial if they can attribute their behaviour to alcohol.

Consequences of alcohol use and abuse

Alcohol abuse is involved in many violent crimes, including assault, rape, spouse abuse and murder, but precisely how alcohol contributes to aggression is not entirely clear (see Bushman, 1997; Bushman &

Cooper, 1990). One theory suggests that it disengages normal inhibitions; that is, alcohol contributes to aggression 'not by stepping on the gas but rather by paralysing the brakes' (Muehlberger, 1956, cited in Bushman & Cooper, 1990, p. 342). A related theory suggests that alcohol facilitates aggression by derailing other psychological processes that normally decrease the likelihood of aggression, such as the ability to assess risks accurately. A third theory suggests that violence-prone individuals drink so that they can have an excuse for aggression, particularly since they tend to believe that alcohol makes them aggressive. All three processes can operate together. An angry, violent person may drink in part to dull his conscience and to provide himself with an excuse for his actions.

Long-term ingestion of alcohol produces physical changes in the brain that can seriously affect cognitive functioning, sometimes to the point of dementia (confusion and disorientation) or Korsakoff's syndrome. Imaging techniques such as CAT scans reveal that roughly half of alcoholics show cerebral atrophy, and many show subcortical damage as well. Some of the behavioural changes associated with these physiological changes appear to be reversible, however, if the person stops drinking (Bowden, 1990).

Research, both in Australia and overseas, has demonstrated a high level of alcohol use and misuse by criminal offenders before they are imprisoned (Bushnell & Bakker, 1997; Doyle, Grant, & Christian, 1996; Indermaur & Upton, 1988; Putnins, 1995; Stathis, Eyland, & Bertram, 1991; Wright, 1993). Surveys of prisoners have shown that many drink greater amounts of alcohol than the rest of the population, with between 32 percent and 50 percent of offenders classified as alcohol dependent (Bushnell & Bakker, 1997; Indermaur & Upton, 1988). In one New South Wales study of prisoners, almost half had been drinking in the 24 hours before their most serious offence and 25 percent blamed alcohol for being in jail (Stathis et al., 1991). The same study also found that alcohol was involved in 42 percent of homicides.

Australian research on alcohol-related homicide indicates that alcohol consumption increases the number of homicides (Australian Institute of Criminology, 2009a). Additionally, the research highlighted the crucial role situational and environmental factors play in precipitating alcohol-related homicide. A key finding was that alcohol is equally likely to be implicated in intimate-partner homicides as it is in all other homicides. However, homicides involving women killing male intimate partners were far more likely to involve alcohol consumption by victim or offender or both, and the overwhelming majority of Indigenous Australian intimate-partner homicides were alcohol related.

Stimulants

Stimulants are drugs that increase alertness, energy and autonomic reactivity (such as heart rate and blood pressure). These drugs range from commonly used substances such as nicotine and caffeine to more potent ones such as amphetamines and cocaine.

Nicotine increases heart rate and blood pressure while often decreasing emotional reactivity. Thus, cigarette smokers often report that smoking increases their arousal and alertness while also providing a soothing effect. The reason is that nicotine has receptors in both branches of the autonomic nervous system — sympathetic (which increases arousal) and parasympathetic (which reduces it). When one of these branches is active, nicotine tends to produce stronger effects in the other — thus both arousing the slothful and soothing the stressed. Over the long term, however, smoking can cause cancer, heart disease and other life-threatening conditions.

A recent National Drug Strategy Household Survey showed that the average age at which Australian smokers took up tobacco smoking was 15 (AIHW, 2007f). It was estimated that approximately 3.6 million Australians aged 14 years or older were smokers and one in five Australians (19.5 percent) aged 14 years or older smoked daily (AIHW, 2007f). The short-term effects produced by tobacco smoking include a rise in blood pressure and heart rate; brain and central nervous system activity which is stimulated then reduced; dizziness, nausea, and watery eyes; and weakened appetite, taste, and smell (AIHW, 2007f). Long-term effects of tobacco smoking include shortness of breath; persistent coughing; increased risk of heart disease, stroke, colds, and chronic bronchitis; and emphysema (AIHW, 2007f).

Smoking during pregnancy can affect the unborn child. Babies are more likely to miscarry, to be of low birth weight, to be premature, and to be stillborn (AIHW, 2007f). Passive smoking occurs when one breathes in the tobacco smoke of others. Passive smoking has been shown to contribute to lung damage, and has been linked to cancer and heart disease. Children exposed to passive smoke are especially susceptible, having more respiratory and ear infections, and suffering from higher levels of these infections, as well as more severe asthma.

While many people have a love affair with coffee, frequent consumption of the drink can lead to feelings of anxiousness brought on by the caffeine it contains.

Caffeine is found in coffee, tea, chocolate, soft drinks and some non-prescription drugs (such as aspirin products, decongestants and sleep suppressants). Whereas moderate amounts of caffeine can help a person stay awake, high doses can produce symptoms indistinguishable from anxiety disorders, such as 'the jitters' or even panic.

Amphetamines lead to hyperarousal and a feeling of 'speeding', where everything seems to move quickly. The molecular structure of amphetamines is similar to that of the neurotransmitters dopamine and norepinephrine. Stimulation of norepinephrine receptors appears to produce alertness, while stimulation of dopamine receptors produces euphoria and increased motor activity. Amphetamines can induce psychosis in vulnerable individuals, death by overdose or ill health in chronic users, who essentially circumvent the normal signals sent by the brain to protect the body from fatigue and overuse.

In one national survey, more than 9 percent of Australians aged 14 and over indicated they had used amphetamines at some stage in their lifetime, and 3 percent had used amphetamines in the past 12 months (Australian Institute of Criminology, 2009b). According to the Australian Crime Commission, there is an increase in the number of young recreational drug users smoking crystal methamphetamine. Research also indicated an increase in use of methamphetamine, which occurred around the same time as the heroin shortage in Australia in 2000–01. People aged 20–29 years were more likely than those in the other age groups to have used methamphetamine (AIHW, 2007f). The average age at which Australians first used methamphetamine was 20.9 years. The vast majority (95 percent) of secondary school students had never used amphetamines. By the age of 17, a small percentage of students reported having had some experience with amphetamines (National Drug Strategy, 2006).

Various Australian studies have shown that drivers of heavy vehicles — such as buses, semitrailers and road trains — have a higher rate of amphetamine use and impairment (Parliamentary Travelsafe Committee, 1998). Drivers reportedly use 'speed' and other stimulants to keep themselves awake on long trips. This trend is extremely worrying from a road traffic safety point of view. Using stimulants increases the risk of greater fatigue and tiredness when their effects wear off, thus increasing the possibility of falling asleep at the wheel and causing an accident. Indeed, long driving hours and excessive fatigue have been identified as factors in many heavy vehicle accidents.

Cocaine has held an attraction for people since about AD 500, when the Inca in Peru learned about the powers of the coca leaf, from which cocaine is derived. The Inca used the coca leaf in religious ceremonies and even treated it as money to compensate labourers (not a strategy recommended for future industrialists, since it also leads to absenteeism and ill health). In the late 1800s, doctors discovered cocaine's anaesthetic properties; soon many medicines and elixirs were laced with cocaine, as was Coca-Cola.

Cocaine causes hyperarousal, leading to a 'rush' that can last a few minutes to several hours. Cocaine is one of the most potent pleasure-inducing substances, as well as one of the most addictive, ever discovered. Experimental animals will press a lever thousands of times to receive a single dose (Siegel, 1990). Like other stimulants, it appears to increase the activity of norepinephrine and dopamine. Chronic use depletes these neurotransmitters and can cause chronic depression similar to the crash that occurs when the initial high is over (GAP, 1991).

Cocaine produces diminished judgement and an inflated sense of one's own abilities. Regular use can also produce paranoia. One study found that 68 percent of cocaine-dependent men in a rehabilitation program reported paranoid experiences on cocaine that lasted several hours, long after the cocaine high was over (Satel, Southwick, & Gawin, 1991). Moreover, 38 percent of the patients who reported paranoia actually responded by arming themselves with guns or knives. A study found that two-thirds of the assailants in domestic violence cases had consumed both cocaine and alcohol on the day they beat their spouse or children (Brookoff, O'Brien, Cook, & Thompson, 1997). In Australia, in 1998, illicit drug use caused more than 1000 deaths and about 7 percent of all hospital admissions (Australian Bureau of Statistics, 2001). Cocaine accounted for 10 percent of these deaths related to illicit drugs (Miller & Draper, 2000). A study of 200 cocaine users in Sydney found that 42 percent reported adverse psychological events associated with the use of the drug. The most common symptoms reported were paranoia, anxiety and panic (Kaye & Darke, 2003).

In Australia, cocaine is most commonly available as cocaine hydrochloride, a white powder, although it can found as an alkaloid form for smoking or in the form of small crystals known as 'crack'. Cocaine is a stimulant, increasing the speed of central nervous system activity. The effects of cocaine include increased body temperature and heart rate, reduced appetite and heightened levels of energy and alertness. Although cocaine can cause euphoria and increased confidence, it may cause anxiety and panic. In larger doses or if used repeatedly over hours, cocaine can lead to extreme agitation, panic, paranoia, hallucinations, dizziness, trembling, nausea and heart attack. Concentration and coordination may deteriorate. Unlike use of most other drugs surveyed, recent cocaine use increased by almost 2 percent between 2004 and 2007 (AIHW, 2007e). In 2007, over one million Australians aged 14 years or older had used cocaine and almost 300 000 had used it in the previous 12 months. The highest levels of cocaine use were seen in the 20–29 years age group (AIHW, 2007e). Cocaine is referred to as coke, crack, okey dokey, charlie, nose candy, big C, blow, marching powder, snow, white lady, ceci, and candi.

Hallucinogens

Hallucinogens derive their name from ***hallucinations*** — sensations and perceptions that occur in the absence of external stimulation. ***Hallucinogens*** alter sensory data to produce bizarre or unusual perceptions. While under the influence of hallucinogens, people may experience time as speeding up or slowing down or sense colours bursting from the sky, walls moving or ants crawling under their skin.

Humans have used hallucinogens for thousands of years, but their impact and cultural meaning differ dramatically. In many cultures, people use hallucinogens largely during cultural rituals such as when Australian Aboriginal boys ingest hallucinogenic plants during ceremonies initiating them into manhood (Grob & Dobkin de Rios, 1992). In these settings, the meaning of the hallucinations is established by the elders, who consider the drugs essential for bringing the young into the community of adults. In the contemporary West, individuals ingest these substances for recreation and with minimal social control, so the effects are more variable and vulnerability to addiction is high.

Hallucinogenic drug use in Europe and North America dramatically increased in the 1960s with the discovery of the synthetic hallucinogen lysergic acid diethylamide (LSD). By the late 1970s, concern over the abuse of LSD and other drugs, such as PCP ('angel dust') and hallucinogenic mushrooms ('magic mushrooms'), intensified, and with good scientific reason. Chronic use of LSD is associated with psychotic symptoms, depression, paranoia, lack of motivation and changes in brain physiology (Kaminer & Hrecznyj, 1991; Smith & Seymour, 1994). Some chronic users repeatedly experience strange visual phenomena, such as seeing trails of light or images as they move their hands. Even when they are not experiencing these symptoms, their EEGs show a pattern of abnormal firing of neurons in visual pathways of the brain (Abraham & Duffy, 1996). The long-term effects of even occasional use of LSD are not entirely clear, although tragic events have occurred with LSD use, such as people walking out of windows and falling to their deaths.

According to the 2007 National Drug Strategy Household Survey, 8 percent of the Australian population reported using hallucinogens at some time, with 1 percent having used them in the previous 12 months (AIHW, 2007a). Popular forms of the drug in Australia are 'tabs' — pieces of blotting paper soaked in the drug and taken orally — and one of the 20 varieties of 'magic mushrooms' found in the country. Users reported a variety of reactions to taking hallucinogens, ranging from elation to terror.

Ecstasy — otherwise known as 'E', 'eccy' or 'Disco biscuits' — is now a popular hallucinogenic stimulant. The National Drug Strategy Household survey (AIHW, 2007a) found that among Australians aged 14 years or older, recent use of ecstasy (3.5 percent) was second only to marijuana (9.1 percent) of all illicit drugs surveyed. About 600 000 people had used ecstasy in the previous 12 months. Males aged 20–29 years were more likely than others to use ecstasy. On average, recent users took 1.6 pills when they used the drug and were most likely to consume them at a rave or dance party. Most recent ecstasy users also consumed alcohol at the same time they used ecstasy. Those aged 20–29 years were more likely than those in the other age groups to have used ecstasy. Its use is mainly associated with the dance culture and so it is often perceived as a 'party' drug. However, ecstasy interferes with the concentration and action of serotonin in our brains, resulting in a change of mood, repression of libido and appetite, mental stimulation and increased body temperature (Australian Drug Foundation, 2006a). Many of the side effects users encounter with ecstasy are similar to those found with the use of amphetamines and cocaine. They include an increased heart rate and blood pressure, nausea, blurred vision, faintness, chills and sweating. Psychological problems such as confusion, depression, insomnia, severe anxiety, paranoia and psychotic episodes can also occur (chapter 15).

As part of the National Drugs Campaign, the Australian government actively promotes anti-drug messages to the community via impacting print, radio and television advertisements.

An Australian study by Allott and Redman (2006) examined the harm-reduction practices employed by ecstasy users. They concluded that ecstasy users are aware of the potential harm associated with ecstasy use and actively employ strategies to attempt to minimise this. Although ecstasy is not physically or psychologically addictive, the long-term effects of ecstasy use are largely unknown and require further investigation.

In New Zealand, Schenk, Gittings, Johnstone, and Daniela (2003) found that rats would self-administer ecstasy when given the chance, indicating that ecstasy has the potential to become addictive and lead to chronic use, similar to cocaine. This finding is of concern, and research that examines how to reverse the cognitive deficits that follow acute exposure to ecstasy is warranted (see Harper, Hunt, & Schenk, 2006).

Marijuana

The use of marijuana has been a subject of controversy for decades. It continues to be among the most widely used recreational drugs across all age groups in Australia. In 2007, for example, over 5.5 million people aged 14 years or older (33.5 percent) had used marijuana/cannabis in their lifetime (AIHW, 2007a). Cannabis was most commonly consumed within private homes and most commonly obtained through friends or acquaintances. Cannabis was also the most commonly used illicit substance among secondary school students, with 18 percent of all secondary school students aged between 12 and 17 years reporting the use of cannabis at some time in their life (National Drug Strategy, 2006). A recent Australian study found that 60 percent of participants had used cannabis by the age of 20 and that 7 percent were daily users at that point (Patton et al., 2002). Debate continues about the extent to which marijuana causes health problems (Degenhardt, Hall, & Lynskey, 2001).

Marijuana produces a state of being high, or 'stoned', during which the individual may feel euphoric, giddy, uninhibited or contemplative. During a marijuana high, judgement is moderately impaired, problem solving becomes less focused and efficient, and attention is more difficult to direct; some people report paranoia or panic symptoms.

For decades, people have speculated about the detrimental effects of marijuana, but few credible scientific studies have documented negative effects from occasional recreational use (Castle & Ames, 1996). In fact, the most definitive study in this area, a longitudinal follow-up of young adults observed since early childhood, actually found occasional marijuana users and experimenters to be healthier psychologically than either abusers *or* abstainers (Shedler & Block, 1990). Other research finds that marijuana abuse, but not occasional use, is a risk factor for use of harder drugs (Kouri, Pope, Yurgelun-Todd, & Gruber, 1995).

Nevertheless, marijuana, like harder drugs, artificially manipulates dopamine reward circuits in the brain (Wickelgren, 1996) and can produce unwanted consequences. For example, residual effects on attention, working memory and motor abilities can make users unaware of subtle impairment at work, at school or at the wheel (Pope, Gruber, & Yurgelun-Todd, 1995). Chronic or heavy use, particularly beyond adolescence, is a symptom of psychological disturbance (chapter 15) and can contribute to deficits in social and occupational functioning. In New Zealand, studies have found that cannabis use among teenage girls is associated with increased levels of health problems, and that cannabis dependence is associated with increased rates of psychotic symptoms in young people, even when pre-existing symptoms and other background factors are taken into account (Fergusson, Horwood, & Swain-Campbell, 2003). As with other drugs, smoking during pregnancy may have risks for the developing foetus (see Chandler, Richardson, Gallagher, & Day, 1996; Fried, 1995).

In summary, like alcohol, the extent to which marijuana has negative psychological consequences probably depends on whether or not it is abused.

INTERIM SUMMARY

The most common way people alter their state of consciousness is by ingesting ***psychoactive substances***, drugs that operate on the nervous system to alter mental activity. Drugs have their effects not only physiologically but also through cultural beliefs and expectations. ***Depressants*** such as alcohol slow down, or depress, the nervous system. ***Stimulants***, such as amphetamines and cocaine, increase alertness, energy and autonomic reactivity. ***Hallucinogens*** such as LSD produce ***hallucinations***, sensations and perceptions that occur without external sensory stimulation. Marijuana is a controversial drug that produces a 'high' that may include a mixture of pleasurable feelings and a sense of calm or panic and paranoia.

Religious experiences in cross-cultural perspective

Religious experiences are subjective experiences of being in contact with the divine or spiritual. They range from relatively ordinary experiences, such as listening passively to a sermon, to altered states of consciousness in which a person feels at one with nature or the supernatural. In his classic work, *The Varieties of Religious Experience*, William James (1902/1958) describes the more dramatic forms of religious experience. In this state, the person experiences a sense of peace and inner harmony, perceives the world and self as having changed dramatically in some way, and has 'the sense of perceiving truths not known before' (p. 199). James quotes the manuscript of a clergyman (1902/1958, p. 67):

> I remember the night, and almost the very spot on the hilltop where my soul opened out, as it were, into the Infinite, and there was a rushing together of the two worlds, the inner and the outer . . . The ordinary sense of things around me faded . . . It was like the effect of some great orchestra when all the separate notes have melted into one swelling harmony.

Experiences people consider spiritual occur in a wide variety of settings and may or may not involve organised religion (Wolman, 2001). In most societies, however, dramatic religious experiences occur in the context of ritualised religious practices. For example, in a possession trance, the person who is 'possessed' believes another person or a supernatural being enters his soul. The altered state typically occurs through drumming, singing, dancing and crowd participation (Bourguignon, 1979). Many born-again Christian churches include possession trances as part of their regular religious practices (e.g. see Griffith, Young, & Smith, 1984).

The use of ritualised altered states dates back at least to the time of the Neanderthals. Graves of prehistoric human remains in northern Iraq contained medicinal substances that are still used today to induce trancelike states. The 'vision quest' of some Native American tribes frequently included religious trance states. During these states, a young person being initiated into adulthood would come in contact with ancestors or a personal guardian and emerge as a full member of adult society (Bourguignon, 1979). John Lame Deer, a Sioux medicine man, describes an experience that in certain respects resembles that of the Western clergyman quoted by James (Lame Deer & Erdoes, 1972, pp. 14–15):

> I was still lightheaded and dizzy from my first sweatbath in which I had purified myself before going up the hill. Even now, an hour later, my skin still tingled. But it seemed to have made my brain empty . . . Blackness was wrapped around me like a velvet cloth. It seemed to cut me off from the outside world, even from my own body. It made me listen to voices within me. I thought of my forefathers, who had crouched on this hill before me . . . I thought I could sense their presence . . . I trembled and my bones turned to ice.

Like James' clergyman, Lame Deer describes a breakdown in the normal boundaries of the inner and outer worlds. Both men also describe a sense of being touched by a presence beyond themselves and an altered experience of reality, perception and consciousness.

Ritualised religious experiences are simultaneously cultural and psychological phenomena. For individuals, they offer a sense of security, enlightenment and oneness with something greater than themselves. For the group, they provide a sense of solidarity, cohesiveness and certainty in shared values and beliefs. The individual is typically swept away in the experience, losing the self-reflective component of consciousness and experiencing a dissolution of the boundaries between self and non-self.

The French sociologist Emile Durkheim (1915) described this phenomenon as 'collective effervescence', in which the individual's consciousness seems dominated by the 'collective consciousness'. Most readers have probably experienced collective effervescence, either during religious ceremonies or in less profound circumstances, such as rock concerts and sporting events. Collective events of this sort, many of which involve chanting or rhythmic movement and speech, seem to tap into a basic human capacity for this kind of altered state.

Central question revisited

◆ Perspectives on consciousness

Like the attentional mechanisms that direct the consciousness of individuals, scientific communities have mechanisms that bring phenomena in and out of focus at various times. In the heyday of behaviourism, consciousness was relegated to the periphery of psychological awareness. As we have seen, recent developments in cognitive science have generated renewed interest in the roles of conscious and unconscious processes.

This renewed interest may actually contribute to integration across some of the theoretical perspectives in psychology. Interest in unconscious processes brings the field squarely back to one of the central tenets of psychoanalytic theory, that much of mental life is unconscious, including thoughts, feelings and motivations — but this time on a much firmer scientific foundation. Paradoxically, the growing literature on unconscious processes has also produced new interest in learning that occurs without awareness, a central focus of behavioural research. We may discover that the conditioned emotional responses of the behaviourist and the unconsciously triggered emotional reactions of the psychoanalyst are not as far apart as they once seemed — and they may have much in common with associations between emotions and memories studied by cognitive psychologists.

Researchers studying consciousness have also increasingly relied on a functionalist approach common to both William James and current evolutionary psychologists. In this view, consciousness serves the functions of monitoring and controlling the self and the environment. It allows us to examine and sometimes override automatic procedures, unconscious motives, dysfunctional conditioned emotional responses and operant responses normally triggered outside awareness.

Issues of consciousness and unconsciousness have become a central focus of psychological attention in the early twenty-first century just as they were a century ago. This time, however, we may have the tools to test and refine our hypotheses in previously unimagined ways — and perhaps to synthesise a unitary experience from the parallel lines of investigation that previously divided the consciousness of the psychological community.

◆

SUMMARY

1 The functions of consciousness

- ***Consciousness*** refers to the subjective awareness of percepts, thoughts, feelings and behaviour. It performs two functions: monitoring the self and environment and controlling thought and behaviour. ***Attention*** is the process of focusing awareness, providing heightened sensitivity to a limited range of experience requiring more extensive information processing. ***Divided attention*** means splitting attention between two or more stimuli or tasks.
- Psychologists study the flow of consciousness through ***experience-sampling*** techniques, such as ***beeper studies***. Even such a private experience as consciousness is in part shaped by cultural practices and beliefs, which influence aspects of subjective awareness, such as the experience of time and the focus on internal psychological states.

2 Perspectives on consciousness

- Freud distinguished among conscious, preconscious and unconscious processes. ***Conscious mental processes*** are at the centre of subjective awareness. ***Preconscious mental processes*** are not presently conscious but could be readily brought to consciousness. Dynamically unconscious processes — or the system of mental processes Freud called the ***unconscious*** — are thoughts, feelings and memories that are inaccessible to consciousness. They are inaccessible because they have been kept from awareness because they are threatening. Research over several decades has demonstrated that subliminal presentation of stimuli can influence conscious thought and behaviour. Emotional and motivational processes can also be unconscious or implicit.
- The ***cognitive unconscious*** refers to information-processing mechanisms that occur outside of awareness, notably unconscious procedures or skills and preconscious associational processes such as those that occur in priming experiments. Cognitive theorists have argued that consciousness is a mechanism for flexibly bringing together quasi-independent processing modules that normally operate in relative isolation and for solving problems that automatic processes cannot optimally solve.
- Hindbrain and midbrain structures, notably the reticular formation, play a key role in regulating states of wakefulness and arousal. Like most psychological functions, consciousness appears to be distributed across a number of neural pathways, involving a circuit running from the reticular formation through the thalamus, from the thalamus to the cortex (particularly the prefrontal cortex), and back down to the thalamus and midbrain regions of the reticular formation.

3 Sleep and dreaming

- The sleep–wake cycle is a ***circadian rhythm***, a cyclical biological process that evolved around the daily cycles of light and dark. Sleep proceeds through a series of stages that cycle throughout the night. Most dreaming occurs during REM sleep, named for the bursts of darting eye movements.
- Freud distinguished between the ***manifest content***, or story line, and the ***latent content***, or underlying meaning, of dreams. Freud believed the latent content is always an unconscious wish, although most contemporary psychodynamic psychologists believe that wishes, fears and current concerns can underlie dreams. Cognitive theorists suggest that dreams express thoughts and current concerns in a distinct language with its own rules of transformation. Some biological theorists contend that dreams have no meaning; in this view, dreams are cortical interpretations of random neural impulses generated in the midbrain. Others focus on the role of sleep and dreaming in memory consolidation. These three approaches to dreaming are not necessarily incompatible.

4 Altered states of consciousness

- In ***altered states of consciousness***, the usual conscious ways of perceiving, thinking and feeling are changed. ***Meditation*** is an altered state in which the person narrows consciousness to a single thought or expands consciousness to focus on stimuli that are usually at the periphery of awareness. ***Hypnosis***, characterised by deep relaxation and suggestibility, appears to be an altered state, but many hypnotic phenomena can be produced under other conditions. In altered states that occur during ***religious experiences***, the person feels a sense of oneness with nature, others or the supernatural and experiences a breakdown in the normal boundaries between self and non-self.
- ***Psychoactive substances*** are drugs that operate on the nervous system to alter patterns of perception, thought, feeling and behaviour. ***Depressants***, the most widely used of which is alcohol, slow down the nervous system. ***Stimulants*** (such as nicotine, caffeine, amphetamines and cocaine) increase alertness, energy and autonomic reactivity. ***Hallucinogens*** create ***hallucinations***, in which sensations and perceptions occur in the absence of any external stimulation. Marijuana leads to a state of being high — euphoric, giddy, uninhibited or contemplative. ***Psychoactive substances*** alter consciousness biologically, by facilitating or inhibiting neural transmission at the synapse, and psychologically, through expectations shaped by cultural beliefs.

KEY TERMS

altered states of consciousness, *p. 205*
attention, *p. 188*
beeper studies, *p. 190*
circadian rhythm, *p. 197*
cognitive unconscious, *p. 192*
conscious mental processes, *p. 191*
consciousness, *p. 187*
daydreaming, *p. 190*
depressants, *p. 209*
dichotic listening, *p. 189*
divided attention, *p. 189*
experience sampling, *p. 190*
hallucinations, *p. 213*
hallucinogens, *p. 213*
hypnosis, *p. 205*
hypnotic susceptibility, *p. 205*
insomnia, *p. 199*
latent content, *p. 202*
manifest content, *p. 202*
meditation, *p. 205*
non-REM (NREM) sleep, *p. 200*
preconscious mental processes, *p. 191*
psychoactive substances, *p. 209*
rapid eye movement (REM) sleep, *p. 200*
religious experiences, *p. 215*
selective inattention, *p. 188*
states of consciousness, *p. 186*
stimulants, *p. 211*
subliminal perception, *p. 191*
unconscious mental processes, *p. 191*

REVIEW QUESTIONS

1. Define consciousness and describe the two main functions it serves.
2. Distinguish between the psychodynamic and cognitive perspectives of consciousness.
3. Describe the neural structures involved in the experience of consciousness.
4. Define rapid-eye-movement (REM) sleep and contrast it with the four stages of non-REM sleep.
5. Describe the main characteristics of hypnosis.

DISCUSSION QUESTIONS

1. Is 'counting sheep' a fail-safe way to put yourself to sleep at night?
2. Hypnosis is not real, or is it?
3. Is drug taking becoming more socially accepted than it used to be?

APPLICATION QUESTIONS

1. Read the following dream scenario, and attribute each interpretation that follows to a particular psychological perspective.

   Bridget dreamed she was canoeing down a river, admiring the scenery. There was a young child in a canoe nearby. Suddenly, a strong current took hold of their canoes and Bridget started to panic. She grabbed hold of a tree branch over the river and pulled herself to shore. But the child missed the branch and before Bridget knew it, the canoes were heading straight for a waterfall. The child was screaming for help. Bridget ran along the shore, but she could not reach the child's canoe. The canoes went over the waterfall, and she heard a loud crash. Bridget stood at the edge of the waterfall but she could not see any trace of the child or the canoes. The bottom of the waterfall looked surprisingly peaceful. Some people were having a picnic on the bank, and others were swimming in a rock pool. Bridget called out to them, but they could not hear her. She was trying to attract their attention when she woke up.

   (a) This dream has great significance. It reflects Bridget's unresolved relationship with her daughter — she has always felt the need to form a closer bond with her daughter, and would love to spend more time with her in the future.
   (b) This dream is of no significance. It merely reflects the cortical interpretations of random neural signals arising from the midbrain during REM sleep.
   (c) The dream has significance. It represents Bridget's concern that life is passing by too quickly and her belief that she should relax more and take life easier.
2. For each of the five scenarios listed below, identify the type of drug that is *most* likely being abused.
   (a) Amy appears very happy and is full of energy. She moves quickly around the room, sometimes knocking things over as she goes. At one point she jumps up on top of a table because she believes a giant monster is coming to get her.
   (b) Tariq is feeling down and has no energy to get up from his chair. He holds his hands out in front of him, and watches the trail of light that follows as he moves his hands.
   (c) Phuong has not eaten or slept for days because she has no time to stop for such trivial things. Life is too busy, and besides, she is on a mission to find the perfect weapon to stop anybody who tries to end her quest for eternal happiness.
   (d) Shane has trouble remembering where he puts things and sometimes suffers from blackouts. He is no longer able to drive a car because he often becomes disoriented while driving and is concerned that he will not be able to stop the car in time should any pedestrians unexpectedly walk out in front of him.
   (e) Nita feels very happy and relaxed. She is lost in thought, but sometimes yells out random words when strangers walk by her on the street. After a short time, she begins to feel giddy and cannot make sense of the things around her.

The solutions to the application questions can be found on page 834.

MULTIMEDIA RESOURCES

The *Cyberpsych* multimedia resource is available *as an option* to accompany this textbook to further develop your understanding of many key psychology concepts. *Cyberpsych* contains a wealth of rich media content and activities, and for this chapter includes:

- video clips on shift workers and sleep, meditation, sleep disorders, teenage sleeping, and dream and sleep patterns
- a video case study on the pressure to sleep less in our 24/7 society
- a concept animation on what happens when we sleep.

Learning

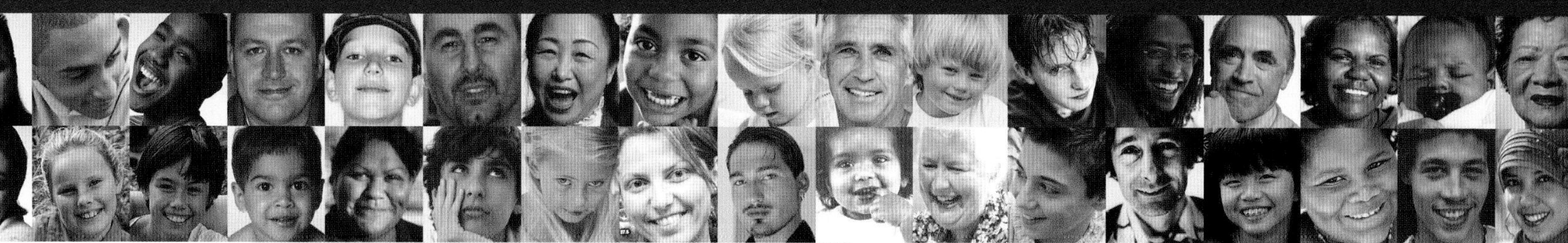

LEARNING OBJECTIVES

After studying this chapter you should be able to:

1 define learning

2 describe the basic principles underlying classical conditioning

3 describe the basic principles underlying operant conditioning

4 explain the basic premise of cognitive–social theory.

Learning refers to any enduring change in the way an organism responds based on its experience.

Classical conditioning

- In *classical conditioning*, an environmental stimulus leads to a learned response, through pairing of an *unconditioned stimulus (UCS)* with a previously neutral *conditioned stimulus (CS)*, or learned reflex. Any *unconditioned response (UCR)* is a response that does not have to be learned. Pavlov noticed that if a stimulus, such as a bell ringing, repeatedly occurred just as a dog was about to be fed, the dog would start to salivate when it heard the bell, even if the food was not presented. The dog had learned to associate the bell with food, and because food produced the reflex of salivation, the bell also came to produce the reflex.

UCS → UCR

||

CS → CR

- *Conditioned responses*, such as taste aversions and immune responses, are learned reflexes that can produce both adaptive and maladaptive responses.
- *Stimulus generalisation* occurs when an organism learns to respond to stimuli that resemble the CS with a similar response. *Stimulus discrimination* occurs when an organism learns to respond to a restricted range of stimuli.
- *Extinction* occurs when a CR is weakened by presentation of the CS without the UCS.
- Several factors influence classical conditioning, including the *interstimulus interval*, the degree to which the presence of the CS is predictive of the UCS, the individual's learning history and *prepared learning*.
- Precisely what organisms learn when in classical conditioning is a matter of debate.

Operant conditioning

- *Operant conditioning* means learning to operate on the environment and produce a consequence. *Operants* are behaviours that are emitted rather than elicited by the environment.
- *Reinforcement* refers to a consequence that increases the probability that a response will recur.
- *Punishment* decreases the probability that a response will recur.
- *Extinction* occurs if enough trials pass in which the operant is not followed by the consequences previously associated with it.
- Learning occurs in a broad context and operant conditioning offers a most comprehensive explanation for a wide range of human and animal behaviour. Operant conditioning is influenced by cultural factors and the characteristics of the learner.

Cognitive–social theory

- *Cognitive–social theory* incorporates concepts of conditioning from behaviourism but adds cognition and social learning.
- Humans develop mental images of, and expectations about, the environment, and these cognitions influence their behaviour.
- *Social learning* refers to learning that occurs through social interaction.

Central questions: what have we learned about learning?

- Skinner's principles of learning remain central to our understanding of behaviour. Today, many psychologists disagree with Skinner's belief that scientific explanation is incompatible with interpretations of mental processes.

THE cane toad is one of the most prolific (and ugliest) pests ever introduced to Australia. Initially imported into Queensland from South America to help control the cane beetle, the toad has become a greater nuisance by far than the insect it was supposed to eradicate. Cane toads are spreading into other states of Australia and have already entered Kakadu National Park in the Northern Territory. One reason for its successful spread is the fact that the toad has poison glands on its back. In its native land, several species of snake can tolerate the toxin and thus help control the toad's numbers. Predator species in Australia, however, lack this tolerance and so are poisoned when they attempt to eat the cane toad.

This has not stopped the cunning crow from learning how to make a feast of the pest animal. Crows in many areas have learnt by bitter experience to avoid the poison glands on the toad's back by turning it over and attacking via its soft (and toxin-free) underbelly. Let us hope the crows of the Northern Territory pick up this technique in a hurry. The fact that crows have discovered how to avoid the toad's toxin illustrates the powerful impact of ***learning***, which refers to any enduring change in the way an organism responds based on its experience. In humans, as in other animals, learning is central to adaptation. Knowing how to distinguish edible from inedible foods, or friends from enemies or predators, is essential for survival. The range of possible foods or threats is simply too great to be prewired into the brain. Learning is essentially about prediction — predicting the future from past experience, and using these predictions to guide behaviour.

For example, even the simplest organisms respond to the environment with reflexes. A ***reflex*** is a behaviour that is elicited automatically by an environmental stimulus, such as the knee-jerk reflex elicited by a doctor's rubber hammer. (A ***stimulus*** is something in the environment that elicits a response.) In perhaps the simplest form of learning, habituation, organisms essentially learn what they can ignore. ***Habituation*** refers to the decreasing strength of a reflex response after repeated presentations of the stimulus. For instance, the loud clang of an old radiator may initially be startling, but repeated clangs produce a steadily decreasing response, until we barely even notice them anymore. Similarly, a novel stimulus initially gains the attention of a newborn. But the more that same stimulus is presented, the weaker the baby's response to that stimulus becomes. As we saw in chapter 4, this kind of simple sensory learning makes sense, because it helps us screen out information that does not predict anything useful to us.

Theories of learning generally share three assumptions. The first is that experience shapes behaviour. Particularly in complex organisms such as humans, the vast majority of responses are learned rather than innate. The migration patterns of whales along Australia's eastern seaboard may be instinctive, but the migration of university students to the beach during the summer break is not. Second, learning is adaptive. Just as nature eliminates organisms that are not well suited to their environments, the environment naturally selects those behaviours in an individual that are adaptive and weeds out those that are not (Skinner, 1977). Behaviours useful to the organism (such as avoiding fights with larger members of its species) will be reproduced because of their consequences (safety from bodily harm). A third assumption is that careful experimentation can uncover laws of learning, many of which apply to human and non-human animals alike.

Learning theory is the foundation of the behaviourist perspective, and the bulk of this chapter explores the behavioural concepts of classical and operant conditioning (known together as associative learning). The remainder examines cognitive approaches that emphasise the role of thought and social experience in learning. What unites these two approaches is a common philosophical ancestor: the concept of association. More than 2500 years ago, Aristotle proposed a set of ***laws of association*** — conditions under which one thought becomes connected, or associated, with another — to account for learning and memory. The most important was the ***law of contiguity***, which proposes that two events will become connected in the mind if they are experienced close together in time (such as thunder and lightning). Another was the ***law of similarity***, which states that objects that resemble each other (such as two people with similar faces) are likely to become associated.

The philosophical school of thought called associationism built upon the work of Aristotle, asserting that our most complex thoughts — which allow us to use equations, program computers and write symphonies — are ultimately nothing but elementary perceptions that become associated and then recombined in the mind. As we will see over the next few chapters, principles of association are fundamental to behaviourist theories of learning as well as to cognitive theories of memory, and neuroscientists have now begun to understand their neural basis — down to changes at the synapse.

Throughout this chapter, three questions are worth keeping in mind. First, to what extent are humans like other animals in the way they learn? Second, what constraints and possibilities has evolution placed on what we can learn? Has natural selection 'wired' us to learn some things more readily than others? And if so, to what degree can experience override innate tendencies? Third, to what extent can we understand learning without reference to mental processes? As we saw in chapter 1, a fundamental aspect of the behaviourist agenda was to rid psychology of terms such as 'thoughts' and 'motives'. The aim was to create a science of behaviour that focused on what could be directly observed. As we will see, decades of behavioural research have produced extraordinary progress in our understanding of learning, as well as substantial challenges to some of the assumptions that generated that research.

Central questions

- To what extent are humans like other animals in the way they learn?
- How has evolution constrained the way we learn?
- To what extent can we understand learning without reference to mental processes?

INTERIM SUMMARY

Learning refers to any enduring change in the way an organism responds based on its experience. ***Habituation*** refers to the decreasing strength of a reflex response after repeated presentations of the stimulus. Learning theories assume that experience shapes behaviour, that learning is adaptive and that only systematic experimentation can uncover laws of learning. Principles of association are fundamental to most accounts of learning.

Classical conditioning

Classical conditioning (sometimes called Pavlovian or respondent conditioning) was the first type of learning to be studied systematically. In the late nineteenth century, the Russian physiologist Ivan Pavlov (1849–1936) was studying the digestive systems of dogs (research for which he won a Nobel Prize). During the course of his work, he noticed a peculiar phenomenon. Like humans and other animals, dogs normally salivate when presented with food, which is a simple reflex. Pavlov noticed that if a stimulus, such as a bell or tuning fork ringing, repeatedly occurred just as a dog was about to be fed, the dog would start to salivate when it heard the bell, even if food was not presented. As Pavlov understood it, the dog had learned to associate the bell with food, and because food produced the reflex of salivation, the bell also came to produce the reflex. This phenomenon is called classical conditioning. Classical conditioning occurs when we learn to identify a relationship between two different stimuli. For example, if you are involved in a serious car accident, you would probably feel very tense the next time you get behind the wheel, especially if the car in front of you brakes suddenly.

Pavlov's model

An innate reflex such as salivation to food is an unconditioned reflex. ***Conditioning*** is a form of learning; hence, an ***unconditioned reflex*** is a reflex that occurs naturally, without any prior learning. The stimulus that produces the response in an unconditioned reflex is called an ***unconditioned stimulus (UCS)***. In this case the UCS was food. An unconditioned stimulus activates a reflexive response without any learning having taken place; thus, the reflex is unlearned, or unconditioned. An ***unconditioned response (UCR)*** is a response that does not have to be learned.

Pavlov's basic experimental setup is illustrated in figure 6.1 (see overleaf). Shortly before presenting the UCS (the food), Pavlov presented a neutral stimulus — a stimulus (in this case, ringing a bell) that normally does not elicit the response in question. After the bell had been paired with the unconditioned stimulus (the food) several times, the sound of the bell alone came to evoke a conditioned response, salivation (figure 6.2). A ***conditioned response (CR)*** is a response that has been learned. By pairing the UCS (the food) with the sound of a bell, the bell became a ***conditioned stimulus (CS)*** — a stimulus that, through learning, has come to evoke a conditioned response. This initial stage of learning, in which the conditioned response becomes associated with the conditioned stimulus, is known as ***acquisition***. Figure 6.3 summarises the classical conditioning process.

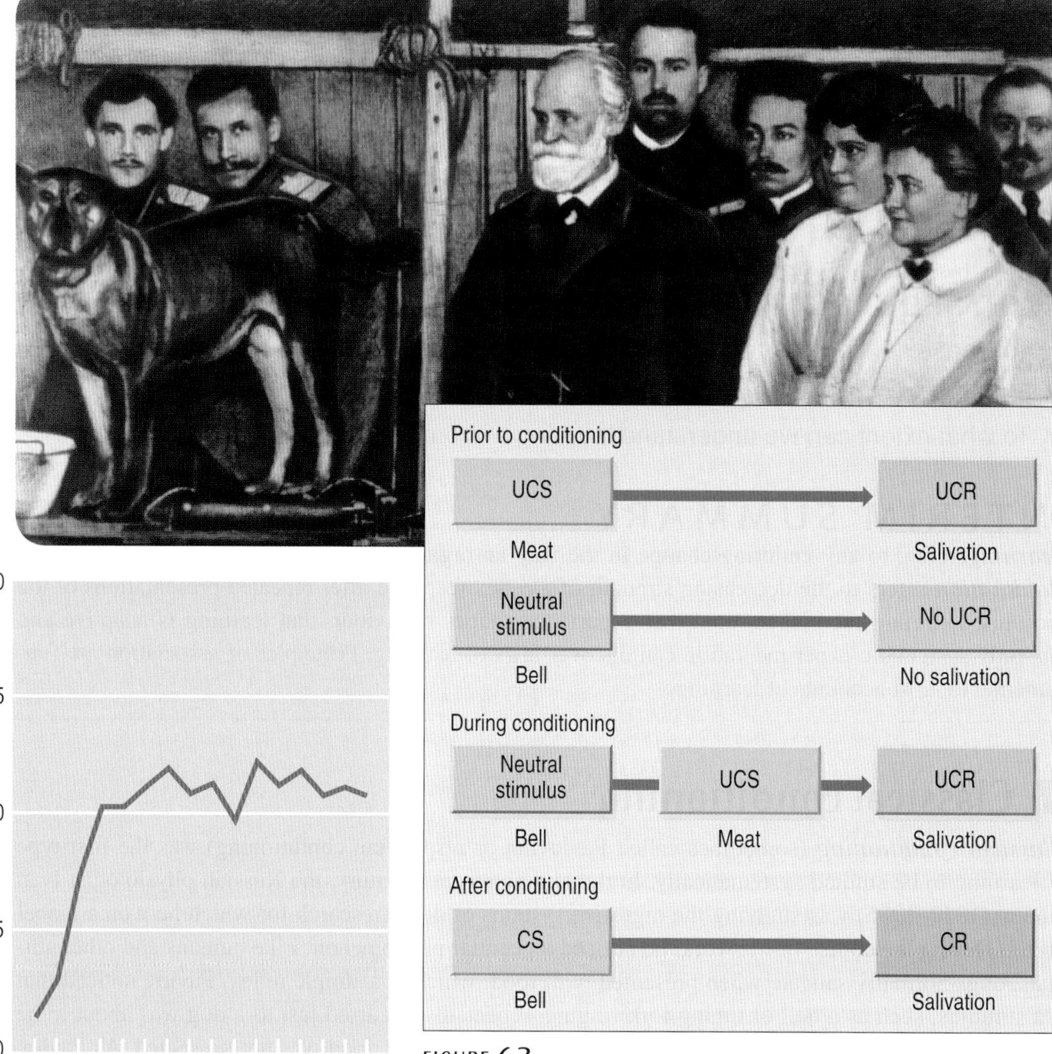

FIGURE 6.1
Pavlov's dog experiments. Pavlov's research with dogs documented the phenomenon of classical conditioning. Actually, his dogs became conditioned to salivate in response to many aspects of the experimental situation and not just to bells or tuning forks; the sight of the experimenter and the harness, too, could elicit the conditioned response.

SOURCE: The Granger Collection, New York.

FIGURE 6.2
Acquisition of a classically conditioned response. Initially, the dog did not salivate in response to the sound of the bell. By the third conditioning trial, however, the conditioned stimulus (the bell) had begun to elicit a conditioned response (salivation), which was firmly established by the fifth or sixth trial.

SOURCE: Pavlov (1927).

FIGURE 6.3
Classical conditioning. In classical conditioning, an initially neutral stimulus comes to elicit a conditioned response.

Why did such a seemingly simple discovery earn Pavlov a central place in the history of psychology? The reason is that classical conditioning can explain a wide array of learned responses outside the laboratory as well. For example, a house cat that was repeatedly sprayed with flea repellent squinted reflexively as the repellent got in its eyes. Eventually it came to squint (CR) whenever its owner used an aerosol spray (CS). The same cat, like many household felines, also came to associate the sound of an electric can opener with the opening of its favorite delicacies and would salivate whenever its owner opened any can, whether cat food or green beans.

If you are beginning to feel somewhat superior to the poor cat wasting all that salivating and squinting on cans of deodorant and vegetables, consider whether you have ever been at your desk, engrossed in work, when you glanced at the clock and discovered that it was dinner time. If so, you probably noticed some physiological responses — mouth watering, feelings of hunger — that had not been present seconds earlier. Through repeated pairings of stimuli associated with a particular time of day and dinner, you have been classically conditioned to associate a time of day indicated on a clock (the CS) with food (the UCS).

Pavlovian conditioning — why bother?

By Professor Ottmar Lipp, University of Queensland

So, dogs will drool if presented with a tone followed by food. Big deal. Surely drooling in response to food is a rather basic reflex, and basic reflex learning is of little relevance to the behaviour of an organism as complex as a human being. So, why is this important? Well, there are at least two good reasons that come to mind.

There is now a relatively well-established consensus that the acquisition of anxiety-related disorders, like phobias and post-traumatic stress disorder, involve Pavlovian learning (Mineka & Zinbarg, 2006). Thus, it is not surprising that the most efficient evidence-based treatment for anxiety disorders, cognitive–behavioural therapy, involves exposure training — an element derived from Pavlovian extinction training. Extinction is very efficient in reducing conditioned responses in the short term, but does not generalise beyond the extinction context. Basic research in non-human animals by Bouton (2002), and others, has revealed that extinction does not eradicate prior fear learning; but leads to the acquisition of new learning, which exists in parallel to the original learning. Thus, a conditional stimulus becomes ambiguous after extinction, and may or may not elicit fear, depending on the circumstances of a particular situation. This is not satisfactory for a client who wants to control an anxiety disorder or a therapist. Recent research in rodents (Monfils, Cowansage, Klann, & LeDoux, 2009) and humans (Schiller et al., 2010) suggests that fear memories may become vulnerable, and are subject to reconsolidation for a short period of time after retrieval. If this initial observation is borne out in subsequent studies, it offers a very promising avenue to enhance the effectiveness of exposure-based therapies, as it suggests that fear learning can indeed be eliminated.

Second, Pavlovian conditioning offers a well-controlled set of procedures that can be applied to the investigation of phenomena, such as racial prejudice. Olsson, Ebert, Banaji, and Phelps (2005) for instance, have shown that, like fear conditioned to stimuli related to animal fear (e.g. snakes and spiders), fear conditioned to members of a racial outgroup is resistant to extinction relative to fear conditioned to members of the racial ingroup. In brief, European and African-American participants participated in a fear conditioning experiment involving the pairing of European and African-American faces with an aversive event. In both participant groups, faces of the racial outgroup elicited fear-related physiological responses for longer during extinction than did faces of the racial ingroup. This suggests that fear of members of a racial outgroup, which may be at the heart of racial prejudice, reflects evolutionary prepared learning (Seligman, 1971) — enhanced learning to stimuli that, in the evolutionary past, posed a survival threat. Research from a laboratory (Mallan, Sax, & Lipp, 2009) has confirmed the finding of resistance to extinction of fear conditioned to racial outgroup faces in a group of Australian students, using Caucasian and Chinese faces. However, it has also been shown (Mallan et al., 2009) that verbal instruction does abolish this 'fear of people who look different' — suggesting that it is not a reflection of prepared learning, but is actually malleable to cognitive intervention.

Thus, Pavlovian conditioning is far from an old hat. Research on the basic mechanisms of Pavlovian learning can inform the design of effective new therapies, and the methodology of Pavlovian conditioning can be harnessed to investigate other psychological phenomena.

Conditioned responses

Pavlov was heavily influenced by Darwin and recognised that the ability to learn new associations is crucial to adaptation. Conditioned aversions to particular tastes help us avoid foods that could poison us. Conditioned emotional responses lead us to approach or avoid objects, people or situations associated with satisfaction or danger — as when an infant learns to associate feelings of warmth, security and pleasure with his parents' presence. Here we will explore three kinds of conditioned responses — and see how learning can produce both adaptive and maladaptive responses.

APPLY + DISCUSS

Watch the brief video clip about classical conditioning that should be available via your university course website for this subject.

- What is classical conditioning?
- How can classical conditioning be used to change behaviour?

Conditioned taste aversions

The case of the crow and the cane toad, which opened this chapter, is an example of a conditioned taste aversion — a learned aversion to a taste associated with an unpleasant feeling, usually nausea. From an evolutionary perspective, connecting tastes with nausea or other unpleasant visceral ('gut') experiences is crucial to survival for an animal that forages for its meals. The capacity to learn taste aversions appears to be hundreds of millions of years old and is present in some very simple invertebrates, like slugs (Garcia, Lasiter, Bermudez-Rattoni, & Deems, 1985; Schafe & Bernstein, 1996). As further evidence of its ancient roots, conditioned taste aversion does not require cortical involvement in humans or other vertebrates. Rats with their cortex removed can still learn taste aversions (Inui, Shimura, & Yamamoto, 2006), and even animals completely anaesthetised while nausea is induced can learn taste aversions, as long as they are conscious during presentation of the CS.

Although conditioned taste aversions normally protect an organism, anyone who has ever developed an aversion to a food eaten shortly before getting the flu knows how irrational — and long lasting — these aversions can sometimes be. Cancer patients undergoing chemotherapy often develop aversions to virtually all food (and may lose dangerous amounts of weight) because a common side effect of chemotherapy is nausea (Docherty, Sandelawski, & Preisser, 2006). To put this in the language of classical conditioning, chemotherapy is a UCS that leads to nausea, a UCR; the result is an inadvertent association of any food eaten (CS) with nausea (the CR). This conditioned response can develop rapidly, with only one or two exposures to the food paired with nausea (Bernstein, 1991). Some patients even begin to feel nauseous at the sound of a nurse's voice, the sight of the clinic or the thought of treatment, although acquisition of these CRs generally requires repeated exposure (Bovbjerg et al., 1990).

Conditioned emotional responses

APPLY + DISCUSS

Humans can develop strong emotional reactions to symbols, such as the Red Cross.

- To what extent can these responses be understood in terms of classical conditioning?
- To what extent can these responses be understood without respect to mental processes, such as empathy for others or a capacity to use symbols, as in language?

One of the most important ways classical conditioning affects behaviour is in the conditioning of emotional responses. Consider the automatic smile that comes to a person's face when hearing a special song, or the sweaty palms, pounding heart and feelings of anxiety that arise when an instructor walks into a classroom and begins handing out a test. Conditioned emotional responses occur when a formerly neutral stimulus is paired with a stimulus that evokes an emotional response (either naturally or through prior learning).

Perhaps the most famous example of classical conditioning is the case of little Albert. The study was performed by John Watson, the founder of American behaviourism, and his colleague, Rosalie Rayner (1920). The study was neither methodologically nor ethically beyond reproach, but its provocative findings served as a catalyst for decades of research (see Harris, 1979; Christopher Green explores how experimental evidence is needed to support the notion of conditioning various types of emotional response). A link to his research should be available via your university course website for this subject.

Albert was nine months old when Watson and Rayner presented him with a variety of objects, including a dog, a rabbit, a white rat, a Santa Claus mask and a fur coat. Albert showed no fear of these objects; in fact, he played regularly with the rat — a budding behaviourist, no doubt. A few days later, Watson and Rayner tested little Albert's response to a loud noise (the UCS) by banging on a steel bar directly behind his head. Albert reacted by jumping, falling forward and whimpering.

About two months later, Watson and Rayner selected the white rat to be the CS in their experiment and proceeded to condition a fear response in Albert. Each time Albert reached out to touch the rat, they struck the steel bar, creating the same loud noise that had initially startled him. After only a few pairings of the noise and the rat, Albert learned to fear the rat.

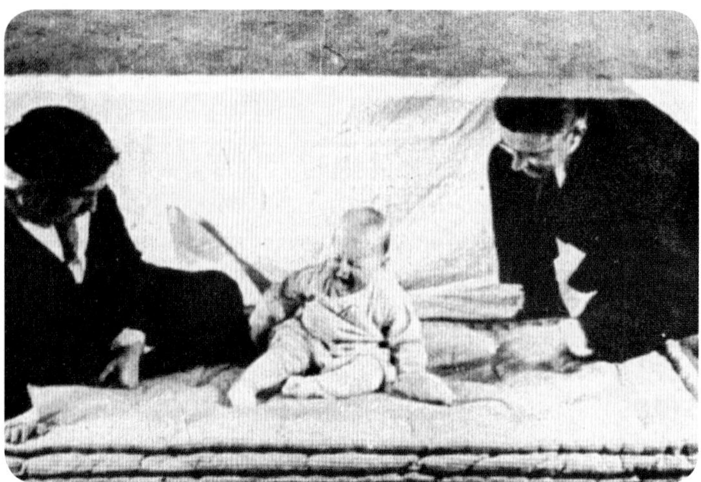

Through classical conditioning, little Albert developed a fear of rats and other furry objects — even Santa's face (a disabling phobia for a child, indeed).
Courtesy of Benjamin Harris.

Studies since Watson and Rayner's time have proposed classical conditioning as an explanation for some human ***phobias***, that is, irrational fears of specific objects or situations (Ost, 1991; Rauhut, Thomas, Ayres, 2001; Wolpe, 1958). For example, many people develop severe emotional reactions (including fainting) to hypodermic needles through exposure to injections in childhood. Knowing as an adult that injections are necessary and relatively painless usually has little impact on the fear, which is elicited automatically. For example, an Australian study of needle phobias showed that chemotherapy outpatients reported strong feelings of 'fear, disgust or discomfort' towards the sight of blood, receiving injections or both (Carey & Harris, 2005). Athletes such as football players often amuse nurses in student health centres with their combination of fearlessness on the field and fainting at the sight of a tiny needle. Many such fears are acquired and elicited through the activation of subcortical neural pathways (pathways below the level of the cortex; chapter 3) between the visual system and the amygdala (LeDoux, 1995). Adult knowledge may be of little use in counteracting them because the crucial neural circuits are outside cortical control and are activated before the cortex even gets the message.

APPLY + DISCUSS

- What are some ways a person might develop a phobia of flying?
- Could fear of flying arise in some other way?
- Can flying phobias be explained through principles of classical conditioning?

Conditioned immune responses

Classical conditioning can even affect the ***immune system***, the system of cells throughout the body that fights disease (Abrous, Rodriquez, le Moal, Moser, & Barneoud, 1999; Ader, 2003; Ader & Cohen, 1985). For example, aside from causing nausea, chemotherapy for cancer has a second unfortunate consequence: it decreases the activity of cells in the immune system that normally fight off infection. Can stimuli associated with chemotherapy, then, become CSs that suppress cell activity?

One study tested this possibility by comparing the functioning of immune cells in cancer patients at two different times (Bovbjerg et al., 1990). The first time was a few days prior to chemotherapy; the second was the morning the patient checked into the hospital for treatment. The investigators hypothesised that exposure to hospital stimuli associated with prior chemotherapy experiences (CS) would suppress immune functioning (CR), just as chemotherapy (UCS) reduces the activity of immune cells (UCR). They were right: blood taken the morning of hospitalisation showed weakened immune functioning when exposed to germs. Researchers have since tried to see whether they can actually *strengthen* immune functioning using classical conditioning (Alvarez-Borda, Ramirez-Amaya, Perez-Montfort, & Bermudez-Rattoni, 1995; Ramirez-Amaya & Bermudez-Rattoni, 1999).

The principles of classical conditioning have been used in research in association with drug tolerance and dependence. Research by Siegel, Baptista, Kim, McDonald, and Weise-Kelly (2000) showed that environmental cues present when drugs are administered typically become associated with the response to those drugs. However, if those environmental cues are presented but the drugs are not administered, drug-compensatory responses can still occur. Thus, the environmental cues present when the drug is administered contribute to tolerance (MacRae, Scoles, & Siegel, 1988).

INTERIM SUMMARY

In ***classical conditioning***, an environmental stimulus leads to a learned response, through pairing of an ***unconditioned stimulus*** with a previously neutral ***conditioned stimulus***. The result is a ***conditioned response***, or learned reflex. Conditioned taste aversions are learned aversions to a taste associated with an unpleasant feeling (usually nausea). Conditioned emotional responses occur when a conditioned stimulus is paired with a stimulus that evokes an emotional response. Conditioned immune responses can occur when a conditioned stimulus is paired with a stimulus that evokes a change in the functioning of the ***immune system*** (the system of cells in the body that fights disease).

Stimulus generalisation and discrimination

Once an organism has learned to associate a CS with a UCS, it may respond to stimuli that resemble the CS with a similar response. This phenomenon, called ***stimulus generalisation***, is related to Aristotle's principle of similarity. For example, you are at a sporting event and you stand for the national anthem.

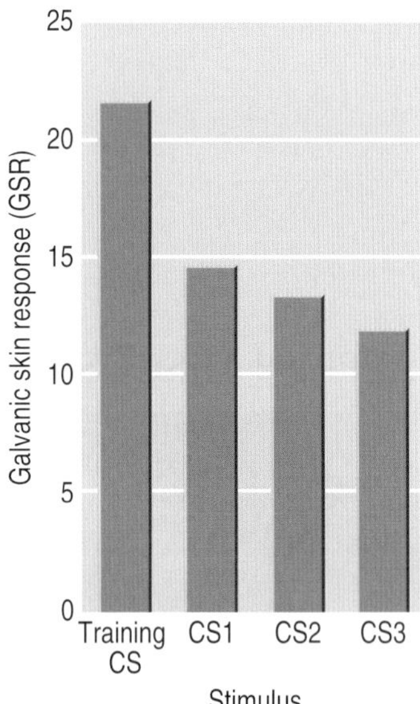

FIGURE 6.4
Stimulus generalisation. Galvanic skin response (a measure of physiological arousal) varies according to the similarity of the CS to the training stimulus. In this case, the training stimulus was a tone of a particular frequency. CS-1 is most similar to the training stimulus; CS-3 is least similar to it.

SOURCE: Hovland (1937).

You suddenly well up with pride in your country (which you now, of course, recognise as nothing but a classically conditioned emotional response). But the song you hear, familiar as it may sound, is not exactly the same stimulus you heard the last time you were at a game. It is not in the same key, and this time the tenor took a few liberties with the melody. So how do you know to respond with the same emotion?

Many years ago researchers demonstrated that the more similar a stimulus is to the CS, the more likely generalisation will occur (Hovland, 1937). In a classic study, the experimenters paired a tone (the CS) with a mild electrical shock (the UCS). With repeated pairings, participants produced a conditioned response to the tone known as a ***galvanic skin response***, or ***GSR*** (an electrical measure of the amount of sweat on the skin, associated with arousal or anxiety). The experimenter then presented tones of varying frequencies that had not been paired with shock and measured the resulting GSR. Tones with frequencies similar to the CS evoked the most marked GSR, whereas dissimilar tones evoked progressively smaller responses (figure 6.4).

A major component of adaptive learning is knowing when to generalise and when to be more discriminating. Maladaptive patterns in humans often involve inappropriate generalisation from one set of circumstances to others, as when a person who has been frequently criticised by a parent responds negatively to all authority figures.

Much of the time, in fact, we are able to discriminate among stimuli in ways that foster adaptation. ***Stimulus discrimination*** is the learned tendency to respond to a restricted range of stimuli or only to the stimulus used during training. In many ways, stimulus discrimination is the opposite of stimulus generalisation. Pavlov's dogs did not salivate in response to just *any* sound, and people do not get hungry when the clock reads four o'clock even though it is not far from six o'clock. Organisms learn to discriminate between two similar stimuli when these stimuli are not consistently associated with the same UCS.

Extinction

In the acquisition, or initial learning, of a conditioned response, each pairing of the CS and UCS is known as a conditioning trial. What happens later, however, if the CS repeatedly occurs without the UCS? For example, suppose Watson and Rayner (1920) had, on the second, third and all subsequent trials, exposed little Albert to the white rat without the loud noise?

Albert's learned fear response would eventually have been extinguished, or eliminated, from his behavioural repertoire. ***Extinction*** in classical conditioning refers to the process by which a CR is weakened by presentation of the CS without the UCS. If a dog has come to associate the sounding of a bell with food, it will eventually stop salivating at the bell tone if the bell rings enough times without the presentation of food. The association is weakened — but not obliterated. If days later the dog once more hears the bell, it is likely to salivate again. This is known as ***spontaneous recovery*** — the re-emergence of a previously extinguished conditioned response. The spontaneous recovery of a CR is typically short-lived, however, and will rapidly extinguish again without renewed pairings of the CS and UCS.

Many people have irrational fears or phobias. The wolf spider is usually harmless to humans, but the sight of its spindly form might elicit feelings of intense fear in a person with a spider phobia. Psychologists use their understanding of classical conditioning to help people extinguish their arachnophobia — a fear of spiders. The treatment of psychological disorders is discussed in depth in chapter 16.

INTERIM SUMMARY

Stimulus generalisation occurs when an organism learns to respond to stimuli that resemble the CS with a similar response. ***Stimulus discrimination*** occurs when an organism learns to respond to a restricted range of stimuli. ***Extinction*** occurs when a CR is weakened by presentation of the CS without the UCS. ***Spontaneous recovery*** is the short-lived re-emergence of a previously extinguished CR.

Factors affecting classical conditioning

Classical conditioning does not occur every time a bell rings, a baby startles or a crow eats a poisonous toad. Several factors influence the extent to which classical conditioning will occur. These include the interstimulus interval, the individual's learning history and the organism's preparedness to learn (see Wasserman & Miller, 1997).

Interstimulus interval

The ***interstimulus interval*** is the time between presentation of the CS and the UCS. Presumably, if too much time passes between the presentation of these two stimuli, the animal is unlikely to associate them, and conditioning is less likely to occur. For most responses, the optimal interval between the CS and UCS is very brief, usually a few seconds or less. The optimal interval depends, however, on the stimulus and tends to bear the imprint of natural selection (Hollis, 1997; Ylioja, Carlson, Raij, & Pertovaara, 2006). A CS that occurs about half a second before a puff of air hits the eye has the maximum power to elicit a conditioned eyeblink response in humans (Ross & Ross, 1971). This makes evolutionary sense because we usually have very little warning between the time we see or hear something and the time debris reaches our eyes.

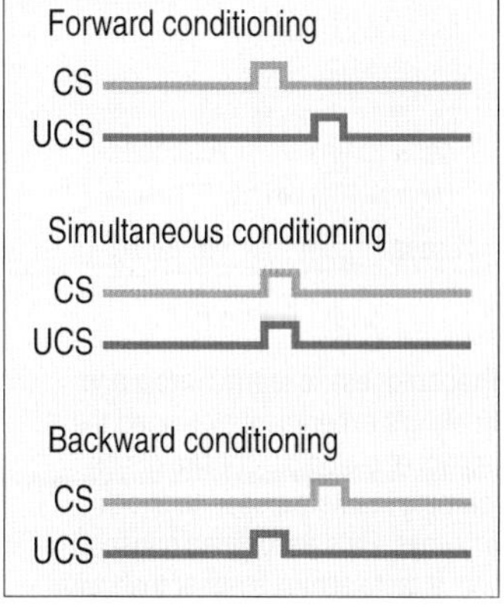

FIGURE 6.5
Forward, simultaneous and backward conditioning. In forward conditioning, the type studied most extensively by Pavlov, the onset of the CS occurs before the UCS. In simultaneous conditioning, the CS is presented at the same time as the UCS. In backward conditioning, the CS is presented after the onset of the UCS. Forward conditioning is most likely to lead to learning.

At the other extreme, conditioned taste aversions do not occur when the interstimulus interval is less than ten seconds, and learning often occurs with intervals up to several hours (Schafe & Bernstein, 1996). Given that nausea or stomach pain can develop hours after ingesting a toxic substance, the capacity to associate tastes with feelings in the gut minutes or hours later clearly fosters survival. However, nausea is the only reflex in which conditioning occurs after such a lengthy interstimulus interval — that is why it is such an important evolutionary reflex for survival. Thus, just as in perception (chapter 4), our brains appear to be attuned to the patterns that exist in nature.

The temporal order of the CS and the UCS — that is, which one comes first — is also crucial (figure 6.5). Maximal conditioning occurs when the CS precedes the UCS. This, too, makes evolutionary sense: a CS that consistently occurs after a UCS offers little additional information, whereas a CS that precedes a UCS allows the organism to 'predict' and hence to prepare.

The individual's learning history

Another factor that influences classical conditioning is the individual's learning history. An extinguished response is usually easier to learn the second time around, presumably because the stimulus was once associated with the response. A previously extinguished nausea response to the taste of bacon can be easily reinstated — and difficult to extinguish — if bacon and nausea ever occur together again. This suggests that neuronal connections established through learning may diminish in strength when the environment no longer supports them, but they do not entirely disappear. Later learning can build on old 'tracks' that have been covered up but not obliterated.

In other circumstances, prior learning can actually *hinder* learning. Suppose a dog has learned to salivate at the sound of a bell (conditioned stimulus 1, or CS1). The researcher now wants to teach the dog to associate food with a flash of light as well (CS2). If the bell continues to sound even occasionally in learning trials pairing the light (CS2) with food (the UCS), the dog is unlikely to produce a conditioned response to the light. This phenomenon is known as blocking. ***Blocking*** refers to the failure of a stimulus (such as a flash of light) to elicit a CR when it is combined with another stimulus that already elicits the response (Fanselow, 1998; Kamin, 1969). If a bell is already associated with food, a flashing light is of little consequence unless it provides additional, non-redundant information.

A similar phenomenon occurs in ***latent inhibition***, in which initial exposure to a neutral stimulus without a UCS slows the process of later learning the CS–UCS association and developing a CR (Lubow & Gewirtz, 1995). Thus, if a bell repeatedly sounds without presentation of meat, a dog may be slower to learn the connection after the bell *does* start to signal mealtime. Similarly, people often take a while to change their attitude towards a colleague who has previously been relatively silent but suddenly starts making useful comments as he becomes more comfortable speaking his mind.

Preparedness to learn: an evolutionary perspective

A third influence on classical conditioning is the organism's readiness to learn certain associations. Many early behaviourists, such as Watson, believed that the laws of classical conditioning could link virtually any stimulus to any response. Yet subsequent research has shown that some responses can be conditioned much more readily to certain stimuli than to others.

This was demonstrated in a classic study by Garcia and Koelling (1966). The experimenters used three conditioned stimuli: light, sound and taste (flavoured water). For one group of rats, these stimuli were paired with the UCS of radiation, which produces nausea. For the other group, the stimuli were paired with a different UCS, electric shock. The experimenters then exposed the rats to each of the three conditioned stimuli to test the strength of the conditioned response to each.

The results are shown in figure 6.6. Rats that experienced nausea after exposure to radiation developed an aversion to the flavoured water but not to the light or sound cues. In contrast, rats exposed to electric shock avoided the audiovisual stimuli but not the taste cues. In other words, the rats learned to associate sickness in their stomachs with a taste stimulus and an aversive tactile stimulus (electrical shock) with audiovisual stimuli.

	Conditioned stimulus (CS)		
Unconditioned stimulus (UCS)	Light	Sound	Taste
Shock (pain)	Avoidance	Avoidance	No avoidance
X-rays (nausea)	No avoidance	No avoidance	Avoidance

FIGURE 6.6
Preparedness to learn. Garcia and Koelling's experiment examined the impact of biological constraints on learning in rats exposed to shock or x-rays. Rats associated nausea with a taste stimulus rather than with audiovisual cues; they associated an aversive tactile event with sights and sounds rather than with taste stimuli. The results demonstrated that animals are prepared to learn certain associations more readily than others in classical conditioning.

SOURCE: Adapted from Garcia and Koelling (1966).

Prepared learning refers to the biologically wired readiness to learn some associations more easily than others (Bjorklund & Pellegrini, 2002; Ohman, Esteves, & Soares, 1995; Seligman, 1971). From an evolutionary perspective, natural selection has favoured organisms that more readily associate stimuli that tend to be associated in nature and whose association is related to survival or reproduction. An animal lucky enough to survive after eating a poisonous caterpillar is more likely to survive thereafter if it can associate nausea with the right stimulus. For most land-dwelling animals, a preparedness to connect taste with nausea allows the animal to bypass irrelevant associations to the hundreds of other stimuli it might have encountered between the time it dined on the offending caterpillar and the time it got sick hours later.

In contrast, most birds do not have well-developed gustatory systems and thus cannot rely heavily on taste to avoid toxic insects. In support of the evolutionary hypothesis, research on quail and other birds finds that, unlike rats, they are more likely to associate nausea with visual than gustatory stimuli (Hollis, 1997). Garcia and Robertson (1985) theorise that vertebrate animals have evolved two defence systems, one attending to defence of the gut (and hence favouring associations between nausea and sensory cues relevant to food) and the other attending to defence of the skin (and usually predisposing the animal to form associations between pain and sights and sounds that signal dangers such as predators).

Humans show some evidence of biological preparedness as well. Phobias of public speaking and snakes are more common than phobias of flowers or telephones (Marks, 1969; Ohman, Frederikson, Hugdahl, & Rimmon, 1976). Readers of this book, for example, are much more likely to have snake or spider phobias than car phobias, despite the fact that they are more than 10 000 times more likely to die at the wheel of a car than at the mouth of a spider — or to have experienced a car accident rather than a snakebite.

Biological preparedness, of course, has its limits, especially in humans, whose associative capacities are almost limitless (McNally, 1987). One study, for example, found people equally likely to develop a fear of handguns as of snakes (Honeybourne, Matchett, & Davey, 1993). Where biological predispositions leave off, learning begins as a way of naturally selecting adaptive responses.

What do organisms learn in classical conditioning?

In some ways, contrasting innate with learned responses is setting up a false dichotomy, because the capacity to learn — to form associations — is itself a product of natural selection. Precisely what organisms learn when they are classically conditioned, however, has been a topic of considerable debate.

Most theorists would agree that organisms learn associations, but associations between what? According to Watson and other early behaviourists, the organism learns a stimulus–response, or S–R, association. In other words, the organism learns to associate the CR with the CS. Pavlov, in contrast, argued that the organism learns to associate the CS with the UCS — a stimulus–stimulus, or S–S, association. Pavlov (1927) hypothesised that in classical conditioning the CS essentially becomes a signal to an organism that the UCS is about to occur. Although both kinds of processes probably occur, the weight of the evidence tends to favour Pavlov's theory (Rescorla, 1973).

Another question is just how far we can take Aristotle's law of contiguity, which, as we have seen, proposes that organisms should associate stimuli that repeatedly occur together in time. Data from animal learning studies suggest that this principle is not quite right, although it was a monumental step in the right direction. If contiguity were the whole story, order of presentation of the UCS and CS would not matter — yet as we have seen, a CS that precedes a UCS produces more potent learning than a CS that follows or occurs simultaneously with the UCS. Similarly, if contiguity were all there were to learning, blocking would not occur: if two stimuli occur together frequently enough, it should make no difference whether some other CS is 'coming along for the ride' — the organism should still associate the new CS with the UCS or CR.

On the basis of these and other findings, Rescorla and Wagner (1972) proposed the ***law of prediction*** to replace the law of contiguity. This law states that a CS–UCS association will form to the extent that the presence of the CS predicts the appearance of the UCS. As we will see, this law moved the field substantially in a cognitive direction, suggesting that animals are not blindly making connections between any two stimuli that come along. Rather — and in line with evolutionary theory as well — rats, humans and other animals are making connections between stimuli in ways that are likely to guide adaptive responding. More recent research suggests, in fact, that animals learn not only about the connection between stimuli in classical conditioning but about their timing (Gallistel & Gibbon, 2000). Thus, a dog in a Pavlovian experiment learns not only that meat will follow the toll of a bell but also how long after the bell the meat (and hence salivation) is likely to occur.

APPLY + DISCUSS

- Why are public speaking phobias so common?
- Does this reflect prepared learning? Or does it simply reflect people's unpleasant experiences with public speaking?

A third question is the extent to which the CR and UR are really the same response. According to Pavlov, following classical conditioning, the organism responds to the CS as if it were the UCS and hence produces the same response. Pavlov proposed a neurological mechanism for this, hypothesising that repeated pairings of the UCS and the CS lead to connections between them in the brain, so that the two stimuli eventually trigger the same response. Although Pavlov was probably right in broad strokes, subsequent research suggests that the CR and the UCR, though usually similar, are rarely identical. Dogs typically do not salivate as much in response to a bell as to the actual presentation of food, which means that the CS is not triggering the exact same response as the UCS.

Sometimes the CR is even the opposite of the UCR, as in ***paradoxical conditioning***, in which the CR is actually the body's attempt to counteract the effects of a stimulus that is about to occur. For example, the sight of drug paraphernalia in heroin addicts can activate physiological reactions that reduce the effect of the heroin they are about to inject (Caggiula, Epstein, Antelman, Seymour, & Taylor, 1991; Siegel, 1984). This produces a conditioned tolerance, or decreased sensitivity, to the drug with repeated use as the body counteracts dosages that were previously effective.

This CR may be involved in the processes that force addicts to take progressively higher doses of a drug to achieve the same effect. One study of paradoxical conditioning in opiate addicts compared the effects of self-injection, which involved exposure to drug paraphernalia (the CS), with an intravenous injection provided by the researchers, which did not (Ehrman, Ternes, O'Brien, & McLellan, 1992). Only the bodies of addicts who self-injected showed efforts to counteract the drug.

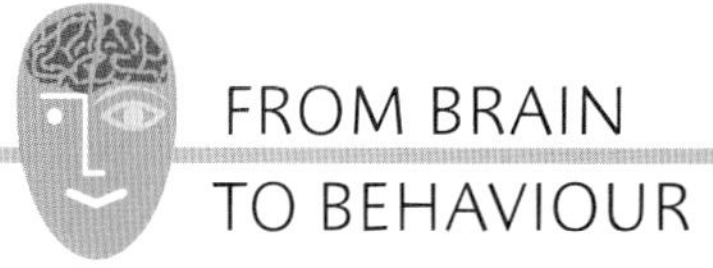

The neural basis of classical conditioning

Research has, however, confirmed Pavlov's speculation that classical conditioning alters the action of neurons that ultimately link stimuli with responses (Bailey & Kandel, 1995; Martinez & Derrick, 1996). For years, Eric Kandel and his colleagues have studied the cellular basis of learning in the marine snail, *Aplysia*. This simple and seemingly unremarkable organism is ideally suited to the study of associative learning because reflex learning in *Aplysia* involves a very small number of large neurons. Thus, researchers can actually observe what is happening at all the relevant synapses as *Aplysia* learns. (In humans, in comparison, thousands or millions of neurons may be activated in a simple instance of classical conditioning.)

Learning at the synapse

In *Aplysia*, classical conditioning and similar forms of learning occur through changes at synapses that link sensory neurons (activated by the CS) to neurons that trigger a motor reflex. Changes occur in both the presynaptic neuron, which releases neurotransmitters more readily with additional conditioning trials, and the postsynaptic neuron, which becomes more easily excited with additional trials. A small number of trials produces changes that last minutes or hours, whereas a larger number of trials can produce changes that last for days.

Kandel and his colleagues have discovered some differences at the cellular level between short-term and longer-term learning of this sort. For example, in short-term learning, the presynaptic neuron uses proteins already available within the cell to facilitate release of neurotransmitters. More frequent pairings of the CS and UCS, however, generate new proteins that lead to the sprouting of new dendritic connections between the presynaptic and postsynaptic neuron. This strengthens the connections between the two cells, creating a long-lasting neural association. (In 2000, Kandel won the Nobel Prize for his research on *Aplysia*.)

Other researchers have studied a similar phenomenon called long-term potentiation in more complex animals (Bliss & Lomo, 1973; Guzowski et al., 2000; Jeffery, 1997). ***Long-term potentiation (LTP)*** refers to the tendency of a group of neurons to fire more readily after consistent stimulation from other neurons (Teyler et al., 2005), as presumably occurs in classical conditioning. Its name refers to a heightened potential for neural firing ('potentiation') that lasts much longer than the initial stimulus. Thus, even after the CS is no longer present, cellular changes at the synapse are. To what extent LTP is involved in various forms of learning is currently a topic of debate among neuroscientists. For example, Teyler et al. (2005) suggest that it is possible to non-invasively induce and measure LTP in humans and establish its behavioural consequences in a variety of sensory and cognitive processes. Similarly, Abraham, Logan, Greenwood, and Dragunow (2002), behavioural scientists at Otago University in New Zealand, suggest that LTP can, under appropriate conditions, remain stable for more than a year, supporting the notion that LTP plays a role in persistent memory function.

Like the work on *Aplysia*, research on LTP supports a hypothesis proposed by the neurologist Donald Hebb (1949) years before the technologies existed to test it: 'When an axon of cell A is near enough to excite cell B and repeatedly or persistently takes part in firing it, some . . . process . . . takes place in one or both cells such that A's efficiency, as one of the cells firing B, is increased.' In other words, when the activation of one set of neurons repeatedly leads to activation of another, the strength of the connection between the two neurons increases — a neural translation of the principles of association first formulated by Aristotle.

Neural circuits and classical conditioning

While Kandel and others have made great strides in understanding learning at the synaptic level, other researchers are focusing on the larger neural circuits that allow humans and other animals to learn conditioned responses. By selectively damaging rats' brains, researchers have been able to determine which parts of the brain are involved in different aspects of fear conditioning. As we will see in chapter 10 on emotion, perhaps the most important discovery has been circuits involving the amygdala that play a central role in the capacity to associate fear with a new stimulus, which is crucial for survival (Fanselow & LeDoux, 1999; LeDoux, 2000).

Unlike lesions of the amygdala, lesions of the hippocampus, which plays a key role in memory (chapter 7), do not disrupt simple fear conditioning — but they do have a very specific effect on learning to fear. In classical conditioning experiments, animals often learn not only the simple association between a CS and a US, such as the association between a tone and shock, but also that being in the experimental chamber (rather than their own cage) predicts shock. This additional learning is called contextual learning (learning about the context). Hippocampal lesions disrupt ***contextual learning*** — as if the rat can no longer remember the broader context in which negative events happen because it cannot remember the specific events at all (Fanselow, 1998; Kim & Fanselow, 1992; LeDoux, 1998).

The distinction between the kinds of learning disrupted by damage to the amygdala and to the hippocampus in animals such as rats appears to have a clear parallel in humans. Humans with lesions to the amygdala have difficulty learning to fear a novel stimulus at all — even if they consciously *know* that every time a tone sounded they received a shock. They can 'talk the talk', but they cannot 'walk the walk'. In contrast, patients with lesions to the hippocampus respond with fear to a conditioned stimulus — even if they cannot remember having ever seen it before (Bechara et al., 1995). Their intact amygdala produces the fear response, even though they have no idea why it is there.

INTERIM SUMMARY

Several factors influence classical conditioning, including the ***interstimulus interval*** (the time between presentation of the CS and the UCS), the degree to which the presence of the CS is predictive of the US, the individual's learning history (such as prior associations between the stimulus and other stimuli or responses) and ***prepared learning*** (the evolved tendency of some associations to be learned more readily than others). Precisely what organisms learn in classical conditioning is a matter of debate. Research on the marine snail *Aplysia* and on ***long-term potentiation*** in more complex animals suggests that learning occurs through changes in the strength of connections between neurons. Research on fear conditioning implicates neural circuits involving the amygdala.

Operant conditioning

In 1898, Edward Thorndike placed a hungry cat in a box with a mechanical latch and then placed food in full view just outside the box. The cat meowed, paced back and forth and rubbed against the walls of the box. In so doing, it happened to trip the latch. Immediately, the door to the box opened and the cat gained access to the food. Thorndike repeated the experiment and, with continued repetitions, the cat became more adept at tripping the latch. Eventually, it was able to leave its cage almost as soon as food appeared.

Thorndike proposed a law of learning to account for this phenomenon, which he called the ***law of effect***: an animal's tendency to reproduce a behaviour depends on that behaviour's effect on the environment and the consequent effect on the animal. If tripping the latch had not helped the cat reach the food, the cat would not have learned to keep brushing up against the latch. More simply, the law of effect states that behaviour is controlled by its consequences.

Thorndike's cat exemplifies a second form of conditioning, known as instrumental or operant conditioning. Thorndike used the term instrumental conditioning because the behaviour is instrumental to achieving a more satisfying state of affairs. B. F. Skinner, who spent years experimenting with the ways in which behaviour is controlled by the environment, called it ***operant conditioning***, which means learning to operate on the environment to produce a consequence.

Although the lines between operant and classical conditioning are not always hard and fast, the major distinction regards which comes first, something in the environment or some behaviour from the organism. In classical conditioning, an environmental stimulus initiates a response, whereas in operant conditioning, a behaviour (or operant) produces an environmental response. ***Operants*** are behaviours that are emitted (spontaneously produced) rather than elicited by the environment. Thorndike's cat spontaneously emitted the behaviour of brushing up against the latch, which resulted in an effect that conditioned future behaviour. Skinner emitted the behaviours of experimenting and writing about his results, which brought him the respect of his colleagues and hence influenced his future behaviour. Had his initial experiments failed, he probably would not have persisted, just as Thorndike's cats did not continue emitting behaviours with neutral or aversive environmental effects. In operant conditioning — whether the animal is a cat or a psychologist — the behaviour precedes the environmental event that conditions future behaviour. By contrast, in classical conditioning, an environmental stimulus (such as a bell) precedes a response.

The basic idea behind operant conditioning, then, is that behaviour is controlled by its consequences. In this section, we explore two types of environmental consequence that produce operant conditioning: ***reinforcement***, which increases the probability that a response will occur, and ***punishment***, which diminishes its likelihood.

Reinforcement

Reinforcement means just what the name implies: something in the environment fortifies, or reinforces, a behaviour. A ***reinforcer*** is an environmental consequence that occurs after an organism has produced a response and makes the response more likely to recur. Psychologists distinguish two kinds of reinforcement, positive and negative.

Positive reinforcement

Positive reinforcement is the process whereby presentation of a stimulus (a reward or pay-off) after a behaviour makes the behaviour more likely to occur again. For example, in experimental procedures pioneered by B. F. Skinner (1938, 1953), a pigeon was placed in a cage with a target mounted on one side. The pigeon spontaneously pecked around in the cage. This behaviour was not a response to any particular stimulus; pecking is simply innate avian (bird) behaviour. If, by chance, the pigeon pecked at the target, however, a pellet of grain dropped into a bin. If the pigeon happened to peck at the target again, it was once more rewarded with a pellet. The pellet is a ***positive reinforcer*** — an environmental consequence that, when presented, strengthens the probability that a response will recur. The pigeon would thus start to peck at the target more frequently because this operant became associated with the positive reinforcer. Rats, along with pigeons, were one of Skinner's most reinforcing subjects (see figure 6.7).

FIGURE 6.7
B. F. Skinner experiments with a rat placed in a Skinner box, in which pressing a bar may result in reinforcement. The box is an apparatus for operant conditioning.

Positive reinforcement is not limited to pigeons. In fact, it controls much of human behaviour. Students learn to exert effort studying when they are reinforced with praise and good grades, salespeople learn to appease obnoxious customers and laugh at their jokes because this behaviour yields them commissions, and people learn to go to work each day because they receive a paycheque. Reinforcement can also be used creatively to initiate change at a community level. For example, in New Zealand positive reinforcement procedures were used to reduce the incidence of unsafe driving behaviours (see Hutton, Sibley, Harper, & Hunt, 2002; Sibley, Hunt, & Harper, 2002) and to reduce the number of instances of unwelcome graffiti (Craw, Leland, Bussell, Munday, & Walsh, 2006).

Although positive reinforcement (and operant conditioning more generally) usually leads to adaptive responding, nothing guarantees that organisms make the 'right' connections between behaviours and their consequences. Just as humans and other animals can develop phobias by forming idiosyncratic associations, they can also erroneously associate an operant and an environmental event, a phenomenon Skinner (1948) labelled ***superstitious behaviour***. For example, in one study, pigeons received grain at regular time intervals, no matter what behaviour the pigeons happened to perform. As a result, each pigeon developed its own idiosyncratic response. One turned counterclockwise about the cage, another repeatedly thrust its head in an upper corner of the cage and a third tossed its head as if lifting an invisible bar (Skinner, 1948). Skinner compared these behaviours to human actions such as wearing a lucky outfit to a football match or tapping the ground three times when up to bat in cricket. According to Skinner, such behaviours develop because the delivery of a reinforcer strengthens whatever behaviour an organism is engaged in at the time.

Negative reinforcement

Just as presenting an animal with a rewarding environmental consequence can reinforce a behaviour, so, too, can eliminating an aversive consequence. This is known as ***negative reinforcement*** — the process whereby termination of an aversive stimulus makes a behaviour more likely to occur. ***Negative reinforcers*** are aversive or unpleasant stimuli that strengthen a behaviour by their removal. Hitting the snooze button on an alarm clock is negatively reinforced by the termination of the alarm; cleaning the kitchen is negatively reinforced by the elimination of unpleasant sights, smells and whining by housemates.

Negative reinforcement occurs in both escape learning and avoidance learning. In ***escape learning***, a behaviour is reinforced by the elimination of an aversive state of affairs that already exists; that is, the organism escapes an aversive situation. For example, a rat presses a lever and terminates an electric shock or an overzealous sunbather applies lotion to her skin to relieve sunburn pain. ***Avoidance learning*** occurs as an organism learns to prevent an expected aversive event from happening. In this case, avoidance of a potentially aversive situation reinforces the operant. For example, a rat jumps a hurdle into a safe chamber when it hears a tone that signals that a shock is about to occur, and the sunbather puts on sunscreen before going out in the sun to avoid a sunburn.

Punishment

Reinforcement is one type of environmental consequence that controls behaviour through operant conditioning; the other is punishment (figure 6.8). Whereas reinforcement always increases the likelihood of a response, either by the presentation of a reward or the removal of an aversive stimulus, punishment decreases the probability that a behaviour will recur. Thus, if Skinner's pigeon received an electric shock each time it pecked at the target, it would be less likely to peck again because this operant resulted in an aversive outcome. Parents intuitively apply this behavioural technique when they 'ground' a teenager for staying out past curfew. The criminal justice system also operates on a system of punishment, attempting to discourage illicit behaviours by imposing penalties.

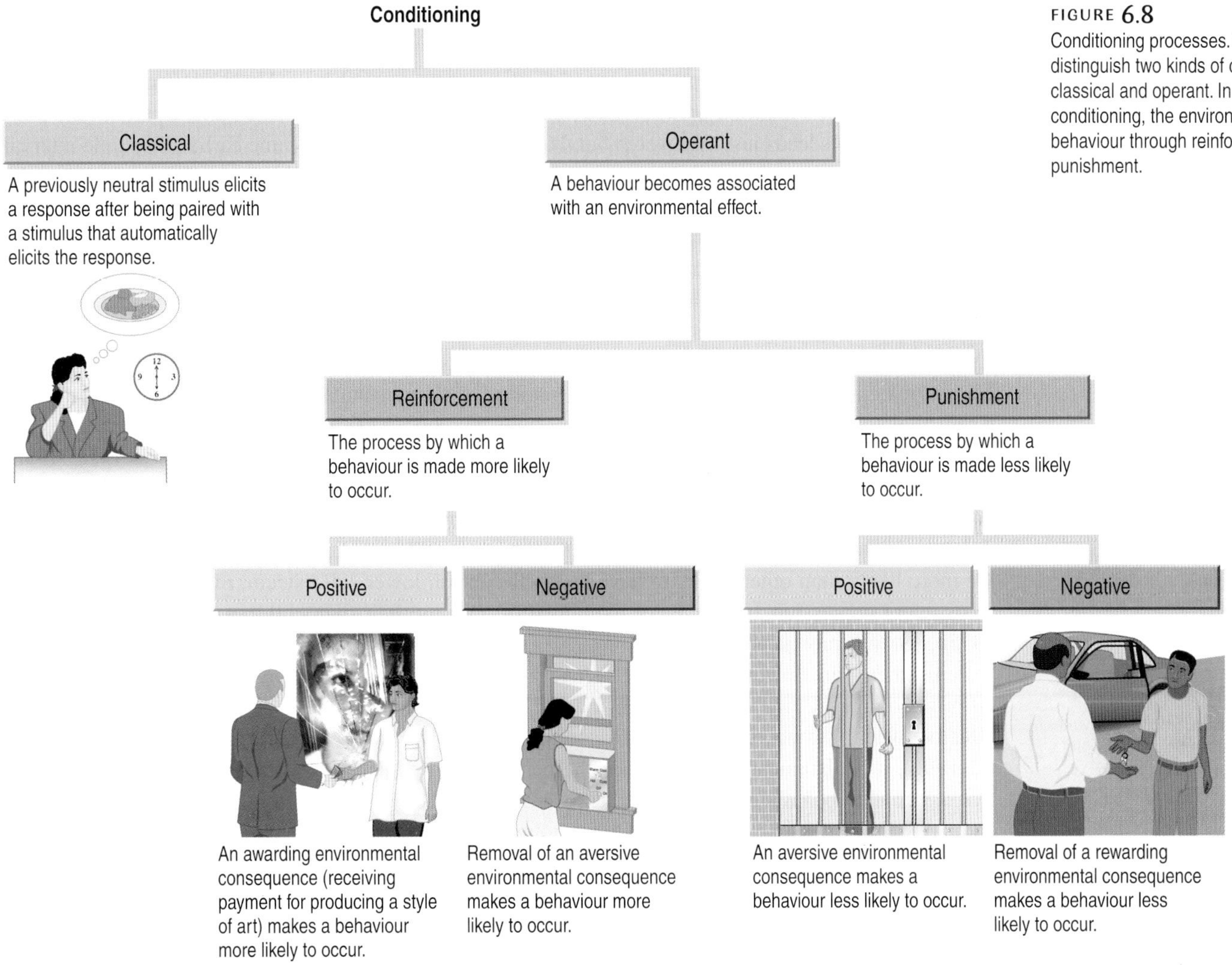

Conditioning

Classical

A previously neutral stimulus elicits a response after being paired with a stimulus that automatically elicits the response.

Operant

A behaviour becomes associated with an environmental effect.

Reinforcement

The process by which a behaviour is made more likely to occur.

Punishment

The process by which a behaviour is made less likely to occur.

Positive

An awarding environmental consequence (receiving payment for producing a style of art) makes a behaviour more likely to occur.

Negative

Removal of an aversive environmental consequence makes a behaviour more likely to occur.

Positive

An aversive environmental consequence makes a behaviour less likely to occur.

Negative

Removal of a rewarding environmental consequence makes a behaviour less likely to occur.

FIGURE 6.8
Conditioning processes. Behaviourists distinguish two kinds of conditioning: classical and operant. In operant conditioning, the environment influences behaviour through reinforcement and punishment.

Like reinforcement, punishment can be positive or negative. 'Positive' and 'negative' here do not refer to the feelings of the participants, who rarely consider punishment a positive experience. Positive simply means something is presented, whereas negative means something is taken away. In positive punishment, such as spanking, exposure to an aversive event following a behaviour reduces the likelihood of the operant recurring. Negative punishment involves losing, or not obtaining, a reinforcer as a consequence of behaviour, as when an employee fails to receive a pay increase because of frequent lateness.

Punishment is commonplace and essential in human affairs, because reinforcement alone does not inhibit many undesirable behaviours, but punishment is frequently applied in ways that render it ineffective (Chance, 1988; Goodman, 2006; Laub & Sampson, 1995; Lewis, 2006; Skinner, 1953). One problem in using punishment with animals and young children is that the learner may have difficulty distinguishing which operant is being punished. People who yell at their dog for coming after it has been called several times are actually punishing good behaviour — coming when called. The dog is more likely to associate the punishment with its action than its inaction — and is likely to adjust its behaviour accordingly, by becoming even less likely to come when called!

A second and related problem associated with punishment is that the learner may come to fear the person meting out the punishment (via classical conditioning) rather than the action (via operant conditioning). A child who is harshly punished by his father may become afraid of his father instead of changing his behaviour.

APPLY + DISCUSS

- Do humans differ from animals such as cats and dogs in their ability to anticipate punishment and hence to avoid behaviours that have never been punished?
- How would a behaviourist explain this phenomenon?

Third, punishment may not eliminate existing rewards for a behaviour. In nature, unlike the laboratory, a single action may have multiple consequences, and behaviour can be controlled by any number of them. A teacher who punishes the class clown may not have much success if the behaviour is reinforced by classmates. Sometimes, too, punishing one behaviour (such as stealing) may inadvertently reinforce another (such as lying).

Fourth, people typically use punishment when they are angry, which can lead both to poorly designed punishment (from a learning point of view) and to the potential for abuse. An angry parent may punish a child for misdeeds just discovered but that occurred a considerable time earlier. The time interval between the child's action and the consequence may render the punishment ineffective because the child does not adequately connect the two events. Parents also frequently punish depending more on their mood than on the type of behaviour they want to discourage, making it difficult for the child to learn what behaviour is being punished, under what circumstances and how to avoid it.

Finally, aggression that is used to punish behaviour often leads to further aggression. The child who is beaten typically learns a much deeper lesson: that problems can be solved with violence. Research in Australia has found that aggressive parents tend to have aggressive children (National Committee on Violence, 1990). In fact, the more physical punishment parents use, the more aggressively their children tend to behave at home and at school (Dodge, Lochman, Harnish, Bates, & Pettit, 1997; Dodge, Pettit, Bates, & Valente, 1995; Larzelere, Schneider, Larson, & Pike, 1996; Straus & Mouradian, 1998; Weiss, Dodge, Bates, & Pettit, 1992). Correlation does not, of course, prove causation; aggressive children may provoke punitive parenting. Nevertheless, the weight of evidence suggests that violent parents tend to create violent children. Adults who were beaten as children are more likely than other adults to have less self-control, lower self-esteem, more troubled relationships, more depression and a greater likelihood of abusing their own children and spouses (Rohner, 1975b, 1986; Straus & Kantor, 1994).

Punishment can, however, be used effectively and is essential for teaching children to control inappropriate outbursts, manipulative behaviour, disruptive behaviour and so forth. Punishment is most effective when it is accompanied by reasoning — even with two- and three-year-olds (Larzelere et al., 1996). It is also most effective when the person being punished is also reinforced for an alternative, acceptable behaviour. Explaining helps a child correctly connect an action with a punishment, and having other positively reinforced behaviours to draw on allows the child to generate alternative responses.

A longitudinal study of Australian children found that punishment styles had a significant impact on child development. For instance, the study indicated that outgoing children were more likely to develop behavioural problems if parents used high levels of punishment but were more likely to be well adjusted if they received parenting which channelled their energy and exuberance in positive ways (Hempill & Sanson, 2001).

ETHICAL DILEMMA

A trained psychologist works as part of an Allied Health team in a local hospital. The team proposes to use punishment to treat self-harming behaviours in autistic children. Specifically, autistic children with head-banging problems are targeted for inclusion in their treatment program. These children are to receive a mild electric shock as punishment when they bang their heads — the health team proposes that the shock itself is less damaging than the head-banging behaviours.

- Is the use of a mild electric shock justified here?
- How would informed consent be obtained?

ONE STEP FURTHER

Two-process learning theory and the unforgettable Grim Reaper

By Doctor Steve Provost, Southern Cross University

It is important to be able to distinguish between the two important forms of learning described in figure 6.8 (on the previous page). In the real world, however, it is unlikely that these forms of learning will influence behaviour independently. Two-process learning theory, first described by Mowrer (1960), provides an explanation of how classical and operant conditioning work together to produce profound, and sometimes problematic, changes in behaviour.

Two-process learning theory has been most useful in providing an explanation for, and suggesting ways of treating, human phobias. The first component of the acquisition of phobias is the conditioning of some strong affective response, such as fear. The example provided in the text is of fear of needles (the CS), which has been conditioned when they have been paired with the pain of an injection, sometimes long ago in the past. This is not really a problem, however, until the second form of learning, operant conditioning, comes into effect. This occurs when the fear elicited by the needle becomes a source of negative reinforcement for behaviours (such as never going to the dentist). The operant behaviour (avoidance) is the major problem, since it is likely to lead to disease and pain in the longer run, but its occurrence depends on the establishment of a source of reinforcement through the classical conditioning having taken place first. Treatment could thus focus on reducing fear of needles (a gentle dentist is a good first-step), finding sources of reinforcement for attending a dentist (e.g. 'How good will my Facebook picture look after I've had my teeth fixed?'), or both.

Two-process learning theory is not only important for explaining extreme forms of behaviour, such as phobias and post-traumatic stress disorder. The operation of classical and operant conditioning permeates everyday life. This has allowed the advertising industry to capitalise on what are referred to as 'fear appeals'. Fear appeal advertising has become extremely popular in recent years, although it has existed for at least as long as Palmolive decided to call its soap 'Lifebouy'. In fear appeals, the consumer is first motivated to feel afraid (germs on hands cause disease), and is then given a way to eliminate that fear (this soap kills germs) by purchasing a product. Perhaps the best known, and possibly most effective, fear appeal in the public health arena has been the 'Grim Reaper' advertisements that were televised in Australia when people were just becoming aware in the late 1980s of the danger posed by Acquired Immune Deficiency Syndrome (AIDS). The advertisement began with an image of the Grim Reaper at a bowling alley, sending gigantic bowling balls hurtling towards a group of people (his skittles). The voice-over informed the viewer that homosexuals and drug users were not the only people at risk from AIDS. The camera then focused on a variety of people, including women and children. This is classical conditioning at work, as the image of the Grim Reaper, which is strongly associated with death in Western culture, and the message that *all* people are at risk of this deadly disease were designed to instil fear. At the close of the advertisment, the voice-over provided the source of reinforcement for operant behaviour: 'If you have sex, have just one safe partner or always use condoms . . . always.' So, the viewer could be safe and eliminate their fear by observing the simple steps that were provided. This advertisement went to air with a massive public health effort to provide clean needles and condoms, particularly in areas in which highest-risk individuals were likely to be found.

The Grim Reaper AIDS campaign worked within a two-process learning framework: instilling fear and providing a behaviour message. If acted upon, this behaviour message promised a reduction in fear: making people less likely to acquire AIDS.

The success of the Grim Reaper advertisements depended on it working well within a two-process framework — eliciting fear and providing a clear behavioural message that could be reinforced by the reduction of that fear.

Extinction

As in classical conditioning, learned operant responses can be extinguished. Extinction occurs if enough conditioning trials pass in which the operant is not followed by the consequence previously associated with it. A child may study less if hard work no longer leads to reinforcement by parents (who may, for example, start taking good grades for granted and only comment on weaker grades), just as a manufacturer may discontinue a product that is no longer profitable.

Knowing how to extinguish behaviour is important in everyday life, particularly for parents. Consider the case of a 21-month-old boy who had a serious illness requiring around-the-clock attention (Williams, 1959). After recovering, the child continued to demand this level of attention. At bedtime, he screamed and cried unless a parent sat with him until he fell asleep, which could take up to two hours.

Relying on the principle that unreinforced behaviour will be extinguished, the parents, with some help from a psychologist, began a new bedtime regimen. In the first trial of the extinction series, they spent a relaxed and warm goodnight session with their son, closed the door when they left the room, and refused to respond to the wails and screams that followed. After 45 minutes, the boy fell asleep, and he fell asleep immediately on the second trial (figure 6.9). The next several bedtimes were accompanied by tantrums that steadily decreased in duration, so that by the tenth trial, the parents fully enjoyed the sound of silence.

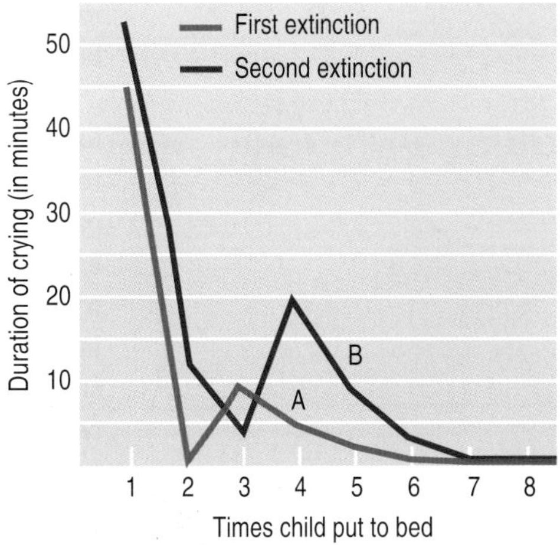

FIGURE 6.9
Extinction of tantrum behaviour in a 21-month-old child. As shown in curve A, the child initially cried for long periods of time, but very few trials of non-reinforced crying were required to extinguish the behaviour. In curve B, the behaviour was again quickly extinguished following its spontaneous recovery.

SOURCE: Williams (1959, p. 269).

As in classical conditioning, spontaneous recovery (in which a previously learned behaviour recurs without renewed reinforcement) sometimes occurs. In fact, the boy cried and screamed again one night when his aunt attempted to put him to bed. She inadvertently reinforced this behaviour by returning to his room; as a result, his parents had to repeat their extinction procedure.

INTERIM SUMMARY

Operant conditioning means learning to operate on the environment to produce a consequence. ***Operants*** are behaviours that are emitted rather than elicited by the environment. ***Reinforcement*** refers to a consequence that increases the probability that a response will recur. ***Positive reinforcement*** occurs when the environmental consequence (a reward or pay-off) makes a behaviour more likely to occur again. ***Negative reinforcement*** occurs when termination of an aversive stimulus makes a behaviour more likely to recur. Whereas reinforcement increases the probability of a response, ***punishment*** decreases the probability that a response will recur. Punishment is frequently applied in ways that render it ineffective. ***Extinction*** in operant conditioning occurs if enough trials pass in which the operant is not followed by the consequence previously associated with it.

Operant conditioning of complex behaviours

Thus far we have discussed relatively simple behaviours controlled by their environmental consequences — pigeons pecking, rats pressing and people showing up at work for a pay cheque. In fact, operant conditioning offers one of the most comprehensive explanations for the range of human and animal behaviour ever produced.

Schedules of reinforcement

In the examples described so far, an animal is rewarded or punished every time it performs a behaviour. This situation, in which the consequence is the same each time the animal emits a behaviour, is called a ***continuous reinforcement schedule*** (because the behaviour is continuously reinforced). A child reinforced for altruistic behaviour on a continuous schedule of reinforcement would be praised every time she shares, just as a rat might receive a pellet of food each time it presses a lever. Such consistent reinforcement, however, rarely occurs in nature or in human life.

More typically, an action sometimes leads to reinforcement but other times does not. Such reinforcement schedules are known as ***partial*** or ***intermittent schedules of reinforcement*** because the behaviour is reinforced only part of the time, or intermittently. (These are called schedules of reinforcement, but the same principles apply with punishment.)

Intuitively, one would think that continuous schedules would be more effective. Although this tends to be true during the initial learning (acquisition) of a response — presumably because continuous reinforcement makes the connection between the behaviour and its consequence clear and predictable — partial reinforcement is usually superior for maintaining learned behaviour. For example, suppose you have a relatively new car, and every time you turn the key, the engine starts. If, however, one day you try to start the car 10 times and the engine will not turn over, you will probably give up and call a towing company. Now suppose, instead, that you are the proud owner of a rusted-out 1972 Kingswood and are accustomed to 10 turns before the car finally cranks up. In this case, you may try 20 or 30 times before enlisting help. Thus, behaviours maintained under partial schedules are usually more resistant to extinction (Miller & Capaldi, 2006; Rescorla, 1999).

Intermittent reinforcement schedules may be either ratio schedules or interval schedules (Ferster & Skinner, 1957; Skinner, 1938):

- In ***ratio schedules***, pay-offs are tied to the number of responses emitted; only a fraction of 'correct' behaviours receive reinforcement, such as one out of every five.
- In ***interval schedules***, rewards (or punishments) are delivered only after some interval of time, no matter how many responses the organism emits.

Figure 6.10 illustrates the four reinforcement schedules we will now describe: fixed ratio, variable ratio, fixed interval and variable interval.

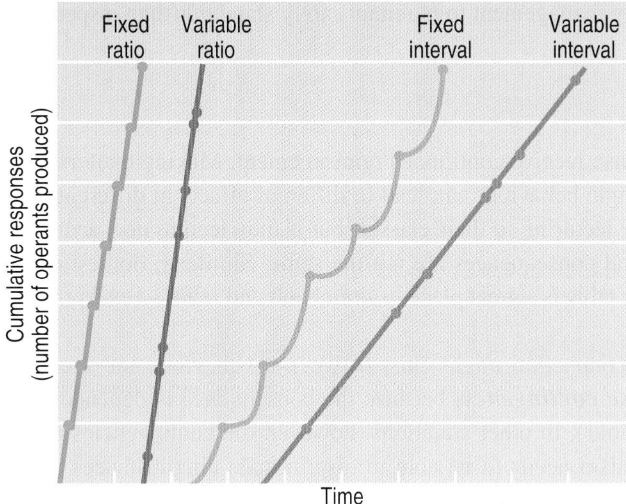

FIGURE 6.10
Schedules of reinforcement. An instrument called a cumulative response recorder graphs the total number of responses that a participant emits at any point in time. As the figure shows, different schedules of reinforcement produce different patterns of responding.

Fixed-ratio schedules

In a ***fixed-ratio (FR) schedule***, an organism receives reinforcement for a fixed proportion of the responses it emits. Piecework employment uses a fixed-ratio schedule of reinforcement: a worker receives payment for every bushel of apples picked (an FR-1 schedule) or for every 10 scarves woven (an FR-10 schedule). Workers weave the first nine scarves without reinforcement; the pay-off occurs when the tenth scarf is completed. As shown in figure 6.10, FR schedules are characterised by rapid responding, with a brief pause after each reinforcement.

Variable-ratio schedules

In ***variable-ratio (VR) schedules***, an animal receives a reward for some percentage of responses, but the number of responses required before reinforcement is unpredictable (that is, variable). Variable-ratio schedules specify an average number of responses that will be rewarded. Thus, a pigeon on a VR-5 schedule may be rewarded on its fourth, seventh, 13th and 20th responses, averaging one reward for every five responses. Variable-ratio schedules generally produce rapid, constant responding and are probably the most common in daily life (figure 6.10). For example, when fishing, you are not likely to be rewarded each time you cast your line into the water. However, on some occasions you will be.

APPLY + DISCUSS

- What kind of reinforcement schedule is involved in gambling and why is it so effective?

Fixed-interval schedules

In a ***fixed-interval (FI) schedule***, an animal receives reinforcement for its responses only after a fixed amount of time. On an FI-10 schedule, a rat gets a food pellet whether it presses the bar 100 times or one time during that 10 minutes, just as long as it presses the bar at some point during each 10-minute interval.

An animal on an FI schedule of reinforcement will ultimately learn to stop responding except towards the end of each interval, producing the scalloped cumulative response pattern shown in figure 6.10. Fixed-interval schedules affect human performance in the same way. For example, workers whose boss comes by only at two o'clock are likely to relax the rest of the day. Schools rely heavily on FI schedules; as a result, some students procrastinate between exams and pull 'all-nighters' when reinforcement (or punishment) is imminent. Politicians, too, seem to resemble rats in their response patterns (which would probably come as no surprise to many voters). The lead-up to election time in Australia and New Zealand is accompanied by both the government and opposition announcing new policies at a rapid rate, producing the same scalloped fixed-interval curve seen in figure 6.10.

Variable-interval schedules

A ***variable-interval (VI) schedule*** ties reinforcement to an interval of time, but unlike a fixed-interval schedule, the animal cannot predict how long that time interval will be. Thus, a rat might receive reinforcement for bar pressing, but only at five, six, 20 and 40 minutes (a VI-10 schedule — a reinforcer that occurs, on average, every 10 minutes). In the classroom, unexpected tests make similar use of VI schedules. Variable-interval schedules are more effective than fixed-interval schedules in maintaining consistent performance. Random, unannounced governmental inspections of working conditions in a factory are much more effective in getting management to maintain safety standards than inspections at fixed intervals.

Discriminative stimuli

In everyday life, then, rarely does a response receive continuous reinforcement. Making matters even more complicated for learners is that a single behaviour can lead to different effects in different situations. Professors receive a paycheque for lecturing to their classes, but if they lecture new acquaintances at a cocktail party, the environmental consequences are not the same. Similarly, domestic cats learn that the dining room table is a great place to stretch out and relax — except when their owners are home.

In some situations, a connection might exist between a behaviour and a consequence (called a ***response contingency***, because the consequence is dependent, or contingent, on the behaviour). In other situations, however, the contingencies might be different, so the organism needs to be able to discriminate circumstances under which different contingencies apply. A stimulus that signals the presence of particular contingencies of reinforcement is called a ***discriminative stimulus*** (S^D). In other words, an animal learns to produce certain actions only in the presence of the discriminative stimulus. For the professor, the classroom situation signals that lecturing behaviour will be reinforced. For the cat on the dinner table, the presence of humans is a discriminative stimulus signalling punishment. For the rats in one study, reinforcement occurred if they turned clockwise when they were placed in one chamber but counterclockwise when placed in another (Richards, Sabol, & Freed, 1990).

Stimulus discrimination is one of the keys to the complexity and flexibility of human and animal behaviour. Behaviour therapists, who apply behaviourist principles to maladaptive behaviours (chapter 16), use the concept of stimulus discrimination to help people recognise and alter some very subtle triggers for maladaptive responses, particularly in relationships (Kohlenberg & Tsai, 1994). For example, one couple was on the verge of divorce because the husband complained that his wife was too passive and indecisive, and the wife complained that her husband was too rigid and controlling. A careful behavioural analysis of their interactions suggested some complex contingencies controlling their behaviour. At times, the woman would detect a particular 'tone' in her husband's voice that she had associated with his getting angry; upon hearing this tone, she would 'shut down' and become more passive and quiet. Her husband found this passivity infuriating and would then begin to push her for answers and decisions, which only intensified her 'passivity' and his 'controlling' behaviour. She was not, in fact, always passive, and he was not always controlling. Easing the tension in the marriage thus required isolating the discriminative stimuli that controlled each of their responses.

APPLY + DISCUSS

There is sometimes a fine line between aggression on the sports field that is praised and aggression that is punished.

- How do people learn when aggression is likely to be reinforced or punished?
- Why do people sometimes produce responses destined to lead to aversive consequences?

INTERIM SUMMARY

In everyday life, ***continuous reinforcement schedules*** (in which the consequence is the same each time an animal emits a behaviour) are far less common than ***partial*** or ***intermittent reinforcement schedules*** (in which reinforcement occurs in some ratio or after certain intervals). A ***discriminative stimulus*** signals that particular contingencies of reinforcement are in effect, so that the organism only produces the behaviour in the presence of the discriminative stimulus.

Context

Thus far, we have treated operants as if they were isolated behaviours, produced one at a time in response to specific consequences. In fact, however, learning usually occurs in a broader context (see Herrnstein, 1970; Kordaki & Balomenou, 2006; Premack, 1965; Singer, 2006; Srinivasan & Hilty, 2006).

Costs and benefits of obtaining reinforcement

In real life, reinforcement is not infinite, and attaining one reinforcer may affect both its future availability and the availability of other reinforcers. Researchers studying the way animals forage in their natural habitats note that reinforcement schedules change because of the animal's own behaviour: by continually eating fruit from one tree, an animal may deplete the supply, so that remaining fruit must be obtained with more work (Stephens & Krebs, 1986).

Psychologists have simulated this phenomenon by changing contingencies of reinforcement based on the number of times rats feed from the same 'patch' in the laboratory (Collier, Johnson, & Berman, 1998; Shettleworth, 1988). Thus, a rat may find that the more it presses one lever, the less reward it receives at that lever but not at another. Researchers using this kind of experimental procedure have found that rats make 'choices' about how long to stay at a patch depending on variables such as its current rate of reinforcement, the average rate of reinforcement they could obtain elsewhere, and the amount of time required to get to a new 'patch'. Rats, it turns out, are good economists.

Obtaining one reinforcer may also adversely affect the chances of obtaining another. An omnivorous animal merrily snacking on some foliage must somehow weigh the benefits of its current refreshments against the cost of pursuing a source of protein it notices scampering nearby. Similarly, a person at a restaurant must choose which of many potential reinforcers to pursue, knowing that each has a cost and that eating one precludes eating the others.

The cost–benefit analysis involved in operant behaviour has led to an approach called behavioural economics, which weds aspects of behavioural theory with economics (Bickel, Green, & Vuchinich, 1995; Green & Freed, 1993; Rachlin, Green, Kagel, & Battalio, 1976). For example, some reinforcers, such as two brands of petrol, are relatively substitutable for each other, so that as the cost of one goes down, its consumption goes up and the consumption of the other decreases. Other reinforcers are complementary, such as meat pies and tomato sauce, so that if the cost of meat pies skyrockets, consumption of tomato sauce will decrease.

Psychologists have studied principles of behavioural economics in some ingenious ways in the laboratory using rats and other animals as subjects. For example, they put animals on a 'budget' by only reinforcing them for a certain number of lever presses per day; thus, the animals had to 'conserve' their lever presses to purchase the 'goods' they preferred (Rachlin et al., 1976). In contrast, decreasing the cost of food relative to water had much less effect on consumption. In the language of economics, the demand for water is relatively 'inelastic'; that is, it does not change much, regardless of the price.

Social and cultural context

We have spoken thus far as if reinforcement and punishment were unilateral techniques, in which one person (a trainer) conditions another person or animal (a learner). In fact, in human social interactions, each partner continuously uses operant conditioning techniques to mould the behaviour of the other. When a child behaves in a way his or her parents find upsetting, the parents are likely to punish the child. But the parents' behaviour is itself being conditioned: the operant of punishing the child will be negatively reinforced if it causes the child's bad behaviour to cease. Thus, the child is negatively reinforcing the parents' use of punishment just as the parents are punishing the child's behaviour! From this point of view, people reinforce and punish each other in nearly all their interactions (Homans, 1961).

The reliance on different operant procedures varies considerably cross-culturally. In part, this reflects the dangers that confront a society. The Gusii of Kenya, with a history of tribal warfare, face threats not only from outsiders but also from natural forces, including wild animals. Gusii parents tend to rely more on punishment and fear than on rewards in conditioning social behaviour in their children. Caning, food deprivation and withdrawing shelter and protection are common forms of punishment. One Gusii mother warned her child, 'If you don't stop crying, I shall open the door and call a hyena to come and eat you!' (LeVine & LeVine, 1963, p. 166). Death from wild animals is a real fear, so this threat gains compliance from Gusii children. In Judeo-Christian cultures, parents have often instilled the 'fear of God' in children to keep their behaviour in line.

By contrast, traditional Aboriginal communities did not rely as much on fear and punishment in teaching their children. In these societies, all members of the wider society were considered to play a part in the disciplining and education of children. The role of adults was to teach the child right and wrong, not to punish them for being wrong. Children were not taught to fear punishment for making a mistake because they knew they could trust their parents, teachers and the community to keep them safe (National Association for Prevention of Child Abuse and Neglect, 2004). This reflected the communal nature of hunter-gatherer Aboriginal societies, which placed greater emphasis on social identity and group membership than on individual identities (chapter 19). Cooperation was essential to survival (Bourke, Bourke, & Edwards, 1998).

Characteristics of the learner

An additional set of factors that increase the complexity of operant conditioning has to do less with the environment than with the learner. Environmental contingencies operate on an animal that already has behaviours in its repertoire, enduring ways of responding and species-specific learning patterns.

Capitalising on past behaviours: shaping and chaining

The range of behaviours humans and other animals can produce is made infinitely more complex by the fact that existing behaviours often serve as the raw material for novel ones. This occurs as the environment subtly refines them or links them together into sequences.

It is unusual to see a monkey wakeboard, and also to drink Pepsi, but these behaviours can be introduced by the process of shaping.

A procedure used by animal trainers, called ***shaping***, produces novel behaviour by reinforcing closer and closer approximations to the desired response. The key is to begin by reinforcing a response the animal can readily produce. Skinner (1951) described a shaping procedure that can be used to teach a dog to touch its nose to a cupboard door handle. Skinner's experiment demonstrates the use of ***successive approximations*** to produce the required shaping procedure. Successive approximations is the process of rewarding those behaviours that move the subject progressively closer to the desired behaviour. Trying to teach the dogs immediately the rather complex (for the canine world) association between touching the cupboard door handle and food would be difficult. Using successive approximations helps to gradually reach the goal step-by-step. The first step is to bring a hungry dog (in behavioural terms, a dog that has been deprived of food for a certain number of hours) into the kitchen and immediately reward him with food any time he happens to face the cupboard; the dog will soon face the cupboard most of the time. The next step is to reward the dog whenever it moves towards the cupboard, then to reward it when it moves its head so that its nose comes closer to the cupboard, and finally to reward the dog only for touching its nose to the cupboard handle. This shaping procedure should take no more than five minutes, even for a beginner.

With humans, shaping occurs in all kinds of teaching. Psychologists have used shaping with considerable success in helping autistic children (who tend to be socially unresponsive and uncommunicative and seem to 'live in their own worlds') speak and act in more socially appropriate ways (Greenberg, Seltzer, Hong, & Orsmond, 2006; Lovaas, 1977). The psychologist begins by initially rewarding the child for any audible sounds. Over time, however, the reinforcement procedure is refined until the child receives reinforcement only for complex language and behaviour. In one study, over 40 percent of autistic children achieved normal scores on IQ tests following this shaping procedure, in comparison to 2 percent of children in a control group (Lovaas, 1987). More recently, researchers in New Zealand have examined how autistic behaviours can be treated with behavioural analytic techniques based on control of stimulus and reinforcer (e.g. Mudford, 2004).

Shaping can allow psychologists to condition responses that most people would never think of as 'behaviours'. In ***biofeedback***, psychologists feed information back to patients about their biological processes, allowing them to gain operant control over autonomic responses such as heart rate, body temperature and blood pressure. As patients monitor their physiological processes on an electronic device or computer screen, they receive reinforcement for changes such as decreased muscle tension or heart rate.

Biofeedback can help patients reduce or sometimes eliminate problems such as high blood pressure, headaches and chronic pain (Arena & Blanchard, 1996; Gauthier, Ivers, & Carrier, 1996; Linden & Moseley, 2006; Nakao et al., 1997). For example, patients treated for chronic back pain with biofeedback in one study showed substantial improvement compared to control participants, and they maintained these benefits at follow-up over two years later (Flor, Haag, & Turl, 1986).

Whereas shaping leads to the progressive modification of a specific behaviour to produce a new response, ***chaining*** involves putting together a sequence of existing responses in a novel order. A psychologist tells the story of his brother using a variant of this operant technique. For several weeks, the brother awakened at four o'clock in the morning and, while everyone else slept soundly, trained the family cat to wake his brother by licking his face. This trick does not come naturally to most felines and required several steps to accomplish. The cat already knew how to climb, jump and lick, so the goal was to get the cat to perform these behaviours in a particular sequence. First, the 'trainer' placed pieces of cat food on the stairs leading up to his brother's bedroom. After several trials, the cat learned to climb the stairs. To reinforce the operant of jumping onto his brother's bed, the trainer again used a few judiciously placed bits of cat food. The same reward, placed gently in the proper location, was enough to train the cat to lick the brother's face. Once this occurred several times, the cat seemed to be reinforced simply by licking the brother's cheek.

Enduring characteristics of the learner

Not only do prior learning experiences influence operant conditioning, but so, too, do enduring characteristics of the learner. In humans as in other species, individuals differ in the ease with which they can be conditioned (Corr, Pickering, & Gray, 1995; Eysenck, 1990; Hooks, Jones, Juncos, Neill, & Justice, 1994). Individual rats vary, for example, in their tendency to behave aggressively or to respond with fear or avoidance in the face of aversive environmental events (e.g., Ramos, Berton, Mormede, & Chaouloff, 1997). Rats can also be selectively bred for their ability to learn mazes (Innis, 1992; van der Staay & Blokland, 1996).

MAKING CONNECTIONS

Humans, like other animals, differ in their 'conditionability'. Many individuals with **antisocial personality disorder**, who show a striking disregard for society's standards, are relatively unresponsive to punishment. Their lack of anxiety when confronted with potential punishment renders them less likely to learn to control behaviours that other people learn to inhibit (chapter 15).

The role of the learner is especially clear in an experiment that attempted to teach three octopi (named Albert, Bertram and Charles) to pull a lever in their saltwater tanks to obtain food (Dews, 1959). The usual shaping procedures worked successfully on Albert and Bertram, who were first rewarded for approaching the lever, then for touching it with a tentacle, and finally for tugging at it. With Charles, however, things were different. Instead of pulling the lever to obtain food, Charles tugged at it with such force that he broke it. Charles was generally a surly subject, spending much of his time 'with eyes above the surface of the water, directing a jet of water at any individual who approached the tank' (p. 62).

Species-specific behaviour and preparedness

Operant conditioning is influenced not only by characteristics of the individual but also by characteristics of the species. Just as some stimulus–response connections are easier to acquire in classical conditioning, certain behaviours are more readily learned by some species in operant conditioning — or may be emitted despite learning to the contrary. This was vividly illustrated in the work of Keller Breland and Marian Breland (1961), who worked with Skinner for a time. The Brelands went on to apply operant techniques in their own animal training business but initially with mixed success. In one case, they trained pigs to deposit wooden coins in a large 'piggy bank' in order to obtain food. After several months, however, the pig would lose interest in the trick, preferring to drop the coin, push it along the way with his snout, toss it in the air, push it, drop it, push it and so on. This pattern occurred with pig

APPLY + DISCUSS

Conditioning a rat to press a lever to avoid an electric shock may be difficult because a rat's natural response to shock is either to crouch and freeze or to run away, both of which interfere with bar pressing.

- To what extent do the same processes apply when humans 'freeze' while taking an exam or speaking in public?
- Do humans have innate tendencies to respond in certain ways when faced with threats?

after pig. The pigs' pushing, or 'rooting', behaviour eventually replaced the conditioned behaviour of depositing coins in the bank so completely that the hungry pigs were not getting enough food.

The Brelands had similar experiences with cats that stalked their food slots and raccoons that tried to wash the tokens they were to deposit in banks. All these operants were more closely related to instinctive, species-specific behaviours than the operants the Brelands were attempting to condition. Species-specific behavioural tendencies, like prepared learning in classical conditioning, make sense from an evolutionary perspective: pigs' rooting behaviour normally allows them to obtain food from the ground, and cats in the wild do not usually find their prey in bowls.

INTERIM SUMMARY

Learning occurs in a broader context than one behaviour at a time. Humans and other animals learn that attaining one reinforcer may affect attainment of others. Cultural factors also influence operant conditioning, as different cultures rely on different operant procedures. Characteristics of the learner influence operant conditioning, such as prior behaviours in the animal's repertoire, enduring characteristics of the learner (such as the tendency to respond with fear or avoidance in the face of aversive environmental events) and species-specific behaviour (the tendency of particular species to produce particular responses).

Cognitive–social theory

By the 1960s, many researchers and theorists had begun to wonder whether a psychological science could be built strictly on observable behaviours without reference to thoughts. Most agreed that learning is the basis of much of human behaviour, but some were not convinced that classical and operant conditioning could explain *everything* people do. From behaviourist learning principles thus emerged ***cognitive–social theory*** (sometimes called cognitive–social learning or cognitive–behavioural theory), which incorporates concepts of conditioning but adds two new features: a focus on cognition and a focus on social learning.

Learning and cognition

According to cognitive–social theory, the way an animal construes the environment is as important to learning as actual environmental contingencies. That is, humans and other animals are always developing mental images of, and expectations about, the environment, and these cognitions influence their behaviour.

Latent learning

Some of the first research to question whether a science of behaviour could completely dispense with thought was conducted by the behaviourist Edward Tolman. In a paper entitled 'Cognitive maps in rats and men', Tolman (1948) described learning that occurred when rats were placed in a maze without any reinforcement, similar to the kind of learning that occurs when people learn their way around a city while looking out the window of a bus. In one experiment, Tolman let rats wander through a maze in 10 trials on 10 consecutive days without any reinforcement (Tolman & Honzik, 1930). A control group spent the same amount of time in the maze, but these rats received food reinforcement on each trial.

The rats that were reinforced learned quite rapidly to travel to the end of the maze with few errors; not surprisingly, the behaviour of the unreinforced rats was less predictable. On the 11th day, however, Tolman made food available for the first time to the previously unreinforced rats and recorded the number of errors they made. As figure 6.11 shows, his findings were striking: these rats immediately took advantage of their familiarity with the maze and obtained food just as efficiently as the rats who had previously received reinforcement. A third group of rats who still received no reinforcement continued to wander aimlessly through the maze.

To explain what had happened, Tolman suggested that the rats who were familiar with the maze had formed ***cognitive maps*** — mental representations or images — of the maze, even though they had received no reinforcement. Once the rats were reinforced, their learning became observable. Tolman called learning that has occurred but is not currently manifest in behaviour, ***latent learning***. To cognitive–social theorists, latent learning is evidence that knowledge or beliefs about the environment are crucial to the way animals behave. So began the effort to look inside the black box that lies between behaviours and environmental events while still maintaining a scientific, experimental approach to behaviour.

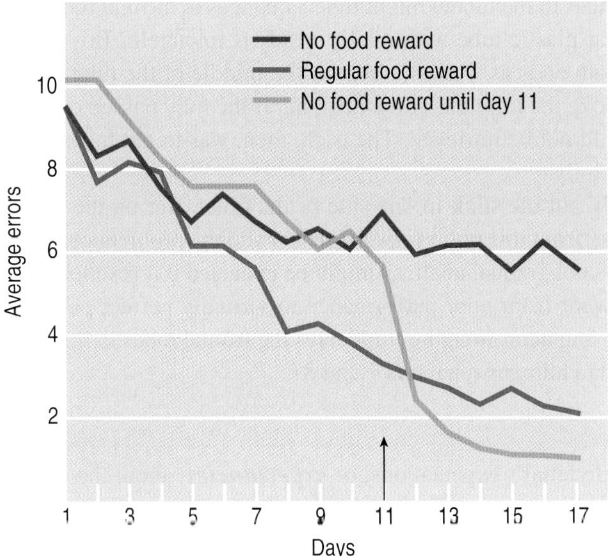

FIGURE 6.11
Latent learning. Rats that were not rewarded until the 11th trial immediately performed equally with rats that had been rewarded from the start. This suggests that they were learning the maze prior to reinforcement and were forming a cognitive map that allowed them to navigate it as soon as they received reinforcement.

SOURCE: Tolman and Honzik (1930, p. 267).

Conditioning and cognition

Many learning phenomena have been reinterpreted from a cognitive perspective. For example, in classical fear conditioning, why does an organism respond to a previously neutral stimulus with a conditioned response? A cognitive explanation suggests that the presence of the CS alerts the animal to prepare for a UCS that is likely to follow. In other words, as suggested earlier, the CS predicts the presence of the UCS. If a CS does not routinely predict a UCS, it will probably not draw a CR. Thus, when a UCS (such as electric shock) frequently occurs in the absence of a CS (a tone), rats are unlikely to develop a conditioned fear response to the CS, regardless of the number of times the CS has been paired with the UCS (Rescorla, 1988; Rescorla & Holland, 1982; Rescorla & Wagner, 1972).

In cognitive language, rats will not become afraid of a stimulus unless it is highly predictive of an aversive event. This does not imply that rats are conscious of these predictions; it simply means that their nervous systems are making these predictions. This was, in fact, an argument offered by Pavlov himself, who described these predictions as 'unconscious' (Pavlov, 1927). From a cognitive point of view, stimulus discrimination and generalisation similarly reflect an animal's formation of a concept of what 'counts' as a particular type of stimulus, which may be relatively general (any furry object) or relatively specific (a white rat).

Operant conditioning phenomena can also be reinterpreted from a cognitive framework. Consider the counterintuitive finding that intermittent reinforcement is more effective than continuous reinforcement in maintaining behaviour. From a cognitive standpoint, exposure to an intermittent reinforcement schedule (such as an old car that starts after five or 10 turns of the ignition) produces the expectation that reinforcement will only come intermittently. As a result, lack of reinforcement over several trials does not signal a change in environmental contingencies. In contrast, when the owner of a new car suddenly finds the engine will not turn over, he has reason to stop trying after only three or four attempts because he has come to expect continuous reinforcement.

Insight in animals

Insight is the sudden understanding of the relation between a problem and a solution. For most of this century, researchers have debated whether animals other than humans have the capacity for insight or whether other animals must always learn associations slowly through operant and classical conditioning (Boysen & Himes, 1999; Kohler, 1925; Thorndike, 1911).

Research with a chimpanzee named Sheba suggests that insight may not be restricted to humans. In one study, Sheba was shown into a room with four pieces of furniture that varied in kind and colour (Kuhlmeier, Boysen, & Mukobi, 1999). She was then taken from the room and shown a small-scale model of the room that contained miniature versions of the furniture, each in its appropriate location. The experimenter then allowed Sheba to watch as a miniature soft-drink can was hidden behind a miniature piece of furniture in the model. Upon returning to the full-sized room, Sheba went immediately to where the soft-drink can had been in the model and retrieved the real soft-drink that had been hidden there. Sheba had immediately formed the insight that changes in the model might reflect changes in the real room.

In another study, Sheba was shown a clear plastic tube with a lolly inside (Limongelli, Boysen, & Visalberghi, 1995). The tube had holes at both ends as well as a hole in the middle of the tube on the bottom surface. Sheba was given a stick to poke the lolly out of the tube, but if the lolly passed over the hole in the middle, it fell into a box and could not be retrieved. The trick, then, was to put the stick in the end of the tube that was farther from the lolly.

For the first several days, Sheba randomly put the stick in one side or the other. But on the eighth day, Sheba apparently had an insight, because from this point forward she solved the problem correctly 99 percent of the time. Her improvement was not gradual at all, as might be expected if it resulted from simple conditioning processes; rather, she went from poor performance to virtually perfect performance in an instant. As we will see, research using neuroimaging implicates the frontal lobes in this kind of 'thoughtful' mental activity in both apes and humans (chapters 7 and 8).

Expectancies

Cognitive–social theory proposes that an individual's expectations, or ***expectancies***, about the consequences of a behaviour are what render the behaviour more or less likely to occur. If a person expects a behaviour to produce a reinforcing consequence, she is likely to perform it as long as she has the competence or skill to do so (Mischel, 1973).

Julian Rotter (1954), one of the earliest cognitive–social theorists, distinguished expectancies that are specific to concrete situations ('If I ask this lecturer for an extension, he will refuse') from those that are more generalised ('You can't ask people for anything in life — they'll always turn you down'). Rotter was particularly interested in ***generalised expectancies*** — expectancies that influence a broad spectrum of behaviour. He used the term ***locus of control of reinforcement*** (or simply locus of control) to refer to the generalised expectancies people hold about whether or not their own behaviour can bring about the outcomes they seek (Rotter, 1954, 1990). Individuals with an ***internal locus of control*** believe they are the masters of their own fate. For example, an Australian study showed that people with an internal locus of control developed high quality relationships with their manager. This, in turn, predicted more favourable work-related outcomes and group relations (Martin, Thomas, Charles, Epitropaki, & McNamara, 2005). People with an ***external locus of control*** believe their lives are determined by forces outside (external to) themselves. Figure 6.12 shows items in Rotter's questionnaire for assessing locus of control. People who believe they control their own destiny are more likely to learn to do so, in part simply because they are more inclined to make the effort.

I more strongly believe that

1. Promotions are earned through hard work and persistence.	**OR**	Making a lot of money is largely a matter of getting the right breaks.
2. In my experience I have noticed that there is usually a direct connection between how hard I study and the grades I get.	**OR**	Many times the reactions of teachers seem haphazard to me.
3. I am the master of my fate.	**OR**	A great deal that happens to me is probably a matter of chance.

FIGURE 6.12
Items from Rotter's locus-of-control questionnaire, called the *Internal–External Scale*. The scale presents participants with a series of choices between two responses, one of which is internal and the other external.

SOURCE: Rotter (1971).

Learned helplessness and explanatory style

The powerful impact of expectancies on the behaviour of non-human animals was dramatically demonstrated in a series of studies by Martin Seligman (1975). Seligman harnessed dogs so that they could not escape electric shocks. At first the dogs howled, whimpered and tried to escape the shocks, but eventually they gave up; they would lie on the floor without struggle, showing physiological stress responses and behaviours resembling human depression. A day later Seligman placed the dogs in a shuttlebox from which they could easily escape the shocks. Unlike dogs in a control condition who had not been previously exposed to inescapable shocks, the dogs in the experimental condition made no effort to escape and generally failed to learn to do so even when they occasionally did escape. The dogs had come to expect that they could not get away; they had learned to be helpless. ***Learned helplessness*** consists of the expectancy that one cannot escape aversive events and the motivational and learning deficits that result from this belief.

Seligman argued that learned helplessness is central to human depression as well. In humans, however, learned helplessness is not an automatic outcome of uncontrollable aversive events. Seligman and his colleagues observed that some people have a positive, active coping attitude in the face of failure or disappointment, whereas others become depressed and helpless (Peterson, 2000a, 2000b; Peterson & Seligman, 1984). They demonstrated in dozens of studies that ***explanatory style*** — the way people make sense of bad events — plays a crucial role in whether or not they become, and remain, depressed (see also Wise & Rosqvist, 2006).

Individuals with a depressive or ***pessimistic explanatory style*** blame themselves for the bad things that happen to them. In the language of helplessness theory, pessimists believe the causes of their misfortune are internal rather than external, leading to lowered self-esteem. They also tend to see these causes as stable (unlikely to change) and global (broad, general and widespread in their impact). When a person with a pessimistic style does poorly on a biology exam, he may blame it on his own stupidity — an explanation that is internal, stable and global. Most people, in contrast, would offer themselves explanations that permit hope and encourage further effort, such as 'The exam was ridiculous'.

Whether optimists or pessimists are more accurate in these inferences is a matter of debate. Several studies suggest that pessimistic people are actually more accurate than optimists in recognising when they lack control over outcomes. According to this view, people who maintain positive illusions about themselves and their ability to control their environment are less accurate but tend to be happier and report fewer psychological symptoms such as depression and anxiety (Taylor & Brown, 1988; Taylor, Kemeny, Reed, Bower, & Gruenewald, 2000).

Other researchers have challenged these findings, however, showing that people who deny their problems or substantially overestimate their positive qualities tend to be more poorly adjusted socially than people who see themselves as others see them (Colvin, Block, & Funder, 1995; Shedler, Mayman, & Manis, 1993). Optimism and positive illusions about the self are probably useful up to a point, because confidence can spur action (Carver et al., 2005). However, when optimism verges on denial of obvious realities, it is likely to be neither healthy nor useful.

Whether or not pessimists are accurate in their beliefs, they clearly pay a price for their explanatory style. Numerous studies document that pessimists have a higher incidence of depression and lower achievement in school than optimists (Peterson & Seligman, 1984). As we will see (chapter 14), pessimists are also more likely to become ill and to die earlier than people who find other ways of finding meaning in bad events.

MAKING CONNECTIONS

People's **expectancies** — about what they can and cannot accomplish, about societal barriers to their goals (e.g. **prejudice**) and so forth — influence all aspects of their lives, from how hard they work to whether they feel hopeful or **depressed** (chapters 10, 12, 15 and 19).

The Anzac soldiers landing at Gallipoli in 1915 continued to move up the beach despite the high likelihood of death at the hands of Turkish soldiers shooting from the hills above. Their expectancies about how a soldier is supposed to behave and about their individual chance of survival played a part in ensuring they kept moving forward.

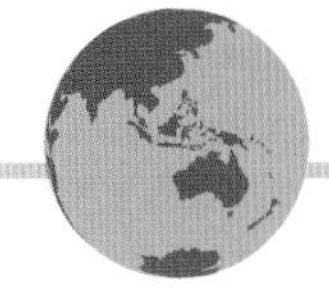

A GLOBAL VISTA

Optimism, pessimism and expectancies of control in cross-cultural perspective

Expectancies arise within a social and cultural context. Cultural belief systems offer individuals ways of interpreting experience that influence their beliefs in what they can and cannot control as well as their reactions to unpleasant events. For example, in the United States, people from fundamentalist religious backgrounds (both Christian and Jewish) tend to have more optimistic explanatory styles than non-fundamentalists (Sethi & Seligman, 1993). They believe their fate is in God's hands, which can be extremely comforting in the face of illness or death.

People who live in a society also share common experiences that lead to shared beliefs and expectancies. We often speak of 'culture' as if it were a single variable. However, cultural beliefs and practices only influence individual thought and action through specific shared experiences (Sapir, 1949; Strauss & Quinn, 1997).

Studies comparing people from East and West Berlin before the fall of the Berlin Wall demonstrate the impact of social, political and cultural factors on expectancies of control and optimism (Baltes & Staudinger, 2000; Oettingen, Little, Lindenberger, & Baltes, 1994; Oettingen & Seligman, 1990). Berliners shared a common culture until 1945, when the city was divided. Thereafter, West Berliners lived in an affluent, thriving country, in which individual initiative was rewarded through free enterprise. East Berliners, under Soviet domination, were much poorer and had fewer freedoms. Inefficient bureaucracies controlled many aspects of their daily lives, from the clothes that were available to the books they were allowed to read. These realities were reflected in a more pessimistic explanatory style and more external locus of control among East Berliners, patterns that could be observed as early as the school years.

Other studies document substantial cultural differences in expectancies. One study compared white American, Chinese American and mainland Chinese college students (Lee & Seligman, 1997). The mainland Chinese were much more pessimistic than white Americans; Chinese Americans were intermediate between the other two groups. White Americans tended to attribute their successes to themselves and their failures to others. Although obviously biased, this self-serving way of interpreting events is probably useful for people who live in a technologically developed, capitalist society that emphasises competition and achievement, because it keeps people going through the tough times. In contrast, mainland Chinese tended to attribute both positive and negative events to forces outside their control — a pattern much more common cross-culturally (Kluckhohn & Strodtbeck, 1961).

These results probably reflect both recent Chinese history, with its emphasis on communical work and communal values, as well as long-standing cultural differences between China and the United States. For hundreds of years of Chinese history, people have lived with their families in densely populated agricultural areas. In such environments, as elsewhere in Asia, excessive pride and self-centredness are disruptive and discouraged. Attributing successes to one's personal characteristics is likely to be neither adaptive nor accurate, since much labour in agricultural societies is communal, and families and villagers tend to share much of their fate. Chinese who immigrated to the United States appear to have begun to acquire more typically American patterns while retaining some of their cultural heritage in their explanatory style.

In traditional Aboriginal Australian society, there is a strong emphasis on collectivist values.

Traditional Aboriginal societies in Australia also featured much more of an emphasis on communal life and values than the individualistic orientation of contemporary Australians. In these hunter-gatherer societies, cooperation was essential to daily living, so a strong group identity helped all members survive. That communal view was also reflected in Aboriginal belief systems. In the Aboriginal world view, there is no division between the spiritual world and the material world (Bourke et al., 1998). The same spirits that inhabit and inspire the land and the animals it contains also give people their life force. Everything in the universe is connected. With this philosophy, individual life takes on much less importance than it does within European cultures (Bourke, 1989). Harmony with the natural world is stressed, rather than the approach of 'man controlling nature' which has characterised European notions of progress.

INTERIM SUMMARY

Cognitive–social theory incorporates concepts of conditioning from behaviourism but adds cognition and social learning. Many learning phenomena can be reinterpreted from a cognitive perspective. For example, intermittent reinforcement is more effective than continuous reinforcement because of the expectations, or ***expectancies***, humans and other animals develop. In humans, ***locus of control*** (generalised beliefs about their ability to control what happens to them) and ***explanatory style*** (ways of making sense of bad events) play important roles in the way people behave and make sense of events.

Social learning

As this discussion suggests, learning does not occur in an interpersonal vacuum. Cognitive–social theory proposes that individuals learn many things from the people around them, with or without reinforcement, through ***social learning*** mechanisms other than classical and operant conditioning.

A major form of social learning is ***observational learning*** — learning by observing the behaviour of others. The impact of observational learning in humans is enormous — from learning how to feel and act when someone tells an inappropriate joke, to learning what kind of clothes, haircuts or foods are fashionable. Albert Bandura (1967), one of the major cognitive–social theorists, provides a tongue-in-cheek example of observational learning in the story of a lonesome farmer who bought a parrot to keep him company. The farmer spent many long hours trying to teach the parrot to repeat the phrase 'Say uncle', but to no avail. Even hitting the parrot with a stick whenever it failed to respond correctly had no effect. Finally, the farmer gave up; in disgust, he relegated the parrot to the chicken coop. Not long afterward, the farmer was walking by the chicken coop when he heard a terrible commotion. Looking in, he saw his parrot brandishing a stick at the chickens and yelling, 'Say uncle! Say uncle!' The moral of the story is that the lesson intended in observational learning is not always the lesson learned.

Observational learning in which a person learns to reproduce behaviour exhibited by a model is called ***modelling*** (Bandura, 1967). The most well known modelling studies were done by Bandura, Ross, and Ross (1961, 1963) on children's aggressive behaviour. In these studies, children observed an adult model interacting with a large inflatable doll named Bobo. One group of children watched the model behave in a subdued manner, while other groups observed the model verbally and physically attack the doll in real life, on film or in a cartoon. A control group observed no model at all. Children who observed the model acting aggressively displayed nearly twice as much aggressive behaviour as those who watched the non-aggressive model or no model at all (figure 6.13). The likelihood that a person will imitate a model depends on a number of factors, such as the model's prestige, likeability and attractiveness. An Australian study showed toddlers a rubber snake and spider paired alternatively with either negative or positive facial expressions by their mothers. Gerull and Rapee (2002) showed that the children showed greater fear expressions and avoidance of stimuli following negative reactions from their mothers.

APPLY + DISCUSS

In Bandura's classic Bobo studies, children learned by observation.

- To what extent does watching aggressive television shows make children more aggressive?
- How could a psychologist design a study to find out? What kind of practical and ethical obstacles might the psychologist face?

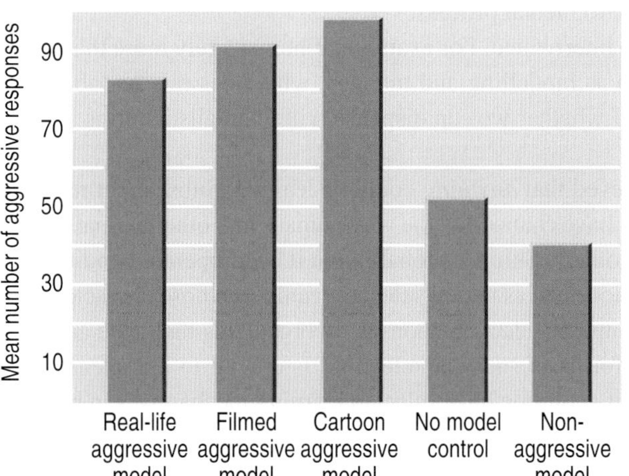

FIGURE 6.13
Social learning of aggressive behaviour through modelling. This figure shows the average number of aggressive responses made by children after observing an adult model playing with an inflatable doll in each of five experimental conditions: real-life aggressive model, filmed aggressive model, cartoon aggressive model, no model control and non-aggressive model. As can be seen, children tend to perform the behaviours of adult models.

SOURCE: Bandura (1967, p. 45).

Whether an individual actually performs modelled behaviour also depends on the behaviour's likely outcome. This outcome expectancy is, itself, often learned through an observational learning mechanism known as vicarious conditioning. In ***vicarious conditioning***, a person learns the consequences of an action by observing its consequences for someone else. For example, adolescents' attitudes towards high-risk behaviours such as drinking and having unprotected sex are influenced by their perceptions of the consequences of their older siblings' risk-taking behaviour (D'Amico & Fromme, 1997).

In a classic study of vicarious conditioning, Bandura et al. (1963) had pre-school children observe an aggressive adult model named Rocky. Rocky took food and toys that belonged to someone named Johnny. In one condition, Johnny punished Rocky; in the other, Rocky packed all of Johnny's toys in a sack, singing, 'Hi ho, hi ho, it's off to play I go' as the scene ended. Later, when placed in an analogous situation, the children who had seen Rocky punished displayed relatively little aggressive behaviour. In contrast, those who had seen Rocky rewarded behaved much more aggressively. Because Rocky's aggressive behaviour exemplified what the children had previously learned was bad behaviour, however, even those who followed his lead displayed some ambivalence when they saw his behaviour rewarded. One girl voiced strong disapproval of Rocky's behaviour but then ended the experimental session by asking the researcher, 'Do you have a sack?'

Another form of social learning is direct ***tutelage*** — teaching concepts or procedures primarily through verbal explanation or instruction. This is a central mechanism involved in formal education — and is (hopefully) occurring at this very moment. At times, conditioning processes, direct tutelage and observational learning can influence behaviour in contradictory ways. For example, most children receive the direct message that alcohol is harmful to their health (tutelage). At the same time, they learn to associate alcohol with positive images through advertising (classical conditioning) and may see high-status peers or parents smoking (modelling). In many cases, however, social learning processes, such as learning from a textbook (tutelage), work in tandem with conditioning processes. Most readers have been reinforced for completing reading assignments — and may also be reinforced by noticing that this chapter is almost over.

INTERIM SUMMARY

Social learning refers to learning that occurs through social interaction. ***Observational learning*** occurs as individuals learn by watching the behaviour of others. Learning to reproduce behaviour exhibited by a model is called ***modelling***. ***Vicarious conditioning*** means learning by observing the consequences of a behaviour for someone else. ***Tutelage*** occurs when people learn through direct instruction.

Central questions revisited

◆ What have we learned about learning?

We began with three questions: To what extent are humans like other animals in the way they learn? What constraints and possibilities has evolution placed on what we can learn? And to what extent can we understand learning without reference to mental processes?

In many respects, these three questions are intertwined. For example, if humans rely more than other animals on social learning mechanisms such as modelling and tutelage, what does this say about the evolution of learning or about the question of whether we can dispense with mentalistic terms such as thoughts and motives?

Watson and many early behaviourists believed that *anything* could be learned. Subsequent research showed, however, that evolutionary pressures have channelled the way humans and other animals learn, facilitating some associations and inhibiting others. Skinner probably put it best: operant conditioning is nothing but a continuation of natural selection. Just as nature selects organisms whose characteristics are adaptive to their environment, the environment selects responses by organisms that have adaptive consequences. The link between these two forms of 'natural selection' is crucial to a contemporary understanding of learning: millions of years of evolution have selected learning mechanisms in humans and other animals that themselves facilitate adaptation.

An even more fundamental shift has occurred in psychologists' conceptions of learning itself. Skinner and others who called themselves radical behaviourists argued that the best way to keep psychology scientific is to focus on what can be directly observed: behaviours and environmental events. Today, researchers from a more cognitive perspective view learning not primarily as a set of behavioural tendencies evoked by different situations but as the accumulation and mental organisation of knowledge (see Canfield & Ceci, 1992; Rescorla, 1999; Solmon, 2006). Psychologists now speak more freely of thoughts, emotions, motives, goals and stresses that interact to produce behavioural outcomes. Many contemporary behaviourists even refer to psychological processes such as thoughts and feelings as private behaviours, to which the same laws of learning can be applied.

Skinner and other behaviourists wanted to avoid mentalistic explanations for a reason. Two thousand five hundred years of philosophical speculation about the mind had led to hundreds of great ideas — but no way to test them. Skinner's argument was simple and compelling: we cannot test what we cannot observe, and we cannot observe what is in other people's heads. In less than a century, behaviourally oriented researchers have, through systematic experimentation, produced a body of generalisations about conditioning processes that will undoubtedly be a permanent legacy to psychology. Psychologists armed with principles of learning generated in the laboratory have been able to use these principles to improve people's lives (e.g. by helping individuals overcome phobias or uncontrollable panic attacks; chapter 16). Perhaps as significant as its contributions to the understanding of learning is another important legacy of behaviourism: a hard-nosed attitude towards psychological observation and explanation and a sceptical attitude towards speculation without empirical support.

Today, many psychologists disagree with Skinner's belief that scientific explanation is incompatible with mentalistic explanation, particularly now that we can watch the brain in action as people look at objects, recall past experiences or solve mathematical problems. Nevertheless, the principles of learning he and his colleagues discovered remain central to our understanding of behaviour, and Skinner will no doubt be remembered as one of the greatest minds — or, as he might prefer, one of greatest emitters of scientifically important verbal behaviour — in the history of the discipline.

◆

SUMMARY

1 Learning

- ***Learning*** refers to any enduring change in the way an organism responds based on its experience. Learning theories assume that experience shapes behaviour, that learning is adaptive and that uncovering laws of learning requires systematic experimentation.

2 Classical conditioning

- ***Conditioning*** is a type of learning studied by behaviourists. ***Classical conditioning*** refers to learning in which an environmental stimulus produces a response in an organism. An innate reflex is an ***unconditioned reflex***. The stimulus that produces the response in an unconditioned reflex is called an ***unconditioned stimulus*** or ***UCS***. An ***unconditioned response (UCR)*** is a response that does not have to be learned. A ***conditioned response (CR)*** is a response that has been learned. A ***conditioned stimulus (CS)*** is a stimulus that, through learning, has come to evoke a conditioned response.
- Once an organism has learned to produce a CR, it may respond to stimuli that resemble the CS with a similar response. This phenomenon is called ***stimulus generalisation***. ***Stimulus discrimination*** is the learned tendency to respond to a very restricted range of stimuli or to only the one used during training. ***Extinction*** in classical conditioning refers to the process by which a CR is weakened by presentation of the CS without the UCS; that is, the response is extinguished.
- Factors that influence classical conditioning include the ***interstimulus interval*** (the time between presentation of the CS and the UCS), the individual's learning history and ***prepared learning***.
- Neuroscientists have begun to track down the neural processes involved in classical conditioning. Research on the marine snail *Aplysia* and on ***long-term potentiation (LTP)*** in more complex animals suggests that learning involves an increase in the strength of synaptic connections through changes in the presynaptic neuron (which more readily releases neurotransmitters), changes in the postsynaptic neuron (which becomes more excitable) and probably an increase in dendritic connections between the two.

3 Operant conditioning

- Thorndike's ***law of effect*** states that an animal's tendency to produce a behaviour depends on that behaviour's effect on the environment. Skinner elaborated this idea into the concept of ***operant conditioning***, which means learning to operate on the environment to produce a consequence. ***Operants*** are behaviours that are emitted rather than elicited by the environment. A consequence is said to lead to ***reinforcement*** if it increases the probability that a response will recur. A ***reinforcer*** is an environmental consequence that occurs after an organism has produced a response, which makes the response more likely to recur.
- ***Positive reinforcement*** is the process whereby presentation of a stimulus (a reward or pay-off) after a behaviour makes the behaviour more likely to occur again. A ***positive reinforcer*** is an environmental consequence that, when presented, strengthens the probability that a response will recur.
- ***Negative reinforcement*** is the process whereby termination of an aversive stimulus (a negative reinforcer) makes a behaviour more likely to recur. ***Negative reinforcers*** are aversive or unpleasant stimuli that strengthen a behaviour by their removal. Whereas the presentation of a positive reinforcer rewards a response, the removal of a negative reinforcer rewards a response.
- Reinforcement always increases the probability that a response will recur. In contrast, ***punishment*** decreases the probability of a response, through either exposure to an aversive event following a behaviour (positive punishment) or losing or failing to obtain reinforcement previously associated with behaviour (negative punishment). Punishment is commonplace in human affairs but is frequently applied in ways that render it ineffective.
- ***Extinction*** in operant conditioning occurs if enough conditioning trials pass in which the operant is not followed by its previously learned environmental consequence.
- Four phenomena in particular help explain the power of operant conditioning: schedules of reinforcement, ***discriminative stimuli*** (stimuli that signal to an organism that particular contingencies of reinforcement are in effect), the behavioural context and characteristics of the learner.
- In a ***continuous schedule of reinforcement***, the environmental consequence is the same each time an animal emits a behaviour. In an ***intermittent schedule of reinforcement***, reinforcement does not occur every time the organism emits a particular response. In a ***fixed-ratio (FR) schedule of reinforcement***, an organism receives reinforcement at a fixed rate, according to the number of operant responses emitted. As in the fixed-ratio schedule, an animal on a ***variable-ratio (VR) schedule*** receives a reward for some percentage of responses, but the number of responses required before each reinforcement is unpredictable. In a ***fixed-interval (FI) schedule***,

an animal receives reinforcement for its responses only after a fixed amount of time. In a ***variable-interval (VI) schedule***, the animal cannot predict how long that time interval will be.

- The operant conditioning of a given behaviour occurs in the context of other environmental contingencies (such as the impact of obtaining one reinforcer on the probability of obtaining another) and broader social and cultural processes. Characteristics of the learner also influence operant conditioning, such as prior behaviours in the animal's repertoire, enduring characteristics of the learner and species-specific behaviour.
- Operant and classical conditioning share many common features, such as extinction, prepared learning, discrimination, generalisation and the possibility of maladaptive associations. Although operant conditioning usually applies to voluntary behaviour, it can also be used in techniques such as ***biofeedback*** to alter autonomic responses, which are usually the domain of classical conditioning. In everyday life, operant and classical conditioning are often difficult to disentangle because most learned behaviour involves both.

4 Cognitive–social theory

- ***Cognitive–social theory*** incorporates concepts of conditioning from behaviourism but adds two additional features: a focus on cognition and on social learning. Tolman demonstrated that rats formed ***cognitive maps*** or mental images of their environment and that these were responsible for ***latent learning*** — learning that has occurred but is not currently manifest in behaviour. Many classic learning phenomena have been reinterpreted from a cognitive perspective, including stimulus discrimination and generalisation.
- According to cognitive–social theory, the way an animal construes the environment is as important to learning as actual environmental contingencies. Cognitive–social theory proposes that expectations or ***expectancies*** of the consequences of behaviours are what render behaviours more or less likely to occur. ***Locus of control*** refers to the generalised expectancies people hold about whether or not their own behaviour will bring about the outcomes they prefer. ***Learned helplessness*** involves the expectancy that one cannot escape aversive events and the motivational and learning deficits that accrue from it. ***Explanatory style*** refers to the way people make sense of bad events. Individuals with a depressive or ***pessimistic explanatory style*** see the causes of bad events as internal, stable and global. Expectancies such as locus of control and explanatory style differ across cultures, since cultural belief systems offer people ready-made ways of interpreting events, and people who live in a society share common experiences (such as work and schooling) that lead to shared beliefs and expectancies.
- Psychologists have studied several kinds of ***social learning*** (learning that takes place as a direct result of social interaction), including ***observational learning*** (learning by observing the behaviour of others) and ***tutelage*** (direct instruction). Observational learning in which a human (or other animal) learns to reproduce behaviour exhibited by a model is called ***modelling***. In ***vicarious conditioning***, a person learns the consequences of an action by observing its consequences for someone else.

KEY TERMS

REVIEW QUESTIONS

1. Describe the differences between an unconditioned stimulus (UCS) and a conditioned stimulus (CS), and between an unconditioned response (UCR) and a conditioned response (CR).
2. Distinguish between stimulus generalisation and stimulus discrimination.
3. Explain the differences between positive and negative reinforcement and positive and negative punishment, using examples to illustrate.
4. Describe the processes involved in extinction and spontaneous recovery in both classical conditioning and operant conditioning.
5. Describe how social learning is important in the cognitive social theory of learning.

DISCUSSION QUESTIONS

1. Is punishment an effective way to discipline children?
2. Why do people develop superstitious behaviours?
3. Is it better to have an internal or external locus of control?

APPLICATION QUESTIONS

1. Test your understanding of classical conditioning by identifying the unconditioned stimulus (UCS), unconditioned response (UCR), conditioned stimulus (CS) and conditioned response (CR) in each of the examples below. Use the spaces provided below for your answers.
   (a) Alicia lived in Darwin when Cyclone Tracy destroyed the city. On the night of the cyclone, she was in a house that had its roof torn off. She was terrified. Now, whenever she hears a weather person on the television talking about a cyclone, she starts to tremble.

   UCS ______________ → UCR ______________
   ||
   CS ______________ → CR ______________

   (b) Every now and then, an ice-cream truck that plays the *Play School* theme song drives past little Benjamin's house. Whenever Benjamin eats ice-cream from the truck, he gets excited. One morning, his sister Emily turned on the television and the *Play School* theme song started to play. Benjamin jumped around excitedly repeating the word 'ice-cream'.

   UCS ______________ → UCR ______________
   ||
   CS ______________ → CR ______________

   (c) Tricia lives near a seafood restaurant where they have an 'all you can eat' offer every Tuesday night. The walls of the restaurant are painted bright blue. Unfortunately, Tricia was sick one Tuesday night after eating the seafood special. Now whenever she enters a room with bright blue walls, she starts to feel sick in the stomach.

   UCS ______________ → UCR ______________
   ||
   CS ______________ → CR ______________

   (d) Yuri used to work in a bakery. One day, his right arm was badly burned when it was caught in the oven that bakes the bread. He was in severe pain for several weeks and still has burn scars on that arm. While Yuri was out shopping with his wife the other day, he passed a bakery. As soon as he smelled the fresh bread, he started to have a panic attack.

   UCS ______________ → UCR ______________
   ||
   CS ______________ → CR ______________

   (e) Mai and Tran went to a restaurant to have lunch. The song *Unforgettable* played softly in the background. While they were there, Tran looked lovingly into Mai's eyes and asked her to marry him. Mai was ecstatic and said yes right away. The next day, Mai turned on the car radio on her way to work. As soon as she heard the song *Unforgettable*, she felt all warm and tingly inside.

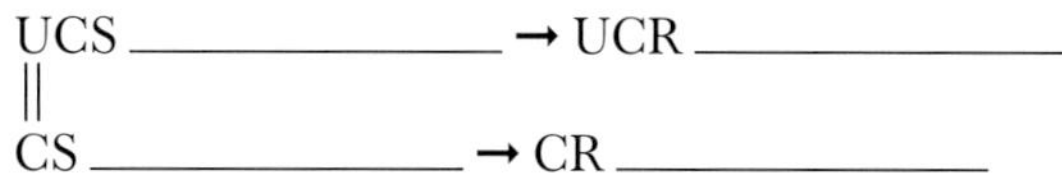

2. Complete the following exercises to test your understanding of (a) the various types of consequences that can occur in operant conditioning, (b) the schedules of reinforcement in operant conditioning and (c) the differences between classical conditioning, operant conditioning and social learning.
   (a) Indicate whether each of the examples below involve positive reinforcement (PR), negative reinforcement (NR), punishment (P) or extinction (E).
      (i) A student fails an assignment because the marker found evidence of plagiarism. ______________
      (ii) Daniel gives an employee a bonus because of their increased productivity. ______________

(iii) Vesna puts up an umbrella so that she will not get wet during a storm. ____________

(iv) Giovanni enjoys being the centre of attention at a party. He likes to tell jokes and make everybody laugh. Unfortunately, he has been telling inappropriate jokes during morning tea time at work. His colleagues decide to ignore his jokes instead of laughing at them. ____________

(b) Indicate whether each of the examples below involve continuous reinforcement (CR), fixed-ratio (FR), variable-ratio (VR), fixed-interval (FI) or variable-interval (VI) schedules.

(i) Every time Tirta puts money in the chocolate machine, he gets a chocolate. ____________

(ii) Dean likes to visit the casino to play the pokies. Sometimes, he wins money after putting in just a few coins. Other times, he has to put in $20 worth of coins before he wins any money. ____________

(iii) Bruce is a retired professional athlete. He signs a contract that allows him to provide expert commentary at the Olympic Games every four years. ____________

(iv) Yasmin is studying for a mathematics exam. To motivate herself to study, she decides to reward herself with a Tim Tam biscuit for every five problems she completes. ____________

(v) Timiko earns her pay by performing at local cultural events held approximately every two weeks. ____________

(c) Indicate whether each of the following examples illustrates principles of classical conditioning (CC), operant conditioning (OC) or social learning (SL).

(i) Every time Nola feeds her cat, she tinkles a spoon on the can of cat food. Eventually, her cat starts meowing whenever he hears a tinkling sound in the kitchen. ____________

(ii) Murray's girlfriend was about to arrive for dinner, when Murray remembered that he had not prepared any dessert. He quickly whipped up a sponge pudding, remembering how to make it from watching his mother. ____________

(iii) *Joe in the Big Smoke* is a hit television show with a string of television drama awards to the producer's credit. During the past year, the producer decided to sway from the show's usual story plots and try something different. The show did not receive high ratings and failed to win the 'best drama' award for the first time in three years. The following year, the producer reverted to the old story plots. ____________

(iv) Lucienne has worked as an apprentice chef for the past three years. The new head chef is delighted with her culinary skills and constantly praises her in front of the other apprentices. After a couple of weeks of constant praise, Lucienne starts to feel happy as soon as she arrives at work. She begins to work longer hours more often because she really enjoys the supportive work environment. ____________

The solutions to the application questions can be found on page 834.

MULTIMEDIA RESOURCES

The *Cyberpsych* multimedia resource is available *as an option* to accompany this textbook to further develop your understanding of many key psychology concepts. *Cyberpsych* contains a wealth of rich media content and activities, and for this chapter includes an interactive module on classical conditioning.

7 Memory

LEARNING OBJECTIVES

After studying this chapter you should be able to:

1. describe memory and outline the model of information processing
2. describe working memory
3. outline the major types of long-term memory
4. describe how information is encoded and organised in long-term memory
5. explain why remembering, misremembering and forgetting occur.

Memory and information processing

- For information to come back to mind after it is no longer present, it has to be represented. ***Sensory representations*** store information in a sensory mode; ***verbal representations*** store information in words.
- The standard model of memory is predicated on the metaphor of the mind as a computer; it distinguishes three memory stores: ***sensory memory***, ***short-term memory (STM)*** and ***long-term memory (LTM)***.

Varieties of long-term memory

- ***Declarative memory*** refers to memory for facts and events; it can be ***semantic*** or ***episodic***. ***Procedural memory*** refers to 'how to' knowledge of procedures or skills.
- ***Explicit memory*** refers to conscious recollection. ***Implicit memory*** refers to memory that is expressed in behaviour.
- ***Everyday memory*** refers to memory as it occurs in daily life.

Encoding and organisation of long-term memory

- To be retrieved from memory, information must be ***encoded***, or cast into a representational form or 'code' that can be readily accessed.
- ***Mnemonic devices*** are systematic strategies for remembering information.
- Knowledge stored in memory forms ***networks of association*** — clusters of interconnected information.
- LTM is organised in terms of schemas, organised knowledge structures or patterns of thought.

Working memory

- ***Working memory*** refers to the temporary storage and processing of information that can be used to solve problems, respond to environmental demands or achieve goals.
- Baddeley and Hitch's (1974) model proposed rehearsal, reasoning and making decisions about how to balance two tasks are the work of a limited-capacity central executive system.
- Most contemporary models distinguish between a visual store (the visuospatial sketchpad) and a verbal store.
- Working memory and LTM are distinct from one another in both their functions and neuroanatomy, but interact to help enhance memory capacities.

Remembering, misremembering and forgetting

- Psychologists often distinguish between the availability of information in memory and its accessibility.
- People make memory errors for a variety of reasons.
- Psychologists have proposed several explanations for why people forget, including decay, interference and motivated forgetting.
- Memories recovered in therapy cannot be assumed to be accurate, but they also cannot be routinely dismissed as false.
- Specific kinds of distortion can also occur within the memories of people whose brains have been affected by illness or injury. ***Anterograde amnesia*** involves the inability to retain new memories. By contrast, ***retrograde amnesia*** involves losing memories from a period before the time that a person's brain was damaged.

A visual overview of memory

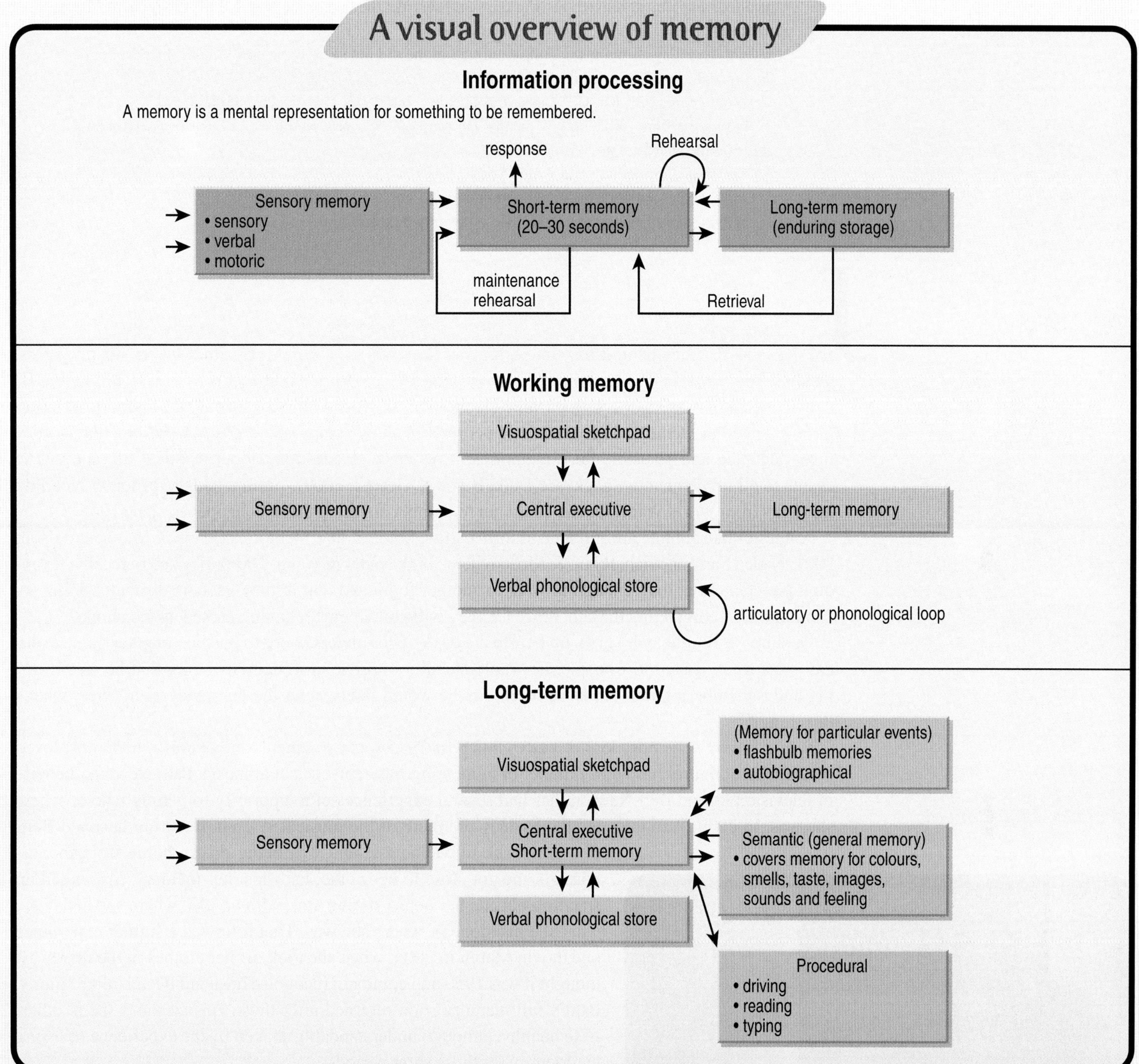

Central questions: what is memory?

- The concept of memory is expanding and we are beginning to see an integration among the differing psychological perspectives.

Jimmie, a healthy and handsome 49-year-old, was a fine-looking man with curly gray hair. He was cheerful, friendly and warm.

'Hi, Doc!' he said. 'Nice morning! Do I take this chair here?'

He was a genial soul, very ready to talk and to answer any question I asked him. He told me his name and birth date, and the name of the little town in Connecticut where he was born . . . He recalled, and almost relived, his war days and service, the end of the war and his thoughts for the future . . .

With recalling, Jimmie was full of animation; he did not seem to be speaking of the past but of the present . . . A sudden, improbable suspicion seized me.

'What year is this, Mr. G.?' I asked, concealing my perplexity in a casual manner.

'Forty-five, man. What do you mean?' He went on, 'We've won the war, FDR's dead, Truman's at the helm. There are great times ahead.'

'And you, Jimmie, how old would you be?'

Oddly, uncertainly, he hesitated a moment as if engaged in calculation.

'Why, I guess I'm nineteen, Doc. I'll be twenty next birthday.'

Sacks (1970, pp. 21–23).

JIMMIE was decades behind the times: he was nearly 50 years old. His amnesia, or memory loss, resulted from Korsakoff's syndrome, a neurodegenerative condition that occurs as a result of vitamin B_1 deficiency and is associated with chronic alcoholism. In Korsakoff's syndrome, the subcortical structures involved in memory deteriorate, and people can show symptoms of ***confabulation***; that is, they invent detailed and plausible false memories in response to questions about personal life and public events to fill in the memory gaps (see Dalla Barba & Decaix, 2009). Jimmie had no difficulty recalling incidents from World War II, but he could not remember anything that had happened since 1945.

Amnesics like Jimmie are still able to form certain kinds of new memories (Knott & Marlsen-Wilson, 2001; Nadel, Samsonovich, Ryan, & Moscovitch, 2000; Nader & Wang, 2006). If asked to recall a seven-digit phone number long enough to walk to another room and dial it, they have no difficulty doing so. A minute after completing the call, however, they will not remember having picked up the phone.

Or suppose Jimmie, who grew up before the days of computers, were to play a computer game every day for a week. Like most people, he would steadily improve at it, demonstrating that he was learning and remembering new skills.Yet each day he would likely greet the computer with, 'Gee, what's this thing?'

While Jimmy's memory loss of key events post-1945 was permanent, one of Australia's most loved entertainment figures has had a number of more temporary episodes of amnesia. Patti Newton, the wife of television legend Bert Newton, has had several experiences of temporarily forgetting who or where she was. In 2009, Patti attended the Sydney premiere of the musical *Wicked*, featuring husband Bert. She flew back to Melbourne and was being driven home from the airport. As she got close to her home, Patti lost her memory. She ended up standing outside her house staring at it, with no idea where she had been, what she had done or where she was. That followed a similar experience one day in March in 2006, when she took off her clothes in the driveway, thought it was 1950 and could not recognise husband Bert. Unlike Jimmy, Patti's full memory soon returned after those episodes and she is otherwise healthy, although understandably shaken by the experience of losing her identity for those short periods.

Matt Damon's character Jason Bourne successfully evaded numerous killers in the popular *Bourne* trilogy of films, remembering how to survive even with memory loss.

While Patti Newton's memory loss was very much a real-life experience, amnesia is often depicted in movies and on television. The extremely popular trilogy of movies about Jason Bourne features actor Matt Damon as a former assassin who has lost his identity and is on a mission to put his life back together. While he cannot remember his name or his past, Jason Bourne has not forgotten how to survive — a skill that comes in extremely handy as he eludes numerous potential killers on his way to uncovering his past. Similarly, in the popular children's movie *Finding Nemo*, one of the characters, a reef fish called Dory, has a profound memory deficit that prevents her from learning or retaining any new information, remembering names, or knowing where she is going (see Baxendale, 2004).

Case studies of neurologically impaired patients and experimental studies of normal subjects have demonstrated that memory is not a single function that a person can have or lose. Rather, memory is composed of several systems. Just how many systems, and how independently they function, are questions at the heart of contemporary research.

The previous chapter was dominated by the behaviourist perspective; this one and the next focus primarily on the cognitive perspective. We begin by considering some of the basic features of memory and an evolving model of information processing that has guided research on memory for over three decades. We then explore the memory systems that allow people to store information temporarily and permanently, and examine why people sometimes forget and misremember. Along the way, we consider the implications of memory research for issues such as the accuracy of eyewitness testimony in court and the existence of repressed memories in victims of childhood sexual abuse.

Two questions form the backdrop of this chapter. The first is deceptively simple: What does it mean to remember? Is memory simply the recollection of 'facts'? Or does memory extend to the activation (or reactivation) of goals, emotions and behaviours — as when we effortlessly 'remember' how to drive, even while deeply engrossed in conversation? Second, what is the relationship between the kind of learning described in the last chapter, which emphasised behaviours and emotional responses, and memory?

Central questions

- What does it mean to remember?
- What is the relationship between learning and memory?

Memory and information processing

Memory is so basic to human functioning that we take it for granted. Consider what was involved the last time you performed the seemingly simple task of remembering a friend's phone number. Did you bring to mind a visual image (a picture of the number), an auditory 'image' (pronouncing a series of numbers out loud in your mind) or simply a pattern of motor movements as you punched the numbers on the phone? How did you bring to mind this particular number, given that you probably have a dozen other numbers stored in memory? Once a number was in your mind, how did you know it was the right one? And were you aware as you reached for the phone that you were remembering at that very moment how to use a phone, what phones do, how to lift an object smoothly to your face, how to push buttons and who your friend is?

This example suggests how complex the simplest act of memory is. Memory involves taking something we have observed, such as a written phone number, and converting it into a form we can store, retrieve and use. We begin by briefly considering the various ways the brain can preserve the past — the 'raw material' of memory — and an evolving model of information processing that has guided psychologists' efforts to understand memory for the last quarter of a century.

MAKING CONNECTIONS

Although olfactory memory is less 'accurate' than visual memory, it is far more emotionally charged. The smell of freshly cut grass can evoke powerful emotional memories from childhood. The scent of a favourite perfume may elicit recognition from grandmother, even in the last stages of Alzheimer's. Thus, **smell** (chapter 4) and **emotion** (chapter 11) are strongly linked by memory.

Mental representations

For a sound, image or thought to return to mind when it is no longer present, it has to be represented in the mind — literally, re-presented, or presented again — this time without the original stimulus. As we saw in chapter 4, a mental representation is a psychological version or mental model of a stimulus or category of stimuli. In neuropsychological terms, it is the patterned firing of a network of neurons that forms the neural 'code' for an object or concept, such as 'dog' or 'sister'.

Representational modes are like languages that permit conversation within the mind (see Jackendoff, 1996). The content of our thoughts and memories — a bird, an angry friend, a beautiful sunset — can be described or translated into many 'languages' — images, sounds, words and so forth — but some languages cannot capture certain experiences the way others can. Fortunately, we are all 'multilingual' and frequently process information simultaneously using multiple representational codes (chapter 3).

Some kinds of representation are difficult to conceptualise and have received less attention from researchers. For example, people store memories of actions, such as how to press the buttons on a phone or how to squeeze the last drops of tomato sauce out of the bottle, which suggests the existence of motoric representations, or stored memories of muscle movements. The most commonly studied representations are sensory and verbal.

Fans of pop star Pink would likely find it easier to 'hear' one of her songs than to describe it.

Sensory representations

Sensory representations store information in a sensory mode, such as the sound of a dog barking or the image of a city skyline. The cognitive maps discovered in rats running mazes (chapter 6) probably include visual representations. People rely on visual representations to recall where they left their keys last night or to catch a ball that is sailing towards them through the air. Visual representations are like pictures that can be mentally scrutinised or manipulated (Burton, 2003; Burton & Fogarty, 2003; Kosslyn, 1983).

The auditory mode is also important for encoding information (Thompson & Paivio, 1994). Some forms of auditory information are difficult to represent in any other mode. For instance, most readers would be able to retrieve a tune by Powderfinger, Pink or Guy Sebastian with little difficulty, but would have much more trouble describing the melody than 'hearing' it in their minds.

Other types of sensory information have their own mental codes as well. People can identify many objects by smell, a finding that suggests that they are comparing current sensory experience with olfactory knowledge (Degel, Piper, & Koster, 2001; Schab & Crowder, 1995). Olfactory representations in humans are, however, far less reliable than visual representations in identifying even common objects (de Wijk, Schab, & Cain, 1995). For example, if exposed to the smell of a lemon, people often misidentify it as an orange, whereas people with an intact visual system rarely confuse the two fruits visually. More recent research indicates that two odours need to be presented initially as a mixture, rather than as two separate odours, to increase participants' similarity ratings of the two odours in each pair. This perceptual learning effect is rapid and resistant to interference (Stevenson, Case, & Boakes, 2005).

Verbal representations

Although many representations are stored in sensory modes, much of the time people think using ***verbal representations***, or information stored in words. Try to imagine what 'liberty' or 'mental representation' means without thinking in words. Other experiences, in contrast, are virtually impossible to describe or remember verbally, such as the smell of bacon. In fact, using words to describe things about which one has little verbal knowledge can actually disrupt sensory-based memory.

Neuroimaging studies confirm that verbal representations are in fact distinct from sensory representations. Consider what happens when researchers present participants with a string of X's versus a word (Menard, Kosslyn, Thompson, Alpert, & Rauch, 1996). Both stimuli lead to activation of the visual cortex, since both are processed visually. Presentation of the word, however, leads to additional activation of a region at the juncture of the left occipital, parietal and temporal lobes that appears to be involved in transforming the visual representation into a verbal or semantic one.

INTERIM SUMMARY

For information to come back to mind after it is no longer present, it has to be represented. ***Sensory representations*** store information in a sensory mode; ***verbal representations*** store information in words. People also store knowledge about actions as motoric representations.

Information processing: an evolving model

Psychologists began studying memory in the late nineteenth century, although interest in memory waned under the influence of behaviourism until the 'cognitive revolution' of the 1960s. In 1890, William James proposed a distinction between two kinds of memory, which he called primary and secondary memory. Primary memory is immediate memory for information momentarily held in consciousness, such as a telephone number. Secondary memory is the vast store of information that is unconscious except when called back into primary memory, such as the 10 or 20 phone numbers a person could bring to mind if he wanted to call various friends, family members, shops and so forth. James' distinction is embodied in what we will call the standard model of memory. This model has guided research on memory and cognition since the 1960s (Atkinson & Shiffrin, 1968; Healy & McNamara, 1996).

The standard model is predicated on the metaphor of the mind as a computer, which places information into different memory stores (the system's 'hardware') and retrieves and transforms it using various programs ('software'). According to this model (figure 7.1), memory consists of three stores:

sensory registers, short-term memory (James' primary memory) and long-term memory (James' secondary memory). Storing and retrieving memories involve passing information from one store to the next and then retrieving the information from long-term memory.

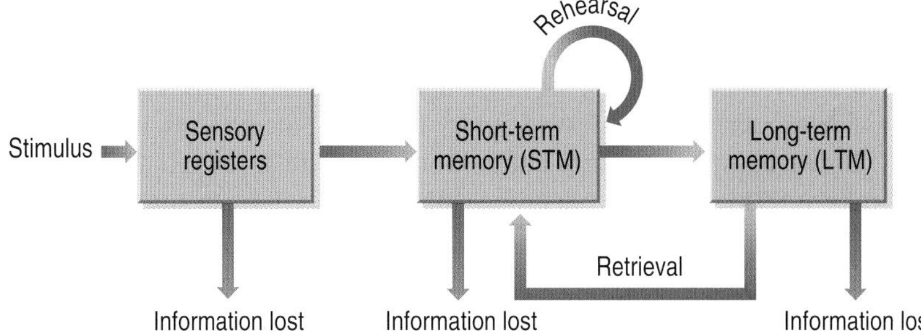

FIGURE 7.1
Standard model of memory. Stimulus information enters the sensory registers. Some information enters STM and is then passed on for storage in LTM. Information can be lost from any of the sensory stores, usually if it is not very important or if a traumatic event has occurred that interferes with memory consolidation or retrieval.

Sensory registers

Suppose you grab a handful of coins (say, six or seven) from your pocket at the laundromat and, while looking away, stretch out your hand so that all of the coins are visible. If you then glance for a second at your hand but look away before counting the change, you are still likely to be able to report accurately the number of coins in your hand because the image is held momentarily in your visual sensory register. ***Sensory registers*** hold information about a perceived stimulus for approximately half a second after the stimulus disappears, allowing a mental representation of it to remain in memory briefly for further processing (figure 7.2) (Sperling, 1960).

Display	Tone	Response
M Q T Z	High	
R F G A	Medium	If low tone was sounded
N S L C	Low	"N, S, L, C"

FIGURE 7.2
Visual sensory register. In a classic experiment, participants briefly viewed a grid of 12 letters and then heard a tone after a short delay. They had been instructed to report the top, middle or bottom row, depending on whether a high, medium or low tone sounded. If the tone sounded within half a second, they were 75 percent accurate, by reading off the image in their mind (iconic storage). If the tone sounded beyond that time, their accuracy dropped substantially because the visual image had faded from the sensory register.

SOURCE: Sperling (1960).

Most research has focused on visual and auditory sensory registration. The term ***iconic storage*** describes momentary memory for visual information. For a brief period after an image disappears from vision, people retain a mental image (or 'icon') of what they have seen. This visual trace is remarkably accurate and contains considerably more information than people can report before it fades (Baddeley & Patterson, 1971). The duration of icons varies from approximately half a second to two seconds, depending on the individual, the content of the image and the circumstances (Neisser, 1976). The auditory counterpart of iconic storage is called ***echoic storage***, momentary memory for auditory information (Battacchi, Pelamatti, Umilta, & Michelotti, 1981; Neisser, 1967).

APPLY + DISCUSS

- In what ways is the mind like a computer?
- In what ways does the computer metaphor fail to capture important aspects of human psychological functioning?

Short-term memory

According to the standard model, then, the first stage of memory is a brief sensory representation of a stimulus. Many stimuli that people perceive register for such a short time that they drop out of the memory system without further processing, as indicated in figure 7.1 ('information lost'). Other stimuli make a greater impression. Information about them is passed on to ***short-term memory (STM)***, a memory store that holds a small amount of information in consciousness — such as a phone number — for roughly 20 to 30 seconds, unless the person makes a deliberate effort to maintain it longer by repeating it over and over (Waugh & Norman, 1965). See Nairne (2002) for a review of recent research that identifies the conceptual and empirical problems of the standard model of STM. Nairne argues that STM is cue driven, much like long-term memory, and that neither rehearsal nor decay is likely to explain short-term forgetting.

Limited capacity

Short-term memory has limited capacity — that is, it does not hold much information. To assess STM, psychologists often measure participants' digit span; that is, how many numbers they can hold in mind at once. On average, people can remember about seven pieces of information at a time, with a normal range of from five to nine items (Miller, 1956). That phone numbers in most countries are five to seven digits long is no coincidence.

Hermann Ebbinghaus (1885/1964) was the first to note the seven-item limit to STM. Ebbinghaus pioneered the study of memory using the most convenient and agreeable subject he could find — himself — with a method that involved inventing some 2300 nonsense syllables (such as *pir* and *vup*). Ebbinghaus randomly placed these syllables in lists of varying lengths and then attempted to memorise the lists; he used nonsense syllables rather than real words to try to control the possible influence of prior knowledge on memory. Ebbinghaus found that he could memorise up to seven syllables, but no more, in a single trial. The limits of STM seem to be neurologically based, as they are similar in other cultures, including those with very different languages (Yu et al., 1985).

(a) **7638826**
(b) 7638826 (20 seconds later)
(c) **918**8326 (25 seconds later)

FIGURE 7.3
Short-term memory. In an experimental task, the participant is presented with a string of seven digits (a). Without rehearsal, 20 seconds later, the representations of the digits have begun to fade but are still likely to be retrievable (b). At 25 seconds, however, the experimenter introduces three more digits, which 'bump' the earliest of the still-fading digits (c).

Because of STM's limited capacity, psychologists often liken it to a lunch counter (Bower, 1975). If only seven stools are available at the counter, some customers will have to get up before new customers can be seated. Similarly, new information 'bumps' previous information from consciousness. Figure 7.3 illustrates this bumping effect.

Rehearsal

Short-term memory is not, however, a completely passive process of getting bumped off a stool. People can control the information stored in STM. For example, after looking up a phone number, most people will repeat the information over and over in their minds — a procedure called ***rehearsal*** — to prevent it from fading until they have dialled the number. This kind of mental repetition in order to maintain information in STM is called ***maintenance rehearsal***.

Rehearsal is also important in transferring information to long-term memory, a finding that will not surprise anyone who has ever memorised a poem or a maths formula by repeating it over and over. As we will see, however, maintenance rehearsal is not as useful for storing information in long-term memory as actively thinking about the information while rehearsing, a procedure known as ***elaborative rehearsal***. Remembering the words to a poem, for example, is much easier if the person really understands what it is about, rather than just committing each word to memory by rote.

INTERIM SUMMARY

The standard model of memory is predicated on the metaphor of the mind as a computer. It distinguishes three memory stores: sensory memory (or sensory registers), short-term memory and long-term memory. ***Sensory registers*** hold information about a perceived stimulus for approximately half a second after the stimulus disappears. From the sensory registers, information is passed on to a limited-capacity ***short-term memory (STM)***, which holds up to seven pieces of information in consciousness for roughly 20 to 30 seconds unless the person makes a deliberate effort to maintain it by repeating it over and over (***maintenance rehearsal***). ***Elaborative rehearsal***, which involves actually thinking about the material while committing it to memory, is more useful for long-term than for short-term storage.

Long-term memory

Just as relatively unimportant information drops out of memory after brief sensory registration, the same is true after storage in STM. An infrequently called phone number is not worth cluttering up the memory banks. More important information, however, goes on to ***long-term memory (LTM)***, in which representations of facts, images, thoughts, feelings, skills and experiences may reside for as long as a lifetime. According to the standard model, the longer information remains in STM, the more likely it is to make a permanent impression in LTM. Recovering information from LTM, known as ***retrieval***, involves bringing it back into STM (which is often used in information-processing models as a synonym for consciousness).

Why did researchers distinguish short-term from long-term memory? One reason was simple: short-term memory is brief, limited in capacity and quickly accessed, whereas LTM is enduring, virtually limitless, but more difficult to access (as anyone knows who has tried to recall a person's name or a term on an exam without success).

Another reason emerged as psychologists tested memory using free-recall tasks. In free-recall tasks, the experimenter presents participants with a list of words, one at a time, and then asks them to recall as many as possible. When the delay between presentation of the list and recall is short, participants demonstrate a phenomenon known as the ***serial position effect***: a tendency to remember information towards the beginning and end of a list rather than in the middle (figure 7.4).

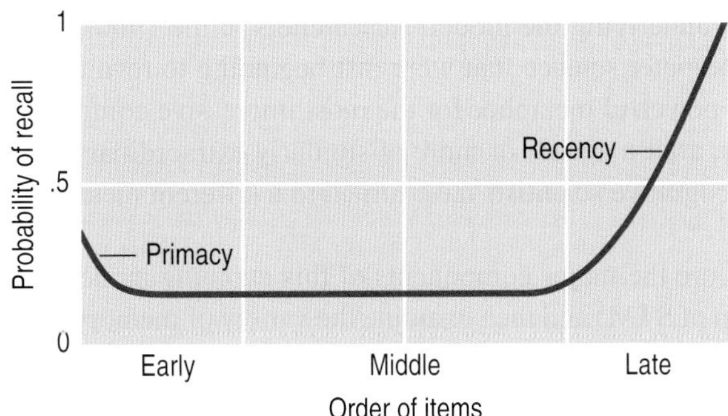

FIGURE 7.4
Serial position effect. Items earlier in a list and those at the end show a heightened probability of recall in comparison to those in the middle.

SOURCE: Atkinson and Shiffrin (1968).

Evolution of the model

Although the standard model provides a basic foundation for thinking about memory, in the last decade it has evolved in four major respects. First, the standard model is a serial processing model: it proposes a series of stages of memory storage and retrieval that occur one at a time (serially) in a particular order, with information passing from the sensory registers to STM to LTM. For information to get into LTM, it must first be represented in each of the prior two memory stores, and the longer it stays in STM, the more likely it is to receive permanent storage in LTM.

Subsequent research suggests that a serial processing model cannot provide a full account of memory. Most sensory information is never processed consciously (i.e. placed in STM), but it can nevertheless be stored and retrieved — an explanation for the familiar experience of finding oneself humming a tune that was playing in the background at a store without ever having noticed consciously that it was playing.

Further, the process of selecting which sensory information to store in STM is actually influenced by LTM; that is, LTM is often activated *before* STM rather than after it. The function of STM is to hold important information in consciousness long enough to use it to solve problems and make decisions. But how do we know what information is important? The only way to decide which information to bring into STM is to compare incoming data with information stored in LTM that indicates its potential significance (Logie, 1996). Thus, LTM must actually be engaged *before* STM to figure out how to allocate conscious attention (chapter 5).

A second major shift is that researchers have come to view memory as involving a set of ***modules*** — discrete but interdependent processing units responsible for different kinds of remembering. These modules operate simultaneously (i.e. in parallel), rather than serially (one at a time) (Fodor, 1983; Rumelhart, McClelland, & the PDP Research Group, 1986). This view fits with neuropsychological theories suggesting that the central nervous system consists of coordinated but autonomously functioning systems of neurons.

For instance, when people simultaneously hear thunder and see lightning, they identify the sound using auditory modules in the temporal cortex and identify the image as lightning using visual modules in the occipital and lower (inferior) temporal lobes (the 'what' pathway), and pinpoint the location of the lightning using a visual–spatial processing module (the 'where' pathway) that runs from the occipital lobes through the upper (superior) temporal and parietal lobes (chapter 4). When they remember the episode, however, all three modules are activated at the same time, so they have no awareness that these memory systems have been operating in parallel.

Similarly, researchers have come to question whether STM is really a single memory store. As we will see shortly, experimental evidence suggests that STM is part of a working memory system that can briefly keep at least three different kinds of information in mind simultaneously so that the information is available for conscious problem solving (Baddeley, 1992, 1995).

Third, researchers once focused exclusively on conscious recollection of word lists, nonsense syllables and similar types of information. Cognitive psychologists now recognise other forms of remembering that do not involve retrieval into consciousness. An amnesic like Jimmie (whose case opened this chapter) who learns a new skill, or a child who learns to tie a shoe, is storing new information in LTM. When this information is remembered, however, it is expressed directly in skilled behaviour rather than retrieved into consciousness or STM. Further, researchers are now paying

APPLY + DISCUSS

At times, we all have trouble remembering certain things, such as a friend's birthday. But, what about remembering to remember? If I put a shirt in the dryer to dry for only 20 minutes, I need to remember in a short time to take the shirt out of the dryer.

- What part of the memory system do you think is related to remembering to remember?
- During the 20-minute interval that the shirt is drying, do most people constantly rehearse in their minds that they need to take the shirt out? Do they use external memory aids, such as a timer?
- How successful are you at remembering to remember?

closer attention to the kinds of remembering that occur in everyday life, as when people remember emotionally significant events or try to remember to pick up several items at the supermarket on the way home from work.

The fourth change is a shift in the metaphor underlying the model. Researchers in the 1960s were struck by the extraordinary developments in computer science that were just beginning to revolutionise technology, and they saw in the computer a powerful metaphor for the most impressive computing machine ever designed: the human mind. Today, after a decade or more of similarly extraordinary progress in unravelling the mysteries of the brain, cognitive scientists have turned to a different metaphor: mind as brain.

In the remainder of this chapter we will explore the major components of this evolving model. We begin with working memory (the current version of STM) and then examine the variety of memory processes and systems that constitute LTM.

INTERIM SUMMARY

In ***long-term memory (LTM)***, representations of facts, images, thoughts, feelings, skills and experiences may reside for as long as a lifetime. Recovering information from LTM, or ***retrieval***, involves bringing it back into STM. The ***serial position effect*** is a tendency to remember information towards the beginning and end of a list rather than from the middle. Although the standard model still provides a foundation for thinking about memory, in the last decade it has evolved in four major ways. First, the assumption that a serial processing model can account for all of memory no longer seems likely. Second and related, researchers have come to view memory as involving a set of ***modules*** — discrete but interdependent processing units responsible for different kinds of remembering that operate simultaneously (in parallel) rather than sequentially (one at a time). Third, the standard model overemphasises conscious memory for relatively neutral facts and underemphasises other forms of remembering, such as skill learning and everyday remembering. Fourth, the underlying metaphor has changed, from mind as computer to mind as brain.

ONE STEP FURTHER

The accuracy of memory testing

By Professor Craig Speelman, Edith Cowan University

All theories of memory are designed to explain the performance of people on some memory test. Typically, a group of people, or even several groups of people, are tested in a similar manner, and their data is averaged. This average data is the target of explanations for these theories. But how accurate is this average data as an indicator of performance?

An illustration of how problematic averaged data can be comes from Heathcote, Brown, and Mewhort (2000). The target of their investigation was the ‘power law of learning’. This refers to the observation that improvement in the speed of performing a task with practice has a characteristic pattern: performance improves by large amounts early in practice, but these increments in performance get smaller as practice proceeds. The smooth trend in these learning curves can, more often than not, be described well by a power function. Such curves have been observed in fields as disparate as cigar rolling (Crossman, 1959), reading mirror-reversed text (Kolers, 1976) and implicit memory (Kirsner & Speelman, 1996), and are similar to retention and forgetting curves in memory (Ebbinghaus, 1885/1964). So ubiquitous is this observation that it has been said to comprise one of the few laws in psychology (Newell & Rosenbloom, 1981), and to be the one fact that requires explanation by any credible theory of skill acquisition. Heathcote et al., however, called into question the lawfulness of this relationship between performance speed and practice. They demonstrated that power functions result from averaging any group data with a downward trend. The important point here is that power functions can appear in averaged data, even when they do not occur in individual data. Certainly if individual data is inspected, smooth learning curves are rarely observed. Although performance usually gets faster with practice on a task, performance from trial to trial almost never follows a smooth downward trend. So, why should theories attempt to explain power function learning if it does not actually exist in individual performance? The assumption of many cognitive theorists appears to be that individual performance does not reflect the real behaviour they wish to explain; averaging is required over many trials, and many people need to remove the noise from the data in order for the real pattern to emerge. In the case of the 'power law of learning', it appears that skill acquisition theorists assume that learning is smooth and follows a power function; therefore, their theories must posit a learning mechanism that produces power function learning curves. It is possible, though, that this assumption is misguided. Rather than assuming that learning must follow a smooth trajectory, with average data needing to be used to observe this smoothness, why not accept that the noise in data is an accurate reflection of the cognitive processes underlying performance? One theory of skill acquisition (Speelman & Kirsner, 2005) does take this position, and considers noise in the data as the outcome of competition between cognitive processes striving to control performance. The lesson for all theories of memory and other cognitive processes, then, is that proposing mechanisms to explain mean performance may provide explanations of behaviour that does not exist.

Working memory

Because people use STM as a 'workspace' to process new information and to call up relevant information from LTM, many psychologists now think of STM as a component of working memory. ***Working memory*** refers to the temporary storage and processing of information that can be used to solve problems, respond to environmental demands or achieve goals (see Baddeley, 1992, 1995; Richardson, 1996a, 1996b).

Working memory is active memory: information remains in working memory only as long as the person is consciously processing, examining or manipulating it. Like the older concept of STM, working memory includes both a temporary memory store and a set of strategies, or control processes, for mentally manipulating the information momentarily held in that store. These control processes can be as simple as repeating a phone number over and over until we have finished dialling it — or as complex as trying to solve an equation in our heads.

Researchers initially believed that these two components of working memory — temporary storage and mental control — competed for the limited space at the lunch counter. In this view, rehearsing information is an active process that itself uses up some of the limited capacity of STM. Researchers also tended to view STM as a single system that could hold a maximum of about seven pieces of information of *any* kind, whether numbers, words or images.

More recent research suggests, instead, that working memory consists of multiple systems and that its storage and processing functions do not compete for limited space. According to one prominent model, working memory consists of three memory systems: a visual memory store, a verbal memory store and a 'central executive' that controls and manipulates the information these two short-term stores hold in mind (Baddeley, 1992, 1995). We begin by discussing the central executive and then examine the memory stores at its disposal.

Processing information in working memory: the central executive

In 1974, Alan Baddeley and Graham Hitch challenged the view of a single all-purpose working memory by presenting participants with two tasks simultaneously, one involving recall of a series of digits and the other involving some kind of thinking, such as reasoning or comprehending the meaning of sentences. They reasoned that if working memory is a single system, trying to remember seven or eight digits would fill the memory store and eliminate any further capacity for thinking.

The investigators *did* find that performing STM and reasoning tasks simultaneously slowed participants' ability to think. In one study, holding a memory load of four to eight digits increased the time participants took to solve a reasoning task (figure 7.5). However, a memory load of three items had no effect at all on reasoning speed, despite the fact that it should have consumed at least three of the 'slots' in STM. Further, performing the two tasks simultaneously had no impact on the number of errors participants made on the thinking task, suggesting that carrying out processes such as reasoning and rehearsal does not compete with storing digits for 'workspace' in a short-term store.

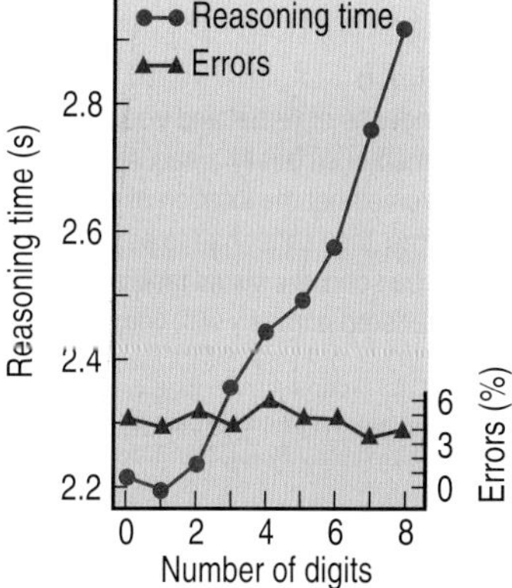

FIGURE 7.5
Speed and accuracy of reasoning as a function of number of digits to remember. Having to remember up to eight digits slowed the response time of participants as they tried to solve a reasoning task, but it did not lead to more errors. Keeping one to three digits in mind had minimal impact on reasoning time or speed.

SOURCE: Adapted from Baddeley (1986). Copyright © 1986 by Oxford University Press. Used by permission of Oxford University Press.

Research suggests there is a strong relationship between working memory and children's cognitive functioning.

These and other data led Baddeley and his colleagues to propose that storage capacity and processing capacity are two separate aspects of working memory. Processes such as rehearsal, reasoning and making decisions about how to balance two tasks simultaneously are the work of a central executive system that has its own limited capacity, independent of the information it is storing or holding momentarily in mind. Other researchers have found that working memory as a whole does seem to have a limited capacity — people cannot do and remember too many things at the same time — but working memory capacity varies across individuals and is related to their general intellectual ability (chapter 9) (Baddeley, 2001; Daneman & Merikle, 1996; Just & Carpenter, 1992; Logie, 1996). Indeed, children also demonstrate working memory limitations. For example, Halford and his colleagues at the University of Queensland's Cognition and Human Reasoning Laboratory have investigated the role of learning and information processing limitations in shaping children's cognitions. They have found evidence for a capacity limitation in young infants, and their research indicates that the complexity of information processed by children increases with age (Halford, Maybery, & Bain, 1986; Halford, Wilson, & Phillips, 1998). Similarly, a study of 144 Year 1 children from Queensland state primary schools showed a strong relationship between working memory and children's cognitive functioning (O'Connor, Spencer, & Patton, 2003).

Visual and verbal storage

Most contemporary models of working memory distinguish between at least two kinds of temporary memory: a visual store and a verbal store (Baddeley, 1995; Baddeley, Gathercole, & Papagno, 1998). Evidence that these are indeed distinct components comes from several lines of research (figure 7.6).

The visual store (also called the visuospatial sketchpad) is like a temporary image the person can hold in mind for 20 or 30 seconds. It momentarily stores visual information such as the location and nature of objects in the environment, so that, for example, a person turning around to grab a mug at the sink will remember where she placed a tea bag a moment before. Images in the visual store can be mentally rotated, moved around or used to locate objects in space that have momentarily dropped out of sight.

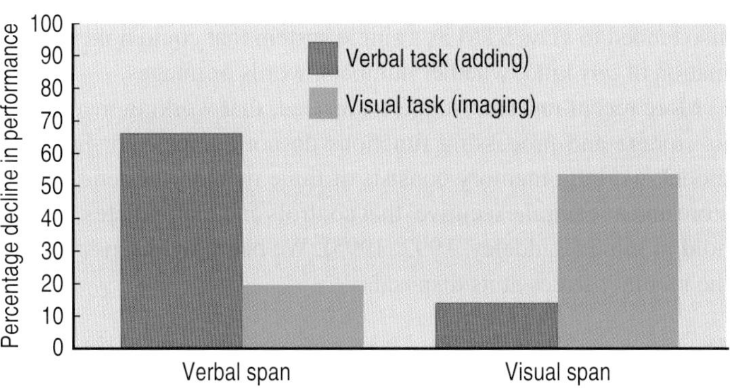

FIGURE 7.6
Independence of verbal and visual working memory storage. In one task, participants had to memorise briefly a sequence of letters ('verbal span'), whereas in another they had to remember the location of an extra grey block on a grid ('visual span'). At the same time, they either had to perform a verbal task (adding) or a visual one (imaging). As can be seen, the visual task interfered primarily with visual span, whereas the verbal task interfered primarily with verbal span.

SOURCE: Adapted from Logie, R., 'The seven ages of working memory', from 'Working memory and Human Cognition' by John T. E. Richardson et al., © 1996 by Oxford University Press, Inc. Used by permission of Oxford University Press, Inc.

The verbal (or phonological) store is the familiar short-term store studied using tasks such as digit span. Verbal working memory is relatively shallow: words are stored in order, based primarily on their sound (phonology), not their meaning. Tehan and Humphreys (1995) demonstrated the importance of phonemic codes in working memory by manipulating the strength of phonemic codes in target words. They suggested that phonemic information helps to make items more distinctive and thus easily discriminable from other target items.

Researchers learned about the 'shallowness' of verbal working memory by studying the kinds of words that interfere with each other (Baddeley, 1986; see also Lange & Oberauer, 2005). A list of similar-sounding words (such as *man*, *mat*, *cap* and *map*) is more difficult to recall than a list of words that do not sound alike. Similarity of meaning (e.g. *large*, *big*, *huge*, *tall*) does not similarly interfere with verbal working memory, but it *does* interfere with LTM. These findings suggest that verbal working memory and LTM have somewhat different ways of storing information.

INTERIM SUMMARY

Many psychologists now refer to STM as ***working memory*** — the temporary storage and processing of information that can be used to solve problems, respond to environmental demands or achieve goals. Working memory includes both a storage capacity and a processing capacity. According to the model proposed by Baddeley and his colleagues, processes such as rehearsal, reasoning and making decisions about how to balance two tasks simultaneously are the work of a limited-capacity central executive system. Most contemporary models distinguish between at least two kinds of temporary memory — a visual store (the visuospatial sketchpad) and a verbal store.

The neuropsychology of working memory

Recently researchers have begun tracking down the neuropsychology of working memory. The emerging consensus is that working memory is 'orchestrated', or directed, by the prefrontal cortex, a region of the brain long known to be involved in the most high-level cognitive functions (Kane & Engle, 2002). When information is temporarily stored and manipulated, the prefrontal cortex is activated along with whichever posterior regions (i.e. regions towards the back of the brain) normally process the kind of information being held in memory, such as words or images (D'Esposito et al., 1997; Faw, 2003; Goldman-Rakic, 1996; Smith, 2000).

Activation of the prefrontal cortex seems to provide access to consciousness to representations normally processed in other parts of the cortex, so that the person can temporarily hold the information in mind and manipulate it. Evidence for the pivotal role of the prefrontal cortex began to accumulate when researchers designed working memory tasks for monkeys and observed the activity of neurons in this region (Fuster, 1989, 1997; Goldman-Rakic, 1995).

Similar studies have now been conducted with humans. In one study, the researchers used fMRI (functional magnetic resonance imaging) to study the activation of different cortical regions while participants tried to remember faces or scrambled faces (a meaningless visual stimulus) (Courtney, Ungerleider, Keil, & Haxby, 1997). The results were striking. Relatively meaningless visual information activated posterior regions of the occipital lobes involved in the early stages of processing visual stimuli. Facial stimuli activated areas of the visual cortex in the occipital and temporal lobes involved in processing and identifying meaningful visual stimuli (and perhaps faces in particular). Anterior regions of the frontal lobes, that is, the prefrontal cortex, were most active during the delay period in which the faces and scrambled faces were removed and had to be held in working memory.

Research also demonstrates the independence of different components of working memory. For example, neuroimaging studies confirm that verbal and visual working memory activate different cortical regions (Smith, Jonides, & Koeppe, 1996). Studies even document the existence of two distinct kinds of visual working memory, processed in different areas of the prefrontal cortex: memory for location and memory for objects (Courtney, Petit, Ungerleider, Maisog, & Haxby, 1998; Rao, Rainier, & Miller, 1997). This finding makes sense in the light of research described in chapter 4 that distinguishes between two visual pathways involved in perception, the 'what' pathway (involved in identifying what objects are) and the 'where' pathway (involved in identifying where they are in space). Researchers have even begun tracking down the anatomical location of the central executive.

Using fMRI, one team of researchers identified a region of the prefrontal cortex that may be involved in functions such as managing the demands of two simultaneous tasks (D'Esposito et al., 1997). The researchers presented participants with two tasks that do not involve short-term storage, one verbal (making simple decisions about some words) and the other visual (mentally rotating images).

As expected, the verbal task activated the left temporal cortex, whereas the visual task activated the occipital and parietal cortex. Neither task alone activated the prefrontal cortex. However, when participants had to complete both tasks at the same time, regions of the prefrontal cortex became active — a suggestion that prefrontal working memory circuits are indeed activated when people have to make 'executive decisions' about how to manage the limited workspace in working memory (see also Adcock, Constable, Gore, & Goldman-Rakic, 2000; Bunge, Klingberg, Jacobsen, & Gabrieli, 2000).

APPLY + DISCUSS

Originally, researchers used the term short-term memory (which eventually became working memory) and consciousness as synonyms.

- Are there aspects of consciousness that are not represented in working memory?
- Is everything of which we are consciously aware held in working memory?
- Are there aspects of working memory that are not conscious?

The relationship between working memory and long-term memory

What can we conclude from these various studies about working memory? First, consistent with the original concept of STM, working memory appears to be a system for temporarily storing and processing information, a way of holding information in mind long enough to use it. Second, working memory includes a number of limited-capacity component processes, including a central executive system, a verbal storage system, and at least one and probably two or three visual storage systems (one for location, one for identification of objects and perhaps another that stores both simultaneously). Third, working memory is better conceived as a conscious workspace for accomplishing goals than as a way station or gateway to storage in LTM, because information can be stored in LTM without being represented in consciousness, and information in LTM is often accessed prior to its representation in working memory (Logie, 1996).

How distinct are working memory and long-term memory?

Are working memory and LTM really distinct? In some ways, yes. As we have seen, working memory is rapidly accessed and severely limited in capacity. Imagine if our LTM allowed us to remember only seven pieces of verbal information, seven objects or faces and seven locations!

Some of the strongest evidence for a distinction between working memory and LTM is neurological. Patients like Jimmie with severe amnesia can often store and manipulate information for momentary use with little trouble. They may be able, for example, to recall seven digits and keep them in mind by rehearsing them. The moment they stop rehearsing, however, they may forget that they were even trying to recall digits, an indication of a severe impairment in LTM. Researchers have also observed patients with the opposite problem: severe working memory deficits (such as a memory span of only two digits) but intact LTM (Caplan & Waters, 1990; Shallice & Warrington, 1970).

Interactions of working memory and long-term memory

Working memory and LTM may be distinct, but much of the time they are so intertwined that they can be difficult to distinguish. (Baddeley, 2002; Burgess & Hitch, 2005; Tehan, Hendry, & Kocinski, 2001). For example, when people are asked to recall a sequence of words after a brief delay, their performance is better if the words are semantically related (such as *chicken* and *duck*), presumably because they recognise the link between them and can use the memory of one to cue the memory of the other from LTM (Wetherick, 1975). Similarly, words are more easily remembered than nonsense syllables (Hulme, Maughan, & Brown, 1991; Roodenrys, Hulme, & Brown, 1993). These findings suggest that working memory involves the conscious activation of knowledge from LTM, since without accessing LTM, the person could not tell the difference between words and non-words.

Indeed, from a neuroanatomical standpoint, working memory appears to become engaged when neural networks in the frontal lobes become activated along with (and linked to) networks in the occipital, temporal and parietal lobes that represent various words or images. These mental representations of words or images themselves reflect an interaction between current sensory data and stored knowledge from LTM, such as matching a visual pattern with a stored image of a particular person's face. In this sense, working memory in part involves a special kind of activation of information stored in LTM (see Cowan, 1994; Ericsson & Kintsch, 1995).

APPLY + DISCUSS

On your university course website for this subject, you should be able to access a website that contains many interactive presentations of phenomena in memory and cognition, including verbal rehearsal, elaboration and short-term memory decay, as well as many others.

- How does working memory help us to remember?
- How does rehearsal and/or chunking help us to remember?
- What strategies best help you to remember things?

Chunking

Perhaps the best example of the interaction between working memory and LTM in daily life is a strategy people use to expand the capacity of their working memory in particular situations (Ericsson & Kintsch, 1995). We have noted that the brain holds a certain number of units of information in consciousness at a time. But what constitutes a unit? A letter? A word? Perhaps an entire sentence or idea?

Consider the working memory capacity of a skilled waiter in a restaurant. How can a person take the order of eight people without the aid of a notepad, armed only with a mental sketchpad and a limited-capacity verbal store? One way is to use ***chunking***, a memory technique that uses knowledge stored in LTM to group information in larger units than single words or digits. Chunking is essential in everyday life, particularly in cultures that rely upon literacy, because people are constantly called upon to remember telephone numbers, written words and lists.

Now consider the following sequence of letters: ASXBHPASICSMH. This string would be impossible for most people to hold in working memory, unless they are interested in business and recognise some meaningful chunks: ASX for Australian Securities Exchange; BHP for Broken Hill Proprietary; ASIC for Australian Securities and Investments Commission; SMH for *Sydney Morning Herald*. In this example, chunking effectively reduces the number of pieces of information in working memory from 13 to 4, by putting three or four customers on each stool. People tend to use chunking most effectively in their areas of expertise, such as waiters who know a menu 'like the back of their hands'. Similarly, knowledge of area codes allows people to store 10 or 11 digits at a time, since 61 (the telephone country code for Australia) or 64 (the telephone country code for New Zealand) can become a single chunk rather than two 'slots' in verbal working memory.

MAKING CONNECTIONS

Psychologists once viewed memory as a warehouse for stored ideas. Today, however, many cognitive neuroscientists believe that memory involves the activation of a previously activated network to create a similar experience. Because the activated network is never identical to the original one, however, multiple opportunities for error exist (chapter 2).

INTERIM SUMMARY

Working memory and LTM are distinct from one another in both their functions and neuroanatomy because patients with brain damage can show severe deficits on one but not the other. Working memory appears to occur as frontal lobe neural networks become activated along with and linked to networks in the occipital, temporal and parietal lobes that represent various words or images. Working memory clearly interacts with LTM systems, as occurs in ***chunking*** — using knowledge stored in LTM to group information in larger units than single words or digits and hence to expand working memory capacity in specific domains.

Varieties of long-term memory

Most readers have had the experience of going into the refrigerator looking for a condiment such as mustard. Our first pass at 'remembering' where the mustard is seems more like habit than memory — we automatically look in a particular place, such as the side door, where we have found it many times. If the bottle is not there, we typically employ one of two strategies. The first is to think about where we usually put it, drawing on our general knowledge about what we have done in the past — do we usually put it in the door or on the top shelf? The second is to try to remember a specific episode, namely the last time we used the mustard.

This simple example reveals something not so simple: that LTM comes in multiple forms, such as automatic 'habits', general knowledge and memory for specific episodes. Researchers do not yet agree on precisely how many systems constitute LTM, but developments in neuroimaging over the last decade have made clear that the three different ways of finding the mustard represent three very different kinds of memory, each with its own neuroanatomy. In this section, we explore some of the major types of LTM.

Declarative and procedural memory

In general, people store two kinds of information: declarative and procedural. ***Declarative memory*** refers to memory for facts and events, much of which can be stated or 'declared' (Squire, 1986). ***Procedural memory*** refers to 'how to' knowledge of procedures or skills.

When we think of memory, we usually mean declarative memory: knowledge of facts and events. Remembering that Edmund Barton was the first Prime Minister of Australia and Henry Sewell was the first Premier of New Zealand, or calling up a happy memory from the past, requires access to declarative memory.

Declarative memory can be semantic or episodic (Tulving, 1972, 1987). ***Semantic memory*** refers to general world knowledge or facts, such as the knowledge that winters are cold in Dunedin or that NaCl is the chemical formula for table salt (Tulving, 1972). The term is somewhat misleading because semantic implies that general knowledge is stored in words, whereas people know many things about objects, such as their colour or smell, that are encoded as sensory representations. For this reason, many psychologists now refer to semantic memory as ***generic memory***.

Episodic memory consists of memories of particular events, rather than general knowledge (Tulving, 2002). Episodic memory allows people to travel mentally through time, to remember thoughts and feelings (or in memory experiments, word lists) from the recent or distant past, or to imagine the future (Wheeler, Stuss, & Tulving, 1997).

In everyday life, episodic memory is often autobiographical, as when people remember what they did on their eighteenth birthday or what they ate yesterday (see Howe, 2000). It is also closely linked to semantic memory (Menon, Boyett-Anderson, Schatzberg, & Reiss, 2002), since when people experience similar episodes over time (such as 180 days a year in school or hundreds of thousands of interactions with their father), they gradually develop generic memories of what those situations were like (e.g. 'I used to love weekends with my father').

Declarative memory is the most obvious kind of memory, but another kind of memory is equally important in daily life: procedural memory, also referred to as skill or habit memory. People are often astonished to find that even though they have not skated for 20 years, the skills are reactivated easily, almost as if their use had never been interrupted. When people put a backspin on a tennis ball, speak grammatically or drive a car, they are drawing on procedural memory. Other procedural skills are less obvious, such as reading, which involves a set of complex procedures for decoding strings of letters and words.

Although procedural memories often form without conscious effort (as in conditioning procedures with rats, who presumably do not carefully think out their next move in a maze), at other times procedural memories are 'residues' of prior conscious knowledge and strategies, which have become automatic and highly efficient. For example, when we first learn to type, we study the layout of the keyboard, trying to form declarative memories. As we are typing our first words, we also hold in working memory the sequence of keys to hit and knowledge about which fingers to use for each key. Over time, however, our speed and accuracy improve, while conscious effort diminishes. This process reflects the formation of procedural memory for typing. In the end, we think only of the words we want to type and would have difficulty describing the layout of the keyboard (declarative memory), even though our fingers 'remember'. As we will see, this shift from conscious, effortful memory to automatic procedural memory occurs as regions of the cortex 'pass the torch' of memory to subcortical regions in the basal ganglia.

Explicit and implicit memory

For much of the last century, psychologists studied memory by asking subjects to memorise word lists, nonsense syllables or connections between pairs of words and then asking them to recall them. These tasks all tap ***explicit memory***, or conscious recollection. Recently, however, psychologists have recognised another kind of memory: implicit memory (Graf & Schacter, 1987; Roediger, 1990; Schacter & Buckner, 1998). ***Implicit memory*** refers to memory that is expressed in behaviour but does not require conscious recollection, such as tying a shoelace.

Some psychologists use explicit and implicit memory as synonyms for declarative and procedural memory. Although there is clearly some overlap, the declarative–procedural dichotomy refers more to the type of knowledge that is stored (facts versus skills), whereas the explicit–implicit distinction refers more to the way this knowledge is retrieved and expressed (with or without conscious awareness). As we will see, people's knowledge of facts (declarative knowledge) is often expressed without awareness (implicitly). Figure 7.7 provides a model of the different dimensions of LTM.

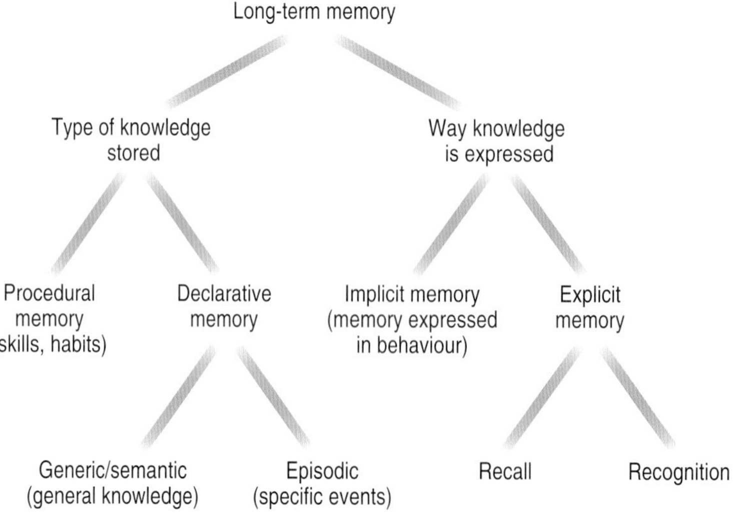

FIGURE 7.7
Key distinctions in long-term memory

Explicit memory

Explicit memory involves the conscious retrieval of information. Researchers distinguish between two kinds of explicit retrieval: recall and recognition. ***Recall*** is the spontaneous conscious recollection of information from LTM, as when a person brings to mind memories of her wedding day or the name of the capital of Egypt. Neuroimaging studies show that recall activates parts of the brain that are also activated during working memory tasks involving the central executive (Nolde, Johnson, & Raye, 1998). This makes sense given that recall requires conscious effort.

Although recall occurs spontaneously, it generally requires effortful use of strategies for calling the desired information to mind. When efforts at recall fail, people sometimes experience the ***tip-of-the-tongue phenomenon***, in which the person knows the information is 'in there' but is not quite able to retrieve it (Brown & McNeill, 1966). Recent research suggests that this phenomenon stems from problems linking the sounds of words (which are arbitrary — a table could just as easily have been called a blah) with their meanings (Merriman, Marazita, Jarvis, Evey-Burkey, & Biggins, 1996). Thus, using the word 'prognosticate' in a conversation with someone who has the word 'pontificate' on the tip of his tongue can lead to sudden recall (and a feeling of relief!).

If asked to name the majority of the members of Australia's 2007 World Cup winning cricket team (a *recall* task), even ardent cricket fans may have some difficulty. If, however, they were shown this team photo (a *recognition* task), many fans would readily and correctly come up with names such as Matthew Hayden, Andrew Symonds, Glenn McGrath, Nathan Bracken, Stuart Clark and Brad Hogg.

Recognition refers to the explicit sense or recollection that something currently perceived has been previously encountered or learned. Researchers often test recognition memory by asking participants whether a word was on a list they saw the previous day. Recognition is easier than recall (as any student knows who has answered multiple-choice items that simply require recognition of names or concepts), because the person does not have to generate the information, just make a judgement about it.

Implicit memory

Implicit memory is evident in skills, conditioned learning and associative memory (i.e. associations between one representation and another). It can be seen in skills such as turning the wheel in the correct direction when the car starts to skid on a gravel road (which skilled drivers in country regions do before they have even formed the thought 'I'm skidding') as well as in responses learned through classical and operant conditioning, such as avoiding a food that was once associated with nausea, whether or not the person has any explicit recollection of the event.

Implicit associative memory emerges in experiments on ***priming effects***, in which prior exposure to a stimulus (the prime) facilitates or inhibits the processing of new information. Participants in memory experiments show priming effects even when they do not consciously remember being exposed to the prime (Bowers & Schacter, 1990; Tulving, Schachter, & Stark, 1982). For example, they might be exposed to a list of words that are relatively rarely used in everyday conversation, such as assassin. A week later, they may have no idea whether assassin was on the list (a test of explicit recognition memory), but if asked to fill in the missing letters of a word fragment such as A--A--IN, they are more likely to complete it with the word assassin than control participants who studied a different list the week earlier. Priming effects appear to rely on activation of information stored in LTM, even though the person is unaware of what has been activated.

INTERIM SUMMARY

Types of LTM can be distinguished by kind of knowledge stored (facts versus skills) and the way this knowledge is retrieved and expressed (with or without conscious awareness). People store two kinds of information, declarative and procedural. ***Declarative memory*** refers to memory for facts and events; it can be ***semantic*** (general world knowledge or facts) or ***episodic*** (memories of particular events). ***Procedural memory*** refers to 'how to' knowledge of procedures or skills. Knowledge can be retrieved explicitly or implicitly. ***Explicit memory*** refers to conscious recollection, whereas ***implicit memory*** refers to memory that is expressed in behaviour. Researchers distinguish between two kinds of explicit retrieval: ***recall*** (the spontaneous retrieval of material from LTM) and ***recognition*** (memory for whether something currently perceived has been previously encountered or learned). Implicit memory is evident in skills, conditioned learning and associative memory (associations between one representation and another).

The neuropsychology of long-term memory

How distinct are these varieties of long-term memories? Are researchers simply splitting hairs, or are they really 'carving nature at its joints', making distinctions where distinctions truly exist?

Some of the most definitive data supporting distinctions among different types of memory are neuroanatomical studies, including case studies of patients with neurological damage, brain imaging with normal and brain-damaged patients and experimental studies with animals (Gabrieli, 1998; Gluck & Myers, 1997; Squire, 1992, 1995). Researchers discovered the distinction between implicit and explicit memory in part by observing amnesic patients who have trouble storing and retrieving new declarative information (such as their age or the name or face of their doctor) but show minimal impairment on implicit tasks (Schacter, 1995a). Consider the case of H. M., who had most of his medial temporal lobes (the region in the middle of the temporal lobes, including the hippocampus and amygdala) removed because of uncontrollable seizures (figure 7.8). Following the operation, H. M. had one of the deepest, purest cases of amnesia ever recorded, leading to the conclusion that medial temporal structures play a central role in the consolidation (i.e. encoding and 'solidification') of new explicit memories. Despite his inability to store new memories, however, H. M. was able to learn new procedural skills, such as writing words upside down. Each new time H. M. was asked to perform this task, his speed improved, but he had no recollection that he had ever performed it before. Sadly, H. M. died on 2 December 2008, aged 82. His survival of ill-conceived brain surgery enabled researchers to identify how and where memories are formed in the brain. His form of anterograde amnesia prevented him from collecting any new memories and he lived in a pre-1953 world. H. M. is to be remembered and saluted for all that he has contributed to the scientific community.

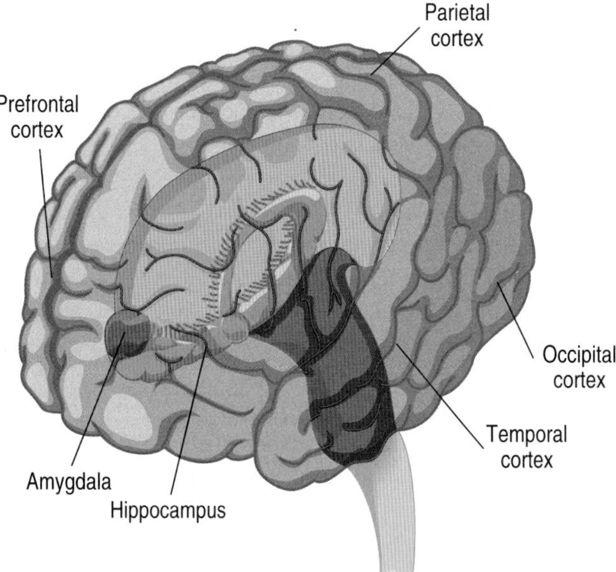

FIGURE 7.8
Anatomy of memory. The medial temporal region (inside the middle of the temporal lobes), particularly the hippocampus, plays a key role in consolidation of explicit, declarative information. The frontal lobes play a more important role in working memory, procedural memory and aspects of episodic memory, such as dating memories for the time at which they occurred. Posterior regions of the cortex (occipital, parietal and temporal cortex) are involved in memory just as they are in perception, by creating mental representations.

Lesion research with monkeys and imaging research with humans have demonstrated that the hippocampus and adjacent regions of the cortex are central to the consolidation of explicit memories (Eichenbaum, 1997; McGaugh, 2000; Squire & Zola-Morgan, 1991). In contrast, the fact that amnesics like H. M. often show normal skill learning and priming effects suggests that the hippocampus is not central to implicit memory.

In daily life, of course, implicit and explicit memory are often intertwined. For example, people learn through conditioning to fear and avoid stimuli that are painful, but they are also frequently aware of the connection between various stimuli or behaviours and their effects. Thus, a child might learn by touching a stove that doing so is punishing (conditioning) but also might be able explicitly to recall the connection between the two events: 'If I touch the stove, I get an ouchie!'

Neurologically speaking, however, implicit and explicit memory rely on separate mechanisms (Bechara et al., 1995). For example, fear conditioning and avoidance learning require an intact amygdala. In a classical conditioning procedure in which a particular sound (the conditioned stimulus or CS) is paired with an electric shock (the unconditioned stimulus or UCS), patients with an intact hippocampus but a damaged amygdala can explicitly state the connection between the CS and the UCS — that is, they consciously know that the tone is associated with shock. However, their nervous system shows no signs of autonomic arousal (e.g. increased heart rate) or behavioural expressions of fear when exposed to the CS. They *know* the connection but cannot *feel* it. In contrast, patients with an intact amygdala but a damaged hippocampus may have no conscious idea that the CS is associated with electric shock — in fact, they may have no recollection of ever having encountered the stimulus before — but nonetheless they show a conditioned fear response to it, including autonomic arousal (see chapters 3 and 6).

Subsystems of implicit and explicit memory

Implicit and explicit memory are themselves broad categories that include neurologically distinct phenomena. The two kinds of explicit memory, semantic and episodic, rely on different neural mechanisms. Patients with damage to the frontal lobes have little trouble retrieving semantic knowledge but often show deficits in episodic memory (Shimamura, 1995; Wheeler, Stuss, & Tulving, 1995, 1997). They may, for example, have trouble remembering the order of events in their lives (Swain, Polkey, Bullock, & Morris, 1998), or they may vividly recall events that never occurred because they have difficulty distinguishing true from false memories of events (Schacter, 1997). Positron emission tomography (PET) studies show greater activation of prefrontal regions when recalling episodic rather than semantic information (Nyberg, 1998). However, other studies have since failed to replicate this finding (see Menon et al., 2002).

Implicit memory also likely comprises at least two systems. Patients with damage to the cortex caused by Alzheimer's disease may have normal procedural memory but impaired performance on priming tasks. In contrast, patients with Huntington's disease, a fatal, degenerative condition that affects the basal ganglia, show normal priming but impaired procedural learning (Butters, Heindel, & Salmon, 1990).

Recent brain imaging data on normal participants have provided insight into the way knowledge that at first requires considerable effort becomes procedural, as the brain essentially transfers the processing of the task from one network to another (see Poldrack, Desmond, Glover, & Gabrieli, 1998). For example, after practice at reading words backward in a mirror, people show *decreased* activity in visual pathways but *increased* activity in verbal pathways in the left temporal lobe. This switch suggests that they are more rapidly moving from the visual task of mentally turning the word around to the linguistic task of understanding its meaning.

INTERIM SUMMARY

Implicit and explicit memory are neuroanatomically distinct. The hippocampus and adjacent regions of the cortex are centrally involved in consolidating explicit memories. Amnesics with hippocampal damage often show normal skill learning, conditioning and priming effects, suggesting that the hippocampus is not central to implicit memory. Different kinds of explicit memory, notably episodic and semantic, also appear to constitute distinct memory systems. The same is true of two types of implicit memory, procedural and associative.

Everyday memory

In designing studies, researchers have to strike a balance between the often conflicting goals of maximising internal validity — creating a study whose methods are sound and rigorous and can lead to clear causal inferences — and external validity — making sure the results generalise to the real world (chapter 2). Since Ebbinghaus' studies in the late nineteenth century, memory research has tended to emphasise internal validity, by measuring participants' responses as they memorise words, nonsense syllables and pairs of words, to try to learn about basic memory processes. Increasingly, however, researchers have begun to argue for the importance of studying ***everyday memory*** as well; that is, memory as it occurs in daily life (Ceci & Bronfenbrenner, 1991; Herrmann, McEvoy, Hertzod, Hertel, & Johnson, 1996; Koriat, Goldsmith, & Pansky, 2000; Rogoff & Lave, 1984).

In the laboratory, the experimenter usually supplies the information to be remembered, the reason to remember it (the experimenter asks the person to) and the occasion to remember it (immediately, a week later etc.). Often the information to be remembered has little intrinsic meaning, such as isolated words on a list. In contrast, in daily life, people store and retrieve information because they need to for one reason or another, the information is usually meaningful and emotionally significant, and the context for retrieval is sometimes a future point in time that itself must be remembered, as when a person tries to remember to call a friend later in the day. Thus, researchers are choosing to study everyday memory in its naturalistic setting — such as people's memory for appointments (Andrzejewski, Moore, Corvette, & Hermann, 1991) — as well as to devise ways to bring it into the laboratory.

MAKING CONNECTIONS

Recent research from the Australian National University has challenged the myth that pregnant women and mothers become forgetful. This short-term memory loss is often described as 'baby brain' or 'placenta brain' and has been contested by Professor Christensen and her team in a 20-year population study on health and ageing. Christensen, Leach, and Mackinnon (2010) analysed the memory and cognitive speed of a group of women before and during pregnancy and in the early stages of motherhood, and found no support for the notion that pregnancy and motherhood are related to persistent cognitive deterioration. Their research indicates that memory lapses can happen to any one of us, pregnant or not, and that **cognitive decline** varies across individuals (see chapter 12).

Everyday memory is functional memory

In their daily lives, people typically remember for a purpose, to achieve some goal (Anderson, 1996; Gruneberg, Morris, & Sykes, 1988). Memory, like all psychological processes, is functional. Of all the things we could commit to memory over the course of a day, we tend to remember those that affect our needs and interests.

The functional nature of memory was demonstrated in a set of studies that examined whether men and women would have better recall for stereotypically masculine and feminine memory tasks (Herrmann, Crawford, & Holdsworthy, 1992). In one study, the investigators asked participants to remember a shopping list and a list of travel directions. As predicted, women's memory was better for the shopping list, whereas men had better memory for the directions.

Does this mean that women are born to shop and men to navigate? A second study suggested otherwise. This time, some participants received a 'shopping list' to remember whereas others received a 'hardware list'. Additionally, some received directions on 'how to make a shirt' whereas others received directions on 'how to make a workbench'. In reality, the grocery and hardware lists were identical, as were the two lists of 'directions'. For example, the shopping list included items such as *brush*, *oil*, *chips*, *nuts* and *gum* that could just as easily be interpreted as goods at a supermarket as hardware items. The 'directions' were so general that they could refer to almost anything (e.g. 'First, you rearrange the pieces into different groups. Of course, one pile may be sufficient . . .').

As predicted, women were more likely to remember details about shirt making and grocery lists. The biases in recall for directions for men were particularly strong (figure 7.9). Apparently, 'real men' do not make shirts. These findings demonstrate the importance of noncognitive factors such as motivation and interest in everyday memory: what men define as not relevant, not interesting or threatening to their masculinity does not make a lasting impression on their memory (Colley, Ball, Kirby, Harvey, & Vingelen, 2002).

Other research links some forms of everyday memory to the hippocampus. Researchers tested London taxi drivers' knowledge of the streets of their city. Drivers showed more activation in the hippocampus for a navigation task that required their expertise than for several other memory tasks (Maguire, Frackowiak, & Frith, 1997). In fact, the size of the activated regions of the hippocampus was strongly correlated with the number of years they had been driving, a suggestion that the brain devotes more 'room' in the hippocampus for frequently used information, just as it does in the cortex (Maguire, Mummery, & Buechel, 2000). More recently, research has used virtual reality to further examine the role of the hippocampus in spatial navigation and episodic memory (see Burgess, 2002).

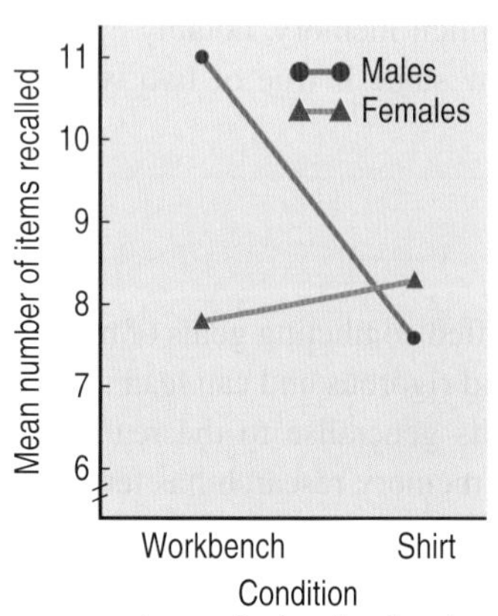

FIGURE 7.9
Gender and everyday memory. The figure shows men's and women's memory, following a distracter task, for a list of directions that they thought were for making either a workbench or a shirt. Women recalled slightly more items when they thought they were remembering sewing instructions. Men's performance was dramatically different in the two conditions: men were much more likely to remember the 'manly' instructions for the workbench.

SOURCE: From Herrmann et al. (1992).

Prospective memory

Most studies of memory have examined ***retrospective memory***, that is, memory for things from the past, such as a list of words encountered 20 minutes earlier. In everyday life, an equally important kind of memory is ***prospective memory***, or memory for things that need to be done in the future, such as picking up some items at the corner shop after work (Brandimonte, Einstein, & McDaniel,

1996; Einstein & McDaniel, 1990; McDaniel, Robinson-Riegler, & Einstein, 1998; Smith, 2003). Prospective memory has at least two components: remembering to remember ('be sure to stop at the corner shop after work') and remembering *what* to remember (e.g. a loaf of bread and milk). In other words, prospective memory requires memory of intent as well as content (Kvavilashvili, 1987; Marsh, Hiscks, & Bink, 1998). Experimental studies suggest that intending to carry out certain acts in the future leads to their heightened activation in LTM (Goschke & Kuhl, 1993, 1996).

Although prospective memory is probably not itself a memory 'system' with its own properties, it does have elements that distinguish it from other kinds of memory (see McDaniel, 1995). One is its heavy emphasis on time. Part of remembering an intention is remembering when to remember it, such as at a specific time (e.g. right after work) or an interval of time (tonight, tomorrow, sometime over the next few days).

Another unique feature of remembered intentions is that the person has to remember whether they have been performed so they can be 'shut off'. This facet of prospective memory is more important with some tasks than with others. Inadvertently hiring a DVD that you already watched a month ago is clearly less harmful than taking medication you did not remember taking an hour earlier.

INTERIM SUMMARY

Everyday memory refers to memory as it occurs in daily life. Everyday memory is functional, focused on remembering information that is meaningful. One kind of everyday memory is ***prospective memory***, memory for things that need to be done in the future.

Encoding and organisation of long-term memory

We have now completed our tour of the varieties of memory. But how does information find its way into LTM in the first place? And how is information organised in the mind so that it can be readily retrieved? In this section, we explore these two questions. The focus is on the storage and organisation of declarative knowledge, since it has received the most empirical attention.

Encoding

For information to be retrievable from memory, it must be ***encoded***, or cast into a representational form, or 'code,' that can be readily accessed. The manner of encoding — how, how much and when the person tries to learn new information — has a substantial influence on its accessibility (ease and ability of retrieval — i.e. how readily it can be accessed).

Levels of processing

Anyone who has ever crammed for a test knows that rehearsal is important for storing information in LTM. As noted earlier, however, the simple, repetitive rehearsal that maintains information momentarily in working memory is not optimal for LTM. Usually, a more effective strategy is to attend to the meaning of the stimulus and form mental connections between it and previously stored information.

Some encoding is deliberate, such as studying for an exam, learning lines for a play or theatre production or trying to remember a joke. However, much of the time encoding simply occurs as a by-product of thought and perception — a reason why people can remember incidents that happened to them 10 years ago even though they were not trying to commit them to memory.

MAKING CONNECTIONS

As the philosopher of science Thomas Kuhn argued, a **paradigm** (or perspective in psychology) includes a set of propositions that constitute a model, an underlying metaphor, and a set of agreed-upon methods (chapter 1). In the last few years, all these have changed in cognitive psychology. We have moved from three sequential memory stores to multiple-memory systems operating in parallel; from a computer metaphor to a brain metaphor; and from a set of methods (such as memorising word pairs) that tended to study memory divorced from meaning to more diverse methods, including those that can examine memory in its natural habitat — everyday life.

Deep and shallow processing

The degree to which information is elaborated, reflected upon and processed in a meaningful way during memory storage is referred to as the depth or ***level of processing*** (Craik & Lockhart, 1972; Lockhart & Craik, 1990). Information may be processed at a shallow, structural level (focusing on physical characteristics of the stimulus); at a somewhat deeper, phonemic level (focusing on simple characteristics of the language used to describe it); or at the deepest, semantic level (focusing on the meaning of the stimulus).

For example, at a shallow, structural level, a person may walk by a restaurant and notice the type face and colours of its sign. At a phonemic level, she may read the sign to herself and notice that it sounds Italian. Processing material deeply, in contrast, means paying attention to its meaning or significance, noticing, for instance, that this is the restaurant a friend has been recommending for months.

Processing information at a deep, semantic level is also positively related to academic success in first-year studies, with a shallow learning approach predicting poor achievement (Burton, Taylor, Dowling, & Lawrence, 2009). In a related Australian study, results from 134 pre-service teacher education students at a rural university in New South Wales indicated that modifications to teaching methods, task requirements, and assessment processes can help minimise a shallow learning approach and encourage in students a deep learning approach (Gordon & Debus, 2002).

Australian performer Hugh Jackman's prefrontal cortex was activated when he used deliberate techniques to learn his lines and the choreography for his role as Peter Allen in the stage production of *The Boy From Oz*.

Different levels of processing activate different neural circuits. As one might guess, encoding that occurs as people make judgements about the meaning of words (such as whether they are concrete or abstract) leads to greater activation of the left temporal cortex, which is involved in language comprehension, than if they attend to qualities of the printed words, such as whether they are in upper- or lowercase letters (Gabrieli et al., 1996). Deliberate use of strategies to remember (such as remembering to buy bread and bottled water by thinking of a prisoner who is fed only bread and water) activates regions of the prefrontal cortex involved in other executive functions such as manipulating information in working memory (Kapur, Tulving, Cabeza, & McIntosh, 1996). Subsequent research has even shown that the amount of activity in the prefrontal and temporal cortices predicts the extent to which participants are likely to remember studied material successfully (Brewer, Zhao, Desmond, Glover, & Gabrieli, 1998; Wagner et al., 1998). Otten, Henson, and Rugg (2001) further extended this finding, showing that episodic encoding for words in a semantic task involves a subset of the regions activated by deep processing.

Encoding specificity

Advocates of depth-of-processing theory originally thought that deeper processing is always better. Although this is generally true, subsequent research shows that the best encoding strategy depends on what the person later needs to retrieve (see Anderson, 1995). If a person is asked to recall shallow information (such as whether a word was originally presented in capital letters), shallow encoding tends to be more useful.

The fact that ease of retrieval depends on the match between the way information is encoded and later retrieved is known as the ***encoding specificity principle*** (Tulving & Thomson, 1973). For example, a student who studies for a multiple-choice test by memorising definitions and details without trying to understand the underlying concepts may be in much more trouble if the lecturer decides to include an essay question, because the student has encoded the information at too shallow a level.

Why does the match between encoding and retrieval influence the ease with which people can access information from memory? According to several theorists, memory is not really a process distinct from perception and thought; rather, it is a by-product of the normal processes of perceiving and thinking, which automatically lay down traces of an experience as it is occurring. When people remember, they simply reactivate the same neural networks that processed the information in the first place (Crowder, 1993; Lockhart & Craik, 1990). If the circumstances at encoding and retrieval are similar, the memory is more easily retrieved because more of the neural network that represents it is activated. To put it another way, a new thought, feeling or perception is like a bushwalker who has to create a new trail through the bush. Each time another traveller takes that path, that is, each time a similar event occurs, the trail becomes more defined and easier to locate.

APPLY + DISCUSS

Research in New Zealand (Harper, 2000; Parkes & White, 2000; White & Ruske, 2002) into the effect of drugs that decrease acetylcholine activity in the brain suggests that memory loss is related to a problem at the initial encoding of the stimulus rather than to a problem with later recall.

- Is information processed at a deep level easier to retrieve than information processed at a shallow level?
- When might shallow information be more useful than deep processing?
- Why is a memory more easily retrieved when the circumstances at encoding emulate those at retrieval?

Context and retrieval

According to the encoding specificity principle, the contexts in which people encode and retrieve information can also affect the ease of retrieval. One study presented scuba divers with different lists of words, some while the divers were under water and others while they were above (Godden & Baddeley, 1975). The divers had better recall for lists they had encoded under water when they were under water at retrieval; conversely, lists encoded above water were better recalled above water. An Australian study (Pearse, Powell, & Thomson, 2003) also found context is important in recall for young children. The study participants took part in the same staged event four times, with some details varied each time (e.g. the colour of a coat). Three days later, the children were asked to recall those details. During the interview process, contextual cues were given to some of the children — such as a different person undertaking one of the tests, or a new watch that the interviewer wore. Those children who were given a contextual cue performed better in recalling details of the events.

The same phenomenon appears to occur with people's emotional state at encoding and retrieval, a phenomenon called state-dependent memory: being in a similar mood at encoding and retrieval (e.g. angry while learning a word list and angry while trying to remember it) can facilitate memory, as long as the emotional state is not so intense that it inhibits memory in general (see Bower, 1981; Keenly, 1997). Having the same context during encoding and retrieval facilitates recall because the context provides ***retrieval cues***, stimuli or thoughts that can be used to facilitate recollection.

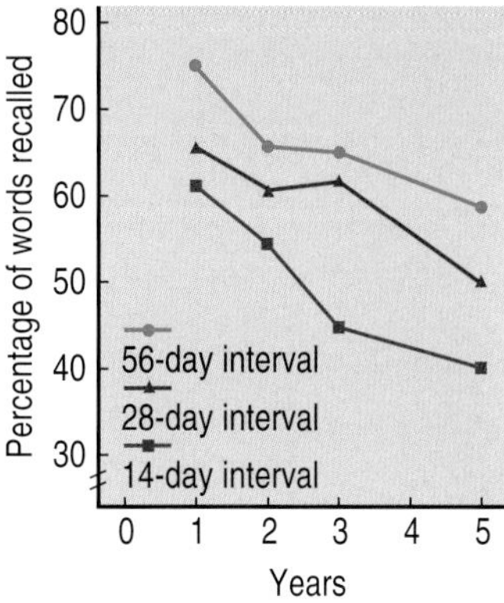

FIGURE 7.10
Impact of spacing on memory retention over five years. Longer intervals between rehearsal sessions for English–foreign language word pairs predicted higher long-term retention of the information one, two, three and five years after the last training session.

SOURCE: Bahrick et al. (1993)

Spacing

Another encoding variable that influences memory is of particular importance in educational settings: the interval between study sessions. Students intuitively know that if they cram the night before a test, the information is likely to be available to them when they need it the next day. They also tend to believe that massed rehearsal (i.e. studying in one long session or several times over a short interval, such as a day) is more effective than spaced, or distributed, rehearsal over longer intervals (Zechmeister & Shaughnessy, 1980). But is this strategy really optimal for long-term retention of the information?

In fact, it is not (Bruce & Bahrick, 1992; Dempster, 1996; Ebbinghaus, 1885/1964). Massed rehearsal seems superior because it makes initial acquisition of memory slightly easier, since the material is at a heightened state of activation in a massed practice session. In the long run, however, research on the ***spacing effect*** — the superiority of memory for information rehearsed over longer intervals — demonstrates that spacing study sessions over longer intervals tends to double long-term retention of information.

In one study, the Bahrick family tested the long-term effects of spaced rehearsal on the study of 300 foreign language vocabulary words (Bahrick, Bahrick, Bahrick, & Bahrick, 1993). The major finding was that, over a five year period, 13 training sessions at intervals of 56 days apart increased memory retention rates compared to 26 sessions spaced at 14-day intervals (figure 7.10). These results are robust across a variety of memory tasks, even including implicit memory (Perruchet, 1989; Toppino & Schneider, 1999).

These and related findings have important implications for students and teachers (Bruce & Bahrick, 1992; Herbert & Burt, 2004; Rea & Modigliani, 1988). Students who want to remember information for more than a day or two after an exam should space their studying over time and avoid cramming. Medical students, law students and others who intend to practise a profession based on their course work should be particularly wary of all-nighters.

Moreover, much as students might protest, cumulative exams over the course of a semester are superior to exams that test only the material that immediately preceded them. Cumulative exams require students to relearn material at long intervals, and the tests themselves constitute learning sessions in which memory is retrieved and reinforced. In fact, research on spacing is part of what led the authors of this text to include both interim summaries and a general summary at the end of each chapter, since learning occurs best with a combination of immediate review and spaced rehearsal.

Representational modes and encoding

The ability to retrieve information from LTM also depends on the modes used to encode it. In general, the more ways a memory can be encoded, the greater the likelihood that it will be accessible for later retrieval. Storing a memory in multiple representational modes — such as words, images and sounds — provides more retrieval cues to bring it back to mind (see Paivio, 1991).

For instance, many people remember phone numbers not only by memorising the digits but also by forming a mental map of the buttons they need to push and a motoric (procedural) representation of the pattern of buttons to push that becomes automatic and is expressed implicitly. When pushing the buttons, they may even be alerted that they have dialled the wrong number by hearing a sound pattern that does not match the expected pattern, suggesting auditory storage as well.

APPLY + DISCUSS

- What are the best ways to study material so that it 'sinks in'?
- What forms of rehearsal and spacing are likely to lead to long-term retention of information?
- Are the same methods useful in procedural learning? What methods would be most useful in remembering a new tennis serve, or learning to type?

INTERIM SUMMARY

For information to be retrievable from memory, it must be ***encoded***, or cast into a representational form that can be readily accessed from memory. The degree to which information is elaborated, reflected upon and processed in a meaningful way during memory storage is referred to as the depth or ***level of processing***. Although deeper processing tends to be more useful for storing information for the long term, ease of retrieval depends on the match between the way information is encoded and the way it is later retrieved, a phenomenon known as the ***encoding specificity principle***. Similar contexts during encoding and retrieval provide ***retrieval cues*** — stimuli or thoughts that can be used to facilitate recollection. Aside from level of processing, two other variables influence accessibility of memory, the ***spacing*** of study sessions and the use of multiple representational modes.

Mnemonic devices

The principles of encoding we have just been describing help explain the utility of many ***mnemonic devices*** — systematic strategies for remembering information (named after the Greek word *mneme*, which means 'memory'). People can use external aids (such as note taking or asking someone else) to enhance their memory, or they can rely on internal aids, such as rehearsal and various mnemonic strategies (Harris, 1980). Most mnemonic devices draw on the principle that the more retrieval cues that can be created and the more vivid these cues are, the better memory is likely to be. Generally, mnemonic devices are most useful when the to-be-remembered information lacks clear organisation.

Method of loci

One mnemonic strategy is the ***method of loci***, which uses visual imagery as a memory aid. The ancient Roman writer Cicero attributed this technique to the Greek poet Simonides, who was attending a banquet when he was reportedly summoned by the gods from the banquet hall to receive a message. In his absence, the roof collapsed, killing everyone. The bodies were mangled beyond recognition, but Simonides was able to identify the guests by their physical placement around the banquet table. He thus realised that images could be remembered by fitting them into an orderly arrangement of locations (Bower, 1970).

To use the method of loci, you must first decide on a series of 'snapshot' mental images of familiar locations. For instance, locations in your bedroom might be your pillow, your wardrobe, the top of your dresser and under the bed. Now, suppose that you need to do the following errands: pick up vitamin C, buy milk, return a book to the library and make plans with one of your friends for the weekend. You can remember these items by visualising each in one of your loci, making the image as vivid as possible to maximise the likelihood of retrieving it. Thus, you might picture the vitamin C pills as spilled all over your pillow, a bottle of milk poured over the best outfit in your wardrobe, the book lying on top of your dresser and your friend hiding under your bed until Friday night. Often, the more ridiculous the image, the easier it is to remember. While you are out doing your errands, you can mentally flip through your imagined loci to bring back the mental images.

SQ4R method

A strategy specifically developed to help students remember information in textbooks is called the ***SQ4R method***, for the six steps involved in the method: survey, question, read, recite, review and write (Martin, 1985; Robinson, 1961). The SQ4R method fosters active rather than passive learning while reading. In brief, the steps of this method are as follows:

- *Survey* Skim through the chapter, looking at headings and the summary. This will help you organise the material more efficiently as you encode.
- *Question* When you begin a section, turn the heading into a question; this alerts you to the content and makes reading more interesting. For example, for the subheading, 'Long-term memory systems', you might ask yourself, 'What evidence could demonstrate the existence of separate memory systems? Could patients with different brain lesions have one kind of LTM intact and another disrupted?'
- *Read* As you read, try to answer the questions you posed.
- *Recite* Mentally (or orally) answer your questions and rehearse relevant information before going on to the next section.
- *Review* When you finish the chapter, recall your questions and relate what you have learned to your experiences and interests.
- *wRite* As you read or listen to lectures, actively write answers to questions and take notes.

Recital is a key component of the SQ4R method.

INTERIM SUMMARY

Mnemonic devices are systematic strategies for remembering information. The ***method of loci*** associates new information with a visual image of a familiar place. The ***SQ4R method*** helps students study textbook material efficiently by encouraging them to survey, question, read, recite, review, and write.

Networks of association

One of the reasons mnemonics can be effective is that they connect new information with information already organised in memory. This makes the new information easier to access because a 'trail' blazed in the neural woods by prior knowledge can be more easily spotted than a new, barely worn path. As William James proposed over a century ago (1890, p. 662, italics deleted):

> The more other facts a fact is associated with in the mind, the better possession of it our memory retains. Each of its associates becomes a hook to which it hangs, a means to fish it up by when sunk beneath the surface. Together, they form a network of attachments by which it is woven into the entire tissue of our thought. The 'secret of a good memory' is thus the secret of forming diverse and multiple associations with every fact we care to retain.

James' comments bring us back once again to the concept of association, which, as we saw in chapter 6, is central to many aspects of learning. Associations are crucial to remembering because the pieces of information stored in memory form ***networks of association***, clusters of interconnected information. For example, for most people the word *dog* is associatively linked to characteristics such as barking and fetching (figure 7.11). It is also associated, though less strongly, with *cat* because cats and dogs are both household pets. The word or image of a dog is also linked to more idiosyncratic personal associations, such as an episodic memory of being bitten by a dog in childhood.

Each piece of information along a network is called a ***node***. Nodes may be thoughts, images, concepts, propositions, smells, tastes, memories, emotions or any other piece of information. That one node may have connections to many other nodes leads to tremendously complex networks of association. One way to think of a node is as a set of neurons distributed throughout the brain that fire together (see chapter 3). Their joint firing produces a representation of an object or category such as dog, which integrates visual, tactile, auditory, verbal and other information stored in memory. To search through memory means you go from node to node until you locate the right information. In this sense, nodes are like cities, which are connected to each other (associated) by roads (Reisberg, 1997).

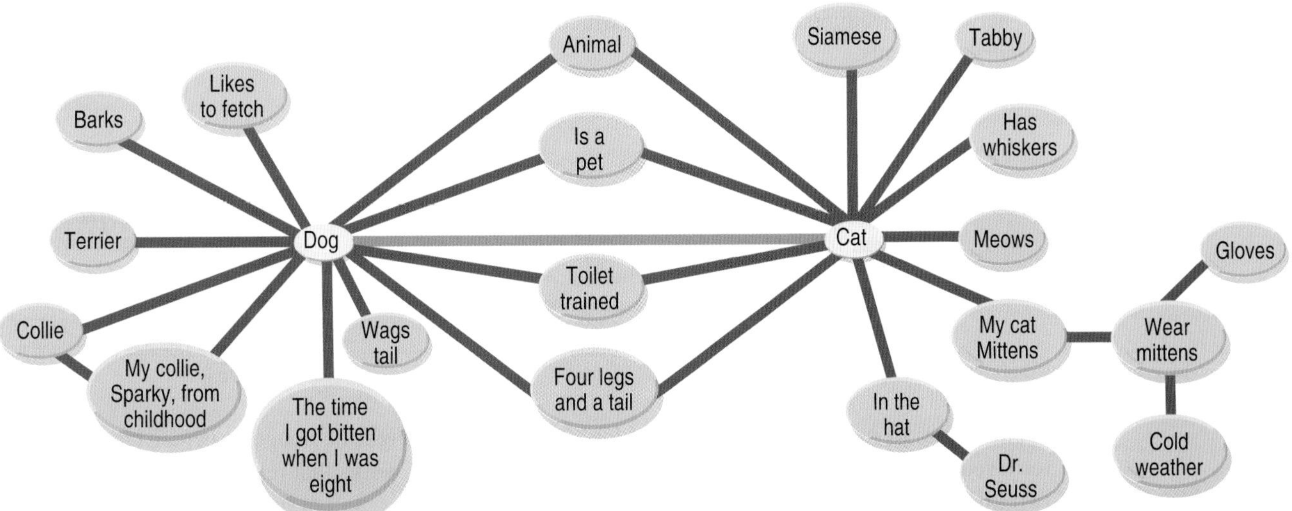

FIGURE 7.11
Networks of association. Long-term knowledge is stored in networks of association, ideas that are mentally connected with one another by repeatedly occurring together.

Not all associations are equally strong; *dog* is more strongly connected to *barks* than to *cat* or *animal*. To return to the cities analogy, some cities are connected by superhighways, which facilitate rapid travel between them, whereas others are connected only by slow, winding country roads. Other cities have no direct links at all, which means that travel between them requires an intermediate link. The same is true of associative networks: in figure 7.11 *cat* is not directly associated to *cold weather*, but it is through the intermediate link of *my cat Mittens*, which is semantically related to *wear mittens*, which is in turn linked to the *cold weather* node.

The neural processes underlying memory involve synaptic activity. No pun intended, but memories are formed by neurons making connections, or by breaking connections. Those **synapses** that are used repeatedly retain and strengthen their dendritic spines (site of synaptic connections), whereas others develop but are lost if not used frequently (chapter 3).

From a neuropsychological perspective, if two nodes without a direct link become increasingly associated through experience, a 'road' between them is built; and if the association continues to grow, that road will be 'widened' to ensure rapid neural transit between one and the other. If, on the other hand, a neural highway between two nodes falls into disuse because two objects or events stop occurring together (such as the link between the word *girlfriend* and a particular girlfriend months after the relationship has ended), the highway will fall into disrepair and be less easily travelled. The old road will not likely disappear completely: occasionally a traveller may wander off the main road down the old highway, as when a person accidentally calls his new girlfriend by his old girlfriend's name.

Spreading activation

One theory that attempts to explain the workings of networks of association involves spreading activation (Collins & Loftus, 1975; Collins & Quillian, 1969). According to ***spreading activation theory***, activating one node in a network triggers activation in closely related nodes. In other words, presenting a stimulus that leads to firing in the neural circuits that represent that stimulus spreads activation, or energy, to related information stored in memory.

Spreading activation does not always start with a stimulus such as a spoken word. Activation may also begin with a thought, fantasy or wish, which in turn activates other nodes. For example, a psychotherapy patient trying to decide whether to divorce his wife found the song *We can work it out* coming to mind on days when he leaned towards reconciliation. On days when he was contemplating divorce, however, he found himself inadvertently singing a different tune, *Fifty ways to leave your lover*.

Considerable research supports the theory of spreading activation. In one study, the experimenters presented participants with word pairs to learn, including the pair *ocean–moon* (see Nisbett & Wilson, 1977). Later, when asked to name a laundry detergent, participants in this condition were more likely to respond with Tide than control participants, who had been exposed to a different list of word pairs. You would expect similar findings if you replaced Tide with Surf in a comparative sample of Australian participants — Surf is a popular laundry detergent in Australia — although the connection would probably not be as strong.

The researchers offered an intriguing explanation (figure 7.12): the network of associations that includes *ocean* and *moon* also includes *tide*. Priming with *ocean–moon* thus activated other nodes on the network, spreading activation to *tide*, which was associated with another network of associations, laundry detergents.

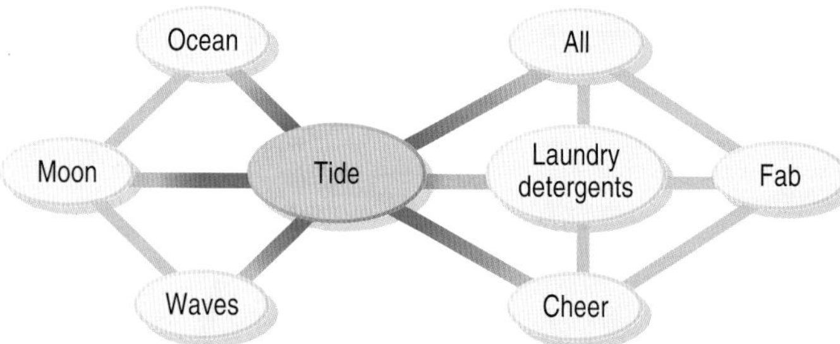

FIGURE 7.12
Spreading activation. Tide stands at the intersection of two activated networks of association and is thus doubly activated. In contrast, other brands only receive activation from one network. (This experiment, of course, only works in places where Tide has a substantial market share.)

According to many contemporary models, each time a thought or image is perceived, primed or retrieved from memory, the level of activation of the neural networks that represent it increases. Thus, two kinds of information are likely to be at a high state of activation at any given moment: recently activated information (such as a news story seen a moment ago on television) and frequently activated information (such as a doctor's knowledge about disease). For example, a person who has just seen a documentary on cancer is likely to identify the word *leukaemia* faster than someone who tuned in to a different channel; a doctor is similarly likely to identify the word quickly because *leukaemia* is at a chronically higher state of activation.

Hierarchical organisation of information

Although activating a *dog* node can trigger some idiosyncratic thoughts and memories, networks of association are far from haphazard jumbles of information. Efficient retrieval requires some degree of organisation of information so that the mind can find its way through dense networks of neural trails.

Some researchers have compared LTM to a filing cabinet, in which important information is kept towards the front of the files and less important information is relegated to the back of our mental archives or to a box in the attic. The filing cabinet metaphor also suggests that some information is filed hierarchically; that is, broad categories are composed of narrower subcategories, which in turn consist of even more specific categories.

For example, a person could store information about *animals* under the subcategories *pets*, *farm animals* and *wild animals*. Under *farm animals* are *cows*, *horses* and *chickens*. At each level of the hierarchy, each node will have features associated with it (such as knowledge that chickens squawk and lay eggs) as well as other associations to it (such as roasted chicken, which is associated with a very different smell than is the generic 'chickens').

Hierarchical storage is generally quite efficient, but it can occasionally lead to errors. For instance, when asked, 'Which is farther north, Perth or Sydney?' many people say Sydney. In fact, Perth is farther north. People mistakenly assume that Sydney is north of Perth because they go to their general level of knowledge about Western Australia and New South Wales. They remember that Perth is right at the bottom of the west coast of Australia, while Sydney is a significant distance up the east coast. In reality, the east coast of Australia extends much further south than the west coast.

Perth

Sydney

INTERIM SUMMARY

Knowledge stored in memory forms ***networks of association*** — clusters of interconnected information. Each piece of information along a network is called a ***node***. According to ***spreading activation theory***, activating one node in a network triggers activation in closely related nodes. Some parts of networks are organised hierarchically, with broad categories composed of narrower subcategories, which in turn consist of even more specific categories.

Schemas

The models of associative networks and spreading activation we have been discussing go a long way towards describing the organisation of memory, but they have limits. For example, psychologists have not yet agreed on how to represent propositions like 'The dog chased the cat' using network models, since if *dog* and *cat* are nodes how is the link between them (*chased*) represented? Further, activation of one node can actually either increase or inhibit activation of associated nodes, as when a person identifies an approaching animal as a dog and not a wolf and hence 'shuts off' the *wolf* node.

Psychologists have argued for over a century about the adequacy of principles of association in explaining memory (Bahrick, 1985). Some have argued that we do not associate isolated bits of information with each other but instead store and remember the 'gist' of facts and events. They note that when people remember passages of prose rather than single words or word pairs, they typically remember the general meaning of the passage rather than a verbatim account.

According to this view, when confronted with a novel event people match it against schemas stored in memory. Schemas are patterns of thought, or organised knowledge structures, that render the environment relatively predictable. When students walk into a classroom on the first day of class and a person resembling a professor begins to lecture, they listen and take notes in a routine fashion. They are not surprised that one person has assumed control of the situation and begun talking because they have a schema for events that normally transpire in a classroom. Proponents of schema theories argue that memory is an active process of reconstruction of the past. Remembering means combining bits and pieces of what we once perceived with general knowledge that helps us fill in the gaps. In this view, memory is not like taking snapshots of an event; it is more like taking notes.

Schemas affect the way people remember in two ways: by influencing the information they encode and by shaping the way they reconstruct data that they have already stored (Davidson, 1996; Rumelhart, 1984).

APPLY + DISCUSS

- If people's memories for events are, in part, driven by schemas, what implications would this have for people recalling details of crime scenes (Tuckey & Brewer, 2003)?
- Might their memory for those details be influenced by a 'crime schema'?
- What role would such schemas play in eyewitness testimony?

Schemas and encoding

Schemas influence the way people initially understand the meaning of an event and thus the manner in which they encode it in LTM. Harry Triandis (1994) relates an account of two Englishmen engaged in a friendly game of tennis in nineteenth-century China. The two were sweating and panting under the hot August sun. As they finished their final set, a Chinese friend sympathetically asked, 'Could you not get two servants to do this for you?' Operating from a different set of schemas, their Chinese friend encoded this event rather differently than would an audience at Wimbledon.

FIGURE 7.13
Influence of schemas on memory. Participants asked to recall this graduate student's office frequently remembered many items that actually were not in it but were in their office schemas.

SOURCE: Brewer and Treyens (1981).

Schemas and retrieval

Schemas not only provide hooks on which to hang information during encoding, but they also provide hooks for fishing information out of LTM. Many schemas have 'slots' for particular kinds of information (Minsky, 1975). A person shopping for a DVD player who is trying to recall the models she saw that day is likely to remember the names Sony and Pioneer but not Paul Collins (the salesman at one of the stores). Unlike Sony, Paul Collins does not fit into the slot 'brand names of DVD players'.

The slots in schemas often have default values, standard answers that fill in missing information the person did not initially notice or bother to store. When asked if the cover of this book gives the authors' names, you are likely to report that it does (default value = yes) even if you never really noticed, because the authors' names normally appear on a book cover. In fact, people are generally unable to tell which pieces of information in a memory are truly remembered and which reflect the operation of default values.

One classic study demonstrated the reconstructive role of schemas using a visual task (Brewer & Treyens, 1981). The experimenter instructed university student participants to wait (one at a time) in a 'graduate student's office' similar to the one depicted in figure 7.13 while he excused himself to check on something. The experimenter returned in 35 seconds and led the student to a different room. There, he asked the participant either to write down a description of the graduate student's office or to draw a picture of it, including as many objects as could be recalled.

The room contained a number of objects (e.g. bookshelves, coffeepot, desk) that would fit most participants' schema of a graduate student's office. Several objects, however, were conspicuous — or rather, inconspicuous — by their absence, such as a filing cabinet, a coffee cup, books on the shelves, a window, pens and pencils, and curtains. Many participants assumed the presence of these default items, however, and 'remembered' seeing them even though they had not actually been present.

Without schemas, life would seem like one random event after another, and efficient memory would be impossible. Yet as the research just described shows, schemas can lead people to misclassify information, to believe they have seen what they really have not seen and to fail to notice things that might be important.

Now is the time for all good men to to come to the aid of their countrymen.

The extra 'to' at the beginning of the second line is easily overlooked because of the schema-based expectation that it is not there. Students often fail to notice typographical errors in their papers for the same reason.

INTERIM SUMMARY

One way psychologists describe the organisation of LTM is in terms of schemas, organised knowledge about a particular domain. Proponents of schema theories argue that memory involves reconstruction of the past, by combining knowledge of what we once perceived with general knowledge that helps fill in the gaps. Schemas influence both the way information is encoded and the way it is retrieved.

A GLOBAL VISTA

Cross-cultural variation in memory — better, worse or just different?

The account of memory presented thus far is based almost exclusively on studies of participants in Western, technologically advanced societies. Do the general principles of memory from these samples apply cross-culturally, or do memory and thought differ depending on the cultural, historical and ecological context?

Memory and adaptation

Studies comparing memory processes across cultures (such as large industrial versus small tribal societies) often produce inconsistent findings, largely because people tend to do better on tasks that resemble the demands of their everyday lives (see Cole, Gay, Glick, & Sharp, 1971). Thus, members of hunter-gatherer societies are better at remembering the location of edible berries than people in industrial societies, who have superior recall for strings of digits (e.g. phone numbers).

Not everyone in a culture is the same, however, and different subgroups confront different ecological or environmental demands. For example, a study in Zambia (Africa) compared the ability of urban schoolboys and rural women to recall information from stories relevant to time (Deregowski, 1970). Whereas the day of a Zambian schoolboy is precisely structured by the clock (as in the West), the daily life of rural Zambian women is regulated primarily by cycles of night and day and is not driven by specific units of time. The experimenters found no differences between the two groups in their ability to recall information in general. However, the schoolboys were significantly more likely to recall aspects of the stories related to when things happened. Across and within cultures, people tend to remember information that matters to them, and they organise information in memory to match the demands of their environment.

A particularly important influence on memory that varies across cultures is literacy. Literacy increases the role played by verbal representations, since it converts many visual experiences to verbal experiences. In preliterate societies, the human brain is the means of storing memories, and people rely on oral history and tradition, such as storytelling, to pass on collective knowledge. Literate societies, on the other hand, store information in many ways that extend the limits of memory, from magazines, textbooks and computers, to simple devices such as lists, which can expand memory capacity exponentially (Goody, 1977).

Cultural models

Throughout this chapter, we have described memory as if it occurs in isolated information processors (see Cole, 1975). However, ***cultural models***, or shared cultural concepts, organise knowledge and shape the way people think and remember (chapter 19; D'Andrade, 1992; Moore & Mathews, 2001; Strauss & Quinn, 1997). Imagine, for example, how much more difficult the task of remembering how a neuron works might be for someone whose culture lacked the concept of cells.

Years ago, Frederic Bartlett (1932) demonstrated the impact of cultural models on retrieval. British participants read a North American Indian folk tale, waited 15 minutes and then attempted to reproduce it verbatim. Their errors were systematic: participants omitted or reworked unfamiliar details to make the story consistent with their own culturally shaped schemas.

INTERIM SUMMARY

Across and within cultures, people tend to remember information that matters to them, and they organise information in memory to match the demands of their environment. Shared cultural concepts, or ***cultural models***, also shape the way people think and remember.

Remembering, misremembering and forgetting

We could not do without our memories, but sometimes we wish we could. According to Daniel Schacter (1999), who has spent his life studying memory, human memory systems evolved through natural selection, but the same mechanisms that generally foster adaptation can regularly cause memory failures. He describes 'seven sins of memory' that plague us all:

- *transience* (the fact that memories fade)
- *absent-mindedness* (the failure to remember something when attention is elsewhere)
- *misattribution* (misremembering the source of a memory — something advertisers rely on when they tell half-truths about competing brands and people remember the half-truth but forget its source)
- *suggestibility* (thinking we remember an event that someone actually implanted in our minds)
- *bias* (distortions in the way we recall events that often tell the story in a way we would rather remember it)

- *persistence* (memories we wish we could get rid of but which keep coming back)
- ***forgetting*** (the inability to remember).

Although at first glance these 'sins' all seem maladaptive, many stem from adaptive memory processes that can go awry. For example, if memory were not transient or temporary, our minds would overflow with irrelevant information.

Perhaps the cardinal sin of memory is forgetting. Over a century ago, Ebbinghaus (1885/1964) documented a typical pattern of forgetting that occurs with many kinds of declarative knowledge: rapid initial loss of information after learning and only gradual decline thereafter (figure 7.14). Researchers have since refined Ebbinghaus' forgetting curve slightly to make it more precise — finding, in fact, that the relation between memory decline and length of time between learning and retrieval is logarithmic and hence predictable by a very precise mathematical function (Wixted & Ebbesen, 1991). This logarithmic relationship is very similar to Stevens' power law for sensory stimuli (chapter 4).

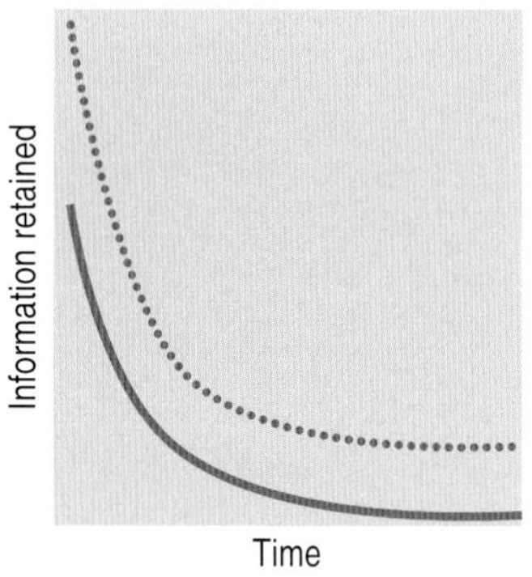

FIGURE 7.14
Rate of forgetting. Forgetting follows a standard pattern, with rapid initial loss of information followed by more gradual later decline. Increasing initial study time (the dotted line) increases retention, but forgetting occurs at the same rate. In other words, increased study shifts the curve upward but does not change the rate of forgetting or eliminate it.

This forgetting curve seems to apply whether the period of time is hours or years. For example, the same curve emerged when researchers studied people's ability to remember the names of old television shows: they rapidly forgot the names of shows cancelled within the last seven years, but the rate of forgetting trailed off after that (Squire, 1989).

How long is long-term memory?

When people forget, is the information no longer stored or is it simply no longer easy to retrieve? And is some information permanent, or does the brain eventually throw away old boxes in the attic if it has not used them for a number of years?

The first question is more difficult to answer than the second. Psychologists often distinguish between the availability of information in memory — whether it is still 'in there' — and its accessibility — the ease with which it can be retrieved. The tip-of-the-tongue phenomenon, like the priming effects shown by amnesics, is a good example of information that is available but inaccessible.

In large part, accessibility reflects level of activation, which diminishes over time but remains for much longer than most people would intuitively suppose. Memory for a picture flashed briefly on a screen a year earlier continues to produce some activation of the visual cortex, which is expressed implicitly even if the person has no conscious recollection of it (Cave, 1997). And most people have vivid recollections from their childhood of certain incidents that occurred once, such as the moment they heard the news that a beloved pet died. But what about the other hundreds of millions of incidents that they cannot retrieve? To what degree these memories are now unavailable, rather than just inaccessible, is unknown.

Studies of very long-term memory suggest, however, that if information is consolidated through spacing over long learning intervals, it will last a lifetime, even if the person does not rehearse it for half a century (Bahrick & Hall, 1991). Eight years after having taught students for a single semester, university lecturers will forget the names and faces of most of their students (sorry!), but 35 years after graduation people still recognise 90 percent of the names and faces from their high school yearbook.

The difference is in the spacing: the lecturer teaches a student for only a few months, whereas high school students typically know each other for at least three or four years. Similarly, people who take university mathematics courses that require them to use the knowledge they learned in high school algebra show nearly complete memory for algebra 50 years later even if they work as artists and never balance their chequebook. People who stop at high school algebra remember nothing of it decades later.

How accurate is long-term memory?

Aside from the question of *how long* people remember is the question of *how accurately* they remember. The short answer is that memory is both functional and reconstructive, so that most of the time it serves us well, but it is subject to a variety of errors and biases.

For example, the normal associative processes that help people remember can also lead to memory errors (see Robinson & Roediger, 1997; Schacter, Verfaellie, Aries, & Racine, 1998). In one set of studies the researchers presented participants with a series of words (such as *slumber*, *nap* and *bed*) that were all related to a single word that had *not* been presented (*sleep*). This essentially primed the word 'sleep' repeatedly (Roediger & McDermott, 1995). Not only did most participants remember having heard the multiply primed word, but the majority even remembered which of two people had read the word to them. Some participants refused to believe that the word had not been presented even after hearing an audiotape of the session!

Emotional factors can also bias recall. The investigators in one study asked university student participants to recall their maths, science, history, English and foreign language grades from high school and then compared their recollections to their high school transcripts (Bahrick, Hall, & Berger, 1996). Students recalled 71 percent of their grades correctly, which is certainly impressive.

More interesting, however, was the pattern of their errors (figure 7.15). Participants rarely misremembered their A's, but they rarely correctly remembered their D's. In fact, a D was twice as likely to be remembered as a B or C than as a D. Approximately 80 percent of participants tended to inflate their remembered grades, whereas only 6 percent reported grades lower than they had actually achieved. (The remaining 14 percent tended to remember correctly.)

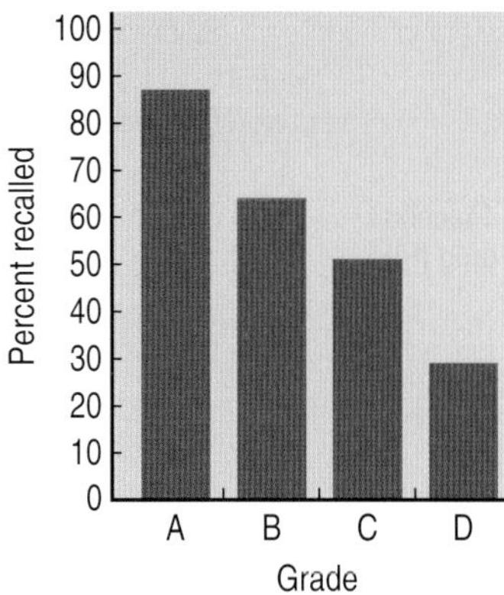

FIGURE 7.15
Distortion in memory for high school grades. The lower the grade, the less memorable it seems to be, demonstrating the impact of motivation and emotion on memory.

SOURCE: Adapted from Bahrick et al. (1996).

Flashbulb memories

If remembering is more like consulting an artist's sketch than a photograph, what do we make of ***flashbulb memories***, that is, vivid memories of exciting or highly consequential events (Brown & Kulik, 1977; Conway, 1995; Winograd & Neisser, 1993)? Many people can recall precisely where and when they first heard the news of the September 11 attacks on the United States in 2001, almost as if a camera had recorded that moment in time. People report similarly vivid memories of the announcement that Sydney had been awarded the 2000 Olympic Games, as well as personal events such as the death of a loved one or a romantic encounter (Rubin & Kozin, 1984).

Flashbulb memories are so clear and vivid that we tend to think of them as totally accurate; however, considerable evidence suggests that they are often not of snapshot clarity or accuracy and can even be entirely incorrect (Neisser, 1991). For example, on the day following the *Challenger* space shuttle disaster in the United States in 1986, people reported where they were when they heard the space shuttle had disintegrated. Three years later when they were again asked where they were, not a single person recalled with complete accuracy where they had been, and a third of the respondents were completely incorrect in their recall (McCloskey, Wible, & Cohen, 1988; Neisser & Harsch, 1992).

Do you remember where you were when you heard that Crocodile Hunter Steve Irwin had died?

Emotional arousal and memory

In trying to understand 'flashbulb' memories, Cahill, Prins, Weber, and McGaugh, (1994) designed an elegant experiment that manipulated both the emotional content of the material to be remembered and adrenalin (the fight-or-flight hormone, chapter 3) (see figure 7.16 overleaf). First, they developed two series of 12 slides depicting a little boy leaving for school, having an unusual experience and then returning home. In the middle section of slides, the unusual experience differed for the two series. In the control or neutral condition, the little boy goes on a field trip to the hospital and sees a disaster drill. In the experimental or arousal condition, the little boy is in a tragic accident in which his feet are severed from his legs and a concussion leads to bleeding in the brain. Miraculously, the doctors are able to reattach the boy's feet and control the brain bleeding.

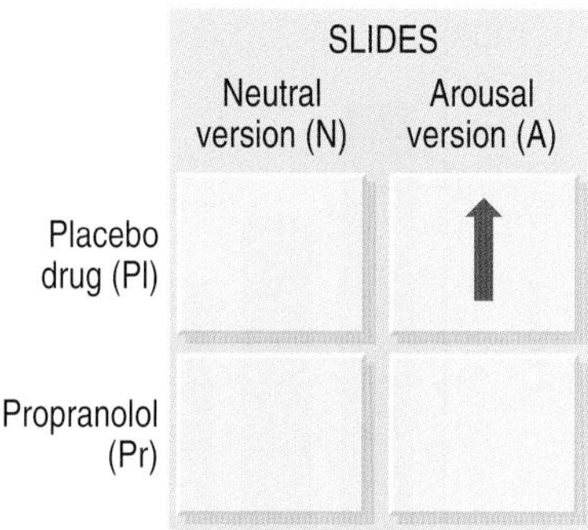

FIGURE 7.16
In an investigation of the relationship between emotional arousal and memory, researchers found that memory was higher for participants in the arousal condition who had not received propranolol, relative to the other three conditions.

Half the participants were shown the neutral slide series; the other half were shown the arousal slide series. The second manipulation, that of adrenalin activity, was created by giving a drug that antagonises the actions of adrenalin (propranolol) to half the participants in each group. The propranolol blocked any effect of adrenalin that the arousal slides produced. In this two-by-two design, two factors were studied: (1) neutral or arousal slide versions, and (2) placebo drug or the adrenalin antagonist propranolol. Thus, there were four groups (see figure 7.16) — NPl: neutral, placebo drug; NPr: neutral, propranolol; APl: arousal, placebo drug; and APr: arousal, propranolol.

The researchers hypothesised that the memory for all groups, when tested one week later, would be the same, except for the APl group, for which memory of the middle set of slides (when the boy was in the accident) would be better than the other groups. That is, they hypothesised that the emotionally arousing slides, which triggered adrenalin release, would lead to enhanced memory of those slides. Neither of the neutral groups would have any adrenalin release (thus, the propranolol would not have any adrenalin to antagonise) and the arousal group whose adrenalin activity was antagonised by propranolol would not have enhanced memory, even though they saw the arousing slides. The results supported their hypothesis.

These results support the notion that our 'flashbulb' memories for emotionally arousing events are dependent on the fight-or-flight hormone, adrenalin. It is important to note that memory was enhanced *only* for the arousal slides, not for the neutral beginning and ending slides. Thus, emotional arousal, via adrenalin activity in the brain, leads to enhanced memory.

Eyewitness testimony

Research on the accuracy of memory has an important real-life application in the courtroom: how accurate is eyewitness testimony (see Melinder, Scullin, Gunnerod, & Nyborg, 2005; Schacter, 1995b; Sporer, Malpass, & Koehnken, 1996; Wells et al., 2000; Wells & Olson, 2003)? Numerous studies have explored this question experimentally, usually by showing participants a short film or slides of an event such as a car accident (Wells & Loftus, 1984; Zaragosta & Mitchell, 1996). The experimenter then asks participants specific questions about the scene, sometimes introducing information that was not present in the actual scene, asking leading questions or contradicting what participants saw.

These studies show that seemingly minor variations in the wording of a question can determine what participants remember from a scene. One study simply substituted the definite article *the* for the indefinite article *a* in the question 'Did you see the/a broken headlight?' Using *the* instead of *a* increased both the likelihood that participants would recall seeing a broken headlight and their certainty that they had, even if they never actually observed one (Loftus & Palmer, 1974; Loftus & Zanni, 1975).

One Australian study (Dietze & Thomson, 1993) explored the accuracy of child witness testimony by showing participants a film and then asking them questions about it under three conditions: first, where the film was being viewed at the time; second, using a series of specific questions; and third, using free recall. The correctness of recall was better when the film was being viewed in context or when specific questions were asked, as compared to free recall. Thus retrieval of memories was affected by the way in which the participants were asked to recall details of a past event.

A more recent Australian study by Tuckey and Brewer (2003) examined how schemas, or expectations, for a crime influenced the types of information eyewitnesses remembered and forgot over time. Their results showed that when a witness reports details that are common to that type of crime (i.e. which are expected of that crime), the schema-consistent details are likely to be accurate and recalled at subsequent interviews.

These findings have clear implications both in the courtroom and in the way police interrogate witnesses. However, individuals vary in their susceptibility to misleading information (Loftus, Levidow, & Diensing, 1992; see also Melinder, Goodman, Eilertsen, & Magnussen, 2004). Further, some aspects of a memory may be more reliable than others. The emotional stress of witnessing a traumatic event can lead to heightened processing of (and hence better memory for) core details of the event but less extensive processing of peripheral details (Christianson, 1992). A sharp barrister could thus attack the credibility of a witness's entire testimony by establishing that her memory of peripheral details is faulty, even though she clearly remembers the central aspects of the event. Consequently, an emerging field is the study of methods for evoking and assessing traumatic memories. The aim is to better determine the processes and contents of memory retrieval in traumatised individuals (see Hopper & van der Kolk, 2001).

ETHICAL DILEMMA

A seven-year-old boy witnesses a brutal assault on his mother by a home invader in the early hours of the morning. The house is dark and the attacker leaves unaware of the child's presence. The boy is the only witness to the assault and has to come to the aid of his mother after the assault. The police later arrest a suspect and need evidence to secure a conviction when the case goes to trial. Eyewitness testimony identifying the culprit would certainly help.

- Should the young boy be allowed to testify at trial? Why or why not?
- How accurate is the child's testimony likely to be?
- Discuss the ethical issues most relevant to this case.

INTERIM SUMMARY

The flipside of memory is ***forgetting***. Many kinds of declarative knowledge show a similar forgetting curve, which is initially steep and then levels off. Psychologists often distinguish between the availability of information in memory — whether it is still 'in there' — and its accessibility — the ease with which it can be retrieved. People tend to make memory errors for a variety of reasons, some cognitive and some emotional. ***Flashbulb memories*** — vivid memories of exciting or highly consequential events — are sometimes extremely accurate but sometimes completely mistaken. Eyewitness testimony is also subject to many biases and errors.

Why do people forget?

The reconstructive nature of remembering — the fact that we have to weave together a memory from patches of specific and general knowledge — leaves memory open to a number of potential errors and biases. But why do people sometimes forget things entirely? Psychologists have proposed several explanations, including decay, interference and motivated forgetting.

Decay theory

Decay theory explains forgetting as a result of a fading memory trace. Having a thought or perception produces changes in synaptic connections, which in turn create the potential for remembering if the neural circuits that were initially activated are later reactivated. According to decay theory, these neurophysiological changes fade with disuse, much as a path in the forest grows over unless repeatedly trodden. The decay theory is difficult to corroborate or disprove empirically. However, it fits with many observed memory phenomena. Further, some studies do show a pattern of rapid and then more gradual deactivation of neural pathways in the hippocampus (which is involved in memory consolidation), which suggests a possible physiological basis for decay (see Anderson, 1995).

Interference theory

A prime culprit in memory failure is ***interference***, the intrusion of similar memories on each other, as when students confuse two theories they learned around the same time or two similar-sounding words in a foreign language. Finding the right path in the neural wilderness is difficult if two paths are close together and look alike. Or to use the filing cabinet metaphor, storing too many documents under the same heading makes finding the right one difficult. Cognitive psychologists distinguish two kinds of interference. ***Proactive interference*** refers to the interference of previously stored memories with the retrieval of new information, as when a person calls a new romantic partner by the name of an old one (a common but dangerous memory lapse). In ***retroactive interference***, new information interferes with retrieval of old information, as when people have difficulty recalling their home phone numbers from past residences. One reason children take years to memorise multiplication tables, even though they can learn the names of cartoon characters or classmates with astonishing speed, is the tremendous interference that is involved, because every number is paired with so many others (Anderson, 1995).

APPLY + DISCUSS

Most people cannot explicitly remember events before about age four, a phenomenon known as childhood amnesia.

- What is your earliest memory?
- Why might we be unable to retrieve memories from before age three or four? What aspects of the way we represent, store and retrieve information might affect our capacity to recall early memories?
- What neurological factors might limit access to early episodic memories?

Motivated forgetting

Another cause of forgetting is ***motivated forgetting***, or forgetting for a reason. People often explicitly instruct themselves or others to forget, as when a person stops in the middle of a sentence and says, 'Oops — forget that. That's the wrong address. The right one is . . .' (Bjork & Bjork, 1996). At other times, the intention to forget is implicit, as when a person who parks in a different parking space every day implicitly remembers to forget where she parked the day before so it does not interfere with memory for where she parked today (Bjork, Bjork, & Anderson, 1998).

Experimental evidence suggests that goal-directed forgetting requires active inhibition of the forgotten information, which remains available but inaccessible. Researchers have demonstrated this by using directed forgetting procedures: participants learn a list of words but are told midway to forget the words they just learned and remember only the last part of the list. This procedure reduces recall for the words in the first part of the list and decreases proactive interference from them, so that participants can more easily remember words in the last half of the list. This outcome suggests that the procedure is in fact inhibiting retrieval of the to-be-forgotten words. This procedure does not, however, decrease recognition of, or implicit memory for, the to-be-forgotten words, and they remain available, just less accessible.

Other studies show that instructing a person not to think about something can effectively keep the information from consciousness, but that deliberately suppressing information in this way creates an automatic, unconscious process that 'watches out' for the information and hence keeps it available (Wegner, 1992). For example, when people are instructed to suppress an exciting thought about sex, they remain physiologically aroused even while the thought is outside awareness. In fact, they remain just as aroused as participants instructed to think about the sexual thought (Wegner, Shortt, Blake, & Page, 1990). In a sense, goal-directed forgetting is like a form of prospective memory, in which the intention is to forget something in the future rather than to remember it. In this situation, forgetting is actually a form of remembering! In real life, people often try to inhibit unpleasant or anxiety-provoking thoughts or feelings (chapter 11). They often forget things they do not want to remember, such as 'overlooking' a dentist appointment.

False memories and repressed memories

The concept of repression has always been controversial in psychology (Holmes, 1990), but it is now the centrepiece of controversy (Sivers, Schooler, & Freyd, 2002). It is at the heart of claims of childhood sexual abuse and counterclaims of false memories raised by alleged perpetrators. The alleged perpetrators claim that the charges of sexual abuse against them have been invented by incompetent clinicians who have convinced their patients of the existence of events that never occurred (Del Monte, 2001; Howe, 2000; Pezdek & Banks, 1996).

The question of implanting false memories is exceedingly difficult to address scientifically for a number of reasons. First, distinguishing true from false allegations is difficult in all legal circumstances, but it is even more difficult when the events may have occurred 15 years ago. Second, a cardinal feature of sexual abuse is that the perpetrator does everything possible to maintain secrecy (including threatening the victim) and to discredit the victim if she or he ever tells the story — a situation not unlike what often occurs with rape, political torture and genocide (Herman, 1992). Third, some number of innocent people are unfairly accused: divorcing parents sometimes accuse former spouses as a tactic in custody disputes, and some poorly trained therapists look for (and 'find') abuse whenever an adult female patient steps into their office complaining of anxiety or depression (Loftus, 1993).

Evidence of false memories

Data from numerous laboratory studies suggest that people can sometimes be led to create compelling memories of things that did not happen (Loftus, 1997a; Payne, Nevschate, Lampien, & Lynn, 1997). As we have seen, presenting people with a series of words semantically related to a target word that was not presented can produce high rates of false recognition of the target, and people can be quite firm in their beliefs about these false memories. Women reporting a recovered memory of childhood sexual abuse are more likely than other women to recognise a target word (*sweet*) mistakenly as having been present in an earlier list of related words (*sugar*, *candy*, *honey*) (Clancy, Schachter, McNally, & Pitman, 2000). Women who report remembering abuse all along (as opposed to recovering it) do not show this bias.

In another experimental design that bears on false memories, researchers obtain detailed information from parents of university students about events that actually occurred when their children were younger and then present the students with several real memories and one false one, such as getting lost in a shopping centre at age five and being found by an elderly woman (Loftus, 1997b). The investigators then interview participants about each event, ask them if they remember it, and ask them to recall what they remember. In these studies, roughly 15 to 25 percent of participants can be induced to recall a false memory over the course of two or three interviews. More recent research from New Zealand indicates that drawing things related to false information while being questioned may promote false memories in children (see Strange, Garry, & Sutherland, 2003). Furthermore, Sharman, Manning, and Garry (2005) found that asking adults to explain earlier events inflated their confidence and memory for those events. Other research has demonstrated the role of sociolinguistic cues on memory. For example,

Vornik, Sharman, and Garry (2003) found that people are likely to be misled by an inaccurate narration if the narrator is high (rather than low) on social attractiveness.

For most people, however, the vulnerability to recall false memories is not without limit. When one researcher tried to induce memories more like those of sexual abuse victims (in this case, memory of a rectal enema in childhood), none of the participants created a false memory (Pezdek, cited in Loftus, 1997b). There is obviously a need for caution in extending the findings of these experimental studies to the creation of false memories of sexual abuse, a highly traumatic and evocative event.

Scepticism and discounting misinformation

By Professor Stephan Lewandowsky, University of Western Australia

People are often exposed to information that later turns out to be false. Not too long ago, some segments of the media were abuzz with apparent 'errors' in the latest Assessment Report of the Intergovernmental Panel on Climate Change (IPCC). Aside from one typo — referring to the year 2035 rather than the likely intended year of 2350 — the reports of 'errors' have been found to have little or no basis in fact. In one well-known instance, the UK *Sunday Times* newspaper issued a retraction and apologised to a scientist whose views it had misrepresented.

What is the long-term fate in memory of tentative, or outright false, information? What happens when a media story is corrected? Do people also correct their memories and update the memorised information? If people accurately updated their memory, then the retraction of earlier misinformation — if provided by a high-credibility source — should lead to its discounting. People who are aware of the *Sunday Times*' retraction of their claim about the IPCC should no longer believe the earlier alleged 'error'.

However, there is much laboratory-based evidence that people continue to rely on misinformation, even if they demonstrably remember and understand a subsequent retraction or correction (e.g. Johnson & Seifert, 1994, 1998; Wilkes & Reynolds, 1999). For example, when people read a story about a hypothetical jewellery theft, they continued to infer the guilt of a person initially presented as a suspect, even though the story later provided an alibi. This persistent reliance on misinformation occurs even when participants correctly recall the alibi (Johnson & Seifert, 1994). Misinformation is discounted only if the retraction also provides people with an *alternative* to the initial message, either by direct suggestion or by inducing suspicions about the ulterior motives underlying the misinformation. For example, if the jewellery theft story concludes with an alternative culprit being arrested, people no longer consider the original suspect to be guilty. Likewise, discounting is also possible if suspicions are raised about the motives underlying misinformation; for example, by noting that it might represent a deliberate attempt at manipulation (Fein, McCloskey, & Tomlinson, 1997). It is probable, thus, that readers of the *Sunday Times* who were sceptical of the motives underlying the very vigorous media attack on the IPCC were more aware of the initially reported information being wrong than readers who were not sceptical of the media's motives.

In an earlier study (Lewandowsky, Stritzke, Oberauer, & Morales, 2005), it was confirmed that cognitive mechanisms also apply to processing of information related to very public events (in the instance of this study, to the Iraq War of 2003). The effects of correction of misinformation on people's memory and beliefs for war-related events in two coalition countries (Australia and the United States), and one that opposed the war (Germany), were investigated as part of the study. Of greatest interest were responses to events that were initially presented as fact, but which were subsequently retracted (of which there were at least as many as the number of spurious reports about the 'errors' made by the IPCC). Only those people who were suspicious of the motives underlying the conflict successfully discounted misinformation; those who believed in the primary official reason for the war — that it was fought to destroy WMDs — failed to discount the discredited versions of events. Because they were less suspicious overall, participants in the United States showed less sensitivity to the correction of misinformation than those in Australia and Germany. Importantly, scepticism was not shown to be related to how people process information that is true. Scepticism is, hence, not just general cynicism, but a crucial tool that permits people to differentiate between truth and falsehood.

Evidence of repressed memories

Other studies call into question the charge that most psychotherapy patients who believe they have been sexually abused invent these memories. The majority of victims of repeated or severe sexual abuse in childhood have at least some memories of the abuse prior to psychotherapy, although their memories are often fragmented (Herman, 1992). Their recollection of childhood events tends to have gaps of months or years, and the memories of traumatic experiences they do recall frequently come to them in flashbacks, in physical forms (such as the sensation of gagging that initially attended the experience of being forced to perform oral sex), or in nightmares.

Several studies document that periods of amnesia for sexual abuse are common (see Briere & Conte, 1993; Loftus, Polonsky, & Fullilove, 1994), just as in other traumatic events such as combat or rape (Arrigo & Pezdek, 1997). Perhaps the clearest empirical evidence for repressed memories comes from a study that tracked down women who had been treated at a hospital for sexual molestation when they were children (Williams, 1994). Seventeen years after their documented abuse, 38 percent were amnesic for the incident. When asked if any family members had ever gotten into trouble for their sexual behaviour, one participant, who denied sexual abuse, reported that before she was born an uncle had apparently molested a little girl and was stabbed to death by the girl's mother. Examination of newspaper reports 17 years earlier found that the participant herself had been one of the uncle's two victims and that the mother of the other victim had indeed stabbed the perpetrator.

Perhaps the moral of the story is that psychologists should always attend both to the phenomenon they are studying — in this case, repressed memories — and to their own needs, fears and cognitive biases. For example, research demonstrates that people with abuse histories are more likely to see or hear themes of abuse in ambiguous situations (Nigg, Lohr, Westen, Gold, & Silk, 1992). Thus, clinicians with painful memories of their own childhood should be particularly careful to avoid jumping to conclusions or subtly influencing patients with leading questions.

On the other hand, researchers who may have had little or no exposure to real sexual abuse victims should be circumspect about overstepping the limits of their vantage point. Researchers and clinicians alike need to look carefully at their own cognitive and motivational biases before attempting to rewrite — or write off — the life histories of others.

INTERIM SUMMARY

The ***decay theory*** explains forgetting as a result of a fading memory trace; disuse of information leads to a gradual decrease in the strength of neural connections. ***Interference*** of similar information is another cause of forgetting. ***Proactive interference*** refers to the interference of previously stored memories with the retrieval of new information, whereas ***retroactive interference*** refers to the interference of new information with retrieval of old information. Another cause of forgetting is ***motivated forgetting***, or forgetting for a reason. The final word has not yet been written about repressed memories of childhood sexual abuse, although the data suggest caution on both sides: memories recovered in therapy cannot be assumed to be accurate, but they also cannot be routinely dismissed as false.

Disordered memories

We have seen that distortion can occur within the memories of people with normal brain function. Specific kinds of distortion can also occur within the memories of people whose brains have been affected by illness or injury. These are called disordered memories. There are two main types of disordered memories — anterograde and retrograde.

Anterograde amnesia

Anterograde amnesia involves the inability to retain new memories. This amnesia is typically caused by damage in the temporal lobe, particularly in the hippocampus and subcortical region (Mishkin & Appenzeller, 1987). People with this condition often have no problem retrieving memories stored before their brains were damaged, but cannot learn anything new (Gleitman, Fridlund, & Reisberg, 1999). The brain simply does not retain or retrieve fresh information. Anterograde amnesia is a symptom that is typically associated with Alzheimer's disease (chapter 12).

Retrograde amnesia

By contrast, ***retrograde amnesia*** involves losing memories from a period before the time that a person's brain was damaged. Brain tumours and strokes often cause this form of amnesia. Severely depressed or manic patients may also experience a brief period of retrograde amnesia following electroconvulsive therapy (Andreason & Black, 1996) — they have no memory of the treatment or of the events directly preceding it (chapter 16). Commonly the amnesia covers only a short period (although this can be up to several years) before the injury or illness damaged the brain — older memories and new memories are not affected. The reasons why this occurs are still being debated (see Squire, 1987).

INTERIM SUMMARY

Specific kinds of distortion can also occur within the memories of people whose brains have been affected by illness or injury. ***Anterograde amnesia*** involves the inability to retain new memories. By contrast, ***retrograde amnesia*** involves losing memories from a period before the time that a person's brain was damaged.

Central questions revisited

◆ What is memory?

We began this chapter with a central question: what is the nature of memory? Is memory the recollection of facts? Or are the feelings that return with the episodic memory of our first kiss (or the procedural memory of *how* to kiss after a long dry spell!) rightly considered memory phenomena? And what is the relationship between learning and memory?

To answer these questions requires a consideration of the perspectives that have guided our inquiry into memory. We have focused in this chapter primarily on the cognitive perspective, just as the previous chapter on learning focused on the behaviourist perspective. But as the concept of memory has expanded to include phenomena such as implicit memory, we are beginning to see an integration of perspectives that would have seemed unimaginable just 10 years ago, as cognitive psychologists move into terrain traditionally viewed as the 'turf' of other perspectives.

Take, for example, the relationship between learning and memory. Whatever happened to classical and operant conditioning in the standard model of memory? Surely an animal must be remembering something when it produces an adaptive response based on prior experience? But behaviourists emphasised that these forms of learning do not require conscious attention (that is, retrieval into STM) and often involve emotional learning (as when a rat learns to avoid situations associated with fear-inducing stimuli). A preliminary answer has begun to emerge: conditioning is a form of associative memory that is expressed implicitly rather than retrieved as explicit, declarative memory.

Our expanding understanding of memory has also begun to narrow the gulf between cognitive, psychodynamic and evolutionary approaches. The standard model assumed that information had to be processed consciously (in STM) before being stored in LTM and that remembering required conscious retrieval. Psychoanalysis, in contrast, proposed that most mental processes occur outside awareness, are processed in parallel and can be expressed in behaviour without ever becoming conscious. Freud, like most contemporary cognitive theorists, was schooled in classical associationist thought, and he proposed a network theory of the mind and a mechanism similar to spreading activation a century ago (see Erdelyi, 1985; Freud, 1895/1966; Pribram & Gill, 1976). He argued that networks of association operate unconsciously, leading people to think, feel and behave in ways they may not understand. Freud and later psychodynamic theorists thus developed an approach to treating psychological problems that involves trying to map these networks, so that the person can begin to recognise the implicit triggers for ideas, feelings and behaviour patterns that lead to problems such as repeated struggles with bosses or other authority figures.

Finally, the standard model viewed the capacity for memory and thought as essentially independent of content; that is, as applying to any kind of information. The mind was a general information-processing machine that could take almost any input, manipulate it and remember it with appropriate encoding and rehearsal. But an increasingly modular conception of the brain and memory systems has made contemporary cognitive models more compatible with a view of cognition emerging in evolutionary circles. This view maintains that the brain has evolved content-specific mechanisms that facilitate the remembering and processing of very particular kinds of information (Tooby & Cosmides, 1992). It is no accident that we have the capacity to perceive and recognise faces that differ in what are objectively some incredibly trivial ways. (To a possum, we all look alike.) Knowing who we are dealing with is incredibly important from an adaptive perspective, so it is perhaps not surprising that we are born with specialised neural circuits that help us recognise faces.

In sum, as cognitive neuroscience has expanded the domain of memory, it has led to an unforeseen potential for integration among cognitive, behavioural, psychodynamic and evolutionary perspectives. Perhaps someday we will not remember the differences among them so clearly.

◆

SUMMARY

1 Memory and information processing

- Case studies of neurologically impaired patients and experimental studies of normal participants have demonstrated that memory is composed of several systems.
- For information to return to mind after it is no longer present, it has to be put into a mental code, or representation. The major forms of representations studied by psychologists are ***sensory representations*** and ***verbal representations***. People also store memory for actions as motoric representations.
- The standard model of memory views the mind as a computer, which stores, transforms and retrieves information processing. It includes three sequential memory stores or stages of memory. The first is the ***sensory register***, the split-second mental representation of a perceived stimulus that remains very briefly after that stimulus disappears. ***Iconic storage*** describes visual sensory registration; ***echoic storage*** describes auditory sensory registration.
- ***Short-term memory (STM)*** stores information for roughly 20 to 30 seconds, unless the information is maintained through ***rehearsal*** (repeating the information again and again). This form of rehearsal, which merely maintains information in STM, is called ***maintenance rehearsal***. ***Elaborative rehearsal*** — thinking about and elaborating on the information's meaning — tends to be superior for storing information in long-term memory.
- Important information is passed along to ***long-term memory (LTM)***, where representations may last as long as a lifetime. Recovering information from LTM, or ***retrieval***, brings it back into STM, or consciousness.
- In recent years, this model has been changing substantially. Instead of viewing memory exclusively in terms of serial processing (which assumes that information passes through a series of stages, one at a time and in order), researchers now view memory as involving a set of ***modules*** that operate simultaneously (in parallel) rather than sequentially (one at a time). Researchers now recognise that not all remembering is expressed by retrieving information into consciousness, or STM, and they rely less on the metaphor of mind as computer than mind as brain.

2 Working memory

- Psychologists now refer to STM as ***working memory***, the temporary storage and processing of information that can be used to solve problems, respond to environmental demands or achieve goals. According to one prominent model, control processes such as rehearsal, reasoning and making decisions about how to balance two tasks simultaneously are the work of a limited capacity central executive system; whereas storage involves at least two limited-capacity systems, a visual store (also called the visuospatial sketchpad) and a verbal store.
- The existence of neurological patients who show deficits in either working memory or LTM but not both suggests that these memory systems are neurologically distinct, although in everyday life they work together, as frontal working memory networks provide a special form of activation to networks in the posterior parts of the cortex that represent current perceptions and information stored in LTM. One way to expand the capacity of working memory in particular domains is ***chunking***; that is, grouping information into larger units than single words or digits. The roughly seven pieces of information stored in visual or auditory working memory can represent larger, more meaningful pieces of information.

3 Types of long-term memory

- Types of long-term memory can be distinguished by the kind of knowledge stored and the way this knowledge is retrieved and expressed. People store two kinds of information, declarative and procedural. ***Declarative memory*** refers to memory for facts and events and is subdivided into ***semantic*** or ***generic memory*** (general world knowledge or facts) and ***episodic memory*** (memories of particular events). ***Procedural memory*** refers to 'how to' knowledge of procedures or skills.
- Information can be retrieved either explicitly or implicitly. ***Explicit memory*** refers to conscious recollection, expressed through ***recall*** (the spontaneous retrieval of material from LTM) or ***recognition*** (memory for whether something currently perceived has been previously encountered or learned). ***Implicit memory*** is expressed in behaviour rather than consciously retrieved.
- Neurological data suggest that different kinds of memory form discrete memory systems. The hippocampus and adjacent regions of the cortex are central to the consolidation of explicit memories but do not appear to play an important role in either implicit memory or working memory.
- ***Everyday memory*** — memory as it occurs in daily life — tends to be functional (focused on remembering information that is meaningful) and emotionally significant. ***Prospective memory*** is memory for things that need to be done in the future.

4 Encoding and organisation of long-term memory

- For information to be retrievable from memory, it must be ***encoded***, or cast into a representational form, or 'code,' that can be readily accessed from memory.
- Among the factors that influence later accessibility of memory are the degree to which information is elaborated, reflected upon and processed in a meaningful way during encoding (***level of processing***); the presence of ***retrieval cues*** (stimuli or thoughts that can be used to facilitate recollection); the ***spacing*** of study sessions (with longer intervals between rehearsal sessions tending to be more effective);

and the use of multiple and redundant representational modes to encode the information, which provides more cues for its retrieval. ***Mnemonic devices***, or systematic strategies for remembering information, can also be useful for remembering, as can external memory aids such as notes.

- Information stored in memory forms networks of association — clusters of interconnected units of information called ***nodes***. According to spreading activation theory, activating one node in a network triggers activation in closely related nodes. Some information is organised hierarchically, with broad categories composed of narrower subcategories, which in turn consist of even more specific categories.
- Schemas are organised knowledge about a particular domain. According to schema theory, memory is an active, reconstructive process that involves reactivation of both the initial representations of an event and general knowledge that helps fill in the gaps. Schemas facilitate memory by organising information at both encoding and retrieval.
- Many schemas are shaped by culture, from beliefs about foods that are appropriate to eat to beliefs about the meaning of life. Across cultures, people tend to remember what matters to them.

5 Remembering, misremembering and forgetting

- Ebbinghaus discovered a forgetting curve that applies to many kinds of declarative memory, in which considerable information is initially lost but ***forgetting*** then tapers off.
- Memory is a reconstructive process that mingles representations of actual experiences with general knowledge. Although memory is functional and tends to work well most of the time, misremembering is common, even in ***flashbulb memories*** (vivid memories of exciting or highly consequential events) and eyewitness testimony, which can be biased by even seemingly minor changes in the way questions are asked.
- Three theories attempt to account for forgetting: ***decay theory*** (which explains forgetting as a result of a fading memory trace); ***interference*** of new and old information with retrieval of the other; and ***motivated forgetting*** (forgetting for a reason, which leads to inhibition of retrieval).
- Specific kinds of distortion can also occur within the memories of people whose brains have been affected by illness or injury. ***Anterograde amnesia*** involves the inability to retain new memories. By contrast, ***retrograde amnesia*** involves losing memories from a period before the time that a person's brain was damaged.

KEY TERMS

anterograde amnesia, *p. 290*
chunking, *p. 268*
confabulation, *p. 258*
cultural models, *p. 283*
decay theory, *p. 287*
declarative memory, *p. 269*
echoic storage, *p. 261*
elaborative rehearsal, *p. 262*
encoded, *p. 275*
encoding specificity principle, *p. 276*
episodic memory, *p. 269*
everyday memory, *p. 273*
explicit memory, *p. 270*
flashbulb memories, *p. 285*
forgetting, *p. 284*
generic memory, *p. 269*
iconic storage, *p. 261*
implicit memory, *p. 270*
interference, *p. 287*
level of processing, *p. 275*
long-term memory (LTM), *p. 262*
maintenance rehearsal, *p. 262*
method of loci, *p. 278*
mnemonic devices, *p. 278*
modules, *p. 263*
motivated forgetting, *p. 287*
networks of association, *p. 279*
node, *p. 279*
priming effects, *p. 271*
proactive interference, *p. 287*
procedural memory, *p. 269*
prospective memory, *p. 274*
recall, *p. 271*
recognition, *p. 271*
rehearsal, *p. 262*
retrieval, *p. 262*
retrieval cues, *p. 277*
retroactive interference, *p. 287*
retrograde amnesia, *p. 291*
retrospective memory, *p. 274*
semantic memory, *p. 269*
sensory registers, *p. 261*
sensory representations, *p. 260*
serial position effect, *p. 263*
short-term memory (STM), *p. 261*
spacing effect, *p. 277*
spreading activation theory, *p. 280*
SQ4R method, *p. 278*
tip-of-the-tongue phenomenon, *p. 271*
verbal representations, *p. 260*
working memory, *p. 265*

REVIEW QUESTIONS

1. Describe the characteristics of working memory, short-term memory and long-term memory.
2. Distinguish between procedural, declarative, explicit and implicit memories, and between the two kinds of explicit retrieval.
3. Explain how information is encoded in long-term memory using deep and shallow processing.
4. Describe techniques for retrieving information from long-term memory.
5. Outline the seven characteristics of human memory systems that can regularly cause memory failures.

DISCUSSION QUESTIONS

1. Why is context important to retrieval from memory?
2. Is the eyewitness on trial when giving evidence in legal cases?
3. How accurate are repressed memories?

APPLICATION QUESTIONS

1. Test your understanding of the different memory types discussed in this chapter by matching each of the scenarios listed here with one of the following: declarative memory, episodic memory, explicit memory, implicit memory, flashbulb memory, everyday memory, procedural memory, prospective memory, retrospective memory and semantic memory.
   (a) Although it has been quite a few years since George had ridden his bike, he is able to pedal down the road after a bit of a wobbly start.

(b) In a tutorial, Yin can recognise a number of word pairs she memorised from a word list that was provided in the lecture.
(c) While going through some old honeymoon photos, Tricia recalls how beautiful and blue the ocean looked in the full moonlight.
(d) Antonio shuts down his computer before leaving work for the day.
(e) Carla intends to stop at the nursery and buy some trees and shrubs to plant in the garden this weekend.
(f) Goran recalls with confidence that Sir Edmund Barton was the first Prime Minister of Australia.
(g) Rodney reminds himself to phone his friend Himesh to wish him a happy birthday.
(h) Maria is 80 years old but clearly recalls the fond memory of her first kiss, as though it happened yesterday.
(i) Sharon recalls precisely where and when she was when she first heard the news of Princess Diana's death in 1997.
(j) Chris was introduced to Russell, Abdul and Mischa at a conference but cannot remember their names when he runs into them at another function the next day.

2. Test your understanding of why forgetting occurs by identifying the theory of forgetting in each of the following scenarios. Choose from decay theory, proactive interference, retroactive interference and motivated forgetting.
   (a) Jung does not like presenting in front of others and forgets when she is scheduled to give a class presentation.
   (b) Michelle has just moved house and is constantly confusing her old home phone number with her new one.
   (c) Matthew flicks through his baby album on his twenty-first birthday and is amazed by how much he has forgotten about his early milestones. His earliest remaining memory is that he loved riding his tricycle when he was three years old.
   (d) Six-year-old Sharif goes to swimming lessons and learns the freestyle kick, shortly followed by the butterfly kick. At swimming lessons the next day, he confuses the butterfly kick with the freestyle kick.

The solutions to the application questions can be found on page 834.

MULTIMEDIA RESOURCES

The *Cyberpsych* multimedia resource is available *as an option* to accompany this textbook to further develop your understanding of many key psychology concepts. *Cyberpsych* contains a wealth of rich media content and activities, and for this chapter includes:

- a video clip on memory storage
- video case studies on the memory of events and eyewitness testimony
- interactive modules on declarative versus procedural memory, amnesia and enhancing memory.

Thought and language

LEARNING OBJECTIVES

After studying this chapter you should be able to:

1. describe the various units of thought
2. distinguish between reasoning, problem solving and decision making
3. describe the role of explicit and implicit cognition in everyday thinking
4. define language and outline its basic elements
5. explain how language develops.

Units of thought

- *Thinking* means manipulating mental representations for a purpose. Much of the time people think using words, *mental images* and *mental models*.
- A *concept* is a mental representation of a class of objects, ideas or events that share common properties. *Categories* are groupings based on common properties.

Explicit and implicit thinking

- Much of the time people rely on cognitive shortcuts, or *heuristics*, that allow them to make rapid judgements but can sometimes lead to irrational choices.
- *Explicit cognition* involves conscious manipulation of representations. *Implicit cognition* refers to cognition outside awareness.
- Motivation and emotion play a substantial role in everyday cognition; they may substantially influence the way people assess risks.
- *Connectionism* asserts that most cognitive processes occur simultaneously through the action of multiple, activated networks.

Reasoning, problem solving and decision making

- *Reasoning* is the process by which people generate and evaluate arguments and beliefs.
- *Problem solving* is the process of transforming one situation into another to meet a goal:
  1. Compare the initial state with the goal state to identify precise differences between the two.
  2. Identify possible operators (actions performed to solve the problem) and select one that seems most likely to reduce the differences.
  3. Apply the operator/s, responding to challenges by establishing subgoals.
  4. Continue using the operator/s until all differences between the initial state and the goal state are eliminated.
- *Decision making* is the process by which an individual weighs the pros and cons of different alternatives in order to make a choice.

Language

- *Language* is the system of symbols, sounds, meanings and rules for their combination that constitutes the primary mode of communication among humans.
- According to the *Whorfian hypothesis of linguistic relativity*, language shapes thought. Thought also shapes language, and language evolves to express new concepts.
- People use grammatical rules to transform sounds and symbols into meaningful sentences.
- Psychologists who study the *pragmatics* of language study the way language is used and understood in everyday life. *Discourse* is the way people ordinarily speak, hear, read and write in interconnected sentences.

Language development

- How children acquire language so quickly has been a matter of considerable theoretical debate.
- For many years, psychologists have debated the existence of a critical period for language learning. The first three years of life seem to be the optimal time to attain native fluency.
- Language development progresses through a series of stages.
- Before infants can start to acquire vocabulary or syntax, they have to learn to segment the continuous streams of speech they hear into units. They then have to learn to classify words into syntactic categories.
- Babies' first recognisable speech sounds occur as *babbling* in the first year. Sometime in the second year they begin to speak in one-word utterances. Young children use *telegraphic speech*, leaving out all but the essential words. By age four, most of the sentences children produce are grammatical.
- Some researchers have taught chimpanzees to use language skills such as sign language. The question of whether or not non-human primates have the capacity to acquire the rules of human language remains the subject of much debate.

Central questions: what is so rational about reason?

- Perhaps we will ultimately find that what is distinctly human is the ability to link motives, emotions and reason in pursuit of our goals.

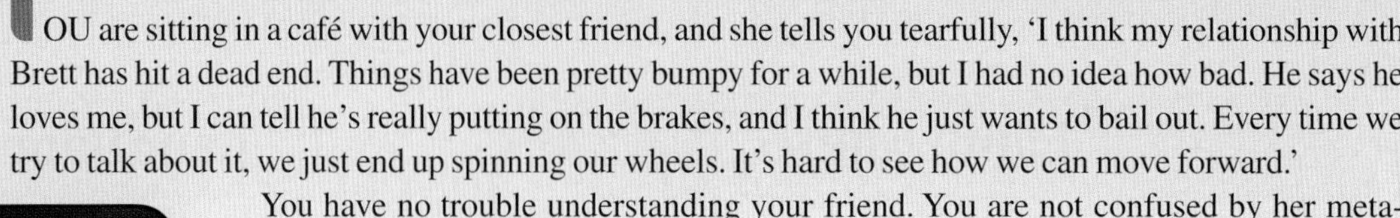

YOU are sitting in a café with your closest friend, and she tells you tearfully, 'I think my relationship with Brett has hit a dead end. Things have been pretty bumpy for a while, but I had no idea how bad. He says he loves me, but I can tell he's really putting on the brakes, and I think he just wants to bail out. Every time we try to talk about it, we just end up spinning our wheels. It's hard to see how we can move forward.'

You have no trouble understanding your friend. You are not confused by her metaphors — the relationship hitting a *dead end*, things being *bumpy*, her boyfriend *putting on the brakes* and wanting to *bail out*, the two of them *spinning their wheels* and having trouble *moving forward*. Your friend is not a poet, yet she communicates her problem through a single controlling metaphor that you understand implicitly: lovers are like travellers on a journey trying to reach a common destination, and their relationship is the vehicle for this journey. With the exception of *bailing out* (an aeronautical metaphor), your friend is describing her relationship as a car travelling on a bumpy road and reaching a dead end, and she is unsure whether the vehicle can go forward under these circumstances (Lakoff, 1980, 1989, 1997).

Several features of this scenario in the café are striking. First, your friend is not Shakespeare — *Love is a car* would probably not have played well at the Globe Theatre. Yet the two of you both understand what she is saying because you share a metaphor rooted in your culture.

Second, in transforming her experience into words, she is manipulating representations — knowledge about cars and relationships — and mapping one knowledge domain onto another (a rough time in a relationship is a bumpy road; feeling 'stuck' in a relationship despite efforts to talk is like spinning your wheels trying to get out of soft sand). She is essentially speaking in highly evocative poetry — and you are able to understand it — without a second's thought and without any likely awareness on your part or hers of the metaphor guiding your thinking.

Finally, and perhaps most importantly, through words, a set of thoughts and feelings in one person's mind enters another's.

This chapter is about thought and language — the ways we transform and manipulate mental representations to navigate our way through life (another journey metaphor) and interact with others using words. We begin by exploring the basic units of thought, such as mental images and concepts, and the way people manipulate these units to reason, solve problems and make decisions. Next we examine explicit and implicit cognition and everyday thinking, exploring how people solve problems and make judgements outside of awareness, often relying on emotion as well as cognition. Then we turn to language, the system of symbols that forms the medium for much of human thought and communication. Could we think in metaphor without language? When we have an idea, do we translate it into language, or are complex thoughts inherently linguistic? Finally, we examine the way children learn language, and address the question of whether evolution has created a brain specifically attuned to linguistic information.

Throughout the chapter, we address a central question: what does it mean to be 'rational'? Under what conditions does rationality mean carefully thinking things through and conducting a careful cost–benefit analysis before taking action? And under what conditions does a 'reasonable' person trust his or her intuition?

Central question

- What does it mean to be rational?

Units of thought

In many ways, thought is simply an extension of perception and memory. When we perceive, we form a mental representation. When we remember, we try to bring that representation to mind. When we think, we use representations to try to solve a problem or answer a question. ***Thinking*** means manipulating mental representations for a purpose.

Manipulating mental representations

People can manipulate virtually any kind of representation in their minds. You may not have realised it, but the last time you sniffed the milk and decided it was spoiled, you were thinking with your nose (actually, with olfactory representations). Or consider what happens when people harmonise while singing along with the radio in a car.

Although their companions in the car may not appreciate it, they are engaged in an impressive act of musical thinking, unconsciously manipulating auditory representations and using sophisticated rules of harmonic structure, probably with no awareness whatsoever.

Thinking in words and images

Much of the time, humans think using words and images. When people try to figure out whether they have enough money with them to buy an extra bag of potato chips or how to tell an unwanted suitor they are not interested, they usually think in words. At other times they rely on ***mental images***, visual representations such as the image of a street or a circle.

Psychologists once disagreed about whether people actually think in images or whether they convert visual questions into verbal questions in order to solve them. For example, to figure out how to carry a large desk through a narrow doorway, do people somehow rotate a visual image of the desk in their minds, or do they convert the problem into statements (e.g. 'the desk won't fit if it isn't turned sideways')?

A classic study addressed this question by showing participants pictures of a stimulus such as a capital R, rotated between 0 and 360 degrees (figure 8.1). The participants had to decide whether the letter was shown normally or in mirror image. The results were clear: the amount of time participants took to answer varied directly with the degree of rotation from upright. In other words, the greater the rotation, the longer the reaction time. This indicated that participants were actually mentally rotating an image of the letter to come to a conclusion (Cooper, 1976; Cooper & Shepard, 1973). Supporting these findings, recent PET studies show that perceiving, remembering and mentally manipulating visual scenes all involve activation of the visual cortex (Farah, 2000; Kosslyn et al., 1993).

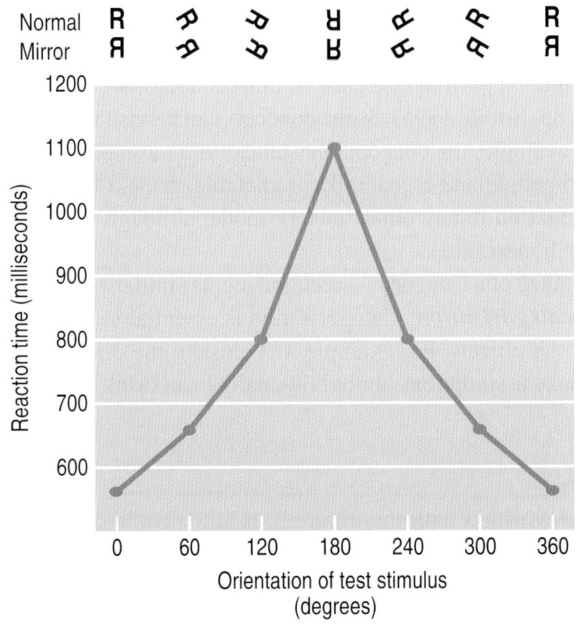

FIGURE 8.1
The manipulation of visual representations. The investigators asked participants to determine whether the 'R' they saw at different degrees of rotation was forward or backward. The dependent variable was the amount of time required to accomplish the task. The figure graphs reaction time as a function of degree of rotation. As can be seen, the more participants had to rotate the letter mentally, the longer they took to complete the task. Peak reaction time was at 180 degrees, which requires the furthest rotation.

SOURCE: Adapted from Cooper and Shepard (1973).

As we saw in chapter 6, humans are not the only animals that use mental images or mental maps. In fact, other animals seem to understand geometry! In one study, the investigators consistently hid birdseed midway between two pipes on a wall, but they moved the pipes different distances from each other so that nutcrackers flying around the room had to keep finding the new midpoint (Kamil & Jones, 1997, 2000). Remarkably, the birds were consistently able to locate the midpoint to find the seed.

They also appeared to be mentally drawing a straight line between the two pipes, which were always placed one above the other, since they tended to land right on the line that intersected them rather than to the right or left.

Mental models

People also frequently think using ***mental models***, representations that describe, explain or predict the way things work (Johnson-Laird, 1999; Johnson-Laird, Legrenzi, Girotto, & Legrenzi, 2000). Mental models may be quite simple, like most people's understanding of cars (if the car doesn't start, there's a problem somewhere under the bonnet) or a child's understanding of what a 'cavity' is (a bad thing in the mouth that requires a trip to the dentist). On the other hand, they can be quite complex, such as the mental models used by mechanics to troubleshoot a car or a dentist's conception of the processes that produce cavities.

Although mental models often include visual elements (such as the dentist's visual representations of different kinds of teeth and what erosion in a tooth looks like), they always include descriptions of the relationships among elements. For example, the dentist may have a causal model of how build-up of food residues leads to bacterial action that eats away at a tooth.

APPLY + DISCUSS

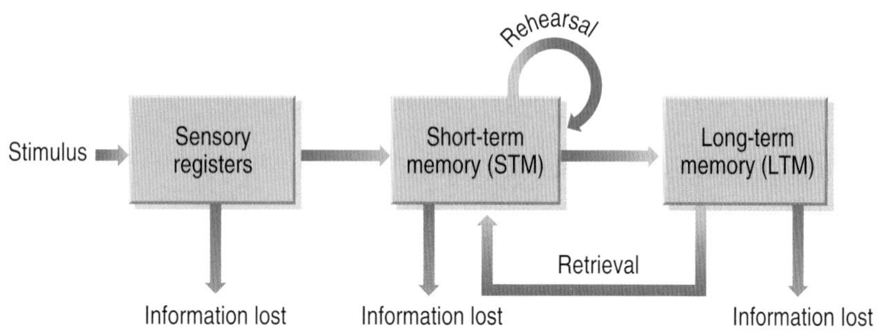

The standard model of memory is an example of a mental model.

- To what extent is it visual?
- What nonvisual elements does the model include?

INTERIM SUMMARY

Thinking means manipulating mental representations for a purpose. Much of the time people think using words, ***mental images*** (visual representations) and ***mental models*** (representations that describe, explain or predict the way things work).

Concepts and categories

Before people can think about an object, they usually have to classify it so that they know what it is and what it does. An approaching person is a friend or a stranger; a piece of fruit on the table is an apple or an orange; a politician is right- or left-wing.

People and things fall into groupings based on common properties called ***categories***. A ***concept*** is a mental representation of a category; that is, an internal portrait of a class of objects, ideas or events that share common properties (Murphy & Medin, 1985; Smith, 1995). Some concepts can be visualised, but a concept is broader than its visual image. For example, the concept *car* stands for a class of vehicles with four wheels, seating space for at least two people and a generally predictable shape. Other concepts, like *honest*, defy visualisation or representation in any other sensory mode, although they may have visual associations (such as an image of an honest face).

The process of identifying an object as an instance of a category — recognising its similarity to some objects and dissimilarity to others — is called ***categorisation***. Categorisation is essential to thinking, because it allows people to make inferences about objects. For example, if I classify the drink in my glass as an alcoholic beverage, I am likely to make assumptions about how many I can drink and what I will feel like afterwards.

Defining features and prototypes

For years, philosophers and psychologists have wrestled with the question of how people categorise objects or situations (Medin, Lynch, & Solorman, 2000; Medin & Smith, 1981). How do they decide that a crab is not a spider, even though crabs look like big hairless tarantulas?

Defining features

One possibility is that people compare the features of objects with a list of ***defining features*** — qualities that are essential, or necessarily present, in order to classify the object as a member of the category. For some concepts this strategy could work. Concepts like salt, water or triangle are ***well-defined concepts*** — they have properties clearly setting them apart from other concepts. A triangle can be defined as a two-dimensional geometric figure with three sides and three angles, and anything that does not fit this definition is not a triangle.

Most of the concepts used in daily life, however, are not easily defined (Rosch, 1978). Consider the concept *good*. This concept takes on different meanings when applied to a meal or a person: few of us look for tastiness in a person or honesty and sensitivity in a meal. Similarly, the concept *adult* is fuzzy around the edges, at least in Western cultures: at what point does a person stop being an adolescent and become an adult? Is a person an adult at voting age? At drinking age? At marriage?

Prototypes

Even where concepts are well defined, consulting a list of defining features is, in psychological time (i.e. milliseconds), a rather slow procedure. As we saw in chapter 4, a person flipping through television stations with a remote control can recognise scenes and classify the objects in them far faster than anyone could possibly go through a list of defining features.

People typically classify objects rapidly by judging their similarity to concepts stored in memory (Estes, 1994; Hahn & Ramscar, 2001; Robertson, Davidoff, & Braisby, 1999; Tversky, 1977). For example, if asked whether Toowoomba, Queensland, is a city, most people compare it with their image of a crowded, bustling, typical example of a city, such as Sydney, or with a generalised portrait extracted from experience with several cities, such as Auckland, Melbourne, New York and London.

APPLY + DISCUSS

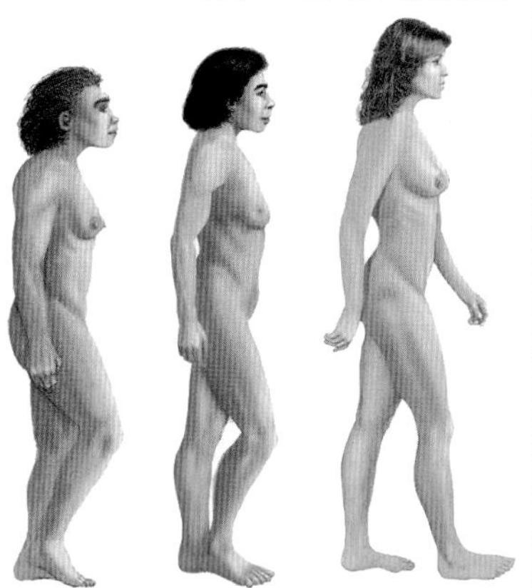

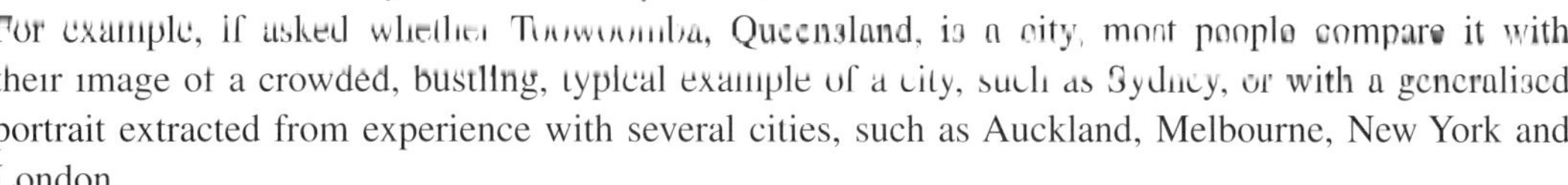

- At what point did humans become categorised as 'humans' (as opposed to apes)?
- What principles do we use to make that decision? Does the concept *human* have defining features?

Researchers have learned how people use similarity in classification by measuring their speed of responding to visual and verbal categorisation tasks. In visual categorisation tasks, the experimenter states the name of a target category (e.g. *bird*) and then presents a picture and asks whether it is a member of the category. In verbal categorisation tasks, the target category is followed by a word instead of a picture (e.g. *sparrow*); the task for the participant is to judge whether the second word is an instance of the category. People rapidly recognise that a parrot is a bird but take 100 to 200 milliseconds longer to classify a penguin (see Smith, 1995). The reason is that a parrot is a more prototypical bird; that is, it shares more of the characteristic features of the concept (Rosch, 1978).

People readily recognise magpies as birds. Categorising penguins takes a little more thought — and hence measurably more time.

A ***prototype*** is an abstraction (based on shared features or functions) across many instances of a category (such as magpies, parrots and sparrows). It represents a typical example of a category of things. When people construct a prototype in their minds, they essentially abstract out the most important common features of the objects in a category. Thus, the prototype of a bird does not look exactly like any particular bird the person has ever seen; it is more like an airbrushed photograph that smooths out idiosyncratic features.

When people judge similarity in visual tasks, they rely primarily on shape. When they judge similarity verbally, they tend to rely on characteristic or prototypical features; that is, qualities typically found in members of a category. For example, most birds fly, chirp and lay eggs. People classify parrots quickly because they do all three. Penguins take longer to classify because they lay eggs but do not share many other features of birds, except for having wings (see Malt & Smith, 1984).

Most concepts include both visual information and information about characteristic features, so that in everyday categorisation, people often use some combination of the two. People may also compare an object to an exemplar; that is, a particularly good example of the category (such as a parrot), rather than an abstract prototype (Medin & Schaffer, 1978; Smith, 1998).

Categorisation is functional

Are these two views of categorisation — one based on defining features and the other on similarity — irreconcilable? People probably represent information in multiple ways that they use flexibly in different categorisation tasks (figure 8.2). As with other psychological processes, categorisation is functional. Rapid, implicit categorisation usually relies primarily on similarity. However, if a person has difficulty implicitly classifying a novel object based on similarity or if the classification task is complex, she may switch to explicit categorisation based on defining features (or on features that may not be defining but are nevertheless useful or diagnostic).

Shape	Defining features	Characteristic features	Exemplars
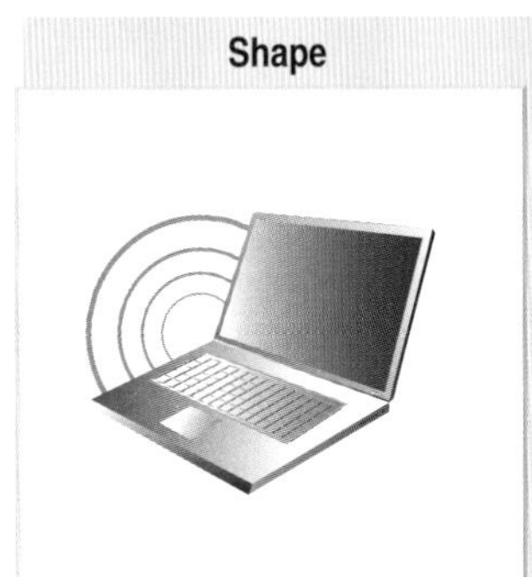	• Electronic device • Has a particular architecture, or operating design • Uses digital processor to perform computations	• Has a keyboard • Has a screen • Can be used for word processing and web browsing • Can store information on hard drive or USB devices	• Apple iMac • IBM Pentium

FIGURE 8.2
Multiple ways concepts can represent information

Complex classification tasks generally require careful, explicit evaluation of the data. A doctor will not diagnose appendicitis in a patient whose symptoms appear similar to a textbook case of appendicitis (a prototype) or cases she has seen before (exemplars) unless a laboratory test shows an abnormal white blood cell count. The symptoms of appendicitis are similar to those of food poisoning and the flu, so that rapid similarity judgements may not be precise enough to start sharpening the scalpel.

The strategies people use to categorise also depend on what they are told and what they think will be most useful. For example, when given a rule (e.g. 'sort the stones into light and dark'), people tend to use rule-based (defining features) categorisation, but in the absence of a rule, they tend to rely on similarity judgements (Allen & Brooks, 1991). Neuroimaging studies confirm that people often carry out both kinds of categorisation and that these two types activate different neural circuits (Smith, Patalano, & Jonides, 1998).

INTERIM SUMMARY

A ***concept*** is a mental representation of a class of objects, ideas or events that share common properties. ***Categorisation*** is the process of identifying an object as an instance of a category. Although people sometimes categorise objects by comparing them with a list of ***defining features***, people typically classify objects rapidly by judging their similarity to ***prototypes*** (abstract representations of a category) stored in memory.

Hierarchies of concepts

Many concepts are hierarchically ordered, with subconcepts at varying levels of abstraction. We categorise all pets that pant, slobber and bark as dogs, but we can further subdivide the concept *dog* into more specific categories such as *blue heeler* and *kelpie*. Similarly, *dog* is itself an instance of larger, more general categories such as *mammal* and *vertebrate* (figure 8.3).

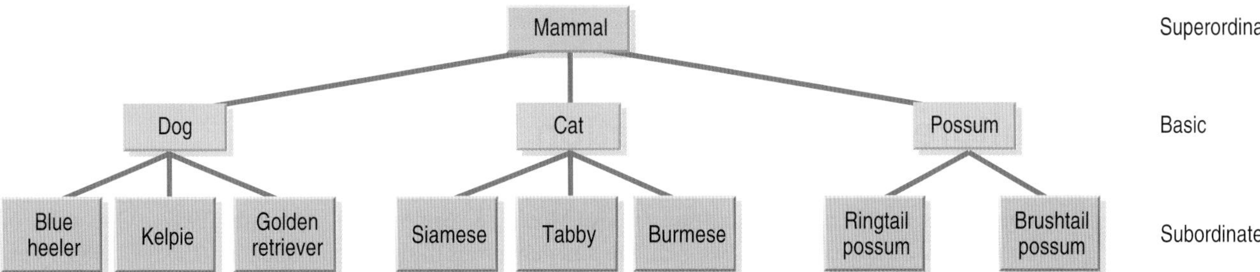

FIGURE 8.3
Superordinate, basic and subordinate levels of categorisation

Efficient thinking requires choosing the right level of abstraction. A woman walking down the street in a bright purple raincoat belongs to the categories *mammal*, *vertebrate* and *human* just as clearly as she belongs to the category *woman*. Yet we are more likely to say 'Look at that woman in the purple raincoat' than 'Look at that vertebrate in brightly coloured apparel'.

The basic level of categorisation

The level people naturally tend to use in categorising objects is known as the ***basic level***: the broadest, most inclusive level at which objects share common attributes that are distinctive of the concept (i.e. attributes that 'stand out') (Rosch, 1978). The basic level is the level at which people categorise most quickly; it is thus the 'natural' level to which the mind gravitates. Thus, *woman* is a basic-level category; so are *dinner*, *car* and *bird*.

At times, however, people categorise at the ***subordinate level***, the level of categorisation below the basic level in which more specific attributes are shared by members of a category. Thus, people on a nature hike distinguish between magpies and butcherbirds. The natural level at which people tend to classify an unusual instance of a category, such as penguin, is often the subordinate level (Jolicoeur, Gluck, & Kosslyn, 1984; see also Scott, Tanaka, Sheinberg, & Curran, 2006).

People also sometimes classify objects at the ***superordinate level***, an abstract level in which members of a category share few common features. A farmer, for example, may ask, 'are the animals in the barn?' rather than running down a list including chickens, horses and so forth. The superordinate level is one level more abstract than the basic level, and members of this class share fewer specific features (figure 8.3).

The metaphors people use tend to be mapped at the superordinate, rather than the basic, level (Lakoff, 1997). In the example that opened this chapter, the underlying metaphor was that *love is a journey*, and hence a *relationship is a vehicle*. Since the richest, most evocative information is stored at the basic level, using the superordinate level allows the mapping of multiple rich concepts onto the current situation. Thus, the listener was not surprised when the woman talking about her relationship seemingly mixed metaphors in likening her relationship to a car but throwing in a metaphor based on a different kind of vehicle, an aeroplane ('he just wants to *bail out*'). She could also have used the metaphor of a boat: initially the relationship had been *smooth sailing*, but now it is *on the rocks* or has *veered off course*.

MAKING CONNECTIONS

The self-concept, like other concepts, appears to be hierarchically organised. For example, we often have a general view of ourselves but more specific views of what we are like with our friends and with our parents (which might include subordinate concepts of self-with-mother and self-with-father) (chapter 17).

Basic-level categories vary to some extent across cultures (Medin, Ross, Atran, Burnett, & Blok, 2002; Robertson et al., 2002). While *love* is a basic-level concept for most Westerners, the Native American Utku have two basic-level concepts for love: love for those who need protection, and love for those who are charming or admired (Russell, 1991).

Neuroimaging research suggests that categorising at different levels actually activates different cognitive processes and neural networks. In one study, the experimenters presented participants with line drawings of objects followed by a word (Kosslyn, Thompson, Kim, & Alpert, 1995). The participant was to decide whether the object was an instance of the category. Some of the words were at the basic level (such as *shirt*), whereas others were subordinate (*dress shirt*) or superordinate (*clothing*).

The researchers reasoned that identifying an object at the superordinate level requires a memory search using language (e.g. mentally 'looking up' whether a shirt is a kind of clothing). In contrast, an object at a subordinate level requires a perceptual search of the object to see if it has particular features (e.g. does the shirt have the characteristic collar of a dress shirt?).

The results were as hypothesised: categorising at the superordinate level activated a region of the left prefrontal cortex involved in verbal memory retrieval. In contrast, categorising at the subordinate level activated the right prefrontal cortex along with circuits involved in paying visual attention to the object.

A GLOBAL VISTA

Culture and categorisation

To a large extent, culture shapes not only the categories people consider basic but also the way they group things together (Lopez, Atran, Coley, Medin, & Smith, 1997; Mishra, 1997). One tribe of Aboriginal Australians includes women, fire and dangerous things in one category (Lakoff, 1985). This category would make little sense to members of other societies, but to the members of the Aboriginal tribe it seems perfectly natural. In their mythology, the sun — a woman — is the wife of the moon. Because the sun gives off heat, it is associated with fire, and since fire is dangerous, both the sun and women are linked to dangerous things. Although this way of classifying may seem peculiar to the Western ear, consider the difficulty a Christian might have explaining to an aboriginal Papuan how Jesus could simultaneously be a man, a god, a spirit and the Son of God.

One study examined the influence of culture on categorisation, comparing 100 university students from New Mexico with 80 illiterate Manu farmers from a small village in Liberia, Africa (Irwin, Schafer, & Fieden, 1974). To assess people's ability to categorise and think abstractly, psychologists in the West often use card-sorting tasks. The psychologist presents participants with a deck of cards showing different geometric forms (squares, triangles etc.). The geometric forms vary in colour and number. The task is to figure out the three dimensions on which the cards vary and sort them by category (i.e. by form, colour and number). The participant has a certain amount of time (in this study, five minutes) in which to sort the cards in all three correct ways. Previous studies had found that preliterate people often did poorly on this task, which psychologists attributed to their lack of formal education.

APPLY + DISCUSS

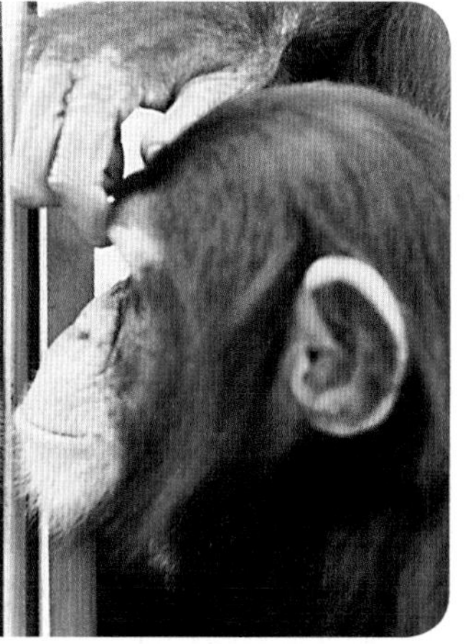

Scientists have discovered that some non-human animals also have a sense of self. For example, both dolphins and chimpanzees who have learned to identify themselves in a mirror, notice (and try to remove) marks placed on their foreheads.

- To what extent do these findings indicate that dolphins and chimpanzees can 'think' about the self?
- To what extent is self-identification a characteristic of humans, and why do so few other animals share it?

The experimenters in this study wondered, however, whether the apparent superiority of Western participants on this task would disappear if the task involved materials more familiar to the Manu. An extremely familiar object in Manu culture is rice, which comes in different forms that the Manu readily distinguish. Thus, the experimenters adapted the sorting task to fit Manu experience by presenting participants with bowls of rice. The bowls varied in amount of rice, type (long grain and short grain) and texture (polished versus unpolished). The task, then, was to sort the rice using each of these three categories. The researchers hypothesised that Manu participants would do better on the rice task, whereas participants from a Western culture would do better on the card sort task.

In fact, Western participants performed much better and faster on the card-sorting task, which is more familiar to them, than on rice sorting. The opposite was true for the Manu, whose performance was substantially better when sorting rice than sorting cards. Interestingly, though, Western participants were faster on both tasks than the Manu, and their performance was generally superior. This probably reflects both the effects of education, which teaches children to think in systematic ways, and greater exposure to tests, particularly timed ones.

Culture can also affect the extent to which people rely on similarity or defining features in categorising objects. East Asians tend to use exemplar- and prototype-based categorisation relying on similarity. People from Western cultures such as Australia, New Zealand and North America, are more likely to look for rules (Nisbett, Peng, Choi, & Norenzayan, 2001). This difference is consistent with a general tendency in Eastern cultures to favour holistic over analytical thinking (Peng & Nisbett, 1999). Whether this reflects primarily a cultural difference or the longer history of industrialisation in the West (which requires breaking things down into their component parts, as in creating an assembly line or software program) is not yet clear.

Thus, to what extent do principles of categorisation vary across cultures? Categorisation is constrained by the nature of reality, which leads to cross-cultural universals. People everywhere group some things together simply because that is the way they are. At the same time, people tend to categorise in ways that help them solve problems (Medin, Lynch, Coley, & Atran, 1997), and these problems differ across cultures and individuals (Medin & Atran, 2004).

INTERIM SUMMARY

Many concepts are hierarchically ordered. The level people naturally tend to use in categorising objects is known as the ***basic level***. One level up is the ***superordinate*** level and one level down is the ***subordinate*** level. Culture shapes not only the categories people consider basic but also the way they group things together. Categorisation, like most cognitive processes, is functional, so that people tend to categorise in ways that help them solve problems.

Reasoning, problem solving and decision making

Mental images, mental models and concepts are the building blocks of thought. In this next section, we explore how people manipulate current information with information stored in memory to reason, solve problems and make decisions.

Reasoning

Reasoning refers to the process by which people generate and evaluate arguments and beliefs (Anderson, 1985; Holyoak & Spellman, 1993), typically to try to solve problems. Philosophers have long distinguished two kinds of reasoning: inductive and deductive. We examine each separately here. We then explore one of the most powerful mechanisms people use to make inferences, particularly about novel situations: reasoning by analogy.

Inductive reasoning

Kissing and casual contact (such as handshakes) do not transmit HIV, which causes AIDS. How do we know this? Early in the epidemic, scientists interviewed a large number of people who had casual contact with HIV-positive individuals. Whereas people who had sexual intercourse with people with HIV had an increased likelihood of themselves testing positive, those who had not did not. Thus, scientists concluded that casual contact does not, as a rule, cause HIV infection. This kind of thinking is called ***inductive reasoning*** — reasoning from specific observations to more general propositions (Heit, 2000; Holland, Holyoak, Nisbett, & Thagard, 1986).

Inductive reasoning relies on probabilities. It involves inferring a conclusion based on probabilities rather than certainties. Thus, an inductive conclusion is based on the evidence available and is not necessarily true because its underlying premises are only probable, not certain. A few people who reported kissing a person with HIV did come down with AIDS, but whether they had contracted the virus some other way or had been unwilling to admit more than kissing was not absolutely certain.

Inductive reasoning is clearly fallible. One four-year-old child, for example, used inductive reasoning to reinforce her fear of the bogeyman: if Santa can come down the chimney, she reasoned, so can the bogeyman! Nevertheless, inductive reasoning is essential in daily life. Every time we categorise an object, we are using a form of inductive reasoning. When we classify a novel animal as a cat, we assume that a particular body shape, whiskers and feline body movements imply 'cat-hood'. In reality, the animal could turn out to be an unusual rabbit or a species with which we are unfamiliar.

Deductive reasoning

Deductive reasoning is logical reasoning that draws a conclusion from a set of assumptions or premises that are based on the rules of logic. In contrast to inductive reasoning, it starts with an idea rather than an observation. In some ways, deduction is the flipside of induction: whereas induction starts with specifics and draws general conclusions, deduction starts with general principles and makes inferences about specific instances. For example, if you understand the general premise that all dogs have fur and you know that Barkley is a dog, then you can deduce that Barkley has fur, even though you have never made Barkley's acquaintance.

This kind of deductive argument is referred to as a syllogism. A ***syllogism*** consists of two premises that lead to a logical conclusion. If it is true that

(A) all dogs have fur and

(B) Barkley is a dog,

then there is no choice but to accept the conclusion that

(C) Barkley has fur.

Unlike inductive reasoning, deductive reasoning can lead to certain rather than simply probable conclusions, as long as the premises are correct and the reasoning is logical.

The influence of content on deductive reasoning

Although deductive reasoning seems completely 'logical', in everyday life both the form (abstract or concrete) and content of deductive reasoning problems influence how easily people solve them (Cosmides, 1989; Wilkins, 1982). Consider the card problem presented in figure 8.4. Participants are shown four cards and told that each card has a letter on one side and a number on the other. They are also told that the cards conform to the following rule: *if a card has an A on one side, then it has a 3 on the other side*. The task: turn over only those cards necessary to discover whether the rule is true or false (Johnson-Laird, Legrenzi, & Legrenzi, 1972; Wason, 1968).

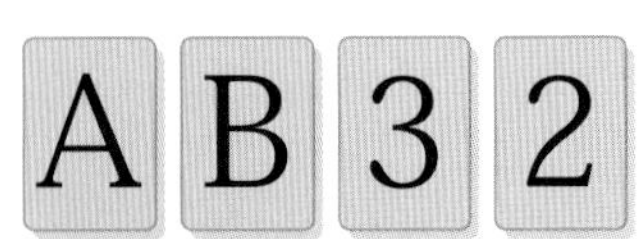

FIGURE 8.4
Card selection task. If each card has a number on one side and a letter on the other, which cards must be turned over to verify or disprove the rule, 'If a card has an A on one side, then it has a 3 on the other'?

SOURCE: Wason (1968).

While most people correctly conclude that they must turn over the card with the *A* on it (a number other than 3 would falsify the rule), few also realise that they must turn over the 2 card: finding an *A* on the opposite side of this card would disprove the rule just as surely as would turning over the *A* card and finding something other than a 3. Most participants also think they have to turn over the 3 card, which is irrelevant: if an *A* is not on the other side, it has no bearing on the rule *If A, then 3*. (If your self-esteem has just plummeted, take heart, most people do not get this right on the first try.) If the same problem is posed with more familiar contents, deductive reasoning is much easier (figure 8.5).

In a crackdown against drunk drivers, South Australian law enforcement officials are revoking liquor licences left and right. You are a bouncer in an Adelaide bar, and you'll lose your job unless you enforce the following law:

> If a person is drinking beer, then he or she must be at least 18 years old.

In front of you are four cards belonging to four patrons of your bar. Each card has the person's age on one side and what she or he is drinking on the other. Which cards must you turn over to ensure that the law is being followed?

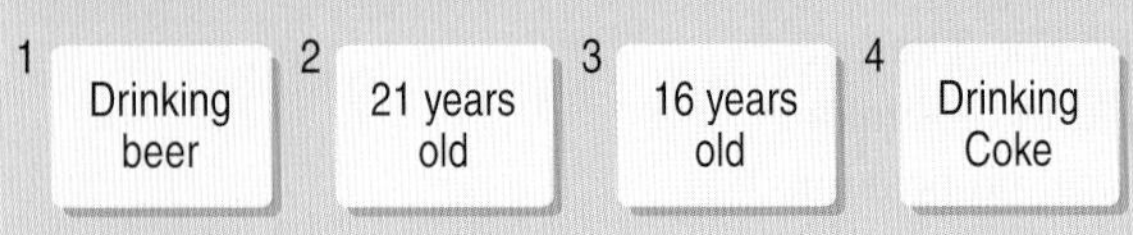

FIGURE 8.5
Card selection task with familiar content

SOURCE: Adapted from Griggs and Cox (1982).

Answer: 1 and 3

If deductive reasoning depends in part on the content of the premises, do people really solve deductive problems by mentally manipulating abstract propositions? According to one theory, deduction is actually less about formal rules of inference (about *A*s and *B*s) than about forming mental models of each of the premises, which allows the person to draw reasonable judgements about the conclusion (Johnson-Laird, 1995).

For example, if asked to solve a syllogism of the form, 'If *A* is on the left of *B*, and *B* is on the left of *C*, then . . .', people typically visualise the scene, creating a mental model that combines the premises. According to this view, people make both inductive and deductive inferences by imagining scenarios or scenes and the relationships among their elements and then imagining what they are, could be or could not be like.

Is deductive reasoning universal?

Deductive reasoning seems as if it would follow similar principles everywhere. However, research suggests that Eastern and Western cultures may follow somewhat different rules of logic — or at least have different levels of tolerance for certain kinds of inconsistency (Norenzayan & Nisbett, 2000; Peng & Nisbett, 1999). The tradition of logic in the West, extending from Ancient Greece to the present, places an enormous premium on the law of non-contradiction: two statements that contradict each other cannot both be true. This law is central to solving syllogisms.

In the East, in contrast, people often view contradictions with much more acceptance, and often believe them to contain great wisdom — like principles of *yin* and *yang*. Consider the statements, 'People are the same over time' and 'People are never the same from one moment to the next'. Each statement has considerable truth. In the West, the law of non-contradiction leads us to try to resolve paradoxes such as these — to find ways to resolve the contradiction, by qualifying one statement or the other, integrating the two or deciding that one is not true after all. In the East, in contrast, the focus is instead on finding the truth that each statement provides — relishing rather than resolving paradox.

APPLY + DISCUSS

Research has indicated that hearing-impaired individuals show reasoning deficits, particularly in the areas of inductive reasoning and cognitive flexibility (Passig & Eden, 2003).

- Why would this be?
- What role would different sensory modalities play in one's ability to think?

Reasoning by analogy

Deductive and inductive reasoning are central to human intelligence. So is reasoning by analogy — ***analogical reasoning*** — the process by which people understand a novel situation in terms of a familiar one (Gentner & Holyoak, 1997).

People use analogies to categorise novel situations, make inferences and solve problems. They also try to influence the inferences other people will make and the conclusions they will reach by using analogies that suit their own goals. For example, then Australian Labor Party leader Mark Latham likened Australia's involvement in the ongoing occupation of Iraq in 2004 to its involvement in the

Vietnam War four decades earlier. This followed almost daily attacks on the United States and other armed forces in Iraq more than a year after then US president George Bush had announced that major conflict in the country was over. Latham used the analogy in outlining a proposal to bring Australian troops home from Iraq — a proposition that was likely to strike a chord with generations of Australians still haunted by the Vietnam experience.

The linking of the Iraqi conflict and the Vietnam War also carried with it echoes of the World War II analogies that helped shape foreign policy in the West for three decades. When communist governments began coming to power in Asia in the late 1940s and 1950s, policy makers in the West had the analogy of pre-war Germany squarely in mind: to 'lose' another country to communism was like letting another country fall to Hitler.

As a consequence, in the 1960s the United States entered into war against the communists in North Vietnam. Australia fell into line behind the United States and also committed troops to the conflict. The war had disastrous consequences for both the United States and Australia — thousands of dead soldiers on both sides, thousands of dead civilians in Vietnam, as well as a devastated environment and infrastructure in that country. The conflict helped create a new analogy as powerful to a younger generation of Australians as World War II had been to their elders. Australia was seen to have been drawn into an unnecessary and unwinnable military intervention in a foreign country, largely due to its close relationship with the United States.

A key aspect of analogies of this sort is that the familiar situation and the novel situation must each contain a system of elements that can be mapped onto one another (Gentner, 1983, Gentner & Markman, 1997). For an analogy to take hold, the two situations need not literally resemble each other. For example, the Iraqi deserts were a far cry from the jungles of Vietnam. However, the elements of the two situations must relate to one another in a way that explains how the elements of the novel situation are similar to those of the familiar situation. In the case of the Iraq conflict, there were many similarities to the Vietnam War. In both cases, the United States led military action against another country to intervene against a perceived potential threat. In both cases, Australia supported the United States by committing troops to the conflict as well. But the real impact of the analogy is the emotional response. If we accepted the analogy that the Iraqi conflict was like the Vietnam War, then the continued commitment and potential death of Australian troops could be seen as pointless. The futility of having soldiers die in 'another Vietnam' would be seen as ample justification for bringing them home.

INTERIM SUMMARY

Reasoning is the process by which people generate and evaluate arguments and beliefs. ***Inductive reasoning*** means reasoning from specific observations to more general propositions that seem likely to be true. ***Deductive reasoning*** means drawing a conclusion from a set of assumptions that is true if the premises are true. Both the form (abstract or concrete) and content of deductive reasoning problems such as syllogisms influence how easily people solve them. ***Analogical reasoning*** is the process by which people understand a novel situation in terms of a familiar one. Analogical reasoning is influenced by the similarity of the situations, the ease of mapping of their elements and the reasoner's goals.

Problem solving

Life is a series of problems to solve. How much should you pay for a new house? How are you going to be able to afford a new car? How do you decide what your university major will be?

Problem solving refers to the process of transforming one situation into another to meet a goal (Gilhooly, 1989; Greeno, 1978). The aim is to move from a current, unsatisfactory state (the initial state) to a state in which the problem is resolved (the goal state) (figure 8.6). To get from the initial state to the goal state, the person uses operators, mental and behavioural processes aimed at transforming the initial state until it eventually approximates the goal (Miller, Galanter, & Pribram, 1960; Newell & Simon, 1972).

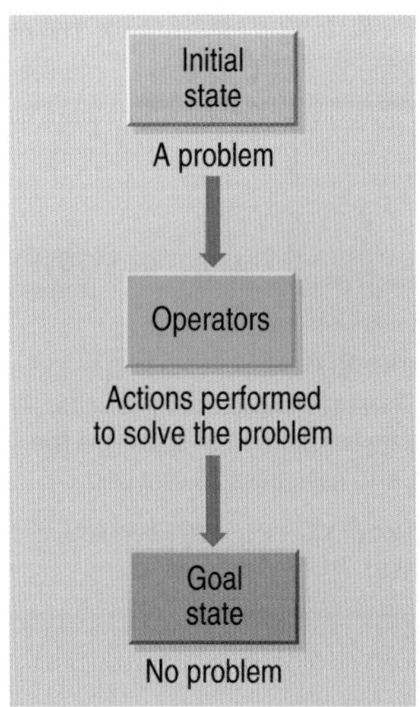

FIGURE 8.6
The problem-solving process. Problem solving means transforming an initial problem state, using operators, to attain a goal state.

Few problems are so straightforward in real life. Ill-defined problems occur when both the information needed to solve them and the criteria for determining when the goal has been met are vague (Jonassen, 2000; Schraw, Dunkle, & Bendixen, 1995; Simon, 1978; Sternberg, 2001). For example, a manager trying to raise morale among his employees faces an ill-defined problem, since he may not know the extent of the problem or whether his efforts to solve it have been successful. Therefore, to solve the problem, the manager needs to move from the initial state to the goal state, by devising strategies (operators) to respond to challenges or barriers, and by establishing ***subgoals*** — minigoals on the way to achieving the broader goal. (This is why business executives often call in organisational psychologists as consultants, to help them identify and measure problems, goal states, strategies for solving them and criteria for assessing change.)

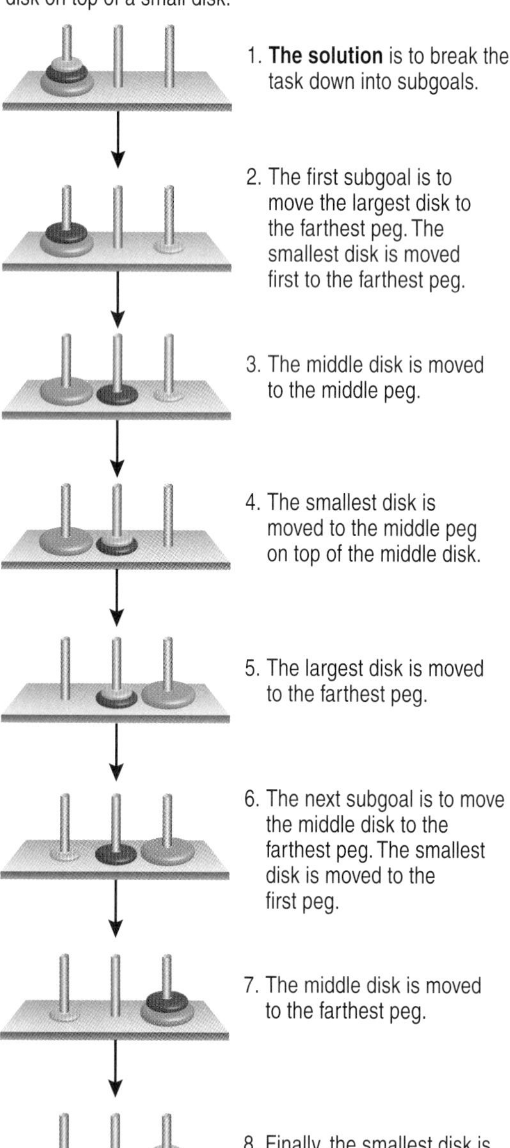

FIGURE 8.7
The Tower of Hanoi problem. You can simulate this problem by stacking a five cent, a 10 cent and a 20 cent coin.

SOURCE: Gazzaniga, Heatherton, and Halpern (2010).

Solving a problem, once it has been clarified, can involve a series of steps or subgoals. Consider the classic Tower of Hanoi problem (figure 8.7), where the task is to move the three disks to the peg on the other end, moving only one disc at a time, and never placing a larger disc on top of a small disk. Solving this problem requires breaking the task into subgoals. The first step is to compare the initial state with the goal state to identify precise differences between the two. Thus, the goal state is to move the ordered stack of three discs to the peg on the other end. The next step is to identify possible operators and select the one that seems most likely to reduce the differences. In this case, one possible strategy is to move the smallest disk to the farthest peg. Another strategy is to then move the middle disk to the middle peg, and so on. The final step is to continue using operators until all differences between the initial state and the goal state are eliminated.

Problem-solving strategies

Problem solving would be impossible if people had to try every potential operator in every situation until they found one that worked. Instead, they employ ***problem-solving strategies***, techniques that serve as guides for solving a problem (Demorest, 1986; Reimann & Chi, 1989).

For example, ***algorithms*** are systematic procedures that inevitably produce a solution to a problem (Anderson, 1995). Computers use algorithms in memory searches, as when a spell-check command compares every word in a file against an internal dictionary. Humans also use algorithms to solve some problems, such as counting the number of guests coming to a barbeque and multiplying by two to determine how many sausages to buy.

Algorithms are guaranteed to find a solution as long as one exists, but they are generally only practical for solving relatively simple problems. Imagine solving for the square root of 16 129 by methodically squaring 1, then 2, then 3 and so forth, each time checking to see if the answer is 16 129. (You would eventually arrive at the right answer, but only on your 127th try.)

One of the most important problem-solving strategies is ***mental simulation*** — imagining the steps involved in solving a problem mentally before actually undertaking them. People conduct mental simulations of this sort every day, such as imagining precisely how they will tell their boss about the holiday they want to take during the busy season, or picturing alternative routes to get to three different stores after work before the shops close.

Although many self-help books encourage people to visualise desired outcomes (the 'power of positive thinking'), mentally simulating the steps to achieving those outcomes is usually more beneficial (Taylor, Pham, Rivkin, & Armor, 1998). One study demonstrated this with introductory psychology students facing a midsemester examination. Students in one condition were told to visualise in detail the things they needed to do to get a good grade — for example, picturing themselves on their beds reviewing lecture notes. Students in the 'positive-thinking' condition were instructed, instead, to visualise themselves receiving the grade they wanted and how good they would feel. Students who imagined the steps to achieving a good grade studied more hours and scored better on the exam than students in the positive-thinking group, who actually did worse than students in a control condition who did not visualise anything (figure 8.8).

However, this is not to say that positive thinking is unrelated to academic success. A recent Australian longitudinal study by Leeson, Ciarrochi, and Heaven (2008) showed that intelligence, gender and positive thinking each play a unique role in predicting academic performance in youth. Their research showed that hope, or self-belief in one's ability to identify potential routes to obtain desired goals, was positively related to academic success across three years of study at high school.

Outcome	Mental simulation	Positive thinking	Control
Number of hours studying	16.1	11.6	14.5
Grade (% of questions correct)	80.6	72.6	77.7

FIGURE 8.8
Effects of mental simulation on exam performance. Students who mentally simulated the steps involved in solving the problem of getting a good grade studied harder and were more successful than students who either visualised success ('positive thinking') without the steps or did not imagine anything.

MAKING CONNECTIONS

Another problem-solving strategy is hypothesis testing — making an educated guess about what might solve the problem and then testing it. Hypothesis testing is not only common in everyday life but is also the basis of **scientific method** (chapter 2).

In a related Australian study, Frydenberg and Lewis (2009) found a positive relationship between self-perceived efficacy of problem solving and productive coping strategies for male adolescents (and to a lesser extent, female adolescents). This implies that teaching effective problem solving to adolescents is valuable. Helping young people to set goals, identify ways to achieve goals, feel in control of their learning, work independently and feel accountable can ensure they experience success after applying the skills to stressors in their everyday lives (Frydenberg & Lewis, 2009). However, this relationship is generally not the case for adults. Adults who perceive themselves as poor problem solvers are likely to use a range of maladaptive coping strategies, including worry, self-blame, wishful thinking and keeping to self (e.g. Belzer & D'Zurilla, 2002). Problem solving for adults might therefore involve various coping mechanisms that help them deal with stressful events (chapter 14).

Barriers to problem solving

Most of us muddle through our lives solving problems relatively well. However, human problem solving is far from perfect. One common problem is ***functional fixedness***, the tendency for people to ignore other possible functions of an object when they have a fixed function in mind. In a classic experiment, participants were asked to mount a candle on a wall so that, when lit, no wax would drip on the floor (Duncker, 1946). On a table lay a few small candles, some tacks and a box of matches (figure 8.9). The tendency, of course, was to see a matchbox as only a matchbox. If the matches were out of the box, however, participants solved the problem more easily (figure 8.11; see overleaf).

FIGURE 8.9
The candle problem. Use the objects on the table to mount a candle on the wall so that when it is lit, no wax drips on the floor. (Solution is overleaf in figure 8.11.)

This is very similar to another obstacle to problem solving known as ***mental set***, the tendency to keep using the same problem-solving techniques that have worked in the past. People blindly continue to apply a proven strategy even when better alternatives should be obvious. Figure 8.10 demonstrates a mental set, adapted from Luchins' (1942) jar problem. You need to obtain the specified volume of liquid shown in column one by using jars with the volumes shown in the next three columns. In the first problem you have to get 210 millilitres using jars that can hold 80 millilitres, 350 millilitres and 30 millilitres, respectively. The solution is to fill Jar B (350 millilitres), then use it to fill Jar A (80 millilitres). That leaves 270 millilitres in Jar B. Then use Jar B to fill Jar C to capacity twice, leaving 210 millilitres in Jar B [270 millilitres – (2 × 30 millilitres) = 210 millilitres]. In mathematical terms, the solution is $B - A - 2C$. The same approach will also solve the rest of the problems in figure 8.10. However, problem 7 is different. You probably did not realise there is a much simpler solution, $A + C$. That is a mental set in action — the tendency to continue using old patterns of problem solving on new problems.

Volume	Jar A	Jar B	Jar C
1. 210 millilitres	80	350	30
2. 100 millilitres	60	180	10
3. 190 millilitres	50	320	40
4. 210 millilitres	200	570	80
5. 180 millilitres	80	400	70
6. 60 millilitres	70	170	20
7. 150 millilitres	120	330	30

FIGURE 8.10
The Luchins jar problem

SOURCE: From Berstein, *Psychology*, 4/E AIE, 4/E. © 1997 Wadsworth, a part of Cengage Learning, Inc. Reproduced by permission. www.cengage.com/permissions.

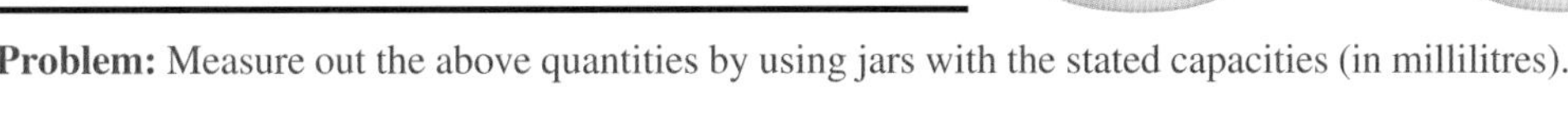

Problem: Measure out the above quantities by using jars with the stated capacities (in millilitres).

FIGURE 8.11
Solution to the candle problem

Another common error in problem solving is ***confirmation bias***, the tendency for people to search for confirmation of what they already believe (see Klayman & Ha, 1989; Nickerson, 1998). In one study, the experimenters presented participants with three numbers (2, 4 and 6) and asked them to discover the rule used to construct this sequence of numbers by generating their own sets of numbers (Wason, 1960). Each time the participant generated a set of numbers, the experimenters responded as to whether the participant's numbers correctly illustrated the rule.

In fact, the rule was quite simple: any three numbers, arranged from smallest to largest. However, the way most people tried to solve the problem kept them from finding the rule. Instead of testing a variety of sequences — such as 3, 12, 428 or 7, –4, 46 — until only one rule remained plausible, most participants did just the opposite. Early on, they formed a hypothesis such as 'add 2 to each number to form the next number' and repeatedly generated one sequence after another that confirmed this rule until they were satisfied they were right. Confirmation bias can be a particular problem for experts in a field; for example, scientists studying a topic may only test hypotheses and use methods that fit with current thinking (Sternberg, 1996).

Overcoming barriers to problem solving

To overcome a barrier to problem solving, we often need to rethink the problem rather than persist with previous strategies or mental sets. One way is to restructure the problem, or represent it in a novel way. For example, in Sheerer's (1963) nine-dot problem (figure 8.12), the task is to connect the dots using at most four straight lines (and without lifting the pencil off the page). One solution is to extend the lines beyond the boundary formed by the dots. Another solution is to use one very wide line that covers all nine dots. Thus, restructuring the problem (by thinking outside the square!) helped to eliminate assumed constraints.

(a) *The task* is to connect the dots using at most four straight lines. Most participants consider only solutions that fit within the square formed by the dots.

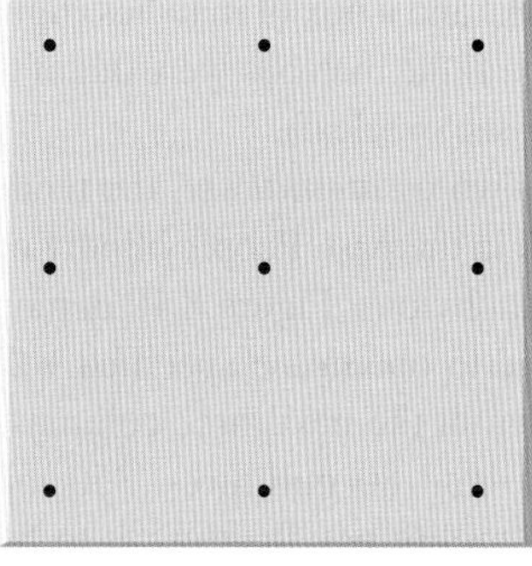

(b) *One solution* is to extend the lines beyond the boundary formed by the dots.

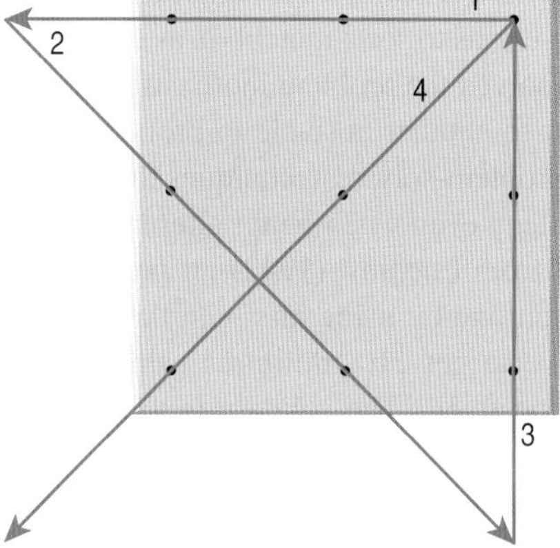

FIGURE 8.12
Sheerer's nine-dot problem. The task is to connect all nine dots using at most four straight lines.

INTERIM SUMMARY

Problem solving means transforming an initial state into a more satisfying goal state using operators. People frequently rely on ***problem-solving strategies*** that serve as guides for solving problems, such as ***algorithms*** (systematic procedures that inevitably produce a solution) and ***mental simulations*** (imagining the steps involved in solving a problem before actually trying them out). Restructuring a problem can help to overcome ***mental sets*** (whereby you continue to use strategies that have worked in the past).

Decision making

Just as life is a series of problems to solve, it is also a series of decisions to make, from the mundane ('Should I buy the cheaper brand or the one that tastes better?') to the consequential ('What career should I choose?'). ***Decision making*** is the process by which an individual weighs the pros and cons of different alternatives in order to make a choice.

We all make many decisions every day — some big, some small. To reach any of the choices we make, we all wc go through a decision-making process. Often that happens sub consciously for those small everyday decisions, and we are not even aware of how we get to the final choice. But the fact is that whether you are at the sandwich counter deciding whether to go for ham or chicken, or whether you are deciding whether or not to accept a job offer in a different city, the basics of decision making are the same.

A simple way of understanding the decision-making process is to break it down into a number of steps, as follows:

1. *Defining the problem* — understand exactly what the decision is that you have to make. For example, 'what will you have for lunch today?'
2. *Defining the alternatives* — work out what different options you have available. For example, you might be able to choose a sandwich, a wrap or a salad, and you can choose different fillings in each.
3. *Deciding on the criteria* — what are the factors that you have to consider in making your decision? For example, how much time will it take to prepare each option; what is the cost; what is your favourite flavour; and what is the healthiest option?
4. *Weighing up the pros and cons* — take each of the options and examine them according to the criteria. For example, you have only $5 in your pocket and you are running late for work, so the options that score best on the time and cost criteria will figure more highly in your thinking.
5. *Making the decision* having weighed up the pros and cons, you make a choice. Today it will be a pre-prepared salad on special for $4.99 out of the deli fridge.

Of course, summarising the process that way makes decision making seem simple. But, we all know how agonising it can be. How do you weigh up the pros and cons of different choices?

According to one information-processing model, when people make decisions, they consider two things: first, the utility (value to them) of the outcomes of different options; and second, the probability (estimated likelihood) of each outcome (Edwards, 1977; Edwards & Newman, 1986). Under this model, you identify the criteria on which to make a choice, and then assign different weighting to each, according to their importance. So, in making a decision, you look at each of the choices and score how well they meet each of the criteria. You then multiply this score by the weighting that you gave each of the criteria. This gives you a ***weighted utility value***, which indicates not just how well an option met a certain criteria, but how important that criteria is to making your decision. Thus, the weighted utility value reflects the importance of each criteria and the extent to which a given option satisfies it. For instance, in making a decision on your lunch order, the fact that you have only $5 in your pocket means that the cost of the different options had to be given a higher weighting, as that was extremely important in making your decision.

In reality, of course, as Rolling Stones lead singer Mick Jagger pointed out many years ago, 'You can't always get what you want', and aiming for an unattainable goal may carry heavy costs. For example, the salad special might be such good value that they are all sold out and you have no chance of purchasing it. Therefore, to make a rational decision, you must determine each option's ***expected utility***, a combined judgement of the weighted utility and the expected probability of obtaining that outcome.

INTERIM SUMMARY

Decision making is the process by which an individual weighs the pros and cons of different alternatives in order to make a choice. According to one information-processing model, when people make decisions, they consider both the utility of outcomes of different options and their probability. A ***weighted utility value*** is a combined judgement of the importance of an attribute and the extent to which a given option satisfies it. ***Expected utility*** is a combined judgement of the weighted utility and the expected probability of obtaining an outcome.

How rational are we?

Cognitive psychologists wonder just how rational we humans really are. Some have pointed to the cognitive shortcuts people use that can lead them to make less than optimal decisions, whereas others have suggested that the concept of rationality itself may be limited (Mellers, Schwartz, & Cooke, 1998).

APPLY + DISCUSS

Under what circumstances do people employ rational cost–benefit analyses to maximise expected utility?

- When do people not make decisions this way?
- Is failing to weigh the costs and benefits in a systematic, 'rational' way always irrational?

■ Explicit and implicit thinking

Explicit cognition involves conscious manipulation of representations. From a behaviourist perspective, the pros and cons of different courses of action — their environmental consequences — determine the decisions people make, whether or not they think about these consequences.

From a psychodynamic perspective, most problem solving and decision making involves motivation and emotion. A child with a learning disability who suffers repeated setbacks in school might 'solve' this problem by convincing himself that he does not care about success or failure, and hence he might stop making any effort. Further, some of the motives that underlie decisions are unconscious or implicit, a hypothesis that has now received considerable empirical support (chapter 10).

Heuristics

The assault on human rationality in psychology began when researchers noticed the extent to which people rely on ***heuristics***, cognitive shortcuts for selecting among alternatives without carefully considering each one. Heuristics allow people to make rapid, efficient but sometimes irrational judgements (Dawes, 1997; Nisbett & Ross, 1980). One example is the ***representativeness heuristic***, in which people categorise by matching the similarity of an object or incident to a prototype but ignore information about its probability of occurring. Consider the following personality description (Tversky & Kahneman, 1974, p. 1124):

> Steve is very shy and withdrawn, invariably helpful, but with little interest in people or in the world of reality. A meek and tidy soul, he has a need for order and structure and a passion for detail.

Is Steve most likely a farmer, a salesman, an airline pilot, a librarian or a doctor? Most people think he is probably a librarian, even if they are told that librarians are much less common in the population from which Steve has been drawn than the other occupations. Although Steve's attributes seem typical or representative of a librarian, if the population has 50 salesmen for every librarian, the chances are high that Steve is a salesman.

Another example is the ***availability heuristic***, in which people infer the frequency of something on the basis of how readily it comes to mind (Tversky & Kahneman, 1973). That is, people essentially assume that events or occurrences they can recall easily are common and typical. For example, in one study, participants were presented with a list of 26 names, half male and half female (McKelvie, 1996). Some of the names were famous, whereas others were not. When asked how many of the names were male or female, participants overestimated the gender that had more famous names, because famous names were more salient and hence available to consciousness.

The availability heuristic is generally adaptive because things that 'stick in our minds' tend to be important; familiar or vivid occurrences come to mind more readily than less familiar or less striking events. Availability can, however, lead to biased judgements when striking or memorable events are in fact infrequent.

A dangerous real-life consequence of this heuristic occurs when parents choose not to have their children vaccinated because of fear of vaccine-induced death. Although news stories about children who die from adverse reactions to vaccines are far more common and memorable than stories about the number of children who no longer die of smallpox or polio, in fact, the likelihood of death from vaccines for childhood illnesses is many times smaller than the likelihood of death without these vaccines (Ritov & Baron, 1990).

Bounded rationality

Researchers studying heuristics challenged the rational models described earlier by suggesting that human thought is highly susceptible to error. An emerging perspective takes this critique of pure reason one step further, arguing that because people rarely have complete information and limitless time, they are often better off using strategies for making inferences and decisions that might seem less than optimal to a philosopher (Gigerenzer & Goldstein, 1996). This view essentially places thought in its ecological context: people tend to do the best they can given the demands of the task and the cognitive resources they have available (Simon, 1990).

Underlying this view is the notion of ***bounded rationality***, that people are rational within the bounds imposed by their environment, goals and abilities. Thus, instead of making optimal judgements, people typically make good-enough judgements. Herbert Simon (1956) called this *satisficing*, a combination of satisfying and sufficing. When we choose a place to have dinner, we do not go through every restaurant in the phone book; rather, we go through a list of the restaurants that come to our minds and choose the one that seems most satisfying at the moment.

APPLY + DISCUSS

Most people believe that driving to a family holiday gathering a few hours away is safer than flying to another country for a holiday. Statistically, however, the chances of fatality are much greater driving on a holiday.

- What might lead to this example of the availability heuristic?

According to one theory, when people are called upon to make rapid inferences or decisions, they often use the strategy 'take the best, ignore the rest' (Gigerenzer & Goldstein, 1996). Thus, instead of weighing all the information possible, they begin with a quick yes/no judgement; if that works, they stop and assume their inference is good enough. If it does not work, they go on to the next quickest judgement and down the list until they get a 'satisficing' answer.

For example, when people are asked, 'Which city is larger, Townsville in Queensland or Bendigo in Victoria?' the first judgement they make is whether they have heard of them both. If they have heard only of Townsville, they assume it is bigger (since, presumably, they would have heard about a large city). This assumption has the paradoxical consequence that people who know fewer cities may be more accurate in answering this sort of question. If they have heard of both, they go to the next judgement. For a basketball fan, it might be 'Do both have a team in the National Basketball League (NBL)?'. In this case, the answer is no: Townsville has the Crocodiles, whereas Bendigo does not boast an NBL team. Thus, the conclusion is 'Townsville'.

INTERIM SUMMARY

Explicit cognition (cognition that involves conscious manipulation of representations) is only one form of thinking. Much of the time people rely on cognitive shortcuts, or ***heuristics***, that allow them to make rapid judgements but can sometimes lead to irrational choices. Some psychologists argue that the classical model of rationality that has guided much research on explicit cognition needs to be amended to recognise the extent to which people do, and should, practice a ***bounded rationality*** constrained by their goals, their cognitive resources and environmental demands.

Implicit cognition

The classical model of rationality emphasises conscious reflection. Yet many of the judgements and inferences people make occur outside of awareness. Try to recall the last time you said to yourself, 'I think I'd like Chinese food for dinner'. How did you come to that conclusion? Did you scan long-term gustatory memory, weigh various potential tastes, calculate the expected utility of each and reflect on the probability of making it to the Golden Dragon in time for dinner? In fact, most of the time judgements like this just 'come to us', which is a shorthand for saying that they are a form of ***implicit cognition***, or cognition outside of awareness.

Implicit learning

People learn, generalise and discriminate stimuli all the time without conscious thought (Reber, 1992). Most learning occurs outside awareness, as people implicitly register regularities in their environment or learn to behave in particular ways with little or no explicit instruction (Reber, 1992, 1993; Seger, 1994; Stadler & Frensch, 1998). For example, men in many cultures turn their eyes away from an attractive woman if her partner notices them looking. No-one ever teaches boys the rule, 'You have to stop looking at an attractive woman if her boyfriend catches you', but they learn it nonetheless. Generally, rules of gaze (such as how long to look someone in the eye while speaking before breaking eye contact, or where to look in a crowded elevator) are rarely taught explicitly, yet people implicitly learn to follow them and notice immediately if someone does not understand 'the rules'.

Implicit problem solving

Another form of implicit cognition can be seen in 'aha' experiences, when people set aside a seemingly insoluble problem only to find hours or days later that the answer suddenly comes to them (as in, 'Aha! I know the answer!'). Implicit problem solving of this sort probably occurs through the activity of associational networks, as information associated with unresolved problems remains active outside awareness (Bowers, Regenr, Balthazard, & Parker, 1990; Siegler, 2000; Zeigarnik, 1927).

Information related to unsolved problems appears to remain active for extended periods. Over time, other cues in the environment or thoughts that occur during the day are likely to spread further activation to parts of the network. If enough activation reaches a potential solution, it will 'jar' the answer free, catapulting it into consciousness (Yaniv & Meyer, 1987). This might explain what happens when people wake up from a dream with the answer to a problem, since elements of the dream can also spread activation to networks involving the unsolved problem.

Emotion, motivation and decision making

Alongside the recognition of the role of implicit processes, a second shift in psychologists' views of thinking has been a recognition of the substantial role played by motivation and emotion in everyday judgements, inferences and decisions (Mellers, Schwartz, & Ritov, 1999).

APPLY + DISCUSS

When choosing a mate, people often have criteria in mind, but their choices are guided as much by their 'heart' and 'gut' as by their head.

- When is this rational and when is it irrational?

Reason and emotion

For 2000 years, philosophers have bemoaned the way reason can be derailed by emotion (chapter 10). Numerous studies have, in fact, pointed to ways emotional processes can produce illogical responses. For example, people are much more likely to be upset if they miss a winning lottery ticket by one digit than by all six because they feel like they 'just missed it' (Kahneman & Tversky, 1982). In reality, missing by one digit has exactly the same consequences as missing every digit (except, of course, where lotteries give prizes for near misses).

On the other hand, thinking can sometimes interfere with sound judgement. In one study, participants looked at five art posters and rated the extent to which they liked each (Wilson et al., 1993). The investigators asked participants in the experimental group to list their reasons for liking or disliking each poster before rating them; participants in the control group simply rated the posters. Afterward, participants were allowed to choose a poster to take home.

A few weeks later, the experimenters contacted them and asked how satisfied they were with their choice. Participants who had analysed the reasons for their preferences were significantly less satisfied with their choice of poster than participants who had chosen without reflection. Conscious thinking appears to have overridden automatic, unconscious reactions, which proved to be a better guide.

Assessing risk

Many of the decisions people make in everyday life stem from their emotional reactions and their *expected* emotional reactions. This is often apparent in the way people assess risks (Kahneman & Tversky, 1979; Mellers, Schwartz, & Cooke, 1998; Mellers, Schwartz, Ho, & Ritov, 1997). Judging risk is a highly subjective enterprise, which leads to some intriguing questions about precisely what constitutes 'rational' behaviour. For example, in gambling situations, losses tend to influence people's behaviour more than gains, even where paying equal attention to the two would yield the highest average pay-off (Coombs & Lehner, 1984). Is this irrational?

Consider the following scenario. A person is offered the opportunity to bet on a coin flip. If the coin comes up heads, she wins $100; if tails, she loses $99. From the standpoint of expected utility theory, the person should take the bet, because on average, this coin flip would yield a gain of $1. However, common sense suggests otherwise. In fact, for most people, the prospect of losing $99 is more negative than winning $100 is positive. Any given loss of X dollars has greater emotional impact than the equivalent gain.

Prospect theory suggests that the value of future gains and losses to most people is in fact asymmetrical, with losses having a greater emotional impact than gains (Kahneman & Tversky, 1979).

Unlike expected utility theory, prospect theory describes the way people *actually* value different outcomes, rather than how they *should* value outcomes if they are behaving like the rational actors of economic theory. Prospect theory also predicts that people should be more willing to take a risk to avoid a loss than to obtain a gain.

Of course, how averse people are to risk depends in part on their circumstances. People tend to be more likely to take risks when the chips are down than when they are up (Tversky & Kahneman, 1981). For example, in a simulated tax collection experiment, participants who expected to receive a tax refund were less likely to write off questionable expenses than those who thought their deductions would not cover their taxes. These findings have practical implications for policy makers: if the government deducted more from people's pay packets during the year and gave it back to them in refunds, taxpayers would write off fewer questionable expenses (Robben, Webley, Weigel, & Warneryd, 1990).

Given the ambiguity of risk, it is not surprising that motivational and emotional factors play an important role in the way people assess it. Scientists who work in corporate research laboratories tend to find the risk of potential cancer-causing agents much smaller than scientists who work at universities (Kraus, Malmfors, & Slovic, 1992). The difference depends upon who pays their salaries and hence what they are motivated to find.

Although prospect theory and other approaches to risk assessment describe the average person, people actually differ substantially in their willingness to take risks — and, in fact, in their enjoyment of risky behaviour (Zuckerman, 1994). Some people are motivated more by fear, whereas others are motivated more by pleasure. These differences appear in part to reflect differences in whether their nervous systems are more responsive to norepinephrine, which regulates many fear responses, or dopamine, which is involved in pleasure seeking (chapter 10).

INTERIM SUMMARY

Implicit cognition refers to cognition outside of awareness. Much of learning is implicit, as people implicitly recognise patterns in the environment even though they may not be able to articulate these patterns explicitly. Problem solving can also occur implicitly, as in 'aha' experiences. Motivation and emotion play a substantial role in everyday cognition. Although emotion can disrupt cognition, it can also sometimes be a better guide for behaviour. Motives and emotions substantially influence the way people assess risks. Given the ambiguity involved in risk assessment, there may be no single 'rational' assessment that is free of emotional influences.

Connectionism

As we saw in chapter 7, psychology is in the midst of a 'second cognitive revolution', which has challenged the notion of the mind as a conscious, one-step-at-a-time information processor that functions like a computer. One of the major contributors to this revolution is an approach to perception, learning, memory, thought and language called ***connectionism***, or ***parallel distributed processing (PDP)***, which asserts that most cognitive processes occur simultaneously through the action of multiple activated networks (Holyoak & Simon, 1999; Rumelhart, McClelland, & the PDP Research Group, 1986; Smolensky, 1988). Like traditional cognitive psychologists, connectionists use computer models to test their theories, but their explicit metaphor for cognitive processing is the mind as a set of neurons that activate and inhibit one another, rather than the mind as a computer with memory stores.

Parallel distributed processing

The easiest way to get a grasp of PDP models is to understand what is meant by the terms *parallel* and *distributed*. First and foremost, PDP models emphasise parallel rather than serial processing. Human information processing is simply too fast and the requirements of the environment too instantaneous for serial processing (bringing information into working memory a piece at a time) to be our primary mode of information processing.

For example, in typing the word *vacuum*, the right hand does nothing until the first *u*, yet high-speed recordings of skilled typists find that the right hand has moved into position to hit the *u* by the time the left hand is typing the *v*. This happens so quickly that the typist cannot possibly be aware of it. Thus, even while the typist is focusing on the action of the left hand, recognition of the word 'vacuum' has activated parallel systems that prepare the right hand for action (Rumelhart et al., 1986).

APPLY + DISCUSS

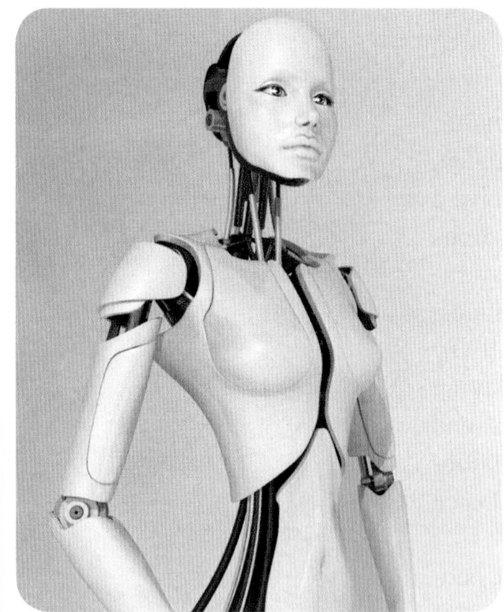

Artificial intelligence refers to the use of computers and robots to mimic human thinking and 'intelligence'. Movies, such as Steven Spielberg's *A. I.*, and conferences devoted to the study of artificial intelligence, have been on the rise.

- What role do you see artificial intelligence playing in the next decade?
- Do you think that ultimately computers or robots will completely mimic the human brain and be able to do all things humans can do?

Second, according to PDP models, the meaning of a representation is not contained in some specific locus in the brain. Rather, it is spread out, or distributed, throughout an entire network of processing units (nodes in the network) that have become activated together through experience. Each node attends to some small aspect of the representation, and none alone 'stands for' the entire concept. For instance, when a person comes across a barking dog, her visual system will simultaneously activate networks of neurons that have previously been activated by animals with two ears, four legs and a tail. At the same time, auditory circuits previously 'turned on' by barking will become active. The simultaneous activation of all these neural circuits identifies the animal with high probability as a dog. The person is not aware of any of this. All she consciously thinks is that she has come upon a dog.

These examples indicate how connectionist models explain categorisation based on similarity. Current perceptions activate neural networks. A concept stored in memory is nothing but a series of nodes that become activated together and hence constitute a network; thus, if current perceptual experience (such as seeing the shape of a dog and hearing barking) activates a large enough number of those nodes, the stimulus will be classified as an instance of that concept.

However, several concepts may be activated simultaneously because many animals have four legs and a tail. According to connectionist models, the concept that 'wins out' is the one that best matches current perceptions; that is, the one with the most nodes in common with current perceptual input. Connectionist models offer a deceptively simple and compelling explanation of memory as well: remembering a visual scene, such as a sunset, entails activation of a substantial part of the visual network that was active when the sunset was initially perceived.

The brain metaphor

According to the connectionist view, then, the brain represents knowledge through the interaction of hundreds, thousands or millions of neurons, which constitute nodes in a neural network. Perception, memory, categorisation and inference lie in the connections among these nodes, hence the term connectionism.

When neurons interact, they may either excite or inhibit other neurons, through the action of excitatory and inhibitory neurotransmitters (chapter 3). Connectionist models postulate similar cognitive mechanisms. Consider the simple perceptual problem posed in figure 8.13. Although the letters are ambiguous, either because they are slanted or because pieces are blotted out, you were probably unaware that your brain was performing some complex 'computations' to determine what the letters and words were. Instead, the meaning of the words just seemed obvious.

FIGURE 8.13
Parallel distributed processing. People are able to decipher ambiguous or distorted messages by simultaneously processing parts (such as letters) and wholes (words and phrases).

SOURCE: Rumelhart (1984, p. 8).

The incomplete letters shown in figure 8.13 are actually the norm in handwriting, where letters are never perfectly drawn. People can read handwriting rapidly because they simultaneously process information about the letters and the words. For example, in the top line of figure 8.13, the second letter of each word could either be an *a* or an *h*. Both letters are thus activated by information-processing units whose job is letter recognition. At the same time, however, a word recognition processing unit recognises that an *a* would render the first word a non-word and an *h* would do the same for the second word. The two processing modules interact, so that extra activation spreads to the *h* option in *the*, and the impossibility of *tae* as a word leads to inhibition of *a* as an option in that word.

On an even broader level, the phrase *the cat* is also being processed, and because no other phrase is possible using that configuration of letters, the brain is even more likely to come to the 'decision' that the first word is *the* (because what else would precede cat and has three letters?), further spreading activation to the *h* in *the*. Similar processes account for the fact that we decode the second word in the figure as *RED*, even though substantial pieces of the letters are covered.

Parallel constraint satisfaction

As figure 8.13 suggests, categorising, making inferences, reading and other cognitive processes actually require substantial 'decision making' at an implicit level. The brain has to decide whether a letter is an *a* or an *h* or whether a four-legged animal with a tail is a dog or a cat. According to connectionist models, implicit decision making of this sort happens rapidly, automatically and without awareness through a process of parallel constraint satisfaction.

Constraint satisfaction refers to the tendency to settle on a cognitive solution that satisfies as many constraints as possible in order to achieve the best fit to the data. A four-legged creature with a tail could be a dog or a cat, but if it starts barking, barking will further activate the *dog* concept and inhibit the *cat* concept, because the neurons representing barking spread activation to networks associated with dogs and spread inhibition to networks associated with cats.

Similarly, in reading the words in figure 8.13, the brain has to satisfy constraints imposed by the structure of the word *t_e* as well as by the structure of the phrase *t_e c_t*, which will increase the activation of some possibilities and decrease the activation of others. To put it slightly differently, the nodes in a PDP network are like *hypotheses* about the presence or absence of a given feature, such as whether a letter is an *a* or an *h* (Read, Vanman, & Miller, 1997). Parallel distributed processing is an implicit everyday form of hypothesis testing, in which the brain weeds out hypotheses that data do not support and converges on hypotheses that best fit the data in the light of multiple constraints processed in parallel.

The connections between nodes in a connectionist network are weighted according to the strength of the association between them and whether they excite or inhibit one another. The presence of barking is strong negative evidence for the 'cat' hypothesis and strong positive evidence that the animal is a dog. Thus, the weight between *barks* and *cats* is strongly negative, whereas the weight that connects barking with dogs is strongly positive. These weights simply reflect the extent to which the two nodes have been activated together in the past, and they increase and decrease with experience, which accounts for learning. Thus, if a person bought an unusual species of cat that made a barking sound, the weight between *bark* and *cat* would become more positive, at least for this particular type of cat.

We can also use connectionist models to explain complex phenomena such as analogies and inferences (Golden & Rumelhart, 1993; Holyoak & Thagard, 1995). Consider the vignette that began this chapter, in which a woman was beginning to infer that her boyfriend wanted to end their relationship. Figure 8.14 presents a simplified connectionist model of how she might have come to that judgement. She observed two things: he says he loves her, but he seems to be avoiding her. Direct observations carry a lot of weight when making inferences and hence receive high activation values (as indicated by the heavy blue lines, which represent strong positive weights) (Kunda & Thagard, 1996). His saying 'I love you', however, could have two interpretations: either he wants to stay with her, or he is trying to let her down easy. 'I love you' has a positive connection to both hypotheses. Wanting to 'let her down easy' is associated with wanting to split up, which is also strongly associated with his avoiding her. The *wants to split up* node is doubly activated — directly by the *avoiding me* node and indirectly by the *'I love you'* node — through its connection to the *wants to let me down easy* node. The *wants to stay together* node is relatively weakly activated in comparison because its only positive input is from the *'I love you'* node. Thus, the system is likely to settle on the solution with the highest activation: he wants to leave.

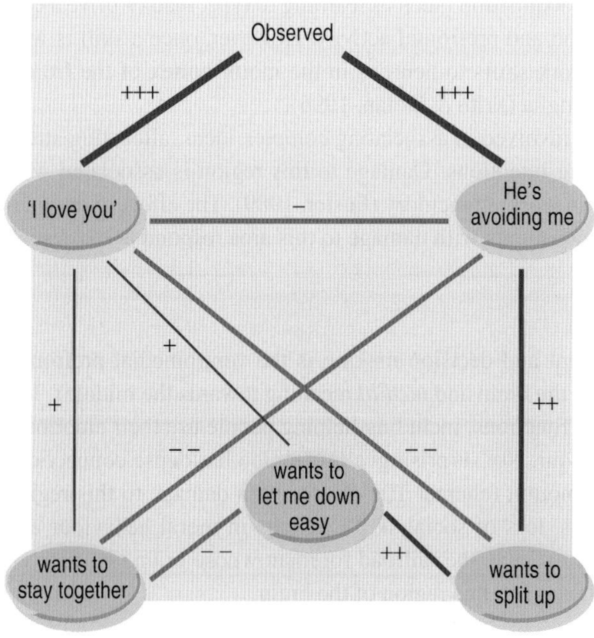

FIGURE 8.14
A connectionist model of inference. Positive weights are indicated in blue, whereas negative weights (inhibitory associations) are indicated in red. Strength of the associative connection (either positive or negative) is indicated by the width of the lines. The woman has observed two behaviours by her boyfriend that are mutually incompatible (indicated by the thick red line connecting them): he says he loves her, and he is avoiding her. Each of these nodes is connected to multiple other nodes. Simultaneous processing of all of these connections leads to the conclusion that he wants to split up, since it has higher activation than the 'wants to stay together' node.

INTERIM SUMMARY

According to ***connectionist*** or ***parallel distributed processing (PDP)*** models, most cognitive processes occur simultaneously (in parallel) through the action of multiple activated networks. The meaning of a representation is distributed throughout a network of processing units (nodes) that are activated together through experience. Knowledge thus lies in the connections between these nodes — in the extent to which they are positively or negatively associated with one another. When perceiving, remembering, categorising or performing other cognitive tasks, the brain settles on a cognitive solution that satisfies as many constraints as possible in order to achieve the best fit to the data through a process of parallel constraint satisfaction.

The neuropsychology of thinking

Connectionist models treat the brain as a powerful metaphor. Other cognitive scientists are studying the brain itself to try to uncover the mysteries of thought.

Like other psychological functions, thought processes are both distributed — spread out through large networks of neurons — as well as localised — carried out through specialised processing units in particular regions of the brain. For explicit reasoning, problem solving and decision making, these regions largely lie in the frontal lobes.

Unlike the other lobes, the frontal lobes receive no direct sensory input. Instead, they receive their input from other parts of the brain. Just as the other lobes combine sensations into perceptions, the frontal lobes combine perceptions into complex ideas. Researchers distinguish two broad regions of the prefrontal cortex that perform different cognitive functions: the dorsolateral and ventromedial prefrontal cortex (figure 8.15) (Damasio, 1994; Frith & Dolan, 1996; Fuster, 1989; Robin & Holyoak, 1995).

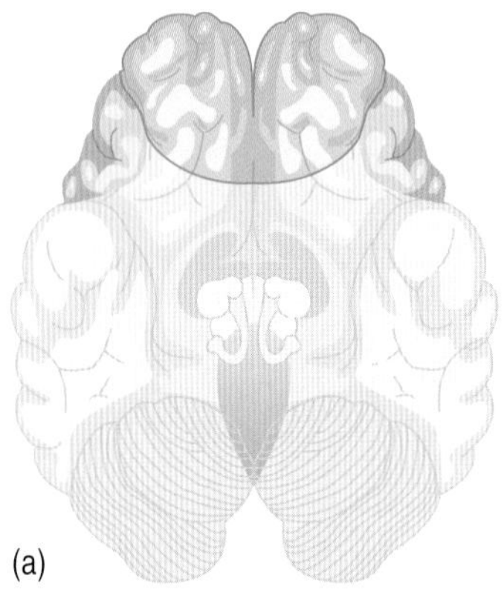

(a)

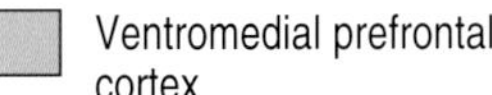

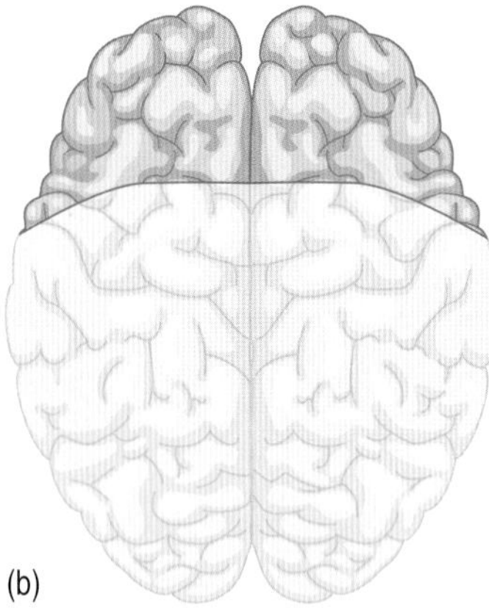

(b)

FIGURE 8.15
Prefrontal cortex and thinking. The drawings show two major regions in the frontal lobes involved in thinking, the dorsolateral and ventromedial prefrontal cortex, (a) from underneath the brain, and (b) from the top of the brain.

Dorsolateral prefrontal cortex

The ***dorsolateral prefrontal cortex*** plays a central role in working memory and explicit manipulation of representations (conscious thought). (Recall that *dorsal* means towards the top of the brain and *lateral* means to the sides; thus, this region encompasses the upper and side regions of the prefrontal cortex.) This area of the brain has many connections to other regions of the cortex (occipital, temporal and parietal) as well as to the basal ganglia. The connections to posterior cortical regions (regions towards the back of the brain) allow people to integrate information from multiple senses and to hold multiple kinds of information in mind while solving problems.

Links to the basal ganglia allow people to form and carry out complex sequences of behaviour and to develop skills (Ashby & Waldron, 2000). Skill acquisition (such as learning to type, read or drive a car) at first requires considerable conscious attention and prefrontal activity. However, once a skill is well learned and becomes automatic, the mental work shifts to neurons in the motor cortex of the frontal lobes and in subcortical circuits in the basal ganglia (Frith & Dolan, 1996).

Dorsolateral prefrontal circuits appear to be involved in associating complex ideas, allocating attention, making plans, and forming and executing intentions. Damage to this region is associated with impaired planning, distractibility and deficits in working memory (Fuster, 1989). The effect of dorsolateral prefrontal damage can be seen in the way patients with damage to this area respond to tasks such as the Tower of London problem (figure 8.16).

Ventromedial prefrontal cortex

Another part of the cortex crucial to judgement and decision making is the ventromedial prefrontal cortex (*ventral* meaning towards the bottom of the brain and *medial* meaning towards the middle). The ***ventromedial prefrontal cortex*** serves many functions, including helping people use their emotional reactions to guide decision making and behaviour. Not surprisingly, this region has dense connections with parts of the limbic system involved in emotion (chapter 10). People with damage to this region show difficulty inhibiting thoughts and actions, loss of social skills, deficits in moral behaviour and disturbances in personality functioning. Phineas Gage, the railroad foreman whose brain was pierced by an iron rod in 1848 (chapter 3), suffered damage to this region of the brain.

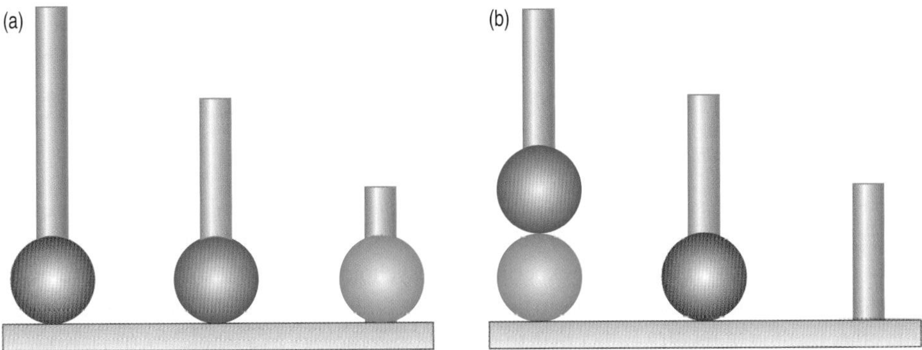

FIGURE 8.16
The Tower of London problem. Participants are presented with pegs holding one, two or three balls (a). They have to manipulate the placement of the balls in their minds so that they can produce the desired solution (b) because they are allowed to move only one ball at a time. While mentally performing these manipulations, participants show activation of dorsolateral prefrontal circuits in the same region involved in 'central executive' working memory tasks, such as managing multiple simultaneous tasks. This makes sense because the task requires the person to hold visual information in memory while mentally arranging a sequence of behaviours.

SOURCE: Frith and Dolan (1996).

Neurologist Antonio Damasio (1994) has studied many patients with damage to this region. Like Gage, these patients often seem cognitively intact: they can solve problems, manipulate information in working memory and recall events from the recent and distant past. Nevertheless, something is terribly wrong. Damage to this region demonstrates the importance of feeling — and of the ability to connect feelings with thoughts — in making sound decisions (Damasio, 1994).

In one study, Damasio and his colleagues showed patients with ventromedial prefrontal lesions a set of neutral images interspersed with disturbing pictures. Individuals with no brain damage or damage to other parts of the brain showed emotional arousal on viewing the upsetting images, as assessed by measuring skin conductance (sweating). In contrast, patients with lesions to the ventromedial prefrontal cortex showed no emotional reaction at all. One patient acknowledged that the pictures *looked* distressing but did not make him *feel* distressed.

Damasio relates another incident with one of these patients that suggests that reason may not be independent of emotion or motivation. The patient came in for testing on a winter day when icy roads were causing many accidents. Damasio asked him if he had had any trouble driving in. The patient responded, casually, that it was no different than usual, except that he had had to take proper procedures to avoid skidding. The patient mentioned that on one especially icy patch, the car ahead of him had spun around and skidded off the road. Unperturbed, the patient simply drove through the same patch with no particular concern.

The next day, Damasio and the patient were scheduling their next appointment, and the patient had the choice of two days. For the next 30 minutes the patient performed a careful cost–benefit analysis of every possible reason for choosing one day over the other, ranging from possible other engagements to potential weather conditions. He seemed unable to satisfice. Without the emotional input that would have told him that this decision was not worth 30 minutes, he behaved like a 'rational problem solver' trying to optimise weighted utility. In this sense, emotion may be the 'on–off switch' for explicit thought, letting us know when we can simply settle on a good-enough decision.

INTERIM SUMMARY

The frontal cortex plays a substantial role in explicit thought. Circuits in the ***dorsolateral prefrontal cortex*** are involved in associating complex ideas, allocating attention, making plans, and forming and executing intentions. The ***ventromedial prefrontal cortex*** is involved in emotional control over decision making and many aspects of social functioning.

Many paradigms do not necessarily lead to clarity

By Doctor Damian P. Birney, University of New South Wales

Lee Cronbach's (1957) presidential address to the American Psychological Association presented the strongest argument of the time for what he perceived to be a rupture in psychology. He warned against considering differential psychology and experimental psychology as two distinct scientific disciplines, and announced that 'Psychology continues to this day to be limited by the dedication of its investigators to one or the other method of inquiry, rather than to scientific psychology as a whole' (p. 671). Now, 50 years on, the resistance to combining differential and experimental paradigms within the field of reasoning and intelligence is still apparent. Working memory (WM), executive function (EF), and fluid intelligence (Gf) are constructs that all capture what is thought of as reasoning at some level. They are similar in that they all reflect cognitive processes that are not contingent on the specific content of the information being processed. However, there is a real risk that these constructs are inappropriately considered synonymous (Birney, Bowman, & Pallier, 2006; Blair, 2006). Working memory is an interesting case in point, because it straddles research investigating the trait-like attributes of Gf and the processes-like attributes of EF. Yet, a clear consensus regarding the nature of WM remains elusive (Conway, Jarrold, Kane, Miyake, & Towse, 2007). Part of the confusion results from the varied paradigms used to conceptualise and study cognition. Experimental psychology, neurosciences and differential psychology all conceptualise cognitive processes somewhat differently. Working memory theory was developed within the experimental paradigm, frequently using dual-task methodologies to dissociate storage and processing systems. Fluid intelligence has developed meaning from patterns of correlations between reasoning tasks studied within differential psychology. Executive function has a more recent history and has been pursued most actively by cognitive neuropsychology (with clinical and/or brain-imaging emphasis) (Jonides et al., 1997).

The cognitive tasks used in these related, yet distinct research paradigms have typically been developed with different purposes in mind. Hence, it is not always clear how theorising within one paradigm should be compared and integrated with theorising in another; it is not always clear how core processes identified using different methodologies in different paradigms can be compared (e.g. dual-task versus correlational methods) and it is not always clear how task- and paradigm-specific differences might obscure or conflate the detection of common underlying processes. As an interesting case in point, the *n-back* task has been labelled a continuous WM task in the neurosciences literature. However, its status as a WM measure has recently been questioned by differential psychologists (Kane, Conway, Miura, & Colflesh, 2007) on the grounds that it does not correlate well enough with other measures of WM (i.e. it lacks *construct validity* — a core criterion for classifying construct-relevant tasks within the differential paradigm). Despite the *n-back* task having the process hallmarks of WM (e.g. elementary cognitive operations including, encoding, storage and rehearsal, and controlled inhibition), correlations between it and other WM tasks are often low. So, what is to be done? If a task looks like, feels like and smells like a WM task, but is not correlated with other WM tasks, is it still a WM task?

To progress *scientific psychology as a whole*, careful investigation is required to build a common frame of reference between paradigms studying cognition. Theories must be integrated so that strong predictions about shared and unique processes can be tested. However, such practices are rare and, in their stead, findings from different paradigms have often been used to bolster theoretical claims for one construct without any real attempt to synthesise theory from other paradigms. Critical tests are needed that are more precise and 'risky' than the typical hypotheses based, for instance, on a predicted pattern of correlations between loosely defined constructs compared against an empirical bed of roughly significant (convergent) and non-significant (divergent) correlations (Birney et al., 2006).

Language

We humans do so much thinking with words that understanding thought is impossible without understanding language. Try, for instance, to solve an arithmetic problem without thinking with words or symbols, to think about the concept *justice* without relying on words, or to do something so seemingly simple as order from a menu without knowing how to read words.

In the remainder of this chapter, we will discuss ***language***, the system of symbols, sounds, meanings and rules for their combination that constitutes the primary mode of communication among humans. We begin by considering the ways language and thought shape each other. We then examine the elements of language, how people use language in everyday life, and how children acquire the capacity to think and communicate with words. In so doing, we enter into one of the most intriguing debates in all of psychology: the extent to which the capacity to acquire language is innate. We conclude by considering whether we are alone among species in the capacity to use symbols to think.

Language and thought

Australia is a culturally diverse nation. People from about 200 countries have migrated to Australia and about 22 percent of the population was born overseas (ABS, 2006c). More than 200 languages are spoken in Australia, including 45 indigenous languages. In 2008, about one in nine (11 percent) indigenous peoples aged 15 years and over spoke an Aboriginal or Torres Strait Islander language as their main language at home (ABS, 2008e). Additionally, almost four in nine (42 percent) people living in remote areas spoke an indigenous language as their main language at home (ABS, 2008e). While English is the dominant language, about 16 percent of the population speaks more than one language at home. Italian, Greek, Cantonese, Arabic and Vietnamese are the most commonly spoken languages other than English.

Research suggests that a higher proportion of people living in remote areas use an indigenous language at home. It is likely that these indigenous children will have different language experiences in the home to many non-indigenous children.

This diversity is significant because language plays an important role in the way people think. The language that you use can influence your approach to reasoning, problem solving and decision making — the basics of thought. The fact that there are so many different languages in Australia means there are many different approaches to the way people perceive and think about the world. Indeed, not only do people take different approaches to problem solving, but individuals who are ***bilingual*** (able to speak another language with approximately equal facility as one's native language) might also be able to draw on different types of thought processes, depending on which language they are using at a particular time.

For example, the Hanunoo people of the Philippines have 92 names for rice (Anderson, 1985). Does this mean that the Hanunoo can think about rice in more complex ways than Australians and New Zealanders, who are hard pressed to do much better than 'white rice' and 'brown rice'? This line of reasoning led Benjamin Whorf (1956) and others to formulate what came to be called the ***Whorfian hypothesis of linguistic relativity***, the idea that language shapes thought (Gumperz & Levinson, 1996; Maffi & Hardin, 1997).

According to the Whorfian hypothesis, people whose language provides numerous terms for distinguishing subtypes within a category actually *perceive* the world differently from people with a more limited linguistic repertoire. In its most extreme version, this hypothesis asserts that even what people can think is constrained by the words and grammatical constructions in their language.

Although Whorf's hypothesis has some substantial grains of truth, subsequent research has not supported its more extreme forms. For example, colour is universal in all cultures, but the number of words for colours is not constant. The Dani people of New Guinea, for example, have only two basic colour words: *mola* for bright, warm shades and *mili* for dark, cold hues (Anderson, 1985). To what extent, then, does the presence or absence of linguistic labels affect the way people perceive colours?

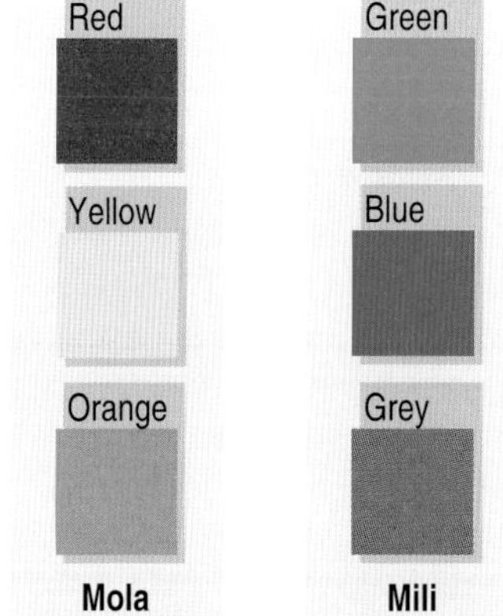

FIGURE 8.17
Language and colour. Although the Dani can remember the hue of different-coloured chips, they will call the three chips on the left mola and the three on the right mili.

A series of experiments with Dani and English-speaking participants explored this question (Rosch, 1973). In one experiment, researchers briefly showed participants a colour chip and then asked them 30 seconds later to select a chip of the same colour from an array of 160 chips (figure 8.17). The hypothesis was that English-speaking participants would perform better if the chip were one of the basic colours for which their language provides a primary name (for instance, a clear, bright red) than if it were an in-between shade, such as magenta or taupe — and indeed they did. Contrary to the Whorfian hypothesis, however, the Dani participants, too, correctly selected basic colours more often than less distinctive shades, even though their language had no names for them.

Other research suggests that the way people in different cultures think about visual scenes does mirror aspects of the language — such as whether they use phrases such as 'it's on my right' versus 'it's to the east' (Danziger, 1999). Further, with complex concepts language does appear to play a role in shaping thought. Having certain concepts, such as *freedom* or *capitalism*, would be impossible without language. Reasoning deductively would certainly be difficult if people could not construct propositions verbally and draw conclusions based on verbally represented premises.

Different languages also call attention to different information. For example, the English language draws attention to a person's gender. English speakers cannot avoid specifying gender when using possessive pronouns; if someone asks 'Whose car is that?' the answer is either 'his' or 'hers'. Many languages have different words for *you* that indicate the relative status of the person being addressed. The more polite, formal form is *usted* in Spanish, *vous* in French and *Sie* in German. The Japanese have many more gradations of respect, and Japanese professionals often exchange business cards immediately upon meeting so they will know which term to use (Triandis, 1994).

APPLY + DISCUSS

- If language influences thought, do people who are fluent in more than one language think differently when they are speaking different languages?

People with political agendas certainly believe language can influence thinking. In the 1960s and 1970s, feminists attempted to raise consciousness about condescending attitudes towards women by objecting to the use of the word *girl* to describe an adult female. Groups for and against abortion rights try to take the moral high ground by referring to themselves as *pro-choice* and *pro-life*.

Although language is an important medium for thought and can sometimes influence it, thought can certainly occur independent of language. Consider the common experience of starting to say something and then correcting it because it did not accurately convey the intended thought, or remembering the 'gist' of what was said in a conversation without remembering the exact words (Pinker, 1994). Patients with strokes that damage left-hemisphere language centres can become very frustrated trying to get ideas and intentions across without words, as can young toddlers.

Furthermore, people often mentally visualise activities or behaviours without putting thoughts about those activities into language. For example, professional athletes often mentally rehearse the steps involved in swinging a golf club or serving a tennis ball. Many professional musicians similarly mentally practise playing a piece of music before a performance, for example (Garfield, 1986). In these cases, the thought appears to be independent of any particular words.

The converse of Whorf's hypothesis — that thought shapes language — is, however, at least as valid. Because rice is critically important to the Hanunoo, it is no accident that their language provides words to describe distinctions in its appearance, texture and use. We can see the 'evolution' of vocabulary in the West, where terms such as *road rage* and *cyberspace* have emerged to describe what previously did not exist. Conversely, words describing phenomena that are no longer part of everyday life (such as *hippie*) fall into disuse.

INTERIM SUMMARY

Language is the system of symbols, sounds, meanings and rules for their combination that constitutes the primary mode of communication among humans. According to the ***Whorfian hypothesis of linguistic relativity***, language shapes thought. Subsequent research has not generally supported the hypothesis, although language is central to many abstract concepts and many forms of reasoning. Thought also shapes language, and language evolves to express new concepts.

Transforming sounds and symbols into meaning

One of the defining features of language is that its symbols are arbitrary. The English language could just as easily have called cats *dogs* and vice versa. In this next section, we examine how sounds and symbols are transformed into meaningful sentences, beginning with the basic elements of language. We then explore the grammatical rules people implicitly follow as they manipulate these elements to produce meaningful utterances.

Elements of language

Language is processed hierarchically, from the small units of sound people produce through their mouths and noses to the complex combinations of words and sentences they produce to convey meaning (table 8.1). The smallest units of sound that constitute speech, called ***phonemes***, are strung together to create meaningful utterances. In the English language, phonemes include not only vowels and consonants but also the different ways of pronouncing them (such as the two pronunciations of the letter *a* in *at* and *ate*).

TABLE 8.1 **Elements of language**

Element	Definition	Examples
Phonemes	Smallest units of sound that constitute speech	th, s, ā, ă
Morphemes	Smallest units of meaning	anti-, house, the, -ing
Phrases	Groups of words that act as a unit and convey a meaning	in the den, the rain in Spain, ate the lolly
Sentences	Organised sequences of words that express a thought or intention	The house is old. Did you get milk?

A string of randomly connected phonemes, however, does not convey any message. To be meaningful, strings of phonemes must be combined into ***morphemes***, the smallest units of meaning in language. Words, suffixes and prefixes are all morphemes, such as *pillow*, *horse*, *the*, *pre-* and *-ing*. The word *cognition*, for example, consists of two morphemes: *cognit-*, from the Latin *cogito* (part of the verb 'to know'), and *-ion*, meaning 'the act of.'

Morphemes are combined into ***phrases***, groups of words that act as a unit and convey a meaning. In the sentence 'When people speak, they make many sounds', the words 'when people speak' and 'many sounds' are phrases. Words and phrases are combined into ***sentences***, organised sequences of words that express a thought or intention. Some sentences are intended as statements of fact or propositions; others ask questions or make requests (e.g. 'Bill, come here!')

Syntax: the rules for organising words and phrases

Speakers of a language intuitively know that they cannot place words or phrases wherever they want in a sentence. A native English speaker would never ask, 'Why you did come here today?' because it violates implicit rules of word placement. Consider, in contrast, the pseudosentence *The sten befted down the flotway*. Although the individual words have no meaning, readers will intuitively recognise it as essentially grammatical: *sten* is clearly a noun and the subject of the sentence; *befted* is a verb in the past tense (as indicated by the morpheme *-ed*) and *flotway* is the direct object. This pseudo-sentence 'feels' grammatical to an English speaker because it conforms to the ***syntax*** of the language, the rules that govern the placement of words and phrases in a sentence.

Linguists (people who study the way languages operate) and psycholinguists (psychologists who study the way people use and acquire language) map the structure of sentences using diagrams such as the one presented in figure 8.18 to analyse *The young woman kissed her anxious date*. Two aspects of this mapping are worth noting. The first is the extent to which rules of syntax determine the way people create and comprehend linguistic utterances. Much of the way psychologists think about syntax in sentences like this reflects the pioneering work of the linguist Noam Chomsky (1957, 1965). Chomsky views ***grammar*** (which includes syntax) as a system for generating acceptable language utterances and identifying unacceptable ones. According to Chomsky, the remarkable thing about language is that by acquiring the grammar of their linguistic community, people can generate an infinite number of sentences they have never heard before; that is, grammar is generative.

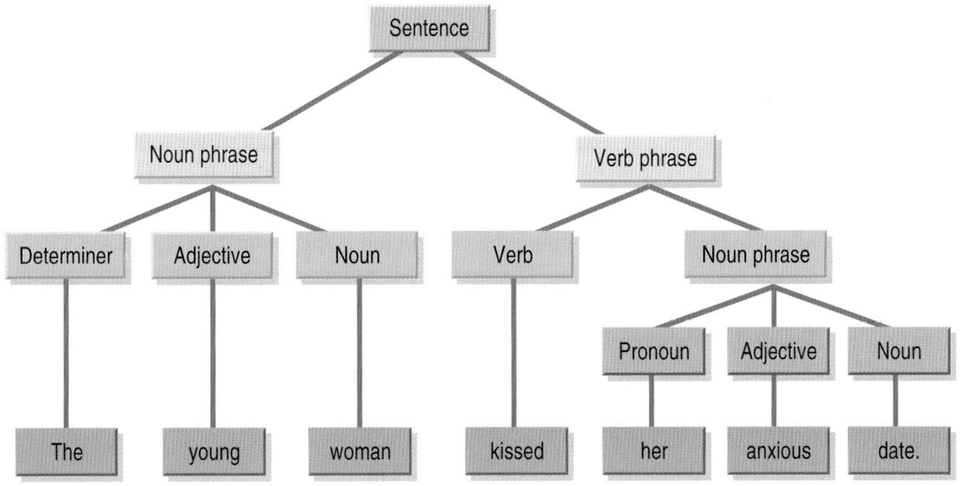

FIGURE **8.18**
A syntactic analysis of sentence and phrase structure. Sentences can be broken down through treelike diagrams, indicating noun phrases and verb phrases and their component parts. One of the regularities in language that makes learning syntax easier is that the same principles apply to phrase structures anywhere in the sentence. Thus, the same syntactical rules apply to noun phrases whether they describe the subject (the young woman) or the direct object (her anxious date).

People can also readily transform one sentence into another with the same underlying meaning despite a very different apparent syntactic construction, or surface structure, of the sentence. For example, instead of stating 'The young woman kissed her anxious date', a speaker could just as easily say 'The anxious date was kissed by the young woman'.

A second feature of this mapping worth noting is the interaction of syntax and ***semantics*** — the rules that govern the meanings (rather than the order) of morphemes, words, phrases and sentences — in understanding what people say. For example, the word *date* has multiple meanings. Perhaps the woman who kissed the date could really love fruit. The presence of *anxious* as a modifier, however, constrains the possible interpretations of *date* and thus makes the fruity interpretation unlikely. But to recognise this semantic constraint, the reader or listener has to recognise a syntactic rule, namely that an adjective preceding a noun typically modifies the noun. The interaction between syntax and semantics (which roughly maps onto Broca's area in the prefrontal cortex and Wernicke's area of the temporal lobes, respectively; chapter 3) is particularly useful in resolving the meaning of ambiguous sentences. For example, semantics comes into play on the television show *Talkin' 'bout your Generation*, with contestants from Generation Y, Generation X and the Baby Boomers responding to questions from host Shaun Micallef based on their understanding of the meaning of different words.

Semantics comes into play on the television show *Talkin' 'bout your Generation*, with contestants from Generation Y, Generation X and the Baby Boomers responding to questions based on their understanding of the meaning of different words. Television personality Jolene Anderson has participated on the show, which is hosted by comedian Shaun Micallef.

The remarkable thing about this interaction of semantic and syntactical knowledge is how quickly and unconsciously it takes place. People do not consciously break sentences down into their syntactic structures and then scan memory for the meanings of each word. Rather, both syntactic and semantic analyses proceed simultaneously, in parallel, and create a set of constraints that lead the reader or listener to settle on the most likely meaning of the sentence. Even this last sentence understates the role of parallel constraint satisfaction in language comprehension, since the person is simultaneously breaking the stream of sound down into phonemes, morphemes, words, phrases and sentences; processing each level of meaning; and using information at one hierarchical level to inform decisions at other levels. We tend to become aware of one level or another only if we have trouble coming to an implicit solution (e.g. if a word does not seem to fit or a phrase has multiple potential meanings that cannot be resolved without conscious attention). As with induction, understanding language probably relies on a combination of formal rules (in this case, of syntax) and general knowledge (semantics, or the meanings of words).

INTERIM SUMMARY

The smallest units of sound that constitute speech are ***phonemes***, which are combined into ***morphemes***, the smallest units of meaning. Morphemes, in turn, are combined into ***phrases***, groups of words that act as a unit and convey a meaning. Words and phrases are combined into ***sentences***, organised sequences of words that express a thought or intention. The rules that govern the placement of words and phrases within a language are called its ***syntax***. Syntax is an aspect of ***grammar***, the system for generating acceptable language utterances and identifying unacceptable ones. To understand what people are saying, people often use information about both syntax and ***semantics*** — the rules that govern the meanings of morphemes, words, phrases and sentences.

The use of language in everyday life

Two people catch each others' eyes at a party. Eventually, one casually walks over to the other and asks, 'Enjoying the party?' A linguist could easily map the syntax of the question: it is a variant of the proposition *You are enjoying the party*, constructed by using a syntactic rule that specifies how to switch words around to make a question (and dropping the *you*, which is the understood subject).

But that would completely miss the point. The sentence is not a question at all, and its meaning has nothing to do with the party. The real message is, 'We've caught each other's eyes several times and I'd like to meet you'. Psychologists interested in the ***pragmatics*** of language — the way language is used and understood in everyday life — are interested in how people decode linguistic messages of this sort (Blasko, 1999; Fussel & Krauss, 1992; Gibbs, 1981).

For years, Chomsky was such a towering figure in linguistics that his research, much of it on grammar and syntax, set the agenda for psychologists studying language. More recently, some researchers have begun to focus on levels of linguistic processing broader than the isolated sentence. Rather than studying the elements of language from the bottom up, they have turned to the analysis of ***discourse*** — the way people ordinarily speak, hear, read and write in interconnected sentences (Carpenter, Miyaka, & Just, 1995; Graesser, Millis, & Zwaan, 1997; McKoon & Ratcliff, 1998; Rubin, 1995). Discourse analysts point out that the meaning (and even the syntactic structure) of every sentence reflects the larger discourse in which it is embedded. The question 'Enjoying the party?' made sense to both people because of the context of the party and some significant nonverbal communication.

Multiple levels of discourse

According to many discourse analysts, people mentally represent discourse at multiple levels (Graesser et al., 1997; van Dijk & Kintsch, 1983). At the lowest level is the exact wording of the phrases and sentences written or spoken, which is retained in memory only briefly while the rest of the sentence is processed.

When later called upon to remember a sentence (such as *Mario went in for a check-up*), however, people generally remember the *gist*, or general meaning (e.g. Mario went to have his physical health examined). They also make inferences, which are largely automatic and implicit (e.g. that he was going to see a doctor for his check-up). These inferences influence both what people 'hear' and what they remember (Bransford, Barclay, & Franks, 1972). Consider the inferences involved when a person reads the familiar instructions, 'Wet hair, apply shampoo, lather, rinse, repeat' (Pinker, 1994). If the person did not think beyond the words on the bottle — did not make inferences — she would wet her hair again after each rinse cycle and repeat endlessly (since the instructions never say to stop!).

At the next level, the speaker or narrator asks the audience to enter a certain situation. Consider the vignette that opened this chapter, which began with the words 'You are sitting in a café with your closest friend'. The aim is to paint an evocative picture that allows readers to suspend reality and enter into a different time and place.

One step higher is the communication level, which reflects what the communicator is trying to do, such as impart ideas in a textbook or tell a story. Finally, at the broadest level is the general type of discourse, such as a story, a news report, a textbook, a joke or a comment at a party intended to start a conversation.

Principles of communication

When people talk or write, their communications are guided not only by syntactic rules that shape the way they put words together but also by a set of shared rules of conversation that are implicit in the minds of both participants (Grice, 1975). For example, people keep track of what their listener knows, and when they introduce a new term or idea, they typically signal it with a change in syntax and embellish it with examples or evocative language.

People also use various cues to signal important information. In writing, they usually put the topic sentence of a paragraph first so that readers know what the main point is. In public speaking, people often use intonation (tone of voice) to make particular points forcefully or use phrases such as 'the point to remember here is . . . '

These literary devices of everyday life may seem obvious, but what is remarkable is how effortlessly people use and understand them. Consider again the opening line of the vignette with which this chapter began: 'You are sitting in a café with your closest friend, and she tells you tearfully, "I think my relationship with Brett has hit a dead end".' By switching to a narrative mode more characteristic of fiction, we were signalling to the reader that something different was happening — that we were 'setting the stage' for a chapter and a new set of ideas. We also introduced a second-person construction ('You are . . .'), seldom used in this book, which also served as a syntactic cue that this material was somehow different. We suspect, however, that most readers were no more aware of the 'rules' we were using to direct their attention than we were in using them.

APPLY + DISCUSS

- To what extent does email communication lose aspects of language that express emotions, intentions or subtle messages? In what ways can email lead to misunderstandings?
- How have people learned to communicate some of these aspects of language by email? What do people do to communicate emotion or emphasis?
- On the other hand, what about email communications leads some people to develop rapid, intimate relationships by email?

Nonverbal communication

People communicate verbally through language, but they also communicate nonverbally, and aspects of speech other than nouns and verbs often speak louder than words. When a parent calls a child by her whole name, it may be to chastise or to praise, depending on the inflection and intonation

('Jennifer Marie Lar*son* [rising tone on last syllable]? *Stop teasing your brother.*' versus '*Jennifer Marie Larson* [lowering tone on last syllable of last word]. *You are so cute.*') Even when no words are spoken, clenched fists and a tense look convey a clear message.

The facial expression, body posture, hands on hips and other nonverbal cues of US President Barack Obama help communicate the message that he is relaying in this situation.

Nonverbal communication includes a variety of signals: body language, gestures, touch, physical distance, facial expressions and nonverbal vocalisations (such as sighs or throat clearings) (DePaulo & Friedman, 1998; Dil, 1984; Schachner, Shaver, & Mikulincer, 2005). Being conversant in the grammar of nonverbal communication can be just as important in interpersonal relations as understanding the grammar of verbal language. When a person sits too close on a bus or stands too close when talking, the effect can be very unsettling. Like other grammars, this one is largely unconscious.

Just how important is nonverbal communication? In one study, participants were shown 30-second video clips of graduate-student teaching assistants (TAs) at the beginning of a term. Participants rated the TAs using a number of adjectives, such as *accepting*, *active*, *competent* and *confident*. The investigators wanted to know whether these brief ratings from only part of a lecture would predict student evaluations of the teacher at the end of the term. The investigators added one extra difficulty: they turned off the sound on the videotapes, so that participants could rely only on nonverbal behaviour (Ambady & Rosenthal, 1993).

The findings were extraordinary. Many of the correlations between initial nonverbal ratings and eventual student evaluations were as near perfect as one finds in psychology, in the range of .75 to .85. Teaching assistants who initially appeared confident, active, optimistic, likable and enthusiastic in their nonverbal behaviour were rated much better teachers months later. Correlations remained substantial (though somewhat lower) when judges were asked to rate two-second film clips! Nonverbal communication also contributes to language learning. How, for example, does a child of 12 to 18 months figure out which of the hundreds of objects in sight is connected with a new word, as when a parent just says, 'Birdie!' Research suggests that children spontaneously recognise very early that they need to follow the gaze of the speaker to figure out the object to which the speaker is referring. This does not appear to be the case for autistic children, who in many ways are isolated in their own mental worlds and often use their own private languages to refer to objects (Baron-Cohen, Baldwin, & Crowson, 1997; Bauminger, 2002; Carpenter, Pennington, & Rogers, 2001). Autistic children seem unable to recognise that the speaker's gaze is an index of the speaker's intention to refer to something. Instead, these children often associate the word with the object in their own gaze.

INTERIM SUMMARY

Psychologists interested in the ***pragmatics*** of language study the way language is used and understood in everyday life. Rather than studying the elements of language from the bottom up, many researchers have turned to the analysis of ***discourse***, the way people ordinarily speak, hear, read and write in interconnected sentences. People mentally represent and discourse simultaneously at multiple levels, from the exact sentences and phrases of a text all the way up to the type of discourse (e.g. news story or joke). When people converse or write, they are guided not only by syntactic rules that shape the way they put their words together but also by implicit rules of conversation. People also use ***nonverbal communication***, such as body language, touch, gestures, physical distance, facial expressions and nonverbal vocalisations.

Language development

For most people who have ever studied a foreign language and then visited a country where that language is the native tongue, watching five-year-olds speak is a humbling experience. Without benefit of years of coursework and hours of rote memorisation, these tiny creatures with their half-baked cortices typically run linguistic circles around their fumbling foreign elders. How do they do it?

In this final section, we consider the mystery of how children acquire language so quickly and effortlessly. We begin by exploring the roles of nature and nurture in language development and then examine stages of language acquisition. We conclude by inquiring into the linguistic abilities of our nearest neighbours on the evolutionary tree.

Nature and nurture in language development

Children develop linguistic competence with astonishing speed. For the first year of life, most babies are lucky if they can rattle off *dadadadada*, but four years later, children have mastered the basics of verbal communication. By young adulthood, the average person knows the meaning of around 60 000 words. A central question for decades has been the extent to which this remarkable capacity for language acquisition depends on nature or nurture. As we will see, as in so many other areas of psychology, nature appears to have selected a brain that is remarkably responsive to particular kinds of nurture, so that the question of nature versus nurture needs to be reframed.

The case for nurture

The behaviourist B. F. Skinner (1957) explained verbal behaviour using the same conditioning principles that apply to other forms of behaviour, notably reinforcement, punishment, generalisation and discrimination. According to Skinner, language development requires no special principles. A baby who happens to gurgle *Muh* after his mother says 'say Mummy' will receive tremendous positive reinforcement from his delighted mother. Consequently, the baby will be more likely to say *Muh* in the future and to imitate the sounds his mother produces and subsequently reinforces. Later, his mother will be pickier about what she reinforces, shaping the baby's verbal responses to approximate adult speech more closely. She and other adults will also reinforce the child for grammatical constructions, which he will then generalise to create new sentences. The child will also learn to respond appropriately to the verbal behaviour of others.

Children clearly do learn language in part by imitation, suggesting a substantial role for social learning in language acquisition (see Bohannon & Bonvillian, 1997). And parents do frequently 'recast' their children's non-grammatical statements into more grammatical forms, which shapes the way children speak (Farrar, 1992; Saxton, 1998). On the other hand, parents tend to focus less on the grammar than on the content of their young children's speech, providing corrective feedback more often when they are entirely unable to understand their children's utterances (Brown & Hanlon, 1970; Hoff-Ginsberg & Shatz, 1982; Marcus, 1993). In addition, some children who have never spoken a word are nevertheless able to comprehend language and understand complex rules of syntax (Stromswold, 1995). This is difficult to explain using a model that presumes that language use and comprehension reflect the same processes of shaping and reinforcement as other learning.

APPLY + DISCUSS

An Australian mother, Priscilla Dunstan, believes she has discovered a universal language spoken by babies (Infants crying a universal language: Listen Mum, baby's sounds make sense, 2006). Ms Dunstan spent numerous hours listening to her son and other youngsters and isolated five distinct 'words' or sounds that infants use to communicate their needs to their parents: *neh* (hungry), *owh* (tired), *eh* (needs a burp), *eairh* (wind pain) and *heh* (uncomfortable).

- Do Ms Dunstan's findings support the case for nature, nurture, or both?
- What research evidence is required to establish whether these five sounds or words are universal?
- What are the practical implications for Ms Dunstan's findings?

The case for nature

Whereas Skinner championed nurture, Chomsky took the side of nature. According to Chomsky (1959, 1986), children could not possibly learn the rules of grammar and thousands of words within such a few short years simply through reinforcement mechanisms. Children effortlessly use grammatical rules far earlier than they can learn less complicated mental operations, such as multiplication, or even less complicated behaviours, such as turning a door knob. Further, they acquire language in similar ways and at a similar pace across cultures, despite very different learning environments. Deaf children show similar developmental patterns in learning sign language as well (Bonvillian, 1999).

An innate grammar?

The similarities of grammar that appear in languages across cultures led Chomsky instead to propose a ***universal grammar*** — an innate, shared set of linguistic principles — that underlies the grammatical forms found in all cultures. In this view, to get from the universal grammar to any particular language is like flipping a series of 'switches'. For example, in English, the switch that indicates whether to include a pronoun before a verb (such as *I have*) is set to 'yes'. In contrast, in Spanish, the same switch is set to 'no' (e.g. *tengo*), since the form of the verb (in this case, first person singular) already indicates the subject, and a pronoun would be redundant.

According to Chomsky, humans are born with a ***language acquisition device (LAD)***, an innate set of neural structures for acquiring language. Through the operation of this device, children are born 'knowing' the features that are universal to language, and language learning in childhood 'sets the switches' so that children speak their native tongue rather than some other. As evidence, Chomsky noted that children routinely follow implicit rules of grammar to produce utterances they have never heard before. For example, most English-speaking four-year-olds use the pronoun *hisself* instead of *himself*, even though this usage has never been reinforced (Brown, 1973). Children essentially invent 'hisself' by applying a general rule of English grammar.

In fact, children exposed to language without proper grammar will infuse their language with grammatical rules they have never been taught! This has been demonstrated in research with deaf children exposed to sign language by their hearing-unimpaired parents, whose ability to sign is often very limited (Goldin-Meadow & Mylander, 1984, 1998; Newport, 1990). These children typically become much better sign language users than their parents even before they enter school, using grammatical constructions their parents do not know. These data strongly support Chomsky's view of a universal grammar, or, to use the more recent term proposed by the linguist Steven Pinker (1994), a 'language instinct'.

Some equally striking evidence for a language instinct comes from a 'natural experiment' that occurred when the Sandinista government came to power in Nicaragua in 1979 and opened schools for the deaf a year later (Senghas, 1996; cited in Bonvillian, 1999). Although their efforts to teach lip reading instead of sign language largely failed, the schools brought together for the first time a group of children who had never spent much time with other deaf children. Outside their classrooms, these children learned to communicate with each other through gestures, most of which involved pantomiming actions rather than the more symbolic gestures of American Sign Language.

Something remarkable, however, occurred when the next generation of deaf children arrived: they effortlessly transformed the primitive sign language of the playground into a real language. They introduced grammatical constructions such as distinctions between nouns and verbs, 'spoke' more fluidly and quickly, and developed a system of symbols that were arbitrary rather than pantomimic. In fact, this new Nicaraguan Sign Language was similar in many ways to existing sign languages. Perhaps these children had flipped some switches in a novel way on Chomsky's universal grammar.

Specialised neural circuits

Specialised neural circuits exist in the left frontal lobe for processing grammar and in the left temporal lobe for processing word meaning. This further suggests that the tendency to follow syntactic rules and to learn word meanings is an innate potential in humans (chapter 3). At birth, language regions of the temporal cortex are already larger in the left than the right hemisphere, and neurons in the left hemisphere are more sensitive to speech sounds than neurons in corresponding regions on the right (Stromswold, 1995).

Precisely how language first evolved in humans is a matter of considerable speculation (Deacon, 1996; Petitto, 2000). Some recent data suggest that grammar may have evolved through the evolution of neural circuits involved in imitation. Recent primate studies have found that the area equivalent to Broca's area in monkeys responds when a person manipulates an object and the monkey then manipulates it in the same way (Rizzolatti & Arbib, 1998). Neuroimaging studies indicate that Broca's area in humans is also activated by imitative matches. This suggests that language may develop in part as children learn to reproduce the meaning of the behaviour of others (Rizzolatti et al., 1996). Some researchers suggest that language may actually have emerged from hand gestures — which could explain why sign languages activate similar parts of the brain as spoken languages.

Additional evidence for innate linguistic capacities comes from individuals with dyslexia, a language-processing impairment that makes tasks such as spelling and arithmetic difficult. The specific left-hemisphere regions activated during certain linguistic tasks (such as rhyming) in non-dyslexic people are not activated in people with the disorder, suggesting that certain innate circuits are not functioning normally (Paulesu et al., 1996; Shaywitz et al., 1998). This problem is only apparent, however, if the person grows up in a literate culture. Otherwise, the deficit would probably never be expressed, because people with dyslexia do not differ in other ways intellectually from other people (and are often highly intelligent, although the disorder often makes them feel incompetent, particularly in primary school).

From an evolutionary perspective, the brain evolved modules to process specialised linguistic information just as the visual system developed specialised cells in the occipital cortex that respond to particular features of the physical world such as angles (Tooby & Cosmides, 1992). In other words, the brain adapted to regular features of the linguistic environment, just as it gradually changed its structure to match the structure of nature. The only difference is that the evolution of language capacities fed its own development, as increasing linguistic capacities allowed progressively more complex communication, which required further neural adaptation (see Deacon, 1996; Kimura, 1993).

MAKING CONNECTIONS

Birds often process the squawks or chirps of other members of their own species in the left hemisphere, much as humans tend to process the 'squawking' of members of their own species in the left **hemisphere** (chapter 3).

Interactions of nature and nurture: an emerging view

Can we conclude that Chomsky was right, that language is innate? In one sense, yes. Today, no-one can make a credible case that language is completely learned, any more than one can argue that the organisation of other organs, such as the kidneys, results completely from experience (Chomsky, 1980; Pinker, 1994). On the other hand, the concept of a language acquisition device is not well fleshed out. What is the nature of this device, and how do children actually learn to flip the switches so that they speak the language of their parents? Are children literally born with knowledge of syntax? And if so, how could rules of syntax be encoded in DNA?

An alternative view suggests that humans are, indeed, born with a particular sensitivity to certain properties of speech, such as intonation, duration of syllables and so forth, but that connectionist principles used to explain other aspects of thought and memory can account for language given these innate tendencies (MacWhinney, 1998; Prince & Smolensky, 1997; Seidenberg, 1997). Chomsky argued that rules of language are so perfect and abstract that children could never learn them given the imperfections of the actual sentences they have heard spoken. Recently, however, connectionist models have shown how people can implicitly learn abstractions from very imperfect cases. Categories (in this case, syntactic categories, such as nouns or verbs) share certain properties, which are encoded in neural networks. When enough of a network representing a syntactic category (such as *verb*) is activated by a given word, the word will be classified as that part of speech. Qualities associated with that part of speech (such as the fact that the past tense of most verbs in English is constructed by adding *-ed*) will then be assumed to apply to a novel word that fits into the category. This could explain both how children learn to apply grammatical rules correctly to new words as well as why they overgeneralise (e.g. *he goed away*) until they learn rules that apply only to specific cases.

INTERIM SUMMARY

How children acquire language so quickly has been a matter of considerable debate. Skinner argued that verbal behaviour, like all behaviour, is selected by its consequences, although empirical data have not generally supported this view. Chomsky argued that the speed and similarity of language acquisition around the world suggest a shared set of linguistic principles, or ***universal grammar***, that is innate. When children converse with others, they spontaneously develop linguistic constructions that resemble other languages even if their parents do not provide them. The existence of specialised neural circuits for language also supports a strong innate component to language acquisition. Recent connectionist thinking proposes that language emerges in children from the interaction of innate tendencies and implicit learning.

A critical period for language development?

The interplay of nature and nurture in language development has led to another hotly debated question among psychologists and linguists: does a critical period exist for language learning; that is, is the brain maximally sensitive to language acquisition at a certain point in development (Lenneberg, 1967)?

Readers who have tried to learn a foreign language as teenagers or young adults have probably found that language acquisition is not so easy at later stages of life. As we have seen (chapter 3), the development of the brain depends on certain kinds of environmental enrichment, and neurons and neuronal connections not used at age-appropriate times may die or disappear. Exposure to language may be necessary for normal lateralisation of linguistic processes to the left hemisphere, which is typically completed between ages two and five (Kinsbourne & Smith, 1974; Marcotte & Morere, 1990).

> **APPLY + DISCUSS**
>
> Children who grow up in abnormal social environments, such as orphanages, in their first few years may have lifelong difficulties forming and maintaining relationships.
>
> - Do humans have a critical period for the capacity for forming intimate relationships?
> - Will these children never express their potential to form loving attachments?

Similarly, exposure to particular phonemes in the first three years may be required in order to attain native fluency in a second language, particularly if that language is very different from one's own (such as Chinese and English). Learning a second language becomes steadily more difficult after age three, up until at least age 12. After that point, people are seldom able to attain even near-native fluency, and the brain appears to recruit different neural circuits to carry out linguistic tasks than it uses to process first languages (McDonald, 1997).

Perhaps the most convincing evidence of critical periods comes from the study of deaf children whose parents did not know sign language and who did not become exposed to sign language until enrolled in schools for the deaf as late as adolescence (Mayberry & Eichen, 1991; McDonald, 1996). Late learners generally do not catch up to early learners in their ability to use sign language, particularly if they begin in adolescence. They have more trouble learning to comprehend the language fluently and to produce signs as rapidly and effortlessly, suggesting that they 'speak with an accent', much like adults who try to learn a second language. Even after 30 years of using sign language, native signers outperform people who learned to sign later in childhood, who in turn outperform later learners (Newport, 1990).

Researchers have also examined a handful of cases of children who were not exposed early to language because they were raised in extreme isolation. The most famous case was a child known as Genie. Authorities found Genie at age 13; she had been living in a tiny room tied to a chair from the time she was 20 months. Her abusive father rarely spoke to her except for occasional screaming. After Genie was discovered, linguists and psychologists worked with her intensively. She acquired a reasonable vocabulary and learned to combine words into meaningful phrases, but she never progressed beyond sentences like 'Genie go' (Curtiss, 1977, 1989). She also did not appear to have the normal left-hemisphere lateralisation for language.

INTERIM SUMMARY

For many years psychologists have debated the existence of a critical period for language learning. The first three years of life seem to be the optimal time to attain native fluency. After age 12, even near-native fluency is difficult to achieve, and language appears to be processed using different neural circuits than in native speakers.

What infants know about language

Although psychologists disagree about the relative roles of nature and nurture in language development, no-one doubts that children learn language with extraordinary speed, often showing individual differences in the exact ages at which they achieve each developmental milestone (see table 8.2). First, however, they must learn to segment the continuous streams of speech they hear into units so they can distinguish one phoneme, morpheme, word or phrase from another. As anyone knows who has ever travelled to a country with an unfamiliar language, this is no easy task, because native speakers talk rapidly and do not typically 'brake' for learners.

TABLE 8.2 **Language development in children**

Age	General characteristics
Months	
1–5	*Reflexive communication:* vocalises randomly, coos, laughs, cries, engages in vocal play, discriminates language from nonlanguage sounds
6–18	*Babbling:* verbalises in response to speech of others; responses increasingly approximate human speech patterns
10–13	*First words:* uses words; typically to refer to objects
12–18	*One-word sentence stage:* vocabulary grows slowly; uses nouns primarily; over-extensions begin
18–24	*Vocabulary spurt:* fast-mapping facilitates rapid acquisition of new words
Years	
2	*Two-word sentence stage:* uses telegraphic speech; uses more pronouns and verbs
2.5	*Three-word sentence stage:* modifies speech to take listener into account; over-regularisations begin
3	Uses complete simple active sentence structure; uses sentences to tell stories that are understood by others; uses plurals
3.5	*Expanded grammatical forms:* expresses concepts with words; uses four-word sentences
4	Uses imaginary speech; uses five-word sentences
5	*Well-developed and complex syntax:* uses more complex syntax; uses more complex forms to tell stories
6	Displays metalinguistic awareness

NOTE: Children often show individual differences in the exact ages at which they display the various developmental achievements outlined here.

SOURCE: From Weiten, *Psychology*, 8E. © 2010 Wadsworth, a part of Cengage Learning, Inc. Reproduced by permission www.cengage.com/permissions.

Infants use a number of cues to segment speech, such as pauses, pitch and duration. By the time they are nine months old, they already show a preference for speech interrupted at the boundaries of phrases (Jusczyk, Houston, & Newsome, 1999; McDonald, 1997). They can also recognise recurring patterns in a string of uninterrupted syllables (such as *badigo* in *badigotabitabadigo*) (Saffran, Aslin, & Newport, 1996).

Although infants must learn to segment speech, they appear to have an innate sensitivity to distinctions among the phonemes that make up human languages long before they even start speaking (Cohen, Diehl, Oakes, & Loehlin, 1992; Miller & Eimas, 1995). Researchers have documented this ability by measuring the rate at which one- and four-month-old infants suck on a pacifier as they listen to various sounds (Eimas, 1985; Eimas, Siqueland, Jusczyk, & Vigorito, 1971). Infants have a preference for novel stimuli, and over time, they will suck faster on a specially wired pacifier when presented with a new stimulus when they realise that their sucking controls what they see. This allows psychologists to learn how infants think and perceive (chapter 12). Recent Australian research has also examined tone perception and discrimination in infants aged six to nine months of age (see Mattock & Burnham, 2006).

One classic study found that a change in phonemes that could signal a different meaning if used in a word (e.g. from a *b* to a *p*) produced a much greater increase in sucking rate than a similar change that carried no potential linguistic meaning (Eimas, 1985). Interestingly, though, humans are not alone in their capacity to distinguish linguistic sounds. Newborn human infants can distinguish Dutch from Japanese — but so can cotton-top tamarin monkeys (Ramus, Hauser, Miller, Morris, & Mehler, 2000)! Human language seems to take advantage of sound processing mechanisms present in other animals (Bonvillian, personal communication, 2000).

The ongoing debate about how to teach reading has seen phonics return as the fundamental method for early reading instruction in Australian schools (Badcock, Hammond, Gillam, Brewer, & Andrews, 2007). Research has established that phonics is essential to learning to read — children need to be taught the relationship between letters and sounds (see Castles & Coltheart, 2004; Rayner, Foorman, Perfetti, Pesetsky, & Seidenberg, 2001, 2002).

Once infants learn to segment speech, one of the next tasks is to classify words into syntactic categories, such as nouns, verbs and noun phrases (McDonald, 1997). That young children implicitly classify words into parts of speech by noticing regularities in their use can be seen in the tendency of preschoolers to overgeneralise (to generalise rules that normally apply to irregular instances). For example, just as they create words such as *hisself*, they also create sentences such as *she hitted me*.

From babbling to bantering

Babies' first recognisable speech sounds are called ***babbling***. These utterances, such as 'lalala' or 'baba,' begin sometime between six months and one year. However, by the end of this period, even before they speak their first words, their language development bears the imprint of their culture. Babies' innate attention to phonemic distinctions becomes markedly limited to phonemes in the language they habitually hear, so that their babbling sounds resemble their parents' language sounds (Eimas, 1985; Miller & Eimas, 1995).

Using words

Sometime between about one and one and a half years, babbling gives way to a stage in which children utter one word at a time. Children's first words refer to concrete things or action, such as 'mama', 'ball' or 'go'. So, too, do the non-linguistic symbolic gestures children often develop even before they have words, such as a knob-turning motion that means 'I want to go out' (Goodwyn & Acredolo, 1998).

Sometime after the first year of life, children utter a single word at a time, often pointing to things.

At about 18 to 20 months, toddlers begin to form two-word phrases. From that point, the number of morphemes they combine in their utterances steadily increases. The use of grammatical niceties such as articles, prepositions and auxiliary verbs expands as well.

Young children characteristically use ***telegraphic speech***, utterances composed of only the most essential words for meaning (as in a telegram). Thus, 'Dog out' might stand for 'The dog is outside'. The words they tend to omit are words like *if*, *the* and *under*. Although they tend not to use these words in speech, children as young as two actually comprehend some of these words, responding more accurately to sentences that include them (Gerken & McIntosh, 1993). By age four, the vast majority of children's sentences are fully grammatical (Stromswold, 1995). Table 8.3 illustrates the progression from telegraphic to grammatical speech in five children whose language was studied intensively.

TABLE 8.3 **Progression from telegraphic speech to complete sentences in children ages 25.5 to 35.5 months**

	Imitations of spoken sentences				
Model sentence	**Eve, 25.5**	**Adam, 28.5**	**Helen, 30**	**Ian, 31.5**	**June, 35.5**
1. It goes in a big box.	Big box.	Big box.	In big box.	It goes in the box.	C
2. Read the book.	Read book.	Read book.	—	Read a book.	C
3. I will not do that again.	Do again.	I will that again.	I do that.	I again.	C
4. I do not want an apple.	I do apple.	I do a apple.	—	I do not want apple.	I don't want apple.
5. Is it a car?	't car?	Is it car?	Car?	That a car?	C
6. Where does it go?	Where go?	Go?	Does it go?	Where do it go?	C

SOURCE: Brown and Fraser (1963).

NOTE: — indicates no intelligible imitation was obtained; C indicates imitation was correct

Children's vocabulary increases exponentially after they achieve their first 50 to 100 words. Their repertoire of words blossoms to several thousand by the time they are six years old (Bloom, 1993; MacWhinney, 1998).

Influences on language development

Although the stages of language development are virtually universal, children acquire language at widely different rates (Goldfield & Snow, 1989; Richards, 1990). These differences in part stem from genetic predispositions, but they also reflect environmental influences. Probably the most important environmental factor is the day-to-day input and feedback that children get from their caregivers.

One way caregivers facilitate infants' language development is by speaking 'Motherese'. Everyone is familiar with this dialect, as it is virtually irresistible when talking to a baby. Motherese is characterised by exaggerated intonation, a slow rate of speech and high pitch (Fernald & Kuhl, 1987). Among other things, the exaggerated style of Motherese may help infants recognise where phrases and sentences begin and end (Gleitman, Gleitman, Landau, & Warner, 1988; Morgan, 1986). With young babies, people often speak 'multimodal motherese', which combines motion or touch with words (Gogate, Bahrick, & Watson, 2000).

The content of the primary caregiver's speech is also important in language acquisition. When parents repeat themselves ('Shall we go to the shop? Let's go to the shop') and expand on their children's telegraphic utterances (e.g. responding to 'dog out' with 'Is the dog out?'), their children tend to develop earlier in their ability to use verbs correctly. In contrast, merely acknowledging what the child has said without adding any new information ('That's right') is associated with delayed syntax development (Hoff-Ginsberg, 1990; Newport, Gleitman, & Gleitman, 1977).

Accent on language development: using dialects to trace how children come to recognise spoken words

By Professor Catherine T. Best, University of Western Sydney, and Doctor Christine Kitamura, University of Western Sydney

Words are often pronounced differently across English accents ('dialects'), which can cause word misperceptions. Real-life cases include a Sydney waiter who replied 'we don't serve dog here!' when a Scottish customer asked for *duck* curry, and a Californian lifeguard who replied 'Bigger wives than ... huh?' when a pair of Australian surfers asked him which local beach had bigger *waves*. But such mistakes are relatively rare. Adults generally understand words across a wide range of pronunciations, assisted by their lexical and grammatical knowledge and their understanding of context.

Infants and toddlers, however, are language novices. They have very little lexical or grammatical knowledge to draw upon and a very restricted sense of conversational contexts, and their experience is mostly restricted to the accent spoken at home. Given this, can they recognise familiar words spoken in a very different accent? Indeed, do they even know that a talker with an unfamiliar accent is speaking the same language as their parents? Importantly, what does the development of these skills reveal about children's emerging grasp of the linguistic structure of their language?

Variations in pronunciation are pervasive. Thus, it is crucial for children to understand that words, and the native language itself, remain constant despite that variability. Many variations reflect non-linguistic characteristics of the talker: individual identity, gender, emotional state and speech style (e.g. formal, casual, infant-directed). However, the pronunciation patterns that define an accent are *linguistically* systematic; that is, they also define the phonological structure of spoken words (i.e. their consonant–vowel composition). To acquire a language, children must learn that while some differences are critical to distinguishing words (e.g. b*ea*k from b*a*ke, and *p*at from *b*at), other variations leave word identity intact (e.g. sh*ar*k is the same word, even though an Australian and an American pronounce the '*ar*' very differently). The complementary principles of *phonological distinctiveness* and *phonological constancy* determine, respectively, which variations change a word and which variations leave it intact. To become efficient language users, children must discover how both principles apply to any word they hear.

These two principles are central to current research on the development of children's early word representations. Virtually all studies on this issue have focused on phonological distinctiveness; that is, children's recognition that changing one consonant or vowel in a word changes the identity of the word (e.g. that *v*aby is categorically different from *b*aby). But, as we explained, word recognition also depends crucially on phonological constancy. Therefore, we exploited accent variation to assess toddlers' recognition of the phonological constancy of words. Specifically, we gave 15- and 19-month-olds two tests of listening preferences between sets of words that are familiar to toddlers over sets of unfamiliar adult words. In one test, the words were spoken in the infants' native accent (American English); in the other, they were spoken in a non-native accent with very different pronunciation patterns (Jamaican English). Toddlers of both ages significantly preferred the familiar over the unfamiliar word set in the native accent test. Importantly, only older toddlers showed a familiar-word preference in the Jamaican accent test, indicating that they recognised the constancy of the words despite the unfamiliar accent (Best, Tyler, Gooding, Orlando, & Quann, 2009).

Our studies with Australian toddlers, where we increased the variability (multiple talkers, more words), showed that familiar-word preferences are clearly correlated with vocabulary development. Children with expressive vocabularies of less than 25 words failed to show a familiar-word preference even with the Australian accent, but 17-month-olds with vocabularies of more than 50 words show a familiar-word preference with the Australian accent. Only 19-month-olds with vocabularies of more than 100 words showed a familiar-word preference with the Jamaican accent (Best, Tyler, Kitamura, & Bundgaard-Nielsen, 2010; Best, Tyler, Kitamura, Notley, & Bundgaard-Nielsen, 2008).

Evidently, the older toddlers had come to realise that a word has a constant structure, despite being spoken in a different accent. However, this means they must already know the other accent belongs to their native language. So, when do infants generalise across accents to recognise the constant form of the language? To examine this question, we tested infants' listening preferences for sentences spoken in Australian versus two non-native English accents. At three months, infants significantly preferred Australian over both non-native accents, but by nine months this preference disappeared. The decline occurs earlier (six months) for a non-native accent that infants are passively exposed to (American English on Australian television), than for one that is rarely if ever heard in their environment (South African English). Thus, exposure to a non-native accent may accelerate, but is not necessary for, infants' recognition that the accent belongs to their native language (Kitamura, Panneton, & Notley, 2006; Kitamura, Panneton, Notley, & Best, 2006). This is an ability that is evident well before the first birthday.

Young children recognise fairly early on that systematic variations in speech provide evidence about the structure of their native language. The complementary abilities to recognise phonological distinctiveness and phonological constancy in words both fall into place around the time that toddlers' vocabularies reach about 100 words (at around 19 months of age). Together, the two skills likely contribute to the increased rate of word learning that emerges around that point in language development.

INTERIM SUMMARY

Language development progresses through a series of stages. Before infants can start to acquire vocabulary or syntax, they have to learn to segment the continuous streams of speech they hear into units. They then have to learn to classify words into syntactic categories. Babies' first recognisable speech sounds occur as ***babbling*** in the first year. Sometime in the second year they begin to speak in one-word utterances. Young children use ***telegraphic speech***, leaving out all but the essential words. By age four, most of the sentences children produce are grammatical. Although the stages of language development are virtually universal, children acquire language at widely different rates depending on environmental input.

Is language distinctly human?

Tim: Lana want apple.
Lana: Yes. (Thereupon Tim went to the kitchen and got one.) You give this to Lana.
Tim: Give what to Lana.
Lana: You give this which is red.
Tim: This. (Tim held up a red piece of plastic as he responded.)
Lana: You give this apple to Lana.
Tim: Yes. (And gave her the apple.)

Rumbaugh and Gill (1977, p. 182).

This conversation is not between two humans but between a human and a chimpanzee named Lana. Apes lack the physiological equipment to speak as humans do, but psychologists have trained several chimpanzees and other primates (such as bonobos, another close relative of humans) to use nonverbal symbols to communicate with humans. Lana learned a computer language called 'Yerkish' (named for the Yerkes Regional Primate Research Center in Atlanta where the research took place). Yerkish uses geometric symbols, or lexigrams, to represent concepts and relationships. Other apes have learned to use signs from American Sign Language or other systems using lexigrams.

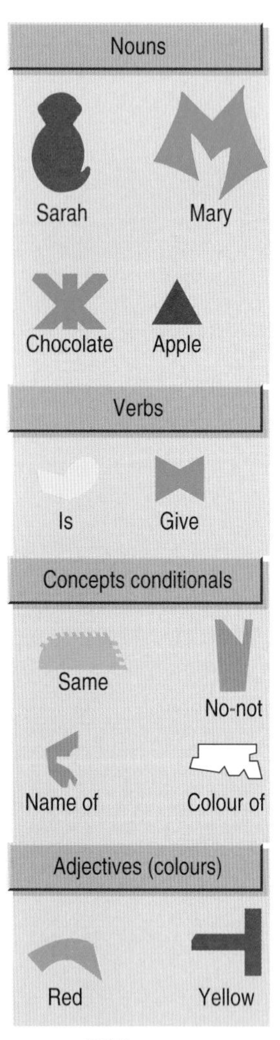

FIGURE 8.19
Sarah's plastic symbols. Researchers provided Sarah, a chimpanzee, with plastic symbols that varied in colour, shape and size. The symbols were backed with metal so that Sarah could arrange them on a magnetic board. Each symbol stood for a single word or concept. (Sarah preferred to write her sentences vertically from top to bottom.)

SOURCE: From Premack and Premack (1972).

Teaching language to apes

Some simian linguists are quite accomplished. A chimpanzee named Sarah learned a vocabulary of about 130 plastic symbols, which she used with 75 to 80 percent accuracy (figure 8.19) (Premack & Premack, 1972). Chimpanzees have also used symbols taught to them by their trainers to communicate with each other (figure 8.20) (Savage-Rumbaugh, Pate, Lawson, Smith, & Rosenbaum, 1983; Savage-Rumbaugh, Rumbaugh, & Boysen, 1978). A chimpanzee named Nim Chimpsky reportedly expressed feelings through signs, saying 'angry' or 'bite' instead of actually committing angry acts (Terrace, 1979).

Do such findings mean that the chimpanzee is, as one researcher put it, 'a creature with considerable innate linguistic competence who has, by accident of nature, been trapped inside a body that lacks the proper [structure for] vocal output' (Savage-Rumbaugh et al., 1983)? Several investigators have questioned whether language is really monkey business. After five years, Nim Chimpsky's utterances ranged from only 1.1 to 1.6 signs, compared with children's progressively longer word combinations (Terrace, 1979). Furthermore, chimpanzees tend to use symbols for purely pragmatic purposes (to request an object) or to imitate their trainers' communications, whereas children use language for many purposes (Seidenberg & Petitto, 1987). Some researchers have compared the linguistic abilities of chimpanzees and other apes to human children at the stage of telegraphic speech (Gardner & Gardner, 1975).

Other psychologists are more convinced by the accomplishments of our primate brethren. Researchers from the Yerkes Center describe a bonobo named Kanzi who spontaneously began to use symbols to communicate (Rumbaugh, 1992; Savage-Rumbaugh, McDonald, Sevcik, Hopkins, & Rupert, 1986). Kanzi was an infant when his mother became the subject of language training. While researchers taught her to communicate by pushing geometric symbols on a keyboard, Kanzi played nearby or got into mischief, leaping on the keyboard or snatching food treats.

Two years later, when the mother was away, Kanzi spontaneously began using the keyboard to ask for specific fruits. When presented with apples, bananas and oranges, he would choose the fruit he had requested, demonstrating that he did indeed know what he was asking. In comparing Kanzi to Nim Chimpsky, the researchers suggested that Nim may have been a bit dim, so that his limited accomplishments did not adequately reflect the language capacities of apes. Unlike Nim, over 80 percent of Kanzi's communications occurred spontaneously. Kanzi also used language to point out objects to the researchers and to announce his intentions (e.g. pushing 'ball' on the keyboard and then going to search for his ball).

FIGURE 8.20
Two chimpanzees communicating. Sherman and Austin learned to communicate with each other using symbols taught to them by their trainers. In this sequence, (a) Sherman requests M&Ms using his symbol board, while Austin watches (b). Austin then hands the M&Ms to Sherman (c).

The evolution of language in non-humans

Psychologists who study language in non-human primates continue to disagree as to whether apes are capable of human language (although no-one has definitively shown that humans can be taught to use chimpanzee communication systems, either). Chimps apparently have the capacity to use symbolic thought under the right conditions, and lowland gorillas use some forms of symbolic gestures to communicate as well (Tanner & Byrne, 1996).

Perhaps the most distinctive feature of human language, however, is not the capacity to use symbols to stand for objects but the creation of a system of symbols whose meaning lies primarily in their relation to one another, not to any concrete realities (Deacon, 1996). This is what allows people to imagine what could be and to create objects in their minds that they then create in the world. And in this, we are alone.

Linguist Steven Pinker (1994) suggests that the question of whether other primates possess language has actually been badly framed, based on the misconception that humans are the highest and latest rung on an evolutionary ladder that runs from orangutans to gorillas to chimpanzees to *Homo sapiens*. Rather than a ladder, the proper analogy is a bush, with a common trunk but multiple branches. Gorillas, chimps, humans and other living primates shared a common ancestor 5 to 10 million years ago, at which point their evolutionary paths began to diverge like branches on a bush. Somewhere after that point, language began to evolve in the now-extinct ancestors of *H. sapiens*, such as *H. erectus*. Natural selection has pruned the bush dramatically — roughly 99 percent of all species become extinct — so that the bush is now quite sparse, leading to the misconception that the species left on the bush are close relatives rather than distant cousins. Pinker (1994) draws a simple conclusion from the debate about language in other primates: 'Other species undoubtedly have language. Unfortunately, they're all dead'.

The jury remains out on whether other species, particularly primates, have language. However, what seems clear is that primates do not have *our* language. While they may learn to use symbols and words borrowed from our language, their ability to create nuance, understand syntax and develop context remains limited. That is not to say, however, that our primate friends do not *communicate*. They can certainly use a variety of media and messages to create shared meaning. But for the moment, the human language remains ours alone.

ETHICAL DILEMMA

A researcher has proposed an experiment to help teach chimpanzees to use sign language. A number of single words have been printed on large cards. The researcher will ask a question and the chimpanzee will have to choose the card that has the correct response printed on it. A correct response is to be rewarded with food. An incorrect response is to be punished with a mild electric shock.

- What ethical issues does this research proposal pose?
- Should the study go ahead?

INTERIM SUMMARY

Some researchers have taught chimpanzees to use language skills such as sign language. The question of whether or not non-human primates have the capacity to acquire the rules of human language remains the subject of much debate.

Central question revisited

◆ What is so rational about reason?

We began this chapter with the question of what it means to be 'rational', and along the way we have encountered some surprising twists and turns on the road to reason. Cold, hard, conscious calculations can be essential to good decision making, but they can also lead us to ignore things we have learned implicitly that have registered in our feelings and intuitions.

Nor are the goals we pursue themselves 'rational' in any meaningful sense of the word. We would be hard-pressed to make a logical case for self-preservation, given that we are all headed for the grave anyway. At their core, most of our basic strivings — for self-preservation, status, love, children — are evolutionary imperatives that set the 'cognitive agenda' for our lives. Much of the time it is our feelings that alert us to the importance of a goal and channel our most sophisticated thought processes.

It has been said that humankind has suffered three major blows to its exalted conception of itself. First, Copernicus showed that we are not at the centre of the universe, that we are just one species on one planet revolving around the sun. When humans persisted in seeing themselves as a privileged species separate from all other animals, Darwin suggested that we are little more than hairless monkeys — remarkable ones, but animals nonetheless. After Darwin, humans prided themselves on being distinguished from other animals by reason and consciousness — until Freud argued that reason and consciousness are a thin veneer covering our animal heritage (Freud, 1925/1952). After Freud, what was left to defend as uniquely human? Some still turned to the remarkable computational powers of the human mind — until, of course, computers began to beat chess masters at their own game.

Perhaps we will ultimately find that what is distinctly human is neither the passions we share with other animals nor the capacity for complex computations we share with computers. The ability to link passion and reason in pursuit of our goals may be the crowning achievement of the human intellect.

◆

SUMMARY

1 Units of thought

- ***Thinking*** means representing mental representations for a purpose. Much of the time people think using words, ***mental images*** (visual representations) and ***mental models*** (representations that describe, explain or predict the way things work).
- A ***concept*** is a mental representation of a category; that is, an internal portrait of a class of objects, ideas or events that share common properties. The process of identifying an object as an instance of a category — recognising its similarity to some objects and dissimilarity to others — is called ***categorisation***. Concepts that have properties that clearly set them apart from other concepts are relatively ***well defined***; many concepts, however, are not easily defined by a precise set of features.
- People typically classify objects rapidly by judging their similarity to concepts stored in memory. They often do this by comparing the observed object they are trying to classify with a ***prototype***, an abstraction across many instances of a category, or a good example, called an exemplar. When people rapidly categorise, they probably rely heavily on prototype matching. Complex, deliberate classification tasks often require more explicit evaluation of the data, such as consulting lists of ***defining features***.
- In categorising objects, people naturally tend to use the ***basic level***, the broadest, most inclusive level at which objects share common attributes that are distinctive of the concept. The way people categorise is partially dependent on culture, expertise and their goals.

2 Reasoning, problem solving, and decision making

- ***Reasoning*** refers to the process by which people generate and evaluate arguments and beliefs. ***Inductive reasoning*** means reasoning from specific observations to more general propositions that seem likely to be true. ***Deductive reasoning*** is logical reasoning that draws conclusions from premises and leads to certainty if the premises are correct. ***Analogical reasoning*** is the process by which people understand a novel situation in terms of a familiar one.
- ***Problem solving*** is the process of transforming one situation into another to meet a goal, by identifying discrepancies between the initial state and the goal state and using various operators to try to eliminate the discrepancies. ***Problem-solving strategies*** are techniques that serve as guides for solving a problem. One of the most important problem-solving strategies is ***mental simulation*** — imagining the steps involved in solving a problem mentally before actually undertaking them.
- ***Decision making*** is the process by which people weigh the pros and cons of different alternatives in order to make a choice. According to one information-processing model, a rational decision involves a combined assessment of the value and probability of different options, which provides an estimate of its ***expected utility***.

3 Explicit and implicit cognition and everyday thinking

- Psychologists have recently begun to question whether the kind of rationality seen in ***explicit cognition*** (cognition that involves conscious manipulation of representations) models is always optimal. In everyday life, people make use of cognitive shortcuts, or ***heuristics***, that allow them to make rapid judgements. Because people rarely have complete information and limitless time, they often practise ***bounded rationality***, or rationality within limits imposed by the environment, their goals and so forth.
- Much of human behaviour reflects ***implicit cognition***, or cognition outside of awareness, including implicit learning and implicit

problem solving. Researchers are increasingly recognising the role of motivation and emotion in everyday judgements, inferences and decisions.

- ***Connectionist***, or ***parallel distributed processing (PDP)***, models propose that many cognitive processes occur simultaneously (in parallel) and are spread (distributed) throughout a network of interacting neural processing units. Connectionist models differ from traditional information-processing models by limiting the importance of serial processing and shifting from the metaphor of mind as computer to mind as brain. These models suggest that perception, memory and thought occur through processes of ***constraint satisfaction***, in which the brain settles on a solution that satisfies as many constraints as possible in order to achieve the best fit to the data.
- The frontal lobes play a particularly important role in thinking. Two regions of the frontal lobes involved in thinking are the ***dorsolateral prefrontal cortex***, which is involved in associating complex ideas, allocating attention, making plans, and forming and executing intentions; and the ***ventromedial prefrontal cortex***, which is involved in emotional control over decision making, inhibiting actions that lead to negative consequences and many aspects of social functioning.

4 Language

- ***Language*** is the system of symbols, sounds, meanings and rules for their combination that constitutes the primary mode of communication among humans. Thought and language shape one another, but thought and language are to some extent separable.
- The smallest units of sound that constitute speech are ***phonemes***. Phonemes are combined into ***morphemes***, the smallest units of meaning. Morphemes are combined into phrases, groups of words that act as a unit and convey a meaning. Words and phrases are combined into ***sentences***, organised sequences of words that express a thought or intention. The rules of ***syntax*** govern the placement of words and phrases within a language.
- Psychologists interested in the ***pragmatics*** of language are interested in the way language is used and understood in everyday life. ***Discourse*** — the way people ordinarily speak, hear, read and write in interconnected sentences — occurs at multiple levels, such as the exact wording of sentences and the gist of the sentence. ***Nonverbal communication*** relies on tone of voice, body language, gestures, physical distance, facial expressions and so forth.
- Some researchers have taught chimpanzees to use language skills such as sign language. The question of whether or not non-human primates have the capacity to acquire the rules of human language remains the subject of much debate.

5 Language development

- Language development reflects an interaction of nature and nurture, although Chomsky appears to be right that the brain is constructed to make language learning easy. According to Chomsky, all language derives from an innate ***universal grammar***. Chomsky explains the speed with which children develop language by arguing that the human brain includes a ***language acquisition device (LAD)***, an innate set of neural structures for acquiring language.
- For years researchers have debated the existence of a critical period for language learning. The first three years of life seem to be the optimal time to attain native fluency. After age 12, even near-native fluency is difficult to achieve.
- Cross-culturally, children go through similar stages of language development. They begin by ***babbling*** in the first year and produce one-word utterances towards the beginning of the second year. Young children's speech is ***telegraphic speech***, omitting all but the essential words. By age four, children's sentences largely conform to the grammar of their language. The stages of language development are virtually universal; however, the precise timing and course of individual language development depend on both nature and nurture.

KEY TERMS

algorithms, *p. 308*
analogical reasoning, *p. 306*
availability heuristic, *p. 312*
babbling, *p. 331*
basic level, *p. 303*
bilingual, *p. 321*
bounded rationality, *p. 312*
categories, *p. 300*
categorisation, *p. 300*
concept, *p. 300*
confirmation bias, *p. 310*
connectionism, *p. 315*
constraint satisfaction, *p. 316*
decision making, *p. 310*
deductive reasoning, *p. 305*
defining features, *p. 300*
discourse, *p. 325*
dorsolateral prefrontal cortex, *p. 318*
expected utility, *p. 311*
explicit cognition, *p. 312*
functional fixedness, *p. 309*
grammar, *p. 323*
heuristics, *p. 312*
implicit cognition, *p. 313*
inductive reasoning, *p. 305*
language, *p. 321*
language acquisition device (LAD), *p. 327*
mental images, *p. 299*
mental models, *p. 300*
mental set, *p. 309*
mental simulation, *p. 308*
morphemes, *p. 323*
nonverbal communication, *p. 326*
parallel distributed processing (PDP), *p. 315*
phonemes, *p. 322*
phrases, *p. 323*
pragmatics, *p. 324*
problem solving, *p. 307*
problem-solving strategies, *p. 308*
prototype, *p. 301*
reasoning, *p. 305*
representativeness heuristic, *p. 312*
semantics, *p. 324*
sentences, *p. 323*
subgoals, *p. 308*
subordinate level, p. 303
superordinate level, *p. 303*
syllogism, *p. 305*
syntax, *p. 323*
telegraphic speech, *p. 331*
thinking, *p. 298*
universal grammar, *p. 327*
ventromedial prefrontal cortex, *p. 318*
weighted utility value, *p. 311*
well-defined concepts, *p. 300*
Whorfian hypothesis of linguistic relativity, *p. 321*

REVIEW QUESTIONS

1. Distinguish between the superordinate, basic and subordinate levels of categorisation.
2. Explain how people consider both the utility of outcomes of different options and their probability when making decisions.
3. Describe the key assumptions in connectionism or parallel distributed processing (PDP).
4. Describe the grammatical rules people implicitly follow to transform sounds and symbols into meaning.
5. Distinguish among the multiple levels of discourse.

DISCUSSION QUESTIONS

1. Why do people settle for decisions that are 'good-enough' instead of aiming for the best possible decision?
2. Why are are people more likely to take risks when things are going badly than when they are going well?
3. Are apes capable of understanding human language?

APPLICATION QUESTIONS

1. Test your understanding of reasoning and decision making by matching the scenarios listed below with the following reasoning types and heuristics: inductive reasoning, deductive reasoning, analogical reasoning, representativeness heuristic and availability heuristic.
   (a) Susanne enjoys living in the city of Melbourne and takes a car trip into the country every second weekend to help her relax, but is afraid to fly to Cairns for a holiday because of a potential cyclone. ______________
   (b) Six-year-old Lim proudly told his teacher that his bird Sammy had feathers because 'All birds have feathers, and my Sammy is a bird.' ______________
   (c) In a group counselling session, Sorcha likened her self-discovery to the joy and freedom she experienced when she first learned to drive a car. ______________
   (d) Mahmood, a child at Rachel's preschool, became sick with a bout of chickenpox. Rachel's mother became concerned that her daughter would also soon catch chickenpox because she often played closely with Mahmood while at preschool. ______________
   (e) People are very surprised to learn that Graham, who is a professional football player, was also dux of his senior year in high school. They assumed he had focused more on his sporting talents than on his scholastic abilities. ______________
2. Test your understanding of problem solving by attempting the following.
   String problem: How would you tie together two strings that are hanging from the ceiling but are too far apart to allow somebody to hold one piece of string and walk to the other? A nearby toolbox contains a screwdriver, some nails, a spirit level and a cleaning rag.
   Have you found a solution to the string problem? Allow yourself enough time to solve the problem before checking your answer against the solution provided on page 834. Then identify the problem-solving strategy or barrier to problem solving illustrated in each of the following scenarios. Choose from developing subgoals, using algorithms, applying mental simulation, using implicit problem solving, experiencing a mental set, experiencing functional fixedness and undergoing confirmation bias.
   (a) If you had set aside the string problem for a period of time and then 'Aha! You knew the answer!' this illustrates______________.
   (b) If you were not able to solve the problem because you focused on using the screwdriver as a tool instead of as a weight for the pendulum, this illustrates______________.
   (c) If you thought the answer might have something to do with the solution for the candle problem in figures 8.9 and 8.11, where you had to use the matchbox for a function other than holding the matches, this illustrates______________.
   (d) If you had continually reverted to using an old problem solving strategy to try and solve the current string problem, this illustrates______________.
   (e) If you first imagined the steps involved in solving the problem before actually attaching the screwdriver to one of the strings, this illustrates______________.
   (f) If you came up with an initial solution to the string problem and then tried to find evidence to support it, this illustrates______________.
   (g) If while working on the problem you thought about how you might use some of the items in the nearby toolbox, this illustrates______________.

The solutions to the application questions can be found on page 834.

MULTIMEDIA RESOURCES

The *Cyberpsych* multimedia resource is available *as an option* to accompany this textbook to further develop your understanding of many key psychology concepts. *Cyberpsych* contains a wealth of rich media content and activities, and for this chapter includes:

- a video clip on how monkeys and humans communicate
- an interactive module on knowing a language and problem solving
- a concept animation on problem solving.

Intelligence

9

LEARNING OBJECTIVES

After studying this chapter you should be able to:

1 describe the nature of intelligence

2 explain how intelligence is measured

3 distinguish among the different approaches to intelligence

4 discuss the extent to which intelligence is inherited or learned.

The nature of intelligence

- ***Intelligence*** refers to the application of cognitive skills and knowledge to learn, solve problems and obtain ends that are valued by an individual or culture.
- Intelligence is multifaceted and functional, and directed at problems of adaptation.
- It is also to some extent culturally shaped and culturally defined, since cultural practices support and recognise intellectual qualities that are useful in the social and ecological context.

Intelligence testing

- Alfred Binet (1904) developed the first intelligence tests for the purpose of identifying intellectually disabled children. His scale assigned an individual child a ***mental age (MA)***, which refers to the average age at which children can be expected to achieve a particular score.

- Terman brought intelligence testing to North America, adapted the concept of the ***intelligence quotient (IQ)*** and expanded the meaning of the IQ from a predictor of school success to a broader index of intellectual ability.

$$\mathbf{IQ = (MA/CA) \times 100}$$

- ***Intellectual impairment*** refers to significantly below average general intellectual functioning (IQ less than 70) with deficits in adaptive functioning that are first evident in childhood and appear in more than one realm. Individuals classified as ***gifted*** show exceptional talents in social, musical or athletic realms.

- The ***validity*** of IQ tests depends on the purpose to which they are put, and they should always be supplemented by other measures; ***reliability*** refers to a measure's ability to produce consistent results.

Approaches to intelligence

- The *psychometric approach* examines which intellectual abilities tend to correlate statistically with one another. This approach uses *factor analysis* to identify common factors that underlie performance across a variety of tasks.
- The *information-processing or cognitive approach* aims to describe and measure the specific cognitive processes that underlie intelligent behaviour, including the following: speed of processing, knowledge base, and the ability to learn and apply mental strategies.
- Current multifactor theories of intelligence include Sternberg's *triarchic theory* and Gardner's *theory of multiple intelligences.*

Heredity and intelligence

- IQ reflects a complex interplay of nature and nurture.
- Studies of the influence of home environment and socioeconomic status suggest that racial differences are probably primarily environmental, although at this point no firm conclusions can be drawn.
- Intelligence test scores can potentially reflect some combination of causes, including genetics, and other related environmental risk factors including poverty, test-taking attitudes and motivation, and cultural expectations about success.

Central questions: what is intelligence and how can we measure it?

- Intelligence is probably best viewed as multifaceted, although we still do not know precisely what its facets are, how many 'general intelligences' humans really have or how to measure many of them. Indeed, some facets of intelligence, such as general problem-solving ability, may be universal, whereas others depend on cultural and historical developments. Perhaps intelligence is as much the match between a person and a time as a quality of a single individual.

THE amazing life story of classical pianist David Helfgott was told to a worldwide audience through Scott Hicks' award-winning movie *Shine*. Born in Melbourne in 1947, Helfgott moved to Perth with his family at age five and was soon demonstrating extraordinary talent as a pianist. His 'child prodigy' status brought him to the attention of music aficionados at an early age. They urged him to move overseas in his early teens to gain more experience and tutelage. However, it was not until 1966, at age 19, that Helfgott won a bursary to study at the Royal College of Music in London.

The future seemed bright for the prodigiously gifted young musician. But the years he spent studying in London also saw the emergence of the first signs of what would become a debilitating mental illness. He returned to Perth in 1970 where his condition worsened and he spent several years institutionalised in a local mental hospital.

The extraordinary talent of Australian classical pianist David Helfgott, who has previously been hospitalised for mental illness, raises questions about categorising and defining intelligence.

Helfgott was eventually released from hospital, but his ability to function within mainstream society was impaired in many ways by his mental illness. For instance, he spoke with a rapid-fire and rambling speech pattern that few could understand. He smoked incessantly, showered many times a day and neglected his own health.

Yet, seat David Helfgott in front of a piano, and he became a master. Helfgott's abilities as a pianist were unaffected by his mental illness. He could not only remember and play many of the most difficult piano arrangements ever written, but also he could imbue them with his own sense of passion and emotion. Helfgott has returned to the concert stage and continues to play to sell-out audiences around the world.

David Helfgott's case points to a number of questions that are central to understanding intelligence. First, what is intelligence? Can a man who can barely speak coherently but can play classical piano pieces flawlessly be described as intelligent? Second, how can we measure intelligence, and how accurate are commonly used measures? David Helfgott would score very poorly on IQ tests, yet he maintains a sense of humour as well as other capacities reflecting intelligent thinking. Third, is intelligence a broad trait that cuts across most areas of a person's life, or do people possess different kinds of intelligence, such as one that facilitates verbal conversation and another that allows a person's fingers to dance deftly across the ivories?

This chapter explores each of these questions in turn. We begin by discussing the nature of intelligence and the methods psychologists have devised to measure it. Next, we examine theoretical approaches to intelligence, from those that centre on the kinds of abilities that best predict school success to those that include aptitudes in domains such as music and sports. We then address the controversial question of the heritability of intelligence — the extent to which differences between people reflect differences in their genetic endowment.

Central questions

- What is intelligence?
- How can we measure intelligence?
- Is intelligence a general trait, or is it specific to particular domains?

The nature of intelligence

The concept of intelligence so successfully eluded definition for years that one psychologist long ago somewhat sarcastically defined intelligence as 'what intelligence tests measure' (Boring, 1923). When asked what intelligence means, most people emphasise problem-solving abilities and knowledge about the world; they also sometimes distinguish between academic intelligence and social intelligence or interpersonal skill (Sternberg & Wagner, 1993). In recent years, psychologists have come to recognise that intelligence is many-faceted, functional and culturally defined.

Intelligence is multifaceted and functional

Intelligence is multifaceted; that is, aspects of it can be expressed in many domains. Most readers are familiar with people who excel in academic and social tasks and are equally adept at changing spark plugs and concocting an exquisite meal (without a cookbook, of course). Yet other people excel in one realm while amazing those around them with their utter incompetence in other domains, such as their apparent lack of practical intelligence (see Sternberg et al., 2000). One psychologist with a national reputation in his field was equally well known among his friends and students as the prototypical absent-minded professor. He once drove to a conference out of town, forgot he had driven and accepted a ride home with a colleague. As we will see, speaking of 'intelligence' may be less useful than speaking of 'intelligences'.

Intelligence is also functional. Intelligent behaviour is always directed towards accomplishing a task or solving a problem. According to Sternberg (2004a), 'successful' intelligence involves an ability to adapt to, shape and select environments so as to achieve various goals. Thus, intelligence may be defined as 'the capacity for goal-directed adaptive behaviour' (Sternberg & Salter, 1982, p. 3). From an evolutionary perspective, intelligent behaviour solves problems of adaptation, and hence facilitates survival and reproduction. From a cognitive perspective, intelligence is applied cognition — that is, the use of cognitive skills to solve problems or obtain desired ends.

A GLOBAL VISTA

The cultural context of intelligence

If the function of intelligence is to help people manage the tasks they confront in their lives, then intelligent behaviour is likely to vary cross-culturally, because the circumstances that confront people differ from one society to the next. In fact, the kinds of thinking and behaviour recognised as intelligent vary considerably (Sternberg, 2000a).

Among the Kipsigi of Kenya, for example, the word *ng'om* is the closest approximation to the English word *intelligent*. The concept of *ng'om*, however, carries a number of connotations that Westerners do not generally associate with intelligence, including obedience and responsibility (Super & Harkness, 1980). The Cree Indians of northern Ontario consider someone a 'good thinker' if she is wise and respectful, pays attention, thinks carefully and has a good sense of direction (Berry & Bennet, 1992).

The attributes a culture considers intelligent are not arbitrary. The personal qualities, skills and cognitive styles cultures value and foster tend to be related to their ecology and social structure (see Benson, 2003; Mistry & Rogoff, 1985). Cultural practices teach people efficient ways of solving everyday problems, and these strategies become part of the way individuals think (Miller, 1997; Vygotsky, 1978; Wertsch & Kanner, 1992). Western views of intelligence emphasise verbal ability (such as the ability to comprehend a written passage) and the kinds of mathematical and spatial abilities useful in engineering or manufacturing. This view of intelligence (which, perhaps not incidentally, defines the kinds of questions on intelligence tests developed in the West) makes sense in a literate, technologically developed capitalist society. According to Nisbett (2003), people in Western cultures view intelligence as a means for individuals to devise categories and to engage in rational debate. In contrast, people in Eastern cultures view intelligence as a way for members of a community to recognise contradiction and complexity and to play their social roles successfully (Nisbett, 2003). For example, Sternberg and Yang (1997) found that Taiwanese-Chinese conceptions of intelligence emphasise understanding and relating to others. Such differences between Eastern and Westerns views of intelligence reflect differences in the basic cognitive processes of people in the two cultures (Nisbett, 2003).

The practical skill of tracking is associated with intelligence in traditional Aboriginal society, with better trackers being more likely to locate food.

Many cultures define intelligence in terms of practical abilities (Serpell, 1989). Western observers have noted that many members of the !Kung tribe of Africa's Kalahari Desert have an almost encyclopedic knowledge of animal behaviour, which is adaptive for a people who must hunt and avoid dangerous animals (Blurton-Jones & Konner, 1976). In Australia, the ability of Aboriginal trackers to find lost children or escaped fugitives in barren bushland is legendary. Former Northern Territory police officer Graham McMahon explains why the cultural background of Indigenous Australians assists in developing these skills: 'They read tracks like we read books.

They are taught to track game from a very early age. It means food. Consequently, like schooling, there are exceptional trackers — you could probably equate them to professors' (Australian Broadcasting Corporation, 2002). Eckermann (1995) noted that people in traditional Aboriginal societies enhanced their standing through being 'good hunters, dancers, singers, weapon makers etc. but most prestige was attached to religious leaders — men and women who had outstanding knowledge in the areas of ritual and myth' (p. 46).

Similarly, cultural groups who depend on the sea for their livelihood often show an extraordinary ability to remember relevant landmarks or calculate locations in navigating the ocean (Gladwin, 1970). Sir Francis Galton, a pioneer in research on intelligence, described an Eskimo (Werner, 1948, p. 147, in Berry & Irvine, 1986):

> With no aid except his memory . . . [the Eskimo] drew a map of a territory whose shores he had but once explored in his kayak. The strip of country was 1100 miles [1770 km] long as the crow flies, but the coastline was at least six times this distance. A comparison of the Eskimo's rude map with an Admiralty chart printed in 1870 revealed a most unexpected agreement.

APPLY + DISCUSS

- What, if any, is the relationship between intelligence and wisdom?
- Are people who are wiser more intelligent?
- Are wisdom and intelligence just two words for the same construct?

Is intelligence, then, a property of individuals, or is it simply a social construction or value judgement? To put it another way, is intelligence solely in the eye of the beholder? Probably not. Some attributes, such as mental quickness or the ability to generate solutions when confronted with novel problems, are valued in any culture; and among cultures at a similar level of technological development, concepts of intelligence tend to share many elements because demands on individuals are similar. An intelligent Norwegian is not very different from an intelligent Australian, although the Norwegian is likely to know more languages — itself an aspect of intelligence in a small country surrounded by countries with many languages. As Australia increasingly depends on trading partners around the world, particularly in Asia, the lack of fluency in other languages characteristic of most Australians will probably be increasingly defined as unintelligent.

We can thus provisionally define ***intelligence*** as the application of cognitive skills and knowledge to learn, solve problems and obtain ends that are valued by an individual or culture (see Gardner, 1983). As we will see in the section that follows, intelligence was not always so broadly defined. Only in recent years has the concept been expanded to include much more than what intelligence tests measure.

INTERIM SUMMARY

Intelligence refers to the application of cognitive skills and knowledge to learn, solve problems and obtain ends that are valued by an individual or culture. Intelligence is multifaceted and functional, directed at problems of adaptation. It is also to some extent culturally shaped and culturally defined, since cultural practices support and recognise intellectual qualities that are useful in the social and ecological context.

Intelligence testing

APPLY + DISCUSS

On your university course website for this subject, you should be able to access an interactive map of the key historical influences in the development of intelligence theories.

- How has our understanding of intelligence changed over time?
- How might we progress our understanding of intelligence in the future?

Measuring psychological qualities such as intelligence is not as straightforward as stepping on a bathroom scale. Psychologists use ***psychometric instruments*** — tests that quantify psychological attributes such as personality traits or intellectual abilities — to see how people differ from and compare with each other on psychological 'scales'. Although scientists usually design measures to fit the construct they are trying to quantify (e.g. scales to measure weight or mass), almost the opposite has occurred with the Western concept of intelligence, in which the measures came first and the construct largely evolved to fit the measures. ***Intelligence tests*** are measures designed to assess an individual's level of cognitive capabilities compared to other people in a population.

Historians credit Sir Francis Galton (1822–1911) of England with the first systematic effort to measure intelligence. A relative of Charles Darwin and a member of his society's aristocracy, Galton set out to evaluate the implications of the theory of evolution for human intelligence (Berg, 1992).

He was convinced that intelligence and social pre-eminence were products of the evolutionary process of 'survival of the fittest' and that intelligence runs in families. Galton believed that the building blocks of intelligence are simple perceptual, sensory and motor abilities. Like his German contemporary Wilhelm Wundt (chapter 1), Galton argued that by studying the 'atoms' of thought one could make inferences about the way they combine into larger intellectual 'molecules'.

To test his theory, Galton set up a laboratory at London's 1884 International Exposition, where, for threepence, some 10 000 people underwent tests of reaction time, memory, sensory ability and other intellectual tasks. (Today psychologists pay participants, not vice versa!) To his surprise, performance on these elementary tasks did not correlate with much of anything, including social class. Galton is remembered not only as the first to attempt to test mental abilities but also as a pioneering statistician who discovered how to express the relationship between two variables (such as the intelligence of one member of a twin pair and that of the other) using the correlation coefficient (chapter 2).

Binet's scale

The most direct ancestor of today's intelligence tests was developed in 1905 in France by Alfred Binet (1857–1911). Unlike Galton, Binet believed that a true measure of intelligence is an individual's performance on *complex* tasks of memory, judgement and comprehension (Kail & Pellegrino, 1985; Mackintosh, 1998). Binet was also less interested in comparing intellectual functioning in adults than in measuring intellectual potential in children.

Binet's purpose was, in fact, quite practical. In 1904, an education commission in France recommended the establishment of special schools for intellectually impaired children. This project required some objective way of distinguishing these children from their intellectually normal peers (Tuddenham, 1962). Binet and his associate, Theodore Simon, noted that problem-solving abilities increase with age, so they constructed a series of tasks ranging in difficulty from simple to complex to capture the ability of children at different ages. A seven-year old could explain the difference between paper and cardboard, for instance, whereas a typical five-year-old could not.

To express a child's level of intellectual development, Binet and Simon (1908) introduced the concept of mental age. ***Mental age (MA)*** is the average age at which children achieve a particular score. A child with a chronological (or actual) age of five who can answer questions at a seven-year-old level has a mental age of seven. A five-year-old who can answer the questions expected for his own age but not for higher ages has a mental age of five. Thus, for the average child, mental age and chronological age coincide. From this standpoint, an intellectually impaired child is just what the term implies: intellectually impaired, or slowed, in cognitive development. An intellectually impaired seven-year-old might miss questions at the seven- and six-year-old levels and be able to answer only some of the five-year-old items.

APPLY + DISCUSS

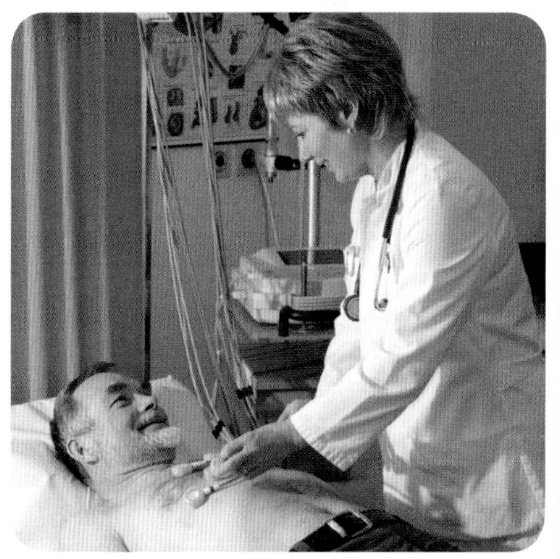

- Can the same psychological yardstick be used to measure the intelligence that underlies the abilities of a skilled mechanic and a doctor?

Tests of intelligence

Binet's intelligence test was translated and extensively revised by Lewis Terman of Stanford University, whose revision was known as the Stanford-Binet scale (1916). Perhaps the most important modification was the ***intelligence quotient***, or ***IQ***, a score meant to quantify intellectual functioning to allow comparison among individuals. To arrive at an IQ score, Terman relied on a formula for expressing the relationship between an individual's mental age and chronological age developed a few years earlier in Germany. The formula derives a child's IQ by dividing mental age by chronological age (CA) and multiplying by 100:

$$IQ = (MA/CA) \times 100.$$

Thus, if an eight-year-old performs at the level of a 12-year-old (i.e. displays a mental age of 12), the child's IQ is (12/8) × 100, or 150. Similarly, a 12-year-old-child whose test score is equivalent to that expected of an eight-year-old has an IQ of 66; and a 12-year-old who performs at the expected level of a 12-year-old has an IQ of 100. By definition, then, a person of average intelligence has an IQ of 100.

When intelligence testing came to the United States, another modification occurred that was seemingly subtle but profound in its implications. Binet had developed intelligence testing for a purpose — to predict school success — and for that purpose intelligence testing was, and is, highly successful. But in the US, people became preoccupied with IQ as a measure of general intellectual ability that could predict their children's success in life, like a deck of psychological tarot cards.

Group tests

Terman's adaptation of Binet's scale gained rapid use, for the intelligence test filled a number of pressing social needs. One of the most important was military (Weinberg, 1989). At the time of Terman's revision (1916), the United States was involved in World War I, and the army needed to recruit hundreds of thousands of soldiers from among millions of men, many of them recent immigrants. IQ testing promised a way of determining quickly which men were mentally fit for military service and, of those, which were likely to make good officers.

FIGURE 9.1
Selected items from the Army Beta test for non-literate adults. In this task, participants are asked to name the part of each picture that is missing.

The army appointed a committee that included Terman to adapt mental testing to these needs. The result was two tests, the Army Alpha for literate adults and the Army Beta for men who were either illiterate or did not speak English (figure 9.1). Unlike the Stanford-Binet, which required one-on-one administration by trained personnel, the army tests were group tests, paper-and-pencil measures of intelligence that can be administered to a roomful of people at a time. Between September 1917 and January 1919, over 1.7 million men took the Army Alpha test.

Today, the Monitoring Standards in Education (MSE) assessment materials are used by government schools in Western Australia to track student performance. These assessment materials use standardised tests and are based on the Curriculum Framework and Outcomes and Standards Framework. The MSE materials are primarily designed to assess learning for students in years 3, 7 and 10. They may be used by schools to diagnose individual students' cognitive strengths and weaknesses, to determine the mean level performance of a class and/or cohort and to assist teachers when designing assessment tasks and criteria (Western Australian Department of Education and Training, 2004). However, like many other standardised tests, the MSE has the potential to encourage schools to 'teach to the test'; that is, students learn how to do well on the MSE, perhaps at the expense of other types of learning, such as creative problem solving.

Wechsler intelligence scales

Although the Army Beta tried to circumvent the problem of language, the intelligence tests used early in the last century were linguistically and culturally biased towards native-born English speakers. David Wechsler attempted to minimise these biases by creating a new instrument, the Wechsler-Bellevue tests (Wechsler, 1939). The latest renditions of these tests are the ***Wechsler Adult Intelligence Scale, Fourth Edition***, or ***WAIS-IV*** (2008), and the child version (appropriate through age 16), the ***Wechsler Intelligence Scale for Children, Fourth Edition***, or ***WISC-IV*** (2003). As measured by the WAIS-IV and WISC-IV, IQ is derived from a number of subtests, which largely attempt to measure four index scales: verbal comprehension, perceptual reasoning, working memory and processing speed. The subtests within a scale are used to derive the corresponding index score (see figure 9.2). Verbal IQ (VIQ) and Performance IQ (PIQ) from the WAIS-III have been replaced with a Verbal Comprehension Index (VCI) and Perceptual Reasoning Index (PRI), respectively. In addition to a single, Full Scale IQ score, the WAIS-IV yields the General Ability Index (GAI) as an optional composite score. The GAI is derived from the sum of scaled scores for the three verbal comprehension and three perceptual reasoning subtests, providing a summary score that minimises the influence of working memory and processing speed.

As shown in figure 9.2, the *Verbal Comprehension Index (VCI)* includes three core subtests and one supplemental subtest. These subtests require facility with symbolic thought and language, such as knowledge of general information and the ability to comprehend and verbally express vocabulary (e.g. how well the person thinks using language) and to deal with abstract rules and expressions. The *Perceptual Reasoning Index (PRI)* includes three core subtests and two supplemental subtests. These subtests require facility with spatial perception and visual abstract problem solving and reflect inductive reasoning skills that do not depend heavily on verbal thinking. For example, the picture completion subtest involves finding missing elements in a picture (see figure 9.2). The *Working Memory Index (WMI)* includes two core subtests and one supplemental subtest. These subtests require ability to hold and manipulate numbers in working memory and reflect arithmetic skills. The *Processing Speed Index (PSI)* includes two core subtests and one supplemental subtest. These subtests measure visual–perceptual speed and visual–motor coordination skills.

Testing several aspects of intelligence this way allows psychologists to identify specific problem areas or strengths. David Helfgott, the musician from the opening vignette, would probably not receive an abnormally low score on the perceptual reasoning subtests, since his visual processing appeared to be intact and his understanding of social scenarios did not seem impaired except when language problems interfered. On the similarities subtest, however, which requires abstract verbal reasoning (e.g. how is a cup similar to a saucer?), his performance is unlikely to be as good.

Verbal Comprehension Index

The Verbal Comprehension Index includes four tests:

- **Similarities:** Abstract verbal reasoning (e.g. 'In what way are an apple and a pear alike?')
- **Vocabulary:** The degree to which one has learned, been able to comprehend and can verbally express vocabulary (e.g. 'What is a guitar?')
- **Information:** Degree of general information acquired from culture (e.g. 'Who is the president of Russia?')
- **Comprehension [Supplemental]:** Ability to deal with abstract social conventions, rules and expressions (e.g.'What does "Kill 2 birds with 1 stone" metaphorically mean?')

Perceptual Reasoning Index

The Perceptual Reasoning Index comprises five tests:

- **Block design:** Spatial perception, visual abstract processing and problem solving 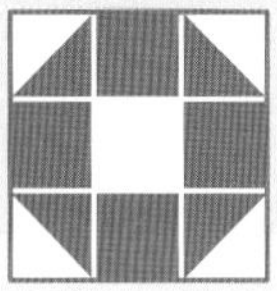
- **Matrix reasoning:** Nonverbal abstract problem solving, inductive reasoning, spatial reasoning
- **Vicual puzzles:** nonverbal reasoning
- **Picture completion [Supplemental]:** Ability to quickly perceive visual details 
- **Figure weights [Supplemental]:** quantitative and analogical reasoning

Processing Speed Index

The Processing Speed Index includes three tests:

- **Symbol search:** Visual perception, speed
- **Coding:** Visual–motor coordination, motor and mental speed

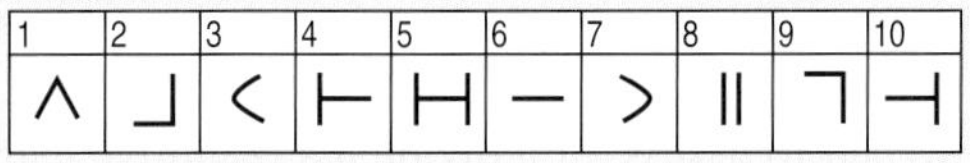

1	2	3	4	5	6	7	8	9	10
∧	⅃	<	⊢	H	—	>	‖	⅂	⊣

- **Cancellation [Supplemental]:** visual–perceptual speed

Demonstration item A

Sample item A

Cancellation

'When I say go, draw a line though each pink square and blue triangle.'

Working Memory Index

The Working Memory Index is obtained from three tests:

- **Digit span:** attention, concentration, mental control (e.g. Repeat the numbers 1-2-3 in reverse sequence)
- **Arithmetic:** Concentration while manipulating mental mathematical problems (e.g. 'How many 45-cent stamps can you buy for a dollar?')
- **Letter–number sequencing [Supplemental]:** attention and working memory (e.g. Repeat the sequence Q-1-B-3-J-2, but place the numbers in numerical order and then the letters in alphabetical order)

FIGURE 9.2
Sample items similiar to those on selected WAIS-IV subtests

SOURCE: Wechsler (2008).

Frequency distribution of IQ scores

Wechsler was responsible for another important innovation in IQ testing. The original formula for deriving IQ [(MA/CA) × 100)] was useful in assessing children's test performance, but it was logically inconsistent when applied to adult test scores. As people grew older, the denominator (chronological age) in the formula grew larger, while the numerator (mental age) remained relatively constant. Thus, participants seemed to become less intelligent with age. Although this supports the intuitive theories held by many teenagers about their parents, as we will see in chapter 13, it is not really true.

APPLY + DISCUSS

By definition, half the people on the average jury are likely to have below-average IQ.

- To what extent is high IQ useful or necessary for making competent legal judgements?

Wechsler remedied this problem by abandoning the concept of mental age and calculating IQ as an individual's position relative to peers of the same age on a frequency distribution. A frequency distribution (chapter 2) describes the frequency of various scores in the population. Like the distributions for weight, height and many other human traits, the distribution for IQ takes the form of a normal, bell-shaped curve (figure 9.3). When a frequency distribution approximates a normal curve, the vast majority of participants receive scores close to the mean, while a progressively smaller percentage falls within ranges that deviate farther from the norm, producing the familiar bell shape. In the case of IQ, extremely high scores, such as 150, are relatively rare, as are extremely low scores, such as 50. Most people's scores fall within the average range, between about 85 and 115.

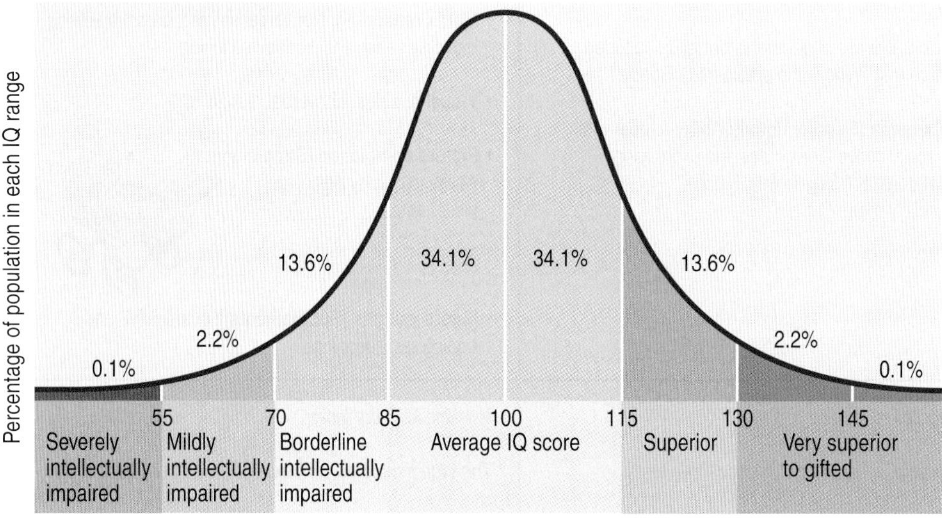

FIGURE 9.3
Frequency distribution of IQ scores. The frequency distribution for IQ takes the form of a bell-shaped curve.

SOURCE: Anastasi and Urbina (1997).

INTERIM SUMMARY

Intelligence tests are ***psychometric instruments*** designed to assess an individual's cognitive capabilities relative to others in a population. Binet developed the ancestor of modern intelligence tests for the purpose of identifying children with an intellectual impairment. His scale assigned an individual child a ***mental age (MA)***, which refers to the average age at which children can be expected to achieve a particular score. Terman brought intelligence testing to North America, adapted the concept of the ***intelligence quotient (IQ)***, and expanded the meaning of IQ from a predictor of school success to a broader index of intellectual ability. IQ was initially calculated by dividing mental age by chronological age and multiplying by 100, but Wechsler abandoned the concept of mental age. Instead, he used a frequency distribution to describe an individual's IQ relative to the scores of peers of equivalent age. The Wechsler scales (the ***WAIS-IV*** for adults and the ***WISC-IV*** for children) yield an overall full-scale IQ score as well as four composite index scale scores (e.g. VCI, PRI, WMI and PSI) and a General Ability Index (GAI).

The extremes of intelligence

If individual differences in intelligence can be located on a frequency distribution, what about those whose intelligence is on one extreme or the other of the distribution? Researchers have paid particular attention to the extremes of intelligence — intellectual impairment and giftedness — as well as the related phenomenon of creativity.

Intellectual impairment

On the extreme left-hand side of the normal distribution of intelligence is intellectual impairment. ***Intellectual impairment*** refers to significantly below average general intellectual functioning (IQ less than 70), with deficits in adaptive functioning that are first evident in childhood and appear in more than one realm, such as communicating with others, living autonomously, interacting socially, functioning in school or work, and maintaining safety and health. Although low IQ is a component of the definition, IQ is not enough to diagnose intellectual impairment (Baroff & Gregory, 1999; Wechsler, 1997).

The most recent research available indicates that almost 600 000 Australians (3 percent of the population) have an intellectual impairment and a majority (61 percent) of those people have a severe or profound limitation in 'core' activities of daily living (AIHW, 2008d). By far the largest number of people classified as intellectually impaired (about 75 to 90 percent) fall in the mild to moderate range (IQ between 50 and 70). The most recent research available indicates that 45 percent of students with intellectual impairment attend ordinary school classes, compared to 95 percent of students with physical disability (AIHW, 2008d). Children with mild intellectual impairment are frequently not diagnosed until they reach school age, when their difficulties become more apparent (AIHW, 2003, 2004; Richardson & Koller, 1996; see also Verri et al., 2004). People with mild to moderate intellectual impairment can, however, usually learn to read and write at a primary school level, and as adults they are capable of self-supporting activities, although often in supervised environments.

Only about 10 percent of intellectually impaired individuals are classified as severely to profoundly impaired (IQ below 50). Many are diagnosed early because of obvious neurological or medical symptoms. Wide-set eyes, flattened facial features and stunted body shape characterise individuals with Down syndrome, a genetic disorder most frequently caused by an extra chromosome 21 (Cody & Kamphaus, 1999). However, many individuals with Down syndrome fall above the severely intellectually impaired range.

Most cases of severe intellectual impairment reflect biological causes (Simonoff, Bolton, & Rutter, 1998). One such cause, phenylketonuria (PKU), is a genetic disorder that illustrates how a highly heritable condition may be neither immutable (unchangeable) nor free of environmental influence. In PKU, the body does not produce sufficient quantities of an enzyme that converts the amino acid phenylalanine into another amino acid. Left in its original form, the phenylalanine is toxic and damages the infant's developing central nervous system. If detected early, however, PKU is treatable by minimising phenylalanine in the child's diet. Thus, in the case of PKU, a highly heritable condition leads to intellectual impairment only in the presence of certain environmental (dietary) conditions.

Not all causes of intellectual impairment are genetic. Some environmental causes are biological, such as brain damage to the foetus early in pregnancy because of exposure to alcohol and other drugs, such as cocaine (Jacobson, Jacobson, Sokol, & Martier, 1993; Lewis & Bendersky, 1995). For example, alcohol is a ***teratogen***, a harmful environmental agent that can cause malformation or death of a foetus. Mothers who seriously abuse alcohol during pregnancy may give birth to babies with ***foetal alcohol syndrome (FAS)*** (Elliott & Bower, 2004; Peterson, 2004; chapter 12). FAS babies have malformations of the nose and eyes, together with a restricted intelligence and an agitated personality (Abel, 1998; O'Leary, 2004).

Other environmental causes are psychosocial. Children in the mild to moderately intellectually impaired range often have parents and siblings with low IQs, and they come disproportionately from families who live in poverty (Richardson & Koller, 1996; Stromme & Magnus, 2000). In the development of mild intellectual impairment, environmental circumstances appear to be more influential than genetic variables.

Giftedness

At the other end of the bell-shaped distribution of intelligence are people classified as ***gifted***, or exceptionally talented. Like definitions of intelligence, definitions of giftedness depend on whatever skills or talents a society labels as gifts (Gardner, 2000; Mistry & Rogoff, 1985). In the West, with its emphasis on academic aptitude as measured by psychometric tests, giftedness is often equated with an IQ exceeding 130, although common definitions often extend to other forms of talent, such as social, musical or athletic ability (Porath, 2000; Winner, 2000).

Giftedness can manifest itself in any of a number of different ways. Melissa Wu only took up diving in 2003, but became the youngest Australian to win an Olympic medal in the sport when she clinched silver with teammate Briony Cole in the synchonised 10 metre platform at the 2008 Beijing Olympics.

A common notion — at least since the days of the Roman Empire — is that extreme intelligence is associated with maladjustment. Is this simply wishful thinking on the part of the rest of us? Apparently so. In 1921, Lewis Terman began a longitudinal study of over 1000 Californian children with IQs above 140; researchers have followed up this sample for decades (Terman, 1925; Tomlinson-Keasey & Little, 1990;

APPLY + DISCUSS

American inventor Thomas Edison said 'genius is 1 percent inspiration and 99 percent perspiration'. Research evidence supports this notion, indicating that genius or giftedness happens because an individual takes a special talent and invests an incredible amount of time and effort to maximise that talent (Ericsson, Charness, Feltovich, & Hoffman, 2006). However, gifted individuals almost always have very supportive environments and are guided by mentors.

- To what extent is giftedness 'born' or learned?
- Is it fairer to say that genius is 1 percent inspiration, 29 percent instruction and encouragement, and 70 percent perspiration?
- If so, does this therefore imply that even the most ordinary among us can achieve great things?

Vaillant & Vaillant, 1990). The data suggest that gifted people tend to have average or above-average adjustment, slightly better chances of marital success, and far greater likelihood of achieving vocational success than the general population (Terman & Oden, 1947). On the other hand, recent research following up the 'Termites' in their eighties finds that being labelled gifted early in life may have later costs. Those who had learned early that they had been labelled intellectually gifted were more likely to feel they had failed to live up to expectations by their forties and report less psychological wellbeing by their eighties (Holahan & Holahan, 1999).

In an Australian longitudinal study of exceptionally gifted children of IQ 160+, Gross (1999) described how such children could also suffer from social isolation in regular schooling environments. Their greater maturity often meant they had little in common with their same age peers and were unable to form friendships, leaving them lonely and isolated. Her study supported the need for academic enrichment for gifted students.

Creativity and intelligence

A quality related to giftedness is ***creativity***, the ability to produce valued outcomes in a novel way (Sternberg, 1998). Creativity is moderately correlated with intelligence (Sternberg & O'Hara, 2000), but not all people who are high in intelligence are high in creativity. In the 40-year follow-up of Terman's study of children with superior levels of intelligence, none had produced highly creative works (Terman & Oden, 1959). The skills and personality traits that predispose people towards creativity may not be common among even intellectually gifted children (Winner, 2000).

Because people do not express creativity in any uniform way (otherwise, they would not be creative), creativity can be extremely difficult to measure. Thus, researchers have tried to study creativity in many ways. Some researchers have turned to the study of eminent people, such as Einstein and Darwin, to learn about the nature and origins of creativity (Simonton, 1994, 1997). According to one theory, creativity is not simply a property of individuals but of the match between fertile minds and ripe times.

APPLY + DISCUSS

Researchers have debated whether creativity is a form of intelligence, whether intelligence and creativity overlap, or whether the two constructs have any relationship at all (Sternberg & O'Hara, 2000).

- Can a person who is not intelligent in a domain (e.g. art or science) be creative in that domain?
- Can a person be creative in one domain but not in others? If so, how general a trait is creativity?
- Are creative people necessarily gifted?

Other researchers have attempted to devise laboratory measures of creativity. One strategy is to measure ***divergent thinking***, the ability to generate multiple possibilities in a given situation, such as describing all the possible uses of a paper clip. Whether Mozart or Einstein would have distinguished themselves in finding uses for a paper clip, however, will never be known.

Other tests of creativity focus on creativity as a personality or cognitive trait (Eysenck, 1983, 1993). Research has linked creativity to such personality traits as high energy, intuitiveness, independence, self-acceptance, a willingness to take risks and an intensely passionate way of engaging in certain tasks for the sheer pleasure of it (Amabile, 1996; Barron & Harrington, 1981).

INTERIM SUMMARY

Intellectual impairment refers to significantly below average general intellectual functioning (IQ less than 70), with multiple deficits in adaptive functioning (e.g. very poor communication and social skills) that are first evident in childhood. At the other end of the bell-shaped distribution of intelligence are people classified as ***gifted***, or exceptionally talented. Giftedness is often equated with an extremely high IQ (>130), although common definitions extend to other forms of talent, such as social, musical or athletic ability. Giftedness is related to ***creativity***, the ability to produce valued outcomes in a novel way. Although creativity is difficult to measure, some researchers have devised tests of ***divergent thinking*** (the ability to generate multiple possibilities in a given situation) to measure this construct.

FROM BRAIN TO BEHAVIOUR

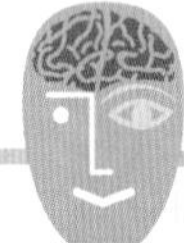

Is bigger better?

The field of phrenology advanced the perspective that the size of people's heads correlated with their intelligence, leading to the idea that the bigger one's head, the better. Is bigger, in fact, better? If we look at the size of the human brain along the course of evolution, we observe a positive correlation between brain size and intelligence. There is, however, an exception: the Cro-Magnon. These humanoids, who inhabited parts of what are now Spain and France, represented an evolutionary dead end. Their skulls were larger than the more successful Neanderthal.

Similarly, if we look at modern humans, brain size does not correlate with intelligence. Einstein donated his brain to science. Scientists found Einstein's brain to be of merely average size, with the only detectable difference compared to other 'average' brains being a slight increase in the size of the temporal lobe. Indeed, what is critical to intelligence is the quality of the connections between the nerves, rather than the existence of more neurons. During early development, the brain makes many more neurons than we will have as adults. What happens is a selective 'pruning' of neurons, in which only the best and the strongest survive.

Paul Erdos, a famous mathematician, had only half of his brain: the right side, or the so-called non-logical side. How did he come to have only half a brain? He had hydrocephalus — that is, the cerebrospinal fluid in one of the ventricles of his brain had become trapped and, therefore, could not drain. As the brain continued to make cerebrospinal fluid, some of the brain tissue gave way. Nevertheless, even with half a brain, this man became a famous mathematician.

Autistic savants provide additional support for the idea that bigger is not necessarily better. People with ***savant syndrome*** have low overall intelligence but an extraordinary talent in one particular realm of ability (Snyder et al., 2003; Young, 2001). Perhaps the most well-known autistic savant portrayed in the media was the character of Raymond Babbitt in the movie *Rain Man*. Among other things, he knew more than 7600 books by heart and could list all United States area codes, zip codes and television stations. These abilities are often thought of as right-brain strengths, such as music and art. This phenomenon occurs more frequently in males than in females, suggesting that the disorder is linked to the Y chromosome.

The character of Raymond Babbitt, brought to life by Dustin Hoffman in the movie *Rain Man* (left), was inspired by the late Kim Peek (right), a famous savant who could recall several thousand books from memory.

More recently, researchers have suggested that autistic savants may have experienced an insult to their brain during development. The right cortex of the brain matures earlier than the left cortex. The left cortex houses the areas of the brain specialised for language. Thus, if brain growth is inhibited, the left brain may not mature fully. Males are more vulnerable than females because testosterone slows cortical neurogenesis (new neurons). Thus, if there is an insult to the brain and a person is male, the combination of insult and testosterone may lead to the autistic savant syndrome.

Validity and reliability of IQ tests

As we have seen (chapter 2), two key attributes of a psychological test are its validity and reliability. The validity of a psychological test refers to its ability to assess the construct it was designed to measure. If 'intelligence' means the kind of mental ability that allows people to succeed in school, then intelligence tests have considerable validity.

ETHICAL DILEMMA

You are working in the human resources department of a large corporation. The company is hiring a new senior manager and wants to give all applicants an IQ test as part of the selection process. One of the applicants has recently emigrated from Russia and speaks English as a second language. The applicant has impressive qualifications and a good track record in the type of managerial position you are filling.

- Will the standard IQ test give a true indication of the person's ability to do the job?
- Should the results of the IQ test determine which applicant gets the job?

To assess the validity of a measure, psychologists usually correlate its results with a relevant external measure or criterion. IQ, measured from intelligence tests, is strongly related to school grades, showing a correlation coefficient between .60 and .70 (where 1.0 is a perfect correlation and 0 is no correlation at all) (Brody, 1992; Wilkinson, 1993). In psychological research, this is as strong a correlation as can usually be found and is equivalent to the correlation between height and weight!

Reliability refers to a measure's ability to produce consistent results (chapter 2). Thus, an individual should receive approximately the same score on a test given at two different times, assuming that the individual's level of ability has not changed in the interim. As with validity, tests of intelligence such as the WAIS-IV have very high reliability. Even over three-year periods in childhood during which children make significant developmental advances, scores on the WISC-IV tend to be very stable (Canivez & Watkins, 1998). Nevertheless, IQ testing has drawn criticism and controversy for many years, largely for two reasons: the lack of a theoretical basis and the potential for cultural bias.

Lack of a theoretical basis

In many respects, IQ tests have been tests in search of a construct. As one psychologist noted, 'social needs have seemed to lead, and theoretical developments to follow, the changes in mental tests over the last half century' (Tuddenham, 1962, p. 515). Most IQ tests only partially address memory, reasoning, problem solving and decision making — the domains studied by cognitive scientists. Only in its most recent version has the *Wechsler Scale*, for example, begun to reflect developments in the scientific study of cognition, such as the recognition of the importance of working memory (which relies heavily on the prefrontal cortex). What, then, do intelligence tests measure? In other words, what is the theoretical meaning of intelligence?

One question raised by this lack of theoretical clarity is whether the kinds of abilities required for academic performance, which IQ assesses with considerable validity, can be equated with general intellectual ability. Critics argue that intelligence tests provide little insight into the kind of practical intelligence involved in achieving goals in everyday life (Scribner, 1986; Sternberg, 2000b). Nor do IQ tests assess creativity, interpersonal skill or, as in Mr. Helfgott's case, the ability to play a tune (Gardner, 1983, 1999). Binet himself actually never considered his test a measure of native ability but only a means of diagnosing performance deficits in school (Fass, 1980).

Are IQ tests culturally biased?

A second concern frequently raised about IQ tests is that they are prone to racial, ethnic or cultural biases (see Blanton, 2000; Jencks, 1998). Indeed, some critics argue that they are designed to favour the white middle class in order to justify social inequality (Garcia, 1979; Weinberg, 1989). Not only do whites tend to outperform most other ethnic groups, but also IQ is associated with social class (see Williams & Ceci, 1997). Thus, critics charge, using IQ and similar tests for placing school-age children into classes based on ability or for admissions decisions at universities leads to biases that perpetuate current inequalities.

Harris (1980) in his study of tradition and education in Australia's Arnhem Land made the point that traditional learning among the Indigenous Australians of that community was done by observation rather than by verbalisation. The emphasis on learning by verbalisation, so central to Western-style school learning, was absent. Watching other people perform daily survival skills was a better style of learning in that type of environment. This approach meant many significant differences in the approach to learning. For example, questioning or verbally curious attitudes were discouraged, as children focused on the task at hand rather than solving hypothetical future scenarios. Indigenous Australians from this type of background are therefore highly likely to perform poorly on a Western-style IQ test, framed as it is in such a totally alien language and learning context.

In an interesting exercise, James Wilson-Miller (1982), the Curator of Koori History and Culture at Sydney's Powerhouse Museum, turned the tables on Australia's non-indigenous population by developing what he called the Koori IQ Test. The term *Koori* is a tongue-in-cheek acronym for Knowledge of Operative Reflective Intelligence, as well as a name that some Indigenous Australians use to identify themselves. The 20-question test is what an IQ test might be like if it were designed by indigenous people in Australia within an indigenous cultural framework. Wilson-Miller first designed the test in 1982 and has revised it several times since then. The aim is to show how the value of knowledge is culturally constructed and what it is like to be assessed and graded on the basis of alien criteria — something that Indigenous Australians have had to contend with for decades (chapter 19).

APPLY + DISCUSS

You should be able to access the Koori IQ Test on your university course website for this subject. After taking the test, answer these questions:

- How did your language and cultural background influence your performance on the test?
- Can an intelligence test ever be free of culture?
- What are the implications for the practice of psychological testing?

Are IQ tests valid?

Given the controversies, are IQ tests invalid, useless and dangerous? The answer is not yes or no. IQ tests are some of the most valid, highly predictive tests psychologists have ever devised, and they can be useful in targeting children on both ends of the bell curve who require special attention. Comparing members of markedly different cultures or subcultures can be problematic. However, studying intelligence in different cultures can help challenge conventional Western ideas about intelligence and offer alternative, culturally appropriate methods of assessing skills and abilities (Benson, 2003).

Further, despite their biases, IQ tests do evaluate areas of intelligence that are important in a literate industrial society, such as the ability to think abstractly, to reason with words and to perceive spatial relationships quickly and accurately. Whereas for years psychologists accepted the conclusion that intelligence tests predicted very little outside of the classroom, more recent evaluations of the evidence suggest, in contrast, that intelligence tests can be powerful predictors of job performance and occupational achievement (Barrett & Depinet, 1991). An evaluation of 85 years of research in industrial/organisational psychology on personnel selection found that tests of general mental ability were essential for prediction of job performance and were particularly useful when used in combination with work samples, tests of integrity or interviews (Schmidt, 2002). Academic controversies aside, few critics of IQ testing would choose a doctor with a low IQ if their child needed treatment for leukaemia.

Asking whether IQ tests are valid is in some ways the wrong question. Validity only has meaning in relation to a goal, and it is always enhanced by matching the test to the goal and adding additional measures that can enhance prediction. If the aim is to predict school success, IQ tests and the like are highly valid. Nevertheless, all tests include a substantial component of error (Potosky, Bobko, & Roth, 2005), so that they over-predict performance in some cases (e.g. predicting that a particular student with a high IQ score will do much better in school than he actually does) and under-predict in others. That is why admissions committees should never rely exclusively on standardised test scores. If the goal is to predict a complex outcome such as occupational performance, the best strategy is often to combine a measure of intelligence with other measures that more closely mirror the requirements of the job, such as measures of competence at the particular task, motivation and social skills if the job involves getting along with people. For instance, many Western intelligence tests reward speed. Completing more questions quickly can deliver a higher score, even if a few mistakes are made along the way. However, not all cultures value speed as highly. People from some cultures prefer to be deliberate and attempt to answer each answer correctly, even if this does take a bit longer. As a result, this cultural difference can produce a lower IQ score.

Attempts have been made to design an IQ test that eliminates these cultural anomalies — a so-called ***culture free test***. The aim was to strip away items in which cultural difference could affect performance. Attempts were also made to develop a ***culture fair test*** — using only those items that would measure skills and knowledge common across cultures. These tests had limited success, as the reality is that cultural influences can never be effectively removed (Lopez, 1995; see also APS, 2007b). The cultural backgrounds of both the people designing the test and those taking the test will always have some impact on the results (Sternberg, 2004b). According to Serpell (2007), it is not sufficient to simply translate a Western test into the local language. Instead, it is critical to tailor each test to the needs and values of the specific culture in which it is to be used.

In summary, IQ tests can measure some aspects of intelligence but should always be considered in the appropriate environmental and cultural context. They can be useful in predicting some aspects, such as academic success in the Western world, but are not an overall measure of a person's intelligence or ability to succeed in everyday life (Sternberg, 1985b, 2004b).

APPLY + DISCUSS

In one minute's time, name as many brilliant men as you can think of, historically speaking. Now do the same exercise but this time name brilliant women.

- Was there a difference in the number of brilliant male and female historical figures that came to mind?
- Can *brilliance* be equated with *intelligence*?
- Given research evidence showing that IQ tests have frequently been biased, is it also possible that there is a gender bias in IQ tests?
- Alternatively, is there no gender bias in intelligence testing, but rather a gender difference in intelligence?

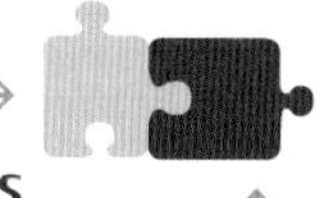

MAKING CONNECTIONS

All tests include some component of **error**. That is why cricket relies on the results of a series rather than just one match, and admissions committees usually rely not only on **standardised** scores but on other predictors of future performance, such as past marks (chapter 2).

INTERIM SUMMARY

Critics charge that IQ tests lack a theoretical basis, fail to capture other kinds of intelligence such as practical intelligence and creativity and have cultural biases. ***Culture free tests*** were designed to eliminate cultural differences that could impact on performance. ***Culture fair tests*** were designed to measure skills and knowledge common across cultures. However, these tests had limited success because the reality is that cultural influences can never be effectively removed. Intelligence tests and similar instruments are highly predictive of school performance and, to a lesser degree, occupational success. Their validity depends on the purpose to which they are put, and they should always be supplemented by other measures.

Approaches to intelligence

IQ tests place individuals on a continuum of intelligence but do not explain what intelligence is. Three approaches that aim to define intelligence are the psychometric approach, the information-processing approach and the contemporary theories of practical and multiple intelligences.

The psychometric approach

The ***psychometric approach*** tries to identify groups of items in a test that correlate highly with one another in order to discover underlying skills or abilities. If participants perform multiple tasks, strong performance on some tasks is likely to predict strong performance on others. For example, people with good vocabularies tend to have strong verbal reasoning skills (e.g. working out the meaning of unfamiliar proverbs). Because vocabulary and verbal reasoning are highly correlated, a person's score on one will usually predict her score on the other.

The primary tool of the psychometric approach is ***factor analysis***, a statistical procedure for identifying common elements, or ***factors***, that underlie performance across a set of tasks. Using factor analysis, researchers set up a table, or matrix, that shows how scores on tests of different abilities correlate with one another. The aim is to reduce 10, 50 or 100 scores to a few combined 'mega-variables' (factors). Once psychologists identify a factor empirically, they examine the various items that comprise it to try to discover the underlying attribute it is measuring, such as verbal intelligence or arithmetical ability.

For example, if researchers tested a diverse sample of people on four kinds of athletic ability and correlated the scores for each measure, the result might look something like the matrix presented in table 9.1. The correlations between each pair are moderate to strong. People who are good sprinters tend to be good at weightlifting (a correlation of +.35), and so on. A *common factor* shared by all these variables that accounts for the positive correlations may be physical conditioning or athletic ability. The extremely high correlation between weightlifting ability and number of chin-ups probably reflects a more specific factor, muscle strength.

TABLE 9.1 **Identifying a common factor**

	Sprint	Weights	Chin-ups	Sit-ups
Sprint	—	.35	.45	.41
Weights	—	—	.70	.52
Chin-ups	—	—	—	.57
Sit-ups	—	—	—	—

Spearman's two-factor theory

The English psychologist Charles Spearman (1863–1945) was the first to apply factor analysis to intelligence tests. Spearman (1904, 1927) set up a matrix of correlations to see how children's test scores on various measures were related to their academic ranking at a village school in England. He proposed a ***two-factor theory of intelligence***, which distinguished two types of factors — general and specific.

Spearman called the first factor the ***g-factor***, or general intelligence. Children with the highest academic ranking tended to score well on arithmetical ability, general knowledge and vocabulary, suggesting a general intelligence factor. Spearman believed the *g*-factor explained why almost any two sets of items assessing intellectual functioning tend to correlate with one another.

Yet Spearman also noted that participants who performed well or poorly on maths tests did not *necessarily* score equally well or poorly on other measures. The correlations among different subtests on a correlation matrix were far from uniform, just as the correlation between weightlifting and number of chin-ups was far higher than the correlation between weightlifting and sprinting speed in table 9.1. Spearman therefore proposed another type of factor, called an *s*-factor ('s' for specific), to explain the differences in correlations between different pairs of measures. According to Spearman, ***s-factors*** reveal specific abilities unique to certain tests or shared only by a subset of tests. Individuals vary in overall intellectual ability (the *g*-factor), but some people are better at mathematical tasks and others are better at verbal tasks (*s*-factors).

Positron emission tomography (PET) research supports Spearman's hypothesis of a *g*-factor that cuts across at least verbal and visual tasks (Duncan et al., 2000). The researchers presented participants with tasks that either correlated highly with tests of general intelligence or did not, using both verbal and visual stimuli (figure 9.4). They then watched to see what areas of the brain 'lit up' during *g* tasks. The results were striking. Tasks associated with general intelligence consistently led to activation of areas of the frontal lobes (particularly the dorsolateral prefrontal cortex) previously shown to be involved in working memory and problem solving (chapters 5 and 6). This was true whether the tasks were visual or verbal, suggesting that differences in *g* may reflect differences in frontal networks.

Which figure does not belong with the others?

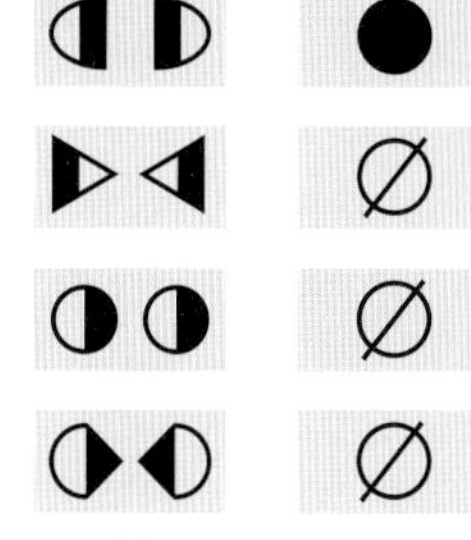

FIGURE 9.4
Low-*g* and high-*g* visual tasks. The task shown in (a) is highly correlated with general intelligence; it requires careful conscious effort to discover that the third pair, unlike the others, is asymmetrical, with the dark part of the geometric forms on the same rather than opposite sides. The task in (b) is much simpler and 'jumps out' with minimal conscious effort. Tasks requiring focused problem solving, which correlated strongly with *g*, activated areas of the frontal lobes, particularly the dorsolateral prefrontal cortex.

SOURCE: Adapted from Duncan et al. (2000). Reprinted with permission from AAAS.

Other factor theories

Factor analysis has proven useful in identifying common factors in the mountains of statistical data produced by intelligence tests. However, both the number of factors and the types of mental ability revealed through factor analysis can vary depending on who is doing the analysis. For example, in table 9.1, we noted a somewhat stronger correlation between weightlifting and chin-ups and suggested that the factor common to the two might be muscle strength. Another factor analyst, however, might conclude that upper body strength is the *s*-factor — since we did not directly assess strength of lower body muscles, except in sprinting — or perhaps even motivation to develop strong upper body muscles, which we did not assess either.

Differing interpretations

Factor analysis can thus yield many varying interpretations of the same findings, and it cannot rule out the possibility that different factors might have emerged if other tasks had been included. The results of factor analysis depend on the categories used by the analyst. For example, consider the words orange, lemon, banana, grapefruit, pear, apple and lime. How would you categorise these words? You could define citrus fruits (orange, grapefruit, lime and lemon) versus non-citrus fruits (apple, banana and pear). Alternatively, you could define yellow fruit (lemon, grapefruit, banana and pear) versus non-yellow fruits (orange, lime and apple). Or you could use some other categories.

In fact, when other psychologists applied Spearman's factor-analytic technique, they arrived at different interpretations. For example, L. L. Thurstone (1938, 1962) argued against the existence of an overriding *g*-factor, finding instead seven primary factors in intelligence: word fluency, comprehension, numerical computation, spatial skills, associative memory, reasoning and perceptual speed.

The most comprehensive re-analysis of over 400 data sets collected from 1927 to 1987 produced a hierarchical, three-level solution that in some ways resembles a compromise between Spearman's and Thurstone's models (Carroll, 1993). At the highest level is a *g*-factor shared by all lower level abilities. At the middle level are more specific factors similar to those Thurstone discovered. At the bottom level of the hierarchy are simple processes, such as speed of recognising objects, that are ultimately necessary for producing any intelligent action.

Gf–Gc theory

Another major approach, called Gf–Gc theory, also proposes a hierarchical model, with specific factors embedded within more general ones (Cattell, 1957; Horn, 1968, 1988; Horn & Noll, 1994; Horn & Stankov, 1982). However, instead of a single *g*-factor, ***Gf–Gc theory*** distinguishes two general intelligence factors — fluid intelligence and crystallised intelligence — and seven more specific factors. Many would argue that this is the most robust psychometric model of intelligence (see Stankov, Boyle, & Cattell, 1995).

Fluid intelligence refers to intellectual capacities that have no specific content but are used in processing information and approaching novel problems, such as the ability to draw inferences, find analogies or recognise patterns. ***Crystallised intelligence*** refers to people's store of knowledge, such as vocabulary and general world knowledge. At a lower hierarchical level are seven more specific factors: short-term memory, long-term memory, visual processing, auditory processing, processing speed on simple tasks, decision speed (processing speed on more difficult tasks, such as solving problems) and quantitative knowledge (mathematical reasoning).

APPLY + DISCUSS

Emotional intelligence refers to a person's ability to perceive and accurately interpret emotions (Salovey, Mayer, & Caruso, 2002).

- Is there any relationship between intelligence as measured by an intelligence scale and emotional intelligence?
- What kind of relationship do you think might exist?

Although considerable controversy remains about whether the data support one *g*-factor or two, Gf–Gc theory has two advantages. First, it makes theoretical sense in the light of research in cognitive science on the components of information processing, such as the distinction between long-term and working memory. Second, it distinguishes components of intelligence that change independently over the life span (figure 9.5; see overleaf). Whereas *g* holds constant over many years, crystallised intelligence rises, fluid intelligence falls, and specific factors rise, fall or remain stable, depending on the factor. Other researchers, including Stankov (1988), have suggested that changes in attentional processes — such as concentration, clerical speed, and divided and selective attention — play an important part in the ageing of human cognitive abilities. Proponents of Gf–Gc theory therefore suggest that relying solely on *g* considerably understates the complexity of cognitive changes through the life span.

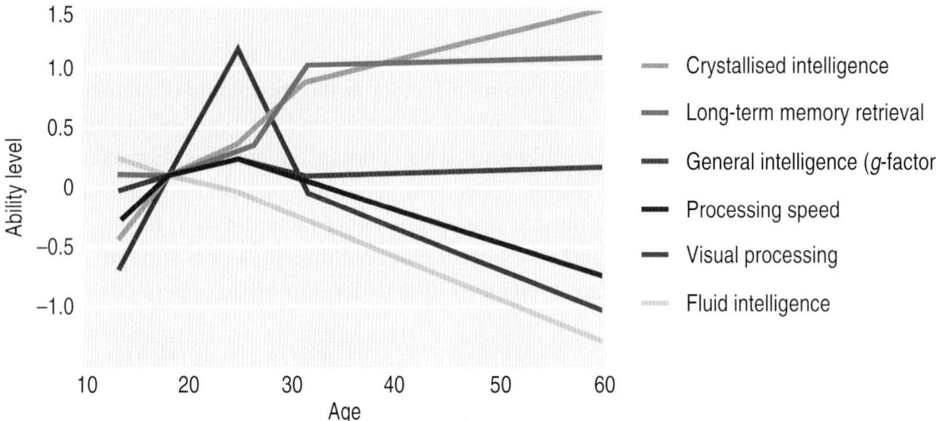

FIGURE 9.5
General and specific intelligence factors over the life span. Whereas *g* remains stable over time, crystallised intelligence tends to increase through at least age 60, whereas fluid intelligence decreases. The capacity to consolidate and retrieve long-term memories increases until age 30 and then levels off. Processing speed and visual processing ability decline steadily after about age 25.

SOURCE: Adapted from Horn and Noll (1997).

ONE STEP FURTHER

Beyond the *g* factor: the search for new cognitive abilities

By Doctor Richard D. Roberts, Educational Testing Service

The 1980s and 1990s saw a resurgence in the theoretical attention that was given to specific intelligences (Gardner, 1993; Sternberg, 1985c). For many years, some scientists argued that general intelligence (or *g*) could suffice to represent an individual's many cognitive abilities in predicting occupational, educational and life success (e.g. Jensen, 1998). Although the *g* factor is a plainly powerful and efficient index of cognitive ability, the idea that one construct could have such universal significance has been hotly debated (Roberts & Lipnevich, 2010).

In the late 1990s and mid 2000s, researchers began to explore, via empirical studies, some of the specific intelligences that interested theorists in the 1980s and early 1990s. Among research conducted by Australian psychologists were studies of tactile-kinaesthesia (e.g. Roberts, Stankov, Pallier, & Dolph, 1997), olfaction (e.g. Danthiir, Pallier, Roberts, & Stankov, 2001), spatial abilities (e.g. Burton & Fogarty, 2003), mental speed (e.g. Danthiir, Wilhelm, Schulze, & Roberts, 2005; McPherson & Burns, 2007), and metacognition (e.g. Kleitman & Stankov, 2007). More recently, there has been a particularly strong focus, both in Australia and abroad, on hot intelligences, such as emotional, social and practical intelligence.

Emotional intelligence describes mental abilities that are primarily focused on perceiving, understanding and managing emotions (e.g. Mayer, Roberts, & Barsade, 2008). By contrast, social intelligence includes capacities to appraise and understand human relationships (e.g. Weis & Süß, 2005). Practical intelligence involves the ability to understand often unstated rules (technically, tacit information) that surround us (e.g. Wagner, 2000).

The investigation of many of these new cognitive abilities is advancing in promising fashion, with some Australian researchers leading the way with unique measurement approaches (see MacCann, 2010). However, significant hurdles need to be bridged in order to give these fields the credibility that intelligence assessment has come to enjoy. For example, self-report assessments of these measures often overlap dramatically with personality and, in any event, can be easily faked (Roberts, MacCann, Matthews, & Zeidner, 2010). In addition, determining the correct answers to questions concerning how best to resolve an argument, comfort a close friend, or deal with a rival love interest is not straightforward; rather, the solutions depend on the context (see Stough, Saklofske, & Parker, 2009). It is likely that research investigating these new intelligence constructs will occupy scientists for several decades, and perhaps for even longer. There is certainly a lifelong career in this field for the budding researcher, and the effort would appear well worth it. Conceivably, these new cognitive abilities will add to the prediction of critical life outcomes — such as academic and work performance — and provide important clues on how to cope with stress, manage social relationships and improve quality of life.

INTERIM SUMMARY

The ***psychometric approach*** examines which intellectual abilities tend to correlate with one another statistically. The primary tool of the psychometric approach is ***factor analysis***, a statistical technique for identifying common factors that underlie performance across a variety of tasks. Spearman's ***two-factor theory*** distinguishes a ***g-factor***, or general intelligence, from ***s-factors***, or specific abilities. ***Gf–Gc theory*** is another hierarchical model of intelligence that argues for the presence of two overarching types of intelligence — ***fluid intelligence*** (intellectual capacities that have no specific content but are used in processing information) and ***crystallised intelligence*** (people's store of knowledge) — as well as more specific intellectual skills, such as short-term (working) memory.

The information-processing approach

The psychometric approach aims to quantify basic abilities and to compare individuals with respect to these abilities. In contrast, the information-processing or cognitive approach tries to understand the *processes* that underlie intelligent behaviour (Sternberg, 1999, 2000b). In other words, the information-processing approach looks at the 'how' of intelligence and not just the 'how much'. It defines intelligence as a process rather than a measurable quantity and suggests that individual differences in intelligence reflect differences in the cognitive operations people use in thinking (Brody, 1992; Ceci, 1990).

A cognitive psychologist interested in intelligence might test participants on various information processing abilities, such as working memory or speed of processing. The aim would be to see which of the many 'bell curves' of ability — such as ability to encode memories visually, ability to hold information in working memory and ability to retrieve declarative information from long-term memory — best predicts some criterion of achievement, such as academic performance or success at engineering, and whether some combination of these abilities is necessary for success in particular endeavours.

Researchers from this perspective have focused on three variables of particular importance in explaining the individual differences seen on intelligence tests: speed of processing, knowledge base and ability to acquire and apply mental strategies (see Anderson, 2005; Badcock, Williams, Anderson, & Jablensky, 2004).

MAKING CONNECTIONS

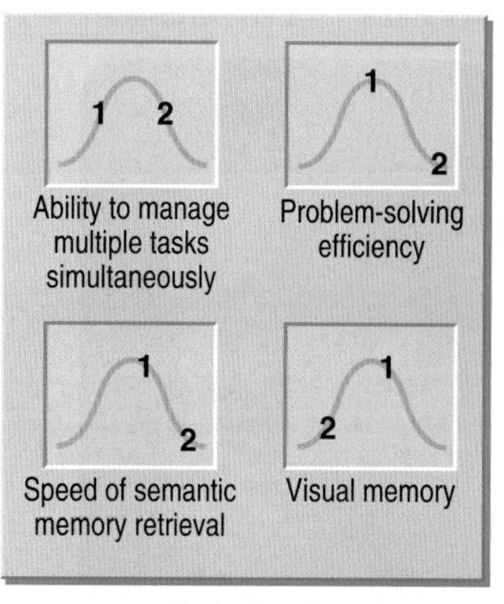

Memory and problem-solving abilities

People have different degrees of ability, and hence fall on different points of multiple bell-shaped curves on various components of **information processing**. Participant 2 is superior to participant 1 in **problem-solving** ability, the central executive functions of **working memory** and **semantic memory**. Participant 1, however, is superior in visual memory (chapters 7 and 8).

Speed of processing

We commonly use the adjective *slow* to describe people who perform poorly in school or on similar tasks, and describe more skilled performers as *quick*. In fact, processing speed is an important aspect of intelligence and a strong correlate of IQ (Badcock et al., 2004; Ryan, Sattler, & Lopez, 2000; Vernon & Weese, 1993).

One ingenious way of measuring processing speed presents participants with pairs of letters and measures the amount of time they take to decide whether the letters are identical physically (e.g. *AA*) or identical in name (e.g. *Aa*). To judge whether two letters have the same name even though they do not look alike (*Aa*), the participant must first judge whether they look the same (which they do not) but must then perform an additional step: search long-term memory for the name of each letter form.

The difference in response time between *AA* and *Aa* provides an index of the speed of memory search (Posner, Boies, Eichelman, & Taylor, 1969).

Supporting the view of 'mental quickness' as a component of intelligence, response time in tasks such as this correlates with measures of academic achievement. Children and university students with above-average scholastic abilities perform this kind of task more rapidly than their peers (Campione, Brown, & Ferrara, 1982; Lindley & Smith, 1992). Conversely, individuals who are intellectually impaired respond much more slowly on a variety of tasks (Nettelbeck & Wilson, 1997). Studies using geometric figures (figure 9.6) document a similar correlation between achievement and visual processing speed (Mumaw & Pellegrino, 1984).

FIGURE 9.6
Spatial transformation problems. Can the figure on the left be constructed from the pieces on the right?

SOURCE: Mumaw and Pellegrino (1984).

Answers: 1 — yes; 2 — no; 3 — yes; 4 — yes; 5 — no.

Knowledge base

Variation among individuals in intellectual functioning also reflects variation in their ***knowledge base*** — the information stored in long-term memory. Differences in knowledge base include the amount of knowledge, the way it is organised, and its accessibility for retrieval (Schauble & Glaser, 1990).

People who have expertise in a particular knowledge domain have well-developed schemas that facilitate encoding, retrieval and mental manipulation of relevant information (Chi, Glaser, & Rees, 1982). People with a broad knowledge base are likely to appear intelligent when talking about their area of expertise because they have a ready way of categorising and retrieving information, such as the jazz aficionado who can hear the first bar of a tune and know who played it, even if he has never heard the particular piece or version of it before.

APPLY + DISCUSS

According to some components of the information processing approach to intelligence, such as knowledge base, we might expect a direct relationship between age and intelligence. On the other hand, other components, such as speed of processing, might lead us to hypothesise an inverse relationship between intelligence and age.

- What do you think the relationship between intelligence and age is?
- Do people get more intelligent as they age, or is intelligence a static characteristic of the person?

Ability to acquire and apply cognitive strategies

A third variable that correlates with many measures of intelligence is the ability to acquire mental strategies (ways of solving problems) and apply them to new situations. Cognitive strategies are essential for many everyday tasks, from remembering grocery lists to calculating a 15 percent public holiday surcharge to a bill (e.g. taking 10 percent and then adding half that amount again to total 15 percent).

Efficient use of cognitive strategies distinguishes children from adults and individuals with differing IQ levels from their peers. For example, children are less likely than adults to apply mnemonic strategies (chapter 7) spontaneously, such as rehearsal in memorising information (Flavell & Wellman, 1977). Their performance improves considerably, however, if they are taught and encouraged to use them (Best, 1993).

INTERIM SUMMARY

Information-processing approaches to intelligence attempt to describe and measure the specific cognitive *processes* that underlie intelligent behaviour. They tend to be more interested in 'how' than 'how much' in studying intelligence. Three variables on which people differ, and which correlate with IQ and achievement, are speed of processing, ***knowledge base***, and the ability to learn and apply mental strategies.

Current multifactor theories of intelligence

In recent years, a very different approach has expanded the scope of thinking about intelligence. Intelligence tests may measure the kinds of intellectual abilities that foster success in school, but what about practical intelligence (the ability to put plans into action in real life) or ***emotional intelligence*** (the ability to read people's emotions and use one's own emotional responses adaptively) (Mayer & Salovey, 1997; Sternberg, 1985a)?

Sternberg's triarchic theory of intelligence

Sternberg's (2003; Sternberg et al., 2008) ***triarchic theory of intelligence*** identifies three types of intelligence: analytical intelligence, creative intelligence and practical intelligence. ***Analytical intelligence*** reflects the ability to put together the mental processing 'components' needed when applying intelligence to a problem normally measured on an IQ test, and it is needed for success in an academic setting. This type of intelligence relates to the internal processing of information needed for the straightforward tasks and problems that we confront in everyday life. ***Creative intelligence*** is the ability to come up with new ideas and novel solutions to problems. This component requires the ability to judge what approach is going to be the most effective in differing situations. Some situations are novel and require a special way of thinking (i.e. creativity) to bring about successful results. ***Practical intelligence*** is the ability to deal with everyday problems and find practical, commonsense solutions. This component of intelligence reflects the ability to adapt to new situations and different tasks, and to quickly learn automatic responses to these novel problems. Practical intelligence has different meanings in different contexts, and practical thinking helps us adapt to or change our everyday environments to achieve success.

According to Sternberg, we use *knowledge acquisition components* to learn new facts, we use *performance components* to develop problem-solving strategies and we use *metacognitive components* for selecting problem-solving strategies and evaluating progress. Together, these three components provide the ability to recognise a problem, devise a strategy to solve it, implement that strategy and then consider the result. Thus, according to Sternberg's model, intelligence is related to the successful interaction among these three types of intelligence: the analytical, the creative and the practical components (see figure 9.7). We balance between adapting to, shaping and selecting problems encountered in our everyday worlds.

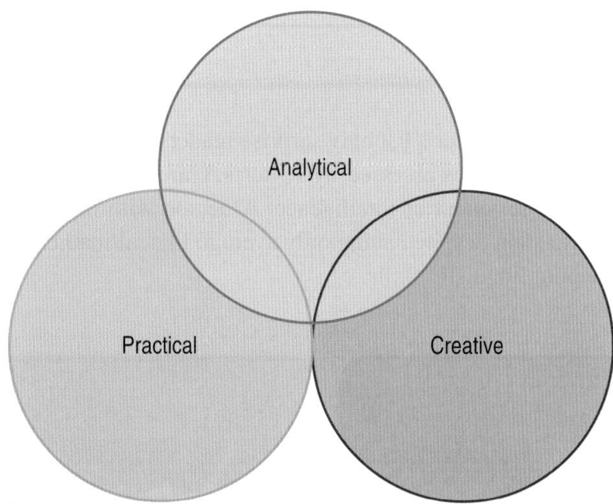

FIGURE 9.7
Sternberg's triarchic theory of intelligence comprises three interacting components: the analytical, the creative and the practical.

SOURCES: Sternberg et al., 2008; Sternberg, 2003.

Gardner's theory of multiple intelligences

Another view of intelligence that addresses questions about practical intelligence is Howard Gardner's theory of multiple intelligences (Gardner, 1983, 1999). Gardner views intelligence as 'an ability or set of abilities that is used to solve problems or fashion products that are of consequence in a particular cultural setting' (Walters & Gardner, 1986, p. 165). The ***theory of multiple intelligences*** identifies seven intelligences: musical, bodily/kinaesthetic (such as the control over the body and movement that distinguishes great athletes and dancers), spatial (the use of mental maps), linguistic or verbal, logical/mathematical, intrapersonal (self-understanding) and interpersonal (social skills). Subsequent research by Gardner led to naturalistic intelligence (understanding patterns and processes in environments) being added as another basic type of intelligence (Gardner, 1999). Table 9.2 (see overleaf) outlines the eight types of intelligence in Gardner's theory of multiple intelligences. As shown in this table, Gardner has also suggested the possibility for a spiritual intelligence and an existential intelligence. To put it another way, Gardner's theory suggests that there is no such thing as a single, unified intelligence. Rather, there are multiple and independent intelligences linked to different areas of the brain (Gardner, 2008). Someone could be a brilliant mathematician but demonstrate low capacity for musical or interpersonal intelligence.

TABLE 9.2 Gardner's theory of multiple intelligences

Type of intelligence	Characteristics	Possible vocations
Linguistic	Sensitivity to the sounds and meaning of words	Author, journalist, teacher
Logical/mathematical	Capacity for scientific analysis and logical and mathematical problem solving	Scientist, engineer, mathematician
Musical	Sensitivity to sounds and rhythm; capacity for musical expression	Musician, composer, singer
Spatial	Ability to perceive spatial relationships accurately	Architect, navigator, sculptor, engineer
Bodily/kinaesthetic	Ability to control body movements and manipulate objects	Athlete, dancer, surgeon
Interpersonal	Sensitivity to the emotions and motivations of others; skilful at managing others	Manager, therapist, teacher
Intrapersonal	Ability to understand one's self and one's strengths and weaknesses	Leader in many fields
Naturalistic	Ability to understand patterns and processes in nature	Biologist, naturalist, ecologist, farmer
(*Possible*) Spiritual/existential	Ability to focus on spiritual issues and the meaning of life	Philosopher, theologian

SOURCE: Adapted from Gardner (1993).

Some of the intelligences on Gardner's list may surprise readers accustomed to equating intelligence with the logical and linguistic abilities assessed by IQ tests. Gardner argues, however, that traditional IQ tests are limited in their assessment of intelligence. A person with high interpersonal intelligence may become a superb salesperson despite having only average logical/mathematical abilities, or a brilliant composer may have poor linguistic skills.

According to Gardner's theory of multiple intelligences, these two individuals each have a different kind of intelligence. Singer–songwriter Missy Higgins displays musical intelligence, whereas Wallaby halfback Will Genia displays bodily/kinaesthetic intelligence.

Gardner's interpersonal and intrapersonal intelligences each relate to emotional intelligence — a person's ability to accurately feel and interpret emotions (Mayer, Caruso, & Salovey, 2000). People high in emotional intelligence can not only understand and regulate their own emotions but they can also understand what other people are feeling. They are 'in tune' with themselves and others. For these reasons, emotional intelligence has become popular as a measure for identifying effective leadership skills in organisational contexts. For example, a study of 41 Australian senior executives showed that emotional intelligence contributed to leadership — effective leaders were able to monitor and manage emotions both within themselves and others (Rosete & Ciarrochi, 2005). Thus, managers with high emotional intelligence are able to use their emotions in beneficial ways, to lead and motivate their subordinates to achieve common goals.

Research efforts have also been directed at attempting to locate emotional intelligence within the traditional psychometric domain of intelligence (see Carroll, 1993; Mayer, Salovey, & Caruso, 2000a, 2000b). Some Australian theorists have argued that emotional intelligence, like crystallised intelligence, develops through experience and social interaction and thus constitutes a separate primary mental ability (Davies, Stankov, & Roberts, 1998). However, emotional intelligence is a diverse construct that covers aspects of personality and ability, and measurement problems need to be addressed before emotional intelligence can be established as a reliable and valid predictor of individual differences in behaviour (see Roberts, Zeidner, & Matthews, 2001).

Bastian, Burns, and Nettlebeck (2005) examined the relationships between emotional intelligence and various life skills in a sample of first-year students at the University of Adelaide. Bastian et al. found emotional intelligence related to higher life satisfaction, better perceived problem-solving and coping abilities and lower anxiety. However, they recognised that the concept of emotional intelligence is relatively new and called for a review of how emotional intelligence is conceptualised and assessed. More recently, Roberts, Schulze, and MacCann (2008) argued that self-reports of emotional intelligence are generally unrelated to intelligence, and that both conceptually and empirically, self-reports of emotional intelligence assess constructs closely aligned with existing personality traits (chapter 11). Consequently, self-reports of emotional intelligence should be researched more fully within the personality domain, and emotional intelligence, when referred to as an ability-based concept, should be assessed using maximum performance measures (Roberts et al., 2008).

Gardner acknowledges that one can never develop 'a single irrefutable universally acceptable list of human intelligences' (1983, p. 60). On what basis, then, did he choose each of his eight intelligences?

One criterion was whether an intelligence could be isolated neuropsychologically. According to Gardner's view, people have multiple intelligences because they have multiple neural modules (chapter 3). Each module has its own modes of representation, its own rules or procedures, and its own memory systems. As in the case of David Helfgott in the opening vignette, mental disability may impair one system without necessarily damaging others. An intellectual skill that can be specifically affected or spared by brain damage qualifies as an independent intelligence. The modularity of intelligences also means that a person's ability in one area does not predict ability in another (Gardner, 1983, 1999).

APPLY + DISCUSS

To recognise the existence of multiple forms of intelligence, Gardner recommends a simple exercise. Instead of asking 'How smart are you?' try asking 'How are you smart?' (Chen & Gardner, 1997). Try to map your answers on Gardner's domains and see how well his intelligences cover yours.

- Musical
- Bodily/kinaesthetic
- Spatial
- Linguistic or verbal
- Logical/mathematical
- Intrapersonal
- Interpersonal
- Naturalistic.

Another criterion was the existence of savants or prodigies with talents in specific domains. Savants are individuals with extraordinary ability in one area but low ability in others. For example, a young man with an IQ in the intellectually impaired range could memorise lengthy and complex piano pieces in only a few hearings (Sloboda, Hermelin, & O'Connor, 1985). Prodigies are individuals with extraordinary and generally early-developing genius in one area but normal abilities in others. For example, Howard (2008) studied eight international chess prodigies and found they likely had great natural talent at an early age. Howard suggests that practice is important and that chess prodigies can become eminent if they persist. Thus, the presence of extraordinary intelligence in one area suggests a distinct form of intelligence.

A third criterion for selecting an intelligence is its distinctive developmental course from childhood to adulthood. The fact that one domain may develop more quickly or slowly than others supports the notion of multiple intelligences. Children learn language and mathematics at very different paces. The existence of prodigies is again instructive. If Mozart could write music before he could even read, then the neural systems involved in musical intelligence must be separate from those involved in processing language.

Recent research examined national differences in lay conceptions of intelligence by evaluating self-estimates from several models of intelligences, including Gardner's multiple intelligences, Sternberg's

APPLY + DISCUSS

- Is the ability to paint or draw an intelligence?
- To what extent can intelligence be taught or learned?

triarchic theory of intelligence and Goleman's emotional intelligence. Von Stumm, Chamorro-Premuzic, and Furnham (2009) showed that people across 12 nations (Australia, Austria, Brazil, France, Iran, Israel, Malaysia, South Africa, Spain, Turkey, the United Kingdom and the United States) have similar concepts of intelligence that focus on traditional components, such as logical and verbal abilities. Men consistently awarded themselves higher overall self-estimates of intelligence than women, and further research is needed to explain this sex difference.

INTERIM SUMMARY

Sternberg's ***triarchic theory*** of intelligence identifies three types of intelligence: ***analytical intelligence***, ***creative intelligence*** and ***practical intelligence***. Analytical intelligence reflects the mental processing components needed to solve problems as measured by IQ tests, creative intelligence involves finding novel solutions to problems and practical intelligence involves finding commonsense solutions to problems. Gardner's ***theory of multiple intelligences*** proposes that intelligence is not one capacity but many. The theory distinguishes eight kinds of intelligence: musical, bodily/kinaesthetic, spatial, linguistic or verbal, logical/mathematical, intrapersonal, interpersonal and naturalistic. Gardner argues that intelligences can be isolated based on a number of criteria, including their neurological independence, the presence of savants (who are severely deficient in major intellectual respects but have pockets of giftedness) and their different developmental courses. ***Emotional intelligence*** is the ability to read people's emotions and use one's own emotional responses adaptively; it corresponds to Gardner's intrapersonal and interpersonal intelligences.

Heredity and intelligence

Having some concept of what intelligence is and how to measure it, we are now prepared to address the most controversial issue surrounding the concept of intelligence: its origins. To what degree is intelligence inherited or learned?

Individual differences in IQ

The influence of both nature and nurture on individual differences in intelligence is well established (see Sternberg, 1997, 2000a). With respect to environmental effects, as we saw in chapter 3, early enrichment of the environments of rats not only makes them better learners but also actually increases their brain mass (see Bors & Forrin, 1996). In humans, some of the best predictors of a child's performance on tests of IQ and language in the toddler and preschool years include an enriched home environment, positive mother–child interactions that foster interest and exploration, and maternal knowledge about child rearing and child development (Bee, 1982; Benasich & Brooks-Gunn, 1996; Hart & Risley, 1992; Landau & Weissler, 1993).

In one longitudinal study (a study following individuals over time), the investigators examined the relationship between the number of risk factors to which the child was exposed in early childhood and the child's IQ at ages four and 13 (Sameroff, Seifer, Baldwin, & Baldwin, 1993). Among these risk factors were maternal lack of education, maternal mental illness, minority status (associated with, among other things, low standard of living and inferior schools) and family size. As figure 9.8 shows, the more risk factors, the lower the child's IQ. More recently, an Australian longitudinal study by Bor, McGee, and Fagan (2004) investigated early risk factors for adolescent antisocial behaviour, using data from over 8000 participants involved in the Mater-University Study of Pregnancy in Brisbane. Bor et al. found that children's prior problem behaviour, including aggression and attention/restlessness problems at five years of age, and marital instability more than doubled the chances of delinquency at age 14. These findings highlight the need for further research to inform prevention programs that target these identified risk factors for Australian youth.

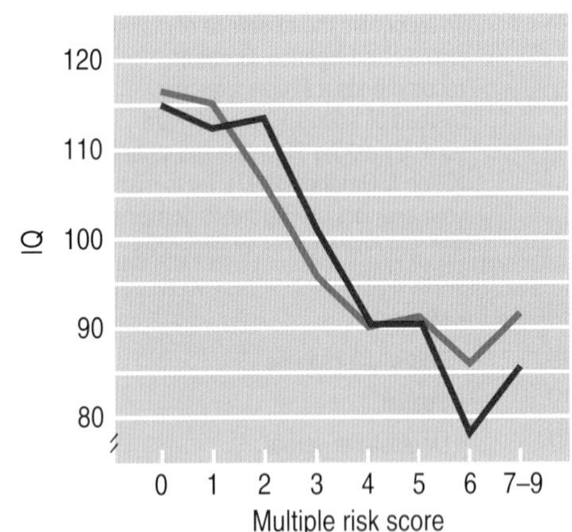

FIGURE 9.8
The impact of the environment on IQ. The figure shows the correlation between number of risk factors and child IQ at ages four and 13. By and large, each of several risk factors was highly predictive of IQ on its own, but the combination predicted IQ with a correlation near –.70 at both ages four and 13.

SOURCE: Sameroff et al. (1993, p. 89).

An Australian study has also found that socioeconomic status is directly related to poorer learning behaviours in boys at age seven (Childs & McKay, 2001). However, this study also found that the persistence of teachers' initial negative perceptions about boys from lower socioeconomic backgrounds might have contributed to that lower level of performance. So, not only were the children disadvantaged by relative poverty, but also by teachers' negative beliefs about their behaviours.

Twin, family and adoption studies

Twin studies can help researchers to draw conclusions about how genetics influence IQ.

Although results such as these are striking, they cannot definitively tease apart the relative contributions of heredity and environment. For example, maternal IQ, which is a strong predictor of a child's IQ, could exert an influence genetically or environmentally, and it could indirectly influence some environmental risk factors, such as low maternal education level. Twin, family and adoption studies can more clearly distinguish some of the influences of nature and nurture. The logic of these studies is to examine participants whose genetic relatedness is known and to see whether degree of relatedness predicts the size of the correlation between their IQs. If the size of the correlation varies with the degree of relatedness, the effect is likely genetic.

As described in chapter 3, siblings, dizygotic (DZ) twins, and parents and their children are all genetically related by .50. Monozygotic (MZ) twins are genetically identical (degree of relatedness 1.0), whereas adoptive relatives are unrelated (degree of relatedness 0). Thus, if genetic factors are important in IQ, MZ twins should be more alike than DZ twins, siblings, and parents and their off-spring. Biological relatives should also be more alike than adopted children and their adoptive parents or siblings. The data across dozens of studies suggest that IQ, like nearly every psychological trait on which individuals differ, reflects a combination of heredity and environment (table 9.3). On the one hand, the data clearly suggest an environmental impact. Being born at the same time (and presumably being treated more alike than siblings who are not twins) produces a higher correlation between DZ twins (.62) than between siblings (.41), even though both are related by .50.

TABLE 9.3 Heritability studies of intelligence examine the degree of relatedness between pairs of people, reared together or apart, and the extent to which they correlate on a measure of intelligence

Relationship	Rearing	Degree of relatedness	Correlation	Number of pairs
Same individual		1.0	.87	456
Monozygotic twins	Together	1.0	.86	1417
Dizygotic twins	Together	.50	.62	1329
Siblings	Together	.50	.41	5350
Siblings	Apart	.50	.24	203
Parent–child	Together	.50	.35	3973
Parent–child	Apart	.50	.31	345
Adoptive parent–child	Together	0	.16	1594
Unrelated children	Together	0	.25	601
Spouses	Apart	0	.29	5318

Identical twins score as similarly as the same person taking the test on two occasions.

The IQ of adoptive parents has little association with the IQ of their adopted children.

The environment appears to have a substantial impact, as dizygotic twins and siblings have the same degree of relatedness but different IQ correlations.

SOURCE: Adapted from Henderson (1982).

NOTE. The table summarises the results from family studies comparing IQs among multiple pairs of individuals, contrasting the degree of relatedness with correlation of intelligence scores. For 'same individual', the correlation refers to the same person taking the test at two different times.

On the other hand, the data on MZ twins suggest an even stronger genetic effect. The higher correlation between MZ than DZ twins reared together does not in itself prove a genetic effect; parents tend to treat identical twins more similarly than fraternal twins, which could also influence the size of the correlations between their IQs (Beckwith, Geller, & Sarkar, 1991; Kamin, 1974). However, most data suggest that the genetic effect is more powerful (Byrne et al., 2007; Kendler, Neale, Kessler, & Heath, 1993; Plomin, Willerman, & Loehlin, 1976). For example, identical twins reared apart show an average IQ correlation of about .75, which is even larger than DZ twins reared together (Bouchard, Lykken, McGue, & Segal, 1990; Newman, Freeman, & Holzinger, 1937; Plomin & DeFries, 1980; Shields, 1962; Thompson et al., 2001).

MAKING CONNECTIONS

A hotly debated issue among intelligence theorists centres on the heritability of intelligence. Although research has clearly demonstrated that the IQ scores of biologically related individuals are more similar than those of unrelated individuals or those of more distantly related biological relatives, the question remains regarding the extent to which intelligence is inherited versus influenced by the environment. Although some aspects of intelligence are clearly inherited, the most heritable aspect of intelligence appears to be vocabulary (Rowe, Jacobson, & Van den Oord, 1999; Rowe & Rodgers, 2002). In case this strikes you as odd, given that people can simply sit down and memorise vocabulary words, the ability to do so is dependent upon brain structures and memory ability (chapters 3 and 7).

Plomin (1997, 1999) examined the relationship between genes and intelligence. He compared 37 markers on chromosome 6 in two groups of children: average IQ of 103 and average IQ of 136. He found significant differences in the gene at one of the sites on chromosome 6. The gene is that for a hormone receptor that may be involved in learning and memory (Plomin & DeFries, 1998; Plomin & Rutter, 1998). In 1999, he reported on three genes on chromosome 4 that are correlated with differences in intelligence. However, each of these genes predicts only 1 to 3 percent of the variance in IQ. Thus, even Plomin acknowledges that parental IQ will be a better predictor of IQ than genetic identification, at least for the foreseeable future. The potential value of genetic studies of intelligence lies more in understanding the neural development that enhances IQ, and thus the potential for a better understanding of how environmental effects modify the outcome.

Adoption studies are particularly important in assessing the relative impact of heredity and environment. Most of these studies compare the IQ of adopted children with other members of their adoptive family, their biological family and a control group matched for the child's age, sex, socioeconomic status and ethnic background.

From the earliest adoption studies conducted in the first half of the twentieth century, researchers have found genetic influences to be the primary determinant of differences between individuals on IQ, with environmental circumstances serving to limit or amplify inborn tendencies (Burks, 1928, 1938; Loehlin, Horn, & Willerman, 1989; Scarr & Carter-Saltzman, 1982; Skodak & Skeels, 1949; Turkheimer, 1991; Weiss, 1992). In one classic study, researchers tested the IQ of each biological mother in the sample at the time of delivery with the Stanford-Binet test and found an average IQ of 86 (Skodak & Skeels, 1949). Thirteen years later, they tested the children, who were reared by adoptive parents (often of higher socioeconomic status), using the same test.

The children scored an average of 107, over 20 points higher than their biological mothers, providing strong evidence for environmental influences on intelligence. However, in this study as in others (e.g. Dudley, 1991; Dumaret, 1985; Schiff, Duyme, Dumaret, & Tomkiewicz, 1982), the correlation between the IQ of adopted children and that of their biological parents was considerably larger than the correlation with their adoptive parents' IQ. Similarly, researchers have found that the correlation between the IQs of adopted (biologically unrelated) siblings reared together is below .20, compared with .50 for biological siblings reared together (Segal, 1997). Thus, blood runs thicker than adoption papers in predicting IQ.

MAKING CONNECTIONS

This early learning classroom is an example of an enriched environment. Studies have shown that an enriched environment not only makes young rats better learners but actually increases the mass of their brains, suggesting that environmental events influence intellectual development (chapter 9). The same is probably true in humans, who require certain kinds of stimulation to turn on certain 'natural' capacities.

In another landmark study, the Texas Adoption Project, psychologists tested 1230 members of 300 Texas families that adopted one or more children from a home for unwed mothers (Horn, Loehlin, & Willerman, 1979, 1982; Loehlin & Horn, 1997). Many of the birth mothers had taken IQ tests while at the home during their pregnancy, and the researchers had access to these scores as well. At the time the project began, the adopted children were between three and 14 years old. At this initial assessment, the correlations between the IQs of the adoptive parents and their adopted children were similar to the correlations between the IQs of the adoptive parents and their biological children, suggesting relatively equal contributions of heredity and environment. When the researchers located and retested many of the participants 10 years later, however, the data presented a very different picture. The only correlations that remained above .20 were between biological relatives (Loehlin et al., 1989).

The results of the Texas Adoption Project, like the findings of several other studies (Loehlin, Horn, & Willerman, 1997; Scarr & Weinberg, 1976; Segal, 1997), suggest that although genes and environment both influence IQ in childhood, the impact of the family environment decreases with age as the impact of genetics increases. Similarities among the IQs of family members appear to reflect their shared genes more than their shared environment (Brody, 1992).

Are differences between individuals largely genetic? Two caveats

Before leaving this discussion, two caveats (cautions) are important. First, the formulae used to assess heritability were developed 60 years ago, in the field of 'agricultural eugenics', for the purpose of breeding high-quality cattle. Built into them are some assumptions that do not hold in any of the data sets discussed here (Hirsch, 1997). One important assumption is that cows do not choose their environments or their mates.

Humans, however, are very different. If people choose mates whose IQs and cultural experience are similar to their own, and if they choose environments that fit their talents and interests, heritability coefficients will be inflated. In the West, where these studies have largely been conducted, people do both. Indeed, some researchers who have been carefully examining the assumptions of heritability studies argue that shared environment plays a much larger role than heritability statistics suggest (Stoolmiller, 1999).

Second, heritability coefficients apply only to a particular population, and they cannot be generalised outside that population (chapter 3). The most decisive studies of the heritability of IQ — twin studies — have nearly all used middle-class samples (Neisser et al., 1998). Their results are thus only generalisable to individuals from middle-class homes. If these studies were to include people from an urban ghetto — or from Liberia or Guatemala — heritability estimates would probably drop substantially because the environments would be so much more varied.

We know, for example, that schooling plays a crucial role in shaping intellectual skills, such as the ability to think abstractly (chapter 8). Because twin studies have only included literate people, they have eliminated a substantial environmental effect — presence or absence of schooling — before calculating heritability. Recent research suggests, in fact, that genetic influences are substantially smaller (and effects of shared environment between siblings larger) in shaping IQ among children of less educated parents, for whom lack of environmental enrichment and decreased opportunities may limit the expression of innate potential (Rowe et al., 1999).

These comments are not intended to suggest that the findings of these studies should be dismissed. The point is simply that nature and nurture interact in complex ways, and psychological findings must always be understood in the context of the methods that produce them.

MAKING CONNECTIONS

The term 'virtual twins' has been used to describe unrelated siblings of the same age who are reared together from infancy (Segal, 2000). Thus, virtual twins have no genetic relationship but share a common rearing environment. In a study of 90 such sibling pairs, the IQ correlation was only .26. Although **statistically significant** (chapter 2), this relationship is far below the reported correlations for MZ twins (.86), DZ twins (.62) and full siblings (.41). It suggests that, although the environment influences IQ, genetic influences remain strong (chapter 9).

Group differences: race and intelligence

Nowhere has controversy loomed larger in psychology than in the attempt to understand group differences in intelligence (see Jencks & Phillips, 1998). Researchers have consistently found a 15-point difference between the average IQ scores of white Americans and African Americans. Rushton and Skuy (2000) reported that African students in South Africa routinely obtained lower scores on intelligence tests than Euro-American students. Ennis (1989) also documented lower performance levels by Indigenous Australian students in similar tests. Arthur Jensen (1973) created a storm of controversy over 25 years ago when he argued, based on the available data, that 'between one-half and three-fourths of the average IQ difference between American Negroes and whites is attributable to genetic factors' (p. 363; see also Jensen, 1969). Many denounced Jensen's interpretation of the data as blatantly racist, questioning both his science and his politics. Echoes of such sentiments can be found in Australia. In 1961, the New South Wales Aboriginal Welfare Board attributed poor retention rates among Aboriginal school students to the fact that Aboriginal children did not possess an IQ comparable to that of white children (Pollard, 1988). The Royal Commission into Aboriginal Deaths in Custody in 1991 noted that IQ tests continued to be applied to indigenous students, despite a demonstrated cultural bias (Wootten, 1991). As a result of such spurious testing, considerable numbers of Aboriginal students were being wrongly labelled as intellectually impaired.

Although the data at this point are inconclusive, several lines of evidence militate against a primarily genetic explanation for group difference in IQ (Scarr & Carter-Saltzman, 1982, p. 864). One study examined the IQ of children of various races adopted by white middle-class families (Scarr & Weinberg, 1976, 1983). Black children who had been adopted in the first year of life scored an average IQ of 110, at least 20 points higher than that of comparable children raised in the black community, where economic deprivation was much more common. When the researchers retested as many of the adoptees as they could locate 10 years later, the IQ scores of black adoptees remained above the average IQ of blacks raised in the black community, although their mean IQ was somewhat below the mean IQ for whites in the sample (Weinberg, Scarr, & Waldman, 1992).

Another study capitalised on the fact that many African Americans have mixed ancestry (Scarr, Pakstis, Katz, & Barker, 1977). If a substantial portion of racial IQ differences is attributable to genetics, then IQ levels should rise and fall in direct proportion to the degrees of African and European ancestry. In fact, the researchers found no correlation between ancestry and IQ.

Perhaps most important are data on changes in IQ scores over time (Neisser et al., 1998). An early study found that black children whose families had moved north to Philadelphia between World Wars I and II gained between 0.5 and 0.7 IQ points for each year they were enrolled in Philadelphia schools

(Lee, 1951). More recent research suggests that the average difference in standardised achievement test scores between blacks and whites in the United States has diminished in recent decades as educational opportunities have expanded and African Americans have climbed up the socioeconomic ladder (Williams & Ceci, 1997).

Further, across all the industrialised countries, IQ appears to be rising about three points a decade, so that a person who is of only average IQ today would have been above average in comparison to other people 50 years ago (Flynn, 1987, 1999). Although the reasons for this increase are unclear, it probably reflects the greater complexity of the occupational and technical tasks required of people today than in their grandparents' day (Neisser, 1998; Neisser et al., 1998). These data suggest that social and environmental conditions can lead to changes in IQ as large as the average difference between blacks and whites.

How can genetic factors be so important in accounting for individual differences in intelligence while environmental factors play such an important role in group differences (see Gould, 1981, 1994)? The answer becomes clear through an analogy. In 1913, Australian Rules football teams Fitzroy and Collingwood played a semi-final in Melbourne where they were reported to be almost evenly matched in height and weight. The players on both teams stood, on average, 175 centimetres tall. Their ruckmen were about eight centimetres taller. Despite the evenness in height, Fitzroy won decisively. In April 2004 — 91 years later — the two teams played again. While Fitzroy won once more, many other things were different about the modern encounter, not the least being the height of the players. In 2004, the average height of the players was 186 centimetres — 11 centimetres more than in 1913. The shortest player on each team was three centimetres taller than the average height of 1913.

Similarly, a study of Australian soldiers at the infamous battleground of Gallipoli in World War I found that just one in five stood taller than 175 centimetres (Blair, 2001). Today, the average height of Australian men is 178 centimetres. Then, as now, tall fathers tended to beget tall sons, although 'tall' in the early twentieth century would be short or average today. If researchers were to assess the men who fought in the Iraq conflict almost 100 years later, they would find high heritability, but the average height would be several centimetres taller. In both samples — from the same country almost a century apart — heritability is high, but the difference between the average height in 1914 and 2004 is entirely environmental, largely resulting from nutritional differences. Similarly, genetic differences could account for many of the observed differences between individuals in IQ, while environmental effects could account for observed differences between groups.

The science and politics of intelligence

It is tempting to conclude that group differences in intelligence can be explained in terms of environmental differences, such as social disadvantage, nutrition and quality of education. Although the studies described here seem to refute genetic explanations for racial differences in intelligence, a few words of caution are in order.

The question of genetic versus environmental components of intelligence is a highly emotional issue, particularly with respect to racial differences. The notion that a mental attribute as highly valued in the West as intelligence could be genetically influenced goes against the grain of many of our most fundamental beliefs and values, including the view that we are all created equal (see Fletcher, 1990). Furthermore, claims of racial superiority have a long and sordid history in human affairs, certainly in the last century. Hence, any psychologist who argues for a genetic basis to any racial differences is immediately suspect, and the psychological community has, by and large, been much less critical of studies that claim to refute genetic or racial differences.

Australian researchers have debated the value of different scientific approaches, including genetics, to the study of intelligence (see Bates & Stough, 2000; Stankov, 1998, 2000). A consensus is that researchers should continue to 'be careful and sensitive when conducting research on topics that may be of social and political significance' (Stankov, 2000, p. 75) and that 'open and wide-ranging research is the preferable method to minimise the adoption of false theories of human nature' (Bates & Stough, p. 68).

Some of the major conclusions on the question of group differences can be summarised as follows (Neisser et al., 1998). First, intelligence tests are highly predictive of school success, with the average correlation about .50. Other variables contribute to academic success as well, such as persistence, interest in school and supportive attitudes of parents or peers. Intelligence tests are not, however, biased against particular groups, since these tests predict outcomes such as school performance within as well as between groups.

Second, the heritability of IQ in children is about .45 but reaches about .75 in adulthood; thus, a substantial percentage of the difference in IQ between most individuals is genetic. Heritability does not imply immutability. Every genetic effect acts within an environmental circumstance, and changing the environment, such as placing a poor child in a middle-class home, can have a substantial impact on IQ.

Third, Aboriginal Australians tend to score lower on IQ tests than non-Aboriginal Australians. The lower average score potentially reflects a combination of causes, including poverty and related environmental risk factors, test-taking attitudes and motivational patterns shaped by generations of discrimination, or aspects of Aboriginal culture and genetics. McCarthy, Dyer, and Hunter (2002) note that IQ test results suffer because many aspects of Aboriginal culture, custom and lifestyle differ markedly from those of Australia's white settlers. For example, Aboriginal culture and custom were traditionally passed down via the spoken word, with no tradition of written language. Yet many IQ tests are based on the written word. Thus, psychologists may have unwittingly been party to using intelligence tests that discriminate against minority groups such as Indigenous Australians because those tests conform to different cultural norms (chapter 19).

INTERIM SUMMARY

IQ reflects a complex interplay of nature and nurture. Twin, family and adoption studies suggest that genetic factors are more important in explaining differences among individuals. Studies of the influence of home environment and socioeconomic status suggest that racial differences are likely primarily environmental, although at this point no firm conclusions can be drawn. Intelligence test scores can potentially reflect some combination of causes, including genetics, and other related environmental risk factors including poverty, test-taking attitudes and motivation, cultural expectations about success and so on.

Understanding the neurobiological basis of intelligence

By Professor Con Stough, Swinburne University of Technology, and Professor Timothy C. Bates, University of Edinburgh

The modern intelligence quotient (IQ) test is over a century old, dating back to Binet and Simon. Research on intelligence predates this — being traceable at least to the 1880s, with the pioneering research of Sir Francis Galton (1883). Having perhaps the most reliable and stable measure of any psychological trait, intelligence research has built progressively over recent decades, accelerating with the advent of modern imaging technologies.

Progress in understanding the biology of human intelligence has, however, been slow compared to both the central success of intelligence in terms of practical usage (IQ tests) and the importance of general cognitive ability in educational and work settings. From a construct perspective, Eysenck (1988) asserted that any psychological construct has to have a firm basis in biology if it is to be regarded as possessing validity. Thus, biological advances may be expected to accelerate the generation of additional breakthroughs, and it may be that intelligence is on this cusp — where understanding fosters interest and research in a virtuous cycle.

Three main types of research have cast light on the biology of intelligence: genetics, pharmacology and neuropsychology (especially neuropsychology that is based on brain imaging). These approaches are complementary.

Clinical neuropsychology commonly works by studying the behavioural dissociations revealed subsequent to damage to the brain — such as in the case of closed head injuries after road accidents, or damage to the brain after a stroke or a tumour. Consistent findings from this field link verbal intelligence with functioning of the left hemisphere (particularly the frontal and temporal cortical areas); spatial or performance intelligence with the right hemisphere (particularly the parietal cortex); and reasoning, working memory and executive functioning with the frontal cortex. This maps onto psychometric models of intelligence that is most widely known from Vernon's Hierarchical Model and the synthesis of intelligence provided by Carroll (1997). To understand the biochemistry of intelligence, complimentary brain imaging and pharmacological studies must be examined.

Functional and structural imaging studies are revealing the importance of white matter connectivity, and are coalescing around the parieto-frontal integration theory (P-FIT) model (see Jung & Haier, 2007). Biochemically, the roles of energetic function, as well as specific neurotransmitters (such as acetylcholine) are becoming more prominent.

Human behavioural psychopharmacology is the science of studying interrelationships between neurochemicals, neurotransmitters and individual differences in intelligence. This research is conducted experimentally, with drugs being administered to participants using double-blind, placebo-controlled trial methodologies. The drugs modify the activity and concentration of specific neurotransmitters and neural receptors. The approach is to assess individual differences in intelligence before and after such changes to brain neurochemistry. This research, much of which has been done at Swinburne University in Melbourne, has shown the importance of different neurotransmitters on different aspects of intelligence. For instance, the neurotransmitter acetylcholine is intimately involved in individual differences in perceptual speed or information processing; whereas serotonin may be more involved in attention, and dopamine in working memory. Stough, Thompson, Bates, and Nathan (2001) were able to propose a neurochemical model of intelligence. This model may be important in understanding intelligence at a micro-level, which focuses on differences in neurochemicals; rather than at a macro-level, which focuses on differences in functioning of large areas of the brain.

Central questions revisited

◆ What is intelligence and how can we measure it?

We began with three questions regarding intelligence: what it is, how to measure it and whether it is one trait or many. We have clearly come a long way since Professor Boring's quip that 'intelligence is what intelligence tests measure'.

Although science seems like a search for answers, it is really a process, not a set of answers — and the 'answer' at any given point in time is often the question for the next era. We now know that both the way psychologists conceived of intelligence and the ways they measured it for much of the last century had substantial limitations. Intelligence clearly includes 'what intelligence tests measure', but it must also include much more than that. Intelligence is *applied cognition*, and we apply our cognitive processes to many domains, some of which cannot be measured using pencil-and-paper tests.

Although intelligence is probably best viewed as multifaceted, we still do not know precisely what its facets are, how many 'general intelligences' humans really have (whether one, two, eight or more) or how to measure many of them (such as musical intelligence). Indeed, some facets of intelligence, such as general problem-solving ability, may be universal, whereas others depend on cultural and historical developments. Who would have known 50 years ago that the wealthiest Australians would include business tycoons such as Gerry Harvey, entertainers such as Kylie Minogue and athletes such as Greg Norman? Would Gerry Harvey have excelled as a hunter-gatherer in the nomadic lifestyle of an Australian Aboriginal tribe before colonisation? Would Kylie Minogue have become a household name in the 1890s, before film and sound recordings were a reality? Would Greg Norman have risen to prominence in a society where organised sport was nonexistent?

Perhaps intelligence is as much the match between a person and a time as a quality of a single individual.

◆

SUMMARY

1 The nature of intelligence

- Intelligence is the application of cognitive skills and knowledge to learn, solve problems and obtain ends that are valued by an individual or culture. Intelligence is multifaceted, functional and culturally defined. Some aspects of intelligence are universal, whereas others depend on the tasks of adaptation in a particular society.

2 Intelligence testing

- ***Intelligence tests*** are ***psychometric instruments*** designed to assess an individual's cognitive capabilities compared to others in a population. The ancestor of modern IQ tests was invented by Binet for the specific purpose of identifying children with intellectual impairment. Binet developed the concept of ***mental age (MA)***, the average age at which children can be expected to achieve a particular score.
- The ***intelligence quotient***, or ***IQ***, is a score meant to represent an individual's intellectual ability, which permits comparison with other individuals. It was initially calculated by dividing mental age by chronological age and multiplying by 100.
- Wechsler abandoned the concept of mental age and calculated IQ as an individual's position relative to peers of the same age by using a frequency distribution. The Wechsler scales (the ***WAIS-IV*** and the ***WISC-IV*** for children) include four index scales: Verbal Comprehension, Perceptual Reasoning, Working Memory, and Processing Speed.
- Intelligence tests are highly predictive of scholastic success, and they also predict occupational success. Critics argue that they lack a theoretical basis, are culturally biased and fail to capture other kinds of intelligence.

3 Approaches to intelligence

- The ***psychometric approach*** derives the components and structure of intelligence empirically from statistical analysis of psychometric test findings. The primary tool of the psychometric approach is ***factor analysis***, a statistical technique for identifying common ***factors*** that underlie performance on a wide variety of measures. Spearman's ***two-factor theory*** distinguishes the ***g-factor***, or general intelligence, from ***s-factors***, or specific abilities. Other models derived from factor analysis have provided different lists of factors, such as ***Gf–Gc theory***, which distinguishes between content-free fluid intelligence and knowledge-based crystallised intelligence.
- The information-processing approach tries to understand the specific cognitive processes that underlie intelligent behaviour. Three of the most important variables on which people differ are speed of processing, ***knowledge base***, and ability to learn and apply mental strategies. Unlike the psychometric approach, the information-processing approach is theory driven, drawing on research in cognitive science.
- Sternberg's ***triarchic theory*** identified three types of intelligence: ***analytical intelligence*** (as measured by IQ tests), ***creative intelligence*** (finding novel solutions to problems) and ***practical intelligence*** (finding commonsense solutions to everyday problems).
- Gardner's ***theory of multiple intelligences*** distinguishes eight kinds of intelligence that are relatively independent, neurologically distinct and show different courses of development. These include musical, bodily/kinaesthetic, spatial, linguistic or verbal, logical/mathematical, intrapersonal, interpersonal and naturalistic intelligences.
- ***Emotional intelligence*** is the ability to read people's emotions and use one's own emotional responses adaptively; it corresponds to Gardner's intrapersonal and interpersonal intelligences.

4 Heredity and intelligence

- A central question in the study of intelligence is the extent to which environment and heredity shape intelligence. To examine the heritability of IQ, studies have correlated the IQ scores of participants with the differing degrees of genetic relatedness of biological and adoptive family members. Twin, family and adoption studies suggest that heredity, environment and their interaction all contribute to IQ but that individual differences in IQ are highly heritable.
- Research does not support the hypothesis that differences among racial or ethnic groups are primarily genetic; at this point, the data are inconclusive. A definitive study will likely require several generations of individuals from multiple ethnic groups who have experienced similar levels of socioeconomic status and opportunity — a study likely to be decades away.

KEY TERMS

analytical intelligence, *p. 359*
creative intelligence, *p. 359*
creativity, *p. 350*
crystallised intelligence, *p. 355*
culture fair test, *p. 353*
culture free test, *p. 353*
divergent thinking, *p. 350*
emotional intelligence, *p. 358*
factor analysis, *p. 354*
factors, *p. 354*
fluid intelligence, *p. 355*
foetal alcohol syndrome (FAS), *p. 349*
g-factor, *p. 354*
Gf–Gc theory, *p. 355*
gifted, *p. 349*
intellectual impairment, *p. 349*
intelligence, *p. 344*
intelligence quotient (IQ), *p. 345*
intelligence tests, *p. 344*
knowledge base, *p. 358*
mental age (MA), *p. 345*
practical intelligence, *p. 359*
psychometric approach, *p. 354*
psychometric instruments, *p. 344*
savant syndrome, *p. 351*
s-factors, *p. 354*
teratogen, *p. 349*
theory of multiple intelligences, *p. 359*
triarchic theory of intelligence, *p. 359*
two-factor theory of intelligence, *p. 354*
Wechsler Adult Intelligence Scale, Fourth Edition (WAIS IV), *p. 346*
Wechsler Intelligence Scale for Children, Fourth Edition (WISC IV), *p. 346*

REVIEW QUESTIONS

1. Define the concept of intelligence.
2. Describe the uses of IQ tests.
3. Distinguish between the concepts of intellectual impairment and giftedness.
4. Describe the psychometric approach to intelligence.
5. Describe the information-processing approach to intelligence.

DISCUSSION QUESTIONS

1. Are IQ tests valid and reliable measures of intelligence?
2. How is creativity linked to intelligence?
3. What factors other than intelligence contribute to academic success?

APPLICATION QUESTIONS

1. Test your understanding of intelligence by matching each of the scenarios listed with the different intelligence types in Gardner's theory of multiple intelligences: musical, bodily/kinaesthetic, spatial, linguistic/verbal, logical/mathematical, intrapersonal, interpersonal and naturalistic.
   (a) Robert is visiting friends in a city he has never been to before. He wishes to spend the next day sightseeing and studies a map of the city to learn where the sights are located. The next day he is able to find his way to all the top tourist locations without needing to refer back to the city map.
   (b) Jiao is personable and has many friends. She recently completed her psychology degree and now works as a school counsellor.
   (c) Trina is a gifted public speaker who enjoys talking to many different people at important social events.
   (d) Shozo does not do very well at school but he can play a song on the guitar after hearing it only once.
   (e) Joseph enjoys doing crossword puzzles and never needs to use a calculator for simple arithmetic problems. Whenever he goes shopping, he can correctly add up the total of his grocery bill in his head and have the right money ready to pay the checkout operator.
   (f) Leila is a professional basketball player who always shoots more goals than any other player on the court.
   (g) Anita has a deep understanding of who she is and always feels comfortable within herself, regardless of the situation.
   (h) Ka Wing specialises in identifying and classifying plants, including the causes and cures of plant diseases.
2. Test your understanding of intelligence by matching each of the scenarios listed with the following components of Sternberg's triarchic theory of intelligence: analytical, creative, and practical.
   (a) Nova is the service manager of a large supermarket. Despite the complaints people make about a particular product, she is able to quickly adjust to the situation and handle herself (and the store's reputation) appropriately.
   (b) Hong is in an exam and reads the first question. She identifies the problem immediately and chooses an appropriate strategy to solve it.
   (c) Paul is the coach of a football team. He knows when set plays are working and when he needs to teach the team a new move.

The solutions to the application questions can be found on page 834.

MULTIMEDIA RESOURCES

The *Cyberpsych* multimedia resource is available *as an option* to accompany this textbook to further develop your understanding of many key psychology concepts. *Cyberpsych* contains a wealth of rich media content and activities, and for this chapter includes:

- an interactive module on cultural bias in intelligence testing
- a video case on giftedness and talent
- a video case on IQ.

Motivation and emotion

10

LEARNING OBJECTIVES

After studying this chapter you should be able to:

1 distinguish among the different theoretical perspectives on motivation

2 describe how eating behaviours are regulated

3 describe how sexual motivation involves hormones and social and cultural factors

4 distinguish between the two clusters of psychosocial motives: relatedness and agency needs

5 distinguish between the different theories of emotion.

Motivation is the driving force behind behaviour that leads us to pursue some things and avoid others.

Perspectives on motivation

- The ***psychodynamic perspective*** distinguishes between conscious (explicit) and unconscious (implicit) motives.
- The ***behaviourist perspective*** asserts that humans are motivated to repeat behaviours that lead to reinforcement and to avoid behaviours associated with punishment.
- The ***cognitive perspective*** asserts that people are motivated to perform behaviours that they value and that they believe they can attain.
- The ***humanistic perspective*** asserts a theory of self-actualisation; Maslow's hierarchy of needs ranges from needs that are basic to survival to needs that guide behaviour only once the person has fulfilled needs lower down the hierarchy.
- The ***evolutionary perspective*** asserts that evolution selects animals that maximise their inclusive fitness.
- Social and cultural practices play a substantial role in shaping motives.

Eating

- ***Metabolism*** is the process by which the body transforms food into energy; ***homoeostasis*** refers to the body's tendency to maintain a relatively constant state that permits cells to live and function.
- Feelings of hunger derive from falling levels of glucose and lipids in the bloodstream, which are detected by receptors in the liver and brainstem.
- ***Satiety*** occurs through a number of mechanisms, including tastes and smells, but primarily through detection of nutrients in the stomach and intestines.
- ***Obesity*** involves having a body weight more than 15 percent above the ideal for a person's height and age.

Sexual motivation

- Sexual motivation and behaviour are highly variable across cultures and individuals.
- The ***sexual response cycle*** refers to the pattern of physiological changes that takes place in both women and men during sex.
- ***Sexual orientation*** refers to the direction of a person's enduring sexual attraction, to members of the same or opposite sex.

Psychosocial motives

- ***Relatedness needs*** refer to motives for connectedness with others, such as attachment, intimacy and affiliation.
- ***Agency needs*** include motives for achievement, autonomy, mastery, power and other self-oriented goals; the ***need for achievement*** refers to the need to succeed and to avoid failure.

Emotion

- ***Emotion*** is an evaluative response that typically includes physiological arousal, subjective experience and behavioural or emotional expression.
- The ***James–Lange theory*** asserts that emotions originate in peripheral nervous system responses, which the central nervous system then interprets. The ***Cannon–Bard theory*** argues that emotion-inducing stimuli simultaneously elicit both an emotional experience and bodily responses.
- The subjective experience of emotion refers to what the emotion feels like to the individual.
- ***Emotional expression*** refers to the overt behavioural signs of emotion.
- ***Basic emotions*** — such as anger, fear, happiness, sadness and disgust — are common to the human species and include characteristic physiological, subjective and expressive components.
- ***Emotion regulation*** refers to efforts to control emotional states.

Perspectives on emotion

- The ***psychodynamic perspective*** asserts that people can be unconscious of their emotional experience and can act on emotions even when they lack subjective awareness of them.
- ***Cognitive perspectives***, such as the ***Schachter–Singer theory***, assert that emotion occurs as people interpret their physiological arousal.
- The ***evolutionary perspective*** asserts that emotion serves an important role in communication between members of a species, and can be a powerful source of motivation.

Central questions: the nature and causes of human motives and emotions

- Everything we do and feel is rooted in biology and shaped by culture and experience. Thoughts provide the direction or goals of a motive; feelings provide the strength or force behind it. Both motivation and emotion work together to influence behaviour.

WEST Australian mother-of-three Alison Braun was obese. The then 35-year-old weighed in for the 2008 series of the Network Ten television series *The Biggest Loser* at a hefty 121 kilograms, about double the healthy weight range for a woman of her 167 centimetre height. So, why was she overweight? Was it a lack of willpower? Was it genetic? Was it a medical condition?

There are some physiological differences that affect the rate at which people gain or lose weight. Some people can eat more than others and still maintain a lower body weight. Look at models and athletes. They have particular body shapes and metabolic rates that help them stay slimmer. Some people have disorders such as diabetes or hypothyroidism, each of which is genetically based and which can lead to obesity. But medical conditions are not the reason why an increasing number of people in the Western world are overweight or obese.

Many people lack the motivation to change behaviours and lead a healthier lifestyle. Food may be solace for some from other issues in their life, such as depression or social isolation. Others may simply have fallen into a pattern of unhealthy eating and little exercise, and cannot find a way out. They may understand how their obesity is endangering their physical health, but still are unable to summon the motivation to change.

So, how can people find their motivation? The answer to this question is neither simple nor global. The reason people lack the motivation to lose weight is also different for everyone. For example, if depression is the reason for a lack of motivation, then the primary issue of the depression must be treated first to alleviate the secondary problem of overeating for short-term emotional comfort.

For Alison Braun, the experience of being on *The Biggest Loser* was the catalyst for overcoming her lack of motivation. Alison said she had become obese by falling into a cycle of physical inactivity, eating too much, and putting the needs of her family ahead of her own personal health.

As much as her time on the show taught her about exercise techniques and healthy food choices, it was the mental change that made the difference. Alison says she discovered on the show just how disciplined, determined, focused and driven she could be. The end result was amazing — she lost 55 kilograms during the course of the show and weighed in at the end at just 66 kilograms. Importantly, she made a guest appearance two years later on the 2010 edition of *The Biggest Loser* and had maintained her weight, despite also having to cope with the suicide of her husband in 2009.

The Biggest Loser contestant Alison Braun was motivated to push through physical pain and resist food temptations while on the show, losing 55 kilograms in the process. Despite the recent suicide of her husband, Alison maintained her weight loss and made a motivational guest appearance on the 2010 edition of the program.

This chapter focuses on ***motivation***, the driving force behind behaviour which leads us to pursue some things and avoid others; and on ***emotion***, which is a positive or negative feeling (or response) that typically includes some combination of physiological arousal, subjective experience and behavioural expression. In fact, the words 'motivation' and 'emotion' share the same Latin root, *movere*, which means to move. We first examine the major perspectives on motivation and then consider some of the most important motives that guide human behaviour across cultures. Finally, we explore the physiological, subjective and neural basis of emotion.

Throughout this chapter, several basic issues repeatedly emerge. The first is the extent to which people are driven by internal needs or pulled by external goals or stimuli. Does the arrival of a savoury pizza increase the likelihood of feeling hungry, or is a person only hungry when in absolute need of calories? A second and related issue is the extent to which human motivation is rooted in biology or influenced by culture and environment. Do the motives of a Western corporate executive and those of a tribal chief in the Sudan differ dramatically, or do both individuals rise to their position out of similar needs for power or achievement?

A third issue is the relative importance of thoughts, emotions and arousal in motivation. Can a person be motivated simply by a thought or goal, or must goals be connected with emotion or arousal to be motivating? In other words, what transforms a thought or daydream into an intention that directs behaviour? A final issue is the function of emotion. What role does emotion really play in people's everyday life? When do emotions guide behaviour in adaptive directions, and when do they lead us astray?

INTERIM SUMMARY

Motivation refers to the driving force behind behaviour that leads us to pursue some things and avoid others. Motives can be divided into biological needs and psychosocial needs (such as needs for dominance, power, achievement and relatedness to others), although few motives are strictly biological or learned. ***Emotion*** is an evaluative response that typically includes physiological arousal, subjective experience and behavioural or emotional expression.

Central questions

- To what extent are we driven by internal needs or pulled by external stimuli?
- To what extent does human motivation reflect biological, environmental and cultural influences?
- What are the roles of thoughts, emotions and arousal in motivation?
- To what extent does emotion guide behaviour in adaptive ways?

Perspectives on motivation

Motivation has two components: what people want to do (the goals they pursue) and how strongly they want to do it. A number of perspectives, presented in their chronological order here, offer insight into both of these components.

Psychodynamic perspective

The psychodynamic perspective emphasises the biological basis of motivation. Humans are animals, and their motives reflect their animal heritage. According to Freud, humans, like other animals, are motivated by ***drives***, internal tension states that build up until they are satisfied. He proposed two basic drives: sex and aggression. The sexual drive includes desires for love, lust and intimacy, whereas the aggressive drive includes not only blatantly aggressive or sadistic impulses but desires to control or master other people and the environment. These drives may express themselves in subtle ways. Aggression, for example, can underlie sarcastic comments or enjoyment of violent movies.

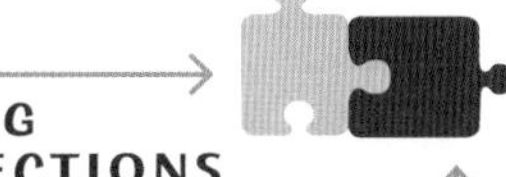

MAKING CONNECTIONS

Few psychologists (or even psychoanalysts) now accept Freud's theory of **aggression** as an **instinct** that builds up until discharged. However, the ethnic warfare in Eastern Europe, the Middle East and Africa in our own times may lead us to think carefully before discarding the idea that a readiness for aggression is an innate human characteristic (chapter 18).

Changing views of motivation: what are our basic motives?

Initially Freud had proposed self-preservation and sex as the two basic drives, much like the evolutionary concept of reproductive success, which includes survival and reproduction. His decision to change from self-preservation to aggression stemmed in part from living through World War I and witnessing the beginning of World War II in Europe. If aggression on such a massive scale kept breaking through in the most 'civilised' societies, he reasoned, it must be a basic motivational force.

Psychodynamic views of motivation have advanced considerably since Freud's death in 1939. In addition to sexual and aggressive desires, psychodynamic theorists now emphasise two other motives in particular: the need for relatedness to others (independent of sexual desires) and the need for self-esteem (feeling good about oneself) (Aron, 1996; Bowlby, 1969, 1973; Kohut, 1977; Mitchell, 1988; see also Frank, 2001; Shaver & Mikulincer, 2005).

Just as psychodynamic theorists have moved away from Freud's dual-instinct theory (sex and aggression), many have also moved away from his abstract notion of 'drives' to two concepts that seem closer to the data of clinical observation: wishes and fears (Brenner, 1982; Holt, 1976). A wish is a representation of a desired state that is associated with emotion or arousal. Wishes range from the obvious and commonplace, such as the desire to be promoted at work, to the less obvious and unconscious, such as competitive desires that the individual would feel guilty to acknowledge. Once a wish is achieved, it may become temporarily deactivated or less intense. A fear is a representation of an undesired state that is associated with unpleasant feelings. Fears, too, range from the obvious, such as a child's fear of being punished, to the less obvious, the child's fear that if she misbehaves her mother will not love her anymore.

Unconscious motivation

Perhaps the most distinctive aspect of the psychodynamic theory of motivation is the view that motives can be unconscious. An individual may be tremendously competitive in school or sports but vehemently assert that 'I'm only competitive with myself'. The child of an abusive alcoholic parent may desperately want to avoid an alcoholic mate but just keeps 'finding' herself in relationships with abusive alcoholic men. Until recently, the evidence for unconscious motivation was largely clinical and anecdotal. However, laboratory evidence now supports the distinction between unconscious motives and the conscious motives people can self-report (Bargh & Chartrand, 1999; McClelland, Koestner, & Weinberger, 1989; Westen, 1998; see also Riketta & Dauenheimer, 2003; Vollmer, 2001).

To study unconscious motives, researchers often use the Thematic Apperception Test (Morgan & Murray, 1935). The ***Thematic Apperception Test (TAT)*** consists of a series of ambiguous pictures about which participants make up a story. Researchers then code the stories for motivational themes. Do the stories describe people seeking success or achievement? Power? Affiliation with other people? Intimacy in a close relationship? The motives researchers code from people's TAT stories are, in fact, highly predictive of their behaviour over time. Studies have found that the number of times an individual's stories express themes of achievement predicts success in business over many years (McClelland et al., 1989). Similarly, the number of intimacy themes expressed in stories at age 30 predicts the quality of marital adjustment almost 20 years later (McAdams & Vaillant, 1982). More recently, an Australian study by Van Tran and Woodside (2009) used the TAT to measure how unconscious motives influence travellers' interpretations and preferences of alternative tours and hotels. They found that people with a high need for achievement prefer a travel experience with adventure as a motivation; people with a high need for affiliation prefer an experience based on cultural values and hotels that are conveniently located. In contrast, people with a high need for power prefer expensive holidays but good value for their money.

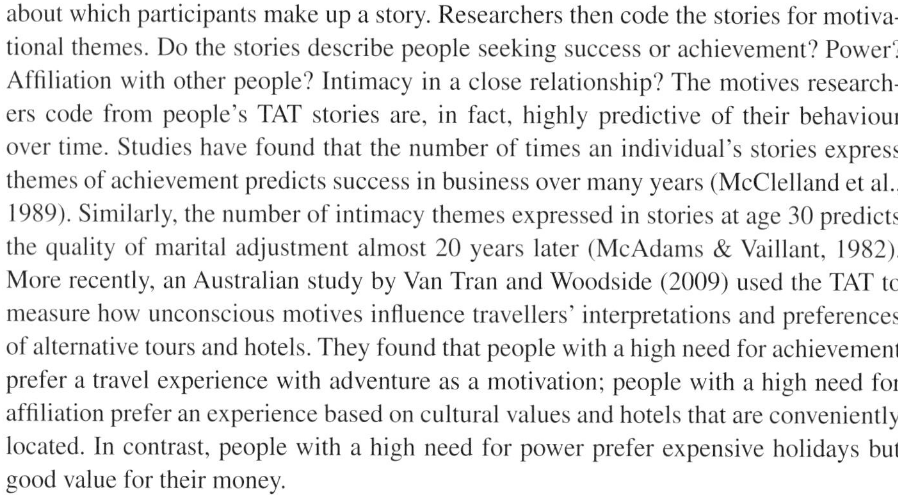

Research suggests that people with a high need for achievement prefer adventurous holidays.

Another way to measure motives is simply to ask people: 'Is achievement important to you? Is power? Is intimacy?' The correlation between conscious, self-reported motives and the inferred motives expressed in TAT stories is typically zero. People who demonstrate high achievement motivation in their stories, for example, do not necessarily report high motivation to achieve.

Although the discrepancy could simply mean that one of the two assessment methods is invalid; in fact, each type of measure predicts different kinds of behaviour. For instance, achievement motivation assessed by the TAT is far more predictive of long-term entrepreneurial success than the same motive assessed by self-report. However, if participants in the laboratory are told they must do well on a task they are about to undertake, self-reported achievement motivation is far more predictive of effort and success than TAT-expressed motivation. How can both types of measure predict achievement behaviour but not predict each other?

David McClelland et al. (1989) found a solution to this paradox, making a distinction similar to that between implicit and explicit memory (chapter 7). The TAT taps implicit (unconscious) motives, whereas self-reports reflect explicit (conscious) motives. Implicit or unconscious motivation is expressed over time without conscious effort or awareness, whereas explicit or self-reported motivation becomes activated when people focus conscious attention on tasks and goals. Conscious motives, which are more flexible and controllable, can override unconscious motives, but often only temporarily, as anyone knows who has ever made — and broken — a New Year's resolution.

Further research suggests that the two kinds of motives, implicit and explicit, reflect different kinds of child-rearing experiences. For example, parental demands for control, mastery and autonomy in early life (e.g. early and rigid feeding schedules or toilet training) predict implicit need for achievement decades later. In contrast, parents' explicit teaching about values (such as the importance of doing well) predicts later explicit motives (Koestner, Zuroff, & Powers, 1991; McClelland & Pilon, 1983; see also Schultheiss & Brunstein, 2005).

INTERIM SUMMARY

Freud argued that humans are motivated by two ***drives*** — internal tension states that build up until they are satisfied — sex and aggression. Contemporary psychodynamic theorists emphasise other needs as well, notably self-esteem and relatedness, and conceptualise motives in terms of wishes and fears. The most distinctive aspect of the psychodynamic approach is its distinction between conscious (explicit) and unconscious (implicit) motives, which is receiving increasing empirical support.

Behaviourist perspective

Although behaviourists usually prefer to avoid terms such as *motivation* that suggest a causal role for internal states, the theory of operant conditioning offers (if only 'implicitly') one of the clearest and most empirically supported views of motivation. Humans, like other animals, are motivated to produce behaviours rewarded by the environment and to avoid behaviours that are punished.

Learning theorists recognised many years ago, however, that the internal state of the organism influences reinforcement. A pellet of food will reinforce a hungry rat but not a sated one. Clark Hull (1943, 1952) and other behaviourists addressed this issue through their own concept of drive. All biological organisms have needs, such as those for food, drink and sex. Unfulfilled needs lead to drives, defined by these theorists as states of arousal that motivate behaviour. ***Drive-reduction theorists*** propose that motivation stems from a combination of drive and reinforcement, and is based on the concept of homeostasis — a tendency of the body to maintain itself in a state of balance or equilibrium (see figure 10.1).

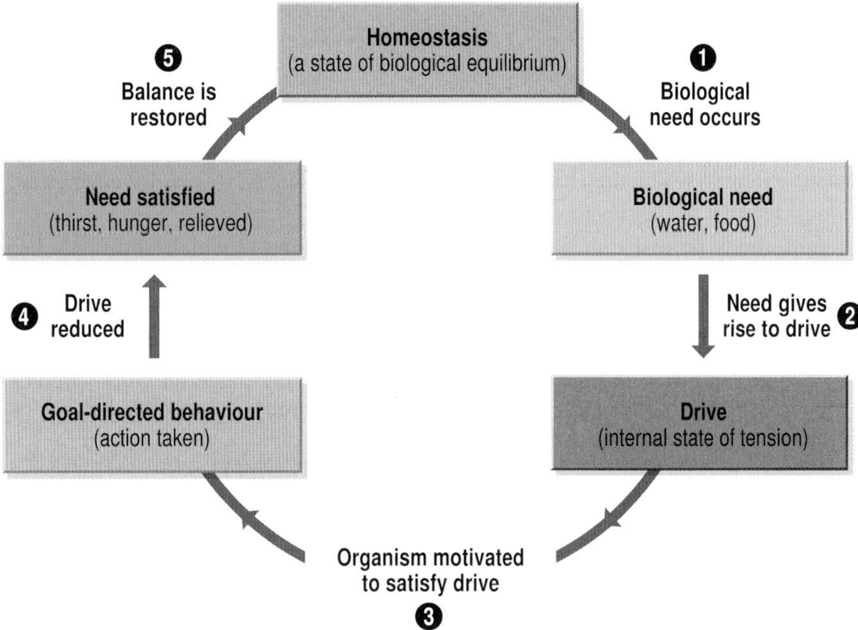

FIGURE 10.1
Drive-reduction theory asserts that deprivation of basic (or biological) needs creates an unpleasant state of tension, motivating us to produce a behaviour that reduces that tension and returns our body to a normal state of equilibrium.

According to this view, deprivation of basic needs creates an unpleasant state of tension; as a result, the animal begins producing behaviours. If the animal in this state happens to perform an action that reduces the tension (as when a hungry dog finds food on the dinner table), it will associate this behaviour with drive reduction. Hence, the behaviour will be reinforced (and the family may have to set another plate). In this example, the drive is a ***primary drive*** — that is, an innate (or biological) drive such as hunger, thirst and sex. Most human behaviours, however, are not directed towards fulfilling primary drives. Especially in wealthier societies, people spend much of their waking time in activities such as earning a living, playing or studying. The motives for these behaviours are secondary, or acquired, drives. A ***secondary drive*** is a drive learned through conditioning and other learning mechanisms such as modelling. An originally neutral stimulus comes to be associated with drive reduction and thus itself becomes a motivator.

For example, in many cultures the desire for money is a secondary drive that ultimately permits the satisfaction of many other primary and secondary drives. Although drive-reduction theories explain a wide range of behaviours, they leave others unexplained. Why, for instance, do people sometimes stay up until 3 am to finish a riveting novel, even though they are exhausted? And why are some people, such as contestants on the reality television series *The Biggest Loser*, initially unable to refuse dessert, even after a filling meal? Such behaviours seem motivated more by the presence of an external stimulus or reward — called an ***incentive*** — than by an internal need state.

Incentives control much of human behaviour, as when a person not previously hungry is enticed by the smells of a bakery or an individual not previously sexually aroused becomes excited by an attractive, scantily clad body on a beach. In these cases, stimuli *activate* drive states rather than eliminate them. Drive-reduction theories also have difficulty explaining motives to create stimulation, encounter novelty or avoid boredom, which are present to varying degrees in different individuals (Zuckerman, 1994) and even in other animal species (Premack, 1962).

INTERIM SUMMARY

Implicit in the theory of operant conditioning is that humans and other animals are motivated to repeat behaviours that lead to reinforcement and to avoid behaviours associated with punishment. Some behavioural theorists have proposed ***drive-reduction theories***, which assert that deprivation of basic needs creates an unpleasant state of tension; if the animal produces a behaviour that reduces that tension, the behaviour is reinforced. Some drives, called ***primary drives***, are innate, whereas others, called ***secondary drives***, are learned through their association with primary drives.

Cognitive perspective

Cognitive theories provide an alternative approach to motivation. One such theory is expectancy–value theory. Expectancy–value theories view motivation as a joint function of the value people place on an outcome and the extent to which they believe they can attain it. That is, we are driven to attain goals that matter a lot to us but that we also believe we can accomplish.

A considerable body of research has demonstrated the extent to which children's beliefs about their abilities influence their motivation (and subsequent achievement) in school (Wigfield & Eccles, 2000). Students of similar *actual* ability levels often differ tremendously in their success, depending on their *perceived* ability. Similarly, research finds that unemployed workers' expectancies about their likelihood of success in job seeking, together with the value they place on work, predict the probability that they will hold a job a year later (Lynd-Stevenson, 1999; Vansteenkiste, Lens, De Witte, & Feather, 2005).

Australian teenager Jessica Watson retained a positive outlook during tough times and overcame the elements to achieve her goal of becoming the youngest person to sail solo and unassisted around the world.

Goal-setting theories

Cognitive approaches to motivation often focus on ***goals*** — desired outcomes established through social learning — such as getting good marks or making a good impression at a party (Bandura, 1999; Cantor, 1990). A cognitive theory widely used by organisational psychologists interested in worker motivation is goal-setting theory (Locke, 1996; Locke & Latham, 1990). The core proposition of ***goal-setting theory*** is that conscious goals regulate much of human behaviour, especially performance on work tasks (Locke, 1991, p. 18). Goals represent desired outcomes that differ in some way from a person's current situation. A salesperson may set a goal of selling 100 computers next month, which is 15 more than she sold last month. Two Australians who have achieved difficult goals in recent years are solo sailor Jessica Watson and wheelchair racer Kurt Fearnley. While Jessica achieved her goal of becoming the youngest person to sail unassisted around the world, Kurt crawled the Kokoda Trail in 2009, finishing the epic journey in 10 days. Goals activate old solutions that have worked in the past and encourage efforts to create new solutions if the old ones fail.

Research using this theory suggests that maximum job performance occurs only under certain conditions (Locke, 1991; Smith, Hauenstein, & Buchanan, 1996). The person must (a) experience a discrepancy between what she has and wants; (b) define specific goals (e.g. 'I've got to improve my serve') rather than general ones (e.g. 'I have to play better'); (c) receive continuing feedback that allows her to gauge her progress towards the goal; (d) believe she has the ability to attain the goal; (e) set a high enough goal to remain motivated (so that the goal is not met too early or too easily); and (f) have a high degree of commitment to the goal.

Students can readily apply this theory to improve their classroom performance. Suppose, for example, they want to learn the material in this textbook. If so, they should set specific goals, such as finishing a section of a chapter before a certain time. To give themselves feedback, they should then glance at the words in bold in the interim summary and see if they can define them all before reading the definitions. If they do not understand a term, they should go back to that section of the text and re-read it. If they have momentary failures along the way, they should remind themselves of prior successes rather than jumping to global conclusions about their incompetence. If they find their motivation flagging, they might set themselves more challenging goals, such as responding to the features in the margins that require them to apply the material (see Latham & Brown, 2006).

Self-determination theory and intrinsic motivation

Thirty years ago, Edward Deci began exploring a paradox that has captured psychologists' attention ever since. Thousands of studies from a behaviourist point of view had shown that rewarding people for performing behaviours increases the likelihood that they will perform them in the future. But does reward increase people's ***intrinsic motivation*** — their enjoyment of and interest in an activity for its own sake — or does it simply make them more likely to perform the behaviour when they can expect an external (or 'extrinsic') reward (Deci, Koestner, & Ryan, 1999)? This question has profound implications for school, work and parenting. Do we increase a child's interest in mathematics by rewarding him for good grades or does rewarding him inadvertently extinguish his intrinsic interest in the subject?

MAKING CONNECTIONS

Expectancies — expectations about the things we value and the behaviours necessary to produce them — are central to cognitive accounts of **learning**, **motivation** and **personality**. For children in minority groups with a history of **discrimination**, **role models** (such as Preston Campbell) shape expectancies about what is possible or impossible and about what they imagine they can and cannot accomplish (chapters 6, 11, 18 and 19). Campbell captained the Indigenous All Stars in their inaugural match against the NRL All Stars in 2010. The Indigenous team won the match, which generated pride and excitement in the indigenous community, particularly among children.

Deci offered a controversial and counterintuitive prediction — that reward can actually stifle intrinsic pleasure in learning — a prediction largely supported by available data (Deci et al., 1999; Rawsthorne & Elliot, 1999). The most recent version of the theory, called ***self-determination theory***, suggests that people have three innate needs — competence, autonomy and relatedness to others — and that intrinsic motivation flourishes when these needs are fulfilled rather than compromised (Ryan & Deci, 2000).

Rewards (as well as threats, such as strict deadlines accompanied with stiff consequences) tend to compromise people's sense of autonomy. As a result, even though they may develop competence in a domain (such as maths or science), they are likely to see the motivation as forced on them and hence to lose intrinsic interest. Thus, the effects of a reward on motivation depend on how the individual perceives the situation. If the person views the reward as compromising her self-determination, intrinsic motivation will decline. If she perceives a reward (such as praise) as an indicator of her competence and not as a bribe or threat, the reward is likely to increase intrinsic motivation.

In many respects, this theory places motives in a social context. A supportive social environment that encourages autonomy and independence is likely to be fertile ground for the development of intrinsic motivation. Thus, when possible, parents who want to foster intrinsic motivation in school would do well to praise and support their children's interests and successes. If they do reward success (e.g. with cash for a good report card), they should emphasise the child's *competence* rather than her *compliance*.

Similarly, losing weight takes time, commitment and motivation. Committing to a healthy lifestyle comprising a nutritious diet and regular exercise is important to avoid weight regain. Support from family and friends is also important. Contestants like Alison Braun from *The Biggest Loser* need to ensure they can maintain their weight loss in the real world, and intrinsic motivation, such as wanting to be a good role model for one's family, can ensure they make meaningful and long-lasting lifestyle changes.

Implicit motives: a cognitive perspective on unconscious motivation

Although self-determination theory is a cognitive theory, it has drawn heavily from other perspectives. For example, Deci derived his theory that children have innate needs for challenge and mastery from the psychoanalyst Robert White (1959), and the theory is certainly compatible with many humanistic approaches to personality that focus on innate needs for growth or self-development (chapter 11).

Another cognitive approach to motivation that 'crosses theoretical lines' is the work of Jonathan Bargh on ***implicit motives***, motives that can be activated and expressed outside of awareness. According to Bargh, just as well-learned cognitive procedures can become automatic and occur without conscious awareness (see chapter 8), so, too, can well-learned goals. Drawing upon principles of association, Bargh argues that if an individual frequently chooses the same goal in a certain situation (e.g. trying to look smart in school), that goal will become associated with the situation. As a result, whenever that situation arises (as when a teacher or lecturer asks a question in class), the goal state will be activated and guide behaviour, whether or not the person has any conscious awareness of the intention (Bargh & Barndollar, 1996, p. 8).

In a series of studies, Bargh and his colleagues tested this hypothesis using priming techniques usually used to assess implicit memory (see Bargh, 1997). They primed participants by having them make words out of scrambled letters, under one of two conditions. In one condition, the words were related to achievement (e.g. 'strive'); in the other, the words were related to affiliation (e.g. 'friend'). Next, they informed participants that the study was over but asked if they could help an experimenter down the hall who was allegedly conducting an entirely separate experiment.

In this 'second experiment,' participants found themselves in a situation of motivational conflict. Each was assigned an incompetent partner (a confederate of the experimenters) and given a puzzle task on which they would receive a joint score reflecting their work as a team. Thus, participants could succeed — by essentially ignoring what the partner had to say and probably making their partner feel humiliated and stupid — or they could be more interpersonally sensitive but receive a lower score.

As predicted, participants who had been primed with achievement words outperformed participants primed with affiliation words (as well as control participants who had been exposed to neutral primes). When debriefed at the end of the study, none of the participants had any idea of the connection between the two 'experiments'. Thus, similar to the conclusions reached by David McClelland et al. (1989), Bargh suggests that motives, like other psychological processes, can be activated either implicitly or explicitly and can guide our behaviour even when we have no idea how (or whether) they became active.

APPLY + DISCUSS

A website that links to various historically significant public domain documents, including Maslow's original article 'A theory of human motivation' should be available for you to access via your university course website.

- How has our understanding of motivation changed over time?
- How might we progress our understanding of motivation in the future?

INTERIM SUMMARY

According to expectancy–value theories, people are motivated to perform a behaviour to the extent that they value the potential outcome and believe they can attain it. ***Goal-setting theory*** argues that conscious goals regulate much of human action. ***Intrinsic motivation*** refers to enjoyment of, and interest in, an activity for its own sake. According to ***self-determination theory***, people have innate needs for competence, autonomy and relatedness, and intrinsic motivation flourishes when these needs are fulfilled. ***Implicit motives*** are motives that can be activated and expressed outside of conscious awareness.

MAKING CONNECTIONS

Paralympic champion, Kurt Fearnley, from Newcastle (pictured in the concept map at the start of the chapter), knows all about pushing his body to the limit. He finished a recent year with marathon wins in Seoul, Paris, London, Sydney, Chicago and New York. He also embraced the toughest challenge of his life — crawling the gruelling 96 km Kokoda Track in Papua New Guinea in support of the charity initiative *Movember.* Fearnley lost a male family member to depression and was motivated to undertake the track using only his hands to raise awareness of men's health issues. He believes that men must support each other and ask for help when they need it (chapters 14 and 15).

Humanistic perspective

An alternative approach to motivation was advanced by Abraham Maslow (1962, 1970). Humanistic psychologists such as Maslow emphasise dignity, individual choice and self-worth as playing key roles in explaining human behaviour. Maslow believed that people are motivated by the desire for personal growth, and will often overcome many obstacles in order to achieve personal fulfilment. He developed a needs hierarchy that has become famous in psychology and other disciplines for explaining why people strive to reach their full potential.

A hierarchy of needs

According to Maslow's ***hierarchy of needs***, lower level needs, beginning with basic survival, must be fulfilled before higher level needs guide a person's behaviour (figure 10.2). At the most basic level are physiological needs, such as those for water and food. Next are safety needs, for security and protection. Having satisfied physiological and safety needs to some extent, people are motivated to pursue closeness and affiliation with other people, or what Maslow calls belongingness needs. Next in the hierarchy are esteem needs, including both self-esteem and the esteem of others.

At the highest level are ***self-actualisation needs***, motives to express oneself and grow, or to actualise one's potential. Self-actualisation needs differ from all the previous levels in that they are not deficiency needs; that is, they are not generated by a lack of something (food, shelter, closeness, the esteem of others). Rather, they are growth needs — motives to expand and develop one's skills and abilities.

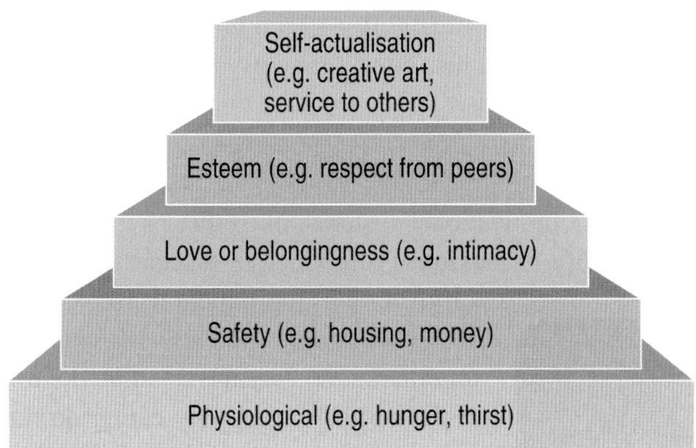

FIGURE 10.2
Maslow's hierarchy of needs. Except for self-actualisation, all of Maslow's needs are generated by a lack of something, such as food or shelter.

Many behaviours reflect multiple needs. Going to work, for example, can 'bring home the bacon' as well as satisfy needs for esteem, affiliation and self-actualisation. According to Maslow, however, people can spend their lives focused on motives primarily at one level and not develop beyond it. People who are starving are unlikely to think much about art, and motives for self-expression may take a back seat in people who desperately need the esteem of others. In contrast, self-actualised individuals are no longer preoccupied with where they will get their dinner or who will hold them in esteem, and are thus free to pursue moral, cultural or aesthetic concerns. Examples of self-actualised people include Mahatma Gandhi, Martin Luther King, Jr and Mother Teresa. Maslow believed that few people reach this level of self-actualisation.

Maslow's theory of self-actualisation has proven difficult to test (Neher, 1991). However, one organisational psychologist, Clayton Alderfer, refined and applied aspects of Maslow's model to motivation in the workplace (Alderfer, 1972, 1989). Alderfer was a consultant to a small manufacturing company that was having trouble motivating its workers. In interviewing the employees, he noticed that their concerns seemed to fall into three categories: material concerns such as pay, fringe benefits and physical conditions in the plant; relationships with peers and supervisors; and opportunities to learn and use their skills on the job. His observations led to ***ERG theory***, which essentially condenses Maslow's hierarchy to three levels of need: existence, relatedness and growth (hence ERG).

According to ERG theory, worker satisfaction and motivation vary with the extent to which a job matches a given worker's needs. Workers whose primary concern is pay are unlikely to appreciate attempts to give them more training to expand their skills. In general, however, the best job provides good pay and working conditions, a chance to interact with other people and opportunities to develop one's skills, thus satisfying the major needs. This theory offers testable hypotheses, although the empirical evidence for it remains sketchy.

APPLY + DISCUSS

- To what extent does factory work on this production line satisfy the motives described by Maslow and ERG theory?
- What could employers do to increase employee satisfaction in jobs such as this?

INTERIM SUMMARY

Maslow proposed a ***hierarchy of needs*** — from needs that are basic to survival to needs that guide behaviour only once the person has fulfilled needs lower down the hierarchy. The hierarchy includes physiological needs, safety needs, belongingness needs, esteem needs and ***self-actualisation needs*** (needs to express oneself and grow). ***ERG theory***, which applied Maslow's model to the workplace, proposes that workers are motivated by three kinds of needs: existence, relatedness and growth.

Evolutionary perspective

In the early part of the twentieth century, psychologists assumed that most motivated behaviour in humans, as in other animals, was a result of ***instincts***, relatively fixed patterns of behaviour produced without learning (Tinbergen, 1951). An example is the mating ritual of the ring dove, which must perform an elaborate, stereotyped sequence of behaviours in exactly the right manner to attract a mate. If the male does not bow and coo at the proper point in the ritual, the female will not be receptive (Lehrman, 1956).

Most psychologists eventually abandoned instinct theory, for a number of reasons. First, human behaviour varies so substantially across cultures that the motives that seemed 'instinctive' in one culture (such as motives for wealth in the West) did not seem so powerful in others. Perhaps more importantly, one of the most distinctive features of human behaviour is its flexibility — seen in our ability to find novel ways to solve problems or to bow and coo when it suits us. Thus, many psychologists came to argue that learning, not instinct, motivates behaviour in humans.

Maximising inclusive fitness

Contemporary evolutionary psychologists contend that motivational systems, like other psychological attributes, have been selected by nature for their ability to maximise reproductive success — that is, survival and reproduction (see Buss, 1999). For some motives, this claim is unremarkable. Organisms that do not replenish their energy by eating do not survive and reproduce. Nature has thus designed humans and other animals with intricate systems for maintaining basic life-support processes.

Some evolutionary explanations, however, are much more controversial. As we saw in chapter 1, evolutionary theorists have argued that evolution selects animals that maximise their inclusive fitness, which refers to their own reproductive success in addition to their influence on the reproductive success of genetically related individuals (Hamilton, 1964). This theory makes mathematical sense. The probability that any given gene of an individual who protects his child will be available in the gene pool in the next generation is 50 percent because his child shares half his genes. The probability jumps to 75 percent for someone who protects his child *plus* his niece (one-half from his child and one-quarter from his niece). Over many generations, this difference becomes substantial.

APPLY + DISCUSS

Many animals have elaborate courting rituals that precede mating.

- To what extent do human 'rituals' and those of other animals reflect common evolutionary roots?
- Are the similarities just accidental (and amusing) or do they reflect similar evolutionary histories?

Evolutionary psychologists are generally careful to distinguish the theory that evolution *favours* organisms that maximise their inclusive fitness from the assumption that organisms deliberately *seek* to maximise their inclusive fitness, as if they carry inclusive fitness calculators in their pockets. Nevertheless, some basic motivational mechanisms presumably evolved to help organisms select courses of action that foster survival, reproduction and the care and protection of kin. These mechanisms should guide their behaviour so that their degree of investment is roughly proportional to their degree of relatedness.

How then do organisms — whether bees or humans — know who their sons, brothers or cousins are? Recent research suggests that some species are actually endowed with chemical mechanisms (pheromones) for kin recognition. Pheromones are similar to hormones, except that they allow cell-to-cell communication *between* rather than *within* organisms (figure 10.3). They are typically detected by specialised neural circuits in the olfactory system (chapter 4) and may have the same or similar effects as hormones (Sorensen, 1996).

FIGURE 10.3
Pheromonal communication. Pheromones activate sexual and other responses much as hormones do, except that they are secreted by other animals instead of by the animal's own endocrine system.

Whether pheromonal communication leads to increased investment in close relatives is unknown, but it does help members of some species avoid mating with members of other species (which wastes precious mating time) and avoid incest, which can produce genetically defective offspring and hence reduce reproductive success (Blaustein & Waldman, 1992; Wilson & Bossert, 1996). In one study, the experimenter allowed female crickets to choose where they would spend their time in an area divided into four territories (Simmons, 1990). Potential male mates were not present, but the experimenter marked each territory with the scent (from droppings) of a male who was a full sibling, a half sibling, a cousin or an unrelated cricket. Thus, the females could spend time in the territory of male crickets related to them by .5, .25, .125 or 0, respectively.

The results were striking. The amount of time females spent in each territory was inversely proportional to degree of relatedness; that is, the more distant the relation, the more time spent 'in the neighbourhood'. The mechanism for kin recognition proved to be chemical, since female crickets whose pheromone receptors were covered with wax showed no preference for unrelated males.

Humans probably do not rely on pheromones for kin recognition; however, as suggested in chapter 1, they probably make use of other mechanisms, such as degree of familiarity, particularly from childhood. Throughout the course of much of human evolution, people who grew up together were more than likely family members, so long-time familiarity, particularly from childhood, would be a rough index of degree of kinship, if an imperfect one. In fact, just as crickets avoid sexual contact with other crickets with the scent of family, marriage among children who grow up together in Israeli communal living arrangements, or *kibbutzim*, is almost nonexistent (Shepher, 1978).

> **APPLY + DISCUSS**
> - To what degree does familiarity influence caretaking behaviour in humans? In other words, do we tend to care about (and for) people with whom we interact regularly?
> - Has the fact that people in technologically developed societies may live hundreds or thousand of kilometres from their families derailed the evolutionary mechanisms that lead people to care for blood relatives (chapters 15 and 18)?

INTERIM SUMMARY

Early on, psychologists assumed that humans and other animals had ***instincts***, with fixed patterns of behaviour produced without learning. According to contemporary evolutionary theory, evolution selects animals that maximise their inclusive fitness (their own reproductive success plus their influence on the reproductive success of genetically related individuals). Maximising inclusive fitness entails a range of motives, such as selecting and competing for mates, taking care of offspring, caring about other genetically related individuals, forming useful alliances and maintaining one's own survival through eating, drinking, keeping the body warm and so on.

Multiple motivational systems

From an evolutionary point of view, humans and other animals are likely to have multiple motivational systems — innate response tendencies, many with their own distinct neural circuitry — that evolved to solve particular problems of adaptation. The motives that shape the ways we think and behave have developed over millions of years in response to evolutionary pressures.

Central to evolutionary accounts is the notion that organisms evolve through natural selection in directions that maximise survival and reproduction, and this should be no less true of motives than any other psychological functions. The primary motives that emerge in cross-cultural research are power and love, which is not surprising from an evolutionary perspective (Buss, 1991). Power allows animals to dominate potential rivals, establish status (which females tend to find attractive in males) and protect their 'turf'. Indeed, competition for status is nearly universal among animals, and certainly among primates, where baboon males can be seen to jockey for power in the bush much as human executives jockey in the boardroom. That 'love' is a basic motive across cultures also makes evolutionary sense. Love is involved in caring for offspring, mates, kin and friends who can be counted on 'like a brother' or 'like a sister'. The fact that we use phrases like these to describe close friends may not be accidental.

Not all motives for intimacy, of course, are brotherly or sisterly. The amount of time we spend on activities related to mating or making ourselves attractive to potential mates — and the number of poems, novels and movies with a central theme of 'boy meets girl', 'meeting Mr Right', unfaithful lovers and so on — is a testimony to the power of natural selection. Motives related to mating include sexual motivation, competition for desirable partners, making sure our mates are faithful (chapter 16) and a host of others. Other motives related to reproduction involve motives for parental care, which exist in nearly every animal species. That parents awakened in the middle of the night by a crying baby generally respond with affection rather than aggression is a true testimony to the power of natural selection!

A key evolutionary assumption is that psychological systems — whether motivational, cognitive or otherwise — serve functions that may have evolved independently in response to particular evolutionary pressures (Buss, 1991, 2000; Cosmides & Tooby, 1995). Just as specialised neural circuits in the cortex and amygdala allow us to recognise the meaning of facial expressions (warning us, for example, that someone is angry and potentially threatening), specific circuits also regulate sexual desire or probably our attunement (and response) to the auditory frequency of a baby's cry.

Applying the perspectives on motivation

How might the different theoretical approaches to motivation explain the puzzling scenario of the apparent lack of motivation for protection against HIV infection many people demonstrate in sexual situations?

From an evolutionary perspective, one answer lies in the discrepancy between the current environment and the circumstances in which our ancestors evolved. Humans have neural programs for sexual arousal that were engineered over millennia; AIDS, like other deadly venereal diseases (notably syphilis), is a new disease (in evolutionary time). Thus, these neural programs do not include momentary breaks for condoms. Distaste for condoms should be particularly high among males, who can lose erections while searching for or wearing condoms, whose reproductive success may be compromised by their application, who face less risk of AIDS transmission than do females from heterosexual intercourse and who in many cultures attract females through apparent bravery ('Nothing scares me, babe').

From a psychodynamic perspective, sex is a basic human motivation, and people are prone to self-deception and wishful thinking; the fact that people frequently deny the risk of unprotected sex to themselves should thus come as no surprise. Furthermore, any sexual encounter reflects multiple motives, and the balance of these motives can sometimes override good judgement. For example, people have casual sex for many reasons beyond biological drive. These include self-esteem motives (to feel desirable), wishes to feel physically or emotionally close to someone and motives for dominance (the feeling of conquest). Casual, unprotected sex may also reflect blatantly self-destructive motives, as was the case with a suicidal young gay man who regularly attended bathhouses at the time when media attention was most focused on the epidemic.

From a behaviourist perspective, sexual behaviour, like all behaviour, is under environmental control. If condom use is punishing (because it 'breaks the mood', decreases genital sensations or leads to whining by male partners), it will diminish over time. Partners who consent to unsafe sex may also be negatively reinforced for doing so by the cessation of complaining or cajoling and positively reinforced by praise or enjoyable sex.

From a cognitive perspective, people's expectancies about the probable outcomes of high-risk behaviour can simply be wrong because of misinformation or inattention to media messages. Moreover, because HIV may not lead to symptoms of AIDS for many years, unprotected sexual contact produces no immediate feedback to deter its continued practice. In fact, the absence of immediate consequences probably bolsters erroneously optimistic expectancies.

From Maslow's perspective, sexual behaviour can satisfy both physiological and belongingness needs, so it is a powerful source of motivation. When the behaviour is life threatening, safety needs should be activated; however, the absence of any obvious negative impact of high-risk behaviour for several years could provide a false sense of safety and allow other motives to be expressed in behaviour.

APPLY + DISCUSS

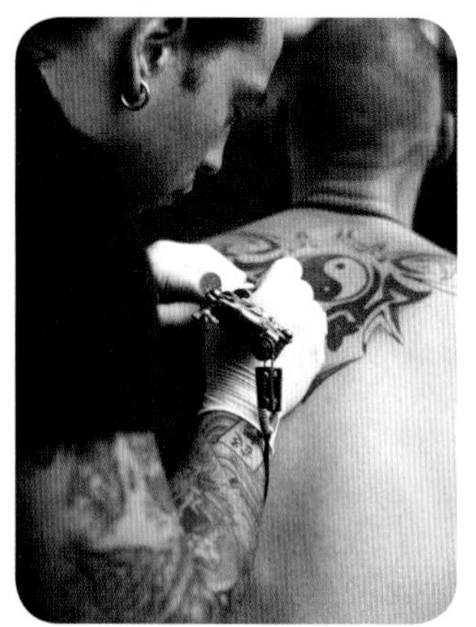

- How might the different theoretical approaches explain the self-inflicted pain people endure in order to sport a tattoo or pierced body parts?
- How would Maslow account for such behaviour?

A GLOBAL VISTA

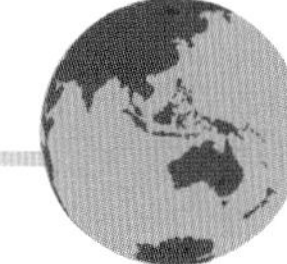

Cultural influences on motivation

Although the major approaches to motivation take the individual as their starting point, cross-cultural work suggests that culture plays a substantial role in shaping motivation (Benedict, 1934). For example, some societies, such as Australia and New Zealand, view the personal accumulation of material wealth as a worthy end of individual endeavour and even celebrate wealthy people (especially people from humble backgrounds who have 'self-made' success stories). In contrast, other cultures disapprove of accumulating material goods for oneself or one's family, considering it a crime against the community or a mark of poor character. The Kapauka Papuans of New Guinea strictly punish individual wealth (Pospisil, 1963). Disapproval or sanctions against individual consumption are common in agricultural or peasant societies, where resources tend to be limited and people tend to be oriented more to the good of the community (Foster, 1965).

Interestingly, it can also be argued that there are conflicting views on high achievement in Australian culture. This reflects the so-called 'tall poppy' syndrome which is part of Australian folklore. That is, on the one hand, high achievers are valued and praised, and seen as important for the nation's progress; but on the other hand, they are seen as 'tall poppies' who should be cut down and brought back to a common level (Feather, 1994; Peeters, 2004).

Psychologist Erich Fromm (1955) argued that a culture's socioeconomic system shapes people's motivations so that they *want* to act in ways that the system *needs* them to act. In other words, for an economic system to work, it must create individuals whose personal needs match the needs of the system. A capitalist economy such as our own depends on workers and consumers to be materialistic. If advertisements for digital cameras or rewriteable CD drives did not motivate people, entrepreneurs would not create them and ultimately the economy would stagnate.

The impact of culture can be seen in the conditions that foster intrinsic motivation in children. Contemporary Western cultures are highly individualistic and hence place a high premium on autonomy and self-direction. In contrast, most non-Western cultures are much more group centred. In these cultures, getting along with others, honouring one's family and parents and participating in the life of the community tend to be more highly valued (chapter 18). For example, in contemporary Aboriginal culture in Australia, primacy is often given to 'social' capital over 'economic' capital — that is, relationships with family and other community members are prized more highly than material wealth (Broadbent & Boyle, 2005; Broadbent, Boyle, & Carmody, 2006; Martin & Liddle, 1997).

Cultural influences can also be seen in the different characteristics and approaches of students in different countries. Research has found that Western students tend to be more self-directed and independent while students from the Asia Pacific region tend to be more passive and dependent on direction from their teacher (Biggs, 1999; Smith & Smith, 1999). In their research on students in Australian universities, Volet and Ang (1998) identified a lack of interaction between Australian students and international students from Asian backgrounds. They found that Chinese-ethnic students had a collectivist approach to study while Australian students tended to be more individualistic. This reflects the social values of the cultures these students originated from. Smith and Smith also investigated the varied approaches to study among Malaysian–Chinese, Singaporean and Hong Kong university students studying in Australia. They found students from Hong Kong were motivated by a fear of failure, Singaporean students were deeper and more efficient learners and Malaysian–Chinese students had less developed study skills. These differences in study approaches and motivations were also related to differences in cultural background.

INTERIM SUMMARY

Social and cultural practices play a substantial role in shaping motives. Influences on what children come to find intrinsically motivating may be very different depending on whether they come from a culture that emphasises individualism and personal control over choices or one that emphasises collectivism and group identity.

Eating

Having explored the major perspectives in motivation, we now turn to specific motives, beginning with eating. At its most basic level, the motivation to eat is biologically based, but the story is not that simple. We often eat in advance of severe caloric depletion. We eat because it smells good; we eat because a friend says 'How about lunch?'; we eat in response to a vast variety of signals, many of which are not related to need. However, in general the function of eating is not to relieve anxiety, frustration or boredom but to convert what were once the cells of other living organisms into energy.

Metabolism refers to the processes by which the body transforms food into energy for moving muscles, maintaining body heat, operating the nervous system, and building and maintaining organ tissue. Much of that energy comes from glucose, a simple sugar. What makes metabolism a complex process is that the body has to maintain energy at all times, even though we cannot be eating at all times.

Metabolism thus has two phases (figure 10.4; see overleaf): absorptive and fasting. In the ***absorptive phase***, the person is ingesting food. During this phase, the body 'runs' on some of the food it is absorbing but puts additional reserves into short- and long-term stores. The short-term 'fuel tanks' store carbohydrates by converting glucose to a more complex sugar (glycogen), which is stored throughout the body but particularly in the liver. The long-term energy tanks, located under the skin and in the abdomen, contain primarily fats (lipids). Fat cells are capable of expanding enormously when reserves are high. From an evolutionary perspective, the ability to store fat served our ancestors well. When winter came and food was scarce, they had both extra reserves of body fuel and an extra layer of warmth.

The second phase of metabolism, the ***fasting phase***, occurs when a person is not eating, as the body converts its short- and long-term reserves into energy. In starvation, both these sources of fuel become depleted, and the body starts converting proteins into fuel, often breaking down muscle.

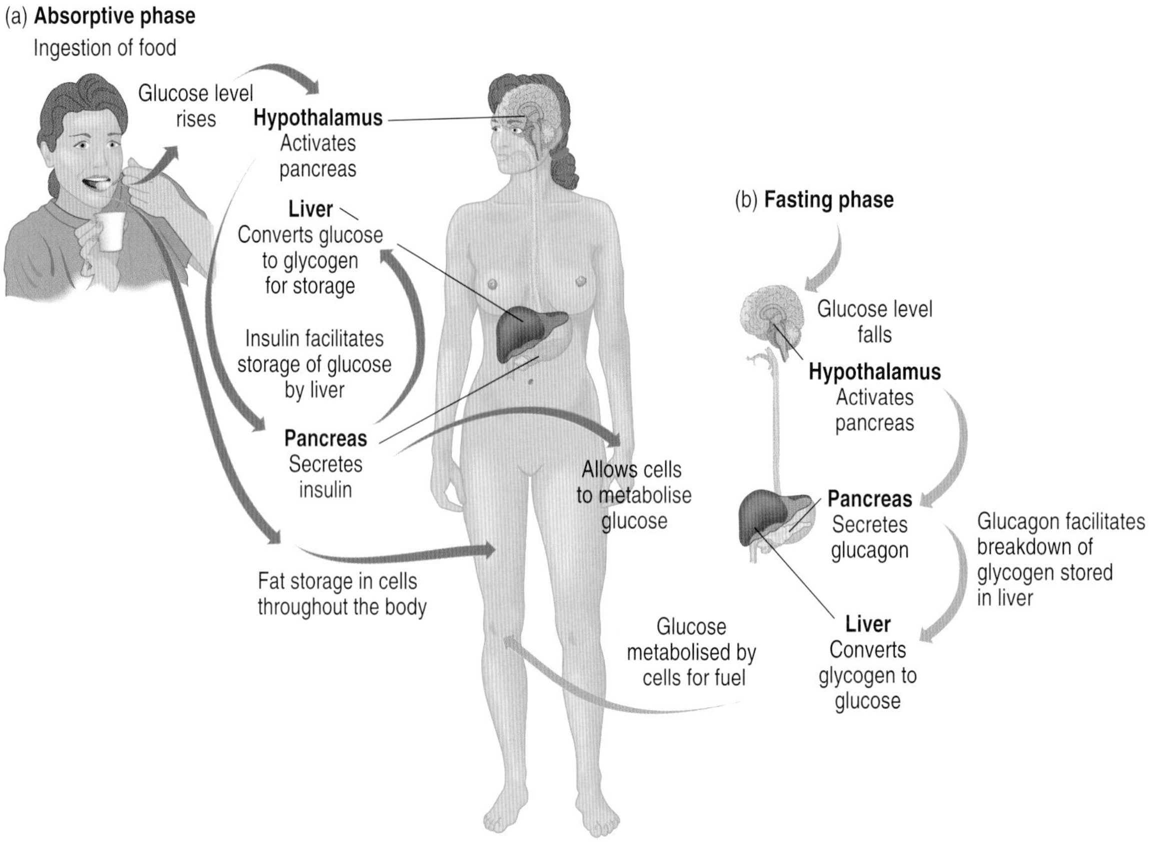

FIGURE 10.4
Metabolism. During the absorptive phase (a), the person ingests food. The hypothalamus detects rising glucose rates in the bloodstream and activates the pancreas, which secretes insulin. Insulin allows cells to absorb and convert glucose into energy for their use. Insulin also is required for the liver to convert glucose into glycogen to provide a short-term energy reservoir. In the fasting phase (b), when the individual is not eating, the hypothalamus detects falling glucose levels and activates the pancreas. The pancreas now secretes glucagon, which helps convert the glycogen in the liver into glucose, which the cells in the body can metabolise.

Homoeostasis

Biological functions such as eating, drinking and sleeping are regulated by a process called ***homoeostasis***, which refers to the body's tendency to maintain a relatively constant state that permits cells to live and function. Homoeostasis literally means 'standing still' (or, more accurately, 'standing similarly'). Homoeostasis requires mechanisms for both *detecting* the state of the system (e.g. determining whether the body has enough nutrients) and *correcting* the situation to restore the system to the desired state (e.g. searching for food).

Cells in the body can live only within a fairly narrow range of conditions (e.g. at the right temperature and bathed in the right amount of water). Thus, humans, like other animals, evolved systems for regulating these conditions. These systems work much like a thermostat in a house. If the thermostat ('the detector') is set at 25 degrees, the heating remains off if the temperature inside meets or exceeds 25 degrees. When the temperature drops below that point, a circuit running from the system's thermometer switches on the heating long enough to restore the temperature to 25 degrees (the correcting mechanism). Once feedback from the thermostat signals that the goal is attained, the heating is again deactivated.

Eating is part of a complex homoeostatic process. Energy reserves become depleted, and the person becomes hungry and eats. As the fuel tanks become full, ingestion stops, until reserves again become depleted. Like other homoeostatic systems, the system that regulates food intake includes several features. First, the system has mechanisms that act like a ***set point*** (or set points), a biologically optimal level the system strives to maintain (in this case, nutrients that provide fuel for cells to do their work). Second, the system must have ***feedback mechanisms*** that provide information regarding the state of the system with respect to the variables being regulated. Thus, the body contains receptors that monitor, for example, how much sugar is in the bloodstream and provide feedback to the brain. Finally, the system must have ***corrective mechanisms*** that restore the system to its set point when needed (in this case, finding and ingesting food).

Two features of this description of homoeostatic process are worth noting. First, although homoeostatic processes most obviously apply to biological needs (e.g. for food, water and air), similar mechanisms are involved in regulating many motives, such as maintaining closeness to people to whom we are deeply attached (Bowlby, 1969; Pittman & Zeigler, 2006). Similar processes occur with regulation of emotional states as well. For example, an unemployed person who feels stressed after two unsuccessful months on the job market may work even harder to find a job or may start drinking to kill the emotional pain. Both are mechanisms aimed at turning off a painful 'feedback' signal (distress), although one is more likely to restore financial security and self-esteem.

Second, in many motivational systems, particularly physiological ones such as hunger and thirst, there may be a substantial lag between the time corrective mechanisms have kicked in to restore the system to homoeostasis and the time the system registers their effects. For example, by the time a hungry person has eaten enough to restore his energy reserves, only a small part of this food has actually been digested — the receptors designed to detect nutrient levels do not yet have all the 'data' necessary to turn off eating. Thus, the body has evolved two separate systems: hunger, for 'turning on' eating; and ***satiety mechanisms***, for turning off ingestive behaviour. The satiety mechanisms are designed to make us feel sated so we will close our mouths long enough to let the food 'sink in'.

INTERIM SUMMARY

Metabolism, the processes by which the body transforms food into energy, has two phases: the ***absorptive phase***, in which the person is ingesting food, and the ***fasting phase***, during which the body converts its short- and long-term stores into energy. ***Homoeostasis*** refers to the body's tendency to maintain a relatively constant state that permits cells to live and function. Homoeostatic processes, including those involved in eating, have several common features. These include a ***set point***, or optimal level the system strives to maintain; ***feedback mechanisms*** that provide the system with information regarding the state of the system with respect to the set point; and ***corrective mechanisms*** that restore the system to its set point when needed. ***Satiety mechanisms*** turn off ingestive behaviour.

What turns hunger on?

Feelings of hunger caused by physiological need ultimately derive from dropping levels of glucose and lipids in the bloodstream as the body draws increasingly on its long-term stores. Because the nervous system can use glucose (and cannot, like the rest of the body, metabolise fats), it has its own glucose detectors (located on the 'brain' side of the blood–brain barrier) that detect falling blood-sugar levels (Carlson, 1999). The body has additional detectors that monitor both glucose and fats, located in the liver, which send specific signals to the brain (Woods, Schwartz, Baskin, & Seeley, 2000). Signals from both liver and brain receptors appear to converge in the brainstem and together play a significant role in feelings of hunger.

Although most people think they become hungry because their stomachs feel empty, glucose levels probably play the most important role in producing feelings of hunger. Even people whose stomachs have been removed because of cancer nonetheless report feeling hunger (Janowitz & Grossman, 1949).

Although we cannot ask rats how hungry they are, injecting small amounts of glucose into their bloodstream when glucose levels begin to drop delays feeding behaviour (Campfield, Brandon, & Smith, 1985). In humans, subjective sensations of hunger increase as glucose levels decrease. In a study that compared the reported sensations of hunger in two groups of well-fed participants, one of which received an injection of a drug that suppresses blood glucose levels, the experimental group felt hungrier, even after a meal (Thompson & Campbell, 1977; see also Ciampolini & Bianchi, 2006). In another study, the investigators continuously recorded participants' glucose levels, subjective ratings of hunger and requests for food (Campfield, Arthur, Francoise, Rosenbaum, & Hirsch, 1996). Just after momentary decreases in glucose levels, participants tended to feel hungry and ask for food.

The role of the hypothalamus

Above the brainstem, the hypothalamus (figure 10.5; see overleaf) plays a key role in hunger and eating, as it does in virtually all homoeostatic processes (Lawrence, Turnbull, & Rothwell, 1999). Researchers once believed that one section of the hypothalamus — the lateral hypothalamus — was the 'on' switch for eating, whereas another region — the ventromedial hypothalamus — was the 'off' switch (Anand &

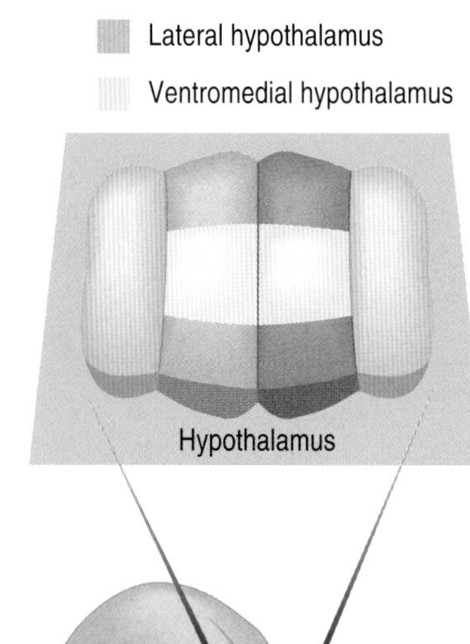

FIGURE 10.5
The hypothalamus and eating. Decades ago, researchers began studying the roles of the ventromedial hypothalamus (*ventral* meaning towards the bottom of the brain, and *medial* meaning towards the middle) and lateral hypothalamus (*lateral* meaning on the sides) in eating. Destruction of the ventromedial hypothalamus can lead to obesity in rats.

Brobeck, 1951; Teitelbaum, 1961). They based this theory in part on the fact that lesions to the lateral hypothalamus led rats to stop eating, and lesions to the ventromedial hypothalamus led them to eat ravenously.

The theory turned out to have several problems. For example, rats with damage to the lateral hypothalamus show deficits in other motivated behaviours, such as thirst and sex. More recent research suggests that eating, like virtually all psychological functions, reflects the action of neural circuits that run throughout the brain, and that, although the hypothalamus plays a central role, it is not the brain's 'eating centre' (Sakurai et al., 1998; Winn, 1995).

The lateral hypothalamus does, however, play a central role in initiating eating. A neurotransmitter found in this region, called neuropeptide Y, is particularly important in turning on eating, whereas the ventromedial hypothalamus is particularly important in producing off signals. Both regions of the hypothalamus, however, contain chemicals that can turn eating off *and* on, and both require substantial input from brainstem circuits that integrate information about blood glucose levels, taste and smell. The hypothalamus also feeds information to the cortex, particularly the frontal cortex, which regulates the motor behaviours involved in finding and ingesting food.

The role of external cues in eating

Hunger is the prime motivator for eating, but external factors also influence the inclination to eat. In fact, desire for a food can be motivated either by hunger or simply by its palatability, or taste. Moreover, these two sources of eating motivation are mediated by different neural pathways and neurotransmitters (Berridge, 1996). Palatability plays an important role (Sorensen, Moller, Flint, Martens, & Raben, 2003), even in animals not known for their gourmet tastes (Capaldi & VandenBos, 1991; Warwick, Hall, Pappas, & Schiffman, 1993). Rats, like humans, like variety in their diets, and as pet owners can attest, dogs and cats may grow tired of a brand of food and walk away from a delightful and nutritious bowl of horse meat or tuna innards even if they are hungry. Some taste preferences are inborn, such as the preference of human infants and baby rats for sweet tastes, while others depend on exposure and learning.

Some researchers argue that learned factors of this sort play a larger role in arousal of hunger than do homoeostatic processes (Woods, Schwartz, Baskin, & Seeley, 2000). For example, rats fed consistently at particular times of day will develop classically conditioned hormonal and other chemical responses that prepare the body for food and 'turn on' eating behaviour. Much of eating is also regulated by learning and habit, as people learn to eat at particular times of day or in particular situations.

Another external factor that influences the motive to eat is the presence of other people. One study gave participants pocket-sized cards on which they were to record both their food intake and dining companions for seven consecutive days (de Castro & Brewer, 1992). The more people present, the more participants ate. Meals eaten with a large group of people were 75 percent larger than meals eaten alone.

What turns hunger off?

Although hunger and satiety signals certainly interact, the mechanisms that stop eating are not the same ones that start it. The signals that stop eating begin with tastes and smells, some learned and some innate, that signal that certain food is better left alone. And noticing that our plate is empty or that other people are no longer eating can certainly signal that dinnertime is over.

Feelings of satiety (fullness, or satiation), however, usually begin in the stomach and intestines. Not only does the stomach wall have stretch receptors that send messages to the brain signalling that enough is enough, but even more important are receptors in the stomach and intestines that detect levels of nutrients. For example, rats will eat more when their stomachs are full of saline solution than of a high-calorie liquid, a suggestion that glucose receptors are involved in feelings of satiety as well as hunger (Angel, Hauger, Giblin, & Paul, 1992; Deutsch & Gonzalez, 1980). Over the long run, knowing when to stop is also regulated by a protein, called leptin, which is secreted by well-stocked fat cells (chapter 14).

APPLY + DISCUSS

- Do people differ in the extent to which their eating behaviour reflects feelings (e.g. taste and mood), cognitions (e.g. knowledge about calories and body image) and arousal (hunger)?
- How might these differences develop?

INTERIM SUMMARY

Feelings of hunger derive from dropping levels of glucose and lipids in the bloodstream, which are detected by receptors in the liver and brainstem. This information is transmitted to regions of the hypothalamus involved in both hunger and satiety. Eating is also influenced by external cues, such as palatability, time of day and presence of other people. Satiety occurs through a number of mechanisms, including tastes and smells but primarily through detection of nutrients in the stomach and intestines.

Obesity

Obesity is one of the easiest to recognise, and most difficult to treat, physical or medical conditions (Devlin, Yanovski, & Wilson, 2000; Elfhag & Rossner, 2005; Teixeira, Going, Sardinha, & Lohman, 2005). ***Obesity*** is defined as body weight 15 percent or more above the ideal for one's height and age. In Australia, about 25 percent of the adult population can be considered obese, and a further 37 percent can be considered overweight (Australian Bureau of Statistics [ABS], 2009d). New Zealand shows comparable results. There has been a dramatic increase in the proportion of overweight and obese Australians, with men more likely than women to be overweight. From 1995 to 2007–08, for people aged 18 years and over, the proportion of overweight or obese women increased from 49 to 55 percent, and the proportion of overweight or obese men increased from 64 to 68 percent (ABS, 2009d). Some 68 percent of Australian males and 55 percent of Australian females consider themselves overweight or obese (ABS, 2009d). These rates are higher in older age groups. For example, 75 percent of people in the 65–74 age group were either overweight or obese. However, the results for children are still alarming. For children aged 5–17 years, 17 percent were classified as overweight and 8 percent were classified as obese (ABS, 2009d).

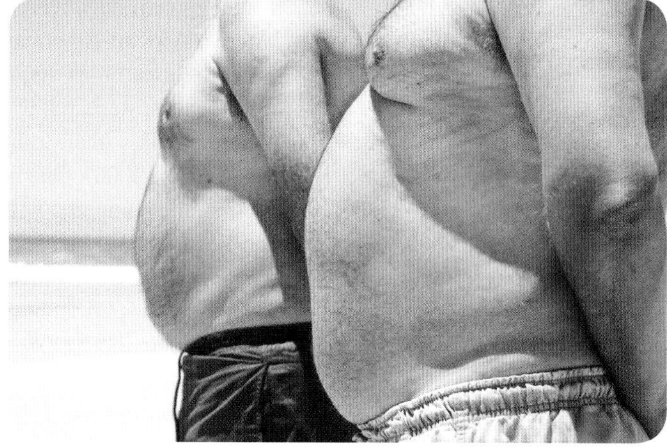

About 62 percent of Australian adults are overweight or obese, increasing their risk of developing type 2 diabetes, heart disease and some cancers.

In industrialised countries, fatness tends to be inversely correlated with socioeconomic status; that is, people in lower social classes tend to be more obese. In developing nations, the direction of this correlation is reversed: the richer, the fatter (at least for women) (Sobal & Stunkard, 1989). The situation in the developing world probably approximates the state of affairs through most of human evolution. Particularly for women, whose pregnancies could extend into times of scarcity, larger internal food reserves were adaptive in the face of variable external reserves. In fact, societies in which food is scarce tend to associate beauty with bulk, since women who are healthy and have more resources tend to be heavier (Triandis, 1994). From an evolutionary point of view, human eating behaviour evolved in conditions of scarcity and unpredictability, leading to evolved mechanisms that probably influence us to eat at our physiological limits when food is available (Pinel, Assanand, & Lehman, 2000). These mechanisms may not be so adaptive when people have to hunt for food on menus instead of in forests.

Obesity places people at increased risk for a number of medical problems, such as heart disease, high blood pressure and diabetes (Brownell & Rodin, 1994; Pinel et al., 2000). The mortality rates of overweight people are up to four times higher than in people of normal weight (Foreyt, 1987; Malnick & Knobler, 2006; Woo, Ho, Yuen, Yu, & Lau, 1998). More than 1000 New Zealanders die each year from obesity-related diseases — twice the number that die on the nation's roads (New Zealand Ministry of Health, 2004). Australian studies have found that mortality and morbidity are also associated with the amount of weight gained in adult life. For example, a weight gain of 10 kilograms or more since young adulthood is associated with increased mortality, coronary heart disease, hypertension, stroke and Type 2 diabetes (Department of Health and Ageing, 2004). On the other hand, the ways people try to lose weight — such as over-reliance on 'diet pills', semi-starvation diets and self-induced vomiting — can also lead to health risks (Berg, 1999). In Australia, frequent dieting (five or more diets in a one-year period) was associated significantly with poorer mental and physical health (Kenardy, 1997b; see also Kenardy, Brown, & Vogt, 2001). Obesity and the health risks associated with it are often preventable through an active lifestyle, and reality shows like *The Biggest Loser* are intended to kick-start a healthy lifestyle for contestants.

Culture, gender and conceptions of weight and obesity

Although obesity can be defined objectively, the subjective experience of being overweight can vary considerably by individual, gender and culture. Western societies are preoccupied with thinness, particularly for women. At any given moment, two-thirds of high school girls in the United States report that they are trying to lose weight (Rosen & Gross, 1987). From age nine to 14, girls (unlike boys) show steady increases in concerns about their weight as well as tendencies to binge at least once a month, probably reflecting their efforts to keep their weight down by overly restricting food intake (Field et al., 1999). A study in Australia found that almost 50 percent of women aged 18 to 22 had dieted to lose weight in the previous 12 months (Kenardy, 1997b). Further, 20 percent of women considered underweight (body mass index <18.5) were dieting to lose as well. In Western cultures, stereotypes about the obese are extremely negative (Crandall, 1994) and begin as early as kindergarten (Hsu, 1989; Rothblum, 1992). Children who are overweight are teased and often develop both lowered self-esteem and negative expectations about the way others will treat them (Miller & Downey, 1999).

Whereas most white women complain about their weight even when their weight is biologically in the 'ideal' range, African-American culture has different norms (Rand & Kuldau, 1990). In one study, African-American women were heavier than their white counterparts, but they were more satisfied with their weight and less likely to find weight on other people (particularly women) unattractive (Harris, Walters, & Waschull, 1991). Overall, men were more concerned about the weight of their dates than women were, but African-American men were less likely than white men to refuse to date a woman because of her weight. Other research finds that white women rate heavier women (especially other white women) negatively on multiple dimensions (such as attractiveness, intelligence and popularity), whereas African-American women do not (Hebl & Heatherton, 1998).

More research is required to understand cross-cultural differences in eating and body image disturbances. Research by colleagues in Australia and New Zealand indicates that to date, findings are mixed, and it is unclear the extent to which an eating disorder differs across cultures (see Soh, Touyz, & Surgenor, 2006). One Australian study looked at attitudes towards body shape among women born in Australia compared with women who had migrated to Australia. It found that young migrant Asian and European women had greater satisfaction with their body weight and shape than Australian-born women (Kenardy, 1997a). However, an interesting finding was the way attitudes changed over time. The longer the period the migrant women had been in Australia, the more similar their attitudes to body shape were to those of Australian-born women.

Views of beauty and obesity vary not only across and within cultures but also historically. Compared to the 'Rubenesque' view of beauty of just a few centuries ago (expressed in the art and culture of the period, in which the artist Rubens was painting nudes that might today be used in advertisements for weight-loss programs!), the prototypes of feminine beauty portrayed in the mass media today look emaciated. The standards have even changed considerably since the 1950s, when the ideal was the voluptuous beauty of Marilyn Monroe, replete with large breasts and slightly protruding abdomen.

Cultures set standards for body types that are considered attractive and unattractive. In Renoir's time in the late nineteenth and early twentieth centuries, beautiful meant bountiful. Even in the 1950s and 1960s, the standard of beauty was considerably plumper than it is now. Marilyn Monroe, for example, would probably be considered chubby today — and might well have difficulty making it in Hollywood. A study of *Playboy*'s centrefolds found a 10 percent decrease in the ratio of weight to height from the late 1950s to the late 1970s. This trend was paralleled by a dramatic increase in the number of articles on dieting in popular women's magazines (Garner et al., 1980, cited in Hsu, 1989).

The way others behave towards obese people in our culture may actually lead them to *behave* less attractively. In one study, obese and non-obese women conversed on the phone with other participants who did not know them and could not see them (Miller, Rothblum, Barbour, & Brand, 1990). University student raters, unaware of the participants' weights (or even of what the study was about), then listened to the recorded conversations and rated the women on their social skills, likeability and probable physical attractiveness. Not only did the raters view the obese women more negatively on all dimensions, but correlations between kilograms overweight and every other variable suggested that coders could judge physical appearance from purely auditory cues. The heavier the participant, the less socially skilled, likeable and physically attractive she was perceived to be.

We will discuss other aspects of obesity in detail in chapter 14.

APPLY + DISCUSS

- Given that virtually all women in the West are exposed to the same skinny models, why do some women develop eating disorders while others do not?
- How firm is the line between eating disorders and the preoccupation with issues of food and weight shown by many girls and women in the West?

INTERIM SUMMARY

Obesity — having a body weight more than 15 percent above the ideal for one's height and age — is highly prevalent in some countries, particularly Australia. Attitudes about weight vary considerably by culture, class, ethnic group and level of affluence of a society. The causes of obesity lie in both nature and nurture.

Sexual motivation

Like hunger, sex is a universal drive based in biology, but its expression varies considerably from culture to culture and from person to person. In fact, sexual motivation is even more variable than hunger. Most people eat two or three meals a day, whereas sexual appetites defy generalisations. Sexual behaviour is driven as much by fantasies as by hormones; indeed, the primary sexual organ in humans is arguably not the genitals but the brain.

Although psychoanalysis broke down many of the Victorian taboos against discussing sexuality, sex did not become a respectable area of scientific research until Alfred Kinsey and his colleagues published two massive volumes on the sexual behaviour of the human male and female (Kinsey, Pomeroy, & Martin, 1948; Kinsey, Pomeroy, Martin, & Gebhard, 1953). Many of Kinsey's findings, based on interviews with thousands of adults, provoked shock and outrage. For instance, some 37 percent of males and 13 percent of females reported having engaged in homosexual activity at some time in their lives. Research in Australia finds slightly lower rates of male homosexual activity, but otherwise paints a similar picture (Grulich, de Visser, Smith, Rissel, & Richters, 2003). More recently, the Australian Research Centre in Sex, Health and Society at La Trobe University found that in 2004, both young women and young men were more likely to be attracted exclusively to the same sex and to identify as gay, homosexual, or lesbian than in 1998, perhaps reflecting greater acceptance within society (Hillier, Turner, & Mitchell, 2005). The average sexually active person in Australia reports having intercourse approximately twice a week and becomes sexually active between ages 17 and 19, although many start earlier or later (Australian Research Centre in Sex, Health & Society, 2004). The Australian Study of Health and Relationships conducted by researchers from La Trobe University, the University of Sydney and the University of New South Wales reported that Australians are having sex at a younger age and with more partners than their parents. It was further found that the majority of respondents (aged 16 to 59) believed that sex before marriage was acceptable. A similar trend is evident in New Zealand: the age of starting sexual activity is decreasing while the number of sexual partners is increasing (New Zealand Ministry of Health, 2001). Furthermore, Durex's global sex survey results indicate that 57 percent of New Zealand men and women are putting themselves at risk by continuing to practise unsafe sex (Durex, 2007). This is more than 20 percent higher than the global average of 35 percent. Most of the New Zealanders surveyed (22 percent) reported having sex three to four times per week.

Since the time of the Kinsey report, and especially since the sexual revolution of the 1960s and 1970s, sexual attitudes and practices in Western cultures have become much more liberal. For example, in a study that used the original Kinsey data for comparison, both white and black women reported earlier age at first intercourse, a wider range of sexual practices, a larger number of sexual partners, and reduced likelihood of marrying their first lover (Wyatt, Peters, & Guthrie, 1988a, 1988b). In Australia, the average age of first intercourse for men has dropped from around 18 to 16 during the past 30 years. Today, the majority of Year 12 students will have already started sexual activity (Australian Research

About half of all Year 12 students will have had sex before they finish their schooling.

Centre in Sex, Health & Society, 2003; see also Smith, Agius, Mitchell, Barrett, & Pitts, 2009). For example, a national survey of almost 2500 students in Years 10 and 12 from all school sectors found that in Year 10, 27.8 percent of male students and 24.2 percent of female students reported having had sex, while in Year 12, the rates were 48.3 percent for male students and 45.7 percent for female students (Australian Research Centre in Sex, Health & Society, 2003).

The fourth National Survey of Secondary Students and Sexual Health conducted in Australia in 2008 involved nearly 3000 Year 10 and Year 12 students from more than 100 secondary schools, including government, Catholic and independent schools from across the country. The results show that the proportion of students who had experienced sexual intercourse has increased between the 2002 and 2008 surveys. In 2002, 35 percent of students reported having sexual intercourse, with this proportion increasing to 40 percent in 2008 (Smith et al., 2009). In this time, there has also been an increase in students' confidence in talking with their parents about sex, and in the use of contraception, such as the birth control pill (Smith et al., 2009).

The sexual response cycle

A major step forward in the scientific study of sex was William Masters and Virginia Johnson's (1966) path-breaking book, *Human Sexual Response*. By observing several hundred women and men in the laboratory, Masters and Johnson discovered that similar physiological changes take place during sex in both women and men, a pattern they termed the ***sexual response cycle*** (figure 10.6).

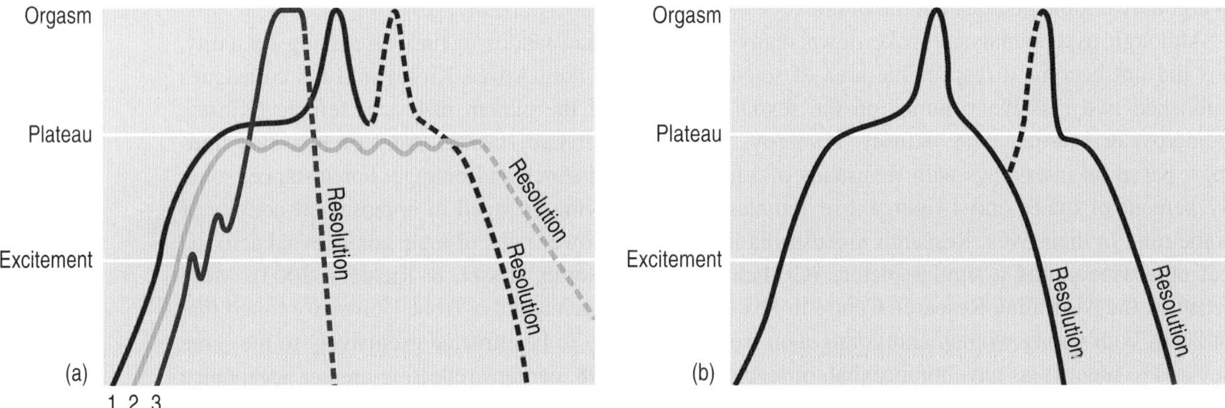

FIGURE 10.6
Sexual response cycles. Part (a) depicts the variations of sensation in women's sexual response. Part (b) illustrates the typical male sexual response cycle. The two are practically indistinguishable, except for the greater variability in women's experience.

SOURCE: Masters and Johnson (1966, p. 5).

The sexual response cycle begins with a phase of excitement, characterised by increased muscle tension, engorgement of blood vessels in the genitals causing erection of the penis and lubrication of the vagina and often a skin flush. Maximum arousal occurs during the second, or plateau, phase. During this stage, heart rate, respiration, muscle tension and blood pressure reach their peak. The third phase, orgasm, is characterised by vaginal contractions in females and expulsion of semen in males. During the fourth phase, resolution, physiological and psychological functioning gradually return to normal.

The subjective experience of orgasm is very similar in men and women. When given written descriptions of orgasms, psychologists, medical students and gynaecologists are unable to distinguish men's from women's if not told the writer's gender (Vance & Wagner, 1976). This finding makes some sense, given that women and men experience similar rhythmic muscular contractions during orgasm.

However, the female sexual response cycle does seem to be more variable. Women describe a few different types of orgasm, from mild pulsations to a sharp climax to repeated sensations of orgasm (Bardwick, 1971). In addition, many women do not reach orgasm with every sexual encounter (figure 10.7), but they do report a sense of sexual release even without experiencing orgasm (Butler, 1976).

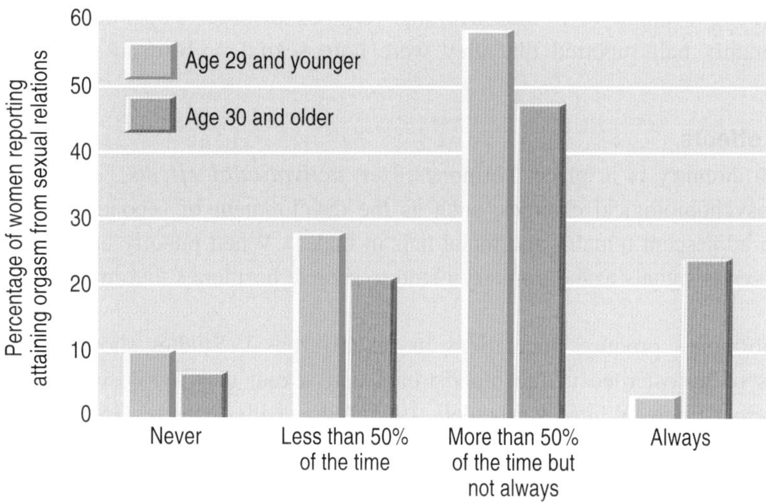

FIGURE 10.7
Female orgasm. Most women achieve orgasm most of the time during sex with male partners, but women over 30 have learned to do so more often.

SOURCE: Butler (1976).

In many animal species, females and males are genetically programmed to follow very specific, stereotyped mating rituals, with attraction and mating behaviour often controlled by pheromones. In the American cockroach, pheromone detection leads the male to touch its antennae to the female's antennae, spread its wings, and turn 180 degrees in a courtship dance (Seelinger & Schuderer, 1985). Even in species less reliant on pheromonal communication, mating behaviour is often rigidly instinctive.

Humans do not have the same kinds of genetically based mating rituals or mating seasons as other animals. However, biological influences on human dating and mating are obvious, from the 'plumage' displayed by both sexes at a party, to scents with names such as 'Passion' and 'Musk', to the simple fact that most humans choose to mate only with members of their own species.

APPLY + DISCUSS

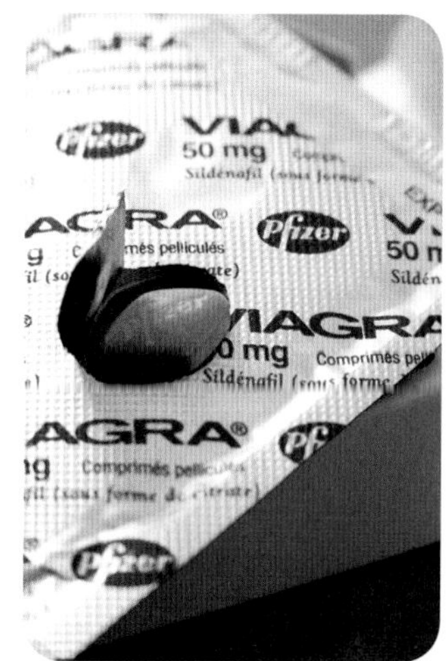

Many people have problems with sexual functioning at some point in their lives. These include trouble getting and keeping an erection, premature ejaculation, inhibited desire and sexual inhibitions of other sorts that lead to reduced sexual satisfaction or to marital distress.

- How freely should doctors dispense Viagra without thoroughly examining a patient and his or her partner psychologically as well as physically?

Biology and sexual motivation

Many key aspects of sexual behaviour in humans and other animals are under hormonal control. Hormones have two effects on the nervous system and behaviour: organisational and activational.

Organisational effects

Hormones exert ***organisational effects*** on the circuitry, or 'organisation', of the brain and thereby influence sexual behaviour. In humans, these effects occur prenatally. Foetuses will develop into females unless something very particular happens. This 'something particular' is the presence of two kinds of hormones secreted in the third month of pregnancy. One hormone 'turns off' female development. The other set of hormones, called androgens (of which the most important is testosterone), 'turns on' male development. Doctors can often tell the sex of a foetus by the fourth month using ultrasound. Other hormones, such as estrogen, appear to have organisational effects that lead to non-reproductive differences between males and females, such as cognitive differences (McEwen, Alves, Bulloch, & Weiland, 1998; chapter 3).

The fact that some hormones turn male development on while others turn female development off explains some otherwise perplexing syndromes (Money, 1987; Money & Ehrhardt, 1972). In ***androgen insensitivity syndrome***, a genetic male develops female genitalia. The testes secrete androgens, but a genetic defect leads to an absence of androgen receptors. Thus, the body responds as if no androgen were present. The child is reared as a girl, usually leading a perfectly normal life, except that she does not develop internal female organs (and hence is sterile) because the hormone secreted by the testes that *turns off* female development continues to function. People with this disorder, who are by all outward appearances female, are rarely attracted to other females, even though they have testes instead of ovaries. (Their testicles are not externally visible.)

A very different course of development occurs in ***congenital adrenal hyperplasia***, a condition in which the adrenal glands secrete too much androgen, leading to masculinisation of the genitals in females. The result is an enlarged clitoris and labia that may resemble a penis and scrotum. (In utero, the tissue that becomes the scrotum in males will become labia if the testes do not secrete androgens.) Among a sample of women with this very rare disorder who would discuss their sexual orientation, roughly half reported that they were homosexual or bisexual (Money, Schwartz, & Lewis, 1984).

Activational effects

Once the brain circuitry is in place, hormones exert ***activational effects***, activating brain circuits that produce psychobiological changes, such as the development of secondary sex characteristics (e.g. breasts in adolescent females and facial hair in males). When puberty begins, for example, the hypothalamus sends signals to the pituitary gland to secrete hormones that in turn activate the testes and ovaries.

In males, hormones produce fluctuations in sexual arousal. Studies show a direct association between levels of testosterone in the bloodstream and sexual activity, desire and arousal in men (Schiavi, Schreiner-Engle, White, & Mandeli, 1991; Udry, Billy, Morris, Groff, & Raj, 1985). One study demonstrated the relationship experimentally by administering doses of testosterone to adult males (Alexander, Swerdloff, Wang, & Davidson, 1997). During the time in which their testosterone levels were chemically inflated, the men reported more sexual desire and enjoyment when presented with erotic auditory stimulation. They also showed increased attention to sexual words presented in the unattended channel in a dichotic listening task. The data are less clear for women (see Hedricks, 1994; Regan, 1996).

APPLY + DISCUSS

- Are most males innately wired to find the female form appealing, or is this attraction primarily learned behaviour?

Culture and sexual behaviour

Although biology plays an important role in sexual motivation, anthropological studies show enormous cultural diversity in both the ways people carry out sexual acts and the types of behaviours they consider acceptable (Davis & Whitten, 1987; see also Ember & Ember, 2004). Among the Basongye people of the Congo, for instance, the conventional position for intercourse is for partners to lie facing each other with the woman on her left side and the man on his right; the woman lifts her right leg to allow the man to enter (Merriam, 1971). In many parts of Melanesia and India, the woman typically lies on her back as the man squats between her legs (Gebhard, 1971), whereas in Western cultures the male lying prone on top of the female is more typical.

Cultures also differ in their conceptions of male and female sexuality. Western cultures view men as having greater sexual needs. Other cultures believe just the opposite (Gordon & Shankweiler, 1971; Griffitt, 1987).

INTERIM SUMMARY

Sexual motivation and behaviour are highly variable across cultures and individuals. Masters and Johnson discovered a common pattern of physiological changes that takes place in both women and men during sex called the ***sexual response cycle***. Hormones influence sexual behaviour through both ***organisational effects***, which influence the developing circuitry of the brain, and ***activational effects***, in which hormones activate those circuits.

Sexual orientation

Sexual orientation refers to the direction of a person's enduring sexual attraction: to members of the same sex, the opposite sex or both. Determining a person's sexual orientation is not as easy as it may seem. Many people report having occasional homosexual fantasies or encounters even though they are not homosexual. Stigma, discrimination, religious values and violence directed against homosexuals lead some people whose sexual motives and fantasies are primarily homosexual to behave heterosexually or to abstain from sex, to deny their homosexuality or to take on the trappings of a heterosexual lifestyle, such as marriage to a member of the opposite sex. Roen (2004) has argued that some people do not fit neatly into the two dominant sex categories (i.e. heterosexual or homosexual) and that cultural insistencies that they do tends to marginalise such people.

Prevalence of homosexuality

In contemporary Western societies, approximately 2 to 7 percent of men and 1 percent of women consider themselves to be homosexual, although the numbers vary depending on how researchers phrase the questions.

An exclusive homosexual orientation is rare among animals, but homosexual behaviours occur frequently among many species, from lizards to chimpanzees (Money, 1987; Srivastava, Borries, & Sommer, 1991). The incidence of homosexuality has varied substantially historically and cross-culturally (Adams, 1985; Herdt, 1997). In a large part of the world, stretching from Sumatra throughout Melanesia, males almost universally participate in homosexual activities several years before they reach marriageable age (Herdt, 1984, 1997; Money & Ehrhardt, 1972). Yet even in some of these cultures, in which homosexual activity is normative during a particular time in life, the concept of homosexuality as a permanent state does not exist (Herdt, 1997).

In contemporary Western societies, approximately 2 to 7 percent of men and 1 percent of women consider themselves homosexual, although the numbers vary depending on how researchers phrase the questions (see Ellis & Ames, 1987; Pillard, Poumadere, & Carretta, 1981). In Australia, one study found that 1.6 percent of men and 0.8 percent of women identified themselves as homosexual, although 8.6 percent of men and 15.1 percent of women reported some same-sex sexual activity or attraction (Australian Research Centre in Sex, Health & Society, 2004).

Until relatively recently, both laypeople and the psychiatric community considered homosexuality a disorder; in fact, the official diagnostic manual of the American Psychiatric Association classified it as a disorder until 1973. People harbour many misperceptions about homosexuality, but one of the most pervasive is that homosexuality is a sexual *preference*. Psychologist John Money (1987), who has conducted some of the best-known research on homosexuality (and on sexuality in general), argues that people no more choose their sexual orientation than they select their native language or decide to be right handed.

Early markers of homosexual orientation

An accumulating body of research demonstrates that children who prefer to dress or act in ways typically associated with the opposite sex are more likely to become homosexual than other children; this is especially true in males (Bailey & Zucker, 1995). In fact, the best predictor of male homosexuality in adulthood is the presence in childhood of marked behavioural characteristics of the opposite sex (Bell, Weinberg, & Hammersmith, 1981; Green, 1987). Although this pattern applies only to a subset of homosexual men, and cross-gender behaviour is present in some boys who do not become homosexual, it is a strong predictor nonetheless.

Consider an example described in an interview with the mother of an eight-year-old boy (Green, 1987, pp. 2–3):

> *Mother:* He acts like a sissy. He has expressed the wish to be a girl. He doesn't play with boys. He's afraid of boys, because he's afraid to play boys' games. He used to like to dress in girls' clothing. He would still like to, only we have absolutely put our foot down. And he talks like a girl, sometimes walks like a girl, acts like a girl.
>
> *Interviewer:* What was the very earliest thing that you noticed?
>
> *Mother:* Wanting to put on a blouse of mine, a pink and white blouse which if he'd put it on it would fit him like a dress. And he was very excited about the whole thing, and leaped around and danced around the room. I didn't like it and I just told him to take it off and I put it away. He kept asking for it.
>
> *Interviewer:* You mentioned that he's expressed the wish to be a girl. Has he ever said, 'I am a girl'?
>
> *Mother:* Playing in front of the mirror, he'll undress for bed, and he's standing in front of the mirror and he took his penis and he folded it under, and he said, 'Look, Mommy, I'm a girl'.

A cross-cultural study reported the same finding in females. A major characteristic distinguishing homosexual and heterosexual females in Brazil, Peru, the Philippines and the United States was cross-gendered childhood behaviour (Whitam & Mathy, 1991). Lesbians in all four cultures were more interested in boys' toys and clothes and less interested in 'girl things' as defined by their cultures than were their heterosexual peers.

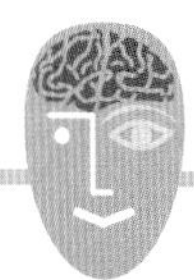

The biology of homosexuality

If sexual orientation is not a matter of conscious choice, what are its causes? Homosexuality is probably the end result of many causes, some environmental and some biological. However, most environmental hypotheses (such as absent or weak fathers and dominant mothers) have received little empirical support.

Researchers who emphasise the nature side of the nature–nurture question have had more success, particularly in explaining male homosexuality (figure 10.8). One study found differences in the neuroanatomy of homosexual and heterosexual men (LeVay, 1991). The investigator compared the brains of homosexual men (who died of AIDS complications) with men and women presumed to be heterosexual. He found that one specific set of nuclei in the hypothalamus was twice as large in heterosexual men as in women and homosexual men.

A more recent study compared the EEG patterns of heterosexual and homosexual men and women while performing a mental rotation task (at which men usually excel) and a verbal task (at which women usually outperform men). Heterosexual and lesbian women did not differ substantially from each other on either task. However, gay men's EEG patterns looked more like those of heterosexual women than heterosexual men on the mental rotation task (Wegesin, 1998). Across a number of studies, a clear finding has also emerged that homosexual men and women are more likely than heterosexuals to be left handed. This suggests early differences between heterosexuals and homosexuals (or, more likely, a subset of homosexual men and women) in the organisation of the brain (Lalumiere, Blanchard, & Zucker, 2000).

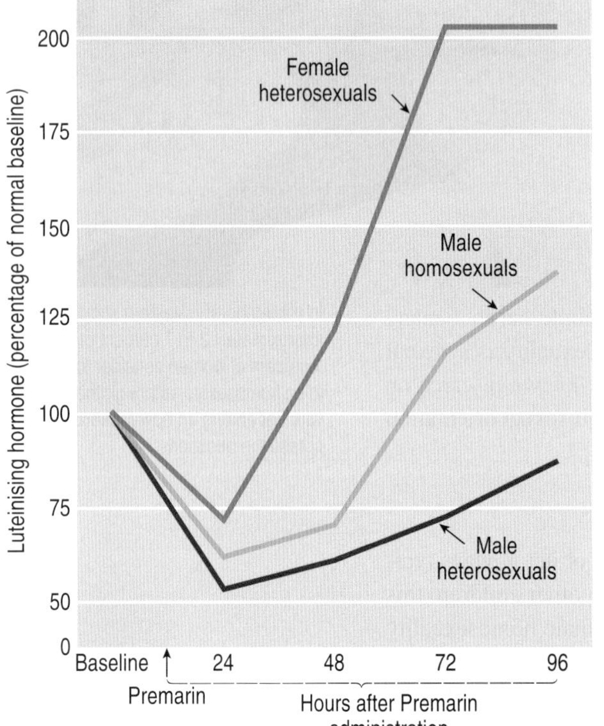

FIGURE 10.8
Hormonal response in male homosexuals. The graph shows the changes in the amount of luteinising hormone (LH) as a response to injections of the drug Premarin. Premarin increases LH in women and increases testosterone in men. Heterosexual men and women showed the expected hormonal responses to Premarin injection. The response of homosexual males, however, was intermediate between heterosexual men and women.

SOURCE: From Gladue, Green, and Hellman (1984). Reprinted with permission from AAAS.

The behavioural genetics of homosexuality

What causes these differences? An increasing body of evidence from behavioural genetics suggests that homosexuality in both men and women is highly heritable (Bailey et al., 1999). Several studies have found a higher incidence of homosexuality among male relatives of male homosexuals than in the general population (Buhrich, Bailey, & Martin, 1991). Whereas rates of homosexuality in the general population are estimated at 2 to 7 percent, nearly 25 percent of brothers of male homosexuals in one study were reportedly homosexual (Pillard et al., 1981, 1982).

The most definitive study to date found concordance rates for homosexuality much higher among identical than fraternal twins and adoptive brothers (Bailey & Pillard, 1991). Concordance for homosexuality was 52 percent for monozygotic twins, 22 percent for dizygotic twins, and 11 percent for adoptive brothers, with heritability estimated somewhere between .31 and .74.

The same research group conducted one of the only studies of heritability of homosexuality in women and found a similar pattern: 48 percent concordance for monozygotic twins, 16 percent for dizygotic and 6 percent for adoptive sisters, with heritability estimates ranging from .27 to .76 (Bailey, Pillard, Neale, & Agyei, 1993). Other research similarly finds increased rates of lesbianism among the biological relatives of homosexual women (Pattatucci & Hamer, 1995).

The data thus suggest that homosexuality is influenced by genetics. If, as appears to be the case, sexual orientation is in part a preference exercised by our genes instead of our souls, this has substantial implications for public policy and attitudes.

APPLY + DISCUSS

- If homosexuality is substantially influenced by genetics, is there any difference between intolerance towards homosexuality and persecution of people with blue eyes or diabetes (both of which also show considerable heritability)?

INTERIM SUMMARY

Sexual orientation refers to the direction of a person's enduring sexual attraction, to members of the same or opposite sex. Attitudes towards homosexuality differ substantially across cultures. The causes of homosexuality are likely numerous, but particularly for males, mounting evidence suggests that homosexuality is highly heritable and does not likely reflect a 'choice'.

Psychosocial motives

Unlike sex, ***psychosocial needs*** (personal and interpersonal motives for achievement, power, self-esteem, affiliation, intimacy and the like) are less obviously biological; however, many of these needs are strongly influenced by evolved tendencies rooted in our biology. Human infants, like the young of other species, have an inborn tendency to form intense social bonds with their primary caretakers, and toddlers spontaneously exhibit joy at their achievements and frustration at their failures. Once again, nature and nurture jointly weave even the most socially constructed fabrics.

Two major clusters of goals people pursue everywhere are ***relatedness*** (sometimes called 'communion', referring to motives for connectedness with others) and ***agency*** (motives for achievement, autonomy, mastery, power and other self-oriented goals) (Bakan, 1966; McAdams, 1999; Woike, Gershkovich, Piorkowski, & Polo, 1999).

Needs for relatedness

Human beings have a number of interpersonal needs (Andersen, Chen, & Carter, 2000; Baumeister & Leary, 1995; Weiss, 1986). The earliest to arise in children are related to attachment (chapter 13). ***Attachment motivation*** refers to the desire for physical and psychological proximity (closeness) to another person, so that the individual experiences comfort and pleasure in the other person's presence. Attachment motives form the basis for many aspects of adult love (Cassidy & Shaver, 1999; Main, Kaplan, & Cassidy, 1985; Roisman, Collins, Sroufe, & Egeland, 2005).

A related need common among adults and older children in some cultures is ***intimacy***, a special kind of closeness characterised by self-disclosure, warmth and mutual caring (Cassidy, 2001; McAdams, Hoffman, Mansfield, & Day, 1996; Reis & Shaver, 1988). Intimacy needs are often satisfied in adult attachment relationships and deep friendships.

Another social motive is the need for ***affiliation***, or interaction with friends or acquaintances. Most people need to be with and communicate with other people, whether that means obtaining support after an upsetting experience, sharing good news or playing sports together. Individuals differ in the extent to which they seek intimate versus affiliative relationships. Some people have many friends and acquaintances but have little need for intimacy. Others desire one or two intimate friends and have little need for a broad social network (Reis & Shaver, 1988; Weiss, 1986).

Social relationships, particularly with people in whom one can confide, are important for both physical and mental health (chapter 14). For example, women who report having at least one confidante are 10 times less likely to suffer depression following a stressful event than women who do not have someone in whom they can confide (Brown, Bhrolchain, & Harris, 1975). Lack of supportive relationships is a risk factor for mortality as well (Lyyra & Heikkinen, 2006; Murata et al., 2005).

ETHICAL DILEMMA

A researcher hypothesises that women who have a strong social support network will experience less distress following a traumatic event than women who have little or no support structure. He proposes to interview a number of victims of domestic violence about their experiences.

- How might the researcher ensure that the study does not compromise the dignity and welfare of participants?
- Explain the procedures for ensuring the confidentiality of the study's results.

INTERIM SUMMARY

Two clusters of ***psychosocial needs*** pursued cross-culturally are ***relatedness*** and ***agency*** (achievement, autonomy, mastery, power and other self-oriented goals). Needs for relatedness include ***attachment***, ***intimacy*** and ***affiliation***. Although relatedness needs are psychosocial, the failure to fulfil them can have powerful biological effects, such as sickness or mortality.

Achievement and other agency motives

Motives for power, competence, achievement, autonomy and self-esteem form a second cluster of motives common to humans throughout the world. As early as the second year of life, infants seem to have a desire to be competent and effective, even when they are not rewarded by their parents (Kagan, Kearsley, & Zalazo, 1978). This can be clearly seen in the persistence and pride shown by young children as they learn to walk.

Pride at mastery appears to emerge spontaneously in the second year of life.

According to some theorists (e.g. Epstein, 1998; White, 1959) humans have an innate need to know and understand the world around them and to feel competent in the exercise of their knowledge. Pleasure in knowing and displeasure in feeling uncertain may have evolved as mechanisms that foster exploration of the environment.

Another self-oriented motive is self-esteem. Theorists of many theoretical persuasions — psychodynamic (Kohut, 1971), humanistic (Rogers, 1959) and cognitive–social (Moretti & Higgins, 1999), among others — view self-esteem motivation, the need to view oneself in a positive light, as a fundamental motivator of behaviour (chapter 17).

Need for achievement

The ***need for achievement*** — to do well, to succeed and to avoid failure — is the best researched psychosocial motive. That is not surprising in view of Western cultures' emphasis on personal achievement in school, sports, careers and practically every domain in which our actions can be described in terms of success and failure.

People high in achievement motivation tend to choose moderately difficult tasks (those with about a 50/50 chance of success) over very easy or very difficult tasks (Atkinson, 1977; Slade & Rush, 1991). They enjoy being challenged and take pleasure in accomplishing a difficult task but are often motivated to avoid failure. In one classic study, participants played a ringtoss game and were free to choose their own distance from the target (Atkinson & Litwin, 1960). Those who scored high in achievement motivation selected distances that were challenging but not impossible. In contrast, participants who scored low in achievement motivation and had a high fear of failure stood either very close to the target or impossibly far, positions that guaranteed either success or a good excuse for failing.

How do experimental findings such as these translate into everyday behaviours? People with a high need for achievement tend to work more persistently than others to achieve a goal, and they take more pride in their accomplishments when they succeed (Atkinson, 1977). Not surprisingly, they are consequently more likely to succeed. They also tend to attribute their past successes to their abilities and their past failures to forces beyond their control, which increases confidence and persistence in the face of adverse feedback (Dweck, 1975; Weiner, 1974, 1986). Students with high achievement motivation are likely to select a major that suits their abilities, commit to a study schedule that is rigorous but not impossible, and work hard to succeed within those limits. The consequences of achievement motivation extend far beyond the classroom (Alderman, 2004; Tollefson, 2000).

In an economically depressed area of India, where government programs had been ineffective in raising the standard of living, psychologist David McClelland undertook an experiment with far-reaching consequences. He taught local businessmen to fantasise about high achievement and to problem solve ways to succeed (McClelland, 1978; McClelland & Winter, 1969). Over time, the local businessmen began new businesses and employed new workers at a much higher rate than businessmen in a comparable town in the same region. In Western cultures, achievement motivation predicts not only occupational success but also people's earnings as much as 25 years later (Dunifon & Duncan, 1998; see also Collins, Hanges, & Locke, 2004).

Components of achievement motivation

As with other motives, people do not express achievement motivation in every domain. For example, an achievement-oriented science student may place little value in succeeding in literature courses and may be undisturbed by her failure to bake a fluffy soufflé. From a cognitive perspective, motives may be expressed selectively because they are hierarchically organised, with some sections of the hierarchy carrying more motivational weight than others (figure 10.9).

Achievement goals themselves appear to reflect a blend of at least three motives: performance-approach, performance-avoidance and mastery (Elliot & Harackiewicz, 1996; Rawsthorne & Elliot, 1999). ***Performance goals*** are motives to achieve at a particular level, usually a socially defined standard, such as getting an A for an assignment (Dweck, 1986). The emphasis of performance goals is on the *outcome* — on success or failure in meeting a standard.

Some people are more motivated to attain a goal (***performance-approach goals***), whereas others are more motivated by the fear of not attaining it (***performance-avoidance goals***). Thus, if I am skiing, I may be motivated by the desire to know (and tell people) I skied a blackdiamond slope — a slope of considerable difficulty. Skiing a tough slope is a performance-approach goal. Alternatively, I may stay on the baby slopes to avoid skiing down the hill on my buttocks, a performance-avoidance goal.

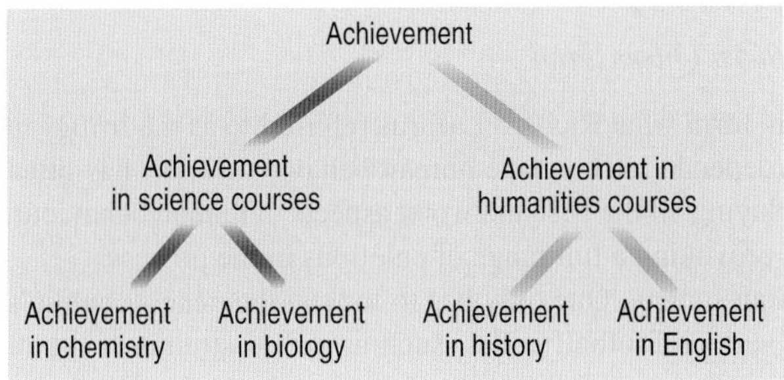

FIGURE 10.9
Cognitive structure of achievement motivation. A science student attaches different motivational weights to different sections of the hierarchy. Red lines indicate strong motivation; blue lines indicate weaker motivation.

MAKING CONNECTIONS

Performance-approach goals and **performance-avoidance goals** are related to both operant **conditioning** and emotion.

- Performance-approach goals are linked to **positive reinforcement** and positive (pleasurable) emotions, such as pride and excitement.
- Performance-avoidance goals are linked to **punishment**, **negative reinforcement** (avoidance of aversive consequences) and negative (unpleasant) emotions such as anxiety, guilt, shame and sadness (chapter 6).

Performance goals, whether for approach or avoidance, are about achieving a concrete outcome — obtaining success or avoiding failure. In contrast, ***mastery goals*** are motives to increase one's competence, mastery or skill. If I am motivated by mastery goals, my interest is in developing my skill or technique — enjoying the sheer pleasure of skiing more quickly or competently — not in being able to brag about my exploits or to avoid the snickers of little children passing me by.

The three types of goals underlying achievement actually predict different outcomes. For example, children with high performance-approach goals tend to get good grades, but they may or may not develop intrinsic interest in the material (Elliot & Church, 1997). Students with high performance-avoidance goals tend to get both low grades and less intrinsic pleasure from what they are doing, presumably because of their preoccupation with fears of failure. Children motivated by mastery goals often get good grades as well as develop intrinsic interest in the material.

In the future, researchers are likely to tease apart fine-grained distinctions such as these in most motivational systems. In fact, multiple motives probably underlie most behaviour. Asking someone out for dinner may reflect needs for affiliation, attachment, food, sex, altruism and self-esteem — and a central task of the person being asked out may involve figuring out which motives are primary.

Parenting, culture and achievement

The need for achievement is primarily a learned motive, which numerous studies have linked to patterns of child rearing. Children with high achievement motivation tend to have parents who encourage them to attempt new tasks slightly beyond their reach, praise success when it occurs, encourage independent thinking, discourage complaining and prompt their children to try new solutions when they fail (McClelland, 1985; see also Gonzalez-Pienda et al., 2002; Weiss & Schwarz, 1996; Winterbottom, 1953).

Parenting always occurs within a cultural context, and motivation for achievement varies considerably across cultures and historical periods. David McClelland and his colleagues spent years exploring the links among culture, child rearing and achievement. One hypothesis, based on the theory that cultures teach motives through the stories they tell, is that a culture's myths, folktales and children's stories should be related to its child-rearing practices and level of economic development. A prominent children's story in our own achievement-oriented society is *The Little Engine That Could*. From a psychological standpoint, the moral of this story is simple: Those who expect success and strive for it despite adversity will succeed ('I think I can, I think I can . . .').

Differences in child-rearing practices are based on different assumptions and beliefs of the cultural group towards the nature of children (Brown, 2000). According to Kearins (1984), the child-rearing practices of many non-Aboriginal Australians derive from a northern European pastoral background, as opposed to the hunter-gatherer backgrounds of Indigenous Australian cultures. These varying backgrounds result in different approaches to child rearing. In non-Aboriginal societies, children are raised to be obedient and defer to authority figures. Historically, this obedience was required in the much more structured pastoral farming societies typical of northern Europe, where many people were required to work together in a hierarchical way to achieve success. However, children in Aboriginal societies are typically raised to be much more independent and autonomous. This reflects the needs of hunter-gather societies, where everyone was expected to exhibit initiative and capacity for individual decision making, with much less direction (chapter 19).

Sport: a microcosm of society

By Professor Peter Terry, University of Southern Queensland

Motivation and emotion, along with cognition, form what Richard Lazarus referred to as the *trilogy of mind*: sharing complex interactions and interdependence to shape human behaviour. Sport has often been proposed as a *microcosm of society*, displaying all the best and worst aspects of human behaviour, testing motivational resources to the core and provoking a full range of emotions in the process.

Sport holds a very special place in Australian society. One only has to look at the general public's interest in athletes and teams competing in various football codes, such as the Australian Football League and National Rugby League, and on the world stage, in events such as the Olympics and the FIFA World Cup. Australian sporting champions from the past, such as cricketer Don Bradman and tennis great Rod Laver, are revered through generations, and are a part of Australian folklore. Sport acts as a vehicle for the development of values and behaviours that are seen as fundamental to the Australian way of life — mateship, commitment, discipline, courage, teamwork, integrity and fun.

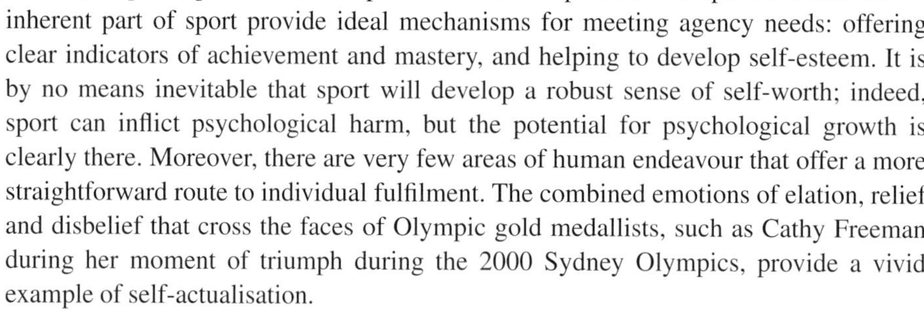

Sport also provides a means of meeting a wide range of psychosocial motives. Team sports offer many opportunities for connectedness — promoting social bonds that often last a lifetime. The physical and psychological closeness of a cohesive team addresses the affiliation needs, and even some of the intimacy needs, of participants. The interpersonal and intrapersonal comparisons that are an inherent part of sport provide ideal mechanisms for meeting agency needs: offering clear indicators of achievement and mastery, and helping to develop self-esteem. It is by no means inevitable that sport will develop a robust sense of self-worth; indeed, sport can inflict psychological harm, but the potential for psychological growth is clearly there. Moreover, there are very few areas of human endeavour that offer a more straightforward route to individual fulfilment. The combined emotions of elation, relief and disbelief that cross the faces of Olympic gold medallists, such as Cathy Freeman during her moment of triumph during the 2000 Sydney Olympics, provide a vivid example of self-actualisation.

The euphoria or despair shown by professional athletes and their supporters is ample testimony to the emotional cauldron that sport creates. Emotions and moods are closely linked to sport — impacting upon and subsequently being influenced by performance outcomes. Athletes intuitively develop strategies to regulate emotions and mood responses, often using music, warm-up exercises and self-talk to help generate an appropriate mindset. Theoretical developments have emphasised the interactive effects of different mood components — such as the effect of depression on anger (see Terry, 2004) — whereby athletes who report depressed mood tend to turn anger inwardly and be counter-productive, and athletes who are free from depressive symptoms tend to use anger to fuel determination, which usually benefits sports performance. The same principles may apply in other achievement settings, such as examinations and the performing arts.

INTERIM SUMMARY

Agency needs include motives such as power, competence, achievement, autonomy and self-esteem. The ***need for achievement*** — to succeed and to avoid failure — affects the goals people pursue in everyday life, the tasks they choose to tackle and the extent to which they persist in the face of difficulty. Achievement goals themselves reflect a blend of at least three motives: ***performance-approach goals*** (the desire to meet a socially defined standard), ***performance-avoidance goals*** (the desire to avoid failure, particularly when it is publicly observable) and ***mastery goals*** (the desire to master the skill). Parenting practices, which themselves reflect cultural values, substantially affect achievement motivation.

Emotion

In this section we explore the nature of emotion. Everyone has an intuitive sense of what an emotion is, but emotion can be exceedingly difficult to define. Imagine explaining the concept of emotion to someone who has never experienced one. Some people use the terms ***affect*** and ***mood*** to explain emotion. Affect is closely related to emotion, and can be defined as the pattern of observable behaviours that expresses an individual's emotions. Affect is variable, fluctuating in response to changing emotional states. For example, a depressed person with blunted affect shows very little intensity in their emotional expression. Affect is also different to mood, which is generally a longer lasting and more general emotional state (chapter 15). Affect involves visible actions and behaviours, whereas mood may be internalised and unobservable to the outsider. In contrast, emotion is an evaluative response (a positive or negative feeling) that typically includes some combination of physiological arousal, subjective experience and behavioural or emotional expression. We examine each component of emotion in turn.

Theories of emotion: physiological components

Over a century ago, William James (1884) argued that emotion is rooted in bodily experience. According to James, an emotion-inducing stimulus elicits visceral, or gut, reactions and voluntary behaviours such as running or gesturing. The physical experience in turn leads the person to feel aroused, and the arousal stimulates the subjective experience of, for example, fear. In this view, confronting a vicious dog on a walk causes a person to run, and running produces fear.

James thus offered a counterintuitive proposition: we do not run because we are afraid; rather, we become afraid because we run (figure 10.10a). James' theory is sometimes called the peripheral theory of emotion because it sees the origins of emotion in the peripheral nervous system. Recall that the peripheral nervous system controls both muscle movements and autonomic responses such as a racing heart and shortness of breath in the face of fear-eliciting stimuli (see chapter 2). At about the same time that James developed his theory, the Danish physiologist Carl Lange (1885) proposed a similar view. Thus, the ***James–Lange theory*** states that emotions originate in peripheral nervous system responses that the central nervous system then interprets (see Lang, 1994).

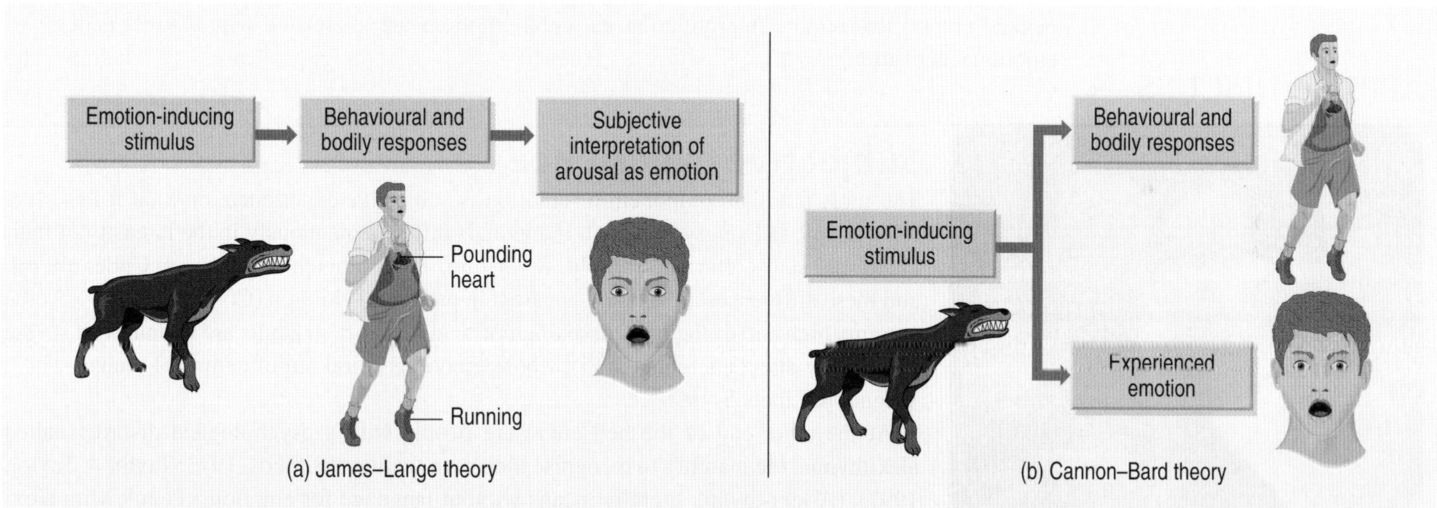

FIGURE **10.10**
The James–Lange and Cannon–Bard theories of emotion. In the James–Lange theory (a), a stimulus leads to a peripheral nervous system response, which in turn is interpreted as an emotion. In the Cannon–Bard theory (b), the stimulus produces simultaneous peripheral responses and subjective experience.

As the James–Lange theory would predict, some emotional experiences — particularly sexual arousal, fear and anger — do appear to be blunted in individuals with spinal cord lesions that prevent them from moving or experiencing gut feelings (Hohmann, 1966; Jasmos & Hakmiller, 1975). One man with a cervical spinal cord lesion (a lesion near the neck, which cuts off almost all autonomic signals) compared his feelings of sexual arousal before and after the accident (Hohmann, 1966, p. 148):

> Before I got hurt . . . I would get a hot, tense feeling all over my body. I've got out and necked a few times since I was hurt, but it doesn't do anything for me. I daydream once in a while about it, and when I'm around a bunch of guys I talk big, but I just don't get worked up anymore.

Other cases of spinal cord injury do not, however, support the James–Lange theory (Bermond, Nieuwenhuyse, Fasotti, & Schuerman, 1991), and the theory was challenged on other grounds over a half century ago by Walter Cannon (1927) and Philip Bard (1934). Cannon and Bard noted that autonomic responses are typically slow, occurring about one to two seconds after presentation of a stimulus. In contrast, emotional responses are immediate and often precede both autonomic reactions and behaviours such as running. Further, many different emotional states are linked to the same visceral responses, so that arousal is too generalised to translate directly into discrete emotional experiences. For instance, muscle tension and quickened heart rate accompany sexual arousal, fear and rage, which people experience as very different emotional states. Thus, the alternative view, known as the ***Cannon–Bard theory***, states that emotion-inducing stimuli simultaneously elicit both an emotional experience, such as fear, and bodily responses, such as sweaty palms (figure 10.10b).

Cannon and Bard's first criticism (about the relative speed of autonomic and emotional responses) continues to be valid. However, their second criticism, that visceral arousal is general, has been challenged by more recent research. In fact, although some forms of arousal are probably general, different emotions are associated with distinct patterns of autonomic activity, such as heart rate acceleration, finger temperature and skin conductance (a measure of sweat on the palms related to arousal or anxiety, also known as galvanic skin response, or GSR) (Ekman, 1992; Levenson, 1992; Levenson, Ekman, & Friesen, 1990). Anger and fear, for example, produce greater heart rate acceleration than does happiness. This finding makes evolutionary sense, because anger and fear are related to fight-or-flight responses, which require the heart to pump more blood to the muscles.

Anger and fear are also distinguishable from each other autonomically. The language we use to describe anger ('hot under the collar') appears to be physiologically accurate. People who are angry get 'heated' in their surface skin temperatures. Data from non-Western cultures such as Indonesia suggest that these links between emotional experience and physiology are similar cross-culturally and appear to be wired into the brain (Levenson, Ekman, Heider, & Friesen, 1992).

INTERIM SUMMARY

Emotion is an evaluative response that typically includes physiological arousal, subjective experience and behavioural or emotional expression. The ***James–Lange theory*** asserts that emotions originate in peripheral nervous system responses, which the central nervous system then interprets. The ***Cannon–Bard theory*** argues that emotion-inducing stimuli simultaneously elicit both an emotional experience and bodily responses. Although people probably experience some forms of general arousal that require interpretation, different emotions are associated with distinct patterns of emotional activation.

APPLY + DISCUSS

After winning the men's singles final at the 2006 Australian Open, tennis great Roger Federer broke down in tears.

- How do you explain that, sometimes, when you are extremely happy, you cry?

Subjective experience

The most familiar component of emotion is subjective experience, or what it feels like to be happy, sad, angry or elated. Individuals differ tremendously in the intensity of their emotional states (Bryant, Yarnold, & Grimm, 1996; Larsen, Billings, & Cutler, 1996), and these differences are already apparent in preschool children (Cole et al., 1997). At the extreme high end of the bell curve of emotional intensity in adults are people with severe personality disorders (chapter 15), whose emotions spiral out of control (Linehan, 1987; Wagner & Linehan, 1999).

At the other end of the bell curve are people with a psychological disorder called alexithymia, the inability to recognise their own feelings (Sifneos, 1973; Taylor & Taylor, 1997). (A-lexi-thymia literally means without language for emotion.) People with alexithymia often report what seem to be meaningful, painful or traumatic experiences with bland indifference. One alexithymic patient told his doctor about a 'strange event' that had occurred the previous day. He had found himself shaking and felt his eyes tearing and wondered if he had been crying. The patient showed no recognition that his tears could have been related to frightening news he had received that morning about the results of a biopsy (D. Hulihan, personal communication, 1992).

Emotional disclosure

Just as being unaware of one's feelings can lead to illness, knowing and attending to them can have a positive impact on health (chapter 2). In one study, Holocaust survivors spoke for one to two hours about their experiences during World War II. The investigators then measured the extent to which they had talked emotionally about traumatic events (Pennebaker, Barger, & Tiebout, 1989). The more emotion they expressed as they recounted the events, the better their health for over a year later. In another study, patients with painful arthritis spoke into a tape recorder for 15 minutes a day about either stressful or trivial events (Kelley, Lumley, & Leisen, 1997). Those who spoke about stressful events were in better emotional and physical shape three months later and, the more unpleasant emotion they experienced while discussing stressful events, the less painful their joints were three months later. The moral of the story? No pain, no gain.

Researchers have been tracking down some of the precise mechanisms through which emotional disclosure affects health (Pennebaker, 1997a, 1997b; Pennebaker & Seagal, 1999). Writing about stressful or unpleasant events has been shown to increase the functioning of specific cells in the immune system (the system of cells in the body that fights off disease). Disclosure also decreases autonomic reactivity that keeps the body on red alert and takes its toll over time.

Perhaps most importantly, disclosure permits a change in cognitive functioning that allows the person to rework the traumatic experience in thought and memory. People who benefit from disclosure tend to begin with disorganised, disjointed narratives about the event, suggesting emotional disruption of their thinking. After writing, their narratives become more coherent. The more complex and coherent people's narratives after disclosing traumatic events, the more their health improves (Suedfeld & Pennebaker, 1997).

Feeling happy

Although psychologists tend to focus on unpleasant emotions such as anxiety and depression, increasingly researchers have begun studying the subjective experience of happiness (Diener, 2000; Myers, 2000; Seligman, 2002). Men and women tend to be equally happy, as do older and younger people (contrary to many people's emotional forecasts about their own sense of wellbeing as they age; see chapter 13). Rates of reported happiness do, however, differ across cultures. The percentage of people who describe themselves as 'very happy' ranges from a low of about 10 percent in some countries to a high of about 40 percent in other countries. Norway topped a list of the most prosperous countries in the world in a recent year (Helman, 2011).

One predictor of happiness is the extent to which a culture is more individualistic or collectivistic. People in individualistic cultures, which focus on the needs and desires of individuals, tend to be happier than people in collectivist cultures, which emphasise the needs of the group. Another predictor is political. The correlation between life satisfaction and the number of uninterrupted years of democracy in a country is .85, which is one of the largest observed correlations ever produced in psychology between two seemingly dissimilar variables (Inglehart, 1991).

Does money buy happiness? Yes and no. Across cultures, the correlation between self-reported happiness and economic prosperity is substantial. Within cultures, however, happiness and income are not highly correlated. Apparently, a decent income is necessary but not sufficient for happiness. Other variables that predict happiness are a large network of close friends and strong religious faith (Myers, 2000).

ONE STEP FURTHER

The strange world of implicit egotism

By Doctor Guy Curtis, Murdoch University

Emotion is intimately linked to liking and disliking. We like things that make us feel good, we want things that we think will make us feel good, and we do not like things that make us feel bad. Self-esteem is, in essence, the extent to which we like, or have positive emotions about, ourselves. Self-esteem has been a focus of theories and research in psychology for a very long time. It influences our thoughts, feelings and behaviour. In recent years, psychologists have distinguished between two types of self-esteem: implicit and explicit self-esteem. Explicit self-esteem is the extent to which we like ourselves that we are aware of and implicit self-esteem is the extent to which we like ourselves that we are not aware of.

Egotism is another word for being self-centred. Implicit egotism is where people like things that are associated with themselves without being aware that they are doing this. People with higher implicit self-esteem tend to show more implicit egotism. One manifestation of implicit egotism is that people tend to like their own name and initials (Nuttin, 1985). Recently, studies have shown that preference for names and initials may even influence significant life choices, such as career decisions and romantic relationships. For example, there are more dentists named Denis and Denise than would be expected by chance (Pelham, Mirenberg, & Jones, 2002), people are more likely to marry someone with the same first initial as themselves than would be expected by chance (Jones, Pelham, Carvallo, & Mirenberg, 2004), and people like consumer brands that have the same starting letter as their first name (Brendl, Chattopadhyay, Pelham, & Carvallo, 2005).

Recently, an Australian study examined whether implicit egotism would influence people's behaviour with other people who do, or do not, share the initials of their name (Kocan & Curtis, 2009). The participants were given a name label with their initials on it and were told that this was their identification for working with another person. When each participant entered the research room they saw a chair with a jacket hanging on it, and on the jacket was a name label containing either the same initials as their own or different initials. The participants were told that the person they will be working with had just stepped out and they should take a seat and wait for them. People tend to approach what they like and avoid what they dislike, so the researchers examined how close participants placed their chair to the chair of the person they thought they would be working with. Participants who were high in implicit self-esteem sat closer to someone who they thought had the same initials as themselves and further away from someone with different initials — indicating they liked someone similar to themselves more than someone different. Interestingly, people with low implicit self-esteem did the opposite. Although the participants' behaviour gave away a subtle indication of their liking, they were unaware that they had shown this behavioural preference.

INTERIM SUMMARY

The subjective experience of emotion refers to what the emotion feels like to the individual. People differ tremendously in emotional intensity. The extent to which people experience happiness is relatively stable across age and gender but differs substantially across cultures.

Emotional expression

A third component of emotion is ***emotional expression***, the overt behavioural signs of emotion. People express feelings in various ways, including facial expressions, posture, gestures and tone of voice.

Facial expression and emotion

In a twist on William James' peripheral hypothesis of emotion, some theorists argue that the face is the primary centre of emotion (Tomkins, 1962, 1980). Whereas James asserted that we feel afraid because we run, these theorists argue that we feel afraid because our face shows fear. In this view, emotion consists of muscular responses located primarily in the face (and, secondarily, muscular and glandular responses throughout the body).

Different facial expressions are, in fact, associated with different emotions (Ekman, 1992; Izard, 1971, 1997; see also Kappas, 2003). The relationship between emotion and facial muscle movements is uniform enough across individuals and cultures that electrodes attached to the face to detect muscle movements allow psychologists to assess directly both the valence (positive or negative tone) and intensity of emotion (Tassinary & Cacioppo, 1992). Some similarity across cultures exists even in the colours people use to describe emotions, such as the association of anger with seeing red — perhaps because anger is associated with facial flushing and an increase in temperature (see Hupka, Zaleski, Otto, Reidl, & Tarabrina, 1997).

Facial expressions not only *indicate* a person's emotional state, they also *influence* the physiological and subjective components of the emotion. In a classic study, researchers gave participants specific directions to contract their facial muscles in particular ways, for instance, as shown in figure 10.11 (Ekman, Levenson, & Friesen, 1983). Although the participants (actors) had not been instructed to show a particular emotion, they created expressions characteristic of fear, anger, sadness, happiness, surprise and disgust. Participants held each expression for 10 seconds, while the experimenters measured their heart rate and finger temperature.

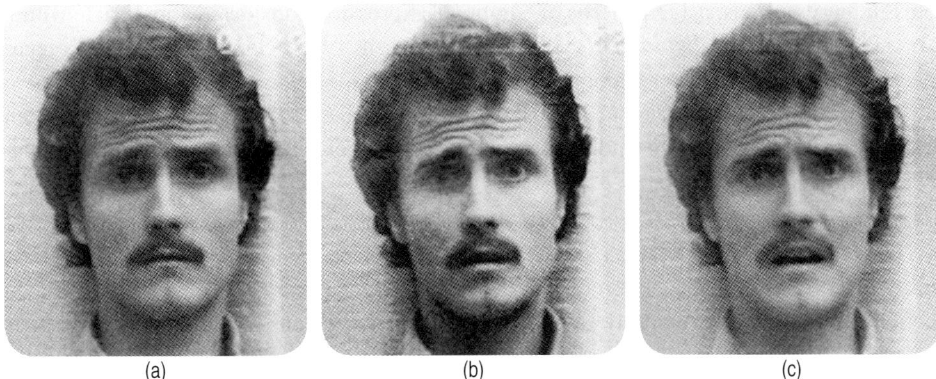

FIGURE 10.11
Creating fear in the face. Participants instructed to (a) raise their eyebrows and pull them together, (b) then raise their upper eyelids and (c) stretch their lips back towards their ears showed physiological changes consistent with fear.

The researchers found a striking causal relationship between the simple act of changing facial expression and patterns of autonomic response (figure 10.12). Subsequent research has found that when people imitate positive and negative expressions in photographs, their own emotions tend to change accordingly (Kleinke, Peterson, & Rutledge, 1998). Still other studies document distinct EEG activity associated with the different posed emotions and changes in subjective experience that accompany them (Ekman & Davidson, 1993; Izard, 1990; Lanzetta, Cartwright-Smith, & Kleck, 1976). Similar effects appear to occur with other nonverbal expressions of emotion. People who receive positive feedback about their appearance experience more pride when they receive the feedback while standing upright rather than hunching over (Stepper & Strack, 1993)!

Not only do emotions differ from one another physiologically, but so do genuine and false emotional displays. True and fake smiles appear to be physiologically different and rely on different sets of muscles (Ekman, 1992; Ekman & Keltner, 1997). True smiles use eye muscles not used in fake smiles. Children actually have some capacity to detect these differences as early as the preschool years (Banerjee, 1997).

Culture and emotional display rules

Before research documented the physiological and anatomical differences among emotions, psychologists and sociologists hotly debated whether people across cultures ascribe the same meaning to a smile or a frown. In fact, some facial expressions are universally recognised (see Ekman & Oster, 1979; Scherer & Wallbott, 1994; see also Fischer, Manstead, Rodriguez Mosquera, & van Vianen, 2004). Participants in one classic study viewed photographs showing the faces of North American actors expressing fear, anger, happiness and other emotions. Participants from diverse cultural groups, ranging from Swedes and Kenyans to members of a preliterate tribe in New Guinea with minimal Western contact, all recognised certain emotions (Ekman, 1971).

Cross-cultural studies have identified six facial expressions recognised by people of every culture that was examined (figure 10.13; see overleaf): surprise, fear, anger, disgust, happiness and sadness (Ekman & Oster, 1979). Shame and interest also may have universal facial expressions (Izard, 1977). These findings suggest that some emotions are biologically linked not only to distinct autonomic states but also to certain facial movements, which people in all cultures can decode. More recently, data from a cross-cultural recognition study examined the relationship between emotion and behaviour. Consedine, Strongman, and Magai (2003) gave participants from four continents (North America, Europe, Australasia and Asia) written descriptions of emotionally driven behaviours and asked them to identify the emotions involved. They found that primary emotions such as happiness,

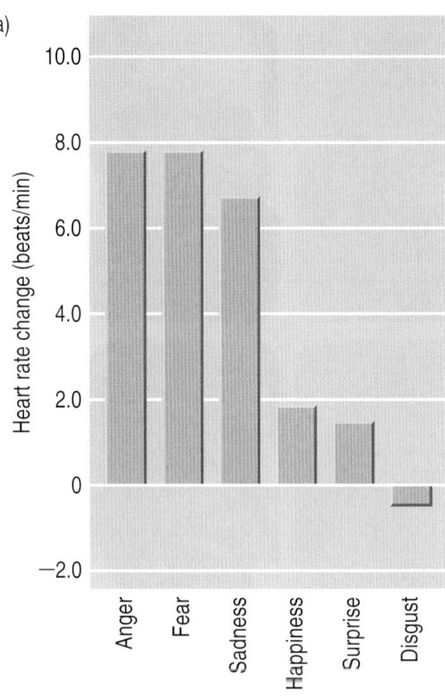

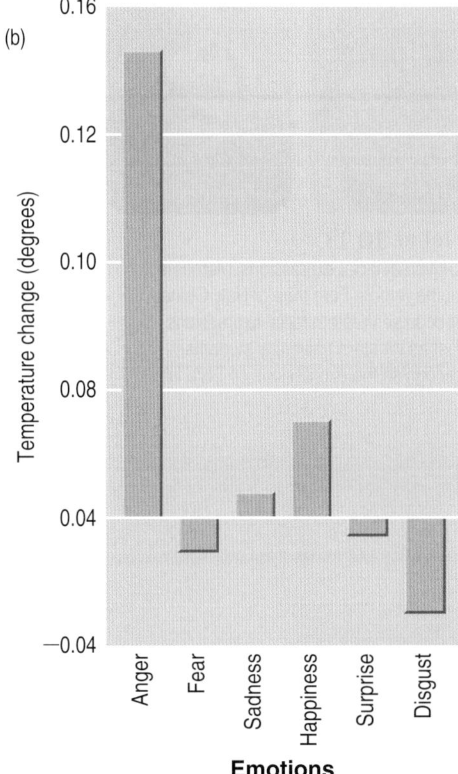

FIGURE 10.12
Facial expression and physiological response. The graphs show changes in heart rate and finger temperature associated with certain emotional expressions. Anger, fear and sadness elevate heart rate, but of these three emotions, only anger also increases temperature. People presumably learn to distinguish these emotions based on subtle physiological cues such as these.

SOURCE: Ekman et al. (1983). Reprinted with permission from AAAS.

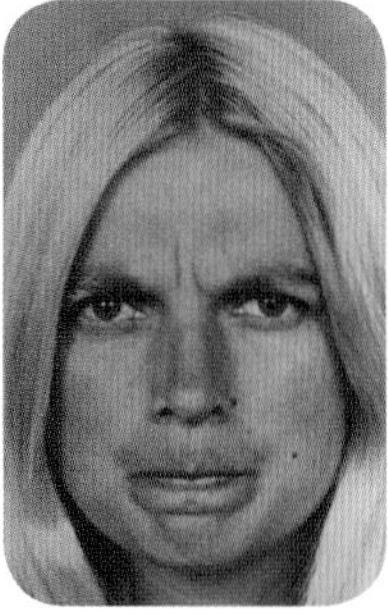

FIGURE 10.13
Universal facial expressions. Members of the remote Fore tribe of New Guinea recognise Western facial expressions, just as Western university students recognise the expressions on Fore faces.

sadness, anger and fear were more readily identified than were complex, socially constructed emotions such as shame, embarrassment, guilt and pride. There were no cross-cultural differences in the recognition rates for the eight emotions studied.

Not all facial expressions, however, are the same from culture to culture. People learn to control the way they express many emotions, using patterns of emotional expression considered appropriate within their culture or subculture, called ***display rules*** (Ekman & Friesen, 1975). Some of these differences appear to reflect such simple variables as geography. A study of a large sample of participants from 26 northern-hemisphere countries found, as many observers and travellers had long believed, that both within and across countries, southerners tend to be more emotionally expressive than northerners (Pennebaker, Mayne, & Francis, 1997).

Gender and emotional expression

Do display rules differ by gender as well as culture? The best evidence available suggests that women probably experience emotion more intensely, are better able to read emotions from other people's faces and nonverbal cues and express emotion more intensely and openly than men (Brody, 1999; Brody & Hall, 2000). For example, a study found that women and men differed in both emotional expression and autonomic arousal while watching emotional films, suggesting that men and women differ in their experience of emotion (Kring & Gordon, 1998; see also Hall & Matsumoto, 2004).

These distinctions apply to children as well. While watching videotapes of emotional interactions, girls show facial expressions that more closely match those of the people on the videos, suggesting greater emotional empathy; they are also better at verbally describing the emotions of the people they view (Strayer & Roberts, 1997). Interestingly, even children as young as three years old recognise that females are more likely to express fear, sadness and happiness and that males are more likely to express anger (Birnbaum, 1983).

The reasons for gender differences in emotion are a matter of debate (Brody, 1999). On the one hand, they may reflect adaptation to the roles that men and women have historically tended to occupy. Women are generally more comfortable with emotions such as love, happiness, warmth, shame, guilt and sympathy, which foster affiliation and caretaking. Men, on the other hand, are socialised to compete and to fight; hence, they avoid 'soft' emotions that display their vulnerabilities to competitors and enemies or discourage them from asserting their dominance when the need arises (Brody & Hall, 2000).

Parents talk to their children differently about emotion from at least the time they are toddlers. They talk more about feelings with girls, implicitly teaching them how — and how much — to think about and express their emotions (Cervantes & Callahan, 1998; Dunn, Bretherton, & Munn, 1987; see also Chaplin, Cole, & Zahn-Waxler, 2005). Little boys, in contrast, often learn that only 'sissies' cry and that feeling scared and showing signs of emotional vulnerability are unmanly. Importantly, however, ethnicity moderates some of these observed gender differences.

Gender differences also make sense from an evolutionary perspective. Nurturing children, for example, requires attention to feelings — which can be dysfunctional for males when they are fighting, defending territory, or competing with other males for mates. This is not, of course, absolute. Men who understand others well, which means being able to read their emotions, are likely to be more socially successful and to compete more successfully for females. Thus, males may have pressures both to feel and not to feel.

APPLY + DISCUSS

Research suggests that moving muscles in the face can lead to changes in emotion. Whoever wrote the lyric about letting a smile be your umbrella on a rainy day may have been a savvy psychologist.

- When is 'putting on a happy face' adaptive? When is it maladaptive?
- In what ways can keeping a stiff upper lip influence the way other people respond, which, in turn, may affect health and happiness?

INTERIM SUMMARY

Emotional expression refers to the overt behavioural signs of emotion. Different facial muscles are associated with different emotions. Facial expressions not only indicate but can influence the subjective experience of emotion. ***Display rules*** are patterns of emotional expression considered appropriate within a culture or subculture. Display rules differ not only by culture but also by gender. Women appear to experience emotions more intensely and to read people's emotions more accurately.

A taxonomy of emotions

Some aspects of emotion, then, are universal, whereas others vary by culture and gender. How many emotions do humans experience, and how many of these are innate?

Basic emotions

Psychologists have attempted to produce a list of ***basic emotions***, emotions common to the human species, with characteristic physiological, subjective and expressive components (Ekman, 1999; Izard & Buechler, 1980). Basic emotions are similar to primary colours in perception. All other emotions and emotional blends are derived from them.

Although theorists generate slightly different lists, and some even argue against the existence of basic emotions (Ortony & Turner, 1990), most classifications include five to nine emotions (Russell, 1991). All theorists list anger, fear, happiness, sadness and disgust. Surprise, contempt, interest, shame, guilt, joy, trust and anticipation are also sometimes included (Plutchik, 1980; Shaver, Schwartz, Kirson, & O'Connor, 1987; Tomkins, 1980). Similar lists of basic emotions were compiled years ago in India (Lynch, 1990) and in China, where an encyclopedia from the first century BC included the following entry (*The Li Chi*, cited in Russell, 1991, p. 426): 'What are the feelings of men? They are joy, anger, sadness, fear, love, disliking, and liking. These seven feelings belong to men without their learning them.'

Beyond the basic emotions, cultures vary in the extent to which they elaborate and distinguish emotional states (Kitayama & Markus, 1994; Mesquita, Frijda, & Scherer, 1997; Russell, 1991). The Tahitian language has 46 different words for anger (much as English has several terms, such as annoyance, frustration and rage) but no word for sadness. The Tahitians do not even have a word for *emotion*. In some African languages, the same word denotes both anger and sadness; members of these cultures seldom seem to distinguish between the two.

Positive and negative affect

A distinction that is perhaps even more basic than the basic emotions is that between ***positive affect*** (pleasant emotions) and ***negative affect*** (unpleasant emotions). Researchers discovered the distinction between positive and negative affect through factor analysis, a statistical procedure that combines variables that are highly correlated with each other into superordinate variables, called factors (chapter 9). Factor analyses of people's ratings of their tendency to experience a variety of emotions suggest that these two factors, positive and negative affect, underlie people's self-reported emotions across cultures (see Watson, 2000; Watson & Clark, 1992; Watson & Tellegen, 1985). Within these two factors, emotions are substantially intercorrelated. In other words, people who frequently experience one negative emotion, such as guilt, also tend to experience others, such as anxiety and sadness.

APPLY + DISCUSS

- Can complex emotions be read from the face?
- What other cues may be necessary to 'read' emotional blends?

Brain imaging studies suggest that positive and negative affect are largely neurologically distinct, although they share *some* neural pathways. In other words, some emotional pathways lead to a general sense of emotional arousal, whereas others add a specific valence (positive or negative) (Lane et al., 1997).

Approach and avoidance

Positive and negative affect appear to motivate different kinds of behaviour and to involve different regions of the cerebral cortex. Positive affect drives pleasure-seeking, approach-oriented behaviour, whereas negative affect leads to avoidance (chapter 6; see also Davidson, 1992; Gray, 1994; Lang, 1995). Approach-oriented feelings and motives are processed to a greater extent in the left frontal lobe, whereas avoidance-oriented feelings and motives are associated with right frontal activation. These circuits appear to be in place by early childhood. For example, four-year-olds who show greater left than right activation by EEG tend to be more socially competent and less interpersonally isolated than four-year-olds who show little difference between the hemispheres or greater right frontal activation (Fox et al., 1995).

Positive and negative affect are regulated by different neurotransmitter systems, leading some researchers to suggest that an individual's tendency to experience one more than the other is related to differences in neurotransmitter functioning (Cloninger, 1998). According to one hypothesis, people who are fear driven have an abundance of or greater reaction to norepinephrine. People who are reward or pleasure driven, in contrast, are slaves to dopamine.

Part of the tendency to experience positive and negative emotions is heritable. For positive affect, estimated heritability (based on studies of twins reared together and apart) is .40. For negative affect, heritability is even higher, at .55 (Gabbay, 1992; Watson & Tellegen, 1985).

Anger

An emotion that does not neatly fit into this distinction between positive and negative affect is anger. Subjectively, anger can feel unpleasant, but anger and aggression can also have pleasurable

APPLY + DISCUSS

Anger is an emotion that gets many people in trouble.

- Why might the tendency to become angry have evolved in humans and other animals?
- Under what circumstances is anger adaptive or maladaptive?
- When we 'talk ourselves out of' being angry, does the emotion really go away?

components, as anyone knows who has ever fantasised about revenge. Anger can sometimes lead to withdrawal, as when people 'swallow it' and say nothing. More often, however, anger is an approach-oriented emotion, because it leads people to approach and attack the object of their anger.

EEG research finds that people who tend to be angry show greater relative activity in the left versus the right frontal lobe, the standard pattern for positive affect (Harmon-Jones & Allen, 1998). This suggests either that anger is more akin to positive affect or that the asymmetry between left and right frontal functioning has less to do with the emotion itself than with the tendency to approach or avoid.

An emotion hierarchy

How can the various theories of emotion be reconciled, with their competing claims about the number of emotions and the relative importance of biology and culture? One solution (figure 10.14) is to organise emotions hierarchically (Fischer, Schaver, & Carnochan, 1990). The most universal categories are positive and negative affect. All cultures make this distinction, and it is the first drawn by young children, who use words such as *nice*, *mean*, *good*, *bad*, *like* and *don't like*. Physiological data (such as EEG responses) suggest that these factors are already distinct in infancy (Belsky, Campbell, Conn, & Moore, 1996).

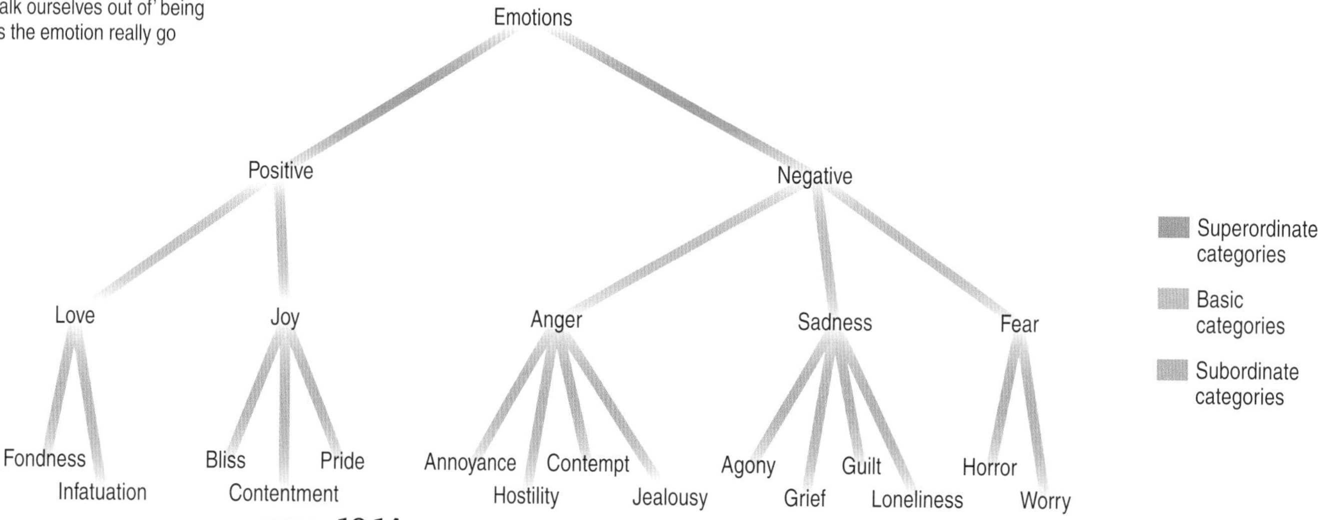

FIGURE 10.14
An emotion hierarchy. Emotions may be arranged hierarchically, with universal categories at the superordinate and basic levels and categories that vary by culture at the subordinate level.

SOURCE: Fischer et al. (1990, p. 90).

The basic emotions at the next level of the hierarchy also apply across cultures. Below this level, however, most emotion concepts are culturally constructed. Western culture, for example, distinguishes different forms of love, such as infatuation, fondness, sexual love, non-sexual love and puppy love. Indian culture, in contrast, distinguishes only two forms of love: *vatsalya bhava*, a mother's love for her child, and *madhurya bhava*, erotic love (Lynch, 1990). Children recognise these culture-specific distinctions much later than they do the basic emotions.

Development of emotion knowledge

Research by Shaver et al. (1987) examined the development of emotion knowledge. Their research suggested that as we move from childhood to maturity, we become increasingly sophisticated in our categorisation of emotions and how we cope with them. Four-year-old children describe a limited repertoire of emotions — happy, sad, mad and scared — and mention love if prompted. They also have limited explicit knowledge of how to control their responses to these emotions. However, by age 10 or 12, children start to recognise a wider range of emotions (often subcategories of the main emotions). They also start to develop strategies for controlling the way they respond to these emotions. In fact, it seems that we need to develop an understanding of the complexity and range of emotions before we are able to exercise self-control over them.

INTERIM SUMMARY

Basic emotions — such as anger, fear, happiness, sadness and disgust — are common to the human species and include characteristic physiological, subjective and expressive components. Beyond the basic emotions, different cultures distinguish different emotional states. Probably the most fundamental distinction is between ***positive affect*** (pleasant emotions) and ***negative affect*** (unpleasant emotions), with positive affect associated with approach-oriented motives and negative affect associated with avoidance-oriented emotions. These emotional systems are to a substantial degree neurologically distinct. Emotions appear to be organised hierarchically, with positive and negative affect at the superordinate level, followed by basic emotions and then more culture-specific emotions.

The neuropsychology of emotion

Poets often locate emotion in the heart, whereas theorists with a less romantic turn of mind locate it in the face or the peripheral nervous system. Still other researchers have searched for the neural circuits underlying emotion in the central nervous system. They have found that affect, like cognition, is distributed throughout the nervous system and not located in any particular region. Three areas of the brain, however, are particularly important: the hypothalamus, limbic system and cortex.

The hypothalamus

Psychologists have known about the role of the hypothalamus in emotion since the 1930s (Papez, 1937). The hypothalamus is a central link in a neural circuit that converts emotional signals generated at higher levels of the brain into autonomic and endocrine responses. (Recall from chapter 3 that the hypothalamus links the brain to the pituitary gland, which in turn activates other glands in the endocrine system.) In some species, motivation is largely controlled by the hypothalamus and hence by instinctive responses and the emotions linked to them. Thus, electrical stimulation of regions of the hypothalamus can produce attack, defence or flight reactions, with corresponding emotions of rage or terror.

The limbic system

In animals such as humans, behaviour is controlled less by instinct than by learning, which is guided by emotional responses to stimuli. Central to emotional reactions are structures in the limbic system, particularly the amygdala (LeDoux, 1989, 1995). Decades ago, researchers discovered that creating lesions in a large temporal region (which later turned out primarily to involve the amygdala) produced a peculiar syndrome in monkeys (Kluver & Bucy, 1939). The monkeys no longer seemed to understand the emotional significance of objects in their environment, even though they had no trouble recognising or identifying them. The animals showed no fear of previously feared stimuli and were generally unable to use their emotions to guide behaviour. They would, for example, eat faeces or other inedible objects that normally elicited disgust or indifference.

Researchers have subsequently found that creating lesions on the neurons connecting the amygdala with a specific sense, such as vision or hearing, makes monkeys unable to register the emotional significance of objects perceived by that sense (LeDoux, 1989). The amygdala, with its dense connections to the hippocampus (which is involved in memory), plays a crucial role in associating sensory and other information with pleasant and unpleasant feelings. This allows humans and other animals to adjust their behaviour based on positive and negative emotional reactions to objects or situations they encounter. For example, in rats, neurons in a region of the amygdala that receives auditory information respond differently to a tone following classical conditioning of an emotional response (fear) to that tone (Rogan, Staeubli, & LeDoux, 1997). In humans, neuroimaging data suggest that the amygdala plays a crucial role in detecting *other* people's emotions as well, particularly from observing their facial expressions (Scott, Young, Calder, & Hellawell, 1997).

Two systems for processing emotion

Recent data from a variety of species point to two distinct circuits involving the amygdala which produce emotional responses, particularly fear (Armony & LeDoux, 2000; LeDoux, 1995). The first circuit is evolutionarily primitive and requires no cortical involvement. The thalamus, which processes and routes sensory information to various parts of the brain, sends some relatively simple sensory information directly to the amygdala. This information can elicit an immediate emotional response (such as fear in response to an approaching snake).

Conditioning can occur through this thalamo-limbic circuit, even when links between the amygdala and the cortex have been severed, as long as the neural connections between the amygdala and the hippocampus are intact. (The hippocampus is involved in forming associations between stimuli and emotional reactions.) Thus, an animal can have a rapid response to a stimulus previously associated with fear or pain even before the cortex 'knows' anything about what is happening. For primitive vertebrates, this simple circuit was probably the sole basis of emotional reaction.

In humans and many other animals, however, the amygdala is also connected to higher processing centres in the cortex. Thus, when the thalamus sends sensory information to the amygdala, it simultaneously routes information to the cortex for more thorough examination. The cortex then transmits signals down to the amygdala. Based on this more complex information processing, a second emotional response may then occur.

Thus, the emotional reaction to a stimulus may occur in two stages, reflecting the semi-independent action of these two pathways (figure 10.15). One is a quick response based on a cursory reaction to gross stimulus features, involving a circuit running from the thalamus to the amygdala. (A dark shadow in the water frightens a swimmer.) The second process is slower, based on a more thorough cognitive appraisal, involving a thalamus-to-cortex-to-amygdala circuit. (The bather realises that the dark shadow is a buoy.) The initial thalamus-to-amygdala response typically occurs faster because it involves fewer synaptic connections; that is, the circuit is shorter and hence faster.

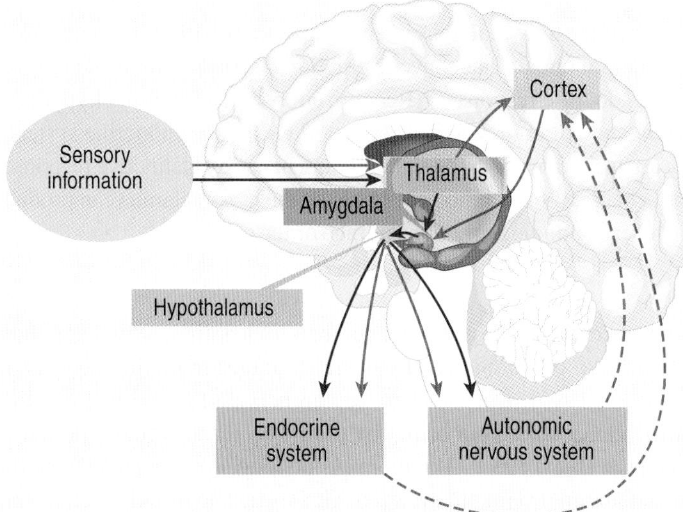

FIGURE 10.15
Two circuits for emotion processing. Emotionally relevant information is relayed from the thalamus simultaneously to the amygdala and the cortex. The first (blue arrows) leads to immediate responses. The second pathway (red solid arrows) allows the person to evaluate the stimulus on the basis of stored knowledge and goals. Both pathways activate the hypothalamus, which produces autonomic and endocrine changes that the cortex must interpret (dashed red arrows, indicating feedback to the cortex).

SOURCE: Adapted from LeDoux (1995).

The existence of two circuits for emotional processing raises fascinating questions about what happens when the affective reactions generated by these two circuits are in conflict. For example, a cancer patient may have an immediate aversive conditioned response to the room in which she receives chemotherapy (chapter 6). At the same time, she recognises that what happens in this room may be key to her survival. As a result of this second reaction, involving higher level cortical processing, she overrides the avoidance behaviour that would ordinarily be elicited by the conditioned emotional response and keeps appearing for her treatments.

The cortex

The cortex plays several roles with respect to emotion (Coricelli et al., 2005). As noted above, it allows people to consider whether a stimulus is safe or harmful. People with damage to the regions of the frontal cortex that receive input from the amygdala have difficulty making choices guided by their emotions (chapter 8) (Damasio, 1994). The cortex has a number of other emotional functions as well. One is its role in interpreting the meaning of peripheral responses, as when a person's shaky knees and dry throat while speaking in front of a group clue her in that she is anxious (Pribram, 1980). The frontal cortex plays a central role, as well, in regulating facial displays of emotion for social purposes, such as amplifying, minimising or feigning an emotion (Borod, 1992; Rinn, 1984; see also Harmer, Thilo, Rothwell, & Goodwin, 2001).

The right and left hemispheres of the cortex appear to be specialised, with the right hemisphere dominant in processing emotional cues from others and producing facial displays of emotion (Borod, 1992). In addition, as discussed earlier, approach-related emotions are associated with activation of the left frontal cortex, whereas avoidance-related emotions are linked to activation of the right frontal lobe (Davidson, 1992; Sutton & Davidson, 1997). People who tend towards more left- than right-hemisphere activation generally experience more positive than negative affect, whereas people who show the opposite pattern of hemispheric activation tend to have more negative mood states (figure 10.16).

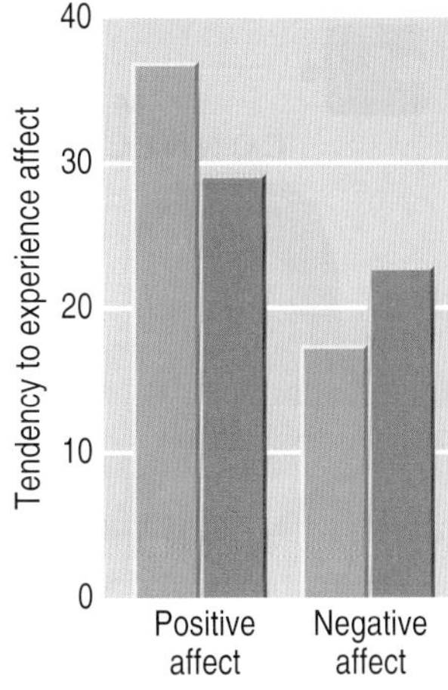

FIGURE **10.16**
Emotional experience and hemisphere activation. The figure shows mean positive and negative affect scores for participants with a strong tendency towards left- versus right-midfrontal activation. Participants with a bias towards left relative to right-hemisphere activation reported more positive and less negative affect.

SOURCE: Adapted from Tomarken, Davidson, Wheeler, and Doss (1992, p. 681).

Emotion regulation

Because emotions feel good or bad and can draw positive or negative responses from other people, people learn to regulate their emotions early in life. ***Emotion regulation*** refers to efforts to control emotional states (Gross, 1999; Kopp, 1989; Westen, Muderrisoglu, Fowler, Shedler, & Koren, 1997; see also Butler, Lee, & Gross, 2007).

People can regulate emotions before or after they occur. Whether they try to regulate an emotion before or after the fact, however, has important psychological and physiological consequences. For example, people often reframe the meaning of an event before it occurs, trying to put it in a perspective that will make them less upset. In contrast, they may try to suppress the emotion after the fact — that is, try not to feel it or show it to others. Although reframing events before they occur often leads to diminished negative feelings, suppression does not. In fact, suppression leads to more sympathetic nervous system activity — that is, arousal — including increased heart rate (Gross, 1998). Suppression also interferes with the ability to engage in other tasks, because it essentially keeps the person 'working overtime' to keep the feeling at bay (Richards & Gross, 2000).

Just as people regulate emotions, they similarly regulate moods, which are relatively extended emotional states. Whereas emotions often grab attention and disrupt ongoing activities, moods provide a background sense of positive or negative wellbeing (Oatley & Jenkins, 1992). Because moods, like emotions, include subjective feelings of pleasure and pain, they also become targets for emotion regulation strategies.

Emotion regulation strategies can be viewed as a form of procedural knowledge (chapter 7); that is, they are procedures people use to try to alter their emotional states (Westen, 1994). Many of these strategies are conscious, as when people exercise to 'blow off steam' or to take their mind off something that is bothering them. Much of the time, however, people learn what regulates their emotions in everyday life as they learn many procedures — implicitly. Some people, for example, regularly handle distress by avoiding awareness of unpleasant emotions (Weinberger, 1990). Stable styles of emotion regulation are already observable by the time children enter preschool (Cole, Zahn-Waxler, Fox, & Usher, 1996; Eisenberg, 2000).

Men and women tend to regulate different emotions. Men more often inhibit expressions of fear and sadness, whereas women are more likely to inhibit anger (Brody & Hall, 2000; Brody, Lovas, & Hay, 1995; see also Evers, Fischer, Manstead, & Rodriguez Mosquera, 2005). This makes sense in the light of gender differences in motivation for power versus motivation to maintain relationships (Fischer, 2000). How much gender differences in regulation of anger are really differences in *display* of anger is not entirely clear, however. Research finds, for example, that women express as much anger as men — but only if the target of the anger is not present. Furthermore, gender differences in emotional expression may reflect simple differences in what is deemed socially acceptable for men and women.

APPLY + DISCUSS

- What is the relationship between reason and desire, or more precisely, between cognition and affect?
- To what extent are psychological processes the same in men and women?

INTERIM SUMMARY

Emotional processes are distributed throughout the nervous system. The amygdala is involved in evaluating the emotional significance of a stimulus. It is also involved in detecting other people's emotions from their facial expression and vocal tone. The emotional reaction to a stimulus appears to occur through two distinct neural pathways: a quick response based on a circuit running from the thalamus to the amygdala and a slower response based on a more thorough cognitive appraisal, based on a thalamus-to-cortex-to-amygdala circuit. In both cases, the amygdala then passes information on to the hypothalamus, which is involved in regulating autonomic responses. The cortex plays multiple roles with respect to emotion, such as interpreting the meaning of events and translating emotional reactions into socially desirable behaviours. ***Emotion regulation*** refers to efforts to control emotional states.

Infants and young children learn to regulate their **emotions** in the context of their primary relationships. Children who feel **secure** in their **relationships** with their parents learn that they can find comfort through closeness. Others, particularly those whose parents are themselves uncomfortable with **intimacy** and physical affection, may learn to 'go it alone' and try to shut off feelings of dependence (chapter 13).

Perspectives on emotion

Having examined the components of emotion and its basis in the nervous system, we now turn to perspectives on emotion. We already explored the behavioural perspective on emotion in some detail in chapter 6, which emphasises conditioned emotional responses, such as fear upon seeing a doctor approaching with a hypodermic needle. Each of the other perspectives offers insight into emotion as well.

Psychodynamic perspective

A growing body of evidence supports a central, and somewhat counter intuitive, contention of psychodynamic theory: that people can be unconscious of their own emotional experience, and that unconscious emotional processes can influence thought, behaviour and even health (Berridge & Winkielman, 2003; Singer, 1990; Winkielman & Berridge, 2004). Researchers from multiple perspectives are increasingly converging on the same view (Westen, 1985, 1998).

Psychodynamic theory also suggests that we regularly delude ourselves about our own abilities and attributes to avoid the unpleasant emotional consequences of seeing ourselves more objectively. A growing body of research supports this hypothesis as well (e.g. Pratkanis, Eskenazi, & Greenwald, 1994; Vaillant, 1992a). One set of studies tested the hypothesis that people who disavow negative thoughts and feelings about themselves will pay a price physiologically (Shedler, Mayman, & Manis, 1993; see also Shedler, Karliner, & Katz, 2003). In the first part of the experiment, participants filled out a questionnaire about their mental health and then described in detail their earliest memories. Participants who self-reported themselves as happy and healthy on the questionnaire but whose early memories were filled with unpleasant emotion (which is empirically associated with psychological disturbance) were categorised as having 'illusory mental health'.

Next, the experimenters presented participants with a potentially anxiety-provoking task, such as making up TAT stories or answering items from an IQ test. Participants with illusory mental health exhibited numerous signs of psychological distress, including elevated heart rate and blood pressure, which are related to heart disease. These participants also consistently scored highest on indirect measures of anxiety, such as sighing and stammering. All the while, however, they consciously reported the *least* anxiety, suggesting the presence of unacknowledged anxiety (figure 10.17). Several other researchers have presented similar data on people who tend to keep themselves unaware of their emotions (e.g. Asendorpf & Scherer, 1983; Bell & Cook, 1998; Brosschot & Janssen, 1998; Weinberger, 1990).

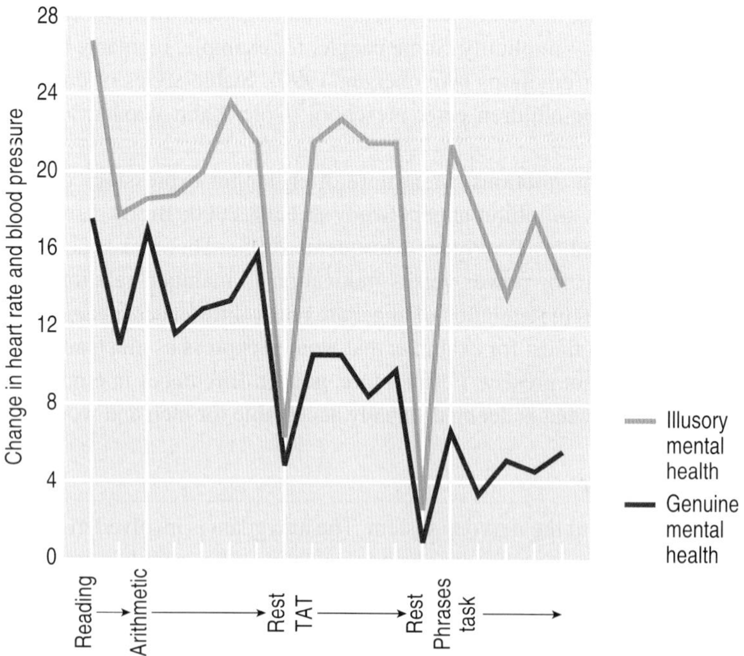

FIGURE 10.17
Illusory mental health. Participants who were judged high but who self-reported themselves to be low in distress showed substantially larger heart rate and blood pressure increases while performing such mildly stressful tasks as solving arithmetic questions and making up stories in response to TAT cards. Note, however, that during resting periods participants who deluded themselves showed as little reactivity as genuinely healthy participants, suggesting that their unconscious anxiety is activated only when performing a potentially threatening task.

SOURCE: Shedler et al. (1993).

Cognitive perspectives

As far back as the fifth century BC, Western thinkers viewed emotion as a disruptive force in human affairs. Plato, for example, believed that reason must rein in the passions, which otherwise distort rational thinking. Today, psychologists study the impact of feelings on cognitive processes such as memory and judgement empirically, as well as studying the reverse — the influence of cognition on emotion (Dalgleish & Bramham, 2001; Dalgleish & Power, 1999).

Another theory of emotion: interpretation and emotion

You have just climbed four flights of stairs to your apartment on a hot, humid day to be confronted by a roommate complaining about dirty dishes in the sink. Your heart is racing, and your face feels flushed. Are you angry? Or is your body simply registering the impact of climbing four flights of stairs in the heat? The way you react may well depend on the ***attributions*** (inferences about causes) you make about these bodily sensations (chapter 17).

In a classic paper, Stanley Schachter and Jerome Singer (1962) argued that a cognitive judgement or attribution is crucial to emotional experience. That is, when people experience a state of non-specific physiological arousal, which could be anger, happiness or any other feeling, they try to figure out what the arousal means. If situational cues suggest that they should be afraid, they interpret the arousal as fear; if the cues suggest excitement, they interpret their arousal as excitement. Thus, according to the ***Schachter–Singer theory***, emotion involves two factors: physiological arousal and cognitive interpretation (figure 10.18).

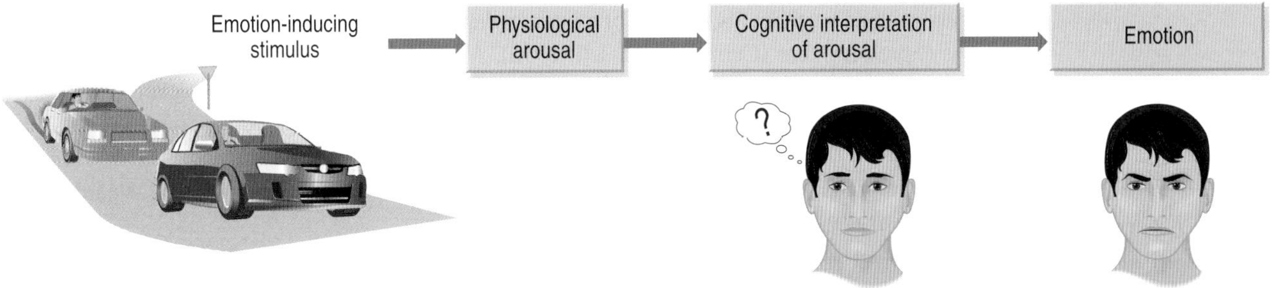

FIGURE **10.18**
The Schachter–Singer theory of emotion. According to Schachter and Singer, people must interpret their arousal (e.g. when cut off by a speeding car) in order to experience a specific emotion.

To test their hypothesis, Schachter and Singer injected participants with either adrenalin (a hormone involved in emotional arousal) or an inert placebo and correctly informed them, misinformed them or told them nothing about the possible effects of the injection. Participants then went to a waiting room, where they were joined by a confederate of the experimenter posing as another participant. The confederate either behaved angrily and stormed out of the room (designed to elicit anger) or playfully threw paper wads into the wastebasket, flew paper aeroplanes and generally enjoyed himself (designed to elicit euphoria).

Schachter and Singer predicted that participants who knew they had been injected with an arousing drug would attribute their arousal to the drug, whereas those who became aroused but did not know why would think they were either angry or euphoric, depending on the condition. The results were as predicted, suggesting that emotional experience is not simply the subjective awareness of arousal. Rather, it is a complex cognitive–affective state that includes inferences about the meaning of the arousal.

APPLY + DISCUSS

- How does the Schachter–Singer theory compare to the James–Lange theory?
- How does it compare to the Cannon–Bard theory?

Schachter and Singer's conclusions have drawn criticism on a number of grounds (see Leventhal & Tomarken, 1986). First, the findings have not been easy to replicate (Maslach, 1979; Mezzacappa, Katkin, & Palmer, 1999). Second, research shows that people can feel anxious or angry even after taking medication that blocks physiological arousal (Cleghorn, Peterfy, Pinter, & Pattee, 1970; Erdmann & Van Lindern, 1980). These data suggest that arousal may intensify emotional experience but may not be necessary for an emotion to occur (Reisenzein, 1983). Perhaps most importantly, as the research reviewed earlier suggests, different emotions have distinct physiological correlates; thus, emotion is not simply the interpretation of general arousal.

Nevertheless, numerous studies support the view that *some* degree of interpretation is involved in the experience of many emotional states. For instance, distinguishing between being tired (or fatigued) and being depressed requires interpretation, because the two physiological states share many common features. Excessive caffeine intake can also lead to arousal, which can be misattributed as anxiety and even contribute to the development of panic attacks (chapter 15).

Cognition and appraisal

In Schachter and Singer's study, participants initially became aroused by a shot of adrenalin. In normal life, however, people typically become aroused by their experiences rather than by injection. According to many cognitive theorists, people's emotions reflect their judgements and appraisals of the situations or stimuli that confront them (Lazarus, 1999b; Scherer, 1999; Smith & Ellsworth, 1985). For example, an event that affects a person's wellbeing in the present can lead to joy or distress, whereas an event that influences the person's potential wellbeing in the future can generate hope or fear (Ortony, Clore, & Collins, 1988).

Many of these cognitive principles operate cross-culturally (Mauro, Sato, & Tucker, 1992; Scherer, 1997). Others, however, depend on cultural conceptions of causality. For example, some preliterate societies believe that prolonged illness is the result of sorcery (Whiting & Child, 1953). Hence, the ill person or his loved ones may direct anger about the illness towards an accused sorcerer. The increased incidence in Australia of malpractice suits against doctors may reflect a similar process, as people look for someone to blame for tragedies.

Cognitive processes also play a central role in interpreting *other* people's emotions. For example, although facial expressions are a major source of information about people's emotions, knowledge about the situation can influence or sometimes override information from the face. In one study, the researchers showed participants the face of a woman that had been unambiguously interpreted in prior studies as expressing fear (Carroll & Russell, 1996). Along with the photograph, however, they told participants that the woman had made a reservation at a fancy restaurant and was kept waiting for over an hour as celebrities and others walked in and were seated immediately. When she reminded the maitre d' of her reservation, he told her that the tables were now full and the wait would probably be over an hour. With this information about the circumstances, the vast majority of participants interpreted the expression as anger, not fear.

These findings suggest that not only emotions but also interpretations of emotion reflect cognitive appraisals. From a connectionist point of view (chapter 8), facial expressions provide a powerful, 'hard-wired' set of constraints that influence the interpretation of another person's emotions. However, they are not the only constraints. In everyday life, knowledge about the situation also constrains inferences and may colour the way a person interprets another's facial expression.

Cognitive appraisals often underlie emotions, but not always. Indeed, emotional responses can sometimes precede complex cognitive evaluations of a stimulus — or, as psychologist Robert Zajonc (1980) put it, 'preferences need no inferences'. Zajonc demonstrated this hypothesis by using a phenomenon called the mere exposure effect, whereby people become more positive about stimuli the more times they are exposed to them. The experimenters briefly exposed participants several times to Japanese ideographs (written characters). When later asked about their preferences for particular characters, as expected from the mere exposure effect, participants preferred characters they had previously seen, even when they did not consciously recognise having seen them (Zajonc, 1980). Zajonc thus concluded that the subjective sense of liking or disliking a stimulus may occur independent of cognitions about that stimulus. At the very least, affect may precede the *conscious* cognitive appraisals proposed by many theorists.

Influence of emotion and mood on cognition

Just as cognition can influence emotion, so, too, can emotion and mood influence ongoing thought and memory. For example, anxiety can reduce working memory capacity and explicit problem solving by distracting the person from the task at hand (Eysenck, 1982; Richardson, 1996a). Mood can also influence the way people make judgements, inferences and predictions (Forgas, 1995; Mayer, Gasche, Braverman, & Evans, 1992; Ochsner & Schacter, 2000). People who are depressed, for example, tend to underestimate the probability of their own success and overestimate the probability of bad events occurring in the future (Beck, 1976, 1991). Once again, anger does not appear to be a classically negative affect. Whereas fear generally leads to pessimistic judgements of the future, anger can actually lead to optimistic judgements (Lerner & Keltner, 2000).

Emotional states influence both the encoding and retrieval of information in long-term memory (Bower, 1989; Kenealy, 1997; Mathews & Macleod, 1994). Individuals in a positive mood tend both to store and to retrieve more positive information (Isen, 1984, 1993). Positive mood also tends to facilitate memory more generally, independent of its emotional quality (Levine & Burgess, 1997). Negative moods also affect encoding and retrieval, but the mechanisms are more complex. Negative mood at retrieval facilitates recall of negative words, because they are associatively linked in memory by the feeling common to both of them (Ochsner, 2000). However, people actively fight negative moods because they are aversive, so they try to retrieve more positive information (Boden & Baumeister, 1997; Josephson, Singer, & Salovey, 1996). Thus, a motivational process (regulating a negative mood) may counteract an automatic cognitive process (recall of information congruent with current thought and mood).

Emotional processes can also have a direct physiological effect on memory (Bremner, 2005). Stressful emotional experiences can alter the structure of the brain (Gould, Tanapat, McEwen, Flugge, & Fuchs, 1998). In one study, monkeys in one condition were exposed to an emotionally threatening encounter — being placed in another monkey's cage, who attacked until the 'intruder' cowered in the corner. Compared to monkeys in a control condition, the traumatised monkeys showed a reduction in neural cells in the hippocampus, a neural structure that plays a crucial role in memory (chapter 7).

Evolutionary perspectives

The evolutionary perspective on emotion derives from Charles Darwin's (1872/1979) view that emotions serve an adaptive purpose. Darwin stressed their communicative function. Animals, including humans, signal their readiness to fight, run or attend to each other's needs through a variety of postural, facial and other nonverbal communications (see Buck, 1986). A baby's cry sends a signal to its parents, just as bared teeth display anger. These communications regulate social behaviour and increase the individual's chances of survival.

Darwin's theory explains why basic emotional expressions are wired into the organism and recognised cross-culturally. In fact, brain-imaging studies demonstrate the existence of hardwired neural circuits that function to recognise emotion in other people. As we have seen, the amygdala includes specific regions that allow people to recognise emotions such as fear and anger from other people's faces.

The similarities in facial expressions of emotions such as anger show their common evolutionary roots.

Emotion and motivation

Evolutionary theorists also view emotion as a powerful source of motivation — an *internal* communication that something must be done (Izard, 1977; Lang, 1995; Plutchik, 1980, 1997; Tomkins, 1962). For example, when people are threatened, they feel fear, which in turn leads them to deal with the threatening situation through either fight or flight. Emotions and drives may also operate in tandem to motivate action, as when excitement accompanies sexual arousal (Tomkins, 1986). Table 10.1 shows how emotional reactions motivate behaviours that promote survival and reproduction (Plutchik, 1980).

TABLE 10.1 Evolutionary links between emotion and behaviour in humans and other animals

Stimulus event	Emotion	Behaviour
Threat	Fear, terror, anxiety	Fight, flight
Obstacle	Anger, rage	Biting, hitting
Potential mate	Joy, ecstasy, excitement	Courtship, mating
Loss of valued person	Sadness, grief	Crying for help
Group member	Acceptance, trust	Grooming, sharing
New territory	Anticipation	Examining, mapping
Sudden novel object	Surprise	Stopping, attending

SOURCE: Adapted from Plutchik (1979). Copyright © 1979 by Pearson Education. Reprinted/adapted by permission of the publisher.

Jealousy: an evolutionary view

An emotion that is less well understood is jealousy. Why do people become jealous in intimate sexual relationships? One series of studies tested evolutionary hypotheses about men's and women's concerns about their partners' fidelity (Buss, Larsen, Westen, & Semmelroth, 1992). From an evolutionary perspective, a female can have only a limited number of children during her lifetime.

APPLY + DISCUSS

At the age of 64, US billionaire Jim Clark wed 29-year-old Australian supermodel Kristy Hinze.

- Why do older men marry younger women?
- Why do men and women become jealous in intimate sexual relationships?

Thus, to maximise her reproductive success, she should seek relationships with males who have resources to contribute to the care of her offspring. In fact, cross-cultural evidence demonstrates that one of the main mate selection criteria used by females is male resources, whether cattle or sports cars (chapter 18). From a female's point of view, then, infidelity by a mate accompanied by emotional commitment to the other woman is a major threat to resources because the male is likely to divert resources or even switch mates.

For males, the situation is different. If a male commits himself to an exclusive relationship with a female, he must be certain that the offspring in whom he is investing are his own. Because a man can never be entirely certain of paternity, the best he can do is prevent his mate from copulating with any other males. In males, then, jealousy should focus less on the female's emotional commitment or resources than on her tendency to give other males sexual access.

Indeed, in species ranging from insects to humans, males take extreme measures to prevent other males from inseminating their mates (Hasselquist & Bensch, 1991). Male birds in some species refuse to let a female out of their sight for days after insemination. In humans, male sexual jealousy is the leading cause of homicides and of spouse battering cross-culturally (Daly & Wilson, 1988).

A study by South Australian researchers found that men were responsible for approximately 94 percent of the homicides of adult women — and the vast majority of these killings occurred within an intimate relationship. They found the main reasons men kill their female partners are jealousy, desertion and the ending of a relationship (Bagshaw & Chung, 2000). In New Zealand, police statistics show that one woman is killed by her partner or ex-partner every five weeks (New Zealand Police, 2004).

To test the evolutionary hypothesis that males and females differ in their reasons for jealousy, university students were asked to 'imagine that you discover that the person with whom you've been seriously involved became interested in someone else' (Buss et al., 1992). Participants were to choose which of two scenarios would upset them more: 'imagining your partner forming a deep emotional attachment to that person' or 'imagining your partner enjoying passionate sexual intercourse with that person'. They were then asked a second question involving similar scenarios contrasting love and sex: 'imagining your partner falling in love with that other person' or 'imagining your partner trying different sexual positions with that other person'.

As figure 10.19 shows, 60 percent of males reported greater distress at the thought of sexual infidelity in response to the first question, compared to only 17 percent of the females, who were more concerned about emotional attachment. The second question yielded similar results, as did a third study in which the investigators measured distress *physiologically* rather than by self-report, using indicators such as pulse and subtle facial movements (such as a furrowed brow, which is associated with negative affect).

The evolutionary interpretation of these findings has not gone unchallenged (DeSteno & Salovey, 1996; Harris & Christenfeld, 1996). For example, the findings could be equally attributed to culture, because these studies were conducted in a single culture. However, cross-cultural researchers have found similar sex differences in countries as diverse as Germany and China, suggesting both cultural and evolutionary influences on feelings of jealousy (Buunk, Angleitner, Oubaid, & Buss, 1996; Geary, Rumsey, Bow-Thomas, & Hoard, 1995; see also Brase, Caprar, & Varacek, 2004).

Percentage reporting more distress to sexual infidelity
70
60
50
40
30
20
10
0
Male
Female
Sexual infidelity versus deep emotional infidelity
Sexual infidelity versus love infidelity

FIGURE 10.19
Jealousy in males and females.
The figure shows the percentage of participants reporting more distress to the sexual infidelity scenario than to imagining their lover either becoming deeply attached to someone else (left) or falling in love with someone else (right). Men are more concerned than women with sexual infidelity, and this is particularly true of those who have actually been in a committed sexual relationship.

SOURCE: Buss et al. (1992).

INTERIM SUMMARY

According to psychodynamic theory, people can be unconscious of their emotional experience and can act on emotions even when they lack subjective awareness of them. According to the ***Schachter–Singer theory***, a cognitive approach to emotion, emotion occurs as people interpret their physiological arousal. Subsequent research suggests that cognitive appraisals influence emotion and that mood and emotion can affect thought and memory. From an evolutionary perspective, emotion serves an important role in communication between members of a species. It is also a powerful source of motivation.

Central questions revisited

◆ The nature and causes of human motives and emotions

Having explored a variety of motives from multiple perspectives, we return to the basic questions with which we began. First, to what extent are people pulled by internal needs or pushed by external stimuli? Examination of the most biological of needs — hunger and sex — makes clear that even where a motive is undeniably rooted in biology, its strength depends in part on whether an appropriate stimulus presents itself, whether the stimulus is a hot fudge sundae or a hot date. A stimulus by itself, however, never motivates behaviour unless the person has acquired some motivational tendency towards it. A hot fudge sundae that calls one person's name will have no effect on another who is indifferent to ice-cream or chocolate.

A second and related question concerns the extent to which human motivation is rooted in biology or in culture and experience. As in nearly every other discussion of nature and nurture in this book, the answer is an intellectually unsatisfying 'yes' to both. Much as doing so might make us more comfortable, we cannot neatly parse motives into biological and psychosocial, because most biological needs are shaped by culture and experience, and most psychosocial motives draw on innate tendencies.

The third question pertains to the roles of thought, emotion and arousal in motivation. Do people act on the basis of cognition? Emotion? Generalised arousal? The most likely answer is that motivation typically requires both cognition and some form of emotional energy or arousal. To put it another way, cognitive representations or thoughts provide the direction or goals of a motive, and feelings provide the strength or force behind it, but neither alone is likely to move anyone anywhere. In neuropsychological terms, the cortex provides the map for life's journeys, but the hypothalamus and limbic system largely provide the fuel.

The final question was about the adaptive function of emotion. When do emotions guide behaviour in adaptive directions, and when do they lead us astray? The answer is not simple. Like other psychological functions, nature has endowed us with emotional responses 'designed' to lead us to approach and avoid people, objects and situations in ways that foster survival and reproduction. We tend to become happy when our goals are met, to be scared when we are in danger, to be anxious when danger could be around the corner and to feel guilty when we have hurt others who matter to us or on whose good graces we rely.

Nothing guarantees, however, that we will draw the 'right' emotional lessons from our experiences. People who have been rejected by someone they love may draw the conclusion, implicitly or explicitly, that they should avoid loving again, rather than that they should choose more wisely or maintain a realistic optimism, and hence deprive themselves of one of the greatest pleasures life affords. In general, emotions provide a compass for guiding our behaviour, but sometimes we need to look at other psychological 'instruments' to chart a more adaptive course.

◆

SUMMARY

1 Perspectives on motivation

- ***Motivation*** refers to the moving force that energises behaviour. It includes two components: what people want to do (the direction in which activity is motivated) and how strongly they want to do it (the strength of the motivation). Although some motives (e.g. eating and sex) are more clearly biologically based and others (e.g. relatedness to others and achievement) are more psychogenic or psychosocial, both types of motives have roots in biology and are shaped by culture and experience.
- Evolutionary psychologists argue that basic human motives derive from the tasks of survival and reproduction. They have expanded the concept of reproductive success to include inclusive fitness, which means that natural selection favours organisms that survive, reproduce and foster the survival and reproduction of their kin. Natural selection has endowed humans and other animals with motivational mechanisms that lead them to maximise their inclusive fitness.
- Freud believed that humans, like other animals, are motivated by internal tension states, or ***drives***, for sex and aggression. Contemporary psychodynamic theorists focus less on drives than on wishes and fears. They emphasise motives for relatedness and self-esteem, as well as sex and aggression, and contend that many human motives are unconscious.
- Behavioural theorists use the term drive to refer to motivation activated by a need state (such as hunger). According to ***drive-reduction theories***, deprivation of basic needs creates an unpleasant state of tension that leads the animal to act. If an action happens to reduce the tension, the behaviour is reinforced. Innate drives such as hunger, thirst and sex are ***primary drives***; with ***secondary drives***, an originally neutral stimulus becomes associated with drive reduction and hence itself becomes a motivator.
- Cognitive theorists often speak of ***goals***, valued outcomes established through social learning. ***Expectancy–value theories*** assert that motivation is a joint function of the value people place on an outcome and the extent to which they believe they can attain it. ***Goal-setting theory*** proposes that conscious goals regulate much of human action, particularly in work tasks. ***Self-determination theory*** suggests that people are most likely to develop ***intrinsic motivation*** (i.e. a genuine interest in the activity for its own sake) in a task or domain when learning is accompanied by feelings of competence, autonomy (i.e. control over their own actions, rather than control by others) and relatedness to others (i.e. a supportive, non-controlling interpersonal environment). Recently, cognitive researchers have begun to apply experimental methods to study ***implicit motives***, which occur outside awareness.
- According to Maslow's ***hierarchy of needs***, basic needs must be met before higher level needs become active. Maslow's hierarchy includes physiological, safety, belongingness, esteem and self-actualisation needs.

2 Regulation of eating

- Many motives, particularly biological motives related to survival, involve ***homoeostasis***, the body's tendency to maintain a relatively constant state, or internal equilibrium, that permits cells to live and function. Homoeostatic systems such as hunger and thirst share a number of common features, including a ***set point*** (a biologically optimal level the system strives to maintain); ***feedback mechanisms*** (which provide the system with information regarding the state of the system with respect to the variables being regulated); and ***corrective mechanisms*** (mechanisms that restore the system to its set point when needed).
- ***Metabolism*** refers to the processes by which the body transforms food into energy. It includes an ***absorptive phase***, in which the body is absorbing nutrients and a ***fasting phase***, in which the body is converting short- and long-term fuel stores into energy useful for the brain and body.
- Eating is regulated both by hunger and by ***satiety mechanisms*** (mechanisms for turning off eating). Hunger increases as glucose (and, to some extent, lipid) levels fall in the bloodstream. These falling levels signal the brain that short- and long-term fuels stores are diminishing. Hunger also reflects external cues, such as the palatability of food, learned meal times and the presence of other people. The body relies on multiple mechanisms to signal satiety (fullness), although the most important are receptors in the intestines that let the body know that the 'fuel tanks' will soon be full.
- ***Obesity*** is a condition characterised by a body weight over 15 percent above the ideal for a person's height and age. Genetic factors and dietary fat intake are strong predictors of body fat.

3 Sexual motivation

- Sexual motivation is driven by both fantasies and hormones and is shaped by culture. Hormones control sexual behaviour in humans and other animals through ***organisational effects*** (influencing the structure of neural circuitry) and ***activational effects*** (activating physiological changes that depend on this circuitry).
- ***Sexual orientation*** refers to the direction of a person's enduring sexual attraction — to members of the same sex, the opposite sex or both. Accumulating evidence on homosexuality suggests a substantial biological influence in both men and women.

4 Psychosocial motives

- ***Psychosocial needs*** are personal and interpersonal motives for such ends as mastery, achievement, power, self-esteem, affiliation and intimacy. Across cultures, the two major clusters of motives are ***agency*** (self-oriented goals, such as mastery or power) and ***relatedness*** (interpersonal motives for connection, or communion, with others).
- The ***need for achievement*** refers to a motive to succeed and to avoid failure, which is heavily influenced by cultural and economic conditions. Underlying achievement motivation are ***performance goals*** (to approach or achieve a socially visible standard) or ***mastery goals*** (to master the skill).
- Even for needs undeniably rooted in biology, such as hunger and sex, the strength of a motive depends in part on whether appropriate stimuli impinge on the organism. Motives also often reflect a subtle blend of innate factors (nature) and learning and culture (nurture). Motivation usually requires both cognition (representations that provide the direction of motivation) and emotional energy or arousal (providing the 'fuel', or strength, of motivation).

5 Theories of emotion

- ***Emotion*** is an evaluative response (a positive or negative feeling state) that typically includes subjective experience, physiological arousal and behavioural expression.
- The ***James–Lange*** theory asserts that the subjective experience of emotion results from bodily experience induced by an emotion-eliciting stimulus. According to this theory, we do not run because we are afraid; we become afraid because we run (and our hearts pound). In contrast, the ***Cannon–Bard*** theory proposes that emotion-inducing stimuli simultaneously elicit both emotional experience and bodily responses. Although both theories have their strengths and

limitations, recent research suggests that different emotions are, as James believed, associated with distinct, innate patterns of autonomic nervous system arousal.

- ***Emotional expression*** refers to facial and other outward indications of emotion, such as body language and tone of voice. Many aspects of emotional expression, particularly facial expression, are innate and cross-culturally universal. Culturally variable patterns of regulating and displaying emotion are called ***display rules***.
- Psychologists have attempted to produce a list of basic emotions, emotions common to the human species from which all other emotions and emotional blends can be derived. Anger, fear, happiness, sadness and disgust are listed by all theorists as basic. An even more fundamental distinction is that between ***positive affect*** and ***negative affect***.
- Emotions are controlled by neural pathways distributed throughout the nervous system. The hypothalamus activates sympathetic and endocrine responses related to emotion. The limbic system, and particularly the amygdala, is part of an emotional circuit that includes the hypothalamus. The cortex plays several roles with respect to emotion, particularly in the appraisal of events.
- The behaviourist perspective on emotion points to approach and avoidance systems associated with positive and negative affect, respectively. According to the psychodynamic perspective, people can be unconscious of their own emotional reactions, which can nonetheless influence thought, behaviour and health.
- From a cognitive perspective, the way people respond emotionally depends on the ***attributions*** they make — that is, their inferences about causes of the emotion and their own bodily sensations. According to the ***Schachter–Singer theory***, emotion involves two factors: physiological arousal and cognitive interpretation of the arousal. Emotion and ***mood*** (relatively extended emotional states that, unlike emotions, typically do not disrupt ongoing activities) have an impact on encoding, retrieval, judgement and decision making.
- The evolutionary perspective on emotion derives from Charles Darwin's view that emotions serve an adaptive purpose. Emotion has both communicative and motivational functions.

KEY TERMS

absorptive phase, *p. 385*
activational effects, *p. 394*
affect, *p. 401*
affiliation, *p. 397*
agency, *p. 397*
androgen insensitivity syndrome, *p. 393*
attachment motivation, *p. 397*
attributions, *p. 413*
basic emotions, *p. 407*
Cannon–Bard theory, *p. 402*
congenital adrenal hyperplasia, *p. 394*
corrective mechanisms, *p. 386*
display rules, *p. 406*
drive-reduction theorists, *p. 377*
drives, *p. 375*
emotion, *p. 374*
emotion regulation, *p. 411*
emotional expression, *p. 404*
ERG theory, *p. 381*
fasting phase, *p. 385*
feedback mechanisms, *p. 386*
goals, *p. 378*
goal-setting theory, *p. 378*
hierarchy of needs, *p. 380*
homoeostasis, *p. 386*
implicit motives, *p. 379*
incentive, *p. 377*
instincts, *p. 381*
intimacy, *p. 397*
intrinsic motivation, *p. 379*
James–Lange theory, *p. 401*
mastery goals, *p. 399*
metabolism, *p. 385*
mood, *p. 401*
motivation, *p. 374*
need for achievement, *p. 398*
negative affect, *p. 407*
obesity, *p. 389*
organisational effects, *p. 393*
performance-approach goals, *p. 398*
performance-avoidance goals, *p. 398*
performance goals, *p. 398*
positive affect, *p. 407*
primary drive, *p. 377*
psychosocial needs, *p. 397*
relatedness, *p. 397*
satiety mechanisms, *p. 387*
Schachter–Singer theory, *p. 413*
secondary drive, *p. 377*
self-actualisation needs, *p. 380*
self-determination theory, *p. 379*
set point, *p. 386*
sexual orientation, *p. 394*
sexual response cycle, *p. 392*
Thematic Apperception Test (TAT), *p. 376*

REVIEW QUESTIONS

1. Distinguish among the following theories of motivation: instinct theory, drive-reduction theory, goal-setting theory and self-determination theory.
2. Describe Maslow's hierarchy of needs and how it relates to the ERG theory.
3. Describe the two phases of metabolism and explain the role of the hypothalamus in eating.
4. Define sexual orientation and outline the four phases of the sexual response cycle.
5. Describe the three components of emotion and outline the six facial expressions recognised by people of every culture.

DISCUSSION QUESTIONS

1. Why is obesity highly prevalent in Western cultures such as Australia?
2. Is sexual orientation dependent primarily on genetic or environmental factors?
3. Why can jealousy be a powerful source of motivation in both males and females?

APPLICATION QUESTIONS

1. Test your understanding of achievement motivation by identifying each of the following scenarios as an example of one of the following three components of achievement motivation: performance-approach goals, performance-avoidance goals and mastery goals.
   (a) Neil is studying a foundation psychology course as part of his degree in general science. He submits all of the necessary assessment tasks by the due date and allows enough time to revise for the final exam. He hopes to receive at least a credit grade for the course.

(b) Lee Xuan is determined to become a professional swimmer. Each weekday she trains both before and after school. She has won her event at the national age swimming titles for the past two years, but continues to focus on refining her start technique at training in order to help her retain her competitive edge. On weekends, she even volunteers her time to help teach toddlers to learn to swim.

(c) Antonio is really worried about his driving test the next day and stays up all night studying the road safety rules. He knows that if he does not pass he will have to catch the bus to university each day instead of driving.

2. Test your understanding of emotion by identifying each of the following scenarios as an example of one of the following three theories of emotion: the James–Lange theory, the Cannon–Bard theory and the Schachter–Singer theory.
   (a) You are happy because you are smiling.
   (b) You are happy because being at a party with your friends explains why you are smiling.
   (c) You are happy because you are smiling and your heart is racing.

The solutions to the application questions can be found on page 834.

MULTIMEDIA RESOURCES

The *Cyberpsych* multimedia resource is available *as an option* to accompany this textbook to further develop your understanding of many key psychology concepts. *Cyberpsych* contains a wealth of rich media content and activities, and for this chapter includes:

- video clips on hormones and appetite, the brain and sexual preference, learning to forget, and robots that can mimic human facial expressions
- an interactive module on the motivation to satisfy hunger
- a concept animation on the polygraph test.

Personality

11

LEARNING OBJECTIVES

After studying this chapter you should be able to:

1. define personality
2. describe the basic assumptions of the psychodynamic theories of personality
3. discuss the basic principles of the cognitive–social theories of personality
4. compare and contrast the major trait theories of personality
5. describe the basic principles of the humanistic theories of personality
6. explain the links between genetics, personality and culture.

Personality refers to the enduring patterns of thought, feeling, motivation and behaviour that are expressed in different circumstances.

Psychodynamic theories

- Freud believed that psychological forces such as wishes, fears and intentions have a direction and an intensity, and that these unconscious motives and forces determine a person's behaviour; Freud's ***topographic model*** divided mental processes into three types: ***conscious, preconscious and unconscious.***
- ***Object relations theories*** focus on interpersonal disturbances and the mental processes that underlie the capacity for relatedness to others.
- Personality assessment involves tapping into a person's unconscious motives and conflicts using ***projective tests.***
- Freud's psychodynamic theory emphasises that human thought and action is laden with meaning. A major limitation is the theory's inadequate basis in scientifically sound observation.

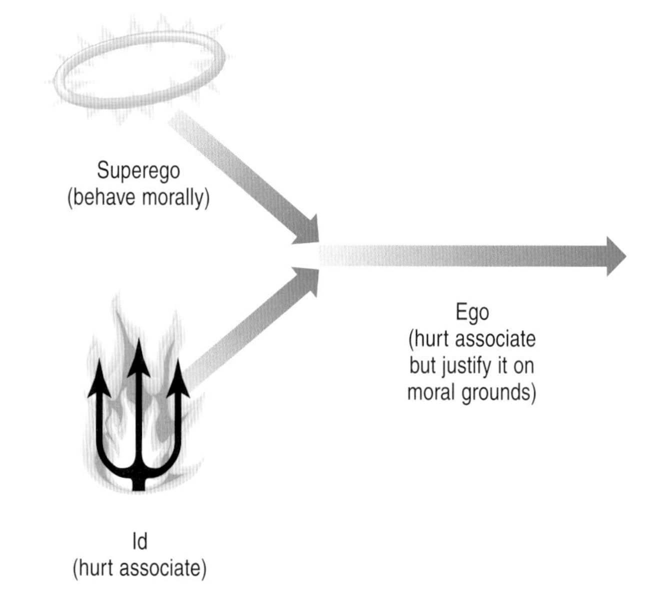

Cognitive–social theories

- ***Cognitive–social theories*** developed from behaviourist and cognitive roots and consider learning, beliefs, expectations and information processing to be central to personality.
- For people to respond to a situation, they must first encode it as relevant. George Kelly proposed that ***personal constructs*** substantially influence people's behaviour. People tend to focus on and select behaviours and situations that have personal value to them, which are relevant to their goals or life tasks.
- People's ***expectancies*** influence the actions they take. A ***behaviour–outcome expectancy*** is a belief that a certain behaviour will lead to a particular outcome. A ***competence*** is a skill used for solving problems.

Trait theories

- ***Traits*** are emotional, cognitive and behavioural tendencies that constitute underlying personality dimensions on which individuals vary.
- Eysenck identified three overarching psychological types, or constellations of traits: extroversion, neuroticism and psychoticism.
- According to the ***five factor model (FFM)***, personality can be reduced to five factors — openness to experience, conscientiousness, extroversion, agreeableness and neuroticism — each of which includes several lower order factors or facets.
- The debate over the extent to which personality is consistent led to recognition of the importance of person-by-situation interactions.
- The trait approach to personality has several advantages, including measurement of traits that help assess the heritability or consistency of personality. Limitations include the reliance on self-report and factor analytic methods. The number of traits necessary to explain personality remains the subject of debate.

Genetics, personality and culture

- Genetic views on personality suggest that many personality traits are inherited; ***heritability*** refers to the proportion of variance in a particular trait that is due to genetic influences.
- ***Interactionist approaches*** view causality as multidirectional, with personality, economics and culture mutually influencing one another.

Humanistic theories

- ***Humanistic approaches*** focus on distinctively human aspects of personality, such as how to find meaning in life or be true to oneself.
- According to Carl Rogers' ***person-centred approach***, psychology should try to understand individuals' ***phenomenal experience*** — the way they conceive of reality and experience themselves and their world — through ***empathy***.
- According to ***existential approaches*** to psychology, people have no fixed nature and must therefore create themselves.
- A major contribution of humanistic psychology is its unique focus on the way humans strive to find meaning in life. A limitation is that it does not offer a comprehensive theory of personality that is testable through empirical research methods.

Central questions: what are the elements of personality and how stable are they?

- Personality lies at the intersection of virtually all psychological processes — cognition, emotion and behaviour — and occurs through the interplay of those processes. Although there are many influences on what a person does at any given moment, we can accurately predict how a person is likely to behave in specific types of situations in the future.

STEVE and Mark Waugh are arguably the best known twins in Australia's sporting history. Both had long and distinguished careers in the Australian cricket team, probably the most hotly contested positions in the country's sporting landscape. What attributes enabled both twins to succeed so well in the same chosen sport? Was there an underlying genetic factor that predisposed both to success in playing cricket? What about personality — surely the secret of their shared success in the same sport came about because they shared the same personality traits? That is not necessarily so. Despite being twins, many argue that Steve and Mark are about as different in personality as two people can be. This difference was typified in their approaches at the batting crease. Steve was renowned as the tough street-fighter, grafting out runs with a minimum of fuss and extravagance. By contrast, Mark was lauded for his elegant stroke-play and his nonchalant attitude at the crease. While they shared the closest possible upbringing and environment, aside from cricket, the pair are said to have very different interests, lifestyles and social circles.

While Steve and Mark Waugh both represented Australia in cricket, the famous twins have very different interests, lifestyles and social circles away from the crease. While Steve (shown left) has launched the Steve Waugh Foundation, an international charity geared towards helping children diagnosed with rare diseases, Mark (pictured right), has pursued a career in the media and has been a keen punter for many years.

Identical twins Bridgitte and Paula Powers, known as the 'Twinnies', run a wildlife refuge together, are practically inseparable and have very similar personalities.

By contrast, consider identical twins Bridgitte and Paula Powers, who run a wildlife refuge on Queensland's Sunshine Coast specialising in caring for injured birdlife. The pair affectionately call themselves the 'Twinnies'. They live together, they dress the same and they finish each other's sentences. They are practically inseparable and share the same passion for rescuing and treating injured marine birds. As well as being physically identical, their personalities are almost the same as well.

Two sets of twins. Why are Mark and Steve Waugh so different in personality, and the 'Twinnies' so similar?

The term *personality* is a part of everyday speech. When people make statements such as 'Paul isn't the best-looking, but he has a nice personality', they typically use the term to denote the manner in which a person acts across a variety of situations. Psychologists use the term to describe not only an individual's reputation — the way the person acts and is known socially — but also the internal processes that create that reputation (Hogan, 1983, 1987). ***Personality*** refers to the enduring patterns of thought, feeling, motivation and behaviour that are expressed in different circumstances.

Personality psychologists have two aims. The first is to construct theories that describe the ***structure of personality*** — that is, the organisation of enduring patterns of thought, feeling, motivation and behaviour. The second aim is to study ***individual differences*** in personality — the way people differ from one another. People are multidimensional and it is unlikely that any one factor will account for complex behaviours. 'But knowing that an underlying pattern of behaviour is typical of one person but not another, and that this pattern may influence a range of abilities is key to understanding individual differences' (O'Connor, 2008, p. 216). Individual differences research provides a framework for studying all the variable behaviours a person may perform over time and in different situations, considering the person and the various person–world interactions (O'Connor, 2008).

Thus, personality psychologists study both how people resemble one another and how they differ. These two dimensions are intimately related. Theories of personality structure specify the central elements of personality, and these are the characteristics on which people differ.

The approach psychologists use to carry out this dual mission depends, once again, on their theoretical perspective. We begin by exploring Freud's models of the mind and the evolution of psychodynamic thinking about personality since his time. We then consider cognitive–social approaches, derived from theories of learning and cognition, which we have already examined in some detail. Next, we explore trait theories, which use everyday language to describe personality, and examine the extent to which personality traits are inherited, as suggested by the case of the 'Twinnies'. We then turn to humanistic theories, which focus on the way people wrestle with fundamental human concerns, such as mortality and meaning in life. We conclude by considering the extent to which personality differs across cultures.

Each of these theories differs in what its proponents believe to be the basic elements of personality: motives, thoughts, feelings, traits, behaviour. As you will see, no single answer has emerged to that question; in fact, it is one of the most hotly debated issues in the field of personality psychology. What psychologists do agree about is that personality lies at the intersection of virtually all psychological processes — cognition, emotion, behaviour — and occurs through the interplay of those processes. Our personality is not just our motives; nor is it just the way we solve problems or the ways we interact with other people. Personality is the way our motives, emotions and ways of thinking about ourselves, others and the world interact in particular situations to produce ways of responding that are characteristically 'ours'.

Throughout, we address two questions. First, what are the basic elements of personality? In other words, what are the components of personality that endure over time and give each of us our own distinct psychological 'fingerprint'? Second, how stable is personality? To what extent is an individual 'the same person' over time and across situations? And how much of this stability, as in the case of the 'Twinnies', reflects genetic influences?

INTERIM SUMMARY

Personality refers to the enduring patterns of thought, feeling, motivation and behaviour that are expressed in different circumstances. Personality psychologists construct general theories of the ***structure of personality*** (the way personality processes are organised) and ***individual differences*** (the way people vary in their personality characteristics).

Central questions

- What are the basic elements of personality?
- To what extent is personality stable over time and across situations?

Psychodynamic theories

Sigmund Freud developed the first comprehensive theory of personality. As a neurologist practising in the 1880s before the advent of psychiatry and clinical psychology, Freud encountered patients with a wide range of psychological disturbances. A particularly perplexing disorder was hysteria, in which a number of patients, most of them women, suffered from paralysis, numbness and fainting spells, with no apparent biological origin.

In seeking a treatment for the disorder, Freud was particularly influenced by the work of Jean Martin Charcot. Charcot, a French neurologist, demonstrated that hysterical symptoms could be produced — and alleviated, at least temporarily — through hypnosis. Paralysed patients could walk again under the influence of a hypnotic suggestion, but the symptoms usually returned before long. These patients *wanted* to walk, but something seemed to override their conscious determination or will, much as many individuals today with bulimia nervosa cannot stop binging and purging.

Freud reasoned that if a symptom is not of physiological origin and the patient is consciously trying to stop it but cannot, then opposing the conscious will must be an unconscious counter-will of equal or greater magnitude. This basic assumption was the centrepiece of Freud's theory of ***psychodynamics***, psychological dynamics analogous to dynamics among physical forces. According to Freud, psychological forces such as wishes, fears and intentions have a direction and an intensity. When several such motives collide and conflict, the balance of these forces determines the person's behaviour, as in the case of a patient suffering from a hysterical paralysis, whose will to move her leg is unconsciously overridden.

Freud's models

Why would a counter-will be unconscious? And what balance of unconscious forces could lead to paralysis or to a need to starve or drink oneself to death? Freud tried to answer these questions throughout his career by developing a series of models. Before turning to Freud's models and those of later psychodynamic theorists, a brief comment about method is in order. Many of the data presented in the next several pages are different from the laboratory data to which you are by now accustomed. Although we will emphasise laboratory evidence for psychodynamic theories, the basis for these theories has largely been observations during clinical sessions with patients.

Many critics have rightly pointed out the problems with case study data of this sort. They cannot easily be observed by other scientists, they are filtered through the biases of the investigator and they do not easily permit generalisation from one to another. Nevertheless, clinical observation has led to the discovery of many important phenomena, such as unconscious processes, that for up to a century were ignored or rejected by advocates of other perspectives for want of reliable methods to study them. As we have seen, psychological science cannot survive on a steady diet of case studies, but such studies can be extremely useful in formulating hypotheses (chapter 2).

Topographic model

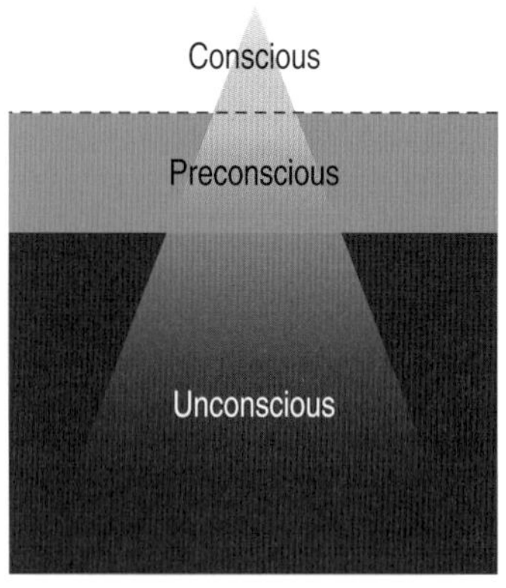

FIGURE 11.1
Freud's topographic model divided mental processes into three types: conscious, preconscious and unconscious. Freud believed that human behaviour was largely influenced by unconscious processes.

SOURCE: Adapted from McAdams (2000).

Freud's (1900/1965) first model, the ***topographic model***, used a spatial metaphor (the mind as split into sectors) that divided mental processes into three types: conscious, preconscious and unconscious (chapter 5). ***Conscious mental processes*** are rational, goal-directed thoughts at the centre of awareness. ***Preconscious mental processes*** are not conscious but could become conscious at any point, such as knowledge of the colour of robins. Finally, ***unconscious mental processes*** are irrational, organised along associative lines rather than by logic. As shown in figure 11.1, they are inaccessible to consciousness because they have been repressed — that is, kept from consciousness to avoid emotional distress.

Unconscious processes, while barred from consciousness, are not inert. Because they are not consciously acknowledged, they may leak into consciousness and affect behaviour in unexpected and often unwelcome ways, as in slips of the tongue. For example, a woman in her late thirties who was dating a man several years her junior was asked about the age difference. She replied, 'Oh, I don't think it really mothers'. Apparently, a part of her was not so sure. Freud also used the topographic model to understand dreams, distinguishing between their story line — the manifest content — and their underlying message — the latent content (chapter 5).

Conflict and ambivalence

A central feature of Freud's theory of psychodynamics was its emphasis on ***ambivalence*** — conflicting feelings or motives. From childhood on, we constantly interact with people who are important to us, but those interactions include both pleasant and unpleasant experiences. The same people who teach us how to love invariably teach us about frustration and rage.

For example, a patient named Bill was terrified that he would someday marry a woman who would treat him in the same harsh and belittling way that he felt his mother had treated his father. Unfortunately, Bill's most ingrained unconscious models of femininity and marital interaction were profoundly shaped by observing his parents as a child.

Years later, Bill and his friend Pete were in a pub, where they noticed two women. Pete thought they looked somewhat severe, that their gestures and facial expressions seemed harsh or angry, and that they were sending clear signals that they had no interest in being disturbed. Bill laughingly disagreed and insisted that he and Pete introduce themselves. Within ten minutes, both men felt, in Bill's words, like 'bananas in a blender'; the women spoke to them with sarcasm and barely veiled hostility for about five minutes and then simply turned back to each other and ignored them. Shortly afterwards, Bill asked his friend, 'How could you tell they'd treat us that way?' Pete replied, 'The more interesting question is, how could you *not* tell?'

Bill's behaviour reflects a classic psychodynamic ***conflict***, a tension or battle between opposing motives. On the one hand, he is consciously determined to avoid women like his mother; on the other, he is unconsciously compelled to provoke hostility or to pursue hostile women, which he has done on many occasions. Bill may not recall incidents from his childhood in which he came to associate excitement, love, sensuality and sexuality with a woman's scorn, but his behaviour nonetheless reflects those unconscious associations. In contemporary cognitive language, Bill's explicit, declarative beliefs and desires do not match the implicit, procedural tendencies expressed in his behaviour.

Research on ambivalence suggests that excessive conflict among competing motives can, in fact, exact a toll — in psychological symptoms, negative emotions and even ill health. For example, one study asked students to list 15 of their 'personal strivings' or goals, defined as objectives 'that you are typically trying to accomplish' (Emmons & King, 1988). To generate a measure of motivational conflict, the investigators then asked participants to rate the extent to which each striving conflicted with every other striving. Participants also reported how *unhappy* they would be if they were successful at each striving (a direct measure of ambivalence).

MAKING CONNECTIONS

Although the emphasis on ambivalence was once unique to psychodynamic approaches, today researchers studying **attitudes** recognise the ambivalence characteristic of many attitudes, such as mixed feelings about donating blood or donating their organs (chapter 16).

To see whether motivational conflict and ambivalence are associated with negative outcomes, the researchers then measured participants' mood twice a day over 21 consecutive days. They also had participants report any bodily ailments such as headaches, coughing and acne as well as number of visits to the health service. The results were striking. The more conflict and ambivalence, the more anxiety, depression, physical complaints and trips to the doctor.

Compromise formations

According to Freud, a single behaviour or a complex pattern of thought and action, as in Bill's case, typically reflects compromises among multiple and often conflicting forces. The solutions people develop to maximise fulfilment of conflicting motives simultaneously are called ***compromise formations*** (Brenner, 1982, 1994; Peterson, 2002; Rothstein, 2005).

Compromise formations occur in normal as well as abnormal functioning. For example, people are constantly faced with the conflicting motives of seeing themselves accurately and maintaining their self-esteem (Bosson & Swann, 1999; Morling & Epstein, 1997; Peterson, 2002; Swann, 1997). Understanding ourselves has obvious adaptive value, since it allows us to know what we can and cannot accomplish, what strategies we can use that will be likely to succeed and so on. On the other hand, few of us can withstand too close a look in the mirror.

Thus, a psychodynamic theorist would predict that, when faced with a conflict between accuracy and self-enhancement, people compromise, creating a distorted self-portrait that allows them a balance of satisfaction of both motives. Empirical research supports this view (see chapter 16). For example, when extroverted people are induced to believe that introversion is a predictor of academic success, they come to view themselves as less extroverted, but they will not completely deny their extroversion (see Kunda, 1990).

APPLY + DISCUSS

- If, as Freud suggests, people's behaviour is motivated by unconscious forces, to what degree are people actually responsible or accountable for their actions?
- If the unconscious is behind the behaviour, can it be fair to say that the person 'intended' to act in a particular way?
- Were Hitler, seen here after announcing the occupation of Austria, or Saddam Hussein responsible for their actions, or was their behaviour simply dictated by unconscious motives and drives?

INTERIM SUMMARY

Freud's ***topographic model*** divided mental processes into ***conscious*** (rational, goal-directed thoughts at the centre of awareness), ***preconscious*** (not conscious but could become conscious at any point) and ***unconscious*** (irrational, organised along associative lines and repressed). In this view, ***ambivalence*** (conflicting feelings or motives) and ***conflict*** (a tension or battle between opposing forces) are the rule in mental life. People resolve conflicts through ***compromise formations***, which try to maximise fulfilment of conflicting motives simultaneously.

Drive model

Freud's topographic model addressed conflict between conscious and unconscious motives. His second model, the ***drive***, or ***instinct model***, focused on what drives or motivates people. Influenced by the work of Charles Darwin, Freud stressed the continuity of human and non-human behaviour. He hypothesised that humans are motivated by drives, or instincts, in the same way as other animals.

Freud (1933/1965) proposed two basic drives: sex and aggression. He defined the sexual drive, or ***libido***, more broadly than its colloquial usage. Libido refers as much to pleasure seeking, sensuality and love as it does to desires for sexual intercourse. Expressions of libido may be as varied as daydreaming about sex or romance, enjoying a close friendship or selecting a career likely to attract a potential spouse because of its status or income potential. People also express aggression in various ways, some socially acceptable and others not. We see aggression on the sports field, in the corporate boardroom and in just about every video game on the market. Freud would not have been surprised by two criteria often used to determine whether television shows and movies are acceptable for general viewing — the amount of sex and the amount of aggression — because these are the same things that individuals regulate and censor in themselves.

Developmental model

Freud (1933/1965) considered the development of the libidinal drive the key to personality development and hence proposed a theory of ***psychosexual stages*** — stages in the development of personality, sexuality and motivation (table 11.1). The psychosexual stages define Freud's ***developmental model***, his model of how children develop. These stages reflect the child's evolving quest for pleasure and growing realisation of the social limitations on this quest. At each stage, libido is focused on a particular part of the body, or erogenous zone (region of the body that can generate sexual pleasure).

TABLE 11.1 **Freud's psychosexual stages**

Stage	Age	Conflicts and concerns
Oral	0–18 months	Dependency
Anal	2–3 years	Orderliness, cleanliness, control, compliance
Phallic	4–6 years	Identification with parents (especially same sex) and others, Oedipus complex, establishment of conscience
Latency	7–11 years	Sublimation of sexual and aggressive impulses
Genital	12+ years	Mature sexuality and relationships

To understand these stages, we must view them both narrowly and broadly. That is, the stages describe specific bodily experiences, but they also represent broader psychological and psychosocial conflicts and concerns (Erikson, 1963). Freud's psychosexual stages may sound preposterous at first, but if you try to imagine yourself a child at each stage — sucking your mother's breast for nourishment, fighting with your parents about toilet training (a fight that can go on for a year), or sobbing and shrieking as your parents leave you alone in your room at night — the broader issues may seem less absurd than at first glance.

Oral stage

During the ***oral stage*** (roughly the first 18 months of life), children explore the world through their mouths. Many parents are aghast to observe that their infants literally put anything that is not nailed down into their mouths. During the oral stage, sucking the breast or bottle is the means by which infants gain nourishment, but it is also a prime avenue for *social* nourishment — that is, warmth and closeness.

From a broader standpoint, in the oral stage children develop wishes and expectations about dependence because they are totally dependent on their caretakers. Difficulties (such as chronic dissatisfaction or discomfort) during the oral stage — or any of the stages — can lead to ***fixations***, conflicts or concerns that persist beyond the developmental period in which they arise. According to Freud, people with fixations at the oral stage may be extremely clingy and dependent, with an exaggerated need for approval, nurturance and love. More concretely, the soothing and pleasure associated with mouthing and sucking during this stage may lead to fixated behaviour such as thumb sucking and nail biting.

Anal stage

The ***anal stage*** (roughly ages two to three) is characterised by conflicts with parents about compliance and defiance, which Freud linked to conflicts over toilet training. Freud argued that these conflicts form the basis of attitudes towards order and disorder, giving and withholding, and messiness and cleanliness. Imagine a toddler, having scarcely been told 'no' to anything, who finds himself barraged by rules during his second year, with the ultimate insult of being told to control his own body! This is the age during which the child learns to do unto others what they are now constantly doing unto him: saying *no*.

More concretely, Freud proposed that in the anal stage the child discovers that the anus can be a source of pleasurable excitation. If this seems preposterous, ask any childcare worker or parent about the way young children seem to enjoy this part of the body and its warm, squishy contents. Within a few short years the anal region is experienced as so disgusting that we cannot even touch it without the intervention of a piece of paper. Paradoxically, however, anal elements often enter into adult sexual interest and arousal ('Nice bum!'), foreplay (looking at or touching the buttocks or anus) and intercourse. Freud would suggest that apparent contradictions of this sort — is it disgusting or erotically arousing? — point to the presence of conflict, between impulses for pleasure and prohibitions against them.

People with anal fixations exhibit a variety of behavioural tendencies. On the one hand, they may be overly orderly, neat and punctual or, on the other, extremely messy, stubborn or constantly late. They may have conflicts about giving and receiving or about compliance versus non-compliance with other people's demands. Research finds that people with these character traits tend to find anal humour particularly compelling (O'Neill, Greenberg, & Fisher, 1992)! Children can also regress to anal issues, particularly in times of stress. Regression means reverting to conflicts or modes of managing emotion characteristic of an earlier stage; such as when young children whose parents are undergoing a divorce suddenly start soiling themselves again (an anal regression) or sucking their thumbs (regression to the oral stage).

APPLY + DISCUSS

Many people doubt Freud's depiction of the anal region as an erogenous zone. However, some celebrities, such as actress Jennifer Lopez, as well as other high-profile personalities, are renowned for their appealing buttocks.

- Are buttocks an object of desire in Western culture? If so, why?
- What other theories might account for how desires for pleasure involving the buttocks are learned?

Phallic stage

During the ***phallic stage*** (roughly ages four to six), children enjoy the pleasure they can obtain from touching their genitals and even from masturbating. Preschool teachers can attest that children commonly masturbate while rocking themselves to sleep at naptime, and during bathroom visits little boys can be seen comparing the size of their penises. During this stage children also become very aware of differences between boys and girls and mummies and daddies.

More broadly, during the phallic stage the child identifies with significant others, especially the same-sex parent. ***Identification*** means making another person part of oneself: imitating the person's behaviour, changing the self-concept to see oneself as like the person and trying to become more like the person by adopting his or her values and attitudes. According to Freud, much of adult personality is built through identification, as the child internalises motives, behaviours, beliefs and ideals.

A longitudinal study of children's attitudes towards themselves provides some empirical support for Freud's theory of identification (Koestner, Zuroff, & Powers, 1991). The extent to which girls were self-critical at age 12 correlated with observer ratings of their mothers as restrictive and rejecting at age five. For boys, self-criticism correlated with these same behaviours manifested by their fathers, not their mothers. This suggests that boys' and girls' attitudes towards themselves may be strongly influenced by identification with the same-sex parent, although, of course, children identify with both parents.

Identification has many roots. Freud emphasised its link to the Oedipus complex, named after the character in a Greek legend who unknowingly killed his father and slept with his mother. The ***Oedipus complex*** refers to Freud's hypothesis that little boys want an exclusive relationship with their mothers, and little girls want an exclusive relationship with their fathers. From a young boy's perspective, 'Why should Mummy spend the night alone with Daddy? Why can't I go in there instead?' (Many children manage a compromise by finding ways to spend the night in the middle.) Children sometimes

The prevelance of older men dating younger women, and older women dating younger men (popularised as the 'cougar' phenomenon) might have an association with the Oedipus complex. Actor Ashton Kutcher is closer in age to the oldest daughter of his wife, Demi Moore, than he is to her, but their relationship has remained strong despite a 15-year age difference.

make astoundingly Oedipal comments. One four-year-old matter-of-factly declared to his mother, 'Mummy, Daddy has to leave. I don't like him anymore'. When the child's mother asked why, the boy bluntly acknowledged, 'He has a bigger penis than I do!'

Thus, according to Freud, children learn about love and sensual gratification from their parents, and they desire an exclusive sexual relationship with the parent of the opposite sex (bearing in mind the broad meaning of 'sexual' in Freud's theory). At the same time, these wishes are so threatening that they are quickly repressed or renounced (consciously given up). Boys unconsciously fear that their father, their ultimate rival, will castrate them because of their desires for their mother (the ***castration complex***). The fear is so threatening that they repress their Oedipal wishes and identify with their father. In other words, they internalise a moral prohibition against incest as a way of preventing themselves from acting on their wishes, which would be dangerous, and they instead become like their father in the hope of someday obtaining someone like their mother. Girls, too, renounce their secret wishes towards their father and identify with their mother because they fear losing her love.

According to Freud, during the phallic stage, girls develop ***penis envy***, the belief that because they lack a penis they are inferior to boys. Taken on a metaphorical level, penis envy refers to the envy a girl develops in a society in which men's activities seem more interesting and valued (Horney, 1926). Given the concreteness of childhood cognition, that a five-year-old might symbolise this in terms of having or not having a penis would not be surprising. Parents often report that their daughters cry when bathing with brothers, who have 'one of those things'.

Latency stage

During the ***latency stage*** (roughly ages seven to 11), children repress their sexual impulses and continue to identify with their same-sex parent. They also learn to channel their sexual and aggressive drives into socially acceptable activities such as school, sports and art. Whereas people fixated at the phallic stage may be preoccupied with attracting mates or take on stereotypical characteristics of their own or the opposite gender, individuals fixated at the latency stage may seem totally asexual.

APPLY + DISCUSS

If you run down a list of obscenities — taboo words — you will find that most reflect one or another of Freud's stages. Indeed, perhaps the most vulgar thing someone can call another person in our society has a distinctly Oedipal ring (you can figure this one out on your own), and its originators were surely not psychoanalysts.

- How might Freud have explained this?
- What other explanations could make sense of this phenomenon?

Genital stage

During the ***genital stage*** (approximately age 12 and beyond), conscious sexuality resurfaces after years of repression, and genital sex becomes the primary goal of sexual activity. At this stage, people become capable of relating to and loving others on a mature level and carrying out adult responsibilities such as work and parenting. Prior elements of sexuality do not disappear — most people's foreplay continues to have oral and anal components — but these 'pre-genital' elements become integrated into patterns of sexual activity involving genital satisfaction. This stage was probably least elaborated by Freud, who believed that the major aspects of personality become firmly established in childhood and may require considerable effort to change thereafter.

Experimental data provide surprising support for some aspects of Freud's psychosexual theories, such as his theory of the Oedipus complex (see Fisher & Greenberg, 1985, 1996). For example, in one study researchers asked parents of children aged three to six to record the number of affectionate and aggressive acts the children displayed towards their same- and opposite-sex parents over a seven-day period (Watson & Getz, 1990). As predicted by Freud, affection towards the opposite-sex parent and aggression towards the same-sex parent were significantly more common than the reverse pattern.

Even the notion of castration anxiety, perhaps Freud's most seemingly outlandish concept, may account for certain observations. In the men's dressing room of a department store, two boys aged about five were struggling with a curtain that would not quite close — pulling the curtain one way only seemed to open up the other side — when one of them was overheard saying, 'You've got to make sure it closes so no-one can come in and steal your ding'. Surely no-one had warned the child to protect his 'ding' at the department store.

INTERIM SUMMARY

According to Freud's ***drive*** or ***instinct model***, people have two instincts, sex and aggression. His ***developmental model*** proposed a series of ***psychosexual stages***. During the ***oral stage***, pleasure is focused on the mouth, and children wrestle with dependence. During the ***anal stage***, children derive pleasure from the anus and wrestle with issues of compliance, orderliness and cleanliness. During the ***phallic stage***, children's personalities develop through ***identification*** with others. They also experience the Oedipus complex, in which they want an exclusive relationship with their opposite-sex parent. In the ***latency stage*** children repress their sexual impulses. In the ***genital stage*** they develop mature sexuality and a capacity for emotional intimacy.

Structural model

The final model Freud developed was his ***structural model***, which described conflict in terms of desires on the one hand and the dictates of conscience or the constraints of reality on the other (Freud, 1923, 1933/1965). Previously, Freud had seen conflict in terms of conscious versus unconscious forces, but he came to believe that conflicts between what we want and what we believe is moral lead to most psychological distress.

Id, ego and superego

The structural model posits three sets of mental forces, or structures: id, ego and superego. The ***id*** is the reservoir of sexual and aggressive energy. It is driven by impulses and, like the unconscious of the topographic model, is characterised by ***primary process thinking***: wishful, illogical and associative thought. The id works according to the ***pleasure principle***, seeking immediate satisfaction and gratification, with little or no consideration for the longer term ramifications.

To counterbalance the 'untamed passions' of the id (Freud, 1933/1965, p. 76), the ***superego*** acts as a conscience and source of ideals. The superego is the parental voice within the person, established through identification.

The ***ego*** is the structure that must somehow balance desire, reality and morality. Freud described the ego as serving three masters: the id, the external world and the superego. Unlike the id, the ego is capable of ***secondary process thinking***, which is rational, logical and goal directed. The ego obeys the ***reality principle***, recognising that the immediate desire for pleasure needs to be offset against the reality of what the consequences might be. The ego brings pleasure-seeking impulses in line with the real world. The ego is thus responsible for cognition and problem solving (Hartmann, 1939). It is also responsible for managing emotions (chapter 10) and finding compromises among competing demands.

To demonstrate how conflict among these forces plays out, consider an example taken from the psychotherapy of an angry, somewhat insecure junior partner at a law firm who felt threatened by a promising young associate. The partner decided to give the associate a poor job performance evaluation, even though the associate was one of the best lawyers the firm had ever had. The partner convinced himself that he was justified because the associate could be working harder, and he wanted to send a message that laziness would get the young lawyer nowhere — an admirable goal indeed!

From the perspective of the structural model (figure 11.2), the perceived threat activated aggressive wishes (id) to hurt the associate (give him a poor evaluation). The partner's conscience (superego), on the other hand, would not permit such a blatant display of aggression and unfairness. Hence, he unconsciously forged a compromise (ego). He satisfied his aggression by giving the poor evaluation, but he cloaked his action in the language of the superego, claiming to be helping the young associate by discouraging his laziness, and hence satisfying his own conscience.

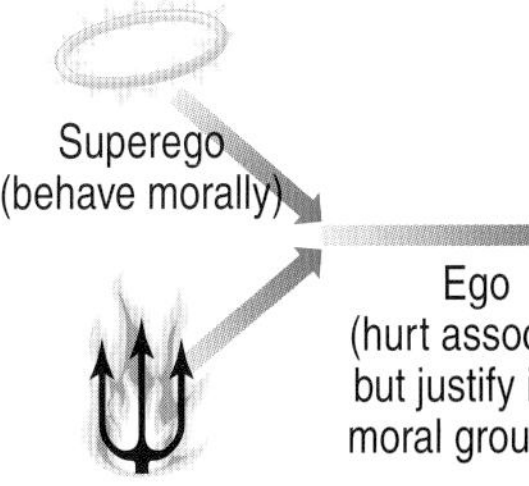

FIGURE 11.2
Freud's structural model as applied to the law firm described. Conflict among various forces leads to a compromise forged by the ego.

Defence mechanisms

When people confront problems in their lives, they typically draw on problem-solving strategies that have worked for them in the past, rather than inventing new solutions to every problem (chapter 8). The same is true of emotional problem solving. According to psychodynamic theory, people regulate their emotions and deal with their conflicts by employing ***defence mechanisms*** — unconscious mental processes aimed at protecting the person from unpleasant emotions (particularly anxiety) or bolstering pleasurable emotions. Psychodynamic psychologists have identified a number of defence mechanisms, many of which have been studied empirically (Cramer, 1996, 2006; Freud, 1936; Kwon, 1999; Vaillant & Vaillant, 1998).

One defence we have encountered before is ***repression***, in which a person keeps thoughts or memories that would be too threatening to acknowledge from awareness (chapter 7). A similar mechanism is ***denial*** in which a person refuses to acknowledge external realities or emotions (such as anxiety). Denial is at work when an individual notices a peculiar skin growth but concludes that 'it's nothing'. Much of the time it *is* nothing, but this defence can lead to failure to seek treatment for a potentially life-threatening cancer (see Cramer, 2002, 2007; Strauss, Spitzer, & Muskin, 1990; Zervas, Augustine, & Fricchione, 1993).

Projection is a defence mechanism by which a person attributes his own unacknowledged feelings or impulses to others. The hard-driving businessman who thinks his competitors, suppliers and customers are always trying to cheat him may in fact be the one with questionable ethics. To recognise his own greed and lack of concern for others would conflict with his conscience, so instead he sees these traits in others.

Research suggests a cognitive mechanism through which projection may occur (Newman, Duff, & Baumeister, 1997). Paradoxically, keeping a thought out of awareness keeps it chronically activated at an implicit level. To stop a thought from attaining consciousness, the mind essentially sets up an automatic mechanism to 'keep a look-out' for the thought; this process has the unintended by-product of keeping the thought active (Wegner, 1992). Thus, when a person is trying not to see himself as dishonest, the concept of dishonesty remains active implicitly. When someone else then behaves in a way that could be interpreted as either accidental or dishonest, the concept dishonesty is already activated and is thus more likely to be used to interpret the person's behaviour.

Reaction formation is a defence mechanism whereby a person fails to acknowledge unacceptable impulses and overemphasises their opposites. For example, a sibling might overpraise her sister's accomplishment even though she is resentful.

APPLY + DISCUSS

The Internet Encyclopedia of Philosophy provides an interesting overview of Freud's theory of the unconscious and psychoanalysis as therapy. It should be available to access via your university course website for this subject. Even people who are vehemently opposed to Freud's theorising find themselves using his terminology in their everyday speech and his defence mechanisms in their everyday behaviour.

- Which of the defence mechanisms discussed in this section have you engaged in? Why?
- What circumstances or feelings prompted you to use a defence mechanism? Do you tend to favour one mechanism over another?
- Is it easier to identify the use of a defence mechanism in yourself or in other people? Why or why not?

Sublimation is a defence that involves converting sexual or aggressive impulses into socially acceptable activities. A young boy may turn his feelings of competition with his father or brother into a desire to excel in competitive sports or to succeed in business when he is older.

Rationalisation is a defence in which the person explains away actions in a seemingly logical way to avoid uncomfortable feelings, especially guilt or shame. A student who plagiarises her assignment and justifies her actions by saying that passing the course will help her earn her public policy degree and serve the community is using rationalisation to justify her dishonesty.

Displacement is a defence that involves people directing their emotions, especially anger, away from the real target to a substitute. People may choose to vent their emotions on another object, animal or person instead of the real target of their feelings. This defence is often used when the real target is seen as too threatening or upsetting to confront directly. For example, a man may take out his anger on a punching bag following a heated argument with his wife.

Regression is a defence that involves a person reverting back to an earlier stage of psychological development, typically when under a period of great stress or hardship. For example, a politician under the heat of intense scrutiny on the floor of parliament may revert to name calling in response to taunts from other politicians.

Another defence mechanism, ***passive aggression***, is the indirect expression of anger towards others. One administrator frustrated everyone around him by 'sitting on' important documents that required a fast turnaround. To be actively aggressive would run afoul of his moral standards and potentially lead to a reprimand from his boss, so he accomplished the same goal — frustrating co-workers and thus satisfying his aggressive impulses — in a way that allowed him to disavow any intention or responsibility.

Using defences is neither abnormal nor unhealthy. In fact, some degree of defensive distortion may be useful, such as the tendency for people to see themselves more positively than is warranted by reality (Norem, 1998; Taylor & Armor, 1996; Taylor & Brown, 1988). A bit of denial can also be essential to surmounting seemingly insurmountable odds, as when an aspiring novelist persists despite repeated rejection and suddenly gets a break.

Defence mechanisms are generally considered properties of individuals, but some defences are patterned at a cultural level (Spiro, 1965). In the Kerala province of India, where cattle are considered sacred and cannot be killed, an anthropologist observed that the mortality rate for male cattle was twice as high as for females (Harris, 1979). Although all the farmers espoused the Hindu prohibition against slaughtering cattle, they were essentially starving the males to death because males cannot give milk and were a drain on scarce economic resources.

INTERIM SUMMARY

Freud's ***structural model*** focuses on conflict among the ***id*** (the reservoir of instincts or desires), ***superego*** (conscience) and ***ego*** (the structure that tries to balance desire, reality and morality). The id operates according to the ***pleasure principle***, while the ego operates according to the ***reality principle***. People regulate their emotions and deal with their conflicts by employing ***defence mechanisms***, unconscious mental processes aimed at protecting the person from unpleasant emotions (particularly anxiety) or bolstering pleasurable emotions.

Object relations theories

During Freud's lifetime, psychodynamic theory evolved from an 'id psychology' to an 'ego psychology'. Freud began with a focus on motivation and instinct (his drive theory, which formed the basis of his theory of the id). Later, he and other psychoanalysts turned their attention to the ways people cope with their feelings (defences) and adapt to reality while trying to fulfil their needs (ego functions).

Perhaps the most important theoretical development in psychoanalysis since Freud's death has been the emergence of object relations theories. When once asked what the healthy person should be able to do, Freud responded, 'to love and to work'. Object relations theories attempt to account for the difficulties of people with high impairment in both domains (love and work), who may show an extreme inability to maintain commitment or trust in relationships, a disavowal of any wish for intimate human contact at all or an inability to sustain employment because of chronic interpersonal conflicts with co-workers and employers. ***Object relations*** refers to enduring patterns of behaviour in intimate relationships and to the motivational, cognitive and affective processes that produce those patterns. (The term comes from Freud's view that an instinct has an aim, which is some kind of gratification, and an object, which is usually a person. Thus, object relations theories are about people's relationships with others.)

Of particular importance are people's representations of self, significant others and relationships (Bowlby, 1982; Jacobson, 1964; Sandler & Rosenblatt, 1962). Empirically, people who have difficulty maintaining relationships tend to view themselves and others in more negative ways, frequently expecting abuse or malevolence in relationships (Calabrese, Farber, & Westen, 2005; Nigg, Lohr, Westen, Gold, & Silk, 1992). They also have trouble maintaining *constancy* of their representations; that is, they have difficulty holding in mind positive representations of people they love during the inevitable interpersonal conflicts that friends, family members and lovers experience (Baker, Silk, Westen, Nigg, & Lohr, 1992; Kernberg, 1984). As a result, they may break off or irreparably damage their relationships while angry.

Instead of explaining such behaviour in terms of neurotic compromise solutions to unconscious conflicts, object relations theorists explain severe interpersonal problems in terms of maladaptive interpersonal patterns laid down in the first few years of life. Whereas Freud described development as a sequence of psychosexual stages, object relations theorists describe it as a progressive movement towards more mature relatedness to others. Like defensive processes, many aspects of object relations theory have been studied empirically (Ackerman, Hilsenroth, Clemence, Weatherill, & Fowler, 2000; Blatt, Auerbach, & Levy, 1997; Masling & Bornstein, 1994; Stricker & Healey, 1990; Westen, 1991, 1992).

A recent outgrowth of object relations theories, called relational theories, extends this line of thinking to people who are less troubled, arguing that for all individuals adaptation is primarily adaptation to other people (Aron, 1996; Mitchell, 1988; Mitchell & Aron, 1999). According to ***relational theories***, the need for relatedness is a central motive in humans, and people will distort their personalities to maintain ties to important people in their lives. Like object relations theorists, relational theorists also argue that many of the ways adults interact with one another, particularly in intimate relationships, reflect patterns of relatedness learned in childhood.

MAKING CONNECTIONS

The psychoanalyst Erik Erikson proposed a **psychosocial model of development**, which stresses the interpersonal nature of human development, to complement Freud's psychosexual model. For example, alongside Freud's oral stage, Erikson proposed a more interpersonal stage, in which the child wrestles with how much she can trust people. Similarly, adolescence is a time of discovering a sense of **self**, or **identity**, and not just maturing sexually (chapters 12 and 17).

INTERIM SUMMARY

Object relations theories focus on interpersonal disturbances and the mental processes that underlie the capacity for relatedness to others. ***Relational theories*** argue that for all individuals adaptation is primarily adaptation to other people.

Assessing unconscious patterns

The core assumption of all psychodynamic approaches, that many personality processes are unconscious, raises a difficult question: how can one assess what one cannot directly access? This dilemma led to a number of methods of personality assessment, including indirect methods called projective tests.

Life history methods

Life history methods aim to understand the whole person in the context of his life experience and environment (see Alexander, 1990; McAdams, 2001; McAdams & de St. Aubin, 1998; McAdams & West, 1997; Runyan, 1984). They are the bread and butter of psychodynamic investigation, typically involving case studies in which the psychologist studies an individual in depth over an extended time. Information may be gathered through psychotherapy, historical or biographical sources, or research interviews.

Projective tests

Projective tests present participants with an ambiguous stimulus and ask them to give some kind of definition to it, to 'project' a meaning into it. The assumption is that in providing definition where none exists in reality, people will fill in the gaps in a way that expresses some of their characteristic ways of thinking, feeling and regulating emotions — that is, aspects of their personalities.

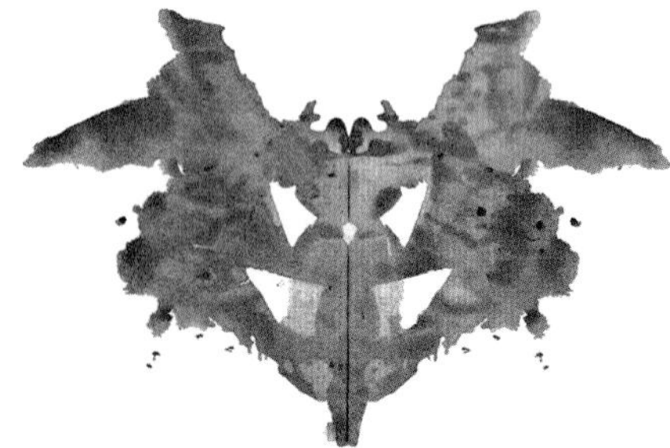

FIGURE 11.3
The Rorschach inkblot test. Participants' responses provide insight into their subconscious perceptual, cognitive and emotional processes. (Reproduced with permission. This inkblot is not part of the Rorschach test.)

Developed by Swiss psychiatrist Hermann Rorschach in 1921, the ***Rorschach inkblot test*** asks a participant to view a set of inkblots and tell the tester what each one resembles. For example, a teenager whose parents were divorcing and battling for custody of her was shown an inkblot similar to the one reproduced in figure 11.3. The participant saw a girl being torn apart down the middle, 'with feelings on each side', just as she felt torn by her parents' conflict.

In another projective test, the Thematic Apperception Test, or TAT (chapter 10), the participant is asked to make up a story about each of a series of ambiguous drawings, most of which depict people interacting. The assumption is that in eliminating the ambiguity, the individual will create a story that reflects her own recurring wishes, fears and ways of experiencing relationships.

Consider the TAT story of a participant with a borderline personality disorder, which typically manifests itself in unstable relationships, repeated suicide attempts and difficulty controlling rage, anxiety and sadness (chapter 15). When shown a TAT card depicting a man and woman similar to the one in figure 11.4, the participant responded (Westen et al., 1991):

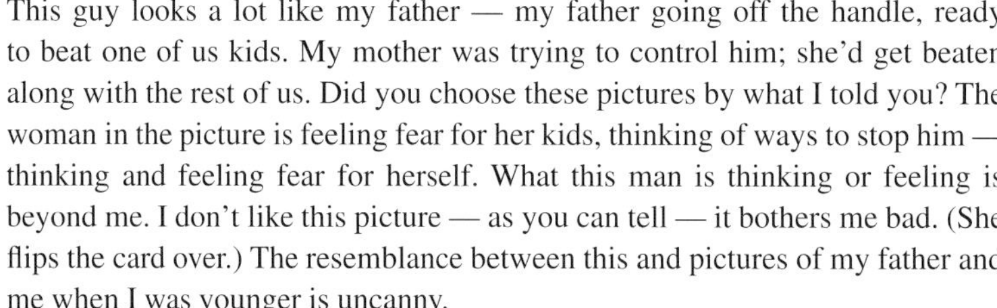

> This guy looks a lot like my father — my father going off the handle, ready to beat one of us kids. My mother was trying to control him; she'd get beaten along with the rest of us. Did you choose these pictures by what I told you? The woman in the picture is feeling fear for her kids, thinking of ways to stop him — thinking and feeling fear for herself. What this man is thinking or feeling is beyond me. I don't like this picture — as you can tell — it bothers me bad. (She flips the card over.) The resemblance between this and pictures of my father and me when I was younger is uncanny.

FIGURE 11.4
Thematic Apperception Test (TAT). This is an artist's rendering of a TAT-like image. The actual card is not reproduced to protect the valid use of the test.

The participant brings in themes of abuse, which is typical of the stories of borderline patients, many of whom were abused as children (Herman, Perry, & Van der Kolk, 1989; Ogata, Voshii, & Narahashi, 1989; Zanarini, 1997). Further, while most people generate stories that are independent of themselves, this participant cannot keep herself out of the cards, a sign of egocentrism or self-preoccupation characteristic of the TAT responses of patients with this disorder (Westen, Lohr, Silk, Gold, & Kerber, 1990). After another card also reminded her of herself, the participant later wondered whether these cards were chosen just for her, demonstrating a degree of paranoia consistent with her personality disorder.

Psychologists have criticised projective tests for years, citing various inadequacies (Mischel, 1968; Wood, Lilienfeld, Garb, & Nezworski, 2000; see also Hibbard, 2003). Projective tests are often less useful in predicting behaviour than simple demographic data such as the participant's age, sex and social class (Garb, 1984); they are frequently used idiosyncratically by clinicians, who may offer very different interpretations of the same response; and they have sometimes been misused to make predictions about behaviours for which the tests are not valid, such as potential job performance.

Other evidence suggests, however, that projective tests can be used with high reliability and validity for *particular purposes*, such as for assessing disturbances in thinking and in object relations and distinguishing patients with particular kinds of disorders (and even their biological relatives) (e.g. Coleman, Levy, Lenzenweger, & Holzman, 1996; Loevinger, 1976, 1985; see also Hibbard, 2003; Leibowitz, Ramos-Marcuse, & Arsenio, 2002). For example, one study asked four- and five-year-olds to complete 10 story stems (stories that the investigators started and asked children to finish) (Oppenheim, Nir, Warren, & Emde, 1997). The more a child's stories included themes of positive interaction and non-abusive discipline, the less depressed, misbehaving and aggressive the child's mother reported him to be. Conversely, the presence of themes such as physical or verbal abuse strongly predicted troubles with aggression and misbehaviour. From a cognitive perspective, projective tests tap implicit processes (chapter 7), such as implicit associational networks, particularly those in which emotional elements are prominent (Westen et al., 1991).

INTERIM SUMMARY

According to psychodynamic theory, personality assessment involves tapping into a person's unconscious motives and conflicts. Personality can be measured by life history methods and indirect methods such as projective tests. ***Life history methods*** aim to understand the whole person in the context of his or her life experience and environment. ***Projective tests*** such as the ***Rorschach inkblot test*** and the Thematic Apperception Test (TAT) present participants with an ambiguous stimulus and ask them to give some kind of definition to it, to 'project' a meaning into it.

APPLY + DISCUSS

A common criticism of projective test methods is that they do not deliver hard empirical data. This is one reason that their level of usage within the psychology profession has fluctuated in past years. University of Ballarat lecturer, Dr Petah Gibbs, believes the criticism is misplaced to a degree. He says that projective tests are a qualitative technique and simply should not be made to fit quantitative standards of data. Rather, he advocates using a variety of tools and methods to assess personality, with projective testing being one of the ways to obtain a richer and deeper understanding of an individual (P. Gibbs, personal communication, December 3, 2007). For example, Gibbs has developed a sport-specific projective technique called the **Athlete Apperception Technique** in an attempt to better explore personality factors that may influence athletes in sporting settings.

- How might projective test techniques help athletes to better understand personality traits that affect their sporting performance?
- Explain how projective measures might complement the data provided by self-report questionnaires.

Contributions and limitations of psychodynamic theories

Although many of Freud's original formulations are, as we might expect, somewhat dated a century after he began his work, the tradition he initiated emphasises five aspects of personality that have now received widespread empirical support. These include the importance of (1) unconscious cognitive, emotional and motivational processes; (2) ambivalence, conflict and compromise; (3) childhood experiences in shaping adult interpersonal patterns; (4) mental representations of the self, others and relationships; and (5) the development of the capacity to regulate impulses and to shift from an immature dependent state in infancy to a mutually caring, interdependent interpersonal stance in adulthood (Westen, 1998). Perhaps most importantly, psychodynamic approaches emphasise that human thought and action are laden with meaning, and that interpreting the multiple meanings of a person's behaviour requires 'listening with a third ear' for ideas, fears and wishes of which the person himself may not be aware.

A major limitation of psychodynamic theory is its inadequate basis in scientifically sound observation (see Crews, 1998; Fonagy & Target, 2000; Grunbaum, 1984; Mischel, 1973; Wallerstein, 1988). Scientific research usually requires a hypothesis that can be tested empirically, which is often difficult to achieve in relation to psychodynamic ideas. Many of them relied on the subjective thoughts of individuals such as Freud. Given the difficulties in testing these theories, there is also a lack of hard empirical data in the body of research evidence used to support psychodynamic theories.

APPLY + DISCUSS

What are the basic components of personality from a psychodynamic perspective? Apply this model to yourself or someone you know well.

- How would you describe your own wishes, fears, conflicts, compromises, desires or thoughts you would rather not admit, fixations or regressions, ego functions (including defences) and object relations?
- To what extent are these elements of personality stable over time? Could a person change them, and if so, how?

Sexism is also a major criticism that has been levelled at psychodynamic theories, with some aspects particularly problematic, such as Freud's theory of female development. The psychodynamic approach is quite male-centred, viewing women as inferior to men in a number of ways. Freud's theory of drives has also not stood the test of time (Holt, 1985). Aggression does not appear to be a bodily need in the same way as sex or hunger, and the theory generally overemphasises sexual motivation. Still other critics charge that psychodynamic theory pays too much attention to childhood experiences and not enough to adult learning.

In evaluating psychodynamic theory, you should keep in mind what it is *not*. Psychodynamic theory is no longer a single theory forged by a single thinker, Sigmund Freud. Most contemporary psychodynamic psychologists think about motivation in terms of wishes and fears, not sexual and aggressive drives, although they agree with Freud that many motives, such as sex and love, are biologically rooted and fundamentally shaped in childhood. Contemporary psychodynamic psychologists also tend to rely on concepts such as conflict, compromise, mental representation and self-esteem, rather than id, ego and superego.

Although Freud developed psychoanalysis as a method of exploring and interpreting meaning, and not of predicting behaviour, there can be little doubt that psychodynamic theories would be much further along today if psychoanalysts had taken more interest in testing and refining their ideas empirically. However, many other theories offer little help in interpreting meaning. Prediction and interpretation should both be central aims of any approach to personality.

It is also true to say that the work Freud and others carried out in psychodynamics blazed a new path in the study of psychology. Psychodynamics has been one of the most influential and provocative fields of study in psychology and has helped usher in a new way of thinking about human behaviour.

Cognitive–social theories

Cognitive–social theories offered the first comprehensive alternative to psychodynamic theories of personality. First developed in the 1960s, these theories go by several names, including social learning theory, cognitive–social learning theory and social–cognitive theory. Cognitive–social theories developed from behaviourist and cognitive roots; we have already examined several aspects of these theories in some detail (chapter 6).

From a behaviourist perspective, personality consists of learned behaviours and emotional reactions that are relatively specific and tied to particular environmental stimuli or events. Many of these behaviours are selected through operant conditioning on the basis of their rewarding or aversive consequences. Cognitive–social theories share the behaviourist belief that learning (rather than instinct, conflict or defence) is the basis of personality and that personality dispositions tend to be relatively specific and shaped by their consequences. However, they also focus on beliefs, expectations and information processing.

According to this approach, personality reflects a constant interplay between environmental demands and the way the individual processes information about the self and the world. Thus, people's actions reflect an interaction between the requirements of the situation (e.g. in school people are expected to work hard, come to class on time and follow the directives of teachers) and the person's learned tendencies to behave in particular ways under particular circumstances. These tendencies reflect their knowledge and beliefs.

For example, Albert Bandura (1986, 1999) argues that people are not driven by inner forces, as proposed by many psychodynamic theories, nor are they automatically shaped and controlled by external stimuli, as asserted by behaviourists such as B. F. Skinner. Rather, people's actions reflect the schemas they use in understanding the world, their expectations of what will happen if they act in particular ways, and the degree to which they believe they can attain their goals. Whereas psychodynamic theory centres on the irrational, cognitive–social theories tend to be eminently rational. Whereas behaviourists downplay the role of thought in producing behaviour, cognitive–social theorists emphasise it.

According to cognitive–social theories, several conditions must be met for a behaviour to occur (figure 11.5) (Bandura, 1977b, 1986, 1999, 2001; Mischel & Shoda, 1998). The person must encode the current situation as relevant to her goals or current concerns, and the situation must have enough personal meaning or value to initiate goal-driven behaviour. The individual must believe that performing the behaviour will lead to the desired outcome and that she has the ability to perform it. The person must also actually have the ability to carry out the behaviour. Finally, the person must be able to regulate ongoing activity in a way that leads to goal fulfilment — perhaps by monitoring behaviour at each step of the way until she fulfils the goal, as in decision-making theories, or changing the goal if she cannot fully achieve it. If any of these conditions is not met, the behaviour will not occur.

To illustrate, imagine you have just been stood up for a date (the stimulus). When you realise what has happened (encoding as personally relevant), your self-esteem plummets, you see that your plans for the evening are ruined, and you would like to make the person feel bad and think twice before standing you up again (personal value). You therefore decide to confront your date (behavioural plan).

In formulating a behavioural plan, however, you must decide whether any action you take will actually achieve the desired result (expectation of link between behaviour and outcome). Will your date simply ignore you and make up an excuse? On top of that, your expectations and beliefs must be accurate. You must actually be able to respond quickly (competence) or you will produce the wrong behaviour, such as saying, 'Oh, that's OK. I found something else to do. Do you want to get together some other time?' Finally, as you begin to execute the action, you will need to monitor progress towards your goal — is your date squirming enough yet? — as you go along.

We now examine each of these components in more detail.

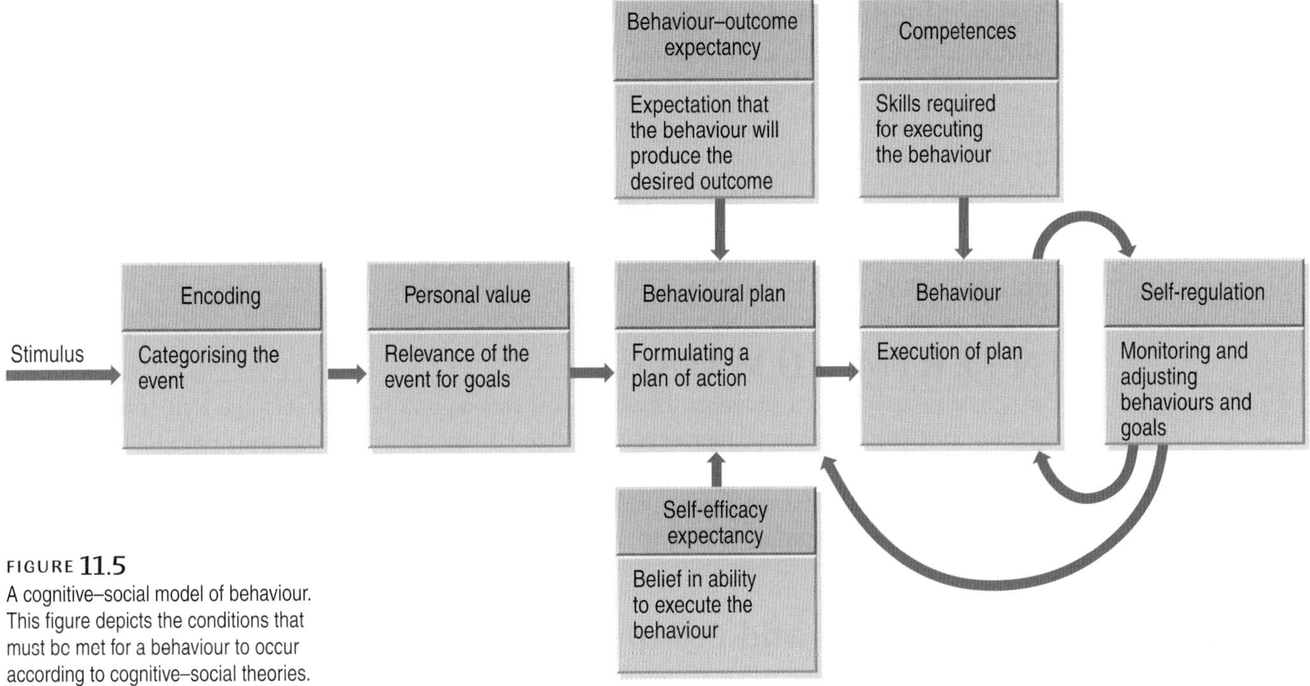

FIGURE 11.5
A cognitive–social model of behaviour. This figure depicts the conditions that must be met for a behaviour to occur according to cognitive–social theories.

INTERIM SUMMARY

Cognitive–social theories developed from behaviourist and cognitive roots and consider learning, beliefs, expectations and information processing to be central to personality. For a behaviour to occur, several conditions must be met. The person must encode the current situation as relevant, endow the situation with personal meaning or value, believe performing the behaviour will lead to the desired outcome, believe she has the ability to perform it, have the ability to carry out the behaviour, and regulate ongoing activity in a way that leads towards fulfilling the goal.

Encoding and personal relevance

For people to respond to a situation, they must first encode its meaning and determine its relevance to them. Responding to a situation is difficult if we cannot categorise it, and responding is unnecessary if it is not demanded by the situation or relevant to our goals.

Encoding

George Kelly (1955) developed an early cognitive approach to personality that focused on ***personal constructs*** — mental representations of the people, places, things and events that are significant to a person. According to Kelly, people can understand and interpret the world in many different ways, which defines their personality. Kelly looked for the roots of behaviour not in motivation, as in psychodynamic theory, but in cognition. For example, if a delinquent or maladjusted boy is accidentally bumped by a peer, he may punch his unwitting assailant because he encoded the bump as deliberate (Crick & Dodge, 1994).

People are not always able to articulate their personal constructs when asked. Thus, Kelly and his colleagues developed a technique for assessing them indirectly, called the repertory grid technique (Blowers & O'Connor, 1996). Participants are asked to describe the dimensions on which important people in their lives resemble and differ from one another (e.g. 'How is your father like your sister? In what ways are they unlike your mother?') By eliciting enough comparisons, the psychologist can discover the constructs that the participant implicitly uses in thinking about people.

Nancy Cantor and John Kihlstrom (1987; Kihlstrom & Cantor, 2000) combined Kelly's emphasis on personal constructs with information-processing theory to create a cognitive theory of personality. They argue that the way people conceive of themselves and others and encode, interpret and remember social information is central to who they are. In this view, individuals who have more accurate and well-organised schemas about people and relationships have greater social intelligence and should be more effective in accomplishing their interpersonal goals, such as making friends and getting desirable jobs.

Personal value and goals

Individuals have elaborate schemas about people and situations that have relevance or personal value to them. ***Personal value*** refers to the importance individuals attach to various outcomes or potential outcomes (Mischel, 1979). Whether a situation or anticipated action has a positive or negative value for an individual often depends on the person's goals.

Cantor and Kihlstrom (1987) define motivation in terms of ***life tasks***, the conscious, self-defined problems people attempt to solve. For a university student, salient life tasks may involve establishing independence from parents, getting good grades, or making and keeping friends (Cantor, 1990; Cantor & Blanton, 1996).

INTERIM SUMMARY

For people to respond to a situation, they must first encode it as relevant. George Kelly proposed that ***personal constructs*** — mental representations of the people, places, things and events that are significant to a person — substantially influence their behaviour. People tend to focus on and select behaviours and situations that have ***personal value*** to them, and that are relevant to their goals or ***life tasks*** (conscious, self-defined problems people try to solve).

Expectancies and competences

Whether people carry out various actions depends substantially on both their ***expectancies***, or expectations relevant to desired outcomes (chapter 6), and their competence to perform the behaviours that would solve their problems or achieve their goals.

Expectancies

Research shows that self-defence training has significant effects on improving women's belief that they could escape from or disable a potential assailant or rapist (Weitlauf, Cervone, Smith, & Wright, 2001).

Of particular importance are behaviour–outcome expectancies and self-efficacy expectancies. A ***behaviour–outcome expectancy*** is a belief that a certain behaviour will lead to a particular outcome. A ***self-efficacy expectancy*** is a person's conviction that she can perform the actions necessary to produce the desired outcome (Bandura, 1997). For example, a person will not start a new business unless she believes both that starting the business is likely to lead to desired results (such as wealth or satisfaction) *and* that she has the ability to get a new business off the ground. Similarly, a person will not quit smoking unless he believes that quitting will decrease his likelihood of developing lung cancer and that he can actually quit smoking successfully (chapter 14).

Bandura (1977a, 1982, 1995) argues that self-efficacy expectancies are generally the most important determinant of successful task performance. Research in a number of areas documents that people who are confident in their abilities are more likely to act, and ultimately succeed, than those plagued by self-doubts. Australian children's author Jeni Mawter tells of receiving more than 123 rejection letters (she stopped counting at that point!) before her first book was accepted for publication in 2000. A prominent psychologist was once told that 'one is no more likely to find the phenomenon [that he eventually discovered and documented] than bird droppings in a cuckoo clock' (Bandura, 1989, p. 1176).

An Australian study by Netz and Raviv (2004) applied cognitive–social theory to explain an individual's motivation to engage in physical activity. They found that exercise (behaviour) was related to self-efficacy (expectancy). In particular, older individuals felt lower self-efficacy in relation to physical activity and expected fewer benefits from exercising. However, older individuals rated themselves as more active and fit than non-exercisers of their same age and gender. More recently, Cervone (2008) has examined how social–cognitive theories provide explanatory models of personality (see also Boyle, Matthews, & Saklofske, 2008).

Competences

Believing in one's abilities is one thing, but truly having them is another. Thus, another crucial variable that impacts behaviour is ***competences*** — that is, skills and abilities used for solving problems. Social intelligence includes a variety of competences that help people navigate interpersonal waters, such as social skills that allow them to talk comfortably with strangers at a cocktail party, or the ability to end an argument to maintain a friendship (see Cantor & Harlow, 1994; Cantor & Kihlstrom, 1987). Individuals develop highly specific skills for handling particular tasks through operant conditioning, observational learning, practice and deliberate conscious effort.

Self-regulation

The final variable required to execute a behaviour successfully is self-regulation. ***Self-regulation*** refers to setting goals, evaluating performance and adjusting behaviour to achieve these goals in the context of ongoing feedback (Bandura, 1986, 1999; Boekaerts, Pintrich, & Zeidner, 2000; Mischel & Shoda, 1998).

Cognitive–social theorists take a problem-solving or decision-making approach to personality, much like information processing approaches to cognition (chapter 8) and goal-setting and expectancy–value theories of motivation (chapter 10). In other words, people are constantly setting goals, applying their skills to achieve them, and monitoring their thoughts and actions until their goals are reached or have to be modified.

In this view, personality is nothing more or less than the problem-solving efforts of people trying to fulfil their life tasks (Harlow & Cantor, 1994; see also Boekaerts et al., 2000). Successful problem solving requires constant feedback, which people use to self-regulate. Feedback on performance can help people solve problems if it focuses their attention on the problem and ways to achieve a solution. However, feedback can *diminish* performance if it leads people to focus on themselves with self-doubt or anxiety (Kluger & DeNisi, 1996).

One study applied a cognitive–social approach to organisational decision making (Wood & Bandura, 1989a). Graduate business students were asked to allocate workers and resources using a computer simulation. The simulation involved 18 decision-making trials, with each trial followed by performance feedback useful for the next. Half the participants (the acquirable-skill group) were told that in 'acquiring a new skill, people do not begin with faultless performance. However, the more they practise, the more capable they become.' Essentially, these participants were encouraged to use the task to develop their skills rather than to evaluate their ability. The other half (the fixed-ability group) were led to believe that the simulation would test their underlying ability as a manager, a basic competence they either did or did not have.

The researchers wanted to know how this manipulation would affect participants' perceived self-efficacy, goal setting, efficiency in problem solving and managerial success in running the simulated company. Self-efficacy was assessed by regularly asking participants how confident they were of achieving production goals following feedback on their performance. Performance goals were assessed by asking them after each trial what they were striving for on the next trial. The researchers also measured the efficiency of participants' problem-solving strategies as well as their actual level of performance on the task (figure 11.6).

MAKING CONNECTIONS

Our **expectancies** about what we can accomplish and how well things will turn out influence virtually everything we do, such as how much we are willing to take risks. Our specific expectancies (such as whether now is the time to invest in technology stocks) reflect not only our personalities but also our knowledge and experience (chapter 6).

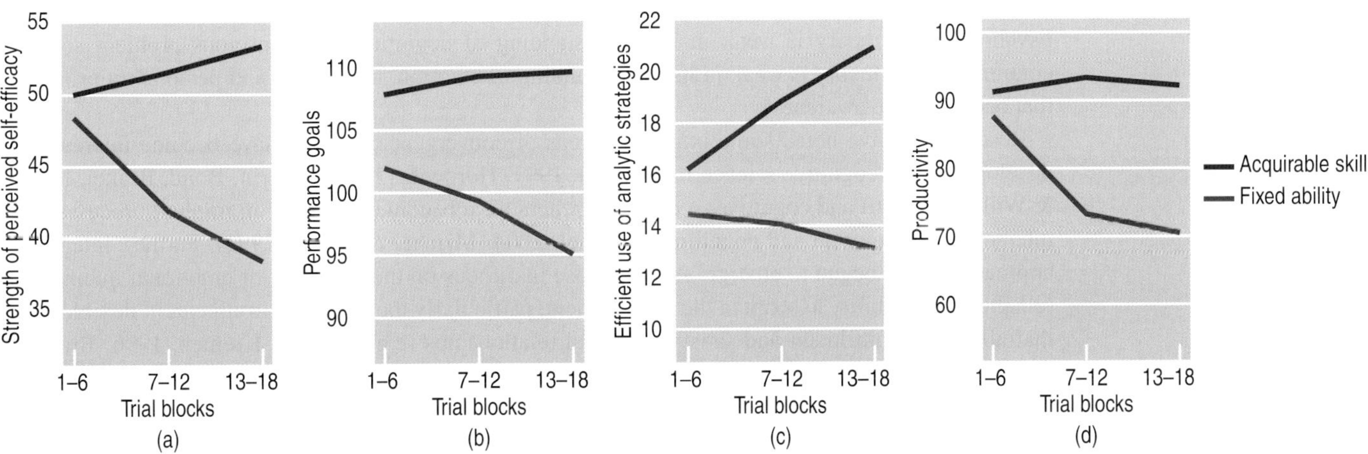

FIGURE **11.6**

An experimental study in self-regulation. Participants who believed they could learn from the task showed consistent increases in perceived self-efficacy, unlike participants who believed their ability to be fixed (a). The latter showed a steady decline in performance goals (b), efficiency of problem solving (c) and actual performance (d).

SOURCE: Wood and Bandura (1989, pp. 411–413).

Participants who believed they could learn from the task showed consistent increases in perceived self-efficacy, unlike those who believed their ability was fixed. The fixed-ability group showed a steady decline in self-efficacy performance goals, efficiency of problem solving and actual performance.

Essentially, in confronting a difficult task, the group that believed their skills were fixed steadily lowered their estimates of their efficacy and their level of aspiration, and their performance steadily declined. In other words, managers are much more likely to be successful if they *believe* they can be successful.

INTERIM SUMMARY

People's ***expectancies***, or expectations relevant to desired outcomes, influence the actions they take. A ***behaviour–outcome expectancy*** is a belief that a certain behaviour will lead to a particular outcome. A ***self-efficacy expectancy*** is a person's conviction that she can perform the actions necessary to produce a desired outcome. A ***competence*** is a skill used for solving problems. ***Self-regulation*** refers to setting goals, evaluating performance and adjusting behaviour to achieve these goals in the context of ongoing feedback.

Contributions and limitations of cognitive-social theories

APPLY + DISCUSS

A young lawyer receives feedback from her boss that her work is of a high calibre, but that she is not producing enough because she is working too slowly. In fact, she is a perfectionist who refuses to turn in a brief until she is absolutely certain she has it 'right.'

- What are the basic elements of the young lawyer's personality from a cognitive–social perspective?
- How might each element — from the way the young lawyer encodes the situation to the way she self-regulates — be involved in her work performance?
- What would need to change for her to turn the situation around and get a better review the next time?

Cognitive–social theories have contributed substantially to the study of personality, bringing into focus the role of thought and memory in personality. The way people behave clearly reflects the expectations and skills they have developed, which are encoded in memory and activated by particular situations. Furthermore, unlike psychodynamic theory, which can be difficult to test, cognitive–social theory is readily testable through experimentation.

Cognitive–social approaches are limited, however, in two respects. First, they tend to emphasise the rational side of life and underemphasise the emotional, motivational and irrational. If personality is really reducible to cognitive processes (Cantor, 1990), one would have difficulty accounting for the psychological abnormalities of a man like Adolph Hitler. Because Hitler was tremendously adept at getting people to follow him and had an extraordinary sense of self-efficacy, one would have to rate him high on several dimensions of social intelligence. Yet his social motives and his ways of dealing with his emotions were clearly disturbed.

A related problem is the tendency to assume that people consciously know what they think, feel and want and hence can report it. Would most of us accept Hitler's self-report of his life task of bettering the world by creating a master race? Or would we suspect that his dreams of world domination and his program of genocide reflected thoughts, feelings and motivations that he could not easily have described?

In some ways, psychodynamic and cognitive–social approaches each offer what the other lacks. Psychodynamic theory is weak in its understanding of cognition and conscious problem solving; cognitive–social theory is weak in its understanding of emotion, motivation and personality processes that occur outside awareness.

Researchers have noted some important areas of convergence, as they have become interested in developments in cognitive science (e.g. Bucci, 1997; Horowitz, 1988; Shevrin, Bond, Brakel, Hertel, & Williams, 1996) and cognitive–social researchers have become interested in implicit processes and interactions of emotion and cognition (Mischel, 2004; Mischel & Shoda, 1995). Further, integrative approaches have begun to emerge, such as those that focus on the construct of emotional intelligence (chapter 9), the ability to adapt to the environment, particularly the social environment, in flexible ways that allow goal fulfilment and satisfying social relationships (e.g. Block & Kremen, 1996; Brackett, Mayer, & Warner, 2004; Goleman, 1995; Mayer, Caruso, & Salovey, 2000).

FROM BRAIN TO BEHAVIOUR

Driving Mr Albert

Cognitive–social theories suggest that the way people encode, process and think about information determines their personality. A question that, as yet, remains unanswered is whether individual differences in cognitive processing can be related to differences in the structure or function of people's brains. Answering this question is the role of cognitive neuroscientists.

But it is not scientists alone who are interested in such questions. A book by Paterniti entitled *Driving Mr Albert: A Trip Across America with Einstein's Brain* reveals the interest of the lay public in the relationship between brain functioning and personality. The author recounts his cross-country travels with the pathologist Dr Thomas Harvey, who in 1955 had examined Einstein's brain. Accompanying the two men in the car is a container holding parts of Einstein's brain, hence the title of the book. The question with which the pathologist is confronted is whether Einstein's genius could be located in his brain. Some evidence seemed to suggest that this was the case. An article published in 1999 indicated that the part of Einstein's cerebral cortex associated with mathematical ability was larger than that of normal individuals (Witelson, Kigar, & Harvey, 1999), suggesting that a personality trait could be linked to a specific brain structure.

Evidence from functional magnetic resonance imaging (fMRI) shows different patterns of brain activation associated with different types of cognitive activity. However, as discussed by Pervin (2003), two factors are worth noting. First, even though specific areas of the brain are activated with particular cognitive tasks, most cognitive activity involves activation of multiple areas of the brain, so that any particular type of cognitive activity is unlikely to be localised solely in a single area of the brain. Second, even though there are genetic influences on brain structure that could account for differences in cognitive functioning, brain structure and function can also be influenced by cognitive activity.

Trait theories

When people talk about traits, they are referring to the words people use to describe themselves and others in their everyday lives, beginning with adjectives such as *shy*, *devious*, *manipulative*, *open* or *friendly*. ***Traits*** are emotional, cognitive and behavioural tendencies that constitute underlying personality dimensions on which individuals vary. Characterising people according to traits is a descriptive approach — an attempt to describe people according to the underlying attributes and tendencies they have.

According to Gordon Allport (1937; Allport & Odbert, 1936), who developed the trait approach to personality, the concept of trait has two separate but complementary meanings. On the one hand, a trait is an observed tendency to behave in a particular way. On the other, a trait is an inferred, or hypothesised, underlying personality disposition that generates this behavioural tendency. Presumably, a tendency to be cheerful (an observed trait) stems from an enduring pattern of internal processes, such as a tendency to experience positive affect, to think positive thoughts or to wish to be perceived as happy (inferred dispositions).

How can we measure traits? The most straightforward way is the same way people intuitively assess other people's personalities. Observe their behaviour over time and in different situations. Because extensive observation of this sort can be very cumbersome and time consuming, however, psychologists often use two other methods. One is to ask people who know the participant well to fill out questionnaires about the person's personality. The second, more commonly used method is to ask participants themselves to answer self-report questionnaires. For example, self-report personality inventories are often used in non-clinical settings, such as schools and organisations, and test for traits such as sociability, responsibility and sense of wellbeing. They may also be used in clinical settings. For example, the scales used to examine personality on the Minnesota Multiphasic Personality Inventory (MMPI) were based on data from psychiatric patients suffering from depression, schizophrenia and paranoia (Dahlstrom, 1993; Hathaway & McKinley, 1940, 1943).

To describe personality from a trait perspective, we must know not only how to measure traits but also which ones to measure. With literally thousands of different ways to classify people, choosing a set of traits that definitively describes personality seems like a Herculean task. Allport and Odbert (1936) compiled a list of some 18 000 words from Webster's unabridged dictionary that could be used to distinguish one person from another. Many of these words denote similar characteristics, however, so over the years trait psychologists have collapsed the list into fewer and fewer traits.

Raymond Cattell (1957, 1990) reduced the list to just 16 traits, such as warm, emotionally stable, intelligent, cheerful, suspicious, imaginative, sensitive and tense. To select these key traits, Cattell relied on factor analysis (chapter 9) to group together those adjectives on Allport's and Odbert's list

APPLY + DISCUSS

Most early personality theories began with in-depth interviewing, usually of patients seeking help. In contrast, trait theories arose from the study of words in the English language that describe personality and relied, at least initially, on normal samples.

- What are the advantages of deriving hypotheses about personality from indepth interviews, case studies and patient samples? What are the disadvantages?
- What are the advantages and disadvantages of relying on everyday language and people's self-reports for trait descriptions?

that were highly correlated with each other. Factor analysis allows researchers to find underlying traits by grouping together adjectives that assess similar qualities (e.g. *angry* and *hostile*) into overarching factors.

In addition to reducing the vast number of traits identified by Allport to a much more manageable number, Cattell is also known for his investigations into how much heredity and the environment contribute to the development of specific traits. Cattell and his colleagues (Hundleby, Pawlik, & Cattell, 1965) concluded that two-thirds of the development of traits is determined by the environment, with the remaining third being determined by heredity. Cattell's research in this area laid the groundwork for the field of behavioural genetics.

Eysenck's theory

One of the best-researched trait theories was developed by Hans Eysenck (1953, 1990). By distinguishing traits and types, with types or super-traits representing a higher order organisation of personality, Eysenck differed from Cattell in the number of traits he believed described personality (figure 11.7). In his view, individuals produce specific behaviours, some of which are frequent or habitual (i.e. they are habits). A trait is a group of correlated habits — a person who has one of these habits tends to have the other habits that constitute the trait. For example, avoiding attention in a group, not initiating conversation and avoiding large social gatherings are habitual behaviours of people with the trait of shyness. A type or super-trait is a group of correlated traits. People who are shy, rigid and inward-looking are introverts.

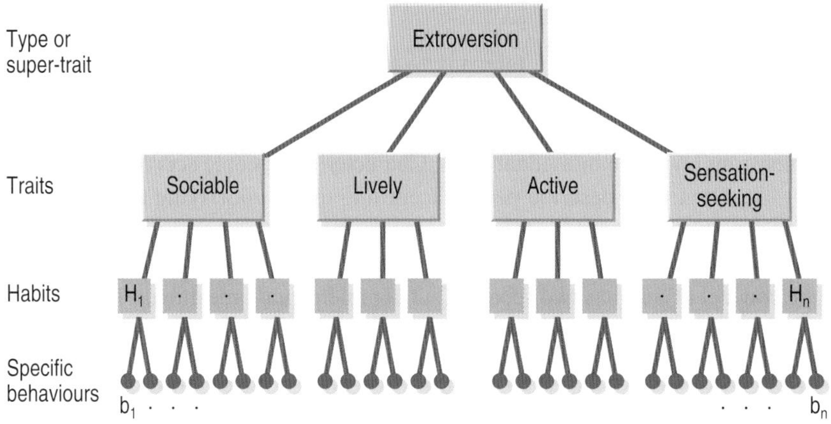

FIGURE 11.7 Eysenck's model of personality. Extroversion–introversion is a supertrait, a group of traits that correlate highly with one another. Sociable, lively and so on are traits — groups of correlated behavioural tendencies (habits). Habits are abstractions derived from observations of specific instances of behaviour.

SOURCE: Data derived from Eysenck (1967).

On the basis of thousands of studies conducted over a half century, Eysenck identified three overarching psychological super-traits: extroversion–introversion, neuroticism–emotional stability and psychoticism–impulse control. ***Extroversion*** refers to a tendency to be sociable, active and willing to take risks. Introverts, who score at the low end of the extroversion scale, are characterised by social inhibition, seriousness and caution. ***Neuroticism*** defines a continuum from emotional stability to instability. It is closely related to the construct of negative affect (chapter 10). People high on neuroticism report feeling anxious, guilty, tense and moody, and they tend to have low self-esteem.

Psychoticism describes people who are aggressive, egocentric, impulsive and antisocial. People low on psychoticism are empathic and able to control their impulses. Like Cattell, Eysenck was also interested in the respective contributions of nature and nurture to the development of traits, but his primary focus was on the biological underpinnings of traits and the evolutionary significance of particular traits.

Eysenck believed that differences in traits, particularly those traits associated with the extroversion–introversion super-trait, could be traced to underlying differences in cortical arousal, which is regulated by the ascending reticular activating system (ARAS). He argued that extroverts, who constantly seek arousal through interacting with people and novel situations, have a lower resting level of ARAS than introverts, who avoid arousal by sticking to solitary activities and familiar surroundings. Thus, introverts are more alert (cortically aroused) than extroverts and prefer situations with lower levels of stimulation to avoid arousal.

Other researchers have taken this theory further. English researcher Jeffrey Gray (1990) proposed that brain structures had evolved in response to reinforcement and punishment. The ***behavioural approach system (BAS)*** is the structure that is attuned to rewards, and leads people to seek out stimulation and arousal. The ***behavioural inhibition system (BIS)*** is the structure that is attuned to punishment, and leads people to avoid potential dangerous or painful experiences. Under this model (see figure 11.8), extroverts are thought to have a stronger BAS than BIS, so they are more influenced by potential rewards than by potential losses. People with a stronger BAS are the ones who go double or nothing on a bet at the roulette table. On the other hand, introverts have a stronger BIS, so are influenced more by the possibility of failure or harm than the possibility of gaining a reward. People with a stronger BIS are more likely to cash in their chips and go home, or not to risk a bet in the first place.

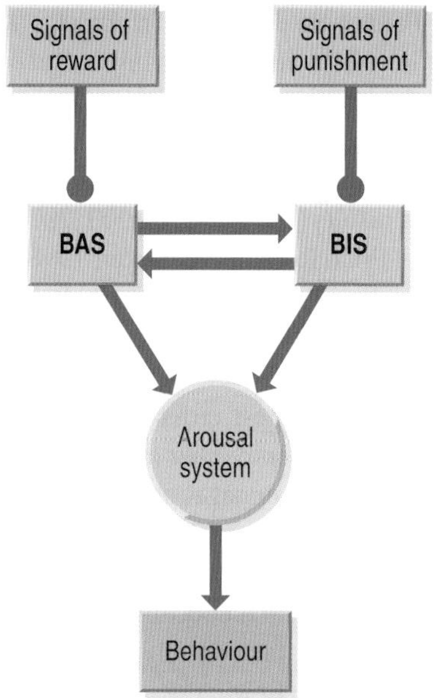

FIGURE 11.8
The BIS is attuned to punishment and inhibits behaviour. In contrast, the BAS is attuned to rewards and activates behaviour.

SOURCE: Gazzaniga and Heatherton (2003, p. 509).

The five factor model

Most theorists who have used factor analysis to arrive at a taxonomy of traits have found that their long lists boil down to five superordinate personality traits, known as the 'big five' factors, or the ***five factor model (FFM)*** (Goldberg, 1993; McCrae & Costa, 1997; Norman, 1963; see also McCrae et al., 2004; Saucier, 2002). Different studies yield slightly different factors, and theorists label them in different ways, but the lists are strikingly consistent. Today, the FFM remains the most widely accepted model of personality structure, examining relations between traits to explain individual differences in behaviour (McCrae & Costa, 2008). Costa and McCrae (1990, 1997) use the labels openness to experience, conscientiousness, extroversion, agreeableness and neuroticism. (A good acronym to remember them is OCEAN.) Each of the five factors represents an amalgam of several more specific traits. For example, as table 11.2 shows, people high on neuroticism tend to be anxious, depressed, impulsive and so on. These lower order traits are called 'facets' of the FFM.

TABLE 11.2 **The five factor model and its facets**

Neuroticism	Extroversion	Agreeableness	Conscientiousness	Openness
Anxiety	Warmth	Trust	Competence	Fantasy (active fantasy life)
Angry hostility	Gregariousness	Straightforwardness	Order	Aesthetics (artistic interests)
Depression	Assertiveness	Altruism	Dutifulness	Feelings (emotionally open)
Self-consciousness	Activity	Compliance	Achievement striving	Actions (flexible)
Impulsivity	Excitement seeking	Modesty	Self-discipline	Ideas (intellectual)
Vulnerability	Positive emotion	Tenderness	Deliberation	Values (unconventional)

SOURCE: Adapted from McCrae and Costa (1997, p. 513).

NOTE: These are the higher order and lower order traits ('facets') that constitute the five factor model. Within each factor, traits are highly correlated; across factors, they are not.

The delineation of basic factors in personality initially arose from the assumption that important individual differences are likely to show up in language, so that classifying hundreds of adjectives into a small group of higher order trait descriptions would generate an adequate taxonomy of traits (Goldberg, 1981). Interestingly, the same five factors seem to appear almost regardless of the specific data used, including adjectives, antonym pairs or statements such as 'I often feel . . .' (Goldberg, 1993; John, 1990). The five factors even emerged in a cross-cultural study using a *nonverbal* personality test

(Paunonen, Jackson, Trzebinski, & Forsterling, 1992). Participants in Canada, Finland, Poland and Germany viewed drawings of people engaged in behaviours related to various traits and rated how often they engage in similar behaviours. Once again, five traits seemed to encompass the spectrum of personality dispositions they ascribed to themselves.

Is the FFM cross-culturally universal? Research in multiple countries has produced remarkably similar results (see Church, 2000, 2001a; John & Srivastava, 1999; McCrae & Costa, 1997; McCrae, Costa, del Pilar, Rolland, & Parker, 1998; McCrae et al., 2004; Rossier, Dahourou, & McCrae, 2005; Somer & Goldberg, 1999; Stumpf, 1993). This is particularly impressive because of the wide array of languages from different linguistic families that have reproduced the FFM, from English and German to Turkish and Korean (Saucier, 2002; Saucier & Goldberg, 2001).

The strongest cross-cultural confirmations of the FFM occur when researchers translate Western instruments into other languages. Findings are not quite as clear when researchers draw adjectives from the native language, as in a study of university students in Taiwan (Kuo-shu & Bond, 1990). In this study, participants described people they knew well using two sets of adjectives: adjectives included in Cattell's inventory (reflecting Western concepts), and adjectives culled from Chinese newspapers (to represent native conceptions of personality). Factor analysis of the Western words produced the FFM. In contrast, factor analysis of the Chinese-derived words produced only three factors with some similarity to the FFM.

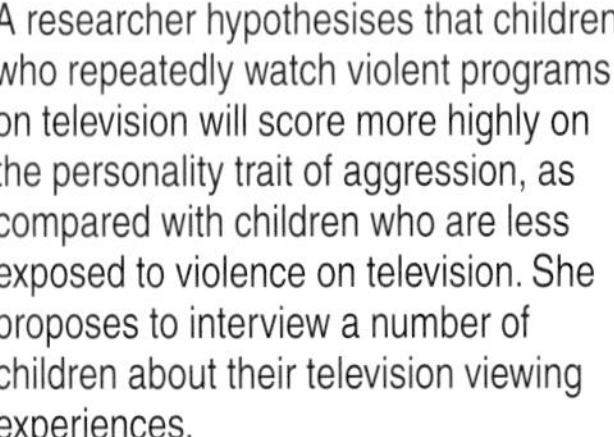

A researcher hypothesises that children who repeatedly watch violent programs on television will score more highly on the personality trait of aggression, as compared with children who are less exposed to violence on television. She proposes to interview a number of children about their television viewing experiences.

- How might the researcher obtain informed consent from her participants?
- Explain the procedures for ensuring the confidentiality of the study's results.

A study that factor-analysed personality descriptions taken from interviews and open-ended questionnaires in the Philippines similarly produced a factor structure that only partially mapped onto the FFM (Katigbak, Church, & Akamine, 1996). Factors resembling conscientiousness, agreeableness and openness emerged, but the other factors could not be mapped onto neuroticism and extroversion. Thus, whether the same five factors emerge cross-culturally depends in part on the culture from which the list of objectives or statements originally came.

Boyle (2008) provides a recent critique of the FFM, outlining a number of problems with the model, including that (a) it provides a static account of personality, (b) the construct validity of the model and the underlying genetic determinants of the traits remains questionable and (c) the utility of the FFM in applied areas of psychology (e.g. clinical practice and organisational psychology) is uncertain. Boyle argues that the FFM provides a 'descriptive account of presumed regularities in behaviour' (p. 305) and argues that a more 'dynamic' model of personality is needed that considers how social learning experiences and enculturation can shape personality over time.

Personality: beyond the five factor model?

By Doctor Carolyn MacCann, University of Sydney, and Doctor Richard D. Roberts, Educational Testing Service

Although psychoanalytic, behavioural, social-learning, and situational theories of personality have dominated the field at one time or another, a near consensual model of personality has emerged over the past three decades (Digman & Inouye, 1986). Five broad personality traits consistently emerge across testing methods, assessments, cultures and diverse languages (e.g. Costa & McCrae, 1992; McCrae et al., 1998; Saucier, 2008; Saucier & Goldberg, 2001; Schulze & Roberts, 2006). These traits are extroversion, agreeableness, conscientiousness, neuroticism, and openness to experience. From the late 1990s to the present, several research groups have suggested additions to this basic model, either extending the model to include further factors, or narrowing the focus to the specific facets within each dimension.

One intriguing suggestion is that social attitudes captured by 'ism' words (e.g. authoritarianism, conservatism) explain parts of personality not covered by the traditional five factors, and should be included in personality models (Saucier, 2000). Another suggestion for extending the five factor model is to add a sixth trait representing 'spirituality' (Piedmont, 1999). Though this six factor model was not widely adopted, an alternative six factor model is now gaining currency. The HEXACO model (honesty/humility, emotionality, extroversion, agreeableness, conscientiousness, and openness to experience) includes a sixth factor representing a blend of honesty and humility (Ashton et al., 2004). The HEXACO model emerged from cross-cultural studies that suggested that a sixth factor may be needed to describe personality in languages outside of the Indo-European family.

Advances in personality theory may also come from a more detailed focus that further delineates the five factors into their composite parts. For example, Costa and McCrae (1995) suggested that conscientiousness could be conceptually divided into six facets (competence, order, dutifulness, achievement striving, self-discipline and deliberation). MacCann, Duckworth, and Roberts (2008) empirically derived eight separate facets of conscientiousness that showed different relationships to educational criteria. Other research suggests that narrow facets of personality are more predictive than broad domains, showing stronger relationships to outcomes such as job performance, academic achievement, health and life satisfaction (e.g. Paunonen & Ashton, 2001; Schimmack, Oishi, Furr, & Funder, 2004). In addition, personality facets from the same broad domain may show different heritability estimates and different developmental trajectories across the life span, suggesting that these should be considered separately (Jackson et al., 2009; Jang, McCrae, Angleitner, Riemann, & Livesley, 1998).

Expansions to the five factor model are potentially useful to more accurately capture differences between people, and thus provide greater accuracy when used for selection, training and diagnosis. However, the nearly universal use and understanding of the five factor model gives researchers a common scientific framework to ground research and build theories. There is a risk that rapidly changing the boundaries of personality to include additional domains or different delineations may fragment researchers into particular camps, making their work inaccessible to the broader scientific and practitioner communities. Thus, even if there may be some worthy emendations, the five factor model serves the pragmatic purpose of providing a common language for personality researchers (and their students) to describe, interpret and disseminate their findings.

INTERIM SUMMARY

Traits are emotional, cognitive and behavioural tendencies that constitute underlying personality dimensions on which individuals vary. Eysenck identified three overarching psychological types, or constellations of traits: ***extroversion*** (tendency to be sociable, active and willing to take risks), ***neuroticism*** (emotional stability or negative affect) and ***psychoticism*** (tendency to be aggressive, egocentric, impulsive and antisocial). According to the ***five factor model (FFM)***, personality can be reduced to five factors — openness to experience, conscientiousness, extroversion, agreeableness and neuroticism — each of which includes several lower order factors or facets. Many of these factors appear to be cross-culturally universal.

Is personality consistent?

The concept of personality traits described thus far implies that personality has some degree of consistency. If John is an honest person, we can assume he is likely to behave honestly in various situations and to be honest two years from now. No-one is honest all the time, however, and people do change. Furthermore, a particular personality trait can manifest itself in different types of behaviour. Thus, two questions arise. Is personality consistent from one situation to another, and is personality consistent over time?

Consistency across situations

In 1968, Walter Mischel touched off a 30-year debate by arguing that ***situational variables*** — the circumstances in which people find themselves — largely determine their behaviour. In other words, what people do largely reflects where they find themselves, not who they are. In an influential book, he marshalled considerable evidence of the inconsistency of people's behaviour across situations and showed that most personality tests had only modest correlations with particular behaviours in the real world. For example, trait measures tended to be far less predictive of whether a psychiatric patient would require future hospitalisation than the weight of the patient's psychiatric chart!

APPLY + DISCUSS

Although Cricket Australia banned the Mexican wave in 2007, defiant fans continue to support the wave.

- What happens to people's personality in a group? Can personality be 'overridden' by a group?
- Does personality just 'disappear' in group situations, or do people's actions still reflect something about who they are — that is, about their personality?

Mischel believed that the inconsistency of behaviour explained a lack of validity in personality tests. Correlations among behavioural measures that supposedly relate to the same trait are often low (+.30 to +.40 and below) or nonexistent (Mischel, 1968; Nisbett, 1980). The reason is that such tests may measure behaviour in one situation, but the criteria by which the test is validated may measure behaviour in a different context. As consistency across situations is low, so too is validity.

Mischel almost single-handedly slew the mighty field of personality. If personality is not consistent, psychologists have nothing to measure, so they might as well pack up their questionnaires and go home. Indeed, the field of personality languished for years after Mischel's critique.

Several psychologists, however, challenged Mischel's arguments. Seymour Epstein (1979, 1986, 1997) pointed out that any single behaviour has multiple causes, so that trying to predict a single behaviour from a personality trait is virtually impossible. No measure of 'honesty', for example, can predict whether a child will cheat on an examination on a particular occasion. However, averaging across multiple occasions, measures of honesty do predict whether or not a child will cheat. Using the ***principle of aggregation***, researchers such as Epstein concluded that 'a trait does not refer to a specific behaviour in a specific situation but rather to a class of behaviours over a range of situations' (Pervin, 2003, p. 60).

Other psychologists argued that psychologists cannot predict what all people will do all of the time, but they *can predict what some people will do some of the time* (Bem & Allen, 1974; Biesanz, West, & Graziano, 1998; Kenrick & Stringfield, 1980). The key is to figure out which people tend to be consistent on which traits, and which traits are relevant for which people. For example, people's self-descriptions tend to be highly predictive of the way others see them on traits they view as central to their personality (Zuckerman et al., 1988). Further, some people are more open and easy to 'read'; their behaviour is thus easier for people who know them well to predict (Colvin, 1993).

Consistency over time

Researchers have now also documented considerable consistency in many aspects of personality over long periods of time, a factor referred to as the stability of personality (Caspi, 1998, 2000; Graziano, 2003; Johnson, McGue, & Krueger, 2005; Mischel & Shoda, 1995). When we use phrases such as 'He's a dishonest person' or when psychologists describe a person as 'low in conscientiousness', we are making statements about what we can expect from the person over time and across situations. One example is inhibition to the unfamiliar, a cluster of attributes in children that includes shyness and anxiety in the face of novelty (Gest, 1997; Kagan, 1989). Inhibition to the unfamiliar appears to be an aspect of ***temperament*** — that is, a basic personality disposition heavily influenced by genes (Chess & Thomas, 1987; Ullrich, Carroll, Prigot, & Fagen, 2002). Infants who are inhibited (roughly 10 percent of the population) show a distinct pattern of crying and motor behaviour as early as four months of age when confronted with unfamiliar stimuli. These infants continue to show more fear responses than uninhibited children at 9, 14 and 21 months when confronted with novel stimuli (such as an unfamiliar room, application of painless electrodes to the skin or application of liquid through a dropper to the mouth or eye). At seven and a half years of age, inhibited children also have significantly more fears outside the laboratory about attending school camp, public speaking, remaining alone at home and so on.

Infants who are inhibited show a distinct pattern of crying and motor behaviour from as early as four months of age. These infants continue to show more fear responses than uninhibited children as they get older.

Psychologists have documented consistency from childhood through early adulthood on various traits as well. A well-known longitudinal study in Dunedin, New Zealand, which has traced the development of a group of 1000 children born in the mid-1970s, has found remarkable consistency between traits evident at an early age and behaviours in adulthood. For instance, as shown in figure 11.9, those classified as 'difficult' at age three were more likely to have problems with alcohol or show a range of other antisocial behaviours as adults. Those who were classified as 'inhibited' at age three were much more likely to suffer from depression as adults (Silva & Stanton, 1996).

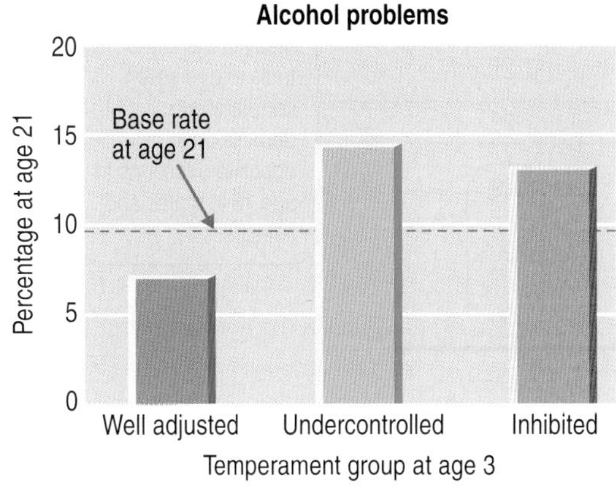

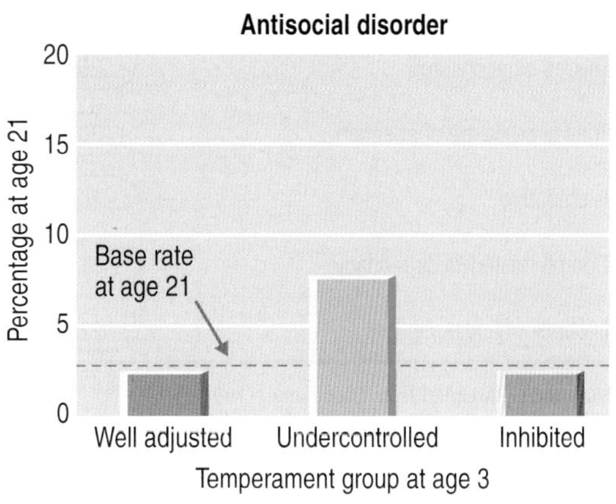

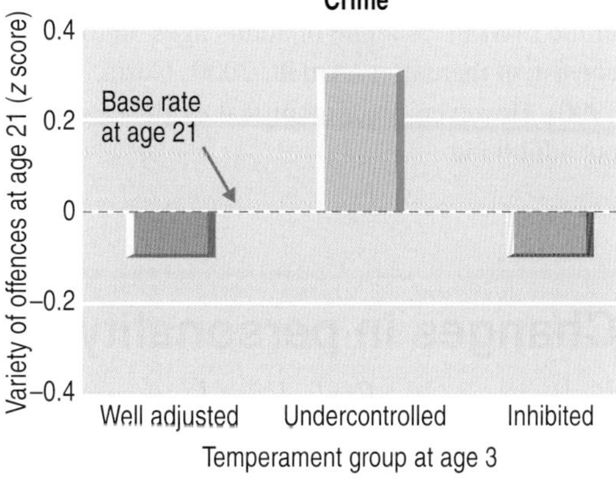

FIGURE 11.9
Temperament group at age three predicts a variety of behaviours at age 21, including criminal activity, alcohol problems and antisocial personality disorder.

SOURCE: Caspi (2000).

In another study, children described as inhibited at age three were more likely than others to be depressed at age 21, whereas children described at age three as impulsive were more likely to be diagnosed as antisocial (aggressive, lacking guilt and so on) at age 21 (Moffit, Caspi, Dickson, Silva, & Stanton, 1996). A Swedish study similarly found that children (particularly boys) rated as aggressive at ages 10 and 13 by their teachers were disproportionately represented among criminals (especially perpetrators of violent crime) at age 26 (Stattin & Magnusson, 1989).

One of the most important studies to document consistency over time examined the childhood personality antecedents of depressive tendencies in 18-year-olds (Block, Gjerde, & Block, 1991). Several preschool teachers rated aspects of the children's behaviour and personality at ages three and four. The same participants were then observed in depth at ages seven, 11, 14 and 18 by various teachers and psychologists.

The investigators offered a more complex hypothesis than simply that depression in childhood would predict depression in adulthood. Their previous research suggested that an important variable that could influence the results was gender. Based on their knowledge of research on the way boys and girls are socialised (boys to be autonomous and girls to be more attuned to social demands), they hypothesised that the personality antecedents of depression in males and females might be quite different.

The results supported their hypothesis:

- Boys who later showed depressive tendencies were characterised when young as aggressive, self-aggrandising and unable to control their impulses. Girls who later became depressed, in contrast, showed almost the opposite attributes in childhood. They were shy, obedient, conscientious and unassuming.
- Boys who were less bright were also more prone to depression at age 18, whereas girls who were *more* intelligent were more likely to report depression at age 18.

Table 11.3 (see overleaf) shows some of the correlations between personality at age seven and depression at age 18. The table clearly shows that many of the same traits at age seven correlate with depression in opposite directions at age 18 in males and females.

TABLE 11.3 **Gender differences in selected personality traits at age seven that correlate with depressive symptoms at age 18**

	Correlation with depression at age 18	
Trait at age seven	**For males**	**For females**
Characteristically stretches limits	.37	−.22
Teases other children	.25	−.32
Tries to be centre of attention	.30	.29
Is empathic	−.30	.29
Can be trusted; is dependable	−.37	.20
Is obedient and compliant	−.22	.30

Many of the same traits at age seven correlate with depression in opposite directions at age 18 in males and females.

SOURCE: Adapted from Block et al. (1991).

NOTE: The table reports the correlations between personality dimensions assessed at age seven with degree of depression reported at age 18. As can be seen, on many dimensions, predictors of depression in males and females differed considerably.

Some research suggests that personality shows considerable stability *throughout* adulthood. A study of the FFM in a sample of adults ages 30 to 96 found that personality stabilises by age 30 and remains consistent thereafter (Ardelt, 2000; Costa, Herbst, McCrae, & Siegler, 2000; Costa & McCrae, 1988, 1990). However, other empirical evidence suggests that personality traits continue to change throughout adulthood.

Changes in personality traits in adulthood

By Professor Greg Boyle, Bond University

Historically, personality traits have been defined as fixed, immutable dispositions. For example, the FFM views personality constructs simply as a set of *static* dispositions that remain unaffected by social experience. (Since Costa and McCrae's related NEO–PI–R items were derived from a top-down approach, the instrument is unable to provide adequate coverage of primary personality trait structure.) Proponents of the FFM have asserted that throughout middle and old age, personality traits remain stable (Costa & McCrae, 1994). In fact, as a result of situational learning, personality traits continue to exhibit considerable developmental changes throughout the adult years, although there are wide individual and cultural differences (Cattell, 1983; Cattell, Boyle, & Chant, 2002; Roberts, Walton, & Viechtbauer, 2006a). Thus, mounting empirical evidence reveals that personality traits exhibit only *relative stability* across the life span (Boyle et al., 2008).

In order to provide a brief empirical illustration of structured personality learning in adulthood, 12 separate item parcels measuring Factors B (Intelligence), C (Ego Strength), and E (Dominance) of the Sixteen Personality Factor Questionnaire (16PF) (Form A) were administered to undergraduates across a one-month test–retest interval (Cattell et al., 2002). The resulting 12 × 12 inter-correlation matrices for the pre- and post-learning data were subjected to separate iterative, maximum-likelihood factor analyses, plus direct oblimin simple structure rotation. Significant increases in Ego Strength provided further evidence suggesting the dynamic nature of certain personality traits during adulthood. Extension of this approach to all 16 normal personality trait dimensions, measured in the 16PF, plus the 12 abnormal personality trait dimensions measured in the Clinical Analysis Questionnaire (CAQ), may provide additional insights into personality changes in adulthood.

Fraley and Roberts (2005) pointed out that inferences about changes in personality traits can only be drawn from examining multiple test–retest data of varying intervals across the life span (including adulthood). Roberts et al. (2006a) carried out an extensive meta-analysis of 92 longitudinal studies to ascertain mean-level trait changes at various chronological ages. They found that in young to middle adulthood, individuals exhibit increases in social dominance, conscientiousness and emotional stability, followed in old age by decreases in vitality and openness, and increases in agreeableness. Had they measured a greater diversity of personality trait constructs (such as those included in either the 16PF or CAQ, covering the normal and abnormal trait spheres, respectively), rather than just the few broad FFM dimensions, evidence of trait change might have been even more revealing. Nevertheless, Roberts et al. (2006a, p. 21) 'provided definitive evidence for the continued plasticity of personality traits beyond age 30 and well into old age in the case of specific traits, such as social vitality, agreeableness, conscientiousness, and openness to experience'.

Finally, as Roberts, Walton and Viechtbauer (2006b) pointed out, 'accepting the fact that personality traits change in adulthood highlights the inadequacies of almost all theoretical positions found in personality psychology and personality development'. They concluded that 'a new vision of personality psychology that is more dynamic' and is 'inclusive of both person and environmental variables' is required. Presumably, personality trait changes during adulthood (including middle and old age) may come about not only as a result of positive learning, but also as a function of traumatic experiences, serious illnesses and medical conditions, including conditions that result in neuropsychological changes in brain integrity and function.

It is also quite possible that personality is much more consistent across situations than Mischel theorised. Epstein (1980) argued that the studies which apparently showed low cross-situational consistency only examined a small range of behaviours, making the assessment unreliable. Determining conclusively whether people behaved consistently across situations would require measuring them on a number of occasions, not just once, as many of the early studies did.

The interaction between personality and situation

If personality shows substantial consistency across situations and over time, was Mischel wrong? The answer is not a simple yes or no. On the one hand, Mischel clearly overstated the case for the role of situations in behaviour and understated the case for personality variables. A 21-year-old man who was impulsive and undercontrolled at age three is more likely to be aggressive when someone accidentally bumps into him on the street and to steal from a store than a man who was better adjusted in preschool.

On the other hand, Mischel forced personality psychologists to move beyond simple statements such as 'John is an aggressive person' to more complex statements about the *circumstances* under which John will be aggressive. In other words, Mischel's critique of traits led to a recognition of ***person-by-situation interactions*** — that is, people express particular traits in particular situations.

In fact, in his most recent statements of his approach, Mischel argues that personality lies in *if–then* patterns — stable ways in which particular situations trigger specific patterns of thought, feeling and behaviour (Mischel & Shoda, 1995, 1998). For example, one man may become aggressive when another man appears to be threatening or humiliating him; another may become aggressive when he feels vulnerable with his wife, which leads him to feel unmasculine. Both men may be equally aggressive when their behaviour is averaged across situations, but the difference between them lies in the circumstances (the 'if') that elicit the response (the 'then'). One of the exciting aspects of this approach is that Mischel explicitly attempts to integrate his own cognitive–social theory with both trait theory (arguing for enduring personality dispositions) and psychodynamic theory (focusing on personality dynamics that get activated under particular conditions, often outside of awareness).

Mischel's research, like that of other psychologists who have been tracking down the nature of person-by-situation interactions (e.g. Funder & Colvin, 1991), supports a contention of early trait theorists that seemed to get lost for many years: consistency is most likely to emerge in similar situations

MAKING CONNECTIONS

Social psychologists study how the presence of others can alter people's behaviour, often focusing on the **situational causes** of behaviour (rather than causes residing in the individual) (chapter 18). In groups, for example, people often behave in ways that are violent, antisocial or very different from the way they usually respond alone.

For example, in Australia, displays of patriotism have devolved into shows of overt nationalism on some occasions, including during the Cronulla riots in 2005. On Australia Day in 2009, crowds formed into mobs at Manly Beach in Sydney, ruining the festivities by damaging cars and intimidating police and other patrons.

(Allport, 1937; Mischel, 2004; Rotter, 1990). A person who is generally quite low on neuroticism may nevertheless tend to become extremely distressed when criticised. Her difficulty coping with criticism is just as much a part of her personality as her generally placid nature; the only difference is that the circumstances that activate neurotic behaviour are much more specific than those that activate its opposite.

INTERIM SUMMARY

Personality demonstrates many consistencies across time and situations. The debate over the extent to which personality is consistent led to a recognition of the importance of ***person-by-situation interactions*** — ways in which people express personality dispositions only under specific circumstances. According to Mischel, personality lies in *if–then* patterns — stable ways in which particular situations trigger specific patterns of thought, feeling and behaviour.

1. You have a great need for other people to like and admire you.
2. You have a tendency to be critical of yourself.
3. You have a great deal of unused capacity, which you have not turned to your advantage.
4. While you have some personality weaknesses, you are generally able to compensate for them.
5. Your sexual adjustment has presented problems for you.
6. Disciplined and self-controlled outside, you tend to be worried and insecure inside.
7. You have found it unwise to be too frank in revealing yourself to others.
8. At times you are extroverted, affable, sociable, while at other times you are introverted, wary, reserved.

FIGURE 11.10
The Barnum effect is likely to be produced from the following personality sketch.

SOURCE: Forer (1949), cited in Gleitman, Fridlund, and Reisberg (1999, p. 677).

Contributions and limitations of trait theories

The trait approach to personality has several advantages. Traits lend themselves to measurement and hence to empirical investigation through questionnaires. Without the trait approach, we would not have been able to assess the heritability or consistency of personality. Further, trait theories are not committed to theoretical assumptions that may be valid for some people but not for others. Psychodynamic and cognitive–social theories offer universal answers to questions such as 'Are humans basically aggressive?' or 'Are people basically rational?' Trait theories, in contrast, offer a very different answer: 'Some people are, some aren't, and some are in between' (McCrae & Costa, 1990). The trait approach has also enabled the development of an appropriate taxonomy for the categorisation of personality attributes. A number of taxonomies have been developed, with perhaps the most widely accepted being the identification of the 'big five' dimensions: extroversion, neuroticism, agreeableness, conscientiousness and openness to experience. The 'big five' factors have been widely used in psychological studies as a conceptual framework through which to examine the structure of personality. This model is not without its critics, however. Some say five factors are too few to describe the huge variations possible in human personality. Another criticism is that the model is purely descriptive and does nothing to explain how personality traits develop. Alternative categorisations have been developed, such as one proposed by Eysenck, which features two main dimensions — neuroticism–emotional stability and extroversion–introversion. Perhaps for these reasons the trait approach, and the FFM in particular, has breathed new life into personality as an important and scientifically sound area of psychological research.

Like all approaches, however, trait approaches have limitations (see Block, 1995, 2001; McAdams, 1992; Westen, 1995). First, they rely heavily on self-reports, and people may not always give an accurate assessment of themselves. For example, people who consider themselves psychologically healthy may deny statements about themselves that are true but threaten their self-concept (Hergovich, Sirsch, & Felinger, 2002; MacDonald & Standing, 2002; Shedler, Mayman, & Manis, 1993). Others may fall victim to what is called the ***Barnum effect*** — when an interpretation of a personality test is so broad it could apply to anyone, so people are willing to accept the results as fact (see figure 11.10). A horoscope in a daily newspaper is an example of the Barnum effect in action — often the forecasts for each star sign are so broad that the readers can interpret them as being valid for their individual circumstances. The term gets its name from infamous circus operator P. T. Barnum who coined the phrase 'There's a sucker born every minute'.

Second, as in factor-analytic studies of intelligence, the factor structure that emerges depends in part on the items that are included and a number of highly subjective decisions made by the factor analyst. Although most personality researchers have converged on the FFM, others have repeatedly found three or four factors (e.g. Boyle, Stankov, & Cattell, 1995; Di Blas & Forzi, 1999; Eysenck, 1990; Stallings, Hewitt, Cloninger, Heath, & Eaves, 1996), and some have found seven (e.g. Benet-Martinez & Waller, 1997).

Third, trait psychology does not examine the dynamic nature of personality (see Boyle, 2008). It focuses on the descriptors that people use to label other people (or themselves) and their behaviour, but it does nothing to explain the underpinnings of that behaviour — why the person behaves the way he does.

Fourth, although there does appear to be cross-cultural consistency in the five factors used to describe personality, these factors may not mean precisely the same thing in different cultures, and their role in affecting behaviour may also vary across cultures. Specifically, people in collectivist cultures, such as

APPLY + DISCUSS

One of the issues with which trait psychologists have struggled regards how many traits are needed to describe the core of people's personalities. Eysenck believed there were three basic personality traits (introversion–extroversion, neuroticism and psychoticism). Cattell identified 16 personality traits measured in his personality test, the Sixteen Personality Factors or 16PF. Proponents of the five factor model obviously endorse the perspective that five traits are central to describing people's personalities.

- How many traits do you think are necessary to describe personality?
- Can you think of traits that the five factor model may have omitted?
- How many traits can you think of to describe yourself?

Japan, where the emphasis is more on the collective or the community rather than the individual, may place less emphasis on traits than do people from more individualistic Western cultures (Church, 2000).

Finally, trait theories often provide more insight into the *how much* of personality than the *how* or the *why* (Block, 1995). A person may rank high in aggressiveness, but this ranking says little about the internal processes that occur when the person is behaving aggressively or why he behaves aggressively in some circumstances but not in others. Trait approaches that attempt to provide causal mechanisms — for example, by linking traits to underlying biology and genetics — tend to be more powerful.

Humanistic theories

During the 1950s and especially the 1960s, an approach to personality emerged as an alternative to psychoanalysis and behaviourism. Unlike these approaches, humanistic approaches to personality focus on aspects of personality that are distinctly human, not shared by other animals. How do people find meaning in life, and how can they remain true to themselves in the midst of pressures they experience from the first days of life to accommodate other people's wishes and preconceptions? Many humanistic psychologists argue that scientific methods borrowed from the natural sciences are inappropriate for studying people, whose actions, unlike those of fish or asteroids, reflect the way they understand and experience themselves and the world.

Although humanistic psychology has its roots in the European philosophical thinking of the late nineteenth century, the humanistic approach to personality emerged during the 1960s, a decade that challenged traditional values. People were tired of fitting into roles others set for them and instead sought ways to be true to themselves and their personal beliefs (see M. B. Smith, 1978, 1988, 1994). Here we examine representative humanistic theories: the person-centred approach of Carl Rogers and existential theories of personality.

APPLY + DISCUSS

Some personality traits are specific to particular situations, whereas others are probably more general, or global.

- Is 'character' a specific or a general trait?
- How might a personality psychologist make sense of golfing superstar Tiger Woods' behaviour? Golf is a game steeped in tradition, etiquette and ethical standards of behaviour. Woods was the undisputed number one player in the world and a married father of two when news of his affairs with multiple women made international headlines.
- Can a person be extremely honourable in one domain and dishonourable in another?

Rogers' person-centred approach

The most widely used humanistic theory of personality is Carl Rogers' ***person-centred approach*** (1951, 1959). Philosophically, Rogers descended from the French philosopher Jean-Jacques Rousseau, who two centuries earlier wrote that 'man is born free but everywhere he is in chains' (Rousseau, 1762/1972). Rousseau meant that people are innately free and compassionate to their fellows but through the effect of living in modern society, they become mean-spirited, selfish and trapped by convention.

Rogers similarly believed that human beings are basically good but their personalities become distorted by interpersonal experiences, especially in childhood. In his view, psychology should try to understand individuals' ***phenomenal experience*** — that is, the way they conceive of reality and experience themselves and their world. According to Rogers and other humanistic psychologists, psychologists should not be studying people as *objects* of their investigations but as *subjects* who construct meaning. Thus, the fundamental tool of the psychologist is not a projective test, an experiment or a questionnaire but ***empathy***, the capacity to understand another person's experience cognitively and emotionally.

Rogers, like other humanistic theorists, postulated that individuals have a ***true self*** — a core aspect of being, untainted by the demands of those around them — but that they often distort this into a ***false self*** — a mask they wear and ultimately mistake to be their true psychological 'face'. According to Rogers, the false self emerges because of people's natural desire to gain the positive regard of other people. As children develop, they learn that to be loved they must meet certain standards; in the process of internalising these ***conditions of worth***, they distort themselves into being what significant others want them to be.

According to Rogers, the self, or ***self-concept***, is an organised pattern of thought and perception about oneself. When the self-concept diverges too much from the ***ideal self*** (the person's view of what she should be like), the individual may distort her behaviour or the way she sees herself to avoid this painful state. Thus, people's internalised expectations of what others want them to be may lead them to abandon their own talents or inclinations and ignore their own needs and feelings. The artistic student who becomes an accountant because that is what his father always wanted him to be is, in Rogers' view, sacrificing his true self to meet internalised conditions of worth.

Rogers proposed that the primary motivation in humans is an ***actualising tendency***, a desire to fulfil the full range of needs that humans experience, from the basic needs for food and drink to the needs to be open to experience and to express one's true self. These needs were similarly described by Maslow, another humanistic psychologist (chapter 10). Opposing the actualising tendency, however, are the needs for positive regard from others and for positive self-regard, which often requires distorting the self to meet imposed standards.

INTERIM SUMMARY

Humanistic approaches focus on distinctively human aspects of personality, such as how to find meaning in life or be true to oneself. According to Carl Rogers' ***person-centred approach***, psychology should try to understand individuals' ***phenomenal experience*** — the way they conceive of reality and experience themselves and their world — through ***empathy***. Rogers defines the self, or ***self-concept***, as an organised pattern of thought and perception about oneself, which can diverge from the ***ideal self***, leading to distortions in personality.

Existential approaches to personality

Existentialism is a school of twentieth-century philosophy that similarly focused on subjective existence. According to many existentialist philosophers, the individual is alone throughout life and must confront what it means to be human and what values to embrace. According to the existential philosopher Jean-Paul Sartre (1971), unlike other animals and physical objects, people have no fixed nature and must essentially *create themselves*.

Existential questions

Sartre argued that the meaning we find in life is essentially our own invention and dies along with us. The paradox inherent in the human condition is that we must find meaning in our lives by committing ourselves to values, ideals, people and courses of action while simultaneously recognising that these things are finite and have no intrinsic meaning, that we have simply endowed them with meaning in order to make our lives seem worthwhile.

Sartre would object to the idea that we have a personality at all, if personality implies a static or unchanging set of traits. What distinguishes humans, he asserted, is that we are ever-changing and free to alter our course of action at any time. Thus, we have no essence, no personality, except if we choose to delude ourselves into believing that we have no choice.

According to existential psychologists, the dilemmas at the heart of existential philosophy are central to personality. Although many different theoretical perspectives have developed within existential psychology (Frankl, 1959; May, 1953; May, Angel, & Ellenberger, 1958), they converge on several key issues:

- the importance of subjective experience
- the centrality of the human quest for meaning in life
- the dangers of losing touch with what one really feels
- the hazards of conceiving of oneself as thing-like, rather than as a changing, ever-forming, creative source of will and action.

Chief among the problems humans face is ***existential dread***, the recognition that life has no absolute value or meaning and that, ultimately, we all face death. People spend their lives denying their mortality and the nothingness hidden behind their values and pursuits (Becker, 1973; Brown, 1959).

Experimental investigations of death anxiety

Many existential and humanistic psychologists have avoided testing their hypotheses or developing methods of personality assessment because of their concern about methods that turn people into objects to be studied rather than subjects to be understood. Nevertheless, a team of creative researchers has been systematically testing an existential theory developed by Ernest Becker (1973) that proposes that cultural beliefs and values serve to protect people from facing the reality of their mortality.

According to Becker's theory, an unfortunate by-product of the evolution of human intelligence is that people can imagine their own death and the death of those they love. To avoid the anxiety that would result from facing this tragic reality, we create and embrace cultural beliefs and values that symbolically deny death and allow hope in the face of mortality and meaninglessness (Solomon, Greenberg, & Pyszczynski, 1991, p. 96).

The researchers testing Becker's theory have demonstrated across a series of studies that, when confronted with experimental procedures designed to stimulate death anxiety (such as a questionnaire asking participants to think about their own death), people cling more tenaciously to their cultural values (Greenberg, Pyszczynski, Solomon, Simon, & Breus, 1994; Mikulincer, Florian, Birnbaum, & Malishkevich, 2002; Solomon et al., 1991). For example, in one study, municipal court judges served as participants (Rosenblatt, Greenberg, Solomon, Pyszczynski, & Lyon, 1989). Half the judges received the mortality salience manipulation (the death questionnaire), whereas the other half (the control group) did not. The experimenters then asked the judges to set bond for a prostitute in a hypothetical case. Prostitution was chosen as the crime because of its culturally defined moral overtones. As predicted, judges who filled out the mortality questionnaire were significantly more punitive, setting bond substantially higher than judges in the control group, whose death anxiety had not been activated.

Not only does mortality salience heighten attraction to cultural norms, but these cultural norms can subsequently affect behaviour. People who adhere to valued cultural norms gain social approval, increased self-esteem and, according to existential theorists, a buffer against death anxiety. In a test of this idea, researchers interviewed pedestrians either in front of a funeral home (high mortality salience) or several blocks away from the funeral home (low mortality salience) (Jonas, Schimel, Greenberg, & Pyszczynski, 2002). They then asked the participants their feelings about two different charities that the participants had deemed to be moderately important. Participants for whom mortality was salient expressed more favourable attitudes towards the charities than those for whom death was not made salient (figure 11.11). These results were interpreted in terms of mortality salience heightening attraction to cultural norms of helping those in need, which affected participants' attitudes towards the charitable organisations.

	Death salience		Control	
	M	*SD*	*M*	*SD*
How beneficial is this charity to society?	17.31	2.96	14.73	3.91
How much does society need this charity?	17.37	2.70	15.80	3.62
How desirable is this charity to you personally?	16.06	3.29	13.40	4.12
Favourability composite	50.75	7.60	43.93	10.68

FIGURE **11.11**
Means and standard deviations for participants' ratings of the charities. Participants for whom mortality was made salient gave more favourable ratings to valued charities than those participants for whom death was not salient. Adherence to cultural norms that dictate prosocial behaviour and concern for the needs of others serve as a buffer against the anxiety that arises when mortality is made salient.

SOURCE: Jonas et al. (2002, p. 1343).

More recently, research has turned to the development of close relationships as a means of buffering people against mortality salience (Mikulincer, Florian, & Hirschberger, 2003). People for whom death is salient appear to seek out close relationships with others more readily than those for whom death is not immediately salient. Furthermore, being in close relationships with others seems to buffer people from the salience of reminders of death.

INTERIM SUMMARY

According to ***existential*** approaches to psychology, people have no fixed nature and must essentially create themselves. Sartre argued that people must find meaning in their lives by making commitments while also recognising that these commitments have no intrinsic meaning. ***Existential dread*** is the recognition that life has no absolute value or meaning and that we all face death. Research supports Becker's theory that people deny death by committing to cultural worldviews that give them a sense of meaning and immortality.

Contributions and limitations of humanistic theories

> **APPLY + DISCUSS**
>
> Earlier in this chapter, we discussed projective measures that are used particularly by psychoanalytic theorists to assess personality. Trait theorists, on the other hand, rely on more subjective means, such as self-report measures, to determine personality.
>
> - How might psychoanalytic theorists use projective tests to measure traits as opposed to unconscious motivations.
> - How might trait theorists, for example, use self-report personality inventories to measure underlying motives and urges?

Humanistic psychology has made a number of contributions to the study of personality. Perhaps the most important is its unique focus on the way humans strive to find meaning in life, a dimension other approaches have failed to address. In day-to-day life this need may not be readily observable because culture confers meaning on activities, relationships and values. The salience of this aspect of personality emerges, however, in times of personal crisis or loss (Janoff-Bulman, 1992), when life may seem meaningless. The search for meaning also becomes apparent in times of rapid cultural change (Wallace, 1956), when a culture's values and worldview are breaking down and no longer fulfil their function of making life predictable and meaningful (see also Baumeister, 1991). The humanistic view places more emphasis on a person's own subjective view of reality and the way individuals strive to rise above obstacles and be the best they can. The prevalence of positive psychology proponents today has its origins in the humanist school.

The humanistic approach has two major limitations. First, it does not offer a comprehensive theory of personality in the same way that psychodynamic and cognitive–social theories do. It does not, for example, offer a general theory of cognition, emotion, behaviour and psychological disorder, although different theorists at times address many of these. Second, with some notable exceptions (e.g. Rogers, 1959), humanistic psychology has not produced a substantial body of testable hypotheses and research, in part because of its rejection of empiricism as a philosophy of science (chapter 2). Much of the body of research on this topic is based on theories that have not been comprehensively tested, or are extremely hard to test empirically. For instance, how do you test and measure a concept such as 'personal growth'? Also, critics argue that the humanistic view of human nature is idealistic and probably not attainable in reality.

Genetics, personality and culture

In this section, we will examine the interplay between genetics, personality and culture. First, we will consider the extent to which personality is inherited. Second, we will explore the intricate relationship between personality and culture.

Genetics and personality

Why is one person extroverted and another introverted? Few would doubt the influence of learning and environment on personality. However, a considerable body of evidence supports an idea first proposed by the Greek physician Galen 2000 years ago, that a substantial part of personality is inherited (Krueger, 2000; Plomin & Caspi, 1999). The case of the 'Twinnies' that opened this chapter is not unusual in finding strong similarities among people with shared genes (Jang et al., 1998; Lykken, Bouchard, McGue, & Tellegen, 1993; McGue, Bacon, & Lykken, 1993; Tellegen et al., 1988; Vierikko, Pulkkinen, Kaprio, Viken, & Rose, 2003). Despite the fact that adopted children may have lived with their adoptive family from birth, biological relatives tend to be more similar than adoptive relatives, even if they have had no contact with one another (Loehlin, Willerman, & Horn, 1988; Plomin & Caspi, 1999). Some heritable personality traits emerge quite early in development. Extroversion, task orientation and activity level already show high heritability in one- and two-year-olds (Braungart, Plomin, DeFries, & Fulker, 1992; Rowe, 1999). ***Heritability*** refers to the proportion of variance in a particular trait that is due to genetic influences (Pervin, 2003; see figure 11.12 opposite).

The most definitive studies in this area compare twins reared together and twins reared apart, a procedure that can distinguish cleanly between genetic and environmental influences (chapter 9). A Minnesota study (Tellegen et al., 1988) examined 217 monozygotic (MZ) and 114 dizygotic (DZ) adult twin pairs who had been reared together and 44 MZ and 27 DZ adult twin pairs who had been reared apart (average age 22). Table 11.4 (opposite) displays the correlations between MZ and DZ twins reared together and apart on a personality test measuring such traits as wellbeing, achievement, aggression and traditionalism. The MZ twins reared together showed substantially higher correlations (averaging .51) than DZ twins reared together (averaging .23) on almost every trait. Even more interesting was that almost identical results were found for twins who were reared apart and had been separated for many years. The correlations averaged +.50 for MZ twins and +.21 for DZ twins. Given the identical twins were raised in totally different family environments, it might have been expected that the correlations between their personality traits would have been much lower. The fact that the results were virtually identical is a strong further argument for heritability (Bouchard, 1984; Bouchard, Lykken, McGue, & Segal, 1990; Tellegen et al., 1988).

A series of studies of Swedish adoptees with a much larger sample but a higher mean age of participants (in their fifties rather than their twenties) also found considerable evidence for genetic influences but yielded lower heritability estimates, averaging about .27 (see Plomin, Chipuer, & Loehlin, 1990). The correlations for MZ twins reared together were considerably larger than those reared apart, demonstrating substantial environmental influences on personality. In this study, two factors from the FFM, agreeableness and conscientiousness, showed minimal heritability (low correlations for MZ twins reared apart) but substantial environmental influence (contrastingly high correlations for MZ twins reared together). Openness was largely heritable, while extroversion and neuroticism showed substantial genetic *and* environmental impact (see also McCrae, 1996; Viken, Rose, Kaprio, & Koskenvuo, 1994). In their study of more than 100 sets of identical and fraternal twins, Jang, Livesley, and Vernon (1996) found that estimates of genetic influence for the 'big five' traits ranged from 40 to 60 percent. Identical twins are more alike than fraternal twins on various personality attributes in just about every case (e.g. Buss & Plomin, 1984; Zuckerman, 1987) and to about the same extent on each of the scales (Rushton, Fulker, Neale, Nias, & Eysenck, 1986). A Swedish study of more than 12 000 sets of twins found average correlations of +.50 between MZ twins on scores of Eysenck's introversion–extroversion and neuroticism–emotional stability traits, compared with correlations of +.21 and +.23 for DZ twins (Floderus-Myrhed, Pedersen, & Rasmuson, 1980). The evidence of these studies seems irrefutable — hereditary factors make a sizeable contribution to differences in personality. Other research suggests that some of the specific facets of the FFM are moderately heritable, such as self-discipline and self-consciousness (Jang et al., 1998; Loehlin, McCrae, Costa, & John, 1998).

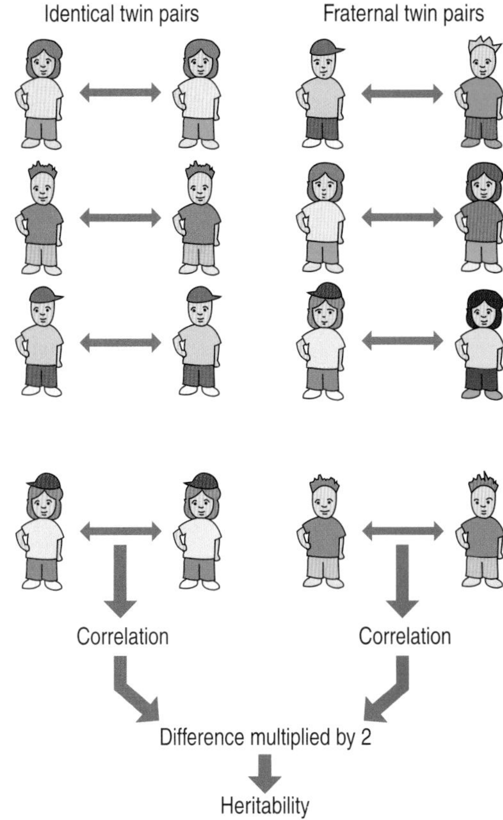

FIGURE 11.12
The twin study method examines pairs of identical and same-sex fraternal twins. The members of each pair are compared on the variable of interest, and a separate correlation is computed for each type of twin. One of these correlations is then subtracted from the other. Multiplying this difference by 2 gives an index of the heritability of the characteristic, an estimate of the variance in it that is accounted for by inheritance.

SOURCE: From Carver and Scheier (1992). Copyright © 1992 by Pearson Education. Reprinted by permission of the publisher.

TABLE 11.4 **Correlations between Minnesota twins reared together and apart on a multidimensional personality measure**

	Reared apart		Reared together	
	MZ	*DZ*	*MZ*	*DZ*
Wellbeing	.48	.18	.58	.23
Achievement	.36	.07	.51	.13
Social closeness	.29	.30	.57	.24
Stress reaction	.61	.27	.52	.24
Alienation	.48	.18	.55	.38
Aggression	.46	.06	.43	.14
Traditionalism	.53	.39	.50	.47
Positive emotionality	.34	−.07	.63	.18
Negative emotionality	.61	.29	.54	.41
Constraint	.57	.04	.58	.25

Substantial differences between MZ and DZ twins suggest a genetic effect.

Substantial differences between MZ twins reared apart and together suggest an environmental effect.

SOURCE: Tellegen et al. (1988, p. 1035).

To what extent do differences between families influence the way a child's personality develops? For instance, does the socioeconomic status or religion of the parents shape the personality of the child? If these differences were influential, you would expect studies of adopted siblings to produce a good correlation on their trait scores. However, this has not proven the case. Plomin and Daniels (1987) found the average correlation between adopted siblings was +.04, and the correlation with their adoptive parents was just +.05. Similarly, Loehlin (1992) found that between-family differences had negligible influence on the 'big five' traits.

The evidence thus points to heritability estimates in the range of 15 to 50 percent for most personality traits, with the balance attributable to the environment (Loehlin, Neiderhiser, & Reis, 2003; Saudino & Plomin, 1996). Despite this strong environmental influence, the same family does not necessarily produce children with similar personalities. Adoptive siblings, for example, tend to share few personality traits, and even natural siblings show great variations. While this may be surprising in one sense, in another, it may simply attest to the flexibility with which human beings can respond to similar circumstances. In a family with erratic alcoholic parents, for example, one sibling may cope by turning inward, becoming introverted and studious, while another may cope by becoming wild, poorly controlled and eventually alcoholic. In both cases, their personalities have been shaped by a similar environment, even though they took very different roads. Each sibling in a family also has different experiences within that family and outside of it, and these unshared experiences can be important in shaping personality. Plomin and Daniels (1987) identify key environmental differences encountered by different children in the same family. They include birth order; age gaps between siblings; treatment by parents; changing economic situation of the family; geographical relocation; differences in peer groups, teachers and friends; hobbies; and significant injuries or accidents. All these factors contribute to differences found between children within the same family. They might also help to explain why twins Mark and Steve Waugh have different personalities.

Birth order and the age gap between siblings are two of several factors that have been identified that contribute to the differences between them.

Behavioural geneticists are increasingly examining the complexities of genetic transmission of psychological characteristics. For example, some inherited traits may only find behavioural expression if each sibling has *several* genes that interact to produce it or if both siblings have the same dominant gene (see Saudino, 1997). Some genes that control personality may, for example, be dominant, like genes for brown eyes. Thus, identical twins with the gene will be highly similar, whereas non-identical twins or other siblings will be entirely different if they do not both inherit the dominant gene or if they do not inherit the constellation of genes required to produce the trait.

Genetic tendencies may also trigger a cascade of events that include *environmental* responses that lead to highly heritable traits. If there are genetic differences between children within the same family, this leads to different behavioural tendencies, which necessarily influences the environment that develops around them. A social and active infant is likely to create greater social interaction than one who is shy and withdrawn. A child who is aggressive and rebellious may evoke harsher treatment and greater levels of punishment from parents, often reinforcing that initial behaviour. For example, in a longitudinal study from Finland, aggression at age eight predicted chronic unemployment 30 years later (Kokko & Pulkkinen, 1997). Although aggression in childhood can reflect in part genetic influences, the data suggested that aggressive children developed problems at school and problems with substance abuse by adolescence. These difficulties, in turn, began to shape their lives and foreclose employment options as they moved into adulthood.

Children may unconsciously mould their environments through their behavioural tendencies at a young age. More overt changes occur as children grow older and are able to seek out and have more control over the environments they inhabit — for instance, what sporting clubs they belong to, what part-time jobs they take up and what people they associate with. According to Scarr (1992), all of these factors combine to produce a correlation between our genetic predispositions and the environment we come to live in. Overall, the research evidence suggests a strong genetic influence on personality.

INTERIM SUMMARY

Genetic views on personality suggest that many personality traits are inherited. Heritability refers to the proportion of variance in a particular trait that is due to genetic influences. Evidence in support of a genetic basis of personality has relied primarily on twin studies comparing monozygotic (MZ) and dizygotic (DZ) twins. Data from studies of behavioural genetics suggest that most personality variables are 15 to 50 percent heritable.

Personality and culture

Two things are notable about the relationship between personality and culture. First, although there is an incredible amount of variability in personality among individuals, there is also a remarkable degree of consistency in many of the traits and behaviours that characterise people across cultures (Leary, 1999; McCrae, 2004; Oishi, 2004; see also Stankov & Lee, 2008). People in all cultures experience anxiety, embarrassment and threats to their self-esteem. Everyone, regardless of their cultural background, fears particular things, whether they be an upcoming speech or death. Most normal individuals have a yearning for unconditional positive regard as recommended by Rogers, and for inclusion in individual or group relationships with others. Thus, in spite of the wide range of individual differences that can be observed, there are some universals to personality that extend across cultures and across people (Barkow, Cosmides, & Tooby, 1992; Foster, Campbell, & Twenge, 2003; Hong & Mallorie, 2004).

Second, the theories we have explored in this chapter represent our own culture's most sophisticated attempts to understand personality. Other cultures, however, have alternative views. Thus, although there are universals in personality, the explanations offered by particular cultures to account for personality vary. In fact, every culture has some implicit, commonsense conception of personality.

Traditional Aboriginal societies in Australia featured complex creation stories that are now known as 'The Dreaming'. Eckermann (1995) describes the Dreaming as the time when the great heroes of the past inhabited the earth and created every natural feature and animal. They turned themselves into rivers, waterholes or animals at will, disappearing and reappearing constantly, and ascending to the sky to become constellations. The spirits of the great heroes live on in the sites where they touched the earth. Everything on earth — the land itself, as well as animals and people — is connected. Each person is connected to a number of creation sites and this gives individuals both a spiritual and social identification. Thus personality is, in part, related to the ancestral spirits that have connection to individuals.

Unlike contemporary Western theories, traditional Aboriginal cultures did not believe that individual personalities could be divorced from the spiritual context in which people lived. In those cultures, everything — people, rain, sky, stars, wind, land and animals — were thought to belong to a spiritual and social whole (Eckermann, 1995).

Traditional Aboriginal cultures believe that everything — people, rain, sky, stars, wind, land and animals — belong to a spiritual and social whole. This painting is of a fish from 'The Dreaming'.

Approaches to culture and personality

Although most Western theories of personality have been constructed with Western people in mind, the complex interactions of personality and culture have intrigued psychologists and anthropologists since the early part of the twentieth century (see Church & Lonner, 1998; LeVine, 1982). Do cultures with harsh child-rearing practices create hostile or paranoid personalities? And how do cultural practices help individuals satisfy psychological needs, such as escaping from death anxiety? We briefly consider three approaches to culture and personality: Freud's, the culture pattern approach and interactionist approaches.

Freud's approach

Freud viewed cultural phenomena as reflections of individual psychodynamics. The Freudian method of analysing cultures is the same method applied to dreams, neurotic symptoms and conscious beliefs in individuals. Look beneath manifest content to find latent content (see Spain, 1992).

Freud thought cultural phenomena such as myths, moral and religious beliefs, and games to be expressions of the needs and conflicts of individuals.

Freud (1928) similarly argued that institutions such as religion can be understood in terms of their functions for individuals. Should one be surprised to find representations in Western culture of a Holy Father and a Holy Mother? The monotheistic concept of God in many religions is remarkably similar to a young child's conception of his father: a strong, masculine, frightening figure who can be both loving and vengeful. (Interestingly, empirical research suggests that people's concepts of God actually tend to resemble their descriptions of their mothers, particularly when they are closer to their mother than to their father; see Wulff, 1997.) A Freudian might also note that the virgin mother of Christian theology is a perfect resolution of Oedipal conflict. No child wants to think that his parents have sex, and the best way of keeping mother pure is to imagine that she could have had a virgin birth.

The culture pattern approach

A second approach asserts that individual psychology reflects cultural practices, not the other way around. The ***culture pattern approach*** sees culture as an organised set of beliefs, rituals and institutions that shape individuals to fit its patterns. Some cultures stress community and pursuit of the common good, and their members generally internalise these values. Others foster a paranoid attitude, which individuals express in their relationships with neighbours or outsiders, such as the Nuer of the Sudan (Evans-Pritchard, 1956) or the Aymaya of South America (LaBarre, 1966). As the American anthropologist Ruth Benedict (1934, p. 2) put it, 'The life history of the individual is first and foremost an accommodation to the patterns and standards traditionally handed down in the community'.

From the standpoint of the culture pattern approach, culture is a great sculptor that chisels the raw biological material of an individual from infancy until it conforms to the sculptor's aesthetic ideal. Some slabs of humanity, however, are very difficult to chisel and are labelled deviant or thrown back into the quarry after being deformed by the hand of the frustrated artist. Those whose temperament and personality patterns do not readily conform to culture patterns may thus find themselves ostracised or incarcerated, viewed in various societies as sinners, criminals, dissidents or mentally ill.

Interactionist approaches to personality and culture

The approaches described thus far reduce one broad set of variables to another: personality to economics, culture to personality or personality to culture. More complex approaches, however, combine the virtues of each. These ***interactionist approaches*** to personality view causality as multidirectional (LeVine, 1982; Whiting & Whiting, 1975; see also Church, 2001b; Poortinga & Van Hermert, 2001). Personality must certainly accommodate to economic and cultural demands, but cultural and economic processes themselves are in part created to fulfil psychological needs. These in turn are shaped by cultural and economic practices, so that causality runs in more than one direction.

For example, societies that treat children more abusively tend to have more aggressive myths and religious beliefs (Rohner, 1975a). From an interactionist perspective, this should not be surprising. On the one hand, the schemas or representations that children develop about relationships in childhood colour their understanding of supernatural relationships. Thus, children with hostile or abusive parents are likely to respond emotionally to images of evil or sadistic gods when they grow older. Indeed, one could argue that in the West, as child-rearing practices have become less harsh since the Middle Ages, the image of God has shifted from a vengeful, angry father to a loving, nurturant one.

On the other hand, causality runs in the opposite direction as well, from aggressive myths to abusive child-rearing practices. Societies use myths and religious beliefs to train people to behave in ways valued by the culture. People reared on a steady diet of myths depicting aggressive interactions are likely to treat their children more aggressively, which in turn produces children who resonate with the aggression in the myths they will teach their own children.

Other interactionist approaches consider historical as well as cultural factors. The psychoanalyst Erik Erikson (1969) examined the lives of powerful leaders such as Gandhi and Hitler and explored the intersection of their personality dynamics, the needs of their followers, and cultural and historical circumstances. Erikson argued, for example, that Hitler's strong need for power and his grandiosity, sensitivity to humiliation, and disgust for anyone he saw as weak contributed to the development of Nazi ideology, which stressed the greatness of Germany (with which Hitler identified) and the need to destroy groups Hitler perceived as either powerful (and hence threatening) or powerless. This ideology appealed to a nation that had been humiliated in World War I and forced to pay reparations to its adversaries, and it appealed to members of a culture whose child-rearing patterns left them vulnerable to feeling humiliated and unable to express their rage (chapter 17).

INTERIM SUMMARY

Freud reduced culture to personality, seeing cultural phenomena as reflections of individual psychodynamics. The ***culture pattern approach*** sees culture as an organised set of beliefs, rituals and institutions that shape individuals to fit its patterns. ***Interactionist approaches*** view causality as multi-directional, with personality, economics and culture mutually influencing one another.

Central questions revisited

◆ What are the elements of personality, and how stable are they?

We began with two central questions about the nature and stability of personality. First, what are the basic elements of personality? Motives? Thoughts? Feelings? Traits? Behaviour? No single answer has emerged to that question; in fact, it is one of the most hotly debated issues in the field of personality psychology. What psychologists do agree on is that personality lies at the intersection of virtually all psychological processes — cognition, emotion, behaviour — and occurs through the interplay of those processes. Our personality is not just our motives; nor is it just the way we solve problems or the ways we interact with other people. Personality is the way our motives, emotions and ways of thinking about ourselves, others and the world interact in particular situations to produce ways of responding that are characteristically 'ours'.

That leads to the question of stability. When we use phrases such as 'he's a dishonest person' or when psychologists describe a person as 'low in conscientiousness', we are making statements about what we can expect from the person over time and across situations. For a psychopath — an individual who lacks any conscience at all (chapter 15) — this may be very informative.

For most people, however, such a statement will tell us little about how the person will respond the next time we see him, because there are so many influences on what a person does at any given moment that generalised traits will play only a small role in predicting behaviour. But that does not mean generalised trait descriptions do not have substantial value in predicting the person's behaviour in the long run, across many situations. We can, as well, make some highly specific statements about the way a person is likely to react in particular *types* of situations, which may turn out to be the most important things we can say about a person's personality (e.g. 'she can interact comfortably with people at a superficial level, but she has difficulty letting her guard down in intimate relationships'). And we can make some surprisingly accurate predictions about the general shape an individual's personality will take 10, 20 or 30 years later.

◆

SUMMARY

1 Define personality

- ***Personality*** refers to the enduring patterns of thought, feeling and behaviour that are expressed in different circumstances. Personality psychologists study both the ***structure of personality*** (the organisation or patterning of thoughts, feelings and behaviours) and ***individual differences*** in dimensions of personality.

2 Psychodynamic theories

- Freud's theory of ***psychodynamics*** holds that psychological forces such as wishes, fears and intentions determine behaviour. His ***topographic model*** distinguished among ***conscious***, ***preconscious*** and ***unconscious mental processes***. Freud argued that mental conflict is ubiquitous and that ambivalence — conflicting feelings or intentions — is the rule rather than the exception in human experience. The solutions people develop in an effort to maximise fulfilment of conflicting motives simultaneously are called ***compromise formations***.
- Freud's ***drive***, or ***instinct***, ***model*** views sex ***(libido)*** and aggression as the basic human motives. His ***developmental model*** proposed a series of ***psychosexual stages*** — stages in the development of personality and sexuality. These include the ***oral***, ***anal***, ***phallic***, ***latency*** and ***genital stages***. Problematic experiences during a stage can lead to ***fixations*** — prominent conflicts and concerns that are focused on wishes from a particular period — or ***regressions***, in which issues from a past stage resurface. During the phallic stage, the child must resolve the ***Oedipus complex***, the desire for an exclusive, sensual/sexual relationship with the opposite-sex parent.
- Freud's ***structural model*** distinguished among ***id*** (the reservoir of sexual and aggressive energy), ***superego*** (conscience) and ***ego*** (the rational part of the mind that must somehow balance desire, reality and morality). Unconscious strategies aimed at minimising unpleasant emotions or maximising pleasant emotions are called ***defence mechanisms***. Common defence mechanisms include ***repression***, ***denial***, ***projection***, ***reaction formation***, ***sublimation***, ***rationalisation***, ***displacement***, ***regression*** and ***passive aggression***.
- Object relations theories stress the role of representations of self and others in interpersonal functioning and the role of early experience in shaping the capacity for intimacy.
- Psychodynamic approaches usually assess personality using ***life history*** and ***projective methods***, such as the ***Rorschach inkblot test*** and Thematic Apperception Test (TAT), although they also use experimental procedures to test hypotheses.

3 Cognitive–social theories

- Cognitive–social theories argue for the importance of encoding, personal value, expectancies, competencies and self-regulation in personality. The schemas people use to encode and retrieve social information play an important role in personality.
- ***Personal value*** refers to the importance individuals attach to various outcomes or potential outcomes. ***Expectancies*** are expectations relevant to desired outcomes. A ***behaviour–outcome expectancy*** is a belief that a certain behaviour will lead to a particular outcome. ***Self-efficacy expectancies*** are people's beliefs about their ability to perform actions necessary to produce a desired outcome. ***Competences*** are skills and abilities used to solve problems.
- ***Self-regulation*** means setting goals, evaluating performance and adjusting behaviours to achieve goals in the context of ongoing feedback. Cognitive–social theories view personality as problem solving to attain goals.

4 Trait theories

- Trait theories are based on the concept of ***traits***, emotional, cognitive and behavioural tendencies that constitute underlying dimensions of personality on which individuals vary. Using factor analysis, different theorists have proposed different theories of the major factors that constitute personality.
- Eysenck considers the major factors (which he calls types or supertraits) to be ***extroversion***, ***neuroticism*** and ***psychoticism***. The current consensus among trait psychologists is that personality consists of five traits, known as the 'big five' factors or ***five factor model (FFM)*** (openness to experience, conscientiousness, extroversion, agreeableness and neuroticism).
- The heritability of personality traits varies considerably; most are influenced by nature and nurture, but some are highly heritable, with heritability estimates often in the range of 15 to 50 percent.
- A debate about the consistency of personality has raged for the past 30 years, sparked by Mischel's arguments against consistency. Mischel's work sensitised researchers to the complexities of ***person-by-situation interactions***, in which personality processes become activated only in particular situations.

5 Humanistic theories

- ***Humanistic*** theories focus on aspects of personality that are distinctly human, not shared by other animals, such as how to find meaning in life and how to be true to oneself.
- Rogers' ***person-centred approach*** aims at understanding individuals' ***phenomenal experience*** — that is, how they conceive of reality and experience themselves and their world. According to Rogers, individuals have a ***true self*** (a core aspect of being, untainted by the demands of those around them), which is often distorted into a ***false self*** by the desire to conform to social demands. When the ***self-concept*** diverges too much from the individual's ***ideal self*** (the person's view of what she should be like), she may distort the way she behaves or the way she sees herself to avoid this painful state of affairs. Psychological understanding requires ***empathy***.
- ***Existential*** personality theories stress the importance of subjective experience and the individual's quest for meaning in life. Chief among the problems human beings face is ***existential dread***, the recognition that life has no absolute value or meaning and that death is inevitable. The ways people handle issues of meaning, mortality and existential dread are central aspects of personality.

6 Genetics, personality and culture

- Substantial evidence supports the idea that much of personality is inherited. Studies of monozygotic and dyzygotic twins reared together and reared apart show evidence for the ***heritability*** of certain traits.
- Some aspects of personality are probably universal, whereas others are culturally specific. The ***culture pattern approach*** sees personality primarily as an accommodation to culture. According to ***interactionist approaches***, personality is shaped by economic and cultural demands, but cultural and economic processes themselves are in part created to fulfil psychological needs.

KEY TERMS

actualising tendency, *p. 451*
ambivalence, *p. 426*
anal stage, *p. 429*
Barnum effect, *p. 450*
behavioural approach system (BAS), *p. 443*
behavioural inhibition system (BIS), *p. 443*
behaviour–outcome expectancy, *p. 438*
castration complex, *p. 430*
competences, *p. 438*
compromise formations, *p. 427*
conditions of worth, *p. 451*
conflict, *p. 427*
conscious mental processes, *p. 426*
culture pattern approach, *p. 458*
defence mechanisms, *p. 431*
denial, *p. 432*
developmental model, *p. 428*
displacement, *p. 432*
drive (*or* instinct) model, *p. 428*
ego, *p. 431*
empathy, *p. 451*
existential dread, *p. 452*
existentialism, *p. 452*
expectancies, *p. 438*
extroversion, *p. 442*
false self, *p. 451*
five factor model (FFM), *p. 443*
fixations, *p. 428*
genital stage, *p. 430*
heritability, *p. 454*
id, *p. 431*
ideal self, *p. 451*
identification, *p. 429*
individual differences, *p. 425*
interactionist approaches, *p. 458*
latency stage, *p. 430*
libido, *p. 428*
life history methods, *p. 434*
life tasks, *p. 438*
neuroticism, *p. 442*
object relations, *p. 433*
Oedipus complex, *p. 429*
oral stage, *p. 428*
passive aggression, *p. 432*
penis envy, *p. 430*
personal constructs, *p. 437*
personality, *p. 424*
personal value, *p. 438*
person-by-situation interactions, *p. 449*
person-centred approach, *p. 451*
phallic stage, *p. 429*
phenomenal experience, *p. 451*
pleasure principle, *p. 431*
preconscious mental processes, *p. 426*
primary process thinking, *p. 431*
principle of aggregation, *p. 446*
projection, *p. 432*
projective tests, *p. 434*
psychodynamics, *p. 426*
psychosexual stages, *p. 428*
psychoticism, *p. 442*
rationalisation, *p. 432*
reaction formation, *p. 432*
reality principle, *p. 431*
regression, *p. 432*
relational theories, *p. 433*
repression, *p. 432*
Rorschach inkblot test, *p. 434*
secondary process thinking, *p. 431*
self-concept, *p. 451*
self-efficacy expectancy, *p. 438*
self-regulation, *p. 439*
situational variables, *p. 445*
structural model, *p. 431*
structure of personality, *p. 424*
sublimation, *p. 432*
superego, *p. 431*
temperament, *p. 446*
topographic model, *p. 426*
traits, *p. 441*
true self, *p. 451*
unconscious mental processes, *p. 426*

REVIEW QUESTIONS

1. Describe the five psychosexual stages of personality development identified by Freud.
2. Differentiate between the id, ego and superego.
3. Compare and contrast Eysenck's theory with the five factor model of personality.
4. Describe the basic principles in Rogers' person-centred approach to personality.
5. Discuss the contributions and limitations of humanistic theories of personality.

DISCUSSION QUESTIONS

1. How have cognitive–social theories contributed to the study of personality?
2. How stable is your personality over time and across situations?
3. To what extent is your personality shaped by genetics and the environment?

APPLICATION QUESTIONS

1. Test your understanding of Freud's psychodynamic theory by matching the scenarios listed with the following defence mechanisms: repression, projection, reaction formation, sublimation, rationalisation, displacement and regression.
   (a) A teacher who unconsciously does not like a child in his class allows him special privileges during playtime.
   (b) A distressed car crash victim cannot recall the details of the accident that almost took her life.
   (c) Omar showed aggressive impulses when he was a young child. Now in his late teens, he has shown a desire to play competitive football and to be the best player in his team.
   (d) Talia is a very competitive player on the netball court and will do everything she can to win. However, at the end of each game she complains that her opponent player was super-competitive and physically targeted her during play.
   (e) Gillian is an adolescent who sulks in her bedroom when her parents advise her of a midnight curfew.
   (f) A person yells at his dog after finding out his application for promotion was unsuccessful.
   (g) A student plagiarises in an assignment because 'everyone does it' and she has 'never been caught before'.
2. Test your understanding of the 'big five' trait approach by indicating which set of traits would be most useful for describing each of the individuals now described.
   (a) Georgia has a vivid imagination and uses this talent to write children's novels. Although she enjoys meeting people and is well liked by her colleagues, she is always running late for appointments and can never meet her publishing deadlines.

(b) Slava is described as a calm and secure person. He is comfortable in his own company and never seeks out attention when at a party with friends.
(c) Dipesh is a down-to-earth person who always takes the same route to work each day. He becomes very anxious whenever he comes across a road detour on his way to work. He does not like to change the way he does things because he worries that something terrible may happen to him.

The solutions to the application questions can be found on pages 834–5.

MULTIMEDIA RESOURCES

The *Cyberpsych* multimedia resource is available *as an option* to accompany this textbook to further develop your understanding of many key psychology concepts. *Cyberpsych* contains a wealth of rich media content and activities, and for this chapter includes:

- a video clip on shyness
- a concept animation on Freud's defence mechanisms.

Physical and cognitive development

12

LEARNING OBJECTIVES

After studying this chapter you should be able to:

1. describe some of the basic issues in developmental psychology
2. distinguish between the three main types of research design used by developmental psychologists
3. describe how physical development occurs across the life span and discuss its impact on psychological functioning
4. describe how perceptual and cognitive development occurs in infancy, childhood and adolescence
5. describe the cognitive changes associated with ageing.

Issues in developmental psychology

- Nature and nurture both contribute to development, and their roles are not easily separated because environmental events often turn genes on and off.
- Human development is characterised by ***critical periods*** — central to specific types of learning that modify future development.
- A contentious issue is whether development occurs in *stages* (relatively discrete steps through which everyone progresses in the same sequence) or is *continuous* (involving steady and gradual change).

Studying development

- ***Cross-sectional studies*** compare groups of participants of different ages at a single time to provide a picture of age differences.
- ***Longitudinal studies*** assess the same individuals over time, providing the opportunity to assess age changes.
- ***Sequential studies*** minimise cohort effects by studying multiple cohorts longitudinally.

Physical development and its psychological consequences

- The prenatal period is divided into three stages: germinal period, embryonic period and foetal period.
- At birth, infants possess many adaptive ***reflexes***, such as rooting and sucking, which help ensure that the infant will get nourishment; motor development follows a universal sequence.
- Growth rates for girls and boys are roughly equal until age 10. At that point, girls begin a growth spurt that usually peaks at age 12, and boys typically follow suit about two or three years later. Physical growth is virtually complete by the end of adolescence.
- Gradual and less dramatic growth changes occur during adulthood. A gradual decline in physical abilities, including muscular strength and sensory functioning, occurs with ageing.

Cognitive development in infancy, childhood and adolescence

- Infants can perceive subtle differences, such as the sound of their mother's and another woman's voice, from birth.
- Piaget argued that children develop knowledge by constructing reality out of their own experience, mixing what they observe with their own ideas about how the world works. There are four stages of cognitive development:
  - *Sensorimotor:* thought and action are virtually identical, as the infant explores the world with its senses and behaviours; child is ***egocentric***.
  - *Preoperational:* symbolic thought develops; object permanence is firmly established; the child cannot coordinate different physical attributes of objects or consider different perspectives.
  - *Concrete operational:* the child is able to perform reversible mental operations on representations of objects; understanding of conservation develops; the child can apply logic to concrete situations.
  - *Formal operational:* the adolescent (or adult) can apply logic more abstractly; hypothetical thinking develops.
- Vygotsky developed a ***zone of proximal development (ZPD)*** that reflects a continuum of cognitive development, ranging from the child's individual capacity for problem solving to a more advanced and collaboratively based level of cognitive development.
- According to the information-processing approach to cognitive development, changes in processing speed, knowledge base, automatisation and metacognition occur with age.
- ***Neo-Piagetian theorists*** attempt to integrate an understanding of the broad stages of Piaget's theory with an information-processing approach; an important factor in qualitative changes in development is an increasing capacity for ***working memory***.

Cognitive development and change in adultood

- In later life, cognitive declines are shown in the following facilities: processing speed, working memory capacity, explicit memory retrieval, problem-solving strategies and fluid intelligence. Other functions show little or no noticeable decline, including many encoding processes, implicit memory, aspects of everyday memory and crystallised intelligence.
- A small proportion of the population suffers incurable progressive ***dementia*** (e.g. ***Alzheimer's disease***).
- The majority of people maintain sharp mental functioning even through old age.

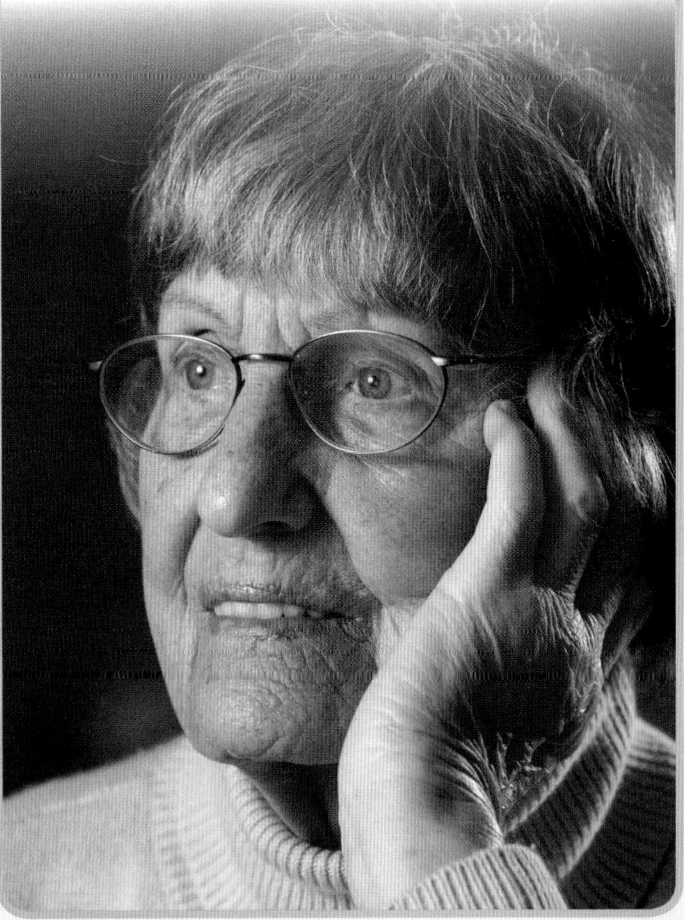

Central questions: the nature of development

- Maturational, cultural and environmental forces interact over time to create an organism capable of responding adaptively to its social and physical environment.

Dear God,

I saw Saint Patrick's Church last week when we went to New York. You live in a nice house.

Frank

FRANK is a young child whose letter was part of a research project studying children's developing ideas about God (Heller, 1986, p. 16). As Frank's letter suggests, young children translate cultural concepts like God into their own 'language'. Frank converted the idea of the church as God's home into his own concrete notion of what constitutes a 'nice house'. Children's drawings similarly reveal the way they translate adult spiritual beliefs into 'childese'.

Children initially have concrete views of God, irrespective of their religious upbringing. One young child, Frank, believed that God lived in Saint Patrick's Church, New York, after visiting the city.

In religious belief as in other areas, children frequently wrestle with concepts beyond their grasp, and their efforts reveal much about childish thought. Consider the mighty task faced by a six-year-old trying to make sense of the relationship between Jesus and God in Christian theology: 'Well, I know Jesus was a president and God is not . . . sort of like David was a king and God is not' (Heller, 1986, p. 40).

Whether children are reared Jewish, Baptist, Catholic, Muslim or Hindu, their views of God, like their understanding of most objects of thought, are initially concrete. By the time they move into adolescence, they are likely to offer abstract conceptions, such as 'God is a force within us all'. If cultural conditions permit, they may also express considerable scepticism about religious notions, since they are able to imagine and reflect on a variety of possible realities.

Changes in the way people understand reality and cultural beliefs are a central focus of ***developmental psychology***, which studies the way humans develop and change over time. For years, psychologists focused largely on childhood and adolescence and tended to consider development complete by the teenage years. More recently, however, psychologists have adopted a life-span developmental perspective that considers both constancy and change, and gains and losses in functioning, that occur at different points over the entire human life cycle (Baltes, 1998).

In this chapter, we first consider three central questions that reverberate throughout all of developmental psychology: the roles of nature and nurture, the importance of early experience and the extent to which development occurs in 'stages'. After addressing the question of how to study development, we focus on the central topics of this chapter: physical development and its impact on psychological functioning (e.g. how does an individual adapt to a changing body during puberty, menopause or old age?), cognitive development (e.g. what can an infant remember?) and cognitive changes associated with ageing (e.g. how do people's minds change with ageing?). The acquisition of language and successively more complex thinking are also discussed.

Central questions

- What roles do nature and nurture play in development?
- How important is early experience in shaping later psychological functioning?
- To what extent does development occur in stages?

Issues in developmental psychology

In this section, we will examine three basic issues relevant to human development. First, to what extent is development the product of nature or nurture? Second, we will discuss evidence for critical periods in psychological development. Third, we will consider whether development occurs in stages or is a continuous, gradual change.

Nature and nurture

For almost as many years as psychologists have been interested in development, they have wrestled with the extent to which changes in individuals over time reflect the influence of genetically programmed maturation (nature) or of learning and experience (nurture). ***Maturation*** refers to biologically based changes that follow an orderly sequence, each step setting the stage for the next step according to an age-related timetable (Wesley & Sullivan, 1986). Infants crawl before they walk, and they utter single syllables and words before they talk in complete sentences. Unless reared in a profoundly deprived environment or physically impaired, virtually all human infants follow these developmental patterns in the same sequence and at roughly the same age, give or take a few months.

Most psychologists believe that development, like intelligence or personality, reflects the action and mutual influence of genes and environment (Loehlin, Horn, & Willerman, 1997; Plomin, Reiss, Hetherington, & Howe, 1994; see also Collins, Maccoby, Steinberg, Hetherington, & Bornstein, 2000; Steinberg & Sheffield Morris, 2001). Nature provides a fertile field for development, but this field requires cultivation. Thus, the question is not which is more important, nature or nurture, or even how much each contributes, but rather how nature and nurture contribute interactively to development (Anastasi, 1958; Spencer et al., 2009).

In fact, in many respects the contrast of nature versus nurture is misplaced, because genetic blueprints do not express themselves without environmental input (Bors & Forrin, 1996; Gottlieb, 1991). Environmental events turn genes on and off. Thus, sensory stimulation is necessary for some genes to become activated, such as genes that shape the functioning of neurons in the occipital lobes involved in vision (Gottlieb, Kusunoki, & Goldberg, 1998). Pigliucci (2010) even suggests that the term *genetic blueprint* is inadequate, and may be better understood in terms of an empirically and theoretically updated concept of *developmental encoding*.

Psychologists now distinguish between the action of genetic and environmental influences (i.e. the way they independently affect development) and two more complex nature–nurture linkages: their interaction and correlation (or correlated action). The interaction of heredity and environment occurs when the effect of having both genetic and environmental vulnerabilities is different from that which would be predicted by simply adding up their independent effects. For example, mounting evidence suggests that both genetic and environmental factors predict later development of anxiety disorders, but that the presence of both multiplies the likelihood of disorders (chapter 15). Gene–environment correlations occur when genes influence the environments people choose or the experiences to which they are exposed. For example, a genetic propensity towards antisocial behaviour can lead a teenager to choose 'bad company', which in turn encourages further antisocial behaviour.

MAKING CONNECTIONS

Language acquisition is much easier in childhood than in adulthood, supporting the view that early experience is central in shaping some aspects of later psychological functioning. When people try to learn new languages as adults, they use different neural circuits than if they had learned the language at age five or six, and they almost always speak with an accent (chapter 8).

The importance of early experience

> Before dawn on January 9, 1800, a remarkable creature came out of the woods near the village of Saint-Sernin in southern France. . . . He was human in bodily form and walked erect. Everything else about him suggested an animal. He was naked except for the tatters of a shirt and showed . . . no awareness of himself as a human person. . . . He could not speak and made only weird, meaningless cries. Though very short, he appeared to be a boy of about eleven or twelve, with a round face under dark matted hair.
>
> Shattuck (1980, p. 5).

The Wild Boy of Aveyron created an immediate sensation in Europe. To scientists, the child was a unique participant for exploring the question of ***critical periods*** in human development, periods of special sensitivity to specific types of learning and sensory stimulation that shape the capacity for future development. Would a boy who was raised, at best, by wolves be able to develop language, interact with other people and develop a conscience? A young doctor named Jean-Marie Itard became the boy's tutor. Itard's efforts met with limited but nonetheless substantial success: the boy became affectionate and learned to respond to some verbal instructions, but he never learned to talk.

Evidence for critical periods

The concept of critical periods initially came from embryology, as researchers discovered that toxic substances could affect the developing foetus but only if the foetus were exposed at very specific points in development. Critical periods in psychological development have been demonstrated in many animal species. The first few hours after hatching are a critical period for goslings. They are biologically prepared to follow whatever moving object they see, usually their mother (Lorenz, 1935).

The concept of critical periods in humans is more controversial. Can a child who does not experience nurturant caretaking in the first five years of life ever develop the capacity to love? Human development is more flexible than development in other animals, but the brain is, in fact, particularly sensitive to certain kinds of environmental input at certain times (see Bornstein, 1989). During some periods, the nervous system is most sensitive to forming new synapses between neurons, given the right environmental stimulus. Equally important is the pruning of neurons: infants are born with an abundance of neural connections, and those that are not used or activated by the environment are gradually lost (Greenough, 1991). A small degree of neuronal pruning is thought to occur in children with autism spectrum disorder, and is implicated as contributing to the increased head circumference noted in young children with this disorder (Autism Victoria, 2010).

Research on non-human animals has documented the importance of early environmental experience on the developing brain. In one study, researchers surgically closed the eyelids of newborn monkeys, depriving them of visual experience for their first 12 months (Carlson, Pertovaara, & Tanila, 1987). Then, over the following 12 months, they tested the monkeys on visual tasks. Although the monkeys could perform some tasks, such as following a large object with their eyes, they had difficulty using vision as a guide in exploring their environment, as shown in figure 12.1.

(a)

(b)

(c)

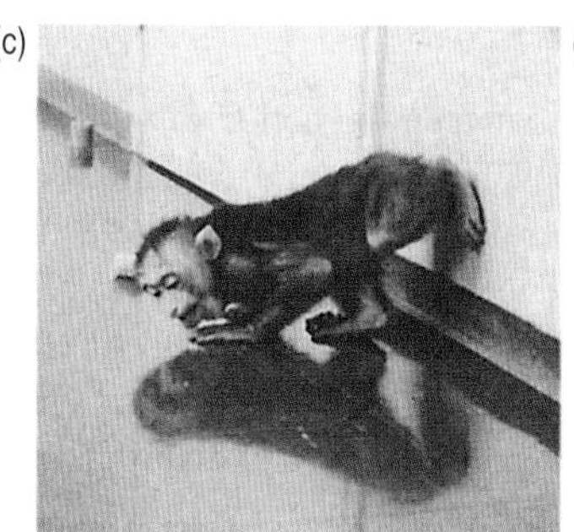

(d)

FIGURE **12.1**

The importance of early environmental experience. Visually deprived monkeys showed a number of peculiarities in the way they explored their environments in the year following deprivation. Photo (a) shows a monkey carefully moving about the floor, in a 'spider walk'; (b) shows a monkey anchoring itself to a chair while exploring with one hand; (c) shows similar anchoring to the wall; and (d) shows a monkey exploring the wall with its hands. Lacking early perceptual experience, these monkeys could not navigate their world visually.

The impact of early abuse or deprivation

As we discussed in chapter 3, the human brain, like that of other mammals, appears to have evolved with many innate potentials that require environmental input to activate. Given appropriate stimulation, most children will learn to speak, think, solve problems and love in ways accepted and encouraged by their culture. In this view, the brain has essentially been 'programmed' by natural selection to expect a range of input. That range is wide, but it is not infinite.

What happens to children whose experience is outside that range? As we saw in chapter 8, one famous case concerned a girl named Genie, who received almost no exposure to language from early in life until she was discovered at age 13 (Fromkin, Krashen, Curtiss, Rigler, & Rigler, 1974; Rymer, 1993). Like the Wild Boy of Aveyron, Genie learned some aspects of language, but her use of syntax never reached normal levels (Fromkin et al., 1974).

Other psychologists, however, have questioned whether the impact of early deprivation is so indelible (Kagan, 1984; Kagan & Zentner, 1996; Lerner, 1991). In one study, children who spent their first 19 months in an overcrowded and understaffed orphanage experienced average IQ gains of 28.5 points after being moved to an environment that provided individual care (Skeels, 1966). Even the case of Genie can be used to counter the notion of critical periods, since she demonstrated remarkable progress in social and intellectual skills in just a few short years (Kagan, 1984). On the other hand, after her initial gains, Genie's functioning stabilised and never approached the levels of a normal adolescent or adult, and she always remained socially awkward.

A similar pattern is emerging from data on severely deprived children from Romanian orphanages who were adopted before age two into homes in the United Kingdom: although all children showed substantial improvement once they left the orphanage, the longer they experienced severe deprivation (e.g. for two years rather than just the first six months of life), the more severe their cognitive impairments remained four to six years later (O'Connor et al., 2000).

Other researchers have found that the consequences of chronic emotional neglect or physical abuse experienced in childhood may be wide-ranging and adverse (Australian Institute of Family Studies [AIFS], 2010). Factors affecting the impact of recurrent neglect/abuse include the child's age and stage of development; the type, severity, frequency and duration of abuse/neglect; and the relationship between child and abuser (AIFS, 2010). Not all children are affected in the same way or in the long-term, with some children being adaptive or resilient to their situation. However, negative outcomes for abused and neglected children may include physical health problems; trauma; behavioural, cognitive and learning difficulties; mental health disorders; youth suicide; drug and alcohol abuse; aggression, violence and criminal activity; and homelessness (AIFS, 2010).

Does the evidence, then, support the notion of critical periods in humans? Probably the most appropriate conclusion to be reached at present is that humans have ***sensitive periods*** — times that are more important to subsequent development than others (O'Connor, 2003). In some domains, such as language, these sensitive periods may actually be critical; appropriate environmental input at certain points may be required or further development is permanently impaired. In most domains, however, sensitive periods are simply sensitive — particularly important but not decisive.

FROM BRAIN TO BEHAVIOUR

The gendered brain

Our genetic sex is determined by whether we have two X chromosomes (female) or one X and one Y chromosome (male). The sexual phenotype (the interaction of genetics and the environment) can be influenced during the early stages of development. One example of this was the masculinisation of a genetic female's brain if her mother took the drug diethylstibesterol (DES) to help reduce the negative symptoms of pregnancy. What does it mean to masculinise the brain? All of us, genetic males and genetic females, will develop a female brain if the brain is not organised to be masculine — that is, the organisation of the brain for gender (sex) in terms of whether at puberty the brain releases sex hormones in a cyclical pattern (the menstrual cycle for females) or noncyclical pattern (the male condition) depends on exposure to sex hormones early in development.

If a mistake occurs, due to one of many different events during development, the brain may remain feminine in a genetic male, or masculine in a genetic female. The female children of mothers who took DES had their brain masculinised: when they reached the age of puberty, they did not start their menstrual periods, because the brain had been masculinised and did not release the sex hormones in a cyclical pattern. Unfortunately, the brain is organised at a critical period, and once that critical period is over the brain is set in its ways. It cannot be changed, at least with the current stage of medical understanding.

Simon LeVay has published some highly controversial data in which he measured the size of the lateral preoptic (LPO) area of the hypothalamus in gay men. Males in general have a smaller LPO than females. The LPOs of the gay men were similar in size to a female's LPO. Does this mean that the LPO determines our sexual identity? Perhaps, or perhaps not. Because the LPO was measured in postmortem tissue, researchers cannot determine whether the LPO was larger from birth, or if a gay lifestyle altered the size of the LPO. In other words, they cannot untangle which is cause and which is effect.

Do such changes mean that the individual's sexual identity is affected? Perhaps. As with all individuals, however, sexual identity depends in part on how many X chromosomes you have, the organisation of the brain that occurs during early development and the rearing conditions (i.e. if little boys are dressed as girls and so on). Further, other genes may influence sexual preference: genes that are not located on the X or Y chromosome, but influence our behaviour in ways similar to shyness, intelligence and aggressiveness. Genetic researchers are also exploring the significance of X chromosome inactivation detected in mothers of some homosexual men, and of new chromosomal regions and linkages as evidence of heritability of sexual orientation (Bocklandt et al., 2006; Mustanski et al., 2005; as cited in Dawood, Bailey, & Martin, 2009). Thus, one's choice of partner is not determined by any one factor, but by multiple factors, from genetic to environmental.

Stages or continuous change?

The third basic issue in development concerns the nature of developmental change (Demetriou & Raftopoulos, 2004). According to one view, development occurs in ***stages***, relatively discrete steps through which everyone progresses in the same sequence. Behaviour in one stage is not just quantitatively different from the next, involving a little less or more of something, but qualitatively different. As we will see, a stage theorist might suggest that the ability to engage in abstract thinking is a novel development in adolescence — not just a gradual refinement of the way younger children think — and that this qualitative difference may reflect maturation of the frontal cortex.

An alternative perspective sees development as continuous, characterised less by major transformations than by steady and gradual change. From this point of view, what may look like a massive change, such as becoming literate between the ages of five and eight or rebellious at 13, may actually reflect a slow and steady process of learning at school or increased reinforcement for independent behaviour. Although the behavioural change may appear to be a new stage, in fact, it may have been practised, and be making an appearance only when 'practice has made perfect'.

Many theorists suggest that development involves both stages and continuous processes (Bidell & Fischer, 1992, 2000; Piaget, 1972; see also Keenan, 2002). Stagelike phenomena are much more obvious in childhood, when the nervous system is maturing. As individuals move into adulthood, they are likely to develop in a number of alternative directions, many of which vary substantially by culture (e.g. whether a culture has a concept of 'retirement').

INTERIM SUMMARY

Developmental psychology studies the way humans develop and change over time. Nature and nurture both contribute to development, and their roles are not easily separated because environmental events often turn genes on and off. Psychologists continue to debate whether human development is characterised by ***critical periods*** (periods central to specific types of learning that modify future development) or ***sensitive periods*** (times that are particularly important but not definitive for subsequent development), and whether development occurs in ***stages*** (relatively discrete steps through which everyone progresses in the same sequence) or is continuous (involving steady and gradual change) is still a matter under discussion.

The three lifesavers shown have Indian, Korean and Afghan heritage respectively, but identify with the relaxed 'Aussie' beach culture. Australia is one of the most multicultural societies in the world today. Cultural diversity can, however, affect the reliability of cross-sectional studies. The results of these studies are most useful to researchers when cohort effects are minimal.

Studying development

At first glance, studying development might seem relatively straightforward: to see if five- and 10-year-olds differ in working memory capacity or in the way they form relationships with peers, simply collect a sample at each age and see how differently they respond. In fact, however, matters are more complex. Psychologists primarily use three types of research designs to study development: cross-sectional, longitudinal and sequential.

Cross-sectional studies

Cross-sectional studies compare groups of participants of different ages at a single time to see whether differences exist among them. For example, a research group studied centenarians — people who have reached 100 years of age — to compare them on a number of dimensions with people in their 60s and 80s (Poon et al., 1992). Cross-sectional studies are useful for providing a snapshot of age differences, or variations among people of different ages.

The major limitation of cross-sectional studies is that they do not directly assess age changes; that is, changes within the same individuals that occur with age. As a result, they are vulnerable to confounding variables (chapter 2), such as cultural change. For example, Australia today is one of the most multicultural societies in the world, with immigrants from many cultures making up its population. In the early years of the twentieth century, most migrants tended to come from Great Britain. The post-World

War II years saw the arrival of migrants from many other European countries. The 1970s ushered in an era of migration from Asian countries such as Vietnam. These different historical experiences could profoundly influence differences among cohorts (groups of people born around the same time) within the Australian population. Cultural changes in education, mass communication and nutrition could also have a profound impact on people's later ways of thinking and acting. Cross-sectional studies are most useful when ***cohort effects*** — differences among age groups associated with differences in the culture — are minimal, as when assessing differences in the self-concepts of four- and six-year-olds.

Longitudinal studies

Longitudinal studies assess the same individuals over time, providing the opportunity to assess age changes rather than age differences. The advantage of longitudinal studies is their ability to reveal differences among individuals as well as changes within individuals over time. Thus, longitudinal research can examine whether the same person becomes more or less conservative, or experiences changes in memory, over time.

Like cross-sectional designs, longitudinal designs are vulnerable to cohort effects. Because they investigate only one cohort, they cannot rule out the possibility that people born at a different time might show different developmental paths or trajectories. For example, the data from four longitudinal studies of gifted women at midlife showed that gifted women born after 1940 scored higher on all measures of psychological wellbeing than gifted women born before that time (Schuster, 1990). The impact of giftedness on women's wellbeing appears to depend in part on cultural attitudes towards women's intelligence and opportunities for achievement.

Sequential studies

Sequential studies minimise cohort effects by studying multiple cohorts longitudinally. In an ideal sequential design, researchers study a group of people at one age and follow them up over time. As the study progresses, a new, younger cohort is added to the study, beginning at the same age at which the first cohort began. Essentially, a sequential design combines cross-sectional and longitudinal comparisons, allowing researchers to distinguish between age effects (differences associated with age) and cohort effects. The design in table 12.1 shows how the effects of the 11 September 2001 terrorist attacks (9/11) on children's development could be controlled for by staggering the study of the changes between ages three and nine across three cohorts, one beginning before 9/11, the other two beginning after 9/11. Only those changes that occurred in all three cohorts, independent of current events such as 9/11, would be considered to be consistent markers of development.

APPLY + DISCUSS

Online social networks such as Facebook, as well as various smartphone technologies, have exploded in popularity — influencing many aspects of our work and social lives. A team of researchers interested in attitudes towards use of the internet and other emerging technologies conducts the following study. They ask thirty Year 3 students, thirty Year 9 students, thirty 21-year-olds, and thirty 60-year-olds to complete an online survey. They ask them to rate their attitudes towards the internet and various emerging technologies, including their perceived usefulness, perceived control or mastery, and intention to use them. They find that all four groups see the benefits of the internet, but the 60-year-olds report a slight disinterest in engaging with the various online social networks and smartphone technologies.

- What kind of design is this: cross-sectional, longitudinal or sequential?
- What can the investigators conclude?
- What can they not conclude, and why?

TABLE 12.1 Example of a sequential study, controlling for age and calendar year

	Cohort 1	Age 3		Age 6		Age 9		
			Cohort 2	Age 3		Age 6	Age 9	
					Cohort 3	Age 3	Age 6	Age 9
Year		2000		2003		2006	2009	2012

Sequential designs solve most of the problems of both cross-sectional and longitudinal designs, but they have one catch: they take years or decades to complete. The moral of the story is that, ideally, psychologists should live a long time; conduct sequential studies, preferably in several cultures; and find successors to carry on their research after they are dead. Short of that, researchers should (and do) try to use the best methods at their disposal and remain aware of the methodological limitations on the generalisability of their results.

INTERIM SUMMARY

Cross-sectional studies compare groups of participants of different ages at a single time to provide a picture of age differences. ***Longitudinal studies*** assess the same individuals over time, providing the opportunity to assess age changes. ***Sequential studies*** minimise ***cohort effects*** by studying multiple cohorts longitudinally.

Physical development and its psychological consequences

Having examined some of the basic issues and methods of developmental psychology, we turn now to physical development and its impact on psychological functioning. Many of those changes are obvious even to the untrained eye. Children develop rapidly during the early years, outgrowing clothes before wearing them out. Some of the most dramatic aspects of physical development, however, cannot be observed directly, because they take place before birth.

Prenatal development

One of the most remarkable aspects of development is that a single cell, forged by the union of a sperm and an egg, contains the blueprint for an organism that will emerge — complete with billions of specialised cells — nine months later. The *prenatal period* (before birth, also called the gestation period) is divided into three stages (figure 12.2). During the germinal period (approximately the first two weeks after conception), the fertilised egg becomes implanted in the uterus. The *embryonic period* (from the beginning of the third week to about the eighth week of gestation) is the most important period in the development of the central nervous system and of the organs. By the end of this stage, the features of the embryo become recognisably human, the rudiments of most organs have formed and the heart has begun to beat. During the foetal period (from about nine weeks to birth), muscular development is rapid. By about 28 weeks, the foetus is capable of sustaining life on its own. (The term foetus is often used more broadly to refer to the organism between conception and birth.)

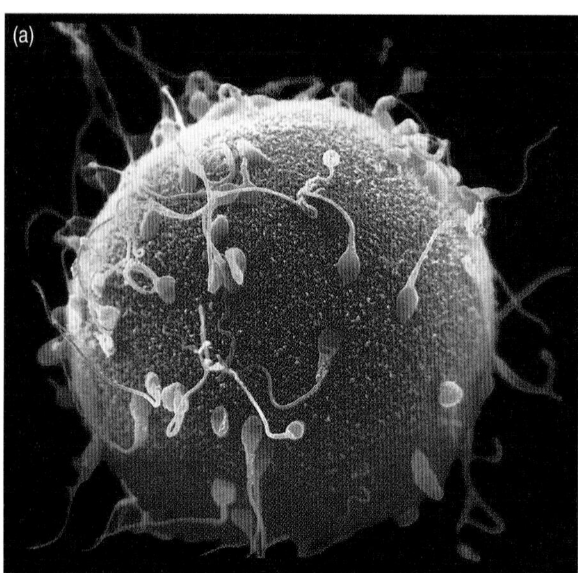

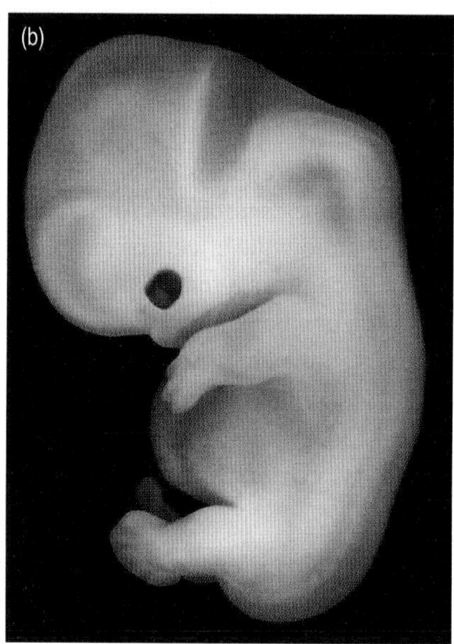

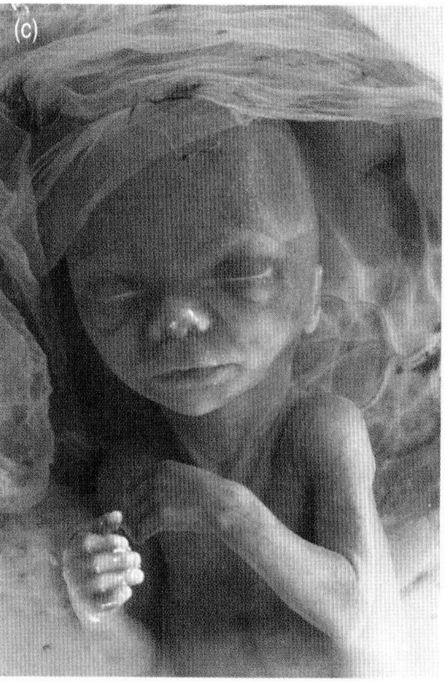

FIGURE 12.2
Prenatal development. The photo in (a) shows a fertilised egg surrounded by sperm. Photo (b) shows a six-week-old embryo. Only six weeks later (c), the foetus is recognisably human.

Mothers often sense that their child is 'wilful' or has a 'personality' before birth. In part, this undoubtedly reflects vivid maternal imagination. Recent research suggests, however, that foetuses of many species can behave and even learn in utero (prenatally) (Robinson & Kleven, 2005; Smotherman & Robinson, 1996). When the young of any species is born, it has to be ready to respond to features of its environment (e.g. that it can eat). The ways human children 'behave' in utero are also highly predictive of the ways they will behave once they are born (DiPietro, Hodgson, Costigan, & Johnson, 1996; DiPietro et al., 2002). For example, foetuses that are more active in the womb tend to be more active and difficult babies at six months.

Environmental influences on prenatal development

Understanding the stages of prenatal development is important to every expectant parent, because at different stages the developing foetus is susceptible to different dangers at different points.

Teratogens are environmental agents that harm the embryo or foetus. They include drugs, radiation, viruses that cause maternal illness such as rubella (German measles) and toxic chemicals. Cigarette smoking during pregnancy, for example, has been linked to a wide range of negative outcomes, ranging from cognitive deficits in childhood to criminality in adulthood (Brennan, Grekin, & Mednick, 1999; Day, Richardson, Goldschmidt, & Cornelius, 2000; Martin, Dombrowski, Mullis, Wisenbaker, & Huttunen, 2006).

One of the most widespread teratogens is alcohol. In the 1970s, researchers identified ***foetal alcohol syndrome (FAS)***, a serious condition affecting up to half the babies born to alcoholic mothers (Jones, Smith, Ulleland, & Streissguth, 1973). More recently, FAS has been identified as one of several adverse health outcomes collectively classified as *foetal alcohol spectrum disorder* (FASD; Department of Health Western Australia [DHWA], 2010). Other FASD conditions include *alcohol-related neuro-developmental disorders* (ARND), *alcohol-related birth defects* (ARBD), *foetal alcohol effects* (FAE), and *partial foetal alcohol syndrome* (PFAS) — each with specific diagnostic criteria (DHWA, 2010). Babies with FAS are born with numerous physical deformities and a wide range of mental abnormalities, including learning disabilities, behaviour problems and attention difficulties (Steinhausen, Willms, & Spohr, 1993; Streissguth, Barr, Johnson, & Kirchner, 1985; Streissguth, Sampson, & Barr, 1989; see also Autti-Ramo, 2002; DHWA, 2010; Steinhausen & Spohr, 1998).

Whether any amount of maternal alcohol ingestion is dangerous or whether alcohol use must cross some threshold is a matter of controversy (see Knupfer, 1991; Passaro & Little, 1997). Research with rhesus monkeys finds that even moderate exposure to alcohol (the monkey equivalent of one to two drinks a day) during pregnancy produces subtle deficits in attention and motor abilities in infant monkeys (Schneider, Roughton, & Lubach, 1997). The most recent research suggests that women who are trying to conceive or who know they are pregnant would do well to abstain from alcohol (Braun, 1996; Hicks & Tough, 2009; New South Wales Department of Health, 2006; Toutain, 2010; Whitehall, 2007).

In Australia, initial reports of FAS were published in the 1980s, with two studies identifying a total of 27 children with FAS (Lipson, Walsh, & Webster, 1983; Walpole & Hockey, 1980). All the mothers of the affected children drank heavily during pregnancy or had a history of chronic alcoholism, and 17.5 percent had Aboriginal parents — reflecting the wider health issue that alcohol misuse poses for some Aboriginal communities in Australia (Brady, 1991). A more recent study in Western Australia found that the rate of FAS among non-Aboriginal children was 0.02 per 1000, compared to the rate for Aboriginal children of 2.76 per 1000 (Bower, Silva, Henderson, Ryan, & Rudy, 2000). The teratogenic effect appears to be highest in the early weeks of pregnancy, often before the woman knows she is pregnant, and increases with greater consumption (Australian Medical Association, 2009; Barr, Streissguth, Darby, & Sampson, 1990).

Another increasingly prevalent teratogen is crack cocaine (Inciardi, Surratt, & Saum, 1997). Prenatal cocaine exposure carries risk of premature birth, malformed internal organs, withdrawal symptoms, respiratory problems, delayed motor development and death (Arendt, Minnes, & Singer, 1996; Bendersky & Lewis, 1998; Wouldes, LaGasse, Sheridan, & Lester, 2004). 'Crack babies' tend to be triply exposed: to the teratogenic effect of cocaine prenatally, to neglectful parenting post-natally, and to poverty and environmental hazards throughout childhood.

One last teratogen is worth noting: maternal stress. Researchers have known for some time that children whose mothers were under significant stress during pregnancy tend to have more problems with attention and motor development. Recent research with rhesus monkeys, who are genetically similar to humans, suggests that the first trimester is a sensitive period during which maternal stress affects the developing nervous system, with decreasing effects through the second trimester (Schneider, Roughton, Koehler, & Lubach, 1999).

Figure 12.3 (overleaf) shows the timing and effects of teratogens during sensitive or critical periods. As shown in figure 12.3, congenital abnormalities may be caused by a combination of genetic and environmental factors that occur during prenatal development. During the first two weeks of gestation, teratogens usually terminate the embryo rather than cause congenital abnormalities. During the embryonic period, teratogens can be especially damaging to the developing central nervous system (brain) and heart. Major damage to eyes, arms and legs is also common during this period. Teratogens tend to have less damaging effects on developing organs and body limbs during the foetal period, which is why most impending parents typically wait until three months after conception before announcing their pregnancy to family and friends.

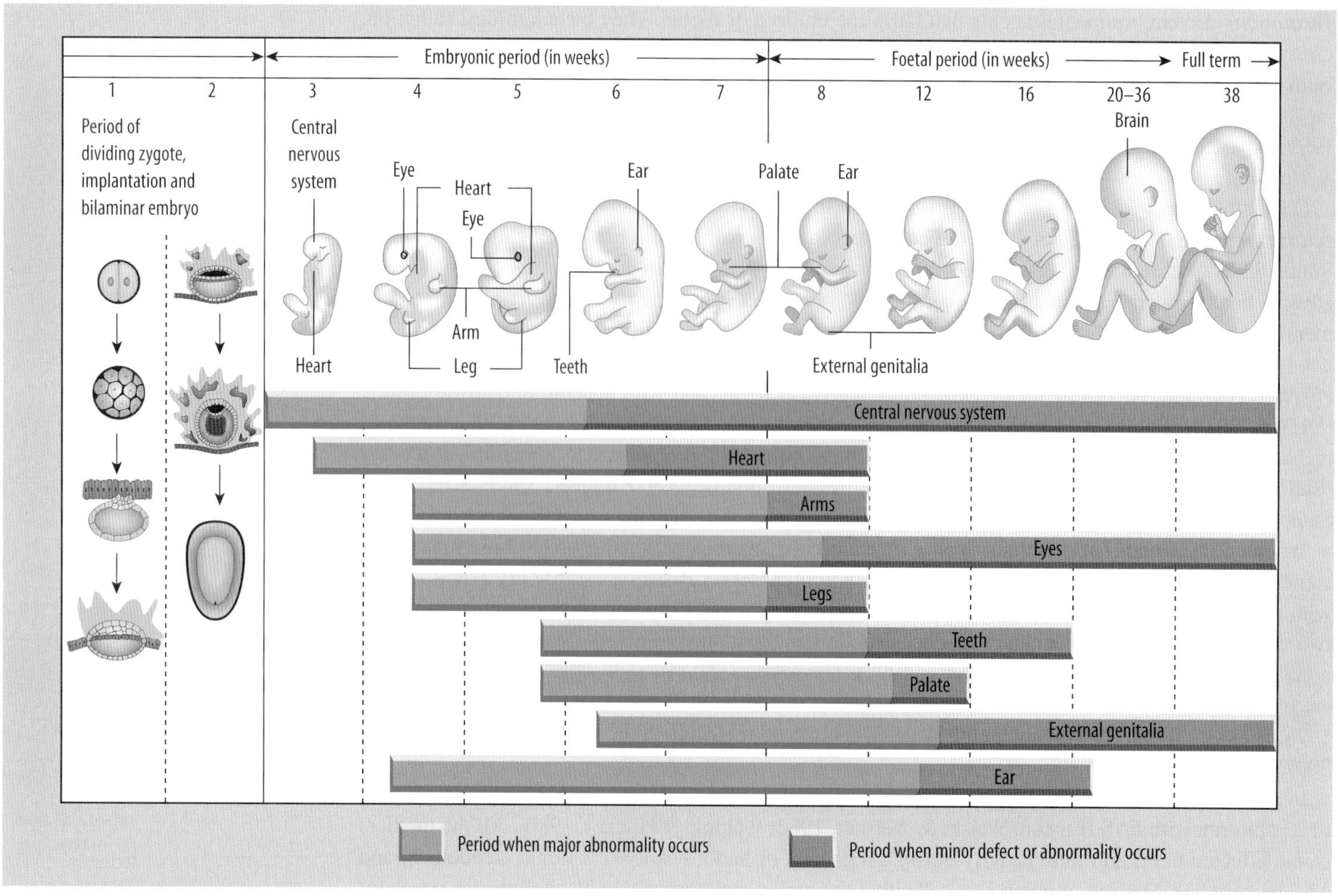

FIGURE 12.3
Timing and effects of teratogens during sensitive or critical periods

INTERIM SUMMARY

The prenatal, or gestational, period is a time of rapid physical and neurological growth that can be disrupted by exposure to ***teratogens***, harmful environmental agents that damage the embryo or foetus. One of the most prevalent teratogens is alcohol. Maternal alcohol abuse can lead to foetal alcohol syndrome (FAS), but increasing evidence suggests that even moderate levels of drinking can impair the developing child. During gestation, neurons develop at the rate of hundreds of thousands per minute. Development continues for years thereafter and also involves considerable pruning of potential neural connections that are not strengthened by environmental input.

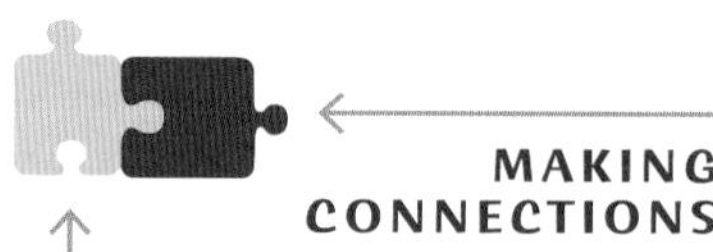

MAKING CONNECTIONS

Similar to **connectionist models** in cognitive science, contemporary models suggest that movement involves the simultaneous coordination of multiple processes outside awareness, as the brain settles on solutions that solve problems by adapting and combining pre-existing skills (chapter 8).

Whereas psychologists once believed that the development of motor control was mostly a matter of maturation of physical 'equipment', today they recognise that 'simple' feats such as walking uphill and downhill require very different muscles, and infants have to learn how to adjust their gait continuously as they move across a surface that is not absolutely level (Thelen, 1995).

Infancy

When asked about their babies, parents almost uniformly begin with motor milestones, such as 'Youla can sit up now by herself' or 'Now that Brandon is crawling, I have to babyproof everything in the house' (Thelen, 1995). How infants move from flailing bundles of flesh to wilful little creatures with radar for breakable objects reflects a complex mixture of nature and nurture (Bertenthal & Clifton, 1998; Thelen, 1995; Thelen & Smith, 1994).

At birth, an infant possesses many adaptive reflexes. For example, the *rooting reflex* helps ensure that the infant will get nourishment: when touched on the cheek, an infant will turn her head and open her mouth, ready to suck. The *sucking reflex* is similarly adaptive: infants suck rhythmically in response to stimulation 3 to 4 centimetres inside their mouths. Many early reflexes disappear within the first six or seven months, as infants gain more control over their movements. In general, motor skills progress from head to toe: infants first master movements of the head, then the trunk and arms and finally the legs (Rallison, 1986).

Motor development in infancy follows a universal sequence, from smiling, turning the head and rolling over, to creeping, walking with support, and ultimately standing alone and walking unaided (figure 12.4). Nevertheless, cross-cultural evidence suggests that environmental stimulation can affect the pace of development. The milestones in infant motor development are influenced by a child's ethnic background. In Australia, for example, Annette Hamilton (1981) discovered that Aboriginal children being reared in a traditional and remote indigenous community developed head and neck muscles much earlier than their Western peers. She found that Aboriginal babies were able to sit without support around the age of two months two weeks as compared with four or five months for Anglo-European infants. Judith Kearins (1986) provided further evidence that the nurturing practices of Aboriginal mothers enhance development of infant head and neck control — Aboriginal mothers tend to carry their infants without offering head and neck support while Anglo-Australian mothers usually provide such support at least until their baby is 20 weeks old. Similarly, the Kipsigis of Kenya teach their infants to sit, stand and walk at an early age. At five or six months, infants are placed in a specially constructed hole in the ground that supports them while they sit upright, and at seven or eight months, their mothers hold them either under the arms or by the hands to help them practise walking. As a result, Kipsigi infants walk at a considerably earlier age than Western infants (Super, 1981).

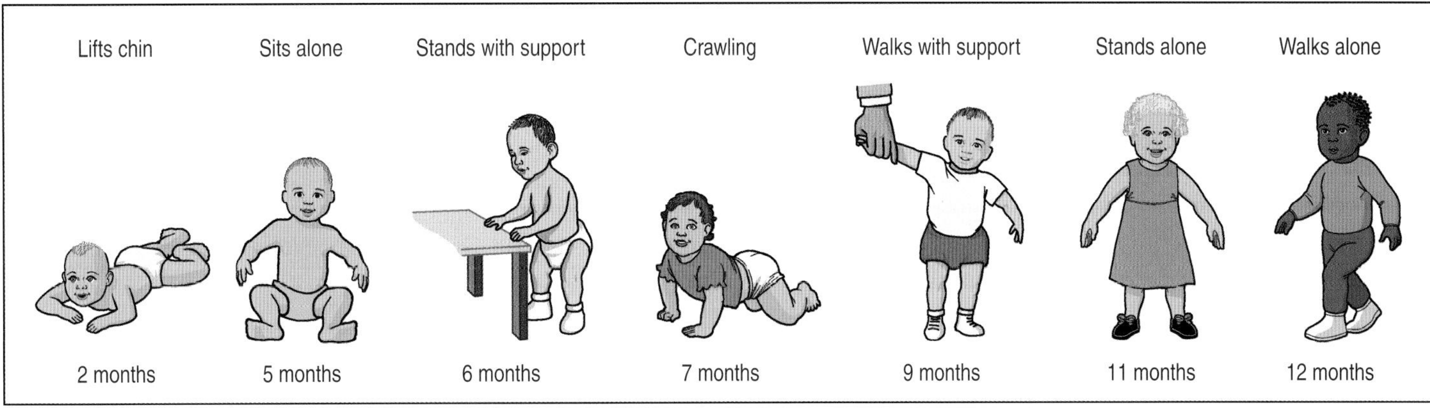

FIGURE 12.4
The maturational sequence of motor development is universal, although the age at which skills are acquired varies. This figure shows average ages at which children reach these milestones.

SOURCE: Adapted from Frankenburg and Dodds (1967); and Berk (2008).

In Australia and the rest of the West, paediatricians are finding that infants are now walking even later than they did 25 years ago. To help prevent death from Sudden Infant Death Syndrome (SIDS), a disease in which the immature brainstem fails to 'jump start' and the infant stops breathing, parents are instructed to put infants to bed on their backs (rather than stomachs) to sleep. An unintended consequence is that infants accustomed to lying on their backs develop crawling skills (and leg muscles) more slowly — and hence walk later.

ONE STEP FURTHER

Can early motor milestones predict later cognitive development?

By Professor Jan Piek, Curtin University

Infancy is a period of rapid development, and motor milestones in infancy are an important indicator of how an infant is tracking in terms of his or her motor development. But how important are these milestones for other aspects of a child's development? Researchers such as Campos et al. (2000) have argued that 'travel broadens the mind', and the ability of infants to explore their environment influences their perceptual, cognitive, social and emotional development. This is supported by studies showing that the development of gross motor milestones in infancy and early childhood can impact on later cognitive development, particularly in relation to processing speed and working memory (Murray et al., 2006; Piek, Dawson, Smith, & Gasson, 2008).

Does this mean that early motor development may be a predictor of later cognitive development? Measures of cognitive development in infancy have generally been found to be unreliable in the prediction of later cognitive development. Strong correlations have been identified between cognitive and motor abilities in infancy and early childhood, although this relationship appears to diminish as the child reaches school age (Dyck, Piek, Kane, & Patrick, 2009). One argument accounting for these strong correlations is that it is difficult to measure cognitive development in infants and young children without including a motor component to the assessment items. Hence, they are measuring both motor and cognitive ability. However, Diamond (2000) has argued that a strong relationship between motor and cognitive ability is not surprising, given that brain imaging has found common brain structures for motor and cognitive performance (suggesting a close functional relationship).

Research suggests early motor development may be just one of many factors that can impact on a child's cognitive development.

Based on the evidence given, it would be easy to assume that if infants have difficulties with achieving their motor milestones, they may develop cognitive deficits. Some support for this assumption comes from research on children with motor deficits, such as developmental coordination disorder. These children have been found to have poorer working memory (e.g. Piek, Dyck, Francis, & Conwell, 2007) and perceptual organisation (e.g. Coleman, Piek, & Livesey, 2001) compared with children without any motor difficulties. But these results do not necessarily provide evidence that early motor ability can predict later cognitive ability.

Many factors impact on a child's cognitive development and it may be that motor development is just one of these factors. As suggested by Bushnell and Boudreau (1993), motor development may act as a 'control parameter', where the achievement of a particular milestone is necessary to engage other perceptual or cognitive functions.

This issue cannot be answered through cross-sectional research, but requires longitudinal studies to follow the path of children from infancy to school age. However, it is clear that there is a relationship between motor and cognitive development. By gaining a better understanding of this relationship, appropriate strategies to ensure children have the best possible environments to maximise their motor and cognitive capabilities will be able to be developed.

Childhood and adolescence

Some of the most important maturational changes that influence psychological development involve changes in the size and shape of the body. A remarkable aspect of human development is the extent to which children can maintain the sense that they are the same person over time despite massive changes in the sheer size of their bodies and the shape of their faces.

Growth rates for girls and boys are roughly equal until about age 10. At that point, girls begin a growth spurt that usually peaks at age 12, and boys typically follow suit about two or three years later. Individuals of both sexes vary, however, in the age at which they enter ***puberty***, the time at which they become capable of reproduction. Girls usually experience the onset of menstruation (known as menarche) at about age 11 to 13. For boys, mature sperm production is somewhat later, at about 14.5 years (Rallison, 1986).

Unusually early or late maturation tends to affect boys and girls differently. Boys whose growth spurt comes early are more likely to excel at athletics and be more popular, relaxed and high in status than late-maturing boys. For girls, early onset of puberty tends to be associated with greater distress and delinquency than later maturation (Caspi, Lynam, Moffitt, & Silva, 1993; Dick, Rose, Viken, & Kaprio, 2000; Ge, Conger, & Elder, 1996; Lynne, Graber, Nichols, Brooks-Gunn, & Botvin, 2007). Parents report more conflict with early-maturing than late-maturing daughters but less conflict with early-maturing than late-maturing sons (Ge et al., 1996; Savin-Williams & Small, 1986). Early maturation in girls may not only be a cause of stress in their families but also a consequence of it: stressful homes tend to trigger the physiological mechanisms that initiate puberty; so, too, does the presence of a male living in the home other than the girl's biological father, such as a stepfather (Ellis & Garber, 2000).

INTERIM SUMMARY

At birth, infants possess many adaptive reflexes, such as *rooting* and *sucking*, which help ensure that the infant will get nourishment. Individuals vary in the age at which they enter puberty, the stage during which they become capable of reproduction. Early pubertal development tends to be associated with positive outcomes for boys but negative outcomes for girls.

Adulthood and ageing

By the end of adolescence, physical growth is virtually complete, and the changes that occur thereafter tend to be gradual and less dramatic. People often gain a few centimetres in height and several more centimetres in fat between ages 18 and 28 — and perhaps some more centimetres in fat with middle age. By their 30s, people are already deteriorating physically, with muscular strength and sensory abilities showing subtle but clear signs of decline (see Spence, 1989; Spirduso & MacRae, 1990; see also Drewing, Aschersleben, & Li, 2006).

Individuals differ tremendously, however, in the extent and pace of these changes, as some 80-year-olds run marathons in seniors' athletics competitions. Whether the variable is muscle strength or intellectual ability, the rule of thumb is use it or lose it: both mental and physical capacities atrophy with disuse.

Midlife changes

For women perhaps the most dramatic physical change of middle adulthood is menopause, the cessation of the menstrual cycle. Menopause usually begins in the 40s or 50s and may last several years. Australian women reach menopause at an average age of 51.3 years (Australian Broadcasting Corporation [ABC], 2000; Science Alert, 2007; Menopause Centre of Australia, 2010), but at least 2 percent have premature menopause before they reach 40, and 7 to 8 percent before they reach 45. The average life expectancy for women in Australia is 82.6 years (Australian Bureau of Statistics, 2010d), which means a woman who goes through menopause at 40 will spend more than half her life in a low-estrogen state.

Some women consider menopause to be traumatic because of the loss of the capacity for child-bearing and symptoms such as 'hot flushes', 'night sweats', aching joints and irritability. However, research now suggests that only the minority of women experience menopause as traumatic (Matthews, 1992; O'Bryant, Palav, & McCaffrey, 2003). Many women enjoy the increased freedom from monthly periods and birth control. A cross-cultural study explored the effects of reported menopause experience of 1743 women. Australian and Japanese women reported similar increases in rates of depression and somatic symptoms at perimenopause (Anderson, Yoshizawa, Gollschewski, Atogami, & Courtney, 2004). However, although most symptoms decreased in Australian women after menopause, they remained high in Japanese women (Anderson et al., 2004). Most of the uncomfortable symptoms can be alleviated medically with hormone replacement therapy (HRT), which compensates for the ovaries' reduced estrogen production (Freedman, 2002; Rymer, Wilson, & Ballard, 2003; Sherwin, 1993; Stewart & Robinson, 1997). Although long-term use of HRT is considered controversial because it increases the risk of breast cancer, heart disease and stroke, current evidence suggests that HRT may also prevent or reduce the symptoms of osteoporosis, and reduce the risk of bowel cancer (National Health & Medical Research Council [NHMRC], 2005; see also Sydney School of Public Health, 2009).

Unlike women, the male reproductive ability does not undergo any specific or dramatic period of physical change. Healthy men can produce sperm and engage in sexual activity as long as they live, although male sexuality does change gradually with age. Sexual desire from the 40s to the 70s shows substantial declines as testosterone levels drop (Schiavi, Schreiner-Engle, Mandeli, Schanzer, & Cohen, 1990; see also chapter 10). As with women, however, individual differences are substantial, and men can enjoy sexuality through their 90s if they live that long and have an available partner.

Gaining a 'beer belly' is a physical change that many men experience (and often accept happily) in midlife.

Later life

As in childhood, some of the most apparent signs of ageing are in physical appearance, such as wrinkled skin and grey hair. Sensory changes are also substantial. Older adults have reduced sensitivity to visual contrasts — for example, climbing stairs can be difficult because they have trouble seeing where one step ends and another begins (Fozard, 1990). Older adults also take a longer time adapting to the dark, which can cause problems driving at night, as oncoming headlights may create temporary flashes of brightness (AARP News Bulletin, 1989; Sigelman & Rider, 2009; McKinney, 2010). Hearing loss is also common. Many older people experience ***presbycusis***, the inability to hear high-frequency sounds (Spence, 1989; Fozard, 1990; National Institute on Deafness and other Communication Disorders, 2010;

Peninsular Hearing Aid Centre, 2010; see also Giri, Phalke, Kishve, Mangla, & Syed, 2010), which can make hearing the telephone ring or understanding high-pitched voices more difficult.

The inability to understand what others are saying can have disturbing psychological consequences. We often lose patience with older adults who constantly ask others to repeat what they have said. Younger people may also inadvertently treat older individuals with hearing loss condescendingly, simplifying their communications instead of speaking more loudly or distinctly.

Deterioration in certain areas of functioning is an inevitable part of ageing, but development throughout the life span is characterised by gains as well as losses (Baltes, 1997). Many Western images of the elderly stem from negative cultural myths and stereotypes, such as the idea that sexuality ends in the 40s or 50s or that senility is inevitable. Gerontologists — scientists who study the elderly — refer to such stereotypes as examples of ***ageism***, or prejudice against old people (Butler, 1969; Schaie, 1988). Although not all negative attitudes towards ageing represent prejudice (older people do, for example, tend to have less physical and mental speed than younger people), ageism can lead not only to condescending treatment of the elderly ('How are we today, Mrs. Jones?') but also to employment discrimination.

Experimental evidence suggests that people in the West process information about the aged in a negative way automatically, without conscious awareness (Perdue & Gurtman, 1990; see also Kite, Stockdale, Whitley, & Johnson, 2005; Nelson, 2005). Using a priming procedure (chapter 7), investigators in one study presented university students with 18 positive adjectives (such as skilful and helpful) and 18 negative adjectives (such as clumsy and impolite) on a computer screen. Immediately prior to presenting each adjective, the computer screen randomly flashed the word old or young briefly enough to register but too briefly to be recognised consciously. The investigators measured participants' reaction time (in milliseconds) in identifying whether each word was positive or negative.

If people differentially associate old and young with positive and negative traits, then flashing 'young' should facilitate responding about positive words, while 'old' should reduce reaction time in identifying negative words. In fact, participants were quicker to identify negative traits when presented with 'old' and substantially faster in identifying positive traits when presented with 'young'.

INTERIM SUMMARY

With ageing comes a gradual decline in physical abilities, including muscular strength, sensory functioning and reaction time. People differ tremendously, however, in their physical competence throughout life. The rule-of-thumb is use it or lose it. For women, the most dramatic physical change of middle adulthood is menopause; for men, sexuality changes more gradually. Deterioration in certain areas of functioning is an inevitable part of ageing, but the extent of deterioration in part reflects internalisation of ***ageist*** stereotypes. It is important to remember that development throughout the life span is also characterised by gains.

Cognitive development in infancy, childhood and adolescence

In a study performed three decades ago, three- and six-year-old children petted a good-natured cat named Maynard (DeVries, 1969). When asked what kind of animal Maynard was, every child responded correctly. In plain sight of the children, the researcher then put a dog mask on Maynard and again asked whether Maynard was a dog or a cat. Unlike the older children, the three-year-old children were confused: most of them said Maynard was now a dog!

How do children learn that physical entities, such as their pets, parents or teddy bears, remain constant over time? This is the kind of question explored by psychologists who study cognitive development. We begin by describing perceptual and cognitive development in infancy and then examine the ways psychologists have conceptualised cognitive development through adolescence.

Perceptual and cognitive development in infancy

For many years, psychologists underestimated the cognitive capacities of infants (Bower, 1982). With neither motor control nor the ability to describe what they are thinking, newborn infants do not appear to be a particularly impressive lot. Infants also have notoriously short attention spans, falling asleep so frequently that a researcher must schedule two hours of laboratory time for every five minutes of useful experimental time (Butterworth, 1978)!

New methods, new discoveries

A very different picture of infancy has emerged, however, as methods to study it have become more sophisticated. Three decades ago, psychologists discovered that they could learn about infant perception and cognition by taking advantage of the orienting reflex, the tendency of humans, even from birth, to pay more attention to novel stimuli than to stimuli to which they have become habituated (chapter 6), or grown accustomed (Fantz, Fagan, & Miranda, 1975). Thus, even though a picture of a face might hold an infant's attention at first, after repeated exposures, the infant will show much less interest.

By recording the amount of time an infant looks at visual stimuli (i.e. the infant's fixation time), researchers can tell when an infant is discriminating between two objects, such as the face of its mother and the face of another woman. For example, if researchers present infants with pictures of cats and horses and then show them novel examples of these categories (e.g. a kind of cat they have not seen before), 10-month-olds will consistently discriminate the two kinds of animals, but seven-month-olds will not (Younger & Fearing, 1999). Thus, we know that by 10 months infants are already forming basic-level categories for animals (chapter 8).

Researchers have subsequently found other ways of assessing infants' knowledge, such as measuring brain wave activity: certain waveforms assessed by EEG (chapter 2) indicate when an infant differentiates between an old stimulus and a new one. Also, because infants prefer novelty, with the use of a simple conditioning procedure they can be conditioned to suck in response to novel stimuli. Sucking rate decreases as the infant habituates to a stimulus (i.e. gets used to it and stops responding; chapter 6) and increases with the presentation of a new one. Thus, researchers can answer some very subtle questions about infant perception, memory and cognition. For example, can infants form abstractions of concepts such as ball? Will they habituate quickly to a red ball they have never seen if they have previously habituated to blue and yellow balls — a response implying that they 'understand' the general concept of a ball?

—APPLY + DISCUSS

The attention infants pay to various objects in their environment is not arbitrary. Infants pay particular attention to human faces and objects with qualities similar to faces — objects that move, are complex, are skin coloured and produce sounds (Siegler, 1991).

- From an evolutionary perspective, how might the tendency to focus on faces have evolved?
- What advantages would this tendency have conferred on infants over the course of human evolution?
- What kinds of information do faces convey?

What can infants sense and perceive?

Infants are born with many sensory capabilities, some better developed than others, such as the sense of hearing. Even before birth, foetal heart rate and movements increase in response to loud sounds, and habituation studies in newborns show that infants hear and recognise their mother's voices before they are born, despite a wall of flesh and an earful of amniotic fluid.

By contrast, vision is not well developed at birth. The visual cortex, retina and some other structures are still immature (Candy, Crowell, & Banks, 1998). At birth, visual acuity is estimated to be approximately 20/500 (i.e. an object 20 metres away looks as clear as an object 500 metres away would look to an adult), but it improves to about 20/100 by six months (Dobson & Teller, 1978). Infants focus best on objects between 18 and 20 centimetres away — approximately the distance between a nursing infant and its mother's face.

Intermodal understanding

Sensory processing occurs in anatomically discrete neural modules (chapter 4). Thus, when infants hear their mothers talking and see their mouths moving, different circuits in the brain become active. How and when do infants connect these sights and sounds? Do infants associate the voice with the visual image, or is the world like a dubbed movie, with lips moving and people talking out of sync? And do infants learn to make these connections across sensory modes, or are these capacities innate?

Research over the last 30 years suggests that infants are far more capable of ***intermodal processing*** — the ability to associate sensations of an object from different senses or to match their own actions to behaviours they have observed visually — than anyone would have expected. Infants show some recognition of the relation between sights and sounds even minutes after birth, turning their eyes towards the direction of a sound (Bower, 1982; Wertheimer, 1961). By three months, infants pay more attention to a person if speech sounds are synchronised with lip movements (Dodd, 1979; Kuhl & Meltzoff, 1988). By four to five months, they follow a conversation by shifting visual attention between two speakers (Horner & Chethik, 1986). Thus, they recognise not only features of objects from different senses but also the temporal order of those features — that is, that events across different senses unfold over time, such as lips moving and sounds of particular sorts coming out of them (Bahrick & Lickliter, 2000; Lewkowicz, 2000).

The newborn's sensory access to the world is surprisingly adult-like in some ways. However, research has shown that there are also identifiable differences in infants' and adults' perceptions. In one study (Slaughter, Heron, & Sim, 2002) infants aged 12, 15 or 18 months were shown line drawings of six distinctive pairs of adult bodies. One member of each pair was always scrambled (e.g. legs where the ears or arms should be) and one member was always anatomically accurate. The younger babies showed no reliable preferences for the body types, while the older infants (aged 18 months) looked significantly longer at the scrambled body types. As the older infants recognised the difference between the scrambled and accurate body types (as assessed by their disparate looking times at the bodies), and the younger infants did not, it would seem that younger infants may not yet perceive the human body as an integrated shape with determined features. It may be that babies are born with an innate predisposition to attend to faces, but must learn about bodies through experience — particularly after learning to walk (Peterson, 2009, as cited in Burton, Westen, & Kowalski, 2009).

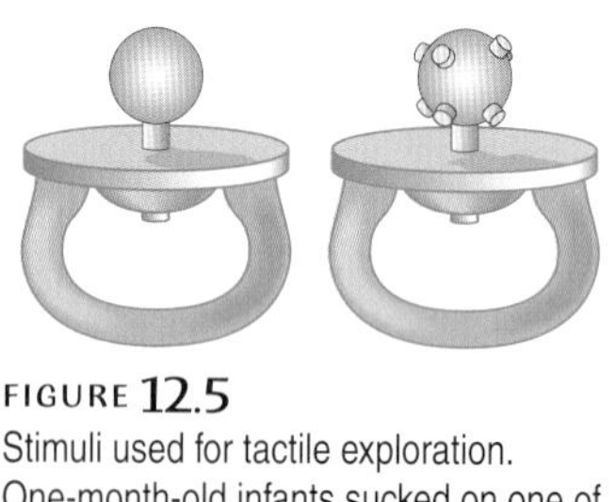

FIGURE 12.5
Stimuli used for tactile exploration. One-month-old infants sucked on one of two dummies like those depicted here. Later, they explored similar objects with their eyes. Most stared longer at the shape they had sucked, demonstrating that they knew with their eyes what they had felt with their mouths.

SOURCE: Reprinted with permission from Macmillan Publishers Ltd. From Meltzoff and Borton (1979). Copyright 1979.

In another study, infants appeared to know by sight something they had explored by touch (Meltzoff, 1990). One-month-old infants sucked on one of two kinds of dummies — smooth, or with nubs — exploring them with their lips and tongues (figure 12.5). The experimenters then visually presented similar objects constructed from orange Styrofoam, reasoning that the infants would fixate on the stimulus they had sucked. In fact, of 32 infants tested, 24 stared longer at the shape they had sucked, demonstrating that they knew with their eyes what they had felt with their mouths. In another study, newborns between 12 and 21 days old were able to imitate the facial gestures of an adult (figure 12.6) (Meltzoff & Moore, 1977).

How does an infant — who has no idea what a tongue is — recognise that she can move her own as an adult model does? Although such capacities are probably in large measure innate, since they have been demonstrated in children as young as 42 minutes old and in many other species (Lewkowicz, 2000), research with other animals suggests that they may also depend in part on experience in utero (Lickliter & Bahrick, 2000).

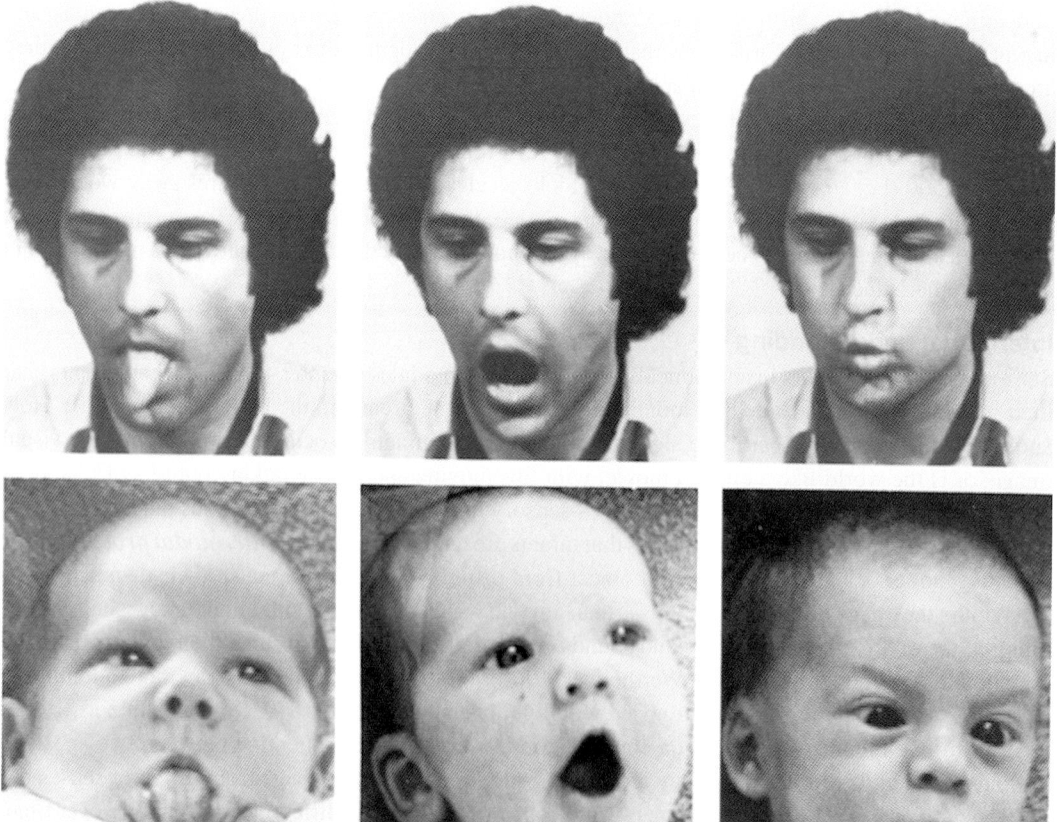

FIGURE 12.6
Imitation in infants. These photographs, published in 1977, show two- to three-week-old infants imitating the facial gestures of an adult. Infants who observed an adult sticking out his tongue were more likely to stick out their own tongue, while those who observed other facial movements, such as opening the mouth, were more likely to perform those behaviours.

SOURCE: From Meltzoff and Moore (1977). Reprinted with permission from AAAS.

Perceiving meaning

Infants may perceive more than psychologists once imagined, but do they attribute meaning to the objects they perceive? According to ecological theorists, who understand perception in its environmental, adaptive context, they do (Gibson, 1984, 1964). Ecological theorists argue that the nervous system is wired to recognise certain dangers, and to recognise the potential 'value' of some stimuli, without prior learning (chapter 4).

Ecological researchers have used looming-object studies to demonstrate their point. As an alert infant sits in a seat, an object suddenly begins moving directly towards the infant at a constant rate. The object may be real, or it may be an expanding shadow. As early as two weeks after birth, infants show a defensive response to the looming object, drawing their heads back, jerking their hands in front of their faces and showing distress (Bower, 1971).

ETHICAL DILEMMA

A psychologist is interested in examining whether or not newborn infants can remember things they experienced during prenatal life. She proposes to examine two groups of babies. The test group will experience auditory stimulation — mothers will be required to read aloud the same passage from a specified children's book each day during the last eight weeks of pregnancy. The control group will not receive any such repeated stimulation. She aims to test their preferences for novel and familiar story passages as read by the mother or a female stranger, a few hours after each baby is born. She proposes to pay each mother $50 for agreeing to participate in her study.

- What steps should the psychologist take to ensure that the welfare of the participants (both mother and child) is not compromised in any way by her study?
- Is it ethical to offer a cash reward to each mother for taking part in the study?

What can infants remember?

Most people completely lack explicit memory for events before age three or four, a phenomenon known as ***infantile amnesia***. This does not imply, however, that experience is lost on infants and young children. What infants remember varies considerably depending on the task and reflects in large part the maturation of neural circuits involved in different kinds of memory (Meltzoff, 1995; Nelson, 1995; Newcombe, Drummey, & Lie, 1995; see also Rovee-Collier, 1999). For example, Hayne (2004) has found that the retention interval over which infants' memories remain accessible to retrieval increases dramatically as a function of age. In particular, infant retention improves dramatically over the first two years of life. Hayne argues that if forgetting occurs within days or weeks during infancy, it is natural to expect that those memories will be unable to be retrieved years or decades later (chapter 7). Over time, however, the forgetting function gradually flattens and a memory becomes easier to retrieve and maintain (Hayne, 2004).

Various forms of implicit memory are present from birth. In one study, six-month-olds exposed once to a stimulus responded faster to it two years later than peers not previously exposed to it (Perris, Myers, & Clifton, 1990). Infants as young as three months old who have been conditioned to kick their legs to make a mobile move will begin kicking their legs sooner than other infants several weeks later, demonstrating implicit memory about the relationship between the behaviour and its consequence (Rovee-Collier, 1990). Some intriguing research finds few differences at all between implicit learning in children as young as four years old and adults, suggesting that the machinery of implicit learning and memory may be 'up and running' very early (Vinter & Perruchet, 2000).

Other research has examined how parents influence their child's memory development. For example, Farrant and Reese (2000) showed that children whose parents adopt a high-elaborative reminiscing style (i.e. asking the children questions that continuously provide and/or require new information) develop an elaborative style of reminiscing of their own. In contrast, children whose parents adopt a low-elaborative reminiscing style (i.e. asking repetitive, closed questions) tend to elaborate less (see Cleveland & Reese, 2005). Reese (2002) argues that children with high-elaborative parents learn what to remember, how to remember it, how to organise recall and how to understand what the memory represents (chapter 7). Reese further suggests that it is possible that memory for events begins at age three or four because this is the time at which memories become useful in how to operate in a social context. Hayne (2004) supports this view, stating that children who can describe an event in words are more likely to recall it later than are children who are unable to use words to describe their experience.

The rudiments of explicit memory are also present from birth, but more complete development of explicit memory depends on maturation of the hippocampi and the temporal lobes sometime between eight and 18 months (Nelson, 1995). In the earliest days of life, infants prefer novel words to those to which they habituated a day before, suggesting recognition memory that lasts at least a day (Swain, Zelano, & Clifton, 1993). EEG recordings suggest that five-month-olds can even tell the difference between tones of two different pitches — preferring the novel one — a day later (Thomas & Lykins, 1995).

MAKING CONNECTIONS

Cognitive psychologists distinguish several kinds of memory, regulated by different neural circuits (chapter 7). Explicit memory refers to memories that can be consciously recalled. Implicit memory is memory expressed in behaviour that may not be represented consciously. Working memory involves information held briefly in consciousness.

- What would be an example of explicit memory in infants?
- What would be an example of implicit memory in infants?
- How could a psychologist measure working memory capacity in infants?

The rudiments of working memory can be seen by six months of age, as infants appear to be able to hold spatial information in mind for three to five seconds (Gilmore & Johnson, 1995). However, working memory appears to be the slowest developing memory system, relying on the maturation of the prefrontal cortex (chapter 7). More recently, research also suggests that working memory deficits may eventuate in some children born prematurely or of low birth weight, due to the impact of damage to, or early disturbance in, cerebral development (Woodward, Edgin, Thompson, & Inder, 2005).

Throwing light on the development of perspective-taking

By Professor Janet Fletcher, University of Western Australia

To function successfully in our dynamic social world, it is essential that we are able to understand the thoughts, feelings and desires of other people. The ability to make these judgements about people's mental states is often referred to as theory of mind. How does this ability develop? Australian researchers have been helping to answer this question by looking at both normally developing children, and children with known disabilities — such as autism, hearing impairment and specific language impairment (e.g. Farrant, Fletcher, & Maybery, 2006; Peterson, Wellman, & Liu, 2005; Slaughter, Peterson, & Mackintosh, 2007).

The existence of theory of mind is typically judged through a variety of tasks, such as those involving 'diverse desires', 'diverse beliefs' and 'false beliefs'. False belief tasks are often taken to be a key exemplar of theory of mind. This type of task usually involves a scenario in which a child is shown an object, such as a pencil case, and is asked what is inside. The child is then shown that it actually contains lollies. They are then introduced to a doll, Mr Jones, who has never seen the pencil case, and are asked what Mr Jones will expect to find in the pencil case. A child who has an understanding of the possibility of false beliefs will answer 'pencils'. Results from many studies over the years have shown that children typically develop this understanding between three and five years (e.g. Astington & Jenkins, 1995; Wimmer & Perner, 1983). But, is this a genetically determined, 'hard-wired' ability that naturally emerges, or is there another possible explanation?

There is converging evidence that language development plays a critical role in the development of theory of mind. Research by Peterson (2003) has shown that deaf children whose language development has been delayed by the lack of a native speaker of sign in their family have substantially delayed theory of mind. In contrast, deaf children who have a native signer in their households, and hence who learn sign language from an earlier age, develop theory of mind as well as do typically developing children. Similarly, children with a specific language impairment (SLI) — that is, a significantly delayed or disordered language accompanied by normal nonverbal intelligence — also display delayed theory of mind (Farrant et al., 2006: Tucker, 2004).

Additional support for the role of language in theory of mind development comes from longitudinal research, such as that of Astington and Jenkins (1999). These researchers found that three-year-olds' language ability significantly predicted their theory of mind ability seven months later (after controlling for their initial theory of mind ability). However, the converse was not true. Training studies also point to the likelihood of a causal link between language development and theory of mind. Lohmann and Tomasello (2003) tested a group of three-year-old children on theory of mind before they participated in one of four training group conditions. The first group were involved in perspective-shifting conversations about deceptive objects. The second group learned the use of mental state verbs (e.g. thinks, believes and so on) and associated syntax (e.g. 'Peter thinks Mummy's home'). Training in the third group combined those of the first two groups in a 'full training' condition. Children in the fourth group were exposed to deceptive objects (e.g. an object that looked like a flower, but was actually a pen, with only a few attention-directing words, such as 'look'). When the children were retested for theory of mind, Lohmann and Tomasello found that all the groups, with the exception of the 'no-language group', made significant improvements. The 'full training' group made the biggest gains.

With language now generally accepted as a major contributor to the development of theory of mind, the task that remains is to determine what aspects of children's language development are critical, and how they might be nurtured. Recent research by Farrant, Maybery and Fletcher (2011) highlights the importance of the language input of mothers.

INTERIM SUMMARY

Although infants have various sensory deficits compared to adults, they are able to perceive subtle differences, such as the sound of their mother's and another woman's voice, from birth. They can also associate sensations of an object from different senses and match their own actions to behaviours they have observed visually, a phenomenon called ***intermodal processing***. Research from an ecological viewpoint suggests that infants innately appreciate the meaning of some experiences important to adaptation. Whereas various forms of implicit memory are present at birth and rudiments of explicit memory also exist in early infancy, explicit memory requires maturation of the hippocampus over at least the first 18 months of life. Working memory is the slowest developing memory system.

Piaget's theory of cognitive development

The first psychologist to trace cognitive development systematically was Jean Piaget (1896–1980). The philosopher of science Thomas Kuhn (1970) observed that major innovations often come from outsiders who have not yet been indoctrinated into the discipline, and this was the case with Piaget. Although Piaget waited until age 21 to complete his doctorate in biology, he published his first paper at the ripe old age of 11 and was offered the curatorship of a Geneva museum's mollusc collection while still in high school. (The offer was rescinded when the museum realised he was a child.) How did this precocious biologist become a world-famous psychologist by age 30?

A philosophical question and a psychological answer

Piaget had a keen interest in epistemology, the branch of philosophy concerned with the nature of knowledge. The British empiricist philosophers, such as John Locke, argued that all knowledge comes from experience. To know what a dog is like, a person has to examine a number of dogs, experience them with the senses and come to some conclusions about their common properties.

In contrast, the German philosopher Immanuel Kant argued that some forms of knowledge do not come from observation but are innate. People impose certain categories of thought — such as space, time and causality — on the data of their senses, but these categories are not derived from experience. Similarly, the rules of logic and mathematics seem to work in the world, yet they are not mere summaries of sensory information. No-one has ever seen the square root of 2 or π, but these concepts have real-world applications, as any engineer or architect can attest. Kant argued that the human propensity for mathematical thinking, like the tendency to use certain categories of thought, is innate.

Kant's ideas were the starting point for Piaget's life work. His hunch was that Kant was both right and wrong. Kant was right that people's understanding of time, space and logic is not simply derived from experience but wrong that people are born with this knowledge. Piaget therefore decided to spend a year or two looking into the way children develop an understanding of time, space and so on — a 'temporary' diversion from philosophy that occupied the next 60 years of his life.

Piaget (1970) proposed that children develop knowledge by inventing, or constructing, reality out of their own experience, mixing what they observe with their own ideas about how the world works. Thus, the preschooler who sees a dog's mask placed on Maynard the cat applies her own rules of logic — 'When things look different, they are different' — to conclude that Maynard is a dog. Similarly, a toddler who notices that a shadow is attached to his feet no matter where he is on a sunny playground may use his own logic to conclude that the shadow is following him. These cognitive constructions are

MAKING CONNECTIONS

Piaget began his career working in Alfred Binet's **intelligence**-testing laboratory (chapter 9). Whereas **Binet** was primarily interested in how well children answered questions, Piaget was interested in how they arrived at their answers. He noticed that children of the same age tended to make the same types of mistakes. They not only gave the same kinds of wrong answers, but when questioned about their reasoning, they provided similar explanations. He concluded that children think in qualitatively different ways at different ages, leading him to a stage theory of cognitive development.

creative, but they are not arbitrary, since they are constrained by both physical realities (such as the fact that cats and dogs usually do not change into one another) and brain development (Brainerd, 1996).

Assimilation and accommodation

Piaget viewed intelligence as the individual's way of adapting to new information about the world. He argued that children cognitively adapt to their environment through two interrelated processes, assimilation and accommodation (Piaget & Inhelder, 1969). ***Assimilation*** involves interpreting actions or events in terms of one's present schemas — that is, fitting reality into one's existing ways of understanding. According to Piaget, a ***schema*** is an organised, repeatedly exercised pattern of thought or behaviour (Flavell, 1992), such as an infant's tendency to suck anything that will fit into its mouth (a nipple, a finger, a dummy etc.). All of these objects can be assimilated — taken in without modifying an existing schema — by sucking. Similarly, a person with a cognitive schema about police can drive into a crowded intersection and immediately understand the role of the person directing traffic.

If humans only assimilated information into existing schemas, no cognitive development would take place. The second process, ***accommodation***, is the modification of schemas to fit reality. At the behavioural level, accommodation takes place when an infant with a sucking schema is presented with a cup: she must modify her existing schema to drink from this new device. At the thought level, accommodation is likely to occur if the reader looks carefully at the spelling of accommodation — it has two c's and two m's, which is highly unusual in English. The word 'accommodation' requires revision of the implicit schema most people hold that would lead them to double only one consonant or the other.

For Piaget, the driving force behind cognitive development is ***equilibration*** — that is, balancing assimilation and accommodation to adapt to the world. When a child comes across something she does not understand, she finds herself in a state of cognitive disequilibrium that motivates her to try to make sense of what she has encountered. She may attempt to fit it into existing schemas (assimilation) or she may combine schemas or construct an entirely new schema to fit the new reality (accommodation). Thus, an infant whose father is holding her in front of a large mirror may not realise that she is the baby at whom she is smiling so broadly, but she has to make sense of the fact that there seem to be two identical daddies in the room, one holding her and one smiling at her in the mirror! Eventually she constructs the understanding that a mirror is a special kind of surface that reflects images.

INTERIM SUMMARY

Piaget argued that children develop knowledge by constructing reality out of their own experience, mixing what they observe with their own ideas about how the world works. They do this through a process of ***equilibration***, which means balancing ***assimilation*** (fitting reality into their existing knowledge) and ***accommodation*** (modifying schemas to fit reality).

Stages of cognitive development

According to Piaget, people assimilate and accommodate when confronted with new information throughout their lives. At each stage of development, however, children use a distinct underlying logic, or ***structure of thought***, to guide their thinking. The same four stages — sensorimotor, preoperational, concrete operational and formal operational — occur in the same sequence for everyone, although the age for each individual may vary somewhat (see table 12.2 on p. 486). A fundamental principle of Piaget's developmental theory is that every stage builds on the next, as children wrestle with problems their old structures will not resolve and work their way towards new solutions by trying out and adjusting schemas currently in their repertoire (Siegler & Ellis, 1996).

Sensorimotor stage

The ***sensorimotor stage***, in which infants think with their hands, mouths and senses, lasts from birth to about two years of age. Sensorimotor thought primarily takes the form of action, as infants learn about the world by mouthing, grasping, watching and manipulating objects. According to Piaget, the practical knowledge infants develop during this period forms the basis for their later ability to represent things mentally.

The label 'sensorimotor' emphasises that infants are bound by their sensations and actions and are capable of little explicit reasoning beyond what they are sensing and doing. They know about an object, such as a toy duck, only in terms of the sensations and actions associated with it, not as an objective reality.

A major achievement of the sensorimotor stage is the development of ***object permanence***, the recognition that objects exist in time and space independent of the child's actions on, or observation of, them. According to Piaget, before the age of about eight to 12 months, an object such as a ball exists for an infant only when it is in sight. If it is hidden from view, it no longer exists. When a child acquires object permanence, he will look for the ball, even when it is hidden from view, and will be delighted to find it. Piaget suggested that the attainment of object permanence lies behind infants' endless fascination with games such as peek-a-boo, which affirm their newfound understanding. Subsequent research suggests that children acquire aspects of object permanence much earlier than Piaget supposed (Baillargeon & DeVos, 1991; see also Moore & Meltzoff, 1999, 2004), even by four or five months, but a comprehensive understanding of the permanence of objects does appear to evolve gradually during infancy (Halford, 1989).

During the sensorimotor stage, children learn with their hands and mouths.

During the sensorimotor stage children are extremely ***egocentric***, thoroughly embedded in their own point of view. When an infant closes her eyes, the whole world becomes dark; when a ball is no longer in view, it ceases to exist. For Piaget, development entails a gradual movement away from egocentrism towards a recognition of alternative points of view (see Flavell, 1996; Selman, 1980).

Preoperational stage

The ***preoperational stage*** begins roughly around age two and lasts until ages five to seven. It is characterised by the emergence of symbolic thought — the ability to use arbitrary symbols, such as words, to represent concepts. Once children learn to manipulate symbols and mental images, thought becomes detachable from action. To put it another way, when children can play with the world in their minds, they no longer have to think exclusively with their hands or mouths. Symbolic thought allows preschool children to converse with other people and imagine solutions to problems before actually doing anything.

Preoperational thought continues, however, to be limited by egocentrism. A classic demonstration of egocentrism at this stage occurs in the *three-mountain task*. A child is seated at a table displaying three model mountains (figure 12.7), with a teddy bear or doll placed on the same table. The child is shown a number of pictures of the table from different perspectives and is asked which view the doll is seeing.

FIGURE 12.7
The three-mountain task. Preoperational children typically do not recognise that the doll 'sees' the mountain from a perspective different from their own, although they can do so if the stimulus is very simple.

Preschool children often answer that the doll sees their own view of the table (Piaget & Inhelder, 1956). They are not egocentric in every situation and can even solve simplified versions of the three-mountain task (Burke, 1975; Ford, 1979; Lempers, Flavell, & Flavell, 1977). Nevertheless, preschoolers are much more likely to make egocentric cognitive errors than older children, like the three-year-old who covers her eyes and declares, 'You can't see me!'

A related limitation of preoperational thought is ***centration***, the tendency to focus, or centre, on one perceptually striking feature of an object without considering other features that might be relevant. When asked which of two chocolate bars is bigger, a long, thin one or a short, thick one, the preschooler is likely to pick the longer one and ignore thickness, even though the amount of chocolate is identical.

Preoperational thinking also tends to be fairly literal. The mother of a three-year-old tried to teach her son the meaning of 'compromise' when he wanted her to read him three bedtime stories instead of the usual one. She suggested they compromise on two. A few days later, they were debating whether he should go to bed at seven or eight o'clock, and the mother asked, 'Billy, do you remember what 'compromise' means?' 'Yes,' he replied earnestly, 'two'. Preschool children's preoperational thought also means they are often much more accepting of happenings that adults may find questionable. In recent years, children's entertainment powerhouse The Wiggles announced the shock news that 'Yellow Wiggle' Greg Page was retiring due to health concerns, with long-term understudy Sam Moran stepping into the yellow skivvy. The change has caused hardly a second thought for many of the group's young fans, who have accepted without question a slightly different-looking Yellow Wiggle. However, the more advanced formal operational stages of cognitive development of teenagers and adults means they often find it much harder to accept such a change without questioning what the impact will be. For example, the decision of rock band INXS to perform with a series of new front men, most recently

J. D. Fortune, picked via a reality television show, after the death of original singer Michael Hutchence has not had the same widespread acceptance among INXS's fans as the new Yellow Wiggle has had among the younger generation.

Perhaps the major limitation of preoperational thought is the feature that gave this stage its name. For Piaget, to know an object is to operate or act on it. ***Operations*** are internalised (i.e. mental) actions the individual can use to manipulate, transform and then return an object to its original state (Piaget, 1972). Alphabetising a list of names is an operation, because a person can put names in alphabetical order and then scramble their order again. Similarly, imagining what one could have said to someone who behaved rudely is an operation. Operations are like actions a person 'tries out' in her head. According to Piaget, the capacity to carry out mental operations of this sort is the defining feature of the next stage of development. Piaget's stages of cognitive development, including the later stages that are discussed shortly, are compared briefly in table 12.2.

TABLE 12.2 **Piaget's stages of cognitive development**

Stage	Approximate ages (years)	Characteristics
Sensorimotor	0–2	Thought and action are virtually identical, as the infant explores the world with its senses and behaviours; object permanence develops; the child is completely egocentric.
Preoperational	2–7	Symbolic thought develops; object permanence is firmly established; the child cannot coordinate different physical attributes of an object or different perspectives.
Concrete operational	7–12	The child is able to perform reversible mental operations on representations of objects; understanding of conservation develops; the child can apply logic to concrete situations.
Formal operational	12+	The adolescent (or adult) can apply logic more abstractly; hypothetical thinking develops.

INTERIM SUMMARY

Piaget argued that cognitive development occurs through a series of stages. During the ***sensorimotor stage***, infants think with their hands and eyes. A major achievement of the sensorimotor stage is ***object permanence***, when infants recognise that objects exist in time and space. During the sensorimotor stage, children are extremely ***egocentric***. The ***preoperational stage*** is characterised by the emergence of symbolic thought, which allows preschool-age children to imagine solutions to problems mentally rather than through action. Children at this stage remain egocentric; they have difficulty imagining reality from other viewpoints, and they have a tendency to centre on one perceptually striking feature of an object.

Concrete operational stage

Piaget called the third stage of cognitive development the ***concrete operational stage***, roughly ages seven to 12. At this point, children are capable of operating on, or mentally manipulating, internal representations of concrete objects in ways that are reversible. In other words, children can imagine performing mental manipulations (operations) on a set of objects and then mentally put them back the way they found them (Piaget, 1972). For example, school-age children are able to imagine different ways of explaining why they came home late from playing with their friends, picture the likely consequences of each and pick the one with the best chance of acceptance. Younger children, in contrast, are more likely to blurt out an obvious lie or the truth, neither of which may satisfy their cognitively more developed parents.

The major achievement of the concrete operational stage is demonstrated in Piaget's classic experiments with conservation problems. According to Piaget, once children reach this third stage, they are able to understand the concept of ***conservation*** — that basic properties of an object or situation remain stable (are conserved) even though superficial properties may be changed.

For example, if preoperational children are shown the three beakers in part (a) of figure 12.8, they easily recognise that the two same-sized beakers contain the same amount of liquid. They will not realise, however, that the tall and short beakers contain the same amount of liquid even if they watch the experimenter pour the liquid from the short to the tall beaker. In contrast, concrete operational children understand that the amount of liquid remains unchanged even though it has been poured into a beaker of a different shape. If asked to justify their answers, they usually say something like, 'You just poured it from one container to another!'. Whereas preoperational thought is characterised by centration on one dimension, concrete operational thinkers are able to *decentre*, that is, to hold in mind multiple dimensions at once.

Two other types of conservation problems, conservation of number and conservation of mass, are shown in parts (b) and (c), respectively, of figure 12.8. Children typically master different kinds of conservation at slightly different ages. Many children understand conservation of number by age six but do not understand conservation of mass until about age eight (Elkind, 1981; Katz & Beilin, 1976).

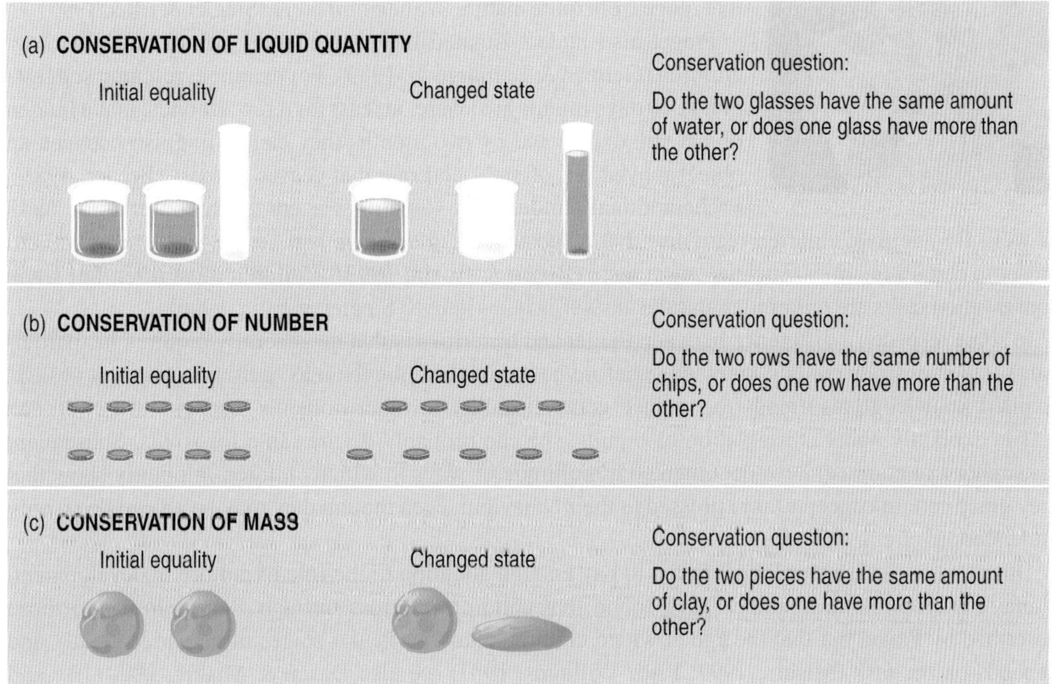

FIGURE 12.8
Conservation. (a) Conservation of liquid quantity: unlike preoperational children, concrete operational children understand that the amount of liquid remains unchanged even though it has been poured into a beaker of a different shape. (b) Conservation of number: preoperational children believe that altering the physical configuration changes the number of objects present. (c) Conservation of mass: preoperational children fail to realise that mass is conserved despite changing the shape of a ball of clay.

At the concrete operational stage children also understand *transitivity* — that if a < b and b < c, then a < c. Although preoperational children can be trained to make some transitive inferences, they have difficulty keeping enough information in mind to solve transitive thinking problems (Bryant & Trabasso, 1971). One transitivity problem asks, 'If Henry is taller than Jack, and Jack is taller than Claude, which boy is the shortest?' Preschoolers are equally likely to pick Jack or Claude because each one is shorter than someone else. They fail to put together the two pieces of information about relative height into a single transitive proposition. In general, before age seven or eight, children have difficulty recognising logical inconsistencies (e.g. that a person cannot be both tall and short, except in relation to different people) (Ruffman, 1999).

Formal operational stage

Piaget's fourth stage, formal operations, begins about ages 12 to 15, when children start to think more abstractly. The ***formal operational stage*** is characterised by the ability to manipulate abstract as well as concrete objects, events and ideas mentally. That is, teenagers can reason about 'formal' propositions (e.g. whether democracy is the best form of government) rather than concrete events. Teenagers are less likely to argue that the two beakers in the conservation task contain the same amount of liquid because they saw the liquid being poured back and forth. They may instead discuss the law of conservation or argue that surface appearances do not always reflect the underlying reality. Another hallmark of formal operational reasoning is the ability to frame hypotheses and figure out how to test them systematically (Inhelder & Piaget, 1958).

APPLY + DISCUSS

Piaget proposed that children's thinking develops in stages.

- If cognition develops in stages, should children show the same level of thinking in all domains, such as maths, science and interpersonal understanding?
- What drives cognitive development? What maturational and social factors might lead a child to move out of sensorimotor into preoperational intelligence, or from the sensorimotor to the preoperational stage?
- When adults learn a new field, such as psychology, does their thinking develop in stages, or do they just gradually build up their knowledge?

Putting Piaget in perspective

Piaget's theory literally defined cognitive development for several decades, and it continues to have a profound influence. Nevertheless, researchers now criticise a number of aspects of his theory.

First, Piaget focused too heavily on the kind of rational thinking typical of scientific or philosophical pursuits and underplayed the extent to which people's thinking is biased, irrational and influenced by motives or emotions. For example, despite their ability to think abstractly, teenagers show the same kinds of biases as adult scientists in weighing arguments against their pet theories (see Klaczynski, 1997, 2000).

APPLY + DISCUSS

- In planning their curriculums, school systems pay attention to what children are capable of thinking at different ages. At what stage should children begin to learn the alphabet? At what stage are children probably ready to learn algebra? Chemistry? Do these stages correspond with the ages at which schools generally teach children their ABCs, x's and y's, and H_2O?

Another criticism concerns Piaget's assumption that a child's thinking tends to be 'at' one stage or another. Cognitive development often progresses unevenly, as the same child shows higher level reasoning in one domain than another (e.g. the ability to think abstractly in science but a lack of complexity in thinking about social relationships) (Case, 1992; Flavell, 1982). Children also exhibit a range of responses on any task and when 'thinking aloud' while solving a problem often provide responses that range from quite mature to quite immature (Siegler & Ellis, 1996).

Piaget also underestimated the capacities of infants and preschool children (Gelman & Baillargeon, 1983). For example, research suggests that at 20 days infants are aware, at least for a few seconds, that a hidden object still exists, and by two months they can distinguish between an object moved out of sight and one that ceases to exist (Breuer, 1985). Preoperational children can sometimes accomplish conservation tasks as well. By age five, children recognise that a substance can dissolve and no longer be seen but still preserve certain qualities, such as sweet taste (Rosen & Rozin, 1993). Children most often fail when conservation tasks are unfamiliar and the answer is quantitative (Siegler & Ellis, 1996).

In some respects, a difference between Piaget and his critics is that he generally required his participants to demonstrate explicit knowledge before he would describe them as 'getting' a concept or task. Explicit knowledge also tends to produce generalisability to other domains, because if a child can reason explicitly about conservation of liquids, she can probably do the same for solids. Subsequent researchers, in contrast, have documented a multitude of ways in which children implicitly show that they grasp certain concepts, as expressed in their behaviour, even though they may be able to do so only under certain circumstances.

Other critics charge that Piaget failed to pay enough attention to the role of culture in development. Numerous cross-cultural studies have found that children progress through stages similar to those described by Piaget but that the age at which children attain particular stages often varies greatly and depends on the task (Mishra, 1997; Price-Williams, 1981; see also Dasen & Mishra, 2000). By and large, cognitive development proceeds more slowly in preliterate societies, although children's abilities tend to reflect their cultural and environmental circumstances. Mexican children of potters show delayed development on the conservation task using beakers, but they demonstrate a relatively early understanding of conservation when asked if a ball of clay has the same volume when it is stretched into an oblong shape (Price-Williams, Gordon, & Ramirez, 1969). Similarly, children in nomadic societies, which travel from location to location for their survival, tend to outperform other children on spatial tasks (Dasen, 1975; Dasen & Heron, 1981).

In sum, Piaget was correct in that children become less egocentric, increasingly able to think symbolically and increasingly able to reason abstractly as they develop (Halford, 1989; see also Feldman, 2004; Sigelman & Rider, 2006). However, development is less uniform and unitary than his model suggests, and infants and young children appear to be more competent — and adults less competent — than Piaget believed (Flavell, 1992).

MAKING CONNECTIONS

Piaget began his work studying **intelligence**, and his theory is fundamentally about the way intelligence develops in children. Researchers studying intelligence have many different theories, ranging from theories that emphasise **general intelligence** — a '*g*-factor' that cuts across all domains — and **specific intelligences**, such as verbal and mathematical (chapter 9).

- Does Piaget's theory presuppose a theory of general intelligence?
- Can Piaget's theory be reconciled with Howard Gardner's theory of multiple intelligences, which proposes that people have many different kinds of intelligence, such as mathematical, musical and interpersonal intelligence?

INTERIM SUMMARY

During the ***concrete operational stage***, children can mentally manipulate representations of concrete objects in ways that are reversible, as can be seen in their understanding of ***conservation*** (that basic properties of an object or situation remain stable even though superficial properties change). The ***formal operational stage*** is characterised by the ability to manipulate abstract as well as concrete representations, to reason about formal propositions rather than concrete events. Many of Piaget's broad principles have withstood the test of time, but many specifics of the theory no longer appear accurate.

Vygotsky's sociocultural theory of cognitive development

Lev Vygotsky (1896–1934) developed a sociocultural theory of cognitive development that emphasises the role of social interaction for the child as motivation for cognitive gains and learning. Vygotsky's model proposes that children collaborate and strive together on tasks to enhance their levels of understanding. Children may also work with significant others such as parents, siblings or teachers to advance their knowledge levels. For example, Vygotsky (1978) believed that children use imitative learning by watching and listening to parents and other people in their social worlds. Children internalise socially conveyed learning through play and interactions with significant others.

Vygotsky developed a ***zone of proximal development (ZPD)*** that reflects a continuum of cognitive development, ranging from the child's individual capacity for problem solving to a more advanced and collaboratively-based level of cognitive development. Thus, the ZPD stretches from sole performance to collaborative cooperation (Peterson, 2004). According to this model, the child will achieve more understanding by socialising cooperatively with a skilled partner (adult or cognitively advanced peer) rather than by working alone. Vygotsky's theory is therefore more explicitly social than Piaget's theory — it focuses more on the child's social interactions with significant others and how the child's cultural background may influence learning. Vygotsky (1997) emphasised the interaction of the individual and the social context, including everything cultural as social.

INTERIM SUMMARY

Lev Vygotsky's sociocultural theory of cognitive development emphasises the role of social interaction in learning. Vygotsky's model proposes children collaborate and strive together on tasks to enhance their levels of understanding. Children also learn by imitating, watching and listening to parents and other significant people in their social worlds. Thus, Vygotsky's ***zone of proximal development (ZPD)*** stretches from sole performance to collaborative cooperation. According to the ZPD, children will achieve more understanding by socialising cooperatively with a skilled partner (adult or cognitively advanced peer) rather than by working alone.

Information-processing approach to cognitive development

The information-processing approach is well suited to sketching some of the finer details of cognitive development. Information-processing researchers have tried to track down the specific processes that account for cognitive development and have focused on continuous, quantitative changes more than the broad, qualitative stages studied by Piaget.

Processing speed

One of the variables that appears to account most for cognitive development is surprisingly simple: processing speed (Kail, 2000; Miller & Vernon, 1997). As we saw in chapter 9, mental quickness is a central aspect of intelligence. As children get older, they are able to do faster a range of cognitive tasks from categorising objects to making decisions (figure 12.9). This increase in speed allows them, among other things, to hold more information in working memory at any given moment and hence to solve problems more effectively. Speed of processing across a wide array of simple and complex tasks increases throughout childhood and levels off around age 15 (Kail, 1991a, 1991b).

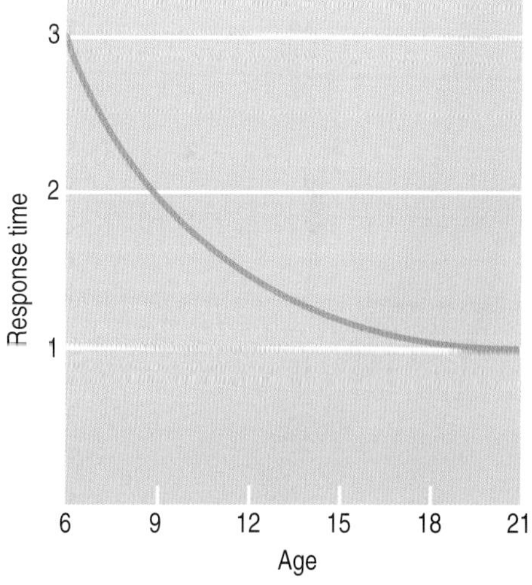

FIGURE 12.9
Processing speed and age. Here, processing speed (scaled as the ratio of children's speed relative to adult speed) follows an exponential function — and can in fact be predicted with mathematical precision (Kail, 1991a, 1991b). In other words, speed increases rapidly from about ages 6 to 12 and starts to level off by age 15.

SOURCE: Adapted from Fry and Hale (1996).

Automatic processing

A second factor that influences children's cognitive skill is their increasing ability to perform cognitive tasks automatically (Chaiken, Kyllonen, & Tirre, 2000; Sternberg, 1984). ***Automatisation*** refers to the process of executing mental processes with increasing efficiency so that they require less and less attention. In many tasks, from performing addition problems to driving a car, increased competence involves shifting from conscious, controlled processing to automatic, or implicit, processing. In reading, for example, children begin by sounding out words bit by bit. As they get more proficient, they immediately recognise common words and only have to sound out new, more complicated words.

Knowledge base

Another factor that influences children's cognitive efficiency is their ***knowledge base***, or accumulated knowledge. Compared to adults, children's knowledge bases are obviously limited because of their comparative inexperience with life. To what extent, then, does the limited size of children's knowledge base, rather than some other factor, account for their cognitive inefficiency compared with adults?

Children can remember the names and personalities of many cartoon characters, some of which may look alike or share similarities with their parents.

One study explored this question by reversing the usual state of affairs, selecting children who were more knowledgeable than their adult counterparts (Chi, 1978). The cognitive task was to remember arrangements of pieces on a chessboard. Child participants (average age 10) were recruited from a local chess tournament; adult participants had no particular skill at chess. That the children easily outperformed the adults demonstrates that knowledge base was more important than age-related factors in this cognitive task. Other studies have corroborated this finding using stimuli such as cartoon characters with which children are more familiar than adults (Lindberg, 1980).

Cognitive strategies

Use of cognitive strategies also develops throughout childhood and adolescence (Siegler, 1996, 2007). In memory tasks, young children tend to rely on simple strategies such as rote repetition. As they get older, children use increasingly sophisticated rehearsal strategies (chapter 7), such as arranging lists into categories before trying to remember the items (see Alexander & Schwanenflugel, 1994; Brown, Bransford, Ferrara, & Campione, 1983). In many respects, cognitive development reflects a process akin to evolution: children try out new 'mutations' (different problem-solving strategies), weed out those that do not work as well, and gradually evolve new strategies depending on changes in the situation (Siegler, 1996).

Metacognition

A final variable involved in cognitive development is ***metacognition*** — thinking about thinking (Bogdan, 2000; Flavell, 1977; Metcalfe & Shimamura, 1994; see also Pintrich, 2002). Metacognition involves cognition that reflects on, monitors and regulates an individual's thinking (Kuhn, 2000). To solve problems, people often need to understand how their mind works — how they perform cognitive tasks such as remembering, learning and solving problems. For example, when asked if they understand something, young children often have trouble discriminating whether they understand something or not, so they simply nod in assent or fail to ask questions (Brown et al., 1983). Similarly, preschoolers do not recognise the importance of 'inner speech' — using words inside one's head — while performing tasks such as mental arithmetic (Flavell, Green, Flavell, & Grossman, 1997). A key factor in the transfer of learning is a child's development of metacognitive skills and thinking; a process defined as metalearning (Fisher, 1998).

An important aspect of metacognition is ***metamemory*** — knowledge about one's own memory and about strategies that can be used to help remember (Flavell & Wellman, 1977; Metcalfe, 2000; see also Perez & Garcia, 2002). Metamemory is impaired in many patients with frontal lobe damage (Shimamura, 1995; see also Pannu, Kaszniak, & Rapcsak, 2005). Not surprisingly, it is also less developed in children, whose frontal lobes remain immature for many years. In one classic study, researchers asked younger and older children to view some pictures and predict how many they could remember. The younger children often predicted total recall (Flavell, Friedrichs, & Hoyt, 1970)! Although metamemory, like metacognition in general, frequently involves explicit processes, many metamemory processes are implicit, such as knowing how, where and how long to search memory (Reder & Schunn, 1996).

INTERIM SUMMARY

Many aspects of information processing change with age. Among the most important are processing speed, children's ***knowledge base*** (store of accumulated knowledge), ***automatisation*** (executing mental processes automatically and relatively effortlessly, with increasing efficiency and decreased attention), more efficient use of cognitive strategies and ***metacognition*** (knowledge about how one's mind works — or cognition about cognition).

Integrative theories of cognitive development

Piaget viewed cognitive development as a progression through qualitatively different stages, whereas the information-processing approach focuses on small-scale, quantitative refinements in children's ability to think and remember. As different as these viewpoints are, they are not mutually exclusive. Cognitive development may be characterised by both qualitative and quantitative changes and general and specific processes (Fischer, 1980; Fischer & Bidell, 1997).

Neo-Piagetian theorists attempt to integrate Piagetian and information-processing theories. With Piaget, they argue that children actively structure their understanding, that knowledge progresses from a preconcrete to a concrete and then to an abstract stage, and that all of these aspects occur in roughly the order reported by Piaget (Bidell & Fischer, 1992; Case, 1998; Fischer, 1980). Like information-processing theorists, however, the neo-Piagetians pay more attention to discrete components of cognitive processing and emphasise domain-specific development — that is, the way cognition can develop in one domain without simultaneously developing in others.

One such theory was proposed by Robbie Case (1992, 1998). Case argues for a general stage theory similar to Piaget's, from a sensorimotor stage to an abstract, complex, formal operational stage. Each stage differs qualitatively from the others in the way children represent problems and strategies for solving them (Case, 1984).

Case's theory differs from Piaget's, however, in some key respects. Case argues that cognitive progress within each stage is possible because humans are innately motivated to solve problems, explore, imitate others and engage in social interaction. Development occurs within each stage as children set goals, formulate problem-solving strategies and evaluate the results of those strategies. They then integrate existing problem-solving strategies to create more elaborate strategies as new situations arise, and they practise those new strategies until they become automatic.

According to Case, development across stages also depends on cultural input, but the most important factor in qualitative changes in development (i.e. movement across stages) is an increasing capacity for working memory. Attending to both length and width in a conservation task is much easier if a child has large enough working memory capacity to hold both dimensions in mind simultaneously while imagining how, for example, a ball of clay might look if those dimensions changed. Research suggests that the central executive function of working memory, which is involved in allocating attention, coordinating different kinds of information held in short-term storage, and handling multiple tasks at once, continues to develop throughout childhood, at least until age 10 (Hale, Bronik, & Fry, 1997).

MAKING CONNECTIONS

Working memory refers to the capacity to hold information in consciousness long enough to use, consider or manipulate it (chapter 7). Working memory capacity expands as children automatise more and more processes that once required conscious attention, such as riding a bike, and become more efficient in their use of cognitive strategies. According to Neo-Piagetian theorists like Case, these developments allow children to keep progressively more things in mind simultaneously and to coordinate previously separate actions and ideas.

Figure 12.10 illustrates the way expanded working memory allows for more complex cognition. Ten- to 18-year-olds were asked to draw a picture of a mother looking out the window to see her son in the park across the street playing peek-a-boo with her (Dennis, 1992, cited in Case, 1992). The youngest participants could keep in mind the image of the mother in the house and the image of the boy in the park, but they could not integrate the two images. This study illustrates the advantages of a neo-Piagetian model over classical Piagetian theory. Certain broad processes, particularly limitations in working memory, constrain the thinking of young children, putting an upper limit on what a child within a given age range can achieve. This leads to qualitative differences in thought at different stages that appear across a variety of domains (such as art, language and mathematics), just as Piaget postulated.

At the same time, neo-Piagetian models recognise that development occurs in specific domains and is influenced by culture and experience (Bidell & Fischer, 2000). By ages eight to 10, children in Western cultures incorporate artistic conventions developed over the past several centuries for depicting perspective (chapter 4), such as representing closer objects as larger. However, a four-year-old with a crayon is unlikely to outperform an adult regardless of culture or experience.

FIGURE 12.10 Artistic skill and working memory. Participants aged 10 to 18 were asked to draw a picture of a mother looking out the window to see her son playing peek-a-boo with her in the park. The 10-year-old who drew this picture accurately depicted both parts of the scene but failed to integrate them, drawing the mother and son both facing the artist instead of each other.

INTERIM SUMMARY

Neo-Piagetian theorists attempt to integrate an understanding of the broad stages of Piaget's theory with an information processing approach. According to Case's theory, the main variable responsible for cognitive development across stages is expansion of working memory capacity.

Cognitive development and change in adulthood

All cultures consider adolescents and adults better decision makers than children, but they differ dramatically in their beliefs about cognition and ageing. Many cultures associate age with wisdom. In contrast, Western cultures associate age with decline. Although real changes in speed of processing and capacity for learning and memory occur cross-culturally (Crook, Youngjohn, Larrabee, & Salama, 1992), as we will see, cognitive decline varies not only across cultures but also across individuals within a single culture.

Cognitive changes associated with ageing

A number of cognitive changes occur with ageing, ranging from changes in psychomotor speed to changes in memory (Craik & Salthouse, 2000; Park & Schwarz, 2000; Salthouse & Davis, 2006).

Psychomotor speed

One of the clearest changes that accompanies ageing is ***psychomotor slowing***, an increase in the time required for processing and acting on information (Park, Smith, Lautenschlager, & Earles, 1996; Salthouse, 1996, 2000). This deceleration actually begins early, around the mid-20s. Psychomotor slowing can be observed both on relatively simple tests, such as pushing a button when a light flashes, and on tests that require more complex thinking (Era, Jokela, & Heikkinen, 1986; Spirduso & MacRae, 1990). In practical terms, psychomotor slowing can be seen in the difficulty older people have relative to younger people when first learning to use a mouse at the computer — particularly double-clicking (Smith, Sharit, & Czaja, 1999)!

At the age of 31, Jamie Dwyer won the 2010 International Hockey Federation Player of the Year, following wins in 2004, 2007 and 2009. In the same year, he captained the Australian men's hockey team to wins in the 2010 Hockey World Cup and the 2010 Commonwealth Games in India. Dwyer continues to have exceptional psychomotor speed, despite the fact that psychomotor slowing generally begins to occur around the age of 25.

For most people, psychomotor slowing is so gradual that it goes unnoticed until the 50s or 60s. For most professional athletes and swimmers, however, increased reaction time means an early retirement age. Some elite competitors, do, however, defy the odds. For example, at age 31, Jamie Dwyer captained Australia in the 2010 Hockey World Cup win in India, and led the Kookaburras to a gold medal in the men's hockey at the 2010 Commonwealth Games. In 2010, Dwyer won the International Hockey Federation (FIH) Player of the Year, following wins in 2004, 2007 and 2009. It is evident that elite athletes can remain on top of their game well into their 30s and have the potential to stage comebacks through extra practice, increased skill and focused strategies.

Does reaction time matter much for the rest of us, whose livelihood does not depend on diving off the blocks or anticipating the direction of a ball heading towards us at 120 kilometres an hour? Actually, it does, because it has indirect effects on all kinds of reasoning and problem-solving abilities (Parkin & Java, 1999). Researchers are just beginning to tease apart the reasons why processing speed appears to matter so much, but two explanations may help to clarify the link between speed and intellectual functioning (Salthouse, 1996).

The first is limited time. If complex mental operations rely on the execution and coordination of many simpler mechanisms, in the brief period of time people have to make most decisions, including implicit decisions, the person will simply have less time to process multiple pieces of information and combine them in complex ways. From a connectionist perspective (chapter 8), if people categorise, perceive and remember through processes of parallel constraint satisfaction (finding the solution that best fits all the constraints active at the moment), people who think quickly can weigh a greater number of constraints and hence come to a more informed conclusion.

A second way decreased processing speed can affect cognitive performance is its influence on working memory. If cognitive processes take longer to execute, less information is available simultaneously in working memory, and relevant information may no longer be available by the time the person needs to think about it.

Memory

A common stereotype is that older people are constantly forgetting things — names of people they have just met, what they did yesterday or where they put their house keys. This stereotype has grains of truth but is far too sweeping. Sometimes even young and otherwise healthy adults do not escape unscathed from this stereotype. For example, cognitive deterioration and memory impairment are commonly held beliefs about pregnant women; sometimes referred to as *baby-brain*. However, findings from a recent Australian prospective cohort study of women in their early 20s suggests these perceptions are unfounded, with no significant cognitive changes determined as a function of pregnancy or motherhood (Christensen, Leach, & MacKinnon, 2010). Despite the good news for young mothers, memory decline is an unfortunate reality for many people, and understanding it requires distinguishing different types of memory (chapter 7).

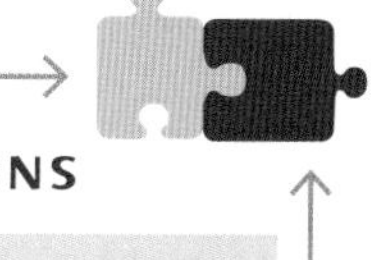

MAKING CONNECTIONS

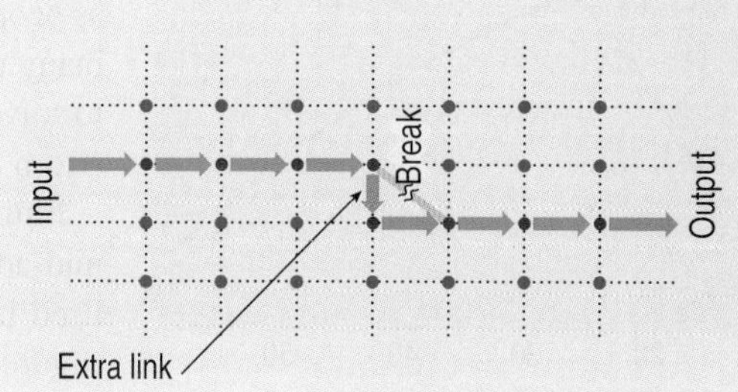

Connectionist models propose that when we perceive, think and remember, we activate networks of neurons that have been activated together in the past (chapter 8). Thus, connectionist models suggest one possible reason for slower reaction time with age: if a mental process or representation is distributed across a number of neurons that form a circuit, any small break that occurs with ageing will require additional steps to recomplete the circuit. Because every synaptic connection adds processing time, the more broken connections that amass over the years, the more time required to find alternative routes to carry out psychological processes.

SOURCE: Cerella (1990, p. 203).

Working memory

Older people do well on simple short-term storage tasks, such as remembering a string of digits (Hultsch & Dixon, 1990; Labouvie-Vief & Schell, 1982; see also Baudouin, Vanneste, Pouthas, & Isingrini, 2006). However, they show substantial deficits in complex working memory tasks, such as repeating a list of digits backwards, dealing with multiple tasks at once or dividing their attention between tasks (Einstein, Smith, McDaniel, & Shaw, 1997; Ponds, Brouwer, & Van Wolffelaar, 1988; Van Gerven, Meijer, & Jolles, 2007). These deficits translate into very practical problems, such as how to keep track of multiple cars at an intersection with a four-way stop. If neo-Piagetian theorists such as Robbie Case are right that the key to cognitive development in childhood is increased working memory capacity, then advanced ageing means development in reverse.

Indeed, neuroimageing studies find not only decreased activation of areas of the prefrontal cortex known to be involved in working memory in people in their 60s and older but also less efficient activation (Reuter-Lorenz & Stanczak, 2000; Rypma & D'Esposito, 2000). For example, older people show activation of both right and left hemispheres in verbal working memory tasks, which are lateralised to the left hemisphere in younger people (chapter 7).

Long-term memory

As for long-term memory, some aspects remain intact throughout the life span, whereas others decline. Although older people take more time to learn new information than younger people, given ample encoding time, their performance approaches that of younger participants (Perlmutter, 1983). Furthermore, if they are healthy, people continue to add to their knowledge base until the day they die; in this sense, people can add to their supply of 'wisdom' until their last breath (Horn & Hofer, 1992; Salthouse, 1992, 2000). Nor is implicit memory impaired with age, as assessed by tasks such as the tendency to complete a word stem (e.g. per-) with a previously primed word (e.g. perfume) (Gaudreau & Peretz, 1999; Russo & Parkin, 1993; Schacter, Cooper, & Valdiserri, 1992).

The problems older people have with long-term memory lie more in retrieving explicit memories than in either encoding new information or in learning or expressing knowledge implicitly. Although some studies find small declines in recognition memory (e.g. 'Did you see the word *dove* on the list presented a few minutes ago?'), older people have particular trouble in recall tasks (e.g. 'What words did you see on that list?').

If older people have trouble retrieving new information, do they 'live in the past'? Interestingly, the years between 10 and 30 seem to be peak years for storing significant episodic (autobiographical) memories (Rubin, Rahhal, & Poon, 1998). When older adults are asked to recall significant episodic memories (memories of events they have experienced), they tend to remember memories from that period more than other memories, and the memories they produce are more vivid. They also show greater semantic knowledge for facts such as current events and who won the Gold Logie or the World Cup during that period.

Everyday memory

Many researchers interested in everyday memory — memory as applied in everyday life (chapter 7) — have wondered whether the somewhat gloomy picture painted by some laboratory studies of memory in older people reflects the realities of their daily lives (see Blanchard-Fields & Chen, 1996).

In everyday tasks, changes in cognition appear to involve both gains and losses (Baltes, 1987, 1998). For example, when asked to remember the events of a story, middle-aged and older participants in one study remembered slightly fewer details of the story but were more likely than late adolescents (age 16 to 19) to get the 'gist' of it — that is, to encode and remember its meaning (Adams, 1991). This can be seen in people's work lives: an analysis of nearly 100 studies with a combined total of more than 38 000 participants found that the correlation between worker productivity and age is essentially zero (McEvoy

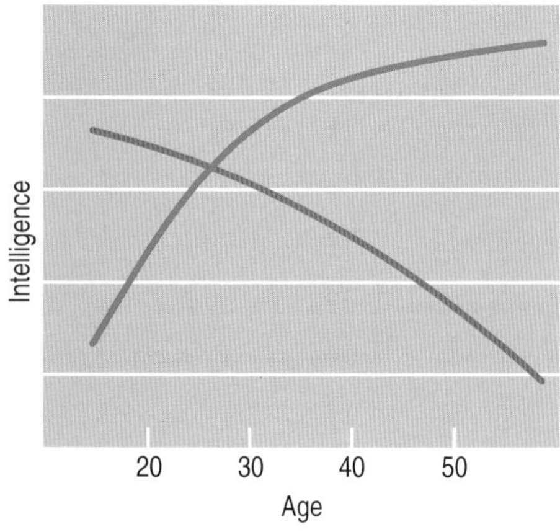

FIGURE 12.11
Fluid and crystallised intelligence throughout the life span. Unlike fluid intelligence, crystallised intelligence increases through at least the 40s and 50s and then levels off.

SOURCE: Horn and Hofer (1992, p. 79).

& Cascio, 1989). Older workers apparently compensate for declines in processing power with a larger knowledge base and alternative strategies for carrying out tasks (Baltes, 1987; Perlmutter et al., 1990).

Intelligence has many facets, and different aspects of intelligence change in different ways as people age. As we saw in chapter 9, fluid intelligence refers to intellectual capacities used in many forms of information processing (assessed by measures of speed of processing, ability to solve analogies etc.), whereas crystallised intelligence refers to people's store of knowledge (Horn & Cattell, 1967; Horn & Hofer, 1992; see also Carroll, 2003).

Fluid intelligence peaks in young adulthood and then levels off and begins declining by mid-adulthood, largely because of a decline in speed of processing. In contrast, crystallised intelligence increases throughout most of life, showing declines only in very old age (figure 12.11) (Horn, 1998; Horn & Hofer, 1992). In sum, intelligence is multifaceted and cumulative, and most of us would do well to be half as productive or creative at 20 or 30 as Picasso was at 90.

Individual differences in ageing and cognition

Many of the studies showing declines with ageing have been cross-sectional. A major limitation of these studies is that they can show, on average, how people fare at different ages, but they cannot show the proportion of people whose cognitive capacities decline. Statistically, if a sizable minority of older people show substantial cognitive deterioration, mean scores for their age group will be lower than for younger groups, leading to an apparent conclusion that intelligence declines with age. But longitudinal studies can ask a different question: of people in different age groups, how many actually deteriorate?

A major longitudinal project, called the Seattle Longitudinal Study (Schaie, 1990, 1994), provides an important corrective to a view of inevitable cognitive decline. The investigators followed a large sample ranging in age from 25 to 81 over several years, administering a battery of cognitive tests. The results were striking: most people do not show significant mental declines. Even on the average, intellectual functioning does not decline until the 60s and 70s (figure 12.12). In fact, cognitive decline can be an indicator of impending death: older people who begin to show signs of substantial psychomotor slowing and declines in crystallised intelligence are more likely to die in the next several years than those whose cognitive functioning remains relatively intact (Bosworth & Schaie, 1999).

APPLY + DISCUSS

Increasing numbers of older people are returning to universities to get or complete their education after retirement.

- Which tasks involved in obtaining a tertiary education would be most difficult for older people?
- At which tasks would they more likely excel?

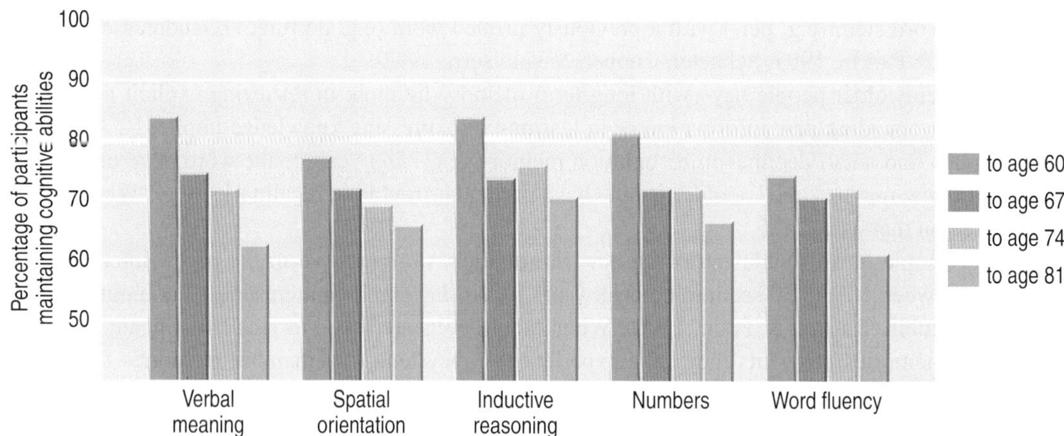

FIGURE 12.12
Cognitive stability over seven-year intervals. On five tests of mental ability, less than 25 percent of participants tested every seven years showed any decline prior to age 60. Even by age 81, over 60 percent of all participants showed stable cognitive functioning rather than decline.

SOURCE: Adapted from Schaie (1990, p. 297).

The Seattle study, like other longitudinal studies, shows that people differ tremendously in the way they age. People who are healthy and mentally active experience fewer mental declines than those who are not (Diamond, 1978; Horn & Meer, 1987; see also Koopman-Boyden & MacDonald, 2003; Salthouse, 2006). The 'use it or lose it' theory applies to mental functioning as much as to physical. B. F. Skinner, Pablo Picasso, Sigmund Freud, Eleanor Roosevelt, Jean Piaget and a host of other septagenarians and octogenarians have shown remarkable cognitive longevity in diverse fields.

Data from an 11-year longitudinal study of a large community sample found that 'using it' early in life may also be important for 'keeping it' later: people who had less than eight years of formal education showed substantially greater cognitive declines than those who had nine or more (Lyketsos, Chen, & Anthony, 1999). Having a certain amount of intellectual training early in life may reduce future deterioration.

The notion that there is wide variation in the experience of ageing is further supported by the results of an Australian longitudinal study of ageing in Adelaide. Andrews, Clark, and Luszez (2002) found that people who age most successfully tend to live longer and experience a better quality of life. Australian centenarian Dorothy De Low is an example of a person who has aged successfully. De Low, a World Veterans table tennis champion, received an Order of Australia medal when she was just shy of her 100th birthday for her service to the sport.

There is a wide variation in the experience of ageing. Centenarian Dorothy De Low, a World Veterans table tennis champion, received an Order of Australia medal after participating in the sport for more than 40 years.

Although most people function well for most or all of their lives, cognitive decline generally escalates in the mid-80s as the brain's hardware begins to wear out (Korten et al., 1997). A prime culprit appears to lie in the frontal lobes (Parkin & Java, 1999; Souchay, Isingrini, & Espagnet, 2000). Most cognitive tasks that involve bringing material to consciousness and manipulating it — from remembering a phone number to figuring out how to solve a novel problem to having that 'feeling of knowing' when asked whether this is the street to turn into — rely on an intact prefrontal cortex. As the frontal lobes begin to function less effectively, not only does working memory become impaired, as we have seen, but explicit memory and decision making decline or at best hold steady if the person finds alternative ways to compensate (see Parkin, Walter, & Hunkin, 1995; West, 1996). Neuroscientists have long suggested a simple maxim that applies to developmental gains in childhood and losses in late life: last in, first out. The frontal lobes are the last to mature in childhood and adolescence, and they seem to be among the first (and most) affected by normal ageing.

Ageing

One of the most pervasive myths about ageing is that old people lose their memory and their ability to think and reason — that is, they become 'senile' (Butler, 1975). In fact, in Australia, only about 1 percent of the population suffers progressive and incurable ***dementia***, a disorder marked by global disturbance of higher mental functions (Morris & Baddeley, 1988; Access Economics, 2009). Another 10 to 15 percent experience mild to moderate memory loss. The majority of people — around 80 percent — retain sharp mental functioning even through old age (Butler, 1984; Schaie, 1990; Wilbert, 2009). Furthermore, longitudinal research from Amsterdam indicates that although women show higher levels of memory functioning than men, there are no gender differences in the decline of cognitive functions (Aartsen, Martin, & Zimprich, 2004).

Organic brain disease, or what people often call senility, is far more prevalent among people in their 80s and 90s than among those in their 60s and 70s. Rates of dementia vary slightly across cultures but are everywhere linked to advancing age (Access Economics, 2006a; van Duijn, 1996). Even among people in their early 80s, however, only about 12 percent of males and 21 percent of females are affected by dementia (Access Economics, 2009).

Dementia has a variety of causes, including reduced blood supplies to the brain and exposure to toxins such as alcohol. Removing the toxic agent or bringing vitamin levels back to normal can help to reverse the dementia (Diagnose Me, 2010). Herbs have low toxicity and can also play a role in the early treatment of dementia (Gaeddert, 2010). Well over half the cases, however, are caused by ***Alzheimer's disease***, a progressive and incurable illness that destroys neurons in the brain, severely impairing memory, reasoning, perception, language and behaviour (see Ashford, Schmitt, & Kumar, 1996; Gilleard, 2000; Mclaughlin et al., 2010; Rosenzweig, 2008). The University of Otago in New Zealand has conducted research into the memory problems of people with Alzheimer's disease (see Smith & Knight, 2002). Although early warning signs (particularly decreased ability to think abstractly and to retain new information) may not be apparent to the naked eye, a longitudinal study of a community sample of more than a thousand people found that those who developed Alzheimer's showed subtle declines on neuropsychological tests a decade before developing overt symptoms (Elias et al., 2000).

Jorm (2001) points out that the ageing nature of Australia's population is highlighting dementia as a health problem. Jorm indicates that in 1995, Australia had a population of 18 million and approximately 130 000 people with dementia. In 2041, it is projected that Australia will have 25 million people, and approximately 460 000 with dementia. As a result, while the total population will have increased by 40 percent, the number with dementia will have grown by more than 350 percent. That is because the 'very elderly' segment — those people most at risk of developing dementia — is the fastest growing segment of the population. By 2050, the number of people with dementia in Australia is expected to exceed 1.13 million — representing 2.9 percent of total population in capital cities, and 3.8 percent of total population in rural and regional areas (Alzheimer's Australia, 2009).

Consequently, the Australian government has initiated various policies and programs designed to address the health-related problems of ageing in a multicultural society. Such reforms are intended to include indigenous people; however, the issues surrounding aged-care provision for Aboriginal and Torres Strait Islanders require careful deliberation (Pollitt, 1997). For example, assessing and diagnosing dementia in indigenous communities, especially among people who follow more traditional ways of life, and providing services to sufferers and their carers need to be managed in a way that ensures the specific mental health needs of indigenous peoples are adequately met (Pollitt, 1997; chapter 19). Of concern in rural and remote areas of Western Australia is a rate of dementia within some indigenous communities of 12.4 percent; more than four times that of the general population rate of dementia, which is 2.6 percent affected (Broe et al., 2009).

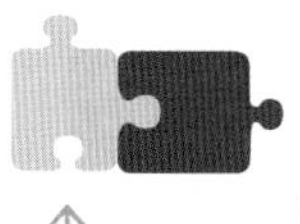

MAKING CONNECTIONS

Numerous myths exist about mental health and ageing. Therefore, in the spirit of the Discovery Channel's series *MythBusters*, it is time to debunk some myths about mental health and ageing.

- *Myth:* Schizophrenia affects only younger people. *Fact:* Although schizophrenia is most commonly diagnosed between the late teens and early 30s, experts agree that approximately 23 percent of all people with schizophrenia have an onset after age 40 (see Ballas, 2007; Hirsch & Weinberger, 2003).
- *Myth:* Mental illness, particularly depression, is more common in older adults. *Fact:* People can experience depression at any stage of their life, with prevalence rates tending to decrease as we get older.
- *Myth:* Older adults do not benefit from treatment. *Fact:* Treatment is tailored to fit the individual case (chapters 15 and 16; Pachana, 2006).

The characteristic changes in brain tissue in Alzheimer's include tangled neurons and protein deposits that disrupt the functioning of cells in the cortex. Alzheimer's patients also have abnormally low levels of several neurotransmitters, most importantly acetylcholine, which plays a central role in memory functioning (Coull & Sahakian, 2000). Recent neuroimaging research has found a direct correlation between the extent of damage in the temporal lobes, particularly the hippocampus and axons connecting it to the cortex, and the degree of cognitive impairment in Alzheimer's patients, which makes sense in the light of the pervasive effects of the disease on explicit memory (Bierer et al., 1995). The result of lesions to this area may be difficulty in remembering what happened moments earlier — or remembering which story the affected individual just told.

Alzheimer's disease may have several different causes, but at least one major form of the disorder is genetic (Coyle, 1991; Nussbaum & Ellis, 2003; Rosenberg, 2003; Williams, 2003; see also Bertram, McQueen, Mullin, Blacker, & Tanzi, 2007). Researchers have isolated genes on at least three chromosomes implicated in the genetic transmission of Alzheimer's. One form of the disease has been linked to a defect on chromosome 21 (Holland & Oliver, 1995; Myllykangas et al., 2005), the chromosome implicated in Down syndrome, a form of mental disability (chapter 9). Down syndrome patients who live into late middle age often develop symptoms and neurological changes similar to Alzheimer's disease.

INTERIM SUMMARY

Cognitive declines in later life tend to be selective rather than global. Processing speed decreases; working memory capacity declines; explicit memory retrieval becomes more difficult; problem-solving strategies become less efficient; and fluid intelligence declines. Other functions show little or no noticeable decline, including many encoding processes, implicit memory, aspects of everyday memory and crystallised intelligence. People also show tremendous variability in the way their minds change with ageing. About 1 percent of the Australian population suffers progressive and incurable ***dementia***, a disorder marked by global disturbance of higher mental functions. The most common cause of dementia is ***Alzheimer's disease***.

Central questions revisited

◆ The nature of development

This chapter began with three questions about development: What are the relative contributions of nature and nurture? To what extent is development characterised by critical or sensitive periods? And to what extent is development stagelike or continuous? All three questions address the way maturational, cultural and environmental forces interact over time to create an organism capable of responding adaptively to its social and physical environment.

Maturational factors provide both the possibilities and limits of physical and cognitive development. Young children cannot think in the abstract ways that adolescents can about justice, God or conservation of matter. Maturation of the frontal lobes permits a new kind of thinking that may well be described as a new 'stage'. Old people cannot think as quickly as their younger counterparts, and in their ninth or tenth decades, they may become much less efficient in their thinking. In both young and old, the nervous system determines the range within which people can function. Except in cases of mental disability or severe neural degeneration, however, that range is extraordinarily large. Experience, genetics and physical health all play a substantial part in determining where in that range people find themselves.

Even this conclusion — that neural hardware constrains the kind of 'software' that can be run on it — does not tell the whole story because, as we have seen, the hardware changes in response to the environment. Although the nervous system establishes certain constraints on and possibilities for cognitive functioning, the nervous system is itself partially a product of its environment. Experience can enrich the developing brain, increasing the connections among neurons that underlie the capacity for complex thought, just as impoverished experience, particularly during sensitive periods of development, can constrain psychological functioning by limiting the processing power of the brain. The human brain evolved to 'assume' certain basic experiences, such as caregivers who speak. Without these experiences, the brain will compensate as best it can, but it is unlikely to do so with the efficiency of a nervous system that got the right environmental input at the right time.

Understanding development thus means living with ambiguities. Perhaps that is a developmental achievement in itself.

◆

SUMMARY

1 Basic issues in developmental psychology

- ***Developmental psychology*** studies the way humans develop and change over time. A life-span developmental perspective examines both constancy and change, and gains and losses in functioning, that occur at different points over the human life cycle.
- Three basic issues confront developmental psychologists. The first concerns the relative roles of nature (particularly genetically programmed ***maturation***) and nurture. The second is the relative importance of early experience and whether human development is characterised by ***critical*** or ***sensitive periods***. The third issue is the extent to which development occurs in ***stages*** — relatively discrete steps through which everyone progresses in the same sequence — or whether it is continuous or gradual.

2 Three types of research design

- Developmental psychologists rely on three types of research design. ***Cross-sectional studies*** compare groups of different-aged participants at a single time to see if differences exist among them. ***Longitudinal studies*** follow the same individuals over time and thus can directly assess age changes rather than age differences. ***Sequential studies*** minimise the confounding variable of cohort by studying multiple cohorts longitudinally.

3 Physical development and its psychological consequences

- Prenatal (before birth) development is divided into three stages: the germinal, embryonic and foetal periods. Prenatal development can be disrupted by harmful environmental agents known as ***teratogens***, such as alcohol.
- Neural development, both prenatally and throughout childhood, proceeds through myelination, trimming back of neurons and increasing dendritic connections.
- Physical development and psychological development are intertwined. At birth, an infant possesses many adaptive reflexes. Motor development follows a universal maturational sequence, although cross-cultural research indicates that the environment can affect the pace of development. By the end of adolescence, physical growth is virtually complete. With ageing comes a gradual decline in physical and sensory abilities with which people must cope psychologically.

4 Cognitive development in infancy, childhood and adolescence

- For many years, psychologists underestimated the substantial abilities of infants. Researchers now know, for example, that babies are capable of ***intermodal*** understanding — the ability to associate sensations about an object from different senses and to match their own actions to behaviours they observe visually — in the earliest days of life.
- Piaget proposed that children develop knowledge by inventing, or constructing, a reality out of their own experience. According to Piaget, people cognitively adapt to their environment through two interrelated processes. ***Assimilation*** means interpreting actions or events in terms of one's present schemas; that is, fitting reality into one's previous ways of thinking. ***Accommodation*** involves modifying schemas to fit reality.
- Piaget proposed a stage theory of cognitive development. During the ***sensorimotor stage***, thought primarily takes the form of perception and action. Gradually, children acquire ***object permanence***, recognising that objects exist in time and space independent of their actions on or observation of them. Sensorimotor children are extremely ***egocentric***, or thoroughly embedded in their own point of view. The ***preoperational stage*** is characterised by the emergence of symbolic thought. Operations are mental actions the individual can use to manipulate, transform and return an object of knowledge to its original state. Piaget called the third stage the ***concrete operational stage*** because at this point children can operate on, or mentally manipulate, internal representations of concrete objects in ways that are reversible. The concrete operational child understands ***conservation*** — the idea that basic properties of an object or situation remain stable even though superficial properties may change. The ***formal operational stage*** is characterised by the ability to reason about formal propositions rather than concrete events.
- In its broadest outlines, such as the movement from concrete, egocentric thought to abstract thought, Piaget's theory appears to be accurate. Psychologists have, however, criticised Piaget for underestimating the capacities of younger children, assuming too much consistency across domains, and downplaying the influence of culture.
- Lev Vygotsky's sociocultural theory of cognitive development emphasises the role of social interaction in learning. Vygotsky's model proposes children collaborate and strive together on tasks to enhance their levels of understanding. Children also learn by imitating, watching and listening to parents and other significant people in their social worlds. Thus, Vygotsky's ***zone of proximal development (ZPD)*** stretches from sole performance to collaborative cooperation. According to the ZPD, children will achieve more understanding by socialising cooperatively with a skilled partner (adult or cognitively advanced peer) than by working alone.
- The information-processing approach to cognitive development focuses on the development of different aspects of cognition. Several variables that develop over time are children's ***knowledge base***, their ***automatisation*** of processing, their ability to use cognitive strategies and their metacognitive abilities (understanding their own thinking processes).
- Integrative, or ***neo-Piagetian***, theories attempt to wed stage conceptions with research on information processing and domain-specific knowledge.

5 Cognitive change in adulthood

- As with muscle strength, the rule-of-thumb with intellectual ability is use it or lose it: mental capacities atrophy with disuse.
- Although many cognitive functions decline in later life, substantial intellectual decline occurs in only a minority of people. The most common declines with age are ***psychomotor slowing***; difficulty with explicit memory retrieval; and decreased speed and efficiency of problem solving. Whereas fluid intelligence (intellectual capacities used in processing many kinds of information) begins to decline gradually in midlife, crystallised intelligence (the person's store of knowledge) continues to expand over the life span.
- ***Dementia*** is a disorder marked by global disturbance of higher mental functions. Well over half the cases of dementia result from ***Alzheimer's disease***, a progressive and incurable illness that destroys neurons in the brain, severely impairing memory, reasoning, perception, language and behaviour.

KEY TERMS

accommodation, *p. 484*
ageism, *p. 478*
Alzheimer's disease, *p. 495*
assimilation, *p. 484*
automatisation, *p. 489*
centration, *p. 485*
cohort effects, *p. 471*
concrete operational stage, *p. 486*
conservation, *p. 486*
critical periods, *p. 467*
cross-sectional studies, *p. 470*
dementia, *p. 495*
developmental psychology, *p. 466*
egocentric, *p. 485*
equilibration, *p. 484*
foetal alcohol syndrome, *p. 473*
formal operational stage, *p. 487*
infantile amnesia, *p. 481*
intermodal processing, *p. 479*
knowledge base, *p. 490*
longitudinal studies, *p. 471*
maturation, *p. 466*
metacognition, *p. 490*
metamemory, *p. 490*
neo-Piagetian theorists, *p. 491*
object permanence, *p. 485*
operations, *p. 486*
preoperational stage, *p. 485*
presbycusis, *p. 477*
psychomotor slowing, *p. 492*
puberty, *p. 476*
schema, *p. 484*
sensitive periods, *p. 469*
sensorimotor stage, *p. 484*
sequential studies, *p. 471*
stages, *p. 470*
structure of thought, *p. 484*
teratogens, *p. 473*
zone of proximal development (ZPD), *p. 489*

REVIEW QUESTIONS

1. Describe the contributions of nature and nurture to development.
2. Differentiate between assimilation and accommodation, providing examples to illustrate.
3. Define the terms *object permanence* and *conservation*, outlining the periods during which each occurs in Piaget's theory of cognitive development.
4. Describe perceptual and cognitive development in infancy.
5. Describe the information-processing approach to cognitive development.

DISCUSSION QUESTIONS

1. What is the impact of early deprivation or abuse on development?
2. Does development occur in stages or is it continuous?
3. Are people destined to lose their memories and faculties in old age?

APPLICATION QUESTIONS

1. Test your understanding of the various research designs used to study development by identifying each of the following scenarios as an example of one of the following studies: cross-sectional, longitudinal or sequential.
   (a) A professor examined the effectiveness of TV quit smoking advertisements in promoting positive health behaviours among teenagers. She examined a group of adolescents at age 13 and followed them up four years later. At the same time, she added another group of 13-year-old teenagers to her sample. She intends to follow up both groups in another four years' time.
   (b) A researcher investigated the effects of divorce on children. She interviewed 1000 mothers with newborn babies in the first week of January 1995, and again in 2005 when their children were 10. Follow-up interviews were done in all families, including intact families and those families that had experienced a separation or divorce. She will interview these same mothers and children again in 2015.
   (c) A professor undertook a nationwide survey of alcohol and marijuana use among adolescents. He compared different samples of teenagers defined by age, gender, ethnicity and geographical location.
2. Test your understanding of Piaget's theory by identifying each of the following scenarios as an example of one of the following stages of cognitive development: sensorimotor, preoperational, concrete operational and formal operational.
   (a) Quan and Luke spend all morning trying to 'crack the code' of a complex, interactive computer game.
   (b) Ryan watches his father transfer orange juice from a tall, skinny glass into a short, round glass. 'Where did all the orange juice go?' asks Ryan.
   (c) Olivia started crying because she thought her father had disappeared, when in fact he had just put on his Santa beard and hat.
   (d) Basmah's grandma shows her a bunch of nine roses and three daisies and asks her, 'Are there more roses or more flowers?' Basmah responds by saying, 'There are more flowers, Grandma.'

The solutions to the application questions can be found on page 835.

MULTIMEDIA RESOURCES

The *Cyberpsych* multimedia resource is available *as an option* to accompany this textbook to further develop your understanding of many key psychology concepts. *Cyberpsych* contains a wealth of rich media content and activities, and for this chapter includes:

- video clips on Alzheimer's disease, painkillers, foetal alcohol syndrome, hearing problems, preschool language comprehension, Down syndrome, genes and MRI scans for memory loss
- video case studies on dementia, teenage brain development and ageing
- an interactive module on Piaget's stages of cognitive development.

Social development

13

LEARNING OBJECTIVES

After studying this chapter you should be able to:

1 explain the importance of attachment in early development

2 describe the socialisation process

3 describe the role of peer relationships in social development

4 explain how social cognition develops across the life span

5 distinguish between the different theories of moral development

6 describe how social development continues throughout life.

Attachment

- *Attachment* refers to the enduring emotional ties children from with their primary caregivers; it includes a desire for proximity to an attached figure, a sense of security derived from the person's presence and feelings of distress when the person is absent.
- Four patterns of infant attachment: ***secure*** (seek comfort from attachment figure), ***avoidant*** (shut off their needs for attachment), ***ambivalent*** (have difficulty being soothed) and ***disorganised*** (behave in contradictory ways that reflect their difficulty predicting or understanding the way their attachment figures will behave).
- Attachment security in infancy predicts social competence as well as school grades from preschool through to adolescence.

Peer relationships

- Friendship patterns develop substantially in childhood and adolescence, from largely same-sex experiences involving mutual play to more intimate interactions in adolescence.
- The way parents behave with their children and relationships with siblings both contribute to a child's socialisation.

Socialisation

- *Socialisation* is the process by which children learn the rules, beliefs, values, skills, attitudes and behaviour patterns of their society.
- Four parenting styles: ***authoritarian*** parents (place high value on obedience and respect for authority), ***permissive*** parents (impose minimal controls on their children), ***authoritative*** parents (enforce standards but explain their views and encourage verbal give-and-take) and ***uninvolved*** parents (consistently place their own needs above the needs of their child).
- Cultural practices affect virtually every aspect of socialisation, such as the relative importance placed on independence and autonomy.
- Among the most powerful roles into which people are socialised are ***gender roles***, which specify the range of behaviours considered appropriate for males and females.

Development of social cognition

- Children develop in their ***social cognition*** — their understanding of themselves, others and relationships — over time.
- Throughout early childhood, children tend to think of themselves and others in relatively concrete ways, such as their age, gender, group membership and possessions. Around age eight, they begin to think more about enduring personality attributes. By adolescence, social cognition is more subtle and abstract.
- ***Perspective-taking*** — the ability to understand other people's perspectives or viewpoints — increases steadily throughout childhood and adolescence.
- ***Gender constancy*** — knowledge that gender cannot be altered by changes in appearance or activities — develops over time.

Moral development

- ***Cognitive theories***, including those of Piaget and Kohlberg, stress the role of thought and learning in moral development.
- Other theories, including the ***psychodynamic theory***, emphasise empathy, or feeling for another person who is hurting.
- Moral development probably reflects an interaction of cognitive and affective changes that allow children to understand and feel for other people as well as inhibit their own wishes and impulses.

Social development across the life span

- Erikson proposed a model of ***psychosocial stages*** — stages in the development of the person as a social being. At each of eight stages, the individual faces a ***developmental task***, a challenge that is normative for that period of life, as follows:
  - *Basic trust versus mistrust* — infants come to trust others or perceive the social world as hostile or unreliable.
  - *Autonomy versus shame and doubt* — toddlers come to experience themselves as independent sources of will and power or feel insecure in their newfound skills.
  - *Initiative versus guilt* — young children develop the capacity to form and carry out plans, but their emerging conscience can render them vulnerable to guilt.
  - *Industry versus inferiority* — school-age children develop a sense of competence but may suffer from feelings of inadequacy.
  - *Identity versus identity confusion* — the task in adolescence is to establish a stable sense of who one is and what one values.
  - *Intimacy versus isolation* — during young adulthood the task is to establish enduring, committed relationships.
  - *Generativity versus stagnation* — middle-aged individuals attempt to pass something on to the next generation.
  - *Integrity versus despair* — people look back on their lives with a sense of satisfaction or sadness and regret.
- In all likelihood, 'crises' in both adolescence and at midlife depend on individual differences and cultural and historical circumstances. Although old age inevitably involves many losses, the realities appear far better than the negative stereotypes of ageing seen in many technologically developed societies.

Central questions: nature and nurture, cognition and emotion

- ◆ Genetics play a commanding role in human development, shaping the way people develop and change in general as well as the way people differ from one another. But genes are only expressed in environmental contexts, and they can be turned on and off by experience.

WHEN 17-year-old Melbourne boy Allem Halkic took his own life in August 2009, it pushed the new phenomenon of cyber bullying firmly into the national spotlight. In the day before his suicide, Allem had been subjected to a series of SMS messages from a former friend, taunting him about his relationship with a girl. That friend subsequently became the first person in Australia charged with cyber stalking, and he received an 18-month community service order for the nasty SMS attacks. That cyber-bullying episode had tragic consequences. Video-sharing websites have also carried numerous examples of schoolchildren filmed bashing and kicking other children in seemingly random attacks, launched purely to be recorded and uploaded to the site. The videos of this bullying behaviour have been proudly overdubbed with music and with graphics glorifying the mindless violence.

Bullying has long been a problem in the schoolyard, but digital technology has opened up a whole new world of communication possibilities and practices that make it even harder for victims to escape. Smartphones give people an instant and uninterrupted connection to the world, via the internet and social media applications, or simply via SMS or mobile phone calls.

Digital technology has opened up a new world of communication possibilities that have coincided with an increase in divergent and pervasive childhood bullying tactics. Some children and adolescents are victimised by their peers via the internet and social media applications.

Being filmed on a mobile phone camera brawling with another child seems like a totally irrational exercise. So why do it? For some, it could be the thought of instant fame, with a video posted for a worldwide audience to see. For others, it may be about creating an image as a tough guy. And why is this phenomenon largely confined to schoolchildren? Why don't groups of middle-aged people and senior citizens demonstrate the same behaviour? The answer lies in what we call ***social development*** — changes in interpersonal thought, feeling and behaviour throughout the life span. Cyber-bullying episodes may be as much about a teenager's attempts to understand and fit in with peer groups as they are about any animosity towards the victim. They may feel it's the way to impress others and show their toughness. On the other hand, middle-aged or senior citizens are much more certain of their place in the world and in their peer relationships.

We begin by discussing the earliest relationships — between an infant and her caregivers — and consider how, and how much, these relationships lay the groundwork for later relationships. Next, we examine how children learn the ways of their culture. For example, how and when do children take on the attributes expected of their gender? Then we explore children's relationships with friends and siblings, their changing conceptions of themselves and others, and their developing capacity for moral judgement and action. We conclude by expanding the focus to the entire life span. Although the range of topics may seem enormous, what unites them is a focus on the types of relationships people form throughout life, from intimate attachments in infancy through to adulthood, to sibling and peer relationships; the development of beliefs and feelings about themselves and others; and the way these beliefs and feelings are expressed in different social contexts.

Throughout, we will address two central questions. The first, raised in chapter 12, has provided a consistent thread across psychological research for over a century: the question of nature and nurture. What are the relative contributions of innate characteristics, culture and experience to social development? How do evolutionary, biological and social pressures converge to create a social person? The second question is, what is the relationship between social development and cognitive development? To what extent does the development of children's experience of friendship, morality or gender depend on their cognitive development?

Central questions

- What are the roles of nature and nurture in social development? How do biology, culture and experience shape the developing person?
- To what extent does social development depend on cognitive development?

Attachment

In the middle of the twentieth century, psychoanalysts observed that children reared in large institutional homes, with minimal stimulation and no consistent contact with a loving caregiver, often became emotionally unstable, lacking in conscience or mentally impaired. Now, many of these children would be classified as suffering from reactive attachment disorder. These observations led to recognition of the importance of ***attachment***, the enduring ties of affection that children form with their primary caregivers (Ainsworth & Bell, 1970; Bowlby, 1969). Attachment includes a desire for proximity to an attachment figure, a sense of security derived from the person's presence and feelings of distress when the person is absent. Attachment is not unilateral; rather, it involves an interaction between two people who react to each other's signals.

Attachment in infancy

For many years, psychoanalysts and behaviourists were in rare agreement on the origins of attachment behaviour, both linking it to feeding. Psychoanalysts assumed that the gratification of oral needs led infants to become attached to people who satisfy those needs. According to behaviourists, mothers became secondary reinforcers through their association with food, which is a primary (innate) reinforcer (chapter 6). Unfortunately, the two theories were similar in one other respect: they were both wrong. Definitive evidence came from a series of classic experiments performed by Harry Harlow (Harlow & Zimmerman, 1959).

Harlow reared infant rhesus monkeys in isolation from their mothers for several months and then placed them in a cage with two inanimate surrogate 'mothers' (chapter 2). One, a wire monkey that provided no warmth or softness, held a bottle from which the infant could nurse. The other was covered with towelling to provide softness, but it had no bottle, so it could not provide food. Baby monkeys spent much of their time clinging to the softer mother. They would also run to the softer surrogate when they were frightened, but they virtually ignored the wire surrogate except when hungry. Harlow's findings established that perceived security, not food, is the crucial element in forming attachment relationships in primates; he referred to the ties that bind an infant to its caregivers as ***contact comfort***. Some infants and children are raised with little or no human contact. These children, called feral children, basically raise themselves in the wild, and show predictable deficits in physical, social and language development. They derive their name from the suggestion that some of these children are 'adopted' by wolves and raised with them. One of the most famous instances of feral children is Victor of Aveyron (Wild Boy of Aveyron).

MAKING CONNECTIONS

Bowlby's model of attachment (discussed later in this section) relies on the concept of **homoeostasis** — the tendency of biological organisms to monitor variables relevant to survival, detect deviations from these goals (feedback) and respond with corrective mechanisms (chapter 10) The child's goal is to remain physically close to the attachment figure. When this goal is threatened, as when a toddler's mother leaves the room, the child experiences a feedback signal: distress. Distress motivates the child to cry or search for his mother. If either behaviour is successful, the child receives a sense of security that temporarily deactivates the attachment system. A similar system operates in adults. For example, social anxiety is viewed as an interrupt mechanism, alerting individuals that they are behaving in ways that may jeopardise the degree to which they are included with (i.e. attached to) others.

Bowlby's theory of attachment

John Bowlby (1969, 1973, 1982), who developed attachment theory, linked Harlow's findings to the psychodynamic literature on children reared in institutional settings. Bowlby was both a psychoanalyst and an ethologist (a scientist interested in comparative animal behaviour), and he proposed an evolutionary theory of attachment. He argued that attachment behaviour is prewired in humans, as is similar behaviour in other animal species, to keep immature animals close to their parents.

Bowlby noted the relationship between human attachment behaviour and a phenomenon studied by the ethologist Konrad Lorenz (1935) called imprinting. ***Imprinting*** is the tendency of young animals of certain species to follow an animal to which they were exposed during a sensitive period early in their lives (figure 13.1; see overleaf). According to Lorenz (1937), imprinting confers an evolutionary advantage: a gosling that stays close to its mother or father is more likely to be fed, protected from predators and taught skills useful for survival and reproduction than a gosling that strays from its parents. Bowlby argued that attachment behaviour in human infants, such as staying close to parents and crying loudly in their absence, evolved for the same reasons.

Normally, imprinting leads young animals to follow an adult member of their species. At times, however, Mother Nature may lead her children astray. Here, geese follow Konrad Lorenz, on whom they imprinted when young.

Thus, when a child feels threatened, the attachment system 'turns on', leading the child to cry or search for its attachment figure. Once the child feels safe again, she is free to play or explore the environment. The attachment figure thus becomes a safe base from which the child can explore

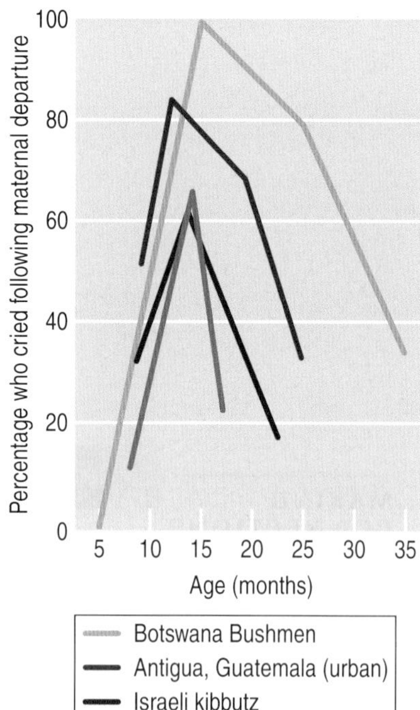

FIGURE 13.1
Separation anxiety across cultures. Separation anxiety, as measured by the percentage of children who cry when separated from their mother, peaks at approximately the same time across various cultures.

SOURCE: Kagan (1983). Copyright © 1983 by Center for Advanced Study in the Behavioral Sciences. Reprinted with permission of The McGraw-Hill Companies.

(Ainsworth, 1979) and to whom he can periodically return for 'emotional refuelling' (Mahler, Pine, & Bergman, 1975). Toddlers who are playing happily often suddenly look around to establish the whereabouts of their attachment figures. Once they locate their caregiver or even run to a comforting lap, they return to play, refuelled for the next period of time. Later in life, a university student's phone calls home may serve a similar function.

The origins of attachment

Attachment behaviour emerges gradually over the first several months of life, peaking some time during the second year and then diminishing in intensity as children become more confident in their independence (Ainsworth, 1967). Among the first precursors of attachment is a general preference for social stimuli (such as faces) over other objects in the environment (Carver et al., 2003). Visual recognition of the mother (the primary caregiver studied in most research) occurs at about three months (Olson, 1981); by five or six months, infants recognise and greet their mothers and other attachment figures from across the room.

At six to seven months, infants begin to show ***separation anxiety***, distress at separation from their attachment figures. Separation anxiety emerges about the same time in children of different cultures (figure 13.1), despite widely different child-rearing practices (Kagan, 1983; see also Kochanska, Aksan, & Joy, 2007). Similarly, blind children show a comparable pattern (although the onset is a few months later), becoming anxious when they no longer hear the familiar sounds of their mother's voice or movements (Fraiberg, 1975). These data suggest a maturational basis for separation anxiety. In fact, separation anxiety emerges about the same time infants begin to crawl, which makes sense from an evolutionary perspective.

Basic attachment mechanisms appear very similar in human and other primates.

INTERIM SUMMARY

Social development involves changes in interpersonal thought, feeling and behaviour throughout the life span. ***Attachment*** refers to the enduring ties children form with their primary caregivers; it includes a desire for proximity to an attachment figure, a sense of security derived from the person's presence and feelings of distress when the person is absent. John Bowlby, who developed attachment theory, argued that attachment, like ***imprinting*** (the tendency of young animals to follow another animal to which they were exposed during a sensitive period), evolved as a mechanism for keeping infants close to their parents while they are immature and vulnerable.

Individual differences in attachment patterns

Bowlby observed that young children typically exhibit a sequence of behaviours in response to separations from their attachment figures. They initially protest by crying or throwing tantrums. However, they may ultimately become detached and indifferent to the attachment figure if they are gone too long.

Attachment patterns

Bowlby's colleague Mary Ainsworth recognised that children vary in their responses to separation: while some seem secure in their relationship with their attachment figure, others seem perpetually stuck in protest or detachment. Ainsworth demonstrated these differences among infants using an experimental procedure called the Strange Situation. In the Strange Situation, the mother leaves her young child (aged 12 to 18 months) alone in a room of toys. Next, the child is joined for a brief time by a friendly stranger. The mother then returns and greets the child (Ainsworth, 1973, 1979, 1991).

Ainsworth found that children tend to respond to their mothers' absence and return in one of three ways, one of which she called secure, and the others, insecure. Infants who welcome the mother's return and seek closeness to her have a ***secure attachment style***. Infants who ignore the mother when she returns display an ***avoidant attachment style***, whereas infants who are angry and rejecting while simultaneously indicating a clear desire to be close to the mother have an ***ambivalent attachment style*** (also sometimes called anxious-ambivalent or resistant). Avoidant children often seem relatively unfazed by their mother's departure, whereas ambivalent children become very upset.

Other research with infants in high-risk samples, such as those who have been maltreated, has uncovered another variant of insecure attachment, called disorganised, or disorganised-disoriented (Lyons-Ruth, Easterbrooks, & Cibelli, 1997; Main & Solomon, 1986; see also Lyons-Ruth & Spielman, 2004). Children with a ***disorganised attachment style*** behave in contradictory ways, indicating helpless efforts to elicit soothing responses from the attachment figure. Disorganised infants often approach the mother while simultaneously gazing away, or appear disoriented, as manifested in stereotyped rocking and dazed facial expressions. Whereas the other attachment patterns seem organised and predictable, the disorganised child's behaviour is difficult to understand and typically comes in the context of parenting that is itself unpredictable, and hence difficult to understand from the infant's point of view (see Carlson, 1998). Research findings suggest that at least 15 percent of infants from *normal* environments develop disorganised attachment behaviour, with much higher percentages likely in cases involving maltreatment (van Ijzendoorn, Schuengel, & Bakermans-Kranenburg, 1999).

Secure attachment is the most commonly observed attachment pattern around the world (see Main, 1990; van Ijzendoorn & Kroonenberg, 1988). Nevertheless, the frequency of different styles of attachment differs substantially across cultures. For example, infants reared on Israeli kibbutzim (collective living arrangements) are much more likely to have ambivalent attachments to their mothers than infants in the West. Other research has highlighted how attachment theory is laden with Western values and meaning. For example, Rothbaum, Weisz, Pott, Miyake, and Morelli's (2000) influential work on cross-cultural studies of attachment showed three core hypotheses of attachment theory — caregiver sensitivity, competence, and secure base — that are culturally specific. Yeo (2003) later examined this theory with Australian Aboriginal children and showed cultural differences in the way these three core hypotheses are expressed. Yeo argued that attachment in Aboriginal children should be defined in terms of the historical context, spirituality and cultural values of the Aboriginal people.

Development is, notably, a lifelong process (see Noller, Feeney, & Peterson, 2001; Peterson, 2009). However, an infant's initial emotional bond of attachment shared with a primary caregiver is of particular importance. The initial infant – primary caregiver bond is pivotal in both promoting optimal relationship development during life and in maximising infant wellbeing (Ainsworth, 1991; Noller et al., 2001; Peterson, 2004). Parental contributions to infants' emotional attachments have been widely studied, with Australian research (Harrison & Ungerer, 2002) showing that maternal sensitivity in the caregiving role is a key determinant of infant attachment security. This research also considered how parental employment and use of childcare influence attachment formation, and a correlation between the timing of the mother's return to paid employment and attachment security was identified. Australian mothers who had returned to work within five months of the birth and who were committed to their work while pregnant were more likely to have securely attached infants.

APPLY + DISCUSS

Separation anxiety appears to rely on evolved mechanisms.

- Under what environmental conditions might separation anxiety not emerge? Would children in orphanages whose caregivers are inconsistent or who do not provide comfort develop separation anxiety?
- If the normal appearance of separation distress requires the presence of an attachment figure, can we call separation anxiety 'innate'? Do innate capacities sometimes — or most of the time — require environmental input to develop?

Internal working models of relationships

MAKING CONNECTIONS

The concept of internal working models of relationships dovetails with other constructs psychologists have used to describe mental representations. **Mental models** are representations of how things work (chapter 8). **Schemas** are enduring ways of processing information about an object of thought, such as the self and relationships (chapters 7 and 17). **Object representations** are representations of self, others and relationships, such as the malevolent representations of relationships that characterise individuals with borderline personality disorder, whose emotions tend to spiral out of control (chapters 11 and 15).

Attachment does not just refer to a pattern of behaviour. Bowlby proposed that infants develop ***internal working models***, or mental representations of attachment relationships that form the basis for expectations in close relationships (Bowlby, 1969, 1982; Bretherton, 1990; Main, 1995; Stevenson-Hinde & Verschueren, 2002; see also Lamb, 2005). For example, a child whose early attachment to her mother is marked by extreme anxiety resulting from inconsistent or abusive caretaking may form a working model of herself as unlovable or unworthy. She may also see significant others as hostile or unpredictable. Her behaviour will appear disorganised or disoriented because she cannot form a coherent working model or representation of her relationship with her mother that both makes sense and provides a feeling of security.

The concept of internal working models may help explain why infants and toddlers who are secure with one caretaker may not be secure with another (Howes & Hamilton, 1992; Verschueren & Marcoen, 1999). A child's experience with one person, such as the mother, may feel secure, while another relationship (such as with a father or preschool teacher) may feel less comfortable or predictable because the child has different internal working models of the relationships. The concept of internal working models may also help explain why attachment classification in infancy predicts not only social but cognitive variables years later, such as the ability to sustain attention: infants who feel safe and secure will have more freedom to explore their environment than insecure infants, whose time and attention are more likely to be consumed by attachment-related thoughts, feelings and motivations.

FROM BRAIN TO BEHAVIOUR

Temperament, experience and their interaction in the development of attachment styles

Why do infants differ in their patterns of attachment? Some researchers emphasise temperament; others emphasise the way caregivers respond to the infant. Both appear to influence attachment security, along with an important interaction between the two: the fit between the child and parent (Belsky & Isabella, 1988; Rosen & Rothbaum, 1993; Seifer, Schiller, Samerof, Resnick, & Riordan, 1996; see also Burgess, Marshall, Rubin, & Fox, 2003; Ferris, McGauley, & Hughes, 2004).

Like all psychological processes, attachment can be understood in part at a psychobiological level. Attachment-related behaviour, such as protest at separation, probably does not occur in the first six months of life because myelination of neurons has not sufficiently progressed in limbic structures that regulate emotional distress, particularly fear and anxiety (Konner, 1991). Protest, distress and despair at separation after that time appear to be mediated by several neurotransmitter systems, notably dopamine, norepinephrine and serotonin, which are involved in arousal, anxiety and depression (Kraemer, 1992). For example, monkeys separated from their mothers show elevated norepinephrine levels, which are consistent with behavioural responses indicating distress. (Attachment is a two-way affair: rhesus monkey mothers separated from their newborn infants similarly show elevated stress hormones for days; Champoux & Suomi, 1994.)

These normal neurotransmitter responses to separation can be altered in monkeys either pharmacologically, using chemicals that disrupt neural transmission, or through abnormal rearing, in which the infant is removed from the mother at birth and reared in isolation or with peers. Abnormal rearing conditions alter neuronal development in the cortex, cerebellum and limbic system in monkeys, a suggestion that environmental events can produce lasting biological changes in the systems that mediate attachment behaviour. These monkeys are particularly vulnerable to despair responses upon later separations (see Suomi, 1999).

The relationship between attachment style and temperament is a matter of controversy. In humans, researchers have identified three infant temperaments — easy, difficult and slow to warm up — which correspond in certain respects to secure, ambivalent and avoidant attachment styles (Chess & Thomas, 1986). Some researchers have argued that attachment security largely reflects temperament (see Kagan, 1984; Mangelsdorf, Gunnar, Kestenbaum, Lang, & Andreas, 1990; see also Burgess et al., 2003;

Finzi-Dottan, Manor, & Tyano, 2006). An inborn tendency to be timid or fearful, for example, could produce anxious behaviour in the Strange Situation (Goldsmith & Alansky, 1987). The temperamental variable most highly predictive of attachment status across several studies is negative affect (chapter 10) — that is, the tendency to experience emotions such as anxiety and depression. The correlation, however, is only 0.30 (Vaughn, Stevenson-Hinde, Waters, & Kotsaftis, 1992), which suggests that temperament is only one determinant of attachment style.

Temperament does not, however, operate in a vacuum. An environmental variable that appears to have a tremendous impact on security of attachment is the mother's sensitivity to her baby's signals (Ainsworth, 1979; Sroufe & Waters, 1977; see also Meins, Fernyhough, Fradley, & Tuckey, 2001). Mothers who are sensitive to their infants enjoy interacting with them, behave in ways that express warmth and encouragement and stimulate their curiosity (De Wolff & van Ijzendoorn, 1997). These interactions tend to be mutually rewarding and produce secure babies. In contrast, infants whose mothers do not respond to their needs form less secure attachment bonds and display more anger, fear and avoidance (De Wolff & van Ijzendoorn, 1997; Pederson et al., 1990; Waters, Hamilton, & Weinfield, 2000). The role of the father in attachment is an area of continued debate (see van Ijzendoorn & De Wolff, 1997), although paternal sensitivity is an important predictor of the parent–child relationship as well.

Both biology and experience thus affect individual differences in attachment. However, the interaction of the two — such as the match between children and their caregivers — may be just as important. For example, infants who are temperamentally prone to distress may be more likely to become insecurely attached if their caretakers are rigid and emotionally controlled (Mangelsdorf et al., 1990). Similarly, infants with an easy temperament may be more likely to become securely attached despite an unresponsive caregiver than would infants with a more difficult temperament.

Implications of attachment for later development

Attachment patterns that begin in infancy can persist and find expression in a wide range of social behaviours throughout the life span (Waters, Hamilton, et al., 2000; Waters, Merrick, Treboux, Crowell, & Albersheim, 2000; Thompson, 2000). Children rated avoidant in infancy tend to be described by their teachers as insecure and detached in preschool and to have difficulty discussing feelings about separation at age six. In contrast, preschoolers who were securely attached as infants tend to have higher self-esteem, are more socially competent, show greater sensitivity to the needs of their peers and are more popular (see DeMulder, Denham, Schmidt, & Mitchell, 2000; LaFreniere & Sroufe, 1985; Waters, Wippman, & Sroufe, 1979).

Security of attachment in infancy predicts a range of behaviours as children grow older, from self-control and peer acceptance to competent behaviour in the classroom (Bretherton, 1990; Howes, Hamilton, & Philiopsen, 1998; Ruschena, Prior, Sanson, & Smart, 2005). Children with a disorganised style in infancy tend to be rated by their teachers in early primary school as impulsive, disruptive and aggressive, particularly if they are also below average intellectually (Lyons-Ruth et al., 1997).

APPLY + DISCUSS

Research on attachment in infancy and early childhood has largely focused on patterns of attachment that children develop through interactions with their parents or other primary caregivers. What role do you think close relationships with pets or the creation of imaginary friends might play in facilitating attachment behaviour in infants and young children? Could children get needs for companionship and connectedness met from these alternative types of relationships? In other words, could pets and/or imaginary friends serve as surrogate attachment figures?

Individual differences in attachment style are also related to different patterns of response in everyday social interactions. Using a diary methodology by which people describe their social interactions each day for a period of weeks, researchers found that securely attached individuals reported more satisfying daily interactions with others and felt that others were more responsive to them than insecurely attached individuals (Kafetsios & Nezlek, 2002). Based on the results of this study, attachment styles affect not only long-term patterns of relating, but also daily satisfaction with those social interactions.

The theory of internal working models helps make sense of why attachment security with parents predicts the quality of peer relationships years later, particularly close peers, as well as with later attachment figures, notably partners (Cassidy, Kirsh, Scolton, & Parke, 1996; Lieberman, Doyle, & Markiewicz, 1999; see also Trebous, Crowell, & Waters, 2004). Children who are secure with their parents have more positive expectations about what they can expect from relationships. This security leads them to be more trusting and engaging with peers and lovers, who are then more likely to respond to them positively. As a result, they then form more positive representations of peer and love relationships — creating a self-reinforcing cycle, in which positive initial working models foster good relationships, which maintain those models.

Temperament and later life

Children's behaviour is influenced by many factors. An Australian longitudinal study by Bor, Brennan, Williams, Najman, and O'Callaghan (2003) found that negative attitudes of mothers towards their six-month-old infants predicted behavioural problems in the children at age five. While attachment style is predictive of later behaviour, temperament in early childhood is also remarkably stable in later life. An Australian longitudinal study by Lewis (1993) found that the temperament dimension of negative mood tone (anger and distress) at three months of age predicted poor cognitive performance at four years. In New Zealand, a longitudinal study of more than 800 boys and girls also revealed remarkable continuity in temperament (Caspi & Silva, 1995). Toddlers who were rough, easily distracted and prone to mood swings carried these traits into their teens. Those who lacked control at age three were likely to be risk takers or sensation seekers as they grew older. These data suggest children may have hereditary dispositions towards a certain temperament, but also tend to select an environment that matches.

INTERIM SUMMARY

Researchers have discovered four patterns of infant attachment: ***secure***, ***avoidant***, ***ambivalent*** and ***disorganised***. Whereas secure infants are readily comforted by their attachment figures, insecure infants tend to shut off their needs for attachment (avoidant), have difficulty being soothed (ambivalent) or behave in contradictory ways that reflect their difficulty predicting or understanding the way their attachment figures will behave (disorganised). Infant attachment patterns reflect a combination of temperament, parental responsiveness and the interaction of the two. Attachment security in infancy predicts social competence as well as school marks from preschool through adolescence.

Adult attachment

Some of the infants first assessed in longitudinal studies using the Strange Situation are just reaching adulthood, and evidence suggests that early attachment patterns remain influential in adult life (Waters, Merrick, et al., 2000). ***Adult attachment*** refers to ways of experiencing attachment relationships in adulthood. Researchers study adult attachment by interviewing participants and coding the way they describe and recall their relationships with their parents (Main, 1995; Main, Kaplan, & Cassidy, 1985; see also Roisman, Tsai, & Kuan-Hiong, 2004) or by measuring the ways they describe their experiences with attachment figures such as spouses on self-report questionnaires (Brennan, Clark, & Shaver, 1998).

Patterns of adult attachment

As already outlined, the development of attachment is a lifelong process (Peterson, 2009). Just as in infancy, a secure attachment style is favourable in adulthood — contributing to optimal relational and psychological development in the long term (Noller et al., 2001; Peterson, 2004). Adults with *secure* adult attachment styles speak freely and openly about their relationships with their parents. People with *ambivalent* styles appear preoccupied with and ambivalent about their parents. *Avoidant* adults dismiss the importance of attachment relationships or offer idealised generalisations about their parents but are unable to back them up with specific examples. When asked about times when they felt rejected or mistreated or were separated from their parents in childhood, adults with an avoidant style tend to deny having such experiences — all the while spiking on measures of physiological reactivity indicating emotional distress (Dozier & Kobak, 1992).

Individuals with an attachment style characterised as *unresolved* (similar to the disorganised style seen in infancy) have difficulty speaking coherently about attachment figures from their past and have generally been unable to cope with losses or other traumatic experiences from their past. As a result, their narratives are often confused and confusing, and they send conflicting signals to their own children, particularly when their own unmet attachment needs get activated under stress.

Predicting behaviour from adult attachment patterns

Attachment patterns in adults predict a range of phenomena, from whether people want to have children (Rholes, Simpson, Blakely, Lanigan, & Allen, 1997), to how they balance the needs of those children with the needs of work (Vasquez, Durik, & Hyde, 2002), to how they cope with stressful life events (Mikulincer

& Florian, 1997; Myers & Vetere, 2002), to how upset they get at airports when separating from their romantic partner (Fraley & Shaver, 1998) and to how troublesome they find the increasing independence of their adolescent children to be (Hock, Eberly, Bartle-Haring, Ellwanger, & Widaman, 2001). Perhaps most importantly, adults' attachment patterns in relation to their own parents, as assessed by interviews, predict their own children's attachment styles with remarkable accuracy (Main, 1995; Steele, Steele, & Fonagy, 1996; van Ijzendoorn, 1995; see also Leerkes & Siepak, 2006). For example, mothers who are uncomfortable or avoidant in describing their own attachment to their mothers tend to have avoidant infants and children (Fonagy, Steele, & Steele, 1991; Main et al., 1985; see also Kretchmar & Jacobvitz, 2002).

Considerable evidence suggests that mothers whose early attachment experiences were disrupted — through death of a parent, divorce, abuse or neglect, or long-term separation from their parents — are more likely to have difficulty forming close attachment relationships with their own infants and to have infants with a disorganised attachment pattern (Lyons-Ruth et al., 1997; Ricks, 1985; Rutter, Quinton, & Liddle, 1983; Zeanah & Zeanah, 1989). Mothers who have insecure attachment relationships with their own mothers are less responsive and have more difficulty maintaining physical proximity to their infants and young children (Crowell & Feldman, 1991).

Stability of early attachment patterns

Is history destiny? Can a person ever overcome a bad start in childhood or infancy? In an Australian study of foster carers by Thorpe and Caltabiano (2004) it was found that carers' own childhood traumas and attachment styles did not predict performance in their role, suggesting that problems experienced in childhood had no appreciable negative impact on job performance. However, problematic early attachments substantially increase vulnerability to subsequent difficulties. Disturbances in childhood attachment relationships predict later difficulties in childhood and adolescence (Bowlby, 1969; Ricks, 1985; Spitz, 1945). Disrupted attachments are associated with severe personality disturbances (Ludolph et al., 1990; Zanarini, Gunderson, Marino, Schwartz, & Frankenberg, 1989), depression (Brown, Andrews, Harris, & Adler, 1986), antisocial behaviour and adjustment problems (Tizard & Hodges, 1978; see also Ward, Lee, & Polan, 2006), and difficulty behaving appropriately as a parent (Ricks, 1985). Childhood experiences such as parental neglect or mistreatment or even parental divorce make people more vulnerable to insecure attachment in adulthood (Mickelson, Kessler, & Shaver, 1997).

All generalisations such as these, however, are probabilistic statements — that is, statements about probabilities or increased risk. Early attachment experiences are not the only determinant of later functioning. Some children are remarkably resilient in the face of neglectful or abusive life experiences (Anthony & Cohler, 1987; Luthar, Cicchetti, & Becker, 2000). Furthermore, as circumstances change, so do patterns of attachment (Lewis, Feiring, & Rosenthal, 2000). Indeed, some of Harlow's monkeys who had been raised in isolation and were extremely socially maladapted showed marked improvement in social interactions after developing a close relationship with a normal monkey who served as a simian 'therapist' (Chamove, 1978; Novak & Harlow, 1975). Longitudinal research suggests that childhood risk factors such as parental loss or divorce, life-threatening illness of parent or child and child abuse can turn securely attached infants into insecurely attached adults (Waters, Merrick, et al., 2000; Weinfield, Sroufe, & Egeland, 2000).

One study provides dramatic evidence of the possibilities for altering problematic patterns of attachment in the opposite direction. The investigators provided a group of high-risk infants and mothers with a weekly home visitor. The mothers were poor, often depressed and exhibited enough signs of inadequate caretaking to warrant referrals from health, educational or social service professionals (Lyons-Ruth, Connell, Grunebaum, & Botein, 1990). The home visitor offered support and advice, modelled positive and active interactions with the infant, and provided a trusting relationship for the mother. The results were compelling: compared to an untreated control group, infants in the intervention group scored 10 points higher on an infant IQ measure and were twice as likely (roughly 60 versus 30 percent) to be classified as securely attached at 18 months.

APPLY + DISCUSS

Some people, like Australian burns victim Jandamarra O'Shane, display resilience in overcoming highly traumatic childhood experiences. O'Shane was doused in petrol and set alight by a male who trespassed on his school grounds when he was just six years old. He suffered burns to 70 percent of his body. Now, more than ten years later, O'Shane says he has forgiven his attacker and moved on with his life — even though he still remembers the attack (Davis, 2007).

- What factors are likely to make some people resilient in the face of illness, neglect or other experiences in childhood that increase people's risk for later social and emotional problems?
- Can anyone be truly 'unscarred' by physical or emotional abuse in childhood? How could researchers design studies to find out? What kind of subtle measures would they need to include?

Cultural variations in temperament

Problematic attachments are seemingly able to be altered, but what about temperament? Different cultures have different perceptions of what is and is not a desirable temperament for their children, which result in different approaches to child-rearing, discipline and socialisation. These variations in parental belief systems across cultures could conceivably influence child temperament (Goodnow, 1996). The multicultural city of Melbourne was used by Kyrios, Prior, Oberklaid, and Demetriou (1989) to study how cultural beliefs influence infant development. They compared temperaments of children from Anglo-Australian families to those of Greek-Australian families. The children were carefully matched in factors such as age, family income, education, health and other variables. Despite the similar demographics, the Greek-Australian infants were more likely than Anglo-Australian infants to display a difficult temperament. They had more negative moods on average, were also less adaptable, less easily distracted and less positive in mood and approach than their Anglo-Australian peers. Cross-cultural research suggests that temperament and culture should not be considered in isolation (Prior, Sanson, Smart, & Oberklaid, 2000). In a comparison study of Australian, American, Greek and Chinese infants in the first year of life, the temperament of Australian children was found to be less negative than Greek and Chinese infants in terms of mood, approach–withdrawal, distractibility and adaptability. Chinese infants were also comparatively more reactive and intense. Australian and American infants had the most similar temperaments. Similarly, Freedman (1974) found a link between culture and temperament in his study comparing Aboriginal and Anglo-Australian infants. Aboriginal newborns were more quietly alert, were much less tense and irritable, were happier, were more responsive to cuddling and were more adept at comforting themselves after bouts of crying. Aboriginal newborns also have better muscular control over their necks, backs and legs than Anglo-Australian babies, despite smaller body mass on average (Hamilton, 1981; chapter 12). While there may be some hereditary and genetic factors involved, the different cultural approach to child-rearing also seems likely to have played a part in developing different temperaments.

INTERIM SUMMARY

Researchers studying ***adult attachment*** find that the majority of people appear to have a secure attachment style. Parents tend to produce children with an attachment style similar to their own. Attachment patterns have considerable stability because internal working models tend to change slowly, but as life circumstances change, so can attachment styles.

Socialisation

Attachment relationships provide the child's first social experiences and serve as a model for many future relationships, but they are only one avenue for initiating the child into the social world. To function as adults, children must learn the rules, beliefs, values, skills, attitudes and behaviour patterns of their society, a process called ***socialisation***. Children learn from a variety of socialisation agents, individuals and groups that transmit social knowledge and values to the child.

Before we consider research on socialisation, several caveats are in order. First, socialisation is not a one-way process in which adults fill children's minds with values and beliefs. Rather, it is a two-way street, or transactional. Children are active participants in their own socialisation, who must construct an understanding of social rules and gradually come to experience cultural beliefs and values as their own (Bell, 1968; Kochanska, 1997; Maccoby, 1992; Sapir, 1949; see also Kochanska et al., 2007). Although we tend to think of socialisation as a process through which parents and other adults 'leave their mark' on children, from an evolutionary perspective, children are also biologically prepared to be socialised (Bugental & Goodnow, 1998). Children come prepared to experience emotions such as shame and guilt that render them readily shaped by parents into the kinds of people who will one day be accepted in their society.

MAKING CONNECTIONS

Children who live in abnormal social environments, such as orphanages, in their first few years may have lifelong difficulties forming and maintaining relationships. This has raised questions about whether humans have a critical period for the capacity for forming intimate **relationships** (chapter 18) and whether these children will ever express their potential to form loving relationships.

Children also have innate temperaments that influence attempts to shape them. Inherited tendencies tend to increase in their expression throughout adolescence. Thus, the quality of parent–child relationships continues to be shaped not just by infant temperament but by genetic predispositions that may become most apparent many years afterward (Elkins, McGue, & Iacono, 1997). Indeed, the way children behave shapes the way their parents respond. Children who are impulsive and poorly controlled elicit ineffective parenting, just as ineffective parents can create troubled children (Stice & Barrera, 1995; see also Aksan, Kochanska, & Ortmann, 2006).

A second point to remember in thinking about socialisation is that socialisation is a lifelong process. Individuals learn throughout their lives to play different roles, such as student, parent, friend, wage-earner or retiree, and roles change from one phase of life to the next.

Finally, socialisation always occurs within a broader social and economic context (Bronfenbrenner, 1998; McLoyd, 1989; Parke & Buriel, 1998; see also Caughy, O'Campo, Nettles, & Lohrfink, 2006). The way parents behave with their children depends on cultural values and practices (Harkness & Super, 2002; Harwood, Schoelmerich, Ventura-Cook, Schulze, & Wilson, 1996). Although deliberate teaching is important, much of socialisation is implicit, as when children learn about the importance of being on time by the regular sounding of school bells between classes (see Strauss & Quinn, 1997). Economic stresses and marital satisfaction also affect the way parents parent and the extent to which their children function well socially and academically (Brooks-Gunn, Duncan, & Aber, 1997; Conger et al., 1993; Fincham, 1998; see also Fishman & Meyers, 2000).

ONE STEP FURTHER

Resiliency and schools

By Doctor Julie-Ann Pooley, Edith Cowan University

The concept of resilience is widely associated with vulnerable children and adolescents, and has been researched since Werner's longitudinal study in Kauai in 1955. Hundreds of factors were examined in hundreds of children, and some forty years later, much has been said about the complexity of risk, resilience and recovery (Werner & Smith, 1989). One thing that is very clear is that resilience is nurtured through multiple levels (individual, family, community) and within contexts. It is for this reason that schools are an important resource and opportunity for children and adolescents (Pike, Cohen, & Pooley, 2008).

Schools are more than just places to learn the 'three Rs' of *r*eading, w*r*iting and a*r*ithmetic — they provide opportunities for children to understand what it is like to be in a community, to feel a sense of community and to develop community mindedness. To understand how young children are able to grapple with the abstract concept of 'community', researchers in Perth, Western Australia, embarked on a number of studies related to children and the community (Pooley, Breen, Pike, Drew, & Cohen, 2007; Pooley, Pike, Drew, & Breen, 2002). The researchers interviewed 46 children aged from 9 to 12 years to see what they understood about their school as a community, and how this related to their broader view of the community in which they lived. For these children, the salient aspects of their school community were the *people* (friends, teachers and the principal), the *places* for activities and interaction (facilities for formal and informal activities), how safe it was (personal safety and environmental safety), school community cooperation (a sense of working together), that they could have influence (getting things done or changed) and the functional aspect of the school community (that the school had facilities and processes to develop its community identity). In developing their understanding of the wider community, the children identified that people in their community were important to them. People identified were those they had access to in different aspects of their lives (their families and their neighbours) and those with whom they were able to form relationships and attachments (their parents and neighbours). *Place* was also a central theme in the children's depiction of community. Places that they identified were both natural, such as parks and the beach; and built, such as the school and their surrounding suburb. These places were recognised as being important as they facilitated *interaction*. Interactions in the form of activities were very important to the process of developing a sense of community as the children described. Through a 'resilience lens', schools provide the context and opportunity for children to gain and use both internal and external resources.

Children derive much of their understanding of their broader community from seeing their school as a community. Students at Northfield Primary School in Adelaide, South Australia, which has students from 41 different countries, held their own multinational soccer tournament to celebrate the 2010 FIFA World Cup.

For children today, school and education take up a large part of the day; school is also a place that children attend for many years. Children derive much of their understanding of their broader community from seeing their school as a community. Schools provide children with opportunities to experience, to connect with other individuals, to feel integrated, to feel good, and to develop competencies in a community context. Schoolchildren can learn about their school community and about the relationship between their school community and the wider community. In this respect, children are not only socialised in the school community, but are also socialised in the wider community. Adults can see the importance of community, and through research, they can understand how children actively seek to construct a positive sense of community. Adults (parents, teachers, neighbours) can aid in the construction of community for children. They can do this by actively engaging with people in different places to form attachments through interactions with others in the community. For children, this creates opportunities for developing community-mindedness, and it is probably not a bad idea for adults as well. In terms of understanding, the concept of resilience has been defined as 'the potential to exhibit resourcefulness by using available internal and external recourses, in response to different contextual and developmental challenges' (Pooley & Cohen, 2010).

The role of parents

The question of how important parents are to development is now hotly debated (Collins, Maccoby, Steinberg, Hetherington, & Bornstein, 2000; Harris, 1998, 2000). For years, psychologists assumed that parenting is the most important determinant of personality and social development. In the last decade, this point of view has been challenged by a steady stream of behavioural genetic studies. These studies suggest that the family environment shared by siblings has little impact on personality, social or cognitive traits, particularly when compared with genetic influences and environmental influences not shared by siblings, such as experiences with peers (chapters 9 and 11). Judith Harris (1998) created a storm of controversy when she published a book challenging the idea that parents matter much at all. The available data suggest, she argued, that genetic and peer influences primarily determine who we are.

Can it be true that our parents, who socialise us from the beginning and whose homes we inhabit and whose rules and attitudes govern our behaviour for the first 18 years of our lives (and in many cultures, long after), have little influence on our subsequent development? The data clearly do not support the old view that parenting is the central determinant of individual differences in personality and social development, but neither do they support the swing of the pendulum in the other direction.

The problems with the 'parenting doesn't matter' hypothesis are complex, but many hinge on the way researchers interpret data on heritability (see Collins et al., 2000). As we have seen (chapters 1 and 9), the size of heritability coefficients is highly dependent on the samples researchers use in their studies. A sample that consists primarily of white middle-class people in Australia has already eliminated many of the most important parenting effects — such as the differences between parental behaviour in Uganda and Perth, which are likely to be far greater than any differences among white middle-class parents in Perth. The tendency of human children to use language is clearly rooted in our genes, but no-one would similarly argue that parents have little influence on the language their children speak. Further, two children in the same family will elicit different patterns of parenting. Although these are often interpreted as genetic effects, they actually reflect transactions between the child's genes and the ways parents respond.

What about the argument that peers are more important than parents? As we will see, peers play a substantial role in development, and their influence can be seen in problems such as delinquency or substance abuse in adolescence. However, adolescents choose their peers, and both the peers they choose and their susceptibility to 'bad company' depend heavily on the social skills, expectations and capacities for intimacy they developed at home in their attachment relationships (Collins et al., 2000; Ladd, 1999). Children with histories of maltreatment by their parents, for example, tend to have poor peer relationships (Bolger, Patterson, & Kupersmidt, 1998; see also McCloskey & Stuewig, 2001).

Perhaps most importantly, when researchers carefully measure parenting, they typically find substantial effects on personality and social development (Bates, Luster, & Vandenbelt, 2003; Kremen & Block, 1998; Westen, 1998). These effects are most apparent when parents behave in unusual or damaging ways, such as abusing their children, but they also appear with more subtle differences in parenting styles.

Some time ago, Diana Baumrind (1967, 1971, 1991) discovered three styles of parenting, distinguished by the extent to which parents control their children's actions and respond to their feelings. ***Authoritarian*** parents place high value on obedience and respect for authority. They do not encourage discussion of why particular behaviours are important or listen to the child's point of view. Rather, they impose a set of standards to which they expect their children to adhere, and they are likely to punish their children frequently and physically. In contrast, ***permissive*** parents impose virtually no controls on their children, allowing them to make their own decisions whenever possible. Permissive parents tend to accept their children's impulsive behaviours, including angry or aggressive ones, and rarely dole out punishments. ***Authoritative*** parents set standards for their children and firmly enforce them, but they also encourage give and take and explain their views while showing respect for their children's opinions.

A fourth style of parenting that has been proposed more recently is ***uninvolved*** parents who consistently place their own needs above the needs of their child. (See figure 13.2 for a comparison of how the four parenting styles differ along the dimensions of nurturing and control.) Although children's genetic endowments clearly influence parenting styles, the data also suggest that different parenting styles tend to produce different kinds of children. The most self-controlled, independent, curious, academically competent and sociable children tend to have authoritative parents (Baumrind, 1987; Steinberg, Lamborn, Darling, & Mounts, 1994; Weiss & Schwarz, 1996; see also Mayseless, Scharf, & Sholt, 2003; Neal & Frick-Horbury, 2001). Authoritarian parenting has been linked, however, to low independence, vulnerability to stress, low self-esteem and an external locus of control (a sense that one has little control over what happens in life) (Buri, Louiselle, Misukanis, & Mueller, 1988; Loeb, Horst, & Horton, 1980; Steinberg et al., 1994). Children with permissive parents tend to be low in self-reliance and impulse control (Martin, Maccoby, Baran, & Jacklin, 1981; Olweus, 1980) and to have more trouble with substance abuse in adolescence (Baumrind, 1991; see also Patock-Peckham, Cheong, Balhorn, & Nagoshi, 2001). Children of uninvolved parents typically display low self-esteem and aggressive behaviour (Bukatko & Daehler, 2004; Hatfield, Ferguson, & Alpert, 1967; Loeb et al., 1980; see also Bronte-Tinkew, Moore, & Carrano, 2006). The match between a child's temperament and parenting styles is also important: difficult, hard-to-manage children tend to have fewer behaviour problems later on if their parents are firm with rules (Bates, Pettit, Dodge, & Ridge, 1998).

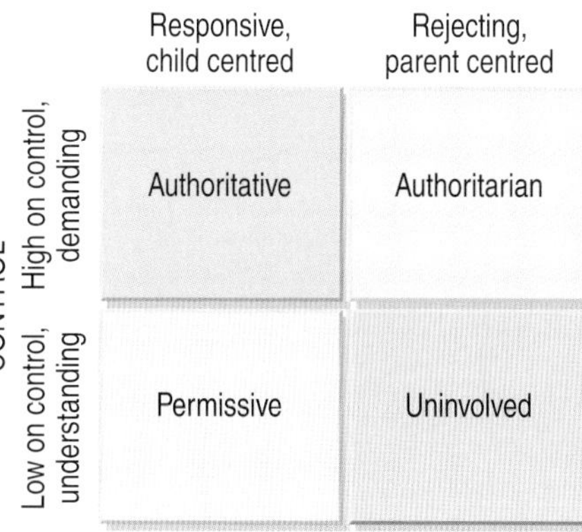

FIGURE 13.2
Variations in nurturing and control as a function of parenting style. As this figure illustrates, each style of parenting represents its own unique combination of nurturance and control. Not surprisingly, these different combinations are expected to influence the kind of children who subsequently develop.

SOURCE: From Bukatko/Daehler. *Child Development, A Thematic Approach*, 5E. © 2004 Wadsworth, a part of Cengage Learning, Inc. Reproduced by permission. www.cengage.com/permissions.

Which style of parenting is best? Every child and every circumstance is different of course, so there is no easy answer to that question. However cross-cultural research by Poole, Sundberg, and Tyler (1982) indicates that democratic–authoritative households provide more positive outcomes for adolescents than authoritarian households. Poole et al. compared parenting styles and their effects on teenagers from rural towns in India, Australia and the United States. They found that those adolescents from democratic homes tended to be more outgoing, assertive and independent, while those from authoritarian homes tended to be conforming, dependent and submissive.

Scott et al. (1991) compared the effects of parenting styles in 2000 families from Australia, Canada, Hong Kong, Japan, Taiwan and the United States. They found that parental affection was related to adolescent self-esteem in all cultures. However, they also came across an interesting finding in relation to punitive parenting styles. In cultures where such a punitive approach was accepted, this practice tended to produce better-adjusted adolescents. But in cultures where a democratic parenting was more common, the authoritarian approach produced relatively low results in terms of adolescent wellbeing. Same approach but a different outcome — that finding is a perfect example of how important cultural context can be in the way we develop. More recently, Lansford et al. (2005) reported that the practice of physical discipline of children varied to a high degree across cultures in China, India, Italy, Kenya and the Philippines. For example, physical discipline was not the norm in Thailand, but it was expected and practised to a high degree in Kenya. However, in *all* countries, regardless of cultural norms, higher use of physical discipline of children was associated with more aggression and anxiety.

Current parenting advice recommends a ***guidance approach*** to raising children, whereby parents help their children to manage their emotions, cooperate with others and think about the effects of their behaviour on others. The ultimate goal is for the child to learn considerate behaviour (Porter, 2005). Parents should not praise their children's achievements, nor should they punish imperfect behaviours as children need to learn from their mistakes. Rather, parents should acknowledge the skills involved in their child's achievements, emphasising how the child went about a task rather than judging what was produced. For example, instead of saying 'Good girl, that's a beautiful painting' (praise), you would say 'Wow, look what you did! Did you know you could do that?' (The discipline dance, 2006, p. 9).

INTERIM SUMMARY

Socialisation is the process by which children learn the rules, beliefs, values, skills, attitudes and behaviour patterns of their society. Socialisation is a transactional and lifelong process. Socialisation also always occurs in a broader social context. ***Authoritarian*** parents place high value on obedience and respect for authority. ***Permissive*** parents impose minimal controls on their children. ***Authoritative*** parents enforce standards but explain their views and encourage verbal give-and-take. ***Uninvolved*** parents consistently place their own needs above the needs of their child. The ***guidance approach*** involves parents helping their children to manage their emotions and learn considerate behaviours.

The role of culture

Although authoritative parenting tends to produce outcomes most people in the West would consider 'better', two qualifications are worth noting. First, good parenting is flexible parenting and changes as children mature. For example, preschoolers and their siblings tend to get along much better if their parents intervene before their squabbles turn into brawls. In contrast, school-age children tend to develop better sibling relationships if their parents let them resolve their own disputes (Kramer, Perozynski, & Chung, 1999).

Second, an authoritative parenting style is rare or nonexistent in many cultures and is probably not the most adaptive pattern everywhere (Whiting & Edwards, 1988; Whiting & Whiting, 1973, 1975). Agricultural societies usually value obedience far more than autonomy or independence. Among the Mayan Zinacanteco Indians of Mexico, for example, an entire family shares a single-room hut, just 60 metres square, and every member contributes to the family's survival by farming (Brazelton, 1972). In this culture, where people have no real choice in the roles they will fill, socialisation for independence and free choice would often prove frustrating or counterproductive.

Training for independence versus embeddedness in kin or clan begins in the first days of life, through implicit forms of learning that predict adult personality and social characteristics (Harwood, Schoelmerich, Schulze, & Gonzalez, 1999; Whiting, 1964). For example, infants in most cultures sleep in the same beds, or at least the same rooms, as their mothers. In Australia, most middle-class parents give infants their own rooms by three to six months. Thus, Australian children learn early that they are, and can be, on their own.

Parents from different cultures often have very different views and practices when it comes to child development. Goodnow, Cashmore, Cotton, and Knight (1984) compared the expectations of Anglo–Australian mothers to those of migrant Lebanese–Australian mothers about the age they believed their child would obey them and be polite to other adults. Mothers from Japan and the United States were also studied for comparison. Interestingly, the Lebanese-Australian mothers expected their children to continue misbehaving at considerably later ages than all the other mothers.

A GLOBAL VISTA

Parental acceptance and rejection in cross-cultural perspective

One of the most important ways parents vary across and within cultures is the extent to which they are accepting or rejecting of their children (Rohner, 1975a, 1986; Veneziano & Rohner, 1998; see also Rohner, Khaleque, & Cournoyer, 2005). Parents can express acceptance verbally through praise, compliments and support, or nonverbally through hugging, approving glances and smiling. Like acceptance, parents can express rejection verbally (bullying or harsh criticism) or nonverbally (hitting, smacking, shaking or simply neglecting).

Parental acceptance and rejection were once considered polar opposites of a single dimension, and they are clearly related. However, like positive and negative affect (chapter 10), they can be measured independently and have somewhat independent effects. A parent who is often loving can also sometimes be harsh or even abusive (Pettit, 1997).

In general, findings both within the West and across cultures show that parental acceptance is quite consistently associated with high self-esteem, independence and emotional stability, whereas the opposite is true of parental rejection (MacKinnon-Lewis, Starnes, Volling, & Johnson, 1997; Rohner & Britner, 2002; see also Erkman & Rohner, 2006). One longitudinal study with a Western sample found that individuals who had a warm or affectionate parent are more likely, 35 years later, to have a long and happy marriage, children and close friendships in middle age (Franz, McClelland, & Weinberger, 1991).

A converging body of data suggests that parents (particularly mothers) who interact with their infants and preschoolers in ways that show mutual responsiveness and 'connectedness' tend to have children with better peer relationships, greater empathy for others and accelerated moral development (Clark & Ladd, 2000; Kochanska, Murray, & Harlan, 2000). Conversely, multiple studies find that abused children and adults with childhood histories of abuse are more likely than their nonabused peers to view the world as a dangerous place, have poor self-esteem and have difficulty maintaining close relationships (see Bolger, 1998; Finkelhor, 1994; Gelinas, 1983).

A large cross-cultural study correlating parental acceptance–rejection with personality traits in children and adults demonstrated that these patterns are indeed universal (Rohner, 1975a). Cultures in which parents were more rejecting (as rated from anthropological reports) produced children who were more hostile and dependent and adults who were less emotionally stable than cultures with more benign parenting practices.

The Alorese, who inhabit a Pacific island off Java, exemplify a culture with highly rejecting parenting practices (see DuBois, 1944; Rohner, 1975b). According to DuBois, Alorese women return to the fields within two weeks of childbirth. After a brief initial period of benign and playful caretaking, Alorese infants receive very inconsistent care, such as sporadic feeding. Alorese children are constantly teased for sport by older children and adults. Parents threaten children with abandonment and send them to live with relatives if they are too difficult.

Generalisations about an entire people are, of course, always overgeneralisations, because individual differences exist in all cultures. Nevertheless, anthropologists such as DuBois describe Alorese adults as hostile, aggressive and distrustful, characteristics that make sense in the context of Alorese child rearing. In Alor, as elsewhere, patterns of child rearing reflect cultural beliefs and values, and parents tend to harvest what they sow.

Socialisation of gender

Among the most powerful roles into which people are socialised are ***gender roles***, which specify the range of behaviours considered appropriate for males and females (see Martin, Ruble, & Szkrybalo, 2002). The distinction between sex and gender is not always clear, but in general, sex refers to a biological categorisation based on genetic and anatomical differences. ***Gender***, in contrast, refers to the psychological meaning of being male or female, which is influenced by learning.

When a new baby is born, people greet its arrival with one of two announcements: 'It's a girl!' or 'It's a boy!' This response rests on a relatively small anatomical feature, but it has important consequences for the way the person will come to think, feel and behave (Archer & Lloyd, 1985). The process by which children acquire personality traits, emotional responses, skills, behaviours and preferences that are culturally considered appropriate to their sex is called ***sex typing*** (Perry & Bussey, 1979).

Differential treatment of boys and girls begins at the very beginning. In one study, first-time mothers of young infants were asked to play with a six-month-old baby (not their own) for 10 minutes (Smith & Lloyd, 1978). Several toys were available. Some, like a squeaky hammer and a stuffed rabbit wearing a bow tie and trousers, were typical masculine toys; others, like a doll and a squeaky Bambi, were more feminine. The mothers did not know the babies were cross-dressed — that the six-month-old in the little boy's outfit was actually a little girl and the baby in the pink dress was a boy. The mothers tended to offer the infants 'gender-appropriate' toys and to encourage more physical activity in the 'boys'. Similar results emerge from experimental studies with older children: adults tend to compliment and encourage girls more, particularly in nurturance play, such as taking care of dolls. They hold higher expectations for boys and provide them with more reinforcements for meeting goals (Day, cited in Block, 1978).

Differential treatment of boys and girls often begins very early in life. While this little girl is playing dress ups as a fairy, this young boy is focused on completing a task-oriented activity.

Naturalistic investigations of parents' behaviour with their children indicate that, throughout childhood, parents (especially fathers) tend to encourage traditional sex-typed behaviour, discouraging play with toys that are typical of the opposite gender (Langlois & Downs, 1980; see also Lindsey & Mize, 2001). The extent to which fathers are more traditional in their attitudes towards gender plays a particularly important role in shaping children's sex-typed attitudes and behaviours (McHale, Crouter, & Tucker, 1999). Boys in Australia and other Western countries receive more encouragement to compete, more punishment and more pressure not to cry or express feelings from both parents. Girls receive more warmth, affection and trust, although they are kept under closer surveillance than boys (Block, 1978). Mothers tend to talk more and speak in more supportive ways to their daughters than their sons (Leaper, Anderson, & Sanders, 1998).

Gender-role socialisation is not, however, limited to parents. Teachers also contribute to the socialisation of males and females to engage in gender-appropriate behaviours (Whitt, Pascarella, Nesheim, Marth, & Pierson, 2003). Although the tide is turning, males have traditionally been encouraged to pursue careers in construction, science, maths and engineering. Girls, on the other hand, are socialised to pursue careers (if they pursue them at all) in disciplines such as the humanities. Educators, even unwittingly, create a 'chilly classroom climate' for girls, whereby they are given less verbal feedback, praise, and encouragement than their male peers (Whitt, Edison, Pascarella, Nora, & Terenzini, 1999), with subsequent effects on the self-esteem, cognitive outcomes and career strivings of male and female students.

Males have traditionally been encouraged to pursue careers in certain fields, such as construction and engineering.

Teachers are having to cope with the need to change traditional practices in order to keep up with the changing needs of boys and girls. Teachers surveyed at a national education symposium in Sydney in 2001 identified Year 9 boys as the most difficult of all students to teach — with their ability to meet the changing needs of boys a key reason (Admin, 2002a). Educators are now striving to make the curriculum more attractive to boys and to teach them in ways that are more effective, such as the use of meaningful and practical projects. The needs of girls, too, are receiving special attention. There is a fear that girls are in danger of being left behind in the technology-dominated world of the future. Schools, universities and TAFE colleges in Australia are now working on strategies to meet the learning needs of girls in the technology area (Admin, 2002b).

Children are also socialised towards stereotypical gender roles by their peers, beginning as early as preschool (Witt, 2000). Boys and girls are rewarded and punished, respectively, by their peers for engaging in gender-appropriate and gender-inappropriate behaviour. Thus, boys who play with dolls or girls who play with trucks are likely to be teased and ridiculed by members of their peer group for playing with toys 'of the other sex' (Fagot & Patterson, 1969; Lamb, Easterbrooks, & Holden, 1980; Lamb & Roopnarine, 1979). Gender roles are also portrayed through the mass media and electronic games, frequently as stereotypes. In many video games, for example, men are shown to be forceful and strong, with characters requiring aggression and violence for success; in contrast, women are often portrayed in more submissive roles (Dietz, 1998).

INTERIM SUMMARY

Cultural practices affect virtually every aspect of socialisation, such as the relative importance placed on independence and autonomy. Parental acceptance and rejection also differ substantially across cultures. Rejection and abuse have negative effects on children everywhere. Among the most powerful roles into which people are socialised are ***gender roles***, which specify the range of behaviours considered appropriate for males and females.

APPLY + DISCUSS

Given the importance of parents, teachers and peers to a child's social development, how might these respective influences change as a child matures?

- Does the role of parents diminish and the role of peers increase?
- What about the continuity of the role of other authority figures, such as teachers, across the life span?

Socialisation and learning

Gender-role socialisation occurs in different ways across different cultures, resulting in considerable variance in gender roles. Similarly, different cultures socialise people into different expectations of the way children are expected to learn. For example, Aboriginal cultures expect children to become independent and self-directed at a much earlier age than Western societies. Aboriginal children are expected to learn by observation and direct participation in activities, the responsibility for learning being on the child (Bavin, 1993). They are not protected from potential danger, or fussed over if they are crying, to the same degree as children in Anglo-Australian households. Socialisation of these expectations begins early and Aboriginal children soon learn what is expected of them.

Peer relationships

We have focused thus far primarily on children's relationships with their parents and other adults. Equally important, however, are peer relationships. The need for peer relationships appears so strong that children who do not have natural peers — first-born and only children — are more likely to invent 'imaginary companions' to accompany them (Gleason, 2002; Gleason, Sebanc, & Hartup, 2000). The presence of friends can protect children from some of the negative effects of child abuse (Schwartz, Dodge, Pettit, & Bates, 2000), just as social support can steel adults against the effects of major stressors such as loss (chapter 11). Here we focus on two important kinds of peers: friends and siblings.

Friendships

Children's friendships are almost exclusively same-sex friendships. Children simply like same-sex peers better (Bukowski, Gauze, Hoza, & Newcomb, 1993). Cross-sex relationships account for only about 5 percent of friends in childhood (Hartup, 1989). In fact, in one large study, only 0.3 percent of children had a best friend of the opposite sex (Kovacs, Parker, & Hoffman, 1996). Part of the preference for peers of the same sex results from the gender segregation of activities in childhood. Boys are encouraged to play with boys and engage in 'boy' activities, and girls are encouraged to play with girls and engage in 'girl' activities. In this way, appropriate gender-role socialisation can more easily be assured.

A qualifier is, however, in order. Although children do show a preference for friends of the same sex, this stated preference depends on the context in which the friends will play together. In one study, preadolescent and adolescent boys and girls were asked whether they would prefer a same-sex or an other-sex partner for a project at school and whether or not they would prefer a same-sex or an other-sex friend to play with at home. Preadolescent children showed the strongest preferences, although not always for the same sex. These children indicated that they would prefer to work on the project with a same-sex friend at school, but would prefer other-sex friends when playing at home (Strough & Marie-Covatto, 2002).

The development of friendship

Friendships marked by commitment and reciprocity (sharing and give and take) begin to emerge around age three (see Hartup, 1989). Even these preschool friendships have remarkable stability, with friendships typically enduring unless one member of the pair moves away (see Collins & Gunnar, 1990).

Particularly during early childhood, children show a marked preference for interactions with same-sex playmates.

The meaning of friendship, however, changes throughout childhood (Damon, 1977; Selman, 1980). Young children describe friends as people who give them things or let them play with their toys. By middle childhood, children recognise some of the longer term pay-offs of specific friendships. When asked why one girl was her friend, an eight-year-old responded, 'Because ... she cheers me up when I'm sad, and she shares. ... I share so she'll share' (Damon, 1977, pp. 159–160). Adolescents express more concern with intimacy in friendships (mutual self-disclosure and empathy) (Buhrmester, 1990). Girls tend to self-disclose more than boys, and when boys self-disclose, they generally do so with girls (Youniss & Haynie, 1992; see also Rose, 2002).

The role of friends, siblings and parents changes over the course of social development. The experience of relationships as sources of conflict and support also changes during this period (Blos, 1967). Research indicates that mothers and fathers are the primary sources of support for nine-year-olds, but this wanes during adolescent years, when conflict with parents is at its peak. Friends loom much larger as sources of support during late childhood and adolescence, but are gradually replaced by romantic partners in early adulthood. In a 2010 national survey of young Australians, all people aged 11–24 years of age ranked family relationships as most highly valued (Mission Australia, 2010). Around 60 percent of young people aged 11–19 years also highly valued friendships, compared with about 45 percent of 20 to 24 year olds (Mission Australia, 2010).

These patterns of friendship are not, however, the same everywhere (see Arnett, 1999; Ladd, 1999). In much of the West, where individualism is strong, parents socialise their children for independence, and they often get more than they asked for in adolescence. In more collectivist cultures, where autonomy from parents is not such a strong value, the shift from parents to friends and lovers is much less apparent (DeRosier & Kupersmidt, 1991). In Japan, for example, children are socialised from birth to accommodate to others, not to separate from them (Rothbaum, Pott, Azuma, Miyake, & Weisz, 2000). Japanese parents spend time in skin-to-skin contact with their infants, often bathing with them, and they are more likely to have their infants and young children sleep in their bed. By adolescence, Japanese children have learned that closeness to parents is an important value and do not show the same kind of 'radical separatism' seen in many Western societies.

MAKING CONNECTIONS

Cyber bullying is on the increase, with high school students posting to YouTube videos of fighting in the classroom and on the school grounds. In October 2010, the Queensland Government appointed psychologist Dr Michael Carr-Greg as its first anti-bullying adviser, in part due to the rise in cyber bullying. Dr Carr-Greg, who specialises in adolescents, believes banning mobiles at schools will help stop the violence (Elsworth, 2009). He has also called for parents to 'grow a digital spine' and to do more to set boundaries, as well as to monitor and supervise their children's use of mobile phones (Hurst, 2010). Other youth experts, such as Associate Professor Alan McKee from the Queensland University of Technology (QUT), believe we need to promote change within society and socially influence the perception of what it means to be masculine (Elsworth, 2009; see also chapter 18). Associate Professor Marilyn Campbell, also from QUT, believes we need to build a social network around vulnerable children and to educate bullies (Chilcott, 2009). Similarly, Professor Donna Cross from Edith Cowan University believes parents of children who bully need to engage in anti-bullying courses to change this intergenerational behaviour (Chilcott, 2009).

Peer status

Most primates are hierarchical animals, and humans are no exception. From preschool onward, children assume positions in status hierarchies. Most readers can probably remember and pinpoint their peers' relative positions in status hierarchies in high school with remarkable accuracy. In fact, researchers rely on peer reports of 'who is in' and 'who is out' to study peer status in children.

Children differ substantially in the way they form relationships and the way other children respond to them (Ladd, 1999; Rubin, Rahhal, & Poon, 1998; see also van Lier, Vitaro, Wanner, Vuijk, & Crijnen, 2005). Children who are disliked by their peers are called ***rejected children***. Some rejected children are teased and ostracised by their peers; others are bullies. Still other children, called ***neglected children***, are ignored by their peers. Researchers study peer acceptance using peer nomination methods: they ask students in a class, for example, to write down the names of children they really like and dislike. Rejected children are those whose names frequently show up on the 'disliked' list; neglected children receive no mention at all.

Children develop reputations among their peers by the time they are in preschool, and these reputations affect the way other children behave towards them (Denham & Holt, 1993; see also Walker & Irving, 1998). Personality characteristics and peer responses can produce a vicious cycle, in which children who are unhappy, aggressive or socially unskilled elicit peer rejection, which in turn intensifies their low self-esteem and awkward social behaviour, leading to further rejection (Hodges & Perry, 1999). Not all children who develop early negative reputations maintain this status throughout the rest of their school careers. But children who are actively disliked by peers (rejected) tend to have low self-esteem and other difficulties later in life, such as higher incidence of school dropout and delinquency in adolescence and more troubles at work and in relationships in adulthood (Dunn & McGuire, 1992; Parker & Asher, 1987; Richards, Crowe, Larson, & Swarr, 1998). Neglected children, however, often perform better academically than more popular peers, as they immerse themselves into their school work. Rejected children tend to do poorly in school, but only if they are also aggressive (Wentzel & Asher, 1995).

Quality of friendship

Children's friendships differ not only in the quantity — in how many friends a child has and how readily other children 'take' to him — but also in their quality (Hartup, 1996; see also Dunn, Cutting, & Fisher, 2002). Whereas having friends is typically a good thing, research supports the commonsense notion that having the wrong kinds of friends — alienated, angry and delinquent — can be detrimental to development, particularly for children who are already at risk (Vitaro, Tremblay, Kerr, Pagani, & Bukowski, 1997).

Increased access to mobile phones, email, internet chat rooms, and online social-networking sites has resulted in friendships of a different kind being developed or maintained through text- and data-based communication. While the number of *cyber friends* a child has may be plentiful, there are also potentially harmful consequences associated with technology-based relationships. For example, cyber bullying is a form of abuse, whereby derogatory messages and/or images are transmitted electronically with the intent of threatening or humiliating another person. The reported incidence of cyber bullying is on the increase globally (Campbell, 2005), and the long-term effects of this relatively new form of peer abuse are not yet known.

Beyond the company they keep, another important dimension of children's friendship is the way they interact with one another (Bukowski et al., 1993; Hartup, 1996). Some children tend to have relatively negative, hostile, angry interactions with their friends. Others have more mutually pleasurable, supportive interactions. As in the study of emotion, these aspects of children's friendships are surprisingly independent: as in adult relationships, people can have passionate friendships that are high on both positive and negative affect.

Sibling relationships

Until the 1980s, relationships with siblings received almost no attention from researchers. This is surprising, given that children often spend as much time with siblings as with parents.

Sibling relationships involve rivalry and conflict as well as warmth and companionship (Collins & Gunnar, 1990). From an evolutionary perspective, we would expect both conflict and love between siblings. On the one hand, siblings are genetically related by half, so the welfare of each influences the inclusive fitness of the other (chapter 10). Thus, natural selection should have selected mechanisms encouraging humans and other animals to care for their siblings.

Identical twins, who share 100 percent of their genetic make-up, should, from the perspective of evolutionary theory, be even more inclined than fraternal twins or non-twin siblings to look after the welfare of one another.

On the other hand, particularly in childhood, siblings compete for precious parental resources, which can mean the difference between life and death when conditions are scarce (see Trivers, 1972). As they mature, they may compete for familial resources that attract mates. Squabbling over an estate is, in fact, a major source of conflict among adult siblings cross-culturally. For example, among the Gabbra of Kenya, a nomadic people, the number of camels in a household predicts reproductive success for males but not females (Mace, 1996). Not surprisingly, sibling competition for resources is much higher in Gabbra society among males, for whom resources are a central component of status.

The birth of a sibling can be a difficult event for children. Parents report a wide range of responses, such as increased dependency, anxiety, bed-wetting, toilet 'accidents' and aggressiveness (Dunn & McGuire, 1992; see also Dunn, 2002). The younger the child's age at the birth, the more difficulty the child has with being displaced (Kramer & Gottman, 1992). Not knowing whether to express hostility or nurturance, young children often alternate between the two. Consider, for example, this description of a toddler coping with the birth of his little sister: 'My son is heroic in his efforts to be the "big man" and big brother, who offered to buy his new sister a birthday truck, though on a few occasions, he has broken down and uttered the most heart-rending sobs imaginable, pleading that we put her back in my belly, take her back to the hospital, or at least put her away somewhere. Mostly, he pats her gently, though sometimes gets a good jab in.'

APPLY + DISCUSS

Love, hate, care and rivalry are all part of the sibling experience.

- From the point of view of a first born, is there an 'optimal' age for a second child to come along? What about from the point of view of later borns and parents?
- What are the advantages and disadvantages of spacing children close together (e.g. two years) versus farther apart?

INTERIM SUMMARY

Friendship patterns develop substantially in childhood and adolescence, from largely same-sex experiences involving mutual play to more intimate interactions in adolescence. ***Rejected children*** are teased, ostracised or disliked by their peers. ***Neglected children*** are ignored. Children develop reputations among their peers by preschool. Children also differ in both the company they keep and the extent to which their friendships are characterised by positive and negative interactions. Sibling relationships involve rivalry and conflict as well as warmth, both of which make sense from an evolutionary standpoint.

Development of social cognition

The changing nature of children's friendships results in part from children's emotional and motivational development, such as an increasing concern with intimacy and an expanding capacity to commit to relationships despite momentary ups and downs. Children's friendships also change as their understanding of themselves, others and relationships — that is, their ***social cognition*** — develops. Fitness and Case (2003) assert that emotions play an integral role in shaping the social mind and that further consideration of the social functions of emotions can enrich our understanding of various mental disorders, including schizophrenia (chapter 15).

The evolving self-concept

One of the initial tasks of social–cognitive development is acquiring a sense of self as a distinct entity with its own physical qualities and psychological processes (Samuels, 1985; Stern, 1985; see also Cole et al., 2001). As adults, we tend to assume that we have always had a ***self-concept***, an organised view of ourselves or way of representing information about the self. However, children are not born knowing that other people have thoughts and feelings or that their own experience is not the centre of the universe. How do we evolve from foetuses — who are capable of sensation and learning but have no idea that their 'world' is in someone else's body or that the voice they can recognise in the womb belongs to someone else, their mother — to beings who understand that their own thoughts and feelings are theirs?

Self-concept in infants and young children

Because infants cannot talk about themselves, researchers have had to devise indirect methods to learn how the self-concept develops in the first few years. One of the most reliable methods, first developed to assess the self-concept of chimpanzees (Gallup, 1972), is to put rouge on the child's nose and observe the way the child responds to its image in a mirror (Amsterdam, 1972; Asendorpf & Baudonniere, 1993; Lewis & Brooks-Gunn, 1979). Infants of different ages respond very differently to the image they see. Children younger than 15 months rarely touch their noses, unlike the vast majority of two-year-olds, who recognise a discrepancy between the way they look and the way they should look. Thus, infants appear to develop a visual self-concept between 15 and 24 months.

Development of the visual self-concept is, however, not complete by two years. When investigators secretly place a sticker on the forehead of three-year-olds and then show them a videotape of themselves from a week or a few minutes earlier, they do not touch their foreheads. Four- and five-year-olds, in contrast, only touch their foreheads after watching the tape of themselves from a few minutes earlier, a suggestion that that they know what they generally do and do not look like (Povinelli & Simon, 1998).

During the toddler years, children begin to categorise themselves on various dimensions, especially age and gender (Damon & Hart, 1988). Throughout early childhood, the categories they use are largely concrete (Bornholt & Piccolo, 2005). When asked to describe themselves, they refer to their membership in groups ('I live with my mummy and my daddy'), material possessions ('I have a pretty room'), things they can do ('I can tie my shoes') and appearance.

These global categories do not imply, however, that the self-concept of young children is entirely devoid of subtlety. Even preschoolers can sometimes observe consistencies in their own behaviours that resemble adult categories of personality, such as extroversion ('I usually play with my friends' versus 'I usually play by myself'). However, they have difficulty making generalisations about their enduring feelings, such as 'I don't usually get mad' or 'I don't like myself' (Eder, 1990; Harter, 1998, 1999).

Self-concept in childhood and adolescence

Around age eight, children begin to define themselves based on internal, psychological attributes as much as on the obviously perceptible qualities or appearances that dominate all cognition in early childhood (Broughton, 1978; Damon & Hart, 1988; Harter, 1999; see also Shapka & Keating, 2005). In other words, they start to think about their abilities, their likes and dislikes, and the ways they tend to feel and think — namely, their personality. Conceiving the self at this point often involves comparisons with other children ('I'm good at maths' or 'I'm the best skateboarder in my school'). Children at this age also begin to describe themselves more relationally, saying things such as 'I'm smarter than anyone else in my class', or 'I'm more helpful around the house than my brother' (Harter, 1999).

In adolescence, representations of the self become much more subtle (figure 13.3) (Harter, 1998; Harter & Monsour, 1992). For example, a 17-year-old interviewed for a research project on the development of children's representations of self and others described herself as follows, 'I seem really shy on the outside, but inside I'm really involved when I'm with people, thinking a lot about what they are saying and doing. And with people I'm comfortable with, I probably don't seem shy at all' (Westen et al., 1991).

Although we have focused here on developmental trends that apply to most children, an important influence on individual differences in self-concept (and self-esteem) that increases as children age is genetics (McHale, Crouter, & Tucker, 1999). As with other attributes such as intelligence (chapter 9), heritability coefficients for self-concept and self-esteem tend to increase during adolescence, as genetic influences that were less apparent in childhood express themselves in behaviour.

Nine-year-old: My name is Jack C. I have brown eyes. I have brown hair. I have brown eyebrows. I'm nine years old. I LOVE! sport. I have seven people in my family. I have GREAT! eyesight. I have lots of friends. I live at 31 Lake Drive. I'm going on 10 in March. I'm a boy. I have an uncle that is almost 2 metres tall. My school is Highfields. My teacher is Mrs V. I play cricket! I am almost the smartest boy in the class. I LOVE! food. I love fresh air. I LOVE school.

Seventeen-year-old: I am a human being. I am a girl. I am an individual. I don't know who I am. I am a Pisces. I am a moody person. I am an indecisive person. I am an ambitious person. I am a very curious person. I am not an individual. I am a loner. I am an Australian. I am a liberal person. I am a radical. I am a conservative. I am a pseudoliberal. I am an atheist. I am not a classifiable person (i.e. I don't want to be).

FIGURE 13.3
Self-concept in childhood and adolescence. School-age children most frequently mention activities, significant others and attitudes when describing themselves, as in this excerpt from an interview with a nine-year-old boy. With age, the self-concept becomes more abstract and complex, as in the response by a 17-year-old girl.

SOURCE: Adapted from Montemayor and Eisen (1977, pp. 317–318).

In addition, gender plays a role not only in the attributes that children and adolescents use to describe themselves, but also in the evaluations that they assign to these attributes. As shown in figure 13.4, females evaluate themselves as weaker on appearance and athletics than males (Harter, 1999). This gender difference has been observed across a range of different cultures.

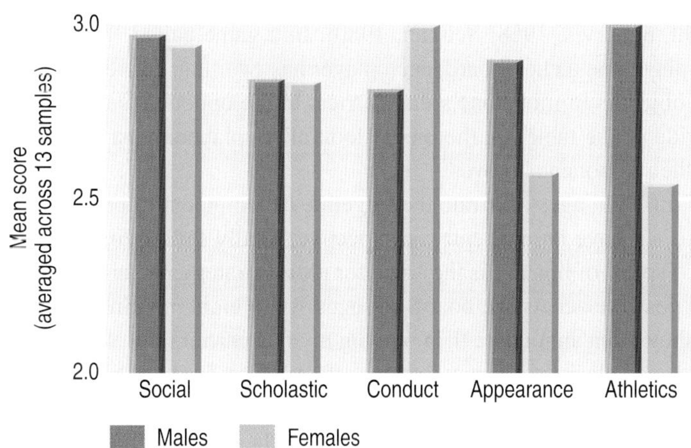

FIGURE 13.4
Gender and the self. Contributing to individual differences in the self-concept is gender. Males and females do not always evaluate themselves equally along different dimensions. As shown in this figure, females rate themselves lower on the categories of appearance and athletics than males. Ratings for each dimension were made along a 4-point scale.

SOURCE: From Bukatko/Daehler. *Child Development, A Thematic Approach*, 5E. © 2004 Wadsworth, a part of Cengage Learning, Inc. Reproduced by permission. www.cengage.com/permissions.

Concepts of others

Coming to understand other people, like coming to understand the self, is a lengthy developmental process (Flavell & Miller, 1998). In infancy, a central accomplishment is the recognition that social interactions are reciprocal — that other people's actions depend on one's own. By the third or fourth month, infants learn that smiling brings playful responses from caregivers, whereas crying usually means being picked up and held.

Infants also learn to read emotions in people's faces. As early as 12 months, an infant 'consults' the mother by looking to her for reassurance when introduced to a new toy. If the mother's face shows concern, the infant approaches the mother rather than the toy (Klinnert, Campos, Sorce, Emde, & Svejda, 1983; Saarni, 1998). If the infant receives a smile from one parent but a fearful look from the other, the child becomes confused and distressed (Hirshberg, 1990).

From early childhood until about age eight, children tend to focus on relatively simple, concrete attributes of other people, such as the way they look or the roles they perform (Shantz, 1983). For instance, a typical seven-year-old described a neighbour she liked as follows: 'she is very nice because she gives my friends and me toffee. She lives by the main road' (Livesley & Bromley, 1973, p. 214). Around age eight, however, children's representations of others begin to change, and they become more complex through adolescence.

Perspective-taking and theory of mind

An important social–cognitive ability that develops throughout childhood and adolescence, and probably beyond, is ***perspective-taking***, the ability to understand other people's viewpoints or perspectives. Taking other people's perspectives — from visualising what they see, as in Piaget's three-mountains task, to understanding in the midst of an argument why the other person is angry — involves moving out of egocentrism and representing the other person's mind in one's own.

A prerequisite to perspective-taking is the development of a ***theory of mind*** — an implicit set of ideas about the existence of mental states, such as beliefs and feelings, in oneself and others (Flavell, 1999; Gopnik, 1993). Researchers have argued about precisely when children develop a coherent theory of mind, but it appears to arise somewhere in the toddler years, between ages two and four. Before that time, children have trouble understanding that people can hold false beliefs, because they have trouble recognising that thought and reality can differ.

Precursors to a theory of mind can be seen, however, in infancy. For example, as early as the middle to end of the first year, infants appear to understand that people's actions reflect their goals, such as grabbing a particular object (Woodward & Sommerville, 2000). Infants also engage in joint visual attention, when their parents look at something and point to it — recognising that they should look at the object and not the parent (Deak, Flom, & Pick, 2000; Flavell, 1999). By the middle of the second year, children can infer from the face an experimenter makes after eating a food that the experimenter does not want it — even if the child likes that food (Repacholi & Gopnik, 1997).

Theory of mind and perspective-taking also develop considerably beyond the preschool years. Early school-age children, for example, do not clearly understand that certain activities, such as listening, pretending or deliberately performing mental or physical actions, require consciousness and cannot occur while people are asleep (Flavell, Green, Flavell, & Lin, 1999). One ingenious technique researchers have devised for assessing perspective-taking involves observing the way children play games of strategy (Flavell, Botkin, Fry, Wright, & Jarvis, 1968; Selman, 1980). In a game called 'Decoy and Defender' (Selman, 1980), which is played on a chessboard, each player has two 'flag carriers' as well as several less valuable tokens. The object is to move one's flag carriers to the opponent's side of the board. Because, from the opposite side of the table, all the pieces look alike, players must figure out which pieces to block by observing their opponents' moves.

The strategies used by children of different ages illustrate the stagelike development of perspective-taking ability. Children aged three to six have an egocentric perspective, totally failing to take their opponent's perspective into account. Typical of this age is the 'rush for glory' strategy: the child simply moves her flag carrier as quickly as possible across the board. By ages six to eight, children become craftier but in a transparent fashion: they often announce, 'I'm moving my flag carrier now' while moving an unimportant token. (They may even clear their throat first for effect.) They are beginning to recognise that to win they must influence the beliefs of their opponents. Other research similarly indicates that by age five children start to recognise the value of trying to influence other people's mental states in order to alter their behaviour (Peskin, 1992).

By ages eight to 10, children show more sophistication. For example, in the 'double-take' strategy, they might advance their flag carrier with considerable fanfare, expecting that the other player would not think they would be so stupid. Behind this strategy is a more complex perspective-taking process: 'He's thinking that I'm thinking . . .' The subtlety and complexity of this kind of back-and-forth thinking expand throughout adolescence.

INTERIM SUMMARY

Children develop in their ***social cognition***, their understanding of themselves, others and relationships. Researchers studying children's ***self-concept*** have found that children are not born with self-knowledge; even learning to represent their physical appearance is an achievement of the toddler years. Throughout early childhood, children tend to think of themselves and others in relatively concrete ways, such as their age, gender, group membership and possessions. Around age eight, they begin to think more about enduring personality attributes. By adolescence, social cognition, like all cognition, is much more subtle and abstract. ***Perspective-taking*** also increases steadily throughout childhood and adolescence, beginning with children's development of a ***theory of mind*** — an implicit set of ideas about the existence of mental states in the self and others.

Children's understanding of gender

Children's social cognition thus develops in complexity and abstractness, much as cognition does in non-social domains (chapter 12). The same is true of children's understanding of what gender is and how it applies to them, which changes dramatically over the first few years of life and continues to evolve throughout the life span.

One cognitive–developmental theory proposes that children progress through three stages in understanding gender (Kohlberg, 1966). In the first stage, usually attained by age two, children acquire ***gender identity***, the ability to categorise themselves (and others) as either male or female (Slaby & Frey, 1976). Precursors to gender knowledge of this sort can be seen as early as six to nine months of age, when habituation studies show that infants can discriminate males and females (see Martin & Ruble, 1997).

The second stage, ***gender stability***, occurs when children understand that their gender remains constant over time. Girls learn that they will never grow up to be Batman, Superman or even a garden-variety father, and boys learn that they will not become Wonder Woman, Kylie Minogue or a mother. Even after they recognise that they will never change their sex, however, children are not absolutely certain that this is also true of other people. Before age six or seven, some children believe that boys who wear dresses may eventually become girls and girls may metamorphose into boys if they do enough boyish things (Marcus & Overton, 1978; McConaghy, 1979). For example, when a four-year-old saw his father dressed as a woman for Halloween, he exclaimed, 'Two mummies!' In general, children know things about their own gender earlier than they can generalise this knowledge to others.

The third stage, ***gender constancy***, occurs when children learn that a person's gender cannot be altered by changes in appearance or activities (except, of course, in exceptional circumstances). Gender constancy may seem a simple achievement to us, but it does not necessarily come easily. One psychologist tells the story of a four-year-old boy who wore a barrette (hairband) to preschool. When another little boy called him a girl, the first child pulled down his pants to demonstrate that he was indeed still a boy. The other child, however, found this unconvincing. In a 'you can't fool me' tone of voice, he responded, 'Everyone has a penis; only girls wear barrettes' (Bem, 1983, p. 607).

APPLY + DISCUSS

With gender constancy, children understand that gender does not change with changes in appearance. In both social and non-social cognition, children around age seven or eight develop the capacity to distinguish between the 'essence' of a person or thing and its momentary appearance.

- How is the development of gender constancy related to a major cognitive achievement that occurs around the same time: understanding conservation of physical properties such as mass?
- Do gender schemas persist across the life span?

Gender schemas

While some researchers have focused on the structure (e.g. the level of complexity) of children's thinking about gender, others have turned their attention to the content of children's knowledge. Cross-culturally, children begin to show an awareness of their culture's beliefs about gender by the age of five; by middle childhood they share many of the stereotypes common in their society (Best et al., 1977; Huston, 1983). They encode and organise information about their culture's definitions of maleness and femaleness in ***gender schemas***, mental representations that associate psychological characteristics with each sex (Bem, 1985).

Gender schemas can be quite persistent across the life span. Consider the following scenario, familiar to any female doctor, reported by a colleague, a psychologist:

> 'Is Dr. Williams in?'
> 'Yes, speaking.'
> 'I'm calling regarding one of the doctor's patients. May I speak with the doctor please?'
> 'This is the doctor.'
> 'No, I need to speak with the doctor, Dr. Williams.'
> 'This is Dr. Williams.'

Because the caller's gender schema associates doctors with masculinity, the person has difficulty recognising that the doctor is, indeed, on the phone. Interestingly, the caller was female.

Gender schemas across the globe show considerable similarities as well as differences. One team of researchers gave an adjective checklist with 300 items (e.g. aggressive, arrogant, artistic, bossy) to university students in 25 countries and asked them to rate whether the words were more characteristic of men, women or neither (Best & Williams, 1998; Williams & Best, 1982). Although many adjectives were categorised differently in different countries, a number were almost universally associated

TABLE 13.1 Adjectives associated with males and females across cultures

Male	Female
Active	Affectionate
Adventurous	Attractive
Aggressive	Dependent
Clear thinking	Emotional
Coarse	Fearful
Courageous	Gentle
Cruel	Sensitive
Dominant	Sentimental
Egotistical	Sexy
Forceful	Submissive
Hardhearted	Weak
Lazy	
Self-confident	
Unemotional	
Wise	

SOURCE: Williams and Best (1982, p. 77).

NOTE: For these adjectives, over 20 of 25 countries share the gender stereotype.

with men or with women. Broadly speaking, people everywhere consider men more active, aggressive and dominant, and perceive women as more affectionate, emotional and sensitive (table 13.1).

The consistency of these findings is striking, although two qualifications are in order. First, technological change is reducing the distinctions between the sexes. Using a similar method, in a follow-up to their initial investigation the researchers examined ***sex-role ideology***, beliefs about appropriate behaviours of the sexes, in 14 countries (Williams & Best, 1990). Technologically developed, urban, individualistic societies tended to have more egalitarian sex roles, with less divergent views of appropriate behaviours for men and women. Protestant countries were also more likely to be egalitarian, while people in predominantly Muslim countries tended to believe men should be dominant and women, submissive.

A second qualification is that gender differences are average differences (Maccoby & Jacklin, 1974; Williams, 1983). For most traits, such as aggressiveness or sensitivity, the bell-shaped curves for males and females overlap substantially. Thus, within a culture, some women score higher than some men even on 'masculine' traits, and vice versa, although the typical member of each sex is higher on gendered traits than the average member of the opposite sex (figure 13.5). For example, women and men differ on the importance they attach to a vast number of criteria when selecting jobs, but the differences tend to be relatively small (Konrad, Ritchie, Edgar, Lieb, & Corrigall, 2000).

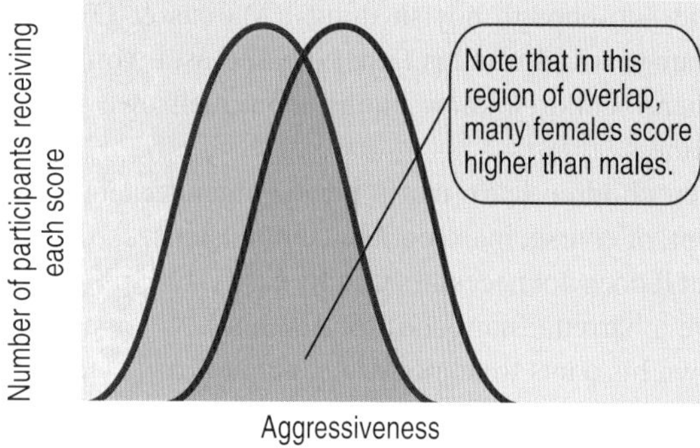

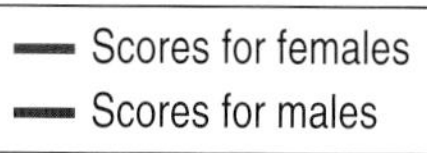

FIGURE 13.5
Aggressiveness in men and women. In this hypothetical distribution of scores on a measure of aggressiveness, one for men and one for women, the male curve is shifted to the right, signifying that most men are more aggressive than most women. Note the significant region of overlap, however, in which many women score higher than many men.

Cross-cultural gender stereotypes

Why are gender stereotypes so similar cross-culturally? As early as age two, Western boys prefer blocks and transportation toys such as trucks and cars, and girls prefer dolls and soft toys (Best, 2004; Chick, Heilman-Houser, & Hunter, 2002). Boys play more actively at manipulating objects and are more likely to engage in forbidden activities (Fagot, 1985; Smith & Daglish, 1977), whereas girls are more likely to play dress-up and dance. Girls also tend to talk earlier than boys (Schachter, Shore, Hodapp, Chalfin, & Bundy, 1978). Cross-cultural research with a large sample of preindustrial societies shows that the vast majority socialise boys from early childhood to be brave and self-reliant and girls to be responsible, self-restrained, obedient and sexually restrained (Low, 1989).

Why do so many cultures socialise children in similar ways? As we saw in exploring the links between gender differences and brain structures in chapter 3, where nature lays a foundation, culture tends to adorn, embellish and reshape it. This is likely to be the case with the most well-documented difference between the sexes, that males are more aggressive and females more nurturant (see Clinchy & Norem, 1998; Jacklin, 1989; Maccoby & Jacklin, 1974). These differences occur across cultures and species and are evident well before children begin school. Boys display higher rates of aggression in virtually every society and are far more likely to engage in rough-and-tumble play (Edwards & Whiting, 1983). Girls have never been found to be more prone to initiate aggressive encounters in any society (Maccoby & Jacklin, 1980).

Biology and evolution

The male hormone testosterone appears to be related to aggression in both males and females (chapter 18). Highly suggestive data come from studies of girls with adrenogenital syndrome, a malfunction of the adrenal glands that exposes the female foetus to unusually high levels of male hormones (chapter 10). The result is not only an increase in aggressiveness but also a general increase in 'tomboy' behaviour during childhood (Erhardt & Baker, 1974; Money & Erhardt, 1972). From an evolutionary perspective, sex differences in aggression and nurturance are products of natural selection. In many species, including most primates, males compete for sexual access to females, often physically establishing dominance over other males by fighting. Hence, males' tendency to exhibit aggressive behaviour and to practise such behaviour in childhood would optimise reproductive success. Behavioural differences would probably have been selected alongside physical differences such as the greater body mass in males of most species, including humans. Females, in contrast, carry infants in their uterus for nine months and hence have already made substantial investments in their offspring by birth. In the context of these sex differences, a division of labour may have evolved in which males tend to fight for status and protect the group and females tend to care for infants and young children.

APPLY + DISCUSS

Women, like men, respond emotionally when people violate gender stereotypes. History was made when the Australian Labor Party (ALP) deposed its leader, Kevin Rudd, during his first term as Prime Minister of Australia. Julia Gillard was elected ALP leader, becoming Australia's first female Prime Minister. She was sworn in by Quentin Bryce, the first female Governor-General of Australia. Many people reacted with surprise and disdain at Gillard's controversial appointment, and at the role she played in removing Kevin Rudd from office.

- To what extent do men's and women's reactions to Prime Minister Julia Gillard reflect the discrepancy between her behaviour as a politician and cultural views on the way 'ladies' should behave?
- Unlike the salaries of Governor-General Bryce and Prime Minister Gillard, average wages for women in Australia are presently only about 82 percent of the average wages for men (ABS, 2010c). How much does this depend on explicit discrimination versus implicit expression of gender stereotypes?

Culture and social learning

A strictly biological version of this hypothesis about sex differences would be difficult to sustain because research finds that males are quite capable of nurturant behaviour (Fogel, Melson, & Mistry, 1986). In fact, changing gender roles now allow fathers to care for infants and young children in ways that would have been considered 'unnatural' decades ago, and children whose fathers are more involved and nurturant with them tend to benefit psychologically in multiple ways (e.g. Black, Dubowitz, & Starr, 1999).

A social learning interpretation of sex differences holds that most behavioural differences observed between women and men result not primarily from innate differences but from expectancies, which, in turn, reflect the way society is organised (Eagly, 1983; Eagly & Wood, 1999). Women and men frequently find themselves in hierarchical relationships in which men are in positions of power and status and women are subordinate (e.g. doctor/nurse, executive/administrative assistant). Because these occur so often, people see them as natural and generalise to other situations, even where status is presumably equal, such as dinner-table discussions of politics. That they also adapt themselves to the roles in which they are likely to find themselves leads to substantial gender differences in behaviour.

Nature and nurture: an integrative view

Although the social learning hypothesis is compelling, it does not account for the fact that such similar social structures have emerged across cultures. Nor does it account for the finding that boys are more active in utero than girls, even before their parents have begun to push them towards more rough-and-tumble play (DiPietro, Hodgson, Costigan, & Johnson, 1996).

A more integrated account considers the interaction between biological evolution, cultural evolution and learned expectations. (In fact, advocates of both evolutionary and social learning approaches tend to acknowledge the importance of both evolution and learning but focus on one side or the other, e.g. Eagly & Wood, 1999.) From an integrative standpoint, biological evolution produced motivational 'pulls' that diverge in various ways for the two sexes, such as a tendency towards aggressive behaviour in males and nurturant behaviour in females, along with physical differences such as body size and strength. Based on these biological differences, nearly all cultures create a division of labour between the sexes and amplify innate tendencies. Simply noting the differences in size and strength between the average man and woman, for example, most cultures would be expected to enlist men and not women in warfare.

As ecological conditions shift (such as the disappearance of hand-to-hand combat or the ability of women to compete on an equal footing in the workplace), cultural ideology changes, and so do socialisation practices. In fact, cross-cultural data document that where women have more power (where they control resources such as property), girls are taught to be less submissive and more aggressive, although they still remain less aggressive than males (Low, 1989). It is important to note, as well, that evolutionary pressures would not likely select men and women to have completely divergent behavioural tendencies. Women in all cultures need aggression in their behavioural repertoire, just as men need nurturance to maximise their reproductive success. Evolution has undoubtedly selected for flexibility in human behaviour.

The politics and science of gender

One of the great difficulties of drawing conclusions about gender differences is the extent of passion and politics involved (Eagly, 1995). The systematic study of gender differences emerged in the 1970s with the rise of the feminist movement, which attempted to use psychological findings to discredit pervasive stereotypes that devalued women. Yet more recent research challenges the view that gender differences tend to be small. Men and women differ substantially in a number of ways, particularly in their relative attraction to and ability for verbal versus mathematical tasks and their tendency to be nurturant or aggressive (e.g. Feingold, 1994). Whereas the first wave of feminist influence on the understanding of gender attempted to show that gender differences are actually small, more recent thinking suggests that men and women do differ in some important respects, but that the problem lies less in those differences than in our tendency to devalue the things at which women excel.

INTERIM SUMMARY

Children's understanding of their own and other people's gender begins in the toddler years, when they start to classify themselves and others according to gender. Over time, they develop ***gender constancy***, the knowledge that gender cannot be altered by changes in appearance or activities. Children encode and organise information about their culture's definitions of maleness and femaleness in ***gender schemas***. People everywhere share certain stereotypes about men and women, which appear to be rooted in both evolved differences between the sexes and social and cultural practices and beliefs.

Moral development

Interviewer: Should boys get more? Why should they get more?
Four-year-old boy: Because they always need more.
Interviewer: Why do they need more?
Boy: Because that's how I want it.

Damon (1977, p. 121).

Fortunately, children's thinking about what is fair (and why) changes dramatically over the years, so that older children and adults do not operate at the same level of morality as this four-year-old (or they do it with more subtlety and conviction borne of biased reasoning). Researchers who study the development of morality — the set of rules people use to balance the conflicting interests of themselves and others — have focused on the roles of cognition and emotion in children's evolving sense of right and wrong (see Rest, 1983; Turiel, 1998).

The role of cognition

Several theories focus on cognition in moral development. These include cognitive–developmental, cognitive–social and information-processing theories.

Cognitive-developmental theories

The cognitive–developmental models of Jean Piaget and Lawrence Kohlberg focus on moral reasoning. These models propose that moral development proceeds through a series of stages that reflect cognitive development.

Piaget's theory

Piaget observed a simple type of event — games of marbles among children — and noted important differences in the way younger and older children thought about the rules (Piaget, 1932/1965). The youngest children, who were essentially pre-moral, arbitrarily altered the rules to enhance their enjoyment of the game and their chances of winning. Once children accepted the notion of rules, however, they would stick staunchly to them. If asked where the rules for playing marbles came from, they would reply with answers like, 'they just are', 'from Daddy' or 'from God!'.

Piaget called this first stage of moral judgement, in which children believe that morals are absolute, the ***morality of constraint***. This form of moral reasoning is typical of children before the age of nine or 10. Piaget described this morality as one 'of duty pure and simple', in which children conform to societal rules that are viewed as unchanging and unchangeable (1932/1965, p. 335). When judging the actions of others, children in this stage tend to centre on the most salient characteristic of the act — its severity — and have difficulty simultaneously keeping in mind other aspects of the act, such as the intention behind it.

Consider what happens when a child is asked to decide who is more blameworthy, a boy who went to steal a cookie from the kitchen and broke a glass while reaching into the cookie jar or another boy who accidentally slipped and broke five glasses. In line with the tendency of preoperational children to focus on only one salient attribute at a time (chapter 12), a five-year-old is likely to reason that the boy who broke more glasses has committed the worse offence, even though his 'crime' was accidental.

Older children and adults focus more on their inferences about others' intentions. They also tend to view rules as means to ends, as strategies for keeping social interactions safe, fair and comfortable. In this ***morality of cooperation***, moral rules can be changed if they are not appropriate to the occasion, as long as the people involved agree to do so. Older children playing marbles may thus change the rules by mutual consent without believing they are violating something sacred.

APPLY + DISCUSS

During the 1980s, Carol Gilligan suggested that males and females differ in the types of moral reasoning or 'voices' they are most likely to use. She suggested that men advocate a voice of justice ('Who is right?'), whereas women operate according to a voice of care ('Is anyone likely to be hurt by this moral dilemma?'). Since Gilligan's research first appeared, however, little support for gender differences in moral reasoning have been obtained.

- Do you think that men and women differ in their levels of moral reasoning? Why or why not?
- What levels of moral reasoning do you think men and women are most likely to use?

Kohlberg's theory

Lawrence Kohlberg shared two of Piaget's central convictions about moral development. The first is that changes in moral reasoning result from basic changes in cognitive structures — that is, changes in ways of thinking. For example, as children's thinking becomes more abstract, so, too, does their moral reasoning. Second, Kohlberg conceptualised children as active constructors of their own moral reality, not passive recipients of social rules.

Kohlberg (1976; Kohlberg & Kramer, 1969) proposed a sequence of three levels of moral development, each comprising of two stages. He assessed moral development by presenting participants with hypothetical dilemmas and asking them how these dilemmas should be resolved and why. Each dilemma forces a person to choose between violating the law and helping another person in need. An example is the dilemma of Heinz and the druggist (pharmacist) (Kohlberg, 1963, p. 19).

> In Europe, a woman was near death from a special kind of cancer. There was one drug that the doctors thought might save her. It was a form of radium that a druggist in the same town had recently discovered. The drug was expensive to make, but the druggist was charging ten times what the drug cost him to make. He paid $200 for the radium and charged $2,000 for a small dose of the drug. The sick woman's husband, Heinz, went to everyone he knew to borrow the money, but he could only get together about $1,000, which is half of what it cost. He told the druggist that his wife was dying and asked him to sell it cheaper or let him pay later. But the druggist said, 'No, I discovered the drug, and I'm going to make money from it.' So Heinz got desperate and broke into the man's store to steal the drug for his wife. Should the husband have done that?

Kohlberg's example of Heinz and the druggist turned out years later to be a real-life moral dilemma that found its way into the courtroom, when the South African government tried to compel the Western pharmaceutical industry to sell medications for life-threatening illnesses such as AIDS to people who could not otherwise afford them.

The level of moral development a person shows in answering this question depends not on the particular answer (to steal or not to steal) but on the reasoning behind the response (table 13.2; see overleaf). At the first level, ***preconventional morality***, children follow moral rules either to avoid punishment (stage 1) or to obtain reward (stage 2). A preconventional child might conclude that Heinz should steal the drug 'if he likes having his wife around'. At the second level, ***conventional morality***, children (and adults whose moral reasoning remains conventional) define what is right and wrong by the standards they have learned from other people, particularly respected authorities such as their parents. People with conventional morality justify their choice of moral actions on the basis of their desire to gain the approval or avoid the disapproval of others (stage 3) or on the need to maintain law and order (e.g. 'if everyone stole whenever he wanted to, what would this world come to?') (stage 4).

The third level, ***postconventional morality***, is a morality of abstract, self-defined principles that may or may not match the dominant morals of the times. A postconventional adult, like a preconventional child, might condone stealing the drug, but for a very different reason, such as 'the value of a human life far exceeds any rights of ownership or property'. (Distinctions between two postconventional stages originally outlined by Kohlberg have not proven empirically useful and will thus not be described here.) Only about 5 percent of people actually reach the postconventional level (Colby & Kohlberg, 1984).

TABLE 13.2 **Kohlberg's levels of moral development**

Level	Reasons to steal the drug	Reasons not to steal the drug
Preconventional: Morality centres on avoiding punishment and obtaining reward.	He should steal it if he likes her a lot; if he gets caught, he won't get much of a jail term, so he'll get to see her when he gets out.	He'll get caught; he shouldn't have to pay with jail time for his wife's problem.
Conventional: Morality centres on meeting moral standards learned from others, avoiding their disapproval and maintaining law and order.	If he doesn't steal it, everyone will think he's a terrible person; it's his duty to care for his wife.	If he steals it, everyone will think he's a criminal; he can't just go stealing things whenever he wants to — it isn't right.
Postconventional: Morality centres on abstract, carefully considered principles.	If he has to run from the police, at least he'll know he did the right thing; sometimes people have to break the law if the law is unjust.	If he steals it, he'll lose all respect for himself; other people might say it was okay, but he'll have to live with his conscience, knowing he's stolen from the druggist.

The basic logic of Kohlberg's theory is that at the preconventional level, the person accepts moral standards only if doing so is personally advantageous; this is an ethic of hedonism or self-interest. The child is preconventional in the sense that he has not yet come to accept society's conventions in their own right as rules that good people should follow. At the conventional level, the individual believes in the moral rules he has learned. The person with postconventional morality, in contrast, views the values of the time as conventions — rules established by social contract rather than by any absolute or divine power — and hence as both potentially fallible and changeable. Virtually all normal children progress to the conventional level of morality (stage 3) by the age of 13. Beyond stages 3 and 4, however, the development of moral reasoning is not related to age and is more a matter of individual differences and culture.

Cognitive-social theories

Cognitive–social theories (chapters 6 and 11) focus less on moral reasoning than on moral behaviour. According to behaviourist and cognitive–social theories, moral behaviours, like other behaviours, are learned through processes such as conditioning and modelling (Bandura, 1977b; Mischel & Mischel, 1976; see also Arsenio & Lemerise, 2004). Cognitive–social researchers measure moral development in terms of ***prosocial behaviour*** — behaviour that benefits other individuals or groups (Holmgren, Eisenberg, & Fabes, 1998; Mischel & Mischel, 1976). Anyone who has ever watched (or been) a child knows how powerful the words 'good boy!' or 'good girl!' can be in shaping prosocial behaviour.

From this point of view, morality develops as children come to discover through trial and error and deliberate instruction that certain actions will be reinforced or punished. Thus, children learn that stealing is wrong because they are punished for it, see someone else punished (vicarious conditioning) or are told they will be punished (direct tutelage). They acquire expectancies about the outcome of their behaviours under different circumstances (whether they will or will not be punished), and they develop conditioned emotional responses (such as anxiety or guilt) to behaviours that are regularly punished. They also generalise from one situation to the next, recognising, for example, that talking in one library is no more acceptable than talking in another.

Clear cultural differences in how altruistically children behave towards others have been observed (Whiting & Edwards, 1988; see also Hart & Carlo, 2005). Children raised in more individualistic cultures, such as Australia and New Zealand, behave more selfishly and with less concern for the needs and wellbeing of others. In more collectivist cultures, however, where the needs of the group are emphasised and children are required to contribute to the family income, empathy and concern for others is much more apparent. Kearins (2000) points out that in Australian Aboriginal societies, with a history of a more collectivist hunter-gatherer approach, children do act differently from those in Western societies. 'They normally are willing participants in family tasks and within the wider community, caring for younger children, collecting firewood, helping in food-getting, shopping, household tasks and so on; but there is rarely coercion' (p. 169). By contrast, children in Western cultures are more often directed and instructed by adults.

Information-processing theories

An alternative cognitive view of moral development is an information-processing approach (Darley & Shultz, 1990; Grusec & Goodnow, 1994; Nelson & Crick, 1999; see also Arsenio & Lemerise, 2004). Information-processing theories do not postulate broad stages of moral development. Rather, they break moral thinking down into component processes and examine the way each of these processes changes during childhood.

According to one such view (Schultz & Schliefer, 1983), when adults make decisions about whether an act is immoral and whether it deserves punishment, as in jury deliberations, they make a series of sequential judgements. As figure 13.6 shows, the first question concerns cause: did the person cause or contribute to the damage? If so, the next question is one of moral responsibility, which rests on intentions (did he mean to?) and judgement (could he have foreseen the results?).

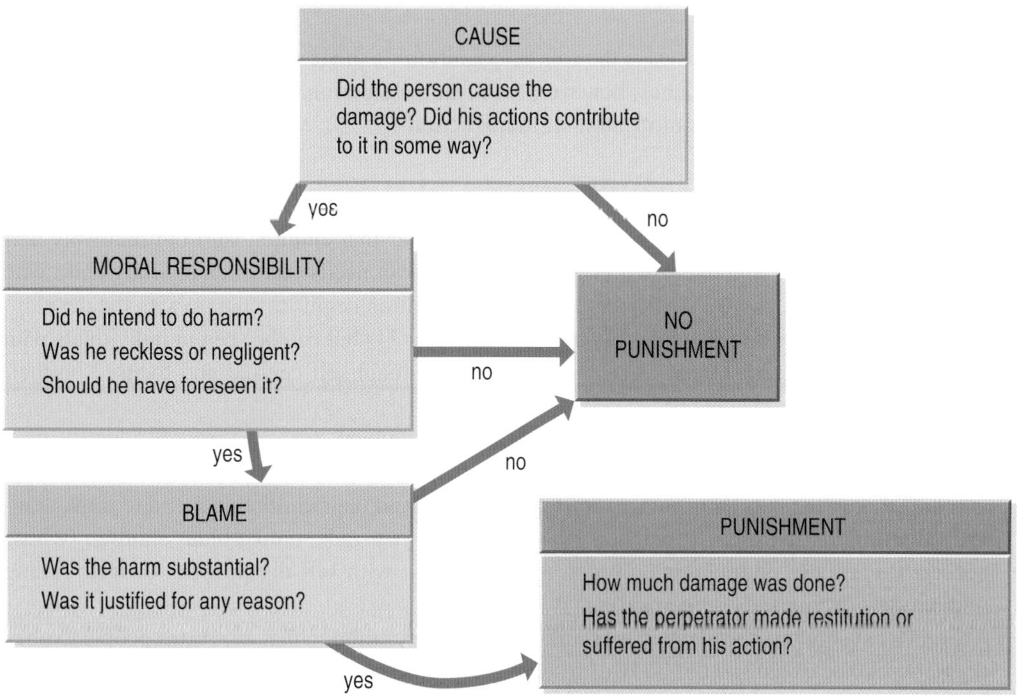

FIGURE 13.6
An information-processing model of moral decision making. According to this model, when people make decisions about whether an act is immoral and whether it deserves punishment, they make a series of sequential judgements, such as whether the person caused the event, was morally responsible, is blameworthy and deserves punishment.

SOURCE: Adapted from Darley and Shultz (1990, p. 532).

ETHICAL DILEMMA

A couple have a young child with a rare terminal illness. The only hope for survival is a transplant from a close relative with matching bone marrow. However, all the child's close relatives are screened and none is a match. Doctors suggest one other alternative — that the couple conceive a child and use artificial genetic programming to produce the right type of bone marrow. When the baby is old enough, that marrow can be transplanted to save the life of its sibling.

- Can this process be carried out in a way that does not compromise the dignity and welfare of everyone involved — including the unborn child?
- Do you think a young child would agree with the doctors' suggestion?

If the individual is morally responsible, the next question is whether he is blameworthy — that is, did he do significant harm and were his actions justified in some way? For example, jurors often make very different judgements about blameworthiness of defendants who attacked someone who molested their child. Finally, if the person caused unjustified harm, what should be his punishment? People in the West tend to determine appropriate punishment, whether in a jury trial or in the discipline of their children, according to three criteria: the extent of the damage, whether the perpetrator has already made appropriate restitution (e.g. by apologising) and whether the perpetrator has suffered as a result of his actions.

From an information-processing view, then, understanding moral development means understanding changes in the way children answer these multiple questions. For example, when do children come to understand the difference between directly causing someone to suffer (e.g. taking something from them) as opposed to taking an action that, combined with someone else's action, produces suffering (e.g. forgetting to lock a door, which contributed to a theft)? According to this view, global stage theories cannot capture developmental changes in the multiple components of moral reasoning, which often occur at different times.

INTERIM SUMMARY

Cognitive theories stress the role of thought and learning in moral development. According to Piaget, children at first believe moral rules are immutable but ultimately come to understand that they are the product of convention. Young children also tend to centre on consequences rather than intentions in making moral judgements. Kohlberg distinguished three levels of moral development: ***preconventional morality*** (people follow moral rules either to avoid punishment or to obtain rewards), ***conventional*** (individuals define what is right by the standards they have learned from other people, particularly respected authorities) and ***postconventional*** (people reason using abstract, self-defined moral principles that may not match conventional moral beliefs). Cognitive–social approaches measure moral development in terms of ***prosocial behaviour***. Information-processing approaches examine changes in the component processes involved in moral thinking.

The role of emotion

The theories discussed thus far emphasise the role of cognition — judgement and decision making — in moral development. Other approaches, however, focus on the emotional side (see Eisenberg, 2000), particularly on guilt and empathy as motivators of moral action.

APPLY + DISCUSS

Family dynasties are commonplace in Australia's ruthless media industry. For example, James Packer took over the business built up by his media tycoon father, Kerry, who himself took over an empire founded by his father, Sir Frank Packer. Despite diversifying, James Packer maintains media interests as part of his family company's portfolio. David Gyngell is in charge of the Nine Network, a position once held by his father, Bruce. Ryan Stokes is part of the executive team at the Seven Network, which is owned and run by his father, Kerry. Moral values tend to be highly similar in fathers and sons.

- Explain why this may be so, using each of the psychodynamic, behaviourist and cognitive perspectives.
- To what extent could behavioural genetics play a part in this phenomenon, via transmitting personality traits such as ruthlessness (chapters 3 and 11)?

Psychodynamic theories

The psychodynamic view of moral development proposes that children start out relatively narcissistic (self-centred and interested in gratifying their own needs), as when a young child who wants an extra piece of cake simply grabs it. This orientation begins to change with the development of a conscience between ages two and five (chapter 11) but can be seen in individuals with narcissistic and antisocial personality disorders, who remain self-centred and focused on their own needs as adults (chapter 15).

From a psychodynamic perspective, moral development occurs through identification or internalisation: children take in the values of their parents, which are at first external, and gradually adopt them as their own. Empirically, parents and their children do tend to think similarly about moral questions (Speicher, 1994), and four-year-olds, unlike older children (whose conscience is more internalised), do not associate lying with self-disapproval, or truth-telling with positive feelings about themselves (Bussey, 1999).

From a psychodynamic perspective, guilt is the primary emotion that motivates people to obey their conscience. A substantial body of research supports the role of guilt in moral development and behaviour (Eisenberg, 2000; see also Koenig, Cicchetti, & Rogosch, 2004). Guilt arises from discrepancies between what people feel they should do and what they contemplate or observe themselves doing. When toddlers are learning about morals, they may feel anxious or ashamed at being caught. Yet they do not experience genuine guilt until they actually internalise their parents' values as their own — that is, until they not only know these values but also believe in them.

Young children's moral beliefs are very concrete and specific and are often tied directly to a mental image of a parent. Toddlers may thus be observed telling themselves 'No!' even as they follow a forbidden impulse, or repeating their parents' admonitions as a way of stopping themselves from doing something they have been told is wrong ('Don't make a mess!'). Research suggests that as children get older, they rely less on an internalised parent 'sitting on their shoulder' and more on abstract moral demands integrated from their parents and the wider culture (see Williams & Bybee, 1994).

Empathy

Unpleasant emotions such as guilt, anxiety and shame are not the only emotions involved in moral behaviour. Some theorists emphasise the motivational role of ***empathy*** or feeling for another person who is hurting (see Holmgren et al., 1998). Empathy has both a cognitive component (understanding what the person is experiencing) and an emotional component (experiencing a similar feeling). Research supports the view that empathy contributes to prosocial behaviour, although empathising too much emotionally can actually make people self-focused and hence less helpful (Strayer, 1993).

According to one theory (Hoffman, 1978, 1998), the ability to respond empathically changes considerably over the course of development. During the first year, infants experience global empathy; that is, they feel the same distress as the other person but cannot separate whose distress is whose. An

11-month-old who witnesses another child fall and cry may put her thumb in her mouth and bury her head in her mother's lap as if she were hurt herself.

As children become better able to distinguish their own thoughts and feelings from those of others, they begin to experience genuine ***empathic distress*** — feeling upset for another person — which motivates moral or prosocial behaviour. As early as the second year of life, children can recognise when someone is hurting, feel bad for that person and try to take action to make the person feel better (Zahn-Waxler, Radke-Yarrow, Wagner, & Chapman, 1992). The response may nonetheless be egocentric: a 13-month-old may give a sad-looking adult his own favourite stuffed animal or bring his own mother over to comfort a crying playmate, reflecting the immature perspective-taking ability of the young child.

As children get older, they respond more accurately to cues about what other people are feeling. By adolescence, a more mature form of empathy emerges, as individuals begin to think about suffering that exists beyond the immediate moment and hence become concerned about broader issues such as poverty or moral responsibility.

If empathy leads to prosocial actions, what type of actions does an individual who lacks empathy display? Do they try to hurt others or are they simply unaware of the needs and feelings of others? The answer appears to favour the former. For example, children with conduct disorder display violent and aggressive behaviour directed towards other people and/or animals. They may also destroy property and lie. In short, they display behaviours that clearly run counter to the social norms of society. Although a number of explanations have been offered to explain the origins of conduct disorder, one recent hypothesis suggests that people with conduct disorder lack empathy. To test this idea, levels of empathy among individuals with conduct disorder and normal individuals were compared. The adolescents viewed videotaped vignettes portraying people in distress. They then completed a series of questionnaires assessing their reactions to the vignettes. Indeed, the individuals with conduct disorder showed significantly less empathy than did the normal controls to whom they were compared (Cohen & Strayer, 1996).

Making sense of moral development

Cognitive and emotional approaches to moral development each present part of the picture, but none alone covers the entire landscape.

Cognitive approaches

The strength of the cognitive–social approach is its emphasis on precisely what is missing from most other approaches, namely, moral or prosocial behaviour. Thinking about morality is irrelevant if it does not affect action. Research does not, in fact, show particularly strong correlations between moral reasoning and prosocial behaviour in older children and adults; correlations between empathy and prosocial behaviour tend to be relatively small as well (e.g. see Eisenberg, Miller, Shell, McNalley, & Shea, 1991; Miller, Eisenberg, Fabes, & Shell, 1996).

The cognitive–social approach, however, tends to assume that certain behaviours are prosocial and generally does not address situations that require choices between imperfect moral options. For example, during the Vietnam War, people agonised over the question of what was moral or 'prosocial'. Was it moral to answer the draft, even though many considered the war immoral or nonsensical? Evade the draft and let other people die instead? Protest the war? These kinds of questions are the essence of moral decision making.

Cognitive–developmental models have advantages and disadvantages as well. Kohlberg's theory highlights a phenomenon that no other theory addresses — that moral development may go beyond the internalisation of society's rules. This has been the principle of many moral leaders, from Jesus to Gandhi to Martin Luther King.

At the same time, Kohlberg's theory has drawn considerable criticism. People at the higher stages of moral reasoning do not necessarily behave any differently from people who are conventional in their moral reasoning. The philosopher Martin Heidegger, who reflected deeply and abstractly on a range of human experiences, found ways to rationalise cooperation with the Nazi regime, which many more 'ordinary' Europeans did not (chapter 18).

Relatedly, moral reasoning does not always translate into moral behaviour. Indeed, as noted earlier, Kohlberg was less concerned with the ultimate decision a person makes and more with the reasoning processes by which they arrive at that decision. Thus, according to the model, morality is clearly determined by the level of reasoning rather than the behaviour itself.

Other critics argue that Kohlberg's model overlooks the role of educational level in influencing moral reasoning. People with higher educational levels display higher levels of moral reasoning than people with less education, but this characteristic does not necessarily mean that they are more moral. Rather, they are more articulate in their reasoning abilities (Eckensberger, 1994). Furthermore, people do not always display the same level of moral reasoning in different situations (Fishkin, Keniston, & MacKinnon, 1973). In other words, in the face of one moral dilemma, a person's reasoning may be at the conventional level; when confronted with another moral dilemma, the person may reason at the postconventional level of morality.

Yet other critics, notably Carol Gilligan (1982, 1996), contend that Kohlberg's theory is gender biased. In Kohlberg's early studies, women rarely transcended stage 3 morality, which equates goodness with pleasing or helping others. Men more often reached stage 4, which focuses on maintaining social order. Does this mean women are morally inferior? Gilligan thinks not — and a glance around the globe at most of the perpetrators of violence supports her view. According to Gilligan, women and men follow divergent developmental paths, with one no less mature than the other. Women's moral concerns, she argues, more likely centre on care and responsibility for specific individuals, whereas men tend to favour the justice orientation emphasised by Kohlberg. A meta-analysis (a review that summarises the data across dozens or hundreds of studies quantitatively, by averaging their findings; chapter 16) found that women and men do tend towards care and justice orientations, respectively, but that the differences are relatively small (Jaffee & Hyde, 2000).

Both Gilligan's and Kohlberg's theories may require some modification when applied to cultures in which concepts of duty and caring are different and less gender based than in the West — that is, where both men and women show a greater orientation towards relationships and community than in the West (Miller, 1994). For example, when six-year-olds in the United States and China tell stories in response to pictures or describe emotional memories, Chinese children show a greater concern with social engagement and obedience to authority, whereas Western children's stories show more themes related to autonomy (Wang & Leichtman, 2000).

The information-processing approach to moral development fills in and clarifies many of the broad strokes painted by stage theories. Nevertheless, it leaves many questions unanswered, particularly about the way motivation influences moral reasoning and behaviour. Why do children accept values in the first place, when doing so produces guilt? Why are they willing to control their impulses at all? How do their judgements about their own guilt or responsibility differ from their judgements about others'? Asking people to make judgements about what other people have done is very different from understanding their own struggles to remain faithful to their lovers, to report their income honestly to the Tax Office or to resist saying something unkind behind a friend's back.

Emotional approaches

Perspectives that focus on the emotional side of morality fare better in answering these questions. Because morality so often requires self-sacrifice and self-restraint, an emotional counterweight such as anxiety or guilt seems essential to balance out the net losses in gratification. Empathy adds a further source of motivation for moral behaviour: helping other people leads to a sense of satisfaction and reduces the empathic distress that comes from observing someone else's suffering (chapter 18).

Emotional approaches, however, also have their pitfalls. Why children internalise moral values is unclear. Freud linked identification with the father to the fear of castration in boys (chapter 12). This seems a rather unlikely impetus for the development of morality and cannot account for moral development in females. Moreover, research indicates that mothers are more responsible for moral training in most Western families (Hoffman & Saltzstein, 1967; see also Walker, Hennig, & Krettenauer, 2000) and that internalisation of values is associated with the extent to which mothers engage in an emotionally responsive, reciprocal relationship with their children (Kochanska et al., 2000). Identification with the father is probably not as central as Freud supposed, although research on moral reasoning does show particularly strong links between fathers' level of moral reasoning and the moral reasoning of both their sons and daughters (Speicher, 1994).

Empathy theories do not provide insight into specifically moral questions, which arise when people's needs are in conflict. Prosocial responses are common by 18 to 20 months when infants witness other people's distress but not when they cause the distress themselves (Zahn-Waxler, Robinson, & Emde, 1992). Infants as young as 12 to 18 months often share toys with other children or with their parents, but by age two they are less likely to share if it means giving up their toys (Hay, Caplan, Castle, & Stimson, 1991).

Perhaps not incidentally, by this age most children have mastered the word 'mine'. Prosocial responses aimed at making up for a transgression emerge around two years, precisely when theorists have argued for the beginnings of moral conscience fuelled by guilt.

Research suggests that the roots of conscience may lie in both the fear emphasised by Freud and the empathy emphasised by other researchers (Kochanska, 1997). For children who have a fearful temperament, gentle discipline by mothers predicts conscience at age four. For children who have a fearless temperament and are less responsive to discipline, positive mother–child interactions appear to predict conscience development. These data make sense in the light of research suggesting that some people are more driven by fear, whereas others are more pulled by rewards (chapter 10). What is interesting is the possibility that these basic temperamental variables may affect the way children internalise moral values as well.

An integrated view

An integrated account of moral development would spell out the interactions of cognition, affect and motivation that are involved when children and adults wrestle with moral questions. Infants and toddlers have many selfish impulses, but they also have prosocial impulses based on an innate capacity for empathy. When self-centred and other-centred motives clash, young children tend to opt for the most gratifying course of action.

This behaviour probably changes over time for a number of reasons. Children mature in their capacity to love and care about other people and to understand the perspectives of others. They also become more able to regulate their impulses as neural circuits in the frontal lobes mature and as expanding cognitive abilities allow them to transform situations in their minds.

Furthermore, through social learning, children come to associate actions such as sharing with positive reinforcement and hitting and lying with punishment. By identifying with people they fear and admire, children's fear of punishment gradually becomes transformed into fear of their own internal monitor of right and wrong — and hence into guilt. Eventually, they reflect more abstractly about moral questions and try to integrate the moral feelings and beliefs they have accrued over the course of their development.

APPLY + DISCUSS

- How might different approaches to moral development account for the actions of committed Jemaah Islamiah terrorists, who killed civilians in their effort to be heard?
- Would all people drawn to terrorist organisations receive similar explanations? What might draw people to support the activities of the Al-Qaeda terrorist organisation?

INTERIM SUMMARY

Emotion, like cognition, is central to moral development. Psychodynamic theories emphasise the role of guilt in moral development and argue that conscience arises through identification with parents. Other theories emphasise ***empathy***, or feeling for another person who is hurting. Moral development probably reflects an interaction of cognitive and affective changes that allow children to understand and feel for other people as well as to inhibit their own wishes and impulses.

Social development across the life span

In discussing social development, we have thus far focused on the first quarter of the life span. Like physical and cognitive development, however, social development continues throughout life. In this section, we begin by examining the most widely known theory of life-span development, formulated by Erik Erikson (1963). We then examine central aspects of life-span development from adolescence through old age.

Erikson's theory of psychosocial development

Erikson's is not the only model of adult development, but it has three important features. First, it is culturally sensitive, reflecting Erikson's experience living in and studying several cultures, from Denmark and Germany to a Sioux reservation. Research since Erikson's time suggests that when and where people develop is crucial to the way they grow and change throughout their lives, even within a single culture (Elder, 1998). For example, people who were young children during the Great Depression never forgot the lessons of poverty, even when they were financially secure years later.

Second, Erikson's theory integrates biology, psychological experience and culture by grounding development simultaneously in biological maturation and changing social demands (chapter 1). For example, like his mentor, the psychoanalyst Anna Freud (1958), Erikson observed that adolescents wrestle with questions about who they are and what they believe during puberty, a time in which teenagers have a surge of new feelings and impulses. Reconstituting a self-concept that now includes the self as a sexual being is a major task spurred by biological maturation. The extent to which adolescents find this conflictual, however, depends on the beliefs, values, rituals and sexual practices of their culture (Mead, 1928).

Third, although Erikson's theory offers a very broad framework, many aspects of his developmental model have received empirical support in cross-sectional, longitudinal and sequential studies (e.g., Bradley & Marcia, 1998; Marcia, 1987, 1999; McAdams, Hart, & Maruna, 1998; Whitbourne, Zuschlag, Elliot, & Waterman, 1992; see also Slater, 2003).

Erikson intended his model of ***psychosocial stages*** — stages in the development of the person as a social being — to supplement Freud's psychosexual stages (see table 13.3). Thus, the toddler years are not only a time of toilet training but also, more generally, a time of learning what it means to submit to authority, to control impulses and to assert one's own autonomy. At each of the eight stages, the individual faces a ***developmental task***, a challenge that is normative for that period of life. Each successive task provokes a crisis — an opportunity for steaming ahead or a danger point for psychological derailment. These alternative 'tracks' at each juncture are not, of course, absolute. No infant, for example, ever feels totally trusting or mistrusting, and people have many opportunities over the course of development to backtrack or take a new route.

TABLE 13.3 **Erikson's psychosocial stage model of development**

Psychosocial stage (approximate age)	Developmental task
0 to 18 months	Basic trust versus mistrust
1 to 2 years	Autonomy versus shame and doubt
3 to 6 years	Initiative versus guilt
7 to 11 years	Industry versus inferiority
Teenage years (adolescence)	Identity versus identity confusion
20s and 30s (young adulthood)	Intimacy versus isolation
40s to 60s (midlife)	Generativity versus stagnation
60s on	Integrity versus despair

Childhood

APPLY + DISCUSS

- How might an infant's innate temperament and early experiences together shape her sense of trust or mistrust — or, in the language of attachment theory, her attachment security?
- How might an insecure or mistrustful infant or young child behave in ways that actually reinforce her view of relationships?

During the first stage, ***basic trust versus mistrust***, infants come to trust others or to perceive the social world as hostile or unreliable. This stage comprises roughly the first 18 months of life, when infants are developing their earliest internal working models of relationships.

By age two, children have learned to walk and talk — a result of biological maturation that has profound psychological consequences. Now they can say what they want and move where they want. This is the time of the 'terrible twos', in which toddlers regularly assert their will. Erikson calls the period from around ages two to three ***autonomy versus shame and doubt***, because toddlers at this stage learn to feel secure in their independence or to experience doubt in their newfound skills and shame at their failures.

Empirically, some of the feelings of excitement and shame children experience at this age are self-generated, whereas others can be traced to the ways their parents respond to their successes, failures and efforts at mastery. During the second year, children spontaneously set standards for themselves and experience pride in their accomplishments (Kagan, 1984). Yet research also finds that two-year-olds whose mothers are critical and controlling as they attempt to teach their toddlers achievement-related tasks in the laboratory tend to demonstrate more shame and less persistence at similar tasks a year later (Kelley, Brownell, & Campbell, 2000).

The third stage, roughly between ages three and six, is called ***initiative versus guilt***. The poles of this stage are a sense of goal-directness and responsibility versus a rigid, tyrannical conscience. Initiative enables a child to follow through with ideas and goals. Children who have difficulty with this stage, in contrast, may be highly self-critical, or may become rigid and constricted to avoid acting on feelings and impulses they have learned to think of as 'bad'.

The next stage, which occurs roughly between ages seven and 11, is ***industry versus inferiority***. In this stage, children develop a sense of competence (industriousness) or of inadequacy, as they begin to develop and practise skills they will use for a lifetime in productive work. In literate cultures, children enter school during this stage, and their experiences of academic and social success or failure shape both their self-concepts and the strategies they use to protect their self-esteem. Some children become caught in a vicious cycle, in which a sense of inferiority leads them to give up quickly on tasks, which in turn increases the probability of further failure (chapter 14).

Adolescence

According to Erikson, the developmental crisis of adolescence is ***identity versus identity confusion***. ***Identity*** refers to a stable sense of who one is and what one's values and ideals are (Erikson, 1968). For example, in the 2010 National Survey of Young Australians, between 24 to 30 percent of young people aged 11–19 years highly valued their independence (Mission Australia, 2010). ***Identity confusion*** occurs when the individual fails to develop a coherent and enduring sense of self and has difficulty committing to roles, values, people or occupational choices. Empirically, individuals differ in the extent to which they explore and maintain commitments to ideologies, occupational choices and interpersonal values (Marcia, 1987). Some establish an identity after a period of soul searching, while others commit early without exploration, foreclosing identity development. Still others remain perpetually confused or put off identity consolidation for many years while trying on various roles throughout their twenties.

These different paths to identity depend heavily on culture (Erikson, 1968; Schlegel & Barry, 1991). Many traditional cultures have ***initiation rites***, ceremonies during adolescence that initiate the child into adulthood and impose a socially bestowed identity. A period of identity confusion occurs primarily in technologically more advanced societies or in cultures that are undergoing rapid change, as in much of the contemporary world.

Sometimes adolescents have trouble establishing a positive identity; they may be doing poorly in school or lack models of successful adulthood with whom to identify. As a result, they may develop a ***negative identity***, defining themselves as *not* something or someone (such as a parent) or taking on a role society defines as bad. This is a path often taken by gang members and chronic delinquents, who seemingly revel in their 'badness'.

Failure to form a cohesive identity beyond adolescence can signify problems later on. Girls who have difficulty forming an identity in late adolescence are more likely than their peers to experience marital disruption at midlife. Boys with late-adolescent identity problems are more likely to remain single and be unsatisfied with their lives in middle age (Kahn, Zimmerman, Csikszentmihalyi, & Getzels, 1985; see also Stein & Newcomb, 1999). Identity disturbances are common in certain forms of personality disorder in adulthood (chapter 15), such as borderline personality disorder (Wilkinson-Ryan & Westen, 2000).

New community-based initiatives to provide alternative senior schooling for marginalised youth are helping practitioners to respond to significant social issues, including those affecting younger and older people. For example, the Toowoomba Flexi School (http://www.centheigshs.eq.edu.au/flexischool_site/index.htm) partnered with The Older Men's Network (TOMNET; www.tomnet.org.au) to win the 2010 Schools First national award. This was based on the intergenerational mentoring program; whereby TOMNET volunteers are trained to mentor the Flexi School students — helping them to develop important life skills, including information and literacy skills (Cafarella, 2010). The students benefit by developing social and literacy skills and positive relationships with the broader community. The older men's self-worth is also enhanced from partnering with the students, reflecting their re-engagement with, and positive contribution to, the community.

Adulthood

Erikson was one of the first theorists to take seriously the notion of development after adolescence. He describes the developmental task confronting young adults as ***intimacy versus isolation***, establishing enduring, committed relationships or withdrawing and avoiding commitment. The task applies to friendships as well as romantic relationships.

Erikson describes the crisis of midlife as ***generativity versus stagnation***, in which people begin to leave some kind of lasting legacy or feel alienated from relationships and community. ***Generativity*** means concern for the next generation as well as an interest in producing (generating) something of lasting value to society. People express their generative impulses through rearing children, participating in culturally meaningful institutions such as churches or civic organisations, mentoring younger workers, or creating something that will last beyond them, such as a work of art. Empirically, people in midlife express more generative themes than younger adults when describing their lives and they report more generative activities (de St Aubin, McAdams, & Kim, 2004; McAdams, de St Aubin, & Logan, 1993; McAdams et al., 1998). As Erikson hypothesised, individuals also differ in the extent to which they maintain an active, generative stance during middle age (Bradley & Marcia, 1998). People who have difficulty with generativity experience ***stagnation***, a feeling that the promise of youth has gone unfulfilled. Stagnation may be expressed as dissatisfaction with a marital partner, alienation from one's children or chronic feelings of boredom or unhappiness.

A much higher proportion of elderly females live alone in Australia, largely due to being widowed at this stage of life.

Erikson's final stage is ***integrity versus despair***, a time in which individuals look back on their lives with a sense of having lived them well or with despair and regret. In Australia, the number of men and women living as lone persons has been increasing for the past two decades. Some 25 percent of all households now consist of just one person and this figure is expected to increase to as high as 34 percent within the next 20 years (ABS, 2008d). While the majority of lone persons were females (55 percent), males outnumbered females in all age groups up to and including the age group 45–54 years. For the age group 65 years and over, females outnumbered males by almost three to one. This is largely due to the high number of females aged 85 and over who are widowed (AIHW, 2007d). Thus, members of both sexes, but particularly women, face the death of a spouse (because women tend to live longer and to marry older men) while dealing with the gradual health declines of ageing themselves.

INTERIM SUMMARY

Erikson proposed a life-span model of ***psychosocial stages*** — stages in the development of the person as a social being. In ***basic trust versus mistrust***, infants come to trust others or perceive the social world as hostile or unreliable. In ***autonomy versus shame and doubt***, toddlers come to experience themselves as independent sources of will and power or feel insecure in their newfound skills. In ***initiative versus guilt***, young children develop the capacity to form and carry out plans, but their emerging conscience can render them vulnerable to guilt. In ***industry versus inferiority***, school-age children develop a sense of competence but may suffer from feelings of inadequacy. Erikson described adolescence as a period of ***identity versus identity confusion***, in which the task is to establish a stable sense of who one is and what one values. The crisis of young adulthood is ***intimacy*** (establishing enduring, committed relationships) ***versus isolation***. In ***generativity versus stagnation***, middle-aged individuals attempt to pass something on to the next generation. In ***integrity versus despair***, people look back on their lives with a sense of satisfaction or sadness and regret.

Development from adolescence to old age

Erikson's theory provides a backdrop for empirical research on social development throughout the life span. Here we focus on some of the central issues in the study of development from adolescence to old age.

Adolescence

Psychologists have offered two conflicting views of adolescent social and personality development (Arnett, 1999; Westen & Chang, 2000). One approach emphasises that as adolescents grow less dependent on their parents and try out new values and roles, they often become rebellious and moody, shifting from compliance one moment to defiance the next. According to this ***conflict model***, put forth at the turn of the twentieth century (Hall, 1904) and later elaborated by psychodynamic theorists (Blos, 1962; Freud, 1958), conflict and crisis are normal in adolescence. Conflict theorists argue that adolescents need to go through a period of crisis to separate themselves psychologically from their parents and to carve out their own identity. Beeper studies (which page or 'beep' participants at random intervals over the course of a day to measure what they are thinking or feeling at the moment; chapter 9) show that adolescents do, in fact, experience a wider range of moods over a shorter period of time than adults (Csikszentmihalyi & Larson, 1984). Longitudinal studies find decreases in hostility and negative emotionality and increases in diligence, self-control and congeniality as teenagers move into early adulthood (see McGue, Bacon, & Lykken, 1993).

Other theorists argue, however, that the stormy, moody, conflict-ridden adolescent is the exception rather than the rule (Compas, Hinden, & Gerhardt, 1995; Douvan & Adelson, 1966; Offer, Ostrov, Howard, & Atkinson, 1990). According to the ***continuity model***, adolescence is not a turbulent period but is essentially continuous with childhood and adulthood. Research supporting this view finds that roughly 80 percent of adolescents show no signs of severe storm and stress (Offer & Offer, 1975).

How do we reconcile these two views of adolescence? Adolescence is a time of enormous individual differences, with many alternative paths that vary according to the individual, culture and historical period (see Hauser & Safyer, 1994). As we will see, researchers have increasingly moved away from models of life-span development that propose a single pathway to 'normal' or 'successful' development, particularly in adolescence and adulthood, when biological maturation is not the driving force it is in childhood and cultural differences make generalisations much more difficult. Thus, adolescence may not inherently be a stormy era, but 'storm and stress' is more likely in adolescence than in either childhood or adulthood, as suggested by data on adolescents' conflicts with parents, mood disruptions and high-risk behaviour (Arnett, 1999).

Aside from individual differences, children show some increasing gender differences in adolescence. For example, across a number of domains, boys tend to become more confident and less dissatisfied with themselves over time, whereas the opposite occurs for girls. Already by third or fourth grade, and increasingly through at least early adolescence, boys tend to overestimate their scholastic ability, and girls underestimate it (Cole, Martin, Peeke, Seroczynski, & Fier, 1999). Similarly, at age 13, boys and girls show similar levels of body dissatisfaction (figure 13.7), but after that point their paths diverge, at least in Western cultures (Rosenblum & Lewis, 1999).

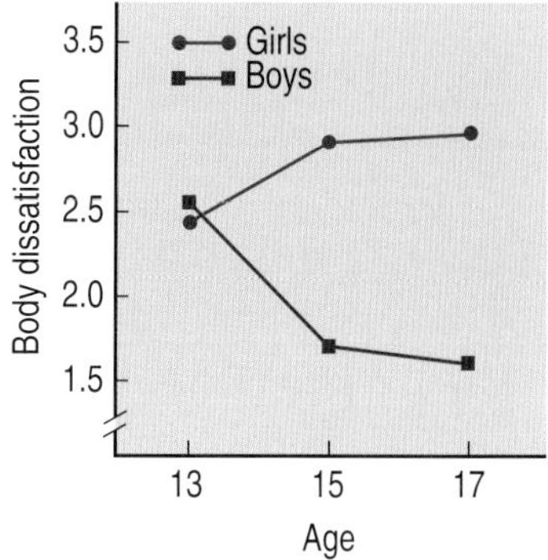

FIGURE 13.7
Body dissatisfaction in boys and girls. At age 13, girls and boys show similar levels of satisfaction with their bodies. By age 15, however, gender differences are substantial.

SOURCE: Rosenblum and Lewis (1999, p. 54).

Risk factors for body dissatisfaction

By Professor Susan Paxton, La Trobe University

The study of risk factors involves understanding what makes some individuals more vulnerable than others to a health problem. A causal risk factor is one that precedes the disorder in a causal manner, and is not merely associated with the onset of the problem (Kraemer et al., 1997). It is very important to understand risk factors for mental health problems, as it is likely that if frequencies of occurrence of risk factors in the community were reduced, the prevalence and severity of the problem would also be reduced.

An important mental health problem in the Australian community, especially among adolescent girls and young women, is that of body dissatisfaction. Body dissatisfaction is a source of distress, but it is also a risk factor for low self-esteem, depressive symptoms, disordered eating behaviours (e.g. use of extreme weight loss behaviours and binge eating) and clinical eating disorders (e.g. anorexia and bulimia nervosa) (Neumark-Sztainer, Paxton, Hannan, Haines, & Story, 2006; Paxton, Neumark-Sztainer, Hannan, & Eisenberg, 2006; Stice, 2002). Mission Australia (2007) reported that 35 percent and 27 percent of young females and young males respectively ranked body image as their issue of greatest concern.

Social risk factors for body dissatisfaction include media, family and peer environments that emphasise the importance of conformity to appearance ideals (Smolak, 2009). In girls, exposure to idealised female media images increases body dissatisfaction (Dohnt & Tiggemann, 2006; Durkin, Paxton, & Sorbello, 2007), although this effect does not seem so strong in boys (Hargreaves & Tiggemann, 2002; Humphreys & Paxton, 2004). Exposure to family and peer subcultures, in which thinness and appearance are highly valued, have also been implicated as risk factors (Paxton, Schutz, Wertheim, & Muir, 1999; Rodgers, Paxton, & Chabrol, 2009). Perceived peers' desire for thinness in girls aged 5 to 8 years of age (Dohnt & Tiggemann, 2006), friend dieting in early adolescent girls (Paxton, Eisenberg, & Neumark-Sztainer, 2006) and weight and shape teasing in girls and boys (e.g. Paxton et al., 2006; Wertheim, Koerner, & Paxton, 2001) have been shown to be risk factors for body dissatisfaction.

Psychological factors are also risk factors for body dissatisfaction. High personal endorsement of media appearance ideals (Smolak, 2009) and a high tendency to compare one's own body with others (Myers & Crowther, 2009) are important risk factors for body dissatisfaction. Low self-esteem in early adolescent girls and depression in middle adolescent boys have been shown to be risk factors for the development of body dissatisfaction (Paxton et al., 2006). Higher body size is also typically found to be a risk factor for body dissatisfaction in girls and boys (Paxton et al., 2006). However, this relationship is not likely to be due to larger body size *per se*, but, rather, to negative feedback received as a consequence of it in society (Wertheim, Paxton, & Blaney, 2004).

Understanding causal risk factors is essential to the development of effective prevention interventions. Research suggests that targeting social pressures to conform to unrealistic appearance ideals, especially from media, is a promising strategy in the prevention of body dissatisfaction and disordered eating (e.g. Richardson & Paxton, 2010; Wilksch & Wade, 2009).

Early adulthood and middle age

Erikson described the central task of young adulthood as the development of intimacy — establishing lifelong friendships and settling down and beginning to have a family of one's own. Empirically, Erikson was probably right to name a stage of adult development 'intimacy' and to tie it to finding a long-term mate. As Peterson (2004) says, couplehood is a fact of life for most young adults, and most Australians and New Zealanders do get married. The marriage rate, however, has been steadily declining in recent decades. A major reason for this trend is the growing number of de facto relationships. While many de facto couples do eventually marry, many do not. Another reason for the declining marriage rate is that many people who do get married are choosing to do so at an older age (on average, age 30 for women and 32 for men in Australia, and 30 for women and 33 for men in New Zealand, an increase of about 3 years in the past decade). However, not all marriages last. Approximately 50 000 divorces are granted each year in Australia, while the number in New Zealand is about 10 000 a year (ABS, 2008d; Statistics New Zealand, 2006).

Statistics more recently released by the Australian Bureau of Statistics (2008), however, indicate a jump in the number of marriages. This anomaly mostly reflected a huge number of weddings performed on 8 August 2008, with eight being a favoured number in Chinese culture. There were also fewer divorces in 2008, perhaps reflecting the continuing trend for couples to delay the age at which they marry, and to live together first. The ABS (2008) statistics further indicate that more long-term marriages of 20 years or longer are also now ending in divorce, implying that unhappy couples are deciding to quit the marriage after the children leave the family home.

APPLY + DISCUSS

- Does personality develop over the course of adulthood, as it does through childhood, or does it simply change, as the person encounters different situations and developmental tasks?
- What does it mean to say that personality, morality or cognition develops?
- Can any theory of adult change or development apply to the range of circumstances cross-culturally? Do some universal principles exist, as they do in memory and cognition? If so, what might account for them?

Marital intimacy does not come easily: in Western cultures, marital distress actually increases over the first three years of marriage, and maintaining intimate relationships in the face of conflict and disillusionment is a challenge that requires continuous negotiation and compromise (Gottman, 1998). Over half of all divorces occur in the first three years of marriage (Whitbourne, 2001). Marital conflict is at its peak when children are young, when housework doubles, financial pressures mount and intimate time alone is difficult to find (Belsky & Hsieh, 1998; Belsky & Pensky, 1988; Berman & Pedersen, 1987).

Women's satisfaction with marriage appears to suffer more than men's after the birth of a child (Cowan & Cowan, 1992). Motherhood usually involves a redefinition of roles and reallocation of time. The household division of labour tends to become more traditional, and women who are used to autonomy and invested in their work suddenly find themselves taking on more and more responsibility at home (Hoffman & Levy-Shiff, 1994). For men, fatherhood means that they are no longer the primary recipients of their wives' attention and love; at the same time, they incur new financial, household and childcare responsibilities (Lamb, 1987).

Precisely when young adulthood ends and middle age begins is difficult to pinpoint. Some observers have described this period as a time of midlife crisis (Jacques, 1965; Levinson, Darrow, Klein, Levinson, & McKee, 1978; Sheehy, 1976). One researcher found that roughly 80 percent of the men he interviewed were in a state of crisis around age 40, as they began to think of themselves as middle-aged instead of young and to question the basic structure of their lives (Levinson, 1978). In Western culture, people are frequently at the height of their careers in their 40s and 50s, enjoying leadership positions at work or in the community. At the same time, however, the death of parents, the occasional jarring death of siblings or contemporaries, and an ageing body inevitably lead people to confront their mortality and to consider how they will live their remaining years.

As with adolescence, however, many psychologists have challenged the view of midlife as a time of crisis and suggest that midlife crisis may be a phenomenon that occurs primarily in upper middle class men (see Rosenberg, Rosenberg, & Farrell, 1999). Empirically, only a minority of people report experiencing a midlife crisis, and in these cases, the crisis usually occurs along with a specific interruption in the normal rhythm of life, such as loss of a job or divorce (Costa & McCrae, 1988; Neugarten, 1977; see also Wethington, 2000).

Old age

The meaning of old age has changed dramatically. In Australia, the average life expectancy of a newborn boy has increased from 55.2 years in 1901 to 78.7 years today. Likewise, the average life expectancy of a newborn girl has increased from 58.8 to 82.6 years during the same period. The increase in life expectancy is due to lower death rates at all ages. As a result, the proportion of the population aged 65 and over has increased markedly, from 4 percent in 1901 to 13 percent in 2006 (ABS, 2002, 2008d) and is expected to reach 26 percent by 2050. Similar life expectancy and ageing trends occur in New Zealand. Disturbingly, longevity projections for Indigenous Australians have not increased to the same degree. Life expectancy for an Aboriginal male is just 67.2 years and for females, 72.9 years — that is, approximately 10 years less than the overall population.

The continuing significant gap in life expectancy, coupled with the low age of death, highlights the inequity in life opportunities experienced by Australia's Aboriginal and Torres Strait Islander population (Australian Medical Association [AMA], 2003). Targets have been set by the Australian government to halve the gap in mortality rates between Indigenous and non-Indigenous children (under five years of age) within a decade and to close the gap in life expectancy at birth between Indigenous and non-Indigenous people within a generation (ABS, 2010a). Australia is slowly making progress towards achieving this goal. In contrast, New Zealand, Canada and the United States have made substantial progress in narrowing the gap between their Indigenous and non-Indigenous populations to between five and seven years, compared with Australia's 10 years (ABS & AIHW, 2002, 2010; Hoy, Baker, Kelly, & Wang, 2000). For example, in New Zealand in the 1950s the life expectancy of the Maori was between 13 and 15 years shorter than non-Indigenous New Zealanders. Improvements in life expectancy appear to have occurred through more adequate provision of primary health care, public health facilities and initiatives relating to social justice. It is important that Australia heed these international experiences (table 13.4; see overleaf) so that continued progress can be achieved (AMA, 2003).

The continuing life expectancy gap between Indigenous and non-Indigenous Australians, coupled with the low age of death for Indigenous Australians, highlights an ongoing inequity in life opportunities.

The demographic shift to longer life spans has produced substantial changes in perceptions of old age. Even three decades ago, people were considered 'old' in their 60s. Today, no-one is surprised to see 70-year-olds on the tennis court. Australians are expected to live long lives. In much of the world, advances in medicine and public health have led to increasing numbers of people who live long lives, and hence to a redefining of the life cycle and concepts of 'old age'.

Technologically developed and Western cultures tend to devalue the elderly more than most cultures and to emphasise the despairing end of the continuum. Contrary to stereotypes, most elderly Australians live in the community, with only about 7 percent of the population aged over 70 requiring government subsidised care in residential facilities (Department of Health and Ageing, 2008). In fact, most people report having more positive and less negative affect as they move towards the end of middle age, and most people cross-culturally report being happy in old age (Diener & Suh, 1998; Helson & Klohnen, 1998; Mroczek & Kolarz, 1998). Why, then, are our stereotypes so negative?

One explanation is that many stereotypes of ageing are built on our emotional forecasts of how we imagine we would feel if we gained weight, lost some hair, greyed and suffered many of the more serious indignities of old age. The reality is that humans have a remarkable capacity for dealing with life's blows with equanimity — for gradually adjusting to realities we cannot change and regaining our emotional equilibrium.

A prime culprit in our negative views of old age may also be technological development (Cowgill & Holmes, 1972). Ironically, the same factor that has prolonged life by decades has undermined the status of the aged by making their jobs obsolete, limiting the applicability of their beliefs and values in a radically changed social and cultural milieu, and eroding the concept of the extended family. The geographical mobility associated with economic development also means that children may live hundreds if not thousands of kilometres from their ageing parents. In contrast, in more traditional societies, the aged are by definition the most knowledgeable because they have lived the longest and accumulated the most information, and mutual ties of affection between the generations are reinforced by daily interaction.

TABLE 13.4 **Top 15 countries by estimated life expectancy for men and women**

Country	Men	Country	Women
Iceland	80	Japan	86
Japan	79	Hong Kong	85
Hong Kong	79	Australia	84
Australia	79	Switzerland	84
Switzerland	79	Spain	84
Sweden	79	France	84
Israel	79	San Marino	84
Macao	79	Iceland	83
Spain	78	Israel	83
Canada	78	Macao	83
Norway	78	Sweden	83
Italy	78	Canada	83
New Zealand	78	Italy	83
Singapore	78	Norway	83
Netherlands	78	Austria	83

SOURCE: AIHW (2010).

APPLY + DISCUSS

At least in the West, parents tend to value their relationship with their adult children more than their adult children value their relationship with their parents (Christensen, 1992).

- Explain this from an evolutionary perspective. Why would parents' investment in their children be greater than their adult children's investment in their ageing parents?

In the face of physical decline, negative stereotypes and the loss of spouse, friends and social roles, what allows an individual to find satisfaction, or what Erikson describes as integrity, in the final years of life? In one study of around 1000 people aged 65 to 72, several variables predicted life satisfaction: close relationships, an active social and community life, continuing recreation, good health and sufficient income (Flanagan, 1978). In general, research suggests that people who find satisfaction in later life tend to be characterised by three factors: lack of significant disease, high cognitive and physical functioning, and an active engagement in productive activity and community with others (Rowe & Kahn, 1997).

Longitudinal studies suggest that earlier factors also predict happiness and physical and mental health in later life (Sears, 1977; Vaillant & Vaillant, 1998). These include marital and career fulfilment as a younger adult, sustained family relationships and long-lived ancestors. Risk factors from young and middle adulthood include defence mechanisms that grossly distort reality (such as projection; see chapter 11), alcoholism and depression before age 50. The quality of old age thus appears to depend to a substantial degree on the quality of youth.

While stereotypes might suggest otherwise, older people in Australia and New Zealand typically engage in social roles for many years after leaving the workforce (Ranzijn, 2002). These roles involve regular contact with family, recreation, church and community service (Feather, 1989). Bereavement often means that living alone becomes more frequent as people get older, but elderly Australians who live completely alone are in the minority (Australian Institute of Family Studies, 2004; Peterson, 1999).

INTERIM SUMMARY

Some researchers adopt a ***conflict model*** of adolescence, arguing that conflict and struggle are normal in adolescence; others propose a ***continuity model***, viewing adolescence as essentially continuous with childhood and adulthood. Each model probably applies to a subset of adolescents. Similarly, researchers disagree on the extent to which midlife crisis is common in middle age. In all likelihood, 'crises' in both adolescence and at midlife depend on individual differences and cultural and historical circumstances. Although old age inevitably involves many losses, the realities appear far better than the negative stereotypes of ageing seen in many technologically developed societies.

Central questions revisited

◆ Nature and nurture, cognition and emotion

We began with two central questions. The first question addressed the roles of nature and nurture in social development. As we have seen, the answers to this question have become more complex as psychologists have gradually come to frame the question in more complex ways.

Genetics play a commanding role in human development, shaping the way people develop and change in general as well as the way people differ from one another. But genes are only expressed in environmental contexts, and they can be turned on or off by experience. Children who spend their first years in a sterile orphanage with a changing cast of characters may never express their potential to form loving attachments. Others with a hardy temperament may find a way to activate the innate neural circuitry for attachment at a later age.

The second question deals with the relationship between social and cognitive development. On the one hand, children's cognitions — their constructions of reality — are in part social constructions. Implicitly and explicitly, parents, peers and other socialisation agents offer children ways of thinking about themselves and the world — from their earliest models of relationships to their understanding of physics (see Cole, 1997; Nelson, 1997). On the other hand, the way children enter into relationships depends on the way they perceive and think about them. A child who can keep a stable mental image of his mother despite a prolonged period of separation, and remember soothing images of his mother when he becomes distressed, will have a much easier time with a separation than one who cannot. And even the way children respond emotionally to moral concerns depends in part on their capacity to represent another person's mind and feelings. Social and cognitive development can be placed in separate chapters of a book, but in reality, they are on the same page.

◆

SUMMARY

- ***Social development*** refers to predictable changes in interpersonal thought, feeling and behaviour over the life span.

1 Attachment in early development

- ***Attachment*** refers to the enduring emotional ties children form with their primary caregivers. ***Separation anxiety*** — distress at separation from attachment figures — occurs around the same time in all human cultures and peaks in the second year of life. Harlow's experiments with monkeys showed that security, not food, is the basis for attachment. Integrating psychodynamic and evolutionary theory, Bowlby proposed that attachment is a mechanism to keep immature animals close to their parents.
- Using a procedure called the Strange Situation, researchers have identified four styles of attachment: ***secure***, ***avoidant***, ***ambivalent*** and ***disorganised***. Early attachment patterns have a powerful impact on later social functioning and form the basis of ***adult attachment*** styles. Infants develop ***internal working models***, or mental representations of attachment relationships, which form the basis for their expectations in later close relationships.

2 Socialisation

- ***Socialisation*** refers to the processes through which individuals come to learn the rules, beliefs, values, skills, attitudes and behaviour patterns of their society. Socialisation is transactional (involving mutual influence of 'teachers' and 'learners'), lifelong and multifaceted. Like all psychological processes, it also occurs within constraints imposed by biology and the broader economic and cultural context.
- Parents are particularly important socialisation agents. Research distinguishes ***authoritarian***, ***permissive***, ***authoritative*** and ***uninvolved*** parenting styles. Each parenting style tends to produce children with different characteristics. Parents vary across and within cultures in the extent to which they are accepting and rejecting of their children. Parental warmth and sensitivity are associated with self-esteem, independence and emotional stability.
- Among the most powerful roles into which people are socialised are ***gender roles***, the range of behaviours considered appropriate for males and females. Unlike sex (a biologically based categorisation), ***gender*** (the psychological meaning of being male or female) is influenced by learning, although evolutionary pressures have probably contributed to gender differences that cultures embellish and magnify. Gender socialisation begins in the first days of life.

3 Peer relationships

- Children differ in the extent to which they are accepted by their peers. ***Rejected children*** are often teased and ostracised, although they may also elicit dislike if they are bullies. ***Neglected children*** are less likely to draw a positive or negative response from their peers and are more likely to be friendless or ignored. Sibling relationships have many dimensions, including both rivalry and closeness.

4 Development of social cognition

- As with cognitive development in non-social domains, children develop in their ***social cognition*** — the way they conceptualise themselves, others and relationships. The ***self-concept*** refers to a person's organised way of representing information about the self. Initially, children lack a distinct concept of self. Their views of themselves, like their views of others, begin concrete and gradually become more abstract. By adolescence, they are much more likely to think about their own and others' internal psychological processes such as feelings and personality traits. An important cognitive–social skill that develops gradually is ***perspective-taking***, the ability to understand other people's viewpoints.
- Children's understanding of what gender is and how it applies to them develops substantially throughout the first several years of life. Children develop ***gender schemas*** — mental representations that associate psychological characteristics with one sex or the other — by integrating cultural beliefs with their personal experiences. Gender schemas share striking similarities across cultures, which appear to reflect an interaction between biology and social learning.

5 Theories of moral development

- Moral development refers to the acquisition of values and rules for balancing the potentially conflicting interests of the self and others. Behaviourist and cognitive–social theories assert that ***prosocial behaviour*** (behaviour that benefits others), like other behaviours, is learned through processes such as operant conditioning and modelling. Cognitive–developmental models focus less on moral behaviours than on moral reasoning. Kohlberg's stage theory distinguishes three levels of moral reasoning: ***preconventional*** (following moral rules to avoid punishment or obtain reward), ***conventional*** (defining right and wrong according to learned cultural standards) and ***postconventional*** (applying abstract, self-defined principles). Information-processing approaches break moral development down into component processes and examine the way each changes during childhood.
- Psychodynamic and other theories suggest that children internalise their parents' values, and that guilt motivates people to obey their conscience. Other research emphasises the role of ***empathy*** (feeling for someone who is hurting) in motivating prosocial behaviour. Recent research suggests that the paths to internalisation of conscience in children depend on an interaction of temperament and parenting styles. Moral development reflects an interaction of cognitive and emotional development.

6 Social development across the life span

- The most widely known theory of life-span development is Erik Erikson's theory of ***psychosocial stages***: ***basic trust versus mistrust***, ***autonomy versus shame and doubt***, ***initiative versus guilt*** and ***industry versus inferiority*** in childhood; ***identity versus identity confusion*** in adolescence; and ***intimacy versus isolation***, ***generativity versus stagnation*** and ***integrity versus despair*** during adulthood.
- Psychologists disagree on the extent to which people experience 'crises' in adolescence and midlife, but in general, there does not appear to be any single path to 'successful ageing'. Nor do the data support a stereotypically bleak view of ageing. People who have high life satisfaction in later life tend to have had fulfilled lives earlier and to be characterised by physical and cognitive health and active engagement with productive activities and other people.

KEY TERMS

adult attachment, *p. 510*
ambivalent attachment style, *p. 507*
attachment, *p. 505*
authoritarian, *p. 514*
authoritative, *p. 514*
autonomy versus shame and doubt, *p. 536*
avoidant attachment style, *p. 507*
basic trust versus mistrust, *p. 536*
conflict model, *p. 538*
contact comfort, *p. 505*
continuity model, *p. 539*
conventional morality, *p. 529*
developmental task, *p. 536*
disorganised attachment style, *p. 507*
empathic distress, *p. 533*
empathy, *p. 532*
gender, *p. 517*
gender constancy, *p. 525*
gender identity, *p. 525*
gender roles, *p. 517*
gender schemas, *p. 525*
gender stability, *p. 525*
generativity, *p. 537*
generativity versus stagnation, *p. 537*
guidance approach, *p. 515*
identity, *p. 537*
identity confusion, *p. 537*
identity versus identity confusion, *p. 537*
imprinting, *p. 505*
industry versus inferiority, *p. 537*
initiation rites, *p. 537*
initiative versus guilt, *p. 536*
integrity versus despair, *p. 538*
internal working models, *p. 508*
intimacy versus isolation, *p. 537*
morality of constraint, *p. 528*
morality of cooperation, *p. 529*
negative identity, *p. 537*
neglected children, *p. 520*
permissive, *p. 514*
perspective-taking, *p. 524*
postconventional morality, *p. 529*
preconventional morality, *p. 529*
prosocial behaviour, *p. 530*
psychosocial stages, *p. 536*
rejected children, *p. 520*
secure attachment style, *p. 507*
self-concept, *p. 521*
separation anxiety, *p. 506*
sex-role ideology, *p. 526*
sex typing, *p. 517*
social cognition, *p. 521*
social development, *p. 504*
socialisation, *p. 512*
stagnation, *p. 538*
theory of mind, *p. 524*
uninvolved, *p. 515*

REVIEW QUESTIONS

1. Define imprinting.
2. Describe the process of socialisation.
3. Explain how children's understanding of gender evolves throughout the life span.
4. Describe how the self-concept evolves from infancy through to adolescence.
5. Distinguish between the models of moral reasoning proposed by Piaget and Kohlberg.

DISCUSSION QUESTIONS

1. Is newborn attachment distinctive?
2. How do parenting styles affect a child's social and emotional development?
3. Is it acceptable to break the law if a life is at stake?

APPLICATION QUESTIONS

1. Test your understanding of attachment patterns displayed by children by identifying each of the following scenarios as an example of one of the following attachment styles — secure, avoidant, ambivalent or disorganised.
   (a) Four-year-old Mark is at family daycare while his mother works full-time. At the end of the day, his mother comes to collect Mark to go home. Upon seeing his mother, Mark calls out 'Mummy!' and runs to give her a big hug hello.
   (b) Three-year-old Sophie is cared for by her grandmother while her mother goes to a doctor's appointment. Sophie ignores her mother when she returns to collect her.
   (c) Three-year-old Habib becomes upset when his mother comes to collect him from daycare after work. Although he runs up to his mother, he acts rejected and does not give her a hug hello.
   (d) Four-year-old Lim is easily distressed and appears to be in a world of her own whenever her mother tries to comfort her. She will often sit on the couch with a dazed expression on her face, gently rocking backward and forward.
2. Test your understanding of Erikson's theory of social development by identifying each of the following scenarios as an example of the conflict or challenge faced by a particular individual at one of the following stages of psychosocial development:
   - basic trust versus mistrust
   - autonomy versus shame and doubt
   - initiative versus guilt
   - industry versus inferiority
   - identity versus identity confusion
   - intimacy versus isolation
   - generativity versus stagnation
   - integrity versus despair.

   (a) Yasmin has just finished high school and is trying to decide what to do with the rest of her life. She cannot decide whether to major in psychology or business at university.
   (b) David loves to play outside in his sandpit. He often builds a row of castles to protect him from the nasty dragons that are hiding in the bushes.
   (c) Tiffanie is learning to walk and talk and proudly says 'Dadda' whenever her father enters the room.

(d) Mohammed feels that he has lived life to the full. He is recently retired and enjoys travelling and spending time with his six great-grandchildren.
(e) Ireland loves going to school and is eager to learn. Each day after school, she enthusiastically completes her homework, making sure her writing is neatly presented and free of any spelling errors.
(f) Six-month-old Mitchell smiles when his mother leans over his cot to pick him up.
(g) Yi Lin, a successful middle-aged businesswoman, serves as a mentor for some of the younger employees in her corporations.
(h) Lachlan and Greta have been in a stable, loving relationship for more than three years and are now thinking about buying a house together.

The solutions to the application questions can be found on page 835.

MULTIMEDIA RESOURCES

The *Cyberpsych* multimedia resource is available *as an option* to accompany this textbook to further develop your understanding of many key psychology concepts. *Cyberpsych* contains a wealth of rich media content and activities, and for this chapter includes:

- a video clip on maternal separation
- a video case study on ageing
- an interactive module on attachment
- concept animations on gender and Kohlberg's stages of moral reasoning.

Health, stress and coping

14

LEARNING OBJECTIVES

After studying this chapter you should be able to:

1 distinguish between the various social–cognitive theories of health behaviour

2 describe the barriers to health promotion and preventive health

3 describe the major sources of stress

4 discuss the nature of the relationship between stress and health

5 describe the major strategies for coping with stress.

Health psychology

- ***Health psychology*** is devoted to understanding psychological influences on how people stay healthy, why they become ill and how they respond when they do get ill.
- Early theorists, believing that illness was caused by evil spirits, engaged in the practice of ***trephination***, drilling holes in the skull to allow the evil spirits to escape. The ***biopsychosocial*** model of health recognises that social and psychological variables in addition to biological underpinnings laid the foundation for health and illness, and guides the field of health psychology today.
- Theories of health behaviour include: the ***health belief model***, the ***protection motivation theory of health***, the ***theory of reasoned action*** and the ***theory of planned behaviour***.
- In spite of knowledge of the negative health consequences that may befall them, people continue to engage in a number of health-compromising behaviours, including obesity, smoking, alcohol abuse and high-risk sexual behaviours.
- Four ***barriers*** to health promotion: ***individual barriers***, ***family barriers***, ***health system barriers*** and ***ethnic barriers***.
- Image can be a major factor in health behaviours — most people are quite concerned about what others think of them and modify their behaviours to create an impression they think will be favourable.

The future of health psychology

- Health psychology will continue to progress in the years to come. Health psychologists will probably persist with the promotion of positive health behaviours and help people to cope better with the consequences of ill health and other health-compromising behaviours.

Stress

- *Stress* refers to a challenge to a person's capacity to adapt to inner and outer demands.
- Stress is a *psychobiological process*, with both physical and psychological components and consequences. For example, Selye's *general adaptation syndrome* consists of three stages: alarm, resistance and exhaustion.
- Stress is also a transaction between the individual and the environment, in which the individual perceives the demands of the environment tax or exceed her psychosocial resources. For example, Lazarus's model identifies two stages in the process of stress and coping: *primary appraisal* and *secondary appraisal*.
- Events that often lead to stress are called *stressors*. For example, life events are stressors that require adaptation and change.
- *Psychoneuroimmunology* examines the influence of psychosocial factors on the functioning of the immune system.
- Stress can affect physical health in two ways: directly, by weakening the *immune system*, and indirectly, by leading to behaviours that weaken the body's defences or lead to exposure to pathogens.

Coping

- *Coping* reflects the ways people deal with stressful situations.
- *Problem-focused coping* involves changing the situation (e.g. deal with the stressor itself); *emotion-focused coping* aims to regulate the emotion generated by a stressful situation (e.g. alter thoughts about the situation, and/or alter the unpleasant emotional consequences of stress).
- Members of minority groups who, for generations, experience a ceiling on their economic prospects because of discrimination sometimes develop a *low-effort syndrome* in which they seemingly stop making the kinds of active efforts that might alleviate some of their hardships.
- *Social support* refers to the presence of others in whom a person can confide and from whom the individual can expect help and concern.

Central questions: promoting good health

- People experience stress when they are unable to adapt to a number of different challenges posed to them. When particularly stressful events occur, social support can help protect people against their potentially harmful effects. For this reason, health psychologists will often involve family members and significant others in their treatment of people with negative health behaviours.

THE amazing comeback of butterfly swimmer Geoff Huegill dominated sporting headlines in Australia during the Delhi Commonwealth Games. Huegill powered his way to a gold medal in the 100 metres butterfly event in a personal best time. At the age of 31, he posted his quickest swim in 10 years. That was a notable effort in itself, but it wasn't the reason the story became so popular. Huegill's efforts amazed the world because just two years earlier he had eaten and drunk his way to morbid obesity — at his heaviest, Huegill nudged 140 kilograms.

Huegill had retired in 2005 after a stellar career that netted Olympic silver and bronze medals, Commonwealth Games gold medals, World Championship medals and world records. After 15 years of slogging up and down the pool, and making difficult physical and social sacrifices to stay at an elite fitness level, Huegill gave it all away — at the age of 26. He indulged in all the excesses he had denied himself during that period, returning home from nightclubs at 4 am instead of getting up at that hour to train. Drinking, eating and not exercising took its toll. By 2008, his weight had ballooned to almost 140 kilograms. Huegill was unrecognisable from his swimming days, when he had been almost as famous for his sculpted physique and abdominal six-pack as he had for his swimming exploits.

Something had to give. After three years of alcohol and pizza, Huegill knew he needed to get his health back on track. He launched a swimming comeback with the 2010 Commonwealth Games in his sights.

There were plenty of sceptics. People had seen the photos of the grossly overweight Huegill and figured there was no way he could return to the kind of shape he had been in during his prime. Regaining fitness and losing weight was tough and demanded supreme discipline.

The doubters started to eat their words when Huegill came out in the Australian Short Course Championships in August 2009 and scored a silver medal. Huegill was back in contention! More good performance saw him force his way into the Australian team for the Delhi Commonwealth Games. After a desperately close second in the 50 metres butterfly, Huegill gained instant acclaim when he powered home to convincingly win the 100 metres butterfly in a personal best time. He followed that with a second gold as part of Australia's 4 by 100 metres medley relay team.

He had shed 40 kilograms and, along the way, discovered his quickest form in 10 years.

Before and after photos of Geoff Huegill's transformation from an overweight partygoer to an elite swimming competitor throw up many questions about the psychology of health and ageing.

The Geoff Huegill story throws up many questions.

How is it that a formerly supremely fit elite athlete could go from peak condition to 138 kilograms within just a few years? What mental and physical changes occurred as he spiralled from super-fit to morbidly obese? How could someone who was so conscious of what it took to reach high levels of physical performance allow himself to slip so far the other way?

And what was it that inspired him to mount the comeback that saw him swim faster than he ever had before? To what extent was his mental health and happiness a product of also being physically fit and healthy? How did he cope with the physical strain of pushing his overweight frame through the demands needed to regain full fitness? How was it that at the age of 31 he was able to not only get back into shape but actually swim a faster time than he had ever swum at the 2010 Commonwealth Games?

Understanding situations and questions such as these is the work of health psychologists. 'Health psychology is the aggregate of the specific educational, scientific and professional contributions of the discipline of psychology to the promotion and maintenance of health, the prevention and treatment of illness, the identification of etiologic and diagnostic correlates of health, illness and related dysfunction, and the analysis and improvement of the health care system and health policy formation' (Matarazzo, 1980, p. 815). Because of changing patterns of illness, global epidemics such as SARS and AIDS, and an increasing emphasis on the role of behaviour in health, health psychology is emerging as one of the leading areas within the field of psychology.

In this chapter, we address three central questions. First, why do people engage in health-compromising behaviours? After considering a brief history of the field of health psychology, we will examine specific health-compromising behaviours that are related to the major causes of death and chronic disease in the world today. Second, what are the barriers to health promotion and prevention? We will then turn our attention to two health-related topics that arguably have received the greatest amount of attention: stress and coping. What causes stress and how do we cope with it?

Central questions

- Why do people engage in health-compromising behaviours?
- What are the barriers to health promotion and preventive health?
- What causes stress and how do people cope with it?

Health psychology

Although people have experienced illness throughout history, until recently psychology played little role in understanding health and illness behaviour. Over the last couple of decades, however, the field of psychology, specifically health psychology, has played an increasingly important role in understanding health and illness. '***Health psychology*** is devoted to understanding psychological influences on how people stay healthy, why they become ill and how they respond when they do get ill' (Taylor, 2003, p. 3). A health psychologist might be interested in why people fail to exercise even though they know the health benefits of doing so. The health psychologist works to understand the reasons why people do not exercise and then designs interventions to increase the likelihood that they will exercise in the future. The health psychologist also tries to answer why some people get sick and others do not, all other factors being equal. She might examine why one person's stressor (e.g. roller coaster rides) is another person's thrill. The health psychologist might also get involved with local, state and federal governments to establish health policies and agendas. And, the health psychologist might work to examine the psychological and social factors that determine whether or not people seek medical care when they believe they are sick, the factors that influence this willingness and how people react when they find out they are sick, particularly with a chronic or terminal illness (Baum & Posluszny, 1999). To understand the importance of health psychology to the study and treatment of health and illness, it is important to examine the aetiology of the field itself.

History of health psychology

The earliest theorists believed that disease arose when evil spirits entered the body. To rid the body of these spirits, a crude type of what today is called neurosurgery was performed using Stone Age tools. This surgery, called ***trephination***, involved drilling holes in the skulls of the diseased individual to allow the evil spirits to escape. Those individuals who managed to survive the procedure were thought to be cured of their illness. (Scar tissue observed in trephinated skulls suggests that, in fact, many people did survive these procedures.)

Some time later, the Greeks abandoned the idea that disease is caused by evil spirits and ascribed illness instead to poor bodily functioning. Hippocrates (460–377 BC), known to many as the father of modern medicine, proposed the ***humoural theory of illness***, which asserts that disease is caused by an imbalance in the four fluids or humours of the body — blood, phlegm, black bile and yellow bile. Fluid imbalance produced both psychological (e.g. personality) and physical (e.g. illness) changes (Lyons & Petrucelli, 1978; Straub, 2002). Balance in the fluids was maintained by health-enhancing behaviours such as appropriate exercise and a balanced diet. This was a very progressive idea for the day.

Hippocrates' original theory was expanded by Galen (AD 129–199) who suggested that four personality types or temperaments were determined by the relative proportions of the four fluids. For example, too much black bile produced a melancholic person who was sad and depressed. Physiologically, an excess of black bile produced ulcers and hepatitis (Straub, 2002). Too much yellow bile produced a person who was quick to anger. Treatments were tailored to the particular fluid that was out of balance. In the case of an excess of black bile, the patient was placed on a special diet and exposed to hot baths. The diets consisted of foods that had characteristics opposite to those of the fluid that was out of balance. For example, black bile was cold and dry, so a person would be prescribed foods that were warm and moist (Clader, 2002). Although the humoural theory has been rejected over time, many of the principles put forth by Hippocrates are suggestive of health enhancement today.

The Middle Ages (c. 476 – c. 1450) saw a return to conceptions of disease as a result of mystical forces, reflecting the dominance of religion at the time. Disease was considered to be God's punishment for wrongdoing. Treatments, generally controlled by the Church, focused on torturing the body to atone for wrongdoing. At this time, humans were viewed as beyond the realm of scientific investigation. Thus, for example, human dissection was forbidden (Straub, 2002; Taylor, 2003). To put these views in perspective, the Middle Ages witnessed a barrage of new and pervasive diseases, including leprosy and the Black Death or bubonic plague. The Black Death is believed to have taken the lives of almost a quarter of the European population (Lyons & Petrucelli, 1978). In just five years after the initial outbreak of the disease, 25 million people died! Thus, it is hardly surprising that such horrific and unexplainable illnesses might have been ascribed to God's punishment for wrongdoing.

MAKING CONNECTIONS

Society continues to have illnesses of epidemic proportions, most notably AIDS (chapter 17). According to the United Nations Programme on HIV/AIDS (UNAIDS) and WHO (2009) report on the global aids epidemic, 33.4 million people are living with HIV worldwide. The total number of people living with the virus in 2008 was more than 20 percent higher than the number in 2000, and the prevalence was roughly threefold higher than in 1990 (UNAIDS & WHO, 2009).

In Australia in 2002, the cumulative total of HIV cases was 22550, while 6272 deaths attributable to AIDS had occurred (ABS, 2004b). However, the 2009 UNAIDS and WHO report states that Australia is beginning to turn the corner, with fewer people in Oceania being infected with HIV and more people having access to treatment. Australia has an estimated HIV prevalence of 0.2 percent, considerably less severe than those of any other high-income country (UNAIDS & WHO, 2009).

In comparison, there is a slow, steady increase in new HIV diagnoses in New Zealand (New Zealand AIDS Epidemiology Group, 2009), and Papua New Guinea accounted for more than 99 percent of reported HIV diagnoses in the Asia–Pacific region in 2007 (Coghlan, Burnet Institute, & Austin Research Institute, 2009). Reported HIV infections are also increasing in Fiji, while the rate of new infections appears to be declining in New Caledonia (Coghlan et al., 2009).

As implied by the name for the era, the Renaissance, beginning in the fifteenth century, witnessed great strides in medical knowledge and treatment. During this period of time, major contributions were made by Leeuwenhock with microscopy and by Morgagni in the area of autopsy (Taylor, 2003). Furthermore, Vesalius resurrected the practice of dissection, and he published a multivolume series on human anatomy. Together, these scientists sounded the death knell for the humoural theory of illness. Rather than viewing disease as the result of an imbalance of bodily fluids (i.e. *humoural theory*), they could now identify biological and anatomical causes of disease (i.e. *anatomical theory*; Straub, 2002). In addition, Descartes (1596–1650) proposed his theory of ***Cartesian dualism***, which contends that the mind and the body are completely separate entities. To understand the body and illness, one must focus on the body alone. At this time, psychology was a long way from being involved in the treatment and prevention of illness.

With technological advances such as those just mentioned, the role of the body (rather than the mind) in disease took precedence. The development of microscopy led to observations of individual cells within the human body, which laid the foundation for the ***cellular theory of illness***, the idea that illness and disease result from abnormalities within individual cells. Not surprisingly, then, doctors took over the care of the body and philosophers took over the care of the mind.

This dualistic view of the mind and the body persisted for hundreds of years and became conceptualised as the biomedical model of health. The ***biomedical model*** takes a reductionistic view of illness, reducing disease to biological causes at the level of individual cells. Psychological and social factors that affect health and illness are virtually ignored in the biomedical model. The biomedical model also adopts an illness-based focus, viewing health as simply the absence of illness rather than as an independent state of wellbeing to be achieved. Although the biomedical model is still the primary model within medicine today, it began to lose some of its punch during the middle of the twentieth century, in large part because of the work of Sigmund Freud.

Freud, who was trained as a physician, realised that some illnesses could not be traced to an underlying biological cause. Based on his work with clients, Freud came to believe that these 'unexplained' physical problems stemmed from unconscious conflicts. He labelled these physical manifestations of psychological issues conversion reactions. This perspective reunited the mind and the body as contributors to illness.

Building on the work of Freud, other individuals extended the link between unconscious conflicts and disease by saying that unconscious conflicts produce physiological changes within the body. These physiological changes tax the body's resources and ultimately lead to the onset of illness. The idea that changes in physiology mediate the relationship between unconscious conflicts and illness constitutes the field of ***psychosomatic medicine***. Although some people continue to this day to endorse psychosomatic medicine, the field has not been without its critics. More modern theorists and researchers argue that the link between unconscious conflicts and illness is a complex one, requiring the presence of any of a number of different factors, such as genetic predispositions to illness or environmental stressors (Taylor, 2003). The origin of psychosomatic medicine within Freudian theory also predicted poorly for the field as psychodynamic theory itself began to be criticised. Nevertheless, both Freudian theory and psychosomatic medicine laid the groundwork for reuniting the mind and body.

This recognition that psychology and physiology mutually influence one another set the stage for the rise of health psychology and the development of the ***biopsychosocial model*** of health, the idea that health and illness stem from a combination of biological, psychological and social factors. There were other indicators, however, that the time was ripe for the field of health psychology to emerge. One of the most prominent of these indicators was the changing illness patterns over the last century. Early in the twentieth century, most people died from acute disorders, such as pneumonia and tuberculosis (Grob, 1983). Over the last few decades, however, illness patterns have changed so that many of the leading causes of death today are largely preventable (see figure 14.1).

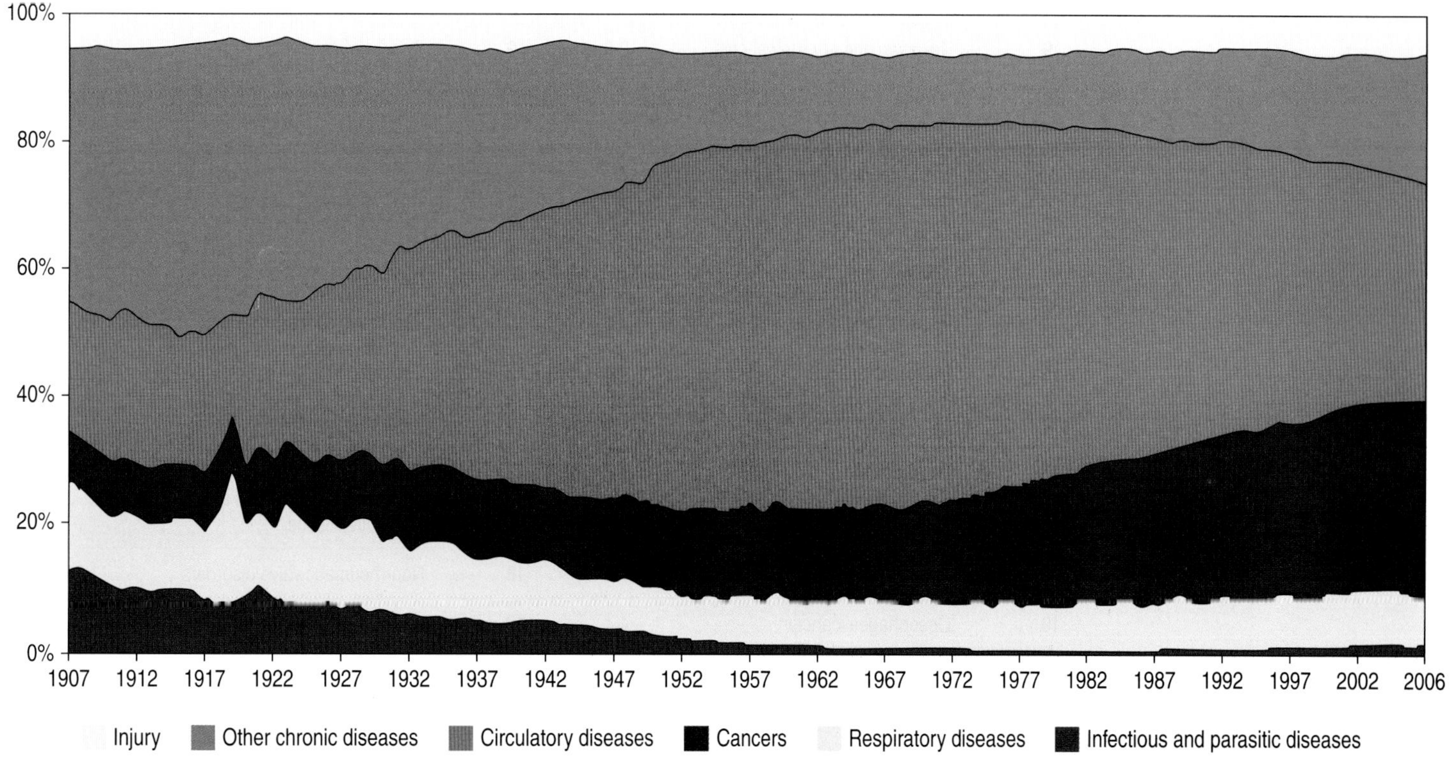

FIGURE **14.1**
100 year trends for major causes of deaths in Australia

In the early 1900s, for example, a leading cause of death was infectious and parasitic diseases. Today, the leading causes of death are cancer, heart disease and strokes (Australian Institute of Health and Welfare [AIHW], 2010). The mortality rates from these illnesses would be largely reduced if people changed one health behaviour, smoking. In fact, statistics indicate that mortality rates from the leading causes of death could be reduced by half if people altered their health behaviour (Centers for Disease Control, 1980). However, there is some good news on the horizon. Death rates are falling for many major health problems, such as cancer, cardiovascular disease, asthma, chronic obstructive pulmonary disease and injuries. The rate of heart attacks is continuing to fall, and survival from them is continuing to improve. Unfortunately, however, the prevalence of diabetes is continuing to increase markedly (AIHW, 2010a). The leading specific causes of death for men and women are shown in table 14.1 (see overleaf).

TABLE 14.1 **Leading underlying specific causes of death, all ages, for men and women**

Male			Female		
Rank	**Cause of death**	**% of deaths***	**Rank**	**Cause of death**	**% of deaths***
1	Coronary heart disease	17.2	1	Coronary heart disease	15.8
2	Lung cancer	6.7	2	Cerebrovascular diseases	10.4
3	Cerebrovascular diseases	6.4	3	Dementia and Alzheimer's disease	7.3
4	Chronic obstructive pulmonary disease	4.2	4	Lung cancer	4.3
5	Prostate cancer	4.2	5	Breast cancer	4.0
6	Dementia and Alzheimer's disease	3.4	6	Chronic obstructive pulmonary disease	3.3
7	Colorectal cancer	3.1	7	Heart failure and complications and ill-defined heart diseases	3.1
8	Diabetes	2.7	8	Diabetes	2.8
9	Unknown primary site cancers	2.6	9	Colorectal cancer	2.8
10	Suicide	2.1	10	Unknown primary site cancers	2.5
11	Heart failure and complications and ill-defined heart diseases	1.9	11	Influenza and pneumonia	2.2
12	Pancreatic cancer	1.7	12	Kidney failure	1.9
13	Kidney failure	1.6	13	Hypertensive diseases	1.6
14	Influenza and pneumonia	1.6	14	Pancreatic cancer	1.5
15	Liver diseases	1.4	15	Ovarian cancer	1.3
16	Land transport accidents	1.3	16	Cardiac arrhythmias	1.2
17	Leukaemia	1.3	17	Diseases of the musculoskeletal system and connective tissue	1.1
18	Melanoma	1.2	18	Non-rheumatic valve disorders	1.0
19	Oesophageal cancer	1.1	19	Accidental falls	0.9
20	Lymphomas	1.1	20	Lymphomas	0.9

*Deaths occurring in the year 2007.

SOURCE: AIHW (2010a).

Lifestyle choices and health-compromising behaviours are major contributors to the leading causes of death today. In addition, an individual with a chronic condition such as cancer may live with that illness for years, with all of the accompanying changes in occupational choices, lifestyle choices and family circumstances. Furthermore, the health status of Aboriginal and Torres Strait Islander peoples is significantly poorer than for Australians as a whole, and more accessible, culturally appropriate primary health care provisions are needed (AMA, 2003; AIHW, 2010a). Clearly, health psychologists are needed to help eliminate health-compromising behaviours and to facilitate health-promoting behaviours, but also to help ill people and their families deal with debilitating health conditions when they arise. People within both the medical profession and public policy are quickly realising the benefits of health psychology to the treatment of illness and the promotion of health, so much so that many primary care facilities now have a full-time health psychologist on board.

Research within the area of health psychology has burgeoned in the last two decades. Health psychologists are involved in examining behavioural and psychological factors that place individuals at risk for illness (e.g. smoking, unsafe sexual practices, alcohol abuse). Because they focus not just on illness, but also on health, health psychologists are also involved in factors that facilitate the development of behaviours that promote health and prevent illness (e.g. exercise, dental hygiene, breast and testicular self-examinations). Finally, health psychologists are increasingly involved in public health policy. What was once a field devoted almost exclusively to research has now become a 'health delivery service' (Marks, Sykes, & McKinley, 2003), with the greatest number of placements of health psychologists in recent years being in two main areas: health promotion and clinical health (Australian Psychological Society, 2004, 2010).

Encouraging health psychology in Australia

By Professor John W. Toumbourou, Deakin University

The professional directions of a number of Australian psychologists were thrown into disarray in a recent year when a new National Registration and Accreditation Scheme was announced that excluded health and community psychology as areas of practice endorsement in Australia. The announcement was surprising, given that the Australian Psychological Society (APS) and many other respected groups had recommended the adoption of all the areas represented within the APS College structure, including health and community psychology.

A solid economic case can be made for ensuring that Australia maintains and expands the health psychology profession. As medical advances have helped to reduce biological and economic causes of death and disease, lifestyle choices and health behaviours have emerged as more dominant influences on health outcomes. Health-compromising behaviours such as poor diet, physical inactivity, tobacco use, harmful alcohol use and maladaptive stress coping strategies are now major contributors to preventable health care costs. There is a trend towards many of these health-compromising behaviours increasing in society. The magnitude of this problem is recognised worldwide. The World Health Organization (2009) has identified the main risk factors responsible for deaths internationally. They include:

- high blood pressure (responsible for 13 percent of deaths)
- tobacco use (responsible for 9 percent of deaths)
- high blood sugar (responsible for 6 percent of deaths)
- physical inactivity (responsible for 6 percent of deaths)
- overweight and obesity (responsible for 5 percent of deaths)
- high cholesterol (responsible for 5 percent of deaths)
- unsafe sex (responsible for 4 percent of deaths)
- alcohol use (responsible for 4 percent of deaths).

A number of these factors also increase the risk of major chronic diseases — including cardiovascular disease, diabetes and cancer.

There is now a substantial evidence base for the effectiveness of health improvement interventions based on psychological theory, research and practice. For this reason, health psychology deserves a high level of recognition within health care funding systems. A meta-analysis of 91 economic studies (Chiles, Lambert, & Hatch, 1999) found that psychological treatments led to an average reduction of about 20 percent in medical costs. Health psychology interventions reduce costs in primary care settings, cancer treatment settings and alcohol abuse treatment settings. They also contribute to future health care cost savings, by preventing injuries and cancers through activities such as tobacco control and sun protection measures.

The Cochrane Collaboration represents an international effort to summarise scientific knowledge of the effectiveness of health care interventions. A Cochrane Collaboration review (Shaw, O'Rourke, Del Mar, & Kenardy, 2005) found that behavioural and cognitive behavioural interventions resulted in significant population reductions in overweight and obesity. Summerbell et al. (2005) found interventions designed to prevent obesity in childhood resulted in improvements in diet and physical activity.

INTERIM SUMMARY

Health psychology is devoted to understanding psychological influences on how people stay healthy, why they become ill and how they respond when they do get ill. Understanding the aetiology of health psychology requires one to go back in history to the earliest theories of illness and its cure. Early theorists, believing that illness was caused by evil spirits, engaged in the practice of ***trephination***, drilling holes in the skull to allow the evil spirits to escape. The role of physiology in illness was identified in the ***humoural theory of illness***, which suggested that physical and psychological problems result from an imbalance of the four fluids: blood, black bile, yellow bile and phlegm. This unity of the mind and body was fractured during the period of the Renaissance by Descartes' theory of ***Cartesian dualism***, the contention that the mind and body are completely separate entities. An increased focus on the body as the source of illness led to the ***cellular theory of illness*** and, subsequently, the ***biomedical model***, the theory that disease can be traced to the level of individual cells. Although still the dominant model of illness within the field of medicine, the biomedical model began to be challenged by Freud and those theorists who endorsed ***psychosomatic medicine***. The recognition that social and psychological variables in addition to biological underpinnings laid the foundation for health and illness set the stage for the ***biopsychosocial model*** of health that guides the field of health psychology today.

APPLY + DISCUSS

All the primary models of health behaviour examine people's attitudes towards positive and negative health behaviours. One of the problems, however, is that people's attitudes are often ambivalent; that is, people hold both positive and negative beliefs about the behaviour in question. Take exercise, for example. Most people believe that exercise will improve health and control weight. However, they also believe that exercise takes too much time, can be done to excess and can result in injury.

- What role do you think attitudinal ambivalence (holding both positive and negative attitudes towards a health behaviour) has on a person's decision to adopt particular health behaviours?
- How would the feelings of a person with ambivalent attitudes compare to those of a person who holds neither positive nor negative attitudes towards exercise or some other health behaviour?

Theories of health behaviour

A number of theories have been proposed to explain why people engage in health-promoting or health-compromising behaviours. These are all social–cognitive theories that focus on the beliefs that individuals hold regarding health threats and their perceived susceptibility to those threats.

Health belief model

One of the earliest theories of health behaviour was the ***health belief model*** (Hochbaum, 1958; Rosenstock, 1966), which suggests that health behaviours are predicted by four factors: the perceived susceptibility to the health threat, the perceived seriousness of the health threat, the benefits and barriers of undertaking particular health behaviours, and cues to action (figure 14.2; see p. 558). ***Perceived susceptibility*** to a health threat refers to a person's perception that he is likely to contract a particular illness. George had an uncle who recently died from lung cancer after years of smoking cigarettes. George is also a smoker and, since his uncle's death, he believes that if he continues to smoke he, too, is likely to develop lung cancer or some other smoking-related illness. Unfortunately, many people experience an ***optimistic bias*** (i.e. unrealistic optimism) by which they believe that they are far less likely than other people to contract particular illnesses (Klein & Helweg-Larsen, 2002; Weinstein, 1980; Weinstein & Klein, 1996). Thus, they rate their own level of susceptibility lower than they rate that of others. George, for example, may believe that, even though his uncle died of lung cancer, his own chances of succumbing to the same fate are remote.

Perceived seriousness or ***severity*** of the health threat refers to an individual's perception of the impact a particular illness would have on her life. For example, the more pain and discomfort associated with a health threat, the more severe it is perceived to be. Similarly, the more disruptive a medical condition is to one's family or current lifestyle, the more severe the illness is rated as being. Having experienced firsthand the death of a close relative due to smoking-induced lung cancer, George has no doubt as to the seriousness of lung cancer.

In deciding whether or not to adopt a health behaviour (e.g. quitting smoking), people evaluate whether the ***benefits*** to be gained from stopping the behaviour (e.g. offsetting a health threat such as lung cancer) outweigh the costs or ***barriers*** associated with the termination of the behaviour (e.g. side effects of withdrawal associated with quitting smoking, weight gain, alienating peers). George can think of a number of benefits associated with quitting smoking, the most notable of which is significantly reducing his chances of contracting lung cancer. On the other hand, not smoking has several negative associations, not the least of which is the discomfort he feels every time he has tried to quit.

Cues to action refer to ancillary factors that influence whether or not a person is willing to begin a healthy behaviour or terminate an unhealthy one. These cues include advice from friends and family, age, gender, socioeconomic status and exposure to media campaigns related to health behaviour, to name a few.

Will George quit smoking? The answer is not a definitive yes or no. According to the health belief model, if George perceives himself to be susceptible to lung cancer, evaluates lung cancer as severe, believes that the health benefits of terminating smoking outweigh any short-term costs, and believes that his decision to quit is supported by his family and friends, then he will be likely at least to attempt to quit. However, the overall effectiveness of the health belief model in predicting health behaviours is mixed — it depends largely on the particular behaviour being examined. The model has done an accurate job predicting preventive dental care (Ronis, 1992), SARS preventive behaviour (Tang & Wong, 2004), sexual risk-taking behaviours (Aspinwall, Kemeny, Taylor, Scheider, & Dudley, 1991; Bakker, Buunk, Siero, & van den Eijnden, 1997), breast self-examination (Champion, 1990, 1994) and mammography screening for women (Tanner-Smith & Brown, 2010). Of the four components of the health belief model, barriers and costs appear to be the best predictor of health-related behaviours.

Protection motivation theory of health

One of the problems with the health belief model is that even those individuals who believe they are susceptible to a health threat, who evaluate the health threat as severe, for whom the benefits of a positive health behaviour outweigh the costs, and for whom the cues to action lead towards health-promoting behaviours may still not alter their behaviour (Janz, Champion, & Strecher, 2002). The reason: they may not believe that they can successfully alter their current health behaviours. For example, if George perceives himself to be susceptible to lung cancer, views lung cancer as severe and sees great benefit in quitting smoking, he will not quit if he does not believe that he can actually quit smoking. Given this, during the 1980s, the health belief model was modified to include the component of ***self-efficacy***, a person's belief in her ability to successfully undertake a particular action or behaviour (Bandura, 1977a).With the addition of self-efficacy, the health belief model assumed a new name: the ***protection motivation theory of health*** (see figure 14.2 overleaf).

Theory of reasoned action

The ***theory of reasoned action***, like the health belief model, takes a social–cognitive view towards health behaviours, broadly stating that behaviours stem from behavioural intentions (Ajzen & Fishbein, 1980; Montano & Kasprzyk, 2002). Although no-one would question that intentions do not always translate into behaviour, certainly intentions to perform a particular behaviour are a necessary first step towards actually performing the behaviour. I intend to do a lot of things that I never really do, but rarely do I do something that I did not have an initial intention to do. Behavioural intentions are a function of two components: attitudes towards the behaviour and the subjective norms surrounding the behaviour (figure 14.2; see overleaf).

Attitudes represent the beliefs one has that a particular behaviour will produce a particular outcome and one's evaluation of those outcomes — for example, the belief that practising safe sex will reduce the likelihood of pregnancy and contracting a sexually transmitted disease; and one's belief that these are favourable outcomes. ***Subjective norms*** reflect someone's perception of how significant other individuals will view the behaviour and the motivation to comply with the desires of those others. For example, if Tran perceives that his parents are opposed to smoking and he wishes to comply with his parents' wishes (and he has favourable beliefs about quitting smoking), then Tran will be more likely to quit smoking. Like the health belief model, the theory of reasoned action has successfully predicted several health behaviours, including participation in mammography screenings (Montano, Thompson, Taylor, & Mahloch, 1997), smoking cessation (Sutton, 1989), condom use to prevent AIDS (Sneed & Morisky, 1998) and a willingness to be an organ donor (Kowalski & Bodenlos, 2003).

MAKING CONNECTIONS

The importance of people's attitudes towards health behaviours has been a major focus of advertising campaigns designed to alter health-compromising behaviours. Thus, it is not surprising that these attitudes are reflected in all four of the theories of health behaviour (chapter 17).

Theory of planned behaviour

Like the health belief model, the theory of reasoned action fails to account for those instances in which behaviour modification does not occur because an individual does not feel he can successfully modify his behaviour. Thus, Ajzen introduced the theory of planned behaviour (figure 14.2; see overleaf). The ***theory of planned behaviour*** includes all the components of the theory of reasoned action plus self-efficacy, sometimes referred to as perceived behavioural control (Ajzen, 1991; Hardeman et al., 2002; Montano & Kasprzyk, 2002). The theory of planned behaviour has met with considerable success in predicting health behaviours, including blood donation (Giles, McClenahan, Cairns, & Mallet, 2004), sunscreen use (Hillhouse, Stair, & Adler, 1996), hand hygiene practice among medical personnel (Jenner, Watson, Miller, Jones, & Scott, 2002), breast (Lierman, Kasprzyk, & Benoliel, 1990) and testicular (Brubaker & Wickersham, 1990) self-examinations, intentions to eat healthy foods (Astrom & Rise, 2001), children's intentions to engage in physical activity (Hagger, Chatzisarantis, Biddle, & Orbell, 2001) and intentions to have mammograms and clinical breast examinations (Godin et al., 2001; see also meta-analytic review conducted by Armitage & Conner, 2001).

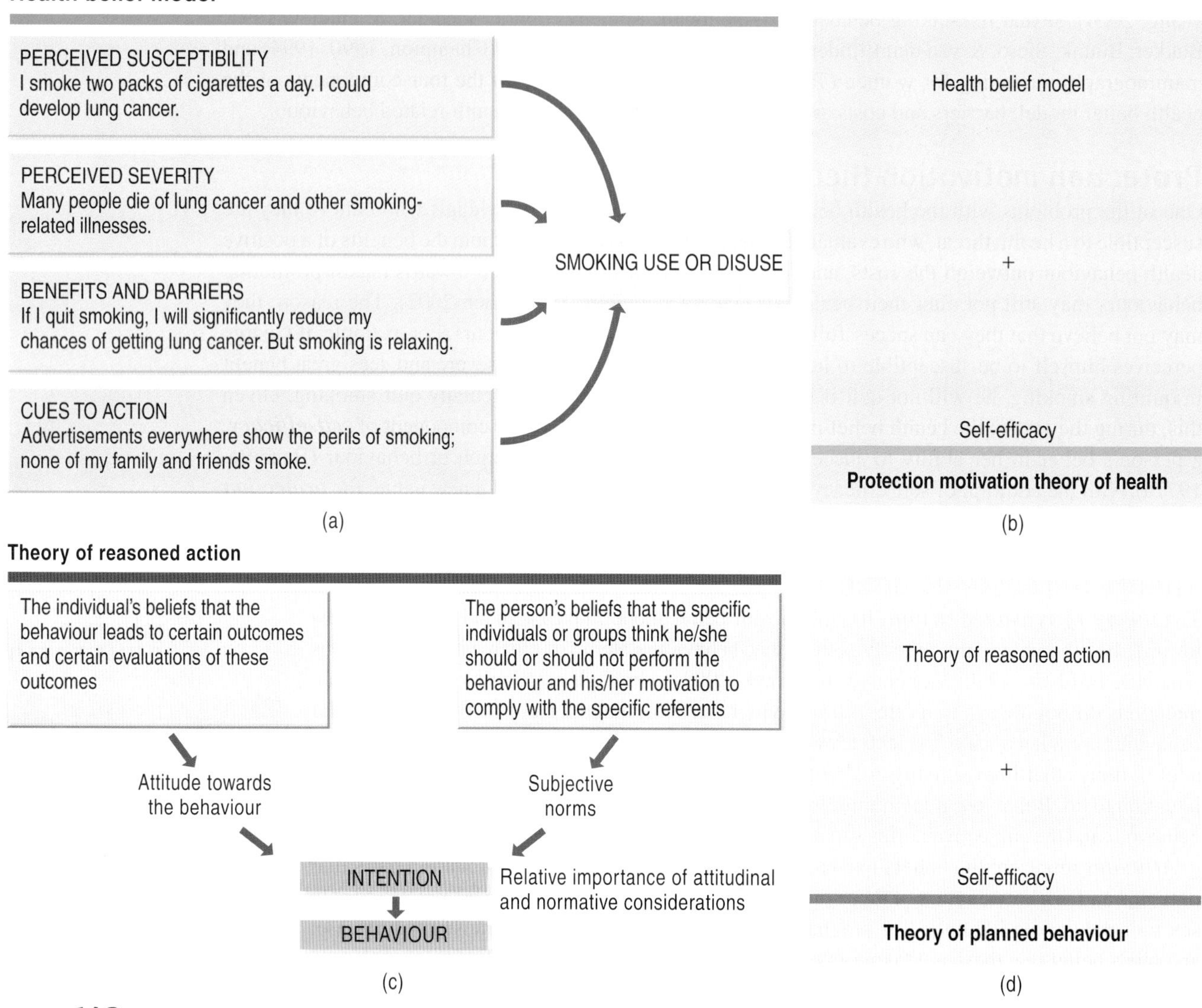

FIGURE 14.2
Theories of health behaviour

INTERIM SUMMARY

Four models of health behaviour have been discussed. The ***health belief model*** theorises that health behaviours are predicted by an individual's perception of his ***perceived susceptibility*** to a health threat (a factor that is undermined by the ***optimistic bias***), the ***perceived seriousness*** of the health threat, the ***benefits*** and ***barriers*** associated with terminating a compromising health behaviour and ***cues to action***. The addition of ***self-efficacy***, or an individual's confidence that she can actually engage in the health behaviour, to the health belief model creates the ***protection motivation theory of health***. The ***theory of reasoned action*** and the ***theory of planned behaviour*** both suggest that behaviour is a function of behavioural intentions. Behavioural intentions are a function of a person's ***attitudes*** towards the health behaviour (i.e. their beliefs that particular outcomes follow from a behaviour and their evaluation of those beliefs), and ***subjective norms*** (i.e. the individual's perception of how significant others feel about the behaviour and the person's motivation to comply with those feelings or desires). These two models differ in the inclusion of self-efficacy into the theory of planned behaviour.

Health-compromising behaviours

Most people can easily list behaviours that are disadvantageous to their health: smoking, excessive alcohol consumption, obesity, lack of sleep and lack of exercise, to name a few. These same people can even tell you many of the negative consequences that follow from engaging in these health-compromising behaviours, including reduced life expectancy, chronic illnesses and poor social relationships. Fewer people, however, can claim that they do not engage in any of these behaviours. And, in all likelihood, people engage in more than one and perhaps several of the health-compromising behaviours.

An AIHW (2010) analysis of a recent National Health Survey revealed that there are correlations between self-assessed health and other health indicators. For example, the analysis showed that people that engage in healthy behaviours — such as not smoking and making healthy dietary choices — are more likely to rate their health as very good or excellent than people who engage in risky behaviour patterns. However, the analysis also showed that high percentages of people who smoked daily, were obese and/or did not eat a healthy diet were also likely to rate their health status favourably (see table 14.2). The presence of a long-term condition or a serious disability was, comparatively, more likely to lead to a person perceiving that they were in fair or poor health (AIHW, 2010a).

TABLE 14.2 **Self-assessed health status and other health indicators**

	Health status (%)		
Indicator	**Excellent/very good**	**Good**	**Fair/poor**
Has a long term condition	54	30	16
Has back pain or a disc disorder	45	32	24
Has cancer	30	28	42
Has diabetes	19	39	42
No long-term condition	74	22	4
Has profound or severe disability	17	23	60
No disability	69	26	5
Healthy weight (BMI 18.5–24.9)	63	25	12
Obese (BMI more than 30)	36	39	25
Daily smoker	39	38	23
Never smoked	62	27	11
Eats four or more serves of vegetables daily	62	25	13
Does not eat vegetables	40	29	31

SOURCE: AIHW (2010a).

In 1999, the AIHW published what it described as the first comprehensive assessment of the health status of the Australian population. The study by Mathers, Vos, and Stevenson (1999) looked at mortality, disability, impairment, illness and injury associated with 176 diseases, injuries and risk factors. The results showed that lifestyle behaviours such as tobacco smoking, physical inactivity, alcohol consumption, poor diet and unsafe sex; physiological states such as obesity, high blood pressure and high cholesterol (often associated with lifestyle choices); as well as societal conditions such as occupational exposure and socioeconomic disadvantage, are responsible for a large part of the burden of disease in Australia.

Fortunately, death rates are falling for many of our major health problems, such as cancer, cardiovascular disease, chronic obstructive pulmonary disease and asthma (AIHW, 2010a). Coronary heart disease causes the largest number of deaths among males aged under 75 years, and breast cancer causes the most among females (AIHW, 2010a). For older people, the main causes of death are heart disease, stroke and cancer (AIHW, 2010). Australian males have a life expectancy of around 79 years; females can expect to live to around 83 (AIHW, 2010a). For Indigenous males, the life expectancy is around

67 years; Indigenous females can expect to live to around 74 years. Australia is slowly closing the gap, but there is still progress to be made. Death rates among children and young people halved between 1987 and 2007, largely due to few deaths from transport accidents (AIHW, 2010a). Although the majority of Australians consider their health status to be very good or excellent, the health and wellbeing among Indigenous Australians, people living in rural and remote areas, and young people suffering socioeconomic disadvantage are identified as areas in need of attention (AIHW, 2010a).

Obesity

Prevalence

Australia is rapidly becoming a nation of overweight and obese people, with three in five adult Australians (61 percent) being overweight or obese in 2007–08 (AIHW, 2010a). Our obesity rates are among the highest in the world, with around one in four Australian adults being obese (AIHW, 2010a). Members of some minority groups are even more at risk. For example, 'Indigenous people are generally less healthy than other Australians, die at much younger ages, and have more disability and a lower quality of life' (AIHW, 2010a, p. 228). Indigenous females are around 1.5 times as likely to be overweight or obese as non-Indigenous females; however, no differences are observed between Indigenous and non-Indigenous males (AIHW, 2010a). These prevalence rates reflect how the traditional low saturated fat and high-fibre, high-protein diet of Indigenous communities has changed to one high in refined carbohydrates and saturated fats (AIHW, 2010a). Similar to Indigenous Australians, people living in rural and remote areas also tend to have higher levels of disease risk factors and illness as compared with their city counterparts (AIHW, 2010a). The increase in prevalence rates of overweight and obese individuals is not limited to adults. One in four children aged 5–17 were overweight or obese in a recent year (AIHW, 2010a). Only one out of every 20 children aged 14–16 consumed the recommended intake of vegetables as part of a healthy diet in the same year (AIHW, 2010a).

Australia is rapidly becoming a nation of overweight and obese people.

Determining whether a person is overweight or obese is typically done by calculating the individual's ***body mass index (BMI)***: the weight in kilograms divided by the height in metres squared: kg/m^2 (AIHW, 2010a; Wadden, Brownell, & Foster, 2002). ***Obesity*** refers to an excessive accumulation of body fat, in excess of 30 percent in women and 20 percent in men (AIHW, 2010a; Lohman, 2002). People are identified as being ***overweight*** if they have a body mass index (BMI) between 25 percent and 30 percent, depending on their gender and age. However, the BMI is flawed because it takes no account of potential differences in muscle mass. Someone with a large amount of lean muscle mass will weigh more than someone of similar height without the muscle. Thus, they will be classified as being overweight but they do not have more fat. Waist circumference can also be used to identify risk of abdominal overweight. Excess fat in the abdominal region (the 'apple' body) is associated with greater health risks than is fat distributed around the body (the 'pear' body; The Australian and New Zealand Obesity Society, 2008). Males should have a waist circumference of less than 94 centimetres; females' waist circumference should be 80 centimetres or less (AIHW, 2010a), though this classification may not be suitable for all ethnic groups.

Consequences

Obesity is not only a pervasive problem in industrialised countries today, but it is also one of the leading contributors to preventable deaths (AIHW, 2010a). For adults, the varied physical problems associated with obesity include musculoskeletal difficulties, cardiovascular disease, high blood pressure, type 2 diabetes, sleep apnoea and certain types of cancer (Department of Health and Ageing [DHA], 2010; The Australian and New Zealand Obesity Society, 2008). Psychosocial consequences can include low self-esteem, body shape dissatisfaction, discrimination, isolation and depression (DHA, 2010; The Australian and New Zealand Obesity Society, 2008). For children, the major issue of concern is the persistence of childhood obesity into adulthood — it is very unlikely that an overweight or obese child will spontaneously revert to a healthy weight in adulthood, thus predisposing them to the health concerns for adults (DHA, 2010). Preventative measures are important for health and wellbeing, and help to prevent the development of overweight and obesity and their associated physical and psychosocial consequences (AIHW, 2010a).

Genes load the gun, the environment pulls the trigger.

(Bray, 1998).

People who are obese often experience psychological difficulties, stemming in large part from the stigma attached to obesity and the subsequent discrimination experienced by obese individuals. The Northern Territory Department of Health and Community Services (2004) has found that overweight children are more likely to have psychological problems such as low self-esteem. As noted by Corsica and Perri (2003, p. 125), 'Obesity may well be the last socially acceptable object of prejudice and discrimination'. People who are obese are considered by many to be lazy and out of control (Crandall, 1994, 1995). Relative to people who are not obese, obese individuals are less likely to marry, get desired jobs, be treated respectfully by doctors and other medical personnel and get into prestigious universities (Corsica & Perri, 2003; Gortmaker, Must, Perrin, Sobol, & Dietz, 1993; Pingitore, Dugoni, Tindale, & Spring, 1994; Wadden, Womble, Stunkard, & Anderson, 2002). They also have lower household incomes, fewer years of education and personal incomes that are more likely to place them at or below the poverty level (Gortmaker et al., 1993). Those who affiliate with or are even in proximity to the obese are also at increased risk of being stigmatised. In a study illustrating this, researchers found that male job applicants were rated more negatively when they were seen seated next to an overweight (as opposed to an average weight) woman (Hebl & Mannix, 2003). Specifically, raters indicated that they would be less likely to hire the job applicant affiliated with an obese individual, and they rated his professional qualities and interpersonal skills more negatively.

The personal rejection and social discrimination experienced by obese individuals can have detrimental effects on their personal wellbeing. A large-scale study involving over 40 000 participants examined the relationship between BMI and depression, suicidal ideation and suicide attempts. Among women, higher BMIs were associated with a higher frequency of major depressive episodes and more suicidal ideation. Among men, however, lower BMIs were associated with depression and suicidal ideation (Carpenter, Hasin, Allison, & Faith, 2000), a clear testament to the different standards of attractiveness to which men and women are held in society.

Obesity also exacts significant economic costs. Treatment for obesity and related illnesses consumes between 2 percent and 7 percent of total health care costs (Caterson, 1999). On top of this are costs associated with lost work hours due to illness and death associated with obesity. The total financial cost of obesity in Australia more than doubled between 2005 and 2008, rising from $3.77 billion to $8.23 billion (Access Economics, 2008). Of this, productivity costs are estimated at $3.6 billion, health system costs at $2 billion and carer costs at $1.9 billion.

APPLY + DISCUSS

At least within Western culture, women are held to different standards of weight than men. Society tells women that thin is in.

- Given the differential treatment of men and women in terms of weight, do you think weight-related discrimination affects men and women differently?
- There are more men than women in both the overweight category and the obese category. Do you think that societal pressures put on women to be thin have influenced their eating behaviours more than those of men?

The genetics of obesity

The multitude of contributors to obesity include both physiological and environmental sources (figure 14.3). Physiologically, both hormones and genes have been implicated in obesity. Genetic influences are estimated to account for up to 40 percent of the aetiology of obesity (Stunkard, Harris, Pederson, & McClearn, 1990; Wadden, Brownell, et al., 2002). Twin studies reveal that both body weight and the amount of fat in a person's body are highly heritable. Body weight of adoptees correlates with the weight of their biological parents but not with their adoptive parents (Allison, Heshka, Neale, & Lykken, 1994; Bouchard, 1989). Heritability for obesity is estimated to range from 30 to 70 percent, which is extremely high (Devlin, Yanovski, & Wilson, 2000). Even the amount a person eats is highly heritable, although family environment during childhood also influences food intake years later (de Castro, 1993; Faith, Rha, Neale, & Allison, 1999).

Tracking down the genes that contribute to obesity is difficult because so many processes influenced by genetics can contribute — such as those regulating hunger, satiety, metabolic rate, fat storage or activity levels. In fact, researchers have already isolated at least 200 genes likely to contribute to normal and abnormal weight (Yager, 2000). Two physiological factors have received attention for many years, both of which show substantial heritability. The first is the number and size of fat cells in the body. Obese people have many more fat cells than average weight individuals, and the cells they do have tend to be larger (Hirsch & Knittle, 1970). Unfortunately, fat cells that develop early in life do not disappear when a person later attempts to lose weight; they only shrink.

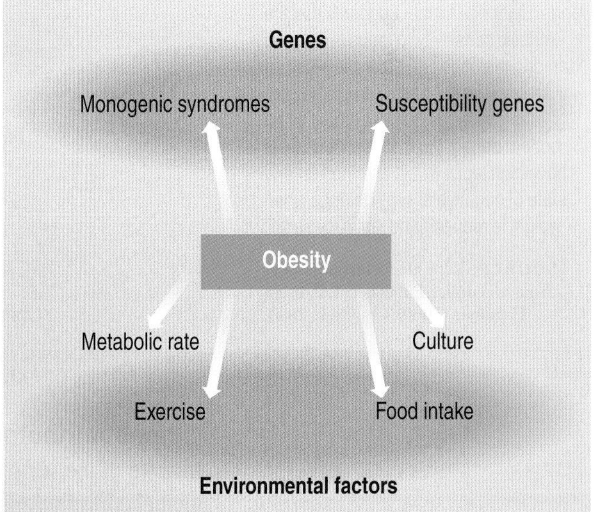

FIGURE 14.3
Factors that influence the development of obesity

SOURCE: Reprinted with permission from Macmillan Publishers Ltd. From Kopelman (2000). Copyright 2000.

One theory suggests that the amount of body fat one has is regulated by the hormone leptin (shown as a monogenic syndrome in figure 14.3). People with higher levels of leptin generally have higher BMIs (Friedman, 2000). Leptin is produced by fat tissue and operates on the hypothalamus to regulate body weight. In order to maintain homoeostasis, decreases in body fat produce decreases in leptin, which triggers the body's desire to take in more food (figure 14.4). Conversely, an increase in body fat increases the level of leptin, which triggers reduced food consumption. It is through this process that many people's weight hovers around a ***set point***, an ideal body weight for each individual. Given this regulator, why does everyone's weight not stay around their set point? The answer again is physiological. Some people, those who become obese, appear to be leptin-resistant (Friedman, 2000). Thus, they are unable to effectively control their weight around their set point. Other individuals do not produce enough leptin and have reduced levels of body fat, almost regardless of what food they might consume. A number of genetic, social and environmental variables can determine how sensitive a particular individual is to leptin. For example, a diet high in fat can lead an individual to become leptin-resistant and thereby increase the likelihood that they will become obese.

Another theory, the ***susceptible gene hypothesis***, suggests that certain genes increase the likelihood of, but do not guarantee, the development of a particular trait or characteristics (e.g. obesity). Animal models, usually mice, have also provided useful information in helping researchers map particular genes that are associated with obesity (Straub, 2002; figure 14.3).

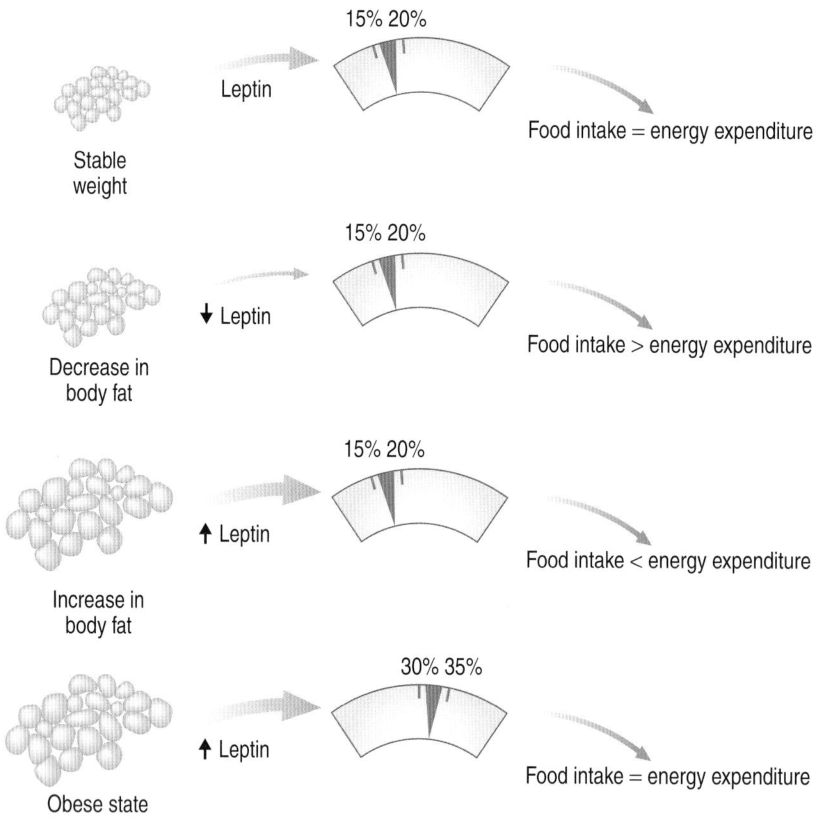

FIGURE **14.4**
Leptin and the regulation of adipose tissue mass. The cloning of the *ob* gene and the characterisation of leptin has indicated that body fat content is under homoeostatic control. The available data suggest that leptin is the afferent signal in a feedback loop regulating adipose tissue mass. At an individual's stable weight (shown as 15–20 percent body fat in this figure, which is the typical fat content of a non-obese person) the amount of circulating leptin elicits a state in which food intake equals energy expenditure. Decreasing leptin levels lead to positive energy balance (food intake > energy expenditure), whereas increasing leptin levels result in negative energy balance (food intake < energy expenditure). These effects maintain constancy of fat cell mass within a relatively narrow range. Evidence further suggests that the intrinsic sensitivity to leptin is reduced among the obese and that the set point for body fat content is thus increased (designated as 30–35 percent in the bottom panel). Most obese individuals have high leptin levels and thus enter a state of negative energy balance when weight is reduced and leptin levels fall.

Other contributors to obesity

In spite of the strong evidence for genetic underpinnings of obesity, it is impossible to rule out environmental contributions to obesity. An example can be found among different Indigenous groups in Australia. Indigenous Australians living a traditional indigenous lifestyle, including fibre-rich, high-protein, and low saturated fat diets, were very lean and obesity was practically nonexistent (Jones & White, 1994; see also AIHW, 2010a). However, other Indigenous Australians living a more Westernised lifestyle have high rates of obesity and associated diseases, such as diabetes (AIHW, 2010a; Burns & Thomson, 2006). Low socioeconomic status is associated with poor health and higher levels of risk factors such as smoking, poor nutrition and obesity (AIHW, 2010a). Unemployment and overcrowded housing have also been linked with poor physical and mental health among Indigenous Australians (AIHW, 2010a). Education is a key factor in closing the gap in life expectancy for Indigenous Australians (AIHW, 2010a). In 2004–05, Indigenous Australians aged 18–34 years who had completed Year 12 were more likely than those with lower education levels to report better health and wellbeing and were less likely to regularly smoke, drink alcohol at high risk levels and be physically inactive (AIHW, 2010a). However, results from the 2006 Census show that almost one-quarter (23 percent) of Indigenous adults completed Year 12 as their highest level of education obtained, compared with almost one half (49 percent) of non-Indigenous adults (ABS, 2008b; AIHW, 2008).

As the last few decades have witnessed an explosion in the incidence of obesity, genes have remained largely the same — clearly genes are not the only factor or even the primary factor involved. Forty-four percent of dogs of obese people are also obese. For non-obese individuals, only 25 percent of the dogs are obese (Mason, 1970). Obesity was once considered a problem only in wealthier, industrialised countries; however, it is now an increasing concern in low- and middle-income countries often concurrently dealing with the effects of undernutrition (AIHW, 2010a). A plethora of high-calorie foods are now readily available across the globe (e.g. at fast food restaurants such as McDonald's). The availability and affordability of these foods is impacting on people's health and lifestyle choices. In addition, as jobs have become increasingly sedentary, energy expenditure has decreased. Complicating matters even further, because of the stigma attached to obesity, many obese individuals feel too embarrassed to be seen exercising in public. The lack of physical activity makes it difficult for many people to maintain their weight at an acceptable level (Access Economics, 2006b).

Women of higher socioeconomic status in technologically developed countries are substantially less obese than women of lower socioeconomic status (Ball & Mishra, 2005). The difference between the two groups appears to reflect environmental factors: diet, efforts to restrain eating and trips to the gym (Garner & Wooley, 1991). Thus, as with IQ, genetics plays a central role in accounting for individual differences in body mass, but group differences may be under greater environmental control.

Other environmental factors substantially affect body weight and obesity. One of the best ways to cut obesity is simply to limit portions and to change expectations about how much food should be on the plate (Hill & Peters, 1998). Another way is to limit the amount of time spent in front of the television. Researchers from the Dunedin Multidisciplinary Health and Development Research Unit in New Zealand have also found that children who watch more than two hours of television a night are at higher risk of becoming overweight, or unfit, or of suffering from high cholesterol as adults (Hancox, Milne, & Poulton, 2004). Reducing TV time would result in greater physical activity and perhaps less snacking. Thus, although DNA plays a key role in obesity, so, too, do Nintendo and potato chips.

The psychological factors involved in obesity are not entirely clear, in part because different people become obese for different reasons (Friedman & Brownell, 1995; Rodin, Schank, & Striegel-Moore, 1989). One frequent psychological correlate of obesity is low self-esteem (Klaczynski, Goold, & Mudry, 2004). Whether self-esteem problems cause or reflect obesity, however, is unclear; the relationship probably runs in both directions, with people sometimes eating to assuage their pain and others feeling bad about themselves because of their weight. Anxiety appears to be another psychological variable relevant to obesity (Greeno & Wing, 1994; Palme & Palme, 1999). Both clinical and experimental data suggest that some people overeat to control anxiety (Ganley, 1989; Slochower, 1987). Further, people who are morbidly obese (at least 50 kg or 100 percent over ideal body weight) are more likely to suffer from depressive, anxiety and personality disorders (Simon et al., 2006).

Another important variable is the motivation to diet or exercise. Exercising is strongly predictive of weight control, but only 15 percent of dieters continue their exercise regimens after reaching their weight goal (Katahn & McMinn, 1990). Health psychologists are attempting to understand the reasons people smoke, eat too much, fail to see the doctor when they are becoming sick and fail to exercise, and are beginning to zero in on some of the reasons for this seemingly 'irrational' behaviour (chapter 10).

Society is also to blame. Society does little to combat obesity in children or adults. The time that children once spent playing outdoors, they now spend playing video games or watching television (Sallis, Prochaska, Taylor, Hill, & Geraci, 1999). Research collected as part of a recent Australian National Children's Nutrition and Physical Activity Survey (AIHW, 2010a) revealed that few children meet recommended limits on participating in screen-based activities (time spent, for example, using a computer, or watching television or DVDs). The survey showed that children aged 9–16 years engage in 223 minutes of screen time on average each day — which equates to nearly four hours of screen time each day, or about 26 hours of screen time a week (AIHW, 2010a). Not only do children exercise less at home, but schools have also reduced their hours of physical education. Thus, caloric intake increases, energy expenditure decreases, and those who are overweight do not exercise for fear of ridicule by others. It is probably no coincidence that increases in sedentary lifestyles, coupled with drive-through food services and remote controls, parallel increases in obesity (Foreyt & Goodrick, 1995; Wadden, Brownell, et al., 2002).

In 2008, the Australian Government announced obesity as a National Health Priority Area to address the increased risk of poor health and psychological wellbeing, including discrimination, victimisation and teasing that stems from excess body weight (AIHW, 2010a). An initial survey to measure nutrition and related physical activity data was due to commence in 2011 as part of the Australian Health Survey 2011–13 (DHA, 2010). The Australian Government is committed to promoting healthy lifestyles through various and diverse initiatives such as:

Children from Kingston Primary School in Hobart are shown here participating in a Walking School Bus program. The program offers children a chance to exercise and socialise as part of a routine of walking to and from school in a group with adult supervision.

- Get set 4 Life — Habits for Healthy Kids
- The Stephanie Alexander Kitchen Garden National Program
- Healthy Spaces and Places
- Community and Schools Grants Program
- Learning from Successful Community Obesity Initiative
- How do you measure up? (DHA, 2010).

Another successful initiative to promote regular physical activity is the Walking School Bus program, a Victorian Health initiative that enables local communities to provide a safe way for children to walk to and from school (TravelSmart Australia, 2007). The program has also been introduced in some other Australian states and territories. A parent 'drives' the walking bus at the front, and another parent supervises at the rear of the bus. The walking bus picks up 'passengers' along the way to school at designated 'bus stops'. A variation on this program is the bicycle train, in which children ride their bikes to school in a group with adult supervision.

Treatment

Australians spend in excess of $500 million a year on commercial weight control measures (Kouris-Blazos & Wahlqvist, 2007; Murphy & Yates, 2005). The newsagents' stands in every town and city bulge with magazines promising the latest in dieting or weight-loss techniques. Weight-loss companies have used celebrities like swimmer Hayley Lewis and comedian Magda Szubanski to advertise their products. People seek treatment for obesity for a number of different reasons. Some individuals need to lose weight because of the health-complicating factors associated with obesity. Others want to lose weight to escape the rejection and ridicule experienced at the hands of others because of their weight. Perhaps because of rejection, others seek help losing weight in order to improve their self-esteem and reduce depression.

Dieting has been and still is the most common step in treating obesity. Many people want a relatively quick fix to their weight problem. Patients who are obese are taught how to restrict their caloric intake and, in addition, how to increase their energy expenditure through physical exercise. However, dietary restrictions are rarely successful in the long term. Estimates are that around 90 percent of people who lose weight via dieting subsequently gain the weight back. As one diet after another is tried (yo-yo dieting), changes in metabolism may actually contribute to the person gaining back even more weight than she started with. This downside does not even include the decreased self-esteem and increased depression resulting from the failure to successfully maintain long-term weight loss that may then lead the person to consume even more 'comfort' food.

Appetite-suppressing drugs may be used to help obese individuals limit their caloric consumption (Bray & Tartaglia, 2000). Two primary problems surround the use of these drugs. First, a few years ago, some of these drugs were removed from the market because of health complications resulting from them. Second, even if the drugs are successful in helping someone lose weight, if the person attributes his success to the drugs, his confidence and self-efficacy about his ability to maintain weight loss are compromised (Rodin, Elias, Silberstein, & Wagner, 1988). Furthermore, the use of diets or appetite-suppressing drugs can complicate health problems that already exist as a result of the obesity or that were worsened as excess body fat accumulated.

For individuals who are at least 100 percent overweight, more extreme measures of treatment are available, including gastroplasty and gastric bypass. Gastroplasty or stomach stapling involves stapling the stomach so that only a small portion of it remains available for processing food. People who have had gastroplasty and consume too much food experience stomach upset and vomiting. Besides obvious complications associated with any type of surgery, two additional issues accompany the use of gastroplasty. First, although the ingestion of anything more than small amounts of food at any one sitting can be aversive, liquids, including high-calorie liquids such as milk shakes, can be more easily accommodated. Second, over time and with the repeated consumption of excess food, the pouch can stretch (Corsica & Perri, 2003).

Gastric bypass is similar to gastroplasty except that, instead of allowing food to move through the remainder of the stomach into the small intestine, a portion of the small intestine is attached directly to the pouch created from the stapling of the stomach. In this way, most of the stomach is 'bypassed'. Very little food is actually absorbed into the body, stimulating weight loss. The ingestion of sweet or high-calorie foods (including high-calorie liquids) produces nausea and vomiting.

None of these methods of controlling obesity will be completely effective unless they are also accompanied by therapeutic interventions to help obese individuals understand the origins of their obesity, their patterns of disordered eating and the consequences of obesity for their health. In recognition of the physical, psychological and social contributions to the accumulation of body fat, some researchers have designed more systematic programs for weight loss that are based on an individual's BMI and current health status (Wadden, Brownell, et al., 2002; see figure 14.5 for an example of one such program). The advantages of such programs are twofold. First, they are tailored to the individual's own needs and physiological states. Second, they recognise the multiple origins of obesity and target most or all of these.

(a)

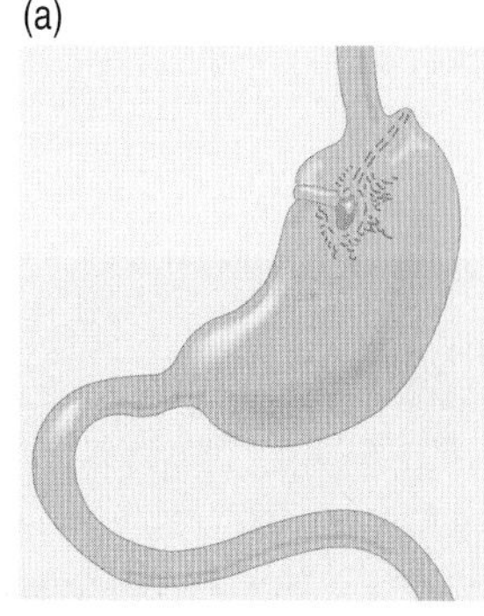

(b)

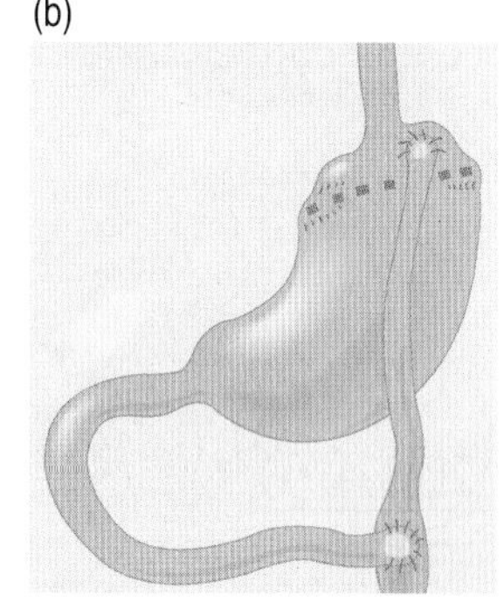

Surgical treatment for obesity
(a) Vertical banded gastroplasty
(b) Roux-en-Y gastric bypass

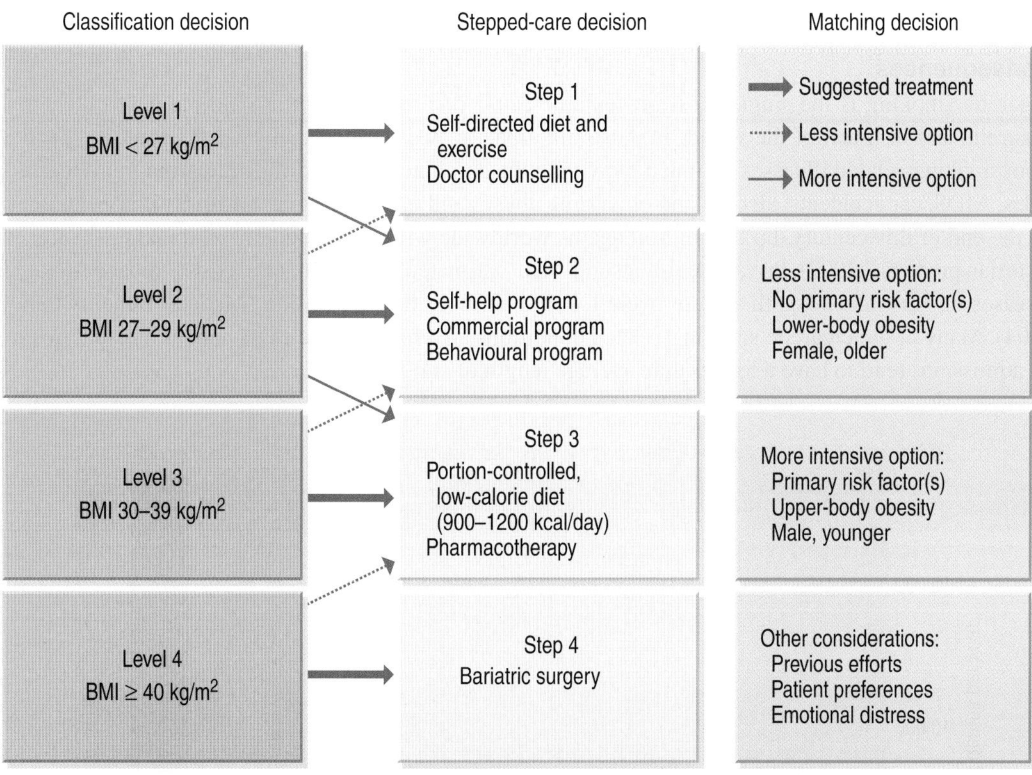

FIGURE 14.5
A conceptual scheme showing a three-stage process for selecting treatment. The first step, the classification decision, divides people into four levels based on body mass index (BMI). This level indicates which of four classes of interventions are likely to be most appropriate in the second stage, the stepped-care decision. All individuals are encouraged to control their weight by increasing their physical activity and consuming an appropriate diet. When this approach is not successful, more intensive intervention may be warranted, with the most conservative treatment (i.e. lowest cost and risks of side-effects) tried next. The thick solid arrow between two boxes shows the class of treatments that is usually most appropriate for an individual when less intensive interventions have not been successful. The third stage, the matching decision, is used to make a final treatment selection, based on the individual's prior weight loss efforts, treatment preferences and need for weight reduction (as judged by the presence of comorbid conditions or other risk factors). The dashed lines point to treatment options for persons with a reduced need for weight reduction because of a reduced risk of health complications. The thin solid arrows show the more intensive treatment options for persons, who despite relatively low BMI levels, have increased risks of health complications. Adjunct nutritional or psychological counselling is recommended for patients who report marked problems with meal planning, depression, body image or similar difficulties.

SOURCE: Wadden, Brownell, et al. (2002, p. 514).

Cigarette smoking

Among the 30 countries of the Organisation for Economic Co-operation and Development (OECD), Sweden has the lowest smoking prevalence rate (14.5 percent), almost three times lower than that for Greece (40 percent; OECD, 2009). Australia had the third lowest daily smoking rate in 2007, behind the United States and Sweden (OECD, 2009). Estimates from the latest National Drug Strategy Household Survey indicate that fewer Australians are smoking each day, with a daily smoking rate of about one in six adults in 2007 (AIHW, 2008). More than half the Australian population (55.4 percent) have never smoked and around a quarter were former smokers (AIHW, 2008). Almost three-quarters (71.8 percent) of people aged 14 years and over who had smoked in the last 12 months had attempted to quit smoking, often due to poor health or fitness reasons or because smoking was too expensive (AIHW, 2008).

Research has shown that Indigenous smokers on average consume six cigarettes per day, compared to the 14 per day average of non-Indigenous smokers.

An encouraging statistic is that Australian teenagers are less likely to smoke than their older counterparts (AIHW, 2008). In 2007, 5.6 percent of 12–19 year olds smoked daily, compared with 16.1 percent for the wider Australian population (AIHW, 2008). However, smoking rates of young Australians increased with age, from 2 percent of 12–15 year olds to 12.6 percent of those aged 18–19 years (AIHW, 2008). This marked increase in smoking in the latter teenage years potentially reflects the strategy of banning sales of cigarettes to people under the age of 18 (AIHW, 2010a). More men (18.0 percent) than women (15.2 percent) report smoking daily and males are more likely to be ex-smokers than females (AIHW, 2008).

Indigenous Australians are more likely to be smokers than non-indigenous Australians. In 2007–08, approximately one in three Indigenous Australians (34.1 percent) were smokers — almost twice the reported rate of the non-Indigenous population (AIHW, 2008).

Consequences

Cigarette smoking is the single most preventable cause of illness, disability and premature death in Australia and in much of the world. In Australia alone, it is estimated that 19 000 people a year die from smoking-related illnesses — much more than the combined number of deaths from murders, suicides, AIDS, car accidents, alcohol and other drug abuses and fires (see figure 14.6). Estimates are that, by the end of this century, up to a billion deaths worldwide will be attributable to smoking ("Science historian predicts," 2002). Private health insurer MBF estimated in 2000 that the cost of tobacco-related diseases on Australia's health system overall would be more than $1 billion (Medical Benefits Fund, 2004). Many of the cigarette smoking-related conditions are chronic conditions and, as a result, hospital admissions tend to have a longer than average length of stay.

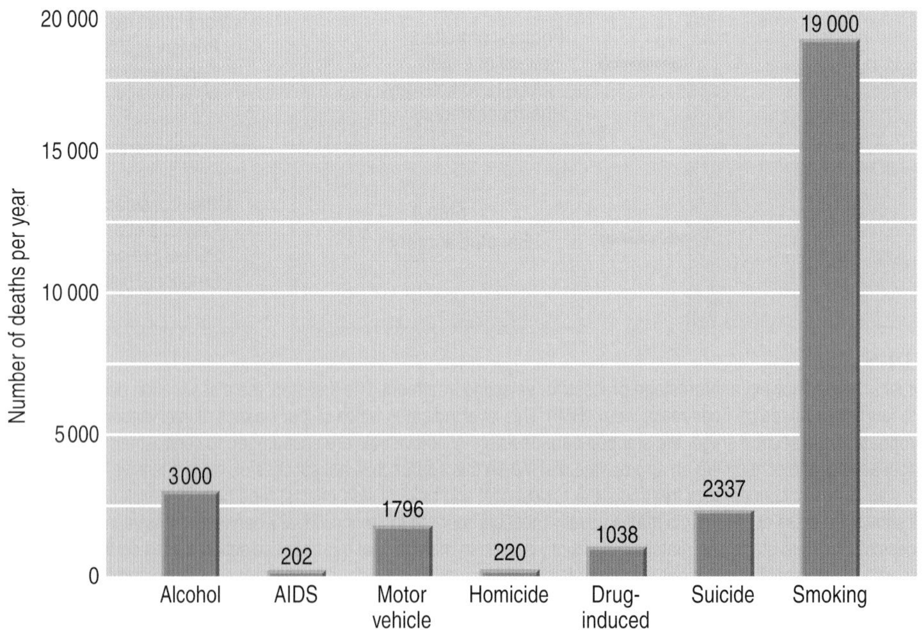

FIGURE 14.6
Comparative causes of annual deaths in Australia

SOURCES: ABS (2004) and AIHW (2009).

Worldwide, 15 billion cigarettes are sold daily — or 10 million every minute (Martin, 2002). Research at the Menzies School of Health Research in Darwin showed that Indigenous Australians averaged about six cigarettes a day, much less than people from the wider Australian community who smoked an average of 14 or more cigarettes a day (Butler, Chapman, Thomas, & Torzillo, 2010). Despite the lower cigarette consumption, Indigenous Australians are more likely to suffer from smoking related illnesses, with one in five Aboriginals dying early due to smoking (ABS, 2009e). Australia should heed this health warning and commit to closing the gap.

In 2004–2005, the federal government collected almost $7 billion from the importation and sale of tobacco products (AIHW, 2007e). Not counting deaths associated with second-hand smoke, estimates are that males lost an average of 13 years and females 14.5 years because of smoking. Each cigarette smoked costs the smoker 12 minutes of his life ('A fistful of', 1996). Each time a cigarette is lit, 4000 chemicals are released (Swan, Hudmon, & Khroyan, 2003).

Not surprisingly, then, smoking is a risk factor for heart disease, lung cancer, emphysema, bronchitis and other respiratory problems, and cancers of the mouth, bladder, oesophagus and pancreas (Newcomb & Carbone, 1992; see also AIHW, 2007b, 2010) (Smoking is associated with approximately 140 infant deaths a year due to low birthweight and Sudden Infant Death Syndrome (SIDS; Mathers et al., 1999). More recent research indicates that neuronal cell death in SIDS cases is evidenced by exposure of the infant to cigarette smoke (Machaalani & Waters, 2008). In addition, children whose mothers smoked during pregnancy are at heightened risk for respiratory problems, lower IQs and attention-deficit hyperactivity disorder (ADHD; Milberger, Biederman, Faraone, Chen, & Jones, 1996). The risks of smoking are not limited to the smokers themselves. People who are around smokers are exposed to second-hand smoke. Referred to as passive smokers, these individuals are also at increased risk of lung cancer and heart disease. Indeed, some refer to passive smoking as the third leading cause of preventable death (Glantz & Parmley, 1991).

Contributors to smoking

Contributors to smoking, as with most other health-related issues, are both genetic and environmental, although the origin of smoking has largely social origins, as will be discussed. Addiction to nicotine is, in part, genetically based. Research indicates that for both males and females, individual differences in smoking initiation were explained by genetic (44 percent), shared environmental (51 percent) and unique environmental (5 percent) influences (Vink, Willemsen, & Boomsma, 2005). In contrast, nicotine dependence was influenced only by genetic (75 percent) and unique environmental (25 percent) factors (Vink et al., 2005). Furthermore, some individuals metabolise nicotine more rapidly than others. Fast metabolisers are less likely than slow metabolisers to experience the negative effects of smoking or to experience smoking as aversive. Thus, fast metabolisers are likely to smoke more than slow metabolisers. The rate at which one metabolises nicotine is genetically determined (Idle, 1990; Swan et al., 2003). Smokers and nonsmokers also appear to differ in a gene related to dopamine. People with the 9-repeat allele gene are less likely to become smokers than people with another form of the gene (Lerman et al., 1999).

In spite of the clear role that dispositional factors play in the onset of cigarette smoking, environmental and social variables play key roles. For example, children and adolescents are likely to model their parents' smoking behaviours (Bradshaw et al., 2007). Most people begin to smoke (or at least try their first cigarette) during adolescence. The main reason: peer pressure and self-presentational concerns (Snow & Bruce, 2003). When asked why he first began to smoke, one young man said 'It's peer pressure. Nobody starts smoking because it feels good or it's the right thing to do' ("Movie stars who smoke linked to teens lighting up," 2003). Many adolescents believe that smoking conveys an image of toughness and rebelliousness, perhaps stemming from the image conveyed by the movies. And, in fact, it may. Smokers are twice as likely as nonsmokers to have had sex, three times more likely to have consumed alcohol and 17 times more likely to have used marijuana (U.S. Department of Health and Human Services, 1994). Australian research has found that adolescents who smoke tend to have a more positive opposite sex self-concept — smoking produces feelings of sexual competence (McInman & Grove, 1991).

These same social variables contribute to why people continue to smoke. The desire to be accepted by a particular peer group and to maintain desired identity images, such as being rebellious, leads many adolescents to become hooked. Contributing to this social addiction is the physiological addiction. At a physiological level, smoking also has rewarding properties. Nicotine increases levels of epinephrine and norepinephrine, producing improved mental acuity, reduced pain sensitivity, reduced feelings of anxiety and feelings of relaxation (Heishman, 1999). Nicotine also increases the release of dopamine in the reward centres of the brain (Nowak, 1994). Forgoing these rewards by quitting smoking is difficult for many people.

Treatment

How do smokers quit? Not easily. Because smoking is so difficult to quit and because the health consequences of smoking are so negative, health psychologists direct much of their attention to programs designed to prevent people from smoking in the first place. Taxes on cigarettes have increased with the idea of making smoking prohibitively expensive for many, particularly adolescents whose funds are already limited. Educational programs intended to inform young people of the hazards of smoking are prevalent in schools. Advertising campaigns have been launched heralding the benefits of a smoke-free lifestyle and highlighting positive peer influence by showing young people who do not smoke and still enjoy satisfactory interactions with others. In Australia, the 2010 National Tobacco Campaign (see www.quitnow.info.au) was launched to educate young Australians about the chemicals they potentially inhale with every smoke, highlighting the long-term damage to their health. The national campaign provided graphic health warnings to encourage people to quit, or avoid smoking in the future. People wanting to quit can phone the Quitline on 131 848 confidentially anywhere in Australia. For the cost of a local call only, they can receive counselling and support. The federal government has continued with various tobacco control measures to discourage smoking. These include bans on most forms of tobacco advertising, including print and electronic media, promoting smoke-free work environments, placing health warnings on tobacco products and revising the taxing of cigarettes.

APPLY + DISCUSS

An article in the medical journal *The Lancet* stated that teens who watch movies in which the actors smoke are three times more likely to smoke than those who do not watch those same movies.

- Do you agree with the journal's finding?
- What other factors might be involved that could possibly distort the findings obtained in this study? How many people do you know who started smoking because of someone they had seen smoking in the movies?

For adults who have been smoking for years and who appear to be immune to media and informational campaigns designed to get them to quit smoking, other methods are available to help with smoking cessation. To curb the physiological urge to smoke, pharmacological treatments, such as the nicotine patch, gum and inhaler, are available. These pharmacological interventions have met with considerable success, particularly if they are paired with some form of behavioural therapy (Swan et al., 2003). Hypnosis is successful for some individuals who desire to quit smoking, as are other types of individual and group therapy. For both pharmacological and non-pharmacological methods of smoking cessation, social support is a critical variable influencing success. One study found that social support increased success in smoking cessation by 50 percent (Fiore et al., 2000). In reality, though, the majority of smokers are unsuccessful in permanently putting out the cigarette. Estimates are that only about 25 percent of people who attempt to quit smoking remain smoke free, although the success rate varies depending on method of quitting. About 10 percent of people who quit unaided will remain non-smokers for 12 months (Sutherland, 2005), and about half the people who abstain for 6 months will quit smoking for the rest of their lives (Phend, 2000). In 2007, about 25 percent of Australians had quit smoking during their lifetime and 61 percent of people who had ever smoked had quit (Victorian Government of Health, 2010).

Alcohol abuse

Consider the following statistics:

- Australia is ranked in the middle of all OECD countries for per capita alcohol consumption, with around 10 litres of alcohol per person per year (OECD, 2009). Australia's consumption peaked in the 1970s and 1980s and has declined over the 1990s and in the early twenty-first century. In comparison, Ireland and the United Kingdom have increased alcohol consumption over the past 40 years (AIHW, 2010a).
- One in five Australians drink at a risky or high level at least once a month. This is mostly evident among young adults, particularly those aged 20–29 (AIHW, 2010a).
- The National Drug Strategy Household Survey conducted in 2007 indicates that most Australians aged 14 years and older drink alcohol (about 83 percent), and about 8 percent drink daily (AIHW, 2008). Almost half the Australian population drinks alcohol at least once a week (AIHW, 2008).
- Drinking to intoxication has become a normalised activity for many Australians and often leads to serious harm, including violence and crime, road crashes, and emotional and verbal abuse (Australian Government Department of Health and Ageing, 2009b, 2009c).
- In one recent financial year, alcohol-related social problems were estimated at a cost of $15.3 million for the Australian economy (Australian Government Department of Health and Ageing, 2009b, 2009c).

- The goal of the National Alcohol Strategy is to prevent and minimise alcohol-related harm to individuals, families and communities and develop safer and healthy drinking cultures in Australia. To reduce the health risks from drinking, it is recommended that both men and women drink no more than two drinks per day (AIHW, 2010a). Young people (under 18 years) and pregnant or breastfeeding women are advised to abstain from alcohol (AIHW, 2010a).
- Each year, excessive alcohol consumption in Australia kills 3200 people and hospitalises 81 000 people (Australian Government Department of Health and Ageing, 2009b, 2009c).

Prevalence

Clearly alcohol can be a problem, but identifying who is an alcoholic, who is a problem drinker and who is a responsible drinker can be difficult at times. A person is identified as having ***alcoholism*** when he or she is physiologically dependent on alcohol, and, therefore, shows withdrawal symptoms when no alcohol has been consumed. ***Problem drinkers*** are not physiologically addicted to alcohol, but still have a number of problems stemming from alcohol consumption, including problems with work and family, and health-related complications. Although there are individual variations in these definitions, problem drinkers appear to have more control over their alcohol consumption than alcoholics.

Alcohol remains a leading cause of death. More than 60 percent of Australian adults aged over 18 drink alcohol at least occasionally (Commonwealth of Australia, 2006). Almost 1.5 million Australians drink alcohol daily, 6.8 million drink weekly and a further 5.5 million drink less than weekly (AIHW, 2007e; McCarthy, 2007). Beer and spirits remain popular drinks, with Australians drinking more light beer than ever before (McCarthy, 2007). However, wine is fast becoming a favoured beverage among Australians (McCarthy, 2007). Among Australians aged 18 years and over, 48 percent of males and 30 percent of females have drunk alcohol at risky or high-risk levels on at least one occasion in the past 12 months (ABS, 2006a). Random breath testing (RBT) has helped to reduce death and injury arising from road traffic accidents by deterring driving under the influence of alcohol (Midford, 2005). RBT is also thought to help undermine peer pressure to drink to excess. More males than females report using alcohol daily (McCarthy, 2007), although there are differences in the drinking patterns of young males and females. Generally, more young females drink at risky or high levels compared with young males, though males can drink more before they are at risk (AIHW, 2008). More 16–17 year-old males (22 percent) drink daily or weekly compared with around 15 percent of girls (AIHW, 2008), with most young Australians preferring to drink spirits.

Random breath testing has deterred people from driving under the influence of alcohol.

Contributors to alcoholism

Where does an addiction to alcohol come from? Although both genetic and environmental factors are important in alcoholism risk, genetic vulnerability clearly plays a role in problem drinking (Enoch, 2006). In some alcoholics, a gene has been identified that alters dopamine receptors. Alcoholics may also inherit a tolerance for the negative effects of alcohol and a sensitivity to the positive effects of alcohol (Straub, 2002). Twin studies show a strong concordance rate for alcoholism. In one study of identical twins, in 76 percent of the cases in which one twin was an alcoholic the other was also (Kendler, Prescott, Neale, & Pedersen, 1997). Children of alcoholics, particularly male children, are at increased risk of abusing alcohol themselves (Plomin, DeFries, & McGuffin, 2001). For both males and females, heritability of alcoholism is estimated to be about 30 percent.

Thus, although genetics is clearly involved, it is not the sole contributor to alcohol abuse. In regards to alcohol, biology is not destiny. Social–cognitive factors also play a contributing role in alcohol abuse. Some people drink to mentally 'escape' from whatever stressors they are currently facing. Because alcohol alters the thought processes of the consumer, they think differently about issues they are facing. Alcohol provides a mechanism for people to escape self-awareness or escape current thoughts and preoccupations, such as that they are a loser or that no one cares about them (Baumeister, 1991; Hull, 1987). Social support can provide a buffer between stressors and alcohol abuse as a way of dealing with those stressors.

Relatedly, people may drink to provide themselves with an excuse for failure in the event that it occurs. In other words, alcohol serves a self-handicapping function. ***Self-handicapping*** is the process by which people set themselves up to fail. If, for example, Jay gets drunk the night before a big test, he can blame failure on the test on the alcohol. On the other hand, if he passes the test in spite of being hung over, then, in his own mind, he must really be a smart guy (Berglas & Baumeister, 1993).

The social environment in which people find themselves also helps to determine the degree to which they abuse alcohol. Children whose parents or peers consume alcohol and who do so during pleasurable social occasions, learn to associate alcohol with pleasure and reward (Taylor, 2003). Thus, they are more likely than people not exposed to 'social' drinking to begin drinking earlier and to have a more favourable association with alcohol. Alcohol consumption among university students is significantly higher while they are enrolled in tertiary studies than when they leave university.

Personality can also influence whether or not one abuses alcohol, reinforcing once again the age-old nature–nurture debate. Personality is determined in part by genetics. People are generally prewired to respond to particular situations in particular ways. However, the situation and environment determine whether or not those genetic underpinnings are realised. For example, people who are high in negative affectivity — that is, people who are chronically in a bad mood — are more likely to consume alcohol than people who are low in negative affectivity or who are high in positive affectivity.

Consequences of alcoholism

The physical and psychological effects of alcohol abuse are many. Because most alcohol that is consumed is metabolised through the liver, damage to the liver is one of the most obvious physiological effects of excessive alcohol consumption over time. In fact, excess alcohol consumption over time is the leading cause of liver damage and death (Van Thiel, 1996). People who rarely drink experience little, if any, damage to their liver. For people who drink excessively and over time, however, the damage can be fatal, as in the case of cirrhosis of the liver. Alcohol is also a risk factor for certain types of cancer including cancer of the mouth, larynx, stomach, colon and breast, and for hypertension, stroke and foetal alcohol syndrome (Day, 2007; Irving, Samokhvalov, & Rehm, 2009). Severe problems with memory and reasoning can also result from long-term alcoholism (National Health Strategy, 2003). Short-term cognitive impairments lead to poor judgement and decision making that can affect non-alcohol-related decisions. For example, because of the disinhibiting effects of alcohol, people, particularly adolescents, engage in high-risk sexual behaviour while under its influence (Weinhardt, Carey, Carey, Maisto, & Gordon, 2001).

APPLY + DISCUSS

Because of the damage that alcohol does to the liver, alcoholics represent one of the populations most in need of liver transplants.

- How would you feel if your liver were donated posthumously to an alcoholic?
- Do you think the individual would drink excessively again and damage 'your' liver as well?

The risk of injury or death is higher for alcoholics than nonalcoholics not only from health-related complications, such as liver disease, associated with alcohol abuse, but also from falls and car accidents (Australian Government Department of Health and Ageing, 2009b, 2009c). Alcohol is the second largest cause of drug-related deaths and hospitalisations in Australia, after tobacco (AIHW, 2005). Alcohol dependence and harmful use was ranked seventeenth in the twenty leading causes of burden of disease and injury for Australia in 2003 (ABS, 2006a). Additionally, alcohol misuse is a large factor in motor vehicle accidents, falls, drowning, burns, suicide, occupational injuries, interpersonal violence, domestic violence and child abuse (Australian Government Department of Health and Ageing, 2009b, 2009c). Estimates are that almost half of the car accidents that occur annually involve alcohol (ABS, 2006a). Although many of the effects of alcohol follow large consumptions, injury risk increases with even very small amounts of alcohol.

Social consequences of alcohol abuse are many. Relationships with family, friends and co-workers are clearly affected by the individual who abuses alcohol, in part because the incidence of intimate and domestic violence, homicide and suicide increases with the use of alcohol (Norton & Morgan, 1989). The economic costs associated with alcoholism are staggering, taking the form of medical costs and lost productivity at work. The estimated economic cost of alcohol misuse to the Australian community totalled $7.6 billion in one recent study (ABS, 2009e). Risky drinkers are more likely to report a mental health illness and high levels of psychological distress as compared with low-risk drinkers (ABS, 2006a; AIHW, 2008), though alcohol use does not always precede mental health issues (AIHW, 2010a).

Treatment

Some people quit drinking or greatly reduce their alcohol intake on their own, without any formal method of intervention, a process called ***spontaneous remission***. Estimates are, however, that only

19 percent of alcoholics and problem drinkers fall within this category (Miller & Hester, 1980). Many of these include university students who engage in binge drinking during their studies when the alcohol is readily available and when the social situation encourages them to do so, but who markedly reduce their alcohol intake once they leave university and the accompanying social scene. Furthermore, people with support from families and friends are more likely to engage in spontaneous remission than people who lack such social support networks.

The remaining 81 percent of alcoholics and problem drinkers require some type of formalised treatment, although the form that the treatment takes is highly variable. Some alcoholics enter rehabilitation centres. The first stage of rehabilitation is ***detoxification*** or the process of drying out. The inpatient setting allows the alcoholic to go through the withdrawal symptoms associated with abstinence from alcohol in a controlled setting and often with the use of medication to alleviate some of the negative side-effects of withdrawal (Ciraulo & Renner, 1991). Detoxification is then followed by a several-week period of intensive inpatient individual and group therapy.

Alcoholics and problem drinkers do not, however, always enter rehabilitation centres; instead, they can receive treatment on an outpatient basis. The purpose of therapy is to allow the individual to see the origins of their drinking behaviour, the effects of that behaviour on other people, and the consequences of their problem to themselves and others. Some outpatient treatments use ***aversion therapy***, or the introduction of something aversive as a means of discouraging the negative health habit. A drug, typically Antabuse, is taken daily by the alcoholic or problem drinker. In the absence of alcohol, the drug has few effects, but if the person consumes alcohol while he is taking the medication, severe nausea and vomiting result. One of the biggest problems associated with the use of Antabuse is that people who really want to continue to drink will simply stop taking the drug. To circumvent this problem, some alcoholics, particularly those in an inpatient treatment setting, go through a series of half-hour sessions during each of which they are administered a drug like Antabuse via injection followed by the consumption of alcohol. Over repeated trials, during each of which the person becomes nauseous and vomits, the appeal of alcohol typically diminishes as the patient quickly forms very negative associations to alcohol (Sarafino, 2002).

Particularly for problem drinkers, cognitive–behavioural types of therapy can be effective. Many problem drinkers begin drinking and continue to drink as a means of coping with stressors at work or home. The goal of therapy, then, is to teach stress management techniques so that the impetus for consuming alcohol is gone.

Perhaps the most well-known treatment is the self-help group known as Alcoholics Anonymous (AA). AA was founded in the United States in 1935 by a group of problem drinkers. Now, thousands of centres have been set up all over the world, including in Australia and New Zealand. The only requirement to be a member of AA is that the individual have a desire to quit drinking. Each member of AA is assigned a sponsor to whom he or she can turn in times of distress. The group meetings provide an open forum in which people can discuss their issues and problems with alcohol. Individual therapy-type meetings are also provided if needed. In addition to providing a forum in which alcoholics can vent their feelings, perhaps the most useful outcome of AA (or related groups such as Al-Anon, for family members of alcoholics, or Alateen, for adolescent children of alcoholics) is the social support that members provide to one another. The overall effectiveness of AA is unknown because the membership is anonymous, but members of the organisation itself claim to have a success rate around 75 percent (Miller & Hester, 1980; see also Crape, Latkin, Laris, & Knowlton, 2002).

APPLY + DISCUSS

Proponents of Alcoholics Anonymous believe that once you are an alcoholic you are always an alcoholic and that even moderate drinking is not possible. Other approaches to treatment, such as some of the cognitive–behavioural approaches, believe that teaching alcoholics and problem drinkers to consume alcohol in moderation is actually a more realistic and successful approach to treatment.

- Which viewpoint do you agree with? Why or why not?

Sexually transmitted diseases

A discussion of sexually transmitted diseases (STDs) takes a slightly different form from a discussion of the other types of health compromising behaviours we have examined. The reason is that the term STDs is a catchphrase for over 20 diseases that are transmitted through intimate or sexual contact (see table 14.3, overleaf, for a partial listing), the most notable of which is infection with the human immunodeficiency virus (HIV). However, sexually transmitted diseases such as chlamydia and syphilis are on the rise in Australia. In 2008, chlamydia was the most frequently reported sexually transmitted infection, at a rate of 238 people per 100 000, up from 57 in 1998 (AIHW, 2008). According to Professor Basil Donovan from the University of New South Wales, 'chlamydia is an easily cured bacterial infection but, if left untreated, can cause long-term fertility problems' (Plambeck, 2008). In addition, women who are pregnant are at risk of transmitting many of the STDs to their unborn child either during pregnancy or during delivery.

TABLE 14.3 Sexually transmitted diseases in Australia

Disease	New cases annually	Primary symptoms
Chlamydia	58 515	Generally asymptomatic
Gonorrhoea	7 675	Discharge from the vagina or penis and painful urination
Syphilis	3 245	Begins as a sore, but left unchecked can affect the central nervous system and the heart
HIV/AIDS	1 094	Originally appears as something resembling a bad case of the flu. Progresses as the virus attacks the immune system, leaving the person vulnerable to opportunistic infections

SOURCE: ABS (2009e).

Unlike other health-compromising behaviours, such as obesity or alcoholism, there is no genetic predisposition for STDs beyond perhaps personality factors, such as impulsivity, that might lead someone to engage in high-risk sexual behaviours. The role of health psychologists is clear: stopping people from engaging in sexual behaviours that put them at risk. The role of the health psychologist goes one step further, however: helping those who have contracted STDs cope with the illness and helping to develop treatments for STDs.

Because of the high mortality rate associated with it, we will focus on HIV/AIDS. When AIDS was first detected in 1980, only a handful of Australians had died from the disease. Just a few decades later, more than 28 000 Australians have been diagnosed with HIV, more than 6700 have died from it, and AIDS had become a leading killer of young adults between 22 and 45 years of age (ABS, 2010h). According to the World Health Organization (WHO), the number of people living with HIV is 33.4 million (WHO, 2010a). Particularly in African nations, the AIDS epidemic is dramatically lowering life expectancy. In some countries, life expectancy is expected to drop by half because of the number of people dying from AIDS (Carey & Vanable, 2003).

Transmission of HIV in Australia continues to be mainly through sexual contact between men (77 percent). This was followed by heterosexual contact (27.1 percent) and injecting drug use (4.4 percent; ABS, 2010g; de Visser, Smith, Rissel, Richters, & Grulich, 2003).

The use of condoms is considered an effective method of preventing transmission of the virus that causes AIDS. However, only 20 percent of sexually active individuals reported using a condom the last time they had intercourse (de Visser et al., 2003). Among those most likely to use condoms were those at greatest risk of being infected with HIV. However, only 70 percent of gay men in Australia used condoms every time they had sex (Australian National Council on AIDS, Hepatitis C and Related Diseases, 2001).

Once a person becomes infected, the disease follows a very predictable course in terms of stages, if not time. A few weeks after being infected, a person will experience symptoms that resemble mononucleosis (popularly known as glandular fever) — fever, fatigue and sore throat. Following this, infected individuals enter an asymptomatic state during which they are symptom free but very capable of infecting others. A number of years can pass before the infected individual develops AIDS. By this time, the person's immune system is so compromised that he or she is open to opportunistic diseases. In fact, people do not die from AIDS itself, but rather from cancers and infections to which the person is now vulnerable. Furthermore, infection with HIV places people at increased risk for contracting other STDs that, in conjunction with HIV, may result in an even shorter life expectancy.

Health psychologists have played an increasingly active role as the AIDS epidemic continues to spread. Of course, their first plan of action is to prevent people from engaging in high-risk sexual behaviours. In some cases, this involves targeting those who are already engaging in such behaviours and working to get them to stop. In other instances, the health psychologist's goal is to reach young people who are not yet sexually active to prevent them from engaging in risky sexual behaviours to begin with. Their efforts on both these levels involve working at both the individual and the community level. Individuals are offered instruction on ways in which they can protect themselves, for example, through the consistent use of condoms. Unprotected sex is on the rise, with only 45 percent of males and 35 percent of females reporting to always use a condom with casual sex partners; less than 10 percent of men and women always use a condom for sexual activity with a regular partner (AIHW, 2008).

Health experts recommend people always use condoms with new partners and urge all young people to get screened for sexually transmitted diseases, particularly chlamydia (Plambeck, 2008). Individuals can be given a personal risk assessment to make them aware of behaviours that are placing them at risk (Carey & Vanable, 2003). Communities, including schools, are encouraged to implement programs and informational campaigns designed to change social norms regarding sexual behaviour.

INTERIM SUMMARY

In spite of knowledge of the negative health consequences that may befall them, people continue to engage in a number of health-compromising behaviours, including obesity, smoking, alcohol abuse, and high-risk sexual behaviours. Obesity is typically measured in terms of ***body mass index (BMI)***. People with a BMI in excess of 30 percent are said to be obese. The prevalence of obesity is even more surprising when examined within the context of ***set point***, the ideal body weight for each individual. However, genetic, social and psychological factors join together to influence someone's ability to regulate his behaviour around the set point. Although genetic influences are strong, the degree to which they manifest themselves is determined in part by the environment, an idea germane to the ***susceptible gene hypothesis***.

As with obesity, the onset, course and termination of smoking behaviour is also determined by biological, social and psychological variables.

The primary distinction between ***alcoholics*** and ***problem drinkers*** is the physiological addiction to alcohol that alcoholics have. Some alcoholics and problem drinkers learn to control their own problem through ***spontaneous remission***. Most, however, require some kind of formal treatment, in some cases even inpatient rehabilitation. The first step in inpatient therapy is ***detoxification***. ***Aversion therapy*** is a method for treating alcoholism that may be used on an inpatient or an outpatient basis.

Many individuals also place themselves at risk of acquiring sexually transmitted diseases. Although over 20 STDs have been identified, the most publicised is HIV/AIDS, which, on an international level, has reached epidemic proportions. Health psychologists have played an active role in encouraging people to alter their high-risk behaviours or to avoid engaging in risky behaviour to begin with.

Barriers to health promotion

Why, given the harmful and even fatal consequences associated with the health-compromising behaviours just described, would someone decide to continue to consume excess fat and calories, smoke or drink? Why, given that many cancers can be effectively treated if detected early enough, would people fail to get regular preventive health screenings, such as for cervical cancer, breast cancer and prostate cancer? The answer to these questions is more complex than it may at first appear, but at least four factors or barriers to health promotion are involved (Straub, 2002).

Individual barriers

People do a lot of things they know they should not do (e.g. smoke) and they do not do a lot of things that they know they should (e.g. receive regular Pap tests). Lack of knowledge is rarely an explanation for people engaging in health-compromising behaviours and failing to engage in preventive health behaviours or health-promoting behaviours. Most people do, in fact, know their negative health behaviours are detrimental to their health. Armed with that knowledge, why would people choose to continue to compromise their health either by engaging in negative health behaviours or by failing to engage in positive health behaviours? One reason is that negative behaviours are rewarding, particularly in the short term. Smoking can reduce anxiety and produce relaxation. Alcohol can allow one to escape intrusive and disturbing thoughts and worries and can, to a point, increase the ease with which one interacts with others. Eating is enjoyable. Who doesn't occasionally want to consume too much pizza, fast food or chocolate cake? Health-promoting behaviours, such as exercise and eating a healthy diet, however, are generally less enjoyable and take considerably more discipline.

In addition, the negative effects of health-compromising behaviours do not occur immediately and are almost always preceded by the positive consequences. Even the negative effects of consuming too much alcohol, including nausea, vomiting, dehydration and headache, follow positive effects of drinking. Most people begin negative health habits, such as smoking, during adolescence. It is difficult to convince most adolescents of anything commonsensical — certainly convincing them that smoking, alcohol, unsafe sex and excessive tanning, for example, will ultimately be detrimental to their health is going to fall on deaf ears. In their own minds, why should they worry about something that might happen 20 or 30 years down the road?

In terms of preventive health care, many people adopt the idea that 'what they don't know won't hurt them'. In fact, it will not just hurt them, it may kill them! One study found that women who believe that they could effectively deal with cancer should they get it are more likely than women who do not share such a belief to receive regular screenings for cancer (Perlman, Clark, Rakowski, & Ehlich, 1999). Relatedly, people who have a realistic sense of their likelihood of contracting cancer or another chronic condition are more likely to receive preventive health screenings than those individuals who are unrealistically optimistic about their health, believing they are less likely than the average other person to contract a chronic condition. People who are the least likely to receive regular preventive health screenings are those who are uneducated, of lower socioeconomic status, who have no access to health care or no money to pay for it, and who have not had preventive screenings recommended by their doctor (*Cancer prevention*, 2002). People who are self-conscious about their bodies or very attuned to the impressions that other people form of them are also less likely to receive preventive health screenings (Kowalski & Brown, 1994).

ETHICAL DILEMMA

A researcher hypothesises that men who regularly exercise will tolerate pain for longer periods of time than men who do not exercise. He proposes to get a sample of 10 athletic men and 10 nonathletic men to run a treadmill for up to one hour each day, for the course of one week and measure how long it takes for them to complain that they are in pain and cannot continue with the exercise. The participants will also indicate the amount of pain they experienced during the exercise by using a Likert-type rating scale.

- What steps should the researcher take to ensure that the welfare of participants is not compromised in any way by his study?
- Can the researcher guarantee that his study will not subject any participant to the risk of physical or emotional harm? If so, how? If not, why not?

One important individual barrier is gender. Women are more likely than men to engage in preventive health behaviours and health-promoting behaviours. According to one group of researchers 'Being a woman may, in fact, be the strongest predictor of preventive and health-promoting behaviour' (Courtenay, McCreary, & Merighi, 2002, p. 220). Men are more likely to engage in risky health behaviours, such as smoking and driving while intoxicated. Men are less likely than women to take care of themselves when they are sick, and they are less likely to seek a doctor's care for illness. Women more than men take a realistic view of their risk of illness and disease, which may account, in part, for men's greater risk-taking behaviours. In short, men are more likely than women to view themselves as invincible and to be overly optimistic about their health outcomes. Ironic, isn't it, given that men have a shorter life expectancy than women?

In one study, university-aged men and women completed a survey examining their health behaviours and attitudes. Six domains of health behaviours were assessed: diet, anger and stress, prevention, medical compliance, substance use, and beliefs about masculinity. The results of the study revealed differences between men and women on five of the six dimensions. Only anger and stress showed no effects of gender. Across the other five health domains, men scored worse than women. Men engaged in riskier dieting behaviours (e.g. were more likely than women to eat red meat, sugar, salt and high-fat foods), displayed fewer preventive health behaviours (e.g. doing regular self-examinations for testicular cancer or breast cancer, getting blood pressure screenings, receiving regular physical and dental exams), displayed more substance use (e.g. smoking cigarettes, chewing tobacco, drinking alcohol), had lower rates of medical compliance (e.g. taking medication as prescribed, getting prescriptions filled) and endorsed riskier health-related attitudes (e.g. a person should always try to control his or her emotions, a person should be physically strong).

Family barriers

Health habits are acquired early, and one of the primary models of health behaviour is parents or caregivers. Children frequently model the health behaviours they see their parents or siblings perform. Thus, parents who smoke or abuse alcohol are more likely to have children who smoke and become problem drinkers. Parents who rarely exercise have a higher likelihood of having children who do not exercise. Parents who are obese tend to have children (and even pets) who are obese. Parents who do not engage in preventive health behaviours have children who also do not engage in preventive behaviours. Indeed, those same parents may be the ones who do not take their young children to their yearly health checks or have their children properly immunised. Although genetics could, and do, account for part of this intergenerational transmission of health habits, they do not account for the entire picture. Children emulate what their parents and older siblings model. Because they see their parents experience immediate rewards from negative health habits, they assume they will as well. Positive health habits, such as regular brushing and flossing, are unlikely to be implemented as adults if the behaviour was not practised regularly as a child.

Health system barriers

As we discussed early in the chapter, the biomedical model has dominated the field of medicine for some time. Doctors are trained to focus on illness, not health. Thus, even when they do ask patients about circumstances leading up to their illness, their primary focus is on treating the illness itself, not the negative health habits that might have contributed to the development of the illness. The situation is compounded by the fact that people often do not go to the doctor when they are well. This practice is unfortunate, both because conditions that could be prevented or treated if caught early go unnoticed and because it is often during these preventive visits to a doctor that time is spent discussing health-compromising and health-promoting behaviours. Breast cancer remains a major health issue for women. According to the Australian Government Department of Health and Ageing (2009a), over 75 percent of breast cancers occur in women aged 50 years and over. Nine out of 10 women who get breast cancer do not have a family history of the disease and the lifetime risk of women developing breast cancer before the age of 75 years is one in 11.

The need to encourage women to take preventative measures against breast cancer has prompted a continuing campaign funded by Australia's state and federal governments, called BreastScreen Australia. This is a national program that provides free screening mammograms at two-year intervals, backed by a comprehensive advertising and awareness campaign. The target audience is particularly women aged 50–69, where screening for breast cancer is particularly important. An evaluation carried out following the 2000–01 BreastScreen Australia awareness campaign found the program had been effective in raising awareness of screening and more positive attitudes towards screening (Department of Health and Ageing, 2004b). For example, while one in three women over 40 has not had a mammogram, the evaluation found that 92 percent of women in the target age range of 50–69 have had a mammogram at some stage in their life. On a further positive note, among all women aged 40 and over, screening numbers have increased from 1.26 million in 1996–97 to 1.62 million in 2002–2003 (AIHW, 2006b), with another 1.63 million women screened in 2005–06 (Australian Government Department of Health and Ageing, 2009a). Breastscreen Australia's aim is to achieve a participation rate of 70 percent among women aged 50–69 years and in 2009, the program was screening 56.9 percent of women in this age group (Australian Government Department of Health and Ageing, 2009a). BreastScreen Australia is an example of the way in which a concerted effort has been required to help change the mind-set of the population to consider preventative measures rather than waiting until illness manifests itself. Publicity generated by some celebrities, such as Kylie Minogue, developing breast cancer; and the work of charities such as the McGrath Foundation (co-founded and chaired by former Australian cricketer Glenn McGrath), has also helped to increase awareness about the illness (Chapman, McLeod, Wakefield, & Holding, 2005).

Kylie Minogue's breast cancer diagnosis at age 36 prompted a 40 percent increase in mammogram screening bookings within two weeks of the news being reported (Chapman et al., 2005). Minogue was still receiving treatment for breast cancer five years after her diagnosis.

Following the success of Breastscreen Australia in reducing deaths from breast cancer, the federal government launched the National Bowel Cancer Screening Program in 2008 to screen eligible Australians. Bowel cancer is one of the most common forms of cancer in Australia, with the risk of developing bowel cancer rising significantly from the age of 50 (Australian Government Department of Health and Ageing, 2009d). Screening every two years can enable an early detection of bowel cancer and reduce the risk of dying by up to one third (Australian Government Department of Health and Ageing, 2009d). Similar to Breastscreen Australia, the National Cervical Screening Program helps to reduce illness and deaths from cervical cancer, encouraging women to have Pap smears every two years. Women should have their first Pap smear around age 18 to 20 or a year or two after first having sex — whichever is the later — and continue having Pap smears throughout their life until around age 70 (Australian Government Department of Health and Ageing, 2009e). The program is successful, with 3.6 million Australian women having pap smears in 2006–07. More than 98 percent of these women were in the target age group of 20–69 years (Australian Government Department of Health and Ageing, 2009e).

One factor inhibiting people from taking preventive health measures is the lack of health insurance. The introduction of the federal government's Medicare scheme in Australia in 1984 has seen the number of Australians with private health cover steadily declining. By 1999, just 31 percent of the population had private health insurance. However, the introduction of the 30 percent rebate on private health cover by the federal government in 2000 saw that percentage jump to approximately 46 percent. Rates have now stabilised and in June 2008, the percentage was around 45 percent (ABS, 2010g).

In a recent year, Australians in the 45–54 and 55–64 year age groups had the highest level of private insurance coverage. In contrast, Australians aged 25–34 and 75 years and over had the lowest coverage (ABS, 2006f). Sadly, one major illness can wipe out an entire family's finances in the absence of health insurance. The alternative is the public hospital system, where there are often long waiting lists for medical procedures, particularly elective surgery.

Yet another health system variable concerns the relationships between patients and practitioners. The ways in which doctors treat and respond to their patients is a major factor influencing the degree to which those patients will hear what the doctor is saying and then comply with the advice that was offered (Bradley, Sparks, & Nesdale, 2001). Patients who feel that their doctor is unresponsive are unlikely to be completely forthcoming about symptoms they are experiencing. Given that up to 80 percent of treatment is based on information provided by patients during consultations with their doctors, this mismatch between patient and provider can be extremely harmful (Straub, 2002). Patients who are uncomfortable with or who feel demeaned by their doctor are also significantly less likely to follow through with treatment regimens recommended by their doctor. Noncompliance is high even among patients who trust and like their doctor. Thus, you can imagine the rates of noncompliance among people who do not trust or who dislike their health care provider. Sadly, people who have one bad experience with a doctor may generalise their negative feelings to other health care providers, increasing the likelihood that they will engage in delay behaviour when future symptoms arise, and decreasing the likelihood that they will go to a doctor for preventive health screenings.

Communication problems between a doctor and patient are compounded even further when they literally do not speak the same language. Trying to understand a patient's complaints in a short period of time is not easy. Add language difficulties and the situation is often futile. Since World War II, Australia has had large numbers of immigrants from non-English speaking backgrounds. English language fluency is only the tip of the iceberg of cultural differences. Such differences appear in beliefs about health and illness, expectations of treatment, and type or intensity of pain behaviours (Allen, 1998). Similar outcomes often follow when doctors are met by patients whom they really do not want to treat, perhaps because of negative experiences with this patient in the past, because of the particular illness the patient has, or because of physical features of the person, such as their gender, race or age.

Importantly, however, doctors are not entirely to blame. With problems in the health care system itself, doctors today are often inundated by paperwork and encouraged to treat as many people as possible. The doctors, too, are overwhelmed with malpractice insurance costs and the ever present threat of a lawsuit. Many practitioners in rural areas of Australia will not deliver babies because of the high cost of insurance premiums against malpractice suits (Caltabiano, Byrne, Martin, & Sarafino, 2002). Furthermore, patients themselves are often at least partly to blame for faulty patient–practitioner interactions. The anxiety they currently feel over the meaning of their symptoms, the fact that they may have been using home remedies to treat their symptoms, and feelings of inferiority relative to the doctor can all create anxiety that makes it difficult for patients to adequately relate their symptoms. Because of the physiological effects of anxiety, it may magnify a patient's symptoms or the anxiety may, in fact, be the reason the patient is seeing the doctor (Graugaard & Finset, 2000). Research has shown that up to two-thirds of visits to doctors are for psychological rather than physical problems (Coyne, Thompson, Klinkman, & Nease, 2002; Taylor, 2003); these are problems that many doctors are unable either to detect or to treat properly if detected. Given this deficiency, it is hardly surprising that many primary care facilities either have or would like to have a health psychologist on staff full-time.

Patient expectations for doctors may also be too high. Beyond the practical expectations, such as that a doctor will see them immediately, patients often expect their doctors to provide them with an immediate solution to whatever ails them; clearly, in most cases, an unrealistic expectation. Nevertheless, unmet expectations may lead patients to be dissatisfied with their doctor and the quality of care provided, which may then affect the degree to which they are willing to comply with the doctor's recommendations (Jackson & Kroenke, 2001). Unrealistic expectations are one of the things that doctors find most frustrating in their interactions with patients (Stein & Kwan, 1999).

Given that children learn from their parents and other caretakers, the role of paediatricians in health promotion is critical. Paediatricians who spend only brief periods of time with their little patients and who fail to relay important information about health promotion to parents of those patients do little to endear themselves to the children whose health they are supposed to be promoting.

Community, cultural and ethnic barriers

People's willingness to engage in preventive health behaviours, to avoid negative health habits and to terminate those negative health habits once they begin is, to a great extent, influenced by the norms of the community in which they live, work and play. People who live and work in environments that encourage the use of alcohol as a means of fitting in will likely initiate or continue alcohol use. As work settings have increasingly become smoke free, the percentage of people who smoke at work where they have to go outside to do so, has decreased. The rise of fitness centres within companies has helped to establish new norms and expectations regarding fitness. Needless to say, more fit workers are a financial boon to the company, manifested in reduced absenteeism and turnover.

Governments in Australia have also played their part in encouraging a healthier lifestyle. The memorable and popular 'Life. Be in it.' program was established in 1975 by the Victorian Government. Because of its popularity and rapid increase in public awareness, the campaign was adopted by the federal government in 1977 and subsequently launched in the rest of the country. The program was designed to encourage recreation and physical fitness in non-threatening ways. The campaign featured the character 'Norm' who appeared on television advertisements encouraging Australians to get up off the couch and become active. Attitudinal studies were undertaken at regular intervals throughout the campaign. The program not only achieved an extremely high level of awareness of leisure activities, but also increased people's involvement in them (Life. Be in it., 2004).

Health disparities are never more evident than when comparing Indigenous Australians to non-Indigenous Australians. On virtually every major index of health status, Indigenous Australians fare worse, and these differences in health occur across the life span. Early this century, the life expectancy for Indigenous Australians was shorter by 21 years for males and 20 years for females, compared with the total population (ABS, 2002a); however, Australia is making progress in closing this gap, with the difference currently averaging around 10 years for females and 12 years for males (ABS, 2010h). Indigenous children aged less than four years die at around twice the rate of non-Indigenous children and progress towards closing the gap might best be achieved by reducing mortality among Indigenous infants (AIHW, 2010a). Cardiovascular disease is a leading cause of death for Aboriginal and Torres Strait Islander peoples (AIHW, 2010a). Indigenous Australians also have much higher rates of smoking, obesity and diabetes (AIHW, 2010a). Indigenous people are also more likely than the total population to die from external causes, such as injuries from accidents and violence; and report very high levels of psychological distress leading to self-harm (AIHW, 2010a).

These disparities are of particular interest to health psychologists because their origin lies, in part, in behaviours that place people within particular minority groups at heightened risk. For example, although Indigenous peoples are considerably less likely to drink alcohol than other Australians, those who drink often do so at risky or high levels (AIHW, 2010a). Indigenous Australian adults are also more than twice as likely as other Australians to be current daily smokers and female Indigenous Australians are more likely to be overweight or obese and sedentary than non-Indigenous females (AIHW, 2010a). However, it is important to recognise that low socioeconomic status is associated with the poor health of Indigenous Australians — they report lower incomes, higher rates of unemployment and lower educational attainment compared with other Australians (AIHW, 2010a). Thus, major improvements are needed in social policy areas such as education, employment and housing to help reduce disadvantage among Indigenous Australians. The Council of Australian Governments (COAG) has agreed to six specific targets and timelines in the National Indigenous Reform Agreement to close the gap, including:

1. Closing the life expectancy gap within a generation (by 2030).
2. Halving the gap in mortality rates for Indigenous children within a decade (by 2018).
3. Ensuring that all Indigenous four-year-olds in remote communities have access to early childhood education within five years (by 2013).
4. Halving the gap for Indigenous students in reading, writing and numeracy within a decade (by 2018).
5. Halving the gap for Indigenous students in Year 12 attainment by 2020.
6. Halving the gap in employment levels within a decade (by 2018).

Comparisons of the health outcomes of people from different racial and ethnic backgrounds and the behavioural, social and environmental factors that place these individuals at risk highlight the role of social and psychological factors in health. Environmental factors include not only physical environmental variables, such as toxins, but also the groups and communities to which people belong, including work, family and peer groups (Taylor, Repetti, & Seeman, 1997). Patterns of interaction within these groups and communities, social norms that characterise them, and the 'social impoverishment' characteristic of them can create risk factors for health-related problems (Taylor et al., 1997, p. 412).

INTERIM SUMMARY

Myriads of reasons exist to account for why people continue to engage in negative health behaviours and why they fail to engage in positive health behaviours. A useful way of compartmentalising these reasons is to group them into four barriers to health promotion: individual barriers, family barriers, health system barriers and community barriers. However, as with most things in life, barriers can be overcome, and the barriers to health promotion presented here are no exception.

Self-presentation and health

Self-presentation (also known as ***impression management***; Leary, 1995; Leary & Kowalski, 1990) refers to people's attempts to control the impressions that others form of them. Much of what people do and don't do, they do and don't do because of concerns with the impressions other people are forming of them. Although self-presentational concerns as they relate to health can be adaptive, as when people exercise to be physically fit and convey positive impressions to others, self-presentational concerns can also be maladaptive for health and lead individuals to engage in health-compromising behaviours or not to engage in health-promoting behaviours because they want to project a particular image of themselves to others (Leary, Tchividjian, & Kraxberger, 1994; Martin, Leary, & O'Brien, 2001). In one study, first year university students were asked, at the end of their first semester at university, the frequency with which they had engaged in a number of health risk behaviours for self-presentational reasons. Seventy-five percent of the university students reported having performed a risky health behaviour at least once during their first semester of university. The most frequently reported behaviours were smoking, drinking and reckless driving. The most frequently cited reason for doing so: to appear cool. A comprehensive review of the maladaptive aspects of self-presentation for health has been written by Leary et al. (1994). Here, we will simply review a few of these.

Condom use

Educators and health practitioners have long advocated the use of condoms to prevent pregnancy and the spread of sexually transmitted diseases (STDs). Beginning in 1999, some television networks allowed condom advertisements to be aired to get information out to teens in particular (Wilke, 2001). In spite of the fact that most people are aware of the effectiveness of condoms, many people still fail to use condoms regularly. In Australia, just 28 percent of sexually active women aged 18 to 49 report using condoms. Usage rates decline from 48 percent of sexually active 18- to 24-year-old women to 12 percent of 45- to 49-year-olds. This may be because condom use may also be linked to the permanency of a woman's sexual relationship (ABS, 2004a). Even people who have had an STD before are no more likely to use condoms than those who have never been diagnosed with an STD ('Even after having', 2003). One reason: self-presentational concerns. People are concerned with what others will think of them if they purchase condoms or what their partners might think of them if they suggest using them.

Residents in local Indigenous communities in Western Australia have had access to 'condom trees' — trees stocked with condoms held in PVC pipes — in recent years. The trees are part of a health initiative designed to overcome potential embarrassment about purchasing condoms and to reduce overall STD prevalence in these areas.

Embarrassment about purchasing condoms is a key factor inhibiting condom use among adolescents and young adults (Hanna, 1989; Herold, 1981), so much so that an estimated 25 percent of sexually active adolescents do not use an effective method of birth control (Sauerwein, 1992). What might people think if they saw them buying condoms? (Probably they would think they were going to have sex — the reason, in fact, why they were buying them, right?) The Condom Tree program, a regional program that seeks to reduce STD prevalence among Indigenous West Australians, has had some success in recent years. As part of the program, condoms are placed inside polyvinyl chloride (PVC) pipes that hang on tree branches at gathering places in local communities in the Kimberley region. Residents are advised of the location of the trees via maps posted at local venues, and access to the condoms is available 24 hours a day. Thousands of condoms were taken by residents from different sites during a three-month period, with tree sites near popular 'hang out' areas for 15–25 year-olds recording the highest usage rates (Australian Indigenous HealthInfoNet, 2010; Shire of Broome, 2006).

Even if condoms are bought, they will not necessarily be used. Sexually active adolescents and young adults report being concerned that their partner will think they worked to seduce them if they suggest using condoms they have with them (Kisker, 1985). Alternatively, many people worry that, if they suggest using condoms, their partner will assume that they must have a sexually transmitted disease themselves. Gay males have reported that they are afraid their partner will view them as a wimp if they suggest using condoms (Leary et al., 1994). Clearly, then, people's concerns with the impressions they might create on others can operate as a deterrent to safe-sex behaviours.

Suntanning and skin cancer

Few people can say that they have not sunbathed or been to a tanning bed with the purpose of improving their appearance (at least in the short term). Although certainly having a tan can make people 'look' healthy, in the long run excessive tanning can have detrimental health consequences — most notably, skin cancer. The incidence of skin cancer has increased significantly in recent years (ABS, 2006b). The prevalence of malignant melanoma (the most serious form of skin cancer) has quadrupled in the last 40 years (Fears & Scotto, 1982; Leary et al., 1994), with the incidence of basal cell carcinoma (the least serious form) increasing at a similar although slightly lower rate. Australia has the highest rate of skin cancer in the world. More than 400 000 Australians are treated for skin cancer every year, and it kills more than 1600 people each year. Approximately two-thirds of all Australians will be diagnosed with some form of skin cancer before the age of 70 (Australian Government Department of Health and Ageing, 2008). The primary cause of skin cancer is too much exposure to ultraviolet radiation. Some people, such as construction workers, are frequently exposed to too much ultraviolet radiation by the nature of their jobs; however, others voluntarily expose themselves to too much sun, either natural or artificial.

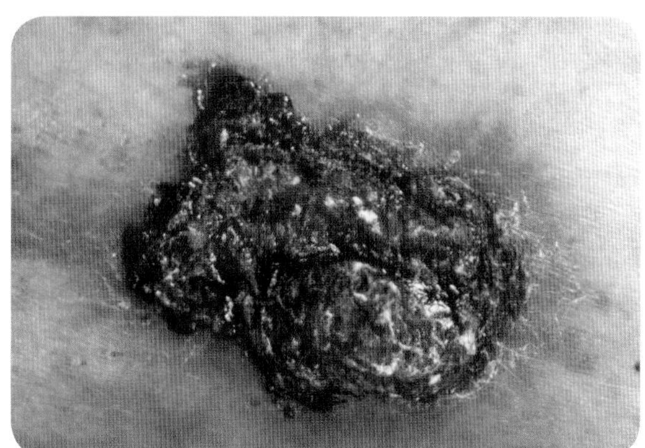

Australia has the highest rate of skin cancer in the world. Many Australians voluntarily expose themselves to too much sun. While activities such as sunbaking on the beach can be enjoyable in the short term, the end result can be life-threatening, especially if a person develops a malignant melanoma — the deadliest form of the disease (pictured left).

Although other factors may influence one's desire to engage in excessive tanning, research has shown impression management concerns to be the best predictor for excessive tanning (Leary & Jones, 1993). People who are concerned with how they appear to others are more likely than those who are less concerned with self-presentation to engage in excessive exposure to ultraviolet radiation. Furthermore, when researchers varied the outcome of tanning, making it clear to participants in the research study, that tanning can ultimately lead to less attractiveness, wrinkled skin and, overall, more negative impressions, people endorsed more safe-sun attitudes (Jones & Leary, 1994).

Smoking, alcohol and illegal drugs

People's concerns with how they are perceived and evaluated by others play a key role in their initial and continued experiences with smoking, alcohol and illegal drugs. How many people do you know had their first cigarette or consumed their first alcoholic beverage alone? The number is very small (Friedman, Lichtenstein, & Biglan, 1985). Rather, peers have a substantial influence on people's initial experiences with nicotine, alcohol or other drugs. Adolescents who smoke, for example, are perceived as tough and rebellious, an image valued by many adolescents trying to establish some independence from their parents. Adolescents begin and continue to drink or use drugs because they perceive those behaviours as valued by their peer group. They want to fit in and be accepted by their peers, so they go along with what they perceive to be normative behaviours (Clayton, 1991).

More recently, research has compared the risk and protective factors that influence youth substance use in Australia and the United States (see Beyers, Toumbourou, Catalano, Arthur, & Hawkins, 2004). Beyers et al. (2004) found that more adolescents in Victoria reported using cigarettes and alcohol, whereas more of the American adolescents reported using marijuana. The Victorian youths also indicated more positive attitudes towards drug use, reflecting more favourable parental attitudes and community norms to drug use.

The use of alcohol and other drugs can allow an individual to control his image not only directly, but also indirectly. Take Nicholas, for example. Nicholas began using alcohol when he was 14 to fit in with his mates. He quickly discovered that alcohol had secondary effects that also helped him create desired impressions on others. Nicholas thought of himself as shy, awkward and socially unskilled. With a little alcohol in his system, however, he became gregarious and, in his mind, much more socially adept. Thus, not only did he fulfil the rebellious image he admired in his friends, but alcohol allowed his social interactions to proceed much more smoothly, allowing him to make a more favourable impression on others when under the influence.

Self-presentational concerns may also be responsible for the difficulty that people have stopping their use of alcohol, nicotine or other drugs. Nicholas may find it very difficult to stop using alcohol because of his feeling that, without alcohol, he will be unable to carry on pleasant interactions with others. Susan, who has smoked for 10 years, may be unwilling to quit smoking for fear that she will gain weight, perhaps compromising the impressions that she makes on others (Klesges & Klesges, 1988).

Exercise

As noted earlier, the desire to make favourable impressions on others can encourage people to exercise. We admire those who are dedicated to exercise, and we think that people who are physically fit look better than those who are not. However, these same self-presentational concerns can actually deter people from engaging in exercise, usually the people who are in most need of exercise. People who are overweight, for example, often fail to exercise because of embarrassment over how they will look when they exercise (Culos-Reed, Brawley, Martin, & Leary, 2002; Hart, Leary, & Rejeski, 1989). One study examining women's experiences with exercise found that 'Although factors such as safety, comfort and quality of instruction affected the women's exercise behaviour, the most powerful influences seemed to be the social circumstances of the exercise setting, especially concerns about visibility, embarrassment and judgement by others' (Bain, Wilson, & Chaikind, 1989, p. 139).

Accidents and injuries

Although certainly people can have accidents and develop injuries that have little if anything to do with self-presentation, a fair number of accidents and injuries stem from self-presentational concerns (Focht & Hausenblas, 2004). People, particularly adolescents, often engage in behaviours that they (a) don't want to do and (b) do not have the skills to do, solely to control the impressions that others form of them. So, people play 'chicken' (the game where two cars race towards one another to see who swerves first) or Russian roulette to avoid being called a coward. People do not wear seatbelts or they drive too fast on the highway to avoid appearing too cautious. From primary school up, children often rebel against wearing helmets and safety gear when they ride skateboards or bikes because it looks wimpy, not cool. Athletes who have been injured often continue to play a game in spite of their injury so that they do not appear weak or unskilled.

Clearly, then, self-presentational processes play a role in inhibiting health-promoting behaviours and in facilitating health-compromising behaviours. Of course, self-presentational factors are not the only factor involved, but such concerns are clearly a major source of influence.

Stress

One of the most frequently researched topics within health psychology is stress (Hobfoll, Schwarzer, & Chon, 1998). ***Stress*** refers to a challenge to a person's capacity to adapt to inner and outer demands. Stressful experiences typically produce physiological and emotional arousal and elicit cognitive and behavioural efforts to cope with the stress.

People cope with stress in different ways.

Stress as a psychobiological process

Stress is a psychobiological process, with both physiological and psychological components and consequences. An early contribution to the understanding of stress was Walter Cannon's (1932) description of the fight-or-flight response (chapter 3), in which an organism prepares for danger with endocrine and sympathetic nervous system activation. If the danger does not abate, however, the organism remains perpetually aroused. This can lead to deteriorating health as the body continues to divert its resources away from everyday maintenance and towards emergency readiness.

Another major contribution to the understanding of stress occurred when a young Canadian scientist, Hans Selye, accidentally uncovered some of the physiological mechanisms of stress. Selye (1936, 1976) was experimenting with what he thought was a new sex hormone, which he injected into rats to test its effects. What he ultimately discovered was that a wide range of stressful events, from injections of various substances (including his 'sex hormone') to fatigue to extreme cold, led the body to respond with a ***general adaptation syndrome*** consisting of three stages: alarm, resistance and exhaustion.

The first stage, *alarm*, involves the release of adrenalin and other hormones such as cortisol as well as activation of the sympathetic nervous system. This is what occurs biologically in fight-or-flight responses: blood pressure, heart rate, respiration and blood sugar rise as blood is diverted from the gastrointestinal tract to muscles and other parts of the body that may be called upon for an emergency response.

The alarm stage cannot last indefinitely, however, and the body may eventually enter the second stage, *resistance*. The parasympathetic nervous system returns respiration and heart rate to normal. However, blood glucose levels remain high (for energy) and some stress-related hormones (including adrenalin and cortisol) continue to circulate at elevated levels. Essentially, the organism remains on red alert, with heightened energy and arousal, but it has begun to adapt to a higher level of stress.

Remaining on red alert takes its toll, making the organism especially vulnerable to illness. Overworked university students in the resistance stage, for example, are susceptible to influenza, glandular fever and whatever garden-variety colds happen to be making the rounds. The situation is analogous to a country that deploys all its military troops to one border to protect against an invasion, leaving its other borders unprotected.

If the resistance phase lasts long enough, the body eventually wears down, and the organism enters a third stage, *exhaustion*. Physiological defences break down, resulting in greatly increased vulnerability to serious or even life-threatening disease. Organs such as the heart that are vulnerable genetically or environmentally (from smoking, too much lifelong cholesterol intake etc.) are the first to go during this stage.

Stress as a transactional process

A major step forward in the study of stress came when Richard Lazarus developed his transactional model of stress. According to this view, stress is typically a transaction between the individual and the environment, rather than a property of either the person or the environment alone (Lazarus, 1981, 1993). Just as the amount of stress on a rope is jointly determined by the quality of the rope and the amount of weight pulling on it, so, too, is the amount of stress people experience a joint function of their internal resources and the external situations 'tugging' at them.

Stress entails an individual's perception that demands of the environment tax or exceed her available psychosocial resources. That is, stress depends on the meaning of an event to the individual. An event that fills one person with excitement, such as a new business opportunity, can make another feel overwhelmed and anxious. The extent to which an event is experienced as stressful, therefore, depends on the person's appraisal of both the situation and her ability to cope with it.

Lazarus' model identifies two stages in the process of stress and coping (neither of which is necessarily conscious). In a ***primary appraisal*** of the situation, the person decides whether the situation is benign, stressful or irrelevant. If she appraises the situation as stressful (e.g. the lecturer who fails to make tenure), she must determine what to do about it. In the second stage, ***secondary appraisal***, the person evaluates the options and decides how to respond (e.g. deciding that she is better off leaving the university to work for an internet firm and make a better living). Both stages involve ***emotional forecasting***, predicting what feelings the situation will produce (primary appraisal) and predicting the likely emotional impact of each potential response (secondary appraisal).

Lazarus distinguishes three types of stress. The first is harm or loss, as when a person loses a loved one or something greatly valued, such as a job. The second is threat, or anticipation of harm or loss.

The third form of stress is challenge, opportunities for growth that may nonetheless be fraught with disruption and uncertainty. Examples of challenges include getting married or entering university. These events can be exceedingly stressful — that is, psychologically and physiologically taxing — because of all the changes and adjustments they entail, even though they are also accompanied by positive affect. Thus, not all stress comes from negative events.

The transition to university

By Professor Keithia Wilson, Griffith University, and Associate Professor Alf Lizzio, Griffith University

The only constant in life is change itself. As this commonly used maxim indicates, the life course can be understood as a 'series of transitions' through stages, social roles and personal situations. There is considerable scholarly and popular literature on some of the 'big transitions' in our lives: starting school, leaving home, becoming a parent, starting a career, moving into retirement. Such transitions are not necessarily orderly or predictable, and they are often challenging (Bloch, 2005).

A transition that you are currently experiencing, or have recently experienced, is the 'transition to university'. The nature of this transition will be quite different depending on your life circumstances. Thus, a transition from high school to university (school leaver) will involve different challenges than a transition from work to university (mature-age student) (Yorke, 1999). International students, students 'coming to the city' or students who are first in their family to come to university often have to manage multiple academic, social and cultural transitions (Collier & Morgan, 2008).

What can you learn from your 'transition to uni' that might be useful in effectively navigating other life transitions ahead of you?

The quite high attrition or drop-out rates among commencing students has stimulated considerable international (Tinto, 1993) and Australian (James, Krause, & Jennings, 2010) research into student transitions. While a complex set of academic, social and personal factors affect student adjustment, there are some practical actions you can take to 'make a good start' at university, or, in psychological terms, enhance your capacity for positive adaptation and resilience (Fergus & Zimmerman, 2005).

First, negotiating a positive *sense of student identity* is a foundational transition task (Stokes & Wyn, 2007). 'Coming to uni' involves more than just the formal process of enrolment in a degree program; it very much involves a change or shift in your identity. What does it mean to be a uni student? How does this change how you and others in your life (family, friends) think about you? How does your student identity 'fit' (complement or compete) with your other roles and identities? How does your idea of what it means to be a uni student (your claimed identity) 'fit' with what the university requires of you or allows you to be (your ascribed identity)?

Second, the extent of your *academic capital or resources* may influence your early success at university. In addition to a positive sense of student identity, the four areas of personal investment that produce payoffs for commencing students have been found to be (Lizzio, 2006):

1. *A sense of connectedness*. This involves building supportive working relationships with your fellow students and staff.
2. *A sense of capability*. This involves developing the academic skills required for university study, and understanding university language and jargon.
3. *A sense of purpose*. This involves having a clear sense of why you are studying your degree — knowing what you want out of it and appreciating how the degree 'hangs together'.
4. *A sense of resourcefulness*. This involves understanding how the university system works; knowing how to seek help; and possessing strategies for managing work, life and study priorities.

Resources such as these function as both *compensatory* (helpful in all university situations) and *protective (*helpful in stressful university situations*)* factors (Gordon Rouse, 2001).

Third, a *capacity to self-regulate* (the metacognitive skill that helps us to 'recognise and read' new or challenging situations, and then to activate or seek the necessary resources to successfully respond) (Hacker, Dunlosky, & Graesser, 2009) appears to be associated with both academic and personal success (Wilson, Charker, Lizzio, Halford, & Kimlin, 2005). Self-regulation is particularly important in managing situations that we have not previously encountered (and where our habitual behaviour doesn't necessarily serve us well) or where the reality does not match our prior expectations (Miller, Bender, & Schuh, 2005). Thus, effective students appear to pay closer attention to deconstructing the demands and expectations of novel academic situations (e.g. a new type of assessment task, a different classroom environment), formulate appropriate strategies, put these into action and monitor the outcomes (Winne & Nesbit, 2010). Thus, the good news is that academic success is a learnable skill!

INTERIM SUMMARY

Stress refers to a challenge to a person's capacity to adapt to inner and outer demands. Stress is a psychobiological process, with both physiological and psychological components and consequences. The ***general adaptation syndrome*** consists of three stages: alarm, resistance and exhaustion. Stress is also a transactional process — a transaction between the individual and the environment, in which the individual perceives that demands of the environment tax or exceed her psychosocial resources. In a ***primary appraisal*** of the situation, the person decides whether the situation is benign, stressful or irrelevant. Part of this process involves ***emotional*** forecasting in which a person evaluates what feelings particular situations will produce. During ***secondary appraisal***, the person evaluates the options and decides how to respond.

Sources of stress

Stress is an unavoidable part of life. Events that often lead to stress are called ***stressors***. Stressors range from the infrequent, such as the death of a parent, to the commonplace, such as a demanding job or a noisy neighbour. Research on stressors has focused on life events, catastrophes and daily hassles.

Life events

One of the most significant sources of stress is change. Virtually any event that requires someone to make a readjustment can be a stressor. The Holmes–Rahe scale, a portion of which is reproduced in table 14.4, measures stress related to 43 common life events that require change and adaptation (Holmes & Rahe, 1967). An important feature of the Holmes–Rahe scale is that it includes both negative items (e.g. death of a spouse) and positive items (e.g. marriage) that can be stressful.

TABLE 14.4 Top 15 stressors on the Holmes–Rahe life events rating scale

Rank	Life event	Mean value
1	Death of spouse	100
2	Divorce	73
3	Marital separation	65
4	Jail term	63
5	Death of a close family member	63
6	Personal injury or illness	53
7	Marriage	50
8	Fired at work	47
9	Marital reconciliation	45
10	Retirement	45
11	Change in health in family member	44
12	Pregnancy	40
13	Sex difficulties	39
14	Gain of new family member	39
15	Business readjustment	39

SOURCE: Holmes and Rahe (1967).

Although the Holmes–Rahe scale offers a good rough estimate of the amount of stress a person is encountering (by summing all the life change units experienced over the past 12 months), it does not take into account the meanings of various experiences for different individuals. Consequently, some researchers have turned, instead, to measures of perceived stress — that is, the extent to which people consider the experiences they have undergone stressful (Blascovich & Mendes, 2000; Karlsen, Dybdahl, & Bitterso, 2006).

Major stressors

One of the most stressful events any individual can experience is the death of a spouse or child — a stress that can take its toll for many years afterwards. For example, a study of people who lost a spouse or child in a car accident indicated that, for many bereaved persons, distress lasts as long as four to seven years after a sudden loss. Symptoms of prolonged distress included depression, sleep disturbances, fatigue, panic attacks, loneliness and increased mortality rate. Additionally, parents who had unexpectedly lost a child were at substantially higher risk for divorce (Lehman, Wortman, & Williams, 1987), especially when the child's cause of death was homicide (Murphy, Johnson, Wu, Fan, & Lohan, 2003).

Striking findings on the relationship between loss and mortality emerged in a study of over one million people from Finland (Martikainen & Valkonen, 1996). Over a five-year period, the investigators charted the mortality rates of individuals who had lost a spouse. Those who lost a spouse were at substantially elevated risk for death by accident, violence and alcohol. Deaths from heart disease doubled — perhaps a confirmation of the popular view that people can 'die of a broken heart'. The relative risk of dying was particularly high within six months of the death of a spouse and was highest in younger people (table 14.5). Other research finds that bereaved spouses displaying a higher proportion of 'fake' smiles to 'real' smiles are at greater risk for depression in the following years (Keltner & Bonanno, 1997; Keltner, Kring, & Bonanno, 1999). Suppressing genuine feelings does not appear to be a particularly healthy strategy, at least not for dealing with loss.

TABLE **14.5** Relative risk of death following death of a spouse

	Cause of death						
	Cancer	Chronic heart disease	Alcohol-related illness	Motor vehicle accidents	Other accidents and violence	Suicide	All causes
Men	1.31	2.08	3.98	1.52	3.05	3.02	1.66
Women	1.04	1.71	2.91	1.52	2.45	2.30	1.25

SOURCE: Adapted from Martikainen and Valkonen (1996).

Another major stressor, unemployment, can also impair physical and mental health, although the effects are generally not as dramatic as the death of a spouse (Jahoda, 1988; Kessler, House, & Turner, 1987). For example, another large Finnish study followed workers for several months after a plant layoff (Viinamaeki, Koskela, & Niskanen, 1996). Those who remained unemployed were at increasing risk for depression, subjective distress and stress-related illnesses as the months wore on.

Major stressors, such as loss of a loved one or unemployment, actually include many specific sources of stress. The effect on a given person depends on the individual's vulnerabilities to these specific stressors (Monroe & Simons, 1991; see also Dollard & Winefield, 2002). For example, unemployment can be devastating because of the financial strain on an individual or a family. It can also lead to marital strain, forced relocation and loss of social contact with friends from work (Bolton & Oatley, 1987; Kessler, Turner, & House, 1989). Thus, even a person who has other sources of income, such as unemployment compensation or savings, may experience lowered self-esteem, loneliness or anxiety following unemployment.

On the other hand, work-related stress can also cause clinical depression and anxiety among young adults (Melchior et al., 2007). The Dunedin Multidisciplinary Health and Development Study at the University of Otago found that almost 14 percent of women and 10 percent of men experience stress at work, despite having no prior mental health problems. Almost half of the cases of depression or generalised anxiety disorder were newly diagnosed at age 32 and were directly related to workplace stress and high job demands. These data signal the need for employers to ensure reasonable steps are taken to eliminate or minimise the risk of stress on the job (Melchior et al., 2007).

Acculturative stress

A severe stressor that is increasingly confronting people throughout the world is acculturative stress (Berry, Dasen, & Saraswathi, 1997; Tartakovsky, 2007; Thomson, Rosenthal, & Russell, 2006). Acculturation means coming into contact with a new, typically dominant culture. Thus, ***acculturative stress*** refers to the stress people experience in trying to adapt to a new culture (chapter 19). Acculturative stress can occur whether people willingly emigrate for better opportunities or flee as refugees. Symptoms may include anxiety, depression, uncertainty and conflict about ethnic identity, and alcohol abuse.

Like other major life stresses, acculturative stress includes many specific stressors. People entering new cultures frequently encounter language difficulties, racial or ethnic prejudice, lower socioeconomic status (such as overseas-trained engineers or doctors working in Australia as labourers because their qualifications were not recognised) and separation from family. Immigrants also face conflicts over preserving their old values and beliefs and adapting to the mores of their new culture — conflicts often played out across the generations, as children shun their parents' Old World attitudes. Finally, many refugees must also come to terms with torture or with the torture or murder of loved ones back home.

Catastrophes

Catastrophes are stressors of massive proportions. Catastrophes may be caused by nature, such as the 2004 Indian Ocean tsunami, or by humans, such as the civil wars in Somalia, Rwanda and the Balkans and the more recent conflict in Libya. The catastrophic 2011 Japanese earthquake and tsunami caused widespread devastation. The earthquake and tsunami were both caused by nature and resulted in many thousands of deaths. The nuclear crisis that unfolded in the aftermath developed into another catastrophe, with potentially devastating effects likely to be experienced over the longer term by people exposed to high radiation levels. Weeks earlier, the scenic city of Christchurch had been hit with an earthquake, with more than 180 deaths recorded. The catastrophe largely destroyed the central business district of the city, which had been hit by another earthquake only months earlier (McDonald, 2011).

On Ash Wednesday in 1983, bushfires destroyed more than 2000 homes and killed 72 people in South Australia and Victoria. A follow-up study of 1500 people affected by the fires found that 40 percent had some psychiatric impairment 12 months later (Leach, 1994). Similarly, people were also affected by the Newcastle earthquake in 1989, which killed 13 people and destroyed thousands of homes and buildings across a 300 000 square kilometre area. Many people needed ongoing counselling for problems such as recurring nightmares, avoidance of recurring thoughts, depression, sleep disturbance, and diminished concentration and interest in life (Carr, Lewin, Carter, & Webster, 1992).

In more recent times, the state of Victoria was affected by widespread bushfires that killed 173 people and destroyed several townships. Thousands of livestock were lost as a result of the fires, and native animal populations were devastated. More than 4500 homes and buildings were also ruined during the crisis, at an estimated cost exceeding $1 billion (Australian Government Attorney-General's Department: Emergency Management Australia, 2009).

While bushfires have been a powerful stressor for people in some Australian communities in recent history, many other Australians have been personally affected by different recent catastrophes. Early in 2011, flooding devastated communities across the states of Queensland, New South Wales, Victoria, Western Australia, South

Catastrophes such as the 2009 Victorian bushfire crisis and the 2011 Queensland flood crisis have a strong impact on the national psyche, causing considerable psychological distress as well as widespread destruction. Health psychologists work with individuals and communities to consider how the ongoing threat and impacts of natural disasters influence quality of life and psychological wellbeing (Morrissey & Reser, 2007).

Australia and Tasmania. Thousands of homes and businesses were destroyed in the crisis, and many people lost their lives. In January 2011, three-quarters of Queensland was declared a disaster zone, with coastal and inland communities both being devastated. The main street in the inland city of Toowoomba was hit by a flash flood that was described by survivors as an 'instant inland tsunami'; people were swept up in floodwaters in the Lockyer Valley; and the capital city of Brisbane recorded near-record flood levels. Only days after thousands of people were cut off by rising floodwaters in New South Wales, the Victorian town of Horsham was hit with a 'one-in-200-year' flood (Lloyd, 2011; Thomas & Callinan, 2011; Brown & Savage, 2011). While the floods were still in the headlines, parts of north Queensland also braced for the arrival of Cyclone Yasi, a category five storm that delivered winds at 290 kilometres an hour and raging high seas. The cyclone caused devastation to some coastal communities, including to a strip of coastline between Cardwell and Innisfail that bore the impact of Cyclone Larry in 2006 (Reilly, 2011).

In 2006, Cyclone Larry caused nearly $1 billion in property damage in north Queensland — destroying many people's homes. The damage bill for Cyclone Yasi was tipped by the Queensland Treasurer to reach $800 million. This bill was expected on top of the $5 billion damage bill from the January floods (AAP, 2011).

At a personal level, many different types of loss were experienced during the floods. ("Govt set to cut spending in flood recovery," 2011). Mental health expert Professor Patrick McGorry said that a high percentage of Australians would require 'psychological first aid' after becoming flood victims. 'There are very intense emotions for the people most directly affected — the grief, the loss, the shock, the numb [feeling]', he said. 'But then it's replaced by other emotions — anger, the sense of terrible loss, even depression' (cited in "Locals urged to doorknock flood-zone homes," 2011). Counsellors working on Lifeline's 24-hour service experienced a surge of calls from people during the flooding. Higher post-traumatic stress disorder and depression rates are expected in the aftermath of the crisis over the longer term (Watson, 2011).

There is considerable scope in how people respond to catastrophes, with proximity to the crisis and the presence of a support network being just two factors that can affect mental health. The type of event can also affect how people respond. A trauma counsellor that worked with victims during both the 2009 Victorian bushfire crisis and in the hard-hit area of Toowoomba after the 2011 floods said the events were like 'chalk and cheese' in terms of the impact that they had on people's mental wellbeing. 'She was expecting it to be similar', said a colleague, 'but at least with a fire it comes and then it leaves often quickly. The floods stir everything up; it bobs up in front of you. It's a different situation altogether' (cited in Watson, 2011). Because of the nature of catastrophes though, and the scope in how people are affected by them, this personal account may differ substantially from the view of a person who experienced considerable personal loss and suffering as a result of the tragic 2009 crisis.

MAKING CONNECTIONS

Catastrophes, such as the Queensland floods, Cyclone Yasi, the Christchurch earthquakes, the Japanese earthquake and tsunami and the Victorian bushfires, sometimes lead to **post-traumatic stress disorder** (PTSD). PTSD includes symptoms such as nightmares, flashbacks to the traumatic event, depression and anxiety. Most severe life events, such as losses, actually do not elicit PTSD. The major exception is rape, which leads to PTSD 80 percent of the time (chapter 15).

One stress of catastrophic proportions, practised by dozens of countries, is torture (Basoglu, 1997). In any given year, over 150 countries in the world practise torture, and between 5 and 35 percent of the world's 14 million refugees have been subjected to at least one episode of torture. The most common psychological effects include anxiety and depression, social withdrawal, problems with memory and attention, sexual dysfunction, nightmares, insomnia and personality changes. A study of torture victims in Turkey found that years later nearly half the survivors continued to suffer from nightmares and other symptoms of post-traumatic stress (Basoglu et al., 1994). The average person was tortured 291 times over four years in captivity, with forms of torture including beating, electric shock, prevention of urination or defecation, rape and twisting of the testicles.

Daily hassles

Although the concept of stressors tends to bring to mind major events such as death, unemployment and catastrophes, more mundane events can be important as well and are often central to the subjective experience of stress (Hahn & Smith, 1999). ***Daily hassles*** are 'the irritating, frustrating, distressing demands that to some degree characterise everyday transactions with the environment' (Kanner, Coyne, Schaefer, & Lazarus, 1981, p. 3). Daily hassles range from interpersonal conflicts to commuting during rush hour. The most common daily hassles include concerns about weight, ill health of a family member, rising prices of common goods, home maintenance, too many things to do, and misplacing or losing things (Kanner et al., 1981; see also Sim, 2000).

INTERIM SUMMARY

Events that often lead to stress are called ***stressors***. Life events are stressors that require change and adaptation. Perceived stress refers to the extent to which people consider the experiences they have undergone stressful. ***Acculturative stress*** refers to the stress people experience in trying to adapt to a new culture. ***Catastrophes*** are stressors of massive proportions, including both natural and human-made disasters. ***Daily hassles*** are minor annoyances of everyday life that contribute to stress.

Stress and health

Stressful events obviously can have a substantial impact on psychological wellbeing. They can also affect other psychological functions, such as memory. Anyone who has ever been in a frightening car accident, suddenly lost a loved one, or even 'pulled an all-nighter' studying for a final exam knows that stress can impair the ability to focus and commit information to memory. Researchers are now beginning to unravel the reasons stressful events can affect memory.

As we discussed in chapter 7, the prefrontal cortex plays a particularly important role in working memory (e.g. momentarily holding in mind a phone number), and the hippocampus is involved in long-term memory (e.g. remembering the number over several weeks or years). Stress interferes with the functioning of both of these structures (Arnsten, 1998; McEwan, 1999). In fact, chronic stress leads to permanent cell death and a reduction in the size of the hippocampus (Bremner, 1999).

Thus, stress can alter the structure and function of the brain. It can also have a substantial effect on physical health and mortality (Kamarack et al., 2005; Kemeny & Laudenslager, 1999; Watkins & Maier, 2000). People under stress often suffer from headaches, depression and other health problems such as influenza, sore throat and backache (Cohen, Tyrrell, & Smith, 1991; DeLongis, Folkman, & Lazarus, 1988). Several studies have linked stress to vulnerability to cancer and have found that psychotherapy aimed at realistically but optimistically facing the cancer and maximising social support may increase life expectancy in some cancer patients (Kiecolt-Glaser, Robles, Heffner, Loving, & Glaser, 2002; Spiegel, 1999; Spiegel & Kato, 1996).

How does stress affect health? Stress can have a direct effect by decreasing the body's capacity to fight illness. It can also affect health indirectly by instigating behaviours that weaken the body's defences or lead to exposure to pathogens and toxic agents that can produce physical illness (figure 14.7). People under stress tend to drink more alcohol, smoke more, sleep less and exercise less than their peers (Cohen & Williamson, 1991; O'Leary, 1992).

APPLY + DISCUSS

Research has shown men and women to be susceptible to different types of stressors. Specifically, women report more stress following interpersonal rejection whereas men report more stress in achievement situations (Stroud, Salovey, & Epel, 2002). What role, if any, might women's susceptibility to interpersonal stressors play in the higher incidence of affective or mood disorders among women?

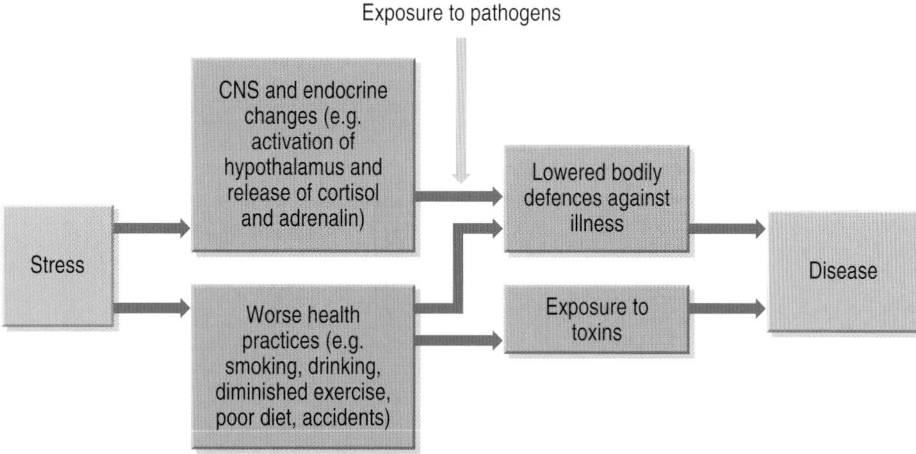

FIGURE 14.7
Pathways linking stress to infectious diseases. Stress can influence the onset of infectious disease in a number of ways. It can lead to central nervous system (CNS) and endocrine responses that diminish immune system functioning, leaving the person vulnerable to infection and illness from random exposure to pathogens such as airborne viruses. Alternatively, stress can lead to non-random exposure to toxins through poor health practices such as smoking.

SOURCE: Adapted from Cohen and Williamson (1991, p. 8).

Other variables can increase or decrease the impact of stress on health. Stress is more likely to affect people's health, for example, if they do not have adequate social support (Cohen & Williamson, 1991; Von Ah, Kang, & Carpenter, 2007). Exercise can also reduce the impact of stress on health. One study compared the number of visits to the health clinic of university students who were either high or low in physical fitness (Brown, 1991). Physically fit participants made fewer visits even when reporting many negative life events. Participants who were less physically fit tended to become ill when stressed.

Stress and the immune system

Psychoneuroimmunology examines the influence of psychosocial factors on the functioning of the immune system (Kiecolt-Glaser, McGuire, Robles, & Glaser, 2002; Stowell, McGuire, Robles, Glaser, & Kiecolt-Glaser, 2003). The ***immune system*** is the body's 'surveillance and security' system, which detects and eliminates disease-causing agents in the body such as bacteria and viruses. Three important types of cells in the immune system are B cells, T cells and natural killer cells.

B cells produce ***antibodies***, protein molecules that attach themselves to foreign invaders and mark them for destruction. Some T cells search out and directly destroy invaders, while others (T-helper cells) stimulate immune functioning. T-helper cells are the primary target of HIV, the virus that causes AIDS. Natural killer cells fight viruses and tumours (Weisse, 1992). Both acute (i.e. short-term) and chronic (i.e. long-term) stress can affect the efficiency and availability of cells in the immune system and hence the body's capacity to fight disease (O'Leary, Brown, & Suarez-Al-Adam, 1997).

When a group of people is exposed to an infectious disease, such as respiratory illness, only some of them actually become sick. Consequently, one way to explore the effects of stress on the immune system is to see whether people under stress are more likely to suffer from infectious diseases. The evidence suggests that they are. For example, one study (Jemmott et al., 1983) investigated the relationship between academic pressure and immunological functioning (specifically, the secretion of an antibody called immunoglobulin A, or IgA). During periods of the academic calendar rated by both the researchers and participants as most stressful, the secretion rate of IgA was lower; that is, the immune response was reduced. Similarly, studies of caregivers of patients with Alzheimer's disease show reduced immunological responses over time (Kiecolt-Glaser, Glaser, Shuttleworth, & Dyer, 1987).

Perhaps the most conclusive study yet of the influence of stress on both immune functioning and illness assessed 394 healthy participants for degree of life stress and then administered nasal drops containing one of five different viruses (Cohen et al., 1991). Participants reporting higher stress showed greater rates of infection for all five viruses (figure 14.8).

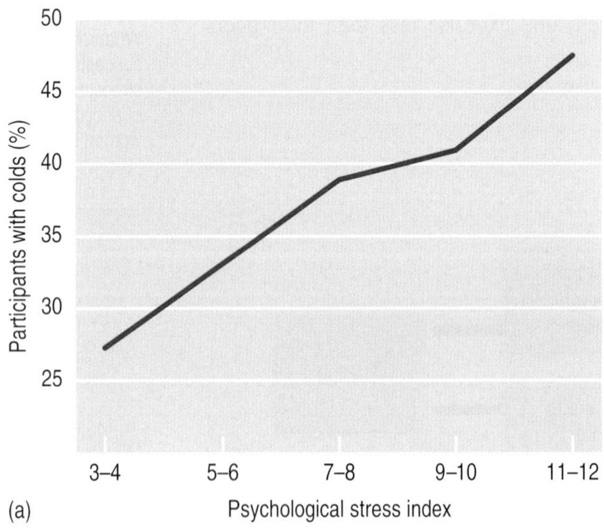

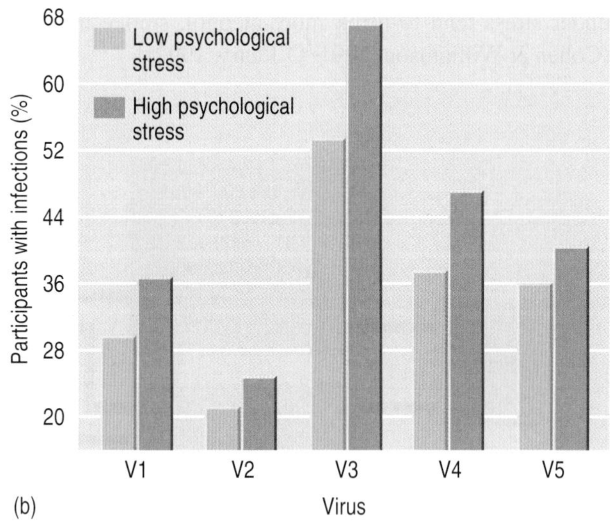

FIGURE 14.8

The relationship between stress and illness following viral exposure. Part (a) shows the relationship between the amount of self-reported psychological stress and the percentage of participants judged by a doctor to have a clinical cold after exposure to a virus. As can be seen, the more stress, the more colds. Part (b) presents data from a biological test of participants' blood for presence of infection. For each of five viruses, participants reporting higher stress showed higher rates of infection.

SOURCE: Cohen et al. (1991, pp. 609–610).

Stress and health-seeking behaviour

Stress can influence health in a more subtle way by influencing the way the person interprets bodily symptoms (Cameron, Levanthal, & Love, 1998; Leventhal & Leventhal, 1993; see also Buitenhuis, de Jong, Jaspers, & Groothoff, 2006). When symptoms are unambiguous and ominous, such as severe stomach pain accompanied by bloody stools, people tend to seek help immediately. Many symptoms, however, are ambiguous, and this ambiguity can lead to several alternative responses.

For example, a middle-aged man might ignore chest pains or take a 'wait-and-see attitude' if they go away. This strategy may represent an effort to cope with the emotion he would likely feel (fear) if he took the symptom seriously. By deciding that 'it's probably nothing', he may be trading short-term reassurance for long-term danger. People's appraisals of health risk also reflect their judgements about the context of the symptom, as when a person who experiences chest pain in the weeks following a job loss decides that 'it's just stress'.

At other times, and for other people, stress can have precisely the opposite effect, leading them to seek medical care for one minor complaint after another, fearing that each new symptom could be a sign of serious disease. In fact, people who are depressed, anxious or recently stressed by experiences such as job loss tend not only to have more physical illnesses but also to interpret their illnesses more seriously and to experience the pain as greater (Leventhal & Leventhal, 1993). Thus, stress can lead people either to take their health too seriously or to not take it seriously enough.

Stress, health and personality

Whether a person under stress remains healthy or becomes ill also depends on the person's enduring personality traits (Kamarack et al., 2005; O'Brien & DeLongis, 1996; Suls, David, & Harvey, 1996). Personality can influence stress and health through the motives people pursue, the way they tend to appraise circumstances (e.g. easily becoming angry or sad), or the way they tend to cope with stress (such as through drinking, cigarette smoking, avoiding doctors or suppressing emotions).

For example, in one study, participants kept a daily diary of their moods and the events of the day (Suls, Green, & Hillis, 1998). The higher participants were in neuroticism — the tendency to experience negative emotions such as depression or anxiety (chapter 11) — the more daily problems they reported, the more reactive they were to stressors, and the more they were distressed by bad things that happened to them.

Another study powerfully demonstrates the impact of personality on both stress and health (Caspi, 2000). A team of investigators has been following a sample of about a thousand people born in Dunedin, New Zealand, during one year in the early 1970s. They have assessed the group repeatedly, beginning at age three. At age 18, they assessed aspects of their personality. Then, three years later, they assessed four high-risk behaviours associated with stress and health: alcohol dependence, violent crime, unprotected sex with multiple partners and dangerous driving habits.

Personality at age 18 was a powerful predictor of high-risk behaviours three years later: those who tended to engage in all four behaviours were lower on traditionalism, concern about avoiding danger, ability to regulate impulses and social closeness. They were also higher on aggression. Perhaps more striking, risk behaviours at age 21 were predictable from the initial assessment of participants at age three. Those who were classified in preschool as undercontrolled — that is, impulsive, poorly behaved and aggressive — were more likely to engage in all four high-risk behaviours than their better controlled (and particularly overcontrolled) peers.

APPLY + DISCUSS

- Why do people engage in behaviours such as smoking and excessive drinking that increase the negative impact of stress on their health?
- Why do people often fail to act in ways that promote health, such as exercising and getting prompt medical attention?

Genetic factors affect stress as well, in two ways: by influencing the probability a person will place herself in stressful situations and by influencing her vulnerability to the stressors she encounters (Kendler, 1995). For example, studies comparing monozygotic and dizygotic twins have found that the likelihood of being robbed, assaulted or confronted with financial difficulties is moderately heritable, with heritability estimated between 30 and 40 percent! The correlation between monozygotic (identical) twins' reports of financial difficulties is .44, whereas for dizygotic (fraternal) twins the correlation is only .12. As we have seen (chapter 11), the tendency to take risks is itself heritable, in large part because people who are fearful take fewer risks and those who are more pleasure-driven take more. Once a person experiences a stressful event, the tendency to experience negative affect, which is also heritable, can then amplify the individual's distress.

Type A behaviour pattern and hostility

One of the most thoroughly researched links between personality and health, which was first observed by two cardiologists and later corroborated by psychological research, is between heart disease and the ***Type A behaviour pattern***, a personality style characterised by impatience, ambition, competitiveness, hostility and a 'hard-driving' approach to life (Friedman & Rosenman, 1959). Type B individuals, on the other hand, are more relaxed, easy-going and less easily angered.

One psychologist illustrated the differences between Type A and Type B behaviour in describing a fishing trip he took with a colleague (Schwartz, 1987, p. 136):

> I baited the hook and dropped the line over in a relaxed fashion, watched the gulls and swayed with the swells. But what really struck [my colleague] was my talking to the fish when they bit the hook: 'That's nice' or 'Take your time, I'm in no rush'.

In contrast to his own Type B pattern, a man fishing in a boat nearby exhibited Type A behaviour (Schwartz, 1987, p. 136):

> He was fishing with two poles, racing back and forth between them and tangling his lines while cursing the fish that happened to be on the line beyond his reach. If the fish eluded him while others caught them, he would pull up the anchor in frustration, start the engine with a roar and race to another part of the bay.

Research suggests that subcomponents of the Type A pattern may be differentially related to heart disease (Myrtek, 2001). In particular, hostility — or the combination of defensiveness, negative affect and suppressed hostility — has been implicated in narrowing of the arteries leading to the heart. Angry people also tend to die slightly younger (Miller, Eisenberg, Fabes, & Shell, 1996).

Optimism/pessimism

Another personality dimension related to immune functioning and health is optimism/pessimism (Carver, 1998; Peterson, 1995; Von Ah et al., 2007). One study found that coronary artery bypass patients who reported higher levels of optimism on a questionnaire recovered more quickly and returned to normal life more easily than pessimistic participants (Scheier et al., 1989). Another found that university students with a pessimistic explanatory style (a tendency to explain bad events in negative, self-blaming ways; see chapter 6) experienced more days of illness and visited doctors more frequently than other students (Peterson, 1988). People who are pessimistic do not take as good care of themselves, do not cope as well and have poorer immune functioning, all of which lead to more illness (Lin & Peterson, 1990).

INTERIM SUMMARY

Psychoneuroimmunology examines the influence of psychosocial factors on the functioning of the immune system. Stress can affect physical health in two ways: directly, by weakening the ***immune system*** (the system of cells that detects and destroys disease-causing agents), and indirectly, by leading to behaviours that weaken the body's defences or lead to exposure to pathogens (toxic agents). Personality factors also affect stress levels and health, such as the tendency to experience negative affect (neuroticism), hostility and suppressed hostility, and pessimism.

APPLY + DISCUSS

Many people strive to achieve work–life balance.

- Why are some people better able to cope with stressful events than others?
- Is having a sense of humour important in coping with stress?
- What impact does culture have on how people respond to stress?

Coping

That people get sick or experience unpleasant emotions in response to stress should come as no surprise. What may seem more surprising is that most people who experience life crises remain healthy (Hobfoll et al., 1998; Moos & Schaefer, 1986). This resiliency in the face of stress reflects the ways people deal with stressful situations, called ways of ***coping*** (or ***coping mechanisms***).

Coping mechanisms

Researchers often distinguish two or three basic types of coping strategies (Folkman & Lazarus, 1980; Folkman & Moskowitz, 2000; Moos & Billings, 1982). Strategies aimed at changing the situation producing the stress are called ***problem-focused coping***, because they try to deal with the stressor itself. Two other types of strategy — efforts to alter thoughts about the situation, and efforts to alter the unpleasant emotional consequences of stress — are called ***emotion-focused coping***. Their aim is to regulate the emotions generated by a stressful experience. Thus, if a person cannot change a stressful situation directly, she can try to change her perception of it or the emotions it produces. Alcohol and drug use are common mechanisms for escaping emotional distress (Kushner, Abrams, & Borchardt, 2000).

Efforts to cope by changing the situation typically involve problem solving (chapter 8). The individual may try to remove the stressor, plan ways of resolving the situation, seek advice or assistance from others to change the situation, or try to avoid the stressor altogether by planning ahead (Aspinwall & Taylor, 1997; Carver, Scheier, & Weintraub, 1989). Children whose mothers have a problem-focused coping style tend to be better adjusted and more socially skilled than their peers (Eisenberg, Fabes, & Murphy, 1996).

A number of studies suggest that religious faith often helps people cope with stressful events, such as contracting a terminal disease or losing a child. Their beliefs allow them to ascribe meaning to the event or strengthen their sense of closeness to the divine (Pargament & Park, 1995). For example, one study found that people who used their religion to cope with a major life stress — such as a kidney transplant — tended to have better outcomes three and 12 months later, as did their significant others, if they relied on their faith (Tix & Frazier, 1998).

A GLOBAL VISTA

The impact of culture on coping styles

The way people respond to stress, as well as the situations they consider stressful, are in part culturally patterned. This is not surprising in the light of data showing that the emphasis on mastering the environment, characteristic of highly technologically developed societies, is relatively new in human history. Most cultures in human history have believed that humans should adjust to nature, not the other way around (Kluckhohn & Strodtbeck, 1961).

These findings suggest possible limits to Western theories and research linking an active coping style (characterised by a sense of mastery, self-efficacy and control) to mental and physical health. In capitalist societies, which are based on entrepreneurship and personal initiative, an active coping style and a strong belief in one's own ability are highly adaptive traits. In societies organised around family, community or tribal ties, such traits may be unrelated to mental and physical health. Coping is always relative to its cultural context, and coping strategies considered useful in one society (such as wailing at a funeral) may engender disapproval, and hence additional stress, in another.

Low-effort syndrome

Understanding patterns of culture and coping may also lead to a better understanding of dilemmas facing minority adolescents in multicultural societies. For years, educators, social scientists and policy makers have wrestled with the large gap between the educational performance of Anglo-Australians and minority groups in Australia, such as Indigenous Australian students, and the absence of such a gap for some immigrant groups, such as Chinese.

John Ogbu (1991) argues that, throughout the world, minority groups who experience a ceiling on their economic prospects over several generations because of job discrimination develop a low-effort syndrome not seen in new immigrants who voluntarily move to a culture in search of a better life. ***Low-effort syndrome*** — the tendency to exert minimal effort to escape stressful social and economic circumstances — is an adaptive coping strategy when social barriers make effort and achievement fruitless and when hard work and academic success would only increase frustration and anger. For instance, immigrant Chinese–Australian students in a Western Australian high school outperform Anglo-Australian students (from a British or Irish heritage) in academic terms (Malik, 1998). The performance of this ethnic group, who moved to Australia in search of a new future, can be contrasted to the performance of Indigenous Australian students, who under-perform compared to Anglo-Australians. Gostin (1996) said that past education practices in Australia demonstrated a fundamental lack of appreciation for the culture and capabilities of Indigenous Australian students, who were not considered capable of instruction at the same level as non-Indigenous students.

Chris Sarra, the first Aboriginal principal of Cherbourg State School in Queensland, was named Queenslander of the Year in 2004 for his efforts in improving the performance of Indigenous Australian students at the school. Sarra said he himself had suffered from low expectations as a student. It was only at teacher's college that he started to understand that 'for many years, because other people in school had limited expectations of my academic ability, I had actually developed limited expectations of my own ability as well' (Sarra, 2004).

Similarly, Chapman (1984) studied a group of 13-year-olds in New Zealand, comparing the attitudes and performance of Maori students against those of non-Maori. The participants had been chosen on the basis of ability and past performance, as well as similarities in socioeconomic status. Chapman found that the Maori children had lower expectations about their chances of academic success and underestimated their own abilities.

Low-effort syndrome is an example of a coping strategy that solves one problem (minimising frustration in the face of racism and barriers to success) but creates another, particularly if opportunities and social attitudes towards race change faster than coping styles developed over several generations. Because Indigenous Australians for years faced impassable barriers to upward mobility, scholastic achievement became defined in many Aboriginal communities as 'white' behaviour. Thus, for many Aboriginal adolescents today the fear of being ridiculed for 'acting white', together with a subcultural ambivalence towards achievement, inhibits scholastic achievement.

INTERIM SUMMARY

Coping mechanisms are the ways people deal with stressful events. Problem-focused coping involves changing the situation. Emotion-focused coping aims to regulate the emotion generated by a stressful situation. The ways people respond to stress, as well as the situations they consider stressful, are in part culturally patterned. Members of minority groups who, for generations, experience a ceiling on their economic prospects because of discrimination sometimes develop a ***low-effort syndrome*** in which they seemingly stop making the kinds of active efforts that might alleviate some of their hardships.

Social support

An important resource for coping with stress is ***social support***, the presence of others in whom one can confide and from whom one can expect help and concern. Social support is as important for maintaining physical health as it is mental health (Bolger & Amarel, 2007; Salovey, Rothman, & Rodin, 1998). A high level of social support is associated with protection against a range of illnesses, from hypertension and herpes to cancer and heart disease (Cohen & Herbert, 1996; Manne, 2003; Sarason, Sarason, & Gurung, 1997; Spiegel & Kato, 1996). The presence of social support enhances the functioning of the immune system whereas the absence of social support compromises the immune system (Stowell et al., 2003).

Furthermore, the number of social relationships a person has, and the extent to which the individual feels close to other people, is a powerful predictor of mortality (House, Landis, & Umberson, 1988; Johnson, Stewart, Hall, Fredlund, & Theorell, 1996). In fact, the evidence supporting the link between social relationships and health is as strong as the data linking smoking and ill health.

Two hypotheses have been advanced to explain the beneficial effects of social support, both of which have received empirical support (Cohen & Wills, 1985; Taylor, 1991). The ***buffering hypothesis*** proposes that social support is a buffer or protective factor against the harmful effects of stress during high-stress periods. In a classic study, urban women who experienced significant life stress were much less likely to become depressed if they had an intimate, confiding relationship with a boyfriend or husband (Brown & Harris, 1978). Among the elderly, social support provides a buffer between the experience of stressful events, such as the loss of a spouse, and the development of depression (Kraaij & Garnefski, 2002). The magnitude of this effect can be seen in the light of the fact that depression is the leading psychological cause of suicide in the elderly.

An alternative hypothesis views social support as a continuously positive force that makes the person less susceptible to stress in the first place. In this view, people with supportive relationships are less likely to make a primary appraisal of situations as stressful, and they are more likely to perceive themselves as able to cope. For example, taking a new job is much more threatening to a person who has no-one in whom to confide and no-one to tell her, 'Don't worry, you'll do well at it'. Another important aspect of social support is the opportunity for emotional disclosure, which, as we have seen, strengthens the immune system.

Although researchers often associate social support with the actual receipt of aid (i.e. received social support), for some individuals merely the perception that social support would be available if needed (i.e. perceived social support) is sufficient to cope with stressful life events (Cobb, 1976). In fact, sometimes the actual provision of aid can interfere with an individual's ability to cope. When Larry's father died, for example, a multitude of people descended on the family home bringing food and words of support and consolation. Although Larry knew these people meant well, and that this was just the way things were done, he wanted this time alone to grieve. Later on, of course, when the funeral was over and Larry really needed a listening ear, all of the people had returned to their own homes and were unavailable.

The flipside of social support — loneliness — is a major source of stress in humans. Loneliness takes a physiological as well as a psychological toll, leading both to increased autonomic arousal during stressful situations and slower recovery from negative emotional states (Cacioppo et al., 2000).

The relationship between social support and stress is not, however, simple or uniform. For example, stress can erode social support, leading to a vicious cycle, particularly if the person under stress responds with anger or helplessness (Lane & Hobfoll, 1992). Severely stressful life events, such as getting cancer, can also overwhelm significant others, who may withdraw because they, too, feel helpless and distressed (Bolger, Foster, Vinokur, & Ng, 1996). Further high-conflict or unsupportive relationships can actually have detrimental effects on health and psychological wellbeing (e.g. Major, Zubek, Cooper, Cozzarelli, & Richards, 1997).

APPLY + DISCUSS

People find social support important in times of sadness and grief.

- How helpful, in the long term, is such immediate social support in helping people to cope with the loss of a loved one?
- How important is it for people to take time alone to grieve?

INTERIM SUMMARY

Social support refers to the presence of others in whom a person can confide and from whom the individual can expect help and concern. In humans and other primates, lack of social support predicts disease and mortality. The buffering hypothesis proposes that social support protects people against the harmful effects of acute stress. An alternative hypothesis suggests that social support is a continuously positive force that makes the person less susceptible to stress. Social support is not, however, uniformly beneficial. Bad relationships do not promote health, and significant others often have difficulty themselves being supportive at times of crisis.

Disclosure and health

The physical and psychological benefits of having other people on whom we can rely are well known. Other people provide a listening ear and a sounding board against which we can bounce ideas and 'hear' ourselves think. People who lack social support and have no-one to whom they can express their thoughts and feelings show reduced psychological and physiological functioning (Stowell et al., 2003). They frequently ruminate about stressors they are experiencing, and they experience heightened bouts of anxiety and depression relative to people who are able to discuss their stressors with others.

Suicide involves the deliberate taking of one's life and continues to be a major health issue that touches families, friends and the community. Many factors can contribute to suicide, including mental health (e.g. depression), drugs and alcohol, family issues, employment and cultural identity, among others. Recent statistics indicate that suicide is the number one cause of death for men and women aged 15 to 34 in Australia (ABS, 2007a) and for men, it remains the leading cause of death up until age 44 (ABS, 2007a). Lifeline Australia receives from 35 to 50 suicidal calls every day to its telephone crisis service and around one call a day where there is an actual suicide in progress (Lifeline, 2009). Currently, the Australian government and local agencies are working together to develop national strategies to address the issue. Lifeline is encouraging people to share their stories on their website (www.lifeline.org.au) to enable them to identify the issues people face and thereby better support those at risk and prevent such tragic deaths (Lifeline, 2010).

One of the leading researchers in this area of emotional disclosure and health, Jamie Pennebaker, has conducted numerous fascinating studies examining the mediating role of emotional expression between experiences of stress and illness (chapter 3). For example, in one study, university students were randomly assigned to one of two conditions. Participants in the trauma group wrote for 20 minutes a day for four consecutive days about the most traumatic event of their life. Participants in the control condition wrote for the same amount of time about different topics assigned by the researcher including their plans for the rest of the day and describing what kind of shoes they were wearing (Pennebaker, Kiecolt-Glaser, & Glaser, 1988). Participants who wrote about traumatic events showed better immune functioning than participants in the non-trauma group as attested to by the fact that those in the trauma condition had significantly fewer visits to the university health centre in the six weeks following the experiment. These effects were most pronounced for participants who had never disclosed the information prior to the experiment.

In a related study, half of the participants were assigned to an experimental group where they wrote about the facts and emotions surrounding a recent romantic breakup (Lepore & Greenberg, 2002). The other half of the participants were assigned to a control group and wrote about innocuous aspects of relationships. Post-experimental comparisons of participants in the two groups revealed that those in the control group experienced significantly more upper respiratory problems, greater levels of fatigue and more intrusive thoughts than those in the experimental group. In addition, the data suggested that those participants in the experimental group were more likely to reunite with their former partner than those in the control group!

In yet another study, Pennebaker interviewed over 60 survivors of the Holocaust who had never talked with anyone about their experiences in the concentration camps. One of the things that emerged from these interviews was the painful memories and intrusive thoughts that these victims had lived with for over 40 years. Many reported remembering numerous times a day horrendous images they had witnessed during that time. In his book *Opening Up*, Pennebaker (1990) recounts one woman's intrusive memory, a memory she sees in her mind several times a day: 'They were throwing babies from the second floor window of the orphanage. I can still see the pools of blood, the screams, and the thuds of their bodies. I just stood there afraid to move. The Nazi soldiers faced us with their guns'. As in his other studies, Pennebaker found both psychological and physical benefits of disclosure among the Holocaust survivors. Over time, those who were labelled high disclosers reported improved affect and fewer illnesses than those who were labelled low disclosers (Pennebaker, Barger, & Tiebout, 1989).

Collectively, these studies highlight the role that emotional disclosure has on physical and psychological health, although the precise mechanism through which emotional expression improves health remains unclear. One possibility is that talking or writing about traumatic or troubling events allows people to cognitively process the event and, thereby, give some meaning to the event (Graybeal, Sexton, & Pennebaker, 2002; Pennebaker, 1990). Others have suggested that talking about troubling events that have produced negative affect and intrusive thoughts reduces the negativity associated with the cognitive intrusions (Lepore, 1997). Alternatively, inhibiting disclosure of traumatic events compromises immune functioning, thereby increasing an individual's susceptibility to illness. It is also possible that people may be motivated to escape the intrusive thoughts associated with inhibition, and may use alcohol or another mind-altering chemical to provide such an escape.

The future of health psychology

When you stop and think about how far the field of health psychology has come in the last 20 to 30 years, the thought is staggering, and there is no reason to think that the same level of progress will not continue in years to come. In spite of media and informational campaigns designed to alter people's negative health behaviours, people will continue to engage in behaviours that put them at risk. As the proportion of the population that constitutes the older generation continues to grow, new issues will arise that are ripe for psychological research and intervention (Siegler, Bastian, Steffans, Bosworth, & Costa, 2002).

Increasingly, the focus of health psychologists will turn to the environment as an influence on people's health behaviours, where the environment includes not only the physical environment in which people live, but also their communities, families and work and peer groups (Keefe, Buffington, Studts, & Rumble, 2002). Part of this focus will examine the effects of 'Westernisation' on the health of immigrant people. Research has consistently shown that, once groups of people live in Western cultures and assume Westernised diets and habits, their health and health habits deteriorate (Daniel, Rowley, McDermott, Mylvaganam, & O'Dea, 1999; deGonzague, Receveur, Wedll, & Kuhnlein, 1999; Eaton & Konner, 1985; Price, Charles, Pettitt, & Knowler, 1993).

Health psychologists who work in clinical settings as therapists will probably increase their attention to the involvement of family members and even peer group members in treatment of people suffering from obesity or drug addiction, for example. This emphasis will also allow psychologists to examine the co-dependent role that family members and friends may play in perpetuating health-related illness and negative health behaviours. In addition, epidemics such as SARS and the possibility of a smallpox outbreak have taken health concerns to an international level. Thus, health psychologists will increasingly be asked to become involved on an international level (Oldenburg, 2002).

Reducing health disparities both within cultures and between cultures is a major priority around the world. In spite of the fact that patterns of illness have changed markedly over the last few decades, major health problems in developing countries still centre around acute and infectious diseases (Oldenburg, 2002; WHO, 1999). 'Among children, diarrhoea, acute respiratory infections, malaria, measles and perinatal conditions account for 21 percent of all deaths in developing countries, compared to 1 percent in developed countries' (Oldenburg, 2002, p. 4). Many of the health disparities throughout the world could be eliminated if one factor were eliminated: poverty.

In 2000, all world leaders at the United Nations Millennium Summit agreed to a global action plan to eradicate extreme poverty and improve social and economic conditions in the world's poorest countries by the year 2015. The eight Millennium Development Goals (www.un.org/millenniumgoals) developed out of the United National Millennium Declaration are summarised as follows:

1. Eradicate extreme poverty and hunger.
2. Achieve universal primary education.
3. Promote gender equality and empower women.
4. Reduce child mortality rate.
5. Improve maternal health.
6. Combat HIV/AIDS, malaria, and other diseases.
7. Ensure environmental sustainability.
8. Develop a global partnership for development.

A Review Summit held in New York in 2010 reviewed progress to date, strengthening the UN's commitment to the global action plan to achieve the eight anti-poverty goals in the remaining five years. There was also a new commitment on women's and children's health and a reinforcement of the need to provide assistance to developing countries.

Technology will also help to advance the use of services provided by health psychologists and the efficiency of those services (Keefe et al., 2002). The computer is increasingly being used as a means of allowing clients to receive information about health services (e.g. pain management information) without having to visit a health clinic (Naylor, Helzer, Naud, & Keefe, 2002). Similarly, health psychologists are increasingly using the internet as a provider of information about health prevention and health promotion (Humphreys & Klaw, 2001; Woodruff, Edwards, Conway, & Elliott, 2001). Instructing people how to tease apart the medically sound advice from the myths found on the internet is another area in which health psychologists will find themselves.

The internet may also be useful as a way of reducing people's self-presentational concerns regarding health behaviours such as condom use. The ability to order condoms online as opposed to having to purchase them face-to-face may facilitate their use. Advances in virtual reality therapy are allowing patients experiencing post-traumatic stress disorder, for example, to confront fear-producing situations in a simulated real world. Virtual reality has also been used as a distraction tool for children who are undergoing painful medical procedures (Hoffman, Doctor, Patterson, Carrougher, & Furness, 2000). In a variation of virtual reality therapy, know as augmented reality, the patient experiences a virtual stressor while in a real-world setting. 'In augmented reality, a mobile patient can learn to confront the virtual world while continuing to interact with people in the real word' (Keefe et al., 2002).

As knowledge continues to advance in all areas of psychology, cross-fertilisation between health psychologists and researchers in other areas of psychology can be expected to increase. For example, health psychologists are trained by receiving a degree in clinical psychology with a health track. Many social psychologists who study topics such as attitudes, self-presentation, self-efficacy and attributions find themselves immersed in applying social psychological theories to health psychology. Health psychologists are increasingly drawing on the work of cognitive psychologists to understand the ways in which people think about events that happen to them (e.g. the development of a chronic illness). Personality psychologists and physiological psychologists have much to offer the area of health psychology, given that virtually all of the health-compromising behaviours are facilitated by particular personality traits and genetic predispositions. And the list goes on and on.

Changes in societal threats and epidemic illness threats will also necessitate increasing interventions by health psychologists. The terrorist attacks in Bali in October 2002 and London in 2006 created fears and stress among many Australians, fears that, for many, continue to this day. Helping people, particularly victims and their families, deal with the stress of those attacks and, for many, the post-traumatic stress disorder they experienced as a result, is the job of health psychologists. Similar fears arise from strange new illnesses that are arising and, in some cases, reaching epidemic proportions. 'Some 30 new diseases have cropped up since the mid-1970s — causing tens of millions of deaths — and forgotten scourges have resurfaced with alarming regularity' (Cowley, 2003). In Africa, Ebola fever is spreading; and polio has broken out in Angola (WHO, 2010g). Cases of avian influenza, or 'bird flu', have caused deaths in Asian countries where the disease has crossed over from poultry to the human population. The outbreaks prompted warnings for people not to travel to the affected countries. The SARS epidemic during the 2000s resulted in many deaths and restricted travel to many affected countries for several months (WHO, 2010h). More recently, a global pandemic of Human Swine Influenza (swine flu) resulted in more than 18 000 deaths worldwide in the year since the virus was first identified in Mexico in April 2009 (WHO, 2010f). In Australia, more than 37 500 confirmed cases of swine flu have been recorded, and almost 200 people have died from complications directly associated with the virus (Queensland Health, 2010). As more and more of these epidemics loom on the horizon, health psychologists will find themselves increasingly involved not only in trying to uncover the aetiology of these diseases, but also in helping people deal with their fears of the illnesses and cope with the consequences should they contract one of these illnesses.

INTERIM SUMMARY

Emotional disclosure plays a key role in physical and psychological health, although the precise mechanism through which emotional expression improves health remains unclear. Health psychology will continue to progress in the years to come. Health psychologists will probably persist with the promotion of positive health behaviours and help people to cope better with the consequences of ill health and other health-compromising behaviours.

Central questions revisited

◆ Promoting good health

We began with three central questions about health psychology. First, we discussed the issue of health-compromising behaviours. Most smokers are well aware that cigarettes kill, yet they continue to light up. Why do people engage in behaviours such as smoking, drinking and over-eating that they know will compromise their health? Image can be a major factor. Most people are quite concerned about what others think of them and modify their behaviours to create an impression they think will be favourable.

A second issue concerned the barriers to health promotion and preventive health. It is also useful to categorise the reasons for indulging in health-threatening behaviours in terms of the barriers people face: individual barriers (bad health behaviours might be more enjoyable than positive health behaviours), family barriers (children model the health behaviour of parents and siblings), health system barriers (doctors treat illness, not poor health practices) and community barriers (norms of the community in which they live, work and play). These barriers can be overcome, but one aspect of life that cannot be avoided is stress.

That leads to the issue of what causes stress and how people cope with stress. People experience stress when they are unable to adapt to a number of different challenges facing them. Stressors can be the irritating and frustrating demands of everyday life (such as juggling full-time work with part-time study), or major life events such as bereavements or divorce. Stressful events can have a substantial impact on psychological wellbeing, can decrease the body's capacity to fight illness, and can instigate behaviours that weaken the body's defences — people under stress tend to drink more alcohol, smoke more, sleep less and exercise less than their peers. While we cannot avoid stress, we do develop coping mechanisms to help deal with it. For example, exercise can reduce the impact of stress on health. When particularly stressful events occur, social support can help protect people against their potentially harmful effects. For this reason, health psychologists will often involve family members and significant others in their treatment of people with negative health behaviours.

SUMMARY

1 Theories of health behaviour

- ***Health psychology*** examines the biological, psychological and social influences on how people stay healthy, why they become ill and how they respond when they do get ill.
- Although the field has taken off only in the last two decades, it has a rich heritage in the fields of medicine and philosophy. This history began with the early theorists and the practice of ***trephination***, continued through the ***humoural theory of illness***, and the Renaissance, and received one of its major boosts from Freud and the field of ***psychosomatic medicine***.
- A number of theories have been created to explain why people engage in positive or negative health habits. Among the most prominent of these are the ***health belief model***, the ***protection motivation theory of health***, the ***theory of reasoned action*** and the ***theory of planned behaviour***.
- ***Obesity*** is second only to nicotine as the primary health threat. Assessments using body mass index indicate that over half of Australians are overweight or obese. Obesity extracts a sizable physical and psychological toll and it does not have a quick fix. The origins of obesity lie in both genetic and environmental influences.
- Cigarette smoking is the most preventable cause of illness today. As with obesity, underlying causes are both genetic (e.g. personality variables) and environmental, although the emphasis is on environmental facilitators of smoking.
- ***Alcoholism*** and ***problem drinking*** are major problems in society today. A number of genetic and environmental variables contribute to the development of alcohol abuse. Some alcoholics enter ***spontaneous remission*** whereas others require more formalised methods of treatment, such as ***aversion therapy***.
- Over 20 sexually transmitted diseases have been identified, most notably HIV/AIDS. Given that behaviour is clearly involved in the transmission of STDs, they are a frequent focus area for health psychologists.

2 Barriers to health promotion and preventative health

- Four broad barriers to health promotion have been identified: individual barriers, family barriers, health system barriers and community barriers.
- People do and do not do a lot of health-related behaviours because of concerns with the impressions other people are forming of them, a process termed ***self-presentation***. Most people who do not wear condoms, who tan excessively and who use alcohol or other drugs, do so, in part, for self-presentational reasons.

3 Stress

- ***Stress*** refers to a challenge to a person's capacity to adapt to inner and outer demands, which may be physiologically arousing and emotionally taxing and call for cognitive and behavioural responses. Stress is a psychobiological process that entails a transaction between a person and her environment. Selye proposed that the body responds to stressful conditions with a ***general adaptation syndrome*** consisting of three stages: alarm, resistance and exhaustion.
- From a psychological standpoint, stress entails a person's perception that demands of the environment tax or exceed his available psychosocial resources. Stress, in this view, depends on the meaning of an event to the individual. Lazarus' model identifies two stages in the process of stress and coping: ***primary appraisal***, in which the person decides whether the situation is benign, stressful or irrelevant; and ***secondary appraisal***, in which the person evaluates the options and decides how to respond.
- Events that often lead to stress are called ***stressors***. Stressors include life events, catastrophes and daily hassles.

4 Stress and health

- Stress has a considerable impact on health and mortality, particularly through its effects on the ***immune system***. Whether a person under stress remains healthy or becomes ill also depends in part on the person's enduring personality dispositions. ***Type A behaviour pattern***, and particularly its hostility component, has been linked to heart disease. Neuroticism (the tendency to experience negative affective states) and optimism/pessimism are other personality traits linked to stress and health.

5 Coping with stress

- The ways people deal with stressful situations are known as strategies for ***coping***; these ***coping mechanisms*** are in part culturally patterned. People cope by trying to change the situation directly, changing their perception of it or changing the emotions it elicits.
- A major resource for coping with stress is ***social support***, which is related to health and mortality.

KEY TERMS

REVIEW QUESTIONS

1. Describe the role of the psychologist in understanding health and illness.
2. Describe the major barriers to health promotion.
3. Define stress as a psychobiological process, outlining the three stages in Selye's general adaptation syndrome.
4. Distinguish between primary appraisal and secondary appraisal in Lazarus' transactional model of stress and coping.
5. Differentiate between Type A behaviour pattern and Type B behaviour pattern.
6. Compare optimistic and pessimistic personality dimensions and describe their relationship to immune functioning and health.

DISCUSSION QUESTIONS

1. What environmental factors contribute to obesity?
2. Why do daily hassles contribute to stress?
3. How can we better cope with stress?

APPLICATION QUESTIONS

1. Test your understanding of health by identifying each of the following scenarios as an example of one of the following theories of health behaviour: health belief model, protection motivation theory of health, theory of reasoned action or theory of planned behaviour.
   (a) Ellen loves to play outdoor sports, but is very aware of the harmful effects of too much sun exposure — her sister Nicola had a melanoma removed from her face. Since this time, Ellen has strongly endorsed a more sun-safe attitude, knowing it could mean the difference between life and death. Each morning, she applies 40-plus sunscreen to her skin, and she never plays outdoors without a protective hat and clothing.
   (b) Voula and Maria are sisters who have a history of breast cancer in their family. They both undergo regular self-examinations and they sometimes book themselves in for mammograms and clinical breast examinations. The sisters provide moral support for each other, knowing that early detection is the best precaution.
   (c) Desmond's father recently died from cirrhosis of the liver after years of drinking alcohol. Desmond also likes a social drink and, since his father's death, he believes that if he continues to drink regularly he, too, is likely to develop cirrhosis of the liver or some other damage to the liver. Desmond therefore decides to cut down on his drinking, consuming no more than three alcoholic drinks at a time in the first month after his father's death. However, within six months, Desmond has reverted to his old habits, drinking alcohol every day of the week.
   (d) Abdul has smoked at least one packet of cigarettes per day for more than twenty years. He likes to smoke whenever he is socialising with friends, and will often light a cigarette while he is chatting on the phone. In recent months, however, he has suffered from continual sore throats, head colds and chesty coughs. His doctor informs him that he will develop lung cancer and emphysema if he does not give up smoking. He knows that he needs to make some lifestyle changes, deciding to cut back his smoking to no more than 10 cigarettes per day in the first six months. He is determined to succeed and believes he can quit smoking within a year and thus increase his chances of a long and healthy life.
2. Test your understanding of coping by identifying each of the following scenarios as an example of one of the following strategies for coping with stress: problem-focused, emotion-focused or social support.
   (a) Dusan normally likes to take the stairs, but decides to take the lift one morning because he is running late for a meeting. The lift becomes jammed and he is stuck in the lift for almost an hour while the mechanical problem is repaired. While in the lift, he focuses on remaining as calm as possible. He makes use of his spare time by working on the papers he was carrying to the meeting.
   (b) Helen's mother passed away last week and her friend, Kyoko, is trying to cheer her up and help her stop feeling so depressed. Helen is very grateful to have such a close friend to help her through this difficult time.
   (c) Bill is an elderly man who lives alone. He needs to choose a specialist for a serious knee operation and so he seeks and studies information about different orthopaedic surgeons prior to making his decision.

The solutions to the application questions can be found on page 835.

MULTIMEDIA RESOURCES

The *Cyberpsych* multimedia resource is available *as an option* to accompany this textbook to further develop your understanding of many key psychology concepts. *Cyberpsych* contains a wealth of rich media content and activities, and for this chapter includes:

- video clips on brain protein, older women and exercise, smoking and pregnancy, quitting smoking, stress and the brain, and having a stronger brain
- video case studies on stress and teenage alcohol use
- a concept animation on the body's stress-response mechanisms.

Psychological disorders

15

LEARNING OBJECTIVES

After studying this chapter you should be able to:

1 define psychopathology

2 explain the cultural context of psychopathology

3 define mental health, mental health problems and mental disorders

4 differentiate between the contemporary approaches to psychopathology

5 understand the classification and diagnostic categories outlined in the latest edition of the DSM

6 outline the key symptoms of some of the major psychopathological syndromes.

The cultural context of psychopathology

- *Psychopathology* refers to problematic patterns of thought, feeling or behaviour that disrupt an individual's sense of wellbeing or social or occupational functioning.
- Many forms of psychopathology are found across cultures; however, cultures differ in the disorders to which their members are vulnerable and the ways they categorise mental illness.

Contemporary approaches to psychopathology

- ***Psychodynamic*** theorists distinguish between three broad classes of psychopathology that form a continuum of functioning: ***neuroses*** (enduring problems in living that cause distress or dysfunction), ***personality disorders*** (chronic, severe disturbances that substantially inhibit the capacity to love and to work), and ***psychoses*** (gross disturbances involving a loss of touch with reality).
- ***Cognitive–behavioural*** clinicians integrate an understanding of classical and operant conditioning with a cognitive-social perspective.
- The ***biological*** approach looks for the roots of mental disorders in the brain's circuitry, such as neurotransmitter dysfunction, abnormalities of specific brain structures or dysfunction anywhere along a pathway that regulates behaviour or mental processes.
- A ***systems*** approach explains an individual's behaviour in the context of a social group, such as a couple, family or larger group.
- ***Evolutionary*** psychologists could explain psychopathology in at least three ways:

  (a) as random variation likely to be weeded out by natural selection
  (b) as the result of broader population pressures that select rates of genes in the population that can be either functional or dysfunctional depending on the other genes an individual inherits
  (c) as the maladaptive environmental 'tuning' of psychological mechanisms that are normally adaptive.

Mental health and mental disorders

- ***Mental health*** is the capacity of individuals to behave in ways that promote their emotional and social wellbeing.
- A ***mental disorder*** implies the existence of a clinically recognisable set of symptoms and behaviours that cause distress to the individual and impair their ability to function as usual.

Descriptive diagnosis and psychopathological syndromes

- A fifth edition of the ***Diagnostic and Statistical Manual of Mental Disorders (DSM-5)*** is due for completion in 2013, with major changes expected to the classification system and diagnostic categories, including fewer axes. It is anticipated that the DSM-5 classifications will be closely aligned to the International Classification of Disease (ICD-10) system endorsed by the World Health Organization (WHO).
- ***DSM-IV*** uses a multiaxial system, placing symptoms in their biological and social context by evaluating patients along five axes: clinical syndromes, personality disorders (and intellectual disability), medical conditions, environmental stressors and global level of functioning.
- Disorders usually first diagnosed in infancy, childhood or adolescence include ***attention-deficit hyperactivity disorder (ADHD)*** and ***conduct disorder***.
- ***Substance-related disorders*** are characterised by continued use of a substance (such as alcohol or cocaine) that negatively affects psychological and social functioning.
- ***Schizophrenia*** is an umbrella term for a number of psychotic disorders that involve disturbances in thought, perception, behaviour, language, communication and emotion.
- ***Mood disorders***, including depression, ***dysthymic disorder*** and ***bipolar disorder***, are characterised by disturbances in emotion and mood, including both depressed and manic states. ***Seasonal affective disorder*** depicts seasonal mood and behavioural changes.
- In ***anxiety disorders***, people experience frequent, intense and irrational anxiety. Examples include ***generalised anxiety disorder***, ***phobia***, ***panic disorder***, ***agoraphobia***, ***obsessive–compulsive disorder*** and ***post-traumatic stress disorder***.

- Eating disorders include ***anorexia nervosa*** and ***bulimia nervosa***.
- ***Dissociative disorders*** are characterised by disruptions in consciousness, memory, sense of identity or perception. In ***dissociative identity disorder***, at least two distinct personalities exist within the person.
- ***Somatoform disorders*** occur when people complain of pain, suffering or illness but no physical problems can be identified to explain their ailments. Examples include ***conversion disorder*** and ***hypochondriasis***.
- ***Personality disorders*** are characterised by enduring maladaptive patterns of thought, feeling and behaviour that lead to chronic disturbances in interpersonal and occupational functioning. Examples include ***borderline personality disorder*** and ***antisocial personality disorder***.
- Although the DSM-IV is often used to describe specific syndromes, most practising clinicians and many researchers question whether psychopathology can be so neatly categorised.

Central questions: when nurture becomes nature

◆ Distinguishing the roles of nature and nurture in the aetiology of psychological disturbance is more difficult than it may first appear. Inherited characteristics typically determine which environmental events are psychologically toxic, and environmental events can translate into changes in the brain.

THE human mind is an amazingly powerful instrument, but there are times when the mind does not quite work as it should. Take the case of Esther McKay, who worked for 15 years as a forensic investigator with the New South Wales police force. She took on the role, aged 23, with little training and support. Esther would be called to serious crime scenes to record what had taken place. This involved witnessing horrific damage at car accidents, murders and suicides, and then often having to relive the experience when giving evidence in court.

As she gained more experience and skills in forensics, Esther also noticed herself changing. She lost her sense of humour; her first marriage broke up; she had trouble sleeping at night; she turned to alcohol; and she developed a phobia of the telephone (Fawcett, 2005). After becoming a mother, she had particular problems coping after attending crime scenes that involved children being killed or injured.

Esther had a breakdown ten years after first noticing symptoms of mental fragility, and she was medically discharged from the police force in 2001. She sought treatment for her condition and was diagnosed with post-traumatic stress disorder (PTSD).

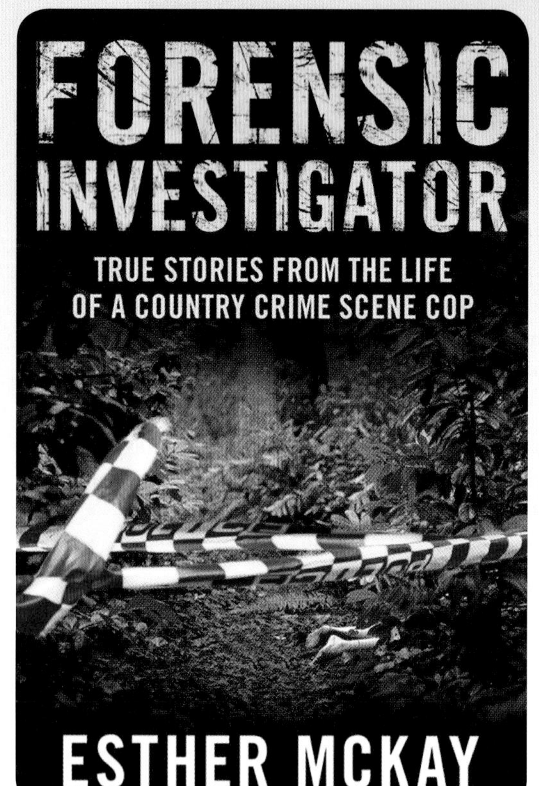

Esther says the condition will always be with her, but she now understands it much better. 'I can see how it happens. A lot of police, for example, don't want to tell their spouse what they've been through when they come home from work. So they have a few drinks, maybe a few too many, and everything simmers away. That's why they call PTSD the speechless terror — people really can't talk about it, and their families really go through hell' (Fawcett, 2005).

Esther has found another outlet for her experiences. She is now a successful author, with her first book, *Crime Scene: True Stories from the Life of a Forensic Investigator,* released in 2005. It was followed by a second book, titled *Forensic Investigator: True Stories from the Life of a Country Crime Scene Cop.*

What is interesting to consider about Esther's case, and the experiences of the other police officers she writes about, is the different ways that they cope with the terrible scenes they have to witness. Why did Esther have such a debilitating reaction? Was there something about her that made her more prone to a breakdown? How do other forensic investigators and police officers cope with witnessing the same sort of horrible incidents without also suffering breakdowns? Did she have a genetic history that made her more predisposed to PTSD? Did she simply witness events that were much more horrific than those that other forensic officers deal with? Or, was it a combination of these factors that triggered her reaction?

In this chapter, we examine ***psychopathology*** (literally, sickness, or pathology, of the mind), or problematic patterns of thought, feeling or behaviour that disrupt an individual's sense of wellbeing or social or occupational functioning. We begin by discussing the cultural context of psychopathology, considering how people like Esther become classified as normal or disordered. Next we examine the differing theoretical viewpoints on psychopathology. Then, in the bulk of the chapter, we turn to a description of the nature and causes of the major forms of psychopathology. Throughout, one key question surfaces. Why do people fall ill psychologically? What are the relative roles of nature and nurture in generating psychological disturbances?

- What are the relative roles of nature and nurture in psychopathology?

The cultural context of psychopathology

Every society has its concept of 'madness', and what a society considers normal or abnormal is constantly changing. The kind of competitive, every-person-for-himself stance taken for granted in many large cities would have been a sign of bad character — or in today's language, personality pathology — by the rural grandparents of many contemporary city-dwellers (and by the vast majority of cultures in human history). Some of the psychopathological syndromes clinicians encounter today were identified and classified as early as 2500 BC by the ancient Sumerians and Egyptians. Over the centuries, Western culture has attributed mental illness to a variety of causes, such as demon possession, supernatural forces, witches and Satan. To what extent does culture shape and define mental illness? And are diagnoses anything but labels a culture uses to brand its deviants?

Culture and psychopathology

Cultures differ both in the disorders they spawn and the ways they categorise mental illness (Brown, 2001; Guarnaccia & Rogler, 1999; Miranda & Fraser, 2002; Sue & Chu, 2003). Prevalence rates (i.e. the percentage of a population with a disorder) vary considerably both across and within cultures. So, too, do the ways people express symptoms of the same disorder (Fabrega, 1994). In rural Ireland, which is almost uniformly Catholic, people with schizophrenia are more likely than other Westerners with the same disorder to have religious delusions, such as the conviction that their body has become inhabited by the Virgin Mary (Scheper-Hughes, 1979).

Cultures also differ on what they consider pathological and how they classify it. For example, one Alaskan Inuit group's concept of 'crazy' includes elements similar to our own, such as talking to oneself or screaming at people who do not exist. However, their definition of severe mental illness also includes some symptoms unusual in Australia, such as believing that a loved one was murdered by witchcraft when no-one else thought so, drinking urine and killing dogs (Murphy, 1976). When European settlers arrived to colonise Australia, they did not recognise examples of people suffering from what they classified as 'insanity' among the Aboriginal population. That is, to them 'madness' involved an illness or disorder in a person's mind, which required certain treatments. The reason for the lack of recognition among Aboriginal communities lay in the spiritual beliefs that underpinned those societies. In these cultures, there was no equivalent to the European concept of insanity. Erratic behaviour was thought to be caused by external factors such as magic from other tribes or evil spirits, rather than by a deficiency in the individual.

APPLY + DISCUSS

Traditional Aboriginal societies are deeply spiritual and believe in both good and bad magic. One of the best-known applications of bad magic in these societies was the ritual 'pointing of the bone'. Aboriginal sorcerers would place a curse on people by pointing a bone at them, and channelling evil spirits through to the recipient. A person who had the bone pointed at them should — and many actually did dic.

- Can clinicians treat or diagnose patients without understanding — or sharing — their cultural backgrounds?
- If an Aboriginal person claimed to have had the bone pointed at them and to be cursed, how could a psychologist distinguish this mental state from a genuine mental disorder?

Is mental illness nothing but a cultural construction?

If definitions of abnormality vary across cultures, can we really speak of mental illness at all? Or, as argued by some prominent researchers and social critics in the 1960s and 1970s, is mental illness simply a construct used by a society to brand and punish those who fail to respect its norms? For example, psychiatrist Thomas Szasz, who wrote a popular book called *The Myth of Mental Illness* (Szasz, 1974), proposed that mental illness is a myth used to make people conform to society's standards of normality. In his view, which was highly influential in changing laws for commitment to mental institutions, people should be treated for mental illness only if they consider their symptoms a problem.

A variation of this view, called ***labelling theory***, similarly argued that diagnosis is a way of stigmatising individuals a society considers deviant (Scheff, 1970). Labelling can be dangerous because it turns people into 'patients', whose subsequent actions are interpreted as part of their 'craziness' and who may face discrimination based on their diagnoses. Labelled individuals may also take on the role of a sick or crazy person and hence actually begin to play the part into which they have been cast — a phenomenon known as a self-fulfilling prophecy (chapter 17).

A case of misdiagnosis?

A classic study raised some of these issues in a dramatic way. Rosenhan (1973) had himself and seven other normal people around the United States admitted to psychiatric hospitals by faking symptoms of schizophrenia, complaining of hearing voices that said 'empty', 'hollow' or 'thud'. All but one of these 'pseudopatients' were subsequently diagnosed with schizophrenia. Once on the psychiatric wards, however, the pseudopatients behaved as they normally would and told staff they no longer heard voices. Psychiatric staff nonetheless interpreted their behaviour as evidence of disturbance. For example, when the pseudopatients took copious notes while on the unit, hospital personnel commented in their psychiatric records about their 'peculiar note-taking behaviour'. When they were finally discharged, which took an average of 19 days, almost all were given the label 'schizophrenia, in remission'. Rosenhan's study set off a wave of controversy, for it appeared to demonstrate that psychiatric illness is in the eye of the beholder and that even trained eyes are not very acute.

Critics argued, however, that the study led to some very dramatic but largely incorrect conclusions (see Spitzer, 1985). Behaviour is meaningful only when it is understood in context. Singing is normal in a chorus but would be very peculiar during a lecture. Similarly, taking notes does appear abnormal for a patient in a psychiatric hospital who has complained of hallucinations. Had the pseudopatients not lied about their initial symptoms, this would have been an appropriate inference. Furthermore, in medical terminology 'in remission' means simply that a patient has previously reported symptoms that are no longer present. One critic concluded that the study did little more than illustrate that people can fool a clinician if they try hard enough (Spitzer, 1985), just as they can trick a neurologist by complaining of all the symptoms of stroke, or a potential employer by creating a false resume.

The myth of the myth of mental illness

Although labelling theory clearly has grains of truth, its claims have not held up well over time. First, many disorders (such as depression and schizophrenia) are recognised cross-culturally — a suggestion of some universality to their occurrence (Sam & Moreira, 2002). Second, although the negative consequences of labelling can indeed be profound, psychologists could neither treat nor research a problem without trying to distinguish those who have it from those who do not. Classification has its pitfalls, particularly when a category is socially undesirable (such as a mental illness) (chapters 8 and 17), but that does not free us from the need to categorise. Third, as described later in this chapter, an accumulating body of evidence suggests that schizophrenia is an illness of the brain, much like Alzheimer's disease, which no one would similarly describe as an 'alternative way of seeing the world'. Finally, the notion of the noble schizophrenic being branded as crazy by a conformist society tends to romanticise mental illness. No-one in his 'right mind' would really want to take on the problems that accompany schizophrenia, such as the inability to trust one's own thoughts and the profound sense of isolation that arises from chronically misunderstanding others and feeling misunderstood.

INTERIM SUMMARY

Psychopathology refers to problematic patterns of thought, feeling or behaviour that disrupt an individual's sense of wellbeing or social or occupational functioning. Many forms of psychopathology are found across cultures; however, cultures differ in the disorders to which their members are vulnerable and the ways they categorise mental illness. One view sees mental illness as a myth used to make people conform to society's standards of normality; ***labelling theory*** similarly argues that diagnosis is a way of stigmatising deviants. Both approaches have some validity but understate the realities of mental illness.

Mental health and mental disorders

What do we mean when we talk about mental health, mental health problems and mental disorders? ***Mental health*** can be thought of as a state of emotional and social wellbeing in which individuals realise their own abilities, can cope with the normal stresses of life, can work productively and can contribute to their community (Australian Institute of Health and Welfare [AIHW], 2007b; WHO, 1998, 2010e).

Mental health problems include the wide range of emotional and behavioural abnormalities that affect people throughout their lives. The spectrum covers cognitive impairment and disabilities, phobias, panic attacks, drug-related harm, anxiety, personality disorders, depressive disorders and psychoses (AIHW, 2007b). A ***mental disorder***, however, implies the existence of a clinically recognisable set of symptoms and behaviours, which usually need treatments (including hospitalisation at times) to be alleviated (WHO, 2010b). A mental disorder can be considered as a serious departure from normal functioning — behaviour that causes distress to the individual and impairs their ability to function as usual (AIHW, 2007b, 2007f). While the two concepts overlap, a mental disorder can be distinguished from a mental health problem by the severity of its impacts. World Mental Health Day is now held annually on 10 October, to raise public awareness about mental health issues and promote open discussion of mental disorders (WHO, 2010d).

In Australia, almost half the population will have a mental disorder at some point in their life (Australian Government Department of Health and Ageing, 2009f). More than three million adults (about one in five) have experienced a mental disorder — most commonly anxiety or mood disorders — within the previous year (DHA, 2009). However, the prevalence of mental disorders varies across population groups. Groups considered at high risk of developing mental health problems or needing special mental health treatments in Australia are children and adolescents, older people, Aboriginal and Torres Strait Islander peoples, rural and remote populations, and people from culturally and linguistically diverse backgrounds (AIHW, 2010). For example, suicide rates in rural and remote centres are significantly higher than in capital cities (Strong, Trickett, Titulaer, & Bhatia, 1998; see also ABS, 2007d). The Aboriginal population suffers from high incarceration rates and entry into the criminal and juvenile justice system, creating issues for mental health and treatment. And about one in five children and adolescents in Australia suffer from a mental health problem or disorder within any six-month period (Zubrick, Silburn, & Garton, 1995; see also ABS, 2007d; AIHW, 2007f).

In New Zealand, the 2003–04 New Zealand Mental Health Survey of people aged 16 years or over was the first of its kind to measure the prevalence of mental disorders in different ethnic groups, including the Maori and the Pacific people (Baxter, Kokaua, Wells, & McGee, 2006). According to the Census, the majority of the New Zealand population are of European ethnicity (almost 72 percent). The Indigenous people of New Zealand, the Maori, make up 15 percent of the population, 6 percent identify as Pacific people and Asian groups comprise 7 percent. Baxter et al. (2006) found that the Maori (29.5 percent), and to a lesser extent the Pacific people (24.4 percent), have had a higher prevalence of mental disorders in the past 12 months than have people of European or Asian descent (19.3 percent). An earlier multidisciplinary health and development study found that up to one-quarter of Dunedin children may have experienced a significant mental health problem between three years of age and adolescence (McGee, Feehan, & Williams, 1996). Indigenous people of New Zealand are also less likely than other non-Indigenous groups to have contact with health services (Baxter et al., 2006). Such findings highlight the need to address ethnic disparities and increase access to and use of mental health services by the Maori and the Pacific people.

As of 1 November 2006, the Australian government introduced new Medicare items for treatment by registered psychologists to enhance access for people living with mental health problems (APS, 2006b; chapter 1). The initial take-up of these services was immense, with more than 1000 therapy sessions being provided by clinical psychologists and about 5500 psychological strategy services being provided by psychologists and other allied health professionals during the first month of the scheme (Franklin, 2007). In 2007–08, almost four million Medicare-subsidised mental health services were provided under this new scheme (ABS, 2010f). These figures indicate that many Australians are now receiving much-needed psychological help for mental health issues.

INTERIM SUMMARY

Mental health is the capacity of individuals to behave in ways that promote their emotional and social wellbeing. ***Mental health problems*** include the wide range of emotional and behavioural abnormalities that affect people throughout their lives. A ***mental disorder*** implies the existence of a clinically recognisable set of symptoms and behaviours that cause distress to the individual and impair their ability to function as usual.

Contemporary approaches to psychopathology

Although few contemporary psychologists view mental illness as a myth (or ascribe its causes to demon possession), they differ considerably in the way they conceptualise the nature and causes of psychological disorders. More recent research suggests that psychopathology is best understood by considering both social motivations and emotions together with social cognition (see Fitness & Case, 2003; chapter 13).

Consider the case of Charlie, a 24-year-old business student with an intense fear of being in groups. Whenever Charlie is at a party, he feels tremendously anxious, avoids making conversation with others and usually ends up leaving shortly after he arrives. In class and in social engagements, he worries that people will laugh at and ostracise him. His mouth becomes dry, his hands become clammy and his stomach knots. Charlie reports that his problem has intensified since he began his university studies. Paradoxically, he feels most anxious when he should feel most confident, as when he has expertise in the topic being discussed. He notes that his father, who never attended university, ridiculed him for his decision to enter postgraduate study ('Why don't you go out and get yourself a job?').

The way different psychologists would understand Charlie's anxiety depends on their theoretical orientation. We first examine psychodynamic and cognitive–behavioural perspectives. Next we consider two very different approaches — biological and systems theories — and then consider what evolutionary theory has to offer to the understanding of psychopathology.

Psychodynamic perspective

Psychodynamic theorists distinguish three broad classes of psychopathology that form a continuum of functioning, from the least to the most disturbed: neuroses, personality disorders and psychoses (figure 15.1). ***Neuroses*** are problems in living, such as phobias, constant self-doubt and repetitive interpersonal problems such as trouble with authority figures. Neurotic problems occur in most, if not all, people at different points in their lives and usually do not stop them from functioning reasonably well. ***Personality disorders*** are characterised by enduring maladaptive patterns of thought, feeling and behaviour that lead to chronic disturbances in interpersonal and occupational functioning.

	Capacities		
Level of disturbance	**Love**	**Work**	**Relation to reality**
Normal to neurotic	Able to maintain relationships May have minor difficulties such as conflicts with significant others or a tendency to be competitive	Able to maintain employment May have difficulties such as rigidity, defensiveness, underconfidence, workaholism, overambition or underachievement	Able to see reality clearly May have minor defensive distortions, such as seeing the self and significant others as better or worse than they really are
Personality disordered	Unable to maintain relationships consistently May avoid relationships, jump into them too quickly or end them abruptly	Difficulty maintaining employment May be grossly underemployed, unable to get along with bosses or likely to terminate employment abruptly	Prone to gross misinterpretations in interpersonal affairs May have chronically idiosyncratic thinking that does not reach psychotic levels
Psychotic	Tremendous difficulty maintaining relationships May be socially peculiar	Unable to maintain employment anywhere near intellectual level Large percentage are chronically unemployed	Unable to distinguish clearly between what is real and what is not Has delusions, hallucinations or other psychotic thought processes

FIGURE 15.1
Continuum of psychopathology. Psychodynamic theorists place disorders on a continuum of functioning, reflecting the maturity and strength of the person's underlying personality structure.

People with personality disorders often have difficulty maintaining meaningful relationships and employment, interpret interpersonal events in highly distorted ways, and may be chronically vulnerable to depression and anxiety. ***Psychoses*** are gross disturbances involving a loss of touch with reality. A person who is psychotic may hear voices telling him to kill himself or believe (without good reason) that the secret service is trying to assassinate him. Neurotic symptoms (such as phobias) may occur in more severely disturbed individuals, and psychotic states can occur episodically (i.e. periodically, in discrete episodes) in people who are otherwise relatively healthy. Many people with bipolar disorder (manic depression), for example, are largely unimpaired between episodes.

According to psychodynamic theorists (e.g. Kernberg, 1984), these three levels of pathology also lie on a continuum with respect to ***aetiology*** (origins of psychological disorders and/or physiological disturbances). Psychoses result primarily from biological abnormalities, with some environmental input. Neuroses and personality disorders stem more from environmental (particularly childhood) experiences, often interacting with biological vulnerabilities (figure 15.2).

To assess psychopathology, a psychodynamic psychologist gathers information about the patient's current level of functioning and life stress, the origins and course of the symptom and salient events in the person's developmental history. The clinician uses all of this information to make a ***psychodynamic formulation***, a set of hypotheses about the patient's personality structure and the meaning of the symptom. This formulation attempts to answer three questions: What does the patient wish for and fear? What psychological resources does the person have at his disposal? And how does he experience himself and others (Westen, 1998; see also Ivey, 2006)?

The first question focuses on the person's dominant motives and conflicts. Psychodynamic clinicians view many neurotic symptoms as expressions of, or compromises among, various motives. In this view, symptoms reflect unconscious conflicts among wishes and fears and efforts to resolve them. Symptoms may also result from beliefs, often forged in childhood (such as the belief that anger is 'wrong'), which lead to conflicts and defences (such as efforts to avoid feeling or acknowledging anger). For example, a psychodynamic clinician might hypothesise that Charlie's symptoms reflect a conflict over success, because his anxiety is strongest when he is in a position to shine and increases as he gets closer to achieving his goals. Charlie wants to be successful and display his abilities, but this desire evokes ridicule by his father (and, we might suspect, an internalised critic who may beat his father to the punch). Charlie might also unconsciously equate success with outdoing his father, who had minimal education, leading to anxiety or guilt.

The second question is about ego functioning – the person's ability to function autonomously, make sound decisions, think clearly and regulate impulses and emotions (see Bellack, Hurvich, & Geldman, 1973; see also Peebles-Kleiger, 2002). A psychodynamic psychologist would want to assess whether Charlie's ability to function and adapt to the environment is impaired in other ways or whether his social phobia is a relatively isolated symptom. For example, is he generally fearful and inhibited? Does he turn to dysfunctional behaviours such as drinking to alleviate his anxiety? Is he able to reflect on his fears and recognise them as irrational?

The third question addresses object relations (chapter 11); that is, the person's ability to form meaningful relationships with others and to maintain self-esteem. Are Charlie's interpersonal problems specific to groups or are they part of a more serious underlying difficulty in forming and maintaining relationships (attachment and object relations)? For example, is he able to develop enduring friendships and love relationships, or are his interpersonal fears so pervasive that he has been unable to form meaningful relationships by his mid-twenties?

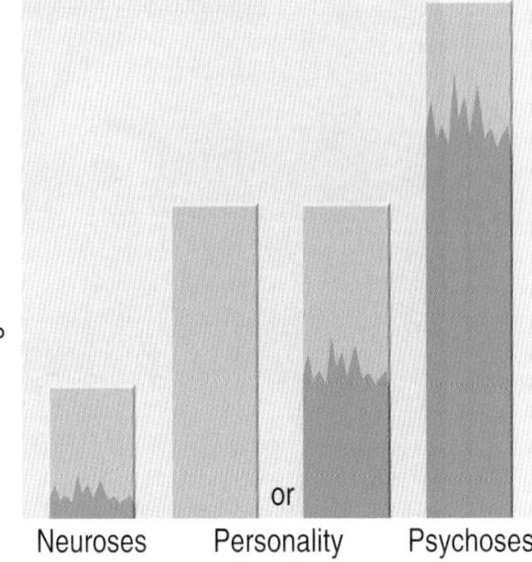

FIGURE 15.2
Heredity and experience in psychopathology. From a psychodynamic point of view, neuroses are often primarily environmental in origin, although they may reflect genetic vulnerabilities. Personality disorders stem either from extreme childhood experiences or from an interaction of genetic and environmental vulnerabilities. Psychoses are primarily genetic in origin, although childhood and adult experiences shape their expression.

INTERIM SUMMARY

Psychodynamic theorists distinguish between three broad classes of psychopathology that form a continuum of functioning: ***neuroses*** (enduring problems in living that cause distress or dysfunction), ***personality disorders*** (chronic, severe disturbances that substantially inhibit the capacity to love and to work) and ***psychoses*** (gross disturbances involving a loss of touch with reality). A ***psychodynamic formulation*** is a set of hypotheses about the patient's personality structure and the meaning of the symptom. It focuses on the person's motives and conflicts, adaptive functioning and ability to form meaningful relationships and maintain self-esteem.

Cognitive-behavioural perspective

In clinical psychology, many practitioners consider themselves ***cognitive–behavioural***, integrating an understanding of classical and operant conditioning with a cognitive–social perspective (Roth & Fonagy, 2005). They focus not on a hypothesised underlying personality structure but on discrete processes, such as thoughts that precede an anxiety reaction or physiological symptoms (e.g. racing heart) that accompany it. From a more behavioural perspective, many of the problems that require treatment involve conditioned emotional responses (chapter 6), in which a previously neutral stimulus has become associated with an emotionally arousing stimulus. For example, a person like Charlie might have had bad experiences in school when he spoke and thus came to associate speaking in groups with anxiety. This anxiety might then have generalised to other group situations. Making matters worse, his fear of groups could then lead to his avoiding them, resulting not only in continued social anxiety but also in poor social skills.

A behaviourally oriented clinician carefully assesses the conditions under which symptoms such as depression and anxiety arise and tries to discover the stimuli that elicit them. What stimuli have become associated with depressed or anxious feelings through classical conditioning? What behaviours is the person engaging in that increase negative emotions, such as negative interactions with a spouse (see Gottman, 1998)? Under what circumstances does the individual become so distressed that she becomes suicidal or tries to hurt herself as a way of controlling the feeling (Linehan, 1993)?

From a more cognitive perspective, psychopathology reflects dysfunctional cognitions, such as low self-efficacy expectancies (chapter 6 and 11), a tendency to believe that situations are hopeless and negative views of the self (Alloy et al., 2000; Beck, 1976; Clark, Beck, & Alford, 1999; Ellis, 2002a, 2002b; Longmore & Worrell, 2007). The clinician thus focuses on irrational beliefs and maladaptive cognitive processes that maintain dysfunctional behaviours and emotions.

APPLY + DISCUSS

- How might a cognitive–behavioural psychologist explain why a teenager has a drug or alcohol problem? What kind of environmental consequences and beliefs might maintain the tendency to abuse substances?
- How might a psychodynamic psychologist explain why a teenager develops a drug or alcohol problem? What kinds of personality might predispose an adolescent to have drug problems?

For example, a number of studies show that patients with different kinds of disorders show attentional biases that may perpetuate their psychopathology (Gilboa & Gotlib, 1997; Lundh, Wikstrom, Westerlund, & Ost, 1999; see also Casey, Newcombe, & Oei, 2005). Depressed people tend to be 'on the lookout' for negative information about themselves. When asked to report the colour in which a set of words is printed (and to ignore the words), they are slowed down by words like 'sad', 'weak' and 'loser', which automatically grab their attention. Patients with anxiety disorders tend to notice potentially threatening stimuli that would not catch other people's attention and to interpret ambiguous information in a threatening way (such as a random comment by a friend that could be interpreted as subtle rejection). People with personality disorders tend to be particularly attuned to threatening interpersonal events, such as ridicule or abandonment (see Korfine & Hooley, 2000).

From a behavioural point of view, Charlie's phobia is a conditioned emotional response (classical conditioning). In addition, the more he avoids the phobic situation, the more his avoidance behaviour is negatively reinforced; in other words, avoidance reduces anxiety, which reinforces avoidance (operant conditioning). Further, Charlie's anxiety may actually make him less socially competent. As a result, others respond less positively to him, which in turn makes him more anxious and avoidant. To try to unravel the conditions eliciting his anxiety, the behaviourally oriented clinician would ask precisely where and when Charlie becomes anxious. Are there group situations in which he does not become anxious? Does he only become anxious when he is expected to talk, or does he become anxious even when he can remain silent?

Working more cognitively, the cognitive–behavioural clinician assesses the thoughts that run through Charlie's mind as his anxiety mounts. For instance, Charlie may erroneously believe that if people laugh at him, he will 'die' of embarrassment or some other calamity will befall him. The clinician examines the way such irrational ideas maintain the phobia. Charlie might feel anxious in any situation that requires him to speak articulately because he does not believe he can do so. Alternatively, he may hold the irrational belief that he must excel in all situations if people are to respect him and consequently become terrified at the possibility of failure.

INTERIM SUMMARY

Cognitive–behavioural clinicians integrate an understanding of classical and operant conditioning with a cognitive–social perspective. From a behavioural perspective, many psychological problems involve conditioned emotional responses, in which a previously neutral stimulus has become associated with unpleasant emotions. Irrational fears in turn elicit avoidance, which perpetuates them and may lead to secondary problems, such as poor social skills. From a cognitive perspective, many psychological problems reflect dysfunctional attitudes, beliefs and other cognitive processes, such as a tendency to interpret events negatively.

Biological approach

To understand psychopathology, mental health professionals often move from a mental to a physiological level. Practitioners from all theoretical perspectives evaluate patients for potential biological contributions to their symptoms, as when they take a family history to assess possible genetic vulnerabilities or inquire about head injuries in childhood to assess possible influences on the developing brain. Some researchers and clinicians, however, believe that biology holds the key to most forms of psychopathology.

Neural circuits

The biological approach looks for the roots of mental disorders in the brain's circuitry (Kalat, 2007). For example, normal anxiety occurs through activation of neural circuits involving, among other structures, the amygdala and frontal lobes (chapter 10). Thus, one might expect pathological anxiety to involve heightened or easily triggered activation of those circuits — a hypothesis supported by neuroimaging studies of many anxiety disorders (Reiman, 1997; see also Cuthbert et al., 2003; Jung et al., 2006). Although, as we will see, abnormal neural firing can have genetic or environmental roots (e.g. people with severe childhood abuse histories may show damage to the hippocampus; Bremner, 1998), a central focus of biological approaches is on the heritability of psychopathology. Thus, like all competent clinicians, biologically oriented clinicians are likely to assess carefully for family history of disorders.

Aside from genetics, biological researchers have searched for the roots of psychopathology primarily in two areas. First, they have examined specific regions of the brain that differ between people with a particular disorder and those without it (Wright et al., 2000). For example, as we will see, a large body of research shows differences in the frontal and temporal lobes between the brains of patients with schizophrenia and the brains of people without the disorder (see Bertolino et al., 2000). This finding makes sense given that the frontal lobes regulate consciousness and thought and the temporal lobes are involved in language — domains of particular difficulty for patients with schizophrenia.

Second, researchers have looked for evidence of neurotransmitter dysfunction in particular disorders, on the assumption that too much or too little neurotransmitter activity could disrupt normal patterns of neural firing. For example, if normal anxiety reactions involve the neurotransmitter norepinephrine (chapter 3), then individuals whose genes predispose them to produce too much of this neurotransmitter or whose receptors are overly sensitive in circuits involving the amygdala are likely to experience pathological anxiety.

Although these efforts will surely continue, recent thinking reflects a view of brain functioning that we have encountered in several other chapters (e.g. chapters 1, 3, 4 and 8). This viewpoint emphasises that mental processes and behaviour typically emerge from the coordination of circuits of neurons distributed throughout the brain, rather than from a single region (Lewis, 2000). Any 'break' in a circuit — such as a circuit regulating thought, attention and consciousness that runs from the frontal lobes through the thalamus and cerebellum — could produce similar symptoms by derailing the functioning of the whole operation (Andreasen, 1999). Thus, many diagnoses, such as schizophrenia, may be heterogeneous categories that apply to people with similar symptoms but whose problems have very different causes. For example, a gene that causes dysfunction of the thalamus could prevent the frontal lobes from working properly if it affects a circuit from the thalamus to the frontal lobes and could thus produce similar symptoms to a gene that directly affects the frontal lobes.

Integrating nature and nurture: the diathesis–stress model

The biological approach is not incompatible with the perspectives described thus far. Charlie's anxiety may indeed be associated with his conflicts about achieving success or he may be caught in a spiral of negatively reinforced avoidance of social situations. Nevertheless, his tendency to become anxious in the first place could reflect a biological predisposition.

Theorists of various persuasions often adopt a ***diathesis–stress model***, which proposes that people with an underlying vulnerability (called a diathesis) may exhibit symptoms under stressful circumstances. The diathesis may be biological, such as a genetic propensity for anxiety symptoms caused by overactivity of norepinephrine; or environmental, stemming from events such as a history of neglect, excessive parental criticism or uncontrollable painful events in childhood (Barlow, 2002; see also Auerbach, Abela, Zhu, & Yao, 2007; Zvolensky, Kotov, Antipova, & Schmidt, 2005). Upsetting events in adulthood, such as the loss of a lover or a failure at work, might then activate the vulnerability.

INTERIM SUMMARY

The biological approach looks for the roots of mental disorders in the brain's circuitry, such as neurotransmitter dysfunction, abnormalities of specific brain structures, or dysfunction anywhere along a pathway that regulates behaviour or mental processes. Theorists of various persuasions often adopt a ***diathesis–stress model***, which proposes that people with an underlying vulnerability (called a diathesis) may exhibit symptoms under stressful circumstances.

Systems approach

A social systems approach looks for the roots of psychopathology in the broader social context. A ***systems approach*** explains an individual's behaviour in the context of a social group, such as a couple, family or larger group (Granic & Hollenstein, 2003). An individual is part of a ***system***, a group with interdependent parts, and what happens in one part of the system influences what happens in others. From this standpoint, diagnosing a problem in an individual without considering the systems in which he operates is like trying to figure out why a car is getting poor fuel economy without considering traffic conditions or the quality of the petrol the car is burning. For example, a study found that roughly one-third of mothers who brought their child in for treatment of depression had a current psychiatric disorder themselves, and that 43 percent had non-diagnosable but clinically recognisable psychopathology (i.e. problems that did not quite meet the 'official' threshold for diagnosis) (Ferro, Verdeli, Pierre, & Weissman, 2000). A child caught in stressful maternal 'traffic' could easily lose some psychological 'horsepower'.

Like the biological approach, a systems approach is not incompatible with other perspectives because it operates at another level of analysis. For example, a child who has problems with aggressive behaviour at school may be part of a broader family system in which violence is a way of life. Nevertheless, in clinical practice, practitioners who take a systems approach frequently consider it their primary theoretical orientation, much as some psychiatrists (medical doctors trained in the treatment of mental illness) view most psychopathology biologically.

Family systems

Most systems clinicians adopt a ***family systems model***, which views an individual's symptoms as symptoms of dysfunction in the family (Hoffman, 1981, 1991; see also Kazak, Simms, & Rourke, 2002). In other words, the identified patient (the person identified as the one who needs help) is the symptom bearer (the person displaying the family's difficulties), but the real problem lies in the family, not primarily in the individual. For example, one couple brought their child to see a psychotherapist because he was disruptive at school and punishment had been ineffective. The psychologist inquired about the parents' marriage and found that it had been very shaky until the child began having difficulties at school. Once the child became symptomatic, the parents worked together to help him, and their marital problems subsided. Thus, the problem was not so much a disruptive child as a disruptive marriage. The child not only expressed his parents' marital problems through his symptom but also helped preserve their marriage by becoming symptomatic. Empirically, marital problems appear to exacerbate a range of psychological and physical conditions, from depression to chronic pain and cancer (Fincham & Beach, 1999).

Systems theorists refer to the methods family members use to preserve equilibrium in a family (such as keeping tension levels down or preserving a marriage) as ***family homoeostatic mechanisms***. These mechanisms operate much like the homoeostatic mechanisms discussed in chapter 10 on motivation. In the case above, marital tension evoked a set of behaviours in the child, which in turn reduced the marital tension, much as a heater turns on until the temperature in a room reaches the temperature set on the thermostat. From this viewpoint, psychological symptoms are actually dysfunctional efforts to cope with a disturbance in the family.

Family systems theorists also focus on the ways families are organised, including family roles, boundaries and alliances (Henry, Robinson, Neal, & Huey, 2006). ***Family roles*** are the parts individuals play in repetitive family 'dramas' — typical interaction patterns among family members. Playing roles is not in itself pathological; it occurs in every social group (chapter 18). For example, one child may take on the role of mediator between two siblings who are often in conflict. In some families, a child and parent may switch roles. This is a phenomenon known as role reversal, in which the child takes care of the parent, attends to the parent's needs and takes on the parent's responsibilities. Empirically, role reversal is more common among people with a history of physical or sexual abuse, and is already apparent in the preschool years (Macfie et al., 1999).

Assessing the family system

In assessing a family, a psychologist with a systems orientation examines the marital subsystem (the relationship between the parents) and the roles different family members play. The clinician may want to explore ***family boundaries***, or physical and psychological limits of the family system and its subsystems (see Goldstein, 1988). Some families are enmeshed — that is, too involved with each other's business — and privacy and autonomy are impossible. Others are disengaged, with minimal contact among family members (see Olson, 1985, 2000). Some families have rigid boundaries with the outside world, punishing their members if they disclose too many family secrets or spend too much time away from home. Others seem to lack internal boundaries, as when a parent refuses to allow a child any privacy.

The systems-oriented psychologist assesses other interaction patterns as well, such as ***family alliances***, or who sides with whom in family conflicts. A child who begins abusing drugs, for example, may be expressing frustration at feeling excluded from or consistently attacked by an alliance between a parent and a sibling who is seen as the 'good' child. The clinician also looks for problematic communication patterns, as when a couple communicates primarily by fighting.

A psychologist working from a systems approach might evaluate Charlie first in one session by himself and then in another with his father or family. Although systems theorists differ considerably in their specific approaches, the clinician might assess the extent to which Charlie is bringing issues from his family of origin into his new relationships (Bowen, 1978, 1991). The systems clinician might observe the way Charlie and his father communicate, looking for mutually unsatisfying patterns in their interactions. The clinician might also try to understand these patterns in the context of the family's subculture, which may have particular ways of regulating emotional expression and communication between the generations. For example, Charlie's conflicts about success may be heightened by the fact that his father is an immigrant who does not approve of Charlie's occupational choice and believes that a son should follow his father's directives.

MAKING CONNECTIONS

Social psychologists emphasise the powerful impact of social situations on behaviour (chapter 18).

- How might family dynamics contribute to a teenager's tendency to abuse drugs or alcohol?
- Can peer influence create problems such as alcoholism in teenagers, or do such problems require a prior vulnerability?

INTERIM SUMMARY

A ***systems approach*** explains an individual's behaviour in the context of a social group, such as a couple, family or larger group. Most systems clinicians adopt a ***family systems model***, which views an individual's symptoms as symptoms of family dysfunction. The methods family members use to preserve equilibrium in a family are called ***family homoeostatic mechanisms***. Family systems theorists focus on the ways families are organised, including ***family roles*** (the parts individuals play in the family), ***boundaries*** (physical and psychological limits of the family and its subsystems) and ***alliances*** (patterns in which family members side with one another). They also focus on problematic communication patterns.

Evolutionary perspective

Although the evolutionary perspective does not offer the kind of comprehensive system for understanding (and treating) psychopathology that we see in the approaches described above, evolutionary psychologists are likely to provide insight into psychopathology in the years ahead (Cosmides & Tooby, 1999; see also Kennair, 2002). In one sense, psychopathology is a paradox from an evolutionary perspective, since psychopathology is maladaptation, and evolution is about natural selection of adaptive traits. Nevertheless, an evolutionary perspective explains psychopathology in at least three ways.

First, nothing in the nature of evolution requires that every organism is well adapted to its environment. In fact, natural selection acts on random variation in genotypes by weeding out those that lead to less adaptive phenotypes. As in all evolutionary analyses, evolutionary pressures are always relative to a specific environment. In some circumstances, a tendency to be anxious could confer an evolutionary advantage by making individuals vigilant to potential dangers; in others, a tendency to be anxious could be socially stigmatising and hence reduce reproductive success.

A challenging question for evolutionary psychologists is how to explain the presence, over several generations, of a stable percentage of the population that has a debilitating mental disorder. How, for example, can an evolutionary theorist explain the worldwide presence of schizophrenia, a disease that clearly diminishes an individual's capacity for both survival and reproduction?

A second evolutionary explanation, though still speculative at this point, uses the analogy of sickle cell anaemia. Sickle cell anaemia is common only in people whose ancestors came from parts of the world where malaria was prevalent. The reason is that people who inherit the sickle cell gene from one parent are protected from malaria. If they inherit the gene from both parents, however, they will die from sickle cell anaemia. Over time a population will evolve a stable percentage of sickle cell genes: if the presence of the gene gets too high in the population, more people die of sickle cell, which reduces its prevalence; if the percentage gets too low, more people die of malaria, and those who survive are more likely to carry the gene.

A similar phenomenon could explain genes for mental disorders such as anxiety disorders or schizophrenia. The mechanisms in some cases may be obvious and intuitive, whereas in others they may be completely unexpected. An obvious example might occur in anxiety disorders, which are to some degree heritable. As we will see, having too little anxiety can contribute to antisocial personality traits and reckless behaviour that lead to premature death. In contrast, having too much anxiety can lead to anxiety disorders. The levels of anxiety in the population attributable to genes could thus reflect a relatively simple mechanism of natural selection that, across the population, maximises survival and reproduction, but produces dysfunction in individuals whose genetic inheritance places them at one extreme or another.

The evolutionary 'trade-offs' that produce a stable percentage of disordered individuals might actually be much less obvious because a single gene or set of genes could also act on two very different traits. For example, the genes that predispose individuals to schizophrenia could also render non-disordered bearers of the gene less vulnerable to some kind of deadly viral infection such as smallpox. The result would be a stable percentage of the population with schizophrenia, just as is the case for sickle cell. Research finding a negative association between schizophrenia and rheumatoid arthritis provides a suggestive example (Narita et al., 2000).

A third evolutionary explanation for psychopathology centres on the interplay of genes and environments. Psychopathology could reflect normal processes gone awry because of abnormal circumstances. Fear is a highly adaptive, inborn mechanism that keeps people away from circumstances associated with danger. However, if those circumstances cannot be avoided or if the person is traumatised by them, he may become preoccupied with fear and less able to function adaptively.

MAKING CONNECTIONS

Australian media mogul and billionaire James Packer, who formerly married a swimsuit model, is in his second marriage; this time to another former model, Erica Baxter. Research suggests that males tend to emphasise youth and physical attractiveness in selecting mates, and females tend to emphasise males' status and resources — a difference evolutionary psychologists attribute to natural selection (chapter 18).

- How might this emphasis influence the disorders females tend to develop? In other words, what kinds of vulnerabilities to specific forms of psychopathology might this produce?
- How might this influence the disorders men tend to develop? To what kinds of problems might competition for status or wealth predispose males?
- May James Packer's decision to twice marry models have been influenced by natural selection? What about his former wife's and current wife's respective decisions to marry him?

INTERIM SUMMARY

Evolutionary psychologists could explain psychopathology in at least three ways: as random variation likely to be weeded out by natural selection; as the result of broader population pressures that select rates of genes in the population that can be either functional or dysfunctional depending on the other genes an individual inherits; and as the maladaptive environmental 'tuning' of psychological mechanisms that are normally adaptive.

Descriptive diagnosis: DSM and psychopathological syndromes

The approaches discussed thus far all assume a particular point of view about the nature and origins of psychopathology. A descriptive approach, in contrast, attempts to be atheoretical, that is, not wedded to any theoretical perspective on aetiology. In ***descriptive diagnosis***, mental disorders are classified in terms of ***clinical syndromes***, or constellations of symptoms that tend to occur together. For example, in a depressive syndrome, depressed mood is often accompanied by loss of interest in pleasurable activities, insomnia, loss of appetite, poor concentration and decreased self-esteem.

Until the early 1950s, psychologists and psychiatrists lacked a standard set of diagnoses. Psychologists from each school of thought used their own preferred terms, and systematic empirical investigation of most psychiatric disorders was impossible (see Nathan, 1998). That changed when the American Psychiatric Association (1994) published the manual of clinical syndromes that researchers and clinicians use to make diagnoses, called the ***Diagnostic and Statistical Manual of Mental Disorders*** (DSM), now in its fourth edition (***DSM-IV***). Almost two decades on, a fifth edition of the DSM (***DSM-5***) is currently being developed by the American Psychiatric Association (APA, 2010) and is due for completion in 2013. There will almost certainly be major changes applied to the current system of classification and diagnostic categories; however, the DSM-IV remains in use until the new edition comes into effect. For the latest information and proposed changes for DSM-5, students should visit the APA DSM-5 Development website (www.dsm5.org). The major diagnostic categories of DSM-IV are listed in table 15.1.

TABLE 15.1 Selected diagnostic categories of DSM-IV*

Category	Description
Disorders usually first diagnosed in infancy, childhood or adolescence	Disorders involving deviations from normal development, such as attention-deficit hyperactivity disorder and conduct disorder
Substance-related disorders	Disorders associated with drug abuse (including alcohol) as well as side effects of medication and exposure to toxins
Schizophrenia and other psychotic disorders	Disorders characterised by loss of contact with reality, marked disturbances of thought and perception and bizarre behaviour
Mood disorders	Disorders characterised by disturbances of normal mood, notably depression, mania or alternating periods of each
Anxiety disorders	Disorders in which anxiety is the main symptom (such as generalised anxiety, panic, phobic, post-traumatic stress and obsessive–compulsive disorders)
Somatoform disorders	Disorders involving physical symptoms that lack a physical basis, such as hypochondriasis (excessive preoccupation with health and fear of disease without a realistic basis for concern)
Dissociative disorders	Disorders characterised by alterations or disruptions in consciousness, memory, identity or perception, such as psychologically induced amnesia
Sexual and gender identity disorders	Disorders of sexuality and gender identity including sexual dysfunctions, paraphilias (sexual urges, fantasies or behaviours involving unusual objects, non-consenting partners, or pain or humiliation, which cause significant distress or dysfunction) and gender identity disorders (such as cross-dressing), that lead to considerable distress or impairment in functioning
Eating disorders	Disorders characterised by severe disturbance in eating behaviour, such as anorexia nervosa and bulimia nervosa
Adjustment disorders	Disorders that are usually relatively mild and transient, in which clinically significant emotional or behavioural symptoms develop as a consequence of some identifiable stressor
Personality disorders	Disorders characterised by long-standing patterns of maladaptive behaviour that deviate from cultural expectations and are pervasive and inflexible, such as borderline and antisocial personality disorders

*DSM-5 is proposed to be released in 2013; please check www.dsm5.org for the latest information and proposed changes.

SOURCE: Adapted from APA (1994).

Descriptive diagnosis allows researchers and clinicians in many different settings to diagnose patients in a similar manner, regardless of their theoretical orientation (Regier, First, Marshall, & Narrow, 2002). In reality, however, not even a descriptive approach can be entirely atheoretical, and psychologists continue to search for alternatives to the DSM approach (see Barron, 1998; Beutler & Malik, 2002). The descriptive approach embodied in DSM-IV tends to be most compatible with a disease model of psychopathology, which presumes that psychological disorders fall into discrete categories, much like medical disorders such as tuberculosis or melanoma. Not surprisingly, then, psychiatrists tend to emphasise descriptive diagnoses more than psychologists, although nearly all mental health professionals use descriptive diagnoses when initially evaluating a patient. A common language is essential, however, if researchers are to study disorders and clinicians are to communicate with one another, and DSM-IV constitutes the best current approximation of a comprehensive diagnostic system. Further, the much anticipated DSM-5 (APA, 2010) will incorporate revised classifications and diagnostic criteria, based on new knowledge gained through decades of scientific advances, increased clinical understanding and research into mental disorders.

DSM-IV uses a ***multiaxial system of diagnosis***, which places symptoms in their biological and social context by evaluating patients along five axes (table 15.2; see overleaf). These axes cover not only symptoms and personality disturbances but also relevant information such as medical conditions and environmental stressors. Axis I lists the clinical syndromes for which a patient seeks treatment, such as depression or schizophrenia. Axis II lists personality disorders and mental retardation. The assumption behind the distinction between the two axes is that Axis I describes state disorders — the patient's current condition, or state — whereas Axis II describes trait disorders — enduring problems with the person's functioning. Thus, a person who is severely depressed (a state disorder, coded on

Axis I) may have an enduring personality disorder that renders him vulnerable to depression, or he may simply have had difficulty coping with the death of a spouse (and hence receive no Axis II diagnosis). (Although Axis II also includes intellectual disability, as a shorthand most researchers treat 'Axis II' and 'personality disorders' as synonyms, since personality disorders are much more prevalent in psychiatric populations.)

TABLE 15.2 Axes of DSM-IV*

Axis	Description
I	Symptoms that cause distress or significantly impair social or occupational functioning
II	Personality disorders and intellectual disability — chronic and enduring problems that impair interpersonal or occupational functioning
III	Medical conditions that may be relevant to understanding or treating a psychological disorder
IV	Psychosocial and environmental problems (such as negative life events and interpersonal stressors) that may affect the diagnosis, treatment and prognosis of psychological disorders
V	Global assessment of functioning — the individual's overall level of functioning in social, occupational and leisure activities

*DSM-5 is proposed to be released in 2013; please check www.dsm5.org for the latest information and changes.

SOURCE: Adapted from APA (1994).

Axis III lists any general medical conditions that may be relevant to understanding the person's psychopathology (such as diabetes or hypothyroidism, which can affect mood). Axis IV is reserved for psychosocial and environmental stressors (life events such as the death of a family member that could be contributing to emotional problems). Axis V rates the patient's current level of functioning (on a scale of 0 to 100) and the highest level of functioning the patient has attained during the past year. Table 15.3 shows how Charlie might be diagnosed using this multiaxial system.

TABLE 15.3 Multiaxial diagnosis of Charlie

Axis	Description
I	Social phobia (disorder marked by fear that occurs when the person is in a social situation)
II	Rule out (possible) avoidant personality disorder (disorder marked by avoidance of interpersonal situations, fear of being disliked or rejected, and view of self as inadequate or inferior)
III	None (no medical conditions)
IV	Business school, father's criticism (current stressors)
V	Global assessment of functioning: 55 (moderate symptoms, on a scale from 0 to 100)

For the new DSM-5, it is proposed that Axes I, II and III may be collapsed onto a single Axis incorporating all general medical and psychiatric diagnoses (APA, 2010). This would bring DSM classifications closer to the International Classification of Disease (ICD-10) system endorsed by the World Health Organization (WHO, 2010c). Similarly, concepts presently covered in Axis IV are being reviewed in terms of possible alignment and consistency with ICD-10 codes and classifications (APA, 2010; WHO, n.d.).

In the sections that follow, we examine some of the major clinical syndromes, starting with disorders that usually become evident in childhood. Before doing so, however, a word of warning is in order. You may have experienced some of these symptoms at one time or another and may start to worry that you have one (or all) of the disorders. This reaction is similar to the 'first-year medical student syndrome' experienced by many doctors in training, who imagine they have whichever disease they are currently studying. Thus, you may recognise yourself or someone you know in many of the symptoms or syndromes described, in part because these disorders are in fact highly prevalent in the population and in part because we all experience anxiety, sadness and interpersonal difficulties at various points in our lives (often appropriately, as at the death of a loved one). Bear in mind that only when symptoms disrupt a person's functioning or sense of wellbeing would a trained mental health professional actually diagnose a disorder, and that most forms of psychopathology can be treated (chapter 16).

How do we know that the current categories of psychiatric disorders are the right ones?

By Professor David Kavanagh, Queensland University of Technology

Since the first version of DSM was released in 1952, there have been many changes to the list of disorders and their definitions. A draft of DSM-5 suggests that many more changes are likely. Are these changes for the better? How can we tell?

The writing of diagnostic criteria is a sociopolitical process, but it is based on data. Early refinements of criteria improved reliability of diagnosis. Recent revisions continue to respond to research advances. In DSM-IV, substance abuse was thought to be less severe than dependence, and abuse could not be diagnosed if dependence had ever been present. However, several dependence criteria (e.g. drinking more than intended) are common, while some abuse features (e.g. neglecting roles and legal problems) are more severe and rare (Hasin & Beseler, 2009). Recent studies suggest that abuse and dependence probably reflect a single disorder (Borges et al., 2010). So, the draft DSM-5 combines these categories. That seems to be a logical change, based on data.

However, there are continuing limitations to diagnostic systems. Over the last 20 years there has been an unprecedented growth in human ability to study neural processes and genetics, but many aspects of disorders remain a mystery, and researchers still rely extensively on symptoms. Many disorders remain 'fuzzy categories'; for example, three people with DSM-IV Schizophrenia may have no symptomatic feature in common! The draft of DSM-5 refines schizophrenia criteria, requiring at least one of three core symptoms, but substantial potential for heterogeneity remains for this and other diagnoses. Criteria for some other disorders may have been too strict: many people only met some criteria for DSM-IV Bulimia Nervosa, and were put into the category of Eating Disorder Not Otherwise Specified. The draft DSM-5 creates a new diagnosis — Binge Eating Disorder — partly to address that problem (Wonderlich, Gordon, Mitchell, Crosby, & Engel, 2009).

Diagnostic categories provide a shorthand description for research and treatment. They help services decide who is treated and receives health insurance. However, this often imposes a cut-off on continua of frequency, severity or symptom numbers. Sometimes, as in alcohol-use disorder, there is no qualitative change at any symptom number (Hasin & Beseler, 2009). People with few features may still have significant psychopathology (Lynskey & Agrawal, 2007) and seek assistance. The DSM-5 draft retains categories, but often also defines severity ratings. This is only a partial answer.

Few researchers now see psychiatric disorders as purely social constructions. However, some diagnoses are highly dependent on social context (e.g. DSM-IV Substance Abuse includes interpersonal problems, which reflect social norms). The WHO derives a competing diagnostic system that is relatively independent of cultural context (the International Classification of Diseases, or ICD). Instead of DSM-IV Substance Abuse, it has Harmful Use — a pattern of use harmful to health. However, violation of social norms is a sign of substance-related problems. How can that phenomenon be captured, while minimising reliance on norms that can be harsh or capricious?

These and other issues are the focus of ongoing debate.

INTERIM SUMMARY

In descriptive diagnosis, mental disorders are classified into ***clinical syndromes***, constellations of symptoms that tend to occur together. The descriptive approach embodied in ***DSM-IV*** tends to be most compatible with a disease model that presumes psychological disorders fall into discrete categories. DSM-IV uses a ***multiaxial system***, placing symptoms in their biological and social context by evaluating patients along five axes: clinical syndromes, personality disorders (and mental retardation), medical conditions, environmental stressors and global level of functioning. The ***DSM-5*** is scheduled for completion in 2013, with major changes expected to the classification system and diagnostic categories, including fewer axes.

Disorders usually first diagnosed in infancy, childhood or adolescence

Several mental disorders typically arise during infancy, childhood or adolescence; these range from disturbances of eating and feeding (such as eating rocks and other inedible objects) to severe separation distress upon leaving home for school. Two of the most common are attention-deficit hyperactivity disorder and conduct disorder.

Attention-deficit hyperactivity disorder

Many children and adolescents are brought to mental health professionals because of behavioural difficulties at school or at home. Consider the case of Jimmy, a six-year-old whose teacher reports that he cannot sit still, does not pay attention and is constantly disturbing his classmates. Jimmy fidgets in his chair, and when his teacher directs him to work, he can only concentrate for a few seconds before becoming disruptive, making noises or throwing paper wads across the room. Jimmy's teacher suspects he has ***attention-deficit hyperactivity disorder (ADHD)***, a disorder characterised by inattention, impulsiveness and hyperactivity inappropriate for the child's age.

Although children with ADHD may exhibit symptoms by age four, the disorder often goes unrecognised until they enter school, since children are not usually required to comply with stringent social demands before that time (Campbell, 1985). Setting a standard for hyperactive behaviour in preschoolers is difficult; in fact, as many as 50 percent of mothers of four-year-old boys believe their son is hyperactive (Varley, 1984)! The exact extent of ADHD in Australia is difficult to determine. Widely different prevalence rates of ADHD have been reported, depending on the methodology used. For example, one Australian study found the prevalence rate of ADHD to be as high as 11.2 percent (Sawyer, Arney, & Baghurst, 2000). However, the authors of this study warned that the high prevalence rates should be viewed with caution, due to possible discrepancies in diagnosis. The prevalence of ADHD is estimated at 5 percent of school-aged children (Rhee, Waldman, Hay, & Levy, 1999). More recently, an Australian study found that more than twice as many boys than girls are diagnosed with ADHD (Graetz, Sawyer, & Baghurst, 2005).

David Hay from Curtin University in Perth has specialised in ADHD through a special study on twins. He has stressed that there are actually a number of distinct types of ADHD, and that the stereotypical hyperactive child portrayed on television current affairs shows is the rarest type — inattention being the most common (ABC, 2004).

Attention-deficit hyperactivity disorder runs in families (Faraone, Biederman, Feighner, & Monuteaux, 2000). In fact, Hay (ABC, 2004b) described ADHD as the most genetic behaviour that he has ever come across in 30 years of studying behaviour genetics. Moreover, families of children with ADHD have a higher incidence of alcoholism and personality disorders in both parents, especially fathers (Pihl, Peterson, & Finn, 1990; Samudra & Cantwell, 1999). Although many cases probably stem from central nervous system dysfunction, the more risk factors a child experiences (such as severe marital discord between parents, low social class, maternal psychopathology and paternal criminality), the more likely he is to develop the disorder (Biederman et al., 1995). On the other hand, parents of ADHD children are thought to experience elevated levels of stress (see Podolski & Nigg, 2001). The University of Otago in New Zealand is actively researching how to support parents and other caregivers of children with ADHD (see Treacy, Tripp, & Baird, 2005; Tripp & Alsop, 2001; Tripp, Ryan, & Peace, 2002).

Data on the extent to which children 'grow out of' this disorder are conflicting (Mannuzza, Klein, Bessler, Malloy, & Lpadula, 1998; Weiss, Hechtman, Milroy, & Perlman, 1985), in part because some of the symptoms, such as hyperactivity, may decline, whereas others, such as inattention, may not (Biederman, Mick, & Faraone, 2000). Nevertheless, children with ADHD are clearly at increased risk for other psychiatric and social problems in adolescence and adulthood, particularly antisocial behaviour and substance abuse (Biederman & Faraone, 2005; Mannuzza et al., 1998).

Conduct disorder

Another relatively common disturbance of childhood is ***conduct disorder***, characterised by persistent violation of societal norms and the rights of others. Symptoms include physical aggression towards people or animals, chronic fighting, vandalism, persistent lying and stealing. Such children are obstinate, resent taking direction, lack empathy and compassion and seldom express remorse for their destructive behaviour. Australian research has found that around 4.5 percent of boys and 1.6 percent of girls aged 6–17 years have conduct disorder (AIHW, 2002).

Both genetic and environmental factors contribute to the aetiology of conduct disorder and delinquent behaviour more generally (Biederman et al., 1995; O'Connor, McGuire, Reiss, Hetherington, & Plomin, 1998), highlighting again the joint contribution of nature and nurture to behaviour. Some children with conduct disorders appear to be relatively unresponsive to conditioning, because they are physiologically less responsive to rewards and especially punishments (Kruesi, Hibbs, Zahn, & Keysor, 1992; Raine & Venables, 1984). Because their autonomic nervous systems are less reactive, they lack the anxiety that motivates other children to adjust their behaviour to avoid threatening consequences. Ineffectively lax or excessively punitive parenting can also lead to delinquent behaviour (see Eysenck, 1982; Patterson & Bank, 1986), although research suggests that poor parenting may itself be partly genetic, reflecting the same genes in parents that predispose their children to develop conduct disorders (Slutske et al., 1997).

There is a complex interplay of nature and nurture in the aetiology of conduct disorders. Both genetic and environmental variables contribute to the likelihood a child will have conduct disorder (Cadoret, Yates, Troughton, Woodworth, & Stewart, 1995). The variables interact, indicating that an unstable home environment is particularly dangerous to children who are genetically vulnerable.

INTERIM SUMMARY

Attention-deficit hyperactivity disorder (ADHD) is characterised by inattention, impulsiveness and hyperactivity inappropriate for the child's age. It is more prevalent in boys and runs in families, apparently for both genetic and environmental reasons. The same is true of ***conduct disorder***, in which a child persistently violates societal norms and the rights of others.

Substance-related disorders

The disorders discussed thus far begin in childhood and often continue in one form or another into adulthood. Both ADHD and conduct disorders predispose individuals to one set of adult disorders, ***substance-related disorders***, which are characterised by continued use of a substance (such as alcohol or cocaine) that negatively affects psychological and social functioning.

The most common substance-related disorder is ***alcoholism*** (abuse of alcohol). As in other Western countries, the misuse of alcohol is one of Australia's greatest health issues. Consider the following interesting statistics about alcohol use in Australia:

- Alcohol abuse is second only to tobacco as a preventable cause of drug-related harm in Australia (Chikritzhs et al., 2007; Pascal, Chikritzhs, & Jones, 2009).
- Alcoholism is a disease that affects roughly one in 20 adults, or approximately 750 000 people in Australia (Wood, 2004).
- The 2007 National Drug Strategy Household Survey found that nine out of every 10 Australians aged 14 years or older had tried alcohol at some time in their lives and around 83 percent had consumed alcohol during the previous 12 months (AIHW, 2008b). About one third of these same Australians had drank alcohol at risky or high risk levels on at least one occasion in the last year (AIHW, 2007f).
- Over 450 000 children in Australia live in households where they are at risk of exposure to binge drinking by at least one adult (Dawes et al., 2007).
- Alcohol misuse costs the Australian community an estimated $15.3 billion each year, taking into account associated crime and violence, treatment costs, loss of productivity and premature death (Collins & Lapsley, 2008).
- The number of Australians hospitalised for alcohol-related injuries and illnesses caused by risky drinking has risen by a third in a decade, causing the death of more than 30 000 Australians aged 15 and older from 1996 to 2005 (Pascal et al., 2009).

According to Professor Chikritzhs from the National Drug Research Institute, 'every week, on average, risky or high risk drinking is killing more than 60 Australians and putting another 1500 people — the equivalent of a small town — in hospital, due to injury or disease that is entirely preventable' (Pascal et al., 2009).

Nature and nurture in the aetiology of substance-related disorders

Why would someone abuse alcohol or other substances when the effects are clearly destructive to relationships, professional ambitions and physical health? As in much research on psychopathology, the major controversy concerns the relative contributions of genetics and environment. Perhaps the best predictor of whether someone will become an alcoholic is a family history of alcoholism (Seljamo et al., 2006). Children of alcoholics are four times as likely to develop alcoholism as children of nonalcoholics (Peele, 1986). Family history, however, could support both genetic and environmental hypotheses.

The best data on the aetiology of addictions support two primary conclusions. First, both genes and environment are involved in the development of substance abuse, with genes playing the major part in use and abuse of some drugs but environmental variables contributing more in others (Kendler, Karkowski, Neale, & Prescott, 2000). Second, most of the genetic and environmental sources of vulnerability to substance abuse are common to all or most drugs. In other words, people who abuse one drug are at risk for abusing several — a suggestion that genes and experience conspire to create a general risk for substance abuse.

On top of this general vulnerability to addiction, however, are some genetic vulnerabilities to particular types of drug abuse, such as heroin and marijuana abuse (e.g. Bierut et al., 1998; Tsuang et al., 1998). The influence of heredity on alcoholism is also well established (Finn, Sharkansky, Brandt, & Turcott, 2000; Prescott & Kendler, 1999). Research carried out in 2004 using data collected from three studies of Australian twins indicated that differences in long-term average alcohol intake were almost entirely due to genetics (Whitfield et al., 2004). As a result, it seems clear that certain people are born with an increased risk of developing alcohol problems. Children whose biological parents are alcoholics may respond differently to alcohol physiologically than children of non-alcoholic parents (Gordis, 1996; Schuckit, 1984, 1994). They may, for example, be predisposed to like the taste, to find alcohol rewarding or to find alcohol emotionally soothing. Alternatively, children could inherit a predisposition to other emotional disorders that indirectly lead to alcoholism, such as anxiety or depression.

Other research suggests multiple routes to alcoholism that involve differing degrees of genetic and environmental influence (Cadoret, O'Gorman, Troughton, & Heywood, 1985; Kendler, Neale, Kessler, Heath, & Eaves, 1994). According to one model, severe, early-onset alcoholism associated with delinquency, antisocial personality disorder and other forms of substance abuse is highly heritable in males; if it is heritable in females, its heritability is low (Kendler et al., 1994; McGue, Pickens, & Svikis, 1992). The more common form of alcoholism, which is less severe and not associated with such significant psychopathology, stems largely from environmental factors shared by family members, such as parents who model alcoholic behaviour or whose parenting leads to poor self-esteem in their children, who are then vulnerable to alcohol as self-medication for depression (Babor et al., 1992; Cloninger, Bohman, & Sigvardsson, 1981; Pickens et al., 1991).

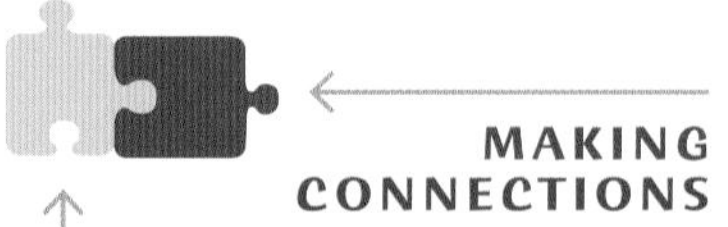

MAKING CONNECTIONS

As an adolescent, Australian actor Matthew Newton was told by a psychologist to 'make sure you never do drugs or alcohol, because you have the sort of personality where it will take over your life'. As an adult, the actor has displayed aggressiveness and battled depression, with his psychologist's forewarning hinting at a genetic predisposition towards antisocial behaviour traits.

Alcohol's effects are both biological and psychological. Alcohol can weaken people's inhibitions and embolden them to take risks through its effects on neurotransmitters, particularly GABA (gamma-aminobutyric acid) and dopamine. Simply believing they have been drinking can have similar effects because of expectancies about alcohol's effects (chapters 5 and 11).

Another model, which applies to other forms of drug abuse as well, is based on studies of children adopted away from their biological parents. This model distinguishes two heritable paths to substance abuse, in addition to the environmental pathway described (Cadoret et al., 1985, 1995). In the first genetic route, a tendency to alcoholism in the biological parent leads directly to the same genetic vulnerability in the child. A second pathway is less direct: a parent with a history of criminality transmits his genes to the child, who is more likely to develop conduct disorder and antisocial traits. Later, the delinquent child becomes involved in substance abuse. This model suggests that some people may be genetically vulnerable to the drug itself, whereas others are vulnerable to becoming antisocial and aggressive — traits leading socially to substance-related disorders, since drug abuse can be a form of antisocial behaviour. Australian actor Matthew Newton, for example, who has twice been accused of assaulting women, and was put on suicide watch and admitted to a treatment facility in 2010, may have a genetic vulnerability that has affected his conduct. In a television interview, Matthew's famous showbiz parents, Bert and Patti, spoke about their son's battle with anger and depression. Patti said that at age 14, Matthew had been told by a psychologist to 'make sure you never do drugs or alcohol, because you have the sort of personality where it will take over your life'. The forewarning suggests that the actor may be predisposed to the aggressive traits that he has displayed in adulthood (Meade, 2010).

When substance use is pathological

Millions of Australians admit to having sampled illegal drugs. In a recent report on drug use, more than one in seven (13.4 percent) of Australians revealed they had used illicit drugs in the preceding 12-month period (AIHW, 2008b). Marijuana was the most commonly used illegal substance, with 9.1 percent of Australians aged over 14 having tried the drug during the previous 12 months; about 2.3 percent had used amphetamines, 3.5 percent had used ecstasy/designer drugs and less than 1 percent had used heroin or cocaine or injected an illegal drug. As shown in table 15.4, rates of marijuana use have decreased in recent years, but marijuana remains the most commonly used illicit drug in Australia, with one in three Australians having tried it at some stage in their lives. In contrast, the use of so-called party drugs, such as ecstasy, has almost doubled.

TABLE **15.4 Comparative summary of illicit drug use in Australia**

	2001			2007		
	Drugs ever used	**Drugs recently used[a]**	**Mean age of initiation**	**Drugs ever used[d]**	**Drugs recently used[a]**	**Mean age of initiation**
Substance/behaviour	**(percentage)**		**(years)**	**(percentage)**		**(years)**
Marijuana	39.1	17.9	18.8	33.5	9.1	18.8
Painkillers/analgesics[b]	11.5	5.2	19.6	4.4	2.5	20.9
Tranquillisers/sleeping pills[b]	6.2	3.0	23.3	3.3	1.4	25.7
Steroids[b]	0.8	0.2	21.4	0.3	—	23.9
Barbiturates[b]	1.6	0.3	19.8	0.9	0.1	19.6
Inhalants	3.9	0.9	17.5	3.1	0.4	19.3
Heroin	2.2	0.8	21.7	1.6	0.2	21.9
Methadone[c]	0.5	0.2	22.1	0.3	0.1	23.3
Other opiates/opioids[c]	—	—	—	0.9	0.2	n.a.
Meth/amphetamine (speed)[e]	8.8	3.7	20.0	6.3	2.3	20.9
Cocaine	4.3	1.4	22.2	5.9	1.6	23.1
Hallucinogens	9.9	3.0	18.4	6.7	0.6	19.6
Ecstasy/designer drugs	4.8	2.4	22.5	8.9	3.5	22.6
Ketamine	—	—	—	1.1	0.2	24.0
GHB	—	—	—	0.5	0.1	24.6
Injected drugs	2.1	0.8	20.7	1.9	0.5	21.3
Any illicit drug	46.4	22.8	18.8	38.1	13.4	19.1
None of the above	7.5	14.7	—	3.2	14.1	—

(a) used in the last 12 months
(b) for non-medical purposes
(c) non-maintenance
(d) used at least once in lifetime
(e) known as 'amphetamines' in the 2001 data

SOURCE: National Drug Strategy Household Survey 1998 in Miller and Draper (2001, p. 18) and AIHW (2007e, p. 22; 2008).

Substance abuse can be a crippling psychological disorder, but the relationship between substance use and abuse is not always clear. Most people drink alcohol, but this does not mean that most people are alcoholics. Similarly, is minor, occasional or experimental use of drugs such as marijuana a sign of mental disorder?

Contrary to popular wisdom, the most definitive study in the area found that late teenagers (age 18) who experimented with marijuana in moderate amounts actually tended to be healthier psychologically than those who either used marijuana frequently or abstained completely (Shedler & Block, 1990). Abstainers were more anxious, emotionally inhibited and lacking in social skills than 'experimenters' (defined as individuals who used marijuana no more than once a month and had tried no more than one other illicit drug). Conversely, frequent users were more impulsive and alienated than experimenters (see figure 15.3). The study suggests that experimentation may be a relatively normal expression of adolescent rebellion and the desire to try new experiences.

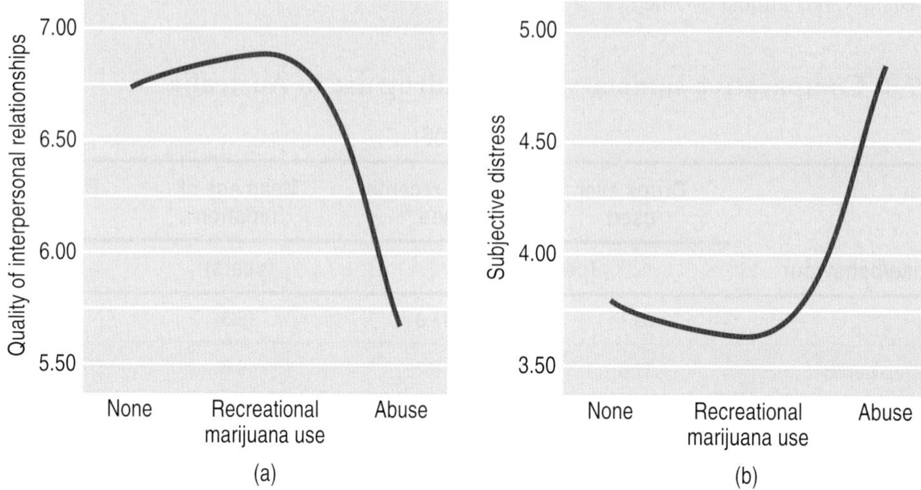

FIGURE 15.3
Relationship between marijuana use and adjustment. The two graphs show the relationships between level of marijuana use and two measures of psychological adjustment: quality of interpersonal relationships (a) and subjective distress (b). The relationship between marijuana use and these variables is clearly not linear; that is, more marijuana use does not uniformly predict worse mental health. No use, mild use and frequent use are qualitatively different, not on a continuum of abuse.

SOURCE: Shedler and Block (1990, p. 624).

The researchers were also able to predict future substance use patterns by watching interactions between participants and their mothers when participants were five years old. The most positive, mutually pleasurable mother–child interactions occurred in the group who later experimented with marijuana but did not abuse it. The mother–child interactions of both abstainers and frequent users at age five were rated as more hostile, more critical, less spontaneous, less relaxed and less enjoyable to the child than the mother–child interactions of those who later experimented with marijuana. Note that the findings of this study did not apply to use of hard drugs such as cocaine or heroin. Marijuana use and hard drug use in this sample appeared to mean very different things (Block, Block, & Keyes, 1988). In girls, for example, marijuana use was not correlated with depression, but hard drug use was. Hard drug use also correlated with mood swings and identity confusion.

What is the message of this and other research on alcoholism and drug abuse? First, for marijuana and alcohol, substance use and abuse are not synonymous. Neither drug is uniformly toxic to people who are not at risk. Second, people with family histories of substance abuse should avoid even casual use or experimentation with any drug. The risks far outweigh the benefits, and the odds that they will follow in their parents' footsteps despite their best intentions are extremely high.

INTERIM SUMMARY

Substance-related disorders are characterised by continued use of a substance (such as alcohol or cocaine) that negatively affects psychological and social functioning. The most common substance-related disorder is ***alcoholism***. Research has clearly demonstrated both environmental and genetic contributions to alcoholism, although researchers are still trying to track down precisely how genetic transmission occurs in different individuals. With marijuana, as with alcohol, substance use and abuse are not synonymous, although for vulnerable individuals, use tends to lead to abuse.

Schizophrenia

Schizophrenia is an umbrella term for a number of psychotic disorders that involve disturbances in nearly every dimension of human psychology, including thought, perception, behaviour, language, communication and emotion. Most forms of schizophrenia begin in the late teens and early twenties.

Table 15.5 shows the subtypes of schizophrenia in DSM-IV. One proposal being considered for DSM-5 is that subtypes be excluded (APA, 2010). This is based on data showing that most subtypes are not used diagnostically, except for paranoid schizophrenia, which applies in 50 to 75 percent of cases. In Australia, approximately 1 in 100 people (about 1 percent of the population) will develop schizophrenia during their lifetime, and it is usually lifelong (Schizophrenia Research Institute, 2010). Many studies find the rate of schizophrenia higher among economically impoverished groups, which may reflect the effect of poverty on people vulnerable to the illness or the fact that individuals with schizophrenia have difficulty holding employment and tend to be downwardly mobile. A review of 188 studies from 46 countries published between 1965 and 2002 revealed no gender differences in the rate of schizophrenia. However, it was found that the prevalence of schizophrenia was higher in migrants than in native-born individuals (Saha, Chant, Welham, & McGrath, 2005). Schizophrenia is a major cause of suicide. About 30 percent of Australians with schizophrenia will attempt suicide and 5 percent will complete suicide (Schizophrenia Research Institute, 2010). The life expectancy of people with schizophrenia is reduced by an average of 10 years (Schizophrenia Research Institute, 2010).

TABLE 15.5 **DSM-IV subtypes of schizophrenia***

Subtype	Characteristics
Paranoid type	Preoccupation with delusion(s) or auditory hallucinations. Little or no disorganised speech, disorganised or catatonic behaviour, or inappropriate or flat affect
Disorganised type	All the following — disorganised speech, disorganised behaviour, and inappropriate or flat affect — are prominent in behaviour, but catatonic-type criteria are not met. Delusions or hallucinations may be present, but only in fragmentary or non-coherent form
Catatonic type	At least two of the following: extreme motor immobility; purposeless excessive motor activity; extreme negativism (motionless resistance to all instructions) or mutism (refusing to speak); peculiar or bizarre voluntary movement; echolalia
Undifferentiated type	Does not fit any of the subtypes above, but meets the symptom criteria for schizophrenia
Residual type	Has experienced at least one episode of schizophrenia, but currently does not have prominent positive symptoms (delusions, hallucinations, disorganised speech or behaviour). However, continues to show negative symptoms and a milder variation of positive symptoms (odd beliefs, eccentric behaviour)

*DSM-5 is proposed to be released in 2013; please check www.dsm5.org/pages/default.aspx for the latest information and proposed changes.

SOURCE: APA (1994).

Although estimates vary, only 10 to 20 percent of individuals with schizophrenia ever fully recover, less than half show even moderate improvement after falling ill, and of those who do improve, almost half fall ill again within a year of leaving the hospital (Carone, Harrow, & Westermeyer, 1991; Hegarty, Baldessarini, Tohen, Waternaux, & Oepen, 1994; Herz et al., 2000). Most people with schizophrenia periodically experience acute phases of the illness and otherwise suffer residual (continuing) impairment in social and occupational functioning throughout life. This pattern appears to hold true cross-culturally (Marengo, Harrow, Sands, & Galloway, 1991). However, relapse rates (percentage of patients who become ill again) and severity of the illness tend to be higher in the industrialised West (Jenkins & Karno, 1992). People with good premorbid social functioning (i.e. social functioning prior to falling ill) are least likely to relapse over time (Robinson et al., 1999; see also Marder & Wirshing, 2003).

Symptoms

Perhaps the most distinctive feature of schizophrenia is a disturbance of thought, perception and language. Individuals with schizophrenia often suffer from ***delusions*** — false beliefs firmly held despite evidence to the contrary (table 15.6; see overleaf). The person may believe the secret service is trying to kidnap him or that his thoughts are being broadcast on the radio. ***Hallucinations*** — perceptual experiences that distort or occur without external stimulation — are also common. Auditory hallucinations (hearing voices) are the most frequent kind of hallucinations in schizophrenia.

TABLE 15.6 Delusions and associated beliefs

Delusion	Associated belief
Persecution	Belief that others are persecuting, spying on or trying to harm them
Reference	Belief that objects, events or other people have particular significance to them
Grandeur	Belief that they have great power, knowledge or talent
Identity	Belief that they are someone else, such as Jesus Christ or the Prime Minister of Australia
Guilt	Belief that they have committed a terrible sin
Control	Belief that their thoughts and behaviours are being controlled by external forces

SOURCE: Gazzaniga and Heatherton (2003, p. 539).

MAKING CONNECTIONS

In many respects, schizophrenia is a disorder of consciousness, in which the normal monitor and control functions of consciousness are suspended. People with schizophrenia have trouble keeping irrelevant associations out of consciousness and controlling the contents of their consciousness to solve problems. In fact, multiple studies have found deficits in focusing and maintaining attention and in using working memory effectively in patients with schizophrenia (chapters 5 and 7) (Cornblatt & Kelip, 1994; Gold, Carpenter, Randolph, Goldberg, & Weinberger, 1997).

Schizophrenic thinking is also frequently characterised by a ***loosening of associations***, the tendency of conscious thought to move along associative lines rather than to be controlled, logical and purposeful. One patient with schizophrenia was talking about her sister April: 'She came in last night from Denver, in like a lion, she's the king of beasts.' Whereas a poet might use a similar metaphor deliberately to express the sentiment that a person is angry or hostile, the individual with schizophrenia often has minimal control over associative thinking and intersperses it with rational thought. In this case, the patient's associations apparently ran from April to March, to a proverb about March coming in like a lion, and then to another network of associations linked to lions. People with schizophrenia may thus speak what sounds like gibberish, as they substitute one word for another associatively connected to it or simply follow a train of associations wherever it takes them.

Schizophrenic symptoms can be categorised into positive and negative symptoms (Crow, 1980; Strauss, Carpenter, & Bartko, 1974). ***Positive symptoms***, such as delusions, hallucinations and loose associations, are most apparent in acute phases of the illness and are often treatable by antipsychotic medications. They are called positive symptoms because they reflect the presence of something not usually or previously there, such as delusions. Research suggests a further distinction between two kinds of positive symptoms: disorganised (inappropriate emotions, disordered thought and bizarre behaviour) and psychotic (delusions and hallucinations) (Andreasen, Arndt, Miller, Flaum, & Nopoulos, 1995).

Negative symptoms (so named because they signal something missing, such as normal emotions) are relatively chronic symptoms of schizophrenia such as flat affect (blunted emotional response), lack of motivation, socially inappropriate behaviour and withdrawal from relationships, and intellectual impairments such as impoverished thought (lack of complex thought in response to environmental events). Positive and negative symptoms appear to involve different neural circuits and to respond to different kinds of medications (chapter 16).

INTERIM SUMMARY

Schizophrenia is an umbrella term for a number of psychotic disorders that involve disturbances in thought, perception, behaviour, language, communication and emotion. ***Positive symptoms*** include disorganised (e.g. disordered thought and bizarre behaviour) and psychotic (e.g. ***delusions*** and ***hallucinations***) symptoms. ***Negative symptoms*** are relatively chronic and include flat affect, lack of motivation, peculiar or withdrawn interpersonal behaviour and intellectual impairments.

Theories of schizophrenia

Over the last century, researchers have advanced several theories to explain the causes of schizophrenia. Most contemporary theorists adopt a diathesis–stress model, hypothesising that people with an underlying biological vulnerability develop the disorder or fall into an episode under stress (Walker & Diforio, 1997; Walker, Kestler, Bollini, & Hochman, 2004). Most of the time this diathesis is genetic, but other cases of schizophrenia probably reflect early damage to the brain (Garver, 1997). Some individuals are probably genetically above threshold for the illness — that is, they will develop schizophrenia regardless of environmental circumstances (figure 15.4). Others are near threshold, requiring only a small environmental contribution. Still others, simply at risk, will not develop the disorder without exposure to substantial pathogenic (disease-causing) experiences (Fowles, 1992).

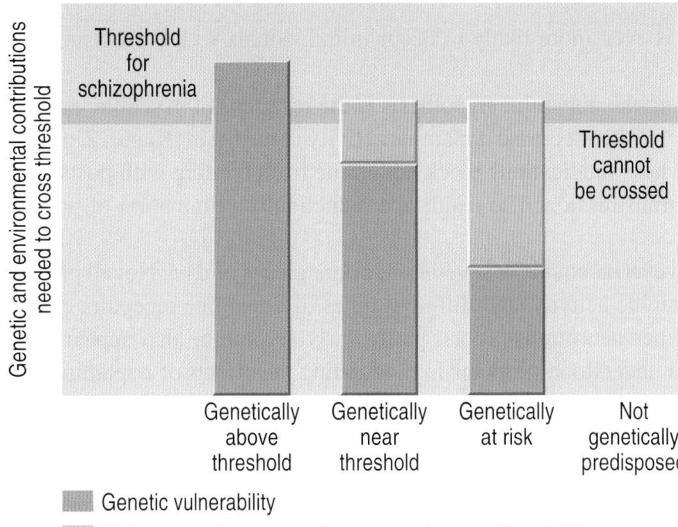

FIGURE 15.4
Diathesis–stress model of schizophrenia. Some individuals probably have a genetic make-up that puts them above threshold for schizophrenia. For others, differing degrees of environmental stress activate the vulnerability or diathesis. People who are not biologically at risk will generally not develop the disorder, regardless of environmental circumstances.

The biology of schizophrenia

Genes undoubtedly play a primary role in the aetiology of schizophrenia (Gottesman, 1991; Kendler, Myers, et al., 2000). A study of all twins born in Finland between 1940 and 1957 estimated heritability at 83 percent (Cannon, Kaprio, Lönnqvist, Huttunen, & Koskenvuo, 1998) — an estimate virtually identical to a study of twins in England in which at least one twin had a history of psychiatric disorder (Cardno, Marshall, et al., 1999).

Table 15.7 shows the risk of developing schizophrenia in people with differing degrees of relatedness to a person with schizophrenia. The table is based on data pooled across over 40 studies conducted over nearly 60 years (Gottesman, 1991). As we would expect for a disorder with a genetic basis, concordance rates between individuals with schizophrenia and their relatives increase with the degree of relatedness; that is, people who share more genes are more likely to share the diagnosis. Also supporting the role of genetics is the fact that the offspring of the healthy twin in a discordant pair of monozygotic twins (i.e. in which one twin has the disorder and the other does not) are just as likely as the offspring of the twin with schizophrenia to develop the disorder (Gottesman & Bertelsen, 1989).

TABLE 15.7 **Risk of schizophrenia and degree of genetic relatedness**

Relationship	Degree of relatedness	Risk (%)
Identical twin	1.0	48
Fraternal twin	.5	17
Sibling	.5	9
Parent	.5	6
Child	.5	13
Second-degree relatives	.25	4

SOURCE: Adapted from Gottesman (1991, p. 96).

Dopamine and glutamate

Precisely how a genetic defect produces schizophrenia is not entirely clear. The ***dopamine hypothesis*** implicates the neurotransmitter dopamine in schizophrenia. Several lines of evidence suggest that the brains of individuals with schizophrenia produce too much dopamine. First, amphetamines increase dopamine activity, and high doses of amphetamines induce psychotic-like symptoms such as paranoia and hallucinations in normal people (Kleven & Seiden, 1991; see also Walker et al., 2004).

An amphetamine-induced psychosis is even more likely to occur in individuals with a predisposition to schizophrenia.

A second line of evidence supporting the dopamine hypothesis is the response of psychotic patients to antipsychotic medications (chapter 16) that decrease dopamine activity in the brain (Kapur, Zipursky, Jones, Remington, & Houle, 2000). These medications block dopamine from binding with postsynaptic receptors, thus preventing neural transmission. The result is a reduction or elimination of positive symptoms such as hallucinations.

An excess of dopamine cannot, however, account for several important pieces of data. Not all patients respond to medicines that block dopamine activity, and different types of dopamine receptors control different psychological processes. Other neurotransmitters, particularly serotonin, also appear to be involved, in ways that are not yet well understood (perhaps in modulating the effects of dopamine).

Another formulation of the dopamine hypothesis suggests that different neural circuits underlie the positive and negative symptoms of schizophrenia (Duval et al., 2003; Kahn, Davidson, & Davis, 1996; Tamminga et al., 1992). Subcortical circuits projecting from the midbrain to the limbic system and basal ganglia have excess dopamine and seem to be responsible for positive symptoms. In contrast, a circuit that projects from the midbrain to the prefrontal cortex seems to be characterised by too little dopamine. This circuit is thought to be responsible for negative symptoms and many of the cognitive deficits seen in schizophrenia, since frontal activation is necessary for emotion, attention and social judgement. This multicircuited view of schizophrenia may explain why most antipsychotic medications, which reduce positive symptoms by diminishing the action of dopamine, do not alleviate negative symptoms and may even exacerbate them.

APPLY + DISCUSS

Although it is, as yet, unclear precisely why many people with schizophrenia show corresponding changes in brain anatomy, one suggestion has been that prenatal trauma may be responsible.

- Could exposure to malnutrition, maternal infection during pregnancy, and birth trauma account for some cases of schizophrenia?
- Would being born during the winter when cases of flu and disease are more common make one more susceptible to schizophrenia?

Although dopamine plays an important role in schizophrenia, another neurotransmitter, glutamate, may be important as well (Farber, Newcomer, & Olney, 1999; Li, Kim, Ichikawa, & Meltzer, 2003). As we have seen, one of the primary pieces of evidence for the dopamine hypothesis is amphetamine-induced psychosis, in which amphetamines produce positive symptoms of schizophrenia by increasing dopamine activity. Researchers have now discovered, however, that phencyclidine hydrochloride (PCP, or 'angel dust') can produce both positive and negative symptoms of schizophrenia. PCP reduces the responsivity of a particular kind of glutamate receptor (see chapter 5).

Precisely how dopamine and glutamate may both be involved is not yet clear. Dopamine can inhibit glutamate, so that too much dopamine could lead to too little glutamate activity. Another possibility is that some cases of schizophrenia reflect a primary dopamine dysfunction, whereas others reflect decreased glutamate activity, which can lead to similar symptoms.

Neural atrophy and dysfunction

Other data point to more global abnormalities in the brains of individuals with schizophrenia. One such abnormality is brain atrophy or neuronal loss, reflected in enlargement of the fluid-filled cavities in the brain called ***ventricles***, indicating that the neural regions surrounding them have degenerated. The brain appears to deteriorate over the course of the illness, with larger ventricles seen in patients with chronic schizophrenia (Zipursky, Lambe, Kapur, & Mikulis, 1998), although neuronal loss is already seen in first-episode schizophrenic patients (Gur, Turetsky, Bilker, & Gur, 1999). Ventricular enlargement and other forms of neuronal loss do not appear to be exclusive to schizophrenia, however, as they have been observed in patients with other psychotic disorders (Andreason, Swayze, Flaum, Alliger, & Cohen, 1990; Weiner, 1985) and even in patients with recurring depression and anxiety disorders (Elkis, Friedman, Wise, & Meltzer, 1995; Szeszko et al., 1999).

Atrophy is most apparent in the temporal and frontal lobes and in neural tissue connecting the frontal lobes to emotion-processing circuits in the limbic system (Goldstein et al., 1999; Sanfilipo et al., 2000). One study found that severity of symptoms (particularly auditory hallucinations) correlated strongly with the degree of atrophy in a region of the left temporal cortex specialised for auditory processing of language (Barta, Pearlson, Powers, Richards, & Tune, 1990). Analyses of dopamine receptors and EEG recordings in the same region have detected abnormalities in patients with schizophrenia (Bruder et al., 1999; Goldsmith, Shapiro, & Joyce, 1997). Atrophy and other cellular abnormalities have also been repeatedly confirmed in the prefrontal cortex (i.e. the most anterior regions of the cortex) of patients with schizophrenia (Gur et al., 2000; Kim et al., 2000; Park & Holzman, 1993). The prefrontal cortex is a particularly likely site for pathology in schizophrenia because one section is involved in working memory (chapter 7) and another in social and emotional functioning (chapter 8).

Relatives of patients with schizophrenia

Several studies have shown a variety of subtle impairments in the perceptual and cognitive functioning of relatives of patients with schizophrenia who do not themselves have the disorder. These impairments resemble the more blatant disturbances in individuals with schizophrenia, such as deficits in working memory and attention, but they are usually much less severe (e.g. Conklin, Curtis, Katsanis, & Iacono, 2000; Faraone, Biederman, & Milberger, 1995; Farmer et al., 2000). One study examined the presence of disordered thinking in adoptive and biological relatives of people with schizophrenia by recording speech samples and later coding them for idiosyncrasies of thinking (Kinney et al., 1997). Biological relatives of patients diagnosed with schizophrenia, particularly their siblings and half-siblings, showed elevated rates of thought disorder compared to relatives of control participants.

Research has even found enlarged ventricles in siblings of schizophrenic patients who do not themselves have the disorder (Staal et al., 2000). Relatives of patients with schizophrenia, like the patients themselves, also show minor physical abnormalities, most often of the head, face, hands or feet, although again these abnormalities are less pronounced than in the affected sibling (Ismail, Cantor-Graae, & McNeil, 1998). Data such as these point to processes in utero that derail both physical and neural development in patients with schizophrenia, which may or may not produce 'soft signs' of disorder in their relatives.

Environmental contributions

Although a biological vulnerability appears to be essential for most or all cases of schizophrenia, environmental variables play an important role in both the onset and course of the disorder. A large body of research focuses on patterns of communication and expression of emotion within the families of schizophrenic patients (Doane, West, Goldstein, Rodnick, & Jones, 1981; Hooley & Hiller, 1998; Wynne & Singer, 1963). Adoption studies show that biological children of individuals with schizophrenia are likely to develop the disorder if their adoptive families have hostile or confusing communication patterns, but not if the adoptive family functions normally (Kety, Rosenthal, Wender, Schulsinger, & Jacobsen, 1975; Tienari, 1991).

A particularly important environmental variable is ***expressed emotion***, the tendency of family interactions to be characterised by criticism, hostile interchanges and emotional overinvolvement or intrusiveness by family members. Researchers study expressed emotion by asking family members to talk about the patient and then coding their responses for comments that indicate criticism, hostility and so forth. Roughly 65 to 75 percent of patients with schizophrenia who return to homes high in expressed emotion relapse relatively quickly, compared to 25 to 35 percent of those whose homes have less intense and less negative emotional climates (Brown, 1985; Brown, Birley, & Wing, 1972; Butzlaff & Hooley, 1998).

A team of researchers in New Zealand has also identified links between child abuse and schizophrenia. Read, Agar, Argyle, and Aderhold (2003) found that psychiatric patients who had been sexually and/or physically abused as a child were four times more likely to experience hallucinations and 15 times more likely to hear voices than patients who had not been abused. A more recent Dutch study also found that people abused as a child were seven times more likely to develop severe psychoses, and that the most severely abused were most likely to become psychotic (Janssen, Krabbendam, Jolles, & van Os, 2004).

Culture and the course of schizophrenia

These findings on expressed emotion, particularly the link between criticism and relapse, have been replicated cross-culturally. High expressed emotion, however, is much less common in families of people with schizophrenia outside the West (Jenkins & Karno, 1992). Although the incidence of schizophrenia is similar across cultures (Jablensky, 1989; Saha, Chant, Welham, & McGrath, 2005), the relapse rate tends to be lower, and the course of the illness more benign, in cultures low in expressed emotion, such as India.

One explanation is that the cultures of developing countries are less individualistic and committed to concepts of personal responsibility than are Western cultures. Thus, they are less likely to assign blame to people with schizophrenia for their actions. Western family members high in expressed emotion tend to have an internal locus of control; that is, they believe they control their own destiny. They

APPLY + DISCUSS

- How are people with mental disorders portrayed in popular film and television?
- What aspect of mental disability is given most attention in the media?
- How do the stereotypes that are applied to people with mental disabilities influence people's perceptions?

also tend to believe their schizophrenic relatives could fight their symptoms if they just exercised more willpower (Hooley, 1998). Theorists in Western cultures generally consider an internal locus of control a sign of positive adjustment, but this view is not universal and probably understates the negative side effects of an individualistic worldview. Believing that people can control their destiny may be destructive when it is not true.

Environmental causes of biological dysfunction

Although the term environmental typically connotes something non-biological, researchers have considered other possible environmental causes of schizophrenia such as birth complications, viruses and malnutrition (Leask, 2004). Events that affect the developing nervous system in utero can later lead to a vulnerability to schizophrenia (Clarke, Harley, & Cannon, 2006). For example, people exposed during the first trimester of pregnancy to rubella (German measles) during an epidemic in 1964 were more likely to develop psychotic disorders than were people unexposed to the disease (Brown, Cohen, Greenwald, & Susser, 2000). Similarly, a Dutch study found that people exposed to famine in utero (particularly during the second trimester of pregnancy) during World War II showed a twofold increase in rates of schizophrenia decades later compared to unexposed individuals born at the same time (Susser et al., 1996). Exposure to famine in the second and third trimesters of pregnancy confers a risk for mood disorders as well (Brown, van Os, Driessens, Hoek, & Susser, 2000).

Birth complications are also more common among individuals who develop schizophrenia, particularly if they result in temporary deprivation of oxygen to the newborn (Rosso et al., 2000; Zornberg, Buka, & Tsuang, 2000). Research comparing monozygotic twins discordant for schizophrenia finds that the affected twin tends to have larger ventricles and a smaller hippocampus. Complications during delivery — particularly prolonged labour — tend to predict whether twin pairs will show these differences in brain structure (McNeil, Cantor-Graae, & Weinberger, 2000).

INTERIM SUMMARY

Most theorists adopt a ***diathesis–stress model*** of schizophrenia. Heritability of schizophrenia is at least 50 percent. According to the ***dopamine hypothesis***, positive symptoms of schizophrenia reflect too much dopamine activity in subcortical circuits involving the basal ganglia and limbic system, whereas negative symptoms reflect too little dopamine activity in the prefrontal cortex. Glutamate may also play a role, at least in some individuals with schizophrenia. Other data implicate abnormalities in the structure and function of the brain, such as enlarged ***ventricles*** and corresponding atrophy (degeneration) in the frontal and temporal lobes. Environmental variables, notably ***expressed emotion*** (criticism, hostile interchanges and emotional overinvolvement by family members), play an important role in the onset and course of the disorder. Prenatal and perinatal events that affect the developing nervous system may also be involved in some cases of schizophrenia.

Mood disorders

Whereas the most striking feature of schizophrenic disorders is disordered thinking, ***mood disorders*** are characterised by disturbances in emotion and mood. In most cases the mood disturbance is negative, marked by persistent or severe feelings of sadness and hopelessness, but a mood disturbance can also be dangerously positive, as in manic states. During ***manic*** episodes, people feel excessively happy or euphoric and believe they can do anything. As a consequence, they may undertake unrealistic ventures such as starting a new business on a grandiose scale.

Depression and mania have been the subject not only of scientific writing but also of many forms of art and poetry. The author William Styron wrote a book about his experience with severe depression. Billy Corgan of The Smashing Pumpkins has described his struggles with depression in his lyrics, and in 'Lithium', Kurt Cobain wrote about the manic and depressive episodes that apparently contributed to his suicide. As we have seen (chapter 9), depression and mania are not uncommon among creative artists, and depression is an experience to which most people can relate. Australian rock and roll pioneer Johnny O'Keefe — 'The Wild One' — was diagnosed with bipolar disorder and schizophrenia (paranoid type) and spent some time in a mental hospital. Actor Ben Stiller has revealed that he has bipolar disorder, and Pete Wentz from the band Fall Out Boy has admitted in an interview to be a manic depressive and taking medication to combat the illness. Mental disorders have also been central to the theme of various movies in recent history. In the 1999 film *Girl, Interrupted*, Angelina Jolie plays a sociopath with a magnetic and rebellious personality. In the 2004 film *The Aviator*, Leonardo DiCaprio displays obsessive compulsive disorder as character Howard Hughes, and in the 2009 film *Adam*, Australian actress Rose Byrne plays the love interest of a man with Asperger syndrome.

Types of mood disorders

Depression was reported as far back as ancient Egypt, when the condition was called melancholia and treated by priests. Occasional blue periods are a common response to life events such as loss of a job, end of a relationship or death of a loved one. In a depressive disorder, however, the sadness may emerge without a clear trigger (or precipitant), continue long after one would reasonably expect or be far more intense than normal sadness, and include intense feelings of worthlessness or even delusions.

Major depressive disorder

The most severe form of depression is ***major depressive disorder***, characterised by depressed mood and loss of interest in pleasurable activities (anhedonia). Major depression also includes disturbances in appetite, sleep, energy level and concentration. People in a major depressive episode may be so fatigued that they sleep day and night or cannot go to work or do household chores. They often feel worthless, shoulder excessive guilt and are preoccupied with thoughts of suicide. Major depressive episodes typically last about five months (see Spijker et al., 2002). Depression is often accompanied by symptoms of anxiety, and a diagnosis of Mixed Anxiety Depression has been proposed for inclusion in the DSM-5 (APA, 2010). Its addition to the DSM-5 would provide clarity and consistency with the disorder as defined in the International Classification of Diseases (ICD-10; WHO, 2010c).

ETHICAL DILEMMA

A psychologist wishes to gather clinical evidence to support the suggested link between depression and suicide risk. She proposes to interview a number of her depressed clients to establish the nature of their suicidal thoughts. However, given the sensitive nature of the issues to be discussed, she has decided not to explain to her clients the true purpose of her research.

- Is deception justified here? Explain why or why not.
- Is it necessary for the clinical psychologist to gain informed consent from her clients?
- What must the clinical psychologist do to respect her clients' rights to confidentiality?

According to the Australian Institute for Health and Welfare (2010), a large number of males (12 percent) and females (27 percent) aged 25–34 years suffer from anxiety and depression. Depression is also common among adolescents, being the most common mental health problem among young Australians aged 12–25 years (AIHW, 2007g). The prevalence of depression among people over 30 also appears to be on the increase (AIHW, 2010; Goldney, Eckert, Hawthorne, & Taylor, 2010). About 6 percent of the Australian population will experience major depression (Wilhelm, Mitchell, Slade, Brownhill, & Andrews, 2003), and about 20 percent of Australians will suffer from depression at some stage in their lives (SANE Australia, 2005). In 2008–09, there was an increase in general practitioners' (GP) management of some chronic diseases, including depression. During this period, depression was the second most common reason for female Australians to see their GP; it was in the top five for male Australians (AIHW, 2010).

What are the risk factors for developing depression? An AIHW (2007g) report into mental health identified numerous factors, including the loss of a loved one, the breakup of a relationship, social isolation, school failure, poverty and unemployment. Depression is more likely to be associated with anxiety than any other disorder but may also co-occur with a range of health-risk behaviours (see Conradi, de Jonge, & Ormel, 2008). For example, depression is linked to tobacco use, illicit drug use, alcohol misuse and dependence, eating disorders and obesity (AIHW, 2010).

In childhood, risk factors for depression include having parents who suffer from depression, parenting style, the loss of a parent, marital discord, physical abuse, neglect and sexual abuse (see Watts & Markham, 2005). Children report much higher rates of depression in Australia than adults, with around 20 percent suffering from depressed mood and 5 percent from a depressive disorder (SANE Australia, 2005).

Rates of depression in Australia also vary depending on a range of factors including ethnicity, health, lifestyle, geographic location and even occupation. The AIHW (2010) report into mental health identified higher rates of mental health problems among Aboriginal and Torres Strait Islander peoples (particularly related high levels of depression, substance abuse and high-risk behaviour); among people living in rural and remote areas; among people with physical illnesses such as cardiovascular disease, cancer and diabetes; and among veterans and defence services personnel.

Depression also has clear links to suicide, which is the largest single cause of injury-related death in Australia. Most people who die from suicide meet the criteria for depressive disorder in the weeks before death (Beyond Blue, 2006). The environmental factors that can influence higher rates of depression can also be linked to higher rates of suicide. For example, suicide rates for men living in rural and remote areas are much higher than for their urban counterparts, especially for those aged 15–24 (AIHW, 2010; see also Caldwell, Jorm, & Dear, 2004; Kilkkinen et al., 2007).

Dysthymic disorder

A less severe type of depression is dysthymic disorder. ***Dysthymic disorder*** (or ***dysthymia***) refers to a chronic low-level depression lasting more than two years, with intervals of normal moods that never last more than a few weeks or months. The effects of dysthymic disorder on functioning may be more subtle, as when people who are chronically depressed choose professions that underutilise their talents because of a lack of confidence, self-esteem or motivation. Dysthymic disorder is a chronic disorder characterised by continuous depression punctuated by bouts of major depression. When followed up over five years, roughly three-quarters of dysthymic patients with no prior history of major depression have their first major depressive episode (Klein, Schwartz, Rose, & Leader, 2000).

Bipolar disorder

A manic episode, or ***mania***, is characterised by a period of abnormally elevated or expansive mood. While manic, a person usually has an inflated sense of self that reaches grandiose proportions. During a manic episode people generally require less sleep, experience their thoughts as racing and feel a constant need to talk. Individuals with ***bipolar disorder*** have manic episodes but often experience both emotional 'poles' of depression and mania. (These symptoms are in contrast to those of ***unipolar depression***, in which the person experiences major depression but not mania.) About 15 to 20 percent of patients who have manic episodes also develop psychotic delusions and hallucinations (Lehmann, 1985).

The risk of developing a bipolar disorder is low. The lifetime prevalence in Australia is about 1.5 percent (Parker, Wilhelm, & Asghari, 1997). It can be one of the most debilitating and lethal psychiatric disorders, with a suicide rate between 10 and 20 percent (Goodwin & Ghaemi, 1998; MacKinnon, Jamison, & DePaulo, 1997). Former rugby league great Andrew Johns stunned the sporting world in mid-2007 by admitting he had battled bipolar disorder and used illicit drugs for much of his career. Johns described how his mental illness would affect him on the playing field — he was sometimes brimming with creativity and excitement, and at other times both withdrawn and apathetic. However, disorders on the bipolar 'spectrum' are much more common if less severe variants of the disorder, in which the individual experiences hypomanic episodes, are included. These episodes have features similar to mania but are less intense (Mitchell, Malhi, & Ball, 2004).

Seasonal affective disorder

Most people show mild seasonal mood changes; however, for some, lack of sunlight in the winter can trigger ***seasonal affective disorder (SAD)***, a depressive syndrome that occurs during a particular season that can be treated by exposing patients to high-intensity fluorescent lights (Terman, Terman, & Ross, 1998). SAD is characterised by mood and behaviour changes with regular seasonal climatic variation. Morrissey, Raggatt, James, and Rogers (1996) examined SAD in tropical north Queensland, where two distinct seasons are typically experienced. The wet season (summer) is characterised by high temperatures, high levels of humidity and monsoonal rainfall. In contrast, the dry season (winter) is characterised by dry weather (it is generally rainless) and mild to warm temperatures. Morrissey et al. (1996) found that at least one in four Townsville residents were adversely affected by the summer wet season — the excessive heat and humidity negatively affected the north Queenslanders' mood and behaviour.

INTERIM SUMMARY

Mood disorders are characterised by disturbances in emotion and mood, including both depressed and manic states (characterised by symptoms such as abnormally elevated mood, grandiosity and racing thoughts). The most severe form of depression is ***major depressive disorder***, characterised by depressed mood and loss of interest in pleasurable activities. ***Dysthymic disorder*** refers to a chronic low-level depression lasting more than two years, with intervals of normal moods that never last more than a few weeks or months. In ***bipolar disorder***, individuals have manic episodes and may also experience intense depression. In ***seasonal affective disorder***, mood and behaviour changes with regular seasonal climatic variation.

Theories of depression

Depression can arise for many different reasons. As in schizophrenia, biological and psychological processes often interact, with environmental events frequently 'igniting' a biological vulnerability. However, unlike schizophrenia, depression is common even among people without a genetic vulnerability.

Genetics

Although heritability is considerably lower than in schizophrenia, genes clearly play a major role in many cases of depression (see Hill & Sahhar, 2006). Most heritability estimates for major depression are in the range of 30 to 40 percent; to put it another way, a family history of depression doubles or triples an individual's risk of a mood disorder.

Bipolar disorder, like schizophrenia, probably requires a biological predisposition (Bowden, 2005). Roughly 80 to 90 percent of individuals with bipolar disorder have a family history of some mood disorder (Andreasen et al., 1987; Winokur & Tanna, 1969). First-degree relatives of bipolar patients have an 11.5 percent risk of developing the disease, which is 15 to 20 times higher than in the general population (Schlesser & Altshuler, 1983). Twin studies provide strong support for the role of genetic factors in the development of the disorder as well, with heritability estimated to be as high as 84 percent (Cardno, Marshall, et al., 1999).

Neural transmission

Serotonin and norepinephrine have been implicated in both major depression and bipolar disorders (Bellivier et al., 1998; Mann et al., 2000, see also Marchand, Dilda, & Jensen, 2005). That is, reduced serotonin levels increase depressive symptoms. This finding makes neurobiological sense because these same neurotransmitters are involved in the capacity to be aroused or energised and in the control of other functions affected by depression, such as sleep cycles and hunger. Drugs that increase the activity of these neurotransmitters decrease the symptoms of depression (and hence are called antidepressants; see chapter 16).

Environmental factors

Environmental factors are important as well, both in creating underlying diatheses for depression such as rejection-sensitivity or depressive ways of viewing the self and the world, and in triggering episodes of major depression (Lewinsohn, Allen, Seeley, & Gotlib, 1999). Early childhood and familial experiences play an important role in the aetiology of depression (Burns, Andrews, & Szabo, 2002; Gilman, Kawachi, Fitzmaurice, & Buka, 2003; Higgins, 2003; Moos, Schutte, Brennan, & Moos, 2005). Depressed adults are more likely than other people to have been raised in disruptive, hostile and negative home environments (Brown & Harris, 1989; Kendler, Neale, Kessler, & Heath, 1993). Depressed children report a greater incidence of negative life events (such as family deaths and divorce) than their non-depressed peers (Nolen-Hoeksema, Girgus, & Seligman, 1992).

Adult experiences also play a significant role. Severe stressors (such as loss of a significant other or a job) tend to occur within six to nine months prior to the onset of depression in roughly 90 percent of people who become depressed (Brown & Harris, 1978; Brown, Harris, & Hepworth, 1994; Frank, Anderson, Reynolds, Ritenour, & Kupfer, 1994). High levels of expressed emotion (especially criticism) in the families of patients with major depression predict relapse, much as in schizophrenia — a finding that has been replicated cross-culturally (Hooley & Teasdale, 1989; Okasha et al., 1994). Lack of an intimate relationship is also a risk factor for depression, particularly in women (Brown & Harris, 1989).

Adult experiences influence the course of bipolar illness as well. In one study, bipolar patients with high life stress were over four times more likely to relapse than those with few significant stressors (Ellicott, Hammen, Gitlin, Brown, & Jamison, 1990). In another study, bipolar patients who experienced severe negative life events took three times as long to recover from an episode as patients with less severe stressors (Johnson & Miller, 1997).

The negative environments of depressed people are not, however, always independent of their actions (Joiner, 2000). Behavioural–genetic analyses suggest that about one-third of the stressors that precipitate depression — such as accidents or alcohol-related injuries — themselves reflect genetic tendencies towards high-risk behaviour (Kendler, Karkowski, & Prescott, 1999). Experimental research also finds that depressed people seek out partners who view them negatively, and they prefer negative to positive feedback (Giesler, Josephs, & Swann, 1996; Swann, Stein-Seroussi, & Giesler, 1992; Swann, Wenzlaff,

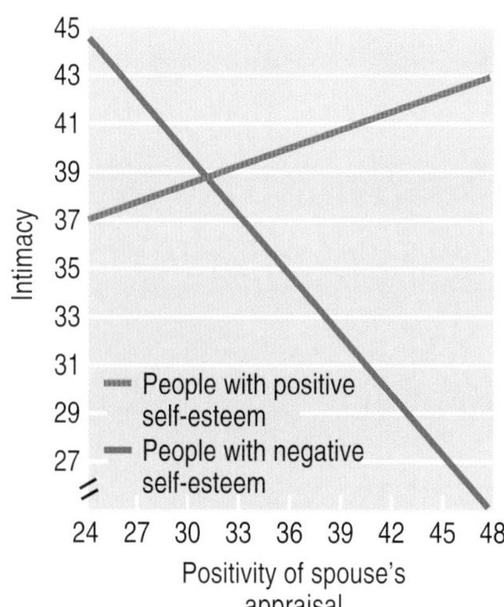

FIGURE 15.5
Intimacy as a function of positivity of spouse's appraisal. The graph shows self-reported intimacy with spouse (intimacy defined in terms of both feelings of closeness and spending time together) for people with positive and negative views of themselves. Unlike people with positive views of themselves, people who view themselves negatively and who are vulnerable to depression report the most intimacy with partners who view them negatively.

SOURCE: De La Ronde and Swann (1998, p. 378).

Krull, & Pelham, 1992). Like other people, depressed individuals seek others who see them as they see themselves (chapter 17) — even when this means being surrounded by people who view them negatively. This characteristic extends to romantic partners as well: people who view themselves negatively report greater intimacy with partners who view them similarly (figure 15.5) (De La Ronde & Swann, 1998).

Cognitive theories

Cognitive theories look for the roots of depression in dysfunctional patterns of thinking (Otto et al., 2007). Learned helplessness theory ties depression to expectancies of helplessness in the face of unpleasant events (chapter 6). According to helplessness theory, the way people feel depends on the way they explain events or outcomes to themselves, particularly aversive events (Abramson, Seligman, & Teasdale, 1978; Peterson & Seligman, 1984). People with a pessimistic explanatory style, who interpret the causes of bad occurrences as internal (their own fault), stable (unchanging) and global (far-reaching), are more likely to become depressed. Upon being jilted by a lover, for example, a person vulnerable to depression may conclude that he is unlovable.

Depressed people differ both in the content of their thinking — how negative their ideas about themselves and the world are — and in their cognitive processes — the ways they manipulate and use information (Hollon, 1988). Aaron Beck (1976, 1991), who developed the major cognitive theory of depression, argues that depressed people interpret events unfavourably, do not like themselves and regard the future pessimistically. Beck calls this negative outlook on the world, the self and the future the ***negative triad***. The negative triad affects mood, motivation and behaviour leading to things such as depressed mood, paralysis of will, avoidance, suicidal wishes and increased dependency (Beck, 1976).

Research suggests that depressed individuals process information about themselves in a negative way automatically and implicitly, perceiving even neutral or positive information negatively (Bargh & Tota, 1988; Mineka & Sutton, 1992). An outgrowth of learned helplessness theory, called hopelessness theory, draws on Beck's observation that depressed people view the future negatively (Abramson, Metalsky, & Alloy, 1989; Alloy et al., 2000). According to this view, depression in some people reflects the loss of hope that things will improve in the future.

Beck (1976) calls the cognitive mechanisms by which a depressed person negatively transforms neutral or positive information ***cognitive distortions***. Consider the following interaction between a therapist and a highly intelligent patient who was afraid to go back to university to pursue a career in law (Beck, 1976):

PATIENT: I can't go back to school. I'm just not smart enough.
THERAPIST: How did you do the last time you were in school?
PATIENT: Um ... I got mostly As. But that was a long time ago. And what have I ever done career-wise that suggests I could handle being a lawyer?
THERAPIST: That's not really a fair question is it? Don't you think your low image of yourself has something to do with why you haven't done anything 'spectacular' career-wise?
PATIENT: I guess you're right. I'm as smart as my sister and she's a lawyer.
THERAPIST: Right.
PATIENT: But what have I ever done career-wise that says I could handle being a lawyer?

The patient repeatedly doubts herself, ignores her past successes and generalises in ways that do not fit the 'data'. At the end, she simply repeats a self-doubting question that she has just admitted is based on a faulty premise.

Beck (1976, 1985) has identified a number of cognitive errors typical of depressed patients. In arbitrary inference, the person draws a conclusion in the absence of supporting evidence or in the presence of contradictory evidence. The patient in the previous dialogue used arbitrary inference when she concluded with little reason that she could not succeed at university despite prior success. Similarly, when faced with contradictory evidence (her prior grades), she arbitrarily dismissed that as 'a long time ago'.

Magnification and minimisation are biases in evaluating the relative importance of events. For example, a man reacted to storm damage to his house by thinking, 'The side of the house is wrecked . . . It will cost a fortune to fix it'. In fact, the damage was minor and cost only about $50 to repair (Beck, 1976). Personalisation occurs when depressed people relate external events to themselves without good reason, as when a student with the highest grades in a class assumed the teacher had a low opinion of him whenever she complimented another student. Overgeneralisation occurs when a person draws a general conclusion on the basis of a single incident. For example, one depressed patient, after a disagreement with his parents, concluded, 'I can't get along with anybody' (Beck, 1985).

Psychodynamic theories

Psychodynamic theorists argue that depression may have a number of roots, such as identification with a depressed or belittling parent or an attachment history that predisposes the person to fear of rejection or abandonment (Blatt & Homann, 1992). Unlike cognitive theories, which focus on faulty cognition, psychodynamic explanations focus on motivation. For example, the patient described by Beck who was afraid to go back to university and denied her prior successes might have been afraid to get her hopes up and thus defended against them with pessimism. If we do not wish, we cannot be disappointed.

From a psychodynamic perspective, depression cannot be isolated from the personality structure of the individual experiencing it (see Kernberg, 1984). A person who has poor object relations (difficulty investing in relationships and maintaining a constant view of the self) may experience depression because he is prone to feeling abandoned, empty and alone. Such patients frequently report feeling that they are totally evil and not just helpless or incompetent. Similarly, a person who is so self-centred and narcissistic that he cannot form deep attachments to other people is likely to become depressed in middle age, when he becomes more aware of his mortality and realises that the grandiose dreams of his youth are not likely to be actualised.

In contrast, a depressed person with a greater capacity for relationships may feel that he is a failure at meeting standards and consequently be vulnerable to feeling guilty or inadequate (Blatt & Zuroff, 1992; Wixom, Ludolph, & Westen, 1993). Psychodynamic and cognitive theorists have recently converged on a distinction between two kinds of vulnerability to depression, one related to interpersonal distress and the other to failure to meet standards. People whose depression focuses on interpersonal issues tend to develop depression in the face of rejection or loss, whereas people whose depression focuses on autonomy and achievement issues tend to become depressed by failures (Bieling, Beck, & Brown, 2000).

Gender and mood disorders

Women are more likely to suffer from mood disorders, including depression, than men in Australia (AIHW, 2010; see also Fullagar & Gattuso, 2002; Wilhelm et al., 2003). Statistics indicate that women are about twice as likely to suffer from depression as men in Australia (Fullagar & Gattuso, 2002; Wilhelm et al., 2003). Results in an Australian mental health survey (ABS, 2007) showed that almost one million people (6.2 percent of the population) reported an affective disorder within the past 12 months, with depression being most prevalent (4.1 percent). The rate of depression was higher among women (5.1 percent) than men (3.1 percent). Men are more likely than women to experience problems with alcohol, antisocial personality disorder and ADHD. Part of this difference may reflect biological differences between men and women.

History and culture, however, seem to discount this explanation. Only in recent history have women seemed to surpass men in the frequency with which they are diagnosed with mood disorders, particularly depression (Unger, 1979). Furthermore, men in developing countries, such as India, are more likely than women to report symptoms associated with depression (Rothblum, 1983).

Even within Australia, ethnic differences in prevalence rates of depression as related to gender have been observed. Many of these differences are related to the country of origin and languages spoken. According to a national survey on mental health and well being in Australia, immigrants born in the main English-speaking countries (USA, Canada, UK, Ireland, South Africa and New Zealand) had higher rates of depression (16 percent) than those born in countries where English is not the main language spoken (14 percent), and the relative differences were higher among males than females (ABS, 1998). Australia is home to many ethnic, religious and language groups and the extent to which various ethnic minority groups experience depression and other mental health problems is difficult to gauge. For example, depression among Chinese people living in traditional Asian regions is low; however, recent research from the University of New South Wales suggests that Chinese immigrants to Australia may be at a greater risk of depression and anxiety if they do not successfully integrate into Australian society (Tang, Dennis, & Comino, 2009). Cultural factors influence how mental illness is experienced, how it affects help-seeking behaviour and whether people adhere and respond to treatment (Minas, Klimidis, & Kokanovic, 2007). Thus, the complex interplay between culture, gender, language and mental health requires further attention to better understand the prevalence of mental health problems in men and women of different ethnic origin.

If biology is not the most viable explanation, perhaps differences in the prevalence rates of different disorders among men and women reflect differences in learning and socialisation. As women internalise things more than men, the frequency of depression and other mood disorders would be expected to be higher among women. As men are socialised to be more active, it is not surprising that psychological disorders in men manifest themselves in more active ways, such as conduct disorder.

Yet again, gender differences in psychological problems may reflect differences in the willingness of men and women to disclose problems they are having and differences in their willingness to seek psychological help. Women are more likely than men both to talk about problems they are having and to seek professional help for those problems. In short, women are more likely to come to the attention of psychologists and psychiatrists than men.

A GLOBAL VISTA

Depression: cross-cultural differences

Depression, like most mental disorders, has equivalents in every culture, but the way people view and experience depression varies considerably. Depressed Nigerians complain that 'ants keep creeping in parts of my brain', whereas Chinese complain that they feel 'exhaustion of their nerves' and that their hearts are being 'squeezed and weighed down' (Good & Kleinman, 1985, p. 4). While people in Western society tend to view depression as originating within themselves, the Maori believe that distressing emotional states such as sadness can be caused by an imbalance in spiritual, mental, physical and family wellbeing (Durie, 2001).

Do these differences imply that the actual subjective experience of depression differs cross-culturally? The answer appears to be yes. Members of less individualistic societies tend to focus more on the behavioural dimensions of depression (such as lethargy, fatigue, loss of appetite and slowness of movement) than on the subjective experience. In contrast, contemporary Westerners are far more attuned to their internal psychological states than people in most cultures in human history. When they suffer from depression, they typically focus on their inner sense of helplessness, hopelessness, guilt and low self-esteem.

Many Indigenous Australians still carry the psychological legacy left by the colonisation of the country and the loss of their traditional cultures. According to McKenna (1990), pre-conquest Aboriginal Australians understood themselves to be in a secure and meaningful cosmos — a security that was obliterated by the arrival of the Europeans. The devastating effects of colonisation have resulted in trauma, grief and loss for successive generations of Indigenous Australians (Swan & Raphael, 1995). The high rates of mental illness, alcoholism and suicide within many Indigenous communities derive from the history of invasion, the ongoing impact of colonisation, loss of land and culture, and the forced separation of children from parents. The unresolved grief associated with such trauma contributes to the manifestation of depression in Aboriginal Australians and other mental health problems in Indigenous communities. In non-Indigenous communities, this level of psychological trauma and abuse can only be found in populations subjected to systematic torture, genocide, concentration camps, or urban or family violence (AIHW, 1999).

Current research reinforces the importance of culture for diagnosis, classification and access to mental health services (Tapsell & Mellsop, 2007). Better understanding how people conceptualise depression within and across cultures is crucial to effective treatment (Johnson, Mayanja, Bangirana, & Kizito, 2009). For example, older Korean American adults hold negative attitudes towards depression, believing it to be a sign of personal weakness and that having a mentally ill family member brings shame to the whole family (Jang, Chiriboga, & Okazaki, 2009). This cultural misconception and stigma about mental disorders also influences attitudes to mental health services (Jang et al., 2009) and highlights the need to develop a culturally competent and contextually relevant model for service delivery (Johnson et al., 2009).

INTERIM SUMMARY

Genetic factors increase the vulnerability to depressive disorders, particularly major depression, and play a central role in the aetiology of bipolar disorder. Serotonin and norepinephrine have been implicated in both major depression and bipolar disorder. Both childhood and adult experiences also play a significant role in the aetiology and course of mood disorders. According to cognitive theories, dysfunctional thought patterns play a crucial role in depression. Depressed people transform neutral or positive information into depressive cognitions through ***cognitive distortions***. According to psychodynamic theory, depressive symptoms, like other psychological symptoms, can be understood only in the context of the individual's personality structure. Depression has equivalents in all cultures, but the way people view and experience it varies considerably.

Anxiety disorders

Anxiety, like sadness, is a normal feeling. Anxiety typically functions as an internal alarm bell that warns of potential danger. In ***anxiety disorders***, however, the individual is subject to anxiety states that may be intense, frequent or even continuous. These 'false alarms' may lead to dysfunctional avoidance behaviour, as when a person refuses to leave the house for fear of a panic attack. Anxiety disorders are one of the most frequently occurring categories of mental disorders in the general population, affecting around 10 percent of the population at any given time (ABS, 2007; see also Somers, Goldner, Waraich, & Hsu, 2006). According to the ABS (2007), women in Australia are more likely than men to experience anxiety disorders (18 percent compared with 11 percent), and this gender difference is evident by age six (Lewinsohn, Gotlib, Lewinsohn, Seeley, & Allen, 1998). Although many anxiety disorders are triggered under particular circumstances, some people (about 2 percent of the population) have a ***generalised anxiety disorder***, characterised by persistent anxiety at a moderate but disturbing level and excessive and unrealistic worry about life circumstances (Stapinski, Abbott, & Rapee, 2010).

As previously mentioned, anxiety disorders are more commonly associated with depression than any other disorder, and a new diagnostic category of Mixed Depression Anxiety is currently being considered for inclusion in DSM-5 (APA, 2010). Half the people with an affective or depressive disorder in one Australian study also reported an anxiety disorder (ABS, 1998; see also Andrews, Henderson, & Hall, 2001). Several other anxiety disorders are also being reviewed for possible inclusion in DSM-5, including Tic Disorder, Hoarding Disorder and Skin Picking Disorder (APA, 2010).

Women have higher rates of anxiety disorders than men at all ages (table 15.8), although the rate of difference between the genders is not constant throughout the life span (ABS, 1998). Women aged 45–54 have much higher rates of anxiety disorders than men, although the gap narrows sharply in older age groups. In a recent national survey of mental health and wellbeing, anxiety disorders were reported by 14 percent of people aged 16 to 85 years (ABS, 2009b). Anxiety disorders were much less common in women over 65 years (6.3 percent) compared to those aged 16–54 years (21 percent).

TABLE 15.8 **Prevalence rates for anxiety disorders (lifetime)**

Anxiety disorder	Males (%)	Females (%)	Persons (%)
Panic disorder	4.6	5.8	5.2
Agoraphobia	4.1	7.9	6.0
Social phobia	8.4	12.8	10.6
Generalised anxiety disorder	4.4	7.3	5.9
Obsessive compulsive disorder	2.3	3.2	2.8
Post-traumatic stress disorder	8.6	15.8	12.2
Any anxiety disorder	20.4	32.0	26.2

SOURCE: ABS (2007), p. 27.

Types of anxiety disorders

In this section, we review the symptoms of some other common anxiety disorders. Although we discuss them separately, people with one anxiety disorder often have others (Barlow, 2002).

Phobia

At any given time, about 5 percent of the population has at least one irrational fear, or ***phobia***, and more than twice that percentage have a phobia at some point in their lifetimes (Graske & Waters, 2005; Ohman & Mineka, 2001). For most people, mild phobic responses to spiders or snakes have minimal effect on their lives. For others with diagnosable phobias, irrational fears can be extremely uncomfortable, such as fear of riding in aeroplanes.

Although plane crashes kill far fewer people than cigarettes, phobias of flying are far more common than cigarette phobias. Learning theorists have proposed that we are biologically prepared to fear certain stimuli, such as extreme heights, darkness and snakes, which posed dangers to our ancestors (chapter 6).

A common type of phobia is ***social phobia***, a marked fear that occurs when the person is in a specific social or performance situation, such as intense public speaking anxiety (see Hofmann & DiBartolo, 2001). The lifetime prevalence for this disorder is almost 15 percent (Magee, Eaton, Wittchen, McGonagle, & Kessler, 1996). Research suggests the potential importance of distinguishing two kinds of social phobias: public speaking phobias, which often occur in people without any other psychiatric problems, and other social phobias, such as intense anxiety at interacting with other people, which typically suggest greater disturbance (Kessler, Stein, & Berglund, 1998).

Panic disorder

Panic disorder is characterised by attacks of intense fear and feelings of doom or terror not justified by the situation. The attacks typically include physiological symptoms such as shortness of breath, dizziness, heart palpitations, trembling and chest pains (Barlow, 2002). Psychological symptoms include fear of dying or going crazy. Lifetime prevalence for panic disorder is in the range of 1.4 to 2.9 percent cross-culturally, in countries as diverse as Canada, New Zealand and Lebanon (Weissman et al., 1997).

Agoraphobia

A related disorder is ***agoraphobia***, a fear of being in places or situations from which escape might be difficult, such as crowded grocery stores or elevators. Between 1 and 2 percent of the population suffer from agoraphobia at some point in their lives (Wilson & Edwards, 1996). Agoraphobia can be extremely debilitating. The person may not leave the house because of intense fears of being outside alone, in a crowd, on a bridge, or travelling in a train, car or bus. Agoraphobia is often instigated by a fear of having a panic attack; ultimately the individual suffering from this disorder may avoid leaving home for fear of having a panic attack in a public place (Royal Australian and New Zealand College of Psychiatrists Clinical Practice Guidelines Team for Panic Disorder and Agoraphobia, 2003).

Obsessive–compulsive disorder

> Mrs. C is a 47-year-old mother of six children who are named in alphabetical order. For 10 years she had been suffering with a compulsion to wash excessively, sometimes 25 to 30 times a day for five- to ten-minute intervals. Her daily morning shower lasts two hours, with rituals involving each part of her body . . . If she loses track of her ritual, she must start at the beginning. Mrs. C's compulsions affect her family as well. She does not let family members wear a pair of underwear more than once and prohibits washing them. The family spends large sums of money buying new underwear for daily use. Mrs. C has hoarded various items such as towels, sheets, earrings and her own clothes for the past two decades.
>
> Prochaska (1980).

Obsessive–compulsive disorder is marked by recurrent obsessions and compulsions that cause severe distress and significantly interfere with an individual's life. ***Obsessions*** are persistent irrational thoughts or ideas, such as the notion that a terrible accident is about to occur to a loved one or that underwear is filled with germs. ***Compulsions*** are intentional behaviours or mental acts performed in response to an obsession and in a stereotyped fashion, often as a magical way of warding off the obsessive thought (e.g. washing every part of the body over and over in the shower in a prescribed order).

People with obsessive–compulsive disorder experience their compulsions as irresistible acts that must be performed, even though they generally recognise them as irrational.

Common compulsions include counting, hand washing and touching; common obsessions are repetitive thoughts of contamination, violence or doubt (Jenike, 1983). Typically, obsessive–compulsive people experience intense anxiety or even panic if they are prevented from performing their rituals. Obsessive–compulsive disorders typically begin during childhood, adolescence or early adulthood (Millet et al., 2004). A longitudinal study found that roughly half of the people with the disorder continued to have it over 40 years later (Skoog & Skoog, 1999).

Post-traumatic stress disorder

A type of anxiety disorder is ***post-traumatic stress disorder (PTSD)***, as evidenced in the story abut Esther that began this chapter. This disorder received more attention following the Vietnam War, and is marked by flashbacks and recurrent thoughts of a psychologically distressing event outside the range of usual human experience. Often the traumatic event is of horrific proportions, such as seeing someone murdered, being raped or losing one's home in an earthquake or other natural disaster. One study examined Cambodian refugees who escaped massive genocide during the 1980s but experienced multiple losses, including uprooting from their homes, torture and rape, as well as immigration to a new country with a new language. Over 80 percent had PTSD (Carlson & Rosser-Hogan, 1991). High rates of PTSD symptoms were similarly found in a large study of ethnic Kosovars, the majority of whom reported having been victims of starvation, violence or rape at the hands of Serbian troops who forced them from their homes in 1998 (Cardozo, Vergara, Agani, & Gotway, 2000).

Even in a country such as Australia, which has never seen war on home soil (save the bombing of Darwin in World War II), PTSD is quite common. For instance, a nurse developed PTSD after counselling relatives and friends of people killed in the Port Arthur massacre. The nurse was called upon to help out in the aftermath of the massacre, including being with relatives while they inspected the bodies of their loved ones for identification, despite having no formal grief counselling training. The woman suffered agoraphobia and insomnia, had frequent panic attacks and flashbacks, and was in and out of psychiatric hospitals since the episode. In August 2004 she won a six-figure payout after a successful lawsuit against her employers. PTSD is not, however, an automatic consequence of trauma. As many as 65 percent of Australians have experienced at least one traumatic life event and it is estimated that around 5 percent of Australians have had PTSD at some point in their lives (The Australian Centre for Posttraumatic Mental Health, 2007).

Post-traumatic stress disorder has a number of symptoms: nightmares, flashbacks, deliberate efforts to avoid thoughts or feelings about the traumatic event, diminished responsiveness to the external world and psychological numbness. Other symptoms include hypervigilance (constant scanning of the environment), an exaggerated startle response (such as jumping when tapped on the shoulder) and autonomic activation when exposed to stimuli associated with the traumatic event. The disorder frequently emerges only some time after the trauma. A longitudinal study of Gulf War veterans found, for example, that rates of PTSD more than doubled between five days and two years after veterans returned home from the war (Wolfe, Erickson, Sharkansky, King, & King, 1999). The disorder can last a lifetime, as demonstrated in research on combat veterans, prisoners of war, torture victims and Holocaust survivors (see Basoglu et al., 1994; Sutker, Winstead, Galina, & Allai, 1991; chapter 11).

INTERIM SUMMARY

In ***anxiety disorders***, people experience frequent, intense and irrational anxiety. ***Generalised anxiety disorder*** is characterised by persistent anxiety and excessive worry about life circumstances. A common type of ***phobia*** (irrational fear) is ***social phobia***, which occurs when the person is in a specific social or performance situation. ***Panic disorder*** is characterised by attacks of intense fear and feelings of doom or terror not justified by the situation. ***Agoraphobia*** involves a fear of being in places or situations from which escape might be difficult. ***Obsessive–compulsive disorder*** is marked by recurrent ***obsessions*** (persistent thoughts or ideas) and ***compulsions*** (stereotyped acts performed in response to an obsession). ***Post-traumatic stress disorder*** is marked by flashbacks and recurrent thoughts of a psychologically distressing event outside the range of usual human experience.

Aetiology of anxiety disorders

As in depression, genetic vulnerability often contributes but is not essential to the development of most anxiety disorders (Carey, 1990; Gorman, Kent, Sullivan, & Coplan, 2000; Kendler, Neale, Kessler, Heath, & Eaves, 1992). Twin and family studies show genetic contributions to many anxiety syndromes, such as panic and simple phobia (Fyer, Mannuzza, Chapman, Martin, & Klein, 1995; Goldstein, Wickramaratne, Horwath, & Weissman, 1997). Obsessive–compulsive disorder shows particularly high heritability, with concordance rates in the range of 85 percent for identical twins and 50 percent for fraternal twins (see Nestadt et al., 2000).

APPLY + DISCUSS

People who suffer from panic attacks are ever vigilant of any signs of arousal, attributing that arousal to the onset of a panic attack.

- Is it possible that these individuals might misattribute the source of their arousal?
- What factors or substances might produce physiological arousal in the body that may be interpreted as a panic attack by individuals who experience them?
- Would chemicals such as caffeine or nicotine produce such arousal?

Stressful life events play an important role in most anxiety disorders as well. Roughly 80 percent of patients suffering from panic attacks report a negative life event that coincided with their first attack, and panic patients report a higher incidence of stressful life events in the months preceding the onset of their symptoms than comparison subjects (Finlay-Jones & Brown, 1981). Stressful events occurring in childhood, such as loss of a parent or childhood sexual abuse, also predispose people to anxiety disorders in adulthood (Barlow, 2002; Brewin, Andrews, & Valentine, 2000). For example, separation from a parent in childhood makes people more likely to develop PTSD after exposure to a traumatic event in adulthood, as does exposure to previous traumas, particularly in childhood (Breslau, Chilcoat, Kessler, & Davis, 1999; Breslau, Davis, Andreski, Peterson, & Schultz, 1997). High expressed emotion in family members is also related to anxiety symptoms (Chambless & Steketee, 1999).

Personality, coping styles and intellectual functioning can predispose people to anxiety disorders as well. For example, one study examined Gulf War veterans at two points after the war (Benotsch et al., 2000). The best predictor of PTSD symptoms at the second assessment (roughly a year after the first) was the use of avoidant coping strategies — that is, efforts to avoid thinking about painful events. These data make considerable sense in the light of research on emotional suppression (chapter 10), which finds that suppression of thoughts or feelings keeps them at a high state of implicit activation. This implicit activation renders people who have experienced traumatic events likely to remain vigilant towards them and to experience unintended 'breakthroughs' of memories or intrusive thoughts.

Another study found that Vietnam veterans with lower IQ (assessed prior to service in the military) were more likely to develop PTSD than veterans with higher IQ when exposed to similar experiences (Macklin et al., 1998). Although the reasons are not entirely clear, a likely explanation is that greater intelligence allows more flexible coping, and greater verbal ability allows people to put traumatic events into words more easily and hence focus on and remember rather than suppress them.

David Barlow (2002), a leading cognitive–behavioural theorist and researcher, has offered a comprehensive model of the development of anxiety disorders, focusing in particular on panic. In Barlow's view, a combination of heritable negative affect and stressful early experiences can generate a vulnerability to anxiety and depression, which provides fertile ground for the development of an initial panic attack. The attack includes autonomic responses such as quickened pulse, pounding heart, difficulty breathing, dry mouth and sweaty palms — responses that then become associated with the panic state through classical conditioning. Thus, whenever the person starts to experience these feelings, she becomes frightened that a panic attack will occur. To put it another way, the individual develops a fear of fear (Goldstein & Chambless, 1978; Kenardy, Evans, & Ian, 1992).

Sufferers of panic attacks can experience symptoms like those experienced by a jogger who is pushing their personal physical limits, such as a racing pulse and sweating.

People with panic disorders thus become especially aware of their autonomic activity and are constantly on the lookout for signals of arousal. Panic patients show heightened awareness of cardiac changes such as rapid heartbeat and palpitations (Schmidt, Joiner, Staab, & Williams, 2003). They are also more likely to panic when exposed to air that contains slightly more carbon dioxide than normal (figure 15.6), presumably because they start to feel short of breath (Rapee, Brown, Antony, & Barlow, 1992). In panic-prone individuals, fear of their own autonomic responses magnifies anxiety and may trigger future attacks (Barlow, 2002). Repeated experiences of this sort may lead them to avoid situations associated with panic attacks or physiological arousal. Thus, people with panic disorders may give up jogging because it produces autonomic responses such as racing pulse and sweating that they associate with panic attacks. Such avoidance behaviour may ultimately lead to agoraphobia.

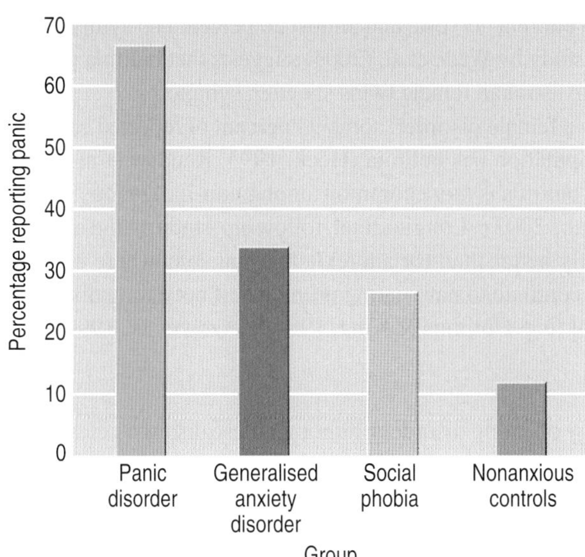

FIGURE 15.6
Precipitation of panic episodes by exposure to carbon dioxide-enriched air. Participants with various anxiety disorders were exposed to air with a slightly elevated carbon dioxide content (5.5 percent elevation), which makes breathing more difficult. Anxiety disordered patients were more likely to panic than normal participants; panic patients were particularly prone to experience panic symptoms.

SOURCE: Rapee et al. (1992, p. 545).

INTERIM SUMMARY

As in other disorders, heredity and environment both contribute to the aetiology of anxiety disorders as do adult and childhood stressors. Behaviourist theories implicate classical conditioning and negative reinforcement of avoidance behaviour in the aetiology and maintenance of anxiety disorders. Cognitive theorists emphasise negative biases in thinking, such as attention to threatening stimuli. A comprehensive cognitive–behavioural model suggests that patients develop classically conditioned fear of their own autonomic responses, which, combined with fearful thoughts, perpetuates anxiety and can trigger panic episodes.

Eating disorders

Some of the most common disorders that afflict women are eating disorders. The two most prevalent are anorexia nervosa and bulimia nervosa. A new disorder currently being considered for inclusion in the DSM-5 is Binge Eating Disorder (APA, 2010).

Anorexia nervosa and bulimia nervosa

Anorexia nervosa is an eating disorder in which the individual starves themself, exercises excessively or eliminates food in other ways (such as vomiting) until they are at least 15 percent below their ideal body weight. Anorexia is a life-threatening illness that can lead to permanent physiological changes (such as brittle bones) and death, usually through heart attack. Patients with anorexia have a distorted body image, often seeing themselves as fat even as they are wasting away (Siegfried, Berry, Hao, & Avraham, 2003). The disorder is about 10 times more prevalent in women than in men, and it typically begins in adolescence or the early adult years. In Australia, the rate of anorexia among young women is estimated to range between 1 and 2 percent (Kenardy, 1997; see also Wade, Bergin, Tiggemann, Bulik, & Fairburn, 2006).

Some variant of anorexia appears to have existed for at least seven centuries — mostly in the form of 'holy fasting' to escape the flesh in the name of God — and clear cases were described in the medical literature in the nineteenth century; however, the incidence appears to have skyrocketed in the late twentieth century (Bell, 1985; Bynum, 1987). The disorder only emerges in cultures and historical periods of relative affluence; people who are starving never develop anorexia (Bemporad, 1996).

Bulimia is characterised by a binge-and-purge syndrome. The person gorges on food (typically massive amounts of carbohydrates such as bags of potato chips) and then induces vomiting, uses laxatives or engages in some other form of behaviour to purge herself or himself of calories. The typical result is a feeling of relief, but it is often accompanied by depression and a sense of being out of control. In a study of 15 000 Australian women aged 18 to 22, Kenardy (1997) found that 4.8 percent might be diagnosed with bulimia nervosa, and almost 20 percent had symptoms of binge eating disorder. However, a more recent study by Wade et al. (2006) suggests that bulimia nervosa is becoming less prevalent, with 2.9 percent of Australian female twins showing symptoms.

Like anorexia, bulimia is almost exclusively a female disorder; some 90 percent of reported cases are female. About 3 to 5 percent of the female population has bulimia (Hoek, 1993; Kendler et al., 1991; see also Wade et al., 2006). Also like anorexia, bulimia is more common among non-Indigenous women than Indigenous women (Striegel-Moore et al., 2003). Longitudinal follow-up studies find that the long-term prognosis for bulimia is substantially better than for anorexia but that somewhere between 30 and 50 percent of women with the disorder continue to have eating problems, if not eating disorders, five to 10 years after initially seeking treatment (e.g. Collings & King, 1994; Herzog et al., 1999).

Aetiology of eating disorders

Researchers are still tracking down the aetiology of eating disorders, although these disorders clearly run in families, with the presence of anorexia or bulimia in a patient substantially increasing the likelihood that relatives will have one or the other disorder (Polivy & Herman, 2002; Strober, Freeman, Lampert, Diamond, & Kaye, 2000). On the biological side, a number of studies have documented genetic links between bulimia on the one hand and mood and anxiety disorders on the other (Kaye, Bulik, Thornton, Barbarich, & Masters, 2004), and have suggested that all three types of disorder share a common problem with serotonin regulation (Brewerton, 1995; Halmi, 1999; Kaye, Gendall, & Stober, 1998).

Many researchers have also emphasised the environmental influence of mass media and cultural norms that equate beauty and thinness. Australians will spend more than $745 million a year trying to lose weight (*Herald Sun*, 2010). Money will be spent on counselling, low-calorie foods and shakes, diet cookbooks and guides, dietary supplements, lap bands, and liposuction. An additional cost includes gyms, personal trainers and other exercise-related expenses (*Herald Sun*, 2010). Kenardy (1997) found that 47.8 percent of Australian women reported dieting to lose weight in the last year. Furthermore 20.9 percent of women who were underweight (BMI < 18.5) were currently dieting to lose weight.

Dieting is also a $100 million industry in New Zealand (Central Region Eating Disorder Services, 2007). According to the New Zealand Ministry of Health (2008), studies have found that 52 percent of females are dissatisfied with their body; in addition, 37 percent of girls have dieted (from as young as seven years old) and 14 percent of boys have dieted. In one group of women, 80 percent of the females were within normal weight limits, but only 18 percent of them thought their weight was normal (New Zealand Ministry of Health, 2008). For some women, obsession with thinness may put them at risk for the development of an eating disorder (Eating Difficulties Education Network, 2010). In this view, culture itself may be a diathesis for the development of a disorder that can be activated by particular stressors.

This cultural approach dovetails with an evolutionary view, which suggests that cultural norms that influence a person's capacity to attract high-status mates should create culture-specific vulnerabilities to psychopathology. Because physical appearance is a criterion males use in selecting mates (chapter 16), cultures that emphasise thinness as a criterion for beauty should generate a preoccupation among females about their weight (see Hamida, Mineka, & Bailey, 1998).

Other researchers have examined personality as a diathesis for the development of anorexia and bulimia. Researchers and clinicians have long noted that women with anorexia are often bright, talented perfectionists who are preoccupied with feeling in control (Bruch, 1973; Casper, Hedeker, & McClough, 1992; Fairburn, Cooper, Doll, & Welch, 1999) and that controlling food intake seems to be a way of maintaining control in general, particularly over impulses (Strauss & Ryan, 1987). Research also supports an observation first made by clinicians working with anorexic patients; namely, that they often have a wish to avoid becoming a physically mature woman (Garner & Garfinkel, 1979; Hick & Katzman, 1999). They are often successful in this aim: severely restricted food intake can stop the development of secondary sex characteristics such as breasts, halt menstruation and make the body look like a prepubescent girl's.

Unlike anorexics, bulimics are not characterised by any particular or consistent set of personality traits (Keel & Mitchell, 1997; Striegel-Moore, Silberstein, & Rodin, 1986), probably because patients who binge and purge are not a homogeneous group. Research suggests, in fact, that patients with eating disorders tend to fall into one of three groups based on their personality profiles (Goldner, Srikameswaran, Schroeder, Livesley, & Birmingham, 1999; Sohlberg & Strober, 1994; Westen & Harnden-Fischer, 2001). One group is high functioning, perfectionistic and self-critical. These patients may have symptoms of either disorder. Patients in the second group, who are more likely to have anorexia than bulimia, are overly controlled, inhibited, avoidant of relationships, depressed and emotionally 'shut down'. Patients who match the profile of the third group, who tend to be bulimic, are undercontrolled — impulsive, sexually promiscuous, frequently suicidal and prone to emotions that spiral out of control.

Research by Overton, Selway, Strongman, and Houston (2005) at the University of Canterbury, New Zealand, has examined the cognitive emotional experiences of women with eating disorders. Overton et al. (2005) found that women with eating disorders experience emotions more frequently than women without such disorders; they also experience higher levels of distress. Their findings indicate that women with eating disorders are adept at using eating to manipulate their emotional states, and the authors recommend that this dynamic be recognised as an important maintenance factor in the aetiology of eating disorders.

INTERIM SUMMARY

Two eating disorders are ***anorexia nervosa***, in which the individual drops below 85 percent of ideal body weight because of refusal to eat, and ***bulimia***, in which the person binges and then purges. Research on aetiology points to vulnerabilities caused by genetics, cultural norms for thinness and personality.

Somatoform disorders

Somatoform disorders occur when people complain of pain, suffering or illness but no physical problems can be identified to explain their ailments. The problems are psychological in nature rather than physical. However, that does not mean people with somatoform disorders are 'faking' their ailments as they genuinely feel the symptoms they describe. Singh (1998) suggests that the prevalence of somatoform disorders in Australia is similar to that of the United States at around 11 percent of the population at some time in their lives.

The two most common forms of this condition are conversion disorder and hypochondriasis. ***Conversion disorder*** is characterised by a loss or significant change in a physical function (such as sight, loss of feeling or the ability to walk) without any physical problem to explain the condition. People with this disorder 'convert' mental distress they are feeling into a physical condition.

Hypochondriasis (commonly called hypochondria) occurs when people believe they are suffering from an illness or ailment, even when there is no medical evidence to support that belief. People with this disorder are often called 'hypochondriacs'. They tend to closely monitor their physical condition and conclude that any tiny alteration from their normal state is evidence of a disease or illness. Hypochondriacs often go doctor shopping — consulting a number of physicians looking for confirmation of the ailments they believe are afflicting them.

Somatoform disorders may also be amended in the DSM-5 to include a new *complex somatic symptom disorder,* comprising hypochondriasis, among others, in this category (APA, 2010).

INTERIM SUMMARY

Somatoform disorders occur when people complain of pain, suffering or illness but no physical problems can be identified to explain their ailments. The two most common forms of this condition are conversion disorder and hypochondriasis. ***Conversion disorder*** is characterised by a loss or significant change in a physical function without any physical problem to explain the condition. ***Hypochondriasis*** occurs when people believe they are suffering from an illness or ailment, even when there is no medical evidence to support that belief.

Dissociative disorders

A central feature of a class of disorders akin to PTSD is ***dissociation***, whereby significant aspects of experience are kept separate and distinct (i.e. disassociated) in memory and consciousness. In ***dissociative disorders***, the individual experiences disruptions in consciousness, memory, sense of identity or perception. The patient may have significant periods of amnesia, find herself in a new city with no recollection of her old life or feel separated from her emotions and experience, as if her mind and body were in two different places. Dissociation is usually a response to overwhelming psychic pain, as when victims of severe physical abuse or rape mentally separate themselves from the situation by experiencing themselves and their feelings as outside of their bodies.

The most severe dissociative disorder is ***dissociative identity disorder*** (popularly known as multiple personality disorder), in which at least two separate and distinct personalities exist within the same person. One patient with this disorder had two lives, including two addresses, two sets of doctors and two lovers who did not understand why she was so often unavailable.

The prevalence of dissociative identity disorder is a matter of controversy. The disorder appears to be quite rare (see Modestin, 1992; Ross, Anderson, Fleisher, & Norton, 1991), despite the attention it has drawn by gripping accounts such as *Sybil* (Schreiber, 1973) and *The Three Faces of Eve* (Thigpen & Cleckley, 1954). Although poorly trained clinicians may overdiagnose the disorder or 'create' it in highly suggestible patients whose sense of identity is already tenuous, some intriguing data suggest that the different personalities in genuine cases may be both psychologically and physiologically distinct. For example, not only do they have access to different memories and look strikingly different on personality tests, but they may also differ in physiological qualities such as muscle tension, heart rate and even allergies (Putnam, 1991). Two different personalities may also differ in handedness (Henninger, 1992).

Individuals with dissociative disorders typically come from chaotic home environments and have suffered physical and sexual abuse in childhood. In fact, a history of extreme trauma, usually sexual abuse, is found in nearly all cases of dissociative disorder (Lewis, Yeager, Swica, Pincus, & Lewis, 1997; Scroppo, Drob, Weinberger, & Eagle, 1998), leading some to view dissociative disorders much like PTSD (Putnam, 1995). Unlike most psychological disorders, twin research suggests that environmental variables account for the disorder with little or no genetic influence (Waller & Ross, 1997). The vast majority of cases are female, probably because of the greater incidence of sexual abuse in females.

Personality disorders

MAKING CONNECTIONS

Personality refers to enduring patterns of thought, feeling, motivation and behaviour that are activated in particular circumstances (e.g. when interacting with peers, authority figures and women; chapter 11). A key feature of personality disorders is that these patterns are often not only socially peculiar or inappropriate but also relatively inflexible, so that the person cannot tailor the way he or she responds to the circumstance.

As we have seen, personality disorders are chronic and severe disturbances that substantially inhibit the capacity to love and to work. For example, people with narcissistic personality disorder have severe trouble in relationships because of a tendency to use people, to be hypersensitive to criticism, to feel entitled to special privileges and to become enraged when others do not respond to them in ways they find satisfying or appropriate to their status. Individuals with this disorder show little empathy for other people. One patient who was asked about the feelings of a woman he had just rejected callously remarked, 'What do I care? What can she do for me anymore? Hey, that's the breaks of the game — sometimes you dump, sometimes you get dumped. Nobody would be crying if this had happened to me.'

Table 15.9 shows the personality disorders in DSM-IV. The prevalence of personality disorders in the general population is unknown, but the best estimates are in the range of 10 percent (Lenzenweger, Loranger, Korfine, & Neff, 1997; see also Zimmerman, Rothschild, & Chelminski, 2005). We examine two of them here — borderline personality disorder, which is more prevalent in women, and antisocial personality disorder, which is more prevalent in men. Major revisions are being proposed for DSM-5 with regard to personality disorders. Under discussion are a new definition of personality disorders and suggestions of different levels for classifying personality functioning and types, including higher order personality trait domains. Several personality disorders currently defined in the DSM-IV may be removed in the subsequent edition (APA, 2010).

TABLE 15.9 DSM-IV Personality disorders*

Personality disorder	Description
Paranoid	Distrust and suspiciousness
Schizoid	Detachment from social relationships; restricted range of emotional expression
Schizotypal	Acute discomfort in close relationships; cognitive or perceptual distortions; eccentricity
Antisocial	Disregard for and violation of the rights of others
Borderline	Impulsivity and instability in interpersonal relationships, self-concept and emotion
Histrionic	Excessive emotionality and attention seeking
Narcissistic	Grandiosity, need for admiration and lack of empathy
Avoidant	Social inhibition and avoidance; feelings of inadequacy; hypersensitivity to negative evaluation
Dependent	Submissive and clinging behaviour and excessive need to be taken care of
Obsessive–compulsive	Preoccupation with orderliness, perfectionism and control

*DSM-5 is proposed to be released in 2013; please check www.dsm5.org for the latest information and proposed changes.

SOURCE: Adapted from APA (1994, p. 629).

Borderline personality disorder

The movie *Fatal Attraction* portrayed a disturbed woman (played by Glenn Close) who took revenge on a married man with whom she had had an affair. This character, with her dramatic suicidal gestures and extreme mood swings, would likely be diagnosed with a severe borderline personality disorder.

Borderline personality disorder is marked by extremely unstable interpersonal relationships, dramatic mood swings, an unstable sense of identity, intense fears of separation and abandonment, manipulativeness and impulsive behaviour. Also characteristic of this disorder is self-mutilating behaviour, such as wrist-slashing, carving words on the arm or burning the skin with cigarettes. Patients with borderline personality disorder tend not only to be highly distressed but to act on it: close to 10 percent of patients with the disorder commit suicide, and between 10 and 30 percent of people who commit suicide carry the diagnosis (Linehan, 2000).

According to SANE Australia (2010), between 2 and 5 percent of the Australian population are affected by borderline personality disorder at some point in their lives. Symptoms usually first appear late adolescence or in early adulthood (SANE Australia, 2010). Women are three times more likely to be diagnosed with borderline personality disorder than men (SANE Australia, 2010).

APPLY + DISCUSS

- Could any person who deliberately orders the murder of hundreds of innocent people be psychologically sound?
- What is the difference between being 'bad' and being 'ill'? How do we draw the line between sin and sickness?

Although people with borderline personality disorder may seem superficially normal, the volatility and insecurity of their attachments become clear in intimate relationships. In part, these reflect the ways they form mental representations of people and relationships. Their representations are often simplistic and one-sided, strongly influenced by their moods and needs (Kernberg, 1975; Kernberg, Selzer, Koenigsberg, Carr, & Appelbaum, 1989; Westen, Lohr, Silk, Gold, & Kerber, 1990). Borderline patients are particularly noted for splitting their representations into all good or all bad — seeing people as either on their side or bent on hurting or leaving them — and rapidly changing from one view of the person to another (Baker, Silk, Westen, Nigg, & Lohr, 1992; Kernberg et al., 1989).

For example, one woman with a borderline personality disorder had been involved with a man for only three weeks before deciding he was 'the only man in the world who could love me'. She began calling him constantly and suggested they live together. He became concerned about the intensity of her feelings and suggested they see each other only on weekends so they could get to know each other a little more slowly. She was furious and accused him of leading her on and using her. This example illustrates another feature of the disorder documented in a number of studies, the proneness to attribute negative or malevolent intentions to other people and to expect abuse and rejection (Bell, Billington, Cicchetti, & Gibbons, 1988; Nigg, Lohr, Westen, Gold, & Silk, 1992).

Antisocial personality disorder

Antisocial personality disorder is marked by irresponsible and socially disruptive behaviour in a variety of areas (see Stoff, Breiling, & Maser, 1997). Symptoms include stealing and destroying property and a lack of empathy and remorse for misdeeds. Individuals with antisocial personality disorder are often unable to maintain jobs because of unexplained absences and harassment of co-workers, lying, stealing, vandalism, impulsive behaviour and recklessness. People with the disorder can be exceedingly charming and are often described as 'con artists'.

Typically, an antisocial personality disorder is evident by age 15. Displaying socially disruptive and antisocial behaviours — such as vandalising another person's property — can be indicative of an antisocial personality disorder.

Typically, an antisocial personality disorder is evident by age 15. The characteristic behaviours are similar to those of childhood conduct disorder. In fact, nearly all adult antisocial personality disorders were conduct disordered as children, although only 40 to 50 percent of conduct-disordered children become antisocial adults (Lytton, 1990). The syndrome is more prevalent in men (3 percent of adult males) than women (less than 1 percent). It is also more commonly found in poor urban areas.

Antisocial individuals rarely take the initiative to seek treatment. Rather, they most commonly wind up in courts, prisons and welfare departments (Vaillant & Perry, 1985; see also Stewart & Harmon, 2004). When they do seek psychiatric treatment, it is usually to avoid some legal repercussion. For example, Mr C was a tall, muscular man with a scruffy beard and steely blue eyes. He came to a clinic complaining of depression and lack of direction in life. He presented a very moving description of a childhood filled with abuse at the hands of his father and neglect by his severely mentally ill mother, which may well have been accurate. He talked about wanting to come to understand why his life was not going well and wanting to work hard to change. He also described chronic depression and feelings of boredom and worthlessness that are common in antisocial personalities.

By the end of the first session, however, Mr C disclosed a troubling history of violence, in which he had escalated several pub brawls by hitting people in the face with empty bottles or pool cues. His casual response when asked about whether they were seriously hurt was, 'You think I stuck around to pick their face up off the floor?' He also had a history of carrying weapons and spoke of a time in his life during which he had his finger on the trigger 'if anybody even looked at me wrong'. When asked why he had finally come in for help now, he admitted that he had been 'falsely accused' of breaking someone's nose at a pub and that his lawyer thought 'seeing a shrink' would help his case — but that this, of course, had nothing to do with his genuine desire to turn his life around.

Theories of personality disorders

Once again, both genetic and environmental factors play a role in the genesis of many personality disorders (Huff, 2004). For many years, psychodynamic theorists suggested that borderline personality disorder originates in highly troubled attachment relationships in early childhood, which render the person vulnerable to difficulties in intimate relationships later in life (Adler & Buie, 1979; Kernberg, 1975; Masterson & Rinsley, 1975). Empirical research supported this view (Ludolph et al., 1990). Several studies also implicate sexual abuse in the aetiology of this disorder, which may account for its prevalence in females (Herman, Perry, & Van der Kolk, 1989; Zanarini, 1997). The best available evidence suggests that a chaotic home life (Golomb et al., 1994), a mother with a troubled attachment history, a male relative who is sexually abusive, and a genetic tendency towards impulsivity and negative affect (chapter 10) provide fertile ground for the development of this syndrome.

In many respects, the aetiology of antisocial personality disorder resembles that of borderline personality disorder, except that physical abuse is more common than sexual abuse and biological contributions to the disorder are better established (see Pollock et al., 1990). Both cognitive–behavioural and psychodynamic approaches implicate physical abuse, neglect and absent or criminal male role models. Young adult experiences can also contribute to the development of the disorder: the extent of combat exposure in Vietnam predicts the extent to which veterans have antisocial symptoms (Barrett et al., 1996), perhaps because men tend to respond to violent traumas with violence.

Adoption studies demonstrate the role of both biological and environmental variables in the aetiology of antisocial personality disorder (Cadoret et al., 1995). An adult adoptee whose biological parent had an arrest record for antisocial behaviour is three times more likely to have problems with aggressive behaviour than a person without a biological vulnerability. A person whose adoptive parent had antisocial personality disorder is also more than three times more likely to develop the disorder, regardless of biological history. Twin studies suggest that environmental factors are more important in predicting antisocial behaviour in adolescence, whereas genetic factors are more important as individuals get older (Lyons, True, Eisen, & Goldberg, 1995). This finding makes sense in the light of other data from behavioural genetics that show that heritability of personality and IQ increase with age — that is, that similarities between biological relatives tend to be stronger as they get older (chapters 9 and 11).

INTERIM SUMMARY

Dissociative disorders are characterised by disruptions in consciousness, memory, sense of identity or perception. In ***dissociative identity disorder***, at least two distinct personalities exist within the person. Dissociative disorders generally reflect a history of severe trauma. ***Personality disorders*** are characterised by enduring maladaptive patterns of thought, feeling and behaviour that lead to chronic disturbances in interpersonal and occupational functioning. ***Borderline personality disorder*** is marked by extremely unstable interpersonal relationships, dramatic mood swings, an unstable sense of identity, intense fears of separation and abandonment, manipulativeness, impulsive behaviour and self-mutilating behaviour. ***Antisocial personality disorder*** is marked by irresponsible and socially disruptive behaviour.

How best to classify a mental disorder?

By Professor Gordon Parker, University of New South Wales

Early modern psychiatric classificatory systems focused on categorical definitions of psychiatric conditions. DSM-III (published in 1980) moved to a mix of categorical and dimensional models, with the latter exemplified by clinical depressive disorders being subcategorised into 'major' and 'minor' expressions.

In the last decade, there has been a greater emphasis on dimensional models for two principal reasons. First, it is likely that some 'conditions' are intrinsically dimensional, with a representative example being the personality disorders which basically capture both personality style dimensions and degrees of disordered functioning. A second and less valid reason for an increasing use of dimensional models probably reflects a general 'expansionist' tendency in psychiatry.

There are predictable problems with the dimensional approach, even if it is validly seeking to capture an intrinsically dimensional condition. First, there has to be a cut-off criterion for 'caseness' — whether based on the number of criterion features, the severity of the overall condition, impairment or another component — and any such imposed cut-off criterion will necessarily risk 'over-diagnosing' and 'under-diagnosing' a percentage of individuals. Dimensionalising psychiatric conditions also raises concerns about pathologising relatively normal states (e.g. sadness as 'clinical depression', shyness as 'social phobia') and inferentially or directly arguing that such conditions then mandate treatment. Adopting a dimensional 'staging model' that includes prodromal states (e.g. psychosis risk syndrome) is also problematic. While having advantages in conceding such states in that they may allow for early intervention, if such prodromal symptoms have limited predictability, there are obvious risks of inappropriate intervention.

There is wisdom in avoiding any single model — be it categorical or dimensional — for classification. First, if consideration is limited to the depressive disorders, it can be reasonably argued that there are certain conditions (e.g. psychotic depression, melancholic depression) that are categorical and disease-like states; that is, they have strong genetic contributions and prototypic phenotypic clinical features, show concomitant evidence of disturbed biological functioning, respond preferentially to physical treatments and show a poor response to placebos. Second, there are some depressed states that are better viewed as 'conditions' or 'syndromes' that meet clinical criteria on the basis of severity and impairment; more reflect contributions of stressful life events and predisposing personality styles, rather than perturbed biological processes; and do not show any preferential response to physical treatments. Third, individuals can develop 'depression' as a normal response to events that diminish their self-esteem or cause existential doubt. In essence, 'depression' can range from pathological to normal and from disease-like state to disorder-like syndrome — supporting the proposition that psychologists should avoid limiting classifications to any single categorical or dimensional model.

The task of classification should be to determine the valid 'model' (be it categorical and/or dimensional), and to then construct classificatory systems that best capture the underpinning structure and allow diagnosis to be made with greater precision.

Are mental disorders really distinct?

Although we have followed the DSM guidelines in describing specific syndromes, most practising clinicians and many researchers question whether psychopathology can be so neatly categorised (Baron, 1998; Beutler & Malik, 2002). One question is whether disorders really fall into discrete categories or whether syndromes such as depression fall along continua of severity (e.g. Kendler & Gardner, 1998; Lewinsohn, Solomon, Seeley, & Zeiss, 2000; Widiger & Sankis, 2000). A major challenge to the categorical approach to diagnosis is the fact that subclinical cases — that is, cases that are clinically significant but are not severe enough to warrant a diagnosis — are as common, if not more common, than the diagnosable cases of mental disorders (Zinbarg, Barlow, Liebowitz, & Street, 1994).

Further, that many people who have one disorder have several raises questions about whether they really suffer from several disorders or from one or two underlying vulnerabilities that can express themselves in multiple ways. For example, depression tends to occur simultaneously with numerous other syndromes, including anxiety, eating and substance-related disorders (Mineka, Watson, & Clark, 1998; see also Krueger & Markon, 2006). Genetic studies show that if one twin has one of these disorders, the other twin is likely to have one or more of the others (Kendler, K. S., Walters, E. E., Neale, M. C., Kessler, R. C., Heath, A. C., & Eaves, L. J. (1995). The structure of the genetic and environmental risk factors for six major psychiatric disorders in women: Phobia, generalised anxiety disorder, panic disorder, bulimia, major depression, and alcoholism. *Archives of General Psychiatry*, 52, 374–383).

Cross-cultural evidence suggests that most non-psychotic disorders involve some mixture of anxiety and depression (Kleinman, 1988), a finding consistent with data on negative affect, which show that people who tend to experience one unpleasant emotion tend to experience others (chapter 10). Indeed, many researchers are coming to the view that anxiety and depression are both expressions of an underlying vulnerability to negative affect (Brown, Chorpita, & Barlow, 1998; Zinbarg & Barlow, 1996). Negative affect, in turn, can lead to other disorders, such as substance abuse, as people who are depressed or anxious turn to alcohol or other substances to help regulate their moods (see Dixit & Crum, 2000).

A particularly problematic diagnostic category is schizoaffective disorder, used to describe individuals who seem to have attributes of both schizophrenia and psychotic depression and may not easily fit the criteria for just one or the other. The disorder appears genetically related to both schizophrenia and major depression (Erlenmeyer et al., 1997) and is too common to be explained as the accidental co-occurrence of the two disorders in the same individual.

Perhaps the most complex questions pertain to the relationship between Axis I disorders and personality disorders (Axis II). Most patients with severe Axis I disorders of all sorts — anxiety, mood, eating, substance use — have concurrent personality pathology, if not diagnosable personality disorders (e.g. Shea, Glass, Pilkonis, Watkins, & Docherty, 1987). Trying to distinguish enduring aspects of personality from specific episodes of illness may be problematic when the personality itself is the wellspring of diverse symptoms. We may also misattribute consequences to disorders such as depression that result from personality pathology such as dysfunction at work or poor parenting skills (see Daley et al., 1999; Ilardi & Craighead, 1999).

ONE STEP FURTHER

Should we change the way we classify mental illnesses?

By Professor Patrick McGorry, University of Melbourne

Professor Patrick McGorry is a leading international clinician, researcher and advocate for youth mental health reform. He was named Australian of the Year in 2010 for his work as a mental health expert.

Current diagnostic systems, including the DSM, were derived from subsets of chronic patients, and therefore describe the endpoint syndromes of the major mental illnesses, without taking into consideration the complex evolution of symptoms that occurs during the onset of illness. These classification systems were designed well before there was any serious scientific interest in the early stages of mental illness. Indeed, until relatively recently, clinicians have tended to think that mental illnesses — particularly more serious forms of mental illness, such as schizophrenia and bipolar disorder — are completely separate disorders with distinct causes and patterns of illness progression, and relatively fixed prognoses. This conceptualisation of mental illness and its diagnosis poses a number of problems. For example, many people suffer clinically significant symptoms and disability, yet their symptoms are not severe enough to allow an official diagnosis to be made. Furthermore, it is very common for people to experience multiple problems, making it difficult to obtain a clear diagnosis due to the complexity of their symptoms. Since the need for clinical care often becomes apparent well before a diagnosis can be made, treatments are often selected on the basis of a patient's symptoms, rather than on the basis of a formal diagnosis. Alternatively, appropriate treatment may be withheld until symptoms evolve and the clinical picture becomes clearer, resulting in unnecessary treatment delay and needless distress for the patient.

Over the last two decades, careful research has shown that mental illnesses develop in overlapping stages, with many shared features and symptoms. These findings have sparked considerable interest in the possibility of reducing the symptoms and disability associated with mental illness; or even preventing the onset of mental illness altogether by intervening very early during the onset of an illness — before the symptoms and their associated disability become entrenched. How should psychologists decide when treatment is necessary? How can they tell if a person's symptoms are simply a transient response to everyday life stresses, or if they are likely to develop into a serious mental disorder? Current diagnostic systems do not allow this. It is not possible to answer this question, since knowledge of how and why symptoms are acquired, intensify and ultimately cohere into full-threshold syndromes is still very limited. Clearly, however, revision of current diagnostic systems is necessary, so that they include a focus on the early stages of the onset of mental illness and recognise the potential for pre-emptive treatment approaches.

What could a revised diagnostic structure in psychiatry look like? A 'clinical staging' model, along the lines of the staging models used for diagnosis in cancer medicine, is one possibility that offers a number of advantages. Clinical staging is a diagnostic tool that defines the progression of a disorder at any given point in time, and thus where a person lies along the continuum of the course of their illness. This approach is particularly useful from a preventive point of view, since it assumes that early treatment may change the course of an illness and prevent its progression to subsequent stages, or even result in remission and cure. This approach also allows for the selection of treatments that are appropriate for the earliest possible stage of illness, while minimising the possibility of harmful side-effects. While knowledge of the risk factors that predict the onset of mental illness is incomplete, a useful staging model in psychiatry can be constructed based on the clinical features seen (type of symptoms and their severity, persistence and recurrence), and the extent of the biopsychosocial impact of the features (associated biological changes and effect on social relationships and employment) on the patient. To represent the full spectrum of illness, this model should include the asymptomatic state, through the early stages of illness as symptoms develop, intensify and become more specific, up to a first episode of a serious illness, and then beyond to remission, relapse or persistence of illness. A staging model will also facilitate the integration of new data on the biological, social and environmental risk and protective factors into the diagnostic infrastructure as this becomes available, all of which will ultimately permit the development of a valid clinicopathological framework in psychiatry. This reform is long overdue to allow a new era of pre-emptive psychiatry.

INTERIM SUMMARY

Using classification systems to diagnose mental illness has been challenged by researchers and theorists in recent years. One reason for this is that people often experience multiple problems simultaneously, making it difficult to apply a single diagnosis. Furthermore, distinguishing the roles of nature and nurture in the aetiology of psychological disturbances is more difficult than it may first appear. Inherited characteristics typically determine which environmental events are psychologically toxic, and environmental events can translate into changes in the brain.

Central questions revisited

◆ When nurture becomes nature

We began with a question that has dominated psychological research in multiple domains: what are the roles of nature and nurture? Just as the gods of abnormality did not create six discrete disorders and rest on the seventh day, they were not particularly careful to separate nature and nurture.

As we have seen, environmental events can activate biological vulnerabilities, so that neither heredity nor environment alone bears the blame. Something as seemingly innocuous as the amount of sunlight to which people are exposed can influence people with the 'right' biological vulnerability. For example, people with seasonal affective disorder show mild seasonal mood and behavioural changes in response to the lack of sunlight in the winter months.

Although SAD has a clear environmental trigger, the tendency to experience it is partly heritable (Madden, Heath, Rosenthal, & Martin, 1996). Thus, the vulnerability to an environmental event is itself inherited! This is likely true of virtually all environmental circumstances that contribute to psychopathology. Sexual abuse, for example, can probably have the damaging effects it can have only because humans have evolved mechanisms that make incest repugnant and traumatising — mechanisms that normally prevent inbreeding.

Psychologically damaging life events can also create changes in the brain that become part of an individual's 'nature' (Kandel, 1999). Monkeys separated from their mothers for prolonged periods show neuropsychological changes — permanent alterations in the number and sensitivity of receptors for neurotransmitters in the postsynaptic membrane (Gabbard, 1992; Suomi, 1999). Similarly, people who experience traumatic events often develop abnormalities in hypothalamic, pituitary and hippocampal functioning (Bremner, 1998). To speak of the causes as completely environmental, however, is not entirely accurate either. Repeated separation from attachment figures only produces biological abnormalities because the brain has evolved to be innately sensitive to attachment-related stimulation. Environmental causes presuppose a nervous system that makes them relevant.

◆

SUMMARY

1 Define psychopathology

- ***Psychopathology*** refers to patterns of thought, feeling or behaviour that disrupt a person's sense of wellbeing or social or occupational functioning.

2 The cultural context of psychopathology

- The concept of mental illness varies historically and cross-culturally. Cultures differ in the ways they describe and pattern psychopathology, but 'mentally ill' is not simply an arbitrary label applied to deviants.

3 Mental health, mental health problems and mental disorders

- ***Mental health*** is the capacity of individuals to behave in ways that promote their emotional and social wellbeing. ***Mental health problems*** include the wide range of emotional and behavioural abnormalities that affect people throughout their lives. A ***mental disorder*** implies the existence of a clinically recognisable set of symptoms and behaviours that cause distress to the individual and impair their ability to function as usual.

4 Contemporary approaches to psychopathology

- Psychodynamic theorists make a general distinction among ***neuroses***, ***personality disorders*** and ***psychoses***, which form a continuum of disturbance. A ***psychodynamic formulation*** involves assessing the person's wishes and fears, cognitive and emotional resources, and experience of the self and others.
- The ***cognitive–behavioural*** perspective integrates principles of classical and operant conditioning with a cognitive perspective. Psychopathology results from environmental contingencies and dysfunctional cognitions.
- Understanding psychopathology often requires shifting to a biological level of analysis. The biological approach proposes that psychopathology stems from faulty wiring in the brain, particularly in the abundance, overreactivity or underreactivity of specific neurotransmitters.
- ***Diathesis–stress models*** of psychopathology propose that people with an underlying vulnerability may become symptomatic under stressful circumstances.
- A ***systems approach*** attempts to explain an individual's behaviour in the context of a social group, such as a couple, family or larger social system. A ***family systems model*** suggests that the symptoms of any individual are really symptoms of dysfunction in a family.
- From an evolutionary perspective, psychopathology can reflect random variation, broader population pressures that can produce stable rates of psychopathology if they confer an offsetting advantage, and normally adaptive mechanisms gone awry.

5 Descriptive diagnosis and psychopathological syndromes

- The ***Diagnostic and Statistical Manual of Mental Disorders (DSM)***, is the official manual of mental illnesses published by the American Psychiatric Association. It is the basis for ***descriptive diagnosis***.
- A fifth edition of the DSM (***DSM-5***) is due for completion in 2013, with major changes expected to the classification system and diagnostic categories, including fewer axes. It is anticipated that the DSM-5 classifications will be closely aligned to the International Classification of Disease (ICD-10) system endorsed by the World Health Organization (WHO).
- Until the DSM-5 comes into effect, mental disorders are classified using the multiaxial system of the ***DSM-IV***. The DSM-IV places symptoms in their biological and social context by evaluating patients along five axes: clinical syndromes, personality disorders (and mental retardation), medical conditions, environmental stressors and global level of functioning.
- One disorder usually first diagnosed in childhood or adolescence is ***attention-deficit hyperactivity disorder***, characterised by inattention, impulsiveness and hyperactivity. Another is ***conduct disorder***, a disturbance in which a child persistently violates the rights of others as well as societal norms.
- ***Substance-related disorders*** refer to continued use of substances that negatively affect psychological and social functioning. Worldwide, ***alcoholism*** is the most common substance use disorder. As with most psychological disorders, the roots of alcoholism lie in genetics, environment and their interaction.
- ***Schizophrenia*** is a disorder or set of disorders in which people lose touch with reality, experiencing both ***positive symptoms*** (such as ***hallucinations***, ***delusions*** and ***loosening of associations***) and ***negative symptoms*** (such as flat affect and poor social skills). Schizophrenia is a highly heritable disease of the brain, although environmental circumstances such as a critical family environment can trigger or worsen it. The DSM-IV subtypes of schizophrenia include: Paranoid, Disorganised, Catatonic, Undifferentiated, and Residual Schizophrenia.
- ***Mood disorders*** are characterised by disturbances in emotion and mood. In ***manic*** states, people feel excessively happy and believe they can do anything. The most severe form of depression is ***major depressive disorder***. ***Dysthymic disorder*** refers to a long-standing, less acute depression of more than two years duration. ***Bipolar disorder*** is a mood disturbance marked by mania, often alternating with major depressive episodes. Genetics contribute to the aetiology of many mood disorders and play a particularly powerful role in bipolar disorders. Environmental and cognitive processes also contribute to the development of depression. ***Seasonal affective disorder (SAD)*** is a depressive syndrome whereby mood and behaviour changes occur with regular seasonal climatic variation.
- ***Anxiety disorders*** are characterised by intense, frequent or continuous anxiety. ***Panic disorders*** are distinguished by attacks of intense fear and feelings of doom or terror not justified by the situation. ***Agoraphobia*** refers to a fear of being in places or situations from which escape might be difficult. ***Obsessive–compulsive disorder*** is marked by recurrent ***obsessions*** (persistent thoughts or ideas) and ***compulsions*** (intentional behaviours performed in response to an obsession and in a stereotyped fashion). ***Post-traumatic stress disorder*** is marked by flashbacks and recurrent thoughts of a psychologically distressing event outside the range of usual human experience. Anxiety disorders, like depression, show substantial heritability but do not require a genetic predisposition. Cognitive–behavioural theories link them to conditioned emotional responses and dysfunctional cognitions.
- The most prevalent eating disorders are anorexia nervosa and bulimia nervosa. ***Anorexia nervosa*** is characterised by a distorted body image and efforts to lose weight that lead to dangerously low body weight. ***Bulimia*** is characterised by a binge-purge syndrome.
- ***Somatoform disorders*** occur when people complain of pain, suffering or illness but no physical problems can be identified to explain their ailments. The two most common forms of this condition are ***conversion disorder*** (a loss or significant change in a physical

function without any physical problem to explain the condition) and ***hypochondriasis*** (people believe they are suffering from an illness or ailment, even when there is no medical evidence to support the belief).

- ***Dissociative disorders*** are characterised by disruptions in consciousness, memory, sense of identity or perception of the environment. The primary feature is ***dissociation***, whereby significant aspects of experience are kept separate and distinct in consciousness. The most severe type is ***dissociative identity disorder***, popularly known as multiple personality disorder.
- ***Personality disorders*** are characterised by maladaptive personality patterns that lead to chronic disturbances in interpersonal and occupational functioning. ***Borderline personality disorder*** is marked by extremely unstable interpersonal relationships, dramatic mood swings, an unstable sense of identity, intense fears of separation and abandonment, manipulativeness, impulsive behaviour and self-mutilating behaviour. ***Antisocial personality disorder*** is marked by a pattern of irresponsible and socially disruptive behaviour in a variety of areas. Genetics plays a role in some personality disorders, as do childhood experiences such as abuse and neglect.

KEY TERMS

aetiology, *p. 606*
agoraphobia, *p. 634*
alcoholism, *p. 617*
anorexia nervosa, *p. 637*
antisocial personality disorder, *p. 641*
anxiety disorders, *p. 633*
attention-deficit hyperactivity disorder (ADHD), *p. 616*
bipolar disorder, *p. 628*
borderline personality disorder, *p. 641*
bulimia, *p. 637*
clinical syndromes, *p. 612*
cognitive–behavioural, *p. 607*
cognitive distortions, *p. 630*
compulsions, *p. 634*
conduct disorder, *p. 616*
conversion disorder, *p. 639*
delusions, *p. 621*
descriptive diagnosis, *p. 612*
Diagnostic and Statistical Manual of Mental Disorders (DSM-IV), *p. 612*
Diagnostic and Statistical Manual of Mental Disorders (DSM-5), *p. 612*
diathesis–stress model, *p. 609*
dissociation, *p. 639*
dissociative disorders, *p. 639*
dissociative identity disorder, *p. 639*
dopamine hypothesis, *p. 623*
dysthymic disorder (dysthymia), *p. 628*
expressed emotion, *p. 625*
family alliances, *p. 611*
family boundaries, *p. 610*
family homoeostatic mechanisms, *p. 610*
family roles, *p. 610*
family systems model, *p. 610*
generalised anxiety disorder, *p. 633*
hallucinations, *p. 621*
hypochondriasis, *p. 639*
labelling theory, *p. 603*
loosening of associations, *p. 622*
major depressive disorder, *p. 627*
mania, *p. 628*
manic, *p. 626*
mental disorder, *p. 604*
mental health, *p. 604*
mental health problems, *p. 604*
mood disorders, *p. 626*
multiaxial system of diagnosis, *p. 613*
negative symptoms, *p. 622*
negative triad, *p. 630*
neuroses, *p. 606*
obsessions, *p. 634*
obsessive–compulsive disorder, *p. 634*
panic disorder, *p. 634*
personality disorders, *p. 606*
phobia, *p. 634*
positive symptoms, *p. 622*
post-traumatic stress disorder (PTSD), *p. 635*
psychodynamic formulation, *p. 606*
psychopathology, *p. 602*
psychoses, *p. 606*
schizophrenia, *p. 620*
seasonal affective disorder (SAD), *p. 628*
social phobia, *p. 634*
somatoform disorders, *p. 639*
substance-related disorders, *p. 617*
system, *p. 610*
systems approach, *p. 610*
unipolar depression, *p. 628*
ventricles, *p. 624*

REVIEW QUESTIONS

1. Define psychopathology.
2. Distinguish between the contemporary approaches to psychopathology: psychodynamic, cognitive–behavioural, biological, systems and evolutionary perspectives.
3. Outline the five axes of diagnosis used by the DSM-IV.
4. Describe the key symptoms of attention-deficit hyperactivity disorder and conduct disorder.
5. Describe the diathesis–stress model of schizophrenia.

DISCUSSION QUESTIONS

1. Why do people become alcoholics?
2. Most people experience anxiety at some point in their lives. When should this anxiety be classified as an anxiety disorder?
3. Why are eating disorders more common in women?

APPLICATION QUESTIONS

1. For each description that follows, indicate the level of disturbance in the behaviour exhibited by using the following classifications: normal, neurotic, personality disordered or psychotic.
   (a) Minh is a young woman who seems to be unlucky in love. She can easily become involved in a relationship, but then often decides to break up whenever things look like becoming more serious — she cannot make a commitment to another person. She has abruptly ended her last three relationships, all within the space of two years.
   (b) Thomas is a happily married man with three grown children. He has worked at a bank for almost 30 years and is looking forward to his retirement. When on holiday, he does not like to be around crowds of people — he enjoys the quiet seclusion of camping in the bush.

(c) Although Carlos has a university degree, he has been unable to hold down a steady position for the past five years. He does not have many friends and is always seen wearing the same black woollen gloves, regardless of the weather. Each day he takes a walk in the park to eat his lunch. He is often seen arguing with himself as he sits there on the park bench, shouting 'Be quiet, I'm not listening to you'.

(d) Vicki is a personable woman who enjoys going out for dinner with friends. She will always try to join into the conversation and make her opinion known. However, often she will later dwell on things that were said at the dinner party and worry that she had said something wrong that would offend one of her friends.

2. Test your understanding of psychopathological syndromes by providing a preliminary diagnosis for each case summary provided.
   (a) Mrs C was hospitalised with complaints of continual fainting. Whenever she recovered consciousness she would assume a new identity, until another fainting incident occurred. At last count, she had three separate and distinct personalities: a newspaper journalist, a preschooler named Isabel, and a supermodel named Fiona.
   (b) Ramon has a persistent mistrust of other people, although such suspicions are always unfounded. For these reasons, he often finds it difficult to maintain meaningful relationships with others.
   (c) Shaye has been feeling up and down for the past two years. When she is on her 'up', she experiences an excessively high state of exhilaration and feels she can conquer the world. When she is on her 'down', she experiences persistent and severe feelings of sadness and hopelessness, and finds it difficult to find a reason to get out of bed each morning.
   (d) Sam suffers from delusions and hallucinations. He will often exhibit both extreme motor immobility and extreme negativism for hours at a time. During such episodes, he refuses to speak to anybody.

The solutions to the application questions can be found on page 835.

MULTIMEDIA RESOURCES

The *Cyberpsych* multimedia resource is available *as an option* to accompany this textbook to further develop your understanding of many key psychology concepts. *Cyberpsych* contains a wealth of rich media content and activities, and for this chapter includes:

- video clips on anorexia, schizophrenia, teenage depression, drugs and the brain
- video case studies on crystal methamphetamine, bipolar disorder and ADHD
- concept animations on professional cognitive behaviour therapy and schizophrenia.

Treatment of psychological disorders

16

LEARNING OBJECTIVES

After studying this chapter you should be able to:

1 outline the mental health services provided by clinical psychologists

2 describe the key principles and techniques of psychodynamic therapies

3 describe the key principles and techniques of cognitive–behavioural therapies

4 distinguish between humanistic, group and family therapies

5 discuss the various biological treatments available for patients with severe mental illness

6 discuss research that has evaluated pharmacotherapy and psychotherapy.

Cognitive-behavioural therapies

- *Cognitive–behavioural therapists* use methods derived from behaviourist and cognitive approaches to learning.
- Behavioural techniques relying on *classical conditioning* include *systematic desensitisation* and *exposure techniques*.
- *Operant* techniques attempt to control maladaptive behaviour by altering its consequences.
- *Social learning* techniques include *participatory modelling* and *skills training*.
- Cognitive therapy focuses on changing dysfunctional cognitions that underlie psychological disorders. Examples include Ellis' *rational–emotive behaviour therapy* and Beck's *cognitive therapy*.

Mental health services

- *Clinical psychologists* often practise in a hospital or other mental health facility settings to treat patients experiencing severe mental disorders, predominantly schizophrenia, bipolar disorder and depression, rather than those with personality disorders.
- The *scientist–practitioner model* adopted by Australian universities has become responsible not only for teaching the science of psychology, but also for training applied psychologists.
- *Multidisciplinary teams* are commonly used in community health facilities and draw together professionals from a range of specialities to carry out the required tasks.
- The most significant recent development in mental health services in Australia has been the shift away from institutionalised care towards community-based care.

Psychodynamic therapies

- *Psychodynamic therapy* rests on two principles: *insight* and the relationship between the patient and therapist.
- To bring about change, therapists rely on three techniques: *free association*, *interpretation* and examination of *transference*.
- The main contemporary forms of psychodynamic treatment are *psychoanalysis* and *psychodynamic psychotherapy*.

Humanistic, group and family therapies

- *Humanistic therapies* focus on the way each person consciously experiences the self, relationships and the world. They aim to help people get in touch with their feelings, their 'true selves' and a sense of meaning in life. For example, Rogers' *client-centred therapy*.
- *Gestalt therapy* tries to help people acknowledge their feelings so they can act in accordance with them.
- In *group therapy*, multiple people meet together to work towards therapeutic goals.
- The aim of *family therapy* is to change maladaptive family interaction patterns.

Evaluating psychological treatments

- Approaches to treatment are bound to our cultural norms, values and beliefs; the concept of what is abnormal and what is functional behaviour in any society is determined to an extent by the cultural context.
- *Pharmacotherapy* is essential for some disorders (such as schizophrenia and bipolar disorder) and can be extremely helpful for others (such as major depression and anxiety disorders). Relapse rates, however, are high when medication is discontinued, and complete cures are uncommon for most disorders.
- Research has provided substantial evidence for the utility of *psychotherapy* for many disorders, with the most successful treatments thus far being cognitive-behaviour treatments for anxiety disorders.
- *Psychotherapy integration* is the use of theory or technique from multiple therapeutic perspectives.

Biological treatments

- *Psychotropic medications* act on the brain to affect mental processes.
- *Antipsychotic medications* treat schizophrenia and other acute psychotic states.
- *Antidepressant medications* can be useful for treating many disorders, particularly depression and anxiety disorders.
- Lithium is the treatment of choice for bipolar disorder.
- Both benzodiazepines and antidepressants can be useful for treating anxiety.
- *Electroconvulsive therapy (ECT)*, also known as electroshock therapy, is currently used in the treatment of major depression.
- Another treatment of last resort, now primarily used for severe cases of obsessive–compulsive disorder, is *psychosurgery*.

Central questions: what works for whom?

- Finding answers to questions — such as what works and for whom — will continue to rely on psychologists both adapting and assessing psychotherapeutic and quasi-experimental research methods.

JENNY was a frail, bright, strong-willed 19-year-old from Melbourne. Had her parents not brought her kicking and screaming to the hospital, she would probably have been dead two weeks later. Jenny was 165 centimetres tall and weighed 32 kilograms — she suffered from anorexia nervosa.

During her 10 weeks in the hospital, Jenny was not the easiest of patients. Like many patients hospitalised for anorexia, she regularly played cat-and-mouse games with her nurses. When weigh-in time came each morning, she had to wear a hospital gown because otherwise she would fill her pockets with coins to fool the scales. Jenny also required a watchful eye at mealtime to make certain she did not skilfully dispose of her food.

In the hospital, Jenny received several forms of treatment. She met with a psychotherapist twice a week to try to understand why she was starving herself. The therapist also set up a behaviour plan to reward Jenny for weight gain, with increased privileges (beginning with walks on the hospital grounds and eventually trips to the movies), and to punish weight loss with increased restrictions. Jenny and her family met twice a week with a family therapist, who explored the role of family dynamics in her disorder. Her mother, a very anxious woman with a severe personality disorder, was dependent on Jenny in many ways. Jenny was her mother's caretaker, sometimes even missing school to stay home with her when her mother was anxious. Jenny's mother was especially anxious about Jenny's sexuality and regularly left Jenny long letters about AIDS, rape, serial killers and so forth. Jenny herself considered sex disgusting and was pleased when she lost so much weight that she stopped menstruating and lost her feminine shape. Jenny's father was preoccupied with her profoundly intellectually impaired sister, whom Jenny always resented for consuming his attention. By becoming so frail herself, Jenny finally caught her father's eye.

In addition to individual and family therapy, Jenny participated in a therapy group for patients with eating disorders. In the group her peers confronted her rationalisations about her eating behaviour; Jenny could also see in the other group members some of the patterns she could not see in herself.

Once Jenny left the hospital, with her weight stabilised, she spent the next four years in psychotherapy. The therapy focused primarily on her need for control over everything (including her body), her discomfort with having any kind of impulses, her fear of her sexuality, her use of starving to regulate feelings of sadness and aloneness, her anger at her sister and her desperate wish for her father to notice her. At one point during her treatment, when she moved out of her family's home for the first time, she became so anxious at being away from her mother that her therapist also recommended medication for a short time.

By the end of her treatment, Jenny's life-threatening disorder had not returned, and she was no longer preoccupied with food. She was now able to deal more appropriately with her mother, was openly able to acknowledge her mixed feelings towards her sister, had a much more satisfying relationship with her father and was happily involved in a romantic relationship (something she could not even imagine at the beginning of treatment).

Jenny's case is unusual because people rarely receive so many different (and such extensive) forms of treatment. In fact, the variety of psychotherapies is astounding — at least 400 different types (see Lambert, 2004) — and the treatment people receive generally depends less on the nature of the disorder than on the theoretical perspective of the therapist. In this chapter, we focus on mental health services provided by clinical psychologists and examine the most widely practised treatments for psychological disorders: psychodynamic, cognitive–behavioural, humanistic, group, family and biological. We will discuss the psychodynamic perspective first, not to emphasise its importance over the other approaches but rather because of its historical chronology. Throughout, we address two key questions. First, what kinds of treatment work and for what kinds of patients? Second, how can we use scientific methods to develop effective psychotherapies?

Central questions

- What works and for whom?
- How can we use scientific methods to study the effects of different kinds of psychotherapy?

Mental health services

There are a variety of treatments and approaches available to people suffering from a mental illness or disorder, delivered by a range of different health care professionals. They can range from private treatment in a psychologist's own office, to specialist treatment in a psychiatric hospital, to nursing services in a community health facility — and many variations in between. For example, counselling psychologists work closely with allied health professionals to assist clients to develop positive psychological characteristics to adapt to change effectively (see Pryor & Bright, 2007). Traditionally, counselling psychologists have helped individuals to deal with acute problems such as marital breakdown, anxiety and depression onset, and support after trauma, but they also help to manage change and transitions at the family and organisational levels (Pryor & Bright, 2007; chapter 15). Different psychological disorders require different approaches and respond to treatment in different ways. In this section, we will look at the types of mental health services commonly delivered in countries such as Australia.

Clinical psychologists

What do we mean by clinical psychology? Psychology can be thought of as both a field of study (the way the human mind works) and a profession (the application of the scientific principles underlying psychology). Clinical psychology is from the applied side of that scale. It can be defined as the branch of the profession that is associated with delivering psychological services in a health care setting.

What do ***clinical psychologists*** actually do? Given the nature of the role, much of the practice takes place in a hospital or mental health facility. An Australian study of clinical psychologists found that 27 percent worked in psychiatric/mental health services; 25 percent in universities; 20 percent in private practice, 6 percent in community/welfare services; 4 percent in intellectual impairment services; and the remainder in settings such as alcohol and drug agencies and prisons (Martin, 1989). Much of the work involves assessment of conditions and the development of intervention strategies.

In recent years in Australia, there has been a move away from institutionalised mental health care to a more community-based system. People with mental health issues are now more likely to be integrated into the community and provided with care in a community mental health facility rather than institutionalised in a mental health facility. The inpatients of a psychiatric hospital tend to be those experiencing severe mental disorders, predominantly schizophrenia, bipolar disorder and depression, rather than those with personality disorders.

Many general hospitals have a psychiatric ward, where people with a wide range of mental health issues can receive short- rather than long-term treatment. The range of mental health disorders encountered in a psychiatric ward can cover the full spectrum. The most common are mood disorders, eating disorders and anxiety disorders; less common are personality disorders, major depression and psychotic disorders such as schizophrenia (Jackson, Robinson, & Pica, 1996). Clinical psychologists in general hospitals are often required to assess and diagnose a patient presenting with mental health issues.

Scientist-practitioner model

The emergence of clinical psychology as a discrete discipline owes a great deal to the ***scientist–practitioner model*** that has been widely adopted in Australia. Under this approach, psychology departments at Australian universities have become responsible for not only teaching the science of psychology, but also training applied psychologists (Birnbrauer, 1996). The focus of the training is science first, practice second — different from many other professions in Australia. As a result, clinical psychologists in Australia take a scientifically-based approach to diagnosis and treatment (see Australian Psychological Society College of Clinical Psychologists, 2006).

Multidisciplinary teams

A common approach in mental health services in Australia today is the multidisciplinary team. This has become more prevalent with the move away from institutionalised care towards more community-based services. ***Multidisciplinary teams*** are commonly used in community health facilities and draw together professionals from a range of specialities to carry out the required tasks. For instance, a clinical psychologist may work in conjunction with a nurse, psychiatrist and social worker as part of a team offering a wide range of services in a community mental health clinic.

Mental health and health care utilisation

It is estimated that 20 percent of Australians experience symptoms of a mental disorder each year (AIHW, 2010c). Findings from a recent national survey of mental health and wellbeing (ABS, 2008f) revealed that almost half of the adult Australian population has had a mental illness at some point in their lifetime (ABS, 2008f). According to Australian Social Trends 2009 report (ABS, 2009c), the most common service used by Australians to help deal with a psychological problem involved visiting a general practitioner (GP), (25 percent) followed by seeing a psychologist (13 percent). Estimates from the 2005–06 Bettering the Evaluation and Care of Health (BEACH) survey of GP activity showed 11.1 percent of all GP encounters involved the management of a mental health problem (Britt et al., 2007). Depression was the fourth most commonly managed problem in general practice (3.6 per 100 encounters) and the second most frequently managed chronic problem, accounting for 7.1 percent of total chronic problems (AIHW, 2008c). Medications such as antidepressants, anti-anxiety drugs and antipsychotics were the most commonly prescribed drug types, accounting for an estimated 21.7 percent of prescriptions written by GPs (AIHW, 2008c). Table 16.1 shows the 10 mental health problems most frequently managed by GPs in Australia.

TABLE 16.1 The 10 mental health-related problems most frequently managed by general practitioners in Australia

Problem managed	Percentage of total mental health-related problems	Percentage of total problems	Rate (per 100 encounters)
Depression	34.3	2.8	4.3
Anxiety	15.6	1.2	1.9
Sleep disturbance	12.6	1.0	1.6
Tobacco abuse	5.7	0.5	0.7
Acute stress reaction	4.9	0.4	0.6
Dementia	4.6	0.4	0.6
Schizophrenia	4.3	0.3	0.5
Drug abuse	3.3	0.3	0.4
Alcohol abuse	2.7	0.2	0.3
Affective psychosis	1.9	0.1	0.2
Other	10.2	0.8	1.3
Total	**100.0**	**8.0**	**12.4**

SOURCE: AIHW (2010c).

History was made on 1 November 2006 when the Australian government launched the 'Better Access to Psychiatrists, Psychologists, and General Practitioners through the Medicare Benefits Scheme' program, to enable all registered psychologists to provide services under Medicare (APS, 2006c). Under the Council of Australian Governments' mental health reforms, specialist clinical psychology services are also available. According to Lyn Littlefield, then Executive Director of the Australian Psychological Society:

> These reforms have given mental health a similar standing to general health in the nation's funded Medicare system, allowing all Australians to have access to effective treatment for mental health problems. The reforms are also a significant recognition of the effectiveness of psychological treatments delivered by psychologists, representing a major milestone for mental health and the profession of psychology. The Medicare initiative has been designed to encourage team-based mental health care in the community, with psychologists working alongside GPs, psychiatrists, mental health nurses and other allied mental health professionals (APS, 2006c, Para. 2).

The Medicare Benefits Scheme program has enabled affordable access to a wider range of mental health services for patients seeking assistance. Encouragingly, during 2008–09, 6.2 million Medicare-subsidised mental health services were provided in Australia (AIHW, 2010c). This included 2.0 million services by psychiatrists, 2.5 million services by psychologists and 1.6 million services by GPs (AIHW, 2010c). During a recent year, the provision of Medicare-subsidised mental health services by psychiatrists, psychologists and other allied health professionals increased by 17.4 percent from the previous year, with about 4.6 million services provided (AIHW, 2010c). Approximately 3.4 percent of the Australian adult population received at least one of these mental health services during that period (AIHW, 2010c). For GPs, the management of patient mental health issues has shown a steady increase of about 5.7 percent each year since 2004–05 (AIHW, 2010c).

INTERIM SUMMARY

There are a variety of treatments and approaches available to people suffering from a mental illness or disorder, delivered by a range of different health care professionals. ***Clinical psychologists*** often practise in a hospital or other mental health facility settings. The inpatients of a psychiatric hospital tend to be those experiencing severe mental disorders, predominantly schizophrenia, bipolar disorder and depression, rather than those with personality disorders. In psychiatric wards, people with a wide range of mental health issues can receive short-term treatment. The ***scientist–practitioner model*** adopted by Australian universities has become responsible for not only teaching the science of psychology, but also for training applied psychologists. ***Multidisciplinary teams*** are commonly used in community health facilities and draw together professionals from a range of specialities to carry out the required tasks. The most significant recent development in mental health services in Australia has been the shift away from institutionalised care towards community-based care.

Psychodynamic therapies

Modern psychotherapy developed in the late nineteenth century out of the work of Sigmund Freud. The psychodynamic approach to therapeutic change rests on two principles: the role of insight and the role of the therapist–patient relationship.

Insight refers to the understanding of one's own psychological processes. According to psychodynamic theory, symptoms result primarily from three sources: maladaptive ways of viewing the self and relationships, unconscious conflicts and compromises among competing wishes and fears, and maladaptive ways of dealing with unpleasant emotions. Therapeutic change requires that patients come to understand the internal workings of their mind and, hence, as one adolescent patient put it, to become 'the captain of my own ship'.

Becoming the captain of one's own ship means acquiring the capacity to make conscious, rational choices as an adult about behaviour patterns, wishes, fears and ways of regulating emotions that may have been forged in childhood. Insight is not, however, a cold cognitive act. Psychodynamic clinicians often speak of 'emotional insight', stressing that knowing intellectually about one's problems is not the same as really confronting intense feelings and fears (such as Jenny's fear that if she did not take care of her mother something terrible might happen).

A second principle of psychodynamic treatment is that the relationship between the patient and therapist is crucial for therapeutic change for three reasons. First, a patient has to feel comfortable with the therapist in order to speak about emotionally significant experiences, a phenomenon called the ***therapeutic alliance*** (Luborsky, 1985). Across all forms of psychotherapy, quality of the therapeutic alliance is in fact predictive of positive outcome (Martin, Ruble, & Szkrybalo, 2000). Second, many psychodynamic (and humanistic) therapists argue that being with someone who listens empathically rather than critically is inherently therapeutic. Third, as we will explore, psychodynamic therapists assume that patients often bring enduring and troubling interpersonal patterns into the relationship with the therapist, which can then be more readily explored and changed.

APPLY + DISCUSS

In an effort to probe for information that a patient may have left unsaid, a psychodynamic therapist might ask questions suggestive of events that may have happened or feelings that the patient may be experiencing but has not yet disclosed.

- Is it possible that such probing may actually plant ideas of events and feelings that did not exist to begin with?
- For example, is it possible that suggestions by the therapist might 'create' memories of childhood sexual abuse when, in fact, no such abuse occurred?

Therapeutic techniques

To bring about therapeutic change, psychodynamic psychotherapies rely on three techniques: free association, interpretation and analysis of transference.

Free association

If a person becomes anxious without knowing why, or starves herself despite a thorough knowledge of the dangers of malnutrition, an important goal is to understand the unconscious events guiding behaviour — or, as Freud put it, 'to make the unconscious conscious'. The patient and his therapist must find a way to map his unconscious networks of association to see what fears or wishes are linked to his symptoms. ***Free association*** is a technique for exploring associational networks and unconscious processes involved in symptom formation. The therapist instructs the patient to say whatever comes to mind — thoughts, feelings, images, fantasies, memories, dreams from the night before or wishes — and to try to censor nothing. The patient and therapist then collaborate to solve the mystery of the symptom, piecing together the connections in what has been said and noting what has not been said (i.e. what the patient may be defending against). As in any good detective story, the most important clues are often those that are concealed, and only by examining gaps in the suspect's account does one find hidden motives and concealed data. The difference, however, is that in psychotherapy the patient is both the co-detective and the prime suspect.

Interpretation

MAKING CONNECTIONS

Research on memory suggests that much of what we know is stored in networks of association — ideas connected to each other — and that these networks are implicit, or unconscious (chapter 7). In this sense, free association is a technique for learning about patients' implicit networks, much like word association tasks used by memory researchers. The difference is that cognitive scientists study associations shared by most people who speak the same language (e.g. between bird and robin), whereas psychodynamic clinicians try to explore the idiosyncratic associations that can produce psychological problems.

Although the patient may work hard to understand her associations, the therapist has two advantages in solving the mystery: the therapist is trained in making psychological inferences and is not personally embroiled in the patient's conflicts and ways of seeing reality. For example, Jenny's aversion to sexuality seemed natural to her until she discovered how she had learned to associate sex and danger from her mother. Thus, a central element of psychodynamic technique is the ***interpretation*** of conflicts, defences, compromise-formations (chapter 11), and repetitive interpersonal patterns, whereby the therapist helps the person understand her experiences in a new light.

One patient, for example, repeatedly had affairs with married men. As she talked about sneaking around the wife of one man in order to see him, her associations led to her parents' divorce. At one point, her mother had refused to allow her to see her father, so the patient had arranged secret meetings with him. The therapist interpreted the connection between the patient's pattern of seeking out married men and sneaking around her mother's back to see her father. The therapist wondered if the rage she felt towards her mother for not letting her see her father was now being directed towards the wives of the men with whom she had affairs, about whom she spoke callously, and which allowed her to rationalise sleeping with their husbands.

An important kind of interpretation addresses ***resistance***, barriers to free association or to the treatment more generally, which the patient creates. As both sleuth and suspect, the patient is consciously on the trail of mental processes she is unconsciously covering up. Resistance emerges because the patient originally developed her symptoms to reduce anxiety; the closer she comes to its source, the more she is motivated to run from it. Jenny, for example, insisted for two years that her attitudes towards sexuality were totally realistic and refused to discuss the matter further.

Analysis of transference

The relationship between the patient and the therapist provides a particularly useful source of information in psychotherapy (Freud, 1912/1958; Gill, 1982; Luborsky & Crits-Christoph, 1990; see also D'Abreu, 2006). Freud observed that patients tend to play out with their therapists many of the same interpersonal scenarios that give them trouble in their lives. For example, a man who came to therapy complaining of problems getting along with people in positions of authority immediately added, 'By the way, I don't believe in this psychotherapy crap'. In so doing, he had already replicated his symptom with a new authority figure — the therapist — in the first moments of the treatment!

The therapy relationship is a very intimate relationship in which the patient communicates personal experiences to someone commonly perceived as an authority or attachment figure. As research documents, this relationship consequently tends to become a magnet for experiences from prior relationships involving intimacy and authority, particularly parental relationships (Luborsky, Barber, & Crits-Christoph, 1990). In fact, the quality of a patient's relationships with his parents is a good predictor of his capacity to form a strong therapeutic alliance with a therapist — which in turn predicts the likely success of the treatment (Hilliard, Henry, & Strupp, 2000).

Transference refers to the process whereby people experience similar thoughts, feelings, fears, wishes and conflicts in new relationships as they did in past relationships. Freud thought of this as the transferring of feelings from childhood relationships onto adult relationships, particularly with the therapist. For example, one patient had experienced his father as extremely critical and impossible to please. In therapy, the patient tended to interpret even neutral comments from the therapist as severe criticism and would then respond by doing things (like missing appointments without calling) that would elicit criticism and hostility in most relationships. By examining such transferential processes, the patient and therapist can learn about the patient's dynamics directly. Freud (1917, p. 454) wrote that the relationship between the patient and therapist creates 'new editions of the old conflicts'. The aim of working with transference is to rewrite the new edition in the light of new information.

Experimental research from a cognitive–social perspective has documented transference processes in everyday relationships. In one study, the investigators asked participants to describe significant others and then embedded pieces of those descriptions in descriptions of fictional characters (Andersen & Cole, 1991). Thus, if a participant described his mother as intelligent, feminine, gentle and courageous, the investigators would create a fictional character who was described, among other things, as gentle. The investigators then presented participants with descriptions of these fictional characters and later asked them to remember them. Upon recall, participants attributed qualities of the significant other (such as courage) to the character, even though these qualities had not been part of the character's initial description. Essentially, participants transferred aspects of one representation to another.

Additionally, researchers have shown that people similarly transfer feelings from significant others onto descriptions of a person who is allegedly in the room next door and that these feelings lead them to either want to meet or avoid the person (Andersen, Reznik, & Manzella, 1996). The same effects occur when descriptions of significant others are embedded in descriptions of hypothetical people and presented subliminally (Glassman & Andersen, 1997). Thus, this research indicates that transference can influence thought, feeling and memory and that it can do so outside awareness.

Varieties of psychodynamic therapy

The main contemporary forms of psychodynamic treatment are psychoanalysis and psychodynamic psychotherapy.

Psychoanalysis

The first kind of psychotherapy developed was ***psychoanalysis***, in which the patient lies on a couch and the analyst sits behind him. The purpose of the couch is to create an environment in which people can simply let associations come to mind. This arrangement can also make disclosing sensitive material easier because the person does not have to look the therapist in the eye. Patients usually undergo psychoanalysis three to five times a week for several years, making it a very intensive, extensive and expensive form of treatment.

MAKING CONNECTIONS

Research on adult **attachment** finds that adults characterised as preoccupied with attachment are afraid of being rejected or abandoned in close relationships and are vulnerable to anxiety (chapter 7).

Psychodynamic psychotherapy

In ***psychodynamic psychotherapy***, the patient and therapist conduct the treatment sitting face-to-face, with the patient in a chair rather than on the couch. The therapy is more conversational than psychoanalysis, although the aim is still exploration of unconscious processes. The techniques are similar to psychoanalysis, but the therapist and patient are usually more goal directed because time is much more limited (Shedler, 2010).

Psychodynamic psychotherapy is particularly appropriate for addressing repetitive interpersonal patterns or difficulties in relationships, such as consistently choosing the wrong kind of lover or fearing vulnerability in close relationships. This kind of treatment proved crucial for Jenny, who initially had trouble maintaining an appropriate weight after she left the hospital. It allowed her to confront her feelings about herself, her intellectually impaired sister, her parents and her sexuality that appeared to have contributed to a life-threatening symptom.

Psychodynamic therapy takes place one to three times a week and, like psychoanalysis, can last several years. (A common misperception about psychodynamic psychotherapy is that the more times a week a person attends a session, the 'sicker' he is. In fact, the purpose of multiple sessions per week is simply to allow more time to explore associational networks, not to 'hold the person together'.) Research suggests that patients who meet twice weekly in long-term psychotherapy get considerably more benefit than those who come once weekly (Freedman, Hoffenberg, Vorus, & Frosch, 1999; see also Perry, Bond, & Roy, 2007).

Since Freud's time, some psychodynamic therapists and researchers have developed short-term therapies (Binder, Strupp, & Henry, 1995; Crits-Christoph, 1992; Davanloo, 1985; Mann, 1982; Sifneos, 1987). Short-term dynamic psychotherapies rely on the same principles as other forms of psychodynamic therapy, but they generally last a year or less (Luborsky, Docherty, Miller, & Barber, 1993; see also Abbass, 2002). Nevertheless, a review of previous research found that these short-term therapies

APPLY + DISCUSS

- What aspects of psychodynamic psychotherapy could be used to alter an attachment style a person has had for 25 years?
- If attachment styles can change with psychotherapy, how quickly or slowly is this likely to occur? Under what conditions is therapy likely to change attachment styles?

can result in significant improvement and symptom reduction in patients across a variety of common mental disorders (Abbass, Hancock, Henderson, & Kisely, 2006). Unlike more intensive psychodynamic treatments, short-term therapies usually have a specific focus, which is formulated in the first few sessions. Formulating the focus entails linking the patient's initial complaint with a hypothesised conflict or dynamic issue, such as unresolved grief, repressed anger or authority conflicts. A brief transcript from a short-term psychodynamic therapy is reproduced in figure 16.1.

Loretta was a woman in her late 30s who sought treatment for long-standing anxiety and depression and an unsatisfying sexual relationship with her husband. Loretta came from a very conservative religious family and described her father as aloof and her mother as extremely critical. In the excerpt below, she describes feeling more relaxed with men, an exciting but still unsettling feeling:

Therapist: How would you experience men before you started feeling this way?
Patient: Sort of avoidance. I didn't — difficulty relating to them . . .
Therapist: Is that different now?
Patient: It's a little different now. In fact, I've noticed it. I can even encounter somebody, a man . . . and I can joke and cut up, and sort of banter back and forth, which has always been a real problem for me . . .
Therapist: It sounds like you have started to feel more comfortable with men. What's bothersome then?
Patient: Well, I guess it's the whole thing of sexual interest, I guess . . . [T]hat part of me that was always taught that sex and intimacy and physicalness was reserved for someone you were very bound to, and were going to spend the rest of your life with. That sort of thing.
Therapist: That sounds like you still believe that. We are talking about your curiosity.
Patient: Well, when I'm in a situation where I'm with a man, with the person I'm supposed to spend my life with, and I should not be having all these sexual feelings about other men . . .
Therapist: Well, do you think that is pretty common?
Patient: Well, this friend and I have, she feels the same way and she and I have had a lot of discussions about that.
Therapist: Then, there are two of you walking around.
Patient: There are two of us. (Laughs)

FIGURE 16.1
Transcript from a short-term psychodynamic psychotherapy. In this excerpt, the therapist helps the patient distinguish between fantasies, for which one need not feel guilty, and actions. The therapist is nonjudgemental and helps Loretta understand that her feelings are normal, through the joke about 'two of you walking around'.

SOURCE: Strupp and Binder (1984).

INTERIM SUMMARY

Psychodynamic therapy rests on two principles: ***insight*** (coming to an understanding of the way one's mind works) and the relationship between the patient and therapist. To bring about change, therapists rely on three techniques: ***free association*** (exploring associational networks by having the patient say whatever comes to mind); ***interpretation*** (efforts to help the patient come to understand her experiences in a new light); and examination of ***transference*** (whereby people transfer thoughts, feelings, fears, wishes and conflicts from past relationships onto the therapist, re-enacting repetitive interpersonal interaction patterns). The main contemporary forms of psychodynamic treatment are ***psychoanalysis*** (in which the patient lies on the couch and meets with the therapist three or more times a week) and ***psychodynamic psychotherapy*** (in which the patient and therapist sit face-to-face and usually meet once or twice a week).

Cognitive–behavioural therapies

Psychodynamic approaches were the first approaches to psychotherapy, and they emerged from clinical practice. In the late 1950s and early 1960s an alternative approach emerged from the laboratory. This approach viewed symptoms as maladaptive learned behaviour patterns that could be changed by applying behaviourist principles of learning (Eysenck, 1952, 1964; Wolpe, 1964). Although many therapists continue to practise behaviour therapy (treatment based primarily on behaviourist learning principles), most who make use of learning principles today are ***cognitive–behavioural*** in their orientation, using methods derived from behaviourist and cognitive approaches to learning.

Basic principles

Cognitive–behavioural therapies are typically short term. Unlike psychodynamic therapies, they are not concerned with exploring and altering underlying personality patterns or unconscious processes (see Eysenck, 1987; Goldfried & Davison, 1994). The focus is on the individual's present behaviour and cognitions, not on childhood experiences or inferred motives. Cognitive–behavioural therapists are much more directive than their psychodynamic counterparts. They suggest specific ways patients should change their thinking and behaviour, assign homework and structure sessions with questions and strategies.

Cognitive–behavioural therapists begin with a careful ***behavioural analysis***, examining the stimuli or thoughts that precede or are associated with a symptom (Kazantzis, 2006; Wright, Basco, Thase, & Gabbard, 2006). They then tailor procedures to address problematic behaviours, cognitions and emotional responses. The effectiveness of this type of therapy lies in its ability to target highly specific psychological processes (Overholser, 2002).

Panic attacks, for example, include physiological arousal, a subjective experience of terror, anxious thoughts and a tendency to avoid stimuli associated with anxiety. Panic patients come to associate autonomic reactions such as a racing heart and a feeling of suffocation with an impending panic attack; they also frequently develop expectancies of helplessness in the face of impending panic and may have catastrophic thoughts such as 'Everyone will be able to see that I am helpless and incompetent' or 'I am about to die' (chapter 14). The therapist addresses different components of the problem with different techniques. These may include paced breathing exercises to deal with feelings of breathlessness (Salkovskis, Jones, & Clark, 1986), repeated exposure to the experience of a racing heart (e.g. through climbing up and down stairs) to extinguish the emotional response, and rational analysis of the accuracy of catastrophic beliefs (Barlow, 2002; Clark, 1994). The success of these treatments in extinguishing fear of autonomic arousal is impressive: exposing panic patients to air heavy in carbon dioxide (which leads to the feeling of breathlessness) leads roughly 75 percent to experience a panic attack prior to treatment but only 20 percent to do so after treatment (Schmidt, Lerew, & Trakowski, 1997; Schmidt, Trakowski, & Staab, 1997).

Classical conditioning techniques

The earliest, and some of the most powerful, cognitive–behavioural techniques emerged from research on classical conditioning. Prominent among these are desensitisation and exposure.

Systematic desensitisation

One of the most widely used cognitive–behavioural techniques is ***systematic desensitisation***, in which the patient gradually confronts a phobic stimulus mentally while in a state that inhibits anxiety (Wolpe, 1958). In classical conditioning of emotional responses (chapter 6), a previously neutral stimulus comes to elicit an emotion when paired with a stimulus that already elicits the emotion. The assumption behind desensitisation is that through classical conditioning phobics have learned to fear what should be a neutral stimulus.

For example, a person who has a car accident feels afraid to drive afterwards because being behind the wheel of a car (conditioned stimulus) is associated with a terrifying experience (unconditioned stimulus). Normally, future encounters with the conditioned stimulus (driving) in the absence of the stimulus that elicited the fear (the accident) will extinguish the response (fear). However, if the person starts walking instead of driving, this short-circuits an adaptive learning process: he avoids the fear by not driving, but because this prevents extinction from occurring, the fear will remain. Thus, phobic responses, like all avoidance responses, become particularly resistant to extinction.

To extinguish irrational fear responses, the patient must confront the feared stimulus. This is the aim of systematic desensitisation, which takes place in four steps. First, the therapist teaches the patient relaxation techniques, such as tensing and then relaxing muscle groups throughout the body or breathing from the diaphragm. Then the therapist questions the patient about his fears and uses this information to construct a hierarchy of feared imagined stimuli from scenes that provoke mild anxiety to those that induce intense fear. For the patient who is afraid of driving, the scenes might range from sitting behind the wheel of a stationary car to driving on a crowded highway on a rainy night (figure 16.2). The third step, which usually begins in the third or fourth session, is desensitisation proper. The patient relaxes, using the techniques he has learned, and is then instructed to imagine

1

Sitting behind the wheel of a nonmoving car in the driveway

2

Driving along an empty, quiet street on a sunny day

3

Driving along a busy street on a sunny day

4

Driving on the same street at night

5

Driving on a busy highway in daylight, in the rain

6

Driving on a busy highway on a rainy night

FIGURE 16.2
Systematic desensitisation. The patient exposes himself to progressively more threatening imagined approximations of the phobic stimulus. Exposure techniques confront the patient with the feared stimulus directly.

vividly the first (i.e. least threatening) scene in the hierarchy. When the patient can imagine this scene comfortably, perhaps with additional relaxation instructions, he then imagines the next scene, and so on up the hierarchy. In the fourth step, the therapist encourages the patient to confront his fears in real life and monitors his progress as he does so, desensitising additional scenes as needed to eliminate anxiety and avoidance.

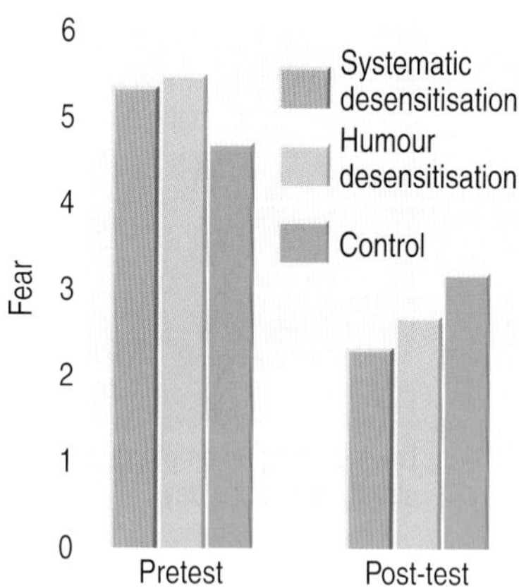

FIGURE 16.3
Humour desensitisation. Ratings of fears of spiders before and after treatment. Ratings were based on 10-point scales. Both desensitisation groups were equally effective at reducing fears of spiders, and more effective than no treatment.

SOURCE: Ventis et al. (2001).

In a variant of systematic desensitisation, researchers in one study compared the role of humour desensitisation to systematic desensitisation (Ventis, Higbee, & Murdock, 2001). Participants who were afraid of spiders were randomly assigned to a humour desensitisation condition, a systematic desensitisation condition or a control condition. Participants in both of the desensitisation groups were asked to rate the fearfulness of different hierarchy scenes depicting spiders. For those participants in the systematic desensitisation group, these scenes were presented in order from least to most fearful and the participants were taught relaxation techniques to help them cope with the scenes presented. Participants in the humour desensitisation group followed the same procedure except their hierarchy scenes were accompanied by humour. Participants in the control condition were not exposed to relaxation techniques or the hierarchy scenes. As shown in figure 16.3, both desensitisation groups were equally effective and both were more effective than was the control group.

Desensitisation has been used to treat a long list of anxiety-related disorders, including phobias, impotence, nightmares, obsessive–compulsive disorders, social anxiety and even fears of death (Lindemann, 1996; McGlynn, Smitherman, & Gothard, 2004). In one striking case, desensitisation was used to help a 20-year-old woman overcome a fear of babies (Free & Beekhuis, 1985). Initially the patient was unable even to look at photographs of babies long enough to establish a hierarchy. By the end of treatment and at a one-year follow-up, she could approach babies without discomfort. This form of therapy is markedly different from a psychodynamic therapy, which would have explored what babies meant to her. Was she feeling guilty about an abortion she had had? Was she a victim of incest who unconsciously associated babies with her childhood fear that she was pregnant? In contrast, the cognitive–behavioural therapist aims to extinguish the fear response, not to search for insight into its origins.

Exposure techniques

A related cognitive–behavioural strategy based on classical conditioning is exposure. ***Exposure techniques*** present patients with the actual phobic stimulus in real life, rather than having them merely imagine it (Powers & Emmelkamp, 2007). Exposure techniques for simple phobias are some of the most successful treatments devised for any disorder (Carter, McIntosh, Joyce, Sullivan, & Bulik, 2003; Hahlweg, Fiegenbaum, Frank, Schroeder, & von Witzleben, 2001; Roth, Fonagy, Parry, & Target, 1996; Rothbaum & Schwartz, 2002). For example, fear of flying affects 10 to 25 percent of the population and can be treated with about 90 percent success with either exposure to aeroplanes or 'virtual exposure' in a virtual reality flight simulator (Rothbaum, Hodges, Smith, Lee, & Price, 2000).

In ***flooding***, the patient confronts the phobic stimulus all at once. The theory behind flooding is that inescapable exposure to the conditioned stimulus eventually desensitises the patient through extinction or related mechanisms. Flooding, like desensitisation, prevents the person from escaping the onset of the conditioned stimulus (such as sitting in the driver's seat of a running car). From a more cognitive perspective, when faced with inescapable exposure, patients eventually recognise that the situation is not really catastrophic and that they have the self-efficacy to confront it. One case report described the use of flooding to treat a young woman with an intense fear of escalators (Nesbitt, 1973). With considerable coaxing from the therapist, the patient rode the escalators in a large department store for hours, first with the therapist and then alone, until the symptom subsided. In another case, a patient who was terrified of driving over speed bumps spent hours driving, with her therapist, over speed bumps on a university campus. As you well know, given the number of speed bumps on a university campus, she received more than her share of exposure.

From the patient's point of view, flooding can be a frightening procedure. A modification of the technique that is less difficult to endure is ***graded exposure***, a procedure in which the patient is gradually exposed to the phobic stimulus. Like flooding, graded exposure uses real stimuli, but like desensitisation, the stimuli are graduated in intensity. One psychologist used graded exposure with a 70-year-old woman who had developed a fear of dogs after having been savagely bitten by one (Thyer, 1980). During the first two sessions, she was exposed to a small dog, first at the other end of the room and then gradually closer until she let it lick her hand. During the third session, she made an hour-long visit to the humane society, where she was exposed to the barking of dozens of dogs. During the fourth and fifth sessions, she repeated the earlier treatments but with large dogs. After five sessions, her symptom disappeared.

Technological advances have altered the ways in which some therapists use graded exposure. Now, therapists can use ***virtual reality exposure therapy*** to treat phobias. Patients are exposed to virtual images of the feared stimulus, as opposed to the actual stimulus. The first study detailing the use of virtual reality therapy was published in 1995 (Rothbaum et al., 1995) and describes the use of virtual reality to treat acrophobia or the fear of heights. Subsequent studies using virtual reality exposure therapy have included Vietnam veterans with post-traumatic stress disorder (Rothbaum, Hodges, Ready, Graap, & Alarcon, 2001), people with a fear of flying (Maltby, Kirsch, Mayers, & Allen, 2002) and children with spider phobias (Dewis et al., 2001). The advantages of virtual reality therapy are that it allows therapists to treat phobias that otherwise would be costly or time-consuming to treat. For example, someone who was agoraphobic would have to be accompanied on excursions outside the confines of their house as they worked to overcome their fear of open spaces. In addition, virtual reality therapy goes beyond simply asking participants to visualise the phobic stimulus. Instead, clients are exposed to virtual images of the feared object or situation (Mahoney, 1997; see also Powers & Emmelkamp, 2007).

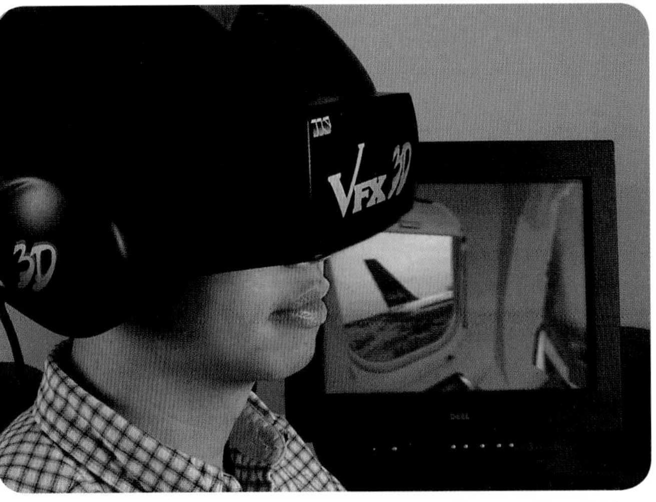

Virtual reality software enables phobic clients to more vividly experience their feared objects and situations, such as flying in an aeroplane during desensitisation.

One therapist who was treating a survivor who had PTSD from the 11 September 2001 terrorist attacks used virtual reality therapy. The client was systematically exposed to 'virtual planes flying over the WTC, jets crashing into the WTC with animated explosions and sound effects, virtual people jumping to their deaths from the burning buildings, towers collapsing and dust clouds' (Difede & Hoffman, 2002, p. 529). Virtual reality exposure therapy represents one of the newest ways to treat phobias. Rather than being exposed to the actual feared stimulus or simply asked to visualise the stimulus in their minds, clients are presented with the stimulus in virtual reality. These treatments have met with considerable success in the treatment of phobias.

Understanding exposure sheds light on not only the treatment but also the nature of many anxiety disorders. For example, people who have PTSD often alternate between numbness and lack of memory for the incident on the one hand and intruding thoughts of it on the other. As we have seen (chapters 2 and 10), disclosure of painful events tends to improve health and psychological functioning, and the reason is probably that disclosure involves exposure. People who have experienced traumatic events and expose themselves to memories of them are more likely to overcome them.

The role of exposure in PTSD was demonstrated by two more recent Australian examples of treatment for combat veterans. Forbes et al. (2003) described a pilot study involving the use of imagery rehearsal therapy (IRT) to treat a group of 12 Australian veterans of the Vietnam War with chronic combat-related PTSD. The 12 month trial of IRT found it had a positive effect in alleviating post-traumatic nightmares, PTSD and broader symptoms in the participants. The other study involved groups of eight Australian World War II veterans and their partners gathering for weekly full-day therapy sessions with a trauma focus to recount their experiences (Bonwick, 2002). The 100 veterans who had been through the program showed improvements in measures of PTSD symptoms, levels of anxiety and depression, alcohol problems, marital satisfaction, physical health, social function and satisfaction with life, as well as anecdotally reporting an improved quality of life.

Dr Katherine Mills, a Senior Lecturer at the UNSW National Drug and Alcohol Research Centre, has discussed how PTSD links strongly with drug use problems based on Australian general population data. Researchers at the Centre have found that PTSD sufferers are about six times more likely to also have a substance use disorder, and that about 25 percent of those with PTSD have a co-occurring substance abuse disorder (ABC Radio National, 2010).

A key component of all exposure techniques is ***response prevention*** — preventing the patient from producing responses that allow avoidance of the feared stimulus. Avoidance can be quite subtle. For example, a person with a social phobia can get himself to go to a party by telling himself that at any moment he can excuse himself to the bathroom or leave. Although this approach seems intuitively sensible, in fact, it is not: for exposure to be successful, the therapist needs to help the patient nail shut all 'escape hatches' that prevent the person from fully confronting the fear.

Response prevention is central to the treatment of obsessive–compulsive disorders, for example, because the patient typically uses various rituals to prevent anxiety (see Martin, Garske, & Davis, 2000). Research has shown that exposure response prevention techniques are effective in reducing obsessive–compulsive symptoms, and maintaining improvements long after completion of treatment (Khodarahimi, 2009).

Operant conditioning techniques

In operant conditioning, behaviour is controlled by its consequences (chapter 6). Therapies based on operant conditioning therefore use reinforcement and punishment to modify unwanted behaviour, as when Jenny, whose case opened this chapter, was rewarded for gaining weight with increased privileges. Operant procedures are used in virtually all psychiatric hospitals and are used unsystematically by all therapists, whether or not they are aware of it, as they reward certain kinds of behaviour and discourage others. Researchers using operant procedures more systematically have found that offering rewards to patients in treatment for alcoholism quadruples the likelihood that they will stay in treatment, which in turn substantially improves outcome (Petry, Martin, Cooney, & Kranzler, 2000).

Operant techniques can be particularly effective in working with children and their parents because parents often intuitively apply rewards and punishments in ineffective or counterproductive ways (see Kendall, 1993). Skilfully managing contingencies of reinforcement can bring unwanted behaviours under control, as in the treatment of a 12-year-old girl who repeatedly scratched herself raw and then picked at the scabs. The behaviour gradually decreased as she was rewarded with 'points' that she could exchange for privileges when she did not pick at herself (Latimer, 1979). Of course, a possible downside of this is that the child or patient comes to depend on the reward, so that adaptive behaviours cease to be performed in the absence of the reward.

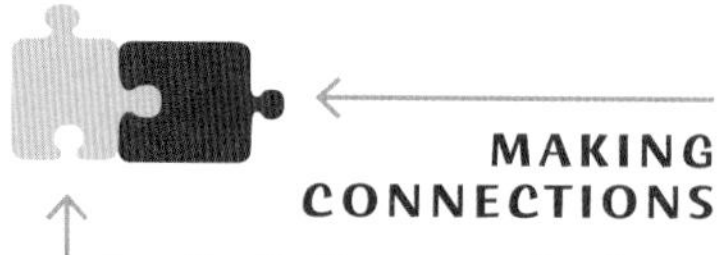

MAKING CONNECTIONS

Even if self-efficacy expectancies are high, people cannot emit a behaviour they lack the competence to perform (chapter 11). Bandura (cited in Goldfried & Davison, 1994) warns that desensitising people who are socially phobic but who actually do lack the ability to interact in socially competent ways produces little more than 'relaxed incompetents'. Thus, cognitive–behavioural therapists use various techniques to teach people skills that can help them cope with stressful events and handle interpersonal problems more effectively.

Modelling and skills training

As learning theory began to broaden its scope in the 1960s to include cognition and social learning (chapter 6) so, too, did behaviour therapists. Two early additions to the therapeutic repertoire of cognitive–behavioural therapists were modelling and skills training.

Modelling

The recognition that people learn not only through their own experiences but also by observing the behaviour of others led psychologists to develop modelling procedures in psychotherapy. In ***participatory modelling***, the therapist models the desired behaviour and gradually induces the patient to participate in it. Bandura, Blanchard, and Ritter (1969) demonstrated the effectiveness of this technique in treating patients with snake phobias. The therapist first handles snakes without showing anxiety and without being harmed. Then the therapist coaxes the patient to handle the snakes.

Watching the therapist handle snakes, the patient begins to recognise that doing so is safe (vicarious conditioning; chapter 6). This then allows the patient to approach the snake (exposure). Participatory modelling also alters self-efficacy expectancies, because observing the model safely approach a snake suggests to the patient that he can, too. Participating with the therapist in snake handling then leads to continued revisions of his expectancies.

Skills training

Another cognitive–behavioural technique, ***skills training***, involves teaching the behaviours necessary to accomplish relevant goals. Skills are a form of procedural knowledge and are typically carried out automatically (chapter 7). Acquiring new skills, however, usually requires that the individual focus conscious awareness on and practise a set of procedures until they gradually become routine (Meichenbaum, 1977, 1990; see also Granholm et al., 2005).

Skills training draws on theories of problem solving and self-regulation (chapters 8 and 11). For example, skills training with impulsive and hyperactive children teaches them to decide what the problem is, divide it into components, develop ways to solve each part and use feedback to determine whether each part (and eventually the entire problem) has been successfully handled (Antshel & Remer, 2003; Meichenbaum, 1977). In one procedure, the therapist teaches impulsive children to ask themselves a series of questions: 'What is my problem?'; 'What can I do about it?'; 'Am I using my plan?'; 'How did I do?'

Social skills training involves teaching new skills to people with specific interpersonal deficits, such as social awkwardness or lack of assertiveness (see Antshel & Remer, 2003). Following assessment, treatment usually begins with direct teaching of skills or modelling of behaviour on film, on videotape or in person. The next stage is rehearsal of the new skills — practising gestures, imagining responses, role playing various scenarios and so forth — which is followed by feedback and renewed practice (Ladd & Mize, 1983).

INTERIM SUMMARY

Cognitive–behavioural therapists use methods derived from behaviourist and cognitive approaches to learning. Treatment begins with a ***behavioural analysis*** of the symptom and the stimuli or thoughts associated with it, which define the targets of treatment. Behavioural techniques relying on classical conditioning include ***systematic desensitisation***, in which the patient mentally confronts a phobic stimulus gradually while in a state that inhibits anxiety, and ***exposure techniques*** that present the patient with the actual phobic stimulus, including ***virtual reality exposure therapy***. Operant techniques attempt to control maladaptive behaviour by altering its consequences. Social learning techniques include ***participatory modelling***, in which the therapist models the desired behaviour and gradually induces the patient to participate in it, and ***skills training***, which involves teaching the behaviours necessary to accomplish relevant goals.

Cognitive therapy

Whereas most cognitive–behavioural techniques try to alter behaviour, ***cognitive therapy*** focuses on changing dysfunctional cognitions presumed to underlie psychological disorders. Cognitive therapies target what Aaron T. Beck (1976, 1993) calls ***automatic thoughts***, the things individuals spontaneously say to themselves and the assumptions they make (see also Ellis, 1962). By questioning the patient's assumptions and beliefs and asking her to identify the data underlying them, the therapist engages the patient in hypothesis testing (Hollon & Beck, 1994). Cognitive therapies also rely on behavioural techniques but largely to induce patients to implement therapeutic suggestions (see Ellis, 1984). Two approaches to combating cognitive distortions are Ellis' rational–emotive behaviour therapy and Beck's cognitive therapy.

Ellis' rational-emotive behaviour therapy

Albert Ellis began as a psychoanalyst but came to believe that psychodynamic treatments take too long and are too often ineffective (Ellis, 1962, 1989). According to Ellis, what people think and say to themselves about a situation affects the way they respond to it. He proposed the ***ABC theory of psychopathology***, where A refers to activating conditions, B to belief systems and C to emotional consequences (Ellis, 1977, 1999). Activating conditions such as loss of a job (A) do not lead directly to consequences such as depression (C). The process that turns unpleasant events into depressive symptoms involves dysfunctional belief systems, often expressed in a person's self-talk, such as, 'I am not a worthy person unless I am very successful' (B).

Ellis thus developed ***rational–emotive behaviour therapy*** (also called rational–emotive therapy), which proposes that patients can rid themselves of most psychological problems by maximising their rational and minimising their irrational thinking (Ellis, 1962, p. 36). The therapist continually brings the patient's illogical or self-defeating thoughts to his attention, shows him how they are causing problems, demonstrates their illogic and teaches alternative ways of thinking (Ellis, 1962, 1977, 1987). If the source of psychological distress is irrational thinking, then the path to eliminating symptoms is increased rationality.

Beck's cognitive therapy

Like Ellis, Aaron T. Beck was a disenchanted psychoanalyst. Also like Ellis, he viewed cognitive therapy as a process of 'collaborative empiricism', in which the patient and therapist work together like scientists testing hypotheses (Beck, 1989). Cognitive therapy began as a treatment for depression, but clinicians now apply cognitive techniques to disorders ranging from anxiety to eating disorders (e.g. Beck, 1992, 2005; Borkovec & Costello, 1993; Chambless & Gillis, 1993; Peterson & Mitchell, 1999).

In therapy sessions, which typically number only 12 to 20, the therapist and patient work on changing maladaptive patterns of thought and behaviour. Often the patient keeps a log, recording thoughts and moods so she can observe the relationship between them and track her progress in therapy. The sessions are highly structured; they begin with setting an agenda. The therapist teaches the patient the theory behind the treatment, often assigning books or articles to read, and trains the patient to fill in the cognitive link between the stimulus that leads to depressed or anxious feelings and the feelings generated in the situation. For example, a patient who felt sad whenever he made a mistake was instructed to focus on his thoughts the next time he made a mistake. At his next session, he reported that he would think, 'I'm a dope' or 'I never do anything right' (Beck, 1976).

The core of Beck's therapy, like Ellis', is challenging cognitive distortions. The therapist questions the data on which the patient's assumptions are based and identifies errors in thinking. A woman who was suicidal believed she had nothing to look forward to because her husband was unfaithful. Underlying her suicidal feelings were the beliefs that she was nothing without her husband and that she could not save her marriage. The dialogue between the therapist and this patient included the following exchange (Beck, 1976):

THERAPIST: You say that you can't be happy without Raymond . . . Have you found yourself happy when you are with Raymond?

PATIENT: No, we fight all the time and I feel worse.

THERAPIST: You say you are nothing without Raymond. Before you met Raymond, did you feel you were nothing?

PATIENT: No, I felt I was somebody.

THERAPIST: If you were somebody before you knew Raymond, why do you need him to be somebody now?

PATIENT: [Puzzled] Hmmm . . .

Eventually, this patient concluded that her happiness did not, in fact, depend on her husband. She divorced him and was able to enjoy a more stable life.

INTERIM SUMMARY

Cognitive therapy focuses on changing dysfunctional cognitions that underlie psychological disorders. Ellis' ***rational–emotive behaviour therapy*** attempts to address the belief systems that mediate between activating conditions and maladaptive emotional reactions. Beck's ***cognitive therapy*** targets cognitive distortions.

Humanistic, group and family therapies

Although psychodynamic and cognitive–behavioural are the most widely practised psychotherapies, clinicians have many other alternatives. The most common are humanistic, group and family therapies.

Humanistic therapies

In the 1960s, a number of therapists took issue with what they perceived as mechanistic and dehumanising aspects of both psychoanalysis and behaviourism. Humanistic therapies, like humanistic personality theories (chapter 11), focus on the phenomenology of the patient — on the way each person consciously experiences the self, relationships and the world. The aim of ***humanistic therapies*** is to help people get in touch with their feelings, with their 'true selves' and with a sense of meaning in life. The two most widely practised humanistic therapies are Gestalt therapy and Carl Rogers' client-centred therapy.

Gestalt therapy

Gestalt therapy is an approach to treatment that emphasises awareness of feelings (Woldt & Toman, 2005). Gestalt therapy developed in response to the belief that people had become too socialised — that they controlled their thoughts, behaviours and even their feelings to conform to social expectations. According to Gestalt therapists, losing touch with one's emotions and one's authentic inner 'voice' leads to psychological problems such as depression and anxiety.

In some respects, Gestalt therapy resembles psychodynamic psychotherapy, although Gestalt therapists try to avoid focusing on explanations of current difficulties, believing that doing so leads people further away from their emotions, not towards them (Perls, 1969, 1989). In this view, understanding why one feels a certain way is far less important than recognising that one feels that way. Gestalt therapy thus focuses on the 'here and now' rather than the 'then and there'.

A technique commonly used by Gestalt therapists is the ***empty-chair technique***: The therapist places an empty chair near the client and asks her to imagine that the person to whom she would like to express her feelings (such as a dead parent) is in the chair. The client can then safely express her feelings by 'talking' with the person without consequences. A variant of this technique is the two-chair technique, in which the patient 'places' two sides of a dilemma in two different chairs and expresses each side while sitting in the appropriate chair.

For example, one woman was torn between staying with her husband, with whom she felt 'dead inside' and leaving him. She desperately wanted to leave but had trouble admitting this to herself because she felt so guilty. In one chair, she described why she wanted to stay with him; in the other, she voiced all her frustrations and disappointments with her husband and their marriage. By the end of the session, what was most striking to her was how passionately she voiced her desires to leave and how weakly she really felt about staying in the marriage.

Client-centred therapy

Carl Rogers was among the first therapists to refer to people who seek treatment as clients rather than patients. He rejected the disease model implied by 'patients' and suggested that people come to therapy seeking help in solving problems, not cures for disorders. ***Client-centred therapy*** is based on Rogers' view that people experience psychological difficulties when their concept of self is incongruent with their actual experience (chapter 11). For example, a man who thought of himself as someone who loved his father came to realise through therapy that he also felt a great deal of rage towards him. He had denied his negative feelings because he learned as a child that he should always be loving and obedient and that feeling otherwise was 'bad'. The aim of client-centred therapy is to help clients experience themselves as they actually are — in this case, for the man to accept himself as a person who can feel both love and rage towards his father and thus to alleviate tension and anxiety (Rogers, 1961; Rogers & Sanford, 1985).

Rogerian therapy assumes that the basic nature of human beings is to grow and mature. Hence, the goal is to provide a supportive environment in which clients can start again where they left off years ago when they denied their true feelings in order to feel worthy and esteemed by significant others. The therapist creates a supportive environment by demonstrating ***unconditional positive regard*** for the client — that is, expressing an attitude of fundamental acceptance towards the client, without any requirements or conditions (Rogers, 1961, 1980) — and by listening empathically. Rogers stressed the curative value of empathy, the process of becoming emotionally in tune with and understanding the client's experience without judging it. Therapeutic change occurs as the client hears his own thoughts and feelings reflected by a caring, empathic, non-judgemental listener. The Rogerian therapist, often called a counsellor, evaluates clients' thoughts and feelings only for their authenticity, not for their unconscious meanings or their rationality (McMillan, 2005).

Based on the Rogerian principle that unconditional positive regard is highly therapeutic, pet therapy has become a widely applied intervention to help reduce the depression of elderly nursing home residents, medically ill people and developmentally disabled individuals. In this approach, individuals interact with various kinds of nonjudgemental animals.

INTERIM SUMMARY

Humanistic therapies focus on the way each person consciously experiences the self, relationships and the world. They aim to help people get in touch with their feelings, their 'true selves' and a sense of meaning in life. ***Gestalt therapy*** tries to help people acknowledge their feelings so they can act in accordance with them. Rogers' ***client-centred therapy*** assumes that problems in living result when people's concept of self is incongruent with their actual experience. Therapeutic change occurs as the therapist empathises with the client's experience, demonstrating ***unconditional positive regard*** (an attitude of fundamental acceptance).

Group therapies

The therapies described thus far all start with the individual. In contrast, group and family therapies treat multiple individuals simultaneously, although they often apply psychodynamic, cognitive–behavioural or humanistic principles.

In ***group therapy***, multiple people meet together to work towards therapeutic goals. Typically five to 10 people meet with a therapist on a regular basis, usually once a week for two hours (Corey & Corey,

2005; Yalom, 1995). As in individual therapy, members of the group talk about problems in their own lives, but they also gain from the nature of the ***group process***, or the way members of the group interact with each other. Some cognitive–behavioural therapy also takes place in groups, particularly where the aim is to teach skills that do not require individual instruction, such as stress management, or where group interaction is itself a form of exposure, as in the treatment of social phobia.

Group therapy is designed to produce benefits that may not arise from individual therapy (Dies, 1992; Yalom, Brown, & Bloch, 1975). For example, for newcomers to a group, the presence of other members who have made demonstrable progress can instill a therapeutic sense of hope. Discovering that others have problems similar to their own may also relieve shame, anxiety and guilt. In addition, the group provides opportunities for members to repeat, examine and alter the types of relationships they experienced with their own families, which they may bring with them to many social situations.

Groups assembled for therapy may be more or less heterogeneous. Heterogeneous therapy groups work on the kinds of problems each person would address in individual therapy, such as anxiety, depression, or trouble finding and maintaining satisfying intimate relationships. Group members typically vary not only in symptoms but also in age, socioeconomic status and gender. In contrast, homogeneous groups usually focus on a common issue or disorder, such as incest, bulimia or borderline personality disorder (Koerner & Linehan, 2000; Linehan, 1993). Group therapy can be quite helpful in part because members can see and confront in other members what they cannot acknowledge in themselves, as when Jenny observed other obviously emaciated anorexics complain that they were fat.

A variation on group therapy is the ***self-help group***, which is not guided by a professional and often has many more than the five to 10 participants in therapist-guided groups (Page, Jones, & Wilson, 2004). Hundreds of thousands of people every year turn to self-help groups in Australia and New Zealand alone; self-help groups tend to flourish when a disease or disorder is stigmatising, such as alcoholism or AIDS (Davison, Pennebaker, & Dickerson, 2000). One of the oldest and best known self-help groups is Alcoholics Anonymous (AA; chapter 14). Others include Parents Without Partners, Weight Watchers, Gamblers Anonymous, and groups for cancer patients or parents who have lost a child.

Psychotherapists frequently refer patients to self-help groups to supplement individual therapy, particularly if the patient has a problem such as overeating or alcoholism. Self-help groups can be effective for many people suffering from alcoholism (Tonigan, Miller, & Connors, 2000) and other psychological and medical problems (Davison et al., 2000). Their main limitation can be a tendency to oversimplify the problem and its causes, leading some members to conclude that all their difficulties can be reduced to being 'co-dependent', an 'adult child of an alcoholic', and so forth.

Treatment method and theoretical orientation of the therapist may also influence how effective self-help groups are for patients. For example, in a study evaluating the combined effectiveness of treatment and self-help groups for substance abuse, researchers found that 12-step and eclectic treatment programs were more effective than cognitive–behavioural therapy in increasing the subsequent level of patient participation in 12-step self-help groups, resulting in more positive psychological outcomes (Humphreys, Huebsch, Finney, & Moos, 1999).

APPLY + DISCUSS

Family therapies are predicated on the view that a family is a system of interdependent parts. In this view, the problem lies in the structure of the system itself rather than in the family member who is merely expressing the symptom (Haley, 1971; Wynne, 1961).

- Can a therapist work successfully with a child without thoroughly evaluating the family? What about an adolescent?
- Adults are often in couples and families, too, but most clinicians never meet adult patients' spouses, parents, siblings or children. When can a clinician assume it is 'safe' to treat a patient as an individual? What are the trade-offs involved in treating an adult — or adolescent — in individual versus family therapy?

Family therapies

The aim of ***family therapy*** is to change maladaptive family interaction patterns (Lebow, 2005). As in group and psychodynamic therapy, the focus of family therapy is often on process as well as content. In other words, the process that unfolds in the therapy hour — a transference reaction to a therapist, a sibling-like competitive relationship in a group, or a round of accusations and counteraccusations between a husband and wife — is as important as the content of what the patient says. In family therapy, the therapist takes a relatively active role and often assigns the family tasks to carry out between sessions.

Approaches to family therapy

Family therapy has many schools of thought. Some approaches (called *structural* and *strategic*) focus on the organisation (structure) of the family system and use active interventions (strategies) to disrupt dysfunctional patterns. Therapists who operate from this standpoint attend to boundaries between generations, alliances and schisms between family members, the hierarchy of power in the family and family homoeostatic mechanisms (Aponte & VanDeusen, 1981; Laroi, 2003; Minuchin, 1974). For example, in one family with an anorexic daughter, the therapist discovered that the father forbade his children to close the doors to their rooms and felt more intimate with his daughter than his wife. Hypothesising that the father–daughter relationship might have contributed to the girl's refusal to eat (particularly since the symptom postponed physical maturation and puberty), the therapist prescribed as a first step that the daughter be allowed to keep her door closed for two hours a day and that the parents spend an hour each evening together in their room with the door closed (Hoffman, 1981).

One assessment technique used widely by family therapists to map family dynamics and to try to understand their origins is a ***genogram***, a map of a family over three or four generations (figure 16.4). The clinician supplements this barebones picture of the family by adding the patient's comments about each person or relationship depicted in the genogram, looking for possible similarities between current difficulties and the family's past (Foster, Jurkovic, Ferdinand, & Meadows, 2002; Milewski-Hertlein, 2001).

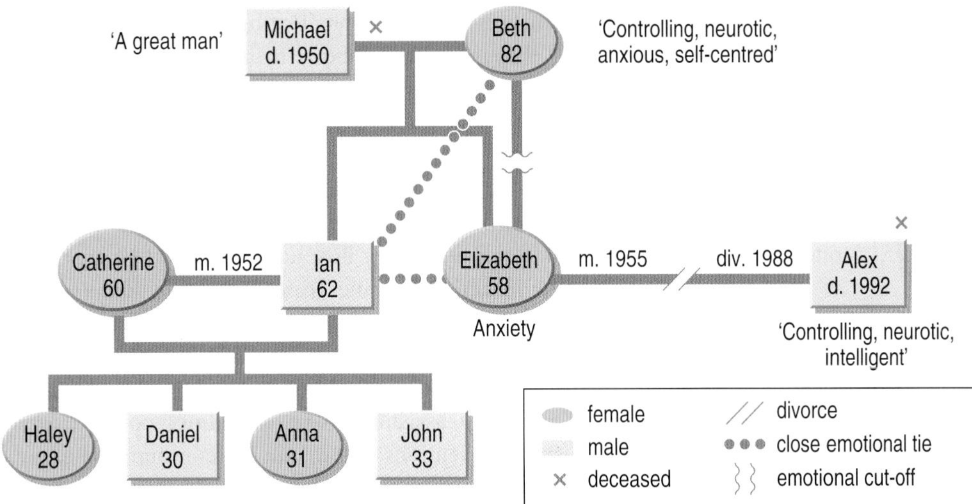

FIGURE 16.4
A genogram. The patient, Elizabeth, sought treatment for anxiety. From the genogram, the therapist could see that she was cut off from her mother, who remained close to her brother, which made Elizabeth feel left out. She also appeared to have married a man somewhat like her mother and to be anxious like her mother.

COMMENTARY

Making an impact with positive parenting programs

By Professor Matthew Sanders, University of Queensland

A wealth of evidence from epidemiological, longitudinal, correlational and experimental studies shows that parenting practices affect children's social and emotional development and overall wellbeing. Many significant mental health problems in children and young people arise in the context of parent–child interactions. Children exposed to harsh, critical and unpredictable parenting are at greater risk of developing behavioural and emotional problems. Therefore, it is not surprising that improving the skills and confidence of parents has become a major focus of efforts to prevent and treat behavioural and emotional problems in children (including conduct problems, delinquency and substance abuse).

There are many different types of parenting programs. However, the programs with the strongest empirical support are based on the application of cognitive–behavioural and social learning principles. Such programs teach parents to use positive parenting skills (e.g. contingent praise and attention) and effective disciplinary routines (e.g. ground rules, clear instructions, planned ignoring, logical consequences, and quiet time or timeout) for dealing with difficult behaviour. Parents are trained through a mixture of written information and guidance, verbal instruction, video or live modelling, behavioural rehearsal, practitioner feedback and homework assignments. These programs can be delivered in a number of different formats, including small group, large group, individual face-to-face, over-the-telephone and completely self-directed formats.

The first behaviourally oriented parenting programs emerged in the mid 1960s, with the seminar work of Gerald Patterson and his colleagues at the Oregon Social Learning Center in the United States. Patterson developed an individually administered parent training program for parents of aggressive school-aged children. Since then, a variety of different programs have been developed that draw on basic behaviour change principles. A wide range of clinical problems have been shown to be amenable to parenting interventions, including child oppositional defiant disorders, attention-deficit hyperactivity disorder, anxiety disorders, feeding disorders, chronic pain syndromes and sleep problems.

A major issue confronting the field is whether parenting programs should target only parents of children at risk of developing behavioural or emotional problems (indicated prevention programs), parents with well-established clinical problems (intervention programs) or all parents in the community (universal prevention programs). The Triple P — Positive Parenting Program developed at the University of Queensland's Parenting and Family Support Centre (see Sanders, 2008) is an example of a program that seeks to concurrently blend universal programming; indicated interventions for vulnerable, or at-risk, children; and interventions for children with well-established problems. The approach is definitely not 'a single size fits all'.

A unique demonstration of the value of implementing this multilevel system of parenting support is visible through a trial funded by the US Center for Disease Control and Prevention (Prinz, Sanders, Shapiro, Whitaker, & Lutzker, 2009). Eighteen US counties were matched for rates of maltreatment, poverty and population size, and were randomly assigned to either Triple P services or services as usual. A multidisciplinary workforce was trained to implement various levels of the Triple P system. After two and a half years, there were significantly lower rates of founded cases of maltreatment, fewer hospitalisations and emergency room visits, and fewer out-of-home placements in the Triple P counties (compared to the comparison counties). This trial demonstrated — for the first time in a randomised design — that wide-scale implementation of Triple P could reduce child maltreatment. The program involved a universal media and communication strategy to normalise and destigmatise seeking assistance with parenting; positive parenting seminars; brief primary care interventions; more intensive group and individual interventions; and enhanced versions of Triple P for complex cases that did not respond to lower levels of intervention.

Triple P, at the time of writing, has been disseminated to 20 countries around the world. It has been translated into 17 languages, and over 56 000 practitioners have been trained to deliver the program. Triple P continues to evolve in light of emerging evidence. New variants and derivative programs are being developed and evaluated in randomised clinical trials, including versions for parents of children with developmental disabilities (Stepping Stones Triple P), parents of overweight and obese children (Lifestyle Triple P), and parents who have been through separation and divorce (Family Transitions Triple P). It is the blending of universal and indicated programs into a multilevel system targeting entire populations that differentiates Triple P from many other parenting programs.

The Triple P — Positive Parenting Program developed at the University of Queensland's Parenting and Family Support Centre offers a multilevel system of support to parents, with the aim of fostering family relationships that allow children to realise their full potential.

Couples therapy

A variant of family therapy, called ***marital*** or ***couples therapy***, focuses on a smaller system, the marital unit or couple (Harway, 2004). The therapist may see the members of the couple individually and/or together.

Many therapists take a family systems approach to couples work, looking for problematic communication or interaction patterns. For example, one couple was trapped in a cycle in which the husband did something, the wife criticised it, and the husband felt angry and helpless and tried to defend himself (Haley, 1971, pp. 275–276). When the therapist pointed out the pattern, the wife responded, 'I have to criticise, because he never does what he should, ' to which the husband replied, 'Well, I try' — which was precisely the pattern repeating itself again.

Marital therapists may also adopt psychodynamic or cognitive–behavioural perspectives. The goal of psychodynamic marital therapy is to help members of the couple recognise and alter patterns of interacting that reflect patterns from the past. A man who complained that his wife was unsupportive repeatedly changed the subject or criticised his wife during therapy sessions every time she was about to do or say something supportive. The therapist hypothesised that he was replaying his experience of his parents' highly critical relationship, which guided his expectations of his wife and their interactions and formed an unconscious internal working model (chapter 12) of relationships.

Behavioural couples therapy rests on the assumption that people stay in relationships when they receive more reinforcement than punishment (Christensen, Atkins, Yi, Baucom, & George, 2006; chapter 18). Thus, behaviour therapists address the ways spouses often control each other's behaviour in ineffective and punishing ways. Empirically, a strong predictor of marital dissatisfaction and divorce is ***negative reciprocity***, the tendency of members of a couple to respond to negative comments or actions by their partner with negative behaviours in return (Gottman, 1998; Sholevar & Schwoeri, 2003). As a result, arguments spiral out of control without resolution. Thus, the marital therapist aims to help couples break these negative spirals.

Researchers also study the role of positive interactions in maintaining marital satisfaction, particularly the extent to which couples engage in behaviour that is accepting or validating (Jacobson, Christensen, Prince, Cordova, & Eldridge, 2000). As in research on positive and negative affect (chapter 10) and on parental rejection and acceptance (chapter 13), the data suggest that negative and positive marital interactions are not simply opposite sides of the same coin. Some couples are high on both accepting and rejecting behaviour towards one another; some are low on both; and others are high on one and low on the other. A couple can be unhappy even if they do not argue much, just as a couple can be happy even if they argue regularly, depending on how much they are also warm and accepting towards one another (Johnson & Jacob, 2000).

Marital therapists strive to help couples overcome difficulties created by behavioural patterns, such as negative reciprocity, that lead to ongoing conflict in personal relationships.

INTERIM SUMMARY

In ***group therapy***, multiple people meet together to work towards therapeutic goals. A variation on group therapy is the ***self-help group***, which is not guided by a professional. The aim of ***family therapy*** is to change maladaptive family interaction patterns. Family therapists often construct a ***genogram*** (a map of a family over three or four generations) to pinpoint recurring family patterns over generations. ***Marital*** or ***couples therapy*** focuses on the relationship between members of a couple and can rely on psychodynamic, systemic, cognitive or behavioural principles.

A GLOBAL VISTA

Culture and psychotherapy

Cross-culturally, as well as within multicultural societies, methods of treatment depend on cultural value systems and beliefs about personality and psychopathology (Kaplan & Sue, 1997; Kleinman, 1988). Psychoanalysis is predicated on the notion that exploring one's own mind is the key to therapeutic change — a view that would probably not have emerged outside the individualistic, industrialised West. Similarly, the role played by the cognitive–behavioural therapist — who acts in many respects like a behavioural engineer repairing malfunctioning psychological machinery — is readily understood and embraced by people in a technologically developed society.

Although psychotherapy is an invention of the twentieth-century West, all known cultures have attempted to understand and treat psychopathology. Many cultures treat psychological disturbances by bringing the community together in healing rituals (Boesch, 1982; Turner, 1969). These rituals give the ill person a sense of social support and solidarity, similar to the healing properties of empathic relationships in many Western therapies. At the same time, by uniting families or extended kin whose conflict may be contributing to the individual's symptoms, community healing rituals perform functions similar to family systems therapy.

Among the Ndembu of north-western Zambia, a ritual doctor thoroughly 'researches' the social situation of a person afflicted with illness, mental or physical (Turner, 1967). He listens to gossip and to the patient's dreams and persuades community members to confess any grudges. In one case, the patient held a position of power in the community but was greatly disliked. During the curing ritual, the patient was required to shed some blood, and members of the community were required to confess their hostilities. In this way, the ritual appeased all parties: the patient paid for his character defects with his blood, and the confession repaired social relationships. At the end of the ritual, the mood was jubilant, and people who had been estranged for years joined hands warmly.

To the extent that successful treatment requires faith in the possibility of help, all psychotherapy — if not all medicine — is to some degree 'faith healing'. The factors that confer faith, however, differ dramatically from culture to culture (Torrey, 1986). Western cultures value academic achievement, and patients tend to respect therapists whose walls are filled with advanced degrees. In non-Western cultures, such as Nigeria, where shamans have practised medicine for generations, family lineage and claims to supernatural powers are more likely to enhance a 'therapist's' prestige.

Biological treatments

The approaches we have examined thus far all use psychological and interpersonal interventions to address psychological problems. A very different type of treatment emerges from the view that psychological disorders reflect pathology of the brain.

Biological treatments use medication to restore the brain to as normal functioning as possible (pharmacotherapy). If medications are ineffective, clinicians may turn to electroconvulsive (shock) therapy (ECT) or, in extreme cases, psychosurgery. (Unlike psychotherapy, which can be administered by psychologists and other mental health practitioners, biological treatments can be administered only by physicians, most commonly psychiatrists.) The therapeutic action of psychotropic medications, as well as the advantages and disadvantages of using such medications in the treatment of mental health issues, is discussed in the next feature.

FROM BRAIN TO BEHAVIOUR

Psychotropic medications

For many years, patients with severe mental illness were sent to state mental hospitals, which provided little more than custodial care in overcrowded wards. But the discovery of ***psychotropic medications*** — drugs that act on the brain to affect mental processes (table 16.2) — changed the care of psychiatric patients dramatically. In 1956, chlorpromazine (trade names Thorazine and Largactil) was introduced to treat schizophrenia. New and better medications have been developed over the ensuing decades. The recent discovery of novel chemical agents, such as clozapine and olanzapine, has led to substantial improvement in a large percentage of psychotic patients who did not respond to chlorpromazine or other medications (Wahlbeck, Cheine, Essali, & Adams, 1999). The benefits of these medications can be so substantial that some researchers are beginning to use them as the treatment of choice for first-episode psychosis (Sanger et al., 1999).

TABLE 16.2 Psychotropic medications

Symptom	Type of medication	Examples
Psychosis	Antipsychotics	Chlorpromazine (Thorazine, Largactil) Clozapine (Clozaril)
Depression	Tricyclic antidepressants	Mianserin (Tolvon) Amitriptyline (Tryptanol, Amitrol) Imipramine (Tofranil)
	MAO inhibitors	Phenelzine (Nardil)
	Selective serotonin reuptake inhibitors	Fluoxetine (Prozac) Paroxetine (Aropax) Sertraline (Zoloft)
Mania	Mood stabilisers	Lithium (Lithicarb)
Anxiety	Anxiolitics Antidepressants	Benzodiazepines (Valium, Xanax) Fluoxetine (Prozac)

Many of the first drugs for treating mental illness were discovered accidentally, when physicians and researchers using them to treat one medical condition noticed that they altered another. For example, when Australian researcher J. F. Cade gave animals a lithium salt as part of his research into animal metabolism and behaviour, he noticed that the animals became calm and quiet. Further investigation showed that lithium was an effective treatment for bipolar disorder.

Most psychotropic medications act at neurotransmitter sites (Kraly, 2006; figure 16.5). Some inhibit overactive neurotransmitters or receptors that are overly sensitive and hence lead neurons to fire too frequently. One way they can do this is by 'locking up' the postsynaptic membrane, binding with receptors that would naturally bind with the neurotransmitter (figure 16.5a). This process renders the postsynaptic neuron unlikely to fire as frequently or at all.

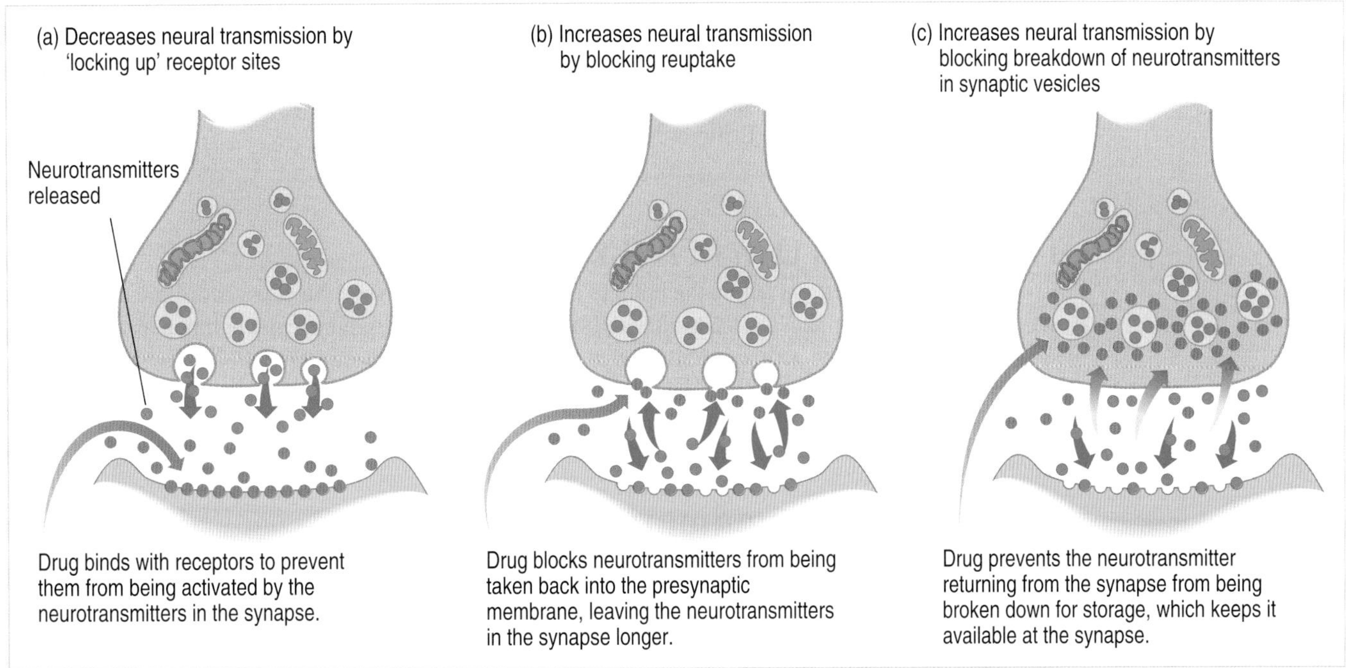

FIGURE 16.5
The therapeutic action of psychotropic medications. This figure depicts three neural mechanisms by which psychotropic medications can reduce symptoms. Psychotropics can decrease neural transmission of overactive neurotransmitters (a), or increase neural transmission where neurotransmitters are depleted (b, c).

Other medications have the opposite effect, increasing the action of neurotransmitters that are underactive or in short supply. They may do this in various ways. Some medications prevent the neurotransmitter from being taken back into the presynaptic membrane, causing the neurotransmitter to remain in the synapse and hence to facilitate further firing (figure 16.5b). Others prevent the neurotransmitter from being broken down once it has returned to the presynaptic neuron, leading to continued availability of the neurotransmitter at the synapse (figure 16.5c).

Alternative theories suggest that some psychotropic medications, particularly for depression, may act at the intracellular level, rather than at the synapse (Duman, Heninger, & Nestler, 1997). They do this by altering the way neurons process information inside the cell. Once a neurotransmitter binds with a receptor, a series of events occurs within the postsynaptic neuron that affects its rate of firing, as chemicals within the cell carry messages from the receptors to the cell's nucleus and activate the cell's DNA (chapter 3). Much of thought and memory appears to reflect changes in the way neurons respond to chronic activation from other neurons (chapter 7; chapter 8). Intracellular mechanisms may help explain why some medications, particularly medications for depression, only begin to have an effect weeks after the person starts to take them: long-term cellular changes take time to occur.

Not all the beneficial effects of psychotropic medications stem from their molecular structure. Because a patient's expectation of cure is influenced by personal and cultural beliefs about the causes and treatment of psychological problems, even drugs or herbal remedies that have no known physiological action can promote health simply because the person has faith that they will work (Torrey, 1986). In the same way, placebo effects (chapter 2) can boost the power of medications that are biologically efficacious. Thus, chemical agents can affect the mind via the brain or they can affect the brain via the mind.

Although psychotropic medications are clearly beneficial and life-saving in many instances, they are not without their downsides. Some psychotropic medications lead to both physical and psychological dependence (Julien, 1998, 2007; see also Mental Health Research Institute, 2005). Barbiturates, for example, which were a key treatment for anxiety disorders for years, can lead to physical addictions, such that termination of the medication can lead to hallucinations and problems with sleeping. Furthermore, because barbiturates reduce anxiety and, thus, create more pleasant feelings, they can lead to psychological dependence and, in the extreme, abuse of the drug. Drugs such as lithium can produce other side effects, including gastrointestinal problems such as nausea and vomiting (Julien, 1998, 2007). Lithium is also associated, in some patients, with memory impairments and weight gain. Not surprisingly, the experience of such side effects leads many people simply to stop taking the medication. Further, the risks and benefits of psychotropic drugs are carefully weighed in a range of other circumstances. For example, medications including benzodiazepines, lithium and chlorpromazine, when used by women during pregnancy, are implicated in an increased rate of congenital abnormalities and neonatal complications (Austin & Mitchell, 1998).

INTERIM SUMMARY

Psychotropic medications act on the brain to affect mental processes. Most psychotropic medications act at neurotransmitter sites. Some bind with postsynaptic receptors, hence preventing neural transmission. Others increase the action of underactive or depleted neurotransmitters, often by preventing them from being taken back into the presynaptic membrane or preventing them from being stored once they do return. Others act at the intracellular level.

Antipsychotic medications

Medications used to treat schizophrenia and other acute psychotic states are called ***antipsychotic medications***. They are also sometimes called major tranquillisers because many are highly sedating, but their efficacy is not reducible to their tranquillising effect. Antipsychotic medications generally inhibit dopamine, which has been implicated in positive symptoms such as hallucinations (Mamo et al., 2004). They are typically much less effective for negative symptoms such as flattened affect and interpersonal difficulties (e.g. Goff, Bagnell, & Perlis, 1999).

Antipsychotic medications are essential in treating schizophrenia and other psychotic states such as psychosis that often accompanies mania (Preston, O'Neal, & Talaga, 2004). However, most of them have significant side effects. Many of these side effects reflect the fact that dopamine exists in multiple regions of the brain and serves many functions. Thus, blocking its overactivity in one region may inhibit its normal functions in another. The most serious side effect is a movement disorder called ***tardive dyskinesia*** (*tardive*, meaning late or tardy in onset, and *dyskinesia*, meaning disorder of movement), in which the patient develops involuntary twitching, typically involving the tongue, face and neck. According to one theory, lowering the amounts of dopamine in the brain leads receptors in motor circuits that require dopamine for normal functioning to become supersensitive. As a result, the neurons in those regions fire too readily.

Tardive dyskinesia does not occur in all patients, and it is more likely to arise in people who have taken antipsychotic medications for many years (Sweet et al., 1995), but it is unpredictable and largely irreversible. Between 30 and 40 percent of patients in a long-term ward of a Montreal hospital who had received antipsychotics on average for 20 years showed symptoms of tardive dyskinesia (Yassa, Nair, Iskandar, & Schwartz, 1990). An Australian study involving a group of 100 patients admitted to a psychiatric unit with a primary psychotic disorder produced a similar result (Sachdev, 2004). All the patients were treated with conventional neuroleptic drugs, with a small number later switching to clozapine. The patients were then tracked longitudinally for a mean period of 41 months, with 78 participants completing the study. Of those patients, 11.5 percent developed symptoms of tardive dyskinesia during the period of the study. Because the side effects of prolonged administration can be so severe, and because antipsychotics are often ineffective for treating the more chronic negative symptoms, they are usually prescribed in high doses during acute phases and lower doses between episodes (Gilbert, Harris, McAdams, & Jeste, 1995). The discovery of multiple types of dopamine receptors in different parts of the brain, however, is leading to the development of drugs that target specific dopamine receptors and avoid tampering with others, which will probably lead to breakthroughs in the treatment of schizophrenia (e.g. Gurevich et al., 1997).

Antidepressant and mood-stabilising medications

Particularly for patients with severe depressions that include physiological symptoms such as sleep disturbance or loss of appetite, antidepressants can also be very effective (Maj, Veltro, Pirozzi, Lobrace, & Magliano, 1992; Montgomery, 1994a, 1994b). ***Antidepressant medications*** increase the amount of norepinephrine, serotonin or both in synapses and appear to reduce depression by correcting for depletion of these neurotransmitters (Preskorn, Feighner, Stanga, & Ross, 2004).

Types of antidepressants

Several different types of medication have proven effective in treating depression. The ***tricyclic antidepressants***, named for their molecular structure, block reuptake of serotonin and norepinephrine into the presynaptic membrane. In other words, they force the neurotransmitter to stay in the synapse longer, compensating for depleted neurotransmitters. Antidepressants (26.4 per 100 mental health-related problems managed) and anxiolytics (anti-anxiety medications — 12.7 per 100) were most commonly prescribed by GPs to manage mental illnesses. Research by Page et al. (2009) showed that total antidepressant use increases with age. For Australians aged 15 years or older, females used antidepressants twice as often as males (Page et al., 2009). Figure 16.6 gives a breakdown of antidepressant use by age group in Australia.

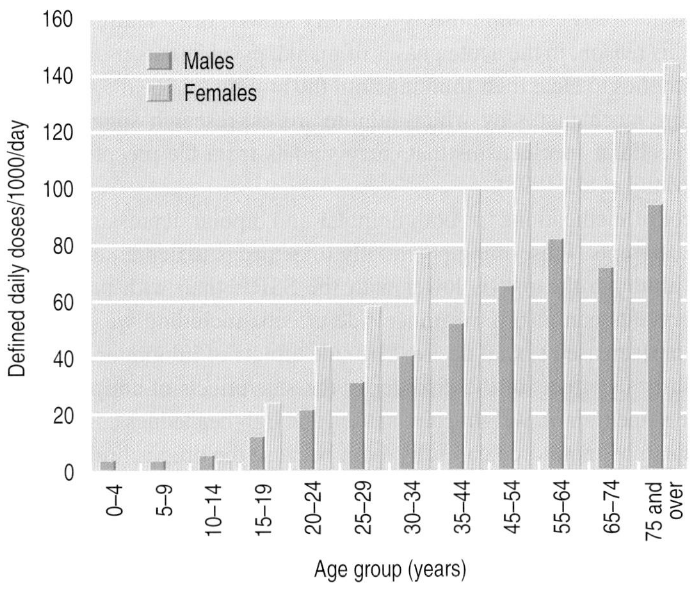

FIGURE **16.6**
Total antidepressant use by age group, Australia

SOURCE: Page, A. N. et al., 'Sociodemographic correlates of antidepressant utilisation in Australia', *MJA* 2009; *190*; 479–483. © 2009. *The Medical Journal of Australia* — reproduced with permission.

Double-blind studies, in which neither the patient nor the doctor knows whether the patient is taking a tricyclic drug or a placebo (chapter 2), have found improvement rates of 70 to 80 percent compared to 20 to 40 percent for the placebo (Maj et al., 1992). Frequently prescribed tricyclics include mianserin (trade name Tolvon), amitriptyline (Elavil) and impramine (Tofranil) (Zohar, Keegstra, & Barrelet, 2003).

Some patients who do not respond well to tricyclics respond to monoamine oxidase (MAO) inhibitors. ***MAO inhibitors*** keep the chemical MAO from breaking down neurotransmitter substances in the presynaptic neuron, and thus make more neurotransmitters available for release into the synapse (Kennedy, Holt, & Baker, 2004). MAO inhibitors are more effective than tricyclics in treating many depressed patients with personality disorders, particularly borderline personality disorders, but doctors rarely prescribe them before trying other antidepressants because they require substantial food restrictions (e.g. no red wine or cheese) and can be lethal if used in a suicide attempt (Cowdry & Gardner, 1988; Gunderson, 1986).

Selective serotonin reuptake inhibitors (SSRIs) are antidepressants designed to target serotonin, so named because they prevent the reuptake of serotonin into the presynaptic neuron and hence keep the neurotransmitter active at the synapse longer. SSRIs have fewer side effects than other antidepressants and are better tolerated over prolonged periods. As a result, they are now the first-line medical treatment against not only depression but a variety of other disorders. In Australia, the total level of antidepressant use (measured as daily doses per 1000 people per day) increased by only 19 percent between 1975 and 1990, when SSRIs first became available. However, between 1990 and 2002, the level of antidepressant use increased by 352 percent, almost all due to SSRIs (Mant et al., 2004).

The best known SSRI is fluoxetine (Prozac), which has vastly expanded the patient population for whom antidepressants are prescribed. Although the side effects for most of the SSRIs are milder than other antidepressants, the one important exception is sexual dysfunction, which often occurs with these medications (e.g. Michelson, Bancroft, Targum, Kim, & Tepner, 2000).

Serotonin reuptake inhibitors (such as Prozac, Aropax and Zoloft) can help some people with chronic low-grade depression, so that people with severe depression are no longer the only candidates for antidepressants (Julien, 1998; Levkovitz, Caftori, Avital, & Richter, 2002; Pinquart, Duberstein, & Lyness, 2006). Furthermore, patients with chronic bouts of depression typically have a smaller hippocampus than patients with intermittent bouts of depression. SSRIs such as Prozac have been shown to protect the brain from the detrimental effects of depression on the hippocampus (Sheline, 2003; Sheline, Mittler, & Mintum, 2002). On the other hand, the routine use of psychotropic medications for people who are not seriously depressed has drawn fire from many critics, particularly when prescribed by primary care doctors, who are not trained in psychiatry or psychology and often prescribe medications without exploring potential psychosocial causes or treatments.

For bipolar disorder, ***lithium*** is the treatment of choice, although antiseizure medications are often effective for manic patients who are not responsive to lithium (Goodwin & Ghaemi, 1997; see also Mental Health Research Institute, 2008). Between 30 and 80 percent of bipolar patients respond to lithium, depending on the sample; however, relapse rates range from 50 to 90 percent (Baldessarini, Tohen, & Tondo, 2000; Gershon & Soares, 1997). Lithium acts relatively slowly, often taking three or four weeks before taking effect. For this reason, in the acute phases of mania, psychiatrists usually treat patients simultaneously with antipsychotics to clear their thinking until the lithium 'kicks in'. Although researchers are still tracking down the mechanisms by which lithium works, research suggests that lithium may operate by altering intracellular mechanisms that carry signals from the receptor to the nucleus of the postsynaptic neuron (Manji et al., 1995).

Perhaps the most serious side effect of medications for both unipolar and bipolar depression is that they can be lethal if used for suicide attempts. Prescribing potentially toxic drugs to depressed people obviously carries risks of overdose although the risk is lower with the SSRIs than with previously developed antidepressants. Antidepressants can also have minor side effects, including weight gain, dry mouth, sweating, blurred vision or decreased sexual desire. The side effects of lithium are usually mild compared to the potentially disastrous effects of the disorder or the side effects of antipsychotic medications; patients may experience a fine tremor, weight gain, nausea and lightheadedness. However, lithium levels in the bloodstream have to be monitored carefully, both because the drug is highly toxic and because if levels drop, the patient may be at risk of relapse.

Antianxiety medications

MAKING CONNECTIONS

Benzodiazepines, such as Valium and Xanax, can be helpful in short-term relief of anxiety. They work by increasing the activity of GABA, a neurotransmitter that inhibits activation throughout the nervous system. Thus, by increasing the activity of an inhibitory neurotransmitter, they reduce anxiety (chapter 3).

Antianxiety medications called ***benzodiazepines*** can be useful for short-term treatment of anxiety symptoms, as with Jenny, who experienced a brief period of intense anxiety. The earliest drug of this class that was widely prescribed was diazepam (Valium); it has since been supplanted by other medications such as alprazolam (Xanax) that are more effective in treating panic symptoms.

Psychiatrists are now more likely to prescribe antidepressants (particularly SSRIs) for anxiety, particularly for panic disorder (Broocks et al., 1998; Varia & Rauscher, 2002). Although the impact on depression generally takes three to four weeks, anxiety symptoms usually respond to antidepressants within a week. The notion of prescribing antidepressants to treat anxiety seems counterintuitive; however, many neurotransmitters have multiple functions. Neurotransmitter systems are also interdependent, so that altering one can lead to widespread effects on others. The use of anxiolytic medications is increasing, with diazepam the most widely used anxiolytic followed by alprazolam and oxazepam (Hollingworth & Siskind, 2010). Medication use is concentrated in those aged 65 years or older, with peak use in those aged 85–89 years (Hollingworth & Siskind, 2010). There is also substantial use of anxiolytics in those aged 30–65 years, with females more likely to use anxioytics than males (Hollingworth & Siskind, 2010).

Antianxiety medications are not without their drawbacks. Patients can become both physiologically and psychologically dependent on them. Many fear that if they get off the medications they will become crippled with panic again. They may in fact be right: the relapse rate after discontinuing antianxiety drugs is very high (Mavissakalian & Perel, 1992; see also Baldwin et al., 2005; Lotufo-Neto et al., 2001; Stein, 2004). Nevertheless, some anxiety symptoms such as recurrent panic attacks can be so unpleasant or debilitating that medications are in order, particularly in combination with psychotherapy or until exposure-based therapies have been initiated.

Electroconvulsive therapy and psychosurgery

Two other biological treatments that were more widely used in previous eras and are now generally seen as treatments of last resort are electroconvulsive therapy and psychosurgery.

Electroconvulsive therapy

Electroconvulsive therapy (ECT), also known as electroshock therapy, is currently used in the treatment of major depression (O'Sullivan & Gilbert, 2003). ECT is also effective in the treatment of patients with delusional depression, bipolar disorder, schizophrenia, and catatonia (Doessel, Scheurer, Chant, & Whiteford, 2006). Patients lie on an insulated cart or bed and are anaesthetised. Electrodes are then placed on their heads to administer an electric shock strong enough to induce a seizure. The mechanisms by which ECT works are not known, although its efficacy appears to require strong enough doses of electricity to produce a seizure (Krystal et al., 2000). Clinical evidence shows that ECT will produce a substantial improvement in about 80 percent of patients with major depression. Furthermore, ECT can show clinical effects after a few treatments, whereas medication can take up to three weeks or longer to be effective (O'Sullivan & Gilbert, 2003).

MAKING CONNECTIONS

An Italian neurologist named Ugo Cerletti was the first person to use electroconvulsive shock therapy. Experimenting with animals first, Cerletti fine-tuned a device that would allow him to deliver electric shocks to induce convulsions. His first work with humans involved individuals with schizophrenia, who showed marked improvements following the procedure (chapter 15).

The use of ECT in Australia declined between 1984 and 1991, but since 2004 usage rates have begun to rise. ECT has sustained a negative image in the general community, and its use remains controversial. There is often resistance to its use (Doessel et al., 2006). The horrifying idea of deliberately shocking a person conjures up images of unscrupulous or overworked mental health professionals using technology to control unruly patients. On the contrary, ECT is not painful as the person is administered a general anaesthetic and muscle relaxant prior to the treatment. ECT has no more complications than any other procedure that uses a general anaesthetic (O'Sullivan & Gilbert, 2003).

ECT may have been used irresponsibly in the past, but today it is considered a safe and effective medical treatment for major depression (Fink, 2001; O'Sullivan & Gilbert, 2003). Previous studies have found that ECT is more effective than antidepressant drugs in treating very severe cases of depression, particularly delusional depressions, which have psychotic features (Goodwin & Roy-Byrne, 1987). More recently, the Royal Australian and New Zealand College of Psychiatrists (RANZCP, 2004) found that for depression with psychosis, ECT or a tricyclic combined with an antipsychotic is equally helpful. As with other therapies for depression, however, relapse rates are high, sometimes requiring readministration a few months later (RANZCP, 2004; Weiner & Coffey, 1988). The main side effect is memory loss (Doessel et al., 2006). This can be lessened, however, by applying electrodes to only one hemisphere of the brain (Abrams, Swartz, & Vedak, 1989). Another side effect is cognitive impairment. For example, an Australian study by Tsourtos, Spong, and Stough (2007) found that ECT temporarily slowed information-processing speed in 12 inpatients diagnosed with major depression.

Those who consider 'shock therapy' a brutal invention of technologically developed Western societies are actually incorrect in another respect. Hieroglyphics on the walls of Egyptian tombs depict the use of electrical fish (such as eels) to numb emotional states, and a number of Greek writers, including Aristotle, refer to the practice. A medieval priest living in Ethiopia observed the use of electrical catfish to drive the devil out of the human body (Torrey, 1986).

Psychosurgery

Another procedure once widely practised is ***psychosurgery***, brain surgery to reduce psychological symptoms. Psychosurgical procedures are typically used for affective or anxiety disorders, such as obsessive-compulsive disorder (Mashour, Walker, & Martuza, 2005). They have been used to treat severe mental disorders that do not respond to other treatments, including major depression (Victorian Government Department of Human Services, 2007). Psychosurgery involves lesioning of neural structures rather than their stimulation (Mashour et al., 2005). Like ECT, psychosurgery is an ancient practice. Fossilised remains from thousands of years ago show holes bored in the skulls, presumably to allow demons to escape from the heads of mentally ill individuals, much the same as in some preliterate cultures studied by anthropologists today.

The most widely practised Western psychosurgery technique was lobotomy, which involved severing tissue in a cerebral lobe, usually the frontal (Valenstein, 1988). Before the development of psychotropic drugs, some clinicians, frustrated in trying to treat the mentally ill patients who jammed the state institutions, embraced psychosurgery as a way of calming patients who were violent or otherwise difficult to manage. One of the leaders of psychosurgery in the middle of the last century, a psychiatrist named Walter Freeman, travelled the United States demonstrating his technique, which involved inserting a cutting tool resembling an ice pick into the socket of each eye and rotating it to cut the fibres at the base of the frontal lobes.

The 'ice-pick lobotomy' technique developed by Walter Freeman, although less time-consuming than traditional methods of lobotomy, nevertheless was met with strong criticism by both the lay public and medical professionals.

Lobotomy reached its peak between 1949 and 1952, during which time neurosurgeons performed about 5000 a year in the United States alone (Valenstein, 1986, 1988). Large numbers of lobotomies were also performed in Australia and New Zealand, though the number fell dramatically after the 1950s, as drugs became available, especially for schizophrenia. Unfortunately, the procedure rarely cured psychosis (Robin, 1958) and often had devastating side effects. Patients became apathetic and lost self-control and the ability to think abstractly (Freeman, 1959), as portrayed in the popular book and film, *One Flew over the Cuckoo's Nest*. Thus, due to the past abuse of psychosurgery, procedures are currently under strict control (see Mashour et al., 2005).

As recently as the 1970s, Australia faced its own controversies surrounding psychosurgery. The ABC current affairs program *Four Corners* launched an exposé of psychotherapy procedures, particularly those used at the Chelmsford Clinic in Sydney where a team of doctors performed psychosurgery on habitual thieves, sex offenders, drug addicts and people with chronic obsessional behaviour (Radio National, 2002). Two commissions of inquiry were conducted in New South Wales into psychosurgery, one in 1973 and another in 1977. Review boards were then established to consider any potential candidates for psychosurgery. Today the only review board active in Australia is in Victoria, where it is a criminal offence to perform psychosurgery without the permission of the Psychosurgery Review Board (see Victorian Government Department of Human Services, 2007). Psychiatrists continue to experiment with a much more limited surgical procedure to treat severely debilitating cases of obsessive–compulsive disorder that do not respond to other forms of treatment (Baer et al., 1995). Furthermore, a multidisciplinary approach with careful regulation is essential to the advancement and ethical administration of psychosurgery for the treatment of mental disorders (Mashour et al., 2005). For example, Anderson and Booker (2006) found that cognitive behaviour therapy coupled with pharmacotherapy, psychoeducation and social skills training effectively treated obsessive–compulsive symptoms following psychosurgery.

INTERIM SUMMARY

Antipsychotic medications treat schizophrenia and other acute psychotic states. ***Antidepressant medications*** can be useful for treating multiple disorders, particularly depression and anxiety disorders. ***Lithium*** is the treatment of choice for bipolar disorder. Both ***benzodiazepines*** and antidepressants can be useful for treating anxiety. ***Electroconvulsive therapy (ECT)***, also known as electroshock therapy, is used to treat major depression. Another neurosurgical procedure, primarily used as a last resort for severe cases of obsessive–compulsive disorder, is ***psychosurgery***.

Evaluating psychological treatments

It is estimated that almost half of all people in Australia and New Zealand will have a mental health problem at some stage in their lives, with one million Australians suffering from a mental disorder at any one time (ABS, 2008f; Oakley Browne, Wells, & Scott, 2006). About one in 5 Australians (approx. 3.2 million) report a long-term mental or behavioural problem, with the highest prevalence being among those aged 16–24 years (26 percent) and the lowest for those aged 75–85 years (5.9 percent). Depression and anxiety-related problems are the most commonly reported conditions (ABS, 2008f) and medications such as antidepressants, anxiolytics and antipsychotics are commonly prescribed (AIHW, 2006a). However, research from the Queensland Centre for Mental Health Research indicates that while Australians under 50 suffer higher rates of depression and anxiety, people aged over 85 are the highest consumers of antidepressant drugs (Rose, 2010). According to the National Health Survey, about 19 percent of respondents aged 18 years or over reported the use of medication for mental health (ABS, 2006d). People with mental and behavioural problems, including depressive disorders (25.9 percent), neurotic and stress-related disorders (16.2 percent), mental and behavioural disorders due to alcohol (10.8 percent), and schizophrenia (9.8 percent), are more likely to be hospitalised than those without these problems (AIHW, 2006a).

Since the implementation of the Better Access to Psychiatrists, Psychologists and GPs through the Medicare Benefits Schedule initiative in November 2006, there has been a significant and sustained increase in the number of Australians accessing services for treatment of mental health-related problems and disorders (AIHW, 2010c). But how well do these treatments at the hands of health professionals work? Psychologists aim to help people to make and sustain successful changes in their behaviour, to alleviate problems and enjoy better health (Montgomery, 2006). According to Montgomery (2006, p. 18), the key ingredients to facilitating successful behavioural change include:

- building self-efficacy while recognising autonomy
- identifying and facilitating readiness to change
- facilitating motivation to change
- helping to prevent and manage relapses
- fostering a good working alliance
- using evidence-based procedures
- providing relevant information and advice
- allowing sufficient time for change.

The treatments of psychological disorders discussed in this chapter are summarised in table 16.3.

TABLE 16.3 Varieties of psychological treatments

Therapy	Description
Psychodynamic	Attempts to change personality patterns through insight (using free association and interpretation) and the therapist–patient relationship (analysis of transference)
Psychoanalysis	Intensive therapy, three to five times per week, in which the patient lies on a couch and talks about whatever comes to mind, using free association
Psychodynamic psychotherapy	Moderately intensive therapy, one to three times per week, in which the patient discusses issues that come to mind while sitting face-to-face with the therapist
Cognitive–behavioural	Attempts to change problematic behaviours and cognitive processes
Systematic desensitisation	Classical conditioning technique in which the therapist induces relaxation and encourages the patient to approach a phobic stimulus gradually in imagination
Exposure techniques	Classical conditioning technique in which the therapist exposes the patient to the feared object in real life, either all at once (flooding) or gradually (graded exposure)
Operant techniques	Therapeutic approach in which the therapist induces change by altering patterns of reinforcement and punishment
Participatory modelling	Cognitive–social technique in which the therapist models behaviour and encourages the patient to participate in it
Skills training	Cognitive–social technique in which the therapist teaches behaviours necessary to accomplish goals, as in social skills or assertiveness training
Cognitive therapy	Therapeutic approach aimed at altering problematic thought patterns that underlie dysfunctional feelings and behaviour
Humanistic	Attempts to restore a sense of genuineness and attunement with inner feelings
Gestalt	Focuses on the 'here and now' and brings out disavowed feelings
Client-centred	Uses empathy and unconditional positive regard to help patients experience themselves as they really are
Family and marital	Attempts to change problematic family or marital patterns, such as communication patterns, boundaries and alliances
Group	Attempts to use the group process and group interaction to help people change problematic patterns, either with the help of a therapist or through self-help
Biological	Attempts to change problematic brain physiology responsible for psychological symptoms

Culture and treatment

It is useful to examine how our approaches to treatment are bound to our cultural norms, values and beliefs (Sue & Sue, 1999; Sue & Zane, 2006). The concept of what is abnormal and what is functional behaviour in any society is determined to an extent by the cultural context (chapter 19). The ability of therapists to assess behaviour is dependent on their knowledge, understanding and appreciation of the cultural context within which that behaviour occurred (Matsumoto & Juang, 2004). Therapists themselves also have their own cultural beliefs and attitudes, which they must acknowledge in the way they interpret behaviour (American Psychological Association, 2002).

Treatment options are also affected by culture. The one-on-one style of treatment favoured by Western therapists may be effective in some cultures but not others (Matsumoto & Juang, 2004). For Western psychologists, focusing on yourself, talking about your feelings, openly expressing your emotions, and being in touch with your inner self are important in understanding and treating distressed individuals.

MAKING CONNECTIONS

Indigenous peoples in Australia and New Zealand experience mental health-related problems at higher rates than non-Indigenous populations (chapter 15). In Australia, many health care services and resources are less accessible in rural and remote Indigenous communities.

Even in urban areas, utilisation of available services by Indigenous Australians is significantly less, despite increased risks and higher prevalence of mental illness (Australian Health Ministers' Advisory Council, 2008). Similar findings were reported for Maori and Pacific populations in the New Zealand Mental Health Survey (Oakley Browne et al., 2006). Culture, cultural differences and traditional belief systems should be considered in the provision of mental health care services to better reflect the complexities involved in assessment, appropriate therapies and meaningful outcomes for Indigenous peoples (see chapter 19; see also Westerman, 2004).

In some Asian countries, however, dwelling on one's thoughts, especially if they are painful, unpleasant or upsetting, is strongly avoided and believed to exacerbate the existing problem. People from collectivist cultures, such as Indigenous Australians, might find this focus on the self unusual and uncomfortable. Nonetheless, the use of psychotherapy has been, and continues to be, implemented with culturally diverse populations within Australia, as well as in other Western countries. It is therefore important to evaluate the efficacy of these treatments with people from different cultural backgrounds (APS, 2006d, 2007c).

Reid, Crofts, and Beyer (2001) examined drug treatment services for ethnic communities in Victoria, Australia. They found that the ethnic communities often did not seek help for drug treatment for various reasons, including a sense of despair or confusion about the services available. They argue that treatment services need to better understand the ethnic family ethos to ensure that the information provided is culturally sensitive and effective (chapter 19).

More recently, a cross-national comparison of youths aged 12–17 in Victoria, Australia, and the states of Oregon and Maine in the United States was conducted to compare the drug policies adopted in the two countries. Toumbourou et al. (2005) found that in contradiction of youth drug and alcohol harm-minimisation objectives in Australia, the Victorian youths, relative to the American youths, demonstrated higher rates of alcohol use, exceeding recommended consumption limits, and daily tobacco use. Furthermore, despite the high prevalence of alcohol and tobacco use by Australians, the management of such problems by general practitioners is relatively lower than that provided for illicit drug use (chapter 14; see Degenhardt, Knox, Barker, Britt, & Shakeshaft, 2005). It is hoped that the Medicare Benefits Scheme will help to address this problem and ensure that all Australians have better access to psychological services for various mental health problems, including those arising from alcohol and drug use. Uutela (2006) recommends that a national prevention agenda of drug use is needed to (a) acknowledge the broad social and structural determinants affecting drug use, and (b) recognise those antecedent circumstances and life experiences that enhance the risk of an individual becoming a drug user (chapter 15).

Pharmacotherapy

The benefits of pharmacotherapy for many disorders are well established. Antipsychotic medication is essential in the treatment of schizophrenia, although full recovery is unusual. Lithium and other mood-stabilising drugs are similarly indispensable for bipolar disorder, although some bipolar patients remain chronically unstable and most are vulnerable to relapse. In addition, as we have seen, medication can be useful in treating many anxiety and mood disorders, particularly major depression, panic and obsessive–compulsive disorder (e.g. Quitkin, Rabkin, Gerald, Davis, & Klein, 2000; Thase & Kupfer, 1996; Van Ameringen, Mancini, Pipe, & Bennett, 2004).

A major problem associated with biological treatments is the high relapse rate when pharmacotherapy is terminated. One way to minimise this drawback is to continue the medication for a considerable length of time after the treatment has succeeded, usually at a lower dosage (see Montgomery, 1994a, 1994b). As shown in figure 16.7, most people who experience a major depressive episode will experience another within five years, but continued preventive use of antidepressants can temper the tendency to relapse (Maj et al., 1992). Another way to minimise relapse is to combine medication with psychotherapy, which can be effective in the treatment of many disorders, such as major depression, bipolar disorder and schizophrenia (Frank et al., 1999; Rosenheck et al., 1999; Scott, 2001; Thase, 2000). However, the question about whether combined treatment is more efficacious than psychotherapy alone depends on the level of severity or chronicity and the stage of treatment (de Maat, Dekker, Schoevers, & de Jonghe, 2007; Otto, Smits, & Reese, 2006).

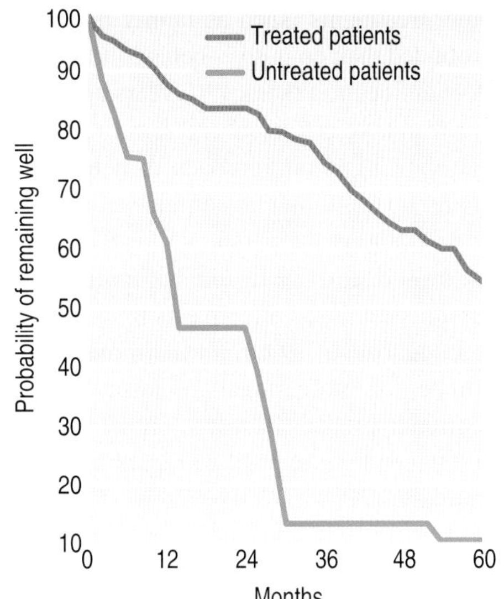

FIGURE 16.7
Relapse rates for major depression with and without medication. The figure shows the effects of the preventive use of antidepressant medication on lithium. Virtually all untreated patients relapsed within three years. Preventive use of medication was clearly helpful, although a substantial number of patients (46 percent) nevertheless relapsed by five years.

SOURCE: Maj et al., (1992). Reprinted with permission from the *American Journal of Psychiatry*, vol. 149, copyright 1992. American Psychiatric Association.

Psychotherapy

People who enter into psychotherapy also fare considerably better than those who try to heal themselves (Gava et al., 2007; Snyder & Ingram, 2000). Researchers have demonstrated this using a statistical technique called ***meta-analysis***, which aggregates, or combines, the findings of diverse studies, to yield a quantified estimate of the average effect of psychotherapy on the average patient. Beginning with a pioneering study in the late 1970s (Smith & Glass, 1977), meta-analyses have shown that the average patient who receives psychotherapy is essentially 25 percent better off than the average control participant, as shown in figure 16.8 (see Landman & Dawes, 1982). In other words, the bell-shaped curve for participants who have been treated is shifted in the direction of mental health, so that a person in the 50th percentile of mental health in the group receiving treatment would be in the 75th percentile of participants if now placed in the control group. This is a substantial shift, equivalent to the difference in reading skill between a Year 3 student who goes to school and one who stays home and gets no instruction for a year (Lambert, Shapiro, & Bergin, 1986).

50th percentile of control

75th percentile of control

Number of participants

Mental health

Control

Treated

FIGURE 16.8
Effectiveness of psychotherapy. Researchers combined the findings of 375 studies to assess the effectiveness of psychotherapy. Participants treated with psychotherapy were, on average, substantially better off than untreated control participants.

SOURCE: Adapted from Smith and Glass (1977).

The efficacy of specific therapies

How successful are the specific psychotherapies we have examined? The answer is more complicated than it seems because of many possible ways to think about success (see Haaga & Stiles, 2000; Kendall, Marrs-Garcia, Nath, & Sheldrick, 1999). For example, a researcher could measure average improvement, percentage of patients who improve, or relapse rate. One treatment might lead to 90 percent improvement but in only 50 percent of patients, whereas another could reduce symptoms by only 50 percent but do so in 90 percent of patients. Still another treatment might be very effective for most people but slow and costly. Another issue is the time frame of assessment of outcome. A long-term follow-up study of marital therapy, for example, found no differences initially between outcome of insight-oriented psychodynamic treatment and behavioural marital therapy. At four-year follow-up, however, only 3 percent of couples treated psychodynamically were divorced, compared with 38 percent of those treated with behavioural techniques (Snyder, Wills, & Grady-Fletcher, 1991).

The efficacy of cognitive–behavioural therapy is much better established than any other form of psychotherapy, especially for anxiety disorders (Butler, Chapman, Forman, & Beck, 2006; Gava et al., 2007; Otto, Smits, & Reese, 2004; Stanley et al., 2003). Some of the most impressive data have come from cognitive–behavioural treatments of panic (Barlow, 2002) and PTSD (Foa et al., 1999; Harvey, Bryant, & Tarrier, 2003). These treatments involve exposing patients to feared thoughts, images and feelings as well as helping them avoid ways of thinking and behaving that perpetuate their anxiety. Considerable research has also demonstrated the efficacy of cognitive therapy in treating depression (Butler et al., 2006; Hollon, Shelton, & Davis, 1993), eating disorders (Agras, Walsh, Fairburn, Wilson, & Kraemer, 2000) and multiple other conditions (Otto, Reilly-Harrington, & Sachs, 2003).

With the exception of a few promising studies (Bateman & Fonagy, 1999; Blatt et al., 1994; Freedman et al., 1999; Wallerstein, 1989), empirically sound studies of long-term psychodynamic treatments are rare. Studies of short-term psychodynamic psychotherapies are much more common (Leichsenring, Rabung, & Leibing, 2004; Piper et al., 1999; Shefler, Dasberg, & Ben-Shakhar, 1995). Humanistic and other treatments (such as family therapy) are, like psychodynamic psychotherapies, less empirically grounded than cognitive–behavioural therapies. Rogers, however, conducted a large number of studies of client-centred therapy 40 years ago, and some treatments drawing on his work are showing promising results (e.g. Greenberg & Safran, 1990; Paivio & Greenberg, 1995). For example, motivational interviewing is an approach to helping patients with alcoholism overcome their ambivalence about giving up drinking that combines a supportive, empathic stance with a realistic appraisal of the impact of drinking on the person's life (Stephens, Roffman, & Curtin, 2000; Yahne & Miller, 1999). One of the most distinctive features of motivational interviewing is its brevity: research suggests that just four sessions can be as effective as treatments that last three times as long (see Babor, Miller, DiClemente, & Longabaugh, 1999). Furthermore, the prevalence of Rogerian therapy is measured in the extensive number of professional organisations, institutes and journals worldwide dedicated to the client-centred approach. Research on therapy outcomes have validated Rogers' core conditions of empathy and unconditional positive regard as being critical to the success of psychotherapy (Kirschenbaum & Jourdan, 2005).

Comparing psychotherapies

Although advocates of different treatments typically argue for the superiority of their own brand, most research finds that, with a few notable exceptions (mostly in the anxiety disorders), different therapies yield comparable effects (Lambert & Bergin, 1994; Litt, Kadden, Cooney, & Kabela, 2003; Smith & Glass, 1977). This is certainly counterintuitive. For example, how could a treatment based on the view that psychopathology stems from unconscious fears or conflicts have the same effect as one that focuses on behaviours or cognitions?

Common factors

One explanation is that, alongside specific mechanisms (such as altering defences, exposing patients to threatening stimuli or inhibiting negative automatic thoughts), most approaches share ***common factors*** — shared elements that produce positive outcomes (Arnkoff, Victor, & Glass, 1993; Frank, 1978; Weinberger, 1995). Such factors include empathy, a warm relationship between therapist and client, and a client's sense of hope or efficacy in coping with the problem (Grencavage & Norcross, 1990).

Methodological challenges in comparing treatments

Other explanations are methodological (see Kendall, 1999; Kendall et al., 1999). Recruiting participants and training therapists to deliver treatments in standardised ways is very difficult. Most studies have relatively small samples, typically around 15 to 20 patients in each experimental condition. Statistically, that is about a quarter of the number required to detect real differences among treatments.

Another complication in comparing treatments is experimenter bias: one of the best predictors of the relative efficacy of one treatment over another in any given study is the strength of the investigator's commitment to that treatment (Smith, Glass, & Miller, 1980). One study found that experimenter allegiance — that is, the experimenter's preference for one treatment or another prior to conducting the study — accounted for over 60 percent of the differences between experimental conditions in even well-conducted double-blind studies, for reasons that have been difficult to detect (Luborsky, McLellan, Diguer, Woody, & Seligman, 1997).

Making matters more complicated, patients differ in their response to different treatments (Beutler, 1991). Even patients who share a diagnosis, such as depression or alcoholism, vary substantially in other respects. Comparing mean outcome scores across treatment groups may thus obscure the fact that different treatments are successful with different patients (see Litt, Babor, DelBoca, Kadden, & Cooney, 1992).

ETHICAL DILEMMA

A community psychologist wishes to gather evidence to support the effectiveness of his new treatment program with adolescent youths in a small rural town. He proposes to collect data from his clients and analyse the results for discussion within the multidisciplinary team that provides health services in the town.

- Is the psychologist responsible for ensuring that his clients fully understand where the information will be discussed and by whom?
- How might the psychologist protect the identity of his clients?

The NIMH collaborative study

The most definitive evidence yet collected about the relative efficacy of different treatments comes from a non-partisan study of depression conducted by the National Institutes of Mental Health (NIMH; Elkin, Shea, Watkins, & Imber, 1989). The NIMH project studied the treatment of 250 patients, a very large sample compared to most prior studies. It compared three treatments for patients with major depression: cognitive therapy, interpersonal therapy (a short-term offshoot of psychodynamic psychotherapy) and imipramine (an antidepressant) combined with supportive clinical management (regular meetings with a concerned doctor). A fourth group (the control group) received a placebo with supportive clinical management. The purpose of giving supportive management to the latter two groups, particularly the placebo group, was to determine whether the effectiveness of psychotherapy is reducible simply to providing regular and kind attention. The study was conducted at several treatment sites, and collaborators from different perspectives administered treatments according to standardised treatment manuals in order to minimise any biases imposed by investigator allegiances.

For all intents and purposes, the three treatments fared equally well. At the end of treatment, none of the treatments worked significantly better than the others. A more sobering picture emerged, however, when patients were followed up two years later. Most patients were less depressed than when they began treatment, but relapse was common across all groups, and only a minority met criteria for full recovery (Shea, Elkin, Imber, & Sotsky, 1992). In fact, a more recent meta-analysis found similar results across studies of depression: most treatments tested in the laboratory initially work for about half of patients, but at 18-month to two-year follow-up, only half of these patients — or 25 percent of patients who enter treatment — remain well (Westen & Morrison, 2001). A study by Ellis and Smith (2002) in New Zealand showed that the best outcomes occur when a good therapeutic alliance is formed between the patient and the health care professional. Ellis and Smith (2002) recommended that therapy should continue for (a) at least one year following a first episode of depression, and (b) at least two years for repeated episodes or where there are other risk factors for relapse. They believed that choice of treatment is less important than continuation of therapy: 'it is not so much what you do but that you keep doing it' (p. S81).

In Australia, the national depression initiative beyondblue aims to educate people about depression and provides evidence-based treatment guidelines for the various depressive disorders (www.beyondblue.org.au). The internet is shaping as a key player in the delivery of self-help treatments for a range of mental disorders, including depression and anxiety, alcohol misuse (Griffiths, Farrer, & Christensen, 2006), and body dissatisfaction and disordered eating (Paxton, Ellis, & McLean, 2006). However, future research is needed to investigate the efficacy of internet-based therapy as an adjunct to clinical practice (Griffiths et al., 2006). In contrast, Professor David Kavanagh has taken a proactive approach to help rural people to cope with depression and suicide during the drought. He established 'On Track', a program that involves mailing a series of letters to rural people to help them identify warning signs before depression sets in (www.uq.edu.au/ontrack). The 'On Track' website provides easy access to resources for both people experiencing mental health issues and practitioners. Participants can also be recruited through the website for ongoing research.

In Australia, the national depression initiative beyondblue aims to educate people about depression and provides evidence-based treatment guidelines for various depressive disorders.

Efficacy versus effectiveness: the consumer reports study

Researchers distinguish between efficacy and effectiveness studies of psychotherapy (Seligman, 1995). ***Efficacy studies*** assess treatment outcome under highly controlled conditions: random assignment of patients to different treatment or control groups, careful training of therapists to adhere to a manual that prescribes the ways they should address patients' problems, standardised length of treatment and so forth. ***Effectiveness studies*** assess treatment outcome under less controlled circumstances, as practised by clinicians in the field. Efficacy studies emphasise internal validity — the validity of the experimental design — and allow researchers to draw strong causal inferences about the effects of receiving one kind of treatment or another (chapter 2). Effectiveness studies emphasise external validity — that is, applicability of the therapy to patients in everyday clinical practice.

Martin Seligman (1995) published a controversial article on the findings of a large *Consumer Reports* survey on the effectiveness of psychotherapy. Seligman described how this survey, involving 2900 respondents who had undergone psychotherapy, led him to reverse his opinion on the superiority of short-term treatments developed and tested in efficacy studies. Perhaps the most important finding of the *Consumer Reports* study concerned length of treatment. The most successful treatments — those in which respondents reported the greatest decline in symptoms, improvement in overall level of functioning and general satisfaction — were psychotherapies lasting more than two years. In fact, degree of consumer satisfaction was directly related to length of treatment. These findings matched those of other effectiveness studies (Bovasso, Eaton, & Armenian, 1999; Howard, Kopta, Krause, & Orlinsky, 1986; Howard, Orlinsky, & Lueger, 1994; see also Hunkeler et al., 2006), but they drew fire from many researchers because of methodological problems inherent in naturalistic and correlational studies (chapter 2).

INTERIM SUMMARY

Pharmacotherapy is essential for some disorders (such as schizophrenia and bipolar disorder) and can be extremely helpful for others (such as major depression and anxiety disorders). Relapse rates, however, are high when medication is discontinued, and complete cures are uncommon for most disorders. Research has provided substantial evidence for the utility of psychotherapy for many disorders, with the most successful treatments thus far being cognitive–behavioural treatments for anxiety disorders. An important distinction is between ***efficacy studies*** that assess treatment outcome under controlled experimental conditions and ***effectiveness studies*** that assess treatment as practised by clinicians in the community.

Psychotherapy integration

Although theory and research have focused largely on the 'brand-name' psychotherapies described here, in everyday practice about twice as many psychologists report crossing over 'party lines' in their work with patients as those who report staying within one of the two most prevalent orientations, psychodynamic and cognitive–behavioural (Norcross, Karg, & Prochaska, 1997). ***Psychotherapy integration*** — the use of theory or technique from multiple therapeutic perspectives — comes in two forms (Arkowitz, 1997; Stricker, 1996; Westen, 2000).

Eclectic psychotherapy

The first is ***eclectic psychotherapy***, in which clinicians combine techniques from different approaches, often to fit the particular case. One recent study, for example, examined the efficacy of an intensive, comprehensive treatment for schizophrenia that combined education about the disorder, medication, weekly group therapy, family therapy and close monitoring of symptoms to allow active intervention at the first signs of relapse (Herz et al., 2000; see also Louw & Straker, 2002). Compared with treatment as normally practised in the community, the treatment cut relapse rates 18 months later from roughly 40 to 20 percent.

Integrative psychotherapy

The second form of psychotherapy integration is less about picking and choosing among strategies from different approaches than about developing an approach to treating patients based on theories that cut across theoretical lines. This approach to treatment, usually called ***integrative psychotherapy***, is intuitively appealing but difficult in practice, because the assumptions, methods and techniques of the various approaches are so different (Arkowitz & Messer, 1984; Messer & Winokur, 1980; see also Scaturo, 2001, 2005). How can a clinician integrate principles of therapy based on theories of unconscious conflict and compromise with others that focus on classical and operant conditioning or cognitive distortions?

The best example of an integrative approach is the work of Paul Wachtel (1977, 1993, 1997). One of his most important contributions is the concept of cyclical psychodynamics, in which people's fears and expectations create self-reinforcing behaviours that often lead them to get precisely what they fear. A considerable body of evidence has documented just such processes experimentally (e.g. Swann, Stein-Seroussi, & Giesler, 1992; Swann, Wenzlaff, Krull, & Pelham, 1992). For example, one team of researchers studied couples in which one or both partners were high in rejection-sensitivity; that is, who fear rejection and are chronically 'on the lookout' for signs of it (Downey, Freitas, Michaelis, & Khouri, 1998). Not only were the relationships of rejection-sensitive people more likely to dissolve — confirming their fear of rejection — but in laboratory sessions with their partners they tended to elicit more rejecting behaviour from their partners by behaving more negatively in discussing conflicts in the relationship.

How might a clinician practising from an integrative perspective treat complex patterns of this sort, in which people unwittingly elicit what they fear? According to Wachtel, insight into the problem is an important first step, but behavioural techniques can be invaluable in encouraging the patient to confront the problem and develop the skills to master it. For example, consider a patient who reports never feeling angry but who 'somehow' finds himself embroiled in one conflict after another with everyone around him, after which everyone else is furious and he feels misunderstood. Empirically, patients like this are relatively common in clinical practice (Westen & Shedler, 1999). Suppose the patient has begun to recognise that he is afraid to acknowledge his anger and has begun to realise how he evokes anger in other people. He may still be unable to confront people, because the anxiety associated with doing so is a conditioned emotional response that motivates avoidance. The therapist may thus need to take a more active stance, encouraging the patient, applying operant techniques (such as rewarding confrontive behaviour with praise) and examining instances in which the patient avoids becoming angry at the therapist (e.g. for 'pushing' him to be more open with his anger).

A case study to illustrate

The treatment of Jenny, whose case began this chapter, provides a good example of both eclectic and integrative therapy. The treatment she received in the hospital was eclectic, bringing together behavioural, psychodynamic, systems and group approaches to try to address multiple aspects of a life-threatening disorder. Her individual psychotherapy as an outpatient was integrative, combining behavioural and psychodynamic principles. For example, after she left the hospital, Jenny's weight was at first precarious, so her therapist required her to weigh in at her doctor's office each week and bring a slip to therapy reporting her weight. Because Jenny found this acutely embarrassing, her therapist made a behavioural contract with her: if she maintained her weight for several weeks, he would stop asking to see her weight unless she obviously appeared to be losing again. Aside from promoting a healthy weight through negative reinforcement (removal of an aversive consequence), this arrangement led to exploration of Jenny's need to be in control (and her anger at feeling controlled by her therapist). It also led to examination of her feelings about her body as she kept her weight at a normal level and once again began to look like a woman instead of a child.

INTERIM SUMMARY

Psychotherapy integration is use of theory or technique from multiple therapeutic perspectives. In ***eclectic psychotherapy***, clinicians combine techniques from different approaches, often to fit the particular case. ***Integrative psychotherapy*** involves developing an approach to treating patients based on theories that cut across theoretical lines.

Theories of the development of emotional disorders

By Associate Professor Louise Sharpe, University of Sydney

Theories of the development of emotional disorders, such as anxiety disorders and mood disorders, have emphasised the role not only of the content of anxious and depressive thinking, but also of the way in which individuals with different emotional disorders process information. For example, there is now good evidence that patients with anxiety disorders over-attend to threatening stimuli, using the gold standard dot-probe paradigm to assess attentional biases (Bar-Haim, Lamy, Pergamin, Bakermans-Kranenburg, & van Ijzendoorn, 2007). Similarly, evidence suggests that patients with depression are more likely to ruminate about negative situations, and hence elaborate memories more and recall more negative information (see Mathews & McLeod, 2005, for a review). Recent research has moved on to the intriguing possibility that interventions that target these information processing styles may have positive outcomes (Koster, Fox, & MacLeod, 2009). McLeod, Rutherford, Campbell, Ebsworthy, and Holker (2002) first demonstrated in a university sample that training individuals to attend away from threats resulted in less anxiety when individuals were faced with a subsequent stressful situation.

In a special issue of the *Journal of Abnormal Psychology*, a series of studies investigated the efficacy of a range of different methods of modifying cognitive biases (see Koster et al., 2009). These articles collectively showed positive outcomes in a range of different mood-related variables relevant to differing psychopathologies. For example, training in perspective taking was found to reduce affective symptoms following the observation of a distressing film (Schartau, Dalgleish, & Dunn, 2009), training worried individuals in allocating benign meanings to ambiguous scenarios reduced worry (Hirsch, Hayes, & Mathews, 2009) and imaginal rehearsal of positive meanings protected individuals from subsequent mood induction (Holmes, Lang, & Shah, 2009). Importantly, cognitive bias modification, based on the dot-probe task (MacLeod, Mathews, & Tata, 1986), was used as a treatment in two anxious clinical samples. The results demonstrated that repeated training of individuals to attend away from threatening information was not only effective in reducing the responses of highly anxious individuals to subsequent stressful situations (See, MacLeod, & Bridle, 2009), but also resulted in large and clinically significant improvements for patients with generalised anxiety disorder (Amir, Beard, Burns, & Bomyea, 2009) and social anxiety disorder (Schmidt, Richey, Buckner, & Timpano, 2009). Indeed, in the Schmidt et al. (2009) study, 72 percent of those with social anxiety no longer met criteria following cognitive bias modification, in comparison with only 11 percent who took part in the placebo condition.

These results are extremely encouraging and have enormous potential clinical promise for a number of reasons. First, these cognitive bias modification paradigms utilise standardised computer programs; hence, they can be made easily available and require minimal time and effort. Second, there are many other areas of clinical psychology where information processing biases have been identified. Two of these areas are eating disorders (e.g. Reiger et al., 1998) and chronic and acute pain conditions (e.g. Dehghani, Sharpe, & Nicholas, 2003; Haggman, Sharpe, Nicholas, & Refshauge, 2010; Khatibi, Dehghani, Sharpe, Asmundson, & Pouretemad, 2009; Sharpe et al., 2009). Already there are trials in analogue populations for both disturbed eating attitudes and the way in which people approach painful situations (McGowan, Sharpe, Refshauge, & Nicholas, 2009) which show that cognitive bias modification results in important changes to people's attitudes and behaviours. The potential for these technologies to support existing therapies is enormous, and is likely to be a key development in the treatment of emotional disorders over the next decade.

Central questions revisited

◆ What works for whom?

These debates bring us back to the central questions with which we began: what works for whom, and how can we use scientific methods to find out? We suspect that the current controversy over empirically supported therapies, efficacy versus effectiveness, and the *Consumer Reports* study reflects in some respects a tension that has long existed between clinicians and researchers (chapter 1). Despite a burgeoning experimental literature on psychotherapy outcomes, clinicians tend to practise without empirical guidance (Beutler, Williams, Wakefield, & Entwistle, 1995), dismissing research findings as irrelevant to their practice. Conversely, researchers often view clinicians as undisciplined and unscientific in their thinking, which limits the kind of cross-talk that might foster mutual feedback and learning on both sides.

We have some very important and suggestive findings. Cognitive–behavioural treatments for anxiety can be highly efficacious for anxiety disorders, particularly simple phobia, social phobia, panic, obsessive–compulsive disorder and PTSD. Longer-term treatments may be more suitable for multisymptom problems seen by many clinicians in the community, particularly those that involve repetitive interpersonal patterns, which sometimes can take weeks or months to pinpoint, let alone to target for change. This may explain why effectiveness studies support longer treatments. But we are a long way from knowing which patients with PTSD or bulimia — such as those with sexual abuse histories or troubled early attachment relationships — are likely to respond or not respond to different interventions.

Empirical questions — such as what works and for whom — require empirical answers. We need not abandon scientific methods to assess a complex clinical phenomenon such as response to psychotherapy. The key is to adapt these methods and use multiple research designs to try to converge on the most accurate conclusions. When internal and external validity sharply collide, as they have in psychotherapy research, the best strategy is not to err consistently on one side or the other but to conduct studies that err on each side, with some aiming to assess causality with the rigour of tightly controlled experimentation and others using quasi-experimental and correlational designs (chapter 2) that sacrifice control for greater generalisability.

◆

SUMMARY

1 Mental health services

- ***Clinical psychologists*** often practise in a hospital or in other mental health facility settings. The inpatients of a psychiatric hospital tend to be those experiencing severe mental disorders, predominantly schizophrenia, bipolar disorder and depression, rather than those with personality disorders. In psychiatric wards, people with a wide range of mental health issues can receive short-term treatment.
- The ***scientist–practitioner*** model adopted by Australian universities has become responsible for not only teaching the science of psychology, but also for training applied psychologists.
- ***Multidisciplinary teams*** are commonly used in community health facilities and draw together professionals from a range of specialities to carry out the required tasks.
- The most significant recent development in mental health services in Australia has been the shift away from institutionalised care towards community-based care.

2 Psychodynamic therapies

- Psychodynamic therapy is predicated on the notion that ***insight*** — understanding one's own psychological processes — is important for therapeutic change, as are aspects of ***therapeutic alliance***.
- ***Free association*** is a technique designed to explore associational networks and unconscious processes. Another central element of psychodynamic therapy is the ***interpretation*** of conflicts, defences, compromise formations and transference reactions. ***Transference*** in psychotherapy refers to the experience of thoughts, feelings, fears, wishes and conflicts from past relationships, particularly childhood, in the patient's relationship with the therapist.
- The main contemporary forms of psychodynamic treatment are ***psychoanalysis*** (which is very intensive and long term) and ***psychodynamic psychotherapy*** (which relies on the same principles but is more conversational).

3 Cognitive–behavioural therapies

- ***Cognitive–behavioural*** therapies are relatively short term and directive, and focus on specific symptoms. They rely on operant and classical conditioning as well as cognitive–social and more strictly cognitive interventions.
- In ***systematic desensitisation***, the patient gradually approaches feared stimuli mentally while in a relaxed state. ***Exposure techniques***, like desensitisation, rely on classical conditioning, but they present the patient with the actual phobic stimulus in real life rather than having the patient merely imagine it. Therapies based on operant conditioning apply rewards and punishments to modify unwanted behaviour.
- In ***participatory modelling***, the therapist not only models the desired behaviour but also gradually encourages the patient to participate in it. ***Skills training*** teaches the procedures necessary to accomplish relevant goals; ***social skills training*** helps people with specific deficits in interpersonal functioning.
- ***Cognitive therapy*** attempts to replace dysfunctional cognitions with more useful and accurate ones. Ellis, who developed ***rational–emotive behaviour therapy***, proposed an ***ABC theory of psychopathology***; A refers to activating conditions, B to belief systems and C to emotional consequences. Beck's cognitive therapy similarly proposes that correcting cognitive distortions is crucial to therapeutic change.

4 Humanistic, group and family therapies

- ***Humanistic therapies*** focus on the phenomenal (experiential) world of the patient. ***Gestalt*** therapy emphasises an awareness of feelings. Rogers' ***client-centred therapy*** aims at helping individuals experience themselves as they really are, through therapeutic empathy and ***unconditional positive regard***.
- Group, family and marital therapies treat multiple individuals simultaneously. ***Group therapy*** focuses on both individual dynamics and group process. A variation on group therapy is the ***self-help group***, which is not guided by a professional. ***Family therapy*** presumes that the roots of symptoms lie in the structure of the family system, so that therapy should target family interaction patterns. A variant of family therapy, ***marital*** or ***couples therapy***, treats the couple as a unit and may employ systems, psychodynamic, behavioural or cognitive–behavioural techniques.

5 Biological treatments

- The aim of biological treatments is to alter the functioning of the brain. Pharmacotherapy, the use of medications to treat psychological disorders, is the major type of biological treatment.
- ***Psychotropic medications*** affect mental processes by acting at neurotransmitter sites or at the intracellular level. ***Antipsychotic medications*** are useful in treating psychotic symptoms, particularly the positive symptoms of schizophrenia. ***Tricyclic antidepressants***, ***MAO inhibitors*** and ***selective serotonin reuptake inhibitors (SSRIs)*** can be useful in treating depression, while ***lithium*** is the treatment of choice for bipolar disorder. Both ***benzodiazepines*** (antianxiety medications) and certain kinds of antidepressants can be useful in treating anxiety.
- ***Electroconvulsive therapy (ECT)***, or shock therapy, is currently used to treat major depression. ***Psychosurgery*** is used as a last resort for treating obsessive–compulsive disorder.

6 Evaluating psychological treatments

- Pharmacotherapy is well established as an effective treatment for schizophrenia, bipolar disorder and many other forms of psychopathology. The two major problems with pharmacotherapy are relapse rates and side effects.
- Researchers have found that all psychotherapies are relatively effective, although some treatments are better for some disorders than others. Cognitive–behavioural treatments have received the most empirical attention and support in ***efficacy studies*** (carefully controlled experimental studies with relatively homogeneous samples and highly standardised therapeutic procedures). The long-term ***effectiveness*** (usefulness in clinical settings with a more heterogeneous population) of short-term treatments is more controversial than that for long-term treatments.
- ***Psychotherapy integration*** is the use of theory or technique from multiple therapeutic perspectives. In ***eclectic psychotherapy***, clinicians combine techniques from different approaches, often to fit the particular case. ***Integrative psychotherapy*** involves developing an approach to treating patients based on theories that cut across theoretical lines.

KEY TERMS

ABC theory of psychopathology, *p. 665*
antidepressant medications, *p. 675*
antipsychotic medications, *p. 674*
automatic thoughts, *p. 665*
behavioural analysis, *p. 661*
benzodiazepines, *p. 676*
client-centred therapy, *p. 667*
clinical psychologists, *p. 655*
cognitive–behavioural, *p. 660*
cognitive therapy, *p. 665*
common factors, *p. 682*
culture, *p. 680*
eclectic psychotherapy, *p. 684*
effectiveness studies, *p. 683*
efficacy studies, *p. 683*
electroconvulsive therapy (ECT), *p. 677*
empty-chair technique, *p. 667*
exposure techniques, *p. 662*
family therapy, *p. 668*
flooding, *p. 662*
free association, *p. 658*
genogram, *p. 669*
Gestalt therapy, *p. 666*
graded exposure, *p. 662*
group process, *p. 668*
group therapy, *p. 667*
humanistic therapies, *p. 666*
insight, *p. 657*
integrative psychotherapy, *p. 684*
interpretation, *p. 658*
lithium, *p. 676*
MAO inhibitors, *p. 675*
marital (*or* couples) therapy, *p. 670*
meta-analysis, *p. 681*
multidisciplinary teams, *p. 655*
negative reciprocity, *p. 670*
participatory modelling, *p. 664*
psychoanalysis, *p. 659*
psychodynamic psychotherapy, *p. 659*
psychosurgery, *p. 677*
psychotherapy integration, *p. 684*
psychotropic medications, *p. 672*
rational–emotive behaviour therapy, *p. 665*
resistance, *p. 658*
response prevention, *p. 663*
scientist–practitioner model, *p. 655*
selective serotonin reuptake inhibitors (SSRIs), *p. 675*
self-help group, *p. 668*
skills training, *p. 664*
social skills training, *p. 665*
systematic desensitisation, *p. 661*
tardive dyskinesia, *p. 674*
therapeutic alliance, *p. 657*
transference, *p. 658*
tricyclic antidepressants, *p. 675*
unconditional positive regard, *p. 667*
virtual reality exposure therapy, *p. 663*

REVIEW QUESTIONS

1. Describe the mental health services provided by clinical psychologists.
2. Distinguish between psychoanalysis and psychodynamic psychotherapy.
3. Describe the methods used in psychodynamic psychotherapies to bring about therapeutic change: free association, interpretation and analysis of transference.
4. Compare and contrast Gestalt therapy and client-centred therapy.
5. Describe some of the approaches to family therapy.

DISCUSSION QUESTIONS

1. When might group therapy be used rather than individual psychotherapy?
2. What are some benefits of psychotherapy integration?
3. Does psychotherapy do more good than harm?

APPLICATION QUESTIONS

1. Test your understanding of cognitive–behavioural therapies by matching each of the scenarios listed with the following treatments: cognitive therapy, operant technique, participatory modelling, flooding, social skills training and systematic desensitisation.
   (a) Tanya seeks help for her fear of spiders. Her therapist firstly uses classical conditional techniques to induce relaxation. Tanya is then encouraged to gradually approach her phobic stimulus — the spider — in her imagination.
   (b) Dragan has an intense fear of heights. With the help of his therapist, he goes up the lift in one of the tallest buildings in his city. He goes a little higher each day, first with the therapist and then alone, until his fear of heights subsides.
   (c) Ten-year-old Carmel will never do as she is told by her parents. The family therapist recommends rewarding Carmel with 'points' for each chore that she successfully completes on time, without any prompting. Carmel can exchange these points for various privileges. Carmel soon learns to do her daily chores without having to be asked by her parents.
   (d) Fong King's therapist models the desired behaviour and over time, encourages Fong King to behave the same way.
   (e) A therapist teaches eight-year-old Alessandra the behaviours necessary to accomplish her goals. Specifically, she learns to identify a problem, develop ways to solve the problem, and use feedback to determine whether it has been successfully handled.
   (f) Patrick's therapist teaches him to identify his self-defeating thoughts. She shows Patrick how they are linked to his problems, and teaches him to replace this negative self-talk with more positive and rational ways of thinking.
2. Test your understanding of biological treatments by matching each of the scenarios listed with its appropriate type of treatment or medication. Choose from the following: electroconvulsive therapy, psychosurgery, antianxiety medication, antipsychotic medication, antidepressant medication and mood stabilising medication.
   (a) Hayley suffers from schizophrenia and takes this type of medication to alleviate her positive symptoms such as hallucinations.

(b) Christopher has obsessive–compulsive disorder. He feels compelled to repeatedly scratch himself, sometimes up to 30 times a day for three to five minutes at a time. His skin is raw from excessive scratching on the same spot. No other medications have worked and this type of treatment is used as a last resort.

(c) Bernadette has bipolar disorder and alternates between extended periods of elevated highs and lows. The doctor prescribes Bernadette with this type of medication, but it can take up to four weeks before any real effect is evident in her behaviour.

(d) Timothy suffers from physiological symptoms such as sleep disturbance and loss of appetite. He takes this type of medication to help him better cope with the troubles in his life.

(e) Swee Seng suffers from severe depression. This type of treatment is used as a last resort to try to bring her prolonged suffering to an end.

(f) Prajol suffers from panic attacks and takes this type of medication to alleviate his intense worries about what will happen when he leaves the house.

The solutions to the application questions can be found on page 835.

MULTIMEDIA RESOURCES

The *Cyberpsych* multimedia resource is available *as an option* to accompany this textbook to further develop your understanding of many key psychology concepts. *Cyberpsych* contains a wealth of rich media content and activities, and for this chapter includes:

- video clips on human speech disorders, antidepressants, post-traumatic stress disorder, and exercise and depression medication
- interactive modules on cognitive therapy and the goals of psychotherapy.

Attitudes and social cognition

17

LEARNING OBJECTIVES

After studying this chapter you should be able to:

1. define social psychology
2. define attitudes and their role in predicting behaviour
3. describe the social–cognitive processes people use to try to understand themselves and others
4. describe how the self-concept guides the way we think about and remember information relevant to ourselves.

Attitudes

- An *attitude* is an association between an act or object and an evaluation.
- *Attitude strength* refers to the durability and impact of an attitude on behaviour. It is influenced by both *attitude importance* and *attitude accessibility*, or the ease with which an attitude comes to mind.
- *Persuasion* refers to deliberate efforts to change an attitude. Characteristics of the source, message, channel, context and receiver all affect the effectiveness of persuasive appeals. Persuasion can occur through a *central route*, inducing the message recipient to think about the argument, or a *peripheral route*, appealing to less thoughtful processes.
- According to the *elaboration likelihood model*, the central route to attitude persuasion is more effective when the person is both motivated and able to think about the arguments, whereas the peripheral route is more effective when the likelihood that the person will engage in high-effort cognitive processing is low.
- *Conservation psychology* involves studying the reciprocal relationships between humans and nature, with a focus on changing attitudes and behaviours to encourage conservation of the environment.
- *Cognitive dissonance* occurs when a person experiences a discrepancy between an attitude and a behaviour or between an attitude and a new piece of information.

Social cognition

- *Social cognition* refers to the processes by which people make sense of themselves, others, social interactions and relationships.
- *First impressions* can have an important influence on subsequent information processing.
- *Stereotypes* are characteristics attributed to people based upon their membership of groups. *Prejudice* means judging people based on (usually negative) stereotypes and *discrimination* involves behaviours that follow from negative attitudes towards particular group members.
- *Attribution* is the process of inferring the causes of one's own and others' mental states and behaviours.
- Social psychologists have identified several biases in social information processing, including:

  1. the *fundamental attribution error*, or correspondence bias, which is the tendency to attribute behaviours to people's personalities and to ignore possible situational causes.
  2. the *self-serving bias*, which is the tendency to see ourselves in a more positive light than we deserve.

- People are not always accurate perceivers of their social world and sometimes jump to conclusions about others on the basis of first impressions. These biases are not limited to the general public, but characterise even the cognitions of people who have been trained to avoid them, such as clinicians.

The self

- The *self* is the person, including mental processes, body and personality characteristics.
- Contemporary ***psychodynamic*** thinking focuses on mental representations of the self, or ***self-representations***, which can be conscious or unconscious, and are typically associated with a variety of feelings. From a ***cognitive*** perspective, the self-concept is a ***self-schema***, which guides thought, attention and memory.
- ***Self-esteem*** is the need to view oneself positively. Self-esteem is maintained and enhanced through such behaviours as downward social comparison, ***self-handicapping***, implicit egotism and basking in reflected glory.
- ***Self-consistency*** is the motive to interpret information to fit existing self-concepts.

- ***Self-presentation*** reflects people's attempts to control the impressions that others form of them. The self that people sometimes present in their interactions with others is the ***actual self*** (how they really are). They may also self present in ways that reflect their ***ideal self*** (the self they would like to be) or the ***ought self*** (the self they feel they should be).

Central questions: social and nonsocial cognition

- Understanding the basic principles of cognition is necessary for understanding social thought and memory, but it is not sufficient. Social cognition differs in a number of ways from non-social cognition; as humans, we are social animals whose experiences and environments help shape the way we think about ourselves and others.

When people think of prejudice, they often think of apartheid in South Africa or Ku Klux Klan rallies in the United States. We think of racial and ethnic stereotypes as beliefs people overtly hold or express about each other based on arbitrary qualities, such as the colour of their skin. However, recent political events in Australia have shown that negative stereotypes can get 'under the skin' in subtle but powerful ways.

One of the key issues in the 2010 Australian federal election campaign was the number of asylum seekers attempting to reach Australia by boat. The issue gained prominence following a surge in the number of boats arriving after the election of the Rudd government in 2007. Many of the asylum seekers were from countries such as Sri Lanka and Afghanistan. The arrival of asylum seekers in Australian waters received extensive coverage in media across the country. Public debate around the issue raised many questions, such as whether the arrivals by boat were 'illegal'; whether they were unfairly trying to 'jump the queue' ahead of other immigrants; whether Australia was being 'swamped' by boat arrivals; whether they were 'genuine' refugees; and whether they were a threat to national security (Phillips, 2010). The asylum seeker issue gained such prominence that Opposition leader Tony Abbott made 'stopping the boats' one of the four key promises of his 2010 election campaign.

What is interesting is that while asylum seekers arriving by boat provoked such a high level of anxiety and political debates about 'illegal immigration', statistics tell a far different story on where the greatest problem might come from. In a recent year, Australia intercepted about 2750 unauthorised people arriving by boat (Department of Immigration and Citizenship, 2010). But in July of that year, the number of people who had arrived by plane and overstayed their visa — thus being in Australia illegally — was approximately 48 720 (Department of Immigration and Citizenship, 2010). In the permanent migration intake in a recent year, 171 320 people came to live in Australia (Department of Immigration and Citizenship, 2010). The Asylum and Refugee Law Project (based at the University of Queensland) estimated recently that at the current rate of arrival, it would take 30 years to fill the Melbourne Cricket Ground with asylum seekers who arrive by boat (Department of Immigration and Citizenship, 2010). Statistically speaking, the number of people arriving by boat is a trickle compared to the planned migration intake and the illegal immigrants who come by plane and then overstay.

So why is it that arrivals by boat create such anger and debate, while visa overstayers go largely unremarked? Perhaps the background of the different groups holds part of the answer. While the boat arrivals are largely people from non-Western countries, the majority of visa overstayers are tourists from Western countries. Do we subconsciously find it easier to feel threatened by a refugee arriving by boat with a different coloured skin, different language and different religion than a British backpacker who simply chose not to go home? Why aren't students from Europe or the United States who overstay their visas targeted in the media to the same degree, and also accused of being 'queue-jumpers'?

Regardless of whether there is an element of prejudice in the treatment of boat arrivals, the fact is that the prominence it gained in the election campaign is indicative of the traction of the issue across wider Australian society. It is also an example of the work of ***social psychology***, which examines the influences of social processes on the way people think, feel and behave (Allport, 1968). Because almost everything people do is social, the subject matter is enormous and varied. In this chapter, we focus on interpersonal thinking. We begin with a discussion of attitudes and how they change. This topic is of central concern to advertisers, who try to shape attitudes towards their products, as well as to politicians, who want to shape — and follow — public opinion. Next we examine the processes by which people make sense of each other, from the first impressions they form to enduring beliefs, including stereotypes. We conclude by considering the way people think about one of the major actors in their social worlds and one of the main directors of social cognition: themselves.

Throughout, we address one central question. To what extent do the principles of thought and memory discovered by cognitive scientists apply to *interpersonal* thought and memory? In other words, when we think about ourselves and others, do we use the same mechanisms as when we learn lists of words or theories of how chemicals combine to form molecules? Or are social thought and memory qualitatively different?

Central question

- In what ways do social thought and memory differ from non-social cognition?

Attitudes

Perhaps more than any topic that falls within the arena of social psychology, attitudes have received the greatest attention. Indeed, at one time, the study of attitudes essentially constituted social psychology. Although research attention to attitudes has diminished since the 1970s, attitudes are still probably the most fundamental concept in social psychology because they are involved in all social behaviour, from political decisions to stereotyping and prejudice (Allport, 1935; Richard, Bond, & Stokes-Zoota, 2003).

The nature of attitudes

An ***attitude*** is an association between an act or object and an evaluation (Ajzen, 2000; Eagly & Chaiken, 1992; Fazio, 1986; Schwarz, 2007). To put it another way, an attitude — whether towards Bonds, King Gee or Osama Bin Laden — is a tendency to evaluate a person, concept or group positively or negatively (Eagly & Chaiken, 1998; Petty, Wegener, & Fabrigar, 1997, Walton & Banaji, 2004). To say that alcohol (an attitude object) is a dangerous drug (evaluation) is to express an attitude. Some psychologists distinguish three components of an attitude: a cognitive component or belief (alcohol contributes to social problems such as traffic fatalities and child abuse); an emotional or evaluative component (alcohol is bad); and a behavioural disposition (alcohol should be avoided).

At first glance, attitudes seem relatively straightforward — a person is either for the choice to have an abortion or against it, favourable or unfavourable towards affirmative action, or more positive towards Woolworths than Coles or vice versa. However, researchers have since discovered a number of variations in attitudes that make them far more complex (see Ajzen, 2001; Eagly & Chaiken, 1998).

Attitude strength

One dimension on which attitudes vary is their strength. Whereas some attitudes are enduring over time and very resistant to change (high attitude strength), others are much less resilient and very susceptible to being changed or discarded (Ajzen, 2001; Bizer & Krosnick, 2001). For example, if you are only minimally interested in cricket, your feelings towards the Australian team are likely to be relatively weak. If the Australian team loses to New Zealand, you do not lose much sleep. Further, your beliefs about the team — the cognitive components of your attitude towards the Australian cricket team — also tend to sway in the wind. If a friend tells you that the Australian cricket team is going to win the next World Cup, you are perfectly happy to believe him and will probably continue believing him until someone else informs you otherwise.

Attitude strength refers to the durability and impact of an attitude (Bassili & Krosnick, 2000; Petty & Krosnick, 1994). An attitude is durable if it tends to persist over time and is resistant to change. An attitude has impact if it affects behaviour and influences the way the person thinks and feels. Using this definition, your attitude towards the Australian cricket team is very weak. It is highly unstable and has minimal impact on what you do on a summer afternoon or how you feel if the team loses. It also has little effect on whether you think the umpire made the right decision.

Although research has shown that many different variables can affect an attitude's strength, two particularly relevant, and related, variables are attitude importance and attitude accessibility. ***Attitude importance*** refers to the personal relevance of an attitude and the psychological significance of that attitude for an individual (Bizer & Krosnick, 2001). The more importance or personal relevance assigned to an attitude, the greater its strength.

For an attitude to have an impact on ongoing thought and behaviour, it must be cognitively accessible — that is, readily pulled from memory. ***Attitude accessibility*** refers to the ease with which an attitude comes to mind (Bizer & Krosnick, 2001; Fazio, 1990, 1995). Highly accessible attitudes come to mind rapidly and automatically when primed by environmental events. For example, a person with positive attitudes towards women may have an immediate and positive initial reaction when the doctor at the clinic who examines her is female. The more accessible an attitude, the more likely it is to affect behaviour and the stronger the attitude is.

Variation in accessibility makes sense from an adaptive (evolutionary) standpoint. The more frequently we encounter something, and the more its potential impact on our lives, the more quickly we should be able to react to it — and the more accessible our attitude towards it is likely to be. A downside of high accessibility, however, is its potential interference with our ability to detect changes in the attitude object (Fazio, Ledbetter, & Towles-Schwen, 2000). A highly accessible attitude towards a politician may make a voter less likely to notice that the politician no longer behaves the way he used to — and hence that the voter should re-evaluate her attitude.

The relationship between attitude importance and attitude accessibility is an interesting and not completely understood one. On one hand, the greater the importance a person attaches to an attitude, the more accessible that attitude is likely to become, a suggestion that attitude importance precedes attitude accessibility. Thus, if you believe that wearing seatbelts is very important and you have a relative who recently suffered major injuries from a car accident in which he was not belted in, your attitude towards seatbelt use is likely to become more accessible. You will think about seatbelt use more frequently and process information related to seatbelt use more completely than someone whose attitude about seatbelts is less strong.

On the other hand, it is possible that attitude accessibility precedes attitude importance. The more easily an attitude comes to mind, the more importance we may assume that attitude holds for us (Bizer & Krosnick, 2001). Thus, if you can easily extract from memory your feelings towards seatbelt use, you may infer that your attitude towards seatbelts is important.

One of the most controversial issues related to attitudes research concerns the heritability of attitudes, with the belief that heritable attitudes are stronger than attitudes that are not inherited (Bourgeois, 2002; Olson, Vernon, Jang, & Harris, 2001; Tesser, 1993). Evidence for the heritability of attitudes can be found in twin studies comparing the attitudes of monozygotic twins and same-sex dizygotic twins. Stronger relationships exist in the attitudes of monozygotic as opposed to dizygotic twins (Olson, Vernon, Harris, & Jang, 2001), and heritable attitudes are more resistant to attitude change than non-heritable attitudes (Tesser, Whitaker, Martin, & Ward, 1998). No-one would suggest that there are specific genes that influence attitudes and, subsequently, behaviour. However, research on the heritability of attitudes looks at biological underpinnings that may account for people's attitudes (chapters 1 and 11).

Implicit attitudes

As with emotions, motives and cognitions, social psychologists are increasingly recognising the importance of distinguishing between explicit (conscious) attitudes and ***implicit attitudes*** — associations between attitude objects and feelings about them that regulate thought and behaviour unconsciously and automatically (Baron & Banaji, 2006; Greenwald et al., 2002; Rudman, 2004). Someone who has just attended a lecture on alcohol-related fatalities is unlikely to stop at the bar on the way home because a conscious attitude is active. He may well, however, over-indulge at a happy hour a few days later when his implicit attitudes towards alcohol — which reflect years of associations between drinking and enjoyment — become active. In fact, implicit attitudes of this sort play a more important role in predicting drug and alcohol use than people's conscious attitudes (Stacy, 1997).

Implicit and explicit attitudes are not necessarily correlated with one another. The attitudes that someone may express publicly to allow him to make a desirable impression on others (explicit attitudes) may differ markedly from those that he holds privately or that are revealed when he fails to devote conscious attention to the attitudes being expressed.

Cognitive complexity

The cognitive components of an attitude vary on a number of dimensions. For example, they can be relatively specific (a large tax cut right now would produce a budget deficit and hurt the economy) or general (tax cuts provide a strong stimulus for the economy in times of recession). An important dimension on which attitudes differ is their ***cognitive complexity*** — the intricacy of thoughts about different attitude objects (Bieri, 1966; Suedfeld & Granatstein, 1995; see also Manajlovic & Nikolic-Popovic, 2005). The beliefs of two people with equally positive attitudes towards a tax cut may have very different levels of complexity. One person might simply believe that 'big government isn't the answer to our problems' and hence always favour tax cuts. Another might believe that large tax cuts foster investment and hence can stimulate a flagging economy. On a simple attitude rating of 1 to 5 (where 1 means the person is very unfavourable to a tax cut and 5 means very favourable), both people might nevertheless rate a 5.

Researchers have used some ingenious methods to assess the complexity of people's attitudes. For example, in one study, researchers read political speeches and coded them for the extent to which the thinking was complex (Tetlock, 1989). They found that people at both political extremes — far right and far left — tended to show less attitudinal complexity than people who were politically more moderate. Many would suggest that during the most recent Australian federal election campaign, few politicians from any party made complex statements on any topic!

Cognitive complexity varies with both gender and culture. Responses to self-report measures of cognitive complexity show females to be more cognitively complex than males (Adams-Webber, 2001), although the same research showed that men and women in close relationships display similar levels of cognitive complexity. Thus, although there may be overall gender differences in cognitive complexity, we are drawn to those at our same level of complexity.

Culture as a mediator of cognitive complexity appears to depend on the nature of the situation being examined. Research with Chinese and Western students showed that students from both backgrounds display cognitively complex attitudes, but typically with different attitudinal objects (Conway, Schaller, Tweed, & Hallett, 2001). Other factors, such as social status, may also affect or be affected by cognitive complexity (Foels & Reid, 2010).

Attitudinal ambivalence

Another dimension on which attitudes differ is the extent to which an attitude object is associated with conflicting feelings. For many years, researchers measured attitudes by asking respondents to rate the extent to which they were for the choice to have an abortion or against it, liked or disliked particular political candidates, and so on. Periodically, however, attitude researchers have wondered whether this focus really captures the complexity of the emotional component of people's attitudes. Think, for example, about how you feel about exercise. More than likely, you have both positive attitudes towards exercise (e.g. exercise can be fun, exercise is good for my health, exercise provides an effective means of controlling weight), and negative attitudes towards exercise (e.g. exercise takes too much time, exercise is boring). If you were asked simply how positively or negatively you felt about exercise, you would probably check the middle score on an attitude scale to reflect the positive and negative feelings you have towards exercise. But this middle score would suggest you have neutral feelings towards exercise, when, in fact, you do not.

Researchers studying ***attitudinal ambivalence*** — the extent to which a given attitude object is associated with conflicting evaluative responses — argue that attitudes include two evaluative dimensions, positive and negative, that are relatively independent (Cacioppo & Gardner, 1999; Hodson, Maio, & Esses, 2001; Priester, 2002). Each of these two components can be relatively weak or relatively strong. Low positive/low negative attitudes will have minimal impact on behaviour because the person is indifferent (i.e. does not care much either way) about the attitude object.

Weakly held attitudes of this sort are very different from highly ambivalent attitudes — high positive/high negative — but they often yield precisely the same (moderate) scores on bipolar attitude measures that assume that attitudes run from negative to positive.

MAKING CONNECTIONS

Positive and negative affect are somewhat independent and rely on different neural circuits (chapter 10). Thus, it is not surprising that a person could associate a single attitude object with both positive and negative feelings — such as mixed feelings towards a food choice that may necessitate an extra trip to the gym.

Determining the degree to which a person holds ambivalent attitudes is important in assessing the relationship between attitudes and behaviour. Most researchers suspect that non-ambivalent attitudes are more predictive of behavioural intentions and, subsequently, actual behaviour, than ambivalent attitudes. If you are completely in favour of organ donation, you are much more likely to become an organ donor, than if you hold very positive attitudes towards organ donation but some negative attitudes as well. Other research, however, found just the opposite — attitudinal ambivalence predicted behavioural intentions better than did non-ambivalence (Clark, Wegener, & Fabrigar, 2008; Jonas, Diehl, & Bromer, 1997; see also Gardner & Cacioppo, 1996, as cited in Cacioppo, Gardner, & Berntson, 1997; Hodson et al., 2001). Participants in one study were provided with consistent versus inconsistent information about fictitious shampoos. Greater consistency between attitudes and behavioural intentions was observed among participants exposed to the evaluatively inconsistent information than the evaluatively consistent information (Jonas et al., 1997). Apparently, attitudinal ambivalence produces more cognitive activity and systematic processing than non-ambivalence (Ajzen, 2001).

Coherence

A final dimension on which attitudes vary is ***attitudinal coherence*** — the extent to which an attitude is internally consistent (Eagly & Chaiken, 1998; see also Crano & Prislin, 2006). Logically, the cognitive and emotional aspects of attitudes should be congruent because an emotional evaluation of an object should reflect a cognitive appraisal of its qualities. That is, we should like things we believe have positive consequences.

INTERIM SUMMARY

An ***attitude*** is an association between an act or object and an evaluation. Attitudes can differ in a number of ways. ***Attitude strength*** refers to the durability and impact of an attitude on behaviour. It is influenced by both ***attitude importance*** and ***attitude accessibility*** or the ease with which an attitude comes to mind. Attitudes can also be either explicit or implicit. ***Implicit attitudes*** regulate thought and behaviour unconsciously and automatically. Attitudes vary in their degree of cognitive complexity as well as the extent to which the attitude object is associated with conflicting evaluative responses (***attitudinal ambivalence***). ***Attitudinal coherence*** refers to the extent to which an attitude (particularly its cognitive and evaluative components) is internally consistent.

Attitudes and behaviour

Logic would suggest that attitudes should predict behaviour. For example, people's attitudes towards exercise should be closely related to how much they exercise. Once again, however, the empirical David is mightier than the logical Goliath. Broad attitudes predict behaviour, but not very well (Ajzen, 1996, 2001; Armitage & Christian, 2003; Fishbein & Ajzen, 1974). People's attitudes towards exercise are not good predictors of the probability that they will exercise, any more than religious attitudes predict attendance at religious ceremonies (Wicker, 1969).

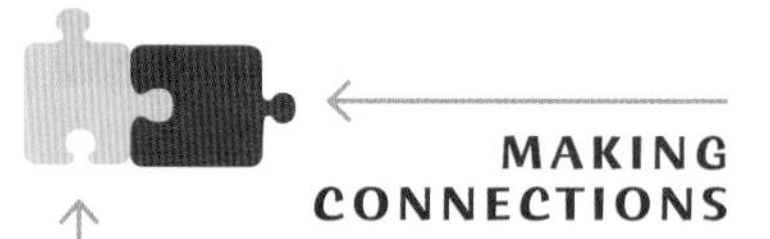

MAKING CONNECTIONS

Because attitudes are only one of the factors that influence behaviour, they may not be useful in predicting who a person will vote for in a particular election; but over the long run they will in fact predict the party the individual tends to endorse at the ballot box. As we saw in chapter 11, human behaviour is so complex that a single variable — whether an **attitude** or a **personality trait** — is rarely likely to predict what a person will do in a specific circumstance.

By aggregating (averaging) across behaviours, however, researchers get a clearer picture of a person's behavioural tendencies. Attitudes, like personality traits, predict behaviour over the long run.

Why are attitudes and behaviours so imperfectly correlated, and what factors affect the link between what we think and feel and how we behave? First, people's attitudes *do* predict their actions if the attitude and action are both relatively specific (Ajzen & Fishbein, 1977; Kraus, 1995). Asking people their attitude towards protecting the environment does not predict whether they will recycle, but asking their attitude towards recycling does (Oskamp, 1991).

Second, and perhaps most importantly, people's attitudes are only one of many influences on what they do (Ajzen & Fishbein, 1977; Fabrigar, Petty, Smith, & Crites, 2006). From a behaviourist perspective, behaviour is under the control of environmental consequences. An environmentally minded person who buys one small bag of groceries a week might re-use her own canvas shopping bag each week and thus contribute to the longevity of tropical rainforests. An equally environmentally conscious person who carries groceries for her family up six flights of stairs might find the convenience of plastic bags such overwhelming reinforcement that she contributes instead to the longevity of landfills.

Third, the consistency between people's attitudes and their behaviour is higher if members of important groups appear to share and endorse similar attitudes (Terry & Hogg, 2001; White, Hogg, & Terry, 2002). Implicit or explicit attitudinal support from group members provides validation for an individual's own attitudes which, subsequently, are more likely to drive behaviour.

Fourth, the recognition that attitudes vary along a number of dimensions points to some previously unrecognised complexities in the way attitudes affect behaviour. As noted earlier, much of behaviour is controlled by implicit procedures (chapter 7), or habits, that people develop through experience, rather than by their explicit (conscious) attitudes (Craeynest et al., 2005; Ouellette & Wood, 1998; Swanson, Rudman, & Greenwald, 2001). Explicit attitudes predict some behaviours, particularly when people are consciously reflecting on them. Much of the time, however, implicit attitudes, which tend to be rapid and automatic, regulate people's actions and reactions, as when a non-indigenous person who thinks she is unprejudiced makes less eye contact with indigenous than non-indigenous strangers.

Similarly, stronger attitudes are more predictive of behaviour than weaker attitudes. In an examination of this, researchers measured participants' attitudes towards Greenpeace and their attitude strength.

A week later, participants were asked if they would be willing to donate money to Greenpeace. Participants with more strongly held attitudes showed a greater willingness to donate than people with more weakly held attitudes (Holland, Verplanken, & van Knippenberg, 2002).

Finally, the way attitudes are acquired influences their impact on behaviour. Attitudes shaped by personal experience are especially likely to influence action (Fazio & Zanna, 1981; Millar & Millar, 1996; Smith & Swinyard, 1983; see also Askew & Field, 2007). For example, one study examined students' attitudes towards a campus housing shortage that forced many to sleep on cots in makeshift quarters for weeks (Regan & Fazio, 1977). Both the affected students and their more comfortably housed peers had negative attitudes towards the situation, but those who were personally affected were much more likely to write letters and sign petitions.

INTERIM SUMMARY

The cognitive, evaluative and behavioural components of an attitude may vary independently of each other. Although attitudes are generally believed to include a behavioural disposition, they often do not predict specific behaviours, for several reasons: the behaviour and the attitude are often at different levels of generality; other variables influence behaviour; and attitudes vary in different ways that make prediction complex, such as the extent to which they are implicit or explicit.

Persuasion

People often have a vested interest in changing others' attitudes, whether they are selling products, running for political office or trying to convince a lover to reconcile one more time. ***Persuasion*** refers to deliberate efforts to change an attitude.

Components of persuasion

Interest in persuasion has a venerable past. Long before modern psychology, Aristotle described rhetoric — the art of persuasive speaking — as a combination of ethos (characteristics of the speaker), pathos (the appeal of the message) and logos (the logic of the argument). Psychologists have expanded Aristotle's view to identify several components of persuasion, including the source, message, channel (the medium in which the message is delivered), context and receiver (Lasswell, 1948; McGuire, 1985; Petty & Wegener, 1998; Petty et al., 1997; see also Crano & Prislin, 2006). Attending to each of these aspects is crucial to the success of a persuasive appeal, whether the goal is to sell a car or get someone to agree to a date.

Source

Speakers tend to be more persuasive when they appear credible (expert and trustworthy), attractive, likeable, powerful and similar to the recipient of the message (Burgoon, Birk, & Pfau, 1990; Chaiken, 1980; Simons, Berkowitz, & Moyer, 1970). For politicians, particularly in countries such as Australia and New Zealand where political candidates must appeal directly to voters, winning votes is often a balancing act in which the candidates must seem likeable but authoritative, and powerful yet able to understand the concerns of everyday citizens.

Message

The type of appeal (e.g. presenting one side of the argument or both) and the way it is delivered also affect attitude change. As we have seen, the match between the recipient's willingness and ability to think about the message and the way the message is delivered is crucial for persuasion. A jingle about a low-fat margarine will not convince someone who has compared the fat content of multiple brands and cares about the difference.

Fear appeals — efforts to induce fear to try to change attitudes — can sometimes be effective, but they can backfire if they induce too much fear and lead people to stop attending to the message and instead to focus on managing their anxiety (Insko, Arkoff, & Insko, 1965; Wood, 2000). For example, messages about AIDS may fall on deaf ears if they are so frightening that people simply deny the realities. Fear can, however, be useful in inducing attitude change if the recipients of the message believe the danger applies to them and that they can do something to avoid it (Dillard & Anderson, 2004; Olson & Zanna, 1993). Anti-smoking ads in Australia are a good example. One memorable ad shows tar being squeezed out of a sponge to represent what happens to a smoker's lungs.

APPLY + DISCUSS

- Identify the basic dimensions on which attitudes towards the environment and recycling might vary.
- Consider your own attitudes towards the environment and recycling. Where do they fall on each of these dimensions? For example, how complex are your feelings towards environmental protection in general, and recycling in particular?
- What factors actually influence whether or not you recycle? How much do your attitudes determine your behaviour on this issue?

Channel

The channel of persuasion is the means by which a message is sent — in words or images, verbally or nonverbally, in person or through media such as telephone or television. Choosing the right channel can be as important as selecting the right message. Because turning someone down for a date is much more difficult face to face than on the telephone, suitors of reluctant 'targets' should make their pitch in person. Emotional appeals to contribute to emergency relief funds are more effective when the target of the communication can see starving children with distended stomachs rather than simply hear about their plight.

In the modern era, text messaging has become the most widely used mobile data service worldwide with access to mobile networks now available in over 90 percent of the global population (International Telecommunication Union [ITU], 2010). Mobile phone users actively use the short message service (SMS), with the number of text messages sent tripling over a recent three years to reach a staggering 6.1 trillion in 2010 (ITU, 2010). This equates to close to 200 000 text messages being sent every second! Its popularity has grown to a sufficient extent that a new style of writing specific to electronic communications has emerged. For example, Weatherall (2004) studied the text messages of school students and young professionals in New Zealand and found that almost half the words in the text messages were not standard (e.g. 'u' and '2' in place of 'you' and 'to'). Weatherall further established that most text messages served a social function; only a small proportion were for practical purposes. Other research supports this finding. Texting is typically used to enhance communication among friends and family, to make plans with one another and to maintain social contact outside of their day-to-day face-to-face conversations (Bryant, Sanders-Jackson, & Smallwood, 2006, par 2). Texting is well-liked by teenagers because it is efficient and less expensive than traditional technologies (Lenhart, Madden, & Hitlin, 2005). Further research is required to determine in what ways using the SMS media channel might change how people of all ages communicate with one another.

Texting has facilitated the use and understanding of abbreviations of many standard words. A New Zealand study found that almost half of the words used in text messages were not standard, such as the use of 'u' and '2' instead of 'you' and 'to'.

Context

The context in which a message is presented can also influence attitude change (Petty & Wegener, 1998). Soft music in the background may lead an ambivalent 'recipient' to agree to a second date, and a roomful of cheering supporters can make a political message seem much more exciting. An important aspect of the context is the presence of competing messages. Things would be easier for Coke if Pepsi did not advertise, and vice versa.

Psychologists and advertisers have devised many methods to increase resistance to contrary appeals. One is to get there first. Being the first to make a pitch renders a persuasive appeal more effective (Insko, 1964; Miller & Campbell, 1959). Another method, called ***attitude inoculation***, involves building up the receiver's 'resistance' to a persuasive appeal by presenting weak arguments for it or forewarning against it (McGuire, 1961; McGuire & Papageorgis, 1962). Thus, much as a vaccine builds the body's defences through exposure to small, inert amounts of a virus, weak and easily assailable arguments supporting the other point of view prompt the person to develop counter-arguments that serve as attitudinal 'antibodies'. Salespeople frequently use this technique when they know a customer is about to visit a competitor ('He'll tell you Sony has better customer service, but don't believe him'). Attitude inoculation methods can be effective in reducing risky behaviours in adolescents, such as smoking and the use of illicit drugs (APA, 2004; see also Ellickson & Bell, 1990; Perry, Killen, Slinkard, & McAlister, 1980).

Receiver

Receiver characteristics — qualities of the person the communicator is trying to persuade — also affect the persuasiveness of a communication. People with strong attitudes on a topic are obviously less likely candidates for attitude change, and some people are simply more difficult to persuade in general (see Haugtvedt & Petty, 1992; Hovland & Janis, 1959). Further, people bias their information processing in order to preserve attitudes they do not want to change (MacCoun, 1998). Coffee drinkers, for example, discount messages about the dangers of caffeine (Liberman & Chaiken, 1992).

Individuals also vary in the extent to which they are likely to attend to and reflect on careful arguments, referred to as the need for cognition (Jarvis & Petty, 1996). People who focus on the substance of the arguments, however, do not necessarily form 'better' attitudes. People can exercise considerable effort in preserving their biases and carefully attacking arguments that do not support their position.

The elaboration likelihood model of persuasion

As helpful as it is to understand all of the different components of persuasion, original models of persuasion that theorised about these components failed to address the question of 'How?' How and when are people persuaded by a speaker's credibility? How do characteristics of the message alter audience members' attitudes? To address the 'how' of persuasion, Richard Petty and John Cacioppo introduced the elaboration likelihood model of persuasion (ELM; Petty & Cacioppo, 1981; Petty & Wegener, 1998). The ELM suggests that there are two routes through which people can be persuaded (Chen & Chaiken, 1999; see also Booth-Butterfield & Welbourne, 2002; O'Keefe, 2002; Petty, Rucker, Bizer, & Cacioppo, 2004; Stephenson, Benoit, & Tschida, 2001).

The first, or ***central route***, involves inducing the recipient of a message to think carefully and weigh the arguments. People who process centrally are highly involved with the issue, tend to be higher in their need for cognition or their need to think about issue-relevant arguments and are attentive to the quality of the arguments that are presented. The second, or ***peripheral route***, appeals to less rational and thoughtful processes. The peripheral route bypasses the cortex and often heads straight for points south, such as the limbic system, the heart or the gut. Most beer commercials, for example, have little to offer in terms of rational persuasion. Thus, people who process persuasive communications peripherally may be influenced not by the quality of the arguments presented but rather by the sheer number of arguments presented or the attractiveness of the communicator.

The ***elaboration likelihood model*** of persuasion posits that knowing how to appeal to people requires figuring out the likelihood that they will think much about (or elaborate on) the arguments (Petty & Cacioppo, 1986). Rational appeals are more likely to change the attitude of a person who both is motivated to think about a topic and has time to consider the arguments. In other words, when elaboration likelihood is high, appeals to logic are most likely to be persuasive.

Much of the time, however, people do not have the time, interest or ability to weigh every argument about every possible attitude object that crosses their paths. Do I buy Dairy Farmers milk or Pauls? If I am a true dairy devotee, I might spend the extra 30 seconds in the aisle at the supermarket pondering the merits of the two brands. However, as we have seen (chapter 8), in everyday cognition people have to choose how to allocate their cognitive resources, because both working memory and time are limited commodities. People often use simple heuristics (cognitive shortcuts or rules of thumb) to make judgements about attitude objects. For example, they may simply follow the majority opinion (hence, laugh tracks on television shows, which tell people that the jokes are funny, in case they did not notice) or accept appeals from unknown experts (e.g. 'nine out of 10 dentists prefer ...') (Chaiken, 1980; Chaiken, Gentner, & Hulse, 1997).

The distinction between central and peripheral routes to attitude change parallels the distinction between explicit and implicit judgement and decision making (chapter 8). Whereas explicit attitude change (the central route) requires conscious deliberation, implicit attitude change (the peripheral route) can occur in several ways. One is through classical conditioning of an object with an emotional response. Beer advertisers populate their commercials with beautiful women and virile men, subtly implying that using their product or drinking their beer will increase consumers' reproductive success (rather than their beer gut).

Another way to influence implicit attitude change is simply to repeat a message enough times that people start to believe it (Arkes, Boehm, & Xu, 1991; Petty, Brinol, & DeMarree, 2007; Petty, Brinol, & Priester, 2009). Politicians are well aware of this — a reason why they often repeat inaccurate information if they can get away with it. Repetition has persuasive effects for several reasons. It produces familiarity, which tends to produce liking (Zajonc, 1968, 1998; see also Weisbuch, Mackie, & Garcia-Marques, 2003); it strengthens the association between the two pieces of information; and it capitalises on the fact that, over time, people tend to forget the source of a message and assume that if they have heard it enough, it must have some credibility.

Thus, changing someone's attitude requires attention to several variables. If the attitude really matters to the person, if the recipient of the message is knowledgeable about the subject, if the recipient has time to evaluate the arguments and if the attitude was initially generated rationally by weighing costs and benefits, then the best appeal is to the head (central processing). In this case, the persuader should avoid distractions (glitzy campaigns, jingles and hoopla) that impede conscious, rational processing and annoy the receiver. If, however, the attitude is not strongly held and is based on minimal knowledge, the best route is usually to the heart or the gut — or, at any rate, as far away from the frontal lobes as possible.

INTERIM SUMMARY

Persuasion refers to deliberate efforts to change an attitude. Characteristics of the source, message, channel, context and receiver all affect the effectiveness of persuasive appeals. Persuasion can occur through a ***central route***, inducing the message recipient to think about the argument, or a ***peripheral route***, appealing to less thoughtful processes. According to the ***elaboration likelihood model***, the central route to attitude persuasion is more effective when the person is both motivated and able to think about the arguments, whereas the peripheral route is more effective when the likelihood that the person will engage in high-effort cognitive processing is low.

Attitudes to the environment

An emerging challenge for the psychology profession — and for the future of humankind on this planet — is climate change. To most objective observers, there seems little doubt that climate change is taking place and that human activities are a major contributing factor. Coal-fired power stations, billions of cars and a global economy that is based on fossil fuels continue to make our planet warmer. The problem of global warming is often labelled as an 'environmental' issue, seemingly far removed from the realms of psychology. But the reality is that psychology is at the heart of what needs to happen if we are to leave our great-grandchildren with a planet that remains as habitable. As Kogan and Winter (2010) say, that's because these 'environmental problems' are really *behavioural* problems. Human behaviour is ultimately responsible for the rapidly deteriorating natural systems on which the survival of the planet depends. Our decisions to drive cars, turn on air-conditioners and rely on coal-fired power stations for cheap electricity create climate change. And we find ways to justify that behaviour and make it seem sensible, even though we also are aware of the damage this is doing to our world.

This situation has seen the emergence of ***conservation psychology***, defined as the 'scientific study of the reciprocal relationships between humans and the rest of nature, with a particular focus on how to encourage conservation of the natural world' (Saunders, 2003, p. 138). Given that human behaviour lies at the heart of the climate change challenge, psychology may hold the answer as to how we can turn that behaviour around before it is too late. Many people profess to be extremely concerned about climate change, and we know that our lifestyles are a major part of the problem, so why do people continue to participate in harmful behaviours? Beattie (2010) says there is no one reason, but a number of contributory factors. One is learned helplessness — the feeling that no matter what we do, the problem is already out of control. Second is the time lag before consequences become apparent. This generation is unlikely to bear the full brunt of climate change — and we know from behavioural studies that for change to occur, the reward or punishment needs to happen immediately after the behaviour. Also, while there is no doubting the logic of the arguments against the impact of our consumerist society, human behaviour can often defy logic.

So what needs to happen to encourage the kind of change that needs to take place? Clayton and Myer (2009) say that both internal and external factors are important to achieve the kind of large-scale behavioural change that our environmental challenges demand. People have to move beyond just specific personal behaviours to a more general way of thinking about consumption and about our impact on the environment. Just as societal norms with regard to smoking, drink-driving and suntans have changed, so too do norms around environmentally destructive behaviours. Moving towards a sustainable society means big changes at both the personal (behavioural, emotional, cognitive and spiritual) and structural (political, economic, and legal) levels, and requires extensive interdisciplinary collaborations (Smith, Positano, Stocks, & Shearman, 2009).

The APA Task Force on the Interface Between Psychology and Global Climate met in 2008–09 to examine the role of psychology in understanding and addressing global climate change. Task force members agreed that the issue of climate change requires interdisciplinary research and practice involving collaborative engagement with communities and other professions (Swim et al., 2009; see also Reser, 2009). Dr Joseph Reser, a social and environmental psychologist at Griffith University in Australia, was a member of the APA Task Force. He recognises the importance of also focusing on climate change and *psychological* adaptation, emphasising the actions people can take in their own lives to make a personally meaningful contribution and be part of the solution to this complex problem (Reser, 2009).

APPLY + DISCUSS

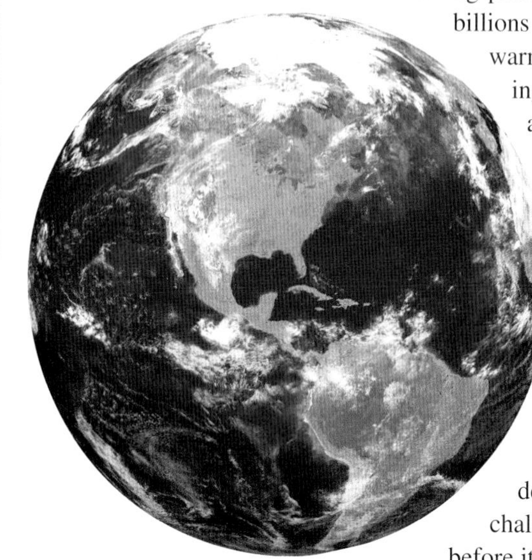

The APA Climate Change Task Force Report (2009) considers psychology's contribution to climate change by addressing the following six questions:

1. How do people understand the risks imposed by climate change?
2. What are the human behavioural contributions to climate change and the psychological and contextual drivers of these contributions?
3. What are the psychosocial impacts of climate change?
4. How do people adapt to and cope with perceived threat and unfolding impacts of climate change?
5. Which psychological barriers limit climate change action?
6. How can psychologists assist in limiting climate change?

Consider these six questions and cross-check your responses against those provided in the APA (2009) report. The report should be available via a link on your university course website for this subject.

Persuasion and climate change

By Associate Professor Niki Harre, Auckland University

In New Zealand and Australia, as in other Western nations, the masters of persuasion are those with something to sell. However, the time is ripe for social psychologists to focus on a much more important target than the latest beauty product or television set — the target of climate change. How can we apply research on social information processing to the task of raising awareness about climate change and its likely causes and solutions?

As psychologists, we know that people are not unbiased when they absorb social information. On the contrary, they filter it through their beliefs about themselves and their position in society. Several studies by Dan Kahan and his colleagues have shown this process at work, something he has called 'cultural cognition' (Kahan, 2010; Kahan, Braman, Lohen, Gastil, & Slovic, 2010; Kahan, Braman, Slovic, Gastil, & Cohen, 2009). They have demonstrated that when you give people balanced information on a current social issue, such as human papillomavirus (HPV) vaccinations, nanotechnology or abortion, they do not objectively consider both sides, but rather latch onto the information that is consistent with their prior beliefs — and ignore or disparage the rest. The result is that they become even more committed to their original viewpoint.

It is likely this process is at work in how people consider information about climate change. Leiserowitz (2005) found that the 7 percent of people who responded to the idea of climate change with 'naysaying' — by using phrases and terms such as 'environmental hysteria', 'hoax' and 'junk science' — also tended to be politically conservative, pro-individualist, pro-hierarchical, distrustful of most organisations and highly religious. On the other hand, the 11 percent who responded with 'alarmist' phrases — such as 'bad . . . bad . . . bad . . . like after nuclear war . . . no vegetation', 'end of the world as we know it' and 'death of the planet' — held pro-egalitarian worldviews and were anti-individualistic, anti-hierarchical and politically liberal. They also strongly supported government actions to mitigate climate change.

Given our understanding of cultural cognition, it is likely that the naysayers differed from the alarmists because taking climate change seriously is connected to a particular political worldview. Almost all climate change mitigation involves regulation of some sort and restrictions on the freedom of business and, in some cases, individuals. If you like the idea of regulating business, then climate change is going to be politically congenial to you — if still terrifying for the planet. If you don't like this idea, then climate change has nothing going for it. Your threshold for 'believing' in it will be high, and you will pay close attention to any flickers of hope that it may all be a socialist plot.

So, how do you persuade people of all political perspectives to take climate change seriously? One way is to ensure the messenger is someone your target audience can identify with. A study by David and Turner (2001) illustrated this. It involved giving logging supporters an anti-logging message from someone who was a member of a bogus organisation called Friends of the Timber Industry. At the same time, anti-logging people received a pro-logging message from another bogus organisation, Friends of the Forest. This meant both groups received a message that went *against* their values, from an organisation whose name indicated they *endorsed* those values. The effect was to make each group shift a little from their original view towards the opposing view. Over time, they shifted even further, suggesting that people continue to consider information long after it has been presented.

Two other strategies come from research on the influence of minority groups (Dreu & Beersma, 2001; Martin, Hewstone, Martin, & Gardikiotis, 2008). The first is to present information that is consistent. I recently attended a Science faculty event at my university that showcased the latest research in climate science. One of the questions posed to the presenters asked them to outline the criticisms of the 'sceptics', and whether any were legitimate concerns. The response from most of the presenters was that the criticisms are 'all over the place' and 'keep shifting'. It was clear that they were meaning that *this is a position you do not need to worry about because they do not have a consistent view.* It is notable that the scientific position is often presented as inconsistent in the media, which may well be one of the problems in getting people to take climate change seriously (although it is becoming increasingly hard to find any credible scientist who doesn't at least agree that warming is occurring).

This brings us to a second strategy suggested by research on minority influence. Emotional appeals work well with people who are already at least partly on our side; however, in persuading those with different values, we may be better off to stick to more objective information. Trying to scare someone who is adamant that climate change isn't happening with images of melting icecaps and forest fires isn't going to work, but systematic data about measured changes is harder to resist. We may not be entirely rational information processors, but few people can resist information that is purely factual for a long time.

Climate change isn't like a lot of social problems psychologists discuss (e.g. poverty, racism, war, crime, violence, drugs) where people can work out that something isn't right just by looking around them. It is a more insidious problem that involves massive shifts in how people think about personal freedom and regulation. But it is, nevertheless, about people as social creatures, which is at the very core of social psychology.

Cognitive dissonance

Although attitude change often involves deliberate efforts at persuasion, another path to attitude change is cognitive dissonance. According to Leon Festinger (1957, 1962), who developed cognitive dissonance theory, attitude change can occur when various objects of thought, which he called 'cognitive elements', are logically inconsistent — that is, when they are dissonant with one another. These objects of thought can be attitudes, behaviours, new information — virtually anything a person can think about. ***Cognitive dissonance*** thus refers to a perceived discrepancy between an attitude and a behaviour or between an attitude and a new piece of information. For example, if a person holds the belief that smoking is dangerous (element 1) but does not smoke (element 2), she does not experience dissonance; the two cognitive elements are consistent. If, on the other hand, she knows that smoking is dangerous (element 1) but also smokes (element 2), she experiences a discrepancy between her beliefs and behaviour.

APPLY + DISCUSS

Advertisers are keenly interested in shaping attitudes towards brands, products and political candidates.

- To what extent can we use the same principles to understand attitudes towards cars and towards political figures?
- Are advertisers wise to rely on the same principles to guide advertising campaigns for a brand of soft drink and a political candidate? If not, what should be different in persuading a consumer versus a voter?

According to Festinger, this kind of discrepancy leads to a state of psychological tension similar to anxiety. The tension, in turn, motivates the individual to change the attitude, the behaviour or the perception of the inconsistent information to eliminate unpleasant arousal or anxiety. For example, if the person knows that smoking is bad but smokes anyway, she may change the belief component of her attitude towards smoking ('It's not really that dangerous — I don't know anyone who has died of lung cancer from smoking') or she may quit smoking. Alternatively, she may add some additional cognitive element that resolves the dissonance (e.g. 'I don't plan to smoke that many years, so it won't hurt me').

In a classic experiment testing the utility of cognitive dissonance theory, Festinger and Carlsmith (1959) had participants perform monotonous tasks for an hour. The experimenters told them that the aim of this procedure was to test their performance, but the actual purpose was to create a negative attitude towards the tasks. The investigators then asked some participants to tell the next 'participant' (who was really a confederate of the experimenter) that the experiment was enjoyable. They paid the participants either $1 or $20 for their compliance.

We might expect that people who received $20 for hyping a boring task would feel more positive towards the task than those paid only $1. In fact, just the opposite occurred. Those who received only $1 rated the experimental tasks as more enjoyable, and they more frequently agreed to participate in a similar experiment again. Although these results seem counterintuitive, they exquisitely matched the predictions of dissonance theory. To say that a boring task is interesting for a meagre payment creates considerable dissonance. Participants who received only $1 either had to change their attitude towards the task or face the dissonance associated with knowing that they had sold their souls rather cheaply. In contrast, those who received $20 reduced their dissonance and thus avoided the need to change their attitude because they could readily explain their behaviour in terms of the payment, a considerable amount in the late 1950s.

In Festinger's terms, participants in both conditions ($1 and $20 payment) experienced a discrepancy between what they believed (cognitive element 1, 'the task is boring') and what they did (cognitive element 2, 'I told this poor sucker that the task is interesting'). When participants in the $1 condition tried to explain this to themselves, they had insufficient justification for their action and hence had to change their attitude towards the task. In contrast, participants paid $20 could add a third cognitive element ('I told the guy it was interesting because they paid me a lot to do it'); a cognition relieved the logical inconsistency between what they believed and what they said.

Two variables that influence the extent to which dissonance arises and requires resolution are the perception of choice and the size of rewards and punishments (Cooper & Fazio, 1984; Jordens & Van Overwalle, 2005; Wood, 2000). A person with a gun to his head will not feel much pressure to cling to attitudes he publicly professed at the time. Coerced statements create little dissonance because they are uttered with minimal choice. Similarly, as in Festinger and Carlsmith's study, the smaller the reward or punishment, the greater the attitude change because larger incentives minimise dissonance.

Dissonance reduction

Cognitive dissonance theory is essentially a drive-reduction theory (chapter 10). That is, reducing an uncomfortable emotional state (a drive) reinforces an attitude change. Suppose, for example, Padma has been dating Justin for a few weeks. She was really interested in him when they began dating, but he has seemed somewhat unenthusiastic, often preferring to go out with his buddies on weekends. Whether Padma is free to date other people is ambiguous; they are involved enough to suggest otherwise, but Justin's level of commitment hardly seems to imply an exclusive relationship.

The plot thickens when Brodie asks her out on Saturday night. Brodie seems like a nice enough guy, and Padma has no intention of spending the evening at home while Justin spends another night out with the boys, so she accepts. Then she begins to worry whether she has made the right choice — a phenomenon called *post-decision regret*. The tension she experiences may lead her to convince herself that Brodie is more attractive than he is — essentially justifying a choice she has made that is inconsistent with another choice, dating Justin. She may also talk to her friends about the situation in a way that solicits a particular answer — for example, talking only to friends who dislike the way Justin has treated her, or 'talking up' Brodie's virtues. These are examples of *post-decision dissonance reduction* — or dissonance reduction after the fact.

MAKING CONNECTIONS

Theories of cognitive dissonance that emphasise motivation resemble models of **stress** and **coping** and **emotion regulation** (chapter 14). The person makes an appraisal of the situation as problematic — whether the problem is logical inconsistency, immorality or the appearance of foolishness — which in turn leads to a negative or stressful emotional state. She then employs coping strategies (such as changing her attitude, changing her behaviour, rationalising her behaviour by adding a third cognitive element or changing the emotion directly by exercising, changing her diet etc.) to reduce the unpleasant feeling.

We can see similar dissonance reduction effects following situations in which people have invested a considerable amount of time and effort only to have their expectations disconfirmed (Aronson & Mills, 1959). Some army recruits endure a great deal of harassment and humiliation as part of a traditional 'welcome' when they first join the service. Once they have survived that initiation into army life, some find that it is not all it was cracked up to be. The result: dissonance or inconsistency between their original expectations or beliefs and the reality. In order to reduce the dissonance, soldiers build up the group in which they have invested so much time and energy. Through this effort justification process, dissonance is reduced and perceptions of the group are favourably influenced.

To what extent is dissonance reduction a conscious process, whereby people change their attitudes or behaviours based on conscious reflection? Recent research with amnesics provides some important clues. If dissonance reduction requires conscious awareness of a discrepancy between present and past attitudes or behaviour, then amnesics who cannot consciously recall their behaviour should show little dissonance reduction when faced with dissonant information. In fact, however, amnesics show *more*, not less, dissonance reduction than people with intact memories (Lieberman, Ochsner, Gilbert, & Schacter, 2001; see also Shultz & Lepper, 1995). This finding suggests that dissonance reduction occurs automatically, without conscious reflection.

Alternative explanations

The original formulation of cognitive dissonance theory explained the results of these experiments in terms of the motivation to reduce dissonance. Not all researchers agree, however, that motivation is necessarily involved. An alternative non-motivational explanation, derived from behaviourism, is self-perception theory. ***Self-perception theory*** holds that individuals infer their attitudes, emotions and other internal states by observing their own behaviour (Bem, 1967, 1972). Thus, if they see themselves telling someone that they like a task and they have received only $1 for doing so, they conclude that they must have liked it or they would not be saying so. According to self-perception theory, the attitudes people report depend on their behaviour; as their behaviour changes (because of changes in reinforcement contingencies) so again will their attitude. No motivation, tension or perceived inconsistency is involved.

Recall the study of Greenpeace in which participants with strongly held attitudes were more willing to donate money than those with weakly held attitudes. By the second week of the study, however, something very different happened. The attitudes of participants with weak attitude strength but not strong attitude strength were affected by their donation behaviour. In other words, participants with weak attitude strength who donated money changed their attitudes towards Greenpeace more than those who did not donate money or those who already held strong attitudes towards Greenpeace.

Other theories provide alternative motivational explanations of the results of dissonance experiments. For example, a self-presentation explanation suggests that what appear to be changes in attitudes in dissonance studies are really changes in reported attitudes (Tedeschi, Schlenker, & Bonoma, 1971). Because people want to present themselves as rational and do not want to look foolish by behaving inconsistently, they report attitudes they do not really hold.

Still another motivational explanation maintains that people feel guilty, ashamed or lacking in integrity after doing something that conflicts with their values, such as lying about a task. Thus, they change their attitudes to minimise their discomfort and preserve their self-esteem (see Abelson, 1983; Scher & Cooper, 1989; Steele, 1988; Stone, 2003).

Most likely, each of the explanations offered to explain the results of cognitive dissonance experiments is applicable at various times. When people do things that do not seem 'like them' but that do not have unpleasant consequences for other people, simple self-perception processes may explain why they change their attitudes. However, experiments measuring physiological responses demonstrate that dissonant information *can* produce emotional arousal that people experience as uncomfortable and that these feelings can indeed be reduced by changing a belief — or by other emotion-regulation strategies (chapter 11). For example, watching a funny movie or misattributing the cause of discomfort to something irrelevant like a pill just taken can all reduce the need to change a dissonant belief (Fried & Aronson, 1995; Zanna & Cooper, 1974). Unpleasant feeling states are most likely to lead to attitude change when the person has done something that leads to shame, guilt or anxiety, such as looking foolish to someone else or breaking a moral standard.

Culture and dissonance

The extent to which cognitive dissonance is universal has been questioned (Fiske, Kitayama, Markus, & Nisbett, 1998; Kitayama, Snibbe, Markus, & Suzuki, 2004). Research with Western participants has shown that giving people positive feedback prior to a dissonance manipulation decreases the motivation to reduce dissonance (because the person is less threatened about his self-worth). In contrast, negative feedback increases attitude change through dissonance reduction because it essentially heightens the person's sense of incompetence, immorality, lack of integrity or similar feelings (Steele, 1988). Westerners are individualistic and independent (chapter 19). To make a bad choice has strong implications for self-esteem, leading to attitude change in dissonance experiments. Asians, on the other hand, tend to be much more collectivist and interdependent in their views of themselves (Fiske et al., 1998; Kitayama et al., 2004; Markus & Kitayama, 1991). Their self-esteem rises and falls more with their ability to meet social expectations and maintain a sense of connection with those around them than it does with individual choices that indicate how smart or savvy they are.

INTERIM SUMMARY

Cognitive dissonance occurs when a person experiences a discrepancy between an attitude and a behaviour or between an attitude and a new piece of information. This leads to a state of tension that can motivate attitude change. According to ***self-perception theory***, attitudes change in dissonance experiments as people observe their own behaviour. Other explanations emphasise self-presentation (trying to look good) or efforts to regulate unpleasant emotions such as guilt and shame. To some extent, cognitive dissonance may presume a particular way of thinking about and evaluating the self that is distinctively Western.

Social cognition

A friend has just told you she has the 'perfect person' for you. She describes the individual as intelligent, witty, engaging and articulate and thinks the two of you would make a great pair. You immediately form an impression of this person, which probably includes traits such as attractive, kind, outgoing and generous. Now suppose instead your friend describes a potential date with precisely the same words — intelligent, witty, engaging and articulate — but first warns that this person is a 'real con artist'. This time your impression probably includes less favourable traits, such as selfish, cold and ruthless.

How does a simple phrase ('perfect for you' versus a 'real con artist') change the meaning of a series of adjectives and lead to an entirely different impression? The answer lies in ***social cognition***, the processes by which people make sense of themselves, others, social interactions and relationships; in other words, how people perceive and think about themselves and other people.

The study of social cognition has closely followed developments in cognitive science, which has provided many of its basic models and metaphors (Macrae & Bodenhausen, 2000). Cognitive psychologists have proposed a number of different models of how information is represented in long-term memory (chapters 6 and 7), which have guided research on social cognition (see Smith, 1998). Some models emphasise principles of association, arguing that memories are stored as interconnected nodes or networks of association. Activation of one node in a network spreads activation to other nodes linked to it through experience.

Other models emphasise schemas, organised patterns of thought that direct attention, memory and interpretation. Activation of a schema (such as a theatre schema) makes a person more likely to hear the word 'play' as referring to a theatre production than as something children do in a playground. Still other models focus on concepts, mental representations of categories, such as birds. In these models, categorising a novel stimulus involves comparing it to an abstract prototype (a generalised image or idea of a class of stimuli), a set of defining features (such as a list of attributes common to all birds) or a salient example or exemplar (such as a magpie).

More recently, supporters of connectionist models have proposed that representations are not so much 'things' that are 'stored' in the brain but patterns of activation in networks of neurons (chapter 8). According to these models, when a person sees an object, multiple neural circuits are activated simultaneously (i.e. in parallel). Somehow the system has to weed out less likely hypotheses about what the object is and settle on a solution. It does this by taking into account the multiple constraints imposed by the data.

Thus, the presence of wings on an animal in the garden activates multiple possible bird representations (magpie, sparrow etc.). At first, the brain automatically favours the most common birds, which begin with the highest level of activation because they are the most frequently encountered. However, the bird's loud chorus of rolling laughter is inconsistent with the calls of garden-variety birds (at least in most parts of Australia), so these representations are inhibited. The representation that is left 'standing' at the end of this battle of competing networks is the one that receives the greatest activation: kookaburra.

These various models, or 'languages', for speaking about representations all continue to be used in research on social cognition. Researchers are just beginning to sort out the extent to which they are compatible or incompatible and the conditions under which one model may be more accurate than another (Smith, 1998). As we will see, however, social psychologists are increasingly applying connectionist models to phenomena that they have previously understood using other models of representation, such as attitudes (Simon & Holyoak, 2002), the self (Humphreys & Kashima, 2002), attributions (Van Overwalle & Van Rooy, 2001) and stereotypes (Kunda & Thagard, 1996).

Because social cognition focuses on how people make sense of themselves, other people and the world, it is a broad encompassing term for a number of more discrete phenomena within social psychology. Among the specific phenomena we will discuss here are person perception, stereotypes and prejudice, attribution, attitudes and the self. As you will see, all these constructs share an emphasis on cognition and the relevance of cognitive processes to social phenomena (Fiske & Taylor, 1991).

APPLY + DISCUSS

Social cognition is all about inference in the face of ambiguity. The most important information — what is going on in another person's mind — is never directly accessible.

- How different is this from our understanding of cars, atoms or other non-human objects?
- How can we know if we have ever really understood another person? What indicators do we have of other people's thoughts and feelings, and how fallible are these indicators?

INTERIM SUMMARY

Social cognition refers to the processes by which people make sense of themselves, others, social interactions and relationships. Changing concepts of representation in cognitive psychology are beginning to lead to similar changes in the study of social cognition, such as the increasing use of connectionist models, which view representations as patterns of activation of networks of neurons operating in parallel.

Perceiving other people

Social cognition is pervasive in everyday life, from the first impressions we form of other people to our more enduring knowledge about people, situations and relationships.

First impressions

Even before the field of social cognition emerged as a distinct discipline, psychologists interested in interpersonal perception studied ***first impressions***, the initial perceptions of another person that affect future beliefs about that person (Asch, 1946; see also Moskowitz, 2005). One early study demonstrated the power of first impressions. Participants read the two passages shown in figure 17.1, but in different order (Luchins, 1957). The order of the material substantially influenced participants' evaluations of the person described. Seventy-eight percent of participants who read paragraph A first considered Jim friendly, compared to only 18 percent who read paragraph B first.

FIGURE 17.1
First impressions. In this classic study, the order of presentation of two paragraphs had a substantial influence on the impression participants formed of Jim.

SOURCE: Luchins (1957, pp. 34–35).

Paragraph A
Jim left the house to get some stationery. He walked out into the sun-filled street with two of his friends, basking in the sun as he walked. Jim entered the stationery store, which was full of people. Jim talked with an acquaintance while he waited for the assistant to catch his eye. On his way out, he stopped to chat with a school friend who was just coming into the store. Leaving the store, he walked towards school. On the way, he met the girl to whom he had been introduced the night before. They talked for a short while, and then Jim left for school.

Paragraph B
After school Jim left the classroom alone. Leaving the school, he started on his long walk home. The street was brilliantly filled with sunshine. Jim walked down the street on the shady side. Coming down the street towards him, he saw the pretty girl whom he had met on the previous evening. Jim crossed the street and entered a café. The café was crowded with students, and he noticed a few familiar faces. Jim waited quietly until the assistant caught his eye and then gave his order. Taking his drink, he sat down at a side table. When he had finished his drink, he went home.

One of the early researchers in this area, Soloman Asch (1946), suggested that first impressions create a frame of reference within which everything else that is learned about a person is interpreted. Thus, if you form an initial impression that another person is hostile and cold, you will interpret anything that he subsequently does in the light of the initial impression. For example, you would perceive a funny comment by this person as sarcastic rather than humorous (see also, Kelley, 1950).

The halo effect can have advantages in business, with the potential for attractive people to be perceived as naturally having other favourable qualities as well, such as intelligence. Research has shown that attractive people earn higher salaries than others who are less pleasing on the eye.

A particularly salient characteristic of first impressions is physical appearance, especially attractiveness. Individuals who are physically attractive benefit from the ***halo effect***, the tendency to assume that positive qualities cluster together. This phenomenon, also referred to as the 'what is beautiful is good' stereotype, refers to the process by which people who are physically attractive are assumed to possess a number of other favourable qualities as well, such as being warm, friendly and intelligent (Dion, Berscheid, & Walster, 1972; Forsterling, Preikschas, & Agthe, 2007). Researchers have found halo effects for physical attractiveness across a wide array of situations. For example, more attractive people get lighter legal sentences and higher salaries (Hamermesh & Biddle, 1994; Lieberman, 2002). Researchers have also found that both young and old alike succumb to the halo effect as it relates to physical attractiveness. Rather than 'outgrowing' the tendency to assign positive traits to attractive individuals, people over 65 continue to demonstrate the halo effect (Larose & Standing, 1998). Given these findings, it is little wonder that the number of people who get plastic surgery for cosmetic reasons has skyrocketed in recent years.

The positive glow of beauty, of course, has its limits (Eagly, Ashmore, Makhijani, & Longo, 1991; Feingold, 1992; Larose & Standing, 1998). Not surprisingly, it is most powerful when people have minimal information about each other. It also extends to some traits more than to others. For example, people typically attribute greater sociability and social competence to attractive people, but they do not expect them to have more integrity, modesty or concern for others. This latter finding, however, is culturally specific, applying primarily to individualistic cultures, such as Australia, New Zealand and the United States. In more collectivist cultures, such as Korea, where an emphasis is placed on group harmony and connections with others, physical attractiveness is more likely to be associated with traits such as integrity and less likely to be associated with traits such as competency (Wheeler & Kim, 1997).

An even more important variable than actual physical attractiveness, however, may be how attractive people *perceive* themselves to be. Individuals who perceive themselves as physically attractive report being more extroverted, socially comfortable and mentally healthy than those who are less comfortable with their appearance (Feingold, 1992). Although they may simply be deluded in every realm of their lives, it is equally likely that seeing themselves as attractive produces a ***self-fulfilling prophecy***, in which feeling attractive leads to behaviours perceived by others as attractive (chapters 6 and 18). In fact, research consistently finds that when people feel and act attractive, others are more likely to see them that way.

Schemas and social cognition

First impressions are essentially the initial schemas people form when they encounter someone for the first time. Schemas — the patterns of thought hypothesised to organise human experience (chapters 4 and 7) — apply in the social realm as in other areas of life (see Fiske, 1993, 1995; Plant & Peruche, 2005; Taylor & Crocker, 1980). We form schemas about specific people or types of people (e.g. extroverts, Asians, women); situations (e.g. how to behave in a classroom or restaurant); and roles and relationships (e.g. how a lecturer, student, parent or friend is supposed to act) (Baldwin, 1992).

As in other cognitive domains, schemas guide information processing about people and relationships. They direct attention, organise encoding and influence retrieval. For example, an employer who suspects that a job candidate may be exaggerating his accomplishments is likely to scrutinise his resume with special care and enquire about details that would normally not catch her eye. If later asked about the candidate, the first thing she may remember is that he described a part-time job as a courier at a radio station as a 'communications consultant'.

People are especially prone to recall schema-relevant social information — behaviours or aspects of a situation related to an activated schema (Hannigan & Tippens-Reinitz, 2001; Higgins & Bargh, 1987). For example, participants presented with a vignette about a librarian are likely a week later to remember information congruent with their librarian schema, such as a bun hairstyle and glasses. They are also prone to remember highly discrepant information, such as her tendency to go out dancing every night. If a librarian schema is active during encoding or retrieval, what people are *least* likely to remember are details irrelevant to the schema, such as her brown hair colour.

INTERIM SUMMARY

First impressions can have an important influence on subsequent information processing. One of the features that strongly affects the way people perceive others upon first meeting is physical attractiveness. We process information about other people and relationships using schemas, which guide information processing by directing attention, organising encoding and influencing retrieval.

Stereotypes and prejudice

Schemas are essential for social cognition. Without them, people would walk into every new situation without knowing how to behave or how others are likely to act. Thus, schemas can be very functional in allowing us to predict some of what will happen in particular situations. Schematic processing can go awry, however, when schemas are so rigidly or automatically applied that they preclude the processing of new information. This often occurs with ***stereotypes***, characteristics attributed to people based on their membership of specific groups.

Stereotypes are often overgeneralised, inaccurate and resistant to new information. Like other schemas, however, they save cognitive 'energy'. In other words, they simplify experience and allow individuals to categorise others quickly and effortlessly (Allport, 1954; Hamilton & Sherman, 1994; Macrae & Bodenhausen, 2001; Macrae, Mitchell, & Pendry, 2002).

Stereotypes arc intimately related to prejudice (chapter 19). ***Prejudice***, which literally means prejudgement, involves judging people based on (either positive or negative) stereotypes. Prejudice involves a person's thoughts or cognitions about another person or group, whereas ***discrimination*** refers to behaviours that follow from evaluations or attitudes towards members of particular groups (Fiske, 1998; see also Ward Schofield & Steers-Wentzell, 2003). Racial, ethnic and religious prejudice has contributed to more bloodshed over the past century than perhaps any other force in human history. Its path of destruction can be traced through the violence and institutionalised discrimination against Aboriginal and Torres Strait Islander peoples in Australia and the Maori people in New Zealand, to the Holocaust, the Arab–Israeli conflict, the tension between Anglophones and Francophones in Quebec, the carnage in

ETHICAL DILEMMA

A researcher wishes to examine whether stereotypes increase biases in perceptions of people. Unbeknownst to a group of undergraduate psychology students, she hands out two versions of a case study on a specific psychological disorder. In one version of the case study, she provides information about the client (e.g. 43-year-old single mother of two children, employed part-time as a waitress). In the second version, she provides non-specific information about the client. She asks the students to diagnose the case study, using all information available to assist them with their interpretation.

- Is it ethical for the researcher to administer two versions of the case study?
- What ethical issues are relevant to this research?

Northern Ireland, the tribal warfare and genocide in Rwanda and other African countries, the civil war and atrocities in Bosnia, other civil wars that erupted after the breakup of the Soviet Union and terrorist activities in the United States and throughout the world. The list is long and grim.

Since the 1930s, psychologists have proposed a number of explanations for prejudice, based on their answers to two central questions: do the roots of prejudice lie in individual psychology (such as personality dynamics or cognition) or in social dynamics (the oppression of one group by another)? And are the causes of prejudice found in cognition or motivation — in the way people think or in the way they *want* to think? As we will see, the absence of a single widely accepted theory of prejudice probably reflects the fact that researchers have often tried to choose among these options (see Duckitt, 1992; Johnston & Miles, 2003).

The authoritarian personality

Around the time of World War II, psychologists turned to psychodynamic theory to explain racism.

A team of researchers who fled Nazi persecution in the middle of the last century suggested that some people are likely to be attracted to racist ideology because of their personality characteristics. Theodore Adorno, Frenkel-Brunswik, Levinson, and Sanford (1950) identified what they called the ***authoritarian personality***, characterised by a tendency to hate people who are different or downtrodden. These individuals tended to have a dominant, stern and sometimes sadistic father and a submissive mother — interestingly, like the family of Adolph Hitler. According to the theory, children in such families fear and hate their fathers, but they would be brutally punished if they expose these feelings, so they repress them. As adults, authoritarian individuals displace or project their rage onto groups such as Jews, indigenous peoples, homosexuals or other people whom they perceive to be different.

Adorno and colleagues thought (and hoped) that authoritarian personality dynamics were limited to, or especially common in, Nazi Germany. However, their research in the United States suggested otherwise. Despite criticism of Adorno's methodology, more recent work supports many of the original findings, such as the link between this personality style and harsh parenting requiring strict obedience (Peterson, Smirles, & Wentworth, 1997; Snyder & Ickes, 1985).

Subtle racism

Recent cognitive approaches to prejudice, specifically racial prejudice, emerged from the observation that racism has changed in the last three decades. Today, overt racial discrimination against ethnic minorities is generally met with public disapproval. Gone are the days of old-fashioned racism, when Indigenous Australians were denied the right to vote, and public places such as pubs and cinemas were segregated. But, racism of a seemingly different kind seems to remain alive and well. Several researchers contend that new, more subtle kinds of racism exist in the wake of old-fashioned racism (Devine, Monteith, Zuwerink, & Elliot, 1991; Dovidio & Gaertner, 1993; Fiske, 1998; Leets, 2003). For example, many people claim not to be racist but in fact hold one attitude after another that 'just happen' to be unfavourable to minorities, such as attitudes towards welfare or immigration (Green, 2007; Jackson, Brown, Brown, & Marks, 2001; McConahay & Hough, 1976) or, as discussed in the opening vignette, asylum seekers (Every & Augoustinos, 2007). Part of this reluctance to admit to racial attitudes in a society that now emphasises political correctness may simply reflect people's desires not to publicly appear untoward in spite of private beliefs to the contrary.

Paralleling the change from old-fashioned racism to subtle racism is a change from old-fashioned sexism to a more subtle brand of sexism (Swim, Aiken, Hall, & Hunter, 1995). Although some people claim that they do not discriminate against women, in reality they continue to do so and to devalue the opinions of women relative to those of men.

Another kind of subtle racism occurs in people who experience a conflict between two attitudes (Katz & Hass, 1988). On the one hand, they believe in what the sociologist Max Weber called the Protestant work ethic, the idea that hard work is the key to 'making it', with the implication that people who are not successful have simply not applied themselves. On the other hand, they believe in equality of opportunity and recognise that all people in their society do not start out at the same place. This ambivalence can lead to extreme responses, both positive and negative, as they sometimes 'land hard' on one side of the ambivalence or the other.

Implicit and explicit racism

Another form of conflict is that between explicit and implicit attitudes towards members of minority groups. Many white people have absorbed negative attitudes towards people of different ethnic background over the course of their lives (Dovidio & Gaertner, 1993). They often express non-bigoted explicit attitudes, but when acting or responding without much conscious attention, unconscious stereotypes slip through the cracks (Devine, Plant, Amodio, Harmon-Jones, & Vance, 2002; Greenwald et al., 2002). For example, in ambiguous situations, non-indigenous people tend to be less helpful to indigenous people than to other non-indigenous people, and they are more likely to impose stiffer penalties for indigenous criminals.

In part, this discrepancy between what people say and what they do reflects a simple cognitive process. When people process information without much conscious thought, they are more likely to rely on stereotypes, to treat people as part of a category rather than as a specific individual (see Olson & Zanna, 1993). Negative stereotypes, like other attitudes, may thus be activated without awareness, as when an Anglo-Australian man automatically checks his wallet after standing next to a young Aboriginal man on the train. Emotional arousal can also render people more susceptible to stereotypic thinking, in part because it draws limited attentional resources away from conscious reflection (Bodenhausen, 1993). The less people make conscious attributions, the more their unreflective, implicit attitudes prevail (Gilbert, 1995).

A growing body of research has begun to demonstrate just how different people's implicit and explicit racial attitudes can be (Devine et al., 2002; Dovidio, Kawakami, & Gaertner, 2000; Greenwald, McGhee, & Schwartz, 1998; Kawakami, Dovidio, Moll, Hermsen, & Russin, 2000). These studies have used priming procedures (chapter 7), activating racial associations and then observing their effects on thought and behaviour.

Another study found that people's implicit and explicit racial attitudes may be completely unrelated to each other — and may control different kinds of behaviour (Fazio, Jackson, Dunton, & Williams, 1995). To measure implicit attitudes, the investigators presented participants with a series of black and white faces followed by either a positive or a negative adjective. The participant's task was simply to press a key indicating whether the adjective was positive or negative. The theory behind the study was that negative attitudes are associatively connected to negative words (because they share the same emotional tone). Thus, the extent to which people have negative associations to blacks should be directly related to how quickly they recognise negative words after exposure to black faces. In other words, the speed with which participants respond to negative adjectives following priming with a black face can serve as a measure of their implicit attitudes towards blacks.

Implicit attitudes did not predict explicit attitudes. For example, many people who denied conscious, explicit racism showed substantial implicit racism as measured by their response to adjectives following black and white primes. But these implicit attitudes did predict something very important: participants' behaviour towards a black confederate of the experimenter who met them at the end of the study and simply rated the extent to which they seemed friendly and interested in what she had to say. Participants who had responded more quickly to negative adjectives after priming with black faces received lower ratings, regardless of what they believed explicitly.

Research demonstrates that there can be a clear difference in a person's implicit and explicit racial attitudes. Actor Mel Gibson implored the public that he wasn't to blame after making anti-Semitic remarks during an earlier arrest, saying: 'Please know from my heart that I am not an anti-Semite. I am not a bigot. Hatred of any kind goes against my faith' (Maddox, 2006).

Recent neuroimaging data suggest that implicit attitudes about race 'run deep'. Recall that the amygdala plays an important role in generating unpleasant emotions, particularly fear, in both rats and humans (chapter 10). In one study, the higher that participants scored on implicit racism, the more their brains showed activation of the amygdala as they looked at pictures of black faces (Phelps et al., 2000). Explicit, conscious attitudes, on the other hand, do predict other conscious attitudes and beliefs, such as beliefs about what should happen to people who commit hate crimes. These findings directly parallel the results of studies distinguishing implicit motives, which predict long-term behavioural trends (such as success in business), from explicit motives, which control behaviour only when people are consciously thinking about them (chapter 10).

Suppressing implicit racism

Implicit racism (or sexism, which shows similar properties; Lepore & Brown, 2002; Skowronski & Lawrence, 2001) may interact with motivational factors. No-one wants to be a hypocrite. When conscious beliefs and values conflict with deep-seated, automatic negative stereotypes, people may alternate between extreme positions, either laying excessive blame at the feet of members of devalued groups or refusing to hold them accountable for their behaviour. Alternatively, they may learn to recognise their unconscious tendencies towards racist thinking and perpetually monitor their reactions to try to prevent racist attitudes from colouring their actions (Devine & Monteith, 1993).

Researchers have examined the conditions under which people will express or suppress their stereotypes. In one series of studies, the investigators used a simple manipulation — the presence of a mirror — to heighten participants' focus on themselves while responding to a questionnaire about the acceptability of stereotypes (Macrae, Bodenhausen, & Milne, 1998). The researchers hypothesised that under conditions of self-focus, people will be more likely to suppress stereotypic attitudes. That is precisely what they found. Participants in the mirror condition considered stereotyping less appropriate than control participants without the mirror.

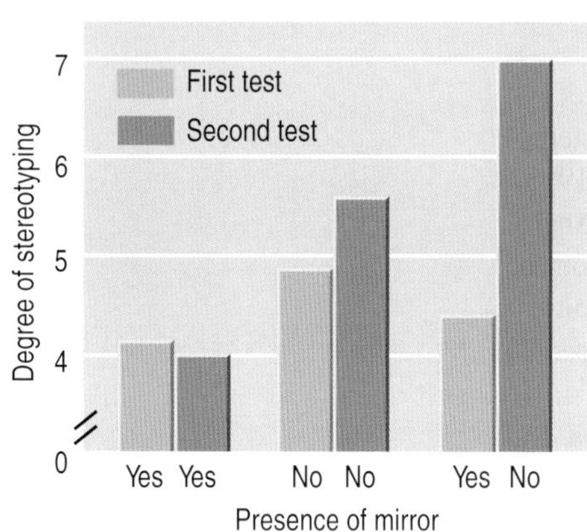

FIGURE 17.2
Stereotype suppression and rebound. Participants who initially suppressed their stereotype because of the presence of a mirror showed a rebound effect if the mirror was not present the second time.

SOURCE: Adapted from Macrae et al. (1998).

Suppressing a stereotype, however, can lead to rebound effects, in which the person later responds even more stereotypically. In another study, the investigators asked participants to evaluate a male hairdresser. After completing the task, the experimenter apologetically told them that some equipment had failed and asked them to do the task again, this time evaluating another male hairdresser. Some participants had the mirror in the room both times, others had the mirror initially but not while evaluating the second hairdresser, and some had no mirror on either occasion.

As predicted, those who had the mirror present initially produced less stereotypical descriptions of the first hairdresser. However, participants who had suppressed the stereotype the first time showed a substantial increase in stereotyping the second time if the mirror was removed (figure 17.2). Thus, fighting a stereotype does not make it go away; in fact, it can intensify its expression when the person least expects it.

Can we fight stereotypes more effectively? One method involves perspective taking. In a study of implicit attitudes towards the elderly (chapter 13), individuals who were asked to imagine the world from the perspective of older people subsequently expressed fewer stereotypes both implicitly and explicitly (Galinsky & Moskowitz, 2000). Conscious efforts to combat stereotypes can also sometimes be effective in sensitising people to their pervasive influence (Kawakami et al., 2000). In fact, simply being aware of the labels one is using can reduce the impact of stereotypes.

INTERIM SUMMARY

Stereotypes are characteristics attributed to people based upon their membership in groups. ***Prejudice*** means judging people based on stereotypes. An early approach to prejudice focused on a personality style called the ***authoritarian personality***, characterised by a tendency to project blame and rage onto specific groups. Cognitive researchers have focused on subtle forms of racism, many of which involve ambivalent attitudes. Of particular importance is implicit racism, which resides in the structure of people's associations towards members of minority groups rather than their explicit attitudes and often controls everyday behaviour.

APPLY + DISCUSS

Prejudice has a grim history, from the forced removal of Aboriginal and Torres Strait Islander children from their parents in Australia in the twentieth century (the 'Stolen Generations') to concentration camps in Bosnia that seemed eerily similar to the Nazi concentration camps a half-century earlier.

- Are some cultures more prone to prejudice than others, or is the belief that they are simply one more example of prejudice?
- What social conditions give rise to prejudice, and what protects against it?
- Is prejudice a personality trait? Would we all become prejudiced if our brother or sister were killed in a civil war based on ethnic or religious divisions?

Prejudice and social conditions

In the late 1950s and 1960s, the civil rights movement in the United States was at its peak, and social scientists were optimistic about eradicating social evils such as poverty and racism. This optimism in part reflected research suggesting that the roots of prejudice lay less in personality dynamics than in social dynamics, particularly in socialisation that teaches children racist attitudes (Duckitt, 1992; Pettigrew, 1958; Sinclair, Dunn, & Lowery, 2005).

Duckitt (2001, 2002) suggests that prejudice is based in early learning experiences. Duckitt's causal model predicts that social situations impact on ideological beliefs through changing people's worldviews and ideological attitudes (see Duckitt & Fisher, 2003). According to this model, social situations and personality (e.g. tough-mindedness and social conformity) each influence individuals' worldviews — the extent to which people view the world as dangerous or competitive. These two worldviews and personality dimensions then impact on ideological attitudes (e.g. authoritarianism and social dominance). Duckitt and Fisher showed that when people were made to think that New Zealand would become more dangerous in 10 years time, their worldview beliefs changed and they became more authoritarian.

Prejudice is indeed transmitted from one generation to the next, and it takes hold early. In India, which has seen continued violence between Muslims and Hindus, children show signs of prejudice by age four or five (Saraswathi & Dutta, 1988). In multi-ethnic societies such as Australia and the United States, children from both minority and majority subcultures tend to express preferences towards the majority culture by the preschool years (Spencer & Markstrom-Adams, 1990; see also Griffiths & Nesdale, 2006). Such culturally patterned associations can later make identity formation difficult for adolescent members of devalued groups, who must somehow integrate a positive view of themselves with negative stereotypes others hold of them.

The roots of prejudice may lie in social conditions in yet another way. Many theorists, from Karl Marx to contemporary sociologists, have argued that prejudiced social attitudes serve a function. They preserve the interests of the dominant classes. Promulgating the view that indigenous people or other minority groups are inferior justifies a social order in which whites hold disproportionate power. Disparities in wealth and property ownership often create the fault lines along which societies crumble with ethnic strife because the haves and have-nots frequently differ in colour, religion or ethnicity.

Attitudes make the world go round

By Professor Stuart C. Carr, Massey University

The International Association of Applied Psychology recently held its first Congress of Applied Psychology in the southern hemisphere. This event was held together with the Australian Psychological Society at its annual conference in Melbourne (International Association of Applied Psychology, 2010). Attitudes were the focus of this global gathering. For example, a Global Special Issue on Psychology and Poverty Reduction was launched at the meeting (Global Special Issue on Psychology and Poverty Reduction, 2010). This unique project brought together eight international journals in psychology, with each producing a special issue focused on their specialism (e.g. health, business, educational psychology) applied to the poverty reduction issue. At the meeting, Professor Elias Mpofu from the University of Sydney spoke about growing up in an African village (Mpofu, 2010). People lived in poverty; faced it on a daily basis. But they did not have poverty 'in' them. They were, and are, extremely resilient. Why then do attitudes towards 'the poor' often stereotype them as 'victims,' rather than people filled with agency and drive?

The professor's story is living proof of that agency and drive. His was a powerful reminder that attitudes are not just 'in the head': they stem from power differentials between richer and poorer — between countries and within. All too often, the privileged implicitly, and unfairly, 'look down on' the less materially well-off. Attitudes are reflections of their own power and privilege. In their theory of social dominance, Jim Sidanius and Felicia Pratto suggest that human beings have an implicit tendency, rooted in social evolution, to favour their own group over others. Even aid and development agencies, which, in principle, seek to remove inequalities and inequities, have latent tendencies to 'lord it' over the poor — to assert their social dominance; to preserve the status quo. These are shocking and unpalatable ideas, but they resonate with some of the criticisms of a 'poverty industry' (MacLachlan, Carr, & McAuliffe, 2010).

What use is it to know about implicit stereotypes of the poor; for example, about social dominance in aid work? One answer is that research raises awareness about the biases, and thereby helps correct them. The literature on bystander intervention, for instance, shows that learning the reasons 'why' people fail to help those in need actually helps them to intervene in future crises. Experimental research by Esther Duflo shows that simply letting parents in low-income countries know about the benefits of education for their child has a big effect on school enrolments. It helps development out of poverty (Duflo, 2010). So research has a social function — especially research on social attitudes!

A major feature of the world today is increased global mobility. People travel, and travel towards us. 'Travel broadens the mind', so the saying goes. But is that really true? Maybe just thinking about issues like immigration is enough to narrow, rather than broaden, some minds — to prejudice attitudes to new settlers, rather than opening them out. And how do new settlers react to such exclusion, if and when it happens? Researchers are currently testing whether, when and how travel broadens, versus narrows, the mind — at conscious, implicit and behavioural levels.

Ingroups and outgroups

Prejudice requires a distinction between ***ingroups*** and ***outgroups*** — people who belong to the group and those who do not (Brewer & Brown, 1998). The impact of ingroups and outgroups was demonstrated in a remarkable classroom experiment. Year 3 teacher Jane Elliott (1977), who taught in a rural, all-white community, one day announced that the brown-eyed children in her class were superior and the blue-eyed children, inferior. Soon the brown-eyed children refused to play with their blue-eyed classmates, and the blue-eyed children began to do poor work because they thought of themselves as stupid and bad. Although this study has been replicated, it has not been without its critics, who state that the results could simply reflect the operation of demand characteristics (chapter 2).

Us and them

Similar ingroup–outgroup behaviour occurs with adults and is particularly powerful in naturally occurring groups such as families, clans and communities. One process that intensifies stereotyping is that people tend to perceive members of outgroups as much more homogeneous than they really are and to emphasise the individuality of ingroup members (Moreland, 1985; Rothgerber, 1997). Thus, people of other races 'all look alike', and are seen to share many core traits — which is highly unlikely, given the tremendous differences in personality that exist within any group of people.

Interpretation of other people's behaviour also depends on their ingroup–outgroup status. A set of studies with Hindu and Muslim students in Bangladesh showed that both groups attributed helpful behaviour of ingroup members to their personal goodness and unhelpful behaviour to environmental causes (Islam & Hewstone, 1993). The reverse applied to outgroup members, who did not similarly receive the benefit of the doubt.

In New Zealand, biculturalism is central to the national philosophy for governance (Sibley & Liu, 2004; chapter 19). According to Sibley and Liu, a distinction between attitudes towards the general principles and the resource-specific aspects of biculturalism is critical to understanding perceptions of policy relating to minority–majority group relations. Motivations for intergroup dominance and superiority (i.e. high social dominance orientation) directly predicts Pakeha (New Zealanders of European descent) opposition towards the symbolic aspects of Maori–Pakeha intergroup relations (Sibley, Robertson, & Kirkwood, 2005). Thus, Pakeha are primarily motivated by realistic threats to material (self-) interests rather than by symbolic threats to identity and values (Sibley & Liu, 2004; Sibley et al., 2005).

Favouring the ingroup and denigrating the outgroup may at first appear to be polar opposites. However, as we have seen elsewhere in this book (chapters 10, 13 and 15), research on a number of seemingly unrelated phenomena — positive and negative affect, parental acceptance and rejection, positive and negative interactions in couples, and positive and negative components of attitudes — has shown an interesting and counterintuitive phenomenon. What look like opposite ends of a single dimension are often actually separate dimensions. The same is true with positive feelings towards ingroups and negative feelings towards outgroups (Brewer & Brown, 1998; Dasgupta, 2004). In most situations, ingroup favouritism is actually more common than outgroup derogation or devaluation.

APPLY + DISCUSS

- Is fear of 'the other' — particularly if the other speaks a different language, looks different, and has different values and beliefs — a tendency that is 'built into' the human psyche, or is it entirely learned?
- Is ethnic pride a threat to the ties that bind a multi-ethnic nation together? How can we maximise the conditions that allow people of different ethnicities to preserve their heritage without fostering ingroup–outgroup antagonism (see the next section)?

In fact, another form of subtle racism or group antagonism may lie less in the *presence* of hostile feelings than in the *absence* of the positive feelings that normally bind people together and lead them to help each other (Pettigrew & Meertens, 1995). The readiness to create and act on ingroup–outgroup distinctions probably rests on both motivational and cognitive processes. From a motivational point of view, casting ingroup members in a positive light gives you a positive glow as a member of the group (Tajfel, 1981). In fact, one study showed that after watching their team win, basketball fans showed an increased belief in their abilities at an unrelated task (Hirt, Zillmann, Erickson, & Kennedy, 1992). From a cognitive perspective, ingroup effects reflect our continuous and automatic efforts to categorise and schematise information.

Although everyone, at times, makes ingroup–outgroup distinctions, those who are most likely to do so are those who derive their primary sense of self or identity from their group memberships. ***Social identity theory*** suggests that people derive part of their identity from the groups to which they belong (Abrams & Hogg, 1999; Hogg, 2001; Tajfel, 1982). Thus, individuals whose identities are based largely on the groups to which they belong will have more of a need to maintain positive feelings for their ingroup and negative feelings for the outgroup.

Not surprisingly, situational events can also enhance the degree to which people define themselves in terms of particular groups and, thus, the degree to which they are likely to display ingroup favouritism and outgroup derogation (Kowalski & Wolfe, 1994). We have only to consider the annual State of Origin rugby league series played between Queensland and New South Wales. For those three matches, supporters in the two states suddenly display a level of parochialism and fervour for their state that is not apparent at any other time of the year. At the same time, anyone declaring allegiance to the other state is denigrated and considered with contempt. Serbian and Croatian tensions are similarly often apparent during the Australian Open, a situational event at which particular group loyalties come to the fore. During the 2007 Australian Open, Serbian and Croatian tennis supporters were involved in a chair-throwing brawl that erupted outside a centre court match involving a Bosnian-born American player and Serbian competitor Novak Djokovic. Unlike the ingroup–outgroup rivalry that is present during State of Origin, the favouritism and derogation shown by Serbian and Croatian supporters has a darker derivation: it is partially inspired by ongoing negative affect that lingers from the Croatian War of Independence. Leering and taunting between Serbian and Croatian fans is an ongoing issue at the Grand Slam.

Ingroup and outgroup distinctions are often more apparent at situational events. During the State of Origin rugby league series, supporters display a level of parochialism for their state that is not seen at other times of the year. Negative affect towards outgroup members can also manifest in more serious forms. Simmering tensions between Serbian and Croatian supporters erupted into a brawl, complete with a chair fight, at an Australian Open tennis championship. In a show of ongoing ingroup favouritism and outgroup aversion, Serbian and Croatian supporters have jeered each other from the comfort of the stands in more recent years.

Reducing group antagonisms

Research on ingroups and outgroups inevitably led to interest in techniques for reducing group antagonisms. In a classic experiment, researchers created friction between two groups of 11-year-old boys, dubbed the Rattlers and the Eagles, at a Boy Scout summer camp (Sherif, Harvey, White, Hood, & Sherif, 1961). Then the experimenters fostered strong ingroup sentiments by instructing the children to give their group a name, wear special clothes and so on. They also encouraged rivalries through competitive activities. Within a short time, the competition became so heated that it degenerated into overt hostility.

Initial attempts to defuse the hostility, such as bringing the groups together for pleasant activities, failed. Another approach was more successful. The experimenters contrived situations that created ***superordinate goals*** — goals requiring the groups to cooperate for the benefit of all. In one instance, the experimenters arranged for a truck transporting food for an overnight trip to stall. Eventually, both groups cooperated in pulling the truck with a rope. Similarly, when the camp's water supply stopped, both groups worked together to solve the problem.

The researchers concluded that contact alone is not enough to reduce conflict; the contact must also involve cooperation (see Sherif & Sherif, 1979). This finding has important implications for social policies such as school desegregation, because it suggests that simply placing children from two different races in the same school may not minimise animosities; it may in fact exacerbate them (Anson, 2000; Stephan, 1987). Compare this to sports teams, where indigenous and non-indigenous players work together for common goals and do not distinguish at the end of a winning game who they will throw their arms around.

Other factors also influence whether contact leads to increased tolerance or animosity. First, individuals must have the opportunity to get to know one another on a one-to-one basis, as in sports teams and musical groups, and to have relatively equal status (Brewer & Brown, 1998). People from different groups also need to have enough shared values, beliefs, interests, culture and skills so that their interactions dissolve stereotypes rather than confirm them. Unfortunately, members of cultures and subcultures often differ on precisely these things, so these characteristics increase the need for superordinate goals and shared or complementary skills that de-emphasise differences and emphasise commonalities (chapter 19).

MAKING CONNECTIONS

In the mid-twentieth century, Australia experienced a wave of migration from many European countries, introducing a range of new cultures and languages. Emphasis was placed on **assimilation** — losing past identities and becoming 'Aussies'. In recent years, however, a different attitude has emerged, placing greater pride and emphasis on cultural backgrounds — the **multicultural society** (chapter 19).

ONE STEP FURTHER

Understanding the 'us-versus-them' divide

By Doctor Stefania Paolini, University of Newcastle

The Australian Socceroos entered the 2010 FIFA World Cup with enthusiasm and bold expectations of success. All of the players' hopes were crushed in the very first opening match in Durban, South Africa, with the Socceroos suffering an embarrassing 4–0 defeat against Germany. Fans and press immediately turned sour, blaming 'the Dutchman' — Pim Verbeek, the team's former coach, and the 'foreign-based players' in the team (including Tim Cahill) — for the disappointing performance.

Socceroos player Tim Cahill, as well as former Socceroos coach Pim Verbeek, were both blamed by fans and the media after the team suffered an embarrassing 4–0 defeat to Germany in the 2010 FIFA World Cup. Cahill controversially received a red card during the match.

When things turn bad, does the 'us-versus-them' divide widen? Is it easier to find in 'foreigners' or, more generally, in members of outgroups, the natural scapegoats and source of all evil? Australian-based research (Paolini, Harwood, & Rubin, 2010) confirms that negativity causes the widening of the 'us-versus-them' divider. When Anglo Australians interacted with a Muslim Australian who had an unpleasant body language, thoughts about 'ethnicity' and 'Anglo versus ethnic differences' popped up in their mind more readily and frequently than when the same Muslim Australian had a pleasant body language. In this line of work, this pattern of response repeated in several other occasions: when the group divider was age — or even membership — in trivial laboratory-created groups; when, rather than engaging in a face-to-face exchange, Anglo Australians just anticipated, recalled or even imagined engaging in such an exchange with 'the other'. This pattern may be so robust and pervasive because, according to Australian export self-categorisation theory (Turner, Hogg, Oakes, Reicher, & Wetherell, 1987; see also Reynolds, Turner, & Haslam, 2000), most people have consolidated expectations that groups to which they do not belong are inherently bad, and that exchanges with outgroup members are likely to be difficult.

Does this mean that humans are destined to undergo a spiral of negative intergroup relations? Do the mechanisms that govern human judgements and behaviours make evil unavoidably stronger than good? The answer to both of these questions is negative. Solid meta-analytic evidence demonstrates that face-to-face contact between members of opposing groups is typically beneficial, even when it is not optimal in nature (Pettigrew & Tropp, 2006). Moreover, European data suggest that positive inter-ethnic contact is far more frequent than negative contact (Christ, Ullrich, & Wagner, 2008; Pettigrew, 2008); thus, as an influential social psychologist and his colleagues candidly put it, 'good may prevail over bad *by superior force of numbers*' (Baumeister, Bratslavsky, Finkenauer, & Vohs, 2001, p. 323).

If the damaging cognitive and behavioural consequences of any automatic or too easy pairing between negativity and wide 'us-versus-them' dividers can indeed be diluted — or even outweighed — by greater availability of positive intergroup contact experiences, then welcome are those media commentators, politicians and educators that remind observers that it was the ethnically diverse Iraqi soccer team that beat Saudia Arabia in the final of the 2007 AFC Asian Cup, that people from different ethnicities and races were cheering together during the joyful closing ceremony of the 2010 FIFA World Cup in South Africa and, more mundanely, that most ordinary interethnic transactions in everyday life go smoothly and have positive outcomes for all the parties involved.

INTERIM SUMMARY

Prejudice lies not only in people's minds but also in social institutions and socialisation practices that foster it. Prejudice requires a distinction between ***ingroups*** and ***outgroups*** (people who belong to the group and those who do not). People often attribute more homogeneity to outgroups than ingroups and make more positive interpretations of the behaviour of ingroup members. Ingroup–outgroup distinctions probably reflect both motivational and cognitive factors. Contact between groups can decrease prejudice and hostility if it is accompanied by shared goals, personal acquaintance with members of the outgroup, relatively equal status, and enough shared values and culture to dissolve stereotypes.

Attribution

Whether trying to understand the causes of inner-city violence or a curt response from a boss, people are constantly thinking about the 'whys' of social interaction. The process of inferring the causes of one's own and others' mental states and behaviours is called ***attribution*** (Gilbert, Fiske, & Lindzey, 1998; Lieberman, Jarcho, & Obayashi, 2005). Attribution plays a central role in virtually every social encounter. For example, an attribution about why a friend did not call back when she said she would can affect the friendship, just as the attributions a student makes for a weak performance on a test can affect her self-esteem and motivation in the future.

Bernard Weiner (1992, 1995) proposed a model of attribution with three elements. First, people seek to understand why certain events happened. For example, a student scores only 60 percent on an assignment and immediately asks why this occurred. Second, people attribute the outcome to a cause. For example, the student may blame a poor teacher or a missing textbook for the bad assignment result. Third, people base their future behaviour on the attributions that they make. For instance, the student may decide to drop out of that teacher's class or to buy the missing textbook, because those factors were seen as the cause of the low score. Changing the attribution can influence subsequent behaviour. For example, the student may identify the decision to spend a weekend at the beach instead of studying as the real reason for the poor score. In that case, rather than dropping out of the class, the student may choose to hit the books instead of the surf the next time an assignment is due.

Intuitive science

People attribute causes by observing the covariation of situations, behaviour and specific people. In other words, they assess the extent to which the presence of one variable predicts the presence of another — that is, whether the two variables co-vary (Heider, 1958; Kelley, 1973, 1992). An employee who receives a terse response from his boss may have noticed that his boss is often brusque when she is stressed by approaching deadlines. Thus, he attributes her behaviour to the situation rather than to her feelings about him.

According to one view, when people make attributions, they are behaving like ***intuitive scientists***. They rely on intuitive theories, frame hypotheses, collect data about themselves and others, and draw conclusions as best they can based on the pattern of data they have observed (Heider, 1958; Ross, 1977). In the language of connectionism, they are essentially trying to settle on a solution that takes into account as many constraints as possible.

Making inferences

Understanding other people's behaviour requires figuring out when their actions reflect demands of the situation, aspects of their personalities (often called personality dispositions) or interactions between the two (the ways specific people behave in particular situations). Thus, people sometimes make ***external attributions***, or attributions to the situation, whereas other times they make ***internal attributions***, attributions to the person (chapter 6; Nisbett & Masuda, 2003). Often they combine the two, as when the employee notices an interaction effect: that his boss tends to become tense and brusque (internal, or dispositional, attribution) when she is stressed by deadlines (external, or situational, attribution).

In making attributions, people rely on three types of information: consensus, consistency and distinctiveness (Kelley, 1973, 1979; see also Ziegler, Diehl, Zigon, & Fett, 2004). ***Consensus*** refers to the way most people respond. If everyone in the organisation responds tersely to his questions, the employee might attribute his boss's brusque behaviour to something situational (such as the organisational culture, or atmosphere of the company). ***Consistency*** refers to the extent to which a person always responds in the same way to the same stimulus. If the boss is frequently brusque, the employee will probably make an internal attribution about her personality. The ***distinctiveness*** of a person's action refers to the individual's likelihood to respond this way to many different stimuli. If the boss treats other people brusquely, the employee is likely to conclude that brusqueness is an enduring aspect of her personality, rather than a reflection of her attitude towards him. Consistency and distinctiveness are the intuitive scientist's versions of the concepts of consistency across time and consistency over situations debated by personality psychologists (chapter 11).

Part of the difficulty in making accurate attributions is that most actions have multiple causes, some situational and some dispositional. In deciding how much to credit or blame a person, people generally adjust for the strength of situational demands through two processes, discounting and augmentation (Trope, 2004; Trope & Liberman, 1996). ***Discounting*** occurs when people downplay (discount) the role of one variable (such as personality, intelligence or skill) because they know that others may be contributing to the behaviour in question (Heider, 1958; McClure, 1998). For example, the employee may discount his boss's bad manners because she is under the strain of an approaching deadline, or because her father recently died. The opposite situation occurs with ***augmentation*** — that is, increasing (augmenting) an internal attribution for behaviour that has occurred despite situational demands. The employee may attribute particular coldness to his boss if she continues to respond tersely to his questions when the workload is low.

Making an attribution is typically a three-step process (Gilbert & Malone, 1995). First, people categorise the behaviour they have observed (e.g. did the boss sound angry?). Then, based on the way they have interpreted the behaviour, they categorise the person's personality (e.g. this is a hostile person). Finally, if the situation seems to have elicited or contributed to the behaviour (e.g. the angry comment was provoked), they may discount the attribution of hostility. Experimental research supporting this theory shows that distracting participants while they are making attributions leads them to make automatic attributions to the person, which they would have discounted if they had had time to think about the situation. In other words, people first jump to conclusions about personality implicitly, and they then correct these attributions if they have the time to think about it. As the first plane flew into one of the towers of the World Trade Center on the morning of 11 September 2001, many people found themselves wondering about the causes of this horrible event. Was something wrong with the plane? Did something happen to the pilot? These initial attributions were quickly dispelled, however, when a second plane flew into the other tower, followed shortly after by a plane flying into the Pentagon in Washington, D.C. Inferences regarding the causes of these events now changed to focus on terrorism.

People differ in the types of attributions they are likely to make and in the implications that these attributions have for the individual. A person's habitual manner of assigning causes to behaviours or events is referred to as his ***attributional style*** (Buchanan & Seligman, 1995; see also Hugelshofer, Kwon, Reff, & Olson, 2006). For example, some people view the world through rose-coloured glasses and typically adopt an optimistic explanatory style. They believe that good events and outcomes are due to internal factors about themselves that are likely to remain stable over time. Conversely, other people take a much darker view of the world and adopt a pessimistic explanatory style. These individuals make attributions for negative events to internal factors that are stable and that will pervade virtually everything that they do. For example, a student with a pessimistic explanatory style will attribute failure on a test to the fact that she is not smart (internal attribution), she will never be smart (stable attribution), and she will probably fail tests in other courses as well (global attribution). Not surprisingly, people who explain events using a pessimistic explanatory style are at greater risk for depression than those who use more optimistic attributional styles (Peterson & Seligman, 1984).

Research conducted six weeks after the 2010 Christchurch earthquake showed that 60 percent of Canterbury residents intended to increase their earthquake preparedness in the next month. The residents' heightened level of preparedness potentially limited the fallout from the subsequent earthquake that caused still more damage and resulted in the loss of over 180 lives in Christchurch in early 2011 (Fisher, 2011).

In New Zealand, a study by McClure, Allen, and Walkey (2001) showed that people are less likely to prepare for earthquakes if they make fatalistic attributions for earthquake damage. Thus, if people hold a fatalistic belief that nothing can be done to prevent earthquake damage, they judge the earthquake outcomes as uncontrollable and are unlikely to take preventative action and prepare for earthquakes. However, if news reports raise awareness that earthquake damage is often selective and the product of building design, then people will learn to attribute the damage to building design and to see the damage as preventable (McClure et al., 2001). Recent research conducted six weeks after a 7.4 Richter scale earthquake devastated Christchurch, New Zealand, in 2010, and also involving Victorian University psychology professor John McClure, showed 60 percent of Canterbury residents intended to increase their earthquake preparedness within the next month. Only 27 percent of residents in Wellington, New Zealand, had the same response (Fisher, 2011). Professor McClure said the 2010 earthquake and the local residents' ensuing preparation measures may have helped limit the fallout from a subsequent earthquake that devastated the region and resulted in over 180 deaths less than a year later.

Researchers have also found cultural variations in the attributions people typically make. Specifically, people in collectivist cultures make more external attributions for others' behaviour than do people from individualistic cultures. Data suggest that people in collectivist cultures take more time before assigning causes to people or events (chapter 19). Thus, they are more likely to take into account all relevant factors, including situational ones, that may have influenced behaviour (Choi, Dalal, Kim, & Park, 2003).

INTERIM SUMMARY

Attribution is the process of inferring the causes of one's own and others' mental states and behaviours. People attribute causes by observing the covariation of social stimuli or events. People are like ***intuitive scientists***, who use intuitive theories, frame hypotheses and try to draw inferences from the data they have collected. They sometimes make ***external attributions*** (attributions to the situation), ***internal attributions*** (attributions to the person), or attributions that reflect the *interaction* of the two. Although people can make any of these attributions in a particular situation, they tend to develop ***attributional styles*** or habitual ways of assigning causes to events.

Biases in social information processing

Although individuals in some sense act like intuitive scientists, their 'studies' often have substantial methodological shortcomings. Indeed, rigorous application of the scientific method is so important in social psychology precisely because it prevents researchers from making the same kinds of intuitive errors we all make in everyday life (chapter 2).

Social psychologists have identified several biases in social information processing. Here we examine two of the most widely studied and then explore the cognitive and motivational roots of biased social cognition.

Fundamental attribution error

One of the most pervasive biases in social cognition, the ***fundamental attribution error***, is the tendency to assume that other people's behaviour corresponds to their internal states rather than external situations — that is, to attribute behaviours to people's personalities and to ignore possible situational causes (Gilbert & Malone, 1995; Heider, 1958; Ross, 1977; Sabini, Siepmann, & Stein, 2001). A good illustration occurs while driving — which in the extreme case can turn into 'road rage'. We may, for example, draw highly sophisticated inferences about a person's character (e.g. 'what a jerk!') from the fact that he is holding us up on our way to work by driving slowly — only to recognise when we see his number plate that he is from another state and probably has no idea where he is going.

The fundamental attribution error (also known as the correspondence bias; Ross, 1977; see also Ehrlinger, Gilovich, & Ross, 2005) occurs primarily when explaining others' behaviour. When explaining our own behaviour, we are far more likely to look for causes outside ourselves. Why does this happen? Carr (2002) says people are often badly positioned to understand the situational influences that lead to the behaviours they observe in others. Observers glimpse only a brief 'slice' of a person's life — not all their intimate details. For example, a manager sees only a staff member arriving late for work — not the flat tyre or bus breakdown that caused that event to happen (Carr, 2002). Thus, we are more likely to make external as opposed to internal attributions for our own behaviour. Researchers have found, however, that this effect can be reversed by getting participants to view their own behaviour much as an outside observer would. Storms (1973) had participants interact with another individual while both were being watched by an observer. When the participant and the observer were asked about the causes of the participant's behaviour, the observer, not surprisingly, made more internal attributions whereas the participant made more external attributions for his own behaviour. When the perspectives were reversed, however, and participants watched themselves on video and then made attributional evaluations of their own behaviour, they, too, made more internal as opposed to external attributions.

Furthermore, the degree to which the fundamental attribution error occurs depends on which culture is being observed. East Asians display the fundamental attribution error less than people from Western cultures (Choi, Nisbett, & Norenzayan, 1999). What is interesting about this finding is that it is not that East Asians do not make dispositional attributions for other people's behaviour; they simply give more attention to situational influences on the person than do people from Western cultures. In other words, they are less likely to discount the role of the situation.

APPLY + DISCUSS

Attributions are central to legal decision making. Suppose, for example, a person is charged with killing another person using a handgun.

- What attributions lead to a charge of murder rather than a lesser charge, such as manslaughter?
- What attributions affect the severity of the sentence once a person has been convicted?

Self-serving bias

Another pervasive bias in social cognition is the ***self-serving bias***, in which people tend to see themselves in a more positive light than others see them (Baumeister, 1998; Epstein, 1992; Greenwald, 1980; von Hippel, Lakin, & Shakarchi, 2005). The self-serving bias takes a number of forms. For example, a majority of people rate themselves as above average on most dimensions. This is, of course, statistically impossible (Taylor & Brown, 1988). People are also more likely to recall positive than negative information about themselves (Kuiper & Derry, 1982; Kuiper, Olinger, MacDonald, & Shaw, 1985; von Hippel et al., 2005) and to see their talents as more striking and unusual than their deficiencies (Campbell, 1986). In addition, they attribute greater responsibility to themselves for a group product than other group members attribute to them (Ross & Sicoly, 1979) and assume that they are less driven by self-interest than those around them (Miller & Ratner, 1998). Finally, people take credit for their successes and attribute failure to external, situational factors (Campbell & Sedikides, 1999).

A sparkling frock, sky-high heels and an eye-catching fascinator are 'must haves' for many of the women who attend the Melbourne Cup. But, irrespective of how they really look and the money that they spend, it is likely that most of the women — as well as their partners and the other men in the crowd — will consider themselves to be smarter, better looking and more personable than the person next to them.

Self-serving biases are not without their limits. Most people will not totally ignore reality (see Kunda, 1990), but they do differ tremendously in their tendency to let their needs for self-enhancement interfere with their objectivity. One study observed MBA students in simulated corporate decision-making meetings over a weekend (John & Robins, 1994). At the conclusion, participants ranked their own performance and that of their peers. The researchers also observed their behaviour and ranked each participant. Participants were fairly objective in ranking their peers' performance. Peer and psychologist rankings correlated at about $r = .50$. However, they were less objective about themselves. The correlation between self-rankings and psychologist rankings was only about $r = .30$. Moreover, 60 percent overestimated their own performance, a finding that suggests a self-serving bias. And those who were rated as more narcissistic by the researchers showed the greatest biases of all! The data indicate that most people wear mildly rose-tinted glasses when they look in the mirror, but that people who are narcissistic keep a pair of opaque spectacles on hand in case the spotlight shines too brightly on their flaws (see also Epley & Dunning, 2000; Robins & Beer, 2001).

Like other biases in social cognition, the self-serving bias may depend in part on culture (Kitayama, Markus, Matsumoto, & Norasakkunkit, 1997). This bias is pervasive in the West but much less so in Eastern and other collectivist cultures, in which people do not define themselves as much in terms of their individual accomplishments. When people from Western countries describe themselves, they tend to list about five times as many positive as negative traits (Holmberg et al., 1995). This pattern is unheard of in cultures such as Japan, where people do not toot their horns so loudly, either in private or in public.

Furthermore, research suggests that as Asians become assimilated into Western culture, their conscious self-descriptions begin to show the Western bias; however, deeper, implicit processes (assessed, for example, by the speed with which they recognise the words *good* and *bad* after priming with the word *me*) may take a generation to change (Kudo & Numazaki, 2003; Lehman, Chiu, & Schaller, 2004; Pelham et al., 1998, as cited in Fiske et al., 1998).

Faulty cognition

What causes biases in processing social information? The answers appear to lie in both cognition and motivation.

Cognitive biases

Some of the errors people make reflect the same kinds of cognitive biases people display in non-social cognition (chapter 8). For example, heuristics can lead to biases in social thinking, as when people assume that 'all politicians are crooks' because of some salient examples that come to mind (the availability heuristic). In fact, one of the main reasons politicians often appear crooked is that their behaviour — including their tax returns, business dealings and so on — is so closely scrutinised.

As in non-social cognition, heuristics can lead people awry, but they are essential to everyday functioning, because they allow us to make decisions and judgements rapidly and without conscious reflection. People frequently lack the time or information they need to make accurate attributions, so they do the best they can. Often, these rapid, good-enough attributions are just that — good enough. On the other hand, phrases like 'I had no idea he would turn out to be that way' or 'I can't believe I didn't see that' express the regrets people feel when they discounted or failed to piece together some initial 'clues' as they employed heuristics that turned out to be not quite good enough.

Motivational biases

Other biases reflect motivation (Fiske, 1992; Kunda, 1990; Tagiuri, Blake, & Bruner, 1953; Westen, 1991, 1998). Schemas and attributions are influenced by wishes, needs and goals. For example, people who are currently involved in romantic relationships tend to perceive opposite-sex peers as less attractive and sexually desirable than people who are uninvolved (Simpson, Gangestad, & Lerma, 1990). This bias is useful because it makes maintaining a monogamous relationship easier.

Motivation can also influence the extent to which people think in a complex way about themselves and others. For example, one study compared people high in need for intimacy with those high in need for power (Woike & Aronoff, 1992). Participants were asked to evaluate potential research assistants by watching them interact with each other on videotape. In one condition, the investigators emphasised the need to be sensitive and empathic towards the applicant. In the other condition, the investigators stressed the importance of taking control of the situation and exercising decision-making power.

After watching the videotapes, the researchers instructed participants to describe the candidates and then coded the complexity of their responses. The investigators reasoned that participants motivated by power would think more deeply and complexly when their power motives were activated, and those high in intimacy motivation would think more complexly when motivated by instructions emphasising intimacy. The findings strongly supported the hypothesis, suggesting that the extent to which people think deeply about others depends on their motivation to do so.

Interactions of cognition and motivation

Although social psychologists have spent many years debating whether particular biases are cognitive *or* motivational in origin, many biases probably reflect both (Tetlock & Levi, 1982). Consider the ***confirmation bias*** — the tendency to seek out information that confirms one's hypotheses. When presented with the task of finding out whether a target person is extroverted, participants tend to ask the person questions that elicit extroverted responses and to fail to ask questions like 'Do you enjoy spending time alone?' (Snyder & Cantor, 1979). People are more likely to commit the confirmation bias when they are not particularly motivated or when they lack the cognitive resources to do a more thorough assessment — for example, if they are distracted by a second task (Liberman & Trope, 1998).

If people are intuitive scientists, research suggests that they could use a basic course in research design. Aside from cognitive errors, social perceivers have many goals besides the scientific objective of seeking truth, and these other agendas often influence their 'findings'. They are interested in looking good, maintaining positive feelings about themselves, believing good things will happen to them, protecting their idealised views of people they care about, and maintaining negative schemas of people (or groups) they dislike. Because motives play a fundamental role in attention, encoding, retrieval and problem solving, social cognition is inherently intertwined with social motivation (see Fiske, 1993).

MAKING CONNECTIONS

People often see what they expect to see and fail to test alternative hypotheses, leading to false confirmation of schemas (chapter 8). When a couple buys a car together, the salesperson often talks primarily to the man, assuming that the man knows more and is more interested in cars — and may not discover, for example, that the woman is more knowledgeable or responsible for making the decision. Gender stereotypes of this sort are widespread and can be highly resistant to change (chapter 13).

Applications

The information on biases in social information processing just presented clearly shows that people are not always accurate perceivers of their social world. People jump to conclusions about others on the basis of first impressions. These first impressions create a frame of reference within which all subsequent information that is learned about a person is interpreted. People use schemas and rely on stereotypes to cognitively process the vast amount of information with which they are confronted on a daily basis. And people succumb to biases, such as the fundamental attribution error, as they interpret the behaviour of others, and the self-serving bias, as they interpret their own. You might think that, with training, the occurrence of errors in social information processing could (and should) be attenuated. Surely, clinical psychologists, for example, are immune from the same social information processing errors that plague the rest of us.

Unfortunately, research shows that clinicians, although perhaps better at overcoming social cognitive errors than members of the public, are still human. Clinicians succumb (although one hopes to a lesser degree) to the social information processing biases that afflict us all. The Rosenhan (1973) study discussed in chapter 15 provides a nice exemplar of these shortcomings.

Social and non-social cognition

Although social psychologists have followed developments in cognitive psychology closely and have borrowed many of their models from cognitive psychology, they also recognise a number of ways in which social cognition differs from non-social cognition (see Fiske, 1995; Zajonc & Markus, 1985). The differences are not black and white, but social and non-social cognition fall on opposite sides of a number of dimensions.

First, a person observing a social interaction is almost always missing the most relevant data: the unspoken intentions, thoughts and feelings of the people involved. Because observers of a social interaction have access only to behaviours, they must infer what those behaviours mean. Ambiguity is thus the rule in social cognition, leaving substantial opportunities for error, bias and idiosyncratic interpretation. Second, social cognition is inherently intertwined with emotion. People either like or dislike their roommate; their psychology lecturer is either interesting or boring; the shop assistant is either courteous or rude. Thinking about chemical formulas, in contrast, may not engender quite so much feeling.

Third, although culture influences many cognitive processes, such as categorisation, it plays a particularly important role in social cognition. An individual who is competitive and driven to accumulate wealth may appear perfectly normal in Western culture and hence draw little attention. The same person may be classified as antisocial or self-centred in many other cultures. Social cognition is inherently infused with cultural value judgements because categories (such as men, nurses or doctors) carry with them implications for how people who fit them *should* behave (Shweder, 1980).

Culture also influences the way people interpret interpersonal events by providing intuitive theories of personality and causality. When children and adults in the West explain their successes and failures, they rely on concepts such as skill, effort and luck (Weiner, 1980). In contrast, Buddhist children from Sri Lanka sometimes attribute achievement and failure to good and bad deeds in past lives. Good deeds from another life lead to good karma, a positive moral force that guides a person's fate (Little, 1987). Finally, social cognition is reciprocal. The 'object' being perceived in social cognition may respond to the perceiver — and change its actions based on how it believes it is being perceived. Getting annoyed at a textbook for being thick and boring does not change it. Getting annoyed at a lecturer for the same reasons, however, may well influence the way he lectures.

Understanding basic principles of thought and memory is thus necessary for understanding social thought and memory, but it is not sufficient. Humans are social animals, and this aspect of human nature has shaped the way we think about ourselves and others. (In the next chapter, we will consider the way humans as social animals *behave*.)

INTERIM SUMMARY

The ***fundamental attribution error*** is the tendency to attribute behaviours to people's personalities and to ignore possible situational causes. The ***self-serving bias*** is the tendency to see oneself in a more positive light than deserved. Biases in social cognition reflect both cognitive factors (such as the use of heuristics) and motivational factors (the impact of wishes, needs and goals). These biases are not limited to the public, but characterise even the cognitions of people who have been trained to avoid them, such as clinicians.

The self

Thus far, we have paid little attention to the social stimulus to which people attend more than any other: the self. The concept of self has a long and rather serpentine history in psychology, slithering in and out of vogue. In some eras, such as the present, psychologists have viewed the self as a central aspect of psychological functioning (Baumeister, 1998; Epstein, 1994; Markus & Cross, 1990; Wheeler, DeMarree, & Petty, 2007). In other eras, particularly during the heyday of behaviourism, psychologists viewed the self as a fuzzy, mushy concept, unobservable and hence scientifically unknowable. Currently, the self is one of the most widely studied topics within social psychology. Many studies on the self have focused on 'how the self directs social cognition and social behaviour' (Banaji & Prentice, 1994, p. 298; see also Guimond, Branscombe, & Brunot, 2007).

As often as the word 'self' is uttered in people's day-to-day conversations (e.g. 'I was just talking to myself'; 'I'm trying to find myself'; 'I have low self-esteem'), understanding what the self is and how it is best conceptualised would seem to be an easy task. However, one of the greatest challenges in describing the self seems to be defining it. Many behaviourists have justifiably complained that psychologists have used the same word to denote dozens of discrete phenomena and hence have failed to provide a coherent, empirically valid construct of the self. For years, theorists of nearly every persuasion have defined the self as the self-concept — the way people see themselves. The problem with this definition is that it is logically impossible. If the self-concept is a concept of something, it must be a concept of the self.

The only logically sensible definition, then, is that the ***self*** is the person, including mental processes, body and personality characteristics. From this definition several others logically follow. The ***self-concept*** is the person's concept of himself, a schema about the self that guides the way we think about and remember information relevant to ourselves (Markus, 1977; Markus & Wurf, 1987; Roger, Kuiper, & Kirker, 1977; see also Ghaderi, 2006). It is a concept like any other (chapter 8), such as wombat, tree or butcher. ***Self-esteem*** refers to a person's evaluation of himself, how much he likes and respects himself (Diehl, 2006). The self-concept could be referred to as the cognitive element of the self (how we think about ourselves), with self-esteem representing the affective element (how we feel about our selves).

Approaches to the self

William James (1890) proposed a fundamental distinction between self as subject and self as object. The self as subject includes the person's experience of self as thinker, feeler and actor. When I feel an emotion or think a thought, it is 'I' — the self as subject — who is feeling or thinking. When I take an action, I have a sense that it is I who has made a choice about how to behave.

In contrast, the self as object is the person's view of the self. This is the self-concept on which people reflect when they take the self as an object of thought. The difference between self as subject and as object can be easily remembered grammatically. The self as subject, which James called the 'I', is the subject who is capable of thinking about the self as object, the 'me'. Thus, the statement 'I am thinking about me' contains both elements of self.

Two perspectives have given increasing prominence to the self: the psychodynamic and the cognitive (see Baumeister, 1998; Westen, 1992; see also Singer, 1992).

APPLY + DISCUSS

- In what ways does cognition about ourselves follow similar principles to cognition about others? To what extent do similar principles of memory apply?
- In what ways is cognition about ourselves different from cognition about others?

Psychodynamic perspective

Contemporary psychodynamic thinking focuses on ***self-representations*** — mental models or representations of the self. Psychodynamic theories assert that people's representations of themselves and others play a key role in personality and psychopathology (chapter 11). Patients with borderline personality disorder, for example, often view themselves as totally unlovable or evil to the core, which can make them vulnerable to suicide (Kernberg, 1975; Waldinger & Gunderson, 1984; Wixom, Ludolph, & Westen, 1993). Thus, the self-concept is an attitude towards the self, which includes beliefs, feelings and tendencies to behave towards oneself in particular ways.

Two characteristics distinguish psychodynamic views of the self. First, they emphasise that people associate the self with many different positive and negative emotions, which are activated under different circumstances (Horowitz, 1988). Second, self-representations can be conscious or unconscious, explicit or implicit (Sandler & Rosenblatt, 1962). These representations can be at odds or even completely contradictory. For example, one patient with a narcissistic personality disorder was furious and deeply depressed when he was passed over for a supervisory position. At some level he worried that his own failings were the cause, but he convinced himself that the only reason he was passed over was because 'mediocrity cannot appreciate true genius'. This consciously grandiose representation seemed to mask a very different unconscious or implicit view of himself. Recent research from a cognitive perspective suggests, in fact, that implicit and explicit feelings about the self can often be very different and that implicit self-esteem, like implicit racism, can predict behaviour in ways that explicit self-esteem cannot (Spalding & Hardin, 1999).

Cognitive perspective

Cognitive theorists focus on the way the self-concept shapes thought and memory (see Higgins, 1999; Markus & Cross, 1990; see also Neisser, 2007). Extending the 'intuitive scientist' view, one theorist has proposed that the self-concept is like a theory of oneself (Epstein, 1973, 1994). Other cognitive theorists propose that the self-concept is a ***self-schema*** — a schema about the self that guides the way we think about and remember information relevant to ourselves (Markus, 1977; Markus & Wurf, 1987; Roger et al., 1977; see also Evans, Heron, & Lewis, 2005; Tanaka, Uji, & Hiramura, 2006). Thus, a person who has a self-schema as incompetent is likely to remember times he failed in exquisite detail and to forget occasions in which he was successful.

Self-schemas may be hierarchically organised (Kihlstrom & Cantor, 1983). At the core of the broader self-schema are fundamental attributes of the self, such as the person's name, sex, physical appearance, relationships to family members and salient personality traits. Below this general level in the hierarchy are schemas of the self in different situations or relationships. Each sub-schema is associated with its own attributes; a person may see herself as annoyed and anxious with her mother but comfortable with friends.

A GLOBAL VISTA

Culture and self

The notion that people have a self-concept and some core of selfhood that distinguishes them from others seems intuitively obvious to people living in twenty-first century Western societies. This view would not, however, be commonsensical to people in most cultures in most historical epochs (Geertz, 1974; Markus & Kitayama, 1991; Shweder & Bourne, 1982). That the term 'the individual' is synonymous with 'the person' in contemporary usage demonstrates how the individualism of our culture is reflected in its language. Not coincidentally, the prefix 'self-', as in 'self-esteem' or 'self-representation', did not evolve in the English language until around the time of the Industrial Revolution.

A relational view of the self

The contemporary Western view of 'the person' is of a bounded individual, distinct from others, who is defined by more or less idiosyncratic attributes. In contrast, most cultures, particularly the nonliterate tribal societies that existed throughout the vast expanse of human history, view the person in her social and familial context, so that the self-concept is far less distinctly bounded.

When the Wintu Indians of North America described being with another person who was closely related to or intimate with them, they would not use a phrase such as 'John and I', but rather, 'John we'. They reserved 'and' to signify distance between people with minimal relationship. When anthropologist Dorothy Lee (1950) tried to elicit an autobiography from a Wintu woman, she received an extensive account of the lives of the woman's ancestors. Only with considerable prompting did the woman eventually discuss 'that which was in my mother's womb'. Cheyenne autobiographies similarly tend to begin with 'My grandfather . . .' (Straus, 1982).

This relational view of selfhood is not confined to North American tribes. It is common among African groups (Comaroff, 1980) and has been observed in many Asian and Indo-Chinese cultures. For example, traditional Hindus in India frequently give their caste and village along with their name when they are asked to identify themselves (De Vos et al., 1985).

Why does the self differ across cultures?

Two factors seem to explain the differences between contemporary Western and other views of the self. First, some cultures are simply more group centred or collectivist and others more individualistic (chapter 19; Fiske et al., 1998; Markus & Kitayama, 2001; Triandis, 1989; see also Cai, Brown, & Deng, 2007; Heine & Hamamura, 2007). Because Japanese culture emphasises cooperation rather than the Western ideal of autonomy, the Japanese experience the self less in terms of internal states than in terms of social relationships (Cousins, 1989; De Vos & Suarez-Orozzo, 1986). Thus, for the Japanese, sincerity describes behaviour that conforms to a person's role expectations (carrying out one's duties), whereas for Westerners it means behaving in accordance with one's inner feelings. Sincere behaviour in Japan may thus be very insincere to an Australian. In general, the Western self tends to be conceptualised as more independent, whereas the Asian self tends to be conceptualised as more *inter*dependent (Heine, Lehman, Markus, & Kitayama, 1999; Kitayama et al., 1998; see also Dietz, 2006; Noguchi, Gohm, Dalsky, & Sakamoto, 2007). The view of the self is complicated and varies not only across cultures, but also within cultures, especially in multicultural countries such as Australia.

A second influence on conceptions of selfhood is technological development (Westen, 1985, 1991). Careful examination of historical documents suggests that only a few centuries ago the Western concept of self was much closer to the non-Western, group-centred view (Baumeister, 1998). The values, attitudes and self-concepts of people in rural Greece, for example, resemble the collectivistic orientation one finds in China more than the individualism of contemporary Athens (see Triandis, 1989).

Ten thousand years ago, before the advent of agriculture, humans lived in bands (small groups). In these band societies, a concept of self distinct from other people and nature was generally absent, and moral values focused on the interests of the clan or band. With the development of agriculture, which allowed accumulation of personal resources and led to social classes, people became more aware of individuality. At the same time, however, this awareness was countered by cultural proscriptions against it.

Around the time of the Industrial Revolution, something remarkable happened. The concept of the individual, free of attachments and duties, was born. And the individual has been born again wherever technological development has taken hold. Technological development seems to facilitate individualism, and with it a more individuated sense of selfhood, for several reasons. The first is geographical mobility. People who remain in a small community, as their kin have before them, tend to view themselves in a different context than people who may relocate hundreds or thousands of kilometres away. In addition, changing work conditions, such as wage labour and work that is not performed communally with kin or clan, lead to a sense of individual competence.

Furthermore, in technologically developed societies people earn much of their status through their actions rather than their family affiliations. They also frequently take up occupations different from those of their parents. When a man is no longer a hunter or farmer like his father, his representations of self and father diverge. Literacy and education also personalise skills and competences, which are no longer experienced as collective knowledge because they may be learned through individual study.

In addition, increased life span and higher standard of living make personal pleasures, desires and interests more important. Factors such as family size and whether children have their own rooms probably have a subtle influence as well. Whether the cultural differences that now divide Japan and the West will remain despite the pressures of industrialisation is a profound psychological question that will probably be resolved over the course of this next century.

Self-esteem

Individuals have multiple motives that guide the way they think about themselves, such as the motive to see themselves accurately (Banaji & Prentice, 1994; Baumeister, 1998; see also Hoyle, 2006; Kirkpatrick & Ellis, 2006; Vignoles, Regalia, & Manzi, 2006). Another primary motive regarding the self, which often competes with accuracy motivation, is the motivation to maintain high self-esteem (chapter 10), sometimes referred to as the motive for self-enhancement. Just as individuals can conjure up a typical or prototypical self-concept, they have a core or global sense of self-esteem (Rosenberg, 1979), a usual way they feel about themselves. They also experience momentary fluctuations in self-esteem, depending on which self-schemas are currently active. An athlete who wins a competition sees herself as a winner and enjoys a momentary boost in self-esteem, regardless of whether being a winner is part of her prototypical self-concept.

Research with Western participants suggests that self-esteem is hierarchically organised, presumably tied to a hierarchically organised view of the self. Thus, nested below a general level of self-esteem, people have feelings about themselves along specific dimensions, such as their morality, physical appearance and competence (Coopersmith, 1967; Harter, Waters, & Whitesell, 1998). A person with generally low esteem for his athletic prowess may nevertheless recognise himself to be a decent tennis player. People generally maintain positive self-esteem by giving greater emotional weight to areas in which they are more successful.

In this way, people can not only maintain their self-esteem, but they can also enhance their self-esteem, at least in areas where they are more successful. People appear to have an almost innate need to maintain a positive sense of self. Although there are a number of possible ways in which people can create this positive self view, one way is by evaluating themselves as better than the average other person. Positive illusions such as this were illustrated quite convincingly in a study in which university students rated themselves and the average other university student of the same sex on 20 positive traits and 20 negative traits. On average, participants rated themselves as better than average on 38 of the 40 traits (Alicke, Klotz, Breitenbecher, Yurak, & Vredenburg, 1995).

Much research that has been done on the self has examined different mechanisms by which people go about trying to maintain high self-esteem. For example, when people compare themselves with other people on a particular dimension, a process termed social comparison, they often use as their comparison group individuals who are worse off than they are (i.e. downward social comparison; Wills, 1981; Wood, 1989). By comparison with these 'downtrodden' individuals, people can maintain a positive view of their own traits and abilities. In addition, people may engage in ***self-handicapping***, a process by which they set themselves up to fail when success is uncertain in order to preserve their self-esteem (Higgins, Snyder, & Berglas, 1990; Jones & Berglas, 1978; see also Eddings, 2003; Rhodewalt & Vohs, 2005; Thomas & Gadbois, 2007; Warner & Moore, 2004). In this way, people can control the attributions that others make for their performance. In the event of failure, other people will attribute the lack of success to the impediment that 'prevented' success. Should success occur in spite of the barrier, then the person must really be talented and worthy of others' praise.

One study tested self-handicapping in an arena in which handicapping is not unfamiliar: golf. Stone (2002) led participants to believe that an athletic test was a measure either of their natural athletic ability or simply of general sports performance. White participants who feared that they would confirm the stereotype of poor white athleticism (i.e. those who thought the test was a measure of their natural ability) self-handicapped by practising less before the actual test (based on golf) than those who did not process the information in terms of a stereotype threat (i.e. people who believed the test was a measure of general sports performance). Should individuals in the former condition not perform well on the test, they, and others, could attribute their poor performance to the lack of practice. Should they succeed on the golf test in spite of the lack of practice, then they must be athletically talented, indeed. Interestingly, this study was conducted during the era of Tiger Woods' dominance over golf. Had he not been such a presence in the sport, white participants may have felt less of a need to self-handicap.

One final means (among many) by which a person may maintain or even enhance her self-esteem is basking in reflected glory or BIRGing (Cialdini et al., 1976). People who BIRG publicly announce their affiliation with another person or group that is successful, even though they had nothing to do with the success of that other person or group. When your football team wins, who do people say won the game? They say '*We* won'! When the team loses, however, the chant changes to '*They* lost'! Thus, we associate ourselves with success and distance ourselves from failure.

Although self-esteem often feels like something we 'have', self-esteem reflects as much a dynamic set of skills for *maintaining* positive feelings about the self as it does the accessibility of positive attitudes towards the self. Individuals with high self-esteem think and behave in ways that lead to positive feelings. When experimentally forced into a bad mood, they tend to problem solve and think positive thoughts, which in turn make them feel better (and better about themselves). In contrast, people with low self-esteem tend to respond to bad moods with negative thoughts (Peden, Hall, Rayens, & Beebe, 2000; Smith & Petty, 1995). Similarly, people with high self-esteem are more likely to help someone out while in a negative mood, which then makes them feel better about themselves (Brown & Smart, 1991).

Self-consistency

A less obvious motive guiding the self is ***self-consistency***, the motive to interpret information to fit the way one already sees oneself and to prefer people who verify rather than challenge that view (Lecky, 1945; Pinel & Swann, 2000; Swann, 1990; see also Brynjulfsen, 2005; Hu, Li, & Wang, 2006). Most of the time, self-consistency and self-esteem motives do not conflict; because most people hold relatively favourable views of themselves, they prefer positive information because it enhances self-esteem and bolsters their existing self-concept.

For people who do not like themselves, however, these two motives can lead in opposite directions. They want to feel better about themselves, but they also dislike evidence that contradicts their self-concept (Swann, Griffin, Predmore, & Gaines, 1987).

Depressed people actually prefer to interact with others — including marital partners — who have a negative view of them (chapter 15). Individuals who perceive themselves negatively appear to avoid people who give them feedback to the contrary for several reasons. They consider the feedback untrue, they feel that the relationship will be smoother and more predictable if the other person understands them and they believe people who view them positively are less perceptive (Swann, Stein-Seroussi, & Giesler, 1992).

Self-presentation

Yet another strategy that people use to gain self-knowledge and maintain favourable views of the self is self-presentation (chapter 14). The self does not exist in a vacuum. Although we all have aspects of ourselves that are known only to us, much of the self is determined and influenced by our interactions with others, what William James referred to as the 'social self'. Indeed, Cooley (1902) coined the term *looking glass self* to refer to the fact that other people are a mirror in which we see ourselves. In other words, much of our self-concept is reflected back to us by other people with whom we interact.

Given the interpersonal side to our 'self', few of us are surprised to discover that people attempt to regulate the way that they present their 'self' in interactions with others. The process by which people attempt to control the impressions that others form of them is called ***self-presentation*** or impression management (Cisek, 2006; Leary, 1995; Leary & Kowalski, 1990; chapter 14). To get a handle on self-presentation, think about all of the behaviours you perform on a given day, at least in part, to influence how other people see you. Before leaving for class each day, you probably shower, brush your teeth and dress in a way that will be approved of by others. You eat with utensils as opposed to your hands, and conduct yourself appropriately and respectfully in class. Although there are multiple reasons why you might perform these behaviours, one of those reasons is self-presentation or your desire to influence how others perceive you.

Although it was once thought that people generally try to make favourable impressions on others, researchers now know that the goal is to create desired impressions, either favourable or unfavourable. Thus, although some people might be motivated to put their best foot forward in their interactions with others, still others want to be perceived as threatening or intimidating. They present themselves in ways that will lead others to perceive them in these desired, albeit negative, ways (Leary, 1995).

Attempts to make impressions, particularly favourable impressions, on others often fail, however. Instances in which our desires to influence the impressions other people form of us fail are termed ***self-presentational predicaments***, and the emotion most frequently experienced in such situations is embarrassment. For example, when people trip on the stairs, the first thing they do is look around to see if anyone saw them fall. Tripping on the stairs creates a self-presentational predicament whereby a person's desire to be seen as a competent, coordinated individual is thwarted. Confronted with such predicaments, people engage in behaviours designed to repair damage to their image. For example, blushing that may follow a fall on the stairs is considered a type of nonverbal apology (Leary, Britt, Cutlip, & Templeton, 1992). People may also try to distance themselves from their own embarrassing behaviour. Age is also no barrier, with older adults motivated to influence the impressions of others in areas such as physical appearance, competence and self-reliance (Martin, Leary, & Rejeski, 2000).

Even though self-presentation is a universal behaviour, some people are more likely to impression manage than others. Individual differences in the degree to which people manage their impressions are referred to as ***self-monitoring*** (Gangestad & Snyder, 2000; Sakaguchi, Sakai, & Ueda, 2007; Snyder, 1974). High self-monitors resemble social chameleons. Who they are and how they present themselves varies with the situation in which they find themselves. Low self-monitors, on the other hand, are much less concerned with the impressions that others form of them.

Australian supermodel, entrepreneur and mum Elle Macpherson, known internationally as 'The Body', has leveraged her good looks into a business empire conservatively valued at over $100 million. In addition to looking youthful in middle-age, she always self-monitors for different situations — whether trying to blend in at the Royal Easter Show in Sydney or stand out at an event in New York.

Gender differences related to self-presentation also exist. Both men and women attempt to regulate the impressions that other people form of them, but they tend to do so in different arenas. In other words, desired identity images for men and women differ. Societal norms dictate that men should present themselves as dominant and assertive (i.e. as masculine individuals). Women, on the other hand, are socialised to present themselves in more feminine ways, such as appearing more nurturing and as more relationship-oriented. Consistent with this, women who desire to make a favourable impression eat 'more lightly' than men, because eating lightly is associated with being feminine (Pliner & Chaiken, 1990). One study showed that this effect was particularly salient when the women thought they were interacting with a man who perceived them as being unfeminine (Mori, Chaiken, & Pliner, 1987). Eating less was a way of restoring a desired and socially accepted social image of being feminine.

FROM BRAIN TO BEHAVIOUR

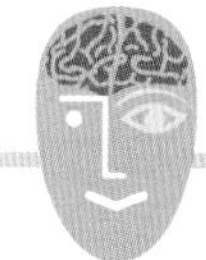

Physical health and views of the self

People have schemas or mental representations not only about the way they are but also about the way they *wish* they were or *fear* becoming (Markus & Nurius, 1986; Niedenthal, Setterlund, & Wherry, 1992). One theory distinguishes three kinds of self-concepts: actual, ideal and ought (Higgins, 1987, 1999). The ***actual self*** refers to people's views of how they actually are. The ***ideal self*** refers to the hopes, aspirations and wishes that define the way the person would like to be. The ***ought self*** includes the duties, obligations and responsibilities that define the way the person should be.

Thus, a person may see himself as a moderately successful businessman (actual self) but hope to become the chief executive officer of a company (ideal self). At the same time, he may volunteer at a soup kitchen at Christmas to satisfy a nagging sense that he is not contributing enough to his community (ought self). People have actual, ideal and ought selves from a number of points of view, including their own and those of significant others. A person may feel she is meeting her 'ought' standards for herself but that she has failed to meet her mother's expectations.

Discrepancies between these various self-schemas are associated with particular types of emotion (Higgins, 1987; Strauman, 1992). When people perceive a discrepancy between their actual self and their ideal self, they tend to feel emotions such as disappointment, dissatisfaction, shame and embarrassment. These are characteristic feelings of individuals who are depressed, who feel their wishes and hopes are unfulfilled.

People who experience a discrepancy between actual self and ought self feel emotions such as anxiety, fear, resentment, guilt, self-contempt or uneasiness. These feelings are characteristic of anxious individuals, who believe they have failed to meet their obligations and hence may be punished.

Research suggests that these schemas may influence not only mood but also physical health. As we have seen (chapter 14), emotional distress can depress immune-system functioning, making a person vulnerable to ill health. Enduring ways of perceiving the self may thus lead to chronic feelings that increase vulnerability to illness.

One remarkable study demonstrated this effect by comparing people who were anxious, depressed or neither (Strauman, Lemieux, & Coe, 1993). The investigators asked participants to describe their actual, ideal and ought selves, thanked them for their participation, and told them the experiment was over. Six weeks later, their research assistants, allegedly conducting a different experiment, primed discrepancies between actual and ideal self in depressed participants and between actual and ought self in anxious participants. They did this by exposing participants to words they had previously mentioned that were related to these discrepancies. For example, the investigators might ask an anxious participant who described his actual self as shy but his ought self as confident to think about the importance of being confident. (They also included words that were irrelevant to the person so that participants would not figure out what was happening.)

A week later, the experimenters exposed participants to a set of entirely irrelevant words (actually, taken from other participants), which they compared against the results of the previous session. Control participants were similarly exposed one day to self-referential words (words taken from their first session) and another day to irrelevant words. After each session, the investigators took blood samples to ascertain levels of natural killer cells, a rough index of immune response. The killer cell activity of control participants, who were neither depressed nor anxious, went up slightly when they were exposed to self-referential words. Depressed participants showed a slight decrease in killer cell activity when exposed to words related to their ideal-self discrepancies, although this was not statistically significant. The most striking finding was that for anxious participants, whose killer cell levels were significantly lower after being exposed to words related to their self-perceived failings (actual/ought discrepancies). Thinking about their unfulfilled obligations or unmet standards made them momentarily more vulnerable to illness. These findings are preliminary, but they suggest that chronic discrepancies between the way one believes one is and the way one ought or ideally should be might have a lasting impact on health.

INTERIM SUMMARY

Considered to be a driving force behind social cognition, the ***self*** is one of the most researched topics in social psychology today. Particular attention has been devoted to people's attempts to maintain and enhance their ***self-esteem*** (the need to view oneself positively) through such behaviours as downward social comparison, self-handicapping, implicit egotism and basking in reflected glory. At times conflicting with the motive to maintain self-esteem is the motive for ***self-consistency*** (the motive to interpret information to fit existing self-concepts). Another strategy for maintaining favourable views of the self is ***self-presentation*** or people's attempts to control the impressions that others form of them. Although much of our behaviour is motivated by self-presentational concerns, at times, ***self-presentational predicaments*** occur that threaten the image we would like to portray. The self that people sometimes present in their interactions with others is the ***actual self*** (how they really are). They may also self-present in ways that reflect their ***ideal self*** (the self they would like to be) or the ***ought self*** (the self they feel they should be).

Central question revisited

◆ Social and non-social cognition

We began this chapter with a fundamental question. To what extent are social and non-social cognition alike? Although social psychologists have followed developments in cognitive psychology closely and have borrowed many of their models from cognitive psychology, they also recognise a number of ways in which social cognition differs from non-social cognition (see Fiske, 1993, 1995; Zajonc & Markus,

1985). The differences are not black and white, but social and non-social cognition fall on opposite sides of a number of dimensions.

First, a person observing a social interaction is almost always missing the most relevant data: the unspoken intentions, thoughts and feelings of the people involved. Because observers of a social interaction have access only to behaviours, they must infer what those behaviours mean. Ambiguity is thus the rule in social cognition, leaving substantial opportunities for error, bias and idiosyncratic interpretation.

Second, social cognition is inherently intertwined with emotion. People either like or dislike their roommate; their psychology lecturer is either interesting or boring; the shop assistant is either courteous or rude. Thinking about chemical formulas, in contrast, may not engender quite so much feeling.

Third, although culture influences many cognitive processes, such as categorisation, it plays a particularly important role in social cognition. An individual who is competitive and driven to accumulate wealth may appear perfectly normal in Western cultures, and hence draw little attention. The same person may be classified as antisocial or self-centred in many other cultures. Social cognition is inherently infused with cultural value judgements because categories (such as men, nurses or doctors) carry with them implications for how people who fit them *should* behave (Shweder, 1980).

Culture also influences the way people interpret interpersonal events by providing intuitive theories of personality and causality. When children and adults in the West explain their successes and failures, they rely on concepts such as skill, effort and luck (Weiner, 1980). In contrast, Buddhist children from Sri Lanka sometimes attribute achievement and failure to good and bad deeds in past lives. Good deeds from another life lead to good karma, a positive moral force that guides a person's fate (Little, 1988).

Finally, social cognition is reciprocal. The 'object' being perceived in social cognition may respond to the perceiver — and change its actions based on how it believes it is being perceived. Getting annoyed at a textbook for being thick and boring does not change it. Getting annoyed at a lecturer for the same reasons, however, may well influence the way he lectures.

Understanding basic principles of thought and memory is thus necessary for understanding social thought and memory, but it is not sufficient. Humans are social animals, and this aspect of human nature has shaped the way we think about ourselves and others. In the next chapter, we turn to the way humans as social animals behave.

◆

SUMMARY

1 Define social psychology

- ***Social psychology*** examines the influence of social processes on the way people think, feel and behave.

2 Attitudes

- An ***attitude*** is an association between an object and an evaluation, which usually includes cognitive, evaluative and behavioural components. These three components can, however, vary independently. Attitudes vary on a number of dimensions, such as their strength, accessibility and complexity; whether they are implicit or explicit; and the extent to which they involve ambivalence. They also differ on their coherence (particularly the fit between cognitive and evaluative components). Broad attitudes tend not to be good predictors of behaviour.
- ***Persuasion*** refers to deliberate efforts to change an attitude. The effectiveness of a persuasive appeal depends on a number of factors related to the source of the communication, the message, the channel (the means by which a message is sent), the context and the receiver. It can occur through either careful, explicit thought (the ***central route***) or less explicit and rational processes (the ***peripheral route***). Persuading people to change their behaviour can also lead them to change their attitudes.
- ***Conservation psychology*** is an emerging field in the discipline involving the scientific study of the reciprocal relationships between humans and nature, with a focus on changing attitudes and behaviours to encourage conservation of the environment.
- ***Cognitive dissonance*** occurs when a person experiences a discrepancy between an attitude and a behaviour or between an attitude and a new piece of information that does not fit with it. Cognitive dissonance can motivate attitude change, although several distinct processes may underlie dissonance phenomena.

3 Social cognition

- ***Social cognition*** refers to the processes by which people make sense of others, themselves, social interactions and relationships.
- ***First impressions*** are the initial representations people form when they encounter someone for the first time. ***Schemas*** — patterns of thought that organise experience — guide attention, encoding and retrieval of information about people, situations and relationships.
- ***Stereotypes*** are characteristics attributed to people based on their membership of specific groups. ***Prejudice*** refers to judging an individual based on stereotypes. Racial and ethnic prejudice has roots both in motivation and cognition, and in the person and the broader social system. Stereotypes can be implicit or explicit. Prejudice typically requires the distinction between ***ingroups*** and ***outgroups*** and ***discrimination*** involves behaviours that follow from negative attitudes towards particular group members.
- The process of making inferences about the causes of one's own and others' thoughts, feelings and behaviour is called ***attribution***. People can make ***external attributions*** (attributions to the situation), ***internal attributions*** (attributions to the person) and attributions about interactions between the person and the situation. In making these attributions, they rely on three types of information: ***consensus*** (how everyone acts in that situation), ***consistency*** (how this person typically reacts in that situation) and ***distinctiveness*** (how this person usually reacts in different situations). ***Discounting*** occurs when people downplay the role of a variable that could account for a behaviour because they know other variables may be contributing to the behaviour in question. The opposite situation occurs with ***augmentation***, which involves increasing an internal attribution for behaviour that has occurred despite situational pressures.
- Social cognition may be biased in a number of ways, including the tendency to attribute behaviour to other people's dispositions even when situational factors could provide an explanation (the ***fundamental attribution error***), and the propensity to see oneself in a more positive light than one deserves (the ***self-serving bias***).

4 The self

- The ***self*** refers to the person. An individual's concept of the self is the ***self-concept***.
- The contemporary Western view of the person is of a bounded individual, distinct from significant others, who is defined by more or less idiosyncratic attributes. In contrast, most cultures have understood the person in social and familial context. Technological development has fostered individualism.
- ***Self-esteem*** refers to a person's feelings towards the self. People's views of themselves are motivated by self-enhancement motivations but also by the need for ***self-consistency***, interpreting information to fit the way they already see themselves.
- As a means of maintaining desired images of the self, people engage in ***self-presentation***, the process by which they try to control the images that other people form of them.

KEY TERMS

actual self, *p. 728*
attitude, *p. 695*
attitude accessibility, *p. 695*
attitude importance, *p. 695*
attitude inoculation, *p. 700*
attitude strength, *p. 695*
attitudinal ambivalence, *p. 697*
attitudinal coherence, *p. 698*
attribution, *p. 717*
attributional style, *p. 718*
augmentation, *p. 718*
authoritarian personality *p. 710*
central route, *p. 701*
cognitive complexity, *p. 696*
cognitive dissonance, *p. 704*
confirmation bias, *p. 721*
consensus, *p. 717*
conservation psychology, *p. 702*
consistency, *p. 717*
discounting, *p. 718*
discrimination, *p. 709*
distinctiveness, *p. 717*
elaboration likelihood model *p. 701*
external attributions, *p. 717*
first impressions, *p. 708*
fundamental attribution error *p. 719*
halo effect, *p. 708*
ideal self, *p. 728*
implicit attitudes, *p. 696*
ingroups, *p. 713*
internal attributions, *p. 717*
intuitive scientists, *p. 717*
ought self, *p. 728*
outgroups, *p. 713*
peripheral route, *p. 701*
persuasion, *p. 699*
prejudice, *p. 709*
self, *p. 723*
self-concept, *p. 723*
self-consistency, *p. 726*
self-esteem, *p. 723*
self-fulfilling prophecy, *p. 709*
self-handicapping, *p. 726*
self-monitoring, *p. 727*
self-perception theory, *p. 705*
self-presentation, *p. 727*
self-presentational predicaments, *p. 727*
self-representations, *p. 723*
self-schema, *p. 724*
self-serving bias, *p. 720*
social cognition, *p. 707*
social identity theory, *p. 714*
social psychology, *p. 694*
stereotypes, *p. 709*
superordinate goals, *p. 715*

REVIEW QUESTIONS

1. Describe attribution.
2. Define cognitive dissonance.
3. Distinguish between the terms *stereotype* and *prejudice*.
4. Describe the different types of information people use in making internal and external attributions for behaviour.
5. Describe the three kinds of self-concept.

DISCUSSION QUESTIONS

1. Do attitudes predict behaviour?
2. How might you be persuaded to change your attitude?
3. How can people act to protect and maintain their high self-esteem?

APPLICATION QUESTIONS

1. Test your understanding of how people make attributions by identifying each of the scenarios that follow as an example of one of the following types of information: consensus, consistency and distinctiveness.
   (a) Alana is an administration manager at a university. Caitlin works temporarily in her office while one of the permanent staff members is on annual leave. During this time Caitlin notices that all employees respond positively to Alana's requests for information relevant to specific work projects. She attributes Alana's excellent management skills to the friendly and supportive office environment.
   (b) Abdul works in human resources at a large organisation. He always keeps to himself and never socialises with his workmates during the lunch break or outside of work hours. He is often described by his colleagues as the 'loner' in their team.
   (c) The sports manager, Ichiro, is always friendly to his new staff members — he welcomes them with a smile and a firm handshake.
2. Test your understanding of stereotypes and other biases in social cognition by identifying each of these scenarios as an example of one of the following biases: fundamental attribution error, self-serving bias and stereotype.
   (a) 'I do not think that the woman who has been working in the library for the past five years is appropriate for the sales position. Although she has the necessary qualifications, I just think she would not be assertive enough. As a former librarian, she would neither have the personality nor the verbal communication skills required to successfully promote the product.'
   (b) You are driving home from work during peak-hour traffic. Out of nowhere, a car cuts in front of you to make a quick left-hand turn off the main highway. You scream out 'What a jerk!', as you hit the brakes. You then notice his number plate and realise he is from another state and probably has no idea where he is going.
   (c) A number of colleagues from a psychology department participated in a three-day skills workshop on time management. At the end of the workshop, the participants ranked both their own performance and that of their peers. The workshop presenters also observed their behaviour and ranked each participant. The participants were fairly objective in ranking their peers' performance, but were less objective when ranking their own performance, overestimating their time management skills.

The solutions to the application questions can be found on page 835.

MULTIMEDIA RESOURCES

The *Cyberpsych* multimedia resource is available *as an option* to accompany this textbook to further develop your understanding of many key psychology concepts. *Cyberpsych* contains a wealth of rich media content and activities, and for this chapter includes an interactive module on attribution theory.

Interpersonal processes

18

LEARNING OBJECTIVES

After studying this chapter you should be able to:

1. describe the factors that attract people to each other
2. distinguish among the theories of altruism
3. describe the theoretical approaches to understanding aggression
4. describe the influence of other people on the way individuals behave.

Relationships

- People ***affiliate***, or seek out and spend time with others, for many reasons.
- Several factors lead to ***interpersonal attraction***, including proximity, interpersonal rewards, similarity and physical attractiveness.
- ***Passionate love*** involves intense physiological arousal and absorption in another person; ***companionate love*** involves deep affection and intimacy.
- Evolutionary theorists emphasise ***sexual strategies***, tactics used in selecting mates, which reflect the different evolutionary selection pressures on males and females.

Altruism

- ***Altruism*** refers to behaviours that help other people with no apparent gain or with potential cost to oneself.
- ***Ethical hedonism*** is the doctrine that *all* behaviour is designed to increase one's own pleasure or reduce one's own pain.
- Evolutionary psychologists propose that people act in ways that maximise their inclusive fitness and are more likely to behave altruistically towards relatives than others.
- Researchers studying ***bystander intervention*** have found that individuals often do not help in a crisis in the presence of other people.

Social influence

- *Social influence* refers to the effects of the presence of others on the way people think, feel and behave.
- *Obedience* refers to compliance with authority. The Milgram experiments demonstrated that most people will obey, without limitations of conscience, when they believe an order comes from legitimate authority.
- *Conformity* means changing attitudes or behaviour to accommodate the standards of peers or groups. The Asch experiments demonstrated that people tend to conform rather than be the lone dissenting voice.
- A *group* is a collection of people whose actions affect the other group members. All groups develop norms, or standards of behaviour.
- The following principles of social influence demonstrate how people are socially influenced by others on a regular basis.
  1. The ***principle of reciprocity*** asserts that people have a compelling need to reciprocate what has been done to them.
  2. The ***principle of commitment*** asserts that because people are concerned with the impressions that others are forming of them, they feel the need to behave consistently with prior impressions or commitments they have made.
  3. The ***principle of liking*** asserts that we do things for people that we like out of a sense of obligation and so that they will continue to like us in return.

Aggression

- *Aggression* refers to verbal or physical behaviour aimed at harming another person or living being.
- The prevalence and forms of aggression vary considerably across cultures.
- Gender differences in aggression are highly consistent across cultures; males rather than females are more likely to commit the majority of criminal and aggressive acts.
- Controversy exists about the origins of aggression. Some theories maintain that the roots of aggression lie in biology and evolution; others look to the environment and social learning.

Central questions: individual, groups and the nature of human nature

- People's behaviour in groups clearly differs qualitatively from their behaviour when they are alone. Culture strongly shapes who we are and influences everything that we do. But cultures are rapidly changing and we are currently witnessing a period of social change that people need to learn to adapt to. One strategy for coping with social change is to synthesise the old and new, to preserve continuity with the past while somehow mooring one's identity in the future.

PICTURE this — it's early in the morning on a beautiful West Australian beach. Suddenly, a swimmer starts thrashing around in agony, calling for help. The reason soon becomes clear — a white pointer shark has attacked him and is still circling around him in the bloodied water. What do you do? Do you stand and watch? Do you call for help? Do you dive into the water and swim out towards the obvious danger?

Joanne Lucas displayed incredible courage while saving a man who was attacked by a white pointer shark at Middleton Beach in Albany, Western Australia. Joanne swam to his aid while the shark was circling nearby, and was later awarded one of Australia's highest bravery awards for her efforts.

This was exactly the situation that faced Joanne Lucas at Middleton Beach, Albany, when she arrived at the surf life saving club early in the morning to prepare for a training session in May 2008. The shark had attacked school teacher Jason Cull and had bitten a large chunk from his leg. His cries for help and agonised thrashing around grabbed Joanne's attention. Even though he was a total stranger, and the shark was still clearly visible close by, Joanne rushed into the surf and swam 80 metres to his rescue. She dragged Jason back to the shore while the shark kept circling. He was quickly whisked into an ambulance and off to safety, while Joanne recovered from both the physical and emotional strain of the rescue.

Joanne was later awarded the Star of Courage, one of Australia's highest bravery decorations, for her amazing rescue. What is it that made Joanne risk her own life to save that of a complete stranger? Why did she perform such an extraordinary act of ***altruism*** — that is, helping another person with no apparent gain, and even potential cost, to oneself?

The altruism of people like Joanne seems to defy theories of moral development (chapter 13). For example, according to cognitive–social theories, reward, punishment and expectancies control behaviour. Everyone standing on the beach that morning faced the same contingencies of reinforcement. To swim out to Jason meant putting their lives in danger; yet, Joanne did so nonetheless. According to cognitive–developmental theories, moral heroism should only occur among people with a high level of moral reasoning. Yet for Joanne, the reaction was instantaneous. She explained, 'I didn't really think "there is a shark out there, don't go in" — it was just completely instinctive that I had to go and save that person' (McPhee, 2009).

What makes people more or less likely to help in such circumstances? People differ on both ***situational variables*** (the situations in which people find themselves) and ***dispositional variables*** (their personalities and attitudes). On the situational side, Joanne just happened to be on the beach right in front of the attack when it took place. She was also a strong swimmer and a volunteer at the local surf life saving club, so she had the required expertise to complete the rescue. On the dispositional side of things, Joanne simply felt obliged to help out a swimmer in danger.

Understanding why some people risk their lives while others do nothing is the work of social psychologists. In the previous chapter we focused on the cognitive processes people use to try to understand themselves and others. In this chapter we will address motives, emotions and behaviours that emerge in social interaction. We begin by examining interpersonal attraction and relationships, from brief encounters through to long-term love relationships. We then turn to two very different forms of social interaction: altruism and aggression. Next we investigate the influence of other people on the way individuals behave and consider what happens when individuals participate in groups. We conclude by placing the psychology of our era in its social and historical context and returning to some of the central themes with which we begin this chapter.

Throughout, we address a central question. To what extent does our behaviour depend on the groups of which we are a part? In other words, do the same psychological principles apply when people are alone as when they are with groups? Can we understand social behaviour through principles of individual psychology, or do people function differently when they are together? And how do social and cultural change affect individual psychology?

Central questions

- To what extent does behaviour depend on the groups of which people are a part?
- Can we understand individual psychology apart from social psychology?

Relationships

People affiliate, or seek out and spend time with others, for many reasons. Sometimes they interact to accomplish instrumental goals, such as raising money for a charity or meeting over dinner to discuss a business deal. Other interactions reflect family ties, shared interests, desires for companionship or sexual interest (Fiske, 1992; Kelman, 2006; Mills & Clark, 1994). Here we focus on two lines of research: one that examines the factors that attract people to each other and another that explores a particular kind of attraction in enduring relationships — love.

APPLY + DISCUSS

Online social networks such as Twitter, Facebook and LinkedIn have exploded in popularity. Using text, video, photographs and quizzes, users build up a personal profile that they project to the world and enmesh themselves in wider social networks by linking with online 'friends'. Users are able to develop networks of people with similar interests and outlooks. They share their moods, thoughts and desires online and develop close ties with 'friends' who may live on the other side of the world. Some people spend several hours each day logged onto social networking sites and have them running in the background whenever they are online.

- Why do you think the new online social networking sites are so popular, particularly among teenagers and young adults?
- Are these new technologies changing the nature of relationships in the modern world? To what extent do you think they are simply a modern manifestation of our innate need to belong?

Factors leading to interpersonal attraction

Although everyone likes to be alone at times, most people thrive on their relationships with others. Indeed, social psychologists believe that humans have a great ***need to belong***, to be involved in relationships with others (Baumeister & Leary, 1995; Pickett, Gardner, & Knowles, 2004). Much of what we do and do not do is to ensure that we remain included by important others and avoid being excluded. Given this intense need to belong, what determines the individuals with whom we choose to be included? What draws us to some people but not to others? According to social psychologists, several key factors determine ***interpersonal attraction***, the reasons people choose to spend time with other people.

Proximity

Sometimes the reason people spend time with particular others is as simple as proximity. Numerous studies have documented that people tend to choose their friends and lovers from individuals nearby.

Proximity plays an equally important role in romantic relationships. As one observer wryly commented, 'Cherished notions about romantic love notwithstanding, the chances are about 50–50 that the "one and only" lives within walking distance' (Eckland, cited in Buss & Schmitt, 1993, p. 205). Social–psychological research has repeatedly shown that situational influences such as proximity (or merely being the first on the scene of a traffic accident) have a remarkably strong impact on behaviour.

Of course, people neither become friends nor fall in love *simply* because the other person is within walking distance. Rather, proximity allows people to get to know one another. It also sets the stage for familiarity, and familiarity tends to breed affection (Zajonc, 1968, 1998). From an evolutionary perspective, the link between familiarity and liking may be part of our genetic endowment. People who are familiar are likely to be safe, and they are likely to be relatives or alliance partners.

Increased proximity and familiarity with someone initially disliked, however, can lead to increasing dislike over time if nothing changes to 'dislodge' the initial impression (Festinger, Schachter, & Back, 1950; Klinger & Greenwald, 1994). At the same time, proximity may lead to negative feelings even for those we initially liked, a phenomenon referred to as environmental spoiling (Ebbesen, Kjos, & Konecni, 1976). Being in close proximity to others exposes us to their bad habits and qualities as well as their good ones. If the bad outweigh the good, environmental spoiling occurs.

Although previous research has shown a strong relationship between proximity and interpersonal attraction, it is evident that it is interaction accessibility, rather than close physical proximity, that really determines attraction (Berscheid & Reis, 1998). With the widespread use of the internet, interaction accessibility takes on a whole new meaning. Defining proximity in terms of the accessibility of others widens the scope of people to whom a person might be attracted.

Interpersonal rewards

A second factor that influences interpersonal attraction is the degree to which interaction with another person is rewarding. From a behaviourist point of view, the more people associate a relationship with reward, the more likely they are to affiliate (Byrne & Murnen, 1988; Clark & Pataki, 1995; Newcomb, 1956).

One ingenious experiment tested a classical conditioning theory of attraction: that children should prefer other children they meet under enjoyable conditions (Lott & Lott, 1974). The investigators placed Year 1 and Year 3 students in groups of three. They gave some of the children a chance to succeed on a task, rewarding them for it, and rigged the task so that others would fail. Later, they asked the children to name a classmate they would like to take on a family holiday. One out of four children in the success condition chose a child who had participated in the study with them, compared to only one in 20 children in the failure condition.

Social exchange theories, based on behaviourist principles, consider reciprocal reward the foundation of relationships (Homans, 1961). In this view, in the social as in the economic 'market', people try to maximise the value they can obtain with their resources (Kenrick, Groth, Trost, & Sadalla, 1993; Li, Bailey, Kenrick, & Linsenmeier, 2002). Or to put it another way, choosing a relationship is like trying to get the maximum return on your investment. The resources (products available for 'investment') in social relationships are personal assets: physical attractiveness, wit, charm, intelligence, material goods and the like. In romantic relationships, people tend to choose others of similar value (as culturally defined) because both partners are trying to maximise the value of their mate.

Similarity

A third factor that influences attraction is similarity. People tend to choose casual acquaintances, as well as mates and best friends, on the basis of shared attitudes, values and interests. One study periodically assessed the attitudes and patterns of affiliation of incoming male university transfer students assigned to the same dormitory (Newcomb, 1961). Over the course of the semester, as the students had a chance to learn one another's attitudes, friendship patterns began to match initial attitude profiles. Surrounding oneself with like-minded others seems to be rewarding, leading to the kind of interpersonal reinforcement described by social exchange theorists.

Folk wisdom that 'birds of a feather flock together' thus tends to have more than a grain of truth. Thus, what do we make of the opposite adage, that 'opposites attract'? Although people tend to like others who share their values and attitudes, they often prefer being with people whose resources, needs or behavioural styles complement their own (Dryer & Horowitz, 1997; Markey & Markey, 2007; Pilkington, Tesser, & Stephens, 1991). For example, dominant people tend to prefer to interact with others who are more submissive, and vice versa.

Physical attractiveness

A final factor that influences interpersonal attraction is physical attractiveness (chapter 17). Even in non-sexual relationships, physically attractive people are magnets (Berscheid & Reis, 1998; Eagly, Ashmore, Makhijani, & Longo, 1991). Attractive premature babies gained more weight and had shorter hospital stays than those perceived as less attractive by nursing staff, perhaps because they received more nurturing from carers (Badr & Abdallah, 2001). Attractive children tend to be more popular among their peers and are treated more leniently by adults (Clifford & Walster, 1973; Dion & Berscheid, 1974). Attractive adults receive more cooperation and assistance from others (Sigall, Page, & Brown, 1971), better job recommendations (Cash, Gillen, & Burns, 1977) and higher pay (Hamermesh & Biddle, 1994) than do less attractive people. They also rate their interactions with others on a daily basis as more pleasant than do people who are less attractive (Reis, Nezlek, & Wheeler, 1980).

The matching hypothesis suggests that people choose partners of equal attractiveness.

Not surprisingly, physical attractiveness tends to have a greater impact on romantic than non-romantic relationships (Fletcher, Simpson, Thomas, & Giles, 1999; Sprecher & Regan, 2002; see also Shackelford, Schmitt, & Buss, 2005). Attractiveness is a major, if not *the* major, criterion university students use in judging initial attraction (e.g. Curran & Lippold, 1975; Walster, Aronson, Abrahams, & Rottman, 1966). One study asked students to indicate whether they were attracted to strangers pictured in photographs. The experimenters gave another group the same photographs but stapled them to surveys showing the strangers' attitudes. Information about the strangers' attitudes had virtually no effect (Byrne, London, & Reeves, 1968). At first meeting, attraction appears to be skin deep.

Given that only a small percentage of people can occupy the choice locations on the bell curve of attractiveness, how do the rest of us ever get a date? In reality, people follow the ***matching hypothesis***, choosing partners they perceive to be equally attractive to themselves, not necessarily the most beautiful or handsome (Berscheid, Dion, Walster, & Walster, 1971; Yela & Sangrador, 2001). One set of studies clarified how and why this happens. In one condition, male participants were told that a number of different women would gladly date them; in the other condition, they were offered no such assurance. Men in the second condition chose less attractive partners. By doing so, they were apparently trying to maximise the beauty of their partner while minimising their risk of rejection (see Huston, 1973).

Across a number of studies, the average correlation between rated attractiveness of members of a couple is around $r = .50$, suggesting that people do indeed tend to find someone of equivalent attractiveness (Feingold, 1988). In economic terms, one of the major 'assets' people take on the dating 'market' is their appearance, and they tend to exchange 'goods' of relatively equal value.

Standards of physical attractiveness vary tremendously from culture to culture (and from individual to individual; Berscheid & Reis, 1998). Nevertheless, views of beauty are not entirely culture specific. People across the world tend to rate facial attractiveness in similar ways (Berscheid & Reis, 1998; Cunningham, Roberts, Barbee, Druen, & Wu, 1995; Dion, 2002; Wheeler & Kim, 1997), with correlations between raters across cultures generally exceeding .60. Several studies have also found that infants in the West who have not yet been socialised to norms of physical beauty gaze longer at faces rated attractive by adults. This occurs whether the faces are of adults or infants, males or females, and regardless of race (Langlois, Ritter, Roggman, & Vaughn, 1991). At an American Psychological Society Annual Convention, Professor Judith Langlois argued that both children and adults can more quickly perceive and categorise attractive faces, like those of Miss Universe contestants, than unattractive ones. Langlois suggested that this phenomenon may explain why we associate positive attributes with beauty and lay the foundation for later, social preferences for attractive people (Dingfelder, 2006).

Infants and adults prefer to look at beautiful faces, like that of celebrity chef Curtis Stone. At least some of the success that Curtis has enjoyed as a media personality may be because of his naturally good looks. Here, he is shown on Hamilton Island in Queensland with US talk show host Oprah Winfrey.

Why does physical attractiveness play such a role in interpersonal attraction? Research in neuroscience suggests that eye contact with a physically attractive individual activates an area in the brain called the ventral striatum (Kampe, Frith, Dolan, & Frith, 2001). When the eye contact is broken, activity in this area of the brain decreases. This particular area of the brain is associated with reward. Thus, eye contact with an attractive person stimulates activity in a reward centre of the brain, whereas loss of eye contact with an attractive other decreases activity and thus reward.

Just how shallow are we?

The research on interpersonal attraction described thus far suggests that we humans are a shallow lot indeed. What we most desire is someone a few doors down, who brings us a cold drink on a warm afternoon, reminds us of ourselves, and looks at least as equally as good as we do. It also won't hurt if they share physical similarities with a model or Miss Universe contestant, or facial features not too dissimilar to those of celebrity chef Curtis Stone.

We may be shallow creatures, but probably not quite that shallow. An important caveat about this body of research is that most studies were conducted in brief laboratory encounters between university students who did not know each other. Although all the identified factors are probably important, the extent to which each influences interpersonal attraction outside this special circumstance is not clear. People tend to emphasise physical attractiveness more during the late teens and early twenties than in any other life stage. Concerns about identity in late adolescence also probably promote a preference for peers who are similar because they reinforce the individual's sense of identity (Sears, 1986).

University students may not be representative for research on relationships. Studies using broader community samples have found that marital satisfaction is typically high initially, lower during child-rearing years (especially when children are toddlers) and higher again once the children leave home, particularly during retirement (Sillars & Zietlow, 1993; Tsang, Harvey, Duncan, & Sommer, 2003).

Love

Researchers aware of these limitations have turned their attention to long-term adult love relationships (Berscheid & Reis, 1998) in an attempt to convert this enigmatic experience from sonnets to statistics, or from poetry to *p* values.

APPLY + DISCUSS

A defining feature of some severe personality disorders is indifference to social contact.

- Are humans 'born to love' — that is, do we innately need other people?
- Are people who do not seek relationships genuinely disordered, or is this simply a cultural value judgement?

Classifying love

At considerable risk to themselves from Cupid's arrows, some researchers have tried to classify love. One important distinction is that between passionate and companionate love (Hatfield, 1988). ***Passionate love*** is a wildly emotional condition, marked by intense physiological arousal and absorption in another

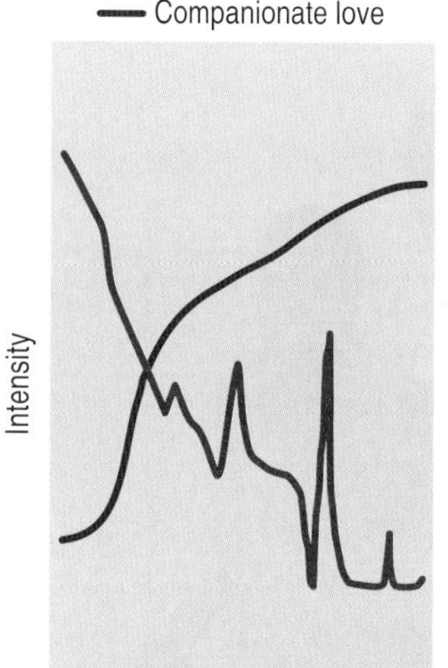

FIGURE 18.1
Passionate and companionate love in a long-term relationship. The figure depicts the intensity of two kinds of love over time. Passionate love is high at the beginning of a relationship but tends to diminish over time, with periodic resurgences, or 'peaks'. Companionate love usually grows over time.

person. It is the stuff of Hollywood movies, sleepless nights and daytime fantasies. In contrast, ***companionate love*** involves deep affection, friendship and emotional intimacy. It grows over time through shared experiences and increasingly takes the place of passionate love — which, alas, does not last forever. However, the two kinds of love generally coexist (figure 18.1), and people experience resurgences of passionate love throughout long relationships (Baumeister & Bratslavsky, 1999).

Another classification, the triangular theory of love, divides love into three components: intimacy (feelings of closeness), passion (sensual arousal) and commitment (dedication to the other person and to the relationship) (Sternberg, 1988a, 1998b). According to this view, relationships can differ in the extent to which they are based on one component or another. Some, for example, are all passion with little intimacy or commitment. Others involve mixtures of all three (see figure 18.2).

TAXONOMY OF KINDS OF LOVE

Kind of love	*Intimacy*	*Passion*	*Decision/ commitment*
Non-love	–	–	–
Liking	+	–	–
Infatuated love	–	+	–
Empty love	–	–	+
Romantic love	+	+	–
Compassionate love	+	–	+
Fatuous love	–	+	+
Consummate love	+	+	+

FIGURE 18.2
The triangular theory of love, + = component present; – = component absent. These kinds of love represent idealised cases based on the triangular theory. Most loving relationships will fit between categories, because the components of love occur in varying degrees, rather than being simply present or absent.

SOURCE: Sternberg (1987).

Yet another conceptualisation views love as a story that reflects a person's expectations and beliefs about love (Sternberg, 1998a, 2001b). At least 25 different love stories exist, including the travelling story (e.g. love is a journey that begins when you first meet someone), the gardening story (e.g. relationships must not be left unattended or they will die), and the horror story (e.g. love involves one or both partners being afraid of one another). No one love story necessarily predicts greater success in a relationship than another. Rather, people who enjoy the greatest satisfaction in their relationships are those whose love stories are similar to one another. Two people who both define love as a journey will be likely to feel more compatible than a couple in which one individual views love as a horror story and the other sees love as a gardening story.

An evolutionary perspective

From an evolutionary perspective, the feelings and behaviours we associate with the concept of love are evolved mechanisms that tend to lead to reproductive success (Birnbaum & Reis, 2006; Buss & Kenrick, 1998). Caring for offspring (parental love), courtship, sexual intimacy and concern for family all maximise the likelihood that we, and those related to us, will reproduce (and survive to reproduce in the future). Romantic love, in this view, is an adaptation that fostered the reproductive success of our ancestors by bonding two people likely to become parents of an infant who would need their reliable care (Hazan & Shaver, 1987).

Neither love nor lust, however, inevitably leads to monogamous marriage. In fact, a relatively permanent union of two individuals is just one mating strategy that occurs across species (Widmer, Treas, & Newcomb, 1998). Even among humans, 80 percent of cultures have practised polygamy, which permits men multiple wives or mistresses. In Western cultures, premarital sex is virtually ubiquitous, and roughly half of married people at some point have extramarital affairs (Buss & Schmitt, 1993).

Sexual strategies

Evolutionary psychologists have studied the ***sexual strategies*** (tactics used in selecting mates) people use in different kinds of relationships, from brief romantic liaisons to marriages (Buss & Kenrick, 1998; Buss & Schmitt, 1993; see also Bozon, 2001). Whereas many researchers studying interpersonal attraction and relationships generalise across genders, evolutionary theorists argue that males and females face very different selection pressures and hence have evolved different sexual strategies. Because a man can have a virtually infinite number of offspring if he obtains enough willing partners, he can maximise his reproductive success by spreading his seed widely, inseminating as many fertile females as possible. In contrast, women can bear only a limited number of children, and they make an enormous initial investment in their offspring during nine months of gestation. As a result, women should be choosier about their mating partners and select only those who can and will commit resources to them and their offspring.

Is love unique to humans?

From these basic differences ensues a battle of the sexes. Females maximise their reproductive success by forcing males with resources to commit to them in return for sexual access. The short- and long-term mating strategies of females should be relatively similar.

For males, in contrast, short- and long-term sexual strategies may be very different. In the short term, the female with the greatest reproductive value is one who is both fertile (young) and readily available for copulation. In the long run, committed relationships provide exclusive sexual access to a female, which allows the male to contribute resources to offspring without uncertainty about paternity (chapter 1). Long-term relationships also bring potential alliances and resources from the woman's family. Thus, for long-term relationships, men should prefer less promiscuous partners who are young enough to produce many offspring and attractive enough to elicit arousal over time and increase the man's status. Men should also be choosier in long-term than in short-term encounters because the women chosen for a long-term relationship will provide half the genes of the offspring in whom they invest.

Aspects of this portrait of male and female sexual strategies probably sound familiar to anyone who has ever dated, although, of course, cultural and historical factors have substantial influences on sexual behaviour as well (chapter 10). Consider the Casanova who professes commitment and then turns out a few months later not to be ready for it; the man who gladly sleeps with a woman on a first date but then does not want to see her again, certainly not for a long-term relationship; or the woman who only dates men of high status and earning potential. From an evolutionary perspective, these are well-known figures because they exemplify common mating strategies.

Furthermore, it appears that traditional gender differences in mate selection remain robust in modern Western cultures. For example, Fletcher, Tither, O'Loughlin, Friesen, and Overall (2004) from the University of Canterbury, New Zealand, examined the mating preferences of 100 male and 100 female students. Half the sample were currently involved in a long-term heterosexual relationship, while the other half were currently not sexually active. Fletcher et al. (2004) found that both men and women rate warmth/trustworthiness in their partners as important, regardless of the length of the relationship. Consistent with previous research, Fletcher et al. (2004) further found that women (relative to men) prefer warmth/trustworthiness and status/resources in a potential mate and rate attractiveness/vitality as less important. Importantly, Fletcher et al. (2004) showed that the relationship context is important in mate selection — both men and women prefer to live in a permanent relationship with a warm and homely person as opposed to a cold and attractive person. However, in the short-term 'fling' relationship, both men and women prefer high levels of attractiveness and vitality.

A recent survey that looked at the dating habits of 7000 Australians revealed some interesting results (Nielsen, 2010). A high percentage of Australians have used online dating sites to find a partner, and the top five criteria for finding a mate are considered to be (in order of importance): (1) personality, (2) sense of humour, (3) morals, (4) manners and (5) sexual chemistry. The survey confirmed gender differences in mate selection, with looks being of higher importance to men (86 percent of men considered looks to be important, versus only 69 percent of women) and a partner's career success being more highly valued by women (rated as important by 69 percent of women, versus only 47 percent of men). Women also rated income as being comparatively more important in finding their 'Mr Right' (considered important by 69 percent of women but only 33 percent of men).

The empirical evidence

How well do the data support these evolutionary predictions? Although the differences between the sexes are not always enormous, they tend to be consistent. For example, Fisman, Iyengar, Kamenica, and Simonson (2006) examined gender differences in mate selection using a speed-dating experiment and found that females put greater weight on the intelligence and race of the partner, while men prefer

APPLY + DISCUSS

According to a recent survey, 25 percent of Australians have used an online dating site (Nielsen, 2010). Over 1.6 million Australians are members of the nation's largest online dating site, RSVP (RSVP, 2010), and more online dating sites are being created for tailored demographic groups (e.g. people looking for a partner with a particular religious affiliation and so on). Social networking sites, such as Facebook, also offer opportunities for creating an online profile that can lead to love.

Some researchers have examined the content of personal advertisements to test the evolutionary view of men as success objects and women as sex objects (Baize & Schroeder, 1995; Davis, 1990; Mills, 1995).

- To what extent do personal ads support or not support evolutionary hypotheses? Would your own personal ad fit evolutionary theory?
- How else could gender differences in ads be explained? What other factors affect the qualities potential suitors 'advertise' and seek?

physical attractiveness in their partner. They further observed that men do not value women's intelligence when it is judged to exceed their own. As expected, women prefer men from affluent neighbourhoods. Similarly, a study of 37 cultures found that in all but one, males tended to value the physical attractiveness of their mates more than females, whereas females were more concerned than males about the resources a spouse could provide (Buss & Angleitner, 1989; see also Buss, 2006). Males also consistently prefer females who are younger and hence have greater reproductive potential. Females prefer males who are older and hence are more likely to possess resources (Buss & Schmitt, 1993; Kenrick & Keefe, 1992; Kenrick et al., 1993). Figure 18.3 shows the results of some tests of evolutionary hypotheses in several cultures.

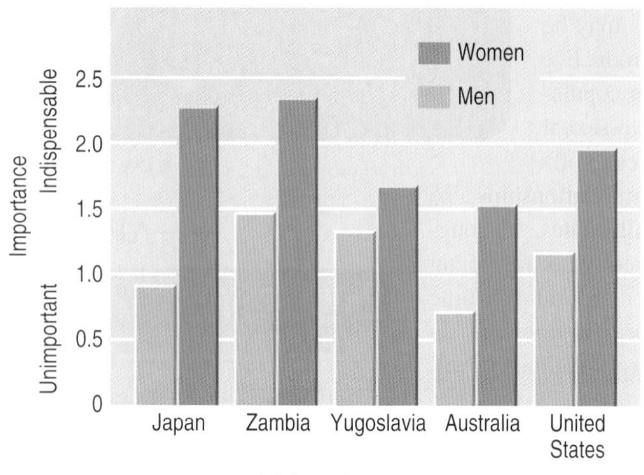

(a) Good financial prospect

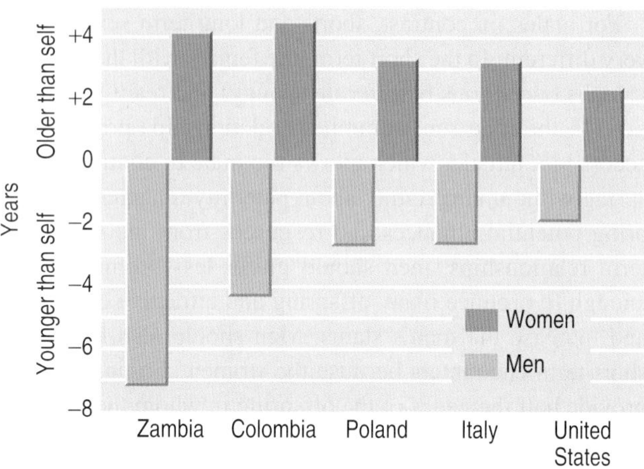

(b) Age difference preferred between self and spouse

FIGURE 18.3
Preferred characteristics of mates across cultures. Across cultures, financial prospects are more important to females than males in choosing a mate (a). Nearly everywhere, males prefer females who are younger, while females prefer males who are older (b).

SOURCE: Buss and Schmitt (1993, pp. 204–232).

More recently, Fieder and Huber (2007) of the University of Vienna examined a database of more than 10 000 Swedish men and women and found that both men and women have more children when the father is a few years older than the mother. On average, men prefer a partner who is 5.92 years younger than them, and women prefer a partner who is 3.97 years older (Fieder & Huber, 2007). These statistics are consistent with global averages and support the notion that evolution is involved when it comes to sex and marriage (Henderson, 2007).

These evolutionary hypotheses are, of course, controversial and some of the assertions regarding sexual infidelity and jealousy have not gone unchallenged (see Grice & Seely, 2000; Hanko, Master, & Sabini, 2004). Some critics argue that they could be used to justify a double standard ('Honey, I couldn't help it, it's in my genes') or date rape (i.e. males have an 'innate' tendency to see women as sexually more interested in them than they are). Others argue that the social learning of gender roles could produce similar results (see chapter 13). From this point of view, increasing gender equality in a given culture should erode gender differences in mate preferences, a hypothesis that has received some empirical support (Eagly & Wood, 1999), but which is vigorously challenged by other research (Gangestad, Haselton, & Buss, 2006; Schmitt, 2007).

Further, evolutionary theory does not adequately explain the large numbers of extramarital affairs among females, the choice to limit family size or remain childless among couples in Western cultures with plenty of resources or homosexuality (although evolutionary theorists have attempted to offer explanations for all these apparently 'evolutionarily maladaptive' phenomena). Nevertheless, evolutionary theory offers some very challenging explanations for phenomena that are not otherwise easily explained. When tempered by a recognition of the role of culture in channelling evolved reproductive tendencies, evolutionary theory provides a powerful source of testable hypotheses.

MAKING CONNECTIONS

Attachment theorists argue that people pattern their adult love relationships on the mental models they constructed of earlier attachment relationships. Thus, the way individuals love as adults — particularly whether they are secure or insecure in their attachments — tends to reflect the way they loved and were loved as children (chapter 13).

Romantic love as attachment

Another theory of love based on evolutionary principles comes from attachment theory. Romantic love relationships share several features with attachment relationships in infancy and childhood (Hazan & Diamond, 2000; Kafetsios & Nezlek, 2002; Shaver, Collins, & Clark, 1996). Adults feel security in their lover's arms, desire physical proximity to them and experience distress when their lover is away for a considerable period or cannot be located (Shaver, Hazan, & Bradshaw, 1988). Adults respond to wartime and job-related marital separations with much the same pattern of depression, anger and anxiety as that observed in childhood separations, suggesting that attachment processes continue into adulthood (Vormbrock, 1993). Romantic love also brings security, contentment and joy, like the satisfaction an infant feels in its mother's arms.

The bond between lovers does, of course, differ from infant attachment. Care for offspring and sexuality are components of adult romantic love absent from infant attachment. Nevertheless, the love between infant and mother and between two lovers may have more in common than may first appear.

Attachment styles may be especially evident in adults when they are under stress because the attachment system is activated by threats to security. One study examined coping mechanisms among Israeli university students during the Gulf War, when Iraq was bombarding civilian areas of Israel (Mikulincer, Florian, & Hirschberger, 1993). Participants who lived in areas directly threatened by missile attacks differed from one another in the ways they coped with the danger. Securely attached participants tended to seek support from others and generally experienced less distress from the bombings. Avoidantly attached people used distancing strategies (such as 'I tried to forget about the whole thing'). Their distress was manifested primarily in physical symptoms, as might be expected given their difficulty experiencing emotional distress consciously. Ambivalently attached participants used coping strategies aimed at calming themselves and quelling their emotions, which makes sense given their high level of conscious distress.

A GLOBAL VISTA

Love in cross-cultural perspective

Western theorists were not the first to recognise a link between infant and adult love. The Japanese have a concept of love that combines the experience of attachment and dependence, called *amae*, derived from the word for 'sweet' (Doi, 1992). *Amae* is both what infants desire with their mothers and what adults feel in the presence of their beloved.

Although adult romantic love may have its origins in the biological proclivity of infants to form attachments, by the time people have participated in relationships for 15 to 20 years, their manner of loving as adults is highly influenced by their culture (Dion & Dion, 1996). Many societies have arranged marriages, which are as much economic bonds linking families or clans as personal and sexual bonds between lovers. In parts of India where marriages have traditionally been arranged, people may experience passionate love, but they typically hide it (Traiwick, 1990). Public displays of affection are avoided, although they are tolerated more between an unmarried than a married couple.

Chinese culture, too, has historically expected couples to consider their obligations to family in choosing a marriage partner: 'Westerners ask, "How does my heart feel?" A Chinese asks, "What will other people say?" ' (Hsu, 1981, p. 50). Indeed, in Chinese culture, love is so secondary to family obligations that the term *love* does not refer to a legitimate, socially sanctioned relationship between a man and a woman but connotes an illicit, shameful affair (see also Dion & Dion, 1988). In feudal China, passionate love was likely to constitute a reason why a couple should *not* marry. The female protagonist in Chinese love stories was more likely to be a concubine than a woman eligible for marriage. The marriage contract was signed by the fathers of the bride and groom; the engaged couple was not required to endorse the contract (Lang, 1946).

Does the passionate, romantic love seen on movie screens exist everywhere, or is it a Western (or Hollywood) creation? Recent Australian research (Nielsen, 2010) showed that 74 percent of all Australians aspire to spend the rest of their lives with just one person. Jackson and Cram (2003) found that young New Zealand women tend to believe they will meet 'Prince Charming' and live happily ever after — a fairytale expectation of love. Romantic, passionate love probably does not exist *everywhere*, but it is common across cultures. A study using data from 42 hunter-gatherer societies from around the globe (compiled by anthropologists over the last century) found evidence of romantic love in 26 of them, or about 60 percent (Harris, 1995). Only six cultures allowed pure individual choice of marital partners, however; the other 36 required some degree of parental control, either in the form of veto power or arranged marriages.

Why is the concept of romantic love so central to contemporary Western cultures that it fills our fairy tales (e.g. *Cinderella*, *Sleeping Beauty*) and movie screens? In a paradoxical way, the *individualism* of countries such as Australia may in part explain our preoccupation with passionate coupling. Contemporary Western cultures are unique in their focus on individual satisfaction as a valued end. This orientation extends into relationships, which are viewed as vehicles for personal gratification. Just 30 years ago, marriage in the West was something people entered and rarely exited. Today, if a marriage is unsatisfying, people often opt to leave and seek passion or satisfaction elsewhere. Romantic love may be a human potential, but cultures shape the ways we love — and leave.

Maintaining relationships

Maintaining a relationship over time is no easy task. Oscar Wilde once quipped that the chains of matrimony are so heavy that it often takes three to carry them. Relationships pass through many phases (Borden & Levinger, 1991; Huston, 1994), and the majority of marriages in Australia and some other Western countries now end in divorce. The real question may not be what causes relationships to end but what allows some to last for 50 years or more! Indeed, Robyn Parker from the Australian Institute of Family Studies examined how to create and maintain long and enduring marriages. Parker (2002) argued that lasting marriages can be conceptualised as reflecting (a) characteristics of the couple and their marriage, and (b) how the couple has dealt with everyday hassles and unusual stressors encountered throughout the marriage. Parker suggested that 'in addition to the basic elements of love, trust and respect, characteristics common to lasting marriages include: commitment to the spouse and the relationship; willingness to adapt, change and compromise; sharing, friendship and liking; containment and resolution of conflict; mutuality, reciprocity and fairness; having children, and physical and psychological intimacy' (p. 23). The distinguishing feature of enduring marriages is the sense of 'coupleness': both spouses are committed to making the marriage work, and both are willing to invest time and effort in preserving the emotional intimacy that attracted them to each other in the first place (Parker, 2002).

In part, people decide whether to stay in a relationship by weighing its relative costs and benefits (Kelley & Thibaut, 1978; Levinger, 1976; Rusbult & Van Lange, 2003; Wieselquist, Rusbult, Foster, & Agnew, 1999). Whether a person remains committed over time depends on the balance of pleasure and discomfort it brings. Commitment to a relationship also depends on how much the person has invested in it and what the alternatives look like (Rusbult & Van Lange, 2003). People will tend to stay in a relatively unhappy marriage if they feel they have put so much into it that they cannot leave and if they do not think they can do any better. The top reasons that Australians break up with a partner include growing apart and having nothing in common, having different aspirations and values, and a partner being unfaithful. Recent Australian research suggests that men are more inclined than women to end a relationship because of a lack of sexual chemistry/attraction, while women are more inclined to end a relationship because their partners don't want to make a commitment or get married (Nielsen, 2010).

A couple's wedding day is like a fairytale come true, but maintaining a relationship over time is no easy task.

Researchers interested in long-term relationships have attempted to track down the causes of marital satisfaction, dissatisfaction and dissolution (Gottman, 1998; see also Parker, 2002). For example, people with successful relationships know how to stop spirals of negative reciprocity, in which one person's hostile or aversive behaviour (e.g. sarcastic criticism) provokes a counterattack, leading to an escalation of conflict (Rusbult, Verette, Whitney, Slovik, & Lipkus, 1991; chapter 16). One of the most characteristic features of marriages that last is the ability to stop such cycles and to avoid the simmering feelings of hatred and disgust they tend to breed.

People in satisfying relationships also tend to make relatively benign attributions of their partners' actions, giving them the benefit of the doubt in difficult situations (Fletcher, 2002; Karney & Bradbury, 2000). People in satisfying relationships also frame their thinking about how to change the relationship in terms of how to approach a better relationship ('How can we become closer?') than how to escape a bad one ('How can we stop drifting apart?') (Gable & Reis, 1999). If anything unites these factors, it is probably the tendency both to accept the other person as he or she is, and to avoid repetitive and spiralling aversive encounters.

People whose relationships are stable also tend to overlook or 'reframe' each other's faults. Studies of both dating and married couples across cultures find that people report greater satisfaction with — and stay longer in — relationships when they have a somewhat idealised or moderately unrealistically positive perception of their partner (Endo, Heine, & Lehman, 2000; Murray & Holmes, 1997, 1999). These findings make sense in the light of research on 'positive illusions', which suggests that people often enhance their sense of wellbeing by holding mildly positive illusions about who they are and what they can accomplish (chapter 10).

Most people reap substantial rewards from their partners' slightly idealised views of them. However, people with low self-esteem (chapter 17) have difficulty taking advantage of their partners' illusions. Despite the fact that their partners tend to hold idealised views of them, people with low self-esteem have difficulty basking in the warm glow of spousal unreality and instead assume that their own negative view of themselves is shared by their partner (Murray, Holmes, & Griffin, 2000). When threatened, people with low self-esteem tend to doubt their partner's regard even more; in contrast, those with high self-esteem respond by inflating their beliefs about their partners' regard for them and hence use the relationship to insulate themselves from negative feelings, particularly about themselves (Murray, Holmes, MacDonald, & Ellsworth, 1998).

Psychology as a profession is adopting preventive action in the form of relationship education. In Australia, inventory programs such as PREPARE/ENRICH and FOCUS are widely used. They typically involve sessions with an 'educator' such as a psychologist, social worker, counsellor or religious leader and may also include some skills training (Bradley, 2002). An example of a skills-based program is the Prevention and Relationship Enhancement Program (PREP) co-developed by Professor Howard Markman. According to Markman (as cited in Bradley, 2002, p. 16), the PREP curriculum teaches couples 'simple tools for problem-solving and for identifying common hidden issues in their relationships. They also learn how to protect, preserve and restore fun, friendship, love and sensuality in their relationships — a powerful set of principles for sacrificing, forgiveness and commitment.'

Predicting relationship satisfaction — perception or reality?

By Doctor Bruce Findlay, Swinburne University of Technology

There is a considerable body of research on the predictors of relationship satisfaction, dissatisfaction and dissolution. Couples come to relationships with considerable psychological 'baggage'. This includes, but is not limited to, their experiences in their family of origin; their experiences of previous relationships, not only in their own relationships but also in those of others close to them; their intelligence; and their personality.

One aspect of personality that has been widely studied by social and personality psychologists is called attachment style (see chapter 13). Research suggests that the pattern of attachment in infancy and early childhood persists into adulthood and is applied to interactions with romantic partners. Modern conceptualisations of adult attachment include the argument that underlying secure, avoidant and anxious attachment styles are the primary factors of anxiety about relationships and avoidance of intimacy. In relationship research, these factors tend to be measured using self-report questionnaires, such as the Experiences in Close Relationships Scale (Fraley, Waller, & Brennan, 2000).

Another characteristic that couples bring to relationships is emotional intelligence (EI) — the ability to recognise their own and others' feelings and to use this knowledge to manage their own and others' behaviour. There is ongoing controversy among researchers about whether EI is an aspect of intelligence or of personality. Many of the most popular measures consider it to be a mix both of these, and to tell more about an individual than any one single measure of either intelligence or personality. Such measures are also usually quantified via self-report questionnaires.

A third characteristic that couples bring to relationships is how they deal with conflict. In even the best relationships, conflict, or at least disagreement, is bound to occur. Such disagreements are not bad in themselves; it is how they are dealt with that affects the success of the relationship. A good deal of research has found that successful conflict resolution is strongly predictive of successful relationships.

Karen Johnson (2010), a Doctor of Psychology student at Swinburne University of Technology, Melbourne, examined the attachment styles, conflict resolution styles, emotional intelligence and relationship satisfaction of 111 heterosexual couples in long-term marital relationships with dependent children. Their mean length of relationship was 17 years. What was particularly interesting about Karen's study was that while she asked participants to complete measures of their own attachment, EI, conflict strategies, and relationship satisfaction, she also asked them to complete measures of their perception of their partner's EI and conflict strategies.

Unsurprisingly, individuals' attachment security correlated positively with their relationship satisfaction, and poor conflict strategies correlated negatively with it. In particular, avoidance of intimacy was one of the strongest predictors of low relationship satisfaction, as was ineffective arguing. Interestingly, when it came to emotional intelligence, both husbands' and wives' relationship satisfaction was best predicted by how emotionally intelligent they perceived their partner to be.

There are several important implications of Karen's study for relationship counsellors. One is that the aspect of attachment that best predicts possible problems in relationships is avoidance of intimacy. Together with ineffective arguing styles, this suggests that not engaging with a partner when differences arise is not good for the relationship. It may be because a partner has not learnt effective ways of dealing with differences. It may also be because the level of intimacy required in dealing with things that are important to an intimate partner, but are different from what is of personal importance, is too threatening. In either case, a therapist can hone in on important aspects of couple behaviour that, with appropriate help, can allow a couple to improve their relationship.

Another implication of Karen's study is that thinking that a partner is emotionally intelligent, whether they are or not, is good for a relationship. This confirms research on the 'rose-coloured glasses' effect, which has found that in other aspects of relationships, it is good to be slightly unrealistic in favour of a partner. Karen's work shows this to be true well beyond the usual 'honeymoon' phase of relationships, especially in the important area of emotional behaviour.

The dark side of relationships

Alas, not everyone is able to hold on to idealised perceptions of their partner or to put a positive spin on repetitive, annoying behaviours. People often meet their greatest criticism and experience their deepest hurts within their close relationships.

> On any given day, 44% of us are likely to be annoyed by a close relational partner . . . On average, young adults encounter 8.7 aggravating hassles in their romantic relationships *each week* . . . Most people (66%) get angry at somebody in any given week . . ., and every seven days *most* young adults will be distressed by different encounters with a lover's (a) criticism, (b) stubbornness, (c) selfishness, *and* (d) lack of conscientiousness, at least once . . . Over time, people are meaner to their intimate partners than to anyone else they know.
>
> Miller (1997, p. 15).

People would not dare criticise the foods their neighbour prepared, yet they quickly point out to their spouses the deficits in their cooking.

The types of annoyances that people perpetrate and experience within their close relationships include complaining, teasing, ostracism, guilt-induction, intentional embarrassment, arrogance, gossip and swearing to name a few (Kowalski, 1997, 2001). On one hand, this behaviour makes sense. Close friends and romantic partners are the people with whom we are closest, with whom we spend the majority of our time and around whom we feel we can be ourselves (including our less appealing selves). On the other hand, many of the pet peeves that people ultimately develop with relationship partners and that, over time, chip away at the relationship are things that initially were appealing or funny (Miller, 1997). A partner's silliness when dating becomes a sign of immaturity five years into the relationship. Furthermore, positive illusions held early in a relationship may become tarnished over time.

MAKING CONNECTIONS

Research across a number of areas consistently finds that negative and positive feelings not only are physiologically distinct but also have independent effects on a variety of outcomes (chapter 10). Parental warmth and hostility each have an impact on a growing child's self-esteem and psychological health, just as the tendency of spouses to display acceptance and warmth towards one another contributes to marital satisfaction independently of the extent to which the couple fights (chapter 17). Some couples with good marriages have 'knock-down-drag-out' arguments but are genuinely loving towards each other most of the time. Others with bad marriages are too indifferent to one another to fight.

In spite of the fact that people can and do list hundreds of annoyances that they have with relationship partners, friends or family (simply type in pet peeve as a search term on the internet and you will find ample evidence of this; Kowalski, Ellis, Hamby, Ritchie, & Starkovich, 2002), some of the most intriguing research centres on ostracism. Within the context of close relationships, ostracism can take the form of the silent treatment, in which one partner refuses to interact with the other, treating him as if he does not exist. The fear of being ostracised or excluded from close relationships motivates much of people's behaviour as they work to maintain their inclusionary status in those relationships (Leary, 2001).

In one study, participants sat in a room with two confederates, or accomplices, of the experimenter. The three individuals could not talk among themselves. However, while the experimenter left the room looking for a fourth participant, one of the confederates discovered a ball and proceeded to throw it to the other two individuals. In the inclusion condition, all three individuals continued to throw the ball to each other for five minutes. In the ostracism condition, the two confederates initially threw the ball to the participant but then begin throwing the ball only to one another, ostracising the participant. Not surprisingly, the participants in the ostracism condition experienced distress, bewildered as to why these other two individuals would choose to exclude them. Some of these individuals simply disengaged from what was going on, whereas others undertook different types of activities, such as fiddling with their hair or looking through their wallets (Williams, 2001).

Whether the behaviour is ostracism, failing to put the toilet seat down or leaving lights on throughout the house, annoyances will always characterise close relationships. The challenge to the couple is to find ways in which they can learn to accommodate one another's pet peeves in constructive and accommodating ways as opposed to destructive and belittling ways.

INTERIM SUMMARY

Several factors lead to interpersonal attraction, including proximity, interpersonal rewards, similarity and physical attractiveness. One taxonomy of love contrasts ***passionate love*** (intense physiological arousal and absorption in another person) with ***companionate love*** (love that involves deep affection and intimacy). Some theorists argue that romantic love is a continuation of attachment mechanisms that first emerge in infancy. Evolutionary theorists emphasise ***sexual strategies***, tactics used in selecting mates, which reflect the different evolutionary selection pressures on males and females. Love appears to be rooted in attachment but is shaped by culture and experience. Maintaining relationships over time is a difficult task. People in satisfying long-term relationships tend to avoid negative spirals, give their partners the benefit of the doubt and hold slightly idealised views of their partners. Nevertheless, all relationships have a dark side characterised by pet peeves and annoyances.

Altruism

One behaviour that appears to have few negative associations and brings people together is ***altruism*** — behaviour that helps other people with no apparent gain or with potential cost to oneself. A person who donates blood, volunteers in a soup kitchen or risks death (like rescuer Joanne Lucas; see the opening vignette) is displaying altruism. Many forms of altruistic behaviour are so common that we take them for granted — holding open a door, giving a stranger directions or trying to make someone feel comfortable during a conversation. According to the Giving Australia Project (Lyons, McGregor-Lowndes, & O'Donoghue, 2006), 13.4 million adult Australians (87% of all adults) gave $5.7 billion to organisations, including mostly private, not-for-profit organisations, in one recent year. Such donations given by individual Australians is greater than those given by Canadians and equivalent to those given by the British, but less than half the proportion given in the United States (Lyons & Passey, 2005). However, analysis of where donations go suggests that such giving is not always altruistic. Lyons and Passey found that most people give to organisations with which they have a prior affiliation, and many such donations would be eligible for a tax deduction. In the 2007–08 income year, individual taxpayers claimed $2346 million worth of gifts, an increase of 24.5 percent from the previous year (Philanthropy Australia, 2010). Lyons et al. (2006) further suggest that a common myth is that giving is spontaneous, although the way Australians and New Zealanders have responded to natural disasters such as the Victorian bushfire crisis, the Queensland floods and the recent Christchurch earthquakes definitely helps support this claim.

Australians give billions of dollars every year to various not-for-profit organisations, and rally behind campaigns to support the victims of natural disasters. Here, a Collingwood footballer lends his support to an appeal held in response to the Victorian bushfire crisis.

We begin this section by examining theories of altruism. We then consider experimental research on a particular form of altruism, bystander intervention.

Theories of altruism

For centuries, philosophers have debated whether any prosocial act — no matter how generous or unselfish it may appear on the surface — is truly altruistic. When people offer money to a homeless person on the street, is their action motivated by a pure desire to help, or are they primarily alleviating their own discomfort? Contemporary research on prosocial behaviour is broad in scope, but can be understood to occur on three levels: micro, meso and macro. At the *micro* level, altruistic tendencies and individual differences are considered primarily in terms of biological processes, developmental and personality factors, or evolutionary theory. At the *meso* level, behaviours of helper–recipient dyads are studied according to specific situations. Prosocial actions at the *macro* level are examined within the context of groups and large organisations, such as volunteering (Penner, Dovidio, Piliavin, & Schroeder, 2005). Various theories underpin our understanding of altruism.

Ethical hedonism

Many philosophers argue for ***ethical hedonism***, the doctrine that all behaviour, no matter how apparently altruistic, is — and should be — designed to increase one's own pleasure or reduce one's own pain. As one observer put it, 'scratch an "altruist" and watch a hypocrite bleed' (Gheslin; cited in Batson, 1995).

APPLY + DISCUSS

During the 2011 Queensland flood crisis, thousands of volunteers signed up to help out people in affected areas in the capital city of Brisbane. Here, residents and volunteers are shown helping with the clean-up effort in the hard-hit suburb of Fairfield. In addition to performing heavy lifting tasks, many of the volunteers faced difficult conditions — smelly, muddy streets were lined with debris; there was the possibly of dangerous snakes, such as brown snakes, getting into people's homes from waterways; and there was a high risk of infection.

Research suggests that people can have many different motivations for engaging in altruism.

- What motivated volunteers in the 2011 Queensland flood crisis to participate in the clean-up effort around Brisbane and in other areas of the state?
- Can you think of any factors (e.g. suburb of residence) that may have affected whether or not some people were at least partially motivated by guilt avoidance in offering to help out?

People have many selfish reasons to behave selflessly (Batson, 1991, 1998). People are frequently motivated by their emotions (chapter 10), and behaving altruistically can produce positive emotions and diminish negative ones. Prosocial acts can also lead to material and social rewards (gifts, thanks and the esteem of others) as well as to positive feelings about oneself that come from meeting ideal-self standards (Penner et al., 2005; Wedekind & Milinski, 2000). Helping may also be motivated by efforts to avoid the guilt associated with not helping (Batson, Ahmed, Lishner, & Tsang, 2002).

Some theorists adopt the aversive-arousal reduction model and explain the motivation to act on another's behalf in terms of empathic distress. Helping relieves the negative feelings aroused through empathy with a person in distress (Batson et al., 2002; Hoffman, 1982). This mechanism does not appear to be unique to humans. In one study, researchers trained rhesus monkeys to pull a chain to receive food (Masserman, Wechkin, & Terris, 1964). Once the monkeys learned the response, the investigators placed another monkey in an adjacent cage, who received an electric shock every time they pulled the chain. Despite the reward, the monkeys stopped pulling the chain, even starving themselves for days to avoid causing the other monkey to suffer. Research with humans suggests, however, that non-altruistic motives for helping take precedence over empathy-based motivations, calling into question, again, whether true altruism really exists (Maner et al., 2002).

Empathising with others apparently does involve actually *feeling* some of what they feel. In one experiment, participants watched videotaped interactions between spouses and were asked to rate the degree of positive or negative affect one of the spouses was feeling at each instant (Levenson & Ruef, 1992). To assess the accuracy of these ratings, the experimenters correlated participants' ratings with the spouses' own ratings of how they felt at each point. Participants who accurately gauged these feelings showed a pattern of physiology similar to the person with whom they were empathising, such as a similar level of skin conductance — but only for unpleasant emotions. In other words, when people 'feel for' another's pain, they do just that — feel something similar, if less intensely — and use this feeling to gauge the other person's feeling. With positive emotions, people apparently use their head instead of their gut.

To the degree that people are genuinely altruistic, they should help regardless of momentary personal or situational variations, such as mood or modelling others' helping. However, these variables do influence helping behaviour, lending additional support to the theory of ethical hedonism (Tsang, 2006). Moods, both good and bad, have a significant effect on helping behaviour. People who are in a good mood help to maintain the positive feelings they have (Salovey, Mayer, & Rosenhan, 1991). People in mild to moderately bad moods help to alleviate their negative mood state (Cialdini & Kenrick, 1976). Even odours have an effect on helping. People provided with the opportunity to help a same-sex individual in a shopping mall by picking up a dropped pen or providing change for a dollar were more likely to help if the incident occurred in the presence of a pleasant fragrance, such as cookies baking or coffee roasting (Baron, 1997).

Genuine altruism

An alternative philosophical position is that people can be genuinely altruistic. Jean-Jacques Rousseau, the French philosopher, proposed that humans have a natural compassion for one another and that the only reason they do not always behave compassionately is that society beats it out of them. Adam Smith, an early capitalist economist, argued that people are generally self-interested but have a natural empathy for one another that leads them to behave altruistically at times. For instance, people across the world, particularly in nearby countries such as Australia, responded with extremely generous aid efforts following the Indian Ocean tsunami disaster in December 2004.

Some experimental evidence suggests that Rousseau and Smith may have been right. People who have the opportunity to escape empathic distress by walking away, or who are offered rewards for doing so, still frequently choose to help someone in distress (Batson, 1991, 2002; Batson & Moran, 1999). People also may behave altruistically for the benefit of a group, usually one with which they identify. Numerous stories of altruism and bravery surfaced following the tragic Bali bombing in October 2002. For example, Jay Solomon and Blake Neate were two of the many young revellers at the Sari Club when the explosions occurred. In the ensuing panic, they were able to climb a wall and helped pull people up and over to safety. They then leaped onto the rafters of an adjoining building and helped two distressed women across the gap, before leaping to safety themselves. The two went out of their way to assist total strangers, despite the risk of injury and possibly even death.

The difficulty in defining an instance of helping as motivated by selfish or selfless motives is in assessing the motives themselves, particularly given that both types of motives may be operative at any one time. Whether or not something is 'true' altruism is missing the point. Even if other motives are operating, if a person's ultimate goal in helping another is to benefit that other person, then the behaviour should be considered altruism (Batson, 2002).

An evolutionary perspective

Evolutionary psychologists have taken the debate about altruism a step further by redefining self-interest as reproductive success (McAndrew, 2002). By this definition, protecting oneself and one's offspring is in an organism's evolutionary 'interest'.

Evidence of this type of altruistic behaviour abounds in the animal kingdom. Some mother birds will feign a broken wing to draw a predator away from their nest, at considerable potential cost to themselves (Wilson, 1975). Chimpanzees 'adopt' orphaned chimps, particularly if they are close relatives (Batson, 1995). If reproductive success is expanded to encompass inclusive fitness (chapter 10), we would expect humans and other animals to care preferentially for themselves, their offspring and their relatives. Organisms that paid little attention to the survival of related others, or animals that indiscriminately invested in kin and non-kin alike, would be less represented in the gene pool with each successive generation. The importance of these evolutionary mechanisms has been documented in humans, who tend to choose to help related others, particularly those who are young (and hence still capable of reproduction), in life-and-death situations (Burnstein, Crandall, & Kitayama, 1994; McAndrew, 2002).

Why, then, do people sometimes behave altruistically towards others unrelated to them? Was Mother Teresa an evolutionary anomaly?

To answer such questions, evolutionary theorists invoke the concept of ***reciprocal altruism***, which holds that natural selection favours animals that behave altruistically if the likely benefit to each individual over time exceeds the likely cost (Caporael & Baron, 1997; Penner et al., 2005). In other words, if the dangers are small but the gains in survival and reproduction are large, altruism is an adaptive strategy.

The same applies to humans. Social organisation for mutual protection, food gathering and so on permits far greater reproductive success for each member on the average than a completely individualistic approach that loses the safety of numbers and the advantages of shared knowledge and culture.

INTERIM SUMMARY

Altruism refers to behaviours that help other people with no apparent gain or with potential cost to oneself. Philosophers and psychologists disagree as to whether an act can be purely altruistic or whether all apparent altruism is really intended to make the apparent altruist feel better (***ethical hedonism***). Evolutionary psychologists propose that people act in ways that maximise their inclusive fitness and are more likely to behave altruistically towards relatives than others. Natural selection also favours animals that behave altruistically towards unrelated others if the likely benefit to each individual over time exceeds the likely cost, a phenomenon known as ***reciprocal altruism***.

Bystander intervention

Although philosophers and evolutionists may question the roots of altruism, apparent acts of altruism are so prevalent that their *absence* can be shocking. A case in point was the brutal 1964 murder of Kitty Genovese in Queens, New York. Arriving home from work at 3 am, Genovese was attacked over a half-hour period by a knife-wielding assailant. Twice he left, only to return again to stab her. Although her screams and cries brought 38 of her neighbours to their windows, not one came to her assistance or even called the police, until some time after she was already dead. These bystanders put on their lights, opened their windows and watched while Genovese was repeatedly stabbed.

The phenomenon is by no means confined to the United States. Carr (2002) reports a case in the Northern Territory in 1998, where a woman was raped beside a busy Darwin road in broad daylight as she walked home from work during peak-hour traffic. Carr also describes the murder of Kylie Jones, a 23-year-old Auckland journalist, who was raped and stabbed in a reserve just 80 metres from her home in 2000. Despite her screams, no residents of nearby homes went to her aid. In Australia, approximately 60 percent of deaths resulting from drug overdoses occur in the presence of other people. Most of the time, people do not intervene or offer assistance when witnessing a drug overdose, despite recognising the symptoms of a health crisis or the impending death of the drug user (National Heroin Overdose Strategy, 2001). 'Doing nothing' is also evident in certain situations involving children. For example, in a Canadian study examining peer involvement in 53 videotaped episodes of bullying on the school playground, it was found that more than half the recorded time was spent by other children passively observing the episode, without any intervention or seeking help for the victims (O'Connell, Pepler, & Craig, 1999).

To understand how a group of law-abiding citizens could fail to help someone who was being murdered, social psychologists John Darley and Bibb Latané (1968) designed several experiments to investigate ***bystander intervention***, or helping a stranger in distress. Darley and Latané were particularly interested in whether being part of a group of onlookers affects an individual's sense of responsibility to take action.

In one experiment, male university students arrived for what they thought would be an interview (Darley & Latané, 1968). While the students waited, either by themselves or in groups of three, the investigators pumped smoke into the room through an air vent. Students who were alone reported the smoke 75 percent of the time. In contrast, only 38 percent of the students in groups of three acted, and only 10 percent acted when in the presence of two confederates who behaved as if they were indifferent to the smoke.

A model of bystander intervention

Based on their experiments, Darley and Latané developed a multi-stage model of the decision-making process that underlies bystander intervention. Bystanders must notice the emergency, interpret it as one, assume personal responsibility to intervene, decide how to intervene and then actually intervene (figure 18.4). At any point in this process, a bystander may make a decision that leads to inaction.

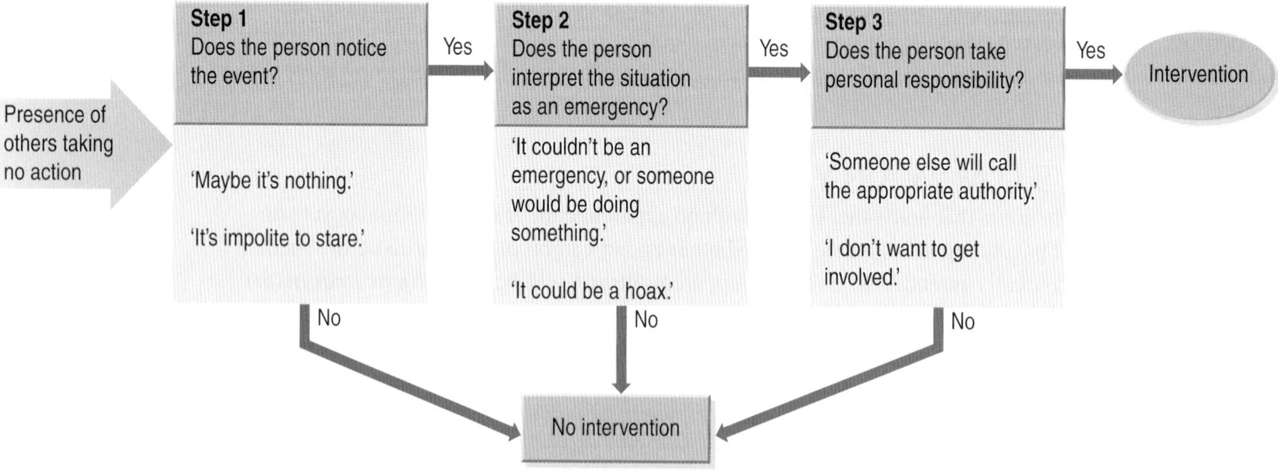

FIGURE 18.4
A decision-making model of bystander intervention. In the first stage, the bystander must notice the emergency. In stage 2, the bystander must interpret the incident as an emergency. In stage 3, the bystander must assume responsibility. Once the bystander accepts responsibility, he must then decide what to do and try to do it.

SOURCE: Adapted from Darley and Latané (1968, pp. 70–71).

This model helps explain why the presence of others can foster action or inaction. In the first two stages (noticing the emergency and interpreting it as one), other people serve as both a source of information ('Is there a crisis here or isn't there?') and a source of reassurance if they do not react strongly. At the next stage, the presence of others leads to a ***diffusion of responsibility*** — a diminished sense of personal responsibility to act because others are seen as equally responsible. At this point people also consider the consequences of action and are less willing to intervene (and more likely to justify inaction) if it jeopardises their own safety or if they fear they might look foolish if they have misinterpreted the situation. Bystanders who are anonymous, such as Kitty Genovese's neighbours, are less likely to help.

The findings of these studies actually support a long tradition of sociological theory suggesting that the anonymity of city life reduces individuals' sense of personal responsibility for the welfare of others. Research comparing the responses of urban and rural participants largely supports this view (see Solomon, Solomon, & Maiorca, 1982). Population density — the number of people crammed into a small urban space — also predicts rates of altruism. The more densely populated a city, the less people help (Levine, Martinez, Brase, & Sorenson, 1994). For example, Levine, Norenzayan, and Philbrick (2001) found large cross-cultural variation in helping behaviours, ranging from an overall rate of 93 percent in Rio de Janeiro, Brazil, to 40 percent in Kuala Lumpur, Malaysia. Levine, Norenzayan, et al. (2001) suggest that *simpatia* cultures, such as Spanish and Latin American cultures, where social harmony and respecting and understanding others' feelings is strongly valued, are more likely to be helpful towards strangers than are non-*simpatia* cultures.

How bleak is this picture?

Most of the bystander studies described so far involved simulated emergencies in laboratory settings. Under other experimental conditions, however, the results are sometimes quite different. One study examined whether bystanders are more likely to respond to an emergency in a natural setting where their compatriots are friends rather than strangers. The investigators staged a rape in a campus parking lot (Harari, Harari, & White, 1985). When unsuspecting male bystanders observed the female victim struggling with her attacker and heard her cries for help, 85 percent of those walking in groups of two or three responded, versus 65 percent of those walking alone. In this study, the presence of several people increased, rather than decreased, bystander intervention — probably because the naturalistic setting, the clarity of the victim's plight, the ability of group members to see and talk to one another and the reality of strength in numbers made intervention more likely.

Situational variables, such as the presence or absence of other people, aside, some people are simply more likely to help those in need than others. The reason: personality traits (chapter 11). People who are higher in empathy feel more responsible for helping. Those high in self-efficacy or the feeling that they will be able to do something in an emergency, more readily identify ways to help. High self-monitors, who are concerned with the impressions that others are forming of them, help when doing so will make themselves look good to others. Individuals high in emotionality more readily interpret a situation as an emergency than those low in emotionality (Bierhoff, Klein, & Kramp, 1991).

Evidence regarding the role of gender and helping is somewhat mixed. When the type of help needed involves potentially dangerous situations such as aiding a stranded motorist, men are more likely than women to intervene. However, when little danger is involved, such as helping out with children, women are more likely than men to help (Eagly & Crowley, 1986). What remains unclear are the factors that motivate men and women to help and whether there are differences between the sexes in these motives (Vogel, Wester, Heesacker, & Madon, 2003). On average, women are more likely than men to be motivated by feelings of empathy (George, Carroll, Kersnick, & Calderon, 1998), but there could also be a social desirability bias operating such that men are less willing than women to admit empathic feelings for those in need.

INTERIM SUMMARY

Researchers studying ***bystander intervention*** have found that individuals often do not help in a crisis in the presence of other people. To intervene, a person must notice the event, define it as an emergency and assume personal responsibility for intervening. ***Diffusion of responsibility***, a diminished sense of personal responsibility to act, is one important reason people do not intervene. Situational determinants of whether or not people will help interact with individual difference variables, such as gender, to determine when helping will occur.

Aggression

Aggression — verbal or physical behaviour aimed at harming another person or living being — is at least as characteristic of human interaction as altruism (Anderson & Bushman, 2002).

Aggression is often elicited by anger, as when someone lashes out at a perceived injustice, and it is referred to as ***hostile aggression***. However, aggression can also be carried out for practical purposes without anger, as when a driver leans on the horn to protest reckless lane-changing that could cause an accident.

Calm, pragmatic aggression, called ***instrumental aggression***, is often used by institutions such as the judicial system to punish wrongdoers (Anderson & Bushman, 2002; Geen, 1998, 2001). Aggressive acts are also frequently mixed with other motives. The behaviour of kamikaze pilots during World War II, terrorists who carry out suicide bombings and many soldiers in wartime involve blends of aggression and altruism, depending upon one's point of view.

Violence and culture

The prevalence and forms of aggression vary considerably across cultures. Among technologically developed countries, the United States has the highest rates of aggression. Indeed, violence has overtaken communicable diseases as the leading cause of death among the young (McAlister, 2006), and the murder rate in some major US cities dwarfs the annual number of murders in all of Canada. In Canada, roughly 600 people a year die from homicides, compared with roughly 15 500 in the United States (Disaster Center, 2010). Taking into account the larger population in the United States, the murder rate in Canada (1.49 per 100 000) is almost one-third that of the United States (5.60 per 100 000), although the gap in crime rates between these two countries is narrowing, with homicide rates in the United States declining at a faster rate than those in Canada (Statistics Canada, 2010; Disaster Center). Cross-cultural data have demonstrated that much of the difference in murder rates is attributable to the ready availability of firearms in the United States (Archer, 1994; see also McAlister, 2006; United States Department of Justice, 2005). Canada's homicide rate is roughly equivalent to the rate in England and Wales (1.40 per 100 000), but slightly higher than the rate in Australia (1.20 per 100 000; ABS, 2008a; Home Office Research Development Statistics, 2010). In New Zealand, violent crime increased in the period 1990–2000, and in 2009 the homicide rate in New Zealand was 0.3 per 10 000, although over a 25 year period, the murder rate is flat (New Zealand Crime Statistics, 2010).

Across and within societies, cultural differences play an important role in violence and aggression. Cultural factors can influence not only how people feel, think and act when confronted with a situation that could potentially lead to violence, but also how they respond physiologically (Cohen, Nisbett, Bowdle, & Schwartz, 1996).

Violence and gender

Gender differences in aggression are remarkably consistent across cultures. In most societies, males commit the majority of criminal and aggressive acts, over 90 percent. Male adolescents are particularly likely to be the perpetrators; in fact, fluctuations in crime rates in most countries can be predicted simply from the proportion of adolescent males in the population (see Segall, 1988).

Violence perpetrated by men against men has been so universal that until recently it drew little attention from either psychologists or policy makers (Goodman et al., 1993). The number of women battered by their male partners is unknown because many women do not report domestic violence. Research indicates that most batterers do not begin abusing their partners until the woman has made an emotional commitment to them, and attacks are most likely to occur during pregnancy or upon separation or divorce (Russell, 1991; see also WHO, 2005). In New Zealand, researchers are proactively examining societal aspects of physical and sexual abuse to better understand violence against women (see Fanslow & Robinson, 2004; Gavey, 2005; Morgan & O'Neill, 2001).

Gender differences also exist in the types of aggression most likely to be perpetrated by men and women (WHO, 2005). Whereas men engage in more direct aggression, women perpetrate aggression more indirectly. For example, adolescent males are more likely to bully their peers through verbal or physical aggression. Adolescent females, on the other hand, are more likely to socially exclude or ostracise the target of their bullying (Eagly & Steffen, 1986; Simmons, 2002). In children, boys tend to be more physically aggressive and are more likely to join in with the bully; whereas girls are more likely to support the victim of bullying (O'Connell et al., 1999). Prominent child psychologist, Michael Carr-Gregg, founding member of the National Centre Against Bullying, said bullies were buoyed from bystander support. To stamp out bullying in schools, victims and witnesses need to stand up to the aggressors (Hurst, 2010).

INTERIM SUMMARY

Aggression refers to verbal or physical behaviour aimed at harming another person or living being. Rates of violence vary cross-culturally, but across cultures, males tend to be more aggressive than females. Researchers are increasingly recognising the prevalence of male violence perpetrated against women.

The roots of violence

The universality of aggression and the individual differences seen in aggressive behaviour have led to considerable controversy about its origins. Some theories maintain that the roots of aggression lie in biology and evolution; others look to the environment and social learning. In this section we explore instinctual, evolutionary, cognitive neoassociation and cognitive–social approaches (which integrate cognitive and behavioural perspectives). We also examine the biopsychological processes that underlie aggressive behaviour, and offer a tentative integration of multiple standpoints.

Instinctual perspective

Some theorists view aggression and aggressive drives as instinctual. For example, Freud viewed aggression as a basic instinct in humans (chapter 10), related to *thanatos* or the death instinct. Although most psychodynamic psychologists no longer accept this theory, they still view aggression as an inborn behavioural potential that is usually activated by frustration and anger. In fact, in every human society ever observed, socialisation to control aggressive impulses is one of the most basic tasks of parenting (see Whiting & Child, 1953). Infants and toddlers bite, scratch and kick when they do not get what they want; as children get older, they show less overt aggression (Hartup, 1977, 1998). This change in behaviour suggests that societies have to teach children to *inhibit* aggression, rather than that aggression is primarily learned. (As we will see, other theories take the opposite perspective.)

Perhaps the most distinctive aspect of the psychodynamic approach to aggression regards the role of consciousness. From a psychodynamic perspective, aggressive motives may blend with other motives to produce behaviour not consciously intended as sadistic, as in 'good-humoured' teasing among friends, enjoyment of aggressive movies or sports or 'forgetting' to pick up the dry cleaning after an argument with one's spouse (passive aggression). Aggressive motives may also blend with other motives, such as achievement or altruism, in choice of occupation, such as a career in the military (or the Australian Taxation Office!).

The triggers for aggression can also be unconscious. For example, James Gilligan spent years working with violent prisoners and conducted extensive interviews with a sample of men incarcerated for violent crimes (Gilligan, 1996). Asked to tell the stories of the acts that landed them behind bars, one after another told stories in which they lashed out after feeling 'dissed' — treated with perceived disrespect. Gilligan concluded that one of the major triggers for violence is the feeling of shame in individuals prone to feeling inadequate or disrespected.

Recent research points to the importance of implicit shame in activating aggression. One study compared the tendency to experience shame in men with histories of sexual abuse who either did or did not go on to perpetrate sexual violence themselves (Conklin, 1999). Those who became abusers reported minimal shame on self-report questionnaires — they were consciously shameless. But the responses they gave to the Thematic Apperception Test (TAT), an instrument used to assess implicit motives and emotions (chapter 10), told a different story. Their responses were filled with themes of shame. Men who went on to become perpetrators appeared to suffer from unacknowledged shame.

APPLY + DISCUSS

Many horror films, as well as films with high levels of violence, gain a cult following. Alfred Hitchcock's 1960 thriller *Psycho* has had two sequels, a prequel, a remake and a television movie spin-off. The ghastly character Freddie Krueger has also appeared in several films as part of the *A Nightmare on Elm Street* series.

- Why are we so captivated by horror and violence in films? What psychological functions do scary or violent movies serve?
- Is pleasure in watching violence in the movies a learned response? Or is fascination with violence part of our genetic heritage?

Sharing in common only certain features with the psychodynamic approach, Konrad Lorenz also viewed aggression as instinctual. According to Lorenz and other ethologists, aggression gradually builds up over time. Unless this aggression is released by triggers or sign stimuli, the aggression will ultimately spill over, much like water that is not controlled will ultimately spill over a dam. One problem with Lorenz's theory, however, is that it suggests that everyone periodically feels the need to behave aggressively, which most people would discount. Furthermore, it fails to account for individual differences in aggression. To the degree that aggression is instinctive, then all members of a particular species should behave similarly, and we know they do not.

An evolutionary perspective

Theorists who viewed aggression as instinctual often did not specifically address the evolutionary adaptations of aggression. Aggression, including killing members of one's own species, occurs in all animals. From an evolutionary standpoint, the capacity for aggression evolved because of its value for survival and reproduction (Lore & Schultz, 1993; see also Johnson, Burk, & Kirkpatrick, 2007). Males typically attack other males to obtain access to females and to keep or take over territory. In many animal species, including some lions and monkeys, a male who takes over a 'harem' from another male kills all the infants so that the females will breed with him and devote their resources only to *his* offspring, maximising his reproductive success. Females often try to fight back in these circumstances. Across species, overt female aggression is elicited largely by attacks on their young.

Contemporary evolutionary psychologists believe that humans, like other animals, have evolved aggressive mechanisms that can be activated when circumstances threaten their survival, reproduction, the reproductive success of their kin or the survival of alliance partners. In this view, aggression is like a pilot light that is always on but can burst into flames if conditions threaten reproductive success (Buss & Shackelford, 1997; de Waal, 1989).

Primates, including humans, have a variety of appeasement techniques to avoid violence, notably facial expressions, vocalisations and gestures (de Waal, 1989). Unfortunately, humans are unique in their capacity to override evolved mechanisms for inhibiting aggression, particularly when divided by nationality, ethnicity or ideology. Furthermore, as Konrad Lorenz noted, humans have developed the ability to kill one another from a distance. Not seeing our victims suffer prevents activation of natural inhibitions against killing members of the species, such as empathic distress responses, which are probably involved in both inhibiting aggression and promoting altruism.

FROM BRAIN TO BEHAVIOUR

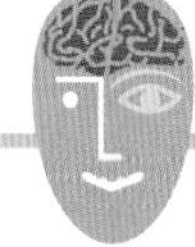

Biological foundations of aggression

Instinctual and evolutionary psychologists presume that aggression is built into the human behavioural repertoire. If a tendency to behave aggressively is innate, it must be rooted in the nervous system and perhaps in the endocrine system as well. Mounting evidence in animals and humans supports this view.

Neural systems

The neural systems that control aggression, like those involved in other forms of behaviour, are hierarchically organised. Neurons in evolutionarily primitive structures such as the hypothalamus are part of circuits regulated by more recent (in evolutionary time) structures, notably the cortex (figure 18.5). As we have seen (chapters 3, 10 and 14), the amygdala and hypothalamus are involved in emotional reactions and drive states. When researchers electrically stimulate regions of the lateral hypothalamus of a normally non-predatory cat or rhesus monkey, the animal immediately attacks (Egger & Flynn, 1963; Robinson, Alexander, & Bowne, 1969). Similar results occur in humans when electrodes are implanted in the amygdala during surgery. With electrical stimulation, a normally submissive, mild-mannered woman became so hostile and aggressive that she tried to strike the experimenter — who was able to control the outburst by switching off the current (King, 1961).

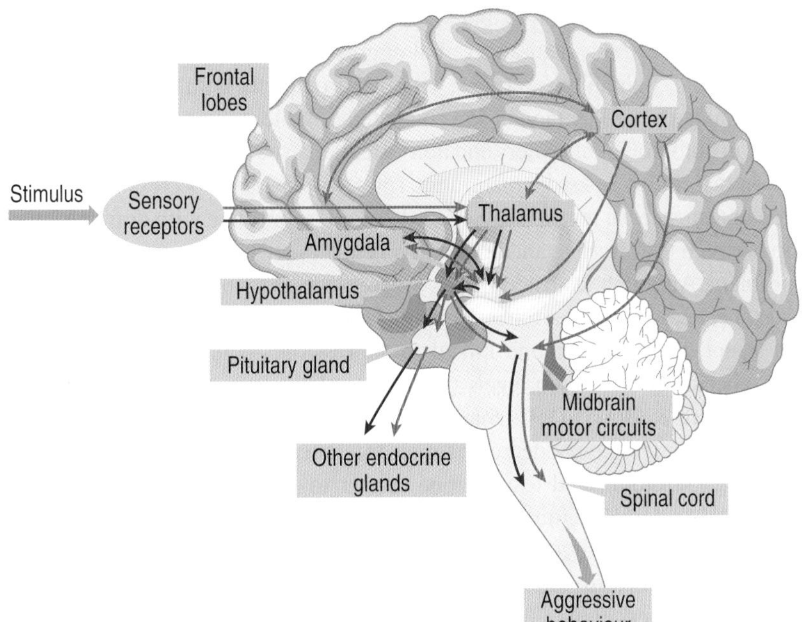

FIGURE 18.5
Areas of the brain involved in aggressive behaviour. Stimulus information (e.g. a threatening gesture) is relayed via the thalamus to the amygdala and hypothalamus for immediate action. The information is also relayed from the thalamus to the cortex for more careful consideration. One or both of these pathways can generate an aggressive response, which may activate midbrain motor mechanisms involved in species-specific aggressive responses. Limbic structures, particularly the amygdala, assess the emotional significance of the stimulus and activate the hypothalamus. The hypothalamus then triggers endocrine responses, which in turn affect arousal and readiness for action. Limbic structures also activate the frontal lobes, which integrate cognitive and emotional responses to stimuli (chapter 8).

Creating lesions in parts of the midbrain can also eliminate an animal's ability to respond with species-typical aggressive motor movements (such as hissing and bared teeth in cats), suggesting a substantial role for midbrain structures in aggression (Carlson, 1999). Brain scans of incarcerated murderers with no history of abuse and of individuals with antisocial personality disorder showed that the prefrontal cortex of the incarcerated murderers was 14 percent less active than normal and 15 percent smaller in the antisocial individuals, suggesting, again, that neural systems play a critical role in at least some forms of aggression (Raine et al., 1998; Raine, Lenez, Bihrle, LaCasse, & Colletti, 2000).

Although sensory information (e.g. a threatening gesture) processed by the thalamus can probably trigger responses directly, in humans aggression is under substantial cortical control. Sophisticated processing at the cortical level can either inhibit or facilitate aggression. A threatening gesture, for example, can be interpreted as either an attack or a joke, and a person with intact frontal lobes (chapters 3 and 7) can usually decide to 'hold back' rather than lashing out physically or verbally.

Testosterone and serotonin

Hormones play a substantial role in the tendency to behave aggressively. In species after species, males are more aggressive than females, and these sex differences appear linked to action of the hormone testosterone both before birth and during development (Archer & Lloyd, 1985; see also Johnson et al., 2007). Recall that hormones both *organise* and *activate* neural circuits (chapter 10). With respect to organisational effects (i.e. influences on the development of the brain), female rats and monkeys that receive testosterone in utero exhibit increased play fighting after birth (Meaney & McEwen, 1986). Similarly, prenatal exposure to synthetic hormones can lead to increased aggression in childhood and adolescence (Reinisch, 1981).

With respect to activational effects (i.e. direct influences of hormones on behaviour), studies with rats find that the amount of aggressive behaviour displayed by both sexes correlates with circulating blood testosterone levels (with additional hormones involved in females) (Albert, Jonik, & Walsh, 1991). Testosterone does not, however, tend to cause aggression in the absence of environmental triggers, such as competition between males for females, or repeated exposure to unfamiliar members of the same species.

MAKING CONNECTIONS

Correlational studies show that higher levels of testosterone in men are associated with higher levels of aggression. However, these studies cannot definitively show whether circulating testosterone levels cause violent behaviour or whether aggression leads to heightened testosterone levels. The reason is that correlation cannot demonstrate **causation**. When two variables correlate highly, one could cause the other, or some third variable could explain the link between them (chapter 2).

The data on humans are less definitive, but several studies provide suggestive evidence. One examined the relationship between physical and verbal aggression and levels of testosterone in adolescent boys (Olweus, Mattsson, Schalling, & Loew, 1980). Participants with higher levels of testosterone tended to be more impatient and irritable. Men convicted of violent crimes also tend to have higher testosterone levels than non-violent offenders and non-offenders (see Archer, 1991). The dramatic increase in male aggression that occurs at sexual maturation (puberty) in many species and cultures is also likely related to a surge in testosterone levels (see Segall, 1988). The problem with drawing conclusions about the relationship between testosterone and aggression is that the two constructs represent something of a chicken–egg problem. Although testosterone may increase aggression, behaving aggressively can also increase testosterone (see, however, Archer, Birring, & Wu, 1998).

Testosterone is not the only hormone linked to aggression. A number of studies in humans and other animals implicate low serotonin levels (which are also associated with depression; chapter 15; Bernhardt, 1997; Cleare & Bond, 1997; Suomi, 2000). In addition, intentionally lowering serotonin levels of participants in a laboratory decreases their tolerance for frustration and increases their likelihood of aggressing. Serotonin and testosterone appear to regulate different aspects of aggression. Testosterone is linked to social dominance and thus leads to aggression in the service of maintaining status within a social hierarchy (Olweus, 1988). Serotonin is linked instead to impulsivity (acting without thinking) and thus leads to unprovoked and socially inappropriate forms of aggression (Higley et al., 1992; see also Summers et al., 2005). Further, the modulating role of the serotonergic system in aggressive human behaviour is complex, with different receptors thought to be involved in regulating trait and state aggression (Olivier, 2004).

Thus far, research focused on biochemical influences on aggression has been limited primarily to testosterone, more commonly associated with males. Variations in female hormones, specifically estrogen and progesterone, also show links to more aggressive tendencies (Trainor, Greiwe, & Nelson, 2006). Although the legitimacy of the phenomenon 'premenstrual syndrome' (PMS) is open for debate, women who commit crimes in some countries while experiencing PMS have been given reduced sentences for their crimes (Dalton, 1987; Lewis, 1990). The basis for this defence is that the women's behaviour was under the influence of raging hormones, leading to a state of temporary insanity (see Figert, 2005).

Genetics

Genetic factors also contribute to individual differences in aggressive behaviour. Successful attempts to breed highly aggressive strains of rats, mice and rabbits demonstrate that among these animals, individuals can inherit an aggressive temperament (see Cologer-Clifford, Simon, & Jubilan, 1992; Moyer, 1983). Questionnaire studies comparing monozygotic and dizygotic twin pairs find aggressive behaviour, like other personality traits, to be heritable in humans (Caspi, 1998; DiLalla, 2002). Researchers have also focused attention on a gene on chromosome 11 that is involved in regulating serotonin in the brain (Nielsen, Jenkins, Stefanisko, Jefferson, & Goldman, 1997). Presence of a particular allele at this level of the chromosome is associated with unprovoked aggression as assessed by self-report (Manuck et al., 1999).

INTERIM SUMMARY

Instinctual theorists view aggression as an inborn potential usually activated by frustration or anger. They argue that aggressive motives can blend with other motives and be triggered unconsciously. Evolutionary theorists similarly view aggression as an inborn human potential that gets activated under conditions that affect reproductive success, such as competing for territory or mates and protecting oneself and related others. The neural control of aggression is hierarchically organised, with the amygdala, hypothalamus and cortex (particularly the frontal lobes) playing prominent roles. Aggression is also partially controlled by hormones, particularly testosterone and serotonin.

Cognitive neoassociation theory

People exposed to aversive situations (e.g. frustrations, hot temperatures, annoyances) often experience negative affect and physiological arousal in response to those events. This arousal lays the groundwork for potential aggression by triggering thoughts and behaviours associated with aggression

(Anderson & Bushman, 2002). Thoughts and feelings associated with negative affect and aggression become activated in the presence of aversive events.

In 1939, John Dollard, Neal Miller and their colleagues at Yale University proposed one of the first theories of aggression, the ***frustration–aggression hypothesis***, which states that when people are frustrated in achieving a goal, they may become aggressive. A child who wants a biscuit and is told to wait until after dinner may throw a tantrum, or a university student who had his heart set on a particular graduate school and was rejected may become not only sad but also furious.

This model is simple and intuitively appealing. It was initially hailed as a significant advance towards a comprehensive theory of aggression because it tied aggression to environmental events rather than solely to instincts. However, researchers soon realised that not all aggression results from frustration and not all frustration leads to aggression. Physical pain may cause aggression, and frustrated goals can lead one person to become aggressive, another to become depressed and still another to become more determined.

A reformulated frustration–aggression hypothesis suggests that frustration breeds aggression to the extent that a frustrating event elicits an unpleasant emotion (Berkowitz, 1989). As frustrating as blocked goals can be, innumerable other unpleasant experiences can also produce arousal and frustration. Air pollution, tobacco smoke and other noxious odours have all been linked to increases in aggressive behaviour (Rotton, Frey, Barry, Milligan, & Fitzpatrick, 1979; Zillman, Baron, & Tamborini, 1981).

The relationship between heat and aggression is particularly well documented (Anderson, 1989; Rotton & Cohn, 2000). As temperature rises, so do tempers. Current predictions regarding global warming and the inevitable increase in air temperature may, therefore, impact on anger and aggression levels in affected communities, and contribute to an increase in the number of violent crimes (Anderson, 2001). One study found a strong correlation between temperature and the incidence of riots in United States cities between 1967 and 1971 (Carlsmith & Anderson, 1979). Rape, murder, assault and prison unrest all vary with the time of the year, peaking in the hot summer months. Within countries as diverse as Spain, Italy, France and the United States, the southern regions typically have the highest rates of violent crime (Anderson, 1989). Even the number of batters hit by pitches in professional baseball varies with the temperature (Reifman, Larrick, & Fein, 1991)! Carr (2002) describes a malady known as 'mango madness', which strikes residents of Australia's far north during the summer months. Searing temperatures combined with extreme humidity throughout summer are associated with increases in aggressive behaviour. Carr outlines one case where a chef at a five-star resort in the Northern Territory 'blew his top' in the middle of 'mango madness' season and surprised guests by tossing a barbecue and outdoor furniture into a pool. Thus, according to cognitive neoassociation theories, people can become angry and behave aggressively no matter how the underlying emotional state was elicited — whether through an insult, an uncomfortable temperature or an unpleasant memory. However, aroused, negative emotions will activate similar cognitions stored in memory — one reason getting rid of negative emotions is so difficult.

A cognitive-social perspective

The capacity for aggression appears to be innate, but the activation and inhibition of aggression depends on culture and learning. Harsh parental discipline, for example, produces children who are more aggressive than children whose parents spare the rod (Keith, 2010). According to cognitive–social theories, children and adults learn to behave aggressively through social rewards and punishments. They also learn through observational learning such as modelling (Bandura, 2001). In his classic Bobo doll study, Bandura (1967) demonstrated that children who watch adults abusing dolls are much more likely to do so themselves (chapter 6). Cognitive processes, especially the attributions people make for the causes of their misfortunes, play a role in eliciting and controlling aggression as well. Individuals are more likely to become aggressive, for example, if they believe someone has willfully and knowingly inflicted harm (see Geen, 1995).

Research from a cognitive–social perspective has contributed to the public debate about the influence of television and other media violence on aggressive behaviour (Bushman & Anderson, 2001). The Australian Communications and Media Authority (ACMA, 2010) reports that Australian youths aged 8 to 17 years consume an average of 4 hours and 49 minutes of media per day. This includes spending an average of 2 hours and 26 mins watching traditional media such as the television and DVDs (78 percent). During this time they see many violent cartoons, 'blockbuster' movies that feature 'glamourised violence' and real-life violence during news broadcasts (Children's Health Development Foundation, 2004).

With the emergence of the internet and mobile phones, young Australians are also embracing new media platforms and playing games on handheld devices such as Wii, Playstation and Nintendo DS. In 2007, nearly all Australian family households with children and young people had a computer (98 percent) — the vast majority also had the internet (91 percent) and just over three-quarters had broadband (76 percent). In 2009, 79 percent of 5 to 14 year olds accessed the internet, up from 65 percent in 2006 and 64 percent in 2003 (ACMA, 2010). Australian youths aged 8 to 17 years spend an average 1 hour 17 minutes per day on the internet, making going online the second most time-consuming media activity behind watching television. The average time spent online increased with age, with 8 to 11 year olds averaging 30 minutes per day online compared with 15 to 17 year olds averaging 2 hours and 24 minutes online (ACMA, 2010). Girls are more likely to engage in online communication activities such as emailing and instant messaging, while boys are more likely to engage in online games against other players (ACMA, 2010).

Girls are more likely to engage in online communication activities such as emailing and video chatting, while boys are more inclined to engage in online games against other players.

Reports indicate that watching violence on television is associated with increased aggression (see Anderson et al., 2003; Johnson, Cohen, Smailes, Kasen, & Brook, 2002; Media Awareness Network, 2010; Monitor on Psychology, 2007). By watching media violence, children learn aggressive scripts that guide their own behaviour at later times (Huesmann, 1998; see also Monitor on Psychology, 2007). Carr (2002) describes alarming meta-messages that violent video games and cartoon convey. He says the protagonists and combatants in these arenas recover completely from destructive blows that would prove fatal in real life. This delivers the message that violence is enjoyable and easily deliverable, while having no real costs or punishment. Others reject the claim of a relationship between aggression and watching violent television and video games (see Ferguson & Kilburn, 2009; Grech, 2010), suggesting media is only one of a number of variables that put children at risk of aggressive behaviour (Science Daily, 2008) and that the pathway to aggression is largely genetic (see Larsson, Andershed, & Lichtenstein, 2006). It is likely that the effect of media violence on children will continue to be debated.

Estimating the long-term effects of television violence on behaviour is very difficult because people who are aggressive tend to seek out aggressive programs, and they do this from the time they are young. Experimental data show that in the short run, children and adolescents are more likely to behave aggressively immediately after viewing violent television shows, particularly if they are provoked (Singer & Singer, 1981; Smith & Donnerstein, 1998; Wood, Wong, & Chachere, 1991). This could occur because watching television violence increases arousal, decreases inhibition, provides aggressive models or desensitises children to violence by making violent acts seem commonplace (Gunter & McAleer, 1990).

The data are less conclusive for long-term effects (see Gadow & Sprafkin, 1993; McGuire, 1986). Rather than having a global effect on every child or adult, televised violence is likely to have a stronger impact on people who are already highly aggressive. In fact, experimental research suggests that people who test high in aggressiveness not only prefer violent films but also become more angry and

APPLY + DISCUSS

There is conflicting research about the effects of media violence on children. To what extent do you think that exposure to television and other media violence affects the behaviour patterns of young children? Consider contemporary research in your response.

aggressive after watching them (Bushman, 1995; Kiewitz & Weaver, 2001). Thus, the impact of televised violence on aggression likely reflects a person-by-situation interaction (chapter 11) — that is, a tendency of certain people to behave in certain ways under certain conditions — rather than a general phenomenon. Similar results emerge from research assessing the effects of pornography on sexual violence. Viewing pornography does not cause sexual violence, but viewing pornographic *aggression* appears to desensitise men to the brutality of rape and other sexual crimes against women (see Malamuth & Donnerstein, 1982). As with television violence, pornographic aggression may affect a person's emotional response to violence or slightly weaken inhibitions in deviant individuals with poor internal controls. Nonetheless, most people will not kill or rape after watching a violent or pornographic movie.

The general aggression model

The general aggression model (GAM) was created to give meaning to the myriad theories that currently exist to explain aggression. Incorporating what researchers viewed as the best of each of the earlier theories of aggression, the GAM examines how person and situation input variables influence aggression through the cognitions, emotions and arousal they generate. In short, person variables, such as personality traits, genetics, attitudes, values and scripts interact with situational variables, including aggressive cues, provocation and aversive situations, to produce particular cognitions and feelings. Thus, if a highly aggressive individual is placed in a situation where guns are present, the guns will activate aggressive scripts (that are probably easily accessible because of the individual's underlying aggressive personality) that will subsequently drive aggressive behaviour, referred to as the output (Anderson & Bushman, 2002).

Research on self-esteem and aggression provides support for this model. Most people assume that low self-esteem is more closely allied with aggression than high self-esteem, but this assumption is unconfirmed. In fact, narcissists and individuals with high self-esteem react more aggressively when they receive negative evaluations than individuals with low self-esteem (Baumeister, Smart, & Boden, 1996; Bushman & Baumeister, 2002; Stucke & Sporer, 2002). However, low self-esteem is linked with aggression in a series of recent studies involving large samples of American and New Zealand adolescents and college students. Research found that although narcissistic individuals were prone to aggression, the significant effect of low self-esteem on aggressive thoughts, feelings and behaviours was completely independent of narcissism, and could not be discounted (Donnellan, Trzesniewski, Robins, Moffitt, & Caspi, 2005). Defined as threatened egotism, this relationship among self-esteem (a person variable), negative evaluations (situational inputs) and aggression (output) lends support to the general aggression model.

Not all people with high self-esteem are more likely to behave aggressively. People with stable high self-esteem (i.e. people whose self-esteem is rarely influenced by situational variables) are no more likely to behave aggressively than anyone else. People with unstable high self-esteem, however, do behave more aggressively when their shaky sense of self is threatened with negative evaluations. Participants in one study were either insulted or praised for an essay they had written. They were then given the opportunity to aggress against the evaluator by giving a noxious blast of noise to that person (Bushman & Baumeister, 1998). Narcissistic individuals exhibited the highest levels of aggression as a reaction to the ego threat.

INTERIM SUMMARY

According to cognitive–social theories, the roots of aggressive behaviour lie in social rewards and punishments, and cognitive processes such as attributions and observational learning. The general aggression model states that person variables interact with situational inputs to determine aggressive output. The capacity for aggression appears to be innate, but the activation and inhibition of aggression depends on culture and learning.

Social influence

By the late nineteenth century, sociologists and philosophers had recognised that people behave differently in crowds than they do as individuals and that a crowd is more than the mere sum of its parts. In a classic book published in 1895, called *The Crowd*, Gustave Le Bon argued that people in a crowd may lose their personal identities and ability to judge right from wrong, a phenomenon now referred to as *deindividuation*. They become anonymous and no longer consider themselves accountable for their behaviour. Le Bon had in mind events of the eighteenth and nineteenth centuries, such as the frenzied mobs of the French Revolution, but his reflections could equally apply to the behaviour of the patrons of the Star Hotel in the New South Wales city of Newcastle during an infamous riot in 1979. The Star Hotel had been the city's main venue for live rock music, but was set to close with one final gig on Wednesday, 19 September 1979. The crowd of revellers became rowdy, and when the police arrived to halt the unrest, the anger boiled over. Police cars were overturned and burnt, while other cars were attacked. The scene became a mass riot that lasted for a number of hours. The riot was later commemorated in a song by Australian rock band Cold Chisel. In December 2005, a series of ethnically motivated riots occurred in and around the Sydney beach suburb of Cronulla. The episode was sparked by an attack on three lifesavers. A week later a crowd of about 5000 people gathered to protest against such violent behaviour, but the gathering ended in the assault of a number of people of Middle Eastern appearance. There were several violent assaults over the following few nights, resulting in a police lockdown of beaches.

Since Le Bon's time, social psychologists have examined a number of forms of ***social influence***, effects of the presence of others on the way people think, feel and behave. Social influence processes can be remarkably subtle. For example, Robert Rosenthal and his colleagues discovered decades ago that teachers' expectations of students — their beliefs about their abilities — can have a profound impact on students' performance (Rosenthal & Jacobson, 1966). Teachers who are led to believe that a particular student is smarter than he appears will tend to behave in ways that lead the student to perform better. Similarly, teachers who hold negative implicit attitudes towards particular minority groups (chapter 17) are likely to respond to student members of those groups in ways that lead them to underachieve.

The influence of implicit and explicit expectations of this sort provides the basis for ***self-fulfilling prophecies***, in which false impressions of a situation evoke behaviour that, in turn, makes these impressions become true (Merton, 1957). Snyder, Tanke, and Berscheid (1977) conducted a classic study of self-fulfilling prophecies, in which pairs of male and female university students conversed from separate rooms through an intercom system. The students had never met, but each male student thought he knew what his partner looked like from a photograph.

Actually, the photo was not of her. Half the participants received a picture of a young woman rated by other students as physically very attractive, and the other half received an unattractive mugshot. Not surprisingly, males who believed their partners were attractive were more sociable and sexually warm towards them. However, the more interesting finding came from studying the responses of the females. Judges who listened to the taped conversation with the male's comments edited out rated the women in the attractive photograph condition more friendly, sociable, witty and appealing. Conversely, women who were treated as if they were unattractive actually behaved unattractively.

In this section we focus on three forms of social influence that are pervasive in social life: obedience, conformity and group processes. We then turn to a discussion of social influence processes in everyday life.

Obedience

In 1978, in the small community of Jonestown, located in a Guyana jungle, over 900 members of the People's Temple cult drank cyanide-laced soft drink to commit mass suicide. The cult's leader, Jim Jones, told his people that a 'revolutionary suicide' would dramatise their dedication. According to the few survivors, some people resisted, but most took their lives willingly, with mothers giving cyanide to their children and then drinking it themselves. An equally grisly example of misplaced obedience was the mass suicide of Californian Heaven's Gate cult members who believed salvation was just around the corner with the arrival of the Hale–Bopp comet in 1997.

Psychological research on ***obedience***, or compliance with authority, increased dramatically following World War II, primarily as an attempt to understand the horrors committed by the Third Reich. Many American social psychologists were refugees from the Nazis who presumed that the blind obedience they had witnessed was an aberration or anomaly caused by flaws in the German character or by the political, social and economic upheaval that left Germany in ruin after World War I.

The Milgram experiments

In the 1960s, Stanley Milgram (1963, 1974) conducted a series of classic studies on obedience at Yale University that took many people, including psychologists, by surprise. The results of his investigations suggested that the philosopher Hannah Arendt may have been right when she said that the horrifying thing about the Nazis was not that they were so deviant but that they were 'terrifyingly normal'.

The basic design of the studies was as follows. The experimenter told participants they were participating in an experiment to examine the effect of punishment on learning. Participants were instructed to punish a 'learner' (actually a confederate of the researcher) in the next room whenever the learner made an error, using an instrument they believed to be a shock generator. Panel switches were labelled from 15 volts (slight shock) to 450 volts (danger: severe shock). The experimenter instructed the participants to begin by administering a slight shock and increase the voltage each time the learner made an error. The learner actually received no shocks, but participants had no reason to disbelieve what they were told — especially since they heard protests and, later, screaming from the next room as they increased the punishment.

Milgram was not actually studying the impact of punishment on learning. Rather, he wanted to determine how far people would go in obeying orders. Before conducting the study, Milgram had asked various social scientists to estimate how many participants would go all the way to 450 volts. The experts estimated that a very deviant subsample — well below 5 percent — might administer the maximum.

They were wrong. As you can see in figure 18.6, approximately *two-thirds* of participants administered the full 450 volts, even though the learner had stopped responding (screaming or otherwise) and was apparently either unconscious or dead. Many participants were clearly distressed by the experience, but each time they asked if they should continue to administer the shocks, the experimenter told them that the experiment required that they continue. If they enquired about their responsibility for any ill effects the learner might be experiencing, the experimenter told them that he was responsible, and that the procedure might be painful but it was not dangerous. The experimenter never overtly tried to coerce participants to continue; all he did was remind them of their obligation.

To Milgram, the implications were painfully clear. People will obey, without limitations of conscience, when they believe an order comes from a legitimate authority (Milgram, 1974).

APPLY + DISCUSS

The story of Australian soldier Harry 'Breaker' Morant's execution in South Africa in 1902 became well known after it was immortalised in film in 1980. Morant was one of numerous Australian soldiers fighting on the side of the British forces against Boer commandos in South Africa. Breaker's best friend, Captain Percy Hunt, was wounded, captured, tortured and finally killed by Boer soldiers. Morant and several other soldiers retaliated with a dawn raid, capturing a Boer soldier whom they found using Hunt's trousers as a pillow. Morant ordered the soldier to be shot and killed. In the next few weeks, Morant and his colleagues shot another 11 Boer soldiers, claiming they had been placed under verbal orders to 'take no prisoners'. The British Army court-martialled Morant and three of his fellow soldiers. Morant and one other were then shot by a firing squad. The death caused controversy in Australia, with many believing the execution was a cover-up to prevent the instruction to 'take no prisoners' from coming to light.

- Do soldiers relinquish their ability — or duty — to judge right and wrong when receiving orders?
- Can the military function if soldiers make independent moral judgements? How can the military maximise the likelihood that soldiers will both respect their commanders and respect human rights?

Shock level	Verbal designation and voltage level	Number of participants who refused to go further	Shock level	Verbal designation and voltage level	Number of participants who refused to go further	Shock level	Verbal designation and voltage level	Number of participants who refused to go further
	Slight shock			**Very strong shock**			**Danger: severe shock**	
1	15		13	195		25	375	1
2	30		14	210		26	390	
3	45		15	225		27	405	
4	60		16	240		28	420	
	Moderate shock			**Intense shock**			XXX	
5	75		17	255		29	435	
6	90		18	270		30	450	26
7	105		19	285				
8	120		20	300	5			
	Strong shock			**Extreme intensity shock**				
9	135		21	315	4			
10	150		22	330	2	Mean maximum shock level		27.0
11	165		23	345	1	Percentage obedient participants		65.0 percent
12	180		24	360	1			

FIGURE 18.6
Data from the original Milgram experiment. The numbers correspond to the number of people who refused to administer shocks beyond that point. So, for example, five individuals administered shocks at an intensity of 300 volts, but refused to go further.

SOURCE: Milgram (1974, p. 35).

Factors that influence obedience

By varying the experimental conditions, Milgram discovered several factors that influence obedience. One is the proximity of the victim to the participant. Obedience declined substantially if the victim was in the room with the participant, if a voice replaced pounding on the wall and if the participant had to force the victim's hand onto a shock plate to administer further punishments (figure 18.7; see overleaf).

APPLY + DISCUSS

Experience the Milgram experiment which demonstrates obedience to authority by linking to a YouTube video that replicates the original experiment. This video should be available via your university course website for this subject.

- Why do people obey authority figures?
- How confident are you that you can predict your own behaviour if placed in a similar situation?

Proximity to the experimenter also affected the decision to obey. The closer the participant was to the experimenter, the more difficult was disobedience; when the experimenter sat in another room, obedience dropped sharply. Subsequent research implicates personality variables such as authoritarianism and hostility that can influence the likelihood of obedience as well (Blass, 1991, 2000). Conversely, gender had little effect on obedience in Milgram's studies — women were as likely to comply with the experimenter as were men.

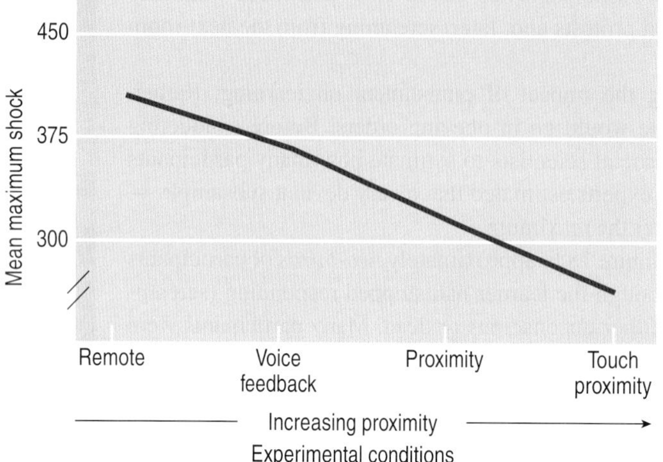

FIGURE 18.7
Effects of proximity on maximum shock delivered. Participants in the Milgram experiments generally obeyed, but the closer they were to the victim, the less they tended to obey.

SOURCE: Milgram (1963, p. 376).

The results of the Milgram studies are in sharp contrast to what most of us believe about ourselves — that is, that we would never obey in such a situation. The disjunction between our beliefs about how we would behave and the way most of us would *actually* behave highlights a consistent finding in social psychology — that is, our blindness to the power of situations over our own behaviour. The effects of powerful situations tend to be implicit and hence to occur automatically and without conscious awareness (Epley & Gilovich, 1999; Wegner & Bargh, 1998). Thus, when we predict our own behaviour, we tend to picture what we would *consciously* think and feel and to underestimate the power of implicit situational 'pulls'.

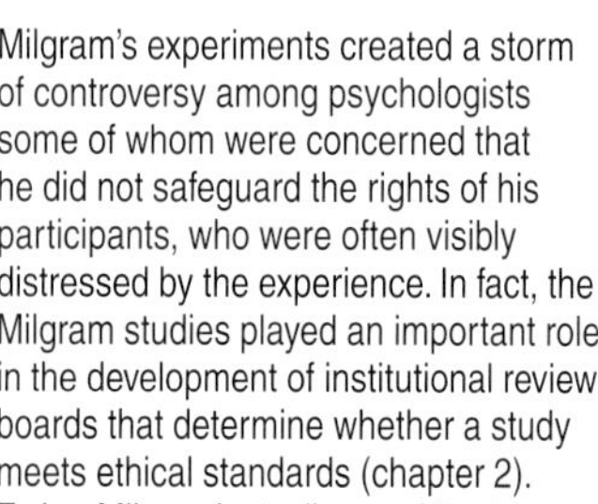

ETHICAL DILEMMA

Milgram's experiments created a storm of controversy among psychologists some of whom were concerned that he did not safeguard the rights of his participants, who were often visibly distressed by the experience. In fact, the Milgram studies played an important role in the development of institutional review boards that determine whether a study meets ethical standards (chapter 2). Today, Milgram's studies could not be conducted.

- Milgram debriefed his participants at the end of the experiment to minimise any impact the experience might have had on them, and none reported regretting their participation. Did the knowledge generated by these experiments outweigh the costs to participants?
- Could we possibly know what we now know had Milgram not performed his experiments?
- Could a different, less stressful, research design have led to such important results?

One of the issues surrounding Milgram's obedience studies was the ethics of the study. Was it ethical to deceive participants in this way and to cause them visible distress? Although many people immediately denounced the study as inherently unethical, research suggests that perceptions of the ethics of the Milgram obedience study and related experiments rest not so much on the design of the study but rather on the study's outcome. Participants asked to judge the ethics of Milgram's obedience study decried its ethics more when they thought obedience was high compared to when they thought obedience was low. If the study itself was unethical, no differences in perceptions of its ethics would exist. If, however, ethical decisions are made on the basis of the outcomes obtained, differences may exist as they did in these studies (Bickman & Zarantonello, 1978; Schlenker & Forsyth, 1977).

More recently, Slater et al. (2006) used a similar paradigm to that used by Milgram within an immersive virtual environment to examine the extent to which participants would respond to extreme social situations as if the environment were real, in spite of their knowledge that they were operating in a virtual space. Slater et al. (2006) found that participants experienced stress in response to their increasing the voltage of shock to a virtual human. Thus, it is possible to establish virtual reality environments where individuals will comply with requests to follow instructions that appear to cause another person to suffer. Such scenarios, in turn, cause discomfort to the individuals concerned because their perceptions in that situation develop an implicit knowledge that their actions are causing pain to another (chapters 3 and 8).

Conformity

Whereas obedience refers to compliance with the demands of an authority, ***conformity*** means changing attitudes or behaviour to accommodate the standards of peers or groups. The pressure to conform can be immense, even if subtle. Wearing a thin tie when wide is in vogue makes many men uncomfortable, as does wearing the wrong brand of sneakers for many teenagers.

The Asch studies

A series of classic studies by Solomon Asch (1955, 1956) documented the power of conformity, much as Milgram's studies established the power of obedience. Asch assembled groups of seven to nine university students and told them they were participating in an experiment on visual judgement. All but one of the students were actually confederates, so their responses were planned in advance.

The experimenter asked the 'participants' to match the lines on two white cards. The first card had one line printed on it; the second had three lines, one of which clearly matched the line on the first card in length (see figure 18.8). The participant's task was to select the line on the second card that matched the line on the first.

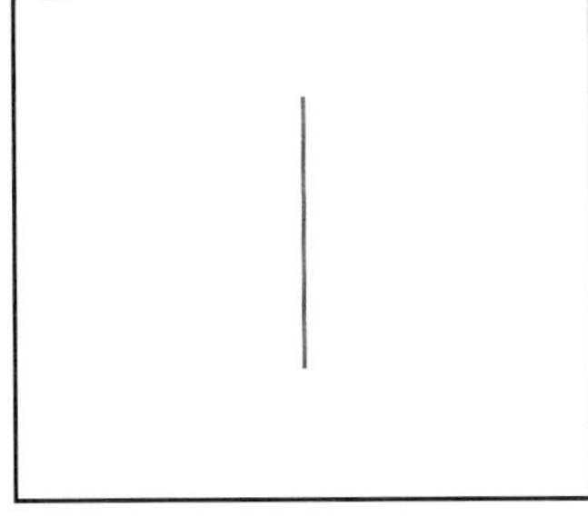

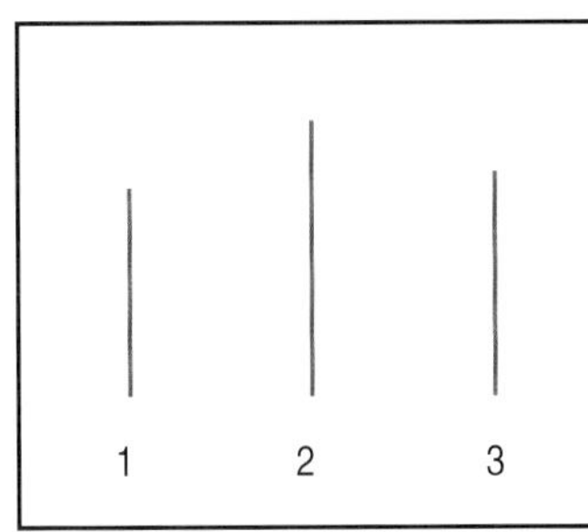

FIGURE 18.8
The Asch conformity experiments. Participants in Asch's experiment on conformity were asked which of the three lines in the box on the right matched the one on the left. Pressure to conform swayed their responses.

SOURCE: Asch (1955, p. 193).

On the first and second trials, everyone — participant and confederates alike — gave the right answer. On subsequent trials, however, the confederates (who went first) unanimously chose a line that was obviously incorrect. Their answers placed the participant in the uncomfortable position of having to choose between publicly opposing the view of the group or answering incorrectly.

Without peer pressure to conform, participants chose the wrong line less than 1 percent of the time. However, when faced with a unanimous (but incorrect) opinion of the confederates, participants made the same incorrect choice as the confederates 36.8 percent of the time. Up to a point, the more confederates, the greater the tendency to conform. Participants only conformed, however, if the confederates all gave the same answer. If at least one confederate gave a different answer from that of the others, participants followed their own judgement most of the time. Apparently, opposing the majority is extremely difficult without at least one other dissenter.

The Asch studies powerfully demonstrate the power of situations to influence behaviour and attitudes. Personality factors, however, also influence the tendency to conform. Individuals with low self-esteem and those who are especially motivated by a need for social approval are more likely to conform (Crowne & Marlowe, 1964; Dittes, 1959; Moeller & Applezweig, 1957; Strang, 1972; see also Twenge & Im, 2007).

To what extent participants actually alter their beliefs in the Asch studies rather than simply comply with situational demands to avoid disapproval is a matter of debate. Many of Asch's participants reported that they believed their (incorrect) answers, perhaps because of cognitive dissonance or a desire not to look foolish. Nevertheless, the main implication of these studies is that many people will change at least the public expression of their beliefs when confronted with a group that disagrees with them.

Conformity and culture

Conformity varies by culture and appears to be linked to the way people earn their livelihood (Price-Williams, 1985). People in hunter-gatherer societies exercise more independent judgements than people in agricultural societies (Berry, 1979). Agricultural societies depend heavily on communal organisation and coordinated action; too much independent judgement can be counterproductive during planting and harvest times, when work needs to be done. Agricultural societies also have much higher population densities, whereas hunter-gatherer societies are often highly dispersed across a territory, and may thus require less compliance with social norms (see Barry, Bacon, & Child, 1957).

In general, conformity is higher in collectivist than in more individualistic cultures (Bond & Smith, 1996; Jetten, Postmes, & McAuliffe, 2002). One study with an East Asian sample found that participants preferred to conform rather than to be different even when 'independence' had no cost (Kim & Markus, 1999). When given a choice among pens, Americans overwhelmingly chose the one pen that was a different colour from the others; East Asians preferred a pen of the same colour as all the others (Kim & Markus, 1999).

Conformity also varies *within* cultures in systematic ways. In both North America and Australia, low-income and rural parents tend to emphasise obedience and conformity in their child-rearing practices as compared with urban and middle-class parents (Cashmore & Goodnow, 1986; Peterson & Peters, 1985). Middle-class parents are likely to value self-direction and believe that children should have freedom in and around the home, while working-class parents are likely to believe that children should be expected to conform to rules (Tudge, Hogan, Snezhkova, Kulakova, & Etz, 2000). This finding, too, makes adaptive sense because parents typically prepare their children for work similar to their own (LeVine, 1982), and labourers have less autonomy than professionals.

Conformity and gender

Gender differences in conformity and susceptibility to social influence are a matter of debate. Much of the early research in social psychology (along with most people's commonsensical notions) suggested that women are more open to influence than men (Asch, 1955). Lay stereotypes suggest that women's desire to maintain harmony in social relationships leads them to go along publicly with the opinions and decisions of others. However, a closer look at the data indicates that these stereotypes are wrong. A meta-analysis looking at the overall effect size of this gender difference showed it to be very small (Eagly & Carli, 1981). In most instances, women are only slightly, if at all, more likely to succumb to social influence than men, with one notable exception. When women are placed in a situation where their responses are public and involve face-to-face interactions, they are more likely to conform than men (Eagly, 1978). Although it is possible that women are simply more gullible than men, it is also possible that men are simply more resistant to social influence tactics in public settings (Cialdini & Trost, 1998).

INTERIM SUMMARY

Social influence refers to the effects of the presence of others on the way people think, feel and behave. ***Obedience*** refers to compliance with authority. The Milgram experiments demonstrated that most people will obey, without limitations of conscience, when they believe an order comes from a legitimate authority. ***Conformity*** means changing attitudes or behaviour to accommodate the standards of peers or groups. The Asch experiments demonstrated that people tend to conform rather than to be the lone dissenting voice. Conformity varies across and within cultures, and tends to reflect economic and ecological demands. In spite of commonsensical notions, few, if any, gender differences in conformity exist.

Group processes

The Asch conformity experiments illustrate just how powerful group processes can be. A ***group*** is a collection of people whose actions affect the other group members. When a collection of people congregate for even relatively short periods of time, their interactions tend to become patterned in various ways; the same is true of more enduring social institutions such as families and corporations.

Characteristics of groups

The behaviour of people in groups is dictated in large part by the norms operating within particular groups and the roles that individual members of the group play. ***Norms***, or standards for behaviour, guide thought, feeling and behaviour, from the way people dress to their attitudes about sex, politics and lawyers. Sometimes norms are explicit (e.g. a written dress code), but much of the time they are implicit (men do not wear dresses; peers do not issue commands to each other). Different groups have different norms, and particularly in complex societies, people must pick and choose the norms to obey at any given moment because they belong to many groups, which may have conflicting norms. Adolescents, for example, frequently find themselves choosing between the norms of adults and peers.

Friends are an important reference group for teenagers.

The way people respond to norms depends on their attitude towards the groups with which the norms are associated. Groups whose norms matter to an individual, and hence have an impact on the individual's behaviour, are known as ***reference groups***. In other words, these are the groups to which a person *refers* when taking action.

A reference group can be positive or negative. A reference group is considered *positive* if the person tries to emulate its members and meet their standards. When a teenage boy gets drunk on weekends because his friends do, his friends are a positive reference group (but not necessarily a positive influence). A reference group is *negative* if a person rejects its members and disavows their standards. If a teenager gets drunk every weekend to establish her independence from her teetotalling parents, her parents are a negative reference group. In both cases, the reference group is influencing the teenager's behaviour (which they each might be loath to admit).

The norms operating in groups determine, in part, the roles that individual group members play. A ***role*** is a position in a group that has norms specifying appropriate behaviour for its occupants (see Merton, 1957; Parsons, 1951). Roles are essentially norms that are specific to particular people or subgroups.

Roles reflect shared expectations about how particular members of a group are supposed to behave. They tend to be flexible, allowing the individual to make decisions about specific actions, much like roles in improvisational theatre. A mother can decide how she will care for her child in a given circumstance, but her culture provides general guidelines for acceptable maternal behaviour, such as whether she should stay home with her child or what forms of discipline she should employ.

Individuals internalise roles as role schemas, which direct their behaviour when they are in a particular role and lead them to expect certain responses from people with complementary roles (such as husband and wife, teacher and student). Several roles routinely emerge in groups, even in brief, unstructured ones (see Bales, 1953). When strangers enter into groups in the laboratory and are asked to solve problems, the group members who take responsibility for seeing that the group completes its tasks are called ***task leaders***, or ***instrumental leaders***. Others, called ***social–emotional leaders***, try to keep the group working cohesively and with minimal animosity.

Because people often define themselves by their roles, roles can have a profound impact on behaviour. One of the most dramatic illustrations of the influence of roles on social behaviour occurred in a study by Philip Zimbardo (1972, 1975). Twenty-two male Stanford University student volunteers played the roles of prisoners and guards in a simulated prison. To make the experiment as realistic as possible, students designated as prisoners were arrested at their homes and searched, handcuffed, fingerprinted and booked at a police station. They were then blindfolded and driven to the simulated prison where they were stripped, sprayed with a delousing preparation (actually a deodorant spray) and told to stand alone naked in the cell yard. After a short time, they were given a uniform and placed in a cell with two other 'prisoners'. The guards received minimal instructions and were free to devise their own rules. The only prohibition was against physical punishment.

APPLY + DISCUSS

Experience a re-creation of the Stanford prison experiment that demonstrates characteristics of groups by linking to a YouTube video clip that should be available via your university course website for this subject.

- Why do people so readily slip into roles, such as prisoners and guards?
- Why are social processes so compelling that they can seemingly override individuals' normal ways of behaving and responding morally?

Soon after the experiment began, Zimbardo noted marked differences between the behaviour of the guards and the prisoners. The guards became increasingly aggressive, treating the prisoners as less than human, seldom using their names (instead calling them by number, if referring to them as individuals at all), and subjecting them to roll calls that could last for hours. Many acted with clear sadistic pleasure.

The prisoners, for their part, initiated progressively fewer actions and appeared increasingly depressed. Half the prisoners (five participants) suffered such extreme depression, anxiety or psychosomatic illness that they had to leave the experiment. The prisoners talked almost exclusively about prison life, maintaining the illusion of their roles. By the fifth day, those who remained were brought before a mock parole board, which would determine whether or not they would be released. Most were willing to forfeit all the money they had earned in the experiment if they could be released. When their requests for parole were denied, they obediently returned to their cells.

The study was originally designed to last two weeks, but the shocking results led Zimbardo to abort it after only six days. The study provides a powerful demonstration of the way roles structure people's behaviour and ultimately their emotions, attitudes and even their identities. Although participants were, in reality, university students randomly assigned to be prisoners or guards, within days they had *become* their roles — in action, thought and feeling.

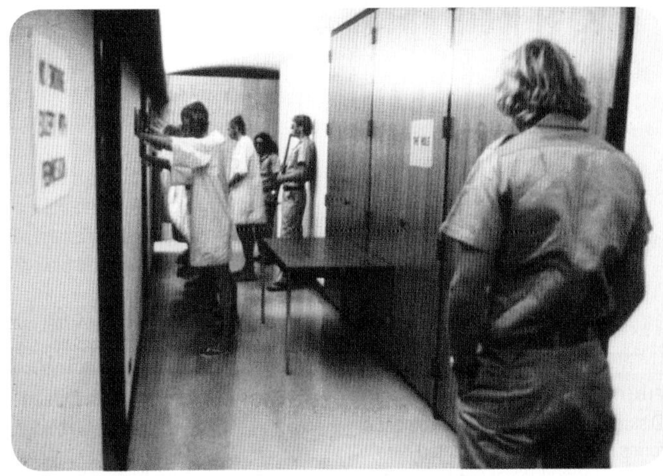

Zimbardo's Stanford University prison study showed how powerful the demands of roles and situations can be on individual behaviour.

Group social influence

Being part of a group can exert a substantial influence on the behaviour of individual group members (see Carron, Burke, & Prapavessis, 2004). The presence of other people can either help or hurt individual performance, a process called ***social facilitation*** (Triplett, 1898). When people are performing dominant, well-learned behaviours, the presence of other people can facilitate performance. On the other hand, when people are performing non-dominant behaviours, or behaviours with which they are unfamiliar, the presence of others can hurt performance (Zajonc, 1965). Driving a car, particularly with a manual transmission, provides a good example of the difference between dominant and non-dominant responses. When a person is first learning to drive a car with manual transmission, he turns the radio off, does not want to engage in conversation, and certainly does not eat, drink or smoke while driving. During the learning phase, driving is a non-dominant response. Other tasks, such as talking to other people, are distracting. However, once the person practises driving so that driving a manual transmission becomes a well-learned behaviour, he can change gears, talk, listen to music, eat and drink all at the same time (although that is definitely not recommended!). Driving with a manual transmission is now a dominant response.

The facilitative effects of other people on performance have their limitations, however, as demonstrated most aptly with the *choking under pressure* phenomenon. In spite of the fact that playing sport in front of a home audience would seem to be an advantage (i.e. home ground advantage), this does not appear to be the case. The pressure to win key games, particularly in front of a home crowd, can be so great that team players become increasingly self-conscious and what was once a dominant response (e.g. playing football or tennis) resembles a non-dominant response. For example, no Australian man has won the Australian Open tennis title since 1975, despite Pat Cash, Pat Rafter and Lleyton Hewitt winning other Grand Slam events during that time.

Furthermore, the facilitative effects of group membership depend on the type of task (Steiner, 1972). Participation in a tug-of-war, for example, is certainly enhanced by the more people present; however, not as much as you would think. If we could determine how much each individual involved in a tug-of-war could pull, the group output would, in fact, be less than the sum of these individual inputs. The more people involved in a task, the harder it is to coordinate efforts — to say nothing of the fact that people in a group frequently rely on others to pick up the slack for them. This process by which people exert less effort when in a group is referred to as ***social loafing*** (Williams, Harkins, & Latane, 1981; see also Hoigaard, Säfvenbom, & Tonnessen, 2006; Piezon & Donaldson, 2005).

On yet other tasks, some individuals will perform at least as well alone as when part of a group (see also Lücken & Simon, 2005). Tasks in which there is a single answer (e.g. yes/no) are referred to as disjunctive tasks (see figure 18.9). The individual in a group who can solve the problem would perform just as well alone as she would as part of the group. Although she might benefit from group discussions that lead to the solution of the problem, the presence of other people could also be distracting, such that the time to completion of the task is actually lengthened.

DISJUNCTIVE PUZZLES

Disjunctive tasks come in two varieties: Eureka and non-Eureka. When we are told the answer to a Eureka problem, we are very certain that the answer offered is correct. It fits so well, we react with an 'Aha!' or 'Eureka'. The answers to non-Eureka problems, in contrast, are not so satisfying. Even after arguing about them, we often wonder if the recommended answer is the correct answer. Examples of both types of problems are listed below, and their answers can be found at the end of the chapter.

1. What is the next letter in the following sequence?

   OTTFFSS

2. A man bought a horse for $60 and sold it for $70. Then he bought it back for $80 and again sold it for $90. How much money did he make in the horse-trading business? (*Source:* Maier & Solem, 1952)
3. Three missionaries and three cannibals are on one side of a river. They want to cross to the other side by means of a boat that can only hold two persons at a time. All the missionaries but only one cannibal can row. For obvious reasons, the missionaries must never be outnumbered by the cannibals, under any circumstances or at any time, except where no missionaries are present at all. How many crossings will be necessary to transport the six people across the river? (*Source:* Shaw, 1932)
4. Isaac is staying at a motel when he runs short of cash. Checking his finances, he discovers that in 23 days he will have plenty of money, but until then he will be broke. The motel owner refuses to let Isaac stay without paying his bill each day, but since Isaac owns a heavy gold chain with 23 links, the owner allows Isaac to pay for each of the 23 days with one gold link. Then, when Isaac receives his money, the motel owner will return the chain. Isaac is very anxious to keep the chain as intact as possible, so he doesn't want to cut off any more of the links than absolutely necessary. The motel owner, however, insists on payment each day, and he will accept no advance payment. How many links must Isaac cut while still paying the owner one link for each successive day? (*Source:* Marquart, 1955)

FIGURE **18.9**
Disjunctive tasks can take a number of forms. The problems presented here will give you some idea of what is meant by a disjunctive task, and the difficulty inherent in solving some of these tasks.

SOURCE: From Forsyth. Group Dynamics 2E. © 1990 Wadsworth, a part of Cengage Learning, Inc. Reproduced by permission. www.cengage.com/permissions.

Group decision making

We all make individual decisions every day of our lives — for instance, what to have for breakfast, or what radio station to listen to in our car. But what about decisions that we make as part of a group — for instance, which movie to go to see, or what type of pizza to order? Are decisions that we make as part of a group different to those we might make alone? To answer that, we need to look at the nature of group decision making. As a start, a model of groupthink discussed later in this section is represented visually in figure 18.10.

Conventional wisdom seems to suggest that decisions made by a group would be characterised as mainstream — that is, neither too conservative nor too radical. In fact, research shows that groups decisions are rarely 'middle of the road' but are normally either at one extreme or the other — either conservative or risky. This is known as ***group polarisation***, a movement towards a decision that is at the extreme position (Kamalanabhan, Sunder, & Vasanthi, 2000). Why does it occur? One possibility is that the group members become exposed to new information argued in a persuasive manner. This convinces the group members to move decisively in one direction or another. Another reason could be ***group cohesiveness***, whereby people tend to cluster together to be viewed even more favourably by members of their ingroup (Hogg, Turner, & Davidson, 1990; see also Hewstone, Rubin, & Willis, 2002; Petersen, Dietz, & Frey, 2004). A further theory is that responsibility for decisions made in a group can be diffused more readily. Once you make a decision as an individual, there is no-one left to blame if something goes wrong. However, blame can be shared and diluted if that same decision was made as part of a group.

Computer-based technologies utilised in the workplace have also been shown to impact on group polarisation. Results from one study found that a reduction in social presence through use of computer-mediated, rather than face-to-face, communication was associated with increased group polarisation (Sia, Tan, & Wei, 2002).

Another characteristic of group decision making is what has become known as ***groupthink***, a concept originated by Irving Janis (1972). Groupthink occurs when members of a group make decisions based more on maintaining group harmony and cohesiveness than a critical analysis of the realities of a situation (Park, 2000). In these circumstances, individuals seek concurrence and censor dissenting opinions. Rather than making an objective examination of the facts and coming to a rational decision, members tend to ignore all their options and fall into line behind each other. Groupthink is common in groups with a charismatic and strong leader, as well as in groups that are under extreme stress. External opposition to the group tends to hardens its position, developing an entrenched 'us against them' attitude. Figure 18.10 outlines Janis' (1982) model of groupthink, showing the link between antecedents (e.g. a strong need for cohesiveness), symptoms of groupthink (e.g. illusion of invulnerability) and symptoms of poor decision making (e.g. failure to examine risks of preferred choice).

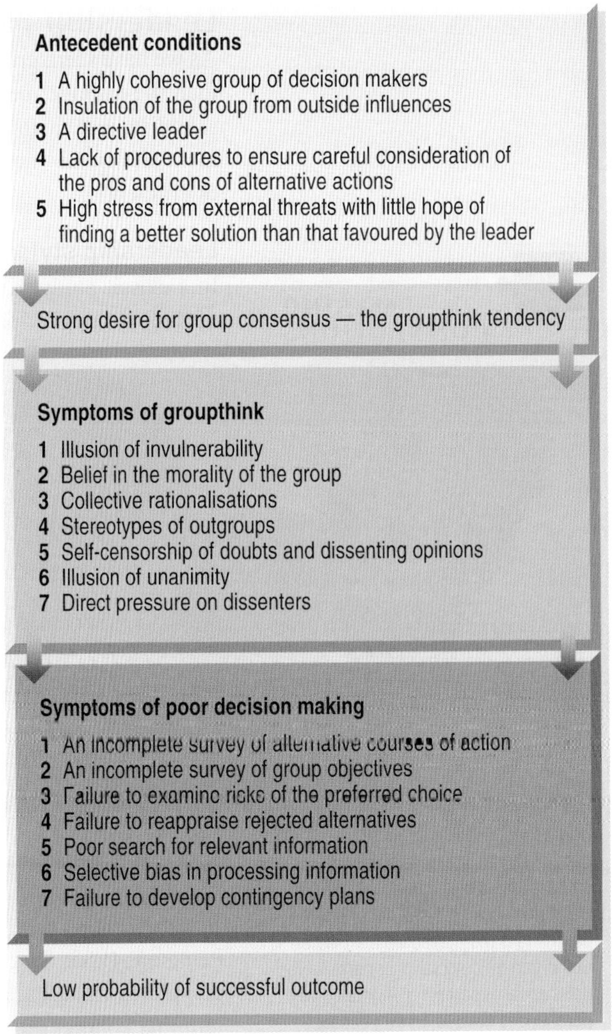

Antecedent conditions

1. A highly cohesive group of decision makers
2. Insulation of the group from outside influences
3. A directive leader
4. Lack of procedures to ensure careful consideration of the pros and cons of alternative actions
5. High stress from external threats with little hope of finding a better solution than that favoured by the leader

Strong desire for group consensus — the groupthink tendency

Symptoms of groupthink

1. Illusion of invulnerability
2. Belief in the morality of the group
3. Collective rationalisations
4. Stereotypes of outgroups
5. Self-censorship of doubts and dissenting opinions
6. Illusion of unanimity
7. Direct pressure on dissenters

Symptoms of poor decision making

1. An incomplete survey of alternative courses of action
2. An incomplete survey of group objectives
3. Failure to examine risks of the preferred choice
4. Failure to reappraise rejected alternatives
5. Poor search for relevant information
6. Selective bias in processing information
7. Failure to develop contingency plans

Low probability of successful outcome

FIGURE **18.10**
Janis' 1982 model of groupthink shows the link between antecedent conditions (top box), symptoms of groupthink (middle box) and symptoms of poor decision making (bottom box).

SOURCE: From Janis, Irving L., Groupthink: Psychological Studies of Policy Decisions and Fiascoes, 2E. © 1982 Wadsworth, a part of Cengage Learning, Inc. Reproduced by permission. www.cengage.com/permissions.

INTERIM SUMMARY

A ***group*** is a collection of people whose actions affect the other group members. All groups develop ***norms***, or standards for behaviour. People also frequently play particular ***roles*** in groups (positions in the group that have norms specifying appropriate behaviour for their occupants). Roles can have a dramatic influence on behaviours, as demonstrated in Zimbardo's prison experiment, which had to be aborted because people became immersed too deeply in their assigned roles. The influence of groups on individuals can be seen readily in studies investigating ***social facilitation*** and individual performance in groups working on a variety of tasks. Decisions made by a group tend to be either conservative or risky. This is known as ***group polarisation***, a movement towards a decision that is at the extreme position. Group decisions may also reflect the ***group cohesiveness***, whereby people tend to cluster together to be viewed even more favourably by members of their ingroup. ***Groupthink*** is another characteristic of group decision making. Groupthink occurs when members of a group make decisions based more on maintaining group harmony and cohesiveness than a critical analysis of the realities of a situation.

Leadership

As we have seen, groups tend to have formal or informal ***leaders***, people who exercise greater influence than the average member. A major initial impetus to research on leadership was Adolf Hitler. Social scientists were astonished that an individual so manifestly disturbed could arouse such popular sentiment and create such a well-oiled war machine. Could democratic forms of leadership be as effective or efficient?

Leadership styles

In a classic study, Kurt Lewin and his colleagues (1939) randomly assigned 10-year-old boys to one of three groups for craft activities after school. Each group was led by an adult who took one of three leadership styles: he made all the decisions (an *autocratic* leadership style); involved himself in the group and encouraged members to come to decisions themselves (a *democratic* style); or simply let things happen, intervening as little as possible (a *laissez-faire* style).

Boys with an autocratic leader produced more crafts, but they were more likely to stray from the task when the leader left the room, and their products were judged inferior to those produced in the democratic condition. Boys in the democratic group expressed greater satisfaction and displayed less aggression than the others. Laissez-faire leadership led to neither satisfaction nor efficiency. Lewin and his colleagues concluded that autocratic leadership breeds discontent but can be efficient, whereas democratic leadership seems to be both efficient and motivating.

Lewin's leadership categories parallel Diana Baumrind's findings on parenting styles (chapter 13). Baumrind showed that authoritative parenting is more effective than either authoritarian (autocratic) or permissive (laissez-faire) parenting. Authoritative parenting is not democratic, because it recognises the limits of children's judgement, but it is participatory and allows input by 'citizens' of the family.

Industrial/organisational (I/O) psychologists have conducted much of the research on leadership, trying to translate theory and research on effective leadership into interventions to make organisations more efficient. Contemporary organisational psychologists emphasise two dimensions on which leaders vary: *task orientation* and *relationship orientation* (see Blake & Mouton, 1964; Burke et al., 2006; Hersey & Blanchard, 1982; Misumi & Peterson, 1985; Stogdill & Coons, 1957). ***Task leaders*** take responsibility for seeing that the group completes its tasks; ***social–emotional leaders*** try to keep the group working cohesively and with minimal conflict. In other words, leaders differ in the extent to which they focus on efficiency and on the feelings of their employees. The distinction is similar to the two major clusters of psychosocial motives found cross-culturally, agency and communion (chapter 10).

Cultural values and norms also guide leadership styles (see Ardichvili & Kuchinke, 2002; Gerstner & Day, 1994). Managers in societies such as Greece and India tend to prefer autocratic leadership styles with passive subordinates; by contrast, leaders in societies such as Australia, the United States, Canada and England prefer subordinates who are active and participatory (Barrett & Franke, 1969; Negandhi, 1973). A study of managers in the United States, Hong Kong and China found American managers more concerned with worker productivity and Chinese managers more concerned with maintaining a harmonious work environment (Ralston, Gustafson, Elsass, & Cheung, 1992). Managers in Hong Kong expressed moderate concerns about both productivity and harmony, presumably reflecting Hong Kong's economic similarity to the United States and cultural similarity to China.

Gender differences in leadership styles continue to be a hotly debated topic for which there is no universal agreement (see Eagly & Johannesen-Schmidt, 2001). Leadership style and effectiveness may also depend on the leader's personality (Hogan, Curphy, & Hogan, 1994; see also Andersen, 2006; Kornor & Nordvik, 2004). Research on the five factor model and similar dimensions of personality (chapter 11) finds that successful leaders tend to be high on extroversion (including dominance, energy and orientation towards status), agreeableness and conscientiousness. Thus, effective leaders tend to be outgoing, energetic, powerful, kind, hard working and attentive to the task at hand. Ineffective leaders tend to be perceived as arrogant, untrustworthy, selfish, insensitive and overambitious — in a word, narcissistic.

These generalisations, however, require the same caveat as all generalisations about personality traits. They are more likely to apply in some situations than in others (chapter 11). Situational factors that influence the effectiveness of a particular management style include the motivation and ability of employees, the extent to which tasks require autonomy and creativity, the leader's position in the organisational hierarchy, the degree of pressure to produce, the type of organisation and the extent to which the environment is competitive (Dipboye, 1997). A good leader is one who can adjust her leadership style to the context in which she leads — and, where appropriate, to adjust the context in the process of leading.

Interactional models of leadership

Although much of the theoretical and empirical work on leadership has focused on leadership styles, more recent attention has been devoted to a leader's ability to adapt the leadership style to particular situations. Interactional theories suggest that effective leaders can adapt their leadership styles to match the needs of the followers and of the situation. One of the most prominent of these theories is Fiedler's (1978, 1981) contingency theory.

Fiedler determined leadership style by having participants complete the *Least Preferred Co-Worker (LPC) Scale*. Participants think of the individual with whom they found it most difficult to work. They then rate this person on 20 bipolar adjectives (e.g. good–bad, pleasant–unpleasant). A person who found it difficult to work with this individual yet who still accords them high ratings is predominantly relationship-oriented. Those who assign negative ratings are primarily task-oriented.

According to Fielder, whether a task- or a relationship-oriented leader is most effective depends on three situational variables: task structure (i.e. the task is either very structured and clear or very unstructured and unclear); leader–member relationships, which can range on a continuum from very good to very bad; and position power (i.e. the status accorded to the leader by the followers). Under highly favourable conditions (i.e. leader–member relationships are good, the task is structured and the leader has strong power over the followers) or under highly unfavourable conditions (i.e. leader–member relationships are poor, the task is unstructured and the leader has little power over group members), a task-oriented leader is best. Under moderately favourable situational conditions, a relationship-oriented leader is more effective.

INTERIM SUMMARY

Leaders are people who exercise greater influence than the average member of a group. Leaders tend to vary in the extent to which they are task oriented or relationship oriented. ***Task leaders*** take responsibility for seeing that the group completes its tasks; ***social–emotional leaders*** try to keep the group working cohesively and with minimal conflict. Leadership styles that are optimal or considered appropriate in one culture or setting may not be optimal in others. Leadership style (and effectiveness) differs across cultures as well as across individuals. At least in the West, effective leaders tend to be extroverted, agreeable and conscientious. The most effective leadership style is one that is matched to particular situational demands. Fiedler's contingency theory of leadership outlines three situational variables that together influence what style of leadership will be most effective: task structure, leader–member relationships and position power.

Everyday social influence

When we read about social influence processes such as the blind obedience to authority described earlier with the Milgram study, it is easy to distance ourselves from such findings by telling ourselves that we would never shock another person who had stopped responding. Though we may not realise it, we are all victims of social influence on a daily basis. In a compelling book called *Influence*, Robert Cialdini discusses various principles of social influence or ways in which people are taken in by others on a regular basis.

One of the first principles of social influence is the principle of *reciprocity*. Most people have a compelling need to reciprocate that which has been done to them. Indeed, most people are socialised to behave this way. A compelling demonstration of this involved two researchers who sent Christmas cards to a group of randomly selected strangers (Kunz & Woolcott, 1976). The response rate in the form of return Christmas cards was overwhelming. Only six individuals who replied indicated that they did not remember the sender.

Although perhaps not as extreme as the Christmas card example, the number of examples of the principle of reciprocity are limitless, with all of them pointing to the fact that we all find ourselves victims of social influence on a regular basis. No-one wants to be perceived as a freeloader, so people reciprocate.

The principle of reciprocity is so strong that it lies at the heart of an everyday social influence tactic, the ***door-in-the-face technique***, when we intentionally make a request that we know will be turned down, so that when we back down from our request, the other individual should reciprocate with a concession.

We should not think that our need to reciprocate extends only to positive situations. Indeed, we also feel the need to reciprocate negative things that people do to us. If someone cuts us off in traffic, we feel the need to reciprocate in kind. If someone plays a practical joke on us (that they may find funny, but we do not), we feel it necessary to play a practical joke on them in return. Reciprocity of negative behaviours constitutes the essence of revenge.

A second principle of social influence that allows us to be influenced is the principle of *commitment*. Because people are concerned with the impressions that others are forming of them (chapter 17), they feel the need to behave consistently with prior impressions or commitments they have made. Thus, if someone can get you to make an initial commitment, no matter how small, they have generally got you. The ***foot-in-the-door technique*** refers to this process by which people who get us to commit to a small request are much more likely to get us to commit to a larger request (Burger, 1999).

In a demonstration of the foot-in-the-door technique, Freedman and Fraser (1966) went door-to-door asking people if they would be willing to have a billboard placed in their yard that said 'Drive carefully'. After viewing a picture showing that the billboard would obscure the house, only 17 percent of the participants in one group agreed. Another group of individuals, however, had been previously asked if they would place a three-inch sign in their window that said 'Be a safe driver'. When the people in this group were subsequently asked whether or not they would put the billboard in their front yard, 76 percent complied! The enormous difference in compliance rates of the two groups of individuals can be explained only by the fact that those people in the second group had committed to a small request before they were asked the larger request — they had become victims of the foot-in-the-door technique.

The principle of commitment also underlies a second specific technique of social influence — ***low-balling***. People who low-ball others get a commitment to a request and then they change the conditions of the request (Cialdini & Goldstein, 2004). Car dealers are infamous for low-balling their customers.

The principle of liking means that people usually buy items at Tupperware parties, even if they do not need them.

One final principle of social influence that gets us all is the principle of *liking*. The Tupperware party is a common example in Australia. People who attend these parties usually buy items, even if they do not need them. The principle of liking makes us feel obligated to buy costly products we normally would not buy. We do things for people that we like out of a sense of obligation and so that they will continue to like us in return.

As we discussed earlier in the chapter, a number of variables, such as physical attractiveness and similarity, determine those to whom we are attracted. People who use the principle of liking as a social influence tool capitalise on some of these features. For example, car salespersons often look for points of similarity with their customers, to create a more likeable impression. Infant car seats indicate that the customer has children, golf clubs that he likes golf. These observations can then be used as points of similarity whereby the salesperson can talk about her own fondness for golf, a point of similarity that breeds liking and that, in this case, translates into a sale. Marketers also frequently use this social psychology principle to enhance the success of their products in the online environment. Tools such as referral programs and news feeds that encourage consumers to follow and share information about what brands they like on social networking sites such as Twitter, Facebook and YouTube are examples of how liking can be used to increase consumer interest in products and services.

Reading about social influence leads us to ask why we are so easily influenced by others. Why can't we be more resilient in the face of interpersonal pressure? Although there are many answers to this question, one of the simplest is *mindlessness*. Each day we are inundated with innumerable stimuli vying for our attention. Obviously, no-one can process everything with which he is confronted on a daily basis, so some of what we say and do follows from mindless processing. In a clever demonstration of mindlessness, Ellen Langer and her colleagues (1978) asked a favour of people using a photocopier.

They established three different conditions in the study. In the first condition, people using the copier were approached with the request, 'Excuse me, I have five pages. May I use the Xerox machine because I'm in a rush?' Ninety-four people complied with this request. In a second condition, however, compliance rates were lower (only 60 percent). These individuals were simply asked, 'Excuse me, I have five pages. May I use the Xerox machine?'

Although these results might be expected, the third condition was the most surprising. Participants in the third condition were approached with the request, 'Excuse me, I have five pages. May I use the Xerox machine because I have to make some copies?' In the latter case, 93 percent of the people complied! As the researchers expected, simply providing a reason for the request being made was sufficient to induce compliance even if the reason was ridiculous — of course the person had to make copies. Why else would he be using a copier? Hearing the word 'because' alerted participants to the fact that a reason was to follow. What that reason was apparently didn't matter and was simply tuned out.

Who benefits from the psychology of interpersonal processes?

By Professor Stuart C. Carr, Massey University

Social psychologists have spent a lot of time and valuable resources studying the dynamics of social influence: relationships, helping versus hurting, individuals in groups and groups in the individual. What is the point of studying and learning about them? Some might say it helps individuals to gain more control over what they do. Others might instead stress the social good (i.e. benefits to others). Yet both of these perspectives link gaining knowledge about people to empowerment. Empowerment brings risks. To paraphrase Lord Acton, empowerment might corrupt, and absolute empowerment corrupts absolutely. Knowing what motivates others can be used to *dis*empower them (i.e. to manipulate them). Psychologists risk becoming what Baritz called 'servants of power'. Servitude is an evergreen issue for psychologists in organisations. Management pays their wages, not labour. So, they could end up finding ways to influence workers to take more pressure. Social psychologists may find themselves working for a government whose real agenda is to befriend other countries, and then to simply exploit them later on.

Social scientists need to stay vigilant against doing more harm than good. This is a social responsibility; an ethical obligation. There are codes of ethics for the profession of psychology in both Australia and New Zealand (Australian Psychological Society, 2007; New Zealand Psychological Society, 2002). These codes of ethical conduct provide extensive guidance on how to decide who is the client, and how to identify and resolve issues like conflicts of interest (e.g. between serving management versus serving labour). Underpinning the codes are human values, which vary from culture to culture and context to context. There is literature on how people resolve moral and other dilemmas across cultures in cross-cultural psychology (chapter 19). The key point for the moment, however, is that codes of ethics are a psychologist's friend — not their enemy: they are there to enable better decisions in the implementation of professional and personal values in everyday psychological practice.

On a grander scale, psychology has a responsibility to address issues of global importance. Take, for example, the issues of human poverty, climate change, gender equity and conflict. These issues are affected by influence processes. It is people who drive business development, consume and recycle environmental resources, construct glass ceilings and negotiate in good faith for peace. This chapter and others address some of these issues, but there is always more to be done.

Not everyone wants to be a career psychologist or a social activist. Yet, being aware of influence processes has a part in everyday life too. Being aware of the dynamics of similarity–attraction can help job selectors make fairer decisions (e.g. among candidates who are culturally diverse and are different from the self) (chapter 19). Awareness about the psychology of bystander intervention can help in an everyday emergency. Being aware of Milgram and Asch's work on obedience and conformity might not only influence, but also improve the results achieved during an upcoming work meeting.

Central questions revisited

◆ Individuals, groups and the nature of human nature

We began this chapter with a central question. To what extent does our behaviour depend on the groups of which we are a part? The data from a century of social–psychological research are clear: we are social animals. As we saw in the last chapter, the cultures, groups and families of which we are a part get 'under our skin' — they become part of the way we think, feel and behave, from the attitudes we hold to the ways we view ourselves. And as we have seen in this chapter, the tendency to behave in groups in ways that seem 'out of character' appears to be very much a part of our character. Much as we might look with horror and astonishment at the participants in Milgram's studies, the only difference between them and us is that they know the truth about themselves.

In this sense, people's behaviour in groups clearly differs qualitatively from their behaviour when they are alone. A group is more than a sum of its parts. In another sense, however, we are never actually alone at all. We are always living with mental representations of the people who matter to us — people we love, hate, admire and interact with every day. We are always in the presence of real or imagined others.

These are very special times to study psychology, because the cultures that get 'under our skin' and so powerfully influence everything we do are so rapidly changing. In the twentieth century, we witnessed the most momentous period of social change in human history, as the vast majority of the world's people shifted from agricultural, nomadic or hunter-gatherer societies to industrial nation states. Not since the rise of agriculture thousands of years ago has the structure of human society changed so dramatically, and never as rapidly as in the present epoch. A century ago, most people lived with their extended families and believed in the values of their parents and ancestors. Within a few brief generations, traditional values and beliefs have broken down and technology has advanced beyond anyone's wildest predictions.

People cope with social change in many ways. Some embrace new ideologies, technologies and values. Others, coping with spiritual unease or feelings of envy, inferiority and hatred of the dominant cultures that swept away their traditions, search for the future in the past, embracing fundamentalist ideologies that rigidly define good and evil, eliminate ambiguity and offer a blueprint for how to live (Lifton, 1963). Another route to personal meaning lies in transferring loyalties from family and clan to large nation states (see Geertz, 1963). Unfortunately, this process can produce the kind of fervent nationalism that left so many dead in the twentieth century, from Nazi Germany to Bosnia. Still another strategy for coping with social change is to synthesise the old and the new, to preserve a continuity with the past while somehow mooring one's identity in the future, as was Gandhi's path.

These psychological responses to the social and political realities of our age lie at the intersection of brain, behaviour and culture. The aggression that fuels conflicts between nations, like the powerful feelings of kinship and solidarity that unite people and give their lives meaning, springs from a brain constructed to make possible the passions that divide and unite. We all share a core of human nature rooted in biology. But the way that nature develops and expresses itself is as diverse as the cultures and individuals who populate the globe.

◆

SUMMARY

1 Attraction

- Several factors lead to ***interpersonal attraction***, including proximity, similarity, rewards and physical attractiveness. ***Social exchange theory*** holds that the foundation of relationships lies in reciprocal rewards.
- Psychologists studying love distinguish the factors that produce initial attraction from those that maintain or corrode relationships over time. Two kinds of love seen in long-term relationships are ***passionate love*** (marked by intense physiological arousal and absorption in another person) and ***companionate love*** (love that involves deep affection, friendship and emotional intimacy).
- Evolutionary theorists understand love in terms of contributions to reproductive success. From this point of view, romantic love shares many features of attachment, and may have evolved to bind parents together to take care of their children. ***Sexual strategies***, tactics used in selecting mates, vary by gender and reflect the different evolutionary selection pressures on males and females. The capacity for love is rooted in biology, but its specific nature is shaped by culture.
- As desirable as relationships with others are, they also have a dark side. People experience their greatest criticisms and most painful hurts in the context of close relationships, as anyone who has ever been ostracised by someone close can attest.

2 Altruism

- ***Altruism*** means behaving in a way that helps another person with no apparent gain or with potential cost to oneself. Philosophers and psychologists disagree as to whether any act can be genuinely altruistic or whether all apparent altruism is really aimed at making the apparent altruist feel better (***ethical hedonism***). Altruistic behaviour probably reflects a blend of selfish and unselfish motives.
- Evolutionary psychologists propose that people act in ways that maximise their inclusive fitness and hence are most likely to behave altruistically towards their relatives. Natural selection favours animals that behave altruistically towards unrelated members of the species if the likely benefit to each individual over time exceeds the likely cost, a phenomenon known as ***reciprocal altruism***.
- Researchers studying ***bystander intervention*** have found that in the presence of other people who do not take action, people often do not help in a crisis. In part this reflects a ***diffusion of responsibility*** (a diminished sense of personal responsibility to act).

3 Aggression

- ***Aggression*** refers to verbal or physical behaviour aimed at harming another person or living being. Across cultures, males tend to be more aggressive than females. Researchers are increasingly recognising the prevalence of male violence perpetrated against females.
- Instinctual and evolutionary psychologists view aggression as rooted in biology. The neural control of aggression is hierarchically organised, with the amygdala, hypothalamus and frontal lobes playing prominent roles. Aggression is also partially controlled by hormones, particularly testosterone.
- Cognitive neoassociation theories suggest that exposure to aversive stimuli triggers thoughts and behaviours associated with aggression. One exemplar of this model is the ***frustration–aggression hypothesis***, which suggests that aggressive behaviour arises from frustrated needs or desires. A reformulated version of this hypothesis suggests that frustrating or unpleasant circumstances are likely to evoke aggression if they elicit unpleasant emotion. Cognitive–social approaches explain aggressive behaviour as a result of rewards and punishments, cognitive processes (such as attributions about people's intentions) and social learning (such as modelling).
- The general aggression model unifies the multitude of theories created to explain aggression. According to the GAM, person and situational input variables combine to determine the presence or absence of aggressive output.

4 Social influence

- ***Social influence*** refers to the influence of the presence of other people on thought, feeling and behaviour. ***Obedience*** is a social influence process whereby individuals follow the dictates of an authority. The Milgram studies demonstrated that most people will obey without limitations of conscience if they believe the authority is legitimate.
- ***Conformity*** is the process by which people change their attitudes or behaviour to accommodate the standards of peers or groups. Asch's studies demonstrated that a substantial number of people will conform when confronted by a group with a consensus opinion, even if the opinion is manifestly wrong. Conformity is highest in agricultural societies with dense populations, where independence may be less adaptive than in hunter-gatherer or urban, technologically developed societies.
- A ***group*** is a collection of people whose actions affect the other group members. Naturally occurring groups routinely have ***norms*** (standards for the behaviour of group members), ***roles*** (socially patterned positions within a group that define appropriate behaviour for the people occupying them) and ***leaders*** (people who exercise greater influence than the average member).
- The presence of others in a group substantially influences the behaviour of individual group members, as illustrated with ***social facilitation***, whereby the presence of others can either facilitate or inhibit individual performance. The degree to which groups influence individual performance is influenced, in part, by the nature of the task. Frequently, people will engage in ***social loafing***, where they will exert less effort when in a group as opposed to when alone.
- In spite of the fact that people like to view themselves as immune to social influence attempts, everyone falls victim to social influence on a regular basis. Common social influence tactics to which people succumb include the ***door-in-the-face*** technique (asking for a large request that we know will be turned down and then backing down from that request to induce similar behaviour in another), the ***foot-in-the-door*** technique (asking for a small commitment to ensure agreement with a larger commitment at a later time) and ***low-balling*** (getting a commitment and then changing the conditions).
- People behave differently in the presence of others, although they also carry 'others' with them all the time in the form of mental representations. The massive social changes in the last century, such as rapid technological development and the breakdown of traditional family structures and values, have created profound psychological changes and dilemmas for coping.

KEY TERMS

aggression, *p. 752*
altruism, *pp. 736, 747*
bystander intervention, *p. 750*
companionate love, *p. 740*
conformity, *p. 762*
diffusion of responsibility, *p. 751*
dispositional variables, *p. 736*
door-in-the-face technique, *p. 770*
ethical hedonism, *p. 748*
foot-in-the-door technique, *p. 770*
frustration–aggression hypothesis, *p. 757*
group, *p. 764*
group cohesiveness, *p. 767*
group polarisation, *p. 767*
groupthink, *p. 767*
hostile aggression, *p. 752*
instrumental aggression, *p. 752*
instrumental leaders, *p. 765*
interpersonal attraction, *p. 737*
leaders, *p. 768*
low-balling, *p. 770*
matching hypothesis, *p. 738*
need to belong, *p. 737*
norms, *p. 764*
obedience, *p. 760*
passionate love, *p. 739*
reciprocal altruism, *p. 749*
reference groups, *p. 764*
role, *p. 765*
self-fulfilling prophecies, *p. 760*
sexual strategies, *p. 740*
situational variables, *p. 736*
social–emotional leaders, *pp. 765, 768*
social exchange theories, *p. 738*
social facilitation, *p. 766*
social influence, *p. 760*
social loafing, *p. 766*
task leaders, *pp. 765, 768*

REVIEW QUESTIONS

1. Differentiate between passionate love and companionate love.
2. Define altruism.
3. Explain how the presence of others influences bystander intervention.
4. Describe the factors that influence obedience and conformity.
5. Describe the characteristics of groups.

DISCUSSION QUESTIONS

1. What factors attract people to each other?
2. Is television violence linked to aggression?
3. Why might groupthink lead to poor decision making?

APPLICATION QUESTIONS

1. Test your understanding of group processes by identifying each of the following scenarios as an example of one of the main leadership styles: autocratic, democratic and laissez-faire.
   (a) The work group is given a set of tasks to be completed by the end of the week. The leader closely examines the task list and asks each team member for input on how to achieve each objective. He encourages each person to decide for themselves how they should proceed to complete the tasks on time.
   (b) The work group is given a set of tasks to be completed by the end of the week. The leader closely examines the task list and allocates a separate team member to achieve each objective. He has decided that this is the best way to achieve the goal. He informs each person how they should proceed to complete their set task on time.
   (c) The work group is given a set of tasks to be completed by the end of the week. The leader gets the team together but offers little advice on how the group should achieve each objective. He believes that when all is said and done, the tasks will be completed if he just lets things happen over time.
2. Test your understanding of social influence processes by identifying each of these scenarios as an example of one of the following techniques of social influence: door-in-the-face, foot-in-the-door and low-balling.
   (a) John was keen to buy a new car, and reached an agreement with the car salesperson on the price of one particular car. However, just before John signed the paperwork, the salesperson reminded him that floor mats were not included in the price of the car and would cost another $100.
   (b) A researcher approached university students and asked if they would chaperone a group of primary-school-aged children to the zoo for a day. Eighty-five percent of the students refused the request. When the researcher approached a second group of students, the researcher first asked if they would be willing to spend two hours a week for the next two years working as mentors for primary-school-aged children. Not surprisingly, the vast majority of participants refused this large request. Subsequently, the researcher asked this group of participants if they would be willing to chaperone a group of primary-school-aged children on a day trip to the zoo. Compared to the first group of students, four times more participants indicated that they would be willing to comply with this request.
   (c) Dr Coorey asked a mental health colleague if she would be willing to help her work on a research project that involved interviewing 100 nursing students about their attitudes to various mental health issues. Although the colleague was reluctant to help because the interviews would be a very time-consuming process, she agreed to interview 10 students. Six months later, after the research data had been collected and collated, this same colleague agreed to help analyse the data.

The solutions to the application questions can be found on page 835.

MULTIMEDIA RESOURCES

The *Cyberpsych* multimedia resource is available *as an option* to accompany this textbook to further develop your understanding of many key psychology concepts. *Cyberpsych* contains a wealth of rich media content and activities, and for this chapter includes:

- video clips on gender and love, and male versus female brains
- a video case on shopping habits.

ANSWERS TO DISJUNCTIVE PUZZLES (p. 766)

1. The answer to this Eureka problem is E. The letters are the first letters of the first eight digits: One, Two, Three, Four, Five, Six, Seven and Eight
2. This non-Eureka puzzle is known as the Horse-Trading Problem. The answer is $20.
3. The missionary/cannibal problem is a non-Eureka problem. The entire process requires the following 13 crossings of the missionaries (M1, M2 and M3), the two non-rowing cannibals (C1 and C2), and the cannibal who can row (RC).
   1. M1 and C1 cross
   2. M1 returns
   3. RC and C2 cross
   4. RC returns
   5. M1 and M2 cross
   6. M1 and C1 return
   7. RC and M1 cross
   8. M1 and C2 return
   9. M1 and M3 cross
   10. RC returns
   11. RC and C1 cross
   12. RC returns
   13. RC and C2 cross
4. The chain puzzle is a Eureka puzzle. Many groups answer 11, since that would involve cutting only every other link. The correct answer, however, is 2. If the 4th and 11th links are cut, all the values from 1 to 23 can be obtained by getting 'change' back from the motel owner. Separate links (the 4th and the 11th) are given on Days 1 and 2, but on Day 3 the 3-link unit is given to the owner, who returns the separate links. These links are then used to pay on Days 4 and 5, but on Day 6 the 6-link unit is used, and the owner returns the others as change. This process can be continued for 23 days.

SOURCE: Reprinted from Forsyth (1990, pp. 266–267).

Cross-cultural and indigenous psychology

19

LEARNING OBJECTIVES

After studying this chapter you should be able to:

1 define culture and outline some of the methodological problems in the study of culture

2 outline the dimensions along which cultural groups may be distinguished

3 describe cross-cultural relations in multicultural societies

4 describe how culture has shaped the identities of indigenous peoples in New Zealand and Australia

5 discuss the approaches taken by psychologists to promote cross-cultural interactions.

Culture and psychology

- *Culture* refers to the shared rules that govern behaviour; it is a filter through which we see and understand our current reality. *Cultural psychologists* study the way in which people are affected by their culture. *Cross-cultural psychologists* compare the similarities and differences in behaviour across cultures.
- Psychologists use a number of different approaches to study culture and face a number of unique challenges in the process of conducting such research. The *emic perspective* focuses on specific psychological aspects of a culture. The *etic perspective* involves the search for commonalities or differences across cultures.

Cross-cultural relations

- *Multiculturalism* refers to those situations where multiple cultures exist within a country. *Pluralism* supports both the coexistence of different cultural groups and their right to retain their cultural heritage. Both are features of Australia and New Zealand and many countries in the Asia–Pacific region, where immigration policies have resulted in the blending and co-existence of many cultural groups.
- Many Australians are proud of their ethnic composition, mutual tolerance and social cohesion and view multiculturalism as positive for both social and economic development. However cultural diversity can also be a source of conflict, including *racism* and *prejudice*.

Promoting cross-cultural interactions

- Education systems need to create inclusive learning environments to ensure that teachers are both aware of and sensitive to the histories, cultures, languages and learning styles of students with different cultural backgrounds.
- Cultural differences may influence all aspects of the communication process and cause misunderstandings and miscommunication across cultures.
- *Cultural competence* refers to a psychologist's effectiveness in communicating and behaving appropriately with people from another culture, both in terms of understanding and being understood.

Understanding culture and its context

- Every culture has a set of unwritten rules that are handed down from generation to generation, and that everyone within the culture learns to abide by. Often, those rules are not apparent to people from other cultures.
- The dimensions of culture cover such things as the attitude towards time, how much emotion is displayed and how much interpersonal space is appropriate during conversations. They also cover how much attention is paid to nonverbal behaviours, how much deviation from cultural norms is tolerated, and whether people are *individualist* (emphasise the primacy of the individual over the group) or *collectivist* (emphasise the group over individuals) in their outlook.

Indigenous psychology

- ***Indigenous psychology*** promotes psychologies that are not imposed, that are influenced by the cultural contexts in which people live, that are developed from within the culture, and that result in locally relevant psychological knowledge.
- Aboriginals are the original inhabitants of Australia's mainland. Contemporary Aboriginal identity is extremely diverse, reflecting the impacts of colonisation and also cultural heritage of pre-European life. Aboriginal people have retained and maintained important cultural practices and share a common philosophical and historical bond that make them feel as one people.
- The Torres Strait Islander people are the original inhabitants of the group of small islands located in the Torres Strait. Cultural identity remains extremely important to Torres Strait Islanders, and many continue to identify as a group through shared cultural practices, languages and traditions.
- The Maori are the original inhabitants of New Zealand, and their sense of identity was severely affected by European colonisation. Today, many Maori people identify with an *iwi* (tribal) group as well as feeling a common ethnic identity that reflects their experience of British occupation and changed social conditions such as urbanisation.

Central questions: psychological universals versus culture-specific behaviours

- The discipline of psychology is a product of the European and North American cultural environment and most psychological theories and practices have been developed in Western countries. Consequently, the way psychologists understand human behaviour is bound and limited by these same cultural contexts. It therefore remains debatable whether these theories are totally relevant to people from other cultures.

TANIA Major grew up a proud Kokoberra woman in the remote community of Kowanyama in Cape York, Queensland. She grew up with a strong connection to her land and her community. She also grew up as a bright and gifted student, always at the top of the class. But educational opportunities in Kowanyama were not great. At age 15, she grabbed the offer to attend a private boarding school in Brisbane to complete her secondary schooling. After leaving school, Tania completed a degree in criminology at Griffith University — becoming the first person from Kowanyama to gain a university degree. She has since recently completed a Masters degree in Public Policy at Sydney University.

But while Tania physically left her community to further her education, her connection with her land and her people has never weakened. She has returned to work in and on behalf of Aboriginal communities, and has forged a path as a passionate advocate for Indigenous Australians and as a campaigner in the ongoing battle to close the gulf of disadvantage that they face.

She has spoken out tirelessly to make mainstream Australia aware of the daily realities and barriers faced by Indigenous people, particularly those living in communities in remote areas such as Cape York. She has also worked with Indigenous Australians to break the cycle of welfare dependency and open up opportunities that they cannot currently grab.

Former Young Australian of the Year Tania Major has achieved success academically and has demonstrated a commitment to narrowing the gap between Indigenous and non-Indigenous Australians. Today, Tania works tirelessly to raise awareness about the daily realities and barriers that many Indigenous Australians still face in contemporary society.

For her efforts, Tania was named Young Australian of the Year in January 2007. Tania's life is a striking example of how one person can successfully juggle conflicting cultural identities. She was born the child of an Indigenous mother and a white father. She grew up in a remote Aboriginal community, yet was able to transition to an elite Brisbane private school and then to university life in urban settings far removed from the rivers and creeks of Kowanyama. Her story of succeeding across cultures is the message she is now sending to young Indigenous people across Australia. It is a message she explained to Andrew Denton when she appeared on his television show *Enough Rope* in 2007:

> I just decided that the only way we're going to change is by working with the kids and impregnating hope in their minds, saying, 'Hey the colour of your skin doesn't mean that you're going to end up in prison or you're going to die and commit suicide at a very young age.' You know, 'There's so much to life'. You know, 'Look what I've done, look where I've gone to, I've had dreams beyond Kowanyama, I wanted to go to New York, I ended up in New York and I still come back home'. And there's this thinking that just because they're black they can't go anywhere.

It is also the message Tania continues to spread in her role as a key spokesperson for *GenerationOne*, the ambitious project launched in 2010 with the aim of bringing all Australians together to end the disparity between Indigenous and non-Indigenous Australians. *GenerationOne* was launched on 24 October 2010, when Madeleine Madden, the 13-year-old granddaughter of Indigenous activist Charles Perkins, gave an impassioned plea to all Australians to help 'close the gap' of Indigenous disadvantage in a two-minute address shown on all free-to-air television stations. *GenerationOne* is a not-for-profit organisation founded by mining entrepreneur Andrew Forrest and his wife Nicola, and supported by other prominent Australians, including James Packer, Kerry Stokes, and the Lowy and Fox families. The goal is to 'close the gap' by focusing on education, training, mentoring and employment, and by engaging all Australians in the quest to achieve real change.

For Tania Major, the work of *GenerationOne* is a chance to succeed where government policymaking has not in overcoming Indigenous inequality. But the solutions are not just in economic benefits — they are also about identity, as Tania wrote in a *Sydney Morning Herald* essay in July 2010:

> The solutions seemed obvious: education, better housing, employment, establishment of real economies and restoration of social order in our communities. But I also knew that to heal ourselves we needed more than these enabling structures. We needed to regain our connection with our lands, re-awaken our cultures and re-establish our identities. Without the former, we would continue to languish in poverty and despair; without the latter we will simply become another minority in a country full of minorities (Major, 2010).

In this chapter, we focus on cross-cultural, Indigenous Australian and indigenous New Zealand psychology. We begin with a discussion of the roles of cultural and cross-cultural psychologists and outline the research methods they use in studying culture. Next, we discuss culture and its context, examining the dimensions of difference between cultures. We then examine the cross-cultural relationships in multicultural societies and explore why prejudice and stereotyping occur (chapter 17). Next we consider how culture has shaped the identities of indigenous peoples in New Zealand and Australia. We conclude by discussing the approaches that have been taken by psychologists to promote cross-cultural interactions.

The growing appreciation of the pervasive influence of culture raises a number of issues. Throughout, we address one central question: to what extent are psychological theories and findings universal and to what extent are they influenced by culture? In other words, how does culture shape your thoughts, feelings and behaviours; to what extent is the interpretation of those behaviours universal; and to what extent does a person's own cultural background influence how thoughts, feelings and behaviours are interpreted?

Central question

- How universal versus culture-specific are psychological theories and findings?

Culture and psychology

The word 'culture' is used in many ways to describe many things. It is often (mis)used as a substitute for the words race, nationality or ethnicity. Here, ***culture*** will be defined as the shared rules that govern the behaviour of a group of people and enable the members of that group to co-exist and survive. Schein (1992) says culture lies at the level of basic assumptions and beliefs. Culture involves shared values, beliefs, attitudes and behaviours that distinguish members of one group from members of others (Lehman, Chiu, & Schaller, 2004). It is something you learn, perhaps even subconsciously, and it shapes your awareness of the world around you. Samuels, a psychologist specialising in life-span development, describes this process of subconsciously absorbing cultural norms, mores and expectations as 'the cultural trance' (personal communication, June 18, 2004). Culture uses artefacts, rituals and text to develop and reinforce a shared sense of identity among members. It is the filter through which we see and understand our current reality (Edgar, 1980). These are the structures of identity that help people organise and make sense of everyday life (Wark, 1997). They also establish boundaries between different groups (Oyserman & Lee, 2007).

APPLY + DISCUSS

A central focus of psychology has been to identify ways of thinking and behaving that are universal (i.e. that remain the same no matter what cultural environment people come from).

- What behaviours do you think remain constant across the human race, regardless of culture?
- To what extent do you think culture influences the way a universal action or behaviour is expressed?

Culture has numerous facets, which makes it difficult to neatly describe. Historical influences help to shape the culture in which you live, and the 'unwritten rules' of culture are handed down from generation to generation through tradition. Examples of cultural rules include the types of food that you eat, clothes that you wear and houses that you live in. Culture also includes structural elements of society such as types of government; it involves social elements such as family structures and recreational activities; and it involves individual values and behaviours, such as following a sport or belonging to a particular social club. All these various facets of culture are interrelated — affect one facet and all others are affected as well. For instance, the introduction of Christianity to the Torres Strait meant changes to traditional song and dance; and the introduction of muskets to Maori tribes in the 1800s changed social structures and intertribal relationships.

Culture is also a difficult construct to identify because it is not homogeneous. Individuals and groups within a culture may differ in the extent to which they participate in a shared value or behaviour. No individual embodies all the characteristics that are said to relate to a particular culture. For instance, New Zealand is often considered a nation where rugby union enjoys mass appeal. However, there are many New Zealanders who have little or no interest in rugby and their numbers are increasing as more immigrants from countries with no tradition of rugby, such as Korea and Croatia, enter New Zealand.

Culture is relatively stable from one generation to the next, but it is still dynamic to a degree, changing and evolving slowly over time. That evolution comes about because culture is something that people construct through their daily life, not something that remains unchanged throughout the ages. For instance, living together before marriage and getting divorced were both quite rare in Australia and New Zealand 50 years ago. Today, about 78 percent of Australian couples live together prior to marriage (ABS, 2009a), and at least 40 percent of marriages are likely to end in divorce (de Vaus, 2004). A cultural shift has occurred during that period.

Cultural and cross-cultural psychology

Importantly, culture is *learned* behaviour. Culture is not genetically imprinted in the same way that sexual instincts are. None of us leave the womb knowing how to shake hands as a greeting, what type of clothes to wear to a funeral or why monogamy is expected in marriage (in the Western world). The process of absorbing and internalising the rules of the culture we live in can be described as ***enculturation***. Historically, psychologists have been indifferent to culture and context as they went looking for universal laws of human behaviour (Goldberger & Veroff, 1995). The discipline's focus was on distilling psychological processes and behaviours that were common across humanity. Only recently has it become more generally accepted by most in the psychology profession that culture can have a major influence on our psychological development.

With increasing attention on culture in mainstream theory and research, cultural psychology has emerged as a recognised discipline with specialist practitioners. There are two main areas of interest in this field — cultural psychology and cross-cultural psychology.

Cultural psychologists study the ways in which people are affected by the culture they live in (van de Vijver & Leung, 2000). They emphasise the belief that individual psychological processes are shaped by cultural context (Fiske & Taylor, 1991). For example, how does the culture you live in influence your self identity?

Cross-cultural psychologists compare the similarities and differences in behaviour across different societies or cultures. The aim is to see how the cultural context affects psychological processes, to identify commonalities and contrasts (Kim, Park, & Park, 2000). For example, cross-cultural psychologists might study several cultures to determine whether Kohlberg's levels of moral reasoning are universal (chapter 12), or whether people from different cultures respond differently to stressful events (chapter 14).

APPLY + DISCUSS

Your identity comes not just from the cultural environment in which you live today, but from the historical influences that have shaped that culture. The way you develop depends not only on your innate personal characteristics but also on the interplay with the cultural surrounds that envelop everything in your life. Think of the food you eat, the language you speak, your appearance, the sports you play or the way you celebrate birthdays. Think of the social groups you are involved with, the family traditions you observe.

- To what extent are these facets of your life influenced by culture?
- How might your life be different if you were raised in a different cultural environment?

INTERIM SUMMARY

Culture refers to the shared rules that govern behaviour; it is a filter through which we see and understand our current reality. ***Cultural psychologists*** study the way in which people are affected by their culture. ***Cross-cultural psychologists*** compare the similarities and differences in behaviour across cultures.

Research methods in cultural and cross-cultural psychology

Research in cultural and cross-cultural psychology uses a number of approaches (Matsumoto, 2001). One approach is the ***emic perspective***, which is culture-specific. It involves focusing on a specific cultural group and examining particular psychological aspects of that group. This perspective involves a cultural psychologist taking a particular theory and applying it to an individual culture. Another approach is the ***etic perspective***, which is more cross-cultural. It involves the search for commonalities or differences across cultures. Under this perspective, the aim is to see whether a particular theory fits across different cultures. Goldberger and Veroff (1995) described the approaches to cultural research slightly differently, using three categories.

1. The study of individual cultures to determine relationships between the structures, values, belief systems, language and practices of a culture and the behaviour of people living within that culture.
2. The comparison of human behaviour across different cultures.
3. The study of the interaction between cultures that co-exist in a larger societal context.

Ember and Ember (2001) stated that cross-cultural research relies on the assumption that comparison is possible because identifiable patterns of behaviour can be observed. Further, they indicated that to understand why a particular group is the way it is, it must be compared to others.

Within the broad framework of cross-cultural research, a number of different methods are used to test hypotheses (van de Vijver & Leung, 2000). ***Cross-cultural comparison studies*** involve comparing two or more different cultures in relation to a particular psychological variable. For example, locus of control might be a variable under examination (chapter 6). Researchers could compare the extent to which people from different cultures believed they controlled their own future (internal locus of control) or that others controlled their destiny (external locus of control). ***Cross-cultural validation studies*** examine whether a psychological variable in one culture can be applied and have meaning in another culture. For instance, the concept of monogamy underpins marriage in Western cultures. But to what extent does this apply in other cultures? ***Unpackaging studies*** try to explain why cultural differences occur, looking at the range of variables that might account for divergence on a particular aspect. For example, the hunter-gatherer approach to food accumulation in traditional Aboriginal cultures helped develop very different social structures to those found in the agrarian societies of Europe. The communal aspects of gathering and preparing food in an Aboriginal community encouraged interdependence and adherence to group values. By contrast, the agrarian practices that developed in Europe relied on demarcation of roles and individual activities, encouraging a more individualistic social structure.

Challenges in cross-cultural research

As noted in chapter 2, good psychological research encompasses four characteristics: a *theoretical framework*, a *standardised procedure*, *generalisability* and *objective measurement*. A cultural psychologist, for example, might first frame a hypothesis about how the 'tall poppy syndrome' leads to Australians cutting down those who are perceived as 'superior' to them. A cross-cultural psychologist may wish to compare evidence for this syndrome in different cultures, including people from Australia and other Western countries like the United States and New Zealand in their samples. Each psychologist would design their studies in ways that protect against bias so that the results provide a clear indication of the impact of their experimental manipulation. However, satisfying the final two characteristics of objective measurement and generalisability from a sample presents five challenges for psychologists studying culture.

1. *The problem of research methods.* Psychologists aim to include multiple measures in their studies to ensure their results are both reliable and valid (chapter 2). However, there is the difficulty of ensuring that data gathered from different cultures can be interpreted on an equivalent basis. Consider, for example, a written test to be completed by people from a number of cultures with different languages. The researcher needs to ensure that the test items will have the same meanings when translated into different languages. The translations may affect the interpretations the participants make and therefore the responses they provide. Do cultural differences mean participants respond differently to particular test research methods? Can we validly compare the results from the different participants? These measurement issues need to be addressed as part of the overall research process and are related to the problem of comparing data from different cultural groups.
2. *The problem of equivalent samples.* Cultural psychologists need to ensure their samples will provide meaningful data for the cultural groups under current investigation. Especially in cross-cultural studies, researchers need to take a great deal of care to ensure equivalence across cultures, and also to ensure that the sample does represent the culture being studied. For instance, how would you draw together a sample that would truly reflect an 'Australian' culture, considering the multicultural nature of Australian society today? Many psychological researchers use samples drawn from the ranks of university students and these student samples may not be representative of the wider population. Consequently, the extent to which the results may be generalised to represent specific cultural groups remains questionable.

   In selecting their samples, cross-cultural psychologists therefore need to divide the culture into a number of different aspects: cultures, communities within the cultures, individuals within the communities, and behavioural aspects of the individuals (Lonner & Malpass, 1994b). Additionally, many cross-cultural psychologists use matched samples to match individuals from different cultural groups on those variables not under specific investigation. ***Matched samples*** therefore ensure that individuals from one culture reflect the same characteristics of individuals from another culture. The different samples of people are similar in all aspects of their lives, except their cultural background.
3. *The problem of interpreting results.* Interpreting the results requires knowledge of the cultural frameworks in which behaviours take place. The same behaviours in two different cultures may have completely different meanings. For example, men kissing each other on the cheek is a widespread form

APPLY + DISCUSS

How well do you understand what it is like to walk in another person's shoes? Some would say it is impossible; that we can never truly know someone else's reality, particularly someone from a different culture. As an exercise, interview five people who come from cultural backgrounds different from your own. Talk to them about their lifestyles, their aspirations and their expectations. Ask them to identify the obstacles and barriers they face in life.

- How do their responses differ from the answers you would give to the same questions?

of greeting in Italian culture; in countries such as Australia, New Zealand and the United States, it is not customary. Additionally, generalising the findings of research becomes problematic in multicultural societies. Not all members of a culture or society behave the same way. Researchers comparing two cultures are often describing the average differences between two groups of people from different cultures. Such researchers should therefore not be tempted to generalise across a culture by reverting to a stereotype (chapter 17).

4. *The problem of researcher bias.* Researchers need to acknowledge that the theoretical approach they adopt and judgements they make are influenced by their own cultural background. Thus, the choice of hypotheses and research methods reflects the researcher's own background, upbringing, education and influences.
5. *The problem of sensitive issues.* Research on cultural differences can often be quite sensitive. It identifies points of difference between cultural groups, which can become the basis for conflict and misunderstanding. For example, Aboriginal Australians are over-represented in jails compared with other cultural groups in Australia. On the face of it, this could lead to adverse assumptions about Aboriginal people. However, other factors such as socioeconomic disadvantage, prejudice, literacy levels and a legacy of cultural dispossession should also be considered as part of the analysis.

The challenges to cultural research reflect the fact that culture is such a difficult construct to define. However, recent work in the conceptualisation of culture has made it easier to measure (Matsumoto & Juang, 2004). The most popular way of measuring cultural variability is the ***individualism–collectivism continuum***, which looks at the extent to which cultures favour individual goals compared to communal goals (Hofstede, 1980). These differences are outlined in table 19.1.

TABLE 19.1 **Some differences between individualist and collectivist cultures**

Individualist cultures	Collectivist cultures
The concept of self is defined as separate and independent from the group.	The concept of self is defined only in relation to the group.
The interests of the individual are given priority.	The interests of the group are given priority.
The independence and autonomy of the individual are emphasised.	The interdependence and solidarity of people within the group are emphasised.
The pursuit and fulfilment of individual goals are expected.	The pursuit of group happiness and harmony is expected.
Behaviour is explained in terms of individual decisions and attributes.	Behaviour is explained in terms of adherence to group norms.
Accumulation of individual wealth and possessions is the norm.	Collective ownership of resources is the norm.
Leadership, competitiveness, aggression and achievement are normal.	Group conformity, obligation and sense of duty are normal.

Redefining cross-cultural research

Cross-cultural research, particularly in relation to indigenous people, is being redefined. Traditionally, research has been something that is 'done' on indigenous people by outsiders. The results of that research are described from the cultural perspective of the researcher, rather than the people being studied. Davidson, Sanson, and Gridley (2000) describe the underlying narratives of previous psychological research on Indigenous Australians as a contributor to oppression and racism. They advocate a re-examination by Australian psychologists of their approach, which involves close collaboration with indigenous people to identify research needs from their perspective. That way, psychology in future might conduct research and provide services that fulfil the social objectives of indigenous people (Davidson et al., 2000).

Similarly, Maori author Linda Tuhiwai Smith (1999) has called for the 'decolonising' of research on indigenous people and advocated its retelling from the indigenous perspective. Smith says it is presumptuous of Western researchers to think they can understand and explain the Maori reality on the basis of brief encounters using Eurocentric research methods.

The National Health and Medical Research Council (2003) published guidelines for ethical conduct in Aboriginal and Torres Strait Islander health research. As shown in figure 19.1, the six values that underpin these guidelines are:

1. *Reciprocity.* The researcher needs to respect the values and cultures of the people involved and balance the benefits to be gained against any potential risks to participants.
2. *Respect.* The researcher needs to affirm the right of people to have different beliefs, customs and aspirations, and show regard for their personal welfare and cultural heritage.
3. *Equality.* The researcher needs to appreciate and respect cultural differences, treating all participants as equals.
4. *Responsibility.* The researcher needs to work with the people and communities involved, ensuring that the research does no harm to participants or to their cultural belief systems.
5. *Survival and protection.* The research needs to reinforce the strong social and cultural bonds between indigenous people and their communities, respecting their right to assert a cultural distinctiveness.
6. *Spirit and integrity.* An overarching value is that the research respects and unites the values and integrity of indigenous people and communities with their cultural heritage.

According to this model, the 'spirit and integrity' value is central to binding together the other five values over time.

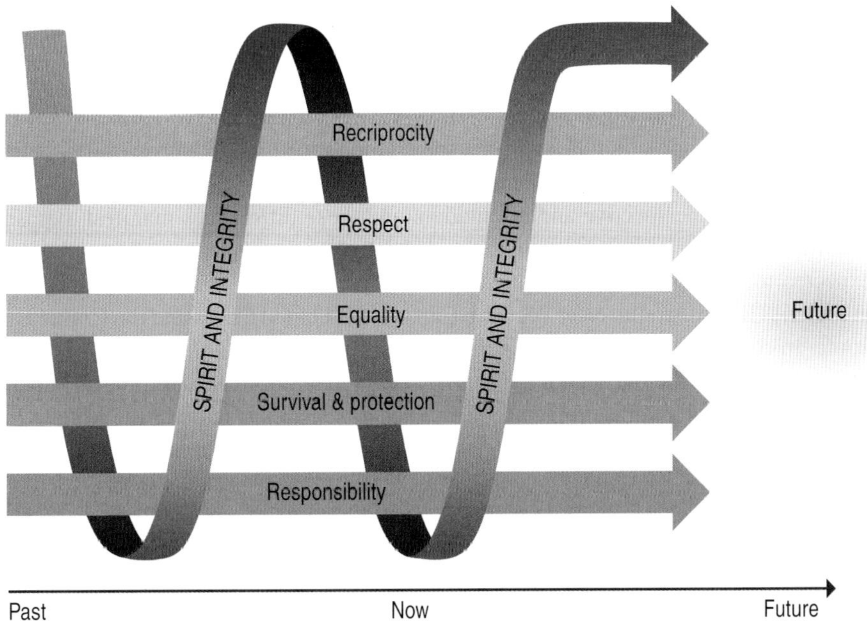

FIGURE 19.1
The six values relevant to research with indigenous people

SOURCE: NHMRC (2003, p. 9).

INTERIM SUMMARY

Psychologists use a number of different approaches to study culture and face a number of unique challenges in the process of conducting such research. The ***emic perspective*** focuses on specific psychological aspects of a culture. The ***etic perspective*** involves the search for commonalities or differences across cultures. Current initiatives promote close collaboration with indigenous people to identify research needs from their perspective. Six values underpin guidelines for ethical conduct of research with Aboriginal Australians and Torres Strait Islanders: reciprocity, respect, equality, responsibility, survival and protection, and spirit and integrity.

Understanding culture and its context

The impact of culture is played out in many different ways in our daily lives. Every culture has a set of unwritten rules that are handed down from generation to generation, by which everyone within a culture learns to abide. Often, those rules are not apparent to people from other cultures. But in today's increasingly multicultural world, where people are much more mobile and globalisation is shrinking the distance

APPLY + DISCUSS

Over time, we all learn the appropriate way to display emotions in certain situations. These 'display rules' are framed by our culture. Think of all the different scenarios in which we find ourselves — attending a business meeting, a university lecture, a barbecue, a football match or a funeral, or having a night out clubbing with friends. Think of the range of emotions we may feel at all those events — sadness, anger, surprise, happiness, fear, disgust. And think of the 'display rules' that govern how we express those emotions at each of those events.

- To what extent are those 'display rules' dependent on culture?
- Think of instances where different cultures apply different rules to the display of emotion in the situations outlined above. How difficult would it be for someone from another culture to know when and where the 'display rules' apply?

between cultures, we all face the challenge of learning to interact effectively with people from disparate cultural backgrounds. For people entering a new culture, such as migrants, adapting to the new environment can involve a period of culture shock. As people adapt, they must also develop and maintain a number of identities — including their personal identity, their social identity (or identities) and their ethnic identity.

The dimensions of culture

Every culture has a set of dimensions, protocols and practices that guide daily life. They are not written down anywhere but everyone within a culture knows what they are; they are the product of implicit learning (chapter 8). These 'unwritten rules' form significant aspects of culture that set different groups of people apart. They are also the source of many misunderstandings and misperceptions when people of different cultures come together. The dimensions of culture cover such things as the attitude towards time, how much emotion is displayed and how much interpersonal space is appropriate during conversations (see Trenholm & Jensen, 2007). They also cover how much attention is paid to nonverbal behaviours, how much deviation from cultural norms is tolerated, and whether people are individualist or collectivist in their outlook.

Time and culture

A difference in attitudes towards time is one area that separates cultures (see Nonis, Teng, & Ford, 2005). While a minute, an hour and a day take the same amount of time to elapse everywhere on the globe, people from different cultures experience time in different ways. Hall (1973) identified that cultures differ in their time perspective and orientation, and these differences manifest themselves in behaviours. In ***monochronic cultures***, time is divided into linear segments and closely regulated. People are expected to be punctual and activities are scheduled to occur at specific and regular intervals. Western societies like Australia, New Zealand, Canada, the United States and the United Kingdom are monochronic. In contrast, in ***polychronic cultures*** time is much more fluid and less closely regulated. These time differences are outlined in table 19.2. People are not expected to be as punctual and precise, and pay less attention to observing strict deadlines or schedules. Parts of the Middle East and South America, as well as traditional Aboriginal and Maori societies, are polychronic.

TABLE 19.2 Some differences between monochronic and polychronic cultures

Monochronic cultures	Polychronic cultures
Attention is focused on one task at a time.	Multiple tasks can be carried out at the same time.
Time commitments are treated seriously and deadlines/appointments are always met.	Time commitments are considered flexible and deadlines/appointments are not always met.
The schedule rules; activities and interactions with others are organised according to the clock.	Activities and interactions with others rule; sticking to the clock is less important.
Time is rigid, divisible and inflexible.	Time is fluid and can move in different cycles.
Future oriented — no living in the past.	The past and its legacy are viewed as important.

Emotion and culture

Displays of *emotion* differ across cultures (chapter 10; see Albert & Ha, 2004; Matsumoto, 2007). Emotions are the feelings and reactions we experience in response to our situations — such as happiness, sadness, fear, anger and anxiety. Ekman and Friesen (1975) put forward the theory of ***cultural display rules***, reasoning that cultures differ in relation to rules on the appropriateness of displaying certain emotions in particular social circumstances. People from southern European cultures, such as Greece or Italy, tend to be much more expressive and emotional than those from English backgrounds. Greeks and Italians who came to Australia in a wave of post-World War II migration found themselves in a mainstream culture where emotions were not openly expressed to the same degree.

Interpersonal space

Cultures also vary on the dimension of interpersonal space. Hall (1966) identified three broad types of interpersonal space 'zones' that apply in different circumstances:

1. *Intimate space.* This is the closest 'bubble' of space surrounding a person. Getting this close to a person is normally acceptable only for close friends, lovers and family.
2. *Social and consultative space.* This refers to the amount of space people feel comfortable with when interacting socially with acquaintances as well as strangers.
3. *Public space.* This refers to the distance apart at which people find it hard to interact with others, or perceive interactions as largely impersonal.

Cultural expectations on what distances apply in each of these circumstances vary widely (Beaulieu, 2004). For example, ***conversational distance*** refers to how close people stand to each other when they are talking, and is related to the idea of intimate space. In some cultures, people prefer to get 'up close and personal' when talking to anyone. In other cultures, people only get that close when talking with a lover.

Cultural differences in interpersonal space dimensions can cause misunderstandings in intercultural interactions. For example, Morrison and Conaway (2000) say that growing up in densely populated environments can reduce the amount of social and public space considered appropriate. As a result, another person entering an elevator in the Philippines may stand right next to you. In an Indian movie theatre with many empty seats, an Indian is likely to choose the seat next to you. And in Indonesia, if you are on an empty escalator, an Indonesian may move to stand on the same step. This sort of behaviour often drives people from less crowded environments like Australia to distraction, but it is considered appropriate in many parts of the world (Morrison & Conaway, 2000).

Context and culture

The attention people pay to context — the circumstances in which something occurs — is also a significant dimension of culture. High-context cultures support considerable differences in behaviours and actions, depending on the prevailing circumstance, whereas low-context cultures emphasise consistency and stability across contexts (Matsumoto & Juang, 2004). ***High-context cultures*** tend to pay close attention to nonverbal signs like body language and conversational difference to decode the real meaning behind words or actions. People in these cultures emphasise interpersonal relationships and rely more on intuition and interpretation than pure logic. Much of the Middle East, Asia, Africa and South America can be considered high-context. ***Low-context cultures*** tend to pay close attention to what people actually say or do and interpret that literally, without as much regard to the accompanying circumstances. People from these cultures rely on fact and logic and are less concerned with relationships. They say exactly what they mean. North America, Australia and much of Western Europe can be considered low-context.

These differences can be the source of misunderstandings. For instance, consider an Australian or New Zealand business operator in a meeting with a trade contact from Japan, attempting to negotiate an export deal. The Westerner might become annoyed at the lack of factual and definite responses to questions; while the Japanese contact might consider the Westerner's straightforward and explicit statements rude. Without an understanding of the differing perspectives, the deal may never be done.

Tight versus loose cultures

Triandis (1995) identifies a distinction between tight cultures and loose cultures. In ***tight cultures***, group members are expected to closely adhere to cultural norms and expectations. Deviation from group norms is not tolerated. In ***loose cultures***, norms are either unclear or deviance from norms is tolerated. For example, Triandis (1995) describes how Japanese children who return home after spending time living in the West, are often criticised for deviations from cultural norms (such as eating Western food for lunch rather than Japanese food). Japanese cultures are tight; Western cultures less so. Thailand is a country with a loose culture, where differences are accepted. For example, Thai locals will overlook many culturally inappropriate behaviours from tourists, such as wearing swimming attire or going shirtless in public places away from the beach or pool, often using the expression *main bin rai* (never mind).

Individualism versus collectivism

As shown previously in table 19.1 (p. 784), one of the most significant differences that can be identified between cultures is the extent to which they are individualist or collectivist (Hofstede, 1980; see also Oyserman, Coon, & Kemmelmeier, 2002). ***Individualist cultures*** emphasise the primacy of the individual over the group. People define themselves in terms of individual attributes, and view their individual identity and needs as more important than group identity and needs. Individual achievement is admired and rewarded. People from these cultures tend to be more self-reliant and competitive. By contrast, ***collectivist cultures*** emphasise the group over individuals. People define themselves in terms of group attributes, and see themselves primarily as part of a group and focus on group needs and identity, rather than focusing on their individual needs and identity. Group- and community-oriented achievement is more highly regarded. Conformity, interdependence and collective responsibility are hallmarks of these cultures.

Write down 20 things that describe you as a person, each starting with the words 'I am . . .'. You have just taken part in an exercise devised by Brislin (1988) to determine where you sit on the individualism–collectivism continuum. Review the list and decide which items imply membership of a group or a social response (e.g. I am a member of a tennis club) as opposed to an individualist response (I am smart). People from collectivist cultures emphasise relationships with others in defining who they are, while those from individualist cultures focus more on personal attributes. In this exercise, people with more than 20 percent of the items on the list showing a group or social response can consider themselves collectivist.

Traditional Aboriginal communities in Australia and Maori communities in New Zealand are collectivist in nature. Prior to white occupation in 1788, Aboriginal people lived as hunter-gatherers in small groups and inhabited their own sections of land. Survival depended on a collectivist approach to gathering food and sharing with other members of the group. Group members shared resources openly rather than keeping them as individuals. The concept of individual ownership of land was foreign. Instead, members of language groups collectively 'belonged' to certain areas of country, and had certain rights and obligations towards it. Land was not only a source of sustenance, but a materialisation of the journeys of ancestors from the Dreamtime (or Creation Time; Dudgeon, Garvey, & Pickett, 2000). In New Zealand, the traditional way for Maori people to introduce themselves is to first state the landmarks of the area to which their tribal groups belong (mountain and river), the name of the canoe on which the founders of their tribal group came to New Zealand (*waka*), the name of their tribal meeting place (*marae*), the name of the tribal group itself, and possibly some names of family members too, all before giving their own individual name.

Western societies such as modern Australia, New Zealand and the United States are more individualist. People strive for individual achievements and accumulate individual wealth and material possessions. Sharing of resources is much less common. For example, land is seen as a commodity to be bought and sold individually, rather than as a collective resource. Research by Hofstede (2001) found the United States, Australia, Great Britain, Canada, the Netherlands and New Zealand to be the most individualist cultures; Venezuela, Colombia, Pakistan, Peru and Taiwan were the least individualist.

COMMENTARY

Culture and schooling: looking beyond individualism and collectivism

By Doctor Dennis M. McInerney, The Hong Kong Institute of Education, and Doctor Gregory Arief D. Liem, The University of Sydney

Teachers in a multicultural classroom often observe that students from different cultural backgrounds appear to have different attitudes towards their schooling, and are driven by different academic goals and values; that is, psychological factors are suspected to underlie differences in learning approach and academic performance. This observation has spurred cross-cultural educational psychologists to find theoretical and applied models that may shed light on the influence of culture on schooling processes and outcomes. Of particular interest is the notion of individualism and collectivism in differentiating cultures and cultural groups. Triandis (1995) maintains that while individualists emphasise the primacy of the individuals' own identity, needs, goals, and accomplishments, collectivists prioritise those of their in-groups, such as their family or clan.

Within the Australian context, the individualist–collectivist dichotomy has been used to explain differences in the academic performance between Aboriginal Australians and Anglo-Australians — two groups believed to be respectively collectivist and individualist. McInerney and his colleagues (2003, 2008; McInerney, Roche, McInerney, & Marsh, 1997), have found, however, that rather than the expected polarities between the Indigenous- and Anglo-Australian students on achievement-related goals such as affiliation, social concern, social power and extrinsic rewards, all groups are very similar in their motivational profiles. When comparing a range of Indigenous (such as Navajo and Australian Aboriginal) groups with Western groups — and where there are significant differences — the differences are a matter of degree, are of little practical significance and often run counter to stereotypes. For example, findings indicate that while all groups are relatively low on competitiveness, Anglo groups are relatively lower than some Indigenous groups. While all groups are relatively high on social goals, Anglo groups are relatively higher than some Indigenous groups (McInerney et al., 1997).

Furthermore, achievement goals and values based on individualism and collectivism that are stereotypically used to distinguish cultural groups (such as degree of social affiliation) do not appear to be salient in the school contexts studied. Factors considered by many to be important key determinants of Indigenous minority students' poor achievement and dropping out of school, such as supposed mismatches between school and student goals and values are, in general, not supported by the findings. What clearly emerge as universally important predictors of students' academic motivation and achievement are their values, goals and beliefs relating to a positive sense of self (feeling good about themselves as students), a sense of purpose (having a goal of doing well at school and getting ahead in life) and their level of mastery orientation and intrinsic motivation (McInerney, 2003, 2008; McInerney et al., 1997).

A similar trend was found in an international setting. Liem and his co-researchers (Liem, 2007; Liem, Martin, Nair, Bernardo, & Prasetya, 2009; Liem, Nair, Bernardo, & Prasetya, 2008) investigated value orientations predicted to underpin approaches to learning of secondary school students in Australia — as a representation of an individualist society — and those in Singapore, the Philippines and Indonesia (countries deemed as more collectivist). Although Australian students are generally higher than South-East Asian students on value orientations typically associated with individualism (such as self-direction and achievement) and South-East Asian students are generally higher than Australian students on value orientation stereotypically associated with collectivism (such as security and conformity), these students are not markedly different in their approaches to learning. Further, the findings also show no striking difference in the patterns of how these value orientations relate to students' academic motivations and how they go about their learning. For instance, regardless of the cultural context in which the schooling process takes place, achievement values underpin endorsement of the achievement motive, and security and conformity values are associated with the adoption of achieving learning strategies. Thus, it seems that culture plays an influential role on socioculturally internalised and transmitted psychological factors — such as basic value orientations — but not so much on educationally learned attributes, such as learning motives and strategies.

While educational systems everywhere are undoubtedly influenced by the sociocultural milieus in which they operate, schooling provides all students with a 'pancultural' context, in which they can internalise certain goals and values related to their schooling and acquire learning strategies that are adaptive for academic tasks. Schools wash out the impact of culture-specific socialisation practices on students' motivation and learning, as well as on values and goal preferences. In particular, schools do this when it comes to learning and achievement-related goals, as schools in many educational systems throughout the world focus on these goals. Schooling requires the development of a new set of social, cognitive, and motivational attributes in all children. However, some children become socialised to schooling more easily than others. The question is, why? The answer to this does not concern cultural differences *per se*, let alone in the individualist–collectivist dichotomy. These are important, of course, but are not the essential reason why many children do not thrive at school. There is too much contradictory evidence for this to be plausible, such as the many successful minority cultural groups and individuals in Western school settings; and the repeated pattern of students from collectivist cultures, such as Hong Kong and Singapore, outperforming their counterparts from individualist cultures, such as the United States, in international comparative studies of academic attainments. An analogy can also be drawn with socioeconomic status (SES) as a predictor of school achievement. Again, many low SES students thrive in schooling and use schooling to get ahead. So SES, in and of itself, does not explain why some children are successful and others are not. Once cultural differences are dispelled as the essential reason for lack of success (and also, perhaps, SES) the real issues — such as schooling processes that are dysfunctional for lots of children across lots of groups, and the macro sociopolitical factors that make schooling more instrumental for opening up life opportunities for some children (more so than others) — can be examined. Whatever factors are looked at next, it is time to move beyond the individualism–collectivism dichotomy.

INTERIM SUMMARY

Every culture has a set of 'unwritten rules' that every member learns to abide by. These dimensions cover such things as attitude to time, rules about appropriate levels of emotional display and conversational distance, among others. People are often classified as belonging to either ***individualist cultures*** (emphasise the primacy of the individual over the group) or ***collectivist cultures*** (emphasise the group over individuals).

APPLY + DISCUSS

Have you seen the movies *The Tracker* or *Once Were Warriors*? Both told a story from the perspective of a minority culture within mainstream Australia or New Zealand. Think back now on how your own cultural framework influenced your interpretation of the films.

- To what extent did your own cultural norms, attitudes and expectations influence the way you judged the behaviour of characters in these films?
- To what extent did your assumptions and stereotypes about the minority groups shown in the films influence your response?

Cross-cultural relations

How well do people from different cultures interact? In this section, we will look at the increasingly multicultural nature of many societies today, as well as the benefits and the challenges that cultural pluralism involves. We will also examine the psychological reactions that can occur when cultures come into contact — such as cultural stereotypes, culture shock, acculturation and assimilation, ethnocentrism, prejudice and racism. As a profession, psychology is playing an important role in implementing strategies to help minimise prejudice and racism in multicultural societies, and to help people from diverse cultural backgrounds cope with the impacts of adjusting to new environments.

Multiculturalism

Multiculturalism can be defined as a situation where multiple cultures exist within a country and where the number of inhabitants representing those minority cultures is significant (Batorowicz, 1999; Smith, 2004). A concept closely linked to multiculturalism is ***pluralism***, where there is general acceptance not just of the existence of many different cultural and ethnic groups but also of their right to retain their cultural heritage and coexist.

Achieving such harmony can be difficult, especially for people from different cultures entering a new society. Australia is one of the most multicultural communities on earth, made up of people from more than 200 nations. As shown in table 19.3, the cultural diversity of Australia is also increasing. In 1947, only 10 percent of the population was born overseas, and of that group, 81 percent came from the main English-speaking countries (United Kingdom, New Zealand, South Africa, Canada and the United States). By 2000, only 39 percent of the overseas-born population came from those countries (Australian Bureau of Statistics [ABS], 2002b). Now, about one in four Australians is born overseas and more than 40 percent of Australians have one or both parents born overseas (ABS, 2010b).

TABLE 19.3 **Main countries of birth in Australia 1901, 1947, 2000 and 2010**

Country of birth	1901[a] ('000)	1947[a] ('000)	2000[b] ('000)	2009[b] ('000)
United Kingdom and Ireland	679.2	541.3	1164.1[c]	1188.2
New Zealand	25.8	43.6	374.9	529.2
Italy	5.7	33.6	241.7	219.3
Former Yugoslav Republics	n.a.	5.9	210.0	49.7
Vietnam	n.a.	n.a.	174.4	203.8
China	29.9	6.4	168.1	350.9
Greece	0.9	12.3	141.2	128.6
Philippines	n.a.	0.1	123.0	168.5
Germany	38.4	14.6	120.2	128.8
India	7.6	n.a.	110.2	308.5
Malaysia	n.a.	1.0	97.6	129.6

Country of birth	1901[a] ('000)	1947[a] ('000)	2000[b] ('000)	2009[b] ('000)
Netherlands	0.6	2.2	90.6	89.9
South Africa	n.a.	5.9	80.1	149.0
Lebanon	n.a.	n.a.	79.9	89.9
Poland	n.a.	6.6	68.3	59.3
Indonesia	n.a.	n.a.	67.6	69.7
United States of America	7.4	6.2	65.0	81.1
Hong Kong (SAR of China)[d]	0.2	0.8	56.3	88.5
Total overseas-born	852.4	743.2	4517.3	5816.4
Australia	2908.3	6835.2	14639.8	16138.8
Total population[e]	3773.8	7579.4	19157.0	21955.2

NOTE: Columns do not total 100% due to rounding errors.
(a) Census counts.
(b) Estimated resident population at 30 June.
(c) Excludes Ireland.
(d) Incudes Macao.
(e) Includes country of birth 'Not stated' and 'At sea' for 1901 to 1971.

SOURCE: ABS (2002b, 2010b).

Australia, originally inhabited by Aboriginal and Torres Strait Islander people, was colonised by Europeans in 1788. The British dominated the early days of migration, though many came 'down under' reluctantly as prisoners transported to penal settlements.

Migration to Australia continued to be dominated by people from Britain and Europe for many years. However, there were a few exceptions. The gold rush in the 1850s attracted various nationalities, including a large contingent of Chinese settlers, Indians and Afghans. In the period immediately after World War II, a wave of migrants arrived in Australia from European countries including Italy, Greece and Holland. Until the 1960s, the 'White Australia policy' guided the nation's immigration policies, encouraging settlers only from 'white' countries, such as many European states.

In recent years, immigration from Middle Eastern and Asian countries such as Vietnam has increased. More recently, refugees and asylum seekers from countries such as Chile, Sudan, Iraq and China have added to the ethnic mix.

In more than 50 years of planned post-war migration, about six million migrants have arrived in Australia, helping population numbers in Australia swell from seven million to almost 22 million (ABS, 2007c, 2010). When you combine the total number of Australians born overseas with those with at least one parent born overseas, the largest groupings came from the UK (2.5 million), Italy (572 000), New Zealand (491 000), the former Yugoslav Republics (306 000) and Greece (280 000), followed by the Netherlands, Vietnam, Lebanon, Ireland and China (ABS, 2006e).

The multicultural nature of contemporary Australian society was personified in 2011 when Usman Khawaja became the first Pakistan-born player to represent Australia in Test cricket. Khawaja's family emigrated to Australia when he was three years old and he grew up in New South Wales.

In addition, about 463 900 people identify as Aboriginal and 33 100 people identify as Torres Strait Islander, with a further 20 200 being of both Aboriginal and Torres Strait Islander origin (ABS, 2007b).

Australia has a large, vibrant Arab community, with the first arrivals taking place in the 1870s. Estimates place the number of Australians of Arab origin as high as one million (Department of Foreign Affairs and Trade, 2004). Arabic is the fifth most spoken language in Australia, after English, Italian, Chinese and Greek. The Lebanese and Egyptian communities are generally the most established, with immigration from Iraq and Syria increasing in more recent times.

In 1861, Asians comprised nearly 3.5 percent of the Australian population. With the advent of the White Australia policy, that number dropped to 0.4 percent by the middle of the twentieth century (Koo & Lee, 1994). However, the removal of ethnic barriers in the early 1970s saw a rapid influx of Asian immigrants. Today, Asian Australians who migrated to Australia comprise about 6 percent of the Australian population (ABS, 2001, 2006e). Asian immigrants have come to Australia for a variety of reasons, some forced and some voluntary, ranging from political refugees to highly qualified professionals pursuing their careers (Castles, 1993).

A more recent phenomenon in Australia has been the rise in trans-Tasman migration, with the number of New Zealanders moving permanently to Australia quadrupling in the 1990s. New Zealand is now the largest contributor of migrants to Australia. Interestingly, about one-third of those immigrants were born outside New Zealand, particularly in Polynesian or Asian nations.

As shown in figure 19.2, the ethnic make-up of the New Zealand population is also diverse and becoming more so. In 2001, 80 percent of the population identified as being of European descent; 14.7 percent as Maori; 6.6 percent as Asian; and 6.5 percent as Pacific Peoples (Statistics New Zealand, 2002). Other groups represented included Arabs, Iranians, Somalis and Latin Americans. Within those broad groupings, there had been noticeable increases in numbers within particular ethnic groups, particularly those from Croatia, South Africa, Tahiti and Korea. In the 2006 census, New Zealand European and Maori remained the two largest ethnic groups, and there was a jump in the number of people who identified as 'New Zealander' (Statistics New Zealand, 2007).

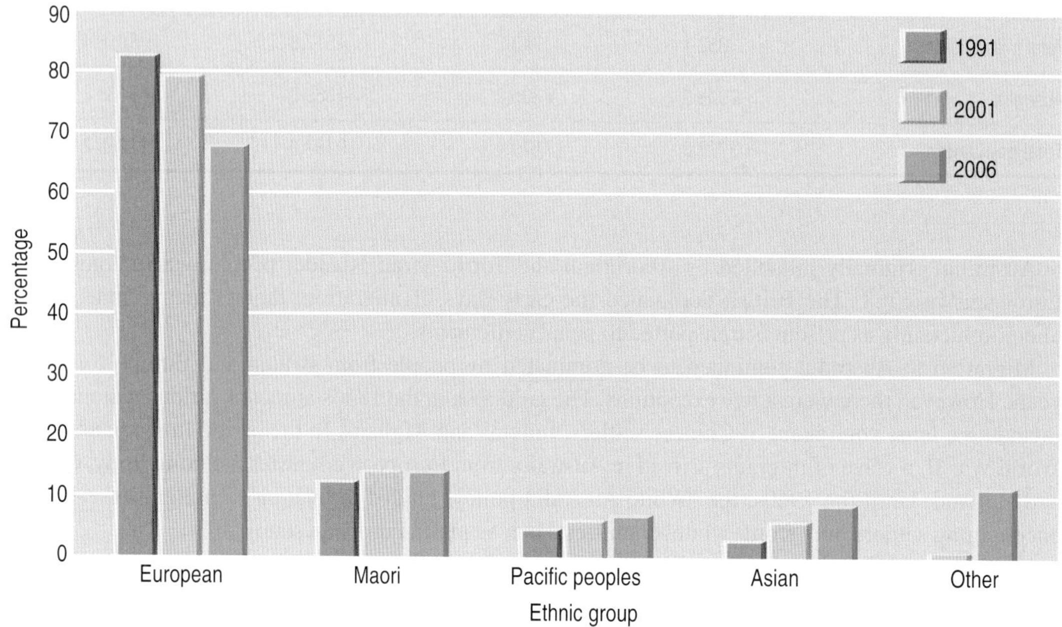

FIGURE 19.2
Ethnic group as a percentage of the total population in New Zealand, 1991, 2001 and 2006

NOTES: The 'other' category in 2006 includes those identifying as 'New Zealander'. Another New Zealand census was planned for 2011 but was deferred due to a national state of emergency and the probable impact on census results after the 2011 Christchurch earthquake. It is recommended that the Statistics New Zealand website (www.stats.govt.nz) is accessed for the most recent information on this topic.

SOURCE: Statistics New Zealand (2002, 2007).

Multiculturalism is a feature of many countries in the Asia–Pacific region. Singapore, for example, has large Chinese, Malay and Indian communities. In Fiji, the Indian population almost outnumbers the indigenous Polynesian people. Indonesia is made up of a lot of different islands, the inhabitants of which come from diverse backgrounds. It is a country without a history of large-scale immigration from outside its national boundary, and boasts considerable cultural diversity. While approximately 45 percent of the population of Indonesia are Javanese, 14 percent are Sundanese, about 7.5 percent are Madurese, another 7.5 percent are coastal Malays, and a further 26 percent of the population is made up of numerous small ethnic groups or minorities from within the country (Central Intelligence Agency, 2007).

Refugees and asylum seekers

Australia currently has a two-pronged immigration approach — a program for skilled migrants and family migrants, and a humanitarian program for refugees and displaced people. In the past 50 years, more than 620 000 people have been resettled in Australia under the humanitarian program. Approximately 12 000 humanitarian migrants a year resettle in Australia. In 2002–03, almost half that number came from African countries, 37 percent from the Middle East and South-West Asia, and 10 percent from Europe (Department of Immigration and Multicultural and Indigenous Affairs, 2004). In 2010–11, the government allocated 6000 places for refugees and made available 7750 places for the Special Humanitarian Program (Department of Immigration and Citizenship, 2009).

A GLOBAL VISTA

Understanding the mental health and wellbeing needs of refugees and asylum seekers

By Emeritus Professor Graham R. Davidson, University of the Sunshine Coast

Behind the often rancorous, self-interested political debate about how Australia should manage the arrival of small vessels carrying humanitarian refugees, there are crucially important questions about the mental health and wellbeing needs of these and other people that need to be asked. In the face of political, religious or cultural persecution, refugees are forced to flee their communities to protect their own and their loved ones' personal safety. Many forced migrants fall under the United Nations 1951 Convention Article 1 definition of a refugee; many others are internally displaced in their own country; and a smaller number seeking refugee status who arrive unannounced in another country are known as asylum seekers. Data published by the United Nations High Commissioner for Refugees (2009) shows there were 42 million forcibly displaced persons worldwide in a recent year, including 15.2 million refugees, 26 million internally displaced persons and 830 000 asylum seekers.

There are crucial questions that need to be asked about the mental health and wellbeing of humanitarian refugees, who, in the face of great persecution, choose to flee their communities to protect their own and their loved ones' personal safety.

Although Australia accepts a relatively small number of refugees and receives a small proportion of asylum applications, its international contribution to refugee resettlement is, nevertheless, important. The number of asylum seekers arriving on Australia's shores by boat also represents a small proportion of forced migrants attempting to enter this country.

Research with refugees and asylum seekers suggests that forced migrants experience higher rates of personal distress than voluntary migrants. They have poorer general health and are at greater risk of mental ill health, including conditions such as post-traumatic stress disorder (PTSD), major depressive disorder, anxiety, dissociation and somatisation. They experience increased likelihood of cognitive disturbances, decreased educational, socioeconomic and work self-efficacy, decreased levels of family and social cohesion, and a reduced sense of belonging (Davidson, Murray, & Schweitzer, 2008). Forced migrants arriving at resettlement destinations are often vulnerable to various forms of exploitation and do not have access to the full range of health, mental health, welfare, educational and employment services available to citizens of those resettlement countries (Davidson & Carr, 2010). Research and professional engagement with asylum seekers arriving in Australia have shown consistently that, by and large, asylum seekers experience greater distress than humanitarian refugees; this has been linked with their experiences of immigration detention and temporary residence status. Unsurprisingly, in all of our summary reviews of mental health (Davidson et al., 2008, 2010; Murray, Davidson, & Schweitzer, 2010), we did not find a single study indicating detention of asylum seekers, or prolongation of their temporary residence status, or withholding economic, housing, educational or health support, was beneficial psychologically or socially for these new arrivals. In all of the research, detainees and temporary visa holders were shown to have poorer initial adjustment outcomes than permanent protection visa holders. Young asylum seekers are particularly at risk of poor mental health adjustment under detention and temporary residence policies (Human Rights and Equal Opportunity Commission, 2004); and young refugees are often very disadvantaged by educational systems that grade them on the basis of their age rather than on the basis of their educational performance and English language ability, resulting in poorer psycho-educational adjustment.

Risk of increased psychological distress and vulnerability is associated with: demographic variables, such as gender, age, rurality and socio-economic status; pre-flight factors, such as magnitude, frequency and type of physical and psychological trauma; and resettlement factors, such as experience of migration processing systems and available resettlement services and support. Forced migrants are often also confronted by negative public opinion, in the form of false beliefs about their intentions, resources and migration methods, and by outright prejudice (Pedersen, Attwell, & Heveli, 2005; Pedersen, Watt, & Hansen, 2006).

Diagnosis, assessment and treatment of psychological distress in refugee and asylum seeker populations raise questions about the universality of Western models of trauma and recovery, as the following examples illustrate. Psychologists have started to question whether a Western, medicalised understanding of PTSD adequately represents refugees' lived experiences of danger, loss and grief, and whether such a diagnosis places too much emphasis on illness and treatment — at the expense of harnessing refugees' resilience and determination to promote positive personal growth and change (Papadopoulos, 2007). Even assessment of PTSD presents a challenge. Bolton (2001) identified local Rwandan culture-specific syndromes of mental trauma and grief that offered explanatory understandings of people's reactions to traumatic events, but which shared only some symptoms with the *Diagnostic and Statistical Manual of Mental Disorders*, 4th edition, (DSM-IV) PTSD and grief syndromes (also see Bolton et al., 2007). Hollifield et al. (2005) developed an expanded 164-item Comprehensive Trauma Inventory for use with refugees who reported on average 150 traumatic events, much higher than the numbers suggested by previous measures. Hollifield et al. (2005) attributed the differential outcomes to limitations in design of previous measures.

There is some evidence that cognitive behaviour therapy (CBT) may be an efficient treatment for some refugee sufferers' traumatic stress and anxiety; however, treatment outcomes are inconsistent, and require further testing with larger samples from other cultural backgrounds. Interventions such as CBT, unless they are to remain a treatment for middle class Westerners (Kelly, 2008), may need to be redesigned in ways that accommodate clients' cultural and linguistic backgrounds, as well as relevant cultural understandings of emotion, suffering, trauma and social support.

International students

Another contributor to the increasingly multicultural nature of today's societies has been growth in the number of international students. In 2003, there were just over 303 000 enrolments by full-fee-paying overseas students in Australia, which is an increase of 10.8 percent from the previous year (Department of Education, Science, and Training, 2004). This number increased to just over 340 000 in 2006 (Department of Education, Science and Training, 2006) and jumped to 631 935 in 2009 (Australian Education International, 2009). In 2002, the majority of international students came from China, Hong Kong, South Korea, Indonesia, Malaysia, Japan, Thailand, India, the United States and Singapore. The year 2009 witnessed a change in the top 10 source countries, with a substantial increase in students from China and India, plus a rise in student numbers from South Korea, Thailand, Nepal, Vietnam, Malaysia, Indonesia, Brazil and Saudi Arabia (Australian Education International, 2009).

In New Zealand, there were 100 000 international students enrolled in 2003, also with the largest proportion coming from China (New Zealand Ministry of Education, 2004). More recently, the number of students coming from New Zealand's main source country, China, has been in decline (Education New Zealand, 2007). However, 2009 witnessed a turnaround, with an increase for the first time in six years. Around 93 500 international students studied in New Zealand in this year (Envisage International Corporation, 2010).

Culture shock

New arrivals to a country often experience a period of 'culture shock' as they adjust to the new environment (Tartakovsky, 2007). ***Culture shock*** is the feeling of disorientation and anxiety that occurs as people from one culture encounter and adapt to the practices, rules and expectations of another culture. The shock arises because people have to cope with different languages, unwritten rules of behaviour, social structures, political and legislative processes and other aspects of daily life. For most, the initial level of culture shock is not a permanent state. Eckermann et al. (2010) describe the four phases or stages of culture shock as:

1. *The honeymoon phase:* initial euphoria and excitement.
2. *The disenchantment phase:* disillusionment and even hostility towards the new culture as values and habits conflict with local attitudes and beliefs.
3. *The beginning resolution phase:* recovery as confidence and understanding of the new culture grows.
4. *The effective functioning stage:* adjustment as the individual learns how to fit into the new cultural environment.

Consider the case of a male student from Malaysia moving to Dunedin in New Zealand to study at university. At first, the new surroundings, scenery and environment are tremendously exciting. He spends the initial days exploring the new campus, looking around the city, and settling into life in the on-campus dormitory. Over the next few weeks, however, that excitement drops away. He finds difficulty adjusting to different teaching methods and student–teacher relationships. The weather is cold. The food is different. The values of the other students are far removed from those of students at home. He has trouble making friends. A few weeks later, he is starting to come to grips with the new surroundings. He has learned to speak up more in his classes. He has made several new friends. He is starting to understand how the different moral values of other students influence their behaviour. By the end of semester, he is enjoying life as a student at Dunedin. His grades are up, his social life is more active and he has even found a Malaysian restaurant that specialises in his favourite Malay foods.

The period of adjustment can be extremely difficult. In 2002 and 2003, a team of researchers in Western Australia investigated the experiences of ethnic groups in Perth, including four African migrant communities — Sudanese, Somali, Eritrean and Ethiopian — primarily in relation to mental health (Tilbury et al., 2004). The participants identified difficulties in adjusting to the different cultural environment in Australia as a significant cause of stress. Specific problems such as learning a new language and using automatic teller machines caused anxiety. But participants reported that the fact their traditional cultures were so distant and removed from mainstream Australian culture produced extreme levels of distress. For example, men from these African countries had grave concerns that mainstream cultural values in Australia were resulting in women and children losing their traditional respect for, and subservience to, men.

MAKING CONNECTIONS

Stress can affect your wellbeing (chapter 14), but stress is not a constant. For example, some people are skilled public speakers, while others feel sick at the thought of talking in front of a crowd. This variation in stress can have a cultural component as well. People can experience high levels of stress — **culture shock** — when visiting or trying to settle in another culture. Imagine the difficulty a person from sparsely settled outback Queensland might experience in adjusting to life in inner-city Sydney!

Access to health services

Another key source of stress for people from different cultural backgrounds is access to health services. Professor Olga Kanitaki from Royal Melbourne Institute of Technology has pointed out that despite Australia being a multicultural society, containing people from many backgrounds, the country's health care system is largely monocultural in nature (Medical Research News, 2004). She said that the health system largely reflected the dominant cultural values, care practices and beliefs of one group — Anglo-Celtic Australians (chapter 14). Consequently, people of diverse cultural and language backgrounds may be at risk of misdiagnosis and incorrect care.

Cultural barriers to the use of health care services include language difficulties and a general lack of recognition of different constructs of health for non-Anglo Australians. A person's cultural background will influence how they interpret and respond to their life experiences and whether they seek support primarily from family and friends or from health professional services (Hunter Institute of Mental Health, 2004). Research indicates that people who immigrate to Australia and are from non-English-speaking backgrounds tend to under-utilise specialist health services (Hollifield et al., 2002) due to a variety of reasons. Of concern are recent findings which suggest that immigrant and multicultural health issues in Australia are essentially unrepresented in health research (Garrett, Dickson, Whelan, & Whyte, 2010). Much needs to be done to ensure that all Australians have access to high quality health care services (Hunter Institute of Mental Health). For example, Henry, Houston, and Mooney (2004) argue that non-Aboriginal Australians must learn to understand and respect Aboriginal culture, including its fundamental philosophy of 'communitarian solidarity', to ensure better access to health services by Aboriginals.

INTERIM SUMMARY

Multiculturalism refers to those situations where multiple cultures exist within a country. ***Pluralism*** supports both the coexistence of different cultural groups and their right to retain their cultural heritage. Both are features of Australia and New Zealand and many countries in the Asia–Pacific region, where immigration policies have resulted in the blending and co-existence of many cultural groups. New arrivals to a country often experience ***culture shock***, a feeling of disorientation and anxiety as they encounter and adapt to the practices, rules and expectations of another culture. If a health system reflects the dominant cultural values, care practices and beliefs, then people of diverse cultural and language backgrounds may be at risk of misdiagnosis and incorrect care provision.

APPLY + DISCUSS

The old saying 'When in Rome, do as the Romans do' recognises that people in different cultures have different ways of doing things. Anyone who has travelled overseas will have encountered behaviours that seemed extremely strange to them, but perfectly natural to the locals.

- Are there any students from other countries studying your course? Can you think of any of your daily activities, or your customs and traditions, which might seem odd to them?

Acculturation and assimilation

The process of acculturation is a growing field of study. International migration, major refugee movements, decolonisation and the globalisation of mass media technologies have brought increased intercultural contact; previously isolated and homogeneous people now have daily contact with people from across the globe, setting in place a process of cultural and psychological adaptation (Berry, 1995). ***Acculturation*** can be defined as the changes that groups and individuals undergo when they come into contact with another culture (Smith Castro, 2003). This can be considered a process of integration, where people adopt and adapt aspects of the new culture they enter, while still retaining many elements of their cultural heritage. The study of acculturation is often applied to the process through which minority ethnic identities in societies like Australia come to identify with and adopt the mainstream culture they are surrounded by. That is not to say that acculturation and ethnic identity are mutually exclusive, though there may certainly be some friction between the two. Some people have difficulty balancing their ethnic identity with the dominant culture. Others accommodate the two with little difficulty.

LaFromboise, Coleman, and Gerton (1993) developed a model that identifies a number of different types of acculturation: ***assimilation***, which involves absorption into the dominant culture and abandonment of their traditional culture; acculturation, which involves competence in a second culture without complete acceptance; ***fusion***, which involves combining two cultures to form a new culture; ***alternation***, which involves bicultural competence; and ***multiculturalism***, which involves maintaining distinct cultural identities within a single multicultural social structure.

Ethnic identity

Within multicultural populations, such as those in Australia and New Zealand, there are many groups of people who define themselves not only by nationality but also by ethnicity. For instance, Australia has large numbers of people who would consider themselves to be of Greek, Italian or Lebanese ethnicity, even though many generations of their families have been born in Australia. While there is no universally accepted definition of ***ethnicity***, the term is commonly used in relation to people who share geographic, language, cultural and religious origins. As such, ethnicity is a narrower concept than race or nationality. For instance, people of the Arabic race may have many different nationalities such as Syrian, Jordanian or Iraqi. However, within the Iraqi group, people may also consider themselves to be of separate ethnicity, depending on exactly where in the country they come from and whether they are of Sunni or Shi'ite religion. Similarly, Italians may consider themselves of the same race but of different ethnicity depending on whether they are of German–Italian, French–Italian or Slovene–Italian origin in the north, or Albanian–Italian or Greek–Italian origin in the south. Most importantly, ethnicity is not defined in isolation but in relation to other groups. ***Ethnic identity*** is where members of an ethnic group identify 'us' in relation to 'them' using aspects of shared culture, language or religion. Thus, ethnicity involves a shared sense of 'peoplehood'.

Within multicultural populations, such as those in Australia and New Zealand, many people define themselves by their ethnicity as well as their nationality.

A sense of ethnic identity can also sit comfortably beside a sense of nationality. Dewhirst (2003) traced the descendants of Giovanni Pulli, who migrated from Italy to Brisbane in 1876 and rose to some prominence in the Italian ethnic community. Five generations of the Pulli family have now been born in Australia. When surveyed, those descendants largely saw themselves as 'Australian' but, equally, most had a strong sense of Italian ethnic identity and a pride in their Italian heritage. Similarly Faria (2001) found that Indian immigrants to Australia had also maintained a strong Indian identity, even when emigrating up to two or three times to different countries within a generation. And those born in Australia retained much the same sense of what it was to be Indian as those who were born in India, through the retention of religious, regional, linguistic and cultural influences.

Personal identity and social identity

We all have a number of different 'identities', depending on the perspective that we adopt. We all have a ***personal identity*** — a sense of who we are as individuals. This personal identity reflects what we feel is unique about us — the combination of our own particular values, traits, abilities, likes, aspirations and life history. Personal identity is very much about us as individuals, whereas social identity is about our sense of belonging to a larger group (Postmes, Baray, Haslam, Morton, & Swaab, 2006). Our ***social identity*** relates to the perception that we are part of a larger social group and share with other group members salient attributes such as values, meanings and goals (Camilleri & Malewska-Peyre, 1997). Our social identity helps define our place in the world, satisfies our need to belong to a wider group, and enables us to feel with other group members a shared sense of difference to others (Brewer & Gardner, 1996). It is possible — in fact, common — for people to have multiple social identities. Different social identities might come from belonging to a particular ethnic group, supporting a particular football team, belonging to a particular church, living in a particular town or suburb, or working in a particular occupation.

Gender and culture

An integral part of our personal identity is our gender. First, it is important to distinguish between 'sex' and 'gender' (see World Health Organization, 2007). ***Sex*** refers to the biological attributes that differentiate males from females. ***Gender*** refers to the roles and behaviours that cultures deem appropriate for men and women. When we are born, we have a sex but no gender — as we grow up within a particular culture, we learn the gender roles considered appropriate within that society. Bem (1981) argues that gender is a fundamental way in which we learn how to understand the world — what behaviours, attitudes, objects and conventions are associated with being male and female in our culture.

There are innate physical and biological differences between men and women, and some common themes in gender roles can be detected across many cultures. For instance, men are traditionally the hunters and the protectors in many societies, whereas women are the nurturers, who care for children, cook and clean. Biology plays a role in these differences — men are physically bigger and stronger, while women are the child-bearers. But biology alone cannot explain the enormous variation of gender roles across the globe. The cultural context has an enormous impact. Research across cultures makes clear that climatic, technological, economic, environmental and social factors all have an impact on how gender roles are defined. The distinction between what can be attributed to biology and what can be attributed to psychological and social factors is the subject of considerable debate in the psychology discipline (Hall & Barongan, 2002). For example, evolutionary theories argue that men are more sexually promiscuous than women because they instinctually look to mate with multiple partners to improve the chances of their genes being passed on. But to what extent is this an innate biological drive, and to what extent is it a result of cultural influences that reinforce promiscuity as an appropriate gender role? The answer perhaps lies somewhere in the middle, with biological, psychological and cultural influences all interacting to help define gender roles in different societies.

MAKING CONNECTIONS

While there are **gender role differences** across cultures, Segall, Dasen, Berry, and Poortinga (1990) found considerable consensus on the stereotypical traits of males and females. Males are considered stronger, more dominant, more aggressive, more achievement oriented and more autonomous. Females are considered more nurturing, more deferent and more communal. Some differences, such as strength, are biological. However, most differences are learned through a process of **socialisation** (chapter 13). The behaviours expected of males and females are heavily influenced by cultural, social and environmental factors. For example, van Leeuwen (1978) argued that cultures based on hunting and gathering encouraged independence and less gender-role specialisation, whereas societies based on farming and grazing emphasised greater gender-role differentiation.

An understanding of sex and gender begins early in life, with most three-year-olds able to tell you whether they are male or female. Children also learn quickly what is expected of different genders. In Western societies, this might mean that girls wear dresses and play with dolls, while boys wear pants and play with toy trucks. It is important to realise that such gender roles are *learned* and are the result of the cultural context children grow up in. The reinforcement of gender roles continues relentlessly throughout our lives.

INTERIM SUMMARY

Acculturation is the process whereby people learn to adopt and adapt aspects of the new culture they enter, while still retaining many elements of their cultural heritage. ***Assimilation*** occurs when a person is completely absorbed into the dominant culture, losing touch with their traditional culture. People have a number of identities: ***ethnic identity*** refers to members of an ethnic group identifying together through a shared sense of culture, language or religion; ***personal identity*** refers to a sense of who we are as individuals; and ***social identity*** refers to our sense of belonging to a larger group.

Impact of multiculturalism

Modern Australia has been built on immigration, and the blending and co-existence of many cultural groups. Multiculturalism is now expressed as a policy goal by government. In the foreword to *A New Agenda for Multicultural Australia*, former Prime Minister John Howard described the country's cultural diversity as one of its most important attributes (Commonwealth of Australia, 1999). He said: 'Our diversity is a source of competitive advantage, cultural enrichment and social stability' (p. 2).

Many would agree that multiculturalism has enriched Australia, from matters as simple as new types of food to higher order improvements such as increased tolerance and understanding. Batorowicz (1999) says many multicultural countries are proud of their ethnic composition, mutual tolerance and social cohesion, and view multiculturalism as positive for both social and economic development. However, he warns that cultural diversity can also be a source of conflict. One such example is the Sydney suburb of Cabramatta, which is the centre of a large Vietnamese community. The murder of local New South Wales MP John Newman in Cabramatta in 1994, and the subsequent conviction of Vietnamese leader and political rival Phuong Ng for the murder, generated a wave of anti-Asian sentiment. The suburb was portrayed as a drug and crime hotspot. Newman's successor in the seat of Cabramatta, Reba Meagher, told the New South Wales Parliament in 1994 that the whole suburb was unfairly spotlighted after the murder, with the Asian community particularly vilified. She said the hype and tabloid headlines the tragedy generated demonstrated the bigotry and racism that were still prevalent in the community (New South Wales Legislative Assembly Hansard, 1994).

The potential for cultural conflict was again realised in Australia in the late 1990s with the rise of the One Nation political party and its founder Pauline Hanson, who campaigned on a platform that Aboriginal Australians were receiving excessive 'handouts' from the government and that Australia was being swamped by Asian immigration. A study by Fraser and Islam (2000) supported the view that One Nation supporters saw themselves as 'real Australians' who supported the belief that Aboriginal Australians and migrants received more than they deserved. While One Nation enjoyed some political success in the mid-1990s, its electoral success since then has been limited. However, many people in Australia were shocked by the racially motivated Cronulla riots that broke out on a Sunday afternoon in December 2005. After weeks of simmering tension, a mob of about 5000 people from Anglo-Saxon backgrounds gathered at Cronulla beach and took over the streets, targeting youths from Lebanese backgrounds. Members of the rioting mob justified their actions as 'reclaiming' the beach for 'real Australians', echoing the sentiments of One Nation supporters.

The attitudes towards Asians and Aboriginal Australians highlighted by the One Nation phenomenon also illustrated the concept of ***xenophobia*** — the fear or hatred of foreigners, or anything foreign and unfamiliar (de Angelis, 2003). The sentiments and fears expressed about these 'foreign' peoples were often irrational or unfounded. Xenophobia is based on a broad stereotype about any cultures different to your own.

APPLY + DISCUSS

What does it mean to be Australian? As an exercise, list all the things (events, attitudes, places etc.) that you believe symbolise Australia and its culture. Now think about that list from the viewpoint of someone from an ethnic or cultural minority living in Australia.

- To what extent would the list be different for people from different ethnic or cultural backgrounds?
- Is there any one list that could encapsulate Australian culture? If not, why is this so?

Cultural stereotypes

Cultural stereotypes are generalised views that we hold about particular groups of people — the belief that all members of a particular cultural group share common traits or behaviours. While the notion of a 'stereotype' these days often has a negative connotation, they can be both positive and negative (chapter 17). A stereotypical view is that German people are hard-working but unemotional; while Italians are passionate and expressive. Some consider the French to be arrogant and Australians to be unsophisticated; others see Maori people as fun-loving and spontaneous, and the Japanese as extremely polite. Stereotypes are not limited to different nationalities. People have stereotypical views about football players, people who drive particular makes of car, politicians and senior citizens. Stereotypes can have a basis in fact but can also be completely untrue. They can also be extremely damaging to intercultural relationships. Stereotypes about Muslim people as 'terrorists' sprang up in many Western countries after the terror attacks in the United States on 11 September 2001. The Bali bombing in 2002 and the bombings in London's public transport system in 2005 further entrenched this stereotype in Australia. Conversely, stereotypes about Australians being racist 'rednecks' also become more apparent across a number of Asian countries following the initial success of the One Nation party in the 1990s. The existence of these stereotypes can act as a barrier to closer relationships between people across cultures (see Terracciano & McCrae, 2007).

A study of attitudes of young Australians towards different cultural groups identified stereotypical views (Islam & Jahjah, 2000, 2001). This study of 139 university students of Anglo-Celtic extraction looked at attitudes towards Aboriginal Australians, Asians and Arabs. The stereotypes that were frequently associated with each of the groups are shown in table 19.4.

TABLE 19.4 **Most frequently elicited stereotypes by Australian university students to Aboriginal Australians, Asians and Arabs**

Aboriginal Australians	Asians	Arabs
Respectful to land	Hardworking	Arrogant
Spiritual	Educated	Aggressive
Bludgers	Ambitious	Nationalistic
Drunken	Industrious	Spiritual

Interestingly, these cultural stereotypes involved a mixture of both positive and negative attributes. But it is unlikely that too many individuals within these cultural groups would fit the stereotype completely because not all members of any culture are the same. Stereotypes do help us to make sense of the world in which we live, but they also lead to three distortions of reality (Judd, Park, Ryan, Brauer, & Kraus, 1995):

1. *Stereotypes accentuate group differences.* Us–them thinking (chapter 17) results in people focusing on the differences between cultural groups and ignoring the similarities that exist between them.
2. *Stereotypes create selective thinking.* People only see what reinforces the cultural stereotype and reject any perceptions that do not fit.
3. *Stereotypes assume homogeneity in other groups.* People recognise dissimilarity between members of their own cultural group but assume that all members of another culture behave the same way.

These distortions apply to all forms of stereotypes, not just cultural stereotypes.

APPLY + DISCUSS

Think of an ethnic minority group living in your country. Can you identify any common stereotypes that have come to be associated with that group? Now, think of any members of that ethnic minority group that you have met personally and interacted with.

- To what extent do those stereotypes apply to the people you have met?
- To what extent do members of ethnic minorities have distinct and different personalities?

Why do we develop stereotypes about groups of people? This phenomenon is actually a quite normal and rational psychological process. Throughout everyday life, we are bombarded with an enormous range of information and new stimuli. Processing and categorising that information, as well as trying to retrieve data stored in our memories, can be a difficult exercise. To make life easier, we use stereotypes as a type of mental categorisation, so we can more efficiently process information. Rather than have to interpret new information and make individual assessments about every person we come across, we use stereotypes as a guide to provide a general context about that person (chapter 17).

Ethnocentrism

How often do you hear people of a particular nationality proclaim that they are from the 'best country in the world'? What leads them to make such a favourable judgement about their homeland? Ethnocentrism is the most likely answer. ***Ethnocentrism*** can be defined as the tendency for a person's own culture to influence the way they view the rest of the world. People from a particular culture use their own values, standards, attitudes and behaviours as a yardstick against which they judge the way other people think and behave. Their own lifestyle is viewed as normal, while the lifestyles of other cultures are viewed as strange and often inferior. This is perhaps natural and understandable. Throughout our life, our culture emphasises particular rules and taboos that we internalise and come to accept as 'normal'. Our enculturation produces filters that colour the way we view the outside world. Our ethnocentrism also strengthens the ties that bind us together. Recent cross-cultural studies have conceptualised ethnocentrism as ethnic group self-centeredness — a multifaceted construct expressed in several ways across groups, such as ingroup preference, superiority, purity and exploitativeness; and expressed within groups as group cohesion and devotion (Bizumic, Duckitt, Popadic, Dru, & Krauss, 2009). Ethnocentrism is often viewed in a negative light, but in reality it is a normal response to growing up in a particular culture (see Cashdan, 2001).

Prejudice and racism

While developing stereotypes and ethnocentrism is quite normal, developing prejudices takes those processes into negative territory. ***Prejudice*** can be defined as having an unreasonable and negative stereotype about members of another group of people. Prejudice is generally taken to mean negatively pre-judging — to make a negative assumption about members of another group simply on the basis of their group membership. The term is commonly used in relation to ***racial prejudice***, where people develop negative stereotypes about members of another racial group or a cultural practice. Aboriginal academic Jackie Huggins tells the story of visiting a local real estate agent in Brisbane wanting to buy a home. On arriving at the counter, she was told 'we don't do rentals here'. The agent had wrongly assumed that she was hoping to rent a home rather than buy one, simply because of her skin colour.

Studies have shown that prejudice is often associated with low self-esteem (Jordan, Spencer, & Zanna, 2005). Self-esteem can be raised by engaging in prejudiced behaviours — people with low self-esteem often try to feel better about themselves by denigrating other groups of people (Islam & Hewstone, 1993b). People also feel a sense of shared identity with others who have the same prejudices. Prejudiced people are often unable to recognise their own ethnocentrism and stereotypical thinking, whereas most of us realise that we do need to put these aside and make individual assessments about others. Prejudice can also be reinforced by parents and other key influencers in our lives (Sinclair, Dunn, & Lowery, 2005).

Pedersen et al. (2005) studied the attitudes of people in Perth towards asylum seekers in Australia. They found that a large proportion of the community expressed negative attitudes towards asylum seekers, which strongly related to falsely held beliefs about them. They found that gender, a lack of education and right-wing political views were significant predictors of negative attitudes. Overall, they concluded that negative attitudes related to societal issues, not simply psychological issues, and that a lot of work was needed in the wider society to dispel misconceptions about asylum seekers before Australia could call itself a 'just and welcoming' multicultural society (p. 158). Xenophobic and hostile attitudes by Australians towards asylum seekers persist throughout some communities, including those in close proximity to immigration detention centres (Klocker, 2004). Inaccurate or inappropriate statements by some federal government representatives have been reported to fuel community false-beliefs about asylum seekers (Pedersen et al., 2006). However, the Western Australian Government has proactively developed an anti-racism strategy to address racial and religious vilification (see Government of Western Australia and Equal Opportunity Commission, 2010).

MAKING CONNECTIONS

Thomas Keneally's book *The chant of Jimmie Blacksmith*, subsequently made into an iconic Australian film, is based on actual events that occurred at the start of the twentieth century. It depicts the impacts of **racism** in colonial Australia (chapter 17). It tells the story of a young Aboriginal man struggling with his identity. The son of an Aboriginal mother and an Anglo-Australian father, Jimmy finds himself torn between two worlds. Though born into the Tullam clan of the Mungindi tribe, he is heavily influenced by a Caucasian Methodist missionary as he grows up. Jimmie leaves the mission and marries a Caucasian girl but finds rejection and exploitation from the dominant Anglo world. Eventually, Jimmie cannot suppress his intense **emotions** and rage (chapter 10) and as a result snaps in a violent and horrific manner.

Racism involves not only the pervasive and systematic assumption of the inferiority of certain groups, but also the different and unfair treatment of those groups on the basis of that assumed inferiority (Sanson et al., 1998; see also Willis-Esqueda, 2008). Ethnic and cultural minorities in many countries continue to be affected by racism — where people use physical or social features to classify and discriminate against those individuals who are different. ***Discrimination*** is the behavioural manifestation of prejudiced attitudes (chapter 17). An example would be a bank refusing to lend money to a person simply on the basis of their ethnic or cultural background. The four most vilified and racially attacked groups in Australia are Aboriginal people, Asians (ethnic Chinese and South-East Asians), Muslims and Jews (Human Rights and Equal Opportunity Council, 1991). Racist attitudes and actions have ebbed and flowed through recent decades along with events such as the rise of the One Nation political party, the arrival of asylum seekers aboard vessels such as the *Tampa*, the September 11 attacks in 2001 and the Bali bombings in 2002 and 2005. Muslim and Arab Australians have reported an increase in experiences of racism in the wake of the September 11 attacks, including physical violence, threats of violence, verbal abuse, and active discrimination in workplaces and other sites (Poynting & Noble, 2004). A study by Schweitzer, Perkoulidis, Krome, Ludlow, and Ryan (2005) found a high prevalence of prejudicial attitudes towards refugees in Australia. Similarly, Pedersen, Clarke, Dudgeon, and Griffiths (2005) reported significant levels of negative attitudes towards both Indigenous Australians and asylum seekers, with false beliefs about them a strong predictor of those negative attitudes. They say this indicates that Australia's multiculturalism is 'conditional' and involves a strong element of 'institutional, cultural, and individual racism' (p. 177).

While the term 'race' is widely used in general society, it is worth noting that it is used much less often today as a variable in psychological research. The concept of race developed historically as a way of differentiating between people based on observable visible features such as skin colour or eye shape. Thus, distinctions were made between 'Caucasians' and 'Asians'. However, as Sanson et al. (1998) point out, there is actually more genetic variation observable *within* racial groupings than *between* racial groupings. Thus, race as a concept is of little value in trying to identify innate differences or patterns of behaviour among people. However, Sanson et al. (1998) state that the concept of race only becomes important when society loads it with cultural significance and differential social value. That is when 'racism', as it is popularly understood, and prejudice occur on the basis of external physical characteristics.

A development in this debate around this topic is the distinction highlighted by Pedersen, Griffith, Contos, Bishop, and Walker (2000) between 'old-fashioned' prejudice, which is expressed overtly and blatantly, and 'modern' prejudice, which is much more subtle and covert. Historically, discrimination against people of particular cultures was expressed and practised openly. For example, employers might have made no secret of denying an applicant a job on the basis of their cultural background. But in many Western countries today, discrimination is less obvious. For example, employers might not openly discriminate on the basis of cultural background, but their refusal to recognise overseas qualifications and their reliance on results obtained through education systems based on Western curricula may discriminate just as effectively.

The change to more subtle forms of prejudice has been influenced by a number of factors. An increased focus on human rights in recent decades and legislation making overt prejudice illegal are among the factors that have made open expressions of racism less socially acceptable. Opponents have labelled such a trend 'political correctness' — saying it undermines free speech in favour of minority rights. However supporters believe the move to less discriminatory language is a strong force in encouraging tolerance and strong intercultural relationships. University of Southern Queensland indigenous academic Stephen Hagan has been waging a long battle to have the 'ES Nigger Brown Stand' sign removed from a Toowoomba sportsground. The stand is named after a white sportsman who was nicknamed 'Nigger'. Hagan considers the sign offensive and believes the reluctance of the sportsground administrators to remove it is a symptom of continuing racism in the community. Hagan's documentary on the issue won an Enhance TV Australian Teachers of Media award in 2007 — ironically, the same year that the grandstand was found to be structurally unsound and requiring demolition.

From the psychology perspective, it is important to note that while people from different cultural backgrounds may no longer suffer overt discrimination (chapter 17) to the extent they once did, many are still subject to more subtle, but still real, forms of prejudice.

Reducing prejudice

An APS position paper by Sanson et al. (1998) outlined a number of recommendations about ways to reduce racism and prejudice in Australian society. These recommendations are aimed at four levels:

1. *The macro level.* Federal and state governments should lead the way in the form of legislation, policy and funding aimed at reducing the incidence of racism. Public statements that condemn racism should be put forward in the media to promote social change.
2. *The institutional level.* Institutions, professions and community groups should review their own policies and practices on racism and conduct anti-racism training programs that promote intercultural understanding.
3. *Psychology.* The discipline and profession of psychology should formally rebut any assertion that reinforces attribution biases or any statement that asserts racial superiority or inferiority on any psychological attribute. APS accredited programs in undergraduate psychology should include courses on cross-cultural issues.
4. *Individual.* Individuals can contribute by becoming active members of groups that encourage tolerance and committing a certain amount of time to these issues.

Psychologists are actively exploring a number of approaches for reducing prejudice and racism. As noted by Sanson et al. (1998), prejudice is the result of many different factors, so there is no single or simple way of eliminating it. A variety of different approaches used in combination will probably achieve the best results (Amir, 1994; Fisher, 1994; Rubin, 1994; see also Case, 2007; Killen & McKown, 2005; Paradies, 2005). The following approaches are consistent with the recommendations made by Sanson et al. (1998).

One approach is through *legislative action* — putting in place laws and punishable offences that make it illegal to discriminate on the basis of racial or ethnic background. The Racial Discrimination Act came into force in Australia in 1975 and puts in place a legislative framework designed to ensure that everyone in the country is treated equally, regardless of their race, colour or ethnic origin. The Human Rights and Equal Opportunities Commission was established in Australia in 1986 to support and protect human rights. Before the establishment of these measures, events like the Freedom Ride in 1965 were needed to highlight the inequity of racial discrimination against Aboriginal people. The Freedom Ride involved 30 students from Sydney University, including Aboriginal activist Charles Perkins, travelling to country towns in New South Wales protesting against racial segregation and other forms of discrimination. It helped move discrimination onto the public agenda and fuel the move towards legislative action. In New Zealand, the *Race Relations Act (1971)* and the *Human Rights Act (1993)* enshrined the rights of all people. The *Human Rights Amendment Act (2001)* merged the Race Relations Office and the Human Rights Commission.

Another approach is through *cooperative tasks*. Getting people from different cultural backgrounds to work cooperatively on learning tasks appears to reduce prejudice (Slavin & Cooper, 1999). This approach has been successful in settings such as schools and universities, as demonstrated through the 'jigsaw' classroom activity used by Aronson (2002). In this activity, each child or group of children is given a separate part of a group task that has been broken up like a jigsaw puzzle. Only by working cooperatively together towards a common goal can the task be completed. Children who have taken part in these activities tend to have greater self-esteem, like their classmates better and show a decrease in prejudice.

One other approach to reducing prejudice is the ***contact hypothesis***. The thinking behind this approach is that the more contact there is between people from different groups, the more they will break down any barriers or prejudices. Mutual cooperation on common goals through informal interpersonal interactions will help to make the contact more successful (Islam & Hewstone, 1993a). While this approach has some supporters, others have found that increased contact, as opposed to the interaction involved in cooperative tasks, does not reduce prejudice and there is still the tendency for people with shared backgrounds to group together (Stephan, 1985).

New work in the field of ***discursive psychology***, particularly in New Zealand, is also examining ways to combat racism by understanding the power of conversation. According to Weatherall (2007), discursive psychology examines the use of psychological phenomena in talk and texts, with 'standard stories' often framing the way ethnic relations are talked about and understood. These standard stories may reinforce the dominant paradigms that can entrench racism and prejudice, but not in an overt way. Kirkwood, Liu, and Weatherall (2005) suggest that the prejudice reinforced by standard stories can be challenged by greater usage of texts illustrating both racism and anti-racism. By becoming aware of the way discourse can covertly reinforce racism, overt strategies can be adopted to influence those discussions. Wilson (2007) says it is vital to understand how discourse can influence relations between people from different backgrounds, as intergroup conflict happens not in the laboratory but in the interactions between individuals and cultures.

Ultimately, it is important to recognise that the stereotypes and prejudices we have about others are *learned* generalisations, and can never apply to every member of a particular group.

Research by Gomersall, Davidson, and Ho (2000) and Augoustinos, Tuffin, and Sale (1999) in Australia has identified a more inclusive social identity as a mechanism for reducing prejudice. That is, strategies can be used to help people change their definition of in group membership to include cultural groups previously excluded. In this case, non-Indigenous Australians were encouraged to think and talk about 'Australians' as a group that included both Indigenous Australians and non-Indigenous Australians, rather than thinking and talking in terms of 'us and them'. Realignment of the in group gave non-indigenous people an opportunity to embrace and celebrate indigenous people, their cultures, uniqueness and significance to the Australian identity (Gomersall et al., 2000).

INTERIM SUMMARY

Cultural stereotypes are beliefs that all members of a particular group share common traits or behaviours. ***Ethnocentrism*** occurs when a person's own culture influences the way they view the rest of the world, and is a normal response to growing up in a particular culture. ***Racial prejudice*** occurs when a person develops an unreasonable and negative stereotype about members of another racial or ethnic group. ***Racism*** involves an assumption of the inferiority of other ethnic groups and the subsequent unfair treatment of those groups on the basis of that assumed inferiority. Psychologists are actively exploring a number of approaches for reducing prejudice and promoting the benefits of cultural diversity in our society.

Indigenous psychology

The term ***indigenous people*** refers to the original inhabitants of a land or country, who in most cases now share their traditional homeland with many other people. Indigenous peoples are found right around the globe. Examples include the Inuit of the Arctic, the Saami of Scandinavia, the Ainu of Japan, the Masai of Kenya, the Indians of the Americas, the Aboriginal and Torres Strait Islander peoples of Australia, and the Maori of New Zealand. Other countries where indigenous peoples are found include Pakistan, Bolivia, Brazil, China, India, Malaysia, Guatemala, Peru and Mongolia.

While indigenous cultures are extremely diverse and varied, there are some common features. Many have a special relationship with their surroundings — a spiritual connection with the sea and the land. Another common experience has been oppression at the hands of colonising forces.

From a psychological viewpoint, many indigenous peoples also share the experience of having an imported psychological framework imposed upon them. In many cases, it has only been in recent years that the concept of 'indigenous psychology', as distinct from Western psychology, has been explored. The objectives of ***indigenous psychology*** are to develop psychologies that are not imposed; that are influenced by the cultural contexts in which people live; that are developed from within the culture; and that result in locally relevant psychological knowledge (Nikora, Levy, Masters, & Waitoki, 2004).

The following sections look at the traditional cultures of the indigenous people of Australia and New Zealand, the impact of European occupation and the contemporary identities of these people.

INTERIM SUMMARY

Indigenous psychology promotes psychologies that are not imposed, that are influenced by the cultural contexts in which people live, that are developed from within the culture, and that result in locally relevant psychological knowledge.

Australian indigenous cultures: Aboriginal peoples and Torres Strait Islanders

There are two distinct groups of indigenous people in Australia — the Aboriginal peoples and the Torres Strait Islanders. The Aboriginal peoples covered the mainland of Australia, living in diverse and varied communities and language groups. The Torres Strait Islander people lived on the group of small islands off the tip of Cape York in Queensland and had a different ethnic background and culture to the Aboriginal peoples of the mainland.

Traditional Aboriginal culture

It is estimated that Aboriginal people had lived in Australia for at least 50 000 years — possibly many more — before Captain James Cook sailed the east coast of Australia, 'discovering' the continent and claiming it for Britain. While it is common to talk about traditional Aboriginal 'culture', as if all Aboriginal people in the country lived the same way, the reality was very different. The Australian continent is twice the size of Europe (excluding Russia) and has a huge range of climatic conditions — ranging from the tropical north, to arid deserts, to snow-prone highlands and everything in between. When you consider the number of cultures that developed in Europe, it is hardly surprising that in the diverse Australian environment there was no homogeneous Aboriginal culture, but a variety of different cultures and social structures. Different language groups occupied geographically well-defined areas of land, with which they had a close and dependent relationship. These environments influenced the types of food they ate and the clothes they wore, as well as the social structures that developed. In traditional Aboriginal communities, where spiritual identity was closely associated with the land and the environment, geography also influenced belief systems and religious practices. At the time the British arrived, Aboriginal people inhabited every part of the Australian continent in hundreds of distinct language groups. Among those language groupings, there were an estimated 250 separate languages and 600 dialect groups spoken (Bourke, Bourke, & Edwards, 1998). Recent research indicates that only 145 Indigenous languages are still spoken in Australia, and about 110 of these are now listed as endangered (Department of Foreign Affairs and Trade, 2008). For example, as of 2010, Kuku Thaypan elder Tommy George, aged 82, was the sole living speaker of his language. Tens of thousands of years of oral history will be lost when he dies and it is estimated that fewer than 100 Aboriginal languages will be left by 2050 (Michael & Gregg, 2009).

Cape York elder Tommy George, the last speaker of the traditional Agu Alaya language in Australia, is pictured. It is estimated that fewer than 100 Aboriginal languages will be left by 2050 (Michael & Gregg, 2009).

Prior to European occupancy, the Aboriginal people had lived in harmony with their environment for thousands of years. Their isolation from the rest of the world, the sustainable use of local resources and the maintenance of complex social structures and spiritual beliefs, had all helped maintain their cultural integrity. They were seasonal hunter-gatherers, and moved throughout their traditional lands as needed to secure food and resources and to maintain spiritual ties and ritual obligations. The spiritual belief systems that underpinned Aboriginal life were based on creation stories today known as 'The Dreaming'. The Dreaming was the period when ancestor spirits wandered the earth creating the land and everything on it. On completing their tasks, some went into the sky and others entered the waterways and the earth, with geographic features such as caves, mountains and rivers marking their place. These became 'sacred sites' and had special significance for particular language groups. The Dreamtime stories were both an explanation of how the world came to be, and a blueprint for how people must conduct their behaviour and social relationships (Broome, 1994).

Their relationship with the land was a key part of their identity. They believed that people were not superior to, or separate from, the environment in which they lived. Rather, the people, the land, the animals, the plants and everything around them were all part of the same fabric and shared a connection to ancestor spirits. The sacred sites found on their 'country' had special spiritual significance and reinforced their connection to the land. As a result, Aboriginal people had no conception of the private ownership of land; instead, people belonged to certain areas of land and had rights and obligations in relation to caring for and maintaining that country.

Aboriginal communities had extremely complex social structures. Kinship was the central focus of communities, with differing kinship relationships carrying with them different rights and responsibilities. Figure 19.3 shows the principles of classificatory kinship in Aboriginal Australian communities. Membership of Aboriginal communities required an understanding of the intricate kinship relationships that existed and the obligations they imposed. Elders played a key leadership role in many communities. Men and women also had carefully differentiated roles, particularly in relation to education and initiation rituals. Sharing and reciprocity were vital factors in all Aboriginal communities, and were normally conducted along kinship and family lines (Dudgeon et al., 2000).

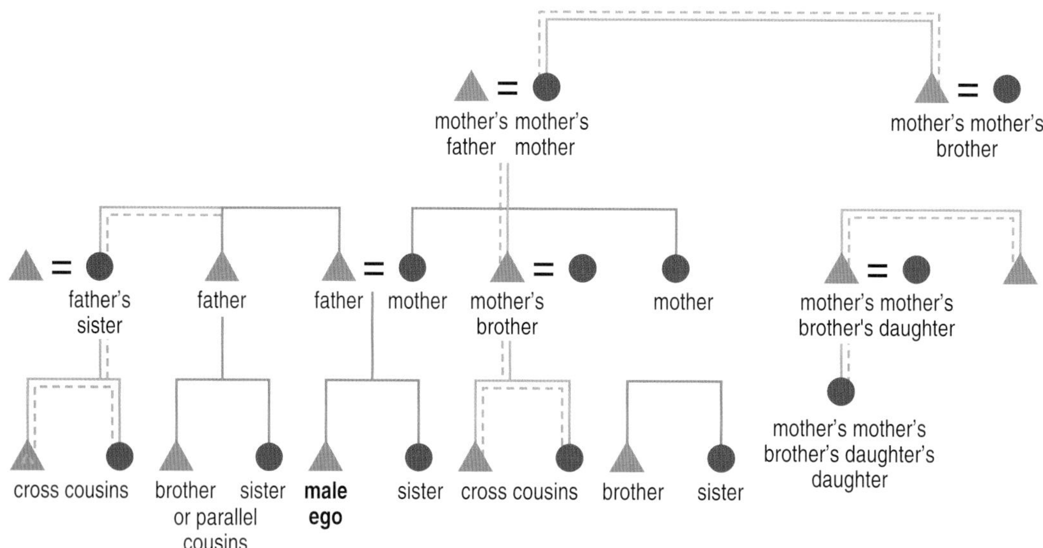

FIGURE 19.3
The principles of classificatory kinship in Aboriginal Australian communities

SOURCE: Eckermann (1995, p. 29).

Each group had its own territory, political system, laws and dialect. Despite this, there were many commonalities in their culture and belief systems. Traditional law was passed on orally and interpreted by elders of both sexes. Traditional law governed aspects of daily life and transgressions were punished.

Art was regarded as an integral part of life, with a functional purpose related to spirituality. Rock and bark paintings in the characteristic red, white, brown and black colours told the stories of The Dreaming. They also recorded details of what was happening in everyday life. Bodies and faces were also painted for ceremonial purposes. Paint was made by grinding coloured rocks and adding water, and jewellery was made of coral, wood, seeds, animals' bones and teeth, and mussel shells. Ceremonial dances were used to explain Aboriginal myths and legends and often involved clapping sticks and didgeridoos.

This painting is an example of contemporary Indigenous art. Historically, art has been an integral part of Aboriginal culture, with a functional purpose related to spirituality.

The European occupation of Australia

The arrival of the First Fleet in 1788 and the subsequent occupation of Australia brought with it the almost total disintegration of traditional Aboriginal lifestyles and cultures. When the British occupants looked at Australia through Eurocentric eyes, they did not see a complex and highly organised society with sophisticated cultures and religious beliefs, living in harmony with its environment. They simply saw a land with no significant buildings or structures, no fences, no agriculture, no technology and no 'civilised' inhabitants. They invoked the principle of 'terra nullius' — the view that the land was not owned or occupied by anyone else — to claim the continent for Britain. The indigenous inhabitants were considered to be inferior, with their lack of attempts to 'improve' the land proof of their primitive society. The proclamation of terra nullius denied that Aboriginal people had a legal system of their own and had strong links with the land they inhabited (Behrendt, 1995). The presumption of 'white superiority' effectively cleared the way for the total disenfranchisement of Aboriginal communities from the lands that sustained them, both physically and spiritually.

This dispossession by the British arrivals highlighted the markedly different beliefs about land between the two cultures. On the one hand was the Aboriginal notion of communal responsibility for certain territories and the sharing of resources among the clan group; on the other hand was the European model of individual ownership and a money economy where the land could be bought and sold (Willis, 1993).

Dudgeon, Oxenham, and Grogan (1996) said that dispossession of land severely dislocated Aboriginal people from the social and cultural links that gave meaning to life, as well as the foods and medicines that sustained them. They said this started a process of massacres, discrimination and oppression that has resulted in the Aboriginal people being the most socially and economically deprived group in Australia.

In the early days of European settlement, battles over land resulted in conflicts and killings. As settlers moved inland from the initial coastal settlements, the Aboriginal inhabitants lost their hunting grounds and waterholes. The superior arms and numbers of the British took a severe toll, as did the ravages of European diseases.

In the mid-nineteenth century, 'social Darwinism' provided a coherent and apparently scientific basis on which to justify the eventual extinction of Aboriginal people (McConnichie, Hollinsworth, & Pettman, 1988). Under this view, there was a struggle for survival in which only the 'fittest' culture would survive — so the extinction of the Aboriginal people was thought not only inevitable, but even beneficial. According to social Darwinian theory, the Aboriginal people were viewed as biologically inferior and on the lowest rung of the civilisation scale.

From around the 1840s, government policies towards Aboriginal people were largely protectionist and segregationalist (Clark, 2000). Large numbers of Aboriginal people were forced to live in reserves and missions, segregated from the non-indigenous population. State governments controlled almost every part of the lives of Aboriginal people, due to the notion that they needed protection from themselves. Governments were even able to define who was Aboriginal and who was not, based on percentiles of blood — 'full blood' as opposed to 'half caste' or 'quarter caste' (Clark, 2000).

Governments in Australia from the 1950s to the 1970s adopted policies of assimilation, so that rather than protection and segregation, the aim was to assimilate Aboriginal people into the wider 'Australian' way of life (Clark, 2000). McConnichie et al. (1988) said that even by the 1960s, when it became clear that Indigenous Australians were not a 'dying race', the belief that Aboriginal people were biologically inferior was deeply entrenched in Australia's social and political structures.

From the 1960s, Aboriginal activism gained momentum, as the indigenous peoples of Australia became more vocal in asserting their rights. In 1965, activists travelled around country towns in New South Wales on what was called the 'Freedom Ride', protesting against racial discrimination such as the segregation of Aboriginal children at local swimming pools. In 1966, members of the Gurindji people at Wave Hill cattle station went on strike, demanding wages and a return of some of their traditional lands. A significant turning point in Aboriginal self-determination was the 1967 referendum, which recognised indigenous peoples as citizens and gave the federal government responsibility for legislation relating to Aboriginal issues. In 1972, the Aboriginal Tent Embassy was established on the lawns outside old Parliament House in Canberra to protest against government policy at the time in relation to mining on traditional lands. The Australian Aboriginal flag designed by Harold Thomas in 1971 was first flown at Victoria Square, Adelaide, and later used at the Tent Embassy in Canberra in 1972 to unite all Aboriginal groups throughout Australia.

The Australian Aboriginal flag is divided horizontally into two equal halves of black (symbolising Aboriginal people) and red (depicting the earth). A yellow circle (representing the sun) appears in the centre.

Land rights became an increasingly important issue for many Aboriginal people from this period. A decade of protest by Eddie Mabo and the Mer islanders of the Torres Strait ended in 1993 when the Australian High Court set aside the principle of 'terra nullius' and agreed that these people had a native title right to their traditional lands. The High Court's decision on the Wik case in 1996 was also significant for native title. The High Court decided that the granting of pastoral leases to graziers for cattle and sheep stations did not extinguish native title rights. That is, the leases gave exclusive rights to graze stock in these areas, but did not confer exclusive ownership. The federal government responded with a '10 Point Plan' which sought to translate that decision into legislation — a plan that was criticised by many Indigenous Australian leaders for effectively extinguishing the native title rights established by Mabo and Wik. The native title debate continues today, as governments and Aboriginal people grapple with the task of translating these High Court decisions into reality. Other issues such as deaths in custody and the 'Stolen Generation' provided additional rallying points for an Aboriginal identity.

The Stolen Generation

The 'Stolen Generation' is an aspect of post-colonisation that encapsulates the ethnocentrism of the non-indigenous community and that has had a profound effect on contemporary Aboriginal identities. *Bringing them home*, the 1997 report of the National Inquiry into the Separation of Aboriginal and Torres Strait Islander Children from their Families, found that between one in 10 and one in three Indigenous Australian children were forcibly removed from their families and communities in the period from approximately 1910 until 1970. The motivations were both misguided attempts to 'save' indigenous children by placing them in 'civilised' white families and institutions and a deliberate attempt to force assimilation by making indigenous people adopt non-indigenous lifestyles. The inquiry found the forced removals were an act of genocide, aimed at wiping out indigenous families, communities and cultures (Human Rights and Equal Opportunity Council, 1991).

The inquiry found that the forced removal of indigenous children had many disturbing consequences. The 'Stolen Generation' children were found to have:

- suffered multiple, continuing and profoundly disabling effects as a result of their removal
- lost their cultures, their languages, their heritage and their lands, as well as their families and communities

- nowhere to belong, no sense of identity
- had damage to their self-esteem and wellbeing, and have had their parenting and relationship skills impaired
- poorer health and are far more likely to be incarcerated than those who had not been removed.

The inquiry found the loss of so many children affected the health and morale of many indigenous communities. Indigenous men and women generally lost their purpose in their families and communities. Individual responses to this loss could result in drinking binges, hospitalisation following accidents or assaults, or behaviour that led to incarceration or premature death. One of the first topics that the Rudd Government promised to address following its election in late 2007 was an apology to the 'Stolen Generation', though it stopped short of promising any financial compensation.

On 13 February 2008, then Prime Minister Kevin Rudd formally apologised to the 'Stolen Generation' for their 'profound grief, suffering and loss'. His speech marks the beginning of the enormous task ahead to reverse the Indigenous disadvantage. For example, as shown in table 19.5, the Council of Australian Governments (COAG) Reform Council reveals that while Australians have one of the highest life expectancy rates in the world, the life expectancy for Indigenous Australians still lags behind that of non-Indigenous Australians. Indigenous men die 11.5 years earlier and Indigenous women 9.7 years earlier than their respective non-Indigenous counterparts (*Sydney Morning Herald*, 2010) and although Indigenous child mortality rates have also dropped in recent years, Aboriginal babies are still three times more likely to die than non-Indigenous infants (James, 2010). Indigenous Australians are also three times more likely to be unemployed than the rest of the nation (ABS, 2006).

APPLY + DISCUSS

In 1931, three children escaped from one of the 'Stolen Generation' settlement camps (the Moore River Native Settlement). They walked nearly 2500 kilometres along a fence built to keep rabbits out of Australian farmlands, to return to their original homes. Doris Pilkington, the daughter of one of the escapees, wrote a book, *Follow the Rabbit-Proof Fence*, which recounted the children's nine-week journey home. This account of the **prejudiced** (chapter 17) treatment of Aboriginal children was later turned into the award-winning Australian film *Rabbit-Proof Fence*, directed by Phillip Noyce.

TABLE 19.5 Disparity between Indigenous and non-Indigenous Australians

	Indigenous	Non-Indigenous
Estimated life expectancy		
Male	67.7 years	79.2 years
Female	74.0 years	83.7 years
Proportion of population who completed Year 12	19.4%	44.9%
Unemployment rate	15.6%	5.1%
Median weekly income	$278	$471
Median household income	$791	$1031
Proportion of households who own or are buying their own home	34.2%	68.9%

SOURCE: Adapted from *The Sydney Morning Herald*, 4 June 2010, with data from the Australian Bureau of Statistics and the Council of Australian Governments.

There are opportunities for all Australians to work together to close the gap and overcome Indigenous disadvantage. For example, Reconciliation Australia has developed the Share Our Pride website (www.shareourpride.org.au) to promote cultural awareness — providing resources for workplaces, schools and individual Australians. The site brings together facts and figures, provides answers to common questions, and documents inspiring stories to help build respectful relationships between Indigenous and non-Indigenous Australians.

Reconciliation Australia (2010) 'acknowledges the traditional owners of country throughout Australia and their continuing connection to land and community. We pay our respect to them and their cultures, and to the elders both past and present'. On a similar note, Indigenous scholar Raelene Ward successfully showed how the community can work together to prevent suicide. The project called Building Bridges: Learning from Experts, is a community-based approach to building resilience, reducing suicide risk and self-harming behaviour and supporting recovery processes among four Indigenous communities in Queensland (Tiller, 2010).

Thousands of Australians gathered to hear the historic apology to the 'Stolen Generation' delivered by then Prime Minister Kevin Rudd on 13 February 2008.

Mr RUDD (Griffith — Prime Minister) — I move:

That today we honour the Indigenous peoples of this land, the oldest continuing cultures in human history.

We reflect on their past mistreatment.

We reflect in particular on the mistreatment of those who were Stolen Generations — this blemished chapter in our nation's history.

The time has now come for the nation to turn a new page in Australia's history by righting the wrongs of the past and so moving forward with confidence to the future.

We apologise for the laws and policies of successive Parliaments and governments that have inflicted profound grief, suffering and loss on these our fellow Australians.

We apologise especially for the removal of Aboriginal and Torres Strait Islander children from their families, their communities and their country.

For the pain, suffering and hurt of these Stolen Generations, their descendants and for their families left behind, we say sorry.

To the mothers and the fathers, the brothers and the sisters, for the breaking up of families and communities, we say sorry.

And for the indignity and degradation thus inflicted on a proud people and a proud culture, we say sorry.

We the Parliament of Australia respectfully request that this apology be received in the spirit in which it is offered as part of the healing of the nation.

For the future we take heart; resolving that this new page in the history of our great continent can now be written.

We today take this first step by acknowledging the past and laying claim to a future that embraces all Australians.

A future where this Parliament resolves that the injustices of the past must never, never happen again.

A future where we harness the determination of all Australians, Indigenous and non-Indigenous, to close the gap that lies between us in life expectancy, educational achievement and economic opportunity.

A future where we embrace the possibility of new solutions to enduring problems where old approaches have failed.

A future based on mutual respect, mutual resolve and mutual responsibility.

A future where all Australians, whatever their origins, are truly equal partners, with equal opportunities and with an equal stake in shaping the next chapter in the history of this great country, Australia.

Apology to Australia's Indigenous Peoples, 13 February 2008, Parliament of Australia.

The Northern Territory intervention

One of the most significant developments in indigenous affairs came in 2007 when the former Howard Government announced an intervention into the running of Aboriginal communities in the Northern Territory. A primary motivation was to halt the alarming incidence of child sexual abuse in the communities. The intervention included measures such as taking control of some indigenous communities for five years, banning alcohol, undertaking medical examinations of all indigenous children under the age of 16, and sending in additional police and army officers to enforce law and order. The reaction to the intervention measures was mixed. To some, they were a necessary 'tough love' response to a situation that could no longer be tolerated. To others, the intervention was a continuation of the paternalistic and assimilationist policies of past governments. What is clear is that a complex set of factors has contributed to communities having unsustainable social and health issues that require attention. The ensuing debate was not so much about whether there was a need to act, but the level of involvement that indigenous people should have in determining how that action was implemented.

In November 2008, COAG endorsed the National Indigenous Reform Agreement, which commits to intergovernmental reform, action and accountability for *closing the gap* in Indigenous disadvantage across key areas of health, childhood development, education and employment (COAG, 2009; COAG Reform Council, 2010a; see also COAG Reform Council, 2010b). In what is a massive undertaking of shared roles and responsibilities across the Commonwealth, states, and territories, the COAG Reform Council will assess and report on performance against six ambitious targets of the National Indigenous Reform Agreement:

1. closing the life expectancy gap within a generation
2. halving the gap in mortality rates for Indigenous children under five within a decade
3. ensuring all Indigenous four-year-olds in remote communities have access to early childhood education within five years
4. halving the gap for Indigenous students in reading, writing and numeracy within a decade
5. halving the gap for Indigenous students in Year 12 attainment or equivalent attainment rates by 2020
6. halving the gap in employment outcomes between Indigenous and non-Indigenous Australians within a decade (COAG, 2008).

Aboriginal identity

In discussing Aboriginal identity, it is important to recognise that for the last 200 or more years, non-indigenous society has sought to impose its own definition of 'Aboriginality' on Australia's indigenous peoples. For many years, the definitions relied on blood fractions, excluding people who were too far removed from 'full blood'. Divergence from pre-European Aboriginal lifestyles was also seen to detract from identity, so that only those following traditional practices were considered 'real' Aboriginals. In discussing identity, non-indigenous people must be mindful that it is up to indigenous people themselves to define and develop their own identities. That principle of self-determination is evident in the most widely accepted definition of ***Aboriginality*** used in Australia today (which also encompasses Torres Strait Islanders): 'An Aboriginal or Torres Strait Islander person is a person of Aboriginal or Torres Strait Islander descent, who identifies as such and is accepted as such by the community in which they live' (Commonwealth of Australia, 1998, p. 60). All three criteria need to be met in order for a person to be accepted as an Indigenous Australian.

It is also important to recognise that to put the present circumstances of Australia's indigenous peoples into context, it is necessary to understand the past (Dudgeon, Oxenham, & Grogan, 1997). The fact and process of colonisation in Australia has profoundly affected the identity of Aboriginal people today. Bourke (1998) makes the point that the colonisation process has forced Aboriginal people to construct identities on terms set by the European colonisers. They encountered dispossession and relocation from their lands, and government policies that set out to eliminate a separate Aboriginal identity and assimilate the people into the mainstream culture. Dispossession and oppression resulted in social disintegration, economic marginalisation, unacceptable health standards and lack of opportunity. Aboriginal people have grown up in a society where the norms and culture of the dominant non-indigenous majority are assumed to be superior and normal. Negative images of Aboriginality have been reinforced through all layers and institutions of society. Since the referendum in 1967 and some 40 years after the recognition of Aboriginal people as citizens, they still experience pervasive overt and covert racism in their daily lives, as they struggle to affirm their place as the original inhabitants of Australia (APS, 1997).

Contemporary Aboriginal identity reflects not only the impacts of colonisation but also the cultural heritage of pre-European life. Despite sometimes overt government policies to extinguish a sense of separate identity, Aboriginal people have retained and maintained important cultural practices. For example, Bourke (1998) highlighted that kinship relationships (and the accompanying obligations and responsibilities) between people who were not necessarily close blood relations continue to be important for Aboriginal identity. Contemporary Aboriginal existence has not been disconnected from traditional values. Rather, communities draw their strength from the body of knowledge, values and wisdom that has emerged from the interaction of tradition and history (National Health & Medical Research

Council, 2003). Prominent Aboriginal leader Mick Dodson, in the 1994 Wentworth Lecture, summed up the importance of heritage in the construction of modern-day identity:

> The right to self-representation includes our right to draw on all aspects of our sense of our Aboriginality, be that our blood, our descent, our history, our ways of living and relation, or any elements of our cultures . . . When we talk about Aboriginality based on the past of our peoples, we are not talking about fabricating an identity based on a past we have rediscovered or dug up; rather, we, the Aboriginal peoples, are already the retelling of the past . . . [W]e re-create Aboriginality in the context of all our experiences, including our pre-colonial practices, our oppression, and our political struggles. It is only a narrowness of vision, or a misconception of culture as a frozen state, which leads people to limit expressions of Aboriginality to the stereotyped pristine. (p. 10)

Contemporary Aboriginal identity is extremely diverse. Aboriginal people do not live homogeneous lifestyles, just as Australians of British backgrounds do not all live the same way. There are considerable differences in lifestyle between Indigenous Australians living in semi-traditional communities and Indigenous Australians in urban centres. Just because urban populations do not overtly fit a picture of 'traditional' Aboriginality does not mean they are not 'real' Aboriginal people (Dudgeon, 2000b). However, Bourke (1998) stresses that despite current differences, and historical language differences, people today identify as Aboriginal because they share a common philosophical and historical bond that makes them feel as one people. Cultural values and practices also prevail within urban populations. For example, kinship and community obligation continue to be a strong part of life for Aboriginal people. While this text uses the terms 'Aboriginal Australians' and 'Indigenous Australians', many within these communities prefer to use terms that better reflect their language group background, such as Kamilaroi, Mamu, Jarowair, Koori, Murri or Nyoongar. These terms better reflect the diversity within the total indigenous community.

A great reclaiming of cultural identity has been in process in recent decades — despite continued prejudice and racism, there is an element of pride in being Aboriginal (Dudgeon, 2000b). According to Hemming (1994), the images that Europeans constructed of Aboriginal people shaped the framework within which Aboriginal history was written, reinforcing negativity. However, he said that in recent decades, Aboriginal people have started an invasion of their own, challenging the dominant 'white' view of Australia and asserting their own perspective. A growing body of Aboriginal literature, greater participation and power in political discourse, and greater recognition through milestones such as the native title decision in the High Court, have contributed to the reclamation of identity.

There is much diversity within Aboriginal peoples. Though Indigenous Australians traditionally lived as separate language groups with distinct cultural practices, Dudgeon and Oxenham (1990) have identified qualities common to contemporary Aboriginal identity. These qualities are unique to all Aboriginal Australians and distinct from the non-indigenous community. They include kindredness, an intuitive sense of spirituality that is shared by Aboriginals and connects them to each other and to their land. Sansom (1982) also identified aspects of a 'pan Aboriginality', including a shared sense of history, a belief in the 'Dreaming' and a sense of humour. Dudgeon and Oxenham proposed that kindredness is the key link that ties together Aboriginal diversity.

Suicide and self-harm

From a psychological perspective, a disturbing aspect of contemporary Aboriginal identity is the growing rate of suicide and self-harm, particularly among young men. Tatz (1999) gathered statistics that showed youth suicide, unknown among Aboriginal Australians 30 years ago, is now treble the rate of suicide among the non-indigenous population. A significant proportion of suicide deaths involved hanging, particularly where the deaths occurred in police custody. Death by suicide accounts for a much higher proportion of all deaths among Aboriginal people than among non-Aboriginal people: suicide accounts for 4.3 percent of all Aboriginal deaths compared with 1.6 percent of deaths for other Australians (Auseinet, 2007).

The psychological factors underlying this dramatic and tragic trend are complex in the extreme. Tatz (1999) identified that many of the risk factors for suicide normally applied in mainstream society did not apply to Aboriginal suicide; that is, Aboriginal suicide was different. Elliott-Farrelly (2004) said there was general acceptance among researchers that it was the product of a complex set of individual, situational and sociocultural factors. Some of the factors identified include an association with psychiatric illness, particularly depression; impulsivity, particularly when intoxicated; impacts associated with loss of culture and racism; a lack of a sense of purpose in life; sexual assault; drug use; illiteracy and the accompanying exclusion and alienation from society; and a persistent cycle of grief due to high death rates in many communities (Elliott-Farrelly, 2004; Hunter, 2002; Reser, 1991; Tatz, 1999; Thomson, 1991). Hunter (2002) stressed that understanding Aboriginal suicide requires an understanding of the historical legacy of cultural destruction and dislocation that Indigenous Australians face.

Aboriginal suicide continues to be one of the most challenging issues facing the psychology profession in Australia. Dr Tracy Westerman from Indigenous Psychological Services at Curtin University of Technology has investigated how Western practices in clinical psychology translate for Aboriginal peoples. As Aboriginal suicide and self-harm are unique phenomena, Westerman (2004) advocates a unique approach from mental health professionals. This means making intervention and training programs culturally relevant — in many cases, incorporating traditional with Westernised methods of treatment. Her approach also involves drawing on the strengths that exist within Aboriginal communities to make intervention methods more successful.

INTERIM SUMMARY

Prior to British occupation, the Aboriginal people had lived in harmony with their land for tens of thousands of years. The spiritual belief system that underpinned Aboriginal life was based on creation stories today known as 'The Dreaming'. The diverse Aboriginal communities had complex social structures and they abided by the principles of classificatory kinship. However, the occupation of the British had a dramatic impact on Australian indigenous culture and all Aboriginal and Torres Strait Islander people have been affected in some way by the 'Stolen Generation', where children were forcibly removed from their families and homes. Contemporary Aboriginal identity is extremely diverse, reflecting the impacts of colonisation and also cultural heritage of pre-European life. Aboriginal people have retained and maintained important cultural practices and share a common philosophical and historical bond that makes them feel as one people. Aboriginal suicide continues to be one of the most challenging issues facing the psychology profession in Australia and current treatment approaches focus on making intervention and training programs culturally relevant.

Torres Strait Islander culture

Torres Strait Islanders are a distinct group of indigenous people who traditionally inhabited the group of small islands located in the Torres Strait. There are about 100 islands in the strait, which bridges the 150-kilometre gap between the northern tip of Queensland's Cape York and the southern coast of Papua New Guinea, although only about 20 are habitable (figure 19.4; see overleaf). While archaeological evidence on the islands themselves is insufficient to determine the pre-history of the people, some conclusions can be drawn from evidence in both Australia and New Zealand. The Torres Strait Islanders are a Melanesian people, similar in ethnicity to other people of the South-West Pacific, and distinct from the Aboriginals of the Australian mainland.

The Torres Strait Islander peoples lived in kinship groups led by an elder or group of elders, who gained leadership status based on age, accomplishments and social standing. Each separate island, or group of small islands, formed an independent community, each containing a number of clans. Each community thought of itself as a separate entity — there was no perception of a single 'Torres Strait Island' identity. The people relied on fishing, hunting and garden cultivation for food. They were highly skilled seafarers. They used dugout canoes and navigated via the stars to trade with other people from nearby islands, with Aboriginals on the mainland and with Papuans from New Guinea. Trade was vital to secure items such as the canoes themselves, as timber was scarce on the islands.

Kinship affiliation was the traditional foundation of community life in the Torres Strait (Wilson, 1993). Elders were the leaders of kinship groups. They regulated many aspects of life such as observance of rituals and enforcement of traditional law. Life was very communal and kinship was not necessarily confined only to blood relatives, but to all who were part of a clan. Kinship structures were complex, and particular relationships carried with them certain important duties and responsibilities. Ritual, spirituality, magic and taboos were very much a part of the social structure and were strictly enforced.

Before colonisation, the people of the Torres Strait Islands lived in discrete communities on different islands, separated by stretches of open water. The different communities were quite warlike and headhunting was a glorified and important part of their way of life (Beckett, 1989). The concept of 'payback' was also the basis of much of the conflict between communities, and contributed to a cycle of revenge killings (Wilson, 1988).

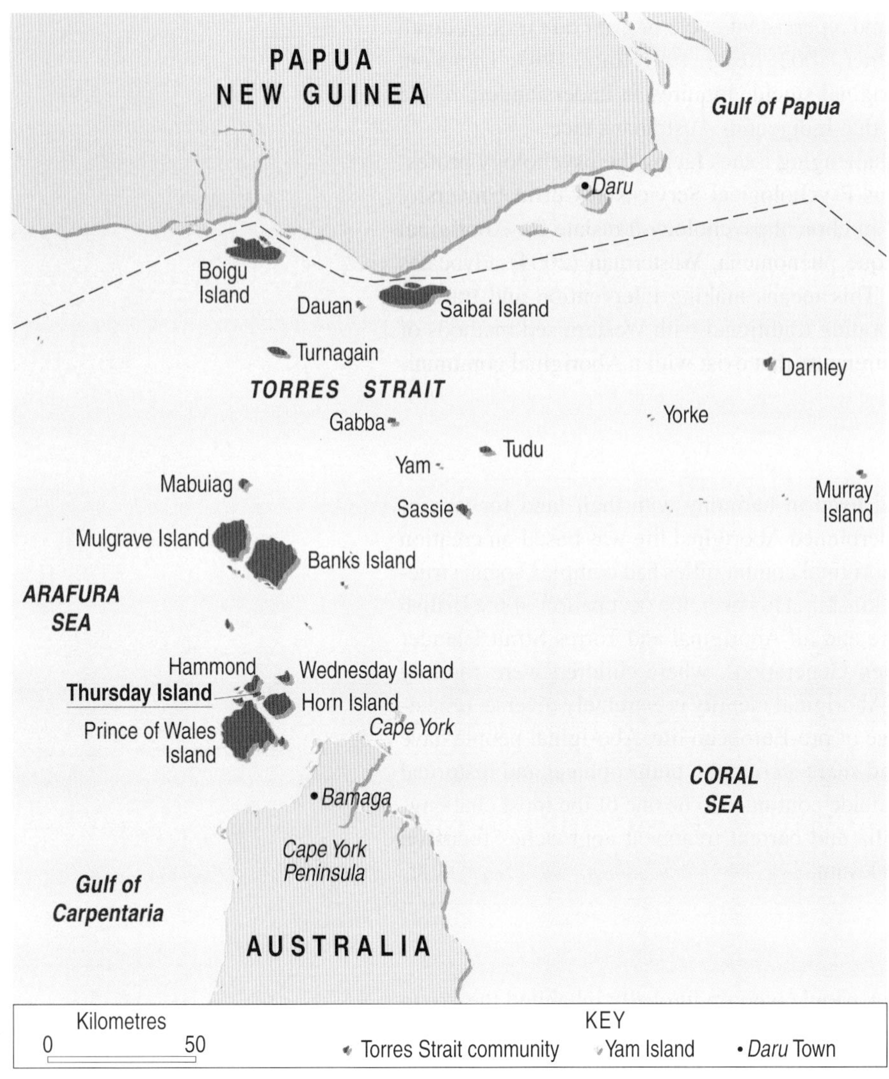

FIGURE 19.4
The Torres Strait Islands

The term 'Ailan Kaston' means 'island custom'. It is used to describe the unique cultures of the islanders. As with many indigenous cultures, there was no division between the spiritual and the secular in everyday life for Torres Strait Islanders. Ancestral spirits were ever present in the land, the sea, the people and the animals. They were present in geographical features and could assume human or animal form at will. Spirits and gods did not exist on a separate, supernatural level, so were within human understanding and were part of everyday life (Wilson, 1998). These spirits also inspired the myths, legends, art and sacred places of the people, passed down through generations in song, dance, story and ceremonial rituals.

There were two main traditional languages in the Torres Strait — one that shared origins with the Melanesian languages found in the Pacific region, the other that was closer to the Aboriginal languages of Cape York. Today, while English is emphasised in the education system, a hybrid vernacular known as Torres Strait Creole, which borrows from a number of languages, is widely spoken. The retention of language by the Torres Strait Islanders is quite different from the Aboriginal experience, where most languages were extinguished by the arrival of white settlers. Keeping traditional languages alive has helped Torres Strait Islanders retain cultural practices, stories and histories that were handed down from generation to generation orally. Elders in the community also emphasise the passing on of their cultural practices to the young.

Traditional island feasts play an important role in Torres Strait Islander life and are used to mark important occasions (Lowah, 1998). These feasts are usually accompanied by singing and dancing (Costigan & Neuenfeldt, 2002). A particularly important occasion is the unique custom of the tombstone opening, which continues today. This is a religious ceremony based on traditional mortuary rites that marks the end of the mourning period after a person's death, and during which the tombstone is unveiled. It is followed by a feast and the performance of traditional songs and dances. Today, it also serves as an affirmation of continuing Torres Strait Islander cultural identity.

The Torres Strait Islanders also have a rich tradition of art and craft work, although the concept of 'art' as Westerners understand it was foreign to them. To them, creating an object only for artistic expression would have been pointless (Wilson, 1988). Art was part of everyday life, whether as part of spiritual and religious observance or to embellish a house or canoe. Women were particularly skilled at weaving textiles and objects such as bags.

The European occupation of the Torres Strait

The first documented white presence in the Torres Strait was the arrival in 1606 of Spanish explorer Luis Vaez de Torres, who passed through the strait from the east with the ships *San Pederico* and *Los Tres Reyes*. Torres recorded details of the islands and described the people he encountered. The next recorded presence was the arrival of Captain James Cook in the *Endeavour* in 1770, claiming the east coast of Australia on Possession Island.

The spread of European settlers and influence in the Torres Strait was slow until the 1860s, when the pearling industry, bêche-de-mer (sea slug) industry and missionaries all started making a greater presence felt. The arrival of commerce and Christianity had a significant impact on island life. The traditional Torres Strait communities had lived as a subsistence economy for thousands of years — hunting, fishing and growing sufficient food to eat, and trading goods with other islanders. There was no monetary economy or wage-based employment. The coming of the pearl shell and bêche-de-mer fishing industries, which employed large numbers of islanders, significantly changed the socioeconomic conditions in the Torres Strait and ushered in a new lifestyle.

The arrival of missionaries from the London Missionary Society in 1871 also heralded significant cultural change. The society used Samoan missionaries to spread the word, aiding the acceptance by their fellow Melanesians. Islanders embraced Christianity remarkably quickly, absorbing the new belief system and adapting their traditional practices to fit. For instance, traditional dancing was replaced by 'happy dance' adapted from South Sea Islander culture; and with the erosion of traditional roles, elders of the community took on senior positions within the Anglican church structure instead of traditional leadership roles (St Augustine's College, 1994). The Torres Strait people now celebrate 1871 as 'The Coming of the Light'.

The Torres Strait Islands were annexed by the Queensland Government in 1879, which effectively took ownership of them, and the people were administered under the Aborigines Protection Act from 1912. It was not until 1939 that the Torres Strait Islanders Act was passed to distinguish the people from Aboriginal Australians. As with the treatment of many Aboriginal communities, the legislation effectively confined the people of the islands to what could be called missions or protectorates. However, unlike the Aboriginals, the Torres Strait Islanders were at least able to remain on their own traditional land. Beckett (1989) makes the point that Europeans came mainly to exploit the region's resources rather than to displace or remove the people and their traditional means of livelihood. Also, the relative remoteness of the Torres Strait Islands and their isolation helped insulate the island communities somewhat from the impact of colonisation, compared with Aboriginal communities on the mainland. However, the Torres Strait Islanders still suffered a significant loss of culture, land and lifestyle.

The decline of the pearl-shelling industry in the 1960s brought further change to the islands. Many Torres Strait Islanders were forced to venture to the mainland looking for work, such as cane cutting in north Queensland. In the 1970s, there was a population drift to Cairns and Townsville in Queensland, and Thursday Island in the strait, due to poor economic circumstances and high unemployment (Synott & Whatman, 1998). Around 31 000 people identified as Torres Strait Islanders in the 2006 census, with the majority of them living on the mainland rather than the islands themselves (ABS, 2008g; see also Human Rights and Equal Opportunity Commission, 2006).

Torres Strait Islander identity

Torres Strait Islanders face many of the same issues in terms of defining and maintaining their identity as do Aboriginal Australians. Their traditional culture was severely dislocated by colonisation and they face similar pressures as a small minority group within a dominant society and culture. While the Torres Strait Islanders were not forcibly removed from their homelands to the same extent that Aboriginal Australians were, their lives were still subjected to similar controls and regulation at the hands of the colonising government.

The Torres Strait Islanders have in the past referred to themselves as 'the forgotten people' (Wilson, 1993). Their relative isolation and small overall number, as well as a lack of self-representation in a political sense, contributed to that perception. Non-indigenous people have also failed to differentiate Torres Strait Islanders from Aboriginals, despite the distinctive differences between the groups. In more recent times, the establishment of bodies such as the Torres Strait Regional Authority has provided a degree of participation in the management of Torres Strait Islander affairs. The Mabo native title claim also helped bring the Torres Strait Islander communities into greater prominence. That case involved a claim by Eddie Mabo for confirmation of traditional land rights to Mer (Murray) Island in the Torres Strait. Since the Mabo case, Torres Strait Islander issues have gained greater recognition in government (Bargh, 2003). The adoption of a unique flag, based on the traditional *dhari* headdress, is also a strong symbol of Torres Strait Islander identity.

The migration of Torres Strait Islanders off their traditional lands and into mainland communities such as Townsville and Cairns is challenging the retention of cultural identity. A generation or more of Torres Strait Islanders has now been born and grown up on the mainland, where they have integrated into largely non-indigenous communities. For them, the continuation of cultural identity is very much a choice. Their predicament is that if their society can survive at all, it is only through the conscious perpetuation of island custom and continual monitoring of its practice (Beckett, 1989). Those on the islands do not need to make such a conscious decision to uphold their cultural identity, living a life much closer to the cultural practices and identity of their ancestors. In urban areas such as Townsville, support groups and networks have been established that help Torres Strait Islanders maintain kinship and cultural links.

Cultural identity remains extremely important to Torres Strait Islanders, according to Professor Martin Nakata, an academic and also a Torres Strait Islander. Professor Nakata (1999) said Torres Strait Islanders need and desire people to respect what they are and they acknowledge that they are different. He said the people of the Torres Strait wanted to maintain their cultural practices, languages and traditions, and identified as a group through shared practices. But the realities of contemporary life meant that Torres Strait Islanders also wanted the same things as other Australians — their land, their own homes, and good jobs, education and health. More recently, Professor Nakata (2007) published a book titled *Disciplining the savages: savaging the disciplines*, in which he critiques the anthropological knowledge gained from the Cambridge Expedition in the late 1890s.

Prominent Torres Strait Islander Eddie Mabo led the fight for traditional land rights for indigenous peoples.

The Torres Strait Islander flag stands for the unity and identity of all Torres Strait Islanders. The green at the top and bottom represents the land. The blue represents the sea. The black lines represent the people. The five-pointed star represents the island groups; the white represents peace. The symbol surrounding the star represents the *dhari* (headdress), a symbol of all Torres Strait Islanders.

INTERIM SUMMARY

The Torres Strait Islander people are the original inhabitants of the group of small islands located in the Torres Strait. Kinship affiliation was the traditional foundation of community life. They have a rich tradition of art and craft work, and, like Aboriginal Australians, their traditional culture was severely dislocated by colonisation. However, cultural identity remains extremely important to Torres Strait Islanders, and many continue to identify as a group through shared cultural practices, languages and traditions.

FROM BRAIN TO BEHAVIOUR

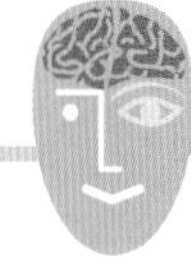

Depth perception in Torres Strait Islanders

In 1895, a research expedition from Cambridge University visited New Guinea and the Torres Strait, primarily to test for differences between the so-called ‘primitive’ cultures in these areas and cultures from the ‘civilised’ Western world. In particular, the expedition set out to test the sense of sight, smell and hearing of the ‘natives’ in these regions, using scientifically-based testing procedures. Along for the trip to help administer these experiments were W. H. R. Rivers and his two research assistants.

Rivers was especially interested in ‘visual acuity’ — how well people can see. He wanted to test anecdotal reports from travellers that ‘savage and semi-civilised races’ had much greater acuteness of sight (as well as hearing and smell) than European races did (Rivers, 1901). This was suspected to be due to the need for Torres Strait inhabitants to see long distances. The results were interesting. At first, the tests seemed to indicate that the people of the Torres Strait did indeed have a much more acute sense of sight when contrasted with Europeans who underwent the same tests. But after reanalysing the tests and trying alternative measures of visual acuity, Rivers found little difference — the visual abilities of the Torres Strait Islanders, though slightly better, were not vastly superior as had been suggested by the anecdotal reports.

Rivers also studied the susceptibility of the Torres Strait Islanders to visual illusions (chapter 4). The same folklore that attributed great eyesight to 'primitive' peoples also suggested that they would be much more easily fooled by illusions than Europeans (Cole, 1996). Rivers used the Müller-Lyer illusion and the horizontal-vertical illusion (shown in figure 4.35, p. 170) both on the Torres Strait Islanders and on a group of English people. What he found surprised many in the Western world. While the Torres Strait Islanders were more susceptible to being fooled by the horizontal-vertical illusion, they were less susceptible to being fooled by the Müller-Lyer illusion (see chapter 4). The results burst the bubble of supposed European mental superiority (Cole, 1998). The effect of the illusion differed by culture, but something besides education was involved — so the researchers concluded that culture must have some effect on the way the world is seen (Matsumoto & Juang, 2004).

This effect has been the subject of much study ever since (see Berry, 1971; Pollack, 1970; Segall, Campbell, & Hersokovitis, 1966). The 'carpentered world' theory offered one explanation. That is, English people were more used to seeing rectangular shapes typical in an environment full of carpenter-built structures, while those from the Torres Strait were more used to irregular shapes and scanning long-distance vistas. Thus the environment in which people live can affect their perception.

However, Pollack and Silvar (1967) offered another explanation. They found that retinal pigmentation affected the ability to detect contours, which is related to the Müller-Lyer illusion. Age also reduced the ability to detect contours. Thus, differences in detecting illusions were thought to have a physiological base. Studies by Stewart (1973) involving children both in the United States and Zambia found some commonalities linking these different theories. Her work indicated that the effect of the visual illusions differed according to how 'carpentered' the environment of the children was, but that the effect declined with age. Thus both cultural background and physiology had an impact on visual perceptions.

Indigenous people in Aotearoa/New Zealand

The Maori are the indigenous people of New Zealand, who occupied Aotearoa (the Maori name for the country, translated as the 'Land of the Long White Cloud') before the settlement of the Europeans in 1839. The Maori people are thought to have arrived in New Zealand from the Polynesian islands to the east over a period of several centuries from about 1000 AD. DNA research suggests that the ancestors of the Maori people may have migrated from China to Polynesia some 5000 years ago (Murray-McIntosh, Scrimshaw, Hatfield, & Penny, 1998).

Traditional Maori culture

The term 'Maori' was originally a word that meant 'natural' or 'original' in the Maori language. It has come to be used to describe the original inhabitants of New Zealand. The Maori people traditionally lived in large tribal or clan groups and were a collectivist culture. They had a stone-age culture, using stones and animal bones to create weapons for hunting game. They developed complex social and family structures, with a strong spiritual connection to the land and the environment. The Maori people had their own language, still in use today, which shared many common elements with other Polynesian languages. While the Maori people had no written language, they passed down their culture from generation to generation through oral history and through song, dance and ritual. For example, the haka was part of the Maori warrior's preparation for battle. The haka means 'to ignite the breath' — to energise the body and inspire the spirit

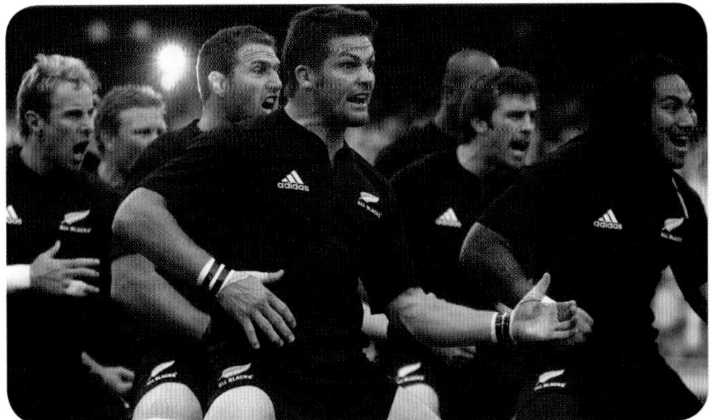

The All Blacks perform the haka before doing battle on the rugby field. *Ka mate* means 'it is death' and *Ka ora* means 'it is life'. This haka is primarily about resilience — the reinvigoration of life after facing death.

(Tu Strategies, 2003). Today, the haka is readily associated as an integral part of the Maori culture of New Zealand. There are many forms of the haka, one being the 'Ka mate ka mate' version performed by the All Blacks as they prepare to do battle on the rugby field.

The Maori people traditionally lived as separate *iwi*, which can be loosely translated to mean 'tribes'. Within the *iwi* were further social divisions — *hapu*, a sub-tribal grouping, and *whanau*, extended family groupings. The *iwi* were located within territorial boundaries. The defence of these boundaries was considered imperative to the Maori warrior culture. In pre-European days, there was no sense of one single Maori identity across the country — identity and allegiance came from the individual *iwi* and from the strata of tribal structures (*iwi*, *hapu* and *whanau*). Tribal location and markers such as mountains and rivers were an intrinsic part of Maori identity, and the Maori people maintained respectful and spiritual connections with the land and with the earth's natural resources (Moeke-Pickering, 1996). *Whanau* (family groups) were centred on the *marae*, the communal meeting place. *Marae* traditions still remain strong today. As with many indigenous cultures, family history and genealogy carried great significance for the Maori people. The term *whakapapa* was used to describe these family ties.

The Maori people had well-defined customs and values, which all fell under *tikanga*, or rules outlining the correct ways to behave. For example, *tapu* was considered the strongest force in Maori life. It could be defined as 'sacredness' — restrictions and rules applied to people, objects and places considered *tapu*. *Mana* was another important concept, relating to prestige and social standing. People built up *mana* through good works and contributions to the group.

Ta moko (tattooing), both facial and of the body, was a widely practised custom among Maori people. Tattooing began when a person reached puberty and was accompanied by elaborate rituals. Men were much more extensively tattooed than women. The tattoos were both a rite of passage for a warrior and an adornment that made him attractive to women. The Maori people were expert carvers and weavers and Maori wood-sculpting skills are world renowned today.

The European occupation of New Zealand

Given New Zealand's geographic isolation, the Maori people lived for hundreds of years without any substantial contact with people from any other country. All that began to change from 1769, when Captain James Cook circumnavigated the coasts of both the north and south islands. Over the ensuing decades, more and more contact with European sailors, missionaries and settlers occurred, and even escaped convicts from Australia surfaced in New Zealand and lived with Maori tribes. By the 1830s, European numbers were still very much in the minority and the social division of the Maori people into large *iwis* remained intact. However, the advent of European contact was having significant repercussions. The acquisition of firearms by *iwi* in close contact with the Europeans upset the balance of inter-tribal warfare and led to a period of bloodshed known as the 'Musket Wars'. European diseases were also killing a large number of Maori people, and missionaries were increasingly active. The leaders of the *iwi* had a number of formal dealings with the representatives of the British Crown in New Zealand and in 1840 a majority of Maori chiefs signed the Treaty of Waitangi.

On 6 February each year, a public holiday in New Zealand marks the anniversary of the signing of the Treaty of Waitangi in 1840. Here, a large crowd has gathered to watch several *waka* (traditional Maori canoes) being paddled ashore as part of the ceremonial re-enactment of this historic event.

The treaty promised that the Maori people retained all rights of land ownership with the Crown acting as the only agent should *iwi* ever desire to sell. All customary rights to land, forest, foul and fisheries were guaranteed, as was Maori social, cultural and organisational leadership, or *Rangatiratanga*. The treaty also accorded Maori the rights of British citizenship and permitted the British government of British settlers. Historians debate the extent to which the Maori chiefs truly understood the terms of the treaty, especially in relation to the European concept of private ownership of land and governance.

Following the signing of the treaty, increasing numbers of settlers began arriving from Britain and Maori *iwi* started losing their traditional lands. The terms of the treaty were often ignored as settlers took over land and built homes. The tension led to an ongoing series of revolts and battles between the Maori people and the colonisers, who were collectively referred to as the ***Pakeha*** or non-Maori. When the conflicts eventually came to an end in 1871, large tracts of tribal land had been confiscated and the *iwi* had been effectively dispossessed. This alienated many Maori people from their ancestral origins and tribal structures. Broughton (1993) described the loss of land as the most traumatic shock, as Maori identity was intimately associated with place and therefore with land. The Maori people entered a period of population and cultural decline.

Moss (2004) however said it was significant for the future of cultural relationships that occupation in New Zealand did not follow the path of virtual extermination of indigenous culture, as in Australia and Canada. For a variety of economic, geographic and chronological reasons, the settlers and the Maori people were able to co-exist to a degree and retain their own cultures. That is not to say Maori culture was without threats. Moeke-Pickering (1996) said that assimilative government policies and the classification of Maori ethnicity by blood quantum undermined Maori identity, increased alienation and reduced opportunities available to Maori people. In the period up to the 1960s, assimilation was the dominant policy and monolingualism and monoculturalism were seen as appropriate for New Zealand by most Pakeha (Walker, 1989). The aim of assimilation was to absorb the Maori people into the mainstream. The Hunn Report written for the Department of Maori Affairs in 1962 introduced a new label for government policy towards Maori people — 'integration' (Thomas & Nikora, 1992). This amounted largely to total assimilation into Pakeha culture. Despite these attempts, the majority of Maori people retained a sense of separate identity.

The 1970s and 1980s ushered in a period of social protest, during which the Maori people became increasingly vocal and political in the assertion of their identity and rights. The Treaty of Waitangi has been a particular focus, with many of the Maori people seeking redress for what they consider was the blatant disregard of the treaty by the colonising British. In 1977, the New Zealand Government established the Waitangi Tribunal to examine any legislation or practices that might have been considered a violation of the treaty. Indigenous identity has become even more explicit in recent years with the official adoption of biculturalism as policy principle, and through the use of Maori art and symbols as national motifs (Moss, 2004). Maori identity has now been built into most spheres of government control, including the adoption of Maori as an official language and the use of it in many official documents, alongside English.

Today, the Maori people make up about 15 percent of the total population of New Zealand (Statistics New Zealand, 2010). A significant development in recent decades has been urbanisation, with about 80 percent of the Maori people today living in urban areas.

Maori identity

The concept of a single Maori ethnic group is a relatively recent construct. Traditionally, group loyalties would have been directed to the *whanau*, *iwi* or *hapu*. A sense of identity for Maori people came from their links to tribal genealogy, traditional lands, tribal and family structures and cultural practices. Colonisation severed these ties for many Maori people. The traditional structures of Maori society broke down and tribal homelands were lost. In addition, because of increasing urbanisation, many Maori people have not been exposed to maintaining and organising themselves primarily around their *whanau* or *hapu* and *iwi* (Moeke-Pickering, 1996). Thus, Maori ethnic identity today is actually a product of occupation and changed social conditions such as urbanisation. The near total breakdown of traditional tribal demarcations between Maori *iwi* has helped develop a pan-Maori sense of identity — a feeling of common identity across Maori people. Many Maori today now feel this common sense of identity while also still retaining links to particular *iwi*.

According to Edwards (2000), the Maori people also faced the process of 'determined identity', through which dominant groups in a society engage in shaping and determining the identity of minority groups, resulting in the oppression of the minority. He said the result was that many Maori came to believe in those negative constructions as 'common sense' and to relinquish their claim on Maori cultural identity. However, he also indicated that a reclamation of Maori cultural identity was possible and desirable. 'It is in the possibility of living a life that incorporates indigenous values and beliefs that the possibility of identity transformation occurs. For many Maori, this is a feature of their lives, an awakening may occur in their cultural lifestyles that adds to the Maori *whakapapa* they were born with. The process of identity reclamation is a tacit project to renew a cultural history in an individual's or group's own terms' (p. 4).

The approach of the government and the Pakeha population in treating the Maori people as a single group as they urbanised also provided a powerful impetus for a Maori ethnic identity (Chapple, 2000). Attempts to assimilate and integrate the Maori lifestyle into the dominant Pakeha culture have also crystallised the desire of the Maori to maintain a separate identity.

That sense of identity has grown stronger in recent times. From the 1960s and 1970s, Maori activists became increasingly vocal and radical, entering a range of political and legal debates. This has helped spark a conscious redefinition of Maori–Pakeha relations in New Zealand, in line with changing attitudes and social values. The changes can be seen as broadly reflecting the decreasing acceptance of assimilation and the increasing acceptance of biculturalism (Sibley & Liu, 2004; Thomas & Nikora, 1992). Linda Tuhiwai Smith (1999) said that a renewal of key cultural concepts such as *iwi*, *hapu* and *whanau*, along with Maori language and customs, was also important in helping give the Maori people a 'purposeful dream'. She said the Treaty of Waitangi provided an organising framework for dialogue with the dominant Pakeha, while issues such as education, health and justice provided more defined sites of struggle. Recent years have seen a revival of *iwi* groups and a rekindling of traditional kinship and cultural ties. As a result, in the 1990s, Maori identity changed to one of confidence (Walker, 1989). Greater recognition by government of biculturalism and Maori rights, and the ability to adapt the frameworks of tribal structures and cultural practices to urban living has played a major role in maintaining the continuity of Maori identity (Thomas & Nikora, 1992).

INTERIM SUMMARY

The Maori are the original inhabitants of New Zealand whose sense of identity nearly became severed upon European colonisation. While many Maori still retain *iwi* links, Maori people today also feel a common ethnic identity that reflects their experience of British occupation and their changed social conditions such as urbanisation.

Promoting cross-cultural interactions

Given the increasing multiculturalism in many countries, psychologists these days are much more likely to be dealing with people from a variety of ethnic and cultural backgrounds. Cultural differences also manifest themselves through education. This section will outline attempts by psychologists to improve cross-cultural relationships, with a specific focus on communicating with indigenous peoples.

MAKING CONNECTIONS

Indigenous Australians tend to score lower on standard **intelligence tests** than do non-Indigenous Australians. Does this indicate a difference in intelligence? No. Australian psychologist Judith Kearins (1976) suggests cultural factors help explain the discrepancy. Standard **IQ tests** have a **cultural bias** against Aboriginal people (chapter 9), because they are designed by and for people from Western society. Kearins' research found that Aboriginal adolescents outperformed Caucasian Australians in all conditions of a visual-spatial memory task.

Education and culture

Education is influenced both by culture and a medium that reinforces culture (see Boulton-Lewis, Marton, Lewis, & Wilss, 2000). Different cultures develop different education systems to meet the needs of their environment. Some are highly formalised, such as the classroom settings of schools and universities in the Western world. Others are informal, such as the 'learning by observing' approach of traditional indigenous cultures in Australia, where education occurred as part of everyday activities. Those systems of education have developed in response to the needs of those cultures. At the same time, education systems also act as one of the most important enculturation mechanisms in any society, reinforcing the values, rules and behaviours of the cultural environment in which they operate.

At this point, it is also worthwhile considering the nature of intelligence and whether it should be defined differently across cultures (chapter 9). Just as education systems teach people what is most important for survival in their culture, Keats (1988) identifies that broad definitions of 'intelligence' also focus on it being an effective adaptation to the environment. That happens differently in different environments. The skills and abilities needed to thrive in a modern post-industrial society are vastly different to those needed in a hunter-gatherer society (Fogarty & White, 2002). These differences underpin how the concept of 'intelligence' is measured and assessed. For example, studies by Kearins (1988) among Aboriginal Australians in Western Australia showed very different conceptions of what it means to be intelligent than those factors measured in common Western tests. Intelligence was most often equated with independence and helpfulness, while lack of intelligence was equated with laziness. To the respondents in this study, intelligence was measured through actions, a quite different concept to measuring intelligence through performance on a written IQ test. Given such differences, Keats (1988) poses the question of whether a pan-cultural view of the nature of intelligence is really possible, or whether there are different intelligences for different people. It is important from a psychological point of view to acknowledge context in any assessments of intelligence, and also to acknowledge that education systems are geared towards different outcomes across cultures.

Cross-cultural comparisons of student performance on tasks such as mathematics have identified noticeable differences. Chinese and Japanese students, for example, tend to outperform their Western counterparts in maths and science (Serpell & Hatano, 1997). The differences are not related to biological differences but are the result of many social and cultural factors, some institutionalised in the education system, others related to parenting styles, others found in personal attributes (Matsumoto & Juang, 2004).

For those involved in the education sector, it is crucial to recognise that the way students respond to their teaching environments reflects the cultural environments in which they are socialised — and that what defines academic success in one culture may not be what defines success in another (McInerney & McInerney, 2002). For example, Lee (1993) identifies a number of cultural reasons why some Aboriginal children may perform to a lower academic level than other children. They include:

- low expectations of their own abilities reinforced by cultural stereotypes and prejudice
- low expectations from teachers in terms of their abilities
- limited use of 'standard' English at home
- the collectivist worldview of indigenous culture contrasting with the individualist framework of the education system
- unfamiliarity with the linguistic system used in reading texts
- unfamiliarity with the structured schooling system
- poverty and socioeconomic disadvantage of indigenous communities affecting ability to study
- limited relevance of content that is geared to 'white' majority population.

Many Maori people are ambivalent towards education for similar reasons to those above and because success in Western schools runs counter to important cultural values, and schools do little to encourage and develop the cultural qualities that Maori people consider important (McInerney & McInerney, 2002).

The increasingly multicultural nature of many countries is placing pressure on their education systems to create more inclusive environments (see Banks & McGee Banks, 2003; Ladson-Billings, 2003; Luchtenberg, 2004). Schools and university campuses are now becoming much more geared to people from non-English-speaking backgrounds. Curriculums and assessment tasks are designed to take more account of cultural differences within student cohorts. An Australian study by Carstairs, Myors, Shores, and Fogarty (2006) compared the performance on cognitive tests of people from both English-speaking backgrounds and non-English-speaking backgrounds. This is particularly relevant in Australia given that around one-quarter of the population was born overseas (ABS, 2005). The study found that people from non-English-speaking backgrounds were disadvantaged on verbal subtests because they lacked proficiency in the language. Furthermore, those people also tended to show a disadvantage on nonverbal subtests, suggesting that there may also be a sociocultural factor affecting performance. Few contemporary societies are insulated from the influence of multiple cultures, and an increasing number of students commute between two or more different worlds in their homes, their neighbourhoods and their schools — as a result, education confronts a new set of responsibilities at the interface between different value systems, languages and practices (Serpell & Hatano, 1997).

MAKING CONNECTIONS

Many theories of personality are based on the belief that our childhood has a crucial role in the development of **personality traits** (chapter 11). For instance, McClelland (1961) reported that parental child-rearing practices are related to the degree of an individual's **achievement motivation** (chapter 10). What, then, is the link between personality and culture? The answer is that the child-rearing practices that influence the development of personality are, in turn, influenced and reinforced by the surrounding cultural environment.

For example, the Department of Education and Training in Queensland issued an updated set of guidelines in 2011 entitled 'Embedding Aboriginal and Torres Strait Islander perspectives in schools'. The guidelines are an excellent demonstration of the challenges that the education system faces in catering for cultural diversity in modern Australian society. The document sets out a context for change which acknowledges that Indigenous communities have distinct and deep cultural views and worldviews that differ from those found in most Western education systems. These views support a different approach to teaching which acknowledges and respects differences in perspectives. 'When Western and Indigenous systems are acknowledged and valued equally, the overlapping or merging of views represents a new way of educating' (Department of Education and Training, 2011, p. 9.) This improves overall outcomes because:

- meeting the educational needs of Indigenous students in practical ways can improve attendance, retention and workplace participation

- providing a more accurate and richer understanding of Australia's history and culture enhances the educational experiences of non-Indigenous students as well.

The guidelines state that weaving the Indigenous story into the fabric of education helps make Indigenous students stronger and more resilient, and improves their educational outcomes. But this also helps to improve overall outcomes for all students and the whole school community as well.

The document states that embedding Indigenous perspectives in the school environment helps in a number of ways. First, there are benefits for school leadership and teachers, including:

- increased cultural competence, including the capacity to interact effectively with people from other cultures
- new opportunities to provide representations and challenge
- a challenge to dominant viewpoints, media representations, negative stereotypes and racism.

Benefits for students include:

- enhancing a strong sense of self-identity and pride for Aboriginal and Torres Strait Islander students
- providing Aboriginal and Torres Strait Islander students with an understanding of how attitudes and perceptions are formed and how to respond to negative attitudes
- providing non-Indigenous students with Aboriginal and Torres Strait Islander viewpoints.

Finally, benefits for the Indigenous community, parents and carers include increased opportunities for Aboriginal and Torres Strait Islander community decision making and engagement in schools.

INTERIM SUMMARY

Education is influenced by culture and different cultures develop different education systems to meet their needs. Consequently, it may not be appropriate to compare performance across different cultural groups. Indeed, it is important that education systems create inclusive learning environments for students, especially in multicultural countries like Australia and New Zealand. Such initiatives will help to ensure that teachers are both aware of and sensitive to the histories, cultures, languages and learning styles of students with different cultural backgrounds.

APPLY + DISCUSS

A number of studies have found that people from ethnic or cultural minorities often fail to seek therapy, or drop out soon after starting.

- What do you think the reasons might be? Do you think they have stereotyped perceptions about people who seek therapy?
- Is the Western-based approach to therapy appropriate to all cultural groups?
- How can psychologists minimise misunderstandings and make therapy more relevant?
- Do people from different cultures have different expectations about therapy?

Indigenous cultures and the psychology discipline

In the past, psychology has been viewed as the search for universal truth about human behaviour. You may question why, as a science, psychology need have any concerns about its applicability to indigenous cultures. Surely, the principles of psychology are equally applicable to people from all cultures? In reality, the discipline of psychology as we know it today is a product of the European and North American cultural environment. Most psychological theories and practices have been developed in Western countries. The 'scientific' basis of psychology — the theories and models we use to understand human behaviour — is constrained by the cultural contexts in which it was derived (Matsumoto & Juang, 2004). Whether it is totally relevant to people from another culture is debatable.

The fact that psychology springs from Western culture is important, because there are fundamental differences in the worldviews of people from Western cultures and those of people from other cultures. Dudgeon and Pickett (2000) identified two fundamental assumptions in the science of psychology that particularly exclude indigenous peoples and realities — the assumptions of individualism and universality. They note that psychology is a discipline centred on the individual rather than the interaction between individuals. They also note that cultural and historical context is ignored. In the Western worldview, humankind is viewed as homogeneous, with universal truths underlying behaviour — differences between individuals and groups are regarded as peripheral. This worldview sets different social priorities from those which indigenous peoples set for themselves, views social issues differently and employs different approaches to the generation of social knowledge (Davidson, 1992). It ignores the reality that social and cultural context is important — the physical, economic and political environments, as well as the language, values, meanings and worldviews of different cultures, do affect behaviour (Wetherell, 1998).

Communication and culture

Why is a consideration of culture important in communication? Communication can be seen as a process that involves four components. First, there is the *sender* — the person or entity that sends out a message. Second, there is the *receiver* — the person or entity to whom the message is sent. Third, there is the *medium* — the channel through which a message is sent. Fourth, there is the content of the message itself. So, a person (sender) texting an SMS (medium) to a friend (receiver) asking them to go to the movies (message) is demonstrating a communication process in action. The sender encodes the message — phrasing and delivering it in a way that gives it a particular meaning. The receiver must then *decode* the message — interpreting the phrasing and delivery to decide what the message means. Communication occurs if the receiver decodes the message to have the same meaning that the sender intended. When people from the same culture communicate, that encoding and decoding process occurs in an environment of shared understanding.

However, cultural differences are important because they can influence all components of the communication process and cause misunderstandings. The fact that the encoding of a message occurs within a sender's own cultural environment, and the decoding of an item occurs within the cultural norms of the receiver, can often lead to miscommunication across cultures (Poyatos, 1988). A cultural clash was a key issue that almost derailed the Indian cricket tour of Australia early in 2008. Both teams made allegations that competing players had made offensive, possibly racist, comments on the field. With the teams arguing about both whether the comments were made and whether they were actually offensive in either or both cultures, the Indian team threatened to abandon the tour.

Difference in language is the most obvious barrier to cross-cultural communication. It is often difficult to translate the exact meaning of words from one culture into those of another. For example, 'The Dreaming' has come to be accepted as the collective English term to represent the wide diversity of spiritual belief systems among Aboriginal Australians, in the absence of an exact translation. The sentence structure and phraseology of languages also differ widely and contain nuances that are not easily transferred to another language.

However, apart from literal differences in the lexicons of languages, the nonverbal behaviours that accompany our interpersonal communication are also the source of considerable cross-cultural confusion. The nonverbal components of the communication process provide much of the information that we need to decode the actual words that are spoken. Nonverbal behaviours include:

1. ***Kinaesics:*** the use of gestures, movements and facial expressions
2. ***Oculesics:*** the use of eye movements and eye contact
3. ***Haptics:*** the use of touch to accompany communication
4. ***Proxemics:*** the use of space between people while communicating
5. ***Chronemics:*** the use of time in communication
6. ***Vocalics:*** the use of vocal cues such as pitch, volume and tempo.

Different cultures have completely different nonverbal behaviours. People from the same culture understand the nonverbal behaviours that accompany the words that others use, which helps them decode the meaning that was intended. The task is much more difficult for people from different cultures, where nonverbal behaviours may mean completely different things. For example:

- In Asian cultures, bowing is a common form of greeting. In Western cultures, a handshake is generally accepted, though a kiss on the cheek may take place when women meet. In Maori culture, the 'hongi' is a form of greeting that involves the touching together of noses.
- In African, Arab and Hispanic cultures, people touch frequently during conversations. In Britain and Australia, such touching is rare.
- In Latin America, people tend to be very close together when they are talking. In Western cultures, such close proximity may be interpreted as hostility or associated with sexual intimacy.
- Some Aboriginal Australians will not use direct eye contact, especially on first meeting a stranger. Arabs, Latin Americans and Southern Europeans usually focus directly on the person to whom they are speaking.

The meanings and nuances of nonverbal behaviours are not something in which we receive much formal training. Rather, we absorb the 'rules' of nonverbal behaviours in our culture through constant exposure to them. We recognise them without conscious thought. From the cross-cultural perspective, it is vital to understand that people from other cultures may have a completely different set of 'unwritten rules' governing nonverbal communication. Understanding these rules is the key to effective communication. It is also important to recognise that we use our own nonverbal behaviours to convey messages, which may hinder communication with people from other cultures.

Communication practices are also at the heart of 'discursive psychology', a relatively new approach that focuses on the spoken and written text as the creator of meaning (see Parker & Bolton Discourse

APPLY + DISCUSS

Interpersonal communication relies on a combination of the words that are spoken and the nonverbal behaviours that accompany those words. It is easy to see how miscommunication can occur across cultures. Both the words and the gestures are liable to misinterpretation. Sometimes, words do not translate perfectly across cultures or the same term may have a different meaning in different cultures. An Australian who asked an American to 'shout' him a beer may not get much response. Gestures can also mean something different. The Western gesture for 'OK', a circle made with thumb and index finger, means 'zero' in Laos.

- Think of a conversation you have had recently with someone from the same culture. Think of the topics you discussed, the phrases you used and the gestures that accompanied the discussion. How difficult would it have been for someone from another culture to understand what you were talking about?

In Asian cultures, bowing is a common form of greeting.

Network, 1999; Potter & Edwards, 1992; Potter & Wetherell, 1987). Discursive psychology treats spoken and written text as contributing to the construction of people's reality, not just a reflection of underlying cognition (Griffin, 2000; see also Herman, 2007). This approach is a departure because it places the qualitative study of text, a practice that is heavily influenced by culture, ahead of the quantitative methods of mainstream positivist psychology. The discursive approach is closely linked to ***social constructionism***, the postmodern theory that there are no universal truths because people are continually constructing knowledge based on their own individual and cultural experiences.

Language and culture

As shown in figure 19.5, language and culture are inextricably linked. Our cultural environment influences the words we use and the way we use them. Our language, in turn, reinforces our cultural beliefs and practices. For example, the English language contains many variations of the word 'I' and is framed around references to individual conceptions of self. This reflects the individualistic nature of Western culture. Other languages, such as Japanese, vary the way an individual is described, depending upon the context and relationships between people. This reflects a more collectivist culture. The words and concepts that people use reflect what is important in their culture, which leads to differences in the number and organisation of words conveying certain concepts (Hall & Barongan, 2002). For example, the Dani people of New Guinea do not have individual words for each different colour — the only differentiation they make in their language is between light and dark. The Dani can recognise different colours if they learn the way Westerners differentiate them — but distinguishing between colours is simply not an important part of their lifestyles.

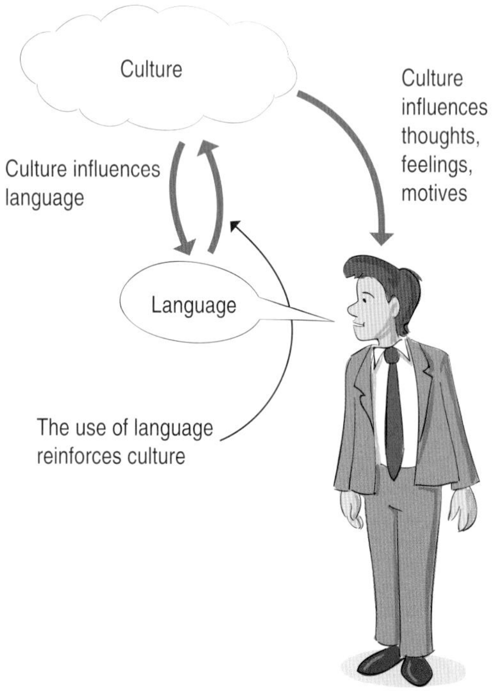

FIGURE 19.5
The relationship between culture and language: culture influences the structures and functions of language and language reflects the manifestation of culture.

SOURCE: The reciprocal relation between culture and language — From Culture and Psychology (with Info Trac) 3rd edition by MATSUMOTO/JUANG. © 2004. Reprinted with permission of Wadsworth, a part of Cengage Learning, Inc. Reproduced by permission. www.cengage.com/permissions.

Language is an essential element in the development of a sense of self (McInerney & McInerney, 2002; chapter 8). The social constructivist theories of Lev Vygotsky (1978) emphasise that individuals do not develop and learn in isolation from their surrounds, but through a process of appropriating culturally relevant behaviour (Kozulin & Presseisen, 1995; chapter 13). Language is a key medium through which culture is transmitted. It reinforces cultural constructs. The cyclical relationships between language and culture, through which language is both influenced by and influences our cultural values and worldviews, suggests that no culture can be fully understood without its language also being understood (Matsumoto & Juang, 2004).

The ***Sapir-Whorf hypothesis***, proposed by Edward Sapir and Benjamin Whorf in the 1950s, suggests that speakers of different languages actually think differently, and do so because of the differences in their languages (Matsumoto & Juang, 2004). That is, people process information differently and interpret things differently because the language they speak has an influence on their thought patterns. There is still considerable debate on the Sapir-Whorf hypothesis, otherwise known as *linguistic relativity*, with subsequent research both supporting and criticising the theory. Advocates for linguistic relativity support the notion that language determines how people conceive their world, providing evidence from studies that compare the thought processes of speakers of different languages on various cognitive tasks (e.g. Bloom, 1981; Lucy, 1992). Critics have challenged the research designs that obtained positive findings, arguing that their results were based on methodological flaws (Pinker, 1995; Takano, 1989). One area that creates difficulties for the theory is where people are multilingual. How do you decide which language is responsible for different thought patterns? Matsumoto and Juang (2004) document the applicability of the theory in bilingual and multilingual populations.

Language enables people to communicate with each other and is one of the major vehicles for preservation of culture (McInerney & McInerney, 2002). Given that role, there is little doubt that loss of language has been a significant contributor to the destruction of traditional Aboriginal cultures in Australia. The early Aboriginal languages were oral rather than written, so their demise has also meant the loss of any coherent record of the history, traditions and practices of these cultures.

INTERIM SUMMARY

Language is the essence of culture; it reinforces our cultural beliefs and practices. The ***Sapir-Whorf hypothesis*** suggests that speakers of different languages think differently because of the differences in their languages.

Communicating with indigenous peoples

For people in the psychology profession, the ability to communicate effectively with people from other cultures is becoming increasingly important. Communication involves not just an understanding of language terms and protocols, such as how to greet someone appropriately. It requires a deeper understanding of how culture can affect the communication process.

For example, Davidson (2000) points out that Australians of Anglo-Celtic origin tend to downplay the importance of emotions in communication, particularly at work or in business. Emotions are not openly displayed. By contrast, Indigenous Australians invest heavily in the emotional component of communication. Displaying an appropriate amount of emotion during interaction sends an important signal about relationships.

Davidson (2000) says that learning to listen, to adjust communicative style and to show appropriate emotion are important skills for psychologists to learn in dealing with Indigenous Australians, and people from other cultures.

As well as that general awareness, there are a number of specific areas that need to be considered in communicating with people from Aboriginal cultures. Several of them are now listed.

1. In some Aboriginal communities, there are specific protocols associated with the use of people's names that are quite different to Western ways. For example, there is a widespread custom that prohibits using the names of dead people, especially during the immediate period after death.
2. Disagreement can often be passive in Aboriginal societies. While Westerners may speak up and make their disagreement clear, Aboriginal people may simply remain quiet to signal their opposition or discomfort. This silence can be misinterpreted as acceptance.
3. Non-Aboriginal people expect that when a commitment is made, such as keeping an appointment or accepting an invitation, it will be kept. Among Aboriginal people, how the commitment is made will determine whether it is kept or not. This is conveyed through a combination of words, tone and body language, and is clearly understood by others within the same culture (Eckermann et al., 1994).

The bottom line is that effective communication requires an understanding of the cultural context in which it takes place. The Queensland Department of Families, Youth and Community Care has developed a guide to proper communication with Torres Strait Islander people, which stresses that the key step is to develop a good understanding of the culture and social system of the Torres Strait (Office of Aboriginal and Torres Strait Islander Affairs, 1997). The guide contains suggestions such as:

- Listening attentively and without interruption is vital to establishing a relationship.
- Asking too many questions is considered impolite.
- Most Torres Strait Islanders speak English but it is often not their first language. Adjust your choice of vocabulary to suit the level of understanding.
- Outsiders should have a participatory role, not a controlling role, in discussions.
- Try not to refuse proposals outright, as this can cause offence.
- Respect religious protocols such as opening and closing meetings with a prayer.
- Avoid talking excessively, particularly in the company of elders.

INTERIM SUMMARY

The discipline of psychology is a product of European and North American cultural environment. Consequently, the theories and models we use to understand human behaviour are constrained by the cultural contexts in which they were derived, and may not be relevant to people from other cultures. Cultural differences may influence all aspects of the communication process and cause misunderstandings and miscommunication across cultures. Psychologists therefore need to understand and respect the cultural context in which such communications take place.

Culturally competent psychologists

Psychological research into indigenous peoples in Australia and New Zealand has a largely paternalistic history. In the early days of European occupation, indigenous peoples were often viewed as objects to be studied. Psychological research was something done to indigenous participants by Western scientists. Early research involved IQ testing and skull measurements, based on Eurocentric assumptions of mental superiority. Garvey, Dudgeon, and Kearins (2000) acknowledge that Australian psychology has a 'black history' but also identify that the relationship between the profession and indigenous peoples has undergone a change in recent decades. The psychology profession is now much more concerned about what indigenous peoples want and receive from the relationship. Similarly, Nikora (2007) says academics took little interest in the Maori world up until the 1940s, and after that were often criticised for doing research 'on' Maori rather than 'with' Maori. However, Nikora says the lack of research on Maori psychology is beginning to change, with work carried out by Professor Mason Durie and by the Maori and Psychology Research Unit at the University of Waikato now leading the way in demonstrating how an indigenous psychology can take shape. Nikora says that 'for psychology, the Maori development agenda is to create psychologies to meet the needs of Maori people in a way that maintains a unique cultural heritage and makes for a better collective Maori future' (p. 82).

Indigenous peoples come from cultures that are distinctly different from the culture in which 'traditional' psychology was born. It is important to recognise that culture does influence the way we think and behave, so an awareness of cultural influences is important when dealing with people from indigenous cultures. So, too, is an appreciation of our own cultural influences. Dudgeon and Pickett (2000, p. 86) described it this way:

> Psychologists need to seek out culturally appropriate practice in interactions with those from different cultural backgrounds — not only indigenous people, but all the cultural groups that make up the multicultural society — so that the practitioner's own conditioned values, assumptions and perspectives of social reality are not imposed on others.

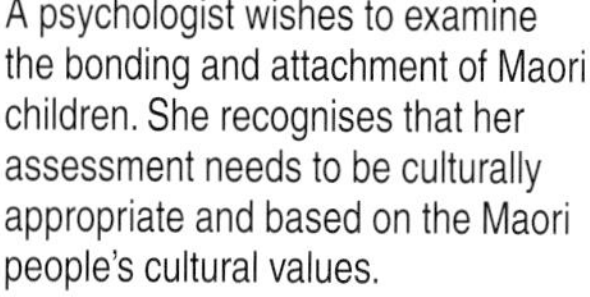

A psychologist wishes to examine the bonding and attachment of Maori children. She recognises that her assessment needs to be culturally appropriate and based on the Maori people's cultural values.

- Should the researcher make the purpose and methodology of her research known to the Maori people she is working with? If so, how might she achieve this?
- Why is it important that the research proposal recognise and respect Maori cultural values and principles?

How can this be done? Sue and Sue (1990) recommended that in dealing with people from another culture, the culturally skilled psychologist should:

- be aware of their own cultural background, heritage and biases
- be aware of the differences that exist between themselves and those of other cultures
- understand and respect that people from other cultures may have different values, attitudes and worldviews
- have an understanding of the client's social and political circumstances, for example, how racism and oppression may have affected them
- be aware of their sociopolitical system and how this affects particular cultural groups.

Thus, according to Sue and Sue (1990), practitioners need to become aware of their own assumptions and biases and be sensitive not to impose their personal values and standards onto the client. Rather than being ethnocentric, the practitioner should recognise that other cultures are legitimate and valuable. In this way, there is respect and appreciation of difference. This active process of self-reflection helps to avoid prejudices and minimise inappropriate labelling and stereotyping. Culturally aware practitioners also recognise that in some instances the client is better served by a referral to another practitioner; and in doing so, acknowledge their own limitations.

Dudgeon et al. (2000) use the term cultural competence to describe what is required of psychologists in dealing with people from another culture. They say ***cultural competence*** is all about a person's effectiveness in communicating and behaving appropriately with people from another culture, both in terms of understanding and being understood. They say it is more than just cultural awareness — it is the practical application of that knowledge. According to Indigenous research and development expert Bronwyn Lumby, co-founder of the Centre for Cultural Competence Australia (CCCA), cultural awareness training should focus on doing, not knowing (HR Daily, 2010). Thus, psychologists need to become both culturally and contextually competent to adapt to ever-changing population demographics. According to Yali and Revenson (2004), *contextual competence* requires considering the various other factors which might impact on health-related issues, including the historic, family, economic and social contexts in which individuals are situated.

Davidson (1999) suggests psychologists need to consider two other aspects of cultural competence. First, he suggests cultural competence is not just a way to work more effectively but is an ethical responsibility for psychologists. That is, in working with people from other cultures, psychologists should be ethically bound to develop cultural competence. Second, he suggests that it is possible to develop a set of generic cultural competencies that can equip a psychologist to operate effectively in multicultural societies. In the Asia–Pacific region, the reality is that practitioners may have to deal on a daily basis with people from all corners of the globe. That poses the question of whether it is possible to gain an in-depth understanding of every cultural group that you might contact. Davidson (1999) suggests that generic competencies can be developed, based on a practitioner's general understanding of how cultures can differ, understanding of their own social and cultural values, and understanding of how to make adjustments that reflect those factors.

More recently, Walker and Sonn (2010) extended the work of Sue and Sue (1990), defining four key aspects of cultural competence of the mental health practitioner working with Indigenous people. They distinguish between *knowledge* (general understandings of cultural differences and worldviews, how colonisation has impacted on Indigenous Australians and the ongoing effects of this), *values* (awareness of how personal values and beliefs are developed and how they might influence their interactions with others from a different cultural group), *skills* (a myriad of high level reasoning skills that enable effective practice), and *attributes* (knowledge and appreciation of the impact of history and understanding the effects of power, privilege and racism in society). Importantly, Walker and Sonn (2010) outline a model for critical reflection to promote cultural competence. Culturally competent practitioners recognise and appreciate cultural difference and actively challenge their own assumptions about those from different cultures (Ranzijn, McConnochie, & Nolan, 2010).

The need for cultural competence was dramatically highlighted in the aftermath of the devastating tsunami that swamped countries on the rim of the Indian Ocean on 26 December 2004 and more recently, on 25 October 2010. The countries affected by the 2004 tsunami included Indonesia, Thailand, Malaysia, Sri Lanka, India, the Maldives and even Somalia on the African continent — widely different cultures but whose people suffered a similar sense of grief and loss. While the first priority for assistance to affected countries was food, water, medical aid and housing, the need for help in overcoming the mental trauma was also high on the agenda. Only days after the tsunami hit in 2004, the Indonesian ambassador to Australia signalled that his government would soon make a formal request to the Australian Government for help from trained psychologists (Banham, 2005). Many of those affected came from the remote province of Aceh, where the people had little previous contact with Westerners. In such circumstances, psychologists need *cultural competence* in order to effectively help the people cope with the tragedy they had experienced.

Similarly, cultural competence and sensitivity were required in the aftermath of the 2011 twin earthquake and tsunami disaster in Japan and the ensuing nuclear crisis in the region. After the tragedy, a Professor of Psychology explained the importance of international counsellors and psychologists considering culture in any interventions. Professor Lilienfeld said, 'There are certainly cultural similarities ... but there are also other cultural differences that have to be respected. Japan tends to be, in a broad generalisation, somewhat more of a collectivist culture. There's often more respect for community and group harmony; group cohesion. There's a danger in people coming in who are not sufficiently culturally sensitive to those kinds of issues. They need to be very careful that [the] interventions they use are culturally attuned' (cited in Szalavitz, 2011).

As well as general competencies in dealing with different cultures, psychologists may also have a need for a greater knowledge of dealing with particular cultural groups. In order to help psychologists improve their interaction with indigenous peoples, the Australian Psychological Society developed a document titled *Guidelines for the provision of psychological services for and the conduct of psychological research with Aboriginal and Torres Strait Islander people* in 1996. The guidelines include recommendations that psychologists should:

- take into account ethnicity and culture when making judgements about and dealing with indigenous clients
- be aware of and show respect for the value systems and authority structures of Indigenous communities
- be aware of sociopolitical factors that might adversely affect indigenous clients or the treatment provided
- be aware of the impact of their own beliefs, stereotypes and communication rules in their interpretation of the way indigenous clients behave
- react appropriately against discrimination or prejudice directed at indigenous clients by others.

The Australian Psychological Society updated these guidelines in 2007. These same principles might also be applied by psychologists who work with people from other cultural backgrounds.

So how do those principles affect the way a psychologist would actually deal with an indigenous client? There are many ways this translation into reality would occur. A key starting point would be familiarisation with the indigenous client's personal history and experience. The applicability of Western-style counselling would be assessed according to individual factors such as the degree of Western acculturation. Kinship structures and social obligations would be considered in assessing behaviour and in determining treatment options. These are just a few of many adjustments that non-indigenous psychologists should make.

MAKING CONNECTIONS

The definition of **abnormal behaviour** depends on the norms, values and expectations of the culture in which it takes place. What is considered abnormal behaviour in one society may be acceptable in another. For example, the Mardujara Aboriginal people practised an initiation rite that involved knocking out the front incisors of boys with stones and sharpened sticks. Facial tattooing was practised by men and women in Maori tribes. And Japanese children often sleep in the same room as their parents well into adolescence. An understanding that abnormality is defined by cultural norms also helps put the **DSM-IV** into context. It can be considered a somewhat culture-specific classification for mental disorders (chapter 15) as it is based largely on Western cultural contexts that may not be relevant to other societies.

MAKING CONNECTIONS

Several cultures use **dreams** to identify and treat **mental disorders** (chapters 5 and 16). Dreams were central to the psychoanalytic techniques Freud developed. Prince (1980) found that therapists in several cultures often treated mental disorders by prescribing long periods of sleep. Prince argued that **altered states of consciousness** are important in many psychotherapeutic techniques, and many therapies use **dream interpretation** to identify underlying problems. In some cultures, a dissociative state is considered therapeutic, as it allows people to act out behaviours that are normally inappropriate. The Zar cult in the Middle East uses a treatment that involves both the client and the therapist entering a dissociative state. This helps identify the 'Zar' — the spirits causing the psychological disorder — and work out a cure (Prince, 1980).

Dudgeon (2000a) summarised the approach by saying that psychologists can play an effective role in helping indigenous clients, but must be aware of both the client's culture and their own cultural biases and values. Gillies (2007, p. 12) says practitioners need to also develop strategies to 'combat assimilationist pressures imposed by Western administrative structures'. However, Dudgeon (2000b) also said that while cultural awareness was important, so too was a respect for the diversity that exists within the indigenous community. Indigenous peoples should not be stereotyped and treated in exactly the same way. The individual needs and experience of the client are still the most important determinant of treatment. Those principles apply equally to dealing with people from other ethnic and cultural groups, as well as indigenous peoples. A recent text edited by Purdie, Dudgeon, and Walker (2010) outlines many of the issues and strategies influencing the mental health and wellbeing of Aboriginal and Torres Strait Islander peoples and provides useful examples of models and programs for practitioners working with different cultural groups.

The Australian Psychological Society (APS) developed a position paper that went further than just providing guidelines on dealing with cultural diversity, but recommended actions that should be taken to proactively reduce prejudice and racism (Sanson et al., 1998). They argued that psychologists have a responsibility to contribute to the process of reconciliation with Aboriginal people and inclusiveness within a multicultural community. This includes steps such as the APS speaking out against assertions that promote racial stereotypes; providing more cross-cultural training; focusing specifically on cross-cultural and indigenous psychology in professional development; encouraging minority group members to train as clinicians; and working in partnership with minority groups to develop and carry out appropriate research. Gabb (2000) suggested that psychologists' role as healers and collective position of strength as a profession, demand a powerful response against signs of cultural and racial division in Australian society.

In 2006, the University of South Australia introduced two new indigenous psychology courses as part of the process of developing greater cultural competence among future practitioners: a compulsory first-year course for all psychology students, and an elective third-year course. The team at the University of South Australia have held national workshops to disseminate the outcomes of this work around Australia. Ranzijn, McConnochie, Nolan, and Day (2007) said the process of developing the courses and teaching materials, then sharing them more widely, has been extremely rewarding. They believe that psychology has a crucial role to play in addressing indigenous disadvantage, 'with the potential to understand the workings of racism and how cultural trauma is perpetuated through the generations' (p. 11). More recently, the Australian Indigenous Psychologists Association (AIPA) was established in 2008 under the auspices of the APS, providing leadership on issues related to the social and emotional wellbeing and mental health of Aboriginal and Torres Strait Islander peoples. AIPA, chaired by Pat Dudgeon as of 2010, provides quality control of workshops and related cultural competence training programs, ensuring that Indigenous Australians have access to high quality psychological help. AIPA also works to ensure that psychology in Australia is responsive to Indigenous cultures, values and belief systems, engaging in research to help generate improved policy and social outcomes for Aboriginal and Torres Strait Islander peoples.

Just as the psychology profession in Australia is redefining its relationship with Indigenous Australians, so too the New Zealand profession is transforming its relationship with the Maori people. Psychology in New Zealand has previously imposed Western-derived concepts, models, theories and practices on to all people on its shores, whether of European, Maori or another ethnic background, with little regard to cultural influences.

That has begun to change in recent times. The constitution of the New Zealand Psychological Society (1993) makes specific reference to the country's cultural diversity and the need to uphold the spirit of the Treaty of Waitangi in relation to the Maori people. Rule three of the constitution states that the society shall 'encourage policies and practices that reflect New Zealand's cultural diversity and shall, in particular, have due regard to the provisions of and to the spirit and intent of, the Treaty of Waitangi' (p. 70). The society has also established a National Standing Committee on Bicultural Issues. The reference to the treaty in the constitution acknowledges the validity of this document, and the fact that in its original form, the treaty negotiated a relationship that allowed for diversity, yet maintained the self-respect and self-determination of all people in New Zealand (National Standing Committee on Bicultural Issues, 1993).

Love (2003) identified three key problems in relation to the psychology profession's fit for Maori and other non-Western people:

1. *cultural knowledge* — a lack of expertise in dealing with Maori people
2. *workforce deficiencies* — Maori people make up just 1.3 percent of psychologists in New Zealand

3. *value bases* — the psychology profession draws on a conception of self, other and the nature of the world that is based on Western culture and is very different to the conceptions held by Maori and many other indigenous peoples.

As shown in table 19.6, Waldegrave (1993) identifies four important differences between Maori culture and Pakeha culture that must be considered in delivering psychological services.

TABLE 19.6 **Differences between Maori and Pakeha (non-Maori) cultures**

Maori culture	Pakeha culture
Communal: a shared group identity	*Individual:* focus on personal or self identity
Spiritual: belief in the sacredness of spirit and religion	*Secular:* worldly and sophisticated; belief that processes evolve slowly over time
Ecological: focus on the complex relationship between the people and their environment	*Consumer:* a user and recipient of goods and services
Consensual: values and symbols derived from a reasoned consensus among community members	*Conflictual:* motives and behaviours are directed towards achievement of individual goals

SOURCE: Based on Waldegrave (1993, p. 6).

Waldegrave (1993) highlights these gaps between Maori culture and Western culture as a critical issue for psychologists in New Zealand (see also New Zealand Psychologists Board, 2006). He points out that for practically all clinical psychological and psychotherapeutic theories, the primary goal of therapy is individual self-worth. That is because Western culture is permeated with the concept of individualism, where self-assertiveness and individual fulfilment is considered the norm. However, for people from a communal or extended family culture, questions of self-exposure and self-assertion are often confusing and even alienating. A counsellor asking detailed questions about self-identity may alienate a client. Waldegrave gives the example of a New Zealander of Samoan heritage who explained how difficult it was responding to direct, personal questions in a therapy session: 'When I'm asked a question like "what do *you* think?" about something in therapy, it is so hard for me to answer that question. I have to think what does my mother think, what does my grandmother think, what does my father think, what does my uncle think, what does my sister think, what is the consensus of those thoughts — ah, that must be what I think' (Waldegrave, 1993, p. 4). Non-indigenous clinicians unconsciously impose the 'correctness' of their Eurocentric culture, which considers individual achievement as more worthy than collectivism and collaboration (Manna, 2002).

Nikora (1993) asserts that everyone involved in the psychology profession in New Zealand has a responsibility to strive for *cultural justice* — ensuring that all facets of the profession and discipline are practised in a way that maintains a balance of justness and rightness for all groups (see also Hodgetts, Barnett, Duirs, Henry, & Schwanen, 2004; Morgan, Coombes, & Campbell, 2006).

In 2005, the *New Zealand Journal of Psychology* devoted a special feature edition to Maori psychological issues. Guest editors Glover and Hirini (2005) said the aim was to critique and reflect on emerging Maori psychological theory, practice and research and showcase Maori psychologists in New Zealand. They said the seven papers identified a common theme, that 'while advances had been made in differentiating Maori psychology from the traditional Western discipline, there was still a long way to go in developing its full potential' (p. 2).

APPLY + DISCUSS

Consider that you are a psychologist dealing with clients from a variety of cultural backgrounds. These clients will come to you with widely different life histories, expectations, beliefs, norms and ailments.

- How would you vary your approach to cater for those differences?
- How would you consider their cultural environment in assessing their problem?
- What are some of the factors that you would have to consider in determining the type of treatment that would be appropriate?

Coming around full circle

By Professor Pat Dudgeon, University of Western Australia

I am calling this article 'Coming around full circle' because the issues we raised more than 20 years ago (see Dudgeon & Pickett, 2000) have the same urgency now as they did then. Recently, a high-profile non-Indigenous supporter/advocate asked a group of around 60 Aboriginal and Torres Strait Islander people in a workshop if they thought things have changed for the better in Indigenous affairs. The response was a resounding no. This triggered some mixed reactions for me. First, I feel that we answered no because that is what our high-profile advocate wanted us to say. We were also in a context where we were discussing a hard issue — support for those frontline workers dealing with Aboriginal and Torres Strait Islander child abuse. The world seemed fairly bleak from that context. I would say that some things have changed for the worse and others have vastly improved for Aboriginal and Torres Strait Islander people. This could also be said for psychology. In 1995, the first Australian Aboriginal keynote speaker presented at the annual Australian Psychological Society conference. That speaker, Rob Riley, delivered an important, historical paper, in the hope that it would make a difference in our discipline. He said:

> How many psychologists have an understanding of Aboriginal people? How many of you . . . have an understanding of Aboriginal culture, history and contemporary issues? For many of you, this work is crucial, given the social conditions and your work environment, in such places as prisons and the welfare sector and where there are large numbers of Aboriginal clients. It is your responsibility to seek that knowledge and understanding now — and to ensure that it is available for future generations of psychologists in psychological training and education programs. (Riley, 1997, pp. 15–16)

This challenge remains for us to address today. His request went beyond reconciliation and demanded that the profession commit to acquiring genuine knowledge, understanding and skills to work with indigenous people; that is, to commit to achieving cultural competence. While I have an indigenous perspective, cultural competence is about the inclusion and celebration of all the cultural groups that make up our nation. As well as understanding other cultural groups, cultural competence requires people to critically reflect on their own beliefs, values and assumptions, so that they can work effectively — and in empowering ways — with people from other cultural backgrounds.

Cultural competence is an important conceptual framework and process. It is not a 'tick a box' or a 'one workshop skill-up', but is rather a lifelong commitment. The commitment to long-term learning that is essential to becoming a culturally competent practitioner should not be underestimated. It involves more than learning about another cultural group — requiring turning one's gaze inwards and critically examining one's own society, history, beliefs and attitudes; a political consciousness; and a commitment to self-determination and to social justice. Indigenous practitioners and researchers acknowledge that 'cultural competence must take a political standpoint that acknowledges the impacts of colonisation, the complexities of racism and the power and privilege that continue to persist in dominant societies' (Dudgeon, Wright, & Coffin, 2010, p. 31).

Cultural competence requires a critical appreciation of cultural difference and national histories. This means understanding a history of colonisation and acknowledging how this has contributed to the psychology of different groups of peoples in Australia: one dominant and the other dominated; one that is based on white privilege and the other that is engaged in a process of survival and cultural reclamation. Cultural competence 'requires a personal honesty and healthy sense of self that is not driven by power and control needs. It requires a commitment to the self-determination, and to the empowerment, of Aboriginal and Torres Strait Islander individuals and communities' (Dudgeon et al., 2010, p. 33).

Recent studies have recognised the need for cultural competence to be explicitly expressed. This reflects the fact that work undertaken by mental health researchers about indigenous people has been largely ineffective; reflecting the norms and values of the dominant Western systems that have failed indigenous people (due to interventions having little or no understanding of indigenous people's realities) (Brown, Morrissey, & Sherwood, 2006; Stanley, 2009). A range of recent reports and frameworks have documented the need for cultural competence training at all levels of engagement so that the needs of indigenous people are properly addressed (Walker & Sonn, 2010).

There has been considerable discussion about cultural competence in recent years, and a realisation that for it to be most effective, it needs to be addressed across a number of levels. *Cultural competence in health: a guide for policy, partnership and participation* (NHMRC, 2006) provides guidelines for cultural competence, and recognises four dimensions — systematic, organisational, professional and individual — to cultural competence. These self explanatory domains 'interrelate, so that cultural competence at an individual and organisational level is underpinned by systemic and organisational commitment and capacity' (p. 4).

Australian psychologists have been involved in discussions about the need for cultural competence for some years. Various dialogues have occurred in higher education and professional bodies (Dudgeon et al., 2000) and a range of different initiatives have been implemented in communities. The formation of the Australian Indigenous Psychologists Association (AIPA) in 2008 and various activities initiated by the AIPA, such as a roundtable discussion on racism and cultural competence workshops across the nation, have provided a catalyst for renewed engagement in the discipline. The Australian Psychological Society's commitment to develop a Reconciliation Action Plan, for example, augurs well for the future.

Despite these promising developments, progress towards addressing cultural competence in the discipline has, overall, been limited. When the handbook for psychologists (Dudgeon et al., 2000) was published, the contributors considered the work of progressive psychologists in the field (see Dudgeon, 2000). These historical discussions (see Sue & Sue, 1990; Walker & Sonn, 2010), as outlined in the body of this chapter, are still relevant in psychology today.

An enhanced cultural awareness about indigenous issues has not been achieved by mental health practitioners to the extent that it should have been by now. Practitioners, however, are still optimistic about the future. In a sense, contemporary psychologists have lived through a time of rapid and unforseen social changes. Looking back, it is fair to say that psychology has gone through considerable changes, and more is yet to come. In both our discipline and in society, things are better in many respects, yet there are still great challenges in other areas. Social problems, such as racism, continue to have a damaging influence, and I believe that contemporary psychologists are well placed to participate in responding to racism and to engage in dialogue about other social problems.

At the turn of the millennium, I wrote that psychologists need to acknowledge that we are an active part of the social fabric and that what we do as individuals and professionals can and does have an impact on society. This statement is still relevant today.

INTERIM SUMMARY

The psychology profession is learning to be more responsive to the needs of different cultural groups. Psychologists need to recognise that culture does influence the way we think and behave and be aware of their own cultural background, heritage and biases. ***Cultural competence*** refers to a psychologist's effectiveness in communicating and behaving appropriately with people from another culture, both in terms of understanding and being understood. This requires psychologists to become familiar with the personal history and cultural experience of people they work with, and to appreciate and respect cultural diversity.

Central question revisited

◆ Psychological universals versus culture-specific behaviours

We began this chapter with one central question: can psychological theories and findings be applied universally across all people or are they culture specific? In other words, to what extent is the interpretation of thoughts, feelings and behaviours universal, and to what extent are your interpretations of the world influenced by your cultural background?

Culture involves shared values, beliefs, attitudes and behaviours. These cultural differences help distinguish one group of people from another. Culture is a learned process, and shapes your awareness of the world around you.

One of the key ways to define cultural variability is the individualism–collectivism continuum. Collectivist cultures emphasise the importance of the group over individuals; individualist cultures emphasise the primacy of the individual over the group. Many indigenous cultures, such as the Aboriginal people of Australia, are collectivist in nature. Western societies are individualist. However, people from all cultures share very similar values, beliefs and goals in relation to academic achievement.

Today, multicultural countries like Australia and New Zealand are based on the blending and coexisting of many cultural groups. Many groups of people define themselves not only by nationality but by ethnicity, a shared sense of 'peoplehood' based on their geographic, language, cultural and religious origins. People continue to identify as Aboriginal because they share a common philosophical and historical bond that makes them feel as one people. For example, many Aboriginal people maintain important cultural practices including kinship relationships and community obligations.

Diversity may result in an increased mutual tolerance and understanding of different ethnic groups that is generally recognised as positive for both social and economic development. However, diversity can also be a source of conflict and a source of prejudice and racism. The Australian Psychological Society has provided guidelines for psychologists in dealing with cultural diversity, recommending actions to proactively reduce prejudice and racism.

The discipline of psychology is a product of the European and North American cultural environment. Most psychological theories and practices have been developed in Western countries. Consequently, the way psychologists understand human behaviour is bound and limited by these same cultural contexts. It therefore remains debatable whether they are totally relevant to people from other cultures. For example, psychology as a discipline is centred on the individual rather than the interaction between individuals. It needs to consider how the physical, economic and political environments, language, values, meanings and world views of different cultures affect behaviour. The psychology profession now recognises the increasing need to communicate effectively with people from other cultures — we need to train culturally competent psychologists who are aware of and show respect for the value systems and authority structures of people from different cultures. They also need to be aware of the impact of their own beliefs, stereotypes and cultural backgrounds in their interpretations of people's behaviour. Cross-cultural research should therefore involve close collaboration with people of different cultural groups to identify research needs from their perspective. The notion of psychological universals in explaining human behaviour highlights the similarities that possibly exist across different cultures. Psychologists need to appreciate the likenesses and value the differences to effectively practise across cultures.

◆

SUMMARY

1 Culture and methodological problems in the study of culture

- ***Culture*** refers to the shared rules that govern behaviour; it is a filter through which we see and understand our current reality. ***Cultural psychologists*** study the way in which people are affected by their culture. ***Cross-cultural psychologists*** compare the similarities and differences in behaviour across cultures.
- Psychologists use a number of different approaches to study culture and face a number of unique challenges in the process of conducting such research.
- Current initiatives promote close collaboration with indigenous peoples to identify research needs from their perspective. Six values underpin guidelines for ethical conduct of research with Aboriginals and Torres Strait Islanders: reciprocity, respect, equality, responsibility, survival and protection, and spirit and integrity.

2 The dimensions of cultural groups

- Every culture has a set of unwritten rules by which every member learns to abide. These rules cover such things as attitude to time, appropriate levels of emotional display and conversational distance, among others.
- People are often classified as belonging to either ***individualist cultures*** (which emphasise the primacy of the individual over the group) or ***collectivist cultures*** (which emphasise the group over individuals).

3 Cross-cultural relations in multicultural societies

- ***Multiculturalism*** refers to those situations where multiple cultures exist within a country. It is a feature of Australia and New Zealand and many countries in the Asia–Pacific region, where immigration policies have resulted in the blending and co-existence of many cultural groups.
- ***Culture shock*** is the feeling of disorientation and anxiety people experience as they encounter and adapt to the practices, rules and expectations of another culture. Such people may experience ***acculturation***, or undergo changes as a result of coming into contact with another culture. ***Assimilation*** occurs when a person is completely absorbed into the dominant culture.
- People have a number of identities: ***ethnic identity*** refers to members of an ethnic group identifying together through a shared sense of culture, language or religion; ***personal identity*** refers to a sense of who we are as individuals; and ***social identity*** refers to our sense of belonging to a larger group.
- ***Cultural stereotypes*** are beliefs that all members of a particular group share common traits or behaviours. ***Ethnocentrism*** occurs when a person's own culture influences the way they view the rest of the world, and is a normal response to growing up in a particular culture. ***Racial prejudice*** occurs when a person develops an unreasonable and negative stereotype about members of another racial or ethnic group. ***Racism*** involves an assumption of the inferiority of other ethnic groups and the subsequent unfair treatment of those groups on the basis of that assumed inferiority.
- Psychologists are actively exploring a number of approaches for reducing prejudice. These include legislative action (laws that make it illegal to discriminate on the basis of racial or ethnic background), cooperative tasks (getting people of different cultural backgrounds to work together) and ***contact hypothesis*** (spending time with people of different cultures). A combination of different approaches, aimed at all levels of society, will likely provide the best results.

4 Cultural identities of indigenous peoples in Australia and New Zealand

- ***Indigenous psychology*** promotes psychologies that are not imposed; that are influenced by the cultural contexts in which people live; that are developed from within the culture; and that result in locally relevant psychological knowledge.

- Aboriginal Australians are the original inhabitants of Australia's mainland. Their traditional communities had complex social structures, such as the kinship system. The occupation of the British had a dramatic impact on Australian indigenous culture and all Aboriginals have been affected in some way by the 'Stolen Generation'. Contemporary Aboriginal identity is extremely diverse, reflecting the impacts of colonisation and also cultural heritage of pre-European life. Aboriginal peoples have retained and maintained important cultural practices and share a common philosophical and historical bond that makes them feel as one people.
- The Torres Strait Islander people are the original inhabitants of the group of small islands located in the Torres Strait. Like Aboriginals, kinship affiliation was the traditional foundation of community life. They have a rich tradition of art and craft work, and like Aboriginal Australians, their traditional culture was severely dislocated by colonisation. However, cultural identity remains extremely important to Torres Strait Islanders, and many continue to identify as a group through shared cultural practices, languages and traditions.
- The Maori are the original inhabitants of New Zealand whose sense of identity was severely affected by the European colonisation. Today, many Maori people identify with an *iwi* (tribal) group as well as feeling a common ethnic identity that reflects their experience of British occupation and their changed social conditions such as urbanisation.

5 Promoting cross-cultural interactions

- Education is influenced by culture. Education systems need to create inclusive learning environments for students, especially in multicultural countries like Australia and New Zealand. Such initiatives will help ensure that teachers are both aware of and sensitive to the histories, cultures, languages and learning styles of students with different cultural backgrounds.
- The discipline of psychology is a product of European and North American cultural environment and psychological theories and methods may not be relevant to people from other cultures.
- Cultural differences may influence all aspects of the communication process and cause misunderstandings and miscommunication across cultures. Psychologists therefore need to understand and respect the cultural context in which such communications take place.
- The psychology profession is learning to be more responsive to the needs of different cultural groups. Psychologists need to recognise that culture does influence the way we think and behave and to be aware of their own cultural background, heritage and biases.
- ***Cultural competence*** refers to a psychologist's effectiveness in communicating and behaving appropriately with people from another culture, both in terms of understanding and being understood. This requires psychologists to become familiar with the personal history and cultural experience of people they work with, and to appreciate and respect cultural diversity.

KEY TERMS

REVIEW QUESTIONS

1. Distinguish between the roles of cultural psychologists and cross-cultural psychologists.
2. Outline some of the methodological challenges in the study of culture.
3. Compare and contrast individualist cultures and collectivist cultures.
4. Explain the difference between personal identity and social identity.
5. Describe the approaches taken by a culturally competent psychologist.

DISCUSSION QUESTIONS

1. Why is culture such a difficult construct to define?
2. How can racial prejudice be reduced?
3. How has culture shaped the identities of Aboriginal people in Australia today?

APPLICATION QUESTIONS

1. Test your understanding of how culture influences perceptions, attitudes and behaviours by identifying each of the following scenarios as an example of one of the following constructs: cultural stereotypes, assimilation, acculturation and ethnocentrism.
   (a) Lillian is a Singaporean student who studied on campus in Australia for a year. She observed that many Australian students were very active in their approaches to learning and would openly challenge teachers' authority. She believed this approach was inferior to the respect displayed by students to teachers back home in Singapore.
   (b) Ten-year-old Marty is a fast runner who enjoys racing at carnivals. However, an Aboriginal boy named Wayne always beats him whenever they race for the age champion trophy. Marty concludes that all Aboriginal children are fast runners.
   (c) Athena was born in Greece but came to live in Australia when she was one. When she is asked, she proudly identifies herself as an Australian and shows little interest in her Greek heritage.
   (d) Hasam emigrated from Lebanon at age 15 and is now undertaking tertiary studies at a metropolitan university in Australia. He maintains a strong loyalty to and interest in Lebanon but is slowing coming to identify with and feel part of the Australian culture by socialising with other Australian students in his class.
2. The following activity is designed to help you identify ways in which ethnicity influences your perceptions of the world (Okun, Fried, & Okun, 1999). To achieve this goal, you should complete the following steps:
   (a) List as many different ethnic groups you can think of.
   (b) For one hour, observe people who frequent a busy public place, such as a coffee shop, a bus or train station, or a park. Then try to label each person into a different 'ethnic' group. What criteria did you use to classify people into different groups? What types of people did you tend to group together? Which types of people were difficult to label? Why?
   (c) Repeat the previous step with a partner who belongs to the same ethnic group as you. Check to see if you agreed on the ethnic categories. Discuss why or why not.
   (d) Repeat the activity with another person who comes from a completely different ethnic group. How much did you agree on the ethnic groupings? Discuss why or why not.

The solutions to the application questions can be found on page 835.

MULTIMEDIA RESOURCES

The *Cyberpsych* multimedia resource is available *as an option* to accompany this textbook to further develop your understanding of many key psychology concepts. *Cyberpsych* contains a wealth of rich media content and activities, and for this chapter includes a video case on the Stolen Generation.

Solutions to application questions

Chapter 1

1. The principal aim of peak bodies such as the Australian Psychological Society (APS) and the New Zealand Psychological Society (NZPsS) is to advance psychology as a discipline and a profession. Other benefits include opportunities for networking, and access to a wide range of resources and support services. Students are also encouraged to become members of these professional associations and you can learn more about the benefits by accessing the following websites on the Internet:
   - www.psychsociety.com.au/aps/
   - www.psychology.org.nz/
2. The career prospects for people with psychology qualifications in Australia are currently very good. You can find out more information about graduate destination and industry employment trends by accessing the following websites on the Internet:
   - *GradsOnline* web site at www.gradlink.edu.au
   - The Department of Education, Science and Training (DEST) site at http://jobguide.dest.gov.au
   - The Australian government's *myfuture* site at http://myfuture.edu.au
   - The Department of Education, Training, and Youth Affairs (DETYA) job guide at www.detya.gov.au/jobguideonline
   - The *Australian Job Search* site at http://jobsearch.gov.au

   The New Zealand government also has a *Kiwi Careers* site at www.careers.co.nz/jop.htm

Chapter 2

1. (a) Experimental research
   (b) Follow the six steps of conceiving and executing an experiment: frame hypothesis; operationalise variables; develop standardised procedures; select and assign participants to conditions; apply statistical techniques to the results; and draw conclusions.
   (c) Independent variable — difficulty of examination questions (e.g. very hard or very easy); Dependent variable — students' evaluations of course.
   (d) Yes, a control group would be important as it would serve as a comparison group (i.e. use an exam containing both hard and easy questions and check study's results against the students' evaluations for this group).
   (e) Demand characteristics could be controlled by using a single-blind study; a double-blind study would also control for experimenter bias.
2. (a) naturalistic observation
   (b) case study
   (c) correlational research
   (d) quasi-experiment
   (e) survey research
   (f) experiment
3. (a) memory is the dependent variable (DV)
   (b) alcohol is the independent variable (IV)
4. (a) Theoretical IV = *Colour of the water*
   (b) Manipulation of IV = *three levels: red, green and blue food colouring*
   (c) Theoretical DV = *rate of water evaporation*
   (d) Measurement of DV: *millimetres of water remaining in the vial after 12 hours*
5. (a) Advantages of experimental research: control over variables can eliminate alternative explanations; able to draw inferences about cause and effect.
   (b) Disadvantages of experimental research: due to practical or ethical reasons some phenomenon cannot be tested in a laboratory; potential detrimental influence of confounding variables; artificial setting not applicable to real life.
6. (a) Naturalistic observation is an in-depth observation of a phenomenon in its natural setting.
   (b) An example of naturalistic observation is sitting behind a tree and observing the behaviour of motorists as they encounter a stop or give way sign.
   (c) Advantages of naturalistic observation: results are more applicable to real life; can be used to study animal and human behaviour.
   (d) Disadvantages of naturalistic observation: difficult to remain undetected which may influence behaviour; cannot control for confounding variables; cannot draw inferences about cause and effect.
7. (a) A case study is an in-depth observation of one person or a small group of individuals. For example, you could conduct an in-depth observation of a person who had been electrocuted and examine the impact that experience had on his or her cognitive abilities.
   (b) Advantage of case studies: provides useful information for rare events and behaviours that are difficult or unethical to reproduce experimentally.
   (c) Disadvantage of case studies: small sample size; susceptible to researcher or observer bias.
8. (a) Survey research involves asking a large sample of people questions, often about attitudes or behaviours using questionnaires or interviews. An example of a large survey using a questionnaire is the Australian census.
   (b) Advantages of survey research: fast collection of large numbers of data; relatively cheap to conduct; can gather data on behaviour and/or thoughts that are difficult to observe.
   (c) Disadvantages of survey research: sample may not reflect the general population; information can be unreliable; cannot draw inferences about cause and effect.

Chapter 2 Supplement

1. Mean = 6.5
   Mode = 8
   Median – 8
2. Standard deviation = 5

Chapter 3

1. (a) basal ganglia
   (b) occipital lobe
   (c) Broca's area, in the left frontal lobe
2. The primary and association areas of all four lobes are involved in this event. The occipital lobe processes your sight of your friend. The temporal lobe processes your calling out his name. The frontal lobe processes your plan to hurry and run to catch up with him. The parietal lobe processes the sensory feedback that adjusts your speed and balance.
3. The response for question 3 is provided at the end of this section on page 836.*

4. • Abstract thinking, planning, social skills — Frontal lobe
   • Necessary for speech production — Broca's area
   • Controls vision — Occipital lobe
   • Touch, spatial orientation, non-verbal thinking — Parietal lobe
   • Receives sensory information — Somatosensory cortex
   • Language, hearing, visual pattern recognition — Temporal lobe
   • Coordinates movement — Cerebellum
   • Speech comprehension — Wernicke's area
   • A relay centre — Thalamus
   • Involved in remembering emotionally significant events — Amygdala
   • Responsible for emotions, motivation, learning, and memory — Limbic system
   • Controls basic life functions — Medulla
   • Necessary for storing new memories — Hippocampus
   • Helps regulates behaviour — Hypothalamus
   • Consists of the tectum and the tegmentum — Midbrain

Chapter 4

1. (a) The absolute threshold for taste is a teaspoon of sugar in about 10 litres of water. Thus, two teaspoons of sugar in a cup of coffee (about 250 millilitres) is above the threshold level, and easily detected by Andrew.
   (b) According to signal detection theory, sensitivity and response bias will influence the judgement about the presence or absence of a stimulus. Karen is more likely to hear a noise in the middle of the night because she has just been burgled.
   (c) According to Weber's Law, when a person compares two stimuli (fish and chips versus razor), the size of the change necessary to produce a just noticeable difference is a constant proportion of the original stimulus. In this case, an extra \$6.00 for the fish and chips is a much larger proportion of \$15.00 than it is of \$90.00, the price of the electric razor. Therefore, Yong Wah spending an extra \$6.00 for the electric razor would not produce a just noticeable difference. Six dollars represents almost half (40 percent) of the price of the fish and chips. A just noticeable different for the electric razor would be 40 percent of the price, or \$36.00.
   (d) Sensory adaptation is a reduction in sensitivity resulting from unchanging, repetitious stimulation. Thus, Giovanni and his friends may not have noticed the smoke and charcoal odour because they had been in the room for a while.
2. (a) Similarity is the tendency to group similar elements together.
   (c) Proximity is the tendency to group together objects that are close to one another.
   (d) Closure is the tendency to perceive incomplete figures as complete.
   (e) Simplicity is the tendency to perceive the simplest pattern possible.

Chapter 5

1. (a) Psychodynamic perspective — the dream represents unconscious thoughts, feelings and wishes.
   (b) Biological perspective — the dream has no significance.
   (c) Cognitive perspective — the dream represents dominant thoughts.
2. (a) Amphetamines
   (b) Lysergic acid diethylamide (LSD)
   (c) Cocaine
   (d) Alcohol
   (e) Marijuana (Note: abusive effects of marijuana use remain controversial)

Chapter 6

1. (a) UCS = Roof torn off in cyclone
   UCR = Feeling terrified
   CS = Weather person on television talking about cyclone
   CR = Trembling
   (b) UCS = Ice cream
   UCR = Gets excited
   CS = *Play School* theme song
   CR = Jumps excitedly and repeats the words 'ice cream'
   (c) UCS = Seafood
   UCR = Being sick
   CS = Bright blue walls
   CR = Feeling sick in the stomach
   (d) UCS = Burning his arm
   UCR = Being in pain
   CS = Smell of fresh bread
   CR = Panic attack
   (e) UCS = Marriage proposal
   UCR = Felt ecstatic
   CS = The song *Unforgettable*
   CR = Felt all warm and tingly inside
2. (a) Punishment; positive reinforcement; negative reinforcement; extinction
   (b) Continuous reinforcement; variable ratio; fixed interval; fixed ratio; variable interval
   (c) Classical conditioning; social learning; operant conditioning; combination of classical conditioning and operant conditioning

Chapter 7

1. (a) procedural memory
   (b) explicit memory
   (c) semantic memory
   (d) implicit memory
   (e) prospective memory
   (f) declarative memory
   (g) everyday memory
   (h) episodic memory
   (i) flashbulb memory
   (j) retrospective memory
2. (a) motivated forgetting
   (c) proactive interference
   (d) decay theory
   (e) retroactive interference

Chapter 8

1. (a) availability heuristic
   (b) deductive reasoning
   (c) analogical reasoning
   (d) inductive reasoning
   (e) representativeness heuristic
2. *String problem solution:* Attach the screwdriver to one string and swing it like a pendulum until it can be reached while holding the other string. Then untie the screwdriver and tie the two strings together.
   (a) implicit problem solving
   (b) functional fixedness
   (c) the use of algorithms
   (d) mental set
   (e) mental simulation
   (f) confirmation bias
   (g) developing subgoals

Chapter 9

1. (a) spatial
   (b) interpersonal
   (c) linguistic/verbal
   (d) musical
   (e) logical/mathematical
   (f) bodily/kinaesthetic
   (g) intrapersonal
   (h) naturalistic
2. (a) practical
   (b) analytical
   (c) creative

Chapter 10

1. (a) performance-approach goals
   (b) mastery goals
   (c) performance-avoidance goals
2. (a) James-Lange theory
   (b) Schachter-Singer theory
   (c) Cannon-Bard theory

Chapter 11

1. (a) reaction formation
   (b) repression
   (c) sublimation
   (d) projection

(e) regression
(f) displacement
(g) rationalisation

2. (a) high Openness to Experience, high Agreeableness, and low Conscientiousness
   (b) low Neuroticism and low Extroversion
   (c) low Openness to Experience and High Neuroticism

Chapter 12

1. (a) sequential
   (b) longitudinal
   (c) cross-sectional
2. (a) formal operational
   (b) preoperational
   (c) sensorimotor
   (d) concrete operational

Chapter 13

1. (a) secure
   (b) avoidant
   (c) ambivalent
   (d) disorganised
2. (a) identity versus identity confusion
   (b) initiative versus guilt
   (c) autonomy versus shame and doubt
   (d) integrity versus despair
   (e) industry versus inferiority
   (f) basic trust versus mistrust
   (g) generativity versus stagnation
   (h) intimacy versus isolation

Chapter 14

1. (a) theory of planned behaviour
   (b) theory of reasoned action
   (c) health belief model
   (d) protection motivation theory of health
2. (a) emotion-focused strategy
   (b) social support
   (c) problem-focused

Chapter 15

1. (a) personality disordered
   (b) normal
   (c) psychotic
   (d) neurotic
2. (a) dissociative identity disorder
   (b) paranoid personality disorder
   (c) bipolar disorder
   (d) catatonic schizophrenia

Chapter 16

1. (a) systematic desensitisation
   (b) flooding
   (c) operant technique
   (d) participatory modelling
   (e) social skills training
   (f) cognitive therapy
2. (a) antipsychotic medication
   (b) psychosurgery
   (c) mood stabilising medication
   (d) antidepressant medication
   (e) electroconvulsive therapy
   (f) antianxiety medication

Chapter 17

1. (a) consensus
   (b) distinctiveness
   (c) consistency
2. (a) stereotype
   (c) fundamental attribution error
   (d) self-serving bias

Chapter 18

1. (a) democratic
   (b) autocratic
   (c) laissez-faire
2. (a) low-balling
   (c) door-in-the-face technique
   (d) foot-in-the-door technique

Chapter 19

1. (a) ethnocentrism
   (b) cultural stereotype
   (c) assimilation
   (d) acculturation
2. There are no set answers to this question as the ethnic groups identified will vary according to the level of cultural diversity in your place of residence. However, you are strongly encouraged to share your answers and experiences with other students in your class.

*Chapter 3 (continued)

The response to question 3 for chapter 3 is shown below.

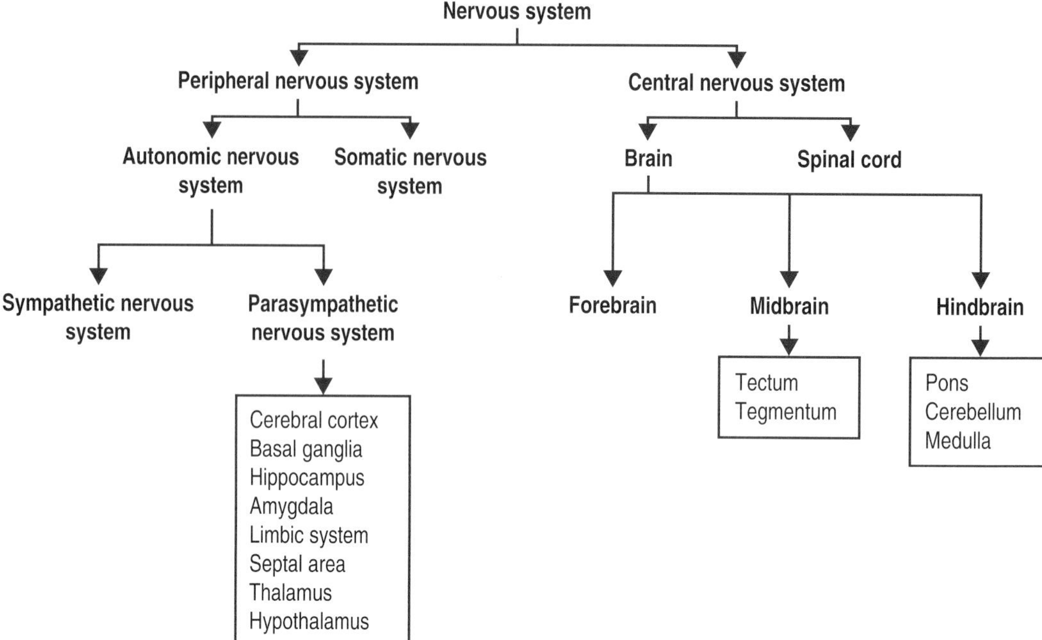

Glossary

A

ABC theory of psychopathology Albert Ellis' theory of psychopathology, in which A refers to activating conditions, B to belief systems and C to emotional consequences (p. 665)

Aboriginality (Australian government definition) An Aboriginal or Torres Strait Islander person is a person of Aboriginal or Torres Strait Islander descent, who identifies as such and is accepted as such by the community in which they live (p. 809)

absolute threshold The minimum amount of physical energy (stimulation) needed for an observer to notice a stimulus (p. 132)

absorptive phase The phase of metabolism during which a person is ingesting food (p. 385)

accommodation In vision, the changes in the shape of the lens that focus light rays; in Piaget's theory, the modification of schemas to fit reality (pp. 138, 484)

acculturation The changes that groups and individuals undergo when they come into contact with another culture. It can also mean competence in a second culture without complete acceptance. (p. 796)

acculturative stress The stress people experience while trying to adapt to a new culture (p. 585)

acetylcholine (ACh) A neurotransmitter involved in muscle contractions, learning and memory (p. 95)

acquisition In classical conditioning, the initial stage of learning in which the conditioned response becomes associated with the conditioned stimulus (p. 224)

action potential A temporary shift in the polarity of the cell membrane, which leads to the firing of a neuron (p. 91)

activational effects Effects of hormones activating brain circuitry to produce psychobiological changes (p. 394)

actualising tendency The primary motivation in humans, according to Carl Rogers, which includes a range of needs that humans experience, from the basic needs for food and drink to the needs to be open to experience and express one's true self (p. 451)

actual self People's views of how they actually are (p. 728)

adaptive traits A term applied to traits that help organisms adjust to their environment (p. 19)

adrenal glands Endocrine glands located above the kidneys that secrete adrenaline and other hormones during emergency situations (p. 96)

adrenaline A hormone that triggers physiological arousal, particularly in potential danger situations (p. 96)

adult attachment Patterns of mental representation, emotion and proximity-seeking in adults related to childhood attachment patterns (p. 510)

aetiology Causes of a disorder (p. 606)

affect The pattern of observable behaviours that express an individual's emotions (p. 401)

affiliation Interaction with friends or acquaintances (p. 397)

ageism A form of prejudice against old people comparable to racism and sexism (p. 478)

agency Motives for achievement, mastery, power, autonomy and other self-oriented goals (p. 397)

aggression Verbal or physical behaviour aimed at harming another person or living being (p. 752)

agoraphobia The fear of being in places or situations from which escape might be difficult (p. 634)

alcoholism The tendency to use or abuse alcohol to a degree that leads to social or occupational dysfunction (pp. 569, 617)

algorithm A systematic problem-solving procedure that inevitably produces a solution (p. 308)

altered states of consciousness Deviations in subjective experience from a normal waking state (p. 205)

alternation Acculturation that involves bicultural competence (p. 796)

altruism Behaving in a way that helps another person with no apparent gain, or with potential cost, to oneself (pp. 736, 747)

Alzheimer's disease A progressive and incurable illness that destroys neurons in the brain, causing severe impairment of memory, reasoning, perception, language and behaviour (p. 495)

ambivalence Conflicting feelings or intentions (p. 426)

ambivalent attachment style Response to separation in which infants who are angry and rejecting simultaneously indicate a clear desire to be close to the mother (p. 507)

amplitude The difference between the minimum and maximum pressure levels in a sound wave, measured in decibels; amplitude corresponds to the psychological property of loudness (p. 149)

amygdala A brain structure associated with the expression of rage and fear and calculation of the emotional significance of a stimulus (p. 106)

analogical reasoning The process by which people understand a novel situation in terms of a familiar one (p. 306)

anal stage The psychosexual phase occurring roughly around ages two to three, which is characterised by conflicts with parents over compliance and defiance (p. 429)

analysis of variance (ANOVA) A statistical procedure used to compare the means of two or more groups (p. 82)

analytical intelligence Abilities measured by IQ tests in academic settings (p. 359)

androgen insensitivity syndrome A condition in which androgens are secreted in utero, but a genetic defect leads to an absence of androgen receptors, so that a genetic male develops female genitalia (p. 393)

anorexia nervosa An eating disorder in which a person refuses to eat, starving themself to the point that physical complications and sometimes death may occur (p. 637)

anterograde amnesia An inability to learn anything new (p. 290)

antibodies Protein molecules that attach themselves to foreign agents in the body, marking them for destruction (p. 588)

antidepressant medications Biological treatment of depression that increases the amount of norepinephrine and/or serotonin available in synapses (p. 675)

antipsychotic medications Medications used to treat schizophrenia and other psychotic states, which have sedating effects and reduce positive symptoms such as hallucinations and delusions (p. 674)

antisocial personality disorder A personality disorder marked by irresponsible and socially disruptive behaviour in a variety of areas (p. 641)

anxiety disorder A disorder characterised by intense, frequent or continuous anxiety, which may lead to disruptive avoidance behaviour (p. 633)

appeals to authority The fallacy that an argument must be true because of the authority or reputation of the person making it (p. 69)

appeals to popularity The fallacy that a popular or widely believed argument is true (p. 69)

arguments directed to the person The fallacy in argument based on attacking the authors of alternative arguments (p. 69)

assimilation (In Piaget's theory of cognitive development) the interpretation of actions or events in terms of one's present schemas (p. 484)

assimilation (In cultural psychology) acculturation that involves absorption into the dominant culture and abandonment of the traditional culture (p. 796)

association areas The areas of cortex involved in putting together perceptions, ideas and plans (p. 109)

attachment Enduring ties of affection that children form with their primary caregivers and that become the basis for later love relationships (p. 505)

attachment motivation The desire for physical and psychological proximity to an attachment figure (p. 397)

attention The process of focusing consciousness on a limited range of experience (p. 188)

attention-deficit hyperactivity disorder (ADHD) A disorder characterised by age-inappropriate inattention, impulsiveness and hyperactivity (p. 616)

attitude An association between an action or object and an evaluation (pp. 557, 695)

attitude accessibility The ease with which an attitude comes to mind or is activated (p. 695)

attitude importance The personal relevance of an attitude and the psychological significance of that attitude for an individual (p. 695)

attitude inoculation Building up a receiver's resistance to an opposing attitude by presenting weak arguments for it or forewarning of a strong opposing persuasive appeal (p. 700)

attitude strength The durability of an attitude (its persistence and resistance to change) and its impact on behaviour (p. 695)

attitudinal ambivalence A condition in which an attitude object is associated with conflicting evaluative responses (p. 697)

attitudinal coherence The extent to which an attitude is internally consistent (p. 698)

attribution The process of making inferences about the causes of one's own and others' thoughts, feelings and behaviour (pp. 413, 717)

attributional style A person's habitual manner of assigning causes to behaviours or events (p. 718)

audition Hearing (p. 147)

auditory nerve The bundle of sensory neurons that transmit auditory information from the ear to the brain (p. 150)

augmentation Attributional phenomenon in which people emphasise an internal explanation for a behaviour because it occurred despite situational pressures (p. 718)

authoritarian A way of parenting that places high value on obedience and respect for authority (p. 514)

authoritarian personality A personality type that is prone to hate people who are different or downtrodden (p. 710)

authoritative A way of parenting that sets standards for children and firmly enforces them but also provides explanations for the parents' actions and encourages verbal give-and-take (p. 514)

automatic thoughts The things people say spontaneously to themselves, which can lead to irrational feelings and behaviours (p. 665)

automatisation The process of executing mental processes with increasing efficiency, so that they require less and less attention (p. 489)

autonomic nervous system The part of the peripheral nervous system that serves visceral or internal bodily structures connected with basic life processes, such as the beating of the heart and breathing. It consists of two parts: the sympathetic nervous system and the parasympathetic nervous system. (p. 97)

autonomy versus shame and doubt In Erikson's theory, the stage in which children begin to walk, talk and get a sense of themselves as independent sources of will and power (p. 536)

availability heuristic A strategy that leads people to judge the frequency of a class of events or the likelihood of something happening on the basis of how easy it is to retrieve from explicit memory (p. 312)

aversion therapy The introduction of something aversive as a means of discouraging a negative health habit (p. 571)

avoidance learning A negative reinforcement procedure in which the behaviour of an organism is reinforced by the prevention of an expected aversive event (p. 234)

avoidant attachment style Response to separation in which infants ignore the mother when she returns (p. 507)

axon The long extension from the cell body of a neuron through which electrical impulses pass (p. 89)

B

babbling A child's earliest language utterances that are spontaneous and incomprehensible (p. 331)

Barnum effect A broad interpretation of personality that is so broad it could apply to anyone, and so is accepted as fact (p. 450)

barriers Costs of terminating a health behaviour (p. 556)

basal ganglia A set of structures located near the thalamus and hypothalamus involved in the control of movement and in judgements that require minimal conscious thought (p. 107)

basic emotions Feeling states common to the human species from which other feeling states are derived (p. 407)

basic level The level of categorisation to which people naturally go; the level at which objects share distinctive common attributes (p. 303)

basic trust versus mistrust In Erikson's theory, the stage in which infants come to trust others or to perceive the social world as unfriendly or unreliable (p. 536)

beeper studies An experience-sampling technique that has provided a more natural window to the flow of consciousness in everyday life (p. 190)

behavioural analysis In cognitive–behavioural therapy, the process of assessing the symptom and the stimuli or thoughts associated with it (p. 661)

behavioural approach system (BAS) The brain structure that is attuned to rewards, and leads people to seek out stimulation and arousal (p. 443)

behavioural genetics A field that examines the genetic and environmental bases of differences among individuals on psychological traits (p. 21)

behavioural inhibition system (BIS) The brain structure that is attuned to punishment, and leads people to avoid potential dangerous or painful experiences (p. 443)

behavioural neuroscience A field of investigation that examines the physical basis of psychological phenomena such as motivation, emotion and stress; also called biopsychology (p. 5)

behaviourism See behaviourist perspective (p. 13)

behaviourist perspective The perspective pioneered by John Watson and B. F. Skinner, which focuses on the relationship between observable behaviours and environmental events or stimuli; also called behaviourism. (p. 13)

behaviour–outcome expectancy Belief that a certain behaviour will lead to a particular outcome (p. 438)

benefits Beneficial consequences associated with terminating a negative health behaviour (p. 556)

benzodiazepines Antianxiety medications that indirectly affect the action of norepinephrine (p. 676)

bilingual Able to speak two different languages (p. 321)

binocular cells Neurons that receive information from both eyes (p. 166)

binocular cues Visual input integrated from two eyes that provides perception of depth (p. 166)

biofeedback A procedure for monitoring autonomic physiological processes and learning to alter them at will (p. 243)

biomedical model A reductionistic view of illness, reducing disease to biological causes at the level of individual cells (p. 552)

biopsychology The field that examines the physical basis of psychological phenomena such as motivation, emotion and stress; also called behavioural neuroscience (p. 5)

biopsychosocial model The idea that health and illness stem from a combination of biological, psychological and social factors (p. 553)

bipolar cells Neurons in the retina that combine information from many receptors and excite ganglion cells (p. 138)

bipolar disorder A psychological disorder marked by extreme mood swings; also called manic-depression (p. 628)

blindsight A phenomenon in which individuals with cortical lesions have no conscious visual awareness but can make discriminations about objects placed in front of them (p. 143)

blind spot The point on the retina where the optic nerve leaves the eye and which contains no receptor cells (p. 138)

blind studies Studies in which participants are kept unaware of or 'blind' to important aspects of the research (p. 52)

blocking When a stimulus fails to elicit a conditioned response because it is combined with another stimulus that already elicits the response (p. 229)

body mass index Statistical index that reflects a person's weight in kilograms divided by the height in metres squared (p. 560)

borderline personality disorder A personality disorder characterised by extremely unstable interpersonal relationships, dramatic mood swings, an unstable sense of identity, intense fears of abandonment, manipulativeness and impulsive behaviour (p. 641)

bottom-up processing Perceptual processing that starts with raw sensory data that feed 'up' to the brain; what is perceived is determined largely by the features of the stimuli reaching the sense organs (p. 173)

bounded rationality The notion that people are rational within constraints imposed by their environment, goals and abilities (p. 312)

Broca's area A brain structure located in the left frontal lobe at the base of the motor cortex, involved in the movements of the mouth and tongue necessary for speech production and in the use of grammar (p. 112)

buffering hypothesis The idea that social support provides a buffer against the harmful effects of stress (p. 592)

bulimia A disorder characterised by a binge-and-purge syndrome in which the person binges on food and then either induces vomiting or uses laxatives to purge (p. 637)

bystander intervention A form of altruism involving helping a person in need (p. 750)

C

Cannon–Bard theory A theory of emotion that asserts that emotion-inducing stimuli elicit both emotional experience and bodily response (p. 402)

Cartesian dualism The doctrine of dual spheres of mind and body (pp. 14, 552)

case study In-depth observation of one participant or a small group of participants (p. 55)

castration complex In Freud's theory, the fear the boy has in the phallic stage that his father will castrate him for his wishes towards his mother (p. 430)

catastrophes Rare, unexpected disasters such as earthquakes, floods and other traumatic events that affect a group of people (p. 585)

categorical variable A variable comprised of groupings, classifications or categories (p. 44)

categorisation The process of identifying an object as an instance of a category, recognising its similarity to some objects and dissimilarity to others (p. 300)

category A grouping based on a common property (p. 300)

cell body The part of the neuron which includes a nucleus containing the genetic material of the cell (the chromosomes), as well as other microstructures vital to cell functioning (p. 89)

cellular theory of illness The idea that illness and disease result from abnormalities within individual cells (p. 552)

central nervous system (CNS) The brain and spinal cord (p. 96)

central route to persuasion A method of persuasion that involves inducing the recipient of a message to think carefully and weigh the arguments (p. 701)

centration (In Piaget's theory of cognitive development) the tendency to focus on one perceptually striking feature of an object without considering other features that might be relevant (p. 485)

cerebellum A large bulge in the dorsal or back area of the brain, responsible for the coordination of smooth, well-sequenced movements as well as maintaining equilibrium and regulating postural reflexes (p. 104)

cerebral cortex The many-layered surface of the cerebrum, which allows complex voluntary movements, permits subtle discriminations among complex sensory patterns and makes symbolic thinking possible (p. 109)

cerebral hemispheres The two halves of the cerebrum (p. 110)

cerebrum The 'thinking' centre of the brain, which includes the cortex and subcortical structures such as the basal ganglia and limbic system (p. 100)

chaining A process of learning in which a sequence of already established behaviours is reinforced step by step (p. 243)

Chi-square (or χ^2) test A test of statistical significance used when both the independent and dependent variables are categorical (p. 82)

chromosomes Strands of DNA arranged in pairs (p. 118)

chronemics The use of time in communication (p. 821)

chunking The process of organising information into small, meaningful bits to aid memory (p. 268)

circadian rhythm Biological rhythm that evolved around the daily cycles of light and dark (p. 197)

classical conditioning A procedure by which a previously neutral stimulus comes to elicit a response after it is paired with a stimulus that automatically elicits that response; the first type of learning to be studied systematically (p. 223)

client-centred therapy A therapeutic approach developed by Carl Rogers, based on the assumption that psychological difficulties result from incongruence between one's concept of self and one's actual experience, and that empathy is curative (p. 667)

clinical psychologist A psychologist who delivers services in a health care setting such as a hospital or mental health facility (p. 655)

clinical syndromes A constellation of symptoms that tend to occur together (p. 612)

closure A Gestalt rule of perception which states that people tend to perceive incomplete figures as complete (p. 162)

cochlea The three-chambered tube in the inner ear in which sound is transduced (p. 150)

cognition Thought and memory (p. 17)

cognitive–behavioural Approach in clinical psychology in which practitioners integrate an understanding of classical and operant conditioning with a cognitive–social perspective (pp. 607, 660)

cognitive complexity The intricacy of thoughts about different attitude objects (p. 696)

cognitive dissonance A phenomenon in which a person experiences a discrepancy between an attitude and a behaviour or between an attitude and a new piece of information incongruent with it, which leads to a state of tension and a subsequent change in attitude, behaviour or perception (p. 704)

cognitive distortions Cognitive mechanisms by which a depressed person transforms neutral or positive information in a depressive direction (p. 630)

cognitive maps Mental representations of visual space (p. 244)

cognitive perspective A psychological perspective that focuses on the way people perceive, process and retrieve information (p. 17)

cognitive–social theory A theory of learning that emphasises the role of thought and social learning in behaviour (p. 244)

cognitive therapy A psychological treatment that focuses on the thought processes that underlie psychological symptoms (p. 665)

cognitive unconscious Information processing mechanisms that operate outside of awareness, such as procedural memory and implicit associative processes, as opposed to the psychodynamic unconscious, which includes information the person is motivated to keep from awareness (p. 192)

cohort effects Differences among age groups associated with differences in the culture (p. 471)

collectivist cultures Cultures that emphasise the group over individuals (p. 788)

colour constancy The tendency to perceive the colour of objects as stable despite changing illumination (p. 169)

common factors Shared elements in psychotherapies that produce positive outcomes (p. 682)

companionate love Love that involves deep affection, friendship and emotional intimacy (p. 740)

competences Skills and abilities used for solving problems (p. 438)

complexity The extent to which a sound wave is composed of multiple frequencies (p. 149)

compromise formations A single behaviour, or a complex pattern of thought and action, which typically reflects compromises among multiple (and often conflicting) forces (p. 427)

compulsion An intentional behaviour or mental act performed in a stereotyped fashion (p. 634)

computerised axial tomography (CAT) scan A brain-scanning technique used to detect lesions (p. 61)

concept A mental representation of a category of objects, ideas or events that share common properties (p. 300)

concrete operational stage Piaget's third stage of cognitive development, which falls between the ages of seven and 12, in which children are capable of mentally manipulating internal representations of concrete objects in ways that are reversible (p. 486)

conditioned response (CR) In classical conditioning, a response that has been learned (p. 224)

conditioned stimulus (CS) A stimulus that the organism has learned to associate with the unconditioned stimulus (p. 224)

conditioning A form of learning (p. 223)

conditions Values or versions of the independent variable that vary across experimental groups (p. 50)

conditions of worth In Carl Rogers' theory, standards children internalise that they must meet in order to esteem themselves (p. 451)

conduct disorder A childhood disorder in which a child persistently violates the rights of others as well as societal norms (p. 616)

cones One of two types of photoreceptors, which are specialised for colour vision and allow perception of fine detail (p. 138)

confabulation Inventing detailed and plausible false memories due to gaps in memory caused by amnesia (p. 258)

confirmation bias The tendency to seek out information that confirms one's hypotheses (pp. 310, 721)

conflict A battle between opposing motives (p. 427)

conflict model Theoretical model of adolescence that holds that conflict and crisis are normal in adolescence (p. 538)

conformity The process of changing attitudes or behaviour to accommodate the standards of a group (p. 762)

confounding variable A variable that produces effects that are confused or confounded with the effects of the independent variable (p. 52)

congenital adrenal hyperplasia A disorder in which the adrenal glands secrete too much androgen, thus masculinising the genitals in females (p. 394)

connectionism A model of human cognitive processes in which many cognitive processes occur simultaneously so that a representation is spread out (i.e. distributed) throughout a network of interacting processing units; also called parallel distributed processing (PDP) (p. 315)

conscious mental processes Processes that involve a subjective awareness of stimuli, feelings or ideas (pp. 191, 426)

consciousness The subjective awareness of mental events (p. 187)

consensus In attribution theory, a normative response in a social group (p. 717)

conservation psychology The study of the reciprocal relationships between humans and nature, with a focus on changing attitudes and behaviours to encourage conservation of the environment (pp. 27, 702)

conservation Recognition that basic properties of an object remain stable even though superficial properties may change (p. 486)

consistency In attribution theory, the extent to which a person always responds in the same way to the same stimulus (p. 717)

constraint satisfaction The tendency to settle on a cognitive solution that satisfies as many constraints as possible in order to achieve the best fit to the data (p. 316)

contact comfort The ties that bind an infant to its caregivers (p. 505)

contact hypothesis The hypothesis that the more contact there is between people from different groups, the more they will break down any barriers or prejudices (p. 802)

context of discovery The part of the scientific process in which phenomena are observed, hypotheses are framed and theories are built (p. 70)

context of justification The part of the scientific process in which hypotheses are tested (p. 70)

contextual learning Learning not only a simple association between a CS and a UCS but also the context for that association (p. 232)

continuity model The theoretical model that holds that adolescence for most individuals is essentially continuous with childhood and adulthood and not distinguished by turbulence (p. 539)

continuous reinforcement schedule When the environmental consequences are the same each time an organism emits a behaviour (p. 238)

continuous variable A variable that can be placed on a continuum, from none or little to much (p. 44)

control group Group of participants in an experiment who receive a relatively neutral condition to serve as a comparison group (p. 54)

conventional morality The level of morality in which individuals define what is right by the standards they have learned from other people, particularly respected authorities (p. 529)

conversational distance How close people stand to each other when they are talking (p. 787)

conversion disorder A disorder characterised by a loss or significant change in a physical function without any physical problem to explain the condition (p. 639)

coping The ways people deal with stressful situations; also called coping mechanisms (p. 590)

coping mechanisms The ways people deal with stressful situations (p. 590)

cornea The tough, transparent tissue covering the front of the eyeball (p. 137)

corpus callosum A band of fibres that connects the two hemispheres of the brain (p. 110)

corrective mechanisms processes that restore a homoeostatic system to its set point (p. 386)

correlate In research, the degree to which two or more variables are related (p. 59)

correlation coefficient An index of the extent to which two variables are related (p. 59)

correlation matrix A table presenting the correlations among several variables (p. 59)

correlational research Research that assesses the degree to which two variables are related, so that knowing the value of one variable can lead to prediction of a second variable (p. 59)

cortex See cerebral cortex (p. 100)

couples therapy Psychotherapy that treats a couple; also called marital therapy (p. 670)

creative intelligence The ability to come up with novel solutions to problems (p. 359)

creativity The ability to produce valued outcomes in a novel way (p. 350)

critical period A period of special sensitivity to specific types of learning that shapes the capacity for future development (p. 467)

critical thinking A skill that involves carefully examining and analysing information to judge its value, assessing both its strengths and its weaknesses, and considering alternative explanations (p. 67)

cross-cultural comparison studies Research that involves comparing two or more different cultures in relation to a particular psychological variable (p. 782)

cross-cultural psychologists Psychologists who compare the similarities and differences in behaviour across different societies or cultures (p. 782)

cross-cultural psychology The field that attempts to test psychological hypotheses in different cultures (p. 7)

cross-cultural validation studies Research that examines whether a psychological variable in one culture can be applied and have meaning in another culture (p. 783)

cross-sectional studies The type of research that compares groups of different aged participants at a single time to see whether differences exist among them (p. 470)

crystallised intelligence People's store of knowledge (p. 355)

cues to action Ancillary factors that influence whether or not a person is willing to begin a healthy behaviour or terminate an unhealthy one (p. 556)

cultural competence A person's effectiveness in communicating and behaving appropriately with people from another culture, both in terms of understanding and being understood (p. 824)

cultural display rules The theory that cultures differ in relation to rules on the appropriateness of displaying certain emotions in particular social circumstances (p. 786)

cultural models Shared cultural concepts, which organise knowledge and shape the way people think and remember (p. 283)

cultural psychologists Psychologists who study the ways in which people are affected by the culture they live in (p. 782)

cultural stereotypes Generalised views that we hold about particular groups of people — the belief that all members of a particular cultural group share common traits or behaviours (p. 798)

culture The shared rules that govern the behaviour of a group of people and enable the members of that group to co-exist and survive (pp. 680, 781)

culture fair test A test that measures skills and knowledge common across cultures (p. 353)

culture free test A test that eliminates cultural difference that could affect performance (p. 353)

culture pattern approach An approach to personality and culture that views culture as an organised set of beliefs, rituals and institutions that shape individuals to fit its patterns (p. 458)

culture shock The feeling of disorientation and anxiety that occurs as people from one culture encounter and adapt to the practices, rules and expectations of another culture (p. 794)

cycle A single round of expansion and contraction of the distance between molecules of air in a sound wave (p. 148)

D

daily hassles The small, but irritating, demands that characterise daily life (p. 586)

daydreaming Turning attention away from external stimuli to internal thoughts and imagined scenarios (p. 190)

decay theory The notion that memories are lost as a result of a fading of the memory trace (p. 287)

deception The deliberate act of not revealing the true purpose of an experiment to a participant before the study commences (p. 65)

decibel (dB) The unit of measure of amplitude (loudness) of a sound wave (p. 149)

decision making The process by which people weigh the pros and cons of different alternatives in order to make a choice among two or more options (p. 310)

declarative memory Knowledge that can be consciously retrieved and 'declared' (p. 269)

Deep learning approach Involves finding meaning in what is being studied to maximise understanding (p. 31)

deductive reasoning The process of reasoning that draws logical conclusions from premises (p. 305)

defence mechanisms Unconscious mental processes aimed at protecting a person from experiencing unpleasant emotions, especially anxiety (p. 431)

defining features Qualities that are essential, or necessarily present, in order to classify an object as a member of a category (p. 300)

degree of relatedness The probability that two people share any particular gene (p. 118)

delusion A false belief firmly held despite evidence to the contrary (p. 621)

demand characteristics The way participants' perceptions of the researcher's goals influence their responses (p. 52)

dementia A disorder marked by global disturbance of higher mental functions (p. 495)

dendrites Branch-like extensions of the neuron that receive information from other cells (p. 89)

denial A defence mechanism in which the person refuses to acknowledge external realities or emotions (p. 432)

dependent variables The responses the experimenter measures to see if the experimental manipulation has had an effect (p. 50)

depressant A drug that slows down the nervous system (p. 209)

depth perception The organisation of perception in three dimensions; also called distance perception (p. 165)

description Involves summarising the relationships between variables in an easily understandable way (p. 49)

descriptive diagnosis A classification of mental disorders in terms of clinical syndromes (p. 612)

descriptive research Research methods that cannot unambiguously demonstrate cause and effect but attempt to describe phenomena as they exist. Methods include case studies, naturalistic observation, survey research and correlational methods. (p. 55)

descriptive statistics Numbers that describe the data from a study in a way that summarises their essential features (pp. 52, 77)

detoxification The process during which an alcoholic dries out (p. 571)

developmental model Freud's model of how children develop, defined by his psychosexual stages (p. 428)

developmental psychology The field that studies the way thought, feeling and behaviour develop throughout the life span (p. 466)

developmental task Challenge that is normative for a particular period of life (p. 536)

Diagnostic and Statistical Manual of Mental Disorders-IV (DSM-IV) The manual of clinical syndromes published by the American Psychiatric Association and used for descriptive diagnosis (p. 612)

diathesis–stress model The model of psychopathology that proposes that people with an underlying vulnerability (also called a diathesis) may develop a disorder under stressful circumstances (p. 609)

dichotic listening A procedure in which different information is presented to the left and right ears simultaneously (p. 189)

difference threshold The smallest difference in intensity between two stimuli that a person can detect (p. 134)

diffusion of responsibility The phenomenon in which the presence of other people leads to a diminished sense of personal responsibility to act (p. 751)

direct perception A theory which states that sensory information intrinsically carries meaning (p. 172)

discounting The attributional phenomenon in which people downplay the role of one variable that might explain a behaviour because they know another may be contributing (p. 718)

discourse The way people ordinarily speak, hear, read and write in interconnected sentences (p. 325)

discrimination The behavioural component of prejudiced attitudes (pp. 709, 800)

discriminative stimulus (S^D) A stimulus that signals that particular contingencies of reinforcement are in effect (p. 240)

discursive psychology An approach to psychology that treats spoken and written text as contributing to the construction of people's reality, not just a reflection of underlying cognition (p. 802)

disorganised attachment style Response to separation in which infants behave in contradictory ways, indicating helpless efforts to elicit soothing responses from the attachment figure (p. 507)

displacement A defence mechanism that involves people directing their emotions, especially anger, away from the real target to a substitute (p. 432)

display rules Patterns of emotional expression that are considered acceptable in a given culture (p. 406)

dispositional variables People's personalities and attitudes (p. 736)

dissociation A disturbance in memory and consciousness in which significant aspects of experience are kept separate and distinct (or disassociated) (p. 639)

dissociative disorders Disorders characterised by disruptions in consciousness, memory, sense of identity or perception of the environment (p. 639)

dissociative identity disorder The most severe dissociative disorder; also known as multiple personality disorder (p. 639)

distinctiveness In attribution theory, the extent to which an individual responds in a particular way to many different stimuli (p. 717)

divergent thinking The ability to generate multiple possibilities in a given situation (p. 350)

divided attention The process by which attention is split between two or more sets of stimuli (p. 189)

dizygotic (DZ,** or **fraternal) twins Twins who, like other siblings, share only about half of their genes, having developed from the union of two sperm with two separate eggs (p. 119)

door-in-the-face technique Everyday social influence tactic whereby people intentionally make a request that they know will be turned down, but follow up on that request with a smaller request. Based on the principle of reciprocity. (p. 770)

dopamine A neurotransmitter with wide-ranging effects in the nervous system, involved in thought, feeling, motivation and behaviour (p. 94)

dopamine hypothesis Hypothesis that implicates an imbalance in the neurotransmitter dopamine in schizophrenia (p. 623)

dorsolateral prefrontal cortex An area in the brain that plays a central role in working memory and explicit manipulation of representations (p. 318)

double-blind study A study in which both participants and researchers are blind to the status of participants (p. 52)

drive According to Freud, an internal tension state that builds up until satisfied; according to behaviourist theory, an unpleasant tension state that motivates behaviour, classified as either primary or secondary (acquired) (p. 375)

drive model Freud's theory of motivation, which held that people are motivated by sexual and aggressive instincts or drives (p. 428)

drive-reduction theories Mid-twentieth century behaviourist theories which proposed that motivation stems from a combination of drive and reinforcement, in which stimuli become reinforcing because they are associated with reduction of a state of biological deficit (p. 377)

DSM-5 A fifth edition of the Diagnostic and Statistical Manual of Mental Disorders is due for completion in 2013, with major changes expected to the classification system and diagnostic categories, including fewer axes. (p. 612)

dysthymia (*or *dysthymic disorder) chronic low-level depression of more than two years' duration, with intervals of normal moods that never last more than a few weeks or months (p. 628)

E

eardrum The thin, flexible membrane that marks the outer boundary of the middle ear; the eardrum is set in motion by sound waves and in turn sets in motion the ossicles; also called the tympanic membrane (p. 149)

echoic storage An auditory sensory registration process by which people retain an echo or brief auditory representation of a sound to which they have been exposed (p. 261)

eclectic psychotherapy Psychotherapy in which psychologists combine techniques from different approaches to fit the particular case (p. 684)

effect size A measure of the magnitude of an experimental effect or the strength of a relationship (p. 81)

effectiveness studies Studies that assess the outcome of psychotherapy as it is practised in the field rather than in the laboratory (p. 683)

efferent neurons See motor neurons (p. 89)

efficacy studies Studies that assess psychotherapy outcome under highly controlled conditions, such as random assignment of patients to different treatment or control groups, careful training of therapists to adhere to a manual, and standardised length of treatment (p. 683)

ego The structure in Freud's model of the mind that must somehow balance desire, reality and morality (p. 431)

egocentric Being thoroughly embedded in one's own point of view (p. 485)

elaboration likelihood model The model of persuasion that proposes that knowing how to appeal to a person requires figuring out the likelihood that he or she will think much about (or elaborate on) the arguments (p. 701)

elaborative rehearsal An aid to long-term memory storage that involves thinking about the meaning of information in order to process it with more depth; see also level of processing (p. 262)

electroconvulsive therapy (ECT) A last-resort treatment for severe depression, in which an electric shock to the brain is used to induce a seizure (p. 677)

electroencephalogram (EEG) A record of the electrical activity towards the surface of the brain, used especially in sleep research and diagnosis of epilepsy (p. 61)

emic perspective a research approach that involves focusing on a specific cultural group and examining particular psychological aspects of that group (p. 782)

emotion A positive or negative feeling state that typically includes arousal, subjective experience and behavioural expression (p. 374)

emotion-focused coping Efforts to regulate the emotions generated by a stressful experience (p. 590)

emotion regulation Efforts to control emotional states; also called affect regulation (p. 411)

emotional expression The overt behavioural signs of emotion (p. 404)

emotional forecasting Predicting emotional reactions to future events (p. 581)

emotional intelligence The ability to read people's emotions and use one's own emotional responses adaptively (p. 358)

empathic distress Feeling upset for another person (p. 533)

empathy The capacity to understand another person's experience, both cognitively and emotionally (pp. 16, 451, 532)

empiricism The belief that the path to scientific knowledge is systematic observation and, ideally, experimental observation (p. 15)

empty-chair technique A technique associated with Gestalt therapy, in which clients practise emotional expression by imagining that the person to whom they would like to speak is seated in an empty chair (p. 667)

encoded Refers to information that is cast into a representational form or 'code', so that it can be readily accessed from memory (p. 275)

encoding specificity principle The notion that the match between the way information is encoded and the way it is retrieved is important to remembering (p. 276)

enculturation The process of absorbing and internalising the rules of the culture we live in (p. 782)

endocrine system The collection of ductless glands that secrete hormones into the bloodstream and control various bodily and psychological functions (p. 96)

endorphins Chemicals in the brain similar to morphine that elevate mood and reduce pain (p. 95)

episodic memory Memories of particular episodes or events from personal experience (p. 269)

equilibration According to Piaget, a balancing of assimilation and accommodation in trying to adapt to the world (p. 484)

ERG theory A theory of worker motivation distinguishing existence, relatedness and growth needs (p. 381)

error That part of a participant's score on a test that is unrelated to the true score (p. 47)

escape learning A negative reinforcement procedure in which the behaviour of an organism is reinforced by the cessation of an aversive event that already exists (p. 234)

estrogens Hormones produced by the female gonads, the ovaries, which control sex drive as well as the development of secondary sex characteristics (p. 96)

ethical hedonism The school of philosophical thought that asserts that all behaviour, no matter how apparently altruistic, is and should be designed to increase one's own pleasure or reduce one's own pain (p. 748)

ethnic identity The characteristic whereby members of an ethnic group identify 'us' in relation to 'them' using aspects of shared culture, language or religion (p. 796)

ethnicity The characteristic of shared geographic, language, cultural and religious origins (p. 796)

ethnocentrism The tendency for a person's own culture to influence the way they view the rest of the world (p. 799)

ethology The field that studies animal behaviour from a biological and evolutionary perspective (p. 20)

etic perspective A research approach that involves the search for commonalities or differences across cultures (p. 782)

everyday memory Memory as it occurs in daily life (p. 273)

evolutionary perspective The viewpoint built on Darwin's principle of natural selection that argues that human behavioural proclivities must be understood in the context of their evolutionary and adaptive significance (p. 19)

evolutionary psychologists Apply evolutionary thinking to a wide range of psychological phenomena (p. 20)

existential dread The recognition that life has no absolute value or meaning, that any meaning that does exist we create for ourselves, and that ultimately, we all face death (p. 452)

existentialism A school of modern philosophy that focuses on each individual's subjective existence or phenomenology and on the way the individual comes to terms with basic issues such as meaning in life and mortality (p. 452)

expectancies Expectations relevant to desired outcomes (pp. 246, 438)

expected utility A combined assessment of the value and probability of different options (p. 311)

experience sampling A research technique whereby participants report on the contents of consciousness at specified times (p. 190)

experimental research A research design in which investigators manipulate some aspect of a situation and examine the impact of this manipulation on the way participants respond (p. 49)

explanatory style The way people make sense of events or outcomes, particularly aversive ones (p. 247)

explicit cognition Thinking that involves conscious manipulation of representations (p. 312)

explicit memory The conscious recollection of facts and events (p. 270)

exposure techniques Behaviour therapy techniques based on classical conditioning in which the patient is confronted with the actual phobic stimulus (p. 662)

expressed emotion The tendency of family interactions to be characterised by criticism, hostile interchanges and emotional overinvolvement or intrusiveness by family members, implicated in the aetiology and maintenance of schizophrenia and other disorders (p. 625)

external attributions An explanation of behaviour that attributes the behaviour to the situation rather than the person (p. 717)

external locus of control The belief that one's life is determined by forces outside (external to) oneself (p. 246)

external validity The extent to which the findings of a study can be generalised to situations outside the laboratory (p. 45)

extinction In classical conditioning, the process by which a conditioned response is weakened by presentation of the conditioned stimulus without the unconditioned stimulus; in operant conditioning, the process by which the connection between an operant and a reinforcer or punishment is similarly broken (p. 228)

extroversion The tendency to be sociable, active and willing to take risks (p. 442)

F

factor analysis A statistical technique for identifying common factors that underlie performance on a wide variety of measures (p. 354)

factors Common elements that underlie performance across a set of tasks (p. 354)

false self A condition in which people mould themselves to other people's expectations and to the demands of the roles they play (p. 451)

family alliances Patterns of taking sides in family conflicts (p. 611)

family boundaries In family systems theory, the physical and psychological limits of a family or system (p. 610)

family homoeostatic mechanisms Methods members use to preserve equilibrium in a family (p. 610)

family roles Parts individuals play in repetitive family interaction patterns (p. 610)

family systems model The model of psychopathology which suggests that an individual's symptoms are really symptoms of dysfunction in a family (p. 610)

family therapy A psychological treatment that attempts to change maladaptive interaction patterns among members of a family (p. 668)

fasting phase The second stage of metabolism, when the body converts glucose and fat into energy (p. 385)

feature detector A neuron that fires only when stimulation in its receptive field matches a particular pattern or orientation (p. 143)

Fechner's law The law of psychophysics proposed by Gustav Fechner, that the subjective magnitude of a sensation grows as a proportion of the logarithm of the stimulus (p. 134)

feedback mechanisms Processes that provide information regarding the state of a homoeostatic system with regard to its set point or steady state (p. 386)

figure–ground perception A fundamental rule of perception described by Gestalt psychology that states that people inherently differentiate between figure (the object they are viewing, sound to which they are listening, etc.) and ground (background) (p. 162)

first impressions Initial perceptions of another person that can be powerful in shaping future beliefs about the person (p. 708)

five factor model (FFM) A trait theory that asserts that personality consists of five traits (openness to experience, conscientiousness, extroversion, agreeableness and neuroticism) (p. 443)

fixations In psychoanalytic theory, prominent conflicts and concerns focused on wishes from a particular period (p. 428)

fixed-interval (FI) schedules of reinforcement When the organism receives rewards for its responses only after a fixed amount of time (p. 239)

fixed-ratio (FR) schedules of reinforcement When the organism receives reinforcement at a fixed rate, according to the number of responses emitted (p. 239)

flashbulb memories Especially vivid memories of exciting or highly consequential events (p. 285)

flooding Cognitive–behavioural technique designed to eliminate phobias, in which the patient confronts the real phobic stimulus all at once (p. 662)

fluid intelligence Intellectual capacities that have no specific content but are used in processing information (p. 355)

foetal alcohol syndrome (FAS) A birth defect caused by alcohol abuse by the mother; FAS babies have facial deformities, restricted intelligence and an agitated personality (pp. 349, 473)

foot-in-the-door technique Persuasive technique often used by salespeople, which involves getting people to comply with a small request in order to induce their compliance with a larger request (p. 770)

forebrain Involved in complex sensory, emotional, cognitive and behavioural processes and consists of the hypothalamus, thalamus and cerebrum (p. 105)

forgetting The inability to retrieve memories (p. 284)

formal operational stage Piaget's fourth stage of cognitive development, which begins at about age 12 to 15, and is characterised by the ability to manipulate abstract as well as concrete objects, events and ideas mentally (p. 487)

form perception The organisation of sensations into meaningful shapes and patterns (p. 161)

fovea The central region of the retina, where light is most directly focused by the lens (p. 138)

free association The therapeutic technique for exploring associational networks and unconscious processes involved in symptom formation (p. 658)

free will versus determinism The philosophical question of whether people act on the basis of their freely chosen intentions, or whether their actions are caused or determined by physical processes in their bodies or in the environment in which they live (p. 8)

frequency In a sound wave, the number of cycles per second, expressed in hertz and responsible for subjective experience of pitch (p. 148)

frequency distribution A method of organising the data to show how frequently participants received each of the many possible scores (p. 77)

frequency theory The theory of pitch that asserts that perceived pitch reflects the rate of vibration of the basilar membrane (p. 151)

frontal lobes Brain structures involved in coordination of movement, attention, planning, social skills, conscience, abstract thinking, memory and aspects of personality (p. 110)

frustration–aggression hypothesis The hypothesis that when people are frustrated in achieving a goal, they may become aggressive (p. 757)

functional fixedness The tendency to ignore other possible functions of an object when one already has a function in mind (p. 309)

functional magnetic resonance imaging (fMRI) A brain-scanning technique used to watch the brain as an individual carries out tasks (p. 62)

functionalism An early school of thought in psychology influenced by Darwinian theory that looked for explanations of psychological processes in terms of their role, or function, in helping the individual adapt to the environment (p. 10)

fundamental attribution error The tendency to assume that people's behaviour corresponds to their internal states rather than external situations; also called correspondence bias (p. 719)

fusion Acculturation that involves combining two cultures to form a new culture (p. 796)

G

GABA Acronym for gamma-aminobutyric acid, one of the most widespread neurotransmitters in the nervous system, which largely plays an inhibitory role in the brain (p. 94)

galvanic skin response (GSR) An electrical measure of the amount of sweat on the skin that is produced during states of anxiety or arousal; also called skin conductance or electrodermal activity (EDA) (p. 228)

ganglion cells Nerve cells in the retina that integrate information from multiple bipolar cells, the axons of which bundle together to form the optic nerve (p. 138)

gate-control theory Theory that emphasises the role of the central nervous system in regulating pain (p. 159)

gender The psychological meaning of being male or female; the roles and behaviours that cultures deem appropriate for men and women (pp. 517, 797)

gender constancy The recognition that people's gender cannot be altered by changes in appearance or activities (p. 525)

gender identity The categorisation of oneself as either male or female (p. 525)

gender roles The range of behaviours considered appropriate by society for males and females (p. 517)

gender schemas Representations that associate psychological characteristics with one sex or the other (p. 525)

gender stability The understanding that one's gender remains constant over time (p. 525)

gene The unit of hereditary transmission (p. 118)

general adaptation syndrome Selye's model of stress that includes the three stages of alarm, resistance and exhaustion (p. 581)

generalisability The applicability of a study's finding to the entire population of interest (p. 45)

generalised anxiety disorder Persistent anxiety at a moderate but disturbing level (p. 633)

generalised expectancies Expectancies that influence a broad spectrum of behaviour (p. 246)

generativity A concern for the next generation as well as an interest in producing something of lasting value to society (p. 537)

generativity versus stagnation In Erikson's theory, the stage in which people in mid-adulthood experience concern for the next generation as well as an interest in producing something of lasting value to society (p. 537)

generic memory General world knowledge or facts; also called semantic memory (p. 269)

genital stage In Freudian theory, psychosexual stage that occurs at approximately age 12 and beyond, when conscious sexuality resurfaces after years of repression (p. 430)

genogram A map of a family over three or four generations, drawn by a therapist to explore possible similarities between current difficulties and the family's past (p. 669)

Gestalt psychology A school of psychology that holds that perception is an active experience of imposing order on an overwhelming panorama of details by seeing them as parts of larger whole (or Gestalts) (p. 35)

Gestalt therapy A psychological treatment based on the assumption that psychological distress results from losing touch with one's emotions and one's authentic inner voice, and that focusing on the 'here and now' is curative (p. 666)

g-factor The general intelligence factor that emerges through factor analysis of IQ tests (p. 354)

Gf–Gc theory A hierarchical model of intelligence that argues for the presence of two overarching types of intelligence — fluid intelligence and crystallised intelligence, as well as more specific intellectual skills, such as short-term memory (p. 355)

gifted Exceptionally talented (p. 349)

glutamate One of the most widespread neurotransmitters in the nervous system, which largely plays an excitatory role; also called glutamic acid (p. 94)

goals Desired outcomes established through social learning (p. 378)

goal-setting theory The theory of motivation that suggests that conscious goals regulate much of human action, particularly performance tasks (p. 378)

gonads Endocrine glands that influence much of sexual development and behaviour (p. 96)

good continuation A Gestalt rule of perception which states that, if possible, the brain organises stimuli into continuous lines or patterns rather than discontinuous elements (p. 162)

graded exposure A modified version of the behaviourist flooding technique for treating anxiety, in which stimuli are real but are presented to the patient in a gradual manner (p. 662)

graded potentials A spreading voltage change that occurs when the neural membrane receives a signal from another cell (p. 91)

grammar A system of rules for generating understandable and acceptable language utterances (p. 323)

group A collection of people, each of whose actions affect the other group members (p. 764)

group cohesiveness People tend to cluster together to be viewed even more favourably by members of their ingroup (p. 767)

group polarisation A movement towards a decision that is at the extreme position (p. 767)

group process The interactions among members of a group (p. 668)

group therapy A treatment method in which multiple people meet together to work towards therapeutic goals (p. 667)

groupthink Members of a group make decisions based more on maintaining group harmony and cohesiveness than a critical analysis of the realities of a situation (p. 767)

guidance approach Parents help children to manage their emotions and learn considerate behaviours (p. 515)

gustation Taste (p. 155)

H

habituation The decreasing strength of a response after repeated presentations of the stimulus (p. 222)

hair cells Receptors for sound attached to the basilar membrane (p. 150)

hallucinations Sensory perceptions that distort, or occur without, an external stimulus (pp. 213, 621)

hallucinogen A drug that produces hallucinations (p. 213)

halo effect A tendency to attribute additional positive characteristics to someone who has one salient quality, such as physical attractiveness (p. 708)

haptics The use of touch to accompany communication (p. 821)

health belief model Theory that states that health behaviours are predicted by the perceived susceptibility to the health threat, the perceived seriousness of the health threat, the benefits and barriers of undertaking particular health behaviours and cues to action (p. 556)

health psychology Field of psychology devoted to understanding psychological influences on how people stay healthy, why they become ill and how they respond when they are ill (p. 551)

heritability The extent to which individual differences in phenotype are determined by genetic factors or genotype (pp. 119, 454)

heritability coefficient The statistic that quantifies the degree to which a trait is heritable (p. 119)

hertz (Hz) The unit of measurement of frequency of sound waves (p. 148)

heuristics In problem solving, cognitive shortcuts or rules of thumb (p. 312)

hierarchy of needs Maslow's theory that needs are arranged hierarchically, from physiological needs, safety needs, belongingness needs and esteem needs, through to self-actualisation needs (p. 380)

high-context cultures Cultures that pay close attention to non-verbal signs like body language and conversational difference to decode the real meaning behind words or actions (p. 787)

hindbrain The part of the brain above the spinal cord that includes the medulla, cerebellum and parts of the reticular formation (p. 103)

hippocampus A structure in the limbic system involved in the acquisition and consolidation of new information in memory (p. 107)

histogram Plots ranges of scores along the x axis and the frequency of scores in each range on the y axis (p. 77)

homoeostasis The body's tendency to maintain a relatively constant state that permits cells to live and function (p. 386)

hormones Chemicals secreted directly into the bloodstream by the endocrine glands (p. 96)

hostile aggression Aggression that is elicited by anger (p. 752)

hue The sensory quality people normally consider colour (p. 145)

humanistic Approaches to personality that focus on aspects of personality that are distinctly human, not shared by other animals (p. 15)

humanistic therapies Psychological treatments that focus on the patient's conscious or lived experience and on the way each person uniquely experiences relationships and the world (p. 666)

humoural theory of illness Theory asserting that disease is caused by an imbalance in the four fluids or humours of the body (p. 552)

hypnosis An altered state of consciousness characterised by deep relaxation and suggestibility which a person voluntarily enters through the efforts of a hypnotist (p. 205)

hypnotic susceptibility The capacity to enter deep hypnotic states (p. 205)

hypochondriasis A disorder that occurs when people believe they are suffering from an illness or ailment, even when there is no medical evidence to support that belief (p. 639)

hypothalamus The brain structure situated directly below the thalamus involved in the regulation of eating, sleeping, sexual activity, movement and emotion (p. 105)

hypothesis A tentative belief or educated guess that purports to predict or explain the relationship between two or more variables (p. 44)

I

iconic storage A visual sensory registration process by which people retain an afterimage of a visual stimulus (p. 261)

id In Freudian theory, the reservoir of sexual and aggressive energy, which is driven by impulses and is characterised by primary process thinking (p. 431)

ideal self A person's view of what she or he would like to be (pp. 16, 451, 728)

identification Making another person part of oneself by imitating the person's behaviour, changing the self-concept to see oneself as more like that person, and attempting to become more like the person by accepting his or her values and attitudes (p. 429)

identity A stable sense of knowing who one is and what one's values and ideals are (p. 537)

identity confusion A condition in which the individual fails to develop a coherent and enduring sense of self, and has difficulty committing to roles, values, people and occupational choices in his or her life (p. 537)

identity versus identity confusion In Erikson's theory, the stage in which adolescents develop a stable sense of who they are and a stable set of values and ideals (p. 537)

immune system A system of cells throughout the body that fights disease (pp. 227, 588)

implicit attitudes Attitudes that regulate thought and behaviour unconsciously and automatically (p. 696)

implicit cognition Thinking that occurs outside awareness (p. 313)

implicit memory Memory that cannot be brought to mind consciously but can be expressed in behaviour (p. 270)

implicit motives Motives that can be activated and expressed outside of awareness (p. 379)

impression management See self-presentation (p. 578)

imprinting The tendency of young animals of certain species to follow an animal to which they were exposed during a sensitive period early in their lives (p. 505)

incentive An external motivating stimulus (as opposed to an internal need state) (p. 377)

inclusive fitness The notion that natural selection favours organisms that survive, reproduce and foster the survival and reproduction of their kin (p. 21)

independent variables The variables an experimenter manipulates, or the effects of which the experimenter assesses (p. 50)

indigenous people The original inhabitants of a land or country (p. 802)

indigenous psychology Promotes psychologies that are not imposed; that are influenced by the cultural contexts in which people live; that are developed from within the culture; and that result in locally relevant psychological knowledge (p. 803)

individual differences The way people resemble and differ from one another in personality or intelligence (p. 425)

individualism–collectivism continuum A dimension of culture measured by the extent to which cultures favour individual goals compared with communal goals (p. 784)

individualist cultures Cultures that emphasise the primacy of the individual over the group (p. 787)

inductive reasoning The process of reasoning from specific observations to generate propositions (p. 305)

industry versus inferiority In Erikson's theory, the stage in which children develop a sense of competence as they begin to practise skills they will use in productive work (p. 537)

infantile amnesia The inability to recall early childhood memories (p. 481)

inferential statistics Procedures for assessing whether the results obtained with a sample are likely to reflect characteristics of the population as a whole (pp. 52, 77)

information processing The transformation, storage and retrieval of environmental inputs through thought and memory (p. 17)

informed consent A participant's ability to agree to participate in a study in an informed manner (p. 65)

ingroups People perceived as belonging to a valued group (p. 713)

initiation rites Ceremonies such as the rites found in many cultures in adolescence, which initiate a person into a new social role, such as adulthood (p. 537)

initiative versus guilt In Erikson's theory, the stage in which children develop a sense of goal-directness and responsibility (p. 536)

insight In learning theory, the ability to perceive a connection between a problem and its solution; in psychodynamic treatments, the understanding of one's own psychological processes (pp. 245, 657)

insomnia The inability to sleep (p. 199)

instinct A relatively fixed pattern of behaviour that animals produce without learning (p. 381)

instinct model Freud's theory of motivation, which held that people are motivated by sexual and aggressive instincts or drives (p. 428)

instrumental aggression Calm, pragmatic aggression that may or may not be accompanied by anger (p. 752)

instrumental leader See task leader (p. 765)

integrative psychotherapy Psychotherapy that uses an approach developed from theories that cut across theoretical lines (p. 684)

integrity versus despair In Erikson's theory, the stage in which older people look back on their lives with a sense of satisfaction that they have lived it well, or with despair, regret and loss for loved ones who have died (p. 538)

intellectual impairment Significantly sub-average general intellectual functioning, existing concurrently with deficits in adaptive behaviour and manifested during childhood (p. 349)

intelligence The application of cognitive skills and knowledge to learn, solve problems and obtain ends that are valued by an individual or culture (p. 344)

intelligence quotient (IQ) A score originally derived by dividing mental age and chronological age and multiplying by 100, but now generally established by comparing the individual's performance to norms of people his or her own age (p. 345)

intelligence test A measure designed to assess an individual's level of cognitive capabilities compared to other people in a population (p. 344)

interactionist approaches Multidirectional view of personality which asserts that personality is shaped by economic and cultural demands but that cultural and economic processes themselves are in part created to fulfil psychological needs (p. 458)

interference The intrusion of similar memories on one another (p. 287)

inter-item reliability See internal consistency (p. 46)

intermittent schedule of reinforcement An operant procedure in which an organism is reinforced only some of the time it emits a behaviour; also called partial schedule of reinforcement (p. 238)

intermodal processing The capacity to associate sensations of an object from different senses, or to match one's own actions to behaviours that are observed visually (p. 479)

internal attributions An explanation of behaviour that attributes it to the person rather than the situation (p. 717)

internal consistency A type of reliability that assesses whether the items in a test measure the same construct; also known as inter-item reliability (p. 46)

internal locus of control The belief that one is the master of one's fate (p. 246)

internal validity The extent to which a study is methodologically adequate (p. 45)

internal working model A mental representation of the attachment relationship, which forms the basis for expectations in close relationships (p. 508)

interneurons Neurons that connect other neurons to each other, found only in the brain and spinal cord (p. 89)

interpersonal attraction The factors that lead people to choose to spend time with other people (p. 737)

interpretation A therapeutic technique whereby the therapist helps the patient understand his or her experiences in a new light (p. 658)

interrater reliability A measure of the similarity with which different raters apply a measure (p. 47)

interstimulus interval The duration of time between presentation of the conditioned stimulus and the unconditioned stimulus (p. 229)

interval schedules of reinforcement Operant conditioning procedures in which rewards are delivered according to intervals of time (p. 238)

interview A research tool in which the investigator asks the participant questions (p. 57)

intimacy A kind of closeness characterised by self-disclosure, warmth and mutual caring (p. 397)

intimacy versus isolation In Erikson's theory, the stage in which young adults establish enduring, committed friendships and romantic relationships (p. 537)

intrinsic motivation The motivation to perform a behaviour for its own sake, rather than for some kind of external (or extrinsic) reward (p. 379)

introspection The method used by Wundt and other structuralists in which trained participants verbally reported everything that went through their minds when presented with a stimulus or task; more generally, refers to the process of looking inward at one's own mental contents or process (p. 10)

intuitive scientists The conception of people as lay scientists who use intuitive theories, frame hypotheses, collect data about themselves and others, and examine the impact of various experimental manipulations when trying to understand themselves and others; also called intuitive psychologists (p. 717)

iris The ring of pigmented tissue that gives the eye its blue, green, or brown colour; its muscle fibers cause the pupil to constrict or dilate (p. 138)

J

James–Lange theory A theory of emotion that asserts that emotion originates with peripheral arousal, which people then label as an emotional state (p. 401)

just noticeable difference (jnd) The smallest difference in intensity between two stimuli that a person can detect (p. 134)

K

kinaesics The use of gestures, movements and facial expressions (p. 821)

kinaesthesia The sense that provides information about the movement and position of the limbs and other parts of the body; receptors in joints transduce information about the position of the bones, and receptors in the tendons and muscles transmit messages about muscular tension (p. 160)

knowledge base Accumulated information stored in long-term memory (pp. 358, 490)

L

labelling theory The theory that psychiatric diagnosis is a way of labelling individuals a society considers deviant (p. 603)

language The system of symbols, sounds, meanings and rules for their combination that constitutes the primary mode of communication among humans (p. 321)

language acquisition device (LAD) The prewired, innate mechanism that allows for the acquisition of language hypothesised by Noam Chomsky (p. 327)

latency stage The psychosexual phase that occurs roughly around ages six to 11, when children repress their sexual impulses (p. 430)

latent content According to Freud's dream theory, the meaning that underlies the symbolism in a dream (p. 202)

latent inhibition A phenomenon in classical conditioning in which initial exposure to a neutral stimulus without a UCS slows the process of later learning the CS–UCS association and developing a CR (p. 229)

latent learning Learning that has occurred but is not currently manifest in behaviour (p. 244)

lateralised Localised on one or the other side of the brain (p. 114)

law of contiguity Two events will become connected in the mind if they are experienced close together in time (p. 222)

law of effect Law proposed by Thorndike which states that the tendency of an organism to produce a behaviour depends on the effect the behaviour has on the environment (p. 233)

law of prediction The CS–UCS association will form such that the presence of the CS predicts the appearance of the UCS (p. 231)

law of similarity Objects that resemble each other are likely to become associated (p. 222)

laws of association First proposed by Aristotle, basic principles used to account for learning and memory, which describe the conditions under which one thought becomes connected, or associated, with another (p. 222)

leader A person who exercises greater influence than the average member of a group (p. 768)

learned helplessness The expectancy that one cannot escape from aversive events (p. 247)

learning Any relatively permanent change in the way an organism responds based on its experience (p. 222)

lens The disk-shaped, elastic structure of the eye that focuses light (p. 138)

level of processing The degree to which information is elaborated, reflected upon or processed in a meaningful way during encoding of memory (p. 275)

libido In Freudian theory, the human sexual drive, which refers as much to pleasure seeking and love as to sexual intercourse (p. 428)

life history method A method of personality assessment which has the aim of understanding the whole person in the context of his or her life experience and environment (p. 434)

life tasks The conscious, self-defined problems people attempt to solve (p. 438)

limbic system Subcortical structures responsible for emotional reactions, many motivational processes, learning and aspects of memory (p. 106)

lithium The drug treatment of choice for bipolar disorder (p. 676)

localisation of function The extent to which different parts of the brain control different aspects of functioning (p. 6)

locus of control of reinforcement Generalised expectancies people hold about whether or not their own behaviour will bring about the outcomes they seek (p. 246)

longitudinal study Type of research that follows the same individuals over time (p. 471)

long-term memory (LTM) Memory for facts, images, thoughts, feelings, skills and experiences that may last as long as a lifetime (p. 262)

long-term potentiation (LTP) The tendency of a group of neurons to fire more readily after consistent stimulation from other neurons (p. 232)

loose cultures Cultures in which norms are unclear or deviance from norms is tolerated (p. 787)

loosening of associations A tendency common in individuals with schizophrenia, in which conscious thought is directed along associative lines rather than by controlled, logical, purposeful processes (p. 622)

loudness The psychological property corresponding to a sound wave's amplitude (p. 149)

low-balling Method of persuasion by which people get a commitment to a request and then change the conditions (p. 770)

low-context cultures Cultures that pay close attention to what people actually say or do and interpret that literally, without as much regard to the accompanying circumstances (p. 787)

low-effort syndrome The tendency to exert minimal effort to escape stressful social and economic circumstance (p. 591)

M

magnetic resonance imaging (MRI) A neuroimaging technique that produces similar results without using x-rays (p. 61)

maintenance rehearsal The process of repeating information over and over to maintain it momentarily in STM (p. 262)

major depressive disorder A form of psychopathology, characterised by depressed mood, loss of interest in pleasurable activities, and disturbances in appetite, sleep, energy level and concentration (p. 627)

mania A period of abnormally euphoric, elevated or expansive mood (p. 628)

manic Relating to a mood disturbance in which people feel excessively happy or euphoric and believe they can do anything (p. 626)

manifest content The obvious storyline of a dream (p. 202)

MAO inhibitors Antidepressant medication that keeps the chemical MAO from breaking down neurotransmitter substances in the presynaptic neuron, which makes more neurotransmitter available for release into the synapse (p. 675)

marital therapy Psychotherapy that treats a couple; also called couples therapy (p. 670)

mastery goals Motives to increase one's competence, mastery or skill (p. 399)

matched samples Samples in which individuals from one culture reflect the same characteristics of individuals from another culture (p. 783)

matching hypothesis Phenomenon whereby people tend to choose as partners people they perceive to be equally attractive to themselves (p. 738)

maturation Biologically based development (p. 466)

mean The statistical average of the scores of all participants on a measure (p. 77)

measure A concrete way of assessing a variable (p. 46)

measures of central tendency Provide an index of the way a typical participant responded on a measure (p. 77)

median The score that falls in the middle of the distribution of scores, with half of participants scoring below it and half above it (p. 78)

meditation A relaxation practice, often associated with religion, characterised by a state of tranquillity (p. 205)

medulla An extension of the spinal cord, essential to life, controlling such vital physiological functions as heartbeat, circulation and respiration (p. 104)

medulla oblongata See medulla (p. 104)

mental age (MA) The average age at which children can be expected to achieve a particular score on an intelligence test (p. 345)

mental disorder The existence of a clinically recognisable set of symptoms and behaviours that cause distress to the individual and impair their ability to function as usual (p. 604)

mental health The capacity of individuals to behave in ways that promote their emotional and social wellbeing (p. 604)

mental health problems Include the wide range of emotional and behavioural abnormalities that affect people throughout their lives (p. 604)

mental image A visual representation of a stimulus (p. 299)

mental models Representations that describe, explain or predict the way things work (p. 300)

mental set The tendency to keep using the same problem-solving techniques that have worked in the past (p. 309)

mental simulation A problem-solving strategy in which people imagine the steps to problem solving mentally before actually undertaking them (p. 308)

meta-analysis A statistical technique that allows researchers to combine findings from various studies and make comparisons between the effects of treatment and no treatment (p. 681)

metabolism The processes by which the body transforms food into energy (p. 385)

metacognition People's understanding of the way they perform cognitive tasks such as remembering, learning or solving problems (p. 490)

metamemory Knowledge about one's own memory and about strategies that can be used to help remember (p. 490)

method of loci A memory aid or mnemonic device in which images are remembered by fitting them into an orderly arrangement of locations (p. 278)

midbrain The section of the brain above the hindbrain involved in some auditory and visual functions, movement, and conscious arousal and activation (p. 104)

mind–body problem The question of how mental and physical events interact (p. 8)

mnemonic devices Systematic strategies for remembering information (p. 278)

mode The most common or most frequent score or value of a variable observed in a sample (p. 78)

modelling A social learning procedure in which a person learns to reproduce behaviour exhibited by a model (p. 249)

modules Discrete but interdependent processing units responsible for different kinds of remembering (p. 263)

monochronic cultures Cultures in which time is divided into linear segments and closely regulated (p. 786)

monocular cues Visual input from a single eye alone that contributes to depth perception (p. 166)

monozygotic (MZ, *or* ***identical) twins*** Twins identical in their genetic make-up, having developed from the union of the same sperm and egg (p. 119)

mood disorder A disorder characterised by disturbances in emotion and mood (p. 626)

moods Relatively extended emotional states that do not shift attention or disrupt ongoing activities (p. 401)

morality of constraint According to Piaget's theory of moral development, the first stage of moral judgement, in which children believe that morals are absolute (p. 528)

morality of cooperation According to Piaget's theory of moral development, the stage at which moral rules can be changed if they are not appropriate to the occasion, as long as the people involved agree to do so (p. 529)

morpheme In language, a basic unit of meaning (p. 323)

motion detectors Ganglion cells that are particularly sensitive to movement (p. 168)

motion parallax A monocular depth cue involving the relative movements of retinal images of objects; nearby objects appear to speed across the field of vision, whereas distant objects barely seem to move (p. 167)

motion perception The perception of movement in objects (p. 168)

motivated forgetting Forgetting for a reason, which leads to inhibition of retrieval (p. 287)

motivation The moving force that energises behaviour (p. 374)

motor cortex The primary zone of the frontal lobes responsible for control of motor behaviour (p. 110)

motor neuron A neuron that transmits commands from the brain to the glands or musculature of the body, typically through the spinal cord; also called efferent neuron (p. 89)

Müller–Lyer illusion A perceptual illusion in which two lines of equal length appear different in size (p. 170)

multiaxial system of diagnosis The system used in DSM-IV that places mental disorders in their social and biological context, assessing the patient on five axes (p. 613)

multiculturalism A situation where multiple cultures exist within a country and where the number of inhabitants representing those minority cultures is significant (pp. 790, 796)

multidisciplinary team Professionals drawn together from a range of specialities to carry out required tasks in a health facility (p. 655)

myelin sheath A tight coat of cells composed primarily of lipids, which serves to insulate the axon from chemical or physical stimuli that might interfere with the transmission of nerve impulses and speeds neural transmission (p. 89)

N

natural selection A theory proposed by Darwin which states that natural forces select traits in organisms that help them adapt to their environment (p. 19)

naturalistic observation The in-depth observation of a phenomenon in its natural setting (p. 56)

nature–nurture controversy The question of the degree to which inborn biological processes or environmental events determine human behaviour (p. 19)

need for achievement A motive to do well, to succeed and to avoid failure (p. 398)

need to belong Strong, possibly innate, need to be involved in relationships with others (p. 737)

negative affect A general category of emotions related to feeling bad (p. 407)

negative correlation A relationship between two variables in which the higher one is, the lower the other tends to be (p. 59)

negative identity Taking on a role that society defines as bad but that nevertheless provides one with a sense of being something (p. 537)

negative reciprocity The tendency of members of a couple to respond to negative comments or actions by their partner with negative behaviours in return (p. 670)

negative reinforcement The process whereby a behaviour is made more likely because it is followed by the removal of an aversive stimulus (p. 234)

negative reinforcer An aversive or unpleasant stimulus that strengthens a behaviour by its removal (p. 234)

negative symptoms Symptoms of schizophrenia such as flat affect, socially inappropriate behaviour and intellectual impairments that reflect a deficit or a loss of something that was once present or should be present (p. 622)

negative triad In Beck's cognitive theory of depression, negative outlook on the world, the self and the future (p. 630)

neglected children Children who are ignored by their peers (p. 520)

neo-Piagetian theories Theories that attempt to wed a stage model of cognitive development with research on information processing and domain-specific knowledge (p. 491)

nervous system The interacting network of nerve cells that underlies all psychological activity (p. 88)

networks of association Clusters of interconnected information stored in long-term memory (p. 279)

neuroimaging techniques Methods for studying the brain that use computer programs to convert the data taken from brain-scanning devices into visual images (p. 61)

neurons Cells in the nervous system (p. 89)

neuroses Problems in living, such as phobias, chronic self-doubts and repetitive interpersonal problems (p. 606)

neuroticism A continuum from emotional stability to emotional instability (p. 442)

neurotransmitter Chemical that transmits information from one neuron to another (p. 93)

node A cluster or piece of information along a network of association (p. 279)

non-REM (NREM) sleep States of sleep in which rapid eye movements (REM sleep) are not present (p. 200)

nonverbal communication Mode of communication that relies on gestures, expressions, intonation, body language and other unspoken signals (p. 326)

noradrenaline A hormone that triggers physiological arousal, particularly in potential danger situations (p. 96)

normal distribution A bell shaped frequency distribution where the scores of most participants fall in the middle and progressively fewer scores fall at either extreme (p. 79)

norms Standards for the behaviour of group members (p. 764)

O

obedience Overt compliance with authority (p. 760)

obesity A condition characterised by a body weight over 15 percent above the ideal for a person's height and age (pp. 389, 560)

objectivity Involves making an impartial judgement about something (p. 67)

object permanence In Piaget's theory, the recognition that objects exist in time and space independent of one's actions on, or observation of, them (p. 485)

object relations Behavioural patterns in intimate relationships and the motivational, cognitive and affective processes that produce them (p. 433)

observational learning Learning that occurs by observing the behaviour of others (p. 249)

observer bias Systematic errors in observation or results caused by the observer's expectations regarding the outcome of the study (p. 55)

obsessions Persistent unwanted thoughts or ideas (p. 634)

obsessive–compulsive disorder A disorder characterised by recurrent obsessions and compulsions that cause distress and significantly interfere with an individual's life (p. 634)

occipital lobes Brain structures located in the rear portion of the cortex, involved in vision (p. 110)

oculesics The use of eye movements and eye contact (p. 790)

Oedipus complex In Freudian theory, process that occurs during the phallic stage of development when the child desires an exclusive, sensual/sexual relationship with the opposite-sex parent (p. 429)

olfaction Smell (p. 153)

olfactory epithelium Thin pair of structures in which transduction of smell occurs (p. 154)

olfactory nerve The bundle of axons from sensory receptor cells that transmits information from the nose to the brain (p. 154)

open-mindedness Considering all sides of an issue, including any alternative explanations that differ from your personal point of view (p. 67)

operant A behaviour that is emitted by the organism rather than elicited by the environment (p. 233)

operant conditioning Learning that results when an organism associates a response that occurs spontaneously with a particular environment effect; also called instrumental conditioning (p. 233)

operation In Piaget's theory, a mental action that the individual can use to manipulate, transform and return an object of thought to its original state (p. 486)

operationalising Turning an abstract concept or variable into a concrete form that can be defined by some set of operations or actions (p. 51)

opponent-process theory A theory of colour vision that proposes the existence of three antagonistic colour systems: a blue–yellow system, a red–green system and a black–white system; according to this theory, the blue–yellow and red–green systems are responsible for hue, while the black–white system contributes to perception of brightness and saturation (p. 146)

optic nerve The bundle of axons of ganglion cells that carries information from the retina to the brain (p. 138)

optimistic bias Unrealistic optimism (p. 556)

oral stage In Freudian theory, the psychosexual phase occurring roughly in the first year of life, when children explore the world through their mouths (p. 428)

organisational effects Effects of hormones that influence the structure of the brain (p. 393)

ought self The duties, obligations and responsibilities that define the way the person should be (p. 728)

outgroups People perceived as not belonging to a valued group (p. 713)

overweight A body mass index between 25 percent and 30 percent, depending on age and gender (p. 560)

P

Pakeha Non-Maori (p. 816)

panic disorder A disorder characterised by attacks of intense fear and feelings of doom or terror not justified by the situation (p. 634)

paradigm A broad system of theoretical assumptions employed by a scientific community to make sense out of a domain of experience (p. 11)

paradoxical conditioning The conditioning that occurs when the CR is the opposite of the UCR (p. 231)

parallel distributed processing (PDP) A model of human cognitive processes in which many cognitive processes occur simultaneously (i.e. in parallel), so that a representation is spread out (i.e. distributed) throughout a network of interacting processing units; also called connectionism (p. 315)

parasympathetic nervous system The part of the autonomic nervous system involved in conserving and maintaining the body's energy resources (p. 98)

parietal lobes Brain structures located in front of the occipital lobes, involved in a number of functions, including sense of touch and the experience of one's own body in space and in movement (p. 110)

Parkinson's disease A disorder characterised by uncontrollable tremors, repetitive movements, and difficulty in both initiating behaviour and stopping movements already in progress (p. 94)

partial schedule of reinforcement An operant procedure in which an organism is reinforced only some of the time it emits a behaviour; also called intermittent schedule of reinforcement (p. 238)

participants The individuals who participate in a study (p. 45)

participatory modelling A cognitive–behavioural technique in which the therapist models desired behaviour and gradually induces the patient to participate in it (p. 664)

passionate love A highly emotional form of love marked by intense physiological arousal and absorption in another person (p. 739)

passive aggression The indirect expression of anger towards others (p. 432)

penis envy In Freudian theory, feeling of envy that emerges in girls, who feel that because they lack a penis they are inferior to boys (p. 430)

perceived seriousness (severity) An individual's perception of the impact a particular illness would have on his life (p. 556)

perceived susceptibility A person's perception that he is likely to contract a particular illness (p. 556)

percentile scores Indicates the percentage of scores that fall below a score (p. 79)

perception The process by which the brain selects, organises and interprets sensations (p. 128)

percepts Meaningful perceptual units, such as images of particular objects (p. 161)

perceptual constancy The organisation of changing sensations into percepts that are relatively stable in size, shape and colour (p. 169)

perceptual illusions Perceptual misinterpretations produced in the course of normal perceptual processes (p. 164)

perceptual interpretation The process of generating meaning from sensory experience (p. 172)

perceptual organisation The process of integrating sensations into meaningful perceptual units (p. 161)

performance-approach goals Goals that centre on approaching or attaining a standard (p. 398)

performance-avoidance goals Goals that centre on avoiding failure, particularly publicly observable failure (p. 398)

performance goals Motives to achieve at a particular level, usually one that meets a socially defined standard (p. 398)

peripheral nervous system (PNS) A component of the nervous system that includes neurons that travel to and from the central nervous system; includes the somatic nervous system and the autonomic nervous system (p. 96)

peripheral route to persuasion A method of persuasion that appeals less to rational and thoughtful processes than to automatic or emotional ones (p. 701)

permissive A way of parenting that imposes few controls on children, allowing the children to make their own decisions whenever possible (p. 514)

personal constructs Mental representations of the people, places, things and events that are significant in a person's life (p. 437)

personal identity A sense of who we are as individuals (p. 796)

personality The enduring patterns of thought, feeling and behaviour that are expressed by individuals in different circumstances (p. 424)

personality disorder A chronic and severe disorder that substantially inhibits the capacity to love and to work (p. 606)

personal value The importance individuals attach to various stimuli and to the outcomes they expect as a result of their behaviour (p. 438)

person-by-situation interaction Process by which some personality dispositions are activated only under certain circumstances (p. 449)

person-centred approach Carl Rogers' therapeutic approach that focuses on the individual's phenomenal world (pp. 16, 451)

perspectives Broad ways of understanding psychological phenomena, including theoretical propositions, shared metaphors and accepted methods of observation (p. 11)

perspective-taking The ability to understand other people's viewpoints or perspectives (p. 524)

persuasion Deliberate efforts to induce attitude change (p. 699)

pessimistic explanatory style A tendency to explain bad events that happen in a self-blaming manner, viewing their causes as global and stable (p. 247)

phallic stage In Freudian theory, the psychosexual phase occurring roughly around ages four to six, when children discover that they can get pleasure from touching their genitals (p. 429)

phantom limbs Misleading 'sensations' from missing limbs (p. 156)

phenomenal experience The way individuals conceive of reality and experience themselves and their world (p. 451)

pheromone A chemical secreted by organisms in some species that allows communication between organisms (p. 153)

phobia An irrational fear of a specific object or situation (pp. 227, 634)

phoneme The smallest unit of speech that distinguishes one linguistic utterance from another (p. 322)

phrase A group of words that acts as a unit and conveys a meaning (p. 323)

pitch The psychological property corresponding to the frequency of a sound wave; the quality of a tone from low to high (p. 148)

pituitary gland Often referred to as the 'master gland' of the endocrine system because many of the hormones it releases stimulate and thus regulate the hormonal action of other endocrine glands (p. 96)

placebo effect A phenomenon in which an experimental intervention produces an effect because participants believe it will produce an effect (p. 52)

place theory A theory of pitch which proposes that different areas of the basilar membrane are maximally sensitive to different frequencies (p. 151)

pleasure principle In Freud's theory, the id seeks immediate satisfaction and gratification, with little or no consideration for the longer term ramifications (p. 431)

pluralism A situation where there is general acceptance not just of the existence of many different cultural and ethnic groups but also of their right to retain their cultural heritage and coexist (p. 790)

polychronic cultures Cultures in which time is much more fluid and less closely regulated (p. 786)

population A group of people or animals of interest to a researcher from which a sample is drawn (p. 45)

positive affect A general category of emotions related to feeling good (p. 407)

positive correlation A relation between two variables in which the higher one is, the higher the other tends to be (p. 59)

positive reinforcement The process by which a behaviour is made more likely because of the presentation of a rewarding stimulus (p. 233)

positive reinforcer A rewarding stimulus that strengthens a behaviour when it is presented (p. 234)

positive symptoms Symptoms of schizophrenia such as delusions and hallucinations that reflect the presence of something that was not there previously and is not normally present (p. 622)

positron emission tomography (PET) A computerised brain-scanning technique that allows observation of the brain in action (p. 61)

postconventional morality In Kohlberg's theory, the level of morality in which individuals follow abstract, self-defined principles which may or may not accord with the dominant mores or morals of the times (p. 529)

post-traumatic stress disorder (PTSD) An anxiety disorder characterised by symptoms such as flashbacks and recurrent thoughts of a psychologically distressing event outside the normal range of experience (p. 635)

practical intelligence The ability to find practical, commonsense solutions to everyday problems (p. 359)

pragmatics The way language is used and understood in everyday life (p. 324)

preconscious mental processes Thoughts that are not conscious but could become conscious at any point, much like information stored in long-term semantic memory (pp. 191, 426)

preconventional morality In Kohlberg's theory, the level of morality in which children follow moral rules either to avoid punishment or to obtain reward (p. 529)

prediction Involves being able to anticipate future events (p. 49)

prejudice Judging people based on negative stereotypes (pp. 709, 799)

preoperational stage Piaget's second stage of cognitive development, beginning roughly around age two and lasting until age five to seven, characterised by the emergence of symbolic thought (p. 485)

prepared learning Responses to which an organism is predisposed because they were selected through natural selection (p. 230)

presbycusis The inability to hear high-frequency sounds, which usually occurs with ageing (p. 477)

primary appraisal The first stage in the process of stress and coping in which the person decides whether the situation is benign, stressful or irrelevant (p. 581)

primary areas The areas of the cortex involved in sensory functions and in the direct control of motor movements (p. 109)

primary drive An innate drive such as hunger, thirst and sex (p. 377)

primary process thinking Associative thinking described by Freud, in which ideas connected in people's minds through experience come to mind automatically when they think about related ideas; primary process thought is also wishful and unrealistic (p. 431)

priming effects The processing of specific information is facilitated by prior exposure to the same or similar information (p. 271)

principle of aggregation Averaging across multiple situations to find evidence of particular personality traits (p. 446)

proactive interference A phenomenon in which old memories that have already been stored interfere with the retrieval of new information (p. 287)

probability value The probability that obtained findings were accidental or just a matter of chance; also called *p* value (p. 80)

problem drinkers People who are not physiologically addicted to alcohol but who still have a number of problems stemming from alcohol consumption (p. 569)

problem-focused coping Efforts to change the situation producing the stress (p. 590)

problem solving The process of transforming one situation into another that meets a goal (p. 307)

problem-solving strategy A technique used to solve problems (p. 308)

procedural memory Knowledge of procedures or skills that emerges when people engage in activities that require them (p. 269)

projection A defence mechanism in which a person attributes his or her own unacknowledged feelings or impulses to others (p. 432)

projective test A personality assessment method in which participants are confronted with an ambiguous stimulus and asked to define it in some way; the assumption underlying these tests is that when people are faced with an unstructured, undefined stimulus, they will project their own thoughts, feelings and wishes into their responses (p. 434)

proprioceptive senses Senses that provide information about body position and movement; the two proprioceptive senses are kinaesthesia and vestibular sense (p. 160)

prosocial behaviour Behaviour that benefits either specific individuals or society as a whole (p. 530)

prospective memory Memory for things that need to be done in the future (p. 274)

protection motivation theory of health The health belief model plus self-efficacy (p. 557)

prototype A typical example of a category of things (p. 301)

proxemics The use of space between people while communicating (p. 821)

proximity A Gestalt rule of perception which states that, other things being equal, the brain groups objects together that are close to each other (p. 162)

psychiatrists Specialists who have medical degrees and prescribe medication to treat mental illness (p. 26)

psychoactive substance Any drug that operates on the nervous system to alter patterns of mental activity (p. 209)

psychoanalysis An intensive therapeutic process in which the patient meets with the therapist three to five times a week, lies on a couch, and uses free association, interpretation and transference (p. 659)

psychodynamic formulation A set of hypotheses about the patient's personality structure and the meaning of a symptom (p. 606)

psychodynamic perspective The perspective initiated by Sigmund Freud that focuses on the dynamic interplay of mental forces (p. 12)

psychodynamic psychotherapy A form of psychotherapy based on psychodynamic principles, in which the patient meets the therapist somewhat less frequently than in psychoanalysis and sits face to face with the therapist (p. 659)

psychodynamics A view analogous to dynamics among physical forces in which psychological forces such as wishes, fears and intentions have a direction and an intensity (pp. 11, 426)

psychological anthropologists People who study psychological phenomena in other cultures by observing people in their natural settings (p. 7)

psychologists Professionals who examine why people behave the way they do; they consider the thought processes that underpin behaviour (p. 26)

psychology The scientific investigation of mental processes and behaviour (p. 5)

psychometric approach An approach to the study of intelligence, personality and psychopathology which tries to derive some kind of theoretical meaning empirically from statistical analysis of psychometric test findings (p. 354)

psychometric instruments Tests that quantify psychological attributes such as personality traits or intellectual abilities (p. 344)

psychomotor slowing An increase in the time required for processing and acting on information that occurs with age (p. 492)

psychoneuroimmunology The study of the interactions among behaviour, the nervous system, the endocrine system and the immune system (p. 588)

psychopathology Problematic patterns of thought, feeling or behaviour that disrupt an individual's sense of wellbeing or social or occupational functioning (p. 602)

psychophysics Branch of psychology that studies the relationship between attributes of the physical world and the psychological experience of them (p. 129)

psychosexual stages Freud's hypothesised stages in the development of personality, sexuality and motivation (p. 428)

psychoses Gross disturbances involving a loss of touch with reality (p. 606)

psychosocial needs Personal and interpersonal motives that lead people to strive for such ends as mastery, achievement, power, self-esteem, affiliation and intimacy with other people (p. 397)

psychosocial stages In Erikson's theory, the stages in the development of the person as a social being (p. 536)

psychosomatic medicine The idea that changes in physiology mediate the relationship between unconscious conflicts and illness (p. 553)

psychosurgery Brain surgery to reduce psychological symptoms (p. 677)

psychotherapy integration The use of theory or technique from multiple theoretical perspectives (p. 684)

psychoticism A dimension on which low end is defined by people who display empathy and impulse control and the high end is defined by people who are aggressive, egocentric, impulsive and antisocial (p. 442)

psychotropic medications Drugs that act on the brain to affect mental processes (p. 672)

puberty The stage at which individuals become capable of reproduction (p. 476)

punishment A conditioning process that decreases the probability that a behaviour will occur (p. 233)

pupil The opening in the centre of the iris that constricts or dilates to regulate the amount of light entering the eye (p. 138)

Q

quasi-experimental designs Research designs that employ the logic of experimental methods but lack absolute control over variables (p. 54)

questionnaire Research tool in which the investigator asks participants to respond to a written list of questions or items (p. 57)

R

racial prejudice Negative stereotypes about members of another racial group or a cultural practice (p. 799)

racism The pervasive and systematic assumption of the inferiority of certain groups and the different and unfair treatment of those groups on the basis of that assumed inferiority (p. 800)

random sample A sample of participants selected from the population in a relatively arbitrary manner (p. 57)

range A measure of variability that represents the difference between the highest and the lowest value on a variable obtained in a sample (p. 78)

rapid eye movement (REM) sleep The period of sleep during which darting eye movements occur, autonomic activity increases, and patterns of brain activity resemble those observed in waking states (p. 200)

rational–emotive behaviour therapy A psychological treatment in which the therapist helps uncover and alter the illogical thoughts that provoke psychological distress (p. 665)

rationalisation A defence mechanism that involves explaining away actions in a seemingly logical way to avoid uncomfortable feelings (p. 432)

rationalist philosophers Emphasise the role of reason in creating knowledge (p. 18)

ratio schedules of reinforcement Operant conditioning procedures in which an organism is reinforced for some proportion of responses (p. 238)

reaction formation A defence mechanism in which the person turns unacceptable feelings or impulses into their opposites (p. 432)

reality principle In Freud's theory, the ego recognises that the immediate desire for pleasure needs to be offset against the reality of what the consequences might be (p. 431)

reasoning The process by which people generate and evaluate arguments and beliefs (p. 305)

recall The explicit (conscious) recollection of material from long-term memory (p. 271)

receptive field A region within which a neuron responds to appropriate stimulation (p. 140)

receptors In neurons, protein molecules in the postsynaptic membrane that pick up neurotransmitters; in sensation, specialised cells of the sensory systems that respond to the environmental stimuli and typically activate sensory neurons (p. 93)

reciprocal altruism The theory that natural selection favours animals that behave altruistically if the likely benefit to each individual over time exceeds the likely cost to each individual's reproductive success (p. 749)

recognition Explicit (conscious) knowledge of whether something currently perceived has been previously encountered (p. 271)

recognition-by-components The theory that asserts that we perceive and categorise objects in our environment by breaking them down into component parts and then matching the components and the way they are arranged against similar 'sketches' stored in memory (p. 163)

reference group The group to which a person refers when taking a particular action (p. 764)

reflexes A behaviour that is elicited automatically by an environmental stimulus (pp. 100, 222)

regression Reverting to conflicts or modes of managing emotion characteristic of an earlier particular stage (p. 432)

rehearsal Repeating or studying information to retain it in memory (p. 262)

reinforcement A conditioning process that increases the probability that a response will occur (p. 233)

reinforcer An environmental consequence that occurs after an organism has produced a response and makes the response more likely to recur (p. 233)

rejected children Children who are disliked by their peers (p. 520)

relatedness Interpersonal motives for connectedness with other people; also called communion motives (p. 397)

relational theories Theories that propose that the need for relatedness is a central motive in humans and that people will distort their personalities to maintain ties to important people in their lives (p. 433)

reliability A measure's ability to produce consistent results (p. 46)

religious experiences Subjective experiences of being in contact with the divine, which can range from relatively ordinary experiences, such as listening passively to a sermon, to altered states of consciousness in which a person feels at one with nature or the supernatural (p. 215)

representative A sample that reflects characteristics of the population as a whole (p. 45)

representativeness heuristic A cognitive shortcut used to assess whether an object or incident belongs in a particular class (p. 312)

repression A defence mechanism in which thoughts that are too anxiety provoking to acknowledge are kept from conscious awareness (p. 432)

reproductive success The capacity to survive and produce offspring (p. 21)

researcher bias Systematic errors in measurement due to the researcher seeing what he or she expects to see (p. 55)

resistance Barriers to psychotherapy created by the patient in an effort to reduce anxiety (p. 658)

response bias In signal detection theory, the participant's readiness to report detecting a signal when uncertain; also called decision criterion (p. 132)

response contingency The connection that exists between a behaviour and a consequence because the consequence is dependent on the behaviour (p. 240)

response prevention Preventing the patient from producing responses that allow avoidance of the feared stimulus (p. 663)

resting potential Condition in which the neuron is not firing (p. 91)

retest reliability Tendency of a test to yield relatively similar scores for the same individual over time (p. 46)

reticular formation A diffuse network of neurons that extends from the lowest parts of the medulla in the hindbrain to the upper end of the midbrain, serving to maintain consciousness, regulate arousal levels, and modulate the activity of neurons throughout the central nervous system (p. 104)

retina The light-sensitive layer of tissue at the back of the eye that transduces light into neural impulses (p. 138)

retrieval Bringing information from long-term memory into short-term, or working, memory (p. 262)

retrieval cues Stimuli or thoughts that can be used to facilitate retrieval (p. 277)

retroactive interference Interference of new information with the retrieval of old information (p. 287)

retrograde amnesia An inability to recall memories for some period prior to the brain injury (p. 291)

retrospective memory Memory for events that have already occurred (p. 274)

rods One of two types of photoreceptors; allow vision in dim light (p. 138)

role A position within a group that defines appropriate behaviour for the person occupying it (p. 765)

Rorschach inkblot test A projective personality test in which a participant views a set of inkblots and tells the tester what each inkblot resembles (p. 434)

S

sample A subgroup of a population likely to be representative of the population as a whole (p. 45)

sampling bias A sampling procedure whereby the sample is not representative of the population as a whole (p. 45)

Sapir–Whorf hypothesis A hypothesis that suggests that speakers of different languages actually think differently, and do so because of the differences in their languages (p. 822)

satiety mechanisms Processes that turn off ingestive behaviour (p. 387)

savant syndrome A condition whereby the person has low overall intelligence but an extraordinary talent in one particular realm of activity (p. 351)

scepticism Not accepting an assertion as true until you have examined the evidence (p. 67)

Schachter–Singer theory The theory that asserts that emotion involves cognitive interpretation of general physiological arousal (p. 413)

schema Integrated pattern of knowledge stored in memory that organises information and guides the acquisition of new information (pp. 176, 484)

schizophrenia Psychotic disorders characterised by disturbances in thought, perception, behaviour, language, communication and emotion (p. 620)

scientific approach This approach to psychology involves using empirical methodologies such as observation and experimentation to gain knowledge (p. 49)

scientist–practitioner model The model whereby psychology students are taught the science of psychology and later trained as applied psychologists (p. 655)

seasonal affective disorder (SAD) A depressive syndrome whereby mood and behaviour changes occur with regular seasonal climatic variation, (p. 628)

secondary appraisal The second stage in the process of stress and coping during which the person evaluates the options and decides how to respond (p. 581)

secondary drive A motive learned through classical conditioning and other learning mechanisms such as modelling; also called acquired drive (p. 377)

secondary process thinking Rational, logical, goal-directed thinking (p. 431)

secure attachment style Response to separation in which infants welcome the mother's return and seek closeness to her (p. 507)

selective inattention The process by which important information is ignored (p. 188)

selective serotonin reuptake inhibitor (SSRI) A class of antidepressant medications, including Prozac, that blocks the presynaptic membrane from taking back serotonin, and hence leaves it acting longer in the synapse (p. 675)

self The person, including mental processes, body and attributes (p. 723)

self-actualisation People are motivated to fulfil the whole range of needs that humans experience (p. 15)

self-actualisation needs In Maslow's theory, the needs to express oneself, grow and actualise, or attain one's potential (p. 380)

self-concept An organised pattern of thought and perception about oneself (pp. 16, 451, 521, 723)

self-consistency The motivation to interpret information to fit the self-concept and to prefer people who verify rather than challenge it (p. 726)

self-determination theory A theory of motivation that proposes that people have three innate needs — competence, autonomy and relatedness to others — and that intrinsic motivation flourishes when these needs are fulfilled rather than compromised (p. 379)

self-efficacy A person's conviction that he or she can perform the actions necessary to produce an intended behaviour (p. 557)

self-efficacy expectancy See self-efficacy (p. 438)

self-esteem The degree to which a person likes, respects or esteems the self (p. 723)

self-fulfilling prophecies False impressions of a situation that evoke behaviour that, in turn, makes impressions become true (pp. 709, 760)

self-handicapping A process by which people set themselves up to fail when success is uncertain to preserve their self-esteem (pp. 569, 726)

self-help groups Groups that are leaderless or guided by a non-professional, in which members assist each other in coping with a specific problem, as in Alcoholics Anonymous (p. 668)

self-monitoring Individual differences in the degree to which people manage their impressions (p. 727)

self-perception theory Alternative explanation of cognitive dissonance phenomena which holds that individuals become aware of their attitudes, emotions and other internal states by observing their own behaviour (p. 705)

self-presentation (Also known as impression management) the process by which people attempt to control the impressions that others form of them (pp. 578, 727)

self-presentational predicaments Instances in which our desires to influence the impressions other people form of us fail (p. 727)

self-regulation Setting goals, evaluating one's own performance, and adjusting one's behaviours flexibly to achieve these goals in the context of ongoing feedback (p. 439)

self-representations Mental models or representations of the self (p. 723)

self-schema A schema about the self that guides the way we think about and remember information relevant to ourselves (p. 724)

self-serving bias A phenomenon in which people tend to see themselves in a more positive light than they deserve (p. 720)

semantic memory General world knowledge or facts; also called generic memory (p. 269)

semantics The rules that govern the meanings, rather than the order, of morphemes, words, phrases and sentences (p. 324)

sensation The process by which the sense organs gather information about the environment (p. 128)

sensitive period Developmental period during which environmental input is especially important, but not absolutely required, for future development in a domain (p. 469)

sensorimotor stage Piaget's first stage of cognitive development, from birth to about two years of age, with thinking primarily characterised by action (p. 484)

sensory adaptation The tendency of sensory systems to respond less to stimuli that continue without change (p. 135)

sensory neurons Neurons that transmit information from sensory cells in the body to the brain (p. 89)

sensory receptors Specialised cells in the nervous system that transform energy in the environment into neural impulses that can be interpreted by the brain (p. 131)

sensory registers Memory systems that hold information for a very brief period of time (p. 261)

sensory representation Information that is represented in one of the sense modalities (p. 260)

sentence A unit of language that combines a subject and predicate and expresses a thought or meaning (p. 323)

separation anxiety Distress at separation from attachment figures (p. 506)

sequential study Type of research in which multiple cohorts are studied over time (p. 471)

serial position effect The phenomenon that people are more likely to remember information that appears first and last in a list than information in the middle of the list (p. 263)

serotonin A neurotransmitter involved in the regulation of mood, sleep, eating, arousal and pain (p. 95)

set point The value of some variable that the body is trying to maintain, such as temperature (pp. 386, 562)

sex The biological attributes that differentiate males from females (p. 797)

sex-role ideology Beliefs about appropriate behaviours of the sexes (p. 526)

sex typing The process by which children come to acquire personality traits, emotional responses, skills, behaviours and preferences that are culturally considered to be appropriate to their sex (p. 517)

sexual orientation The direction of a person's enduring sexual attraction to members of the same sex, the opposite sex or both (p. 394)

sexual response cycle The pattern of physiological changes during sexual stimulation, consisting of four phases: excitement, plateau, orgasm and resolution (p. 392)

sexual strategies Tactics used in selecting mates (p. 740)

s-factors Specific cognitive abilities unique to certain tests or shared only by a subset of tests (p. 354)

shape constancy The perception that an object's shape remains constant despite the changing shape of the retinal image as the object is viewed from varying perspectives (p. 170)

shaping The process of teaching a new behaviour by reinforcing closer and closer approximations of the desired response (p. 242)

short-term memory (STM) Memory for information that is available to consciousness for roughly 20 to 30 seconds; also called working memory (p. 261)

signal detection theory The theory that experiencing a sensation means making a judgement about whether a stimulus is present or absent (p. 132)

similarity A Gestalt rule of perception which states that the brain tends to group similar elements within a perceptual field (p. 162)

simplicity A Gestalt rule of perception which states that people tend to perceive the simplest pattern possible (p. 162)

single-blind study A study in which participants are kept blind to crucial information, notably about the experimental condition in which they have been placed (p. 52)

situational variables Aspects of the situation that interact with aspects of the person to produce behaviour (pp. 445, 736)

size constancy The perception that the shape of objects remains unchanged in spite of the fact that different impressions are made on the retina each time the object is encountered (p. 169)

skills training A technique that involves teaching behaviours or procedures for accomplishing specific goals (p. 664)

social cognition The processes by which people make sense of others, themselves, social interactions and relationships (pp. 521, 707)

social constructionism The postmodern theory that there are no universal truths because people are continually constructing knowledge based on their own individual and cultural experiences (p. 822)

social development Predictable changes in interpersonal thought, feeling and behaviour (p. 504)

social–emotional leader A role that may emerge in a group in which that member seeks to maximise group cohesion and minimise hostility (pp. 765, 768)

social exchange theories Theories based on behaviourist principles that suggest the foundation of relationships is reciprocal reward (p. 738)

social facilitation The phenomenon in which the presence of other people facilitates performance (p. 766)

social identity Our sense of belonging to a larger group (p. 797)

social identity theory Theory suggesting that people derive part of their identity from groups to which they belong (p. 714)

social influence The ways in which the presence of other people influences a person's thought, feeling or behaviour (p. 760)

socialisation The process by which children and adults learn the rules, beliefs, values, skills, attitudes and patterns of behaviour of their society (p. 512)

social learning Learning in which individuals learn many things from the people around them, with or without reinforcement (p. 249)

social loafing A reduction in individual effort when in a group (p. 766)

social phobia A marked fear that occurs when a person is in a specific social or performance situation (p. 634)

social psychology A subdiscipline that examines the influence of social processes on the way people think, feel and behave (p. 694)

social skills training A cognitive–behavioural technique that involves instruction and modelling, and was designed to help people develop interpersonal competence (p. 665)

social support Relationships with others that provide resources for coping with stress (p. 592)

sociobiology A field that explores possible evolutionary and biological bases of human social behaviour (p. 20)

somatic nervous system The division of the peripheral nervous system that consists of sensory and motor neurons that transmit sensory information and control intentional actions (p. 97)

somatoform disorders Disorders that occur when people complain of pain, suffering or illness but no physical problems can be identified to explain their ailments (p. 639)

somatosensory cortex The primary area of the parietal lobes, located behind the central tissue, which receives sensory information from different sections of the body (p. 110)

sound localisation Identifying the location of a sound in space (p. 153)

sound wave A pulsation of acoustic energy (p. 147)

spacing effect The superior long-term retention of information rehearsed in sessions spread out over longer intervals of time (p. 277)

spinal cord The part of the central nervous system that transmits information from sensory neurons to the brain, and from the brain to motor neurons that initiate movement; it is also capable of reflex actions (p. 102)

split brain The condition that results when the corpus callosum has been surgically cut, blocking communication between the two cerebral hemispheres (p. 113)

spontaneous recovery The spontaneous re-emergence of a response or an operant that has been extinguished (p. 228)

spontaneous remission When people quit drinking or greatly reduce their alcohol intake without any formal method of intervention (p. 570)

spreading activation theory The theory that the presentation of a stimulus triggers activation of closely related nodes (p. 280)

SQ4R method A mnemonic device designed to help students remember material from textbooks, which includes five steps: survey, question, read, recite, review and write (pp. 33, 278)

SSRI See selective serotonin reuptake inhibitor (p. 675)

stages Relatively discrete steps through which everyone progresses in the same sequence (p. 470)

stagnation A feeling that the promise of youth has gone unfulfilled (p. 538)

standard deviation (SD) The amount that the average participant deviates from the mean of the sample on a measure (p. 78)

standardised procedures Procedures applied uniformly to participants to minimise unintended variation (p. 44)

states of consciousness Different ways of orienting to internal and external events, such as awake states and sleep states (p. 186)

statistical significance The likelihood that results of a study have occurred simply by chance (p. 80)

stereotypes Schemas about characteristics ascribed to a group of people based on qualities such as race, ethnicity or gender rather than achievements or actions (p. 709)

Stevens' power law A law of sensation proposed by S. S. Stevens, which states that the subjective intensity of a stimulus grows as a proportion of the actual intensity raised to some power (p. 135)

stimulant A drug that increases alertness, energy and autonomic reactivity (p. 211)

stimulus An object or event in the environment that elicits a response in an organism (p. 222)

stimulus discrimination The tendency for an organism to respond to a very restricted range of stimuli (p. 228)

stimulus generalisation The tendency for learned behaviour to occur in response to stimuli that were not present during conditioning but that are similar to the conditioned stimulus (p. 227)

Strategic learning approach Involves being guided by the assessment criteria and enhancing self-esteem through competition (p. 31)

stratified random sample A sample selected to represent subpopulations proportionately, randomising only within groups (such as age or race) (p. 57)

straw man A fallacy in argument based on attacking an opposing argument for the purpose of strengthening one's own argument (p. 69)

stress A challenge to a person's capacity to adapt to inner and outer demands, which may be physiologically arousing, emotionally taxing, and cognitively and behaviourally activating (p. 580)

stressors Situations that often lead to stress, including life events, catastrophes and daily hassles (p. 583)

structuralism An early school of thought in psychology developed by Edward Titchener, which attempted to use introspection as a method for uncovering the basic elements of consciousness and the way they combine with each other into ideas (p. 10)

structural model Freud's model of conflict between desires and the dictates of conscience or the constraints of reality, which posits three sets of mental forces or structures: id, ego and superego (p. 431)

structure of personality The way enduring patterns of thought, feeling and behaviour are organised within an individual (p. 424)

structure of thought In Piaget's theory, a distinct underlying logic used by a child at a given stage (p. 484)

subcortical structures Structures within the cerebrum, such as the basal ganglia and limbic system, which lie below the cortex (p. 105)

subgoals Mini-goals on the way to achieving a broader goal (p. 308)

subjective norms Someone's perception of how significant other individuals will view a particular health behaviour, and the motivation to comply with the desires of those others (p. 557)

subjects The individuals whom a researcher observes in a study; also called participants (p. 45)

sublimation A defence mechanism that involves converting sexual or aggressive impulses into socially acceptable activities (p. 432)

subliminal perception Perception of stimuli below the threshold of consciousness (p. 191)

subordinate level A level of categorisation below the basic level in which more specific attributes are shared by members of a category (p. 303)

substance-related disorders Disorders involving continued use of a substance (such as alcohol or cocaine) that negatively affects psychological and social functioning (p. 617)

successive approximations A process of rewarding those behaviours that move the subject progressively closer to the desired behaviour (p. 242)

superego In Freudian theory, the structure that acts as conscience and source of ideals, or the parental voice within the person, established through identification (p. 431)

superordinate goals Goals requiring groups to cooperate for the benefit of all (p. 715)

superordinate level The most abstract level of categorisation in which members of a category share few common features (p. 303)

superstitious behaviour A phenomenon that occurs when the learner erroneously associates an operant and an environmental event (p. 234)

Surface learning approach Involves investing little time in the academic task and memorising information with rote learning (p. 31)

survey research Research asking a large sample of participants questions, often about attitudes or behaviours, using questionnaires or interviews (p. 57)

susceptible gene hypothesis Certain genes increase the likelihood of, but do not guarantee, the development of a particular trait or characteristic (p. 562)

syllogism A formal statement of deductive reasoning, which consists of two premises that lead to a logical conclusion (p. 305)

sympathetic nervous system A branch of the autonomic nervous system, typically activated in response to threats to the organism, which readies the body for 'fight-or-flight' reactions (p. 97)

synapse The place at which transmission of information between neurons occurs (p. 90)

syntax Rules that govern the placement of specific words or phrases within a sentence (p. 323)

system A group with interdependent parts (p. 610)

systematic desensitisation A cognitive–behavioural procedure in which the patient is induced to approach feared stimuli gradually, in a state that inhibits anxiety (p. 661)

systems approach An approach that explains an individual's behaviour in the context of a social group, such as a couple, family or larger group (p. 610)

T

tardive dyskinesia A serious, unpredictable, irreversible side effect of prolonged use of antipsychotic medications, in which a patient develops involuntary or semivoluntary twitching, usually of the tongue, face and neck (p. 674)

task leader The group member who takes responsibility for seeing that the group completes its tasks; also called instrumental leader (pp. 765, 768)

tastebuds Structures that line the walls of the papillae of the tongue (and elsewhere in the mouth) that contain taste receptors (p. 155)

tectum A midbrain structure involved in vision and hearing (p. 104)

tegmentum Midbrain structure that includes a variety of neural structures, related mostly to movement and conscious arousal and activation (p. 104)

telegraphic speech Speech used by young children that leaves out all but the essential words in a sentence (p. 331)

temperament A basic personality disposition heavily influenced by genes (p. 446)

temporal lobes Brain structures located in the lower side portion of the cortex that are important in audition (hearing) and language (p. 112)

teratogen A harmful environmental agent, such as a drug, irradiation or a virus, that causes maternal illness, which can produce foetal abnormalities or death (pp. 349, 473)

terminal buttons Structures at the end of the neuron that receive nerve impulses from the axon and transmit signals to adjacent cells (p. 90)

testosterone The hormone produced by the male gonads (testes) (p. 96)

thalamus A structure located deep in the centre of the brain that acts as a relay station for sensory information, processing it and transmitting it to higher brain centres (p. 105)

Thematic Apperception Test (TAT) A projective test consisting of a series of ambiguous pictures about which participants are asked to make up a story (p. 376)

theory A systematic way of organising and explaining observations (p. 44)

theory of mind An implicit set of ideas about the existence of mental states, such as beliefs and feelings, in oneself and others that children begin to develop in the toddler years (p. 524)

theory of multiple intelligences Howard Gardner's theory of seven intelligences used to solve problems or produce culturally significant products (p. 359)

theory of planned behaviour The theory of reasoned action plus self-efficacy (p. 557)

theory of reasoned action Behaviours stem from behavioural intentions, which are a function of a person's attitude towards the behaviour, and his perception of the subjective norms surrounding the behaviour (p. 557)

therapeutic alliance The patient's degree of comfort with the therapist, which allows him or her to speak about emotionally significant experiences (p. 657)

thinking Manipulating mental representations for a purpose (p. 298)

thyroid gland Endocrine structure located next to the trachea and larynx in the neck, which releases hormones that control growth and metabolism (p. 96)

tight cultures Cultures in which group members are expected to closely adhere to cultural norms and expectations (p. 787)

timbre The psychological property corresponding to a sound wave's complexity; the texture of a sound (p. 149)

tip-of-the-tongue phenomenon The experience in which people attempting but failing to recall information from memory know the information is 'in there' but are not quite able to retrieve it (p. 271)

top-down processing Perceptual processing that starts with the observer's expectations and knowledge (p. 174)

topographic model Freud's model of conscious, preconscious and unconscious processes (p. 426)

traits Emotional, cognitive and behavioural tendencies that constitute underlying dimensions of personality on which individuals vary (p. 441)

transduction The process of converting physical energy into neural impulses (p. 131)

transference The phenomenon in which the patient displaces thoughts, feelings, fears, wishes and conflicts from past relationships, especially childhood relationships, onto the therapist (p. 658)

trephination The practice of drilling holes in the skull of a diseased individual to allow evil spirits to escape (p. 551)

triarchic theory of intelligence Distinguishes three aspects of intelligence: experiential intelligence, contextual intelligence and componential intelligence (p. 359)

trichromatic theory of colour A theory of colour vision initially proposed by Thomas Young and modified by Herman Von Helmholtz that proposes that the eye contains three types of receptors, each sensitive to wavelengths of light that produce sensations of blue, green and red; by this theory, the colours that humans see reflect blends of the three colours to which the retina is sensitive; also called the Young–Helmholtz theory (p. 145)

tricyclic antidepressant A class of medications for depression that compensates for depleted neurotransmitters (p. 675)

true self A core aspect of being, untainted by the demands of others (p. 451)

t test A test of statistical significance used when comparing the mean scores of two groups (p. 82)

tutelage The teaching of concepts or procedures primarily through verbal explanation or instruction (p. 250)

two-factor theory of intelligence A theory derived by Charles Spearman that holds that two types of factors or abilities underlie intelligence (p. 354)

tympanic membrane see eardrum (p. 149)

Type A behaviour pattern A pattern of behaviour and emotions that includes ambition, competitiveness, impatience and hostility (p. 589)

U

unconditional positive regard An attitude of total acceptance expressed by the therapist towards the client in client-centred therapy (p. 667)

unconditioned reflex A reflex that occurs naturally, without any prior learning (p. 223)

unconditioned response (UCR) An organism's unlearned, automatic response to a stimulus (p. 223)

unconditioned stimulus (UCS) A stimulus that produces a reflexive response without any prior learning (p. 223)

unconscious mental processes In Freud's theory, mental processes that are inaccessible to consciousness, many of which are repressed (pp. 191, 426)

understanding Involves identifying the causes of a phenomenon (p. 49)

uninvolved Parents who consistently place their own needs above the needs of their child (p. 515)

unipolar depression A mood disorder involving only depression; see also bipolar disorder (p. 628)

universal grammar An innate, shared set of linguistic principles (p. 327)

unpackaging studies Studies that try to explain why cultural differences occur, looking at the range of variables that might account for divergence in a particular aspect (p. 783)

V

valid Said of a study which has sound procedures (p. 45)

validation Demonstrating the validity of a measure by showing that it consistently relates to other phenomena in theoretically expected ways (p. 47)

validity The extent to which a test measures the construct it attempts to assess, or a study adequately addresses the hypothesis it attempts to assess (p. 47)

variability The extent to which participants tend to vary from each other in their scores on a measure (p. 78)

variable A phenomenon that changes across circumstances or varies among individuals (p. 44)

variable-interval (VI) schedule of reinforcement An operant conditioning procedure in which an organism receives a reward for its responses after an amount of time that is not consistent (p. 239)

variable-ratio (VR) schedule of reinforcement An organism receives a reward for a certain percentage of behaviours that are emitted, but this percentage is not fixed (p. 239)

ventricles Fluid-filled cavities of the brain that are enlarged in schizophrenics suggesting neuronal atrophy (p. 624)

ventromedial prefrontal cortex An area in the brain that serves many functions, including helping people use their emotional reactions to guide decision making and behaviour (p. 318)

verbal representations Information represented in words (p. 260)

vestibular sense The sense that provides information about the position of the body in space by sensing gravity and movement (p. 160)

vicarious conditioning The process by which an individual learns the consequences of an action by observing its consequences for someone else (p. 249)

virtual reality exposure therapy A treatment for phobias in which virtual images of the feared stimulus are shown, as opposed to the actual stimulus (p. 663)

visual cliff A clear table with a checkerboard directly beneath it on one side and another checkerboard that appears to drop off like a cliff on the other, used especially with human infants in depth perception studies (p. 172)

vocalics The use of vocal cues such as pitch, volume and tempo (p. 821)

W

wavelength The distance over which a wave of energy completes a full oscillation (p. 136)

Weber's law The perceptual law described by Ernst Weber that states that for two stimuli to be perceived as differing in intensity, the second must differ from the first by a constant proportion (p. 134)

Wechsler Adult Intelligence Scale, Fourth Edition (WAIS-IV) An intelligence test for adults that yields scores for both verbal and nonverbal (performance) IQ scores (p. 346)

Wechsler Intelligence Scale for Children, Fourth Edition (WISC-IV) An intelligence test for children up to age 16 that yields verbal and nonverbal (performance) IQ scores (p. 346)

weighted utility value In expectancy value theory, a combined measure of the importance of an attribute and how well a given option satisfies it (p. 311)

well-defined concept A concept that has properties clearly setting it apart from other concepts (p. 300)

Wernicke's area A brain structure located in the left temporal lobe involved in language comprehension (p. 112)

'what' pathway The pathway running from the striate cortex in the occipital lobes through the lower part of the temporal lobes, involved in determining what an object is (p. 144)

'where' pathway The pathway running from the striate cortex through the middle and upper regions of the temporal lobes and up into the parietal lobes, involved in locating an object in space, following its movement and guiding movement towards it (p. 144)

Whorfian hypothesis of linguistic relativity The notion that language shapes thought (p. 321)

working memory Conscious 'work-space' used for retrieving and manipulating information, maintained through maintenance rehearsal; also called short-term memory (p. 265)

X

xenophobia The fear or hatred of foreigners, or anything foreign and unfamiliar (p. 798)

Y

Young–Helmholtz theory A theory of colour vision initially proposed by Young and modified by Helmholtz which proposes that the eye contains three types of receptors, each sensitive to wavelengths of light that produce sensations of blue, green and red; by this theory, the colours that humans see reflect blends of the three colours to which the retina is sensitive; also called trichromatic theory (p. 145)

Z

zone of proximal development (ZPD) A continuum of cognitive development, ranging from the child's individual capacity for problem solving to a more advanced and collaboratively-based level of cognitive development (p. 489)

References

AARP News Bulletin. (1989, January). New study finds older drivers 'capable, safe'. *30*, 14.

Aartsen, M. J., Martin, M., & Zimprich, D. (2004). Gender differences in level and change in cognitive functioning: Results from the longitudinal aging study, Amsterdam. *Gerontology, 50*, 35–38.

Abbass, A. (2002). Intensive short-term dynamic psychotherapy in a private psychiatric office: Clinical and cost effectiveness. *American Journal of Psychotherapy, 56*(2), 225–232.

Abbass, A. A., Hancock, J. T., Henderson, J., & Kisely, S. (2006). Short-term psychodynamic psychotherapies for common mental disorders. *Cochrane Database of Systematic Reviews, 5*(CD004687), 1–58.

ABC Radio National. (2010, June 10). A new approach to treating PTSD and substance abuse. Radio broadcast. *Life Matters*. Retrieved from http://www.abc.net.au/rn/lifematters/stories/2010/2922664.htm

Abel, E. (1998). Fetal alcohol syndrome. *Psychological Bulletin, 87*, 29–50.

Abelson, R. B. (1995). *Statistics as principled argument*. Hillsdale, NJ: Lawrence Erlbaum.

Abelson, R. P. (1983). Whatever became of consistency theory? *Personality and Social Psychology Bulletin, 9*, 37–54.

Abraham, H. D., & Duffy, F. H. (1996). Stable quantitative EEG difference in post-LSD visual disorder by split-half analysis: Evidence for disinhibition. *Psychiatry Research: Neuroimaging, 67*, 173–187.

Abraham, W. C., Logan, B., Greenwood, J. M., & Dragunow, M. (2002). Induction and experience-dependent consolidation of stable long-term potentiation lasting months in the hippocampus. *The Journal of Neuroscience, 22*, 9626–9634.

Abramov, I., & Gordon, J. (1994). Color appearance: On seeing red—or yellow, or green, or blue. *Annual Review of Psychology, 45*, 451–485.

Abrams, D., & Hogg, M. A. (Eds.). (1999). *Social identity and social cognition*. Oxford: Blackwell.

Abrams, D. B., & Wilson, G. T. (1983). Alcohol, sexual arousal, and self-control. *Journal of Personality and Social Psychology, 45*, 188–198.

Abrams, R., Swartz, C. M., & Vedak, C. (1989). Antidepressant effects of right versus left unilateral ECT and the lateralization theory of ECT action. *American Journal of Psychiatry, 146*, 1190–1192.

Abramson, L. Y., Metalsky, G. I., & Alloy, L. B. (1989). Hopelessness depression: A theory-based subtype of depression. *Psychological Review, 96*, 358–372.

Abramson, L. Y., Seligman, M. E. P., & Teasdale, J. D. (1978). Learned helplessness in humans: Critique and reformulation. *Journal of Abnormal Psychology, 87*, 49–74.

Abrous, D. N., Rodriquez, J., le Moal, M., Moser, P. C., & Barneoud, P. (1999). Effects of mild traumatic brain injury on immunoreactivity for the inducible transcription factors c-Fos, c-Jun, JunB, and Krox-24 in cerebral regions associated with conditioned fear responding. *Brain Research, 826*, 181–192.

Access Economics. (2006a). *Dementia prevalence and incidence among Australians who do not speak English at home* (Report by Access Economics Pty Ltd for Alzheimer's Australia). Retrieved from http://www.alzheimers.org.au/upload/NoEnglishAtHome

Access Economics. (2006b). *The economic costs of obesity* (Report by Access Economics Pty Ltd to Diabetes Australia). Canberra, Australia: Access Economics.

Access Economics. (2008). *The growing cost of obesity in 2008: Three years on* (Report by Access Economics Pty Ltd to Diabetes Australia). Retrieved from http://www.accesseconomics.com.au/publicationsreports/showreport.php?id=172

Access Economics. (2009). *Keeping dementia front of mind: Incidence and prevalence 2009–2050* (Final report by Access Economics Pty Ltd for Alzheimer's Australia). Retrieved from http://www.apo.org.au/research/keeping-dementia-front-mind-incidence-and-prevalence-2009-2050

Ackerman, S. J., Hilsenroth, M. J., Clemence, A. J., Weatherill, R., & Fowler, J. C. (2000). The effects of social cognition and object representation on psychotherapy continuation. *Bulletin of the Menninger Clinic, 64*, 386–408.

Adams, B. D. (1985). Age, structure, and sexuality. *Journal of Homosexuality, 11*, 19–33.

Adams, C. (1991). Qualitative age differences in memory for text: A life-span development perspective. *Psychology and Aging, 6*, 323–336.

Adams, H. E., Wright, L. W., & Lohr, B. A. (1996). Is homophobia associated with homosexual arousal? *Journal of Abnormal Psychology, 105*, 440–445.

Adams-Webber, J. R. (2001). Cognitive complexity and role relationships. *Journal of Constructivist Psychology, 14*, 43–50.

Adcock, R. A., Constable, R. T., Gore, J. C., & Goldman-Rakic, P. S. (2000). Functional neuroanatomy of executive processes involved in dual-task performance. *Proceedings of the National Academy of Sciences, USA, 97*, 3567–3572.

Ader, R. (2003). Conditioned immunomodulation: Research needs and directions. *Brain, Behavior and Immunity, 17*(Suppl. 1), S51–S57.

Ader, R., & Cohen, N. (1985). CNS immune system interactions: Conditioning phenomena. *Behavioral and Brain Sciences, 8*, 379–426.

Adler, G., & Buie, D. H. (1979). Aloneness and borderline psychopathology: The possible relevance of child development issues. *International Journal of Psychoanalysis, 60*, 83–96.

Admin, N. (2002a). *Addressing the academic needs of boys*. Retrieved November 16, 2004, from http://www.achieveonline.com.au/article/view/246/1/10/

Admin, N. (2002b). *Girls and technology*. Retrieved November 16, 2004, from http://www.achieveonline.com.au/article/view/197/1/10/

Adolphs, R. (1999). Social cognition and the brain. *Trends in Cognitive Sciences, 3*, 469–479.

Adolphs, R., Damasio, H., Tranel, D., & Damasio, A. R. (1996). Cortical systems for the recognition of emotion in facial expressions. *Journal of Neuroscience, 16*, 7678–7687.

Adorno, T. W., Frenkel-Brunswik, E., Levinson, D., & Sanford, R. N. (1950). *The authoritarian personality*. New York: W.W. Norton.

A fistful of risks. (1996). *Discover, 17*, 82–84.

Aggleton, J. P. (Ed.). (1992). *The amygdala: Neurobiological aspects of emotion, memory, and mental dysfunction*. New York: Wiley-Liss.

Ainsworth, M. D. S. (1967). *Infancy in Uganda*. Baltimore: Johns Hopkins University.

Ainsworth, M. D. S. (1973). The development of infant–mother attachment. In B. Caldwell & H. Ricciuti (Eds.), *Review of child development research: Vol. 3*. Chicago: University of Chicago Press.

Ainsworth, M. D. S. (1979). Infant–mother attachment. *American Psychologist, 34*, 932–937.

Ainsworth, M. D. S. (1991). Attachments and other affectional bonds across the life cycle. In C. M. Parkes, J. Stevenson-Hinde, & P. Marris (Eds.), *Attachment across the life cycle* (pp. 33–51). London: Tavistock/Routledge.

Ainsworth, M. D. S., & Bell, S. M. (1970). Attachment, exploration, and separation: Illustrated by the behavior of one-year-olds in a strange situation. *Child Development, 41*, 49–67.

Ajzen, I. (1991). The theory of planned behavior. *Organizational Behavior and Human Decision Processes, 50*, 179–211.

Ajzen, I. (1996). The directive influence of attitudes on behavior. In P. M. Gollwitzer & J. A. Bargh (Eds.), *The psychology of action: Linking cognition and motivation to behaviour* (pp. 385–403). New York: Guilford Press.

Ajzen, I. (2000). Nature and operation of attitudes. *Annual Review of Psychology, 27*, 27–58.

Ajzen, I. (2001). Nature and operation of attitudes. *Annual Review of Psychology, 52*, 27–58.

Ajzen, I., & Fishbein, M. (1977). Attitude-behavior relations: A theoretical analysis and review of empirical research. *Psychological Bulletin, 84*, 888–918.

Ajzen, I., & Fishbein, M. (1980). *Understanding attitudes and predicting social behavior*. Englewood Cliffs, NJ: Prentice-Hall.

Aksan, M., Kochanska, G., & Ortmann, M. R. (2006). Mutually responsive orientation between parents and their young children: Toward methodological advances in the science of relationships. *Developmental Psychology, 42*, 833–848.

al Absi, M., & Rokke, P. D. (1991). Can anxiety help us tolerate pain? *Pain, 46*, 43–51.

Albert, D. J., Jonik, R. H., & Walsh, M. (1991). Hormone-dependent aggression in the female rat: Testosterone plus estradiol implants prevent the decline in aggression following ovariectomy. *Physiology and Behavior, 49*, 673–677.

Albert, M. K. (1993). Parallelism and the perception of illusory contours. *Perception, 22*, 589–595.

Albert, R. D., & Ha, I. A. (2004). Latino/Anglo-American differences in attributions to situations involving touch and silence. *International Journal of Intercultural Relations, 28*, 253–280.

Alberts, A. C. (1989). Ultraviolet visual sensitivity in desert iguanas: Implications for pheromone detection. *Animal Behaviour, 38*, 129–137.

Alderfer, C. (1972). *Existence, relatedness, and growth: Human needs in organizational settings*. New York: Free Press.

Alderfer, C. P. (1989). Theories reflecting my personal experience and life development. *Journal of Applied Behavioral Science, 25*, 351–365.

Alderman, M. K. (2004). *Motivation for achievement: Possibilities for teaching and learning* (2nd ed.). Mahwah, NJ: Lawrence Erlbaum.

Alexander, G. M., Swerdloff, R. S., Wang, C. W., & Davidson, T. (1997). Androgen-behavior correlations in hypogonadal men and eugonadal men: I. Mood and response to auditory sexual stimuli. *Hormones and Behavior, 31*, 110–119.

Alexander, I. (1990). *Personology: Method and content in personality assessment and psychobiography*. Durham, NC: Duke University Press.

Alexander, J. M., & Schwanenflugel, P. J. (1994). Strategy regulation: The role of intelligence, metacognitive attributions, and knowledge base. *Developmental Psychology, 30*, 709–723.

Alicke, M. D., Klotz, M. L., Breitenbecher, D. L., Yurak, T. J., & Vredenburg, D. S. (1995). Personal contact, individuation, and the better-than-average effect. *Journal of Personality and Social Psychology, 68*, 804–825.

Allen, F. (1998). *Health psychology: Theory and practice*. Sydney, Australia: Allen & Unwin.

Allen, S. W., & Brooks, L. R. (1991). Specializing the operation of an explicit rule. *Journal of Experimental Psychology: General, 120*, 3–19.

Allison, D. B., Heshka, S., Neale, M. C., & Lykken, D. T. (1994). A genetic analysis of relative weight among 4,020 twin pairs, with an emphasis on sex effects. *Health Psychology, 13*, 362–365.

Allott, K., & Redman, J. (2006). Patterns of use and harm reduction practices of ecstasy users in Australia. *Drug and Alcohol Dependence, 82*(2), 168–176.

Alloy, L. B., Abramson, L. Y., Hogan, M. E., Whitehouse, W. G., Rose, D. T., Robinson, M. S., et al. (2000). The Templen-Wisconsin Cognitive Vulnerability to Depression Project: Lifetime history of axis I psychopathology in individuals at high and low cognitive risk for depression. *Journal of Abnormal Psychology, 109*, 403–418.

Allport, G. (1935). Attitudes. In C. Murchison (Ed.), *Handbook of social psychology* (pp. 798–844). Worcester, MA: Clark University Press.

Allport, G. (1937). *Personality: A psychological interpretation*. New York: Henry Holt.

Allport, G. (1954). *The nature of prejudice*. Cambridge, MA: Addison-Wesley.

Allport, G. (1968). The historical background of modern social psychology. In G. Lindzey & E. Aronson (Eds.), *Handbook of social psychology: Vol. I*. Reading, MA: Addison-Wesley.

Allport, G., & Odbert, H. (1936). Trait-names: A psycho-lexical study. *Psychological Monographs, 47*(1, Whole No. 211).

Altamura, A. C., Pioli, R., Vitto, M., & Mannu, P. (1999). Venlafaxine in social phobia: A study in selective serotonin reuptake inhibitor nonresponders. *International Clinical Psychopharmacology, 14*, 239–245.

Alvarez-Borda, B., Ramirez-Amaya, V., Perez-Montfort, R., & Bermudez-Rattoni, F. (1995). Enhancement of antibody production by a learning paradigm. *Neurobiology of Learning and Memory, 64*, 103–105.

Alzheimer's Australia. (2009). *Keeping dementia front of mind: Incidence and prevalence 2009–2050* (Report by Access Economics). Retrieved from http://www.alzheimers.org.au/upload/Access_Exec_Summary-Aug09.pdf

Amabile, T. M. (1996). *Creativity in context. Update to 'the social psychology of creativity'*. Boulder, CO: Westview Press.

Ambady, N., & Rosenthal, R. (1993). Half a minute: Predicting teacher evaluations from thin slices of nonverbal behavior and physical attractiveness. *Journal of Personality and Social Psychology, 64*, 431–441.

American Cancer Society. (2002). *Cancer prevention and early detection facts and figures*. Retrieved from www.cancer.org

American Psychiatric Association. (1994). *Diagnostic and statistical manual of mental disorders* (4th ed.). Washington, DC: Author.

American Psychiatric Association. (2010). *DSM-5 Development*. Retrieved from http://www.dsm5.org

American Psychological Association. (2004). *Have your children had their anti-smoking shots?* Retrieved from http://www.apa.org/research/action/smoking.aspx

Amir, N., Beard, C., Burns, M., & Bomyea, J. (2009). Attention modification program in individuals with generalized anxiety disorder. *Journal of Abnormal Psychology, 118*, 28–33.

Amir, Y. (1994). The contact hypothesis in intergroup relations. In W. J. Lonner & R. Malpass (Eds.), *Psychology and culture*. Needham Heights, MA: Allyn & Bacon.

Amsterdam, B. (1972). Mirror self–image reactions before age two. *Developmental Psychology, 5*, 297 305.

An intro to sleep: What is sleep? (2007). Retrieved from www.talkaboutsleep.com/sleep-disorders/archives/intro.htm

Anand, B., & Brobeck, J. (1951). Hypothalamic control of food intake in rats and cats. *Yale Journal of Biological Medicine, 24*, 123–140.

Anastasi, A. (1958). Heredity, environment, and the question 'how?' *Psychological Review, 65*, 197–208.

Anastasi, A., & Urbina, S. (1997). *Psychological testing* (7th ed.). Upper Saddle River, NJ: Prentice-Hall.

Andersen, J. A. (2006). Leadership, personality and effectiveness. *The Journal of Socio-Economics, 35*, 1078–1091.

Andersen, S., & Cole, S. (1991). Do I know you? The role of significant others in general social perception. *Journal of Personality and Social Psychology, 59*, 384–399.

Andersen, S. M., Chen, S., & Carter, C. (2000). Fundamental human needs: Making social cognition relevant. *Psychological Inquiry, 11*(4), 269–318.

Andersen, S. M., Reznik, L., & Manzella, L. M. (1996). Eliciting facial affect, motivation, and expectancies in transference: Significant-other representations in social relations. *Journal of Personality and Social Psychology, 71*, 1108–1129.

Anderson, C. (1989). Temperature and aggression: Ubiquitous effects of heat on occurrence of human violence. *Psychological Bulletin, 106*, 74–96.

Anderson, C. A. (2001). Heat and violence. *Current Directions in Psychological Science, 10*, 33–38.

Anderson, C. A., Berkowitz, L., Donnerstein, E., Huesmann, L. R., Johnson, J. D., Linz, D., et al. (2003). The influence of media violence on youth. *Psychological Science in the Public Interest, 4*(3), 81–110.

Anderson, C. A., & Bushman, B. J. (2002). Human aggression. *Annual Review of Psychology, 53*, 27–52.

Anderson, D. J., Yoshizawa, T., Gollschewski, S. E., Atogami, F., & Courtney, M. D. (2004). Menopause in Australia and Japan: Effects of country of residence on menopausal status and menopausal symptoms. *Climacteric: The Journal of the International Menopause Society, 7*(2), 165–174.

Anderson, J. (1983). *The architecture of cognition*. Cambridge, MA: Harvard University Press.

Anderson, J. R. (1985). *Cognitive psychology and its implications* (2nd ed.). New York: Freeman.

Anderson, J. R. (1995). *Learning and memory: An integrated approach*. New York: John Wiley.

Anderson, J. R. (1996). ACT: A simple theory of complex cognition. *American Psychologist, 51*, 355–365.

Anderson, M. (2005). Marrying intelligence and cognition: A developmental view. In R. J. Sternberg & J. E. Pretz (Eds.), *Cognition and Intelligence* (pp. 268–287). Cambridge: Cambridge University Press.

Anderson, S. W., & Booker, M. B. (2006). Cognitive behavioral therapy versus psychosurgery for refractory obsessive-compulsive disorder. *Journal of Neuropsychiatry and Clinical Neuroscience, 18*, 129.

Andreasen, N. C. (1999). A unitary model of schizophrenia: Bleuler's 'fragmented phrene' as schizencephaly. *Archives of General Psychiatry, 56*, 781–787.

Andreasen, N. C., Arndt, S., Miller, D., Flaum, M., & Nopoulos, P. (1995). Correlational studies of the scale for the assessment of negative symptoms and the scale for the assessment of positive symptoms: An overview and update. *Psychopathology, 28*, 7–17.

Andreasen, N. C., Rice, J., Endicott, J., Coryell, W., Grove, W. M., & Reich, T. (1987). Familial rates of affective disorder: A report from the National Institute of Mental Health collaborative study. *Archives of General Psychiatry, 44*, 461–469.

Andreason, N. C., Swayze, V., Flaum, M., Alliger, R., & Cohen, G. (1990). Ventricular abnormalities in affective disorder: Clinical and demographic correlates. *American Journal of Psychiatry, 147*, 893–900.

Andreasson, S., & Brandt, L. (1997). Mortality and morbidity related to alcohol. *Alcohol & Alcoholism, 32*, 173–178.

Andrews, G., Clark, M., & Luszez, M. (2002). Successful aging in the Australian longitudinal study of aging: Applying the MacArthur model cross-nationally. *Journal of Social Issues, 58*, 749–765.

Andrews, G., Henderson, S., & Hall, W. (2001). Prevalence, comorbidity, disability and service utilisation. *British Journal of Psychiatry, 178*, 145–153.

Andrzejewski, S. J., Moore, C. M., Corvette, M., & Hermann, D. (1991). Prospective memory skill. *Bulletin of the Psychonomic Society, 29*, 304–306.

Angel, I., Hauger, R., Giblin, B., & Paul, S. (1992). Regulation of the anorectic drug recognition site during glucoprovic feeding. *Brain Research Bulletin, 28*, 201–207.

Antshel, K. M., & Remer, R. (2003). Social skills training in children with attention deficit hyperactivity disorder: A randomized-controlled clinical trial. *Journal of Clinical Child and Adolescent Psychology, 32*(1), 153–165.

Anthony, E., & Cohler, B. (Eds.). (1987). *The invulnerable child*. New York: Guilford Press.

Antoch, M. P., Song, E. J., Chang, A. M., Vitaterna, M. H., Zhao, Y. L., Wilsbacher, L. D., et al. (1997). Functional identification of the mouse circadian clock gene by transgenic BAC rescue. *Cell, 89*, 655–667.

Antrobus, J. (1991). Dreaming: Cognitive processes during cortical activation and high afferent thresholds. *Psychological Review, 98*, 96–121.

Antshel, K. M., & Remer, R. (2003). Social skills training in children with attention deficit hyperactivity disorder: A randomized-controlled clinical trial. *Journal of Clinical Child and Adolescent Psychology, 32*, 153–165.

Antzoulatos, E. G., & Byrne, J. (2004). Learning insights transmitted by glutamate. *Trends in Neurosciences, 27*(9), 555–560.

Aponte, H. J., & VanDeusen, J. M. (1981). Structural family therapy. In A. S. Gurman & D. P. Kniskern (Eds.), *Handbook of family therapy*. New York: Brunner/Mazel.

Applebaum, P. S., Uyehara, L. A., & Elin, M. R. (Eds.). (1997). *Trauma and memory: Clinical and legal controversies*. New York: Oxford University Press.

Archer, D. (1994). American violence: How high and why? *Law Studies, 19*, 12–20.

Archer, J. (1991). The influence of testosterone on human aggression. *British Journal of Psychology, 82*, 1–28.

Archer, J., Birring, S. S., & Wu, F. C. W. (1998). The association between testosterone and aggression among young men. *Aggressive Behavior, 24*, 411–420.

Archer, J., & Lloyd, B. (1985). *Sex and gender* (2nd ed.). New York: Cambridge University Press.

Ardelt, M. (2000). Still stable after all these years? Personality stability theory revisited. *Social Psychology Quarterly, 63*(4), 392–405.

Ardichvili, A., & Kuchinke, K. P. (2002). Leadership styles and cultural values among managers and subordinates: A comparative study of four countries of the former Soviet Union, Germany, and the US. *Human Resource Development International, 5*(1), 99–117.

Arena, J. G., & Blanchard, E. B. (1996). Biofeedback and relaxation therapy for chronic disorders. In R. J. Gatchel & D. C. Turk (Eds.), *Psychological approaches to pain management: A practitioner's handbook* (pp. 179–230). New York: Guilford Press.

Arendt, J., Skene, D. J., Middleton, B., Lockley, S. W., & Deacon, S. (1997). Efficacy of melatonin treatment in jet lag, shift work, and blindness. *Journal of Biological Rhythms, 12*(6), 604–617.

Arendt, R. E., Minnes, S., & Singer, L. T. (1996). Fetal cocaine exposure: Neurologic effects and sensory-motor delays. In L. S. Chandler & S. J. Lane (Eds.), *Children with prenatal drug exposure* (pp. 129–144). New York: Haworth Press.

Arkes, H., Boehm, L., & Xu, G. (1991). Determinants of judged validity. *Journal of Experimental Social Psychology, 27*, 576–605.

Arkowitz, H. (1997). Integrative theories of therapy. In P. L. Wachtel & S. B. Messer (Eds.), *Theories of psychotherapy: Origins and evolution* (pp. 227–288). Washington, DC: American Psychological Association.

Arkowitz, H., & Messer, S. B. (Eds.). (1984). *Psychodynamic therapy and behavior therapy: Is integration possible?* New York: Plenum Press.

Armitage, C. J., & Christian, J. (2003). From attitudes to behaviour: Basic and applied research on the theory of planned behaviour. *Current Psychology: Developmental, Learning, Personality, and Social, 22*(3), 187–195.

Armitage, C. J., & Conner, M. (2001). Efficacy of the theory of planned behaviour: A meta-analytic review. *British Journal of Social Psychology, 40*, 471–499. Retrieved from http://www.uns.ethz.ch/edu/teach/masters/ebcdm/readings/armitage_reviewtbp.pdf

Armony, J. L., & LeDoux, J. E. (2000). How danger is encoded: Toward a systems, cellular, and computational understanding of cognitive emotional interactions in fear. In M. S. Gazzaniga (Ed.), *The new cognitive neurosciences* (2nd ed., pp. 1067–1080). Cambridge, MA: MIT Press.

Arnett, J. J. (1999). Adolescent storm and stress, reconsidered. *American Psychologist, 54*, 317–326.

Arnkoff, D., Victor, B., & Glass, C. (1993). Empirical research on factors in psychotherapeutic change. In G. Stricker & J. Gold (Eds.), *Comprehensive handbook of psychotherapy integration* (pp. 27–42). New York: Plenum Press.

Arnsten, A. F. T. (1998). Catecholamine modulation of prefrontal cortical cognitive function. *Trends in Cognitive Sciences, 2*, 436–447.

Aron, L. (1996). *A meeting of minds: Mutuality in psychoanalysis*. Hillside, NJ: Analytic Press.

Aronson, E. (2002). Building empathy, compassion and achievement in jigsaw classrooms. In J. Aronson (Ed.), *Improving academic achievement: Impact of psychological factors on education* (pp. 209–225). San Diego, CA: Academic Press.

Aronson, E., & Mills, J. (1959). The effect of severity of initiation on liking for a group. *Journal of Abnormal and Social Psychology, 59*, 177–181.

Arrigo, J. A., & Pezdek, K. (1997). Lessons from the study of psychogenic amnesia. *Current Directions in Psychological Science, 5*, 148–152.

Arsenio, W. F., & Lemerise, E. A. (2004). Aggression and moral development: Integrating social information processing and moral domain models. *Child Development, 75*, 987–1002.

Arvey, R. D., McCall, B., & Bouchard, T. J. (1994). Genetic influence on job satisfaction and work values. *Personality and Individual Differences, 17*, 21–33.

Asch, S. E. (1946). Forming impressions of personality. *Journal of Abnormal and Social Psychology, 41*, 258–290.

Asch, S. E. (1955). Opinions and social pressure. *Scientific American, 193*, 31–35.

Asch, S. E. (1956). Studies of independence and conformity: A minority of one against unanimous majority. *Psychological Monographs: General and Applied, 70*, 1–69.

Asendorpf, J., & Baudonniere, P. (1993). Self-awareness and other-awareness: Mirror self-recognition and synchronic imitation among unfamiliar peers. *Developmental Psychology, 29*, 88–95.

Asendorpf, J., & Scherer, K. (1983). The discrepant repressor: Differentiation between low anxiety, high anxiety, and repression of anxiety by autonomic-facial-verbal patterns of behavior. *Journal of Personality and Social Psychology, 45*, 1334–1346.

Ashby, F. G., & Waldron, E. M. (2000). The neuropsychological bases of category learning. *Current Directions in Psychological Science, 9*, 10–14.

Ashford, J. W., Schmitt, F. A., & Kumar, V. (1996). Diagnosis of Alzheimer's disease. *Psychiatric Annals, 26*, 262–268.

Ashton, M. C., Lee, K., Perugini, M., Szarota, P., de Vries, R. E., Di Blas, L., et al. (2004). A six-factor structure of personality-descriptive adjectives: Solutions from psycholexical studies in seven languages. *Journal of Personality and Social Psychology, 86*, 356–366.

Askew, C., & Field, A. P. (2007). Vicarious learning and the development of fears in childhood. *Behaviour Research and Therapy, 45*, 2616–2627.

Aspinwall, L. G., Kemeny, M. E., Taylor, S. E., Schneider, S. G., & Dudley, J. P. (1991). Psychosocial predictors of gay men's AIDS risk-reduction behavior. *Health Psychology, 10*, 432–444.

Aspinwall, L. G., & Taylor, S. E. (1997). A stitch in time: Self-regulation and proactive coping. *Psychological Bulletin, 121*, 417–436.

Astington, J., & Jenkins, J. (1995). Theory-of-mind development and social understanding. *Cognition and Emotion, 9*(2/3), 151–165.

Astington, J., & Jenkins, J. (1999). A longitudinal study of the relation between language and theory-of-mind development. *Developmental Psychology, 35*(5), 1311–1320.

Astrom, A. N., & Rise, J. (2001). Young adults' intention to eat healthy food: Extending the theory of planned behavior. *Psychology and Health, 16*, 223–237.

Atkinson, J. W. (1977). Motivation for achievement. In T. Blass (Ed.), *Personality variables in social behavior* (pp. 25–108). Hillsdale, NJ: Erlbaum.

Atkinson, J. W., & Litwin, G. H. (1960). Achievement motive and test anxiety conceived as motive to approach success and motive to avoid failure. *Journal of Abnormal and Social Psychology, 60*, 52–63.

Atkinson, R. C., & Shiffrin, R. N. (1968). Human memory: A proposed system and its control processes. In K. W. Spence & J. T. Spence (Eds.), *The psychology of learning and motivation: Vol. 2* (pp. 89–195). New York: Academic Press.

Auerbach, R. P., Abela, J. R. Z., Zhu, X., & Yao, S. (2007). A diathesis-stress model of engagement in risky behaviours in Chinese adolescents. *Behaviour Research & Therapy, 45*, 2850–2860.

Augoustinos, M., Tuffin, K., & Sale, L. (1999). Race talk. *Australian Journal of Psychology, 51*, 90–97.

Auseinet. (2007). *Australian suicide statistics, 2005: Key findings*. Retrieved December 16, 2007, from http://www.auseinet.com/suiprev/statistics.php

Australian Broadcasting Corporation. (2000). *Menopause*. Retrieved June 25, 2004, from http://www.abc.net.au/science/menopause/default.htm

Australian Broadcasting Corporation. (2002). *Aboriginal trackers deserve tribute says former NT cop*. Retrieved October 10, 2004, from http://www.abc.net.au/central/stories/s692199.htm

Australian Broadcasting Corporation. (2004). *All in the mind: 19 June 2004 – attention deficit hyperactivity disorder (ADHD) – debate hots up in Western Australia*. Retrieved November 11, 2004, from http://www.abc.net.au/rn/science/mind/stories/s1132023.htm

Australian Bureau of Statistics. (1998). *Mental health and wellbeing: Profile of adults, Australia*. Canberra, Australia: Author.

Australian Bureau of Statistics. (2001). *Australian social trends 2001 –population composition: Asian-born Australians*. Canberra, Australia: AGPS.

Australian Bureau of Statistics. (2002a). *Australian social trends 2002*. Canberra, Australia: Author.

Australian Bureau of Statistics. (2002b). *Yearbook Australia 2002*. Canberra, Australia: Author.

Australian Bureau of Statistics. (2004a). *Australian social trends 2004*. Canberra, Australia: Author.

Australian Bureau of Statistics. (2004b). *Yearbook Australia 2004*. Canberra, Australia: Author.

Australian Bureau of Statistics. (2005). *Migration, Australia 2003–04*. Canberra, Australia: Author.

Australian Bureau of Statistics. (2006a). *Alcohol consumption in Australia: A snapshot, 2004–05*. Canberra, Australia: ABS.

Australian Bureau of Statistics. (2006b). *Cancer in Australia: A snapshot, 2004–05*. Canberra, Australia: Author.

Australian Bureau of Statistics. (2006c). *Cultural diversity overview*. Retrieved January 10, 2010, from http://www.abs.gov.au

Australian Bureau of Statistics. (2006d). *Mental health in Australia: A snapshot, 2004–05*. Canberra, Australia: Author.

Australian Bureau of Statistics. (2006e). *Population characteristics, Aboriginal and Torres Strait Islander Australians, 2006*. Retrieved from http://www.abs.gov.au/ausstats/abs@.nsf/0/6C0A23CD450AD61DCA257718002A8BBC?opendocument

Australian Bureau of Statistics. (2006f). *Private health insurance: A snapshot, 2004–05*. Canberra, Australia: ABS.

Australian Bureau of Statistics. (2007a). *2005 Causes of death: Australia*. Canberra, Australia: ABS.

Australian Bureau of Statistics. (2007b). *4705.0 – Population distribution, Aboriginal and Torres Strait Islander Australians, 2006*. Retrieved from http://www.abs.gov.au/AUSSTATS/abs@.nsf/Lookup/4705.0Main+Features12006?OpenDocument

Australian Bureau of Statistics. (2007c). *Australian social trends. Migration: Permanent additions to Australia's population*. Canberra, Australia: Author.

Australian Bureau of Statistics. (2007d). *National survey of mental health and wellbeing: Summary of results*. Retrieved from http://www.ausstats.abs.gov.au/ausstats/subscriber.nsf/0/6AE6DA447F985FC2CA2574EA00122BD6/$File/43260_2007.pdf

Australian Bureau of Statistics. (2008a). *Australian crime statistics*. Canberra, Australia: Author.

Australian Bureau of Statistics. (2008b). *Health literacy, Australia 2006* (ABS Cat. No. 4233.0). Canberra, Australia: Author.

Australian Bureau of Statistics. (2008c). *Internet activity, Australia, December 2008* (Cat. No. 8153.0). Retrieved from http://www.abs.gov.au/ausstats/

Australian Bureau of Statistics. (2008d). *Marriages and divorces, Australia, 2008*. Retrieved from http://www.abs.gov.au/ausstats/abs@.nsf/mf/3310.0

Australian Bureau of Statistics. (2008e). *National Aboriginal and Torres Strait Islander social survey: Language and culture*. Retrieved January 10, 2010, from http://www.abs.gov.au

Australian Bureau of Statistics. (2008f). *National survey of mental health and wellbeing: Summary of results, 2007* (ABS Cat. No. 4326.0). Canberra, Australia: Author.

Australian Bureau of Statistics. (2008g). *Year Book Australia 2008*. Canberra, Australia: Author.

Australian Bureau of Statistics. (2009a). *3310.0 – Marriages and divorces, Australia, 2008*. Retrieved from http://www.abs.gov.au/ausstats/abs@.nsf/0/AA3E05E646A0D60BCA2576200015A3E5?opendocument

Australian Bureau of Statistics. (2009b). *4102.0 – Australian social trends, March 2009*. Retrieved from http://www.abs.gov.au/AUSSTATS/abs@.nsf/Lookup/4102.0Main+Features30March 2009

Australian Bureau of Statistics. (2009c). *Australian social trends, March 2009*. Retrieved from http://www.ausstats.abs.gov.au/ausstats/subscriber.nsf/0/9B47C077B3B6C1AECA2575830015F1CF/$File/41020_ast_march2009.pdf

Australian Bureau of Statistics. (2009d). *National health survey: Summary of results*. Retrieved from http://abs.gov.au

Australian Bureau of Statistics. (2009e). *Tobacco smoking in the Aboriginal and Torres Strait Islander population, 2004–05*. Retrieved from http://www.abs.gov.au/AUSSTATS/abs@.nsf/Lookup/4724.0.55.002Main+Features42004-05

Australian Bureau of Statistics. (2010a). *1301.0 Yearbook chapter, 2009–10*. Retrieved from http://www.abs.gov.au/AUSSTATS/abs@.nsf/Latestproducts/1301.0Feature%20Article9012009–10?opendocument&tabname=Summary&prodno=1301.0&issue=2009–10&num=&view=

Australian Bureau of Statistics. (2010b). *3412.0 – 2008–09 Migration*. Retrieved from http://www.ausstats.abs.gov.au/Ausstats/subscriber.nsf/0/3A3EB923A8CBB55CCA25776E001762A6/$File/34120_2008-09.pdf

Australian Bureau of Statistics. (2010c). *6302.0 Average weekly earnings, Australia, February 2010*. Retrieved from http://www.ausstats.abs.gov.au/Ausstats/subscriber.nsf/0/DD6063E66BBDCF0DCA25772800193B80/$File/63020_Feb%202010.pdf

Australian Bureau of Statistics. (2010d). *Indigenous disadvantage and selected measures of wellbeing. 1301.0 Yearbook Chapter 2009–10*. Retrieved from http://www.abs.gov.au/AUSSTATS/abs@.nsf/Lookup/1301.0Feature+Article9012009%E2%80%9310

Australian Bureau of Statistics. (2010e). *Internet activity, Australia, June 2010* (Cat. No. 8153.0). Retrieved from http://www.abs.gov.au/ausstats/

Australian Bureau of Statistics. (2010f). *Year Book Australia, 2009–10. Feature article 2: Mental health*. Retrieved from http://www.abs.gov.au/AUSSTATS/abs@.nsf/Lookup/1301.0Chapter11082009%E2%80%9310

Australian Bureau of Statistics. (2010g). *Year Book Australia, 2009–10. Health care delivery and financing: Private health insurance*. Retrieved from http://abs.gov.au/AUSSTATS/abs@.nsf/Lookup/4ED550A390396D70CA25773700169C8A?opendocument

Australian Bureau of Statistics. (2010h). *Year Book Australia, 2009–10. Health: Communicable diseases*. Retrieved from http://abs.gov.au/AUSSTATS/abs@.nsf/Lookup/E4277318BCD03B96CA25773700169C89?opendocument

Australian Bureau of Statistics and Australian Institute of Health and Welfare. (2002). *Hospital Statistics: Aboriginal and Torres Strait Islander Australians, 1999–2000*. Canberra, Australia: Author.

Australian Centre for Posttraumatic Mental Health. (2007). *Australian guidelines for the treatment of adults with acute stress disorder and posttraumatic stress disorder: Information for people with ASD and PTSD, their families and carers*. Canberra, Australia: NHMRC.

Australian Communications and Media Authority. (2010). *Trends in media use by children and young people. Insights from the Kaiser's Family Foundation's Generation M2 2009 (USA), and results from the ACMA's media and communications in Australian families 2007*. Retrieved from http://www.acma.gov.au/webwr/_assets/main/lib310665/trends_in_media_use_by_children_and_young_people.pdf

Australian Drug Foundation. (2006a). *Ecstasy*. Retrieved December 21, 2006, from http://www.druginfo.adf.org.au/article.asp?ContentID=ecstasy

Australian Drug Foundation. (2006b). *Heroin*. Retrieved December 21, 2006, from http://www.druginfo.adf.org.au/article.asp?ContentID=heroin

Australian Education International. (2009). *2009 Annual international student statistics*. Retrieved from http://www.aei.gov.au/AEI/Statistics/StudentEnrolmentAndVisaStatistics/2009/2009_Annual.htm#1994

Australian Government Attorney-General's Department: Emergency Management Australia. (2009). *EMA disasters database: Victorian bushfires*. Retrieved from http://www.ema.gov.au/ema/emadisasters.nsf/c85916e930b93d50ca256d050020cb1f/99b5a9963369d3e0ca25755b001d41f1?OpenDocument

Australian Government Department of Health and Ageing. (2008). *Key statistics of incidence and mortality of skin cancer in Australia*. Retrieved from http://www.skincancer.gov.au/internet/skincancer/publishing.nsf/Content/fact-2

Australian Government Department of Health and Ageing. (2009a). *Breast screen Australia program*. Retrieved from http://www.cancerscreening.gov.au/

Australian Government Department of Health and Ageing. (2009b). *National alcohol strategy 2006–2011*. Retrieved from http://www.alcohol.gov.au/internet/alcohol/publishing.nsf/Content/nas-06-09

Australian Government Department of Health and Ageing. (2009c). *National alcohol strategy 2006–2009: Towards safer drinking cultures*. Retrieved from http://www.alcohol.gov.au/internet/alcohol/publishing.nsf/Content/nas-06-09

Australian Government Department of Health and Ageing. (2009d). *National bowel cancer screening program*. Retrieved from http://www.medicareaustralia.gov.au/

Australian Government Department of Health and Ageing. (2009e). *National cervical screening program*. Retrieved from http://www.health.gov.au/

Australian Government Department of Health and Ageing. (2009f). *The mental health of Australians 2: Report on the 2007 national survey of mental health and wellbeing, May 2009*. Retrieved from http://www.health.gov.au/internet/mentalhealth/publishing.nsf/Content/8CF8540215E98930CA2574320019D4F8/$File/The%20Mental%20Health%20of%20Australians%202%20A%20report%20on%20the%202007%20NSMHW_May%202009.pdf

Australian Health Ministers' Advisory Council. (2008). *Aboriginal and Torres Strait Islander health performance framework report: 2008 Summary*. Canberra, Australia: Author.

Australian Indigenous HealthInfoNet. (2010). *The condom tree program (2010)*. Retreived from http://www.healthinfonet.ecu.edu.au/health-resources/programs-projects?pid=515

Australian Institute of Criminology. (2009a). *Alcohol and homicide in Australia*. Retrieved October 3, 2009, from http://www.aic.gov.au/publications/current%20series/tandi/361-380/tandi372.aspx

Australian Institute of Criminology. (2009b). *Amphetamines*. Retrieved October 3, 2009, from http://www.aic.gov.au/crime_types/drugs_alcohol/drug_types/amphetamines.aspx

Australian Institute of Family Studies. (2004). *Diversity and change in Australian families: Statistical profiles*. Retrieved from http://www.aifs.gov.au/institute/pubs/diversity/09livingalone.pdf

Australian Institute of Family Studies. (2010). *Effects of child abuse and neglect for children and adolescents* (Resource sheet). Retrieved from http://www.aifs.gov.au/nch/pubs/sheets/rs17/rs17.html

Australian Institute of Health and Welfare. (1999). *National health priority areas report: Mental health 1998. A report focusing on depression*. Canberra, Australia: Author.

Australian Institute of Health and Welfare. (2002). *Mental health services in Australia 2000–01*. Canberra, Australia: Author.

Australian Institute of Health and Welfare. (2003). *Disability prevalence and trends* (AIHW Cat. No. DIS 34). Canberra, Australia: Author.

Australian Institute of Health and Welfare. (2004). Estimates of prevalence of intellectual disability in Australia. *Journal of Intellectual & Developmental Disability, 29*(3), 284–289.

Australian Institute of Health and Welfare. (2005). *2004 National drug strategy household survey: First results* (Drug Statistics Series 13). Canberra, Australia: Author.

Australian Institute of Health and Welfare. (2006a). *Australia's health 2006. The tenth biennial health report of the Australian Institute of Health and Welfare*. Canberra, Australia: Author.

Australian Institute of Health and Welfare. (2006b). *Breast cancer in Australia: An overview, 2006*. Canberra, Australia: Author.

Australian Institute of Health and Welfare. (2007a). *2007 National drug strategy household survey*. Retrieved October 3, 2009, from http://www.aihw.gov.au/publications/phe/ndshs07-df/ndshs07-df.pdf

Australian Institute of Health and Welfare. (2007b). *Chronic diseases mortality*. Retrieved from http://www.aihw.gov.au/cdarf/data_pages/mortality/index.cfm

Australian Institute of Health and Welfare. (2007c). *Mental health services in Australia, 2004–2005* (Mental Health Series No. 9, AIHW Cat. No. HSE 47). Canberra, Australia: Author.

Australian Institute of Health and Welfare. (2007d, November). *Older Australians at a glance*. Retrieved from http://www.aihw.gov.au/publications/age/oag04/oag04.pdf

Australian Institute of Health and Welfare. (2007e). *Overview: The status of drug use in 2007*. Retrieved October 3, 2009, from http://www.aihw.gov.au/publications/phe/ndshs07-fr/ndshs07-fr-c02.pdf

Australian Institute of Health and Welfare. (2007f). *Statistics: Consumption patterns (2007) for tobacco, alcohol, drugs*. Retrieved October 10, 2009, from http://www.aihw.gov.au/publications/phe/ndshs07-fr/ndshs07-fr-c03.pdf

Australian Institute of Health and Welfare. (2007g). *Young Australians: Their health and wellbeing 2007*. Canberra, Australia: Author.

Australian Institute of Health and Welfare. (2008a). *2007 National drug strategy household survey: Detailed findings* (Drug Statistics Series No. 22, Cat. No. PHE 107). Canberra, Australia: Author.

Australian Institute of Health and Welfare. (2008b). *2007 National drug strategy household survey: First results* (Drug Statistics Series No. 20, Cat. No. PHE 98). Canberra, Australia: Author. Retrieved from http://www.aihw.gov.au/publications/index.cfm/title/10579

Australian Institute of Health and Welfare. (2008c). *Australia's health 2008* (Cat. No. AUS 99). Canberra, Australia: Author. Retrieved from http://www.aihw.gov.au/publications/index.cfm/title/10585

Australian Institute of Health and Welfare. (2008d). *Disability in Australia: Intellectual disability* (Bulletin 67). Retrieved from http://www.aihw.gov.au/publications/

Australian Institute of Health and Welfare. (2010a). *Australia's health 2010. The twelfth biennial health report of the Australian Institute of Health and Welfare*. Canberra, Australia: Author. Retrieved from http://www.aihw.gov.au/publications/index.cfm/title/11374

Australian Institute of Health and Welfare. (2010b). *Life expectancy: How Australia compares*. Retrieved from http://www.aihw.gov.au/mortality/life_expectancy/compares.cfm

Australian Institute of Health and Welfare. (2010c). *Mental health services in Australia 2007–08* (Mental Health Series No. 12). Retrieved from http://www.aihw.gov.au/publications/hse/88/11415.pdf

Australian Medical Association. (2003). *Public report card 2003. Aboriginal and Torres Strait Islander health. Time for action*. Australia: Author.

Australian Medical Association. (2009). *Alcohol use and harms in Australia: Information paper*. Retrieved from http://www.ama.com.au/node/4762

Australian National Council on AIDS, Hepatitis C and Related Diseases. (2001). *HIV incidence among gay men: Could there be an increase?* Retrieved July 31, 2004, from http://www.ancahrd.org/pubs/bulletins/01/20_hiv_incidence.pdf

Australian National Hypnotherapy Register. (2009). Retrieved October 3, 2009, from http://anhregister.org.au/

Australian Psychological Society. (1997). *Racism and prejudice: Psychological perspectives: APS position paper*. Melbourne, Australia: Author.

Australian Psychological Society. (2002). *Code of ethics*. Retrieved August 8, 2003, from http://www.aps.psychsociety.com.au/

Australian Psychological Society. (2003). *Code of ethics*. Melbourne, Australia: Author.

Australian Psychological Society. (2004). *Health psychologists*. Retrieved August 2, 2004, from http://www.psychsociety.com.au/psych/special_areas/2.4_7.asp

Australian Psychological Society. (2006a). *Medicare announcement of new psychology items heralds new ear for mental health services in Australia*. Retrieved October 9, 2006, from http://www.psychology.org.au/news/media_releases/10.1_171.asp

Australian Psychological Society. (2006b). *APS fact sheet: Better access to psychologists through the Medicare Benefits Schedule (MBS)*. Retrieved November 30, 2007, from http://www.psychology.org.au

Australian Psychological Society. (2006c). *Medicare: New psychology medicare items*. Retrieved September 14, 2007, from http://www.psychology.org.au/

Australian Psychological Society. (2006d). *Clinical college guidelines*. Retrieved October 3, 2007, from http://www.psychology.org.au/

Australian Psychological Society. (2007a). *Code of ethics*. Melbourne, Australia: Author.

Australian Psychological Society. (2007b). *Guidelines for the provision of psychological services for and the conduct of psychological research with Aboriginal and Torres Strait Islander people of Australia*. Retrieved March 11, 2007, from http://www.aps.psychsociety.com.au

Australian Psychological Society. (2007c). *Undergraduate guidelines*. Retrieved October 3, 2007, from http://www.psychology.org.au/

Australian Psychological Society. (2010a). *Evidence-based psychological interventions in the treatment of mental disorders: A literature review* (3rd ed.). Melbourne, Australia: Author.

Australian Psychological Society. (2010b). *Health psychology*. Retrieved from http://www.psychology.org.au/community/specialist/health/

Australian Psychological Society College of Clinical Psychologists. (2006). *Course approval guidelines. Updated November, 2006*. Retrieved September 9, 2007, from http://www.psychology.org.au/

Australian Research Centre in Sex, Health & Society. (2003). *Sex in Australia: Summary findings of the Australian study of health and relationships*. Retrieved June 1, 2004, from http://www.latrobe.edu.au/arcshs

Autism Victoria. (2010). *Autism spectrum disorders have a neurological basis* (Statement). Retrieved from http://www.autismvictoria.org.au/policy/documents/NeurobiologyStatement.pdf

Autti-Ramo, I. (2002). Foetal alcohol syndrome: A multifaceted condition. *Developmental Medicine and Child Neurology, 44*, 141–144.

Baars, B. (1995). Tutorial commentary: Surprisingly small subcortical structures are needed for the stage of waking consciousness, while cortical projection areas seem to provide perceptual contents of consciousness. *Consciousness and Cognition, 4*, 159–162.

Baars, B. J. (1988). Momentary forgetting as a 'resetting' of a conscious global workspace due to competition between incompatible contexts. In M. J. Horowitz (Ed.), *Psychodynamics and cognition* (pp. 269–293). Berkeley, CA: University of California.

Baars, B. J. (1997). *In the theater of consciousness: The workspace of the mind.* New York: Oxford University Press.

Baars, B. J., & McGovern, K. (1996). Cognitive views of consciousness: What are the facts? How can we explain them? In M. Velmans (Ed.), *The science of consciousness: Psychological, neuropsychological and clinical reviews* (pp. 63–95). London: Routledge.

Babor, T., Hoffman, M., DelBoca, F., Hesselbrock, V., Meyer, R. E., Dolinsky, Z., et al. (1992). Types of alcoholics, I: Evidence for an empirically derived typology based on indicators of vulnerability and severity. *Archives of General Psychiatry*, *49*, 599–608.

Babor, T. F., Miller, W. R., DiClemente, C., & Longabaugh, R. (1999). A study to remember: Response of the project MATCH research group. *Addiction*, *94*, 66–69.

Bach, D. R., Schächinger, H., Neuhoff, J. G., Esposito, F., Di Salle, F., Lehmann, C., et al. (2008). Rising sound intensity: An intrinsic warning cue activating the amygdala. *Cerebral Cortex, 18*, 145–150.

Badcock, D., Hammond, G., Gillam, B., Brewer, N., & Andrews, S. (2007). *Psychology: The science of mind, brain, and behaviour* (Federation of Australian Scientific and Technological Societies (FASTS) Occasional Paper, No. 6). Canberra, Australia: FASTS

Badcock, J., Williams, R., Anderson, M., & Jablensky, A. (2004). Speed of processing and individual differences in IQ in schizophrenia: General or specific cognitive deficits. *Cognitive Neuropsychiatry*, *9*, 233–247.

Baddeley, A. (1986). *Working memory*. New York: Oxford University Press.

Baddeley, A., Gathercole, S., & Papagno, C. (1998). The phonological loop as a language learning device. *Psychological Review*, *105*, 158–173.

Baddeley, A. D. (1992). Working memory. *Science*, *255*, 556–559.

Baddeley, A. D. (1995). Working memory. In M. Gazzaniga (Ed.), *The cognitive neurosciences* (pp. 754–764). Cambridge, MA: Bradford/MIT Press.

Baddeley, A. D. (2001). Is working memory still working? *American Psychologist*, *56*, 849–864.

Baddeley, A. D. (2002). Is working memory still working? *European Psychologist*, *7*(2), 85–97.

Baddeley, A. D., & Patterson, K. (1971). The relation between long-term and short-term memory. *British Medical Bulletin*, *27*, 237–242.

Badr, L. K., & Abdallah, B. (2001). Physical attractiveness of premature infants affects outcome at discharge from the NICU. *Infant Behavior and Development, 24*, 129–133.

Baer, L., Rauch, S. L., Ballantine, H. T., Martuza, R., Cosgrove, R., Cassem, E., et al. (1995). Cingulotomy for intractable obsessive–compulsive disorder: Prospective long-term follow-up of 18 patients. *Archives of General Psychiatry*, *52*, 384–392.

Bagshaw, D., & Chung, D. (2000). *Women, men and domestic violence*. Retrieved May 19, 2004, from http://www.dpmc.gov.au/osw/padv/index.html

Bahrick, H. P. (1985). Associationism and the Ebbinghaus legacy. *Journal of Experimental Psychology: Learning, Memory, & Cognition*, *11*, 439–443.

Bahrick, H. P., Bahrick, L. E., Bahrick, A. S., & Bahrick, P. E. (1993). Maintenance of foreign language vocabulary and the spacing effect. *Psychological Science*, *4*, 316–321.

Bahrick, H. P., & Hall, L. K. (1991). Lifetime maintenance of high school mathematics content. *Journal of Experimental Psychology: General*, *120*, 20–33.

Bahrick, H. P., Hall, L. K., & Berger, S. A. (1996). Accuracy and distortion in memory for high school grades. *Psychological Science*, *7*, 265–271.

Bahrick, L. E., & Lickliter, R. (2000). Intersensory redundancy guides attentional selectivity and perceptual learning in infancy. *Developmental Psychology*, *36*, 190–201.

Bailey, C. H., & Kandel, E. R. (1995). Molecular and structural mechanisms underlying long-term memory. In M. S. Gazzaniga (Ed.), *The cognitive neurosciences* (pp. 19–36). Cambridge, MA: MIT Press.

Bailey, J. M., & Pillard, R. (1991). A genetic study of male sexual orientation. *Archives of General Psychiatry*, *48*, 1089–1096.

Bailey, J. M., Pillard, R. C., Dawood, K., Miller, M. B., Farrer, L. A., Trivedi, S., et al. (1999). A family history study of male sexual orientation using three independent samples. *Behavior Genetics*, *29*, 79–86.

Bailey, J. M., Pillard, R. C., Neale, M. C., & Agyei, Y. (1993). Heritable factors influence sexual orientation in women. *Archives of General Psychiatry*, *50*, 217–223.

Bailey, J. M., & Zucker, K. J. (1995). Childhood sex-typed behavior and sexual orientation: A conceptual analysis and quantitative review. *Developmental Psychology*, *31*, 43–55.

Baillargeon, R., & DeVos, J. (1991). Object permanence in young infants: Further evidence. *Child Development*, *62*, 1227–1246.

Bain, L. L., Wilson, T., & Chaikind, E. (1989). Participant perceptions of exercise programs for overweight women. *Research Quarterly for Exercise and Sport*, *60*, 134–143.

Baize, H. R., & Schroeder, J. E. (1995). Personality and mate selection in personal ads: Evolutionary preferences in a public mate selection process. *Journal of Social Behavior and Personality, 10*, 517–536.

Bakan, D. (1966). *The duality of human existence: An essay on psychology and religion*. New York: Rand McNally.

Baker, L., Silk, K. R., Westen, D., Nigg, J. T., & Lohr, N. E. (1992). Malevolence, splitting, and parental ratings by borderlines. *Journal of Nervous and Mental Disease*, *180*, 258–264.

Bakker, A. B., Buunk, B. P., Siero, F. W., & van den Eijnden, R. J. J. M. (1997). Application of a modified health belief model to HIV preventive behavioural intentions among gay and bisexual men. *Psychology & Health, 12*(4), 481–492.

Baldessarini, R. J., Tohen, M., & Tondo, L. (2000). Maintenance treatment in bipolar disorder. *Archives of General Psychiatry*, *57*, 490–492.

Baldwin, D. S., Anderson, I. M., Nutt, D. J., Bandelow, B., Bond, A., Davidson, J. R. T., et al. (2005). Evidence-based guidelines for the pharmacological treatment of anxiety disorders: Recommendations from the British Association for Psychopharmacology. *Journal of Psychopharmacology*, *19*(6), 567–596.

Baldwin, M. (1992). Relational schemas and the processing of social information. *Psychological Bulletin*, *112*, 461–484.

Bales, R. F. (1953). The equilibrium problem in small groups. In T. Parsons, R. F. Bales, & E. A. Shils (Eds.), *Working papers in the theory of action* (pp. 111–161). Glencoe, IL: Free Press.

Balkwill, L. L., & Thompson, W. F. (1999). A cross-cultural investigation of the perception of emotion in music: Psychophysical and cultural cues. *Music Perception, 17*, 43–64.

Ball, K., & Mishra, G. D. (2005). Whose socioeconomic status influences a woman's obesity risk: Her mother's, her father's, or her own? *International Journal of Epidemiology*, *35*, 131–138.

Ballas, P. (2007). *Answers: Late-onset schizophrenia*. Retrieved November 30, 2007, from http://www.healthcentral.com/schizophrenia/

Baltes, P. (1987). Theoretical propositions of lifespan developmental psychology: On the dynamics between growth and decline. *Developmental Psychology*, *23*, 611–626.

Baltes, P. B. (1997). On the incomplete architecture of human ontogeny: Selection, optimization, and compensation as foundation of developmental theory. *American Psychologist*, *52*, 366–380.

Baltes, P. B. (1998). Theoretical propositions of life-span developmental psychology: On the dynamics between growth and decline. In M. P. Lawton & T. A. Salthouse (Eds.), *Essential papers on the psychology of aging. Essential papers in psychoanalysis* (pp. 86–123). New York: New York University Press.

Baltes, P. B., & Staudinger, U. M. (2000). Wisdom: A metaheuristic (pragmatic) to orchestrate mind and virtue toward excellence. *American Psychologist*, *55*, 122–136.

Banaji, M. R., & Prentice, D. A. (1994). The self in social contexts. *Annual Review of Psychology*, *45*, 297–333.

Bandler, R. (1982). Identification of neuronal cell bodies mediating components of biting attack behavior in the cat: Induction of jaw opening following microinjections of glutamate into hypothalamus. *Brain Research*, *245*, 192–197.

Bandura, A. (1967). The role of modeling personality development. In C. Lavatelli & F. Stendler (Eds.), *Readings in childhood and development* (pp. 334–343). New York: Harcourt Brace Jovanovich.

Bandura, A. (1977a). Self-efficacy: Toward a unifying theory of behavioral change. *Psychological Review*, *84*, 191–215.

Bandura, A. (1977b). *Social learning theory*. Englewood Cliffs, NJ: Prentice-Hall.

Bandura, A. (1982). Self-efficacy mechanisms in human agency. *American Psychologist*, *37*, 122–147.

Bandura, A. (1986). *Social foundations of thought and action: A social cognitive theory*. Englewood Cliffs, NJ: Prentice-Hall.

Bandura, A. (1989). Human agency in social cognitive theory. *American Psychologist*, *44*, 1175–1184.

Bandura, A. (1995). *Self-efficacy in changing societies*. New York: Cambridge University Press.

Bandura, A. (1997). Self-efficacy: Toward a unifying theory of behavioral change. *Psychological Review*, *84*, 191–215.

Bandura, A. (1999). Social cognitive theory of personality. In L. Pervin & O. John (Eds.), *Handbook of personality: Theory and research* (2nd ed., pp. 154–196). New York: Guilford Press.

Bandura, A. (2001). Social cognitive theory: An agentic perspective. *Annual Review of Psychology*, *52*, 1–26.

Bandura, A., Blanchard, E. B., & Ritter, B. (1969). Relative efficacy of desensitization and modeling approaches for inducing behavioral, affective, and attitudinal changes. *Journal of Personality and Social Psychology*, *13*, 173–199.

Bandura, A., Ross, D., & Ross, S. (1961). Transmission of aggression through imitation of aggressive models. *Journal of Abnormal and Social Psychology*, *66*, 3–11.

Bandura, A., Ross, D., & Ross, S. (1963). Vicarious reinforcement and imitative learning. *Journal of Abnormal and Social Psychology*, *67*, 601–607.

Banerjee, M. (1997). Hidden emotions: Preschoolers' knowledge of appearance-reality and emotion display rules. *Social Cognition*, *15*, 107–132.

Banham, C. (2005, January 5). Neighbour in distress badly needs tender care. *Sydney Morning Herald*. Retrieved January 5, 2005, from www.smh.com.au

Banks, J. A., & McGee Banks, C. A. (Eds.). (2003). *Handbook of research on multicultural educations* (pp. 50–65). San Francisco: Jossey-Bass.

Bar, M., & Biederman, I. (1998). Subliminal visual priming. *Psychological Science*, *9*, 464–469.

Barabasz, A., & Watkins, J. G. (2004). *Hypnotherapeutic techniques* (2nd ed.). New York: Brunner-Routledge.

Bard, P. (1934). On emotional expression after desortication with some remarks on certain theoretical views. *Psychological Review*, *41*, 309–328.

Bardwick, J. (1971). *Psychology of women*. New York: Harper & Row.

Bargh, J. (1997). The automaticity of everyday life. In J. S. Wyer Jr. (Ed.), *Advances in social cognition: Vol. 10*. Hillsdale, NJ: Lawrence Erlbaum.

Bargh, J., & Barndollar, K. (1996). Automaticity in action: The unconscious as repository of chronic goals and motives. In P. M. Gollwitzer & J. Bargh (Eds.), *The psychology of action: Linking cognition and motivation to behavior* (pp. 457–481). New York: Guilford.

Bargh, J. A., & Chartrand, T. L. (1999). The unbearable automaticity of being. *American Psychologist*, *54*(7), 462–479.

Bargh, J. A., & Tota, M. E. (1988). Context-dependent automatic depression: Accessibility of negative constructs with regard to self but not others. *Journal of Personality and Social Psychology, 54*, 925–939.

Bargh, M. (2003). *Torres Strait: A new deal*. Retrieved November 16, 2004, from http://www.aotearoa.wellington.net/nz/pasif/tuhinga/tor.htm

Bar-Haim, Y., Lamy, D., Pergamin, L., Bakermans-Kranenburg, M. J., & van Ijzendoorn, M. H. (2007). Threat-related attentional bias in anxious and non-anxious individuals: A meta-analytic study. *Psychological Bulletin, 133*, 1–24.

Barinaga, M. (1997). New imaging methods provide a better view into the brain. *Science, 276*, 1974–1976.

Barkow, J. H., Cosmides, L., & Tooby, J. (1992). *The adapted mind*. New York: Oxford University Press.

Barlow, D. H. (2002). *Anxiety and its disorders: The nature and treatment of anxiety and panic*. New York: Guilford Press.

Baroff, G. S., & Gregory, O. J. (1999). *Mental retardation: Nature, cause, and management*. Bristol, PA: Brunner/Mazel.

Baron, A. S., & Banaji, M. R. (2006). The development of implicit attitudes: Evidence of race evaluations from ages 6 and 10 and adulthood. *Psychological Science, 17*(1), 53–58.

Baron, C. S. (1998). Modularity in developmental cognitive neuropsychology: Evidence from autism and Gilles de la Tourette syndrome. In J. A. Burack & R. M. Hodapp (Eds.), *Handbook of mental retardation and development* (pp. 334–348). New York: Cambridge University Press.

Baron, R. A. (1997). The sweet smell of helping: Effects of pleasant ambient fragrance on prosocial behavior in shopping malls. *Journal of Personality and Social Psychology, 23*(5), 498–503.

Baron-Cohen, S., Baldwin, D. A., & Crowson, M. (1997). Do children with autism use the speaker's direction of gaze strategy to crack the code of language? *Child Development, 68*, 48–57.

Barr, H., Streissguth, A. P., Darby, B., & Sampson, P. (1990). Prenatal exposure to alcohol, caffeine, tobacco, and aspirin: Effects on fine and gross motor performance in 4-year old children. *Developmental Psychology, 26*, 339–348.

Barrett, D. H., Resnick, H. S., Foy, D. W., Dansky, B. S., Flanders, W. D., & Stroup, N. E. (1996). Combat exposure and adult psychosocial adjustment among U.S. army veterans serving in Vietnam, 1965–1971. *Journal of Abnormal Psychology, 105*, 575–581.

Barrett, G. V., & Depinet, R. L. (1991). A reconsideration of testing for competence rather than for intelligence. *American Psychologist, 46*, 1012–1024.

Barrett, G. V., & Franke, R. H. (1969). Communication preference and performance: A cross-cultural comparison. In *Proceedings of the 77th Annual American Psychological Association Convention* (pp. 597–598).

Barron, F., & Harrington, D. M. (1981). Creativity, intelligence, and personality. *Annual Review of Psychology, 32*, 439–476.

Barron, J. W. (1998). *Making diagnosis meaningful: Enhancing evaluation and treatment of psychological disorders*. Washington, DC: American Psychological Association.

Barry, H. M., Bacon, M. K., & Child, I. L. (1957). A cross-cultural survey of some sex differences in socialization. *Journal of Abnormal Social Psychology, 55*, 327–332.

Barta, P., Pearlson, G., Powers, R. E., Richards, S. S., & Tune, L. (1990). Auditory hallucinations and smaller superior temporal gyral volume in schizophrenia. *American Journal of Psychiatry, 147*, 1457–1462.

Bartlett, F. C. (1932). *Remembering: A study in experimental and social psychology*. Cambridge: Cambridge University Press.

Bartoshuk, L. M., & Beauchamp, G. K. (1994). Chemical senses. *Annual Review of Psychology, 45*, 419–449.

Basoglu, M. (1997). Torture as a stressful life event: A review of the current status of knowledge. In T. W. Miller (Ed.), *Clinical disorders and stressful life events* (pp. 45–70). Madison, CT: International Universities Press.

Basoglu, M., Paker, M., Paker, O., Ozmen, E., Marks, I., Sahin, D., & Sarimurat, N. (1994). Psychological effects of torture: A comparison of tortured with nontortured political activists in Turkey. *American Journal of Psychiatry, 151*, 6–81.

Bassili, J. N., & Krosnick, J. A. (2000). Do strength-related attitude properties determine susceptibility to response effects? New evidence from response latency, attitude extremity, and aggregate indices. *Political Psychology, 21*, 107–132.

Bastian, V. A., Burns, N. R., & Nettelbeck, T. (2005). Emotional intelligence predicts life skills, but not as well as personality and cognitive abilities. *Personality and Individual Differences, 39*, 1135–1145.

Bateman, A., & Fonagy, P. (1999). Effectiveness of partial hospitalization in the treatment of borderline personality disorder: A randomized controlled trial. *American Journal of Psychiatry, 156*, 1563–1569.

Bates, J., Pettit, G., Dodge, K., & Ridge, B. (1998). Interaction of temperamental resistance to control and restrictive parenting in the development of externalizing behavior. *Developmental Psychology, 34*, 982–995.

Bates, L., Luster, T., & Vandenbelt, M. (2003). Factors related to social competence in elementary school among children of adolescent mothers. *Social Development, 12*, 107–124.

Bates, M. S. (1987). Ethnicity and pain: A biocultural model. *Social Science and Medicine, 24*, 47–50.

Bates, T. C., & Stough, C. (2000). Intelligence arguments and Australian psychology: A reply to Stankov and an alternative view. *Australian Psychologist, 35*, 68–72.

Batorowicz, K. (1999). Multiculturalism and immigration: The Australian case. In O. Koivukangas & C. Westin (Eds.), *Scandinavian and European migration to Australia and New Zealand* (pp. 11–21). Vammala, Finland: Institute of Migration, Turku, and Centre for Research in International Relations and Ethnic Relations, Sweden.

Batson, C. D. (1991). Evidence for altruism: Toward a pluralism of prosocial motives. *Psychological Inquiry, 2*, 107–122.

Batson, C. D. (1995). Altruism. In A. Tesser (Ed.), *Advanced social psychology*. New York: McGraw-Hill.

Batson, C. D. (1998). Altruism and prosocial behavior. In D. T. Gilbert, S. T. Fiske, & G. Lindzey (Eds.), *The handbook of social psychology: Vol. 2* (4th ed., pp. 282–316). Boston: McGraw-Hill.

Batson, C. D. (2002). Addressing the altruism question experimentally. In S. G. Post, L. G. Underwood, J. P. Schloss, & W. B. Hurlbut (Eds.), *Altruism and altruistic love: Science, philosophy, and religion in dialogue* (pp. 89–105). New York: Oxford University Press.

Batson, C. D., Ahmad, N., Lishner, D. A., & Tsang, J. (2002). Empathy and altruism. In C. R. Snyder & S. J. Lopez (Eds.), *Handbook of positive psychology* (pp. 485–498). New York: Oxford University Press.

Batson, C. D., & Moran, T. (1999). Empathy-induced altruism in a prisoner's dilemma. *European Journal of Social Psychology, 29*, 909–924.

Battacchi, M. W., Pelamatti, G., Umilta, C., & Michelotti, E. (1981). On the acoustic information stored in echoic memory. *International Journal of Psycholonguistics, 8*, 17–29.

Batteau, D. W. (1967). The role of the pinna in human localization. *Proceedings of the Royal Society of London, Series B, 168*, 158–180.

Batuev, A. S., & Gafurov, B. G. (1993). The chemical nature of the hypothalamocortical activation underlying drinking behavior. *Neuroscience of Behavioral Psychology, 23*, 35–41.

Baudouin, A., Vanneste, S., Pouthas, V., & Isingrini, M. (2006). Age-related changes in duration reproduction: Involvement of working memory processes. *Brain and Cognition, 62*, 17–23.

Baum, A., & Posluszny, D. M. (1999). Health psychology: Mapping biobehavioral contributions to health and illness. *Annual Review of Psychology, 50*, 137–163.

Baumeister, R. F. (1991). *Escaping the self*. New York: Basic Books.

Baumeister, R. F. (1998). The self. In D. T. Gilbert, S. T. Fiske, & G. Lindzey (Eds.), *The handbook of social psychology: Vol. 2* (pp. 680–740). New York: McGraw-Hill.

Baumeister, R. F., & Bratlavsky, E. (1999). Passion, intimacy, and time: Passionate love as a function of change in intimacy. *Personality and Social Psychology Review, 3*, 49–67.

Baumeister, R. F., Bratslavsky, E., Finkenauer, C., & Vohs, K. D. (2001). Bad is stronger than good. *Review of General Psychology, 5*, 323–370.

Baumeister, R. F., & Leary, M. R. (1995). The need to belong: Desire for interpersonal attachments as a fundamental human motive. *Psychological Bulletin, 117*, 497–529.

Baumeister, R. F., Smart, L., & Boden, J. M. (1996). Relation of threatened egotism to violence and aggression: The dark side of high self-esteem. *Psychological Review, 103*, 5–33.

Bauminger, N. (2002). The facilitation of social-emotional understanding and social interaction in high-functioning children with autism: Intervention outcomes. *Journal of Autism and Developmental Disorders, 32*(4), 283–298.

Baumrind, D. (1967). Child care practices anteceding three patterns of preschool behavior. *Genetic Psychology Monographs, 75*, 43–88.

Baumrind, D. (1971). Current patterns of parental authority. *Developmental Psychology Monograph, 4*, 1–103.

Baumrind, D. (1987). A developmental perspective on adolescent risk taking in contemporary America. *New Directions for Child Development, 37*, 93–125.

Baumrind, D. (1991). The influence of parenting style on adolescent competence and substance use. *Journal of Early Adolescence, 11*, 56–95.

Bavin, E. (1993). Language and culture: Socialisation in a Warlpiri community. In M. Walsh & C. Yallop (Eds.), *Language and culture in Aboriginal Australia* (pp. 85–96). Canberra, Australia: Aboriginal Studies Press.

Baxendale, S. (2004). Memories aren't made of this: Amnesia at the movies. *British Medical Journal, 329*(7480), 1480–1483.

Baxter, J., Kokaua, J., Wells, J. E., & McGee, M. A. (2006). Ethnic comparisons of the 12 month prevalence of mental disorders and treatment contact in Te Rau Hinengaro: The New Zealand Mental Health Survey. *Australian and New Zealand Journal of Psychiatry, 40*, 905–913.

Beattie, G. (2010). *Why aren't we saving the planet? A psychologist's perspective*. New York: Routledge.

Beaulieu, C. M. J. (2004). Intercultural study of personal space: A case study. *Journal of Applied Social Psychology, 34*(4), 794–805.

Bechara, A., Tranel, D., Damasio, H., Adolphs, R., Rockland, C., & Damasio, A. (1995). Double dissociation of conditioning and declarative knowledge relative to the amygdala and hippocampus in humans. *Science, 29*, 1115–1118.

Beck, A. (1985). *Anxiety disorders and phobias: A cognitive perspective*. New York: Basic Books.

Beck, A. (1989). *Cognitive therapy in clinical practice: An illustrative casebook*. New York: Routledge.

Beck, A. (1991). Cognitive therapy: A 30-year retrospective. *American Psychologist, 46*, 368–375.

Beck, A. (1992). Cognitive therapy: A 30 year retrospective. In J. Cottraux, P. Legeron, & E. Mollard (Eds.), *Which psychotherapies in year 2000? Annual series of European research in behavior therapy: Vol. 6* (pp. 13–28). Amsterdam: Swets & Zeitlinger.

Beck, A. T. (1976). *Cognitive therapy and the emotional disorders*. New York: International Universities Press.

Beck, A. T. (1993). Cognitive therapy: Past, present, and future. *Journal of Consulting and Clinical Psychology, 61*, 194–198.

Beck, J. S. (2005). *Cognitive therapy for challenging problems: What to do when the basics don't work*. New York: Guilford.

Becker, E. (1973). *The denial of death*. New York: Free Press.

Beckett, J. (1989). *Torres Strait Islanders — custom and colonisation*. Sydney, Australia: Cambridge University Press.

Beckwith, J., Geller, L., & Sarkar, S. (1991). Sources of human psychological differences: The Minnesota study of twins reared apart: Comment. *Science*, *252*, 191.

Bee, H. (1982). Prediction of IQ and language skill from perinatal status, child performance, family characteristics, and mother-infant interaction. *Child Development*, *53*, 1134–1156.

Behrendt, L. (1995). *Aboriginal dispute resolution: A step towards self determination and community autonomy*. Annandale, NSW: Federation Press.

Bekesy, G. von. (1959). Synchronism of neural discharges and their demultiplication in pitch perception on the skin and in learning. *Journal of the Acoustical Society of America*, *31*, 338–349.

Bekesy, G. von. (1960). *Experiments in hearing*. New York: McGraw-Hill.

Bekesy, G. von, & Rosenblith, W. A. (1951). The mechanical properties of the ear. In S. S. Stevens (Ed.), *Handbook of experimental psychology*. New York: John Wiley.

Bell, A. J., & Cook, H. (1998). Empirical evidence for a compensatory relationship between dream content and repression. *Psychoanalytic Psychology*, *15*, 154–163.

Bell, A. P., Weinberg, M. S., & Hammersmith, S. (1981) *Sexual preference. Its development in men and women* Bloomington: University of Indiana Press.

Bell, M., Billington, R., Cicchetti, D., & Gibbons, J. (1988). Do object relations deficits distinguish BPD from other diagnostic groups? *Journal of Clinical Psychology*, *44*(4), 511–516.

Bell, R. M. (1985). *Holy anorexia*. Chicago: University of Chicago Press.

Bell, R. Q. (1968). A reinterpretation of the direction of effects in studies of socialization. *Psychological Review*, *75*, 71–85.

Bellack, L., Hurvich, M., & Geldman, H. (1973). *Ego functions in schizophrenics, neurotics, and normals*. New York: John Wiley.

Bellivier, F., Leboyer, M., Courtet, P., Buresi, C., Beufils, B., Samolyk, D., et al. (1998). Association between the tryptophan hydroxylase gene and manic-depressive illness. *Archives of General Psychiatry*, *55*, 33–37.

Belsky, J., Campbell, S. B., Conn, J. F., & Moore, G. (1996). Instability of infant-parent attachment security. *Developmental Psychology*, *32*, 921–924.

Belsky, J., & Hsieh, K. (1998). Patterns of marital change during the early childhood years: Parent personality, coparenting, and division-of-labor correlates. *Journal of Family Psychology*, *12*, 511–528.

Belsky, J., & Isabella, R. (1988). Maternal, infant, and social-contextual determinants of attachment security. In J. Belsky & T. Nezworsky (Eds.), *Clinical implications of attachment* (pp. 41–94). Hillsdale, NJ. Lawrence Erlbaum.

Belsky, J., & Pensky, F. (1988). Marital change across the transition to parenthood. *Marriage and Family Review*, *12*, 133–156.

Belzer, K. D., & D'Zurilla, T. J. (2002). Social problem solving and trait anxiety as predictors of worry in a college student population. *Personality and Individual Differences, 33*, 573–585.

Bem, D. J. (1967). Self perception: An alternative interpretation of cognitive dissonance phenomena. *Psychological Review, 74*, 183–200.

Bem, D. J. (1972). Self-perception theory. In L. Berkowitz (Ed.), *Advances in experimental social psychology: Vol. 6*. New York: Academic Press.

Bem, D. J., & Allen, A. (1974). On predicting some of the people some of the time: The search for cross-situational consistencies in behavior. *Psychological Review*, *81*, 506–520.

Bem, S. L. (1981). Gender schema theory: A cognitive account of sex typing. *Psychological Review*, *88*(4), 354–364.

Bem, S. L. (1983). Gender schema theory and its implications for child development: Raising gender-aschematic children in a gender-schematic society. *Signs, Journal of Women in Culture and Society*, *8*, 354–364.

Bem, S. L. (1985). Androgyny and gender schema theory: A conceptual and empirical integration. In T. B. Sonderegger (Ed.), *Nebraska symposium on motivation: Psychology and gender: Vol. 32*. Lincoln: University of Nebraska Press.

Bemporad, J. R. (1996). Self-starvation through the ages: Reflections on the pre-history of anorexia nervosa. *International Journal of Eating Disorders*, *19*, 217–237.

Benasich, A. A., & Brooks-Gunn, J. (1996). Maternal attitudes and knowledge of child-rearing: Associations with family and child outcomes. *Child Development*, *67*, 1186–1205.

Benbow, C., & Stanley, J. (1983). Sex differences in mathematical reasoning ability: More facts. *Science*, *222*, 1029–1030.

Bendersky, M., & Lewis, M. (1998). Arousal modulation in cocaine-exposed infants. *Developmental Psychology*, *34*, 555–564.

Benedict, R. (1934). *Patterns of culture*. New York: Mentor/New American Library.

Benet-Martinez, V., & Waller, J. G. (1997). Further evidence for the cross-cultural generality of the Big Seven factor model: Indigenous and imported Spanish personality constructs. *Journal of Personality*, *65*, 567–598.

Benotsch, E. G., Brailey, K., Vasterling, J. J., Uddo, M., Constans, J. I., & Sutker, P. B. (2000). War zone stress, personal and environmental resources, and PTSD symptoms in Gulf War veterans: A longitudinal perspective. *Journal of Abnormal Psychology*, *109*, 205–213.

Benson, E. (2003). Intelligence across cultures. *Monitor on Psychology, 34*(2), 56.

Berg, C. (1992). Perspectives for viewing intellectual development throughout the life course. In R. J. Sternberg & C. A. Berg (Eds.), *Intellectual development* (pp. 1–15). New York: Cambridge University Press.

Berg, F. M. (1999). Health risks associated with weight loss and obesity treatment programs. *Journal of Social Issues*, *55*, 277–297.

Berger, R. J., & Phillips, N. H. (1995). Energy conservation and sleep. *Behavioural Brain Research*, *69*, 65–73.

Berglas, S., & Baumeister, R. F. (1993). *Your own worst enemy*. New York: Basic Books.

Berk, L. E. (2008). *Infants, children, and adolescents*. Boston: Allyn & Bacon.

Berkowitz, L. (1989). Frustration-aggression hypothesis: Examination and reformulation. *Psychological Bulletin*, *106*, 59–73.

Berman, P. W., & Pedersen, F. A. (1987). Research on men's transitions to parenthood: An integrative discussion. In P. W. Berman & F. A. Pederson (Eds.), *Men's transitions to parenthood: Longitudinal studies of early family experience*. Hillsdale, NJ: Lawrence Erlbaum.

Bermond, B., Nieuwenhuyse, B., Fasotti, L., & Schuerman, J. (1991). Spinal cord lesions, peripheral feedback, and intensities of emotional feelings. *Cognition and Emotion*, *5*, 201–220.

Bernhardt, P. C. (1997). Influences of serotonin and testosterone in aggression and dominance: Convergence with social psychology. *Current Directions in Psychological Science, 6*, 44–48.

Bernstein, D. A., Clarke-Stewart, A., Roy, E. J., & Wickens, C. D. (1997). *Psychology* (4th ed.). New York: Houghton Mifflin Co.

Bernstein, I. L. (1991). Aversion conditioning in response to cancer and cancer treatment. *Clinical Psychology Review, 11*, 185–191.

Berquier, A., & Ashton, R. (1992). Characteristics of the frequent nightmare sufferer. *Journal of Abnormal Psychology, 101*(2), 246–250.

Berridge, K., & Zajonc, R. (1991). Hypothalamic cooling effects elicit eating: Differential effects on motivation and pleasure. *Psychological Science*, *2*, 184–189.

Berridge, K. C. (1996). Food reward: Brain substrates of wanting and liking [Special issue: Society for the Study of Ingestive Behavior, Second Independent Meeting]. *Neuroscience & Biobehavioral Reviews*, *20*, 1–25.

Berridge, K. C., & Winkielman, P. (2003). What is an unconscious emotion? (The case for unconscious 'liking'). *Cognition and Emotion*, *17*(2), 181–211.

Berry, C. H. (1978, July). Will your smoke detector wake you? *Fire Journal*, *72*(4), 105–108.

Berry, J. W. (1971). Mueller-Lyon susceptibility: Culture, ecology or race? *International Journal of Psychology*, *1*, 207–229.

Berry, J. W. (1979). A cultural ecology of social behavior. In L. Berkowitz (Ed.), *Advances in experimental social psychology: Vol. 12*. New York: Academic Press.

Berry, J. W. (1995). Psychology of acculturation. In N. R. Goldberger & J. B. Veroff (Eds.), *The culture and psychology reader*. New York: University Press.

Berry, J. W., & Bennet, J. A. (1992). Cree conceptions of cognitive competence. *International Journal of Psychology, 27*, 73–88.

Berry, J. W., Dasen, P. R., & Saraswathi, T. S. (Eds.). (1997). *Handbook of cross-cultural psychology: Vol. 2. Basic processes and human development* (2nd ed.). Boston: Allyn & Bacon.

Berry, J. W., & Irvine, S. H. (1986). Bricolage: Savages do it daily. In R. J. Sternberg & R. K. Wagner (Eds.), *Practical intelligence: Nature and origins of competence in the everyday world* (pp. 271–303). New York: Cambridge University Press.

Berry, J. W., Poortinga, Y. H., Segall, M. H., & Dasen, P. R. (1992). *Cross-cultural psychology: Research and applications*. New York: Cambridge University Press.

Berscheid, E., Dion, K., Walster, E., & Walster, G. (1971). Physical attractiveness and dating choice: A test of the matching hypothesis. *Journal of Experimental Social Psychology, 7*, 173–189.

Berscheid, E., & Reis, H. T. (1998). Attraction and close relationships. In D. T. Gilbert, S. T. Fiske, & G. Lindzey (Eds.), *The handbook of social psychology: Vol. 2* (4th ed., pp. 193–281). Boston: McGraw-Hill.

Bersoff, D. N. (Ed.). (1999). *Ethical conflicts in psychology* (2nd ed.). Washington, DC: American Psychological Association.

Bertenthal, B. I. (1996). Origins and early development of perception, action, and representation. *Annual Review of Psychology, 47*, 431–459.

Bertenthal, B. I., & Clifton, R. K. (1998). Perception and action. In W. Damon (Ed. in Chief) & N. Eisenberg (Vol. Ed.), *Handbook of child psychology: Vol. 2* (pp. 51–102). New York: John Wiley.

Bertolino, A., Esposito, G., Callicott, J. H., Mattay, V. S., Van Horn, J. D., Frank, J. A., et al. (2000). Specific relationship between prefrontal neuronal N-acetylaspartate and activation of the working memory cortical network in schizophrenia. *American Journal of Psychiatry, 157*, 26–33.

Bertram, L., McQueen, M. B., Mullin, K., Blacker, D., & Tanzi, R. E. (2007). Systematic meta-analyses of Alzheimer disease genetic association studies. The AlzGene database. *Nature Genetics*, *39*, 17–23.

Best, C. T., Tyler, M. D., Gooding, T. N., Orlando, C. B., & Quann, C. A. (2009). Development of phonological constancy: Toddlers' perception of native- and Jamaican-accented words. *Psychological Science, 20*, 539–542.

Best, C. T., Tyler, M. D., Kitamura, C., & Bundgaard-Nielsen, R. (2010, March). *Vocabulary size at 17 months and the emergence of phonological constancy in word recognition across native and nonnative dialects*. Presented at the International Conference on Infant Studies. Baltimore, MD.

Best, C. T., Tyler, M. D., Kitamura, C., Notley, A., & Bundgaard-Nielsen, R. (2008, March). *Phonetic specificity of early words? Australian toddlers' perception of Australian versus Jamaican English pronunciations*. Presented at the International Conference on Infant Studies, Vancouver, Canada.

Best, D. L. (1993). Inducing children to generate mneumonic organizational strategies: An examination of long-term retention and materials. *Developmental Psychology*, *29*, 324–336.

Best, D. L. (2004). Gender roles in childhood and adolescence. In U. P. Gielen & J. L. Roopnarine (Eds.), *Childhood and adolescence in cross-cultural perspective* (pp. 199–228). Westport, CT: Greenwood Press.

Best, D. L., & Williams, J. E. (1998). Masculinity and femininity in the self and ideal self descriptions of university students in 14 countries. In G. Hofstede (Ed.), *Masculinity and femininity: The taboo dimension of national cultures. Cross-cultural psychology series: Vol. 3* (pp. 106–116). Thousand Oaks, CA: Sage Publications.

Best, D. L., Williams, J. E., Cloud, J. M., Davis, S. W., Robertson, L. S., Edwards, J. R., et al. (1977). Development of sex trait stereotypes among young children in the United States, England, and Ireland. *Child Development, 48,* 1375–1384.

Beutler, L. E. (1991). Have all won and must all have prizes? Revisiting Luborsky et al.'s verdict. *Journal of Consulting and Clinical Psychology, 59,* 226–232.

Beutler, L. E., & Malik, M. L. (2002). *Rethinking the DSM: A psychological perspective*. Washington, DC: American Psychological Association.

Beutler, L. E., Williams, R. E., Wakefield, P. J., & Entwistle, S. R. (1995). Bridging scientist and practitioner perspectives in clinical psychology. *American Psychologist, 50,* 984–994.

Beyers, J. M., Toumbourou, J. W., Catalano, R. F., Arthur, M. W., & Hawkins, J. D. (2004). A cross-national comparison of risk and protective factors for adolescent substance use: The United States and Australia. *Journal of Adolescent Health, 35*(1), 3–16.

Beyond Blue. (2006). *Depression and suicide*. Retrieved from http://www.beyondblue.org.au/

Bickel, W. K., Green, L., & Vuchinich, R. E. (1995). Behavioral economics. *Journal of the Experimental Analysis of Behavior, 64,* 257–262.

Bickman, L., & Zarantonello, M. (1978). The effects of deception and level of obedience on subjects' ratings of the Milgram study. *Personality and Social Psychology Bulletin, 4,* 81–85.

Bidell, T. R., & Fischer, K. W. (1992). Beyond the stage debate: Action, structure, and variability in Piagetian theory and research. In R. Sternberg & C. Berg (Eds.), *Intellectual development* (pp. 100–140). Cambridge: Cambridge University Press.

Bidell, T. R., & Fischer, K. W. (2000). The role of cognitive structure in the development of behavioral control: A dynamic skills approach. In W. J. Perrig & A. Grob (Eds.), *Control of human behavior, mental processes, and consciousness: Essays in honor of the 60th birthday of August Flammer* (pp. 183–201). Mahwah, NJ: Lawrence Erlbaum.

Biederman, I. (1987). Recognition by components: A theory of human image understanding. *Psychological Review, 94,* 115–147.

Biederman, I. (1990). Higher-level vision. In D. N. Osherson, S. M. Kosslyn, & J. M. Hollerbach (Eds.), *Visual cognition and action: An invitation to cognitive science: Vol. 2* (pp. 41–72). Cambridge, MA: MIT Press.

Biederman, I., Glass, A. L., & Stacy, E. W., Jr. (1973). Searching for objects in real-world scenes. *Journal of Exerimental Psychology, 97,* 22–27.

Biederman, I., Mezzanotte, R. J., & Rabinowitz, J. C. (1982). Scene perception: Detecting and judging objects undergoing relational violations. *Cognitive Psychology, 14,* 143–177.

Biederman, I., Mezzanotte, R. J., Rabinowitz, J. C., Francolini, C. M., & Plude, D. (1981). Detecting the unexpected in photo-interpretation. *Human Factors, 23,* 153–164.

Biederman, J., & Faraone, S. V. (2005). Attention-deficit hyperactivity disorder. *Lancet*, *366*, 237–248.

Biederman, J., Mick, E., & Faraone, S. V. (2000). Age-dependent decline of symptoms of attention deficit hyperactivity disorder: Impact of remission definition and symptom type. *American Journal of Psychiatry, 157,* 816–818.

Biederman, J., Milberger, S., Faraone, S. V., Kiely, K., Guite, J., Mick, E., et al. (1995). Family-environment risk factors for attention-deficit hyperactivity disorder: A test of Rutter's indicators of adversity. *Archives of General Psychiatry, 52,* 464–470.

Bieling, P. J., Beck, A. T., & Brown, G. K. (2000). The Sociotropy-Autonomy Scale: Structure and implications. *Cognitive Therapy and Research, 24,* 763–780.

Bierer, L. M., Hof, P. R., Purohit, D. P., Carlin, L., Schmeidler, J., Davis, K. L., et al. (1995). Neocortical neurofibrillary tangles correlate with dementia severity in Alzheimer's disease. *Archives of Neurology, 52,* 81–88.

Bierhoff, H. W., Klein, R., & Kramp, P. (1991). Evidence for the altruistic personality from data on accident research. *Journal of Personality, 59*, 263–280.

Bieri, J. (1966). Cognitive complexity and personality development. In O. J. Harvey (Ed.), *Experience, structure and adaptability*. New York: Springer Publishing Company.

Bierut, L. J., Dinwiddie, S. H., Begleiter, H., Crowe, R. R., Hesselbrock, V., Nurnberger, J. I., Jr., et al. (1998). Familial transmission of substance dependence: Alcohol, marijuana, cocaine, and habitual smoking: A report from the collaborative study on the genetics of alcoholism. *Archives of General Psychiatry, 55,* 982–988.

Biesanz, J., West, S. G., & Graziano, W. (1998). Moderators of self-other agreement: Reconsidering temporal stability in personality. *Journal of Personality and Social Psychology, 75*, 467–477.

Biggs, J. (1999). *Teaching for quality learning at university: What the student does*. London: Open University Press.

Binder, J. L., Strupp, H. H., & Henry, W. P. (1995). Psychodynamic therapies in practice: Time-limited dynamic psychotherapy. In M. B. Bongar & L. E. Beutler (Eds.), *Comprehensive textbook of psychotherapy: Theory and practice. Oxford textbooks in clinical psychology: Vol. 1* (pp. 48–63). New York: Oxford University Press.

Binet, A., & Simon, T. (1908). Le developpement de l'intelligence chez les enfants. *L'Annee Psychologique*, *14*, 1–94.

Birnbaum, D. W. (1983). Preschooler's stereotypes about sex differences in emotionality: A reaffirmation. *Journal of Genetic Psychology, 143*, 139–140.

Birnbaum, G. E., & Reis, H. T. (2006). Women's sexual working models: An evolutionary-attachment perspective. *The Journal of Sex Research*, *43*(4), 328–342.

Birnbrauer, J. S. (1996). Development of clinical psychology in Australia. In P. R. Martin & J. S. Birnbrauer (Eds.), *Clinical psychology: Profession and practice in Australia* (pp. 21–51). Melbourne, Australia: Macmillan Education.

Birney, D. P., Bowman, D. B., & Pallier, G. (2006). Prior to paradigm integration, the task is to resolve construct definitions of gF and WM. *Behavioral and Brain Science, 29*, 127.

Bishop, J. A., & Cook, L. M. (1975). Moths, melanism and clean air. *Scientific American*, *232*, 90–99.

Bizer, G. Y., & Krosnick, J. A. (2001). Exploring the structure of strength-related attitude features: The relation between attitude importance and attitude accessibility. *Journal of Personality and Social Psychology, 81*, 566–586.

Bizumic, B., Duckitt, J., Popadic, D., Dru, V., & Krauss, S. (2009). A cross-cultural investigation into a reconceptualization of ethnocentrism. *European Journal of Social Psychology, 39,* 871–899.

Bjork, E. L., & Bjork, R. A. (1996). Continuing influences of to-be-forgotten information. *Consequences & Cognition: An International Journal, 5,* 176–196.

Bjork, E. L., Bjork, R. A., & Anderson, M. C. (1998). Varieties of goal-directed forgetting. In J. M. Golding & C. M. MacLeod (Eds.), *Intentional forgetting: Interdisciplinary approaches* (pp. 103–137). Mahwah, NJ: Lawrence Erlbaum Associates.

Bjorklund, A., & Gage, F. (1985). Neural grafting of neutrodegenerative diseases in animal models. *Annals of the New York Academy of Sciences*, *457*, 53–81.

Bjorklund, D. F., & Pellegrini, A. D. (2002). *The origins of human nature: Evolutionary developmental psychology*. Washington, DC: American Psychological Association.

Black, M. M., Dubowitz, H., & Starr, R. H. (1999). African American fathers in low income, urban families: Development, behavior, and home environment of their three-year-old children. *Child Development, 70,* 967–978.

Blair, C. (2006). How similar are fluid cognition and general intelligence? A developmental neuroscience perspective on fluid cognition as an aspect of human cognitive ability. *Behavioral and Brain Sciences, 29,* 109–160.

Blair, D. (2001). *Dinkum diggers: An Australian battalion at war*. Carlton, Australia: Melbourne University Press.

Blake, R., & Hirsch, H. V. B. (1975). Deficits in binocular depth perception in cats after alternating monocular deprivation. *Science, 190,* 1114–1116.

Blake, R., & Mouton, J. (1964). *The managerial grid*. Houston, TX: Gulf.

Blakemore, C., & Cooper, G. F. (1970). Development of the brain depends on the visual environment. *Nature, 228*, 477–478.

Blampied, N. M. (1999). A legacy neglected: Restating the case for single-case research in cognitive-behaviour therapy. *Behaviour Change*, *16*, 89–104.

Blanchard-Fields, F., & Chen, Y. (1996). Adaptive cognition and aging. *American Behavioral Scientist, 39,* 231–248.

Blanton, C. K. (2000). 'They cannot master abstractions, but they can often be made efficient workers': Race and class in the intelligence testing of Mexican Americans and African Americans in Texas during the 1920s. *Social Science Quarterly, 81,* 1014–1026.

Blascovich, J., & Mendes, W. B. (2000). Challenge and threat appraisals: The role of affective cues. In J. P. Forgas (Ed.), *Feeling and thinking: The role of affect in social cognition*. New York: Cambridge University Press.

Blasko, D. G. (1999). Only the tip of the iceberg: Who understands what about metaphors. *Journal of Pragmatics, 31,* 1675–1683.

Blass, T. (1991). Understanding behavior in the Milgram obedience experiment: The role of personality, situations, and their interactions. *Journal of Personality and Social Psychology, 60*, 398–413.

Blass, T. (2000). *Obedience to authority: Current perspectives on the Milgram paradigm*. Mahwah, NJ: Lawrence Erlbaum.

Blatt, S., Ford, R., Berman, W., Cook, B., Cramer, P., & Robins, C. E. (1994). *Therapeutic change: An object relations perspective*. New York: Plenum Press.

Blatt, S., & Zuroff, D. (1992). Interpersonal relatedness and self-definition: Two prototypes for depression. *Clinical Psychology Review, 12,* 527–562.

Blatt, S. J., Auerbach, J. S., & Levy, K. N. (1997). Mental representations in personality development, psychopathology, and the therapeutic process. *Review of General Psychology, 1*, 351–374.

Blatt, S. J., & Homann, E. (1992). Parent child interaction in the etiology of dependent and self-critical depression. *Clinical Psychology Review, 12,* 47–91.

Blaustein, A. R., & Waldman, B. (1992). Kin recognition in anuran amphibians. *Animal Behavior, 44,* 207–221.

Bliss, T. V., & Lomo, T. (1973). Long-lasting potentiation of synaptic transmission in the dentate area of the anaesthetized rabbit following stimulation of the perforant path. *Journal of Physiology, 232,* 331–356.

Bloch, D. P. (2005). Complexity, chaos and non-linear dynamics: A new perspective on career development theory. *Career Development Quarterly, 53*, 194–207.

Block, J. (1971). *Lives through time*. Berkeley, CA: Bancroft Books.

Block, J. (1995). A contrarian view of the five-factor approach to personality description. *Psychological Bulletin, 117*, 187–215.

Block, J. (2001). Millenial contrarianism: The five-factor approach to personality description 5 years later. *Journal of Research in Personality, 35*, 98–107.

Block, J., Block, J. H., & Keyes, S. (1988). Longitudinally foretelling drug usage in adolescence: Early childhood personality and environmental precursors. *Child Development, 59*, 336–355.

Block, J., & Kremen, A. (1996). IQ and ego-resiliency: Conceptual and empirical connections and separateness. *Journal of Personality and Social Psychology, 70*, 349–361.

Block, J. H. (1978). Another look at sex differentiation in the socialization behaviors of mothers and fathers. In J. Sherman & F. L. Denmark (Eds.), *The psychology of women: Future directions of research*. New York: Psychological Dimensions.

Block, J. H., Gjerde, P., & Block, J. H. (1991). Personality antecedents of depressive tendencies in 18-year-olds: A prospective study. *Journal of Personality and Social Psychology, 60*, 726–738.

Blokland, A. (1997). Acetylcholine: A neurotransmitter for learning and memory? *Brain Research Reviews, 21*, 285–300.

Bloom, L. (1993). *The transition from infancy to language: Acquiring the power of expression*. New York: Cambridge University Press.

Blos, P. (1962). *On adolescence: A psychoanalytic interpretation*. New York: Free Press.

Blos, P. (1967). The second individuation process of adolescence. *Psychoanalytic Study of the Child, 22*, 162–186.

Blowers, G. H., & O'Connor, K. P. (1996). *Personal construct psychology in the clinical context*. Ottawa, Canada: University of Ottawa Press.

Blum, G. S. (1954). An experimental reunion of psychoanalytic theory with perceptual vigilance and defense. *Journal of Abnormal and Social Psychology, 49*, 94–98.

Blumer, D., & Benson, D. (1984). Personality changes with frontal and temporal lesions. In D. F. Benson & F. Blumer (Eds.), *Psychiatric aspects of neurologic disease*. New York: Grune & Stratton.

Blurton-Jones, N., & Konner, M. (1976). !Kung knowledge of animal behavior. In R. B. Lee & I. De Vore (Eds.), *Kalahari hunter-gatherers* (pp. 326–348). Cambridge, MA: Harvard University Press.

Boden, J. M., & Baumeister, R. F. (1997). Repressive coping: Distraction using pleasant thoughts and memories. *Journal of Personality and Social Psychology, 73*, 45–62.

Bodenhausen, G. (1993). Emotions, arousal, and stereotypic judgments: A heuristic model of affect and stereotyping. In D. Mackie & D. Hamilton (Eds.), *Affect, cognition, and stereotyping: Interactive processes in group perception*. New York: Academic Press.

Boecker, H., Sprenger, T., Spilker, M., Henriksen, G., Koppenhoefer, M., Wagner, K. J., et al. (2008). The runners high: Opioidergic mechanisms in the human brain. *Cerebral Cortex, 18*(11), 2523–2531.

Boekaerts, M., Pintrich, P. R., & Zeidner, M. (Eds.). (2000). *Handbook of self-regulation*. San Diego, CA: Academic Press.

Boesch, E. E. (1982). Ritual und psychotherapie. Zeitschrift fuer klinische. *Psychologie und Psychotherapie, 30*, 214–234.

Bogdan, R. J. (2000). *Minding minds: Evolving a reflexive mind by interpreting others*. Cambridge, MA: MIT Press.

Bogen, J. E. (1995). On the neurophysiology of consciousness: I. An overview. *Consciousness & Cognition: An International Journal, 4*, 52–62.

Bohannon, J. N., & Bonvillian, J. D. (1997). Theoretical approaches to language acquisition. In J. B. Gleason (Ed.), *The development of language* (4th ed., pp. 259–316). Boston: Allyn and Bacon.

Bolger, K. E., Patterson, C. J., & Kupersmidt, J. B. (1998). Peer relationships and self-esteem among children who have been maltreated. *Child Development, 69*, 1171–1197.

Bolger, N., & Amarel, D. (2007). Effects of social support visibility on adjustment to stress: Experimental evidence. *Journal of Personality and Social Psychology, 92*, 458–475.

Bolger, N., Foster, M., Vinokur, A. D., & Ng, R. (1996). Close relationships and adjustment to a life crisis: The case of breast cancer. *Journal of Personality and Social Psychology, 70*, 283–294.

Bolton, P. (2001). Local perceptions of mental health effects of the Rwandan genocide. *Journal of Nervous and Mental Disease, 189*, 243–248.

Bolton, P., Bass, J., Betancourt, T., Speelman, L., Onyango, G., Clougherty, K. F., et al. (2007). Interventions for depression symptoms among adolescent survivors of war and displacement in Northern Uganda: A randomized controlled trial. *Journal of the American Medical Association, 298*, 519–527.

Bolton, W., & Oatley, K. (1987). A longitudinal study of social support and depression in unemployed men. *Psychological Medicine, 17*, 453–460.

Bond, R., & Smith, P. B. (1996). Culture and conformity: A meta-analysis of studies using Asch's (1952b, 1956) line judgment task. *Psychological Bulletin, 119*, 111–137.

Bonebakker, A. E., Bonke, B., Klein, J., & Wolters, G. (1996). Information processing during general anesthesia: Evidence for unconscious memory. *Memory and Cognition, 24*, 766–776.

Bonomo, Y., Coffey, C., Wolfe, R., Lynskey, M., Bowes, G., & Patton, G. (2001). Adverse outcomes of alcohol use in adolescents. *Addiction, 96*(10), 1485–1496.

Bonvillian, J. D. (1999). Sign language development. In M. Barrett (Ed.), *The development of language*. London: UCL Press.

Bonwick, R. (2002). The Australian experience: Post-traumatic stress disorder in the elderly. *International Psychogeriatrics Association Bulletin, 19*(1).

Boon, S. D., & Brussoni, M. J. (1996). Young adults' relationships with their 'closest' grandparents: Examining emotional closeness. *Journal of Social Behavior & Personality, 11*, 1–14.

Booth-Butterfield, S., & Welbourne, J. (2002). The elaboration likelihood model: Its impact on persuasion theory and research. In J. P. Dillard & M. Pfau (Eds.), *The persuasion handbook: Developments in theory and research* (pp. 155–174). Thousand Oaks, CA: Sage.

Bor, W., Brennan, P. A., Williams, G. M., Najman, J. M., & O'Callaghan, M. (2003). A mother's attitude towards her infant and child behaviour five years later. *Australian and New Zealand Journal of Psychiatry, 37*, 748–755. Retrieved from http://www.uq.edu.au/qadrec/Documents/Najman03-mothers-attitude-towards-infant.pdf

Bor, W., McGee, T. R., & Fagan, A. A. (2004). Early risk factors for adolescent antisocial behaviour: An Australian longitudinal study. *Australian and New Zealand Journal of Psychiatry, 38*(5), 365–372.

Borbély, A. (1986). *Secrets of sleep*. New York: Basic Books.

Borden, V. M. H., & Levinger, G. (1991). Interpersonal transformations in intimate relationships. In W. H. Jones & D. Perlman (Eds.), *Advances in personal relationships: A research annual: Vol. 2. Advances in personal relationships* (pp. 35–56). London: Jessica Kingsley Publishers.

Borges, G., Ye, Y., Bond, J., Cherpitel, C. J., Cremonte, M., Moskalewicz, J., et al. (2010). The dimensionality of alcohol use disorders and alcohol consumption in a cross-national perspective. *Addiction, 105*, 240–254.

Boring, E. G. (1923, June 6). Intelligence as the tests test it. *The New Republic*, pp. 35–37.

Boring, E. G. (1930). A new ambiguous figure. *American Journal of Psychology, 42*, 444–445.

Borkovec, T. D., & Costello, E. (1993). Efficacy of applied relaxation and cognitive-behavioral therapy in the treatment of generalized anxiety disorder. *Journal of Consulting and Clinical Psychology, 61*, 611–619.

Bornholt, L. J., & Piccolo, A. (2005). Individuality, belonging, and children's self concepts: A motivational spiral model of self-evaluation, performance, and participation in physical activities. *Applied Psychology: An International Review, 54*, 515–536.

Bornstein, M. H. (1989). Sensitive periods in development: Structural characteristics and causal interpretations. *Psychological Bulletin, 105*, 179–197.

Borod, J. (1992). Interhemispheric and intrahemispheric control of emotion: A focus on unilateral brain damage. *Journal of Consulting and Clinical Psychology, 60*, 339–348.

Bors, D. A., & Forrin, B. (1996). The effects of post-weaning environment, biological dam, and nursing dam on feeding neophobia, open field activity, and learning. *Canadian Journal of Experimental Psychology, 50*, 197–204.

Bosson, J. K., & Swann, W. B., Jr. (1999). Self-liking, self-competence, and the quest for self-verification. *Personality and Social Psychology Bulletin, 25*, 1230–1241.

Bosworth, H. B., & Schaie, K. W. (1999). Survival effects in cognitive function, cognitive style and sociodemographic variables in the Seattle longitudinal study. *Experimental Aging Research, 25*, 121–139.

Bouchard, C. (1989). Genetic factors in obesity. *Medical Clinics of North America, 73*, 67–81.

Bouchard, T. J., Jr. (1984). Twins reared apart and together: What they tell us about human diversity. In S. Fox (Ed.), *The chemical and biological bases of individuality* (pp. 147–184). New York: Plenum.

Bouchard, T. J., Lykken, D. T., McGue, M., & Segal, N. L. (1990). Sources of human psychological differences: The Minnesota study of twins reared apart. *Science, 250*, 223–228.

Boulton-Lewis, G. M., Marton, F., Lewis, D. C., & Wilss, L. A. (2000). Learning in formal and informal contexts: Conceptions and strategies of Aboriginal and Torres Strait Islander university students. *Learning and Instruction, 10*, 393–414.

Bourgeois, M. J. (2002). Heritability of attitudes constrains dynamic social impact. *Personality and Social Psychology Bulletin, 28*, 1063–1072.

Bourguignon, E. (1979). *Psychological anthropology: An introduction to human nature and cultural differences*. New York: Holt, Rinehart & Winston.

Bourke, C. (1989, September). *Cross-cultural communication and professional education: An aboriginal perspective*. Paper presented at the Multicultural Communication Conference.

Bourke, C. (1998). Contemporary Australian Aboriginal identity. In D. Day (Ed.), *Australian IDENTITIES* (pp. 175–185). Melbourne, Australia: Australian Scholarly Publishing.

Bourke, C., Bourke, E., & Edwards, B. (1998). *Aboriginal Australia: An introductory reader in Aboriginal studies* (2nd ed.). Brisbane, Australia: University of Queensland Press.

Bouton, M. E. (2002). Context, ambiguity, and unlearning: Sources of relapse after behavioral extinction. *Biological Psychiatry, 52*, 976–986.

Bovasso, G. B., Eaton, W. W., & Armenian, H. K. (1999). The long-term outcomes of mental health treatment in a population-based study. *Journal of Consulting and Clinical Psychology, 67*, 529–538.

Bovbjerg, D., Redd, W. H., Maier, L. A., Holland, J. C., Leske, L. M., Niedzwiecki, D., et al. (1990). Anticipatory immune suppression and nausea in women receiving cyclic chemotherapy for ovarian cancer. *Journal of Consulting and Clinical Psychology, 58*, 153–157.

Bowd, A. D. (1990). A decade of animal research in psychology: Room for consensus? *Canadian Psychology, 31*, 74–82.

Bowden, C. L. (2005). A different depression: Clinical distinctions between bipolar and unipolar depression. *Journal of Affective Disorders, 84*, 117–125.

Bowden, S. C. (1990). Separating cognitive impairment in neurologically asymptomatic alcoholism from Wernicke-Korsakoff syndrome: Is the neuropsychological distinction justified? *Psychological Bulletin, 107*, 355–366.

Bowen, M. (1978). *Family therapy in clinical practice*. New York: Jason Aronson.

Bowen, M. (1991). Alcoholism as viewed through family systems theory and family psychotherapy. *Family Dynamics of Addiction Quarterly, 1,* 94–102.

Bower, C., Silva, D., Henderson, T. R., Ryan, A., & Rudy, E. (2000). Ascertainment of birth defects: The effect on completeness of adding a new source of data. *Journal of Paediatric Child Health, 36,* 574–576.

Bower, G. (1975). Cognitive psychology: An introduction. In W. K. Estes (Ed.), *Handbook of learning and cognitive processes: Vol. 1. Introduction to concepts and issues* (pp. 25–80). Hillsdale, NJ: Lawrence Erlbaum.

Bower, G. H. (1970). Analysis of a mnemonic device. *American Scientist, 58,* 496–510.

Bower, G. H. (1981). Mood and memory. *American Psychologist, 36,* 129–148.

Bower, G. H. (1989). In search of mood-dependent retrieval. *Journal of Social Behavior & Personality, 4,* 121–156.

Bower, T. G. R. (1971). The object in the world of the infant. *Scientific American, 225,* 30–38.

Bower, T. G. R. (1982). *Development in infancy* (2nd ed.). San Francisco: Freeman.

Bowers, J. S., & Schacter, D. L. (1990). Implicit memory and test awareness. *Journal of Experimental Psychology: Learning, Memory, and Cognition, 16,* 404–416.

Bowers, K. (1976). *Hypnosis for the seriously curious*. Monterey, CA: Brooks/Cole.

Bowers, K., Regenr, G., Balthazard, C., & Parker, K. (1990). Intuition in the context of discovery. *Cognitive Psychology, 22,* 72–110.

Bowlby, J. (1969). *Attachment and loss: Vol. I. Attachment*. New York: Basic Books.

Bowlby, J. (1973). *Separation, attachment, and loss: Vol. 2*. New York: Basic Books.

Bowlby, J. (1982). Attachment and loss: Retrospect and prospect. *American Journal of Orthopsychiatry, 52,* 664–678.

Boyle, G. J. (2008). Critique of the five-factor model of personality. In G. J. Boyle, G. Matthews, & D. H. Saklofske (Eds.), *The Sage handbook of personality theory and assessment: Vol. 1. Personality theories and models* (pp. 295–312). London: Sage Publications.

Boyle, G. J., Matthews, G., & Saklofske, D. (Eds.). (2008). *Handbook of personality theory and assessment* (2 vols.). London: Sage Publications.

Boyle, G. J., Stankov, L., & Cattell, R. B. (1995). Measurement and statistical models in the study of personality and intelligence. In D. H. Saklofske & M. Zeidner (Eds.), *International handbook of personality and intelligence* (pp. 417–446). New York: Plenum.

Boysen, S. T., & Himes, G. T. (1999). Current issues and emerging theories in animal cognition. *Annual Review of Psychology, 50,* 683–705.

Bozon, M. (2001). Sexuality, gender, and the couple: A sociohistorical perspective. *Annual Review of Sex Research*, 12, 1–32.

Brackett, M. A., Mayer, J. D., & Warner, R. M. (2004). Emotional intelligence and its relation to everyday behaviour. *Personality and Individual Differences, 36,* 1387–1402.

Bradley, C. L., & Marcia, J. E. (1998). Generativity-stagnation: A five-category model. *Journal of Personality, 66,* 39–64.

Bradley, G., Sparks, B., & Nesdale, D. (2001). Doctor communication style and patient outcomes: Gender and age as moderators. *Journal of Applied Social Psychology, 31,* 1749–1773.

Bradley, P. (2002). Relationship education: Helping couples live happy, full lives. *Psych, 24*(3), 14–16.

Bradshaw, J., Dwyer, T., Mummery, W. K., Rossi, D., Broadbent, M., & Reid Searl, K. (2007). Smokers' and women's beliefs on the risk of children becoming smokers if parents are smokers. *Australian and New Zealand Journal of Public Health, 31*(3), 291–292.

Brady, M. (1991). *The health of young Aborigines. A report on the health of Aborigines aged 12 to 25. National youth affairs research scheme*. Hobart, Tasmania: University of Tasmania.

Brainerd, C. J. (1996). Piaget: A centennial celebration. *Psychological Science, 7,* 191–195.

Brandao, M., Cardoso, S. H., Melo, L. L., Motta, V., & Coimbra, N. C. (1994). Neural substrate of defensive behavior in the midbrain tectum. *Neuroscience and Biobehavioral Reviews, 18,* 339–346.

Brandimonte, M., Einstein, G. O., & McDaniel, M. A. (Eds.). (1996). *Prospective memory: Theory and applications*. Mahwah, NJ: Lawrence Erlbaum.

Bransford, J. D., Barclay, J. R., & Franks, J. J. (1972). Sentence memory: A constructive versus interpretive approach. *Cognitive Psychology, 3,* 193–209.

Brase, G. L., Caprar, D. V., & Varacek, M. (2004). Sex differences in response to relationship threats to England and Romania. *Journal of Social and Personal Relationships, 21*(6), 763–778.

Braun, A. R., Balkin, T. J., Wesensten, N. J., Gwadry, F., Carson, R. E., Varga, M., et al. (1998). Dissociated pattern of activity in visual cortices and their projections during human rapid movement sleep. *Science, 279,* 91–95.

Braun, S. (1996). New experiments underscore warnings on maternal drinking. *Science, 273,* 738–739.

Braungart, J., Plomin, R., DeFries, J., & Fulker, D. (1992). Genetic influence on tester-rated infant temperament as assessed by Bayley's infant behavior record: Nonadoptive and adoptive siblings and twins. *Developmental Psychology, 28,* 40–47.

Bray, G. A. (1998). *Contemporary diagnosis and management of obesity*. Newton, PA: Handbooks in Health Care.

Bray, G. A., & Tartaglia, L. A. (2000). Medicinal strategies in the treatment of obesity. *Nature, 404,* 672–677.

Brazelton, T. B. (1972). Implications of infant development among the Mayan Indians of Mexico. *Human Development, 15,* 90–111.

Breland, K., & Breland, M. (1961). The misbehavior of organisms. *American Psychologist, 16,* 681–684.

Bremner, J. D. (1998). Neuroimaging of posttraumatic stress disorder. *Psychiatric Annals, 28,* 445–450.

Bremner, J. D. (1999). Does stress damage the brain? *Biological Psychiatry, 45,* 797–805.

Bremner, J. D. (2005). Effects of traumatic stress on brain structure and function: Relevance to early responses to trauma. *Journal of Trauma Dissociation, 6*(2), 51–68.

Brendl, C. M., Chattopadhyay, A., Pelham, B. W., & Carvallo, M. (2005). Name letter branding: Valence transfers when product specific needs are active. *Journal of Consumer Research, 32,* 405–415.

Brennan, K. A., Clark, C. L., & Shaver, P. R. (1998). Self-report measurement of adult attachment: An integrative overview. In J. A. Simpson & W. S. Rholes (Eds.), *Attachment theory and close relationships* (pp. 46–76). New York: Guilford Press.

Brennan, P. A., Grekin, E. R., & Mednick, S. A. (1999). Maternal smoking during pregnancy and adult male criminal outcomes. *Archives of General Psychiatry, 56,* 215–219.

Brenner, C. (1982). *The mind in conflict*. New York: International Universities Press.

Brenner, C. (1994). The mind as conflict and compromise formation. *Journal of Clinical Psychoanalysis, 3,* 473–488.

Breslau, N., Chilcoat, H. D., Kessler, R. C., & Davis, G. C. (1999). Previous exposure to trauma and PTSD effects of subsequent trauma: Results from the Detroit Area Survey of Trauma. *American Journal of Psychiatry, 156,* 902–907.

Breslau, N., Davis, G. C., Andreski, P., Peterson, E. L., & Schultz, L. R. (1997). Sex differences in posttraumatic stress disorder. *Archives of General Psychiatry, 54,* 1044–1048.

Bretherton, I. (1990). Communication patterns, internal working models, and the intergenerational transmission of attachment relationships. *Infant Mental Health Journal, 11,* 237–257.

Breuer, K. (1985). Intentionality and perception in early infancy. *Human Development, 28,* 71–83.

Brewer, J. B., Zhao, Z., Desmond, J. E., Glover, G. H., & Gabrieli, J. D. E. (1998). Making memories: Brain activity predicts how well visual experience will be remembered. *Science, 281,* 1185–1187.

Brewer, M. B., & Brown, R. J. (1998). Intergroup relations. In D. T. Gilbert, S. T. Fiske, & G. Lindzey (Eds.), *The handbook of social psychology: Vol. 2* (4th ed., pp. 554–594). Boston: McGraw-Hill.

Brewer, M. B., & Gardner, W. (1996). Dimensions of adult attachment, affect regulation, and romantic relationship functioning. *Personality and Social Psychology Bulletin, 21,* 267–283.

Brewer, W. F., & Treyens, J. C. (1981). Role of schemata in memory for places. *Cognitive Psychology, 13,* 207–230.

Brewerton, T. D. (1995). Toward a unified theory of serotonin dysregulation in eating and related disorders. *Psychoneuroendocrinology, 20,* 561–590.

Brewin, C. R., Andrews, B., & Valentine, J. D. (2000). Meta-analysis of risk factors for posttraumatic stress disorder in trauma-exposed adults. *Journal of Consulting and Clinical Psychology, 68,* 748–766.

Briere, J., & Conte, J. R. (1993). Self-reported amnesia for abuse in adults molested as children. *Journal of Traumatic Stress, 6,* 21–31.

Brislin, R. (1988). Increasing awareness of class, ethnicity, culture, and race by expanding on student's own experiences. In I. S. Cohen (Ed.), *The G. Stanley Hall lecture series: Vol. 8* (pp. 137–180). Washington, DC: American Psychological Association.

Brislin, R. W., & Keating, C. F. (1976). Cultural differences in the perception of a three-dimensional Ponzo illusion. *Journal of Cross-Cultural Psychology, 7,* 397–412.

British Psychological Society. (2007). *Report on the working party on conducting research on the internet: Guidelines for ethical practice in psychological research online*. Retrieved from http://www.bps.org.uk/downloadfile.cfm?file_uuid=2b3429b3-1143-dfd0-7e5a-4be3fdd763cc&ext=pdf

Britt, H., Miller, G. C., Charles, J., Pan, Y., Valenti, L., Henderson, J., et al. (2007). *General practice activity in Australia 2005–06* (General Practice Series No. 19, AIHW Cat. No. GEP 19). Canberra, Australia: AIHW.

Broadbent, C., & Boyle, M. (2005). What's up? Indigenous families learning together. *Education Links: Building Strength Through Partnership, 69,* 25–29.

Broadbent, C., Boyle, M., & Carmody, M. (2006). *Culture, communication and connectedness: Building social capital within the Indigenous community*. Paper presented at the 46th Annual Conference of Adult Learning Australia. Retrieved April 4, 2007, from http://www.ala.asn.au/conf/2006/papers/refereed%20papers/ALApaper06CBMBMC%20C%20Broadbent_S03_.pdf

Broadbent, D. E. (1958). The hidden preattentive processes. *American Psychologist, 32,* 109–118.

Brody, L., & Hall, J. (2000). Gender, emotion, and expression. In M. Lewis & J. Haviland-Jones (Eds.), *Handbook of emotions* (2nd ed., pp. 338–349). New York: Guilford Press.

Brody, L. R. (1999). *Gender, emotion, and the family*. Cambridge, MA: Harvard University Press.

Brody, L. R., Lovas, G. S., & Hay, D. H. (1995). Gender differences in anger and fear as a function of situational context. *Sex Roles, 32*(1–2), 47–78.

Brody, N. (1992). *Intelligence* (2nd ed.). San Diego, CA: Academic Press.

Broe, G. A., Jackson Pulver, L., Arkles, R., Robertson, H., Kelso, W., Chalkley, S., et al. (2009). *Cognition, ageing and dementia in Australian Aboriginal and Torres Strait Islander peoples: A review of the literature* (Summary Report for Dementia Collaborative Research Centre). Retrieved from http://www.dementia.unsw.edu.au/DCRCweb.nsf/resources/DCRC+Products/$file/Indigenous+People+Literature+Review+Final+300109.pdf

Bronte-Tinkew, J., Moore, K. A., & Carrano, J. (2006). The father-child relationship, parenting styles, and adolescent risk behaviours in intact families. *Journal of Family Issues*, *27*, 850–881.

Broocks, A., Bandelow, A., Pekrun, G., George, A., Meyer, T., Bartmann, U., et al. (1998). Comparison of aerobic exercise, clomipramine, and placebo in the treatment of panic disorder. *American Journal of Psychiatry, 155,* 603–609.

Brookoff, D., O'Brien, K., Cook, C. S., & Thompson, T. D. (1997). Characteristics of participants in domestic violence. *Journal of the American Medical Association*, *277*, 1369–1373.

Brooks-Gunn, J., Duncan, G., & Aber, L. (Eds.). (1997). *Neighborhood poverty: Context and consequences for children*. New York: Russell Sage Foundation.

Broome, R. (1994). *Aboriginal Australians* (2nd ed.). Sydney, Australia: Allen & Unwin.

Brosschot, J. F., & Janssen, E. (1998). Continuous monitoring of affective-autonomic response dissociation in repressors during negative emotional stimulation. *Personality and Individual Differences, 25,* 69–84.

Broughton, J. (1978). Development of concepts of self, mind, reality, and knowledge. *New Directions for Child Development, 1,* 75–100.

Broughton, L. (1993). Being Maori. *New Zealand Medical Journal, 106*(968), 506–508.

Brown, A., Bransford, J., Ferrara, R., & Campione, J. (1983). Learning, remembering, and understanding. In E. M. Markman & J. H. Flavell (Eds.), *Carmichael's manual of child psychology: Vol. III*. New York: John Wiley.

Brown, A., Morrissey, M., & Sherwood, J. (2006). Uncovering the determinants of cardiovascular disease among Indigenous people. *Ethnicity and Health, 11*(2), 191–210.

Brown, A. S., Cohen, P., Greenwald, S., & Susser, E. (2000). Nonaffective psychosis after prenatal exposure to rubella. *American Journal of Psychiatry, 157,* 438–443.

Brown, A. S., van Os, J., Driessens, C., Hoek, H. W., & Susser, E. S. (2000). Further evidence of relation between prenatal famine and major affective disorder. *American Journal of Psychiatry*, *157*, 190–195.

Brown, G., Bhrolchain, M., & Harris, T. (1975). Social class and psychiatric disturbance among women in an urban poulation. *Sociology, 9*, 225–254.

Brown, G. W., Andrews, B., Harris, T. O., & Adler, Z. (1986). Social support, self-esteem, and depression. *Psychological Medicine, 16,* 813–831.

Brown, G. W., Birley, J. L., & Wing, J. K. (1972). Influence of family life on the course of schizophrenic disorders: A replication. *British Journal of Psychiatry*, *121*, 241–258.

Brown, G. W., & Harris, T. O. (1978). *Social origins of depression: A study of psychiatric disorder in women*. New York: Free Press.

Brown, G. W., & Harris, T. O. (1989). Depression. In G. W. Brown & T. O. Harris (Eds.), *Life events and illnesses*. New York: Guilford Press.

Brown, G. W., Harris, T. O., & Hepworth, C. (1994). Life events and endogenous depression: A puzzle reexamined. *Archives of General Psychiatry*, *51*, 525–534.

Brown, I. (2000). The socialisation of the Aboriginal child. In P. Dudgeon, D. Garvey, & H. Pickett (Eds.), *Working with indigenous Australians: A handbook for psychologists* (pp. 177–179). Perth, Australia: Gunada Press.

Brown, J., & Smart, S. A. (1991). The self and social conduct: Linking self-representations to prosocial behavior. *Journal of Personality and Social Psychology, 60*, 368–375.

Brown, J. B. (1991). Staying fit and staying well: Physical fitness as a moderator of life stress. *Journal of Personality and Social Psychology, 61*, 555–561.

Brown, N. O. (1959). *Life against death: The psychoanalytic meaning of history*. Middleton, CT: Wesleyan University Press.

Brown, P. K., & Wald, G. (1964). Visual pigments in single rods and cones in the human retina. *Science, 144*, 45–52.

Brown, R. (1973). *A first language: The early stages*. Cambridge, MA: Harvard University Press.

Brown, R. (2001). Australian Indigenous mental health. *Australian and New Zealand Journal of Mental Health Nursing*, *10*, 33–41.

Brown, R., & Fraser, C. (1963). The acquisition of syntax. In C. N. Cofer & B. Musgrave (Eds.), *Verbal behavior and learning: Problems and processes* (pp. 158–201). New York: McGraw- Hill.

Brown, R., & Hanlon, C. (1970). Derivational complexity and order of acquisition in child speech. In J. R. Hayes (Ed.), *Cognition and the development of language*. New York: John Wiley.

Brown, R., & Kulik, J. (1977). Flashbulb memories. *Cognition, 5,* 73–99.

Brown, R. P., & Josephs, R. A. (1999). A burden of proof: Stereotype relevance and gender differences in math performance. *Journal of Personality and Social Psychology, 76*, 246–257.

Brown, R. W., Galanter, E., Hess, D., & Mandler, G. (1962). *New directions in psychology*. New York: Holt.

Brown, R. W., & McNeill, D. (1966). The tip-of-the-tongue phenomenon. *Journal of Verbal Learning and Verbal Behavior, 5,* 325–337.

Brown, S. L. (1985). Two adolescents at risk for schizophrenia: A family case study: Discussion. *International Journal of Family Therapy, 7,* 149–154.

Brown, T. A., Chorpita, B. F., & Barlow, D. H. (1998). Structural relationships among dimensions of the DSM-IV anxiety and mood disorders and dimensions of negative affect, positive affect, and autonomic arousal. *Journal of Abnormal Psychology, 107,* 179–192.

Brownell, K. D., & Rodin, J. (1994). The dieting maelstrom: Is it possible and advisable to lose weight? *American Psychologist*, *49*, 781–791.

Brubaker, R. G., & Wickersham, D. (1990). Encouraging the practice of testicular self-examination: A field application of the theory of reasoned action. *Health Psychology, 9,* 154–163.

Bruce, D., & Bahrick, H. P. (1992). Perceptions of past research. *American Psychologist, 47,* 319–328.

Bruch, H. (1973). *Eating disorders: Obesity, anorexia nervosa, and the person within*. New York: Basic Books.

Bruck, D. (1999). Non-awakening in children in response to a smoke detector alarm. *Fire Safety Journal*, *32*, 369–376.

Bruck, D. (2001). The who, what, where and why of waking to fire alarms: A review. *Journal of Fire Safety, 36*, 623–639.

Bruck, D., Ball, M., Thomas, I., & Rouillard, V. (2009). How does the pitch and pattern of a signal affect auditory arousal thresholds? *Journal of Sleep Research, 18*, 196–203.

Bruck, D., & Horasan, M. (1995). Non-arousal and non-action with a smoke detector alarm in normal sleepers. *Fire Safety Journal*, *25*(2), 125–139.

Bruck, D., & Thomas, I. (2008). Towards a better smoke alarm signal — an evidence based approach. In B. Karlsson (Ed.), *Proceedings of the 9th International Symposium of the International Association for Fire Safety Science, Karlsruhe, Germany* (pp. 403–414).

Bruder, G., Kayser, J., Tenke, C., Amador, X., Friedman, M., Sharif, Z., et al. (1999). Left temporal lobe dysfunction in schizophrenia: Event-related potential and behavioral evidence from phonetic and tonal dichotic listening tasks. *Archives of General Psychiatry, 56,* 267–276.

Bruner, J. S. (1992). Another look at New Look 1. *American Psychologist*, *47*, 780–783.

Bruyer, R. (1991). Covert face recognition in prosopagnosia: A review. *Brain and Cognition*, *15*, 223–235.

Bryant, F. B., Yarnold, P. R., & Grimm, L. G. (1996). Toward a measurement model of the affect intensity measure: A three-factor structure. *Journal of Research in Personality, 30*, 223–247.

Bryant, J. A., Sanders-Jackson, A., & Smallwood, A. M. K. (2006). IMing, text messaging, and adolescent social networks. *Journal of Computer-Mediated Communication*, *11*(2), article 10. Retrieved from http://jcmc.indiana.edu/vol11/issue2/bryant.html

Bryant, P. E., & Trabasso, T. (1971). Transitive inferences and memory in young children. *Nature, 232,* 456–458.

Brynjulfsen, L. (2005). Self-construct, self-consistency, self-esteem, and well-being. *The Sciences and Engineering*, *66*, 3454.

Bucci, W. (1997). *Psychoanalysis and cognitive science: A multiple code theory*. New York: Guilford Press.

Buchanan, G. M., & Seligman, M. E. P. (Eds.). (1995). *Explanatory style*. Hillsdale, NJ: Lawrence Erlbaum.

Buck, R. (1986). The psychology of emotion. In J. E. LeDoux & W. Hirst (Eds.), *Mind and brain: Dialogues in cognitive neuroscience*. New York: Cambridge University Press.

Bugental, D. B., & Goodnow, J. J. (1998). Socialization processes. In W. Damon (Ed. in Chief) & N. Eisenberg (Vol. Ed.), *Handbook of child psychology: Vol. 3* (pp. 389–462). New York: John Wiley.

Buhrich, N., Bailey, J. M., & Martin, N. G. (1991). Sexual orientation, sexual identity, and sex-dimorphic behaviors in male twins. *Behavior Genetics, 21,* 75–96.

Buhrmester, D. (1990). Intimacy of friendship, interpersonal competence, and adjustment during preadolescence and adolescence. *Child Development, 61,* 1101–1111.

Buitenhuis, J., de Jong, P. J., Jaspers, J. P. C., & Groothoff, J. W. (2006). Relationship between posttraumatic stress disorder symptoms and the course of whiplash complaints. *Journal of Psychosomatic Research*, *61*, 681–689.

Bukatko, D., & Daehler, M. W. (2004). *Child development* (5th ed.). New York: Houghton Mifflin.

Bukowski, W., Gauze, C., Hoza, B., & Newcomb, A. (1993). Differences and consistency between same-sex and other-sex peer relationships during early adolescence. *Developmental Psychology, 29,* 255–263.

Bunge, S. A., Klingberg, T., Jacobsen, R. B., & Gabrieli, J. D. E. (2000). A resource model of the neural basis of executive working memory. *Proceedings of the National Academy of Sciences, USA*, *97*, 3573–3578.

Burger, J. M. (1999). The foot-in-the-door compliance procedure: A multiple-process analysis and review. *Personality and Social Psychology Review*, *3*(4), 303–325.

Burgess, K. B., Marshall, P. J., Rubin, K. H., & Fox, N. A. (2003). Infant attachment and temperament as predictors of subsequent externalizing problems and cardiac physiology. *Journal of Child Psychology and Psychiatry*, *44*, 819–831.

Burgess, N. (2002). The hippocampus, space, and viewpoints in episodic memory. *The Quarterly Journal of Experimental Psychology*, *55A*(4), 1057–1080.

Burgess, N., & Hitch, G. (2005). Computational models of working memory: Putting long-term memory into context. *Trends in Cognitive Science*, *9*(11), 535–541.

Burgess, N., & Hitch, G. J. (1999). Memory for serial order: A network model of the phonological loop and its timing. *Psychological Review*, *106*, 551–581.

Burgoon, J. K., Birk, T., & Pfau, M. (1990). Nonverbal behaviors, persuasion, and credibility. *Human Communication Research, 17,* 140–169.

Buri, J., Louiselle, P., Misukanis, T., & Mueller, R. (1988). Effects of parental authoritarianism on self-esteem. *Personality and Social Psychology Bulletin, 14,* 271–282.

Burke, C. S., Stagl, K. C., Klein, C., Goodwin, G. F., Salas, E., & Halpin, S. M. (2006). What type of leadership behaviors are functional in teams? *The Leadership Quarterly*, *17*, 288–307.

Burke, W., & Cole, A. M. (1978). Extra-retinal influences on the lateral geniculate nucleus. *Review of Physiology, Biochemistry, and Pharmacology, 80,* 105–166.

Burks, B. S. (1928). The relative influence of nature and nurture upon mental development: A comparative study of foster parent-foster child resemblance and true parent-true child resemblance. *27th Yearbook of the National Society for the Study of Education, 27*, 219–316.

Burks, B. S. (1938). On the relative contributions of nature and nurture to average group differences in intelligence. *Proceedings of the National Academy of Sciences, USA, 24*, 276–282.

Burns, J., & Thomson, N. (2006). Overweight and obesity: A major problem for Indigenous Australians. *Australian Indigenous Health Bulletin, 6*(4), 1–10.

Burns, J. M., Andrews, G., & Szabo, M. (2002). Depression in young people: What causes it and can we prevent it? *Medical Journal Australia, 177*, S93–S96.

Burnstein, E., Crandall, C., & Kitayama, S. (1994). Some neo-Darwinian decision rules for altruism: Weighing cues for inclusive fitness as a function of the biological importance of the decision. *Journal of Personality and Social Psychology, 67*, 773–789.

Burton, L. J. (2002). *An interactive approach to writing essays and research reports in psychology*. Brisbane, Australia: John Wiley & Sons.

Burton, L. J. (2003). Examining the relation between visual imagery and spatial ability tests. *International Journal of Testing, 3*(3), 277–291.

Burton, L. J. (2007). *An interactive approach to writing essays and research reports in psychology* (2nd ed.). Milton, Australia: John Wiley & Sons.

Burton, L. J., & Fogarty, G. J. (2003). The factor structure of visual imagery and spatial abilities. *Intelligence, 31*, 289–318.

Burton, L. J., Taylor, J. A., Dowling, D. G., & Lawrence, J. (2009). Learning approaches, personality and concepts of knowledge of first-year students: Mature-age versus school leaver. *Studies in Learning, Evaluation, Innovation and Development, 6*(1), 65–81. Retrieved from http://sleid.cqu.edu.au

Bushman, B. J. (1995). Moderating role of trait aggressiveness in the effects of violent media on aggression. *Journal of Personality and Social Psychology, 69*, 950–960.

Bushman, B. J. (1997). Effects of alcohol on human aggression: Validity of proposed explanations. In M. Galanter (Ed.), *Recent developments in alcoholism: Vol. 13. Alcohol and violence: Epidemiology, neurobiology, psychology, family issues* (pp. 227–243). New York: Plenum Press.

Bushman, B. J., & Anderson, C. A. (2001). Media violence and the American public: Scientific facts versus media misinformation. *American Psychologist, 56*, 477–489.

Bushman, B. J., & Baumeister, R. F. (1998). Threatened egotism, narcissism, self-esteem, and direct and displaced aggression: Does self-love or self-hate lead to violence? *Journal of Personality and Social Psychology, 75*, 219–229.

Bushman, B. J., & Baumeister, R. F. (2002). Does self-love or self-hate lead to violence? *Journal of Research in Personality, 36*, 543–545.

Bushman, B. J., & Cooper, H. M. (1990). Effects of alcohol on human aggression: An integrative research review. *Psychological Bulletin, 107*, 341–354.

Bushnell, E. W., & Boudreau, J. P. (1993). Motor development and the mind: The potential role of motor abilities as a determinant of aspects of perceptual development. *Child Development, 64*, 1005–1021.

Bushnell, J. A., & Bakker, L. W. (1997). Substance use disorders among men in prison: A New Zealand study. *Australian and New Zealand Journal of Psychiatry, 31*(4), 577–581.

Buss, A. H., & Plomin, R. (1984). *Temperament: Early developing personality traits*. Hillsdale, NJ: Erlbaum.

Buss, D. M. (1991). Evolutionary personality psychology. *Annual Review of Psychology, 42*, 459–492.

Buss, D. M. (1999). Human nature and individual differences: The evolution of human personality. In L. A. Pervin & O. P. John (Eds.), *Handbook of personality: Theory and research* (2nd ed., pp. 31–56). New York: Guilford Press.

Buss, D. M. (2000). The evolution of happiness. *American Psychologist, 55*, 15–23.

Buss, D. M. (2006). Strategies of human mating. *Psychological Topics, 15*, 239–260. Retrieved from http://homepage.psy.utexas.edu/homepage/group/busslab/pdffiles/strategies_of_human_mating2006.pdf

Buss, D. M., & Angleitner, A. (1989). Mate selection preferences in Germany and the United States. *Personality and Individual Differences, 10*, 1269–1280.

Buss, D. M., & Kenrick, D. T. (1998). Evolutionary social psychology. In D. T. Gilbert, S. T. Fiske, & G. Lindzey (Eds.), *The handbook of social psychology: Vol. 2* (4th ed., pp. 982–1026). Boston: McGraw-Hill.

Buss, D. M., Larsen, R. J., Westen, D., & Semmelroth, J. (1992). Sex differences in jealousy: Evolution, physiology, and psychology. *Psychological Science, 3*, 251–255.

Buss, D. M., & Schmitt, D. P. (1993). Sexual strategies theory: An evolutionary perspective on human mating. *Psychological Review, 100*, 1–29.

Buss, D. M., & Shackelford, T. K. (1997). Human aggression in evolutionary psychological perspective. *Clinical Psychology Review, 17*, 605–619.

Bussey, K. (1999). Children's categorization and evaluation of different types of lies and truths. *Child Development, 70*, 1338–1347.

Butler, A. B., & Hodos, W. (1996). *Comparative vertebrate neuroanatomy: Evolution and adaptation*. New York: Wiley-Liss.

Butler, A. C., Chapman, J. E., Forman, E. M., & Beck, A. T. (2006). The empirical status of cognitive-behavioral therapy: A review of meta-analyses. *Clinical Psychology Review, 26*, 17–31.

Butler, C. A. (1976). New data about female sexual response. *Journal of Sex and Marital Therapy, 2*, 40–46.

Butler, E. A., Lee, T. L., & Gross, J. G. (2007). Emotion regulation and culture: Are the social consequences of emotion suppression culture-specific? *Emotion, 7*, 30–48.

Butler, R., Chapman, S., Thomas, D. P., & Torzillo, P. (2010). Low daily smoking estimates derived from sales monitored tobacco use in six remote predominantly Aboriginal communities. *Australian and New Zealand Journal of Public Health, 34*, S71–S75.

Butler, R. N. (1969). Ageism: Another form of bigotry. *Gerontologist, 9*, 243–246.

Butler, R. N. (1975). *Why survive? Being old in America*. New York: Harper & Row.

Butler, R. N. (1984). Senile dementia: Reversible and irreversible. *Counseling Psychology, 12*, 75–79.

Butt, A., Testylier, G., & Dykes, R. (1997). Acetylcholine release in rat frontal and somatosensory cortex is enhanced during lactile discrimination learning. *Psychobiology, 25*, 18–33.

Butters, N., Heindel, W. C., & Salmon, D. (1990). Dissociation of implicit memory in dementia: Neurological implications. *Bulletin of the Psychonomic Society, 28*, 359–366.

Butterworth, A. (1978). A review of a primer of infant development. *Perception, 17*, 363–364.

Butzlaff, R. L., & Hooley, J. M. (1998). Expression emotion and psychiatric relapse: A meta-analysis. *Archives of General Psychiatry, 55*, 547–552.

Buunk, B. P., Angleitner, A., Oubaid, V., & Buss, D. M. (1996). Sex differences in jealousy in evolutionary and cultural perspective: Tests from the Netherlands, Germany, and the United States. *Psychological Science, 7*, 359–363.

Bynum, C. W. (1987). *Holy feast and holy fast*. Berkeley: University of California Press.

Byrne, B., Samuelsson, S., Wadsworth, S., Hulslander, J., Corley, R., DeFries, J. C., et al. (2007). Longitudinal twin study of early literacy development: Preschool through Grade 1. *Journal of Reading and Writing, 20*, 77–102.

Byrne, D., London, O., & Reeves, K. (1968). The effects of physical attractiveness, sex, and attitude similarity on interpersonal attraction. *Journal of Personality, 36*, 259–271.

Byrne, D., & Murnen, S. (1988). Maintaining loving relationships. In R. Sternberg & M. L. Barnes (Eds.), *The psychology of love* (pp. 293–310). New Haven, CT: Yale University Press.

Cacioppo, J. T., Ernst, J. M., Burleson, M. H., McClintock, M. K., Malarkey, W. B., Hawkley, L. C., et al. (2000). Lonely traits and concomitant physiological processes: The MacArthur social neuroscience studies. *International Journal of Psychophysiology, 35*, 143–154.

Cacioppo, J. T., & Gardner, W. L. (1999). Emotions. *Annual Review of Psychology, 50*, 191–214.

Cacioppo, J. T., Gardner, W. L., & Berntson, G. G. (1997). Beyond bipolar conceptualizations and measures: The case of attitudes and evaluative space. *Personality and Social Psychology Review, 1*, 3–25.

Cadoret, R. J., O'Gorman, T. W., Troughton, E., & Heywood, E. (1985). Alcoholism and antisocial personality. *Archives of General Psychiatry, 42*, 161–167.

Cadoret, R. J., Yates, W. R., Troughton, E., Woodworth, G., & Stewart, M. A. (1995). Genetic-environmental interaction in the genesis of aggressivity and conduct disorders. *Archives of General Psychiatry, 52*, 916–924.

Cafarella, J. (2010, November 29). Men at work. National win for the gentlemen who change lives. *Sydney Morning Herald*.

Caggiula, A. R., Epstein, L. H., Antelman, S., Seymour, M., & Taylor, S. S. (1991). Conditioned tolerance to the anorectic and corticosterone-elevating effects of nicotine. *Pharmacology, Biochemistry, and Behavior, 40*, 53–59.

Cahill, L., Prins, B., Weber, M., & McGaugh, J. L. (1994). Beta-adrenergic activation and memory for emotional events. *Nature, 371*, 702–704.

Cai, H., Brown, J. D., & Deng, C. (2007). Self esteem and culture: Differences in cognitive self-evaluations or affective self-regard? *Asian Journal of Social Psychology, 10*(3), 162–170.

Calabrese, M. L., Farber, B. A., & Westen, D. (2005). The relationship of adult attachment constructs to object relational patterns of representing self and others. *Journal of the American Academy of Psychoanalysis and Dynamic Psychiatry, 33*(3), 513–530.

Caldwell, T. M., Jorm, A. F., & Dear, K. B. G. (2004). Suicide and mental health in rural, remote and metropolitan areas in Australia. *Medical Journal Australia, 181*(7), S10–S14.

Caltabiano, M. L., Byrne, D., Martin, P. R., & Sarafino, E. P. (2002). *Health psychology: Biopsychosocial interactions. An Australian perspective*. Brisbane, Australia: John Wiley & Sons.

Cameron, L. D., Leventhal, H., & Love, R. R. (1998). Trait anxiety, symptom perceptions, and illness-related responses among women with breast cancer in remission during a Tamoxifen clinical trial. *Health Psychology, 17*, 459–469.

Camilleri, C., & Malewska-Peyre, H. (1997). Socialisation and identity strategies. In J. W. Berry, P. R. Dasen, & T. S. Saraswathi (Eds.), *Handbook of cross-cultural Psychology: Vol. 2. Basic processes and human development* (pp. 41–68). Boston: Allyn & Bacon.

Campbell, D. T., & Stanley, J. C. (1963). *Experimental and quasi-experimental designs for research*. Chicago: Rand McNally.

Campbell, J. D. (1986). Similarity and uniqueness: The effects of attribute type, relevance, and individual differences in self-esteem and depression. *Journal of Personality and Social Psychology, 50*, 281–294.

Campbell, M. A. (2005). Cyber bullying: An old problem in a new guise? *Australian Journal of Guidance and Counselling, 15*(1), 68–76. Retrieved from http://eprints.qut.edu.au/1925/1/1925.pdf

Campbell, S. B. (1985). Hyperactivity in preschoolers: Correlates and prognostic implications. *Clinical Psychology Review, 5*, 405–428.

Campbell, W. K., & Sedikides, C. (1999). Self-threat magnifies the self-serving bias. A meta-analytic integration. *Reviews of General Psychology, 3*, 23–43.

Campfield, L., Arthur, S., Francoise, J., Rosenbaum, M., & Hirsch, J. (1996). Human eating: Evidence for a physiological basis using a modified paradigm [Special issue: Society for the Study of Ingestive Behavior,

Second Independent Meeting]. *Neuroscience & Biobehavioral Reviews, 20*, 133–137.

Campfield, L., Brandon, P., & Smith, F. J. (1985). On-line continuous measurement of blood glucose and meal pattern in free-feeding rats: The role of glucose in meal initiation. *Brain Research Bulletin, 14*, 605–617.

Campione, J. C., Brown, A. L., & Ferrara, R. A. (1982). Mental retardation and intelligence. In R. J. Sternberg (Ed.), *Handbook of human intelligence* (pp. 393–490). New York: Cambridge University Press.

Campos, J. J., Anderson, D. I., Barbu-Roth, M. A., Hubbard, E. M., Hertenstein, M. J., & Witherington, D. (2000). Travel broadens the mind. *Infancy, 1*(2), 149–219.

Campos, J. J., Bertenthal, B. I., & Kermoian, R. (1992). Early experience and emotional development: The emergence of wariness and heights. *Psychological Science, 3*, 61–64.

Candy, T. R., Crowell, J. A., & Banks, M. S. (1998). Optical, receptoral, and retinal constraints on foveal and peripheral vision in the human neonate. *Vision Research, 38*, 3857–3870.

Canfield, R. L., & Ceci, S. J. (1992). Integrating learning into a theory of intellectual development. In R. J. Sternberg & C. A. Berg (Eds.), *Intellectual development*. New York: Cambridge University Press.

Canivez, G. L., & Watkins, M. W. (1998). Long-term stability of the Wechsler Intelligence Scale for children, third edition. *Psychological Assessment, 10*, 285–291.

Cannon, T. D., Kaprio, J., Lönnqvist, J., Huttunen, M., & Koskenvuo, M. (1998). The genetic epidemiology of schizophrenia in a Finnish twin cohort: A population-based modeling study characterization of psychotic conditions. *Archives of General Psychiatry, 55*, 67–74.

Cannon, W. B. (1927). The James-Lange theory of emotions: A critical examination and an alternative theory. *American Journal of Psychiatry, 39*, 106–124.

Cannon, W. B. (1932). *The wisdom of the body*. New York: W.W. Norton.

Cantor, N. (1990). From thought to behavior: Having and doing in the study of personality and cognition. *American Psychologist, 45*, 735–750.

Cantor, N., & Blanton, H. (1996). Effortful pursuit of personal goals in daily life. In P. M. Gollwitzer & J. A. Bargh (Eds.), *The psychology of action: Linking cognition and motivation to behavior* (pp. 338–359). New York: Guilford Press.

Cantor, N., & Harlow, R. (1994). Personality, strategic behavior, and daily-life problem solving. *Current Directions in Psychologial Science, 3*, 169–172.

Cantor, N., & Kihlstrom, J. F. (1987). *Personality and social intelligence*. Englewood Cliffs, NJ: Prentice-Hall.

Capaldi, E., & VandenBos, G. (1991). Taste, food exposure, and eating behavior. *Hospital and Community Psychiatry, 42*, 787–789.

Caplan, D., & Waters, G. S. (1990). Short-term memory and language comprehension: A critical review of the neuropsychological literature. In G. Vallar & T. Shallice (Eds.), *Neuropsychological impairments of short-term memory* (pp. 337–389). Cambridge: Cambridge University Press.

Caplan, P. J., Crawford, M., Hyde, J. S., & Richardson, J. T. E. (1997). *Gender differences in human cognition*. London: Oxford University Press.

Caporael, L. R., & Baron, R. M. (1997). Groups as the mind's natural environment. In J. A. Simpson & D. T. Kenrick (Eds.), *Evolutionary social psychology* (pp. 317–344). Mahwah, NJ: Lawrence Erlbaum.

Cardno, A. G., Marshall, E. J., Coid, B., Macdonald, A. M., Ribchester, T. R., Davies, N. J., et al. (1999). Heritability estimates for psychotic disorders: The Maudsley Twin Psychosis Series. *Archives of General Psychiatry, 56*, 162–168.

Cardozo, B. L., Vergara, A., Agani, F., & Gotway, C. A. (2000). Mental health, social functioning, and attitudes of Kosovar Albanians following the war in Kosovo. *Journal of the American Medical Association, 284*, 569–577.

Carey, C. L., & Harris, L. M. (2005). The origins of blood-injection fear/phobia in cancer patients undergoing intravenous chemotherapy. *Behaviour Change, 22*(4), 212–219.

Carey, G. (1990). Genes, fears, phobias, and phobic disorders. *Journal of Counseling and Development, 68*, 628–632.

Carey, M. P., & Vanable, P. A. (2003). AIDS/HIV. In A. M. Nezu, C. M. Nezu, & P. A. Geller (Eds.), *Handbook of psychology: Health psychology: Vol. 9* (pp. 219–244). Hoboken, NJ: John Wiley & Sons.

Carlsmith, J. M., & Anderson, C. A. (1979). Ambient temperature and the occurrence of collective violence: A new analysis. *Journal of Personality and Social Psychology, 37*, 337–344.

Carlson, E. A. (1998). A prospective longitudinal study of attachment disorganization/disorientation. *Child Development, 69*, 1107–1128.

Carlson, E. B., & Rosser-Hogan, R. (1991). Trauma experiences, posttraumatic stress, dissociation, and depression in Cambodian refugees. *American Journal of Psychiatry, 148*, 1548–1551.

Carlson, N. R. (1999). *Foundations of physiological psychology* (4th ed.). New York: Allyn & Bacon.

Carlson, S., Pertovaara, A., & Tanila, H. (1987). Late effects of early binocular visual deprivation on the function of Brodmann's area 7 of monkeys. *Developmental Brain Research, 33*, 101–111.

Carmagnani, A., & Carmagnani, E.-F. (1999). Biofeedback: Present state and future possibilities. *International Journal of Mental Health, 28*, 83–86.

Carolsfeld, J., Tester, M., Kreiberg, H., & Sherwood, N. M. (1997). Pheromone-induced spawning of Pacific herring: I. Behavioral characterization. *Hormones and Behavior, 31*, 256–268.

Carone, B. J., Harrow, M., & Westermeyer, J. F. (1991). Posthospital course and outcome in schizophrenia. *Archives of General Psychiatry, 48*, 247–253.

Carpenter, K. M., Hasin, D. S., Allison, D. B., & Faith, M. S. (2000). Relationship between obesity and DSM-IV major depressive disorder, suicide ideation, and suicide attempts: Results from a general population study. *American Journal of Public Health, 90*, 251–257.

Carpenter, M., Pennington, B. F., & Rogers, S. J. (2001). Understanding of others' intentions in children with autism. *Journal of Autism and Developmental Disorders, 31*(6), 589–599.

Carpenter, P. A., Miyaka, A., & Just, M. A. (1995). Language comprehension: Sentence and discourse processing. *Annual Review, 46*, 91–120.

Carr, S. (2002). *Social psychology: Context, communication and culture*. Brisbane, Australia: John Wiley.

Carr, V. J., Lewin, T. J., Carter, G. L., & Webster, R. A. (1992). Patterns of service utilisation following the 1989 Newcastle earthquake: Findings from phase 1 of the quake impact study. *Australian Journal of Public Health, 16*(4), 360–369.

Carroll, J. B. (1993). *Human cognitive abilities: A survey of factor-analytic studies*. New York: Cambridge University Press.

Carroll, J. B. (1997). The three-stratum theory of cognitive abilities. In D. P. Flanagan, J. L. Genshaft, & P. L. Harrison (Eds.), *Contemporary intellectual assessment: Theories, tests, and issues* (pp. 122–130). New York: The Guilford Press.

Carroll, J. B. (2003). The higher-stratum structure of cognitive abilities: Current evidence supports g and about ten broad factors. In H. Nyborg (Ed.), *The scientific study of general intelligence: Tribute to Arthur R. Jensen* (pp. 5–22). San Diego, CA: Pergamon.

Carroll, J. M., & Russell, J. A. (1996). Do facial expressions signal specific emotions? Judging emotion from the face in context. *Journal of Personality and Social Psychology, 70*, 205–218.

Carron, A. V., Burke, S. M., & Prapavessis, H. (2004). Self-presentation and group influence. *Journal of Applied Sport Psychology, 16*, 41–58.

Carskadon, M. A., & Dement, W. (1982). Nocturnal determinants of daytime sleepiness. *Sleep, 5*, 73–81.

Carstairs, J. R., Myors, B., Shores, E. A., & Fogarty, G. (2006). Influence of language background on tests of cognitive ability: Australian data. *Australian Psychologist, 41*(1), 48–54.

Carter, F. A., McIntosh, V. V. W., Joyce, P. R., Sullivan, P. F., & Bulik, C. M. (2003). Role of exposure with response prevention in cognitive-behavioral therapy for bulimia nervosa: Three year follow-up results. *International Journal of Eating Disorders, 33*, 127–135.

Cartwright, R. D. (1996). Dreams and adaptation to divorce. In D. Barrett (Ed.), *Trauma and dreams* (pp. 179–185). Cambridge, MA: Harvard University Press.

Carver, C. S. (1998). Resilience and thriving: Issues, models, and linkages. *Journal of Social Issues, 54*, 245–266.

Carver, C. S., & Scheier, M. F. (1992). *Perspectives on personality* (2nd ed.). Boston: Allyn & Bacon.

Carver, C. S., & Scheier, M. F. (2000). *Perspectives on personality* (4th ed.). Boston: Allyn & Bacon.

Carver, C. S., Scheier, M. F., & Weintraub, J. K. (1989). Assessing coping strategies: A theoretically based approach. *Journal of Personality and Social Psychology, 56*, 267–283.

Carver, C. S., Smith, R. G., Antoni, M. H., Petronis, V. M., Weiss, S., & Derhagopian, R. P. (2005). Optimistic personality and psychosocial well-being during treatment predict psychosocial well-being among long-term survivors of breast cancer. *Health Psychology, 24*(5), 508–516.

Carver, L. J., Dawson, G., Panagiotides, H., Meltzoff, A. N., McPartland, J., Gray, J., et al. (2003). Age-related differences in neural correlates of face recognition during the toddler and preschool years. *Developmental Psychobiology, 42*, 148–159.

Case, K. A. (2007). Raising white privilege awareness and reducing racial prejudice: Assessing diversity course effectiveness. *Teaching of Psychology, 34*(4), 231–235.

Case, R. (1984). The process of stage transitions: A neo-Piagetian view. In R. J. Sternberg (Ed.), *Mechanisms of cognitive development*. New York: Freeman.

Case, R. (1992). Neo-Piagetian theories of child development. In R. J. Sternberg & C. A. Berg (Eds.), *Intellectual development* (pp. 161–196). New York: Cambridge University Press.

Case, R. (1998). The development of conceptual structures. In W. Damon (Ed. in Chief) & N. Eisenberg (Vol. Ed.), *Handbook of child psychology: Vol. 2* (pp. 745–800). New York: John Wiley.

Casey, L. M., Newcombe, P. A., & Oei, T. P. S. (2005). Cognitive mediation of panic severity: The role of catastrophic misinterpretation of bodily sensations and panic self-efficacy. *Cognitive Therapy and Research, 29*(2), 187–200.

Casey, M. B., Nuttall, R. L., & Pezaris, E. (1997). Mediators of gender differences in mathematics college entrance test scores: A comparison of spatial skills with internalized beliefs and anxieties. *Development Psychology, 33*, 669–680.

Cash, T. F., Gillen, B., & Burns, D. S. (1977). Sexism and 'beautyism' in personnel consultant decision making. *Journal of Applied Psychology, 62*, 301–310.

Cashdan, E. (2001). Ethnocentrism and xenophobia: A cross-cultural study. *Current Anthropology, 42*(5), 760–765.

Cashmore, J. A., & Goodnow, J. J. (1986). Influences on Australian parents' values: Ethnicity versus socioeconomic status. *Journal of Cross-Cultural Psychology, 17*, 441–454.

Casper, R. C., Hedeker, D., & McClough, J. F. (1992). Personality dimensions in eating disorders and their relevance for subtyping. *Journal of the American Academy of Child and Adolescent Psychiatry, 31*, 830–840.

Caspi, A. (1998). Personality development across the lifespan. In W. Damon (Ed.) & N. Eisenberg (Vol. Ed.), *Handbook of child psychology: Vol. 3. Social, emotional, and personality development* (pp. 311–388). New York: John Wiley & Sons.

Caspi, A. (2000). The child is father of the man: Personality continuities from childhood to adulthood. *Journal of Personality and Social Psychology, 78*, 158–172.

Caspi, A., Lynam, D., Moffitt, T., & Silva, P. (1993). Unraveling girls' delinquency: Biological, dispositional, and contextual contributions to adolescent misbehavior. *Developmental Psychology, 29,* 19–30.

Caspi, A., & Silva, P. (1995). Temperamental qualities at age three predict personality traits in young adulthood: Longitudinal evidence from a birth cohort. *Child Development, 66,* 486–498.

Cassady, J. C. (2004). The impact of cognitive test anxiety on test comprehension and recall in the absence of external evaluative pressure. *Applied Cognitive Psychology, 18,* 311–325.

Cassidy, J. (2001). Truth, lies, and intimacy: An attachment perspective. *Attachment and Human Development, 3*(2), 121–155.

Cassidy, J., Kirsh, S. J., Scolton, K., & Parke, R. D. (1996). Attachment and representations of peer relationships. *Developmental Psychology, 32,* 892–904.

Cassidy, J., & Shaver, P. R. (Eds.). (1999). *Handbook of attachment: Theory, research, and clinical applications.* New York: Guilford Press.

Castle, D. J., & Ames, F. R. (1996). Cannabis and the brain. *Australian and New Zealand Journal of Psychiatry, 30,* 179–183.

Castles, A., & Coltheart, M. (2004). Is there a causal link from phonological awareness to success in learning to read? *Cognition, 91,* 77–111.

Castles, S. (1993). The 'new' migration and Australian immigration policy in Asians in Australia. In I. Inglis, S. Gunasekaran, G. Sullivan, & C. Wu (Eds.), *Institute of Southeast Asian Studies.* Sydney, Australia: Allen & Unwin.

Caterson, I. D. (1999). Obesity and its management. *Australian Prescriber, 22,* 12–16.

Cattell, R. B. (1957). *Personality and motivation: Structure and measurement.* New York: World Book.

Cattell, R. B. (1983). *Structured personality-learning theory: A wholistic multivariate research approach.* New York: Praeger.

Cattell, R. B. (1990). Advances in Cattellian personality theory. In L. Pervin (Ed.), *Handbook of personality: Theory and research* (pp. 101–110). New York: Guilford Press.

Cattell, R. B., Boyle, G. J., & Chant, D. (2002). The enriched behavioral prediction equation and its impact on structured learning and the dynamic calculus. *Psychological Review, 109,* 202–205.

Caughy, M., O'Campo, P. J., Nettles, S. M., & Lohrfink, K. F. (2006). Neighborhood matters: Racial socialization of African-American children. *Child Development, 77,* 1220–1236.

Cave, C. B. (1997). Long-lasting priming in picture naming. *Psychological Science, 8,* 322–325.

Ceci, S. J. (1990). Framing intellectual assessment in terms of a person-process-context model. *Educational Psychologist, 25,* 269–291.

Ceci, S. J., & Bronfenbrenner, U. (1991). On the demise of everyday memory: 'The rumors of my death are much exaggerated' (Mark Twain). *American Psychologist, 46,* 27–31.

Centers for Disease Control. (1980). *Ten leading causes of death in the United States 1977.* Washington, DC: U.S. Government Printing Office.

Central Intelligence Agency. (2007, December). *The world factbook.* Retrieved December 14, 2007, from https://www.cia.gov/library/publications/the-world-factbook/geos/id.html

Central Region Eating Disorder Services. (2007). *Common questions.* Retrieved from http://www.eatingdisorders.org.nz/index.php?id=782

Cervantes, C. A., & Callahan, M. (1998). Labels and explanations in mother-child emotion talk: Age and gender differentiation. *Developmental Psychology, 34,* 88–98.

Chaiken, M. L., Gentner, T. Q., & Hulse, S. H. (1997). Effects of social interaction on the development of startling song and the perception of these effects by conspecifics. *Journal of Comparative Psychology, 111,* 379–392.

Chaiken, S. (1980). Heuristic versus systematic information processing and the use of source versus message cues in persuasion. *Journal of Personality and Social Psychology, 39,* 752–766.

Chaiken, S. R., Kyllonen, P. C., & Tirre, W. C. (2000). Organization and components of psychomotor ability. *Cognitive Psychology, 40,* 198–226.

Chambless, D. C., & Gillis, M. M. (1993). Cognitive therapy of anxiety disorders. *Journal of Consulting and Clinical Psychology, 61,* 248–260.

Chambless, D. L., & Steketee, G. (1999). Expressed emotion and behavior therapy outcome: A prospective study with obsessive–compulsive and agoraphobic outpatients. *Journal of Consulting and Clinical Psychology, 67,* 658–665.

Chamove, A. S. (1978). Therapy of isolate rhesus: Different partners and social behavior. *Child Development, 49,* 43–50

Champion, V. L. (1990). Breast self-examination in women 35 and older: A prospective study. *Journal of Behavioral Medicine, 13,* 523–538.

Champion, V. L. (1994). Strategies to increase mammography utilization. *Medical Care, 32,* 118–129.

Champoux, M., & Suomi, S. J. (1994). Behavioral and adrenocortical responses of rhesus macaque mothers to infant separation in an unfamiliar environment. *Primates, 35,* 191–202.

Chan, R. (2006). Hypnosis and phantom limb pain. *Australian Journal of Clinical and Experimental Hypnosis, 34*(1), 55–64.

Chance, P. (1988). *Learning and behavior* (2nd ed.). Belmont, CA: Wadsworth.

Chandler, L. S., Richardson, G. A., Gallagher, J. D., & Day, N. L. (1996). Prenatal exposure to alcohol and marijuana: Effects on motor development of preschool children. *Alcoholism: Clinical and Experimental Research, 20,* 455–461.

Chaplin, T. M., Cole, P. M., & Zahn-Waxler, C. (2005). Parental socialization of emotion expression: Gender differences and relations to child adjustment. *Emotion, 5,* 80–88.

Chapman, J. W. (1984). The self concept of Maori school pupils revisited: A critique of Ranby's study and some new data. *New Zealand Journal of Educational Studies, 19,* 45–54.

Chapman, S., McLeod, K., Wakefield, M., & Holding, S. (2005). Impact of news of celebrity illness on breast cancer screening: Kylie Minogue's breast cancer diagnosis. *The Medical Journal of Australia, 183*(5), 247–250. Retrieved from http://www.mja.com.au/public/issues/183_05_050905/cha10589_fm.html

Chapple, S. (2000). *Maori socio-economic disparity.* Paper for the Ministry of Social Policy. Retrieved October 26, 2004, from http://www.act.org.nz/content/20887/maorisocioeconomicdisparity.pdf

Chen, J., & Gardner, H. (1997). Alternative assessment from a multiple intelligences theoretical perspective. In D. P. Flanagen, J. L. Genshaft, & P. L. Harrison (Eds.), *Contemporary intellectual assessment: Theories, tests, and issues* (pp. 105–121). New York: Guilford Press.

Chen, S., & Chaiken, S. (1999). The heuristic-systematic model in its broader context. In S. Chaiken & Y. Trope (Eds.), *Dual-process theories in social psychology* (pp. 73–96). New York: Guilford Press.

Chenoweth, P. J., & Sanderson, M. W. (2005). *Beef practice: Cow-calf production medicine.* Ames, IA: Blackwell Publishing.

Cherry, E. C. (1953). Some experiments on the recognition of speech, with one and with two ears. *Journal of the Acoustical Society of America, 25,* 975–979.

Chess, S., & Thomas, A. (1986). *Temperament in clinical practice.* New York: Guilford Press.

Chess, S., & Thomas, A. (1987). *Origins and evolution of behavior disorders: From infancy to early adult life.* Cambridge, MA: Harvard University Press.

Cheyette, S. R., & Cummings, J. L. (1995). Encephalitis lethargica: Lessons for contemporary neuropsychiatry. *Journal of Neuropsychiatry & Clinical Neurosciences, 7,* 125–134.

Chi, M. T. H. (1978). Knowledge structures and memory development. In R. Siegler (Ed.), *Children's thinking: What deficits?* Hillsdale, NJ: Lawrence Erlbaum.

Chi, M. T. H., Glaser, R., & Rees, E. (1982). Expertise in problem solving. In R. J. Sternberg (Ed.), *Advances in the psychology of human intelligence: Vol. 1* (pp. 7–76). Hillsdale, NJ: Lawrence Erlbaum.

Chick, K. A., Heilman-Houser, R. A., & Hunter, M. W. (2002). The impact of child care on gender role development and gender stereotypes. *Early Childhood Education Journal, 29,* 149–154.

Chikritzhs, T., Pascal, R., Gray, D., Stearne, A., Saggers, S., & Jones, P. (2007). *Trends in alcohol-attributable deaths among Indigenous Australians, 1995–2004* (National Alcohol Indicators Bulletin No. 11). Perth, Australia: National Drug Research Institute.

Chilcott, T. (2009, April 4). Cyber bullies warning. *The Courier Mail,* p. 30.

Children's Health Development Foundation. (2004). *Virtually healthy.* Retrieved August 28, 2004, from http://www.chdf.org.au/icms_wrapper?page=653&issurvey=&rand=0.06453862949614003

Childs, G., & McKay, M. (2001). Boys starting school disadvantaged: Implications from teachers' ratings of behaviour and achievement in the first two years. *British Journal of Educational Psychology, 71,* 303–314.

Chiles, J. A., Lambert, M. J., & Hatch, A. L. (1999). The impact of psychological interventions on medical cost offset: A meta-analytic review. *Clinical Psychology: Science and Practice, 6*(2), 214–220.

Chiropractors' Association of Australia. (2009). *Fact sheet.* Retrieved October 3, 2009, from http://www.chiropractors.asn.au/AM/Template.cfm?Section=Sleep&Template=/CM/ContentDisplay.cfm&ContentID=1867

Choi, I., Dalal, R., Kim, P., & Park, H. (2003). Culture and judgment of causal relevance. *Journal of Personality and Social Psychology, 84,* 46–59.

Choi, I., Nisbett, R. E., & Norenzayan, A. (1999). Causal attribution across cultures: Variation and universality. *Psychological Bulletin, 125,* 47–63.

Chomsky, N. (1957). *Syntactic structures.* The Hague, The Netherlands: Mouton.

Chomsky, N. (1959). Review of Skinner's verbal behavior. *Language, 35,* 26–58.

Chomsky, N. (1965). *Aspects of the theory of syntax.* Oxford: MIT Press.

Chomsky, N. (1980a). The new organology. *Behavioral and Brain Sciences, 3,* 42–61.

Chomsky, N. (1980b). *Rules and representations.* Oxford: Blackwell.

Chomsky, N. (1986). *Knowledge of language: Its nature, origins, and use.* New York: Praeger.

Christ, O., Ullrich, J., & Wagner, U. (2008, June). *The joint effects of positive and negative contact on attitudes and attitude strength.* Paper presented at the General Meeting of the European Association of Experimental Social Psychology, Opatija, Croatia.

Christenfeld, N. (1997). Memory for pain and the delayed effects of distraction. *Health Psychology, 16,* 327–330.

Christensen, A., Atkins, D. C., Yi, J., Baucom, D. H., & George, W. H. (2006). Couple and individual adjustment for 2 years following a randomized clinical trial comparing traditional versus integrative behavioural couple therapy. *Journal of Consulting and Clinical Psychology, 74,* 1180–1191.

Christensen, H., Leach, L. S., & MacKinnon, A. (2010). Cognition in pregnancy and motherhood: Prospective cohort study. *The British Journal of Psychiatry, 196,* 126–132.

Christianson, S. A. (1992). Emotional stress and eyewitness memory: A critical review. *Psychological Bulletin, 112*(2), 284–309.

Chrobak, J. J., & Buzsaki, G. (1994). Selective activation of deep layer (V–VI) retrohippocampal cortical neurons during hippocampal sharp waves in the behaving rat. *Journal of Neuroscience, 14,* 1660–1670.

Chung, K. K. K., Martinez, M., & Herbert, J. (2000). c-Fos expression, behavioural, endocrine and autonomic responses to acute social stress in male rats after chronic restraint: Modulation by serotonin. *Neuroscience, 95,* 453–463.

Church, A. T. (2000). Culture and personality: Toward an integrated cultural trait psychology. *Journal of Personality, 68,* 651–703.

Church, A. T. (2001a). Personality measurement in cross-cultural perspective. *Journal of Personality, 69*, 955–978.

Church, A. T. (2001b). Culture and personality: Introduction. *Journal of Personality, 69*(6), 787–801.

Church, A. T., & Lonner, W. J. (1998). The crosscultural perspective in the study of personality: Rationale and current research. *Journal of Cross-Cultural Psychology, 29*, 32–62.

Cialdini, R. B., Borden, R. J., Thorne, A., Walker, M. R., Freeman, S., & Sloan, L. R. (1976). Basking in reflected glory: Three (football) field studies. *Journal of Personality and Social Psychology, 34*, 366–375.

Cialdini, R. B., & Goldstein, N. J. (2004). Social influence: Compliance and conformity. *Annual Review of Psychology, 55*, 591–621.

Cialdini, R. B., & Trost, M. R. (1998). Social influence: Social norms, conformity, and compliance. In D. T. Gilbert & S. T. Fiske (Eds.), *The handbook of social psychology: Vol. 2* (pp. 151–192). New York: McGraw-Hill.

Ciampolini, M., & Bianchi, R. (2006). Training to estimate blood glucose and to form associations with initial hunger. *Nutrition and Metabolism, 3*, 42. Retrieved April 4, 2007, from http://www.pubmedcentral.nih.gov/articlerender.fcgi?artid=1702540

Ciraulo, D. A., & Renner, J. A. (1991). Alcoholism. In D. A. Ciraulo & R. I. Shader (Eds.), *Clinical manual of chemical dependence*. Washington, DC: American Psychiatric Press.

Cisek, S. (2006). Feedback does matter: Perceived effectiveness of self-presentation and the degree of changes in the self-concept. *Polish Psychological Bulletin, 37*(3), 145–153.

Clader, R. (2002). *The humoral theory: How the world was fooled*. Retrieved from http://www.cranfordschools.org/chs/scholars/2002/17c/clader.html

Clancy, S. A., Schacter, D. L., McNally, R. J., & Pitman, R. K. (2000). False recognition in women reporting recovered memories of sexual abuse. *Psychological Science, 11*, 26–31.

Clark, A. S., & Goldman-Rakic, P. (1989). Gonadal hormones influence the emergence of cortical function in nonhuman primates. *Behavioral Neuroscience, 103*, 1287–1295.

Clark, D. A., Beck, A. T., & Alford, B. A. (1999). *Scientific foundations of cognitive theory and therapy of depression*. New York: John Wiley.

Clark, D. M. (1994). Cognitive therapy for panic disorder. In B. E. Wolfe & J. D. Maser (Eds.), *Treatment of panic disorder: A consensus development conference* (pp. 121–132). Washington, DC: American Psychiatric Press.

Clark, J. K., Wegener, D. T., & Fabrigar, L. R. (2008). Attitudinal ambivalence and message-based persuasion: Motivated processing of proattitudinal information and avoidance of counterattitudinal information. *Personality and Social Psychology Review, 34*(4), 565–577.

Clark, K. E., & Ladd, G. W. (2000). Connectedness and autonomy support in parent-child relationships: Links to children's socioemotional orientation and peer relationships. *Developmental Psychology, 36*, 485–498.

Clark, M. S., & Pataki, S. (1995). Interpersonal processes influencing attraction and relationships. In A. Tesser (Ed.), *Advanced social psychology*. New York: McGraw-Hill.

Clark, Y. (2000). The construction of Aboriginal identity in people separated from their families community and culture: Pieces of a jigsaw. *Australian Psychologist, 35*(2), 150–157.

Clarke, M. C., Harley, M., & Cannon, M. (2006). The role of obstetric events in schizophrenia. *Schizophrenia Bulletin, 32*(1), 3–8.

Clarke, S. R. (2005). Home advantage in the Australian football league. *Journal of Sports Sciences, 23*(4), 375–385.

Claustrat, B., Brun, J., David, M., Sassolas, G., & Chazot, G. (1992). Melatonin and jet lag: Confirmatory result using a simplified protocol. *Biological Psychiatry, 32*, 705–711.

Clayton, S. (1991). Gender differences in psychosocial determinants of adolescent smoking. *Journal of School Health, 61*, 15–120.

Clayton, S., & Myers, G. (2009). *Conservation psychology: Understanding and promoting human care for nature*. Oxford, UK: Wiley-Blackwell.

Cleare, A., & Bond, A. (1997). Does central oserotonergic function correlate inversely with aggression? A study using d-fenfluramine in healthy subjects. *Psychiatry Research, 69*, 89–95.

Cleghorn, J. M., Peterfy, G., Pinter, E. J., & Pattee, C. J. (1970). Verbal anxiety and the beta adrenergic receptors: A facilitating mechanism? *Journal of Nervous and Mental Disease, 151*, 266–272.

Clifford, M. M., & Walster, E. (1973). The effect of physical attractiveness on teacher expectations. *Sociological Education, 46*, 248–258.

Clinchy, B. M., & Norem, J. K. (Eds.). (1998). *The gender and psychology reader*. New York: New York University Press.

Cloninger, C. R. (1998). The genetics and psychobiology of the seven factor model of personality. In K. R. Silk (Ed.), *Biology of personality disorders. Review of psychiatry series* (pp. 63–92). Washington, DC: American Psychiatric Association.

Cloninger, C. R., Bohman, M., & Sigvardsson, S. (1981). Inheritance of alcohol abuse. *Archives of General Psychiatry, 38*, 861–868.

COAG Reform Council. (2010a). *Indigenous reform*. Retrieved from http://www.coagreformcouncil.gov.au/agenda/indigenous.cfm

COAG Reform Council. (2010b). *National indigenous reform agreement: Baseline performance report for 2008–09* (Report to the Council of Australian Governments, April 30, 2010). Retrieved from http://www.coagreformcouncil.gov.au/reports/docs/indigenous_reform_agreement_report_2008-09_exec_summary.pdf

Cobb, S. (1976). Social support as a moderator of life stress. *Psychosomatic Medicine, 38*, 300–314.

Cody, H., & Kamphaus, R. W. (1999). Down syndrome. In S. Goldstein & C. R. Reynolds (Eds.), *Handbook of neurodevelopmental and genetic disorders in children* (pp. 385–405). New York: Guilford Press.

Coghlan, B., Burnet Institute, & Austin Research Institute. (2009). *HIV in the pacific: 1984–2007*. Melbourne, Australia: Burnet Institute.

Cohen, D. (1983). *Piaget: Critique and reassessment*. New York: St. Martin's Press.

Cohen, D., Nisbett, R. E., Bowdle, B. F., & Schwarz, N. (1996). Insult, aggression, and the southern culture of honor: An 'experimental ethnography'. *Journal of Personality & Social Psychology, 70*, 945–960.

Cohen, D., & Strayer, J. (1996). Empathy in conduct-disordered and comparison youth. *Developmental Psychology, 32*, 988–998.

Cohen, J. D., & Schooler, J. W. (1997). *Scientific approaches to consciousness*. Mahwah, NJ: Lawrence Erlbaum.

Cohen, L. B., Diehl, R. L., Oakes, L. M., & Loehlin, J. L. (1992). Infant perception of /aba/ versus /apa/: Building a quantitative model of infant categorical discrimination. *Developmental Psychology, 28*, 261–272.

Cohen, S., & Herbert, T. B. (1996). Health psychology: Psychological factors and physical disease from the perspective of human psychoneuroimmunology. *Annual Review of Psychology, 47*, 113–142.

Cohen, S., Tyrrell, D. A. J., & Smith, A. P. (1991). Psychological stress and susceptibility to the common cold. *New England Journal of Medicine, 325*, 606–612.

Cohen, S., & Williamson, G. M. (1991). Stress and infectious disease in humans. *Psychological Bulletin, 109*, 5–24.

Cohen, S., & Wills, T. A. (1985). Stress, social support, and the buffering hypothesis. *Psychological Bulletin, 98*, 310–357.

Colby, A., & Kohlberg, L. (1984). Invariant squence and internal consistency in moral judgment stages. In W. M. Kurtines & J. L. Gewirtz (Eds.), *Morality, moral behavior and moral development*. New York: John Wiley.

Cole, D. A., Martin, J. M., Peeke, L. A., Seroczynski, A. D., & Fier, J. (1999). Children's over- and underestimation of academic competence: A longitudinal study of gender differences, depression, and anxiety. *Child Development, 70*, 459–473.

Cole, D. A., Maxwell, S. E., Martin, J. M., Peeke, L. M., Seroczynski, A. D., Tram, J. M., et al. (2001). The development of multiple domains of child and adolescent self-concept: A cohort sequential longitudinal design. *Child Development, 72*, 1723–1746.

Cole, M. (1975). An ethnographic psychology of cognition. In R. Brislin, S. Boschner, & W. J. Lonner (Eds.), *Cross-cultural perspectives on learning*. New York: Sage Publications.

Cole, M. (1996). *Cultural psychology: A once and future discipline*. Cambridge, MA: Bellknap Press.

Cole, M. (1997). Cultural mechanisms of cognitive development. In E. Amsel & K. A. Renninger (Eds.), *Change and development: Issues of theory, method, and application. The Jean Piaget symposium series* (pp. 245–263). Mahwah, NJ: Lawrence Erlbaum Associates.

Cole, M., Gay, J., Glick, J. A., & Sharp, D. W. (1971). *The cultural context of learning and thinking*. New York: Basic Books.

Cole, P. M., Zahn-Waxler, C., Fox, N. A., & Usher, B. A. (1996). Individual differences in emotion regulation and behavior problems in preschool children. *Journal of Abnormal Psychology, 105*, 518–529.

Coleman, M. J., Levy, D. L., Lenzenweger, M. F., & Holzman, P. S. (1996). Thought disorder, perceptual aberrations, and schizotypy. *Journal of Abnormal Psychology, 105*, 469–473.

Coleman, R., Piek, J. P., & Livesey, D. J. (2001). A longitudinal study of motor ability and kinaesthetic acuity in young children at risk of developmental coordination disorder. *Human Movement Science, 20*, 95–110.

Collett, M., Harland, T., & Collett, T. S. (2002). The use of landmarks and panoramic context in the performance of local vectors by navigating honeybees. *The Journal of Experimental Biology, 205*(6), 807–814.

Collett, T. S., & Baron, J. (1994). Biological compasses and the coordinate frame of landmark memories in honeybees. *Nature, 368*, 137–140.

Colley, A., Ball, J., Kirby, N., Harvey, R., & Vingelen, I. (2002). Gender-linked differences in everyday memory performance: Effort makes the difference. *Sex Roles, 47*, 577–582.

Collier, G., Johnson, D. F., & Berman, J. (1998). Patch choice as a function of procurement cost and encounter rate. *Journal of the Experimental Analysis of Behavior, 69*, 5–16.

Collier, P. J., & Morgan, D. L. (2008). Is that paper really due today? Differences in first generation and traditional college students' understandings of faculty expectations. *Higher Education, 55*, 425–446.

Collings, S., & King, M. (1994). Ten-year followup of 50 patients with bulimia nervosa. *British Journal of Psychiatry, 164*, 80–87.

Collins, A., & Loftus, E. F. (1975). A spreading-activation theory of semantic processing. *Psychological Review, 82*, 407–428.

Collins, A. M., & Quillian, M. R. (1969). Retrieval time from semantic memory. *Journal of Verbal Learning and Verbal Behavior, 8*, 240–247.

Collins, C. J., Hanges, P. J., & Locke, E. A. (2004). The relationship of achievement motivation to entrepreneurial behavior: A meta-analysis. *Human Performance, 17*(1), 95–117.

Collins, R. L., Lapp, W. M., Emmons, K. M., & Isaac, L. M. (1990). Endorsement and strength of alcohol expectancies. *Journal of Studies on Alcohol, 51*, 336–342.

Collins, T., & Lapsley, H. (2008). *The cost of tobacco, alcohol and illicit drug abuse to Australian Society in 2004–2005. Summary version* (National Drug Strategy Monograph Series No. 66). Canberra, Australia: Commonwealth Department of Health & Ageing.

Collins, W. A., & Gunnar, M. R. (1990). Social and personality development. *Annual Review of Psychology, 41,* 387–416.

Collins, W. A., Maccoby, E. E., Steinberg, L., Hetherington, E. M., & Bornstein, M. H. (2000). Contemporary research on parenting: The case for nature and nurture. *American Psychologist, 55,* 218–232.

Cologer-Clifford, A., Simon, N., & Jubilan, B. (1992). Genotype, uterine position, and testosterone sensitivity in older female mice. *Physiology and Behavior, 51,* 1047–1050.

Colvin, C. R. (1993). Judgable people: Personality, behavior, and competing explanations. *Journal of Personality and Social Psychology, 64,* 861–873.

Colvin, C. R., Block, J., & Funder, D. C. (1995). Overly positive self-evaluations and personality: Negative implications for mental health. *Journal of Personality and Social Psychology, 68,* 1152–1162.

Comaroff, J. (1980). Healing and the cultural order: The case of the Barolong boo Ratshidi of Southern Africa. *American Ethnologist, 7,* 637–657.

Commonwealth of Australia. (1998). *As a matter of fact: Answering the myths and misconceptions about Indigenous Australians.* Canberra, Australia: Office of Public Affairs, ATSIC.

Commonwealth of Australia. (1999). *A new agenda for multicultural Australia.* Canberra, Australia: Department of Immigration and Multicultural Affairs.

Commonwealth of Australia. (2006). *National alcohol strategy, 2006–2009. Towards safer drinking cultures.* Canberra, Australia: Commonwealth of Australia.

Compas, B., Hinden, B. R., & Gerhardt, C. (1995). Adolescent development: Pathways and processes of risk and resilience. *Annual Review of Psychology, 46,* 265–293.

Conger, R., Conger, K., Elder, G., Lorenz, F., Simons, R., & Whitbeck, L. (1993). Family economic stress and adjustment of early adolescent girls. *Developmental Psychology, 29,* 206–219.

Conklin, H. M., Curtis, C. E., Katsanis, J., & Iacono, W. G. (2000). Verbal working memory impairment in schizophrenia patients and their first-degree relatives: Evidence from the Digit Span Task. *American Journal of Psychiatry, 157,* 275–277.

Conradi, H. J., de Jonge, P., & Ormel, J. (2008). Prediction of the three-year course of recurrent depression in primary care patients: Different risk factors for different outcomes. *Journal of Affective Disorders, 105,* 267–271.

Consedine, N. S., Strongman, K. T., & Magai, C. (2003). Emotions and behaviour: Data from a cross-cultural recognition study. *Cognition and Emotion, 17*(6), 881–902.

Conway, A. R., Jarrold, C., Kane, M. J., Miyake, A., & Towse, J. N. (Eds.). (2007). *Variation in working memory.* New York: Oxford University Press.

Conway, L. G., Schaller, M., Tweed, R. G., & Hallett, D. (2001). The complexity of thinking across cultures: Interactions between culture and situational context. *Social Cognition, 19,* 228–250.

Conway, M. A. (1995). *Flashbulb memories.* Hillsdale, NJ: Lawrence Erlbaum Associates.

Cooley, C. H. (1902). *Human nature and the social order.* New York: Scribners.

Coombs, C., & Lehner, P. E. (1984). Conjoint design and analysis of the bilinear model: An application to judgments of risk. *Journal of Mathematical Psychology, 28,* 1–42.

Cooper, J., & Fazio, R. H. (1984). A new look at dissonance theory. *Advances in Experimental Social Psychology, 17,* 229–266.

Cooper, L. A. (1976). Demonstration of a mental analog of an external rotation. *Perception and Psychophysics, 19,* 296–302.

Cooper, L. A., & Shepard, R. N. (1973). Chronometric studies of the rotation of mental images. In W. G. Chase (Ed.), *Visual information processing.* New York: Academic Press.

Coopersmith, S. (1967). *The antecedents of self-esteem.* San Francisco: Freeman.

Coricelli, G., Critchley, H. D., Joffily, M., O'Doherty, J. P. O., Sirigu, A., & Dolan, R. J. (2005). Regret and its avoidance: A neuroimaging study of choice behavior. *Nature Neuroscience, 8*(9), 1255–1262.

Cork, R. C. (1996). Implicit memory during anesthesia. In S. R. Hameroff, A. W. Kaszniak, & A. C. Scott (Eds.), *Toward a science of consciousness: The first Tucson discussions and debates. Complex adaptive systems* (pp. 295–302). Cambridge, MA: MIT Press.

Cornblatt, B. A., & Kelip, J. G. (1994). Impaired attention, genetics, and the pathophysiology of schizophrenia. *Schizophrenia Bulletin, 20,* 31–46.

Corr, P. J., Pickering, A. D., & Gray, J. A. (1995). Personality and reinforcement in associative and instrumental learning. *Personality and Individual Differences, 19,* 47–71.

Corsica, J. A., & Perri, M. G. (2003). Obesity. In A. M. Nezu, C. M. Nezu, & P. A. Geller (Eds.), *Handbook of psychology: Health psychology: Vol. 9* (pp. 121–146). Hoboken, NJ: John Wiley & Sons.

Cosmides, L. (1989). The logic of social exchange: Has natural selection shaped how humans reason? Studies with the Wason selection task. *Cognition, 31,* 187–276.

Cosmides, L., & Tooby, J. (1995). From evolution to adaptations to behavior: Toward an integrated evolutionary psychology. In R. Wong (Ed.), *Biological perspectives on motivated activities* (pp. 11–74). Norwood: Ablex Publishing.

Cosmides, L., & Tooby, J. (1999). Toward an evolutionary taxonomy of treatable conditions. *Journal of Abnormal Psychology, 108,* 453–464.

Costa, P. T., Jr., Herbst, J. H., McCrae, R. R., & Siegler, I. C. (2000). Personality at midlife: Stability, intrinsic maturation, and response to life events. *Assessment, 7*(4), 365–378.

Costa, P. T., Jr., & McCrae, R. R. (1988). Personality in adulthood: A six-year longitudinal study of self-reports and spouse ratings on the NEO Personality Inventory. *Journal of Personality and Social Psychology, 54,* 853–863.

Costa, P. T., Jr., & McCrae, R. R. (1990). Personality: Another 'hidden factor' in stress research. *Psychological Inquiry, 1,* 22–24.

Costa, P. T., Jr., & McCrae, R. R. (1992). Four ways five factors are basic. *Personality and Individual Differences, 13,* 653–665.

Costa, P. T., Jr., & McCrae, R. R. (1994). "Set like plaster"? Evidence for the stability of adult personality. In T. Heatherton & J. Weinberger (Eds.), *Can personality change?* (pp. 21–40). Washington, DC: American Psychological Association.

Costa, P. T., Jr., & McCrae, R. R. (1995). Domains and facets: Hierarchical personality assessment using the revised NEO Personality Inventory. *Journal of Personality Assessment, 64,* 21–50.

Costa, P. T., Jr., & McCrae, R. R. (1997). Stability and change in personality assessment: The revised NEO Personality Inventory in the year 2000. *Journal of Personality Assessment, 68,* 86–94.

Costigan, L., & Neuenfeldt, K. (2002). Torres Strait Islander music and dance in informal and formal educational contexts in Australia. *Research Studies in Music Education, 19,* 46–55.

Coull, J. T., & Sahakian, B. J. (2000). Psychopharmacology of memory. In G. E. Berrios & J. R. Hodges (Eds.), *Memory disorders in psychiatric practice* (pp. 75–98). New York: Cambridge University Press.

Council of Australian Governments. (2009). *National indigenous reform agreement (closing the gap).* Retrieved from http://www.coag.gov.au/intergov_agreements/federal_financial_relations/docs/IGA_FFR_ScheduleF_National_Indigenous_Reform_Agreement.pdf

Courtenay, W. H., McCreary, D. R., & Merighi, J. R. (2002). Gender and ethnic differences in health beliefs and behavior. *Journal of Health Psychology, 7,* 219–231.

Courtney, S. M., Petit, L., Ungerleider, L. G., Maisog, J., & Haxby, J. V. (1998). An area specialized for spatial working memory in human frontal cortex. *Science, 279,* 1347–1351.

Courtney, S. M., Ungerleider, L. G., Keil, K., & Haxby, J. V. (1997). Transient and sustained activity in a distributed neural system for human working memory. *Nature, 386,* 608–611.

Cousins, S. (1989). Culture and self-perception in Japan and the United States. *Journal of Personality and Social Psychology, 56,* 124–131.

Cowan, C. P., & Cowan, P. A. (1992). *When partners become parents.* New York: Basic Books.

Cowan, N. (1994). Mechanisms of verbal short-term memory. *Current Directions in Psychological Science, 3,* 185–189.

Cowdry, R. W., & Gardner, D. L. (1988). Pharmacotherapy of borderline personality disorder: Alprazolam, carbamazepine, trifluoperazine, and tranylcypromine. *Archives of General Psychiatry, 45,* 111–119.

Cowgill, D. O., & Holms, L. D. (1972). *Aging and modernization.* New York: Appleton-Century Crofs.

Cowley, G. (2003, May 5). How progress makes us sick. *Newsweek,* pp. 33–35.

Coyle, J. (1991). Molecular biological and neurobiological contributions to our understanding of Alzheimer's disease. In A. Tasman & S. Goldfinger (Eds.), *American psychiatric press review of psychiatry: Vol. 10* (pp. 515–527). Washington, DC: American Psychiatric Press.

Coyne, J. C., Thompson, R., Klinkman, M. S., & Nease, D. E., Jr. (2002). Emotional disorders in primary care. *Journal of Consulting and Clinical Psychology, 70,* 798–809.

Craeynest, M., Crombez, G., De Houwer, J., Deforche, B., Tanghe, A., & De Bourdeaudhuij, I. (2005). Explicit and implicit attitudes towards food and physical activity in childhood obesity. *Behaviour Research and Therapy, 43,* 1111–1120.

Craig, A. D., Reiman, E. M., Evans, A., & Bushnell, M. C. (1996). Functional imaging of an illusion of pain. *Nature, 384,* 258–260.

Craig, J. C., & Rollman, G. B. (1999). Somesthesis. *Annual Review of Psychology, 50,* 305–331.

Craik, F., & Lockhart, R. (1972). Levels of processing: A framework for memory research. *Journal of Verbal Learning and Verbal Behavior, 11,* 671–684.

Craik, F. I. M., Govoni, R., Naveh-Benjamin, M., & Anderson, N. D. (1996). The effects of divided attention on encoding and retrieval processes in human memory. *Journal of Experimental Psychology: General, 125,* 159–180.

Craik, F. I. M., & Salthouse, T. A. (2000). *The handbook of aging and cognition* (2nd ed.). Mahwah, NJ: Lawrence Erlbaum.

Crair, M. C., Gillespie, D. C., & Stryker, M. P. (1998). The role of visual experience in the development of columns in cat visual cortex. *Science, 279,* 566–570.

Cramer, P. (1996). *Storytelling, narrative, and the Thematic Apperception Test.* New York: Guilford Press.

Cramer, P. (2002). Defense mechanisms, behavior and affect in young adulthood. *Journal of Personality, 70*(1), 103–125.

Cramer, P. (2006). *Protecting the self: Defense mechanisms in action.* New York: Guilford Press.

Cramer, P. (2007). Longitudinal study of defense mechanisms: Late childhood to late adolescence. *Journal of Personality, 75*(1), 1–23.

Crandall, C. (1994). Prejudice against fat people: Ideology and self-interest. *Journal of Personality and Social Psychology, 66,* 882–894.

Crandall, C. S. (1995). Do parents discriminate against their heavyweight daughters? *Personality and Social Psychology Bulletin, 21,* 724–735.

Crano, W. D., & Prislin, R. (2006). Attitudes and persuasion. *Annual Review of Psychology, 57*, 345–374.

Crape, B. L., Latkin, C. A., Laris, A. S., & Knowlton, A. R. (2002). The effects of sponsorship in 12-step treatment of injection drug users. *Drug and Alcohol Dependence, 65*, 291–301.

Craw, P. J., Leland, L. S., Jr., Bussell, M. G., Munday, S. J., & Walsh, K. (2006). The mural as graffiti deterrence. *Environment and Behavior, 38*, 422–434.

Crews, F. C. (1998). *Unauthorized Freud: Doubters confront a legend*. New York: Viking Penguin.

Crick, F., & Koch, C. (1998). Consciousness and neuroscience. *Cerebral Cortex, 8*, 97–107.

Crick, F., & Mitchison, G. (1983). The function of dream sleep. *Nature, 304*, 111–114.

Crick, N. R., & Dodge, K. A. (1994). A review and reformulation of social information-processing mechanisms in children's social adjustment. *Psychological Bulletin, 115*, 74–101.

Critchley, H., Daly, E., Phillips, M., Brammer, M., Bullmore, E., Williams, S., et al., (2000). Explicit and implicit neural mechanisms for processing of social information from facial expressions: A functional magnetic resonance imaging study. *Human Brain Mapping, 9*, 93–105.

Crits-Christoph, P. (1992). The efficacy of brief dynamic psychotherapy: A meta-analysis. *American Journal of Psychiatry, 149*, 151–158.

Cronbach, L. J. (1957). The two disciplines of scientific psychology. *American Psychologist, 12*, 671–684.

Crook, T. H., Youngjohn, J., Larrabee, G., & Salama, M. (1992). Aging and everyday memory. *Neuropsychology, 6*, 123–136.

Crossman, E. R. (1959). A theory of the acquisition of speed-skill. *Ergonomics, 2*, 153–166.

Crow, T. J. (1980). Molecular pathology of schizophrenia: More than one disease process? *British Medical Journal, 280*, 66–68.

Crowder, R. (1993). Systems and principles in memory theory: Another critique of pure memory. In A. F. Collins, S. Gathercole, M. A. Conway, & P. E. Morris (Eds.), *Theories of memory* (pp. 139–161). Hillsdale, NJ: Lawrence Erlbaum.

Crowell, J. A., & Feldman, S. S. (1991). Mothers' working models of attachment relationships and mother and child behavior during separation and reunion. *Developmental Psychology, 27*, 597–605.

Crowne, D. P., & Marlowe, D. (1964). *The approval motive: Studies in evaluative dependence*. New York: John Wiley.

Csikszentmihalyi, M., & Larson, R. (1984). *Being adolescent: Conflict and growth in the teenage years*. New York: Basic Books.

Culos-Reed, S. N., Brawley, L. R., Martin, K. A., & Leary, M. R. (2002). Self-presentation concerns and health behaviors among cosmetic surgery patients. *Journal of Applied Social Psychology, 32*, 560–569.

Cummins, R. A., Livesey, P. J., & Evans, J. G. M. (1977). A developmental theory of environmental enrichment. *Science, 197*, 692–694.

Cunningham, M. R., Roberts, A. R., Barbee, A. P., Druen, P. B., & Wu, C. H. (1995). 'Their ideas of beauty are, on the whole, the same as ours': Consistency and variability in the cross-cultural perception of female physical attractiveness. *Journal of Personality and Social Psychology, 68*, 261–279.

Curran, J. P., & Lippold, S. (1975). The effects of physical attraction and attitude similarity on attraction in dating dyads. *Journal of Personality and Social Psychology, 43*, 528–539.

Curtiss, S. (1977). *Genie: A psycholinguistic study of a modern-day wild child*. New York: Academic Press.

Curtiss, S. (1989). The independence and task-specificity of language. In A. Bornstein & J. Bruner (Eds.), *Interaction in human development*. Mahwah, NJ: Lawrence Erlbaum.

Cuthbert, B. N., Lang, P. J., Strauss, C., Drobes, D., Patrick, C. J., & Bradley, M. M. (2003). The psychophysiology of anxiety disorder: Fear memory imagery. *Psychophysiology, 40*, 407–422.

Cyna, A. M., McAuliffe, G. L., & Andrew, M. I. (2004). Hypnosis for pain relief in labour and childbirth: A systematic review [Electronic version]. *British Journal of Anaesthesia, 93*(4), 505–511.

Cytowic, R. E. (2003). *The man who tasted shapes*. Cambridge, MA: MIT Press.

D'Abreu, A. A. (2006). The act of interpretation. *International Journal of Psychoanalysis, 87*, 953–964.

Dahlstrom, W. G. (1993). *The items in the MMPI-2: Alterations in wording, patterns of interrelationships, and changes in endorsements: Supplement to the MMPI-2 manual for administration and scoring*. Minneapolis: University of Minnesota Press.

Daley, S. E., Hammen, C., Burge, D., Davila, J., Paley, B., Lindberg, N., et al. (1999). Depression and axis II symptomatology in an adolescent community sample: Concurrent and longitudinal associations. *Journal of Personality Disorders, 13*, 47–59.

Dalgleish, T., & Bramham, F. (2001). Cognitive perspective. In D. Levinson, J. J. Ponzetti Jr., & P. F. Jorgensen (Eds.), *Encyclopedia of human emotions* (pp. 118–121). New York: Macmillan.

Dalgleish, T., & Power, M. J. (1999). *Handbook of cognition and emotion*. Chichester, England: John Wiley & Sons Ltd.

Dalla Barba, G., & Decaix, C. (2009). 'Do you remember what you did on March 13, 1985?' A case study of confabulatory hypermnesia. *Cortex, 45*, 566–574.

Dalton, K. (1987). Should premenstrual syndrome be a legal defense? In B. E. Ginsburg & B. F. Carter (Eds.), *Premenstrual syndrome: Ethical and legal implications in a biomedical perspective* (pp. 287–300). New York: Plenum Press.

Daly, M., & Wilson, M. (1988). Evolutionary social psychology and family homicide. *Science, 242*, 519–524.

Damasio, A. R. (1994). *Descartes' error: Emotion, reason, and the human brain*. New York: Grosset/Putnam.

D'Amico, E. J., & Fromme, K. (1997). Health risk behaviors of adolescent and young adult siblings. *Health Psychology, 16*, 426–432.

Damon, W. (1977). *The social world of the child*. San Francisco: Jossey-Bass.

Damon, W., & Hart, D. (1988). *Self-understanding in childhood and adolescence*. New York: Cambridge University Press.

D'Andrade, R. G. (1992). Cognitive anthropology. In T. Schwartz, G. M. White, & C. A. Lutz (Eds.), *New directions in psychological anthropology. Publications of the Society for Psychological Anthropology: Vol. 3* (pp. 47–58). Cambridge: Cambridge University Press.

Daneman, M., & Merikle, P. (1996). Working memory and language comprehension: A meta-analysis. *Psychonomic Bulletin and Review, 3*, 422–433.

Daniel, M., Rowley, K. G., McDermott, R., Mylvaganam, A., & O'Dea, K. (1999). Diabetes incidence in an Australian aboriginal population: An 8-year follow-up. *Diabetes Care, 22*, 1993–1998.

Danthiir, V., Pallier, G., Roberts, R. D., & Stankov, L. (2001). What the nose knows: Olfaction within the structure of human cognitive abilities. *Intelligence, 30*, 337–361.

Danthiir, V., Wilhelm, O., Schulze, R., & Roberts, R. D. (2005). Factor structure and validity of paper-and-pencil measures of mental speed: Evidence for a higher-order model? *Intelligence, 33*, 491–514.

Darley, J. M., & Latané, B. (1968). When will people help in a crisis? *Psychology Today, 2*, 54–57, 70–71.

Darley, J. M., & Shultz, T. R. (1990). Moral rules: Their content and acquisition. *Annual Review of Psychology, 41*, 525–556.

Darwin, C. (1859). *The origin of species by means of natural selection, or, the preservation of favoured races in the struggle for life*. London: John Murray.

Darwin, C. (1979). *The expression of the emotions in man and animals*. London: John Murray/Julian Friedmann. (Originally published 1872)

Dasen, P. (1975). Concrete operational development in three cultures. *Journal of Cross-Cultural Psychology, 6*, 156–172.

Dasen, P., & Heron, A. (1981). Cross-cultural tests of Piaget's theory. In H. C. Triandis & A. Heron (Eds.), *Handbook of cross-cultural psychology: Vol. 4. Developmental psychology*. Boston: Allyn & Bacon.

Dasen, P. R., & Mishra, R. C. (2000). Cross-cultural views on human development in the third millennium. *International Journal of Behavioral Development, 24*, 428–434.

Dasgupta, N. (2004). Implicit ingroup favouritism, outgroup favouritism, and their behavioral manifestations. *Social Justice Research, 17*(2), 143–169.

Davanloo, H. (1985). Short-term dynamic psychotherapy. In H. I. Kaplan & B. J. Sadock (Eds.), *Comprehensive textbook of psychiatry* (4th ed.). Baltimore: Williams & Wilkins.

David, B., & Turner, J. C. (2001). Majority and minority influence: A single process self-categorization analysis. In C. K. W. Dreu & N. K. D. Vries (Eds.), *Group consensus and minority influence: Implications for innovation* (pp. 91–121). Oxford: Blackwell.

Davidson, D. (1996). The role of schemata in children's memory. In H. W. Reese (Ed.), *Advances in child development and behavior* (pp. 35–58). San Diego, CA: Academic Press.

Davidson, G. (1992). Toward an applied Aboriginal psychology. *South Pacific Journal of Psychology, 5*, 1–20.

Davidson, G. (1999). Cultural competence as an ethical precept in psychology. In P. R. Martin & W. Noble (Eds.), *Psychology and society* (pp. 162–174). Brisbane, Australia: Australian Academic Press.

Davidson, G. (2000). The importance of interpersonal communication skills in intercultural contacts. In P. Dudgeon, D. Garvey, & H. Pickett (Eds.), *Working with Indigenous Australians: A handbook for psychologists* (pp. 181–184). Perth, Australia: Gunada Press.

Davidson, G., Sanson, A., & Gridley, H. (2000). Australian psychology and Australia's Indigenous people: A decade of action. *Australian Psychologist, 35*(2), 88–91.

Davidson, G. R., & Carr, S. C. (2010). Forced migration, social exclusion and poverty: Introduction. *Journal of Pacific Rim Psychology, 4*, 1–6.

Davidson, G. R., Murray, K. E., & Schweitzer, R. (2008). Review of refugee mental health and wellbeing: Australian perspectives. *Australian Psychologist, 43*(3), 160–174.

Davidson, G. R., Murray, K. E., & Schweitzer, R. D. (2010). Review of refugee mental health assessment: Best practices and recommendations. *Journal of Pacific Rim Psychology, 4*, 72–85.

Davidson, R. (1992). Emotion and affective style: Hemispheric substrates. *Psychological Science, 3*, 39–43.

Davies, M., Stankov, L., & Roberts, R. D. (1998). Emotional intelligence: In search of an elusive construct. *Journal of Personality and Social Psychology, 75*, 989–1015.

Davis, D. L., & Whitten, R. G. (1987). The cross-cultural study of human sexuality. *Annual Review of Anthropology, 16*, 69–98.

Davis, S. (1990). Men as success objects and women as sex objects: A study of personals advertisements. *Sex Roles, 23*, 43–50.

Davis, S. (2007, August 15). A good day: Jandamarra O'Shane celebrates his eighteenth birthday. *ABC News*. Retrieved from http://www.abc.net.au/local/stories/2008/08/15/2336753.htm

Davison, K. P., Pennebaker, J. W., & Dickerson, S. S. (2000). Who talks? The social psychology of illness support groups. *American Psychologist, 55*, 205–217.

Dawes, R. (1997). Judgment, decision making, and interference. In D. Gilbert, S. Fiske, & G. Lindzey (Eds.), *Handbook of social psychology* (pp. 497–549). Boston: McGraw-Hill.

Dawes, S., Frye, S., Best, D., Moss, D., Atkinson, J., Evans, C., et al. (2007). *Drug use in the family: Impacts and implications for children* (ANCD Research Paper No. 13). Canberra, Australia: Australian National Council on Drugs. Retrieved January 30, 2008, from http://www.ancd.org.au/publications/pdf/rp13_drug_use_in_family.pdf

Day, C. P. (2007). Alcohol and the liver. *Medicine, 35*, 22–25.

Day, N. L., Richardson, G. A., Goldschmidt, L., & Cornelius, M. D. (2000). Effects of prenatal tobacco exposure on preschoolers' behavior. *Journal of Developmental and Behavioral Pediatrics, 21,* 180–188.

Dawood, K., Bailey, J. M., & Martin, N. G. (2009). Genetic and environmental influences on sexual orientation. In Y. K. Kim (Ed.), *Handbook of behavior genetics* (pp. 269–279).

Deacon, T. W. (1996). *The making of language*. Edinburgh, UK: Edinburgh University Press.

Deak, G. O., Flom, R. A., & Pick, A. D. (2000). Effects of gesture and target on 12- and 18-month-olds' joint visual attention to objects in front of or behind them. *Developmental Psychology, 36,* 511–523.

de Angelis, R. A. (2003). A rising-tide for Jean-Marie, Jörg, and Pauline? Xenophobic populism in comparative perspective. *Australian Journal of Politics and History*, *49*(1), 75–92.

de Castro, J., & Brewer, M. (1992). The amount eaten in meals by humans is a power function of the number of people present. *Physiology and Behavior, 51*, 121–125.

de Castro, J. M. (1993). Genetic influences on daily intake and meal patterns of humans. *Physiology & Behavior, 53,* 777–782.

Deci, E. L., Koestner, R., & Ryan, R. M. (1999). A meta-analytic review of experiments examining the effects of extrinsic rewards on intrinsic motivation. *Psychological Bulletin, 125*, 627–668.

Degel, J., Piper, D., & Koster, E. P. (2001). Implicit learning and implicit memory for odors: The influence of odor identification and retention time. *Chemistry Senses*, *26*, 267–280.

Degenhardt, L., Hall, W., & Lynskey, M. (2001). Alcohol, cannabis and tobacco use among Australians: A comparison of their associations with other drug use and use disorders, affective and anxiety disorders, and psychosis. *Addiction, 96*(11), 1603–1614.

Degenhardt, L., Knox, S., Barker, B., Britt, H., & Shakeshaft, A. (2005). The management of alcohol, tobacco and illicit drug use problems by general practitioners in Australia. *Drug and Alcohol Review*, *24*(6), 499–506.

deGonzague, B., Receveur, O., Wedll, D., & Kuhnlein, H. V. (1999). Dietary intake and body mass index of adults in 2 Ojibwe communities. *Journal of the American Dietetic Association, 99,* 710–726.

Dehghani, M., Sharpe, L., & Nicholas, M. K. (2003). Selective attention to pain-related information in chronic musculoskeletal pain patients. *Pain, 105*, 37–46.

DeKay, T. (1998). *An evolutionary-computational approach to social cognition: Grandparental investment as a test case*. Unpublished doctoral dissertation, University of Michigan, Ann Arbor.

De La Ronde, C., & Swann, W. B., Jr. (1998). Partner verification: Restoring shattered images of our intimates. *Journal of Personality and Social Psychology, 75,* 374–382.

Del Monte, M. M. (2001). Fact or fantasy? A review of recovered memories of childhood sexual abuse. *Irish Journal of Psychological Medicine, 18,* 99–105.

DeLoache, J. S., Miller, K. F., & Rosengren, K. S. (1997). The credible shrinking room: Very young children's performance with symbolic and nonsymbolic relations. *Psychological Science, 8*, 308–313.

DeLongis, A., Folkman, S., & Lazarus, R. S. (1988). The impact of daily stress on health and mood: Psychological and social resources as mediators. *Journal of Personality and Social Psychology, 54,* 486–495.

de Maat, S. M., Dekker, J., Schoevers, R. A., & de Jonghe, F. (2007). Relative efficacy of psychotherapy and combined therapy in the treatment of depression: A meta-analysis. *European Psychiatry*, *22*(1), 1–8.

Demetriou, A., & Raftopoulos, A. (Eds.). (2004). *Cognitive developmental change: Theories, models, and measurement*. Cambridge, UK: Cambridge University Press.

Demorest, M. E. (1986). Problem solving: Stages, strategies, and stumbling blocks. *Journal of Academic Rehabilitation Audiology, 19,* 13–26.

Dempster, F. N. (1996). Distributing and managing the conditions of encoding and practice. In E. L. Bjork & R. A. Bjork (Eds.), *Memory. Handbook of perception and cognition* (2nd ed., pp. 317–344). San Diego, CA: Academic Press.

DeMulder, E. K., Denham, S., Schmidt, M., & Mitchell, J. (2000). Q-sort assessment of attachment security during the preschool years: Links from home to school. *Developmental Psychology, 36,* 274–282.

Denham, S., & Holt, R. W. (1993). Preschoolers' likability as cause or consequence of their social behavior. *Developmental Psychology, 29,* 271–275.

De Pascalis, V., & Perrone, M. (1996). EEG asymmetry and heart rate during experience of hypnotic analgesia in high and low hypnotizables. *International Journal of Psychophysiology, 21*, 163–175.

Department of Education, Science and Training. (2004). *Australian education international: Student enrolment and visa statistics*. Retrieved December 1, 2004, from http://aei.dest.gov.au/AEI/MIP/Statistics/StudentEnrolmentAndVisaStatistics/Recent.htm#Final

Department of Education, Science and Training. (2006). *AEI releases August 2006 international student enrolment*. Retrieved January 11, 2008, from http://aei.dest.gov.au/AEI/MIP/ItemsOfInterest/06Interest51.htm

Department of Education, Training and the Arts, Queensland. (2006). *Embedding Aboriginal and Torres Strait Islander perspectives in schools (EATSIPS)*. Retrieved January 11, 2008, from http://education.qld.gov.au/schools/indigenous/educators/eatsips-overview.html

Department of Foreign Affairs and Trade. (2004). *Australia in brief: A diverse people*. Retrieved December 12, 2004, from http://www.dfat.gov.au/aib/society.html#1

Department of Foreign Affairs and Trade. (2008). *Indigenous languages*. Retrieved fromh http://www.dfat.gov.au/facts/Indigenous_languages.html

Department of Health and Ageing. (2004a). *About overweight and obesity*. Retrieved May 20, 2004, from http://www.health.gov.au/pubhlth/strateg/hlthwt/obesity.htm#consequences

Department of Health and Ageing. (2004b). *Screening monograph no. 1/2004. Research report: Evaluation report for the 2000/2001 phase of the breast screen Australia campaign, April 2003*. Canberra, Australia: Commonwealth of Australia.

Department of Health and Ageing. (2008). *Evaluation of the impact of accreditation on the delivery of quality of care and quality of life to residents in Australian Government subsidised residential aged care homes - final report*. Retrieved from http://www.health.gov.au/internet/main/publishing.nsf/Content/ageing-iar-final-report.htm~ageing-iar-final-report-3.htm

Department of Health and Ageing. (2010). *A healthy and active Australia: Overweight and obesity in Australia*. Retrieved from http://www.health.gov.au/internet/healthyactive/publishing.nsf/Content/overweight-obesity

Department of Health, Western Australia. (2010). *Fetal alcohol spectrum disorder model of care*. Retrieved from http://www.healthnetworks.health.wa.gov.au/modelsofcare/docs/FASD_Model_of_Care.pdf

Department of Immigration and Citizenship. (2009). *Fact sheet 60 – Australia's refugee and humanitarian program*. Retrieved from http://www.immi.gov.au/media/fact-sheets/60refugee.htm

Department of Immigration and Citizenship. (2010). *Population flows: Immigration aspects 2008–2009*. Canberra, Australia: Commonwealth of Australia. Retrieved from http://www.immi.gov.au/media/publications/statistics/popflows2008-09/pop-flows.pdf

Department of Immigration and Multicultural and Indigenous Affairs. (2004). *Australia's refugee and humanitarian program*. Retrieved November 24, 2004, from http://www.immi.gov.au/facts/60refugee.htm

DePaulo, B. M., & Friedman, H. S. (1998). Nonverbal communication. In D. T. Gilbert, S. T. Fiske, & G. Lindzey (Eds.), *The handbook of social psychology* (4th ed.). New York: McGraw-Hill.

Deregowski, J. B. (1970). Effect of cultural value of time upon recall. *British Journal of Social and Clinical Psychology, 9,* 37–41.

DeRosier, M., & Kupersmidt, J. (1991). Costa Rican children's perceptions of their social networks. *Developmental Psychology, 27,* 656–662.

D'Esposito, M., Detre, J., Aquirre, G., Stallcup, M., Alsop, D., Tippet, L., et al. (1997). A functional MRI study of mental image generation. *Neuropsychologia, 35*, 725–730.

DeSteno, D. A., & Salovey, P. (1996). Genes, jealousy, and the replication of misspecified models. *Psychological Science, 7,* 376–377.

Deutsch, J. A., & Gonzalez, M. E. (1980). Gastric nutrient content signals satiety. *Behavioral and Neural Biology, 30*, 113–116.

DeValois, R. L., & DeValois, K. (1975). Neural coding of color. In E. C. Carterette & M. P. Friedman (Eds.), *Handbook of perception*. New York: Academic Press.

de Vaus, D. (2004). *Diversity and change in Australian families. Statistical profiles* (Chapter 15: Divorce and separation). Retrieved from http://www.aifs.gov.au/institute/pubs/diversity/DiversityAndChange.pdf

Devine, P., Monteith, M., Zuwerink, J., & Elliot, A. (1991). Prejudice with and without compunction. *Journal of Personality and Social Psychology, 60*, 817–830.

Devine, P. G., & Monteith, M. J. (1993). The role of discrepancy-associated affect in prejudice reduction. In D. M. Mackie & D. L. Hamilton (Eds.), *Affect, cognition and stereotyping: Interactive processes in group perception* (pp. 317–344). San Diego, CA: Academic Press.

Devine, P. G., Plant, E. A., Amodio, D. M., Harmon-Jones, E., & Vance, S. L. (2002). The regulation of explicit and implicit race bias: The role of motivations to respond without prejudice. *Journal of Personality and Social Psychology, 82*, 835–848.

de Visser, R. O., Smith, A. M. A., Rissel, C. E., Richters, J., & Grulich, A. E. (2003). Safer sex and condom use among a representative sample of adults. *Australian and New Zealand Journal of Public Health, 27*(7), 223–229.

Devlin, M. J., Yanovski, S. Z., & Wilson, G. T. (2000). Obesity: What mental health professionals need to know. *American Journal of Psychiatry, 157*, 854–866.

DeVos, G., & Suarez-Orozco, M. M. (1986). Child development in Japan and the United States: Prospectives of cross-cultural comparisons. In H. W. Stevenson & H. Azuma (Eds.), *Child development and education in Japan* (pp. 289–298). New York: W. H. Freeman.

deVries, R. (1969). Constancy of generic identity in the years three to six. *Monographs of the Society for Research in Child Development*, *34*(3).

de Waal, F. (1989). *Peacemaking among primates*. Cambridge, MA: Harvard University Press.

Dewhirst, C. (2003, November 21). *Italian roots: Family history, inter-generational experience and identity*. Paper presented to the social change in the 21st Century Conference, Queensland University of Technology, Australia.

de Wijk, R. A., Schab, F. R., & Cain, W. S. (1995). Odor identification. In F. R. Schab & R. G. Crowder (Eds.), *Memory for odors* (pp. 21–37). Mahwah, NJ: Lawrence Erlbaum.

Dewis, L. M., Kirkby, K. C., Martin, F., Daniels, B. A., Gilroy, L. J., & Menzies, R. G. (2001). Computer-aided vicarious exposure versus live graded exposure for spider phobia in children. *Journal of Behavior Therapy and Experimental Psychiatry, 32,* 17–27.

De Witte, P. (1996). The role of neurotransmitters in alcohol dependence: Animal research. *Alcohol and Alcoholism, 31*, 13–16.

De Wolff, M., & van Ijzendoorn, M. H. (1997). Sensitivity and attachment: A meta-analysis on parental antecedents of infant attachment. *Child Development, 68*, 571–591.

Dews, P. B. (1959). Some observations on an operant in the octopus. *Journal of the Experimental Analysis of Behavior, 2*, 57–63.

Diagnose Me. (2010). *Senile dementia*. Retrieved from http://www.diagnose-me.com/cond/C180356.html

Diamond, A. (2000). Close interrelation of motor development and cognitive development and of the cerebellum and prefrontal cortex. *Child Development, 71*, 44–56.

Diamond, M. C. (1978). The aging brain: Some enlightening and optimistic results. *American Psychologist, 66*, 66–71.

Di Blas, L., & Forzi, M. (1999). Refining a descriptive structure of personality attributes in the Italian language: The abridged big three circumplex structure. *Journal of Personality and Social Psychology, 76*, 451–481.

Di Chiara, G., Acquas, E., & Tanda, G. (1996). Ethanol as a neurochemical surrogate of conventional reinforcers: The dopamine-opioid link. *Alcohol, 13*, 13–17.

Dick, D. M., Rose, R. J., Viken, R. J., & Kaprio, J. (2000). Pubertal timing and substance use: Associations between and within families across late adolescence. *Developmental Psychology, 36*, 180–189.

Diehl, M. (2006). Development of self-representations in adulthood. In D. Mroczek & T. Little (Eds.), *Handbook of personality development* (pp. 373–398). Mahwah, NJ: Erlbaum.

Diener, E. (2000). Subjective well-being: The science of happiness and a proposal for a national index. *American Psychologist, 55*, 34–43.

Diener, E., & Suh, M. E. (1998). Subjective well-being and age: An international analysis. In K. W. Schaie & M. P. Lawton (Eds.), *Annual review of gerontology and geriatrics: Vol. 17. Focus on emotion and adult development* (pp. 304–324). New York: Springer.

Dies, R. (1992). The future of group therapy. *Psychotherapy, 29*, 58–64.

Dietz, B. E. (2006). The concept of the independent and the interdependent self and sociological theory: Inter-disciplinary cross-fertilization. In A. P. Prescott (Ed.), *The concept of self in education, family and sports* (pp. 191–206). New York: Nova Science Publishers.

Dietz, T. L. (1998). An examination of violence and gender role portrayals in video games: Implications for gender socialization and aggressive behavior. *Sex Roles, 38*(5/6), 425–442. Retrieved from http://videogames.procon.org/sourcefiles/Dietz.pdf

Dietze, P. M., & Thomson, D. M. (1993). Mental reinstatement of context: A technique for interviewing child witnesses. *Applied Cognitive Psychology, 7*(2), 97–108.

Difede, J., & Hoffman, H. G. (2002). Virtual reality exposure therapy for World Trade Center post-traumatic stress disorder: A case report. *CyberPsychology and Behavior, 5*, 529–535.

Digman, J. M., & Inouye, J. (1986). Further specification of the five robust factors of personality. *Journal of Personality and Social Psychology, 50*, 116–123.

Dil, N. (1984). Nonverbal communication in young children. *Topics in Early Childhood Special Education, 4*, 82–99.

DiLalla, L. F. (2002). Behavior genetics of aggression in children: Review and future directions. *Developmental Review, 22*, 593–622.

Dillard, J. P., & Anderson, J. W. (2004). The role of fear in persuasion. *Psychology and Marketing, 21*(11), 909–926.

Dingfelder, S. F. (2006, October). Pretty faces: Easy on the brain. *Monitor on Psychology, 37*(9), 32–33.

Dion, K., Berscheid, E., & Walster, E. (1972). What is beautiful is good. *Journal of Personality and Social Psychology, 24*, 285–290.

Dion, K. K. (2002). Cultural perspectives on physical attractiveness. In G. Rhodes & L. A. Zebrowitz (Eds.), *Facial attractiveness: Evolutionary, cognitive, and social perspectives. Advances in visual cognition: Vol. 1* (pp. 239–259). Westport, CT: Ablex Publishing.

Dion, K. K., & Berscheid, E. (1974). Physical attractiveness and peer perception among children. *Sociometry, 37*, 1–12.

Dion, K. K., & Dion, K. L. (1996). Cultural perspectives on romantic love. *Personal Relationships, 3*, 5–17.

Dion, K. L., & Dion, K. K. (1988). Romantic love: Individual and cultural perspectives. In R. Sternberg & M. Barnes (Eds.), *The psychology of love*. New Haven, CT: Yale University Press.

Dipboye, R. L. (1997). Organizational barriers to implementing a rational model of training. In M. A. Quinones & A. Ehrenstein (Eds.), *Training for a rapidly changing workplace: Applications of psychological research* (pp. 31–60). Washington, DC: American Psychological Association.

DiPietro, J. A., Bornstein, M. H., Costigan, K. A., Pressman, E. K., Hahn, C.-S., Painter, K., et al. (2002). What does fetal movement predict about behavior during the first two years of life? *Developmental Psychobiology, 40*, 359–371.

DiPietro, J. A., Hodgson, D. M., Costigan, K. A., & Johnson, T. R. B. (1996). Fetal antecedents of infant temperament. *Child Development, 67*, 2568–2583.

Diseth, A. (2003). Personality and approaches to learning as predictors of academic achievement. *European Journal of Personality, 17*, 143–155.

Dittes, J. E. (1959). Effect of changes in self-esteem upon impulsiveness and deliberation in making judgments. *Journal of Abnormal Social Psychology, 53*, 100–107.

Dixit, A. R., & Crum, R. M. (2000). Prospective study of depression and the risk of heavy alcohol use in women. *American Journal of Psychiatry, 157*, 751–758.

Dixon, N. F. (1971). *Subliminal perception: The nature of a controversy*. New York: McGraw-Hill.

Dixon, N. F. (1981). *Preconscious processing*. New York: John Wiley.

Doane, J. A., West, K. L., Goldstein, M. J., Rodnick, E. H., & Jones, J. E. (1981). Parental communication deviance and affective style: Predictors of subsequent schizophrenia spectrum disorders in vulnerable adolescents. *Archives of General Psychiatry, 38*, 679–685.

Dobson, V., & Teller, D. Y. (1978). Visual acuity in human infants: A review and comparison of behavioral and electrophysiological studies. *Visual Research, 18*, 1469–1483.

Docherty, S. L., Sandelowski, M., & Preisser, J. S. (2006). Three months in the symptom life of a teenage girl undergoing treatment for cancer. *Research in Nursing and Health, 29*(4), 294–310.

Dodd, B. (1979). Lip reading in infants: Attention to speech presented in- and out-of-synchrony. *Cognitive Psychology, 11*, 478–484.

Dodge, K., Lochman, J., Harnish, J., Bates, J. E., & Pettit, G. (1997). Reactive and proactive aggression in school children and psychiatrically impaired chronically assaultive youth. *Journal of Abnormal Psychology, 106*, 37–51.

Dodge, K., Pettit, G., Bates, J. E., & Valente, E. (1995). Social information-processing patterns partially mediate the effect of early physical abuse on later conduct problems. *Journal of Abnormal Psychology, 104*, 632–643.

Doessel, D. P., Scheurer, R. W., Chant, D. C., & Whiteford, H. A. (2006). Changes in private sector electroconvulsive treatment in Australia. *Australian and New Zealand Journal of Psychiatry, 40*, 362–367.

Dohnt, H., & Tiggemann, M. (2006). The contribution of peer and media influences to the development of body dissatisfaction and self-esteem in young girls: A prospective study. *Developmental Psychology, 42*(5), 929–936.

Doi, T. (1992). On the concept of amae. *Infant Mental Health Journal, 13*, 7–11.

Dollard, M. F., & Winefield, A. H. (2002). Mental health: Overemployment, underemployment, unemployment and healthy jobs. *Australian e-Journal for the Advancement of Mental Health, 1*(3), 1–26.

Domhoff, G. W. (1996). *Finding meaning in dreams: A quantitative approach*. New York: Plenum Press.

Donnellan, M. B., Trzesniewski, K. H., Robins, R. W., Moffitt, T. E., & Caspi, A. (2005). Low self-esteem is related to aggression, antisocial behavior, and delinquency. *Psychological Science, 16*, 328–335.

Doty, R. L., Green, P. A., Ram, C., & Tandeil, S. L. (1982). Communication of gender from human breath odors: Relationship to perceived intensity and pleasantness. *Hormones and Behavior, 16*, 13–22.

Douvan, E., & Adelson, J. (1966). *The adolescent experience*. New York: John Wiley.

Dovidio, J., & Gaertner, S. (1993). Stereotypes and evaluative intergroup bias. In D. Mackie & D. Hamilton (Eds.), *Affect, cognition, and stereotyping: Interactive processes in group perception*. San Diego, CA: Academic Press.

Dovidio, J. F., Kawakami, K., & Gaertner, S. L. (2000). Reducing contemporary prejudice: Combating explicit and implicit bias at the individual and intergroup level. In S. Oskamp (Ed.), *Reducing prejudice and discrimination: The Claremont Symposium on applied social psychology* (pp. 137–163). Mahwah, NJ: Lawrence Erlbaum.

Downey, G., Freitas, A. L., Michaelis, B., & Khouri, H. (1998). The self-fulfilling prophecy in close relationships: Rejection sensitivity and rejection by romantic partners. *Journal of Personality and Social Psychology, 75*, 545–560.

Doyle, P., Grant, C., & Christian, B. (1996). An overview of drug and alcohol treatment approach in a Queensland prison setting. In *Drugs — policies, programs and people: 1996 winter school in the sun* (pp. 93–96). Brisbane, Australia: Alcohol and Drugs Foundation Queensland

Dozier, M., & Kobak, R. (1992). Psychophysiology in attachment interviews: Converging evidence for deactivating strategies. *Child Development, 63*, 1473–1480.

Drasdo, N. (1977). The neural representation of visual space. *Nature, 266*, 554–556.

Drepper, J., Timmann, D., Kolb, F. P., & Diener, H. C. (1999). Non-motor associative learning in patients with isolated degenerative cerebellar disease. *Brain, 122*, 87–97.

Dreu, C. K. W., & Beersma, B. (2001). Minority influence in organisations. In C. K. W. Dreu & N. K. D. Vries (Eds.), *Group consensus and minority influence: Implications for innovation* (pp. 258–283). Oxford: Blackwell.

Drewing, K., Aschersleben, G., & Li, S. C. (2006). Sensorimotor synchronization across the life span. *International Journal of Behavioral Development, 30*, 280–287.

Dryer, D. C., & Horowitz, L. M. (1997). When do opposites attract? Interpersonal complementarity versus similarity. *Journal of Personality and Social Psychology, 72*, 592–603.

DuBois, C. (1944). *The people of Alor: A social psychological study of an East Indian Island*. Minneapolis: University of Minnesota Press.

Duckitt, J. (1992). Psychology and prejudice: A historical analysis and integrative framework. *American Psychologist, 47*, 1182–1197.

Duckitt, J. (2001). A dual process cognitive-motivational theory of ideology and prejudice. *Advances in Experimental Social Psychology, 33*, 41–113.

Duckitt, J. (2002). The psychological bases of ideology and prejudice: Testing a dual process model. *Journal of Personality and Social Psychology, 83*, 75–93.

Duckitt, J., & Fisher, K. (2003). The impact of social threat on worldview and ideological attitudes. *Political Psychology, 24*, 199–222.

Dudgeon, P. (2000a). Counselling with Indigenous people. In P. Dudgeon, D. Garvey, & H. Pickett (Eds.), *Working with Indigenous Australians: A handbook for psychologists* (pp. 249–270). Perth, Australia: Gunada Press.

Dudgeon, P. (2000b). Diversity in Aboriginal culture. In P. Dudgeon, D. Garvey, & H. Pickett (Eds.), *Working with Indigenous Australians: A handbook for psychologists* (pp. 137–142). Perth, Australia: Gunada Press.

Dudgeon, P., Garvey, D., & Pickett, H. (Eds.). (2000). *Working with Indigenous Australians: A handbook for psychologists*. Perth, Australia: Gunada Press.

Dudgeon, P., & Oxenham, D. (1990). *The complexity of Aboriginal diversity: Identity and kindredness. Monographs of the Aboriginal and Torres Strait Islanders Studies Unit, University of Queensland, No. 1*.

Dudgeon, P., Oxenham, D., & Grogan, G. (1996). Learning identities and differences in feminisms and pedagogies of everyday life. In C. Luke (Ed.), *Feminisms and pedagogies of everyday life*. New York: State University of New York Press.

Dudgeon, P., & Pickett, H. (2000). Psychology and reconciliation: Australian perspectives. *Australian Psychologist, 35*(2), 82–87.

Dudgeon, P., Wright, M., & Coffin, J. (2010). Talking it and walking it: Cultural competence. *Journal of Indigenous Studies Press, 13*(3–4), 31–47.

Dudley, R. (1991). IQ and heritability. *Science, 252,* 191–192.

Duman, R. S., Heninger, G. R., & Nestler, E. J. (1997). A molecular and cellular theory of depression. *Archives of General Psychiatry, 54,* 597–606.

Dumaret, A. (1985). I.Q., scholastic performance and behavior of sibs raised in contrasting environments. *Journal of Child Psychology and Psychiatry and Allied Disciplines, 26*, 553–580.

Duncan, G., & Brooks, G. J. (2000). Family poverty, welfare reform, and child development. *Child Development, 71*, 188–196.

Duncan, J., Seitz, R., Kolodny, J., Bor, D., Herzog, H., Ahmed, A., et al. (2000). A neural basis for general intelligence. *Science, 289,* 457–460.

Duncker, K. (1946). On problem solving. *Psychological Monographs, 158*(5), 270.

Dunifon, R., & Duncan, G. J. (1998). Long-run effects of motivation on labor-market success. *Social Psychology Quarterly, 61*, 33–48.

Dunn, J. (2002). Sibling relationships. In P. Smith & C. H. Hart (Eds.), *Childhood social development* (pp. 223–237). Oxford, UK: Blackwell Publishers.

Dunn, J., Bretherton, I., & Munn, P. (1987). Conversations about feeling states between mothers and their young children. *Developmental Psychology, 23*, 132–139.

Dunn, J., Cutting, A. L., & Fisher, N. (2002). Old friends, new friends: Predictors of children's perspectives on their friends at school. *Child Development, 73*, 621–635.

Dunn, J., & McGuire, S. (1992). Sibling and peer relationships in childhood. *Journal of Child Psychology and Psychiatry, 33*, 67–105.

Durex. (2007). *Global sex survey 2004 results*. Retrieved November 28, 2007, from http://www.durex.com/uk/globalsexsurvey/2004results.asp

Durie, M. (2001). *Mauri ora: The dynamics of Maori health*. Melbourne, Australia: Oxford University Press.

Durkheim, E. (1915). *The elementary forms of the religious life*. New York: Free Press.

Durkin, S. J., Paxton, S. J., & Sorbello, M. (2007). An integrative model of the impact of exposure to idealized female images on adolescent girls' body satisfaction. *Journal of Applied Social Psychology, 37*, 1092–1117.

Duval, F., Mokrani, M. C., Monreal, J., Bailey, P., Valdebenito, M., Crocq, M. A., et al. (2003). Dopamine and serotonin function in untreated schizophrenia: Clinical correlates of the apomorphine and d-fenfluroamine tests. *Psychoneuroendocrinology, 28,* 627–642.

Dweck, C. (1975). The role of expectations and attributions in the alleviation of learned helplessness. *Journal of Personality and Social Psychology, 31*, 674–685.

Dweck, C. (1986). Motivational processes affecting learning. *American Psychologist, 41*, 1040–1048.

Dworkin, R. H., Hartsetin, G., Rosner, H., Walther, R., Sweeney, E. W., & Brand, L. (1992). A high-risk method for studying psychosocial antecedents of chronic pain: The prospective investigation of herpes zoster. *Journal of Abnormal Psychology, 101*, 200–205.

Dyck, M. J., Piek, J. P., Kane, R., & Patrick, J. (2009). How uniform is the structure of ability across childhood? *The European Journal of Developmental Psychology, 6*, 432–454.

Eagly, A. H. (1978). Sex differences in influenceability. *Psychological Bulletin, 85*, 86–116.

Eagly, A. H. (1983). Gender and social influence: A social psychological analysis. *American Psychologist, 38,* 971–981.

Eagly, A. H. (1995). The science and politics of comparing men and women. *American Psychologist, 50,* 145–158.

Eagly, A. H., Ashmore, R., Makhijani, M., & Longo, L. (1991). What is beautiful is good, but: A meta-analytic review of research on the physical attractiveness stereotype. *Psychological Bulletin, 110,* 109–128.

Eagly, A. H., & Carli, L. L. (1981). Sex of researchers and sex-typed communications as determinants of sex differences in influenceability: A meta-analysis of social influence studies. *Psychological Bulletin, 90,* 1–20.

Eagly, A. H., & Chaiken, S. (1992). *The psychology of attitudes*. San Diego, CA: Harcourt Brace.

Eagly, A. H., & Chaiken, S. (1998). Attitude structure and function. In D. T. Gilbert, S. T. Fiske, & G. Lindzey (Eds.), *The handbook of social psychology: Vol. 2* (4th ed., pp. 269–322). Boston: McGraw-Hill.

Eagly, A. H., & Crowley, M. (1986). Gender and helping behavior: A meta-analytic review of the social psychological literature. *Psychological Bulletin, 100*, 283–308.

Eagly, A. H., & Johannesen-Schmidt, M. C. (2001). The leadership styles of women and men. *Journal of Social Issues, 57*, 781–797.

Eagly, A. H., & Steffen, V. (1986). Gender and aggressive behavior: A meta-analytic review of the social psychological literature. *Psychological Bulletin, 100*, 309–330.

Eagly, A. H., & Wood, W. (1999). The origins of sex differences in human behavior: Evolved dispositions versus social roles. *American Psychologist, 54*, 408–423.

Eating Difficulties Education Network. (2010). *Research & statistics*. Retrieved from http://www.eden.org.nz/research-statistics/

Eaton, S. B., & Konner, M. (1985). Paleolithic nutrition: A consideration of its nature and current implications. *The New England Journal of Medicine, 312,* 283–289.

Ebbesen, E. B., Kjos, G. L., & Konecni, V. J. (1976). Spatial ecology: Its effect on the choice of friends and enemies. *Journal of Experimental Social Psychology, 12*, 505–518.

Ebbinghaus, H. (1964). *Memory*. New York: Columbia University/Dover. (Originally published 1885).

Eckensberger, L. H. (1994). Moral development and its measurement across cultures. In W. J. Lonner & R. Malpass (Eds.), *Psychology and culture*. Needham Heights, MA: Allyn & Bacon.

Eckermann, A., Dowd, T., Chong, E., Nixon, L., Gray, R., & Johnson, S. (2010). *Binan Goonji. Bridging cultures in Aboriginal health*. Chatswood, Australia: Elsevier.

Eckermann, A., Dowd, T., Martin, M., Nixon, L., Gray, R., & Chong, E. (1994). *Binan Goonji*. Armidale, Australia: University of New England Press.

Eckermann, A. K. (1995). *Introduction to traditional Aboriginal societies*. Armidale, Australia: University of New England Press.

Eddings, S. K. (2003). Gender differences in self-handicapping: The role of self-construals. *The Sciences and Engineering, 64*, 463.

Edelman, G. (2001). Consciousness: The remembered present. *Annals of the New York Academy of Science, 929*, 111–122.

Edelman, G. M. (1989). *The remembered present: A biological theory of consciousness*. New York: Basic Books.

Eder, R. (1990). Uncovering young children's psychological selves: Individual and developmental differences. *Child Development, 61,* 849–863.

Edgar, D. (1980). *Introduction to Australian society: A sociological perspective*. Sydney, Australia: Prentice-Hall.

Education New Zealand. (2007). *International students: Studying and staying on in New Zealand*. Retrieved from http://www.dol.govt.nz/PDFs/international-students2007.pdf

Edwards, C. P., & Whiting, B. B. (1983). Differential socialization of girls and boys in light of cross-cultural research. In W. Damon (Ed.), *Social and personality development: Essays on the growth of the child*. New York: W.W. Norton.

Edwards, S. (2000, April 3–7). *Identity reclamation: Re-education as empowerment*. Paper presented at the Australian Indigenous Education Conference, Fremantle, Western Australia. Retrieved December 12, 2004, from http://www.kk.ecu.edu.au/sub/schoola/research/confs/aiec/papers/sedward.doc

Edwards, W. (1977). How to use multiattribute utility measurement for social decision making. *IEEE Transactions in Systems Man and Cybernetics, 17,* 326–340.

Edwards, W., & Newman, J. R. (1986). Multiattribute choice. In H. R. Arkes & K. R. Hammond (Eds.), *Judgment and decision making: An interdisciplinary reader*. Cambridge: Cambridge University Press.

Egger, M. D., & Flynn, J. P. (1963). Effect of electrical stimulation of the amygdala on hypothalamically elicited attack behavior in cats. *Journal of Neurophysiology, 26*, 705–720.

Ehrlinger, J., Gilovich, T., & Ross, L. (2005). Peering into the bias blind spot: People's assessments of bias in themselves and others. *Personality and Social Psychology Bulletin, 31*, 680–692.

Ehrman, R., Ternes, J., O'Brien, C. P., & McLellan, A. T. (1992). Conditioned tolerance in human opiate addicts. *Psychopharmacology, 108,* 218–224.

Ehrt, U., & Aarsland, D. (2005). Psychiatric aspects of Parkinson's disease: Depression, anxiety and apathy in Parkinson's disease. *Current Opinion in Psychiatry, 18*(3), 335–341.

Eichenbaum, H. (1997). Declarative memory: Insights from cognitive neurobiology. *Annual Review, 48,* 547–572.

Eight hours work. (2003). Retrieved October 3, 2009, from http://www.8hourday.org.au/pdf/888_fact_03_work_rest_play.pdf

Eimas, P. D. (1985). The equivalence of cues in the perception of speech by infants. *Infant Behavior and Development, 8,* 125–138.

Eimas, P. D., Siqueland, E. R., Jusczyk, P., & Vigorito, J. (1971). Speech perception in infants. *Science, 171,* 303–306.

Einstein, G. O., & McDaniel, M. A. (1990). Normal aging and prospective memory. *Journal of Experimental Psychology: Learning, Memory, & Cognition, 16,* 717–726.

Einstein, G. O., Smith, R. E., McDaniel, M. A., & Shaw, P. (1997). Aging and prospective memory: The influence of increased task demands at encoding and retrieval. *Psychology & Aging, 12,* 479–488.

Eisenberg, N. (2000). Emotion, regulation, and moral development. *Annual Review of Psychology, 51*, 665–697.

Eisenberg, N., Fabes, R. A., & Murphy, B. C. (1996). Parent's reactions to children's negative emotions: Relations to children's social competence and comforting behavior. *Child Development, 67,* 2227–2247.

Eisenberg, N., Miller, P. A., Shell, R., McNalley, S., & Shea, C. (1991). Prosocial development in adolescence: A longitudinal study. *Developmental Psychology, 27,* 849–857.

Ekman, P. (1971). Universals and cultural differences in facial expression. In J. K. Cole (Ed.), *Nebraska symposium on motivation*. Lincoln: University of Nebraska Press.

Ekman, P. (1992a). An argument for basic emotions. *Cognition and Emotion, 6*, 169–200.

Ekman, P. (1992b). Facial expressions of emotion: New findings, new questions. *Psychological Science, 3*, 34–38.

Ekman, P. (1999). Facial expressions. In T. Dalgleish & M. Power (Eds.), *The handbook of cognition and emotion* (pp. 301–320). New York: John Wiley & Sons.

Ekman, P., & Davidson, R. J. (1993). Voluntary smiling changes regional brain activity. *Psychological Science, 4*, 342–345.

Ekman, P., & Friesen, W. V. (1975). *Unmasking the face: A guide to recognizing emotions from facial cues*. Englewood Cliffs, NJ: Prentice-Hall.

Ekman, P., & Keltner, D. (1997). Universal facial expressions of emotion: An old controversy and new findings. In U. C. Segerstrale & P. Molnar (Eds.), *Nonverbal communication: Where nature meets culture* (pp. 27–46). Hillsdale, NJ: Lawrence Erlbaum.

Ekman, P., Levenson, R. W., & Friesen, W. V. (1983). Autonomic nervous system activity distinguishes among emotions. *Science, 221*, 1208–1210.

Ekman, P., & Oster, H. (1979). Facial expressions of emotion. *Annual Review of Psychology, 30*, 527–554.

Elder, G. H., Jr. (1998). The life course as developmental theory. *Child Development, 69*, 1–12.

Eldridge, L., Knowlton, B., & Engel, S. (2000). *Hippocampus selectively encodes episodic memories*. Unpublished manuscript, University of California, Los Angeles.

Elfhag, K., & Rossner, S. (2005). Who succeeds in maintaining weight loss? A conceptual review of factors associated with weight loss maintenance and weight regain. *Obesity Reviews, 6*, 67–85.

Elias, M. F., Beiser, A., Wolf, P. A., Au, R., White, R. F., & D'Agostino, R. B. (2000). The preclinical phase of Alzheimer disease: A 22 year prospective study of the Framingham cohort. *Archives of Neurology, 57*, 808–813.

Elkin, I., Shea, M. T., Watkins, J., & Imber, S. (1989). National Institute of Mental Health Treatment of Depression Collaborative Research Program: General effectiveness of treatments. *American Journal of Psychiatry, 46*, 971–982.

Elkind, D. (1981). Children's discovery of the conservation of mass, weight, and volume: Piaget replications studies II. *Journal of Genetic Psychology, 98*, 37–46.

Elkins, G., Marcus, J., Bates, J., Rajab, M. H., & Cook, T. (2006). Intensive hypnotherapy for smoking cessation: A prospective study. *International Journal of Clinical and Experimental Hypnosis, 54*(3), 303–315.

Elkins, I. J., Mcgue, M., & Iacono, W. G. (1997). Genetic and environmental influences on parent-son relationships: Evidence for increasing genetic influence during adolescence. *Developmental Psychology, 33*, 351–363.

Elkis, H., Friedman, L., Wise, A., & Meltzer, H. Y. (1995). Meta-analyses of studies of ventricular enlargement and cortical sulcall prominence in mood disorders: Comparisons with controls or patients with schizophrenia. *Archives of General Psychiatry, 52*, 735–746.

Ellickson, P. L., & Bell, R. M. (1990). Drug prevention in junior high: A multi-site longitudinal test. *Science, 247*(4948), 1299–1305.

Ellicott, A., Hammen, C., Gitlin, M., Brown, G., & Jamison, K. (1990). Life events and the course of bipolar disorder. *American Journal of Psychiatry, 147*, 1194–1198.

Elliot, A. J., & Church, M. A. (1997). A hierarchical model of approach and avoidance achievement motivation. *Journal of Personality and Social Psychology, 72*, 218–232.

Elliot, A. J., & Harackiewicz, J. M. (1996). Approach and avoidance achievement goals and intrinsic motivation: A mediational analysis. *Journal of Personality and Social Psychology, 70*, 461–475.

Elliott, E. J., & Bower, C. (2004). FAS in Australia: Fact or fiction? *Journal of Paediatric Child Health, 40*, 8–10.

Elliott, J. (1977). The power and pathology of prejudice. In P. G. Zimbardo & F. L. Ruch (Eds.), *Psychology and life* (9th ed.). Glenview, IL: Scott, Foresman.

Elliott-Farrelly, T. (2004). Australian Aboriginal suicide: The need for an Aboriginal suicidology? *Australian e-Journal for the Advancement of Mental Health, 3*(3). Retrieved January 7, 2005, from http://www.auseinet.com/journal/vol3iss3/elliottfarrelly.pdf

Ellis, A. (1962). *Reason and emotion in psychotherapy*. New York: Lyle Stuart.

Ellis, A. (1977). The basic clinical theory of rational-emotive therapy. In A. Ellis & R. Grieger (Eds.), *Handbook of rational-emotive therapy*. New York: Springer.

Ellis, A. (1984). Rational-emotive therapy. In R. J. Corsini (Ed.), *Current psychotherapies* (2nd ed.). Itasca, IL: Peacock Publishers.

Ellis, A. (1987). Cognitive therapy and rational-emotive therapy: A dialogue. *Journal of Cognitive Psychotherapy, 1*, 205–255.

Ellis, A. (1989). *Inside rational-emotive therapy: A critical appraisal of the theory and therapy of Albert Ellis*. New York: Academic Press.

Ellis, A. (1999). Why rational-emotive therapy to rational emotive behavior therapy? *Psychotherapy, 36*, 154–159.

Ellis, A. (2002a). *Overcoming resistance: A rational emotive behavior therapy integrated approach* (2nd ed.). New York: Springer.

Ellis, A. (2002b). The role of irrational beliefs in perfectionism. In G. L. Fleet & P. L. Hewitt (Eds.), *Perfectionism: Theory, research, and treatment* (pp. 217–229). Washington, DC: American Psychological Association.

Ellis, B. J., & Garber, J. (2000). Psychosocial antecedents of variation in girls' pubertal timing: Maternal depression, stepfather presence, and marital and family stress. *Child Development, 71*, 485–501.

Ellis, L., & Ames, M. A. (1987). Neurohormonal functioning and sexual orientation: A theory of homosexuality-heterosexuality. *Psychological Bulletin, 101*, 233–258.

Ellis, P. M., & Smith, D. A. R. (2002). Treating depression: The beyondblue guidelines for treating depression in primary care. *Medical Journal of Australia, 176*, S77–S83.

Elsworth, S. (2009, April 4–5). Attackers lust for web fame. *The Courier Mail*, p. 31.

Ember, C. R., & Ember, M. (2004). *Encyclopedia of sex and gender: Men and women in the world's cultures*. New York: Kluwer/Plenum.

Emmons, R., & King, L. A. (1988). Conflict among personal strivings: Immediate and long-term implications for psychological and physical well-being. *Journal of Personality and Social Psychology, 54*, 1040–1048.

Endo, Y., Heine, S. J., & Lehman, D. R. (2000). Culture and positive illusions in close relationships: How my relationships are better than yours. *Personality and Social Psychology Bulletin, 26*, 1571–1586.

Engel, S., Zhang, X., & Wandell, B. (1997). Colour tuning in human visual cortex measured with functional magnetic resonance imaging. *Nature, 388*, 68–71.

Engen, T. (1982). *The perception of odors*. New York: Academic Press.

Ennis, M. (1989). Testing and assessment of Aboriginal students. *Queensland Journal of Guidance and Counselling, 3*, 39–49.

Enoch, M.-A. (2006). Genetic and environmental influences on the development of alcoholism: Resilience vs. risk. *Annals New York Academy of Science*, 193–201.

Entwistle, N. J., & Peterson, E. R. (2004). Conception of learning and knowledge in higher education — relationships with study behaviour and influences of learning environments. *International Journal of Educational Research, 41*, 407–428.

Envisage International Corporation. (2010). *Foreign student numbers rising in New Zealand*. Retrieved from http://blog.internationalstudent.com/2010/05/foreign-student-numbers-rising-in-new-zealand/

Epley, N., & Dunning, D. (2000). Feeling 'holier than thou': Are self-serving assessments produced by errors in self or social prediction? *Journal of Personality and Social Psychology, 79*, 861–875.

Epley, N., & Gilovich, T. (1999). Just going along: Nonconscious priming and conformity to social pressure. *Journal of Experimental Social Psychology, 35*, 578–589.

Epstein, S. (1979). The stability of behavior: On predicting most of the people much of the time. *Journal of Personality and Social Psychology, 37*, 1097–1126.

Epstein, S. (1980). The stability of behaviour. II. Implications for psychological research. *American Psychologist, 35*, 790–806.

Epstein, S. (1986). Does aggregation produce spuriously high estimates of behavior stability? *Journal of Personality and Social Psychology, 50*, 1199–1210.

Epstein, S. (1992). Coping ability, negative self-evaluation, and overgeneralization: Experiment and theory. *Journal of Personality and Social Psychology, 62*, 826–836.

Epstein, S. (1994). Integration of the cognitive and the psychodynamic unconscious. *American Psychologist, 49*, 709–724.

Epstein, S. (1997). This I have learned from over 40 years of personality research. *Journal of Personality, 65*, 3–32.

Epstein, S. (1998). Cognitive-experiential self-theory. In D. F. Barone, M. Hersen, & V. B. Van Hasselt (Eds.), *Advanced personality. The Plenum series in social/clinical psychology* (pp. 211–238). New York: Plenum Press.

Era, P., Jokela, J., & Heikkinen, E. (1986). Reaction and movement times in men of different ages: A population study. *Perceptual and Motor Skills, 63*, 111–130.

Erdelyi, M. H. (1985). *Psychoanalysis: Freud's cognitive psychology*. New York: Freeman.

Erdmann, G., & Van Lindern, B. (1980). The effects of beta-adrenergic stimulation and beta-adrenergic blockade on emotional reactions. *Psychophysiology, 17*, 332–338.

Erhardt, A. A., & Baker, S. W. (1974). Fetal androgens, human central nervous system differentiation, and behavior sex differences. In R. C. Friedman, R. M. Richart, & R. L. Vande Wiele (Eds.), *Sex differences in behavior*. New York: John Wiley.

Ericsson, A. K., Charness, N., Feltovich, P. J., & Hoffman, R. R. (2006). *The Cambridge handbook of expertise and expert performance*. New York: Cambridge University Press.

Ericsson, K. A., & Kintsch, W. (1995). Long-term working memory. *Psychological Review, 102*, 211–245

Erikson, E. (1963). *Childhood and society*. New York: W. W. Norton.

Erikson, E. (1968). *Identity: Youth and crisis*. New York: W. W. Norton.

Erikson, E. (1969). *Gandhi's truth: On the origin of militant nonviolence*. New York: W. W. Norton.

Erkman, F., & Rohner, R. (2006). Youths' perceptions of corporal punishment, parental acceptance, and psychological adjustment in a Turkish metropolis. *Cross-Cultural Research, 40*, 250–267.

Erlenmeyer, K. L., Adamo, U. H., Rock, D., Roberts, S. A., Bassett, A. S., Squires- Wheeler, E., et al. (1997). The New York high-risk project prevalence and comorbidity of axis I disorders in offspring of schizophrenic parents at 25-year follow-up. *Archives of General Psychiatry, 54*, 1096–1102.

Estes, W. K. (1994). *Classification and cognition*. New York: Oxford University Press.

Euler, H. A., & Weitzel, B. (1996). Discriminative grandparental solicitude as reproductive strategy. *Human Nature, 7*, 39–59.

Evans, I. M. (2002). Clinical psychology in early 21st century Aotearoa/New Zealand: Introduction to the special issue. *New Zealand Journal of Psychology, 31*, 50–52.

Evans, J., Heron, J., & Lewis, G. (2005). Negative self-schemas and the onset of depression in women: Longitudinal study. *British Journal of Psychiatry, 186*(4), 302–307.

Evans, K. K., & Singer, J. A. (1994). Studying intimacy through dream narratives: The relationship of dreams to self-report and projective measures of personality. *Imagination, Cognition & Personality, 14*, 211–226.

Evans-Pritchard, E. E. (1956). *Nuer religion*. Oxford: Clarendon Press.

Evers, C., Fischer, A. H., Manstead, A. S. R., & Rodriguez Mosquera, P. M. (2005). Anger and social appraisal: A 'spicy' sex difference? *Emotion, 5*(3), 258–266.

Everson, C. A. (1997). Sleep deprivation and the immune system. In M. R. Pressman & W. C. Orr (Eds.), *Understanding sleep: The evaluation and treatment of sleep disorders. Application and practice in health psychology* (pp. 401–424). Washington, DC: American Psychological Association.

Every, D., & Augoustinos, M. (2007). Constructions of racism in the Australian parliamentary debates on asylum seekers. *Discourse Society, 18*(4), 411–436.

Eysenck, H. (1987). *Theoretical foundations of behavior therapy*. New York: Plenum Press.

Eysenck, H. J. (1952). The effects of psychotherapy: An evaluation. *Journal of Consulting Psychology, 16*, 319–324.

Eysenck, H. J. (1953). *The structure of human personality*. New York: John Wiley.

Eysenck, H. J. (1964). Psychotherapy or behaviour therapy. *Indian Psychological Review, 1*, 33–41.

Eysenck, H. J. (1967). *The biological basis of personality*. Spingfield, IL: Charles C. Thomas.

Eysenck, H. J. (1982). Development of a theory. In H. J. Eysenck (Ed.), *Personality, genetics and behavior: Selected papers* (pp. 593–595). New York: Praeger.

Eysenck, H. J. (1983). Human learning and individual differences: The genetic dimension. *Educational Psychology, 3*, 169–188.

Eysenck, H. J. (1988). Editorial: The concept of IQ: Useful or useless? *Intelligence, 12*, 1–6.

Eysenck, H. J. (1990). Biological dimensions of personality. In L. A. Pervin (Ed.), *Handbook of personality: Theory and research* (pp. 244–276). New York: Guilford Press.

Eysenck, H. J. (1993). Creativity and personality: Suggestions for a theory. *Psychological Inquiry, 4*, 147–178.

Fabrega, H. (1994). International systems of diagnosis in psychiatry. *Journal of Nervous & Mental Disease, 182*, 256–263.

Fabrigar, L. R., Petty, R. E., Smith, S. M., & Crites, S. L., Jr. (2006). Understanding knowledge effects on attitude-behavior consistency: The role of relevance, complexity, and amount of knowledge. *Journal of Personality and Social Psychology, 90*(4), 556–577.

Fagot, B. I. (1985). Changes in thinking about early sex role development. *Developmental Review, 5*, 83–98.

Fagot, B. I., & Patterson, G. R. (1969). An in vivo analysis of reinforcing contingencies for sex-role behaviors in the preschool child. *Developmental Psychology, 1*, 563–568.

Fairburn, C. G., Cooper, Z., Doll, H. A., & Welch, S. L. (1999). Risk factors for anorexia nervosa: Three integrated case-control comparisons. *Archives of General Psychiatry, 56*, 468–476.

Faith, M. S., Rha, S. S., Neale, M. C., & Allison, D. B. (1999). Evidence for genetic influences on human energy intake: Results from a twin study using measured observations. *Behavior Genetics, 29*, 145–154.

Fanselow, M. S. (1998). Pavlovian conditioning, negative feedback, and blocking: Mechanisms that regulate association formation. *Neuron, 20*, 625–627.

Fanselow, M. S., & LeDoux, J. E. (1999). Why we think plasiticity underlying Pavlovian fear conditioning occurs in the basolateral amygdala. *Neuron, 23*, 229–232.

Fanslow, J., & Robinson, E. (2004). Violence against women in New Zealand: Prevalence and health consequences. *The New Zealand Medical Journal, 117*, 1–12.

Fantz, R. L., Fagan, J. F., III, & Miranda, S. B. (1975). Early visual selectivity. In L. B. Cohen & P. Salapatek (Eds.), *Infant perception: From sensation to cognition: Vol. I. Basic visual processes*. New York: Academic Press.

Farah, M. J. (2000). *The cognitive neuroscience of vision*. Malden, MA: Blackwell Publishers.

Faraone, S. V., Biederman, J., Feighner, J. A., & Monuteaux, M. C. (2000). Assessing symptoms of attention deficit hyperactivity disorder in children and adults: Which is more valid? *Journal of Consulting and Clinical Psychology, 68*, 830–842.

Faraone, S. V., Biederman, J., & Milberger, S. (1995). How reliable are maternal reports of their children's psychopathology? One-year recall of psychiatric diagnoses of ADHD children. *Journal of the American Academy of Child & Adolescent Psychiatry, 34*, 1001–1008.

Farber, N. B., Newcomer, J. W., & Olney, J. W. (1999). Glycine agonists: What can they teach us about schizophrenia? *Archives of General Psychiatry, 56*, 13–17.

Faria, A. I. (2001). The future of Indian ethnicity in Australia: An educational and cultural perspective. *International Education Journal, 2*(4), 134–140.

Farmer, C. M., O'Donnell, B. F., Niznikiewicz, M. A., Voglmaier, M. M., McCarley, R. W., & Shenton, M. E. (2000). Visual perception and working memory in schizotypal personality disorder. *American Journal of Psychiatry, 157*, 781–786.

Farrant, B. M., Fletcher, J., & Maybery, M. T. (2006). Specific language impairment, theory of mind and visual perspective taking: Evidence for simulation theory and the developmental role of language. *Child Development, 77*(6), 1842–1853.

Farrant, B.M., Maybery, M.T. & Fletcher, J. (2011). Language, cognitive flexibility and explicit false belief: Longitudinal analysis in typical development and specific language impairment [Special issue]. *Child Development: Raising Healthy Children, 82*(1). doi: 10.1111/j.1467-8624.2010.01566.x

Farrant, E., & Reese, E. (2000). Maternal style and children's participation in reminiscing: Stepping stones in children's autobiographical memory development. *Journal of Cognition & Development, 1*, 193–225.

Farrar, M. (1992). Negative evidence and grammatical morpheme acquisition. *Developmental Psychology, 28*, 90–98.

Fass, P. S. (1980). The I.Q.: A cultural and historical framework. *American Journal of Education, 88*, 431–458.

Faw, B. (2003). Pre-frontal executive committee for perception, working memory, attention, long-term memory, motor control, and thinking: A tutorial review. *Consciousness and Cognition: An International Journal, 12*, 83–139.

Fawcett, A. (2005, October 6). Health and science section. *Sydney Morning Herald*, p. 3.

Fazio, R. (1990). Multiple processes by which attitudes guide behavior: The MODE model as an integrative framework. In L. Berkowitz (Ed.), *Advances in Experimental Social Psychology* (Vol. 23, pp. 75–109).

Fazio, R., Jackson, J. R., Dunton, B., & Williams, C. J. (1995). Variability in automatic activation as an unobtrusive measure of racial attitudes: A bona fide pipeline? *Journal of Personality and Social Psychology, 69*, 1013–1027.

Fazio, R., & Zanna, M. (1981). Direct experience and attitude-behavior consistency. In L. Berkowitz (Ed.), *Advances in experimental social psychology: Vol. 14*. New York: Academic Press.

Fazio, R. H. (1986). How do attitudes guide behavior? In R. M. Sorrentino & E. T. Higgins (Eds.), *The handbook of motivation and cognition: Foundations of social behavior*. New York: Guilford Press.

Fazio, R. H. (1995). Attitudes as object-evaluation associations: Determinants, consequences, and correlates of attitude accessibility. In R. E. Petty & J. A. Krosnick (Eds.), *Attitude strength: Antecedents and consequences. Ohio State University series on attitudes and persuasion: Vol. 4* (pp. 247–282). Mahwah, NJ: Lawrence Erlbaum.

Fazio, R. H., Ledbetter, J. E., & Towles-Schwen, T. (2000). On the costs of accessible attitudes: Detecting that the attitude object has changed. *Journal of Personality and Social Psychology, 78*, 197–210.

Fears, T. R., & Scotto, J. (1982). Changes in skin cancer morbidity between 1971–1972 and 1977–1978. *Journal of the National Cancer Institute, 69*, 365–370.

Feather, N. T. (1989). Behaviour changes after job loss. *Australian Journal of Psychology, 41*, 175–185.

Feather, N. T. (1994). Attitudes towards high achievers and reactions to their fall: Theory and research concerning tall poppies. *Advances in Experimental Social Psychology, 26*, 1–73.

Fehm-Wolfsdorf, G., Soherr, U., Arndt, R., Kern, W., Fehm, H. L., & Nagel, D. (1993). Auditory reflex thresholds elevated by stress-induced cortisol secretion. *Psychoneuroendocrinology, 18*, 579–589.

Fein, S., McCloskey, A. L., & Tomlinson, T. M. (1997). Can the jury disregard that information? The use of suspicion to reduce the prejudicial effects of pretrial publicity and inadmissible testimony. *Personality and Social Psychology Bulletin 23*, 1215–1226.

Feingold, A. (1988). Matching for attractiveness in romantic partners and same-sex friends: A meta-analysis and theoretical critique. *Psychological Bulletin, 104*, 226–235.

Feingold, A. (1992). Good-looking people are not what we think. *Psychological Bulletin, 111*, 304–341.

Feingold, A. (1994). Gender differences in personality: A meta-analysis. *Psychological Bulletin, 116*, 429–456.

Feldman, D. E., Brainard, M. S., & Knudsen, E. I. (1996). Newly learned auditory responses mediated by NMDA receptors in the owl inferior colliculus. *Science, 271*, 525–528.

Feldman, D. H. (2004). Piaget's stages: The unfinished symphony of cognitive development. *New Ideas in Psychology, 22*, 233–237.

Feldman, M. D., & Ford, C. V. (1994). *Patient or pretender: Inside the strange world of factitious disorders*. Oxford: John Wiley & Sons.

Feng, A. S., & Ratnam, R. (2000). Neural basis of hearing in real-world situations. *Annual Review of Psychology, 51*, 699–725.

Fergus, S., & Zimmerman, M. (2005). Adolescent resilience: A framework for understanding healthy development in the face of risk. *Annual Review of Public Health, 26*, 399–419.

Ferguson, C., & Kilburn, J. (2009). The public health risks of media violence: A meta-analytic review. *Journal of Pediatrics*. Retrieved from http://www.tamiu.edu/~cferguson/MVJPED.pdf

Ferguson, E. D. (2000). *Motivation: A biosocial and cognitive integration of motivation and emotion*. New York: Oxford University Press.

Fergusson, D. M., Horwood, L. J., & Swain-Campbell, N. R. (2003). Cannabis dependence and psychotic symptoms in young people. *Psychological Medicine, 33*(1), 15–21.

Fernald, A., & Kuhl, P. (1987). Acoustic determinants of infant preference for motherese speech. *Infant Behavior and Development, 10*, 279–293.

Fernald, R. D. (1996). Recognition of visual signals: Eyes specialize. In C. F. Moss & S. J. Shettleworth (Eds.), *Neuroethological studies of cognitive and perceptual processes* (pp. 229–249). Boulder, CO: Westview Press.

Ferrie, J. E., Shipley, M. J., Cappuccio, F. P., Brunner, E., Miller, M. A., Kumari, M., et al. (2007). A prospective study of change in sleep duration: Associations with mortality in the Whitehall II cohort. *Sleep, 30*(12), 1659–1666.

Ferris, S., McGauley, G., & Hughes, P. (2004). Attachment disorganization in infancy: Relation to psychoanalytic understanding of development. *Psychoanalytic Psychotherapy, 18*, 151–166.

Ferro, T., Verdeli, H., Pierre, F., & Weissman, M. M. (2000). Screening for depression in mothers bringing their offspring for evaluation or treatment of depression. *American Journal of Psychiatry, 157*, 375–379.

Ferster, C. B., & Skinner, B. F. (1957). *Schedules of reinforcement*. East Norwalk, CT: Appleton-Century-Crofts.

Ferster, D., & Miller, K. D. (2000). Neural mechanisms of orientation selectivity in the visual cortex. *Annual Review of Neuroscience, 23*, 441–471.

Festinger, L. (1957). *A theory of cognitive dissonance*. New York: Harper & Row.

Festinger, L. (1962). Cognitive dissonance. *Scientific American, 107*, 409–415.

Festinger, L., & Carlsmith, J. M. (1959). Cognitive consequences of forced compliance. *Journal of Abnormal and Social Psychology, 58*, 203–210.

Festinger, L., Schachter, S., & Back, K. (1950). *Social pressures in informal groups: A study of human factors in housing*. New York: Harper Bros.

Fieder, M., & Huber, S. (2007, December). Parental age difference and offspring count in humans. *Biology Letters, 3*(6), 689–691.

Fiedler, F. E. (1978). The contingency model and the dynamics of the leadership process. In L. Berkowitz (Ed.), *Advances in experimental social psychology: Vol. 12* (pp. 59–112). New York: Academic Press.

Fiedler, F. E. (1981). Leadership effectiveness. *American Behavioral Scientist, 24*, 619–632.

Field, A. E., Camargo, C. A., Jr., Taylor, C. B., Berkey, C. S., Frazier, L., Gillman, M. W., et al. (1999). Overweight, weight concerns, and bulimic behaviors among girls and boys. *Journal of the American Academy of Child and Adolescent Psychiatry, 38*, 754–760.

Figert, A. E. (2005). Premenstrual syndrome as scientific and cultural artefact. *Integrative Physiological and Behavioral Science, 40*, 102–113.

Fincham, F. D. (1998). Child development and marital relations. *Child Development, 69*, 543–574.

Fincham, F. D., & Beach, S. R. H. (1999). Conflict in marriage: Implications for working with couples. *Annual Review of Psychology, 50*, 47–77.

Fink, M. (2001). Convulsive therapy: A review of the first 55 years. *Journal of Affective Disorders, 63*, 1–15.

Finkelhor, D. (1994). The international epidemiology of child sexual abuse. *Child Abuse and Neglect, 18*, 409–417.

Finlay, B. L., & Darlington, R. (1995). Linked regularities in the development and evolution of mammalian brains. *Science, 268*, 1578–1583.

Finlay-Jones, R., & Brown, G. W. (1981). Types of stressful life event and the onset of anxiety and depressive disorders. *Psychological Medicine, 11*, 803–815.

Finn, P. R., Sharkansky, E. J., Brandt, K. M., & Turcotte, N. (2000). The effects of familial risk, personality, and expectancies on alcohol use and abuse. *Journal of Abnormal Psychology, 109*, 122–133.

Finzi-Dottan, R., Manor, I., & Tyano, S. (2006). ADHD, temperament, and parental style as predictors of the child's attachment patterns. *Child Psychiatry & Human Development, 37*, 103–114.

Fiore, M. C., Bailey, W. C., Cohen, S. J., Dorfman, S. F., Fox, B. J., Goldstein, M. G., et al. (2000). *Treating tobacco use and dependence: Clinical practice guideline*. Rockville, MD: U.S. Department of Health and Human Service.

Fischer, A. H. (Ed.). (2000). *Gender and emotion: Social psychological perspectives*. New York: Cambridge University Press

Fischer, A. H., Manstead, A. S. R., Rodriguez Mosquera, P. M., & van Vianen, A. E. M. (2004). Gender and culture differences in emotion. *Emotion, 4*, 87–94.

Fischer, K. W. (1980). A theory of cognitive development: The control and construction of hierarchies of skills. *Psychological Review, 87*, 477–531.

Fischer, K. W., & Bidell, T. R. (1997). Dynamic development of psychological structures in action and thought. In W. Damon & R. Lerner (Eds.), *Handbook of child psychology. Vol. 1: Theoretical models of human development* (5th ed., pp. 467–561). New York: Wiley.

Fischer, K. W., Shaver, P. R., & Carnochan, P. (1990). How emotions develop and how they organize development. *Cognition and Emotion, 4*, 81–127.

Fiset, P., Paus, T., Daloze, T., Plourde, G., Meuret, P., Bonhomme, V., et al. (1999). Brain mechanisms of propofol-induced loss of consciousness in humans: A positron emission tomographic study. *Journal of Neuroscience, 19*, 5506–5513.

Fishbein, M., & Ajzen, I. (1974). Attitudes towards objects as predictors of single and multiple behavioral criteria. *Psychologial Review, 81*, 59–74.

Fisher, A. (2011, March 1). Many not prepared for big earthquake. *The Dominion Post*. Retrieved from http://www.stuff.co.nz/the-press/news/4714717/Many-not-prepared-for-big-earthquake

Fisher, R. (1998). Thinking about thinking: Developing metacognition in children. *Early Child Development and Care, 141*(1), 1–15.

Fisher, R. J. (1994). Generic principles for resolving intergroup conflict. *Journal of Social Issues, 50*, 47–66.

Fisher, S., & Greenberg, R. P. (1985). *The scientific credibility of Freud's theories and therapy*. New York: Columbia University Press.

Fisher, S., & Greenberg, R. P. (1996). *Freud scientifically reappraised. Testing the theories and therapy*. New York: John Wiley & Sons.

Fishkin, J., Keniston, K., & MacKinnon, C. (1973). Moral reasoning and political ideology. *Journal of Personality and Social Psychology, 27*, 109–119.

Fishman, E. A., & Meyers, S. A. (2000). Marital satisfaction and child adjustment: Direct and mediated pathways. *Contemporary Family Therapy, 22*, 437–452.

Fiske, A. P., Kitayama, S., Markus, H. R., & Nisbett, R. E. (1998). The cultural matrix of social psychology. In D. T. Gilbert & S. T. Fiske (Eds.), *The handbook of social psychology: Vol. 2* (4th ed., pp. 915–981). Boston: McGraw-Hill.

Fiske, S. (1992). Thinking is for doing: Portraits of social cognition from daguerreotype to laserphoto. *Journal of Personality and Social Psychology, 63*, 877–889.

Fiske, S. (1995). Social cognition. In A. Tesser (Ed.), *Constructing social psychology*. New York: McGraw-Hill.

Fiske, S. T. (1993). Social cognition and social perception. *Annual Review of Psychology, 44*, 155–194.

Fiske, S. T. (1998). Stereotyping, prejudice, and discrimination. In D. T. Gilbert, S. T. Fiske, & G. Lindzey (Eds.), *The handbook of social psychology: Vol. 2* (4th ed., pp. 357–411). Boston: McGraw-Hill.

Fiske, S. T., & Taylor, S. E. (1991). *Social cognition* (2nd ed.). New York: McGraw-Hill.

Fisman, R., Iyengar, S. S., Kamenica, E., & Simonson, I. (2006, May). Gender differences in mate selection: Evidence from a speed dating experiment. *The Quarterly Journal of Economics, 673*, 673–697.

Fitness, J., & Case, T. I. (2003). The emotional brain drives the social mind. *Connexions, 6*, 17–20. Retrieved November 30, 2007, from http://www.open.ac.uk/Arts/connex/

Flanagan, J. C. (1978). A research approach to improving our quality of life. *American Psychologist, 33*, 138–147.

Flanagan, O. (2000). *Dreaming souls: Sleep, dreams, and the evolution of the conscious mind*. New York: Oxford University Press.

Flavell, J., Green, F. L., Flavell, E., & Grossman, J. B. (1997). The development of children's knowledge about inner speech. *Child Development, 68*, 39–47.

Flavell, J. H. (Ed.). (1977). *Cognitive development*. Oxford: Prentice-Hall.

Flavell, J. H. (1982). Structures, stages, and sequences in cognitive development. In W. A. Collins (Ed.), *The concept of development: Vol. 15*. Hillsdale, NJ: Lawrence Erlbaum.

Flavell, J. H. (1992). Perspectives on perspective taking. In H. Beilin & P. B. Pufall (Eds.), *Piaget's theory: Prospects and possibilities. The Jean Piaget symposium series* (pp. 107–139). Hillsdale, NJ: Lawrence Erlbaum.

Flavell, J. H. (1996). Piaget's legacy. *Psychological Science, 7*, 200–203.

Flavell, J. H. (1999). Cognitive development: Children's knowledge about the mind. *Annual Review of Psychology, 50*, 21–45.

Flavell, J. H., Botkin, P. T., Fry, C. L., Jr., Wright, J. W., & Jarvis, P. E. (1968). *The development of role-taking and communications skills in children*. New York: John Wiley.

Flavell, J. H., Friedrichs, A. G., & Hoyt, J. D. (1970). Developmental changes in memorization processes. *Cognitive Psychology, 1*, 324–340.

Flavell, J. H., Green, F. L., Flavell, E. R., & Lin, N. T. (1999). Development of children's knowledge about unconsciousness. *Child Development, 70*, 396–412.

Flavell, J. H., & Miller, P. H. (1998). Social cognition. In W. Damon (Ed. in Chief) & N. Eisenberg (Vol. Ed.), *Handbook of child psychology: Vol. 2* (pp. 851–898). New York: John Wiley.

Flavell, J. H., & Wellman, H. M. (1977). Metamemory. In R. V. Kail Jr. & J. W. Hagen (Eds.), *Perspectives on the development of memory and cognition*. Hillsdale, NJ: Lawrence Erlbaum.

Fletcher, G. J. O., Tither, J. M., O'Loughlin, C., Friesen, M., & Overall, N. (2004). Warm and homely or cold and beautiful? Sex differences in trading off traits in mate selection. *Personality and Social Psychology Bulletin, 30*, 659–672.

Fletcher, G. L. (2002). *The new science of intimate relationships*. Malden, MA: Blackwell.

Fletcher, G. O., Simpson, J. A., Thomas, G., & Giles, L. (1999). Ideals in intimate relationships. *Journal of Personality and Social Psychology, 76*, 72–89.

Floderus-Myrhed, B., Pedersen, N., & Rasmuson, L. (1980). Assessment of heritability for personality based on a short form of the Eysenck Personality Inventory: A study of 12,898 twin pairs. *Behaviour Genetics, 10*, 153–162.

Flor, H., Haag, G., & Turl, D. C. (1986). Long-term efficacy of EMG biofeedback for chronic rheumatic back pain. *Pain, 27*, 195–202.

Flooding resupply effort underway in northern NSW. (2011, January). *ABC News*. Retrieved from http://www.abc.net.au/news/stories/2011/01/16/3113804.htm?section=justin

Flynn, J. R. (1987). Massive IQ gains in 14 nations: What IQ tests really measure? *Psychological Bulletin, 101*, 171–191.

Flynn, J. R. (1999). Searching for justice: The discovery of IQ gains over time. *American Psychologist, 54*, 5–20.

Foa, E. B., Dancu, C. V., Hembree, E. A., Jaycox, L. H., Meadows, E. A., & Street, G. P. (1999). A comparison of exposure therapy, stress inoculation training, and their combination for reducing post-traumatic stress disorder in female assault victims. *Journal of Consulting and Clinical Psychology, 67*, 194–200.

Focht, B. C., & Hausenblas, H. A. (2004). Perceived evaluative threat and state anxiety during exercise in women with social physique anxiety. *Journal of Applied Sport Psychology, 16*, 361–368.

Fodor, J. (1983). *The modularity of mind*. Cambridge, MA: MIT Press.

Foels, R., & Reid, L. D. (2010). Gender differences in social dominance orientation: The role of cognitive complexity. *Sex Roles, 62*(9), 684–692.

Fogarty, G., & White, C. (2002). Person-environment fit in higher education: How good is the fit for indigenous students? In D. McInerney & S. Van Etten (Eds.), *Sociocultural influences on motivation and learning* (pp. 129–149). Greenwich, CT: Information Age Publishing.

Fogel, A., Melson, G. F., & Mistry, J. (1986). Conceptualizing the determinants of nurturance: A reassessment of sex differences. In A. Fogel & G. F. Melson (Eds.), *Origins of nurturance*. Hillsdale, NJ: Lawrence Erlbaum.

Folkman, S., & Lazarus, R. S. (1980). An analysis of coping in a middle-aged community sample. *Journal of Health and Social Behavior, 21*, 219–239.

Folkman, S., & Moskowitz, J. T. (2000). Positive affect and the other side of coping. *American Psychologist, 55,* 647–654.

Fonagy, P., Steele, H., & Steele, M. (1991). Maternal representations of attachment during pregnancy predict the organization of infant–mother attachment at one year of age. *Child Development, 62,* 891–905.

Fonagy, P., & Target, M. (2000). The place of psychodynamic theory in developmental psychopathology. *Development and Psychopathology, 12,* 407–425.

Forbes, D., Phelps, A. J., McHugh, A. F., Debenham, P., Hopwood, M., & Creamer, M. (2003). Imagery rehearsal in the treatment of posttraumatic nightmares in Australian veterans with chronic combat-related PTSD: 12-month follow-up data. *Journal of Traumatic Stress, 16,* 509–513.

Ford, J. M., & Mathalon, D. H. (2005). Corollary discharge dysfunction in schizophrenia: Can it explain auditory hallucinations? *International Journal of Psychophysiology, 58,* 179–189.

Ford, M. (1979). The construct validity of egocentrism. *Psychological Bulletin, 86,* 1169–1188.

Foreyt, J. P. (1987). Issues in the assessment and treatment of obesity. *Journal of Consulting and Clinical Psychology, 55,* 677–684.

Foreyt, J. P., & Goodrick, G. D. (1995). The ultimate triumph of obesity. *Lancet, 346,* 134–135.

Forgas, J. P. (1995). Mood and judgment: The affect infusion model (AIM). *Psychological Bulletin, 117,* 39–66.

Forsterling, F., Preikschas, S., & Agthe, M. (2007). Ability, luck, and looks: An evolutionary look at achievement ascriptions and the sexual attribution bias. *Journal of Personality and Social Psychology, 92*(5), 775–788.

Forsyth, D. R. (1990). *Group dynamics* (2nd ed.). Pacific Grove, CA: Brooks/Cole.

Foster, G. (1965). Peasant society and the image of limited good. *American Anthropologist, 67,* 293–315.

Foster, J. D., Campbell, W. K., & Twenge, J. M. (2003). Individual differences in narcissism: Inflated self-views across the lifespan and around the world. *Journal of Research in Personality, 37,* 469–486.

Foster, M. A., Jurkovic, G. J., Ferdinand, L. G., & Meadows, L. A. (2002). The impact of the genogram on couples: A manualized approach. *Family Journal Counseling and Therapy for Couples and Families, 10,* 34–40.

Foulkes, D. (1982). REM-dream perspectives on the development of affect and cognition. *Psychiatric Journal of the University of Ottawa, 7,* 48–55.

Foulkes, D. (1993). Data constraints on theorizing about dream function. In A. Moffitt & M. Kramer (Eds.), *The functions of dreaming* (pp. 11–20). Albany, NY: State University of New York Press.

Fowles, D. C. (1992). Schizophrenia: Diathesis–stress revisited. *Annual Review of Psychology, 43,* 303–336.

Fox, N. (1991). If it's not left, it's right: Electroencephalograph asymmetry and the development of emotion. *American Psychologist, 46,* 863–872.

Fox, N. A., Rubin, K. H., Calkins, S. D., Marshall, T. R., Coplan, R. J., Porges, S. W., et al. (1995). Frontal activation asymmetry and social competence at four years of age. *Child Development, 66,* 1770–1784.

Fozard, J. (1990). Vision and hearing in aging. In J. Birren & K. W. Schaie (Eds.), *Handbook of the psychology of aging* (3rd ed.). New York: Academic Press.

Fraiberg, S. (1975). The development of human attachments in infants blind from birth. *Merrill-Palmer Quarterly, 21,* 315–334.

Fraley, R. C., & Roberts, B. W. (2005). Patterns of continuity: A dynamic model for conceptualizing the stability of individual differences in psychological constructs across the life course. *Psychological Review, 112,* 60–74.

Fraley, R. C., & Shaver, P. R. (1998). Airport separations: A naturalistic study of adult attachment dynamics in separating couples. *Journal of Personality & Social Psychology, 75,* 1198–1212.

Fraley, R. C., Waller, N. G., & Bennan, K. A. (2000). An item response theory analysis of self-report measures of adult attachment. *Journal of Personality and Social Psychology, 78,* 350–365.

Frank, E., Anderson, B., Reynolds, C. F., Ritenour, A., & Kupfer, D. J. (1994). Life events and the research diagnostic criteria endogenous subtype: A confirmation of the distinction using the Bedford College methods. *Archives of General Psychiatry, 51,* 519–524.

Frank, E., Swartz, H. A., Mallinger, A. G., Thase, M. E., Weaver, E. V., & Kupfer, D. J. (1999). Adjunctive psychotherapy for bipolar disorder: Effects of changing treatment modality. *Journal of Abnormal Psychology, 108,* 579–587.

Freud, S. (1958). The dynamics of transference. In J. Strachey (Ed., Trans.), *The standard edition of the complete psychological works of Sigmund Freud: Vol. 12* (pp. 97–108). London: Hogarth. (Originally published 1912)

Freud, S. (1963). The unconscious. In P. Rieff (Ed.), *Freud: General psychological theory*. New York: Collier. (Originally published 1915)

Freud, S. (1963). Mourning and melancholia. In P. Reiff (Ed.), *Freud: General psychological theory*. New York: Collier. (Originally published 1917)

Freud, S. (1965). *New introductory lectures on psychoanalysis*. New York: W.W. Norton. (Originally published 1933)

Freud, S. (1965). *The interpretation of dreams*. New York: Avon. (Originally published 1900)

Freud, S. (1966). Project for a scientific psychology. In J. Strachey (Ed.), *The standard edition of the complete psychological works of Sigmund Freud: Vol. 1*. London: Hogarth Press. (Originally published 1895)

Fried, C. B., & Aronson, E. (1995). Hypocrisy, misattribution, and dissonance reduction. *Personality and Social Psychology Bulletin, 21,* 925–933.

Fried, P. A. (1995). The Ottawa Prenatal Prospective Study (OPPS): Methodological issues and findings: It's easy to throw the baby out with the bath water [Special issue: 1994 International Symposium on Cannabis and the Cannabinoids: Developmental effects]. *Life Sciences, 56,* 2159–2168.

Friedman, J. M. (2000). Obesity in the new millennium. *Nature, 404,* 632–634.

Friedman, L. S., Lichtenstein, E., & Biglan, A. (1985). Smoking onset among teens: An empirical analysis of initial situations. *Addictive Behaviors, 10,* 1–13.

Friedman, M., & Rosenman, R. H. (1959). Association of specific overt behavior pattern with blood and cardiovascular findings — blood cholesterol level, blood clotting time, incidence of arcus senilis, and clinical coronary heart disease. *Journal of the American Medical Association, 162,* 1286–1296.

Friedman, M. A., & Brownell, K. D. (1995). Psychological correlates of obesity: Moving to the next research generation. *Psychological Bulletin, 117,* 3–20.

Frith, C. (2005). The neural basis of hallucinations and delusions. *Comptes Rendus Biologies, 328,* 169–175.

Frith, C., & Dolan, R. (1996). The role of the prefrontal cortex in higher cognitive functions. *Cognitive Brain Research, 5,* 175–181.

Fromkin, V., Krashen, S., Curtiss, S., Rigler, D., & Rigler, M. (1974). The development of language in Genie: A case of language acquisition beyond the critical period. *Brain and Language, 1,* 81–107.

Fromm, E. (1955). *The sane society*. Greenwich, CT: Fawcett Books.

Fry, A. F., & Hale, S. (1996). Processing speed, working memory, and fluid intelligence: Evidence for a developmental cascade. *Psychologial Science, 7,* 237–241.

Frydenberg, E., & Lewis, R. (2009). The relationship between problem-solving efficacy and coping amongst Australian adolescents. *British Journal of Guidance & Counselling, 37*(1), 51–64.

Fullagar, S., & Gattuso, S. (2002). Rethinking gender, risk and depression in Australian mental health policy. *Australian e-Journal for the Advancement of Mental Health, 1*(3), 1–13.

Fulero, S. M., & Wrightsman, L. S. (2009). *Forensic psychology* (3rd ed.). Belmont, CA: Wadsworth.

Funder, D., & Colvin, C. R. (1991). Explorations in behavioral consistency: Properties of persons, situations, and behaviors. *Journal of Personality and Social Psychology, 60,* 773–794.

Fussel, S. R., & Krauss, R. M. (1992). Coordination of knowledge in communication: Effects of speakers' assumptions about what others know. *Journal of Personality and Social Psychology, 62,* 378–391.

Fuster, J. (1989). *The prefrontal cortex* (2nd ed.). New York: Raven.

Fuster, J. M. (1997). Network memory. *Trends in Neurosciences, 20,* 451–459.

Fyer, A. J., Mannuzza, S., Chapman, T. F., Martin, L. Y., & Klein, D. F. (1995). Specificity in familial aggregation of phobic disorders. *Archives of General Psychiatry, 52,* 564–573.

Gabbard, G. (1992). Psychodynamic psychiatry in the 'decade of the brain.' *American Journal of Psychiatry, 149,* 991–998.

Gabbard, G. O., & Atkinson, S. D. (Eds.). (1996). *Synopsis of treatments for psychiatric disorders* (2nd ed.). Washington, DC: American Psychiatric Association.

Gabbay, F. (1992). Behavior-genetic strategies in the study of emotion. *Psychological Science, 3,* 50–55.

Gable, S. L., & Reis, H. T. (1999). Now and then, them and us, this and that: Studying relationships across time, partner, context, and person. *Personal Relationships, 6,* 415–432.

Gabrieli, J. D. (1998). Cognitive neuroscience of human memory. *Annual Review of Psychology, 49,* 87–115.

Gabrieli, J. D., Desmond, J. E., Demb, J. B., Wagner, A. D., Stone, M. V., Vaidya, C. J., et al. (1996). Functional magnetic resonance imaging of semantic memory processes in the frontal lobes. *Psychological Science, 7,* 278–283.

Gadow, K., & Sprafkin, J. (1993). Television violence and children with emotional and behavioral disorders. *Journal of Emotional and Behavioral Disorders, 1,* 54–63.

Gaeddert, A. (2010). *The herbal approaches to treating memory loss, dementia, and Alzheimer's disease*. Retrieved from http://acupuncturetoday.com/mpacms/at/article.php?id=28184

Gaensbauer, T., Chatoor, I., Drell, M., Siegel, D., & Zeanah, C. H. (1995). Traumatic loss in a one-year old girl. *Journal of the American Academy of Child and Adolescent Psychiatry, 34,* 520–528.

Galinsky, A. D., & Moskowitz, G. B. (2000). Perspective-taking: Decreasing stereotype expression, stereotype accessibility, and in-group favoritism. *Journal of Personality and Social Psychology, 78,* 708–724.

Gallistel, C. R., & Gibbon, J. (2000). Time, rate, and conditioning. *Psychological Review, 107,* 289–344.

Gallup, G. H. (1972). It's done with mirrors: Chimps and self-concept. *Psychology Today, 4,* 58–61.

Galton, F. (1883). *Enquires into human faculty and its development*. London: Macmillan.

Gamsa, A. (1990). Is emotional disturbance a precipitator or a consequence of chronic pain? *Pain, 42,* 183–195.

Gangestad, S. W., Haselton, M. G., & Buss, D. M. (2006). Evolutionary foundations of cultural variation: Evoked culture and mate preferences. *Psychological Inquiry, 17,* 75–95.

Gangestad, S. W., & Snyder, M. (2000). Self-monitoring: Appraisal and reappraisal. *Psychological Bulletin, 126,* 530–555.

Ganley, R. (1989). Emotion and eating in obesity: A view of the literature. *International Journal of Eating Disorders, 8,* 343–361.

Gannon, P. J., Holloway, R. L., Broadfield, D. C., & Braun, A. R. (1998). Asymmetry of chimpanzee planum temporale: Human-like pattern of Wernicke's brain language, area homolog. *Science, 279,* 220–222.

Garb, H. N. (1984). The incremental validity of information used in personality assessment. *Clinical Psychological Review, 40,* 641–655.

Garcia, J. (1979). I.Q.: The conspiracy. In J. B. Maas (Ed.), *Readings in psychology today* (4th ed., pp. 198–202). New York: Random House.

Garcia, J., & Garcia y Robertson, R. (1985). Evolution of learning mechanisms. In B. L. Hammonds (Ed.), *The master lecture series. Vol. 4: Psychology and learning* (pp. 191–243). Washington, DC: American Psychological Association.

Garcia, J., & Koelling, R. (1966). Relation of cue to consequence in avoidance learning. *Psychonomic Science, 4,* 123–124.

Garcia, J., Lasiter, P., Bermudez-Rattoni, & Deems, D. (1985). A general theory of aversion learning. *Annals of the New York Academy of Sciences, 443,* 8–21.

Gardner, B. T., & Gardner, R. A. (1975). Evidence for sentence constituents in the early utterances of child and chimpanzee. *Journal of Experimental Psychology: General, 104,* 244–267.

Gardner, H. (1983). *Frames of mind: The theory of multiple intelligences*. New York: Basic Books. Basic Books Paperback, 1985. Tenth Anniversary Edition with new introduction, New York: Basic Books, 1993.

Gardner, H. (1985). *The mind's new science: A history of the cognitive revolution*. New York: Basic Books.

Gardner, H. (1993). *Frames of mind: The theory of multiple intelligences*. New York: Basic Books.

Gardner, H. (1999). *Intelligence reframed: Multiple intelligences for the 21st century*. New York: Basic Books.

Gardner, H. (2000). The giftedness matrix: A developmental perspective. In R. C. Friedman & B. M. Shore (Eds.), *Talents unfolding: Cognition and development* (pp. 77–88). Washington, DC: American Psychological Association.

Gardner, H. (2008). Who owns intelligence? In M. H. Immordino-Yang (Ed.), *The Jossey-Bass reader on the brain and learning* (pp. 120–132). San Francisco: Jossey-Bass.

Garfield, C. (1986). *Peak performers: The new heroes of American business*. New York: Morrow.

Garner, D. M., & Garfinkel, P. E. (1979). The Eating Attitudes Test: An index of the symptoms of anorexia nervosa. *Psychological Medicine, 9,* 273–279.

Garner, D. M., & Wooley, S. (1991). Confronting the failure of behavioral and dietary treatments for obesity. *Clinical Psychology Review, 11,* 729–780.

Garrett, P. W., Dickson, H. G., Whelan, A. K., & Whyte, L. (2010). Representations and coverage of non-English-speaking immigrants and multicultural issues in three major health care publications. *Australia and New Zealand Health Policy, 7,* 1–13.

Garver, D. L. (1997). The etiologic heterogeneity of schizophrenia. *Harvard Review of Psychiatry, 4,* 317–327.

Garvey, D., Dudgeon, P., & Kearins, J. (2000). Australian psychology has a black history. In P. Dudgeon, D. Garvey, & H. Pickett (Eds.), *Working with Indigenous Australians: A handbook for psychologists* (pp. 231–247). Perth, Australia: Gunada Press.

Gaudreau, D., & Peretz, I. (1999). Implicit and explicit memory for music in old and young adults. *Brain & Cognition, 40,* 126–129.

Gauthier, J. G., Ivers, H., & Carrier, S. (1996). Nonpharmacological approaches in the management of recurrent headache disorders and their comparison and combination with pharmacotherapy. *Clinical Psychology Review, 16,* 543–571.

Gava, I., Barbui, C., Aguglia, E., Carlino, D., Churchill, R., De Vanna, M., et al. (2007). Psychological treatments versus treatment as usual for obsessive compulsive disorder (OCD). *Cochrane Database of Systematic Reviews, 2*(CD005333), 1–41.

Gavey, N. (2005). *Just sex? The cultural scaffolding of rape*. London: Routledge.

Gazzaniga, M. (1967). The split brain in man. *Scientific American, 217,* 24–29.

Gazzaniga, M. S., & Heatherton, T. F. (2003). *Psychological science: Mind, brain, and behaviour*. New York: Norton.

Ge, X., Conger, R. D., & Elder, G. (1996). Coming of age too early: Pubertal influences on girls' vulnerability to psychological distress. *Child Development, 67,* 3386–3400.

Geary, D. C., Rumsey, M., Bow-Thomas, C. C., & Hoard, M. K. (1995). Sexual jealousy as a facultative trait: Evidence from the pattern of sex differences in adults from China and the United States. *Ethology and Sociobiology, 16,* 355–383.

Gebhard, P. H. (1971). Human sexual behavior: A summary statement. In D. S. Marshall & R. C. Suggs (Eds.), *Human sexual behavior: Variations in the ethnographic spectrum*. New York: Basic Books.

Geen, R. G. (1995). Human aggression. In A. Tesser (Ed.), *Advanced social psychology*. New York: McGraw-Hill.

Geen, R. G. (1998). Aggression and antisocial behavior. In D. T. Gilbert, S. T. Fiske, & G. Lindzey (Eds.), *The handbook of social psychology: Vol. 2* (4th ed., pp. 317–356). Boston: McGraw-Hill.

Geen, R. G. (2001). *Human aggression* (2nd ed.). New York: Taylor & Francis.

Geertz, C. (1963). The integrative revolution: Primordial sentiments and civil politics in the new states. In C. Geertz (Ed.), *Old societies and new states*. New York: Free Press

Geertz, C. (1974). From the natives' point of view. *American Academy of Arts and Sciences Bulletin, 28,* 26–43.

Geldard, G. A. (1972). *The human senses* (2nd ed.). New York: John Wiley.

Gelinas, D. J. (1983). The persisting negative effects of incest. *Psychiatry, 46,* 312–332.

Gelman, R., & Baillargeon, R. (1983). A review of Piagetian concepts. In J. H. Flavell & E. M. Markman (Eds.), *Handbook of child psychology: Cognitive development: Vol. 3*. New York: John Wiley.

Gentner, D. (1983). Structure-mapping: A theoretical framework for analogy. *Cognitive Science, 7,* 155–170.

Gentner, D., & Holyoak, K. J. (1997). Reasoning and learning by analogy: Introduction. *American Psychologist, 52,* 32–34.

Gentner, D., & Markman, A. B. (1997). Structure mapping in analogy and similarity. *American Psychologist, 52,* 45–46.

George, D., Carroll, P., Kersnick, R., & Calderon, K. (1998). Gender-related patterns of helping among friends. *Psychology of Women Quarterly, 22,* 685–704.

Gerken, L., & McIntosh, B. J. (1993). Interplay of function morphemes and prosody in early language. *Developmental Psychology, 29,* 448–457.

Gershon, S., & Soares, J. C. (1997). Current therapeutic profile of lithium. *Archives of General Psychiatry, 54,* 16–20.

Gerstner, C., & Day, D. V. (1994). Cross-cultural comparison of leadership prototypes. *Leadership Quarterly, 5,* 121–134.

Gerull, F. C., & Rapee, R. M. (2002). Mother knows best: Effects of maternal modelling on the acquisition of fear and avoidance behaviour in toddlers. *Behaviour Research and Therapy, 40*(3), 279–287.

Gest, S. D. (1997). Behavioral inhibition: Stability and associations with adaptation from childhood to early adulthood. *Journal of Personality and Social Psychology, 72,* 467–475.

Ghaderi, A. (2006). The foundation of the self and the assessment of self-esteem. In A. Prescott (Ed.), *The concept of self in psychology* (pp. 69–86). New York: Nova Science Publishers.

Gibbs, R. W., Jr. (1981). Your wish is my command: Convention and context in interpreting indirect requests. *Journal of Verbal Learning and Verbal Behavior, 20,* 431–444.

Gibson, E. J. (1984). Perceptual development from the ecological approach. In M. E. Lamb, A. L. Brown, & B. Rogoff (Eds.), *Advances in developmental psychology: Vol. 3*. Hillsdale, NJ: Lawrence Erlbaum Associates.

Gibson, E. J., & Walk, R. D. (1960). The 'visual cliff.' *Scientific American, 202,* 64–71.

Gibson, J. J. (1966). *The senses considered as perceptual systems*. Boston: Houghton Mifflin.

Gibson, J. J. (1979). *The ecological approach to visual perception*. Boston: Houghton Mifflin.

Giesler, R. B., Josephs, R. A., & Swann, W. B., Jr. (1996). Self-verification in clinical depression: The desire for negative evaluation. *Journal of Abnormal Psychology, 105,* 358–368.

Gigerenzer, G., & Goldstein, D. G. (1996). Reasoning the fast and frugal way: Models of bounded rationality. *Psychological Review, 103,* 650–669.

Gilbert, D. (1989). Thinking lightly about others: Automatic components of the social inference process. In J. S. Uleman & J. A. Bargh (Eds.), *Unintended thought* (pp. 189–211). New York: Guilford Press.

Gilbert, D. T., Fiske, S. T., & Lindzey, G. (1998). *The handbook of social psychology: Vol. 1* (4th ed.). Boston: McGraw-Hill.

Gilbert, D. T., & Malone, P. S. (1995). The correspondence bias. *Psychological Bulletin, 117,* 21–38.

Gilbert, L. (1995). The articulation of circumstance and causal understandings. In D. Sperber & D. Premack (Eds.), *Causal cognition: A multidisciplinary debate* (pp. 557–576). New York: Oxford University Press.

Gilbert, P. L., Harris, M. J., McAdams, L. A., & Jeste, D. V. (1995). Neuroleptic withdrawal in schizophrenic patients: A review of the literature. *Archives of General Psychiatry, 52,* 173–188.

Gilboa, E., & Gotlib, I. H. (1997). Cognitive biases and affect persistence in previously dysphoric and never-dysphoric individuals. *Cognition & Emotion, 11,* 517–538.

Giles, M., McClenahan, C., Cairns, E., & Mallet, J. (2004). An application of the theory of planned behaviour to blood donation: The importance of self-efficacy. *Health Education Research, 19*(4), 380–391. Retrieved from http://her.oxfordjournals.org/cgi/reprint/19/4/380

Gilhooly, K. J. (1989). Human and machine problem solving: Toward a comparative cognitive science. In K. J. Gilhooly (Ed.), *Human and machine problem solving*. New York: Plenum Press.

Gill, M. (1982). *The analysis of transference: Vol. 1. Theory and technique. Psychological issues, monograph, no. 53*. New York: International Universities Press.

Gilleard, C. J. (2000). Is Alzheimer's disease preventable? A review of two decades of epidemiological research. *Aging & Mental Health, 4,* 101–118.

Gillies, C. (2007, February). Institutional safety: An important step towards achieving cultural safety. *InPsych, 29*(1), 12–13.

Gilligan, C. (1982). *In a different voice*. Cambridge, MA: Harvard University Press.

Gilligan, J. (1996). Exploring shame in special settings: A psychotherapeutic study. In C. Cordess & M. Cox (Eds.), *Forensic psychotherapy: Crime, psychodynamics and the offender patient: Vol. 2. Mainly practice. Forensic focus series, no. 1* (pp. 475–489). London: Jessica Kingsley Publishers.

Gilman, S. E., Kawachi, I., Fitzmaurice, G. M., & Buka, S. L. (2003). Family disruption in childhood and risk of adult depression. *American Journal of Psychiatry, 160*(5), 939–946.

Giri, P. A., Phalke, D. B., Kishve, S. P., Mangla, D., & Syed, M. M. A. (2010). Otorhinolaryngological disorders in a geriatric population: A study from a rural tertiary care hospital in India. *Australasian Medical Journal, 1*(5), 291–294.

Gladue, B. A., Green, R., & Hellman, R. E. (1984). Neuroendocrine response to estrogen and sexual orientation. *Science, 225,* 1496–1499.

Gladwin, T. (1970). *East is a big bird. Navigation and logic on Puluwat atoll*. Cambridge, MA: Belknap Press.

Glantz, S. A., & Parmley, W. W. (1991). Passive smoking and heart disease: Epidemiology, physiology, and biochemistry. *Circulation, 83,* 1–12.

Glassman, N., & Andersen, S. (1997). *Activating transference without consciousness: Using significant-other representations to go beyond the subliminally given information*. Unpublished manuscript, Department of Psychology, New York University.

Gleason, T. R. (2002). Social provisions of real and imaginary relationships in early childhood. *Developmental Psychology, 38,* 979–992.

Gleason, T. R., Sebanc, A. M., & Hartup, W. W. (2000). Imaginary companions of preschool children. *Developmental Psychology, 36,* 419–428.

Gleitman, G., Reisberg, D., & Gross, J. (2007). *Psychology* (7th ed.). New York: Norton.

Gleitman, H., Fridlund, A. J., & Reisberg, D. (1999). *Psychology* (5th ed.). New York: Norton.

Gleitman, L. R., Gleitman, H., Landau, B., & Warner, E. (1988). Where learning begins: Initial representations for language learning. In F. Newmeyer (Ed.), *Linguistics: The Cambridge survey. Vol. III. Language: Psychological and biological aspects*. Cambridge: Cambridge University Press.

Global Special Issue on Psychology and Poverty Reduction. (2010, July). *Official launch — a global special issue on psychology and poverty reduction*. Melbourne, Australia: International Congress of Applied Psychology. Retrieved from http://poverty.massey.ac.nz/#global_issue

Glover, M., & Hirini, P. (2005). Maori psychology: A long way from Imago, He Ara Roa Tonu. *New Zealand Journal of Psychology, 34*(1), 1–2.

Glozier, N., Martiniuk, A., Patton, G., Ivers, R., Li, Q., Hickie, I., et al. (2009). Short sleep duration in prevalent and persistent psychological distress in young adults: The DRIVE study. *Sleep, 33*. Retrieved from http://www.journalsleep.org/ViewAbstract.aspx?pid=27892

Gluck, M. A., & Myers, C. E. (1997). Psychobiological models of hippocampal function in learning and memory. *Annual Review, 48,* 481–514.

Glynn, I. (2003). *An anatomy of thought: The origin and machinery of the mind*. New York: Oxford University Press.

Godden, D. R., & Baddeley, A. D. (1975). Context-dependent memory in two natural environments: On land and underwater. *British Journal of Psychology, 66,* 325–331.

Godin, G., Gagne, C., Maziade, J., Moreault, L., Beaulieu, D., & Morel, S. (2001). Breast cancer: The intention to have a mammography and clinical breast examination — application of the theory of planned behavior. *Psychology and Health, 16,* 423–441.

Goff, D. C., Bagnell, A. L., & Perlis, R. H. (1999). Glutamatergic augmentation strategies for cognitive impairment in schizophrenia. *Psychiatric Annals, 29,* 649–654.

Gogate, L. J., Bahrick, L. E., & Watson, J. D. (2000). A study of multimodal motherease: The role of temporal synchrony between verbal labels and gestures. *Child Development, 71,* 878–894.

Gold, J. M., Carpenter, C., Randolph, C., Goldberg, T. E., & Weinberger, D. E. (1997). Auditory working memory and Wisconsin card sorting test performance in schizophrenia. *Archives of General Psychiatry, 54,* 159–165.

Gold, M. S., & Pearsall, H. R. (1983). Hypothyroidism — or is it depression? *Psychosomatics, 24,* 646–656.

Gold, P. E. (2003). Acetylcholine modulation of neural systems involved in learning and memory [Special issue: Acetylcholine: Cognitive and brain functions]. *Neurobiology of Learning and Memory, 80,* 194–210.

Goldberg, L. R. (1981). Language and individual differences: The search for universals in personality lexicons. In L. Wheeler (Ed.), *Review of personality and social psychology*. Beverly Hills, CA: Sage.

Goldberg, L. R. (1993). The structure of phenotypic personality traits. *American Psychologist, 48,* 26–34.

Goldberger, N. R., & Veroff, J. B. (Eds.). (1995). *The culture and psychology reader*. New York: University Press.

Golden, R. M., & Rumelhart, D. E. (1993). A parallel distributed processing model of story comprehension and recall. *Discourse Processes, 16,* 203–237.

Goldfield, B. A., & Snow, C. E. (1989). Individual differences in language acquisition. In J. Berko Gleason (Ed.), *The development of language* (2nd ed.). Columbus, OH: Merrill.

Goldfried, M. R., & Davison, G. C. (1994). *Clinical behavior therapy* (2nd ed.). New York: John Wiley & Sons.

Goldin-Meadow, S., & Mylander, C. (1984). Gestural communication in deaf children: The effects and noneffects of parental input on early language development. *Monographs of the Society for Research in Child Development, 49,* 1–121.

Goldin-Meadow, S., & Mylander, C. (1998). Spontaneous sign systems created by deaf children in two cultures. *Nature, 391,* 279–281.

Goldman-Rakic, P. (1995). Cellular basis of working memory. *Neuron, 14,* 477–485.

Goldman-Rakic, P. (1996). Regional and cellular fractionation of working memory. *Proceedings of the National Academy of Sciences, USA, 93,* 13473–13476.

Goldner, E. M., Srikameswaran, S., Schroeder, M. L., Livesley, W. J., & Birmingham, C. L. (1999). Dimensional assessment of personality pathology in patients with eating disorders. *Psychiatry Research, 85,* 151–159.

Goldney, R. D., Eckert, K. A., Hawthorne, G., & Taylor, A. W. (2010). Changes in the prevalence of major depression in an Australian community sample between 1998 and 2008. *Australian and New Zealand Journal of Psychiatry, 44*(10), 901–910.

Goldsmith, H. H., & Alansky, J. A. (1987). Maternal and infant temperamental predictors of attachment: A meta-analytic review. *Journal of Consulting and Clinical Psychology, 55,* 805–816.

Goldsmith, S. K., Shapiro, R. M., & Joyce, J. N. (1997). Disrupted pattern of D2 dopamine receptors in the temporal lobe in schizophrenia: A postmortem study. *Archives of General Psychiatry, 54,* 649–658.

Goldsmith, T. H. (1994). Ultraviolet receptors and color visions: Evolutionary implications and a dissonance of paradigms. *Vision Research, 34,* 1479–1487.

Goldstein, A. J., & Chambless, D. J. (1978). A reanalysis of agoraphobia. *Behavior Therapy, 9,* 47–59.

Goldstein, E. B. (1989). *Sensation and perception*. Belmont, CA: Wadsworth.

Goldstein, J. M., Goodman, J. M., Seidman, L. J., Kennedy, D. N., Makris, N., Lee, H., et al. (1999). Cortical abnormalities in schizophrenia identified by structural magnetic resonance imaging. *Archives of General Psychiatry, 57,* 537–547.

Goldstein, M. J. (1988). The family and psychopathology. *Annual Review of Psychology, 39,* 283–299.

Goldstein, R. B., Wickramaratne, P. J., Horwath, E., & Weissman, M. M. (1997). Familial aggregation and phenomenology of 'early'-onset (at or before age 20 years) panic disorder. *Archives of General Psychiatry, 54,* 271–278.

Goleman, D. (1995). *Emotional intelligence*. New York: Bantam Books.

Golomb, A., Ludolph, P., Westen, D., Block, M. J., Maurer, P., & Wiss, F. C. (1994). Maternal empathy, family chaos, and the etiology of borderline personality disorder. *Journal of the American Psychoanalytic Association, 42,* 525–548.

Gomersall, A. M., Davidson, G., & Ho, R. (2000). Factors affecting acceptance of Aboriginal reconciliation amongst non-Indigenous Australians. *Australian Psychologist, 35*(2), 118–127.

Gonzalez-Pienda, J. A., Nunez, J. C., Gonzalez-Pumariega, S., Alvarez, L., Roces, C., & Garcia, M. (2002). A structural equation model of parental involvement, motivational and aptitudinal characteristics, and academic-achievement. *The Journal of Experimental Education, 70*(3), 257–287.

Good, B. J., & Kleinman, A. M. (1985). Culture and anxiety: Cross-cultural evidence for the patterning of anxiety disorders. In A. H. Tuma & J. D. Maser (Eds.), *Anxiety and the anxiety disorders* (pp. 297–323). Hillsdale, NJ: Lawrence Erlbaum Associates.

Goodenough, B., & Gillam, B. (1997). Gradients as visual primitives. *Journal of Experimental Psychology: Human Perception and Performance, 23,* 370–387.

Goodman, J. F. (2006). School discipline in moral disarray. *Journal of Moral Education, 35*(2), 213–230.

Goodnow, J. J. (1996). Collaborative rules: How are people supposed to work with one another? In P. B. Baltes & U. M. Staudinger (Eds.), *Interactive minds: Life-span perspectives on the social foundation of cognition*. New York: Cambridge University Press.

Goodnow, J. J., Cashmore, J., Cotton, S., & Knight, R. (1984). Mother's developmental timetables in two cultural groups. *International Journal of Psychology, 19,* 193–205.

Goodwin, F. K., & Ghaemi, S. N. (1997). Future directions in mood disorder research. In A. Honig & H. M. van Praag (Eds.), *Depression: Neurobiological, psychopathological and therapeutic advances. Wiley series on clinical and neurobiological advances in psychiatry: Vol. 3* (pp. 627–643). New York: John Wiley & Sons.

Goodwin, F. K., & Ghaemi, S. N. (1998). Understanding manic-depressive illness. *Archives of General Psychiatry, 55,* 23–25.

Goodwin, F. K., & Roy-Byrne, P. (1987). Treatment of bipolar disorders. In A. J. Frances & R. E. Hales (Eds.), *Psychiatric update annual review: Vol. 6*.

Goodwyn, S. W., & Acredolo, L. P. (1998). Encouraging symbolic gestures: A new perspective on the relationship between gesture and speech. In J. M. Iverson & S. Goldin-Meadow (Eds.), *The nature and functions of gesture in children's communication. New directions for child development, no. 79* (pp. 71–73). San Francisco: Jossey-Bass.

Goody, J. (1977). *The domestication of the savage mind*. Cambridge: Cambridge University Press.

Gopnik, A. (1993). How we know our minds: The illusion of first-person intentionality. *Behavioral and Brain Sciences, 16,* 1–14.

Gordis, E. (1996). Alcohol research: At the cutting edge. *Archives of General Psychiatry, 53,* 199–201.

Gordon, C., & Debus, R. (2002). Developing deep learning approaches and personal teaching efficacy within a preservice teacher education context. *British Journal of Educational Psychology, 72*(4), 483–511.

Gordon, M., & Shankweiler, P. J. (1971). Different equals less: Female sexuality in recent marriage manuals. *Journal of Marriage and the Family, 33,* 459–466.

Gordon Rouse, K. A. (2001). Resilient students' goals and motivation. *Journal of Adolescence, 24,* 461–472.

Gorman, J. M., Kent, J. M., Sullivan, G. M., & Coplan, J. D. (2000). Neuroanatomical hypothesis of panic disorder, revised. *American Journal of Psychiatry, 157,* 493–505.

Gorski, R. A., & Barraclough, C. A. (1963). Effects of low dosages of androgen on the differentiation of hypothalamic regulatory control of ovulation in the rat. *Endocrinology, 73,* 210–216.

Gortmaker, S. L., Must, A., Perrin, J. M., Sobol, A. M., & Dietz, W. H. (1993). Social and economic consequences of overweight in adolescence and young adulthood. *The New England Journal of Medicine, 329,* 1008–1012.

Goschke, T., & Kuhl, J. (1993). Representations of intentions: Persisting activation in memory. *Journal of Experimental Psychology: Learning, Memory, and Cognition, 19,* 1211–1226.

Goschke, T., & Kuhl, J. (1996). Remembering what to do: Explicit and implicit memory for intentions. In M. Brandimonte, G. Einstein, & M. McDaniel (Eds.), *Prospective memory: Theory and applications* (pp. 53–91). Mahwah, NJ: Lawrence Erlbaum Associates.

Gostin, O. (1996). Identity, ownership, and appropriation. Aspect of Aboriginal Australian experience in tertiary education. In B. Saraswati (Ed.), *Interface of cultural identity development*. New Delhi, India: Indira Gandhi National Centre for the Arts.

Goto, H. (1971). Auditory perception by normal Japanese adults of the sounds 'l' and 'r.' *Neuropsychologia, 9,* 317–323.

Gottesman, I. I. (1991). *Schizophrenia genesis: The origins of madness*. New York: Freeman.

Gottesman, I. I., & Bertelsen, A. (1989). Confirming unexpressed genotypes for schizophrenia: Risks in the offspring of Fischer's Danish identical and fraternal discordant twins. *Archives of General Psychiatry, 50,* 527–540.

Gottlieb, G. (1991). Experiential canalization of behavioral development: Theory. *Developmental Psychology, 27,* 4–13.

Gottlieb, J. P., Kusunoki, M., & Goldberg, M. E. (1998). The representation of visual salience in monkey parietal cortex. *Nature, 391,* 481–484.

Gottman, J. (1998). Psychology and the study of marital processes. *Annual Review of Psychology, 49,* 169–197.

Gould, E., Tanapat, P., McEwen, B. S., Flugge, G., & Fuchs, E. (1998). Proliferation of granule cell precursors in the dentate gyrus of adult monkeys is diminished by stress. *Proceedings of the National Academy of Sciences, USA, 95,* 3168–3171.

Gould, S. J. (1981). *The mismeasure of man.* New York: W. W. Norton.

Gould, S. J. (1984). Human equality is a contingent fact of history. *Natural History, 92,* 26–33.

Government of Western Australia and Equal Opportunity Commission. (2010). *The policy framework for substantive equality: 'If you want to treat me equally, you may have to be prepared to treat me differently.'* Retrieved from http://www.eoc.wa.gov.au/Libraries/pdfs/se-The_Policy_Framework_for_Substantive_Equality_-_2010_-_Yvonne_Henderson_-_2010.sflb.ashx

Govt set to cut spending in flood recovery. (2011, January). *Business Spectator.* Retrieved from http://www.businessspectator.com.au/bs.nsf/Article/Australia-says-economic-cost-of-floods-to-top-othe-D72AN?OpenDocument&src=hp13

Gracely, R., Lynch, S., & Bennett, G. J. (1992). Painful neuropathy: Altered central processing maintained dynamically by peripheral input. *Pain, 51,* 175–194.

Graduate Careers Council of Australia. (2009). *Psychology bachelor.* Retrieved from http://svc071.wic016v.server-web.com/GraDSOnline/fos/fos.asp?YR=2007&DL=2&FS=56&SS=

Graesser, A. C., Millis, K. K., & Zwaan, R. (1997). Discourse comprehension. *Annual Review of Psychology, 48,* 163–189.

Graetz, B. W., Sawyer, M. G., & Baghurst, P. (2005). Gender differences among children with DSM-IV ADHD in Australia. *Journal of American Academy of Child and Adolescent Psychiatry, 44*(2), 159–168.

Graf, P., & Schacter, D. L. (1987). Selective effects of interference on implicit and explicit memory for new associations. *Journal of Experimental Psychology: Learning, Memory, & Cognition, 13,* 45–53.

Graham, K. S., Patterson, K., & Hodges, J. R. (1999). Episodic memory: New insights from the study of semantic dementia. *Current Opinion in Neurobiology, 9,* 245–250.

Granholm, E., McQuaid, J. R., McClure, F. S., Auslander, L. A., Perivoliotis, D., Pedrelli, P., et al. (2005). A randomized, controlled trial of cognitive behavioral social skills training for middle-aged and older outpatients with chronic schizophrenia. *American Journal of Psychiatry, 162,* 520–529.

Granic, I., & Hollenstein, T. (2003). Dynamic systems methods for models of developmental psychopathology. *Development and Psychopathology, 15,* 641–669.

Graske, M. G., & Waters, A. M. (2005). Panic disorder, phobias, and generalized anxiety disorder. *Annual Review of Clinical Psychology, 1,* 197–225.

Graugaard, P., & Finset, A. (2000). Trait anxiety and reactions to patient-centered and doctor-centered styles of communication: An experimental study. *Psychosomatic Medicine, 62,* 33–39.

Gray, J. A. (1990). Brain systems that mediate both emotion and cognition. *Cognition and Emotion, 4,* 269–288.

Gray, J. A. (1994). Framework for a taxonomy of psychiatric disorder. In S. H. M. van Goozen & N. E. Van de Poll (Eds.), *Emotions: Essays on emotion theory* (pp. 29–59). Hillsdale, NJ: Lawrence Erlbaum.

Graybeal, A., Sexton, J. D., & Pennebaker, J. W. (2002). The role of story-making in disclosure writing: The psychometric properties of narrative. *Psychology and Health, 17,* 571–581.

Graziadei, P. P. C. (1969). The ultra-structure of vertebrate taste buds. In C. Pfaffman (Ed.), *Olfaction and taste: Vol. 3.* New York: Rockefeller University Press.

Graziano, W. G. (2003). Personality development: An introduction towards process approaches to long-term stability and change in persons. *Journal of Personality, 71*(6), 893–904.

Grech, J. (2010, December 2). Report on video games clears way for R18+ rating. *The Daily Telegraph.* Retrieved from http://www.adelaidenow.com.au/news/report-on-video-games-clears-way-for-r18-rating/story-fn6bqvxz-1225964566577

Green, E. G. T. (2007). Guarding the gates of Europe: A typological analysis of immigration attitudes across 21 countries. *International Journal of Psychology, 42*(6), 365–379.

Green, L., & Freed, D. E. (1993). The substitutability of reinforcers. *Journal of the Experimental Analysis of Behavior, 60,* 141–158.

Green, R. (1987). *The 'sissy boy' syndrome and the development of homosexuality.* New Haven, CT: Yale University Press.

Greenberg, J., Pyszczynski, T., Solomon, S., Simon, L., & Breus, M. (1994). Role of consciousness and accessibility of death-related thoughts in mortality salience effects. *Journal of Personality and Social Psychology, 67,* 627–637.

Greenberg, J. S., Seltzer, M. M., Hong, J., & Orsmond, G. I. (2006). Bidirectional effects of expressed emotion and behavior problems and symptoms in adolescents and adults with autism. *American Journal on Mental Retardation, 111*(4), 229–249.

Greenberg, L. S., & Safran, J. D. (1990). Emotional-change processes in psychotherapy. In R. Plutchik & H. Kellerman (Eds.), *Emotion, psychopathology, and psychotherapy. Vol. 5: Emotion: Theory, research, and experience* (pp. 59–85). San Diego, CA: Academic Press.

Greene, D. M., & Swets, J. A. (1966). *Signal detection theory and psychophysics.* New York: Wiley.

Greeno, C. G., & Wing, R. R. (1994). Stress-induced eating. *Psychological Bulletin, 115,* 444–464.

Greeno, J. G. (1978). Natures of problem-solving abilities. In W. K. Estes (Ed.), *Handbook of learning and cognitive processes: Vol. 5.* Hillsdale, NJ: Lawrence Erlbaum.

Greenough, W. T. (1991). Experience as a component of normal development: Evolutionary considerations. *Developmental Psychology, 27,* 14–17.

Greenwald, A. G. (1980). The totalitarian ego: Fabrication and revision of personal history. *American Psychologist, 35,* 603–618.

Greenwald, A. G., & Banaji, M. (1995). Implicit social cognition: Attitudes, self-esteem, and stereotypes. *Psychological Review, 102,* 4–27.

Greenwald, A. G., Banaji, M. R., Rudman, L. A., Farnham, S. D., Nosek, B. A., & Mellott, D. S. (2002). A unified theory of implicit attitudes, stereotypes, self-esteem, and self-concept. *Psychological Review, 109*(1), 3–25.

Greenwald, A. G., McGhee, D. E., & Schwartz, J. L. K. (1998). Measuring individual differences in implicit cognition: The implicit association test. *Journal of Personality and Social Psychology, 74,* 1464–1480.

Gregory, J. (2003). *Sickened: The memoir of a Munchausen by proxy childhood.* New York: Bantam Books.

Gregory, R. (1978). *Eye and brain: The psychology of seeing* (3rd ed.). New York: McGraw-Hill.

Gregory, R. I. (1970). *The intelligent eye.* New York: McGraw-Hill.

Grencavage, L. M., & Norcross, J. C. (1990). Where are the commonalities among the therapeutic common factors? *Professional Psychology: Research and Practice, 21,* 372–378.

Grice, H. P. (1975). Logic and conversation. In P. Cole & J. L. Morgan (Eds.), *Syntax and semantics: Speech acts* (pp. 41–58). San Diego, CA: Academic Press.

Grice, J. W., & Seely, E. (2000). The evolution of sex differences in jealousy: Failure to replicate previous results. *Journal of Research in Personality, 34,* 348–356.

Griffin, C. (2000). More than simply talk and text: Psychologists as cultural ethnographers. In C. Squire (Ed.), *Culture in psychology* (pp. 17–30). London: Routledge.

Griffith, E. E., Young, J. L., & Smith. (1984). An analysis of the therapeutic elements in a Black church service. *Hospital and Community Psychiatry, 35,* 464–469.

Griffiths, J. A., & Nesdale, D. (2006). In-group and out-group attitudes of ethnic majority and minority children. *International Journal of Intercultural Relations, 30*(6), 735–749

Griffiths, K., Farrer, L., & Christensen, H. (2006). Effective treatments a click away. In L. Littlefield (Ed.), *In psych* (pp. 18–19). Melbourne, Australia: APS.

Griffitt, W. (1987). Females, males, and sexual responses. In K. Kelley (Ed.), *Females, males, and sexuality: Theories and research.* Albany: State University of New York Press.

Griggs, R. A., & Cox, J. R. (1982). The elusive thematic-materials effect in Wason's selection task. *British Journal of Psychology, 73,* 407–420.

Grimshaw, G. M., Bryden, M. P., & Finegan, J. K. (1995). Relations between prenatal testosterone and cerebral lateralization in children. *Neuropsychology, 9,* 68–79.

Grob, C., & Dobkin de Rios, M. (1992). Adolescent drug use in cross-cultural perspective. *Journal of Drug Issues, 22,* 121–138.

Grob, G. N. (1983). Historical origins of deinstitutionalization. *New Directions for Mental Health Services, 17,* 15–29.

Gross, J. J. (1998). Antecedent- and response-focused emotion regulation: Divergent consequences for experience, expression, and physiology. *Journal of Personality and Social Psychology, 74,* 224–237.

Gross, J. J. (1999). Emotion regulation: Past, present, future. *Cognition and Emotion, 13,* 551–573.

Gross, M. (1999). *From 'the saddest sound' to the D major chord: The gift of accelerated progression.* Keynote address presented at the 3rd Biennial Australasian International Conference on the Education of Gifted Students, Melbourne, Australia.

Group for the Advancement of Psychiatry (GAP) Committee on Alcoholism and the Addictions. (1991). Substance abuse disorders: A psychiatric priority. *American Journal of Psychiatry, 148,* 1291–1300.

Grunbaum, A. (1984). *The foundations of psychoanalysis: A philosophical critique.* Berkeley: University of California Press.

Grulich, A. E., de Visser, R. O., Smith, A. M. A., Rissel, C. E., & Richters, J. (2003). Homosexual experience and recent homosexual encounters. *Australia and New Zealand Journal of Public Health, 27,* 155–163.

Gruneberg, M. M., Morris, P. E., & Sykes, R. N. (Eds.). (1988). *Practical aspects of memory: Current research and issues: Vol. 1: Memory in everyday life.* Oxford: John Wiley & Sons.

Grusec, J. E., & Goodnow, J. J. (1994). Summing up and looking to the future. *Developmental Psychology, 30,* 29–31.

Guarnaccia, P. J., & Rogler, L. H. (1999). Research on culture-bound syndromes: New directions. *American Journal of Psychiatry, 156,* 1322–1327.

Gudjonsson, G. H., & Haward, L. R. C. (1998). *Forensic psychology: A guide to practice.* London: Routledge.

Guimond, S., Branscombe, N. R., & Brunot, S. (2007). Culture, gender, and the self: Variations and impact of social comparison processes. *Journal of Personality and Social Psychology, 92*(6), 1118–1134.

Gumperz, J. J., & Levinson, S. C. (Eds.). (1996). *Rethinking linguistic relativity.* Cambridge: Cambridge University Press.

Gunderson, J. G. (1986). Pharmacotherapy for patients with borderline personality disorder. *Archives of General Psychiatry, 43,* 698–700.

Gunter, B., & McAleer, J. (1990). *Children and television: The one eyed monster?* London: Routledge.

Gur, R. E., Cowell, P. E., Latshaw, A., Turetsky, B. I., Grossman, R. I., Arnold, S. E., et al. (2000). Reduced dorsal and orbital prefrontal gray matter volumes in schizophrenia. *Archives of General Psychiatry, 57,* 761–768.

Gur, R. E., Turetsky, B. I., Bilker, W. B., & Gur, R. C. (1999). Reduced gray matter volume in schizophrenia. *Archives of General Psychiatry, 56,* 905–911.

Gurevich, E. V., Bordelon, Y., Shapiro, R. M., Arnold, S. E., Gur, R. E., & Joyce, J. N. (1997). Mesolimbic dopamine D3 receptors and use of antipsychotics in patients with schizophrenia: A postmortem study. *Archives of General Psychiatry, 54,* 225–232.

Guzowski, J. F., Lyford, G. L., Stevenson, G. D., Houston, F. P., McGaugh, J. L., Worley, P. F., et al. (2000). Inhibition of activity-dependent arc protein expression in the rat hippocampus impairs the maintenance of long-term potentiation and the consolidation of long-term memory. *Journal of Neuroscience, 20,* 3993–4001.

Haaga, D. A. F., & Stiles, W. B. (2000). Randomized clinical trials in psychotherapy research: Methodology, design, and evaluation. In C. R. Snyder & R. E. Ingram (Eds.), *Handbook of psychological change: Psychotherapy processes and practices for the 21st century* (pp. 14–39). New York: John Wiley & Sons.

Hacker, D. J., Dunlosky, J., & Graesser, A. C. (2009). *Handbook of metacognition in education*. Mahwah, NJ: Erlbaum.

Hagan, M. M., Castaneda, E., Sumaya, I. C., Fleming, S. M., Galloway, J., & Moss, D. E. (1998). The effect of hypothalamic peptide YY on hippocampal acetylcholine release in vivo: Implications for limbic function in binge-eating behavior. *Brain Research, 805,* 20–28.

Hagger, M. S., Chatzisarantis, N., Biddle, S. J. H., & Orbell, S. (2001). Antecedents of children's physical activity intentions and behaviour: Predictive validity and longitudinal effects. *Psychology and Health, 16,* 391–407.

Haggman, S., Sharpe, L., Nicholas, M. K., & Refshauge, K. (2010). Attentional biases towards sensory pain words in acute and chronic pain patients. *Journal of Pain, 11,* 36–45.

Hahlweg, K., Fiegenbaum, W., Frank, M., Schroeder, B., & von Witzleben, I. (2001). Short- and long-term effectiveness of an empirically supported treatment for agoraphobia. *Journal of Consulting and Clinical Psychology, 69,* 375–382.

Hahn, C., Pawlyk, A. C., Whybrow, P. C., Gyulai, L., & Tejani-Butt, S. M. (1999). Lithium administration affects gene expression of thyroid hormone receptors in rat brain. *Life Sciences, 64,* 1793–1802.

Hahn, S. E., & Smith, C. S. (1999). Daily hassles and chronic stressors: Conceptual and measurement issues. *Stress Medicine, 15,* 89–101.

Hahn, U., & Ramscar, M. (Eds.). (2001). *Similarity and categorization*. New York: Oxford University Press.

Halasz, P. (1993). Arousals without awakening: Dynamic aspect of sleep. *Physiology and Behavior, 54,* 795–802.

Hale, S., Bronik, M., & Fry, A. (1997). Verbal and spatial working memory in school-age children: Differences in susceptibility to interference. *Developmental Psychology, 33,* 364–371.

Haley, J. (1971). Family therapy: A radical change. In J. Haley (Ed.), *Changing families: A family therapy reader*. New York: Grune & Stratton.

Halford, G. (1989). Reflections on 25 years of Piagetian cognitive developmental psychology, 1963–1988. *Human Development, 32,* 325–357.

Halford, G. S., Maybery, M. T., & Bain, J. D. (1986). Capacity limitations in children's reasoning: A dual-task approach. *Child Development, 57*(3), 616–627.

Halford, G. S., Wilson, W. H., & Phillips, S. (1998). Processing capacity defined by relational complexity: Implications for comparative, developmental, and cognitive psychology. *Behaviorial and Brain Sciences, 2*(6), 803–831.

Hall, E. T. (1966). *The hidden dimension*. New York: Doubleday.

Hall, E. T. (1973). *The silent language*. New York: Anchor.

Hall, G. C. N., & Barongan, C. (2002). *Multicultural psychology*. New York: Prentice Hall.

Hall, G. S. (1904). *Adolescence: Its psychology and its relations to physiology, anthropology, sociology, sex, crime, religion, and education: Vols. 1–2*. New York: Appleton-Century-Crofts.

Hall, J. A., & Matsumoto, D. (2004). Gender differences of judgments of multiple emotions from facial expressions. *Emotion, 4,* 201–206.

Halmi, K. A. (1999). Eating disorders: Defining the phenotype and reinventing the treatment. *American Journal of Psychiatry, 156,* 1673–1675.

Hamermesh, D. S., & Biddle, J. E. (1994). Beauty and the labor market. *American Economic Review, 84,* 1174–1195.

Hamida, B. S., Mineka, S., & Bailey, J. M. (1998). Sex differences in perceived controllability of mate value: An evolutionary perspective. *Journal of Personality and Social Psychology, 75,* 953–966.

Hamilton, A. (1981). *Nature and nurture*. Canberra, Australia: Australian Institute of Aboriginal Studies.

Hamilton, D., & Sherman, J. (1994). Stereotypes. In R. S. Wyer Jr. & T. K. Srull (Eds.), *Handbook of social cognition: Vol. 1. Basic processes* (2nd ed., pp. 1–68). Hillsdale, NJ: Lawrence Erlbaum.

Hamilton, R. H., & Pascual-Leone, A. (1998). Cortical plasticity associated with Braille learning. *Trends in Cognitive Neuroscience, 2,* 168–174.

Hamilton, W. D. (1964). The genetical theory of social behavior. *Journal of Theoretical Biology, 6,* 1–52.

Hancox, R. J., Milne, B. J., & Poulton, R. (2004). Association between child and adolescent television viewing and adult health: A longitudinal birth cohort study. *The Lancet, 364,* 257–262.

Hanko, K., Master, S., & Sabini, J. (2004). Some evidence about character and mate selection. *Personality and Social Psychology Bulletin, 30,* 732–742.

Hanna, J. (1989, September 25). Sexual abandon: The condom is unpopular on the campus. *Maclean's*, p. 48.

Hannigan, S. L., & Tippens-Reinitz, M. (2001). A demonstration and comparison of two types of inference-based memory errors. *Journal of Experimental Psychology: Learning, Memory, and Cognition, 27,* 931–940.

Harari, H., Harari, O., & White, R. V. (1985). The reaction to rape by American male bystanders. *Journal of Social Psychology, 125,* 653–658.

Hardeman, W., Johnston, M., Johnston, D. W., Bonetti, D., Wareham, N. J., & Kinmonth, A. L. (2002). Application of the theory of planned behaviour in behaviour change interventions: A systematic review. *Psychology and Health, 17,* 123–158.

Hargreaves, D., & Tiggemann, M. (2002). The effect of television commercials on mood and body dissatisfaction: The role of appearance-schema activation. *Journal of Social and Clinical Psychology, 21,* 287–308.

Harkness, S., & Super, C. M. (2002). Culture and parenting. In M. H. Bornstein (Ed.), *Handbook of parenting: Vol. 2: Biology and ecology of parenting* (2nd ed., pp. 253–280). Mahwah, NJ: Lawrence Erlbaum Associates.

Harlow, H. F., & Zimmerman, R. R. (1959). Affectional responses in the infant monkey. *Science, 130,* 421–432.

Harlow, R., & Cantor, N. (1994). Personality as problem solving: A framework for the analysis of change in daily-life behavior. *Journal of Personality Integration, 4,* 355–386.

Harmer, C. J., Thilo, K. V., Rothwell, J. C., & Goodwin, G. M., (2001). Transcranial magnetic stimulation of medial-frontal cortex impairs the processing of angry facial expressions. *Nature Neuroscience, 4*(1), 17–18.

Harmon-Jones, E., & Allen, J. J. B. (1998). Anger and frontal brain activity: EEG asymmetry consistent with approach motivation despite negative affective valence. *Journal of Personality and Social Psychology, 74,* 1310–1316.

Harper, D. N. (2000). An assessment and comparison of the effects of oxotremorine, D-cycloserine and bicuculline on delayed matching-to-sample performance in rats. *Experimental and Clinical Psychopharmacology, 8,* 207–215.

Harper, D. N., Hunt, M., & Schenk, S. (2006). Attenuation of the disruptive effects of (+/–)3,4-methylene diosymethamphetamine (MDMA) on delaying matching-to-sample performance in the rat. *Behavioral Neuroscience, 120,* 201–205.

Harris, B. (1979). Whatever happened to little Albert? *American Psychologist, 34*(2), 151–160.

Harris, C. R., & Christenfeld, N. (1996). Gender, jealousy, and reason. *Psychological Science, 7,* 364–366.

Harris, J. E. (1980). Memory aids people use: Two interview studies. *Memory and Cognition, 8,* 31–38.

Harris, J. R. (1998). *The nurture assumption: Why children turn out the way they do*. New York: Free Press.

Harris, J. R. (2000). The outcome of parenting: What do we really know? *Journal of Personality, 68,* 625–637.

Harris, M. B., Walters, L. C., & Waschull, S. (1991). Gender and ethnic differences in obesity-related behaviors and attitudes in a college sample. *Journal of Applied Social Psychology, 21,* 1545–1566.

Harris, S. (1980). *Culture and learning: Tradition and education in north-east Arnhem Land*. Canberra, Australia: Australian Institute of Aboriginal Studies.

Harris, Y. H. (1995, June). *The opportunity for romantic love among hunter-gatherers*. Paper presented at the annual convention of the Human Behavior and Evolution Society, Santa Barbara, CA.

Harrison, B. J., Shaw, M., Yqcel, M., Purcell, R., Brewer, W. J., Strother, S. C., et al. (2005). Functional connectivity during Stroop task performance. *NeuroImage, 24,* 181–191.

Harrison, L., & Ungerer, J. (2002). Maternal employment and infant attachment at 12 months postpartum. *Developmental Psychology, 38,* 758–773.

Hart, B., & Risley, T. (1992). American parenting of language-learning children: Persisting differences in family-child interactions observed in natural home environments. *Developmental Psychology, 28,* 1096–1105.

Hart, D., & Carlo, G. (2005). Moral development in adolescence. *Journal of Research on Adolescence, 15,* 223–233.

Hart, E. A., Leary, M. R., & Rejeski, W. J. (1989). The measurement of social physique anxiety. *Journal of Sport and Exercise Psychology, 11,* 94–104.

Harter, S. (1998). The development of self-representations. In W. Damon (Ed. in Chief) & N. Eisenberg (Vol. Ed.), *Handbook of child psychology: Vol. 3* (pp. 553–618). New York: John Wiley & Sons.

Harter, S. (1999). *The construction of the self: A developmental perspective*. New York: Guilford Press.

Harter, S., & Monsour, A. (1992). Development analysis of conflict caused by opposing attributes in the adolescent self-portrait. *Developmental Psychology, 28,* 251–260.

Harter, S., Waters, P., & Whitesell, N. R. (1998). Relational self-worth: Differences in perceived worth as a person across interpersonal contexts among adolescents. *Child Development, 69,* 756–766.

Hartline, H. K. (1938). The response of single optic nerve fibers of the vertebrate eye to illuminate of the retina. *American Journal of Physiology, 121,* 400–415.

Hartmann, H. (1939). *Ego psychology and the problem of adaptation*. New York: International Universities Press.

Hartup, W. (1989). Social relationships and their developmental significance. *American Psychologist, 44,* 120–126.

Hartup, W. W. (1977). Aggression in childhood: Developmental perspectives. In M. Hertherington & D. Ross (Eds.), *Contemporary readings in child psychology*. New York: McGraw-Hill.

Hartup, W. W. (1996). The company they keep: Friendships and their developmental significance. *Child Development, 67,* 1–13.

Hartup, W. W. (1998). Cooperation, close relationships, and cognitive development. In W. M. Bukowski, A. F. Newcomb, & W. W. Hartup (Eds.), *The company they keep: Friendship in childhood and adolescence. Cambridge studies in social and emotional development* (pp. 213–237). New York: Cambridge University Press.

Harway, M. (Ed.). (2004). Setting the stage for working with couples. In M. Harway (Ed.), *Handbook of couples therapy* (pp. 1–4). New York: Wiley.

Harwood, R. L., Schoelmerich, A., Schulze, P. A., & Gonzalez, Z. (1999). Cultural differences in maternal beliefs and behaviors: A study of middle-class Anglo and Puerto Rican mother–infant pairs in four everyday situations. *Child Development, 70,* 1005–1016.

Harwood, R. L., Schoelmerich, A., Ventura-Cook, E., Schulze, P. A., & Wilson, S. P. (1996). Culture and class influence on Anglo and Puerto Rican mothers' beliefs regarding long-term socialization goals and child behavior. *Child Development, 67,* 2446–2461.

Hasin, D. S., & Beseler, C. L. (2009). Dimensionality of lifetime alcohol abuse, dependence and binge drinking. *Drug and Alcohol Dependence, 101*, 53–61.

Hasselquist, D., & Bensch, S. (1991). Trade-off between mate guarding and mate attraction in the polygynous great reed warbler. *Behavioral Ecology and Sociobiology*, *28*, 187–193.

Hatfield, E. (1988). Passionate and companionate love. In R. J. Sternberg & M. L. Barnes (Eds.), *The psychology of love* (pp. 191–217). New Haven, CT: Yale University Press.

Hatfield, J. S., Ferguson, L. R., & Alpert, R. (1967). Mother-child interaction and the socialization process. *Child Development, 38,* 365–414.

Hathaway, S. R., & McKinley, J. C. (1940). A multiphasic personality schedule (Minnesota): I. Construction of the schedule. *Journal of Psychology, 10,* 249–254.

Hathaway, S. R., & McKinley, J. C. (1943). *The Minnesota multiphasic personality inventory* (Rev. ed.). Minneapolis: University of Minnesota Press.

Haugtvedt, C., & Petty, R. (1992). Personality and persuasion: Need for cognition moderates the persistence and resistance of attitude changes. *Journal of Personality and Social Psychology, 63,* 308–319.

Hauser, S. T., & Safyer, A. W. (1994). Ego development and adolescent emotions. *Journal of Research on Adolescence, 4,* 487–502.

Hay, D. F., Caplan, M., Castle, J., & Stimson, C. A. (1991). Does sharing become increasingly 'rational' in the second year of life? *Developmental Psychology, 27,* 987–993.

Haykin, S., & Chen, Z. (2005). The cocktail party problem. *Neural Computation*, *17*(9), 1875–1902.

Hayne, H. (2004). Infant memory development: Implications for childhood amnesia. *Developmental Review*, *24*, 33–73.

Hazan, C., & Diamond, L. M. (2000). The place of attachment in human mating. *Review of General Psychology, 4*, 186–204.

Hazan, C., & Shaver, P. (1987). Romantic love conceptualized as an attachment process. *Journal of Personality and Social Psychology, 57*, 731–739.

Healy, A. F., & McNamara, D. S. (1996). Verbal learning and memory: Does the modal model still work? *Annual Review, 47,* 143–172.

Healy, S. D. (1996). Ecological specialization in the avian brain. In C. F. Moss & S. J. Shettleworth (Eds.), *Neuroethological studies of cognitive and perceptual processes* (pp. 84–110). Boulder, CO: Westview Press.

Heathcote, A. S., Brown, S., & Mewhort, D. J. K. (2000). The power law repealed: The case for an exponential law of practice. *Psychological Bulletin & Review, 7*(2), 185–207.

Hebb, D. O. (1949). *The organization of behavior: A neuropsychological theory*. New York: John Wiley.

Hebl, M. R., & Heatherton, T. F. (1998). The stigma of obesity in women: The difference is black and white. *Personality and Social Psychology Bulletin, 24,* 417–426.

Hebl, M. R., & Mannix, L. M. (2003). The weight of obesity in evaluating others: A mere proximity effect. *Personality and Social Psychology Bulletin, 29,* 28–38.

Heckers, S., Goff, D., Schacter, D. L., Savage, C. R., Fischman, A. J., Alpert, N. M., et al. (1999). Functional imaging of memory retrieval in deficit vs nondeficit schizophrenia.≈*Archives of General Psychiatry, 56,* 1117–1123.

Hedricks, C. A. (1994). Female sexual activity across the human menstrual cycle. *Annual Review of Sex Research, V,* 122–172.

Hegarty, J., Baldessarini, R., Tohen, M., Waternaux, C., & Oepen, G. (1994). One hundred years of schizophrenia: A meta-analysis of the outcome literature. *American Journal of Psychiatry, 151,* 1409–1416.

Heider, F. (1958). *The psychology of interpersonal relations*. New York: John Wiley.

Heine, S. J., & Hamamura, T. (2007). In search of East Asian self-enhancement: Erratum. *Personality and Social Psychology Review*, *11*(1), 1–24.

Heine, S. J., Lehman, D. R., Markus, H. R., & Kitayama, S. (1999). Is there a universal need for positive self-regard? *Psychological Review, 106,* 766–794.

Heinkel, C., Rosenfeld, M., & Sheikh, A. A. (2003). *Imagery in smoking cessation and weight management*. New York: Baywood Publishing.

Heishman, S. J. (1999). Behavioral and cognitive effects of smoking: Relationship to nicotine addiction. *Nicotine & Tobacco Research, 1,* S143–S147.

Heit, E. (2000). Properties of inductive reasoning. *Psychonomic Bulletin & Review*, *7*(4), 569–592.

Heller, D. (1986). *The children's God*. Chicago: University of Chicago Press.

Helman, C. (2011, February). Norway tops list of world's countries. *Forbes*. Retrieved from http://www.msnbc.msn.com/id/41352791/ns/travel-destination_travel/

Helmholtz, H. von (1863). *Die Lehre von den tonempfindungen als physiolgisdne grundlage fur die theorie der musik*. Brunswick, Germany: Vieweg-Verlag.

Helmholtz, H. von (1962). *Treatise on physiological optics*. New York: Dover. (Originally published 1909)

Helson, R., & Klohnen, E. C. (1998). Affective coloring of personality from young adulthood to midlife. *Personality & Social Psychology Bulletin, 24,* 241–252.

Hemming, S. (1994). Changing history: New images of Aboriginal history. In C. Bourke, E. Bourke, & B. Edwards (Eds.), *Aboriginal Australia: An introductory reader in Aboriginal studies* (pp. 17–34). Brisbane, Australia: University of Queensland Press.

Hempill, S., & Sanson, A. (2001). Matching parenting to child temperament: Influences on early childhood behavioural problems. *Family Matters, 59,* 42–47.

Henderson, N. D. (1982). Human behavior genetics. *Annual Review of Psychology, 33,* 403–440.

Henderson, M. (2007, August). Couples like an age gap. *The Times*. Retrieved November 30, 2007, from http://www.theaustralian.news.com.au/story/

Henninger, P. (1992). Conditional handedness: Handedness changes in multiple personality disordered subject reflect shift in hemispheric dominance. *Consciousness and Cognition, 1,* 265–287.

Henry, B. R., Houston, S., & Mooney, G. H. (2004). Institutional racism in Australian healthcare: A plea for decency. *Medical Journal of Australia, 180*(10), 517–520.

Henry, C. S., Robinson, L. C., Neal, R. A., & Huey, E. L. (2006). Adolescent perceptions of overall family system functioning and parental behaviours. *Journal of Child and Family Studies*, *15*, 319–329.

Herald Sun. (2010, June 1). *Slimmers are splurging millions of dollars a year on weight loss aids including surgery*. Retrieved from http://www.heraldsun.com.au/news/australians-spend-millions-of-dollars-on-weight-loss-aides/story-e6frf7jo-1225873713807

Herbert, D. M. B., & Burt, J. (2004). What do students remember? Episodic memory and the development of schematization. *Applied Cognitive Psychology*, *18*, 77–88.

Herbert, W. (2007). *Plumbing the mediocre mind*. Retrieved September 30, 2009, from http://www.psychologicalscience.org/onlyhuman/2007/07/plumbling-mediocre-mind.cfm

Herdt, G. (1997). *Same sex, different cultures: Gays and lesbians across cultures*. Boulder, CO: Westview Press.

Herdt, G. H. (Ed.). (1984). *Ritualized homosexuality in Melanesia*. Berkeley: University of California Press.

Hergovich, A., Sirsch, U., & Felinger, M. (2002). Self-appraisals, actual appraisals and reflected appraisals of preadolescent children. *Social Behavior and Personality*, *30*(6), 603–612.

Hering, E. (1878). *Zur Lehre vom Lichtsinne*. Vienna: Gerold.

Hering, E. (1920). *Grundzuge, der Lehr vs. Lichtsinn*. Berlin: Springer-Verlag.

Heritch, A., Henderson, K., & Westfall, T. (1990). Effects of social isolation on brain catecholamines and forced swimming in rats. *Journal of Psychiatric Research*, *24*, 251–258.

Herman, D. (2007). Storytelling and the sciences of mind: Cognitive narratology, discursive psychology, and narratives in face-to-face interaction. *Narrative*, *15*(3), 306–334.

Herman, J., Perry, J. C., & van der Kolk, B. A. (1989). Childhood trauma in borderline personality disorder. *American Journal of Psychiatry, 146,* 490–495.

Herman, J. L. (1992). *Trauma and recovery: The aftermath of violence—from domestic violence to political terror*. New York: Basic Books.

Herold, E. S. (1981). Contraceptive embarrassment and contraceptive behavior among young single women. *Journal of Youth and Adolescence, 10,* 233–242.

Herrmann, D., McEvoy, C., Hertzod, C., Hertel, P., & Johnson, M. K. (Eds.). (1996). *Basic and applied memory research: Vols. 1–2*. Mahwah, NJ: Lawrence Erlbaum.

Herrmann, D. J., Crawford, M., & Holdsworthy, M. (1992). Gender-linked differences in everyday memory performance. *British Journal of Psychology, 83,* 221–231.

Herrnstein, R. J. (1970). On the law of effect. *Journal of the Experimental Analysis of Behavior, 13,* 243–266.

Hersey, P., & Blanchard, K. (1982). *Management of organizational behavior: Utilizing human resources* (2nd ed.). Englewood Cliffs, NJ: Prentice-Hall.

Herz, M. I., Lamberti, J. S., Mintz, J., Scott, R., O'Dell, S. P., McCartan, L., et al. (2000). A program for relapse prevention in schizophrenia: A controlled study. *Archives of General Psychiatry, 57,* 277–283.

Herzog, D. B., Dorer, D. J., Keel, P. K., Selwyn, S. E., Ekeblad, E. R., Flores, A. T., et al. (1999). Recovery and relapse in anorexia and bulimia nervosa: A 7.5-year follow-up study. *Journal of the American Academy of Child & Adolescent Psychiatry, 38,* 829–837.

Hewstone, M., Rubin, M., & Willis, H. (2002). Intergroup bias. *Annual Review of Psychology*, *53*, 575–604.

Hibbard, S. (2003). A critique of Lilienfeld et al.'s (2000) 'The scientific status of projective techniques'. *Journal of Personality Assessment*, *80*(3), 260–271.

Hick, K. M., & Katzman, D. K. (1999). Self-assessment of sexual maturation in adolescent females with anorexia nervosa. *Journal of Adolescent Health, 24,* 206–211.

Hicks, M., & Tough, S. (2009). Importance of complete abstinence from alcohol during pregnancy: Enough evidence for justification? *Expert Review of Obstetrics & Gynecology, 4*(4), 401–414.

Hicks, R. A., & Pelligrini, R. (1991). The changing sleep habits of college students. *Perceptual and Motor Skills, 72*, 631–636.

Higgins, D. J. (2003). The relationship of childhood family characteristics and current attachment styles to depression and depressive vulnerability. *Australian Journal of Psychology*, *55*(1), 9–14.

Higgins, E. T. (1987). Self-discrepancy: A theory relating self and affect. *Psychological Review, 94,* 319–340.

Higgins, E. T. (1999). Self-discrepency: A theory relating self and affect. In R. F. Baumeister (Ed.), *The self in social psychology. Key readings in social psychology* (pp. 150–181). Philadelphia: Psychology Press/Taylor & Francis.

Higgins, E. T., & Bargh, J. A. (1987). Social cognition and social perception. *Annual Review of Psychology, 38*, 369–425.

Higgins, R. L., Snyder, C. R., & Berglas, S. (Eds.). (1990). *Self-handicapping: The paradox that isn't*. New York: Plenum Press.

Higley, J., Mehlman, P., Taub, D., Higley, S., Suomi, S., Linnoila, M., et al. (1992). Cerebrospinal fluid momoamine and adrenal correlates of aggression in free-ranging rhesus monkeys. *Archives of General Psychiatry, 49*, 436–441.

Hilgard, E. R. (1965). *Hypnotic susceptibility*. New York: Harcourt Brace Jovanovich.

Hilgard, E. R. (1986). *Divided consciousness: Multiple controls in human thought and action*. New York: John Wiley.

Hill, A. (1999). Phantom limb pain: A review of the literature on attributes and potential mechanisms. *Journal of Pain and Symptom Management, 17*, 125–412.

Hill, M. K., & Sahhar, M. (2006). Genetic counselling for psychiatric disorders. *Medical Journal Australia, 185*(9), 507–510.

Hill, J. O., & Peters, J. C. (1998). Environmental contributions to the obesity epidemic. *Science, 280*, 1371–1374.

Hillhouse, J. J., Stair, A. W., III, & Adler, C. M. (1996). Predictors of sunbathing and sunscreen use in college undergraduates. *Journal of Behavioral Medicine, 19*, 543–562.

Hilliard, R. B., Henry, W. P., & Strupp, H. H. (2000). An interpersonal model of psychotherapy: Linking patient and therapist developmental history, therapeutic process, and types of outcome. *Journal of Consulting and Clinical Psychology, 68*, 125–133.

Hillier, L., Turner, A., & Mitchell, A. (2005). *Writing themselves in again: The 2nd national report on the sexuality, health & well-being of same sex attracted young people in Australia* (Monograph Series No. 50). Melbourne, Australia: Australian Research Centre in Sex, Health and Society (ARCSHS), La Trobe University.

Hinde, R. (1982). *Ethology: Its nature and relations with other sciences*. New York: Oxford University Press.

Hirsch, C. R., Hayes, S., & Mathews, A. (2009). Looking on the bright side: Accessing benign meanings reduces worry. *Journal of Abnormal Psychology, 118*, 44–54.

Hirsch, J. (1997). Some history of heredity-vs-environment, genetic inferiority at Harvard (?), and the (incredible) Bell curve. *Genetica, 99*, 207–224.

Hirsch, J., & Knittle, J. L. (1970). Cellularity of obese and nonobese human adipose tissue. *Federation Proceedings, 29*, 1516–1521.

Hirsch, S. R., & Weinberger, D. R. (2003). *Schizophrenia* (2nd ed.). New York: Wiley.

Hirshberg, L. M. (1990). When infants look to their parents: II. Twelve-month-olds' response to conflicting parental emotional signals. *Child Development, 61*, 1187–1191.

Hirst, W. (1994). The remembered self in amnesics. In U. Neisser & R. Fivush (Eds.), *The remembering self: Construction and accuracy in self-narrative* (pp. 252–277). New York: Cambridge University Press.

Hirt, E. R., Zillmann, D., Erickson, G. A., & Kennedy, C. (1992). Costs and benefits of allegiance: Changes in fans' self-ascribed competencies after team victory versus defeat. *Journal of Personality and Social Psychology, 63*, 724–738.

Hittner, J. B. (1997). Alcohol-related outcome expectancies: Construct overview and implications for primary and secondary prevention. *Journal of Primary Prevention, 17*, 297–314.

Hobfoll, S. E., Schwarzer, R., & Chon, K. K. (1998). Disentangling the stress labyrinth: Interpreting the meaning of the term stress as it is studied in a health context. *Anxiety, Stress, and Coping, 11*, 181–212.

Hobson, J. A. (1988). *The dreaming brain*. New York: Basic Books.

Hobson, J. A., & McCarley, R. W. (1977). The brain as a dream state generator: An activation-synthesis hypothesis of the dream process. *American Journal of Psychiatry, 134*, 1335–1348.

Hochbaum, G. (1958). *Public participation in medical screening programs* (DHEW Publication No. 572, Public Health Service). Washington, DC: U.S. Government Printing Office.

Hock, E., Eberly, M., Bartle-Haring, S., Ellwanger, P., & Widaman, K. F. (2001). Separation anxiety in parents of adolescents: Theoretical significance and scale development. *Child Development, 72*, 284–298.

Hodges, E. V. E., & Perry, D. G. (1999). Personal and interpersonal antecedents and consequences of victimization by peers. *Journal of Personality & Social Psychology, 76*, 677–685.

Hodgetts, D., Barnett, A., Duirs, A., Henry, J., & Schwanen, A. (2004). *Media psychology, symbolic power and social justice in Aorearoa*. Retrieved December 12, 2007, from http://researchcommons.waikato.ac.nz/maori_psych/2

Hodson, G., Maio, G. R., & Esses, V. M. (2001). The role of attitudinal ambivalence in susceptibility to consensus information. *Basic and Applied Social Psychology, 23*(3), 197–205.

Hoek, H. W. (1993). Review of the epidemiological studies of eating disorders. *International Review of Psychiatry, 5*, 61–74.

Hoff-Ginsberg, E. (1990). Maternal speech and the child's development of syntax: A further look. *Journal of Child Language, 17*, 85–99.

Hoff-Ginsberg, E., & Shatz, M. (1982). Linguistic input and the child's acquisition of language. *Psychological Review, 92*, 3–26.

Hoffman, H. G., Doctor, J. N., Patterson, D. R., Carrougher, G. J., & Furness, T. A. (2000). Virtual reality as an adjunctive pain control during burn wound care in adolescent patients. *Pain, 85*, 305–309.

Hoffman, H. G., Patterson, D. R., Magula, J., Carrougher, G. J., Zeltzer, K., Dagadakis, S., et al. (2004). Water-friendly virtual reality pain control during wound care. *Journal of Clinical Psychology, 60*(2), 189–195.

Hoffman, L. (1981). *Foundations of family therapy*. New York: Basic Books.

Hoffman, L. (1991). A reflexive stance for family therapy. *Journal of Strategic and Systemic Therapies, 10*, 4–17.

Hoffman, M. A., & Levy-Shiff, R. (1994). Coping and locus of control: Cross-generational transmission between mothers and adolescents. *Journal of Early Adolescence, 14*, 391–405.

Hoffman, M. L. (1978). Psychological and biological perspectives on altruism. *International Journal of Behavioral Development, 1*, 323–339.

Hoffman, M. L. (1982). Development of prosocial motivation: Empathy and guilt. In N. Eisenberg (Ed.), *The development of prosocial behavior*. New York: Academic Press.

Hoffman, M. L. (1998). Varieties of empathy-based guilt. In J. Bybee (Ed.), *Guilt and children* (pp. 91–112). San Diego, CA: Academic Press.

Hoffman, M. L., & Saltzstein, H. D. (1967). Parent discipline and the child's moral development. *Journal of Personality and Social Psychology, 5*, 45–47.

Hoffman, P. (1997). The endorphin hypothesis. In W. P. Morgan (Ed.), *Physical activity and mental health. Series in health psychology and behavioral medicine* (pp. 163–177). Washington, DC: Taylor & Francis.

Hofmann, S., & DiBartolo, P. M. (Eds.). (2001). *From social anxiety to social phobia: Multiple perspectives*. Boston: Allyn & Bacon.

Hofstede, G. (2001). *Culture's consequences: Comparing values, behaviors, institutions, and organizations across nations* (2nd ed.). Thousand Oaks, CA: Sage.

Hogan, R. (1983). What every student should know about personality psychology. In A. M. Rogers & J. Scheirer (Eds.), *G. Stanley Hall lecture series: Vol. 6*. Washington, DC: American Psychological Association.

Hogan, R. (1987). Personality psychology: Back to basics. In J. Aronoff, A. Rabin, & R. Zucker (Eds.), *The emergence of personality*. New York: Springer.

Hogan, R., Curphy, G., & Hogan, J. (1994). What we know about leadership: Effectiveness and personality. *American Psychologist, 49*, 493–304.

Hogg, M. A. (2001). A social identity theory of leadership. *Personality and Social Psychology Review, 5*, 184–200.

Hogg, M. A., Turner, J. C., & Davidson, B. (1990). Polarised norms and social frames of reference: A test of the self-categorisation theory of group polarization. *Basic and Applied Social Psychology, 11*, 77–100.

Hohmann, G. W. (1966). Some effects of spinal cord lesions on experienced emotional feelings. *Psychophysiology, 3*, 143–156.

Hoigaard, R., Säfvenbom, R., & Tonnessen, F. E. (2006). The relationship between group cohesion, group norms, and perceived social loafing in soccer teams. *Small Group Research, 37*(3), 217–232.

Holahan, C. K., & Holahan, C. J. (1999). Being labeled as gifted, self-appraisal, and psychological well-being: A life span developmental perspective. *International Journal of Aging and Human Development, 48*, 161–173.

Holland, A. J., & Oliver, C. (1995). Down's syndrome and the links with Alzheimer's disease. *Journal of Neurology, Neurosurgery & Psychiatry, 59*, 111–114.

Holland, J., Holyoak, K., Nisbett, R., & Thagard, P. (1986). *Induction: Processes of inference, learning, and discovery*. Cambridge, MA: MIT Press.

Holland, R. W., Verplanken, B., & van Knippenberg, A. (2002). On the nature of attitude-behavior relations: The strong guide, the weak follow. *European Journal of Social Psychology, 32*, 869–876.

Hollifield, M., Eckert, V., Warner, T. D., Jenkins, J., Krakow, B., Ruiz, J., et al. (2005). Development of an inventory for measuring war-related events in refugees. *Comprehensive Psychiatry, 46*, 67–80.

Hollifield, M., Warner, T. D., Lian, N., Krakow, B., Jenkins, J., Kesler, J., et al. (2002). Measuring trauma and health status in refugees: A critical review. *Journal of American Medical Association, 288*(5), 611–621.

Hollingworth, S. A., & Siskind, D. J. (2010). Anxiolytic, hypnotic and sedative medication use in Australia. *Pharmacoepidemiological Drug Safety, 19*(3), 280–288.

Hollis, K. L. (1997). Contemporary research on Pavlovian conditioning: A 'new' functional analysis. *American Psychologist, 52*, 956–965.

Hollon, S. (1988). Cognitive therapy. In L. Y. Abramson (Ed.), *Social cognition and clinical psychology: A synthesis* (pp. 204–253). New York: Guilford Press.

Hollon, S. D., & Beck, A. T. (1994). Cognitive and cognitive-behavioral therapies. In A. E. Bergh & S. L. Garfield (Eds.), *Handbook of psychotherapy and behavior change* (4th ed., pp. 428–466). Oxford: John Wiley & Sons.

Holmes, D. (1990). The evidence for repression: An examination of sixty years of research. In J. L. Singer (Ed.), *Repression and dissociation: Implications for personality theory, psychopathology, and health* (pp. 85–102). Chicago: University of Chicago Press.

Holmes, E. A., Lang, T. J., & Shah, D. M. (2009). Developing interpretation bias modification as a vaccine for depressed mood — imagining positive events makes you feel better than thinking about them. *Journal of Abnormal Psychology, 118*, 76–88.

Holmes, T. H., & Rahe, R. H. (1967). The social readjustment rating scale. *Journal of Psychosomatic Research, 11*, 213–218.

Holmgren, R. A., Eisenberg, N., & Fabes, R. A. (1998). The relations of children's situational empathy-related emotions to dispositional prosocial behavior. *International Journal of Behavioral Development, 22*, 169–193.

Holscher, C., Anwyl, R., & Rowan, M. J. (1997). Stimulation on the positive phase of hippocampal theta rhythm induces long-term potentiation that can be depotentiated by stimulation on the negative phase in area C1 in vivo. *Journal of Neuroscience, 17*, 6470–6477.

Holt, R. (1976). Drive or wish? A reconsideration of the psychoanalytic theory of motivation. In M. Gill & P. Holzman (Eds.), *Psychology vs. metapsychology: Psychoanalytic essays in memory of George Klein. Psychological issues, monograph 36, Vol. 9*(4).

Holt, R. R. (1985). The current status of psychoanalytic theory. *Psychoanalytic Psychology, 2*, 289–315.

Holyoak, K. J., & Simon, D. (1999). Bidirectional reasoning in decision making by constraint satisfaction. *Journal of Experimental Psychology: General, 128*, 3–31.

Holyoak, K. J., & Spellman, B. A. (1993). Thinking. *Annual Review of Psychology, 44*, 265–315.

Holyoak, K. J., & Thagard, P. (1995). *Mental leaps: Analogy in creative thought*. Cambridge, MA: MIT Press.

Homans, G. (1961). *Social behavior: Its elementary forms*. London: Routledge & Kegan Paul.

Home Office Research Development Statistics. (2010). *Crime in England and Wales 2009/10: An overview of the findings*. Retrieved from http://rds.homeoffice.gov.uk/rds/pdfs10/hosb1210chap1.pdf

Honeybourne, C., Matchett, G., & Davey, G. (1993). Expectancy models of laboratory preparedness effects: A UCS-expectancy bias in phylogenetic and ontogenetic fear-relevant stimuli. *Behavior Therapy, 24*, 253–264.

Hong, Y. Y., & Mallorie, L. M. (2004). A dynamic constructivist approach to culture: Lessons learned from personality psychology. *Journal of Research in Personality, 38*, 59–67.

Hooks, M. S., Jones, G. H., Juncos, J. L., Neill, D. B., & Justice, J. B. (1994). Individual differences in schedule-induced and conditioned behaviors. *Behavioural Brain Research, 60*, 199–209.

Hooley, J., & Teasdale, J. D. (1989). Predictors of relapse in unipolar depressives: Expressed emotion, marital distress and perceived criticism. *Journal of Abnormal Psychology, 98*, 229–235.

Hooley, J. M. (1998). Expressed emotion and locus of control. *Journal of Nervous & Mental Disease, 186*, 374–378.

Hooley, J. M., & Hiller, J. B. (1998). Expressed emotion and the pathogenesis of relapse in schizophrenia. In M. F. Lenzenweger & R. H. Dworkin (Eds.), *Origins and development of schizophrenia: Advances in experimental psychopathology* (pp. 447–468). Washington, DC: American Psychological Association.

Hooley, M., & Crassini, B. (2008). The behaviour of infants and toddlers at 'falling-off places': Do tactual properties of edges matter? In *EPC 2008: Proceedings for the Australasian Society for Experimental Psychology Conference*. Perth: University of Western Australia.

Hopper, J. W., & van der Kolk, B. (2001). Retrieving, assessing, and classifying traumatic memories: A preliminary report on three case studies of a new standardized method. *Journal of Aggression, Maltreatment & Trauma, 4*(2), 33–71.

Horn, J. (1998). A basis for research on age differences in cognitive capabilities. In J. J. McArdle & R. W. Woodcock (Eds.), *Human cognitive abilities in theory and practice* (pp. 57–91). Mahwah, NJ: Lawrence Erlbaum.

Horn, J. C., & Meer, J. (1987). The vintage years. *Psychology Today, 21*, 76–90.

Horn, J. L. (1968). Organization of abilities and the development of intelligence. *Psychological Review, 75*, 242–259.

Horn, J. L. (1988). Thinking about human abilities. In J. R. Nesselroade & R. B. Cattell (Eds.), *Handbook of multivariate experimental psychology* (2nd ed., pp. 645–685). New York: Plenum Press.

Horn, J. L., & Cattell, R. B. (1967). Age differences in fluid and crystallized intelligence. *Acta Psychologica, 26*, 107–129.

Horn, J. L., & Hofer, S. M. (1992). Major abilities and development in the adult period. In R. J. Sternberg & C. A. Berg (Eds.), *Intellectual development* (pp. 44–99). New York: Cambridge University Press.

Horn, J. L., & Noll, J. (1994). System for understanding cognitive capabilities: A theory and the evidence on which it is based. In D. K. Detterman (Ed.), *Current topics in human intelligence: Vol. IV* (pp. 151–203). New York: Springer-Verlag.

Horn, J. L., & Noll, J. (1997). Human cognitive capabilities: Gf-Gc theory. In D. P. Flanagen, J. L. Genshaft, & P. L. Harrison (Eds.), *Contemporary intellectual assessment: Theories, tests and issues* (pp. 53–91). New York: Guilford Press.

Horn, J. L., & Stankov, L. (1982). Auditory and visual factors of intelligence. *Intelligence, 6*, 165–185.

Horn, J. M., Loehlin, J. C., & Willerman, L. (1979). Intellectual resemblance among adoptive and biological relatives: The Texas Adoption Project. *Behavior Genetics, 9*, 177–207.

Horn, J. M., Loehlin, J. C., & Willerman, L. (1982). Aspects of the inheritance of intellectual abilities. *Behavioral Genetics, 12*, 479–516.

Horner, T. M., & Chethik, L. (1986). Conversation attentiveness and following in 12- and 18-week-old infants. *Infant Behavior and Development, 9*, 203–213.

Horney, K. (1926). The flight from womanhood. *International Journal of Psychoanalysis, 7*, 324–339.

Horowitz, M. (1988). *Introduction to psychodynamics: A synthesis*. New York: Basic Books.

Houpt, K. A. (2004). *Domestic animal behavior*. Chicago: University of Chicago Press.

House, J. S., Landis, K. R., & Umberson, D. (1988). Social relationships and health. *Science, 241*, 540–545.

Hovland, C. (1937). The generalization of conditioned responses: IV. The effects of varying amounts of reinforcement upon the degree of generalization of conditioned responses. *Journal of General Psychology, 21*, 261–276.

Hovland, C. I., & Janis, I. (1959). *Personality and persuasibility*. New Haven, CT: Yale University Press.

Howard, K. I., Kopta, S. M., Krause, M. S., & Orlinsky, D. E. (1986). The dose–effect relationship in psychotherapy. *American Psychologist, 41*, 159–164.

Howard, K. I., Orlinsky, D. E., & Lueger, R. J. (1994). Clinically relevant outcome research in individual psychotherapy: New models guide the researcher and clinician. *British Journal of Psychiatry, 165*, 4–8.

Howard, R. W. (2008). Linking extreme precocity and adult eminence: A study of eight prodigies at international chess. *High Ability Studies, 19*(2), 117–130.

Howe, M. L. (2000). *The fate of early memories: Developmental science and the retention of childhood experiences*. Washington, DC: American Psychological Association.

Howes, C., & Hamilton, C. E. (1992). Children's relationships with child care teachers: Stability and concordance with parental attachments. *Child Development, 63*, 867–878.

Howes, C., Hamilton, C. E., & Philiopsen, L. C. (1998). Stability and comorbidity of child-caregiver and child-peer relationships. *Child Development, 69*, 418–426.

Hoy, W. E., Baker, P. R., Kelly, A. M., & Wang, Z. (2000). Reducing premature death and renal failure in Australian Aboriginals. *Medical Journal of Australia, 172*, 473–478.

Hoyle, R. H. (2006). Self-knowledge and self-esteem. In M. H. Kernis (Ed.), *Self-esteem issues and answers: A sourcebook of current perspectives* (pp. 208–215). New York: Psychology Press.

HR Daily. (2010, October 14). *Cultural-awareness training should focus on doing, not knowing, says expert*. Retrieved from http://www.hrdaily.com.au/

Hsu, F. L. K. (1981). *Americans and Chinese: Passage to difference* (3rd ed.). Honolulu: University Press of Hawaii.

Hsu, L. K. G. (1989). The gender gap in eating disorders: Why are the eating disorders more common among women? *Clinical Psychology Review, 9*, 393–407.

Hu, J., Li, C., & Wang, D. (2006). Relationship between self-esteem and mental health of normal college students. *Chinese Journal of Clinical Psychology, 14*(6), 620–621.

Hubbard, R., Ryan, P. A., Mick, D. G., Stewart, D. W., Kover, A. J., & Winer, R. S. (2000). The historical growth of statistical significance testing in psychology: And its future prospects [Commentaries: Statistical significance with comments by editors of marketing journals]. *Educational and Psychological Measurement, 60*, 661–754.

Hubel, D. H., & Wiesel, T. N. (1959). Receptive fields of single neurons in the cat's striate cortex. *Journal of Physiology, 148*, 574–591.

Hubel, D. H., & Wiesel, T. N. (1963). Single-cell responses in striate cortex of kittens deprived of vision in one eye. *Journal of Neuropsychology, 26*, 1003–1009.

Hubel, D. H., & Wiesel, T. N. (1979). Brain mechanisms of vision. *Scientific American, 241*, 150–162.

Huesmann, L. R. (1998). The role of social information processing and cognitive schema in the acquisition and maintenance of habitual aggressive behavior. In R. G. Geen & E. Donnerstein (Eds.), *Human aggression: Theories, research, and implications for policy* (pp. 73–109). New York: Academic Press.

Huff, C. (2004). A multifaceted research approach is providing more clues to the origins of personality disorders. *Monitor on Psychology: Personality Disorders, 35*(3), 1–42.

Huffmann, K. (2002). *Psychology in action* (6th ed.). New York: John Wiley & Sons.

Huffman, K. (2007). *Psychology in action* (8th ed.). Hoboken: John Wiley & Sons.

Hugelshofer, D. S., Kwon, P., Reff, R. C., & Olson, M. L. (2006). Humour's role in the relation between attributional style and dysphoria. *European Journal of Personality, 20*, 325–336.

Huizinga, M. M., & Peltier, A. (2007). Painful diabetic neuropathy: A management-centered review. *Clinical Diabetes, 25*(1), 6–15.

Hull, C. L. (1943). *Principles of behavior: An introduction to behavior theory*. New York: Oxford University Press.

Hull, C. L. (1952). *A behavior system: An introduction to behavior theory concerning the individual organism*. New Haven, CT: Yale University Press.

Hull, J. G. (1987). Self-awareness model. In H. T. Blane & K. E. Leonard (Eds.), *Psychological theories of drinking and alcoholism* (pp. 272–304). New York: Guilford Press.

Hull, J. G., & Bond, C. F. (1986). Social and behavioral consequences of alcohol consumption and expectancy: A meta-analysis. *Psychological Bulletin, 99*, 347–360.

Hulme, C., Maughan, S., & Brown, G. D. A. (1991). Memory for familiar and unfamiliar words: Evidence for a long-term memory contribution to short-term memory span. *Journal of Memory and Language, 30*, 685–701.

Hultsch, D., & Dixon, R. (1990). Learning and memory in aging. In J. Birren & K. W. Schaie (Eds.), *Handbook of the psychology of aging* (3rd ed.). New York: Academic Press.

Human Rights and Equal Opportunity Commission. (2004). *A last resort: National inquiry into children in immigration detention*. Sydney, Australia: Author.

Human Rights and Equal Opportunity Commission. (2006). *A statistical overview of Aboriginal and Torres Strait Islander peoples in Australia*. Retrieved December 25, 2007, from http://www.hreoc.gov.au/Social_Justice/statistics/index.html#toc2

Human Rights and Equal Opportunity Council. (1991). *Racist violence: Report of the national inquiry into racist violence in Australia*. Canberra, Australia: AGPS.

Humphreys, K., Huebsch, P. D., Finney, J. W., & Moos, R. H. (1999). A comparative evaluation of substance abuse treatment: V. Substance abuse treatment can enhance the effectiveness of self-help groups. *Alcoholism: Clinical and Experimental Research, 23*(3), 558–563.

Humphreys, K., & Klaw, E. (2001). Can targeting nondependent problem drinkers and providing Internet-based services expand access to assistance for alcohol problems? A study of the moderation management self-help/mutual aid organization. *Journal of Studies of Alcohol, 62*, 528–532.

Humphreys, M. S., & Kashima, Y. (2002). Connectionism and self: Distributed representational systems and their implications for self and identity. In Y. Kashima & M. Foddy (Eds.), *Self and identity: Personal, social, and symbolic* (pp. 27–54). Mahwah, NJ: Lawrence Erlbaum.

Humphreys, P., & Paxton, S. J. (2004). Impact of exposure to idealized male images on adolescent boys' body image. *Body Image, 1*(3), 253–266.

Hundleby, J. D., Pawlik, K., & Cattell, R. B. (1965). *Personality factors in objective test devices: A critical integration of a quarter of a century's research*. San Diego, CA: Knapp.

Hunkeler, E. M., Katon, W., Tang, L., Williams, J. W., Kroenke, K., Lin, E. H. B., et al. (2006). Long term outcomes from the IMPACT randomised trial for depressed elderly patients in primary care. *British Medical Journal, 332*, 259–263.

Hunter, E. (2002). Aboriginal and Torres Strait Islander suicide. In J. Healy (Ed.), *Suicide and self-harm: Issues in society: Vol. 166* (pp. 12–14). Sydney, Australia: The Spinney Press.

Hunter, J. E. (1997). Needed: A ban on the significance test. *Psychological Science, 8*, 3–7.

Hunter Institute of Mental Health. (2004). *Multicultural issues and mental health*. Retrieved January 11, 2005, from http://www.responseability.org/Jweb/j%20MIS%2006.htm

Hupka, R. B., Zaleski, Z., Otto, J., Reidl, L., & Tarabrina, N. V. (1997). The colors of anger, envy, fear, and jealousy: A cross-cultural study. *Journal of Cross-Cultural Psychology, 28*, 156–171.

Hurlbert, S. H., & Lombardi, C. M. (2009). Final collapse of the Neyman-Pearson decision-theoretic framework and the rise of the neoFisherian. *Annales Zoologici Fennici, 46*, 311–349.

Huron, D. (2006). *Sweet anticipation: Music and the psychology of expectation*. Cambridge, MA: MIT Press.

Hurst, D. (2010, October 26). Parents told to grow a digital spine. *Brisbane Times*. Retrieved from http://www.brisbanetimes.com.au

Hurvich, L. M., & Jameson, D. (1957). An opponent-process of color vision. *Psychological Review, 64*, 384–404.

Huston, A. C. (1983). Sex-typing. In M. Hetherington (Ed.), *Handbook of child psychology: Vol. 4. Social and personality development*. New York: John Wiley.

Huston, T. L. (1973). Ambiguity of acceptance, social desirability, and dating choice. *Journal of Experimental Social Psychology, 9*, 32–42.

Huston, T. L. (1994). Courtship antecedents of marital satisfaction and love. In R. Erber & R. Gilmour (Eds.), *Theoretical frameworks for personal relationships* (pp. 43–65). Hillsdale, NJ: Lawrence Erlbaum.

Hutton, K. A., Sibley, C. G., Harper, D. N., & Hunt, M. (2002). Modifying driver behaviour with passenger feedback. *Transportation Research, 4*, 257–269.

Hyde, J. S. (1990). Meta-analysis and the psychology of gender differences. *Signs, 16*, 55–73.

Idle, J. R. (1990). Titrating exposure to tobacco smoke using cotinine: A minefield of misunderstandings. *Journal of Clinical Epidemiology, 43*, 313–317.

Ilardi, S. S., & Craighead, W. E. (1999). The relationship between personality pathology and dysfunctional cognitions in previously depressed adults. *Journal of Abnormal Psychology, 108*, 51–57.

Imbrosciano, A., & Berlach, R. G. (2005). The Stroop test and its relationship to academic performance and general behaviour of young students. *Teacher Development, 9*(1), 131–144.

Inciardi, J. A., Surratt, H. L., & Saum, C. A. (1997). *Cocaine-exposed infants: Social, legal, and public health issues*. Thousand Oaks, CA: Sage.

Indermaur, D., & Upton, K. (1988). *Drug abuse screening project* (Monograph). Perth, Australia: Western Australian Department of Corrective Services.

Infants crying a universal language: Listen Mum, baby's sounds make sense. (2006, December 2). *The Courier-Mail*, p. 29.

Inglehart, M. R. (1991). *Reactions to critical life events: A social psychological analysis*. New York: Praeger.

Inhelder, B., & Piaget, J. (1958). *The growth of logical thinking from childhood to adolescence*. New York: Basic Books.

Inkeles, A., & Smith, D. H. (1974). *Becoming modern: Individual change in six developing countries*. Cambridge, MA: Harvard University Press.

Innis, N. K. (1992). Early research on the inheritance of the ability to learn. *American Psychologist, 47*, 190–197.

Insko, C. A. (1964). Primacy versus recency in persuasion as a function of the timing of arguments and measures. *Journal of Abnormal and Social Psychology, 69*, 381–391.

Insko, C. A., Arkoff, A., & Insko, V. M. (1965). Effects of high and low fear-arousing communications upon opinions toward smoking. *Journal of Experimental Social Psychology, 1*, 156–266.

Inui, T., Shimura, T., & Yamamoto, T. (2006). Effects of brain lesions on taste-potentiated odor aversion in rats. *Behavioral Neuroscience, 120*(3), 590–599.

International Association of Applied Psychology. (2010, July). Melbourne, Australia: International Congress of Applied Psychology. Retrieved from http://www.icap2010.com/

International Telecommunication Union. (2010). *The world in 2010: ICT facts and figures*. Retrieved from http://www.itu.int/ITU-D/ict/material/FactsFigures2010.pdf

Irving, H., Samokhvalov, A., & Rehm, J. (2009). Alcohol as a risk factor for pancreatitis. A systematic review and meta-analysis. *Journal of the Pancreas (Online), 10*(4), 387–392.

Irwin, M., Schafer, G., & Fieden, C. (1974). Emic and unfamiliar category sorting of Mano farmers and U.S. undergradutes. *Journal of Cross-Cultural Psychology, 5*, 407–423.

Isen, A. (1984). Toward understanding the role of affect in cognition. In R. S. Wyer Jr. & T. K. Srull (Eds.), *Handbook of social cognition: Vol. 3*. Hillsdale, NJ: Lawrence Erlbaum.

Isen, A. (1993). Positive affect and decision making. In M. Lewis & J. M. Haviland (Eds.), *Handbook of emotions* (pp. 261–277). New York: Guilford Press.

Ishai, A., Ungerleier, L. G., Martin, A., Schouten, J. L., & Haxby, J. V. (1999). Distributed representation of objects in the human ventral visual pathway. *Proceedings of the National Academy of Sciences, USA, 96*, 9379–9384.

Islam, M. R., & Hewstone, M. (1993a). Dimensions of contact as a predictor of outgroup anxiety, perceived outgroup variability, and outgroup attitude: An integrative model. *Personality and Social Psychology Bulletin, 19*, 700–710.

Islam, M. R., & Hewstone, M. (1993b). Intergroup attributions and affective consequences in majority and minority groups. *Journal of Personality and Social Psychology, 64*, 936–950.

Islam, M. R., & Jahjah, M. (2000). *Young Australians, emotions, stereotypes, and attitudes towards Aborigines, Asians and Arabs*. Paper presented at the 2000 National Conference on Reconciliation, Multiculturalism, Immigration and Human Rights, University of Technology, Sydney, Australia.

Islam, M. R., & Jahjah, M. (2001). Predictors of young Australians' attitudes toward Aboriginals, Asians and Arabs. *Social Behaviour and Personality, 29*, 569–580.

Ismail, B., Cantor-Graae, E., & McNeil, T. F. (1998). Minor physical anomalies in schizophrenic patients and their siblings. *American Journal of Psychiatry, 155*, 1695–1702.

Ivey, G. (2006). A method of teaching psychodynamic case formulation. *Psychotherapy: Theory, Research, Practice, Training, 43*(3), 322–336.

Izard, C. (1990). Facial expressions and the regulation of emotions. *Journal of Personality and Social Psychology, 58*, 487–498.

Izard, C. E. (1971). *The face of emotion*. New York: Appleton.

Izard, C. E. (1977). *Human emotions*. New York: Plenum Press.

Izard, C. E. (1997). *Emotions and facial expressions: A perspective from differential emotions theory*. New York: Cambridge University Press.

Izard, C. E., & Buechler, S. (1980). Aspects of consciousness and personality in terms of differential emotions theory. In R. Plutchik & H. Kellerman (Eds.), *Emotion: Theory, research, and experience: Vol. I. Theories of emotion*. New York: Academic Press.

Izquierdo, I., & Medina, J. H. (1997). The biochemistry of memory formation and its regulation by hormones and neuromodulators. *Psychobiology, 25*, 1–9.

Jablensky, A. (1989). Epidemiology and cross-cultural aspects of schizophrenia. *Psychiatric Annals, 19*, 516–524.

Jackendoff, R. (1996). The architecture of the linguistic-spatial interface. In P. Bloom, M. A. Peterson, L. Nadel, & M. Garrett (Eds.), *Language and space* (pp. 1–30). Cambridge, MA: MIT Press.

Jacklin, C. (1989). Female and male: Issues of gender. *American Psychologist, 44*, 127–133.

Jackson, H., Robinson, T., & Pica, S. (1996). State psychiatric hospitals and psychiatric wards in general hospitals. In P. R. Martin & J. S. Birnbrauer (Eds.), *Clinical psychology: Profession and practice in Australia* (pp. 103–128). Melbourne, Australia: Macmillan Education.

Jackson, J. J., Bogg, T., Walton, K., Wood, D., Harms, P. D., Lodi-Smith, J. L., et al. (2009). Not all conscientiousness scales change alike: A multi-method, multi-sample study of age differences in the facets of conscientiousness. *Journal of Personality and Social Psychology, 96*, 446–459.

Jackson, J. L., & Kroenke, K. (2001). The effect of unmet expectations among adults presenting with physical symptoms. *Annals of Internal Medicine, 134*, 889–897.

Jackson, J. S., Brown, K. T., Brown, T. N., & Marks, B. (2001). Contemporary immigration policy orientations among dominant-group members in Western Europe. *Journal of Social Issues, 57*(3), 431–456.

Jackson, S., & Cram, F. (2003). Disrupting the sexual double standard: Young women's talk about heterosexuality. *British Journal of Social Psychology, 42*(1), 113–128.

Jacobson, E. (1964). The self and the object world. *Psychoanalytic Study of the Child, 9*, 75–127.

Jacobson, J. L., Jacobsen, S. W., Sokol, R. J., & Martier, S. S. (1993). Teratogenic effects of alcohol on infant development. *Alcoholism: Clinical and Experimental Research, 17*, 174–183.

Jacobson, N. S., Christensen, A., Prince, S. E., Cordova, J., & Eldridge, K. (2000). Integrative behavioral couple therapy: An acceptance-based, promising new treatment for couple discord. *Journal of Consulting and Clinical Psychology, 68*, 351–355.

Jacoby, L. L., & Kelley, C. M. (1987). Unconscious influences of memory for a prior event. *Personality and Social Psychology Bulletin, 13*, 314–336.

Jacques, E. (1965). Death and the mid-life crisis. *International Journal of Psychoanalysis, 46*, 502–514.

Jaeger, T., & van der Kooy, D. (1996). Separate neural substrates mediate the motivating and discriminative properties of morphine. *Behavioral Neuroscience, 110*, 181–201.

Jaffee, S., & Hyde, J. S. (2000). Gender differences in moral orientation: A meta-analysis. *Psychological Bulletin, 126*, 703–726.

Jahoda, M. (1988). Opening address: The range of convenience of personal construct psychology an outsider's view. In F. Fransella & F. Thomas (Eds.), *Experimenting with personal construct psychology* (pp. 1–14). London: Routledge & Kegan Paul.

James, M. (2010, March 10). Increase in Indigenous babies with low birth weight. *ABC News*. Retrieved from http://www.abc.net.au/news/stories/2010/03/10/2841851.htm

James, R., Krause, K., & Jennings, C. (2010). *The first year experience in Australian Universities: Findings from 1994 to 2009*. Melbourne, Australia: Centre for the Study of Higher Education, The University of Melbourne.

James, W. (1884). What is emotion? *Mind, 19,* 188–205.

James, W. (1890). *Principles of psychology: Vol. 1*. New York: Henry Holt.

James, W. (1958). *Varieties of religious experience*. New York: American Library. (Originally published 1902)

Jang, K. L., Livesley, W. J., & Vernon, P. A. (1996). Heritability of the big five personality dimensions and their facets: A twin study. *Journal of Personality, 64,* 577–591.

Jang, K. L., McCrae, R. R., Angleitner, A., Riemann, R., & Livesley, W. J. (1998). Heritability of facet-level traits in a cross-cultural twin sample: Support for a hierarchical model of personality. *Journal of Personality and Social Psychology, 74,* 1556–1565.

Jang, Y., Chiriboga, D. A., & Okazaki, S. (2009). Attitudes toward mental health services: Age-group differences in Korean American adults. *Aging Mental Health, 13*(1), 127–134.

Jangid, R. K., Vyas, J. N., & Shukla, T. R. (1988). The effects of the transcendental meditation programme on the normal individuals. *Journal of Personality and Clinical Studies, 4,* 145–149.

Janis, I. L. (1972). *Victims of groupthink: A psychological study of foreign-policy decisions and fiascoes*. Boston: Houghton Mifflin.

Janis, I. L. (1982). *Groupthink* (2nd ed.). Boston: Houghton Mifflin.

Janoff-Bulman, R. (1992). *Shattered assumptions: Towards a new psychology of trauma*. New York: Free Press.

Janowitz, H. D., & Grossman, M. I. (1949). Some factors affecting the food intake of normal dogs and dogs with esophagostomy and gastric fistula. *American Journal of Physiology, 159,* 143–148.

Janssen, I., Krabbendam, L., Jolles, J., & Van Os, J. (2004). Alterations in theory of mind in patients with schizophrenia and non-psychotic relatives. *Acta Psychiatry Scandinavia, 108,* 110–117.

Janz, N. K., Champion, V. L., & Strecher, V. J. (2002). The health belief model. In K. Glanz, B. K. Rimer, & F. M. Lewis (Eds.), *Health behavior and health education: Theory, research, and practice* (pp. 45–66). San Francisco: John Wiley & Sons.

Jarvis, W. B. G., & Petty, R. E. (1996). The need to evaluate. *Journal of Personality and Social Psychology, 70,* 172–194.

Jasmos, T. M., & Hakmiller, K. I. (1975). Some effects of lesion level, and emotional cues of affective expression in spinal cord patients. *Psychological Reports, 37,* 859–870.

Jeffery, K. J. (1997). LTP and spatial learning — where to next? *Hippocampus, 7,* 95–110.

Jemmott, J. B., III, Boryseko, J. Z., Borysenko, M., McClelland, D. C., Chapman, R., Meyer, D., et al. (1983). Academic stress, power motivation, and decrease in secretion rate of salivary secretory immunoglobulin A. *Lancet, 1,* 1400–1402.

Jencks, C. (1998). Racial bias in testing. In C. Jencks & M. Phillips (Eds.), *The black-white test score gap* (pp. 55–85). Washington, DC: Brookings Institution.

Jencks, C., & Phillips, M. (1998). *The black-white test score gap*. Washington, DC: Brookings Institution.

Jenike, M. A. (1983). Obsessive compulsive disorder. *Comprehensive Psychiatry, 24,* 99–111.

Jenkins, J. H., & Karno, M. (1992). The meaning of expressed emotion: Theoretical issues raised by cross-cultural research. *American Journal of Psychiatry, 149,* 9–21.

Jenner, E. A., Watson, P. W. B., Miller, L., Jones, F., & Scott, G. M. (2002). Explaining hand hygiene practice: An extended application of the theory of planned behavior. *Psychology, Health, and Medicine, 7,* 311–326.

Jensen, A. R. (1969). How much can we boost IQ and scholastic achievement? *Harvard Educational Review, 39,* 1–123.

Jensen, A. R. (1973). *Educability and group differences*. New York: Harper & Row.

Jensen, A. R. (1998). *The g-factor: The science of mental ability*. London: Praeger.

Jetten, J., Postmes, T., & McAuliffe, B. J. (2002). 'We're all individuals': Group norms of individualism and collectivism, levels of identification and identity threat. *European Journal of Social Psychology, 32,* 189–207.

Jewesbury, E. C. O. (1951). Insensitivity to pain. *Brain, 74,* 336–353.

Jockin, V., McGue, M., & Lykken, D. (1996). Personality and divorce: A genetic analysis. *Journal of Personality and Social Psychology, 71,* 288–299.

John, O., & Robins, R. (1994). Accuracy and bias in self-perception: Individual differences in self-enhancement and the role of narcissism. *Journal of Personality and Social Psychology, 66,* 206–219.

John, O. P. (1990). The big five factor taxonomy: Dimensions of personality in the natural language and in questionnaires. In L. Pervin (Ed.), *Handbook of personality: Theory and research* (pp. 66–100). New York: Guilford Press.

John, O. P., & Srivastava, S. (1999). The big five trait taxonomy: History, measurement, and theoretical perspectives. In L. A. Pervin & O. P. John (Eds.), *Handbook of personality: Theory and research* (2nd ed., pp. 102–138). New York: Guilford Press.

Johnson, J. G., Cohen, P., Smailes, E. M., Kasen, S., & Brook, J. S. (2002). Television viewing and aggressive behaviour during adolescence and adulthood. *Science, 295* (5564). Retrieved November 4, 2007, from Academic Search Premier database.

Johnson, H. M., & Seifert, C. M. (1994). Sources of the continued influence effect: When misinformation in memory affects later inferences. *Journal of Experimental Psychology: Learning, Memory and Cognition, 20,* 1420–1436.

Johnson, H. M., & Seifert, C. M. (1998). Updating accounts following a correction of misinformation. *Journal of Experimental Psychology: Learning, Memory and Cognition, 24,* 1483–1494.

Johnson, J. V., Stewart, W., Hall, E. M., Fredlund, P., & Theorell, T. (1996). Long-term psychosocial work environment and cardiovascular mortality among Swedish men. *American Journal of Public Health, 86,* 324–331.

Johnson, K., Churchill, L., Klitenick, M. A., & Hooks, M. S. (1996). Long-term psychosocial work environment and cardiovascular mortality among Swedish men. *American Journal of Public Health, 86,* 324–331.

Johnson, K. O., & Lamb, G. H. (1981). Neural mechanisms of spatial tactile discrimination: Neural patterns evoked by Braille-like dot patterns in the monkey. *Journal of Physiology, 310,* 117–144.

Johnson, K. T. (2010). *Predicting the relationship satisfaction of couples with dependent children: The impact of attachment, conflict styles and emotional intelligence*. Unpublished doctoral thesis, Swinburne University of Technology, Melbourne, Australia.

Johnson, L. R., Mayanja, M. K., Bangirana, P., & Kizito, S. (2009). Contrasting concepts of depression in Uganda: Implications for service delivery in a multicultural context. *American Journal of Orthopsychiatry, 79*(2), 275–289.

Johnson, M. K., Kim, J. K., & Risse, G. (1985). Do alcoholic Korsakoff's syndrome patients acquire affective reactions? *Journal of Experimental Psychology: Learning, Memory, & Cognition, 11,* 22–36.

Johnson, R. T., Burk, J. A., & Kirkpatrick, L. A. (2007). Dominance and prestige as differential predictors of aggression and testosterone levels in men. *Evolution and Human Behavior, 28,* 345–351.

Johnson, S. L., & Jacob, T. (2000). Sequential interactions in the marital communication of depressed men and women. *Journal of Consulting & Clinical Psychology, 68,* 4–12.

Johnson, S. L., & Miller, I. (1997). Negative life events and time to recovery from episodes of bipolar disorder. *Journal of Abnormal Psychology, 106,* 449–457.

Johnson, W., McGue, M., & Krueger, R. F. (2005). Personality stability in late adulthood: A behavioral genetic analysis. *Journal of Personality, 73*(2), 523–551.

Johnson-Laird, P. N. (1995). Mental models, deductive reasoning, and the brain. In M. S. Gazzaniga (Ed.), *The cognitive neurosciences* (pp. 999–1008). Cambridge, MA: MIT Press.

Johnson-Laird, P. N. (1996). The process of deduction. In D. Steier & T. M. Mitchell (Eds.), *Mind matters: A tribute to Allen Newell. Carnegie Mellon Symposia on cognition* (pp. 363–399). Hollsdale, NJ: Lawrence Erlbaum.

Johnson-Laird, P. N. (1999). Deductive reasoning. *Annual Review of Psychology, 50,* 109–135.

Johnson-Laird, P. N., Legrenzi, P., Girotto, V., & Legrenzi, M. S. (2000). Illusions in reasoning about consistency. *Science, 288,* 531–532.

Johnson-Laird, P. N., Legrenzi, P., & Legrenzi, M. S. (1972). Reasoning and a sense of reality. *British Journal of Psychology, 63,* 395–400.

Johnston, L., & Miles, L. (2003). Responding to the social world: Attributions and stereotype-based judgments. In J. Forgas, K. Williams, & W. von Hippel (Eds.), *Responding to the social world: Implicit and explicit processes in social judgments and decisions* (pp. 364–386). Cambridge, UK: Cambridge University Press.

Joiner, T. E. (2000). Depression's vicious scree: Self-propagating and erosive processes in depression chronicity. *Clinical Psychology — Science and Practice, 7,* 203–218.

Jolicoeur, P., Gluck, M. A., & Kosslyn, S. M. (1984). Pictures and names: Making the connection. *Cognitive Psychology, 16,* 243–275.

Jonas, E., Schimel, J., Greenberg, J., & Pyszczynski, T. (2002). The scrooge effect: Evidence that mortality salience increases prosocial attitudes and behavior. *Personality and Social Psychology Bulletin, 28,* 1342–1353.

Jonas, K., Diehl, M., & Bromer, P. (1997). Effects of attitudinal ambivalence on information processing and attitude-intention consistency. *Journal of Experimental Social Psychology, 33,* 190–210.

Jonassen, D. H. (2000). Toward a design theory of problem solving. *Educational Technology Research & Development, 48*(4), 63–85.

Jones, C., & White, N. (1994). Adiposity in Aboriginal people from Arnhem Land, Australia: Variation in degree and distribution associated with age, sex, and lifestyle. *Annals of Human Biology, 21,* 207–227.

Jones, E. E., & Berglas, S. (1978). Control of attributions about the self through self-handicapping strategies: The appeal of alcohol and the role of underachievement. *Personality and Social Psychology Bulletin, 4,* 200–206.

Jones, E. G. (2000). Cortical and subcortical contributions to activity-dependent plasticity in primate somatosensory cortex. *Annual Review of Neuroscience, 23,* 1–37.

Jones, J. L., & Leary, M. R. (1994). Effects of appearance-based admonitions against sun exposure on tanning intentions in young adults. *Health Psychology, 13,* 86–90.

Jones, J. T., Pelham, B. W., Carvallo, M., & Mirenberg, M. C. (2004). How do I love thee? Let me count the Js: Implicit egotism and interpersonal attraction. *Journal of Personality and Social Psychology, 87,* 665–683.

Jones, K. L., Smith, D. W., Ulleland, C. N., & Streissguth, A. (1973). Pattern of malformation in offspring of chronic alcoholic mothers. *Lancet, 1,* 1267–1271.

Jonides, J., Schumacher, E. H., Smith, E. E., Lauber, E. J., Minoshima, S., & Koeppe, R. A. (1997). Verbal working memory load affects regional brain activation as measured by PET. *Journal of Cognitive Neuroscience, 9,* 462–475.

Jordan, C. H., Spencer, S. J., & Zanna, M. P. (2005). Types of high self-esteem and prejudice: How implicit self-esteem relates to ethnic discrimination among high explicit self-esteem individuals. *Personality and Social Psychology Bulletin, 31,* 693–702.

Jordens, K., & Van Overwalle, F. (2005). Cognitive dissonance and affect: An initial test of a connectionist account. *Psychologica Belgica, 45*(3), 157–184.

Jorm, A. (2001). *Dementia: A major health problem for Australia* (Position paper 1, September). Retrieved from http://www.alzvic.asn.au/jorm.htm

Josephson, B. R., Singer, J. A., & Salovey, P. (1996). Mood regulation and memory: Repairing sad moods with happy memories. *Cognition and Emotion, 10,* 437–444.

Judd, C., Park, B., Ryan, C. S., Brauer, M., & Kraus, S. (1995). Stereotypes and ethnocentrism: Diverging interethnic perceptions of African American and white American youth. *Journal of Personality and Social Psychology, 69,* 460–481.

Julien, R. M. (1998). *A primer of drug action*. New York: Freeman.

Julien, R. M. (2007). *A primer of drug action* (11th ed.). New York: Freeman.

Julius, D., & King, A. J. (2005). Sensory systems: Editorial overview. *Current Opinion in Neurobiology, 15*(4), 379–381.

Jung, R. E., & Haier, R. J. (2007). The parieto-frontal integration theory (P-FIT) of intelligence: Converging neuroimaging evidence. *Behavioral and Brain Sciences, 30*(2), 135–154.

Jung, Y. C., An, S. K., Seok, J. H., Kim, J. E., Oh, S. J., Moon, D. H., et al. (2006). Neural substrates associated with evaluative processing during co-activation of positivity and negativity: A PET investigation. *Biological Psychology, 73*(3), 253–261.

Jusczyk, P. W., Houston, D. M., & Newsome, M. (1999). The beginnings of word segmentation in English-learning infants. *Cognitive Psychology, 39,* 159–207.

Just, M. A., & Carpenter, P. A. (1992). A capacity theory of comprehension: Individual differences in working memory. *Psychological Review, 99,* 122–149.

Kaas, J. H. (1987). Somatosensory cortex. In G. Adelman (Ed.), *Encyclopedia of neuroscience: Vol. 2*. Boston: Birkhauser.

Kafetsios, K., & Nezlek, J. B. (2002). Attachment styles in everyday social interaction. *European Journal of Social Psychology, 32,* 719–735.

Kagan, J. (1983). Stress and coping in early development. In N. Garmezy & M. Rutter (Eds.), *Stress, coping, and development in children*. New York: McGraw-Hill.

Kagan, J. (1984). *The nature of the child*. New York: Basic Books.

Kagan, J. (1989). Temperamental contributions to social behavior. *American Psychologist, 44,* 668–674.

Kagan, J., Kearsley, R. B., & Zelazo, P. R. (1978). *Infancy: Its place in human development*. Cambridge, MA: Harvard University Press.

Kagan, J., & Zentner, M. (1996). Early childhood predictors of adult psychopathology. *Harvard Review of Psychiatry, 3,* 341–350.

Kahan, D. (2010). Fixing the communications failure. *Nature, 463*(21), 296–297.

Kahan, D. M., Braman, D., Lohen, G. L., Gastil, J., & Slovic, P. (2010). Who fears the HPV vaccine, who doesn't and why? An experimental study of the mechanisms of cultural cognition. *Law and Human Behavior*.

Kahan, D. M., Braman, D., Slovic, P., Gastil, J., & Cohen, G. (2009). Cultural cognition of the risks and benefits of nanotechnology. *Nature Nanotechnology, 4,* 87–90.

Kahn, R. S., Davidson, M., & Davis, K. L. (1996). Dopamine and schizophrenia revisted. In S. J. Watson (Ed.), *Biology of schizophrenia and affective disease* (pp. 369–391). Washington, DC: American Psychiatric Press.

Kahn, S., Zimmerman, G., Csikszentmihalyi, M., & Getzels, J. (1985). Relations between identity in young adulthood and intimacy at midlife. *Journal of Personality and Social Psychology, 49,* 1316–1322.

Kahneman, D., & Tversky, A. (1979). Prospect theory: An analysis of decision under risk. *Econometrica, 47,* 263–291.

Kahneman, D., & Tversky, A. (1982). The simulation heuristic. In D. Kahneman, P. Slovic, & A. Tversky (Eds.), *Judgment under uncertainty: Heuristics and biases* (pp. 201–208). New York: Cambridge University Press.

Kail, R. (1991a). Developmental change in speed of processing during childhood and adolescence. *Psychological Bulletin, 109,* 490–501.

Kail, R. (1991b). Processing time declines exponentially during childhood and adolescence. *Developmental Psychology, 27,* 259–266.

Kail, R. (2000). Speed of information processing: Developmental change and links to intelligence. *Journal of School Psychology, 38,* 51–61.

Kail, R., & Pellegrino, J. W. (1985). *Human intelligence: Perspectives and prospects*. New York: Freeman.

Kalat, J. W. (2007). *Biological psychology* (9th ed.). Belmont, CA: Thomson Wadsworth.

Kamalanabhan, T. J., Sunder, D. L., & Vasanthi, M. (2000). An evaluation of the choice dilemma questionnaire as a measure of risk-taking propensity. *Social Behaviour and Personality, 28*(2), 149–156.

Kamarack, T. W., Schwartz, J. E., Shiffman, S., Muldoon, M. F., Sutton-Tyrrell, K., & Janicki, D. L. (2005). Psychosocial stress and cardiovascular risk: What is the role of daily experience? *Journal of Personality, 73,* 1–26.

Kamil, A. C., & Jones, J. E. (1997). The seed-storing corvid Clark's nutcracker learns geometric relationships among landmarks. *Nature, 390,* 276–279.

Kamil, A. C., & Jones, J. E. (2000). Geometric rule learning by Clark's nutcrackers (columbiana). *Journal of Experimental Psychology: Animal Behavior Processes, 26,* 439.

Kamin, L. J. (1969). Predictability, surprise, attention, and conditioning. In B. A. Campbell & R. M. Church (Eds.), *Punishment and aversive behavior*. New York: Appleton-Century-Crofts.

Kamin, L. J. (1974). *The science and politics of I.Q.* Hillsdale, NJ: Lawrence Erlbaum.

Kaminer, Y., & Hrecznyj, B. (1991). Lysergic acid diethylamide-induced chronic visual disturbances in an adolescent. *Journal of Nervous and Mental Disease, 179,* 173–174.

Kampe, K. K. W., Frith, C. D., Dolan, R. J., & Frith, U. (2001). Reward value of attractiveness and gaze. *Nature, 416,* 589.

Kandel, E. R. (1998). A new intellectual framework for psychiatry. *American Journal of Psychiatry, 155,* 457–469.

Kandel, E. R. (1999). Biology and the future of psychoanalysis: A new intellectual framework for psychiatry revisited. *American Journal of Psychiatry, 156,* 505–524.

Kane, M. J., Brown, L. E., McVay, J. C., Silvia, P. J., Myin-Germeys, I., & Kwapil, T. R. (2007). For whom the mind wanders, and when: An experience-sampling study of working memory and executive control in daily life. *Psychological Science, 18,* 614–621.

Kane, M. J., Conway, A. R., Miura, T. K., & Colflesh, G. J. H. (2007). Working memory, attention control, and the N-back task: A question of construct validity. *Journal of Experimental Psychology: Learning, Memory, and Cognition, 33,* 615–622.

Kane, M. J., & Engle, R. W. (2002). The role of prefrontal cortex in working memory capacity, executive attention, and general fluid intelligence: An individual-differences perspective. *Psychonomic Bulletin and Review, 9,* 637–671.

Kanizsa, G. (1976). Subjective contours. *Scientific American, 234,* 48–52.

Kanner, A. D., Coyne, J. C., Schaefer, C., & Lazarus, R. S. (1981). Comparison of two modes of stress measurement: Daily hassles and uplifts versus major life events. *Journal of Behavioral Medicine, 491,* 1–39.

Kanwisher, N., McDermott, J., & Chun, M. M. (1997). The fusiform face area: A module in human extrastriate cortex specialized for face perception. *Journal of Neuroscience, 17,* 4302–4311.

Kaplan, J. S., & Sue, S. (1997). Ethnic psychology in the United States. In D. F. Halpern & A. E. Voiskounsky (Eds.), *States of mind: American and post-Soviet perspectives on contemporary issues in psychology* (pp. 342–369). New York: Oxford University Press.

Kappas, A. (2003). What facial activity can and cannot tell us about emotions. In M. Katsikitis (Ed.), *The human face: Measurement and meaning* (pp. 215–234). Dordrecht: Kluwer Academic.

Kapur, S., Tulving, E., Cabeza, R., & McIntosh, A. R. (1996). The neural correlates of intentional learning of verbal materials: A PET study in humans. *Cognitive Brain Research, 4,* 243–249.

Kapur, S., Zipursky, R., Jones, C., Remington, G., & Houle, S. (2000). Relationship between dopamine D-sub-2 occupancy, clinical response, and side effects: A double-blind PET study of first-episode schizophrenia. *American Journal of Psychiatry, 157,* 514–520.

Kardiner, A. (1945). *The psychological frontiers of society*. New York: Columbia University Press.

Karlsen, E., Dybdahl, R., & Bitterso, J. (2006). The possible benefits of difficulty: How stress can increase and decrease subjective wellbeing. *Scandinavian Journal of Psychology, 47,* 411–417.

Karney, B. R., & Bradbury, T. N. (2000). Attributions in marriage: State or trait? A growth curve analysis. *Journal of Personality and Social Psychology, 78,* 295–309.

Kassin, S., & Kiechel, K. (1996). The social psychology of false confessions: Compliance, internationalization, and confabulation. *Psychological Science, 7,* 125–128.

Katahn, M., & McMinn, M. (1990). Obesity: A biobehavioral point of view. *Annals of the New York Academy of Arts and Sciences, 602,* 189–204.

Katigbak, M., Church, A. T., & Akamine, T. (1996). Cross-cultural generalizability of personality dimensions: Relating indigenous and imported dimensions in two cultures. *Journal of Personality and Social Psychology, 70,* 99–114.

Katz, H., & Beilin, H. (1976). A test of Bryant's claims concerning the young children's understanding of quantitative invariance. *Child Development, 47,* 877–880.

Katz, I., & Hass, R. (1988). Racial ambivalence and American value conflict: Correlational and priming studies of dual cognitive structures. *Journal of Personality and Social Psychology, 55,* 893–905.

Katz, J., & Melzack, R. (1990). Pain 'memories' in phantom limbs: Review and clinical observations. *Pain, 43,* 319–336.

Kaufman, L., & Rock, I. (1989). The moon illusion thirty years later. In M. Hershenson (Ed.), *The moon illusion* (pp. 193–234). Hillsdale, NJ: Lawrence Erlbaum.

Kawakami, K., Dovidio, J. F., Moll, J., Hermsen, S., & Russin, A. (2000). Just say no (to stereotyping): Effects of training in the negation of stereotypic associations on stereotype activation. *Journal of Personality and Social Psychology, 78,* 871–888.

Kaye, S., & Darke, S. (2003). *Non-fatal cocaine overdose and other adverse events among injecting and non-injecting cocaine users*. Sydney, Australia: National Drug and Alcohol Research Centre.

Kaye, W. H., Bulik, C. M., Thornton, L., Barbarich, N., & Masters, K. (2004). Comorbidity of anxiety disorders with anorexia and bulimia nervosa. *American Journal of Psychiatry, 161,* 2215–2221.

Kaye, W. H., Gendall, K., & Strober, M. (1998). Serotonin neuronal function and selective serotonin reuptake inhibitor treatment in anorexia and bulimia nervosa. *Biological Psychiatry, 44,* 825–838.

Kazak, A. E., Simms, S., & Rourke, M. T. (2002). Family systems practice in pediatric psychology. *Journal of Pediatric Psychology, 27*(2), 133–143.

Kazantzis, N. (2006). Theory, research, and practice of cognitive behaviour therapy in special feature. *New Zealand Journal of Psychology, 35*(3), 114–116.

Kazdin, A. E., & Tuma, A. H. (1982). *Single-case research designs*. San Francisco: Jossey-Bass.

Kearins, J. (1976). Skills of desert Aboriginal children. In G. E. Kearney & D. W. McElwain (Eds.), *Aboriginal cognition: Retrospect and prospect*. Canberra, Australia: Australian Institute of Aboriginal Studies Press.

Kearins, J. (1984). *Child-rearing practices in Australia: Variation with lifestyle*. Perth, Australia: Education Department of Western Australia.

Kearins, J. (1986). Visual spatial memory in Aboriginal and white Australian children. *Australian Journal of Psychology, 38*, 203–214.

Kearins, J. (1988). Cultural elements in testing: The test, the tester and the tested. In G. Davidson (Ed.), *Ethnicity and cognitive assessment: Australian perspectives* (pp. 60–70). Darwin, Australia: Darwin Institute of Technology.

Kearins, J. (2000). Children and cultural difference. In P. Dudgeon, D. Garvey, & H. Pickett (Eds.), *Working with Indigenous Australians: A handbook for psychologists* (pp. 167–176). Perth, Australia: Gunada Press.

Keats, D. M. (1988). Cultural concepts of intelligence. In G. Davidson (Ed.), *Ethnicity and cognitive assessment: Australian perspectives* (pp. 37–43). Darwin, Australia: Darwin Institute of Technology.

Keefe, F. J., Buffington, A. L. H., Studts, J. L., & Rumble, M. E. (2002). Behavioral medicine: 2002 and beyond. *Journal of Consulting and Clinical Psychology, 70*, 852–856.

Keel, P. K., & Mitchell, J. E. (1997). Outcome in bulimia nervosa. *American Journal of Psychiatry, 154*, 313–321.

Keenan, T. (2002). *An introduction to child development*. London: Sage.

Keith, K. L. (2010). *My child has a problem — aggression*. Retrieved from http://childparenting.about.com/cs/behaviorproblems/a/aggressivechild.htm

Keller, L. S., & Butcher, J. N. (1991). *Assessment of chronic pain patients with the MMPI-2*. Minneapolis: University of Minnesota Press.

Kelley, H. H. (1950). The warm-cold variable in first impressions of persons. *Journal of Personality, 18*, 431–439.

Kelley, H. H. (1973). The process of causal attribution. *American Psychologist, 28*, 107–128.

Kelley, H. H. (1979). *Personality relationships*. Hillsdale, NJ: Lawrence Erlbaum.

Kelley, H. H. (1992). Common-sense psychology and scientific psychology. *Annual Review of Psychology, 43*, 1–23.

Kelley, H. H., & Thibaut, J. W. (1978). *Interpersonal relations: A theory of interdependence*. New York: Wiley.

Kelley, J. E., Lumley, M. A., & Leisen, J. C. C. (1997). Health effects of emotional disclosure in rheumatoid arthritis patients. *Health Psychology, 16*, 331–340.

Kelley, S. A., Brownell, C. A., & Campbell, S. B. (2000). Mastery motivation and self-evaluative affect in toddlers: Longitudinal relations with maternal behavior. *Child Development, 71*, 1061–1071.

Kelly, G. A. (1955). *Psychology of personal constructs*. New York: W.W. Norton.

Kelly, J. (2008). Teaching us how to American dream? *The Psychologist, 21*, 810–811.

Kelman, H. C. (2006). Interests, relationships, identities: Three central issues for individuals and groups in negotiating their social environment. *Annual Review of Psychology, 57*, 1–26.

Keltner, D., & Bonanno, G. A. (1997). A study of laughter and dissociation: Distinct correlates of laughter and smiling during bereavement. *Journal of Personality and Social Psychology, 73*, 687–702.

Keltner, D., Kring, A. M., & Bonanno, G. A. (1999). Fleeting signs of the course of life: Facial expression and personal adjustment. *Current Directions in Psychological Science, 8*, 18–22.

Kemeny, M. E., & Laudenslager, M. L. (1999). Beyond stress: The role of individual difference factors in psychoneuroimmunology. *Brain, Behavior and Immunity, 13*, 73–75.

Kenardy, J. (1997a). *Dieting, body image and weight: Ethnicity and acculturation*. Paper presented at the Australian Tropical Health and Nutrition Conference, Brisbane, Queensland, Australia.

Kenardy, J. (1997b, September). *The Australian longitudinal study on women's health: Weight, shape, and dieting*. Paper presented at the Challenge the Body Culture Conference, Brisbane, Queensland, Australia.

Kenardy, J., Brown, W. J., & Vogt, E. (2001). Dieting and health in young Australian women. *European Eating Disorders Review, 9*, 242–254.

Kenardy, J., Evans, L., & Tian, P. (1992). The latent structure of anxiety symptoms in anxiety disorders. *American Journal of Psychiatry, 149*, 1058–1061.

Kendall, P. C. (1993). Treating anxiety disorders in children: Results of a randomized clinical trial. *Journal of Consulting and Clinical Psychology, 62*, 100–110.

Kendall, P. C. (1999). Clinical significance. *Journal of Consulting and Clinical Psychology, 67*, 283–284.

Kendall, P. C., Marrs-Garcia, A., Nath, S. R., & Sheldrick, R. C. (1999). Normative comparisons for the evaluation of clinical significance. *Journal of Consulting and Clinical Psychology, 67*, 285–299.

Kendler, K. S. (1995). Adversity, stress and psychopathology: A psychiatric genetic perspective. *International Journal of Methods in Psychiatric Research, 5*, 163–170.

Kendler, K. S., & Gardner, C. O., Jr. (1998). Boundaries of major depression: An evaluation of DSM-IV criteria. *American Journal of Psychiatry, 155*, 172–177.

Kendler, K. S., Gardner, C. O., & Prescott, C. A. (1999). Clinical characteristics of major depression that predict risk of depression in relatives. *Archives of General Psychiatry, 56*, 322–327.

Kendler, K. S., Karkowski, L. M., Neale, M. C., & Prescott, C. A. (2000). Illicit psychoactive substance use, heavy use, abuse and dependence in a U.S. population-based sample of male twins. *Archives of General Psychiatry, 57*, 261–269.

Kendler, K. S., Karkowski, L. M., & Prescott, C. A. (1999). Causal relationship between stressful life events and the onset of major depression. *American Journal of Psychiatry, 156*, 837–848.

Kendler, K. S., MacLean, C., Neale, M., Kessler, R., Heath, A., & Eaves, L. (1991). The genetic epidemiology of bulimia nervosa. *American Journal of Psychiatry, 148*, 1627–1637.

Kendler, K. S., Myers, J. M., O'Neill, F. A., Martin, R., Murphy, B., MacLean, C. J., et al. (2000). Clinical features of schizophrenia and linkage to chromosomes 5q, 6p, 8p, and 10p in the Irish study of high density schizophrenia families. *American Journal of Psychiatry, 157*, 402–408.

Kendler, K. S., Neale, M. C., Heath, A. C., Kessler, R. C., & Eaves, L. J. (1994). A twin-family study of alcoholism in women. *American Journal of Psychiatry, 151*, 707–715.

Kendler, K. S., Neale, M., Kessler, R., Heath, A., & Eaves, L. (1992). The genetic epidemiology of phobias in women: The interrelationship of agoraphobia, social phobia, situational phobia, and simple phobia. *Archives of General Psychiatry, 49*, 273–281.

Kendler, K. S., Neale, M. C., Kessler, R. C., & Heath, A. C. (1993a). A longitudinal twin study of 1-year prevalence of major depression in women. *Archives of General Psychiatry, 50*, 843–852.

Kendler, K. S., Neale, M. C., Kessler, R. C., & Heath, A. C. (1993b). A test of the equal-environment assumption in twin studies of psychiatric illness. *Behavior Genetics, 23*, 21–27.

Kendler, K. S., Prescott, C., Neale, M. C., & Pedersen, N. L. (1997). Temperance Board registration for alcohol abuse in a national sample of Swedish male twins, born 1902 to 1949. *Archives of General Psychiatry, 54*, 178–184.

Kendler, K. S., Walters, E. E., Neale, M. C., Kessler, R. C., Heath, A. C., & Eaves, L. J. (1995). The structure of the genetic and environmental risk factors for six major psychiatric disorders in women: Phobia, generalised anxiety disorder, panic disorder, bulimia, major depression, and alcoholism. *Archives of General Psychiatry, 52*, 374–383.

Kenealy, P. M. (1997). Mood-state-dependent retrieval: The effects of induced mood on memory reconsidered. *Quarterly Journal of Experimental Psychology: Human Experimental Psychology, 50*, 290–317.

Kennair, L. E. O. (2002). Evolutionary psychology: An emerging integrative perspective within the science and practice of psychology. *Human Nature Review, 2*, 17–61.

Kennedy, S. H., Holt, A., & Baker, G. B. (2004). Monoamine oxidise inhibitors. In S. H. Preskorn, J. P. Feighner, C. Y. Stanga, & R. Ross (Eds.), *Antidepressants: Past, present and future* (pp. 209–240). Berlin: Springer-Verlag.

Kenrick, D., Groth, G., Trost, M., & Sadalla, E. (1993). Integrating evolutionary and social exchange perspectives on relationships: Effects of gender, self-appraisal, and involvement level on mate selection criteria. *Journal of Personality and Social Psychology, 64*, 951–969.

Kenrick, D., & Keefe, R. (1992). Age preferences in mates reflect sex differences in human reproductive strategies. *Behavioral and Brain Sciences, 15*, 75–113.

Kenrick, D. T., & Stringfield, D. O. (1980). Personality traits and the eye of the beholder: Crossing some traditional philosophical boundaries in the search for consistency in all of the people. *Psychological Review, 87*, 88–104.

Kernberg, O. (1975). *Borderline conditions and pathological narcissism*. New York: Aronson.

Kernberg, O. (1984). *Severe personality disorders: Psychotherapeutic strategies*. New Haven, CT: Yale University Press.

Kernberg, O. F., Selzer, M. A., Koenigsberg, H. W., Carr, A. C., & Appelbaum, A. H. (1989). *Psychodynamic psychotherapy of borderline patients*. New York: Basic Books.

Kerr, N. H., Foulkes, D., & Jurkovic, G. J. (1978). Reported absence of visual dream imagery in a normally sighted subject with Turner's syndrome. *Journal of Mental Imagery, 2*, 247–264.

Kessler, R. C., House, J. S., & Turner, J. B. (1987). Unemployment and health in a community sample. *Journal of Health and Social Behavior, 28*, 51–59.

Kessler, R. C., Stein, M. B., & Berglund, P. (1998). Social phobia subtypes in the National Comorbidity Survey. *American Journal of Psychiatry, 155*, 613–619.

Kessler, R. C., Turner, J. B., & House, J. S. (1989). Unemployment, reemployment, and emotional functioning in a community sample. *American Sociological Review, 54*, 648–657.

Kety, S. S., Rosenthal, D., Wender, P. H., Schulsinger, F., & Jacobsen, B. (1975). Mental illness in the biological and adoptive families of adopted individuals who have become schizophrenic: A preliminary report based on psychiatric interviews. In E. Fieve, D. Rosenthal, & H. Brill (Eds.), *Genetic research in psychiatry*. Baltimore: Johns Hopkins University Press.

Khatibi, A., Dehghani, M., Sharpe, L., Asmundson, G. J. G., & Pouretemad, H. (2009). Selective attention towards painful faces among chronic pain patients: Evidence from a modified version of the dot-probe. *Pain, 142*, 42–47.

Khodarahimi, S. (2009). Satiation therapy and exposure response prevention in the treatment of obsessive compulsive disorder. *Journal of Contemporary Psychotherapy, 39*(3), 203–207.

Kiecolt-Glaser, J. K., Glaser, R., Shuttleworth, E. C., & Dyer, C. S. (1987). Chronic stress and immunity in family caregivers of Alzheimer's disease victims. *Psychosomatic Medicine, 49*, 523–535.

Kiecolt-Glaser, J. K., McGuire, L., Robles, T. F., & Glaser, R. (2002). Psychoneuroimmunology: Psychological influences on immune function and health. *Journal of Consulting and Clinical Psychology, 70*, 537–547.

Kiecolt-Glaser, J. K., Robles, T. F., Heffner, K. L., Loving, T. J., & Glaser, R. (2002). Psycho-oncology and cancer: Psychoneuroimmunology and cancer. *European Society of Medical Oncology*, 165–169.

Kiewitz, C., & Weaver, J. B., III. (2001). Trait aggressiveness, media violence, and perceptions of interpersonal conflict. *Personality and Individual Differences, 31*, 821–835.

Kihlstrom, J. F. (1987). The cognitive unconscious. *Science, 237*, 1445–1452.

Kihlstrom, J. F., & Cantor, N. (2000). Social intelligence. In R. J. Sternberg (Ed.), *Handbook of intelligence* (pp. 359–379). New York: Cambridge University Press.

Kilkkinen, A., Kao-Philpot, A., O'Neil, A., Philpot, B., Reddy, P., Bunker, S., et al. (2007). Prevalence of psychological distress, anxiety and depression in rural communities in Australia. *Australian Journal of Rural Health, 15*, 114–119.

Killen, M., & McKown, C. (2005). How integrative approaches to intergroup attitudes advance the field. *Applied Developmental Psychology*, *26*, 616–622.

Kim, H., & Markus, H. R. (1999). Deviance or uniqueness, harmony or conformity? A cultural analysis. *Journal of Personality and Social Psychology, 77*, 785–800.

Kim, J. J., & Fanselow, M. S. (1992). Modality-specific retrograde amnesia of fear. *Science, 256,* 675–677.

Kim, J. M. S., Andreasen, N. C., O'Leary, D. S., Watkins, G. L., Ponto, L. L. B., & Hichwa, R. D. (2000). Regional neural dysfunctions in chronic schizophrenia studied with positron emission tomography. *American Journal of Psychiatry, 157,* 542–548.

Kim, U., Park, Y. S., & Park, D. (2000). The challenge of cross-cultural psychology: The role of the indigenous psychologies. *Journal of Cross-Cultural Psychology*, *31*(1), 63–75.

Kimble, D. P. (1992). *Biological psychology* (2nd ed.). Fort Worth: Harcourt Brace Jovanovich.

Kimura, D. (1987). Are men's and women's brains really different? *Canadian Psychology*, *28*, 133–148.

Kimura, D. (1993). *Neuromotor mechanisms in human communication*. Oxford: Oxford University Press.

King, A. J., & Carlile, S. (1995). Neural coding for auditory space. In M. S. Gazzaniga (Ed.), *The cognitive neurosciences* (pp. 279–293). Cambridge, MA: MIT Press.

King, H. E. (1961). Psychological effects of excitation in the limbic system. In D. E. Sheer (Ed.), *Electrical stimulation of the brain*. Austin: University of Texas Press.

Kinney, D. K., Holzman, P. S., Jacobsen, B., Jansson, L., Faber, B., Hildebrand, W., et al. (1997). Thought disorder in schizophrenic and control adoptees and their relatives. *Archives of General Psychiatry, 54,* 475–479.

Kinomura, S., Larsson, J., Gulyas, B., & Roland, P. E. (1996). Activation of attention by the human reticular formation and thalamic intralaminar nuclei. *Science, 271*, 512–515.

Kinsbourne, M., & Smith, W. L. (1974). *Hemispheric disconnection and cerebral function*. Springfield, IL: Charles C. Thomas.

Kinsey, A. C., Pomeroy, W. B., & Martin, C. E. (1948). *Sexual behavior in the human male*. Philadelphia: W. B. Saunders.

Kinsey, A. C., Pomeroy, W. B., Martin, C. E., & Gebhard, P. (1953). *Sexual behavior in the human female*. Philadelphia: W. B. Saunders.

Kirkpatrick, L. A., & Ellis, B. J. (2006). The adaptive functions of self-evaluative psychological mechanisms. In M. H. Kernis (Ed.), *Self-esteem issues and answers: A sourcebook of current perspectives* (pp. 334–339). New York: Psychology Press.

Kirkwood, S., Liu, J. H., & Weatherall, A. (2005). Challenging the standard story of indigenous rights in Aotearoa/New Zealand. *Journal of Community & Applied Social Psychology*, *15*, 493–505.

Kirsch, I., & Lynn, S. J. (1998). Social-cognitive alternatives to dissociation theories of hypnotic involuntariness. *Review of General Psychology, 2*, 66–80.

Kirsch, I., Montgomery, G., & Sapirstein, G. (1995). Hypnosis as an adjunct to cognitive behavioral psychotherapy: A meta-analysis. *Journal of Consulting and Clinical Psychology, 63*, 214–220.

Kirschenbaum, H., & Jourdan, A. (2005). The current status of Carl Rogers and the person-centered approach. *Psychotherapy: Theory, Research, Practice*, *42*, 37–51.

Kirsner, K., & Speelman, C. (1996). Skill acquisition and repetition priming: One principle, many processes. *Journal of Experimental Psychology: Learning, Memory & Cognition, 22*(3), 563–575.

Kisker, E. E. (1985). Teenagers talk about sex, pregnancy, and contraception. *Family Planning Perspectives, 17,* 83–90.

Kitamura, C., Panneton, C., & Notley, A. (2006). Attuning to the native dialect: When more means less. In *Proceedings of the Australasian Speech Science and Technology Association* (pp. 124–129).

Kitamura, C., Panneton, R., Notley, A., & Best, C. T. (2006). Aussie, aussie, aussie, oi-oi-oi: Infants love an Australian accent. *Journal of the Acoustical Society of America, 120*, 3135.

Kitayama, S., & Markus, H. R. (Eds.). (1994). *Emotion and culture: Empirical studies of mutual influence*. Washington, DC: American Psychological Association.

Kitayama, S., Markus, H. R., Matsumoto, H., & Norasakkunkit, V. (1997). Individual and collective processes in the construction of the self: Self-enhancement in the United States and self-criticism in Japan. *Journal of Personality and Social Psychology, 72*, 1245–1267.

Kitayama, S., Snibbe, A. C., Markus, H. R., & Suzuki, T. (2004). Is there any 'free' choice? Self and dissonance in two cultures. *Psychological Science*, *15*(8), 527–533.

Kite, M. E., Stockdale, G. D., Whitley, Jr., B. E., & Johnson, B. T. (2005). Attitudes toward younger and older adults: An updated meta-analytic review. *Journal of Social Issues*, *61*, 241–266.

Klaczynski, P. (1997). Bias in adolescents' everyday reasoning and its relationship with intellectual ability, personal theories, and self-serving motivation. *Developmental Psychology, 33,* 273–283.

Klaczynski, P. (2000). Motivated scientific reasoning biases, epistemological beliefs, and theory polarization: A two-process approach to adolescent cognition. *Child Development, 71,* 1347–1366.

Klaczynski, P. A., Goold, K. W., & Mudry, J. J. (2004). Culture, obesity stereotypes, self-esteem, and the 'thin ideal': A social identity perspective. *Journal of Youth and Adolescence*, *33*(4), 307–317.

Klayman, J., & Ha, Y. (1989). Hypothesis testing in rule discovery: Strategy, structure, and content. *Journal of Experimental Psychology: Learning, Memory, and Cognition, 15,* 596–604.

Klein, C. T. F., & Helweg-Larsen, M. (2002). Perceived control and the optimistic bias: A meta-analytic review. *Psychology and Health, 17,* 437–446.

Klein, D. N., Schwartz, J. E., Rose, S., & Leader, J. B. (2000). Five-year course and outcome of dysthymic disorder: A prospective, naturalistic follow-up study. *American Journal of Psychiatry, 157,* 931–939.

Kleinke, C. L., Peterson, T. R., & Rutledge, T. R. (1998). Effects of self-generated facial expressions on mood. *Journal of Personality and Social Psychology, 74*, 272–279.

Kleinman, A. (1988). *Rethinking psychiatry: From cultural category to personal experience*. New York: Macmillan.

Kleitman, S., & Stankov, L. (2007). Self-confidence and metacognitive processes. *Learning and Individual Differences, 17*, 161–173.

Klesges, R. C., & Klesges, L. M. (1988). Cigarette smoking as a dietary strategy in a university population. *International Journal of Eating Disorders, 7*, 413–417.

Kleven, M., & Seiden, L. (1991). Repeated injection of cocaine potentiates methamphetamine-induced toxicity to dopamine-containing neurons in rat striatum. *Brain Research, 557,* 340–343.

Klinger, M. R., & Greenwald, A. G. (1994). Preferences need no inferences? The cognitive basis of unconscious mere exposure effects. In P. M. Niedenthal & S. Kitayama (Eds.), *The heart's eye: Emotional influences in perception and attention* (pp. 67–85). San Diego, CA: Academic Press.

Klinnert, M. D., Campos, J. J., Sorce, J. F., Emde, R. R., & Svejda, M. (1983). Emotions as behavior regulators: Social reference in infancy. In R. Plutchik & H. Kellerman (Eds.), *Emotion: Theory, research, and experience: Vol. 2. Emotions in early development*. San Diego, CA: Academic Press.

Klocker, N. (2004). Community antagonism towards asylum seekers in Port Augusta, South Australia. *Australian Geographical Studies, 42*, 1–17.

Kluckhohn, F., & Strodtbeck, F. (1961). *Variations in value orientations*. Evanston, IL: Row, Peterson.

Kluger, A., & DeNisi, A. (1996). The effects of feedback interventions on performance: A historical review, a meta-analysis, and a preliminary feedback intervention theory. *Psychological Bulletin, 119*, 254–284.

Kluver, H., & Bucy, P. (1939). Preliminary analysis of functions of the temporal lobe in monkeys. *Archives of Neurology and Psychiatry, 42*, 979–1000.

Knott, R., & Marlsen-Wilson, W. (2001). Does the medial temporal lobe bind phonological memories? *Journal of Cognitive Neuroscience, 13,* 593–609.

Knowlton, B. J., Mangels, J. A., & Squire, L. R. (1996). A neostriatal habit learning system in humans. *Science, 273*, 1399–1402.

Knupfer, G. (1991). Abstaining for foetal health: The fiction that even light drinking is dangerous. *British Journal of Addiction, 86,* 1063–1073.

Kocan, S. E., & Curtis, G. J. (2009). Close encounters of the initial kind: Implicit self-esteem, name-letter similarity, and social distance. *Basic and Applied Social Psychology, 31*, 17–23.

Kochanska, G. (1997). Multiple pathways to conscience for children with different temperaments: From toddlerhood to age 5. *Developmental Psychology, 33,* 228–240.

Kochanska, G., Aksan, N., & Joy, M. E. (2007). Children's fearfulness as a moderator of parenting in early socialization: Two longitudinal studies. *Developmental Psychology*, *43*, 222–237.

Kochanska, G., Murray, K. T., & Harlan, E. T. (2000). Effortful control in early childhood: Continuity and change, antecedents, and implications for social development. *Developmental Psychology, 36,* 220–232.

Koenig, A. L., Cicchetti, D., & Rogosch, F. A. (2004). Moral development: The association between maltreatment and young children's prosocial behaviours and moral transgressions. *Social Development*, *13*, 87–106.

Koerner, K., & Linehan, M. M. (2000). Research on dialectical behavior therapy for patients with borderline personality disorder. *Psychiatric Clinics of North America, 23,* 151–167.

Koestner, R., Zuroff, D., & Powers, T. (1991). Family origins of adolescent self-criticism and its continuity into adulthood. *Journal of Abnormal Psychology, 100,* 191–197.

Kogan, S. M., & Winter, D. D. N. (2010). *The psychology of environmental problems* (3rd ed.). New York: Psychology Press.

Kohlberg, L. (1963). The development of children's orientations toward a moral order. I. Sequence in the development of moral thought. *Vita Humana, 6,* 11–33.

Kohlberg, L. (1976). Moral stages and moralization: The cognitive-developmental perspective. In T. Lickona (Ed.), *Moral development and behavior: Theory, research, and social issues*. New York: Holt, Rinehart & Winston.

Kohlberg, L., & Kramer, R. (1969). Continuities and discontinuities in childhood and adult moral development. *Human Development, 12,* 93–120.

Kohlberg, L. A. (1966). A cognitive-developmental analysis of children's sex-role concepts and attitudes. In E. E. Maccoby (Ed.), *The development of sex differences*. Stanford, CA: Stanford University Press.

Kohlenberg, R. J., & Tsai, M. (1994). Improving cognitive therapy for depression with functional analytic psychotherapy: Theory and case study. *Behavior Analyst, 17,* 305–319.

Kohler, W. (1925). *The mentality of apes*. New York: Harcourt Brace.

Kohut, H. (1971). *The analysis of the self: A systematic approach to the treatment of narcissistic personality disorders*. New York: International Universities Press.

Kohut, H. (1977). *The restoration of the self*. New York: International Universities Press.

Kokko, K., & Pulkkinen, L. (1997). Economical and psychological well-being of the unemployed. *Psykologia, 32*, 349–359.

Kolb, B., & Whishaw, I. Q. (1996). *Fundamentals of neuropsychology*. New York: Freeman.

Kolers, P. A. (1976). Reading a year later. *Journal of Experimental Psychology: Human Learning and Memory, 2*, 554–565.

Konishi, M. (1995). Neural mechanisms of auditory image formation. In M. S. Gazzaniga (Ed.), *The cognitive neurosciences* (pp. 269–277). Cambridge, MA: MIT Press.

Konner, M. (1991). Universals of behavioral development in relation to brain myelination. In K. R. Gibson & A. C. Petersen (Eds.), *Brain maturation and cognitive development: Comparative and cross-cultural perspectives*. New York: Aldine de Gruyter.

Konrad, A. M., Ritchie, J., Edgar, J., Lieb, P., & Corrigall, E. (2000). Sex differences and similarities in job attribute preferences: A meta-analysis. *Psychological Bulletin, 126*, 593–641.

Koo, C., & Lee, G. Y. (1994). *Multiculturalism in Australia: An Asian perspective*. Retrieved October 26, 2004, from http://www.atrax.net.au/userdir/yeulee/NonHmong/Multiculturalism%20in%20Australia.html

Koopman-Boyden, P. G., & MacDonald, L. (2003). Ageing, work performance and managing ageing academics. *Journal of Higher Education Policy and Management, 25*, 29–40.

Kopelman, P. G. (2000). Obesity as a medical problem. *Nature, 404*, 635–643.

Kopp, C. B. (1989). Regulation of distress and negative emotions: A developmental view. *Developmental Psychology, 25*, 343–354.

Kordaki, M., & Balomenou, A. (2006). Challenging students to view the concept of area in triangles in a broad context: Exploiting the features of CABRI-II. *International Journal of Computers for Mathematical Learning, 11*(1), 99–135.

Korfine, L., & Hooley, J. M. (2000). Directed forgetting of emotional stimuli in borderline personality disorder. *Journal of Abnormal Psychology, 109*, 214–221.

Koriat, A., Goldsmith, M., & Pansky, A. (2000). Toward a psychology of memory accuracy. *Annual Review of Psychology, 51*, 481–537.

Korn, J. H., Davis, R., & Davis, S. F. (1991). Historians' and chairpersons' judgments of eminence among psychologists. *American Psychologist, 46*, 789–792.

Kornor, H., & Nordvik, H. (2004). Personality traits in leadership behavior. *Scandinavian Journal of Psychology, 45*, 49–54.

Korten, A. E., Henderson, A. S., Christensen, H., Jorm, A. F., Rodgers, B., Jacomb, P., et al. (1997). A prospective study of cognitive function in the elderly. *Psychological Medicine, 27*, 919–930.

Kosslyn, S. M. (1983). *Ghosts in the mind's machine*. New York: W. W. Norton.

Kosslyn, S. M., Alpert, N. M., Thompson, W. L., Maljokovic, V., Weise, S. B., Chabris, C. F., et al. (1993). Visual imagery activates topographically organized visual cortex: PET investigations. *Journal of Cognitive Neuroscience, 5*, 263–287.

Kosslyn, S. M., Thompson, W. L., Costantini- Ferrando, M. F., Alpert, N. M., & Spiegel, D. (2000). Hypnotic visual illusion alters brain color processing. *American Journal of Psychiatry, 157*, 1279–1284.

Kosslyn, S. M., Thompson, W. L., Kim, I. J., & Alpert, N. M. (1995). Topographical representations of mental images in primary visual cortex. *Nature, 378*, 496–498.

Koster, E. H., Fox, E., & MacLeod, C. (2009). Introduction to the special section on cognitive bias modification in emotional disorders. *Journal of Abnormal Psychology, 118*, 1–4.

Kouri, E., Pope, H. G., Yurgelun-Todd, D., & Gruber, S. (1995). Attributes of heavy vs. occasional marijuana smokers in a college population. *Biological Psychiatry, 38*, 475–481.

Kouris-Blazos, A., & Wahlqvist, M. L. (2007). Health economics of weight management: Evidence and cost. *Asia Pacific Journal of Clinical Nutrition, 16*(Suppl. 1), 329–338.

Kourtzi, Z., & Kanwisher, N. (2000). Activation in human MT/MST by static images with implied motion. *Journal of Cognitive Neuroscience, 12*, 48–55.

Kovacs, D. M., Parker, J. G., & Hoffman, L. W. (1996). Behavioral, affective, and social correlates of involvement in cross-sex friendship in elementary school. *Child Development, 67*, 2269–2286.

Kowalski, R. M. (Ed.). (1997). *Aversive interpersonal behaviors*. New York: Plenum Press.

Kowalski, R. M. (Ed.). (2001). *Behaving badly: Aversive behaviors in interpersonal relationships*. Washington, DC: American Psychological Association.

Kowalski, R. M., & Bodenlos, J. (2003). *Psychosocial predictors of organ donation*. Manuscript under review.

Kowalski, R. M., & Brown, K. (1994). Psychosocial barriers to cervical cancer screening: Effects of self-presentation and social evaluation. *Journal of Applied Social Psychology, 24*, 941–958.

Kowalski, R. M., Ellis, M., Hamby, M., Ritchie, J., & Starkovich, E. (2002). *Perceptions of pet peeves in our relationships with close friends and strangers*. Paper presented at the meeting of the Society for Personality and Social Psychology, Savannah, GA.

Kowalski, R. M., & Wolfe, R. (1994). Collective identity orientation, patriotism, and reactions to national outcomes. *Personality and Social Psychology Bulletin, 20*, 533–540.

Kozulin, A., & Presseisen, B. Z. (1995). Mediated learning experience and psychological tools: Vygotsky's and Feuerstein's perspectives in a study of student learning. *Educational Psychologist, 30*, 67–75.

Kraaij, V., & Garnefski, N. (2002). Negative life events and depressive symptoms in late life: Buffering effects of parental and partner bonding? *Personal Relationships, 9*, 205–214.

Kraemer, G. (1992). A psychobiological theory of attachment. *Behavioral and Brain Sciences, 15*, 493–541.

Kraemer, H. C., Kazdin, A. E., Offord, D. R., Kessler, R. C., Jensen, P. S., & Kupfer, D. J. (1997). Coming to terms with the terms of risk. *Archives of General Psychiatry, 54*, 337–343.

Kraly, F. S. (2006). *Brain science and psychological disorders: Therapy, psychotropic drugs, and the brain*. New York: W. W. Norton.

Kramer, L., & Gottman, J. (1992). Becoming a sibling: 'With a little help from my friends'. *Developmental Psychology, 28*, 685–699.

Kramer, L., Perozynski, L. A., & Chung, T. (1999). Parental responses to sibling conflict: The effects of development and parent gender. *Child Development, 70*, 1401–1414.

Kraus, N., Malmfors, T., & Slovic, P. (1992). Intuitive toxicology: Expert and lay judgments of chemical risks. *Risk Analysis, 12*, 215–232.

Kraus, S. J. (1995). Attitudes and the prediction of behavior: A meta-analysis of the empirical literature. *Personality and Social Psychology Bulletin, 21*, 58–75.

Kraut, R., Olson, J., Banaji, M., Bruckman, A., Cohen, J., & Couper, M. (2003). *Psychological research online: Opportunities and challenges*. Retrieved from http://www.apa.org/science/apainternetresearch.pdf

Kremen, A. M., & Block, J. (1998). The roots of ego-control in young adulthood: Links with parenting in early childhood. *Journal of Personality & Social Psychology, 75*, 1062–1075.

Kretchmar, M. D., & Jacobvitz, D. B. (2002). Observing mother-child relationships across generations: Boundary patterns, attachment, and transmission of caregiving. *Family Process, 41*, 351–374.

Kring, A. M., & Gordon, A. H. (1998). Sex differences in emotion: Expression, experience, and physiology. *Journal of Personality and Social Psychology, 74*, 686–703.

Kripke, D., Simons, R. N., Garfinkel, L., & Hammond, E. C. (1979). Short and long sleep and sleeping pills. *Archives of General Psychiatry, 36*, 103–116.

Krueger, R. F. (2000). Phenotypic, genetic, and nonshared environmental parallels in the structure of personality: A view from the multidimensional personality questionnaire. *Journal of Personality and Social Psychology, 79*, 1057–1067.

Krueger, R. F., & Markon, K. E. (2006). Reinterpreting comorbidity: A model-based approach to understanding and classifying psychopathology. *Annual Review of Clinical Psychology, 2*, 111–133.

Kruesi, M., Hibbs, E., Zahn, T., & Keysor, C. (1992). A 2-year prospective follow-up study of children and adolescents with disruptive behavior disorders: Prediction by cerebrospinal fluid 5-hydroxyindoleacetic acid, homovanillic acid, and autonomic measures? *Archives of General Psychiatry, 49*, 429–435.

Krystal, A. D., Dean, M. D., Weiner, R. D., Tramontozzi, L. A., Connor, K. M., Lindahl, V. H., et al. (2000). ECT stimulus intensity: Are present ECT devices too limited? *American Journal of Psychiatry, 157*, 963–967.

Kubzansky, L. D., Sparrow, D., Vokonas, P., & Kawachi, I. (2001). Is the glass half empty or half full? A prospective study of optimism and coronary heart disease in the normative aging study. *Psychosomatic Medicine, 63*(6), 910–916.

Kudo, E., & Numazaki, M. (2003). Explicit and self-serving bias for success and failure. *Journal of Cross-Cultural Psychology, 34*(5), 511–521.

Kuffler, S. W. (1953). Discharge patterns and functional organization of mammalian retina. *Journal of Neurophysiology, 16*, 37–68.

Kuhl, P. K., & Meltzoff, A. N. (1988). Speech and an intermodal object of perception. In A. Tonas (Ed.), *Minnesota symposium on child psychology: Vol. 20. Perceptual development in infancy*. Hillsdale, NJ: Lawrence Erlbaum.

Kuhlmeier, V. A., Boysen, S. T., & Mukobi, K. L. (1999). Scale-model comprehension by chimpanzees (Pan troglodytes). *Journal of Comparative Psychology, 113*, 396–402.

Kuhn, D. (2000). Metacognitive development. *Current Directions in Psychological Science, 9*, 178–181.

Kuhn, T. S. (1970). *The structure of scientific revolutions* (2nd ed.). Chicago: University of Chicago Press.

Kuiper, N. A., & Derry, P. A. (1982). Depressed and nondepressed content self-reference in mild depression. *Journal of Personality, 50*, 67–79.

Kuiper, N. A., Olinger, L. J., MacDonald, M. R., & Shaw, B. F. (1985). Self-schema processing of depressed and nondepressed content: The effects of vulnerability on depression. *Social Cognition, 3*, 77–93.

Kunda, Z. (1990). The case for motivated reasoning. *Psychological Bulletin, 108*, 480–498.

Kunda, Z., & Thagard, P. (1996). Forming impressions from stereotypes, traits, and behaviors: A parallel-constraint satisfaction theory. *Psychological Review, 103*, 284–308.

Kunz, P. R., & Woolcott, M. (1976). Season's greetings: From my status to yours. *Social Science Research, 5*, 269–278.

Kunzendorf, R. G., Spanos, N. P., & Wallace, B. (Eds.). (1996). *Hypnosis and imagination. Imagery and human development series*. New York: Baywood Publishing.

Kuo-shu, Y., & Bond, M. H. (1990). Exploring implicit personality theories with indigenous or imported constructs: The Chinese case. *Journal of Personality and Social Psychology, 58*, 1087–1095.

Kushner, M. G., Abrams, K., & Borchardt, C. (2000). The relationship between anxiety disorders and alcohol use disorders: A review of major perspectives and findings. *Clinical Psychology Review, 20*, 149–171.

Kvavilashvili, L. (1987). Remembering intention as a distinct form of memory. *British Journal of Psychology, 78*, 507–518.

Kwon, P. (1999). Attributional style and psychodynamic defense mechanisms: Toward an integrative model of depression. *Journal of Personality, 67*(4), 645–658.

Kyrios, M., Prior, M., Oberklaid, F., & Demetriou, A. (1989). Cross-cultural studies of temperament in Greek infants. *International Journal of Psychology, 24*, 585–603.

LaBar, K. S., & LeDoux, J. E. (1996). Partial disruption of fear conditioning in rats with unilateral amygdala damage: Correspondence with unilateral temporal lobectomy in humans. *Behavioral Neuroscience, 110*, 991–997.

LaBarre, W. (1966). The Aymaya: History and world view. *Journal of American Folklore, 79*, 130–144.

Labouvie-Vief, G., & Schell, D. A. (1982). Learning and memory in late life. In B. B. Wolman (Ed.), *Handbook of developmental psychology*. Englewood Cliffs, NJ: Prentice-Hall.

Lack, L. C. (1986). Delayed sleep and sleep loss in university students. *Journal of American College Health, 35*, 105–110.

Ladd, G. W. (1999). Peer relationships and social competence during early and middle childhood. *Annual Review of Psychology, 50*, 333–359.

Ladd, G. W., & Mize, J. (1983). A cognitive-social learning model of social skill training. *Psychologial Review, 90*, 127–157.

Ladson-Billings, G. (2003). New directions in multicultural education: Complexities, boundaries, and critical race theory. In J. A. Banks & C. A. McGee Banks (Eds.), *Handbook of research on multicultural educations* (pp. 50–65). San Francisco: Jossey-Bass.

LaFreniere, P. J., & Sroufe, L. A. (1985). Profiles of peer competence in the preschool: Interrelations between measures, influences of social ecology, and relation to attachment history. *Developmental Psychology, 21*, 56–69.

Laing, D. G., Prescott, J., Bell, G. A., & Gilmore, R. (1993). A cross-cultural study of taste discrimination with Australians and Japanese. *Chemical Senses, 18*, 161–168.

Lakoff, G. (1985). *Women, fire, and dangerous things*. Chicago: University of Chicago Press.

Lakoff, G. (1989). A suggestion for a linguistics with connectionist foundations. In D. Touretzky, G. E. Hinton, & T. Sejnowski (Eds.), *Proceedings of the 1988 Connectionist Models Summer School* (pp. 301–314). San Mateo, CA: Morgan Kaufmann.

Lakoff, G. (1997). How unconscious metaphorical thought shapes dreams. In D. J. Stein (Ed.), *Cognitive science and the unconscious. Progress in psychiatry* (No. 52, pp. 89–120). Washington, DC: American Psychiatric Press.

Lalor, D. (2002). *A memory scanning study*. Unpublished manuscript, University of Southern Queensland, Australia.

Lalumiere, M. L., Blanchard, R., & Zucker, K. J. (2000). Sexual orientation and handedness in men and women: A meta-analysis. *Psychological Bulletin, 126*, 575–592.

Lamb, M. E. (1987). Introduction: The emergent American father. In M. E. Lamb (Ed.), *The father's role: Cross-cultural perspective*. Hillsdale, NJ: Lawrence Erlbaum.

Lamb, M. E. (2005). Attachments, social networks, and developmental contexts. *Human Development, 48*, 108–112.

Lamb, M. E., Easterbrooks, M. A., & Holden, G. (1980). Reinforcement and punishment among preschoolers: Characteristics and correlates. *Child Development, 51*, 1230–1236.

Lamb, M. E., & Roopnarine, J. L. (1979). Peer influences on sex-role development in preschoolers. *Child Development, 50*, 1219–1222.

Lambert, M. J. (2004). *Bergin and Garfield's handbook of psychotherapy and behavior change* (5th ed.). New York: John Wiley & Sons.

Lambert, M. J., & Bergin, A. E. (1994). The effectiveness of psychotherapy. In A. E. Bergin & S. L. Garfield (Eds.), *Handbook of psychotherapy and behavior change* (4th ed., pp. 143–189). Oxford: John Wiley & Sons.

Lambert, M. J., Shapiro, D. A., & Bergin, A. E. (1986). The effectiveness of psychotherapy. In S. L. Garfield & A. E. Bergin (Eds.), *Handbook of psychotherapy and behavior change*. New York: John Wiley.

Lame Deer, J., & Erdoes, R. (1972). *Lame Deer, seeker of visions*. New York: Simon & Schuster.

Lamond, N., Dorrian, J., Roach, G. D., McCulloch, K., Holmes, A. L., Burgess, H. J., et al. (2003). The impact of a week of simulated night work on sleep, circadian phase, and performance. *Occupational and Environmental Medicine, 60*(11), e13.

Landau, E., & Weissler, K. (1993). Parental environment in families with gifted and nongifted children. *Journal of Psychology, 127*, 129–142.

Landman, J. T., & Dawes, R. M. (1982). Psychotherapy outcome: Smith and Glass' conclusions stand up under scrutiny. *American Psychologist, 37*, 504–516.

Lane, C., & Hobfoll, S. E. (1992). How loss affects anger and alienates potential supporters. *Journal of Consulting and Clinical Psychology, 6*, 935–942.

Lane, R. D., Reiman, E. M., Bradley, M. M., Lang, P. J., Ahern, G. L., Davidson, R. J., et al. (1997). Neuroanatomical correlates of pleasant and unpleasant emotion. *Neuropsychologia, 35*, 1437–1444.

Lang, O. (1946). *Chinese family and society*. New Haven, CT: Yale University Press.

Lang, P. (1995). The emotion probe: Studies of motivation and attention. *American Psychologist, 50*, 372–385.

Lang, P. J. (1994). The varieties of emotional experience: A meditation on James-Lange theory. *Psychological Review, 101*, 212–221.

Lange, E. B., & Oberauer, K. (2005). Overwriting of phonemic features in serial recall. *Memory, 13*(3/4), 333–339.

Lange, C. G. (1922). The emotions: A psychophysiological study. In C. G. Lange & W. James (Eds.), *Psychology classics: Vol. I*. Baltimore: Williams & Wilkins. (Originally published 1885, I. A. Haupt, Trans.)

Langer, E. J. (1978). Rethinking the role of thought in social interaction. In J. H. Harvey, W. I. Ickes, & R. F. Kidd (Eds.), *New directions in attribution research: Vol. 2* (pp. 35–58). Hillsdale, NJ: Lawrence Erlbaum.

Langlois, J., Ritter, J. M., Roggman, L., & Vaughn, L. S. (1991). Facial diversity and infant preferences for attractive faces. *Developmental Psychology, 27*, 79–84.

Langlois, J. H., & Downs, A. C. (1980). Mothers, fathers, and peers as socialization agents of sex-typed play behaviors in young children. *Child Development, 51*, 1217–1247.

Lansford, J. E., Chang, L., Dodge, K. A., Malone, P. S., Oburu, P., Palmérus, K., et al. (2005). Physical discipline and children's adjustment: Cultural normativeness as a moderator. *Child Development, 76*(6), 1234–1246.

Lanzetta, J. T., Cartwright-Smith, J., & Kleck, R. E. (1976). Effects of nonverbal dissimulation on emotional experience and autonomic arousal. *Journal of Personality and Social Psychology, 33*, 354–370.

Large, E. W., & Jones, M. R. (1999). The dynamics of attending: How people track time-varying events. *Psychological Review, 106*, 119–159.

Laroi, F. (2003). The family systems approach to treating families of persons with brain injury: A potential collaboration between family therapist and brain injury professional. *Brain Injury, 17*, 175–187.

Larose, H., & Standing, L. (1998). Does the halo effect occur in the elderly? *Social Behavior and Personality, 26*, 147–150.

Larsen, R. J., Billings, D. W., & Cutler, S. E. (1996). Affect intensity and individual differences in informational style. *Journal of Personality, 64*, 185–207.

Larson, R. W. (1997). The emergence of solitude as a constructive domain of experience in early adolescence. *Child Development, 68*, 80–93.

Larsson, H., Andershed, A., & Lichtenstein, P. (2006). A genetic factor explains most of the variation in the psychopathic personality. *Journal of Abnormal Psychology, 115*(2), 221–230.

Larzelere, R. E., Schneider, W. N., Larson, D. B., & Pike, P. L. (1996). The effects of discipline responses in delaying toddler misbehavior recurrences. *Child and Family Behavior Therapy, 18*, 35–57.

Lasswell, H. D. (1948). The structure and function of communication in society. In L. Bryson (Ed.), *Communication of ideas*. New York: Harper-Collins.

Latham, G. P., & Brown, T. C. (2006). The effect of learning vs. outcome goals on self-efficacy, satisfaction and performance in an MBA program. *Applied Psychology, 55*(4), 606–623.

Latimer, P. R. (1979). The behavior treatment of self-excoriation in a twelve-year-old girl. *Journal of Behavioral Therapy and Experimental Psychiatry, 10*, 349–352.

Laub, J. B., & Sampson, R. J. (1995). The long-term effect of punitive discipline. In J. McCord (Ed.), *Coercion and punishment in long-term perspectives* (pp. 247–258). New York: Cambridge University Press.

Lavie, P. (1996). *The enchanted world of sleep* (A. Berris, Trans.). New Haven, CT: Yale University Press.

Lawrence, C. B., Turnbull, A. V., & Rothwell, N. J. (1999). Hypothalamic control of feeding. *Current Opinion in Neurobiology, 9*, 778–783.

Lazarus, R. (1981). The stress and coping paradigm. In C. Eisdorfer, D. Cohen, A. Kleinman, & P. Maxim (Eds.), *Models for clinical psychopathology*. New York: Spectrum.

Lazarus, R. S. (1993). From psychological stress to the emotions: A history of changing outlooks. *Annual Review of Psychology, 44*, 1–21.

Lazarus, R. S. (1999a). *Stress and emotion: A new synthesis*. New York: Springer.

Lazarus, R. S. (1999b). The cognition-emotion debate: A bit of history. In T. Dalgleish & M. Power (Eds.), *The handbook of cognition and emotion* (pp. 3–20). New York: John Wiley & Sons.

Lazarus, R. S., & McCleary, R. A. (1951). Autonomic discrimination without awareness: A study of subception. *Psychological Review, 58*, 113–122.

Leach, J. (1994). *Survival psychology*. London: Macmillan.

Leaper, C., Anderson, K. J., & Sanders, P. (1998). Moderators of gender effects on parents' talk to their children: A meta-analysis. *Developmental Psychology, 34*, 3–27.

Leary, M. R. (1995). *Self-presentation: Impression management and social behavior*. Duguque, IA: Brown & Benchmark.

Leary, M. R. (1999). The scientific study of personality. In V. J. Derlega, B. A. Winstead, & W. H. Jones (Eds.), *Personality: Contemporary theory and research* (pp. 3–26). Chicago: Nelson-Hall.

Leary, M. R. (Ed.). (2001). *Interpersonal rejection*. London: Oxford University Press.

Leary, M. R., Britt, T. W., Cutlip, W. D., & Templeton, J. D. (1992). Social blushing. *Psychological Bulletin, 107*, 446–460.

Leary, M. R., & Jones, J. L. (1993). The social psychology of tanning and sunscreen use: Self-presentational motives as a predictor of health risk. *Journal of Applied Social Psychology, 23*, 1390–1406.

Leary, M. R., & Kowalski, R. M. (1990). Impression management: A literature review and two-component model. *Psychological Bulletin, 107*, 34–47.

Leary, M. R., Tchividjian, L. R., & Kraxberger, B. E. (1994). Self-presentation can be hazardous to your health: Impression management and health risk. *Health Psychology, 13*, 461–470.

Leask, S. J. (2004). Environmental influences in schizophrenia: The known and the unknown. *Advances in Psychiatric Treatment, 10*, 323–330.

Lebow, J. L. (2005). In J. L. Lebow (Ed.), *Handbook of clinical family therapy* (pp. 1–14). New York: Wiley.

Lecky, P. (1945). *Self-consistency: A theory of personality*. New York: Island Press.

LeDoux, J. (1995). Emotion: Clues from the brain. *Annual Review of Psychology, 46*, 209–235.

LeDoux, J. (1998). Fear and the brain: Where have we been, and where are we going? *Biological Psychiatry, 44*, 1229–1238.

LeDoux, J. E. (1989). Cognitive-emotional interactions in the brain. *Cognition and Emotion, 3*, 267–289.

LeDoux, J. E. (2000). Emotion circuits in the brain. *Annual Review of Neuroscience, 23*, 155–184.

LeDoux, J. E., Wilson, D. H., & Gazzaniga, M. S. (1977). Manipulo-spatial aspects of central lateralization. *Neuropsychologia, 15*, 743–750.

Lee, D. (1950). The conception of the self among the Wintu Indians. In D. Lee (Ed.), *Freedom and culture*. Englewood Cliffs, NJ: Prentice-Hall, 1959.

Lee, E. (1951). Negro intelligence and selective migration: A Philadelphia test of Klineberg's hypothesis. *American Sociological Review, 61*, 227–233.

Lee, R. (1993). Why are Aboriginal children labelled as a special needs group? *The Aboriginal Child at School, 2*(1), 23–31.

Lee, Y., & Seligman, M. E. P. (1997). Are Americans more optimistic than the Chinese? *Personality and Social Psychology Bulletin, 23,* 32–40.

Leerkes, E. M., & Siepak, K. J. (2006). Attachment-linked predictors of women's emotional and cognitive responses to infant distress. *Attachment & Human Development, 8*, 11–32.

Leeson, P., Ciarrochi, J., & Heaven, P. C. (2008). Cognitive ability, personality, and academic performance in adolescence. *Personality and Individual Differences, 45*(7), 630–635.

Leets, L. (2003). Disentangling perceptions of subtle racist speech: A cultural perspective. *Journal of Language and Social Psychology*, *22*(2), 145–168.

Lehman, D. R., Chiu, C., & Schaller, M. (2004). Psychology and culture. *Annual Review of Psychology, 55*, 689–714.

Lehman, D. R., Wortman, C. B., & Williams, A. F. (1987). Long-term effects of losing a spouse or child in a motor vehicle crash. *Journal of Personality and Social Psychology, 52,* 218–231.

Lehmann, H. E. (1985). Affective disorders: Clinical features. In H. I. Kaplan & B. J. Sadock (Eds.), *Comprehensive textbook of psychiatry* (4th ed.). Baltimore: Williams & Wilkins.

Lehrman, D. S. (1956). On the organization of maternal behavior and the problem of instinct. In *L'instinct dans le Comportement des Animaux et de l'homme*. Paris: Masson et Cie.

Leibowitz, J., Ramos-Marcuse, F., & Arsenio, W. F. (2002). Parent-child emotion communication, attachment, and affective narratives. *Attachment & Human Development*, *4*(1), 55–67.

Leichsenring, F., Rabung, S., & Leibing, E. (2004). The efficacy of short-term psychodynamic psychotherapy in specific psychiatry disorders: A meta-analysis. *Archives of General Psychiatry*, *61*, 1208–1216.

Leiserowitz, A. A. (2005). American risk perceptions: Is climate change dangerous. *Risk Analysis, 25*(6), 1433–1442.

Lempers, J. D., Flavell, E. R., & Flavell, J. H. (1977). The development in very young children of tacit knowledge concerning visual perception. *Genetic Psychology Monographs, 95,* 3–53.

Lenhart, A., Madden, M., & Hitlin, P. (2005). *Teens and technology: Youth are leading the transition to a fully wired and mobile nation*. Washington, DC: Pew Internet & American Life Project.

Lenneberg, E. (1967). *The biological foundations of language*. New York: John Wiley.

Lenzenweger, M. F., Loranger, A. W., Korfine, L., & Neff, C. (1997). Detecting personality disorders in a nonclinical population: Application of a 2-stage for case identification. *Archives of General Psychiatry, 54,* 345–351.

Lepore, L., & Brown, R. (2002). The role of awareness: Divergent automatic stereotype activation and implicit judgment correction. *Social Cognition*, *20*(4), 321–351.

Lepore, S. J. (1997). Expressive writing moderates the relation between intrusive thoughts and depressive symptoms. *Journal of Personality and Social Psychology, 73,* 1030–1037.

Lepore, S. J., & Greenberg, M. A. (2002). Mending broken hearts: Effects of expressive writing on mood, cognitive processing, social adjustment, and health following a relationship breakup. *Psychology and Health, 17,* 547–560.

Lepri, J. (2003). *Pheromones and animal behaviour: Communication by smell and taste*. Cambridge, UK: Blackwell.

Lerman, C., Caporaso, N. E., Audrain, J., Main, D., Bowman, E. D., Lockshin, B., et al. (1999). Evidence suggesting the role of specific genetic factors in cigarette smoking. *Health Psychology, 18,* 14–20.

Lerner, R. (1991). Changing organism–context relations as the basic process of development: A developmental contextual perspective. *Developmental Psychology, 27,* 27–32.

Lerner, J. S., & Keltner, D. (2000). Beyond valence: Toward a model of emotion-specific influences on judgment and choice. *Cognition and Emotion, 14*, 473–493.

LeVay, S. (1991). A difference in hypothalamic structure between heterosexual and homosexual men. *Science, 253*, 1034–1037.

Levenson, R., & Ruef, A. (1992). Empathy: A physiological substrate. *Journal of Personality and Social Psychology, 63*, 234–246.

Levenson, R. W. (1992). Autonomic nervous system differences among emotions. *Psychological Science, 3*, 23–27.

Levenson, R. W., Ekman, P., & Friesen, W. (1990). Voluntary facial action generates emotion- specific autonomic nervous system activity. *Psychophysiology, 27,* 363–385.

Levenson, R. W., Ekman, P., Heider, K., & Friesen, W. V. (1992). Emotion and autonomic nervous system activity in the Minangkabau of West Sumatra. *Journal of Personality and Social Psychology, 62*, 972–988.

Leventhal, E. A., Leventhal, H., Shacham, S., & Easterling, D. V. (1989). Active coping reduces reports of pain from childbirth. *Journal of Consulting and Clinical Psychology, 57*, 365–371.

Leventhal, H., & Leventhal, E. A. (1993). Affect, cognition, and symptom perception. In C. R. Chapman & K. M Foley (Eds.), *Current and emerging issues in cancer pain: Research and practice. Bristol-Myers Squibb Symposium on pain research series* (pp. 153–173). New York: Raven.

Leventhal, H., & Tomarken, A. J. (1986). Emotion: Today's problems. *Annual Review of Psychology, 37,* 565–610.

Levine, L. J., & Burgess, S. L. (1997). Beyond general arousal: Effects of specific emotions on memory. *Social Cognition, 15*, 157–181.

LeVine, R. (1982). *Culture, behavior, and personality* (2nd ed.). Chicago: Aldine.

LeVine, R. A., & LeVine, B. B. (1963). Nyasongo: A Gusii community in Kenya. In B. Whiting (Ed.), *Six cultures: Studies in child rearing* (pp. 19–202). New York: John Wiley.

Levine, R. V., Martinez, T., Brase, G., & Sorenson, K. (1994). Helping in 36 U.S. cities. *Journal of Personality and Social Psychology, 67*, 69–82.

Levine, R. V., Norenzayan, A., & Philbrick, K. (2001). Cross-cultural differences in helping strangers. *Journal of Cross Cultural Psychology*, *32*, 543–560.

Levinger, G. (1976). Social psychological perspectives on marital dissolution. *Journal of Social Issues, 32*, 21–47.

Levinson, B. W. (1965). States of awareness during general anaesthesia. Preliminary communication. *British Journal of Anaesthesia, 37*, 544–546.

Levinson, D. (1978). *The seasons of a man's life*. New York: Ballantine Books.

Levinson, D. J., Darrow, C. N., Klein, E. B., Levinson, M. H., & McKee, B. (1978). *The seasons of a man's life*. New York: Alfred A. Knopf.

Levkovitz, Y., Caftori, R., Avital, A., & Richter, L. G. (2002). The SSRI's drug Fluoxetine, but not the noradrenergic tricyclic drug Desipramine, improves memory performance during acute major depression. *Brain Research Bulletin, 58,* 345–350.

Lewandowsky, S., Stritzke, W. G. K., Oberauer, K., & Morales, M. (2005). Memory for fact, fiction, and misinformation: The Iraq War 2003. *Psychological Science, 16*, 190–195.

Lewin, K. (1939). Field theory and experiment in social psychology: Concepts and methods. *American Journal of Sociology, 44,* 868–897.

Lewinsohn, P. M., Allen, N. B., Seeley, J. R., & Gotlib, I. H. (1999). First onset versus recurrence of depression: Differential processes of psychosocial risk. *Journal of Abnormal Psychology, 108,* 483–489.

Lewinsohn, P. M., Gotlib, I. H., Lewinsohn, M., Seeley, J. R., & Allen, N. B. (1998). Gender differences in anxiety disorders and anxiety symptoms in adolescents. *Journal of Abnormal Psychology, 107,* 109–117.

Lewinsohn, P. M., Solomon, A., Seeley, J. R., & Zeiss, A. (2000). Clinical implications of 'subthreshold' depressive symptoms. *Journal of Abnormal Psychology, 109,* 345–351.

Lewis, D. A. (2000). Distributed disturbances in brain structure and function in schizophrenia. *American Journal of Psychiatry, 157,* 1–2.

Lewis, D. O., Yeager, C. A., Swica, Y., Pincus, J. H., & Lewis, M. (1997). Objective documentation of child abuse and dissociation in 12 murderers with dissociative identity disorder. *American Journal of Psychiatry, 154,* 1703–1710.

Lewis, J. A. (2006). Do juvenile drunk driving laws really work? An interrupted time-series analysis of Pennsylvania's zero-tolerance juvenile alcohol law (Ohio). *Dissertation Abstracts International Section A: Humanities and Social Sciences*, *67*(2-A), 731.

Lewis, J. W. (1990). Premenstrual syndrome as a criminal defense. *Archives of Sexual Behavior, 19*, 425–441.

Lewis, M. (1993). Self-conscious emotions: Embarrassment, pride, shame and guilt. In M. Lewis & J. M. Haviland (Eds.), *Handbook of emotions*. New York: Guilford Press.

Lewis, M., & Bendersky, M. (1995). *Mothers, babies, and cocaine: The role of toxins in development*. Hillsdale, NJ: Lawrence Erlbaum.

Lewis, M., Feiring, C., & Rosenthal, S. (2000). Attachment over time. *Child Development, 71,* 707–720.

Lewis, N., & Brooks-Gunn, J. (1979). *Social cognition and the acquisition of self*. New York: Plenum Press.

Lewkowicz, D. J. (2000). The development of intersensory temporal perception: An epigenetic systems/limitations view. *Psychological Bulletin, 126,* 281–308.

Li, N. P., Bailey, J. M., Kenrick, D. T., & Linsenmeier, J. A. W. (2002). The necessities and luxuries of mate preferences: Testing the tradeoffs. *Journal of Personality and Social Psychology*, *82*(6), 947–955.

Li, Z., Kim, C. H., Ichikawa, J., & Meltzer, H. Y. (2003). Effect of repeated administration of phencyclidine on spatial performance in an eight-arm radial maze with delay in rats and mice. *Pharmacology, Biochemistry, and Behavior, 75,* 335–340.

Liberman, A., & Chaiken, S. (1992). Defensive processing of personally relevant health messages. *Personality & Social Psychology Bulletin, 18*, 660–679.

Liberman, N., & Trope, Y. (1998). The role of feasibility and desirability conditions in near and distant future decisions: A test of temporal construal theory. *Journal of Personality and Social Psychology, 75*, 5–18.

Libet, B. (1965). Cortical activation in conscious and unconscious experience. *Perspectives in Biology and Medicine, 9*, 77–86.

Lickliter, R., & Bahrick, L. E. (2000). The development of infant intersensory perception: Advantages of a comparative convergent-operations approach. *Psychological Bulletin, 126,* 260–280.

Lieberman, J. D. (2002). Head over the heart or heart over the head? Cognitive experiential self-theory and extralegal heuristics in juror decision making. *Journal of Applied Psychology, 32*(12), 2526–2553.

Lieberman, M., Doyle, A., & Markiewicz, D. (1999). Developmental patterns in security of attachment to mother and father in late childhood and early adolescence: Associations with peer relations. *Child Development, 70,* 202–213.

Lieberman, M. D. (2000). Intuition: A social cognitive neuroscience approach. *Psychological Bulletin, 126,* 109–136.

Lieberman, M. D., Jarcho, J. M., & Obayashi, J. (2005). Attributional inference across cultures: Similar automatic attributions and different controlled corrections. *Personality and Social Psychology Bulletin*, *31*, 889–901.

Lieberman, M. D., Ochsner, K. N., Gilbert, D. T., & Schacter, D. L. (2001). Do amnesics exhibit cognitive dissonance reduction? The role of explicit memory and attention in attitude change. *Psychological Science*, *12*, 135–140.

Liem, A. D. (2007). Triandis award: Appreciating differences, celebrating similarities – an experience of learning in culturally diverse contexts. *Cross-Cultural Psychology Bulletin, 40*, 31–35.

Liem, A. D., Nair, E., Bernardo, A. B. I., & Prasetya, P. H. (2008). The influence of culture on students' classroom social interactions: Implications for best teaching and learning practice in multicultural and international education. In D. M. McInerney & A. D. Liem (Eds.), *Teaching and learning: International best practice. Vol. 8 in research on sociocultural influences on motivation and learning* (pp. 377–404). Charlotte, NC: Information Age Publishing.

Liem, G. A. D., Martin, A. J., Nair, E., Bernardo, A. B. I., & Prasetya, P. H. (2009). Cultural factors relevant to secondary school students in Australia, Singapore, Philippines and Indonesia: Relative differences and congruencies. *Australian Journal of Guidance and Counselling, 19*, 161–178.

Lierman, L. M., Kasprzyk, D., & Benoliel, J. Q. (1991). Understanding the adherence to breast self-examination in older women. *Western Journal of Nursing Research*, *13*, 46–66.

Life. Be in it. (2004). *Remember norm?* Retrieved August 1, 2004, from http://www.lifebeinit.org/?uri=history/start

Lifeline. (2009). *Suicide statistics not the full picture*. Retrieved July 21, from http://www.lifeline.org.au/learn_more/media_centre/media_releases/2009/suicide_statistics_not_the_full_picture

Lifton, R. J. (1963). *Thought reform and the psychology of totalism: A study of brainwashing in China*. New York: W. W. Norton.

Limongelli, L., Boysen, S. T., & Visalberghi, E. (1995). Comprehension of cause-effect relations in a tool-using task by chimpanzees (Pan troglodytes). *Journal of Comparative Psychology, 109*, 18–26.

Lin, E. H., & Peterson, C. (1990). Pessimistic explanatory style and response to illness. *Behaviour Research and Therapy, 28*, 243–248.

Lindberg, M. (1980). Is knowledge base development a necessary and sufficient condition for memory development? *Journal of Experimental Child Psychology, 30*, 401–410.

Lindemann, C. G. (Ed). (1996). *Handbook of the treatment of the anxiety disorders* (2nd ed.). Northvale, NJ: Jason Aronson.

Linden, W., & Moseley, J. V. (2006). The efficacy of behavioural treatments for hypertension. *Applied Psychophysiology and Biofeedback*, *31*(1), 51–63.

Lindley, R. H., & Smith, W. R. (1992). Coding tests as measures of IQ: Cognitive or motivation? *Personality and Individual Differences, 13*, 25–29.

Lindsey, E. W., & Mize, J. (2001). Contextual differences in parent-child play: Implications for children's gender role development. *Sex Roles*, *44*, 155–176.

Linehan, M. M. (1987a). Dialectical behavior therapy for borderline personality disorder: Theory and method. *Bulletin of the Menninger Clinic, 51*, 261–276.

Linehan, M. M. (1987b). Dialectical behavioral therapy: A cognitive behavioral approach to parasuicide. *Journal of Personality Disorders*, *1*, 328–333.

Linehan, M. M. (1993). *Cognitive-behavioral treatment of borderline personality disorder*. New York: Guilford Press.

Linehan, M. M. (2000). Behavioral treatments of suicidal behaviors: Definitional obfuscation and treatment outcomes. In R. W. Maris & S. S. Canetto (Eds.), *Review of suicidology, 2000* (pp. 84–111). New York: Guilford Press.

Lipp, O. V., Terry, D. J., Chalmers, D., Bath, D., Hannan, G., Martin, F., et al. (2007). *Teaching psychology: Learning outcomes and curriculum development in psychology*. Strawberry Hills, Australia: The Carrick Institute for Learning and Teaching in Higher Education.

Lipson, A. H., Walsh, D. A., & Webster, W. S. (1983). Fetal alcohol syndrome: A great paediatric imitator. *Medical Journal of Australia, 1*, 266–269.

Lisspers, J., & Ost, L. (1990). Long-term follow-up of migraine treatment: Do the effects remain up to six years? *Behaviour Therapy and Research, 28*, 313–322.

Litt, M., Babor, T., DelBoca, F., Kadden, R., & Cooney, N. (1992). Types of alcoholics, II: Application of an empirically derived typology to treatment matching. *Archives of General Psychiatry, 49*, 609–614.

Litt, M. D., Kadden, R. M., Cooney, N. L., & Kabela, E. (2003). Coping skills and treatment outcomes in cognitive-behavioral and interactional group therapy for alcoholism. *Journal of Consulting and Clinical Psychology, 71*, 118–128.

Little, A. (1987). Attributions in cross-cultural context. *Genetic, Social, and General Psychology Monographs, 113*, 61–79.

Littlefield, L., Giese, J., & Katsikitis, M. (2007, April). Special report. Professional psychology training under review. *InPsych, 29*(2), 6–13.

Livesley, W. J., & Bromley, D. B. (1973). *Person perception in childhood and adolescence*. London: John Wiley.

Livingstone, M., & Hubel, D. H. (1988). Segregation of form, color, movement, and depth: Anatomy, physiology, and perception. *Science, 240*, 740–749.

Lizzio, A. (2006). *The five senses of success: Designing effective transition programs for commencing students*. Queensland, Australia: Griffith University.

Lloyd, G. (2011, January 15). An inland tsunami — like a fury from hell. *The Australian*. Retrieved from http://www.theaustralian.com.au/in-depth/queensland-floods/an-inland-tsunami-like-a-fury-from-hell/story-fn7iwx3v-1225988066591

Locals urged to doorknock flood-zone homes. (2011, January). *ABC News*. Retrieved from http://www.abc.net.au/news/stories/2011/01/17/3114505.htm?section=justin

Locke, E., & Latham, G. (1990). *A theory of goal-setting and task performance*. Englewood Cliffs, NJ: Prentice-Hall.

Locke, E. A. (1991). Goal theory vs. control theory: Contrasting approaches to understanding work motivation. *Motivation and Emotion, 15*, 9–27.

Locke, E. A. (1996). Motivation through conscious goal setting. *Applied and Preventive Psychology, 5*, 117–124.

Lockhart, R. S., & Craik, F. (1990). Levels of processing: A retrospective commentary on a framework for memory research. *Canadian Journal of Psychology, 44*, 87–112.

Loeb, R. C., Horst, L., & Horton, P. J. (1980). Family interaction patterns associated with self-esteem in preadolescent girls and boys. *Merill-Palmer Quarterly, 26*, 203–217.

Loehlin, J. (1992). *Genes and environment in personality development*. New York: Guilford Press.

Loehlin, J. C., Horn, J. M., & Willerman, L. (1989). Modeling IQ change: Evidence from the Texas Adoption Project. *Child Development, 60*, 993–1004.

Loehlin, J. C., Horn, J. M., & Willerman, L. (1997). Heredity, environment and IQ in the Texas Adoption Project. In R. J. Sternberg & E. L. Grigorenko (Eds.), *Intelligence, heredity, and environment* (pp. 105–125). New York: Cambridge University Press.

Loehlin, J. C., McCrae, R. R., Costa, P. T., Jr., & John, O. P. (1998). Heritabilities of common and measure-specific components of the big five personality factors. *Journal of Research in Personality*, *32*, 431–453.

Loehlin, J. C., Neiderhiser, J. M., & Reis, D. (2003). The behavior genetics of personality and the NEAD study. *Journal of Research in Personality*, *37*, 373–387.

Loehlin, J. C., Willerman, L., & Horn, J. M. (1988). Human behavior genetics. *Annual Review of Psychology, 39*, 101–133.

Loevinger, J. (1976). *Ego development*. San Francisco: Jossey-Bass.

Loevinger, J. (1985). Revision of the sentence completion test for ego development. *Journal of Personality and Social Psychology, 48*, 420–427.

Loewenstein, W. R. (1960). Biological transducers. *Scientific American*, *203*, 98–108.

Loftus, E. (1993). The reality of repressed memories. *American Psychologist, 48*, 518–537.

Loftus, E. (1997a). Creating false memories. *Scientific American, 277*, 70–75.

Loftus, E. (1997b). Memory for a past that never was. *Current Directions in Psychological Science, 6*, 60–65.

Loftus, E. F. (2000). Remembering what never happened. In E. Tulving (Ed.), *Memory, consciousness, and the brain: The Tallinn Conference* (pp. 106–118). New York: Psychology Press.

Loftus, E. F., Levidow, B., & Duensing, S. (1992). Who remembers best? Individual differences in memory for events that occurred in a science museum. *Applied Cognitive Psychology, 6*, 93–107.

Loftus, E. F., & Palmer, J. C. (1974). Reconstruction and automobile destruction. An example of the interaction between language and memory. *Journal of Verbal Learning and Verbal Behavior, 13*, 585–589.

Loftus, E. F., Polonsky, S., & Fullilove, M. T. (1994). Memories of childhood sexual abuse: Remembering and repressing. *Psychology of Women Quarterly, 18*, 67–84.

Loftus, E. F., & Zanni, G. (1975). Eyewitness testimony: The influence of the wording of a question. *Bulletin of the Psychonomic Society, 5*, 86–88.

Logie, R. (1996). The seven ages of working memory. In J. T. E. Richardson, R. W. Engle, L. Hasher, R. Logie, E. Stoltzfus, & R. Zacks (Eds.), *Working memory and human cognition* (pp. 31–65). New York: Oxford University Press.

Lohman, T. G. (2002). Body composition. In K. D. Brownell & C. G. Fairburn (Eds.), *Eating disorders and obesity: A comprehensive handbook* (2nd ed., pp. 62–66). New York: Guilford Press.

Lohmann, H., & Tomasello, M. (2003). The role of language in false belief understanding: A training study. *Child Development, 74*(4), 1130–1144.

Longmore, R. J., & Worrell, M. (2007). Do we need to challenge thoughts in cognitive behavior therapy? *Clinical Psychology Review*, *27*(2), 173–187.

Lonner, W., & Malpass, R. (Eds.). (1994a). *Readings in psychology and culture*. Boston: Allyn & Bacon.

Lonner, W. J., & Malpass, R. (1994b). *Psychology and culture*. Needham Heights, MA: Allyn & Bacon.

Lopez, A., Atran, S., Coley, J. D., Medin, D. L., & Smith, E. E. (1997). The tree of life: Universal and cultural features of folkbiological taxonomies and inductions. *Cognitive Psychology, 32*, 251–295.

Lopez, S. R. (1995). Testing ethnic minority children. In B. B. Wolman (Ed.), *The encyclopedia of psychology, psychiatry, and psychoanalysis*. New York: Henry Holt.

Lore, R., & Schultz, L. A. (1993). Control of human aggression: A comparative perspective. *American Psychologist, 48*, 16–25.

Lorenz, K. (1935). The companion in the bird's world. The fellow-member of the species as releasing factor of social behavior. *Journal fuer Ornithologie, 83*, 137–213.

Lorenz, K. (1937). Ueber den Begriff der Instinkthandlung [The concept of instinctive action]. *Folia Biotheoretica, 2*, 17–50.

Lorenz, K. (1979). *King Solomon's ring*. New York: Harper-Collins.

Lott, A., & Lott, B. (1974). The role of reward in the formation of positive interpersonal attitudes. In T. Huston (Ed.), *Foundations of interpersonal attraction*. New York: Academic Press.

Lotufo-Neto, F., Bernik, M., Ramos, R. T., Andrade, L., Gorenstein, C., Cordas, T., et al. (2001). A dose-finding and discontinuation study of clomipramine in panic disorder. *Journal of Psychopharmacology*, *15*(1), 13–17.

Louw, F., & Straker, G. (2002). An integration of cognitive therapy and psychodynamic therapy. *Journal of Psychotherapy Integration, 12*, 190–217.

Lovaas, O. I. (1977). *The autistic child*. New York: John Wiley.

Lovaas, O. I. (1987). Behavioral treatment and normal educational and intellectual functioning in young autistic children. *Journal of Consulting and Clinical Psychology, 55,* 3–9.

Love, C. (2003). *Keynote address in the Proceedings of the National Maori Graduates of Psychology Symposium 2002*. Hamilton, New Zealand: The Maori and Psychology Research Unit, University of Waikato.

Low, B. S. (1989). Cross-cultural patterns in the training of children: An evolutionary perspective. *Journal of Comparative Psychology, 103,* 311–319.

Lu, C., Shaikh, M. B., & Siegel, A. (1992). Role of NMDA receptors in hypothalamic facilitation of feline defensive rage elicited from the midbrain pariaqueductal gray. *Brain Research, 581,* 123–132.

Luborsky, L. (1985). Therapist success and its determinants. *Archives of General Psychiatry, 42,* 602–611.

Luborsky, L., Barber, J. P., & Crits-Christoph, P. (1990). Theory-based research for understanding the process of dynamic psychotherapy. *Journal of Consulting and Clinical Psychology, 58,* 281–287.

Luborsky, L., & Crits-Christoph, P. (1990). *Understanding transference: The core conflictual relationship theme method*. New York: Basic Books.

Luborsky, L., Docherty, J. P., Miller, N. E., & Barber, J. P. (1993). What's here and what's ahead in dynamic therapy research and practice? In N. E. Miller, L. Luborsky, J. Barber, & J. Docherty (Eds.), *Psychodynamic treatment research: A handbook for clinical practice* (pp. 536–553). New York: Basic Books.

Luborsky, L., McLellan, A. T., Diguer, L., Woody, G., & Seligman, D. A. (1997). The psychotherapist matters: Comparison of outcomes across twenty-two therapists and seven patient samples. *Clinical Psychology — Science & Practice, 4,* 53–65.

Lubow, R. E., & Gewirtz, J. C. (1995). Latent inhibition in humans: Data, theory, and implications for schizophrenia. *Psychological Bulletin, 117,* 87–103.

Luchins, A. (1957). Primacy-recency in impression formation. In C. Hovland (Ed.), *The order of presentation in persuasion* (pp. 33–61). New Haven, CT: Yale University Press.

Luchins, A. S. (1942). Mechanisation in problem solving: The effect of Einstellung. *Psychological Monographs, 54*(248), 1–95.

Luchtenberg, S. (Ed.). (2004). *Migration, education and change*. London: Routledge.

Lucken, M., & Simon, B. (2005). Cognitive and affective experiences of minority and majority members: The role of group size, status, and power. *Journal of Experimental Social Psychology, 41,* 396–413.

Ludolph, P. S., Westen, D., Misle, B., Jackson, A., Wixom, J., & Wiss, F. C. (1990). The borderline diagnosis in adolescents: Symptoms and developmental history. *American Journal of Psychiatry, 147,* 470–476.

Lumer, E. D., & Rees, G. (1999). Covariation of activity in visual and prefrontal cortex associated with subjective visual perception. *Proceedings of the National Academy of Sciences, USA, 96,* 1669–1673.

Lumley, M. A., & Provenzano, K. M. (2003). Stress management through written emotional disclosure improves academic performance among college students with physical symptoms. *Journal of Educational Psychology, 93*(3), 641–649.

Lundh, L., Wikstrom, J., Westerlund, J., & Ost, L. (1999). Preattentive bias for emotional information in panic disorder with agoraphobia. *Journal of Abnormal Psychology, 108,* 222–232.

Luria, A. R. (1973). *The working brain*. Harmondsworth, UK: Penguin.

Luthar, S. S., Cicchetti, D., & Becker, B. (2000). Research on resilience: Response to commentaries. *Child Development, 71,* 573–575.

Lyketsos, C. G., Chen, L., & Anthony, J. C. (1999). Cognitive decline in adulthood: An 11.5-year follow-up of the Baltimore Epidemiologic Catchment Area Study. *American Journal of Psychiatry, 156,* 58–65.

Lykken, D. T., Bouchard, T. J., McGue, M., & Tellegen, A. (1993). Heritability of interests: A twin study. *Journal of Applied Psychology, 78,* 649–661.

Lynch, O. M. (1990). The social construction of emotion in India. In O. M. Lynch (Ed.), *Divine passions: The social construction of emotion in India* (pp. 3–34). Berkeley: University of California Press.

Lynd-Stevenson, R. M. (1999). Expectancy-value theory and predicting future employment status in the young unemployed. *Journal of Occupational and Organizational Psychology, 72,* 101–106.

Lynn, S. J., Lock, T., Myers, B., & Payne, D. G. (1997). Recalling the unrecallable: Should hypnosis be used to recover memories in psychotherapy? *Current Directions in Psychological Science, 6,* 79–83.

Lynne, S. D., Graber, J. A., Nichols, T. R., Brooks-Gunn, J., & Botvin, G. J. (2007). Links between pubertal timing, peer influences, and externalizing behaviors among urban students followed through middle school. *Journal of Adolescent Health, 40,* 181.e7–181.e13.

Lynskey, M. T., & Agrawal, A. (2007). Psychometric properties of DSM assessments of illicit drug abuse and dependence: Results from the National Epidemiologic Survey of Alcohol and Related Conditions (NESARC). *Psychological Medicine, 37,* 1345–1355.

Lyons, A. S., & Petrucelli, R. J., III. (1978). *Medicine: An illustrated history*. New York: Harry Abrams.

Lyons, M., McGregor-Lowndes, M., & O'Donoghue, P. (2006). Researching giving and volunteering in Australia. *Australian Journal of Social Issues, 41*(4), 385–397.

Lyons, M., & Passey, A. (2005). *Australians giving and volunteering, 2004. Giving Australia: Research on philanthropy in Australia*. Canberra, Australia: Department of Family and Community Services. Retrieved from http://www.partnerships.gov.au/philanthropy/philanthropy_research.shtml#FinalReports

Lyons, M. J., True, W. R., Eisen, S. A., & Goldberg, J. (1995). Differential heritability of adult and juvenile antisocial traits. *Archives of General Psychiatry, 52,* 906–915.

Lyons-Ruth, K., Connell, D., Grunebaum, H., & Botein, S. (1990). Infants at social risk: Maternal depression and familiy support services as mediators of infant development and security of attachment. *Child Development, 61,* 85–98.

Lyons-Ruth, K., Easterbrooks, M. A., & Cibelli, C. D. (1997). Infant attachment strategies, infant mental lag, and maternal depressive symptoms. Predictors of internalizing and externalizing problems at age 7. *Developmental Psychology, 33,* 681–692.

Lyons-Ruth, K., & Spielman, E. (2004). Disorganised infant attachment strategies and helpless-fearful profiles of parenting: Integrating attachment research with clinical intervention. *Infant Mental Health Journal, 25,* 318–335.

Lytton, H. (1990). Child and parent effects in boys' conduct disorder: A reinterpretation. *Developmental Psychology, 26,* 683–697.

Lyyra, T. M., & Heikkinen, R. L. (2006). Perceived social support and mortality in older people. *The Journals of Gerontology Series B: Psychological Sciences and Social Sciences, 61,* S47–S152.

MacCann, C. (2010). Further examination of emotional intelligence as a standard intelligence: A latent variable analysis of fluid intelligence, crystallized intelligence, and emotional intelligence. *Personality and Individual Differences, 49,* 490–496.

MacCann, C., Duckworth, A. L., & Roberts, R. D. (2008). Empirical identification of the main factors of conscientiousness. *Learning and Individual Differences, 19,* 451–458.

Maccoby, E. (1992). The role of parents in the socialization of children: An historical overview. *Developmental Psychology, 28,* 1006–1017.

Maccoby, E. E., & Jacklin, C. N. (1974). *The psychology of sex differences*. Stanford, CA: Stanford University Press.

Maccoby, E. E., & Jacklin, C. N. (1980). Sex differences in aggression: A rejoinder and reprise. *Child Development, 51,* 964–980.

MacCoun, R. J. (1998). Biases in the interpretation and the use of research results. *Annual Review of Psychology, 49,* 259–287.

MacDonald, A. W., Cohen, J. D., Stenger, V. A., & Carter, C. S. (2000). Dissociating the role of the dorsolateral prefrontal and anterior cingulate cortex in cognitive control. *Science, 288,* 1835–1838.

MacDonald, D. J., & Standing, L. G. (2002). Does self-serving bias cancel the Barnum effect? *Social Behaviour and Personality, 30*(6), 625–630.

Mace, R. (1996). Biased parental investment and reproductive success in Gabbra pastoralists. *Behavioral Ecology & Sociobiology, 38,* 75–81.

Macfie, J., Toth, S. L., Rogosch, F. A., Robinson, J., Emde, R. N., & Cicchetti, D. (1999). Effect of maltreatment on preschoolers' narrative representations of responses to relieve distress and of role reversal. *Developmental Psychology, 35,* 460–465.

Machaalani, R., & Waters, K. A. (2008). Neuronal cell death in the Sudden Infant Death Syndrome brainstem and associations with risk factors. *Brain, 131*(1), 218–228.

MacKinnon, D. F., Jamison, K. R., & DePaulo, J. R. (1997). Genetics of manic-depressive illness. *Annual Review of Neuroscience, 20,* 355–373.

MacKinnon-Lewis, C., Starnes, R., Volling, B., & Johnson, S. (1997). Perceptions of parenting as predictors of boys' sibling and peer relations. *Developmental Psychology, 33,* 1024–1031.

Mackintosh, N. J. (1998). *IQ and human intelligence*. New York: Oxford University Press.

Macklin, M. L., Metzger, L. J., Litz, B. T., McNally, R. J., Lasko, N. B., Orr, S. P., et al. (1998). Lower precombat intelligence is a risk factor for posttraumatic stress disorder. *Journal of Consulting & Clinical Psychology, 66,* 323–326.

MacLachlan, M., Carr, S. C., & McAuliffe, E. (2010). *The aid triangle: Recognising the human dynamics of dominance, justice and identity*. New York: Zed Books.

MacLean, P. D. (1982). On the origin and progressive evolution of the triune brain. In E. Armstrong & D. Falk (Eds.), *Primate brain evolution*. New York: Plenum Press.

MacLean, P. D. (1990). A reinterpretation of memorative functions of the limbic system. In E. Goldberg (Ed.), *Contemporary neuropsychology and the legacy of Luria. Institute for research in behavioral neuroscience* (pp. 127–154). Hillsdale, NJ: Lawrence Erlbaum.

MacLeod, C., Mathews, A., & Tata, P. (1986). Attentional bias in emotional disorders. *Journal of Abnormal Psychology, 95,* 15–20.

MacLeod, C., Rutherford, E., Campbell, L., Ebsworthy, G., & Holker, L. (2002). Selective attention and emotional vulnerability: Assessing the causal basis of their association through the experimental manipulation of attentional bias. *Journal of Abnormal Psychology, 111,* 107–123.

Macrae, C. N., & Bodenhausen, G. V. (2000). Social cognition: Thinking categorically about others. *Annual Review of Psychology, 51,* 93–120.

Macrae, C. N., & Bodenhausen, G. V. (2001). Social cognition: Categorical person perception. *British Journal of Psychology, 92,* 939–955.

Macrae, C. N., Bodenhausen, G. V., & Milne, A. B. (1998). Saying no to unwanted thoughts: Self-focus and the regulation of mental life. *Journal of Personality and Social Psychology, 74,* 578–589.

Macrae, C. N., Mitchell, J. P., & Pendry, L. F. (2002). What's in a forename? Cue familiarity and stereotypical thinking. *Journal of Experimental Social Psychology, 38,* 186–193.

MacRae, J. R., Scoles, M. T., & Siegel, S. (1988). The contribution of Pavlovian conditioning to drug tolerance and dependence. *British Journal of Addiction, 82,* 371–380.

MacWhinney, B. (1998). Models of the emergence of language. *Annual Review of Psychology, 49,* 199–227.

Madden, P. A. F., Heath, A. C., Rosenthal, N. E., & Martin, N. G. (1996). Seasonal changes in mood and behavior: The role of genetic factors. *Archives of General Psychiatry, 53,* 47–55.

Maddox, G. (2006, August 3). Will we want to see Mel Gibson's next movie? [Entertainment blog]. *The Sydney Morning Herald*. Retrieved from http://blogs.smh.com.au/entertainment/archives/box_office/005391.html

Magee, W. J., Eaton, W. W., Wittchen, H., McGonagle, K. A., & Kessler, R. C. (1996). Agoraphobia, simple phobia, and social phobia in the National Comorbidity Survey. *Archives of General Psychiatry, 53,* 159–168.

Maguire, E. A., Frackowiak, R. S. J., & Frith, C. D. (1997). Recalling routes around London: Activation of the right hippocampus in taxi drivers. *Journal of Neuroscience, 17,* 7103–7110.

Maguire, E. A., Mummery, C. J., & Buechel, C. (2000). Patterns of hippocampal-cortical interaction dissociate temporal lobe memory subsystems. *Hippocampus, 10,* 475–482.

Mahler, M., Pine, F., & Bergman, A. (1975). *The psychological birth of the human infant: Symbiosis and individualization*. New York: Basic Books.

Mahoney, D. P. (1997, December). Virtual therapy nets real results. *Computer Graphics World, 20,* 52–56.

Main, M. (1990). Cross-cultural studies of attachment organization: Recent studies, changing methodologies, and the concept of conditional strategies. *Human Development, 33,* 48–61.

Main, M. (1995). Recent studies in attachment: Overview, with selected implications for clinical work. In S. Goldberg, R. Muir, & J. Kerr (Eds.), *Attachment theory: Social, developmental, and clinical perspectives* (pp. 407–474). Hillsdale, NJ: Analytic Press.

Main, M., Kaplan, N., & Cassidy, J. (1985). Security in infancy, childhood, and adulthood: A move to the level of representation. In I. Bretherton & E. Waters (Eds.), *Growing points of attachment theory and research. Monographs of the society for research in child development, 50* (No. 1–2, pp. 67–104).

Main, M., & Solomon, J. (1986). Discovery of a new, insecure-disorganized/disoriented attachment pattern. In T. Brazelton & M. Yogman (Eds.), *Affective development in infancy* (pp. 95–124). Norwood, NJ: Ablex.

Maj, M., Veltro, F., Pirozzi, R., Lobrace, S., & Magliano, L. (1992). Pattern of recurrence of illness after recovery from an episode of major depression: A prospective study. *American Journal of Psychiatry, 149,* 795–800.

Major, B., Zubek, J. M., Cooper, M. L., Cozzarelli, C., & Richards, M. C. (1997). Mixed messages: Implications of social conflict and social support within close relationships for adjustment to a stressful life event. *Journal of Personality & Social Psychology, 72,* 1349–1363.

Major, T. (2010, July 28). Remembering history. *Sydney Morning Herald*. Retrieved from http://www.smh.com.au/federal-election/remembering-history-20100727-10t9o.html

Malamuth, N. M., & Donnerstein, E. (1982). The effects of aggressive-pornographic mass media stimuli. In L. Berkowitz (Ed.), *Advances in experimental social psychology: Vol. 15*. New York: Academic Press.

Malik, R. S. (1998). *Accounting for the differential academic performance: A case of the Chinese-Australian and Anglo-Australian children*. Paper presented at the Australian Association for Research in Education Conference, Adelaide, Australia.

Mallan, K. M., Sax, J., & Lipp, O. V. (2009). Verbal instruction abolishes fear conditioned to racial out-group faces. *Journal of Experimental Social Psychology, 45,* 1303–1307.

Malnick, S. D. H., & Knobler, H. (2006). The medical complications of obesity. *Quarterly Journal of Medicine: An International Journal of Medicine, 99*(9), 565–579.

Malpass, R. S., & Devine, P. G. (1980). Realism and eyewitness identification research. *Law and Human Behavior, 4,* 347–358.

Malt, B., & Smith, E. E. (1984). Correlated properties in natural categories. *Journal of Verbal Learning and Verbal Behavior, 23,* 250–269.

Maltby, N., Kirsch, I., Mayers, M., & Allen, G. J. (2002). Virtual reality exposure therapy for the treatment of fear of flying: A controlled investigation. *Journal of Consulting and Clinical Psychology, 70,* 1112–1118.

Mamo, D., Remington, G., Nobrega, J., Hussey, D., Chirakal, R., Wilson, A. A., et al. (2004). Effect of acute antipsychotic administration on dopamine synthesis in rodents and human subjects using 6-[18F]-L-m-tyrosine. *Synapse, 52,* 153–162.

Manajlovic, S., & Nikolic-Popovic, J. (2005). Cognitive complexity of paranoid patients. *Medicine and Biology, 112*(2), 113–117.

Mandler, G. (1997). *Human nature explored*. New York: Oxford University Press.

Mandler, G., & Nakamura, Y. (1987). Aspects of consciousness. *Personality and Social Psychology Bulletin, 13,* 299–313.

Maner, J. K., Luce, C. L., Neuberg, S. L., Cialdini, R. B., Brown, S., & Sagarin, B. J. (2002). The effects of perspective taking on motivations for helping: Still no evidence for altruism. *Personality and Social Psychology Bulletin, 28,* 1601–1610.

Mangelsdorf, S., Gunnar, M., Kestenbaum, R., Lang, S., & Andreas, D. (1990). Infant proneness-to-distress temperament, maternal personality, and mother-infant attachment: Associations and goodness of fit. *Child Development, 61,* 820–831.

Manji, H. K., Chen, G., Shimon, H., Hsiao, J. K., Potter, W. Z., & Belmaker, R. H. (1995). Guanine nucleotide-binding proteins in bipolar affective disorder: Effects of long-term lithium treatment. *Archives of General Psychiatry, 52,* 135–144.

Mann, J. (1982). *A casebook in time-limited psychotherapy*. New York: McGraw-Hill.

Mann, J. J., Huang, Y., Underwood, M. D., Kassir, S. A., Oppenheim, S., Kelly, T. M., et al. (2000). A serotonin transporter gene promoter polymorphism (5-HTTLPR) and prefrontal cortical binding in major depression and suicide. *Archives of General Psychiatry, 57,* 729–738.

Manna, L. (2002). Biculturalism in practice 'Te Pounamu': Integration of a Maori mode with traditional clinical assessment processes. In *Proceedings of the National Maori Graduates of Psychology Symposium 2002*. Hamilton, New Zealand: The Maori and Psychology Research Unit, University of Waikato.

Manne, S. (2003). Coping and social support. In A. M. Nezu, C. M. Nezu, & P. A. Geller (Eds.), *Handbook of psychology: Health psychology: Vol. 9* (pp. 51–74). Hoboken, NJ: John Wiley & Sons.

Mannuzza, S., Klein, R. G., Bessler, A., Malloy, P., & Lpadula, M. (1998). Adult psychiatric status of hyperative boys grown up. *American Journal of Psychiatry, 155,* 493–498.

Mant, A., Rendle, V. A., Hall, W. D., Mitchell, P. B., Montgomery, W. S., McManus, P. R., et al. (2004). Making new choices about antidepressants in Australia: The long view 1975–2002. *Medical Journal of Australia, 181,* 21–24.

Manuck, S. B., Flory, J. D., Ferrell, R. E., Dent, K. M., Mann, J. J., & Muldoon, M. F. (1999). Aggression and anger-related traits associated with a polymorphism of the tryptophan hydroxylase gene. *Biological Psychiatry, 45,* 603–614.

Maquet, P., Peters, J., Aerts, J., & Delfiore, G. (1996). Functional neuroanatomy of human rapid-eye-movement sleep and dreaming. *Nature, 383,* 163–166.

Marcel, A. J. (1983). Conscious and unconscious perception: Experiments on visual masking and word recognition. *Cognitive Psychology, 15,* 197–237.

Marchand, W. R., Dilda, D. S., & Jensen, C. R. (2005, September). Neurobiology of mood disorders. *Hospital Physician, 43,* 17–26.

Marcia, J. (1987). The identity status approach to the study of ego identity development. In T. Honess & K. Yardley (Eds.), *Self and identity: Perspectives across the lifespan* (pp. 161–171). Boston: Routledge & Kegan Paul.

Marcia, J. E. (1999). Representational thought in ego identity, psychotherapy, and psychosocial developmental theory. In I. E. Sigel (Ed.), *Development of mental representation: Theories and applications* (pp. 391–414). Mahwah, NJ: Lawrence Erlbaum.

Marcotte, A., & Morere, D. (1990). Speech lateralization in deaf populations: Evidence for a developmental critical period. *Brain & Language, 39,* 134–152.

Marcus, D. E., & Overton, W. E. (1978). The development of cognitive gender constancy and sex role preferences. *Child Development, 49,* 434–444.

Marcus, G. F. (1993). Negative evidence in language acquisition. *Cognition, 46,* 53–85.

Marder, S. R., & Wirshing, D. A. (2003). Maintenance treatment. In S. R. Hirsch & D. R. Weinberger (Eds.), *Schizophrenia* (2nd ed., pp. 474–488). Malden, MA: Blackwell Publishing.

Marengo, J., Harrow, M., Sands, J., & Galloway, C. (1991). European versus U.S. data on the course of schizophrenia. *American Journal of Psychiatry, 148,* 606–611.

Margolis, S., & Swartz, K. L. (2001). *Depression and anxiety. Johns Hopkins white papers*. Baltimore: Johns Hopkins Medical Institutions.

Margolskee, R. (1995). Receptor mechanisms in gustation. In R. L. Doty (Ed.), *Handbook of olfaction and gustation*. New York: Marcel Dekker.

Marieb, E. N., & Hoehn, K. (2007). *Human anatomy and physiology* (7th ed.). San Francisco: Pearson.

Markey, P. M., & Markey, C. N. (2007). Romantic ideals, romantic obtainment, and relationship experiences: The complementarity of interpersonal traits among romantic partners. *Journal of Social and Personal Relationships, 24*(4), 517–533.

Marks, D. F., Sykes, C. M., & McKinley, J. M. (2003). Health psychology: Overview and professional issues. In A. M. Nezu, C. M. Nezu, & P. A. Geller (Eds.), *Handbook of psychology: Health psychology: Vol. 9* (pp. 5–26). Hoboken, NJ: John Wiley & Sons.

Marks, I. M. (1969). *Fears and phobias*. New York: Academic Press.

Markus, H. (1977). Self-schemata and processing information about the self. *Journal of Personality and Social Psychology, 35,* 63–78.

Markus, H., & Cross, S. (1990). The interpersonal self. In L. Pervin (Ed.), *Handbook of personality: Theory and research* (pp. 576–608). New York: Guilford Press.

Markus, H., & Kitayama, S. (1991). Culture and the self: Implications for cognition, emotion, and motivation. *Psychological Review, 98,* 224–253.

Markus, H. R., & Kitayama, S. (2001). The cultural construction of self and emotion: Implications for social behavior. In W. G. Parrott (Ed.), *Emotions in social psychology: Essential readings* (pp. 119–137). New York: Psychology Press.

Markus, H., & Nurius, P. (1986). Possible selves. *American Psychologist, 41,* 954–969.

Markus, H., & Wurf, E. (1987). The dynamic selfconcept: A social psychological perspective. *Annual Review of Psychology, 38,* 299–337.

Marsh, R. L., Hiscks, J. L., & Bink, M. L. (1998). Activation of completed, uncompleted, and partially completed intentions. *Journal of Experimental Psychology: Learning, Memory and Cognition, 24,* 350–361.

Marshall, D. A., & Moulton, D. G. (1981). Olfactory sensitivity to a-ionone in humans and dogs. *Chemical Senses, 6,* 53–61.

Martikainen, P., & Valkonen, T. (1996). Mortality after the death of a spouse: Rates and causes of death in a large Finnish cohort. *American Journal of Public Health, 86,* 1087–1093.

Martin, C. L., & Ruble, D. N. (1997). A developmental perspective of self-construals and sex differences: Comment on Cross and Madson. *Psychological Bulletin, 122,* 45–50.

Martin, C. L., Ruble, D. N., & Szkrybalo, J. (2002). Cognitive theories of early gender development. *Psychological Bulletin, 128,* 903–933.

Martin, D. J., Garske, J. P., & Davis, M. K. (2000). Relation of the therapeutic alliance with outcome and other variables: A meta-analytic review. *Journal of Consulting and Clinical Psychology, 68,* 438–450.

Martin, D. F., & Liddle, L. (1997). *Money business and culture: Issues for Aboriginal economic policy*. Retrieved May 28, 2004, from http://www.anu.edu.au/caepr/briefs/brief18.php

Martin, J., & Sugarman, J. (1999). *The psychology of human possibility and constraint*. Albany: State University of New York Press.

Martin, J. A., Maccoby, E. E., Baran, K. W., & Jacklin, C. N. (1981). Sequential analysis of mother-child interaction at 18 months: A comparison of microanalytic methods. *Developmental Psychology, 17,* 146–157.

Martin, K. A., Leary, M. R., & O'Brien, J. (2001). Role of self-presentation in the health practices of a sample of Irish adolescents. *Journal of Adolescent Health, 28,* 259–262.

Martin, K. A., Leary, M. R., & Rejeski, W. J. (2000). Self-presentational concerns in older adults: Implications for health and well-being. *Basic and Applied Social Psychology, 22*(3), 169–179.

Martin, M. A. (1985). Students' applications of self-questioning study techniques: An investigation of their efficacy. *Reading Psychology, 6,* 69–83.

Martin, P. R. (1989). The scientist–practitioner model and clinical psychology: Time for a change? *Australian Psychologist, 24,* 71–92.

Martin, R., Hewstone, M., Martin, P. Y., & Gardikiotis, A. (2008). Persuasion from majority and minority groups. In W. D. Crano & R. Prislin (Eds.), *Attitudes and attitude change* (pp. 361–384). New York: Psychology Press.

Martin, R., Thomas, G., Charles, K., Epitropaki, O., & McNamara, R. (2005). The role of leader-member exchanges in mediating the relationship between locus of control and work reactions. *Journal of Occupational and Organizational Psychology, 78*(1), 141–147.

Martin, R. P., Dombrowski, S. C., Mullis, C., Wisenbaker, J., & Huttunen, M. O. (2006). Smoking during pregnancy: Association with childhood temperament, behavior, and academic performance. *Journal of Pediatric Psychology, 31,* 490–500.

Martin, T. (2002). *Global smoking statistics for 2002*. Retrieved from http://quitsmoking.about.com/cs/antismoking/a/statistics.htm

Martinez, J., Charles, R., & Forgatch, M. S. (2002). Adjusting to change: Linking family structure with parenting and boys' adjustment. *Journal of Family Psychology, 16*(2), 107–117.

Martinez, J. L., & Derrick, B. E. (1996). Long-term potentiation and learning. *Annual Review, 47,* 173–203.

Mashour, G. A., Walker, E. E., & Martuza, R. L. (2005). Psychosurgery: Past, present, and future. *Brain Research Reviews, 48,* 409–419.

Maslach, C. (1979). Negative emotional biasing of unexplained arousal. *Journal of Personality and Social Psychology, 37,* 953–969.

Masling, J. M., & Bornstein, R. F. (Eds.). (1994). *Empirical perspectives on object relations theory*. Washington, DC: American Psychological Association.

Maslow, A. H. (1962). *Toward a psychology of being*. Princeton, NJ: Van Nostrand.

Maslow, A. H. (1970). *Motivaiton and personality* (2nd ed.). New York: Harper & Row.

Mason, E. (1970). Obesity in pet dogs. *Veterinary Record, 86,* 612–616.

Masserman, J. H., Wechkin, S., & Terris, W. (1964). 'Altruistic' behavior in rhesus monkeys. *American Journal of Psychiatry, 121,* 584–585.

Masters, W., & Johnson, V. (1966). *Human sexual response*. Boston: Little, Brown.

Masterson, J. F., & Rinsley, D. B. (1975). The borderline syndrome: The role of the mother in the genesis and psychic structure of the borderline personality. *International Journal of Psychoanalysis, 56,* 163–177.

Matarazzo, J. D. (1980). Behavioral health and behavioral medicine: Frontiers for a new health psychology. *American Psychologist, 35,* 807–817.

Mathers, C., Vos, T., & Stevenson, C. (1999). *The burden of disease and injury in Australia*. Canberra, Australia: AIHW.

Mathews, A., & Macleod, C. (1994). Cognitive approaches to emotion. *Annual Review of Psychology, 45,* 25–50.

Mathews, A., & MacLeod, C. (2005). Cognitive vulnerability to emotional disorders. *Annual Review of Clinical Psychology, 1,* 167–195.

Matlin, M. M. (1983). *Perception*. Boston: Allyn & Bacon.

Matsumoto, D. (Ed.). (2001). *Handbook of culture and psychology*. Cary, NC: Oxford University Press.

Matsumoto, D. (2007). Emotion judgments do not differ as a function of perceived nationality. *International Journal of Psychology, 42,* 207–214.

Matsumoto, D., & Juang, L. (2004). *Culture and psychology* (3rd ed.). Belmont, CA: Wadsworth/Thomson Learning.

Matsuoka, S. (1990). Theta rhythms: State of consciousness. *Brain Topography, 3,* 203–208.

Matthews, K. A. (1992). Myths and realities of the menopause. *Psychosomatic Medicine, 54,* 1–9.

Mattock, K., & Burnham, D. (2006). Chinese and English infants' tone perception: Evidence for perceptual reorganization. *Infancy, 10*(3), 241–265.

Mauro, R., Sato, K., & Tucker, J. (1992). The role of appraisal in human emotions: A cross-cultural study. *Journal of Personality and Social Psychology, 62,* 301–317.

Mavissakalian, M., & Perel, J. (1992). Protective effects of imipramine maintenance treatment in panic disorder with agoraphobia. *American Journal of Psychiatry, 149,* 1053–1057.

May, R. (1953). *Man's search for himself*. New York: Signet Books.

May, R., Angel, E., & Ellenberger, H. F. (1958). *Existence: A new dimension in psychiatry and psychology*. New York: Basic Books.

Mayberry, R., & Eichen, E. B. (1991). The long-lasting advantage of learning sign language in childhood: Another look at the critical period for language acquisition. *Journal of Memory and Language, 30,* 486–512.

Mayer, J., Gasche, Y., Braverman, D., & Evans, T. (1992). Mood-congruent judgment is a general effect. *Journal of Personality and Social Psychology, 63,* 119–132.

Mayer, J., Roberts, R. D., & Barsade, S. G. (2008). Human abilities: Emotional intelligence. *Annual Review of Psychology, 59,* 507–536.

Mayer, J. D., Caruso, D., & Salovey, P. (2000). Emotional intelligence meets traditional standards for an intelligence. *Intelligence, 27,* 267–298.

Mayer, J. D., & Salovey, P. (1997). What is emotional intelligence? In P. Salovey & D. Sluyter (Eds.), *Emotional development and emotional intelligence: Implications for educators*. New York: Basic Books.

Mayer, J. D., Salovey, P., & Caruso, D. (2000a). Models of emotional intelligence. In R. J. Sternberg (Ed.), *Handbook of human intelligence* (2nd ed., pp. 396–420). New York: Cambridge University Press.

Mayer, J. D., Salovey, P., & Caruso, D. (2000b). Emotional intelligence as zeitgeist, personality, and as a mental ability. In R. Bar-On & J. D. A. Parker (Eds.), *The handbook of emotional intelligence* (pp. 92–117). New York: Jossey-Bass.

Mayseless, O., Scharf, M., & Sholt, M. (2003). From authoritative parenting practices to an authoritarian context: Exploring the person-environment fit. *Journal of Research on Adolescence, 13,* 427–456.

McAdams, D. (1992). The five-factor model in personality: A critical appraisal. *Journal of Personality, 60,* 329–361.

McAdams, D., & Vaillant, G. (1982). Intimacy motivation and psychosocial adjustment: A longitudinal study. *Journal of Personality Assessment, 46,* 586–593.

McAdams, D., & West, S. G. (1997). Introduction: Personality psychology and the case study. *Journal of Personality, 65,* 757–783.

McAdams, D. P. (1999). Motives. In V. J. Derlega, B. A. Winstead, & Jones, W. H. (Eds.), *Personality: Contemporary theory and research. Nelson-Hall series in psychology* (2nd ed., pp. 162–194). Chicago: Nelson-Hall.

McAdams, D. P. (2000). *The person: An integrated introduction to personality psychology*. Orlando, FL: John Wiley & Sons.

McAdams, D. P. (2001). The psychology of life stories. *Review of General Psychology, 5*(2), 100–122.

McAdams, D. P., & de St. Aubin, E. (1998). *Generativity and adult development: How and why we care for the next generation*. Washington, DC: American Psychological Association.

McAdams, D. P., de St. Aubin, E., & Logan, R. L. (1993). Generativity among young, midlife, and older adults. *Psychology and Aging, 8,* 221–230.

McAdams, D. P., Hart, H. M., & Maruna, S. (1998). The anatomy of generativity. In D. P. McAdams & E. de St. Aubin (Eds.), *Generativity and adult development: How and why we care for the next generation* (pp. 7–43). Washington, DC: American Psychological Association.

McAdams, D. P., Hoffman, B. J., Mansfield, E. D., & Day, R. (1996). Themes of agency and communion in significant autobiographical scenes. *Journal of Personality, 64,* 339–377.

McAlister, A. L. (2006). Acceptance of killing and homicide rates in nineteen nations. *European Journal of Public Health, 16*(3), 259–265.

McAndrew, F. T. (2002). New evolutionary perspectives on altruism: Multilevel- selection and costly-signaling theories. *Current Directions in Psychological Science, 11*(2), 79–82.

McCarthy, K., Dyer, S., & Hunter, M. (2002). A comparison of WAIS-III profiles of Australian and American adolescents with special education needs: A preliminary report from an ongoing study. *Australian Journal of Educational & Developmental Psychology, 2,* 49–58.

McCarthy, P. (2007). *Alcohol consumption in Australia*. Canberra, Australia: DrinkWise Australia.

McCaul, K. D., & Malott, J. M. (1984). Distraction and coping with pain. *Psychological Bulletin, 95,* 516–533.

McClelland, D. C. (1961). *The achieving society*. Princeton, NJ: Van Nostrand.

McClelland, D. C. (1978). Managing motivation to expand human freedom. *American Psychologist, 33,* 201–210.

McClelland, D. C. (1985). *Human motivation*. Glenview, IL: Scott, Foresman.

McClelland, D. C., Koestner, R., & Weinberger, J. (1989). How do self-attributed and implicit motives differ? *Psychological Review, 96,* 690–792.

McClelland, D. C., & Pilon, D. A. (1983). Sources of adult motives in patterns of parent behavior in early childhood. *Journal of Personality and Social Psychology, 44,* 564–554.

McClelland, D. C., & Winter, D. G. (1969). *Motivating economic achievement*. New York: Free Press.

McClelland, J. L. (1995). Constructive memory and memory distortions: A parallel-distributed processing approach. In D. L. Schacter (Ed.), *Memory distortions: How minds, brains, and societies reconstruct the past* (pp. 69–90). Cambridge, MA: Harvard University Press.

McClintock, M. K. (1971). Menstrual synchrony and suppression. *Nature, 229,* 244–245.

McCloskey, L. A., & Steuwig, J. (2001). The quality of peer relationships among children exposed to family violence. *Development and Psychopathology, 13*(1), 83–96.

McCloskey, M., Wible, C. G., & Cohen, N. J. (1988). Is there a special flashbulb-memory mechanism? *Journal of Experimental Psychology: General, 117,* 171–181.

McClure, J. (1998). Discounting causes of behavior: Are two reasons better than one? *Journal of Personality and Social Psychology, 74,* 7–20.

McClure, J., Allen, M. W., & Walkey, F. (2001). Countering fatalism: Causal information in news reports affects judgments about earthquake damage. *Basic and Applied Social Psychology, 23,* 109–121.

McConaghy, N. (1979). Maternal deprivation: Can its ghost be laid? *Australian and New Zealand Journal of Psychiatry, 13,* 209–217.

McConahay, J., & Hough, J. (1976). Symbolic racism. *Journal of Social Issues, 32,* 23–45.

McConkey, K. M. (1995). *Hypnosis, memory, and behavior in criminal investigation*. New York: Guilford Press.

McConkey, K. M. (2008). Generations and landscapes of hypnosis: Questions we've asked, questions we should ask. In M. R. Nash & A. J. Barnier (Eds.), *The Oxford handbook of hypnosis: Theory, research and practice* (pp. 53–77). Oxford: Oxford University Press.

McConnichie, K., Hollinsworth, D., & Pettman, J. (1988). *Race and racism in Australia*. Sydney, Australia: Social Science Press.

McCrae, R. R. (1996). Social consequences of experiential openness. *Psychological Bulletin, 120,* 323–337.

McCrae, R. R. (2004). Personality and culture revisited: Linking traits and dimensions of culture. *Cross-Cultural Research, 38*(1), 52–88.

McCrae, R. R., & Costa, P. T., Jr. (1990). *Personality in adulthood*. New York: Guilford Press.

McCrae, R. R., & Costa, P. T., Jr. (1997). Personality trait structure as a human universal. *American Psychologist, 52,* 509–516.

McCrae, R. R., & Costa, P. T., Jr. (2008). Empirical and theoretical status of the five-factor model of personality traits. In G. J. Boyle, G. Matthews, & D. H. Saklofske (Eds.), *The Sage handbook of personality theory and assessment: Vol. 1. Personality theories and models* (pp. 273–294). London: Sage Publications.

McCrae, R. R., Costa, P. T., Jr., del Pilar, G. H., Rolland, J. P., & Parker, W. D. (1998). Cross-cultural assessment of the five-factor model: The revised NEO personality inventory. *Journal of Cross-Cultural Psychology, 29,* 171–188.

McCrae, R. R., Costa, P. T., Jr., Martin, T. A., Oryol, V. E., Rukavishnikov, A. A., Senin, I. G., et al. (2004). Consensual validation of personality traits across cultures. *Journal of Research in Personality, 38,* 179–201.

McDaniel, M. A. (1995). Prospective memory: Progress and processes. In D. L. Medin (Ed.), *The psychology of learning and motivation: Advances in research and theory: Vol. 33* (pp. 191–227). San Diego, CA: Academic Press.

McDaniel, M. A., Robinson-Riegler, B., & Einstein, G. O. (1998). Prospective remembering: Perceptually driven or conceptually driven processes? *Memory and Cognition, 26,* 121–134.

McDonald, A. S. (2001). The prevalence and effects of test anxiety in school children. *Educational Psychologist, 21,* 89–98.

McDonald, J. L. (1997). Language acquisition: The acquisition of linguistic structure in normal and special populations. *Annual Review of Psychology, 48,* 215–241.

McDonald, P. (2011, March 18). Memorial held for victims of Christchurch earthquake [Radio broadcast episode]. *The World Today.* Ultimo: Australian Broadcasting Corporation.

McEvoy, G. M., & Cascio, W. F. (1989). Cumulative evidence of the relationship between employee age and job performance. *Journal of Applied Psychology, 74,* 11–17.

McEwan, D. (1998). Recognizing Munchausen's syndrome. *AORN Journal*. Retrieved from http://findarticles.com/p/articles/mi_m0FSL/is_n2_v67/ai_20651296/pg_3/?tag=content;col1

McEwen, B. S. (1999). Stress and hippocampal plasticity. *Annual Review of Neuroscience, 22,* 105–122.

McEwen, B. S., Alves, S. E., Bulloch, K., & Weiland, N. G. (1998). Clinically relevant basic science studies of gender differences and sex hormone effects. *Psychopharmacology Bulletin, 34,* 251–259.

McGaugh, J. L. (2000). Memory: A century of consolidation. *Science, 287,* 248–251.

McGee, R., Feehan, M., & Williams, S. (1996). Mental health. In P. A. Silva & W. R. Stanton (Eds.), *From child to adult. The Dunedin multidisciplinary health and development study* (pp. 136–154). Auckland, New Zealand: Oxford University Press.

McGlynn, F. D., Smitherman, T. A., & Gothard, K. D. (2004). Comment on the status of systematic desensitization. *Behavior Modification, 28*(2), 194–205.

McGowan, N., Sharpe, L., Refshauge, K., & Nicholas, M. (2009). The effect of attentional re-training and threat expectancy in response to acute pain. *Pain, 142,* 42–47.

McGue, M., Bacon, S., & Lykken, D. (1993). Personality stability and change in early adulthood: A behavior genetic analysis. *Developmental Psychology, 29,* 96–109.

McGue, M., & Bouchard, T. J. (1998). Genetic and environmental influences on human behavioral differences. *Annual Review of Neuroscience, 21,* 1–24.

McGue, M., Pickens, R. W., & Svikis, D. (1992). Sex and age effects on the inheritance of alcohol problems: A twin study. *Journal of Abnormal Psychology, 101,* 3–17.

McGuire, W. (1986). The myth of massive media impact: Savagings and salvagings. In G. Comstock (Ed.), *Public communication and behavior: Vol. 1*. New York: Academic Press.

McGuire, W. J. (1961). The effectiveness of supportive and refutational defenses in immunizing and restoring beliefs against persuasion. *Sociometry, 24,* 184–197.

McGuire, W. J. (1985). Attitudes and attitude change. In G. Lindzey & E. Aronson (Eds.), *Handbook of social psychology*. Reading, MA: Addison-Wesley.

McGuire, W. J., & Papageorgis, D. (1962). Effectiveness of forewarning in developing resistance to persuasion. *Public Opinion Quarterly, 26,* 24–34.

McHale, S. M., Crouter, A. C., & Tucker, C. J. (1999). Family context and gender role socialization in middle childhood: Comparing girls to boys and sisters to brothers. *Child Development, 70,* 990–1004.

McInerney, D. M. (2003). Motivational goals, self-concept and sense of self — what predicts academic achievement? Similarities and differences between Aboriginal and Anglo Australians in high school settings. In H. W. Marsh, R. G. Craven, & D. M. McInerney (Eds.), *International advances in self research: Vol. 1*. Greenwich, CT: Information Age Publishing.

McInerney, D. M. (2008). Personal investment, culture and learning: Insights into the most salient influences on school achievement across Anglo, Indigenous, Asian and Lebanese-background students in Australia. *International Journal of Psychology, 43,* 870–879.

McInerney, D. M., & McInerney, V. (2002). *Educational psychology: Contructing learning*. Sydney, Australia: Prentice Hall.

McInerney, D. M., Roche, L., McInerney, V., & Marsh, H. W. (1997). Cultural perspectives on school motivation: The relevance and application of goal theory. *American Educational Research Journal, 34,* 207–236.

McInman, A. D., & Grove, J. R. (1991). Multidimensional self concept, smoking, and intentions to smoke in adolescents. *Australian Psychologist, 26*(3), 192–196.

McKenna, A. (1990). The black death. *New Internationalist, Issue 209*. Retrieved October 8, 2004, from http://www.newint.org/issue209/asylum.htm

McKinney, S. (2010). *Night vision and driving: How safe are older motorists?* Retrieved from http://www.allaboutvision.com/over40/night-driving.htm

McKoon, G., & Ratcliff, R. (1998). Memory-based language processing: Psycholinguistic research in the 1990s. *Annual Review of Psychology, 49,* 25–42.

McLaughlin, T., Feldman, H., Fillit, H., Sano, M., Schmitt, F., Aisen, P., et al. (2010). Dependence as a unifying construct in defining Alzheimer's disease severity. *Alzheimer's & Dementia: The Journal of the Alzheimer's Association, 6*(6), 482–493.

McLoyd, V. (1989). Socialization and development in a changing economy: The effects of paternal job and income loss on children. *American Psychologist, 44,* 293–302.

McMillan, M. (2005). *The person-centered approach to therapeutic change*. Thousand Oaks, CA: Sage.

McNally, R. (1987). Preparedness and phobias: A review. *Psychologial Bulletin, 101,* 283–303.

McNeil, T. F., Cantor-Graae, E., & Weinberger, D. R. (2000). Relationship of obstetric complications and differences in size of brain structures in monozygotic twin pairs discordant for schizophrenia. *American Journal of Psychiatry, 157,* 203–212.

McPhee, L. (2009, August 17). Shark attack rescue to receive star of courage. *The West Australian*. Retrieved from http://www.thewest.com.au/

McPherson, J., & Burns, N. (2007). Gs invaders: Assessing a computer game-like test of processing speed. *Behavior Research Methods, 39,* 876–883.

McVay, J. C., Kane, M. J., & Kwapil, T. R. (2009). Tracking the train of thought from the laboratory into everyday life: An experience-sampling study of mind wandering across controlled and ecological contexts. *Psychonomic Bulletin and Review, 16*(5), 857–863.

Mead, M. (1928). *Coming of age in Samoa: A psychological study of primitive youth for Western civilization*. New York: Morrow & Co.

Meade, A. (2010, August 31). Matthew Newton wants to kill himself: Patti. *The Australian*. Retrieved from http://www.theaustralian.com.au/news/nation/matthew-newton-wants-to-kill-himself-patti/story-e6frg6nf-1225912185559.

Meaney, M., & McEwen, B. (1986). Testosterone implants into the amygdala during the neonatal period masculinize the social play of juvenile female rats. *Brain Research, 398,* 324–328.

Media Awareness Network. (2010). *Research on the effects of media violence*. Retrieved from http://www.media-awareness.ca/english/issues/violence/effects_media_violence.cfm

Medical Benefits Fund. (2004). *Call for urgent upgrading of health warnings on cigarette packets*. Retrieved August 1, 2004, from http://www.mbf.com.au/about/mediareleases/upgradingwarnings.html

Medical Research News. (2004). *Health care and cultural differences at centre of Australian study*. Retrieved January 11, 2005, from http://www.news-medical.net/print_article.asp?id=1471

Medin, D. L., & Atran, S. (2004). The native mind: Biological categorization and reasoning in development and across cultures. *Psychological Review, 111*(4), 960–983.

Medin, D. L., & Heit, E. (1999). Categorization. In B. M. Bly & D. E. Rumelhart (Eds.), *Cognitive science: Handbook of perception and cognition* (2nd ed., pp. 99–143). San Diego, CA: Academic Press.

Medin, D. L., Lynch, E. B., Coley, J. D., & Atran, S. (1997). Categorization and reasoning among tree experts: Do all roads lead to Rome? *Cognitive Psychology, 32,* 49–96.

Medin, D. L., Lynch, E. B., & Solormon, K. O. (2000). Are there kinds of concepts? *Annual Review of Psychology, 51,* 121–147.

Medin, D. L., Ross, N., Atran, S., Burnett, R. C., & Blok, S. V. (2002). Categorization and reasoning in relation to culture and expertise. In B. H. Ross (Ed.), *The psychology of learning and motivation: Advances in research and theory: Vol. 41* (pp. 1–41). San Diego, CA: Academic Press.

Medin, D. L., & Schaffer, M. M. (1978). Context theory of classification learning. *Psychological Review, 85,* 207–238.

Medin, D. L., & Smith, E. E. (1981). Strategies and classification learning. *Journal of Experimental Psychology: Human Learning and Memory, 7,* 241–253.

MedlinePlus, United States. (2004). *Breast milk*. Retrieved November 2, 2006, from http://www.nlm.nih.gov/medlineplus/ency/article/002451.htm

Meichenbaum, D. (1977). *Cognitive-behavior modification: An integrative approach*. New York: Plenum Press.

Meichenbaum, D. (1990). Cognitive perspective on teaching self-regulation. *American Journal of Mental Retardation, 94,* 367–369.

Meins, E., Fernyhough, C., Fradley, E., & Tuckey, M. (2001). Rethinking maternal sensitivity: Mothers' comments on infants' mental processes predict security of attachment at 12 months. *Journal of Child Psychology & Psychiatry, 42,* 637–648.

Melchior, M., Caspi, A., Milne, B. J., Danese, A., Poulton, R., & Moffitt, T. E. (2007). Work stress precipitates depression and anxiety in young working women and men. *Psychological Medicine, 37,* 1119–1130.

Melinder, A., Goodman, G. S., Eilertsen, D. E., & Magnussen, S. (2004). Beliefs about child witnesses: A survey of professionals. *Psychology, Crime & Law, 10*(4), 347–365.

Melinder, A., Scullin, M. H., Gunnerod, V., & Nyborg, E. (2005). Generalizability of a two-factor measure of young children's suggestibility in Norway and the USA. *Psychology, Crime, & Law, 11*(2), 123–145.

Mellers, B., Schwartz, A., & Cooke, A. D. J. (1998). Judgment and decision making. *Annual Review of Psychology, 49,* 447–477.

Mellers, B., Schwartz, A., Ho, K., & Ritov, I. (1997). Decision affect theory: Emotional reactions to the outcomes of risky options. *Psychological Science, 8,* 423–429.

Mellers, B., Schwartz, A., & Ritov, I. (1999). Emotion-based choice. *Journal of Experimental Psychology: General, 128,* 332–345.

Meltzoff, A. (1990). Towards a developmental cognitive science: The implications of cross-modal matching and imitation for the development of representation and memory in infancy. *Annals of the New York Academy of Sciences, 608,* 1–7.

Meltzoff, A. N. (1995). What infant memory tells us about infantile amnesia: Long-term recall and deferred imitation [Special issue: Early memory]. *Journal of Experimental Child Psychology, 59,* 497–515.

Meltzoff, A. N., & Borton, R. W. (1979). Intermodal matching by human neonates. *Nature, 282,* 403–404.

Meltzoff, A. N., & Moore, M. K. (1977). Imitation of facial and manual gestures by human neonates. *Science, 198,* 75–78.

Meltzoff, J. (1998). *Critical thinking about research: Psychology and related fields.* Washington, DC: American Psychological Association.

Melzack, R. (1970). Phantom limbs. *Psychology Today,* 63–68.

Melzack, R. (1993). Pain: Past, present and future. *Canadian Journal of Experimental Psychology, 47,* 615–629.

Melzack, R., & Wall, P. D. (1983). *The challenge of pain.* New York: Basic Books.

Menard, M. T., Kosslyn, S., Thompson, W. L., Alpert, N. M., & Rauch, S. L. (1996). Encoding words and pictures: A positron emission tomography study. *Neuropsychologia, 34*(3), 185–194.

Mendola, J. D., Dale, A. M., Fischl, B., Liu, A. K., & Tootell, R. B. H. (1999). The representation of illusory and real contours in human cortical visual areas revealed by functional magnetic resonance imaging. *Journal of Neuroscience, 19,* 8560–8572.

Mendoza, S. P., & Mason, W. A. (1997). Attachment relationships in New World primates. In C. S. Carter, I. I. Lederhendler, & B. Kirkpatrick (Eds.), *The integrative neurobiology of affiliation: Vol. 807* (pp. 203–209). New York: New York Academy of Sciences.

Menon, V., Boyett-Anderson, J. M., Schatzberg, A. F., & Reiss, A. L. (2002). Relating semantic and episodic memory systems. *Cognitive Brain Research, 13,* 261–265.

Menopause Centre of Australia. (2010). *What is menopause?* Retrieved from http://www.menopausecentre.com.au/

Merriam, A. P. (1971). Aspects of sexual behavior among the Bala (Basongye). In D. S. Marshall & R. C. Suggs (Eds.), *Human sexual behavior: Variations in the ethnographic spectrum.* New York: Basic Books.

Merriman, W. E., Marazita, J. M., Jarvis, L. H., Evey-Burkey, J. A., & Biggins, M. (1996). What can be learned from something's not being named. *Child Development, 66,* 1890–1908.

Merton, R. K. (1957). *Social theory and social structure.* Glencoe, IL: Free Press.

Mesquita, B., Frijda, N. H., & Scherer, K. R. (1997). Culture and emotion. In J. W. Berry & P. R. Dasen (Eds.), *Handbook of cross-cultural psychology: Vol. 2. Basic processes and human development* (2nd ed., pp. 255–297). Boston: Allyn & Bacon.

Messer, S., Sass, L. H., & Woolfolk, R. L. (Eds.). (1988). *Hermeneutics and psychologial theory.* New Brunswick, NJ: Rutgers University Press.

Messer, S., & Winokur, M. (1980). Some limits to the integration of psychodynamic and behavior therapy. *American Psychologist, 35,* 818–827.

Metcalfe, J. (2000). Metamemory: Theory and data. In E. Tulving & F. I. Craik (Eds.), *The Oxford handbook of memory* (pp. 197–211). New York: Oxford University Press.

Metcalfe, J., & Shimamura, A. P. (Eds.). (1994). *Megacognition: Knowing about knowing.* Cambridge, MA: MIT Press.

Mezzacappa, E. S., Katkin, E. S., & Palmer, S. N. (1999). Epinephrine, arousal, and emotion: A new look at two-factor theory. *Cognition and Emotion, 13,* 181–199.

Michael, P., & Gregg, N. (2009, June 19). Aboriginal elder the last speaker of his language. *Courier Mail,* p. 4.

Michelson, D., Bancroft, J., Targum, S., Kim, Y., & Tepner, R. (2000). Female sexual dysfunction associated with antidepressant administration: A randomized, placebo-controlled study of pharmacologic intervention. *American Journal of Psychiatry, 157,* 239–243.

Mickelson, K. D., Kessler, R. C., & Shaver, P. R. (1997). Adult attachment in a nationally representative sample. *Journal of Personality & Social Psychology, 73,* 1092–1106.

Midford, R. (2005). Australia and alcohol: Living down the legend. *Addiction, 100*(7), 891–896.

Mikulincer, M., & Florian, V. (1997). Are emotional and instrumental supportive interactions beneficial in times of stress? The impact of attachment style. *Anxiety, Stress & Coping: an International Journal, 10,* 109–127.

Mikulincer, M., Florian, V., Birnbaum, G., & Malishkevich, S. (2002). Reminders of death-thought accessibility. The death-anxiety buffering function of close relationships: Exploring the effects of separation. *Personality and Social Psychology Bulletin, 28,* 287–299.

Mikulincer, M., Florian, V., & Hirschberger, G. (2003). The existential function of close relationships: Introducing death into the science of love. *Personality and Social Psychology Review, 7,* 20–40.

Mikulincer, M., Florian, V., & Weller, A. (1993). Attachment styles, coping strategies, and posttraumatic psychological distress: The impact of the Gulf War in Israel. *Journal of Personality and Social Psychology, 64,* 817–826.

Milberger, S., Biederman, J., Faraone, S. V., Chen, L., & Jones, J. (1996). Is maternal smoking during pregnancy a risk factor for attention deficit hyperactivity disorder in children? *American Journal of Psychiatry, 153,* 1138–1142.

Milewski-Hertlein, K. A. (2001). The use of a socially constructed genogram in clinical practice. *American Journal of Family Therapy, 29,* 23–38.

Milgram, S. (1963). Behavioral study of obedience. *Journal of Abnormal and Social Psychology, 67,* 371–378.

Milgram, S. (1974). *Obedience to authority: An experimental view.* New York: Harper & Row.

Millar, M. G., & Millar, K. U. (1996). The effects of direct and indirect experience on affective and cognitive responses and the attitude-behavior relation. *Journal of Experimental Social Psychology, 32,* 561–579.

Miller, C. T., & Downey, K. T. (1999). A meta-analysis of heavyweight and self-esteem. *Personality and Social Psychology Review, 3,* 68–84.

Miller, C. T., Rothblum, E. D., Barbour, L., & Brand, P. A. (1990). Social interactions of obese and nonobese women. *Journal of Personality, 58,* 365–380.

Miller, D. T., & Ratner, R. K. (1998). The disparity between the actual and assumed power of self-interest. *Journal of Personality and Social Psychology, 74,* 53–62.

Miller, G. A. (1956). The magical number seven, plus or minus two: Some limits in our capacity for processing information. *Psychological Review, 63,* 81–97.

Miller, G. A., Galanter, E., & Pribram, K. H. (1960). *Plans and the structure of behavior.* New York: Holt, Rinehart & Winston.

Miller, I. J., Jr. (1995). Anatomy of the peripheral taste system. In R. L. Doty (Ed.), *Handbook of olfaction and gustation.* New York: Marcel Dekker.

Miller, J. G. (1994). Cultural diversity in the morality of caring: Individually oriented versus duty-based interpersonal moral codes. *Cross-Cultural Research, 28,* 3–39.

Miller, J. G. (1997). A cultural-psychology perspective on intelligence. In R. J. Sternberg & E. L. Grigorenko (Eds.), *Intelligence, heredity, and environment* (pp. 269–302). New York: Cambridge University Press.

Miller, J. L., & Eimas, P. (1995). Speech perception: From signal to word. *Annual Review of Psychology, 46,* 467–492.

Miller, L. T., & Vernon, P. A. (1997). Developmental changes in speed of information processing in young children. *Developmental Psychology, 33,* 549–554.

Miller, M., & Draper, G. (2000). *Statistics on drug use in Australia.* Canberra, Australia: Australian Institute of Health and Welfare.

Miller, M., & Draper, G. (2001). *Statistics on drug use in Australia 2000* (Drug Statistics Series No. 8). Canberra, Australia: AIHW.

Miller, N., & Campbell, D. T. (1959). Recency and primacy in persuasion as a function of the timing of speeches and measurement. *Journal of Abnormal and Social Psychology, 59,* 1–9.

Miller, N. E. (1985). The value of behavioral research on animals. *American Psychologist, 40,* 423–440.

Miller, P. A., Eisenberg, N., Fabes, R., & Shell, R. (1996). Relations of moral reasoning and vicarious emotion to young children's prosocial behavior toward peers and adults. *Developmental Psychology, 32,* 210–219.

Miller, R. M., & Capaldi, E. J. (2006). An analysis of sequential variables in Pavlovian conditioning employing extended and limited acquisition training. *Learning and Motivation, 37*(4), 289–303.

Miller, T. E., Bender, B. E., & Schuh, J. H. (2005). *Promoting reasonable expectations: Aligning student and institutional views of the college experience.* San Francisco: Jossey Bass.

Miller, T. W., & Kraus, R. F. (1990). An overview of chronic pain. *Hospital and Community Psychiatry, 41,* 433–440.

Miller, W. A., Ratliff, F., & Hartline, H. K. (1961). How cells receive stimuli. *Scientific American, 215,* 222–238.

Miller, W. R., & Hester, R. K. (1980). Treating the problem drinker: Modern approaches. In W. R. Miller (Ed.), *The addictive behaviors: Treatment of alcoholism, drug abuse, smoking, and obesity.* New York: Pergamon.

Millet, B., Kochman, F., Gallard, T., Krebs, M. O., Demonfaucon, F., Barrot, I., et al. (2004). Phenomenological and comorbid features associated in obsessive-compulsive disorder: Influence of age of onset. *Journal of Affective Disorders, 79,* 241–246.

Millman, R. P. (2005). Excessive sleepiness in adolescents and young adults: Causes, consequences, and treatment strategies. *Pediatrics, 115*(6), 1774–1786.

Mills, J., & Clark, M. S. (1994). Communal and exchange relationships: Controversies and research. In R. Erber & R. Gilmour (Eds.), *Theoretical frameworks for personal relationships* (pp. 29–42). Hillsdale, NJ: Lawrence Erlbaum.

Mills, M. (1995, June). *Characteristics of personals ads differ as a function of publication readership SES.* Paper presented at the annual convention of the Human Behavior and Evolution Society, Santa Barbara, CA.

Milner, B., Corkin, S., & Teuber, H. L. (1968). Further analysis of the hippocampal amnesic syndrome: Fourteen year follow-up study of H.M. *Neuropsychologia, 6,* 215–234.

Milner, P. (1991). Brain-stimulation reward: A review. *Canadian Journal of Psychology, 45*, 1–36.

Minas, H., Klimidis, S., & Kokanovic, R. (2007). Depression in multicultural Australia: Policies, research and services. *Australia and New Zealand Health Policy, 4*, 16.

Mineka, S., & Sutton, S. K. (1992). Cognitive biases and the emotional disorders. *Psychological Science, 3*, 65–69.

Mineka, S., Watson, D., & Clark, L. A. (1998). Comorbidity of anxiety and unipolar mood disorders. *Annual Review of Psychology, 49*, 377–412.

Mineka, S., & Zinbarg, R. (2006). A contemporary learning theory perspective on the etiology of anxiety disorders: It's not what you thought it was. *American Psychologist, 61*, 10–26.

Minsky, M. (1975). A framework for representing knowledge. In P. H. Winston (Ed.), *The psychology of computer vision*. New York: McGraw-Hill.

Minuchin, S. (1974). *Families and family therapy*. Cambridge, MA: Harvard University Press.

Miranda, A. O., & Fraser, L. D. (2002). Culture-bound syndromes: Initial perspectives from individual psychology. *Journal of Individual Psychology, 58*, 422–433.

Mischel, W. (1968). *Personality and assessment*. New York: John Wiley.

Mischel, W. (1973). Toward a cognitive social learning reconceptualization of personality. *Psychological Review, 39*, 351–364.

Mischel, W. (1979). On the interface of cognitive and personality: Beyond the person-situation debate. *American Psychologist, 34*, 740–754.

Mischel, W. (1990). Personality dispositions revisited and revised: A view after three decades. In L. A. Pervin (Ed.), *Handbook of personality: Theory and research* (pp. 111–134). New York: Guilford.

Mischel, W. (2004). Toward an integrative science of the person. *Annual Review of Psychology, 55*, 1–22.

Mischel, W., & Mischel, H. N. (1976). A cognitive social-learning approach to morality and self-regulation. In T. Lickona (Ed.), *Moral development and behavior: Theory, research, and social issues*. New York: Holt, Rinehart & Winston.

Mischel, W., & Shoda, Y. (1995). A cognitive-affective system theory of personality: Reconceptualizing situations, dispositions, dynamics, and invariance in personality structure. *Psychological Review, 102*, 246–268.

Mischel, W., & Shoda, Y. (1998). Reconciling processing dynamics and personality dispositions. *Annual Review of Psychology, 49*, 229–258.

Mishkin, M., & Appenzeller, T. (1987). The anatomy of memory. *Scientific American, 256*, 80–89.

Mishra, R. C. (1997). Cognition and cognitive development. In J. W. Berry, P. R. Dasen, & T. S. Swanaswathi (Eds.), *Handbook of cross-cultural psychology: Vol. 2. Basic processes and human development* (2nd ed., pp. 143–175). Boston: Allyn & Bacon.

Mission Australia. (2007). *National survey of young Australians 2007*. Author.

Mission Australia. (2010). *National survey of young Australians 2010*. Retrieved from http://www.missionaustralia.com.au/downloads/national-survey-of-young-australians/271-2010

Mistry, J., & Rogoff, B. (1985). A cultural perspective on the development of talent. In F. D. Horowitz & M. O'Brien (Eds.), *The gifted and talented: Developmental perspectives* (pp. 125–144). Washington, DC: American Psychological Association.

Misumi, J., & Peterson, M. F. (1985). The performance-maintenance (PM) theory of leadership: Review of a Japanese research program. *Administrative Science Quarterly, 30*, 198–223.

Mitchell, P. B., Malhi, G. S., & Ball, J. R. (2004). Major advances in bipolar disorder. *Medical Journal Australia, 181*(4), 207–210.

Mitchell, S. A. (1988). *Relational concepts in psychoanalysis: An integration*. Cambridge, MA: Harvard University Press.

Mitchell, S. A., & Aron, L. (Eds.). (1999). *Relational psychoanalysis: The emergence of a tradition*. Hillsdale, NJ: Analytic Press.

Modestin, J. (1992). Multiple personality disorder in Switzerland. *American Journal of Psychiatry, 149*, 88–92.

Moeke-Pickering, T. (1996). *Maori identity within Whanau: A review of literature*. Retrieved December 15, 2004, from http://psychology.waikato.ac.nz/mpru/pubs/paps-sums/moeke-pickering-2.html

Moeller, G., & Applezweig, M. M. (1957). A motivational factor in conformity. *Journal of Abnormal Social Psychology, 55*, 114–120.

Moffit, T. E., Caspi, A., Dickson, N., Silva, P., & Stanton, W. (1996). Childhood-onset versus adolescent-onset antisocial conduct problems in males: Natural history from ages 3 to 18 years. *Development and Psychopathology, 8*, 399–424.

Mogil, J. S., Yu, L., & Basbaum, A. I. (2000). Pain genes? Natural variation and transgenic mutants. *Annual Review of Neuroscience, 23*, 777–811.

Moloney, D. P., Bouchard, T., & Segal, N. (1991). A genetic and environmental analysis of the vocational interests of monozygotic and dizygotic twins reared apart. *Journal of Vocational Behavior, 39*, 76–109.

Money, J. (1987). Sin, sickness, or status? Homosexual gender identity and psychoneuroendocrinology. *American Psychologist, 42*, 384–399.

Money, J., & Ehrhardt, A. A. (1972). *Man and woman. Boy and girl*. Baltimore: Johns Hopkins University Press.

Money, J., Schwartz, M., & Lewis, V. G. (1984). Adult heterosexual status and fetal hormonal masculinization and demasculinization. *Psychoneuroendocrinology, 9*, 405–414.

Monfils, M.-H., Cowansage, K. K., Klann, E., & LeDoux, J. E. (2009). Extinction-reconsolidation boundaries: Key to persistent attenuation of fear memories. *Science, 324*, 951–955.

Monitor on Psychology. (2007). TV violence harms children, APA member testifies to congress. *Monitor on Psychology, 38*(8). Retrieved from http://www.apa.org/monitor/sep07/tvviolence.aspx

Monk, T. H. (1997). Shift work. In M. R. Pressman & W. C. Orr (Eds.), *Understanding sleep: The evaluation and treatment of sleep disorders. Application and practice in health psychology* (pp. 249–266). Washington, DC: American Psychological Association.

Monroe, S. M., & Simons, A. D. (1991). Diathesis — stress theories in the context of life stress research: Implications for the depressive disorders. *Psychological Bulletin, 110*, 406–425.

Montano, D. E., & Kazprzyk, D. (2002). The theory of reasoned action and the theory of planned behaviour. In K. Glanz, B. K. Rimer, & F. M. Lewis (Eds.), *Health behavior and health education: Theory, research, and practice* (pp. 67–98). San Francisco: John Wiley & Sons.

Montano, D. E., Thompson, B., Taylor, V. M., & Mahloch, J. (1997). Understanding mammography intention and utilization among women in an inner city public hospital clinic. *Preventive Medicine, 26*, 817–824.

Montemayor, R., & Eisen, M. (1977). A developmental sequence of self-conceptions from childhood to adolescence. *Developmental Psychology, 13*, 314–319.

Montgomery, B. (2006). The keys to successful behaviour change. In L. Littlefield (Ed.), *In psych* (pp. 18–19). Melbourne, Australia: APS.

Montgomery, S. (1994a). Long-term treatment of depression. *British Journal of Psychiatry, 165*, 31–36.

Montgomery, S. A. (1994b). Antidepressants in long-term treatment. *Annual Review of Medicine, 45*, 447–457.

Moore, C. C., & Mathews, H. F. (Eds.). (2001). *The psychology of cultural experience*. New York: Cambridge University Press.

Moore, M. K., & Meltzoff, A. N. (1999). New findings on object permanence: A developmental difference between two types of occlusion. *British Journal of Psychology, 17*, 563–584.

Moore, M. K., & Meltzoff, A. N. (2004). Object permanence after a 24-hour delay and leaving the locale of disappearance: The role of memory, space, and identity. *Developmental Psychology, 40*, 606–620.

Moos, R. H., & Billings, A. G. (1982). Conceptualizing and measuring coping resources and processes. In L. Goldberger & S. Breznitz (Eds.), *Handbook of stress*. New York: Macmillan.

Moos, R. H., & Schaefer, J. A. (1986). Life transitions and crises. In R. H. Moos & J. A. Schaefer (Eds.), *Coping with life crises: An integrated approach*. New York: Plenum Press.

Moos, R. H., Schutte, K. K., Brennan, P. L., & Moos, B. S. (2005). The interplay between life stressors and depressive symptoms among older adults. *Journals of Gerontology Series B: Psychological Sciences and Social Sciences, 60*, 199–206.

Moreland, R. L. (1985). Social categorization and the assimilation of new group members. *Journal of Personality and Social Psychology, 48*, 1173–1190.

Moretti, M. M., & Higgins, E. T. (1999). Own versus other standpoints in self-regulation. Developmental antecedents and functional consequences. *Review of General Psychology, 3*, 188–223.

Morgan, C. D., & Murray, H. H. (1935). A method for investigating fantasies: The thematic apperception test. *Archives of Neurology and Psychiatry, 34*, 289–306.

Morgan, J. (1986). *From simple input to complex grammar*. Cambridge, MA: MIT Press.

Morgan, M., & O'Neill, D. (2001). Pragmatic poststructuralism (II): An outcomes analysis of a stopping violence programme. *Journal of Community and Applied Social Psychology, 11*, 277–289.

Morgan, M., Coombes, L., & Campbell, B. (2006). *Biculturalism, gender and critical social movements in Aotearoa/New Zealand: Still speaking from psychologies' margins*. Retrieved December 15, 2007, from http://www.discourseunit.com/arcp/arcp5/arNew%20Zealand%20ARCP%205.doc

Mori, D., Chaiken, S., & Pliner, P. (1987). 'Eating lightly' and the self-presentation of femininity. *Journal of Personality and Social Psychology, 53*, 693–702.

Morling, B., & Epstein, S. (1997). Compromises produced by the dialectic between self-verification and self-enhancement. *Journal of Personality and Social Psychology, 73*, 1268–1283.

Morris, J. S., Frith, C. D., Perrett, D. I., Rowland, D., Young, A. W., Calder, A. J., et al. (1996). A differential neural response in the human amygdala to fearful and happy facial expressions. *Nature, 383*, 812–815.

Morris, J. S., Oehman, A., & Dolan, R. J. (1998). Conscious and unconscious emotional learning in the human amygdala. *Nature, 393*, 467–470.

Morris, R. G., & Baddeley, A. D. (1988). Primary and working memory functioning in Alzheimer-type dementia. *Journal of Clinical and Experimental Neuropsychology, 10*, 279–296.

Morrison, T., & Conaway, W. A. (2000). The problems of proxemics. *Industry Week*. Retrieved January 11, 2005, from http://www.industryweek.com/Columns/asp/columns.asp?ColumnID=563

Morrissey, S. A., Raggatt, P. T. F., James, B., & Rogers, J. (1996). Seasonal affective disorder: Some epidemiological findings from a tropical climate. *Australian and New Zealand Journal of Psychiatry, 30*, 579–586.

Morrissey, S. A., & Reser, J. P. (2007). Natural disasters, climate change and mental health considerations for rural Australia. *Australian Journal of Rural Health, 15*, 120–125.

Morse, J. M., & Park, C. (1988). Differences in cultural expectations of the perceived painfulness of childbirth. In K. Michaelson (Ed.), *Childbirth in America: Anthropological perspectives*. South Hadley, MA: Bergin & Garvey.

Moskowitz, G. B. (2005). *Social cognition*. New York: Guilford Press.

Moss, L. (2004). *Cultural diversity and biculturalism: Congruence and contrasts in arts policies and practices between New Zealand and England*. Paper presented at the 3rd International Conference on Cultural Policy Research, Montreal, Canada.

Movie stars who smoke linked to teens lighting up. (2003, June 9). *The Greenville News*.

Mowrer, O. H. (1960). *Learning theory and behavior*. New York: John Wiley & Sons.

Moyer, K. E. (1983). The physiology of motivation: Aggression as a model. In C. J. Scheirer & A. M. Rogers (Eds.), *G. Stanley Hall lecture series: Vol. 3*. Washington, DC: American Psychological Association.

Mpofu, E. (2010, July). *Psychological aspects of poverty alleviation programs*. Melbourne, Australia: International Congress of Applied Psychology.

Mroczek, D. K., & Kolarz, C. M. (1998). The effect of age on positive and negative affect: A developmental perspective on happiness. *Journal of Personality and Social Psychology, 75,* 1333–1349.

Mudford, O. C. (2004). Autism and pervasive developmental disorders. In J. Matson, R. Laud, & M. Matson (Eds.), *Behavior modification for persons with developmental disabilities: Treatments and supports* (Vol. 2, pp. 213–252). New York: NADD Press.

Mulligan, R. (1996). Dental pain. In J. Barber (Ed.), *Hypnosis and suggestion in the treatment of pain: A clinical guide* (pp. 185–208). New York: W. W. Norton.

Mumaw, R., & Pellegrino, J. (1984). Individual differences in complex spatial processing. *Journal of Educational Psychology, 76*, 920–939.

Munk, M., Roelfsema, P., Konig, P., Engel, A. K., & Singer, W. (1996). Role of reticular activation in the modulation of intracortical synchronization. *Science, 272*, 271–274.

Murata, C., Takaaki, K., Hori, Y., Miyao, D., Tamakoshi, K., Yatsuya, H., et al. (2005). Effects of social relationships on mortality among the elderly in a Japanese rural area: An 88-month follow-up study. *Journal of Epidemiology, 15*(3), 78–84.

Murphy, C., & Yates, J. (2005). Economic comparison of weight loss programmes versus drug treatment for the management of obesity. *Asia Pacific Journal of Clinical Nutrition, 14*, 97–105.

Murphy, G. L., & Medin, D. L. (1985). The role of theories in conceptual coherence. *Psychological Review, 92,* 289–316.

Murphy, J. M. (1976). Psychiatric labeling in cross-cultural perspective. *Science, 191,* 1019–1028.

Murphy, S. A., Johnson, L. C., Wu, L., Fan, J. J., & Lohan, J. (2003). Bereaved parents' outcomes 4 to 60 months after their children's deaths by accident, suicide, or homicide: A comparative study demonstrating differences. *Death Studies, 27*, 39–61.

Murphy, S. T., & Zajonc, R. (1993). Affect, cognition, and awareness: Affective priming with optimal and suboptimal stimulus exposures. *Journal of Personality and Social Psychology, 64*, 723–739

Murray, G. K., Veijola, J., Moilanen, K., Miettunen, J., Giahn, D. C., Cannon, T. D., et al. (2006). Infant motor development is associated with adult cognitive categorisation in a longitudinal birth cohort study. *Journal of Child Psychology and Psychiatry, 47*, 25–29.

Murray, K. E., Davidson, G. R., & Schweitzer, R. (2010). Review of refugee mental health interventions: Best practices and recommendations. *American Journal of Orthopsychiatry, 50*, 580–589.

Murray, S. L., & Holmes, J. G. (1997). A leap of faith? Positive illusions in romantic relationships. *Personality and Social Psychology Bulletin, 23*, 586–604.

Murray, S. L., & Holmes, J. G. (1999). The (mental) ties that bind: Cognitive structures that predict relationship resilience. *Journal of Personality and Social Psychology, 77*, 1228–1244.

Murray, S. L., Holmes, J. G., & Griffin, D. W. (2000). Self-esteem and the quest for felt security: How perceived regard regulates attachment processes. *Journal of Personality and Social Psychology, 78*, 478–498.

Murray, S. L., Holmes, J. G., MacDonald, G., & Ellsworth, P. C. (1998). Through the looking glass darkly? When self-doubts turn into relationship insecurities. *Journal of Personality and Social Psychology, 75*, 1459–1480.

Murray-McIntosh, R. P., Scrimshaw, B. J., Hatfield, P. J., & Penny, D. (1998). Testing migration patterns and estimating founding population size in Polynesia by using human mtDNA sequences. *Proceedings of the National Academy of Sciences, USA, 95*(15), 9047–9052.

Murrey, G. J., Cross, H. J., & Whipple, J. (1992). Hypnotically created pseudomemories: Further investigation into the 'memory distortion or response bias' question. *Journal of Abnormal Psychology, 101*, 75–77.

Myers, D. G. (2000). The funds, friends, and faith of happy people. *American Psychologist, 55*, 56–67.

Myers, L. B., & Vetere, A. (2002). Adult romantic attachment styles and health-related measures. *Psychology, Health, and Medicine, 7,* 175–180.

Myers, T. A., & Crowther, J. H. (2009). Social comparison as a predictor of body dissatisfaction: A meta-analytic review. *Journal of Abnormal Psychology, 118*, 683–698.

Myllykangas, L., Wavrant-De, V. F., Polvikoski, T., Notkola, I. L., Sulkava, R., Niinisto, L., et al. (2005). Chromosome 21 BACE2 haplotype associates with Alzheimer's disease: A two-stage study. *Journal of the Neurological Sciences*, *236*, 17–24.

Myrtek, M. (2001). Meta-analyses of prospective studies on coronary heart disease, Type A personality, and hostility. *International Journal of Cardiology*, *79*, 245–251.

Nadel, L., Samsonovich, A., Ryan, L., & Moscovitch, M. (2000). Multiple trace theory of human memory: Computational, neuroimaging, and neuropsychological results. *Hippocampus, 10,* 352–368.

Nader, K., & van der Kooy, D. (1997). Deprivation state switches the neurobiological substrates mediating opiate reward in the ventral tegmental area. *Journal of Neuroscience*, *17*, 383–390.

Nader, K., & Wang, S. (2006). Fading in. *Learning & Memory*, *13*, 530–535.

Nagasako, E. M., Oaklander, A. L., & Dworkin, R. H. (2003). Congenital insensitivity to pain: An update. *Pain*, *101*(3), 213–219.

Nairne, J. S. (2002). Remembering over the short-term: The case against the standard model. *Annual Review of Psychology*, *53*, 53–81.

Nakao, M., Nomura, S., Shimosawa, T., Fujita, T., & Kuboki, T. (1999). Blood pressure biofeedback treatment, organ damage and sympathetic activity in mild hypertension. *Psychotherapy and Psychosomatics*, *68*, 341–347.

Nakao, M., Nomura, S., Shimosawa, T., Yoshiuchi, K., Kumano, H., Kuboki, T., et al. (1997). Clinical effects of blood pressure biofeedback treatment on hypertension by auto-shaping. *Psychosomatic Medicine, 59,* 331–338.

Nakata, M. (1999). History, cultural diversity and English language teaching. In P. Wignell (Ed.), *Double power: English literacy and indigenous education*. Melbourne, Australia: Language Australia.

Nakata, M. (2007). *Disciplining the savages: Savaging the disciplines*. Canberra, Australia: Aboriginal Studies Press.

Narita, K., Sasaki, T., Akaho, R., Okazaki, Y., Kusumi, I., Kato, T., et al. (2000). Human leukocyte antigen and season of birth in Japanese patients with schizophrenia. *American Journal of Psychiatry, 157,* 1173–1175.

Nash, M. R. (1988). Hypnosis as a window on regression. *Bulletin of the Menninger Clinic, 52*, 383–403.

Nathan, P. E. (1998). The DSM-IV and its antecedents: Enhancing syndromal diagnosis. In J. W. Barron (Ed), *Making diagnosis meaningful: Enhancing evaluation and treatment of psychological disorders* (pp. 3–27). Washington, DC: American Psychological Association.

Nathans, J. (1987). Molecular biology of visual pigments. *Annual Review of Physiology, 10*, 163–194.

National Association for Prevention of Child Abuse and Neglect. (2004). *Children are sacred: Child abuse*. Retrieved February 12, 2004, from http://www.napcan.org.au

National Centre in HIV Epidemiology and Clinical Research. (2009, October). The HIV epidemic in Australia. *Australian HIV Surveillance Report, 25*(4). Retrieved from http://www.nchecr.unsw.edu.au/NCHECRweb.nsf/resources/Quart_17/$file/NCHECR_QSROct09.pdf

National Committee on Violence. (1990). *Violence: Directions for Australia*. Canberra, Australia: Australian Institute of Criminology.

National Drug & Alcohol Research Centre. (2009). *Magic mushrooms*. Retrieved October 3, 2009, from http://ndarc.med.unsw.edu.au/ndarcweb.nsf/resources/NDARCFact_Drugs7/$file/Mushroom+fact+sheet.pdf

National Drug Strategy. (2006). *Australian secondary school students' use of over-the-counter and illicit substances in 2005*. Retrieved October 3, 2009, from http://www.nationaldrugstrategy.gov.au/internet/drugstrategy/publishing.nsf/Content/DB31984A46E05D8BCA257225001137F5/$File/mono60.pdf

National Health and Medical Research Council. (1999). *A guide to the development, implementation and evaluation of clinical practice guidelines*. Canberra, Australia: Author.

National Health and Medical Research Council. (2003). *Values and ethics: Guidelines for ethical conduct in Aboriginal and Torres Strait Islander health research*. Canberrra, Australia: Commonwealth of Australia.

National Health and Medical Research Council. (2005). *Hormone replacement therapy for women at or after the menopause: A comprehensive literature review*. Retrieved from http://nhmrc.gov.au/publications/synopses/wh34syn.htm

National Health Strategy. (2003). *Harms associated with alcohol*. Retrieved from http://www.alcohol.gov.au/internet/alcohol/publishing.nsf/Content/01212F447EC2AD34CA257261001F1ACB/$File/alcfs19.pdf

National Health Workforce Taskforce. (2010). *National registration and accreditation scheme*. Retrieved from http://www.ahwo.gov.au/natreg.asp

National heroin overdose strategy. (2001). Retrieved from http://www.nationaldrugstrategy.gov.au/internet/drugstrategy/publishing.nsf/content/3BBC336160FE6CD4CA2575B4001353B7/$File/heroin_strategy.pdf

National Institute on Deafness and other Communication Disorders. (2010). *Presbycusis*. Retrieved from http://www.nidcd.nih.gov/health/hearing/presbycusis.html

National Standing Committee on Bicultural Issues. (1993). *The New Zealand Psychological Society and the Treaty of Waitangi: Proposed implementation plan*. Proceedings of a Symposium held at the Annual Conference of the New Zealand Psychological Society, University of Victoria, Wellington, New Zealand.

Naylor, M. R., Helzer, J. E., Naud, S., & Keefe, F. J. (2002). Automated telephone as an adjunct for the treatment of chronic pain: A pilot study. *Journal of Pain, 3,* 429–438.

Neal, J., & Frick-Horbury, D. (2001). The effects of parenting styles and childhood attachment patterns on intimate relationships. *Journal of Instructional Psychology*, *28*, 178–183.

Negandhi, A. R. (1973). *Management and economic development: The case of Taiwan*. The Hague, The Netherlands: Martinus Nijhoff.

Neher, A. (1991). Maslow's theory of motivation: A critique. *Journal of Humanistic Psychology, 31*, 89–112.

Neisser, U. (1967). *Cognitive psychology*. New York: Appleton-Century-Crofts.

Neisser, U. (1976). *Cognition and reality*. San Francisco: Freeman.

Neisser, U. (1991). A case of misplaced nostalgia. *American Psychologist, 46,* 34–36.

Neisser, U. (Ed.). (1998). *The rising curve: Long-term gains in IQ and related measures*. Washington, DC: American Psychological Association.

Neisser, U. (2007). Ulric Neisser. In G. Lindzey & R. W. M. Gardner (Eds.), *A history of psychology in autobiography, Vol. IX* (pp. 269–301). Washington, DC: American Psychological Association.

Neisser, U., Boodoo, G., Bouchard, T. J., Boykin, A. W., Brody, N., Ceci, S. J., et al. (1998). Intelligence: Knowns and unknowns. In M E. Hertzig & E. A. Farber (Eds.), *Annual progress in child psychiatry and child development: 1997* (pp. 95–133). Bristol, PA: Brunner/Mazel.

Neisser, U., & Harsch, N. (1992). Phantom flashbulbs: False recollections of hearing the news about Challenger. In E. Winograd & U. Neisser (Eds.), *Affect and accuracy in recall: Studies of 'flashbulb' memories*. New York: Cambridge University Press.

Nelson, C. A. (1995). The ontogeny of human memory: A cognitive neuroscience perspective. *Developmental Psychology, 31,* 723–738.

Nelson, D. A., & Crick, N. R. (1999). Rose-colored glasses: Examining the social information-processing of prosocial young adolescents. *Journal of Early Adolescence, 19,* 17–38.

Nelson, K. (1997). Cognitive change as collaborative construction. In E. Amsel & K. A. Renninger (Eds.), *Change and development: Issues of theory, method, and application. The Jean Piaget symposium series* (pp. 99–115). Mahwah, NJ: Lawrence Erlbaum Associates.

Nelson, T. D. (2005). Ageism: Prejudice against our feared future self. *Journal of Social Issues, 61,* 207–221.

Nesbitt, E. B. (1973). An escalator phobia overcome in one session of flooding in vivo. *Journal of Behavior Therapy and Experimental Psychiatry, 4,* 405–406.

Nestadt, G., Samuels, J., Riddle, M., Bienvenu, J., Liang, K., LaBuda, M., et al. (2000). A family study of obsessive-compulsive disorder. *Archives of General Psychiatry, 57,* 358–363.

Nettelbeck, T., & Wilson, C. (1997). Speed of information processing and cognition. In W. E. MacLean Jr. (Ed.), *Ellis' handbook of mental deficiency, psychological theory and research* (3rd ed., pp. 245–274). Hillsdale, NJ: Lawrence Erlbaum.

Netz, Y., & Raviv, S. (2004). Age differences in motivational orientation toward physical activity: An application of social—cognitive theory. *The Journal of Psychology: Interdisciplinary and Applied, 138*(1), 35–48.

Neugarten, B. L. (1977). Personality and aging. In J. E. Birren & K. W. Schaie (Eds.), *Handbook of the psychology of aging*. New York: Academic Press.

Neumark-Sztainer, D., Paxton, S. J., Hannan, P. J., Haines, J., & Story, M. (2006). Does body satisfaction matter? Five-year longitudinal associations between body satisfaction and health behaviors in adolescent females and males. *Journal of Adolescent Health, 39,* 244–251.

Neutra, M., & Leblond, C. P. (1969). The Golgi apparatus. *Scientific American, 220,* 100–107.

Newcomb, P. A., & Carbone, P. P. (1992). The health consequences of smoking. Cancer. *Medical Clinics of North America, 76,* 305–331.

Newcomb, T. M. (1956). The predictions of interpersonal attraction. *American Psychologist, II,* 575–586.

Newcomb, T. M. (1961). *The acquaintance process*. New York: Holt, Rinehart & Winston.

Newcombe, N., & Dubas, J. S. (1992). A longitudinal study of predictors of spatial ability in adolescent females. *Child Development, 63,* 37–46.

Newcombe, N., Drummey, A. B., & Lie, E. (1995). Children's memory for early experience [Special issue: Early memory]. *Journal of Experimental Child Psychology, 59,* 337–342.

Newell, A., & Simon, H. A. (1972). *Human problem solving*. Englewood Cliffs, NJ; Prentice-Hall.

Newman, H. G., Freeman, F. N., & Holzinger, K. J. (1937). *Twins: A study of heredity and environment*. Chicago: University of Chicago Press.

Newman, J. (1995). Thalamic contributions to attention and consciousness. *Consciousness and Cognition, 4,* 172–193.

Newman, L. S., Duff, K., & Baumeister, R. (1997). A new look at defensive projection: Thought suppression, accessibility, and biased person perception. *Journal of Personality and Social Psychology, 72,* 980–1001.

Newport, E. L. (1990). Maturational constraints on language learning. *Cognitive Science, 14,* 11–28.

Newport, E. L., Gleitman, H., & Gleitman, L. R. (1977). Mother, I'd rather do it myself: Some effects and noneffects of maternal speech style. In C. Snow & C. A. Ferguson (Eds.), *Talking to children: Language input and acquisition*. Cambridge: Cambridge University Press.

Newsome, W. T., Britten, K. H., & Movshon, J. A. (1989). Neuronal correlates of a perceptual decision. *Nature, 341,* 52–54.

New South Wales Department of Health. (2006). *National clinical guidelines for drug use in pregnancy*. Sydney, Australia. Commonwealth of Australia.

New South Wales Legislative Assembly Hansard. (1994, December). *Article 42*. Retrieved January 17, 2005, from http://www.parliament.nsw.gov.au/prod/parlment/hansart.nsf/V3Key/LA19941201042

New Zealand AIDS Epidemiology Group. (2009). *AIDS — New Zealand*. Dunedin, New Zealand: University of Otago.

New Zealand Crime Statistics. (2010). *Crime statistics for fiscal year ending 30 June 2010. A summary of recorded and resolved offence statistics*. Retrieved from http://www.police.govt.nz/service/statistics/index.html

New Zealand Ministry of Education. (2004). *Moving forward in international education*. Retrieved October 26, 2004, from http://www.minedu.govt.nz/index.cfm?layout=document&documentid=9597&indexid=6664&indexparentid=6663

New Zealand Ministry of Health. (2001). *New Zealand public health report*. Retrieved November 28, 2007, from http://www.moh.govt.nz/nzphr.html

New Zealand Ministry of Health. (2004). *Obesity in New Zealand*. Retrieved May 21, 2004, from http://www.moh.govt.nz/moh.nsf/wpg_Index/About-Obesity#0

New Zealand Ministry of Health. (2008). *Future directions for eating disorders services in New Zealand*. Retrieved from http://www.moh.govt.nz/moh.nsf/0/87929C23C9EEE217CC25741C007A9866

New Zealand Police. (2004). *Domestic violence*. Retrieved May 18, 2004, from http://www.police.govt.nz/safety/home.domesticviolence.php

New Zealand Psychological Society. (1993). *Rules of the society*. Retrieved June 25, 2004, from http://www.psychology.org.nz/about/rules.html#name

New Zealand Psychological Society. (2002). *Code of ethics for psychologists working in Aotearoa/New Zealand, 2002*. Wellington, New Zealand: Author.

New Zealand Psychologists Board. (2006). *Cultural competencies*. Wellington, New Zealand: Author.

NFPA 72. (2010). *National fire alarm code*. Quincy, MA: Author.

NHMRC (National Health and Medical Research Council). (2006). *Cultural competency in health: A guide for policy, partnership and participation*. Canberra, Australia: Commonwealth of Australia.

Nickerson, R. S. (1998). Confirmation bias: A ubiquitous phenomenon in many guises. *Review of General Psychology, 2,* 175–220.

Niedenthal, P., Setterlund, M., & Wherry, M. B. (1992). Possible self-complexity and affective reactions to goal-relevant evaluation. *Journal of Personality and Social Psychology, 63,* 5–16.

Nielsen. (2010). *RSVP date of the nation report*, commissioned by RSVP, June. PowerPoint presentation. Retrieved from http://www.rsvp.com.au/cms-media/30677.pdf

Nielsen, D. A., Jenkins, G. L., Stefanisko, K. M., Jefferson, K. K., & Goldman, G. (1997). Sequence, splice site, and population frequency distribution analyses of polymorphic human tryptophan hydroxylase intron 7. *Molecular Brain Research, 45,* 145–148.

Nigg, J. T., Lohr, N. E., Westen, D., Gold, L. J., & Silk, K. (1992). Malevolent object representations in borderline personality disorder and major depression. *Journal of Abnormal Psychology, 101,* 61–67.

Nikora, L. W. (1993). *Cultural justice and ethics*. Proceedings of a Symposium held at the Annual Conference of the New Zealand Psychological Society, University of Victoria, Wellington.

Nikora, L. W. (2007). Maori and psychology: Indigenous psychology in New Zealand. In A. Weatherall, M. Wilson, D. Harper, & J. McDowall (Eds.), *Psychology in Aotearoa/New Zealand* (pp. 80–85). Auckland, New Zealand: Pearson Education New Zealand.

Nikora, L. W., Levy, M., Masters, B., & Waitoki, M. (2004). *Indigenous psychologies globally: A perspective from Aotearoa/New Zealand*. Retrieved December 1, 2004, from http://psychology.waikato.ac.nz/mpru/pubs/paps-sums/2004indpsyc.pdf

Nisbett, R. E. (1980). The trait construct in lay and professional psychology. In L. Festinger (Ed.), *Retrospections on social psychology* (pp. 109–130). New York: Oxford University Press.

Nisbett, R. E. (2003). *The geography of thought: How Asians and Westerners think differently...and why*. New York: Free Press.

Nisbett, R. E., & Masuda, T. (2003). Culture and point of view. *Proceedings of the National Academy of Sciences, USA, 100*(19), 11163–11170.

Nisbett, R. E., Peng, K., Choi, I., & Norenzayan, A. (2001). Culture and systems of thought: Holistic versus analytic cognition. *Psychological Review, 108,* 291–310.

Nisbett, R. E., & Ross, L. (1980). *Human inference: Strategies and shortcomings of social judgment*. Englewood Cliffs, NJ: Prentice-Hall.

Nisbett, R. E., & Wilson, T. D. (1977). Telling more than we can know: verbal reports on mental processes. *Psychological Review, 84,* 231–259.

Nober, E. H., Peirce, H., & Well, A. (1981, July). Waking effectiveness of household smoke and fire detection devices. *Fire Journal, 75*(4), 86–91.

Noguchi, K., Gohm, C. L., Dalsky, D. J., & Sakamoto, S. (2007). Cultural differences related to positive and negative valence. *Asian Journal of Social Psychology, 10*(2), 68–76.

Nolde, S. F., Johnson, M. K., & Raye, C. L. (1998). The role of prefrontal cortex during tests of episodic memory. *Trends in Cognitive Sciences, 2,* 399–406.

Nolen-Hoeksema, S., Girgus, J. S., & Seligman, M. E. (1992). Predictors and consequences of childhood depressive symptoms: A 5-year longitudinal study. *Journal of Abnormal Psychology, 101,* 405–422.

Noll, R. (1994). Hypnotherapy for warts in children and adolescents. *Journal of Developmental and Behavioral Pediatrics, 15,* 170–173.

Noller, P., Feeney, J. A., & Peterson, C. (2001). *Personal relationships across the lifespan*. Philadelphia: Taylor & Francis.

Nonis, S. A., Teng, J. K., & Ford, C. W. (2005). A cross-cultural investigation of time management practices and job outcomes. *International Journal of Intercultural Relations, 29,* 409–428.

Norcross, J., Karg, R., & Prochaska, J. (1997). Clinical psychologists in the 1990s: Part 1. *Clinical Psychologist, 50,* 4–8.

Norem, J. K. (1998). Why should we lower our defense about defense mechanisms? *Journal of Personality, 66*(6), 895–917.

Norenzayan, A., & Nisbett, R. E. (2000). Culture and causal cognition. *Current Directions in Psychological Science, 9,* 132–135.

Norman, W. T. (1963). Toward an adequate taxonomy of personality attributes: Replicated factor structure in peer nomination personality ratings. *Journal of Abnormal and Social Psychology, 66,* 574–583.

Northern Territory Department of Health and Community Services. (2004). *Fit kids — a new program for families of overweight and obese children*. Retrieved August 1, 2004, from http://www.nt.gov.au/health/news/2003/fit_kids.shtml

Norton, R. N., & Morgan, M. Y. (1989). The role of alcohol in mortality and morbidity from interpersonal violence. *Alcohol, 24,* 565–576.

Novak, M. A., & Harlow, H. F. (1975). Social recovery of monkeys isolated for the first year of life: Rehabilitation and therapy. *Developmental Psychology, 11,* 453–465.

Nowak, R. (1994). Nicotine research. Key study unveiled — 11 years late. *Science, 264,* 196–197.

Nussbaum, R. L., & Ellis, C. E. (2003). Alzheimer's disease and Parkinson's disease. *New England Journal of Medicine, 348,* 1356–1364.

Nuttin, J. M. (1985). Narcissism beyond Gestalt and awareness: The name letter effect. *European Journal of Social Psychology, 15,* 353–361.

Nyberg, L. (1998). Mapping episodic memory. *Behavioral Brain Research, 90,* 107–114.

Oakley Browne, M. A., Wells, J. E., & Scott, K. M. (Eds.). (2006). *Te Rau Hinengaro — The New Zealand mental health survey: Summary*. Wellington, New Zealand: Ministry of Health. Retrieved from http://www.moh.govt.nz/moh.nsf/pagesmh/5166/$File/mental-health-survey-summary.pdf

Oatley, K., & Jenkins, J. M. (1992). Human emotion: Function and dysfunction. *Annual Review of Psychology, 43,* 55–85.

O'Brien, T. B., & DeLongis, A. (1996). The interactional context of problem-, emotion-, and relationship-focused coping: The role of the Big Five personality factors. *Journal of Personality, 64,* 775–813.

O'Bryant, S. E., Palav, A., & McCaffrey, R. J. (2003). A review of symptoms commonly associated with menopause: Implications for clinical neuropsychologists and other health care providers. *Neuropsychology Review, 13,* 145–152.

Ochsner, K. N. (2000). Are affective events richly recollected or simply familiar? The experience and process of recognizing feelings past. *Journal of Experimental Psychology: General, 129,* 242–261.

Ochsner, K. N., & Schacter, D. L. (2000). A social cognitive neuroscience approach to emotion and memory. In J. C. Borod (Ed.), *The neuropsychology of emotion* (pp. 163–193). New York: Oxford University Press.

O'Connor, B., Spencer, F., & Patton, W. (2003). The relationship between working memory and cognitive functioning in children. In *Proceedings of the 38th Australian Psychological Society Annual Conference, Perth, Australia* (pp. 147–152).

O'Connor, K. P. (2008). Eysenck's model of individual differences. In G. J. Boyle, G. Matthews, & D. H. Saklofske (Eds.), *The Sage handbook of personality theory and assessment: Vol. 1. Personality theories and models* (pp. 215–238). London: Sage Publications.

O'Connell, P., Pepler, D., & Craig, W. (1999). Peer involvement in bullying: Insights and challenges for intervention. *Journal of Adolescence, 22,* 437–452. Retrieved from http://www.bullylab.com/Portals/0/Peer%20involvement%20in%20bullying-%20Insights%20and%20challenges%20for%20intervention.pdf

O'Connor, T. (2003). Early experiences and psychological development: Conceptual questions, empirical illustrations, and implications for intervention. *Development and Psychopathology, 15,* 671–690.

O'Connor, T. G., McGuire, S., Reiss, D., Hetherington, E. M., & Plomin, R. (1998). Co-occurrence of depressive symptoms and antisocial behavior in adolescence: A common genetic liability. *Journal of Abnormal Psychology, 107,* 27–37.

O'Connor, T. G., Rutter, M., Beckett, C., Keaveney, L., Kreppner, J., & the English and Romanian Adoptees Study Team. (2000). The effects of global severe privation on cognitive competence: Extension and longitudinal follow-up. *Child Development, 71,* 376–390.

OECD. (2009). *OECD health data: Statistics and indicators for 30 countries, CD-ROM and online version*. Paris: Author.

Oettingen, G., Little, T. D., Lindenberger, U., & Baltes, P. B. (1994). Causality, agency, and control beliefs in East versus West Berlin children: A natural experiment on the role of context. *Journal of Personality and Social Psychology, 66,* 579–595.

Oettingen, G., & Seligman, M. (1990). Pessimism and behavioral signs of depression in East versus West Berlin. *European Journal of Social Psychology, 20,* 207–220.

Offer, D., & Offer, J. (1975). *From teenage to young manhood: A psychological study*. New York: Basic Books.

Offer, D., Ostrov, E., Howard, K., & Atkinson, R. (1990). Normality and adolescence. *Psychiatric Clinics of North America, 13,* 377–388.

Ogata, N., Voshii, M., & Narahashi, T. (1989). Psychotropic drugs block voltage-gated ion channels in neuroblastoma cells. *Brain Research, 476,* 140–144.

Ogbu, J. (1991). Minority coping responses and school experience. *Journal of Psychohistory, 18,* 434–456.

Ohman, A., Esteves, F., & Soares, J. F. (1995). Preparedness and preattentive associative learning: Electrodermal conditioning to masked stimuli. *Journal of Psychophysiology, 9,* 99–108.

Ohman, A., Fredrikson, M., Hugdahl, K., & Rimmon, P. (1976). The premise of equipotentiality in human classical conditioning. *Journal of Experimental Psychological General, 105,* 313–337.

Ohman, A., & Mineka, S. (2001). Fears, phobias, and preparedness: Toward an evolved module of fear and fear learning. *Psychological Review, 108,* 483–522.

Oishi, S. (2004). Personality in culture: A neo-Allportian view. *Journal of Research in Personality, 38,* 68–74.

Okasha, A., El Akabaw, A. S., Snyder, K. S., Wilson, A. K., Youssef, I., & El Dawla, A. S. (1994). Expressed emotion, perceived criticism, and relapse in depression: A replication. *American Journal of Psychiatry, 151,* 1001–1005.

O'Keefe, D. J. (2002). The elaboration likelihood model. In D. J. O'Keefe (Ed.), *Persuasion: Theory and research* (2nd ed., pp. 137–167). Thousand Oaks, CA: Sage.

Okun, B. F., Fried, J., & Okun, M. L. (1999). *Understanding diversity: A learning-as-practice primer*. Pacific Grove, CA: Brooks/Cole.

Oldenburg, B. (2002). Preventing chronic disease and improving health: Broadening the scope of behavioral medicine research and practice. *International Journal of Behavioral Medicine, 9,* 1–16.

Olds, J., & Milner, P. (1954). Positive reinforcement produced by electrical stimulation of septal areas and other regions of rat brains. *Journal of Comparative and Physiological Psychology, 47,* 419–427.

O'Leary, A. (1992). Self-efficacy and health: Behavioral and stress-physiological mediation. *Cognitive Therapy & Research, 16,* 229–245.

O'Leary, A., Brown, S., & Suarez-Al-Adam, M. (1997). Stress and immune function. In T. W. Miller (Ed.), *Clinical disorders and stressful life events* (pp. 181–215). Madison, CT: International Universities Press.

O'Leary, C. M. (2004). Fetal alcohol syndrome: Diagnosis, epidemiology, and developmental outcomes. *Journal of Paediatric Child Health, 40,* 2–7.

Olivier, B. (2004). Serotonin and aggression. *Annals of the New York Academy of Sciences, 1036,* 382–392.

Olsen, K. N., & Stevens, C. J. (2010). Perceptual overestimation of rising intensity: Is stimulus continuity necessary? *Perception, 39,* 695–704.

Olson, D. (1985). Circumplex model VII: Validation and FACES III. *Family Process, 25,* 337–351.

Olson, D. H. (2000). Circumplex model of marital and family systems. *Journal of Family Therapy, 22,* 144–167.

Olson, G. B. (1981). Perception of melodic contour through intrasensory matching and intersensory transfer by elementary school students. *Journal of Educational Research, 74,* 358–362.

Olson, J. M., Vernon, P. A., Harris, J. A., & Jang, K. L. (2001). The heritability of attitudes: A study of twins. *Journal of Personality and Social Psychology, 80*(6), 845–860.

Olson, J. M., & Zanna, M. (1993). Attitudes and attitude change. *Annual Review of Psychology, 44,* 117–154.

Olsson, A., Ebert, J. P., Banaji, M. R., & Phelps, E. A. (2005). The role of social groups in the persistence of learned fear. *Science, 309,* 785–787.

Olweus, D. (1980). Familial and temperamental determinants of aggressive behavior in adolescent boys: A causal analysis. *Developmental Psychology, 16,* 644–666.

Olweus, D. (1988). Environmental and biological factors in the development of aggressive behavior. In W. Buikhuisen & S. A. Mednick (Eds.), *Explaining criminal behaviour: Interdisciplinary approaches* (pp. 90–120). Leiden, The Netherlands: E. J. Brill.

O'Neill, R. M., Greenberg, R. P., & Fisher, S. (1992). Humor and anality. *Humor: International Journal of Humor Research, 5,* 283–291.

Opacic, T., Stevens, C., & Tillmann, B. (2009). Unspoken knowledge: Implicit learning of structured human dance movement. *Journal of Experimental Psychology: Learning, Memory and Cognition, 35,* 1570–1577.

Oppenheim, D., Nir, A., Warren, S., & Emde, R. N. (1997). Emotion regulation in mother-child narrative co-construction: Associations with children's narratives and adaptation. *Developmental Psychology, 33,* 284–294.

Orne, M. T., Sheehan, P. W., & Evans, F. J. (1968). Occurrence of posthypnotic behavior outside the experimental setting. *Journal of Personality and Social Psychology, 9,* 189–196.

Ornstein, R. E. (1986). *The psychology of consciousness* (2nd ed.). New York: Penguin.

Ortony, A., Clore, G. L., & Collins, A. (1988). *The cognitive structure of emotions*. New York: Cambridge University Press.

Ortony, A., & Turner, T. J. (1990). What's basic about basic emotions? *Psychological Review, 97,* 315–331.

Oskamp, S. (1991). Factors influencing household recycling behavior. *Environment and Behavior, 23,* 494–519.

Ost, L. (1991). Acquisition of blood and injection phobia and anxiety response patterns in clinical patients. *Behavior Research and Therapy, 29,* 323–332.

O'Sullivan, J., & Gilbert, J. (2003). *ECT (Electroconvulsive therapy)*. Brisbane, Australia: Queensland Health.

Otten, L. J., Henson, R. N. A., & Rugg, M. D. (2001). Depth of processing effects on neural correlates of memory encoding: Relationship between findings from across- and within-task comparisons. *Brain, 124,* 399–412.

Otto, M. W., Smits, J. A. J., & Reese, H. E. (2006). Combined psychotherapy and pharmacotherapy for mood and anxiety disorders in adults: Review and analysis. *Focus, 4,* 204–214.

Otto, M. W., Teachman, B. A., Cohen, L. S., Soares, C. N., Vitonis, A. F., & Harlow, B. L. (2007). Dysfunctional attitudes and episodes of major depression: Predictive validity and temporal stability in never-depressed, depressed, and recovered women. *Journal of Abnormal Psychology, 114*(3), 475–483.

Ouellette, J. A., & Wood, W. (1998). Habit and intention in everyday life: The multiple processes by which past behavior predicts future behavior. *Psychological Bulletin, 124,* 54–74.

Overholser, J. C. (2002). Cognitive-behavioral treatment of social phobia. *Journal of Contemporary Psychotherapy, 32,* 125–144.

Overton, A., Selway, S., Strongman, K., & Houston, M. (2005). Eating disorders: The regulation of positive as well as negative emotion experience. *Journal of Clinical Psychology in Medical Settings, 12*(1), 39–56.

Oyserman, D., & Lee, S. W. (2007). Priming culture: Culture as situated cognition. In S. Kitayama & D. Cohen (Eds.), *Handbook of cultural psychology* (pp. 255–279). New York: Guilford Press.

Oyserman, D., Coon, H. M., & Kemmelmeier, M. (2002). Rethinking individualism and collectivism: Evaluation of theoretical assumptions and meta-analyses. *Psychological Bulletin, 128*(1), 3–72.

Pachana, N. (2006, September). *Ageing: Too cool for school (I think not ...)*. Paper presented at the 2006 Joint Conference of the APS and NZPsS, Auckland, New Zealand.

Packwood, J., & Gordon, B. (1975). Steropsis in normal domestic cat, Siamese cat, and cat raised with alternating monocular occlusion. *Journal of Neurophysiology, 38,* 1485–1499.

Page, A. C., Jones, R., & Wilson, F. (2004). Survey of West Australian anxiety support group participants' views on treatment processes and outcomes. *Australian Psychologist, 39*(3), 208–211.

Page, A. N., Swannell, S., Martin, G., Hollingworth, S., Hickie, I. B., & Hall, W. D. (2009). Sociodemographic correlates of antidepressant utilisation in Australia. *The Medical Journal of Australia*. Retrieved from http://www.mja.com.au/public/issues/190_09_040509/pag11449_fm.html

Paivio, A. (1991). Dual coding theory: Retrospect and current status. *Canadian Journal of Psychology, 45*, 255–287.

Paivio, S. C., & Greenberg, L. S. (1995). Resolving 'unfinished business': Efficacy of experimental therapy using empty-chair dialogue. *Journal of Consulting and Clinical Psychology, 63*, 419–425.

Palme, G., & Palme, J. (1999). Personality characteristics of females seeking treatment for obesity, bulimia nervosa and alcoholic disorders. *Personality and Individual Differences, 26*, 255–263.

Pannu, J. K., Kaszniak, A. W., & Rapcsak, S. Z. (2005). Metamemory for faces following frontal lobe damage. *Journal of the International Neuropsychological Society, 11*, 668–676.

Paolini, S., Harwood, J., & Rubin, M. (2010). Negative intergroup contact makes group memberships salient: Explaining why intergroup conflict endures. *Personality and Social Psychology Bulletin, 36*(12), 1723.

Papadopoulos, R. K. (2007). Refugees, trauma and adversity-activated development. *European Journal of Psychotherapy and Counselling, 9*, 301–312.

Papez, J. W. (1937). A proposed mechanism of emotion. *Archives of Neurology and Psychiatry, 38*, 725–743.

Paradies, Y. (2005). Anti-racism and Indigenous Australians. *Analyses of Social Issues and Public Policy, 5*(1), 1–28.

Pargament, K. I., & Park, C. L. (1995). Merely a defense? The variety of religious means and ends. *Journal of Social Issues, 51*, 13–32.

Park, D. C., Smith, A. D., Lautenschlager, G., & Earles, J. L. (1996). Mediators of long-term memory performance across the life span. *Psychology & Aging, 11*, 621–637.

Park, D. C., & Schwarz, N. (2000). *Cognitive aging: A primer*. Philadelphia: Psychology Press/Taylor & Francis.

Park, S., & Holzman, P. S. (1993). Association of working memory deficit and eye tracking dysfunction in schizophrenia. *Schizophrenia Research, 11*, 55–61.

Park, W. W. (2000). A comprehensive empirical investigation of the relationships among variables of the groupthink model. *Journal of Organizational Behavior, 21*, 873–887.

Parke, R. D., & Buriel, R. (1998). Socialization in the family: Ethnic and ecological perspectives. In W. Damon (Ed. in Chief) & N. Eisenberg (Vol. Ed.), *Handbook of child psychology: Vol. 3* (pp. 463–552). New York: John Wiley.

Parker, G., Wilhelm, K., & Asghari, A. (1997). Early onset of depression: The relevance of anxiety. *Social Psychiatry and Psychiatric Epidemiology, 32*, 30–37.

Parker, I., & Bolton Discourse Network. (Eds.). (1999). *Critical textwork: An introduction to varieties of discourse and analysis*. Buckingham: Open University Press.

Parker, J. G., & Asher, S. R. (1987). Peer relations and later personal adjustment: Are low-accepted children at risk? *Psychological Bulletin, 102*, 357–389.

Parker, R. (2002, July). *Why marriages last: A discussion of the literature* (Research Paper No. 28). Melbourne, Australia: Australian Institute of Family Studies.

Parkes, M., & White, K. G. (2000). Glucose attenuation of memory impairments. *Behavioral Neuroscience, 114*, 1–13.

Parkin, A. J., & Java, R. I. (1999). Deterioration of frontal lobe function in normal aging: Influences of fluid intelligence versus perceptual speed. *Neuropsychology, 13*, 539–545.

Parkin, A. J., Walter, B. M., & Hunkin, N. M. (1995). Relationships between normal aging, frontal lobe function, and memory for temporal and spatial information. *Neuropsychology, 9*, 304–312.

Parliamentary Travelsafe Committee. (1998). *Drug driving in Queensland* (Issues Paper No. 3). Retrieved January 28, 2004, from http://www.parliament.qld.gov.au/

Parsons, T. (1951). *The social system*. Glencoe, IL: Free Press.

Pascal, R., Chikritzhs, T., & Jones, P. (2009). *Trends in estimated alcohol attributable deaths and hospitalisations in Australia, 1996–2005* (National Alcohol Indicators, Bulletin No. 12). Perth, Australia: National Drug Research Institute/Curtin University of Technology.

Pascual-Leone, A., & Torres, F. (1993). Plasticity of the sensorimotor cortex representations of the reading finger in Braille. *Brain, 116*, 39–52.

Pascual-Leone, A., Walsh, V., & Rothwell, J. (2000). Transcranial magnetic stimulation in cognitive neuroscience—virtual lesion, chronometry, and functional connectivity. *Current Opinion in Neurobiology, 10*, 232–237.

Passaro, K. T., & Little, R. E. (1997). Childbearing and alcohol use. In R. W. Wilsnack & S. C. Wilsnack (Eds.), *Gender and alcohol: Individual and social perspectives* (pp. 90–113). Rutgers, NJ: Rutgers Center of Alcohol Studies.

Passig, D., & Eden, S. (2003). Cognitive intervention through virtual environments among deaf and hard-of-hearing children. *European Journal of Special Needs Education, 18*, 173–182.

Patock-Peckham, J. A., Cheong, J. W., Balhorn, M. E., & Nagoshi, C. T. (2001). A social learning perspective: A model of parenting styles, self-regulation, perceived drinking control, and alcohol use and problems. *Alcoholism: Clinical and Experimental Research, 25*, 1284–1292.

Pattatucci, A., & Hamer, D. (1995). Development and familiarity of sexual orientation in females. *Behavior Genetics, 25*, 407–420.

Patterson, D. R., Everett, J. J., Burns, G. L., & Marvin, J. A. (1992). Hypnosis for the treatment of burn pain. *Journal of Consulting & Clinical Psychology, 60*, 713–717.

Patterson, D. R., & Ptacek, J. T. (1997). Baseline pain as a moderator of hypnotic analgesia for burn injury treatment. *Journal of Consulting & Clinical Psychology, 65*, 60–67.

Patterson, G. R., & Bank, L. (1986). Bootstrapping your way in the nomological thicket. *Behavioral Assessment, 8*, 49–73.

Patton, G., Coffey, C., Carlin, J. B., Degenhardt, L., Lynskey, M., & Hall, W. (2002). Cannabis use and mental health in young people: Cohort study. *British Medical Journal, 325*(7374), 1195–1198.

Paulesu, E., Frith, U., Snowling, M., Gallagher, A., Morton, J., Frackowiak, R. S. J., et al. (1996). Is developmental dyslexia a disconnection syndrome? Evidence from PET scanning. *Brain, 119*, 143–157.

Paulhus, D., Fridhandler, B., & Hayes, S. (1997). Psychological defense: Contemporary theory and research. In R. Hogan, J. Johnson, & S. R. Briggs (Eds.), *Handbook of personality psychology* (pp. 543–579). San Diego, CA: Academic Press.

Paunonen, S. V., & Ashton, M. C. (2001). Big five predictors of academic achievement. *Journal of Research in Personality, 35*, 78–90.

Paunonen, S. V., Jackson, D. N., Trzebinski, J., & Forsterling, F. (1992). Personality structure across cultures: A multimethod evaluation. *Journal of Personality and Social Psychology, 62*, 447–456.

Pause, B. M., Bernfried, S., Krauel, K., Fehm- Wolfsdorf, G., & Ferstl, R. (1996). Olfactory information processing during the course of the menstrual cycle. *Biological Psychology, 44*, 31–54.

Pavlov, I. P. (1927). *Conditioned reflexes*. New York: Oxford University Press.

Paxton, S. J., Eisenberg, M. E., & Neumark-Sztainer, D. (2006). Prospective predictors of body dissatisfaction in adolescent girls and boys: A five-year longitudinal study. *Developmental Psychology, 42*, 888–899.

Paxton, S. J., Ellis, B., & McLean, S. (2006). Internet therapy for body dissatisfaction and disordered eating: Increasing access to effective treatment. In L. Littlefield (Ed.), *In Psych* (p. 23). Melbourne, Australia: APS.

Paxton, S. J., Neumark-Sztainer, D., Hannan, P. J., & Eisenberg, M. (2006). Body dissatisfaction prospectively predicts depressive symptoms and low self-esteem in adolescent girls and boys. *Journal of Clinical Child and Adolescent Psychology, 35*, 539–549.

Paxton, S. J., Schutz, H. K., Wertheim, E. H., & Muir, S. L. (1999). Friendship clique and peer influences on body image attitudes, dietary restraint, extreme weight loss behaviours and binge eating in adolescent girls. *Journal of Abnormal Psychology. 108*, 255–266.

Payne, D. G., Neuschatz, J. S., Lampien, J. M., & Lynn, S. J. (1997). Compelling memory illusions: The qualitative characteristics of false memories. *Current Directions in Psychological Science, 6*, 56–60.

Pearse, S. L., Powell, M. B., & Thomson, D. M. (2003). The effect of contextual cues on children's ability to remember an occurrence of a repeated event. *Legal and Criminological Psychology, 8*(1), 39–50.

Peden, A. R., Hall, L. A., Rayens, M. K., & Beebe, L. (2000). Negative thinking mediates the effect of self-esteem on depressive symptoms of college women. *Nursing Research, 49*(4), 201–207.

Pedersen, A., Attwell, J., & Heveli, J. (2005). Prediction of negative attitudes toward Australian asylum seekers: False beliefs, nationalism and self-esteem. *Australian Journal of Psychology, 57*(3), 148–160.

Pedersen, A., Clarke, S., Dudgeon, P., & Griffiths, B. (2005). Attitudes toward Indigenous Australians and asylum seekers: The role of false beliefs and other social-psychological variables. *Australian Psychologist, 40*(3), 170–178.

Pedersen, A., Griffith, B., Contos, N., Bishop, B., & Walker, I. (2000). Attitudes toward Aboriginal Australians in city and country settings. *Australian Psychologist, 35*(2), 109–117.

Pedersen, A., Watt, S., & Hansen, S. (2006). The role of false beliefs in the community's and federal government's attitudes toward Australian asylum seekers. *Australian Journal of Social Issues, 41*, 105–124.

Pedersen, D. M., & Wheeler, J. (1983). The Muller-Lyer illusion among Navajos. *Journal of Social Psychology, 121*, 3–6.

Pederson, D. R., Moran, G., Sitko, C., Campbell, K., Ghesquire, K., & Acton, H. (1990). Maternal sensitivity and the security of infant-mother attachment: A q-sort study. *Child Devleopment, 61*, 1974–1983.

Peebles-Kleiger, M. J. (2002). *Beginnings: The art and science of planning psychotherapy*. Hillsdale, NJ: Analytic Press.

Peele, S. (1986). Implications and limitations of genetic models of alcoholism and other addictions. *Journal of Studies on Alcohol, 47*, 63–73.

Peeters, B. (2004). Tall poppies and egalitarianism in Australian discourse. *English World-Wide, 25*(1), 1–25.

Pelham, B. W., Mirenberg, M. C., & Jones, J. T. (2002). Why Susie sells seashells by the seashore: Implicit egotism and major life decisions. *Journal of Personality and Social Psychology, 82*, 469–487.

Pelucchi, B., Hay, J. F., & Saffran, J. R. (2009). Statistical learning in a natural language by 8-month old infants. *Child Development, 80*, 674–685.

Peng, D., & Nisbett, R. E. (1999). Culture, dialectics, and reasoning about contradiction. *American Psychologist, 54*, 741–754.

Peninsular Hearing Aid Centre. (2010). *Presbycusis*. Retrieved from http://www.penhear.com.au/info4.htm

Pennebaker, J., Colder, M., & Sharp, L. K. (1990). Accelerating the coping process. *Journal of Personality and Social Psychology, 58*, 528–537.

Pennebaker, J. W. (1997a). *Opening up: The healing power of expressing emotions* (Rev. ed.). New York: Guilford Press.

Pennebaker, J. W. (1997b). Writing about emotional experiences as a therapeutic process. *Psychological Science, 8*, 162–166.

Pennebaker, J. W., Barger, S. D., & Tiebout, J. (1989). Disclosure of traumas and health among Holocaust survivors. *Psychosomatic Medicine, 51*, 577–589.

Pennebaker, J. W., Kiecolt-Glaser, J., & Glaser, R. (1988). Disclosure of traumas and immune function: Health implications for psychotherapy. *Journal of Consulting and Clinical Psychology, 56*, 239–245.

Pennebaker, J. W., Mayne, T. J., & Francis, M. E. (1997). Linguistic predictors of adaptive bereavement. *Journal of Personality and Social Psychology, 72*, 863–871.

Pennebaker, J. W., & Seagal, J. D. (1999). Forming a story: The health benefits of narrative. *Journal of Clinical Psychology, 55*, 1243–1254.

Pennebaker, J. W., Zech, E., & Rime, B. (2001). Disclosing and sharing emotion: Psychological, social and health consequences. In M. S. Stroebe, R. O. Hansson, W. Stroebe, & H. Schut (Eds.), *Handbook of bereavement research: Consequences, coping, and care* (pp. 517–544). Washington, DC: American Psychological Association.

Penner, L. A., Dovidio, J. F., Piliavin, J. A., & Schroeder, D. A. (2005). Prosocial behavior: Multilevel perspectives. *Annual Review of Psychology, 56*, 365–392.

Perdue, C., & Gurtman, M. (1990). Evidence for the automaticity of ageism. *Journal of Experimental Social Psychology, 26*, 199–216.

Perez, L. M., & Garcia, E. G. (2002). Programme for the improvement of metamemory in people with medium and mild mental retardation. *Psychology in Spain, 6*, 96–101.

Perlman, D. N., Clark, M. A., Rakowski, W., & Ehrich, B. (1999). Screening for breast and cervical cancers: The importance of knowledge and perceived cancer survivability. *Women's Health, 28*, 93–112.

Perlmutter, M. (1983). Learning and memory through adulthood. In M. W. Riley, B. B. Hess, & K. Bond (Eds.), *Aging in society: Selected reviews of recent research*. Hillsdale, NJ: Lawrence Erlbaum.

Perlmutter, M., Dams, C., Berry, J., Kaplan, M., Pearson, D., & Verdonik, J. (1990). Aging and memory. *Annual Review of Gerontology and Geriatrics, 7*, 57–92.

Perls, F. S. (1969). *Ego, hunger and aggression: The beginning of Gestalt therapy*. New York: Random House.

Perls, F. S. (1989). Theory and technique of personality integration. *TACD Journal, 17*, 35–52.

Perris, E. E., Myers, N. A., & Clifton, R. K. (1990). Long-term memory for a single infancy experience. *Child Development, 61*, 1796–1807.

Perrone, J. A. (2004). A visual motion sensor based on the properties of V1 and MT neurons. *Vision Research, 44*, 1733–1755.

Perruchet, P. (1989). The effect of spaced practice on explicit and implicit memory. *British Journal of Psychology, 80*, 113–130.

Perry, C. L., Killen, J., Slinkard, L. A., & McAlister, A. L. (1980). Peer teaching and smoking prevention among junior high students. *Adolescence, 15*, 277–281.

Perry, E., Walker, M., Grace, J., & Perry, R. (1999). Acetylcholine in mind: A neurotransmitter correlate of consciousness? *Trends in Neurosciences, 22*, 273–280.

Perry, G. D., & Bussey, K. (1979). The social learning theory of sex differences: Imitation is alive and well. *Journal of Personality and Social Psychology, 37*, 1699–1712.

Perry, J. C., Bond, M., & Roy, C. (2007). Predictors of treatment duration and retention in a study of long-term dynamic psychotherapy: Childhood adversity, adult personality, and diagnosis. *Journal of Psychiatric Practice, 13*(4), 221–232.

Pervin, L. A. (2003). *The science of personality* (2nd ed.). New York: Oxford.

Peskin, J. (1992). Ruse and representations: On children's ability to conceal information. *Developmental Psychology, 28*, 84–89.

Petersen, L. E., Dietz, J., & Frey, D. (2004). The effects of intragroup interaction and cohesion on intergroup bias. *Group Processes and Intergroup Relations, 7*(2), 107–118.

Petersen, M. R., Beecher, M. D., Zoloth, S., Green, S., Marler, P., Moody, D. B., et al. (1984). Neural lateralization of vocalizations by Japanese Macaques: Communicative significance is more important than acoustic structure. *Behavioral Neuroscience, 98*, 779–790.

Peterson, B. E., Smirles, K. A., & Wentworth, P. A. (1997). Generativity and authoritarianism: Implications for personality, political involvement, and parenting. *Journal of Personality and Social Psychology, 72*(5), 1202–1216.

Peterson, B. S. (2002). Indeterminacy and compromise formation: Implications for psychoanalytic theory of mind. *International Journal of Psychoanalysis, 83*, 1017–1035.

Peterson, C. (1988). Explanatory style as a risk factor for illness. *Cognitive Therapy and Research, 12*, 119–132.

Peterson, C. (1995). Explanatory style and health. In G. M. Buchanan & M. E. P. Seligman (Eds.), *Explanatory style* (pp. 233–246). Hillsdale, NJ: Lawrence Erlbaum.

Peterson, C. (1999). The ticking of the social clock: Adults' beliefs about the timing of transition events. *International Journal of Aging and Human Development, 142*, 189–203.

Peterson, C. (2000a). The future of optimism. *American Psychologist, 55*, 44–55.

Peterson, C. (2000b). Kindred spirits: Influences of siblings' perspectives on theory of mind. *Cognitive Psychology, 15*, 435–455.

Peterson, C. (2003). The social face of theory of mind: The development of concepts of emotion, desire, visual perspective and false belief in deaf and hearing children. In B. Repacholi & V. Slaughter (Eds.), *Individual differences in theory of mind: Implications for typical and atypical development* (pp. 171–196). New York: Psychology Press.

Peterson, C. (2004). *Looking forward through the lifespan: Developmental psychology* (4th ed.). Frenchs Forest, Australia: Pearson Education Australia.

Peterson, C., & Seligman, M. E. P. (1984). Causal explanations as a risk factor for depression: Theory and evidence. *Psychological Review, 91*, 347–374.

Peterson, C. B., & Mitchell, J. E. (1999). Psychosocial and pharmacological treatment of eating disorders: A review of research findings. *Journal of Clinical Psychology, 55*, 685–697.

Peterson, C. C., Wellman, H. M., & Liu, D. (2005). Steps in theory-of-mind development for children with deafness or autism. *Child Development, 76*(2), 502–517.

Peterson, G. W., & Peters, D. F. (1985). The socialization values of low-income Appalachian White and rural Black mothers: A comparative study. *Journal of Comparative Family Studies, 16*, 75–91.

Petitto, L. A. (2000). On the biological foundations of human language. In K. Emmorey & H. Lane (Eds.), *The signs of language revisited: An anthology in honor of Ursula Bellugi and Edward Klima*. Mahwah, NJ: Lawrence Erlbaum Associates.

Petrinovich, L. F. (1999). *Darwinian dominion: Animal welfare and human interests*. Cambridge, MA: MIT Press.

Petry, N. M., Martin, B., Cooney, J. L., & Kranzler, H. R. (2000). Give them prizes and they will come: Contingency management for treatment of alcohol dependence. *Journal of Consulting and Clinical Psychology, 68*, 250–257.

Pettigrew, T. (1958). Personality and socio-cultural factors in intergroup attitudes: A cross-national comparison. *Journal of Conflict Resolution, 2*, 29–42.

Pettigrew, T. F. (2008). Future direction for intergroup contact theory and research. *International Journal of Intercultural Relations, 32*, 187–199.

Pettigrew, T. F., & Meertens, R. W. (1995). Subtle and blatant prejudice in western Europe. *European Journal of Social Psychology, 25*, 57–75.

Pettigrew, T. F., & Tropp, L. R. (2006). A meta-analytic test of intergroup contact theory. *Journal of Personality and Social Psychology, 90*(5), 751–783.

Pettit, G. S. (1997). The developmental course of violence and aggression: Mechanisms of family and peer influence. *Psychiatric Clinics of North America, 20*, 283–299.

Petty, F. (1995). GABA and mood disorders: A brief review and hypotheses. *Journal of Affective Disorders, 34*, 275–281.

Petty, R., & Cacioppo, J. (1981). *Attitudes and persuasion: Classic and contemporary approaches*. Dubuque, IA: W. C. Brown.

Petty, R., & Cacioppo, J. T. (1986). The elaboration likelihood model of persuasion. *Advances in Experimental Social Psychology, 19*, 123–205.

Petty, R., & Krosnick, J. (1994). *Attitude strength: Antecedents and consequences*. Hillsdale, NJ: Lawrence Erlbaum.

Petty, R. E., Brinol, P., & DeMarree, K. G. (2007). The meta-cognitive model (MCM) of attitudes: Implications for attitude measurement, change, and strength. *Social Cognition, 25*, 1–15.

Petty, R. E., Brinol, P., & Priester, J. R. (2009). Mass media attitude change: Implications of the elaboration likelihood model of persuasion. In J. Bryant & M. B. Oliver (Eds.), *Media effects. Advances in theory and research* (pp. 125–164). New York: Routledge.

Petty, R. E., Rucker, D. D., Bizer, G. Y., & Cacioppo, J. T. (2004). The elaboration likelihood model of persuasion. In J. S. Seiter & R. H. Gass (Eds.), *Perspectives on persuasion, social influence, and compliance gaining* (pp. 65–89). Boston: Allyn & Bacon.

Petty, R. E., & Wegener, D. T. (1998). Matching versus mismatching attitude functions: Implications for scrutiny of persuasive messages. *Personality and Social Psychology Bulletin, 24*, 227–240.

Petty, R. E., Wegener, D. T., & Fabrigar, L. R. (1997). Attitudes and attitude change. *Annual Review of Psychology, 48*, 609–648.

Pezdek, K., & Banks, W. P. (Eds.). (1996). *The recovered memory/false memory debate*. San Diego, CA: Academic Press.

Pfizer Australia. (2004a). *Healthy sleep*. Retrieved October 3, 2009, from http://www.healthreport.com.au/Reports/34.pdf

Pfizer Australia. (2004b). *New research finds a good night's sleep for Australians is nothing but a fairy tale*. Retrieved October 3, 2009, from http://www.pfizer.com.au/Media/Sleep.aspx

Phelps, E. A., O'Connor, K. J., Cunningham, W. A., Funayama, E. S., Gatenby, J. C., Gore, J. C., et al. (2000). Performance on indirect measures of race evaluation predicts amygdala activation. *Journal of Cognitive Neuroscience, 12*, 729–738.

Phend, C. (2000, April 3). Gradual cutback with nicotine replacement boosts quit rates. *MedPage Today*. Retrieved from http://www.medpagetoday.com/PrimaryCare/Smoking/13590

Philanthropy Australia. (2010). *Fast facts and statistics on philanthropy*. Retrieved from http://www.philanthropy.org.au/research/fast.html

Phillips, J. (2010). *Asylum seekers and refugees: What are the facts?* Canberra, Australia: Australian Department of Parliamentary Services. Retrieved from http://www.aph.gov.au/library

Phillips, M. L., Young, A. W., Senior, C., Brammer, M., Andrews, C., Calder, A. J., et al. (1997). A specific neural substrate for perceiving facial expressions of disgust. *Nature, 389*, 495–498.

Piaget, J. (1951). *The language and thought of the child*. New York: Humanities Press. (Originally published 1926)

Piaget, J. (1965). *The moral judgment of the child* (M. Gabrain, Trans.). New York: Free Press. (Originally published 1932)

Piaget, J. (1970). Piaget's theory. In P. Mussen (Ed.), *Carmichael's manual of child psychology*. New York: John Wiley.

Piaget, J. (1972). Development and learning. In C. S. Lavatelli & F. Stendler (Eds.), *Readings in child behavior and development* (3rd ed.). New York: Harcourt Brace Jovanovich.

Piaget, J., & Inhelder, B. (1956). *The child's conception of space* (F. J. Langdon & J. L. Lunzer, Trans.). London: Routledge & Kegan Paul.

Piaget, J., & Inhelder, B. (1969). *The psychology of the child*. New York: Basic Books.

Pickens, R., Svikis, D., McGue, M., Lykken, D., Heston, L., & Clayton, P. (1991). Heterogeneity in the inheritance of alcoholism: A study of male and female twins. *Archives of General Psychiatry, 48,* 19–28.

Pickett, C. L., Gardner, W. L., & Knowles, M. (2004). Getting a cue: The need to belong and enhanced sensitivity to social cues. *Personality and Social Psychology Bulletin, 30,* 1095–1107.

Piedmont, R. L. (1999). Does spirituality represent the sixth factor of personality? Spiritual transcendence and the five-factor model. *Journal of Personality, 67,* 985–1013.

Piek, J. P., Dawson, L., Smith, L. M., & Gasson, N. (2008). The role of early fine and gross motor development on later motor and cognitive ability. *Human Movement Science, 27,* 668–681.

Piek, J. P., Dyck, M. J., Francis, M., & Conwell, A. (2007). Working memory, processing speed and set-shifting in children with developmental coordination disorder and attention deficit hyperactivity disorder. *Developmental Medicine & Child Neurology, 49,* 678–683.

Piezon, S. L., & Donaldson, R. L. (2005). Online groups and social loafing: Understanding student-group interactions. *Online Journal of Distance Learning Administration, VIII*(IV).

Pigliucci, M. (2010). Genotype-phenotype mapping and the end of the 'genes as blueprint' metaphor. *Philosophical Transactions of the Royal Society of Biological Sciences, 365,* 557–566.

Pihl, R., Peterson, J., & Finn, P. (1990). Inherited predisposition to alcoholism: Characteristics of sons of male alcoholics. *Journal of Abnormal Psychology, 99,* 291–301.

Pike, L. T., Cohen, L., & Pooley, J. A. (2008). Australian approaches to understanding and building resilience in at risk populations. In L. Liebenberg & M. Unger (Eds.), *Resilience in children and youth* (pp. 264–285). Toronto, Ontario, Canada: University of Toronto Press.

Pilkington, C. J., Tesser, A., & Stephens, D. (1991). Complementarity in romantic relationships: A self-evaluation maintenance perspective. *Journal of Social and Personal Relationships, 8,* 481–504.

Pillard, R. C., Poumadere, J., & Carretta, R. A. (1981). Is homosexuality familial? A review, some data, and a suggestion. *Archives of Sexual Behavior, 10,* 465–473.

Pillard, R. C., Poumadere, J., & Carretta, R. A. (1982). A family study of sexual orientation. *Archives of Sexual Behavior, 11,* 511–520.

Pinel, E. C., & Swann, W. B., Jr. (2000). Finding the self through others: Self-verification and social movement participation. In S. Stryker & T. J. Owens (Eds.), *Self, identity, and social movements. Social movements, protest, and contention: Vol. 13* (pp. 132–152). Minneapolis: University of Minnesota Press.

Pinel, J. P., Assanand, S., & Lehman, D. R. (2000). Hunger, eating, and ill health. *American Psychologist, 55,* 1105–1116.

Pingitore, R., Dugoni, B. L., Tindale, R. S., & Spring, B. (1994). Bias against overweight job applicants in a simulated employment interview. *Journal of Applied Psychology, 79,* 909–917.

Pinker, S. (1994). *The language instinct: How the mind creates language*. New York: Harper-Collins.

Pinquart, M., Duberstein, P. R., & Lyness, J. M. (2006). Treatments for later-life depressive conditions: A meta-analytic comparison of pharmacotherapy and psychotherapy. *American Journal of Psychiatry, 163,* 1493–1501.

Pintrich, P. R. (2002). The role of metacognitive knowledge in learning, teaching, and assessing. *Theory into Practice, 41,* 219–225.

Piper, W. E., Ogrodniczuk, J. S., Joyce, A. S., McCallum, M., Rosie, J. S., O'Kelly, J. G., et al. (1999). Prediction of dropping out in time-limited, interpretive individual psychotherapy. *Psychotherapy, 36,* 114–122.

Pittman, T. S., & Zeigler, K. R. (2006). Basic human needs. In A. Kruglanski & E. Higgins (Eds.), *Social psychology: A handbook of basic principles* (2nd ed.). New York: Guilford.

Plack, C. J. (2005). *The sense of hearing*. Mahwah, NJ: Lawrence Erlbaum.

Plambeck, S. (2008, September 2). *STD rates rising as condom use falls*. Retrieved from http://www.fpq.com.au/pdf/media/STDratesRisingCondomUseFalls.pdf

Plant, E. A., & Peruche, B. M. (2005). The consequences of race for police officers' responses to criminal suspects. *Psychological Science, 16*(3), 180–183.

Pliner, P., & Chaiken, S. (1990). Eating, social motives, and self-presentation in women and men. *Journal of Experimental Social Psychology, 26,* 240–254.

Plomin, R. (1997). Identifying genes for cognitive abilities and disabilities. In R. J. Sternberg & E. L. Grigorenko (Eds.), *Intelligence, heredity, and environment* (pp. 89–104). New York: Cambridge University Press.

Plomin, R. (1999). Genetics and general cognitive ability. *Nature, 402*(Suppl. 6761), C25–C29.

Plomin, R., & Caspi, A. (1999). Behavioral genetics and personality. In L. Pervin & O. John (Eds.), *Handbook of personality: Theory and research* (2nd ed., pp. 251–276). New York: Guilford Press.

Plomin, R., Chipuer, H., & Loehlin, J. C. (1990). Behavioral genetics and personality. In L. Pervin & O. John (Eds.), *Handbook of personality: Theory and research* (pp. 225–243). New York: Guilford Press.

Plomin, R., & Daniels, D. (1987). Why are children from the same family so different from one another? *Behavioural and Brain Sciences, 10,* 1–16.

Plomin, R., & DeFries, J. (1980). Genetics and intelligence: Recent data. *Intelligence, 4,* 15–24.

Plomin, R., & DeFries, J. (1998). Genetics of cognitive abilities and disabilities. *Scientific American, May,* 62–69.

Plomin, R., DeFries, J. C., McClearn, G. E., & Rutter, R. (1997). *Behavioral genetics* (3rd ed.). New York: Freeman.

Plomin, R., Defries, J. C., & McGuffin, P. (2001). *Behavioral genetics* (4th ed.). New York: Worth.

Plomin, R., Reiss, D., Hetherington, E. M., & Howe, G. W. (1994). Nature and nurture: Genetic contributions to measures of the family environment. *Developmental Psychology, 30,* 32–43.

Plomin, R., & Rutter, M. (1998). Child development, molecular genetics, and what to do with genes once they are found. *Child Development, 69,* 1221–1240.

Plomin, R., Willerman, L., & Loehlin, J. C. (1976). Resemblance in appearance and the equal environments assumption in twin studies of personality. *Behavior Genetics, 6,* 43–52.

Plous, S. (1996). Attitudes toward the use of animals in psychological research and education: Results from a national survey of psychologists. *American Psychologist, 51,* 1167–1180.

Plutchik, R. (1979). *Emotion: a psychoevolutionary synthesis*. Boston: Allyn & Bacon.

Plutchik, R. (1980). *Emotions: A psychoevolutionary synthesis*. New York: Harper & Row.

Plutchik, R. (1997). The circumplex as a general model of the structure of emotions and personality. In R. Plutchik & H. R. Conte (Eds.). *Circumplex models of personality and emotions* (pp. 17–45). Washington, DC: American Psychological Association.

Podolski, C.-L., & Nigg, J. T. (2001). Parent stress and coping in relation to child ADHD severity and associated child disruptive behavior problems. *Journal of Clinical Child Psychology, 30,* 503–513.

Poldrack, R. A., Desmond, J. E., Glover, G. H., & Gabrieli, J. D. E. (1998). The neural basis of visual skill learning: An *f*MRI study of mirror reading. *Cerebral Cortex, 8,* 1–10.

Polivy, J., & Herman, C. P. (2002). Causes of eating disorders. *Annual Review of Psychology, 53,* 187–213.

Pollack, R. H. (1970). Mueller-Lyon illusion: Effect of age, lightness, contrast and hue. *Science, 170,* 93–94.

Pollack, R. H., & Silvar, S. D. (1967). Magnitude of the Mueller-Lyon illusion in children as a function of the pigmentation of the fundus oculi. *Psychonomic Science, 8,* 83–84.

Pollard, D. (1988). *Give and take: The losing partnership in Aboriginal poverty*. Sydney, Australia: Hale and Iremonger.

Pollen, D. A. (1999). On the neural correlates of visual perception. *Cerebral Cortex, 9,* 4–19.

Pollitt, P. A. (1997). The problem of dementia in Australian Aboriginal and Torres Strait Islander communities: An overview. *International Journal of Geriatric Psychiatry, 12,* 155–163.

Pollock, V. E., Briere, J., Schneider, L., Knop, J., Mednick, S., & Goodwin, D. W. (1990). Childhood antecedents of antisocial behavior: Parental alcoholism and physical abusiveness. *American Journal of Psychiatry, 147,* 1290–1293.

Ponds, R., Brouwer, W., & Van Wolffelaar, P. (1988). Age differences in divided attention in a simulated driving task. *Journal of Gerontology, 43,* 151–156.

Poole, M., Sundberg, N. D., & Tyler, L. E. (1982). Adolescents' perceptions of family decision-making and autonomy in India, Australia and the United States. *Journal of Comparative Family Studies, 13,* 349–357.

Pooley, J. A., Breen, L., Pike, L. T., Drew, N. M., & Cohen, L. (2007). Critiquing the school community: A qualitative study of children's conceptualizations of their school. *International Journal of Qualitative Studies in Education, 21*(2), 87–98.

Pooley, J.A. & Cohen, L. (2010). Resilience: A definition in context. *Australian Community Psychologist, 22*(1), 30–37.

Pooley, J. A., Pike, L. T., Drew, N. M., & Breen, L. (2002). Inferring children's sense of community: A critical exploration. *Community, Work and Family, 5*(1), 5–22.

Poon, L., Clayton, P. M., Martin, P., Johnson, M. A., Courtenay, B., Sweaney, A., et al. (1992). The Georgia Centenarian study. *International Journal of Aging and Human Development, 34,* 1–17.

Poor sleep affecting accuracy and attitude on the job. (2007). Retrieved from www.bettersleep.org/Pressroom/poor-sleep-pr.asp

Poortinga, Y. H., & Van Hermert, D. A. (2001). Personality and culture: Demarcating between the common and the unique. *Journal of Personality, 69*(6), 1033–1060.

Pope, H. G., Gruber, A. J., & Yurgelun-Todd, D. (1995). The residual neuropsychological effects of cannabis: The current status of research. *Drug and Alcohol Dependence, 38,* 25–34.

Popper, K. (1963). *Conjectures and refutations: The growth of scientific knowledge*. New York: Basic Books.

Porath, M. (2000). Social giftedness in childhood: A developmental perspective. In R. C. Friedman & B. M. Shore (Eds.), *Talents unfolding: Cognition and development* (pp. 195–215). Washington, DC: American Psychological Association.

Porkka-Heiskanen, T., Strecker, R. E., Thakkar, M., & Bjorkum, A. A. (1997). Adenosine: A mediator of the sleep-induced effects of prolonged wakefulness. *Science, 276,* 1265–1268.

Porter, L. (2005). *Children are people too: A parent's guide to young children's behaviour* (4th ed.). Bowden, South Australia: East Street Publications.

Posner, M. I. (1995). Attention in cognitive neuroscience: An overview. In M. S. Gazzaniga (Ed.), *The cognitive neurosciences* (pp. 615–624). Cambridge, MA: MIT Press.

Posner, M. I., & DiGirolamo, G. J. (2000). Attention in cognitive neuroscience: An overview. In M. S. Gazzaniga (Ed.), *The new cognitive neurosciences* (2nd ed., pp. 623–631). Cambridge, MA: MIT Press.

Posner, N. I., & Raichle, M. E. (1996). Precis of image and mind. *Behavioral and Brain Sciences, 18,* 327–383.

Posner, R. M., Boies, S., Eichelman, W. H., & Taylor, R. L. (1969). Retention of visual and name codes of single letters. *Journal of Experimental Psychology, 79,* 1–16.

Pospisil, L. (1963). *Kapauka Papuan political economy* (Publications in Anthropology, No. 67). New Haven, CT: Yale University

Postle, B. R., & D'Esposito, M. (1999). 'What'–then–'where' in visual working memory: An event-related fMRI study. *Journal of Cognitive Neuroscience, 11*, 585–597.

Postmes, T., Baray, G., Haslam, A., Morton, T. A., & Swaab, R. I. (2006). The dynamics of personal and social identity formation. In T. Postmes & J. Jetten (Eds.), *Individuality and the group: Advances in social identity*. London: Sage.

Potosky, D., Bobko, P., & Roth, P. L. (2005). Forming composites of cognitive ability and alternative measures to predict job performance and reduce adverse impact: Corrected estimates and realistic expectations. *International Journal of Selection and Assessment, 13*(4), 304–315.

Potter, J., & Edwards, D. (1992). *Discursive psychology*. London: Sage.

Potter, J., & Wetherell, M. (1987). *Social psychology: Beyond attitudes and behaviour*. London: Sage.

Povinelli, D., & Simon, B. B. (1998). Young children's understanding of briefly versus extremely delayed images of the self: Emergence of the autobiographical stance. *Developmental Psychology, 34*, 188–194.

Powers, M. B., & Emmelkamp, P. M. G. (2007). Virtual reality exposure therapy for anxiety disorders: A meta-analysis [Electronic version]. *Anxiety Disorders*.

Poyatos, F. (1988). New research perspectives in cross-cultural psychology through non-verbal communication studies. In F. Poyatos (Ed.), *Cross-cultural perspectives in non-verbal communication* (pp. 35–69). Toronto, Ontario, Canada: CJ Hogrefe.

Poynting, S., & Noble, G. (2004). *Living with racism: The experience and reporting by Arab and Muslim Australians of discrimination, abuse and violence since 11 September 2001* (Report to the Human Rights and Equal Opportunity Commission). Retrieved November 17, 2004, from http://www.uws.edu.au/ccr

Pratkanis, A. R., Eskenazi, J., & Greenwald, A. G. (1994). What you expect is what you believe (but not necessarily what you get): A test of the effectiveness of subliminal self-help audiotapes. *Basic and Applied Social Psychology, 15*, 251–276.

Premack, A. J., & Premack, D. (1972). Teaching language to an ape. *Scientific American, 227*, 92–99.

Premack, D. (1962). Reversibility of the reinforcement relation. *Science, 136*, 235–237.

Premack, D. (1965). Reinforcement theory. In D. Levine (Ed.), *Nebraska symposium on motivation: Vol. 3* (pp. 123–180). Lincoln: University of Nebraska Press.

Prescott, C. A., & Kendler, K. S. (1999). Genetic and environmental contributions to alcohol abuse and dependence in a population-based sample of male twins. *American Journal of Psychiatry, 156*, 34–40.

Preskorn, S. H., Feighner, J. P., Stanga, C. Y., & Ross, R. (Eds.). (2004). *Antidepressants: Past, present and future*. Berlin: Springer-Verlag.

Preston, J. D., O'Neal, J. H., & Talaga, M. C. (2004). *Handbook of clinical psychopharmacology for therapists*. Oakland, CA: New Harbinger Publications.

Preti, G., Cutler, W. B., Garcia, G. R., Huggins, M., & Lawley, J. J. (1986). Human axillary secretions influence women's menstrual cycles: The role of donor extract from females. *Hormones and Behavior, 20*, 474–482.

Pribram, K. H. (1980). The biology of emotions and other feelings. In R. Plutchik & H. Kellerman (Eds.), *Emotion: Theory, research, and experience: Vol. I. Theories of emotion*. New York: Academic Press.

Pribram, K. H., & Gill, M. M. (1976). *Freud's project reassessed*. New York: Basic Books.

Price, R. A., Charles, M. A., Pettitt, D. J., & Knowler, W. C. (1993). Obesity in Pima Indians: Large increases among post-World War II birth cohorts. *American Journal of Physical Anthropology, 92*, 473–480.

Price-Williams, D. (1981). Concrete and formal operations. In R. H. Munroe, R. L. Munroe, & B. D. Whiting (Eds.), *Handbook of cross-cultural human development*. New York: Garland Press.

Price-Williams, D. (1985). In G. Lindzey & E. Aronson (Eds.), *Handbook of social psychology*. Reading, MA: Addison-Wesley.

Price-Williams, D., Gordon, W., & Ramirez, M. (1969). Skill and conservation: A study of pottery-making children. *Developmental Psychology, 1*, 769.

Priester, J. R. (2002). Sex, drugs, and attitudinal ambivalence: How feelings of evaluative tension influence alcohol use and safe sex behaviors. In W. D. Crano & M. Burgoon (Eds.), *Mass media and drug prevention: Classic and contemporary theories and research* (pp. 145–162). Mahwah, NJ: Lawrence Erlbaum.

Prince, A., & Smolensky, P. (1997). Optimality: From neural networks to universal grammar. *Science, 275*, 1604–1610.

Prince, R. (1980). Variations in psychotherapeutic procedures. In H. C. Triandis & J. G. Draguns (Eds.), *Handbook of cross-cultural psychology: Vol. 6. Psychopathology* (pp. 291–350). Boston: Allyn & Bacon.

Prinz, R. J., Sanders, M. R., Shapiro, C. J., Whitaker, D. J., & Lutzker, J. R. (2009). Population-based prevention of child maltreatment: The US Triple P system population trial. *Prevention Science, 10*, 1–12.

Prior, M., Sanson, A., Smart, D., & Oberklaid, F. (2000). *Pathways from infancy to adolescence: Australian temperament project 1983–2000*. Retrieved from http://192.135.208.240/institute/pubs/resreport4/5.html

Pryor, R. G. B., & Bright, J. E. H. (2007). The current state and future direction of counseling psychology in Australia. *Applied Psychology: An International Review, 56*(1), 7–19.

Puce, A., Allison, T., Asgari, M., Gore, J. C., & McCarthy, G. (1996). Differential sensitivity of human visual cortex to faces, letterstrings, and textures: A functional magnetic resonance imaging study. *Journal of Neuroscience, 16*, 5205–5215.

Puce, A., Alison, T., Bentin, S., Gore, J. C., & McCarthy, G. (1998). Temporal cortex activation in humans viewing eye and mouth movements. *Journal of Neuroscience, 18*, 2188–2199.

Purdie, N., Dudgeon, P., & Walker, R. (Eds.). (2010). *Working together: Aboriginal and Torres Strait Islander mental health and wellbeing principles and practice*. Retrieved from http://www.apo.org.au/node/22487

Putnam, F. W. (1991). Dissociative disorders in children and adolescents: A developmental perspective. *Psychiatric Clinics of North America, 14*, 519–531.

Putnam, F. W. (1995). Rebuttal of Paul McHugh. *Journal of the American Academy of Child and Adolescent Psychiatry, 34*, 963.

Putnam, H. (1973). Reductionism and the nature of psychology. *Cognition, 2*, 131–146.

Putnins, A. L. (1995). Recent drug use and suicidal behaviour among young offenders. *Drug and Alcohol Review, 14*, 151–158.

Queensland Health. (2010). *Pandemic (H1N1) 2009 human swine influenza*. Retrieved from http://www.health.qld.gov.au/swineflu/

Quitkin, F. M., Rabkin, J. G., Gerald, J., Davis, J. M., & Klein, D. F. (2000). Validity of clinical trials of antidepressants. *American Journal of Psychiatry, 157*, 327–337.

Rachlin, H., Green, L., Kagel, J. H., & Battalio, R. C. (1976). Economic demand theory and psychological studies of choice. In G. H. Bower (Ed.), *The psychology of learning and motivation: Vol. 10* (pp. 129–154). New York: Academic Press.

Rack, S. K., & Makela, E. H. (2000). Hypothyroidism and depression: A therapeutic challenge. *Annual Pharmacotherapy, 34*(10), 1142–1145.

Radio National. (2002). *All in the mind: The legacy of the lobotomy*. Retrieved October 15, 2004, from http://www.abc.net.au/rn/science/mind/s468539.htm

Raine, A., & Venables, P. H. (1984). Electrodermal nonresponding, antisocial behavior, and schizoid tendencies in adolescents. *Psychophysiology, 21*, 424–433.

Raine, A., Lenez, T., Bihrle, S., LaCasse, L., & Colletti, P. (2000). Reduced prefrontal gray matter volume and reduced autonomic activity in antisocial personality disorder. *Archives of General Psychiatry, 57*, 119–127.

Raine, A., Meloy, J. R., Birhle, S., Stoddard, J., LaCasse, L., & Buchsbaum, M. S. (1998). Reduced prefrontal and increased subcortical brain functioning assessed using positron emission tomography in predatory and affective murderers. *Behaviour Science and Law, 16*, 319–332.

Rallison, M. (1986). *Growth disorders in infants, children, and adolescents*. New York: John Wiley.

Ralston, D., Gustafson, D., Elsass, P., & Cheung, F. (1992). Eastern values: A comparison of managers in the United States, Hong Kong, and the People's Republic of China. *Journal of Applied Psychology, 77*, 664–671.

Ramachandran, V. S., & Hirstein, W. (1998). The perception of phantom limbs: The D. O. Hebb lecture. *Brain, 121*, 1603–1630.

Ramachandran, V. S., & Hubbard, E. M. (2005, October). Hearing colors, tasting shapes. *Scientific American*. Retrieved September 30, 2009, from http://www.scientificamerican.com/article.cfm?id=hearing-colors-tasting-sh-2005-10

Ramirez-Amaya, V., & Bermudez-Rattoni, F. (1999). Conditioned enhancement of antibody production is disrupted by insular cortex and amygdala but not hippocampal lesions. *Brain, Behavior and Immunity, 13*, 46–60.

Ramos, A., Berton, O., Mormede, P., & Chaouloff, F. (1997). A multiple-test study of anxiety-related behaviours in six inbred rat strains. *Behavioural Brain Research, 85*, 57–69.

Ramus, F., Hauser, M., Miller, C., Morris, D., & Mehler, J. (2000). Language discrimination by human newborns and by cotton-top tamarin monkeys. *Science, 288*, 349–351.

Rand, C. S., & Kuldau, J. M. (1990). The epidemiology of obesity and self-defined weight problem in the general population: Gender, race, age, and social class. *International Journal of Eating Disorders, 9*, 329–343.

Randhawa, B. (1991). Gender differences in academic achievement: A closer look at mathematics. *Alberta Journal of Educational Research, 37*, 241–257.

Ranzijn, R. (2002). Enhancing community quality of life: Links between positive psychology and productive ageing. *Ageing International, 27*(2), 28–53.

Ranzijn, R., McConnochie, K., & Nolan, W. (2010). *Psychology and Indigenous Australians: Foundations of cultural competence*. South Yarra, Australia: Palgrave Macmillan.

Ranzijn, R., McConnochie, K., Nolan, W., & Day, A. (2007, February). Teaching cultural competence in relation to Indigenous Australians: Steps along a journey. *InPsych, 29*(1), 10–11.

Rao, S. C., Rainier, G., & Miller, E. K. (1997). Integration of what and where in the primate prefrontal cortex. *Science, 276*, 821–824.

Rao, S. M., Huber, S. J., & Bornstein, R. A. (1992). Emotional changes with multiple sclerosis and Parkinson's disease. *Journal of Consulting and Clinical Psychology, 60*, 369–378.

Rapee, R. M., Brown, T. A., Antony, M., & Barlow, D. (1992). Response to hyperventilation and inhalation of 5.5% carbon dioxide-enriched air across the DSM-III-R anxiety disorders. *Journal of Abnormal Psychology, 101*, 538–552.

Rashidy-Pour, A., Motaghed-Larijani, Z., & Bures, J. (1995). Reversible inactivation of the medial septal area impairs consolidation but not retrieval of passive avoidance learning in rats. *Behavioural Brain Research, 72*, 185–188.

Rauhut, A. S., Thomas, B. L., & Ayres, J. J. B. (2001). Treatments that weaken Pavlovian conditioned fear and thwart its renewal in rats: Implications for treating human phobias. *Journal of Experimental Psychology: Animal Behavior Processes, 27*(2), 99–114.

Rawsthorne, L. J., & Elliot, A. J. (1999). Achievement goals and intrinsic motivation: A meta-analytic review. *Personality and Social Psychology Review, 3*, 326–344.

Rayner, K., Foorman, B. R., Perfetti, C. A., Pesetsky, D., & Seidenberg, M. S. (2001). How psychological science informs the teaching of reading. *Psychological Science in the Public Interest, 2*, 31–74.

Rayner, K., Foorman, B. R., Perfetti, C. A., Pesetsky, D., & Seidenberg, M. S. (2002). How should reading be taught? *Scientific American, March*, 71–77.

Rea, C. P., & Modigliani, V. (1988). Educational implications of the spacing effect. In M. M. Gruneberg, P. E. Morris, & R. Sykes (Eds.), *Practical aspects of memory: Current research and issues: Vol. 1. Memory in everyday life* (pp. 402–406). New York: John Wiley & Sons.

Read, J., Agar, K., Argyle, N., & Aderhold, V. (2003). Sexual and physical abuse during childhood and adulthood as predictors of hallucinations, delusions and thought disorder. *Psychology and Psychotherapy: Theory, Research and Practice, 76*, 1–22.

Read, S. J., Vanman, E. J., & Miller, L. C. (1997). Connectionism, parallel constraint satisfaction processes, and Gestalt principles: (Re)introducing cognitive dynamics to social psychology. *Personality and Social Psychology Review, 1*, 26–53.

Reber, A. S. (1992). The cognitive unconscious: An evolutionary perspective. *Consciousness and Cognition, 1*, 93–133.

Reber, A. S. (1993). *Implicit learning and tacit knowledge: An essay on the cognitive unconscious*. New York: Oxford University Press.

Reber, A. S., & Reber, E. (2001). *The Penguin dictionary of psychology* (3rd ed.). Camberwell, Australia: Penguin Books Australia.

Recanzone, G. H., Schreiner, C. E., & Merzenich, M. M. (1993). Plasticity in the frequency representation in the primary auditory cortex following discontinuous training in adult owl monkeys. *Journal of Neuroscience, 13*, 87–103.

Rechtschaffen, A., Bergmann, B. M., Everson, C. A., Kushida, C. A., & Gilliland, M. A. (1989). Sleep deprivation in the rat: X. Integration and discussion of the findings. *Sleep, 12*, 68–87.

Reconciliation Australia. (2010). *Welcome to share our pride*. Retrieved from http://www.shareourpride.org.au/topics/welcome-to-share-our-pride

Reder, L. M., & Schunn, C. D. (1996). Metacognition does not imply awareness: Strategy choice is governed by implicit learning and memory. In L. M. Reder (Ed.), *Implicit memory and metacognition* (pp. 45–77). Mahwah, NJ: Lawrence Erlbaum.

Rees, G., Frackowiak, R., & Firth, C. (1997). Two modulatory effects of attention that mediate object categorization in human cortex. *Science, 275*, 835–838.

Regan, D., & Fazio, R. (1977). On the consistency between attitudes and behavior: Look to the method of attitude formation. *Journal of Experimental Social Psychology, 13*, 28–45.

Regan, P. C. (1996). Rhythms of desire: The association between menstrual cycle phases and female sexual desire. *Canadian Journal of Human Sexuality, 5*, 145–215.

Regan, T. (1997). The rights of humans and other animals. *Ethics and Behavior, 7*, 103–111.

Regier, D. A., First, M., Marshall, T., & Narrow, W. E. (2002). The American Psychiatric Association (APA) of mental disorders: Strengths, limitations and future perspectives. In M. Maj, W. Gaebel, J. J. Lopez-Ibor, & N. Sartorius (Eds.), *Psychiatric diagnosis and classification* (pp. 47–75). New York: John Wiley & Sons.

Reid, G., Crofts, N., & Beyer, L. (2001). Drug treatment services for ethnic communities in Victoria, Australia: An examination of cultural and institutional barriers. *Ethnicity & Health, 6*(1), 13–26.

Reifman, A., Larrick, R., & Fein, S. (1991). Temper and temperature on the diamond: The heat-aggression relationship in major league baseball. *Personality and Social Psychology Bulletin, 17*, 580–585.

Reiger, E., Schotte, D. E., Touyz, S. W., Beaumont, P., Griffiths, R., & Russell, J. (1998). Attentional biases in eating disorders: A visual probe detection procedure. *International Journal of Eating Disorders, 23*, 199–205.

Reilly, T. (2011, February 2). The beast roars. *Brisbane Times*. Retrieved from http://www.brisbanetimes.com.au/environment/weather/the-beast-roars-20110202-1adwi.html

Reiman, E. M. (1997). The application of positron emission tomography to the study of normal and pathologic emotions. *Journal of Clinical Psychiatry, 58*, 4–12.

Reimann, P., & Chi, M. T. H. (1989). Human expertise. In K. J. Gilhooly (Ed.), *Human and machine problem solving*. New York: Plenum Press.

Reinisch, J. M. (1981). Prenatal exposure to synthetic progestins increases potential for aggression in humans. *Science, 211*, 1171–1173.

Reis, H. J., & Shaver, P. (1988). Intimacy as an interpersonal process. In S. Duck (Ed.), *Handbook of personal relationships: Theory, relationships and interventions*. New York: John Wiley.

Reis, H. T., Nezlek, J., & Wheeler, L. (1980). Physical attractiveness in social interaction. *Journal of Personality and Social Psychology, 38*, 604–617.

Reisberg, D. (1997). *Cognition: Exploring the science of the mind*. New York: W. W. Norton.

Reisenzein, R. (1983). The Schachter theory of emotion: Two decades later. *Psychological Bulletin, 94*, 239–264.

Remy, P., Doder, M., Lees, A., Turjanski, N., & Brooks, D. (2005). Depression in Parkinson's disease: Loss of dopamine and noradrenaline innervation in the limbic system. *Brain, 128*(6), 1314–1322.

Repacholi, B., & Gopnik, A. (1997). Early reasoning about desires: Evidence from 14- and 18-month-olds. *Developmental Psychology, 33*, 12–21.

Rescorla, R. A. (1973). Second order conditioning: Implications for theories of learning. In F. J. McGuigan & D. B. Lumsden (Eds.), *Contemporary approaches to conditioning and learning*. New York: John Wiley.

Rescorla, R. A. (1988). Pavlovian conditioning: It's not what you think it is. *American Psychologist, 43*, 151–160.

Rescorla, R. A. (1999). Partial reinforcement reduces the associative change produced by nonreinforcement. *Journal of Experimental Psychology: Animal Behavior, 25*, 403–414.

Rescorla, R. A., & Holland, P. C. (1982). Behavioral studies of associative learning in animals. *Annual Review of Psychology, 33*, 265–308.

Rescorla, R. A., & Wagner, A. R. (1972). A theory of Pavlovian conditioning: Variations in the effectiveness of reinforcement and non-reinforcement. In A. H. Black & W. F. Prokasy (Eds.), *Classical conditioning: II. Current research and theory*. New York: Appleton.

Reser, J. (1991). Aboriginal mental health: Conflicting cultural perspectives. In J. Reid & P. Trompf (Eds.), *The health of Aboriginal Australia*. Sydney, Australia: Harcourt Brace Jovanovich.

Reser, J. (2009, June). Joseph Reser: The ecopsychology interview. *Ecopsychology, 1*(2), 57–63.

Rest, J. R. (1983). Morality. In J. H. Flavell & E. M. Markman (Eds.), *Handbook of child psychology: Vol. 3. Cognitive development*. New York: John Wiley.

Reuter-Lorenz, P. A., & Stanczak, L. (2000). Differential effects of aging on the functions of the corpus callosum. *Developmental Neuropsychology, 18*, 113–137.

Reynolds, A. J., Mehana, M., & Temple, J. A. (1995). Does preschool intervention affect children's perceived competence? *Journal of Applied Development Psychology, 16*, 211–230.

Reynolds, K. J., Turner, J. C., & Haslam, S. (2000). When are we better than them and they worse than us? A closer look at social discrimination in positive and negative domains. *Journal of Personality and Social Psychology, 78*, 64–80.

Rhee, S. H., Waldman, I. D., Hay, D. A., & Levy, F. (1999). Sex differences in genetic and environmental influences on DSM-III-R attention-deficit/hyperactivity disorder. *Journal of Abnormal Psychology, 108*, 24–41.

Rhodewalt, F., & Vohs, K. D. (2005). Defensive strategies, motivations, and the self: AA self-regulatory process view. In A. J. Elliot & C. S. Dweck (Eds.), *Handbook of competence and motivation* (pp. 548–565). New York: Guilford Publications.

Rholes, W. S., Simpson, J. A., Blakely, B. S., Lanigan, L., & Allen, E. A. (1997). Adult attachment styles, the desire to have children, and working models of parenthood. *Journal of Personality, 65*, 357–385.

Richard, F. D., Bond, C. F., & Stokes-Zoota, J. J. (2003). One hundred years of social psychology quantitatively described. *Review of General Psychology, 17*(4), 331–363.

Richards, B. J. (1990). *Language development and individual differences: A study of auxiliary verb learning*. Cambridge: Cambridge University Press.

Richards, J. B., Sabol, K. E., & Freed, C. R. (1990). Conditioned rotation: A behavioral analysis. *Physiology and Behavior, 47*, 1083–1087.

Richards, J. M., & Gross, J. J. (2000). Emotion regulation and memory: The cognitive costs of keeping one's cool. *Journal of Personality and Social Psychology, 79*, 410–424.

Richards, M. H., Crowe, P. A., Larson, R., & Swarr, A (1998). Developmental patterns and gender differences in the experience of peer companionship during adolescence. *Child Development, 69*, 154–163.

Richardson, S. M., & Paxton, S. J. (2010). An evaluation of a body image intervention based on risk factors for body dissatisfaction: A controlled study with adolescent girls. *International Journal of Eating Disorders, 43*(2), 112–122.

Richardson, J. T. E. (1996a). Evolving concepts of working memory. In J. T. E. Richardson, R. W. Engle, L. Hasher, R. Logie, E. Stoltzfus, & R. Zacks (Eds.), *Working memory and human cognition* (pp. 3–29). New York: Oxford University Press.

Richardson, J. T. E. (1996b). Evolving issues in working memory. In J. T. E. Richardson, R. W. Engle, L. Hasher, R. Logie, E. S. Stoltzfus, & R. Zacks (Eds.), *Working memory and human cognition* (pp. 121–152). New York: Oxford University Press.

Richardson, S. A., & Koller, H. (1996). *Twenty-two years: Causes and consequences of mental retardation*. Cambridge: Harvard University Press.

Rickard, T. C., Romero, S. G., Basso, G., Wharton, C., Flitman, S., & Grafman, J. (2000). The calculating brain: An fMRI study. *Neuropsychologia, 38*, 325–335.

Ricks, M. H. (1985). The social transmission of parental behavior: Attachment across generations. In I. Bretherton & E. Waters (Eds.), *Growing points of attachment theory and research. Monographs of the Society for Research in Child Development: Vol. 50* (1–2, Serial No. 209, pp. 211–227).

Riedel, G., Platt, B., & Micheau, J. (2003). Glutamate receptor function in learning and memory. *Behavioural Brain Research, 140*(1–2), 1–47.

Riesen, A. H. (1960). The effects of stimulus deprivation on the development and atrophy of the visual sensory system. *American Journal of Orthopsychiatry, 30*, 23–36.

Riketta, M., & Dauenheimer, D. (2003). Anticipated success at unconscious goal pursuit: Consequences for mood, self-esteem, and the evaluation of a goal-relevant task. *Motivation and Emotion, 27*(4), 327–338.

Rinn, W. E. (1984). The neuropsychology of facial expression: A review of the neurological and psychological mechanisms for producing facial expressions. *Psychological Bulletin, 95*, 52–77.

Ritov, I., & Baron, J. (1990). Reluctance to vaccinate: Omission bias and ambiguity. *Journal of Behavioral Decision-Making, 3*, 263–277.

Rivers, W. H. R. (1901). Vision. In A. C. Haddon (Ed.), *Report of the Cambridge anthropological expedition to the Torres Strait: Vol. 2*. Cambridge, UK: Cambridge University Press.

Rizzolatti, G., & Arbib, M. A. (1998). Language within our grasp. *Trends in Neuroscience, 21*, 188–194.

Rizzolatti, G., Fadiga, L., Matelli, M., Bettinardi, V., Paulesu, E., Perani, D., et al. (1996). Localization of grasp representations in humans by PET: 1.

Observation versus execution. *Experimental Brain Research, 111,* 246–252.

Robben, H. S., Webley, P., Weigel, R., & Warneryd, K.-E. (1990). Decision frame and opportunity as determinants of tax cheating: An international experimental study. *Journal of Economic Psychology, 11,* 341–364.

Robbins, T. W. (1997). Arousal systems and attentional processes. *Biological Psychology, 45,* 57–71.

Robbins, T. W., & Everitt, B. J. (1999). Interaction of the dopaminergic system with mechanisms of associative learning and cognition: Implications for drug abuse. *Psychological Science, 10,* 199–202.

Roberts, B. W., Walton, K., & Viechtbauer, W. (2006a). Patterns of mean-level change in personality traits across the life course: A meta-analysis of longitudinal studies. *Psychological Bulletin, 132,* 1–25.

Roberts, B. W., Walton, K., & Viechtbauer, W. (2006b). Personality changes in adulthood: Reply to Costa & McCrae (2006). *Psychological Bulletin, 132,* 29–32.

Roberts, R. D., & Lipnevich, A. (2010). From general intelligence to multiple intelligences: Meanings, models, and measures. In T. Urdan (Ed.), *APA educational psychology handbook: Vol. 2.* Washington, DC: APA.

Roberts, R. D., MacCann, C., Matthews, G., & Zeidner, M. (2010). Emotional intelligence: Towards a consensus of models and measures. *Social & Personality Psychology Compass, 4*(10), 821–840.

Roberts, R. D., Schulze, R., & MacCann, C. (2008). The measurement of emotional intelligence: A decade of progress? In G. J. Boyle, G. Matthews, & D. H. Saklofske (Eds.), *The Sage handbook of personality theory and assessment: Vol. 2. Personality measurement and testing* (pp. 461–482). London: Sage Publications.

Roberts, R. D., Stankov, L., Pallier, G., & Dolph, B. (1997). Charting the cognitive sphere: Tactile and kinesthetic performance within the structure of intelligence. *Intelligence, 25,* 111–148.

Roberts, R. D., Zeidner, M., & Matthews, G. (2001). Does emotional intelligence meet traditional standards for an intelligence? Some new data and conclusions. *Emotion, 1,* 196–231.

Robertson, D., Davidoff, J., & Braisby, N. (1999). Similarity and categorization: Neuropsychological evidence for a dissociation in explicit categorization tasks. *Cognition, 71,* 1–42.

Robertson, L. C., & Rafal, R. (2000). Disorders of visual attention. In M. S. Gazzaniga (Ed.), *The new cognitive neurosciences* (2nd ed., pp. 633–649). Cambridge, MA: MIT Press.

Robin, A. A. (1958). A controlled study of the effects of leucotomy. *Journal of Neurology, Neurosurgery and Psychiatry, 21,* 262–269.

Robin, N., & Holyoak, K. (1995). Relational complexity and the functions of the prefrontal cortex. In M. Gazzaniga (Ed.), *The cognitive neurosciences* (pp. 987–997). Cambridge, MA: MIT Press.

Robins, R. W., & Beer, J. S. (2001). Positive illusions about the self: Short-term benefits and long-term costs. *Journal of Personality and Social Psychology, 80,* 340–352.

Robinson, B. W., Alexander, M., & Bowne, G. (1969). Dominance reversal resulting from aggressive responses evoked by brain telestimulation. *Physiology and Behavior, 4,* 749–752.

Robinson, D., Woerner, M. G., Alvir, J. M. J., Bilder, R., Goldman, R., Geisler, S., et al. (1999). Predictors of relapse following response from a first episode of schizophrenia or schizoaffective disorder. *Archives of General Psychiatry, 56,* 241–247.

Robinson, F. P. (1961). *Effective study.* New York: Harper & Row.

Robinson, K. J., & Roediger, H. L., III. (1997). Associative processes in false recall and false recognition. *Psychological Science, 8,* 231–237.

Robinson, S. R., & Kleven, G. A. (2005). Learning to move before birth. In B. Hopkins & S. P. Johnson (Eds.), *Prenatal development of postnatal functions* (pp. 131–175). Westport, CT: Praeger Publishers.

Rodgers, R. F., Paxton, S. J., & Chabrol, H. (2009). Effects of parental comments on body dissatisfaction and eating disturbance in young adults: A sociocultural model. *Body Image, 6,* 171–177.

Rodin, J., Elias, M., Silberstein, L. R., & Wagner, A. (1988). Combined behavioral and pharmacologic treatment for obesity: Predictors of successful weight maintenance. *Journal of Consulting and Clinical Psychology, 56,* 399–404.

Rodin, J., Schank, D., & Striegel-Moore, R. (1989). Psychological features of obesity. *Medical Clinics of North America, 73,* 47–66.

Rodkin, P., Farmer, T. W., Pearl, R., & Van Acker, R. (2000). Heterogeneity of popular boys: Antisocial and prosocial configurations. *Developmental Psychology, 36,* 14–24.

Rodman, H. R. (1997). Temporal cortex. In G. Adelman & B. Smith (Eds.), *Encyclopedia of neuroscience.* Amsterdam: Elsevier.

Rodman, H. R., & Albright, T. D. (1989). Single-unit analysis of pattern-motion selective properties in the middle temporal visual area (MT). *Experimental Brain Research, 75,* 53–64.

Roediger, H. L. (1990). Implicit memory: Retention without remembering. *American Psychologist, 45,* 1043–1056.

Roediger, H. L., & McDermott, K. B. (1995). Creating false memories: Remembering words not presented in lists. *Journal of Experimental Psychology: Learning, Memory, and Cognition, 21,* 803–814.

Roen, K. (2004). Queerly sexed bodies in clinical contexts: Problematising conceptual foundations of genital surgery with intersex infants. In A. Potts, N. Gavey, & A. Weatherall (Eds.), *Sex and the body* (pp. 89–106). Wellington, New Zealand: Dunmore Press.

Rogan, M. T., Staeubli, U. V., & LeDoux, J. E. (1997). AMPA receptor facilitation accelerates fear learning without altering the level of conditioned fear acquired. *Journal of Neuroscience, 17,* 5928–5935.

Roger, T. B., Kuiper, N. A., & Kirker, W. S. (1977). Self-reference and the encoding of personal information. *Journal of Personality and Social Psychology, 35,* 677–688.

Rogers, C. (1959). A theory of therapy, personality, and interpersonal relationships, as developed in the client-centered framework. In S. Koch (Ed.), *Psychology: A study of a science: Vol. 3.* New York: McGraw-Hill.

Rogers, C. R. (1951). *Client-centered therapy: Its current practice, implications, and theory.* Boston: Houghton Mifflin.

Rogers, C. R. (1961). *On becoming a person: A therapist's view of psychotherapy.* Boston: Houghton Mifflin.

Rogers, C. R. (1980). *A way of being.* Boston: Houghton Mifflin.

Rogers, C. R., & Sanford, M. A. (1985). Client-centered psychotherapy. In H. I. Kaplan & B. J. Sadock (Eds.), *Comprehensive textbook of psychiatry* (4th ed.). Baltimore: Williams & Wilkins.

Rogoff, B., & Lave, J. (Eds.). (1984). *Everyday cognition: Its development in social context.* Cambridge, MA: Harvard University Press.

Rohner, R. (1975a). Parental acceptance-rejection and personality development: A universalist approach to behavioral science. In R. W. Brislin, S. Bochner, & W. J. Lonner (Eds.), *Cross-cultural perspectives on learning* (pp. 251–269). New York: Sage.

Rohner, R. (1975b). *They love me, they love me not.* New Haven, CT: HRAF Press.

Rohner, R. P. (1986). *The warmth dimension: Foundations of parental acceptance-rejection theory.* Beverly Hills, CA: Sage.

Rohner, R. P., & Britner, P. A. (2002). Worldwide mental health correlates of parental acceptance-rejection: Review of cross-cultural and intracultural evidence. *Cross-Cultural Research: The Journal of Comparative Social Sciences, 36,* 15–47.

Rohner, R. P., Khaleque, A., & Cournoyer, D. E. (2005). Parental acceptance-rejection: Theory, methods, cross-cultural evidence, and implications. *Ethos, 33,* 299–334.

Roisman, G. I., Tsai, J. L., & Kuan-Hiong, S. C. (2004). The emotional integration of childhood experience: Physiological, facial expressive, and self-reported emotional response during the adult attachment interview. *Developmental Psychology, 40,* 776–789.

Roisman, G., Collins, A., Sroufe, A., & Egeland, B. (2005). Predictors of young adults' representations of and behavior in their current romantic relationship: Prospective tests of the prototype hypothesis. *Attachment and Human Development, 7*(2), 105–121.

Ronenstein, D., & Oster, H. (2005). Differential facial responses to four basic tastes in newborns. In P. Ekman & E. L. Rosenberg (Eds.), *What the face reveals: Basic and applied studies of spontaneous expression using the facial action coding system (FACS)* (2nd ed., pp. 302–327). New York: Oxford University Press.

Ronis, D. L. (1992). Conditional health threats: Health beliefs, decisions, and behaviors among adults. *Health Psychology, 11,*127–134.

Roodenrys, S., Hulme, C., & Brown, G. (1993). The development of short-term memory span: Separable effects of speech rate and long-term memory. *Journal of Experimental Child Psychology, 56,* 431–442.

Rosch, E. (1973). On the internal structure of perceptual and semantic categories. In T. E. Moore (Ed.), *Cognitive development and the acquisition of language.* New York: Academic Press.

Rosch, E. (1978). Principles of categorization. In E. Rosch & B. Lloyd (Eds.), *Cognition and categorization.* New York: John Wiley.

Rose, A. J. (2002). Co-rumination in the friendships of girls and boys. *Child Development, 73,* 1830–1843.

Rose, D. (2010, May 21). Concern over antidepressant drug use. *The Sydney Morning Herald.*

Roseman, I. J., Dhawan, N., Rettek, S. I., Naidu, R. K., & Thapa, K. (1995). Cultural differences and cross-cultural similarities in appraisals and emotional responses. *Journal of Cross-Cultural Psychology, 26,* 23–48.

Rosen, A. B., & Rozin, P. (1993). Now you see it, now you don't: The preschool child's conception of invisible particles in the context of dissolving. *Developmental Psychology, 29,* 300–311.

Rosen, J. C., & Gross, J. (1987). The prevalence of weight reducing and weight gaining in adolescent girls and boys. *Health Psychology, 6,* 131–147.

Rosen, K. S., & Rothbaum, F. (1993). Quality of parental caregiving and security of attachment. *Developmental Psychology, 29,* 358–367.

Rosenberg, M. (1979). *Conceiving the self.* New York: Basic Books.

Rosenberg, R. N. (2003). Advances in molecular and genetic basis of Alzheimer's disease. In M. F. Weiner & A. M. Lipton (Eds.), *The dementias: Diagnosis, treatment, and research* (3rd ed., pp. 433–452). Washington, DC: American Psychiatric Publishing.

Rosenberg, S. D., Rosenberg, H. J., & Farrell, M. P. (1999). The midlife crisis revisited. In S. L. Willis & J. D. Reid (Eds.), *Life in the middle: Psychological and social development in middle age* (pp. 25–45, 47–73). San Diego, CA: Academic Press.

Rosenblatt, A., Greenberg, J., Solomon, S., Pyszczynski, T., & Lyon, D. (1989). Evidence for terror management theory: I. The effects of mortality salience on reactions to those who violate or uphold cultural values. *Journal of Personality and Social Psychology, 57,* 681–690.

Rosenblum, G. D., & Lewis, M. (1999). The relations among body image, physical attractiveness, and body mass in adolescence. *Child Development, 70,* 50–64.

Rosenhan, D. L. (1973). On being sane in insane places. *Science, 179,* 252–258.

Rosenheck, R., Dunn, L., Peszke, M., Cramer, J., Xu, W., Thomas, J., et al. (1999). Impact of clozapine on negative symptoms and on the deficit syndrome in refractory schizophrenia. *American Journal of Psychiatry, 156,* 88–93.

Rosenstock, I. M. (1966). Why people use health services. *Milbank Memorial Fund Quarterly, 44,* 94–127.

Rosenthal, R., & Jacobson, L. (1966). Teachers' expectancies: Determinants of pupils' IQ gains. *Psychological Reports, 19,* 115–118.

Rosenwald, G. (1988). The multiple case study method. *Journal of Personality, 56*, 239–264.

Rosenzweig, A. (2008). *Alzheimer's disease*. Retrieved from http://alzheimers.about.com/od/glossary/g/Alzheimers.htm

Rosenzweig, M. R., Bennett, E. L., & Diamond, M. C. (1972). Brain changes in response to experience. *Scientific American, 226*, 22–29.

Rosete, D., & Ciarrochi, J. (2005). Emotional intelligence and its relationship to workplace performance outcomes of leadership effectiveness. *Leadership & Organization Development Journal, 26*(5), 388–399.

Ross, C. A., Anderson, G., Fleisher, W., & Norton, G. R. (1991). The frequency of multiple personality disorder among psychiatric inpatients. *American Journal of Psychiatry, 148,* 1717–1720.

Ross, L. (1977). The intuitive psychologist and his shortcomings: Distortions in the attribution process. *Advances in Experimental Social Psychology, 10,* 84.

Ross, M., & Sicoly, F. (1979). Egocentric biases in availability and attribution. *Journal of Personality and Social Psychology, 37,* 322–336.

Ross, S. M., & Ross, L. E. (1971). Comparison of trace and delay classical eyelid conditioning as a function of interstimulus interval. *Journal of Experimental Psychology, 91,* 165–167.

Rossier, J., Dahourou, D., & McCrae, R. R. (2005). Structural and mean-level analyses of the five-factor model and locus of control: Further evidence. *Journal of Cross-Cultural Psychology, 36*, 227–246.

Rosso, I. M., Cannon, T. D., Huttunen, T., Huttunen, M. O., Loennqvist, J., & Gasperoni, T. L. (2000). Obstetric risk factors for early-onset schizophrenia in a Finnish birth cohort. *American Journal of Psychiatry, 157,* 801–807.

Roth, A., & Fonagy, P. (2005). *What works for whom: A critical review of psychotherapy research* (2nd ed.). London: Guildford Press.

Roth, A., Fonagy, P., Parry, G., & Target, M. (1996). *What works for whom? A critical review of psychotherapy research*. New York: Guilford Press.

Rothbaum, B. O., Hodges, L. F., Kooper, R., Opdyke, D., Williford, J., & North, M. M. (1995). Effectiveness of computer-generated (virtual reality) graded exposure in the treatment of acrophobia. *American Journal of Psychiatry, 152,* 626–628.

Rothbaum, B. O., Hodges, L. F., Ready, D., Graap, K., & Alarcon, R. D. (2001). Virtual reality exposure therapy for Vietnam veterans with posttraumatic stress disorder. *Journal of Clinical Psychiatry, 62,* 617–622.

Rothbaum, B. O., Hodges, L., Smith, S., Lee, J. H., & Price, L. (2000). A controlled study of virtual reality exposure therapy for the fear of flying. *Journal of Consulting and Clinical Psychology, 68,* 1020–1026.

Rothbaum, B. O., & Schwartz, A. C. (2002). Exposure therapy for posttraumatic stress disorder. *American Journal of Psychotherapy, 56,* 59–75.

Rothbaum, F., Pott, M., Azuma, H., Miyake, K., & Weisz, J. (2000). The development of close relationships in Japan and the United States: Paths of symbiotic harmony and generative tension. *Child Development, 71,* 1121–1142.

Rothbaum, F., Weisz, J., Pott, M., Miyake, K., & Morelli, G. (2000). Attachment and culture: Security in the United States and Japan. *American Psychologist, 55*, 1093–1104.

Rothblum, E. D. (1983). Sex-role stereotypes and depression in women. In V. Franks & E. D. Rothblum (Eds.), *The stereotyping of women: Its effects on mental health* (pp. 83–111). New York: Springer.

Rothblum, E. D. (1992). The stigma of women's weight: Social and economic realities. *Feminism and Psychology, 2*, 61–73.

Rothgerber, H. (1997). External intergroup threat as an antecedent to perceptions in in-group and out-group homogeneity. *Journal of Personality and Social Psychology, 73*, 1206–1212.

Rothstein, A. (2005). Compromise formation theory: An intersubjective dimension. *Psychoanalytic Dialogues, 15*(3), 415–431.

Rotter, J. (1971). External control and internal control. *Psychology Today,* June, 40–45.

Rotter, J. B. (1954). *Social learning and clinical psychology*. New York: Prentice-Hall.

Rotter, J. B. (1966). Generalized expectancies for internal versus external control of reinforcement. *Psychological Monographs* (Whole No. 609).

Rotter, J. B. (1990). Internal versus external control of reinforcement: A case history of a variable. *American Psychologist, 45,* 489–493.

Rotton, J., & Cohn, E. G. (2000). Violence is a curvilinear function of temperature in Dallas: A replication. *Journal of Personality and Social Psychology, 78,* 1074–1081.

Rotton, J., Frey, J., Barry, T., Milligan, M., & Fitzpatrick, M. (1979). The air pollution experience and physical aggression. *Journal of Applied Social Psychology, 9,* 397–442.

Rousseau, J. J. (1972). *The social contract*. New York: Penguin Classics. (Originally published 1762)

Rovee-Collier, C. (1990). The 'memory system' of prelinguistic infants. In A. Diamond (Ed.), *Development and neural bases of higher cognitive functions* (pp. 517–542). New York: New York Academy of Sciences Press.

Rovee-Collier, C. (1999). The development of infant memory. *Current Directions in Psychological Science, 8*, 80–85.

Rowe, D. C. (1999). Heredity. In V. J. Derlega, B. A. Winstead, & W. H. Jones (Eds.), *Personality: Contemporary theory and research* (pp. 66–100). Chicago: Nelson-Hall.

Rowe, D. C., Jacobson, K. C., & Van den Oord, E. J. C. G. (1999). Genetic and environmental influences on vocabulary IQ: Parental education level as moderator. *Child Development, 70*, 1151–1162.

Rowe, D. C., & Rodgers, J. L. (2002). Expanding variance and the case of historical changes in IQ means: A critique of Dickens and Flynn (2001). *Psychological Review, 109*, 759–763.

Rowe, J. W., & Kahn, R. L. (1997). Successful aging. *Gerontologist, 37,* 433–440.

Royal Australian and New Zealand College of Psychiatrists Clinical Practice Guidelines Team for Panic Disorder and Agoraphobia. (2003). Australian and New Zealand clinical practice guidelines for the treatment of panic disorder and agoraphobia. *Australian and New Zealand Journal of Psychiatry, 37*, 641–656.

Royal Australian and New Zealand College of Psychiatrists Clinical Practice Guidelines Team for Depression. (2004). Australian and New Zealand clinical practice guidelines for the treatment of depression. *Australian and New Zealand Journal of Psychiatry, 38*, 389–407.

Rubin, D. C. (1995). *Memory in oral traditions: The cognitive psychology of epic, ballads, and countingout rhymes*. New York: Oxford University Press.

Rubin, D. C., & Kozin, M. (1984). Vivid memories. *Cognition, 16,* 81–95.

Rubin, D. C., Rahhal, T. A., & Poon, L. W. (1998). Things learned in early childhood are remembered best. *Memory and Cognition, 26,* 3–19.

Rubin, J. Z. (1994). Models of conflict management. *Journal of Social Issues, 50,* 33–45.

Rudman, L. A. (2004). Sources of implicit attitudes. *Current Directions in Psychological Science, 13*(2), 79–82.

Ruffman, T. (1999). Children's understanding of logical inconsistency. *Child Development, 70,* 872–886.

Rumbaugh, D. M. (1992). Learning about primates' learning, language, and cognition. In G. G. Brannigan & M. R. Merrens (Eds.), *The undaunted psychologist: Adventures in research*. New York: McGraw-Hill.

Rumbaugh, D. M., & Gill, T. V. (1977). Lana's acquisition of language skills. In D. M. Rumbaugh (Ed.), *Language learning by a chimpanzee: The Lana project* (pp. 165–192). New York: Academic Press.

Rumelhart, D. (1984). Schemata and the cognitive system. In R. S. Wyer & T. K. Srull (Eds.), *Handbook of social cognition: Vol. 1*. Hillsdale, NJ: Erlbaum.

Rumelhart, D. E., McClelland, J. L., & the PDP Research Group. (1986). *Parallel distributed processing: Explorations in the microstructure of cognition*. Cambridge, MA: MIT Press.

Runyan, W. M. (1984). *Life histories and psychobiography: Explanations in theory and method*. New York: Oxford University Press.

Rusbult, C. E., & Van Lange, P. A. M. (2003). Interdependence, interaction, and relationships. *Annual Review of Psychology, 54*, 351–375.

Rusbult, C. E., Verette, J., Whitney, G. A., Slovik, L. F., & Lipkus, I. (1991). Accommodation processes in close relationships: Theory and preliminary empirical evidence. *Journal of Personality and Social Psychology, 60*, 53–78.

Ruschena, E., Prior, M., Sanson, A., & Smart, D. (2005). A longitudinal study of adolescent adjustment following family transitions. *Journal of Child Psychology & Psychiatry & Allied Disciplines, 46*, 353–363.

Rushton, J. P., Fulker, D. W., Neale, M. C., Nias, D. K. B., & Eysenck, H. J. (1986). Altruism and aggression: The heritability of individual differences. *Journal of Personality and Social Psychology, 50,* 1192–1198.

Rushton, P. J., & Skuy, M. (2000). Performance on Raven's matrices by African and white university students in South Africa. *Intelligence, 28,* 4.

Rushton, W. A. H. (1962). Visual pigments in man. *Scientific American, 207*, 120–132.

Russell, J. A. (1991). Culture and the categorization of emotions. *Psychological Bulletin, 110*, 426–450.

Russell, J. D., & Roxanas, M. (1990). Psychiatry and the frontal lobes. *Australian and New Zealand Journal of Psychiatry, 24*, 113–132.

Russell, M. J. (1976). Human olfactory communication. *Nature, 260*, 520–522.

Russo, R., & Parkin, A. J. (1993). Age differences in implicit memory: More apparent than real. *Memory and Cognition, 21,* 73–80.

Rutter, M., Quinton, D., & Liddle, C. (1983). Parenting in two generations: Looking backwards and looking forwards. In N. Madge (Ed.), *Families at risk* (pp. 60–98). London: Heineman.

Ryan, J. J., Sattler, J. M., & Lopez, S. J. (2000). Age effects on Wechsler Adult Intelligence Scale-III subtests. *Archives of Clinical Neuropsychology, 15*, 311–317.

Ryan, R. M., & Deci, E. L. (2000). Intrinsic and extrinsic motivations: Classic definitions and new directions. *Contemporary Educational Psychology, 25*, 54–67.

Rymer, J., Wilson, R., & Ballard, K. (2003). Making decisions about hormone replacement therapy. *British Medical Journal, 326,* 322–326.

Rymer, R. (1993). *Genie: An abused child's flight from silence*. New York: Harper Collins.

Rypma, B., & D'Esposito, M. (2000). Isolating the neural mechanisms of age-related changes in human working memory. *Nature Neuroscience, 3,* 509–515.

Saarni, C. (1998). Issues of cultural meaningfulness in emotional development. *Developmental Psychology, 34,* 647–652.

Sabini, J., Siepmann, M., & Stein, J. (2001). The really fundamental attribution error in social psychological research. *Psychological Inquiry, 12*, 1–15.

Sachdev, P. (2004). Early extrapyramidal side-effects as risk factors for later tardive dyskinesia: A prospective study. *Australian and New Zealand Journal of Psychiatry, 38,* 445–449.

Sachs, B., Zindrick, M., & Beasley, R. (1993). Reflex sympathetic dystrophy after operative procedures on the lumbar spine. *Journal of Bone and Joint Surgery, 75-A*, 721–725.

Sacks, O. (1970). *Migraine*. London: Faber & Faber.

Sacks, O. (1993, May 10). A neurologist's notebook: To see and not see. *New Yorker*, 59–73.

Saegert, S., & Winkel, G. H. (1990). Environmental psychology. *Annual Review of Psychology, 41*, 441–477.

Saffran, J., Aslin, R., & Newport, E. (1996). Statistical learning by 8-month-old infants. *Science, 274,* 1926–1928.

Saha, S., Chant, D., Welham, J., & McGrath, J. (2005). A systematic review of the prevalence of schizophrenia. *PLoS Medicine, 2*(5), e141. Retrieved from http://www.ncbi.nlm.nih.gov/pubmed/15916472

Sahraie, A., Weiskrantz, L., Barbur, J. L., Simmons, A., Williams, S. C., & Brammer, M. J. (1997). Pattern of neuronal activity associated with conscious and unconscious processing of visual signals. *Proceedings of the National Academy of Sciences, USA, 94*, 9406–9411.

Sakaguchi, K., Sakai, Y., & Ueda, K. (2007). Robust association between sociosexuality and self-monitoring in heterosexual and non-heterosexual Japanese. *Personality and Individual Differences*, *43*(4), 815–825.

Sakurai, T., Amemiya, A., Ishii, M., Matsuzaki, I., Chemelli, R. M., Tanaka, H., et al. (1998). Orexins and orexin receptors: A family of hypothalamic neuropeptides and g protein-coupled receptors that regulate feeding behavior. *Cell, 92*, 573–585.

Salcedo, E., Zheng, L., Phistry, M., Bagg, E. E., & Britt, S. G. (2003). Molecular basis for ultraviolet vision in invertebrates. *The Journal of Neuroscience, 23*(34), 10873–10878.

Salkovskis, P. M., Jones, D. R., & Clark, D. M. (1986). Respiratory control in the treatment of panic attacks: Replication and extension with concurrent measurement of behavior and PCPs. *British Journal of Psychiatry, 148*, 526–532.

Sallis, J. F., Prochaska, J. J., Taylor, W. C., Hill, J. O., & Geraci, J. C. (1999). Correlates of physical activity in a national sample of girls and boys in grades 4 through 12. *Health Psychology, 18*, 410–415.

Salovey, P., Mayer, J., & Caruso, D. (2002). The positive psychology of emotional intelligence. In C. R. Snyder & S. J. Lopez (Eds.), *Handbook of positive psychology* (pp. 159–171). London: Oxford University Press.

Salovey, P., Mayer, J. D., & Rosenhan, D. L. (1991). Mood and healing: Mood as a motivator of helping and helping as a regulator of mood. In M. S. Clark (Ed.), *Prosocial behavior*. Newbury Park, CA: Sage.

Salovey, P., Rothman, A. J., & Rodin, J. (1998). Health behavior. In D. T. Gilbert, S. T. Fiske, & G. Lindzey (Eds.), *The handbook of social psychology: Vol. 2* (4th ed., pp. 633–683). Boston: McGraw-Hill.

Salthouse, T. (1992). The information-processing perspective on cognitive aging. In R. Sternberg & C. Berg (Eds.), *Intellectual development*. Cambridge: Cambridge University Press.

Salthouse, T. A. (1996). General and specific speed mediation of adult age differences in memory. *Journals of Gerontology Series B — Psychological Sciences and Social Sciences, 51B*, P30–P42.

Salthouse, T. A. (2000). Pressing issues in cognitive aging. In D. C. Park & N. Schwarz (Eds.), *Cognitive aging: A primer* (pp. 43–54). Philadelphia: Psychology Press/Taylor & Francis.

Salthouse, T. A. (2006). Mental exercise and mental aging: Evaluating the validity of the 'use it or lose it' hypothesis. *Perspectives on Psychological Science*, *1*, 68–87.

Salthouse, T. A., & Davis, H. P. (2006). Organization of cognitive abilities and neuropsychological variables across the lifespan. *Developmental Review*, *26*, 31–54.

Sam, D. L., & Moreira, V. (2002). The mutual embeddedness of culture and mental illness. In W. J. Lonner, D. L. Dinnel, S. A. Hayes, & D. N. Sattler (Eds.), *Online readings in psychology and culture*. Washington, DC: Center for Cross-Cultural Research, Western Washington University.

Sameroff, A., Seifer, R., Baldwin, A., & Baldwin, C. (1993). Stability of intelligence from preschool to adolescence: The influence of social and family risk factors. *Child Development, 64*, 80–97.

Samudra, K., & Cantwell, D. P. (1999). Risk factors for attention-deficit/hyperactivity disorder. In H. C. Quay & A. E. Hogan (Eds.), *Handbook of disruptive behavior disorders* (pp. 199–220). Dordrecht, The Netherlands: Kluwer.

Samuels, C. A. (1985). Bases for the infant's developing self awareness. *Human Development, 29*, 36–48.

SANE Australia. (2010). *Borderline personality disorder fact sheet*. Retrieved from http://www.sane.org/information/factsheets-podcasts/160-borderline-personality-disorder

SANE Australia. (2005). *Depression*. Retrieved from http://www.sane.org/Information/Factsheets/Depression.html

Sanders, M. R. (2008). The Triple P-Positive Parenting Program as a public health approach to strengthening parenting. *Journal of Family Psychology, 22*(4), 506–517.

Sandler, J., & Rosenblatt, B. (1962). The concept of the representational world. *Psychoanalytic Study of the Child, 17*, 128–145.

Sanfilipo, M., Lafargue, T., Rusinek, H., Arena, L., Loneragan, C., Lautin, A., et al. (2000). Volumetric measure of the frontal and temporal lobe regions in schizophrenia: Relationship to negative symptoms. *Archives of General Psychiatry, 57*, 471–480.

Sanger, T. M., Lieberman, J. A., Tohen, M., Grundy, S., Beasley, C., & Tollefson, G. D. (1999). Olanzapine versus haloperidol treatment in first-episode psychosis. *American Journal of Psychiatry, 156*, 79–87.

Sansgiry, S. S., & Sail, K. (2006). Effect of students' perceptions of course load on test anxiety. *American Journal of Pharmaceutical Education, 70*(2), 1–6.

Sansom, B. L. (1982). The Aboriginal commonality. In R. M. Berndt (Ed.), *Aboriginal sites, rights and resource development*. Perth, Australia: University of Western Australia Press.

Sanson, A., Augoustinos, M., Gridley, H., Kyrios, M., Reser, J., & Turner, C. (1998). Racism and prejudice: An Australian Psychological Society position paper. *Australian Psychologist, 33*(3), 161–182.

Sapir, E. (1949). *Culture, language and personality*. Berkeley: University of California Press.

Sarafino, E. P. (2002). *Health psychology: Biopsychosocial interactions* (4th ed.). Hoboken, NJ: John Wiley & Sons.

Sarason, B. R., Sarason, I. G., & Gurung, R. A. R. (1997). Close personal relationships and health outcomes: A key to the role of social support. In S. Duck (Ed.), *Handbook of personal relationships: Theory, research and interventions* (2nd ed., pp. 547–573). Chichester, England: John Wiley & Sons.

Saraswathi, T., & Dutta, R. (1988). Current trends in developmental psychology: A life span perspective. In J. Pandey (Ed.), *Psychology in India: The state-of-the-art: Vol. 1. Personality and mental processes* (pp. 93–152). London: Sage.

Sarnat, H. B., & Netsky, M. G. (1974). *Evolution of the nervous system*. New York: Oxford University Press.

Sarra, C. (2004). Strong and smart: Aboriginal children are expected to do poorly at school. *New Internationalist, 14*, 364.

Sarter, M., & Markowitsch, H. J. (1985). Involvement of the amygdale in learning and memory: A critical review, with emphasis on anatomical relation. *Behavioral Neuroscience, 99*, 342–380.

Sartre, J. P. (1971). *Being and nothingness: An essay in phenomenological ontology* (H. E. Barnes, Trans.). New York: Citadel Press.

Satel, S. L., Southwick, S. M., & Gawin, F. H. (1991). Clinical features of cocaine-induced paranoia. *American Journal of Psychiatry*, *148*, 495–498.

Saucier, G. (2000). Isms and the structure of social attitudes. *Journal of Personality and Social Psychology, 78*, 366–385.

Saucier, G. (2002). Orthogonal markers for orthogonal factors: The case of the big five. *Journal of Research in Personality*, *36*, 1–31.

Saucier, G. (2008). Measures of the personality factors found recurrently in human lexicons. In G. J. Boyle, G. Matthews, & D. Saklofske (Eds.), *Handbook of personality theory and testing: Vol. 2. Personality measurement and assessment* (pp. 29–54). London: Sage Publications.

Saucier, G., & Goldberg, L. R. (2001). Lexical studies of indigenous personality factors: Premises, products, and prospects. *Journal of Personality, 69*, 847–879.

Saudino, K. (1997). Moving beyond the heritability question: New directions in behavioral genetic studies of personality. *Current Directions in Psychological Science, 6*, 86–89.

Saudino, K. J., & Plomin, R. (1996). Personality and behavioral genetics: Where have we been and where are we going? *Journal of Research in Personality, 30*, 335–347.

Sauerwein, K. (1992, October 21). Too scared to be safe: Teens know they need condoms if they're going to have sex, but they're too freaked out to buy them. *Los Angeles Times*.

Saunders, C. D. (2003). The emerging field of conservation psychology. *Human Ecology Review, 10*, 137–149.

Savage-Rumbaugh, E. S., McDonald, K., Sevcik, R., Hopkins, W., & Rupert, E. (1986). Spontaneous symbol acquisition and communicative use by pygmy chimpanzees (pan paniscus). *Journal of Experimental Psychology: General, 115*, 211–235.

Savage-Rumbaugh, E. S., Pate, J. L., Lawson, J., Smith, S. T., & Rosenbaum, S. (1983). Can a chimpanzee make a statement? *Journal of Experimental Psychology: General, 112*, 457–492.

Savage-Rumbaugh, E. S., Rumbaugh, D. M., & Boysen, S. (1978). Symbolic communication between two chimpanzees. *Science, 201*, 641–644.

Savin-Williams, R. C., & Small, S. A. (1986). The timing of puberty and its relationship to adolescent and parent perceptions of family interactions. *Developmental Psychology, 22*, 342–347.

Sawyer, M., Arney, F. M., & Baghurst, P. A. (2000). *Mental health of young people in Australia*. Canberra, Australia: Commonwealth Department of Health and Aged Care.

Scarr, S. (1992). Developmental theories for the 1990s: Development and individual differences. *Child Development, 63*, 1–19.

Scarr, S., & Carter-Saltzman, L. (1982). Genetics and intelligence. In R. J. Sternberg (Ed.), *Handbook of human intelligence* (pp. 792–896). New York: Cambridge University Press.

Scarr, S., Pakstis, A. J., Katz, S. H., & Barker, W. B. (1977). The absence of a relationship between degree of white ancestry and intellectual skills within a black population. *Human Genetics, 39*, 69–86.

Scarr, S., & Weinberg, R. A. (1976). IQ test performance of black children adopted by white families. *American Psychologist, 31*, 726–739.

Scarr, S., & Weinberg, R. A. (1983). The Minnesota adoption studies: Genetic differences and malleability. *Child Development, 54*, 260–267.

Scaturo, D. J. (2001). The evolution of psychotherapy and the concept of manualization: An integrative perspective. *Professional Psychology: Research and Practice*, *5*, 522–530.

Scaturo, D. J. (2005). *Clinical dilemmas in psychotherapy: A transtheoretical approach to psychotherapy integration*. Washington, DC: American Psychological Association.

Schab, F. R., & Crowder, R. G. (1995). Odor recognition memory. In F. R. Schab & F. R. G. Crowder (Eds.), *Memory for odors* (pp. 9–20). Mahwah, NJ: Lawrence Erlbaum.

Schachner, D. A., Shaver, P. R., & Mikulincer, M. (2005). Patterns of nonverbal behavior and sensitivity in the context of attachment relationships. *Journal of Nonverbal Behavior*, *29*(3), 141–169.

Schachter, F. F., Shore, E., Hodapp, R., Chalfin, S., & Bundy, C. (1978). Do girls talk earlier? Mean length of utterance in toddlers. *Developmental Psychology, 14*, 388–392.

Schachter, S., & Singer, J. (1962). Cognitive, social, and physiological determinants of emotional state. *Psychological Review, 69*, 379–399.

Schacter, D. (1995a). Implicit memory: A new frontier for cognitive neuroscience. In M. Gazzaniga (Ed.), *The cognitive neurosciences* (pp. 815–824). Cambridge, MA: MIT Press.

Schacter, D. (1995b). *Memory and distortion: How minds, brains, and societies recollect the past*. Cambridge, MA: Harvard University Press.

Schacter, D. (1997). False recognition and the brain. *Current Directions in Psychological Science, 6,* 65–70.

Schacter, D., Cooper, L. A., & Valdiserri, M. (1992). Implicit and explicit memory for novel visual objects in older and younger adults. *Psychology and Aging, 7,* 299–308.

Schacter, D. L. (1999). The seven sins of memory: Insights from psychology and cognitive neuroscience. *American Psychologist, 54,* 182–203.

Schacter, D. L., & Buckner, R. L. (1998). Priming and the brain. *Neuron, 20,* 185–195.

Schacter, D. L., Verfaellie, M., Anes, M., & Racine, C. (1998). When true recognition suppresses false recognition: Evidence from amnesic patients. *Journal of Cognitive Neuroscience, 10,* 668–679.

Schafe, G. E., & Bernstein, I. L. (1996). Taste aversion learning. In E. D. Capaldi (Ed.), *Why we eat what we eat: The psychology of eating* (pp. 31–51). Washington, DC: American Psychological Association.

Schaie, K. W. (1988). Ageism in psychological research. *American Psychologist, 43,* 179–183.

Schaie, K. W. (1990). Intellectual development in adulthood. In J. E. Birren & K. W. Schaie (Eds.), *Handbook of the psychology of aging* (3rd ed.). New York: Van Nostrand Reinhold.

Schaie, K. W. (1994). The course of adult intellectual development. *American Psychologist, 49,* 304–313.

Schartau, P. E. S., Dalgleish, T., & Dunn, B. D. (2009). Seeing the bigger picture: Training in perspective broadening reduces self-reported affect and psychophysiological response to distressing films and autobiographical memories. *Journal of Abnormal Psychology, 118,* 15–27.

Schauble, L., & Glaser, R. (1990). Scientific thinking in children and adults. *Contributions to Human Development, 21,* 9–27.

Scheff, T. J. (1970). Schizophrenia as ideology. *Schizophrenia Bulletin, 1,* 15–20.

Scheier, M., & Carver, C. (1993). On the power of positive thinking: The benefits of being optimistic. *Current Directions in Psychological Science, 2,* 26–30.

Scheier, M. F., Matthews, K. A., Owens, J., Magovern, G. J., Lefebvre, R. C., Abbott, R., et al. (1989). Dispositional optimism and recovery from coronary artery bypass surgery: The beneficial effects on physical and psychological well-being. *Journal of Personality and Social Psychology, 57,* 1024–1040.

Schein. E. (1992). Coming to a new awareness of organisational culture. In G. Salaman (Ed.), *Human resource strategies*. London: Sage.

Schenk, S., Gittings, D., Johnstone, M., & Daniela, E. (2003). Development, maintenance and temporal pattern of self-administration maintained by ecstasy (MDMA) in rats. *Psychopharmacology, 169,* 21–27.

Scheper-Hughes, N. (1979). *Saints, scholars, and schizophrenics: Mental illness in rural Ireland.* Berkeley: University of California Press.

Scher, S., & Cooper, J. (1989). Motivational basis of the dissonance: The singular role of behavioral consequences. *Journal of Personality and Social Psychology, 56,* 899–906.

Scherer, K., & Wallbott, H. (1994). Evidence for universality and cultural variation of differential emotion response patterning. *Journal of Personality and Social Psychology, 66,* 310–328.

Scherer, K. R. (1997). Profiles of emotion-antecedent appraisal: Testing theoretical predictions across cultures. *Cognition and Emotion, 11,* 113–150.

Scherer, K. R. (1999). Appraisal theory. In T. Dalgleish & M. Power (Eds.), *The handbook of cognition and emotion* (pp. 637–664). New York: John Wiley & Sons.

Schiavi, R. C., Schreiner-Engle, P., Mandeli, J., Schanzer, H., & Cohen, E. (1990). Healthy aging and male sexual function. *American Journal of Psychiatry, 147,* 766–771.

Schiavi, R. C., Schreiner-Engel, P., White, D., & Mandeli, J. (1991). The relationship between pituitary-gonadal function and sexual behavior in healthy aging men. *Psychosomatic Medicine, 53,* 363–374.

Schiff, M., Duyme, M., Dumaret, A., & Tomkiewicz, S. (1982). How much could we boost scholastic achievement and IQ scores? A direct answer from a French adoption study. *Cognition, 12,* 165–196.

Schiffman, H. R. (1996). *Sensation and perception* (4th ed.). New York: John Wiley.

Schiller, D., Monfils, M.-H., Raio, C. M., Johnson, D. C., LeDoux, J. E., & Phelps, E. A. (2010). Preventing the return of fear in humans using reconsolidation update mechanisms. *Nature, 463,* 49–53.

Schimmack, U., Oishi, S., Furr, F. M., & Funder, D. C. (2004). Personality and life satisfaction: A facet level analysis. *Personality and Social Psychology Bulletin, 30,* 1062–1075.

Schizophrenia Research Institute. (2010). *Schizophrenia: The key facts.* Retrieved from http://www.schizophreniaresearch.org.au/home.php?r=3&menu=About

Schlegel, A., & Barry, H., III. (1991). *Adolescence: An anthropological inquiry.* New York: Free Press.

Schlenker, B. R., & Forsyth, D. R. (1977). On the ethics of psychological research. *Journal of Experimental Social Psychology, 13,* 369–396.

Schlesser, M. A., & Altshuler, K. Z. (1983). The genetics of affective disorder: Date, theory, and clinical applications. *Hospital and Community Psychiatry, 34,* 415–422.

Schmidt, F. L. (2002). The role of general cognitive ability and job performance: Why there cannot be a debate. *Human Performance, 15,* 187–210.

Schmidt, N. B., Richey, J. A., Buckner, J. D., & Timpano, K. R. (2009). Attention training for generalized social anxiety disorder. *Journal of Abnormal Psychology, 118,* 5–14.

Schmidt, N. B., Joiner, T. E., Jr., Staab, J. P., & Williams, F. M. (2003). Health perceptions and anxiety sensitivity in patients with panic disorder. *Journal of Psychopathology and Behavioral Assessment, 25*(3), 139–145.

Schmidt, N. B., Lerew, D. R., & Trakowski, J. H. (1997). Body vigilance in panic disorder: Evaluating attention to bodily perturbations. *Journal of Consulting and Clinical Psychology, 65,* 214–220.

Schmidt, N. B., Trakowski, J. H., & Staab, J. P. (1997). Extinction of panicogenic effects of a 35% CO2 challenge in patients with panic disorder. *Journal of Abnormal Psychology, 106,* 630–640.

Schmitt, D. P. (2007). *Attachment matters: Patterns of romantic attachment across gender, geography, and cultural forms.* Chapter prepared for the 10th Sydney Symposium of Social Psychology, 2007 (pp. 1–54). Retrieved from http://www.sydneysymposium.unsw.edu.au/2007/Chapters/SchmittSSSP07.pdf

Schnapf, J., Kraft, T., Nunn, B., & Baylor, D. (1989). Transduction in primate cones. *Neuroscience Research Supplements, 10,* 9–14.

Schneider, M. L., Roughton, E. C., Koehler, A. J., & Lubach, G. R. (1999). Growth and development following prenatal stress exposure in primates: An examination of ontogenetic vulnerability. *Child Development, 70,* 263–274.

Schneider, M. L., Roughton, E. C., & Lubach, G. R. (1997). Moderate alcohol consumption and psychological stress during pregnancy induce attention and neuromotor impairments in primate infants. *Child Development, 68,* 747–759.

Schneider-Corey, M., & Corey, G. (2005). *Groups: Process and practice.* New York: Thomson Wadsworth.

Schooler, J. W., Reichle, E. D., & Halpern, D. V. (2004). Zoning out while reading: Evidence for dissociations between experience and metaconsciousness. In D. Levin (Ed.), *Thinking and seeing: Visual metacognition in adults and children* (pp. 203–226). Cambridge, MA: MIT Press.

Schraw, G., Dunkle, M. E., & Bendixen, L. D. (1995). Cognitive processes in well-defined and ill-defined problem solving. *Applied Cognitive Psychology, 9,* 523–538.

Schreiber, F. R. (1973). *Sybil.* Chicago: Regnery.

Schreiner, C. E., Read, H. L., & Sutter, M. L. (2000). Modular organization of frequency integration in primary auditory cortex. *Annual Review of Neuroscience, 23,* 501–529.

Schuckit, M. (1984). Relationship between the course of primary alcoholism in men and family history. *Journal of Studies on Alcohol, 45,* 334–338.

Schuckit, M. A. (1994). Low level of response to alcohol as a predictor of future alcoholism. *American Journal of Psychiatry, 151,* 184–189.

Schultheiss, O. C., & Brunstein, J. C. (2005). An implicit motive perspective on competence. In A. J. Elliot & C. Dweck (Eds.), *Handbook of competence and motivation* (pp. 31–51). New York: Guilford.

Schultz, T., & Schliefer, M. (1983). Towards a refinement of attribution concepts. In J. Jaspars, F. Fincham, & M. Hewstone (Eds.), *Attribution theory and research: Conceptual, developmental, and social dimensions* (pp. 37–62). New York: Academic Press.

Schultz, W. (1998). Predictive reward signal of dopamine neurons. *Journal of Neurophysiology, 80,* 1–27.

Schultz, W. (2002). Getting formal with dopamine and reward. *Neuron, 36*(2), 241–263.

Schulze, R., & Roberts, R. D. (2006). Assessing the big-five: Development and validation of the openness conscientiousness extraversion agreeableness neuroticism index condensed (OCEANIC). *Zeitschrift für Psychologie, 214,* 133–149.

Schuster, D. T. (1990). Fulfillment of potential, life satisfaction, and competence: Comparing four cohorts of gifted women at midlife. *Journal of Educational Psychology, 82,* 471–478.

Schwartz, D., Dodge, K. A., Pettit, G. S., & Bates, J. E. (2000). Friendship as a moderating factor in the pathway between early harsh home environment and later victimization in the peer group. *Developmental Psychology, 36,* 646–662.

Schwartz, G. E. (1987). Personality and health: An integrative health science approach. In V. P. Makosky (Ed.), *The G. Stanley Hall lecture series: Vol. 7.* Washington, DC: American Psychological Association.

Schwarz, N. (2007). Attitude construction: Evaluation in context. *Social Cognition, 5,* 638–656.

Schweitzer, R., Perkoulidis, S., Krome, S., Ludlow, C., & Ryan, M. (2005). Attitudes toward refugees: The dark side of prejudice in Australia. *Australian Journal of Psychology, 57*(3), 170–179.

Science Alert. (2007). *Early menopause triggers health risks.* Retrieved from http://www.sciencealert.com.au/

Science Daily. (2008, October 6). *Television viewing and aggression: Some alternative perspectives.* Retrieved from http://www.sciencedaily.com/releases/2008/10/081001145030.htm

Science historian predicts a billion deaths from tobacco by end of the century. (2002). *Bulletin of the World Health Organization, 80,* 80.

Scott, J. (2001). Cognitive therapy as an adjunct to medication in bipolar disorder. *British Journal of Psychiatry, 178,* s164–s168.

Scott, L. S., Tanaka, J. W., Sheinberg, D. L., & Curran, T. (2006). A re-evaluation of the electrophysiological correlates of expert object processing. *Journal of Cognitive Neuroscience, 18*(9), 1453–1465.

Scott, S. K., Young, A. W., Calder, A. J., & Hellawell, D. J. (1997). Impaired auditory recognition of fear and anger following bilateral amygdala lesions. *Nature, 385,* 254–257.

Scott, W. A., Scott, R., Boehnke, K., Shall-Way, C., Kwok, L., & Masamichi, S. (1991). Children's personality as a function of family relations within and between cultures. *Journal of Cross-Cultural Psychology, 22,* 182–208.

Scoville, W. B., & Milner, B. (1957). Loss of recent memory after bilateral hippocampal lesions. *Journal of Neurology, Neurosurgery, and Psychiatry, 20,* 11–21.

Scribner, S. (1986). Thinking in action: Some characteristics of practical thought. In R. J. Sternberg & R. K. Wagner (Eds.), *Practical intelligence: Nature and origins of competence in the everyday world* (pp. 13–40). New York: Cambridge University Press.

Scroppo, J. C., Drob, S. L., Weinberger, J. L., & Eagle, P. (1998). Identifying dissociative identity disorder: A self-report and projective study. *Journal of Psychology, 107,* 272–284.

Searle, J. R. (2000). Consciousness. *Annual Review of Neuroscience, 23,* 557–578.

Sears, D. O. (1986). College sophomores in the laboratory: Influences of a narrow data base on social psychological view of human nature. *Journal of Personality and Social Psychology, 51,* 515–530.

Sears, R. R. (1977). Sources of life satisfactions of the Terman gifted men. *American Psychologist, 32,* 119–128.

See, J., MacLeod, C., & Bridle, R. (2009). The reduction of anxiety vulnerability through the modification of attentional bias: A real-world study using a home-based cognitive bias modification procedure. *Journal of Abnormal Psychology, 118,* 66–75.

Seelinger, G., & Schuderer, B. (1985). Release of male courtship display in Periplaneta americana: Evidence for female contact sex pheromone. *Animal Behaviour, 33,* 599–607.

Segal, N. L. (1997). Same-age unrelated siblings: A unique test of within-family environmental influences on IQ similarity. *Journal of Educational Psychology, 89,* 381–390.

Segal, N. L. (2000). Virtual twins: New findings on within-family environmental influences on intelligence. *Journal of Educational Psychology, 92,* 442–448.

Segall, M. H. (1988). Cultural roots of aggressive behavior. In M. H. Bond (Ed.), *The cross-cultural challenge to social psychology*. Newbury Park, CA: Sage.

Segall, M. H., Campbell, D. T., & Herskovitz, M. J. (1966). *Influence of culture on visual perception*. New York: Bobbs-Merrill.

Segall, M. H., Dasen, P. R., Berry, J. W., & Poortinga, Y. H. (1990). *Human behavior in global perspective: An introduction to cross-cultural psychology*. New York: Pergamon

Seger, C. A. (1994). Implicit learning. *Psychological Bulletin, 115,* 163–196.

Seidenberg, M. S. (1997). Language acquisition and use: Learning and applying probabilistic constraints. *Science, 275,* 1599–1603.

Seidenberg, M. S., & Petitto, L. A. (1987). Communication, symbolic communication, and language: Comment on Savage-Rumbaugh, McDonald, Sevcik, Hopkins, & Rupert (1986). *Journal of Experimental Psychology: General, 116,* 279–287.

Seifer, R., Schiller, M., Samerof, A., Resnick, S., & Riordan, K. (1996). Attachment, maternal sensitivity, and infant temperament during the first year of life. *Developmental Psychology, 32,* 12–25.

Sekuler, R., & Blake, R. (1994). *Perception* (3rd ed.). New York: McGraw-Hill.

Seligman, L. (1975). Skin potential as an indicator of emotion. *Journal of Counseling Psychology, 22,* 489–493.

Seligman, M. E. P. (1971). Phobias and preparedness. *Behavior Therapy, 2,* 307–320.

Seligman, M. E. P. (1995). The effectiveness of psychotherapy: The Consumer Reports study. *American Psychologist, 50,* 965–974.

Seligman, M. E. P. (2002). *Authentic happiness: Using the new positive psychology to realize your potential for lasting fulfilment*. New York: Free Press.

Seljamo, S., Aromaa, M., Koivusilta, L., Rautava, P., Sourander, A., Helenius, H., et al. (2006). Alcohol use in families: A 15-year prospective follow-up study. *Addiction, 101,* 984–992.

Selman, R. L. (1980). *The growth of interpersonal understanding*. New York: Academic Press.

Selye, H. (1936). A syndrome produced by diverse nocuous agents. *Nature, 138,* 32.

Selye, H. (1976). *The stress of life*. New York: McGraw-Hill.

Serjeant, J. (2010, January 26). 'Avatar' becomes highest grossing movie. *Reuters*. Retrieved from http://www.reuters.com/article/idUSTRE60P63Y20100126

Serpell, L., Treasure, J., Teasdale, J., & Sullivan, V. (1999). Anorexia nervosa: Friend or foe? *International Journal of Eating Disorders, 25,* 177–186.

Serpell, R. (1989). Dimensions endogenes de l'intelligence chez les A-chewa et autres peuples africans. In J. Retschitzky, M. Bossel-Lagos, & P. Dasen (Eds.), *La recherche interculturelle*. Paris: L'Harmattan.

Serpell, R. (2007). Bridging between orthodox western higher educational practices and an African sociocultural context. *Comparative Education, 43*(1), 23–51.

Serpell, R., & Hatano, G. (1997). Education, schooling and literacy. In J. W. Berry, P. R. Dasen, & T. S. Sarawathi (Eds.), *Handbook of cross-cultural psychology: Vol. 2. Basic processes and human development*. Boston: Allyn and Bacon.

Sethi, S., & Seligman, M. (1993). Optimism and fundamentalism. *Psychological Science, 4,* 256–259.

Sewall, L., & Wooten, B. R. (1991). Stimulus determinants of achromatic constancy. *Journal of the Optical Society of America, 8,* 1794–1809.

Shackelford, T. K., Schmitt, D. P., & Buss, D. M. (2005). Universal dimensions of human mate preferences. *Personality and Individual Differences, 39,* 447–458.

Shallice, T., & Warrington, E. K. (1970). Independent functioning of verbal memory stores: A neuropsychological study. *Quarterly Journal of Experimental Psychology, 22,* 261–273.

Shantz, C. U. (1983). Social cognition. In J. H. Flavell & E. M. Markman (Eds.), *Handbook of child psychology: Vol. 3. Cognitive development*. New York: John Wiley.

Shapka, J. D., & Keating, D. P. (2005). Structure and change in self-concept during adolescence. *Canadian Journal of Behavioural Science, 37,* 83–96.

Shapley, R. (1995). Parallel neural pathways and visual function. In M. S. Gazzaniga (Ed.), *The cognitive neurosciences* (pp. 315–324). Cambridge, MA: MIT Press.

Sharman, S. J., Manning, C. G., & Garry, M. (2005). Explain this: Explaining events inflates confidence for those events. *Applied Cognitive Psychology, 19,* 67–74.

Shattuck, R. (1980). *The forbidden experiment: The story of the wild boy of Aveyron*. New York: Farrar Straus Giroux.

Shaughnessy, J. J., & Zechmeister, E. B. (1997). *Research methods in psychology* (4th ed.). Singapore: McGraw-Hill.

Shaughnessy, J. J., Zechmeister, E. B., & Zechmeister, J. S. (2000). *Research methods in psychology* (5th ed.). Boston: McGraw Hill.

Shaver, P., Hazan, C., & Bradshaw, D. (1988). Love as attachment. In R. J. Sterberg & M. L. Barnes (Eds.), *The psychology of love*. New Haven, CT: Yale University Press.

Shaver, P., Schwartz, J., Kirson, D., & O'Connor, G. (1987). Emotion knowledge: Further exploration of a prototype approach. *Journal of Personality and Social Psychology, 52,* 1061–1086.

Shaver, P. R., Collins, N., & Clark, C. L. (1996). Attachment styles and internal working models of self and relationship partners. In G. O. Fletcher & J. Fitness (Eds.), *Knowledge structures in close relationships: A social psychological approach* (pp. 25–61). Mahwah, NJ: Lawrence Erlbaum.

Shaver, P. R., & Mikulincer, M. (2005). Attachment theory and research: Resurrection of the psychodynamic approach to personality. *Journal of Research in Personality, 39,* 22–45.

Shaw, K., O'Rourke, P., Del Mar, C., & Kenardy, J. (2005). Psychological interventions for overweight or obesity. *Cochrane Database of Systematic Reviews,* 2(CD003818).

Shaywitz, B. A., Shaywitz, S. E., Pugh, K. R., Constable, R. T., Skudlarski, P., Fulbright, R. K., et al. (1995). Sex differences in the functional organization of the brain for language. *Nature, 373,* 607–609.

Shaywitz, S., Shaywitz, B., Pugh, K. R., Fulbright, R. K., Constable, R. T., Mencl, W. E., et al. (1998). Functional disruption in the organization of the brain for reading in dyslexia. *Proceedings of the National Academy of Sciences, USA, 95,* 2636–2641.

Shea, M., Glass, D., Pilkonis, P., Watkins, J., & Docherty, J. (1987). Frequency and implications of personality disorders in a sample of depressed outpatients. *Journal of Personality Disorders, 1,* 27–42.

Shea, M. T., Elkin, I., Imber, S., & Sotsky, S. (1992). Course of depressive symptoms over follow-up: Findings from the National Institute of Mental Health Treatment of Depression Collaborative Research Program. *Archives of General Psychiatry, 49,* 782–787.

Shearman, L. P., Jin, X., Lee, C., Reppert, S. M., & Weaver, D. R. (2000). Targeted disruption of the *mPer3* gene: Subtle effects on circadian clock function. *Molecular Cell Biology, 20,* 6269–6275.

Shedler, J. (2010). The efficacy of psychodynamic psychotherapy. *Psychotherapy in Australia, 16*(3), 38–51.

Shedler, J., & Block, J. (1990). Adolescent drug use and psychological health: A longitudinal inquiry. *American Psychologist, 45,* 612–630.

Shedler, J., Karliner, R., & Katz, E. (2003). Cloning the clinician: A method for assessing illusory mental health. *Journal of Clinical Psychology, 59*(6), 635–650.

Shedler, J., Mayman, M., & Manis, M. (1993). The illusion of mental health. *American Psychologist, 48,* 1117–1131.

Sheehy, G. (1976). *Passages*. New York: E. P. Dutton.

Shefler, G., Dasberg, H., & Ben-Shakhar, G. (1995). A randomized controlled outcome and follow-up study of Mann's time-limited psychotherapy. *Journal of Consulting and Clinical Psychology, 63,* 585–593.

Sheldon, S. H. (2005). Sleep in infants and children. In T. Lee-Chiong (Ed.), *Sleep: A comprehensive handbook* (pp. 507–510). Hoboken, NJ: John Wiley & Sons.

Sheline, Y. I. (2003). Neuroimaging studies of mood disorder effects on the brain. *Biological Psychiatry, 54*(3), 338–352.

Sheline, Y. I., Mittler, B. L., & Mintum, M. A. (2002). The hippocampus and depression. *European Psychiatry, 17,* 300s–305s.

Shepher, J. (1978). Reflections on the origins of human pair-bonds. *International Journal of Social and Biological Structures, 1,* 253–264.

Sherif, M., Harvey, O. J., White, J., Hood, W. R., & Sherif, C. W. (1961). *Intergroup conflict and cooperation: The Robber's Cave experiment*. Norman: University of Oklahoma Press.

Sherif, M., & Sherif, C. W. (1979). Research on intergroup relations. In W. G. Austin & S. Worchel (Eds.), *The social psychology of intergroup relations*. Monterey, CA: Brooks/Cole.

Sherwin, B. (1993). *Menopause myths and realities*. Washington, DC: American Psychiatric Press.

Shettleworth, S. J. (1988). Foraging as operant behavior and operant behavior as foraging: What have we learned? In G. H. Bower (Ed.), *The psychology of learning and motivation: Advances in research and theory: Vol. 22* (pp. 1–49). San Diego, CA: Academic Press.

Shevrin, H. (1980, April). Glimpses of the unconscious. *Psychology Today*, 128.

Shevrin, H., Bond, J., Brakel, L., Hertel, R., & Williams, W. J. (1996). *Conscious and unconscious processes: Psychodynamic, cognitive, and neurophysiological convergences*. New York: Guilford Press.

Shields, J. (1962). *Monozygotic twins brought up apart and brought together*. London: Oxford University Press.

Shimamura, A. P. (1995). Memory and frontal lobe function. In M. S. Gazzaniga (Ed.), *The cognitive neurosciences* (pp. 803–813). Cambridge, MA: MIT Press.

Shimizu, H., & LeVine, R. A. (Eds.). (2001). *Japanese frames of mind: Cultural perspectives on human development*. New York: Cambridge University Press.

Shiner, R. L. (2000). Linking childhood personality with adaptation: Evidence for continuity and change across time in late adolescence. *Journal of Personality and Social Psychology, 78,* 310–325.

Shire of Broome. (2006, May–August). *Condom tree report*. Retrieved from http://www.broome.wa.gov.au/council/pdf/attach/2006/September/20060928-935.pdf

Sholevar, G. P., & Schwoeri, L. D. (2003). *Textbook of family and couples therapy: Clinical applications*. Washington, DC: APA.

Shore, R. (1997). *Rethinking the brain*. New York: Families and Work Institute.

Shrout, P. E. (1997). Should significance tests be banned? *Psychological Science, 8*, 1–2.

Shultz, T. R., & Lepper, M. R. (1995). Cognitive dissonance reduction as constraint satisfaction. *Psychological Review, 103*, 219–240.

Shweder, R. A. (1980). Scientific thought and social cognition. In W. A. Collins (Ed.), *Development of cognition, affect, and social relations: Minnesota Symposium on Child Development: Vol. 13*. Hillsdale, NJ: Lawrence Erlbaum.

Shweder, R. A., & Bourne, E. J. (1982). Does the concept of the person vary cross-culturally? In A. J. Marsella & G. M. White (Eds.), *Cultural conceptions of mental health and therapy*. Boston: D. Reidel.

Sia, C., Tan, B. C. Y., & Wei, K. (2002). Group polarization and computer-mediated communication: Effects of communication cues, social presence, and anonymity. *Information Systems Research, 13*, 70–90.

Sibley, C. G., & Liu, J. H. (2004). Attitudes towards biculturalism in New Zealand: Social dominance and Pakeha attitudes towards the general principles and resource-specific aspects of bicultural policy. *New Zealand Journal of Psychology, 33*, 88–99.

Sibley, C. G., Hunt, M., & Harper, D. N. (2002). Identifying cross-cultural differences in the effectiveness of an information and free child seat rental program. *Behavior Change, 18*, 224–235.

Sibley, C. G., Robertson, A., & Kirkwood, S. (2005). Pakeha attitudes towards the symbolic and resource-specific aspects of bicultural policy in New Zealand: The legitimizing role of collective guilt for historical injustices. *New Zealand Journal of Psychology, 34*, 171–180.

Siegel, A., Roeling, T. A. P., Gregg, T. R., & Kruk, M. R. (1999). Neuropharmacology of brain-stimulation-evoked aggression. *Neuroscience and Biobehavioral Reviews, 23*, 359–389.

Siegel, R. K. (1990). *Intoxication*. New York: Pocket Books.

Siegel, S. (1984). Pavlonian conditioning and heroin overdose: Reports by overdose victims. *Bulletin of the Psychonomic Society, 22*, 428–430.

Siegel, S., Baptista, M. A. S., Kim, J. A., McDonald, R. V., & Weise-Kelly, L. (2000). Pavlovian psychopharmacology: The associative basis of tolerance. *Experimental and Clinical Psychopharmacology, 8*, 276–293.

Siegfried, Z., Berry, E. M., Hao, S., & Avraham, Y. (2003). Animal models in the investigation of anorexia. *Physiology and Behavior, 79*, 39–45.

Siegler, I. C., Bastian, L. A., Steffans, D. C., Bosworth, H. B., & Costa, P. T. (2002). Behavioral medicine and aging. *Journal of Consulting and Clinical Psychology, 70*, 843–851.

Siegler, R. S. (1991). *Children's thinking* (2nd ed.). Englewood Cliffs, NJ: Prentice-Hall.

Siegler, R. S. (1996). *Emerging minds: The process of change in children's thinking*. New York: Oxford University Press.

Siegler, R. S. (2000). Unconscious insights. *Current Direction in Psychological Science, 9*, 79–83.

Siegler, R. S. (2007). Cognitive variability. *Developmental Science, 10*, 104–109.

Siegler, R. S., & Ellis, S. (1996). Piaget on childhood. *Psychological Science, 7*, 211–215.

Sifneos, P. (1973). The prevalence of alexithymic characteristics in psychosomatic patients. *Psychotherapy and Psychosomatics, 22*, 255–262.

Sifneos, P. (1987). *Short-term dynamic psychotherapy: Evaluation and technique* (2nd ed.). New York: Plenum Press.

Sigall, H., Page, R., & Brown, A. C. (1971). Effort expenditure as a function of evaluation and evaluator attractiveness. *Representative Research in Social Psychology, 2*, 19–25.

Sigelman, C. K., & Rider, E. A. (2006). *Life-span: Human development* (5th ed.). Belmont, CA: Thomson Wadsworth.

Sigelman, C. K., & Rider, E. A. (2009). *Life-span human development* (6th ed.). Belmont, CA: Wadsworth Cengage Learning.

Sillars, A. L., & Zietlow, P. (1993). Investigations of marital communication and lifespan development. In N. Coupland & J. Nussbaum (Eds.), *Discourse and lifespan identity: Language and language behaviors: Vol. 4* (pp. 237–261). Newbury Park, CA: Sage.

Silva, P. A., & Stanton, W. (1996). *From child to adult: The Dunedin study*. Oxford, UK: Oxford University Press.

Sim, H. (2000). Relationship of daily hassles and social support to depression and antisocial behavior among early adolescents. *Journal of Youth and Adolescence, 29*, 647–659.

Simmons, L. W. (1990). Pheromonal cues for the recognition of kin by female field crickets, Gryllus bimaculatus. *Animal Behaviour, 40*, 192–195.

Simmons, R. (2002). *Odd girl out*. New York: Harcourt.

Simon, D., & Holyoak, K. J. (2002). Structural dynamics of cognition: From consistency theories to constraint satisfaction. *Personality and Social Psychology Review, 6*, 283–294.

Simon, G. E., Von Korff, M., Saunders, K., Miglioretti, D. L., Crane, P. K., van Belle, G., et al. (2006). Association between obesity and psychiatric disorders in the US adult population. *Archives of General Psychiatry, 63*, 824–830.

Simon, H. (1990). Invariants of human behavior. *Annual Review of Psychology, 41*, 1–19.

Simon, H. A. (1978). Information-processing theory of human problem solving. In W. K. Estes (Ed.), *Handbook of learning and cognitive processes*. Hillsdale, NJ: Lawrence Erlbaum.

Simonoff, E., Bolton, P., & Rutter, M. (1998). Genetic perspectives on mental retardation. In J. A. Burack, R. M. Hodapp, & E. Zigler (Eds.), *Handbook of mental retardation and development* (pp. 41–79). New York: Cambridge University Press.

Simons, H. W., Berkowitz, N. N., & Moyer, R. J. (1970). Similarity, credibility, and attitude change: A review and a theory. *Psychological Bulletin, 73*, 1–16.

Simonton, D. K. (1994). *Greatness: Who makes history and why?* New York: Guilford Press.

Simonton, D. K. (1997). Creative productivity: A predictive and explanatory model of career trajectories and landmarks. *Psychological Review, 104*, 66–89.

Simpson, J., Gangestad, S., & Lerma, M. (1990). Perception of physical attractiveness: Mechanisms involved in the maintenance of romantic relationships. *Journal of Personality and Social Psychology, 59*, 1192–1201.

Sinclair, S., Dunn, E., & Lowery, B. S. (2005). The relationship between parental racial attitudes and children's implicit prejudice. *Journal of Experimental Social Psychology, 41*, 283–289.

Sinclair-Gieben, A. H., & Chalmers, D. (1959). Evaluation of treatment of warts by hypnosis. *Lancet, 2*, 480–482.

Singer, J. A. (1992). Challenges to the integration of the psychoanalytic and cognitive perspectives on the self. *Psychological Inquiry, 3*(1), 59–61.

Singer, J. L. (1975). *The inner world of daydreaming*. New York: Harper & Row.

Singer, J. L. (1990). *Repression and dissociation: Implications for personality theory, psychopathology, and health*. Chicago: University of Chicago Press.

Singer, J. L. (2006). Epilogue: Learning to play and learning through play. In D. G. Singer, R. M. Michnick, & K. Hirsh-Pasek (Eds.), *Play = learning: How play motivates and enhances children's cognitive and social-emotional growth* (pp. 251–262). New York: Oxford University Press.

Singer, J. L., & Singer, D. G. (1981). *Television, imagination, and aggression: A study of preschoolers*. Hillsdale, NJ: Lawrence Erlbaum.

Singh, B. S. (1998). Managing somatoform disorders. *Medical Journal of Australia, 168*, 572–577.

Sivers, H., Schooler, J., & Freyd, J. J. (2002). Recovered memories. *Encyclopedia of the Human Brain, 4*, 169–184.

Skeels, H. M. (1966). Adult states of children with contrasting early life experiences: A follow-up study. *Monographs of the Society for Research in Child Development, 31*(Serial No. 105), 70.

Skemp, R. R. (1976). Relational understanding and instrumental understanding. *Mathematics Teaching, 77*, 20–26.

Skinner, B. F. (1938). *The behavior of organisms*. New York: Appleton-Century-Crofts.

Skinner, B. F. (1948). *Walden two*. New York: Macmillan.

Skinner, B. F. (1951). How to teach animals. *Scientific American, 185*, 26–29.

Skinner, B. F. (1953). *Science and human behavior*. New York: Macmillan.

Skinner, B. F. (1957). *Verbal behavior*. New York: Appleton-Century-Crofts.

Skinner, B. F. (1977). Hernstein and the evolution of behaviorism. *American Psychologist, 32*, 1006–1012.

Skodak, M., & Skeels, H. M. (1949). A final follow-up study of one hundred adopted children. *Journal of Genetic Psychology, 75*, 85–125.

Skoog, G., & Skoog, I. (1999). A 40-year followup of patients with obsessive-compulsive disorder. *Archives of General Psychiatry, 56*, 121–127.

Skowronski, J. J., & Lawrence, M. A. (2001). A comparative study of the implicit and explicit gender attitudes of children and college students. *Psychology of Women Quarterly, 25*, 155–165.

Slaby, R. G., & Frey, K. S. (1976). Development of gender constancy and selective attention to same-sex models. *Child Development, 46*, 849–856.

Slade, L. A., & Rush, M. C. (1991). Achievement motivation and the dynamics of task difficulty choices. *Journal of Personality and Social Psychology, 60*, 165–172.

Slater, C. L. (2003). Generativity versus stagnation: An elaboration of Erikson's adult stage of human development. *Journal of Adult Development, 10*, 53–65.

Slater, M., Antley, A., Davison, A., Swapp, D., Guger, C., Barker, C., et al. (2006). A virtual reprise of the Stanley Milgram obedience experiments. *PLoS ONE, 1*(1), e39.

Slaughter, V., Peterson, C. C., & Macklntosh, E. (2007). Mind what mother says: Narrative input and theory of mind in typical children and those on the autism spectrum. *Child Development, 78*(3), 839–858.

Slaughter, V. P., Heron, M., & Sim, S. (2002). Development of preferences for the human body shape in infancy. *Cognition, 85*, B71–B81.

Slavin, R. E., & Cooper, R. (1999). Improving intergroup relations: Lessons learned from cooperative learning programs. *Journal of Social Issues, 55*(4), 647–664.

Sleep Disorders Australia. (2006). *Insomnia*. Retrieved October 3, 2009, from http://www.sleepoz.org.au/images/FactSheets/AT04-Insomnia.pdf

Sleep Studies. (2009). *Infant sleep study*. Retrieved October 3, 2009, from http://www.rch.org.au/ccch/research.cfm?doc_id=10629#ISS

Sloboda, J. A., Hermelin, B., & O'Connor, N. (1985). An exceptional music memory. *Music Perception, 3*, 155–169.

Slochower, J. (1987). The psychodynamics of obesity: A review. *Psychoanalytic Psychology, 4*, 145–159.

Slutske, W. S., Heath, A. C., Dinwiddie, S. H., Madden, P. A. F., Bucholz, K. K., Dunne, M. P., et al. (1997). Modeling genetic and environmental influences in the etiology of conduct disorder: A study of 2682 adult twin pairs. *Journal of Abnormal Psychology, 106*, 266–279.

Smith, A. (1759). *A theory of moral sentiments*. Cambridge: Cambridge University Press.

Smith, A., Agius, P., Mitchell, A., Barrett, C., & Pitts, M. (2009). *Secondary students and sexual health: Results of the 4th national survey of Australian secondary students, HIV/AIDS and sexual health* (Monograph Series No. 70). Retrieved from http://www.latrobe.edu.au/arcshs/assets/downloads/reports/SSASH_2008_Final_Report.pdf

Smith, C., & Lloyd, B. (1978). Maternal behavior and perceived sex of infant: Revisited. *Child Development, 49,* 1263–1265.

Smith, C. A., & Ellsworth, P. (1985). Patterns of cognitive appraisal in emotion. *Journal of Personality and Social Psychology, 48,* 813–838.

Smith, D. E., & Seymour, R. B. (1994). LSD: History and toxicity. *Psychiatric Annals, 24,* 145–147.

Smith, E. E. (1995). Concepts and categorization. In E. E. Smith & D. N. Osherson (Eds.), *Thinking: An invitation to cognitive science: Vol. 3* (2nd ed., pp. 3–33). Cambridge, MA: MIT Press.

Smith, E. E. (2000). Neural bases of human working memory. *Current Directions in Psychological Science, 6,* 45–49.

Smith, E. E., Jonides, J., & Koeppe, R. A. (1996). Dissociating verbal and spatial working memory using PET. *Cerebral Cortex, 6,* 11–20.

Smith, E. E., Patalano, A. L., & Jonides, J. (1998). Alternative strategies of categorization. *Cognition, 65,* 167–196.

Smith, E. R. (1998). Mental representation and memory. In D. T. Gilbert, S. T. Fiske, & G. Lindzey (Eds.), *The handbook of social psychology: Vol. 2* (4th ed., pp. 391–445). Boston: McGraw-Hill.

Smith, J. A., Hauenstein, N. M. A., & Buchanan, L. B. (1996). Goal setting and exercise performance. *Human Performance, 9,* 141–154.

Smith, J. A., & Knight, R. G. (2002). Memory processing in Alzheimer's disease. *Neuropsychologia, 40,* 666–682.

Smith, J. W., Positano, S., Stocks, N., & Shearman, D. (2009). *A new way of thinking about our climate crisis: The rational-comprehensive approach.* Lewiston, NY: Edwin Mellen Press.

Smith, L. T. (1999). *Decolonising methodologies: Research and indigenous peoples.* Dunedin, New Zealand: University of Otago Press.

Smith, M. B. (1978). Perspectives on self-hood. *American Psychologist, 33,* 1053–1063.

Smith, M. B. (1988). *Can there be a human science?* Symposium of the American Psychological Association, Atlanta, GA.

Smith, M. B. (1994). Selfhood at risk: Postmodern perils and the perils of postmodernism. *American Psychologist, 49,* 405–411.

Smith, M. L., & Glass, G. V. (1977). Meta-analysis of psychotherapy outcome studies. *American Psychologist, 32,* 752–760.

Smith, M. L., Glass, G. V., & Miller, R. L. (1980). *The benefits of psychotherapy.* Baltimore: John Hopkins University Press.

Smith, M. W., Sharit, J., & Czaja, S. J. (1999). Aging, motor control, and the performance of computer mouse tasks. *Human Factors, 41,* 389–396.

Smith, P. K., & Daglish, L. (1977). Sex differences in parent and infant behavior. *Child Development, 48,* 1250–1254.

Smith, P. J., & Smith, S. N. (1999). Differences between Chinese and Australian students: Some implications for distance educators. *Distance Education, 20*(1), 64–80.

Smith, R. E. (2003). The cost of remembering to remember in event-based prospective memory: Investigating the capacity demands of delayed intention performance. *Journal of Experimental Psychology: Learning, Memory, and Cognition, 29,* 347–361.

Smith, R. E., & Swinyard, W. R. (1983). Attitude–behavior consistency: The impact of product trial versus advertising. *Journal of Marketing Research, 20,* 257–267.

Smith, S. L., & Donnerstein, E. (1998). Harmful effects of exposure to media violence: learning of aggression, emotional desensitization, and fear. In R. G. Geen & E. Donnerstein (Eds.), *Human aggression: Theories, research, and implications for social policy* (pp. 167–202). San Diego, CA: Academic Press.

Smith, S. M., & Petty, R. E. (1995). Personality moderators of mood congruency effects on cognition: The role of self-esteem and negative mood regulation. *Journal of Personality and Social Psychology, 68,* 1092–1107.

Smith, T. B. (Ed.). (2004). Practicing multiculturalism: Affirming diversity in counseling and psychology. *Journal of Rehabilitation, 71*(4), 48–50.

Smith Castro, V. (2003). *Acculturation and psychological adaptation.* London: Greenwood Press.

Smolak, L. (2009). Risk factors for the development of body image, eating problems and obesity. In L. Smolak & J. K. Thompson (Eds.), *Body image, eating disorders, and obesity in youth: Assessment, prevention and treatment* (2nd ed., Chap. 7, pp. 135–155). Washington, DC: American Psychological Association.

Smolensky, P. (1988). On the proper treatment of connectionism. *Behavioral and Brain Sciences, 11,* 1–74.

Smotherman, W. P., & Robinson, S. R. (1996). The development of behavior before birth. *Developmental Psychology, 32,* 425–434.

Sneed, C. D., & Morisky, D. E. (1998). Applying the theory of reasoned action to condom use amongst sex workers. *Social Behavior and Personality, 26*(4), 317–328. Retrieved from http://findarticles.com/p/articles/mi_qa3852/is_199801/ai_n8796585/

Snow, P. C., & Bruce, D. D. (2003). Cigarette smoking in teenage girls: Exploring the role of peer reputations, self-concept and coping. *Health Education Research, 18*(4), 439–452.

Snyder, A. W., Mulcahy, E., Taylor, J. L., Mitchell, D. J., Sachdev, P., & Gandevia, S. C. (2003). Savant-like skills exposed in normal people by suppressing the left fronto-temporal lobe. *Journal of Integrative Neuroscience,* 2(2), 149–158.

Snyder, C. R., & Ingram, R. E. (2000). *Handbook of psychological change: Psychotherapy processes and practices for the 21st century.* New York: Wiley.

Snyder, D. K., Wills, R. M., & Grady-Fletcher, A. (1991). Long-term effectiveness of behavioral versus insight-oriented marital therapy: A 4-year follow-up study. *Journal of Consulting and Clinical Psychology, 59,* 138–141.

Snyder, M. (1974). Self-monitoring of expressive behavior. *Journal of Personality and Social Psychology, 30,* 526–537.

Snyder, M., & Cantor, N. (1979). Testing hypotheses about other people: The use of historical knowledge. *Journal of Experimental Social Psychology, 15,* 330–342.

Snyder, M., & Ickes, W. (1985). In G. Lindzey & E. Aronson (Eds.), *Handbook of social psychology.* Reading, MA: Addison-Wesley.

Snyder, M., Tanke, E. D., & Berscheid, E. (1977). Social perception and interpersonal behavior: On the self-fulfilling nature of social stereotypes. *Journal of Personality and Social Psychology, 35,* 656–666.

Sobal, J., & Stunkard, A. (1989). Socioeconomic status and obesity: A review of the literature. *Psychological Bulletin, 105,* 260–275.

Soh, N. L., Touyz, S. W., & Surgenor, L. J. (2006). Eating and body image disturbances across cultures: A review. *European Eating Disorders Review, 14,* 54–65.

Sohlberg, S., & Strober, M. (1994). Personality in anorexia nervosa: An update and a theoretical integration. *Acta Psychiatrica Scandinavica, 89*(Suppl. 37), 16.

Solmon, M. A. (2006). Goal theory in physical education classes: Examining goal profiles to understand achievement motivation. *International Journal of Sport and Exercise Psychology, 4*(3), 325–346.

Solomon, L. Z., Solomon, H., & Maiorca, J. (1982). The effects of bystander's anonymity, situational ambiguity, and victim's status on helping. *Journal of Social Psychology, 117,* 285–294.

Solomon, S., Greenberg, J., & Pyszczynski, T. (1991). A terror management theory of social behavior: The psychological functions of self-esteem and cultural worldviews. *Advances in Experimental Social Psychology, 24,* 93–159.

Somer, O., & Goldberg, L. (1999). The structure of Turkish traits—descriptive adjectives. *Journal of Personality and Social Psychology, 76,* 431–450.

Somers, J. M., Goldner, E. M., Waraich, P., & Hsu, L. (2006). Prevalence and incidence studies of anxiety disorders: A systematic review of the literature. *Canadian Journal of Psychiatry, 51*(2), 100–113.

Sorensen, L. B., Moller, P., Flint, A., Martens, M., & Raben, A. (2003). Effect of sensory perception of foods on appetite and food intake: A review of studies on humans. *International Journal of Obesity, 27,* 1152–1166.

Sorensen, P. W. (1996). Biological responsiveness to pheromones provides fundamental and unique insight into olfactory function. *Chemical Senses, 21,* 245–256.

Sorrentino, R. M., & Higgins, E. T. (Eds.). (1996). *Handbook of motivation and cognition: Vol. 3. The interpersonal context.* New York: Guilford Press.

Souchay, C., Isingrini, M., & Espagnet, L. (2000). Aging, episodic memory feeling-of-knowing, and frontal functioning. *Neuropsychology, 14,* 299–309.

Spain, D. (Ed.). (1992). *Psychoanalytic anthropology after Freud.* New York: Psyche Press.

Spalding, L. R., & Hardin, C. D. (1999). Unconscious unease and self-handicapping: Behavioural consequences of individual differences in implicit and explicit self-esteem. *Psychological Science, 10,* 535–539.

Spanos, N. P., Burgess, C. A., Wallace-Capretta, S., & Ouaida, N. (1996). Simulation, surreptitious observation and the modification of hypnotizability: Two tests of the compliance hypothesis. *Contemporary Hypnosis, 13,* 161–176.

Spanos, N. P., Stenstrom, R. J., & Johnston, J. C. (1988). Hypnosis, placebo, and suggestion in the treatment of warts. *Psychosomatic Medicine, 50,* 245–260.

Spearman, C. (1904). General intelligence, objectively determined and measured. *American Journal of Psychology, 15,* 201–293.

Spearman, C. (1927). *The abilities of man: Their nature and measurement.* New York: Macmillan.

Speelman, C. P., & Kirsner, K. (2005). *Beyond the learning curve: The construction of mind.* Oxford: Oxford University Press.

Speicher, B. (1994). Family patterns of moral judgement during adolescence and early adulthood. *Developmental Psychology, 30,* 624–632.

Spelke, E., Hirst, W., & Neisser, U. (1976). Skills of divided attention. *Cognition, 4,* 215–230

Spence, A. P. (1989). *Biology of human aging.* Englewood Cliffs, NJ: Prentice-Hall.

Spence, S. A., Liddle, P. F., Stefan, M. D., Hellewell, J. S. E., Sharma, T., Friston, K. J., et al. (2000). Functional anatomy of verbal fluency in people with schizophrenia and those at genetic risk: Focal dysfunction and distributed disconnectivity reappraised. *British Journal of Psychiatry, 176,* 52–60.

Spencer, J. P., Blumberg, M. S., McMurray, B., Robinson, S. R., Samuelson, L. K., & Tomblin, J. B. (2009). Short arms and talking eggs: Why we should no longer abide the nativist-empiricist debate. *Child Development Perspectives, 3*(2), 79.

Spencer, M. B., & Markstrom-Adams, C. (1990). Identity processes among racial and ethnic minority children in America. *Child Development, 61,* 290–310.

Sperling, G. (1960). The information available in brief visual presentations. *Psychological Monographs, 74,* 1–29.

Sperry, R. (1984). Consciousness, personal identity and the divided brain. *Neuropsychologia, 22,* 661–673.

Spiegel, D. (1999). Healing words — emotional expression and disease outcome. *Journal of the American Medical Association, 281,* 1328–1329.

Spiegel, D., & Kato, P. M. (1996). Psychological influences on cancer incidence and progression. *Harvard Review of Psychiatry, 4,* 10–26.

Spijker, J., de Graaf, R., Bijl, R. V., Beekman, R. T. F., Ormel, J., & Nolen, W. A. (2002). Duration of major depressive episodes in the general population: Results from the Netherlands mental health survey and incidence study (NEMESIS). *British Journal of Psychiatry, 181*, 208–213.

Spillman, L. (1994). The Mermann grid illusion: A tool for studying human perceptive field organization. *Perception, 23*, 691–708.

Spirduso, W., & MacRae, P. (1990). Motor performance and aging. In J. E. Birren & K. W. Schaie (Eds.), *Handbook of the psychology of aging* (3rd ed.). New York: Van Nostrand Reinhold.

Spiro, M. (1965). *Context and meaning in cultural anthropology*. New York: Free Press.

Spitz, R. A. (1945). Hospitalism: An inquiry into the genesis of psychiatry conditions in early childhood. *Psychoanalytic Study of the Child, 1*, 53–74.

Spitzer, R. L. (1985). DSM-III and the politics-science dichotomy syndrome: A response to Thomas E. Schacht's 'DSM-III and the politics of truth'. *American Psychologist, 40*, 522–526.

Sporer, S., Malpass, R., & Koehnken, G. (Eds.). (1996). *Psychological issues in eyewitness identification*. Mahwah, NJ: Lawrence Erlbaum.

Sprecher, S., & Regan, P. C. (2002). Liking some things (in some people) more than others: Partner preferences in romantic relationships and friendships. *Journal of Social and Personal Relationships, 19*, 463–481.

Squier, L. H., & Domhoff, G. W. (1998). The presentation of dreaming and dreams in introductory psychology textbooks: A critical examination with suggestions for textbook authors and course instructors. *Dreaming: Journal of the Association for the Study of Dreams, 8*, 149–168.

Squire, L. R. (1986). Mechanisms of memory. *Science, 232*, 1612–1619.

Squire, L. R. (1987). *Memory and brain*. New York: Oxford University.

Squire, L. R. (1989). On the course of forgetting in very long-term memory. *Journal of Experimental Psychology: Learning, Memory, and Cognition, 15*, 241–245.

Squire, L. R. (1992). Declarative and nondeclarative memory: Multiple brain systems supporting learning and memory. *Journal of Cognitive Neuroscience, 4*, 232–243.

Squire, L. R. (1995). Memory and brain systems. In R. D. Broadwell (Ed.), *Neuroscience, memory, and language. Decade of the brain: Vol. 1* (pp. 59–75). Washington, DC: U.S. Government Printing Office.

Squire, L. R., & Zola-Morgan, S. (1991). The medial temporal lobe memory system. *Science, 253*, 1380–1386.

Srinivas, K., Breedin, S. D., Coslett, H. B., & Saffran, E. M. (1997). Intact perceptual priming in a patient with damage to the anterior inferior temporal lobes. *Journal of Cognitive Neuroscience, 9*, 490–511.

Srinivasan, M., & Hilty, D. M. (2006). Teaching and helping others to learn. In L. W. Roberts & D. M. Hilty (Eds.), *Handbook of career development in academic psychiatry and behavioural sciences* (pp. 157–181). Washington, DC: American Psychiatric Publishing.

Srivastava, A., Borries, C., & Sommer, V. (1991). Homosexual mounting in free-ranging female langurs (Presbytis entellus-R). *Archives of Sexual Behavior, 20*, 487–512.

Sroufe, L. A., & Waters, E. (1977). Heart rate as a convergent measure in clinical and developmental research. *Merrill Palmer Quarterly, 23*, 3–27.

Staal, W. G., Hulshoff Pol, H. E., Schnack, H. G., Hoogendoorn, M. L. C., Jellema, K., & Kahn, R. S. (2000). Structural brain abnormalities in patients with schizophrenia and their healthy siblings. *American Journal of Psychiatry, 157*, 416–421.

Stacy, A. W. (1997). Memory activation and expectancy as prospective predictors of alcohol and marijuana use. *Journal of Abnormal Psychology, 106*, 61–73.

Stadler, M. A., & Frensch, P. A. (1998). *Handbook of implicit learning*. London: Sage.

Stallings, M., Hewitt, J., Cloninger, C. R., Heath, A. C., & Eaves, L. J. (1996). Genetic and environmental structure of the tridimensional personality questionnaire: Three or four temperament dimensions? *Journal of Personality and Social Psychology, 70*, 127–140.

Stankov, L. (1988). Aging, attention, and intelligence. *Psychology and Aging, 3*, 59–74.

Stankov, L. (1998). Intelligence arguments and Australian psychology. *Australian Psychologist, 33*, 53–57.

Stankov, L. (2000). Intelligence debates and some Australian confusions. *Australian Psychologist, 35*, 73–76.

Stankov, L., Boyle, G. J., & Cattell, R. B. (1995). Models and paradigms in personality and intelligence research. In D. Saklofske & M. Zeidner (Eds.), *International handbook of personality and intelligence. Perspectives on individual differences* (pp. 15–43). New York: Plenum Press.

Stankov, L., & Lee, J. (2008). Culture: Ways of thinking and believing. In G. J. Boyle, G. Matthews, & D. H. Saklofske (Eds.), *The Sage handbook of personality theory and assessment: Vol. 1. Personality theories and models* (pp. 560–575). London: Sage Publications.

Stanley, F. (2009). *The greatest injustice: Why we have failed to improve the health of Aboriginal people*. Adelaide, Australia: The Bob Hawke Prime Ministerial Centre.

Stanley, M. A., Beck, J. G., Novy, D. M., Averill, P. M., Swann, A. C., Diefenbach, G. J., et al. (2003). Cognitive–behavioral treatment of late-life generalized anxiety disorder. *Journal of Consulting and Clinical Psychology, 71*, 309–319.

Stapinski, L. A., Abbott, M. J., & Rapee, R. M. (2010). Evaluating the cognitive avoidance model of generalised anxiety disorder: Impact of worry on threat appraisal, perceived control and anxious arousal. *Behaviour Research and Therapy, 48*, 1032–1040.

Stathis, H., Eyland, S., & Bertram, S. (1991). *Patterns of drug use amongst NSW prison receptions* (Report No. 23). Sydney, Australia, Department of Corrective Services.

Statistics Canada. (2010). *Homicide offences, number and rate, by province and territory*. Retrieved from http://www.statcan.gc.ca/

Statistics New Zealand. (2002). *2001 Census of population and dwellings: Ethnic groups*. Wellington, New Zealand: Author.

Statistics New Zealand. (2006). *Marriages, civil unions and divorces year ended December 2006*. Wellington, New Zealand: New Zealand Government.

Statistics New Zealand. (2007). *Profile of New Zealander responses, ethnicity questions: 2006 census*. Wellington, New Zealand: New Zealand Government.

Statistics New Zealand. (2010). *New Zealand in profile: 2010*. Retrieved from http://www.stats.govt.nz/browse_for_stats/Corporate/Corporate/nz-in-profile-2010/summary.aspx

Stattin, H., & Magnusson, D. (1989). The role of early aggressive behavior in the frequency, seriousness, and types of later crime. *Journal of Consulting and Clinical Psychology, 57*, 710–718.

Steele, C. M. (1988). The psychology of self-affirmation: Sustaining the integrity of the self. In L. Berkowitz (Ed.), *Advances in experimental social psychology: Vol. 21. Social psychological studies of the self: Perspectives and programs* (pp. 261–302). San Diego, CA: Academic Press.

Steele, H., Steele, M., & Fonagy, P. (1996). Associations among attachment classifications of mothers, fathers, and their infants. *Child Development, 67*, 541–555.

Stein, B. E., & Meredith, M. A. (1990). Multisensory integration: Neural and behavioral solutions for dealing with stimuli from different sensory modalities. *Annals of the New York Academy of Sciences, 608*, 51–70.

Stein, D. J. (Ed.). (2004). *Clinical manual of anxiety disorders*. Washington, DC: APA.

Stein, J. A., & Newcomb, M. D. (1999). Adult outcomes of adolescent conventional and agentic orientations: A 20-year longitudinal study. *The Journal of Early Adolescence, 19*, 39–65.

Stein, T. S., & Kwan, J. (1999). Thriving in a busy practice: Physician–patient communication training. *Effective Clinical Practice, 2*, 63–70.

Steinberg, L., Lamborn, S. D., Darling, N., & Mounts, N. S. (1994). Over-time changes in adjustment and competence among adolescents from authoritative, authoritarian, indulgent, and neglectful families. *Child Development, 65*, 754–770.

Steinberg, L., & Sheffield Morris, A. (2001). Adolescent development. *Annual Review of Psychology, 52*, 83–110.

Steiner, I. D. (1972). *Group processes and productivity*. New York: Academic Press.

Steinhausen, H. C., & Spohr, H. L. (1998). Long-term outcome of children with fetal alcohol syndrome: Psychopathology, behavior, and intelligence. *Alcohol Clinical Experimental Research, 22*, 334–338.

Steinhausen, H. C., Willms, J., & Spohr, H. L. (1993). Long-term psychopathological and cognitive outcome of children with fetal alcohol syndrome. *Journal of the American Academy of Child and Adolescent Psychiatry, 32*, 990–994.

Stephan, W. (1987). Intergroup relations. In G. Lindzey & E. Aronson (Eds.), *Handbook of social psychology: Vol. 2*. New York: Random House.

Stephan, W. G. (1987). The contact hypothesis in intergroup relations. In C. Hendrick (Ed.), *Group processes and intergroup relations. Review of personality and social psychology: Vol. 9* (pp. 13–40). Beverly Hills, CA: Sage.

Stephens, D. W., & Krebs, J. R. (1986). *Foraging theory*. Princeton, NJ: Princeton University Press.

Stephens, R. S., Roffman, R. A., & Curtin, L. (2000). Comparison of extended versus brief treatments for marijuana use. *Journal of Consulting and Clinical Psychology, 68*, 898–908.

Stephenson, M. T., Benoit, W. L., & Tschida, D. A. (2001). Testing the mediating role of cognitive responses in the elaboration likelihood model. *Communication Studies, 52*, 324–337.

Stepper, S., & Strack, F. (1993). Proprioceptive determinants of emotional and nonemotional feelings. *Journal of Personality and Social Psychology, 64*, 211–220.

Stern, D. (1985). *The interpersonal world of the infant*. New York: Basic Books.

Stern, K., & McClintock, M. K. (1998). Regulation of ovulation by human pheromones. *Nature, 392*, 177–179.

Sternbach, R. A. (1968). *Pain: A psychophysiological analysis*. New York: Academic Press.

Sternberg, R. J. (Ed.). (1984). *Mechanisms of cognitive development*. New York: Freeman.

Sternberg, R. J. (1985a). *Beyond IQ: A triarchic theory of human intelligence*. New York: Cambridge University Press.

Sternberg, R. J. (1985b). Implicit theories of intelligence, creativity, and wisdom. *Journal of Personality and Social Psychology, 49*, 607–627.

Sternberg, R. J. (1985c). Human intelligence: The model is the message. *Science, 230*, 1111–1118.

Sternberg, R. J. (1987). *The triangle of love: Intimacy, passion, commitment*. New York: Basic Books.

Sternberg, R. J. (1988a). Triangulating love. In R. Sternberg & M. L. Barnes (Eds.), *The psychology of love*. New Haven, CT: Yale University Press.

Sternberg, R. J. (1988b). *The triarchic mind: A new theory of human intelligence*. New York: Viking.

Sternberg, R. J. (1996). Costs of expertise. In K. A. Ericsson (Ed.), *The road to excellence: The acquisition of expert performance in the arts and sciences, sports, and games* (pp. 347–354). Hinsdale, NJ: Lawrence Erlbaum.

Sternberg, R. J. (1997). The triarchic theory of intelligence. In D. P. Flanagan, J. L. Genshaft, & P. L. Harrison (Eds.), *Contemporary intellectual assessment: Theories, tests, and issues* (pp. 92–104). New York: Guilford Press.

Sternberg, R. J. (1998). *Handbook of creativity*. New York: Cambridge University Press.

Sternberg, R. J. (1999a). Looking back and looking forward on intelligence: Toward a theory of successful intelligence. In M. Bennett (Ed.), *Developmental psychology: Achievements and prospects* (pp. 289–308). Philadelphia: Psychology Press/Taylor & Francis.

Sternberg, R. J. (1999b). The theory of successful intelligence. *Review of General Psychology, 3,* 292–316.

Sternberg, R. J. (2000a). *Handbook of intelligence*. New York: Cambridge University Press.

Sternberg, R. J. (2000b). The concept of intelligence. In R. J. Sternberg (Ed.), *Handbook of intelligence* (pp. 3–15). New York: Cambridge University Press.

Sternberg, R. J. (2001). Teaching problem solving as a way of life. In A. L. Costa (Ed.), *Developing minds: A resource book for teaching thinking*. New York: Association for Supervision and Curriculum Development.

Sternberg, R. J. (2004a). North American approaches to intelligence. In R. J. Sternberg (Ed.), *International handbook of intelligence* (pp. 411–436). New York: Cambridge University Press.

Sternberg, R. J. (2004b). Culture and intelligence. *American Psychologist, 59,* 325–338.

Sternberg, R. J., Forsythe, G. B., Hedlund, J., Horvath, J., Snook, S., Williams, W. M., et al. (2000). *Practical intelligence in everyday life*. New York: Cambridge University Press.

Sternberg, R. J., & O'Hara, L. A. (2000). Intelligence and creativity. In R. J. Sternberg (Ed.), *Handbook of intelligence* (pp. 611–630). New York: Cambridge University Press.

Sternberg, R. J., & Salter, W. (1982). Conceptions of intelligence. In R. J. Sternberg (Ed.), *Handbook of human intelligence* (pp. 3–28). New York: Cambridge University Press.

Sternberg, R. J., & Wagner, R. K. (1993). The geocentric view of intelligence and job performance is wrong. *Current Directions in Psychological Science, 2,* 1–5.

Sternberg, R. J., & Yang, S. (1997). Taiwanese Chinese people's conceptions of intelligence. *Intelligence, 25*(1), 21–36.

Sternberg, S. (1975). Memory scanning: New findings and current controversies. *Quarterly Journal of Experimental Psychology, 27,* 1–32.

Stevens, C. F. (1979). The neuron. *Scientific American, 241,* 54–65.

Stevens, J. R. (2002). Schizophrenia: Reproductive hormones and the brain. *American Journal of Psychiatry, 159*(5), 713–719.

Stevens, S. S. (1956). The direct estimation of sensory magnitudes — loudness. *American Journal of Psychology, 69,* 1–25.

Stevens, S. S. (1961). Psychophysics of sensory function. In W. Rosenblith (Ed.), *Sensory communication* (pp. 1–33). Cambridge, MA: MIT Press.

Stevens, S. S. (1975). *Psychophysics: Introduction to its perceptual, neural, and social prospects*. New York: John Wiley.

Stevens, S. S., & Newman, E. B. (1934). The localization of pure tone. *Proceedings of the National Academy of Sciences, USA, 20,* 593–596.

Stevenson, R. J., Case, T. I., & Boakes, R. A. (2005). Implicit and explicit tests of odour memory reveal different outcomes following interference. *Learning and Motivation, 36,* 353–373.

Stevenson-Hinde, J., & Verschueren, K. (2002). Attachment in childhood. In P. K. Smith & C. H. Hart (Eds.), *Blackwell handbook of childhood social development* (pp. 182–204). Malden, MA: Blackwell.

Stewart, D., & Harmon, K. (2004). Mental health services responding to men and their anger. *International Journal of Mental Health Nursing, 13,* 249–254.

Stewart, D. E., & Robinson, G. E. (1997). *A clinician's guide to menopause*. Washington, DC: Health Press International.

Stewart, V. (1973). Tests of the 'carpentered world' hypothesis by race and environment in America and Zambia. *International Journal of Psychology, 8,* 83–94.

Stice, E. (2002). Risk and maintenance factors for eating pathology: A meta-analytic review. *Psychological Bulletin, 128,* 825–848.

Stice, E., & Barrera, M. (1995). A longitudinal examination of the reciprocal relations between perceived parenting and adolescents' substance use and externalizing behaviors. *Developmental Psychology, 31,* 322–334.

Stickgold, R. (1998). Sleep: Off-line memory reprocessing. *Trends in Cognitive Sciences, 2,* 484–492.

Stickgold, R., Malia, A., Maguire, D., Roddenberry, D., & O'Connor, M. G. (2000). Replaying the game: Hypnagogic images in normals and amnesics. *Science, 290,* 350–353.

Stoff, D. M., Breiling, J., & Maser, J. D. (Eds.). (1997). *Handbook of antisocial behavior*. New York: John Wiley.

Stogdill, R., & Coons, A. (1957). *Leader behavior: Its description and measure*ment. Columbus, OH: Ohio State University Bureau of Business Research.

Stokes, H., & Wyn, J. (2007). Constructing identities and making careers: Young people's perspectives on work and learning. *International Journal of Lifelong Education, 26,* 495–511.

Stone, J. (2002). Battling doubt by avoiding practice: The effects of stereotype threat on self-handicapping in white athletes. *Personality and Social Psychology Bulletin, 28,* 1667–1678.

Stone, J. (2003). Self-consistency for low self-esteem in dissonance processes: The role of self-standards. *Personality and Social Psychology Bulletin, 29,* 846–858.

Stoolmiller, M. (1999). Implications of the restricted range of family environments for estimates of heritability and nonshared environment in behavior-genetic adoption studies. *Psychological Bulletin, 125,* 392–409.

Storms, M. D. (1973). Videotape and the attribution process: Reversing actors' and observers' points of view. *Journal of Personality and Social Psychology, 27,* 165–175.

Stough, C., Saklofske, D. H., & Parker, J. D. A. (Eds.). (2009). *Assessing emotional intelligence: Theory, research, and applications*. New York: Springer.

Stough, C., Thompson, J. C., Bates, T. C., & Nathan, P. J. (2001). Examining neurochemical determinants of inspection time: Development of a biological model. *Intelligence, 29,* 511–522.

Stowell, J. R., McGuire, L., Robles, T., Glaser, R., & Kiecolt-Glaser, J. K. (2003). Psychoneuroimmunology. In A. M. Nezu, C. M. Nezu, & P. A. Geller (Eds.), *Handbook of psychology: Health psychology: Vol. 9* (pp. 75–95). Hoboken, NJ: John Wiley & Sons.

Strang, D. J. (1972). Conformity, ability, and self-esteem. *Representative Research in Social Psychology, 3,* 97–103.

Strange, D., Garry, M., & Sutherland, R. (2003). Drawing out children's false memories. *Applied Cognitive Psychology, 17,* 607–619.

Straub, R. O. (2002). *Health psychology*. New York: Worth.

Strauman, T. (1992). Self-guides, autobiographical memory, and anxiety and dysphoria: Toward a cognitive model of vulnerability to emotional distress. *Journal of Abnormal Psychology, 101,* 87–95.

Strauman, T., Lemieux, A., & Coe, C. (1993). Self-discrepancy and natural killer cell activity: Immunological consequences of negative self-evaluation. *Journal of Personality and Social Psychology, 64,* 1042–1052.

Straus, A. S. (1982). The structure of the self in Northern Cheyenne culture. In B. Lee (Ed.), *Psychosocial theories of the self*. New York: Plenum Press.

Straus, M. A., & Kantor, G. K. (1994). Corporal punishment of adolescents by parents: A risk factor in the epidemiology of depression, suicide, alcohol abuse, child abuse, and wife beating. *Adolescence, 29,* 543–561.

Straus, M. A., & Mouradian, V. E. (1998). Impulsive corporal punishment by mothers and antisocial behavior and impulsiveness of children. *Behavioral Sciences and the Law, 16,* 353–374.

Strauss, C., & Quinn, N. (1997). *A cognitive theory of cultural meaning*. New York: Cambridge University Press.

Strauss, D. H., Spitzer, R. L., & Muskin, P. R. (1990). Maladaptive denial of physical illness: A proposal for DSM-IV. *American Journal of Psychiatry, 147,* 1168–1172.

Strauss, J., Carpenter, W. T., & Bartko, J. (1974). The diagnosis and understanding of schizophrenia, III: Speculations on the processes that underlie schizophrenic symptoms and signs. *Schizophrenia Bulletin, 1,* 61–69.

Strauss, J., & Ryan, R. M. (1987). Autonomy disturbances in subtypes of anorexia nervosa. *Journal of Abnormal Psychology, 96,* 254–258.

Strayer, J. (1993). Children's concordant emotions and cognitions in response to observed emotions. *Child Development, 64,* 188–201.

Strayer, J., & Roberts, W. (1997). Facial and verbal measures of children's emotions and empathy. *International Journal of Behavioral Development, 20,* 627–649.

Streissguth, A., Barr, H., Johnson, M. D., & Kirchner, G. (1985). Attention and distraction at age 7 years related to maternal drinking during pregnancy. *Alcoholism: Clinical and experimental research, 9,* 195.

Streissguth, A., Sampson, P., & Barr, H. (1989). Neurobehavioral dose-response effects of prenatal alcohol exposure in humans from infancy to adulthood. *Annals of the New York Academy of Sciences, 562,* 145–158.

Stricker, G. (1996). Empirically validated treatment, psychotherapy manuals, and psychotherapy integration. *Journal of Psychotherapy Integration, 6,* 217–226.

Stricker, G., & Healey, B. J. (1990). Projective assessment of object relations: A review of the empirical literature. *Psychological Assessment, 2,* 219–230.

Striegel-Moore, R. H., Dohm, F. A., Kraemer, H. C., Taylor, C. B., Daniels, S., Crawford, P. B., et al. (2003). Eating disorders in white and black women. *American Journal of Psychiatry, 160,* 1326–1331.

Striegel-Moore, R. H., Silberstein, L. R., & Rodin, J. (1986). Toward an understanding of risk factors for bulimia. *American Psychologist, 41,* 246–263.

Strober, M., Freeman, R., Lampert, C., Diamond, J., & Kaye, W. (2000). Controlled family study of anorexia nervosa and bulimia nervosa: Evidence of shared liability and transmission of partial syndromes. *American Journal of Psychiatry, 157,* 393–401.

Stromme, P., & Magnus, P. (2000). Correlations between socioeconomic status, IQ and aetiology in mental retardation: A population-based study of Norwegian children. *Social Psychiatry and Psychiatric Epidemiology, 35,* 12–18.

Stromswold, K. (1995). The cognitive and neural bases of language acquisition. In M. S. Gazzaniga (Ed.), *The cognitive neurosciences* (pp. 855–870). Cambridge, MA: MIT Press.

Strong, K. L., Trickett, P. J., Titulaer, I., & Bhatia, K. (1998). *The health in rural and remote Australia*. Canberra, Australia: AIHW.

Stroud, L. R., Salovey, P., & Epel, E. S. (2002). Sex differences in stress responses: Social rejection versus achievement stress. *Biological Psychiatry, 52,* 318–327.

Strough, J., & Marie-Covatto, A. (2002). Context and age differences in same- and other-gender peer preferences. *Social Development, 11,* 346–361.

Strupp, H., & Binder, J. L. (1984). *Psychotherapy in a new key: A guide to time-limited dynamic psychotherapy*. New York: Basic Books.

Stucke, T. S., & Sporer, S. L. (2002). When a grandiose self-image is threatened: Narcissism and self-concept clarity as predictors of negative emotions and aggression following ego threat. *Journal of Personality, 70,* 509–532.

Stumpf, H. (1993). The factor structure of the personality research form: A cross-national evaluation. *Journal of Personality, 61,* 1–26.

Stunkard, A. J., Harris, J. R., Pedersen, N. L., & McClearn, G. E. (1990). The body mass index of twins who have been reared apart. *New England Journal of Medicine, 322,* 1483–1487.

Stuss, D. T., Gow, C. A., & Hetherington, C. R. (1992). 'No longer gage': Frontal lobe dysfunction and emotional changes. *Journal of Counselling and Clinical Psychology, 60*, 349–359.

Suarez-Orozco, M., Spindler, G., & Spindler, L. (1994). *The making of psychological anthropology II*. Fort Worth, TX: Harcourt Brace Jovanovich.

Sue, D. W., & Sue, D. (1990). *Counselling the culturally different: Theory and practice*. New York: John Wiley & Sons.

Sue, D. W., & Sue, D. (1999). *Counselling the culturally different: Theory and practice* (3rd ed.). New York: Wiley.

Sue, S., & Chu, J. Y. (2003). The mental health of ethnic minority groups: Challenges posed by the supplement to the surgeon general's report on mental health. *Culture, Medicine and Psychiatry*, *27*, 447–465.

Sue, S., & Zane, N. (2006). Ethnic minority populations have been neglected by evidence-based practices. In J. C. Norcross, L. E. Beutler, & R. F. Levant (Eds.), *Evidence-based practices in mental health: Debate and dialogue on the fundamental questions* (pp. 338–345, 359–361). Washington, DC: APA.

Suedfeld, P., & Granatstein, J. L. (1995). Leader complexity in personal and professional crises: Concurrent and retrospective information processing. *Political Psychology, 16*, 509–544.

Suedfeld, P., & Pennebaker, J. W. (1997). Health outcomes and cognitive aspects of recalled negative life events. *Psychosomatic Medicine, 59*, 172–177.

Suls, J., David, J. P., & Harvey, J. H. (1996). Personality and coping: Three generations of research. *Journal of Personality, 64,* 711–735.

Suls, J., Green, P., & Hillis, S. (1998). Emotional reactivity to everyday problems, affective inertia, and neuroticism. *Personality & Social Psychology Bulletin, 24,* 127–136.

Suls, J., & Rothman, A. (2004). Evolution of the biopsychosocial model: Prospects and challenges for health psychology. *Health Psychology, 23*(2), 119–125.

Summerbell, C. D., Waters, E., Edmunds, L. D., Kelly, S., Brown, T., & Campbell, K. J. (2005). Interventions for preventing obesity in children. *Cochrane Database of Systematic Reviews, 3*(CD001871).

Summers, C. H., Korzan, W. J., Lukkes, J. L., Watt, M. J., Forster, G. L., Overli, L., et al. (2005). Does serotonin influence aggression? Comparing regional activity before and during social interaction. *Physiological and Biochemical Zoology*, *78*, 679–694.

Suomi, S. J. (1999). Behavioral inhibition and impulsive aggressiveness: Insights from studies with rhesus monkeys. In L. Balter & C. S. Tamis-LeMonda (Eds.), *Child psychology: A handbook of contemporary issues* (pp. 510–525). Philadelphia: Psychology Press/Taylor & Francis.

Suomi, S. J. (2000). A biobehavioral perspective on developmental psychopathology: Excessive aggression and serotonergic dysfunction in monkeys. In A. J. Sameroff & M. Lewis (Eds.), *Handbook of developmental psychopathology* (2nd ed., pp. 237–256). New York: Kluwer Academic/Plenum Publishers.

Super, C. M. (1981). Cross-cultural research on infancy. In H. C. Triandis & A. Heron (Eds.), *Handbook of cross-cultural psychology: Vol. 4. Developmental psychology*. Boston: Allyn & Bacon.

Super, C. M., & Harkness, S. (1980). *Anthropological perspectives on child development*. San Francisco: Jossey-Bass.

Susser, E., Neugebauer, R., Hoek, H. W., Brown, A. S., Lin, S., Labovitz, D., et al. (1996). Schizophrenia after prenatal famine further evidence. *Archives of General Psychiatry, 53,* 25–31.

Sutherland, G. (2005, May 16). *Methods for quitting*. Retrieved from http://www.netdoctor.co.uk/smoking/quitmethods_000505.htm

Sutker, P., Winstead, D., Galina, Z., & Allai, A. (1991). Cognitive deficits and psychopathology among former prisoners of war and combat veterans of the Korean conflict. *American Journal of Psychiatry, 148,* 67–72.

Sutton, S. K., & Davidson, R. J. (1997). Prefrontal brain asymmetry: A biological substrate of the behavioral approach and inhibition systems. *Psychological Science*, *8*, 204–210.

Sutton, S. R. (1989). Smoking attitudes and behavior: Applications of Fishbein and Ajzen's theory of reasoned action to predicting and understanding smoking decisions. In T. Ney & A. Gale (Eds.), *Smoking and human behavior* (pp. 289–312). Chichester, England: Wiley.

Suzuki, H., Uchiyama, M., Tagay, H., Ozaki, A., Kuriyama, K., Aritake, S., et al. (2004). Dreaming during non-rapid eye movement sleep in the absence of prior rapid eye movement sleep. *Sleep: Journal of Sleep and Sleep Disorders Research*, *27*(8), 1486–1490.

Swain, S. A., Polkey, C. E., Bullock, P., & Morris, R. G. (1998). Recognition memory and memory for order in script-based stories following frontal lobe excisions. *Cortex, 34,* 25–45.

Swan, G. E., Hudmon, K. S., & Khroyan, T. V. (2003). Tobacco dependence. In A. M. Nezu, C. M. Nezu, & P. A. Geller (Eds.), *Handbook of psychology: Health psychology: Vol. 9* (pp. 147–168). Hoboken, NJ: John Wiley & Sons.

Swan, P., & Raphael, B. (1995). *Ways forward: National consultancy report on Aboriginal and Torres Strait Islander mental health*. Canberra, Australia: AGPS.

Swann, W. (1990). To be adored or to be known: The interplay of self-enhancement and selfverification. In R. M. Sorrentino & E. T. Higgins (Eds.), *Handbook of motivation and cognition: Vol. 2* (pp. 408–448). New York: Guilford Press.

Swann, W., Griffin, J., Predmore, S., & Gaines, B. (1987). The cognitive-affective crossfire: When self-consistency confronts self-enhancement. *Journal of Personality and Social Psychology, 52*, 881–889.

Swann, W., Stein-Seroussi, A., & Giesler, R. B. (1992). Why people self-verify. *Journal of Personality and Social Psychology, 62,* 392–401.

Swann, W., Wenzlaff, R., Krull, D. S., & Pelham, B. (1992). Allure of negative feedback: Self-verification strivings among depressed persons. *Journal of Abnormal Psychology, 101,* 293–306.

Swann, W. B. (1997). The trouble with change: Self-verification and allegiance to the self. *Psychological Science, 8,* 177–180.

Swanson, J. E., Rudman, L. A., & Greenwald, A. G. (2001). Using the implicit association test to investigate attitude-behaviour consistency for stigmatised behaviour. *Cognition and Emotion*, *15*(2), 207–230.

Sweet, R. A., Mulsant, B. H., Gupta, B., Rifai, A. H., Pasternak, R. E., McEachran, A., et al. (1995). Duration of neuroleptic treatment and prevelence of tardive dyskinesia in late life. *Archives of General Psychiatry, 52,* 478–486.

Swets, J. A. (1992). The science of choosing the right decision threshold in high-stakes diagnostics. *American Psychologist, 47*, 522–532.

Swim, J., Clayton, S., Doherty, T., Gifford, R., Howard, G., Reser, J., et al. (2009). *Psychology and global climate change: Addressing a multi-faceted phenomenon and set of challenges* (A report by the American Psychological Association's Task Force on the interface between psychology and global climate change). Retrieved from http://www.apa.org/science/about/publications/climate-change.aspx

Swim, J. K., Aikin, K. J., Hall, W. S., & Hunter, B. A. (1995). Sexism and racism: Old-fashioned and modern prejudices. *Journal of Personality and Social Psychology, 68*, 199–214.

Sydney Morning Herald. (2010, June 4). *Report reveals indigenous disadvantage*. Retrieved from http://news.smh.com.au/breaking-news-national/report-reveals-indigenous-disadvantage-20100604-xif9.html

Sydney School of Public Health. (2009). *HRT risks and benefits*. Retrieved from http://sydney.edu.au/medicine/public-health/hrt/questions/index.php

Synott, J., & Whatman, S. (1998). United to sea and land: Cultures, histories and education in the Torres Strait. In G. Partington (Ed.), *Perspectives on Aboriginal and Torres Strait Islander education*. Katoomba, NSW: Social Science Press.

Szasz, T. (1974). *The myth of mental illness: Foundations of a theory of personal conduct* (Rev. ed.). New York: Harper & Row.

Szeszko, P. R., Robinson, D., Alvir, J. M. J., Bilder, R. M., Lencz, T., Ashtari, M., et al. (1999). Orbital frontal and amygdala volume reductions in obsessive-compulsive disorder. *Archives of General Psychiatry, 56,* 913–919.

Szymusiak, R., Iriye, T., & McGinty, D. (1989). Sleep-walking discharge of neurons in the posterior lateral hypothalamic area of cats. *Brain Research Bulletin, 23*, 111–120.

Tagiuri, R., Blake, R. R., & Bruner, J. S. (1953). Some determinants of the perception of positive and negative feelings in others. *Journal of Abnormal and Social Psychology, 48*, 585–592.

Tajfel, H. (1981). *Human groups and social categories: Studies in social psychology*. Cambridge: Cambridge University Press.

Tajfel, H. (1982). *Social identity and intergroup relations*. New York: Cambridge University Press.

Tamminga, C., Thaker, G., Buchanon, R., Kirkpatrick, B., Alpha, L., Chase, T., et al. (1992). Limbic system abnormalities identified in schizophrenia using positron emission tomography with fluorodeoxyglucose and neocortical alterations with deficit syndrome. *Archives of General Psychiatry, 49,* 522–530.

Tan, C. C. (1991). Occupational health problems among nurses. *Scandinavian Journal of Work, Environment, and Health, 17*, 221–230.

Tanaka, N., Uji, M., & Hiramura, H. (2006). Cognitive patterns and depression: Study of a Japanese university student population. *Psychiatry and Clinical Neurosciences*, *60*(3), 358–364.

Tandberg, E., Larsen, J. P., Aarsland, D., & Cummings, J. L. (1996). The occurrence of depression in Parkinson's disease: A community-based study. *Archives of Neurology*, *53*, 175–179.

Tang, C. S., & Wong, C. (2004). Factors influencing the wearing of facemasks to prevent the severe acute respiratory syndrome among adult Chinese in Hong Kong. *Preventive Medicine, 39*(6), 1187–1193.

Tang, G. W.-G., Dennis, S., & Comino, E. (2009). Anxiety and depression in Chinese patiences attending an Australian GP clinic. *Australian Family Physician, 38*(7), 552–555.

Tanner, J. E., & Byrne, R. W. (1996). Representation of action through iconic gesture in a captive lowland gorilla. *Current Anthropology, 37,* 162–173.

Tanner-Smith, E. E., & Brown, T. N. (2010). Evaluating the health-belief model: A critical review of studies predicting mammographic and pap screening. *Social Theory & Health, 8*(1), 95–125(31).

Tapsell, R., & Mellsop, G. (2007). The contributions of culture and ethnicity to New Zealand mental health research findings. *International Journal of Social Psychiatry, 53*(4), 317–324.

Tarr, M. J., Buelthoff, H. H., Zabinski, M., & Blanz, V. (1997). To what extent do unique parts influence recognition across changes in viewpoint? *Psychological Science, 8*, 282–289.

Tartakovsky, E. (2007). A longitudinal study of acculturative stress and homesickness: High-school adolescents immigrating from Russia and Ukraine to Israel without parents. *Social Psychiatry, Psychiatry Epidemiology*, *42*, 485–494.

Tassinary, L. G., & Cacioppo, J. (1992). Unobservable facial actions and emotion. *Psychological Science, 3*, 28–33.

Tatz, C. (1999). *Aboriginal suicide is different: A report to the criminology research council on CRC project*. Sydney, Australia: Macquarie University, Centre for Comparative Genocide Studies.

Taylor, G. J., & Taylor, H. L. (1997). Alexithymia. In M. McCallum & W. E. Piper (Eds.), *Psychological mindedness: A contemporary understanding. The LEA series in personality and clinical psychology* (pp. 77–104). Mahwah, NJ: Lawrence Erlbaum.

Taylor, S. (1991). *Health psychology* (2nd ed.). New York: McGraw-Hill.

Taylor, S., & Crocker, J. (1980). Schematic bases of social information processing. In E. T. Higgins, P. Herman, & M. Zanna (Eds.), *Social cognition: The Ontario Symposium*. Hillsdale, NJ: Lawrence Erlbaum.

Taylor, S. E. (2003). *Health psychology* (5th ed.). New York: McGraw-Hill.

Taylor, S. E., & Armor, D. A. (1996). Positive illusions and coping with adversity. *Journal of Personality, 64,* 873–898.

Taylor, S. E., & Brown, J. D. (1988). Illusion and well-being: A social psychological perspective on mental health. *Psychological Bulletin, 103,* 193–210.

Taylor, S. E., Kemeny, M. E., Reed, G. M., Bower, J. E., & Gruenewald, T. L. (2000). Psychological resources, positive illusions, and health. *American Psychologist, 55,* 99–109.

Taylor, S. E., Pham, L., Rivkin, I., & Armor, D. (1998). Harnessing the imagination: Mental stimulation, self-regulation, and coping. *American Psychologist, 53,* 429–439.

Taylor, S. E., Repetti, R. L., & Seeman, T. (1997). Health psychology: What is an unhealthy environment and how does it get under the skin? *Annual Review of Psychology, 48,* 411–448.

Tedeschi, J. T., Schlenker, B. R., & Bonoma, T. V. (1971). Cognitive dissonance: Private ratiocination or public spectacle? *American Psychologist, 26,* 685–695.

Tehan, G., Hendry, L., & Kocinski, D. (2001). Word length and phonological similarity effects in simple, complex and delayed serial recall tasks: Implications for working memory. *Memory, 9*(4–6), 333–348.

Tehan, G., & Humphreys, M. S. (1995). Transient phonemic codes and immunity to proactive interference. *Memory and Cognition, 23*(2), 181–191.

Teitelbaum, P. (1961). Disturbances in feeding and drinking behavior after hypothalamic lesions. In M. R. Jones (Ed.), *Nebraska Symposium on Motivation* (pp. 39–68). Lincoln: University of Nebraska Press.

Teixeira, P. J., Going, S. B., Sardinha, L. B., & Lohman, T. G. (2005). A review of psychosocial pre-treatment predictors of weight control. *Obesity Reviews, 6,* 43–65.

Tellegen, A., Lykken, D. T., Bouchard, T. J., Wilcox, K. J., Segal, N. L., & Rich, S. (1988). Personality of twins reared apart and together. *Journal of Personality and Social Psychology, 54,* 1031–1039.

Terman, L. M. (1916). *The measurement of intelligence*. Boston: Houghton Mifflin.

Terman, L. M. (1925). *Genetic studies of genius: Vol. 1. Mental and physical traits of a thousand gifted children*. Stanford, CA: Stanford University Press.

Terman, L. M., & Oden, M. H. (1947). *Genetic studies of genius: Vol. 4. The gifted child grows up: Twenty-five years' follow-up of a superior group*. Stanford, CA: Stanford University Press.

Terman, L. M., & Oden, M. H. (1959). *Genetic studies of genius: Vol. 5. The gifted group at midlife*. Stanford, CA: Stanford University Press.

Terman, M., Terman, J. S., & Ross, D. C. (1998). A controlled trial of timed bright light and negative air ionization for treatment of winter depression. *Archives of General Psychiatry, 55,* 875–882.

Terracciano, A., & McCrae, R. R. (2007). National character stereotypes. Perceptions of Americans and the Iraq invasion: Implications for understanding national character stereotypes. *Journal of Cross-Cultural Psychology, 38,* 695–710.

Terrace, H. S. (1979). How Nim Chimsky changed my mind. *Psychology Today, 3,* 65–76.

Terry, D. J., & Hogg, M. A. (2001). Attitudes, behavior, and social context: The role of norms and group membership in social influence processes. In J. P. Forgas & K. D. Williams (Eds.), *Social influence: Direct and indirect processes* (pp. 253–270). Philiadelphia: Psychology Press.

Terry, P. C. (2004). Mood and emotions in sport. In T. Morris & J. Summers (Eds.) *Sport psychology: Theory, applications and issues* (2nd ed., pp. 48–73). Brisbane, Australia: Wiley.

Tesser, A. (1993). On the importance of heritability in psychological research: The case of attitudes. *Psychological Review, 100,* 129–142.

Tesser, A., Whitaker, D., Martin, L., & Ward, D. (1998). Attitude heritability, attitude change and physiological responsivity. *Personality and Individual Differences, 24,* 89–96.

Tetlock, P., & Levi, A. (1982). Attributional bias: On the inconclusiveness of the cognitive-motivation debate. *Journal of Experimental Social Psychology, 18,* 68–88.

Tetlock, P. E. (1989). Structure and function in political belief systems. In A. R. Pratkanis, S. J. Breckler, & A. G. Greenwald (Eds.), *Attitude structure and function. The third Ohio State University volume on attitudes and persuasion* (pp. 129–151). Hillsdale, NJ: Lawrence Erlbaum.

Tews, M. C., Shah, S. M., & Gossain, V. V. (2005). Hypothyroidism: Mimicker of common complaints. *Emergency Medicine Clinics of North America, 23*(3), 649–667.

Teyler, T. J., Hamm, J. P., Clapp, W. C., Johnson, B. W., Corballis, M. C., & Kirk, I. J. (2005). Long-term potentiation of human visual evoked responses. *European Journal of Neuroscience, 21,* 2045–2050.

Thase, M. E. (2000). Relapse and recurrence of depression: An updated practical approach for prevention. In K. J. Palmer (Ed.), *Drug treatment issues in depression* (pp. 35–52). Kwai Chung, Hong Kong: Adis International Publications.

Thase, M. E., & Kupfer, D. J. (1996). Recent developments in the pharmacotherapy of mood disorders. *Journal of Consulting & Clinical Psychology, 64,* 646–659.

The Australian and New Zealand Obesity Society. (2008). *What are the consequences of overweight and obesity?* Retrieved from http://www.asso.org.au/profiles/general/faq/consequences

The Australian Centre for Posttraumatic Mental Health. (2007). *Australian guidelines for the treatment of adults with acute stress disorder and posttraumatic stress disorder*. Melbourne, Australia: Author.

The Disaster Center. (2010). *United States crime rates 1960–2009*. Retrieved from http://www.disastercenter.com/crime/uscrime.htm

The discipline dance. (2006, November). *Australian Family*, pp. 6–9.

The Mental Health Research Institute. (2005). *A guide to psychotropic drugs*. Melbourne, Australia: Author. Retrieved from http://www.mhri.edu.au/pdf/A%20GUIDE%20TO%20PSYCHOTROPIC%20DRUGS.pdf

The Mental Health Research Institute. (2008). *Bipolar disorder*. Melbourne, Australia: Author. Retrieved from http://www.mhri.edu.au/documents/FS9_bipolar_2008.pdf

The National Sleep Research Project – 40 amazing facts about sleep. (2000). Retrieved from http://www.abc.net.au/science/sleep/facts.htm

Thelen, E. (1995). Motor development: A new synthesis. *American Psychologist, 50,* 79–95.

Thelen, E., & Smith, L. B. (1994). *A dynamic systems approach to the development of cognition and action*. Cambridge University: MIT Press.

Thigpen, C. H., & Cleckley, H. (1954). *The three faces of Eve*. Kingsport, TN: Kingsport Press.

Thomas, C. R., & Gadbois, S. A. (2007). Academic self-handicapping: The role of self-clarity and students' learning strategies. *British Journal of Educational Psychology, 77*(1), 101–119.

Thomas, D. R., & Nikora, L. W. (1992). From assimilation to biculturalism: Changing patterns in Maori-Pakeha relationships. In D. R. Thomas & A. Veno (Eds.), *Community psychology and social change: Australian and New Zealand perspectives*. Palmerston North, New Zealand: Dunmore.

Thomas, H., & Callinan, R. (2011, January 15). Flood crisis spreads to five states. *The Australian*. Retrieved from http://www.theaustralian.com.au/in-depth/queensland-floods/flood-crisis-spreads-to-five-states/story-fn7iwx3v-1225988077729

Thomas, I., & Bruck, D. (2010). Awakening of sleeping people — a decade of research. *Fire Technology, 46*(3), 743–761.

Thompson, D. A., & Campbell, R. G. (1977). Hunger in humans induced by 2-deoxy-D-glucose: Clucoprivic control of taste preference and food intake. *Science, 198,* 1065–1068.

Thompson, P. M., Cannon, T. D., Narr, K. L., van Erp, T. G. M., Poutanen, V. P., Huttunen, M., et al. (2001). Genetic influences on brain structure, *Nature Neuroscience, 4*(12), 1253–1258.

Thompson, R. A. (2000). The legacy of early attachments. *Child Development, 71*(1), 145–152.

Thompson, V. A., & Paivio, A. (1994). Memory for pictures and sounds: Independence of auditory and visual codes. *Canadian Journal of Experimental Psychology, 48,* 380–398.

Thomson, G., Rosenthal, D., & Russell, J. (2006). *Cultural stress among international students at an Australian university*. Australian International Education Conference 2006. Retrieved June 25, 2006, from http://www.idp.com/aiec

Thomson, N. (1991). A review of Aboriginal health status. In J. Reid & P. Trompf (Eds.), *The health of Aboriginal Australia*. Sydney, Australia: Harcourt Brace Jovanovich.

Thorndike, E. L. (1911). *Animal intelligence: Experimental studies*. New York: Macmillan.

Thorpe, R., & Caltabiano, M. (2004). *Foster carers' adult attachment styles: Preliminary findings from a research study in Queensland*. Poster presented at the International Society for the Prevention of Child Abuse and Neglect World Congress, Brisbane, Australia. Retrieved from http://www.aifs.gov.au/nch/pubs/newsletters/nl2005/summerrt.pdf

Thurstone, L. L. (1938). Primary mental abilities. *Psychometric Monographs: Vol. 1*. Chicago: Chicago University Press.

Thyer, B. A. (1980). Prolonged in vivo exposure therapy with a 70-year-old woman. *Journal of Behavior Therapy and Experimental Psychiatry, 11*.

Tienari, P. (1991). Interaction between genetic vulnerability and family environment: The Finnish adoptive family study of schizophrenia. *Acta Psychiatrica Scandinavica, 84,* 460–465.

Tilbury, F., Slee, R., Clark, S., O'Ferrall, I., Rapley, M., & Kokanovic, R. (2004). Listening to diverse voices: Understandings and experiences of, and interventions for, depression among East African migrants. *Synergy, 2*(5–6), 24–25.

Tiller, M. (2010, October). *Indigenous suicide prevention project receives national award*. Retrieved from http://www.usq.edu.au/newsevents/news/2009/indigenouslifeaward09

Tinbergen, N. (1951). *The study of instinct*. Oxford: Clarendon Press.

Tinto, V. (1993). *Leaving college: Rethinking the causes and cures of student attrition* (2nd ed.). Chicago: The University of Chicago Press.

Tix, A. P., & Frazier, P. A. (1998). The use of religious coping during stressful life events: Main effects, moderation, and mediation. *Journal of Consulting and Clinical Psychology, 66*(2), 411–422.

Tizard, B., & Hodges, J. (1978). The effects of early institutional rearing on the development of eight-year-old children. *Journal of Child Psychology and Psychiatry, 19,* 99–108.

Tollefson, N. (2000). Classroom applications of cognitive theories of motivation. *Educational Psychology Review, 12,* 63–83.

Tolman, E. C. (1948). Cognitive maps in rats and men. *Psychological Review, 55,* 189–208.

Tolman, E. C., & Honzik, C. H. (1930). Insight in rats. *University of California Publications in Psychology, 4,* 215–232.

Tomarken, A. J., Davidson, R. J., Wheeler, R. E., & Doss, R. C. (1992). Individual differences in anterior brain asymmetry and fundamental dimensions of emotion. *Journal of Personality and Social Psychology, 62,* 676–687.

Tomkins, S. S. (1962). *Affect, imagery, consciousness: Vol. 1. The positive affects*. New York: Springer.

Tomkins, S. S. (1980). Affect as amplification: Some modifications in theory. In R. Plutchik & H. Kellerman (Eds.), *Emotion: Theory, research, and experience: Vol. I. Theories of emotion*. New York: Academic Press.

Tomkins, S. S. (1986). Script theory. In J. Aronoff, A. I. Radin, & R. Zucker (Eds.), *The emergence of personality* (pp. 147–216). New York: Springer.

Tomlinson-Keasey, C., & Little, T. D. (1990). Predicting educational attainment, occupational achievement, intellectual skill, and personal adjustment among gifted men and women. *Journal of Educational Psychology, 82*, 442–455.

Tonigan, J. S., Miller, W. R., & Connors, G. J. (2000). Project MATCH client impressions about alcoholics anonymous: Measurement issues and relationship to treatment outcome. *Alcoholism Treatment Quarterly, 18*, 25–41.

Tooby, J., & Cosmides, L. (1992). The psychological foundations of culture. In J. H. Barkow, L. Cosmides, & J. Tooby (Eds.), *The adapted mind: Evolutionary psychology and the generation of culture* (pp. 19–136). New York: Oxford University Press.

Tootell, R. B. H., Reppas, J. B., Dale, A. M., & Look, R. B. (1995a). Visual motion aftereffect in human cortical area MT revealed by functional magnetic resonance imaging. *Nature, 375*, 139–141.

Tootell, R. B. H., Reppas, J. B., Kwong, K. K., & Malach, R. (1995b). Functional analysis of human MT and related visual cortical area using magnetic resonance imaging. *Journal of Neuroscience, 15*, 3215–3230.

Toppino, T. C., & Schneider, M. A. (1999). The mix-up regarding mixed and unmixed lists in spacing-effect research. *Journal of Experimental Psychology: Learning, Memory, & Cognition, 25*, 1071–1076.

Torrey, E. F. (1986). *Witchdoctors and psychiatrists: The common roots of psychotherapy and its future*. New York: Jason Aronson.

Toumbourou, J. W., Beyers, J. M., Catalano, R. F., Hawkins, J. D., Arthur, M. W., Evans-Whipp, T., et al. (2005). Youth alcohol and other drug use in the United States and Australia: A cross-national comparison of three state-wide samples. *Drug and Alcohol Review, 24*(6), 515–523.

Toutain, S. (2010). What women in France say about alcohol abstinence during pregnancy. *Drug and Alcohol Review, 29*, 184–189.

Trainor, B. C., Greiwe, K. M., & Nelson, R. J. (2006). Individual differences in estrogen receptor α in select brain nuclei are associated with individual differences in aggression. *Hormones and Behavior, 50*, 338–345.

Traiwick, M. (1990). The ideology of love in a Tamil family. In O. M. Lynch (Ed.), *Divine passions: The social construction of emotion in India*. Berkeley: University of California Press.

TravelSmart Australia. (2007). *Walking school bus: A guide for parents and teachers*. Retrieved from http://www.travelsmart.gov.au/schools/schools2.html

Treacy, L., Tripp, G., & Baird, A. (2005). Parent stress management training for attention deficit hyperactivity disorder. *Behavior Therapy, 36*, 223–234.

Trebous, D., Crowell, J. A., & Waters, E. (2004). When 'new' meets 'old': Configurations of adult attachment representations and their implications for marital functioning. *Developmental Psychology, 40*, 295–314.

Trenholm, S., & Jensen, A. (2007). *Interpersonal communication* (6th ed.). New York: Oxford University Press.

Trevethan, C. T., Sahraie, A., & Weiskrantz, L. (2007). Can blindsight be superior to 'sighted-sight'? *Cognition, 103*, 491–501.

Triandis, H. (Ed.). (1980). *Handbook of cross-cultural psychology* (6 vols.). Boston: Allyn & Bacon.

Triandis, H. (1989). The self and social behavior in differing cultural contexts. *Psychological Bulletin, 96*, 506–520.

Triandis, H. (1994). *Culture and social behavior*. New York: McGraw-Hill.

Triandis, H. C. (1995). Motivation and achievement in collectivist and individualist cultures. In M. L. Maehr & P. R. Pintrich (Eds.), *Advances in motivation and achievement: Culture, motivation and achievement* (Vol. 9, pp. 1–30). Greenwich, CT: JAI Press.

Triesman, A. (1986). Properties, parts and objects. In K. Boff, L. Kaufman, & J. Thomas (Eds.), *Handbook of perception and human performance: Vol. 2* (pp. 3501–3570). New York: John Wiley.

Triplett, N. (1898). The dynamogenic factors in pacemaking and competition. *American Journal of Psychology, 9*, 507–533.

Tripp, G., & Alsop, B. (2001). Sensitivity to reward delay in children with attention deficit hyperactivity disorder (ADHD). *Journal of Child Psychology & Psychiatry, 42*, 691–698.

Tripp, G., Ryan, J., & Peace, K. (2002). Neuropsychological functioning in children with DSM-IV combined type attention deficit hyperactivity disorder. *Australian and New Zealand Journal of Psychiatry, 36*, 771–779.

Trivers, R. (1972). Parental investment and sexual selection. In B. Campbell (Ed.), *Sexual selection and the descent of man: 1871–1971* (pp. 136–179). Chicago: Aldine.

Trope, Y. (2004). Theory in social psychology: Seeing the forest and the trees. *Personality and Social Psychology Review, 8*, 193–200.

Trope, Y., & Liberman, A. (1996). Social hypothesis testing: Cognitive and motivational mechanisms. In E. T. Higgins & W. Kruglanski (Eds.), *Social psychology: Handbook of basic principles* (pp. 239–270). New York: Guilford Press.

Tsai, G., & Coyle, J. T. (2002). Glutamatergic mechanisms in schizophrenia. *Annual Review of Pharmacology and Toxicology, 42*, 165–179.

Tsang, J. (2006). Gratitude and prosocial behaviour: An experimental test of gratitude. *Cognition and Emotion, 20*(1), 138–148.

Tsang, L. L. W., Harvey, C. D. H., Duncan, K. A., & Sommer, R. (2003). The effects of children, dual earner status, sex role traditionalism, and marital structure on marital happiness over time. *Journal of Family and Economic Issues, 24*(1), 5–26.

Tse, M. M. Y., Ng, J. K. F., Chung, J. W. Y., & Wong, T. K. S. (2002). The effect of visual stimulation via the eyeglass display and the perception of pain. *CyberPsychology & Behavior, 5*(1), 65–75.

Tsourtos, G., Spong, J., & Stough, C. (2007). The effects of electro-convulsive therapy on the speed of information processing in major depression. *Journal of Affective Disorders, 103*, 263–266.

Tsuang, M. T., Lyons, M. J., Meyer, J. M., Doyle, T., Eisen, S. A., Goldberg, J., et al. (1998). Co-occurrence of abuse of different drugs in men: The role of drug-specific and shared vulnerabilities. *Archives of General Psychiatry, 55*, 967–972.

Tu Strategies. (2003). *From earliest times, the haka has inspired and energised generations of Maori in both peace and war*. Retrieved December 15, 2004, from http://www.tu.co.nz/haka.htm

Tucker, L. (2004). *Specific language impairment and theory-of-mind: Is normal language development an essential precursor for on time theory-of-mind development?* Unpublished thesis, University of Western Australia, Perth.

Tuckey, M. R., & Brewer, N. (2003). How schemas affect eyewitness memory over repeated retrieval attempts. *Applied Cognitive Psychology, 17*(7), 785–800.

Tuddenham, R. D. (1962). The nature & measurement of intelligence. In L. Postman (Ed.), *Psychology in the making: Histories of selected research problems* (pp. 469–525). New York: Alfred A. Knopf.

Tudge, J. R. H., Hogan, D., Snezhkova, I. A., Kulakova, N. N., & Etz, K. E. (2000). Parents' child-rearing values and beliefs in the United States and Russia: The impact of culture and social class. *Infant and Child Development, 9*, 105–121.

Tulving, E. (1972). Episodic and semantic memory. In E. Tulving & W. Donaldson (Eds.), *Organization of memory* (pp. 381–403). New York: Academic Press.

Tulving, E. (1987). Multiple memory systems and consciousness. *Human Neurobiology, 6*(2), 67–80.

Tulving, E. (2002). Episodic memory: From mind to brain. *Annual Review of Psychology, 53*, 1–25.

Tulving, E., Schachter, D. L., & Stark, H. A. (1982). Priming effects in word-fragment completion are independent of recognition memory. *Journal of Experimental Psychology: Learning, Memory, and Cognition, 8*, 336–342.

Tulving, E., & Thomson, D. M. (1973). Encoding specificity and retrieval processes in episodic memory. *Psychological Review, 80*, 359–380.

Turiel, E. (1998). The development of morality. In W. Damon (Ed.) & N. Eisenberg (Vol. Ed.), *Handbook of child psychology: Vol. 3. Social, emotional, and personality development* (pp. 863–932). New York: John Wiley & Sons.

Turkheimer, E. (1991). Individual and group differences in adoption studies of IQ. *Psychological Bulletin, 110*, 392–405.

Turner, J. C., Hogg, M. A., Oakes, P. J., Reicher, S. D., & Wetherell, M. S. (1987). *Rediscovering the social group: A self-categorization theory*. New York: Basil Blackwell.

Turner, V. (1969). *The ritual process*. Chicago: Aldine.

Turner, V. W. (1967). *A forest of symbols: Aspects of Ndembu ritual*. Ithaca, NY: Cornell University Press.

Tversky, A. (1977). Features of similarity. *Psychological Review, 84*, 327–352.

Tversky, A., & Kahneman, D. (1973). Availability: A heuristic for judging frequency and probability. *Cognitive Psychology, 5*, 207–232.

Tversky, A., & Kahneman, D. (1974). Judgment under uncertainty: Heuristics and biases. *Science, 185*, 1124–1131.

Tversky, A., & Kahneman, D. (1981). Extensional vs. intuitive reasoning: The conjunction fallacy in probability judgment. *Psychological Review, 90*, 293–315.

Twenge, J. M., & Im, C. (2007). Changes in the need for social approval, 1958–2001. *Journal of Research in Personality, 41*, 171–189.

Udry, J. R., Billy, J. O. G., Morris, N. M., Groff, T. R., & Raj, J. H. (1985). Serum androgenic hormones motivate sexual behavior in adolescent boys. *Fertility and Sterility, 43*, 90–94.

Ullman, S. (1989). Aligning pictorial descriptions: An approach to object recognition. *Cognition, 32*, 193–254.

Ullman, S. (1995). The visual analysis of shape and form. In M. S. Gazzaniga (Ed.), *The cognitive neurosciences* (pp. 339–350). Cambridge, MA: MIT Press.

Ullrich, A., Carroll, M., Prigot, J., & Fagen, J. (2002). Preschoolers' inhibition in their home: Relation to temperament. *The Journal of Genetic Psychology, 163*(3), 340–359.

Ulrich, R. E. (1991). Animal rights, animal wrongs, and the question of balance. *Psychological Science, 2*, 197–201.

Ulrich, R. S. (1984). View through a window may influence recovery from surgery. *Science, 224*, 420–421.

Unger, R. K. (1979). *Female and male: Psychological perspectives*. New York: Harper & Row.

Ungerleider, L. G., & Haxby, J. V. (1994). 'What' and 'where' in the human brain. *Current Opinion in Neurobiology, 4*, 157–165.

United Nations High Commissioner for Refugees. (2009). *2008 Global trends: Refugees, asylum-seekers, returnees, internally displaced and stateless persons*. Geneva: Author.

United Nations Programme on HIV/AIDS and WHO. (2009). *AIDS epidemic update, December 2009*. Retrieved from http://www.unaids.com

United States Department of Justice. (2005). *Bureau of justice. Statistics: Homicide rates recently declined to levels last seen in the late 1960s*. Retrieved November 16, 2007, from http://www.ojp.usdoj.gov/bjs/glance/hmrt.htm

U.S. Department of Health and Human Services. (1994). *Preventing tobacco use among young people: A report of the Surgeon General*. Atlanta, GA: U.S. Department of Health and Human Services.

Uutela, A. (2006). Substance use down under: The prevention of substance use, risk and harm in Australia. *Psychology & Health, 21*(2), 295–296.

Uzum, G., Diler, A. S., Bahcekapili, N., Tasyurekli, M., & Zivlan, Y. Z. (2004). Nicotine improves learning and memory in rats: Morphological evidence for acetylcholine involvement. *International Journal of Neuroscience, 114*(9), 1163–1179.

Vaillant, C., & Vaillant, L. M. (1998). The role of ego mechanisms of defense in the diagnosis of personality disorders. In J. Barron (Ed.), *Making diagnosis meaningful* (pp. 139–158). Washington, DC: American Psychological Association.

Vaillant, G., & Perry, J. C. (1985). Personality disorders. In H. I. Kaplan & B. J. Sadock (Eds.), *Comprehensive textbook of psychiatry* (4th ed.). Baltimore: Williams & Wilkins.

Vaillant, G., & Vaillant, C. (1990). Natural history of male psychology health: XII. A 45-year study of predictors of successful aging at age 65. *American Journal of Psychiatry, 147*, 31–37.

Vaillant, G. E. (Ed.). (1992a). *Ego mechanisms of defense: A guide for clinicians and researchers*. Washington, DC: American Psychiatric Association Press.

Vaillant, G. E. (1992b). The historical origins and future potential of Sigmund Freud's concept of the mechanisms of defence. *International Review of Psycho-Analysis, 19*, 35–50.

Valenstein, E. S. (1986). *Great and desperate cures*. New York: Basic Books.

Valenstein, E. S. (1988). The history of lobotomy: A cautionary tale. *Michigan Quarterly, 27*, 417–437.

Van Ameringen, M., Mancini, C., Pipe, B., & Bennett, M. (2004). Antiepileptic drugs in the treatment of anxiety disorders: Role in therapy. *Drugs, 64*(19), 2199–2220.

Vance, E. B., & Wagner, N. N. (1976). Written descriptions of orgasm: A study of sex differences. *Archives of Sexual Behavior, 5*, 87–98.

van der Staay, F. J., & Blokland, A. (1996). Behavioral differences between outbred Wistar, inbred Fischer 344, Brown Norway, and hybrid Fischer 344 Brown Norway rats. *Physiology & Behavior, 60*, 97–109.

van de Vijver, F. J. R., & Leung, K. (2000). Methodological issues in psychological research on culture. *Journal of Cross-Cultural Psychology, 31*(1), 33–51.

van Dijk, T. A., & Kintsch, W. (1983). *Strategies of discourse comprehension*. New York: Academic Press.

van Duijn, C. M. (1996). Epidemiology of the dementias: Recent developments and new approaches. *Journal of Neurology, Neurosurgery & Psychiatry, 60*, 478–488.

van Essen, D. C., Anderson, C. H., & Felleman, D. J. (1992). Information processing in the primate visual system: An integrated systems perspective. *Science, 255*, 419–423.

Van Gerven, P. W. M., Meijer, W. A., & Jolles, J. (2007). Education does not protect against age-related decline of switching focal attention in working memory. *Brain and Cognition, 64*(2), 158–163.

van Ijzendoorn, M. (1995). Adult attachment representations, parental responsiveness, and infant attachment: A meta-analysis on the predictive validity of the Adult Attachment Interview. *Psychological Bulletin, 117*, 387–403.

van Ijzendoorn, M., & Kroonenberg, P. (1988). Cross-cultural patterns of attachment: A meta-analysis of the strange situation. *Child Development, 59*, 147–156.

van Ijzendoorn, M. H., & De Wolff, M. S. (1997). In search of the absent father — meta-analyses of infant-father attachment: A rejoinder to our discussants. *Child Development, 68*, 604–609.

van Ijzendoorn, M. H., Schuengel, C., & Bakermans-Kranenburg, M. J. (1999). Disorganized attachment in early childhood: Meta-analysis of precursors, concomitants, and sequelae. *Developmental Psychopathology, 11*, 225–249. Retrieved from http://www.psy.miami.edu/faculty/dmessinger/c_c/rsrcs/rdgs/attach/vanIJ.Disorganization.devPsychopath99.pdf

van Leeuwen, M. S. (1978). A cross-cultural examination of psychological differentiation in males and females. *International Journal of Psychology, 13*, 87–122.

van Lier, P. A. C., Vitaro, F., Wanner, B., Vuijk, P., & Crijnen, A. A. M. (2005). Gender differences in developmental links among antisocial behavior, friends' antisocial behavior, and peer rejection in childhood: Results from two cultures. *Child Development, 76*, 841–855.

van Overwalle, F., & Van Rooy, D. (2001). How one cause discounts or augments another: A connectionist account of causal competition. *Personality and Social Psychology Bulletin, 27*, 1613–1626.

Vansteenkiste, M., Lens, W., De Witte, H., & Feather, N. T. (2005). Understanding unemployed people's job search behaviour, unemployment experience and wellbeing: A comparison of expectancy-value theory and self-determination theory. *British Journal of Social Psychology, 44*, 269–287.

van Thiel, D. H. (1996). Liver transplantation for alcoholics with terminal liver disease. *Alcohol Health & Research World, 20*, 261–266.

Van Tran, X., & Woodside, A. G. (2009). How unconscious needs influence traveler's interpretations and preferences of alternative tours and hotels. In *Advances in culture, tourism and hospitality research* (Vol. 3, pp. 215–308). Retrieved from http://www.emeraldinsight.com/10.1108/S1871-3173(2009)0000003010

Varia, I., & Rauscher, F. (2002). Treatment of generalized anxiety disorder with citalopram. *International Clinical Psychopharmacology, 17*, 103–107.

Varley, C. K. (1984). Attention deficit disorder (the hyperactivity syndrome): A review of selected issues. *Developmental and Behavioral Pediatrics, 5*, 254–258.

Vasquez, K., Durik, A. M., & Hyde, J. S. (2002). Family and work: Implications of adult attachment styles. *Personality and Social Psychology Bulletin, 28*, 874–886.

Vaughn, B. E., Stevenson-Hinde, J., Waters, E., & Kotsaftis, A. (1992). Attachment security and temperament in infancy and early childhood: Some conceptual clarifications. *Developmental Psychology, 28*, 463–473.

Velez-Blasini, C. J. (1997). A cross-cultural comparison of alcohol expectancies in Puerto Rico and the United States. *Psychology of Addictive Behaviors, 11*, 124–141.

Vermunt, J. D. (2007). The power of teaching–learning environments to influence student learning [Monograph]. *British Journal of Educational Psychology, 4*, 73–90.

Veneziano, R. A., & Rohner, R. P. (1998). Perceived paternal acceptance, paternal involvement, and youths' psychological adjustment in a rural, biracial southern community. *Journal of Marriage & the Family, 60*, 335–343.

Ventis, W. L., Higbee, G., & Murdock, S. A. (2001). Using humor in systematic desensitization to reduce fear. *Journal of General Psychology, 128*(2), 241–253.

Vernon, P. A., & Weese, S. E. (1993). Predicting intelligence with multiple speed of information-processing tests. *Personality and Individual Differences, 14*, 413–419.

Verri, A. P., Maraschio, P., Uggetti, C., Pucci, E., Ronchi, G., Nespoli, L., et al. (2004). Late diagnosis in severe and mild intellectual disability in adulthood. *Journal of Intellectual Disability Research, 48*(7), 679–686.

Verschueren, K., & Marcoen, A. (1999). Representation of self and socioemotional competence in kindergartners: Differential and combined effects of attachment to mother and father. *Child Development, 70*, 183–201.

Victorian Government Department of Health. (2010). *Smoking statistics*. Retrieved from http://www.betterhealth.vic.gov.au/bhcv2/bhcarticles.nsf/pages/Smoking_statistics

Victorian Government Department of Human Services. (2007). *Psychosurgery: About your rights*. Retrieved September 9, 2007, from http://www.health.vic.gov.au/mentalhealth

Victorian Health. (2010). *Walking school bus*. Victorian Government. Retrieved from http://www.vichealth.vic.gov.au/wsb

Vierikko, E., Pulkkinen, L., Kaprio, J., Viken, R., & Rose, R. J. (2003). Sex differences in gentic and environmental effects on aggression. *Aggressive Behavior, 29*, 55–68.

Vignoles, V. L., Regalia, C., & Manzi, C. (2006). Beyond self-esteem: Influence of multiple motives on identity construction. *Journal of Personality and Social Psychology, 90*(2), 308–333.

Viinamaeki, H., Koskela, K., & Niskanen, L. (1996). Rapidly declining mental well being during unemployment. *European Journal of Psychiatry, 10*, 215–221.

Viken, R. J., Rose, R. J., Kaprio, J., & Koskenvuo, M. (1994). A developmental genetic analysis of adult personality: Extraversion and neuroticism from 18 to 59 years of age. *Journal of Personality and Social Psychology, 66*, 722–730.

Vink, J. M., Willemsen, G., & Boomsma, D. I. (2005). Heritability of smoking initiation and nicotine dependence. *Behavior Genetics, 35*(4), 397–406.

Vinter, A., & Perruchet, P. (2000). Implicit learning in children is not related to age evidence from drawing behavior. *Child Development, 71*, 1223–1240.

Vitaro, F., Tremblay, R. E., Kerr, M., Pagani, L., & Bukowski, W. M. (1997). Disruptiveness, friends' characteristics, and delinquency in early adolescence: A test of two competing models of development. *Child Development, 68*, 676–689.

Vogel, D. L., Wester, S. R., Heesacker, M., & Madon, S. (2003). Confirming gender stereotypes: A social role perspective. *Sex Roles, 48*, 519–528.

Volet, S. E., & Ang, G. (1998). Culturally mixed groups on international campuses: An opportunity for intercultural learning. *Higher Education Research and Development, 17*(1), 5–23.

Volkow, N. D., Fowler, J. S., Wang, G. J., & Swabsib, J. M. (2004). Dopamine in drug abuse and addiction: Results from imaging studies and treatment implications. *Molecular Psychiatry, 9*, 557–569.

Vollmer, F. (2001). The control of everyday behaviour. *Theory & Psychology, 11*(5), 637–654.

Von Ah, D., Kang, D.-H., & Carpenter, J. S. (2007). Stress, optimism, and social support: Impact on immune responses in breast cancer. *Research in Nursing & Health, 30*, 72–83.

von Hippel, W., Lakin, J. L., & Shakarchi, R. J. (2005). Individual differences in motivated social cognition: The case of self-serving information processing. *Personality and Social Psychology Bulletin, 31*, 1347–1357.

Von Senden, M. (1960). *Space and sight. Public health transcript*. New York: Free Press.

Von Stumm, S., Chamorro-Premuzic, T., & Furnham, A. (2009). Decomposing self-estimates of intelligence: Structure and sex differences across 12 nations. *British Journal of Psychology, 100*, 429–442.

Vormbrock, J. (1993). Attachment theory as applied to wartime and job-related marital separation. *Psychological Bulletin, 114*, 122–144.

Vornik, L. A., Sharman, S. J., & Garry, M. (2003). The power of the spoken word: Sociolinguistic cues influence the misinformation effect. *Memory, 11*, 101–109.

Vygotsky, L. (1978). *Mind in society: The development of higher psychological processes*. Cambridge, MA: Harvard University Press

Vygotsky, L. S. (1997). In R. W. Rieber (Ed.), *The collected works of L. S. Vygotsky: Vol. 4. The history of the development of higher mental functions*. New York: Plenum.

Wachtel, P. (1977). *Psychoanalysis and behavior therapy: Toward an integration*. New York: Basic Books.

Wachtel, P. (1993). *Therapeutic communication*. New York: Guilford Press.

Wachtel, P. (1997). *Psychoanalysis, behavior therapy, and the relational world*. Washington, DC: American Psychological Association Press.

Wadden, T. A., Brownell, K. D., & Foster, G. D. (2002). Obesity: Responding to the global epidemic. *Journal of Consulting and Clinical Psychology, 70,* 510–525.

Wadden, T. A., Womble, L. G., Stunkard, A. J., & Anderson, D. A. (2002). Psychsocial consequences of obesity and weight loss. In T. A. Wadden & A. J. Stunkard (Eds.), *Handbook of obesity treatment* (pp. 144–169). New York: Guilford Press.

Wade, T. D., Bergin, J. L., Tiggemann, M., Bulik, C. M., & Fairburn, C. G. (2006). Prevalence and long-term course of lifetime eating disorders in an adult Australian twin cohort. *Australian and New Zealand Journal of Psychiatry*, *40*, 121–128.

Wagner, A. D., Schacter, D. L., Rotte, M., Koutstaal, W., Maril, A., Dale, A. M., et al. (1998). Building memories: Remembering and forgetting of verbal experiences as predicted by brain activity. *Science, 281,* 1188–1191.

Wagner, A. W., & Linehan, M. (1999). Facial expression recognition ability among women with borderline personality disorder: Implications for emotion regulation. *Journal of Personality Disorders, 13,* 329–344.

Wagner, R. K. (2000). Practical intelligence. In R. J. Sternberg (Ed.), *Handbook of intelligence* (pp. 380–395). Cambridge, UK: Cambridge University Press.

Wagstaff, G. F. (1984). The enhancement of witness memory by 'hypnosis': A review and methodological critique of the experimental literature. *British Journal of Experimental and Clinical Hypnosis, 2*, 3–12.

Wahlbeck, K., Cheine, M., Essali, A., & Adams, C. (1999). Evidence of clozapine's effectiveness in schizophrenia: A systematic review and meta-analysis of randomized trials. *American Journal of Psychiatry, 156,* 990–999.

Wakefield, C. E., Homewood, J., & Taylor, A. J. (2004). Cognitive compensations for blindness in children: An investigation using odour naming. *Perception*, *33*, 429–442.

Wald, G. (1968). Molecular basis of visual excitation. *Science, 162*, 230–239.

Waldegrave, C. (1993). The challenges of culture to psychology and post-modern thinking. In L. M. Nikora (Ed.), *Proceedings of a Symposium held at the Annual Conference of the New Zealand Psychological Society, University of Victoria, Wellington, New Zealand, August 23–24, 1993*.

Waldinger, R. J., & Gunderson, J. G. (1984). Completed psychotherapies with borderline patients. *American Journal of Psychotherapy, 38*, 190–202.

Walker, E., Kestler, L., Bollini, A., & Hochman, K. M. (2004). Schizophrenia: Etiology and course. *Annual Review of Psychology*, *55*, 401–430.

Walker, E. F., & Diforio, D. (1997). Schizophrenia: A neural diathesis-stress model. *Psychological Review, 104,* 667–685.

Walker, L. J., Hennig, K. H., & Krettenauer, T. (2000). Parent and peer contexts for children's moral reasoning development. *Child Development*, *71*, 1033–1048.

Walker, R., & Sonn, C. (2010). Working as a culturally competent mental health practitioner. In P. Purdie, P. Dudgeon, & R. Walker (Eds.), *Working together Aboriginal and Torres Strait Islander mental health and wellbeing principles and practice* (pp. 157–180). Canberra, Australia: ACER.

Walker, S., & Irving, K. (1998). The effect of perceived social status on preschool children's evaluations of behaviour. *Australian Research in Early Childhood Education: Journal of Australian Research in Early Childhood Education*, *1*, 94–103.

Wallace, A. F. C. (1956). Revitalization movements. *American Anthropologist, 58*, 264–281.

Wallace, A. F. C. (1959). Cultural determinants of response to hallucinatory experiences. *Archives of General Psychiatry, 1*, 58–69.

Wallace, B. (1993). Day persons, night persons, and variability in hypnotic susceptibility. *Journal of Personality and Social Psychology*, *64*, 827–833.

Wallace, P. (1977). Individual discrimination of humans by odor. *Physiology and Behavior, 19*, 577–579.

Waller, N., Kojetin, B., Bouchard, T., & Lykken, D. (1990). Generic and environmental influences on religious interests, attitudes, and values: A study of twins reared apart and together. *Psychological Science*, *1*, 138–142.

Waller, N. G., & Ross, C. A. (1997). The prevalence and biometric structure of pathological dissociation in the general population: Taxometric and behavior genetic findings. *Journal of Abnormal Psychology, 106,* 499–510.

Wallerstein, J. S., & Corbin, S. B. (1999). The child and the vicissitudes of divorce. In R. M. Galatzer-Levy & L. Kraus (Eds.), *The scientific basis of child custody decisions* (pp. 73–95). New York: John Wiley & Sons.

Wallerstein, R. S. (1988). One psychoanalysis or many? *International Journal of Psycho-Analysis, 69*, 5–22.

Wallerstein, R. S. (1989). The psychotherapy research project of the Menninger Foundations: An overview. *Journal of Consulting and Clinical Psychology, 57,* 195–205.

Walpole, I., & Hockey, A. (1980). Fetal alcohol syndrome: Implications to family and society in Australia. *Australian Paediatric Journal, 16,* 101–105.

Walsh, J. K., & Lindblom, S. S. (1997). Psychophysiology of sleep deprivation and disruption. In M. R. Pressman & W. C. Orr (Eds.), *Understanding sleep: The evaluation and treatment of sleep disorders. Application and practice in health psychology* (pp. 73–110). Washington, DC: American Psychological Association.

Walster, E., Aronson, V., Abrahams, D., & Rottman, L. (1966). The importance of physical attractiveness in dating behavior. *Journal of Personality and Social Psychology, 4*, 508–516.

Walters, J. M., & Gardner, H. (1986). The theory of multiple intelligences: Some issues and answers. In R. J. Sternberg & R. K. Walters (Eds.), *Practical intelligence: Nature and origins of competence in the everyday world*. New York: Cambridge University Press.

Walton, G. M., & Banaji, M. R. (2004). Being what you say: The effect of essentialist linguistic labels on preferences. *Social Cognition*, *22*(2), 193–213.

Wampler, M. A., Hamolsky, D., Hamel, K., Melisko, M., & Topp, S. (2004). Case report: Painful peripheral neuropathy following treatment with docetaxel for breast cancer. *Clinical Journal of Oncology Nursing, 9*, 189–193.

Wang, Q., & Leichtman, M. D. (2000). Same beginnings, different stories: A comparison of American and Chinese children's narratives. *Child Development, 71,* 1329–1346.

Ward, M. J., Lee, S. S., & Polan, H. J. (2006). Attachment and psychopathology in a community sample. *Attachment & Human Development*, *8*, 327–340.

Ward Schofield, J., & Steers-Wentzell, K. L. (2003). Prejudice and discrimination: Exploring their origins and understanding their nature. Essay review of *Peer Prejudice and Discrimination* by Harold Fishbein. *Human Development*, *46*, 331–336.

Wark, M. (1997). *The virtual republic: Australia's culture wars of the 1990s*. Sydney, Australia: Allen & Unwin.

Warner, S., & Moore, S. (2004). Excuses, excuses: Self-handicapping in an Australian adolescent sample. *Journal of Youth and Adolescence*, *33*(4), 271–281.

Warwick, Z. S., Hall, W. G., Pappas, T. N., & Schiffman, S. S. (1993). Taste and smell sensations enhance the satiating effect of both a high-carbohydrate and a high-fat meal in humans. *Physiology and Behavior, 53*, 553–563.

Wason, P. C. (1960). On the failure to eliminate hypotheses in a conceptual task. *Quarterly Journal of Experimental Psychology*, *12*, 129–140.

Wason, P. C. (1968). Reasoning about a rule. *Quarterly Journal of Experimental Psychology, 20,* 273–281.

Wasserman, E. A., & Miller, R. R. (1997). What's elementary about associative learning? *Annual Review, 48,* 573–607.

Watanabe, T., Sasaki, Y., Miyauchi, S., Putz, B., Fujimaki, N., Nielsen, M., et al., (1998). Attention-regulated activity in human primary visual cortex. *Journal of Neurophysiology, 79*, 2218–2221.

Waters, E., Hamilton, C. E., & Weinfield, N. S. (2000). The stability of attachment security from infancy to adolescence and early adulthood: General introduction. *Child Development, 71,* 678–683.

Waters, E., Merrick, S., Treboux, D., Crowell, J., & Albersheim, L. (2000). Attachment security in infancy and early adulthood: A twenty-year longitudinal study. *Child Development*, *71*, 684–689.

Waters, E. Wippman, J., & Sroufe, J. A. (1979). Attachment, positive affect, and competence in the peer group: Two studies of construct validation. *Child Development, 50,* 821–829.

Watkins, L. R., & Maier, S. F. (2000). The pain of being sick: Implications of immune-to-brain communication for understanding pain. *Annual Review of Psychology,* 29–57.

Watson, C. (2011, January). Emotional turmoil will not recede. *The Advertiser*. Retrieved from http://www.adelaidenow.com.au/ipad/emotional-turmoil-will-not-recede/story-fn6bqphm-1225986572226

Watson, D. (2000). *Mood and temperament*. New York: Guilford Press.

Watson, D., & Clark, L. A. (1992). Affects separable and inseparable: On the hierarchical arrangement of the negative affects. *Journal of Personality and Social Psychology, 62,* 489–505.

Watson, D., & Tellegen, A. (1985). Toward a consensual structure of mood. *Psychological Bulletin, 98,* 219–225.

Watson, J. (1925). *Behaviorism*. New York: W.W. Norton, 1970.

Watson, J., & Rayner, R. (1920). Conditioned emotional reactions. *Journal of Experimental Psychology, 3,* 1–14.

Watson, M. W., & Getz, K. (1990). The relationship between Oedipal behaviors and children's family role concepts. *Merrill-Palmer Quarterly, 36*, 487–505.

Watts, S. J., & Markham, R. A. (2005). Etiology of depression in children. *Journal of Instructional Psychology*, *32*(3), 266–270.

Waugh, N. C., & Norman, D. A. (1965). Primary memory. *Psychological Review, 72,* 89–104.

Weale, R. (1982). *Focus on vision*. Cambridge, MA: Harvard University Press.

Weatherall, A. (2004). 'Whr r u?tb?' A preliminary study of language use on young people's text messages. *Wellington Working Papers in Linguistics*, *16*, 78–92.

Weatherall, A. (2007). Language and communication. In A. Weatherall, M. Wilson, D. Harper, & J. McDowall (Eds.), *Psychology in Aotearoa/New Zealand* (pp. 75–79). Auckland, New Zealand: Pearson Education New Zealand.

Wechsler, D. (1939). *Measurement of adult intelligence*. Baltimore: Williams & Wilkins.

Wechsler, D. (1997). *WAIS-III: Administration and scoring manual*. San Antonio, TX: Psychological Corporation.

Wechsler, D. (2008). *WAIS-IV: Administration and scoring manual*. San Antino, TX: Psychological Corporation.

Wedekind, C., & Milinski, M. (2000). Cooperation through image scoring in humans. *Science, 288,* 850–852.

Wegesin, D. J. (1998). A neuropsychologic profile of homosexual and heterosexual men and women. *Archives of Sexual Behavior, 27*, 91–108.

Wegner, D. (1992). You can't always think what you want: Problems in the suppression of unwanted thoughts. *Advances in Experimental Social Psychology, 25,* 193–225.

Wegner, D., Shortt, J., Blake, A. W., & Page, M. S. (1990). The suppression of exciting thoughts. *Journal of Personality and Social Psychology, 58,* 409–418.

Wegner, D. M., & Bargh, J. A. (1998). Control and automaticity in social life. In D. Gilbert, S. T. Fiske, & G. Lindzey (Eds.), *Handbook of social psychology* (4th ed., pp. 446–496). New York: McGraw-Hill.

Wegner, D. M., & Wheatley, T. (1999). Apparent mental causation: Sources of the experience of will. *American Psychologist, 54*, 480–492.

Weinberg, R. A. (1989). Intelligence and IQ: Landmark issues and great debates. *American Psychologist, 44*, 98–104.

Weinberg, R. A., Scarr, S., & Waldman, I. D. (1992). The Minnesota Transracial Adoption Study: A follow-up of IQ test performance at adolescence. *Intelligence, 16*, 117–135.

Weinberger, D. A. (1990). The construct validity of the repressive coping style. In J. L. Singer (Ed.), *Repression and dissociation: Implications for personality, psychopathology and health*. Chicago: University of Chicago Press.

Weinberger, J. (1995). Common factors aren't so common: The common factors dilemma. *Clinical Psychology — Science and Practice, 2*, 45–69.

Weinberger, J. (2004). Heart and head: Are they one? In H. Kurtzman (Ed.), *Cognition and psychodynamics*. New York: Oxford University Press.

Weinberger, J., & Hardaway, R. (1990). Subliminal separating science from myth in subliminal psychodynamic activation. *Clinical Psychological Review, 10*, 727–756.

Weiner, B. (1974). *Achievement motivation and attribution theory*. Morristown, NJ: General Learning Press.

Weiner, B. (1986). *An attributional theory of motivation and emotion*. New York: Springer-Verlag.

Weiner, B. (1992). *Human motivation. Metaphors, theories and research*. Newbury Park, CA: Sage.

Weiner, B. (1995). *Judgments of responsibility: A foundation for a theory of social conduct*. New York: Guilford.

Weiner, H. (1985). The psychobiology and pathophysiology of anxiety and fear. In A. H. Tuma & J. D. Maser (Eds.), *Anxiety and the anxiety disorders* (pp. 333–354). Hillsdale, NJ: Lawrence Erlbaum Associates.

Weiner, M. J. (1980). The effect of incentive and control over outcomes upon intrinsic motivation and performance. *Journal of Social Psychology, 112*, 247–254.

Weiner, R. D., & Coffey, C. E. (1988). Indications for use of electroconvulsive therapy. In A. J. Frances & R. E. Hales (Eds.), *Review of psychiatry: Vol. 7*. Washington, DC: American Psychiatric Press.

Weinfield, N. S., Sroufe, L. A., & Egeland, B. (2000). Attachment from infancy to early adulthood in a high-risk sample: Continuity, discontinuity, and their correlates. *Child Development, 71*, 695–702.

Weinhardt, L. S., Carey, M. P., Carey, K. B., Maisto, S. A., & Gordon, C. M. (2001). The relation of alcohol use to sexual HIV risk behavior among adults with a severe and persistent mental illness. *Journal of Consulting and Clinical Psychology, 69*, 77–84.

Weinstein, N. D. (1980). Unrealistic optimism about future life events. *Journal of Personality and Social Psychology, 39*, 306–320.

Weinstein, N. D., & Klein, W. M. (1996). Unrealistic optimism: Present and future. *Journal of Social and Clinical Psychology, 15*, 1–8.

Weis, S., & Süß, H.-M. (2005). Social intelligence: A review and critical discussion of measurement concepts. In R. Schulze & R. D. Roberts (Eds.), *Emotional intelligence: An international handbook* (pp. 204–230). Cambridge, MA: Hogrefe & Huber.

Weisbuch, M., Mackie, D. M., & Garcia-Marques, T. (2003). Prior source exposure and persuasion: Further evidence for misattributional processes. *Personality and Social Psychology Bulletin, 29*, 691–700.

Weiskrantz, L. (1997). *Consciousness lost and found: A neuropsychological exploration*. England: Oxford University Press.

Weiskrantz, L., Warrington, E., Sanders, M. D., & Marshall, J. (1974). Visual capacity in the hemianopic field following a restricted occipital ablation. *Brain, 97*, 709–728.

Weiss, B., Dodge, K., Bates, J., & Pettit, G. (1992). Some consequences of early harsh discipline: Child aggression and a maladaptive social information processing style. *Child Development, 63*, 1321–1335.

Weiss, G., Hechtman, L., Milroy, T., & Perlman, T. (1985). Psychiatric status of hyperactives as adults: A controlled prospective 15-year follow-up of 63 hyperactive children. *Journal of the American Academy of Child Psychiatry, 24*, 211–220.

Weiss, L. H., & Schwarz, J. C. (1996). The relationship between parenting types and older adolescents' personality, academic achievements, adjustment, and substance use. *Child Development, 67*, 2101–2114.

Weiss, R. S. (1986). Continuities and transformations in social relationships from childhood to adulthood. In W. W. Hartup & Z. Rubin (Eds.), *Relationships and development* (pp. 95–110). Hillsdale, NJ: Lawrence Erlbaum.

Weiss, V. (1992). Major genes of general intelligence. *Personality and Individual Differences, 13*, 1115–1134.

Weisse, C. S. (1992). Depression and immunocompetence: A review of the literature. *Psychological Bulletin, 111*, 475–489.

Weissman, M. M., Bland, R. C., Canino, G. J., Faravelli, C., Greenwald, S., Hwu, H., et al. (1997). The cross-national epidemiology of panic disorder. *Archives of General Psychiatry, 54*, 305–309.

Weitlauf, J. C., Cervone, D., Smith, R. E., & Wright, P. M. (2001). Assessing generalizations in perceived self-efficacy: Multidomain and global assessments of the effects of self-defense training for women. *Personality & Social Psychology Bulletin, 27*(12), 1683–1691.

Wells, G. L., & Loftus, E. F. (Eds.). (1984). *Eyewitness testimony: Psychological perspectives*. Cambridge, England: Cambridge University Press.

Wells, G. L., Malpass, R. S., Lindsay, R. C. L., Fisher, R. P., Turtle, J. W., & Fulero, S. M. (2000). From the lab to the police station: A successful application of eyewitness research. *American Psychologist, 55*(6), 581–598.

Wells, G. L., & Olson, E. A. (2003). Eyewitness testimony. *Annual Review of Psychology, 54*, 277–295.

Wenderoth, P., & Johnstone, S. (1988). The different mechanisms of the direct and indirect tilt illusions. *Vision Research, 28*, 301–312.

Wentzel, K. R., & Asher, S. R. (1995). The academic lives of neglected, rejected, popular, and controversial children. *Child Development, 66*, 754–763.

Werner, E., & Smith, R. (1989). *Vulnerable but invincible: A longitudinal study of resilient children and youth*. New York: Adams, Bannister, and Cox.

Werner, H. (1948). *Comparative psychology of mental development* (Rev. ed.). Chicago: Follett.

Wertenbaker, L. (1981). *The eye: Window to the world*. Washington, DC: U.S. News books.

Wertheim, E. H., Koerner, J., & Paxton, S. J. (2001). Longitudinal predictors restrictive eating and bulimic behavior in adolescent girls. *Journal of Youth and Adolescence, 30*, 69–81.

Wertheim, E. H., Paxton, S. J., & Blaney, S. (2004). Risk factors for body image dissatisfaction. In J. K. Thompson (Ed.), *Handbook of eating disorders and obesity* (Chap. 23, pp. 463–494). Hoboken, NJ: John Wiley & Sons.

Wertheimer, M. (1961). Psychomotor coordination of auditory and visual space at birth. *Science, 134*, 1692.

Wertsch, J., & Kanner, B. (1992). A sociocultural approach to intellectual development. In R. Sternberg & C. A. Berg (Eds.), *Intellectual development* (pp. 328–349). New York: Cambridge University Press.

Wesley, F., & Sullivan, E. (1986). *Human growth and development: A psychological approach* (2nd ed.). New York: Human Sciences Press.

West, R. L. (1996). An application of prefrontal cortex function theory to cognitive aging. *Psychological Bulletin, 120*, 272–292.

Westen, D. (1985). *Self and society: Narcissism, collectivism, and the development of morals*. New York: Cambridge University Press.

Westen, D. (1991). Social cognition and object relations. *Psychological Bulletin, 109*, 429–455.

Westen, D. (1992). The cognitive self and the psychoanalytic self: Can we put our selves together? *Psychological Inquiry, 3*, 1–13.

Westen, D. (1994). Toward an integrative model of affect regulation: Applications to social-psychological research. *Journal of Personality, 62*, 641–647.

Westen, D. (1995). A clinical-empirical model of personality: Life after the Mischelian ice age and the Neolithic era. *Journal of Personality, 63*, 495–524.

Westen, D. (1998). The scientific legacy of Sigmund Freud: Toward a psychodynamically informed psychological science. *Psychological Bulletin, 124*, 333–371.

Westen, D. (2000). Integrative psychotherapy: Integrating psychodynamic and cognitive-behavioral theory and technique. In C. R. Snyder & R. E. Ingram (Eds.), *Handbook of psychology change: Psychotherapy processes and practices for the 21st century* (pp. 217–242). New York: John Wiley & Sons.

Westen, D., & Chang, C. (2000). Personality pathology in adolescence: A review. In A. H. Esman, L. T. Flaherty, & T. Lois (Eds.), *Adolescent psychiatry: Developmental and clinical studies: Vol. 25. The Annals of the American Society for Adolescent Psychiatry* (pp. 61–100). Hillsdale, NJ: Analytic Press.

Westen, D., & Gabbard, G. (1999). Psychoanalytic approaches to personality. In L. Pervin & O. John (Eds.), *Handbook of personality: Theory and research* (2nd ed., pp. 57–101). New York: Guilford Press.

Westen, D., & Harnden-Fischer, J. (2001). Classifying eating disorders by personality profiles: Bridging the chasm between axis I and axis II. *American Journal of Psychiatry, 158*, 1767–1771.

Westen, D., Klepser, J., Ruffins, S., Silverman, M., Lifton, N., & Boekamp, J. (1991). Object relations in childhood and adolescence: The development of working representations. *Journal of Consulting and Clinical Psychology, 59*, 400–409.

Westen, D., Lohr, N., Silk, K., Gold, L., & Kerber, K. (1990). Object relations and social cognition in borderlines, major depressives, and normals: A TAT analysis. *Psychological Assessment: A Journal of Consulting and Clinical Psychology, 2*, 355–364.

Westen, D., & Morrison, K. (2001). *A meta analytic investigation of empirically supported treatments for depression, anxiety, and generalized anxiety disorder*. Unpublished manuscript, Boston University.

Westen, D., Muderrisoglu, S., Fowler, C., Shedler, J., & Koren, D. (1997). Affect regulation and affective experience: Individual differences, group differences, and measurement using a Q-sort procedure. *Journal of Consulting and Clinical Psychology, 65*, 429–439.

Westen, D., & Shedler, J. (1999). Revising and assessing axis II, part II: Toward an empirically based and clinically useful classification of personality disorders. *American Journal of Psychiatry, 156*, 273–285.

Westerman, T. G. (2004). Engagement of Indigenous clients in mental health services: What role do cultural differences play? *Australian e-Journal for the Advancement of Mental Health, 3*(3), 1–7. Retrieved from www.auseinet.com/journal/vol3iss3/westermaneditorial.pdf

Western Australian Department of Education and Training. (2004). *Monitoring standards in education*. Retrieved November 4, 2004, from http://www.eddept.wa.edu.au/mse/materials.html

Wetherell, M. (1998). Defining social psychology. In R. Sapsford, A. Still, M. Wetherell, D. Miell, & R. Stevens (Eds.), *Theory and social psychology*. London: Sage.

Wetherick, N. (1975). The role of semantic information in short-term memory. *Journal of Verbal Learning and Verbal Behavior, 14*, 471–480.

Wethington, E. (2000). Expecting stress: Americans and the 'midlife crisis'. *Motivation and Emotion, 24*, 85–103.

Whalen, P. J., Rauch, S. L., Etcoff, N. L., McInerney, S. C., Lee, M. B., & Jenike, M. A. (1998). Masked presentations of emotional facial expressions modulate amygdala activity without explicit knowledge. *Journal of Neuroscience, 18*(1), 411–418.

Wheeler, L., & Kim, Y. (1997). What is beautiful is culturally good: The physical attractiveness stereotype has different content in collectivistic cultures. *Personality and Social Psychology Bulletin, 23*, 795–800.

Wheeler, M. A., Stuss, D. T., & Tulving, E. (1995). Frontal lobe damage produces episodic memory impairment. *Journal of the International Neuropsychological Society, 1*, 525–533.

Wheeler, M. A., Stuss, D. T., & Tulving, D. (1997). Toward a theory of episodic memory: The frontal lobes and autonoetic consciousness. *Psychological Bulletin, 121*, 331–354.

Wheeler, S. C., DeMarree, K. G., & Petty, R. E. (2007). Understanding the role of the self in prime-to-behavior effects: The active-self account. *Personality and Social Psychology Review, 11*(3), 234–261.

Whipple, B., Josimovich, J. B., & Komisaruk, B. R. (1990). Sensory thresholds during the antepartum, intrapartum and postpartum periods. *International Journal of Nursing Studies, 27*, 213–221.

Whitam, F., & Mathy, R. (1991). Childhood cross-gender behavior of homosexual females in Brazil, Peru, the Philippines, and the United States. *Archives of Sexual Behavior, 20*, 151–170.

Whitbourne, S. K. (2001). *Adult development and aging: Biopsychosocial perspectives*. New York: John Wiley & Sons.

Whitbourne, S. K., Zuschlag, M. K., Elliot, L. B., & Waterman, A. S. (1992). Psychosocial development in adulthood: A 22-year sequential study. *Journal of Personality & Social Psychology, 63*, 260–271.

White, K. G., & Ruske, A. C. (2002). Memory deficits in Alzheimer's disease: The encoding hypothesis and cholinergic function. *Psychonomic Bulletin & Review, 9*, 426–437.

White, K. M., Hogg, M., & Terry, D. J. (2002). Improving attitude-behavior correspondence through exposure to normative support from a salient ingroup. *Basic and Applied Social Psychology, 24*, 91 103.

White, R. W. (1959). Motivation reconsidered: The concept of competence. *Psychological Review, 66*, 297–333.

Whitehall, J. S. (2007). National guidelines on alcohol use during pregnancy: A dissenting opinion. *The Medical Journal of Australia, 186*, 35–37.

Whitfield, J. B., Zhu, G., Madden, P. A., Neale, M. C., Heath, A. C., & Martin, N. G. (2004). The genetics of alcohol intake and of alcohol dependence. *Alcoholism: Clinical & Experimental Research, 28*, 1153–1160.

Whiting, B. B., & Edwards, C. P. (1988). *Children of different worlds: The formation of social behavior*. Cambridge, MA: Harvard University Press.

Whiting, B. B., & Whiting, J. W. M. (1975). *Children of six cultures: A psychocultural analysis*. Cambridge, MA: Harvard University Press.

Whiting, J. (1964). The effects of climate on certain cultural practices. In W. Goodenough (Ed.), *Explorations in cultural anthropology: Essays in honor of George Peter Murdock* (pp. 511–544). New York: McGraw-Hill.

Whiting, J. W. M., & Child, I. L. (1953). *Child training and personality: A cross-cultural study*. New Haven, CT: Yale University Press.

Whiting, J. W. M., & Whiting, B. B. (1973). Altruistic and egoistic behavior in six cultures. In L. Nader & T. W. Marekzki (Eds.), *Cultural illness and health: Essays in human adaptation*. Washington, DC: American Anthropological Association.

Whitt, E. J., Edison, M. I., Pascarella, E. T., Nora, A., & Terenzini, P. T. (1999). Women's perceptions of a 'chilly climate' and cognitive outcomes in college: Additional evidence. *Journal of College Student Development, 40*, 163–177.

Whitt, E. J., Pascarella, E. T., Nesheim, B. S. E., Marth, B. P., & Pierson, C. T. (2003). Differences between women and men in objectively measured outcomes, and the factors that influence those outcomes, in the first three years of college. *Journal of College Student Development, 44*. Retrieved June 6, 2007, from http://findarticles.com/p/articles/mi_qa3752/is_200309/ai_n9258805

WHO (World Health Organization). (n.d.). *The ICD-10 classification of mental and behavioural disorders: Clinical descriptions and diagnostic guidelines*. Retrieved from http://www.who.int/classifications/icd/en/bluebook.pdf

WHO. (1998). *Primary prevention of mental health, neurological and psychological disorders*. Geneva, Switzerland: Author.

WHO. (1999). *World health report: Making a difference*. Geneva, Switzerland: Author.

WHO. (2005). *Summary report: WHO multi-country study on women's health and domestic violence. Initial results on prevalence, health outcomes and women's responses*. Geneva, Switzerland: Author.

WHO. (2007). *What do we mean by 'sex' and 'gender'?* Retrieved December 12, 2007, from http://www.who.int/gender/whatisgender/en/index.html

WHO. (2009). *Global health risks: Mortality and burden of disease attributable to selected major risks*. Geneva, Switzerland: Author.

WHO. (2010a). *A global view of HIV infection in 2008: 33.4 million people living with HIV*. Retrieved from http://www.who.int/hiv/data/global_data/en/index.html

WHO. (2010b). *Health topics: Mental disorders*. Retrieved from http://www.who.int/topics/mental_disorders/en/

WHO. (2010c). *International classification of diseases (ICD)*. Retrieved from http://www.who.int/classifications/icd/en/

WHO. (2010d). *Mental health*. Retrieved from http://www.who.int/mental_health/en/

WHO. (2010e). *Mental health: Strengthening our response* (Fact sheet No. 220). Retrieved from http://www.who.int/mediacentre/factsheets/fs220/en/

WHO. (2010f). *Pandemic (H1N1) 2009 – update 109*. Retrieved from http://www.who.int/csr/don/2010_07_16/en/index.html

WHO. (2010g). *Polio in Angola – high risk of international spread*. Retrieved from http://www.who.int/csr/don/2010_07_19/en/index.html

WHO. (2010h). *Severe acute respiratory syndrome (SARS)*. Retrieved from http://www.who.int/csr/sars/en/

Whorf, B. L. (1956). *Language, thought, and reality*. Cambridge, MA: MIT Press.

Wicker, A. W. (1969). Attitudes versus action: The relationship of verbal and overt behavioral responses to attitude objects. *Journal of Social Issues, 25*, 41–78.

Wickelgren, I. (1996). Marijuana: Harder than thought? *Science, 276*, 1967–1968.

Widiger, T. A., & Sankis, L. M. (2000). Adult psychopathology: Issues and controversies. *Annual Review of Psychology, 51*, 377–404.

Widmer, E. D., Treas, J., & Newcomb, R. (1998). Attitudes toward nonmarital sex in 24 countries. *The Journal of Sex Research, 35*(4), 349–358.

Wiesel, T. N. (1982). Postnatal development of the visual cortex and the influence of environment. *Nature, 299*, 583–591.

Wiesel, T. N., & Hubel, D. H. (1960). Receptive fields of ganglion cells in the cat's retina. *Journal of Physiology, 153*, 583–594.

Wieselquist, J., Rusbult, C. E., Foster, C. A., & Agnew, C. R. (1999). Commitment, pro-relationship behavior, and trust in close relationships. *Journal of Personality and Social Psychology, 77*, 942–966.

Wigfield, A., & Eccles, J. S. (2000). Expectancy-value theory of achievement motivation. *Contemporary Educational Psychology, 25*, 68–81.

Wilbert, C. (2009). *People who maintain mental acuity in their 70s and 80s are more likely to exercise, shun smoking*. Retrieved from http://www.webmd.com/healthy-aging/news/20090609/how-to-stay-sharp-in-old-age

Wilhelm, K., Mitchell, P., Slade, T., Brownhill, S., & Andrews, G. (2003). Prevalence and correlates of DSM-IV major depression in an Australian national survey. *Journal of Affective Disorders, 75*, 155–162.

Wilke, M. (2001). Changing standards: Condom advertising on American television. *Kaiser Daily Reproductive Health Report*.

Wilkes, A. L., & Reynolds, D. J. (1999). On certain limitations accompanying readers' interpretations of corrections in episodic text. *Quarterly Journal of Experimental Psychology: Human Experimental Psychology, 52A*, 165–183.

Wilkins, M. C. (1982). The effect of changed material on ability to do formal syllogistic reasoning. *Archives of Psychology, 16*, 1–83.

Wilkinson, L., & Task Force on Statistical Inference. (1999). Statistical methods in psychology journals: Guidelines and explanations. *American Psychologist, 54*, 594–604.

Wilkinson, S. C. (1993). WISC-R profiles of children with superior intellectual ability. *Gifted Child Quarterly, 37*, 84–91.

Wilkinson-Ryan, T., & Westen, D. (2000). Identity disturbance in borderline personality disorder: An empirical investigation. *American Journal of Psychiatry, 157*, 528–541.

Wilksch, S. M., & Wade, T. D. (2009). Reduction of shape and weight concern in young adolescents: A 30-month controlled evaluation of a media literacy program. *Journal of American Academy for Child and Adolescent Psychiatry, 48*, 652–661.

Williams, C., & Bybee, J. (1994). What do children feel guilty about? Developmental and gender differences. *Developmental Psychology, 30*, 617–623.

Williams, C. D. (1959). The elimination of tantrum behavior by extinction procedures. *Journal of Abnormal and Social Psychology, 59*, 269.

Williams, J. (2003). Dementia and genetics. In R. Plomin, J. C. DeFries, I. W. Craig, & P. McGuffin (Eds.), *Behavioral genetics in the postgenomic era* (pp. 503–527). Washingon, DC: American Psychological Association.

Williams, J. E., & Best, D. L. (1982). *Measuring sex stereotypes: A thirty-nation study*. Beverly Hills, CA: Sage.

Williams, J. E., & Best, D. L. (1990). *Measuring sex stereotypes: A multination study*. Newbury Park, CA: Sage.

Williams, J. H. (1983). The emergence of gender differences. In W. Damon (Ed.), *Social and personality development*. New York: W. W. Norton.

Williams, K. B. (2001). *Ostracism: The power of silence*. New York: Guilford Press.

Williams, K. B., Harkins, S., & Latane, B. (1981). Identifiability as a deterrent to social loafing: Two cheering experiments. *Journal of Personality and Social Psychology, 40*, 303–311.

Williams, L. M. (1994). Recall of childhood trauma: A prospective study of women's memories of child sexual abuse. *Journal of Consulting and Clinical Psychology, 62*, 1167–1176.

Williams, W. M., & Ceci, S. J. (1997). Are Americans becoming more or less alike? Trends in race, class, and ability differences in intelligence. *American Psychologist, 52*, 1226–1235.

Willis, A. (1993). *Illusions of identity: The art of nation*. Sydney, Australia: Hale & Iremonger.

Willis-Esqueda, C. (Ed.). (2008). *Motivational aspects of prejudice and racism*. New York: Springer.

Wills, T. A. (1981). Downward comparison principles in social psychology. *Psychological Bulletin, 90*, 245–271.

Wilshire, C. E., & Saffran, E. M. (2005). Contrasting effects of phonological priming in aphasic word production. *Cognition, 95*, 31–71.

Wilson, A., Bekiaris, J., Gleeson, S., Papasavva, C., Wise, M., & Hawe, P. (1993). The good heart, good life survey: Self reported cardiovascular disease risk factors among Greek-Australians in Sydney. *Australian Journal of Public Health, 17*(3), 215–221.

Wilson, E. O. (1975). *Sociobiology: A new synthesis*. Cambridge, MA: Harvard University Press.

Wilson, E. O., & Bossert, W. H. (1996). Chemical communication among animals. In L. D. Houck & L. C. Drickamer (Eds.), *Foundations of animal behavior: Classic papers with commentaries* (pp. 602–645). Chicago: University of Chicago Press.

Wilson, K. L., Charker, J., Lizzio, A. J., Halford, W. K., & Kimlin, S. (2005). Assessing how much couples work at their relationships: The behavioral self-regulation for effective relationships scale. *Journal of Family Psychology, 19*, 385–393.

Wilson, L. (1988). *Thathilgaw Emeret Lu: A handbook of traditional Torres Strait Islands material culture*. Brisbane, Australia: Department of Education.

Wilson, L. (1993). *Kerkar Lu: Contemporary artefacts of the Torres Strait Islanders*. Brisbane, Australia: Department of Education.

Wilson, M. (2007). Social psychology and group processes. In A. Weatherall, M. Wilson, D. Harper, & J. McDowall (Eds.), *Psychology in Aotearoa/New Zealand* (pp. 59–63). Auckland, New Zealand: Pearson Education New Zealand.

Wilson, M. A., & McNaughton, B. L. (1994). Reactivation of hippocampal ensemble memories during sleep. *Science, 265*, 676–679.

Wilson, P. H., & Edwards, C. J. (1996). Clinic-based mental health services. In P. R. Martin & J. S. Birnbrauer (Eds.), *Clinical psychology: Profession and practice in Australia* (pp. 129–158). Melbourne, Australia: Macmillan Education.

Wilson, T. D., Lindsey, S., & Schooler, T. Y. (2000). A model of dual attitudes. *Psychological Review, 107*, 101–126.

Wilson-Miller, J. (1982). *Koori IQ test*. Retrieved September 9, 2004, from http://www.sbs.com.au/australianeye/index2.html?id=88

Wimmer, H., & Perner, J. (1983). Beliefs about beliefs: Representation and constraining function of wrong beliefs in young children's understanding of deception. *Cognition, 13*(1), 103–128.

Winer, R. S. (2000). Comment on 'the historical growth of statistical significance testing in psychology — and its future prospects'. *Educational and Psychological Measurement, 60*(5), 693–696.

Winkielman, P., & Berridge, K. C. (2004). Unconscious emotion. *Current Directions in Psychological Science, 13*(3), 120–123.

Winn, P. (1995). The lateral hypothalamus and motivated behavior: An old syndrome reassessed and a new perspective gained. *Current Directions in Psychological Science, 4*, 182–187.

Winne, P. H., & Nesbit, J. C. (2010). The psychology of academic achievement. *Annual Review of Psychology, 61*, 653–678.

Winner, E. (2000). The origins and ends of giftedness. *American Psychologist 55*, 159–169.

Winograd, E., & Neisser, U. (Eds.). (1993). *Affect and accuracy in recall: Studies of 'flashbulb' memories*. New York: Cambridge University Press.

Winokur, G., & Tanna, V. L. (1969). Possible role of X-linked dominant factor in manic depressive disease. *Diseases of the Nervous System, 30*, 89–94.

Winson, J. (1985). *Brain and psyche: The biology of the unconscious*. New York: Anchor.

Winterbottom, M. R. (1953). *The relation of childhood training in independence to achievement motivation*. Unpublished doctoral dissertation, Univerisity of Michigan, Ann Arbor.

Wise, D., & Rosqvist, J. (2006). Explanatory style and well-being. In J. C. Thomas, D. L. Segal, & M. Hersen (Eds.), *Comprehensive handbook of personality and psychopathology, Vol. 1: Personality and everyday functioning* (pp. 285–305). Hoboken, NJ: John Wiley & Sons.

Wispe, L. G., & Drambarean, N. C. (1953). Physiological need, word frequency, and visual deviation thresholds. *Journal of Experimental Psychology, 46*, 25–31.

Witelson, S. F., Kigar, D. L., & Harvey, T. (1999). The exceptional brain of Albert Einstein. *Lancet, 353*, 2149–2153.

Witt, S. D. (2000). The influence of peers on children's socialisation to gender roles. *Early Child Development and Care, 162*, 1–7.

Wixom, J., Ludolph, P., & Westen, D. (1993). Quality of depression in borderline adolescents. *Journal of the American Academy of Child and Adolescent Psychiatry, 32*, 1172–1177.

Wixted, J., & Ebbesen, E. (1991). On the form of forgetting. *Psychological Science, 2*, 409–415.

Woike, B., & Aronoff, J. (1992). Antecedents of complex social cognitions. *Journal of Personality and Social Psychology, 63*, 97–104.

Woike, B., Gershkovich, I., Piorkowski, R., & Polo, M. (1999). The role of motives in the content and structure of autobiographical memory. *Journal of Personality and Social Psychology, 76*, 600–612.

Woldt, A. L., & Toman, S. M. (Eds.). (2005). *Gestalt therapy: History, theory, and practice*. Thousand Oaks, CA: Sage.

Wolfe, J., Erickson, D. J., Sharkansky, E. J., King, D. W., & King, L. A. (1999). Course and predictors of posttraumatic stress disorder among Gulf War veterans: A prospective analysis. *Journal of Consulting and Clinical Psychology, 67*, 520–528.

Wolman, R. (2001). *Thinking with your soul: Spiritual intelligence and why it matters*. New York: Harmony Books.

Wolpe, J. (1958). *Psychotherapy by reciprocal inhibition*. Stanford, CA: Stanford University Press.

Wolpe, J. (Ed.). (1964). *The conditioning therapies: The challenge in psychotherapy*. New York: Holt, Rinehart & Winston.

Wonderlich, S. A., Gordon, K. H., Mitchell, J. E., Crosby, R. D., & Engel, S. G. (2009). The validity and clinical utility of binge eating disorder. *International Journal of Eating Disorders, 42*, 687–705.

Wong, P., Shevrin, H., & Williams, W. J. (1994). Conscious and nonconscious processes: An ERP index of an anticipatory response in a conditioning paradigm using visually masked stimuli. *Psychophysiology, 31*, 87–101.

Woo, J., Ho, S. C., Yuen, Y. K., Yu, L. M., & Lau, J. (1998). Cardiovascular risk factors and 18-month mortality and morbidity in an elderly Chinese population aged 70 years and over. *Gerontology, 44*, 51–55.

Wood, J. M., Lilienfeld, S. O., Garb, H. N., & Nezworski, M. T. (2000). 'The Rorschach test in clinical diagnosis': A critical review, with a backward look at Garfield (1947). *Journal of Clinical Psychology, 56*, 395–430.

Wood, J. V. (1989). Theory and research concerning social comparisons of personal attributes. *Psychological Bulletin, 106*(2), 231–248.

Wood, M. (2004). *Alcohol: A killer in our midst*. Retrieved October 1, 2004, from http://www.enhancetv.com.au/features/health/alcohol/0204alcohol_2.htm

Wood, R., & Bandura, A. (1989a). Impact of conceptions of ability on self-regulatory mechanisms and complex decision-making. *Journal of Personality and Social Psychology, 56*, 407–415.

Wood, R., & Bandura, A. (1989b). Social cognitive theory of organizational management [Special issue: Theory development forum]. *Academy of Management Review, 14*, 361–384.

Wood, W. (2000). Attitude change: Persuasion and social influence. *Annual Review of Psychology, 51*, 539–570.

Wood, W., Wong, F., & Chachere, J. G. (1991). Effects of media violence on viewers' aggression in unconstrained social interaction. *Psychologial Bulletin*, 109, 371–383.

Woodruff, S. I., Edwards, C. C., Conway, T. L., & Elliott, S. P. (2001). Pilot test of an Internet virtual world chat room for rural teen smokers. *Journal of Adolescent Health, 29*, 239–243.

Woods, S. C., Schwartz, M. W., Baskin, D. G., & Seeley, R. J. (2000). Food intake and the regulation of body weight. *Annual Review of Psychology, 51*, 255–277.

Woodward, A. L., & Sommerville, J. A. (2000). Twelve-month-old infants interpret action in context. *Psychological Science, 11*, 73–77.

Woodward, L. J., Edgin, J. O., Thompson, D., & Inder, T. E. (2005). Object working memory deficits predicted by early brain injury and development in the preterm infant. *Brain, 128*, 2578–2587. Retrieved from http://www.medscape.com/medline/abstract/16150850

Woody, E., & McConkey, K. M. (2003). What we don't know about the brain and hypnosis, but need to: A view from the Buckhorn Inn. *International Journal of Clinical and Experimental Hypnosis, 51*, 309–338.

Woody, E. Z., Barnier, A. J., & McConkey, K. M. (2005). Multiple hypnotizabilities: Differentiating the building blocks of hypnotic response. *Psychological Assessment, 17*, 200–211.

Wootten, J. H. (1991). *Regional report of inquiry in New South Wales, Victoria, and Tasmania: Royal commission into Aboriginal deaths in custody*. Retrieved September 9, 2004, from http://www.austlii.edu.au/au/other/IndigLRes/rciadic/regional/nsw-vic-tas/186.html

Worthington, E. L., Jr., Martin, G. A., Shumate, M., & Carpenter, J. (1983). The effect of brief Lamaze training and social encouragement on pain endurance in a cold pressor tank. *Journal of Applied Social Psychology, 13*, 223–233.

Wouldes, T., LaGasse, L., Sheridan, J., & Lester, B. (2004). Maternal methamphetamine use during pregnancy and child outcome: What do we know? *Journal of the New Zealand Medical Association, 117*, 1206.

Wright, J. H., Basco, M. R., Thase, M. E., & Gabbard, G. O. (Eds.). (2006). *Learning cognitive-behavior therapy*. Washington, DC: American Psychiatric Publishers.

Wright, I. C., Rabe-Hesketh, S., Woodruff, P. W. R., David, A. S., Murray, R. M., & Bullmore, E. T. (2000). Meta-analysis of regional brain volumes in schizophrenia. *American Journal of Psychiatry, 157*, 16–[illegible].

Wright, K. N. (1993). Alcohol use by prisoners. *Alcohol Health & Research World, 17*(2), 157–65.

Wulff, D. M. (1997). *Psychology of religion: Classic and contemporary* (2nd ed.). New York: John Wiley & Sons.

Wyatt, G. E., Peters, S. D., & Guthrie, D. (1988a). Kinsey revisited: I. Comparisons of the sexual socialization and sexual behavior of white women over 33 years. *Archives of Sexual Behavior, 17*, 201–239.

Wyatt, G. E., Peters, S. D., & Guthrie, D. (1988b). Kinsey revisited: II. Comparisons of the sexual socialization and sexual behavior of black women over 33 years. *Archives of Sexual Behavior, 17*, 289–332.

Wynne, L. C. (1961). The study of intrafamilial alignments and splits in exploratory family therapy. In N. Ackerman, F. L. Beatman, & S. N. Sherman (Eds.), *Exploring the base for family therapy*. New York: Family Service Association of America.

Wynne, L. C., & Singer, M. T. (1963). Thought disorder and family relations of schizophrenics. *Archives of General Psychiatry, 9*, 191–198.

Yadin, E., & Thomas, E. (1996). Stimulation of the lateral septum attenuates immobilization-induced stress ulcers. *Physiology & Behavior, 59*, 883–886.

Yager, J. (2000). Weighty perspectives: Contemporary challenges in obesity and eating disorders. *American Journal of Psychiatry, 157*, 851–853.

Yahne, C. E., & Miller, W. R. (1999). Enhancing motivation for treatment and change. In B. S. McCrady & E. E. Epstein (Eds.), *Addictions: A comprehensive guidebook* (pp. 235–249). New York: Oxford University Press.

Yali, A. M., & Revenson, T. A. (2004). Changes in population demographics will impact health psychology: Incorporating a broader notion of cultural competence into the field. *Health Psychology, 23*, 147–155.

Yalom, I. D. (1995). *The theory and practice of group psychotherapy* (4th ed.). New York: Basic Books.

Yalom, I., Brown, S., & Bloch, S. (1975). The written summary as a group psychotherapy technique. *Archives of General Psychiatry, 32*, 605–613.

Yaniv, I., & Meyer, D. (1987). Activation and metacognition of inaccessible stored information: Potential bases for incubation effects in problem solving. *Journal of Experimental Psychology: Learning, Memory, and Cognition, 13*, 187–205.

Yassa, R., Nair, N., Iskandar, H., & Schwartz, G. (1990). Factors in the development of severe forms of tardive dyskinesia. *American Journal of Psychiatry, 147,* 1156–1163.

Yasi damage bill to top $800 million. (2011, February 16). *AAP*. Retrieved from http://www.heraldsun.com.au/news/breaking-news/yasi-damage-bill-to-top-800-million/story-e6frf7kf-1226006886166

Yates, P. M., Edwards, H. E., Nash, R. E., Walsh, A. M., Fentiman, B. J., Skerman, H. M., et al. (2002). Barriers to effective cancer pain management: A survey of hospitalised cancer patients in Australia. *Journal of Pain and Symptom Management, 23*(5), 393–405.

Yee, B., Campbell, A., Beasley, R., & Neill, A. (2002). Sleep disorders: A potential role in New Zealand motor vehicle accidents. *Internal Medicine Journal, 32*(7), 297–304.

Yela, C., & Sangrador, J. L. (2001). Perceptions of physical attractiveness throughout loving relationships. *Current Research in Social Psychology, 6*(5), 57–75.

Yeo, S. S. (2003). Bonding and attachment of Australian Aboriginal children. *Child Abuse Review, 12,* 292–304.

Ylioja, S., Carlson, S., Raij, T. T., & Pertovaara, A. (2006). Localization of touch versus heat pain in the human hand: A dissociative effect of temporal parameters on discriminative capacity and decision strategy. *Pain, 121*(1–2), 6–13.

Yorke, M. (1999). *Leaving early: Undergraduate non-completion in higher education*. London: Falmer Press.

Young, A. J., MacLeod, H. A., & Lawrence, A. B. (1994). Effect of manipulation design on operant responding in pigs. *Animal Behavior, 47,* 1488–1490.

Young, G. B., & Pigott, S. E. (1999). Neurobiological basis of consciousness. *Archives of Neurology, 56,* 153–157.

Young, R. (2001). Current research in the area of autism and savant syndrome. *International Education Journal, 2*(4), 329–333.

Younger, B. A., & Fearing, D. D. (1999). Parsing items into separate categories: Developmental change in infant categorization. *Child Development, 70,* 291–303.

Youniss, J., & Haynie, D. (1992). Friendship in adolescence. *Developmental and Behavioral Pediatrics, 13,* 59–66.

Yu, B., Zhang, W., Jing, Q., Peng, R., Zhang, G., & Simon, H. A. (1985). STM capacity for Chinese and English language materials. *Memory and Cognition, 13,* 202–207.

Zadra, A., & Donderi, D. C. (2000). Nightmares and bad dreams: Their prevalence and relationship to well-being. *Journal of Abnormal Psychology, 109,* 273–281.

Zahn-Waxler, C., Radke-Yarrow, M., Wagner, E., & Chapman, M. (1992). Development of concern for others. *Developmental Psychology, 28,* 126–136.

Zahn-Waxler, C., Robinson, J., & Emde, R. (1992). The development of empathy in twins. *Developmental Psychology, 28,* 1038–1047.

Zajonc, R. B. (1965). Social facilitation. *Science, 149,* 269–274.

Zajonc, R. B. (1968). The attitudinal effects of mere exposure. *Journal of Personality and Social Psychology, 9,* 1–27.

Zajonc, R. B. (1980). Feeling and thinking: Preferences need no inferences. *American Psychologist, 35,* 151–175.

Zajonc, R. B. (1998). Emotions. In D. T. Gilbert, S. T. Fiske, & G. Lindzey (Eds.), *The handbook of social psychology: Vol. 2* (4th ed., pp. 591–632). Boston: McGraw-Hill.

Zajonc, R. B., & Markus, H. (1985). Must all affect be mediated by cognition? *Journal of Consumer Research, 12,* 363–364.

Zanarini, M. C. (Ed.). (1997). *Role of sexual abuse in the etiology of borderline personality disorder*. Washington, DC: American Psychiatric Press.

Zanarini, M. C., Gunderson, J. G., Marino, M. F., Schwartz, E. D., & Frankenburg, F. R. (1989). Childhood experience of borderline patients. *Comprehensive Psychiatry, 30,* 18–25.

Zanarini, M., Gunderson, J., Marino, M., Schwartz, E., & Frankenburg, F. (1990). Psychiatric disorders in the families of borderline outpatients. In P. Links (Ed.), *Family environment and borderline personality disorder* (pp. 69–84). Washington, DC: American Psychiatric Press.

Zanna, M. P., & Cooper, J. (1974). Dissonance and the pill: An attribution approach to studying the arousal properties of dissonance. *Journal of Personality and Social Psychology, 9,* 703–709.

Zaragosta, M., & Mitchell, K. J. (1996). Repeated exposure to suggestion and the creation of false memories. *Psychological Science, 7,* 294–300.

Zatzick, D. F., & Dimsdale, J. E. (1990). Cultural variations in response to painful stimuli. *Psychosomatic Medicine, 52,* 544–557.

Zeanah, C. H., & Zeanah, P. D. (1989). Intergenerational transmission of maltreatment: Insights from attachment theory and research. *Psychiatry, 52,* 177–196.

Zechmeister, E. B., & Shaughnessy, J. J. (1980). When you know that you know and when you think that you know but you don't. *Bulletin of the Psychonomic Society, 15,* 41–44.

Zeki, S., Aglioti, S., McKeefry, D., & Berlucchi, G. (1999). The neurological basis of conscious color perception in a blind patient. *Proceedings of the National Academy of Sciences, USA, 96,* 14124–14129.

Zervas, I. M., Augustine, A., & Fricchione, G. L. (1993). Patient delay in cancer: A view from the crisis model. *General Hospital Psychiatry, 15,* 9–13.

Ziegler, R., Diehl, M., Zigon, R., & Fett, T. (2004). Source consistency, distinctiveness, and consensus: The three dimensions of the Kelley ANOVA model in persuasion. *Personality and Social Psychology Bulletin, 30,* 352–364.

Zigler, E., & Styfco, S. J. (2000). Pioneering steps (and fumbles) in developing a federal preschool intervention. *Topics in Early Childhood Special Education, 20,* 67–70, 78.

Zillman, D., Baron, R. A., & Tamborini, R. (1981). Special costs on smoking: Effects of tobacco smoke on hostile behavior. *Journal of Applied Social Psychology, 11,* 548–561.

Zimbardo, P. G. (1972). Pathology of imprisonment. *Society, 6,* 4–8.

Zimbardo, P. G. (1975). Transforming experimental research into advocacy for social change. In M. Deutsch & H. A. Hornstein (Eds.), *Applying social psychology: Implications for research, practice, and training*. Hillsdale, NJ: Lawrence Erlbaum.

Zimmerman, M., Rothschild, L., & Chelminski, I. (2005). The prevalence of DSM-IV personality disorders in psychiatric outpatients. *American Journal of Psychiatry, 162,* 1911–1918.

Zinbarg, R. E., & Barlow, D. H. (1996). Structure of anxiety and the anxiety disorders: A hierarchical model. *Journal of Abnormal Psychology, 105,* 181–193.

Zinbarg, R., Barlow, D., Brown, T., & Hertz, R. (1992). Cognitive–behavioral approaches to the nature and treatment of anxiety disorders. *Annual Review of Psychology, 43,* 235–267.

Zinbarg, R. E., Barlow, D. H., Liebowitz, M., & Street, L. (1994). The DSM-IV field trial for mixed anxiety-depression. *American Journal of Psychiatry, 151,* 1153–1162.

Zipursky, R. B., Lambe, E. K., Kapur, S., & Mikulis, D. J. (1998). Cerebral gray matter volume deficits in first episode psychosis. *Archives of General Psychiatry, 55,* 540–546.

Zohar, J., Keegstra, H., & Barrelet, L. (2003). Fluvoxamine as effective as clomipramine against symptoms of severe depression: Results from a multicentre, double-blind study. *Human Psychopharmacology: Clinical and Experimental, 18,* 113–119.

Zornberg, G. L., Buka, S. L., & Tsuang, M. T. (2000). Hypoxic-ischemia-related fetal/neonatal complications and risk of schizophrenia and other nonaffective psychoses: A 19-year longitudinal study. *American Journal of Psychiatry, 157,* 196–202.

Zubrick, S. R., Silburn, S. R., & Garton, A. F. (1995). *Western Australian child health survey: Developing health and wellbeing in the nineties*. Perth, Australia: ABS.

Zuckerman, M. (1987). A critical look at three arousal constructs in personality theories: Optimal levels of arousal, strength of the nervous system, and sensitivities to signals of reward and punishment. In J. Strelau & H. J. Eysenck (Eds.), *Personality dimensions and arousal: Perspectives on individual differences* (pp. 217–230). New York: Plenum.

Zuckerman, M. (1994). *Behavioral expression and biosocial bases of sensation seeking*. New York: Cambridge University Press.

Zuckerman, M., Koestner, R., DeBoy, T., Garcia, T., Maresca, B., & Sartois, J. (1988). To predict some of the people some of the time. A reexamination of the moderator variable approach in personality theory. *Journal of Personality and Social Psychology, 54,* 1006–1019.

Zvolensky, M. J., Kotov, R., Antipova, A. V., & Schmidt, N. B. (2005). Diathesis stress model for panic-related distress: A test in a Russian epidemiological sample. *Behaviour Research and Therapy, 43,* 521–532.

Name index

A

B

C

D

E

F

G

H

I

J

K

L

M

N

O

P

Q

R

S

T

U

V

W

X

Y

Z

Subject index

B

C

D

E

F

G

H

I

N

O

P

Q

R

S

T

U

V

W

X

Y

Z